KIBBLE AND TIDBITS FROM
Vacationing With Your Pet

WHERE TO STAY

A comprehensive guide to pet-friendly accommodations, Eileen's award-winning directory includes more than 25,000 hotels, motels, inns and B&Bs in the United States and Canada that welcome you and your pet.

- Fluff Fido's pillow at the Four Seasons Hotel in Beverly Hills (page 143).

- Do the River Walk with Rover when you stay at the Plaza San Antonio in Texas (page 570).

- Fill your eyes with starry skies ¡- ¯ the Westward Look Re˳⁻

- Window shop till y˵ weary paws at the H˲ ˳ ˳ew York City (page 432).

- Fall hard for autumn colors with furface in Vermont at the award-winning Topnotch at Stowe Resort (page 592).

- Take your sun-loving pet on a journey to the Grove Isle Resort in Miami (page 223).

WHERE TO STAY

- Let your Sandy have her way on the sandy shores of Cannon Beach, Oregon when you stay at the Tolovana Inn (page 479).

- Enjoy a winter wonderland with your snow-sniffing wagalong at The Little Nell in Aspen, Colorado (page 184).

- Maybe the sniffmeister can unearth some silver trinkets at the Inn on the Alameda in Santa Fe (page 423).

- Better than an igloo, cozy into Alaska Auntie's B&B (Bed & Biscuit?) in Anchorage (page 106).

- Don't be sleepless in Seattle, hightail it to The Alexis Historic Hotel (page 620).

- People and pooch watch under the famous clock at San Francisco's historic Westin St. Francis Hotel (page 173).

- Give Bowser something to bark home about from the Fairmont Royal York in Toronto, Ontario (page 692).

- Have a howl of a good time at the Chateau Versailles in Montreal, Quebec (page 696).

HOW TO DO IT

Increase your travel know-how with some handy traveling tips.

- How to Pack For Your Pet (page 38).
- 29 Tips For Travel Safety (page 57).
- 27 "On-the-Road Tips" (page 61).

Old dogs can learn new tricks.

- Training Do's and Don'ts (page 33).
- Prevent Aggression in Your Dog (page 36).
- Get Crate Smart (page 34).

Make a night of it.

- Hotel and Motel Policies (page 17).
- Travel by Car (page 42).
- Travel by Plane (page 49).

Kitty comes along.

- What About Cats (page 25).
- Cat Travel Tips (page 27).

Directories by Eileen Barish

DOIN' ARIZONA WITH YOUR POOCH

DOIN' CALIFORNIA WITH YOUR POOCH

DOIN' NEW YORK WITH YOUR POOCH

DOIN' TEXAS WITH YOUR POOCH

DOIN' THE NORTHWEST WITH YOUR POOCH

VACATIONING WITH YOUR PET

THE GUIDE TO LODGING IN ITALY'S MONASTERIES

THE GUIDE TO LODGING IN SPAIN'S MONASTERIES

THE GUIDE TO LODGING IN FRANCE'S MONASTERIES

Novels by Eileen Barish

ARIZONA TERRITORY
AS TIME GOES BY

EILEEN'S DIRECTORY OF PET-FRIENDLY LODGING IN THE UNITED STATES & CANADA

VACATIONING WITH YOUR PET

Over 25,000 Listings of
Hotels, Motels, Inns, Ranches
and B&Bs that Welcome
Guests with Pets

Pet-Friendly Publications
P.O. Box 8459, Scottsdale, AZ 85252

VACATIONING WITH YOUR PET
by Eileen Barish

Pet-Friendly Publications
P.O. Box 8459, Scottsdale, AZ 85252
Tel: (800) 638-3637

ISBN #1-884465-24-6
Library of Congress Catalog Card Number: 2006930173
Printed and bound in the United States of America.
Sixth Edition

S P E C I A L   E D I T I O N S

Eileen's directories are available at special discounts when purchased in
bulk for premiums and special sales promotions as well as for fund-
raising or educational use. Special editions or book excerpts can also be
created to specification. For details, call 1-800-638-3637.

CREDITS

Author & Managing Editor — Eileen Barish

Associate Editor — Harvey Barish

Lodging & Research Editor — Phyllis Holmes

Research/Writing Staff — Alison Dufner
Tiffany Geoghegan
Courtney Mechling

Illustrator — Gregg Myers
Graphic Designer — Tawni Hensley
Photographer — Ken Friedman

ACKNOWLEDGEMENTS

Phyllis, I am grateful for your tireless dedication and extraordinary thoroughness. Your efforts meant the difference between good and great.

For Nona, Kenny and Chris for being so supportive and especially for Harvey who makes it all come together, who's always up for the often demanding challenge and more than ready for the next adventure.

In memory of Sam, the "best friend" who started it all. And for Rosie and Max who continued the legacy of loving dogs. They will always be missed.

Cover photo
NACHO
By Patricia Marroquin

TABLE OF CONTENTS

Traveling with your pet can be a rewarding experience.
How to use this directory.
No more sneaking Snoopy.
Do hotel and motel policies differ regarding pets?
Not just for vacationers.
Lodging guidelines for you and your pet.
Can my dog be left alone in the room?
Pooch rules and regulations.

Vacationing with pets.
Samson.
Life goes on....Rosie and Maxwell.
Sooo...we took them along.
Is my pet vacation-friendly?
A socialized pooch is a sophisticated traveler.
Just ordinary dogs.

A walk in the park!
One step at a time.
Follow the leader.
Cat travel tips 1, 2 and 3.

TRAVELING BY PLANE (cont.)

How will my pet feel about a kennel?
What about identification?
How can I make plane travel comfortable for my pet?
Will there automatically be room on board for my pet?
What will pet travel cost?
What about food and water?
What about tranquilizers?
What about after we land?
Pets who shouldn't fly.
Health certificates - will I need one?

Allergies.
Bites and stings.
Bleeding.
Burns.
Earache.
Eye scratches or inflammation.
Falls or impact injuries.
Fleas.
Heatstroke.

UNITED STATES DIRECTORY OF
PET-FRIENDLY LODGING

CANADIAN DIRECTORY OF PET-FRIENDLY LODGING

Traveling With Your Pet Can Be A Rewarding Experience

You never have to leave your best friend home or kenneled in a small cage while you vacation. Bring your four-legged buddy along. Double your enjoyment and increase your safety. If your pet is a great companion at home, he can be just as companionable when you travel.

HOW TO USE THIS DIRECTORY
No more sneaking Snoopy

Whether you're a seasoned pet traveler or a first-time explorer, ***Vacationing With Your Pet*** will make traveling with your pet easier and more enjoyable.

At a glance, you'll locate thousands of accommodations in the United States and Canada that welcome people traveling with their pets.

Choose lodging from hotels, B&Bs (aka Bed & Biscuits), motels, resorts, inns and ranches that welcome you and your pet *through the front door.* Arranged in an easy-to-use alphabetical format, ***Vacationing With Your Pet*** covers the United States and Canada. Within each state or province, cities are also arranged in alphabetical order. Each listing includes the name of the lodging, address, zip code and phone number. Wherever available, the high/low range of room rates and toll-free 800-numbers are provided.

Do hotel and motel policies differ regarding pets?

Yes, but all the accommodations in *Vacationing With Your Pet* allow pets. Policies can vary on charges and sometimes on pet size or type. Some might require a damage deposit while some combine their deposit with a daily and/or one-time charge. Others may restrict pets to specific rooms, perhaps cabins or cot-

tages. Residence-type inns which cater to long-term guests often charge a long-term fee. Some also require advance notice. But most accommodations do not charge a fee or have restrictive policies. As with all travel arrangements, it is recommended that you call in advance to confirm policies and room availability. Be aware that hotel policies may change. At the time your reservations are made, determine the pet-policy of your lodging choice.

Not just for vacationers, this is a "must-have" reference for anyone who has a pet.

Increase your travel horizons and give your best friend a new leash on life. Owning a copy of *Vacationing With Your Pet* means you won't have to leave your trusted companion at home when you travel. Containing a comprehensive overview of practical, hands-on information, this directory to make your travel experiences safer and more pleasurable. Training do's and don'ts, crate use and selection, driving tips, pet etiquette, travel manners, what and how to pack for your pet, first-aid advice and a pet identification form are just some of the topics covered. See the Table of Contents for a complete listing of travel, training and pet care information.

A word about area codes.

Area codes keep changing all over the country and every attempt has been made to keep up with these changes. To help you, we have included toll-free numbers wherever available. If a local phone number doesn't go through, check for a new area code.

Lodging Guidelines For You and Your Pet

Conduct yourself in a courteous manner and you'll continue to be welcome anywhere you travel. Never do anything on vacation with your pet that you wouldn't do at home. Some quick tips follow that can make traveling with your pet more pleasurable.

1. If your pet is accustomed to sleeping on the bed with you, take along a sheet or favorite blanket and put that on top of the bedding provided by your lodging.

2. Place a towel or small mat under your pet's food and water dishes and feed your pet in the bathroom where clean-up is easier should an accident occur.

3. Try to keep your pet off the furniture. Pack a lint and hair remover to eliminate unwanted hairs.

4. Always keep your dog on a leash on the hotel and motel grounds and carry plastic bags and/or paper towels for clean-up.

5. Keep your cat's litter box in the bathroom. Clean it often, flushing away waste.

Can my dog be left alone in the room?

Only you know the answer to that. If your dog isn't destructive, if he doesn't bark incessantly and if the hotel allows unattended dogs, try leaving him in the room for short periods of time — say when you dine out. Hang the "Do Not Disturb" sign on your door to alert the chambermaid or hotel staff members that your room shouldn't be entered.

Before leaving your dog unattended, the following suggestions might prove helpful:

1. Walk or otherwise exercise your pooch. An exercised dog will fall asleep more easily.

2. Provide a favorite toy as a distraction.

3. Turn on the TV or radio for audio/ visual companionship.

4. Be certain that there is an ample supply of fresh water available.

5. Calm your dog with a reassuring goodbye and a stroke of your hand.

Pooch Rules & Regulations

BE A
RESPONSIBLE
DOG OWNER
AND OBEY
THE RULES.

- Clean up after your dog even if no one has seen him do his business.
- Leash your dog in areas that require leashing.
- Train your dog to be well behaved.
- Control your dog in public places so that he's not a nuisance to others.

Note: When leashes are required, they must be six feet or less in length. Leashes should be carried at all times. They are prudent safety measures .

FIDO FACT:

- *Problems with dogs in many recreation areas have increased in recent years. The few rules that apply to dogs are meant to assure that you and other visitors have enjoyable outdoor experiences.*

INTRODUCTION

Vacationing with your pet can be a fun-filled adventure. It doesn't require special training or expertise. Just a little planning and a little patience. This directory is filled with information to make traveling with your pet easier and more satisfying. From training tips to what to take along, to the do's and don'ts of travel, virtually all of your questions will be answered.

Vacationing with pets.

Not something I thought I'd ever do. But as the adage goes, necessity is the mother of invention. What began as a necessity turned into a lifestyle. A lifestyle that has improved every aspect of my vacation and travel time.

Although my family had dogs on and off during my childhood, it wasn't until my early thirties that I decided it was time to bring another dog into my life. And the lives of my young children. I wanted them to grow up with a dog; to know what it was like to have a canine companion, a playmate, a friend who would always be there, to love you, no questions asked. A four-legged pal who would be the first to lick a teary face or a bloody knee. Enter Samson, our family's first Golden Retriever.

Samson.

For nearly fifteen years, Sammy was everything a family could want from their dog. Loyal, forgiving, sweet, funny, neurotic, playful, sensitive, smart, too smart, puddle loving, fearless, strong and cuddly. He could melt your heart with a woebegone expression or make your hair stand on end with one of his pranks. Like the time he methodically opened the seam on a bean bag chair and then cheerfully spread the beans everywhere. Or when he followed a jogger and ended up in a shelter more than 20 miles from home.

As the years passed, Sam's face turned white and one by one our kids headed off to college. Preparing for the inevitable, my husband Harvey and I decided that when Sam died, no other dog would take his place. We wanted our freedom, not the responsibility of another dog.

Sammy left us one sunny June morning with so little fanfare that we couldn't believe he was actually gone. Little did we realize the void that would remain when our white-faced Golden Boy was no longer with us.

Life goes on...Rosie and Maxwell.

After planning a two-week vacation through California, with an ultimate destination of Lake Tahoe, Harvey and I had our hearts stolen by two Golden Retriever puppies, Rosie and Maxwell. Two little balls of fur that would help to fill the emptiness Sam's death had created. The puppies were ready to leave their mom and come home with us only weeks before our scheduled departure. What to do? Kennel them? Hire a pet sitter? Neither felt right.

Sooo...we took them along.

Oh, the fun we had. And the friends we made. Both the two-legged and four-legged variety. Having dogs on our trip made us more a part of the places we visited. We learned that dogs are natural conversation starters. Rosie and Maxwell were the prime movers in some lasting friendships we made during that first trip together. Now when we revisit Lake Tahoe, we have old friends to see as well as new ones to make. The locals we met made us feel at home, offering insider information on little known hikes, wonderful restaurants and quiet neighborhood parks. This knowledge enhanced our vacation and filled every day with wonder.

Since that first trip, our travels have taken us to many places. We've visited national forests, mountain resorts, seaside villages, island retreats, big cities and tiny hamlets. We've shared everything from luxury hotel rooms to rustic cabin getaways. We've experienced good times together and always come home with wonderful memories. I can't imagine travel that doesn't include our dogs.

When I watch Rosie and Maxwell frolic in a lake or when they accompany us on a hike, I stop and think of Sammy and remember the legacy of love and friendship he left behind. So for those of you who regularly take your pet along and those who would if you knew how, come share my travel knowledge. And happy trails and tails to you.

Is my pet vacation-friendly?

Most pets can be excellent traveling companions. It stands to reason that if you accustom your pet to travel at an early age, he will adapt more quickly. That doesn't mean that an older pet won't love vacationing with you. And it doesn't mean that the training period has to be a difficult one.

Even if your dog hasn't traveled with you in the past, chances are he'll make a wonderful companion. And chances are that this unique time will result in a closer relationship with your animal and fill your travels with memories to last a lifetime.

A socialized pooch is a sophisticated traveler.

Of course, every dog is different. And you know yours better than anyone. To be sure that he will travel like a pro, accustom him to different situations. Take him for long walks around your neighborhood. Let him accompany you while you do errands. If your chores include stair climbing or using an elevator, take him with you. The more exposure to people, places and things, the better. Make your wagger worldly. The sophistication will pay off in a better behaved, less frightened pet. It won't be long until he will happily share travel and vacation times with you.

Just ordinary dogs.

Rosie and Maxwell, my traveling companions, are not exceptional dogs to anyone but me. Their training was neither intensive nor professionally rendered. They were trained with kindness, praise, consistency and love. And not all of their training came about when they were puppies. I too had a lot to learn. And as I learned what I wanted of them, their training continued. It was a sharing and growing experience. Old dogs (and humans too) can learn new tricks. Rosie and Maxwell never fail to surprise me. Their ability to adapt to new situations has never stopped. So don't think you have to start with a puppy. Every dog, young and old, can be taught to be travel friendly.

Rosie and Maxwell know when I begin putting their things together that another holiday is about to begin. Their excitement mounts with every phase of preparation. They stick like glue - remaining at my side as I organize their belongings. By the time I've finished, they can barely contain their joy. Rosie grabs her leash and prances about the kitchen holding it in her mouth while Max sits on his haunches and howls. If they could talk, they'd tell you how much they enjoy traveling. But since they can't, trust this directory to lead you to a different kind of experience. One that's filled with lots of love and an opportunity for shared adventure. So with an open mind and an open heart, pack your bags and pack your pooch. Slip this handy book into your suitcase or the glove compartment of your car and let the fun begin.

WHAT ABOUT CATS?

When people learn about my book and the fact that I travel with my two Golden Retrievers, they often say, "well, you travel with dogs, but I have cats."

Well cat lovers, rejoice! You too can enjoy the companionship of your feline when you vacation or travel. Of course, not every cat is going to adapt to travel. That's a decision only you can make. But if you'd like to give it a try, the following should prove helpful.

A walk in the park!

Perhaps one of the biggest obstacles cat owners face when they think of taking their cats along is what to do with them; how to include a feline friend on something as simple as a walk in the park. Although you don't often see people walking cats, it's not because it can't be done. It can. According to my cat-loving friends, it's not that difficult and they maintain it's worth the effort; not to mention the novelty of the sight and the friendly encounters it can provoke.

One step at a time.

Walking your kitty is not something that can be hurried. Before you begin, you'll need a well-made, lightweight harness and leash. Don't even think of using a collar with just a piece of rope. Too tight and your cat will be uncomfortable and dread her walks. Too loose and she might squirm away. A properly fitted harness is a necessity. As a rule of thumb, if you can slip the width of two fingers between the harness and your cat's neck and between the harness and her belly, you've got a good fit.

Begin slowly…as you would with a baby. Once you buy the harness and leash, let her sniff it. Leave it next to her until she becomes accustomed to its sight and smell. When she appears relaxed, gently slip on the harness. Let her wear it. You'll know when she's feeling comfortable. At that point, attach the leash and again wait for her to feel at ease. Let her walk around with it, feel the weight trailing behind. During these times, remain with your cat to supervise her. You know her better than anyone. When you sense she's ready, pick up the leash and walk around the house. Take along a handful of treats. As you walk, talk reassuringly to her, stopping every so often to praise her efforts. Give her a treat to reinforce your pleasure. Let her know how happy you are with her progress. Continue this "practice walking" until you feel confident she's up to the next step…the great outdoors. Remember she is apt to feel ill at ease and somewhat vulnerable. She'll look to you for protection. Once you're outdoors, be alert to your surroundings. If you sense anything that might frighten your cat, scoop her up in your arms. Reinforce the sense of security that being with you provides.

Follow the leader.

Make your outings fun. Praise your feline and reward her with a treat as she follows your lead. Or if you prefer, let her choose the direction and pace of your walk. Or try a combination of both approaches.

Training kitty to walk can be the first step to more shared times and a closer relationship. Not only will you be getting exercise and fresh air, but you'll be spending unique, quality time together. And don't overlook the social benefits that having your cat with you can mean. You're bound to attract other cat lovers who share the same interests.

Once you make the decision to try, proceed slowly and be generous with praise. Patience, love and a treat or two can mean success as well as a new way of life for you and your furry friend.

CAT TRAVEL TIP #1:

Several weeks before your journey, have your cat examined by your vet. If shots are due, have them done early and avoid the possibility of side effects at the time of your trip. If your cat has a tendency to carsickness, ask your vet about sedatives.

CAT TRAVEL TIP #2:

Cats should always be confined to a kennel when in a car — for their safety and yours. Cats love to jump and perch and a kennel will eliminate the potential for accidents. Make your cat's kennel as comfortable as you can by including a small scratch post or a favorite toy. Put some soft bedding on the floor of the kennel as well. Shortly before you plan to leave on your vacation, fill your cat's home litter box with fresh litter. Generally this will prompt your cat to answer nature's call before your departure. You can then begin your trip knowing your cat has already voided.

CAT TRAVEL TIP #3:

If you have more than one cat and they're companionable, buy a larger carrier and let them share the accommodations. At home or on the road, it's comforting for friendly felines to curl up together. Being in the same crate also means that your cats can continue to groom one another, a sure antidote to anxiety.

TRAVEL TRAINING

A well-trained, well-behaved dog is easy to live with and especially easy to travel with. There are basics other than sit, down and stay which you might want to incorporate into your training routine. Whenever you begin a training session, remember that your patience and your dog's attention span are the key elements to success.

Training sessions should be 5-10 minutes each. Even if the results are initially disappointing, don't become discouraged. Stick with it. After just a few lessons, your canine will respond. Dogs love to learn, to feel productive and accomplished. Training isn't punishment. It's a gift. A gift of love. You'll quickly see the difference training can make in your animal. Most of all, keep a sense of humor. It's not punishment for you either.

Throughout this section, several references are made to puppies. But it's never too late for training to begin. The adage that you can't teach an old dog new tricks just isn't true. Patience and consistency combined with a reward system will provide excellent results.

Let's get social.

When it comes to travel training, not enough can be said about the benefits of socialization. The lessons of socialization are the foundation of a well-trained, well-behaved dog.

Socialize your dog at an early age. Allow your puppy to be handled by different people. Include men and children since puppies are inherently more fearful of both. When your puppy is three months old, join an obedience/ training class. These classes are important because they provide puppies with the experience of being with other dogs. Your puppy will have the opportunity of putting down other dogs without inflicting harm and he'll also learn how to bounce back after being put down himself. Socialization can continue with walks around your neighborhood, visits to parks frequented by other dogs and children and by working with friends who have dogs they want to socialize.

FIDO FACT:

- *Dog ownership is a common bond and the basis of impromptu conversations as well as lasting friendships.*

It's very natural for a puppy to pull at his leash. Instead of just pulling back, stop walking. Hold the leash to your chest. If your dog lets the leash slacken, say GOOD DOG. If he sits, say GOOD SIT. Then begin your walk again. Stop every ten feet or so and tell your dog to sit. Knowing he'll only be told to sit if he pulls, he'll eventually learn to pay attention to the next command. It makes sense to continue your training while on walks because your dog will learn to heed your commands under varying conditions. This will prove especially important when traveling together. Eliminating the "tug of war" factor can mean the difference between enjoying or disliking the company of your pooch at home or away.

Chewing.

Most dogs chew out of boredom. Eliminate destructive chewing by teaching your dog to chew on chew toys. An easy way to interest him in chewing is to stuff a hollow, nonconsumable chew toy with treats such as peanut butter, kibble or a piece of hard cheese. Once the toy is stuffed, attach a string to it and tempt your dog's interest by pulling the toy along. He'll take it from there.

Until you're satisfied that he won't be destructive, consider confining your pooch to one room or to his crate with a selection of chew toys. This is a particularly important training tool for dogs who must be left alone for long periods of time, and for dogs who travel with their owners. If your pooch knows not to chew destructively at home, those same good habits will remain with him on the road.

Bite inhibition.

The trick here is to keep a puppy from biting in the first place, not break the bad habit after it's formed, although that too can be accomplished. Your puppy should be taught to develop a soft mouth by inhibiting the force of his bites. As your dog grows into adolescence, he should continue to be taught to soften his bite and as an adult dog should learn never to mouth at all.

Allow your puppy to bite but whenever force is exhibited, say OUCH! If he continues to bite, say OUCH louder and then leave the room. When you return to the room, let the puppy come to you. Your pup will begin to associate the bite and OUCH with the cessation of playtime and will learn to mouth more softly. Even when your puppy's bites no longer hurt, pretend they do. Once this training is finished, you'll have a dog that will not mouth. A dog who will not accidentally injure people you meet during your travels.

Jumping dogs.

Dogs usually jump on people to get their attention. A fairly simple way to correct this habit is to teach your dog to sit and stay until released. When your dog is about to meet new people, put him in the sit/stay position. Be sure to praise your dog for obeying the command and then pet him to provide the attention he craves. Ask friends and visitors to help reinforce the command.

Come.

The secret to this command is to begin training at an early age. But older dogs can also learn. It might just take a little longer. From the time your pup's brought home, call him by name and say COME every time you're going to feed him. The association will be simple. He'll soon realize that goodies await if he responds to your call. Try another approach as well. During training sessions, call to your dog every few minutes. Reward him with praise and sometimes with a treat. And take advantage of normally occurring circumstances, such as your dog approaching you. Whenever you can anticipate that your dog is coming toward you, command COME as he nears you. Then reward him with praise for doing what came naturally.

NEVER order your dog to COME for punishment. If he's caught in the act of negative behavior, walk to him to reprimand.

Pay attention.

Train your dog to listen to you. For example, when your dog is at play in the yard, call him to you. When he comes, have him sit and praise him. Then release him to play again. Your dog will soon understand that obeying does not mean the end of playtime. Instead it means that he'll be petted and praised and then allowed to resume play.

Communication - talking to your dog.

Training isn't just about teaching your dog to sit or give his paw. Training is about teaching your pooch to become an integral part of your life. To fit into your daily routine and into your leisure time. Take notice of how your dog studies you, anticipates your next move. Incorporate his natural desire to please into your training. Let him know what you're thinking, how you're feeling. Talk to him as you go about your daily chores. He'll eventually recognize and understand changes in your voice, facial expressions, hand movements and body language. He'll know when you're happy or angry with him or with anyone else. If you want him to do something, get his attention and then speak to him. For example, if you want him to fetch his ball, ask him in an emphatic way, stressing the word ball. He won't understand at first, so fetch it yourself and tell him ball. Put the ball down and then repeat the command. This training method can be used in both play related activities and general obedience. It won't be long until you increase your dog's vocabulary and his understanding of numerous commands.

Training do's & don'ts.

- Never hit your dog.

- Praise and reward your dog for good behavior. Don't be embarrassed to lavish praise upon a dog who's earned it.

- Unless you catch your dog in a mischievous act, don't punish him. He will not understand what he did wrong. And when you do punish, go to your dog. Never use the command COME for punishment.

- Don't repeat a command. Dogs have excellent hearing. Say the command once in a firm voice. If he doesn't obey it's not because he hasn't heard you. Return to the training method for the disobeyed command.

- Don't be too eager or too reticent to punish. Most of all, be consistent.

- Don't encourage fearfulness. If your dog has a fear of people or places, work with him to overcome this fear rather than ignoring it, or believing it can't be changed.

- Don't ignore or encourage aggression.

- Don't use food excessively as a reward.

- Don't become discouraged if your initial attempts at training are unsuccessful. Try other approaches. Every dog can be trained.

CRATE TRAINING IS GREAT TRAINING

Many people erroneously equate the crate to jail. But that's only a human perspective. To a dog who's been properly crate trained, the crate represents a private place where your dog will feel safe and secure. It is much better to prevent behavioral problems by crate training than to give up on an unruly dog.

4 reasons why crate training is good for you.

1. You can relax when you leave your dog home alone. You'll know that he is safe, comfortable and incapable of destructive behavior.

2. You can housebreak your pooch faster. Confinement to a crate encourages control and helps establish a regular walk time routine.

3. You can safely confine your dog to prevent unforeseen situations. For example, if he's sick, if you have workers or guests that are either afraid of or allergic to dogs, or if your canine becomes easily excited or confused when new people enter the scene, the crate provides a reasonable method of containment.

4. You can travel with your pooch. Use of a crate in your automobile eliminates the potential for distraction. It also assures that your dog will not get loose during your trip.

FIDO FACT:

- *Want to register your puppy or locate a breeder? The American Kennel Club's customer service line is (919) 233-9767.*

5 reasons why crate training is good for your dog.

1. He'll have an area for rest when he's tired, stressed or sick.

2. He'll be exposed to fewer bad behavior temptations which can result in punishment.

3. He'll have an easier time learning to control calls of nature.

4. He'll feel more secure when left alone.

5. He'll be able to join you in your travels.

Some do's and don'ts.

- DO exercise your dog before and after crating.

- DO place the crate in a well-used, well-ventilated area of your home.

- DO make sure that you can always approach your dog while he is in his crate. This will insure that he does not become overly protective of his space.

- DON'T punish your dog in his crate or banish him to the crate.

- DON'T leave your pooch in the crate for more than four hours at a time.

- DON'T let curious kids invade his private place. This is his special area.

- DON'T confine your dog to a crate if he becomes frantic or completely miserable.

- DON'T use a crate without proper training.

10
Ways To Prevent Aggression in Your Dog

1. Socialize him at an early age.

2. Set rules and stick to them.

3. Under your supervision, expose him to children and other animals.

4. Never be abusive towards your dog by hitting or yelling at him.

5. Offer plenty of praise when he's behaving himself.

6. Be consistent with training. Make sure your dog responds to your commands before you do anything for him.

7. Don't handle your dog roughly or play aggressively with him.

8. Neuter your dog.

9. Contact your veterinarian to deal with persistent behavior problems.

10. Your dog is a member of the family. Treat him that way. Tied to a pole is not a life.

Take your dog's temperament into account.

- Is he a pleaser?
- Is he the playful sort?
- Does he love having tasks to perform?
- Does he like to retrieve? To carry?

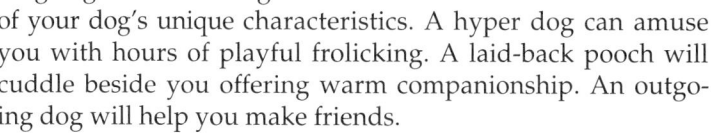

Dogs, like people, have distinct personalities... mellow, hyper, shy or outgoing. Take advantage of your dog's unique characteristics. A hyper dog can amuse you with hours of playful frolicking. A laid-back pooch will cuddle beside you offering warm companionship. An outgoing dog will help you make friends.

If you can combine what you know of your dog's personality with what you want to teach, your dog will train more easily. Together you will achieve a fulfilling compatibility.

<u>FIDO FACT:</u>

- *Staying at a hotel for a few days or more? Here's an easy way to identify your pet's temporary home. Staple one of the hotel's matchbook covers to your pet's collar. Be sure to remove the matches first.*

WHAT AND HOW TO PACK FOR YOUR POOCH

Be prepared.

Dogs enjoy the adventure of travel. If your dog is basically well behaved and physically fit, he should make an excellent traveling companion. But traveling times will be more successful with just a little common sense and preparation.

Just as many children (and adults I might add) travel with their own pillow, your pooch will also enjoy having his favorites with him. Perhaps you'll want to include the blanket he sleeps with or his favorite toy. Not only will a familiar item or toy make him feel more at ease, but it will keep him occupied as well.

I restock Max and Rosie's travel bags at the end of each trip. That way I'm always prepared for our next adventure. "My Pooch's Packing List" is found on page 41. Consider including some or all of the items that follow.

- A blanket to cover the back seat of your vehicle.
- Two or three old towels for emergencies.
- Two bowls, one for water, the other for food.
- Plastic clean-up bags (supermarket produce bags work well).
- Paper towels — for spills, clean-up and everything in between.
- A long line of rope. You'll be surprised how often you'll use this very handy item.
- An extra collar and lead.
- Can opener and spoon.
- Flashlight.
- An extra flea and tick collar.
- Dog brush.
- Small scissors.
- Blunt end tweezers — great for removing thorns and cactus needles.
- Chew toys, balls, frisbees, treats — whatever your pooch prefers.
- Nightlight.
- A room deodorizer.
- A handful of zip-lock bags in several sizes.
- Pre-moistened towelettes. Take along two packs. Put one in your suitcase, the other in the glove compartment of your car.
- Dog food, enough for a couple of days. Although most brands are available throughout the country, either at pet stores, supermarkets or veterinary offices, you'll want to pack enough and eliminate having to find dog food the first night or two of your vacation.
- Water — a full container from home. Top off as needed and gradually accustom your dog to his new water supply.

People packing made easy...12 tips.

No matter where your travels take you, whether it's to the local park or on a cross-country trip, never leave home without your dog's leash and a handful of plastic bags or pooper scooper. I clearly remember those awful moments when I ended up without one or both.

1. Consolidate. Even if you're traveling as a family, one tube of toothpaste and one hair dryer should suffice.

2. Avoid potential spills by wrapping perfume, shampoo and other liquids together and placing them in large zip-lock plastic bags.

3. When packing, layer your clothing using interlocking patterns. You'll fit more into your suitcase and have less shifting and wrinkling.

4. Write out your itinerary, including flight info, car rental confirmation numbers, travel agent telephone numbers and lodging info. Keep one copy with you and put a duplicate in a safe place.

5. Take along a night light, especially if you're traveling with a child. A flashlight always comes in handy too.

6. Stash a supply of zip-lock plastic bags, moist towelettes, trash bags, an extra leash (or rope) and a plastic container in an accessible place.

7. If you plan to hike with children, give each a whistle; they're great for signaling help.

8. Include a can opener and some plastic utensils.

9. Comfortable walking shoes are a must. If you plan on hiking, invest in a sturdy pair of hiking boots, but be sure to break them in before your trip. Take an extra pair of socks with you whenever you hike.

10. Don't forget to include first aid-kits. One for dogs and one for people.

11. Pack an extra pair of glasses or contact lenses.

12. Keep medications in separate, clearly marked containers.

MY POOCH'S PACKING LIST

1 _____   16 _____

2 _____   17 _____

3 _____   18 _____

4 _____   19 _____

5 _____   20 _____

6 _____   21 _____

7 _____   22 _____

8 _____   23 _____

9 _____   24 _____

10 _____   25 _____

11 _____   26 _____

12 _____   27 _____

13 _____   28 _____

14 _____   29 _____

15 _____   30 _____

TRAVEL BY CAR

"Kennel Up"...the magical, all-purpose command.

When Rosie's and Maxwell's training began, I used a metal kennel which they were taught to regard as their spot, their sleeping place. Whenever they were left at home and then again when they were put to bed at night, I used the simple command, "Kennel Up," as I pointed to and tapped their kennel. They quickly learned the command. As they outgrew the kennel, the laundry room became their "kennel up" place. As full-grown dogs, the entire kitchen became their "kennel up" area. Likewise, when they began accompanying me on trips, I reinforced the command each time I told them to jump into the car. They soon understood that being in their "kennel up" place meant that I expected them to behave, whether they were at home, in the car or in a hotel room. Teaching your dog the "kennel up" command will make travel times easier and more pleasurable.

Old dogs can learn new tricks.

When we first began vacationing with Rosie and Max, some friends decided to join us on a few of our local jaunts. Their dog Brandy, a ten year-old Cocker Spaniel, had never traveled with them. Other than trips to the vet and the groomer, she'd never been in the car. The question remained... would Brandy adjust? We needn't have worried. She took to the car immediately. Despite her small size, she quickly learned to jump in and out of the rear of the station wagon. She ran through the forests with Rosie and Max, playing and exploring as if she'd always had free run. To her owners and to Brandy, the world took on new meaning. Nature as seen through the eyes of their dog became a more exciting place of discovery.

Can my dog be trained to travel?

Dogs are quite adaptable and responsive and patience will definitely have its rewards. Your pooch loves nothing more than to be with you. If it means behaving to have that privilege, he'll respond.

Now that you've decided to travel and vacation with your dog, it's probably a good idea to get him started with short trips. Before you go anywhere, remember two of the most important items for happy dog travel, a leash for safety and the proper paraphernalia for clean-up. There's nothing more frustrating or scary than a loose, uncontrolled dog. And nothing more embarrassing than being without clean-up essentials when your dog unexpectedly decides to relieve himself.

Make traveling a pleasant experience. Stop every so often and do fun things. But when you do stop to let him out, leash him before you open the car doors. When the walk or playtime is over, remember the "Kennel Up" command when you tell your pooch to get into the car or into his kennel. And use lots of praise when he obeys.

You'll find that your dog will most likely be lulled to sleep by the motion of the car. Rosie and Maxwell fall asleep after less than fifteen minutes. I stop every few hours, give them water and let them "stretch their legs." They've become accustomed to these short stops and anticipate them. The moment the car is turned off and the hatch-back popped open, they anxiously await their leashes. When our romping time is over and we're back at the car, a simple "kennel up" gets them into their travel area.

To kennel or not to kennel.

Whether or not you use a kennel for car travel is a personal choice. Safety should be your primary concern. Yours and your dog's. Whatever method of travel you choose, be certain that your dog will not interfere with your driving. If you plan to use a kennel, line the bottom with an old blanket, towel or shredded newspaper and include a favorite toy. When you're vacationing by car and not using a kennel, consider a car harness.

If you're not going to use a kennel or harness, consider confining your dog to the back seat and commanding him to "kennel up." Protect your upholstery by covering the seat with an old blanket. This will make clean-up easier at the end of your trip. To keep my car fresh smelling and free from doggie odors, I stash a deodorizer under the front seat.

How often should I stop?

Many people think that when their dogs are in the car, they have to "go" more often. Not true. Whenever you stop for yourself, let your pooch have a drink and take a walk. It's not necessary to make extra stops along the way unless your dog has a physical problem and must be walked more often. Always pull your car out of the flow of traffic so you can safely care for your pooch. Never let your dog run free. Use a leash at all times.

Can my pet be left alone in the car?

Weather is the main factor to consider in this situation. Even if you think you'll only be gone a few minutes, that's all it takes for an animal to become dehydrated in warm weather. Even if all the windows are open, even if your car is parked in the shade, even when the outside temperature is only 85°, the temperature in a parked car can reach 100° to 120° in just minutes. Exposure to high temperatures, even for short periods, can cause your pet's body temperature to skyrocket.

NEVER LEAVE YOUR DOG UNATTENDED IN WARM WEATHER.

During the winter months, be aware of hypothermia, a life threatening condition when an animal's body temperature falls below normal. In particular, short-haired dogs and toys are very susceptible to illness in extremely cold weather.

What about carsickness?

Just like people, some dogs are queasier than others. And for some reason, puppies suffer more frequently from motion sickness. It's best to wait a couple of hours after your dog has eaten before beginning your trip. Or better yet, feed your dog after you arrive at your destination. Keep the windows open enough to allow in fresh air. If your pooch has a tendency to be carsick, sugar can help. Give your dog a tablespoon of  honey or a small piece of candy before beginning your trip (**NO CHOCOLATE**). That should help settle his stomach. If you notice that he still looks sickly, stop and allow him some additional fresh air or take him for a short walk. In time most dogs will outgrow carsickness.

What about identification if my dog runs off?

As far as identification, traveling time is no different than staying at home. Never allow your pooch to be anywhere without proper identification. ID tags should provide your dog's name, your name, address and phone number. Most states require dog owners to purchase a license every year. The tag usually includes a license number that is registered with your state. If you attach the license tag to your dog's collar and you become separated, your dog can be traced. There are also local organizations that help reunite lost pets and owners. The phone numbers of these organizations can be obtained from local police authorities.

Use the form on the following page to record your pooch's description so that the information will be handy should the need arise.

MY POOCH'S IDENTIFICATION

In the event that your dog is lost or stolen, the following information will help describe your pooch. Before leaving on your first trip, take a few minutes to fill out this form, make a duplicate, and then keep them separate but handy.

Answers to the name of: _____

Breed or mix: _____

Sex: _____ Age: _____ Tag ID#: _____

Description of hair (color, length and texture): _____

_____

Indicate unusual markings or scars: _____

_____

TAIL: ❏ Short ❏ Screw-type ❏ Bushy ❏ Cut

EARS: ❏ Clipped ❏ Erect ❏ Floppy

Weight: _____ Height: _____

If you have a recent photo of your pet, attach it here.

TRAVEL BY PLANE

Quick takes:

- Always travel on the same flight as your pet. Personally ascertain that your pet has been put on board before you board the plane.

- Book direct, nonstop flights.

- Upon boarding, inform a flight attendant that your pet is traveling in the cargo hold.

- Early morning or late evening flights are best in the summer, while afternoon flights are best in the winter.

- Fill the water tray of your pet's travel carrier with ice cubes rather than water. This will prevent spillage during loading.

- Clip your pet's nails to prevent them from hooking in the crate's door, holes or other openings.

Carriers/kennels.

Most airlines require pets to be in specific carriers. Airline regulations vary and arrangements should be made well in advance of travel. Some airlines allow small pets to accompany their owners in the passenger cabins. The carrier must fit under the seat and the pet must remain in the carrier for the duration of the flight. These regulations also vary and prior arrangements should be made.

Airlines run hot and cold on pet travel.

Many airlines won't allow pets to travel in the cargo hold if the departure or destination temperatures are over 80°. The same holds true if the weather is too cold. Check with the airlines to ascertain specific policies.

What about the size of the carrier?

Your pet should have enough room to stand, lie down, sit and turn around comfortably. Larger doesn't equate to more comfort. If anything, larger quarters only increase the chances of your pet being hurt because of too much movement. Just as your pet's favorite place is under your desk, a cozy, compact kennel will suit him much better than a spacious one.

Should anything else be in the carrier?

Cover the bottom with newspaper sheets and cover that with shredded newspaper. This will absorb accidents and provide a soft, warm cushion for your pet. Include a blanket or an old flannel shirt of yours; some article that will remind your pet of home and engender a feeling of security. You might want to include a hard rubber chew, but forget toys, they increase the risk of accidents.

How will my pet feel about a kennel?

Training and familiarization are the key elements in this area. If possible, buy the kennel (airlines and pet stores sell them) several weeks before your trip. Leave it in your home in the area where your animal spends most of his time. Let him become accustomed to its smell, feel and look. After a few days, your pet will become comfortable around the kennel. You might even try feeding him in the kennel to make it more like home. Keep all the associations friendly. Never use the kennel for punishment. Taking the time to accustom your pet to his traveling quarters will alleviate possible problems and make vacationing more fun.

What about identification?

The kennel should contain a tag identifying your pet and provide all pertinent information including the pet's name, age, feeding and water requirements, your name, address and phone number and your final destination. In addition, it should include the name and phone number of your pet's vet. A "luggage-type" ID card will function well. Use a waterproof marker. Securely fasten the ID tag to the kennel. Your pet should also wear his state ID tag. Should he somehow become separated from his kennel, the information will travel with him. Using a waterproof pen, mark the kennel "LIVE ANI-MAL" in large letters of at least an inch or more. Indicate which is the top and bottom with arrows and more large lettering of "THIS END UP."

How can I make plane travel comfortable for my pet?

If feasible make your travel plans for weekday rather than weekend travel. Travel during off hours. Direct and nonstop flights reduce the potential for problems and delays. Check with your airline to determine how much time they require for check in. Limiting the amount of time your pet will be in the hold section will make travel time that much more comfortable. Personally ascertain that your pet has been put on board your flight before you board the aircraft.

Will there automatically be room on board for my pet?

Not always. Airline space for pets is normally provided on a first-come, first-served basis. As soon as your travel plans are decided, contact the airline and confirm your arrangements.

What will pet travel cost?

Prices vary depending on whether your pet travels in the cabin or whether a kennel must be provided in the hold. Contact the airlines to determine pricing policies.

What about food and water?

It's best not to feed your pet at least six hours before departure; water two hours.

What about tranquilizers?

Opinions vary on the subject. Discuss this with your vet. But don't give your pet any medication not prescribed by a vet. And be aware that dosages for animals and humans are not the same.

What about after we land?

If your pooch has not flown in the passenger cabin with you, you will be able to pick him up in the baggage claim area. Since traveling in a kennel aboard a plane is an unusual experience, your dog may react strangely. Leash him before you let him out of the kennel to avoid mishaps. Once he's leashed, provide a cool drink of water and walk him ASAP. Cats should remain in their kennel until you arrive at your destination, but provide water upon landing.

Pets who shouldn't fly.

In general, very young puppies, females in heat, sickly, frail or pregnant pets should not be flown. In addition to the stress of flying, changes in altitude and cabin pressure might adversely effect your animal. Also, pug-nosed pets are definite "no flys" in the cargo section. These pets have short nasal passages and the noxious fumes in the cargo area can severely limit their supply of oxygen, leaving them highly susceptible to illness.

Health certificates - will I need one?

Although you may never be asked to present a health certificate, it's a good idea to have one with you. Your vet can supply a certificate listing the inoculations your pet has received, including rabies. Keep this information with your travel papers.

Airlines have specific regulations regarding animal flying rights. Make certain you know your pet's rights.

37
WAYS TO HAVE A BETTER VACATION WITH YOUR PET

Some tips and suggestions to increase your enjoyment when you and your pet hit the road.

1. Don't feed or water your animal just before starting on your trip. Feed and water your pet at least two hours before you plan to depart. Better still, if it's a short trip, wait until you arrive at your destination.

2. Exercise your dog before you leave. A tired pet will fall off to sleep more easily and adapt more readily to new surroundings.

3. Take a large container of water to avoid potential stomach upset. Your pet will do better drinking from his own water supply for the first few days. Having water along also means you can stop wherever you like and not worry about finding water. Gradually accustom your pet to the new water source by topping off the container with local water.

4. Plan stops along the way. Just like you, your animal will enjoy stretching his legs. As you travel, you'll find many areas conducive to a leisurely walk or a bit of playtime. If you make the car ride an agreeable part of the journey, your vacation will begin the moment you leave home - not just when you reach your ultimate destination.

5. While driving, keep windows open enough to allow the circulation of fresh air but not enough for your dog to jump out. If you have air conditioning, that will keep your pet cool enough.

6. Don't let your dog hang his head out of the window. Eyes, ears and throats can become inflamed.

7. Use a short leash when walking your pooch through public areas — he'll be easier to control.

8. Pack your pet's favorite toy or chew. If it entertains him at home, it'll entertain him on the road.

9. Before any trip, allow your pooch to relieve himself.

10. Cover your back seat with an old blanket or towel to protect the upholstery.

11. A room freshener under the seat of your car will keep it smelling fresh. Take an extra one for your room.

12. If your dog has a tendency to be carsick, keep a packet of honey in the glove compartment or carry a roll of hard candy like Lifesavers. Either remedy might help offset queasiness.

13. Use a flea and tick collar on your pet.

14. When traveling in warm weather months, drape a damp towel over your pet's crate. Adding moisture to the air will reduce the heat.

15. Before you begin a trip, expose your animal to experiences he will encounter while traveling; such as crowds, noise, people, elevators, walks along busy streets and stairs (especially those with open risers).

16. Shade moves. If you must leave your pet in the car for a short period of time, make sure the shade that protects him when you park will be there by the time you return. As a general rule though, it's best not to leave your pet in a parked car. <u>NEVER LEAVE YOUR PET IN THE CAR DURING THE WARM SUMMER MONTHS</u>. In the colder months, beware of hypothermia, a life threatening condition that occurs when an animal's body temperature falls below normal. Short-haired dogs and toys are very susceptible to illness in extremely cold weather.

17. Pack a clip-on minifan for airless hotel rooms.

18. When packing, include a heating pad, ice pack and a few safety pins.

19. A handful of clothespins will serve a dozen purposes, from clamping together motel curtains to sealing a bag of potato chips.

20. A night light will help you find the bathroom in the dark.

21. Don't forget that book you've been meaning to read.

22. Include a journal and record your travel memories.

23. Pack a roll of duct tape. Use it to repair shoes, patch suitcases or strap lunch onto the back of a rented bicycle.

24. Never begin a vacation with a new pair of shoes.

25. Pooper scoopers make clean-up simple and sanitary. Plastic vegetable bags from the supermarket are great too.

26. FYI, in drier climates, many lodging accommodations have room humidifiers available for guest use. Arrange for one when you make your reservation.

27. Use unbreakable bowls and storage containers for your pet's food and water.

28. Don't do anything on the road with your pet that you wouldn't do at home.

29. Brown and grey tinted sun lenses are the most effective for screening bright light. Polarized lenses reduce the blinding glare of the sun.

30. Before you leave on vacation, safeguard your home. Ask a neighbor to take in your mail and newspapers, or arrange with your mail carrier to hold your mail and stop newspaper delivery. Use timers so that a couple of lights go on and off. Unplug small appliances and electronics. Lock all doors and windows. Place steel bars or wooden dowels in the tracks of sliding glass doors and windows. Ladders or other objects that can be used to gain entry into your home should be stored in your garage or inside your home. Arrange to have your lawn mowed. And don't forget to take out the garbage.

31. Pack some snacks and drinks in a small cooler.

32. As a precaution when traveling, once you arrive at your final destination, check the yellow pages for the nearest vet and determine emergency hours and location.

33. It is unsafe for your dog to travel in the bed of a pickup truck. If you must use this means of transportation, there are safety straps available at auto supply stores that can offset the danger to your animal. Never use a choke chain, rope or leash around your dog's neck to secure him in the bed of a pickup.

34. Pack a spray bottle of water. A squirt in your dog's mouth will temporarily relieve his thirst.

35. Heavy duty zip-lock type bags make terrific traveling water bowls. Just roll down the edges to form a bowl and fill with water. They fold up into practically nothing. Keep one in your purse, jacket pocket or fanny pack and another in your glove compartment.

36. Arrange with housekeeping at your lodging choice to have your room cleaned either while you're in the room to supervise your pet or while you're out with your pet.

37. Traveling with children too? Keep them occupied with colored pencils and markers. Avoid crayons — they can melt in the sun. Question cards from trivia games as well as a pack of playing cards are handy amusements. Travel size magnetic games like checkers and chess are also good diversions. Don't forget those battery operated electronic games either. Include a book of crossword puzzles, a pair of dice and a favorite stuffed animal for cuddling time. In the car, games can include finding license plates from different states, spotting various makes or colors of cars, saying the alphabet backwards, or completing the alphabet from roadsigns.

29
TIPS FOR TRAVEL SAFETY

Whether you're just running errands at home or on a travel adventure, practice travel safety. A healthy dose of common sense can go a long way towards preventing you from becoming a statistic, no matter where you are.

1. When returning to your room late at night, use the main entrance of your hotel.

2. Don't leave your room key within sight in public areas, particularly if it's numbered instead of coded.

3. Store valuables in your room safe or in a safety-deposit box at the front desk.

4. Don't carry large amounts of cash, use traveler's checks and credit cards instead.

5. Avoid flaunting expensive watches and jewelry.

6. When visiting a public attraction like a museum or amusement park, decide where to meet should you become separated from your traveling companions.

7. Use a fanny pack and not a purse when touring.

8. Make use of the locks provided in your room. In addition to your room door, be certain all sliding glass doors, windows and connecting doors are locked.

9. If someone comes to your room, the American Hotel and Motel Association advises guests to ascertain the identity of the caller before opening the door. If you haven't arranged for room service or requested a delivery, call the front desk and determine if someone has been sent to your room before opening the door.

10. Carry your money (or preferably traveler's checks) separately from credit cards.

11. Use your business address on luggage tags, not your home address.

12. Be alert in parking lots and underground garages.

13. Check the back seat of your car before getting inside.

14. In your car, always buckle up. Seatbelts save lives.

15. Keep car doors locked.

16. When you stop at traffic lights, leave enough room (one car length) between your vehicle and the one in front so you can quickly pull away.

17. AAA recommends that if you're hit from behind by another vehicle, motion the other driver to a public place before getting out of your car.

18. When driving at night, stay on main roads.

19. Fill your tank during daylight hours. If you must fill up at night, do so at a busy, well-lit service station.

20. If your vehicle breaks down, tie a white cloth to the antenna or the raised hood of your car to signal other motorists. Turn on your hazard lights. Remain in your locked car until police or road service arrive.

21. Don't pull over for flashing headlights. Police cars have red or blue lights.

22. Lock video cameras, car phones and other expensive equipment in your trunk. Don't leave them in sight.

23. Have car keys ready as you approach your car.

24. At an airport, allow only uniformed airport personnel to carry your bags or carry them yourself. Refuse offers of transportation from strangers. Use the airport's ground transportation center or a uniformed taxi dispatcher.

25. Walk purposefully.

26. When using an ATM, choose one in a well-lit area with heavy foot traffic. Look for machines inside establishments - they're the safest.

27. Avoid poorly lit areas, shrubbery or dark doorways.

28. When ordering food from an outside source, have it delivered to the front desk rather than to your room.

29. Trust your instincts. If a situation doesn't feel right - it probably isn't.

11
WAYS TO TAKE THE STRESS OUT OF VACATIONS

Vacations are intended to be restful occasions but sometimes the preparations involved in "getting away from it all" can prove stressful. The tips on the following page are proven stress reducers to help you cope before, during and after your trip.

1. Awaken fifteen minutes earlier each day for a couple of weeks before your trip and use that extra time to plan your day and do vacation chores.

2. Write down errands to be done. Don't rely on your memory. The anticipation of forgetting something important can be stressful.

3. Don't procrastinate. Whatever has to be done tomorrow, do today. Whatever needs doing today, do now.

4. Take stock of your car. Get car repairs done. Have your car washed, your journey will be more pleasant in a clean car. Fill up with gas the day before your departure and check your tires and oil gauge. Summertime travel, check your air conditioning. In the winter, be certain your heater and defroster work. Make sure wiper blades are also in good working condition.

5. Learn to be more flexible. Not everything has to be perfect. Compromise, you'll have a happier life.

6. If you have an unpleasant task to do, take care of it early in the day.

7. Ask for help. Delegating responsibility relieves pressure and stress. It also makes others feel productive and needed.

8. Accept that we are all part of this imperfect world. An ounce of forgiveness will take you far.

9. Don't assume responsibility for more tasks than you can readily accomplish.

10. Think positive thoughts and eliminate negativism, like, "I'm too fat, I'm too old, I'm not smart enough."

11. Take 5-10 minutes to stretch before you begin your day or before bedtime. Breathe deeply and slowly, clearing your mind as you do.

27
ON-THE-ROAD TIPS

1. Keep your pet confined with either a crate, barrier or harness.

2. To avoid sliding in the event of sharp turns or sudden stops, be certain that your luggage, as well as your pet's crate are securely stored or fastened.

3. Ascertain that your vehicle is in good working order. Check brakelights, turn signals, hazard and headlights. Clean the windshield and top off washer fluid whenever you fill up. Since you'll be driving in unfamiliar territory, so keep an eye on the gas gauge. Fill up during daylight hours or at well-lit service stations.

4. When packing, include a flashlight, tool kit, paper towels, an extra leash, waterproof matches, a first-aid kit, blanket and a supply of plastic bags. During the winter months, keep an ice scraper, snow brush and small shovel in your trunk.

5. Never drive tired. Keep the music on and the windows open. Fresh air can help you remain alert.

6. Keep your windshield clean, inside and out.

7. Avoid using sedatives or tranquilizers when driving.

8. Don't drink and drive.

9. Never drive and read a map at the same time. If you're driving alone, pull off at a well-lit gas station or roadside restaurant and check the map. If you're unsure of directions, ask for assistance from a safe source.

10. Wear your seatbelt, they save lives.

11. Keep car doors locked.

12. Good posture is especially important when driving. Do your back a favor and sit up straight. For lower back pain, wedge a small pillow between your back and the seat.

13. If you're the driver, eat frequent small snacks rather than large meals. You'll be less tired that way.

14. Don't use high beams in fog. The light will bounce back into your eyes as it reflects off the moisture.

15. When pulling off to the side of the road, use your flashers to warn away other cars.

16. Before beginning your drive each day, do a car check. Tire pressure okay? Leakage under car? Windows clean? Signals working? Mirrors properly adjusted? Gas tank full?

17. Roads can become particularly slippery at the onset of rain, the result of water mixing with dust and oil on the pavement. Slow down and exercise caution in wet weather.

18. Every so often, turn off your cruise control. Overuse can lull you into inattention.

19. If you'll be doing a lot of driving into the sun, put a towel over the dashboard. It will provide some relief from the heat and brightness.

20. Even during the cooler months, your car can become stuffy. Keep the windows or sun roof open and let fresh air circulate.

21. Kids coming along? A small tape or CD player can amuse youngsters. Hand-held video games are also entertaining. And action figures are a good source for imaginary games. Put together a travel container and include markers or colored pencils, stamps, stickers, blunt safety scissors, and some pads of paper, both colored and lined.

22. If your car trip requires an overnight stay on route to your destination, pack a change of clothing and other necessities in a separate bag. Keep it in an accessible location.

23. When visiting wet and/or humid climates, take along insect repellent.

24. Guard against temperature extremes. Protect your skin from the effects of the sun. Hazy days are just as dangerous to your skin as sunny ones. Pack plenty of sunscreen. Apply in the morning and then again in the early afternoon. The sun is strongest midday so avoid overexposure at that time. To remain comfortable in warm weather, wear lightweight, loose fitting cotton clothing. Choose light colors, dark ones attract the sun. In dry climates, remember to drink lots of liquids. Because the evaporation process speeds up in arid areas, you won't be aware of how much you're perspiring.

25. In cold climes, protect yourself from frostbite. If the temperature falls below 32° fahrenheit and the wind chill factor is also low, frostbite can occur in a matter of minutes. Layer your clothing. Cotton next to your skin and wool over that is the best insulator. Wear a hat to keep warm - body heat escapes very quickly through your head.

26. Changes in altitude can cause altitude sickness. Whenever possible, slowly accustom yourself to an altitude change. Don't overexert yourself either. Symptoms of high altitude sickness occur more frequently over 8,000 feet and include dizziness, shortness of breath and headaches.

27. Store your maps, itinerary and related travel information in a clear plastic container (shoe box storage type with a lid works best). Keep it in the front of your vehicle in an easy-to-reach location.

FIDO FACT:

• *If your pooch is becoming too aggressive or is misbehaving, try startling him. Dogs dislike loud, grating noises. Load an empty soda can with pebbles or coins and keep it handy. When your pooch starts to act up, a firm "No" and a vigorous shaking of the can should prove to be an excellent deterrent to bad behavior. Be firm but not terrifying. And remember, corrective training must be administered immediately following the offending act.*

WHAT YOU SHOULD KNOW ABOUT DRIVING IN THE DESERT

Water: Check your radiator before journeying into the desert. Other than metropolitan areas, service stations are few and far between, even on major roads. Always carry extra water.

Gasoline: Since you'll be traveling through sparsely populated areas, fill up before beginning any desert adventure. When your vehicle has half a tank or less, refuel at the first service station.

Flash floods: Summer thunderstorms in the desert can wreak havoc, especially where roads dip into washes. The runoff quickly fills the washes, creating hazardous driving conditions and impassable roads. Heed the warning signs which pinpoint flash flood areas.

Dust storms: When a dust storm approaches, pull your vehicle off the road as far as possible, switch off your headlights and wait until the storm passes.

Breakdowns: Use your hazard lights or raise the hood. Remain in your vehicle until help arrives. Keep doors locked and do not open doors except for police officers. If you break down on a secluded back road and must seek help, retrace your route. Don't take any short cuts.

FIDO FACT:

- *Never leave your dog unattended in the car during very warm or very cold weather.*

Desert survival.

Anyone can end up lost or stranded in the desert. All it takes is a flat tire or a wrong turn and suddenly you're faced with a dire situation which requires survival skills. Remain calm. Think through your options. Use common sense and keep focused. Survivalists recommend that you stay with your vehicle. Do not attempt to walk through the desert. Dehydration, exposure and exhaustion are killers.

Prepare yourself before traveling into a desert environment by considering the following:

- Plan your excursion and familiarize yourself with the area.
- Know where water sources exist.
- Determine local weather conditions and forecasts before hand.
- If you're hiking, carry a topographical map of the area and avoid the intense desert heat with an early morning outing.
- Never overestimate your hiking abilities - know your limits.
- Don't take sidetrips, they may cause you to lose your bearings.
- Carry as much drinking water as possible, it can save your life.
- If you're planning an overnight, establish camp near water.
- Inform a third party of your plans and when you'll be home. Contact that person upon your return.

Heat Stroke / Exhaustion.

Early heat exhaustion indicators include weakness, pale skin, dizziness, nausea, dehydration, muscle cramping and profuse sweating. Heat stroke symptoms include the preceding as well as hot, dry, red skin. In either case, seek shade, cool off by fanning yourself and apply damp cloths to face, neck and ears. Cases of heat stroke demand immediate medical attention.

Hypothermia.

Although hypothermia is a serious medical condition most commonly associated with mountain hiking, desert hikers and campers are also susceptible. Temperatures do not have to dip below freezing for exposure to occur. In fact, hypothermia strikes most often in the 30-50° temperature range - a common temperature for winter nights in the desert. Damp clothing and a cool breeze can sometimes be enough to cause the body to lose heat faster than it can be replaced - causing cold shivers. If you experience unstoppable shivering, it's imperative that you put on dry clothes, wrap yourself in a blanket and drink hot liquids. Without these precautions, you can lapse into the second, and sometimes fatal stage of hypothermia. When that occurs, there is little chance of the body rewarming itself without the aid of conventional heating methods and immediate medical attention.

Keep your cool.

- When traveling with your animal, it's a good idea to keep a cooler of cold towels in the car. Cold towels can help to bring down a dog's body temperature after a long afternoon of hiking.

- A wet bandana wrapped around your neck, and another around your dog's neck, can keep you both comfortably cool while hiking.

FIRST-AID EMERGENCY TREATMENT

Having a bit of the Girl Scout in me, I like being prepared. Over the years, I've accumulated information regarding animal emergency treatment. Although I've had only one occasion to use this information, once was enough. I'd like to share my knowledge with you.

Whether you're the stay-at-home type who rarely travels with your pet, or a gadabout who can't sit still, every pet owner should know these simple, but potentially lifesaving procedures.

The following are only guidelines to assist you during emergencies. Whenever possible, seek treatment from a vet if your animal becomes injured and you are unprepared to administer first aid.

Allergies: One in five pets suffers from some form of allergy. Sneezing and watery eyes can be an allergic reaction caused by pollen and smoke. Inflamed skin can indicate a sensitivity to grass or to chemicals used in carpet cleaning. See your vet.

Bites and stings: Use ice to reduce swelling. If your animal has been stung in the mouth, immediately take him to the vet. Swelling can close the throat. If your pet experiences an allergic reaction, an antihistamine may be needed. For fast relief from a wasp or bee sting, dab the spot with plain vinegar and then apply baking soda. If you're in the middle of nowhere, a small mud pie plastered over the sting will provide relief. Snake bites, seek veterinary attention ASAP.

Bleeding: If the cut is small, use tweezers to remove hair from the wound. Gently wash with soap and water and then bandage (not too tightly). Severe bleeding, apply direct pressure and seek medical attention ASAP.

Burns: <u>First degree burns:</u> Use an ice cube or apply ice water until the pain is alleviated. Then apply vitamin E, swab with honey or cover with a freshly brewed teabag.

<u>Minor burns:</u> Use antibiotic ointment.

<u>Acid:</u> Apply dampened baking soda.

<u>Scalds:</u> Douse with cold water. After treatment, bandage all burns for protection.

Earache: A drop of warm eucalyptus oil in your pet's ear can help relieve the pain.

Eye scratches or inflammation: Make a solution of boric acid and bathe eyes with soft cotton.

Falls or impact injuries: Limping, pain, grey gums or prostration need immediate veterinary attention. The cause could be a fracture or internal bleeding.

Fleas: Patches of hair loss, itching and redness are common signs of fleas, particularly during warm months. Use a flea bath and a flea collar to eliminate and prevent infestation. Ask your vet about new oral medication now available for flea control.

Heatstroke: Signs include lying prone, rapid or difficult breathing and heartbeat, rolling eyes, panting, high fever, a staggering gait. Quick response is essential. Move your animal into the shade. Generously douse with cold water or if possible, partially fill a tub with cold water and immerse your pet. Remain with him and check his temperature. Normal for dogs and cats: 100°-102°. Don't let your pet's temperature drop below that.

Prevent common heatstroke by limiting outdoor exercise in hot or humid weather and providing plenty of fresh, cool water and access to shade. Never leave your pet in a car on a warm day, even for "just a few minutes."

Heartworm: Mosquitos can be more than pests when it comes to the health of your dog. They are the carriers of heartworm disease, which can be life threatening to your furry friend. There is no vaccine. However, daily or monthly pills can protect your pet from infection. In areas with high mosquito populations, use a heartworm preventative. Contact your local veterinarian about testing and medication. In the case of heartworm, "an ounce of prevention equals a pound of cure."

Poisons: Gasoline products, antifreeze, disinfectants, and insecticides are all poisonous. Keep these products tightly closed and out of reach. Vomiting, trembling and convulsions can be symptoms of poisoning. If your pet suffers from any of these symptoms, get veterinary attention. (See listings on Poison Control Centers in section "Everything You Want to Know About Pet Care...")

Poison ivy: Poison ivy or oak on your pet's coat will not bother him. But the poison can be passed on to you. If you believe your pet has come in contact with poison ivy or oak, use rubber gloves before handling your animal. Rinse him in salt water, then follow with a clear water rinse. Shampoo and rinse again.

Shock: Shock can occur after an accident or severe fright. Your animal might experience shallow breathing, pale gums, nervousness or prostration. Keep him still, quiet and warm and have someone drive you to a vet.

FIDO FACT:

• *Got a fussy eater?*

Although missing a meal isn't unhealthy, you don't want meal times to become problem times. Never beg your dog to eat. Put the food down and leave the area. If the food hasn't been eaten in an hour, pick it up and save it for the next feeding. Your dog will eventually get the message. And no table scraps, they only encourage bad eating habits.

Skunks: The following might help you avoid a smelly encounter.

1. Don't try to scare the skunk away. Your actions might provoke a spray.

2. Keep your dog quiet. Skunks have an unforgettable way of displaying their dislike of barking.

3. Begin an immediate retreat.

If you still end up in a stinky situation, try this home remedy.

1. The recipe consists of three common household items which are probably in most homes.

The ingredients for a 40-50 pound dog are:

1 qt. 3% hydrogen peroxide
1/4 cup baking soda
1 tsp. liquid soap

2. Wet the dog down with a hose. Mix all the ingredients in a container and slowly pour the mixture over the dog while rubbing it into the fur.

3. After the solution bath, rinse dog with the hose. The dog should be odor free.

4. The ingredients are not dangerous but take care to keep the solution out of dog's eyes, ears and mouth.

Remember that hydrogen peroxide may bleach clothing and hair.

Snake bites: Immobilization and prompt medical attention are the key elements in handling a poisonous snake bite. Immediate veterinary care (within 2 hours) is essential to recovery. If the bite occurs in a remote area, immediately immobilize the bitten area and carry your pet to the vehicle. Don't allow your pet to walk, the venom will spread more quickly. Most snake bites will be to the head or neck area, particularly the nose. The second most common place will be a pet's front leg.

Severe swelling within 30 to 60 minutes of the bite is the first indication that your pet is suffering from a venomous snake bite. Excessive pain and slow, steady bleeding are other indicators. Hemotoxins in the venom of certain snakes prevent blood from clotting. If your pet goes into shock or stops breathing, begin CPR. Cardiopulmonary resuscitation for pets is the same as for humans. Push on your pet's chest to compress his heart and force blood to the brain. Then hold his mouth closed and breathe into his nose.

When treating a snake bite:

- DO NOT apply ice to the bite - venom constricts the blood vessels and ice only compounds the constriction.

- DO NOT use a tourniquet - the body's natural immune system fights off the venom. By cutting off the blood flow, you'll either minimize or completely eliminate the body's natural defenses.

- DO NOT try to clean the bite or administer medication.

Ticks: Use lighter fluid (or other alcohol) and loosen by soaking. Then gently tweeze out. Make sure you get the tick's head.

Winter woes: Rock salt and other commercial chemicals used to melt ice can be very harmful to your animal. Not only can they burn your pet's pads, but ingestion by licking can result in poisoning or dehydration. Upon returning from a walk through snow or ice, wash your pet's feet with a mild soap and then rinse. Before an outdoor excursion, spray your pet's paws with cooking oil to deter adherence.

FITNESS FOR FIDO

A daily dose of exercise is as important for the pooch's health as it is for yours. A 15-30 minute walk twice daily is a perfect way to build muscles and stamina and get you and the dogster in shape for more aerobic workouts. In the summertime, beat the heat by walking in the early hours of the morning or after sundown. Keep in mind that dogs don't sweat, so if you notice your pooch panting excessively or lagging behind, stop in a cool shaded area for a water break.

If your dog is overweight or still a puppy, consult with your vet to determine an appropriate exercise program. Overweight canines may have other health problems which must be considered. Young dogs are still developing their bone structure and may not be ready for a rigorous program.

FIDO FACT:

- *Fido's fitness counts towards insuring a longer, healthier life. The most common cause of ill health in canines is obesity. About 60% of all adult dogs are or will become overweight due to lack of physical activity and overfeeding.*

MASSAGE, PETTING WITH A PURPOSE

Treat your dog to some special quality time. Give him the attention he craves while also doing something healthful for him. The simple procedures that follow require only 10 to 15 minutes of your time.

1. Gently stroke your animal's head.
2. Caress around his ears in a circular fashion.
3. Rub down both his neck and shoulders, first on one side of the spine, and then the other, continuing down to the rump.
4. Turn your dog over and gently knead his abdominal area.
5. Rub his legs.
6. Caress the area between his paw pads.

After the massage, offer your pooch plenty of fresh, cool water which will flush out the toxins released from the muscles.

Massages are also therapeutic for dogs recovering from surgery and/or suffering from hip dysplasia, circulatory disorders, sprains, chronic illness and old age. Timid and hyperactive pooches can benefit as well.

FIDO FACT:

- *Is your pooch pudgy? Place both thumbs on your dog's backbone and then run your fingers along his rib cage. If the bony part of each rib cannot be easily felt, your dog may be overweight. Another quickie test - stand directly over your dog while he's standing. If you can't see a clearly defined waist behind his rib cage, he's probably too portly.*

STEPS TO BETTER GROOMING

Grooming is another way of saying "I love you" to your pooch. As pack animals, dogs love grooming rituals. Make grooming time an extension of your caring relationship. Other than some breeds which require professional grooming, most canines can be kept well-groomed in about 10 minutes a day.

1. Designate a grooming place, preferably one that is not on the floor. If possible, use a grooming table. Your dog will learn to remain still and you won't trade a well-groomed pooch for an aching back.

2. End every grooming session with a small treat. When your dog understands that grooming ends with a goodie, he'll behave better.

3. Brush out your dog's coat before washing. Wetting a matted coat only tightens the tangles and makes removal more difficult.

4. Using a soft tissue, wipe around your dog's eyes daily, especially if his eyes tend to be teary.

5. When bathing a long-haired dog, squeeze the coat, don't rub. Rubbing can result in snarls.

6. To gently clean your dog's teeth, slip your hand into a soft sock and go over each tooth.

FIDO FACT:
- ***Stroke a dog instead of patting it. Stroking is soothing. Patting can make a dog nervous.***

Grooming tips...sticky problems

Chewing gum: There are two methods you can try. Ice the gum for a minimum of ten minutes to make it more manageable and easier to remove. Or use peanut butter. Apply and let the oil in the peanut butter loosen the gum from the hair shaft. Leave on about 20 minutes before working out the gum.

Tar: This is a tough one. Try soaking the tarred area in vegetable or baby oil. Leave on for an hour or more and then bathe your dog. The oil should cause the tar to slide off the hair shaft. Since this method can be messy, shampoo your dog with Dawn dishwashing soap to remove the oil. Follow with pet shampoo to restore the pH balance.

Oil: Apply baby powder or cornstarch to the oily area. Leave on 20 minutes. Shampoo with warm water and Dawn. Follow with pet shampoo to restore the pH balance.

Burrs:

1. Burrs in your dog's coat may be easier to remove if you first crush the burrs with pliers.

2. Slip a kitchen fork under the burr to remove.

3. Soften the burrs with vegetable or baby oil before working them out.

Keep cleaning sessions as short as possible. Your dog will not want to sit for hours. If your dog's skin is sensitive, you might want to simply remove the offending matter with a scissors. If you don't feel competent to do the removal yourself, contact a grooming service in your area and have them do the job for you.

FIDO FACT:
- ***Inflamed skin can indicate a sensitivity to grass or chemicals used in carpet cleaning. Patches of hair loss, itching and redness are common signs of fleas, particularly during warm months.***

12

TIPS ON MOVING WITH YOUR PET

Every year, one out of five Americans will move. Of those, nearly half will be moving with their pets. If you're part of the "pet half", be aware that your pet can experience the same anxiety as you. The following tips can make moving less stressful for you and your animal.

1. Although moving companies provide information on how to move your pet, they are not permitted to transport animals. Plan to do so on your own.

2. Begin with a visit to your vet. Your vet can provide a copy of your pet's medical records and possibly recommend a vet in the city where you'll be moving.

3. If you'll be traveling by plane, contact the airlines ASAP. Many airlines offer in-cabin boarding for small pets but only on a first-come, first-served basis. The earlier you make your reservations, the better chance you'll have of securing space.

4. If you'll be driving to your new home, *Vacationing With Your Pet* will assist you with your lodging reservations. By planning ahead, your move will proceed more smoothly .

5. Buy a special toy or a favorite chew that's only given to your pet when you're busy packing.

6. Don't feed or water your animal for several hours before your departure. The motion of the ride might cause stomach upset.

7. Keep your pet kenneled up on moving day to avoid disasters. Never allow your pet to run free when you're in unfamiliar territory.

8. Pack your pet's dishes, food, water, treats, toys, leash and bedding in an easy-to-reach location. Take water and food from home. Drinking unfamiliar water or eating a different brand of food can cause digestion problems. And don't forget those plastic bags for clean-up.

9. Once you're moved in and unpacked, be patient. Your animal may misbehave. Like a child, he may resent change and begin acting up. Deal with problems in a gentle and reassuring manner. Spend some extra time with your pet during this upheaval period and understand that it will pass.

10. If your pet requires medication or prescription diet, pack plenty for your journey and keep a copy of your pet's medical records with you.

11. Always carry your current veterinarian's phone number. You never know when an emergency may arise or when your new veterinarian will need additional health information

12. Learn as much as you can about your new area, including common diseases, local laws and required vaccinations.

10
REASONS WHY PETS
ARE GOOD FOR YOUR HEALTH

Adding a pet to your household can improve your health and that of your family. In particular, pets seem to help the very young and seniors. The following is based on various studies.

1. People over 40 who own pets have lower blood pressure. 20% have lower triglyceride levels. Talking to pets has been shown to lower blood pressure as well.

2. People who own pets see their doctor less than those who don't.

3. Pets have been shown to reduce depression, particularly in seniors.

4. It's easier to make friends when you have a pet. Life is more social with them.

5. It's healthier too. Seniors with pets are generally more active because they walk more.

6. Pets are friends. Here again, seniors seem to benefit most.

7. Pets can help older people deal with the loss of a spouse. Seniors are less likely to experience the deterioration in health that often follows the stressful loss of a mate.

8. Pets ease loneliness.

9. Perhaps because of the responsibility of pet ownership, seniors take better care of themselves.

10. Pets provide a sense of security to people of all ages.

FIDO FACTS

The following facts, tidbits and data will enhance your knowledge of our canine companions.

- Gain the confidence of a worried dog by avoiding direct eye contact or by turning away, exposing your back or side to the dog.

- When dogs first meet, it's uncommon for them to approach each other head on. Most will approach in curving lines. They'll walk beyond each other's noses sniffing at rear ends while standing side by side.

- Dog ownership is a common bond and the basis of impromptu conversations as well as lasting friendships.

- Chemical salt makes sidewalks less slippery but can be harmful to your dog's footpads. Wash your dog's paws after walks to remove salt. Don't let him lick the salt either, it's poisonous.

- Vets warn that removing tar with over-the-counter petroleum products can be highly toxic.

- Although a dog's vision is better than humans in the dark, bright red and green are the easiest colors for them to see.

- Puppies are born blind. Their eyes open and they begin to see at 10 to 14 days.

- The best time to separate a pup from his mother is seven to ten weeks after birth.

- It's a sign of submission when a dog's ears are held back close to his head.

- Hot pavement can damage your dog's sensitive footpads. In the summer months, walk your pooch in the morning or evening or on grassy areas and other cool surfaces.

- Never leave your dog unattended in the car during the warm weather months or extremely cold ones.

- Always walk your dog on a leash on hotel/motel grounds.

- Want to register your puppy, or locate a breeder in your area? The American Kennel Club has a new customer service line at (919) 233-9767. Their interactive voice processing telephone system is open twenty-four hours a day, seven days a week. Information is available on dog and litter registrations. You can also use the number to order registration materials, certified pedigrees, books and videos. If you want to speak with a customer service rep, call during business hours.

- Stroke a dog instead of patting it. Stroking is soothing. Patting can make some dogs nervous.

- If your dog is lonely for you when he's left alone, try leaving your voice on a tape and let it play during your absence.

- When a dog licks you with a straight tongue, he's saying "I Love You."

- Don't do anything on the road with your dog that you wouldn't do at home.

- Never put your dog in the bed of a pickup truck as a means of transportation.

- Black dogs and dark colored ones are more susceptible to the heat.

- When traveling, take a spray bottle of water with you. A squirt in your dog's mouth will temporarily relieve his thirst.

- Changing your dog's water supply too quickly can cause stomach upset. Take along a container of water from home and replenish with local water, providing a gradual change.

- One in five dogs suffers from some form of allergy. Sneezing and watery eyes can be an allergic reaction caused by pollen or smoke.

- Inflamed skin can indicate a sensitivity to grass or chemicals used in carpet cleaning.

- Patches of hair loss, itching and redness are common signs of fleas, particularly during warm months.

- Normal temperature for dogs: 100° to 102°.

- No matter how much your dog begs, do not overfeed him.

- Housebreaking problems can sometimes be attributed to diet. Consult with your vet about one good dog food and be consistent in feeding. A change in your dog's diet can lead to digestive problems.

- Spay/neuter your dog to prevent health problems and illnesses that plague the intact animal. Contrary to popular belief, spaying/neutering your canine will not result in weight gain. Only overfeeding and lack of exercise can do that.

- Spend ample quality time with your canine every day. Satisfy his need for social contact.

- Obedience train your dog; it's good for his mental well being and yours.

- If you make training fun, your dog will learn faster.

- Always provide cool fresh drinking water for your dog.

- If your pooch lives outdoors, make sure he has easy access to shade and plenty of water.

- If your pooch lives indoors, he'll need access to cool moving air and ample fresh water.

- In the summertime, avoid exercising your dog during the hottest parts of the day.

- Never tie your dog or let him run free while he's wearing a choke collar. Choke collars can easily hook on something and strangle him.

- The Chinese Shar-Pei and the Chow have blue-black tongues instead of pink ones.

- The smallest breed of dog is the Chihuahua.

- Poodles, Bedlington Terriers, Bichon Frises, Schnauzers and Soft-Coated Wheaten Terriers don't shed.

- Terriers and toy breeds usually bark the most.

- The Basenji is often called the barkless dog.

- Labs and Golden Retrievers are fast learners, making them easy to train.

- Climate counts when deciding on a breed. Collies and Pugs will be unhappy in hot, humid climates. But the Italian Greyhound and Chihuahua originated in hot climes. The heat won't bother them, but winter will. They'll need insulation in the form of dog apparel to protect them from the cold. And as you might think, heavy-coated dogs like the Saint Bernard, Siberian Husky and the Newfy thrive in cooler weather.

- Apartment dwellers, consider the Dachshund and Cairn Terrier. Both can be content in small quarters.

- Fido's fitness counts towards insuring a longer, healthier life. In this arena, you're the one in control. The most common cause of ill health in canines is obesity. Approximately 60% of all adult dogs are overweight or will become overweight due to lack of physical activity and overfeeding. Much like humans, the medical consequences of obesity include liver, heart and orthopedic problems. As little as a few extra pounds on a small dog can lead to health-related complications.

- Is your pooch pudgy? Place both thumbs on your dog's backbone and then run your fingers along his rib cage. If the bony part of each rib cannot be easily felt, your dog may be overweight. Another quickie test - stand directly over your dog while he's standing. If you can't see a clearly defined waist behind his rib cage, he's probably too portly.

- The infamous Red Baron owned a Great Dane named Moritz who lived on the military base with the pilot. The Red Baron fondly referred to Moritz as his "little lapdog."

- Frederick the Great owned an estimated 30 Greyhounds. His love of these animals led him to coin the saying: "The more I see of men, the more I love my dogs."

- It's easier than you might think to help your dog lose those extra pounds. Begin by eliminating unnecessary table scraps. Cut back a small amount on the kibble or canned dog food you normally feed your pooch. If he's accustomed to two full cups each day, reduce that amount to 1 3/4 cups instead. If you normally give your pooch biscuits every day, cut the amount in half. And don't feel guilty. Stick with the program and you'll eventually see a reduction in weight. Slow and steady is the best approach. And don't let yourself imagine that your dog is being deprived of anything. Even when he looks at you with a woebegone expression, remember you're doing him a favor by helping him reduce and you're adding years of good health to his life.

- Exercise. Not enough can be said about the benefits. Establish a daily exercise routine. Awaken twenty minutes earlier every morning and take a brisk mile walk. Instead of watching TV after dinner, walk off some calories. Your pooch's overall good health, as well as your own, will be greatly enhanced.

- According to a survey, 90% of dog owners speak to their dogs like humans, walk or run with their dogs and take pictures of them; 72% take their pups for car rides; 51% hang Christmas stockings for their dogs; 41% watch movies and TV with their pooches; 29% sign Rover's name to greeting cards and more than 20% buy homes with their dogs in mind, carry photos of Fido with them and arrange the furniture so FiFi can see outside.

- Lewis and Clark traveled with a 150-pound Newfoundland named "Seamen." The pooch was a respected member of the expedition and his antics were included in the extensive diaries of these famous explorers.

- The English have a saying: The virtues of a dog are its own, its vices those of its master.

- Lord Byron, in his eulogy to his dog Boatswain, wrote, "One who possessed beauty without vanity, strength without insolence, courage without ferocity, and all the virtues of man without his vices."

- "Be Kind To Animals Week" (May 7-13) was established in 1915. Recognized by Congress, it is the oldest week of its kind in the nation.

- The "Always Faithful" Memorial, which honors Dogs of War, was unveiled on June 20, 1994. It now stands on the US Naval Base in Orote Point, Guam.

- During WWII, Dobermans were official members of the US Marine Corps combat force.

- The domestic dog dates back more than 50,000 years.

- Ghandi once said, "The greatness of a nation and its moral progress can be judged by the way its animals are treated."

- England's Dickin Medal is specifically awarded to dogs for bravery and outstanding behavior in wartime.

- Napoleon's wife, Josephine, had a Pug named Fortune. She relied on the animal to carry secret messages under his collar to Napoleon while she was imprisoned at Les Carnes.

- Former First Lady Barbara Bush said: "An old dog that has served you long and well is like an old painting. The patina of age softens and beautifies, and like a master's work, can never be replaced by exactly the same thing, ever again."

- Dogs and Halloween don't mix. Even the mellowest of pooches can become frightened and overexcited by all the commotion. Save the candy collecting and chocolate for the kids and leave the dog at home.

- Most outdoor dogs suffer from unnoticed parasites like fleas.

- In winter, the water in an outdoor dog dish can freeze within an hour.

- In summer, dogs consume large quantities of water. Bowls need frequent refilling.

EVERYTHING YOU WANT TO KNOW ABOUT PET CARE AND WHO TO ASK

Whether you've always had a pet or you're starting out with your first, the following organizations and hotlines can provide information on the care, feeding and protection of your loyal companion.

Pet behavior information.

Tree House Animal Foundation: If you are concerned with canine aggression, nipping, biting, housebreaking or other behavioral problems, the Tree House Animal Foundation will try to help. But don't wait until the last minute. Call for advice early on and your animal's problems will be easier to correct. Consultation is free, except for applicable long distance charges. Call (773) 784-5488, 9AM to 5PM CST, seven days a week.

Pet Loss Helpline - 630-325-1600: The Chicago Veterinary Medical Association is a non-profit organization that promotes the health and well being of animals through veterinary care. Veterinarians, by their concern for and knowledge of animal health and behavior, help pet owners and their pets enjoy long and rewarding relationships. There is no charge. These services are funded primarily by donation. If you wish to make a donation in the name of your pet it would be greatly appreciated. We would also be interested in poems, drawings, prose or any creative expression of the love for your pet. CVMA, 120 East Ogden Avenue, Suite 22, Hinsdale, IL 60521

Animal Behavior Helpline: This organization is sponsored by the San Francisco Society for the Prevention of Cruelty to Animals. It will assist you in solving canine behavioral problems. Staffed by volunteers, you may reach a recorded message. However, calls are returned within 48 hours by volunteers trained in animal behavior. Problems such as chewing, digging and barking are cited as the most common reasons dog owners call. Housebreaking tips, how to deal with aggression and other topics are covered. Callers are first asked to speak about the problem and describe what steps have been taken to correct inappropriate behavior. After evaluating the information, specific advice is given to callers. The consultation is free, except for applicable long distance charges or collect call charges when a counselor returns your call. Messages can be left any time. Call (415) 554-3075.

Poison Control Center: There are two telephone numbers for this organization. The 800 number is an emergency line for both veterinarians and pet owners for poisoning control information. Calls are taken by the veterinarian-staffed National Animal Poison Control Center at the University of Illinois. When calling the 800 number, there is a charge of $30 per case. Every call made to the 800 number is followed up by the NAPCC.

When calling the NAPCC, be prepared to provide your name and address and the name of the suspected poison (be specific). If the product is manufactured by a company that is a member of the Animal Product Safety Service - the company may pay the charge.

In all other cases, you pay for the consultation. You must also provide the animal species, breed, sex, and weight. You will be asked to describe symptoms as well as unusual behavior. This detailed information is critical - it can mean the difference between life or death for your animal.

For emergencies only, call (800) 548-2423. Major credit cards are accepted. The Poison Control Center offers poison control information by veterinarians 24 hours a day, 7 days a week.

Poinsettias and other toxic plants... pretty but deadly.

During the Christmas holidays, the risk of poisoning and injury is greater for your pet. If eaten, poinsettias and holly berries for example, can be fatal. Although there are conflicting reports on the effects of mistletoe, play it safe and keep your pet away from this plant. Be alert - swallowed tree ornaments, like ribbon and tinsel can cause choking and/or intestinal problems.

Christmas wiring is another potential problem. Your pet can be electrocuted by chewing on it. And don't forget about the dangers of poultry bones. The same goes for aluminum foil including the disposable pans that are used at holiday time.

Keep your trash inaccessible. And remember that the holidays are a source of excitement and stress to both people and animals. Maintain your pet's feeding and walking schedules and provide plenty of TLC and playtime. Then everyone, including your animal, will find the holidays more enjoyable.

FYI...
common plants* that are toxic to pets

Amaryllis (bulbs)
Appleseeds (cyanide)
Azalea
Boxwood
Caladium
Cherry Pits (cyanide)
Climbing Lily
Daffodil (bulb)
Delphinium
Dumb Cane
English Ivy
Foxglove
Holly
Hydrangea
Japanese Yew
Jerusalem Cherry
Laburnum
Laurel
Marigold
Mistletoe (berries)
Mushrooms
Nightshade
Peach
Poinsettia
Privet
Rhubarb
Stinging Nettie
Tobacco
Walnuts
Yew

Andromeda
Arrowgrass
Bittersweet
Buttercup
Castor Bean
Chokecherry
Crown of Thorns
Daphne
Dieffenbachia
Elephant Ear
Elderberry
Hemlock
Hyacinth (bulbs)
Iris (bulb)
Jasmine (berries)
Jimsonweed
Larkspur
Locoweed
Marijuana
Monkshood
Narcissus (bulb)
Oleander
Philodendron
Poison Ivy
Rhododendron
Snow on the Mountain
Toadstool
Tulip (bulb)
Wisteria

NOTE: This is only a partial list.

PET POEMS, PROCLAMATIONS, PRAYERS...& DOG BISCUITS

Ode to Travel with Pets

We're all set to roam

Going far from home

With doggies in tow

Off shall we go

To wander and gadabout

Since travel we're mad about

With Rosie and Max by my side

We'll all go for a ride

As we travel for miles

And bring about smiles

Rosie will grin

Max will chime in

Driving into the sunset

Odometers all set

But enough of these word rhymes

Let's roll with the good times!

— Eileen Barish, November 1994

Alone Again

I wish someone would tell me what it is
      That I've done wrong.
Why I have to stay chained up and
      Left alone so long.
They seemed so glad to have me
      When I came here as a pup.
There were so many things we'd do
      While I was growing up.
They couldn't wait to train me as a
      Companion and a friend.
And told me how they'd never fear
      Being left alone again.
The children said they'd feed me and
      Brush me every day.
They'd play with me and walk me
      If only I could stay.
But now the family "Hasn't time,"
      They often say I shed.
They do not even want me in the house
      Not even to be fed.
The children never walk me.
      They always say "Not now!"
I wish that I could please them.
      Won't someone tell me how?
All I had, you see, was love.
      I wish they would explain
Why they said they wanted me
      Then left me on a chain?

— Anonymous

A Dog's Bill of Rights

I have the right to give and receive
        unconditional love.
I have the right to a life that is beyond
        mere survival.
I have the right to be trained so I do not become
        the prisoner of my own misbehavior.
I have the right to adequate food and
        medical care.
I have the right to fresh air and green grass.
I have the right to socialize with people
        and dogs outside my family.
I have the right to have my needs
        and wants respected.
I have the right to a special time with
        my people .
I have the right to only be bred
        responsibly if at all.
I have the right to be foolish and silly, and
        to make my person laugh.
I have the right to earn my person's trust
        and be trusted in return.
I have the right to be forgiven.
I have the right to die with dignity.
I have the right to be remembered well.

A Dog's Prayer

Treat me kindly, my beloved master, for no heart in all the world is more grateful for kindness, than the loving heart of mine.

Do not break my spirit with a stick, for though I should lick your hand between the blows, your patience and understanding will more quickly teach me the things you would have me do.

Speak to me often, for your voice is the world's sweetest music as you must know by the fierce wagging of my tail when your footstep falls up on my waiting ear.

When it is cold and wet, please take me inside...for I am now a domesticated animal, no longer used to bitter elements...and I ask no greater glory than the privilege of sitting at your feet beside the hearth...though had you no home, I would rather follow you through ice and snow, than rest upon the softest pillow in the warmest home in all the land...for you are my God...and I am your devoted worshipper.

Keep my pan filled with fresh water, for although I should not reproach you were it dry, I cannot tell you when I suffer thirst. Feed me clean food, that I may stay well, to romp and play and do your bidding, to walk by your side, and stand ready willing and able to protect you with my life, should your life be in danger.

And beloved master, should the Great Master see fit to deprive me of my health or sight, do not turn away from me. Rather hold me gently in your arms, as skilled hands grant me the merciful boon of eternal rest...and I will leave you knowing with the last breath I draw, my fate was ever safest in your hands.

Rainbow Bridge

There is a bridge connecting Heaven and Earth. It is called the Rainbow Bridge because of its many colors. Just this side of the Rainbow Bridge there is a land of meadows, hills and valleys with lush green grass.

When a beloved pet dies, the pet goes to this place. There is always food and water and warm spring weather. The old and frail animals are young again. Those who are maimed are made whole again. They play all day with each other.

There is only one thing missing. They are not with their special person who loved them on Earth. So each day they run and play until the day comes when one suddenly stops playing and looks up! The nose twitches! The ears are up! The eyes are staring! And this one suddenly runs from the group!

You have been seen, and when you and your special friend meet, you take him or her in your arms and embrace. Your face is kissed again and again, and you look once more into the eyes of your trusting pet.

Then you cross Rainbow Bridge together, never again to be separated.

— Anonymous

FIDO FACT:
• *Lord Byron, in his eulogy to his dog Boatswain, wrote, "One who possessed beauty without vanity, strength without insolence, courage without ferocity, and all the virtues of man without his vices."*

Homemade dog biscuits
(Makes about 8 dozen biscuits)

Ingredients

3 1/2 cups all-purpose flour

2 cups whole wheat flour

1 cup rye flour

1 cup cornmeal

2 cups cracked wheat bulgur

1/2 cup nonfat dry milk

4 tsp. salt

1 package dry yeast

2 cups chicken stock or other liquid

1 egg and 1 tbsp. milk (to brush on top)

Combine all the dry ingredients except the yeast. In a separate bowl, dissolve the yeast in 1/4 cup warm water. To this, add the chicken stock. (You can use bouillon, pan drippings or water from cooking vegetables.) Add the liquid to the dry ingredients. Knead mixture for about 3 minutes. Dough will be quite stiff. If too stiff, add extra liquid or an egg. Preheat oven to 300 degrees. Roll the dough out on a floured board to 1/4" thickness, then immediately cut into shapes with cookie cutters. Place on an ungreased cookie sheet and brush with a wash of egg and milk. Place in oven. After 45 minutes, turn off the heat and leave biscuits overnight in the oven to get bone hard.

In Memory of Max and Rosie

It seems like it was just yesterday...

MAXWELL
MAY 1991 - July 2000

ROSIE
MAY 1991 - MARCH 2001

UNITED STATES DIRECTORY OF PET-FRIENDLY LODGING

ALABAMA

ABBEVILLE
BEST WESTERN
1237 Hwy 431 S
(36310)
Rates: $46-$100
(334) 585-5060
(800) 528-1234

ALBERTVILLE
JAMESON INN
315 Martling Rd
(25950)
Rates: $49-$104
(256) 891-2600
(800) 526-3766

KINGS INN MOTOR MOTEL
7080 Hwy 431 N
(35950)
Rates: $35-$70
(256) 878-6550
(800) 490-8589

TWIN HOUSE B&B
705 Baltimore Ave
(35950)
Rates: $70-$90
(256) 878-7499

ALEXANDER CITY
JAMESON INN
4335 Hwy 280
(35010)
Rates: $49-$104
(256) 234-7099
(800) 526-3766

ANDALUSIA
BEST WESTERN OF ANDALUSIA
305 W Bypass
(36420)
Rates: $45-$60
(334) 222-9999
(800) 528-1234

BUDGET INN
Hwy 29 N (36420)
Rates: $28-$42
(334) 222-7929

DAYS INN
1604 HWY 84 E
Bypass (36420)
Rates: $46-$90
(334) 427-0050
(800) 329-7466

SCOTTISH INN
1421 MLK Jr
Expwy (36420)
Rates: $25-$50
(334) 222-7511

TOWN LINE INN
1106 Hwy 29
Bypass W (36420)
Rates: $25-$32
(334) 222-3191

ANNISTON
LENLOCK INN
6210 McClellan
Blvd (36206)
Rates: $36-$144
(256) 820-1515

ARAB
JAMESON INN
706 N Brindlee
Mtn Pkwy (35016)
Rates: $49-$104
(256) 586-5777
(800) 526-3766

ARDMORE
BUDGET INN
I-65 & Hwy 53
(35739)
Rates: $40-$70
(256) 423-6699

ATHENS
BEST WESTERN
1329 Hwy 72 East
(35611)
Rates: $49-$99
(256) 233-4030
(800) 321-0122

BOMAR INN
1101 Hwy 31 S
(35611)
Rates: $34-$41
(256) 233-6944
(800) 824-6834

COUNTRY HEARTH INN
1500 Hwy 72 E
(35611)
Rates: $54-$99
(256) 232-1520
(888) 443-2784

DAYS INN
1322 Hwy 72 E
(35611)
Rates: $40-$85
(256) 233-7500
(800) 329-7466

HAMPTON INN
1488 Thrasher
Blvd (35611)
Rates: $61-$85
(256) 232-0030
(800) 426-7866

SLEEP INN
1115 Audubon Ln
(35611)
Rates: $49-$89
(256) 232-4700
(800) 424-6423

SUPER 8 MOTEL
1325 Hwy 72
(35611)
Rates: $49-$69
(256) 233-1446
(800) 800-8000

ATTALLA
ECONO LODGE
507 Cherry St
(35954)
Rates: $44-$150
(256) 538-9925
(800) 424-6423

HOLIDAY INN EXP
801 Cleveland Ave
(35954)
Rates: $56+
(256) 538-7861
(800) 465-4329

AUBURN
ARBOR SUITES
1188 Commerce
Dr (36830)
Rates: $39-$79
(334) 826-1123

AUBURN UNIVERSITY HOTEL & DIXON CONFERENCE CTR
241 S College St
(36830)
Rates: $89-$205
(334) 821-8200
(800) 228-2876

BEST WESTERN UNIV CONV CTR
1577 S College St
(36830)
Rates: $62-$300
(334) 821-7001
(800) 282-8763

ECONO LODGE
2145 S College
(36830)
Rates: $60-$160
(334) 826-8900
(800) 424-6423

HEART OF AUBURN INN
333 South College
(36830)
Rates: $49-$89
(334) 887-3462
(800) 843-5634

JAMESON INN
1212 Mall Pkwy
(36830)
Rates: $49-$104
(334) 502-5020
(800) 526-3766

BAY MINETTE
BAY INN & SUITES
1402 Hwy 31 S
(36507)
Rates: $40
(251) 937-9521
(800) BAY-STAY

BESSEMER
BEST WESTERN HOTEL & SUITES
5041 Academy Dr
(35022)
Rates: $84-$250
(205) 481-1950
(800) 528-1234
(877) 741-3232

COMFORT INN
5051 Academy Dr
(35022)
Rates: $79-$120
(205) 428-3999
(800) 424-6423

JAMESON INN
5021 Academy Dr
(35022)
Rates: $49-$104
(205) 428-3194
(800) 526-3766

MASTERS ECONOMY INN
1113 9th Ave SW
(35022)
Rates: $34+
(205) 424-9690
(800) 633-3434

MOTEL 6
1000 Shiloh Ln
(35020)
Rates: $37-$53
(205) 426-9646
(800) 466-8356

BIRMINGHAM
AMERISUITES INVERNESS
4686 Hwy 280 E
(35242)
Rates: $69-$129
(205) 995-9242
(800) 333-1516

BAYMONT INN
513 Cahaba Park
Circle (35203)
Rates: $59-$64
(205) 995-9990
(877) 229-6668

BEST INN & SUITES
9225 Parkway E
(35206)
Rates: $55-$85
(205) 836-5400
(866) 237-8001

BEST WESTERN MEDICAL CTR
800 11th St S
(35205)
Rates: $70-$110
(205) 933-1900
(800) 528-1234

BEST WESTERN MT BROOK
4627 Hwy 280 E
(35242)
Rates: $70-$200
(205) 991-9977
(800) 528-1234

CANDLEWOOD SUITES
600 Corporate
Ridge Dr (35242)
Rates: $69-$104
(205) 991-0272
(888) 226-3539

COMFORT INN
195 Oxmoor Rd
(35209)
Rates: $49-$159
(205) 941-0990
(800) 424-6423

COMFORT INN
1485 Montgomery
Hwy (35216)
Rates: $49-$69
(205) 823-4300
(800) 424-6423

DAYS INN
5101 Airport Hwy
(35212)
Rates: $58-$200
(205) 592-6110
(800) 329-7466

**DELUXE INN &
SUITES/MOTEL**
7905 Crestwood
Blvd (35210)
Rates: $55-$145
(205) 956-4440

**DRURY INN
& SUITES**
3510 Grandview
Pkwy (35210)
Rates: $62-$102
(250) 967-2450
(800) 378-7946

**EASTWOOD
MOTEL**
1813 Crestwood
Blvd (35210)
Rates: $41-$56
(205) 956-3650

EMBASSY SUITES
2300 Woodcrest Pl
(35209)
Rates: $129-$229
(205) 879-7400
(800) 362-2779

HOLIDAY INN
5000 Richard
Arrington Blvd
(35212)
Rates: $75-$90
(205) 591-6900
(800) 465-4329

**HOMESTEAD
STUDIO SUITES
HOTEL**
12 Perimeter Park
South (35243)
Rates: $49-$64
(205) 967-3800
(888) 782-9473

LA QUINTA INN
905 11th Ct
(35201)
Rates: $67-$75
(205) 324-4510
(800) 687-6667

**LA QUINTA INN
& SUITES
HOMEWOOD**
60 State Farm
Pkwy (35209)
Rates: $79-$99
(205) 290-0150
(800) 687-6667

**LA QUINTA INN &
SUITES-HOOVER/
RIVERCHASE**
120 Riverchase
Pkwy E (35201)
Rates: $65-$95
(205) 403-0096
(800) 687-6667

MICROTEL
251 Summit Pkwy
(35205)
Rates: $35-$55
(205) 945-5550
(888) 771-7171

PARK INN-AIRPORT
7901 Crestwood
Blvd (35210)
Rates: $94-$114
(205) 951-0700

PICKWICK HOTEL
1023 20th St S
(35205)
Rates: $92-$114
(205) 933-9555
(800) 255-7304

RELAX INN
6101 1st Ave N
(35212)
Rates: $43-$55
(205) 591-5575

**RESIDENCE INN
BY MARRIOTT**
3 Green Hill Pkwy
(35242)
Rates: $115-$125
(205) 991-8686
(800) 331-3131

**RESIDENCE INN
WILDWOOD**
50 State Farm
Pkwy (35209)
Rates: $119-$145
(205) 943-0044
(800) 331-3131

SLEEP INN
1259 Greenmor Dr
(35210)
Rates: $45-$169
(205) 424-0000
(800) 753-3746

SUPER 8-NORTH
624 Decatur Hwy
(35068)
Rates: $36-$55
(205) 841-2200
(800) 800-8000

**THE TUTWILER-
A WYNDHAM
GRAND HOTEL**
2021 Park Place
N (35205)
Rates: $99-$169
(205) 322-2100
(800) 845-3426

BOAZ
KEY WEST INN
10535 Alabama
Hwy 168 (35957)
Rates: $44-$90
(256) 593-0800
(866) 253-9937

RODEWAY INN
751 Hwy 431 S
(35957)
Rates: $40-$100
(256) 593-8410
(800) 424-6423

BREMEN
**BREMEN
LAKEVIEW
RESORT**
1940 CR 143
(35033)
Rates: $44
(256) 287-0023

BREWTON
**COLONIAL
MANOR MOTEL**
643 South Blvd
(36427)
Rates: $33
(251) 867-5421

CALERA
**BEST WESTERN
SUITE LIFE**
11960 Hwy 25
(35040)
Rates: $59-$79
(205) 668-0222
(800) 528-1234
(800) 254-1267

HOLIDAY INN EXP
357 Hwy 304
35040
Rates: $63-$89
(205) 668-3641
(800) 465-4329

CAMDEN
DAYS INN
39 Camden
Bypass (36726)
Rates: $47-$57
(334) 682-4555
(800) 329-7466

CEDAR BLUFF
**J. R.'S MARINA
& MOTEL**
CR 102 (35959)
Rates: $40-$50
(256) 779-6461

**LIGHTHOUSE
& MOTEL**
Hwy 68 (35959)
Rates: $40-$60
(256) 779-8400

RIVERSIDE MOTEL
1210 CR 131
(35959)
Rates: $20-$65
(256) 779-6117
(800) 292-9324

CLANTON
BEST WESTERN
801 Bradberry Ln
(35046)
Rates: $55-$85
(205) 280-1006
(800) 528-1234

**GUESTHOUSE
INTL' INN**
946 Lake Mitchell
Rd (35045)
Rates: $48-$58
(205) 280-0306
(800) 214-8378

COLLINSVILLE
**HOWARD
JOHNSON INN**
Hwy 68 W (35961)
Rates: $46-$54
(256) 524-2114
(800) 446-4656

COLUMBIANA
ALABAMA 4 H
892 4-H Rd
(35051)
Rates: $50-$60
(205) 669-4281

CULLMAN
**BEST WESTERN
FAIRWINDS INN**
1917 Commerce
Ave NW (35055)
Rates: $49-$98
(256) 737-5009
(800) 528-1234
(888) 559-0549

COMFORT INN
5917 SR 157 NW
(35058)
Rates: $59-$149
(256) 734-1240
(800) 424-6423

DAYS INN
1841 4th St SW
(35055)
Rates: $45-$60
(256) 739-3800
(800) 329-7466

ECONO LODGE
1655 CR 437
(35056)
Rates: $40-$99
(256) 734-2691
(800) 424-6423

**MCQUEENS
COTTAGE**
8786 CR 813
(35057)
Rates: $70
(256) 736-1153

**SMITH LAKE
FISHING RESORT**
175 CR 312
(35057)
Rates: $55+
(256) 734-1598

DADEVILLE
**HEART OF DIXIE
MOTEL**
1775 E South St
(36853)
Rates: $28-$40
(256) 825-4236

DALEVILLE
**GREEN HOUSE
INN & LODGE**
761 S Daleville
Ave (36322)
Rates: $36-$60
(334) 598-1475

THE LODGE
444 N Daleville
Ave (36322)
Rates: $45-$55
(334) 598-6304

AREA CODES - If the local number doesn't connect, check for a new area code.

DAPHNE

EASTERN SHORE MOTEL
29070 Hwy 98 (36526)
Rates: $50
(251) 626-6601

MICROTEL INN & SUITES
29050 Hwy 98 (36526)
Rates: $49-$89
(251) 621-8707
(888) 771-7171

DAUPHIN ISLAND

GULF BREEZE MOTEL
1512 Cadillac Ave (36528)
Rates: $49-$79
(251) 861-7344
(800) 286-0296

HARBOR LIGHTS INN
1506 Cadillac Ave (36528)
Rates: $59-$79
(251) 861-7344
(800) 286-0296

DECATUR

COMFORT INN
3239 Point Mallard Pkwy (35601)
Rates: $79-$125
(256) 355-1037
(800) 424-6423

COMFORT INN
2212 Danville Rd SW (35601)
Rates: $69-$89
(256) 355-1999
(888) 424-6423

JAMESON INN
2130 Jameson Pl SW (35601)
Rates: $49-$104
(256) 355-2229
(800) 526-3766

MICROTEL INN & SUITES
3429 Hwy 31 S (35601)
Rates: $49-$81
(256) 355-9995
(888) 771-7171

RAMADA LIMITED
1317 E Hwy 67 (35602)
Rates: $44-$70
(256) 353-0333
(800) 272-6232

DEMOPOLIS

HERITAGE MOTEL
1324 Hwy 80 (36732)
Rates: $30-$40
(334) 289-1175

RIVERVIEW INN
110 Yacht Basin Dr (36732)
Rates: $50+
(334) 289-0690

DOTHAN

AMERICAN INN
3118 E Main St (36301)
Rates: $23-$35
(334) 793-4688

BEE LINE MOTEL
733 N Oates St (36303)
Rates: $30
(334) 794-8631

BEST VALUE INN & SUITES
2901 Ross Clark Cir (36301)
Rates: $40-$45
(334) 793-5200

COMFORT INN
3595 Ross Clark Cir, NW (36303)
Rates: $71-$97
(334) 793-9090
(800) 424-6423

DAYS INN
2841 Ross Clark Cir (36301)
Rates: $40-$51
(334) 793-2550
(800) 329-7466

DOTHAN NATIONAL GOLF CLUB & HOTEL
7410 Hwy 231 S (36301)
Rates: $39-$59
(334) 677-3321
(800) 214-1150

EASTGATE INN
1080 Ross Clark Cir (36301)
Rates: $29-$48
(334) 794-6643

ECONO LODGE
2910 Ross Clark Cir SW (36301)
Rates: $36-$61
(334) 673-8000
(800) 424-6423

HOLIDAY INN EXP
3071 Ross Clark Cir (36301)
Rates: $55-$98
(334) 671-3700
(800) 465-4329

HOLIDAY INN SOUTH
2195 Ross Clark Cir (36301)
Rates: $70-$90
(334) 794-8711
(800) 465-4329

HOWARD JOHN-SON EXPRESS INN
2244 Ross Clark Cir (36301)
Rates: $59-$69
(334) 792-3339
(800) 446-4656

MOTEL 6
2907 Ross Clark Cir SW (36301)
Rates: $29-$47
(334) 793-6013
(800) 466-8356

QUALITY INN
3053 Ross Clark Cir (36301)
Rates: $55-$90
(334) 794-6601
(800) 424-6423

RAMADA INN
3011 Ross Clark Cir (36301)
Rates: $50-$89
(334) 792-0031
(800) 272-6232

TOWN TERRACE INN
251 N Oates St (36303)
Rates: $25-$40
(334) 792-1135

ELBA

RIVIERA MOTEL
154 Yelverton (36323)
Rates: $32-$45
(334) 897-2204

ENTERPRISE

COMFORT INN
615 Boll Weevil Cir. (36330)
Rates: $75-$140
(334) 393-2304
(800) 424-6423

HOLIDAY INN EXP HOTEL & SUITES
9 North Pointe Blvd (36330)
Rates: $39-$64
(334) 347-2211
(800) 465-4329

EQUALITY

REAL ISLAND MARINA
2700 Real Island Rd (36026)
Rates: $69
(334) 857-2741

EUFAULA

COMFORT SUITES
12 PaulLee Pkwy (36027)
Rates: $70-$96
(334) 616-0114
(800) 424-6423

JAMESON INN
136 Towne Center Blvd (36027)
Rates: $49-$104
(334) 687-7747
(800) 541-3268

LAKE EUFAULA MOTOR LODGE
620 E Barbour St (36027)
Rates: $35-$85
(334) 687-4811

LAKESIDE MOTOR LODGE
1010 N Eufaula Ave (36027)
Rates: $35-$85
(334) 687-2477

RAMADA INN
631 E Barbour St (36027)
Rates: $55+
(334) 687-2021
(800) 272-6232

EVERGREEN

COMFORT INN
83 Ted Bates Rd (36401)
Rates: $55-$75
(334) 578-4701
(800) 424-6423

DAYS INN
901 Liberty Hill Dr (36401)
Rates: $35-$85
(251) 578-2100
(800) 329-7466

FAIRHOPE

BARONS "ON THE BAY" INN
701 S Mobile Ave (36532)
Rates: $34-$65
(251) 928-8000

KEY WEST INN
231 S Greeno Rd (36532)
Rates: $50-$150
(251) 990-7373
(800) 833-0555

OAK HAVEN COTTAGES
355 S Mobile St (36532)
Rates: $55-$75
(251) 928-5431

THE PARKER HOUSE
413 N Section St (36532)
Rates: $25-$75
(251) 928-8472

FAYETTE

JOURNEY'S INN
2502 Temple Ave N (35555)
Rates: $40-$60
(205) 932-6727

FLORALA

MAGNOLIA INN B&B
706 5th St (36442)
Rates: $55-$65
(334) 858-2143

FLORENCE

DAYS INN
1915 Florence Blvd (35630)
Rates: $45-$85
(256) 766-2620
(800) 329-7466

DOUBLEHEAD RESORT
145 CR 134, Town Creek (35672)
Rates: $150-$275
(256) 685-9267
(800) 685-9267

HOMESTEAD EXECUTIVE INN
505 S Court St (35630)
Rates: $35-$79
(256) 766-2331
(800) 248-5336

JAMESON INN
115 Ana Dr (35630)
Rates: $49-$104
(256) 764-5326
(800) 526-3766

SUPER 8 MOTEL
101 Hwy 72 & 43 E (35631)
Rates: $42-$86
(256) 757-2167
(800) 800-8000

FOLEY
CORNERSTONE LODGE OF AMERICA
126 CR 20 W (36535)
Rates: $50-$90
(251) 943-3339
(800) 572-4225

HOLIDAY INN EXP
2682 S McKenzie St (36535)
Rates: $68-$143
(251) 943-9100
(800) 465-4329
(800) 962-1833

KEY WEST INN
2520 S McKenzie St (36535)
Rates: $59-$139
(251) 943-1241
(800) 833-0555

FORESTDALE
TRAVELER'S REST MOTEL
1066 Forestdale Blvd (35214)
Rates: n/a
(205) 798-3831

FORT PAYNE
ADAMS OUTDOORS
6102 Mitchell Rd NE (35967)
Rates: $20-$120
(256) 845-2988

DAYS INN
1416 Glen Blvd SW (35967)
Rates: $54-$119
(256) 845-2085
(800) 329-7466

ECONO LODGE
1312 Glen Blvd SW (35967)
Rates: $45-$65
(256) 845-4013
(800) 424-6423

FORT PAYNE INN
1828 Gault Ave N Fort (35967)
Rates: $45-$65
(245) 845-0481

FULTONDALE
DAYS INN
616 Decatur Hwy (35068)
Rates: $51-$89
(205) 849-0111
(800) 329-7466

GADSDEN
DAYS INN
1612 W Grand Ave (35901)
Rates: $48-$160
(256) 442-7913
(800) 329-7466

MOTEL 6
1600 Rainbow Dr (35901)
Rates: $35-$45
(256) 543-1105
(800) 466-8356

GAYLESVILLE
THE LIGHTHOUSE MOTEL
Hwy 68 (35973)
Rates: $40-$55
(256) 779-8400

GRANT
MANY SPARROWS B&B
5605 Main St (35747)
Rates: $69-$95
(256) 728-4147

GREENVILLE
BEST VALUE INN
941 Fort Dale Rd (36037)
Rates: $45-$55
(334) 382-2651
(888) 315-2378

BEST WESTERN
56 Cahaba Rd (36037)
Rates: $50-$85
(334) 382-9200
(800) 528-1234

COMFORT INN
1029 Fort Dale Rd (36037)
Rates: $50-$85
(334) 383-9595
(800) 424-6423

ECONO LODGE
946 Fort Dale Rd (36037)
Rates: $45-$70
(334) 382-3118
(800) 424-6423

JAMESON INN
71 Jameson Ln (36037)
Rates: $49-$104
(334) 382-6300
(800) 526-3766

THRIFTY INN
105 Greenville Bypass (36037)
Rates: $39-$49
(334) 382-6671

GULF SHORES
COMFORT INN
3049 W 1st St (36542)
Rates: $50-$290
(251) 968-8604
(800) 424-6423

GULF PINES MOTEL
245 E 22nd Ave (36542)
Rates: $29-$99
(251) 968-7911
(888) 878-9575

RAMADA LIMITED
610 W Beach Blvd (36542)
Rates: n/a
(251) 948-8141
(800) 272-6232

RIVERSIDE INN
5587 CR 6 (36542)
Rates: $45-$70
(251) 968-7478

GUNTERSVILLE
COVENANT COVE LODGE & MARINA
7001 Val-Monte Dr (35976)
Rates: $55-$300
(256) 582-1000
(888) 288-2683

DAYS INN
14040 Hwy 431 S (35976)
Rates: $46-$109
(256) 582-3200
(800) 329-7466

HOLIDAY INN
2140 Gunter Ave (35976)
Rates: n/a
(256) 582-2220
(800) 465-4329

SUPER 8 MOTEL
14341 Hwy 431 S (35976)
Rates: $41-$49
(256) 582-8444
(800) 800-8000

HAMILTON
DAYS INN
1849 Military St S (35570)
Rates: $49-$109
(205) 921-1790
(800) 329-7466

HOMEWOOD
LA QUINTA INN
60 State Farm Pkwy (35209)
Rates: $69-$120
(205) 290-0150
(800) 687-6667

MICROTEL
2251 Summit Pkwy (35209)
Rates: $35-$45
(205) 945-5550
(888) 771-7171

RAMADA INN
226 Summit Pkwy (35223)
Rates: $65-$149
(205) 916-0464
(800) 272-6232

RED ROOF INN
151 Vulcan Rd (35209)
Rates: $38-$59
(205) 942-9414
(800) 843-7663

RESIDENCE INN BY MARRIOTT
50 State Farm Pkwy (35209)
Rates: n/a
(205) 943-0044
(800) 331-3131

SUPER 8 MOTEL
140 Vulcan Rd (35223)
Rates: $39-$53
(205) 945-9888
(800) 800-8000

TOWNEPLACE SUITES
500 Wildwood Cir (35209)
Rates: $75-$119
(205) 943-0114
(800) 257-3000

HOOVER
AMERISUITES RIVERCHASE
2980 Hwy 150 (35244)
Rates: $99-$159
(205) 988-8444
(800) 833-1516

LA QUINTA INN
120 Riverchase Pkwy E (35244)
Rates: $60-$110
(205) 403-0096
(800) 687-6667
(800) 221-4731

HUNTSVILLE
BAYMONT INN & SUITES
4890 University Dr NW (35816)
Rates: $59-$79
(256) 830-8999
(877) 229-6668

CANDLEWOOD SUITES
201 Exchange Pl (35806)
Rates: $72-$92
(256) 830-8222
(888) 226-3539

EXECUTIVE STAY AMERICA
3100 University Dr (35816)
Rates: $25-$42
(256) 433-0610

FEDERAL SQUARE MOTEL & SUITES
8781 Madison Blvd (35816)
Rates: $40-$88
(256) 772-8470
(800) 458-1639

GUESTHOUSE SUITES PLUS
4020 Independence Dr (35816)
Rates: $65-$105
(256) 837-8907
(800) 214-8378

HILTON HOTEL
401 Williams Ave (35801)
Rates: $79-$158
(256) 533-1400
(800) 445-8667

LA QUINTA INN RESEARCH PARK
4870 Univeristy Dr (35816)
Rates: $60-$91
(256) 830-2070
(800) 687-6667

LA QUINTA INN SPACE CENTER
3141 Univeristy Dr (35816)
Rates: $60-$86
(256) 533-0756
(800) 687-6667

MOTEL 6
8995 Madison Blvd (35824)
Rates: $33-$43
(256) 772-7479
(800) 466-8356

IRONDALE
BEST WESTERN RIME GARDEN INN & SUITES
5320 Beacon Dr (35210)
Rates: $89-$99
(205) 951-1200
(800) 528-1234
(888) 828-1768

JACKSON
ECONO LODGE
3680 N College Ave (36545)
Rates: $49-$51
(800) 424-6423

JASPER
JAMESON INN
1100 Hwy 78 E (35501)
Rates: $49-$104
(205) 387-7710
(800) 526-3766

TRAVEL-RITE INN
200 Mallway Dr (35501)
Rates: $26-$39
(205) 221-1161

UNCLE MORT'S WARRIOR RIVER MOTEL
30 Hwy 78 Loop (35501)
Rates: $38
(205) 483-9212

LAFAYETTE
MAPLE HILL GARDENS & GUEST HOUSE
215 LaFayette St N (36862)
Rates: n/a
(334) 864-0970

LEEDS
DAYS INN
1835 Ashville Rd (35094)
Rates: $54-$140
(205) 699-9833
(800) 329-7466

LEESBURG
LEESBURG LODGE
5915 Weiss Lake Blvd (35983)
Rates: $33-$52
(256) 526-7378
(800) 209-3219

LIVINGSTON
LIVINGSTON MOTEL
713 N Washington St (35479)
Rates: $32
(205) 652-9621

LOXLEY
LOXLEY MOTEL
4000 S Hickory St (36551)
Rates: $30-$75
(251) 964-5094
(251) 964-5095

ROYAL MOTEL
Hwy 59 S (36551)
Rates: $30-$65
(251) 964-5094
(251) 964-5516

WIND CHASE INN
13156 N Hickory St (36551)
Rates: $50
(251) 964-4444

MADISON
MOTEL 6
8995 Hwy 20 W (35758)
Rates: $36-$51
(256) 772-7479
(800) 466-8356

MARION
GATEWAY INN
1615 Hwy 5 S (36756)
Rates: $49-$58
(334) 683-9166

MENTONE
MENTONE SPRINGS HISTORICAL HOTEL
6114 Hwy 117 (35984)
Rates: $54-$125
(256) 634-4040
(800) 404-0100

MOBILE
ASHBURY HOTEL & SUITES
600 S Beltline Hwy (36608)
Rates: $59-$99
(251) 344-8030
(800) 752-0398

BEST SUITES OF AMERICA
150 Beltline Hwy S (36608)
Rates: $52-$150
(251) 343-4949

BEST WESTERN BATTLESHIP INN
2701 Battleship Pkwy (36601)
Rates: $61-$99
(334) 432-2703
(800) 528-1234

COMFORT SUITES
70 Springdale Blvd (36606)
Rates: $69-$95
(251) 471-1515
(800) 424-6423

DAYS INN
5480 Inn Dr (36619)
Rates: $39-$99
(251) 661-8181
(800) 329-7466

DRURY INN
824 Beltline Hwy S (36609)
Rates: $60-$100
(251) 344-7700
(800) 378-7946

ECONO LODGE
156 Beltline Hwy S (36608)
Rates: $45-$65
(251) 343-4911
(800) 424-6423

GUEST HOUSE INN
3132 Government Blvd (36606)
Rates: $40-$65
(251) 471-2402
(888) 811-9246

GUESTHOUSE INT'L INN
5472-A Inn Rd (36619)
Rates: $49-$69
(251) 660-1520
(800) 552-4667

HOLIDAY INN-BELLINGRATH GARDENS
5465 Hwy 90 W (36619)
Rates: $60-$80
(251) 666-5600
(800) 465-4329

LA QUINTA INN
816 W I-65 Service Rd (36609)
Rates: $60-$95
(251) 343-4051
(800) 687-6667

LAFAYETTE PLAZA HOTEL
301 Government St (36619)
Rates: $59-$99
(251) 694-0100
(800) 692-6662

MOTEL 6- TILL-MANS CORNER
5488 Inn Rd (36619)
Rates: $34-$42
(251) 660-1483
(800) 466-8356

OLSSON'S MOTEL
4137 Government Blvd (36693)
Rates: $35-$55
(251) 661-5331
(800) 332-1004

RAMADA INN
850 W I-65 Service Rd (36609)
Rates: $59-$85
(251) 342-3220
(800) 272-6232

RAMADA INN
5472A Inn Rd (36619)
Rates: $65-$93
(251) 660-1520
(800) 272-6232

RED ROOF INN N
33 I-65 Service Rd E (36606)
Rates: $36-$61
(251) 476-2004
(800) 843-7663

RED ROOF INN SOUTH
5450 Coca Cola Rd (36619)
Rates: $37-$60
(251) 666-1044
(800) 843-7663

RESIDENCE INN BY MARRIOTT
950 S Beltline Hwy (36609)
Rates: $105-$139
(251) 304-0570
(800) 331-3131

TOWNEPLACE SUITES
1075 Montlimar Dr (36609)
Rates: $79-$119
(251) 345-9588
(800) 257-3000

AREA CODES - If the local number doesn't connect, check for a new area code.

MONROE-VILLE

DAYS INN
4389 S Alabama
Ave (36460)
Rates: $52-$69
(251) 743-3297
(800) 329-7466

HOLIDAY INN EXP
120 Hwy 21 S
(36460)
Rates: $55-$85
(251) 743-3333
(800) 465-4329

MONROEVILLE INN
1750 S Alabama
Ave (36460)
Rates: $28-$36
(251) 575-3312

MONTGOMERY

BAYMONT INN
5225 Carmichael
Rd (36106)
Rates: $64-$79
(334) 277-6000
(877) 229-6668

BEST INN & SUITES
5135 Carmichael
Rd (36106)
Rates: $59-$99
(334) 270-9199
(800) 237-8466

BEST INN & SUITES
977 W South Blvd
(36106)
Rates: $42-$48
(334) 288-5740
(800) 237-8466

**BEST WESTERN
MONTICELLO INN**
5837 Monticello
Dr (36117)
Rates: $55-$70
(334) 277-4442
(800) 528-1234

COLISEUM INN
1550 Federal Dr
(36107)
Rates: $31-$39
(334) 265-0586

**COLONEL'S
REST B&B**
11091 Atlanta
Hwy (36117)
Rates: $60+
(334) 215-0380
(800) 461-3758

DAYS INN
2625 Zelda Rd
(36107)
Rates: $49-$79
(334) 269-9611
(800) 329-7466

DAYS INN
4470 N Chase
Blvd (36109)
Rates: $96
(334) 396-6501
(800) 329-7466

**GOVERNORS
HOUSE HOTEL
& CONF CTR**
2705 E South Blvd
(36116)
Rates: $55-$72
(334) 288-2800
(800) 334-8459

HOLIDAY INN
1185 Eastern Blvd
Bypass (36117)
Rates: $69-$119
(334) 272-0370
(800) 465-4329

INN SOUTH
I-65 & South Blvd,
Exit 168 (36117)
Rates: $29-$34
(334) 288-7999
(800) 642-0890

LA QUINTA INN
1280 East Blvd
(36117)
Rates: $60-$90
(334) 271-1620
(800) 687-6667

MOTEL 6
1051 Eastern
Bypass (36117)
Rates: $37-$55
(334) 277-6748
(800) 466-8356

REGENCY INN
1771 Cong. W L
Dickinson Dr
(36109)
Rates: $48+
(334) 260-0444
(888) 301-2992

**RESIDENCE INN
BY MARRIOTT**
1200 Hilmar Ct
(36117)
Rates: $121-$145
(334) 270-3300
(800) 331-3131

**TOWNEPLACE
SUITES**
5047 Towneplace
Dr (36106)
Rates: $94-$119
(334) 396-5505
(800) 257-3000

MOODY

SUPER 8 MOTEL
2451 Moody Pkwy
(35004)
Rates: $52-$62
(205) 640-7091
(800) 800-8000

NORTHPORT

THREE BEARS B&B
2415 5th St (35476)
Rates: $85
(205) 752-2534

ONEONTA

**BEST WESTERN
COLONIAL INN**
293 Valley Rd
(35121)
Rates: $60-$70
(205) 274-2200
(800) 528-1234

OPELIKA

DAYS INN
1014 Anand Ave
(36801)
Rates: $45-$125
(334) 749-5080
(800) 329-7466

**GUESTHOUSE
INN**
1520 Columbus
Pkwy (36801)
Rates: $45
(334) 742-0270
(800) 214-8378

MOTEL 6
1015 Columbus
Pkwy (36804)
Rates: $31-$37
(334) 745-0988
(800) 466-8356

TRAVELODGE
1002 Columbus
Pkwy (36804)
Rates: $37-$150
(3340 749-1461
(800) 578-7878

OPP

EXECUTIVE INN
812 Forala Hwy
(36467)
Rates: $55
(334) 493-6399

TRAVEL INN
702 Florala Hwy
(36467)
Rates: $45-$50
(334) 493-3551

*ORANGE
BEACH*

**SLEEP INN GULF
FRONT RESORT**
25400 Perdido
Beach Blvd
(36561)
Rates: $45-$189
(251) 981-6722
(800) 424-6423

ORRVILLE

**RIVER OAKS
LANDING B&B**
100 Breland Ln
(36767)
Rates: n/a
(334) 996-3601
(866) 996-3601

OXFORD

BEST WESTERN
Hwy 78 & SR 21
S (36203)
Rates: $49-499
(256) 831-3410
(800) 528-1234
(866) 8886654

DAYS INN
#1 Recreation Dr
(36203)
Rates: $55-$85
(256) 835-0300
(800) 329-7466
(800) 266-8694

ECONO LODGE
25 Elm St (36203)
Rates: $43-$51
(256) 831-9480
(800) 424-6423

**HOWARD
JOHNSON EXP**
Hwy 78 & 21
South (36203)
Rates: $36-$49
(256) 835-3988
(800) 446-4656

JAMESON INN
161 Colonial Dr
(36204)
Rates: $49-$104
(256) 835-2170
(800) 526-3766

MOTEL 6
202 Grace St
(36203)
Rates: $35-$51
(256) 831-5463
(800) 466-8356

OZARK

**ALL AMERICAN
OZARK INN**
Hwy 231 S (36360)
Rates: $50-$58
(334) 774-5166
(866) 768-5970

BAYWOOD SUITES
305 Newton Ave
(36360)
Rates: $135 wkly
(334) 774-4470

BUDGET INN
1610 Hwy 231S
(36360)
Rates: $25-$40
(334) 774-5105

JAMESON INN
1360 Hwy 231 S
(36360)
Rates: $49-$104
(334) 774-0233
(800) 526-3766

OZARK MOTEL
Hwy 231 N
(36360)
Rates: $27
(334) 774-8335

QUALITY INN
151 Hwy 231 N
(36360)
Rates: $70-$140
(334) 774-7300
(800) 424-6423

PELHAM

**BEST WESTERN
OAK MOUNTAIN**
100 Bishop Cir
(35124)
Rates: $59-$69
(205) 982-1113
(800) 528-1234

AREA CODES - If the local number doesn't connect, check for a new area code.

COMFORT INN
110 Cahaba Valley
Pkwy (35124)
Rates: $69-$130
(205) 444-9200
(800) 424-6423

PELL CITY
**BEST WESTERN
RIVERSIDE INN**
11900 Hwy 78
(35135)
Rates: $49-$79
(205) 338-3381
(800) 528-1234

PHENIX CITY
HOLIDAY INN EXP
1700 E 280 Bypass
(36867)
Rates: $60-$70
(334) 298-9321
(800) 465-4329

PHIL CAMPBELL
**DISMALS CANYON
CABINS**
901 Hwy 8
(35581)
Rates: $120-$196
(205) 993-4559

PIEDMONT
LAMONT MOTEL
Hwy 278 E (36272)
Rates: $35-$45
(256) 447-6002

PIKE ROAD
SCOTTISH INNS
7237 Troy Hwy
(36064)
Rates: n/a
(334) 288-1501
(800) 251-1962

PINE APPLE
**TURKEY HOLLOW
"MAN" HUNTING
LODGE**
Rt 2, Box 57
(36768)
Rates: n/a
(334) 746-2159

PRATTVILLE
JAMESON INN
104 Jameson Ct
(36067)
Rates: $49-$104
(334) 361-6463
(800) 526-3766

JUPITER INN
1940 Hwy 82 W
(36067)
Rates: $40-$50
(334) 361-0499

PINE MOTEL
I-65 N, Exit 186
(36067)
Rates: $40
(334) 365-3311

PRICEVILLE
DAYS INN
63 Marco Dr
(35603)
Rates: $59-$99
(256) 355-3297
(800) 329-7466

ROANOKE
BEST WESTERN
2983 Hwy 431
(36274)
Rates: $46-$79
(334) 863-2100
(800) 528-1234
(888) 893-6896

ROGERSVILLE
ECONOMY INN
Hwy 72 (35652)
Rates: $38-$48
(256) 247-5416

SARALAND
BAMBOO MOTEL
1113 Hwy 43
(36571)
Rates: $34
(251) 675-5691

DAYS INN
1101 Industrial
Pkwy (36571)
Rates: $40-$110
(251) 675-7800
(800) 329-7466

**PLANTATION
MOTEL**
1010 Saraland
Blvd (36571)
Rates: $35-$65
(251) 675-5511

SCOTTSBORO
BEST WESTERN
46 Micah Way
(35768)
Rates: $45-$64
(256) 259-4300
(800) 528-1234

JAMESON INN
208 Micah Way
(35768)
Rates: $49-$104
(256) 574-6666
(800) 526-3766

**WOODY'S
LODGE-CABINS**
4334 Hwy 79
(35768)
Rates: $100
(256) 574-1761

SELMA
**THE BRIDGE
TENDER'S
HOUSE B&B**
2 Lafayette Park
(36701)
Rates: $65-$75
(334) 875-5517
(866) 382-5517

BUDGET INN
601 Highland Ave
(36701)
Rates: $35-$49
(334) 872-3451

COMFORT INN
1812 Hwy 14 E
(36701)
Rates: $55-$95
(334) 875-5700
(800) 424-6423

**GRAYSTONE
MOTEL**
1200 W Highland
Ave (36701)
Rates: $35-$45
(334) 874-6681

HOLIDAY INN
1710 W Highland
Ave (36701)
Rates: $60-$65
(334) 872-0461
(800) 465-4329

JAMESON INN
2420 Broad St
(36701)
Rates: $49-$104
(334) 874-8600
(800) 526-3766

**RESIDENCE
SUITES**
2006 W Highland
Ave (36701)
Rates: $44-$54
(334) 875-1200

SHEFFIELD
HOLIDAY INN
4900 Hatch Blvd
(35660)
Rates: $99-$125
(256) 381-4710
(800) 465-4329

SHORTER
DAYS INN
450 Main St
(36075)
Rates: $40-$79
(334) 727-6034
(800) 329-7466

SPANISH FORT
**LAS BRISAS
ON THE BAY**
1525 Battleshi
Rates: $49-$59
(251) 626-7200

STEVENSON
**BUDGET
HOST INN**
42973 Hwy 72
(35772)
Rates: $35-$55
(256) 437-2215

**CROW CREEK
COTTAGE B&B**
361 CR 287
(35772)
Rates: $65-$100
(256) 437-1847
(888) 344 -5573

SYLACAUGA
**SUPER 8 MOTEL/
JAY VILISH TOWN
HOUSES**
40770 Hwy 280
(35150)
Rates: $42-$150
(256) 249-4321
(800) 800-8000

TOWNE INN
Hwy 280 (35150)
Rates: $33-$52
(256) 249-3821

THEODORE
RIVERHOUSE B&B
13285 Rebel Rd
(36590)
Rates: $110-$140
(251) 973-2233
(800) 552-9791

THOMASVILLE
DAYS INN
424 Hwy 43 N
(36784)
Rates: $34-$46
(334) 636-5467
(800) 329-7466

TROY
HOLIDAY INN
Hwy 231 at Hwy
29 (36081)
Rates: $58-$62
(334) 566-1150
(800) 465-4329

HOLIDAY INN EXP
Hwy 231 &
Hwy 29 (36081)
Rates: $59-$62
(334) 670-0012
(800) 465-4329

TRUSSVILLE
JAMESON INN
4730 Norrell Dr
(35173)
Rates: $49-$104
(205) 661-9323
(800) 526-3766

TUSCALOOSA
BEST VALUE INN
3501 McFarland
Blvd (35405)
Rates: $49-$150
(205) 556-7950

JAMESON INN
5021 Oscar Baxter
Rd (35405)
Rates: $49-$104
(205) 345-5018
(800) 5413268

LA QUINTA INN
4122 McFarland
Blvd E (35405)
Rates: $52-$81
(205) 349-3270
(800) 687-6667

MASTERS INN
3600 McFarland
Blvd (35405)
Rates: $39-$103
(205) 556-2010

MOTEL 6
4700 McFarland
Blvd E (35405)
Rates: $35-$53
(205) 759-4942
(800) 466-8356

TUSCUMBIA
KEY WEST INN
1800 Hwy 72 W
(35674)
Rates: $47-$55
(256) 383-0700
(866) 253-9937

TUSKEGEE
WHITE OAK PLANTATION
5215 CR 10
(36082)
Rates: $85+
(334) 727-9258

UNION SPRINGS
MASTER RACK LODGE
13096 CR 14
(36089)
Rates: $35-$500
(334) 474-3600

VANCE
WELLESLEY INN & SUITES
11170 Will Walker
Rd (35490)
Rates: $79-$109
(2050 556-3606
(800) 444-8888

VESTAVIA HILLS
HAMPTON INN
1466 Montgomery
Hwy (35216)
Rates: $79-$104
(205) 822-2224
(800) 426-7866

WETUMPKA
KEY WEST INN
4225 Hwy 231 N
(36093)
Rates: $47-$65
(334) 567-2227
(800) 833-0555

YORK
DAYS INN
17700 Hwy 17
(36925)
Rates: $44-$79
(205) 392-9675
(800) 329-7466

AREA CODES - If the local number doesn't connect, check for a new area code.

ALASKA

ANCHOR POINT

ANCHOR RIVER INN
P. O. Box 154
(99556)
Rates: $50-$85
(800) 435-8531

ANCHORAGE

A COMFORT B&B
8501 Brookridge
Dr (99504)
Rates: n/a
(907) 338-0453

A COUSIN OF MINE
4406 Forest Rd
(99517)
Rates: n/a
(907) 248-3462

ADAMS PLACE B^B
5701 E 97th Ave
(99516)
Rates: n/a
(907) 346-3604

ALASKA AUNTIE'S B&B
1206 W 47th Ave
(99503)
Rates: n/a
(907) 562-7626

ANCHORAGE EAGLE NEST HOTEL
4110 Spenard Rd
(99517)
Rates: $40-$170
(907) 243-3433
(800) 848-7852

ARCTIC INN MOTEL
842 W Int'l
Airport Rd (99518)
Rates: n/a
(907) 561-1328

AURORA WINDS B&B RESORT
7501 Upper
O'Malley (99516)
Rates: $105-$250
(907) 346-2533

BEAR DEN B&B
3002 154th St
(99516)
Rates: n/a
(907) 345-4012

BEST WESTERN BARRATT INN
4616 Spenard Rd
(99517)
Rates: $59-$199
(907) 243-3131
(800) 528-1234
(800) 221-7550

BIG TIMBER MOTEL
2037 E 5th Ave
(99501)
Rates: n/a
(907) 272-2541

COMFORT INN SHIP CREEK
111 Ship Creek
Ave (99501)
Rates: $59-$169
(907) 277-6887
(800) 424-6423

CREEKWOOD INN
2150 Gambell St
(99503)
Rates: $53-$159
(800) 478-6008

DAYS INN DOWNTOWN
321 E 5th Ave
(99501)
Rates: $75-$300
(907) 276-7226
(800) 329-7466

DIAMOND HOUSE B&B
2201 W. 48th Ave
(99517)
Rates: n/a
(907) 245-8080

DUKES 8TH AVENUE HOTEL
630 W 8th Ave
(99520)
Rates: $79-$165
(907) 274-6213
(800) 478-4837

ECONO LODGE
642 E 5th Ave
(99510)
Rates: $40-$70
(907) 274-1515
(800) 424-6423

EXECUTIVE SUITE HOTEL
4360 Spenard Rd
(99517)
Rates: $89-$289
(907) 243-6366
(800) 770-6366

FERNBROOK B&B
8120 Rabbit Creek
Rd (99516)
Rates: $75-$95
(907) 345-1954

LONG HOUSE ALASKAN HOTEL
4335 Wisconsin
St (99517)
Rates: $69-$199
(907) 243-2133
(888) 243-2133

MERRILL FIELD INN
420 Sitka St
(99501)
Rates: $55-$136
(907) 276-4547
(800) 898-4547

MICROTEL INN & SUITES
5205 Northwood
Dr (99517)
Rates: $69-$149
(907) 245-5002
(888) 771-7171

MILLENNIUM HOTEL
4800 Spenard Rd
(99517)
Rates: $150-$305
(907) 243-2300
(800) 544-0553

MOTEL 6
5000 A St (99503)
Rates: $59-$149
(907) 677-8000
(800) 466-8356

PUFFIN INN
4400 Spenard Rd
(99517)
Rates: $64-$209
(907) 243-4044
(800) 478-3346

QUPQUIGIAQ B&B
3801 Spenard Rd
(99517)
Rates: n/a
(907) 562-5681

RAMADA INN
115 E Third Ave
(99501)
Rates: $79-$239
(907) 272-7561
(800) 272-6232

REGAL ALASKAN HOTEL
4800 Spenard Rd
(99517)
Rates: $119-$310
(907) 243-2300
(800) 544-0553

RESIDENCE INN BY MARRIOTT
1025 E 35th Ave
(99508)
Rates: $129-$334
(907) 563-9844
(877) 729-0197

SHERATON HOTEL
401 E 6th Ave
(99510)
Rates: $89-$290
(907) 276-8700
(800) 325-3535

6 BAR E RANCH B&B
11401 Totem Rd
(99516)
Rates: n/a
(907) 346-2665

SIXTH & B BED & BREAKFAST
145 W Sixth Ave
(99501)
Rates: $38-$105
(907) 279-5293

SOURDOUGH VISITORS LODGE
801 E Erickson St
(99520)
Rates: $69-$125
(907) 279-4148
(800) 777-3716

SPRINGHILL SUITES
3401 A St (99503)
Rates: $89-$199
(907) 562-3247

SUPER 8 MOTEL
3501 Minnesota
Dr (99503)
Rates: $60-$147
(907) 276-8884
(800) 800-8000

12TH & L B&B
1134 L St (99501)
Rates: $45
(907) 276-1225

VALARIAN VISIT B&B
1536 Valarian St
(99508)
Rates: $50-$75
(907) 274-5760

WESTMARK ANCHORAGE HOTEL
720 W 5th St
(99501)
Rates: $109-$209
(907) 276-7676

ANGOON

KOOTZENAHOO INLET LODGE
P. O. Box 91
(99820)
Rates: $55-$65
(907) 788-3615

BETTLES

BETTLES LODGE WILDERNESS TRIPS & CABINS
P. O. Box 27-VP
(99726)
Rates: $95-$145
(907) 692-5111
(800) 770-5111

BIG LAKE
BIG LAKE MOTEL
P. O. Box 520728
(99652)
Rates: $65-$75
(907) 892-7976

CANTWELL
**BACKWOODS
LODGE**
MP 210 George
Parks Hwy
(99729)
Rates: $90-$130
(907) 768-2232

**REINDEER
MOUNTAIN
LODGE**
MP 210 George
Parks Hwy
(99729)
Rates: n/a
(907) 768-2420

**CIRCLE
SPRINGS**
**CIRCLE HOT
SPRINGS RESORT**
P. O. Box 254
(99730)
Rates: n/a
(907) 520-5113

**COOK INLET
WEST SIDE**
**CHINITNA BAY
LODGE**
P. O. Box 233032
(Anchorage 99523)
Rates: $1100/
Three days
(907) 522-2715

**COOPER
LANDING**
GWIN'S LODGE
14865 Sterling
Hwy (99572)
Rates: $59-$149
(907) 595-1266

**SUNRISE INN
MOTEL**
MP 45-A, Sterling
Hwy (99572)
Rates: $39-$99
(907) 595-1222

**DELTA
JUNCTION**
ALASKA 7 MOTEL
3548 Richardson
Hwy (99737)
Rates: $65-$75
(907) 895-4848

**BLACK SPRUCE
LODGE**
2740 Old
Richardson Hwy
(99737)
Rates: n/a
(907) 895-4668

**DELTA NT'L
HOSTEL**
Main St. USA
North (99737)
Rates: n/a
(907) 895-5074

**SUMMIT LAKE
LODGE**
Mile 195
Richardson Hwy
(99737)
Rates: n/a
(907) 822-3969

**DENALI
NATL PARK
& PRESERVE**
**DENALI GRIZZLY
BEAR CABINS &
CAMPGROUND**
P. O. Box 7-VP
(99755)
Rates: $49-$168
(907) 683-2696

**DENALI PARK
HOTEL**
MP 247, Parks
Hwy (99755)
Rates: $85-$119
(907) 683-1800
(866) 683-1800

**DENALI RV PARK
& MOTEL**
MP 245, George
Parks Hwy
(99755)
Rates: $54-$119
(800) 478-1501

**DENALI WEST
LODGE**
Box 40-VP (Lake
Minchumina
99757)
Rates: Package
(907) 674-3112

**EARTHSONG
LODGE**
P. O. Box 89
(Healy 99743)
Rates: $95-$115
(907) 683-2863

**MCKINLEY
CHALET RESORT**
MP 238, Parks
Hwy (99755)
Rates: $179-$239
(907) 683-8200

**MCKINLEY/
DENALI
PRIVATE
CABINS**
P. O. Box 90
(99755)
Rates: $65-$115
(907) 683-2733

**MT. MCKINLEY
MOTOR LODGE**
P. O. Box 77
(99755)
Rates: $98
(907) 683-1240

**SOURDOUGH
CABINS**
P. O. Box 118
(99755)
Rates: $80-$144
(907) 683-2773

**VALLEY VISTA
BED & BREAKFAST**
P. O. Box 395
(Healy 99743)
Rates: $70-$120
(877) 683-2841

EAGLE RIVER
**EAGLE RIVER INN
& SUITES**
13049 Old Glenn
Hwy (99577)
Rates: $59-$139
(907) 622-3232

**EAGLE RIVER
MOTEL**
11111 Old Eagle
River Rd (99577)
Rates: $49-$90
(907) 694-5000
(866) 256-6835

MICROTEL
13409 Old Glenn
Hwy (99577)
Rates: $79-$149
(907) 622-6000

**MOUNTAIN AIR
B&B**
HC83, Box 1652
(99577)
Rates: $40-$60
(907) 696-3116

**SHOOTING STAR
B&B**
19211 Upper
Skyline Dr (99577)
Rates: n/a
(907) 696-1748

ELFIN COVE
TANAKU LODGE
P. O. Box 72
(99825)
Rates: n/a
(800) 482-6258

FAIRBANKS
AAAA CARE B&B
557 Fairbanks St
(99709)
Rates: $75-$150
(907) 479-2447
(800) 478-2705

A PIONEER B&B
1119 Second Ave
(99701)
Rates: $55-$85
(907) 452-5393

ALASKA MOTEL
1546 Cushman St
(99701)
Rates: $45-$70
(907) 456-6393

**BEST WESTERN
FAIRBANKS INN**
1521 S Cushman
St (99701)
Rates: $59-$179
(907) 456-6602
(800) 528-1234
(877) 456-6602

CAPTAIN BARTLETT
1411 Airport Way
(99701)
Rates: $130-$139
(907) 452-1888
(800) 544-7528

**CHENA HOT
SPRINGS RESORT**
MP 56.5 Chena
Hot Springs Rd
(99701)
Rates: $105-$175
(907) 451-8104
(800) 478-4681

**CHENA RIVER
B&B**
1001 Dolly Varden
Ln (99709)
Rates: $50-$100
(907) 479-2532

COMFORT INN
1908 Chena
Landings Lp
(99701)
Rates: $59-$169
(907) 479-8080
(800) 424-6423

FOX CREEK B&B
2498 Elliott Hwy
(99712)
Rates: $54-$70
(907) 457-5494

**GOLDEN
NORTH HOTEL**
4888 Old Airport
Rd (99709)
Rates: $49-$99
(907) 479-6201
(800) 447-1910

HILLSIDE B&B
310 Rambling
Road (99712)
Rates: $35-$55
(907) 457-2664

**NORTH WOODS
LODGE & CABINS**
P. O. Box 83615
(99708)
Rates: $20-$87
(907) 479-5300
(800) 478-5305

**OLD F. E. GOLD
CAMP**
5550 Old Steese
Hwy N (99712)
Rates: n/a
(907) 389-2414

**PIKE'S
WATERFRONT
LODGE**
1850 Hoselton Rd
(99709)
Rates: $99-$235
(907) 456-4500
(877) 774-2400

**REGENCY
FAIRBANKS
HOTEL**
95 Tenth Ave
(99701)
Rates: $89-$169
(907) 452-3200
(800) 348-1340

AREA CODES - If the local number doesn't connect, check for a new area code.

SOURDOUGH B&B
1146 Gilmore Tr.
(99708)
Rates: $75-$90
(907) 457-6684

SUCH A DEAL B&B
P. O . Box 82527
(99708)
Rates: $45-$65
(907) 474-8159

SUPER 8 MOTEL
1909 Airport Way
(99701)
Rates: $75-$139
(907) 451-8888
(800) 800-8000

GAKONA

GAKONA JUNCTION VILLAGE
P. O. Box 222
(99586)
Rates: $55-$98
(800) 962-1933

GLENNALLEN

THE NEW CARIBOU HOTEL
P. O. Box 329
(99588)
Rates: $79-$115
(907) 822-3302
(800) 478-3302

GUSTAVUS

A PUFFIN'S B&B
(1/4 Mile Logging Rd) Box 3 (99826)
Rates: $85-$125
(907) 697-2260

GLACIER BAY'S BEAR TRACK INN
255 Rink Creek Rd
(99826)
Rates: $352-$704 (weekly)
(907) 697-3017
(888) 697-2284

TRI B & B
P. O. Box 214
(99826)
Rates: $90
(907) 697-2425

HAINES

CAPTAIN'S CHOICE MOTEL
108 2nd Ave
(99827)
Rates: $80-$115
(907) 766-3111
(800) 478-2345

EAGLE'S NEST MOTEL
1069 Haines Hwy
(99827)
Rates: $60-$95
(907) 766-2891
(800) 354-6009

FORT SEWARD LODGE & SALOON
39 Mud Bay Rd
(99827)
Rates: $40-$95
(907) 766-2009
(800) 478-7772

FORT WM. H. SEWARD B&B
House #1, Box 5
(99827)
Rates: $58-$125
(907) 766-2856
(800) 615-6676

THUNDERBIRD MOTEL
242 Dalton St
(99827)
Rates: $58-$68
(800) 327-2556

HATCHER PASS

HATCHER PASS LODGE
P. O. Box 763
(Palmer 99645)
Rates: $95-$125
(907) 745-5897

HOMER

ALASKA BY THE SEA S&B
58901 East End Rd (99603)
Rates: $40-$150
(907) 235-2716
(877) 374-2716

ANNA'S GUEST HOUSE
460 Bonanza Ave
(99603)
Rates: $55-$99
(907) 235-2716
(877) 374-2716

BEST WESTERN BIDARKA INN
575 Sterling Hwy
(99603)
Rates: $69-$179
(907) 235-8148
(800) 528-1234
(866) 685-5000

BRIGITTE'S BAVARIAN B&B
P. O. Box 2391
(99603)
Rates: $115
(907) 235-6620

DRIFTWOOD INN
135 W Bunnell Ave (99603)
Rates: $45-$130
(907) 235-8019
(800) 478-8019

HERITAGE HOTEL & LODGE
147 E. Pioneer Ave
(99603)
Rates: $50-$80
(907) 235-7787

HOME B&B/ SEEKINS
P. O. Box 1264
(99603)
Rates: $50-$80
(907) 235-8996

HOME SEASIDE COTTAGES
206 Bunnell Ave
(99603)
Rates: $125-$175
(907) 235-6836

LAKEWOOD INN
984 Ocean Dr #1
(99603)
Rates: n/a
(907) 235-6144

OCEAN SHORES MOTEL
3500 Crittenden Dr (99603)
Rates: $65-$165
(907) 235-7775
(800) 770-7775

PATCHWORK FARM B&B
P. O. Box 1654
(99603)
Rates: n/a
(907) 235-7368

SEASIDE FARM HOSTEL & CABINS
58335 E End Rd
(99603)
Rates: $65
(907) 235-7850

SUNDMARKS B&B
East Hill Rd
(99603)
Rates: n/a
(907) 235-5188

HOPE

BEAR CREEK CABINS
P O Box 64 (99605)
Rates: $75-$95
(907) 782-3730
(800) 360-8498

INDIAN

CABIN COMFORT B&B
HC 52, Box 8802
(99540)
Rates: n/a
(907) 653-7726

JUNEAU

BEST WESTERN COUNTRY LANE INN
9300 Glacier Hwy
(99801)
Rates: $90-$130
(907) 789-5005
(800) 528-1234

THE DRIFTWOOD LODGE
435 Willoughby Ave (99801)
Rates: $49-$115
(907) 586-2280
(800) 544-2239

FRONTIER SUITES AIRPORT HOTEL
9400 Glacier Hwy
(99801))
Rates: $90-$144
(800) 544-2250

JAN'S VIEW B&B
P. O. Box 32245
(99803)
Rates: $40-$65
(907) 463-5897

PROSPECTOR HOTEL
375 Whittier St
(99801)
Rates: $75-$155
(907) 586-3737
(800) 331-2711

SUPER 8 MOTEL
2295 Trout St
(99801)
Rates: $70-$114
(907) 789-4858
(800) 800-8000

WATERFRONT BREAKWATER INN
1711 Glacier Ave
(99801)
Rates: $99-$119
(800) 544-2250

WESTMARK BARANOF
127 N Franklin St
(99801)
Rates: $139-$159
(907) 586-2660

KENAI

CAPT. BLIGH'S BEAVER CREEK LODGE & GUIDES
P. O.Box 4300
(Soldotna 99669)
Rates: Package
(907) 262-7919
(907) 283-7550

THE FISH HUT CHARTERS & LODGING
1125 Angler Dr
(99611)
Rates: $120-$240
(877) 827-2675

HI-LO CHARTERS & RIVERSIDE LODGE
1105 Angker Dr
(99611)
Rates: $60-$250
(800) 757-9333

KENAI KINGS INN
P. O. Box 1080
(99611)
Rates: $74-$104
(907) 283-6060

AREA CODES - If the local number doesn't connect, check for a new area code.

MERIT INN
260 S Willow
(99611)
Rates: $50-$90
(907) 283-6131
(800) 227-6131

KENAI PENINSULA

ALASKA MOUNTAIN VIEW CABINS
P. O. Box 423
(Sterling 99672)
Rates: $75-$175
(907) 262-4827

ANGLER'S LODGE & FISH CAMP
P. O. Box 508-VG
(Sterling 99672)
Rates: $49-$150
(907) 262-1747

KENAI MAGIC LODGE
2440 E Tudor Rd #205
(Anchorage 99507)
Rates: $99-$158
(888) 262-6644

KENAI PENINSULA CONDOS
P. O. Box 3416
(Soldotna 99669)
Rates: $79-$99
(800) 362-1383

KENAI WILDERNESS LODGE
3074 Commercial Dr (Anchorage 99501)
Rates: $40+
(907) 262-4390

MORGAN'S LANDING CABIN RENTALS
P. O. Box 422
(Sterling 99672)
Rates: $65-$140
(907) 262-8343

KETCHIKAN

BEST WESTERN LANDING HOTEL
3434 Tongass Ave
(99901)
Rates: $110-$197
(907) 225-5166
(800) 528-1234
(800) 428-8304

THE GILMORE HOTEL
P. O. Box 6814
(99901)
Rates: $65-$110
(907) 225-9423
(800) 275-9423

INGERSOLL HOTEL
303 Mission St
(99901)
Rates: $57-$99
(907) 225-2124
(800) 478-2124

MILLAR STREET HOUSE B&B
P. O. Box 7281
(99901)
Rates: $55-$80
(907) 225-1258
(800) 287-1607

SUPER 8 MOTEL
2151 Sea Level Dr
(99901)
Rates: $82-$135
(907) 225-9088
(800) 800-8000

KING SALMON

KING SALMON GUIDES B&B
P O Box 602
(99613)
Rates: $180
(800) 976-2202

KODIAK

BEST WESTERN KODIAK INN
236 Rezanof Dr, W
(99615)
Rates: $74-$199
(907) 486-5712
(800) 528-1234
(888) 563-4254

BUSKIN RIVER INN
1395 Airport Way
(99615)
Rates: $125-$135
(907) 487-2700
(800) 544-2202

KALSIN BAY INN
P. O. Box 1696
(99615)
Rates: n/a
(907) 486-2659

KODIAK B&B
308 Cope St
(99615)
Rates: $70-$82
(907) 486-5367

NORTHLAND RANCH RESORT
P. O. Box 2376
(99615)
Rates: Package
(907) 486-5578

SHELIKOF LODGE
211 Thorsheim Ave (99615)
Rates: $65-$85
(907) 486-4141

LAKE LOUISE

LAKE LOUISE LODGE
(HC01 Box 1716, Glenallen 99588)
Rates: $45-$105
(907) 822-3311

MOOSE PASS

TRAIL LAKE LODGE
MM 29.5 Seward Hwy (99631)
Rates: $59-$105
(907) 288-3101

PALMER

HATCHER PASS B&B
HC01, Box 6797-D
(99645)
Rates: $55
(907) 745-4210

PETERSBURG

NARROWS INN
P. O. Box 1048
(99833)
Rates: $70
(907) 772-4284

SCANDIA HOUSE HOTEL
P. O. Box 689
(99833)
Rates: $90-$175
(907) 772-4281

SALCHA

SALCHA RIVER LODGE
P. O. Box 111
(99714)
Rates: n/a
(907) 488-2233

SEWARD

BREEZE INN
P. O. Box 2147
(99664)
Rates: $49-$218
(888) 224-5237

NEW SEWARD HOTEL
P. O. Box 670C
(99664)
Rates: $50-$96
(907) 224-8001
(800) 478-1774

TAROKA INN
P. O. Box 2448
(99664)
Rates: $45-$105
(907) 224-8975

"THE FARM" B&B
P. O. Box 305
(99664)
Rates: $65-$110
(907) 224-2300

SITKA

BARANOF WILDERNESS LODGE
P. O. Box 2187-VP
(99835)
Rates: Package
(800) 613-6551

SUPER 8 MOTEL
404 Sawmill Creek Rd (99835)
Rates: $94-$129
(907) 747-8804
(800) 800-8000

SKAGWAY

SARGEANT PRESTONS LODGE
6th Ave & State St
(99840)
Rates: $70+
(907) 983-2521

WESTMARK INN
3rd & Spring Sts
(99840)
Rates: $99-$119
(907) 983-2291
(800) 544-0970

SOLDOTNA

BED & BREAKFST COTTAGES
General Del
(99669)
Rates: $60-$80
(800) 582-7829

KENAI PENINSULA CONDOS
P. O. Box 3416A
(99669)
Rates: $86-$135
(888) 811-6433
(800) 362-1383

RAVEN MTN FARM B&B
P. O. Box 344
(Kasilof 99610)
Rates: $45-$76
(907) 262-9186

SOARING EAGLE LODGE
HC01, Box 1203
(99669)
Rates: $50-$100
(907) 337-1223

TALKEETNA

ALASKA LOG CABIN B&B
#1A Beaver Rd
(99676)
Rates: $55-$85
(907) 733-2668

LATITUDE 62 LODGE
P. O. Box 478
(99676)
Rates: n/a
(907) 733-2262

TOK

CLEFT OF THE ROCK B&B
5 Sundog Trail
(99780)
Rates: $60-$135
(907) 883-4219
(800) 478-5646

SNOWSHOE MOTEL
P. O. Box 559
(99780)
Rates: $42-$78
(907) 883-4511
(800) 478-4511

AREA CODES - If the local number doesn't connect, check for a new area code.

STAGE STOP B&B
P. O. Box 69
(99780)
Rates: $40-$85
(907) 883-5338

TOK LODGE
P. O. Box 135
(99780)
Rates: $50-$80
(907) 883-2851

WESTMARK INN
Alaska Hwy &
Glenn Hwy
(99780)
Rates: $129
(907) 883-5174
(800) 544-0970

YOUNG'S MOTEL
MP 1313,
Box 482,
Alaska Hwy
(99780)
Rates: $55-$79
(907) 883-4411

TRAPPER CREEK

GATE CREEK CABINS
Mile 10.5
Petersville Rd
(99683)
Rates: $90-$125
(907) 733-1393

MCKINLEY FOOTHILLS B&B
P. O. Box 13089
(99683)
Rates: $80+
(907) 773-1454

VALDEZ

BEST WESTERN VALDEZ HARBOR INN
100 Harbor Dr
(99686)
Rates: $79-$179
(907) 835-3434
(800) 528-1234

TIEKEL RIVER LODGE
Richardson Hwy
Mile 56, (99686)
Rates: $45-$85
(907) 822-3259

TOTEM INN
P. O. Box 648
(99686)
Rates: $69-$154
(907) 835-4443

WASILLA

BEST WESTERN LAKE LUCILLE INN
1300 W Lake
Lucille Dr (99654)
Rates: $79-$219
(907) 373-1776
(800) 528-1234

GRANDVIEW INN & SUITES
2900 E Parks Hwy
(99654)
Rates: $70-$160
(907) 357-7666

KOZEY CABINS
351 E Spruce Ave
(99654)
Rates: $85-$100
(907) 376-3190

PIONEER RIDGE B&B
2221 Yukon Cir
(99654)
Rates: $79-$155
(907) 376-7472

WILLOW

ALASKAN HOST B&B
MP 66.5 Old Parks
Hwy (99688)
Rates: $70-$115
(907) 495-6800

SHEEP CREEK LODGE
Mile 88, Parks
Hwy (99688)
Rates: n/a
(907) 495-6227

WOODTIKCHIK STATE PARK

MAURICE'S FLOATING LODGE
P. O. Box 1261
(Dillingham
99576)
Rates: Package
(800) 356-2844

WRANGELL

BRUCE HARDING'S OLD SOURDOUGH LODGE
P. O. Box 1062
(99929)
Rates: $75-$195
(800) 874-3613

AREA CODES - If the local number doesn't connect, check for a new area code.

ARIZONA

AHWATUKEE

CLARION HOTEL TECH CENTER
5121 E La Puente Ave (85044)
Rates: $49-$134
(480) 893-3900
(800) 424-6423

HOLIDAY INN EXPRESS & SUITES
15221 S 50th St (85044)
Rates: $99-$119
(480) 785-8500
(800) 465-4329

AJO

LA SIESTA MOTEL
2561 N Ajo-Gila Bend Hwy (85321)
Rates: $36-$62
(520) 387-6569

MARINE MOTEL
1966 N 2nd Ave (85321)
Rates: $38-$69
(520) 387-7626

ALPINE

CORONADO TRAILS CABINS
25302 Hwy 191 (85920)
Rates: $45+
(928) 339-4772

HANNAGAN MEADOW LODGE CABINS
HC 61, P.O. Box 335 (85920)
Rates: $70-$150
(928) 428-2225

SPORTSMANS LODGE
42627 W Hwy 180 (85920)
Rates: $50-$75
(928) 339-4576
(888) 202-1033

TAL-WI-WI LODGE
40 County Road 2220 (85920)
Rates: $65-$95
(928) 339-4319

ANTHEM

HAMPTON INN
42415 N 41st Dr (85086)
Rates: $49-$129
(623) 465-7979
(800) 426-7866

APACHE JUNCTION

APACHE JUNCTION MOTEL
1680 W Apache Trail (85219)
Rates: $34-$66
(480) 982-7702

GOLD CANYON GOLF RESORT
6100 S Kings Ranch Rd (Gold Canyon 85219)
Rates: $135-$310
(480) 982-9090
(800) 624-6445

SUPER 8 MOTEL
251 E 29th Ave (85219)
Rates: $55-$109
(480) 288-8888
(800) 800-8000

APACHE LAKE

APACHE LAKE MARINA & RESORT
Hwy 88 (Tortilla Flat 85290)
Rates: $55-$65
(928) 467-2511

ASH FORK

ASH FORK INN
1137 W Hwy 66 (86320)
Rates: $22-$39
(928) 637-2514

BELLEMONT

MICROTEL INN
12380 W I-40 (86015)
Rates: $34-$79
(928) 556-9599
(888) 771-7171

BENSON

BEST WESTERN QUAIL HOLLOW INN
699 N Ocotillo St (85602)
Rates: $60-$70
(520) 586-3646
(800) 528-1234
(800) 322-1850

MOTEL 6
637 S Whetstone Commerce Dr (85602)
Rates: $39-$56
(520) 586-0066
(800) 466-8356

SUPER 8 MOTEL
855 N Ocotillo Rd (85602)
Rates: $42-$59
(520) 586-1530
(800) 800-8000

BISBEE

AUDREY'S INN
20 Brewery Ave (85603)
Rates: $85-$455
(520) 227-6120
(888) 437-4263

CALUMET & ARIZONA GUEST HOUSE
608 Powell (85603)
Rates: $45-$80
(520) 432-4815

81 OK STREET GUEST HOUSE
81 OK St (85603)
Rates: $65
(520) 432-7482

EL RANCHO MOTEL
1104 Hwy 92 (85603)
Rates: $55-$125
(520) 432-2293

HOTEL LAMORE/ THE BISBEE INN
45 OK St (85603)
Rates: $60-$155
(520) 432-5131
(888) 432-5131

INN AT CASTLE ROCK
112 Tombstone Canyon (85603)
Rates: $47-$150
(520) 432-4449
(800) 566-4449

120 NACO ROAD RENTALS
120 Naco Rd (85603)
Rates: $125-$245
(520) 432-5439
(800) 728-8537

PARK PLACE B&B
200 E Vista in Warren (85603)
Rates: $50-$70
(520) 432-3054
(800) 388-4388

SAN JOSE LODGE
1002 Naco Hwy (85603)
Rates: $59-$105
(520) 432-5761

SLEEPY DOG GUEST HOUSE- OLD BISBEE
212A Opera Dr (85603)
Rates: $95
(520) 432-3057

220A OPERA RENTALS HOME
220A Opera Dr (85603)
Rates: $115-$495
(520) 432-5439
(800) 728-8537

BUCKEYE

DAYS INN
25205 W Yuma Rd (85326)
Rates: $69-$199
(623) 386-5400
(800) 329-7466

BULLHEAD CITY

(Also see Laughlin, NV)

ARIZONA BLUFFS
2220 Rancho Colorado Blvd (86442)
Rates: $192 Wkly
(928) 763-3839

BEST WESTERN BULLHEAD CITY
1124 Hwy 95 (86429)
Rates: $44-$99
(928) 754-3000
(800) 528-1234
(800) 634-4463

COLORADO RIVER RESORT
434 Riverglen Dr (86440)
Rates: $36-$68
(928) 754-4101

DAYS INN & SUITES
2200 Rancho Colorado Blvd (86442)
Rates: $35-$200
(928) 758-1711
(800) 329-7466

DESERT RANCHO MOTEL
1041 Hwy 95 (86430)
Rates: $30-$45
(928) 754-2578

LA PLAZA INN
1978 Hwy 95 (86442)
Rates: $26-$35
(928) 763-8080

LAKE MOHAVE RESORT & MARINA
At Katherine Landing (86430)
Rates: $80-$110
(928) 754-3245
(800) 752-9669

LODGE ON THE RIVER MOTEL
1717 Hwy 95 (86442)
Rates: $26-$64
(928) 758-8080
(888) 200-7855

RIVER QUEEN RESORT
125 Long Ave (86430)
Rates: $35-$53
(928) 754-3214

SHANGRI-LA LODGE/VILLAGER LODGE
1767 Georgia Ln (86442)
Rates: $33-$71
(928) 758-1117

SUNRIDGE HOTEL & CONF CENTER
839 Landon Dr (86429)
Rates: $49-$89
(928) 754-4700
(800) 977-4242

SUPER 8 MOTEL
1616 Hwy 95 (86442)
Rates: $35-$45
(928) 763-1002
(800) 800-8000

CAMERON

CAMERON TRADING POST MOTEL
US 89 (86020)
Rates: $49-$119
(928) 679-2231
(877) 675-0614

CAMP VERDE

COMFORT INN
340 N Industrial Dr (86322)
Rates: $49-$139
(928) 567-9000
(800) 424-6423

DAYS INN & SUITES
1640 W Finnie Flat Rd (86322)
Rates: $49-$129
(928) 567-3700
(800) 329-7466

FORT VERDE MOTEL
628 S Main St (86322)
Rates: $35+
(928) 567-3486

LODGE AT CLIFF CASTLE
333 Middle Verde Rd (86322)
Rates: $59-$82
(928) 567-6611
(800) 524-6343

CAREFREE

THE BOULDERS RESORT & GOLDEN DOOR SPA
34631 N Tom Darlington Rd (85377)
Rates: $169-$495
(480) 488-9009
(800) 553-1717
(800) 996-3426

CAREFREE RESORT & VILLAS
37220 Mule Train Rd (85377)
Rates: $75-$700
(480) 488-5300
(800) 949-1994

CASA GRANDE

BEST WESTERN CASA GRANDE SUITES
665 Via Del Cielo (85222)
Rates: $59-$145
(520) 836-1600
(800) 528-1234

DAYS INN
5300 N Sunland Gin Rd (85222)
Rates: $49-$89
(520) 426-9240
(800) 329-7466

HOLIDAY INN
777 N Pinal Ave (85222)
Rates: $83-$99
(520) 426-3500
(800) 465-4329
(800) 858-4499

MOTEL 6
4965 N Sunland Gin Rd (85222)
Rates: $31-$63
(520) 836-3323
(800) 466-8356

SE-TAY MOTEL
901 N Pinal Ave (85222)
Rates: $29-$40
(520) 836-7489

SUNLAND INN
7190 S Sunland Gin Rd (85222)
Rates: $32-$38
(520) 836-5000

SUPER 8 MOTEL
2066 E Florence Blvd (85222)
Rates: $49-$150
(520) 836-8800
(800) 800-8000

CATALINA

SUPER 8 MOTEL
15691 N Oracle Rd (85739)
Rates: $47-$75
(520) 818-9500
(800) 800-8000

CAVE CREEK

CAVE CREEK TUMBLEWEED HOTEL
6333 E Cave Creek Rd (85327)
Rates: $99-$199
(480) 488-3668

CHAMBERS

BEST WESTERN CHIEFTAIN INN
I-40 & Jct US 191, Exit 333 (86502)
Rates: $58-$150
(520) 688-2611
(800) 528-1234
(800) 657-7632

CHANDLER

COMFORT INN
255 N Kyrene (85226)
Rates: $59-$99
(280) 705-8882
(800) 424-6423

HAWTHORN SUITES LTD
5858 W Chandler Blvd (85226)
Rates: $85-$165
(480) 705-8881
(800) 527-1133

HOMEWOOD SUITES
7337 W Detroit St (85226)
Rates: $94-$129
(480) 753-6200
(800) 225-5466

LA QUINTA INN & SUITES
15241 S 50th St (85224)
Rates: $60-$116
(480) 961-7700
(800) 687-6667
(800) 221-4731

PRIME HOTEL & SUITES
7475 W Chandler Blvd (85226)
Rates: $59-$149
(480) 961-4444
(800) 889-8846

RED ROOF INN
7400 W Boston St (85226)
Rates: $43-$66
(480) 857-4969
(800) 843-7663

RESIDENCE INN-CHANDLER FASHION SQ.
200 N Federal St (85226)
Rates: $79-$179
(480) 782-1551
(800) 331-3131

SHERATON SAN MARCOS GOLF &
1 San Marcos Place (85224)
Rates: $85-$119
(480) 812-0900
(800) 325-3535
(800) 528-8071

SOUTHGATE MOTEL
7445 W Chandler Blvd (85226)
Rates: $40-$80
(480) 940-0308

SUPER 8 MOTEL
7171 W Chandler Blvd (85226)
Rates: $44-$65
(480) 961-3888
(800) 800-8000

WELLESLEY INN & SUITES
5035 E Chandler Blvd (85226)
Rates: $59-$109
(480) 753-6700
(800) 444-8888

WINDMILL SUITES
3535 W Chandler Blvd (85226)
Rates: $79-$129
(480) 812-9600
(800) 547-4747
(866) 645-4725

CHINLE

BEST WESTERN CANYON DE CHELLY INN
100 Main St (86503)
Rates: $69-$139
(928) 674-5874
(800) 528-1234
(800) 327 0354

CLAY SPRINGS

DEER SPRINGS INN
Hwy 260, MP 320.9 (85923)
Rates: n/a
(928) 368-5229
(928) 528-7350

COCHISE

STRAWBALE MANOR BED & BREAKFAST
114 Kaibab Way (85606)
Rates: $65-$85
(520) 825-3077
(888) 414-3077

COTTONWOOD

BEST WESTERN COTTONWOOD INN
993 S Main St (86326)
Rates: $69-$99
(928) 634-5575
(800) 528-1234
(800) 350-0035

BUDGET INN & SUITES
189 Hwy 260 (86326)
Rates: $45-$99
(928) 634-3678
(888) 720-1719

LITTLE DAISY MOTEL
34 S Main St (86326)
Rates: $48-$125
(928) 634-7865

THE PINES MOTEL
920 S Camino Real (86326)
Rates: $44-$64
(928) 634-9975

QUALITY INN
301 W Hwy 89A (86326)
Rates: $59-$109
(928) 634-4207
(800) 424-6423

THE VIEW MOTEL
818 S Main St (86326)
Rates: $36-$50
(928) 634-7581

DOUGLAS

MOTEL 6
111 16th St (85607)
Rates: $33-$42
(520) 364-2457
(800) 466-8356

PRICE CANYON GUEST RANCH
P. O. Box 1065 (85607)
Rates: $85-$170
(520) 558-2383
(800) 727-0065

EAGAR

BEST WESTERN SUNRISE INN
128 N Main St (85925)
Rates: $59-$99
(928) 333-2540
(800) 528-1234

EHRENBERG

BEST WESTERN FLYING J MOTEL
Flying J Travel Plaza, S Frontage Rd (85334)
Rates: $45-$149
(928) 923-9711
(800) 528-1234
(800) 292-9711

ELOY

SUPER 8 MOTEL
3945 W Houser Rd (85231)
Rates: $55-$73
(520) 466-7804
(800) 800-8000

FLAGSTAFF

AMERISUITES
2455 S Beulah Blvd (86001)
Rates: $79-$129
(928) 774-8042
(800) 833-1516

ARIZONA MOUNTAIN INN
4200 Lake Mary Rd (86001)
Rates: $85-$205
(928) 774-8959
(800) 239-5236

BEST WESTERN KINGS HOUSE MOTEL
1560 E Rt 66 (86001)
Rates: $34-$99
(928) 774-7186
(800) 528-1234
(888) 577-7186

BUDGET HOST SAGA MOTEL
820 W Rt 66 (86001)
Rates: $28-$46
(928) 779-3631
(800) 283-4678

CANYON INN
510 S Milton Rd (86001)
Rates: $26-$125
(928) 774-7301
(888) 822-6966

COMFORT INN
2355 S Beulah Blvd (86001)
Rates: $59-$139
(928) 774-2225
(800) 424-6423

DAYS INN EAST
3601 E Lockett Rd (86004)
Rates: $35-$119
(928) 527-1477
(800) 329-7466

DAYS INN- ROUTE 66
1000 W Rt 66 (86001)
Rates: $39-$169
(928) 774-5221
(800) 329-7466

ECONO LODGE
2480 E Lucky Ln (86004)
Rates: $59-$129
(928) 774-7701
(800) 424-6423

ECONO LODGE UNIVERSITY
914 S Milton Rd (86001)
Rates: $43-$99
(928) 774-7326
(800) 424-6423

FRONTIER MOTEL
1700 E Rt 66 (86001)
Rates: $18-$80
(928) 774-8993

HAMPTON INN
3501 E Lockett Rd (86004)
Rates: $59-$179
(928) 526-1885
(800) 426-7866

HANFORD HOTEL
2200 E Butler Ave (86004)
Rates: $30-$99
(928) 779-6944

HOLIDAY INN FLAGSTAFF/ GRAND CANYON
2320 E Lucky Ln (86004)
Rates: $69-$129
(928) 526-1150
(800) 465-4329

HOWARD JOHNSON INN
3300 E Rt 66 (86004)
Rates: $29-$99
(928) 526-1826
(800) 446-4656
(800) 437-7137

INNSUITES HOTEL
1008 E Rt 66 (86001)
Rates: $53-$139
(928) 774-7356
(888) 235-2478
(800) 898-9124

LA QUINTA INN & SUITES
2015 S Beulah Blvd (86001)
Rates: $65-$126
(928) 556-8666
(800) 687-6777

MOTEL 6
2010 E Butler Ave (86004)
Rates: $33-$56
(928) 774-1801
(800) 466-8356

MOTEL 6
2440 E Lucky Ln (86004)
Rates: $30-$52
(928) 774-8756
(800) 466-8356

MOTEL 6
2745 S Woodlands Village Blvd (86001)
Rates: $34-$56
(928) 779-3757
(800) 466-8356

PARKSIDE FAMILY INN & SUITES
121 S Milton Rd (86001)
Rates: $18-$139
(928) 774- 8820

PINECREST MOTEL
2818 E Rt 66 (86001)
Rates: $24-$54
(928) 526-1950

QUALITY INN
2000 S Milton Rd (86001)
Rates: $29-$74
(928) 774-8771
(800) 424-6423

QUALITY INN LUCKY LANE
2500 E Lucky Ln (86004)
Rates: $35-$79
(928) 226-7111
(800) 424-6423

RADISSON WOODLANDS PLAZA HOTEL
1175 W Rt 66 (86001)
Rates: $79-$179
(928) 773-8888
(800) 333-3333

RAMADA LIMITED LUCKY LANE
2350 E Lucky Ln (86004)
Rates: $69-$129
(928) 779-3614
(800) 272-6232

RAMADA LIMITED WEST
2755 S Woodlands Vlge Blvd (86001)
Rates: $44-$129
(928) 773-1111
(800) 272-6232

RED ROOF INN
2520 E Lucky Ln (86004)
Rates: $42-$79
(928) 779-5121
(800) 843-7663
(800) 545-5525

RELAX INN MOTEL
1416 E Santa Fe (86001)
Rates: $35-$44
(928) 774-5123

RESIDENCE INN BY MARRIOTT
3440 N Country Club Dr (86004)
Rates: $89-$209
(928) 526-5555
(800) 331-3131

AREA CODES - If the local number doesn't connect, check for a new area code.

RODEWAY INN
2650 E Rt 66
(86004)
Rates: $29-$99
(928) 526-2200
(800) 424-6423

ROYAL INN
2140 E Rt 66
(86001)
Rates: $52-$120
(928) 774-7308

SLEEP INN
2765 S Woodlands
Vlge Blvd (86001)
Rates: $49-$109
(928) 556-3000
(800) 753-3746

SUPER 8 MOTEL
602 W Rte 66
(86004)
Rates: $42-$125
(928) 774-4581
(800) 800-8000
(800) 654-4667

SUPER 8 MOTEL
3725 Kasper Ave
(86004)
Rates: $53-$79
(928) 526-0818
(800) 800-8000
(888) 324-9131

TOWN HOUSE MOTEL
122 W Route 66
(86001)
Rates: $24-$49
(928) 774-5081

TRAVEL INN
801 W Rt 66
(86001)
Rates: $26-$70
(928) 774-3381

TRAVELODGE
2610 E Rt 66
(86001)
Rates: $29-$99
(928) 526-1399
(800) 578-7878

WESTERN HILLS MOTEL
1580 E Rt 66
(86001)
Rates: $20-$65
(928) 774-6633

FLORENCE
RANCHO SONORA INN
9198 N Hwy 79
(85232)
Rates: $50-$150
(520) 868-8000
(800) 205-6817

FOREST LAKES
FOREST LAKES LODGE
876 Hwy 260,
MP 288.6 (85931)
Rates: $42-$74
(928) 535-4727

FOUNTAIN HILLS
ARIZONA TRAILS RESERVATION SERVICE
P. O. Box 18998
(85269)
Rates: $65-$625
(480) 837-4284
(888) 799-4284

FREDONIA
CRAZY JUG MOTEL
465 S Main (86022)
Rates: $38-$49
(928) 643-7752

SHIP ROCK MOTEL
337 S Main (86022)
Rates: n/a
(928) 643-7355

GILA BEND
AMERICAS CHOICE INN & SUITES
2888 Butterfield
Trail (85337)
Rates: $60-$70
(928) 883-6311

BEST WESTERN SPACE AGE LODGE
401 E Pima St
(85337)
Rates: $60-$109
(928) 683-2273
(800) 528-1234

YUCCA MOTEL
836 E Pima St
(85337)
Rates: $30-$50
(928) 683-2211

GLENDALE
BEST WESTERN INN GLENDALE
5940 W Grand
Ave (85301)
Rates: $49-$99
(623) 939-9431
(800) 528-1234
(800) 333-7172

RAMADA LIMITED AT ARROWHEAD MALL
7885 W
Arrowhead
Towne Center Dr
(85308)
Rates: $62-$71
(623) 412-2000
(800) 272-6232

GLOBE
BELLE AIRE MOTEL
1600 N Broad St
(85501)
Rates: $22-$47
(928) 425-4406

CEDAR HILL B&B
175 E Cedar St
(85501)
Rates: $25-$50
(928) 425-7530

COMFORT INN AT ROUND MTN PARK
1515 South St
(85501)
Rates: $59-$159
(928) 425-7575
(800) 424-6423

DAYS INN
1630 E Ash St
(85501)
Rates: $55-$89
(928) 425-5500
(800) 329-7466

ECONOMY INN
1105 N Broad St
(85501)
Rates: $28-$36
(928) 425-5736

EL RANCHO MOTEL
1300 E Ash St
(85501)
Rates: $22-$45
(928) 425-5757

HIDEAWAY B&B
7719 Ice Hosue
Canyon Rd
(85501)
Rates: $45-$95
(928) 402-0454
(888) 692-3369

MOTEL 6
1699 E Ash St
(85501)
Rates: $40-$90
(928) 425-5741
(800) 466-8356

TRAVELODGE
2119 Hwy 60
(85501)
Rates: $65-$99
(928) 425-7008
(800) 578-7878

WILLOW MOTEL
792 N Willow St
(85501)
Rates: $20-$30
(928) 425-9491

GOODYEAR
BEST WESTERN GOODYEAR INN
55 N Litchfield Rd
(85338)
Rates: $59-$159
(623) 932-3210
(800) 528-1234
(888) 449-3330

HAMPTON INN & SUITES
2000 N Litchfield
Rd (85338)
Rates: $89-$179
(623) 536-1313
(800) 426-7866

HOLIDAY INN EXP
1313 Litchfield Rd
(85338)
Rates: $89-$169
(623) 535-1313
(800) 465-4329

RAMADA INN
1770 N Dysart Rd
(85338)
Rates: n/a
(623) 932-9191
(800) 272-6232

SUPER 8 MOTEL
1710 N Dysart Rd
(85338)
Rates: $38-$65
(623) 932-9622
(800) 800-8000

WINGATE INN & SUITES
1188 N Dysart Rd
(85338)
Rates: $99-$169
(623) 547-1313

GRAND CANYON NAT'L PARK (SOUTH RIM)
(Canyon hotels
& lodges do not
allow pets in
rooms. Contact
the Grand Canyon
Kennels at
(928) 638-0534.)

BRIGHT ANGEL LODGE & CABINS
P. O. Box 699
(86023)
Rates: $60-$115
(928) 638-2631
(303) 297-2757

EL TOVAR HISTORIC HOTEL
P. O. Box 699
(86023)
Rates: $137-$308
(928) 638-2631
(303) 297-2757

GRAND HOTEL
SR 64, P. O. Box
3319 (86023)
Rates: $99-$149
(928) 638-3333
(888) 63-GRAND

KACHINA LODGE
P. O. Box 699
(86023)
Rates: $128-$138
(928) 638-2631
(303) 297-2757

MASWIK LODGE
P. O. Box 699
(86023)
Rates: $66-$127
(928) 638-2631
(303) 297-2757

QUALITY INN & SUITES
Hwy 64
(Tusayan 86023)
Rates: $78-$188
(928) 638-2673
(800) 424-6423

AREA CODES - If the local number doesn't connect, check for a new area code.

RODEWAY RED FEATHER LODGE
Hwy 64,US 80
(Tusayan 86023)
Rates: $54-$139
(928) 638-2414
(800) 424-6423
(800) 538-2345

THUNDERBIRD LODGE
P. O. Box 699
(86023)
Rates: $128-$138
(928) 638-2631
(303) 297-2757

YAVAPAI LODGE
P. O. Box 699
(86023)
Rates: $66-$110
(928) 638-2631
(303) 297-2757

GRAY MOUNTAIN

ANASAZI INN-GRAY MOUNTAIN
P. O. Box 29100
(86016)
Rates: $40-$70
(928) 679-2214
(800) 867-2214

GREEN VALLEY

BAYMONT INN & SUITES
60 W Esperanza
Blvd (85614)
Rates: $70-$139
(520) 399-3736
(800) 301-0200
(877) 229-6668

BEST WESTERN GREEN VALLEY INN
111 S La Canada
Dr (85614)
Rates: $79-$120
(520) 625-2250
(800) 528-1234
(800) 344-1441

HOLIDAY INN EXP
19200 Frontage
Rd, Ex 69 (85614)
Rates: $66-$110
(520) 625-0900
(800) 465-4329

GREER

ANTLER RIDGE CABINS
87 Main St (85927)
Rates: n/a
(928) 735-7288
(888) 563-7337

BIG TEN CABINS
P. O. Box 124
(85927)
Rates: n/a
(928) 735-7578

MOLLY BUTLER LODGE & CABINS
109 Main St
(85927)
Rates: $55-$90
(928) 735-7232
(866) 288-3167

SNOWY MOUNTAIN INN
38721 SR 373
(85927)
Rates: $150-$350
(928) 735-7576
(888) 766-9971

WHITE MT LODGE
140 Main St
(85927)
Rates: n/a
(928) 735-7568
(888) 493-7568

HAPPY JACK

HAPPY JACK LODGE & CABINS
P. O. Box 19569
(86024)
Rates: n/a
(928) 477-2805

HEBER

BEST WESTERN SAWMILL INN
1877 Hwy 260
(85928)
Rates: $56-$89
(928) 535-5053
(800) 528-1234
(800) 372-9564

HEREFORD

CASA DE SAN PEDRO
8933 S Yell Ln
(85615)
Rates: $129-$149
(520) 366-1300
(888) 257-2050

SAN PEDRO RIVER INN
8326 S Hereford
Rd (85615)
Rates: $105
(520) 366-5532

HOLBROOK

BEST INN
2211 E Navajo
Blvd (85026)
Rates: $35-$52
(938) 524-2654
(800) 237-8466

BEST WESTERN ADOBE INN
615 W Hopi Dr
(86025)
Rates: $40-$58
(928) 524-3948
(800) 528 1234
(877) 524-3948

BEST WESTERN ARIZONAN INN
2508 E Navajo
Blvd (86025)
Rates: $45-$89
(928) 524-2611
(800) 528-1234
(877) 280-7300

COMFORT INN
2602 E Navajo
Blvd (86025)
Rates: $46-$79
(928) 524-6131
(800) 424-6423

ECONO LODGE
2596 E Navajo
Blvd (86025)
Rates: $40-$60
(928) 524-1448
(800) 424-6423

HOLBROOK INN
235 W Hopi Dr
(86025)
Rates: $22-$34
(928) 524-3809

HOLIDAY INN EXP
1308 E Navajo
Blvd (86025)
Rates: $69-$85
(928) 524-1466
(800) 465-4329

MOTEL 6
2514 E Navajo
Blvd (86025)
Rates: $31-$34
(928) 524-6101
(800) 466-8356

RAMADA LTD
2608 E Navajo
Blvd (86025)
Rates: n/a
(928) 524-2566
(800) 272-6232

RELAX INN
2418 E Navajo
Blvd (86025)
Rates: $30-$40
(928) 524-6815

JEROME

CONNOR HOTEL OF JEROME
164 Main St
(86331)
Rates: $90-$125
(928) 634-5006
(800) 523-3554

GHOST CITY INN B&B
541 Main St
(86331)
Rates: $90-$135
(928) 634-4678
(888) 634-4678

THE SURGEON'S HOUSE B&B
101 Hill St (86331)
Rates: $100-$200
(928) 990-0682
(800) 639-1452

KAYENTA

ANASAZI INN-TSEGI CANYON
Hwy 160 (86033)
Rates: $70-$90
(928) 697-3793

HAMPTON INN OF MONUMENT VALLEY
Hwy 160 (86033)
Rates: $55-$115
(928) 697-3170
(800) 426-7866

KEARNY

GENERAL KEARNY INN
301 Alden Rd
(85237)
Rates: $39-$75
(520) 363-5505

KINGMAN

BEST WESTERN WAYFARER'S INN
2815 E Andy
Devine (86401)
Rates: $62-$150
(928) 753-6271
(800) 528-1234
(800) 548-5695

BEST WESTERN KING'S INN & SUITES
2930 E Andy
Devine (86401)
Rates: $62-$105
(928) 753-6101
(800) 528-1234
(800) 750-6101

BRUNSWICK HOTEL
315 E Andy
Devine (86401)
Rates: $25-$115
(928) 718-1800

DAYS INN WEST
3023 E Andy
Devine (86401)
Rates: $29-$89
(928) 753-7500
(800) 329-7466

DAYS INN
3381 E Andy
Devine (86401)
Rates: 30-$70
(928) 757-7337
(800) 329-7466

ECONO LODGE
3421 E Andy
Devine (86401)
Rates: $40-$55
(928) 757-7878
(800) 424-6423

HIGH DESERT INN
2803 E Andy
Devine (86401)
Rates: $25-$75
(928) 753-2935

HILL TOP MOTEL
1901 E Andy
Devine (86401)
Rates: $34-$85
(928) 753-2198

MOTEL 6 EAST
3351 W Andy
Devine (86401)
Rates: $31-$36
(928) 757-7151
(800) 466-8356

AREA CODES - If the local number doesn't connect, check for a new area code.

MOTEL 6 WEST
424 W Beale St
(86401)
Rates: $35-$55
(928) 753-9222
(800) 466-8356

QUALITY INN
1400 E Andy
Devine (86401)
Rates: $48-$65
(928) 753-4747
(800) 424-6423
(800) 869-3252

SUPER 8 MOTEL
3401 E Andy
Devine (86401)
Rates: $29-79
(928) 757-4808
(800) 800-8000

LAKE HAVASU CITY

**BEST WESTERN
LAKE PLACE INN**
31 Wing's Loop
(86403)
Rates: $49-$99
(928) 855-2146
(800) 528-1234
(800) 258-8558

**BRIDGEVIEW
MOTEL**
101 London
Bridge Rd (86403)
Rates: $35-$110
(928) 855-5559

EZ-8 MOTEL
41 S Acoma Blvd
(86403)
Rates: $25-$40
(928) 855-4023

HAMPTON INN
245 London
Bridge Rd (86403)
Rates: $73-1111
(928) 855-4071
(800) 426-7866
(888) 428-2465

**ISLAND INN
HOTEL**
1300 W
McCulloch Blvd
(86403)
Rates: $59-$220
(928) 680-0606
(800) 243-9955

ISLAND SUITES
236 S Lake
Havasu Ave
(86403)
Rates: $45-$95
(928) 855-7333

LAKEVIEW MOTEL
440 London
Bridge Rd (86403)
Rates: $25-$45
(928) 855-3605

MOTEL 6
111 London
Bridge Rd (86403)
Rates: $35-$52
(928) 855-3200
(800) 466-8356

**PECOS II
CONDOMINIUMS**
451 N Lake
Havasu Ave
(86403)
Rates: $385 Wk
(928) 855-7444

RAMADA INN
271 S Lake
Havasu (86403)
Rates: n/a
(928) 855-1111
(800) 272-6232

SANDMAN INN
1700 N McCulloch
Blvd (86403)
Rates: $30-$90
(928) 855-7841
(800) 835-2410

SUPER 8 MOTEL
305 London
Bridge Rd (86403)
Rates: $36-$96
(928) 855-8844
(800) 800-8000

TRAVELODGE
480 London
Bridge Rd (86403)
Rates; $59-$149
(928) 680-9202
(800) 578-7878

WINDSOR INN
451 London
Bridge Rd (86403)
Rates: $26-$49
(928) 855-4135
(800) 245-4135

**LAKE MEAD
AREA**

**TEMPLE BAR
RESORT**
1 Main St (Temple
Bar Marina 86443)
Rates: $80-$115
(928) 767-3211
(800) 752-9669

LAKESIDE

COMFORT INN
1637 W White Mtn
Blvd (85929)
Rates: $45-$89
(928) 368-6600
(800) 424-6423
(800) 843-4792

**FOREST HOUSE
MOTEL**
2990 W White Mtn
Blvd (85929)
Rates: $30-$55
(928) 368-6628
(888) 440-2220

**LAKE OF THE
WOODS RESORT**
2244 W White Mtn
Blvd (85929)
Rates: $43-$83
(928) 368-5353

**LAZY OAKS
RESORT
COTTAGES**
1075 Larson Rd
(85929)
Rates: $67-$82
(928) 368-6203

**MOONRIDGE
LODGE & CABINS**
P. O. Box 1058
(85929)
Rates: $35-$135
(928) 367-1906

**OLD ARIZONA
HOMESTAY
CABINS**
551 Billy Creek Dr
(85929)
Rates: $85-$185
(928) 367-0232
(877) 301-3850

**THE PLACE
RESORT CABINS**
Rt 3, Box 2675
(85929)
Rates: $66-$74
(928) 368-6777

**RAINBOW'S END
RESORT**
2677 Trout Rd
(85929)
Rates: n/a
(928) 368-9004

**WOLF'S BIDE-
A-WEE CABINS**
1401 W Rim Rd
(85929)
Rates: n/a
(928) 368-5134

**LITCHFIELD
PARK**

**THE WIGWAM
RESORT**
300 Wigwam Blvd
(85340)
Rates: $205-$489
(623) 935-3811
(800) 327-0396

MARANA

RAMADA LTD
6020 W Hospitality
Rd (85743)
Rates: $55-$140
(520) 572-4235
(800) 272-6232

RED ROOF INN N
4940 N Ina Rd
(85743)
Rates: $42-$78
(520) 744-8199
(800) 843-7663

SUPER 8 MOTEL
8351 N Cracker
Barrel Rd (85743)
Rates: $39-$110
(520) 572-0300
(800) 800-8000

**MARBLE
CANYON**

**CLIFF DWELLERS
LODGE**
N Hwy 89A
(86036)
Rates: n/a
(928) 355-2221
(800) 433-2543

LEES FERRY LODGE
HC67, Box 1
(Vermillion
Cliffs 86036)
Rates: $47+
(928) 355-2231
(800) 962-9755

**MARBLE CANYON
LODGE**
Hwy 89A (86036)
Rates: $50-$135
(928) 355-2225
(800) 726-1789

MESA

AAA MOTEL
6763 E Main St
(85203)
Rates: n/a
(480) 985-1112

**ARIZONA
GOLF RESORT
& CONF CENTER**
425 S Power Rd
(85206)
Rates: $99-$199
(480) 832-3202
(800) 528-8282

BEST INNS
1750 E Main St
(85203)
Rates: $49-$99
(480) 969-3600

**BEST WESTERN
DOBSON RANCH
INN RESORT**
1666 S Dobson Rd
(85202)
Rates: $55-$180
(480) 831-7000
(800) 528-1234
(800) 528-1356

**BEST WESTERN
MESA INN**
1625 E Main St
(85203)
Rates: $49-$115
(480) 964-8000
(800) 528-1234

**BEST WESTERN
MEZONA INN**
250 W Main St
(85201)
Rates: $54-$129
(480) 834-9233
(800) 528-1234
(800) 528-8299

**BEST WESTERN
SUPERSTITION
SPRINGS INN**
1342 S Power Rd
(85206)
Rates: $49-$139
(480) 641-1164
(800) 528-1234

AREA CODES - If the local number doesn't connect, check for a new area code.

BUDGET SUITES MOTEL
537 S Country Club Dr (85210)
Rates: n/a
(480) 969-5248

COLONADE SUITES
5440 E Main St (85201)
Rates: n/a
(480) 981-8888
(800) 645-3702

DAYS INN
333 W Juanita Ave (85210)
Rates: $49-$119
(480) 844-8900
(800) 329-7466

HOLIDAY INN EXPRESS HOTEL & CONF CENTER
5750 E Main St (85205)
Rates: $55-$129
(480) 985-3600
(800) 465-4329
(800) 888-9561

HOLIDAY INN HOTEL & SUITES
1600 S Country Club Dr (85210)
Rates: $59-$119
(480) 964-7000
(800) 465-4329
(800) 917-2010

HOMESTEAD STUIO SUITES HOTEL
1920 W Isabella Ave (85202)
Rates: $38-$91
(480) 752-2266
(888) 782-9473

LA QUINTA INN & SUITES
902 W Grove Ave (85210)
Rates: $60-$110
(480) 844-8747
(800) 687-6777

LA QUINTA INN & SUITES EAST
6530 E Superstition Spgs Blvd (85208)
Rates: $60-$126
(480) 654-1970
(800) 687-6777

MARRIOTT HOTEL
200 N Centennial Way (85201)
Rates: $59-$110
(480) 898-8300
(800) 228-9290
(800) 456-6372

MILES MOTEL
5911 E Main St (85201)
Rates: n/a
(480) 985-2200
(800) 645-3702

MOTEL 6 MAIN
630 W Main St (85201)
Rates: $37-$52
(480) 969-8111
(800) 466-8356

MOTEL 6 NORTH
336 W Hampton Ave (85210)
Rates: $37-$52
(480) 844-8899
(800) 466-8356

MOTEL 6 SOUTH
1511 S Country Club Dr (85210)
Rates: $39-$63
(480) 834-0066
(800) 466-8356

QUALITY INN
951 W Main St (85201)
Rates: $49-$130
(480) 833-1231
(800) 424-6423

RAMADA INN
1410 S Country Club Dr (85210)
Rates: n/a
(480) 964-2897
(800) 272-6232

RESIDENCE INN BY MARRIOTT
941 W Grove Ave (85210)
Rates: $85-$209
(480) 610-0100
(800) 331-3131

SAN DEE MOTEL
6649 E Apache Tr (85205)
Rates: $45-$58
(480) 985-1912

SLEEP INN
6347 E Southern Ave (85206)
Rates: $49-$119
(480) 807-7760
(800) 424-6423
(888) 275-3374

SUPER 8 MOTEL
1550 S Gilbert Rd (85204)
Rates: $46-$66
(480) 545-0888
(800) 800-8000

TRAVELODGE SUITES
4244 E Main (85205)
Rates: $39-$124
(480) 832-5961
(800) 578-7878

WINDEMERE HOTEL
5750 E Main St (85205)
Rates: $59-$139
(480) 985-3600
(800) 888-3561

MIAMI

COPPER HILLS INN & SUITES
4805 E Hwy 60 (85539)
Rates: $57-$84
(928) 425-7151
(877) 909-4455

DELVAN'S DRAW-ING ROOM B&B
55 Chisholm Ave (85539)
Rates: 50-$125
(928) 473-9045

MORMON LAKE

MONTEZUMA LODGE
HC 31, Box 342 (86038)
Rates: $105-$125
(928) 354-2220

MORMON LAKE LODGE
I-17, Exit 339, Main St, P. O. Box 38012 (86038)
Rates: $45-$145
(928) 354-2227

MUNDS PARK

MOTEL IN THE PINES
80 W Pinewood Rd (86017)
Rates: $35-$89
(928) 286-9699
(800) 574-5080

NEW RIVER

HAMPTON INN AT ANTHEM
42415 N 41st Dr (85086)
Rates: $49-$139
(623) 465-7979
(800) 426-7866

NOGALES

A ROOM WITH A VIEW
HC 2, Box 282 (85621)
Rates: n/a
(520) 397-9297
(877) 533-8439

AMERICANA MOTOR HOTEL
639 N Grand Ave (85621)
Rates: $45-$65
(520) 287-7211
(800) 874-8079

BEST WESTERN SIESTA MOTEL
673 N Grand Ave (85621)
Rates: $45-$65
(520) 287-4671
(800) 528-1234
(888) 215-4783

CP RANCH B&B
15 Duquesne Rd (85621)
Rates: $100-$125
(520) 287-0073
(866) 277-2624

HOLIDAY INN EXP HOTEL & SUITES
850 W Shell Rd (85621)
Rates: $75-$95
(520) 281-0123
(800) 465-4329

MOTEL 6
141 W Mariposa Rd (85621)
Rates: $38-$44
(520) 281-2951
(800) 466-8356

SUPER 8 MOTEL
547 W Mariposa Rd (85621)
Rates: $55-$79
(520) 281-2242
(800) 800-8000

PAGE

BASHFUL BOB'S MOTEL
760 N Navajo (86040)
Rates: $39+
(928) 645-3919

BEST WESTERN ARIZONA INN
716 Rimview Dr (86040)
Rates: $47-$119
(928) 645-2466
(800) 528-1234
(800) 826-2718

BEST WESTERN PAGE INN & SUITES
207 N Lake Powell Blvd (86040)
Rates: $49-$195
(928) 645-2451
(800) 528-1234
(888) 637-9183

BUDGET HOST ECONOMY INN
121 S Lake Powell Blvd (86040)
Rates: $55-$69
(928) 645-2488
(800) 283-4678

CANYON COLORS B&B
225 S Navajo (86040)
Rates: $85-$95
(928) 645-5979
(800) 536-2530

DAYS INN & SUITES
961 N Hwy 89 (86040)
Rates: $49-$109
(928) 645-2800
(800) 329-7466

EMPIRE HOUSE MOTEL
100 S Lake Powell Blvd (86040)
Rates: $50-$62
(928) 645-2406
(800) 551-9005

AREA CODES - If the local number doesn't connect, check for a new area code.

LAKE POWELL RESORT
100 Lakeshore Dr,
Hwy 89 N (86040)
Rates: $65-$199
(928) 645-2433
(800) 645-LAKE

LINDA'S LAKE POWELL CONDOS
1019 Tower Butte
(86040)
Rates: $78-$115
(928) 645-3222
(800) 525-3189

LINDA'S LAKE POWELL SUITES
89N Greenhaven
(86040)
Rates: $88-$121
(928) 353-4591
(800) 525-3189

LULU'S SLEEP EZZE MOTEL
105 8th Ave
(86040)
Rates: $39-$52
(928) 608-0273

MOTEL 6 PAGE/ LAKE POWELL
637 S Lake Powell
Blvd (86040)
Rates: $29-$69
(928) 645-5888
(800) 466-8356

QUALITY INN PAGE /LK POWELL
287 N Lake Powell
Blvd (86040)
Rates: $39-$104
(928) 645-8851
(800) 424-6423

RED ROCK MOTEL
114 8th Ave
(86040)
Rates: $39-$85
(928) 645-0062

SUNRISE VIEW B&B
1633 San Juan Ct
(86040)
Rates: $85-$95
(928) 608-4763
(866) 205-8443

WAHWEAP LODGE LAKE POWELL
100 Lake Shore Dr
(86040)
Rates: $89-$160
(928) 645-2433
(602) 331-5226
(800) 528-6154
(888) 272-3161

PARADISE VALLEY

DOUBLETREE LA POSADA RESORT
4949 E Lincoln Dr
(85253)
Rates: $59-$225
(602) 952-0420
(800) 222-8733

HERMOSA INN
5532 N Palo Cristi
Rd (85253)
Rates: $115-$695
(602) 955-8614
(800) 241-1210

MARRIOTT'S CAMELBACK INN
5402 E Lincoln Dr
(85253)
Rates: $129-$490
(480) 948-1700
(800) 242-2635

SANCTUARY ON CAMELBACK MOUNTAIN
5700 E McDonald
Dr (85253)
Rates: $225-$850
(480) 948-2100
(800) 245-2051

PARKER

BEST WESTERN PARKER INN
1012 Geronimo
Ave (85344)
Rates: $49-$110
(928) 669-6060
(800) 528-1234
(877) 297-6667

EL RANCHO MOTEL
709 California
Ave (85344)
Rates: $35+
(928) 669-2231

HAVASU SPRINGS RESORT
2581 Hwy 95
(85344)
Rates: $95-$200
(928) 667-3361

MOTEL 6
604 California
Ave (85344)
Rates: $42-$65
(928) 669-2133
(800) 466-8356

PATAGONIA

DOS PALMAS VACATION HOMES
362 Duquesne
(85624)
Rates: n/a
(866) 394-8056

STAGE STOP INN
303 McKeown Ave
(85624)
Rates: $49-$95
(520) 394-2211
(800) 923-2211

PAYSON

BEST VALUE INN- TRAILS END MOTEL
811 S Beeline Hwy
(85541)
Rates: $35-$99
(928) 474-2283
(800) 474-2283

BEST WESTERN INN OF PAYSON
801 N Beeline
Hwy (85541)
Rates: $69-$149
(928) 474-3241
(800) 528-1234
(800) 247-9477

BUDGET INN & SUITES
302 S Beeline Hwy
(85541)
Rates: n/a
(928) 474-2201

CHRISTOPHER CREEK LODGE & MOTEL
Star Rt Box 119
(85541)
Rates: $40-$75
(928) 478-4300

COMFORT INN
809 E Hwy 260
(85541)
Rates: $49-$139
(928) 474-5241
(800) 424-6423
(800) 888-9828

DAYS INN & SUITES
301-A S Beeline
Hwy (85541)
Rates: $59-$129
(928) 474-9800
(800) 329-7466
(877) 474-9800

GREY HACKLE LODGE
Hwy 260 (85541)
Rates: $40-$95
(928) 478-4392

KOHL'S RANCH LODGE
Hwy 260 (85541)
Rates: $82-$275
(928) 478-4211
(800) 331-5645

MAJESTIC MOUNTAIN INN
602 E Hwy 260
(85541)
Rates: $62-$150
(928) 474-0185
(800) 408-2442

MOTEL 6
101 W Phoenix St
(85541)
Rates: $35-$85
(928) 474-4526
(800) 466-8356

MOUNTAIN MEADOWS CABINS
Colcord Rd
(85541)
Rates: n/a
(928) 478-4415

PAYSONGLO LODGE
1005 S Beeline
Hwy (85541)
Rates: $65-$140
(928) 474-2382
(800) 872-9766

YE OLE COUNTRY INN
Hwy 260,
Mathews Lane
(85541)
Rates: n/a
(928) 478-4426

PEARCE

SUNGLOW GUEST RANCH IN THE CHIRICAHUAS
14066 S Sunglow
Rd (85625)
Rates: $119-$350
(520) 824-3334
(866) 786-4569

PEORIA

COMFORT SUITES
8473 W Paradise
Ln (85382)
Rates: $59-$159
(623) 334-3992
(800) 424-6423

HOLIDAY INN EXP HOTEL & SUITES
16771 N 84th Ave
(85345)
Rates: $47-$124
(623) 853-1313
(800) 465-4329

LA QUINTA INN & SUITES
16321 N 83rd Ave
(85345)
Rates: $66-$156
(623) 487-1900
(800) 687-6777

RESIDENCE INN BY MARRIOTT
8435 W Paradise
Ln (85382)
Rates: $69-$279
(623) 979-2074
(800) 331-3131

PHOENIX
(and Vicinity)

AMERISUITES METRO CENTER
10838 N 25th Ave
(85029)
Rates: $69-$139
(602) 997-8800
(800) 833-1516

ARIZONA BILTMORE RESORT & SPA
2400 E Missouri
(85016)
Rates: $195-$520
(602) 955-6600
(800) 950-0086

AREA CODES - If the local number doesn't connect, check for a new area code.

BEST WESTERN AIRPORT INN
2425 S 24th St
(85034)
Rates: $59-$130
(602) 273-7251
(800) 528-1234
(800) 528-8199

BEST WESTERN BELL HOTEL
17211 N Black Cyn Hwy (85023)
Rates: $49-$119
(602) 993-8300
(800) 528-1234
(877) 263-1290

BEST WESTERN INNSUITES HOTEL
1615 E Northern Ave (85020)
Rates: $79-$159
(602) 997-6285
(800) 528-1234
(800) 752-2204

BEST WESTERN PHOENIX WEST
1241 N 53rd Ave
(85043)
Rates: $49-$139
(602) 269-1919
(800) 528-1234

CANDLEWOOD SUITES
11411 N Black Canyon Hwy
(85029)
Rates: $49-$109
(602) 861-4900
(888) 226-3539

COMFORT INN
5050 N Black Canyon Hwy
(85017)
Rates: $61-$80
(602) 242-8011
(800) 424-6423

COMFORT INN TURF PARADISE
1711 W Bell Rd
(85023)
Rates: $49-$139
(602) 866-2089
(800) 424-6423

COMFORT SUITES
10210 N 26th Dr
(85021)
Rates: $49-$129
(602) 861-3900
(800) 424-6423

CROWNE PLAZA METRO CENTER
2532 W Peoria Ave
(85029)
Rates: $59-$119
(602) 943-2341
(800) 227-6963

DAYS INN AIRPORT
3333 E Van Buren St (85008)
Rates: $45-$109
(602) 244-8244
(800) 329-7466

ECONO LODGE/ LOS OLIVOS HOTEL & SUITES
202 E McDowell Rd (85004)
Rates: $59-$149
(602) 528-9100
(800) 424-6423
(800) 776-5560

EMBASSY SUITES AIRPORT WEST AT 44TH STREET
1515 N 44th St
(85008)
Rates: $79-$229
(602) 244-8800
(800) 362-2779

EMBASSY SUITES AIRPORT WEST AT 24TH STREET
2333 E Thomas Rd
(85016)
Rates: $69-$189
(602) 957-1910
(800) 362-2779

EMBASSY SUITES BILTMORE
2630 E Camelback St (85016)
Rates: $89-$269
(602) 955-3992
(800) 362-2779

EMBASSY SUITES PHOENIX NORTH
2577 W Greenway Rd (85023)
Rates: $129-232
(602) 375-1777
(800) 362-2779

E-Z 8 MOTEL
1820 S 7th St
(85034)
Rates: $30-$36
(602) 254-9787

HAMPTON INN I-17/METRO CTR
8101 N Black Canyon Hwy
(85021)
Rates: $59-$99
(602) 864-6233
(800) 426-7866

HAMPTON INN I-10 WEST
5152 W Latham St
(85043)
Rates: $59-$149
(602) 484-7000
(800) 426-7866

HAWTHORN SUITES
2990 W Thunderbird Rd
(85053)
Rates: $49-$129
(602) 564-8000
(800) 527-1133

HILTON GARDEN INN / AIRPORT
3422 E Elwood Dr
(85040)
Rates: $69-$209
(602) 470-0500
(800) 445-8667

HILTON SUITES PHOENIX PLAZA
10 E Thomas Rd
(85012)
Rates: $79-$229
(602) 222-1111
(800) 445-8667

HOLIDAY INN EXPRESS & SUITES
15221 S 50th St
(85044)
Rates: $99-$119
(602) 785-8500
(800) 465-4329

HOLIDAY INN EXPRESS & SUITES
3401 E University Dr (85034)
Rates: $69-$169
(602) 453-9900
(800) 465-4329

HOLIDAY INN SELECT AIRPORT
4300 E Washington St
(85034)
Rates: $64-$125
(602) 273-7778
(800) 465-4329

HOLIDAY INN W
1500 N 51st Ave
(85043)
Rates: $129-$179
(602) 484-9009
(800) 465-4329

HOMESTEAD STUDIO SUITES
2102 W Dunlap Ave (85021)
Rates: $40-$90
(602) 944-7828
(888) 782-9473

HOMEWOOD SUITES BILTMORE
2001 E Highland Ave (85016)
Rates: $89-$184
(602) 508-0937
(800) 225-5466

HOMEWOOD SUITES HOTEL
2536 W Beryl Ave
(85021)
Rates: $62-$99
(602) 674-8900
(800) 225-5466

HOWARD JOHNSON/ AIRPORT INN
124 S 24th St
(85034)
Rates: $40-$90
(602) 220-0044
(800) 446-4656
(866) 813-4738

LA QUINTA INN COLISEUM
2725 N Black Canyon Hwy
(85009)
Rates: $54-$96
(602) 258-6271
(800) 687-6667
(800) 221-4731

LA QUINTA PHOENIX AIRPORT NORTH
4727 E Thomas Rd
(85018)
Rates: $59-$109
(602) 956-6500
(800) 687-6667

LA QUINTA PHOENIX NORTH
2510 W Greenway Rd (85023)
Rates: $52-$115
(602) 993-0800
(800) 687-6667
(800) 221-4731

MOTEL 6 AIRPORT
214 S 24th St
(85034)
Rates: $39-$54
(602) 244-1155
(800) 466-8356

MOTEL 6
5315 E Van Buren St (85008)
Rates: $38-$52
(602) 267-8555
(800) 466-8356

MOTEL 6
1530 N 52nd Dr
(85043)
Rates: $38-$54
(602) 272-0220
(800) 466-8356

MOTEL 6
8152 N Black Canyon Hwy
(85051)
Rates: $39-$52
(602) 995-7592
(800) 466-8356

MOTEL 6
4130 N Black Canyon Hwy
(85017)
Rates: $38-$49
(602) 277-5501
(800) 466-8356

MOTEL 6
2330 W Bell Rd
(85023)
Rates: $40-$54
(602) 993-2353
(800) 466-8356

MOTEL 6
2735 W Sweetwater Ave
(85029)
Rates: $39-$52
(602) 942-5030
(800) 466-8356

PARKWAY INN- METROCENTER
8617 N Black Canyon Hwy
(85021)
Rates: $39-$89
(602) 995-9500

PHOENIX SUNRISE MOTEL
3644 E Van Buren St (85008)
Rates: $29-$46
(602) 275-7661
(800) 432-6483

AREA CODES - If the local number doesn't connect, check for a new area code.

PREMIER INNS
10402 N Black
Canyon Hwy
(85051)
Rates: $44-$109
(602) 943-2371
(800) 786-6835

PRIME HOTEL & SUITES AIRPORT
427 N 44th St
(85008)
Rates: $101-$147
(602) 220-4400
(866) 937-7746

RAMADA INN NORTH
12027 N 28th Dr
(85029)
Rates: $49-$159
(602) 866-7000
(800) 272-6232

RED ROOF INN CAMELBACK
502 W Camelback
Rd (85013)
Rates: $49-$85
(602) 264-9290
(800) 843-7663

RED ROOF INN NORTH
17222 N Black
Canyon Hwy
(85023)
Rates: $43-$76
(602) 866-1049
(800) 843-7663

RED ROOF INN WEST
5215 W Willetta
(85043)
Rates: $43-$71
(602) 233-8004
(800) 843-7663

RESIDENCE INN BY MARRIOTT
8242 N Black
Canyon Fwy
(85051)
Rates: $69-$188
(602) 864-1900
(800) 331-3131

RESIDENCE INN BY MARRIOTT/ AIRPORT
801 N 44th St
(85008)
Rates: $80-$179
(602) 273-9220
(800) 331-3131

RODEWAY INN AIRPORT
3541 E Van Buren
(85008)
Rates: $40-$91
(602) 273-7121
(800) 424-6423

ROYAL PALMS RESORT & SPA
5200 E Camelback
Rd (85018)
Rates: $179-$525
(602) 840-3610
(888) 654-8655

SHERATON CRESCENT HOTEL
2620 W Dunlap
Ave (85021)
Rates: $69-$269
(602) 943-8200
(800) 423-4126

SHERATON WILD HORSE PASS RESORT & SPA
5594 W Wild
Horse Pass Blvd
(85070)
Rates: $199-$580
(602) 225-0100
(866) 837-4156

SIERRA SUITES HOTEL/BILTMORE
5235 N 16th St
(85016)
Rates: $59-$189
(602) 265-6800
(800) 474-3772

SIERRA SUITES HOTEL/METRO CENTER
9455 N Black Cyn
Hwy (85021)
Rates: $49-$124
(602) 395-0900
(800) 474-3772

SLEEP INN/ SKY HARBOR AIRPORT
2621 S 47th Place
(85023)
Rates: $49-$110
(480) 967-7100
(800) 424-6423

SLEEP INN NORTH
18235 N 27th Ave
(85053)
Rates: $40-$120
(602) 504-1200
(800) 424-6423

SOUTH MTN VILLAGE VACATION APT
113 E La Mirada
Dr (85042)
Rates: $85 per
night/$400 wk
(602) 243-3452

SPRINGHILL SUITES/ METRO CENTER
9425 N Black Cyn
Hwy (85021)
Rates: $59-$150
(602) 943-0010

STUDIO 6/ DEER VALLEY
18405 N 27th Ave
(85023)
Rates: $43-$73
(602) 843-1151
(888) 897-0202

SUNSHINE HOTEL & SUITES
3600 N 2nd Ave
(85013)
Rates: $39-$145
(602) 248-0222

SUPER 8 MOTEL
1242 N 53rd Ave
(85043)
Rates: $42-$85
(602) 415-0888
(800) 800-8000

TOWNPLACE SUITES
9425-B N Black
Canyon Hwy
(85021)
Rates: $79-$179
(602) 943-9510
(800) 257-3000

TRAVELERS INN
5102 W Latham St
(85043)
Rates: $42-$68
(602) 233-1988

TRAVELODGE
1624 N Black
Canyon Hwy
(85008)
Rates: $50-$80
(602) 269-6281
(800) 578-7878

VILLAGER PREMIER ROYAL SUITES
10421 N 33rd Ave
(85051)
Rates: $49-$85
(602) 942-1000

WELLESLEY INN & SUITES AIRPORT
4357 E Oak St
(85008)
Rates: $59-$109
(602) 225-2998
(800) 444-8888

WELLESLEY INN & SUITES METROCENTER
11211 N Black Cyn
Hwy (85029)
Rates: $39-$49
(602) 870-2999
(800) 444-8888

WELLESLEY INN & SUITES PARK CENTRAL
217 W Osborn Rd
(85013)
Rates: $69-$159
(602) 279-9000
(800) 444-8888

WINGATE INN
2520 N Central
Ave (85003)
Rates: $69-$149
(602) 716-9900

PINE

PINE CREST B&B
P. O. Box 2004
(85544)
Rates: n/a
(928) 476-4265

PINETOP

BEST WESTERN INN OF PINETOP
404 S White Mtn
Blvd (85935)
Rates: $59-$109
(928) 367-6667
(800) 528-1234

BONANZA MOTEL
858 E White Mtn
Blvd (85935)
Rates: n/a
(928) 367-4440
(888) 577-4440

BUCK SPRINGS RESORT COTTAGES
P. O. Box 130
(85935)
Rates: $65-$145
(928) 369-3554

DOUBLE B LODGE & CABINS
1075 E White Mtn
Blvd (85935)
Rates: $34-$100
(928) 367-2747

GRETCHEN'S BED & BREAKFAST
1184 Malapai Dr
(85935)
Rates: n/a
(928) 367-0867

HOLIDAY INN EXP
431 E White Mtn
Blvd (85935)
Rates: $79-$109
(928) 367-6077
(800) 465-4329

LAKESIDE INN
1637 E White Mtn
Blvd (85935)
Rates: $59-$142
(928) 368-6600

MEADOW VIEW LODGE
P. O. Box 325
(85935)
Rates: $48+
(928) 367-4642

MOUNTAIN HACIENDA LODGE
1023 E White Mtn
Blvd (85935)
Rates: $35-$79
(928) 367-4146
(888) 567-4148

NINE PINES MOTEL
2089 E White Mtn
Blvd (85935)
Rates: n/a
(928) 367-2999
(888) 597-4637

NORTHWOODS RESORT
165 E White Mtn
Blvd (85935)
Rates: $79-$149
(928) 367-2966
(800) 813-2966

AREA CODES - If the local number doesn't connect, check for a new area code.

SUPER 8 MOTEL
1202 E White Mtn
Blvd (85935)
Rates: $65-$85
(928) 367-3161
(800) 800-8000

**TIMBER LODGE
MOTEL**
1078 E White Mtn
Blvd (85935)
Rates: $35-$85
(928) 367-4463

**WHISPERING
PINES RESORT
CABINS**
P. O. Box 1043
(85935)
Rates: n/a
(928) 367-4386
(800) 840-3867

**WOODLAND
INN & SUITES**
458 E White Mtn
Blvd (85935)
Rates: $69-$139
(928) 367-3636
(866) 746-3867

PRESCOTT
**ANTELOPE
RESORT ESTATES**
6200 N Hwy 89
(86301)
Rates: 2 month
rental/$2950
(928) 776-2600

APACHE MOTEL
1130 E Gurley St
(86301)
Rates: $39-$59
(928) 445-1422

**AZ VACATION
LODGING**
555 Onyx Dr
(86303)
Rates: $110-$200
(928) 778-9573

**BEST WESTERN
PRESCOTTONIAN**
1317 E Gurley St
(86301)
Rates: $54-$125
(928) 445-3096
(800) 528-1234

CASCADE MOTEL
805 White Spar Rd
(86303)
Rates: $30-$80
(928) 445-1232

COMFORT INN
1290 White Spar
Rd (85303)
Rates: $70-$100
(928) 778-5770
(800) 424-6423

HERITAGE HOUSE
819 E Gurley St
(86301)
Rates: $36-$85
(928) 445-9091

HI-ACRE RESORT
1001 White Spar
Rd (86303)
Rates: $29-$110
(928) 445-0588

**LYNX CREEK FARM
BED & BREAKFST**
5555 Onyx Dr
(86302)
Rates: $75-$170
(928) 778-9573

MOTEL 6
1111 E Sheldon St
(86301)
Rates: $42-$58
(928) 776-0160
(800) 466-8356

9 PINES COTTAGE
P. O. Box 2099
(86302)
Rates: $55-$85
(928) 778-3620

PINE VIEW MOTEL
500 Copper Basin
Rd (86303)
Rates: $20-$60
(928) 445-4660

**PRESCOTT
SIERRA INN**
809 White Spar Rd
(86303)
Rates: $34-$95
(928) 445-1250

**QUALITY INN
& SUITES**
4499 Hwy 69
(86301)
Rates: $79-$199
(928) 777-0770
(800) 424-6423

SENATOR INN
1117 E Gurley St
(86301)
Rates: $35-$145
(928) 445-1440

SKYLINE MOTEL
523 E Gurley St
(86301)
Rates: $32-$65
(928) 445-9963

SUPER 8 MOTEL
1105 E Sheldon St
(86301)
Rates: $45-$69
(928) 776-1282
(800) 800-8000

*PRESCOTT
VALLEY*
DAYS INN
7875 E Hwy 69
(86314)
Rates: $59-$99
(928) 772-8600
(800) 329-7466

MOTEL 6
8383 E Hwy 69
(86314)
Rates: $45-$72
(928) 772-2200
(800) 466-8356

**PRESCOTT VALLEY
MOTEL**
8350 E Hwy 69
(86314)
Rates: $35-$85
(928) 772-9412

QUARTZSITE
SUPER 8 MOTEL
2050 W Dome
Rock Rd (85359)
Rates: $59-$134
(928) 927-8080
(800) 800-8000

RIO RICO
**ESPLENDOR
RESORT**
1069 Camino
Caralampi (85648)
Rates: $99-$159
(520) 281-1901
(800) 288-4746

SAFFORD
**BEST WESTERN
DESERT INN**
1391 W Thatcher
Blvd (85546)
Rates: $63-$74
(928) 428-0521
(800) 528-1234
(800) 707-2336

COMFORT INN
1578 W Thatcher
Blvd (85546)
Rates: $56-$69
(928) 428-5851
(800) 424-6423

DAYS INN
520 E Hwy 70
(85546)
Rates: $55-$95
(928) 428-5000
(800) 329-7466

ECONO LODGE
225 E Hwy 70
(85546)
Rates: $42-$60
(928) 348-0011
(800) 424-6423

**QUALITY INN
& SUITES**
420 E Hwy 70
(85546)
Rates: $55-$110
(928) 428-3200
(800) 424-6423
(877) 726-2328

SAHUARITA
**SANTA RITA
LODGE- MADERA
CANYON**
HC 70, Box 5444
(85629)
Rates: n/a
(520) 625-8756

ST. JOHNS
DAYS INN
125 E Commercial
St (85936)
Rates: $34-$48
(928) 337-4422
(800) 329-7466

SUPER 8 MOTEL
75 E Commercial
St (85936)
Rates: $45-$79
(928) 337-2990
(800) 800-8000

SALOME
**INTERNATIONAL
INN**
67600 E Hwy 60
(85348)
Rates: n/a
(928) 859-3452

SCOTTSDALE
**ADOBE
APARTMENT
HOTEL**
3635 N 68th St
(85251)
Rates: $54-$89
(480) 945-3544

**AMERISUITES
CIVIC CENTER/
OLD TOWN**
7300 E 3rd Ave
(85251)
Rates: $64-$169
(480) 423-9944
(800) 833-7576

**BEST WESTERN
PAPAGO INN &
RESORT**
7017 E McDowell
Rd (85257)
Rates: $59-$149
(480) 947-7335
(800) 528-1234
(866) 806-4400

**BEST WESTERN
SCOTTSDALE
AIRPARK SUITES**
7515 E Butherus
Dr (85260)
Rates: $49-$149
(480) 951-4000
(800) 528-1234
(800) 344-1977

**CHAPARRAL
SUITES RESORT**
5001 N Scottsdale
Rd (85250)
Rates: $89-$209
(480) 949-1414
(800) 528-1456

**COMFORT
SUITES-
OLD TOWN**
3275 N
Drinkwater Blvd
(85251)
Rates: $49-$149
(480) 946-1111
(800) 424-6423

**COUNTRY INN
& SUITES BY
CARLSON**
10801 N 89th Pl
(85260)
Rates: $61-$119
(480) 314-1200
(800) 456-4000

AREA CODES - If the local number doesn't connect, check for a new area code.

DOUBLETREE PARADISE VALLEY RESORT
5401 N Scottsdale Rd (85250)
Rates: $69-$249
(480) 947-5400
(800) 222-8733
(877) 445-6677

FAIRMONT SCOTTSDALE PRINCESS RESORT
7575 E Princess Dr (85255)
Rates: $179-$589
(480) 585-4848
(800) 527-4727
(800) 441-1414

FOUR SEASONS RESORT AT TROON NORTH
10600 E Crescent Moon Dr (85255)
Rates: $195-$4000
(480) 515-5700
(800) 332-3442
(800) 365-8611
(888) 207-9696

HAMPTON INN OLD TOWN/ FASHION SQ.
4415 N Civic Center Blvd (85251)
Rates: $49-$159
(480) 941-9400
(800) 426-7866

HILTON SCOTTSDALE RESORT & VILLAS
6333 N Scottsdale Rd (85250)
Rates: $69-$299
(480) 948-7750
(800) 445-8667

HOLIDAY INN EXP HOTEL & SUITES
3131 N Scottsdale Rd (85251)
Rates: $69-$199
(480) 675-7665
(800) 465-4329
(800) 401-7666

HOMESTEAD STUDIO SUITES HOTEL
3560 N Marshall Way (85251)
Rates: $42-$123
(480) 994-0297
(888) 782-9473

HOSPITALITY SUITE RESORT
409 N Scottsdale Rd (85257)
Rates: $49-$119
(480) 949-5115
(800) 445-5115

THE INN AT PIMA SUITE HOTEL
7330 N Pima Rd (85258)
Rates: $49-$268
(480) 948-3800
(800) 344-0262

INNSUITES OF SCOTTSDALE AT EL DORADO PARK
7707 E McDowell Rd (85257)
Rates: $45-$100
(480) 941-1202
(800) 238-8851

IVY AT THE WATERFRONT- A HAWTHORN SUITE HOTEL
7445 E Chaparral Rd (85250)
Rates: $85-$425
(480) 994-5282
(877) 284-3489
(800) 527-1133

KIERLAND VILLAS CONDOMINIUMS
15221 N Clubgate (85254)
Rates: n/a
(480) 515-2300

LA QUINTA INN
8888 E Shea Blvd (85260)
Rates: $60-$139
(480) 614-5300
(800) 687-6667

MILLENNIUM RESORT- MCCORMICK RANCH
7401 N Scottsdale Rd (85253)
Rates: $69-$299
(480) 948-5050
(800) 243-1332

MIRA VISTA CONDOMINIUMS
9550 E Thunderbird Rd (85260)
Rates: n/a
(480) 515-2300

MOTEL 6
6848 E Camelback Rd (85251)
Rates: $40-$65
(480) 946-2280
(800) 466-8356

THE PHOENICIAN RESORT
6000 E Camelback Rd (85251)
Rates: $179-$725
(480) 941-8200
(800) 888-8234

RENAISSANCE SCOTTSDALE RESORT
6160 N Scottsdale Rd (85253)
Rates: $79-$349
(480) 991-1414
(800) 835-6205

RESIDENCE INN BY MARRIOTT
6040 N Scottsdale Rd (85253)
Rates: $55-$189
(480) 948-8666
(800) 331-3131

RESIDENCE INN SCOTTSDALE NORTH
17011 N Scottsdale Rd (85255)
Rates: $89-$269
(480) 563-4120
(800) 331-3131

RODEWAY INN
7110 E Indian School Rd (85251)
Rates: $59-$119
(480) 946-3456
(800) 424-6423

SAN ANTIQUA IN MCCORMICK RANCH CONDOS
8311 E Via de Ventura (85258)
Rates: n/a
(480) 948-1997

SCOTTSDALE LINKS RESORT
16858 N Perimeter Dr (85260)
Rates: n/a
(480) 563-0500

SCOTTSDALE MARRIOTT AT MCDOWELL MTS
16770 N Perimeter Dr (85260)
Rates: $89-$289
(480) 502-3836
(800) 228-9290

SCOTTSDALE PARK APTS. & INN
1251 N Miller Rd (85257)
Rates: $60-$129
(480) 949-8637

SCOTTSDALE RESORT ACCOM- MODATIONS
7025 E Greenway Pkwy, Ste 250 (85254)
Rates: n/a
(480) 515-2300
(888) 868-4378

SCOTTSDALE SIESTA SUITES
7601 E 2nd St (85251)
Rates: $50-$110
(480) 947-7244
(888) 990-1326
(800) 346-6663

SHERATON'S DESERT OASIS
17700 N Hayden Rd (85255)
Rates: $259
(480) 515-5888
(800) 325-3535

SIERRA SUITES HOTEL
10660 N 69th St (85254)
Rates: $49-$129
(480) 483-1333

SLEEP INN
16630 N Scottsdale Rd (85254)
Rates: $47-$139
(480) 998-9211
(800) 424-6423

SUMMERFIELD SUITES HOTEL
4245 N Drinkwater Blvd (85251)
Rates: $89-$209
(480) 946-7700
(800) 833-4353
(800) 996-3426

SUN DESTINATIONS SCOTTSDALE RENTALS
7552 E Camelback Rd (85251)
Rates: n/a
(480) 946-2384
(800) 527-4059

TOWNEPLACE SUITES BY MARRIOTT
10740 N 90th St (85260)
Rates: $59-$159
(480) 551-1100
(800) 257-3000

THE WESTIN KIERLAND RESORT, SPA & VILLAS
6902 E Greenway Pkwy (85254)
Rates: $109-$599
(480) 624-1000
(800) 228-3000
(800) 354-5892

SECOND MESA

HOPI CULTURAL CENTER INN
P. O. Box 67 (86030)
Rates: n/a
(928) 734-2401

SEDONA

A TOUCH OF THE SOUTHWEST SUITES
410 Jordan Rd (86336)
Rates: $109-$175
(928) 282-4747

BELL ROCK INN & SUITES
6426 Hwy 179 (86351)
Rates: $59-$139
(928) 282-4161
(800) 881-7625

BEST WESTERN INN OF SEDONA
1200 Hwy 89A (86336)
Rates: $85-$160
(928) 282-3072
(800) 528-1234
(800) 292-6344

AREA CODES - If the local number doesn't connect, check for a new area code.

DESERT QUAIL INN
6626 Hwy 179
(86336)
Rates: $69-$169
(928) 284-1433
(800) 385-0927
(800) 284-3965

EL PORTAL SEDONA B&B
95 Portal Lane
(86336)
Rates: $200-$400
(928) 203-9405

FOREST HOUSES- ON THE CREEK IN OAK CREEK CANYON
9275 N Hwy 89A
(86336)
Rates: $75-$120
(928) 282-2999

GRACES SECRET GARDEN B&B
1240 Jacks Canyon
Rd (86351)
Rates: $110-$200
(928) 284-2340
(800) 579-2340

HILTON SEDONA RESORT & SPA- OAK CREEK
90 Ridge Trail Dr
(86351)
Rates: $109-$229
(928) 284-4040
(800) 445-8667
(800) 916-2221
(877) 273-3762

IRIS GARDEN INN
390 Jordan Rd
(96336)
Rates: $69-$99
(928) 282-2552

L'AUBERGE DE SEDONA
301 L'Auberge
Lane (86336)
Rates: $225-$595
(928) 282-1661
(800) 272-6777

LA VISTA MOTEL
500 N Hwy 89A
(86336)
Rates: $40-$125
(928) 282-7301
(800) 896-7301

LODGE AT SEDONA - A LUXURY B&B INN
125 Kallof Pacel
(86336)
Rates: $150-$205
(928) 204-1942
(800) 619-4467

LO LO MAI SPRINGS CABINS
Page Springs Rd
(86336)
Rates: $45-$150
(928) 634-4700

MATTERHORN MOTOR LODGE
230 Apple Ave
(86336)
Rates: $79-$119
(928) 282-7176

OAK CREEK TERRACE RESORT
4548 N Hwy 89A
(86336)
Rates: $72-$165
(928) 282-3562
(800) 224-2229

QUAIL RIDGE RESORT
120 Canyon Circle
Dr (86351)
Rates: $79-$136
(928) 284-9327

QUALITY INN- MOTOR HOTEL
771 Hwy 179
(86339)
Rates: $80-$160
(520) 282-7151
(800) 424-6423

RED ROCK INN
66 E Cortez Dr
(86351)
Rates: $59-$135
(928) 284-2487

SEDONA REAL INN
95 Arroyo Pinon
(86340)
Rates: $87-$270
(928) 282-1414
(877) 785-5489

SKY RANCH LODGE MOTEL
SR 89A, Airport
Rd (86336)
Rates: $80-$225
(928) 282-6400
(888) 708-6400

SUGAR LOAF LODGE
1870 W Hwy 89A
(86340)
Rates: $36-$60
(928) 282-9451
(877) 282-0632

SUPER 8 MOTEL
2545 W Hwy 89A
(86336)
Rates: $55-$95
(928) 282-1533
(800) 800-8000
(877) 832-6408

VILLAGE LODGE- OAK CREEK
105 Bell Rock Blvd
(86336)
Rates: $45-$59
(928) 284-3626
(800) 890-0521

SELIGMAN
CANYON SHADOWS MOTEL
114 E Chino Ave
(86337)
Rates: $35+
(928) 422-3255
(800) 700-5054

HISTORIC ROUTE 66 MOTEL
500 W Hwy 66
(86337)
Rates: $47-$67
(928) 422-3204

STAGECOACH 66 MOTEL
639 E Chino Ave
(86337)
Rates: n/a
(928) 422-3470

SUPAI MOTEL
134 W Chino
(86337)
Rates: $35+
(928) 422-4153

SHOW LOW
BEST WESTERN PAINT PONY LODGE
581 W Deuce of
Clubs Ave (85901)
Rates: $64-$140
(928) 537-5773
(800) 528-1234

DAYS INN
480 W Deuce of
Clubs Ave (85901)
Rates: $59-$80
(928) 537-4356
(800) 329-7466

KIVA MOTEL
261 E Deuce of
Clubs Ave (85901)
Rates: $40-$55
(928) 537-4542

MOTEL 6
1941 E Deuce of
Clubs Ave (85901)
Rates: $46-$62
(928) 537-7694
(800) 466-8356

SLEEP INN
1751 W Deuce of
Clubs Ave (85901)
Rates: $63-$72
(928) 532-7323
(800) 424-6423
(800) 753-3746

SNOWY RIVER MOTEL
1640 E Deuce of
Clubs Ave (85901)
Rates: $34-$39
(928) 537-2926

SIERRA VISTA
BELLA VISTA MOTEL
1101 E Fry Blvd
(85635)
Rates: $30-$40
(520) 458-6737

BEST WESTERN MISSION INN
3460 E Fry Blvd
(85635)
Rates: $55-$79
(520) 458-8500
(800) 528-1234
(877) 937-8386

MOTEL 6
1551 E Fry Blvd
(85635)
Rates: $36+
(520) 459-5035
(800) 466-8356

QUALITY INN
1631 S Hwy 92
(85635)
Rates: $49-$68
(520) 458-7900
(800) 424-6423

SIERRA SUITES
391 E Fry Blvd
(85635)
Rates: $79-$99
(520) 459-4221

SUPER 8 MOTEL
100 Fab Ave
(85635)
Rates: $49-$70
(520) 459-5380
(800) 800-8000

VISTA INN
201 W Fry Blvd
(85635)
Rates: $29+
(520) 458-6711

WINDMERE HOTEL & CONF CENTER
2047 S Hwy 92
(85635)
Rates: $69-$195
(520) 459-5900
(800) 825-4656

SNOWFLAKE
COMFORT INN
2055 S Main
(85937)
Rates: $49-$129
(928) 536-3888
(800) 424-6423

SONOITA
RAINBOW'S END B&B/ APARTMENT
3088 Hwy 83
(85637)
Rates: $110
(520) 455-0202

SONOITA INN
3243 Hwy 82
(85637)
Rates: n/a
(520) 455-5935
(800) 696-1006

THE OLD BENTON PLACE CABINS
P. O. Box 129
(85637)
Rates: n/a
(520) 455-9303

SPRINGERVILLE
EL-JO MOTOR INN
425 E Main St
(85938)
Rates: $26-$40
(928) 333-4314

REED'S MOTOR LODGE
514 E Main St (85938)
Rates: $28-$45
(928) 333-4323
(800) 814-6451

RODE INN & SUITES
242 E Main St (85938)
Rates: $60-$145+
(928) 333-4365
(877) 220-6553

SUPER 8 MOTEL
138 W Main (85938)
Rates: $45-$60
(928) 333-2655
(800) 800-8000

STAR VALLEY

LAZY "D" RANCH MOTEL & RESORT
Hwy 260 (85541)
Rates: n/a
(928) 474-2442

STAR VALLEY RESORT MOTEL
255450 E Hwy 260 (85541)
Rates: n/a
(928) 474-5182

STONEMAN LAKE

STONEMAN LAKE LODGE B&B
I-17 N, Stoneman Lake exit 306 (c/o 736 E Loyola Dr, Tempe, AZ 85282)
Rates: $99-$210
(480) 239-0254
(866) 878-6636

STRAWBERRY

CABINS ON STRAWBERRY HILL
Hwy 87 (85544)
Rates: n/a
(928) 476-4252
(480) 575-7866

STRAWBERRY LODGE
HCR 1, Box 331 (85544)
Rates: $42-$52
(928) 476-3333

SURPRISE

DAYS INN & SUITES
12477 W Bell Rd (85374)
Rates: $49-$119
(623) 933-4000
(800) 329-7466

THE LODGE AT SUN RIDGE
12129 W Bell Rd (85374)
Rates: $44-$138
(623) 583-0993
(800) 337-6667

WINDMILL INN AT SUN CITY WEST
12545 W Bell Rd (85374)
Rates: $99-$129
(623) 583-0133
(800) 547-4747
(866) 645-4725

TACNA

CHAPARRAL MOTEL
Arizona Ave & Hwy A (85352)
Rates: n/a
(928) 785-4510

TAYLOR

SILVER CREEK INN
825 N Hwy 77 (85939)
Rates: $50-$69
(928) 536-2600
(888) 246-5440

TEMPE

AMERISUITES/ AIRPORT
1413 W Rio Salado Pkwy (85281)
Rates: $59-$129
(480) 804-9544
(800) 833-1516

AMERISUITES ARIZONA MILLS MALL
1520 W Baseline Rd (85283)
Rates: $59-$129
(480) 831-9800
(800) 833-1516

BEST WESTERN INN AT ASU
670 N Scottsdale Rd (85281)
Rates: $59-$129
(480) 784-2233
(800) 528-1234
(800) 784-2698

THE BUTTES- A WYNDHAM RESORT
2000 Westcourt Way (85282)
Rates: $89-$448
(480) 225-9000
(800) 996-3429

CANDLEWOOD SUITES
1335 W Baseline Rd (85283)
Rates: $59-$109
(480) 777-0440
(888) 226-3539

COUNTRY INN & SUITES BY CARLSON
1660 W Elliot Rd (85283)
Rates: $50-$110
(480) 345-8585
(800) 456-4000

FIESTA INN RESORT
2100 S Priest Dr (85282)
Rates: $79-$250
(480) 967-1441
(480) 804-5266
(800) 528-6481

HAMPTON INN & SUITES/ASU
1429 N Scottsdale Rd (85281)
Rates: $59-$119
(480) 675-9799
(800) 426-7866

HAWTHORN SUITES LTD
2301 E Southern Ave (85282)
Rates: $59-$99
(480) 633-2744
(800) 527-1133

HOLIDAY INN EXP
5300 S Priest Dr (85283)
Rates: $59-$109
(480) 820-7500
(800) 465-4329

HOLIDAY INN TEMPE/ASU
915 E Apache Blvd (85281)
Rates: $59-$139
(480) 968-3451
(800) 465-4329
(800) 553-1826

HOMESTEAD TUDIO SUITES
2165 W 15th St (85281)
Rates: $53-$104
(480) 557-8880
(800) 225-5466

INNSUITES HOTEL AIRPORT
1651 W Baseline Rd (85283)
Rates: $59-$105
(480) 897-7900
(800) 841-4242

LA QUINTA INN
911 S 48th St (85281)
Rates: $49-$112
(480) 967-4465
(800) 687-6667

MOTEL 6
513 W Broadway Rd (85282)
Rates: $38-$52
(480) 967-8696
(800) 466-8356

MOTEL 6
1720 S Priest Dr (85281)
Rates: $38-$52
(480) 968-4401
(800) 466-8356

MOTEL 6
1612 N Scottsdale Rd (85281)
Rates: $38-$52
(480) 945-9506
(800) 466-8356

QUALITY INN TEMPE/ASU
1375 E University (85281)
Rates: $69-$109
(480) 774-2500
(800) 424-6423

RAMADA LTD
1701 W Baseline Rd (85253)
Rates: $42-$86
(480) 413-1188
(800) 272-6232

RAMADA LTD
1915 E Apache Blvd (85281)
Rates: n/a
(480) 736-1700
(800) 272-6232

RED ROOF INN AIRPORT
2135 W 15th St (85281)
Rates: $41-$89
(480) 449-3205
(800) 843-7663

RESIDENCE INN BY MARRIOTT
5075 S Priest Dr (85282)
Rates: $69-$159
(480) 756-2122
(800) 331-3131

RODEWAY INN AIRPORT EAST
1550 S 52nd St (85281)
Rates: $69-$89
(480) 967-3000
(800) 424-6423

SERENITY RENTALS
1445 E Guadalupe Rd, Ste 107 (85283)
Rates: n/a
(800) 645-9061

SHERATON PHOENIX AIR-PORT HOTEL
1600 S 52nd St (85281)
Rates: $119-$229
(480) 967-6600
(800) 325-3535

STUDIO 6
4909 S Wendler Dr (85282)
Rates: $43-$52
(602) 414-4470
(888) 897-0202

SUPER 8 MOTEL
1020 E Apache Blvd (85281)
Rates: $49-$109
(480) 967-8891
(800) 800-8000

TEMPE MISSION PALMS HOTEL-OLD TOWN/ASU
60 E 5th St (85281)
Rates: $95-$375
(480) 894-1400
(800) 547-8705

AREA CODES - If the local number doesn't connect, check for a new area code.

TRAVELODGE UNIVERSITY
1005 E Apache
Blvd (85281)
Rates: $49-$99
(480) 968-7871
(800) 578-7878
(800) 831-4667

TWIN PALMS HOTEL
225 E Apache
Blvd (85281)
Rates: $79-$159
(480) 967-9431

TOMBSTONE

BEST WESTERN LOOKOUT LODGE
Hwy 80 W (85638)
Rates: $79-$90
(520) 457-2223
(800) 528-1234
(877) 652-6772

HOLIDAY INN EXP
1001 N Hwy 80
(85638)
Rates: $79-$149
(520) 457-9507
(800) 465-4329

TOMBSTONE MOTEL & CONV CENTER
502 E Fremont St
(85638)
Rates: $49-$149
(520) 457-3478
(888) 455-3478

TRAIL RIDERS INN
13 N 7th St (85638)
Rates: $35-$45
(520) 457-3573
(800) 574-0417

TUBA CITY

QUALITY INN NAVAJO NATION
Main & Moenave
Ave (86045)
Rates: $89-$109
(928) 283-4545
(800) 424-6423
(800) 644-8383

TUBAC

MI SUEÑO B&B
2036 W Frontage
Rd (85646)
Rates: $100-$205
(520) 398-0775

TUBAC GOLF RESORT
One Otero Rd
(85646)
Rates: $85-$255
(520) 398-2211
(800) 848-7893

TUCSON

AMERISUITES AIRPORT
6885 S Tucson
Blvd (85706)
Rates: $79-$149
(520) 295-0405
(800) 833-1516

ARIZONA PLAZA HOTEL
1601 N Oracle Rd
(85705)
Rates: $59-$99
(520) 740-0123

BAYMONT INN NORTH
1560 W Grant Rd
(85745)
Rates: $55-$65
(520) 624-3200
(800) 789-4103
(877) 229-6668

BED & BAGELS OF TUCSON B&B
10402 E Glenn St
(85749)
Rates: n/a
(520) 760-5595
(520) 603-1580

BEST VALUE INN
810 E Benson
Hwy (85713)
Rates: $36-$120
(520) 884-5800
(888) 315-2378

BEST WESTERN EXECUTIVE INN
333 W Drachman
(85705)
Rates: $42-$117
(520) 791-7551
(800) 528-1234
(800) 255-3371

BEST WESTERN INNSUITES CATALINA FOOTHILLS
6201 N Oracle Rd
(85704)
Rates: $69-$179
(520) 297-8111
(800) 528-1234
(800) 554-4535

CHATEAU SONATA
550 S Camino Seco
(85710)
Rates: $59-$239
(520) 886-2468
(800) 597-8483

CLARION HOTEL-RANDOLPH PARK
102 N Alvernon
(85711)
Rates: $59-$120
(520) 795-0330
(800) 252-7466

CLARION SANTA RITA HOTEL
88 E Broadway
(85701)
Rates: $99-$159
(520) 622-4000
(800) 252-7466
(877) 526-7737

COMFORT SUITES
515 W Auto Mall
Dr (85705)
Rates: $59-$135
(520) 888-6676
(800) 424-6423

COUNTRY INN & SUITES BY CARLSON
7411 N Oracle Rd
(85704)
Rates: $59-$139
(520) 575-9255
(800) 456-4000

DAYS INN
222 S Freeway
(85745)
Rates: $39-$69
(520) 791-7511
(800) 329-7466

DOUBLETREE HOTEL/REID PARK
445 S Alvernon
Way (85711)
Rates: $56-$179
(520) 881-4200
(800) 222-8733

ECONO LODGE
1136 N Stone Ave
(85705)
Rates: $42-$109
(520) 622-6714
(800) 424-6423

EMBASSY SUITES AIRPORT
7051 S Tucson
Blvd (85706)
Rates: $149-$209
(520) 573-0700
(800) 362-2779

FLAMINGO HOTEL
1300 N Stone Ave
(85705)
Rates: $44-$142
(520) 770-1910
(800) 300-3533

GHOST RANCH LODGE
801 W Miracle
Mile (85705)
Rates: $42-$106
(520) 791-7565
(800) 456-7565

THE GOLF VILLAS AT ORO VALLEY
10950 N La
Canada Dr (85737)
Rates: $89-$499
(520) 498-0098
(888) 388-0098

HACIENDA DEL SOL GUEST RANCH RESORT
5601 N Hacienda
Del Sol Rd (85718)
Rates: $79-$465
(520) 299-1501
(800) 728-6514

HAMPTON INN N
1375 W Grant Rd
(85745)
Rates: $79-$149
(520) 206-0602
(800) 426-7866

HAWTHORN SUITES
7007 E Tanque
Verde Rd (85715)
Rates: $69-$139
(520) 298-2300
(800) 527-1133

HILTON TUCSON EL CONQUISTADOR
10000 N Oracle Rd
(85737)
Rates: $89-$325
(520) 544-5000
(800) 325-7832

HOLIDAY INN EXP HOTEL & SUITES TUCSON AIRPORT
2548 E Medina Rd
(85706)
Rates: $70-$110
(520) 889-6600
(800) 465-4329

HOTEL CONGRESS
311 E Congress
(85701)
Rates: $29-$58
(520) 622-8848
(800) 722-8848

HOWARD JOHNSON EXP
1010 S Freeway
(85745)
Rates: $44-$129
(520) 622-5871
(800) 446-4656

INNSUITES TUCSON AT ST. MARY'S
475 N Granada
Ave (85701)
Rates: $59-$199
(520) 622-3000
(800) 446-6589

JUNCTION INN
755 E Benson
Hwy (85713)
Rates: $40-$50
(520) 622-4614

KNIGHTS INN
720 W 29th St
(85713)
Rates: $99-$119
(520) 624-8291
(800) 843-5644

LA POSADO LODGE/CASITAS
5900 N Oracle Rd
(85704)
Rates: $99-$229
(520) 887-4800

LA QUINTA INN E
6404 E Broadway
(85710)
Rates: $59-$121
(520) 747-1414
(800) 687-6667

LA QUINTA INN & SUITES AIRPT
7001 S Tucson
Blvd (85706)
Rates: $60-$136
(520) 573-3333
(800) 687-6667

LA QUINTA INN DOWNTOWN
750 Starr Pass
Blvd (85713)
Rates: $49-$109
(800) 687-6667

THE LODGE AT
VENTANA CANYON
6200 N Clubhouse
Ln (85750)
Rates: $95-$497
(520) 577-4000

THE LODGE
ON THE DESERT
306 N Alvernon
Way (85711)
Rates: $79-$289
(520) 325-3366
(800) 456-5634

LOEWS VENTANA
CANYON RESORT
7000 N Resort Dr
(85750)
Rates: $99-$485
(520) 299-2020
(800) 234-5117

MOTEL 6
960 S Freeway
(85745)
Rates: $32-$51
(520) 628-1339
(800) 466-8356

MOTEL 6
4630 W Ina Rd
(85741)
Rates: $35-$56
(520) 744-9300
(800) 466-8356

MOTEL 6
1222 S Freeway
(85713)
Rates: $32-$51
(520) 624-2516
(800) 466-8356

PARK INN
TUCSON
AIRPORT
2803 E Valencia
Rd (85706)
Rates: $49-$119
(520) 294-2500

RADISSON HOTEL
CITY CENTER
181 W Broadway
(85701)
Rates: $98-$134
(520) 624-8711
(800) 333-3333

RADISSON SUITES
TUCSON
6555 E Speedway
Blvd (85710)
Rates: $59-$146
(520) 721-7100
(800) 333-3333

RAMADA INN &
SUITES/AIRPORT
5251 S Julian Dr
(85706)
Rates: $49-$99
(520) 294-5250
(800) 272-6232

RAMADA INN
FOOTHILLS
RESORT
6944 E Tanque
Verde Rd (85715)
Rates: $49-$139
(520) 886-9595
(800) 272-6232

RAMADA LTD
665 N Frwy
(85706)
Rates: $59-$115
(520) 622-6491
(800) 272-6232

RED ROOF INN S
3700 E Irvington
Rd (85714)
Rates: $38-$74
(520) 571-1400
(800) 843-7663

RESIDENCE INN
BY MARRIOTT
6477 E Speedway
Blvd (85710)
Rates: $79-$199
(520) 721-0991
(800) 331-3131

RIVERPARK INN
350 S Freeway
(85745)
Rates: $59-$159
(520) 622-6611
(800) 551-1466

RODEWAY INN
1365 W Grant Rd
(85745)
Rates: $44-$89
(520) 622-7791
(800) 424-6423

SHERATON
TUCSON HOTEL
& SUITES
5151 E Grant Rd
(85712)
Rates: $79-$229
(520) 325-3535

SMUGGLER'S
INN MOTEL
6350 E Speedway
Blvd (85710)
Rates: $59-$139
(520) 296-3292
(800) 525-8852

STUDIO 6
EXTENDED STAY
4950 S Outlet
Center Rd (85706)
Rates: $59-$73
(520) 746-0030
(888) 897-0202

SUPER 8 MOTEL
1000 S Freeway
(85745)
Rates: $35-$109
(520) 622-8089
(800) 800-8000

SUPER 8 MOTEL
1248 N Stone St
(85705)
Rates: $42-$99
(520) 622-6446
(800) 800-8000

TOWNEPLACE
SUITES BY
MARRIOTT
405 W Rudasil Rd
(85704)
Rates: $54-$139
(520) 292-9697
(800) 257-3000

UNIVERSITY INN
950 N Stone Ave
(85705)
Rates: $32-$59
(520) 791-7503

VAGABOND
PLAZA HOTEL
1601 N Oracle Rd
(85705)
Rates: $45-$89
(520) 740-0123

WAYWARD WINDS
LODGE
707 W Miracle
Mile (85705)
Rates: $69-$99
(520) 791-7526
(800) 791-9503

WESTIN
LA PALOMA
3800 E Sunrise Dr
(85718)
Rates: $99-$469
(520) 742-6000
(800) 937-8461

WESTWARD
LOOK RESORT
245 E Ina Rd
(85704)
Rates: $85-$549
(520) 297-1151
(800) 722-2500

WINDMILL INN
AT ST. PHILLIP'S
PLAZA
4250 N Campbell
Ave (85718)
Rates: $75-$130
(520) 577-0007
(800) 547-4747
(800) 645-4725

WICKENBURG
AMERICINN
MOTEL
850 E Wickenburg
Way (85390)
Rates: $58-$95
(928) 684-5461
(800) 634-3444

BEST WESTERN
RANCHO GRANDE
MOTOR HOTEL
293 E Wickenburg
Way (85390)
Rates: $61-$119
(928) 684-5445
(800) 528-1234
(800) 854-7235

SUPER 8 MOTEL
975 N Tegner Rd
(85930)
Rates: $65-$105
(928) 684-0808
(800) 800-8000

WESTERNER MOTEL
680 W
Wickenburg Way
(85358)
Rates: $35-$50
(928) 684-2493

WILLCOX
BEST WESTERN
PLAZA INN
1100 W Rex Allen
Dr (85643)
Rates: $69-$99
(520) 384-3556
(800) 528-1234
(800) 262-2645

DAYS INN
724 N Bisbee Ave
(85643)
Rates: $47-$52
(520) 384-4222
(800) 329-7466

MOTEL 6
921 N Bisbee Ave
(85643)
Rates: $33-$42
(520) 384-2201
(800) 466-8356

ROYAL WESTERN
LODGE
590 S Haskell Ave
(85643)
Rates: $24-$38
(520) 384-2266

WILLIAMS
A WESTERNER
MOTEL
530 W Rt 66
(86046)
Rates: $24-$48
(928) 635-4312
(800) 385-8608

BIG SIX MOTEL
134 E Rt 66 (86046)
Rates: $25+
(928) 635-4591

BUDGE HOST INN
620 W Rt 66
(86046)
Rates: $20-$49
(928) 635-4415
(800) 283-4678
(800) 745-4415

CANYON MOTEL
1900 E Rodeo
Rd/Rt 66 (86046)
Rates: $50-$90
(928) 635-9371

DAYS INN
2488 W Rt 66
(86046)
Rates: $52-$82
(928) 635-4051
(800) 329-7466

DOWNTOWNER
HOTEL
201 E Rt 66 (86046)
Rates: $30+
(928) 635-4041

EL RANCHO
MOTEL
617 E Rt 66 (86046)
Rates: $26-$63
(928) 635-2552
(800) 228-2370

FAMILY INN
200 E Rt 66 (86046)
Rates: $17-$50
(928) 635-2562

GATEWAY MOTEL
219 E Rt 66 (86046)
Rates: $25-$40
(928) 635-4601

AREA CODES - If the local number doesn't connect, check for a new area code.

GRAND MOTEL
234 E Rt 66 (86046)
Rates: $24-$40
(928) 635-4601

HIGHLANDER MOTEL
533 W Rt 66
(86046)
Rates: $30-$48
(928) 635-2541
(800) 800-8288

HOLIDAY INN
950 N Grand
Canyon Blvd
(86046)
Rates: $49-$109
(928) 635-4114
(800) 465-4329

MOTEL 6-EAST
710 E Rt 66 (86046)
Rates: $36-$67
(928) 635-4464
(800) 466-8356

MOTEL 6-WEST
831 W Rt 66
(86046)
Rates: $38-$69
(928) 636-9000
(800) 466-8356

MOUNTAINSIDE INN-GATEWAY TO THE GRAND CANYON
642 E Rt 66 (86046)
Rates: $49-$99
(928) 635-4431
(800) 462-9381

QUALITY INN MT RANCH & RESORT
6701 E Mtn Ranch
Rd (86046)
Rates: $59-$102
(928) 635-2693
(800) 424-6423

RODEWAY INN
750 N Grand Cyn
Rd (86046)
Rates: $30-$79
(928) 639-9127
(800) 424-6423
(888) 895-0997

ROUTE 66 INN
128 E Rt 66 (86046)
Rates: $22-$65
(928) 635-4791
(888) 786-6956

TRAVELODGE
430 E Rt 66 (86046)
Rates: $49-$169
(928) 635-2651
(800) 578-7878
(888) 635-5132

WINDOW ROCK

NAVAJO NATION INN
48 W Hwy 264
(86515)
Rates: $72-$77
(928) 871-4108
(800) 662-6189

WINSLOW

BEST WESTERN ADOBE INN
1701 N Park Dr
(86047)
Rates: $62-$120
(928) 289-4638
(800) 528-1234

DAYS INN
2035 W Old Rt 66
(86047)
Rates: $45-$75
(928) 289-1010
(800) 329-7466

ECONO LODGE
1706 N Park Dr
(86047)
Rates: $39-$109
(928) 289-4687
(800) 424-6423

HOLIDAY INN EXP
816 Transcon Ln
(86047)
Rates: $79-$99
(928) 289-2960
(800) 465-4329

LA POSADA HISTORIC HOTEL
303 E 2nd st
(86047)
Rates: $79-$129
(928) 289-4366

MOTEL 6
520 W Desmond
St (86047)
Rates: $35-$57
(928) 289-9581
(800) 466-8356

MOTEL 10
725 W Third St
(86047)
Rates: $29-$40
(928) 289-3211
(800) 675-7478

SUPER 8 MOTEL
1916 W Third St
(86047)
Rates: $39-$78
(928) 289-4606
(800) 800-8000

TRAVELODGE
1914 W Third St
(86047)
Rates: $40-$52
(928) 289-4611
(800) 578-7878

YOUNGTOWN

BEST WESTERN INN & SUITES OF SUN CITY
11201 Grand Ave
(85363)
Rates: $56-$125
(623) 933-8211
(800) 528-1234
(800) 253-2168

MOTEL 6
11133 Grand Ave
(85363)
Rates: $56-$72
(623) 977-1318
(800) 466-8356

YUMA

BEST WESTERN CORONADO MOTOR HOTEL
233 4th Ave
(85364)
Rates: $62-$145
(928) 783-4453
(800) 528-1234
(877) 234-5667

BEST WESTERN INNSUITES HOTEL
1450 S Castle
Dome Ave (85365)
Rates: $79-$159
(928) 783-8341
(800) 528-1234
(800) 922-2034

COMFORT INN
1691 S Riley
(85365)
Rates: $70-$115
(5928 782-1200
(800) 424-6423

COURTESY OASIS MOTEL
10574 Fortuna Rd
(85365)
Rates: $25-$43
(928) 342-6565

HACIENDA MOTEL
2150 S 4th Ave
(85364)
Rates: n/a
(928) 782-4316

HOLIDAY INN EXP
3181 S 4th Ave
(85364)
Rates: $64-$92
(928) 344-1420
(800) 465-4329

INTERSTATE 8 INN
2730 S 4th Ave
(85364)
Rates: $33+
(928) 726-6110
(800) 821-7465

LA FUENTE INN & SUITES
1513 E 16th St
(85365)
Rates: $89-$165
(928) 329-1814
(800) 841-1814

MARTINEZ LAKE RESORT
Star Rt 4 (85365)
Rates: n/a
(928) 783-9589
(800) 876-7704

MICROTEL INN & SUITES
11274 S Fortuna
Rd (85367)
Rates: $47-$97
(928) 345-1777
(888) 777-7171

MOTEL 6-
1640 S Arizona
Ave (85364)
Rates: $32-$45
(928) 782-6561
(800) 466-8356

OAK TREE INN
1731 S Sunridge
Dr (85365)
Rates: $59-$89
(928) 539-9000
(888) 897-9647

QUALITY INN AIRPORT
711 E 32nd St
(85365)
Rates: $64-$104
(928) 726-4721
(800) 424-6423
(800) 835-1132

RADISSON SUITES
2600 S 4th Ave
(85364)
Rates: $79-$189
(928) 726-4830
(800) 333-3333

RAMADA INN CHILTON CONF CENTER
300 E 32nd St
(85364)
Rates: $59-$99
(928) 344-1050
(800) 272-6232

ROYAL MOTOR INN
2941 S 4th Ave
(85364)
Rates: $40-$110
(928) 344-0550
(800) 729-0550

SHILO INN
1550 S Castle
Dome Ave (85365)
Rates: $84-$289
(928) 782-9511
(800) 222-2244

SUPER 8 MOTEL
1688 S Riley Ave
(85365)
Rates: $65-$99
(928) 782-2000
(800) 800-8000

TORCH LITE LODGE
2501 S 4th Ave
(85364)
Rates: n/a
(928) 344-1600

TROPICANA MOTEL
2115 S 5th Ave
(85364)
Rates: n/a
(928) 782-0600

YUMA CABANA MOTEL
2151 S 4th Ave
(85364)
Rates: $34-$69
(928) 783-8311
(800) 874-0811

YUMA INN
260 S 4th Ave
(85364)
Rates: n/a
(928) 782-4592

AREA CODES - If the local number doesn't connect, check for a new area code.

ARKANSAS

ALMA

ALAMA INN & SUITES
439 Hwy 71 N
Rates: $49-$70
(479) 632-4141

DAYS INN
250 N US Hwy 71
(72921)
Rates: $45-$70
(479) 632-4595
(800) 329-7466

ARKADELPHIA

BEST WESTERN CONTINENTAL INN
136 Valley St
(71923)
Rates: $45-$89
(870) 246-5592
(800) 528-1234

COMFORT INN
100 Crystal Palace Dr (71923)
Rates: $50-$75
(870) 246-3800
(800) 424-6423

DAYS INN
137 Valley Dr,
Hwy 67 N (71923)
Rates: $49-$58
(870) 246-3031
(800) 329-7466

HOLIDAY INN EXP
150 Valley St
(71923)
Rates: $65-$75
(870) 230-1506
(800) 465-4329

MOTEL 6
106 Crystal Palace Dr (71923)
Rates: $34-$45
(870) 246-2333
(800) 466-8356

SUPER 8 MOTEL
118 Valley St
(71923)
Rates: $52-$65
(870) 246-8585
(800) 800-8000

BATESVILLE

RAMADA INN
1325 N St. Louis St
(72501)
Rates: $62-$69
(870) 698-1800
(800) 272-6232

BEEBE

DAYS INN
100 Tammy Ln
(72012)
Rates: $44-$150
(501) 882-2008
(800) 329-7466

BENTON

BEST INN OF BENTON
1221 Hot Springs Rd (72015)
Rates: $33-$55
(501) 776-1515

BEST WESTERN
17036 I-30 (72015)
Rates: $39-$70
(501) 778-9695
(800) 528-1234

DAYS INN
17701 I-30 (72015)
Rates: $42-$55
(501) 776-3200
(800) 329-7466

RAMADA INN
16732 I-30 (72015)
Rates: $44-$80
(501) 776-1900
(800) 272-6232

BENTONVILLE

TOWNEPLACE SUITES
3100 SE 14th St
(72712)
Rates: $59-$169
(479) 621-0202
(800) 257-3000

BISMARCK

DEGRAY LAKE-VIEW COTTAGES
Rt 3, Box 450
(71929)
Rates: n/a
(501) 865-3389

MORRISON'S COTTAGES
Rt 3 (71929)
Rates: n/a
(501) 865-4872

BLYTHEVILLE

BEST WESTERN
1101 Kari St
(72315)
Rates: $50-$63
(870) 762-5200
(800) 528-1234

COMFORT INN
1520 E Main St
(72316)
Rates: $50-$77
(870) 763-7081
(800) 424-6423

DAYS INN
I-55 & SR 18 E
(72316)
Rates: $45-$70
(870) 763-1241
(800) 329-7466

DELTA K MOTEL
P. O. Box 1472
(72316)
Rates: $25-$36
(870) 763-1410

HOLIDAY INN
1121 E Main St
(72316)
Rates: $79-$109
(870) 763-5800
(800) 465-4329

PEAR TREE INN
239 N Service Rd
(72315)
Rates: $50-$74
(870) 763-2300
(800) 282-8733

BOLES

Y-C MOUNTAIN INN
HCR 69, Box 199
(72926)
Rates: n/a
(501) 577-2211

BRINKLEY

BEST WESTERN
1306 Hwy 17 N
(72021)
Rates: $49-$69
(870) 734-1650
(800) 528-1234

DAYS INN
2203 N Main (72021)
Rates: $45-$95
(870) 734-1052
(800) 329-7466

BRYANT

BEST VALUE INN & SUITES
407 W Commerce St (72022)
Rates: $45-$59
(501) 653-7800

SUPER 8 MOTEL
201 Dell Dr (72022)
Rates: $69-$90
(501) 847-7888
(800) 800-8000

BULL SHOALS

BULL SHOALS WHITE RIVER LANDING
P. O. Box 748
(72619)
Rates: n/a
(501) 445-4166

DOGWOOD LODGE
505 Shorecrest Dr
(72619)
Rates: n/a
(501) 445-4311
(800) 883-4311

DRIFTWOOD RESORT
P. O. Box 75
(72619)
Rates: n/a
(501) 445-4455
(800) 424-1129

MAR-MAR RESORT
Shorecrest Dr &
Hwy 178 (72619)
Rates: n/a
(501) 445-4444
(800) 332-2855

CABOT

DAYS INN
1114 W Main
(72023)
Rates: $47-$95
(501) 843-0145
(800) 329-7466

SUPER 8 MOTEL
15 Ryeland Dr
(72023)
Rates: $51-$70
(501) 941-3748
(800) 800-8000

CADDO GAP

ARROWHEAD CABINS
HC 65, Box 2
(71935)
Rates: n/a
(501) 356-2944

CALICO ROCK

FOREST HOME LODGE & CABINS
HC 61, Box 72
(72519)
Rates: n/a
(501) 297-8211

JENKINS MOTEL
605 Hwy 56 E
(72519)
Rates: n/a
(501) 297-8987

WISEMAN MOTEL
Box 546, Hwy 5
(72519)
Rates: n/a
(501) 297-3733

CAMDEN

HOLIDAY INN EXP
1450 Hwy 278 W
(71701)
Rates: $75-$99
(870) 838-8100
(800) 465-4329

CARLISLE

BEST WESTERN INTERSTATE INN
I-40 & Hwy 13
(72024)
Rates: $49-$79
(870) 552-7566
(800) 528-1234

AREA CODES - If the local number doesn't connect, check for a new area code.

CLARKRIDGE

TREASURE COVE RESORT
902 County Rd 470 (72623)
Rates: n/a
(501) 425-4325

CLARKSVILLE

BEST WESTERN SHERWOOD MOTOR INN
1200 S Rogers St (72830)
Rates: $39-$59
(479) 754-7900
(800) 528-1234

COMFORT INN
1167 S Rogers Ave (72830)
Rates: $53-$110
(479) 754-3000
(800) 424-6423

DAYS INN
2600 W Main St (72830)
Rates: $39-$65
(479) 754-8555
(800) 329-7466

CLINTON

BEST WESTERN HILLSIDE INN
1025 Hwy 65B (72031)
Rates: $44-$64
(501) 745-4700
(800) 528-1234

CONWAY

BEST WESTERN
I-40 & US 64 East (72032)
Rates: $45-$79
(501) 329-9855
(800) 528-1234
(800) 800-6298

COMFORT INN
150 Hwy 65 N (72033)
Rates: $55-$75
(501) 329-0300
(800) 424-6423

DAYS INN
1002 E Oak St (72032)
Rates: $45-$100
(501) 450-7575
(800) 329-7466

MOTEL 6
1105 Hwy 65 N (72032)
Rates: $33-$49
(501) 327-6623
(800) 466-8356

RAMADA INN
815 E Oak St (72032)
Rates: $52-$65
(501) 329-8392
(800) 272-6232

COTTER

CHAMBERLAIN'S TROUT DOCK
Denton Ferry Rd, Rt 1, Box 620 (72626)
Rates: n/a
(501) 435-6535

RAINBOW DRIVE RESORT
Rainbow Dr, Rt 1, Box 1185 (72626)
Rates: n/a
(501) 430-5217

WHITE SANDS MOTEL
P. O. Box 116 (72626)
Rates: n/a
(501) 435-2244

CROSSETT

THE ASHLEY INN
Hwy 72 E (71635)
Rates: n/a
(501) 364-4911
(800) 276-7738

DARDANELLE

WESTERN FRONTIER MOTEL
I-40, Exit 81 (72834)
Rates: $36-$46
(501) 229-4118

DEER

THE PINEY INN
Hwy 7, P. O. Box 10 (72628)
Rates: n/a
(501) 428-5878

DEVALLS BLUFF

PALAVER PLACE BED & BREAKFAST
Rt 1, Box 29-A (72041)
Rates: n/a
(501) 998-7206

DEWITT

SAHARA MOTEL
Hwy 1, Box 309 (72042)
Rates: n/a
(870) 946-3581

DOGPATCH

ERBIE LODGE
HCR 73, Box 145 (72648)
Rates: $90+
(501) 446-5851

DOVER

MACK'S PINES
22816 SR 7 N (72837)
Rates: n/a
(501) 331-3261

DRASCO

TANNEBAUM RESORT & GOLF CLUB
1329 Tannebaum (72530)
Rates: n/a
(501) 362-3075

DUMAS

EXECUTIVE INN
310 Hwy 65 S (71639)
Rates: n/a
(501) 382-5115

PENDLETON INN
Rt 1 (71639)
Rates: n/a
(501) 382-4215

EL DORADO

BEST WESTERN KINGS INN CONF CTR
1920 Junction City Rd (71730)
Rates: $59-$79
(870) 862-5191
(800) 528-1234

EL DORADO INN MOTEL
3019 N West Ave (71730)
Rates: n/a
(870) 862-6676

FLAMINGO MOTEL
420 S West Ave (71730)
Rates: n/a
(870) 862-4201

LA QUINTA INN
2303 Junction City Rd (71730)
Rates: $50-$70
(870) 863-6677
(800) 687-6667

WHITEHALL MOTEL
840 W Hillsboro (71730)
Rates: n/a
(870) 863-4136

ELIZABETH

HOLIDAY HILLS RESORT
Rt 1, Box 22 (72531)
Rates: n/a
(501) 488-5303

KELLER'S KOVE RESORT
Rt 1, Box 45 (72531)
Rates: n/a
(501) 488-5360

EUREKA SPRINGS

CLIFF COTTAGE, B&B INN
42 Armstrong Dr (72632)
Rates: $120-$195
(5479 253-7409

ALPEN-DORF MOTEL
Rt 4, Box 580 (72632)
Rates: $48-$89
(479) 253-9475
(800) 776-9865

BASIN PARK HOTEL
12 Spring St (72632)
Rates: $89-$149
(479) 253-7837
(800) 643-4972

BEST WESTERN OZARKS INN
Hwy 62 W (72632)
Rates: $44-$149
(479) 253-9768
(800) 528-1234
(800) 552-3785
(800) 813-8373

CARRIAGE HOUSE
75 Lookout Ln (72632)
Rates: n/a
(479) 253-5259

CHALET INN
Rt 6, Box 156 (72632)
Rates: $32-$48
(479) 253-9687

COLONIAL MANSION INN
154 Huntsville (72632)
Rates: $38-$98
(479) 253-7300

COTTAGE INN B&B
Rt 6, Box 115 (72632)
Rates: $65
(479) 253-5282

DAYS INN
120 W Van Buren (72632)
Rates: $44-$150
(479) 253-8863
(800) 329-7466

DOGWOOD COTTAGES
RR 1, Box 168 (72632)
Rates: n/a
(479) 253-8897

DOGWOOD INN
170 Huntsville Rd (72632)
Rates: $48-$58
(479) 253-7200

1876 INN
Rt 6, Box 247 (72632)
Rates: $30-$71
(479) 253-7183
(800) 643-3030

1886 CRESCENT HOTEL & SPA
75 Prospect Ave (72632
Rates: $99-$179
(479) 253-9766
(888) 891-9766

EUREKA SUNSET COTTAGES
10 Dogwood Ridge (72632)
Rates: n/a
(479) 253-9565
(888) 253-9565

FOUR RUNNERS INN
RR 4, Box 306 (72632)
Rates: n/a
(479) 253-6000

HARVEST HOUSE B&B
104 Wall (72632)
Rates: n/a
(479) 253-9363
(800) 293-5665

HIDDEN VALLEY GUEST RANCH
777 Hidden Valley Ranch (72632)
Rates: n/a
(479) 253-9777

HILLSIDE COTTAGE BED & BREAKFAST
23 Hillside (72632)
Rates: n/a
(479) 253-8688

HOWARD JOHNSON EXP
4042 E Van Buren St (72632)
Rates: $39-$110
(479) 253-6665
(800) 446-4656

INDIAN MT LODGE & CABINS
Rt 4, Box 570 (72632)
Rates: n/a
(479) 253-5221

JOY MOTEL
216 W Van Buren St (72632)
Rates: $39-$93
(479) 253-9568

KATIE WILLOW COTTAGES
Rt 6, Box 354 (72632)
Rates: n/a
(479) 253-8199

KINGS HI-WAY INN
92 Kings Hwy (72632)
Rates: n/a
(479) 253-7311

LAKE LEATHER-WOOD PARK
Hwy 62 W (72632)
Rates: n/a
(479) 253-8624

LAKE LUCERNE RESORT
P. O. Box 441 (72632)
Rates: n/a
(479) 253-8085

LAZEE DAZE LOG CABIN RESORT
5432 Hwy 23 South (72632)
Rates: $105-$135
(479) 253-7026
(800) 760-7413

LOG CABIN INN MOTEL
42 Kings Hwy (72632)
Rates: n/a
(479) 253-9400
(800) 254-9411

MARIPOSA INN
3 Echols (72632)
Rates: n/a
(479) 253-9169

MOTEL 6
3169 E Van Buren (72632)
Rates: $39-$60
(479) 253-5600
(800) 466-8356

OAK CREST COTTAGES
Rt 6, Box 126 (72632)
Rates: $30-$45
(479) 253-9493
(800) 262-6255

OLD HOMESTEAD
82 Armstrong St (72632)
Rates: n/a
(479) 253-7501

PINE LODGE
Rt 2, Box 18 (72632)
Rates: n/a
(479) 253-8065

PINE TOP LODGE
Rt 6, Box 265 (72632)
Rates: $24-$56
(479) 253-7331
(800) 643-2233

POINTE WEST RESORT
Rt 2, Box 87 (72632)
Rates: n/a
(479) 253-9050

POTTER'S HOUSE MOTEL
Passion Play Rd (72632)
Rates: n/a
(479) 253-7398

PURPLE IRIS INN
RR 6, Box 339 (72632)
Rates: n/a
(800) 831-4747

REGENCY 7
62E Passion Play Rd (72632)
Rates: n/a
(800) 470-5959

ROADRUNNER INN
3034 Mundell Rd (72632)
Rates: $49-$70
(479) 253-8166
(888) 253-8166

ROGUE'S MANOR AT SWEET SPRINGS BED & BREAKFAST
124 Spring St (72632)
Rates: n/a
(479) 253-4911
(800) 764-8376

SCANDIA INN BED & BREAKFAST
33 Ave, Hwy 62 W (72632)
Rates: n/a
(479) 253-8922
(800) 523-8922

SHERWOOD COURT
27 Glenn Ave (72632)
Rates: n/a
(479) 253-8920
(800) 268-8920

STATUE ROAD INN MOTEL
Rt 1, Box 965 (72632)
Rates: n/a
(479) 253-9163
(800) 501-7666

STUDIO GUEST HOUSE
120 N Main (72632)
Rates: n/a
(479) 253-8773

SWISS VILLAGE INN
Rt 6, Box 5 (72632)
Rates: $44-$65
(479) 253-9541
(800) 447-6525

TAYLOR-PAGE INN B&B
33 Benton St (72632)
Rates: n/a
(479) 253-7315

TRADEWINDS MOTEL
77 Kings Hwy (72632)
Rates: $26-$80
(479) 253-9774
(800) 242-1615

TRAVELERS INN
2044 E Van Buren (72632)
Rates: $28-$58
(479) 253-8386
(800) 643-5566

TRAVELODGE
110 Huntsville Dr (72632)
Rates: $32-$120
(479) 253-8992
(800) 578-7878

WHISPERING OAKS MOTEL
Rt 6, Box 338 (72632)
Rates: n/a
(479) 253-9459

WHITE DOVER MANOR B&B
8 Washington St (72632)
Rates: n/a
(479) 253-6151
(800) 261-6151

WILDFLOWER COTTAGES
22 Hale St (72632)
Rates: n/a
(479) 253-9173

EVENING SHADE

THE TURMAN HOUSE B&B
P. O. Box 146 (72532)
Rates: n/a
(870) 266-3405
(800) 257-3405

FAYETTEVILLE

BEST WESTERN WINDSOR SUITES
1122 S Futrail Dr (72701)
Rates: $55-$200
(479) 587-1400
(800) 528-1234

COMFORT INN
735 S Shiloh Dr (72704)
Rates: $49-$125
(479) 587-8300
(800) 424-6423

DAYS INN
2402 N College Ave (72703)
Rates: $50-$125
(479) 443-4323
(800) 329-7466

HOLIDAY INN EXP
1251 N Shiloh Dr (72701)
Rates: $70-$95
(479) 444-6006
(800) 465-4329

THE INN OF FAYETTEVILLE
1000 Hwy 71 (72701)
Rates: $38-$44
(479) 442-3041
(800) 290-3041

MOTEL 6
2980 N College Ave (72703)
Rates: $37-$40
(479) 443-4351
(800) 466-8356

QUALITY INN
523 S Shiloh Dr (72704)
Rates: $60-$100
(479) 444-9800
(800) 424-6423

RADISSON HOTEL
70 N East Ave (72701)
Rates: $69-$135
(479) 442-5555
(800) 333-3333

SLEEP INN
728 Millsap Rd (72703)
Rates: $49-$125
(479) 587-8700
(800) 424-6423

AREA CODES - If the local number doesn't connect, check for a new area code.

SUPER 8 MOTEL
1075 S Shiloh Dr
(72701)
Rates: $47-$75
(479) 521-8866
(800) 800-8000

FLIPPIN

SEAWRIGHT'S MOTEL
1st & Sunset Sts
(72634)
Rates: n/a
(870) 453-2555

SHADY OAKS COTTAGES
HC 62, Box 128
(72634)
Rates: $50-$65
(870) 626-5474
(800) 467-6257

SPORTSMAN'S RESORT
HCR 62, Box 96
(72634)
Rates: n/a
(870) 453-2424
(800) 626-5474

WHITE HOLE RESORT
HCR 62, Box 100
(72634)
Rates: n/a
(870) 453-2913

WILDCAT SHOALS RESORT
P. O. Box 1032
(72634)
Rates: n/a
(870) 453-2321

FORDYCE

A-OK MOTEL
2403 Hwy 167 &
79 (71742)
Rates: n/a
(501) 352-3197

ANTLERS INN MOTEL
2400 Bypass (71742)
Rates: n/a
(501) 352-5174

FORREST CITY

BEST WESTERN COLONY INN
2333 N Washington
(72335)
Rates: $65-$100
(870) 633-0870
(800) 528-1234

COMFORT INN
115 Barrow Hill
Rd (72335)
Rates: $45-$85
(870) 633-0042
(800) 424-6423

DAYS INN
350 Barrow Hill
Rd (72335)
Rates: $50-$110
(870) 633-777
(800) 329-7466

ECONO LODGE
204 Holiday Dr
(72335)
Rates: $49-$84
(870) 633-6900
(800) 424-6423

HOLIDAY INN
200 Holiday Dr
(72335)
Rates: $65-$68
(870) 633-6300
(800) 465-4329

LUXURY INN
315 Barrow Hilll
Rd (72335)
Rates: $33-$39
(870) 633-8990

FORT SMITH

ASPEN HOTEL & SUITES
2900 S 68th St
(72903)
Rates: $89-$120
(479) 452-9000

BAYMONT INN & SUITES
2123 Burnham Rd
(72903)
Rates: $54-$74
(479) 484-5770
(877) 229-6668

BEST WESTERN KINGS ROW INN
5801 Rogers Ave
(72903)
Rates: $58-$73
(479) 452-4200
(800) 528-1234
(800) 531-5464

COMFORT INN
2120 Burnham Rd
(72903)
Rates: $60-$90
(479) 474-2223
(800) 424-6423

DAYS INN
1021 Garrison Ave
(72901)
Rates: $36-$65
(479) 783-0548
(800) 329-7466

DENNIS MOTEL
5100 Midland
Blvd (72904)
Rates: n/a
(479) 782-4064

FIFTH SEASON MOTOR INN
2219 S Waldron
Rd (72903)
Rates: $59-$79
(479) 452-4880
(800) 643-4567

HOLIDAY INN CIVIC CENTER
700 Rogers Ave
(72901)
Rates: $89-$109
(479) 783-1000
(800) 465-4329

HOLIDAY INN EXP
6813 Phoenix Ave
(72903)
Rates: n/a
(479) 452-7500
(800) 465-4329

MOTEL 6
6001 Rogers Ave
(72903)
Rates: $35-$53
(479) 484-0576
(800) 466-8356

RESIDENCE INN BY MARRIOTT
3005 S 74th St
(72903)
Rates: $99-$139
(479) 478-8300
(800) 331-3131

SUPER 8 MOTEL
3810 Towson Ave
(72901)
Rates: $45-$60
(479) 646-3411
(800) 800-8000

GAMALIEL

BAYOU RESORT
HC 66, Box 390
(72537)
Rates: n/a
(870) 467-5277

CASTAWAYS RESORT
Hwy 101 (72537)
Rates: n/a
(870) 467-5348

DRIFTWOOD RESORT
HC 66, Box 6000
(72537)
Rates: n/a
(870) 467-5330

LAKESIDE RESORT
Koeller Rd, CR
801 (72537)
Rates: n/a
(870) 467-5196

LUCKY 7 RESORT
HC 66, Box 1345
(72537)
Rates: n/a
(870) 467-5451

SHADY VALLEY RESORT
HC 66, Box 220
(72537)
Rates: n/a
(870) 467-5350

TWIN GABLES RESORT
HC 66, Box 1385
(72537)
Rates: $55-$67
(870) 467-5686

GASSVILLE

RED BUD DOCK MOTEL
Rt 2, Box 541
(72635)
Rates: n/a
(501) 435-6303

GATEWAY

HOLIDAY HILL MOTEL
Hwy 62 E
Gateway (72733)
Rates: n/a
(501) 656-3395

GENTRY

APPLE CREST INN B&B
12758 S Hwy 59
(72734)
Rates: $85-$165
(479) 736-8201

GENTRY MOTEL
P. O. Box 177 (72734)
Rates: n/a
(479) 736-8006

GILBERT

BUFFALO CAMP-ING & CANOEING
P. O. Box 45 (72636)
Rates: n/a
(870) 439-2888

GENERAL STORE CABINS
1 Frost St (72636)
Rates: n/a
(501) 439-2386

GILLETT

RICE PADDY MOTEL
P. O. Box 536
(72055)
Rates: n/a
(501) 548-2223

GLENWOOD

CADDO RIVER MOTEL
Rt 2, Box 786
(71943)
Rates: n/a
(870) 356-4117

OUACHITA MTN INN
Box 32, Hwy 70
Bypass (71943)
Rates: n/a
(870) 356-3737

RIVERWOOD INN
363 Hwy 70 E
(71943)
Rates: $50-$70
(870) 356-4567

GREERS FERRY

COLE'S OZARK MOTEL
7650 Edgemont
Rd (72067)
Rates: n/a
(501) 825-6607

NARROW'S INN
7910 Edgemont
Rd (72067)
Rates: n/a
(501) 825-6246

RED BIRD INN
9174 Edgemont
Rd (72067)
Rates: n/a
(501) 825-6256

AREA CODES - If the local number doesn't connect, check for a new area code.

HAMPTON

SMITH'S MOTEL
P. O. Box 823
(71744)
Rates: n/a
(501) 798-2755

HARDY

FRONTIER MOTOR LODGE
Rt 1, Box 62
(72542)
Rates: n/a
(501) 966-3377

HIDEAWAY INN B&B
Rt 1, Box 199
(72542)
Rates: n/a
(501) 966-4770
(888) 966-4770

MOTOR CENTER MOTEL
Rt 1, Box 57-A
(72542)
Rates: n/a
(501) 856-3282

RAZORBACK MOTEL
Rt 1, Box 234
(72542)
Rates: n/a
(501) 856-2465

WEAVER MOTEL
Rt 1, Box 2 (72542)
Rates: n/a
(501) 856-3224

HARRISON

AIRPORT MOTEL
1605 Hwy 62-65 N
(72601)
Rates: n/a
(870) 741-5900

COMFORT INN
1210 Hwy 62/65
N (72601)
Rates: $55-$89
(870) 741-7676
(800) 424-6423

CRESTHAVEN INN
825 N Main
(72601)
Rates: n/a
(870) 741-9522

FAMILY BUDGET INN
401 S Main Hwy
65B (72601)
Rates: $33-$40
(870) 743-1000

HARRISON HOTEL & SUITES
816 N Main
(72601)
Rates: $52-$61
(870) 741-2391

HOLIDAY INN EXP HOTEL & SUITES
117 Hwy 43 E
(72601)
Rates: $55-$86
(870) 741-3636
(800) 465-4329

LITTLE SWITZERLAND
Jasper Star Rt,
Hwy 7 (72601)
Rates: n/a
(870) 446-2693
(800) 510-0691

MERRY OTTER BED & BREAKFAST
103 W South St
(72601)
Rates: n/a
(870) 743-9010

ROCK CANDY MTN
Hwy 7 South
(72601)
Rates: n/a
(870) 743-1531

SCENIC 7 MOTEL
Rt 1, Box 16
(72601)
Rates: n/a
(870) 741-9648

SUPER 8 MOTEL
1330 Hwy 62/65
N (72601)
Rates: $45-$75
(870) 741-1741
(800) 800-8000

HAZEN

SUPER 8 MOTEL
2809 Hwy 63
(72064)
Rates: $45-$65
(870) 255-2888
(800) 800-8000

HEBER SPRINGS

ARKANSAS INN
2233 Hwy 25 NB
(72543)
Rates: n/a
(501) 362-2500
(800) 530-7740

BARNETT MOTEL
616 W Main St
(72543)
Rates: $36-$47
(501) 362-8111

LAKE & RIVER INN
2322 Hwy 25B
(72543)
Rates: $35-$45
(501) 362-3161

LAKESHORE RESORT MOTEL
801 Case Ford Rd
(72543)
Rates: $42+
(501) 362-2315

OZARK TRAIL MOTEL
1631 Hwy 25 B
(72543)
Rates: n/a
(501) 362-3102

PINES MOTEL
1819 25 B (72543)
Rates: n/a
(501) 362-3176

HELENA

RIVERBLUFF HOTEL
Box 730 (72342)
Rates: $40-$75
(501) 338-6431
(800) 543-5352

HENDERSON

CRYSTAL COVE RESORT
HC 66, Box 845
(72544)
Rates: n/a
(501) 488-5373

HINDSVILLE

FOXFIRE CAMP RESORT
Rt 1, Box 198
(72738)
Rates: n/a
(501) 789-2122

HOPE

BEST WESTERN INN OF HOPE
Jct I-30 & SR 4,
Exit 30 (71801)
Rates: $50-$70
(870) 777-9222
(800) 528-1234
(800) 429-4494

DAYS INN
1600 N Hervey Rd
(71801)
Rates: $44-$70
(870) 722-1904
(800) 329-7466

ECONO LODGE
2504 N Hazel St
(71801)
Rates: $44-$70
(870) 777-0777
(800) 424-6423

FRIENDLY INN
P. O. Box 930
(71801)
Rates: n/a
(870) 777-4665

HOLIDAY INN EXP
2600 N Hervey
(71801)
Rates: $61-$70
(870) 722-6262
(800) 465-4329

SUPER 8 MOTEL
I-30 & Hwy 4
(71801)
Rates: $29-$39
(870) 777-8601
(800) 800-8000

HORSESHOE BEND

BOXHOUND RESORT & MARINA
1313 Tri-Lake Dr
(72512)
Rates: n/a
(870) 670-4496

HOT SPRINGS

APPLE TREE INN
805 E Grand
(71901)
Rates: n/a
(501) 624-4672
(800) 782-7753

CLARION RESORT ON THE LAKE
4813 Central Ave
(71913)
Rates: $59-$205
(501) 525-1391
(800) 424-6423

EL RANCHO MOTEL
1611 Central Ave
(71901)
Rates: n/a
(501) 624-1273

EMBASSY SUITES
400 Convention
Blvd (71901)
Rates: $149-$199
(501) 624-9200
(800) 362-2779

FOUNTAIN MOTEL
1622 Central Ave
(71901)
Rates: n/a
(501) 624-1262

HOT SPRINGS RESORT
1871 E Grand
(71901)
Rates: n/a
(501) 623-8824
(800) 238-4891

HOWARD JOHNSON
400 W Grand Ave
(71901)
Rates: $40-$80
(501) 624-4441
(800) 446-4656

KING'S INN MOTEL
2101 Central Ave
(71901)
Rates: n/a
(501) 623-8824
(800) 235-8824

LAKE HAMILTON RESORT
2803 Albert Pike
Rd (71901)
Rates: $84-$160
(501) 767-8606

MAJESTIC HOTEL
Park & Central
Ave (71901)
Rates: $45-$65
(501) 623-5511

MARGARETE MOTEL
217 Fountain St
(71901)
Rates: $65-$120
(501) 623-1192

MOUNTAIN SPRINGS INN
1127 Central Ave
(71901)
Rates: n/a
(501) 624-7131

PARK HOTEL
211 Fountain St
(71901)
Rates: $65-$125
(501) 624-5323

PATTON'S LAKE RESORT
100 San Carlos
Point (71913)
Rates: n/a
(501) 525-1678

QUALITY INN
1125 E Grand Ave
(71901)
Rates: $60-$135
(501) 624-3321
(800) 424-6423

ROYALE VISTA INN
2204 Central Ave
(71901)
Rates: n/a
(501) 624-5551

SHAMROCK MOTEL
508 Albert Pike
(71913)
Rates: n/a
(501) 624-3833

TAYLOR ROSAMOND MOTEL
316 Park Ave
(71901)
Rates: n/a
(501) 624-1255

TOWN HOUSE MOTEL
100 Cove (71901)
Rates: n/a
(501) 624-9271

TRAVELIER INN
1045 E Grand Ave
(71901)
Rates: $36-$62
(501) 624-4681

VAGABOND MOTEL
4708 Central Ave
(71913)
Rates: n/a
(501) 525-2769

VELDA ROSE HOTEL & SPA
217 Park Ave
(71901)
Rates: $76-$85
(501) 623-3311

WILLOW BEACH RESORT
260 Lake
Hamilton (71913)
Rates: n/a
(501) 525-1362
(800) 874-1385

WOODBINE HOLLOW B&B
213 Woodbine
(71901)
Rates: n/a
(501) 624-3646

HOT SPRINGS NATIONAL PARK

AVANELLE MOTOR LODGE
1204 Central Ave
(71901)
Rates: $44-$70
(501) 321-1332

BUENA VISTA RESORT
201 Abernia
(71913)
Rates: $45-$120
(800) 255-9030

HAMILTON INN RESORT
106 Lookout Point
(71913)
Rates: $45-$58
(501) 525-5666

LAKE HAMILTON RESORT
2803 Albert Pike
Rd (71913)
Rates: $99-$150
(501) 767-5511

MARGARETE MOTEL
217 Fountain St
(71901)
Rates: $33-$48
(501) 623-1192

SHORECREST RESORT
360 Lakeland Dr
(71901)
Rates: $41-$52
(800) 447-9914

TRAVELIER INN
1045 E Grand Ave
(719019)
Rates: $29-$52
(501) 624-4681

HUTTIG

TRACKS INN MOTEL
1141 K Ave (71747)
Rates: n/a
(501) 943-2943

JACKSONVILLE

DAYS INN
1414 John Harden
Dr (72076)
Rates: $45-$65
(501) 982-1543
(800) 329-7466

OXFORD INN
920 Hwy 161
(72076)
Rates: n/a
(501) 982-1976

SANDS MOTEL
1008 S Hwy 161
(72076)
Rates: n/a
(501) 985-0266

JASPER

LOOKOUT MTN LOG CABINS
HCR 31, Box 90
(72641)
Rates: n/a
(870) 446-6224
(800) 596-5409

MOCKINGBIRD MOTEL
HCR 31, Box 64-B
(72641)
Rates: n/a
(870) 446-2643

JESSIEVILLE

OUACHITA MOTEL
6127 N Hwy 7
(71949)
Rates: n/a
(501) 984-5363

JONESBORO

BEST WESTERN
2901 Phillips Dr
(72401)
Rates: $47-$69
(870) 932-6600
(800) 528-1234

COMFORT INN & SUITES
2911 Gilmore Dr
(72401)
Rates: $59-$119
(870) 972-9000
(800) 424-6423

ECONO LODGE
2406 Phillips Dr
(72401)
Rates: $37-$60
(870) 932-9339
(800) 424-6423

HOLIDAY INN EXP
2407 Phillips Dr
(72401)
Rates: $74-$80
(870) 932-5554
(800) 465-4329

JAMI BEE MOTEL
3423 E Nettleton
Ave (72401)
Rates: n/a
(870) 932-1611

JONESBORO MOTEL
403 S Gee St
(72401)
Rates: n/a
(870) 932-6615

MOTEL 6
2300 S Caraway
Rd (72401)
Rates: $29-$38
(870) 932-1050
(800) 466-8356

RAMADA LIMITED
3000 Apache Dr
(72401)
Rates: $54-$82
(870) 932-5757
(800) 272-6232

WILSON INN
2911 Gilmore Dr
(72401)
Rates: $35-$55
(870) 972-9000

KIRBY

DAISY MOTEL
HC 71, Box 255
(71950)
Rates: n/a
(501) 398-5173

LAKESIDE GROCERY & MOTEL
HC 71, Box 67
(71950)
Rates: n/a
(501) 398-5304

LAKE VILLAGE

LA VILLA MOTEL
Hwys 65 & 82
(71653)
Rates: n/a
(870) 265-2277

LAKE SHORE MOTEL
P. O. Box 231
(71653)
Rates: n/a
(870) 265-2238

PLAZA MOTEL
Hwys 65 & 82 S
(71653)
Rates: n/a
(870) 265-5341

RAMADA LIMITED
912 Hwy 65 &
82 S (71653)
Rates: n/a
(870) 265-4545
(800) 272-6232

LAKEVIEW

BAY BREEZE RESORT
Box 185, Hwy 178
(72642)
Rates: n/a
(870) 431-5261

CEDAR OAKS RESORT
Rt 1, Box 694
(72642)
Rates: $45-$75
(870) 431-5351

GASTON'S WHITE RIVER RESORT
1 River Rd (72642)
Rates: $57-$105
(870) 431-5202

AREA CODES - If the local number doesn't connect, check for a new area code.

LAST RESORT
P. O. Box 144
(72642)
Rates: n/a
(870) 431-5681
(800) 799-5253

NEWLAND FLOAT TRIPS & LODGE
Rt 1, River Rd
(72642)
Rates: n/a
(870) 431-8620
(800) 334-5604

TWIN FIN RESORT
P. O. Box 218 (72642)
Rates: n/a
(870) 431-5377
(800) 622-6291

LEAD HILL
BON TERRE INN
Hwy 281 N
(72644)
Rates: n/a
(501) 436-7318

HILL TOP COTTAGES
Rt 1, Box 280
(72644)
Rates: n/a
(501) 436-5365

LITTLE ROCK
AMERISUITES
10920 Financial
Center Pkwy
(72209)
Rates: $89-$119
(501) 225-1075
(800) 833-1516

BAYMONT INN
1010 Breckenridge
Rd (72205)
Rates: $56-$63
(501) 225-7007
(877) 229-6668

COMFORT INN & SUITES DOWNTOWN
707 Interstate 30
(72202)
Rates: $60-$130
(501) 687-7700
(800) 424-6423

DAYS INN SOUTH
2600 W 65th St
(72209)
Rates: $32-$60
(501) 562-1122
(800) 329-7466

DAYS INN & SUITES
3200 Bankheard
Dr (72206)
Rates: $48-$70
(501) 490-2010
(800) 329-7466

EMBASSY SUITES
11301 Financial
Ctr Pkwy (72211)
Rates: $109-$199
(501) 312-9000
(800) 362-2779

HAMPTON INN
6100 Mitchell Dr
(72209)
Rates: $72-$74
(501) 562-6667
(800) 426-7866

HOLIDAY INN SELECT
201 S Shackelford
(72211)
Rates: $99$114
(501) 223-3000
(800) 465-4329

JACK'S MOTEL
9515 Hwy 365
(72206)
Rates: n/a
(501) 897-4951

KNIGHTS INN
9709 I-30 (72209)
Rates: $33-$40
(501) 568-6800
(800) 843-5644

LA QUINTA INN
200 S Shackleford
Rd (72211)
Rates: $62-$81
(501) 224-0900
(800) 687-6667

LA QUINTA INN
11701 I-30 (72209)
Rates: $59-$85
(501) 455-2300
(800) 687-6667

LA QUINTA INN
901 Fair Park Blvd
(72204)
Rates: $60-$91
(501) 664-7000
(800) 687-6667

LEGACY HOTEL
625 W Capitol
(72201)
Rates: n/a
(501) 374-0100

MARKHAM INN
5120 W Markham
(72205)
Rates: n/a
(501) 666-0161
(800) 654-0161

MOTEL 6-S EAST
7501 I-30 (72209)
Rates: $33-$40
(501) 568-8888
(800) 466-8356

MOTEL 6-WEST
10524 Markham St
(72205)
Rates: $37-$46
(501) 225-7366
(800) 466-8356

RESIDENCE INN BY MARRIOTT
1401 S Shackeford
Rd (72211)
Rates: $89-$150
(501) 312-0200
(800) 331-3131

WILSON INN
4301 E Roosevelt
(72206)
Rates: $34-$54
(501) 376-2466

LONOKE
DAYS INN
105 Dee Dee Ln
(72086)
Rates: $55-$70
(501) 656-5138
(800) 329-7466

SUPER 8 MOTEL
102 Dee Dee Ln
(72086)
Rates: $55-$69
(501) 676-8880
(800) 800-8000

MAGNOLIA
BEST WESTERN COACHMAN'S INN
420 E Main (71753)
Rates: $69-$79
(870) 234-6122
(800) 528-1234
(800) 237-6122

CASTLE INN MOTEL
912 E Main
(71753)
Rates: n/a
(501) 234-2262

FLAMINGO MOTEL
100 N Vine (71753)
Rates: n/a
(501) 234-4752

MAMMOTH SPRING
RIVERVIEW MOTEL
P. O. Box 281
(72554)
Rates: n/a
(870) 625-3218

MARBLE FALLS
ERBIE LODGE
HCR 73, Box 145
(72648)
Rates: $90+
(870) 446-5851

MARION
BEST WESTERN REGENCY MOTOR INN
3635 I-55 (72364)
Rates: $50-$80
(870) 739-3278
(800) 528-1234

MARSHALL
ROSE MOTEL
P. O. Box 913
(72650)
Rates: n/a
(501) 448-2596

SUNSET MOTEL
P. O. Box 205
(72650)
Rates: n/a
(501) 448-3348

MAUMELLE
COMFORT SUITES
14322 Frontier Dr
(72113)
Rates: $69-$149
(501) 851-8444
(800) 424-6423

QUALITY INN
14325 Frontier Dr
(72113)
Rates: $59-$79
(501) 851-3500
(800) 424-6423

MCGEHEE
BEST WESTERN
1202 Hwy 65 N
(71654)
Rates: $53-$64
(870) 222-3564
(800) 528-1234

SENATOR MOTEL
222 Hwy 65
(71654)
Rates: n/a
(501) 222-5511

MENA
AERIE B&B
Hwy 375 (71953)
Rates: n/a
(501) 394-6473

HOLIDAY MOTEL
1162 US 71 S
(71953)
Rates: n/a
(501) 394-2611

NANA'S COUNTRY INN
203 US 71 N
(71953)
Rates: n/a
(501) 394-6433

OZARK INN
2102 US 71 S
(71953)
Rates: $28-$35
(501) 394-1100

MIDWAY
HOLIDAY SHORES RESORT
943 Howard
Creek Rd (72651)
Rates: n/a
(870) 431-5370
(800) 365-4089

HOWARD CREEK RESORT
RR 1, Box 282
(72651)
Rates: n/a
(870) 431-5371

RED ARROW RESORT
Rt 1, Box 281
(72651)
Rates: n/a
(870) 431-5375
(800) 548-8724

SUNSET POINT RESORT
354 Westview Rd
(72651)
Rates: n/a
(870) 431-5372
(800) 336-8113

AREA CODES - If the local number doesn't connect, check for a new area code.

MONTICELLO

HIWAY HOST INN
617 W Gaines
(71655)
Rates: n/a
(501) 367-8555

MORRILTON

DAYS INN
1506 N SR 95
(72110)
Rates: $40-$65
(501) 354-5101
(800) 329-7466

SCOTTISH INNS
356 Hwy 95 & I-40
(72110)
Rates: n/a
(501) 354-0181
(800) 251-1962

MOUNT IDA

COLONIAL MOTEL
HC 63, Box 306
(71957)
Rates: n/a
(501) 867-2431

DENBY POINT LODGE & MARINA
SR 1, Box 241
(71957)
Rates: $35-$90
(501) 867-3651

MOUNT IDA MOTEL
HC 67, Box 67-X
(71957)
Rates: n/a
(501) 867-3456

MOUNTAIN HOME

BEST WESTERN CARRIAGE INN
963 Hwy 62 E
(72653)
Rates: $50-$85
(870) 425-6001
(800) 528-1234
(877) 425-6001

BLACKBURNS RESORT
Rt 6, Box 280
(72653)
Rates: n/a
(870) 492-5115

BLUE PARADISE RESORT
Rt 6, Box 379-CC
(72653)
Rates: $29-$46
(870) 492-5113

BUNGALOW RESORT
Rt 4, Box 439
(72653)
Rates: n/a
(870) 492-5105

BUZZARD ROOST INN
4271 Buzzard
Roost Rd (72653)
Rates: $39
(870) 492-5187

CHIT-CHAT-CHAW RESORT
9476 Promise
Land Rd (72653)
Rates: n/a
(870) 431-5584

DURBON'S NOE CREEK RESORT
Rt 1, Box 128
(72653)
Rates: n/a
(870) 431-5574
(800) 264-5574

EDGEWATER RESORT & LODGE
10108 Promise
Land Rd (72653)
Rates: n/a
(870) 431-5222

FISH & FIDDLE RESORT
Rt 10, Box 430
(72653)
Rates: n/a
(870) 491-5161

GENE'S TROUT FISHING RESORT
Rt 3, Box 348
(72653)
Rates: n/a
(870) 499-5381
(800) 256-3625

HOLIDAY INN EXP HOTEL & SUITES
1005 Coley Dr
(72654)
Rates: n/a
(870) 425-6200
(800) 465-4329

LASALLE RESORT
Rt 4, Box 485-C
(72653)
Rates: n/a
(870) 492-5133

MOCKINGBIRD BAY RESORT
Rt 3, Box 183-MH
(72653)
Rates: n/a
(870) 491-5112

MT HOME MOTEL
411 S Main (72653)
Rates: n/a
(870) 425-2171
(800) 413-2171

OZARKS OAKS MOTEL
147 S Main (72653)
Rates: n/a
(870) 425-4881

PEAL'S RESORT
Rt 3, Box 252
(72653)
Rates: n/a
(870) 499-5215

PROMISE LAND RESORT
323 CR 107
(72653)
Rates: n/a
(870) 431-5576
(888) 730-3799

RAMADA INN
1127 NE Hwy 62
(72653)
Rates: n/a
(870) 425-9191
(800) 272-6232

RIM SHOALS TROUT RESORT
Rt 2, Box 594
(72653)
Rates: n/a
(870) 435-6695

ROCKING CHAIR RANCH
Rt 6, Box 445
(72653)
Rates: $39-$95
(870) 492-5157

ROCKY RIDGE RESORT
Rt 10, Box 610
(72653)
Rates: n/a
(501) 491-5665

ROYAL MOTEL RESORT
Rt 6, Box 500
(72653)
Rates: $33-$80
(870) 492-5288

SCOTT VALLEY RESORT & GUEST RANCH
P. O. Box 1447
(72653)
Rates: $77-$175
(870) 425-5136
(888) 855-7747

SILVER SADDLE APARTMENTS & MOTEL
128 N College St
(72653)
Rates: n/a
(870) 425-9998

SISTER CREEK RESORT
9833 Promise
Land Rd (72653)
Rates: n/a
(870) 531-5587

SPRING VALLEY MOTEL
548 Hwy 62 NE
(72653)
Rates: n/a
(870) 425-3717

SUNRISE POINT RESORT
Rt 10, Box 620-CC
(72653)
Rates: n/a
(870) 491-5188

TEAL POINT RESORT
715 Teal Point Rd
(72653)
Rates: $66-$126
(870) 492-5145

WATERTREE INN
Rt 4, Box 495
(72653)
Rates: n/a
(870) 492-6477

Y CABINS
Hwy 5 S & Hwy
177 (72653)
Rates: n/a
(870) 499-5294

MOUNTAIN VIEW

BEST WESTERN FIDDLERS INN
601 Sylamore Ave
(72560)
Rates: $50-$90
(870) 269-2828
(800) 528-1234
(866) 301-0470

DAYS INN
Hwys 5, 9 & 14
(72560)
Rates: $40-$75
(870) 269-3287
(800) 329-7466

HIDDEN VALLEY CABINS
P. O. Box 740
(72560)
Rates: n/a
(870) 269-2655

JACK'S FISHING RESORT & MOTEL
Hwy 5 N (72560)
Rates: n/a
(870) 585-2211

SYLAMORE LODGES
P. O. Box 1378
(72560)
Rates: n/a
(870) 585-2221
(800) 538-2221

MURFREES-BORO

AMERICAN HERITAGE INN
705 N Washington
(71958)
Rates: n/a
(501) 285-2131

LITTLE SHAMROCK MOTEL
919 N Washington
(71958)
Rates: n/a
(501) 285-2342

RIVERSIDE COTTAGE MOTEL
RFD 1 (71958)
Rates: n/a
(501) 285-2255

NASHVILLE
HOLIDAY MOTOR LODGE
Hwy 27-B S (71852)
Rates: n/a
(501) 845-2953

NEWPORT
LAKESIDE INN
203 Malcolm Ave (72112)
Rates: n/a
(870) 523-2787

NEWPORT MOTEL
1504 Hwy 67 N (72112)
Rates: n/a
(870) 523-2768

PARK INN INTL
901 Hwy 67 N (72112)
Rates: $58-$63
(870) 523-5851
(800) 437-7275

NORFOLK
WOODSMAN'S MOTEL
HC 61, Box 461 (82658)
Rates: n/a
(501) 499-7454

NORTH LITTLE ROCK
BAYMONT INN
4311 Warden Rd (72116)
Rates: $59-$66
(501) 758-8888
(877) 229-6668

COMFORT SUITES
14322 Frontier Dr (72113)
Rates: $62-$199
(501) 851-8444
(800) 424-6423

COMFORT INN I-40 EAST
5710 Pritchard Dr (72117)
Rates: $50-$90
(501) 955-9453
(800) 424-6423

DAYS INN
5800 Pritchard Dr N (72117)
Rates: $45-$95
(501) 945-4100
(800) 329-7466

DAYS INN
7200 Bicentennial Rd (72118)
Rates: $49-$110
(501) 851-3297
(800) 329-7466

HAMPTON INN
500 W 29th St (72114)
Rates: $59-$70
(501) 771-2090
(800) 426-7866

LA QUINTA INN
4100 E McCain Blvd (72117)
Rates: $62-$85
(501) 945-0808
(800) 687-6667

MOTEL 6-NORTH
400 W 29th St (72114)
Rates: $29-$33
(501) 758-5100
(800) 466-8356

RED ROOF INN
5571 Pritchard Dr (72117)
Rates: $50-$60
(501) 945-0080
(800) 843-7663

RESIDENCE INN BY MARRIOTT
4110 Healthcare Dr (72117)
Rates: $114-$150
(501) 945-7777
(800) 331-3131

SUPER 8 MOTEL
1 Gray Rd (72117)
Rates: $45-$51
(501) 945-0141
(800) 800-8000

TRAVELODGE
3100 N Main (72116)
Rates: $45-$60
(501) 758-8110
(800) 578-7878

OAKLAND
BLACK OAK RESORT
P. O. Box 100 (72661)
Rates: n/a
(870) 431-8363

FIN 'N' FEATHER RESORT
Rt 1, Box 14 (72661)
Rates: n/a
(870) 431-5621

HENRY'S RESORT
Rt 1, Box 16 (72661)
Rates: n/a
(870) 431-5626

HIDDEN BAY RESORT
Rt 1, Box 320 (72661)
Rates: n/a
(870) 431-8121

PERSIMMON POINT RESORT
Rt 1, Box 169 (72661)
Rates: n/a
(870) 431-8877

SOUTHERN COMFORT RESORT
Rt 1, Box 40 (72661)
Rates: n/a
(870) 431-8470

OLA
MIMA'S MOTEL
P. O. Box 157 (72853)
Rates: n/a
(501) 489-5611

OMAHA
AUNT SHIRLEY'S SLEEPING LOFT
Rt 1, Box 84-D (72662)
Rates: n/a
(501) 426-5408

OZARK
DAYS INN
105 Airport Rd (72949)
Rates: $44-$54
(479) 667-2540
(800) 329-7466

OXFORD INN
305 N 18th St (72949)
Rates: $40-$45
(479) 667-1131

PARAGOULD
LINWOOD MOTEL
1611 Linwood Dr (72450)
Rates: n/a
(870) 236-7671

RAMADA INN
2310 W Kings Hwy (72450)
Rates: $77-$88
(870) 239-2121
(800) 272-6232

PARIS
BLAKELY INN
2010 E Walnut St (72855)
Rates: n/a
(501) 963-2400

PARTHENON
A CABIN IN THE WOODS
HCR 72, Box 134 (72666)
Rates: n/a
(501) 446-2293

PEA RIDGE
BATTLEFIELD INN MOTEL
14753 Hwy 62 E (72751)
Rates: n/a
(501) 451-1188

PERRYVILLE
COFFEE CREEK MOTEL
Harrisbrake (72126)
Rates: n/a
(501) 889-2745

PIGGOTT
OPEN ROADS MOTEL
148 Independent St (72454)
Rates: n/a
(501) 598-5941

PINE BLUFF
CLASSIC INN
4125 Rhinehart Rd (71601)
Rates: n/a
(870) 535-1200

HAMPTON INN
3103 E Market St (71601)
Rates: $60-$70
(870) 850-0444
(800) 426-7866

HOLIDAY INN EXP HOTEL & SUITES
3620 Camden Rd (71603)
Rates: $80
(870) 879-3800
(800) 465-4329

POCAHONTAS
DAYS INN & SUITES
2805 Hwy 67 S (72455)
Rates: $75
(870) 892-9500
(800) 329-7466

PONCA
LOST VALLEY CANOE & LODGING
Hwy 43, Buffalo National River (72670)
Rates: n/a
(870) 861-5522

PRESCOTT
BROADWAY HOTEL
123 W 1st (71857)
Rates: n/a
(870) 887-5446

ECONO LODGE
1703 Hwy 371 W (71857)
Rates: $40-$80
(870) 887-6641
(800) 424-6423

ROGERS
AMERISUITES
4610 W Walnut (72756)
Rates: $119-$139
(479) 633-8555
(800) 833-1516

BEAVER LAKE LODGE
14733 Dutchman Dr (72756)
Rates: $50-$56
(479) 925-2313
(800) 367-4513

EMBASSY SUITES
3303 Pinnacle Hills Pky (72758)
Rates: $89-$289
(479) 254-8400
(800) 362-2779

AREA CODES - If the local number doesn't connect, check for a new area code.

HARTLAND LODGE
2931 W Walnut
(72756)
Rates: n/a
(479) 631-6000
(800) 451-1588

HIWAY HOST INN
915 S 8th (72756)
Rates: n/a
(479) 636-9400

JAN-LIN MOTOR INN
1601 71-B S
(72756)
Rates: n/a
(479) 636-1733

RESIDENCE INN BY MARRIOTT
4611 W Locust St
(72756)
Rates: $129-$159
(479) 636-5900
(800) 331-3131

SECOND HOME BEAVER LAKE
100 W Locust
(72756)
Rates: n/a
(501) 530-1773

TANGLEWOOD LODGE
Rt 6 (72756)
Rates: n/a
(501) 925-2100

RUSSELLVILLE
BEST WESTERN INN
2316 N Arkansas
Ave (72802)
Rates: $52-$58
(479) 967-1000
(800) 528-1234

COMFORT INN
3019 E Parkway
Dr (72802)
Rates: $45-$65
(479) 967-7500
(800) 424-6423

DAYS INN
204 Lakefront Dr
(72802)
Rates: $46-$99
(479) 968-5511
(800) 329-7466

HOLIDAY INN
2407 N Arkansas
Ave (72801)
Rates: $65-$70
(479) 968-4300
(800) 465-4329

HOLLEY JOHNSON MOTEL
1206 E Main St
(72801)
Rates: n/a
(479) 968-4959
(800) 465-4329

LAKESIDE RESORT MOTEL
3320 N Arkansas
Ave (72801)
Rates: n/a
(479) 968-9715

MERRICK MOTEL
1320 E Main St
(72801)
Rates: n/a
(479) 968-6332

MOTEL 6
215 W Birch St
(72801)
Rates: $29-$34
(479) 968-3666
(800) 466-8356

PARK MOTEL
2615 W Main St
(72801)
Rates: $26-$44
(479) 968-4862

SUNRISE INN
154 E Aspen Rd
(72801)
Rates: n/a
(479) 968-7200

SUPER 8 MOTEL
2404 N Arkansas
(72811)
Rates: $46-$59
(479) 968-8898
(800) 800-8000

WOODY'S CLASSIC INN
1522 E Main St
(72801)
Rates: n/a
(479) 968-7774

SEARCY
HAMPTON INN
3204 E Race Ave
(72143)
Rates: $59-$74
(501) 268-0654
(800) 426-7866

ROYAL INN
2203 E Race Ave
(72143)
Rates: $40-$59
(501) 268-3511

SILOAM SPRINGS
EASTGATE MOTOR LODGE
1951 Hwy 412
(72761)
Rates: n/a
(479) 524-5157

SUPER 8 MOTEL
1800 Hwy 412 W
(72761)
Rates: $60-$65
(479) 524-8898
(800) 800-8000

SPRINGDALE
BAYMONT INN & SUITES
1300 S 48th St
(72764)
Rates: $51-$57
(479) 751-2626
(877) 229-6668

BEST WESTERN HERITAGE INN
1394 W Sunset
(72764)
Rates: $59-$130
(479) 751-3100
(800) 528-1234

COMFORT SUITES
1099 Rieff St
(72764)
Rates: $72-$85
(479) 725-1777
(800) 424-6423

HAMPTON INN & SUITES
1700 S 48th
(72762)
Rates: $79-$106
(479) 756-3500
(800) 426-7866

HOLIDAY INN
1500 S 48th St
(72762)
Rates: $159-$199
(479) 751-8300
(800) 465-4329

RESIDENCE INN BY MARRIOTT
1740 S 48th St
(72762)
Rates: $119-$149
(479) 872-9100
(800) 331-3131

ST. JOE
MAPLEWOOD MOTEL
P. O. Box 1 (72675)
Rates: n/a
(501) 439-2525

STAMPS
LAFAYETTE MOTEL
Hwy 72 E (71860)
Rates: n/a
(501) 533-4333

STAR CITY
SUPER 8 MOTEL
1308 N Lincoln St
(71667)
Rates: $64-$69
(870) 628-6883
(800) 800-8000

STORY
AQUA MOTEL
HC 64, Box 105
(71970)
Rates: n/a
(501) 867-2123

STUTTGART
BEST WESTERN DUCK INN
704 W Michigan
(72160)
Rates: $57-$104
(870) 673-2575
(800) 528-1234

HOLIDAY INN EXP
708 W Michigan
(72160)
Rates: $69-$124
(870) 673-3616
(800) 465-4329

WALKER MOTOR INN
405 E Michigan
(72160)
Rates: n/a
(501) 673-2671

TEXARKANA
BAYMONT INN & SUITES
5012 N State Line
Ave (75502)
Rates: $50-$55
(870) 773-1000
(877) 229-6668

BEST WESTERN KINGS ROW INN
4200 N State Line
Ave (71854)
Rates: $58-$70
(870) 774-3851
(800) 528-1234
(800) 643-5464

FOUR STATES INN
4300 N State Line
Ave (75502)
Rates: $34-$42
(870) 773-3144

HOLIDAY INN
5100 N State Line
Ave (75503)
Rates: $68-$78
(870) 774-3521
(800) 465-4329

QUALITY INN
5210 N State Line
Ave (75504)
Rates: $59-$69
(870) 772-0070
(800) 424-6423

TRUMANN
WEEM'S MOTEL
404 Hwy 63 N
(72472)
Rates: n/a
(501) 483-6331

VAN BUREN
COMFORT INN
3131 Cloverleaf St
(72956)
Rates: $55-$90
(479) 474-2223
(800) 424-6423

HOLIDAY INN EXP
1903 N 6th St
(72956)
Rates: $68
(479) 474-8100
(800) 465-4329

MOTEL 6
1716 Fayetteville
Rd (72956)
Rates: $37+
(479) 474-8001
(800) 466-8356

SUPER 8 MOTEL
106 N Plaza Ct
(72956)
Rates: $49-$69
(479) 471-8888
(800) 800-8000

WALNUT RIDGE
ALAMO COURT MOTEL
Hwy 67 S (72476)
Rates: $30-$95
(501) 886-2441
(800) 633-9575

PHILLIPS MOTEL
501 Hwy 67 N
(72476)
Rates: n/a
(501) 886-6767

WARREN
ECONOMY INN
108 E Church St
(71671)
Rates: n/a
(870) 226-5881

SUPER 8 MOTEL
1408 E Curch St
(71671)
Rates: $44-$59
(870) 226-9888
(800) 800-8000

TOWN HOUSE MOTEL
201 E Church St
(71671)
Rates: n/a
(870) 226-5822

WEST HELENA
HARBOR INN MOTEL
Hwy 49-B (72390)
Rates: n/a
(870) 572-2597

SANDS MOTEL
Hwy 49-B (72390)
Rates: n/a
(870) 572-6774

WEST MEMPHIS
BEST WESTERN W. MEMPHIS INN
3401 Service Loop
Rd (72302)
Rates: $48-$95
(870) 735-7185
(800) 528-1234

COMFORT INN
1300 Ingram Blvd
(72301)
Rates: $49-$94
(870) 732-0044
(800) 424-6423

EXPRESS INN
3700 E Service Rd
(72301)
Rates: n/a
(870) 732-5688

MOTEL 6
2501 S Service Rd
(72301)
Rates: $35-$42
(870) 735-0100
(800) 466-8356

WHEATLEY
RAMADA LIMITED
129 Lawson Rd
(72392)
Rates: $46-$55
(870) 457-2202
(800) 272-6232

WHITE HALL
DAYS INN
8006 Sheridan Rd
(71602)
Rates: $55-$80
(870) 247-1339
(800) 329-7466

WOOSTER
PATTON HOUSE BED & BREAKFAST
Hwy 25, P. O. Box
61 (72181)
Rates: n/a
(501) 679-2975

WYNNE
NATION WIDE 9 MOTEL
706 Hwy 64 E
(72396)
Rates: n/a
(501) 238-9399

YELLVILLE
SILVER RUN CABINS
14 Silver Run
Lane (72687)
Rates: n/a
(870) 449-6355
(800) 741-2022

WILD BILL'S OUTFITTERS- MOTEL & CABINS
23 Hwy 268E
(72687)
Rates: n/a
(870) 449-6235
(800) 554-8657

AREA CODES - If the local number doesn't connect, check for a new area code.

CALIFORNIA

ADELANTO
DAYS INN
11628 Bartlett Ave (92301)
Rates: $45-$89
(760) 246-8777
(800) 329-7466

AGOURA HILLS
RADISSON HOTEL
30100 Agoura Rd (91301)
Rates: $79+
(818) 707-1220
(800) 333-3333

AHWAHNEE
SILVER SPUR B&B
44625 Silver Spur Tr (93601)
Rates: $45-$60
(209) 683-2896

ALAMEDA
ISLANDER LODGE MOTEL
2428 Central Ave (94501)
Rates: $44-$59
(510) 865-2121

ALMANOR
ALMANOR LAKE-SIDE RESORT
325 Peninsula Dr (96137)
Rates: $95-$375
(530) 598-4530

ALTURAS
BEST WESTERN TRAILSIDE INN
343 N Main St (96101)
Rates: $65-$75
(530) 233-4111
(800) 528-1234

DRIFTERS INN
395 Lake View Rd (96101)
Rates: $40+
(530) 233-2428

ESSEX MOTEL
1216 N Main St (96101)
Rates: $36-$42
(530) 233-2821

FRONTIER MOTEL
1033 N Main St (96101)
Rates: $28-$43
(530) 233-3383

HACIENDA MOTEL
201 E 12th St (96101)
Rates: $26-$45
(530) 233-3459

ANAHEIM
BEST WESTERN ANAHEIM STAR-TUDST
1057 W Ball Rd (92802)
Rates: $59-$119
(714) 774-7600
(800) 528-1234

CLARION HOTEL
616 Convention Way (92802)
Rates: $59-$159
(714) 750-3131
(800) 424-6423

COAST ANAHEIM HOTEL
1855 S Harbor Blvd (92802)
Rates: $69-$199
(714) 750-1811
(800) 663-1144

EMBASSY SUITES HOTEL
3100 E Frontera (92806)
Rates: $119-$204
(714) 632-1221
(800) 362-2779

HAWTHORN SUITES
1752 S Clementine St (92802)
Rates: $85-$139
(714) 635-5000
(800) 527-1133
(800) 992-4884

HILTON ANAHEIM
777 Convention Way (92802)
Rates: $99-$299
(714) 750-4321
(800) 233-6904

HOLIDAY INN HOTEL & SUITES
1240 S Walnut St (92802)
Rates: $69-$99
(714) 535-0300
(800) 465-4329

LA QUINTA INN & SUITES
1752 S Clementine St (92802)
Rates: $75-$139
(714) 635-5000
(800) 687-6667

MARRIOTT HOTEL
700 W Convention Way (92802)
Rates: $129-$199
(714) 750-8000
(800) 228-9290

MOTEL 6-FULLERTON EAST
1440 N State College (92806)
Rates: $39-$52
(714) 956-9690
(800) 466-8356

PLAZA HOTEL & SUITES
1700 S Harbor Blvd (92802)
Rates: $89-$119
(714) 772-5900
(800) 522-6415

QUALITY INN MAINGATE
2200 S Harbor Blvd (92802)
Rates: $59-$119
(714) 750-5211
(800) 424-6423

RED ROOF INN-MAINGATE
100 Disney Way (92802)
Rates: $59-$71
(714) 520-9696
(800) 843-7663

RESIDENCE INN BY MARRIOTT
1700 S Clementine St (92801)
Rates: $119-$269
(714) 533-3555
(800) 331-3131

SHERATON ANAHEIM HOTEL
900 S Disneyland Dr (92802)
Rates: $85-$105
(714) 778-1700
(800) 325-3535

STAYBRIDGE SUITES
1855 S Manchester Ave (92802)
Rates: $109-$229
(714) 748-7700
(800) 238-8000

TOWNEPLACE SUITES BY MARRIOTT
1730 S State College (92805)
Rates: $69-$129
(714) 939-9700

VAGABOND INN EXECUTIVE
2145 S Harbor Blvd (92802)
Rates: $59-$109
(714) 971-5556
(800) 522-1555

ANAHEIM HILLS
BEST WESTERN ANAHEIM HILLS INN
5710 E La Palma (92807)
Rates: $64-$129
(714) 779-0252
(800) 528-1234
(800) 346-6662

ANDERSON
AMERIHOST INN
2040 Deschutes Rd (96007)
Rates: $59-$139
(530) 365-6100
(800) 434-5800

ANDERSON VALLEY INN
2861 McMurry Dr (96007)
Rates: $45-$65
(530) 365-2566

BEST WESTERN KNIGHTS INN
2688 Gateway Dr (96007)
Rates: $55-$80
(530) 365-2753
(800) 528-1234

ANGELS CAMP
ANGELS HACIENDA B&B
4871 Hunt Rd (Farmington 95230)
Rates: n/a
(209) 785-8533

ANGELS INN MOTEL
600 N Main St (95221)
Rates: $75-$105
(209) 736-4242
(888) 753-0226

BEST WESTERN CEDAR INN & SUITES
444 S Main St (95221)
Rates: $89-$189
(209) 736-4000
(800) 528-1234
(800) 767-1127

JUMPING FROG MOTEL
330 Murphys Grade Rd (95221)
Rates: $60-$150
(209) 736-2191

ANTIOCH
BEST WESTERN HERITAGE INN
3210 Delta Fair Blvd (94509)
Rates: $78-$85
(925) 778-2000
(800) 528-1234

APPLEGATE
ORIGINAL FIREHOUSE MOTEL
17855 Lake Arthur Rd (95703)
Rates: $34-$43
(916) 878-7770

AREA CODES - If the local number doesn't connect, check for a new area code.

APTOS

APPLE LANE INN BED & BREAKFAST
6265 Soquel Dr (95003)
Rates: $120-$200
(831) 475-6868
(800) 649-8988

MANGELS HOUSE BED & BREAKFAST
570 Aptos Creek Rd (95003)
Rates: $105-$135
(831) 688-7982

ARCADIA

MOTEL 6
225 Colorado Place (91007)
Rates: $47-$60
(626) 446-2660
(800) 466-8356

RESIDENCE INN BY MARRIOTT
321 E Huntington Dr (91006)
Rates: $149-$168
(626) 446-6500
(800) 331-3131

ARCATA

BEST WESTERN ARCATA INN
4827 Valley West Blvd (95521)
Rates: $69-$150
(707) 826-0313
(800) 528-1234
(888) 646-6514

COMFORT INN
4701 Valley West Blvd (95521)
Rates: $55-$150
(707) 826-2827
(800) 424-6423

HOTEL ARCATA
708 9th St (95521)
Rates: $120-$200
(707) 826-0217
(800) 344-1221

MOTEL 6
4755 Valley West Blvd (95521)
Rates: $39-$58
(707) 822-7061
(800) 466-8356

QUALITY INN
3535 Janes Rd (95521)
Rates: $59-$149
(707) 822-0409
(800) 424-6423

SUPER 8 MOTEL
4887 Valley West Blvd (95521)
Rates: $45-$90
(707) 822-8888
(800) 800-8000

ARNOLD

EBBETT'S PASS LODGE
1173 Hwy 4, PO Box 2591 (95223)
Rates: $42-$59
(209) 795-1563
(800) 225-3764

RELIABLE VACATION RENTALS
P. O. Box 869 (95223)
Rates: $140-$200
(209) 795-4111

SIERRA VACATION RENTALS
P. O. Box 1080 (95223)
Rates: $130-$170
(209) 795-2422

WEHE'S MEADOWMONT LODGE
2011 Hwy 4 (95223)
Rates: $47-$58
(209) 795-1394
(800) 225-3764

ARROYO GRANDE

BEST WESTERN CASA GRANDE INN
850 Oak Park Rd (93420)
Rates: $69-$219
(805) 481-7309
(800) 528-1234
(800) 475-9777

PREMIER INNS
555 Camino Mercado (93420)
Rates: $39-$119
(805) 481-4774

ARTESIA

QUALITY INN & SUITES
16905 S Pioneer Blvd (90701)
Rates: $74
(562) 402-2202
(800) 424-6423

ATASCADERO

MOTEL 6
9400 El Camino Real (93422)
Rates: $37-$65
(805) 466-6701
(800) 466-8356

AUBURN

BEST WESTERN GOLDEN KEY MOTEL
13450 Lincoln Way (95603)
Rates: $75-$115
(530) 885-8611
(800) 528-1234
(800) 201-0121

COMFORT INN CENTRAL
1875 Auburn Ravine Rd (95603)
Rates: $79-$129
(530) 885-1800
(800) 424-6423

FOOTHILLS MOTEL
13431 Bowman Rd (94503)
Rates: $55-$105
(430) 885--8444

HOLIDAY INN
120 Grass Valley Hwy (95603)
Rates: $109-$149
(530) 887-8787
)800) 465-4329

MOTEL 6
1819 Auburn Ravine Rd (95602)
Rates: $55-$62
(530) 888-7829
(800) 466-8356

TRAVELODGE
13490 Lincoln Way (95603)
Rates: $60-$85
(530) 885-7025
(800) 478-7878

AVALON

(Catalina Island)

BEST WESTERN CATALINA CANYON HOTEL & SPA
888 Country Club Dr (90704)
Rates: $79-$299
(310) 510-0325
(800) 528-1234
(888) 478-7829

BADGER

BADGER INN MOTEL
49496 Hwy 245 (93603)
Rates: $75-$85
(559) 337-0022
(800) 223-4374

BAKER

BUN BOY MOTEL
72155 Baker Blvd (92309)
Rates: $51-$73
(760) 733-4363

BAKERSFIELD

BEST INN
200 Trask St (93312)
Rates: $49-$59
(661) 764-5221
(800) 237-8466

BEST WESTERN CRYSTAL PALACE INN & SUITES
2620 Buck Owens Blvd (93308)
Rates: $52-$135
(661) 327-9651
(800) 528-1234
(800) 424-4900

BEST WESTERN HERITAGE INN
253 Trask St (93312)
Rates: $60-$80
(661) 764-6268
(800) 528-1234

BEST WESTERN HILL HOUSE INN
700 Truxtun Ave (93301)
Rates: $54-$139
(661) 327-4064
(800) 528-1234
(800) 300-4230

DAYS INN
4500 Buck Owens Blvd (93308)
Rates: $79-$109
(661) 324-5555
(800) 329-7466

DOUBLETREE HOTEL
3100 Camino Del Rio Ct (93308)
Rates: $135-$250
(661) 323-7111
(800) 222-8733

HOLIDAY INN SELECT
801 Truxtun Ave (93301)
Rates: $85-$119
(661) 323-1900
(800) 465-4329

HOWARD JOHNSON EXP INN
2700 White Ln (93304)
Rates: $60-$65
(661) 396-1425
(800) 446-4656

LA QUINTA INN
3232 Riverside Dr (93308)
Rates: $75-$87
(661) 325-7400
(800) 687-6667

LIBERTY INN MOTEL
8230 E Brundate Ln (93307)
Rates: $46-$55
(661) 366-1630

MOTEL 6 AIRPORT
5241 Olive Tree Ct (93308)
Rates: $31-$37
(661) 392-9700
(800) 466-8356

MOTEL 6 CONV CENTER
1350 Easton Dr (93309)
Rates: $36-$44
(661) 327-1686
(800) 466-8356

MOTEL 6 EAST
8223 E Brundage Ln (93307)
Rates: $37-$42
(661) 366-7231
(800) 466-8356

MOTEL 6 SOUTH
2727 White Lane
(93304)
Rates: $36-$44
(661) 834-2828
(800) 466-8356

QUALITY INN
1011 Oak St
(93304)
Rates: $62-$110
(661) 325-0772
(800) 424-6423

RAMADA LTD
830 Wible Rd
(93304)
Rates: $60-$100
(661) 831-1922
(800) 272-6232

RED LION HOTEL
2400 Camino Del
Rio Ct (93308)
Rates: $90-$160
(661) 327-0681
(800) 733-5466

**RESIDENCE INN
BY MARRIOTT**
4241 Chester Ln
(93309)
Rates: $124-$146
(661) 321-9800
(800) 331-3131

**RIO BRAVO
RESORT**
11200 Lake Ming
Rd (93306)
Rates: $85-$119
(661) 872-5000
(800) 282-5000

ROYAL OAK INN
889 Oak St (93304)
Rates: $38-$80
(661) 324-9686

SUPER 8 MOTEL
901 Real Rd
(93309)
Rates: $49-$70
(661) 322-1012
(800) 800-8000

**TRAVEL RITE
HOTEL**
818 Real Rd
(93309)
Rates: $50-$67
(661) 324-6666

VAGABOND INN N
6100 Knudsen Dr
(93308)
Rates: $36-$42
(661) 392-1800
(800) 522-1555

**VAGABOND INN
SOUTH**
6501 Colony St
(93307)
Rates: $36-$42
(661) 831-9200
(800) 522-1555

BALDWIN PARK
MOTEL 6
14510 Garvey Ave
(91706)
Rates: $39-$54
(626) 960-5011
(800) 466-8356

BANNING
DAYS INN
2320 W Ramsey St
(92220)
Rates: $57-$165
(909) 849-0092
(800) 329-7466

SUPER 8 MOTEL
1690 W Ramsey St
(92220)
Rates: $65-$199
(909) 849-8888
(800) 800-8000

TRAVELODGE
1700 W Ramsey St
(92220)
Rates: $57-$199
(909) 849-1000
(800) 578-7878

BARSTOW
BEST MOTEL
1281 E Main St
(92311)
Rates: $30-$36
(760) 256-6836

DAYS INN
1590 Coolwater
Ln (92311)
Rates: $45-$55
(760) 256-1737
(800) 329-7466

ECONO LODGE
1230 E Main St
(92311)
Rates: $29-$99
(760) 256-2133
(800) 424-6423

EXECUTIVE INN
1261 E Main St
(923118
Rates: $30-$60
(760) 256-7581

GATEWAY MOTEL
1630 E Main St
(92311)
Rates: $31-$85
(760) 256-8931

HOLIDAY INN EXP
1861 W Main St
(92311)
Rates: $69-$109
(760) 256-1300
(800) 465-4329

**HOLIDAY INN EXP
HOTEL & SUITES**
2700 Lenwood Rd
(92311)
Rates: $89-$159
(760) 253-9200
(800) 465-4329

MOTEL 6
150 N Yucca Ave
(92311)
Rates: $34-$51
(760) 256-1752
(800) 466-8356

OAK TREE INN
35450 Yemo Rd
(92398)
Rates: $60-$70
(760) 254-1148

QUALITY INN
1520 E Main St
(92311)
Rates: $62-$83
(760) 256-6891
(800) 424-6423

RAMADA INN
1511 E Main St
(92311)
Rates: $79-$99
(760) 256-5673
(800) 272-6232

SUPER 8 MOTEL
170 Coolwater Ln
(92311)
Rates: $58-$72
(760) 256-8443
(800) 800-8000

BASS LAKE
FORK'S RESORT
39150 Rd 222
(93604)
Rates: $75-$125
(209) 642-3737

**THE LAKEHOUSE
B&B**
39131 Lake Dr
(93604)
Rates: $115-$195
(209) 683-8220

BEAUMONT
BEST VALUE INN
625 E 5th St
(92223)
Rates: $55-$95
(909) 845-2185

**BEST WESTERN
EL RANCHO
MOTOR INN**
480 E 5th St
(92223)
Rates: $55-$120
(909) 845-2176
(800) 528-1234

BELLFLOWER
MOTEL 6
17220 Downey
Ave (90706)
Rates: $39-$54
(562) 531-3933
(800) 466-8356

BELMONT
MOTEL 6
1101 Shoreway Rd
(94002)
Rates: $53-$56
(650) 591-1471
(800) 466-8356

**SUMMERFIELD
SUITES BY
WYNDHAM**
400 Concourse Dr
(94002)
Rates: $79-$129
(650) 591-8600
(800) 833-4353

BEN LOMOND
ECONO LODGE
9733 Hwy 9
(95005)
Rates: $69-$169
(831) 336-2292
(800) 424-6423

**TYROLEAN INN
& COTTAGES**
9600 Hwy 9
(95005)
Rates: $43-$60
(831) 336-5188

BENICIA
**BEST WESTERN
HERITAGE INN**
1955 E 2nd St
(94510)
Rates: $85-$120
(707) 746-0401
(800) 528-1234

**THE PAINTED
LADY B&B**
141 East F St
(94510)
Rates: $70-$85
(707) 746-1646

BERKELEY
BEAU SKY HOTEL
2520 Durant Ave
(94704)
Rates: $60-$85
(510) 540-7688

**BEST VALUE
GOLDEN BEAR
INN**
1620 San Pablo
Ave (94702)
Rates: $60-$119
(510) 525-6770
(800) 525-6770

BERRY CREEK
**LAKE OROVILLE
BED & BREAKFST**
240 Sunday Dr
(95916)
Rates: $125-$175
(530) 589-0700
(800) 455-5253

BEVERLY HILLS
(Also see Los
Angeles)

AVALON HOTEL
9400 W Olympic
Blvd (90212)
Rates: $209-$269
(310) 277-5221

**THE BEVERLY
HILLS HOTEL &
BUNGALOWS**
9641 Sunset Blvd
(90210)
Rates: $420-$530
(310) 276-2251

BEVERLY HILTON
9876 Wilshire Blvd
(90210)
Rates: $175-$330
(310) 274-7777
(800) 922-5432

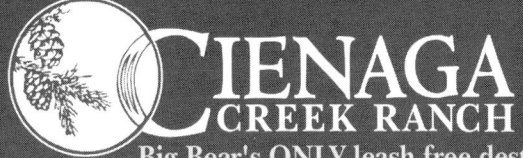

Leave your pooper scooper at home

when visiting Cienaga Creek Ranch,
southern california's premier pet friendly destination.

*Enjoy a secluded luxury cottage on 50 acres surrounded
by private and national forests. Bring your best friend
and hike from your cabin door on the pacific crest trail
and a miriad of other scenic trails. Surround yourself in
sunsets, mountain views, scent of pine and starry nights
in this peaceful and picturesque spot.*

CIENAGA CREEK RANCH

Big Bear's ONLY leash free destination.

1-888-336-2891

reserve online: www.mountaincottage.com

FOUR SEASONS BEVERLY HLLS
300 S Doheny Dr (90048)
Rates: $335-$1300
(310) 273-2222
(800) 332-3442

HOTEL SOFITEL
8555 Beverly Blvd (90048)
Rates: $299-$329
(310) 278-5444
(800) 521-7772

LE MERIDIEN AT BEVERLY HILLS
465 S La Cienega Blvd (90048)
Rates: $290-$450
(310) 247-0400

LUXE HOTEL RODEO DRIVE
360 N Rodeo Dr (90210)
Rates: $350-$400
(310) 273-0300

THE MOSAIC HOTEL
125 S Spalding Dr (90212)
Rates: $209-$229
(310) 278-0303

PENINSULA BEVERLY HILLS
9882 S Santa Monica Blvd (90212)
Rates: $395-$3000
(310) 551-2888

RAFFLES/ L'ERMITAGE BEVERLY HILLS
9291 Burton Way (90210)
Rates: $418-$448
(310) 278-3344

THE REGENT BEVERLY WILSHIRE
9500 Wilshire Blvd (90212)
Rates: $385-$7500
(310) 275-5200
(800) 421-4354

RESIDENCE INN BY MARRIOTT-BEVERLY HILLS
1177 S Beverly Dr (90035)
Rates: $119-$159
(310) 277-4427
(800) 331-3131

BIG BEAR LAKE
ALPINE VILLAGE SUITES LODGE
546 Pine Knot Ave (92315)
Rates: $89-$189
(909) 866-5460
(877) 224-4232

BEAR CLAW CABINS
586 Main St (92315)
Rates: $55-$94
(909) 866-7633

BEAR VALLEY MTN HOMES
1301 E Big Bear Blvd (92314)
Rates: $45+
(909) 585-0500

BEST WESTERN BIG BEAR CHATEAU
42200 Moonridge Rd (92315)
Rates: $79-$289
(909) 866-6666
(800) 528-1234
(800) 232-7466

BIG BEAR FRONTIER LODGE & MOTEL
40472 Big Bear Blvd (92315)
Rates: $79-$500
(909) 866-5888
(800) 457-6401

BIG BEAR LAKEFRONT LODGE
40360 Lakeview Dr (92315)
Rates: $65-$450
(909) 866-8271

BLACK FOREST LODGE
P. O. Box 156 (92315)
Rates: $45-$125
(909) 866-2166
(800) 255-4378

BOULDER CREEK RESORT
Box 92 (92315)
Rates: $45-$500
(909) 866-2665
(800) 244-2327

CAL-PINE CABINS
41545 Big Bear Blvd (92315)
Rates: $59-$175
(909) 866-2574

CIENEGA CREEK RANCH
PO BOX 2773 (92314)
888.336.2891
SEE OUR AD ON OPPOSITE PAGE 142

EAGLE'S NEST B&B
41675 Big Bear Blvd (92315)
Rates: $110-$160
(909) 866-6465
(888) 866-6465

GOLDEN BEAR COTTAGES
39367 Big Bear Blvd (92315)
Rates: $79-$799
(909) 866-2010

GREY SQUIRREL RESORT
39372 Big Bear Blvd (92315)
Rates: $85-$675
(909) 866-4335

THE GRIZZLY INN
39756 Big Bear Blvd (92315)
Rates: $55+
(800) 423-2742

HAPPY BEAR VACATION RNTLS
41592 Big Bear Blvd (92315)
Rates: n/a
(909) 866-7744
(800) 766-9776

HAPPY BEAR VILLAGE RESORT
40154 Big Bear Blvd (92315)
Rates: $65-$165
(909) 866-2415
(800) 352-8581

HONEY BEAR LODGE
40994 Pennsylvania (92315)
Rates: $49-$269
(909) 866-7825
(800) 628-8714

MAJESTIC MOOSE LODGE
39328 Big Bear Blvd (92315)
Rates: $79-$209
(909) 866-2435

MOTEL 6
42899 Big Bear Blvd (92315)
Rates: $39-$70
(909) 585-6666
(800) 466-8356

PINE KNOT GUEST RANCH
908 Pine Knot Ave (92315)
Rates: $89-$189
(909) 866-6500

QUAIL COVE LODGE
39117 N Shore Dr (Fawnskin 92315)
Rates: $115-$125
(909) 866-5957
(800) 595-3683

SLEEPY FOREST COTTAGES
P. O. Box 3706 (92315)
Rates: $39-$199
(909) 866-7444
(800) 544-7454

SMOKETREE RESORT
40210 Big Bear Blvd (92315)
Rates: $49-$167
(909) 866-2415
(800) 352-8581

SNUGGLE CREEK LODGE
40440 Big Bear Blvd (92315)
Rates: $79-$109
(909) 866-2555

STAGE COACH LODGE COTTAGES
652 Jeffries (92315)
Rates: $89-$369
(909) 878-3008
(800) 756-9871

TIMBER HAVEN LODGE
877 Tulip Ln (92315)
Rates: $59-$189
(909) 866-3568

TIMBERLINE LODGE
39921 Big Bear Blvd (92315)
Rates: $89-$276
(909) 866-4141
(800) 803-4111

WILDWOOD RESORT COTTAGES
40210 Big Bear Blvd (92315)
Rates: $66-$148
(909) 876-2178

BIG PINE
BIG PINE MOTEL
370 S Main (93515)
Rates: $36-$62
(760) 938-2282

BRISTLECONE MOTEL
101 N Main (93513)
Rates: $36-$68
(760) 938-2067

BISHOP
BEST WESTERN HOLIDAY SPA LODGE
1025 N Main St (93514)
Rates: $69-$99
(760) 873-3543
(800) 528-1234
(800) 576-3543

COMFORT INN
805 N Main St (93514)
Rates: $70-$99
(760) 873-4284
(800) 576-4080
(800) 424-6423

DAYS INN
724 W Line St (93514)
Rates: $55-$130
(760) 872-1095
(800) 329-7466

HOLIDAY INN EXP HOTEL & SUITES
636 N Main St (93514)
Rates: $99-$159
(760) 872-2423
)800) 465-4329

AREA CODES - If the local number doesn't connect, check for a new area code.

MOTEL 6
1005 N Main St
(93514)
Rates: $39-$89
(760) 873-8426
(800) 466-8356

RAMADA LTD
155 E Elm St
(93514)
Rates: $59-$89
(760) 872-1771
(800) 272-6232

RODEWAY INN
150 E Elm St
(93514)
Rates: $70-$150
(760) 873-3564
(800) 424-6423

THUNDERBIRD MOTEL
190 W Pine St
(93514)
Rates: $50-$150
(760) 873-4215

VAGABOND INN
1030 N Main St
(93514)
Rates: $81-$90
(760) 873-6351
(800) 522-1555

BLAIRSDEN
FEATHER RIVER PARK RESORT
Hwy 89, Box 37
(96103)
Rates: $82-$182
(530) 836-2328

GRAYEAGLE LODGE
Gold Lake Rd
Box 38 (96103)
Rates: $190-$230
(530) 836-0916
(800) 635-8778

LAYMAN RESORT
Hwy 70, Box 8
(96103)
Rates: $48-$55
(530) 836-2511
(800) 635-8788

RIVER PINES RESORT
8296 Hwy 89
(96103)
Rates: $70-$90
(530) 836-2552
(800) 696-2551

BLYTHE
BEST WESTERN SAHARA MOTEL
825 W Hobsonway
(92225)
Rates: $69-$149
(760) 922-7105
(800) 528-1234

COMFORT SUITES
545 E Hobsonway
(92225)
Rates: $50-$159
(760) 922-9209
(800) 424-6423

DAYS INN
9274 E Hobsonway
(92225)
Rates: $50-$85
(760) 922-5101
(800) 329-7466

HOLIDAY INN EXP
600 W Donion St
(92225)
Rates: $79-$159
(760) 921-2300
(800) 465-4329

LEGACY INN
903 W
Hobsonway
(92225)
Rates: $45-$115
(760) 922-4146

MOTEL 6
500 W Donlon St
(92225)
Rates: $37-$50
(760) 922-6666
(800) 466-8356

SUPER 8 MOTEL
550 W Donion St
(92225)
Rates: $40-$140
(760) 922-8881
(800) 800-8000

TRAVELERS INN EXPRESS
1781 E
Hobsonway
(92225)
Rates: $50-$129
(760) 922-3334

BODEGA BAY
BODEGA COAST INN
521 SR 1 N (94923)
Rates: $129-$299
(707) 875-2217
(800) 346-6999

BOLINAS
PARROT'S COVE VACATION RENTALS
P O Box 86 (94924)
Rates: $100-$150
(415) 868-9588
(888) 844-8255

BORREGO SPRINGS
BORREGO SPRINGS RESORT
1112 Tilting T Dr
(9204)
Rates: $94-$135
(760) 767-5700

STANLUNDS DESERT MOTEL
2771 Borrego
Springs Rd
(92004)
Rates: $50-$65
(760) 767-5501

BRAWLEY
BRAWLEY INN
575 W Main St
(92227)
Rates: $60-$120
(760) 344-1199

BREA
HOMESTEAD STUDIO SUITES
3050 E Imperial
Blvd (92621)
Rates: $69-$95
(714) 528-2500
(888) 782-9473

HYLAND MOTEL
727 S Brea Blvd
(92621)
Rates: $50-$60
(714) 990-6867

WOODFIN SUITE HOTEL
3100 E Imperial
Hwy (92621)
Rates: $115-$165
(714) 579-3200
(800) 237-8811

BRIDGEPORT
BEST WESTERN RUBY INN
333 Main St
(93517)
Rates: $80-$150
(760) 932-7241
(800) 528-1234

REDWOOD MOTEL
425 Main St
(93517)
Rates: $45-$175
(760) 932-7060
(888) 932-3292

SILVER MAPLE INN
310 Main St
(93517)
Rates: $70-$120
(760) 932-7383

WALKER RIVER LODGE
100 Main St
(93517)
Rates: $50-$145
(760) 932-7021
(800) 688-3351

BRISBANE
HOMEWOOD SUITES
2000 Shoreline Ct
(94005)
Rates: $119-$189
(650) 589-1600
(800) 225-5466

BROOKDALE
BROOKDALE LODGE
11570 Hwy 9
(95007)
Rates: $44-$60
(408) 338-6433

BUELLTON
MOTEL 6
333 McMurray Rd
(93427)
Rates: $41-$83
(805) 688-7797
(800) 466-8356

QUALITY INN
630 Ave of Flags
(93427)
Rates: $70-$130
(805) 688-0022
(800) 424-6423

BUENA PARK
MOTEL 6-KNOTTS BERRY FARM/ DISNEYLAND
7051 Valley View
(90620)
Rates: $37-$48
(714) 522-1200
(800) 466-8356

BURBANK
BURBANK AIRPORT HILTON & CONV CENTER
2500 Hollywood
Way (91505)
Rates: $99-$270
(818) 843-6000
(800) 445-8667

THE COAST ANABELLE HOTEL
2011 W Olive Ave
(91506)
Rates: $116-$169
(818) 845-7800

THE GRACIELA BURBANK
322 N Pass Ave
(91505)
Rates: $190-$240
(818) 842-8887

SAFARI INN - A COAST HOTEL
1911 W Olive Ave
(91506)
Rates: $83-$169
(818) 845-8586
(800) 782-4373

BURLINGAME
CROWNE PLAZA
1177 Airport Blvd
(94010)
Rates: $79-$150
(650) 342-9200
(800) 227-6963

DOUBLETREE HOTEL- AIRPORT
835 Airport Blvd
(94010)
Rates: $79-$179
(650) 344-5500
(800) 222-8733

EMBASSY SUITES- SF AIRPORT
150 Anza Blvd.
(94010)
Rates: $119-$194
(650) 342-4600
(800) 362-2779

MARRIOTT SF AIRPORT
1800 Old Bayshore
Hwy (94010)
Rates: $99-$219
(650) 692-9100
(800) 228-9290

AREA CODES - If the local number doesn't connect, check for a new area code.

RED ROOF INN
777 Airport Blvd
(94010)
Rates: $54-$164
(650) 342-7772
(800) 843-7663

SHERATON GATE-WAY HOTEL
600 Airport Blvd
(94010)
Rates: $139-$189
(650) 340-8500
(800) 325-3535

VAGABOND INN SF AIRPORT
1640 Old Bayshore
Hwy (94010)
Rates: $69-$99
(650) 692-4040
(800) 522-1555

BURNEY
BURNEY MOTEL
37448 Main St
(96013)
Rates: $39-$69
(530) 335-4500

CHARM MOTEL
37363 Main St
(96013)
Rates: $39-$89
(530) 335-2254

GREEN GABLES MOTEL
37385 Main St
(96013)
Rates: $47-$82
(530) 335-2264

SHASTA PINES MOTEL
37386 Main St
(96013)
Rates: $42-$116
(530) 335-2201

SLEEPY HOLLOW LODGE
36898 Main St
(96013)
Rates: $30-$60
(530) 335-2285

BUTTON WILLOW
MOTEL 6
20638 Tracy Ave
(93206)
Rates: $30+
(661) 764-5153
(800) 466-8356

SUPER 8 MOTEL
20681 Tracy Ave
(93206)
Rates: $37-$49
(661) 764-5117
(800) 800-8000

CALIMESA
CALIMESA INN MOTEL
1205 Calimesa
Blvd (92320)
Rates: $55-$70
(909) 795-2536

CALIPATRIA
CALIPATRIA INN & SUITES
700 N Sorenson
(92233)
Rates: $61-$150
(760) 348-7348

CALISTOGA
MEADOWLARK COUNTRY HOUSE
601 Petrified
Forest Rd (94515)
Rates: $125-$150
(707) 942-5651

TRIPLE "S" RANCH
4600 Mtn Home
Ranch Rd (94515)
Rates: $42-$59
(707) 942-6730

WASHINGTON STREET LODGING
1605 Washington
St (94515)
Rates: $96-$325
(707) 942-6968

CALPINE
SIERRA VALLEY LODGE
Box 115 (96124)
Rates: $38-$42
(530) 994-3367
(800) 858-0322

CAMARILLO
MOTEL 6
1641 E Daily Dr
(93010)
Rates: $39-$56
(805) 388-3467
(800) 466-8356

CAMBRIA
CAMBRIA SHORES INN
6276 Moonstone
Beach Dr (93428)
Rates: $105-$180
(805) 927-8644
(800) 433-9179

FOG CATCHER INN
6400 Moonstone
Beach Dr (93428)
Rates: $119-$359
(805) 927-1400

MARINERS INN BY THE SEA
6180 Moonstone
Beach Dr (93428)
Rates: $79-$239
(805) 927-4624

SEA OTTER INN
6656 Moonstone
Beach Dr (93428)
Rates: $99-$259
(805) 927-5888

CAMERON PARK
BEST WESTERN CAMERON PARK
3361 Coach Ln
(95682)
Rates: $79-$149
(530) 677-2203
(800) 528-1234
(800) 601-1234

CAMINO
CAMINO HOTEL-SEVEN MILE HOUSE B&B
4103 Carson Rd
(95709)
Rates: $86-$119
(530) 644-7740

CAMPBELL
CAMPBELL INN
675 E Campbell
Ave (95008)
Rates: $89-$109
(408) 374-4300

MOTEL 6
1240 Camden Ave
(95008)
Rates: $59-$70
(408) 371-8870
(800) 466-8356

RESIDENCE INN BY MARRIOTT
2761 S Bascom
Ave (95008)
Rates: $149-$179
(408) 559-1551
(800) 331-3131

CANOGA PARK
MOTEL 6
7132 De Soto Ave
(91303)
Rates: $49-$55
(818) 346-5400
(800) 466-8356

SUPER 8 MOTEL
7631 Topanga
Canyon Blvd
(91304)
Rates: $49-$73
(818) 883-8888
(800) 800-8000

CAPITOLA
BEST WESTERN CAPITOLA BY-THE-SEA INN & SUITES
1435 41st Ave
(95010)
Rates: $79-$199
(831) 477-0607
(800) 528-1234
(800) 621-8115

CAPITOLA INN
822 Bay Ave
(95010)
Rates: $75-$175
(831) 462-3004

EL SALTO BY THE SEA B&B
620 El Salto Dr
(95010)
Rates: $100-$185
(831) 462-6365

CARLSBAD
FOUR SEASONS RESORT AVIARA
7100 Four Seasons
Point (92009)
Rates: $405-$525
(760) 603-6800
(800) 332-3442

INNS OF AMERICA
751 Raintree Dr
(92009)
Rates: $89-$129
(760) 931-1185
(800) 826-0778

MOTEL 6
1006 Carlsbad
Vllge Dr (92008)
Rates: $45-$60
(760) 434-7135
(800) 466-8356

MOTEL 6 EAST
6117 Paseo del
Norte (92009)
Rates: $45-$60
(760) 438-1242
(800) 466-8356

MOTEL 6 SOUTH
750 Raintree Dr
(92009)
Rates: $45-$60
(760) 431-0745
(800) 466-8356

CARMEL
BEST WESTERN CARMEL MISSION INN
3665 Rio Rd
(93922)
Rates: $79-$379
(831) 624-1841
(800) 528-1234
(800) 348-9090

CARMEL COUNTRY INN B&B
Dolores & 3rd Ave
(93921)
Rates: $150-$325
(831) 625-3263
(800) 215-6343

CARMEL FIREPLACE INN B&B
San Carlos St &
4th Ave (93923)
Rates: $99-$285
(831) 624-4862
(866) 626-1171

CARMEL GARDEN COURT B&B
4th Ave & Torres
St (93921)
Rates: $150-$245
(831) 624-6926
(800) 313-7770

CARMEL RIVER INN COMPLEX
Carmel River
Bridge at Oliver
Rd (93921)
Rates: $125-$250
(831) 624-1575
(800) 882-8142

CARMEL TRADEWINDS INN
Mission & 3rd Ave (93921)
Rates: $195-$575
(831) 624-2776
(800) 624-6665

CASA DE CARMEL INN
Ocean & 7th Ave (93921)
Rates: $115-$125
(831) 624-2429
(800) 262-1262

COACHMAN'S INN
San Carlos St & 7th Ave (93921)
Rates: $135-$425
(831) 624-6421
(800) 336-6421

CYPRESS INN
Lincoln St & 7th Ave (93921)
Rates: $125-$550
(831) 624-3871
(800) 443-7443

LAMPLIGHTER'S INN
Ocean & Camino Real (93921)
Rates: $119-$259
(831) 624-7372

LINCOLN GREEN INN
Carmelo between 15th/16th (93921)
Rates: $185
(831) 624-7738
(831) 624-1880
(800) 262-1262

SUNSET HOUSE BED & BREAKFAST
Ocean on Camino Real (93921)
Rates: $190-$230
(831) 624-4884

VAGABOND HOUSE INN B&B
Dolores & 4th Ave (93921)
Rates: $95-$205
(831) 624-7738
(800) 262-1262

WAYSIDE INN
Mission & 7th Ave (93921)
Rates: $99-$305
(831) 624-5336
(800) 433-4732

CARMEL VALLEY

BLUE SKY LODGE
10 Flight Rd (93924)
Rates: $149-$219
(831) 659-2256
(800) 733-2160

CARMEL VALLEY LODGE
8 Ford Rd (93924)
Rates: $149-$219
(831) 659-2261
(800) 641-4646

CARMEL VALLEY RANCH
1 Old Ranch Rd (93923)
Rates: $265-$750
(831) 625-9500
(800) 541-3113

LOS LAURELES LODGE
313 W Carmel Valley Rd (93924)
Rates: $85-$595
(831) 659-2233

QUAIL LODGE RESORT & GOLF
8205 Valley Greens Dr (93923)
Rates: $295-$1350
(831) 624-2888
(888) 828-8787
(800) 538-9516

CARPTINERIA

HOLIDAY INN EXP HOTEL & SUITES
5606 Carpinteria Ave (93013)
Rates: $75-$124
(805) 566-9499
(800) 465-4329

MOTEL 6-NORTH
4200 Via Real (93013)
Rates: $44-$68
(805) 684-6921
(800) 466-8356

MOTEL 6-SOUTH
5550 Carpinteria Ave (93013)
Rates: $44-$68
(805) 684-8602
(800) 466-8356

CARSON

ECONO LODGE
1325 E Carson St (90745)
Rates: $62-$115
(310) 830-8044
(800) 424-6423

CASSEL

BURNEY MTN GUEST RANCH
22800 Hat Creek Powerhouse #2 (96016)
Rates: $175
(530) 335-4087

CASTAIC

COMFORT INN-MAGIC MTN AREA
31558 Castaic Rd (91384)
Rates: $49-$89
(661) 295-1100
(800) 424-6423

CASTRO VALLEY

HOLIDAY INN EXP
2532 Castro Valley Blvd (94546)
Rates: $105
(510) 538-9501
(800) 465-4329

CASTROVILLE

CASTROVILLE MOTEL
11656 Merritt St (95012)
Rates: $36-$48
(831) 633-2502

CATALINA ISLAND

(See Avalon)

CATHEDRAL CITY

COMFORT SUITES
69-151 E Palm Canyon Dr (92234)
Rates: $49-$199
(760) 324-5939
(800) 424-6423

DORAL DESERT PRINCESS RESORT PALM SPRINGS
67-967 Vista Chino (92234)
Rates: $69-$149
(760) 322-7000
(888) 386-4677

FRANCONIA COURT HOTEL
69-375 Ramon Rd (92234)
Rates: $95-$125
(760) 324-4521

CAYUCOS

CAYUCOS BEACH INN
333 S Ocean Ave (93430)
Rates: $85-$135
(805) 995-2828

CYPRESS TREE MOTEL
125 S Ocean Ave (93430)
Rates: $39-$97
(805) 995-3917
(800) 241-4289

DOLPHIN INN
399 S Ocean Ave (93430)
Rates: $49-$159
(805) 995-3810
(800) 540-4726

ESTERO BAY MOTEL
25 S Ocean Ave (93430)
Rates: $49-$145
(805) 995-3614
(800) 736-1292

SHORELINE INN
1 N. Ocean Ave (93430)
Rates: $80-$160
(805) 995-3681

CAZADERO

CAZANOMA LODGE
100 Kid Creek Rd (95421)
Rates: $80-$115
(707) 632-5255

CEDARVILLE

SUNRISE MOTEL
54889 Hwy 299 (96104)
Rates: $50-$65
(530) 279-2161

CERRITOS

SHERATON CERRITOS HOTEL AT TOWNE CENTER
12725 Center Court Dr (90703)
Rates: $279-$550
(562) 809-1500
(800) 325-3535

CHATSWORTH

RAMADA INN
21340 Devonshire St (91311)
Rates: $65-$79
(818) 998-5289
(800) 272-6239

STAYBRIDGE SUITES
21902 Lassen St (91311)
Rates: $130-$160
(818) 773-0707
(800) 238-8000

SUMMERFIELD SUITES BY WYNDHAM
21902 Lassen St (91311)
Rates: $119-$159
(818) 773-0707
(800) 833-4353

CHESTER

THE BIDWELL HOUSE B&B
1 Main St (96020)
Rates: $100-$200
(530) 258-3338

CEDAR LODGE MOTEL
Hwy 36, Box 677 (96020)
Rates: $29-$53
(530) 258-2904

CHESTER MANOR MOTEL
306 Main St (96020)
Rates: $75-$105
(530) 258-2441

SENECA MOTEL
Cedar & Martin Box 504 (96020)
Rates: $35-$47
(530) 258-2815

TIMBER HOUSE LODGE
First & Main Box 1010 (96020)
Rates: $35-$60
(530) 258-2729

CHICO

BUDGET INN
1717 Park Ave (95928)
Rates: $45-$95
(530) 342-9472

AREA CODES - If the local number doesn't connect, check for a new area code.

DELUXE INN
2507 Esplanada (95926)
Rates: $39-$89
(530) 342-8386

HERITAGE INN EXPRESS
725 Broadway (95928)
Rates: $74-$80
(530) 343-4527

HOLIDAY INN
685 Manzanita Ct (95926)
Rates: $109-$200
(530) 345-2491
(800) 465-4329

MOTEL 6
665 Manzanita Ct (95926)
Rates: $39-$52
(530) 345-5500
(800) 466-8356

MUSIC EXP INN
1145 El Monte Ave (95928)
Rates: $67-$125
(530) 345-8376

OXFORD SUITES
2035 Business Lane (95928)
Rates: $95-$159
(530) 899-9090
(800) 870-7848

SAFARI GARDEN MOTEL
2352 Esplanada (95926)
Rates: $45-$55
(530) 343-3201

SUPER 8 MOTEL
655 Manzanita Ct (95926)
Rates: $50-$150
(530) 345-2533
(800) 800-8000

CHINO
MOTEL 6
12266 Central Ave (91710)
Rates: $43-$52
(909) 591-3877
(800) 466-8356

CHOWCHILLA
DAYS INN
220 E Robertson Blvd (93610)
Rates: $40-$68
(559) 665-4821
(800) 329-7466

CHULA VISTA
LA QUINTA INN
150 Bonita Rd (91910)
Rates: $100-$125
(619) 691-1211
(800) 687-6667

MOTEL 6
745 "E" St (91910)
Rates: $43-$58
(619) 422-4200
(800) 466-8356

CITRUS HEIGHTS
OLIVE GROVE SUITES
6143 Auburn Blvd (95621)
Rates: $85-$125
(916) 725-0100

CLAREMONT
RAMADA INN
840 S Indian Hill Blvd (91711)
Rates: $59-$80
(909) 621-4831
(800) 272-6232

CLEAR CREEK
CLEAR CREEK MOTEL
667-150 Hwy 147 (96137)
Rates: $35-$45
(916) 256-3166

CLEARLAKE
SHIP 'N SHORE RESORT
13885 Lakeshore Dr (95422)
Rates: $30-$75
(707) 994-2248

SUNSET LODGE
13961 Lakeshore Dr (95422)
Rates: $40-$85
(707) 994-6642

CLEARLAKE OAKS
BLUE FISH COVE RESORT
10573 E Hwy (95423)
Rates: $35-$95
(707) 998-1769

LAKE HAVEN MOTEL
100 Short St (95423)
Rates: $36-$53
(707) 998-3908

TWENTY OAKS COURT
10503 E Hwy 20 (95423)
Rates: $40
(707) 998-3012

CLIO
MOLLY'S B&B
276 Lower Main St (96106)
Rates: $90-$110
(530) 836-4436

WHITE SULPHUR SPRINGS RANCH B&B
2200 Hwy 89, PO Box 136 (96106)
Rates: $85-$140
(530) 836-2387
(800) 854-1797

CLOVERDALE
ABRAMS HOUSE INN B&B
314 N Main St (95425)
Rates: $60-$125
(707) 894-2412
(800) 764-4466

CLOVERDALE OAKS INN
123 S Cloverdale Blvd (95425)
Rates: $55-$129
(707) 894-2404

COALINGA
BEST WESTERN BIG COUNTRY INN
25020 W Dorris Ave (93210)
Rates: $59-$109
(559) 935-0866
(800) 528-1234
(800) 836-6835

THE INN AT HARRIS RANCH
24505 W Dorris Ave (93210)
Rates: $110-$250
(559) 935-0717
(800) 942-2333

MOTEL 6-EAST
25008 W Dorris Ave (93210)
Rates: $39-$44
(559) 935-1536
(800) 466-8356

COFFEE CREEK
BONANZA KING RESORT
Rt 2, Box 4790 (96091)
Rates: $65-$70
(530) 266-3305

COLEVILLE
ANDRUSS MOTEL
Walker Rte, Box 64 (96107)
Rates: $36-$42
(530) 495-2216

MEADOWCLIFF MOTEL
Rte 1, Box 126 (96107)
Rates: $32-$45
(530) 495-2255

COLTON
DAYS INN
2830 Iowa Ave (92324)
Rates: $60-$119
(909) 788-9900
(800) 329-7466

HAMPTON INN
250 N 9th St (92324)
Rates: $89-$179
(909) 370-2424
(800) 426-7866

COLUMBIA
COLUMBIA GEM MOTEL
22131 Parrotts Ferry Rd (95310)
Rates: $79-$139
(209) 532-4508

COMMERCE
RAMADA INN
7272 Gage Ave (90040)
Rates: $59-$70
(562) 806-4777
(800) 272-6232

CONCORD
BEST WESTERN HERITAGE INN
4600 Clayton Rd (94521)
Rates: $69-$109
(925) 686-4466
(800) 528-1234

HOLIDAY INN
1050 Burnett Ave (94520)
Rates: $79-$149
(925) 687-5500
(800) 465-4329

PREMIER INNS
1581 Concord Ave (94520)
Rates: $49-$74
(925) 674-0888

SHERATON CONCORD HOTEL
45 John Glen Dr (94520)
Rates: $79-$179
(925) 825-7700
(800) 325-3535

CORNING
BEST WESTERN
2165 Solano St (96021)
Rates: $55-$89
(530) 824-2468
(800) 528-1234
(800) 221 2230

COMFORT INN
910 Hwy 99 W (96021)
Rates: $69-$109
(530) 824-5200
(800) 424-6423

DAYS INN
3475 Hwy 99 W (96021)
Rates: $45-$110
(530) 824-2000
(800) 329-7466

HOLIDAY INN EXP HOTEL & SUITES
3350 Sunrise Way (96021)
Rates: $55-$109
(530) 824-6400
(800) 465-4329

AREA CODES - If the local number doesn't connect, check for a new area code.

CORONA

DYNASTY SUITES MOTEL
1805 W 6th St (91720)
Rates: $66-$78
(909) 371-7185
(800) 842-7899

MOTEL 6
200 N Lincoln (91719)
Rates: $39-$46
(909) 735-6408
(800) 466-8356

CORONADO

CORONADO ISLAND MARRIOTT RESORT
2000 2nd St (92118)
Rates: $229-$304
(619) 435-3000
(800) 228-9290

CROWN CITY INN
520 Orange Ave (92118)
Rates: $99-$259
(619) 435-3116
(800) 422-1173

LOEWS CORONADO BAY RESORT
4000 Coronado Bay Rd (92118)
Rates: $155-$425
(619) 424-4000
(800) 815-6397

CORTE MADERA

MARIN SUITES HOTEL
45 Tamal Vista Blvd (94925)
Rates: $154-$204
(415) 924-1502
(800) 777-9670

COSTA MESA

COMFORT INN
2430 Newport Blvd (92626)
Rates: $53-$80
(949) 631-7840
(800) 424-6423

COSTA MESA MARRIOTT SUITES
500 Anton Blvd (92626)
Rates: $179-$189
(714) 957-1100
(800) 228-9290

HILTON COSTA MESA
3050 Bristol St (92626)
Rates: $89-$154
(949) 540-7000
(800) 445-8667

LA QUINTA INN
1515 S Coast Dr (92626)
Rates: $66-$86
(714) 957-5841
(800) 687-6667

MOTEL 6
1441 Gisler Ave (92626)
Rates: $45-$62
(714) 957-3063
(800) 466-8356

RAMADA LIMITED & SUITES
1680 Superior Ave (92627)
Rates: $89-$124
(949) 645-2221
(800) 272-6232

RESIDENCE INN BY MARRIOTT
881 W Baker St (92626)
Rates: $139-$199
(714) 241-8800
(800) 331-3131

VAGABOND INN
3205 Harbor Blvd (92626)
Rates: $60-$89
(714) 557-8360
(800) 522-1555

WESTIN SOUTH COAST PLAZA
686 Anton Blvd (92626)
Rates: $320
(714) 540-2500
(800) 937-8461

WYNDHAM ORANGE COUNTY AIRPORT
3350 Ave of the Arts (92626)
Rates: $84-$144
(714) 751-5100
(800) 996-3426

COULTERVILLE

YOSEMITE GOLD COUNTRY MOTEL
10407 Hwy 49 (95311)
Rates: $43-$59
(209) 878-3400

COVELO

WAGON WHEEL MOTEL
75860 Covelo Rd (95428)
Rates: $32-$39
(707) 983-6717

CRESCENT CITY

BEST VALUE INN
440 Hwy 101 N (95531)
Rates: $59-$72
(707) 464-4141
(800) 323-7917

HAMPTON INN & SUITES
100 "A" St (94116)
Rates: $109-$139
(707) 465-5400
(800) 426-7866

HIOUCHI MOTEL
2097 Hwy199 (95531)
Rates: $60-$80
(707) 458-3041

JADE RIVER LODGE
180 Oak St (95531)
Rates: $60-$70
(707) 464-4003

RIVER RETREAT VACATION RENTALS
4901 North Bank Rd (95531)
Rates: $100+
(707) 458-3231

ROYAL INN MOTEL
102 L St. (95531)
Rates: $33-$70
(707) 464-4113

SUPER 8 MOTEL
685 Hwy 101 S (95531)
Rates: $40-$100
(707) 464-4111
(800) 800-8000

CRESTLINE

CREST LODGE MTN RESORT
23508 Lake Dr (92325)
Rates: $55-$150
(909) 338-2418

CROMBERG

LONG VALLEY RESORT COTTAGES
59532 Hwy 70 (96103)
Rates: $75-$85
(530) 836-0754

CULVER CITY

FOUR POINTS BY SHERATON
5990 Green Valley Cir (90230)
Rates: $89+
(310) 641-7740
(800) 325-3535

RADISSON HOTEL LA WESTSIDE
6161 Centinela Ave (90230)
Rates: $105-$129
(310) 649-1776
(800) 333-3333

CUPERTINO

CYPRESS HOTEL
10050 S De Anza Blvd (95014)
Rates: $189-$279
(408) 253-8900
(800) 499-1408

CYPRESS

HOMESTEAD STUDIO SUITES HOTEL
5990 Corporate Ave (90630)
Rates: $79-$104
(714) 761-2766
(800) 225-5466

WOODFIN SUITE HOTEL
5905 Corporate Ave (90630)
Rates: $89-$179
(714) 828-4000
(800) 237-8811

DANA POINT

CAPISTRANO SEASIDE INN
1515 S Coast Dr (92626)
Rates: $66-$83
(714) 957-5841
(800) 531-5900

LAGUNA CLIFFS MARRIOTT RESORT
25135 Park Lantern (92629)
Rates: $298-$418
(949) 661-5000
(800) 533-9748

THE ST. REGIS MONARCH BEACH RESORT & SPA
One Monarch Beach Resort (92629)
Rates: $405-$875
(949) 234-3200

DANVILLE

DANVILLE INN
803 Camino Ramon (94526)
Rates: $65-$80
(925) 838-8080
(800) 654-1050

DARDANELLE

DARDANELLE RESORT
Hwy 108 (95314)
Rates: $49-$65
(209) 965-4355

DAVIS

BEST WESTERN UNIVERSITY LODGE
123 "B" St (95616)
Rates: $65-$99
(530) 756-7890
(800) 528-1234

HOWARD JOHNSON
4100 Chiles Rd (95616)
Rates: $79-$169
(530) 792-0800
(800) 446-4656

MOTEL 6
4835 Chiles Rd (95616)
Rates: $39-$48
(530) 753-3777
(800) 466-8356

DEATH VALLEY NATIONAL MONUMENT

STOVE PIPE WELLS VILLAGE
SR 190 (92328)
Rates: $79-$99
(760) 786-2387

DEL MAR

BEST WESTERN STRATFORD INN
710 Camino Del
Mar (92014)
Rates: $79-$229
(858) 755-1501
(800) 528-1234
(888) 478-7829

DEL MAR INN-A CLARION CARRIAGE HOUSE INN
720 Camino Del
Mar (92014)
Rates: $79-$194
(858) 755-9765
(800) 424-6423

DOUBLETREE HOTEL DEL MAR
11915 El Camino
Real (92130)
Rates: $99-$249
(858) 481-5900
(800) 222-8733

DELANO

COMFORT INN
2211 Girard St
(93215)
Rates: $52-$70
(661) 725-1022
(800) 424-6423

DESERT HOT SPRINGS

ATLAS HI LODGE
18-336 Avenida
Hermosa (92240)
Rates: $28-$39
(760) 329-5446

BROADVIEW LODGE
12-672 Eliseo Rd
(92240)
Rates: $25-$45
(760) 329-8006

CARAVAN SPA
66-810 E 4th St
(92240)
Rates: $38+
(760) 329-7124

EL REPOSO MOTEL
66-334 W 5th St
(92240)
Rates: $35-$75
(760) 329-6632

KISMET LODGE
13-340 Mountain
View Rd (92240)
Rates: $45-$65
(760) 329-6451

LAS PRIMAVERAS RESORT SPA
66-659 6th St
(92240)
Rates: $45-$75
(760) 251-1677
(800) 400-1677

MINERAL SPRINGS RESORT
11-000 Palm Dr
(92240)
Rates: $29-$125
(760) 329-6484

ROYAL PALMS INN B&B
12-885 Eliseo Rd
(92240)
Rates: $45-$65
(760) 329-7975
(800) 755-9538

SAN MARCUS INN
66-540 San Marcus
Rd (92240)
Rates: $32-$64
(760) 329-5304

STARDUST SPA MOTEL
66-634 5th St
(92240)
Rates: $48-$63
(760) 329-5443
(800) 482-7835

SUNSET INN
67-585 Hacienda
Ave (92240)
Rates: $45-$125
(760) 329-4488

TAMARIX SPA
66-185 Acoma
(92240)
Rates: $25-$60
(760) 329-6615

DINUBA

REEDLEY COUN-TRY INN B&B
43137 Rd 52
(Reedley 93654)
Rates: $85-$95
(559) 638-2585

DIXON

BEST WESTERN DIXON INN
1345 Commercial
Way (95620)
Rates: $80-$135
(707) 678-1400
(800) 528-1234

DOUGLAS CITY

INDIAN CREEK LODGE
Hwy 299 E.,
PO Box 100
(96024)
Rates: $28-$75
(530) 623-6294

DOWNEY

EMBASSY SUITES
8425 Firestone
Blvd (90241)
Rates: $139-$182
(562) 861-1900
(800) 362-2779

DOWNIEVILLE

DOWNIEVILLE RIVER INN RESORT
121 River St
(95936)
Rates: $85-$225
(530) 289-3308
(800) 696-3308

LURE RESORT
100 Lure Bridge
Ln (95936)
Rates: $55-$220
(530) 289-3465
(800) 671-4084

RIVERSIDE INN
206 Commercial St
(96936)
Rates: $70-$79
(530) 289-1000

DOYLE

7W CAFE & MOTEL
434-455 Doyle
Loop (96109)
Rates: $22-$33
(530) 827-3331

MIDWAY MOTEL
Doyle Loop
(96109)
Rates: $28+
(530) 827-2208

DUBLIN

AMERISUITES
4950 Hacienda Dr
(94568)
Rates: $109
(925) 828-9006
(800) 833-1516

RADISSON HOTEL
6680 Regional St
(94568)
Rates: $69-$129
(925) 828-7750
(800) 333-3333

DUNNIGAN

BEST VALUE INN
3930 Rd 89 (95937)
Rates: $49-$99
(530) 724-3333

BEST WESTERN COUNTRY INN
3930 Rd 89 (95937)
Rates: $59-$129
(530) 724-3471
(800) 528-1234

BUDGET 8 MOTEL
4930 CR 99 W
(95937)
Rates: $49-$65
(530) 724-3411

DUNSMUIR

BEST CHOICE INN
4221 Siskiyou Ave
(96025)
Rates: $30-$80
(530) 235-0930

CABOOSE MOTEL-RAILROAD PARK RESORT
100 Railroad Park
Dr (96025)
Rates: $80-$115
(530) 235-4440

CAVE SPRINGS RESORT
4727 Dunsmuir
Ave (96025)
Rates: $37-$49
(530) 235-2721

CEDAR LODGE MOTEL
4201 Dunsmuir
Ave (96025)
Rates: $49-$125
(530) 235-4331

OAK TREE INN MOTEL
6604 Dunsmuir
Ave (96025)
Rates: $48-$96
(530) 235-2884
(877) 235-2884

RIVERWALK INN B&B
4300 Dunsmuir
Ave (96025)
Rates: $49-$71
(530) 235-4300
(800) 954-4300

EL CAJON

BEST WESTERN COURTESY INN
1355 E Main St
(92021)
Rates: $66-$140
(619) 440-7378
(800) 528-1234

MOTEL 6
550 Montrose Ct
(92020)
Rates: $39-$50
(619) 588-6100
(800) 466-8356

EL CENTRO

BARBARA WORTH GOLF COURSE
2050 Country
Club Dr
(Holtville 92250)
Rates: $87-$99
(760) 356-2806
(800) 356-3806

BRUNNER'S MOTEL
215 N Imperial
Ave (92243)
Rates: $69-$149
(760) 352-6431

COMFORT INN & SUITES
2354 S Fourth St
(92243)
Rates: $84-$135
(760) 335-3502
(800) 424-6423

DAYS INN
1425 Adams Ave
(92243)
Rates: $45-$120
(760) 352-5511
(800) 329-7466

AREA CODES - If the local number doesn't connect, check for a new area code.

MOTEL 6
395 Smoketree Dr
(92243)
Rates: $39+
(760) 353-6766
(800) 466-8356

VACATION INN
2015 Cottonwood
Cir (92243)
Rates: $54-$69
(760) 352-9700

EL CERRITO
FREEWAY MOTEL
11645 San Pablo
Ave (95430)
Rates: $38-$58
(510) 234-5581

EL MONTE
MOTEL 6
3429 Peck Rd
(91731)
Rates: $39-$52
(626) 448-6660
(800) 466-8356

EL PORTAL
YOSEMITE VIEW
LODGE
11156 Hwy 140
(95318)
Rates: $85-$269
(209) 379-2681
(800) 321-5261

EL SEGUNDO
EMBASSY SUITES
HOTEL LAX
1440 E Imperial
Ave (90245)
Rates: $99-$209
(310) 640-3600
(800) 362-2779

HOMESTEAD
STUDIO SUITES
1910 E Mariposa
Ave (90245)
Rates: $74-$99
(310) 607-4000
(888) 782-9473

SUMMERFIELD
SUITES BY
WYNDHAM/LAX
810 S Douglas Ave
(90245)
Rates: $99-$159
(310) 725-0100
(800) 833-4353

ELK
GREENWOOD
PIER INN
5938 Hwy One
(95432)
Rates: $120-$235
(707) 877-9997

EMERYVILLE
WOODFIN SUITE
HOTEL-SF BAY
BRIDGE
5800 Shellmound
St (94608)
Rates: $149
(510) 601-5880
(800) 237-8811

ENCINITAS
BEST WESTERN
ENCINITAS INN
MOONLIGHT BCH
85 Encinitas Blvd
(92024)
Rates: $89-$229
(760) 942-7455
(800) 528-1234
(866) 362-4648

HOLIDAY INN EXP
607 Leucadia Blvd
(92024)
Rates: $109-$149
(760) 944-3800
(800) 465-4329

ESCONDIDO
BEST WESTERN
ESCONDIDO
1700 Seven Oaks
Rd (92026)
Rates: $79-$169
(760) 740-1700
(800) 528-1234

COMFORT INN
1290 W Valley
Pkwy (92029)
Rates: $69-$109
(760) 489-1010
(800) 424-6423

MOTEL 6
900 N Quince St
(92025)
Rates: $39-$54
(760) 745-9252
(800) 466-8356

RODEWAY INN
250 W El Norte
Pkwy (92026)
Rates: $49-$125
(760) 746-0441
(800) 424-6423

WELK RESORT-
SAN DIEGO
8860 Lawrence
Welk Drive
(92026)
Rates: $120-$375
(760) 749-3000
(800) 932-9355

ETNA
BRADLEYS'
ALDERBROOK
MANOR
836 Main St
(96027)
Rates: $20-$60
(530) 467-3917

MOTEL ETNA
317 Collier Way
(96027)
Rates: $39-$44
(530) 467-5330

EUREKA
A WEAVER'S INN
BED & BREAKFAST
1440 B St (95501)
Rates: $80-$140
(707) 443-8119
(800) 992-8119

BAYVIEW MOTEL
2844 Fairfield St
(95501)
Rates: $75-$150
(707) 442-1673

BEST WESTERN
BAYSHORE INN
3500 Broadway
(95501)
Rates: $70-$165
(707) 268-8005
(800) 528-1234
(888) 268-8005

EUREKA INN
HISTORIC HOTEL
518 7th St (95501)
Rates: $88-$250
(707) 442-6441
(800) 862-4906

FIRESIDE INN
5th & R Sts
(95501)
Rates: $30-$55
(707) 443-6312

LAMPLIGHTER
MOTEL
4033 S Broadway
(95501)
Rates: $35-$50
(707) 443-5001

MOTEL 6
1934 Broadway
(95501)
Rates: $39-$56
(707) 445-9631
(800) 466-8356

PINE MOTEL
2411 Broadway
(95501)
Rates: $25-$45
(707) 441-9204

QUALITY INN
1209 4th St (95501)
Rates: $58-$200
(707) 443-1601
(800) 424-6423

RAMADA LIMITED
270 5th St (95501)
Rates: $65-$90
(707) 443-2206
(800) 272-6232

RED LION INN
1929 4th St (95501)
Rates: $109-$129
(707) 445-0844
(800) 733-5466

ROYAL INN
1137 5th St (95501)
Rates: $30-$42
(707) 442-2114

SAFARI
BUDGET 6 MOTEL
801 Broadway
(95501)
Rates: $30-$58
(707) 443-4891

SANDPIPER
MOTEL
4055 Broadway
(95501)
Rates: $34-$45
(707) 443-7394

SUNRISE INN
129 4th St (95501)
Rates: $39-$85
(707) 443-9751

TOWN HOUSE
MOTEL
933 4th St (95501)
Rates: $45-$125
(707) 443-4536
(800) 445-6888

TRAVELODGE
4 Fourth St (95501)
Rates: $56-$175
(707) 443-6345
(800) 578-7878

FAIRFIELD
ECONO LODGE
INN & SUITES
4625 Central Way
(94533)
Rates: $54-$99
(707) 864-2426
(800) 424-6423

MOTEL 6
1473 Holiday Ln
(94533)
Rates: $49-$66
(707) 425-4565
(800) 466-8356

FALL RIVER
MILLS
HI-MONT MOTEL
43021 Bridge St
(96028)
Rates: $55-$96
(530) 336-5541

LAVA CREEK LODGE
One Island Rd
(96028)
Rates: $75-$135
(530) 336-6288

PIT RIVER LODGE
24500 Pit One
Powerhouse Rd
(96028)
Rates: n/a
(530) 336-5005

FALLBROOK
BEST WESTERN
FRANCISCAN INN
1635 S Mission Rd
(92028)
Rates: $75-$145
(760) 728-6174
(800) 528-1234

FERNDALE
COLLINGWOOD
INN B&B
831 Main St
(95536)
Rates: $115-$205
(707) 786-9219
(800) 469-1632

SHAW HOUSE
B&B INN
703 Main St
(95536)
Rates: $115-$275
(707) 786-9958

FIREBAUGH

**BEST WESTERN
APRICOT INN**
46290 W Panoche
Rd (93622)
Rates: $49-$99
(559) 659-1444
(800) 528-1234

FISH CAMP

**APPLE TREE INN
AT YOSEMITE**
1110 Hwy 41
(93623)
Rates: $99-$249
(559) 683-5111
(888) 683-5111

**THE NARROW
GAUGE INN**
48571 Hwy 41
(93623)
Rates: $79-$195
(559) 683-7720
(888) 644-9050

FOLSOM

**RESIDENCE INN
BY MARRIOTT**
2555 Iron Point Rd
(95630)
Rates: $144-$175
(916) 983-7289
(800) 331-3131

FONTANA

**AMERIHOST INN
& SUITES**
13500 Baseline
Ave (92336)
Rates: $89-$101
(909) 463-5900
(800) 434-5800

ECONO LODGE
17133 Valley Blvd
(92335)
Rates: $75-$95
(909) 822-5411
(800) 424-6423

MOTEL 6
10195 Sierra Ave
(92335)
Rates: $43-$56
(909) 823-8686
(800) 466-8356

FORT BIDWELL

FT. BIDWELL HOTEL
Main St, PO Box
100 (96112)
Rates: $35-$45
(916) 279-2050

FORT BRAGG

**BEACH HOUSE
INN**
100 Pudding
Creek Rd (95437)
Rates: $89-$175
(707) 961-1700
(888) 559-9992

**BEACHCOMBER
MOTEL**
1111 N Main St
(95437)
Rates: $59-$250
(707) 964-2402
(800) 440-7873

**CLEONE
GARDENS INN**
24600 N Hwy 1
(95437)
Rates: $86-$140
(707) 964-2788
(800) 400-2189 (CA)

COAST MOTEL
18661 Hwy 1
(95437)
Rates: $38-$64
(707) 964-2852

**DELAMERE SEASIDE
COTTAGE**
16821 Ocean Dr
(95437)
Rates: $125
(707) 964-9188

**THE EMERALD
DOLPHIN INN**
1211 S Main St
(95437)
Rates: $45-$180
(707) 964-6699

**OLD STEWART
HOUSE INN B&B**
511 Stewart St
(95437)
Rates: $100-$150
(707) 961-0775
(800) 287-8392

SEABIRD LODGE
191 South St
(95437)
Rates: $66-$118
(707) 964-4731

**TRADEWINDS
LODGE**
400 S Main St
(95437)
Rates: $59-$150
(707) 964-4761
(800) 524-2244

**WISHING WELL
COTTAGES**
31430 Hwy 20
(95437)
Rates: $65-$75
(707) 961-5450

FORTUNA

**BEST WESTERN
COUNTRY INN**
2025 River Walk
Dr (95540)
Rates: $62-$115
(707) 725-6822
(800) 528-1234
(800) 679-7511

HOLIDAY INN EXP
1859 Alamar Way
(95540)
Rates: $75-$169
(707) 725-5500
(800) 465-4329

6 RIVERS MOTEL
531 S Fortuna
Blvd (95540)
Rates: $30-$58
(707) 725-1181

SUPER 8 MOTEL
1805 Alamar Way
(95540)
Rates: $55-$105
(707) 725-2888
(800) 800-8000

TRAVEL INN
275 12th St (95540)
Rates: $49-$89
(707) 725-6993

FOUNTAIN VALLEY

RAMADA LTD
9125 Recreation
Cir (92708)
Rates: $79-$89
(714) 847-3388
(800) 272-6232

**RESIDENCE INN
BY MARRIOTT**
9930 Slater Ave
(92708)
Rates: $149-$199
(714) 965-8000
(800) 331-3131

FREESTONE

GREEN APPLE INN
520 Bohemian
Hwy (95472)
Rates: $85-$92
(707) 874-2526

FREMONT

AMERISUITES
3101 W Warren
Ave (94538)
Rates: $94
(510) 623-6000
(800) 833-1516

**BEST WESTERN
GARDEN COURT**
5400 Mowry Ave
(94538)
Rates: $79-$139
(510) 792-4300
(800) 528-1234
(800) 541-4909

ECONO LODGE
46101 Warm
Springs Blvd
(94539)
Rates: $55-$75
(510) 656-2800
(800) 424-6423

**HOMESTEAD
STUDIO SUITES**
46080 Fremont
Blvd (94538)
Rates: $67-$87
(510) 353-1664
(888) 782-9473

ISLANDER MOTEL
4101 Mowry Ave
(94538)
Rates: $35-$53
(510) 796-8200

LA QUINTA INN
46200 Landing
Pkwy (94538)
Rates: $80-$120
(510) 445-0808
(800) 687-6667

MARRIOTT HOTEL
46100 Landing
Pkwy (94538)
Rates: $74-$139
(510) 413-3700
(800) 228-9290

**MISSION PEAK
LODGE**
43643 Mission
Blvd (94539)
Rates: $29-$50
(510) 656-2366

MOTEL 6-NORTH
34047 Fremont
Blvd (94536)
Rates: $39-$43
(510) 793-4848
(800) 466-8356

MOTEL 6-SOUTH
46101 Research
Ave (94539)
Rates: $34-$40
(510) 490-4528
(800) 466-8356

**RESIDENCE INN
BY MARRIOTT**
5400 Farwell Pl
(94536)
Rates: $189-$209
(510) 794-5900
(800) 331-3131

FRESNO

COMFORT INN
5455 W Shaw Ave
(93722)
Rates: $75-$200
(559) 275-2374
(800) 424-6423

DAYS INN
1101 N Parkway
Dr (93728)
Rates: $52-$84
(559) 268-6211
(800) 329-7466

ECONO LODGE
445 N Parkway Dr
(93706)
Rates: $42-$50
(559) 485-5019
(800) 424-6423

**HOLIDAY INN EXP
HOTEL & SUITES**
5046 N Barcus Rd
(93722)
Rates: $99-$119
(559) 277-5700
(800) 465-4329

KNIGHTS INN
3093 N Parkway
Dr (93722)
Rates: $45-$69
(559) 275-7766
(800) 843-5644

LA QUINTA INN
2926 Tulare St
(93721)
Rates: $66-$82
(559) 442-1110
(800) 687-6667

MOTEL 6
1240 Crystal Ave
(93728)
Rates: $36-$42
(559) 237-0855
(800) 466-8356

AREA CODES - If the local number doesn't connect, check for a new area code.

MOTEL 6 NORTH
4245 N Blackstone
Ave (93726)
Rates: $37-$46
(559) 221-0800
(800) 466-8356

MOTEL 6 SOUTH
4080 N Blackstone
Ave (93726)
Rates: $35-$44
(559) 222-2431
(800) 466-8356

RADISSON HOTEL
2233 Ventura St
(93722)
Rates: $99-$154
(559) 268-1000
(800) 333-3333

RED ROOF INN
5021 N Barcus Ave
(93722)
Rates: $45-$59
(559) 276-1910
(800) 843-7663

RED ROOF INN
6730 N Blackstone
Ave (93710)
Rates: $45-$80
(559) 431-3557
(800) 843-7663

**RESIDENCE INN
BY MARRIOTT**
5322 N Diana Ave
(93710)
Rates: $119-$124
(559) 222-8900
(800) 331-3131

SUPER 8 MOTEL
1087 N Parkway
Dr (93728)
Rates: $49-$85
(559) 268-0741
(800) 800-8000

SUPER 8 MOTEL
2127 Inyo St
(93721)
Rates: $60-$95
(559) 268-0621
(800) 800-8000

**TOWNEPLACE
SUITES BY
MARRIOTT**
7127 N Fresno St
(93720)
Rates: $69-$129
(559) 435-4600
(800) 257-3000

TRAVELODGE
3093 N Parkway
Dr (93722)
Rates: $59-$119
(559) 276-7745
(800) 578-7878

UNIVERSITY INN
2655 E Shaw Ave
(93710)
Rates: $43-$85
(559) 294-0224

VALLEY INN
933 N Parkway Dr
(93728)
Rates: $32-$45
(559) 233-3913

FULLERTON
**FOUR POINTS BY
SHERATON**
1500 S Raymond
Ave (92831)
Rates: $75-$115
(714) 635-9000
(800) 325-3535

FULLERTON INN
2601 W Orange-
thorpe Ave (92633)
Rates: $55-$75
(714) 773-4900

**MARRIOTT HOTEL
CAL STATE UNIV**
2701 E Nutwood
Ave (92831)
Rates: $79-$149
(714) 738-7800
(800) 228-9290

GALT
ROYAL DELTA INN
1040 N Lincoln
Way (95632)
Rates: $43-$53
(209) 745-9181

GARBERVILLE
**BEST WESTERN
HUMBOLDT
HOUSE INN**
701 Redwood Dr
(95542)
Rates: $75-$125
(707) 923-2771
(800) 528-1234
(800) 862-7756

**GARBERVILLE
MOTEL**
948 Redwood Dr
(95542)
Rates: $39-$79
(707) 923-2422

**SHERWOOD
FOREST MOTEL**
814 Redwood Dr
(95542)
Rates: $60-$100
(707) 923-2721

GARDEN GROVE
**CANDLEWOOD
SUITES ANAHEIM
SOUTH**
12901 Garden
Grove Blvd (92843)
Rates: $110-$170
(714) 539-4200
(888) 226-3539

**HOLIDAY INN EXP
HOTEL & SUITES**
12867 Garden
Grove Blvd
(92843)
Rates: $89
(714) 539-3535
(800) 465-4329

**HOMEWOOD
SUITES**
12005 Harbor
Blvd (92840)
Rates: $139
(714) 740-1800
(800) 225-5466

MARRIOTT SUITES
12015 Harbor
Blvd (92840)
Rates: $119-$299
(714) 750-1000
(800) 228-9290

**RESIDENCE INN
ANAHEIM**
11931 Harbor
Blvd (92840)
Rates: $129-$369
(714) 591-4000
(800) 681-0174

GEORGETOWN
**AMERICAN RIVER
INN B&B**
Main & Orlean Sts
(95643)
Rates: $89-$105
(530) 333-4499
(800) 245-6566

GILROY
LEAVESLEY INN
8430 Murray Ave
(95020)
Rates: $55-$75
(408) 847-5500
(800) 624-8225

**MOTEL 6
EXTENDED STAY**
6110 Monterey
Hwy (95020)
Rates: $45-$60
(408) 842-6061
(800) 466-8356

GLEN AVON
**CIRCLE INN
MOTEL**
9220 Granite Hill
Dr (92509)
Rates: $29-$36
(909) 360-1132

GLENDALE
DAYS INN
600 N Pacific Ave
(91203)
Rates: $99-$194
(818) 956-0202
(800) 329-7466

**HOMESTEAD
STUDIO SUITES**
1377 W Glenoaks
Blvd (91201)
Rates: $90-$115
(818) 956-6665
(888) 782-9473

VAGABOND INN
120 W Colorado St
(91204)
Rates: $79-$94
(818) 240-1700
(800) 522-1555

GLENHAVEN
**INDIAN BEACH
RESORT**
9945 E Hwy 20
(95443)
Rates: $35-$100
(707) 998-3760

GLENNVILLE
**THE BUNKHOUSE
MOTEL**
12044 Hwy 15 S
(93226)
Rates: $65-$85
(661) 536-9100

GOLETA
MOTEL 6
5897 Calle Real
(93117)
Rates: $51-$86
(661) 964-3596
(800) 466-8356

GORMAN
ECONO LODGE
49713 Gorman Post
Rd (93243)
Rates: $59-$99
(661) 248-6411
(800) 424-6423

GRASS VALLEY
**ALTA SIERRA
VILLAGE INN**
11858 Tammy Way
(95949)
Rates: $69-$190
(530) 273-9102
(800) 992-5300

**BEST WESTERN
GOLD COUNTRY**
11972 Sutton Way
(95945)
Rates: $85-$119
(530) 273-1393
(800) 528-1234

**COACH N' FOUR
MOTEL**
628 S Auburn St
(95945)
Rates: $58-$124
(530) 273-8009

**GOLDEN CHAIN
RESORT MOTEL**
13413 SR 49
(95949)
Rates: $42-$102
(530) 273-7279

**GRASS VALLEY
COURTYARD
SUITES**
210 N Auburn St
(94945)
Rates: $125-$290
(530) 272-7696

HOLIDAY LODGE
1221 E Main St
(95948)
Rates: $60-$80
(530) 477-2878
(800) 742-7125

**STAGECOACH
MOTEL**
405 S Auburn St
(94945)
Rates: $50-$110
(530) 272-3701

AREA CODES - If the local number doesn't connect, check for a new area code.

GREENVILLE

HIDEAWAY RESORT MOTEL
101 Hideaway Rd (95947)
Rates: $42-$45
(530) 284-7915

OAK GROVE MOTOR LODGE
700 Hwy 89 (95947)
Rates: $40-$47
(530) 284-6671

SIERRA LODGE
303 Main St, Box 578 (95947)
Rates: $24-$40
(530) 284-6565

SPRING MEADOW RESORT MOTEL
18964 Hwy 89 (95947)
Rates: $53+
(530) 284-6768

GRIDLEY

GRIDLEY INN
1490 Hwy 99, Suite A (95948)
Rates: $59-$69
(530) 846-4520

PACIFIC MOTEL
1308 Hwy 99 (95948)
Rates: $50-$65
(530) 846-4580

GROVELAND

BEST VALUE YOSEMITE WESTGATE BUCKMEADOWS LODGE
7633/7647 Hwy 120 (95321)
Rates: $69-$179
(209) 962-5281
(800) 253-9673
(888) 315-2378

GROVELAND HISTORIC COUNTRY INN
18767 Main St (95321)
Rates: $145-$260
(209) 962-4000
(800) 273-3314

MTN RIVER MOTEL
12655 Jacksonville Rd (95321)
Rates: $35
(209) 984-5071

YOSEMITE INN
31191 Hardin Flat Rd (95321)
Rates: $28-$55
(209) 962-0103

GUALALA

GUALALA COUNTRY INN
47955 Center St (95445)
Rates: $95-$165
(707) 884-4343
(800) 564-4466

SURF MOTEL
39170 Hwy 1 (95445)
Rates: $95-$179
(707) 884-3571
(888) 451-7873

GUERNEVILLE

FERNGROVE COTTAGES
16650 Hwy 16 (95446)
Rates: $89-$239
(707) 869-8105

HACIENDA HEIGHTS

MOTEL 6
1154 S 7th Ave (91745)
Rates: $39-$54
(626) 968-9462
(800) 466-8356

HALF MOON BAY

HARBOR VIEW INN
51 Ave Alhambra (94018)
Rates: $76-$186
(650) 726-2329

HOLIDAY INN EXP
230 S Cabrillo Hwy (94019)
Rates: $69-$149
(650) 726-3400
(800) 465-4329

MIRAMAR LODGE
2930 N Cabrillo Hwy (94019)
Rates: $79-$159
(650) 712-1999

RITZ-CARLTON
1 Miramontes Point Rd (94019)
Rates: $295-$395
(650) 712-7000
(800) 241-3333

ZABALLA HOUSE INN B&B
324 Main St (94019)
Rates: $75-$250
(650) 726-9123

HANFORD

SEQUOIA INN MOTEL
1655 Mall Dr (92320)
Rates: $65-$105
(559) 582-0338

HAPPY CAMP

FOREST LODGE MOTEL
63712 Hwy 96 (96039)
Rates: $40-$55
(530) 493-5424

HARBOR CITY

MOTEL 6
820 W Sepulveda Blvd (90710)
Rates: $47-$60
(310) 549-9560
(800) 466-8356

HAWTHORNE

TOWNEPLACE SUITES BY MARRIOTT
14400 Aviation Blvd (90250)
Rates: $79-$119
(310) 725-9696
(800) 257-3000

HAYWARD

COMFORT INN
24997 Mission Blvd (94544)
Rates: $69+
(510) 538-4466
(800) 424-6423
(800) 835-6159

LA QUINTA INN & SUITES
20777 Hesperian Blvd (94541)
Rates: $84-$103
(510) 732-6300
(800) 687-6667

MAINSTAY SUITES
835 West A St (94541)
Rates: $69-$129
(510) 731-3571
(800) 424-6423

MOTEL 6
30155 Industrial Pkwy SW (94544)
Rates: $42-$45
(510) 489-8333
(800) 466-8356

HEALDSBURG

BEST WESTERN DRY CREEK INN
198 Dry Creek Rd (95448)
Rates: $85-$199
(707) 433-0300
(800) 528-1234
(800) 222-5784

DUCHAMP COTTAGES
421 Foss St (95448)
Rates: $275-$450
(707) 431-1300

FAIRVIEW MOTEL
74 Healdsburg Ave (95448)
Rates: $59-$139
(707) 433-5548

HEMET

BEST WESTERN INN OF HEMET
2625 W Florida Ave (92545)
Rates: $64-$94
(909) 925-6605
(800) 528-1234
(800) 605-0001

COACH LIGHT MOTEL
1640 W Florida Ave (92545)
Rates: $45-$59
(909) 65 8-3237
(800) 678 -0124

MOTEL 6
3885 W Florida Ave (92545)
Rates: $44-$50
(909) 929-8900
(800) 466-8356

HERMOSA BEACH

QUALITY INN & SUITES
901 Aviation Blvd (90254)
Rates: $79-$139
(310) 374-2666
(800) 424-6423

HESPERIA

DAYS INN SUITES
14865 Bear Valley Rd (92345)
Rates: $59-$159
(760) 948-0600
(800) 329-7746

HOLIDAY IN EXP HOTEL & SUITES
9750 Key Pointe Ave (92345)
Rates: $69-$149
(760) 244-7674
(800) 465-4329

LA QUINTA INN & SUITES
12000 Mariposa Rd (92345)
Rates: $90-$150
(760) 949-9900
(800) 687-6667

SUPER 8 MOTEL
12033 Oakwood Ave (92345)
Rates: $49-$89
(760) 949-3231
(800) 800-8000

HOLLYWOOD

BEST WESTERN HOLLYWOOD HILLS
6141 Franklin Ave (90028)
Rates: $79-$249
(323) 464-5181
(800) 528-1234
(800) 287-1700

ECONO LODGE
777 N Vine St (90038)
Rates: $64-$79
(323) 463-5671
(800) 424-6423

MOTEL 6
1738 N Whitley Ave (90028)
Rates: $49-$76
(323) 464-6006
(800) 466-8356

AREA CODES - If the local number doesn't connect, check for a new area code.

RAMADA INN & CONF CENTER
1160 N Vermont Ave (90029)
Rates: $89-$109
(323) 315-1800
(800) 272-6232
(800) 800-9733

HOPE VALLEY

SORENSON'S RESORT
14255 Hwy 88 (96120)
Rates: $80-$450
(530) 694-2203

HUNTINGTON BEACH

HILTON WATERFRONT BEACH RESORT
21100 Pacific Coast Hwy (92648)
Rates: $189-$329
(714) 845-8000
(800) 445-8667

HUNTINGTON LAKE

LAKEVIEW COTTAGES
58374 Huntington Lodge Rd (93634)
Rates: $45-$93
(559) 893-2330

HYAMPOM

ZIEGLER'S TRAILS' END
1 Main St (96046)
Rates: $50-$80
(530) 628-4929
(800) 566-5266

IDYLLWILD

FIRESIDE INN
54540 N Circle Dr (92549)
Rates: $65-$130
(951) 659-2966

IMPERIAL

IMPERIAL VALLEY INN
1093 Airport Blvd (92251)
Rates: $48-$100
(760) 355-4500
(800) 232-2378

IMPERIAL BEACH

BEACH FRONT RENTALS
716 Ocean Lane (91932)
Rates: n/a
(619) 423-9958

INDEPENDENCE

INDEPENDENCE COURTHOUSE MOTEL
157 N Edwards (93526)
Rates: $47-$72
(800) 801-0703

MT. WILLIAMSON MOTEL
515 S Edwards (93526)
Rates: $47-$64
(760) 878-2121

RAY'S DEN MOTEL
405 N Edwards (93526)
Rates: $57-$72
(760) 878-2122

INDIO

BEST WESTERN DATE TREE HOTEL
81-909 Indio Blvd (92201)
Rates: $49-$159
(760) 347-3421
(800) 528-1234
(800) 292-5599

HOLIDAY INN EXP HOTEL & SUITES
84-096 Indio Spgs Pkwy (92201)
Rates: n/a
(760) 342-6344
(800) 465-4329

INDIAN PALMS COUNTRY CLUB & RESORT
48-630 Monroe St (92201)
Rates: $84-$169
(760) 775-444
(800) 778-5288

MOTEL 6
82-195 Indio Blvd (92201)
Rates: $39-$49
(760) 342-6311
(800) 466-8356

PALM SHADOW INN
80-761 Hwy 111 (92201)
Rates: $59-$144
(760) 347-3476

QUALITY INN
43-505 Monroe St (92201)
Rates: $59-$149
(760) 347-4044
(800) 424-6423

ROYAL PLAZA INN
82-347 Hwy 111 (92201)
Rates: $49-$129
(760) 347-0911
(800) 228-9559

SUPER 8 MOTEL
81-753 Hwy 111 (92201)
Rates: $55-$120
(760) 342-0264
(800) 800-8000

INDUSTRY

PACIFIC PALMS CONFERENCE RESORT
One Industry Hills Pkwy (91744)
Rates: $159-$1050
(626) 810-4455

INGLEWOOD

ECONO LODGE
439 W Manchester Blvd (90301)
Rates: $65-$100
(310) 674-8596
(800) 424-6423

MOTEL 6 INT'L AIRPORT
5101 W Century Blvd (90304)
Rates: $49-$60
(310) 419-1234
(800) 466-8356

INVERNESS

COTTAGES ON THE BEACH
12790 Sir Frances Drake (94937)
Rates: n/a
(415) 663-9696

MANKA'S INVERNESS LODGE
P. O. Box 1110 (94937)
Rates: $65-$160
(415) 669-1034

ROSEMARY COTTAGE B&B
75 Balboa Ave (94937)
Rates: $180-$245
(415) 663-9338
(800) 808-9338

INYOKERN

THREE FLAGS INN
1233 Brown Rd (93527)
Rates: $30-$120
(760) 377-3300

IRVINE

CANDLEWOOD SUITES
16150 San Canyon Ave (92618)
Rates: $79-$149
(949) 788-0500
(888) 226-3539

HILTON HOTEL-AIRPORT
18800 MacArthur Blvd (92612)
Rates: $149-$234
(949) 833-9999
(800) 445-8667

LA QUINTA INN-IRVINE SPECTRUM
14972 Sand Canyon Ave (92618)
Rates: $80-$110
(949) 551-0909
(800) 687-6667

MARRIOTT HOTEL
18000 Van Karman Ave (92612)
Rates: $189-$209
(949) 553-0100
(800) 228-9290

RESIDENCE INN BY MARRIOTT
10 Morgan St (92618)
Rates: $149-$199
(949) 380-3000
(800) 331-3131

ISLETON

HOTEL DEL RIO & CASINO
207-11 2nd St (95641)
Rates: $35-$75
(916) 777-6033

JACKSON

BEST WESTERN AMADOR INN
200 S Hwy 49 (95642)
Rates: $75-$105
(209) 223-0211
(800) 528-1234
(800) 543-5221

EL CAMPO CASA RESORT MOTEL
12548 Kennedy Flat Rd (95642)
Rates: $56-$106
(209) 223-0100

JACKSON GOLD LODGE
850 N Hwy 49 (95642)
Rates: $54-$80
(209) 223-0486
(888) 777-0380

LINDA VISTA MOTEL
10708 N Hwy 49 (95642)
Rates: $40-$60
(209) 223-1096

JAMESTOWN

COUNTRY INN SONORA
18730 Hwy 108 (95327)
Rates: $59-$179
(209) 984-0315
(800) 847-2211

1859 HISTORIC NAT'L HOTEL-COUNTRY INN
18183 Main St (95327)
Rates: $95-$150
(209) 984-3446
(800) 894-3446

JAMESTOWN RAILTOWN MOTEL
10301 Willow St (95327)
Rates: $49-$85
(209) 984-3332

AREA CODES - If the local number doesn't connect, check for a new area code.

JENNER

JENNER INN & COTTAGES
10400 Hwy 1 (95450)
Rates: $98-$278
(707) 865-2377
(800) 732-2377

STILLWATER COVE RANCH
22555 Coast Hwy 1 (95450)
Rates: $50-$155
(707) 847-3227

JOSHUA TREE

HIGH DESERT MOTEL
61310 29 Palms Hwy (92252)
Rates: $45+
(760) 366-1978

JOSHUA TREE INN B&B
61259 29 Palms Hwy (92252)
Rates: $95-$150
(760) 366-1188

JULIAN

THE JULIAN HOMESTEAD B&B
4924 Hwy 79 (92036)
Rates: $135-$200
(760) 765-1536

JUNCTION CITY

BIGFOOT CAMPGROUND
Hwy 299 (96048)
Rates: $69
(530) 623-6088
(800) 422-5219

JUNE LAKE

DOUBLE EAGLE RESORT & SPA
5587 Hwy 158 (93529)
Rates: $287-$319
(760) 648-7004

GULL LAKE LODGE
132 Leonard Ave (93529)
Rates: $65-$149
(760) 648-7516
(800) 631-9081

KELSEYVILLE

CREEKSIDE LODGE
7990 Hwy 29 (95451)
Rates: $45-$72
(707) 279-9258
(800) 279-1380

EDGEWATER RESORT SODA BAY
6420 Soda Bay Rd (95451)
Rates: $25-$85
(707) 279-0208
(800) 396-6224

KERNVILLE

RIVER VIEW LODGE
2 Sirretta St (93238)
Rates: $69-$129
(760) 376-6019

KETTLEMAN CTY

BEST WESTERN
33410 Powers Dr (93239)
Rates: $72-$159
(559) 386-0804
(800) 528-1234
(800) 381-1116

SUPER 8 MOTEL
33415 Powers Dr (93239)
Rates: $50-$65
(559) 386-9530
(800) 800-8000

KING CITY

COURTESY INN
4 Broadway Circle (93930)
Rates: $43-$119
(831) 385-4646
(800) 350-5616

DAYS INN
1130 Broadway Circle (93930)
Rates: $45-$110
(831) 385-6508
(800) 329-7466

MOTEL 6
3 Broadway Circle (93930)
Rates: $35-$46
(831) 385-5000
(800) 466-8356

KINGS BEACH

STEVENSON'S HOLIDAY INN
8742 N Lake Blvd (96143)
Rates: $59-$129
(530) 546-2269
(800) 634-9141

KINGSBURG

SWEDISH INN
401 Conejo St (93631)
Rates: $58-$129
(559) 897-1022
(800) 834-1022

KLAMATH

CAMP MARIGOLD GARDEN CTGS
16101 Hwy 101 (95548)
Rates: $42-$165
(707) 482-3585
(800) 621-8513

MOTEL TREES
15495 Hwy 101 N (95548)
Rates: $45-$86
(707) 482-3152

TREES OF MYSTERY AND SKYTRAIL
15500 Hwy 101 (95548)
Rates: $48-$98
(800) 638-3389

KYBURZ

KYBURZ RESORT MOTEL
13668 Hwy 50 (95720)
Rates: $49-$99
(530) 293-3382

LA JOLLA

LA JOLLA COVE SUITES
1155 Coast Blvd (92037)
Rates: $239-$599
(858) 459-2621
(888) 525-6552

LA JOLLA VILLAGE LODGE
1141 Silverado St (92037)
Rates: $70-$220
(858) 551-2001
877-551-2001

LA VALENCIA HOTEL
1132 Prospect St (92037)
Rates: $300-$2000
(858) 454-0771

MARRIOTT LA JOLLA
4240 La Jolla Village Dr (92037)
Rates: $179-$219
(858) 587-1414
(800) 228-9290

RESIDENCE INN BY MARRIOTT
8901 Gilman Dr (92037)
Rates: $149-$199
(858) 587-1770
(800) 331-3131

LA MESA

MOTEL 6
7621 Alvarado Rd (91941)
Rates: $41-$60
(619) 464-7151
(800) 466-8356

LA MIRADA

RESIDENCE INN BY MARRIOTT
14419 Firestone Blvd (90638)
Rates: $149-$189
(714) 523-2800
(800) 331-3131

LA PALMA

LA QUINTA INN
3 Centerpointe Dr (90623)
Rates: $90-$130
(714) 670-1400
(800) 687-6667

LA QUINTA

LA QUINTA RESORT & CLUB
49-499 Eisenhower Dr (92253)
Rates: $199-$229
(760) 564-4111
(800) 854-1271

LAGUNA BEACH

BEST WESTERN LAGUNA BRISAS SPA HOTEL
1600 S Coast Hwy (92651)
Rates: $99-$289
(949) 497-7272
(800) 528-1234
(888) 296-6834

THE CARRIAGE HOUSE B&B
1322 Catalina St (92651)
Rates: $140-$180
(949) 494-8945
(888) 335-8945

CASA LAGUNA INN B&B
2510 S Coast Hwy (92651)
Rates: $105-$350
(949) 494-2996

LA CASA DEL CAMINO
1289 S Coast Hwy (92651)
Rates: $79-$299
(949) 497-2446
(888) 367-5232

LAKE ALMANOR

ALMANOR LAKESIDE LODGE
3747 Eastshore Dr (96137)
Rates: $70
(530) 284-7376
(800) 238-3924

KNOTTY PINE RESORT
430 Peninsula Dr (96137)
Rates: n/a
(530) 596-3348

LAKE ALMANOR RESORT
2706 Big Springs Rd (96137)
Rates: $47-$90
(530) 596-3337

LAKE ARROWHEAD

ARROWHEAD SADDLEBACK HISTORIC COUNTRY INN
SR 173 & 189 (92352)
Rates: $89-$218
(909) 336-3571

LAKE ARROWHEAD RESORT
27984 Hwy 189 (92352)
Rates: $129-$209
(909) 336-1511

AREA CODES - If the local number doesn't connect, check for a new area code.

**STORYBOOK
INN B&B**
28717 SR 18 (Sky
Forest 28717)
Rates: $79-$299
(909) 337-0011

*LAKE
FOREST*
**CANDLEWOOD
SUITES**
3 S Pointe Dr
(92630)
Rates: $75-$169
(949) 598-9105
(888) 226-3539

COMFORT SUITES
20768 Lake Forest
Dr (92630)
Rates: $89-$119
(949) 900-1288
(800) 424-6423

*LAKE
SAN MARCOS*
**QUAIL INN
HOTEL**
1025 La Bonita Dr
(92069)
Rates: $99-$299
(760) 744-0120
(800) 447-6556

*LAKE TAHOE
AREA*

(Kings Beach)

**STEVENSON'S
HOLLIDAY INN**
8742 N Lake Blvd
(96143)
Rates: $59-$129
(530) 546-2269
(800) 634-9141

(Lake Tahoe Area-
South Lake
Tahoe)

ALDER INN
1072 Ski Run Blvd
(96150)
Rates: $42-$125
(530) 544-4485
(800) 544-0056

ALPENROSE INN
4074 Pine Blvd
(95729)
Rates: $49-$99
(530) 544-2985

BLUE JAY LODGE
4133 Cedar Ave
(96150)
Rates: $59-$129
(530) 544-5232
(800) 258-3529

**DAYS INN-CASINO
AREA-STATELINE**
968 Park Ave
(96150)
Rates: $39-$249
(530) 541-4800
(800) 329-7466

**ECHO CREEK
RANCH**
P. O. Box 20088
(96151)
Rates: $100+
(530) 544-5397
(800) 462-5397

**HARRAH'S LAKE
TAHOE HOTEL
& CASINO**
15 Hwy 50
(Stateline, NV
89449)
Rates: $179-$269
(775) 588-6611
(800) 427-7247
(Kennels provided)

**HIGH COUNTRY
LODGE**
1227 Emerald Bay
Rd (96150)
Rates: $25-$150
(530) 541-0508

**INN AT HEAVENLY
VALLEY B&B**
1261 Ski Run Blvd
(96150)
Rates: $75-$395
(530) 544-4244
(800) 692-2246

LA BAER INN
4133 Lake Tahoe
Blvd (96150)
Rates: $49-$109
(530) 544-2139
(800) 544-5575

**MATTERHORN
MOTEL**
2187 Lake Tahoe
Blvd (96157)
Rates: $40-$185
(530) 541-0367

**MONTGOMERY
INN**
966 Modesto Ave
(96151)
Rates: $49-$69
(530) 544-3871
(800) 624-8224

SUPER 8 MOTEL
3600 Lake Tahoe
Blvd (96150)
Rates: $44-$118
(530) 544-3476
(800) 237-8882
(800) 800-8000

**TAHOE HACIENDA
MOTEL**
3820 Lake Tahoe
Blvd (96150)
Rates: $35-$85
(530) 541-3805

**TAHOE KEYS
RESORT**
599 Tahoe Keys
Blvd (96150)
Rates: $108-$440
(530) 544-5397
(800) 438-8246

**TAHOE
SUNDOWNER
MOTEL**
1211 Emerald Bay
(96150)
Rates: $30-$140
(530) 541-2282

**TAHOE
TROPICANA
LODGE**
4132 Cedar Ave
(96154)
Rates: $40-$70
(530) 541-3911

**TAHOE VALLEY
LODGE**
2241 Lake Tahoe
Blvd (96150)
Rates: $95-$195
(530) 541-0353
(800) 669-7544

(Lake Tahoe Area
-Tahoe Vista)

**BEESLEY'S
COTTAGES**
6674 N Lake Blvd
(96148)
Rates: $70-$140
(530) 546-2448

HOLIDAY HOUSE
7276 N Lake Blvd
(96148)
Rates: $95-$145
(530) 546-2369
(800) 294-6378 (CA)

RUSTIC COTTAGES
7449 N Lake Blvd
(96148)
Rates: $49-$139
(530) 546-3523

(Lake Tahoe Area
-Tahoma)

**NORFOLK
WOODS
COUNTRY INN**
6941 W Lake Blvd
(96142)
Rates: $100-$170
(530) 525-5000

**TAHOE LAKE
COTTAGES**
7030 W Lake Blvd
(96142)
Rates: $125-$185
(530) 525-4411
(800) 824-6348

TAHOMA LODGE
7018 W Lake Blvd
(96142)
Rates: $45-$115
(530) 525-7721
(800) 824-6348

(Lake Tahoe Area
-Truckee)

**ALPINE VILLAGE
MOTEL**
12660 Deerfield
Dr (96161)
Rates: $50-$79
(530) 587-3801
(800) 933-1787

**THE INN AT
TRUCKEE**
11506 Deerfield Dr
(96161)
Rates: $89-$139
(530) 587-8888
(888) 773-6888

RICHARDS MOTEL
15758 Donner
Pass Rd (96160)
Rates: $60-$110
(530) 587-3662

LAKEHEAD
**ANTLERS RESORT
& MARINA**
P. O. Box 140
(96051)
Rates: $90-$170
(800) 238-3924

**SUGARLOAF
COTTAGES**
19667 Lakeshore
Dr (96051)
Rates: $64-$218
(530) 238-2448
(800) 953-4432

TSASDI RESORT
19990 Lakeshore
Dr (96051)
Rates: $75-$250
(530) 238-2575
(800) 995-0291

LAKEPORT
**LAKE VACATION
RENTALS**
1855 S Main St
(95453)
Rates: $125-$325
(707) 263-7188

RAINBOW MOTEL
2569 Lakeshore
Blvd (95453)
Rates: $34-$55
(707) 263-4309

LAKESHORE
**LAKESHORE
RESORT**
61953 Huntington
Lake Rd (93634)
Rates: $77-$150
(559) 893-3193

**LAKEVIEW
COTTAGES**
58374 Huntington
Ldge Rd (93634)
Rates: $45-$80
(310) 697-6556

LAKEWOOD
CRAZY 8 MOTEL
11535 E Carson St
(90715)
Rates: $34-$42
(562) 860-0546

LANCASTER

BEST WESTERN
ANTELOPE
VALLEY INN
44055 N Sierra
Hwy (93534)
Rates: $89-$132
(661) 948-4651
(800) 528-1234
(800) 810-9430

DESERT INN HOTEL
44219 N Sierra
Hwy (93534)
Rates: $72-$112
(661) 942-8401

MOTEL 6
43540 17th St W
(93534)
Rates: $41-$50
(661) 948-0435
(800) 466-8356

OXFORD INN
1651 W Ave K
(93534)
Rates: $89-$119
(661) 949-3423

**LASSEN
VOLCANIC
NATIONAL PARK**

DRAKESBAD
GUEST RANCH
CR Chester-
Warner Valley
(96020)
Rates: $119-$230
(530) 529-1512

LATHROP

DAYS INN
14750 S Harlan Rd
(95350)
Rates: $60-$81
(209) 982-1959
(800) 329-7466

LAYTONVILLE

THE RANCH
MOTEL
P. O. Box 1535
(95454)
Rates: $26-$45
(707) 984-8456

LEBEC

BEST REST
FLYING J INN
51541 N Peace
Valley Rd (93243)
Rates: $49-$75
(661) 248-2700
(800) 766-9009

RAMADA LTD
COUNTRY INN
9000 Countryside
Court (93243)
Rates: $70-$90
(661) 248-1530
(800) 272-6232

LEE VINING

MURPHEY'S
MOTEL
51493 Hwy 395
(93541)
Rates: $48-$108
(760) 647-6316
(800) 334-6316

LEMOORE

BEST WESTERN
VINEYARD INN
877 East D St
(93245)
Rates: $68-$80
(559) 924-1261
(888) 924-7384

LINDSAY

SUPER 8 MOTEL
390 N Hwy 65
(93247)
Rates: $55-$95
(559) 562-5188
(800) 800-8000

LITTLE RIVER

AUBERGE
SEASIDE
COTTAGES
8200 N Hwy 1
(95456)
Rates: $99-$325
(707) 937-0088

INN AT
SCHOOLHOUSE
CREEK
7051 N. HWY 1
(95456)
800.731-5525
SEE OUR AD
ON FOLLOWING
PAGE 158

LITTLE RIVER INN
P. O. Drawer B
(95456)
Rates: n/a
(707) 937-5942

S S SEAFOAM
LODGE
6751 N Hwy 1
(95456)
Rates: $95-$150
(707) 937-1827
(800) 606-1827

LIVERMORE

MOTEL 6
4673 Lassen Rd
(94550)
Rates: $46-$50
(925) 443-5300
(800) 466-8356

RAMADA LTD
7600 Southfront
Rd (94551)
Rates: $69-$169
(925) 456-5422
(800) 272-6232

RESIDENCE INN
BY MARRIOTT
1000 Airway Blvd
(94550)
Rates: $149-$194
(925) 373-1800
(800) 331-3131

LODI

EL RANCHO
MOTEL
603 N Cherokee
Ln (95240)
Rates: $45-$60
(209) 368-0651

LOMPOC

BEST VALUE INN
1200 North H St
(93436)
Rates: $39-$199
(805) 735-3737

DAYS INN-
VANDENBERG
VILLAGE
3955 Apollo Way
(93436)
Rates: $79-$139
(805) 733-5000
(800) 329-7466

MOTEL 6
1521 North H St
(93436)
Rates: $37-$55
(805) 735-7631
(800) 466-8356

QUALITY INN
& EXEC SUITES
1621 North H St
(93436)
Rates: $79-$119
(805) 735-8555
(800) 424-6423

VAGABOND INN
1122 North H St
(93436)
Rates: $59-$129
(805) 735-7744
(800) 522-1555

LONE PINE

BEST WESTERN
FRONTIER MOTEL
1008 S Main St
(93545)
Rates: $44-$103
(760) 876-5571
(800) 528-1234

DOW VILLA
MOTEL
310 S Main St
(93545)
Rates: $75-$105
(760) 876-5521
(800) 824-9317

LONE PINE
BUDGET INN
MOTEL
138 W Willow St
(93545)
Rates: $39-$99
(760) 876-5655

NATIONAL 9
TRAILS MOTEL
633 S Main St
(93545)
Rates: $39-$99
(760) 876-5555

LONG BEACH

THE COAST
LONG BEACH
HOTEL
700 Queensway
Dr (90802)
Rates: $105-$135
(562) 435-7676

DAYS INN CITY
CENTER
1500 E Pacific
Coast Hwy (90806)
Rates: $60-$100
(562) 591-0088
(800) 329-7466

GUESTHOUSE
HOTEL
5325 E Pacific
Coast Hwy
(90804)
Rates: $79-$89
(562) 597-1341
(800) 214-8378
(800) 990-9991

HILTON HOTEL
Two World Trade
Center (90831)
Rates: $94-$295
(562) 983-3400
(800) 445-8667

HOLIDAY INN-
AIRPORT/
CONV CENTER
2640 N Lakewood
Blvd (90815)
Rates: $79-$129
(562) 597-4401
(800) 465-4329

MOTEL 6
5665 E 7th St
(90804)
Rates: $53-$73
(562) 597-1311
(800) 466-8356

MOTEL 6
1121 E Pacific
Coast Hwy
(90806)
Rates: $48-$70
(562) 591-3321
(800) 466-8356

RENAISSANCE
LONG BEACH
HOTEL
111 E Ocean Blvd
(90802)
Rates: $94-$219
(562) 437-5900

VAGABOND INN
150 Alamitos Ave
(90802)
Rates: $55-$89
(562) 435-7621
(800) 522-1555

THE WESTIN
LONG BEACH
333 E Ocean Blvd
(90802)
Rates: $299-$460
(562) 436-3000
(800) 228-3000

**LOS
ALAMITOS**

RESIDENCE INN
BY MARRIOTT
4931 Katella Ave
(90720)
Rates: $139-$189
(800) 331-3131

LOS ALAMOS

SKYVIEW MOTEL
9150 Hwy 101
(93440)
Rates: $75-$125
(805) 344-3770

AREA CODES - If the local number doesn't connect, check for a new area code.

LOS ALTOS

**RESIDENCE INN
BY MARRIOTT**
4460 El Camino
Real (94022)
Rates: n/a
(650) 559-7890
(800) 331-3131

LOS ANGELES

(Find additional
L A area lodging in
the following cities:
Beverly Hills,
Hollywood, West
Hollywood and
Westwood)

**BEST WESTERN
DRAGON GATE
INN**
818 N Hill St
(90012)
Rates: $99-$169
(213) 617-3077
(800) 528-1234
(800) 282-9999

**BEVERLY HILLS
PLAZA HOTEL**
10300 Wilshire
Blvd (90024)
Rates: $135-$385
(323) 275-5575
(800) 800-1234

**BEVERLY LAUREL
MOTOR HOTEL**
8018 Beverly Blvd
(90048)
Rates: $80-$94
(323) 651-2441
(800) 962-3824

**CENTURY
WILSHIRE HOTEL**
10776 Wilshire
Blvd (90029)
Rates: $65-$85
(800) 421-7223

**CHATEAU
MARMONT HOTEL**
8221 Sunset Blvd
(90046)
Rates: $160-$550
(323) 656-1010
(800) 242-8328

COMFORT INN
1710 W 7th St
(90017)
Rates: $69-$210
(213) 616-3000
(800) 424-6423

**FOUR POINTS BY
SHERATON LAX**
9750 Airport Blvd
(90045)
Rates: $79-$179
(310) 645-6400
(800) 529-4683

FURAMA HOTEL
8601 Lincoln Blvd
(90045)
Rates: $59-$89
(310) 670-8111

**HILTON &
TOWERS/LAX**
5711 W Century
Blvd (90045)
Rates: $148-$168
(310) 410-4000
(800) 445-8667

**HOLIDAY INN-
BRENTWOOD/
BEL AIR**
170 N Church
Ln (90049)
Rates: $99-$119
(310) 476-6411
(800) 465-4329

HOTEL BEL-AIR
701 Stone Canyon
Rd (90077)
Rates: $384-$575
(310) 472-1211

**LUXE HOTEL-
SUNSET
BOULEVARD**
11461 Sunset Blvd
(90049)
Rates: $250
(310) 476-6571

**MARRIOTT
HOTEL/LAX**
5855 W Century
Blvd (90045)
Rates: $99-$259
(310) 641-5700
(800) 228-9290

**OMNI LOS
ANGELES HOTEL**
251 S Olive St
(90012)
Rates: $110-$199
(213) 617-3300
(800) 843-6664

**QUALITY
HOTEL-LAX**
5249 W Century
Blvd (90045)
Rates: $79-$109
(310) 645-2200
(800) 266-2200

**QUALITY INN
& SUITES
DOWNTOWN**
1901 W Olympic
Blvd (90006)
Rates: $79-$109
(213) 385-7141
(800) 424-6423

**RADISSON
HOTEL/LAX**
6225 W Century
Blvd (90045)
Rates: $99-$210
(310) 670-9000
(800) 333-3333

ST. REGIS HOTEL
2055 Ave of the
Stars (90067)
Rates: $485-$650
(310) 277-6111

**SHERATON GATE-
WAY HOTEL**
6101 W Century
Blvd (90045)
Rates: $269-$500
(310) 642-1111
(800) 325-3535

**TRAVELODGE
HOTEL/LAX**
5547 W Century
Blvd (90045)
Rates: $54-$89
(310) 649-4000
(800) 578-7878

**VAGABOND
INN/USC**
3101 S Figueroa St
(90007)
Rates: $75-$85
(213) 746-1531
(800) 522-1555

**W LOS ANGELES
HOTEL**
930 Hilgard Ave
(Westwood
Village 90024)
Rates: $279-$419
(310) 208-8765
(800) 421-2317

**THE WESTIN
CENTURY PLAZA
HOTEL AND SPA**
2025 Avenue of
the Stars (90067)
Rates: $409-$429
(310) 277-2000
(800) 228-3000

**THE WESTIN
HOTEL/LAX**
5400 W Century
Blvd (90045)
Rates: $89-$239
(310) 216-5858
(800) 937-8461

**WESTWOOD
VILLAGE SUITE
HOTEL**
930 Hilgard Ave
(90024)
Rates: $279-$419
(310) 208-8765

WILSHIRE MOTEL
12023 Wilshire
Blvd (90025)
Rates: $50-$60
(323) 478-3545

LOS BANOS

**BEST WESTERN
EXECUTIVE INN**
301 W Pacheco
Blvd (93635)
Rates: $56-$86
(209) 827-0954
(800) 528-1234

DAYS INN
2169 E Pacheco
Blvd (93635)
Rates: $39-$79
(209) 826-9690
(800) 329-7466

REGENCY INN
349 W Pacheco
Blvd (93635)
Rates: $39-$55
(209) 826-3871

LOS GATOS

**LOS GATOS
LODGE**
50 Saratoga Los
Gatos Rd (95032)
Rates: $89-$159
(408) 354-3300

LOS OSOS

**SEA PINES GOLF
RESORT**
1945 Solano St
(93402)
Rates: $99-$139
(805) 528-5252

LOST HILLS

DAYS INN
14684 Aloma St
(93249)
Rates: $35-$129
(661) 797-2371
(800) 329-7466

MOTEL 6
14685 Warren St
(93249)
Rates: $33-$38
(661) 797-2346
(800) 466-8356

LUCERNE

**BEACHCOMBER
RESORT**
6345 E Hwy 20
(95458)
Rates: $40-$85
(707) 274-6639

STARLITE MOTEL
5960 E Hwy 20
(95458)
Rates: $40-$85
(707) 274-5515

MADERA

**BEST WESTERN
MADERA VALLEY
INN**
317 North G St
(93637)
Rates: $65-$150
(559) 664-0100
(800) 528-1234

MOTEL 6
22683 Ave 18 1/2
(93637)
Rates: $49-$85
(559) 675-8697
(800) 466-8356

SUPER 8 MOTEL
1855 W Cleveland
Ave (93637)
Rates: $55-$65
(559) 661-1131
(800) 800-8000

MAMMOTH LAKES

**CONVICT LAKE
RESORT**
Rt 1, Box 204
(93546)
Rates: $65-$350
(760) 934-3800
(800) 992-2260

AREA CODES - If the local number doesn't connect, check for a new area code.

DISCOVERY 4 CONDOS
25 Lee Rd (93546)
Rates: $132-$308
(760) 934-6410

ECONO LODGE WILDWOOD INN
3626 Main St
(93546)
Rates: $59-$149
(760) 934-6855
(800) 424-6423
(800) 845-8764

MAMMOTH SKI & RACQUET CLUB
248 Mammoth
Slopes Dr (93546)
Rates: $105-$322
(760) 934-7368

MOTEL 6
3372 Main St
(93546)
Rates: $49-$80
(760) 934-6660
(800) 466-8356

RODEWAY INN SIERRA NEVADA
164 Old
Mammoth Rd
(93546)
Rates: $89-$429
(760) 934-2515
(800) 424-6423

SHILO INN
2963 Main St
(93546)
Rates: $99-$219
(760) 934-4500
(800) 222-2244

SIERRA LODGE
3540 Main St
(93546)
Rates: $59-$199
(760) 934-8881
(800) 356-5711

SWISS CHALET MOTEL
3776 Viewpoint
Rd (93546)
Rates: $65-$120
(760) 934-2403

ZWART HOUSE, THE FAMILY LODGE
76 Lupine St
(93546)
Rates: $50-$80
(760) 934-2217

MANHATTAN BEACH
RESIDENCE INN BY MARRIOTT
1700 N Sepulveda
Blvd (90266)
Rates: $278-$299
(310) 546-7627
(800) 331-3131

MANTECA
BEST WESTERN EXEC INN & SUITES
1415 E Yosemite
Ave (95336)
Rates: $65-$85
(209) 825-1415
(800) 528-1234

MARINA
HERITAGE MARINA DAYS INN
416 Reservation
Rd (93933)
Rates: n/a
(831) 384-9784
(800) 329-7466

MOTEL 6
100 Reservation
Rd (93933)
Rates: $43-$73
(831) 384-1000
(800) 466-8356

MARIPOSA
BEST VALUE MARIPOSA LODGE
5052 Hwy 140
(95338)
Rates: $49-$129
(209) 966-3607
(800) 966-8819

BEST WESTERN YOSEMITE WAY STATION
4999 S Hwy 140
(95338)
Rates: $44-$96
(209) 966-7545
(800) 528-1234
(800) 321-5261

MINERS INN
5181 Hwy 49 N
(95338)
Rates: $45-$159
(209) 742-7777
(800) 321-5261

MARKLEEVILLE
J. MARKLEE TOLL STATION HOTEL
14856 Hwy 89
(96120)
Rates: $40
(530) 694-2507

THE MOUNTAIN & GARDEN B&B
250 Old Pony
Express Rd
(96120)
Rates: n/a
(530) 694-0012

MARYSVILLE
BEST VALUE INN
904 E St (95901)
Rates: $45-$80
(530) 743-1531

MCKINLEYVILLE
SEA VIEW MOTEL
1186 Central Ave
(95521)
Rates: $35-$125
(707) 839-1321

MENDOCINO
ABIGAIL'S BED & BREAKFAST
951 Ukiah St
(95460)
Rates: $99-$299
(707) 937-0934

BLACKBERRY INN
44951 Larkin Rd
(95460)
Rates: $105-$215
(707) 937-5281
(800) 950-7806

THE GRINDLE GUEST HOUSE
44800 Little Lake
Rd (95460)
Rates: n/a
(707) 937-4143
(800) GRINDLE

HILL HOUSE INN
10701 Pallette Dr
(95460)
Rates: $121-$250
(707) 937-0554

THE INN AT SCHOOLHOUSE CREEK B&B
7051 N Hwy 1
(95460)
Rates: $130-$235
(707) 937-5525
(800) 731-5525

MACCALLUM HOUSE INN
45020 Albion St
(95460)
Rates: $120-$325
(707) 937-0289
(800) 609-0492

MCELROY'S INN B&B
998 Main St
(95460)
Rates: $85-$115
(707) 937-1734

MENDOCINO SEASIDE COTTAGE B&B
10940 Lansing St
(95460)
Rates: $145-$391
(707) 485-0239
(800) 94-HEART

SALLIE & EILEEN'S PLACE FOR WOMEN ONLY
P.O. Box 409
(95460)
Rates: $65-$80
(707) 937-2028

STANFORD INN BY THE SEA
44850 Comptche-
Ukiah Rd (95460)
Rates: $215-$475
(707) 937-5615
(800) 331-8884

MERCED
MOTEL 6-NORTH
1410 V St (95340)
Rates: $39-$50
(209) 384-2181
(800) 466-8356

PS HAPPY INN
740 Motel Dr
(95340)
Rates: n/a
(209) 722-6291

SAN JOAQUIN MOTEL
1439 W 16th St
(95340)
Rates: n/a
(209) 722-2761

SANDPIPER LODGE
1001 Motel Dr
(95340)
Rates: $36-$58
(209) 723-1034

SIERRA LODGE
951 Motel Dr
(95340)
Rates: n/a
(209) 722-3926

SLUMBER MOTEL
1315 W 16th St
(95340)
Rates: n/a
(209) 722-5783

TRAVELODGE
1260 Yosemite
Pkwy (95340)
Rates: $45-$75
(209) 722-6224
(800) 578-7878

MI-WUK VILLAGE
MI-WUK VILLAGE INN & RESORT
24680 Hwy 108
(95346)
Rates: $99-$160
(209) 586-3031
(800) 341-8000

MIDPINES
HOMESTEAD GUEST RANCH
P. O. Box 113 (95345)
Rates: $95-$130
(209) 966-2820

LION'S DEN RETREAT
5125 Chamberlain
Rd (95345)
Rates: $75-$110
(209) 966-5254

MUIR LODGE HOTEL
6833 Hwy 140
Midpines (95345)
Rates: $28-$78
(209) 966-2468

MILL CREEK
CHILDS MEADOW ALL SEASON RESORT
41500 Hwy 36 E
(96061)
Rates: $50-$240+
(530) 595-3383

MILLBRAE
CLARION HOTEL SF AIRPORT
401 E Millbrae
Ave (94030)
Rates: $69-$179
(650) 692-6363
(800) 424-6423

AREA CODES - If the local number doesn't connect, check for a new area code.

WESTIN SF AIRPORT
1 Old Bayshore Hwy (94030)
Rates: $189
(650) 692-3500
(800) 937-8461

MILPITAS
BEST WESTERN BROOKSIDE INN
400 Valley Way (95035)
Rates: $59-$139
(408) 263-5566
(800) 528-1234
(800) 995-8834

CANDLEWOOD SUITES
40 Ranch Dr (95035)
Rates: $59-$179
(408) 719-1212
(888) 226-3539

HOMESTEAD STUDIO SUITES
330 Cypress Dr (95035)
Rates: $79-$99
(408) 433-9700
(888) 782-9473

INNS OF AMERICA
270 S Abbott Ave (95035)
Rates: $79+
(408) 946-8889
(800) 826-0778

RESIDENCE INN BY MARRIOTT
1501 California Cir (95035)
Rates: $89-$159
(408) 941-9222
(800) 331-3131

SHERATON SAN JOSE AT SILICON VALLEY
1801 Barber Ln (95035)
Rates: $59-$189
(408) 943-0600
(800) 325-3535

TOWNEPLACE SUITES
1428 Falcon Dr (95035)
Rates: $59-$129
(408) 719-1959
(800) 257-3000

MIRANDA
MIRANDA GARDENS RESORT
6766 Avenue of the Giants (95553)
Rates: $95-$225
(707) 943-3011

MISSION HILLS
BEST WESTERN MISSION HILLS INN
10621 Sepulveda Blvd (91345)
Rates: $64-$85
(818) 891-1771
(800) 528-1234
(800) 352-5670

MODESTO
BEST WESTERN TOWN HOUSE LODGE
909 16th St (95354)
Rates: $70-$85
(209) 524-7261
(800) 528-1234

DOUBLETREE HOTEL
1150 9th St (95354)
Rates: $69-$169
(209) 526-6000
(800) 733-5466

HOWARD JOHNSON EXP INN
1672 Herndon Rd (95307)
Rates: $60-$90
(209) 537-4821
(800) 446-4656

MICROTEL INN & SUITES
1760 Herndon Rd (95307)
Rates: $64-$99
(209) 538-6466

MOTEL 6
1920 W Orangeburg Ave (95350)
Rates: $43-$60
(209) 522-7271
(800) 466-8356

RED LION HOTEL
1612 Sisk Rd (95350)
Rates: n/a
(209) 521-1612
(800) 733-5466

TRAVELODGE
722 Kansas Ave (95351)
Rates: $45-$70
(209) 524-3251
(800) 578-7878

MOJAVE
BEST VALUE INN
16352 Sierra Hwy (93501)
Rates: $50-$80
(661) 824-9317

BEST WESTERN DESERT WINDS
16200 Sierra Hwy (93501)
Rates: $69-$82
(661) 824-3601
(800) 528-1234
(800) 969-3601

DESERT INN
1954 Hwy 58 (93501)
Rates: $42-$54
(661) 824-2518
(800) 305-1625

ECONO LODGE
2145 Hwy 58 (93501)
Rates: $36-$129
(661) 824-2463
(800) 424-6423

MARIAH COUNTRY INN & SUITES
1385 Hwy 58 (93501)
Rates: $90-$95
(661) 824-4980

MOTEL 6
16958 Hwy 58 (93501)
Rates: $36+
(661) 824-4571
(800) 466-8356

MONROVIA
HOMESTEAD STUDIO SUITES HOTEL
930 S Fifth Ave (91016)
Rates: $81-$106
(626) 256-6999
(888) 782-9473

MONTARA
FARALLONE INN BED & BREAKFAST
1410 Main St (94037)
Rates: $75-$150
(415) 728-8200
(800) 350-9777

MONTE RIO
ANGELO'S RESORT
20285 River Blvd (95462)
Rates: $50-$150
(707) 865-9080

HIGHLAND DELL INN B&B
21050 River Blvd (95462)
Rates: $85-$250
(707) 865-1759
(800) 767-1759

MONTECITO
SAN YSIDRO RANCH
900 San Ysidro Ln (93108)
Rates: $195-$995
(805) 969-5046
(800) 368-6788

MONTEREY
BAY PARK HOTEL
1425 Munras Ave (93940)
Rates: $79-$259
(831) 649-1020
(800) 338-3564

BEST WESTERN THE BEACH RSRT
2600 Sand Dunes Dr (93940)
Rates: $99-$389
(831) 394-3321
(800) 528-1234
(800) 242-8627

BEST WESTERN VICTORIAN INN
487 Foam St (93940)
Rates: $119-$439
(831) 373-8000
(800) 528-1234
(800) 232-4141

EL ADOBE INN
936 Munras Ave (93940)
Rates: $49-$199
(831) 372-5409
(800) 433-4732

HYATT REGENCY MONTEREY RESORT
1 Old Golf Course Rd (93940)
Rates: $139-$249
(831) 372-1234
(800) 233-1234

MONTEREY BAY LODGE
55 Camino Aguajito (93940)
Rates: $89-$319
(831) 372-8057
(800) 588-1900

MONTEREY FIRESIDE LODGE
1131 10th St (93940)
Rates: $59-$309
(831) 373-4172

MOTEL 6
2124 N Fremont St, Old Hwy 1 (93940)
Rates: $51-$90
(831) 646-8585
(800) 466-8356

MONTEREY PARK
DAYS INN & SUITES
434 Potrero Grande Dr (91755)
Rates: $56-$129
(323) 728-8444
(800) 329-7466

MORENO VALLEY
COMFORT INN
23330 Sunnymead Blvd (92553)
Rates: $59-$109
(909) 242-0699
(800) 424-6423

ECONO LODGE
24412 Sunnymead Blvd (92553)
Rates: $60-$140
(909) 247-6699
(800) 424-6423

MORGAN HILL
BEST WESTERN COUNTRY INN
16525 Condit Rd (95037)
Rates: $65-$119
(408) 779-0447
(800) 528-1234
(888) 434-1444

AREA CODES - If the local number doesn't connect, check for a new area code.

RESIDENCE INN BY MARRIOTT
18620 Madrone Pkwy (95037)
Rates: $119-$149
(408) 782-8311
(800) 331-3131

MORRO BAY

BEST WESTERN EL RANCHO INN
2460 Main St (93442)
Rates: $59-$149
(805) 772-2212
(800) 528-1234
(800) 628-3500

COFFEY BREAK B&B
213 Dunes St (93442)
Rates: $75-$125
(805) 772-4378

DAYS INN
1095 Main St (93442)
Rates: $59-$249
(805) 772-2711
(800) 329-7466

GOLDEN PELICAN
3270 N Main St (93442)
Rates: $40-$125
(805) 772-7135

MORRO BAY SANDPIPER/ KEYSTONE INN
540 Main St (93442)
Rates: $49-$169
(805) 772-7503

MORRO HILLTOP HOUSE
1200 Morro Ave (93442)
Rates: $40-$75
(805) 772-1890

MOTEL 6
298 Atascadero Rd (93442)
Rates: $35-$75
(805) 772-5641
(800) 466-8356

PLEASANT INN MOTEL
235 Harbor St (93442)
Rates: $35-$89
(805) 772-8521
(888) 772-8521

SUNDOWN MOTEL
640 Main St (93442)
Rates: $36-$135
(805) 772-7381
(800) 696-6928

VILLAGER MOTEL
1098 Main St (93442)
Rates: $40-$199
(805) 772-1235

MOUNT SHASTA

A-1 CHOICE INN
1340 S Mt Shasta Blvd (96067)
Rates: $59-$99
(530) 926-4811

BEST WESTERN TREE HOUSE MOTOR INN
111 Morgan Way (96067)
Rates: $91-$159
(530) 926-3101
(800) 528-1234
(800) 545-7164

ECONO LODGE
908 S Mt. Shasta Blvd (96067)
Rates: $49-$145
(530) 926-3145
(800) 424-6423

MOUNT SHASTA RANCH B&B
1008 W A Barr Rd (96067)
Rates: $60-$125
(530) 926-3870

MOUNTAIN AIR LODGE
1121 S Mt. Shasta Blvd (96067)
Rates: $42-$125
(530) 926-3411

SHASTA LODGE MOTEL
724 N Mt. Shasta Blvd (96067)
Rates: $29-$55
(530) 926-2815
(800) 742-7821

SHELDON HOUSE & COTTAGE RENTAL
624 S Mt. Shasta Blvd (96067)
Rates: $75-$250
(530) 926-0619

SWISS HOLIDAY LODGE
2400 S Mt. Shasta Blvd (96067)
Rates: $40-$80
(530) 926-3446

TRAVEL INN
504 S Mt. Shasta Blvd (96067)
Rates: $24-$60
(530) 926-4617

VILLAS VACATION RENTAL/CABINS
P. O. Box 344 (96067)
Rates: $30-$125
(530) 926-3313

WAGON CREEK INN B&B
1239 Woodland Park Dr (96067)
Rates: $65-$75
(530) 926-0838
(800) 995-9260

MOUNTAIN VIEW

HOMESTEAD STUDIO SUITES
190 E El Camino Real (94040)
Rates: $79-$99
(650) 962-1500
(888) 782-9473

QUALITY INN
5 Fairchild Dr (94043)
Rates: $89-$179
(650) 934-0155
(800) 424-6423

TROPICANA LODGE
1720 El Camino Real W (94040)
Rates: $70-$105
(650) 961-0220
(888) 961-0502

MURPHYS

THE CHURCH STREET COTTAGE
485 Church St (95247)
Rates: $125-$155
(209) 736-9372

THE LITTLE YEL-LOW COTTAGE
541 S Algiers St (95247)
Rates: $125-$155
(209) 736-9372

THE PARKSIDE COTTAGE
549 S Algiers St (95247)
Rates: $125-$155
(209) 736-9372

MYERS FLAT

LOG CHAPEL INN
P. O. Box 195 (95554)
Rates: $35-$50
(707) 943-3315

NAPA

THE CHABLIS INN
3360 Solano Ave (94558)
Rates: $100-$235
(707) 257-1944
(800) 443-3490

THE NAPA INN B&B
1137 Warren St (94558)
Rates: $120-$295
(707) 257-1444

NAPA RIVER INN
500 Main St (94558)
Rates: $159-$499
(707) 251-8500
(877) 251-8500

NAPA VALLEY REDWOOD INN
3380 Solano Ave (94558)
Rates: $67-$150
(707) 257-6111
(877) 872-6272

NATIONAL CITY

RED LION INN & SUITES
810 National City Blvd (91950)
Rates: $69-$139
(619) 336-1100
(800) 733-5466

NEEDLES

BEST WESTERN COLORADO RIVER INN
2371 W Broadway (92363)
Rates: $50-$150
(760) 326-4552
(800) 528-1234

BEST WESTERN ROYAL INN
1111 Pashard St (92363)
Rates: $45-$75
(760) 326-5660
(800) 528-1234

DAYS INN & SUITES
1215 Hospitality Ln (92363)
Rates: $35-$175
(760) 326-5836
(800) 329-7466

IMPERIAL 400 MOTOR INN
644 W Broadway (92363)
Rates: $28-$48
(760) 326-2145

MOTEL 6-NORTH
1420 J St. (92363)
Rates: $35-$46
(760) 326-3399
(800) 466-8356

OLD TRAILS INN BED & BREAKFAST
304 Broadway (92363)
Rates: $40-$65
(760) 326-3523

OVERLAND INN
712 W Broadway (92363)
Rates: $25-$30
(760) 326-8808

RIVER VALLEY MOTOR LODGE
1707 W Broadway (92363)
Rates: $23-$35
(760) 326-3839
(800) 346-2331

SUPER 8 MOTEL
1102 E. Broadway (92363)
Rates: $44-$59
(760) 326-4501
(800) 800-8000

TRAVELERS INN
1195 3rd St Hill (92363)
Rates: $30-$65
(760) 326-4900

AREA CODES - If the local number doesn't connect, check for a new area code.

NEVADA CITY

NEVADA CITY INN MOTEL
760 Zion St
(95959)
Rates: $69-$99
(530) 265-2253
(800) 977-8884

NEVADA STREET COTTAGES
690 Nevada St
(95959)
Rates: $60-$100
(530) 265-8071

OUTSIDE INN
575 E Broad St
(95959)
Rates: $55-$120
(530) 265-2233

NEWARK

HOMEWOOD SUITES
39270 Cedar Blvd
(94560)
Rates: $109
(510) 791-7700
(800) 225-5466

MOTEL 6
5600 Cedar Ct
(94560)
Rates: $39-$46
(510) 791-5900
(800) 466-8356

RESIDENCE INN BY MARRIOTT
34566 Dumbarton Ct (94560)
Rates: $99-$199
(510) 739-6000
(800) 331-3131

TOWNEPLACE SUITES
39802 Cedar Blvd
(94560)
Rates: $59-$99
(510) 657-4600
(800) 257-3000

WOODFIN SUITES
39150 Cedar Blvd
(94560)
Rates: $89-$129
(510) 795-1200
(800) 237-8811

NEWBURY PARK

CLARION PALM GARDEN HOTEL
495 N Ventu Park Rd (91320)
Rates: $150+
(805) 716-4200
(800) 424-6423

MOTEL 6
1516 Newbury Rd
(91320)
Rates: $39-$54
(805) 499-0711
(800) 466-8356

PREMIER INNS
2434 W Hillcrest Dr (91320)
Rates: $30-$75
(805) 499-0755

NEWPORT BEACH

BALBOA BAY CLUB & RESORT
1221 West Coast Hwy (92663)
Rates: $225-$500
(949) 645-5000

FOUR SEASONS HOTEL-NEWPORT BEACH
690 Newport Center Dr (92660)
Rates: $295-$355
(949) 759-0808
(800) 268-6282

HYATT NEWPORTER
1107 Jamboree Rd
(92660)
Rates: $125-$185
(949) 729-1234
(800) 233-1234
(800) 532-7496

MARRIOTT HOTEL & TENNIS CLUB
900 Newport Center Dr (92660)
Rates: $159-$189
(949) 640-4000
(800) 228-9290

THE SUTTON PLACE HOTEL
4500 MacArthur Blvd (92660)
Rates: $129-$169
(949) 476-2001
(800) 305-0276

NICE

TALLEY'S FAMILY RESORT
3827 E Hwy 20
(95464)
Rates: $45-$90
(707) 274-1177

NIPINNAWASSEE

DEER VALLEY INN BED & BREAKFAST
45013 Hwy 49
(93601)
Rates: $49-$175
(209) 683-2155

NORCO

HOWARD JOHNSON EXP
1695 Hamner Ave
(91760)
Rates: $35-$70
(909) 278-8886
(800) 446-4656

NORTH FORK

SOUTH FORK MOTEL
57714 Mammoth Pool Rd (93643)
Rates: $38+
(209) 877-2237

NORTH HIGHLANDS

MOTEL 6
4600 Watt Ave
(95660)
Rates: $43-$59
(916) 973-8637
(800) 466-8356

NORTH HILLS

HOWARD JOHNSON
9401 Sepulveda Blvd (91343)
Rates: $45-$79
(818) 892-0751
(800) 446-4656

MOTEL 6
15711 Roscoe Blvd
(91343)
Rates: $45-$63
(818) 894-9341
(800) 466-8356

NORWALK

MOTEL 6
10646 E Rosecrans Ave (90650)
Rates: $47-$60
(562) 864-2567
(800) 466-8356

RAMADA INN
12500 Firestone Blvd (90650)
Rates: n/a
(562) 868-0991
(800) 272-62323

NOVATO

DAYS INN
8141 Redwood Blvd (94945)
Rates: $64-$159
(415) 897-7111
(800) 329-7466

INN MARIN
250 Entrada Dr
(94949)
Rates: $99-$179
(415) 883-5952
(800) 652-6565

TRAVELODGE RUSH CREEK
7600 Redwood Blvd (94945)
Rates: $64-$94
(415) 892-7500
(800) 578-7878

OAKHURST

BEST WESTERN YOSEMITE GATEWAY INN
40530 Hwy 41
(93644)
Rates: $46-$149
(559) 683-2378
(800) 528-1234
(800) 545-5462

COMFORT INN
40489 Hwy 41
(93644)
Rates: $49-$139
(559) 683-8282
(800) 424-6423

PINE ROSE INN B&B
41703 Road 222
(93644)
Rates: $89-$159
(559) 642-2800
(866) 642-2800

OAKLAND

BEST WESTERN INN AT THE SQUARE
233 Broadway
(94607)
Rates: $99-$159
(510) 452-4565
(800) 528-1234

BROWN'S YOSEMITE CABIN
7187 Yosemite Pkwy (94605)
Rates: $55-$75
(510) 430-8466

CLARION SUITES LAKE MERRITT HISTORIC HOTEL
1800 Madison St
(94612)
Rates: $179-$299
(510) 832-2300
(800) 933-4683
(800) 424-6423

HILTON HOTEL OAKLAND AIRPORT
1 Hegenberger Rd
(94614)
Rates: $69-$249
(510) 635-5000
(800) 445-8667

HOMEWOOD SUITES
1103 Embarcadero
(94606)
Rates: $99-$269
(510) 663-2700
(800) 225-5466

MOTEL 6 AIRPORT
8480 Edes Ave
(94612)
Rates: $56+
(510) 638-1180
(800) 466-8356

MOTEL 6 EMBARCADERO
1801 Embarcadero
(94606)
Rates: $69-$76
(510) 436-0103
(800) 466-8356

RAMADA LTD
8471 Enterprise Way (94621)
Rates: n/a
(510) 562-4888
(800) 272-6232

OAKLEY

COMFORT SUITES
5549 Bridgehead Rd (94561)
Rates: $79-$160
(925) 755-1222
(800) 424-6423

OCCIDENTAL

OCCIDENTAL LODGE
3610 Bohemian Hwy (95465)
Rates: $59-$119
(707) 874-3623

UNION HOTEL
3731 Main St (95465)
Rates: $38-$55
(707) 874-3555

OCEANSIDE

LA QUINTA INN
937 N Coast Hwy (92054)
Rates: $71-$125
(760) 450-0730
(800) 687-6667

MOTEL 6
3708 Plaza Dr (92056)
Rates: $45-$60
(760) 941-1011
(800) 466-8356

MOTEL 6 DOWNTOWN
909 N Coast Hwy (92054)
Rates: $59-$87
(760) 721-1542
(800) 466-8356

OJAI

BEST WESTERN CASA OJAI
1302 E Ojai Ave (93023)
Rates: $75-$179
(805) 646-8175
(800) 528-1234
(800) 255-8175

BLUE IGUANA INN
11794 N Ventura Ave (93023)
Rates: $105-$145
(805) 646-5277

OAKRIDGE INN
780 N Ventura Ave (93023)
Rates: $65-$125
(805) 649-4018

OJAI VALLEY INN & SPA
905 Country Club Rd (93023)
Rates: $245-$4000
(805) 646-1111
(800) 422-6524

OLEMA

RIDGETOP INN & COTTAGES
9865 Sir Francis Drake Bl (94950)
Rates: $95-$150
(415) 663-1500

ONTARIO

AMERISUITES
4760 E Mills Cir (91764)
Rates: $79-$159
(909) 980 2200
(800) 833-1516

BAYMONT INN & SUITES
4395 E Ontario Mills Pkwy (91764)
Rates: $81-$117
(909) 987-5940
(877) 229-6668

BEST WESTERN COUNTRY INN
2359 S Grove Ave (91761)
Rates: $79-$129
(909) 923-1887
(800) 528-1234
(800) 770-1887

COUNTRY INN & SUITES BY CARLSON
231 N Vineyard Ave (91764)
Rates: $114-$194
(909) 937-6000
(800) 456-4000

DOUBLETREE HOTEL
222 N Vineyard Ave (91764)
Rates: $94-$254
(909) 937-0900
(800) 222-8733

HILTON ONTARIO AIRPORT
700 N Haven Ave (91764)
Rates: $99-$219
(909) 980-0400
(800) 445-8667

HOLIDAY INN EXP ONTARIO AIRPT
3400 Shelby St (91764)
Rates: $105-$125
(909) 466-9600
(800) 465-4329

LA QUINTA

INN & SUITES
3555 Inland Empire Blvd (91764)
Rates: $90-$140
(909) 476-1112
(800) 687-6667

MOTEL 6 AIRPORT
1560 E 4th St (91764)
Rates: $39-$56
(909) 984-2424
(800) 466-8356

RESIDENCE INN BY MARRIOTT
2025 Convention Center Way (91764)
Rates: $135-$161
(909) 937-6788
(800) 331-3131

ORANGE

HILTON SUITES
400 N State College Blvd (92868)
Rates: $95-$225
(714) 938-1111
(800) 445-8667

MOTEL 6-ANAHEIM STADIUM
2920 W Chapman Ave (92868)
Rates: $39-$56
(714) 634-2441
(800) 466-8356

ORICK

ROLF'S PARK MOTEL
Davidson Rd (95555)
Rates: $29-$35
(707) 488-3841

ORLAND

AMBER LIGHT INN MOTEL
828 Newville Rd (95963)
Rates: $48-$58
(530) 865-7655

ORLAND INN
1052 South St (95963)
Rates: $51-$61
(530) 865-7632

OROVILLE

BEST VALUE INN
580 Oro Dam Blvd (95965)
Rates: $55-$110
(530) 533-7070

COMFORT INN CENTRAL
1470 Feather River Blvd (95965)
Rates: $74-$150
(530) 553-9673
(800) 424-6423

DAYS INN
1745 Feather River Blvd (95965)
Rates: $40-$99
(530) 533-3297
(800) 329-7466

MOTEL 6
505 Montgomery St (95965)
Rates: $36-$42
(530) 532-9400
(800) 466-8356

SUNSET INN
1835 Feather River Blvd (95965)
Rates: $40-$150
(530) 533-8201

OXNARD

BEST WESTERN OXNARD INN
1156 S Oxnard Blvd (93030)
Rates: $89-$109
(805) 483-9581
(800) 469-6273

CASA SIRENA HOTEL & MARINA
3605 Peninsula Rd (93035)
Rates: $79-$170
(805) 985-6311
(800) 447-3529

RESIDENCE IN AT RIVER RIDGE
2101 W Vineyard Ave (93030)
Rates: $128-$167
(805) 278-2200
(800) 331-3131

VAGABOND INN
1245 N Oxnard Blvd (93030)
Rates: $52-$74
(805) 983-0251
(800) 522-1555

VILLA MOTEL
1715 S Oxnard Blvd (93030)
Rates: $49
(805) 487-1370

PACIFIC GROVE

BIDE-A-WEE INN & COTTAGES
221 Asilomar Ave (93950)
Rates: $69-$169
(831) 372-2330

THE GATEHOUSE INN B&B
225 Central Ave (93950)
Rates: $125-$220
(831) 649-8436

OLYMPIA MOTOR LODGE
1140 Lighthouse Ave (93950)
Rates: $110-$180
(831) 373-2777

SEA BREEZE INN & COTTAGES
1100 Lighthouse Ave (93950)
Rates: $69-$179
(831) 372-7771

SEA BREEZE LODGE
1101 Lighthouse Ave (93950)
Rates: $59-$159
(831) 372-3431
(800) 525-3373

PALM DESERT

BEST WESTERN PALM DESERT RESORT
74-635 Hwy 111 (92260)
Rates: $69-$229
(760) 340-4441
(800) 231-8675

CASA LARREA RESORT
73-811 Larrea St (92260)
Rates: $64-$104
(760) 568-0311

COMFORT SUITES
39-585 Washington St (92211)
Rates: $69-$189
(760) 360-3337
(800) 424-6423

DESERT PATCH INN
73-758 Shadow
Mtn Dr (92260)
Rates: $47-$124
(760) 346-9161
(800) 350-9758

**DESERT SPRINGS/
J W MARRIOTT
RESORT & SPA**
74-855 Country
Club Dr (92260)
Rates: $99-$445
(760) 341-2211
(800) 228-9290

**THE INN AT
DEEP CANYON**
74-470 Abronia
Trail (92260)
Rates: $74-$261
(760) 346-8061
(800) 253-0004

MOTEL 6
78100 Varner Rd
(92261)
Rates: $45-$66
(760) 345-0550
(800) 466-8356

**RESIDENCE INN
BY MARRIOTT**
38-305 Cook St
(92211)
Rates: $89-$199
(760) 776-0050
(800) 331-3131

PALM SPRINGS
**A PLACE IN THE
SUN MOTEL**
754 San Lorenzo
Rd (92264)
Rates: $69-$179
(760) 325-0254

**CALIENTE
TROPICS RESORT**
411 E Palm Cyn
Dr (92264)
Rates: $65-$225
(760) 327-1391
(866) 468-9595

**CASA CODY
COUNTRY INN**
175 S Cahuilla Rd
(92262)
Rates: $59-$349
(760) 320-9346
(800) 231-2639

**COMFORT INN
RESORT**
390 S Indian Cyn
Dr (92264)
Rates: $69-$159
(760) 778-3699
(800) 424-6423
(888) 322-1997

**HILTON PALM
SPRINGS RESORT**
400 E Tahquitz
Cyn Way (92262)
Rates: $98-$189
(760) 320-6868
(800) 445-8667
(800) 522-6900

**HOTEL
CALIFORNIA**
424 E Palm Cyn
Dr (92264)
Rates: $69-$135
(760) 322-8855

IRONSIDE HOTEL
310 E Palm Cyn
Dr (92264)
Rates: $35-$75
(760) 325-1995

**LA MANCHA
VILLAS & SPA
RESORT**
444 N Avenida
Caballeros (92262)
Rates: $99-$699
(760) 323-1773

**LA SERENA
VILLAS**
339 S Belardo Rd
(92262)
Rates: $55-$180
(760) 325-3216

**MOTEL 6-
DOWNTOWN**
660 S Palm Cyn Dr
(92264)
Rates: $36-$58
(760) 327-4200
(800) 466-8356

MOTEL 6-EAST
595 E Palm Cyn
Dr (92264)
Rates: $39-$54
(760) 325-6129
(800) 466-8356

MOTEL 6-NORTH
63950 20th Ave
(North Palm
Springs 92258)
Rates: $39-$52
(760) 251-1425
(800) 466-8356

MUSICLAND HOTEL
1342 S Palm Cyn
Dr (92264)
Rates: $29-$99
(760) 325-1326
(800) 428-3939

**PALM GARDEN
RESORT**
950 N Indian Cyn
Dr (92262)
Rates: $35-$149
(760) 323-1328

**PALM SPRINGS
RIVIERA RESORT**
1600 N Indian Cyn
Dr (92262)
Rates: $89-$269
(760) 327-8311
(800) 444-8311

**PALM SPRINGS
VACATION
RENTAL AGENCY**
225 S Civic Dr -#7
(92262)
Rates: $45-$900
(760) 320-7451
(800) 410-3575

**PARK INN
& SUITES**
2000 N Palm Cyn
Dr (92262)
Rates: $69-$119
(760) 320-0555

**THE PARKER
PALM SPRINGS**
4200 E Palm Cyn
Dr (92262)
Rates: n/a
(760) 770-5000

PLAZA RESORT
2601 Golf Club Dr
(92264)
Rates: $79-$169
(760) 324-1802
(800) 438-6493

**QUALITY INN
RESORT**
1269 E Palm Cyn
Dr (92264)
Rates: $49-$109
(760) 323-2775
(800) 424-6423

**RAMADA RESORT
INN & CONF CTR**
1800 E Palm Cyn
Dr (92264)
Rates: $109-$199
(760) 323-1711
(800) 272-6232

**SAN MARINO
HOTEL**
225 W Baristo Rd
(92262)
Rates: $69-$169
(760) 325-6902

SUPER 8 LODGE
1900 N Palm Cyn
Dr (92262)
Rates: $45-$86
(760) 322-3757
(800) 800-8000

VAGABOND INN
1699 S Palm Cyn
Dr (92262)
Rates: $49-$129
(760) 325-7211
(800) 522-1555

**VICEROY
PALM SPRINGS**
415 S Belardo Rd
(92262)
Rates: $165-$265
(760) 320-4117
(800) 237-3687

VILLA ROSA INN
1577 S Indian Tr
(92264)
Rates: $109-$165
(760) 327-5915

**WYNDHAM PALM
SPIRNGS**
888 Tahquitz Cyn
Way (92262)
Rates: $99-$189
(760) 322-6000
(800) 996-3426

PALMDALE
HOLIDAY INN
38630 5th St W
(93551)
Rates: $99-$149
(661) 947-8055
(800) 465-4329

MOTEL 6
407 W Palmdale
Blvd (93551)
Rates: $39-$46
(661) 272-0660
(800) 466-8356

**RESIDENCE INN
BY MARRIOTT**
514 W Ave P
(93551)
Rates: $140-$180
(661) 947-4204
(800) 331-3131

PALO ALTO
CARDINAL HOTEL
235 Hamilton Ave
(94301)
Rates: $70-$200
(650) 323-5101

CORONET MOTEL
2455 El Camino
Real (94306)
Rates: $38-$40
(650) 326-1081

**CROWNE PLAZA
CABANA HOTEL**
4290 El Camino
Real (94306)
Rates: $189-$219
(650) 857-0787
(800) 227-6963

MOTEL 6
4301 El Camino
Real (94306)
Rates: $55-$60
(650) 949-0833
(800) 466-8356

**SHERATON PALO
ALTO HOTEL**
625 El Camino
Real (94301)
Rates: $209-$279
(650) 328-2800
(800) 325-3535

TRAVELODGE
3255 El Camino
Real (94306)
Rates: n/a
(650) 493-6340
(800) 578-7878

**THE WESTIN
PALO ALTO**
675 El Camino
Real (94301)
Rates: n/a
(650) 321-4422
(800) 228-3000

PARADISE
**COMFORT INN
CENTRAL**
5475 Clark Rd
(95969)
Rates: $69-$129
(530) 876-0191
(800) 424-6423

AREA CODES - If the local number doesn't connect, check for a new area code.

LANTERN INN
5799 Wildwood
Ln (95969)
Rates: $50-$90
(530) 877-5553

PARADISE INN
5423 Skyway
(95969)
Rates: $40-$99
(530) 877-2127

**PONDEROSA
GARDENS MOTEL**
7010 Skyway
(95969)
Rates: $68-$95
(530) 872-9094

PARKFIELD
PARKFIELD INN
First & Oak Sts
(93451)
Rates: $41-$65
(805) 463-2323

PASADENA
QUALITY INN
3321 E Colorado
Blvd (91107)
Rates: $59-$175
(626) 796-9291
(800) 424-6423

**RITZ-CARLTON/
HUNTINGTON
HOTEL & SPA**
1401 S Oak Knoll
Ave (91106)
Rates: $325-$3000
(626) 568-3900
(800) 241-3333

**SHERATON
PASADENA
HOTEL**
303 E Cordova St
(91101)
Rates: $129-$209
(626) 449-4000
(800) 325-3535

SUPER 8 MOTEL
2863 E Colorado
Blvd (91107)
Rates: $53-$95
(626) 449-3020
(800) 800-8000

VAGABOND INN
1203 E Colorado
Blvd (91106)
Rates: $68-$95
(626) 449-3170
(800) 522-1555

WESTWAY INN
1599 E Colorado
Blvd (91106)
Rates: $69-$350
(626) 304-9678

PASO ROBLES
**FARMHOUSE
MOTEL**
425 Spring St
(93446)
Rates: $25+
(805) 238-1720

**HAMPTON INN
& SUITES**
212 Alexa Ct
(93446)
Rates: $79-$154
(805) 226-9988
(800) 426-7866

MOTEL 6
1134 Black Oak Dr
(93446)
Rates: $39-$57
(805) 239-9090
(800) 466-8356

**SHAMROCK INN
BED & BREAKFST**
1640 Circle B Rd
(93446)
Rates: $41-$65
(805) 239-8585

**SUBURBAN
LODGE**
1955 Theatre Dr
(93446)
Rates: $40-$65
(805) 238-3814

PEBBLE BEACH
**THE LODGE AT
PEBBLE BEACH**
1700 17-Mile
Drive (93953)
Rates: $555-$935
(831) 624-3811
(800) 654-9300

PETALUMA
MOTEL 6
1368 N McDowell
Blvd (94952)
Rates: $39-$52
(707) 765-0333
(800) 466-8356

QUALITY INN
5100 Montero Way
(94954)
Rates: $89-$175
(707) 664-1155
(800) 424-6423

PETROLIA
**MATTOLE RIVER
RESORT**
42354 Mattole Rd
(95558)
Rates: $45-$90
(707) 629-3445
(800) 845-4607

PHELAN
**BEST WESTERN
CAJON PASS**
8317 Hwy 138
(92371)
Rates: $59-$129
(760) 249 6777
(800) 528-1234
(866) BWCAJON

PICO RIVERA
DAYS INN
6540 S Rosemead
Blvd (90660)
Rates: $45-$149
(562) 942-1003
(800) 329-7466

PINECREST
**PINECREST
CHALET**
P. O.Box 1279
(95364)
Rates: $55-$295
(209) 965 3276

PINOLE
MOTEL 6
1501 Fitzgerald Dr
(94564)
Rates: $49-$68
(510) 222-8174
(800) 466-8356

PIONEERTOWN
**PIONEERTOWN
MOTEL**
5040 Curtis (92268)
Rates: $35-$42
(760) 365-4879

**RIMROCK RANCH
CABINS**
P.O. Box 313 (92268)
Rates: $75-$145
(760) 228-1297

PIRU
**HERITAGE VALLEY
HISTORIC
COUNTRY INN**
631 N Main St
(93040)
Rates: $125-$195
(805) 521-0700

PISMO BEACH
CLIFFS RESORT
2757 Shell Beach
Rd (93449)
Rates: $209-$299
(805) 773-5000
(800) 441-8885

**COTTAGE INN
BY THE SEA**
2351 Price St
(93449)
Rates: $89-$249
(805) 773-4617
(800) 914-6662

MOTEL 6
860 4th St (93449)
Rates: $327$66
(805) 773-2665
(800) 466-8356

**OXFORD SUITES
RESORT**
651 Five Cities Dr
(93449)
Rates: $89-$159
(805) 773-3773
(800) 982-7848

**PISMO BAY
MOTOR LODGE**
371 Pismo St
(93449)
Rates: $40-$85
(805) 773-2554

**SANDCASTLE INN
ON THE BEACH**
100 Stimson Ave
(93449)
Rates: $99-$279
(805) 773-2422
(800) 822-6606

SEA GYPSY MOTEL
1020 Cypress
(93449)
Rates: $45-$165
(805) 773-1801
(800) 592-5923

**SHELL BEACH
MOTEL**
653 Shell Beach
Rd (93449)
Rates: $43-$80
(805) 773-4372
(800) 549-4727

SPYGLASS INN
2705 Spyglass Dr
(93449)
Rates: $79-$249
(805) 773-4855
(800) 824-2612

SURF MOTEL
250 Main St
(93449)
Rates: $45-$120
(805) 773-2070
(800) 472-7873

PITTSBURG
MOTEL 6
2101 Loveridge
Rd (94565)
Rates: $49+
(925) 427-1600
(800) 466-8356

PLACENTIA
**RESIDENCE INN
BY MARRIOTT**
700 W Kimberly
Ave (92870)
Rates: $124+
(714) 996-0555
(800) 331-3131

PLACERVILLE
**MOTHER LODE
MOTEL**
1940 Broadway
(95667)
Rates: $48-$78
(530) 622-0895

PLEASANT HILL
**RESIDENCE INN
BY MARRIOTT**
700 Ellinwood
Way (94523)
Rates: $179-$209
(925) 689-1010
(800) 331-3131

**SUMMERFIELD
SUITES BY
WINDHAM**
2611 Contra Costa
Blvd (94523)
Rates: $99-$179
(925) 934-3343
(800) 833-4353

PLEASANTON
**CANDLEWOOD
SUITES**
5535 Johnson Dr
(94588)
Rates: $119-$129
(925) 463-1212
(888) 226-3539

**CROWNE PLAZA
HOTEL**
11950 Dublin Cyn
Rd (94588)
Rates: $69-$165
(925) 847-6000
(800) 227-6963

AREA CODES - If the local number doesn't connect, check for a new area code.

MOTEL 6
5102 Hopyard Rd
(94588)
Rates: $59+
(925) 463-2626
(800) 466-8356

RAMADA INN
5375 Owens Ct
(94588)
Rates: $69-$95
(925) 463-1300
(800) 272-6232

RESIDENCE IN BY MARRIOTT
11920 Dublin Cyn
Rd (94588)
Rates: $79$159
(925) 227-0500
(800) 331-3131

SIERRA SUITES HOTEL
4555 Chabot Dr
(94588)
Rates: $69-$149
(925) 730-0000

SUMMERFIELD SUITES BY WYNDHAM
4545 Chabot Dr
(94588)
Rates: $89-$174
(925) 730-0070
(800) 833-4353

POINT REYES STATION

BERRY PATCH COTTAGE B&B
P. O. Box 712
(94956)
Rates: $100-$120
(415) 663-1942
(888) 663-1942

GRAY'S RETREAT AT POINT REYES
P. O. Box 547
(94956)
Rates: $135
(415) 663-2000
(800) 887-2880

JASMINE COTTAGE AT POINT REYES
P. O. Box 547
(94956)
Rates: $125
(415) 663-2000
(800) 887-2880

POINT REYES COUNTRY INN & COTTAGES ON THE BEACH
12050 Hwy One
(94956)
Rates: $105-$150
(415) 663-9696

POINT REYES LODGING
P. O. Box 878
(94956)
Rates: $95-$325
(415) 663-1872
(800) 539-1872

THE TREE HOUSE BED & BREAKFST
P.O. Box 1075
(94956)
Rates: $100-$150
(415) 663-8720
(800) 495-8720

THIRTY NINE CYPRESS B&B
39 Cypress Rd
(94956)
Rates: $110-$130
(415) 663-1709

POLLOCK PINES

BEST VALUE WESTHAVEN INN
5658 Pony Express
Trail (95726)
Rates: $70-$90
(530) 644-7800

BEST WESTERN STAGECOACH INN
5940 Pony Express
Tr (95726)
Rates: $89-$129
(530) 644-2029
(800) 528-1234
(800) 622-8802

POMONA

MOTEL 6
2470 S Garey Ave
(91766)
Rates: $39-$53
(909) 591-1871
(800) 466-8356

SHERATON SUITES FAIRPLEX
601 W McKinley
Ave (91768)
Rates: $95-$189
(909) 622-2220
(800) 722-4055

SHILO INN POMONA HOTEL
3200 Temple Ave
(91768)
Rates: $81-$157
(909) 598-0073
(800) 222-2244

PORT HUENEME

SURFSIDE MOTEL
615 E Hueneme
Rd (93041)
Rates: $49
(805) 488-3686

PORTERVILLE

BEST WESTERN INN
350 W Montgomery
Ave (93257)
Rates: $82-$99
(559) 781-7411
(800) 528-1234

MOTEL 6
935 W Morton
Ave (93257)
Rates: $35-$40
(559) 781-7600
(800) 466-8356

PORTOLA

SLEEPY PINES MOTEL
74631 Hwy 70
(96122)
Rates: $56-$91
(530) 832-4291

POWAY

BEST WESTERN POWAY COUNTRY INN
13845 Poway Rd
(92064)
Rates: $75-$129
(858) 748-6320
(800) 528-1234
(800) 648-6320

RAMADA LIMITED
12448 Poway Rd
(92064)
Rates: $59-$109
(858) 748-7311
(800) 272-6232

QUINCY

GOLD PAN MOTEL
200 Cresent
(95971)
Rates: $38-$64
(530) 283-3686
(800) 804-6541

NEW ENGLAND RANCH
2571 Quincy Jct
Rd (95971)
Rates: $85-$105
(530) 283-2223

PINE HILL MOTEL
42075 Hwy 70
(95971)
Rates: $65-$80
(530) 283-1670
(866) 342-2891

RAMONA

RAMONA VALLEY INN
416 Main St (92065)
Rates: $50-$77
(760) 789-6433
(800) 648-4618

RANCHO BERNARD

FOUR POINTS BY SHERATON
11611 Bernardo
Plaza Ct (92128)
Rates: $159-$239
(858) 485-9250
(800) 325-3535

LA QUINTA INN
10185 Paseo
Montril (92129)
Rates: $80-$103
(858) 484-8800
(800) 687-6667

RANCHO BERNARDO INN
17550 Bernardo
Oaks Dr (92128)
Rates: $259-$379
(858) 487-1611
(800) 935-2392

RESIDENCE INN BY MARRIOTT
11002 Rancho
Carmel Dr (92128)
Rates: $139-$219
(858) 673-1900
(800) 331-3131

STAYBRIDGE SUITES-CARMEL MOUNTAIN
11855 Ave of
Industry (92128)
Rates: $159-$200
(858) 487-0900
(800) 238-8000

TRAVELODGE
16929 W Bernardo
Dr (92127)
Rates: $67-$90
(858) 487-0445
(800) 578-7878

RANCHO CORDOVA

AMERISUITES
10744 Gold Center
Dr (95670)
Rates: $79-$126
(916) 633-1516
(800) 833-1516

BEST WESTERN HERITAGE INN
11269 Point East
Dr (95742)
Rates: $85-$109
(916) 635-4040
(800) 528-1234

INNS OF AMERICA
12249 Folsom
Blvd (95742)
Rates: $75-$99
(916) 351-1213
(800) 826-0778

MOTEL 6
10694 Olson Dr
(95670)
Rates: $45-$58
(916) 635-8784
(800) 466-8356

RESIDENCE INN BY MARRIOTT
2779 Prospect
Park Dr (95670)
Rates: $121-$149
(916) 851-1550
(800) 331-3131

WINGATE INN
10745 Gold Center
Dr (95670)
Rates: $69-$109
(916) 858-8680

RANCHO MIRAGE

THE LODGE AT RANCHO MIRAGE
68-900 Frank
Sinatra Dr (92270)
Rates: $195-$425
(760) 321-8282

AREA CODES - If the local number doesn't connect, check for a new area code.

MOTEL 6
69-570 Hwy 111
(92270)
Rates: $39-$60
(760) 324-8475
(800) 466-8356

**RANCHO
LAS PALMAS
MARRIOTT
RESORT & SPA**
41-000 Bob Hope
Dr (92270)
Rates: $175-$325
(760) 568-5845
(800) 458-8766

**THE WESTIN
MISSION HILLS
RESORT**
71-333 Dinah
Shore Dr (92270)
Rates: $89-$450
(760) 328-5955
(800) 228-3000

RANCHO
SANTA FE
**INN AT RANCHO
SANTA FE**
5951 Linea del
Cielo (92067)
Rates: $185-$275
(858) 756-1131
(800) 654-2928
(800) 843-4661

RAVENDALE
**RAVENDALE
LODGE**
Hwy 395 (96123)
Rates: $25-$30
(916) 728-0028

RED BLUFF
**BEST VALUE INN
& SUITES**
30 Gilmore Rd
(96080)
Rates: $50-$90
(530) 529-2028

**DAYS INN
& SUITES**
5 John Sutter
(96080)
Rates: $42-$95
(530) 527-6130
(800) 328-7466

ECONO LODGE
1142 N Main St
(96080)
Rates: $45-$100
(530) 528-8890
(800) 424-6423

**LAMPLIGHTER
LODGE**
210 S Main St
(96080)
Rates: $55-$85
(916) 527-1150

MOTEL 6
20 Williams Ave
(96080)
Rates: $35-$48
(530) 527-9200
(800) 466-8356

**SPORTSMAN
LODGE**
768 Antelope Blvd
(96080)
Rates: $44-$110
(530) 527-2888

SUPER 8 MOTEL
203 Antelope Blvd
(96080)
Rates: $55-$100
(530) 527-8882
(800) 800-8000

TRAVELODGE
38 Antelope Blvd
(96080)
Rates: $55-$90
(530) 527-6020
(800) 578-7878

RED
MOUNTAIN
**OLD OWL INN
COTTAGES & B&B**
701 Hwy 395
(93558)
Rates: $45-$105
(888) 653-6954

REDCREST
**REDCREST
RESORT CABINS**
26459 Ave of the
Giants (95569)
Rates: $50-$140
(707) 722-4208

REDDING
**BEST WESTERN
HOSPITALITY
HOUSE MOTEL**
532 N Market St
(96003)
Rates: $50-$80
(530) 241-6464
(800) 528-1234
(800) 700-3019

**BEST WESTERN
PONDEROSA INN**
2220 Pine St
(96001)
Rates: $49-$70
(530) 241-6300
(800) 528-1234
(800) 626-1900

COMFORT INN
2059 Hilltop Dr
(96002)
Rates: $55-$159
(530) 221-6530
(800) 424-6423

**GRAND MANOR
INN & SUITES**
850 Mistletoe Ln
(96002)
Rates: $68-$117
(530) 221-4472

HOLIDAY INN EXP
1080 Twin View
Blvd (96003)
Rates: $94-$99
(530) 241-5500
(800) 465-4329

LA QUINTA INN
2180 Hilltop Dr
(96002)
Rates: $75-$100
(530) 221-8200
(800) 687-6667

**MOTEL 6-
CENTRAL**
1640 Hilltop Dr
(96002)
Rates: $39-$60
(530) 221-1800
(800) 466-8356

MOTEL 6-NORTH
1250 Twin View
Blvd (96003)
Rates: $41-$60
(530) 246-4470
(800) 466-8356

MOTEL 6-SOUTH
2385 Bechelli Ln
(96002)
Rates: $41-$60
(530) 221-0562
(800) 466-8356

MOTEL 99
533 N Market St
(96001)
Rates: $35+
(530) 241-4942

**NORTH GATE
LODGE**
1040 Market St
(96001)
Rates: $30
(530) 243-4900

OXFORD SUITES
1967 Hilltop Ln
(96002)
Rates: $85-$105
(530) 221-0100
(800) 762-0133

RAMADA LTD
1286 Twin View
Blvd (96003)
Rates: $74-$149
(530) 246-2222
(800) 272-6232

RED LION HOTEL
1830 Hilltop Ln
(96002)
Rates: $80-$107
(530) 221-8700
(800) 733-5466

REDDING LODGE
1135 Market St
(96001)
Rates: $32-$36
(530) 243-5141

RIVER INN
1835 Park Marina
Dr (96001)
Rates: $65-$85
(530) 241-9500
(800) 995-4341

**SARATOGA
MOTEL**
3025 S Market St
(96001)
Rates: $25+
(530) 243-8586

SHASTA LODGE
1245 Pine St
(96001)
Rates: $28-$45
(530) 243-6133

**SILVERTHORN
RESORT**
16250 Silverthorn
Rd (96003)
Rates: n/a
(530) 275-1571
(800) 332-3044

STAR DUST MOTEL
1200 Pine St
(96001)
Rates: $30-$35
(530) 241-6121

**THRIFTLODGE
CASA BLANCA
MOUNTAIN**
413 N Market St
(96003)
Rates: $26-$59
(530) 241-3010
(800) 578-7878

TRAVELODGE
540 N Market St
(96003)
Rates: $62-$99
(530) 243-5291
(800) 578-7878

REDLANDS
**BEST WESTERN
SANDMAN MOTEL**
1120 W Colton
Ave (92374)
Rates: $59-$79
(909) 793-2001
(800) 528-1234

DYNASTY SUITES
1235 W Colton
Ave (92373)
Rates: $66-$78
(909) 793-6648
(800) 842-7899

REDONDO
BEACH
**BEST WESTERN
REDONDO BEACH**
1850 S Pacific
Coast Hwy
(90277)
Rates: $79-$119
(310) 540-3700
(800) 528-1234

REDWAY
**DEAN CREEK
RESORT**
4112 Redwood Dr
(95560)
Rates: $58-$135
(707) 923-2555

REDWOOD
CITY
**SOFITEL SAN
FRANCISCO BAY**
223 Twin Dolphin
Dr (94065)
Rates: $249-$279
(650) 598-9000

AREA CODES - If the local number doesn't connect, check for a new area code.

TOWNEPLACE SUITES
1000 Twin Dolphin Dr (94065)
Rates: n/a
(650) 593-4100
(800) 257-3000

REEDLEY
EDGEWATER INN
1977 W Manning Ave (93654)
Rates: $69-$89
(559) 637-7777
(800) 479-5855

RIALTO
BEST WESTERN EMPIRE INN
475 W Valley Blvd (92376)
Rates: $79-$150
(909) 877-0690
(800) 528-1234
(800) 937-8376

RICHARDSON GROVE
RICHARDSON GROVE LDG/CBNS
Richardson Grove State Pk (95542)
Rates: $55-$65
(707) 247-3415

RIDGECREST
BEST WESTERN CHINA LAKE INN
400 S China Lake Blvd (93555)
Rates: $70-$100
(760) 371-2300
(800) 528-1234

CARRIAGE INN
901 N China Lake Blvd (93555)
Rates: $80-$143
(760) 446-7910

ECONO LODGE
201 Inyokern Rd (93555)
Rates: $53-$90
(760) 446-2551
(800) 424-6423

HERITAGE INN & SUITES
1050 N Norma Dr (93555)
Rates: $75-$88
(760) 446-7951
(800) 843-6543

MOTEL 6
535 S China Lake Blvd (93555)
Rates: $31-$34
(760) 375-6866
(800) 466-8356

QUALITY INN
507 S China Lake Blvd (93555)
Rates: $79-$98
(760) 375-9732
(800) 424-6423

VAGABOND INN
426 China Lake Blvd (93555)
Rates: $65-$75
(760) 375-2220
(800) 522-1555

RIO DELL
HUMBOLDT GABLES MOTEL
40 W Davis St (95562)
Rates: $40-$80
(707) 764-5609

RIO NIDO
RIO NIDO LODGE RESORT
1458 River Rd (95471)
Rates: $50-$80
(707) 869-0821

RIVERSIDE
BEST WESTERN
10518 Magnolia Ave (92505)
Rates: $69-$139
(909) 359-0770
(800) 528-1234

DYNASTY SUITES
3735 Iowa Ave (92507)
Rates: $66-$78
(909) 369-8200
(800) 842-7899

ECONO LODGE
10705 Magnolia Ave (92505)
Rates: $39-$129
(909) 351-2424
(800) 424-6423

ECONO LODGE & SUITES
1971 University Ave (92507)
Rates: $49-$99
(909) 684-6363
(800) 424-6423

MOTEL 6-EAST
1260 University Ave (92507)
Rates: $39-$50
(909) 784-2131
(800) 466-8356

MOTEL 6-SOUTH
3663 La Sierra Ave (92505)
Rates: $37-$50
(909) 351-0764
(800) 466-8356

ROCKLIN
HOWARD JOHNSON HOTEL
4420 Rocklin Rd (95677)
Rates: $89-$169
(916) 624-4500
(800) 446-4656

RAMADA LTD
4480 Rocklin Rd (95677)
Rates: $59-$119
(916) 632-3366
(800) 272-6232

ROHNERT PARK
BEST WESTERN
6500 Redwood Dr (94928)
Rates: $68-$89
(707) 584-7435
(800) 528-1234

MOTEL 6
6145 Commerce Blvd (94928)
Rates: $39-$52
(707) 585-8888
(800) 466-8356

ROSAMOND
DEVONSHIRE INN MOTEL
2076 Rosamond Blvd (93560)
Rates: $54-$69
(661) 256-3454

ROSEMEAD
MOTEL 6
1001 S San Gabriel Blvd (91770)
Rates: $45-$58
(626) 572-6076
(800) 466-8356

ROSEVILLE
BEST WESTERN ROSEVILLE INN
220 Harding Blvd (95678)
Rates: $65-$100
(916) 782-4434
(800) 528-1234

OXFORD SUITES
130 N Sunrise Ave (95661)
Rates: $89-$129
(916) 784-2222

RESIDENCE INN BY MARRIOTT
1930 Taylor Rd (95661)
Rates: $119-$199
(916) 772-5500
(800) 331-3131

ROWLAND HEIGHTS
MOTEL 6
18970 E Labin Ct (91748)
Rates: $39-$52
(626) 964-5333
(800) 466-8356

RUBIDOUX
MOTEL 6
6830 Valley Way (92509)
Rates: $39-$48
(909) 681-6666
(800) 466-8356

RUNNING SPRINGS
GIANT OAKS MOTEL & CABIN
32180 Hilltop Blvd (92382)
Rates: $49-$159
(916) 867-2231
(800) 786-1689

SACRAMENTO
BEST WESTERN EXPO INN
1413 Howe Ave (95825)
Rates: $80-$150
(916) 922-9833
(800) 528-1234
(800) 643-4422

BEST WESTERN HARBOR INN
1250 Halyard Dr (95691)
Rates: $59-$149
(916) 371-2100
(800) 528-1234
(800) 371-2101

CANDLEWOOD SUITES
555 Howe Ave (95825)
Rates: $69-$120
(916) 646-1212
(888) 226-3539

CANTERBURY INN
1900 Canterbury Rd (95815)
Rates: $49-$89
(916) 927-0927
(800) 932-3492

CLARION HOTEL NEAR CALEXPO
2600 Auburn Blvd (95821)
Rates: $79-$179
(916) 487-7600
(800) 424-6423

DOUBLETREE HOTEL
2001 Point West Way (95815)
Rates: $190-$219
(916) 929-8855
(800) 222-8733

ECONO LODGE
711 16th St (95814)
Rates: $49-$109
(916) 443-6631
(800) 424-6423

HOMESTEAD STUDIO SUITES
2810 Gateway Oaks Dr (95833)
Rates: $70-$89
(916) 564-7500
(888) 782-9473

HOST AIRPORT HOTEL
6945 Airport Blvd (95837)
Rates: $80-$140
(916) 922-8071

LA QUINTA INN DOWNTOWN
200 Jibboom St (95814)
Rates: $95-$129
(916) 448-8100
(800) 687-6667

LA QUINTA INN NORTH
4604 Madison Ave (95841)
Rates: $90-$125
(916) 348-0900
(800) 687-6667

MARRIOTT RESIDENCE INN
1530 Howe Ave (95825)
Rates: $89-$179
(916) 920-9111
(800) 331-3131

MOTEL 6-CENTRAL
7850 College Town Dr (95826)
Rates: $44-$59
(916) 383-8110
(800) 466-8356

MOTEL 6-DOWNTOWN
1415 30th St (95816)
Rates: $43-$58
(916) 457-0777
(800) 466-8356

MOTEL 6-NORTH
5110 Interstate Ave (95842)
Rates: $43-$59
(916) 331-8100
(800) 466-8356

MOTEL 6-OLD SACRAMENTO
227 Jibboom St (95814)
Rates: $43-$58
(916) 441-0733
(800) 466-8356

MOTEL 6 SOUTH
7407 Elsie Ave (95828)
Rates: $43-$58
(916) 689-6555
(800) 466-8356

MOTEL 6-SOUTHWEST
7780 Stockton Blvd (95823)
Rates: $43-$58
(916) 689-9141
(800) 466-8356

RADISSON HOTEL
500 Leisure Ln (95815)
Rates: $109-$189
(916) 922-2020
(800) 333-3333

RED LION HOTEL
1401 Arden Way (95815)
Rates: $89-$119
(916) 922-8041
(800) 547-8010

RESIDENCE INN BY MARRIOTT
2410 W El Camino Ave (95833)
Rates: $99-$154
(916) 649-1300
(800) 331-3131

VAGABOND EXECUTIVE INN OLD TOWN
909 3rd St (95814)
Rates: $79-$119
(916) 446-1481
(800) 522-1555

SALINAS

BARLOCKER'S RUSTLNG OAKS RANCH
25252 Limekiln Rd (93908)
Rates: $75-$150
(831) 675-9121

CABANA HOLIDAY CABINS
8710 Prunedale North Rd (93907)
Rates: n/a
(831) 663-2886

EL DORADO MOTEL
1351 N Main St (93906)
Rates: $36-$90
(831) 449-2442
(800) 523-6506

MOTEL 6-NORTH
140 Kern St (93901)
Rates: $39-$54
(831) 753-1711
(800) 466-8356

MOTEL 6-SOUTH
1257 De La Torre Blvd (93905)
Rates: $39-$54
(831) 757-3077
(800) 466-8356

QUALITY INN
181 Kern St (93905)
Rates: $69-$259
(831) 770-1400
(800) 424-6423

RAMADA LTD
109 John St (93901)
Rates: $59-$159
(831) 424-4801
(800) 272-6232

RESIDENCE INN BY MARRIOTT
17215 El Rancho Way (93907)
Rates: $109-$139
(831) 775-0410
(800) 331-3131

VAGABOND INN
131 Kern St (93905)
Rates: $60-$170
(831) 758-4693
(800) 522-1555

SAN ANDREAS

BLACK BART INN & MOTEL
35 Main St (95249)
Rates: $47-$60
(209) 754-3808
(800) 225-3764

COURTYARD B&B INN
334 W St. Charles (95249)
Rates: $65-$90
(209) 754-1518

ROBINS NEST HISTORIC B&B
247 W St. Charles St (95249)
Rates: $85-$155
(209) 754-1076

SAN BERNARDINO

DAYS INN
1386 E Highland Ave (92404)
Rates: $49-$139
(909) 881-1702
(800) 329-7466

E-Z 8 MOTEL
1750 S Waterman Ave (92408)
Rates: $29-$37
(909) 888-4827

LA QUINTA INN
205 E Hospitality Ln (92408)
Rates: $76-$105
(909) 888-7571
(800) 687-6667

MOTEL 6-NORTH
1960 Ostrems Way (92407)
Rates: $39-$50
(909) 887-8191
(800) 466-8356

MOTEL 6-SOUTH
111 Redlands Blvd (92408)
Rates: $37-$48
(909) 825-6666
(800) 466-8356

SANDS MOTEL
606 North H St (92410)
Rates: $40-$49
(909) 889-8391

SAN BRUNO

REGENCY INN
411 E San Bruno Ave (94066)
Rates: $69-$75
(650) 589-7535

STAYBRIDGE SUITES
1350 Huntington Ave (94066)
Rates: $170-$300
(650) 588-0770
(800) 238-8000

SAN CARLOS

FAIRFIELD INN & SUITES
555 Skyway Rd (94070)
Rates: $99-$109
(650) 631-0777
(800) 228-2800

HOMESTEAD STUDIO SUITES
3 Circle Star Way (94070)
Rates: $89-$109
(650) 368-2600
(888) 782-9473

SAN CLEMENTE

CASA DE ELENA B&B
516 Elena Ave (92672)
Rates: $139-$350
(949) 940-9099

HOLIDAY INN
111 S Avenida de Estrella (92672)
Rates: $129-$149
(949) 361-3000
(800) 465-4329

SAN DIEGO

BEST WESTERN LAMPLIGHTER INN & SUITES
6474 El Cajon Blvd (92115)
Rates: $80-$210
(619) 582-3088
(800) 528-1234
(800) 545-0778

THE BRISTOL HOTEL
1055 First Ave (92101)
Rates: $119-$129
(619) 232-6141
(800) 662-4477

BUDGET MOTELS OF AMERICA
133 Encinitas Blvd (92024)
Rates: n/a
(619) 944-0260
(800) 795-6044

BUDGET MOTELS OF AMERICA
641 Camino del Rio South (92108)
Rates: n/a
(619) 295-6886
(800) 624-1257

CLARION HOTEL BAY VIEW
660 K St (92101)
Rates: $69-$209
(619) 696-0234
(800) 424-6423

COMFORT INN AIRPORT AT OLD TOWN
1955 San Diego Ave (92110)
Rates: $69-$159
(619) 543-1130
(800) 424-6423

COMFORT INN GASLAMP
660 G St (92101)
Rates: $79-$169
(619) 238-4100
(800) 424-6423

CROWN POINT VIEW SUITE HOTEL
4088 Crown Point Dr (92109)
Rates: $42-$250
(858) 272-0676
(800) 338-3331

AREA CODES - If the local number doesn't connect, check for a new area code.

DIAMOND HEAD INN MOTEL
605 Diamond St (92109)
Rates: $79-$179
(858) 273-1900

DOUBLETREE CLUB HOTEL-ZOO/SEAWORLD
1515 Hotel Cir (92108)
Rates: $109-$199
(619) 881-6900
(800) 222-8733
(800) 619-1541

DOUBLETREE HOTEL-MISSION VALLEY
7450 Hazard Center Dr (92108)
Rates: $129-$239
(619) 297-5466
(800) 222-8733

HAMPTON INN
3888 Greenwood St (92110)
Rates: $89-$128
(619) 299-6633
(800) 426-7866

THE HILLCREST B&B AT KASA KORBET
4050 Front St (92103)
Rates: $79-$109
(619) 291-3062

HOLIDAY INN ON THE BAY
1355 N Harbor Dr (92101)
Rates: $149-$189
(619) 232-3861
(800) 465-4329

HOMESTEAD STUDIO SUITES MISSION VALLEY
7444 Mission Valley Rd (92108)
Rates: $71-$96
(619) 299-2292
(888) 782-9473

HOMESTEAD STUDIO SUITES
9880 Pacific Hgts Blvd (92121)
Rates: $84-$109
(858) 623-0100
(888) 782-9473

HORTON GRAND HISTORIC HOTEL
311 Island Ave (92101)
Rates: $129-$189
(619) 544-1886
(800) 542-1886

MOTEL 6
2424 Hotel Circle N (92108)
Rates: $49-$76
(619) 296-1612
(800) 466-8356

MOTEL 6-DOWNTOWN
1546 2nd Ave (92101)
Rates: $49-$76
(619) 236-9292
(800) 466-8356

MOTEL 6-NORTH
5592 Clairemont Mesa Blvd (92117)
Rates: $53-$76
(858) 268-9758
(800) 466-8356

OCEAN VILLA INN
5142 W Point Loma Blvd (92107)
Rates: $70-$150
(619) 224-3481
(800) 759-0012

OLD TOWN INN
4444 Pacific Hwy (92110)
Rates: $60-$140
(619) 260-8024
(800) 643-3025

OUTRIGGER MOTEL
1370 Scott St (92106)
Rates: $35-$50
(619) 223-7105

PACIFIC SANDS MOTEL & CONDOS
4449 Ocean Blvd (92109)
Rates: $40-$60
(619) 483-7555

PACIFIC SHORES INN ON THE BEACH
4802 Mission Blvd (92109)
Rates: $59-$159
(858) 483-6300
(800) 622-5871

PREMIER INN
2484 Hotel Circle Pl (92108)
Rates: $39-$124
(619) 291-8252

PREMIER INN
3333 Channel Way (92110)
Rates: $50-$170
(619) 223-9500

QUALITY RESORT MISSION VALLEY
875 Hotel Circle St (92108)
Rates: $99-$139
(619) 298-8282
(800) 424-6423

RADISSON HOTEL
1433 Camino Del Rio S (92108)
Rates: $189-$239
(619) 260-0111
(800) 333-3333

RED LION HANALEI HOTEL
2270 Hotel Circle N (92108)
Rates: $99-$169
(619) 297-1101
(800) 733-5466
(800) 882-0858

RESIDENCE INN BY MARRIOTT DOWNTOWN
1747 Pacific Coast Hwy (92101)
Rates: $159-$219
(619) 338-8200
(800) 331-3131

RESIDENCE INN MISSION VALLEY
1865 Hotel Circle S (92108)
Rates: $139-$359
(619) 881-3600
(800) 331-3131
(800) 522-6431

RESIDENCE INN SAN DIEGO RANCHO BERNARDO/ SCRIPPS POWAY
12011 Scripps Highland Dr (92131)
Rates: $109-$189
(858) 635-5724
(800) 331-3131

RESIDENCE INN SORRENTO MESA
5995 Pacific Mesa Ct (92121)
Rates: $139-$159
(858) 552-9100
(800) 331-3131

SAN DIEGO MARRIOTT HOTEL & MARINA
333 W Harbor Dr (92101)
Rates: $365-$385
(619) 234-1500
(800) 228-9290

SAN DIEGO MARRIOTT HOTEL MISSION VALLEY
8757 Rio San Diego Dr (92108)
Rates: $159-$228
(619) 692-3800
(800) 228-9290

SHELTER POINTE HOTEL & MARINA
1551 Shelter Is. Dr (92106)
Rates: $139-$219
(619) 221-8000
(800) 566-2524

SHERAON SAN DIEGO HOTEL & MARINA
1380 Harbor Is. Dr (92101)
Rates: $169
(619) 291-2900
(800) 325-3535

SHERATON SAN DIEGO HOTEL MISSION VALLEY
1433 Camino del Rio (92108)
Rates: $199-$219
(619) 260-0111
(800) 325-3535

SHERATON SUITES-SAN DIEGO
701 "A" St (92101)
Rates: $369
(619) 696-9800
(888) 627-8067

SOMERSET SUITES HOTEL
606 Washington St (92103)
Rates: $79-$279
(619) 692-5200
(800) 962-9665

STAYBRIDGE SUITES
1110 "A" Street (92101)
Rates: $169-$229
(619) 795-4000
(800) 238-8000

STAYBRIDGE SUITES-SORRENTO MESA
6639 Mira Mesa Blvd (92121)
Rates: $129-$207
(858) 453 5343
(800) 238-8000

U.S. GRANT HISTORIC HOTEL
326 Broadway (92101)
Rates: $175-$195
(619) 232-3121
(800) 237-5029

VAGABOND INN POINT LOMA
1325 Scott St (92106)
Rates: $64-$79
(619) 224-3371
(800) 522-1555

WELK RESORT
8860 Lawrence Welk Drive (Escondido 92026)
Rates: $120-$375
(760) 749-3000
(800) 932-9355

THE WESTIN HORTON PLAZA
910 Broadway Cir (92101)
Rates: $189-$409
(619) 239-2200
(800) 228-3000

SAN DIMAS
MOTEL 6
502 W Arrow Hwy (91773)
Rates: $43-$54
(909) 592-5631
(800) 466-8356

AREA CODES - If the local number doesn't connect, check for a new area code.

AREA CODES - If the local number doesn't connect, check for a new area code.

SAN FRANCISCO

ARGONAUT HOTEL
495 Jefferson St (94109)
Rates: $129-$269
(415) 563-0800
(866) 415-0704

BERESFORD ARMS
701 Post St (94109)
Rates: $92-$185
(415) 673-2600
(800) 533-6533

BEST WESTERN CIVIC CENTER MOTOR INN
364 9th St (94103)
Rates: $89-$149
(415) 621-2826
(800) 528-1234
(800) 444-5829

BEST WESTERN TUSCAN INN AT FISHERMANS WHARF
425 Northpoint Rd (94133)
Rates: $129-$269
(415) 561-1100
(800) 528-1234
(800) 648-4626

CAMPTON PLACE HOTEL
340 Stockton St (94108)
Rates: $335-$470
(415) 781-5555
(800) 235-4300

CARTWRIGHT HOTEL
524 Sutter St (94012)
Rates: $119-$219
(415) 421-2865

CLARION HOTEL COSMO
761 Post St (94109)
Rates: $89-$159
(415) 673-6040
(800) 424-6423

CROWNE PLAZA UNION SQUARE
480 Sutter St (94108)
Rates: $119-$299
(415) 398-8900
(800) 227-6963

DIVA HOTEL
440 Geary St (94012)
Rates: $130
(415) 885-0200

ECONO LODGE
2505 Lombard St (94123)
Rates: $60-$159
(415) 921-2505
(800) 424-6423

EXECUTIVE HOTEL VINTAGE COURT
650 Bush St (94108)
Rates: $99-$139
(415) 392-4666

THE FAIRMONT HOTEL
950 Mason St (94108)
Rates: $189-$379
(415) 772-5000

THE FITZGERALD HOTEL
620 Post St (94109)
Rates: $59-$79
(415) 775-8100
(877) 662-4455

FOUR SEASONS HOTEL
757 Market St (94013)
Rates: $469-$600
(415) 633-3000
(800) 332-3442

HARBOR COURT HOTEL
165 Steuart St (94105)
Rates: $189-$249
(415) 882-1300
(800) 346-0555

HOLIDAY INN CIVIC CENTER
50 8th St (94103)
Rates: $179-$199
(415) 626-6103
(800) 465-4329

HOLIDAY INN SELECT
750 Kearny St (94108)
Rates: $109-$259
(415) 433-6600
(800) 465-4329

HOTEL BERESFORD
635 Sutter St (94102)
Rates: $92-$145
(415) 673-9900
(800) 533-6533

HOTEL METROPOLIS
25 Mason St (94102)
Rates: $95
(415) 775-4600

HOTEL MONACO
501 Geary St (94102)
Rates: $179-$399
(415) 292-0100
(800) 214-4220

HOTEL PALOMAR
12 Fourth St (94103)
Rates: $150-$449
(415) 394-1111
(877) 294-9711
(888) 546-7866

HOTEL TRITON
342 Grant Ave (94108)
Rates: $139-$299
(415) 394-0500
(99) 433-6611

HOTEL UNION SQUARE
114 Powell St (94102)
Rates: $105
(415) 397-3000

THE INN SAN FRANCISCO B&B
943 S Van Ness Ave (94110)
Rates: $85-$225
(415) 641-0188
(800) 359-0913

KENSINGTON PARK HOTEL
450 Post St (94102)
Rates: $105
(415) 788-6400

LA QUINTA INN & SUITES
1050 Van Ness Ave (94109)
Rates: $79-$119
(415) 673-471
(800) 687-6667

THE LAUREL INN
444 Presidio Ave (94115)
Rates: $175
(415) 567-8467
(800) 552-8735

MANDARIN ORIENTAL HOTEL
222 Sansome St (94104)
Rates: $470-$775
(415) 276-9888

MARRIOTT AT FISHERMANS WHARF
1250 Columbus Ave (94133)
Rates: $109-$219
(415) 775-7555
(800) 228-9290

MONTICELLO INN
127 Ellis St (94102)
Rates: $129-$199
(415) 392-8800
(866) 778-6169

OMNI HOTEL
500 California St (94109)
Rates: $84-$129
(415) 677-9494
(800) 843-6664

PACIFIC HEIGHTS INN
1555 Union St (94123)
Rates: $79-$150
(415) 776-3310
(800) 523-1801

PALACE HOTEL
2 New Montgomery St (94105)
Rates: $159-$539
(415) 512-1111

THE PRESCOTT HOTEL
545 Post St (94102)
Rates: $139-$1200
(415) 563-0303
(800) 283-7322

SERRANO HOTEL
405 Taylor St (94102)
Rates: $139-$239
(415) 885-2500
(888) 546-7866

SHERATON AT FISHERMANS WHARF
2500 Mason St (94133)
Rates: $139-$179
(415) 362-5500
(800) 325-3535

SIR FRANCIS DRAKE HOTEL
450 Powell St (94102)
Rates: $129-$129
(415) 392-7755
(800) 227-5480

TRAVELODGE BY THE BAY
1450 Lombard St (94123)
Rates: $62-$109
(415) 673-0691
(800) 578-7878

VILLA FLORENCE HOTEL
225 Powell St (94107)
Rates: $139-$209
(415) 397-7700
(800) 553-4411

THE WESTIN ST. FRANCIS
335 Powell St (94102)
Rates: $129-$599
(415) 397-7000
(800) 937-8461

SAN JACINTO

CROWN MOTEL
138 S Ramona Blvd (92583)
Rates: $37-$43
(909) 654-7133

SAN JOSE

BEST WESTERN GATEWAY INN
2585 Seaboard Ave (95131)
Rates: $109
(408) 435-8800
(800) 528-1234
(800) 437-8855

COMFORT SUITES AIRPORT
1510 N First St (95112)
Rates: $99-$169
(408) 392-9009
(800) 424-6423

AREA CODES - If the local number doesn't connect, check for a new area code.

DOUBLETREE HOTEL
2050 Gateway Pl (95110)
Rates: $89-$229
(408) 453-4000
(800) 222-8733

FAIRMONT SAN JOSE
170 S Market St (95113)
Rates: $119-$250
(408) 998-1900
(800) 527-4727

HILTON
300 Almaden Blvd (95110)
Rates: $89-$269
(408) 287-2100
(800) 445-8667

HOMESTEAD STUDIO SUITES
1560 N First St (95112)
Rates: $79-$99
(408) 573-0648
(888) 782-9473

HOMEWOOD SUITES
10 W Trimble Rd (95131)
Rates: $139-$179
(408) 428-9900
(800) 225-5466

HOTEL DE ANZA
233 W Santa Clara St (95113)
Rates: $109-$399
(408) 286-1000

HOWARD JOHNSON
1215 S First St (95110)
Rates: $69-$169
(408) 280-5300
(800) 446-4656

MOTEL 6-AIRPORT
2081 N First St (95131)
Rates: $49-$56
(408) 436-8180
(800) 466-8356

MOTEL 6-SOUTH
2560 Fontaine Rd (95121)
Rates: $49+
(408) 270-3131
(800) 466-8356

SIERRA SUITES
55 E Brokaw Rd (95112)
Rates: $79-$199
(408) 453-3000

SLEEP INN
2390 Harris Way (95131)
Rates: $69-$149
(408) 434-9330
(800) 424-6423

STAYBRIDGE SUITES
1602 Crane Ct (95122)
Rates: $62-$125
(408) 436-1600
(800) 238-8000

TOWNEPLACE SUITES
440 Saratoga Ave (95129)
Rates: n/a
(408) 984-5903
(800) 257-3000

VAGABOND INN
1488 N First St (95112)
Rates: $69-$99
(408) 453-8822
(800) 522-1555

SAN JUAN BAUTISTA
SAN JUAN INN
410 The Alameda (95045)
Rates: $69-$99
(831) 623-4380

SAN JUAN CAPISTRANO
BEST WESTERN CAPISTRANO INN
27174 Ortega Hwy (92675)
Rates: $89-$179
(949) 493-5661
(800) 528-1234
(800) 441-9438

SAN LEANDRO
ISLANDER LODGE MOTEL
2398 E 14th St (94577)
Rates: $33-$45
(510) 352-5010

SAN LUIS OBISPO
BEST WESTERN ROYAL OAK MOTOR HOTEL
214 Madonna Rd (93405)
Rates: $79-$150
(805) 544-4410
(800) 528-1234
(800) 545-4410

DAYS INN
2050 Garfield St (93405)
Rates: $59-$199
(805) 549-9911
(800) 329-7466

HERITAGE INN B&B
978 Olive St (93405)
Rates: $85-$200
(805) 544-7440

HOLIDAY INN EXP
1800 Monterey St (93401)
Rates: $99-$219
(805) 544-8600
(800) 465-4329

MOTEL 6-NORTH
1433 Calle Joaquin (93401)
Rates: $39-$70
(805) 549-9595
(800) 466-8356

MOTEL 6-SOUTH
1625 Calle Joaquin (93401)
Rates: $39-$70
(805) 541-6992
(800) 466-8356

RAMADA INN OLIVE TREE
1000 Olive St (93405)
Rates: $59-$159
(805) 544-2800
(800) 272-6232
(800) 777-5847

SAN LUIS CREEK LODGE
1941 Monterey St (93401)
Rates: $109-$249
(805) 541-1122

SAN LUIS INN & SUITES
404 Santa Rosa St (93405)
Rates: $55-$200
(805) 544-0881
(800) 447-8080

SANDS SUITES & MOTEL
1930 Monterey St (93401)
Rates: $85-$219
(805) 544-0500
(800) 441-4657

SUPER 8 MOTEL
1951 Montgomery St (93401)
Rates: $49-$129
(805) 544-6888
(800) 800-8000

SAN MARCOS
QUAILS INN AT LAKE SAN MARCOS
1025 La Bonita Dr (92069)
Rates: $139-$225
(760) 744-0120
(800) 447-6556

SAN MATEO
RADISSON VILLA HOTEL
4000 S El Camino Real (94403)
Rates: $129-$289
(650) 341-0966
(800) 333-3333

RESIDENCE INN BY MARRIOTT
2000 Winward Way (94404)
Rates: $109-$219
(650) 574-4700
(800) 331-3131

SAN PEDRO
HOLIDAY INN
111 S Gaffey St (90731)
Rates: $89-$119
(310) 514-1414
(800) 465-4329

MARINA HOTEL SAN PEDRO
2800 Via Cabrillo Marina (90731)
Rates: $199-$209
(310) 514-3344

VAGABOND INN
215 S Gaffey St (90731)
Rates: $64-$69
(310) 831-8911
(800) 522-1555

SAN RAFAEL
CASA SOLDAVINI GUESTHOUSE
531 C St (94901)
Rates: n/a
(415) 454-3140

VILLA INN
1600 Lincoln Ave (94901)
Rates: $69-$95
(415) 456-4975

SAN RAMON
HOMESTEAD STUDIO SUITES
18000 San Ramon Valley Blvd (94583)
Rates: $89-$109
(925) 277-0833
(888) 782-9473

MARRIOTT AT BISHOP RANCH
2600 Bishop Dr (94583)
Rates: $79-$209
(925) 867-9200
(800) 228-9290

RESIDENCE INN BY MARRIOTT
1071 Market Pl (94583)
Rates: $89-$209
(925) 277-9292
(800) 331-3131

SIERRA SUITES HOTEL
2323 San Ramon Valley Blvd (94583)
Rates: $89-$179
(925) 743-1882

SAN SIMEON
MOTEL 6-HEARST CASTLE
9070 Castillo Dr (93452)
Rates: $39-$67
(805) 927-8691
(800) 466-8356

AREA CODES - If the local number doesn't connect, check for a new area code.

SILVER SURF MOTEL
9390 Castillo Dr (93452)
Rates: $63-$176
(805) 927-4661
(800) 621-3999

SAN YSIDRO

BEST WESTERN AMERICANA INN
815 W San Yisdro Blvd (92173)
Rates: $59-$149
(619) 428-5521
(800) 528-1234
(800) 553-3933

ECONOMY INNS OF AMERICA-MEXICAN BORDER
230 Via de San Ysidro (92173)
Rates: $30-$45
(619) 428-6191
(800) 826-0778

MOTEL 6-MEXICAN BORDER
160 E Calle Primera (92173)
Rates: $37-$52
(619) 690-6663
(800) 466-8356

SANTA ANA

CANDLEWOOD SUITES
2600 S Red Hill Ave (92705)
Rates: n/a
(949) 250-0404
(888) 226-3539

COMFORT SUITES JOHN WAYNE AIRPORT
2620 Hotel Terrace Dr (92705)
Rates: $69-$129
(714) 966-5200
(800) 424-6423

MOTEL 6
1623 E First St (92701)
Rates: $40-$56
(714) 558-0500
(800) 466-8356

QUALITY SUITES JOHN WAYNE AIRPORT
2701 Hotel Terrace Dr (92705)
Rates: $99-$189
(714) 957-9200
(800) 424-6423

SANTA BARBARA

BACARA RESORT & SPA
8301 Holister Ave (93117)
Rates: $425-$5000
(805) 968-0100
(877) 422-4245

BEACH HOUSE INN & APARTMENTS
320 W Yanonali St (93101)
Rates: $75-$200
(805) 966-1126

BEST WESTERN BEACHSIDE INN
336 W Cabrillo Blvd (93101)
Rates: $89-$289
(805) 965-6556
(800) 528-1234
(800) 932-6556

BLUE SANDS MOTEL
421 S Milpas (93103)
Rates: $75-$205
(805) 965-1624

CASA DEL MAR INN
18 Bath St (93101)
Rates: $69-$219
(805) 963-4418
(800) 433-3097

FESS PARKERS DOUBLETREE RESORT
633 E Cabrillo Blvd (93103)
Rates: $169-$484
(805) 564-4333
(800) 222-8733
(800) 879-2929

FOUR SEASONS BILTMORE HOTEL
1260 Channel Dr (93108)
Rates: $490-$675
(805) 969-2261
(800) 332-3442

HARBOR HOUSE INN
104 Bath St (93101)
Rates: $99-$275
(805) 962-9745

MARINA BEACH MOTEL
21 Bath St (93101)
Rates: $79-$275
(805) 963-9311
(877) 627-4621

MOTEL 6
3505 State St (93105)
Rates: $49-$86
(805) 687-5400
(800) 466-8356

MOTEL 6-BEACH
443 Corona Del Mar (93103)
Rates: $59-$100
(805) 564-1392
(800) 466-8356

PACIFICA SUITES
5490 Hollister Ave (93111)
Rates: $119-$259
(805) 683-6722
(800) 338-6722

RANCHO OSO GUEST RANCH & STABLES
3750 Paradise Rd (93105)
Rates: $55-$89
(805) 683-5686

SANTA BARBARA INN
901 E Cabrillo Blvd (93103)
Rates: $139-$369
(805) 966-2285
(800) 231-0431

TRAVELER'S MOTEL
3222 State St (93105)
Rates: $75-$125
(805) 687-6009

VILLA ELEGANTE VACATION RENTALS
402 Orilla del Mar (93103)
Rates: $1200/Wkly
(805) 966-4410

SANTA CATALINA ISLAND
(See Avalon)

SANTA CLARA

GUESTHOUSE INT'L INN & SUITES
2930 El Camino Real (95051)
Rates: $79-$150
(408) 241-3010
(800) 214-8378

MARRIOTT HOTEL
2700 Mission College Blvd (95054)
Rates: $89-$265
(408) 988-1500
(800) 228-9290

MOTEL 6
3208 El Camino Real (95051)
Rates: $45-$54
(408) 241-0200
(800) 466-8356

SIERRA SUITES HOTEL
3915 Rivermark Plaza (95054)
Rates: $179-$199
(408) 486-0800

VAGABOND INN
3580 El Camino Real (95051)
Rates: $39-$139
(408) 241-0771
(800) 522-1555

WELLESLEY INN
5405 Stevens Crk Blvd (95051)
Rates: $74-$89
(408) 257-8600
(800) 444-8888

WESTIN HOTEL
5101 Great America Pkwy (95054)
Rates: $99-$259
(408) 986-0700
(800) 937-8461

SANTA CLARITA

BEST WESTERN VALENCIA INN
27413 Tourney Rd (91355)
Rates: $70-$110
(661) 255-0555
(800) 528-1234

RESIDENCE INN BY MARRIOTT
25320 The Old Rd (91381)
Rates: $129-$159
(661) 290-2800
(800) 331-3131

SANTA CRUZ

BAY FRONT INN
325 Pacific Ave (95060)
Rates: $48-$185
(831) 423-8564
(800) 736-2023

COAST SANTA CRUZ HOTEL
175 W Cliff Dr (95060)
Rates: $149-$349
(831) 426-4330

CONTINENTAL INN
414 Ocean St (95060)
Rates: $75-$260
(831) 429-1221

GUESTHOUSE PACIFIC INN
330 Ocean St (95060)
Rates: $49-$199
(831) 425-3722
(800) 214-8378

LAGUNA CREEK INN B&B
2727 Smith Grade (95060)
Rates: $85-$125
(831) 425-0692
(800) 730-5398

MOTEL 6
370 Ocean St (95060)
Rates: $68-$169
(831) 458-9220
(800) 466-8356

AREA CODES - If the local number doesn't connect, check for a new area code.

OCEAN FRONT HOUSE
1600 W Cliff Dr (95060)
Rates: $850-$1230 Weekly
(831) 266-4453
(800) 801-4453

OCEAN PACIFIC LODGE
120 Washington St (95060)
Rates: $77-$160
(831) 457-1234
(800) 995-0289

REDWOOD CROFT B&B
276 Northwest Dr (95060)
Rates: $75
(831) 458-1939

SUNNY COVE MOTEL
2-1610 E Cliff Dr (95062)
Rates: $40-$100
(831) 475-1741

SANTA FE SPRINGS

MOTEL 6
13412 Excelsior Dr (90670)
Rates: $39-$52
(562) 921-0596
(800) 466-8356
(800) 426-3213

SANTA MARIA

BEST WESTERN BIG AMERICA
1725 N Broadway (93454)
Rates: $77-$150
(805) 922-5200
(800) 528-1234
(800) 426-3213

COMFORT INN
210 S Nicholson Ave (93454)
Rates: $89-$129
(805) 922-5891
(800) 424-6423

HISTORIC SANTA MARIA INN
801 S Broadway (93454)
Rates: $119-$149
(805) 928-7777
(800) 462-4276

MOTEL 6
2040 N Preisker Lane (93454)
Rates: $39-$63
(805) 928-8111
(800) 466-8356

SANTA MONICA

THE FAIRMONT MIRAMAR HOTEL
101 Wilshire Blvd (90401)
Rates: $209-$299
(310) 576-7777
(800) 527-4727

THE GEORGIAN
1415 Ocean Ave (90401)
Rates: $235-$285
(310) 395-6333
(800) 538-8147

LE MERIGOT/ J W MARRIOTT BEACH HOTEL AND SPA
1740 Ocean Ave (90401)
Rates: $299-$479
(310) 395-9700

LOEWS SANTA MONICA BEACH
1700 Ocean Ave (90401)
Rates: $240-$405
(310) 458-6700
(800) 235-6397

TRAVELODGE
3102 W Pico Blvd (90405)
Rates: $79-$149
(310) 450-5766
(800) 578-7878
(800) 231-7679

SANTA NELLA

COMFORT INN
28821 W Gonzaga Rd (95322)
Rates: $59-$90
(209) 827-8700
(800) 424-6423

HOLIDAY INN EXP
28976 W Plaza Dr (95322)
Rates: $75-$95
(209) 826-8282
(800) 465-4329

MOTEL 6
12733 S Hwy 33 (95322)
Rates: $37-$46
(209) 826-6644
(800) 466-8356

RAMADA INN MISSION DE ORO
13070 S Hwy 33 (95322)
Rates: $50-$89
(209) 826-4444
(800) 272-6232

SANTA ROSA

BEST WESTERN GARDEN INN
1500 Santa Rosa Ave (95404)
Rates: $75-$125
(707) 546-4031
(800) 528-1234
(800) 929-2771

COMFORT INN
2632 Cleveland Ave (95403)
Rates: $70-$136
(707) 542-5544
(800) 424-6423

COOPERS GROVE RANCH B&B
5800 Sonoma Mtn Rd (95404)
Rates: $110-$185
(707) 571-1928

HILLSIDE INN MOTEL
2901 4th St (95409)
Rates: $78-$98
(707) 546-9353

MOTEL 6-NORTH
3145 Cleveland Ave (95403)
Rates: $45-$62
(707) 525-9010
(800) 466-8356

MOTEL 6-SOUTH
2760 Cleveland Ave (95403)
Rates: $45-$62
(707) 546-1500
(800) 466-8356

SANTA ROSA MOTOR INN
1800 Santa Rosa Ave (95403)
Rates: $60-$90
(707) 523-3480

TRAVELODGE
1815 Santa Rosa Ave (95403)
Rates: $50-$109
(707) 542-3472
(800) 578-7878

SANTA YNEZ

SANTA COTA MOTEL
3099 Mission Dr (93460)
Rates: $75-$125
(805) 688-5525

SANTA YSABEL

APPLE TREE INN
4360 Hwy 78 (92070)
Rates: $55-$79
(760) 765-0222

SANTEE

CARLTON OAKS COUNTRY CLUB
9200 Inwood Dr (92071)
Rates: $50-$80
(619) 448-4242
(800) 831-6757

SCOTTS VALLEY

HILTON SAN JOSE SOUTH
6001 La Madrona Dr (95066)
Rates: $167-$229
(831) 440-1000
(800) 445-8667

SEASIDE

ECONO LODGE BAY BREEZE
2049 Fremont Blvd (93955)
Rates: $49-$260
(831) 899-7111
(800) 424-6423

SELMA

SUPER 8 MOTEL
3142 S Highland Ave (93662)
Rates: $52-$70
(559) 896-2800
(800) 800-8000

SHASTA LAKE CITY

BRIDGE BAY RESORT
10300 Bridge Bay Rd (Redding 96003)
Rates: $78-$103
(530) 275-3021
(800) 752-9669

FAWNDALE LODGE
15215 Fawndale Rd (Redding 96003)
Rates: $59-$91
(530) 275-8000
(800) 338-0941

SHAVER LAKE

DINKEY CREEK INN & CHALETS
53861 Dinkey Creek Rd (93664)
Rates: $85-$100
(559) 841-3435

SHELTER COVE

INN OF THE LOST COAST
205 Wave Dr (95589)
Rates: $105-$135
(707) 986-7521
(888) 870-9676

MARINA MOTEL
533 Machi Rd (95589)
Rates: $52-$62
(707) 986-7595

SIERRA CITY

HERRINGTONS SIERRA PINES
104 Main St (96125)
Rates: $69-$125
(530) 862-1151
(800) 682-9848

SIMI VALLEY

MOTEL 6
2566 N Erringer Rd (93065)
Rates: $59-$70
(805) 526-3533
(800) 466-8356

AREA CODES - If the local number doesn't connect, check for a new area code.

SMITH RIVER
BEST WESTERN SHIP ASHORE MOTEL
12340 Hwy 101 (95567)
Rates: $58-$88
(707) 487-3141
(800) 487-3141

CASA RUBIO BEACH HOUSE
17285 Crissey Rd (95567)
Rates: $68-$98
(707) 487-4313
(800) 357-6199

SEA ESCAPE MOTEL
15370 Hwy 101 N (95567)
Rates: $60-$65
(707) 487-7333

SOLEDAD
BEST WESTERN VALLEY HARVEST INN
1155 Front St (93960)
Rates: $79-$170
(831) 676-3833
(877) 467-2244

PARAISO HOT SPRINGS LODGE
Paraiso Springs Rd (93960)
Rates: $110-$160
(831) 678-2882

SOLVANG
MEADOWLARK INN
2644 Mission Dr (93463)
Rates: $130
(805) 688-4631
(800) 549-4658

ROYAL COPENHAGEN INN
1579 Mission Dr (93463)
Rates: $71-$189
(805) 688-5561

SOMES BAR
MARBLE MTN RANCH CABINS
92520 Hwy 96 (95568)
Rates: $27-$200
(800) 552-6284

SONOMA
BEST WESTERN SONOMA VALLEY INN
550 2nd St W (95476)
Rates: $129-$349
(707) 938-9200
(800) 334-5784

MARTHA'S COTTAGE B&B
19377 Orange Ave (95476)
Rates: $110-$125
(707) 996-6918

STONE GROVE BED & BREAKFAST
240 2nd St E (95476)
Rates: $65-$115
(707) 939-8249

TREE HOUSE B&B
431 2nd St E (95476)
Rates: $125-$150
(707) 938-1628

VILLA CASTILLO BED & BREAKFAST
1100 Castle Rd (95476)
Rates: $150
(707) 996-4616

SONORA
ALADDIN MOTOR INN
14260 Mono Way (95370)
Rates: $68-$102
(209) 533-4971

BEST WESTERN SONORA OAKS MOTOR HOTEL
19551 Hess Ave (95370)
Rates: $79-$149
(209) 553-4400
(800) 532-1944

COUNTRY INN SONORA
18730 Hwy 108 (95327)
Rates: $54-$159
(209) 984-0315

DAYS INN
160 S Washington St (95370)
Rates: $69-$159
(209) 532-2400
(800) 329-7466

HAMMONS HOUSE INN B&B
22963 Robertson Ranch Rd (95370)
Rates: $130-$150
(209) 532-7921
(888) 666-7923

KENNEDY MEADOWS RESORT CABINS
P. O. Box 4010 (95370)
Rates: $52-$105
(209) 965-3900

MINERS MOTEL
18740 Hwy 108 (95370)
Rates: $39-$75
(209) 532-7850
(800) 451-4176

MOUNTAIN VIEW B&B
12980 Mountain View Rd (95370)
Rates: $60-$80
(209) 533-0628
(800) 446-1333

RAIL FENCE MOTEL
19950 Hwy 108 (95370)
Rates: $35-$47
(209) 532-9191

SONORA GOLD LODGE
480 Stockton St (95370)
Rates: $39-$109
(209) 532-3952

SOUTH LAKE TAHOE
(Also See Lake Tahoe area)

ALDER INN
1072 Ski Run Blvd (96150)
Rates: $42-$160
(530) 544-4485
(800) 544-0056

ALPENROSE INN
4074 Pine Blvd (96150)
Rates: $40-$140
(530) 544-2985
(800) 370-4049

AMBASSADOR MOTOR LODGE
4130 Manzanita Ave (96150)
Rates: $55-$110
(530) 544-6461

BEST WESTERN TIMBER COVE LODGE
3411 Lake Tahoe Blvd (96150)
Rates: $69-$209
(530) 541-6722
(800) 972-8558

BLUE JAY LODGE
4133 Cedar Ave (96150)
Rates: $49-$169
(530) 544-5232
(800) 258-3529

BLUE LAKE MOTEL
1055 Ski Run Blvd (96150)
Rates: $50-$80
(530) 541-2399

BUDGET INN
3496 Lake Tahoe Blvd (96150)
Rates: $32-$150
(530) 544-2834

CAL VA RADO MOTEL
988 Stateline Ave (96150)
Rates: $39-$75
(530) 541-3900

CAPRI MOTEL
932 Stateline Ave (96150)
Rates: $55-$110
(530) 544-3665

CEDAR INN & SUITES
890 Stateline Ave (96150)
Rates: $35-$69
(530) 543-0159

CEDAR LODGE
4069 Cedar Ave (96150)
Rates: $40-$340
(530) 544-6453

COLONY INN
3794 Montreal (96150)
Rates: $35-$110
(530) 655-6481
(800) 338-5552

DAYS INN-CASINO AREA
968 Park Ave (95150)
Rates: $42-$275
(530) 541-4800
(800) 448-0754

ECHO CREEK RANCH
P. O. Box 20088 (96151)
Rates: $100+
(530) 544-5397
(800) 462-5397

FIRESIDE LODGE
515 Emerald Bay Rd (96150)
Rates: $69-$155
(530) 542-1717

HARRAH'S LAKE TAHOE HOTEL
US 50 (Stateline, NV 89449)
Rates: $69-$299
(775) 588-6611
(800) 427-7247
(Kennels provided)

HARVEYS CASINO & RESORT
US 50 (Stateline, NV 89449)
Rates: $39-$289
(775) 588-6611
(Kennels provided)

HIGH COUNTRY LODGE
1227 Emerald Bay Rd (96150)
Rates: $30-$715
(530) 541-0508

INN AT HEAVENLY B&B
1261 Ski Run Blvd (96150)
Rates: $75-$395
(530) 544-4244
(800) 692-2246

INN BY THE LAKE
3300 Lake Tahoe Blvd (96150)
Rates: $98-$238
(530) 542-0330
(800) 877-1466

LA BAER INN
4133 Lake Tahoe Blvd (96150)
Rates: $49-$109
(530) 544-2139
(800) 544-5575

AREA CODES - If the local number doesn't connect, check for a new area code.

LAKE VILLAGE RESORT CONDOS
301 Hwy 50 (Stateline, NV 89449)
Rates: $155-$450
(775) 589-6065

LAKEPARK LODGE
4081 Cedar Ave (96150)
Rates: $40-$75
(530) 541-5004

LAMPLITER MOTEL
4143 Cedar Ave (96150)
Rates: $45-$100
(530) 544-2936

MATTERHORN MOTEL
2187 Lake Tahoe Blvd (96150)
Rates: $40-$185
(530) 541-0367

MONTGOMERY INN
966 Modesto Ave (96151)
Rates: $49-$69
(530) 544-3871
(800) 624-8224

MOTEL 6
2375 Lake Tahoe Blvd (96150)
Rates: $39-$63
(530) 542-1400
(800) 466-8356

PARK AVENUE/ MEADOWOOD LODGE
904 Park Ave (96150)
Rates: $70-$100
(530) 544-3503

PISTANTES COY- OTE DEN MOTEL
1211 Emerald Bay Rd (96150)
Rates: $30-$195
(530) 541-2282

RAVEN WOOD HOTEL
4075 Manzanita Ave (96150)
Rates: $52-$169
(800) 659-4185

RIDGEWOOD INN MOTEL
1341 Emerald Bay Rd (96150)
Rates: $49-$135
(530) 541-8589

SAFARI MOTEL
966 LaSalle St (96150)
Rates: $70-$100
(530) 544-2912

SLEEPY RACCOON MOTEL
1180 Ski Run Blvd (96150)
Rates: $40-$70
(530) 544-5890

SOUTH LAKE TAHOE CABIN RENTAL
4 Miles South at Hwy 89 & 50 Jct (96150)
Rates: $120-$250
(619) 246-0678
(888) 818-3283

STATELINE LODGE
913 Friday Ave (96150)
Rates: n/a
(530) 544-3075

TAHOE KEYS RESORT
599 Tahoe Keys Blvd (96150)
Rates: $150-$1500
(530) 544-5397
(800) 698-2463

TAHOE MARINA INN
930 Bal Bijou Rd (96150)
Rates: $79-$140
(530) 541-2180

TAHOE QUEEN MOTEL
932 Poplar St (96157)
Rates: $40-$70
(530) 544-2291

TAHOE SUNDOWNER MOTEL
1211 Emerald Bay (96150)
Rates: $30-$85
(530) 541-2282

TAHOE SUNSET LODGE
1171 Emerald Bay (96150)
Rates: $26-$60
(530) 541-2940

TAHOE TROPICANA LODGE
4132 Cedar Ave (96154)
Rates: $40-$70
(530) 541-3911

TAHOE VALLEY LODGE
2241 Lake Tahoe Blvd (96150)
Rates: $75-$395
(530) 541-0353
(800) 669-7544

TRADE WINDS RESORT
944 Friday Ave (96150)
Rates: $35-$125
(530) 544-6459
(800) 628-1829

SOUTH SAN FRANCISCO

HOWARD JOHNSON EXP INN
222 S Airport Blvd (94080)
Rates: $39-$159
(650) 589-9055
(800) 446-4656

LA QUINTA INN
20 Airport Blvd (94080)
Rates: $99-$125
(650) 583-2223
(800) 687-6667

MOTEL 6- AIRPORT
111 Mitchell Ave (94080)
Rates: $64-$75
(650) 877-0770
(800) 466-8356

SPRING VALLEY

CROWN INN SUITES
9603 Campo Rd (91977)
Rates: $43-$64
(619) 589-1111

STANTON
MOTEL 6
7450 Katella Ave (90680)
Rates: $35-$42
(714) 891-0717
(800) 466-8356

ST. HELENA
EL BONITA MOTEL
195 Main St (94574)
Rates: $89-$289
(707) 963-3216
(800) 541-3284

HARVEST INN
One Main St (94574)
Rates: $255-$675
(707) 963-9463
(800) 950-8466

STINSON BEACH
OCEAN COURT MOTEL
Hwy 1 (94970)
Rates: $95-$200
(415) 868-0212

SEADRIFT CO. VACATION RENTALS
2 Dipsea Rd (94970)
Rates: n/a
(415) 868-1791

STOCKTON
BEST VALUE INN
1707 W Fremont St (95203)
Rates: $58
(209) 466-7777
(888) 315-2378

HOWARD JOHNSON EXP
33 N Center St (95202)
Rates: $70-$100
(209) 948-6151
(800) 446-4656

LA QUINTA INN
2710 W March Ln (95219)
Rates: $76-$92
(209) 952-7800
(800) 687-6667

MOTEL 6
1625 French Camp Tpke Rd (95206)
Rates: $39-$52
(209) 467-3600
(800) 466-8356

MOTEL 6
817 Navy Dr (95206)
Rates: $41-$54
(209) 946-0923
(800) 466-8356

MOTEL 6
6717 Plymouth Rd (95207)
Rates: $43-$56
(209) 951-8120
(800) 466-8356

RESIDENCE INN BY MARRIOTT
3240 W March Ln (95219)
Rates: $119-$139
(209) 472-9800
(800) 331-3131

SUNSHINE INN
8009 N Hwy 99 (95212)
Rates: $25-$50
(209) 956-5200

STRAWBERRY
3 RIVERS RESORT
P. O. Box 81 (95375)
Rates: $85-$185
(209) 965-3278
(800) 514-6777

SUISUN CITY
ECONOMY INNS OF AMERICA
4376 Central Pl (94585)
Rates: $30-$42
(707) 864-1728
(800) 826-0778

SUN CITY
TRAVELODGE
27955 Encanto Dr (92586)
Rates: $59-$69
(909) 679-1133
(800) 578-7878

SUN VALLEY
SCOTTISH INNS
8365 Lehigh Ave (91352)
Rates: $40+
(818) 504-2671
(800) 251-1962

AREA CODES - If the local number doesn't connect, check for a new area code.

SUNNYVALE

CAPTAIN'S COVE MOTEL
600 N Mathilda Ave (94086)
Rates: $59-$61
(800) 322-2683

COMFORT INN
1071 E El Camino Real (94087)
Rates: $69-$139
(408) 244-9000
(800) 424-6423

FOUR POINTS BY SHERATON
1250 Lakeside Dr (94086)
Rates: $129
(408) 738-4888

HOMESTEAD STUDIO SUITES
1255 Orleans Dr (94086)
Rates: $69-$89
(408) 734-3431
(888) 782-9473

MAPLE TREE INN
711 E El Camino Real (94087)
Rates: $59-$150
(408) 720-9700
(800) 423-0243

MOTEL 6 NORTH
775 N Mathilda Ave (94086)
Rates: $50+
(408) 736-4595
(800) 466-8356

MOTEL 6 SOUTH
806 Ahwanee Ave (94086)
Rates: $50+
(408) 720-1222
(800) 466-8356

QUALITY INN
1280 Persian Dr (94089)
Rates: $69-$189
(408) 744-1100
(800) 424-6423

RADISSON INN
1085 E El Camino Readl (94086)
Rates: n/a
(408) 247-0800
(800) 333-3333

RESIDENCE INN BY MARRIOTT
1080 Stewart Dr (94086)
Rates: $199-$239
(408) 720-8893
(800) 331-3131

RESIDENCE INN BY MARRIOTT
750 Lakeway Dr (94086)
Rates: $199-$239
(408) 720-1000
(800) 331-3131

STAYBRIDGE SUITES
900 Hamlin Ct (94089)
Rates: $160-$190
(408) 745-1515
(800) 238-8000

TOWNEPLACE SUITES
606 S Bernardo Ave (94087)
Rates: $69-$149
(408) 733-4200
(800) 257-3000

VAGABOND INN
816 Ahwanee Ave (94086)
Rates: $59-$209
(408) 734-4607
(800) 522-1555

WILD PALMS HOTEL
910 E Fremont St (94087)
Rates: $169
(408) 738-0500

WOODFIN SUITES
635 E El Camino Real (94087)
Rates: n/a
(408) 738-1700
(800) 237-8811

SUSANVILLE

AMERICA'S BEST INNS
2705 Main St (96130)
Rates: n/a
(530) 257-4522

BUDGET HOST FRONTIER INN
2685 Main St (96130)
Rates: $31-$41
(530) 257-4141
(800) 283-4678

COZY MOTEL
2829 Main St (96130)
Rates: $25-$30
(530) 257-2319

DIAMOND VIEW MOTEL
1529 Main St (96130)
Rates: $27-$34
(530) 257-4585

KNIGHTS INN MOTEL
1705 Main St (96130)
Rates: $37-$49
(530) 257-2168
(800) 843-5644

MT. LASSEN HOTEL
27 S Lassen St (96130)
Rates: $37+
(530) 257-6609

RIVER INN MOTEL
1710 Main St (96130)
Rates: $45-$60
(530) 257-6051

SIERRA VISTA MOTEL
1067 Main St (96130)
Rates: $29-$34
(530) 257-6721

SUPER 8 MOTEL
2975 Johnstonville Rd (96130)
Rates: $50-$68
(530) 257-2782
(800) 800-8000

SYLMAR

MOTEL 6
12775 Encinitas Ave (91342)
Rates: $39-$58
(818) 362-9491
(800) 466-8356

TAHOE VISTA

BEESLEY'S COTTAGES
6674 N Lake Blvd (96148)
Rates: $70-$140
(530) 546-2448

HOLIDAY HOUSE
7276 N Lake Blvd (96148)
Rates: $115-$205
(530) 546-2369
(800) 294-6378

RUSTIC COTTAGES
7499 N Lake Blvd (96148)
Rates: $49-$139
(530) 546-3523

TAHOMA

NORFOLK WOODS INN CABINS
6941 W Lake Blvd (96142)
Rates: $100-$180
(530) 525-5000

TAHOE LAKE COTTAGES
7030 W Lake Blvd (96142)
Rates: $125-$185
(530) 525-4411
(800) 824-6348

TAHOMA LODGE
7018 W Lake Blvd (96142)
Rates: $45-$115
(530) 525-7721
(800) 824-6348

TARZANA

ST. GEORGE MOTOR INN
19454 Ventura Blvd (91356)
Rates: $68-$150
(818) 345-6911
(800) 845-8919

TECOPA

DELIGHT'S HOT SPA ROOMS & CABINS
368 Tecopa Hot Springs Rd (92389)
Rates: $32-$50
(760) 852-4343
(800) 854-5007

TEHACHAPI

BEST WESTERN MOUNTAIN INN
416 W Tehachapi Blvd (93561)
Rates: $63-$89
(661) 822-5591
(800) 528-1234

GOLDEN HILLS MOTEL
22561 Woodford-Tehachapi Rd (93561)
Rates: $24-$49
(661) 822-4488
(800) 434-1118

TRAVELODGE TEHACHAPI SUMMIT
500 Steuber Rd (93561)
Rates: $72-$78
(661) 823-8000
(800) 578-7878

TEMECULA

COMFORT INN
27338 Jefferson Ave (92590)
Rates: $69-$169
(909) 296-3788
(800) 424-6423

MOTEL 6- RANCHO CALIFORNIA
41900 Moreno Dr (92590)
Rates: $45-$66
(909) 676-7199
(800) 466-8356

THOUSAND OAKS

MOTEL 6
1516 Newbury Rd (91320)
Rates: $41-$59
(805) 499-0711
(800) 466-8356

PREMIER INN
2434 W Hillcrest Dr (91320)
Rates: $44-$69
(805) 499-0755

THOUSAND OAKS INN
75 W Thousand Oaks Blvd (91360)
Rates: $90-$115
(805) 497-3701

THOUSAND PALMS

RED ROOF INN
72-215 Varner Rd (92276)
Rates: $45-$79
(760) 343-1381
(800) 843-7663

AREA CODES - If the local number doesn't connect, check for a new area code.

THREE RIVERS
BEST WESTERN HOLIDAY LODGE
40105 Sierra Dr (93271)
Rates: $59-$129
(559) 561-4119
(888) 523-9291

BUCKEYE TREE LODGE
46000 Sierra Dr (93271)
Rates: $59-$124
(559) 561-5900

GATEWAY LODGE
45978 Sierra Dr (93271)
Rates: $69-$125
(559) 561-4133

LAZY J RANCH MOTEL
39625 Sierra Dr (93271)
Rates: $75-$119
(559) 561-4449

SEQUOIA VILLAGE INN
45971 Sierra Dr (93271)
Rates: $60-$249
(559) 561-3652

SIERRA LODGE
43175 Sierra Dr (93271)
Rates: $42-$112
(559) 561-3681

TORRANCE
HOMESTEAD STUDIO SUITES HOTEL
3995 Carson St (90503)
Rates: $75-$100
(310) 543-0048
(800) 782-9473

RESIDENCE INN BY MARRIOTT
3701 Torrance Blvd (90503)
Rates: $79-$149
(310) 543-4566
(800) 331-3131

STAYBRIDGE SUITES
19901 Prairie Ave (90503)
Rates: $198-$228
(310) 371-8525
(800) 465-4329

TRACY
BEST WESTERN LUXURY INN
811 Clover Rd (95376)
Rates: $79-$99
(209) 832-0271
(877) 468-7229

MOTEL 6
3810 Tracy Blvd (95376)
Rates: $39-$48
(209) 836-4900
(800) 466-8356

TRINIDAD
BISHOP PINE LODGE
1481 Patrick's Point Dr (95570)
Rates: $80-$90
(707) 677-3314

TRINIDAD INN
1170 Patrick's Pt Dr (95570)
Rates: $90-$150
(707) 677-3349

TRINITY CENTER
BECKER'S BOUNTY LODGE
HCR 3, Box 4659 (96091)
Rates: $400-$650 Weekly
(530) 266-3277

ENRIGHT GULCH CABINS
3500 Hwy 3, P.O. Box 244 (96091)
Rates: $30-$35
(530) 266-3600

RIPPLE CREEK CABINS
Rt 2, Box 4020 (96091)
Rates: $60-$115
(530) 266-3505

WYNTOON RESORT
Hwy 3 (96091)
Rates: $16-$110
(530) 266-3337
(800) 715-3337

TRONA
DESERT ROSE MOTEL
84368 Trona Rd (93562)
Rates: $30-$42
(619) 372-4572

TRUCKEE
ALPINE COUNTRY LODGE
12260 Deerfield Dr (96161)
Rates: $50-$79
(530) 587-3801
(800) 933-1787

THE INN AT TRUCKEE
11506 Deerfield Dr (96161)
Rates: $89-$139
(530) 587-8888
(888) 773-6888

TULARE
BEST WESTERN TOWN & COUNTRY LODGE
1051 N Blackstone Dr (93274)
Rates: $62-$150
(559) 688-7537
(800) 528-1234
(888) 488-5273

CHARTER INN
1016 E Prosperity Ave (93274)
Rates: $69-$119
(559) 685-9500
(888) 457-9100

DAYS INN
1183 N Blackstone Dr (93274)
Rates: $49-$65
(559) 686-0985
(800) 329-7466

MOTEL 6
1111 N Blackstone Dr (93274)
Rates: $37-$46
(559) 686-1611
(800) 446-8356

QUALITY INN SEQUOIA AREA
1010 E Prosperity Ave (93274)
Rates: $60-$150
(559) 686-3432
(800) 424-6423

TULELAKE
ELLIS MOTEL
2238 Hwy 139 (96134)
Rates: $30-$57
(530) 667-5242

TURLOCK
MOTEL 6
250 S Walnut Ave (95380)
Rates: $37-$52
(209) 667-4100
(800) 466-8356

TRAVELODGE
201 W Glenwood Ave (95380)
Rates: $79-$90
(209) 668-3400
(800) 578-7878

TWAIN HARTE
ELDORADO MOTEL
22678 Blackhawk Dr (95383)
Rates: $42-$65
(209) 586-4479

TWENTYNINE PALMS
BEST WESTERN GARDENS INN
71487 Twentynine Palms Hwy (92277)
Rates: $79-$90
(760) 367-9141
(800) 528-1234

CIRCLE "C" LODGE
6340 El Rey Ave (92277)
Rates: $65-$90
(760) 367-7615

MOTEL 6
72562 29 Palms Hwy (92277)
Rates: $39-$43
(760) 367-2833
(800) 466-8356

SUNNYVALE GARDEN SUITES HOTEL
73843 Sunnyvale Dr (92277)
Rates: $69-$89
(760) 361-3939

TWIN PEAKS
ARROWHEAD PINE ROSE CABINS
25994 Hwy 189 (92391)
Rates: $49-$159
(909) 337-2341
(800) 429-7463

UKIAH
BEST VALUE INN
693 S Orchard Ave (95482)
Rates: $49-$89
(707) 468-9167

DAYS INN REDWOODS-WINE COUNTRY
950 N State St (95482)
Rates: $59-$125
(707) 462-7584
(800) 329-7466
(800) 922-3388

HAMPTON INN
1160 Airport Park Blvd (95482)
Rates: $99-$129
(707) 462-6555
(800) 426-7866

MOTEL 6
1208 S State St (95482)
Rates: $39-$57
(707) 468-5404
(800) 466-8356

RODEWAY INN
1050 S State St (95482)
Rates: $55-$139
(707) 462-2906
(800) 424-6423

SUPER 8 MOTEL
1070 S State St (95482)
Rates: $39-$99
(707) 462-6657
(800) 800-8000

UNION CITY
CROWNE PLAZA
32084 Alvarado Niles Rd (94587)
Rates: $108-$199
(510) 489-2200
(800) 227-6963

UPPER LAKE
BLUE LAKES LODGE & RESTAURANT
5135 W Hwy 20 (95485)
Rates: $32-$59
(707) 275-2181
(800) 423-2181

NARROWS LODGE RESORT
5690 Blue Lakes Rd (95485)
Rates: $50-$85
(707) 275-2718

PINE ACRES BLUE LAKE RESORT
5328 Blue Lakes Rd (95485)
Rates: $85+
(707) 275-2811

VACAVILLE
BEST WESTERN HERITAGE INN
1420 E Monte Vista Ave (95688)
Rates: $75-$95
(707) 448-8453
(800) 528-1234

MOTEL 6
107 Lawrence Dr (95687)
Rates: $39-$60
(707) 447-5550
(800) 466-8356

RESIDENCE INN BY MARRIOTT
360 Orange Dr (95687)
Rates: $129-$169
(707) 469-0300
(800) 331-3131

SUPER 8 MOTEL
101 Allison Court (95688)
Rates: $64-$89
(707) 449-8884
(800) 800-8000

VALENCIA
HILTON GARDEN INN-SIX FLAGS
27710 The Old Rd (91355)
Rates: $99-$129
(661) 254-8800
(800) 445-8667

VALLEJO
BEST WESTERN INN AT MARINE WORLD
1596 Fairgrounds Dr (94589)
Rates: $49-$169
(707) 554-9655
(800) 528-1234
(877) 554-9655

HOLIDAY INN NAPA VALLEY GATEWAY
1000 Fairgrounds Dr (94590)
Rates: $84-$119
(707) 644-1200
(800) 465-4329
(800) 533-5753

MOTEL 6 FAIRGROUNDS-MARINE WORLD EAST
458 Fairgrounds Dr (94589)
Rates: $39-$60
(707) 642-7781
(800) 466-8356

MOTEL 6-MARINE WORLD WEST
1455 Marine World Pkwy (94589)
Rates: $45-$63
(707) 643-7611
(800) 466-8356

MOTEL 6 MARITIME NORTH
597 Sandy Beach Rd (94590)
Rates: $46+
(707) 552-2912
(800) 466-8356

RAMADA INN
1000 Admiral Callaghan Ln (94591)
Rates: $99-$119
(707) 643-2700
(800) 272-6232

VALLEY FORD
VALLEY FORD HOTEL
14415 Coast Hwy One (94972)
Rates: $55-$90
(707) 876-3600
(800) 696-6679

VALLEY SPRINGS
10TH GREEN INN BED & BREAKFAST
14 St. Andrews Rd (95252)
Rates: $59-$89
(209) 772-1084

VENTURA
BEST WESTERN VENTURA INN
708 E Thompson Blvd (93001)
Rates: $69-$149
(805) 648-3101
(800) 528-1234
(800) 648-1508

LA MER B & B
411 Poli St (93001)
Rates: n/a
(805) 643-3600

LA QUINTA INN
5818 Valentine Rd (93003)
Rates: $76-$103
(805) 658-6200
(800) 687-6777

MOTEL 6-BEACH
2145 E Harbor Blvd (93001)
Rates: $45-$66
(805) 643-5100
(800) 466-8356

MOTEL 6-SOUTH
3075 Johnson Dr (93003)
Rates: $45-$66
(805) 650-0080
(800) 466-8356

OCEAN VIEW MOTEL
1690 E Thompson Blvd (93001)
Rates: n/a
(805) 648-6440

REX MOTEL
2406 E Thompson Blvd (93001)
Rates: n/a
(805) 643-5681

VAGABOND INN
756 E Thompson Blvd (93001)
Rates: $64-$159
(805) 648-5371
(800) 522-1555

VENTURA BEACH MARRIOTT
2055 Harbor Blvd (93001)
Rates: $229
(805) 643-6000
(800) 228-9290

VICTORIA MOTEL
2350 S Victoria Ave (93003)
Rates: $33-$60
(805) 642-2173

WHITE CAPS MOTEL
1612 E Thompson Blvd (93001)
Rates: n/a
(805) 648-4924

VICTORVILLE
BEST WESTERN GREEN TREE INN & SUITES
14173 Green Tree Blvd (92392)
Rates: $79-$94
(760) 245-3461
(800) 528-1234

BUDGET INN
14153 Kentwood Blvd (92392)
Rates: $37-$47
(760) 241-8010

COMFORT SUITES
12281 Mariposa Rd (92392)
Rates: $69-$169
(760) 245-6777
(800) 424-6423

HOWARD JOHNSON EXP INN
16868 Stoddard Wells Rd (92392)
Rates: $50-$70
(760) 243-7700
(800) 446-4656

MOTEL 6
16901 Stoddard Wells Rd (92392)
Rates: $39-$44
(760) 243-0666
(800) 466-8356

RAMADA INN
15494 Palmdale Rd (92392)
Rates: $85-$90
(760) 245-6565
(800) 272-6232

RED ROOF INN HI DESERT
13409 Mariposa Rd (92392)
Rates: $55-$99
(760) 241-1577
(800) 843-7663

TRAVELODGE
12175 Mariposa Rd (92392)
Rates: $45-$72
(760) 241-7200
(800) 578-7878

VISALIA
BEST WESTERN VISALIA INN
623 W Main St (93277)
Rates: $83-$94
(559) 732-4561
(800) 528-1234

DAYS INN
4645 W Noble Ave (93277)
Rates: $50-$125
(559) 732-5611
(800) 329-7466

HOLIDAY INN HOTEL
9000 W Airport Dr (93277)
Rates: $109-$169
(559) 651-5000
(800) 465-4329

LAMP LITER INN
3300 W Mineral King Ave (93277)
Rates: $69-$109
(559) 732-4511

SUPER 8 MOTEL
4801 W Noble Ave (93277)
Rates: $55-$95
(559) 627-2885
(800) 800-8000

VISTA
LA QUINTA INN
630 Sycamore Ave (92083)
Rates: $80-$112
(760) 727-8180
(800) 687-6667

WALNUT CREEK
HOLIDAY INN
2730 N Main St (94596)
Rates: $79-$199
(925) 932-3332
(800) 465-4329

MOTEL 6
2389 N Main St (94596)
Rates: $59-$75
(925) 935-4010
(800) 466-8356

AREA CODES - If the local number doesn't connect, check for a new area code.

WATSONVILLE

BEST WESTERN ROSE GARDEN INN
740 Freedom Blvd (95076)
Rates: $59-$159
(831) 724-3367
(800) 528-1234
(888) 685-5760

COMFORT INN
112 Airport Blvd (95019)
Rates: $49-$160
(831) 728-2300
(800) 424-6423

COUNTRY SUNRISE B&B
3085 Freedom Blvd (95076)
Rates: $70-$95
(831) 722-4793

EL RANCHO MOTEL
976 Salinas Rd (95076)
Rates: $30-$69
(831) 722-2766

MOTEL 6
125 Silver Leaf Dr (95076)
Rates: $41-$70
(831) 728-4144
(800) 466-8356

RED ROOF INN
1620 W Beach St (95076)
Rates: $49-$84
(831) 740-4520
(800) 843-7663

WAWONA STATION

THE REDWOOD GUEST COTTAGES
P. O. Box 2085 (95389)
Rates: $95-$400
(209) 375-6666

WEAVERVILLE

BEST WESTERN VICTORIAN INN
1709 Main St (96093)
Rates: $59-$279
(530) 623-4432
(800) 528-1234

49ER MOTEL
718 Main St (96093)
Rates: $45-$140
(530) 623-4937

MOTEL TRINITY
1112 Main St (96093)
Rates: $40-$80
(530) 623-2129

RED HILL MOTEL
Red Hill Rd (96093)
Rates: $32-$78
(530) 623-4331

WEED

COMFORT INN CENTRAL
1844 Shastina Dr (96094)
Rates: $69-$123
(530) 938-1982
(800) 424-6423

HOLIDAY INN EXP
1830 Black Butte Dr (96094)
Rates: $69-$120
(530) 938-1308
(800) 465-4329

MOTEL 6
466 N Weed Blvd (96094)
Rates: $35-$50
(530) 938-4101
(800) 466-8356

SIS-Q-INN MOTEL
1825 Shastina Dr (96094)
Rates: $40-$120
(530) 938-4194

STEWART MINERAL SPRINGS CABINS
4617 Stewart Spgs Rd (96094)
Rates: $25-$65
(530) 938-2222
(800) 322-9223

TOWN HOUSE MOTEL
157 S Weed Blvd (96094)
Rates: $35-$38
(530) 938-4431

WEST COVINA

HAMPTON INN
3145 E Garvey Ave N (91791)
Rates: $69-$89
(626) 967-5800
(800) 426-7866

WEST HOLLYWOOD

THE ARGYLE HISTORIC HOTEL
8358 Sunset Blvd (90069)
Rates: $265-$330
(323) 654-7100

THE GRAFTON ON SUNSET
8462 Sunset Blvd (90069)
Rates: $150-$310
(323) 654-4600

LE MONTROSE SUITE HOTEL
900 Hammond St (90069)
Rates: $165-$440
(323) 855-1115
(800) 776-0666

LE PARC SUITE HOTEL
733 N West Knoll Dr (90069)
Rates: $330-$440
(323) 855-8888
(800) 578-4837

MONDRIAN HOTEL
8440 Sunset Blvd (90069)
Rates: $235-$475
(323) 650-8999
(800) 525-8029

SUMMERFIELD SUITES HOTEL
1000 Westmount Dr (90069)
Rates: $115-$129
(310) 657-7400
(800) 833-4353

WYNDHAM BEL AGE HOTEL
1020 N San Vicente Blvd (90069)
Rates: 169-$189
(310) 854-1111
(800) 996-3426

WEST SACRAMENTO

MOTEL 6
1254 Halyard Dr (95691)
Rates: $39-$52
(916) 372-3624
(800) 466-8356

WESTLEY

DAYS INN
7144 McCracken Rd (95387)
Rates: $39-$90
(209) 894-5500
(800) 329-7466

ECONO LODGE
7100 McCracken Rd (95387)
Rates: $50-$90
(209) 894-3900
(800) 424-6423

WESTMINSTER

MOTEL 6 NORTH
13100 Goldenwest St (92683)
Rates: $39-$48
(714) 895-0042
(800) 466-8356

MOTEL 6 SOUTH
6266 Westminster Ave (92683)
Rates: $39-$48
(714) 891-5366
(800) 466-8356

WESTMOR-LAND

SUPER 8 MOEL
351 W Main St (92281)
Rates: $60-$65
(760) 351-7100

WESTPORT

BLUE VICTORIAN INN
38921 N Hwy 1 (95488)
Rates: $75-$130
(707) 964-6310
(800) 466-8356

DE HAVEN VALLEY FARM B&B
39247 N Hwy 1 (95488)
Rates: $94-$151
(707) 961-1660

HOWARD CREEK RANCH B&B
40501 N Hwy 1 (95488)
Rates: $75-$160
(707) 964-6725

WESTPORT INN
37040 N Hwy 1 (95488)
Rates: $45+
(707) 964-5135

WHITTIER

MOTEL 6
8221 S Pioneer Blvd (90606)
Rates: $39-$54
(562) 692-9101
(800) 466-8356

VAGABOND INN
14125 E Whittier Blvd (90605)
Rates: $55-$80
(562) 698-9701
(800) 522-1555

WILLIAMS

COMFORT INN
400 C St (95987)
Rates: $59-$85
(530) 473-2381
(800) 424-6423

GRANZELLA'S INN
391 6th St (95987)
Rates: $80-$110
(530) 473-3310

MOTEL 6
455 4th St (95987)
Rates: $37-$50
(530) 473-5337
(800) 466-8356

STAGE STOP MOTEL
330 7th St (95987)
Rates: $40-$50
(530) 473-2281

WILLITS

BAECHTEL CREEK INN & SPA
101 Gregory Ln (95490)
Rates: $56-$160
(707) 459-9063
(800) 459-9911

ETTA PLACE B&B I
909 Exley Ln (95490)
Rates: n/a
(707) 459-5953

LARK MOTEL
1411 S Main St (95490)
Rates: $30-$40
(707) 459-2421

PEPPERWOOD MOTEL
452 S Main St (95490)
Rates: $30-$50
(707) 459-2231

PINE CONE MOTEL
1350 S Main (95490)
Rates: $29-$32
(707) 459-5044

SKUNK TRAIL MOTEL
500 S Main (95490)
Rates: $38+
(707) 459-2302

WESTERN VILLAGE INN
1440 S Main St (95490)
Rates: $34+
(707) 459-4011

WILLOW CREEK

BIGFOOT MOTEL
39039 Hwy 299 (95573)
Rates: $55-$125
(530) 629-2142

WILLOWS

BEST WESTERN GOLDEN PHEASANT INN
249 N Humboldt Ave (95988)
Rates: $69-$150
(530) 934-4603
(800) 838-1387

BLUE GUM INN
Rt 2637, Road 99 W (95988)
Rates: $32-$48
(530) 934-5401

DAYS INN
475 N Humboldt Ave (95988)
Rates: $54-$120
(530) 934-4444
(800) 329-7466

ECONOMY INN
435 N Tehama (95988)
Rates: $40-$70
(530) 934-4224

GROVE MOTEL
Rt 2, Hwy 99 W (95988)
Rates: $32+
(530) 934-5067

MOTEL 6
452 N Humboldt Ave (95988)
Rates: $37-$68
(530) 934-7026
(800) 466-8356

SUPER 8 MOTEL
457 Humboldt Ave (95988)
Rates: $39-$70
(530) 934-2871
(800) 800-8000

WESTERN MOTEL
601 N Tehama (95988)
Rates: $30+
(530) 934-3856

WISHON

MILLER'S LANDING
37976 Rd 222 (93669)
Rates: $40-$125
(209) 642-3633

WOODLAKE

WICKY-UP RANCH B&B
22702 Ave 344 (93286)
Rates: $80-$100
(559) 564-8898

WOODLAND

DAYS INN
1524 E Main St (95776)
Rates: $50-$99
(530) 666-3800
(800) 329-7466

HOLIDAY INN EXP
2070 Freeway Dr (95776)
Rates: n/a
(530) 662-7750
(800) 465-4329

MOTEL 6
1564 Main St (95776)
Rates: $39-$58
(530) 666-6777
(800) 466-8356

YERMO

OAK TREE INN
35450 Yermo Rd (92398)
Rates: $77-$82
(760) 254-1148

YORKVILLE

SHEEP DUNG ESTATES COTTAGES
P. O. Box 49 (95494)
Rates: $80+
(707) 894-5322

YOSEMITE NATIONAL PARK

THE REDWOODS COTTAGES & RENTALS
8038 Chilnualna Falls Rd (95389)
Rates: $121-$672
(209) 375-6666

YOSEMITE'S FOUR SEASONS
7519 Henness Cir (95389)
Rates: $79-$500
(209) 372-9000
(800) 669-9300

YOUNTVILLE

VINTAGE INN
6541 Washington St (94599)
Rates: $215-$550
(707) 944-1112
(800) 351-1133

YOUNTVILLE INN
6462 Washington St (94599)
Rates: $175-$375
(707) 944-5600
(800) 972-2293

YREKA

AMERIHOST INN
148 Moonlit Oaks Ave (96097)
Rates: $79-$95
(530) 841-1300
(800) 434-5800

BEST WESTERN MINER'S INN
122 E Miner St (96097)
Rates: $65-$99
(530) 842-4355
(800) 528-1234
(800) 444-1320

COMFORT INN
1804 B Fort Jones Rd (96097)
Rates: $45-$105
(530) 842-1612
(800) 424-6423

ECONO LODGE
526 S Main St (96097)
Rates: $49-$75
(530) 842-4404
(800) 424-6423

MOTEL 6
1785 S Main St (96097)
Rates: $36-$48
(530) 842-4111
(800) 466-8356

SUPER 8 MOTEL
136 Montague Rd. (96097)
Rates: $48-$68
(530) 842-5781
(800) 800-8000

YUBA CITY

COMFORT INN
730 N Palora Ave (95991)
Rates: $55-$100
(530) 674-1592
(800) 424-6423

DAYS INN
700 N Palora Ave (95991)
Rates: $55-$85
(530) 674-1711
(800) 329-7466

DAYS INN-SOUTH
4228 S Hwy 99 (95991)
Rates: $48-$150
(530) 674-0210
(800) 329-7466

MOTEL 6
965 Gray Ave (95991)
Rates: $55-$66
(530) 790-7066
(800) 466-8356

YUCCA VALLEY

OASIS OF EDEN INN & SUITES
56377 Twentynine Palms Hy (92284)
Rates: $65-$140
(760) 365-6321
(800) 606-6686

SUPER 8 MOTEL
57096 Twentynine Palms Hy (92284)
Rates: $59-$99
(760) 228-1773
(800) 800-8000

YUCCA INN & SUITES
7500 Camino Del Cielo (92284)
Rates: $34-$149
(760) 365-3311

AREA CODES - If the local number doesn't connect, check for a new area code.

COLORADO

ALAMOSA

BEST WESTERN ALAMOSA INN
2005 Main St (81101)
(Rates: $89-$189
719) 589-2567

COMFORT INN
6301 US 160 (81101)
Rates: $55-$110
(719) 587-9000
(800) 424-6423

DAYS INN
224 O'Keefe Pkwy (81101)
Rates: $33-$65
(719) 589-9037
(800) 329-7466

GRIZZLY INN
1919 W Main St (81101)
Rates: n/a
(719) 589-4788

INN OF THE RIO GRANDE
333 Santa Fe Ave (81101)
Rates: $60-$85
(719) 589-5833
(800) 669-1658

ALMONT

THREE RIVERS RESORT CABINS
130 CR 742 (81210)
Rates: $35-$120
(970) 641-1303
(888) 761-3474

ASPEN

ASPEN MEADOWS RESORT
845 Meadows Rd (81611)
Rates: $99-$300
(970) 925-4240

ASPEN MTN LODGE
311 W Main St (81611)
Rates: $89-$259
(970) 925-7650
(800) 362-7736

BEAUMONT INN
1301 E Cooper Ave (81611)
Rates: $80-$235
(970) 925-7081
(800) 344-3853

HISTORIC HOTEL JEROME
330 E Main St (81611)
Rates: $235-$1360
(970) 920-1000
(800) 331-7213

HOTEL ASPEN
110 W Main St (81611)
Rates: $89-$399
(970) 925-3441

HOTEL LENADO B&B
200 S Aspen St (81611)
Rates: $125-$495
(970) 925-6246
(800) 321-3457

INNSBRUCK INN/ L'AUBERGE CABINS
233 W Main St (81611)
Rates: $101-$200
(970) 925-2980
(866) 925-2980

LIMELITE LODGE
228 E Cooper St (81611)
Rates: $68-$359
(970) 925-3025
(800) 433-0832

THE LITTLE NELL RESORT HOTEL
675 E Durant Ave (81611)
Rates: $250-$550
(970) 920-4600
(800) 525-6200

ST. REGIS ASPEN
315 E Dean St (81611)
Rates: $250-$725
(970) 920-3300

SKY HOTEL
709 E Durant (81611)
Rates: $139-$599
(970) 925-6760
(800) 882-2582

STAY ASPEN SNOWMASS RENTAL SERVICE
425 Rio Grande Place (81611)
Rates: $100-$200+
(970) 925-9000
(800) 26-ASPEN

AURORA

AMERISUITES
16250 E 40th Ave (80012)
Rates: $89-$107
(303) 371-0700
(800) 833-1516

BEST WESTERN GATEWAY INN & SUITES
800 S Abilene St (80012)
Rates: $69-$129
(720) 748-4800
(800) 528-1234

COMFORT INN
14071 E Iliff Ave (80014)
Rates: $80-$140
(303) 755-8000
(800) 424-6423

HEARTHSIDE BY VILLAGER
14090 E Evans (80014)
Rates: $49-$99
(303) 481-0379

HOLIDAY INN
15500 E 40th Ave (80239)
Rates: $85-$119
(303) 371-9494
(800) 465-4329

HOMESTEAD STUDIO SUITES HOTEL
13941 E Harvard Ave (80014)
Rates: $41-$66
(303) 750-9116
(800) 782-9473

LA QUINTA INN
1011 S Abilene (80012)
Rates: $65-$80
(303) 337-0206
(800) 687-6667

MOTEL 6
14031 E Iliff Ave (80014)
Rates: $39-$50
(303) 873-0286
(800) 466-8356

SLEEP INN DENVER INT'L AIRPORT
15900 E 40th Ave (80011)
Rates: $49-$99
(303) 373-1616
(800) 424-6423

WELLESLEY INN & SUITES
14095 E Evans Ave (80014)
Rates: $64-$99
(303) 337-7000
(800) 444-8888

BAYFIELD

BEAR PAW LODGE CABINS
18011 CR 501 (81122)
Rates: $56-$150
(970) 884-2508
(877) 884-2508

BEAVER CREEK

COMFORT INN VAIL/BEAVER CREEK
0161 W Beaver Crk Blvd (81620)
Rates: $79-$299
(970) 949-5511
(800) 424-6423

RITZ-CARLTON BACHELOR GULCH
0130 Daybreak Ridge (81620)
Rates: $195-$700
(970) 748-6200
(800) 241-3333

BOULDER

BEST WESTERN BOULDER INN
770 28th St (80303)
Rates: $74-$119
(303) 449-1800
(800) 528-1234
(800) 233-8469

BOULDER BROKER INN
555 30th St (80303)
Rates: $129-$139
(303) 444-3330
(800) 338-5407

BOULDER MOUNTAIN LODGE
91 Four Mile Canyon Rd (80302)
Rates: $49-$98
(303) 444-0882
(800) 458-0882

BOULDER OUTLOOK HOTEL & SUITES
800 28th St (80303)
Rates: $79-$159
(303) 443-3322
(800) 542-0304

COLORADO CHAUTAUQUA HISTORIC DISTRICT COTTAGES
900 Baseline Rd (80302)
Rates: n/a
(303) 442-3282

DAYS INN
5397 S Boulder Rd (80303)
Rates: $62-$89
(303) 499-4422
(800) 329-7466

AREA CODES - If the local number doesn't connect, check for a new area code.

FOOT OF THE MOUNTAIN MOTEL
200 Arapahoe Ave (80302)
Rates: $60-$85
(303) 442-5688
(866) 773-5489

HOLIDAY INN EXP
4777 N Broadway (80304)
Rates: $94-$109
(303) 442-6600
(800) 465-4329

HOMEWOOD SUITES
4950 Baseline Rd (80303)
Rates: $119-$250
(303) 499-9922
(800) 225-5466

MILLENIUM HARVEST HOUSE BOULDER
1345 28th St (80302)
Rates: $139-$219
(303) 443-3850
(866) 866 8086

PEARL STREET INN B&B
1800 Pearl St (80302)
Rates: $78-$103
(303) 444-5584
(888) 810-1302

QUALITY INN & SUITES
2020 Arapahoe Ave (80302)
Rates: $69-$150
(303) 449-7550
(800) 424-6423
(888) 449-7550

RESIDENCE INN BY MARRIOTT
3030 Center Green Dr (80301)
Rates: $80-$152
(303) 449-5545
(800) 331-3131

SUPER 8 MOTEL
970 28th St (80303)
Rates: $55-$115
(303) 443-7800
(800) 800-8000

BRECKENRIDGE

THE HUNT PLACER INN B&B
275 Ski Hill Rd (80424)
Rates: $149-$270
(970) 453-7573

PARAGON LODGING RENTALS
210 N Main St (80424)
Rates: $200+
(970) 547-2122
(877) 827-2722

WILDWOOD SUITES/CONDOS
120 Sawmill Rd (80424)
Rates: $95-$415
(970) 453-0232
(800) 866-0300

BRIGHTON

COMFORT INN
15150 Brighton Rd (80601)
Rates: $69-$139
(303) 654-1400
(800) 424-6423

BROOMFIELD

OMNI INTERLOCKEN RESORT
500 Interlocken Blvd (80021)
Rates: $199-$239
(303) 438-6600
(800) 843-6664

TOWNEPLACE SUITES BY MARRIOTT
480 Flat Iron Blvd (80021)
Rates: $99-$149
(303) 466-2200
(800) 257-3000

BRUSH

BEST VALUE INN
1208 N Colorado Ave (80723)
Rates: $35-$72
(970) 842-5146

MICROTEL INN
975 N Colorado Ave (80723)
Rates: $46-$72
(970) 842-4241
(888) 771-7171

BUENA VISTA

ALPINE LODGE
12845 Hwy 24 & 285 (81211)
Rates: $40-$65
(719) 395-2415

BEST WESTERN VISTA INN
733 N Hwy 24 (81211)
Rates: $60-$139
(719) 395-8009
(800) 528-1234
(800) 809-3495

THUNDER LODGE
P. O. Box 504 (81211)
Rates: $45-$64
(719) 395-2245
(800) 330-9194

BURLINGTON

CHAPARRAL MOTOR INN
405 S Lincoln (80807)
Rates: $35-$59
(719) 346-5361

COMFORT INN
282 S Lincoln (80807)
Rates: $54-$120
(719) 346-776
(800) 424-6423

SLOAN'S MOTEL
1901 Rose Ave (80807)
Rates: $25-$60
(719) 346-5333
(800) 362-0464

CALHAN

CALHAN INN
15 5th St, Hwy 24 (80808)
Rates: $49-$77
(719) 347-9589
(888) 211-0505

CAÑON CITY

BEST WESTERN ROYAL GORGE
1925 Fremont Dr (81212)
Rates: $39-$109
(719) 275-3377
(800) 528-1234
(800) 231-7317

BUFFALO BILL'S ROYAL GORGE CAMPGROUND CABINS
30 County Rd, 3-A (81212)
Rates: $35-$80
(719) 269-3211

COMFORT INN
311 Royal Gorge Blvd (81212)
Rates: $65-$169
(719) 276-6900
(800) 424-6423

HOLIDAY INN EXP
110 Latigo Lane (81212)
Rates: $79-$125
(719) 275-2400
(800) 465-4329

KNOTTY PINE MOTEL
2990 E Main St (81212)
Rates: $$35-$60
(719) 275-0461

PARK LANE MOTEL
1401 Main St (81212)
Rates: $38-$55
(719) 275-7240

QUALITY INN & SUITES
3075 E Hwy 50 (81212)
Rates: $59-$109
(719) 275-8676
(800) 424-6423
(800) 525-7727

ROYAL GORGE INN
217 N Reynolds Ave (81212)
Rates: $45-$99
(719) 269-1100

CARBONDALE

BRB CRYSTAL RIVER RESORT CABINS
7202 Hwy 133 (81623)
Rates: $60-$85
(970) 963-2341
(800) 963-2341

COMFORT INN & SUITES
920 Cowen Dr (81723)
Rates: $79-$159
(970) 963-8880
(800) 424-6423

DAYS INN
950 Cowen Dr (81723)
Rates: $59-$119
(970) 963-9111
(800) 329-7466

THUNDER RIVER LODGE
179 Hwy 133 (81623)
Rates: $40-$77
(970) 963-2543

CASTLE ROCK

BEST WESTERN INN & SUITES
595 Genoa Way (80104)
Rates: $59-$109
(303) 814-8800
(800) 528-1234

COMFORT INN
200 Wolfensberger Rd (80104)
Rates: $52-$89
(303) 660-2222
(800) 424-6423

COMFORT SUITES
4755 Castleton Way (80109)
Rates: $55-$165
(303) 814-9999
(800) 424-6423
(800) 517-4000

DAYS INN SUITES
4691 Castleton Way (80109)
Rates: $49-$129
(303) 814-5825
(800) 329-7466

HOLIDAY INN EXP
884 Park St (80104)
Rates: $89-$109
(303) 660-9733
(800) 465-4329

CEDAR EDGE

HOWARD JOHNSON EXPRESS INN
530 S Grand Mesa Dr (81413)
Rates: $69-$119
(970) 856-7824
(800) 446-4656

CENTENNIAL

CANDLEWOOD SUITES
6780 S Galena St (80112)
Rates: n/a
(303) 792-5393
(888) 226-3539

EMBASSY SUITES TECH CENTER
10250 E Costilla Ave (80112)
Rates: $79-$199
(303) 792-0433
(800) 362-2779

TOWNEPLACE SUITES-TECH CENTER
7877 S Chester St (80112)
Rates: $47-$85
(720) 875-1113
(800) 257-3000

CHIPITA PARK

CHIPITA LODGE B&B
9090 Chipita Park Rd (80809)
Rates: $100-$200
(719) 684-8454
(877) 244-7484

COLORADO SPRINGS

AIRPORT VALUE INN & SUITES
6875 Space Village Ave (80915)
Rates: $49-$99
(719) 596-5588

AMERISUITES
503 W Garden of the Gods Rd (80907)
Rates: $69-$125
(719) 265-9385
(800) 833-1516

APOLLO PARK EXECUTIVE SUITES
805 S Circle Dr, 2-B (80910)
Rates: $55-$105
(719) 634-0286
(800) 279-3620

BEST WESTERN AIRPORT INN
180 Aeroplaza Dr (80916)
Rates: $59-$99
(719) 574-7707
(800) 528-1234
(866) 840-3824

BEST WESTERN EXECUTIVE INN & SUITES
1440 Harrison Rd (80906)
Rates: $65-$159
(719) 576-2371
(800) 528-1234

BROADMOOR
1 Lake AVe (80906)
Rates: $230-$470
(719) 634-7711
(866) 696-1977

CHIEF MOTEL
1624 S Nevada Ave (80906)
Rates: $27-$65
(719) 473-5228

COMFORT INN NORTH
6450 Corporate Center Dr (80919)
Rates: $59-$129
(719) 262-9000
(800) 424-6423

COMFORT INN SOUTH WORLD ARENA
1410 Harrison Rd (80906)
Rates: $79-$129
(719) 579-6900
(800) 424-6423

COMFORT SUITES
1055 Kelly Johnson Blvd (80920)
Rates: $86-$145
(719) 536-0731
(800) 424-6423

DAYS INN-AIR FORCE ACADEMY
8350 Razorback Rd (80920)
Rates: $45-$139
(719) 266-1317
(800) 329-7466

DOUBLETREE WORLD ARENA
1775 E Cheyenne Mtn Blvd (80906)
Rates: $79-$189
(719) 576-8900
(800) 222-8733

DRURY INN PIKES PEAK
8155 N Academy Blvd (80920)
Rates: $55-$109
(719) 598-2500
(800) 378-7946

ECONO LODGE INN & SUITES WORLD ARENA
1623 S Nevada Ave (80906)
Rates: $39-$119
(719) 632-6651
(800) 424-6423

FIRESIDE SUITES
620 N Murray (80915)
Rates: $45-$90
(719) 597-6207
(800) 597-6202

HOMEWOOD SUITES
9130 Explorer Dr (80920)
Rates: $99-$209
(719) 265-6600
(800) 225-5466

HOMEWOOD SUITES AIRPORT
2875 Zeppelin Rd (80916)
Rates: $90-$190
(719) 574-2701
(800) 225-5466

HOWARD JOHNSON EXPRESS INN
1231 S Nevada Ave (80903)
Rates: $35-$85
(719) 634-1545
(800) 446-4656

LA QUINTA INN GARDEN OF THE GODS
4385 Sinton Rd (80907)
Rates: $60-$90
(719) 528-5060
(800) 687-6667

LA QUINTA INN
2750 Geyser Dr (80906)
Rates: $70-$120
(719) 527-4788
(800) 687-6667

LE BARON HOTEL
314 W Bijou St (80905)
Rates: $71-$98
(719) 471-8680
(800) 477-8610

MOTEL 6
3228 N Chestnut St (80907)
Rates: $30-$60
(719) 520-5400
(800) 466-8356

QUALITY INN GARDEN OF THE GODS
555 W Garden of the Gods Rd (80907)
Rates: $49-$139
(719) 593-9119
(800) 424-6423

QUALITY INN WORLD ARENA
1440 Harrison Rd (80906)
Rates: $54-$139
(719) 576-2371
(800) 424-6423

RADISSON INN & SUITES
1645 Newport Dr (80916)
Rates: $88-$126
(719) 597-7000
(800) 333-3333

RADISSON INN NORTH
8110 N Academy Blvd (80920)
Rates: $79-$169
(719) 598-5770
(800) 333-3333

RAINBOW LODGE & INN
3709 W Colorado Ave (80904)
Rates: $39-$95
(719) 632-4551

RAMADA LIMITED
520 N Murray Blvd (80915)
Rates: $59-$109
(719) 596-7660
(800) 272-6232

RESIDENCE INN BY MARRIOTT
3880 N Academy Blvd (80917)
Rates: $99-$139
(719) 574-0370
(800) 331-3131

RESIDENCE INN BY MARRIOTT NORTH
9805 Federal Dr (80921)
Rates: $99-$249
(719) 388-9300
(800) 331-3131

RESIDENCE INN BY MARRIOTT SOUTH
2765 Geyser Dr (80906)
Rates: $69-$189
(719) 576-0101
(800) 331-3131

RODEWAY INN
2409 E Pikes Peak Ave (80909)
Rates: $39-$139
(719) 471-0990
(800) 424-6423

SHERATON COLORADO SPRINGS HOTEL
2886 S Circle Dr (80906)
Rates: $159-$199
(719) 576-5900
(800) 325-3535

SLEEP INN
1075 Kelly Johnson Blvd (80920)
Rates: $49-$119
(719) 260-6969
(800) 424-6423

AREA CODES - If the local number doesn't connect, check for a new area code.

STAGECOACH MOTEL
1647 S Nevada Ave (80906)
Rates: $45-$69
(719) 633-3894

STAYBRIDGE SUITES-AIR FORCE ACADEMY
7130 Commerce Center Dr (80919)
Rates: $69-$199
(719) 590-7829
(800) 238-8000

SUPER 8 HOTEL/ HWY 24/PAFB
605 Peterson Rd (80915)
Rates: $35-$65
(719) 597-4100
(866) 597-4100

TOWNEPLACE SUITES BY MARRIOTT
4760 Centennial Blvd (80919)
Rates: $69-$149
(719) 594-4447
(800) 257-3000

TRAVEL INN
512 S Nevada Ave (80903)
Rates: $27-$65
(719) 636-3986

TRAVELODGE
2625 Ore Mill Rd (80904)
Rates: $40-$85
(719) 632-4600
(800) 578-7878

WYNDHAM HOTEL
5580 Tech Center Dr (80919)
Rates: $79-$109
(719) 260-1800
(800) 996-3426

COPPER MOUNTAIN

COPPER MOUNTAIN RESORT
0508 Copper Rd (80443)
Rates: $79-$1029
(970) 968-2882
(866) 534-7453

CORTEZ

ANASAZI MOTOR INN
640 S Broadway (81321)
Rates: $46-$71
(970) 565-3773
(800) 972-6232

BEST WESTERN SANDS
1120 E Main St (81321)
Rates: $49-$92
(970) 565-3761
(800) 528-1234

BEST WESTERN TURQUOISE INN & SUITES
535 E Main St (81321)
Rates: $64-$149
(970) 565-3778
(800) 528-1234
(800) 547-3376

BUDGET HOST INN
2040 E Main St (81321)
Rates: $32-$78
(970) 565-3738
(800) 283-4678

CAREFREE INN SANDS MOTEL
1120 E Main St (81321)
Rates: $39-$76
(970) 565-3761

COMFORT INN
2321 E Main St (81321)
Rates: $59-$119
(970) 565-3400
(800) 424-6423

DAYS INN
430 N State Hwy 145 (81321)
Rates: $49-$89
(970) 565-8577
(800) 329-7466

ECONO LODGE
2020 E Main St (81321)
Rates: $37-$89
(970) 565-3474
(800) 424-6423

HOLIDAY INN EXP
2121 E Main St (81321)
Rates: $99-$137
(970) 565-6000
(800) 465-4329

TOMAHAWK LODGE
728 S Broadway (81321)
Rates: $31-$73
(970) 565-8521
(800) 643-7705

TRAVELODGE
440 S Broadway (81321)
Rates: $40-$79
(970) 585-7778
(800) 578-7878

UTE MOUNTAIN MOTEL
531 S Broadway (81321)
Rates: $26-$40
(970) 565-8507

COTOPAXI

ARKANSAS RIVER KOA & LOMA LINDA MOTEL
21435 Hwy 50 (81223)
Rates: $34-$60
(719) 275-9308
(800) 562-2686

CRAIG

BLACK NUGGET MOTEL
2855 W Victory Way (81625)
Rates: $32-$65
(970) 824-8161

COLORADO INN & SUITES
205 E Victory Way (81625)
Rates: $$40-$80
(970) 824-3274

CRAIG MOTEL
894 Yampa Ave (81625)
Rates: $30-$58
(970) 824-4491

DEER PARK INN & SUITES
262 Commerce St (81625)
Rates: $69-$139
(970) 824-9282

HOLIDAY INN HOTEL & SUITES
300 S Hwy 13 (81625)
Rates: $82-$102
(970) 824-4000
(800) 465-4329

CRESTED BUTTE

GRAND LODGE CRESTED BUTTE
6 Emmons Rd (81225)
Rates: $69-$289
(970) 349-8000
(888) 823-4446

OLD TOWN INN
708 6th St (81224)
Rates: $58-$98
(970) 349-6184

THE RUBY OF CRESTED BUTTE B&B
624 Gothic Ave (81224)
Rates: $130-$150
(970) 349-1338
(800) 390-1338

SAN MORITZ CONDOS
18 Hunter Hill Rd (81225)
Rates: n/a
(970) 349-5150
(800) 443-7459

CRIPPLE CREEK

DOUBLE EAGLE HOTEL/CASINO
442 E Bennett Ave (80813)
Rates: $70-$140
(719) 689-5000
(800) 711-7234

DELTA

BEST WESTERN SUNDANCE
903 Main St (81416)
Rates: $75-$95
(970) 874-9781
(800) 528-1234
(800) 626-1994

COMFORT INN
180 Gunnison River Dr (81416)
Rates: $59-$129
(970) 874-1000
(800) 424-6423

SOUTH GATE INNS
2124 S Main St (81416)
Rates: $45-$79
(970) 874-9726
(800) 621-2271

DENVER

BEST WESTERN CENTRAL DENVER
200 W 48th Ave (80216)
Rates: $59-$129
(303) 296-4000
(800) 528-1234

BROWN PALACE HISTORIC HOTEL
321 17th St (80202)
Rates: $189-$199
(303) 297-3111
(800) 321-2599

CAMERON MOTEL
4500 E Evan Ave (80222)
Rates: $42-$55
(303) 757-2100

COMFORT INN DOWNTOWN
401 17th St (80202)
Rates: $99-$119
(303) 296-0400
(800) 424-6423

DAYS INN CENTRAL
620 Federal Blvd (80204)
Rates: $49-$79
(303) 571-1715
(800) 329-7466

DOUBLETREE HOTEL
3203 Quebec St (80207)
Rates: $69-$179
(303) 321-3333
(800) 243-3112
(800) 222-8733

DRURY INN
4380 E Peoria St (80239)
Rates: $62-$92
(303) 373-1983
(800) 378-7946

AREA CODES - If the local number doesn't connect, check for a new area code.

EMBASSY SUITES AIRPORT
4444 N Havana St (80239)
Rates: $109-$179
(303) 375-0400
(800) 362-2779

FOUR POINTS BY SHERATON
1475 S Colorado Blvd (80222)
Rates: $55-$169
(303) 757-8797
(800) 325-3535

FOUR POINTS BY SHERATON SOUTHEAST
6363 E Hampden Ave (80222)
Rates: $199
(303) 758-7000
(800) 325-3535

GUESTHOUSE HOTEL
3737 Quebec St (80207)
Rates: $60-$100
(303) 388-6161
(800) 214-8378

HAMPTON INN & SUITES- TECH CENTER
5001 S Ulster (80239)
Rates: $89-$149
(303) 804-9900
(800) 426-7866

HAMPTON INN DIA
6290 Tower Rd (80249)
Rates: $90-$100
(303) 371-0200
(800) 426-7866

HOLIDAY CHALET VICTORIAN B&B
1820 E Colfax Ave (80218)
Rates: $90-$145
(303) 437-8245
(800) 626-4497

HOLIDAY INN- AIRPORT AREA
15500 E 40th Ave (80239)
Rates: n/a
(303) 371-9494
(800) 465-4329

HOLIDAY INN DENVER CENTRAL
4849 Bannock St (80216)
Rates: $99-$159
(303) 292-9500
(800) 465-4329

HOMESTEAD STUDIO SUITES
4885 S Quebec St (80237)
Rates: $37-$62
(303) 689-9443
(800) 782-9473

HOTEL MONACO
1717 Champa St (80239)
Rates: $159-$269
(303) 296-1717

HOTEL TEATRO
1100 14th St (80202)
Rates: $225-$395
(303) 228-1100

J W MARRIOTT AT CHERRY CREEK
150 Clayton Ln (80206)
Rates: $209-$241
(303) 316-2700
(800) 228-9290

LA QUINTA INN AIRPORT
6801 Tower Rd (80249)
Rates: $70-$110
(303) 371-0888
(800) 687-6667

LA QUINTA INN DOWNTOWN
3500 Park Ave W (80216)
Rates: $73-$100
(303) 458-1222
(800) 687-6667

LA QUINTA INN SOUTH-CHERRY CREEK
1975 S Colorado Blvd (80222)
Rates: $60-$80
(303) 758-8886
(800) 687-6667

MAGNOLIA HOTEL
818 17th St (80202)
Rates: $210-$290
(303) 607-9000

MARRIOTT HOTEL CITY CENTER
1701 California St (80202)
Rates: $152-$169
(303) 297-1300
(800) 228-9290

MARRIOTT HOTEL SOUTHEAST
6363 E Hampden Ave (80222)
Rates: $98-$169
(303) 758-7000
(800) 228-9290

MARRIOTT HOTEL TECH CENTER
4900 S Syracuse St (80237)
Rates: $164
(303) 779-1100
(800) 228-9290

MOTEL 6- AIRPORT
12020 E 39th Ave (80239)
Rates: $35-$46
(303) 371-1980
(800) 466-8356

MOTEL 6- CENTRAL
3050 W 49th Ave (80221)
Rates: $37-$50
(303) 455-8888
(800) 466-8356

QUALITY INN EAST
3975 Peoria Way (80239)
Rates: $49-$89
(303) 371-5640
(800) 424-6423

RADISSON HOTEL STAPLETON PLAZA
3333 Quebec St (80207)
Rates: $69-$95
(303) 321-3500
(800) 333-3333

RAMADA CONTINENTAL HOTEL
2601 Zuni St (80211)
Rates: $69-$129
(303) 433-6677
(800) 272-6232

RAMADA INN
1150 E Colfax Ave (80218)
Rates: 69-$179
(303) 831-7700
(800) 272-6232

RAMADA LIMITED & SUITES
7020 Tower Rd (80249)
Rates: $79-$99
(303) 373-1600
(800) 272-6232

RED LION CENTRAL
4040 Quebec St (80216)
Rates: $89-$139
(303) 321-6666
(800) 733-5466

RED LION HOTEL DOWNTOWN- INVESCO FIELD
1975 Bryant St (80204)
Rates: $109-$129
(303) 433-8331
(800) 733-5466

RED ROOF INN & SUITES
6890 Tower Rd (80249)
Rates: $56-$68
(303) 371-5300
(800) 843-7663

RESIDENCE INN BY MARRIOTT DOWNTOWN
2777 Zuni St (80211)
Rates: $89-$199
(303) 458-5318
(800) 331-3131

STAYBRIDGE SUITES
4220 E Virginia Ave (80246)
Rates: n/a
(303) 321- 5757
(800) 238-8000

TOWNEPLACE SUITES BY MARRIOTT
3696 S Monaco St Pkwy (80237)
Rates: $47-$119
(303) 759-9393
(800) 257-3000

TOWNEPLACE SUITES BY MARRIOTT DOWNTOWN
685 Speer Blvd (80204)
Rates: $59-$149
(303) 722-2322
(800) 257-3000

WARWICK HOTEL
1776 Grant St (80203)
Rates: $149-$210
(303) 861-2000
(800) 525-2588

WESTIN TABOR CENTER HOTEL
1672 Lawrence St (80202)
Rates: $279-$299
(303) 572-9100
(800) 228-3000

DILLON

ANNABELLE'S B&B
276 Snowberry Way (80435)
Rates: $60-$100
(970) 468-8667

BEST WESTERN PTARMIGAN LODGE
652 Lake Dillon Dr (80435)
Rates: $65-$199
(970) 468-2341
(800) 528-1234
(800) 842-5939

SUPER 8 MOTEL
808 Little Beaver Tr (80435)
Rates: $60-$135
(970) 478-8888
(800) 800-8000

DOLORES

DOLORES MOUNTAIN INN
701 Railroad Ave (81323)
Rates: $39-$60
(970) 882-7203
(800) 842-8113

PRIEST GULCH CABINS/LODGE
27646 Hwy 145 (81323)
Rates: $54-$59
(970) 562-3810

AREA CODES - If the local number doesn't connect, check for a new area code.

DURANGO

ADOBE INN
2178 Main Ave
(81301)
Rates: $29-$89
(970) 247-2743

ALPINE INN
3515 N Main Ave
(81301)
Rates: $528$84
(970) 247-4042
(800) 818-4042

CABOOSE MOTEL
3363 Main Ave
(81301))
Rates: $38-$88
(970) 247-1191

COMFORT INN
2930 N Main Ave
(81301)
Rates: $49-$129
(970) 259-5373
(800) 424-6423

DAYS INN
1700 County Rd
203 (81301)
Rates: $55-$124
(970) 259-1430
(800) 329-7466

DOUBLETREE HOTEL
501 Camino Del
Rio (81301)
Rates: $69-$229
(970) 259-6580
(800) 222-8733

DURANGO MOUNTAIN RESORT
49617 Hwy 550 N
(81301)
Rates: $69-$350
(970) 247-9669
(800) 637-7727

HOLIDAY INN
800 Camino Del
Rio (81301)
Rates: $68-$139
(970) 247-5393
(800) 465-4329

IRON HORSE INN
5800 N Main Ave
(81301)
Rates: $59-$109
(970) 259-1010
(800) 748-2990

LELAND HOUSE B&B SUITES
721 E 2nd Ave
(81301)
Rates: $119-$199
(970) 385-1920
(800) 664-1920

THE LODGE AT TAMARRON CONDOS
40292 Hwy 550
(81301)
Rates: n/a
(800) 678-1000

NATIONAL 9 INN
2855 N Main Ave
(81301)
Rates: $39-$89
(970) 247-2653

PINES RENTALS
Hwy 550 N
(81301)
Rates: n/a
(828) 963-5149
(800) 863-5604

QUALITY INN
455 S Camino Del
Rio (81301)
Rates: $69-$149
(970) 259-7900
(800) 424-6423

RESIDENCE INN BY MARRIOTT
21691 Hwy 160 W
(81301)
Rates: $94-$224
(970) 259-6200
(800) 331-3131

ROCHESTER HISTORIC B&B HOTEL
726 E 2nd Ave
(81301)
Rates: $119-$219
(970) 385-1920
(800) 664-1920

RODEWAY INN
2701 N Main Ave
(81301)
Rates: $39-$109
(970) 259-2540
(800) 424-6423

SIESTA MOTEL
3475 N Main Ave
(81301)
Rates: $25-$75
(970) 247-0741

TRAVELODGE
2970 Main Ave
(81301)
Rates: $58-$129
(970) 247-1741
(800) 578-7878

EADS

ECONO LODGE
609 East 15th St
(81036)
Rates: $39-$59
(719) 438-5451
(800) 424-6423

EAGLE

AMERICINN LODGE & SUITES
0085 Pond Rd
(81631)
Rates: $79-$139
(970) 328-5155
(800) 634-3444

BEST WESTERN EAGLE LODGE
200 Loren Ln
(81631)
Rates: $70-$275
(970) 328-6316
(800) 528-1234
(800) 475-4824

HOLIDAY INN EXP
0075 Pond Rd
(81631)
Rates: $70-$129
(970) 328-8088
(800) 465-429

EDGEWOOD

HOLIDAY INN HOTEL & SUITES
7770 S Peoria St
(80112)
Rates: n/a
(303) 790-7770
(800) 465-4329

EDWARDS

INN & SUITES AT RIVERWALK
27 Main St (81632)
Rates: $85-$200
(970) 926-0606

ENGLEWOOD

AMERISUITES TECH CENTER
8300 E Crescent
Pkwy (80111)
Rates: $55-$115
(303) 804-0700
(800) 833-1516

BEST WESTERN DENVER TECH CENTER
9799 E Geddes
Ave (80112)
Rates: $49-$109
(303) 768-9300
(800) 528-1234

DRURY INN TECH CENTER
9445 E Dry Creek
Rd (80112)
Rates: $72-$97
(303) 694-3400
(800) 378-7946

HAMPTON INN-SOUTHEAST TECH CENTER
9231 E Arapahoe
Rd (80112)
Rates: $89-$99
(303) 792-9999
(800) 426-7866

HOLTZE EXECUTIVE VILLAGE
6380 S Boston St
(80112)
Rates: $69
(303) 290-1100

HOMESTEAD STUDIO SUITES-TECH CENTER
9650 E Geddes
Ave (80112)
Rates: $41-$66
(303) 708-8888
(888) 782-9473

QUALITY SUITES
7374 S Clinton St
(80112)
Rates: $59-$89
(303) 858-0700
(800) 424-6423

RESIDENCE INN BY MARRIOTT
6565 S Yosemite St
(80111)
Rates: $99-$139
(303) 740-7177
(800) 331-3131

RESIDENCE INN PARK MEADOWS
8322 S Valley Hwy
(80112)
Rates: $89-$119
(720) 895-0200
(800) 331-3131

TOWNEPLACE TECH CENTER
7877 S Chester St
(80112)
Rates: $49-$85
(720) 875-1113
(800) 257-3000

ESTES PARK

BUDGET HOST FOUR WINDS MOTOR LODGE
1120 Big
Thompson Ave
(80517)
Rates: $43-$130
(970) 586-3313
(800) 283-4678
(800) 527-7509

CASTLE MTN LODGE
1520 Fall River
Rd (80517)
Rates: $70-$215
(970) 586-3664
(800) 689-8252

HOLIDAY INN-ROCKY MTN PARK
101 S St. Vrain Ave
(80517)
Rates: $89-$299
(970) 586-2332
(800) 465-4329

LAKE ESTES INN & SUITES
1650 Big
Thompson Ave
(80517)
Rates: $99-$349
(970) 586-3386
(800) 332-6867

LANE GUEST RANCH/RESORT
P. O. Box 1766
(80517)
Rates: n/a
(303) 747-2493

MACHIN'S COTTAGES IN THE PINES
P O Box 2867
(80517)
Rates: $85-$130
(970) 586-4276

SILVER MOON INN
175 Spruce Dr
(80517)
Rates: $64-$130
(970) 586-6006
(800) 818-6006

AREA CODES - If the local number doesn't connect, check for a new area code.

SKYLINE COTTAGES
2752 Hwy 66
(80517)
Rates: $88-$95
(970) 586-2886

THE STANLEY HOTEL
333 Wonderview
(80517)
Rates: n/a
(907) 577-4000
(800) 976-1377

TIMBER CREEK CHALETS
2115 Fall River
Rd (80517)
Rates: $55-$265
(970) 586-8803

TWO EAGLES RESORT
1372 Big
Thompson Cyn
(80537)
Rates: n/a
(970) 663-5532
(866) 834-4744

YOGI BEAR'S JELLYSTONE PARK CABINS
5495 Hwy 36
(80517)
Rates: n/a
(970) 586-4230
(800) 991-YOGI

EVANS
MOTEL 6
3015 8th Ave
(80620)
Rates: $31-$50
(970) 351-6481
(800) 466-8356

SLEEP INN
3025 8th Ave E
(80620)
Rates: $65-$90
(970) 356-2180
(800) 424-6423

EVERGREEN
QUALITY SUITES
29300 Hwy 40
(80401)
Rates: $70-$159
(303) 526-2000
(800) 424-6423

FAIRPLAY
HAND HOTEL B&B
531 Front St
(80440)
Rates: $45-$95
(719) 836-3595

SOUTH PARK LODGE
801 Main (80440)
Rates: $45-$55
(719) 836-3278

WESTERN INN
490 Hwy 285
(80440)
Rates: $53-$75
(719) 836-2026
(800) 613-1976

FLORENCE
SUPER 8 MOTEL
4540 S State Hwy
67 (81226)
Rates: $45-$76
(719) 784-4800
(800) 800-8000

FORT COLLINS
BEST WESTERN UNIVERSITY INN
914 S College Ave
(80524)
Rates: $74-$125
(970) 484-1984
(800) 528-1234

COMFORT SUITES
1415 Oakridge Dr
(80525)
Rates: $90-$35
(970) 206-4597
(800) 424-6423

DAYS INN
3625 E Mulberry
St (80524)
Rates: $42-$95
(970) 221-5490
(800) 329-7466

HAMPTON INN
1620 Oakridge Dr
(80525)
Rates: $94-$114
(970) 229-5927
(800) 426-7866

HILTON FORT COLLINS
425 W Prospect
Rd (80526)
Rates: $107-$139
(970) 482-2626
(800) 445-8667

MARRIOTT HOTEL
350 E Horsetooth
Rd (80525)
Rates: $75-$127
(970) 226-5200
(800) 228-9290

MOTEL 6
3900 E Mulberry
(80524)
Rates: $39-$60
(970) 482-6466
(800) 466-8356

MULBERRY INN
4333 E Mulberry
St (80524)
Rates: $39-$90
(970) 493-9000

PLAZA INN
3709 E Mulberry
St (80524)
Rates: n/a
(970) 493-7800
(800) 434-5548

QUALITY INN & SUITES
4001 S Mason St
(80525)
Rates: $79-$169
(970) 282-9047
(800) 424-6423

RAMADA INN
3836 E Mulberry
St (80524)
Rates: n/a
(970) 484-4660
(800) 272-6232

RESIDENCE INN BY MARRIOTT
1127 Oakridge Dr
(80525)
Rates: $114-$169
(980) 223-5700
(800) 331-3131

SLEEP INN
3808 E Mulberry
St (80524)
Rates: $50-$120
(970) 484-5515
(800) 424-6423

SUPER 8 MOTEL
409 Centro Way
(80524)
Rates: $40-$105
(970) 493-7701
(800) 800-8000

FORT LUPTON
MOTEL 6
65 S Grand
(80621)
Rates: $34-$39
(303) 857-1800
(800) 466-8356

FORT MORGAN
AFFORDABLE INNS
1409 Barlow Rd
(80701)
Rates: $50-$87
(970) 867-9481

BEST WESTERN PARK TERRACE
725 Main (80701)
Rates: $59-$88
(970) 867-8256
(800) 528-1234
(888) 593-5793

CENTRAL MOTEL
201 N Platte Ave
(80701)
Rates: $39-$61
(970) 867-2401

FRISCO
BEST WESTERN LAKE DILLON LODGE
1202 Summit Blvd
(80443)
Rates: $79-$229
(970) 668-5094
(800) 528-1234
(800) 727-0607

BIGHORN RENTALS
P. O. Box 4037
(80443)
Rates: $90-$200
(970) 668-1666
(800) 826-7706

HOLIDAY INN
1129 N Summit
Blvd (80443)
Rates: $99-$159
(970) 668-5000
(800) 465-4329

HOTEL FRISCO
308 Main St
(80443)
Rates: $59-$169
(970) 668-5009

NEW SUMMIT INN
1205 N Summit
Blvd (80443)
Rates: $40-$145
(970) 668-3220

RAMADA LIMITED
990 Lakepoint Dr
(80443)
Rates: $55-$139
(970) 668-8783
(800) 272-6232

SNOWSHOE MOTEL
521 Main St
(80443)
Rates: $42-$125
(970) 668-3444

FRUITA
BALANCED ROCK MOTEL
126 S Coulson
(81521)
Rates: $35-$55
(970) 858-7333

COMFORT INN
400 Jurrasic Ave
(81521)
Rates: $59-$135
(970) 858-1333
(800) 424-6423

H-MOTEL
333 Hwy 6 & 50
(81521)
Rates: $30-$55
(970) 858-7198

SUPER 8 MOTEL
399 Jurrasic Ave
(81521)
Rates: $39-$70
(970) 858-0808
(800) 800-8000

GEORGETOWN
GEORGETOWN MOUNTAIN INN
1100 Rose St
(80444)
Rates: $54-$79
(303) 569-3201
(800) 884-3201

AREA CODES - If the local number doesn't connect, check for a new area code.

GLENDALE

FOUR POINTS CHERRY CREEK
600 S Colorado Blvd (80246)
Rates: $79-$119
(303) 757-3341
(800) 325-3535

HOMESTEAD STUDIO SUITES HOTEL
4444 Leetsdale Dr (80246)
Rates: $60-$85
(303) 388-3880
(888) 782-9473

LOEWS DENVER HOTEL
4150 E Mississippi Ave (80222)
Rates: $95-$140
(303) 782-9300
(800) 235-6397

STAYBRIDGE SUITES
4220 E Virginia Ave (80246)
Rates: $119-$179
(303) 321-5757
(800) 238-8000

GLENWOOD SPRINGS

CARAVAN INN
1826 Grand Ave (81601)
Rates: $55-$109
(970) 945-7451
(800) 945-5495

HISTORIC HOTEL COLORADO
526 Pine St (81601)
Rates: $145-$169
(970) 945-6511
(800) 544-3998

HOTEL DENVER
402 7th St (81601)
Rates: $85-$150
(970) 945-6565

QUALITY INN & SUITES
2650 Gilstrap Ct (81601)
Rates: $49-$199
(970) 945-5995
(800) 424-6423

RAMADA INN & SUITES
124 W 6th St (81601)
Rates: $69-$149
(970) 945-2500
(800) 272-6232

SILVER SPRUCE MOTEL
162 W 6th St (81601)
Rates: $40-$110
(970) 945-5458
(800) 523-4742

GOLDEN

CLARION GOLDEN HOTEL
800 11th St (80401)
Rates: $99-$259
(303) 279-0100

DAYS INN SUITES WEST
15059 W Colfax Ave (80401)
Rates: $59-$149
(303) 277-0200
(800) 329-7466

HOLIDAY INN
14707 W Colfax Ave (80401)
Rates: $99-$125
(303) 279-7611
(800) 465-4329

LA QUINTA INN
3301 Youngfield Service Rd (80401)
Rates: $63-$80
(303) 279-5565
(800) 687-6667

MARRIOTT WEST
1717 Denver West Blvd (80401)
Rates: $180
(303) 279-9100
(800) 228-9290

RESIDENCE INN BY MARRIOTT
14600 W 6th Ave, Frontage Rd (80401)
Rates: $79-$139
(303) 271-0909
(800) 331-3131

TABLEMTN INN
1310 Washington Ave (80401)
Rates: $99-$172
(303) 277-9898

GRANBY

THE INN AT SILVER CREEK
62927 Hwy 40 (80446)
Rates: $59-$338
(970) 887-2131

SILVERCREEK LODGING
P. O. Box 4222 (80446)
Rates: $101-$200
(970) 887-2131
(800) 926-4386

GRAND JUNCTION

BEST WESTERN HORIZON INN
754 Horizon Dr (81506)
Rates: $49-$79
(970) 245-1410
(800) 528-1234
(800) 544-3782

BEST WESTERN SANDMAN MOTEL
708 Horizon Dr (81506)
Rates: $40-$105
(970) 243-4150
(800) 528-1234

BUDGET HOST INN
721 Horizon Dr (81506)
Rates: $50-$75
(970) 243-6050
(800) 283-4678

DAYS INN
733 Horizon Dr (81506)
Rates: $50-$120
(970) 245-7200
(800) 329-7466

GRAND VISTA HOTEL
2790 Crossroads Blvd (81506)
Rates: $75-$82
(970) 241-8411
(800) 800-7796

HAMPTON INN
205 Main St (81601)
Rates: $85-$95
(970) 243-3222
(800) 426-7866

HAWTHORN SUITES

225 Main St (81501)
Rates: $99-$209
(970) 242-2525
(800) 527-1133

HOLIDAY INN
755 Horizon Dr (81502)
Rates: $79-$84
(970) 243-6790
(800) 465-4329
(888) 489-9796

LA QUINTA INN
2761 Crossroads Blvd (81506)
Rates: $83-$100
(970) 241-2929
(800) 687-6667

MESA INN
704 Horizon Dr (81506)
Rates: $35-$75
(970) 245-3080
(888) 955-3080

MOTEL 6
776 Horizon Dr (81506)
Rates: $31-$54
(970) 243-2628
(800) 466-8356

QUALITY INN
733 Horizon Dr (81506)
Rates: $45-$90
(970) 245-7200
(800) 424-6423

RAMADA INN
752 Horizon Dr (81506)
Rates: $54-$84
(970) 243-5150
(800) 272-6232

SUPER 8 MOTEL
728 Horizon Dr (81506)
Rates: $53-$70
(970) 248-8080
(800) 800-8000

WEST GATE INN
2210 Hwys 6 & 50 (81505)
Rates: $48-$74
(970) 241-3020

GRAND LAKE

SPIRIT LAKE LODGE
829 Grand Ave (80447)
Rates: $55-$160
(970) 627-3344

GREAT SAND DUNES NATIONAL MONUMENT

GREAT SAND DUNES LODGE
7900 Hwy 150 N (81146)
Rates: $79-$85
(719) 378-2900

GREELEY

BEST WESTERN REGENCY HOTEL
701 8th St (80631)
Rates: $55-$105
(970) 353-8444
(800) 528-1234

COUNTRY INN & SUITES
2501 W 29th St (80631)
Rates: $68-$99
(970) 330-3404
(800) 456-4000

HOLIDAY INN EXP
2563 W 29th St (80631)
Rates: $65-$95
(970) 330-7495
(800) 465-4329

SUPER 8 MOTEL
2423 W 29th St (80631)
Rates: $64-$74
(970) 330-8880
(800) 800-8000

GREENWOOD VILLAGE

HAMPTON INN SOUTHEAST
9231 E Arapahoe Rd (80112)
Rates: $79-$89
(303) 792-9999
(800) 426-7866

AREA CODES - If the local number doesn't connect, check for a new area code.

HOMESTEAD STUDIO SUITES
9253 E Costilla St (80112)
Rates: $45-$70
(303) 858-1669
(888) 782-9473

LA QUINTA INN
7077 S Clinton St (80112)
Rates: $70-$100
(303) 649-9969
(800) 687-6667

MOTEL 6-SOUTH TECH CENTER
9201 E Arapahoe Rd (80112)
Rates: $40+
(303) 790-8220
(800) 466-8356

SHERATON DENVER-TECH CENTER
7007 S Clinton St (80112)
Rates: $199
(303) 799-6200
(800) 325-3535

SLEEP INN DENVER-TECH CENTER
9257 E Costilla Ave (80112)
Rates: $49-$69
(303) 662-9950
(800) 424-6423

SUMMERFIELD SUITES-TECH CENTER
9280 E Costilla Ave (80112)
Rates: $68-$260
(303) 706-1945
(800) 833-4353

WOODFIELD SUITES-TECH CENTER
9009 E Arapahoe Rd (80112)
Rates: $79-$129
(303) 799-4555
(800) 338-0008

GUNNISON

ABC MOTEL
212 E Tomichi Ave (81230)
Rates: $42-$69
(970) 641-2400

HYLANDER INN
412 E Tomichi Ave (81230)
Rates: $45-$75
(970) 641-0700

ISLAND ACRES MOTEL
38339 W Hwy 50 (81230)
Rates: $33-$58
(970) 641-1442

RAMADA LIMITED
1011 W Rio Grande (81230)
Rates: n/a
(970) 641-2804
(800) 272-6232

WATER WHEEL INN
37478 W Hwy 50 (81230)
Rates: $49-$99
(970) 641-1650
(800) 642-1650

WILDWOOD MOTEL
1312 W Tomichi Ave (81230)
Rates: n/a
(970) 741-1663

HERMOSA

THE INN AT DURANGO
49617 US 550 N (81301)
Rates: $69-$179
(970) 247-9669

HIGHLANDS RANCH

RESIDENCE INN BY MARRIOTT
93 W Centennial Blvd (80126)
Rates: $134
(303) 683-5500
(800) 331-3131

HOT SULPHUR SPRINGS

CANYON MOTEL
221 Byers Ave (80451)
Rates: $49-$84
(970) 725-3395

HOTCHKISS

HOTCHKISS INN
406 Hwy 133 (81419)
Rates: $51-$65
(970) 872-2200

IDAHO SPRINGS

H & H MOTOR LODGE
2445 Colorado Blvd (80452)
Rates: $54-$84
(303) 567-2838

JULESBURG

BUDGET HOST PLATTE VALLEY INN
15225 Hwy 385 & I-76 (80737)
Rates: $39-$60
(970) 474-3336
(800) 283-4678

KEYSTONE

THE INN AT KEYSTONE
23044 Hwy 6 (80435)
Rates: $138-$336
(970) 496-4825

KREMMLING

HOTEL EASTIN
105 S 2nd St (80459)
Rates: $40-$60
(970) 724-3261

RIVER OF LIFE CABINS
Hwy 40, West End of Town (80459)
Rates: $40-$100
(970) 724-9559
(866) 724-9559

LA JUNTA

HOLIDAY INN EXP
27994 US Hwy 50 (81050)
Rates: $69-$99
(719) 384-2900
(800) 465-4329

MID-TOWN MOTEL
215 E 3rd St (81050)
Rates: n/a
(719) 384-7741

TRAVEL INN
110 E 1st St (81050)
Rates: $30-$48
(719) 384-2504

LAKE CITY

CINNAMON INN
426 Gunnison Ave (81235)
Rates: $60-$85
(970) 944-2641

LAKE CITY RESORT
307 S Gunnison Ave (81235)
Rates: $44-$84
(970) 944-2866
(970) 944-2437

MATTERHORN MOUNTAIN MOTEL
409 Bluff St (81235)
Rates: $60-$79
(970) 944-2210

LAKE GEORGE

UTE TRAIL RIVER RANCH CABINS
21446 CR 77, Tarryall River Vly (80827)
Rates: $50-$90
(719) 748-3015

LAKEWOOD

COMFORT SUITES
11909 W 6th (80401)
Rates: $89
(303) 231-9929
(800) 424-6423

DAYS INN
3440 S Vance St (80215)
Rates: $59-$90
(303) 989-5500
(800) 329-7466

HAMPTON INN SOUTHWEST
3605 S Wadsworth Blvd (80235)
Rates: $69-$79
(303) 989-6900
(800) 426-7866

HOLIDAY INN
7390 W Hampden Ave (80227)
Rates: $59-$79
(303) 980-9200
(800) 465-4329

LA QUINTA INN
7190 W Hampden Ave (80227)
Rates: $70-$90
(303) 969-9700
(800) 687-6667

LAKEWOOD INN
3440 S Vance St (80227)
Rates: $50-$100
(303) 989-5500
(800) 707-5188

MILE HIGH INN & SUITES
11595 W 6th Ave (80215)
Rates: $39-$125
(303) 238-7751

MOTEL 6
480 Wadsworth Blvd (80226)
Rates: $35-$50
(303) 232-4924
(800) 466-8356

QUALITY SUITES SOUTHWEST
7260 W Jefferson Ave (80235)
Rates: $59-$159
(303) 988-8600
(800) 424-6423

RESIDENCE INN BY MARRIOTT
7050 W Hampden Ave (80215)
Rates: $99-$109
(303) 985-7676
(800) 331-3131

SHERATON DENVER WEST HOTEL
360 Union Blvd (80228)
Rates: $69-$99
(303) 987-2000
(800) 325-3535

TOWNEPLACE SUITES BY MARRIOTT
800 Tabor St (80215)
Rates: $89-$112
(303) 232-7790
(800) 257-3000

TRAVELODGE DENVER WEST
11595 W 6th Ave (80215)
Rates: $49-$89
(303) 238-7751
(800) 578-7878

AREA CODES - If the local number doesn't connect, check for a new area code.

LAMAR

BEST WESTERN COW PALACE INN
1301 N Main St (81052)
Rates: $84-$119
(719) 336-7753
(800) 528-1234
(800) 678-0344

BLUE SPRUCE MOTEL
1801 S Main St (81052)
Rates: $45-$69
(719) 336-7454

EL MAR BUDGET HOST MOTEL
1210 S Main St (81052)
Rates: $36-$48
(719) 336-4331

PASSPORT INN
113 N Main St (81052)
Rates: $32-$47
(719) 336-7746

LAS ANIMAS

BEST WESTERN BENT'S FORT INN
East Hwy 50 (81054)
Rates: $49-$69
(719) 456-0011
(800) 528-1234
(877) 236-8738

LEADVILLE

ALPS MOTEL
207 Elm St (80461)
Rates: $49-$109
(719) 486-1223

BEL-AIR MOTEL
Hwy 24 S at Elm (80461)
Rates: n/a
(719) 486-0881

CLUB LEAD
500 E 7th St (80461)
Rates: n/a
(719) 486-2202

LEADVILLE INN
25 Jacktown Pl (80461)
Rates: $40-$50
(719) 486-3637

MOUNTAIN PEAKS MOTEL
1 Harrison Ave (80461)
Rates: n/a
(719) 486-3178

SILVER KING MOTOR INN
2020 N Poplar (80461)
Rates: $42-$59
(719) 486-2610
(800) 871-2610

TIMBERLINE MOTEL
216 Harrison Ave (80461)
Rates: $40-$80
(719) 486-1876
(800) 352-1876

LIMON

BEST WESTERN LIMON INN
925 "T" Ave (80828)
Rates: $45-$105
(719) 775-0277
(800) 528-1234

ECONO LODGE
985 Hwy 24 (80828)
Rates: $45-$99
(719) 775-2867
(800) 424-6423

MIDWEST COUNTRY INN
795 Main St (80828)
Rates: $42-$65
(719) 775-2373

PREFERRED MOTOR INN
158 E Main St (80828)
Rates: $38-$60
(719) 775-2385

SAFARI MOTEL
637 Main St (80828)
Rates: $34-$76
(719) 775-2363

SUPER 8 MOTEL
937 Hwy 24 (80828)
Rates: $38-$68
(719) 775-2889
(800) 800-8000

TYME SQUARE INN
2505 6th St (80828)
Rates: $59-$85
(719) 775-0700
(877) 900-8963

LITTLETON

MARRIOTT DENVER SOUTH
10345 Park Meadows Dr (80124)
Rates: $49-$179
(303) 925-0004
(800) 229-9290

LONE TREE

AMERISUITES
9030 E Westview Rd (80124)
Rates: $99-$109
(303) 662-8500
(800) 833-1516

STAYBRIDGE SUITES
7820 Park Meadows Dr (80124)
Rates: $94-$166
(303) 649-1010
(800) 238-8000

LONGMONT

DAYS INN
3820 Hwy 119 (80504)
Rates: $50-$90
(303) 651-6999
(800) 329-7466

HAWTHORN SUITES
2000 Sunset Way (80501)
Rates: $162-$295
(303) 774-7100
(800) 527-1133

RADISSON HOTEL & CONF CENTER
1900 Ken Pratt Blvd (80501)
Rates: $169
(303) 776-2000
(800) 333-3333

RESIDENCE INN BY MARRIOTT
1450 Dry Creek Dr (80503)
Rates: $99-$149
(303) 702-9933
(800) 331-3131

SUPER 8 MOTEL
10805 Turner Ave (80504)
Rates: $45-$88
(303) 772-0888
(800) 800-8000

LOUISVILLE

COMFORT INN BOULDER COUNTY
1196 Dillon Rd (80027)
Rates: $59-$134
(303) 604-0181
(800) 424-6423

LA QUINTA INN
902 Dillon Rd (80027)
Rates: $70-$110
(303) 664-0100
(800) 687-6667

RESIDENCE INN BY MARRIOTT
845 Coal Creek Cir (80027)
Rates: $116-$134
(303) 665-2661
(800) 331-3131

LOVELAND

BEST WESTERN COACH HOUSE
5542 E Hwy 34 (80537)
Rates: $65-$95
(970) 667-7810
(800) 528-1234
(888) 818-6223

BUDGET HOST EXIT 254 INN
2716 SE Frontage Rd (80538)
Rates: $49-$76
(970) 667-5202
(800) 283-4678

MANCOS

ECHO BASIN GUEST RANCH
43747 Rd M (81328)
Rates: $89-$101
(970) 533-7000
(800) 426-1890

SUNDANCE BEAR LODGE
38890 Hwy 184 (81328)
Rates: n/a
(970) 533-1504
(866) 529-2480

MANITOU SPRINGS

B&B'S OF THE PIKES PEAK AREA
P. O. Box 342 (80829)
Rates: $55-$100
(719) 685-1120
(888) 835-8900

BEST WESTERN SKYWAY INN & SUITES
311 Manitou Ave (80829)
Rates: $49-$119
(719) 685-5991
(800) 528-1234
(800) 938-5991

PARK ROW LODGE
54 Manitou Ave (80829)
Rates: $39-$89
(719) 685-5216

RED WING MOTEL
56 El Paso Blvd (80829)
Rates: $35-$68
(719) 685-5656
(800) 733-9547

SANTA FE MOTEL
3 Manitou Ave (80829)
Rates: $35-$65
(719) 475-8185
(866) 460-3030

SILVER SADDLE MOTEL
215 Manitou Ave (80829)
Rates: $54-$85
(719) 685-5611

SPRING COTTAGES
113 Pawnee Ave (80829)
Rates: $101-$200
(719) 685-9395
(888) 588-9395

UTE PASS MOTEL
1132 Manitou Ave (80829)
Rates: $40-$200
(719) 685-5171

AREA CODES - If the local number doesn't connect, check for a new area code.

MARBLE

CHAIR
MOUNTAIN
RANCH CABINS
0178 CR 3 (81623)
Rates: $25-$100
(970) 963-9522

UTE MEADOWS
INN B&B
2880 CR 3 (81623)
Rates: $119-$159
(970) 963-7088

MEEKER

LOST CREEK
LODGE
2638 CR 12
(81641)
Rates: $85-$120
(970) 878-5214
(800) 522-5187

POLLARD'S UTE
LODGE
393 CR 75 (81641)
Rates: $25-$60
(970) 878-4669
(888) 414-2022

RIMROCK CABINS
73179 Hwy 64
(81641)
Rates: $28-$32
(970) 878-4486

SLEEPY CAT
GUEST RANCH
16064 CR 8
(81641)
Rates: $60
(970) 878-4413

MESA

MESA LAKES
RESORT CABINS
P O Box 230
(81643)
Rates: $20-$130
(970) 268-5467

WAGON WHEEL
MOTEL
1090 Hwy 65
(81643)
Rates: $40-$45
(970) 268-5224

MESA VERDE NATIONAL PARK

FAR VIEW LODGE
IN MESA VERDE
1 Navajo Hill
(81330)
Rates: $93-$123
(970) 529-4421
(800) 449-2288

MOFFAT

WILLOW SPRING
B&B
223 Moffat Way
(81143)
Rates: $45-$95
(719) 256-4116

MONARCH

MONARCH
MOUNTAIN
LODGE
#1 Power Pl
(81227)
Rates: $54-$175
(719) 539-2581
(800) 332-3668

MONTE VISTA

BEST WESTERN
MOVIE MANOR
MOTOR INN
2830 W Hwy 160
(81144)
Rates: $55-$120
(719) 852-5921
(800) 528-1234
(800) 771-9468

COMFORT INN
1519 Grande Ave
(81144)
Rates: $65-$105
(719) 852-0612
(800) 424-6423

MONTROSE

AFFORDABLE
INNS
1480 S Townsend
Ave (81401)
Rates: $41-$86
(970) 249-6644

BEST WESTERN
RED ARROW
1702 E Main St
(81401)
Rates: $69-$109
(970) 249-9641
(800) 528-1234
(800) 468-9323

BLACK CANYON
MOTEL
1605 E Main
(81401)
Rates: $40-$95
(970) 249-3495
(800) 348-3495

BLUE FOX MOTEL
1150 N Townsend
Ave (81401)
Rates: n/a
(970) 249-4595

CANYON
TRAILS INN
1225 E Main
(81401)
Rates: $32-$58
(970) 249-3426
(800) 858-5911

COMFORT INN
2100 E Main St
(81401)
Rates: $55-$99
(970) 240-8000
(800) 424-6423

DAYS INN
1655 E Main St
(81401)
Rates: $39-$69
(970) 249-3411
(800) 329-7466

HOLIDAY INN
EXPRESS HOTEL
1391 S Townsend
Ave (81401)
Rates: $89-$149
(970) 240-1800
(800) 465-4329
(800) 550-9252

QUALITY INN
& SUITES
2751 Commercial
way (81401)
Rates: $49-$109
(970) 249-1011
(800) 424-6423

SAN JUAN INN
1480 S Townsend
(81401)
Rates: $48-$70
(970) 249-6644
(888) 681-4159

UNCOMPAHGRE
BED & BREAKFST
21049
Uncompahgre Rd
(81401)
Rates: $52-$77
(970) 240-4000

WESTERN MOTEL
1200 E Main St
(81401)
Rates: $38-$46
(970) 249-3481
(800) 445-7301

MOSCA

GREAT SAND
DUNES LODGE
7900 Hwy 150 N
(81146)
Rates: $69-$79
(719) 378-2900

INN AT
HISTORICAL
ZAPATA RANCH
5303 Hwy 150
(81146)
Rates: $95-$225
(800) 284-921

NATURITA

RAY MOTEL
123 Main St
(81422)
Rates: $26-$46
(970) 865-2235

NEDERLAND

ARAPAHO
RANCH CABINS
1250 Eldora Rd
(80466)
Rates: $70
(303) 258-3405

BEST WESTERN
LODGE
55 Lakeview Dr
(80466)
Rates: $85-$115
(303) 258-9463
(800) 528-1234
(800) 279-9643

NEDERHAUS
MOTEL
686 Hwy 119
South (80466)
Rates: $38-$90
(303) 444-4705
(800) 422-4629

NEW CASTLE

RODEWAY INN
781 Burning Mtn
Ave (81647)
Rates: $59-$109
(970) 984-2363
(800) 228-2000

NORTHGLENN

DAYS INN NORTH
36 E 120th Ave
(80233)
Rates: $69-$77
(303) 457-0688
(800) 329-7466

HOLIDAY INN
10 E 120th Ave
(80233)
Rates: $94-$114
(303) 452-4100
(800) 465-4329

RAMADA LIMITED
110 W 104th Ave
(80234)
Rates: $72-$87
(303) 451-1234
(800) 272-6232

NORWOOD

ANNIE'S
COUNTRY B&B
551 CR 44ZN
(81423)
Rates: $40
(970) 327-4331

BUCKHORN /
DREAM CATCHER
RANCH
SR 1 (81423)
Rates: $40-$60
(253) 588-7737

LONE CONE ELK
RANCH B&B
P O Box 220
(81423)
Rates: $45
(970) 327-4300

OHIO CITY

BIG HORN GUEST
RANCH
9102 CR 76
(81237)
Rates: $31-$51
(970) 641-1800

OURAY

COMFORT INN
191 5th Ave
(81427)
Rates: $59-$128
(970) 325-7203
(800) 424-6423

OURAY COTTAGE
MOTEL
4th & Main Sts
(81427)
Rates: $45-$115
(970) 325-4370

AREA CODES - If the local number doesn't connect, check for a new area code.

OURAY

VICTORIAN INN
50 3rd Ave (81427)
Rates: $55-$100
(970) 325-7222
(800) 84-OURAY

RIVERS EDGE MOTEL
110 7th Ave
(81427)
Rates: $50-$112
(970) 325-4621
(866) 739-4987

TIMBER RIDGE MOTEL
1515 North Main St (81427)
Rates: n/a
(970) 325-4523

PAGOSA SPRINGS

BE OUR GUEST BED & BREAKFAST
19 Swiss Village Dr (81147)
Rates: $47-$65
(970) 264-6814

BEST VALUE HIGH COUNTRY LODGE
3821 E Hwy 160 (81147)
Rates: $60-$91
(970) 264-4181
(800) 862-3707

BEST WESTERN OAK RIDGE LODGE
158 Hot Springs Blvd (81147)
Rates: $62-$124
(970) 264-4173
(800) 528-1234
(866)-472-4672

BRUCE SPRINGS RANCH & CABINS
Box 296 (81147)
Rates: $33-$48
(970) 264-5374
(800) 622-1346

ECONO LODGE
315 Navajo Trail Dr (81147)
Rates: $59-$109
(970) 731-2701
(800) 424-6423

FIRESIDE INN CABINS
1600 E Hwy 160 (81147)
Rates: $85-$144
(970) 264-9204
(888) 264-9204

INDIAN HEAD LODGE
P O Box 2499 (81147)
Rates: $24-$65
(970) 731-2282
(970) 358-4853

PAGOSA RIVERSIDE CAMPER CABINS
2270 E Hwy 160 (81147)
Rates: $24-$28
(970) 264-5874

PAGOSA SPRINGS INN
519 Village Dr (81147)
Rates: $61-$89
(970) 731-3400

PIEDRA RIVER RESORT
P O Box 4190 (81147)
Rates: $36-$50
(970) 731-4630
(800) 898-2006

SPA MOTEL
P O Box 37 (81147)
Rates: $45-$70
(970) 264-5910
(800) 832-5523

SPORTSMAN'S CAMPGROUND & CABINS
2095 Taylor Ln (81147)
Rates: n/a
(970) 731-2300

SUPER 8 MOTEL
34 Piedra Rd (81147)
Rates: $36-$100
(970) 731-4005
(800) 800-8000

PAONIA

COLORADO GUEST RANCH / CHIPETA RANCH
1938 Hwy 133 (81428)
Rates: $43-$60
(970) 929-6260
(800) 521-4055

PARLIN

7 - 11 RANCH CABINS
5291 CR 76 (81239)
Rates: $30
(970) 641-0666

PUEBLO

BEST WESTERN TOWN HOUSE MOTOR HOTEL
730 N Santa Fe (81003)
Rates: $45-$85
(719) 543-6530
(800) 528-12340

HAMPTON INN
4703 North Freeway (81108)
Rates: $79-$99
(719) 544-4700
(800) 426-7866

HOLIDAY INN
4001 N Elizabeth St (81008)
Rates: $69-$99
(719) 543-8050
(800) 465-4329

LA QUINTA INN
4801 N Elizabeth St (81008)
Rates: $69-$99
(719) 542-35
(800) 687-6667

MICROTEL INN & SUITES
3343 Gateway Dr (81004)
Rates: $54-$74
(719) 242-2020
(888) 771-7171

MOTEL 6
960 Hwy 50 W (81008)
Rates: $33-$50
(719) 543-8900
(800) 466-8356

MOTEL 6 EXTENDED STAY
4103 N Elizabeth St (81008)
Rates: $35-$52
(719) 543-6221
(800) 466-8356

SLEEP INN
3626 North Freeway (81008)
Rates: $49-$109
(719) 583-4000
(800) 424-6423

PUEBLO WEST

INN AT PUEBLO WEST
201 S McCulloch Blvd (81007)
Rates: $47-$74
(719) 547-2111

PURGATORY

SHERATON TAMARRON RESORT
40292 Hwy 550 N (81301)
Rates: $129-$449
(970) 259-2000

RED CLIFF

PANDO CABINS
1088 Hwy 24 (81649)
Rates: $125
(970) 949-4232
(888) 949-6682

RED FEATHER LAKES

BEAVER MEADOWS RESORT RANCH
100 Marmot (80545)
Rates: $39-$150
(800) 462-5870

RED FEATHER RANCH B&B & HORSE HOTEL
3613 CR 68C (80545)
Rates: n/a
(970) 881-3715
(877) 881 5215

TROUT LODGE CABINS
P O Box 126 (80545)
Rates: $49-$99
(970) 881-2964

REDSTONE

AVALANCHE RANCH CABINS
12863 Hwy 133 (81623)
Rates: $70-$155
(970) 963-2846
(877) 963-9339

RIDGWAY

CHIPETA SUN LODGE & SPA
304 S Lena St (81432)
Rates: $95-$215
(970) 626-3737
(800) 633-5868

RIDGWAY- OURAY LODGE & SUITES
373 Palomino Tr (81432)
Rates: $60-$88
(970) 626-5444
(800) 368-5444

RIFLE

RUSTY CANNON MOTEL
701 Taughenbaugh Blvd (81650)
Rates: $50-$76
(970) 625-4004
(866) 625-4004

ROCKY FORD

MELON VALLEY INN
1319 Elm Ave (81067)
Rates: $30-$45
(719) 254-3306

RYE

THE LODGE AT SAN ISABEL
HCR 75, Box 123 (81069)
Rates: $45-$95
(719) 489-2280

SALIDA

ASPEN LEAF LODGE
7350 Hwy 50W (81201)
Rates $39-$69
(719) 539-6733
(800) 759-0338

**BEST WESTERN
COLORADO
LODGE**
352 W Rainbow
Blvd (81201)
Rates: $42-$112
(719) 539-2514
(800) 528-1234
(800) 777-7947

CIRCLE R MOTEL
304 E Rainbow
Blvd (81201)
Rates: $30-$76
(719) 539-6296
(800) 755-6296

DAYS INN
407 E Hwy 50
(81201)
Rates: $39-$89
(719) 539-6651
(800) 329-7466

ECONO LODGE
1310 E Hwy 50
(81201)
Rates: $39-$129
(719) 539-2895
(800) 424-6423

**PIÑON & SAGE
B&B INN**
803 F St (81201)
Rates: $45-$75
(719) 539-3227
(800) 840-3156

RAINBOW INN
105 E Hwy 50
(81201)
Rates: $50-$75
(719) 539-4444
(800) 539-4447

**RANCH HOUSE
LODGE**
7545 W Hwy 40
(81201)
Rates: $32-$68
(719) 539-6655

**REDWOOD
LODGE**
7310 Hwy 50
(81201)
Rates: $42-$79
(719) 539-2528

**SILVER RIDGE
LODGE**
545 W Rainbow
Blvd (81201)
Rates: $35-$85
(719) 539-2553
(877) 268-3320

SUPER 8 MOTEL
525 W Rainbow
(81201)
Rates: $49-$119
(719) 539-6689
(800) 800-8000

TRAVELODGE
7310 Hwy 50
(81201)
Rates: $49-$109
(719) 539-2528
(800) 578-7878

**THE TUDOR ROSE
BED & BREAKFAST**
6720 Paradise Rd
(81201)
Rates: $75-$165
(719) 539-2002
(800) 379-0889

**WOODLAND
MOTEL**
903 W 1st (81201)
Rates: $36-$99
(719) 539-4980
(800) 488-0456

SAPINERO
**LEY-Z-B AT
SAPINERO
CABINS**
16020 W Hwy 50
(81247)
Rates: $25
(970) 641-2340

SILVER CREEK
**THE INN AT
SILVER CREEK**
62927 Hwy 40
(80446)
Rates: $69-$218
(970) 887-2131
(800) 926-4386

SILVERTHORNE
DAYS INN
580 Silverthorne
Ln (80498)
Rates: $55-$200
(970) 468-8661
(800) 329-7466

**FOUR POINTS
BY SHERATON**
560 Silverthorne
Ln (80498)
Rates: $80-$152
(970) 468-6200
(800) 325-3535

I-70 INN
361 Blueriver
Pkwy (80498)
Rates: n/a
(970) 468-5170

**LUXURY INN
& SUITES**
540 Silverthorne
Ln (80498)
Rates: $40-$100
(970) 468-0800
(800) 742-1972

**QUALITY INN
& SUITES**
530 Silverthorne
Ln (80498)
Rates: $49-$279
(970) 513-1222
(800) 424-6423

SILVERTON
**MOLAS LAKE
PARK CAMPER
CABINS**
P O Box 776
(81433)
Rates: $25
(970) 387-5848
(800) 846-2177

**RED MOUNTAIN
MOTEL**
664 Green St
(81433)
Rates: $40-$65
(970) 387-5512
(888) 970-5512

**SILVERTON'S INN
OF THE ROCKIES
HISTORIC ALMA
HOUSE B & B**
220 E 10th St
(81433)
Rates: $80-$130
(970) 387-5336
(800) 267-5336

**VILLA
DALLAVALLE B&B**
1257 Blair (81433)
Rates: $120-$215
(970) 387-5555

**WYMAN HOTEL
& INN B&B**
1370 Greene St
(81433)
Rates: $120-$215
(970) 387-5372
(800) 609-7845

**_SNOWMASS
VILLAGE_**
**SILVERTREE
HOTEL**
100 Elbert Lane
(81615)
Rates: $98-$525
(970) 923-3520
(800) 375-7873

**SNOWMASS
MOUNTAIN
CHALET HOTEL**
115 Daly Lane
(81615)
Rates: $59-$325
(970) 923-3900

**WILDWOOD
LODGE**
40 Elbert Lane
(81615)
Rates: $89-$275
(970) 923-3550
(800) 375-7873

SOMERSET
**CRYSTAL
MEADOWS
RANCH LODGING**
30682 CR 12
(81434)
Rates: $40-$135
(970) 929-5656

SOUTH FORK
**ASPENRIDGE
CABINS**
0710 W Hwy 149
(81154)
Rates: $40-$45
(719) 873-5921

**BLUE CREEK
LODGE & CABINS**
Hwy 149,
MP 11-12,
HC 33 (81154)
Rates: $32-$64
(719) 658-2479
(800) 326-6408

**BUDGET HOST
UTE BLUFF LODGE**
27680 W Hwy 160
(81154)
Rates: $44-$95
(719) 873-5595
(800) 473-0595
(800) 283-4678

COMFORT INN
0182 E Frontage
Rd (81154)
Rates: $59-$150
(719) 873-5600
(800) 424-6423

**COTTONWOOD
COVE LODGE &
CABINS**
Hwy 149, HC 33
(81154)
Rates: $39-$74
(719) 658-2242

**GOODNIGHT'S
LONESOME DOVE
CABINS**
P O Box 157
(81154)
Rates: $55-$65
(719) 873-1072
(800) 551-3683

THE INN MOTEL
30362 West Hwy
160 (81154)
Rates: $26-$75
(719) 873-5514
(800) 233-9723

**LAZY BEAR
CABINS**
29257 W Hwy 160
(81154)
Rates: $40-$100
(719) 873-1443
(877) 873-1443

**RIVEREND
RESORT CABINS**
Box 129 (81154)
Rates: $42-$140
(719) 873-5344
(800) 621-6512

**SOUTH FORK
LODGE**
P O Box 43 (81154)
Rates: $45-$75
(719) 873-5303
(800) 457-9156

**SPRUCE LODGE
B&B AND CABINS**
Box 156 (81154)
Rates: $28-$55
(719) 873-5605
(800) 228-5606

**WOLF CREEK
SKI LODGE**
31042 Hwy W 160
(81154)
Rates: $45-$80
(719) 873-5547
(800) 874-0416

AREA CODES - If the local number doesn't connect, check for a new area code.

SPRINGFIELD

PLUM BEAR RANCH
29461 CR 21 (81073)
Rates: $45-$50
(719) 523-4344

STEAMBOAT SPRINGS

THE ALPINER LODGE
424 Lincoln Ave (80477)
Rates: $89-$139
(970) 879-1430
(800) 538-7519

BEST WESTERN PTARMIGAN INN
2304 Apres Ski Way (80487)
Rates: $79-$295
(970) 879-1730
(800) 528-1234
(800) 538-7519

COMFORT INN
1055 Walton Creek Rd (80477)
Rates: $69-$189
(970) 879-6669
(800) 424-6423

HAMPTON INN & SUITES
725 S Lincoln AVe (80487)
Rates: $109-$339
(970) 871-8900
(800) 426-7866

HOLIDAY INN
3190 S Lincoln Ave (80487)
Rates: $99-$170
(970) 879-2250
(800) 465-4329
(800) 654-3944

IRON HORSE INN
333 S Lincoln Ave (80487)
Rates: $95-$200
(970) 879-6505

RABBIT EARS MOTEL
201 Lincoln Ave (80487)
Rates: $60-$129
(970) 879-1150
(800) 828-7702

SHERATON STEAMBOAT RESORT
2200 Village Inn Court (80477)
Rates: $200+
(970) 879-2220
(800) 325-3535
(800) 848- 8877

STEAMBOAT LOG CABINS AT PERRY MANSFIELD
40755 CR 36 (80487)
Rates: $105-$350
(970) 879-1060
(800) 538-7519

SUPER 8 MOTEL
3195 Hwy 40 E (80487)
Rates: $49-$109
(970) 879-5230
(800) 800-8000

STERLING

BEST WESTERN SUNDOWNER
125 Overland Trail St (80751)
Rates: $79-$129
(970) 522-6265
(800) 528-1234

COLONIAL MOTEL
915 S Division (80751)
Rates: $35-$60
(970) 522-3382

RAMADA INN
I-76 & Hwy 6 E (80751)
Rates: $85-$105
(970) 522-2625
(800) 272-6232

STRASBURG

STRASBURG INN BED & BREAKFAST
1406 Main (80136)
Rates: $35-$50
(303) 622-4314

STRATTON

BEST WESTERN GOLDEN PRAIRIE
700 Colorado Ave (80836)
Rates: $55-$99
(719) 348-5311
(800) 528-1234
(800) 626-0043

SWEETWATER

SWEETWATER LAKE RESORT
3406 Sweetwater Rd (81637)
Rates: $50-$90
(970) 524-7344

TABERNASH

HURD CREEK RANCH LODGE & CABIN RENTAL
P O Box 516 (80478)
Rates: $150-$250
(970) 726-5304
(800) 471-5122

TELLURIDE

CAMEL'S GARDEN RESORT HOTEL
250 W San Juan Ave (81535)
Rates: n/a
(970) 728-9300
(888) 772-2635

HOTEL COLUMBIA
300 W San Juan Ave (81435)
Rates: $175-$450
(970) 728-0660
(800) 201-9505

THE HOTEL TELLURIDE
199 N Cornet St (81435)
Rates: $149-$349
(970) 369-1188
(866) 468-3501

TELLURIDE MOUNTAIN LODGING
P. O. Box 2288 (81435)
Rates: n/a
(970) 728-1950
(888) 728-1950

WYNDHAM PEAKS RESORT & GOLDEN DOOR SPA
136 Country Club Dr (81435)
Rates: $199-$299
(970) 728-6800
(800) 996-3426
(800) 789-2220

TEXAS CREEK

WHISPERING PINES RESORT
24871 Hwy 50 W (81223)
Rates: $35-$45
(719) 275-3827
(888) 275-3827

THORNTON

MOTEL 6
6 W 83rd Pl (80221)
Rates: $37-$56
(303) 429-1550
(800) 466-8356

SLEEP INN
12101 Grant St (80229)
Rates: $69-$104
(303) 280-9819
(800) 424-6423

TRINIDAD

BEST WESTERN TRINIDAD INN
900 W Adams St (81082)
Rates: $49-$109
(719) 846-2215
(800) 528-1234
(800) 955-2215

BUDGET HOST DERRICK MOTEL
10301 Santa Fe Trail Dr (81082)
Rates: $49-$89
(719) 846-3307
(800) 283-4678

BUDGET SUMMIT INN
9800 Santa Fe Trail Dr (81082)
Rates: $44-$119
(719) 846-2251

CHICOSA CANYON B&B
32391 CR 40 (81082)
Rates: $75-$95
(719) 846-6199

HOLIDAY INN
3125 Toupal Dr (81082)
Rates: $129
(719) 846-4491
(800) 465-4329

SUPER 8 MOTEL
1924 Freedom Rd (81082)
Rates: $45-$80
(719) 846-8280
(800) 800-8000

TWIN LAKES

MOUNT ELBERT LODGE & CABINS
10764 Hwy 82 (81251)
Rates: $59-$88
(719) 486-0594
(800) 381-4433

TWIN LAKES NORDIC INN
6435 Hwy 82 (81251)
Rates: $48-$65
(719) 486-1830
(800) 626-7812

TWIN PEAKS CABINS
6889 Hwy 82 (81251)
Rates: $45-$80
(719) 486-2667

VAIL

ANTLERS AT VAIL
680 W Lionshead Place (81657)
Rates: $160-$415
(970) 476-2471
(800) 843-8245

SONNENALP RESORT OF VAIL
20 Vail Rd (81657)
Rates: $200-$975
(970) 476-5656
(800) 654-8312

VALLECITO LAKE

EAGLE'S NEST RENTAL CABINS
18903 CR 501 (Bayfield 81122)
Rates: n/a
(970) 884-2866

SAWMILL POINT LODGE CABINS
14737 CR 501 (Bayfield 81122)
Rates: $50-$125
(970) 884-2669

AREA CODES - If the local number doesn't connect, check for a new area code.

VICTOR
HISTORIC VICTOR HOTEL
397 Victor Ave
(80860)
Rates: $85-$99
(970) 689-3553
(800) 748-0870 (CO)

WALDEN
LAKE JOHN RESORT
2521 CR 7A
(80480)
Rates: $35-$45
(970) 723-3226

NORTH PARK MOTEL
625 Main St
(80480)
Rates: $30-$60
(970) 723-4271

WALSENBURG
ANCHOR MOTEL
1001 Main St
(81089)
Rates: $30-$65
(719) 738-2800

BEST WESTERN RAMBLER MOTEL
457 Hwy 85-87
(81089)
Rates: $62-$97
(719) 738-1121
(800) 528-1234
(866) 224-7016

COUNTRY BUDGET HOST MOTEL
553 Hwy 85-87
(81089)
Rates: $38-$64
(719) 738-3800
(800) 283-4678

WESTCLIFFE
CROSS D BAR TROUT RANCH
2299 CR 328
(81252)
Rates: $80
(719) 783-2007
(800) 453-4379

WESTCLIFFE INN
S Hwy 69 &
Hermit Rd (81252)
Rates: $33-$75
(719) 783-9275
(800) 284-0850

WESTMINSTER
COMFORT SUITES
12085 Delaware St
(80234)
Rates: $54-$124
(303) 429-5500
(800) 424-6423

DOUBLETREE HOTEL
8773 Yates Dr
(80031)
Rates: 59-$169
(303) 427-4000
(800) 222-8733

LA QUINTA INN
10179 Church
Ranch Way
(80234)
Rates: $69-$89
(303) 438-5800
(800) 687-6667

LA QUINTA INN NORTH
345 W 120th Ave
(80234)
Rates: $63-$80
(303) 252-9800
(800) 687-6667

LA QUINTA INN WESTMINSTER MALL
8701 Turnpike Dr
(80230)
Rates: $63-$80
(303) 425-9099
(800) 687-6667

RESIDENCE INN BY MARRIOTT
5010 W 88th Pl
(80031)
Rates: $129
(303) 427-9500
(800) 331-3131

SUPER 8 MOTEL
12055 Melody Dr
(80234)
Rates: $67-$87
(303) 451-7200
(800) 800-8000

THE WESTIN
10600 Westminster
Blvd (80020)
Rates: $99-$219
(303) 410-5000
(800) 228-3000

WHEAT RIDGE
MOTEL 6
9920 W 49th Ave
(80033)
Rates: $33-$50
(303) 424-0658
(800) 466-8356

MOTEL 6
10300 S I-70
Frontage Rd
(80033)
Rates: $33-$46
(303) 467-3172
(800) 466-8356

QUALITY INN
12100 W 44th Ave
(80033)
Rates: $59-$119
(303) 467-2400
(800) 424-6423

WINDSOR
AMERICINN LODGE & SUITES
7645 Westgate Dr
(80528)
Rates: $79-$164
(970) 226-1232
(800) 634-3444

SUPER 8 MOTEL
1265 Main St
(80550)
Rates: $66-$76
(970) 686-5996
(800) 800-8000

WINTER PARK
ALPENGLO PROPERTIES
P. O. Box 35
(80482)
Rates: $100-$200
(970) 726-5294
(800) 541-6130

SITZMARK CHALETS & CABINS
Hwy 40 at King's
Crossing (80482)
Rates: $40-$80
(970) 726-5453

SUPER 8 LODGE
78665 Hwy 40
(80482)
Rates: $35-$85
(970) 726-8088
(888) 726-8088

THE VIKING LODGE
P. O`. Box 89
(80482)
Rates: n/a
(800) 421-4013

THE VINTAGE RESORT HOTEL
100 Winter Park
Dr (80482)
Rates: $101-$200
(970) 726-8801
(800) 472-7017

WINTER PARK MOUNTAIN LODGE
81699 Hwy 40
(80482)
Rates: $50-$300
(970) 726-4211
(866) 726-6642

WOODLAND PARK
TRIPLE B GUEST & ACTIVITY RANCH
27640 N Hwy 67
(80863)
Rates: $101-$200
(719) 687-8899
(877) 687-8899

YAMPA
OAK TREE INN
98 Moffat Ave
(80483)
Rates: $75
(970) 638-1000

VAN CAMP CABINS
P O Box 170
(80483)
Rates: $45-$55
(970) 638-4254

AREA CODES - If the local number doesn't connect, check for a new area code.

CONNECTICUT

BERLIN
HAWTHORNE INN
2387 Berlin Tpke (06037)
Rates: $51-$75
(860) 828-4181

BETHEL
MICROTEL INN & SUITES
80 Benedict Rd (06801)
Rates: $70-$122
(203) 748-8318
(888) 771-7171

BRANFORD
DAYS INN
375 E Main St (06405)
Rates: $59-$199
(203) 488-8314
(800) 329-7466

MOTEL 6
320 E Main St (06405)
Rates: $39-$60
(203) 483-5828
(800) 466-8356

BRIDGEPORT
HOLIDAY INN
1070 Main St (06604)
Rates: $119-$159
(203) 334-1234
(800) 465-4329

BROOKFIELD
TWIN TREE INN
1030 Federal Rd (06804)
Rates: $76-$99
(203) 775-0220

CHAPLIN
PLEASANT VIEW LODGE MOTEL
Rt 6 (06235)
Rates: $30-$50
(860) 455-9588

CHESTER
THE INN & VINEYARD AT CHESTER
318 W Main St (06412)
Rates: $95-$105
(860) 526-9541
(800) 949-7829

CORNWALL BRIDGE
CORNWALL INN
Route 7 (06754)
Rates: $50-$150
(800) 786-6884

COVENTRY
MILLBROOK FARM B & B
110 Wall St (06238)
Rates: $45-$60
(860) 742-5761

CROMWELL
COMFORT INN
111 Berlin Rd (06416)
Rates: $59-$159
(860) 635-4100
(800) 424-6423

RADISSON HOTEL & CONFERENCE CENTER
100 Berlin Rd (06416)
Rates: $99-$149
(860) 635-2000
(800) 333-3333

DANBURY
ETHAN ALLEN HOTEL
21 Lake Ave Extension (06811)
Rates: $129
(203) 744-1776

HOLIDAY INN
80 Newtown Rd (06810)
Rates: $121-$125
(203) 792-4000
(800) 465-4329

MARON HOTEL & SUITES
42 Lake Ave Extension (06810)
Rates: $99-$179
(203) 791-2200

RESIDENCE INN BY MARRIOTT
22 Segar St (06810)
Rates: $129-$149
(203) 797-1256
(800) 331-3131

SHERATON DANBURY
18 Old Ridgebury Rd (06810)
Rates: $89-$189
(203) 794-0600
(800) 325-3535

SUPER 8 MOTEL
3 Lake Ave Extension (06810)
Rates: $64-$74
(203) 743-0064
(800) 800-8000

WELLESLEY INN
116 Newtown Rd (06810)
Rates: $89-$129
(203) 792-3800
(800) 444-8888

DAYVILLE
HOLIDAY INN EXPRESS HOTEL
16 Tracy Rd (06241)
Rates: n/a
(860) 779-3200
(800) 465-4329

EAST HARTFORD
HOLIDAY INN
363 Roberts St (06108)
Rates: $119-$129
(860) 528-9611
(800) 465-4329

SHERATON HARTFORD HOTEL
100 E River Dr (06108)
Rates: $79-$119
(860) 528-9703
(800) 325-3535

EAST WINDSOR
HOLIDAY INN EXP
260 Main St (06088)
Rates: $89-$109
(860) 627-6585
(800) 465-4329

ENFIELD
MOTEL 6
11 Hazard Ave (06082)
Rates: $39-$60
(860) 741-3685
(800) 466-8356

RADISSON HOTEL
1 Bright Meadow Blvd (06082)
Rates: $85-$100
(860) 741-2211
(800) 333-3333

RED ROOF INN
5 Hazard Ave (06082)
Rates: $50-$107
(860) 741-2571
(800) 843-7663

SUPER 8 MOTEL
1543 King St (06082)
Rates: $59-$115
(860) 741-3636
(800) 800-8000

FARMINGTON
CENTENNIAL INN SUITES
5 Spring Ln (06032)
Rates: $129-$210
(860) 677-4647
(800) 852-2052

FARMINGTON INN
827 Farmington Ave (06032)
Rates: $99-$129
(860) 677-2821
(800) 648-9804

HOMEWOOD SUITES
2 Farm Glen Blvd (06032)
Rates: $149
(860) 321-0000
(800) 225-5466

GRISWOLD
AMERICINN LODGE & SUITES
375 Voluntown Rd (06351)
Rates: $69-$179
(860) 376-3200
(800) 634-3444

GROTON
BENHAM MOTEL
107 Benham Rd (06340)
Rates: $76-$99
(860) 449-5700

CLARION INN
156 Kings Hwy (06340)
Rates: $49-$209
(860) 446-0660
(800) 424-6423

HARTFORD
CROWNE PLAZA
50 Morgan St (06120)
Rates: $79-$219
(860) 549-2400
(800) 227-6963

GOODWIN HOTEL
1 Haynes St (06103)
Rates: $79-$228
(860) 246-7500
(800) 922-5006

MOTEL 6
100 Weston St (06120)
Rates: $49-$60
(860) 724-0222
(800) 466-8356

AREA CODES - If the local number doesn't connect, check for a new area code.

**RESIDENCE INN
BY MARRIOTT**
942 Main St
(06103)
Rates: $179-$199
(860) 524-5550
(800) 331-3131

LAKEVILLE
**INN AT IRON
MASTERS**
229 Main St
(06039)
Rates: $95-$145
(860) 435-9844

**INTERLAKEN
INN RESORT**
74 Interlaken Rd
(06039)
Rates: $149-$189
(860) 435-9878
(800) 222-2909

LEDYARD
**THE MARE'S INN
BED & BREAKFAST**
333 Colonel
Ledyard Hwy
(06372)
Rates: $100-$175
(860) 572-7556

LITCHFIELD
**HISTORIC
TOLLGATE HILL
INN**
571 Torrington
Rd (06759)
Rates: $100-$175
(860) 567-1233
(800) 445-3903

LITCHFIELD INN
432 Bantam Rd
(06759)
Rates: $130-$250
(860) 567-4503

MANCHESTER
**CLARION
SUITES INN**
191 Spencer St
(06040)
Rates: $115-$181
(860) 643-5811
(800) 992-4004

RESIDENCE INN
201 Hale Rd
(06040)
Rates: $144-$194
(860) 432-4242
(800) 331-3131

SUPER 8 MOTEL
20 Taylor St
(06040)
Rates: n/a
(860) 643-1864
(800) 800-8000

MERIDEN
**CANDLEWOOD
SUITES**
1511 E Main St
(06450)
Rates: n/a
(203) 379-5048
(888) 226-3539

**FOUR POINTS BY
SHERATON**
275 Research
Pkwy (06450)
Rates: $89-$229
(230) 238-2380
(800) 325-3535

**RESIDENCE INN
BY MARRIOTT**
390 Bee St (06450)
Rates: $174
(203) 634-7770
(800) 331-3131

MIDDLETOWN
**INN AT
MIDDLETOWN**
70 Main St
(06457)
Rates: $89-$159
(860) 854-6300

MILFORD
COMFORT INN
278 Old Gate Ln
(06460)
Rates: $69-$175
(203) 877-9411
(800) 424-6423

RED ROOF INN
10 Rowe Ave
(06460)
Rates: $61-$73
(203) 877-6060
(800) 843-7663

MILLDALE
DAYS INN
1845 Meriden
Waterbury Tpke
(06467)
Rates: $50-$99
(860) 621-9181
(800) 329-7466

MONTVILLE
**CHESTERFIELD
LODGE**
1596 Rt 85
(06370)
Rates: $30-$50
(860) 442-0039

MYSTIC
AMERISUITES
224 Greenmanville
Ave (06355)
Rates: $129-$234
(860) 536-9997
(800) 833-1516

**HARBOUR INNE
&COTTAGE**
15 Edgemont St
(06355)
Rates: $76-$99
(860) 572-9253

**THE INN
AT MYSTIC**
3 Williams Ave
(06355)
Rates: $85-$295
(860) 536-9604

**RESIDENCE INN
BY MARRIOTT**
40 Whitehall aVe
(06355)
Rates: $149-$399
(860) 536-5150
(800) 331-3131

NEW BRITAIN
DAYS INN
65 Columbus
Blvd (06051)
Rates: $49-$149
(860) 224-9161
(800) 329-7466

NEW HAVEN
DAYS INN
270 Foxon Blvd
(06513)
Rates: $70-$160
(203) 469-0343
(800) 329-7466

**ECONO LODGE
& SUITES**
100 Pond Lily
Ave (06525)
Rates: $79-$159
(203) 387-6651
(800) 424-6423

**OMNI NEW
HAVEN HOTEL
AT YALE**
155 Temple St
(06510)
Rates: $189-$239
(203) 772-6664
(800) 843-6664

**RESIDENCE INN
BY MARRIOTT**
3 Long Wharf Dr
(06513)
Rates: $145-$180
(203) 777-5337
(800) 331-3131

NEW LONDON
RED ROOF INN
707 Colman St
(06320)
Rates: $60-$100
(860) 444-0001
(800) 843-7663

NEW MILFORD
**THE
HOMESTEAD INN
B&B**
5 Elm St (06776)
Rates: $95-$165
(860) 354-4080

NEW PRESTON
**ATHA HOUSE
COTTAGE**
Wheaton Rd off
Rt 202 (06777)
Rates: $76-$99
(860) 355-7387

NIANTIC
MOTEL 6
269 Flanders Rd
(06357)
Rates: $39-$80
(860) 739-6991
(800) 466-8356

NORFOLK
**BLACKBERRY
RIVER INN B&B**
536 Greenwoods
Rd W (06058)
Rates: $95-$195
(860) 542-5100
(800) 414-3636

NORTH STONINGTON
**ANTIQUES AND
ACCOMMODA-
TIONS**
32 Main St
(06359)
Rates: $99-$229
(860) 535-1736

BUDGET INN
593 Providence-
New London
Tpke (06359)
Rates: $51-$75
(860) 599-0835

CEDAR PARK INN
85 Norwich
Westerly Rd
(06359)
Rates: $79-$249
(860) 535-7829

**THE INN AT
LOWER FARM
B&B**
119 Mystic Rd
(06359)
Rates: $85-$150
(860) 535-9075

NORWALK
**DOUBLETREE
HOTEL**
789 Connecticut
Ave (06854)
Rates: $79-$169
(203) 853-3477
(800) 222-8733

**GARDEN PARK
MOTEL**
351 Westport Ave
(06851)
Rates: $51-$75
(203) 847-7303

**HOMESTEAD
STUDIO SUITES**
400 Main Ave
(06851)
Rates: $114-$139
(203) 847-6888
(888) 782-9473

NORWICH
RAMADA HOTEL
10 Laura Blvd
(06360)
Rates: $69-$159
(860) 889-5201
(800) 272-6232

AREA CODES - If the local number doesn't connect, check for a new area code.

OLD LYME

OLD LYME INN
85 Lyme St (06371)
Rates: $99-$175
(860) 434-2600
(800) 434-5352

OLD SAYBROOK

SANDPIPER MOTOR INN
1750 Boston Post Rd (06475)
Rates: $65-$135
(860) 399-7973
(800) 323-7973

SAYBROOK POINT INN & SPA
2 Bridge St (06475)
Rates: $179-$649
(860) 395-2000
(800) 243-0212

PLAINFIELD

PLAINFIELD MOTEL
Box 101, RR 2
(Moosup 06354)
Rates: $37-$64
(860) 564-2791

PLAINVILLE

RAMADA INN
400 New Britain Ave (06062)
Rates: $75-$89
(860) 747-6876
(800) 272-6232

PUTNAM

KING'S INN
5 Heritage Rd (06260)
Rates: $62-$78
(860) 928-7961
(800) 541-7304

RIVERTON

OLD RIVERTON INN
436 E River Rd (06065)
Rates: $55-$130
(860) 379-8678
(860) 378-1796

SALISBURY

BARBARA ARDIZONES B&B
62 Main St (06068)
Rates: n/a
(860) 435-3057

SHARON

SHARON MOTOR LODGE
SR 41 (06069)
Rates: $62-$125
(860) 364-0036

SHELTON

AMERISUITES
695 Bridgeport Ave (06484)
Rates: $154
(203) 925-5900
(800) 833-1516

HOMESTEAD STUDIO SUITES
945 Bridgeport Ave (06484)
Rates: $101-$126
(203) 926-6868
(888) 782-9473

RAMADA PLAZA HOTEL
780 Bridgeport Ave (06484)
Rates: $69-$155
(203) 929-1500
(800) 272-6232

RESIDENCE INN BY MARRIOTT
1001 Bridgeport Ave (06484)
Rates: $145-$190
(203) 926-9000
(800) 331-3131

SIMSBURY

IRONHORSE INN
969 Hopmeadow St (06070)
Rates: $79-$89
(860) 658-2216
(800) 245-9938

THE SIMSBURY 1820 HOUSE
731 Hopmeadow St (06070)
Rates: $109-$169
(860) 658-7658
(800) TRY-1820

SOUTHBURY

HILTON HOTEL
1284 Strongtown Rd (06488)
Rates: $136-$151
(203) 598-7600
(800) 445-8667

SOUTHING-TON

MOTEL 6
625 Queen St (06489)
Rates: $39-$50
(860) 621-7351
(800) 466-8356

RESIDENCE INN BY MARRIOTT
778 West St (06489)
Rates: $114-$225
(860) 621-4440
(800) 331-3131

STAMFORD

MARRIOTT HOTEL
Two Stamford Forum (06901)
Rates: $265-$285
(203) 357-9555
(800) 228-9290

RODEWAY INN
19 Clarks Hill Ave (06902)
Rates: $80-$130
(203) 327-4300
(800) 424-6423

SHERATON HOTEL
2701 Summer St (06905)
Rates: $99-$219
(203) 359-1300
(800) 325-3535

SUPER 8 MOTEL
32 Grenhart Rd (06902)
Rates: $89-$109
(203) 324-8887
(800) 800-8000

THE WESTIN STAMFORD
1 First Stamford Place (06902)
Rates: $89-$199
(203) 967-2222
(800) 228-3000

STONINGTON

ANOTHER SECOND PENNY INN B&B
870 Pequot Tr (06378)
Rates: $80-$185
(860) 535-1710

STRATFORD

STAYBRIDGE SUITES
6905 Main St (06497)
Rates: $139
(203) 377-3322
(800) 238-8000

TORRINGTON

DAYS INN
395 Winsted Rd (06790)
Rates: $80-$350
(860) 496-8808
(800) 329-7466

VOLUNTOWN

TAMARACK LODGE
21 Ten Rod Rd (06384)
Rates: $51-$75
(860) 376-0640
(860) 376-0224

WATERBURY

HOUSE ON THE HILL B&B
92 Woodlawn Ter (06710)
Rates: $125-$165
(203) 757-9901

WATERFORD

OAKDELL MOTEL
983 Hartford Tpke (06385)
Rates: $55-$145
(860) 442-9446
(800) 676-7378

RODEWAY INN
211 Waterford Pkwy N (06385)
Rates: $59-$189
(860) 442-7227
(800) 424-6423

WEST GOSHEN

GOSHEN MOTEL
Rt 4 W (06756)
Rates: $30-$50
(860) 491-9989

WEST HAVEN

ECONO LODGE
370 Highland St (06516)
Rates: $49-$139
(203) 934-6611
(800) 424-6423

WESTBROOK

BEACH PLUM INN MOTEL
1935 Boston Post Rd (06498)
Rates: $60-$350
(860) 399-9345

WESTPORT

WESTPORT INN
1595 Post Rd E (06880)
Rates: $139-$189
(203) 259-5236

WETHERS-FIELD

BEST WESTERN CAMELOT INN
1330 Silas Deane Hwy (06109)
Rates: $79-$109
(860) 563-2311
(800) 528-1234

MOTEL 6
1341 Silas Deane Hwy (06109)
Rates: $39-$50
(860) 563-5900
(800) 466-8356

WILLINGTON

ECONO LODGE
327 Ruby Rd (06279)
Rates: $70-$100
(860) 684-1400
(800) 424-6423

WINDSOR

RESIDENCE INN BY MARRIOTT
100 Dunfey Ln (06095)
Rates: n/a
(860) 688-7474
(800) 331-3131

WINDSOR LOCKS

BAYMONT INN & SUITES
64 Ella Grasso Tpk (06096)
Rates: $77-$87
(860) 623-3336
(877) 229-6668

HOMEWOOD SUITES
65 Ella Grasso Tpke (06096)
Rates: $159-$179
(860) 627-8463
(800) 225-5466

AREA CODES - If the local number doesn't connect, check for a new area code.

**MOTEL 6-
BRADLEY
AIRPORT**
3 National Dr
(06096)
Rates: $39-$48
(860) 292-6200
(800) 466-8356

RAMADA INN
5 Ella T Grasso
Tpke (06096)
Rates: $89-$135
(860) 623-9494
(800) 272-6232

**SHERATON
HOTEL AT
BRADLEY INTL
AIRPORT**
1 Bradley Intl
Airport (06096)
Rates: $145-$160
(860) 627-5311
(800) 325-3535

DELAWARE

BEAR

AMERICINN
875 Pulaski Hwy
(19701)
Rates: $75-$100
(302) 326-2500
(800) 634-3444

CAMDEN

**THE ROSE
TOWER B&B**
228 E Camden-
Wyoming Ave
(19934)
Rates: $75-$100
(302) 698-9033
(877) 893-3031

CLAYMONT

**HOLIDAY INN
SELECT**
630 Naamans Rd
(19703)
Rates: $75-$115
(302) 792-2700
(800) 465-4329

DEWEY BEACH

**ATLANTIC
OCEANSIDE
MOTEL**
1700 Hwy 1
(19971)
Rates: $89-$229
(302) 227-8811
(800) 422-0481

**BELLBUOY
MOTEL**
21 Van Dyke St
(19971)
Rates: $65-$165
(302) 227-6000

**BEST WESTERN
GOLD LEAF**
1400 Hwy One
(19971)
Rates: $49-$229
(302) 226-1100
(800) 528-1234
(800) 422-8566

COOL PINES B&B
108 Houston St
(19971)
Rates: $125-$185
(302) 227-8164

SEA ESTA MOTEL
2306 Hwy 1
(19971)
Rates: $49-$139
(302) 227-7666
(800) 436-6591

**SEA ESTA
MOTEL III**
1409 Hwy 1 (19971)
Rates: $55-$179
(302) 227-4343
(800) 436-6591

**SEA ESTA
MOTEL IV**
3101 Hwy 1
(19971)
Rates: $50-$75
(302) 227-5882
(800) 436-6591

DOVER

**LITTLE
CREEK INN**
2623 N Little
Creek Rd (19901)
Rates: $125-$200
(302) 730-1300

RED ROOF INN
642 N DuPont
Hwy (19901)
Rates: $74-$120
(302) 730-8009
(800) 843-7663

FENWICK ISLAND

**ATLANTIC
COAST INN**
Lighthouse Rd &
Coastal Hwy
(19944)
Rates: $59-$179
(302) 539-7673

GEORGETOWN

COMFORT INN
507 N Dupont
Hwy (19947)
Rates: $69-$300
(302) 854-9400
(800) 424-6423

HARRINGTON

**AMERICINN
LODGE & SUITES**
1259 Corn Crib
Rd (19952)
Rates: $75-$120
(302) 398-3900
(800) 644-3444

LEWES

**COUNTRY
LANE B&B**
7 Country Ln
(19958)
Rates: $85-$95
(302) 945-1586

**THE INN AT
CANAL SQUARE**
122 Market St
(19958)
Rates: $125-$185
(302) 644-3377
(888) 644-1911

THE KINGS INN
151 Kings Hwy
(19958)
Rates: $75-$100
(302) 645-6438

RED MILL INN
150 Hwy 1 (19958)
Rates: $45-$75
(302) 645-9736

SLEEP INN,
1595 Hwy One
(19958)
Rates: $59-$249
(302) 645-6464
(800) 424-6423

LONG NECK

**SEA ESTA II
MOTEL**
A19 Long Neck
Rd (19968)
Rates: $42-$139
(302) 945-5900

MILLSBORO

**ATLANTIC INN
MOTEL**
210 E DuPont
Hwy (19966)
Rates: $69-$219
(302) 934-6711

NEW CASTLE

DAYS INN
3 Memorial Dr
(19720)
Rates: $40-$70
(302) 654-5400
(800) 329-7466

DUTCH INN
111 S DuPont
Hwy (19720)
Rates: $55-$60
(302) 328-6246

MOTEL 6
1200 West Ave
(19720)
Rates: $45+
(302) 571-1200
(800) 466-8356

**QUALITY INN
SKYWAYS**
147 N DuPont
Hwy (19720)
Rates: $69-$289
(302) 328-6666
(800) 424-6423

RAMADA INN
Rt 13 N, off I-295
(19720)
Rates: $40-$77
(302) 658-8511
(800) 272-6232

RODEWAY INN
111 S Dupont
Hwy (91720)
Rates: $40-$75
(302) 328-6246
(800) 228-2000

NEWARK

**BEST WESTERN
DELAWARE INN**
260 Chapman Rd
(19702)
Rates: $75-$120
(302) 738-3400
(800) 633-3203

COMFORT SUITES
56 S Old
Baltimore Pike
(19702)
Rates: $89-$249
(302) 266-6600
(800) 424-6423

DAYS INN
900 Churchmans
Rd (19713)
Rates: $59-$129
(302) 368-2400
(800) 329-7466

**HILTON
CHRISTIANA**
100 Continental
Dr (19713)
Rates: $$125-$190
(302) 454-1500
(800) 445-8667

**HOMESTEAD
STUDIO SUITES
HOTEL**
333 Continental
Dr (19713)
Rates: $73-$78
(302) 283-0800
(888) 782-9473

**HOWARD
JOHNSON
HOTEL & SUITES**
1119 S College
Ave (19713)
Rates: $59-$125
(302) 368-8521
(800) 446-4656

**QUALITY INN
UNIVERSITY**
1120 S College
Ave (19713)
Rates: $69-$125
(302) 368-8715
(800) 424-6423

RED ROOF INN
415 Stanton
Christiana Rd
(19713)
Rates: $57-$73
(302) 292-2870
(800) 843-7663

**RESIDENCE INN
BY MARRIOTT**
240 Chapman Rd
(19702)
Rates: $88-$179
(302) 453-9200
(800) 331-3131

AREA CODES - If the local number doesn't connect, check for a new area code.

SLEEP INN
630 S College Ave
(19713)
Rates: $62-$169
(302) 453-1700
(800) 424-6423

TRAVELODGE
268 E Main St
(19711)
Rates: $45-$55
(302) 737-5050
(800) 578-7878

REHOBOTH BEACH

AMERICINN LODGE & SUITES
329 Z Airport Rd
(19971)
Rates: $75-$120
(302) 226-0700
(800) 634-3444

THE ATLANTIS INN
154 Rehoboth
Ave (19971)
Rates: $59-$209
(302) 227-9446

THE BREAKERS HOTEL & SUITES
105 2nd St
(19971)
Rates: $55-$299
(302) 227-6688

LOVE CREEK MOTEL
Rt 24 (19971)
Rates: $48+
(302) 945-8909

MELBOURNE GUEST HOUSE
14 Brooklyn Ave
(19971)
Rates: $35-$70
(302) 227-2007

SEA ESTA IV, III & I
3101 Hwy 1
(19971)
Rates: $39-$169
(302) 227-5882

THREE MAPLES B&B
137 Old Landing
Rd (19971)
Rates: $125-$195
(302) 227-2419

TOWNSEND

PLEASANT HILL MOTEL
3155 S Dupont
Hwy (19734)
Rates: $35-$65
(302) 378-2468

WILMINGTON

BEST WESTERN BRANDYWINE VALLEY INN
1807 Concord
Pike (19803)
Rates: $99-$149
(302) 656-9436
(800) 528-1234
(800) 537-7772

DAYS INN
5209 Concord
Pike (19803)
Rates: $52-$100
(302) 478-0300
(800) 329-7466

SHERATON SUITES
422 Delaware
Ave (19801)
Rates: $99-$225
(302) 654-8300
(800) 325-3535

WYNDHAM WILMINGTON
700 N King St
(19801)
Rates: $99-$149
(302) 655-0400
(800) 996-3426

DISTRICT OF COLUMBIA

WASHINGTON
(Downtown
and vicinity)

**BEST WESTERN-
NEW HAMPSHIRE
SUITES HOTEL**
1121 New
Hampshire Ave
NW (20037)
Rates: $89-$189
(202) 457-0565
(800) 528-1234
(800) 762-3777

**DOUBLETREE
GUEST SUITES**
801 New
Hampshire Ave
NW (20037)
Rates: $109-$279
(202) 785-2000
(800) 222-8733

**THE
FAIRMONT**
2401 M St Nw
(20037)
Rates: $149-$529
(202) 429-2400
(800) 527-4727

**FOUR
SEASONS**
2800 Pennsylvania
Ave NW (20007)
Rates: $550-$1550
(202) 342-0444
(800) 332-3442

**THE GRAND
HYATT**
1000 H St NW
(20001)
Rates: $149-$340
(202) 582-1234
(800) 233-1234

**HAMILTON
CROWNE PLAZA
HOTEL**
1001 14th St NW
(20005)
Rates: $94-$324
(202) 682-0111

HAY-ADAMS
1 Lafayette Sq
(20006)
Rates: $550-$5500
(202) 638-6600

**HILTON
& TOWERS**
1919 Connecticut
Ave NW (20009)
Rates: $99-$369
(202) 483-3000
(800) 445-8667

**HOLIDAY INN
CENTRAL**
1501 Rhode
Island Ave NW
(20005)
Rates: $189-$209
(202) 483-2000
(800) 465-4329

**HOLIDAY INN-
DOWNTOWN**
1155 14th St NW
(20005)
Rates: $159-$229
(202) 737-1200
(800) 465-4329

**THE HOTEL
GEORGE**
15 E St NW
(20001)
Rates: $149-$434
(202) 347-4200

HOTEL HELIX
1430 Rhode
Island NW
(20005)
Rates: $119-$309
(202) 462-9001
(866) 508-0658

HOTEL MADERA
1310 New
Hampshire Ave
NW (20036)
Rates: $149-$349
(202) 296-7600
(800) 368-5691

HOTEL MONACO
700 F St NW
(20004)
Rates: $149-$479
(202) 628-7177

HOTEL ROUGE
1315 16th St NW
(20036)
Rates: $129-$309
(202) 232-8000
(800) 368-5689

**HOTEL
WASHINGTON**
515 15th St NW
(20004)
Rates: $200-$325
(202) 638-5900
(800) 424-9540

**LINCOLN SUITES
DOWNTOWN**
1823 L St NW
(20036)
Rates: $125-$195
(202) 223-4320
(800) 424-2970

**LOEWS
JEFFERSON
HOTEL**
1200 16th St NW
(20036)
Rates: $195-$405
(202) 347-2200
(800) 235-6397

**LOEWS
L'ENFANT
PLAZA HOTEL**
480 L'Enfant
Plaza SW (20024)
Rates: $119-$274
(202) 484-1000
(800) 235-6397

**THE MADISON
HOTEL**
1177 15th St NW
(20005)
Rates: $179-$299
(202) 862-1600

**MANDARIN
ORIENTAL**
1330 Maryland
Ave SW (20024)
Rates: $350-$900
(202) 554-8588

**MARRIOTT
WARDMAN PARK
HOTEL**
2660 Woodley Rd
NW (20008)
Rates: $109-$344
(202) 328-2000
(800) 228-9290

**THE MELROSE
HOTEL**
2430
Pennsylvania
Ave NW (20037)
Rates: $169-$209
(202) 955-6400

MOTEL 6
6711 Georgia Ave
(20012)
Rates: $55-$70
(2020 722-1600
(800) 466-8356

**OMNI
SHOREHAM
HOTEL**
2500 Calvert St
NW (20008)
Rates: $349-$389
(202) 234-0700
(800) 843-6664

**PARK HYATT
WASHINGTON**
1201 124th St NW
(20037)
Rates: $306-$410
(202) 789-1234
(800) 778-7477

RED ROOF INN
500 H St, NW
(20001)
Rates: $90-$150
(202) 289-5959
(800) 843-7663

**RENAISSANCE
MAYFLOWER
HISTORIC HOTEL**
1127 Connecticut
Ave NW (20036)
Rates: $149-$409
(202) 347-3000
(800) 468-3571

**RESIDENCE INN
DUPONT CIRCLE**
2120 P St NW
(20037)
Rates: $149-$299
(202) 466-6800
(800) 331-3131

**RESIDENCE INN
VERMONT AVE**
1199 Vermont
Ave NW (20005)
Rates: $259
(202) 896-1100
(800) 331-3131

**RITZ CARLTON
GEORGETOWN**
3100 South St
NW (20007)
Rates: $260-$550
(202) 912-4100
(800) 241-3333

RITZ CARLTON
1150 22nd St NW
(20037)
Rates: $259-$645
(202) 835-0500
(800) 241-3333

THE RIVER INN
924 25th St NW
(20036)
Rates: $99-$405
(202) 337-7600
(800) 424-2741

THE ST. REGIS
923 16th St NW
(20006)
Rates: $230-$385
(202) 638-2626

**SOFITEL
LAFAYETTE
SQUARE**
806 15th St NW
(20005)
Rates: $300-$480
(202) 730-8800

TOPAZ HOTEL
1733 N St NW
(20036)
Rates: $139-$339
(202) 393-3000
(800) 424-2950

WASHINGTON COURT HOTEL
525 New Jersey Ave NW (20001)
Rates: $119-$359
(202) 628-2100

WASHINGTON SUITES
2500 Pennsylvania Ave NW (20037)
Rates: $148-$248
(202) 333-8060
(877) 736-2500

THE WESTIN EMBASSY ROW
2100 Massachusetts Ave NW (20008)
Rates: $209-$289
(202) 293-2100
(800) 228-3000

WESTIN GRAND
2350 M St NW (20037)
Rates: $209-$289
(202) 429-0100
(800) 228-3000

THE WILLARD INTER-CONTINENTAL
1401 Pennsylvania Ave NW (20004)
Rates: $410-$525
(202) 628-9100
(800) 424-6835

WASHINGTON
(Maryland)

BEST WESTERN WASHINGTON GATEWAY HOTEL
1251 W Montgomery Ave (Rockville 20850)
Rates: $59-$179
(301) 424-4940
(800) 528-1234
(800) 366-1251

COMFORT INN-SHADY GROVE
16216 Frederick (Gaithersburg 20877)
Rates: $59-$129
(301) 330-0023
(800) 424-6423

COMFORT SUITES LAUREL LAKES
14402 Laurel Pl (Laurel 20707)
Rates: $79-$239
(301) 206-2600
(800) 424-6423

DAYS INN
5001 Mercedes Blvd (Camp Springs 20746)
Rates: $49-$84
(301) 423-2323
(800) 329-7466

DAYS INN
11370 Days Ct (Waldorf 20603)
Rates: $49-$109
(301) 932-9200
(800) 329-7466

DOUBLETREE CLUB HOTEL
9100 Basit Ct (Largo 20774)
Rates: $69-$149
(301) 773-0700
(800) 222-8733

ECONO LODGE
3131 Branch Ave (Temple Hills 20748)
Rates: $46-$90
(301) 894-3600
(800) 424-6423

HAMPTON INN
15202 Major Landsdale Blvd (Bowie 20716)
Rates: $89-$139
(301) 809-1800
(800) 426-7866

HAMPTON INN
3750 Crain Hwy (Waldorf 20603)
Rates: n/a
(301) 632-9600
(800) 426-7866

HOLIDAY INN
2 Montgomery Village Ave (Gaithersburg 20879)
Rates: $79-$99
(301) 948-8900
(800) 465-4329

HOLIDAY INN
3400 Ft. Meade Rd (Laurel 20724)
Rates: n/a
(301) 498-0900
(800) 465-4329

HOMESTEAD STUDIO SUITES
2621 Research Dr (Gaithersburg 20850)
Rates: $850$110
(301) 987-9100
(888) 782-9473

HOMESTEAD STUDIO SUITES
20141 Century Blvd (Germantown 20874)
Rates: $72-$97
(301) 515-4500
(888) 782-9473

MOTEL 6
5701 Allentown Rd (Camp Springs 20746)
Rates: $47-$60
(301) 702-1061
(800) 466-8356

MOTEL 6
75 Hampton Park Blvd (Capital Heights 20743)
Rates: $47-$70
(301) 499-0800
(800) 466-8356

MOTEL 6
497 Quince Orchard Rd (Gaithersburg 20879)
Rates: $49-$65
(301) 977-3311
(800) 466-8356

MOTEL 6
3510 Old Annapolis Rd (Laurel 20724)
Rates: $47-$65
(301) 497-1544
(800) 466-8356

QUALITY SUITES SHADY GROVE
3 Research Ct (Rockville 20850)
Rates: $69-$199
(301) 840-0200
(800) 424-6423

QUALITY INN & SUITES
1 Second St (Laurel 20707)
Rates: $79-$250
(301) 725-8800
(800) 424-6423

RAMADA INN
5151 Allentown Rd (Camp Springs 20746)
Rates: $50-$89
(301) 899-7700
(800) 272-6232

RED ROOF INN
9050 Lanham Severn Rd (Lanham 20706)
Rates: $60-$89
(301) 731-8830
(800) 843-7663

RED ROOF INN
12525 Laurel Bowie Rd (Laurel 20708)
Rates: $55-$84
(301) 498-8811
(800) 843-7663

RED ROOF INN
16001 Shady Grove Rd (Rockville 20850)
Rates: $63-$96
(301) 987-0965
(800) 843-7663

RESIDENCE INN
7335 Wisconsin Ave (Bethesda 20814)
Rates: $239-$279
(301) 718-0200
(800) 331-3131

RESIDENCE INN
9721 Washingtonian Blvd (Gaithersburg 20879)
Rates: $99-$179
(301) 590-3003
(800) 331-3131

RESIDENCE INN
6320 Golden Triangle Dr (Greenbelt 20770)
Rates: $129-$249
(301) 982-1600
(800) 331-3131

SHERATON COLLEGE PARK
4095 Powder Mill (Beltsville 20705)
Rates: $89-$139
(301) 937-4422
(800) 325-3535

SUMMERFIELD SUITES
200 Skidmore Blvd (Gaithersburg 20879)
Rates: $135-$175
(301) 527-6000
(800) 833-4353

TOWNPLACE SUITES BY MARRIOTT
212 Perry Pkwy (Gaithersburg 20879)
Rates: $59-$149
(301) 590-2300
(800) 257-3000

WOODFIN SUITES HOTEL
1380 Piccard Dr (Rockville 20850)
Rates: $124
(301) 590-9880
(800) 237-8811

WASHINGTON
(Virginia)

AMERISUITES-DULLES AIRPORT
4994 Westone Plaza Dr (Chantilly 20151)
Rates: $159-$179
(703) 961-8160
(800) 833-1516

AMERISUITES-DULLES AIRPORT
21481 Ridgetop Cir (Sterling 20166)
Rates: $79-$169
(703) 444-3909
(800) 833-1516

BEST WESTERN KEY BRIDGE
1850 N Fort Myer Dr (Arlington, 22209)
Rates: $79-$169
(703) 522-0400
(800) 539-2743

AREA CODES - If the local number doesn't connect, check for a new area code.

BEST WESTERN TYSONS WESTPARK
8401 Wstpark Dr (McLean 22102)
Rates: $59-$149
(703) 723-2800
(800) 528-1234
(800) 533-3301

CANDELWOOD SUITES
45520 E Severn Way (Sterling 20166)
Rates: n/a
(888) 226-3539

CANDELWOOD SUITES
13845 Sunrise Valley Dr (Herndon 20171)
Rates: n/a
(703) 793-7100
(888) 226-3539

COMFORT INN BALLSTON
1211 N Glebe Rd (22201)
Rates: $75-$195
(703) 247-3399
(800) 424-6423

COMFORT INN
6560 Loisdale Ct (Springfield 22150)
Rates: $89-$125
(703) 922-9000
(800) 424-6423

COMFORT INN GUNSTON CORNER
8180 Silverbook Rd (Lorton 22079)
Rates: $85-$109
(703) 643-3100
(800) 424-6423

COMFORT INN TYSONS CORNER
1587 Spring Hill Rd (Vienna 22182)
Rates: $79-$139
(703) 448-8020
(800) 424-6423

COMFORT INN UNIVERSITY CENTER
11180 Main St (Fairfax 22030)
Rates: $79-$149
(703) 591-5900
(800) 424-6423

COMFORT SUITES
13980 Metrotech Dr (Chantilly 20151)
Rates: $79-$199
(703) 263-2007
(800) 424-6423

COMFORT SUITES
7350 Williamson Rd (Manassas 20109)
Rates: $79-$129
(703) 686-1100
(800) 424-6423

DAYS INN-RICHMOND HIGHWAY
6100 Richmond Hwy (Alexandria 22303)
Rates: $55-$85
(703) 329-0500
(800) 329-7466

ECONO LODGE-MT. VERNON
8849 Richmond Hwy (Alexandria 22309)
Rates: $40-$85
(703) 780-0300
(800) 424-6423

ECONO LODGE-WOODBRIDGE
13317 Gordon Blvd (Woodbridge 22191)
Rates: $47-$90
(703) 491-5196
(800) 424-6423

EMBASSY SUITES OLD TOWN
1900 Diagonal Rd (Alexandria 22314)
Rates: $139-$289
(703) 684-5900
(800) 362-2779

HAMPTON INN
6550 Loisdale Ct (Springfield 22150)
Rates: $89-$129
(703) 924-9444
(800) 426-7866

HAMPTON INN
46331 McClellan Way (Sterling 20165)
Rates: $69-$179
(703) 450-9595
(800) 426-7866

HAMPTON INN DULLES AIRPORT
45440 Holiday Dr (Sterling 20166)
Rates: $59-$159
(703) 471-8300
(800) 426-7866

HAWTHORN SUITES HOTEL
420 N Van Dorn St (Alexandria, 22303)
Rates: $99-$179
(703) 370-1000
(800) 527-1133

HAWTHORN SUITES HOTEL
467 Herndon Pkwy (Herndon 20170)
Rates: $99-$185
(703) 437-5000
(800) 527-1133

HILTON HOTEL WASH/DULLES AIRPORT
13869 Park Center Rd (Herndon 22070)
Rates: $67-$307
(703) 478-2900
(800) 445-8667

HILTON OLD TOWN
1767 King St (Alexandria 22314)
Rates: $119-$289
(703) 837-0440
(800) 445-8667

HOLIDAY INN-BATTLEFIELD
10800 Vandor Ln (Manassas 20109)
Rates: $59-$99
(703) 335-0000
(800) 465-4329

HOLIDAY INN DULLES
1000 Sully Rd (Sterling 20166)
Rates: $69-$179
(703) 471-7411
(800) 465-4329

HOLIDAY INN EXP
485 Elden St (Herndon 20170)
Rates: $59-$159
(703) 478-9777
(800) 465-4329

HOLIDAY INN-FAIR OAKS MALL
11787 Lee Jackson Hwy (Fairfax 22033)
Rates: $145
(703) 352-2525
(800) 465-4329

HOLIDAY INN-OLD TOWN
480 King St (Alexandria 22314)
Rates: $161-$171
(703) 549-6080
(800) 465-4329

HOLIDAY INN AT CARRODOC HALL
1500 E Market St (Leesburg 22075)
Rates: $109-$159
(703) 771-9200
(800) 465-4329

HOLIDAY INN HOTEL & SUITES/ HISTORIC DISTRICT
625 First St (Alexandria 22314)
Rates: $109-$239
(703) 548-6300
(800) 465-4329

HOLIDAY INN SELECT
4335 Chantilly Shopping Ctr (Chantilly 20151)
Rates: $99-$199
(703) 815-6060
(800) 465-4329

HOLIDAY INN-TYSONS CORNER
1960 Chain Bridge Rd (McLean 22102)
Rates: $219-$279
(703) 893-2100
(800) 465-4329

HOMESTEAD STUDIO SUITES
200 Blue Stone Rd (Alexandria 22309)
Rates: $105-$130
(703) 329-3399
(888) 782-9473

HOMESTEAD STUDIO SUITES
4504 Brookfield Corporate Dr (Chantilly 20151)
Rates: $91-$116
(703) 263-3361
(888) 782-9473

HOMESTEAD STUDIO SUITES
12104 Monument Dr (Fairfax 22033)
Rates: $80-$105
(703) 273-3444
(888) 782-9473

HOMESTEAD STUDIO SUITES
8281 Willow Oaks Corporate Dr (Fairfax 22031)
Rates: $95-$120
(703) 204-0088
(888) 782-9473

HOMESTEAD STUDIO SUITES
12190 Sunset Hills Rd (Reston 20190)
Rates: $95-$120
(703) 707-9700
(888) 782-9473

HOMESTEAD STUDIO SUITES
45350 Catalina Ct (Sterling 20166)
Rates: $91-$106
(703) 904-7575
(888) 782-9473

AREA CODES - If the local number doesn't connect, check for a new area code.

HOMESTEAD STUDIO SUITES
8201 Old Courthouse Rd (Vienna 22182)
Rates: $110-$135
(703) 356-6300
(888) 782-9473

HOMEWOOD SUITES
8130 Porter Rd (Falls Church 22042)
Rates: $109-$209
(703) 560-6644
(800) 225-5466

HOMEWOOD SUITES
13460 Sunrise Valley Dr (Herndon 20171)
Rates: $109-$219
(703) 793-1700
(800) 225-5466

QUALITY HOTEL COURTHOUSE PLAZA
1200 N Courthouse Rd (Arlington 22201)
Rates: $99-$189
(703) 524-4000
(800) 424-6423

QUALITY INN
17133 Dumfries Rd (Dumfries 22026)
Rates: $69-$109
(703) 221-1141
(800) 424-6423

QUALITY INN IWO JIMA
1501 Arlington Blvd (Arlington 22203)
Rates: $65-$175
(703) 524-5000
(800) 424-6423

QUALITY INN MOUNT VERNON
7212 Richmond Hwy (Alexandria 22306)
Rates: $72-$105
(703) 765-9000
(800) 424-6423

QUALITY INN
1109 Horner Rd (Woodbridge 22191)
Rates: $50-$120
(703) 494-0300
(800) 424-6423

RAMADA INN
4316 Inn St (Triangle 22172)
Rates: n/a
(703) 221-1181
(800) 272-6232

RED ROOF INN
5975 Richmond Hwy (Alexandria 22303)
Rates: $65-$95
(703) 960-5200
(800) 843-7663

RED ROOF INN
10610 Automotive Dr (Manassas 22110)
Rates: $60-$90
(703) 335-9333
(800) 843-7663

RED ROOF INN
6868 Springfield Blvd (Springfield 22150)
Rates: $70-$90
(703) 644-5311
(800) 843-7663

RESIDENCE INN OLD TOWN
1456 Duke St (Alexandria 22314)
Rates: $129-$339
(703) 548-5474
(800) 331-3131

RESIDENCE INN
12815 Fair Lakes Pkwy (Fairfax 22033)
Rates: $170-$209
(703) 266-4900
(800) 331-3131

RESIDENCE INN
8125 Gatehouse Rd (Falls Church 22042)
Rates: $139-$259
(703) 573-5200
(800) 331-3131

RESIDENCE INN
315 Elden St (Herndon 22070)
Rates: $209-$229
(703) 435-0044
(800) 331-3131

RESIDENCE INN TYSONS CORNER
8616 Westwood Center Dr (Vienna 22182)
Rates: $179-$299
(703) 893-0120
(800) 331-3131

RESIDENCE INN TYSONS CORNER MALL
8400 Old Courthouse Rd (Vienna 22182)
Rates: $119-$269
(703) 917-0800
(800) 331-3131

RITZ CARLTON TYSONS CORNER
1700 Tysons Blvd (McLean 22102)
Rates: $409-$599
(703) 506-4300
(800) 241-3333

RODEWAY INN
13964 Jefferson Davis Hwy (Woodbridge 22191)
Rates: $46-$110
(703) 494-4144
(800) 424-6423

SHERATON PENTAGON SOUTH
4641 Kenmore Ave (Alexandria 22304)
Rates: $101-$170
(703) 751-4510
(800) 325-3535

SHERATON SUITES
801 N St. Asaph St (Alexandria 22314)
Rates: $109-$229
(703) 836-4700
(800) 325-3535

SHERATON PREMIERE TYSONS CORNER
8661 Leesburg Pike (Vienna 22182)
Rates: $219-$229
(703) 448-1234
(800) 325-3535

STAYBRIDGE SUITES
3860 Centerview Dr (Chantilly 22021)
Rates: n/a
(800) 238-8000

STAYBRIDGE SUITES
13700 Coppermine Rd (Herndon 20171)
Rates: $205-$265
(703) 713-6800
(800) 238-8000

STAYBRIDGE SUITES-TYSONS CORNER
6845 Old Dominion Dr (McLean 22101)
Rates: $170-$230
(703) 448-5400
(800) 238-8000

TOWNEPLACE SUITES
14036 Thunderbolt Pl (Chantilly 20151)
Rates: $84-$144
(703) 709-0453
(800) 257-3000

TOWNEPLACE SUITES
205 Hillwood Ave (Falls Church 22046)
Rates: $89-$199
(703) 237-6172
(800) 257-3000

TOWNEPLACE SUITES
6245 Brandon Ave (Springfield 22150)
Rates: $149-$199
(703) 569-8060
(800) 257-3000

TOWNEPLACE SUITES-DULLES
22744 Holiday Park Dr (Sterling 22170)
Rates: $69-$179
(703) 707-2017
(800) 257-3000

TOWNEPLACE SUITES
21123 Whitfield Pl (Sterling 20165)
Rates: $59-$199
(703) 421-1090
(800) 257-3000

WASHINGTON SUITES
100 S Reynolds (Alexandria 22304)
Rates: $99-$209
(703) 370-9600
(877) 736-2500

FLORIDA

ALACHUA

COMFORT INN
15920 NW Hwy
441 (32615)
Rates: $60-$150
(386) 462-2414
(800) 424-6423

DAYS INN
16100 NW Hwy
441 (32615)
Rates: $60-$135
(386) 462-3251
(800) 329-7466

QUALITY INN
15960 NW Hwy
441 (32615)
Rates: $60-$95
(386) 462-2244
(800) 424-6423

RAMADA LIMITED
16305 NW 163rd
Ln (32615)
Rates: $65-$140
(386) 462-4200
(800) 272-6232

ALTAMONTE SPRINGS

BEST WESTERN
150 Douglas Ave
(32714)
Rates: $59-$123
(407) 862-8200
(800) 528-1234
(800) 327-5560

CANDLEWOOD SUITES
644 Raymond
Ave (32701)
Rates: $79-$109
(407) 767-5757
(888) 226-3539

CLUB ESPRIT APT SUITES
525 One Center
Blvd (32701)
Rates: $46-$90
(407) 331-3132
(800) 800-3332

DAYS INN
150 S Westmonte
Dr (32714)
Rates: $45-$170
(407) 788-1411
(800) 329-7466

EMBASSY SUITES
225 E Altamonte
Dr (32701)
Rates: $109-$134
(407) 834-2400
(800) 362-2779

HAMPTON INN
151 N Douglas
Ave (32714)
Rates: $69-$95
(407) 869-9000
(800) 426-7866

HOLIDAY INN
230 W State Rd
436 (32714)
Rates: $85-$288
(407) 862-4455
(800) 465-4329

HOMESTEAD STUDIO SUITES
302 S North Lake
Blvd (32701)
Rates: $54-$74
(407) 332-9300
(800) 225-5466

RESIDENCE INN BY MARRIOTT
270 Douglas Ave
(32714)
Rates: $79-$229
(407) 788-7991
(800) 331-3131

ALTOONA

FIDDLERS GREEN RANCH
Demko Road,
(32702)
Rates: n/a
(352) 669-7111
(800) 947-2624

AMELIA ISLAND

1857 FLORIDA HOUSE INN B&B
22 S 3rd St
(32034)
Rates: $99-$219
(904) 261-3300
(800) 258-3301

AMELIA HOTEL & SUITES
1997 Fletcher
Ave (32034)
Rates: n/a
(904) 261-5735
(800) 595-6255

ANNA MARIA ISLAND

ANNA MARIA ISLAND BEACH RESORT
105 39th St
(34217)
Rates: n/a
(947) 778-7477
(877) 632-3224

ANNA MARIA PIRATES DEN
3501 Gulf Dr
(34217)
Rates: $50-$149
(941) 778-4368

ANNA MARIA VILLAS
(515) 42nd St
(34217)
Rates: n/a
(800) 083-1783

HALEY'S MOTEL & RESORT
8102 Gulf Dr N
(34217)
Rates: $50-$150
(941) 778-5405
(800) 367-7824

QUEENS GATE RESORT
1101 Gulf Dr
(34217)
Rates: $50-$135
(941) 778-7153
(800) 310-7153

SAND PEBBLE APARTMENTS & MOTEL
2218 Gulf Dr N
(34216)
Rates: n/a
(941) 778-3053
(800) 500-7263

TORTUGA INN BEACH RESORT
1325 Gulf Dr N
(34217)
Rates: $100-$275
(941) 778-0156
(877) 867-8842

TRADEWINDS RESORT
1603 Gulf Dr N
(34217)
Rates: n/a
(941) 779-0010
(888) 686-6716

APALACHICOLA

APALACHICOLA RIVER INN
123 Water St
(32320)
Rates: n/a
(850) 653-8139

BREAKAWAY MARINA & MOTEL
200 Waddell Rd
(32320)
Rates: $30-$50
(850) 653-8897

FIVE OAKS INN
145 Avenue E
(32320)
Rates: $55-$75
(850) 653-8980

THE HISTORIC GIBSON COUNTRY INN
Market St &
Ave C (32329)
Rates: $90-$160
(850) 653-2191

RAINBOW INN & MARINA
123 Water St
(32320)
Rates: n/a
(850) 653-8139

RANCHO INN
240 Hwy 98
(32320)
Rates: $47-$73
(850) 653-9435

THE RANEY GUEST COTTAGE
46 Avenue F
(32320)
Rates: $190/
Two Nights
(850) 653-2501

WITHERSPOON INN
94 5th St (32320)
Rates: $70-$75
(850) 653-9186

APOLLO BEACH

RAMADA INN ON TAMPA BAY
6414 Surfside
Blvd (33572)
Rates: $65-$150
(813) 641-2700
(800) 272-6232
(800) 67-BEACH

APOPKA

CROSBY'S MOTOR INN
1440 W Orange
Blossom Tr
(32712)
Rates: $50-$69
(407) 886-3220
(800) 821-6685

ARCADIA

BEST WESTERN ARCADIA INN
504 S Brevard
(34266)
Rates: $69-$119
(863) 494-4884
(800) 528-1234
(877) 886-0797

AUBURNDALE

FISH HAVEN LODGE & CABINS
Fish Haven Rd
(33823)
Rates: n/a
(941) 984-1183

AVENTURA

FAIRMONT TURNBERRY ISLE RESORT & SPA
19999 W Country Club Dr (33180)
Rates: $169-$4200
(305) 392-6200

RESIDENCE INN BY MARRIOTT
19900 W Country Club Dr (33180)
Rates: $99-$409
(786) 528-1001
(800) 331-3131

AVON PARK

LAKE BRENTWOOD MOTEL
2060 US 27 N (33825)
Rates: n/a
(863) 453-4358

SIGNUM RESORT LAS PALMAS
600 E Canfield St (33825)
Rates: $80-$165
(863) 452-2020
(800) 528-0823

BAL HARBOUR

SHERATON BAL HARBOUR BEACH RESORT
9701 Collins Ave (33154)
Rates: $165-$320
(305) 865-7511
(800) 325-3535
(800) 998-9898

BALDWIN

BEST WESTERN BALDWIN INN
1088 Hwy 301 (32234)
Rates: $40-$99
(904) 266-9759
(800) 528-1234

BARTOW

DAVIS BROS MOTEL
1035 N Broadway Ave (33830)
Rates: $50-$75
(941) 533-0711
(800) 424-0711

EL JON MOTEL
1460 E Main St (33830)
Rates: $39-$75
(941) 533-8191
(800) 533-8191

BAY HARBOR ISLAND

BAY HARBOR INN
9660 E Bay Harbor Dr (33154)
Rates: $80-$115
(305) 868-4141

BIG PINE KEY

CAPTAIN VARRIEUR'S
P. O. Box 430744 (33043)
Rates: $650-$750 Weekly
(508) 394-4338
(888) 394-4338

OLD WOODEN BRIDGE FISHING CAMP
1791 Bogie Dr (33043)
Rates: $69-$90
(305) 872-2241

PARADISE LODGING
31316 Ave J (33043)
Rates: $75-$100
(305) 872-9009

BLUE MOUNTAIN BEACH

SANDCASTLES BY THE SEA
229 Blue Mountain Rd #101 (32541)
Rates: $115
(504) 845-8126

BOCA GRANDE

GASPARILLA INN & COTTAGES
5th St & Palm Ave (33921)
Rates: n/a
(941) 964-2201

BOCA RATON

DOUBLETREE GUEST SUITES
701 NW 53rd St (33487)
Rates: $99-$259
(561) 997-9500
(800) 222-8733

HOMESTEAD STUDIO SUITES
501 NW 77th St (33487)
Rates: $54-$119
(561) 994-2599
(888) 782-9473

RADISSON SUITE HOTEL
7920 Glades Rd (33434)
Rates: $169-$299
(561) 483-3600
(800) 333-3333

RESIDENCE INN BY MARRIOTT
525 NW 77th St (33487)
Rates: $189-$229
(561) 994-3222
(800) 331-3131

TOWNEPLACE SUITES
5110 NW 8th Ave (33487)
Rates: $54-$199
(561) 994-7232
(800) 257-3000

BONITA SPRINGS

AMERICINN HOTEL & SUITES
28600 Trails Edge Blvd (34134)
Rates: $69-$170
(239) 495-9255
(800) 634-3444

COMFORT INN HOTEL
8900 Bonita Beach Rd (34135)
Rates: $59-$149
(239) 992-5001
(800) 424-6423

STAYBRIDGE SUITES
8900 Brighton Ln (34135)
Rates: $99-$239
(239) 949-5913
(800) 238-8000

BRADENTON

BAHIA COURT
1905 Cortez Rd W (34207)
Rates: $50-$100
(941) 755-2188

BLUE BOY MOTEL
1839 14th St W (34205)
Rates: $50-$100
(941) 748-6909

CHARLIE'S COTTAGES
P. O. Box 671 (34215)
Rates: n/a
(941) 794-5980

COMFORT INN & SUITES
4450 47th St W (34210)
Rates: $79-$149
(941) 795-4633
(800) 424-6423

DAYS INN
3506 1st St W (34208)
Rates: $59-$109
(941) 746-1141
(800) 329-7466

ECONO LODGE AIRPORT
6727 14th St W (34207)
Rates: $49-$99
(941) 758-7199
(800) 424-6423

HOWARD JOHNSON EXP
6511 14th St W (34207)
Rates: $59-$104
(941) 756-8399
(800) 446-4656

MOTEL 6
660 67 St Cir W (34208)
Rates: $39-$67
(941) 747-6005
(800) 466-8356

BRADENTON BEACH

THE BREAKERS
2512 Gulf Drive N (34217)
Rates: n/a
(941) 778-5588

CAPRI INN INTL APTS MOTEL
210 & 300 Gulf Drive S (34217)
Rates: $51-$100
(941) 778-5243

ISLAND BREEZE APARTMENTS
2516 Gulf Dr N (34217)
Rates: $51-$100
(941) 778-9593

PELICAN COVE RESORT CONDO
904 Gulf Dr S (34217)
Rates: n/a
(941) 778-4800
(800) 237-2252

QUEENSGATE APARTMENTS
1101 Gulf Dr N (34217)
Rates: $51-$100
(941) 778-7153

SAND PEBBLE APARTMENTS
2218 Gulf Dr N (34217)
Rates: $49-$140
(941) 778-3053
(800) 500-7263

TORTUGA INN BEACH RESORT
1325 Gulf Dr N (34217)
Rates: $114-$379
(941) 778-6611

TRADEWINDS RESORT
1603 Gulf Dr N (34217)
Rates: $159-$319
(941) 779-0010

BRANDON

BEHIND THE FENCE B&B
1400 Viola Dr (33511)
Rates: $69-$99
(813) 685-8201

HOMESTEAD STUDIO SUITES
330 Grand Regency Blvd (33511)
Rates: $69-$104
(813) 643-5900
(888) 782-9473

LA QUINTA INN & SUITES
310 Grand Regency Blvd (33511)
Rates: $95-$125
(813) 643-0574
(800) 687-6667

BRANFORD
SMOKEHOUSE RANCH B&B
RR 1, Box 518 (32008)
Rates: $50-$100
(386) 935-2662
(877) 258-9686

BROOKSVILLE
BEST WESTERN
30307 Cortez Blvd (34602)
Rates: $75-$99
(352) 796-9481
(800) 528-1234
(888) 568-4060

DAYS INN
6320 Windmere Rd (34602)
Rates: $59-$74
(352) 796-9486
(800) 329-7466

THE OAKS MOTEL
630 S Broad St (34601)
Rates: n/a
(352) 796-4807

SUNRISE MOTEL
250 N Broad St (34601)
Rates: n/a
(352) 796-8634

BUSHNELL
BEST WESTERN GUEST HOUSE INN
I-75 & SR 48 (33513)
Rates: $52-$89
(352) 793-5010
(800) 528-1234

CALLAHAN
SHIP INN
US 1 & 23, 301 N (32011)
Rates: $33-$49
(904) 879-3451

CAPE CORAL
DEL PRADO INN
1502 Miramar St (33904)
Rates: $60-$75
(239) 542-3151
(800) 231-6818

QUALITY INN NAUTILUS
1538 Cape Coral Pkwy (33904)
Rates: $61-$122
(239) 542-2121
(800) 424-6423

CAPTIVA ISLAND
NORTH CAPITVA ISLAND CLUB RESORT
4421 Bartlett Pkwy (33924)
Rates: n/a
(239) 394-1001
(800) 576-7343

TWEEN WATERS INN
15951 Sanibel/ Captiva Rd (33924)
Rates: $150-$250+
(941) 472-5161
(800) 223-5865

CARRABELLE
MOORINGS AT CARRABELLE
1000 US 98 (32322)
Rates: $125-$275
(850) 697-2800

CEDAR KEY
FARAWAY INN
3rd & F Sts (32625)
Rates: $40-$65
(352) 543-5330
(888) 543-5330

MARINA MOTEL
11912 SR 24 (32625)
Rates: $50
(352) 543-6167
(877) 338-3318

MERMAID'S LANDING
12865 Hwy 24 (32625)
Rates: $40-$65
(352) 543-5949
(877) 543-5949

OLD FENIMORE MILL CONDOS
P. O. Box 805 (32625)
Rates: n/a
(352) 543-9803
(800) 767-8354

PARK PLACE MOTEL & CONDOS
211 2nd St Cedar Key (32625)
Rates: $65-$100
(352) 543-5737

PIRATES COVE WATERFRONT COTTAGES
Hwy 24 (32625)
Rates: $40-$55
(352) 543-5141

SEAHORSE LANDING CONDOS
4050 G St (32625)
Rates: $125-$150
(352) 543-5860

CHAMPIONS GATE
OMNI ORLANDO RESORT
8390 Championsgate Blvd (33896)
Rates: n/a
(321) 677-6664
(800) 843-6664

CHARLOTTE HARBOR
BANANA BAY WATERFRONT MOTEL
23285 Bayshore Rd (33980)
Rates: $39-$99
(941) 743-4441

HARBOUR INN
5000 Tamiami Tr (33980)
Rates: $45-$115
(941) 625-6126
(800) 646-6037

CHATTA-HOOCHEE
MORGAN MOTEL
E US 90 (32324)
Rates: $27-$36
(850) 683-4336

CHIEFLAND
BEST WESTERN SUWANNEE VALLEY INN
1125 N Young Blvd (32626)
Rates: $60-$79
(352) 493-0663
(800) 528-1234
(888) 526-4428

HOLIDAY INN EXP
809 NW 21st Ave (32626)
Rates: $65-$91
(352) 493-9400
(800) 465-4329

CHIPLEY
SUPER 8 MOTEL
1700 Main St (32428)
Rates: $45-$75
(850) 638-8530
(800) 800-8000

CHULUOTA
BIG OAKS RANCH
1900 Brumley Rd (32766)
Rates: n/a
(407) 365-8885

CITRA
ORANGE BLOS-SOM MOTEL
17575 N Hwy 301 (32113)
Rates: n/a
(352) 595-8836

CLEARWATER
BELLEVIEW BILTMORE RESORT, GOLF CLUB & SPA
25 Belleview Blvd (33756)
Rates: $169-$209
(727) 373-3000
(800) 237-8947

DAYS INN
3910 Ulmerton Rd (33762)
Rates: $49-$99
(727) 573-3334
(800) 329-7466

HOMESTEAD STUDIO SUITES
2311 Ulmerton Rd (33762)
Rates: $59-$104
(727) 572-4800
(888) 782-9473

HOMEWOOD SUITES
2233 Ulmerton Rd (33762)
Rates: $99-$169
(727)573-1500
(800) 225-5466

LA QUINTA INN AIRPORT
3301 Ulmerton Rd (33762)
Rates: $84-$124
(727) 572-7222
(800) 687-6667

RADISSON HOTEL
20967 Us 19 N (33765)
Rates: $69-$79
(727) 799-1181
(800) 333-3333

RAMADA INN
26508 US 19 N (33761)
Rates: $69-$109
(727) 796-1234
(800) 272-6232

RESIDENCE INN BY MARRIOTT
5050 Ulmerton Rd (33762)
Rates: $115-$225
(727) 573-4444
(800) 331-3131

SUPER 8 AIRPORT
13260 34th St N (33762)
Rates: $49-$119
(727) 572-8881
(800) 800-8000

TOWNEPLACE SUITES BY MARRIOTT
13200 49th St N (33762)
Rates: $62-$116
(727) 299-9229
(800) 257-3000

CLEARWATER BEACH
BEL CREST BEACH RESORT
706 Bayway Blvd (33767)
Rates: $68-$208
(727) 442-4923

AREA CODES - If the local number doesn't connect, check for a new area code.

BEST WESTERN SEA STONE RESORT/SUITE
445 Hamden Dr (34630)
Rates: $59-$189
(727) 441-1722
(800) 528-1234
(800) 444-1919

CLEARWATER BEACH HOTEL
500 Mandalay Ave (33767)
Rates: $125-$225
(727) 441-2425
(800) 292-2295

SHERATON SAND KEY RESORT
1160 Gulf Blvd (33767)
Rates: $219-$299
(727) 595-1611
(800) 325-3535

CLERMONT
FLORIDA PINES
3479 W Vine St (34741)
Rates: $115-$215
(407) 846-1722

HIGHLANDS RESERVE-SUPERI-OR RESORT
9230 Hwy 192 (34711)
Rates: n/a
(863) 424-8411

VACATION VILLAGE RESORT
10301 US Hwy 27 (34711)
Rates: $46-$90
(352) 394-4091
(800) 962-9969

COCOA
BEST WESTERN COCOA INN
4225 W King St (32926)
Rates: $59-$99
(321) 632-1065
(800) 528-1234
(866) 262-6229

ECONO LODGE SPACE CENTER
3220 N Cocoa Blvd (32926)
Rates: $50-$150
(321) 632-4561
(800) 424-6423

HOLIDAY INN EXP HOTEL
301 Tucker Ln (32926)
Rates: $79-$109
(321) 635-9975
(800) 465-4329

RAMADA INN KENNEDY SPACE CTR
900 Friday Rd (32926)
Rates: $69-$119
(321) 631-1210
(800) 272-6232

SPACE COAST MOTEL
860 W Cocoa Blvd (32922)
Rates: $30-$89
(321) 639-8700
(888) 672-4897

SUPER 8 MOTEL
900A Friday Rd (32926)
Rates: $59-$109
(321) 631-1212
(800) 800-8000

COCOA BEACH
BEST WESTERN OCEANFRONT RESORT
5600 N Atlantic Ave (32931)
Rates: $79-$229
(321) 783-7621
(800) 528-1234
(800) 962-0028

CRAWFORD'S COCOA CABANAS
1901 S Atlantic Ave (32931)
Rates: $100-$125
(321) 799-0307

DAYS INN
5500 N Atlantic Ave (32931)
Rates: $69-$179
(321) 784-2550
(800) 329-7466

HOLIDAY INN OCEANFRONT
1300 N Atlantic Ave (32931)
Rates: $119-$229
(321) 783-2271
(800) 465-4329

HOWARD JOHNSON EXP
2082 N Atlantic Ave (32931)
Rates: $59-$79
(321) 783-8855
(800) 446-4656

MOTEL 6
3701 N Atlantic Ave (32931)
Rates: $43-$64
(321) 783-3103
(800) 466-8356

SATELLITE MOTEL ON OCEAN
1600 N Atlantic Ave (32931)
Rates: n/a
(321) 783-7714

SEA ESTA VILLAS
686 S Atlantic Ave (32931)
Rates: n/a
(321) 783-1739
(800) 872-9444

SILVER SANDS MOTEL
225 N Atlantic Ave (32931)
Rates: $50-$99
(321) 783-2415
(800) 647-0761

SOUTH BEACH INN
1701 S Atlantic Ave (32931)
Rates: $70-$150
(321) 784-3333
(800) 548-4244

SURF STUDIO BEACH RESORT
1801 S Atlantic Ave (32931)
Rates: $75-$185
(321) 783-7100

COCONUT GROVE
COMMODORE INN THE GROVE
3162 Commodore Plaza (33133)
Rates: $123-$358
(305) 448-2128
(877) 544-2484

MAYFAIR HOUSE HOTEL &SPA
3000 Florida Ave (33133)
Rates: $199-$649
(305) 441-0000

RESIDENCE INN BY MARRIOTT
2835 Tigertail Ave (33133)
Rates: n/a
(305) 285-9303
(800) 331-3131

CORAL GABLES
BEST WESTERN CHATEAUBLEAU HOTEL
1111 Ponce de Leon Blvd (33194)
Rates: $69-$149
(305) 448-2634
(800) 528-1234
(888) 642-6442

CORAL SPRINGS
LA QUINTA INN
3701 University Dr (33065)
Rates: $69-$135
(954) 753-9000
(800) 687-6667

MARRIOTT HOTEL & GOLF CLUB
11775 Heron Bay Blvd (33076)
Rates: $89-$169
(954) 753-5598
(800) 331-3131

STUDIO 6
5645 University Dr (33067)
Rates: $54-$80
(954) 796-0011
(888) 897-0202

WELLESLEY INN & SUITES
3100 N University Dr (33065)
Rates: $89-$119
(954) 344-2200
(800) 444-8888

CRESCENT BEACH
BEACHER'S LODGE
6970 A1A S (32080)
Rates: $79-$245
(904) 471-8849

CRESCENT CITY
LAKE VIEW MOTEL
1004 N Summit St (32112)
Rates: $48-$75
(386) 698-1090

LEONARD'S LANDING LAKE CRESCENT RESORT
100 Grove Ave (32112)
Rates: n/a
(386) 698-2485

CRESTVIEW
HOLIDAY INN
4050 S Ferdon Blvd (32536)
Rates: $68
(850) 682-6111
(800) 465-4329

JAMESON INN
151 Cracker Barrel Dr (32536)
Rates: $49-$104
(850) 683-1778
(800) 526-3766

SUPER 8 MOTEL
3925 S Ferdon Blvd (32536)
Rates: $38-$63
(850) 682-9649
(800) 800-8000

CROSS CITY
CARRIAGE INN
280 E Main (32628)
Rates: $38-$45
(352) 498-0001
(800) 682-4816

CRYSTAL RIVER
BEST WESTERN CRYSTAL RIVER RESORT
614 NW Hwy 19 (34428)
Rates: $89-$122
(352) 795-3171
(800) 435-4409

AREA CODES - If the local number doesn't connect, check for a new area code.

DAYS INN RESORT
2380 NW Hwy
19 (34428)
Rates: $50-$85
(352) 795-2111
(800) 329-7466

HAYES MOTEL
1151 NW Hwy 19
(34428)
Rates: n/a
(352) 795-2075

KING'S BAY LODGE
506 NW 1st Ave
(34428)
Rates: n/a
(352) 795-2850

PARADISE FOUND ISLAND RETREAT
14195 W
Beachview Dr
(34429)
Rates: n/a
(352) 564-1757
(800 474-1757

CUTLER RIDGE

BAYMONT INN & SUITES
10821 Caribbean
Blvd (33189)
Rates: $55-$94
(877) 229-6668

BEST WESTERN FLORIDIAN HOTEL
10775 Caribbean
Blvd (33189)
Rates: $65-$149
(305) 253-9960
(800) 528-1234
(800) 371-6593

DANIA BEACH

MOTEL 6
825 E Dania
Beach Blvd
(33004)
Rates: $39-$75
(954) 921-5505
(800) 466-8356

SHERATON FT. LAUDERDALE AIRPORT HOTEL
1825 Griffin Rd
(33004)
Rates: $95-$179
(954) 920-3500
(800) 325-3535

DAVENPORT

BEST WESTERN CENTRAL FLORIDA
2425 Frontage Rd
(33837)
Rates: $65-$95
(863) 424-2596
(800) 528-1234

RAMADA INN
5414 US Hwy 27
N (33837)
Rates: n/a
(863) 424-2511
(800) 272-6232

CALABAY PARC-THE FLORIDA STORE
3479 W Vine St
(34741)
Rates: $110-$215
(407) 846-1722

ESPRIT-ABSOLUTE PRE-MIER VACATION HOMES
3160 Vineland
Rd, Ste 1 (34746)
Rates: $111-$249
(407) 396-2401

HAMPTON INN
44117 Hwy 27
(33897)
Rates: $79-$120
(863) 420-9898
(800) 426-7866

ROYAL PALM INN & SUITES
44089 Hwy 27
(33897)
Rates: $39-$69
(863) 424-2811

SOUTHERN DUNES-THE FLORIDA STORE
3479 W Vine St
(34741)
Rates: $115-$215
(407) 846-1722

SUPER 8 MOTEL
5620 US Hwy 27
N (33837)
Rates: $39-$120
(863) 420-8888
(800) 800-8000

DAVIE

HOMESTEAD STUDIO SUITES
7550 SR 84 E
(33316)
Rates: $69-$109
(954) 476-1211
(888) 782-9473

DAYTONA BEACH

ARUBA INN
1254 N Atlantic
Ave (32118)
Rates: $32-$110
(386) 253-5643
(877) 222-5858

ATLANTIC OCEAN PALM INN
3247 S Atlantic
Ave (32118)
Rates: $45-$150
(800) 634-0098

BREAKERS BEACH OCEAN-FRONT MOTEL
27 S Ocean Ave
(32118)
Rates: $45-$99
(386) 252-0863
(800) 441-8459

DAYS INN SPEEDWAY
2900 W Int'l
Speedway Blvd
(32124)
Rates: $49-$249
(386) 255-0467
(800) 329-7466

FOUNTAIN BEACH RESORT
313 S Atlantic
Ave (32118)
Rates: $39-$199
(386) 255-7491
(800) 556-8855

LA QUINTA INN
2725 Int'l
Speedway Blvd
(32114)
Rates: $69-$105
(386) 255-7412
(800) 687-6667

PLAZA OCEAN CLUB
640 N Atlantic
Ave (32118)
Rates: $89-$309
(386) 239-9800
(800) 874-7420

RAMADA INN SPEEDWAY
1798 W Int'l
Speedway Blvd
(32114)
Rates: $89-$325
(386) 255-2422
(800) 272-6232

SCOTTISH INN
1515 S
Ridgewood Ave
(32114)
Rates: $36-$195
(386) 258-5742

SUPER 8 - DAYTONA SANDS MOTEL
2523 S Atlantic
Ave (32118)
Rates: $39-$69
(386) 767-2551
(800) 800-8000

WHITE SANDS MOTEL
1122 N Atlantic
Ave (32118)
Rates: $30-$110
(386) 253-7461

DAYTONA BEACH SHORES

ATLANTIC OCEAN PALM INN
3247 S Atlantic
Ave (32118)
Rates: $39-$109
(386) 761-8450
(800) 634-0098

DAY STAR MOTEL
3811 S Atlantic
Ave (32127)
Rates: $45-$85
(386) 767-3780
(800) 506-5505

JASMIN MOTEL
3621 S Atlantic
Ave (32118)
Rates: n/a
(386) 760-9196

MANATEE SUITES
3167 S Atlantic
Ave (32118)
Rates: $45-$99
(800) 378-6826

PALM CIRCLE VILLAS
2327 S Atlantic
Ave (32118)
Rates: $35-$130
(386) 255-4004
(800) 217-3947

PARADISE INN
335 S Atlantic
Ave (32118)
Rates: $89-$99
(386) 255-8827

QUALITY INN OCEAN PALMS
2323 S Atlantic
Ave (32118)
Rates: $65-$279
(386) 255-0476
(800) 424-6423

SAND CASTLE MOTEL
3619 S Atlantic
Ave (32127)
Rates: $28-$65
(386) 767-3182
(800) 967-4757

DE FUNIAK SPRINGS

BEST WESTERN CROSSROADS INN
2343 Freeport Rd
(32433)
Rates: $69-$99
(850) 892-5111
(800) 528-1234

DAYS INN
472 Hugh Adams
Rd (32433)
Rates: $60-$90
(850) 892-6115
(800) 329-7466

RAMADA LIMITED
326 Green Acre
Dr (32435)
Rates: n/a
(850) 951-9780
(800) 272-6232

DEERFIELD BEACH

COMFORT SUITES
1040 E Newport
Center Dr (33442)
Rates: $69-$160
(954) 570-8887
(800) 424-6423

LA QUINTA INN
351 W Hillsboro
Blvd (33441)
Rates: $59-$131
(954) 421-1004
(800) 687-6667

RAMADA INN
1250 W Hillsboro
Blvd (33442)
Rates: $30-$259
(954) 427-2200
(800) 272-6232

TRAVELERS INN
1401 S Federal
Hwy (33441)
Rates: $55-$149
(954) 421-5000
(800) 283-9946

WELLESLEY INN
100 SW 12th Ave
(33442)
Rates: $49-$119
(954) 428-0661
(800) 444-8888

DELAND

COMFORT INN
400 E Int'l
Speedway Blvd
(32724)
Rates: $65-$235
(386) 736-3100
(800) 424-6423

HOLIDAY INN
350 E Int'l
Speedway Blvd
(32724)
Rates: $59-$209
(386) 738-5200
(800) 465-4329

**RIVIERA RESORT
& MARINA**
2760 Botts
Landing Rd
(32724)
Rates: n/a
(904) 822-5662
(888) 823-4642

UNIVERSITY INN
644 N Woodland
Blvd (32724)
Rates: $59-$175
(386) 734-5711

DELRAY BEACH

**COLONY HOTEL
& CABANA CLUB**
525 E Atlantic
Ave (33483)
Rates: $95-$275
(561) 276-4123
(800) 552-2363

**CRANE'S
BEACHHOUSE**
82 Gleason St
(33483)
Rates: $120-$425
(561) 278-1700
(866) 372-7263

**RESIDENCE INN
BY MARRIOTT**
1111 E Atlantic
Ave (33444)
Rates: $299-$599
(561) 276-7441
(800) 331-3131
(866) 258-7257

DELTONA

**BEST WESTERN
DELTONA INN**
481 Deltona Blvd
(32725)
Rates: $59-$99
(386) 860-3000
(800) 528-1234

DESTIN

DAYS INN
1029 Old Hwy
98 E (32541)
Rates: $45-$200
(850) 837-2599
(800) 329-7466

MOTEL 6
405 Hwy 98 E, #A
(32541)
Rates: $39-$85
(850) 837-0007
(800) 466-8356

RAMADA LIMITED
39 Scenic Gulf Dr
(32550)
Rates: n/a
(850) 837-2378
(800) 272-6232

SLEEP INN
10775 W Emerald
Coast Pkwy
(32550)
Rates: $59-$140
(850) 654-7022
(800) 424-6423

DUNDEE

DAYS INN
339 Hwy 27 N
(33838)
Rates: $59-$119
(863) 439-1591
(800) 329-7466

**MONTICELLO
MOTEL**
28500 Hwy 27
(33838)
Rates: $40-$85
(863) 439-3276

DUNEDIN

**SAILWINDS
WATERFRONT
RESORT**
1414 Bayshore
Blvd (34698)
Rates: $50-$149
(727) 734-8851
(800) 331-2548

DUNNELLON

**THE RAINBOW
RIVERS CLUB**
205100 The
Granada (34432)
Rates: n/a
(352 489-9983

EASTPOINT

**SPORTSMAN'S
LODGE MOTEL**
99 N Bayshore Dr
(32328)
Rates: $36-$46
(850) 670-8423

ELKTON

**COMFORT
INN ST.
AUGUSTINE**
2625 SR 207
(32033)
Rates: $59-$209
(904) 829-3435
(800) 424-6423

ELLENTON

**GUESTHOUSE
INT'L INN**
4915 17th St E
(34222)
Rates: $60-$110
(941) 729-0600
(800) 214-8378

**SLEEP INN,
INN & SUITES
RIVERFRONT**
5605 18th St E
(34222)
Rates: $55-$160
(941) 721-4933
(800) 424-6423

ENGLEWOOD

VERANDA INN
2073 S McCall Rd
(34224)
Rates: $85-$100
(941) 475-6533
(800) 633-8115

**WESTON'S
RESORT**
985 Gulf Blvd
(34224)
Rates: $100-$149
(941) 474-3431

EVERGLADES CITY

**EVERGLADES
VACATION
RENTALS**
201 W Broadway
(34139)
Rates: $50-$149
(239) 695-3151
(888) 431-1977

FERNANDINA BEACH

**AMELIA ISLAND
LODGING**
584 S Fletcher
(32034)
Rates: $50-$250+
(904) 261-4148
(800) 872-8531

**BEST WESTERN
INN-AMELIA
ISLAND**
2707 Sadler Rd
(32034)
Rates: $39-$129
(904) 277-2300
(800) 528-1234

**FLORIDA HOUSE
INN**
22 S 3rd St (32034)
Rates: $70-$160
(904) 261-3300

**HAMPTON INN-
AMELIA ISLAND**
2549 Sadler Rd
(32034)
Rates: $50-$140
(904) 321-1111
(800) 426-7866

FLAGLER BEACH

**BEACH FRONT
MOTEL**
1544 S A1A
(32136)
Rates: $49-$57
(386) 439-0089

**ISLAND
COTTAGE VILLA
BY THE SEA-
OCEANFRONT
INN**

2320 S
Oceanshore Blvd
(32136)
Rates: n/a
(386) 439-0092
(867) 662-6232

**LUXURY ON
THE OCEAN**
2815 S
Oceanshore Blvd
(32136)
Rates: $150
(904) 439-1826

TOPAZ MOTEL
1224 S
Oceanshore Blvd
(32136)
Rates: $55-$175
(386) 439-3301

**WHALE WATCH
MOTEL**
2448 S
Oceanshore Blvd
(32136)
Rates: $50-$99
(386) 439-2545
(877) 635-5535

FLORAL CITY

**MOONRISE
RESORT**
8501 E Moonrise
Ln (34436)
Rates: $60-$85
(352) 726-2553
(800) 665-6701

AREA CODES - If the local number doesn't connect, check for a new area code.

FLORIDA CITY

CORAL ROC MOTEL
1100 N Krome Ave (33034)
Rates: $45-$78
(305) 246-2888

HAMPTON INN
124 E Palm Dr (33034)
Rates: $99+
(305) 247-8833
(800) 426-7866

FORT LAUDERDALE

ADMIRAL'S COURT MOTEL
21 Hendricks Isle (33301)
Rates: $195-$795 Weekly
(954) 462-5072
(800) 248-6669

AMERISUITES
1851 SE 10th Ave (33316)
Rates: $119-$169
(954) 763-7670
(800) 833-1516

BAHAMA HOTEL
401 N Atlantic Blvd (33304)
Rates: $50-$149
(954) 467-7315
(800) 622-9995

BAY PALMS VILLAS
8 Isle of Venice (33301)
Rates: $290-$450 Weekly
(954) 552-2821

BAYMONT INN & SUITES
3800 W Commercial Blvd (33309)
Rates: $50-$149
(954) 485-7900
(877) 229-6668

BIRCH PATIO MOTEL
617 N Birch Rd (33304)
Rates: $35-$105
(954) 563-9540

CORTLEIGH RESORT HOTEL
2100 NE 33rd Ave (33305)
Rates: $50-$149
(954) 564-5868

DOUBLETREE GUEST SUITES
2670 E Sunrise Blvd (33304)
Rates: $69-$269
(954) 565-3800
(800) 222-8733

EIGHTEENTH STREET INN
712 S 18th St (33316)
Rates: $100-$249
(954) 467-7841
(888) 828-4466

ELYSIUM RESORT
552 N Birch Rd (33304)
Rates: $50-$249
(954) 564-9601
(800) 533-4744

FLYING CLOUD MOTEL
533 Orton Ave (33304)
Rates: $49-$135
(954) 563-7062

HAMPTON INN
2301 SW 12th Ave (33315)
Rates: $94-$149
(954) 524-9900
(800) 426-7866

HOLIDAY INN EXP HOTEL
1150 W State Rd Rd 84 (33315)
Rates: $99-$169
(954) 828-9905
(800) 465-4329

HOTEL OCEAN
205 N Atlantic Blvd (33304)
Rates: n/a
(954) 763-3452
(888) 456-2326

LA QUINTA INN CYPRESS CREEK
999 W Cypress Creek Rd (33309)
Rates: $99-$126
(954) 491-7666
(800) 687-6667

MANHATTAN TOWER APT HOTEL
701 Bayshore Dr (33304)
Rates: $125-$250+
(954) 564-1117

MARK 2100 RESORT HOTEL
2100 N Atlantic Blvd (33305)
Rates: $45-$199
(954) 566-8383
(800) 334-6275

MARTINDALE AT THE BEACH RESORT
3016 Bayshore Dr (33304)
Rates: $50-$249
(954) 467-1841
(800) 666 1841

MOTEL 6
1801 SR 84 (33150)
Rates: $41-$77
(954) 760-7999
(800) 466-8356

OCEAN HACIENDA INN
1924 N Atlantic Blvd (33305)
Rates: $50-$275
(954) 564-7800
(800) 562-8467

OCEAN MILE MOTOR LODGE
4101 N Ocean Blvd (33308)
Rates: $35-$99
(954) 565-1691

RED ROOF INN
4800 Powerline Rd (33309)
Rates: $41-$87
(954) 776-6333
(800) 843-7663

ROYAL SAXON APARTMENTS
551 Breakers Ave (33304)
Rates: $55-$125
(954) 566-7424

SEA CHATEAU RESORT MOTEL
555 N Birch Rd (33304)
Rates: $50-$100
(954) 566-8331
(800) 726-3723

SHERATON SUITES CYPRESS CREEK
555 NW 62nd St (33309)
Rates: $89-$329
(954) 772-5400
(800) 325-3535

TOWNEPLACE SUITES
3100 Prospect Rd (33309)
Rates: $54-$189
(954) 484-2214
(866) 211-4607

WESTIN HOTEL-CYPRESS CREEK
400 Corporate Dr (33304)
Rates: $89-$269
(954) 772-1331
(800) 228-3000

WISH YOU WERE HERE INN
7 N Birch Rd (33304)
Rates: $59-$139
(954) 462-0531
(800) 462-0531

FORT MYERS

BEST WESTERN AIRPORT INN
8955 Daniels Pkwy (33912)
Rates: $69-$169
(239) 561-7000
(800) 528-1234
(888) 490-2600

BEST WESTERN CORAL BRIDGE INN
9200 College Pkwy (33919)
Rates: $49-$139
(239) 454-6363
(800) 528-1234

BEST WESTERN ISLAND GTWY
20091 Summerlin Rd SW (33908)
Rates: $99-$199
(239) 466-1200
(800) 528-1234

BEST WESTERN SPRINGS RESORT
18051 S Tamiami Tr (33908)
Rates: $62-$139
(239) 267-7900
(800) 528-1234
(800) 344-9794

COMFORT INN
4171 Boatways Rd (33905)
Rates: $79-$139
(239) 694-9200
(800) 424-6423

COMFORT SUITES AIRPORT
13651-A Indian Paint Lane (33912)
Rates: $59-$159
(239) 768-0005
(800) 424-6423

COUNTRY INN
13901 Shell Point Plaza (33908)
Rates: $99-$179
(239) 454-9292
(800) 456-4000

DAYS INN AIRPORT
11435 Cleveland Ave (33907)
Rates: $39-$199
(239) 936-1311
(800) 329-7466

ECONO LODGE
13301 N Cleveland Ave (33903)
Rates: $42-$125
(239) 995-0571
(800) 424-6423

FOUNTAIN MOTEL
14621 McGregor Blvd (33901)
Rates: n/a
(239) 481-0429

GOLF VIEW MOTEL
3523 Cleveland Ave (33901)
Rates: $42-$80
(239) 936-1858

HOLIDAY INN RIVERWALK
2220 W First St (33901)
Rates: n/a
(239) 334-3434
(800) 465-4329

AREA CODES - If the local number doesn't connect, check for a new area code.

HOMEWOOD SUITES
5255 Big Pine Way (33907)
Rates: $109-$239
(239) 275-6000
(800) 225-5466

LA QUINTA INN
4850 Cleveland Ave (33907)
Rates: $75-$92
(239) 275-3300
(800) 687-6667

MOTEL 6
3350 Marinatown Lane (33903)
Rates: $37-$66
(239) 656-5544
(800) 466-8356

QUALITY HOTEL HISTORIC DISTRICT
2431 Cleveland Ave (33901)
Rates: $65-$155
(239) 332-3232
(800) 424-6423

RAMADA INN & SUITES-AMTEL MARINA
2500 Edwards Dr (33901)
Rates: n/a
(239) 337-0300
(800) 272-6232

RESIDENCE INN BY MARRIOTT
2960 Colonial Blvd (339907)
Rates: $104-$209
(239) 936-0110
(800) 331-3131

ROCK LAKE RESORT
2930 Palm Beach Blvd (33916)
Rates: n/a
(239) 334-3242
(800) 325-7596

RUSTY'S RESORT
309 San Carlos (33916)
Rates: n/a
(239) 463-4691

SLEEP INN AIRPORT
13661-B Indian Paint Ln (33912)
Rates: $49-$159
(239) 561-1117
(800) 424-6423

STONES THROW APARTMENTS
183 Washington Ave (33916)
Rates: n/a
(239) 463-0052

SUBURBAN EXTENDED STAY HOTEL
10150 Metro Pkwy (33901)
Rates: $50-$130
(239) 938-0100
(800) 265-0363

TA KI-KI MOTEL
2631 1st St (33916)
Rates: $58-$105
(239) 334-2135
(866) 453-0016

WYNSTAR INN & SUITES
10150 Daniels Pkwy (33913)
Rates: $69-$179
(239) 791-5000

FORT MYERS BEACH

ANCHOR INN COTTAGES
285 Virginia Ave (33931)
Rates: $330-$1085 Weekly
(239) 463-2630

BEST WESTERN BEACH RESORT
684 Estero Blvd (33931)
Rates: $119-$239
(239) 463-6000
(800) 528-1234
(800) 336-4045

CASA PLAYA BEACH RESORT
510 Estero Blvd (33931)
Rates: $199-$305
(239) 765-0510
(800) 569-4876

DAYS INN-ISLAND BEACH RESORT
1130 Estero Blvd (33931)
Rates: $68-$198
(941) 463-9759
(800) 329-7466

HOWARD JOHNSON BEACHFRONT
1100 Estero Blvd (33931)
Rates: $134-$240
(800) 544-4592

LIGHTHOUSE ISLAND RESORT
1051 5th St (33931)
Rates: $62-$275
(239) 463-9392
(800) 778-7748

RAMADA INN BEACHFRONT
1160 Estero Blvd (33931)
Rates: $69-$255
(239) 463-6158
(800) 272-6232

SILVER SANDS VILLAS
1207 Estero Blvd (33931
Rates: $79-$187
(239) 463-2755
(800) 603-0501

SUN DECK RESORT
1051 Third St (33931)
Rates: $49-$235
(239) 463-1842

FORT PIERCE

DAYS INN
6651 Darter Ct (34945)
Rates: $59-$99
(772) 466-4066
(800) 329-7466

ECONO LODGE
3236 S Hwy 1 (34982)
Rates: $49-$110
(772) 461-2323
(800) 424-6423

HOLIDAY INN EXP
7151 Okeechobee Rd (34945)
Rates: $79-$159
(772) 464-5000
(800) 465-4329

MOTEL 6
2500 Peters Rd (34945)
Rates: $39-$65
(772) 461-9937
(800) 466-8356

FT WALTON BEACH

MARINA MOTEL & MARINA
1345 Miracle Strip Pkwy E (32548)
Rates: $50-$100
(850) 244-1129
(800) 237-7021

RODEWAY INN
314 Miracle Strip Pkwy (32548)
Rates: $59-$129
(850) 243-6162
(800) 424-6423

GAINESVILLE

BAYMONT INN & SUITES
3905 SW 43rd St (32608)
Rates: $77-$119
(352) 376-0004
(877) 229-6668

BEST WESTERN GATEWAY GRAND
4200 NW 97th Blvd (32606)
Rates: $79-$99
(352) 331-3336
(800) 528-1234
(877) 464-2378

BUDGET LODGE
6901 NW 8th Ave (32605)
Rates: n/a
(352) 331-1601

COMFORT INN UNIVERSITY
2435 SW 13th Ave (32608)
Rates: $55-$65
(352) 373-6500
(800) 424-6423

COMFORT INN WEST
3440 SW 40th Blvd (32608)
Rates: $69-$199
(352) 264-1771
(800) 424-6423

ECONO LODGE-U OF FL
2649 SW 13th St (32608)
Rates: $38-$115
(352) 373-7816
(800) 424-6423

HOLIDAY INN WEST
7417 Newberry Rd (32608)
Rates: $78-$109
(352) 332-7500
(800) 465-4329

LA QUINTA INN
920 NW 69th Terr (32601)
Rates: $69-$105
(352) 332-6466
(800) 687-6667

MAGNOLIA PLANTATION B&B INN
309 SE 7th St (32601)
Rates: $50-$250+
(352) 375-6653
(800) 201-2379

MOTEL 6-U OF FL
4000 SW 40th Blvd (32608)
Rates: $36-$46
(352) 373-1604
(800) 466-8356

QUALITY INN
3455 SW Williston Rd (32608)
Rates: $70-$196
(352) 378-2405
(800) 424-6423

RAMADA LTD
7413 Newberry Rd (32605)
Rates: $55-$79
(352) 332-8001
(800) 272-6232

RED ROOF INN
3500 SW 42nd St (32608)
Rates: $59-$75
(352) 336-3311
(800) 843-7663

GEORGE TOWN

GEORGETOWN MARINA & LODGE
1533 CR 309 (32139)
Rates: $50-$135
(866) 325-2003

AREA CODES - If the local number doesn't connect, check for a new area code.

GRASSY KEY

GULF VIEW WATERFRONT RESORT
58743 Overseas Hwy (Marathon 33050)
Rates: $50-$250
(305) 289-1414

GREENVILLE

TARTARUGA CREEK RESORT
Rt 2 (32331)
Rates: n/a
(904) 997-0036
(800) 465-2958

HAINES CITY

BEST WESTERN LAKE HAMILTON
605 B Moore Rd (33844)
Rates: $59-$99
(863) 421-6929
(800) 528-1234
(800) 421-6928

HOWARD JOHNSON INN
33224 Hwy 27 S (33844)
Rates: $49-$69
(863) 422-8621
(800) 446-4656

HERNANDO

BEST WESTERN CITRUS HILL LODGE
350 E Norvell Bryant Hwy (34442)
Rates: $78-$105
(352) 527-0015
(800) 528-1234
(888) 424-5634

HERNANDO BEACH

HERNANDO BEACH MOTEL & CONDOS
4291 Shoal Line Blvd (34607)
Rates: n/a
(352) 596-2527

HIALEAH

DAYS INN
1950 W 49th St (33012)
Rates: $49-$109
(305) 823-2121
(800) 329-7466

HOBE SOUND

RED CARPET INN
8605 SE Federal Hwy (33455)
Rates: n/a
(561) 546-3600
(800) 251-1962

HOLIDAY

TAHITIAN RESORT
2337 US 19 (34691)
Rates: $49-$99
(727) 937-4121

HOLLYWOOD

COMFORT INN AIRPORT/CRUISE PORT SOUTH
2520 Stirling Rd (33020)
Rates: $59-$169
(954) 922-1600
(800) 333-1492
(800) 424-6423

DAYS INN AIRPORT SOUTH
2601 N 29th Ave Hollywood (33020)
Rates: $69-$199
(954) 923-7300
(800) 329-7466

ECONO LODGE INN & SUITES PRESIDENT'S CIRCLE
4900 Hollywood Blvd (33021)
Rates: $49-$189
(954) 981-1800
(800) 424-6423

GREEN SEAS MOTEL
1419 S Federal Hwy Hollywood (33020)
Rates: $37-$99
(954) 923-6564

GRENIER'S ON THE BEACH
326 Nebraska St (33019)
Rates: $50-$125
(954) 981-9556
(800) 922-3157

HOWARD JOHNSON EXP

2900 Polk St (33020)
Rates: $45-$99
(954) 923-1516
(800) 446-4656

LA QUINTA INN & SUITES
2620 N 26th Ave (33019)
Rates: $89-$145
(954) 922-2295
(800) 687-6667

MIRADOR RESORT MOTEL
901 S Ocean Dr (33019)
Rates: $195-$860 Weekly
(954) 922-7581

MONTREAL INN
324-336 Balboa St (33019)
Rates: $50-$99
(954) 925-4443
(800) 217-2637

SANDY SHORES MOTEL & FAMILY LODGING
342 Van Buren St (33019)
Rates: $55-$95
(954) 923-3750

SUNRISE VIEW MOTEL
327 Pierce St (33019)
Rates: $50-$99
(954) 921-0572
(888) 364-9596

THREE PALM MOTEL
930 N 17th Ct (33020)
Rates: n/a
(954) 923-7683

HOLMES BEACH

AQUARIUS BEACH RESORT
105 39th St (34217)
Rates: $50-$150
(941) 778-7477

GULF DRIVE APTS

6505 Gulf Drive N (34217)
Rates: $30-$50
(941) 251-2952

HALEYS MOTEL
8102 Gulf Dr (34217)
Rates: $30-$100
(941) 778-5405
(800) 367-7824

THE INN BETWEEN MOTEL
105 66th St (34217)
Rates: $310-$525 Weekly
(941) 778-0751

ISLAND WEST EFFICIENCIES
3605 Gulf Dr (34217)
Rates: $30-$100
(941) 778-6569

PELICAN COVE RESORT CONDO
901 Gulf Dr S (34217)
Rates: n/a
(941) 778-4800
(800) 237-2252

HOMESTEAD

DAYS INN
51 S Homestead Blvd (33030)
Rates: $55-$124
(305) 245-1260
(800) 329-7466

EVERGLADES MOTEL
605 S Krome Ave (33030)
Rates: $39-$68
(305) 247-4117

KATY'S PLACE BED & BREAKFAST
31850 SW 195th Ave (33030)
Rates: n/a
(305) 246-0783
(800) 428-3438

HOMOSASSA SPRINGS

PARK INN
4076 S Suncoast Blvd (34448)
Rates: $69-$89
(352) 628-4311
(800) 670-7275

HUDSON

GULFCOVE WATERFRONT RESORT
6525 Clark St (34667)
Rates: n/a
(800) 600-1955

INDIALANTIC

CASABLANCA INN
1805 N A1A Hwy (32903)
Rates: $60-$80
(321) 728-7188
(800) 333-7273

GUESTHOUSE INTERNATIONAL
2900 N A1A Hwy (32903)
Rates: $59-$149
(321) 779-9994
(800) 760-6031

HILTON MELBOURNE BEACH OCEANFRONT
3003 N SR A1A (32903)
Rates: $119-$249
(321) 777-5000
(800) 445-8667

OCEANFRONT COTTAGES
612 Wavecrest Ave (32903)
Rates: $99-$125
(321) 725-8474
(800) 785-8080

QUALITY SUITES OCEANFRONT HOTEL
1665 N SR A1A (32903)
Rates: $119-$219
(321) 723-4222
(800) 424-6423

INDIAN HARBOUR BEACH

WELLESLEY INN
1894 S Patrick Dr (32937)
Rates: $79-$119
(321) 773-0325
(800) 444-8888

AREA CODES - If the local number doesn't connect, check for a new area code.

INDIAN ROCKS BEACH

ARBORS SEASIDE COTTAGES
218 Gulf Blvd
(33785)
Rates: n/a
(727) 517-7222
(800) 873-0224

BEACH TRAIL COTTAGES
726 Gulf Blvd
(33785)
Rates: n/a
(727) 734-3956

GULF BREEZE INN
2008 Gulf Blvd
(33785)
Rates: $50-$99
(888) 422 4853

SEA STAR MOTEL & APTS
1805 Gulf Blvd
(33785)
Rates: $60-$90
(727) 596-2525

INDIAN SHORES

CASA CHICA COTTAGES
19000 Gulf Blvd
(34635)
Rates: n/a
(727) 596-1602
(800) 562-5335

EDGEWATER BEACH RESORT
19130 Gulf Blvd
(34635)
Rates: $50-$100
(727) 595-4028

FLORENTINE APARTMENTS
19722 Gulf Blvd
(34635)
Rates: n/a
(727) 595-8820

HOLIDAY VILLAS II CONDO
19610 Gulf Blvd
(34635)
Rates: $50-$149
(727) 596-4852
(800) 428-4852

INDIAN PASS APARTMENTS
19417 Gulf Blvd
(34635)
Rates: n/a
(727) 595-5444

LA REGINA MOTEL
19600 Gulf Blvd
(34635)
Rates: n/a
(727) 595-8067

SAND GLO VILLAS
19316 Gulf Blvd
(34635)
Rates: $100-$275
(727) 320-9720
(800) 816 1970

THE SUN BURST INN
19204 Gulf Blvd
(34635)
Rates: 49-$149
(727) 596-2500
(877) 384-8067

VICTORIA APTS & COTTAGES
19738 Gulf Blvd
(34635)
Rates: n/a
(727) 595-4004

INVERNESS

VAN DER VALK VACATION HOMES
4555 E Windmill Dr (34453)
Rates: $1130-$1300 Weekly
(352) 637-1140

ISLAMORADA

CASA MORADA
136 Madeira Rd
(33036)
Rates: $140-$250+
(305) 664-0044
(888) 881-8080

COCONUT COVE RESORT/ MARINA
84801 Old Hwy
(33036)
Rates: $65-$125
(305) 664-0123
(800) 801-1079

LOOKOUT LODGE RESORT
87770 Overseas Hwy (33036)
Rates: $69-$159
(305) 852-9915
(800) 870-1772

OCEAN DAWN LODGE
82885 Old Hwy
(33036)
Rates: $65-$115
(305) 664-4844

PORT OF CALL TOWNHOMES
136 Aregood Lane (33036)
Rates: $100-$250
(305) 232-3569

SANDS OF ISLAMORADA RESORT
80051 Overseas Hwy (33036)
Rates: $99-$275
(305) 664-2791
(888) 741-4518

WHITE GATE COURT
76010 Overseas Hwy (33036)
Rates: $98-$200
(305) 664-4136
(800) 645-4283

JACKSONVILLE

AMERISUITES/ BAY MEADOWS
8277 Western Way Cir (32256)
Rates: $89-$149
(904) 737-4477
(800) 833-1516

BAYMONT INN & SUITES
3199 Hartley Rd
(32257)
Rates: $54-$75
(904) 268-9999
(877) 229-6668

BEST WESTERN HOTEL JTB/ SOUTHPOINT
4660 Salisbury Rd (32256)
Rates: $55-$159
(904) 281-0900
(800) 528-1234
(800) 842-1348

CANDLEWOOD SUITES
4990 Belfort Rd
(32256)
Rates: $99-$399
(904) 296-7785
(888) 226-3539

HAMPTON INN
1170 Airport Entrance Rd
(32218)
Rates: $64-$99
(904) 741-4980
(800) 426-7866

HOLIDAY INN
9150 Baymeadows Rd
(32256)
Rates: $64-$99
(904) 737-1700
(800) 465-4329

HOLIDAY INN AIRPORT
14670 Duvall Rd
(32218)
Rates: $119-$139
(904) 741-4404
(800) 465-4329

HOMESTEAD STUDIO SUITES
10020 Skinner Lake Dr (32246)
Rates: $59-$84
(904) 642-9911
(888) 782-9473

HOMESTEAD STUDIO SUITES
8300 Western Way (32256)
Rates: $69-$84
(904) 739-1881
(888) 782-9473

HOMESTEAD STUDIO SUITES
4693 Salisbury Rd (32256)
Rates: $74-$104
(904) 296-0661
(888) 782-9473

HOMEWOOD SUITES
8737 Baymeadows Rd
(32256)
Rates: $135-$200
(904) 733-9299
(800) 225-5466

INN 2000
14585 Duval Rd
(32218)
Rates: n/a
(904) 741-1133

JAMESON INN
7030 Bonneval Rd (32216)
Rates: $49-$104
(904) 296-0968
(800) 526-3766

LA QUINTA INN
4868 Lenoir Ave S (32216)
Rates: $89-$109
(904) 296-0703
(800) 687-6667

LA QUINTA INN
8555 Blanding Blvd (32244)
Rates: $79-$93
(904) 778-9539
(800) 687-6667

LA QUINTA INN NORTH
812 Dunn Ave
(32218)
Rates: $79-$105
(904) 751-6960
(800) 687-6667

LA QUINTA INN-BAYMEADOWS
8255 Dix Ellis Tr (32256)
Rates: $79-$99
(904) 731-9940
(800) 687-6667

MASTERS INN JT BUTLER
4940 Mustang Rd (32216)
Rates: $44-$59
(904) 281-2244

MOTEL 6 AIRPORT
10885 Harts Rd
(32218)
Rates: $36-$44
(904) 757-8600
(800) 466-8356

MOTEL 6-SOUTHEAST
8285 Dix Ellis Tr
(32256)
Rates: $35-$40
(904) 731-8400
(800) 466-8356

MOTEL 6-SOUTHWEST
6107
Youngerman Cir
(32244)
Rates: $36-$46
(904) 777-6100
(800) 466-8356

RAMADA INN MANDARIN
3130 Hartley Rd
(32257)
Rates: $77-$82
(904) 268-8080
(800) 272-6232

RED ROOF INN AIRPORT
14701 Airport
Entrance Rd
(32218)
Rates: $45-$73
(904) 741-4488
(800) 843-7663

RED ROOF INN SOUTH
6099
Youngerman Cir
(32244)
Rates: $45-$61
(904) 777-1000
(800) 843-7663

RESIDENCE INN BY MARRIOTT
8365 Dix Ellis
Trail (32256)
Rates: $69-$189
(904) 733-8088
(800) 331-3131

RESIDENCE INN BY MARRIOTT
10551 Deerwood
Park Blvd (32256)
Rates: $74-$169
(904) 996-8900
(800) 331-3131

STUDIO 6
8765
Baymeadows Rd
(32256)
Rates: $199-$259
(9040 731-7317
(888) 897-0202

JACKSONVILLE BEACH

SURFSIDE INN
1236 N 1st St
(32250)
Rates: $69-$179
(904) 246-1583

JASPER

DAYS INN
8182 SR 6 W
(32052)
Rates: $35-$80
(386) 792-1987
(800) 329-7466

JENNINGS

JENNINGS HOUSE INN
SR 143 (32053)
Rates: $20-$25
(904) 938-3305

JENSEN BEACH

RIVER PALM COTTAGES & FISH CAMP
2325 NE Indian
River Dr (34957)
Rates: $79-$199
(561) 334-0401
(800) 305-0511

JUNO BEACH

HOLIDAY INN EXP
13950 US Hwy 1
(33408)
Rates: $69-$400
(561) 622-4366
(800) 465-4329

JUPITER

JUPITER BEACH RESORT
5 N A1A (33477)
Rates: $129-$559
(561) 746-2511
(800) 228-8810

WELLESLEY INN
34 Fishermans
Wharf (33477)
Rates: $69-$149
(561) 575-7201
(800) 444-8888

KEY LARGO

BAY HARBOR LODGE
97702 Overseas
Hwy (33037)
Rates: $50-$149
(305) 852-5695
(800) 385-0986

COCONUT BAY RESORT
97770 Overseas
Hwy (33037)
Rates: $50-$149
(305) 852-5695
(800) 385-0986

HOWARD JOHNSON
102400 Overseas
Hwy (33037)
Rates: $139-$349
(305) 451-1400
(800) 446-4656

MARINA DEL MAR OCEANSIDE RESORT/MARINA
527 Caribbean
Dr, MM 100
(33037)
Rates: $99-$289
(305) 451-4107
(800) 451-3483

SEA TRAIL MOTEL
Rt 5 (33037)
Rates: $35-$55
(305) 852-8001

KEY WEST

AMBROSIA TOO B&B
622 Fleming St
(33040)
Rates: $120-$425
(305) 296-9838
(800) 535-9838

ARCHER HOUSE SUITES
425 Frances St
(33040)
Rates: $150-$250
(877) 295-0900

ATLANTIC SHORES RESORT
510 South St
(33040)
Rates: n/a
(305) 296-2492
(800) 526-3559

BOATHOUSE RESORT & MARINA
1445 S Roosevelt
Blvd (33040)
Rates: $170-$300
(305) 292-0017
(800) 958-2128

CARIBBEAN HOUSE MOTEL
226 Petronia St
(33040)
Rates: $39-$79
(305) 296-1600

CASA ALANTE COTTAGES B&B
1435 S Roosevelt
Blvd (33040)
Rates: $60-$150
(305) 293-0702
(800) 688-3942

CENTER COURT HISTORIC INN & COTTAGES B&B
916 Center St
(33040)
Rates: $98-$598
(305) 296-9292
(800) 797-8787

CHELSEA HOUSE HISTORIC B&B
707 Truman Ave
(33040)
Rates: $89-$275
(305) 296-2211
(800) 845-8859

COURTNEY'S PLACE HISTORIC COTTAGES
720 Whitmarsh
Ln (33040)
Rates: $79-$249
(305) 294-3480
(800) 869-4639

THE CUBAN CLUB SUITES APT MOTEL
1102-1108 Duval
St (33040)
Rates: $179-$399
(305) 296-0465
(800) 432-4849

CURRY MANSION INN B&B
511 Caroline St
(33040)
Rates: $175-$325
(305) 294-5349
(800) 253-3466

DEJA VU RESORT
611 Truman Ave
(33040)
Rates: $100-$249
(305) 292-9339
(800) 724-5351

DOUGLAS GUEST HOUSE
419 Amelia St
(33040)
Rates: $88-$275
(305) 294-5269
(800) 833-0372

FRANCES STREET BOTTLE INN B&B
535 Frances St
(33040)
Rates: $89-$189
(305) 294-8530
(800) 294-8530

THE GRAND HISTORIC B&B
1116 Grinnell St
(33040)
Rates: $88-$188
(305) 294-0590

HALFRED MOTEL
512 Truman Ave
(33040)
Rates: $65-$143
(305) 296-5565

HIDEAWAY COTTAGES
6531 Maloney
Ave (33040)
Rates: $125+
(305) 296-0294
(800) 484-8777

INCENTRA CARRIAGE HOUSE
729 Whitehead St
(33040)
Rates: $59-$290
(305) 296-5565

JABOUR'S CABINS
223 Elizabeth St
(33040)
Rates: n/a
(305) 294-5723

MAHOGANY HOUSE
812 Simongton St
(33040)
Rates: $45-$175
(305) 293-9464

NASSAU HOUSE
1016 Fleming St
(33040)
Rates: $49-$199
(305) 296-8513
(800) 296-8513

OLD CUSTOMS HOUSE INN
124 Duval St
(33040)
Rates: $50-$200
(305) 294-8507

AREA CODES - If the local number doesn't connect, check for a new area code.

OLIVIA BY DUVAL HOTEL
511 Olivia St
(33040)
Rates: $40-$249
(305) 296-5169
(800) 413-1978

THE PALMS HOTEL HISTORIC B&B
820 White St
(33040)
Rates: $95-$250
(305) 294-3146
(800) 558-9374

PIER HOUSE RESORT & SPA
One Duval St
(33040)
Rates: $200-$460
(305) 296-4600
(800) 327-8340

RED ROOSTER B&B
709 Truman Ave
(33040)
Rates: $79-$250+
(305) 296-6558
(800) 845-8854

SEA ISLE RESORT
915 Windsor Ln
(33040)
Rates: $65-$140
(305) 294-5188

SEA SHELL MOTEL
718 South St
(33040)
Rates: $45-$95
(305) 296-5719

SEASCAPE TROPICAL INN & COTTAGES
420 Olivia St
(33040)
Rates: n/a
(305) 296-7776
(800) 765-6438

SPEAK EASY INN
1117 Duval St
(33040)
Rates: $70-$163
(305) 296-2680

SUITE DREAMS ALL SUITES
1001 Von Phister
(33040)
Rates: $100-$249
(305) 296-5169
(800) 730-2483

SUNRISE SUITES RESORT
3685 Seaside Dr
(33040)
Rates: n/a
(305) 296-6661
(888) 723-5200

TRAVELERS PALM INN B&B
915 Center St
(33040)
Rates: $98-$308
(305) 294-9560

WHISPERS BED & BREAKFAST INN
409 William St
(33040)
Rates: $69-$150
(305) 294-5969
(800) 856-7444

WILLIAM HOUSE
1317 Duval St
(33040)
Rates: $83-$170
(305) 294-8223

KISSIMMEE
AMERISUITES
4991 Calypso
Cay Way (34746)
Rates: $79-$169
(407) 997-1300
(800) 833-1516

BEST WESTERN MAINGATE EAST HOTEL & SUITES
4018 W Vine St
(34741)
Rates: $52-$149
(407) 870-2000
(800) 528-1234
(877) 444-2407

BEST WESTERN EASTGATE
5565 W Irlo
Bronson Hwy
(34746)
Rates: $49-$109
(407) 396-0707
(800) 528-1234
(800) 223-5361

CLARION SUITES RESORT WORLD
2800 N Poinciana
Blvd (34746)
Rates: $89-$199
(407) 997-5000
(800) 424-6423

CLEAR CREEK- THE FLORIDA STORE
3479 W Vine St
(34741)
Rates: $110-$215
(407) 846-1722

COUNTRY INN & SUITES
5001 Calypso
Cay Way (34746)
Rates: $69-$149
(407) 997-1400
(800) 456-4000

DAYS INN
2095 E Irlo
Bronson Hwy
(34744)
Rates: $35-$169
(407) 846-7136
(800) 329-7466

DAYS INN MAIN GATE-E. WALT DISNEY WORLD
5840 W Irlo
Bronson Hwy
(34746)
Rates: $30-$129
(407) 396-7969
(800) 329-7466

EASTGATE INN
5565 W Irlo
Bronson Hwy
(34746)
Rates: $42-$138
(407) 396-0707

ECONO LODGE HAWAIIAN RESORT
7514 W Irlo
Bronson Hwy
(34747)
Rates: $30-$79
(407) 396-2000
(800) 424-6423

ECONO LODGE POLYNESIAN
5335 Irlo Bronson
Hwy (34746)
Rates: $29-$35
(407) 396-2121
(800) 424-6423

FANTASY WORLD CLUB VILLAS
3000 Hart Ave
(34746)
Rates: $99-$195
(407) 396-1808
(800) 874-8047

FLAMINGO INN
801 E Vine St
(34744)
Rates: $27-$60
(407) 846-1935
(800) 780-7617

HAMPTON LAKES- THE FLORIDA STORE
3479 W Vine St
(34741)
Rates: $105-$215
(407) 846-1722

HOLIDAY INN- MAINGATE WEST /THEME PARK AREA
7601 Black Lake
Rd (34747)
Rates: $89-$189
(407) 396-1100
(800) 465-4656

HOMEWOOD SUITES
3100 Parkway
Blvd (34747)
Rates: $69-$129
(407) 396-2229
(800) 225-5466
(800) 225-4543

HOWARD JOHNSON EXP
4311 W Vine St
(34746)
Rates: $40-$70
(407) 396-7100
(800) 446-4656
(800) 388-7698

HOWARD JOHNSON HOTEL
2323 Hwy 192 E
(34744)
Rates: $40-$89
(407) 846-4900
(800) 446-4656

HOWARD JOHN- SON MAINGATE RESORT WEST
8660 W Irlo
Bronson Hwy
(34747)
Rates: $39-$00
(407) 396-4500
(800) 446-4656

INDIAN CREEK- VACATION HOMES
3160 Vineland
Rd, Ste 1 (34746)
Rates: $111-$249
(407) 396-2401

INDIAN CREEK- THE FLORIDA STORE
3479 W Vine St
(34741)
Rates: $110-$215
(407) 846-1722

LA QUINTA INN & SUITES
3484 Polynesian
Isle Blvd (34746)
Rates: $59-$139
(407) 997-1700
(800) 687-6667

LA QUINTA INN LAKESIDE
7769 W Irlo
Bronson Hwy
(34747)
Rates: $59-$129
(407) 396-2222
(800) 687-6667

MAINSTAY SUITES MAINGATE
4786 W Irlo
Bronson Hwy
(34746)
Rates: $69-$229
(407) 396-2056
(800) 424-6423

MASTERS INN
5367 W Irlo
Bronson Hwy
(34746)
Rates: $37-$79
(407) 396-4020

MASTERS INN- MAINGATE
2945 Entry Point
Blvd (34747)
Rates: $39-$99
(407) 396-7743

MOTEL 6
5731 W Irlo
Bronson Hwy
(34746)
Rates: $29-$65
(407) 396-6333
(800) 466-8356

MOTEL 6- DISNEYWORLD MAIN GATE
7455 W Irlo
Bronson Hwy
(34747)
Rates: $29-$65
(407) 396-6422
(800) 466-8356

AREA CODES - If the local number doesn't connect, check for a new area code.

PARK INN MAINGATE EAST
6075 W Irlo
Bronson Hwy
(34747)
Rates: $39-$89
(407) 396-6100
(800) 670-7275

RAMADA INN DOWNTOWN
2009 W Vine St
(34741)
Rates: $69-$99
(407) 846-2713
(800) 272-6232

RAMADA INN RESORT EASTGATE
5150 Hwy 192 W
(34746)
Rates: $45-$99
(407) 396-1111
(800) 272-6232

RAMADA PLAZA GATEWAY
7470 Hwy 192 W
(34747)
Rates: $59-$129
(407) 396-4400
(800) 272-6232

RED ROOF INN
4970 Kyng's
Heath Rd (34746)
Rates: $40-$68
(407) 396-0065
(800) 843-7663

RODEWAY INN MAINGATE
5995 W Irlo
Bronson Hwy
(34747)
Rates: $35-$90
(407) 396-4300
(800) 424-6423
(800) 223-1584

SUMMERFIELD CONDO RESORT
2422 Summerfield
Way (34741)
Rates: $99-$159
(407) 847-7222
(800) 207-9582

SUNSET LAKES-VACATION HOMES
3160 Vineland
Rd, Ste 1 (34746)
Rates: $111-$249
(407) 396-2401

SUPER 8 MOTEL
5875 W Irlo
Bronson Hwy
(34746)
Rates: $40-$70
(407) 396-8883
(800) 800-8000

TRADITION HOTEL & SUITES
5678 W Irlo
Bronson Hwy
(34746)
Rates: $59-$129
(407) 396-4488

TRAVELODGE MAINGATE E.
5711 W Irlo
Bronson Hwy
(32744)
Rates: $49-$129
(407) 396-4222
(800) 578-7878

TROPICAL PALMS FUN RESORT
2650 Holiday Trail
(34746)
Rates: n/a
(407) 396-4595
(800) 64-PALMS

WINDSOR PALMS-VACATION HOMES
3160 Vineland Rd,
Ste 1 (34746)
Rates: $111-$249
(407) 396-2401

LABELLE
THE RIVER'S EDGE MOTEL
285 N River Rd
(33935)
Rates: $45+
(941) 675-6062

LADY LAKE
HOLIDAY INN EXP HOTEL
1205 Avenida
Central N (32159)
Rates: $92-$97
(352) 750-3888
(800) 465-4329

MICROTEL INN & SUITES
850 Hwy 27/441
(32159)
Rates: $49-$94
(352) 259-0184

LAKE BUENA VISTA
COMFORT INN
8442 Palm Pkwy
(32830)
Rates: $49-$89
(407) 996-7300
(800) 424-6423

DAYS INN LAKE BUENA VISTA HOTEL
12799 Apopka-
Vineland Rd
(32836)
Rates: $65-$129
(407) 239-4441
(800) 329-7466
(800) 224-5058

EMBASSY SUITES HOTEL
8100 Lake Ave
(32836)
Rates: $109-$229
(407) 239-1144
(800) 362-2779
(800) 257-8483

HOLIDAY INN-SUNSPREE RESORTS
13351 SR 535
(32821)
Rates: $89-$189
(407) 239-4500
(800) 465-4329
(800) 366-6299

SHERATON SAFARI HOTEL
12205 Apopka-
Vineland Rd
(32836)
Rates: $109-$209
(407) 239-0444
(800) 325-3535
(800) 423-3297

LAKE CITY
BEST WESTERN LAKE CITY INN
3598 Hwy 90 W
(32055)
Rates: $45-$95
(386) 752-3801
(800) 528-1234
(800) 718-0244

DAYS INN
3430 N Hwy 441
(32055)
Rates: $50-$85
(386) 758-4224
(800) 329-7466

DRIFTWOOD MOTEL
2764 Hwy 90 W
(32055)
Rates: $28-$49
(386) 755-3545

ECONO LODGE SOUTH
Rt 2, Box 6008
(32024)
Rates: $35-$100
(286) 755-9311
(800) 424-6423

JAMESON INN
285 SW Commerce
Blvd (32025)
Rates: $49-$104
(386) 758-8440
(800) 526-3766

KNIGHTS INN
Rt 13, Box 201
(32055)
Rates: $23-$60
(386) 752-7720
(800) 843-5644

MOTEL 6
3835 W Hwy 90
(32055)
Rates: $29-$32
(386) 755-4664
(800) 466-8356

PINEY WOODS LODGE
Rt 13 (32055)
Rates: $20-$45
(386) 752-8334

QUAIL HEIGHTS COUNTRY CLUB
SR 247 (32025)
Rates: n/a
(386) 752-3339

QUALITY INN
3072 W Hwy 90
(32055)
Rates: $89-$125
(386) 755-5770
(800) 424-6423

RODEWAY INN
205 SW Commerce
Blvd (32025)
Rates: $30-$70
(386) 755-5203
(800) 424-6423

SCOTTISH INNS
4450 W Hwy 90
(32055)
Rates: $29-$59
(386) 755-0230

LAKE MARY
CANDLEWOOD SUITES
1130 Greenwood
Blvd (32746)
Rates: $89
(407) 585-3000
(888) 226-3539

HOMESTEAD STUDIO SUITES
1040 Greenwood
Blvd (32746)
Rates: $64-$79
(407) 829-2332
(800) 225-5466

LA QUINTA INN & SUITES
1060 Greenwood
Blvd (32746)
Rates: $99-$125
(407) 805-9901
(800) 687-6667

LAKE PLACID
RAMADA INN
2165 US 27 S
(33852)
Rates: $59-$89
(863) 465-3133
(800) 272-6232

LAKE WALES
A PRINCE OF WALES MOTEL
513 S Scenic Hwy
(33853)
Rates: $45-$99
(863) 676-1249

LAKE WORTH
LAGO MOTOR INN
714 S Dixie Hwy
(33460)
Rates: $50-$75
(561) 585-5246

THE PARADOR OF THE PALM BEACHES
100 S Federal
Way (33466)
Rates: $75-$150
(561) 540-1443

LAKELAND
AMERISUITES LAKELAND CTR
525 W Oange St
(33815)
Rates: $79-$159
(863) 413-1122
(800) 833-1515

AMPAK LAKE-LAND MALL INN
3520 Hwy 98 N (33809)
Rates: $50-$145
(888) 499-3434

BAYMONT INN & SUITES
4315 Lakeland Park Dr (33809)
Rates: $49-$129
(863) 815-0606
(877) 229-6668

COMFORT INN
3520 N Hwy 98 (33809)
Rates: $59-$149
(863) 859-0100
(800) 424-6423

JAMESON INN
4375 Lakeland Park Dr (33809)
Rates: $49-$104
(863) 858-9070
(800) 526-3766

LA QUINTA INN & SUITES
1024 Crevasse St (33809)
Rates: $79-$124
(863) 859-2866
(800) 687-6667

MOTEL 6
3120 US Hwy 98 N (33809)
Rates: $39-$52
(863) 682-0643
(800) 466-8356

RESIDENCE INN BY MARRIOTT
3701 Harden Blvd (33803)
Rates: $130-$350
(863) 680-2323
(800) 331-3131

SUPER 8 MOTEL
601 E Memorial Blvd (33801)
Rates: $49-$70
(863) 683-5961
(800) 800-8000

LANTANA

MOTEL 6
1310 W Lantana Rd (33462)
Rates: $39-$73
(561) 585-5833
(800) 466-8356

LAUDERDALE BY THE SEA

THE PIER POINT RESORT
4320 El Mar Dr (33308)
Rates: $59-$259
(954) 776-5121

LEESBURG

SUPER 8 MOTEL
1392 N Blvd W (34748)
Rates: $39-$99
(352) 787-6363
(800) 800-8000

LEHIGH ACRES

ADMIRAL LEHIGH GOLF RESORT
225 E Joel Blvd (33936)
Rates: $69-$135
(888) GOLF-222

LIVE OAK

BEST WESTERN SUWANNEE RIVER INN
6819 US 129 (320642
Rates: $39-$130
(386) 362-6000
(800) 528-1234

ECONO LODGE
6811 N US 129 & I-10 (32060)
Rates: $45-$89
(386) 362-7459
(800) 424-6423

LONGBOAT KEY

CEDARS TENNIS RESORT
645 Cedars Court (34228)
Rates: $50-$149
(941) 383-4621
(800) 433-4621

HILTON LONGBOAT KEY BEACHFRONT RESORT
4711 Gulf of Mexico Dr (34228)
Rates: $155-$600
(941) 383-2451
(800) 282-3046

RIVIERA BEACH MOTEL
5451 Gulf of Mexico Dr (34228)
Rates: $700-$1300 Weekly
(941) 383-2552

ROLLING WAVES COTTAGES
6351 Gulf of Mexico Dr (34228)
Rates: $90-$202
(941) 383-1323

LONGWOOD

COMFORT INN
2025 W SR 434 (32779)
Rates: $79-$89
(407) 862-4000
(800) 424-6423

MACCLENNY

ECONO LODGE
151 Woodlawn Rd (32063)
Rates: $43-$90
(904) 259-3000
(800) 424-6423

MADEIRA BEACH

BEACH SUITES RESORT
14560 Gulf Blvd (33708)
Rates: $79-$129
(727) 319-6393
(866) 621-8300

ISLAND PARADISE COTTAGES
13115 2nd St E (33708)
Rates: n/a
(727) 395-9751

LIGHTHOUSE MOTEL & APTS
13355 Second St E (33708)
Rates: n/a
(727) 391-0015

SANDY SHORES CONDOS
12924 Gulf Blvd (33708)
Rates: $77-$101
(727) 392-1281
(877) 994-0500

SCHOONER MOTEL
14500 Gulf Blvd (33708)
Rates: $40-$249
(727) 392-5167
(800) 573-5187

SEA DAWN MOTEL
13733 Gulf Blvd (33708)
Rates: $27-$60
(727) 391-7500

SNUG HARBOR WATERFRONT BED&BREAKFAST
SEE OUR AD ON PAGE 234
13655 Gulf Blvd (33708)
Rates: $49-$265
(727) 395-9256
(866) 395-9256

STARGAZER ON THE GULF
14048 Gulf Blvd (33708)
Rates: n/a
(727) 393-7200
(800) 775-3732

WAVES MOTEL
13343 Gulf Blvd (33708)
Rates: $35-$45
(727) 391-3641

MADISON

DAYS INN
I-10 & Ex 258, SR 53 (32340)
Rates: $49-$64
(850) 973-3330
(800) 329-7466

DEERWOOD RESORT MOTEL
I-10 Exit 37 (32340)
Rates: $50-$99
(850) 973-2504

MAITLAND

HOMEWOOD SUITES
290 Southhall Lane (32751)
Rates: $129-$143
(407) 875-8777
(800) 225-5466

HOTEL ORLANDO NORTH
600 N Lake Destiny Dr (32751)
Rates: $59-$285
(407) 660-9000

MANALAPAN

RITZ CARLTON PALM BEACH
100 S Ocean Blvd (33462)
Rates: $225-$2500
(561) 533-6000
(800) 241-3333

MARATHON

FARO BLANCO MARINE RESORT
1996 Overseas Hwy (33050)
Rates: $55-$233
(305) 743-2918

GRASSY KEY BEACH MOTEL
Rt 1, Box 357 (33050)
Rates: $45-$95
(305) 743-0533

LAGOON RESORT
7200 Aviation Blvd (33050)
Rates: $49-$129
(305) 743-5463

PEACE INN
7931 US 1 Hwy (33050)
Rates: $30-$55
(305) 743-5124

PELICAN MOTEL
Rt 1 (33050)
Rates: $34-$78
(305) 289-0011

RAINBOW BEND RESORT
Rt 1 (33050)
Rates: $120-$210
(305) 289-1505
(800) 929-1505

RAMADA INN OCEANVIEW
13351 Overseas Hwy (33050)
Rates: $69-$399
(305) 743-8550
(800) 272-6232

AREA CODES - If the local number doesn't connect, check for a new area code.

SEA COVE MOTEL
12685 Overseas
Hwy (33050)
Rates: $24-$99
(305) 289-0800

**SEASHELL
BEACH**
Resort Rt 1
(33050)
Rates: $39-$49
(305) 289-0265

**SEAWARD
RESORT MOTEL**
8700 US 1 (33050)
Rates: $35-$80
(305) 754-5711

SIESTA MOTEL
7425 Overseas
Hwy (33050)
Rates: $40-$99
(305) 743-5671

MARCO ISLAND

**BOAT HOUSE
MOTEL**
1180 Edington Pl
(34145)
Rates: $66+
(239) 642-2400
(800) 528-6345

LAKESIDE INN
1551 1st Ave
(34145)
Rates: $100-$149
(239) 394-1161
(800) 729-0216

**MORAN'S BARGE
MARINA & MOTEL**
3200 SR 92
(34146)
Rates: n/a
(239) 642-1920
(800) 642-1921

MARIANNA

**BEST WESTERN
MARIANNA INN**
2086 Hwy 71
(32448)
Rates: $54-$69
(850) 526-5666
(800) 528-1234

COMFORT INN
2175 Hwy 71 S
(32446)
Rates: $55-$89
(850) 526-5600
(800) 424-6423

RAMADA LTD
4655 Hwy 90
(32448)
Rates: n/a
(850) 526-3251
(800) 272-6232

MATLACHA

**BRIDGEWATER
INN**
4331 Pine Island
Rd (33993)
Rates: $50-$245
(239) 283-2423
(800) 378-7666

MAYO

**JIM HOLLIS'
RIVER RNDVOUZ
CABINS**
Rt 2 (32066)
Rates: n/a
(904) 294-2510
(800) 533-5276

MELBOURNE

**BAYMONT INN
& SUITES**
7200 George T
Edwards Dr
(32940)
Rates: $70-$110
(321) 242-9400
(877) 229-6668

**BEST WESTERN
HARBORVIEW**
964 S Harbor City
Blvd (32901)
Rates: $54-$99
(727) 724-4422
(800) 528-1234
(888) 329-8901

**CASABLANCA
INN**
1805 N A1A Hwy
(32903)
Rates: $39-$79
(321) 728-7188
(800) 333-7273

**CRANE CREEK
INN WATER-
FRONT B&B**
907 E Melbourne
Ave (32901)
Rates: $100-$175
(321) 768-6416

DAYS INN
1423 S Harbor
City Blvd (32901)
Rates: $45-$100
(321) 727-2950
(800) 329-7466

**HILTON AT
RIALTO PLACE**
200 Rialto Pl
(32901)
Rates: $99-$249
(321) 768-0200
(800) 445-8667

HOLIDAY INN
964 S Harbor
City Blvd (32901)
Rates: $63-$80
(321) 724-4422
(800) 465-4329

**QUALITY SUITES
OCEANSIDE**
1665 SR A1A N
(32903)
Rates: $99-$219
(321) 723-4222
(800) 424-6423

RAMADA INN
420 S Harbor City
Blvd (32901)
Rates: $45-$95
(321) 723-5320
(800) 272-6232

**RIO VISTA
MOTEL**
1046 S Harbor
City Blvd (32901)
Rates: $29-$49
(321) 727-2818

SUPER 8 MOTEL
1515 S Harbor
City Blvd (32901)
Rates: $49-$79
(321) 723-4430
(800) 800-8000

MELBOURNE BEACH

**HILTON
OCEANFRONT**
3003 N Hwy A1A
(32903)
Rates: $100-$300
(321) 777-5000
(877) 843-8786

**RADISSON
SUITES HOTEL
OCEANFRONT**
3101 N Hwy A1A
(32903)
Rates: $100-$249
(321) 73-9260
(800) 333-3333

MEXICO BEACH

**OCEAN BREEZE
LODGE**
4103 Hwy 98 &
42nd St (34210)
Rates: n/a
(850) 648-4800

**PELICAN POINT
MOTEL**
4001 40th St
(34210)
Rates: n/a
(850) 648-4361

**SANDMAN
MOTEL & APTS**
2303 Hwy 98
(34210)
Rates: n/a
(850) 648-8244

MIAMI

AMERISUITES
11520 SW 88th St
(33176)
Rates: $50-$149
(305) 279-8688
(800) 833-1516

**AMERISUITES
AIRPORT**
3655 NW 82nd
Ave (33166)
Rates: $84-$159
(305) 718-8292
(800) 833-1516

**AMERISUITES
BLUE LAGOON**
6700 NW 7th St
(33126)
Rates: $109-$129
(305) 265-0144
(800) 833-1516

**BAYMONT INN
& SUITES**
3501 NW
LeJeune Rd
(33142)
Rates: n/a
(305) 871-1777
(877) 229-6668

**BAYMONT INN
& SUITES**
10821 Caribbean
Blvd (33189)
Rates: n/a
(305) 278-0001
(877) 229-6668

**BEST INN
AIRPORT**
7330 NW 36th St
(33166)
Rates: $49-$75
(305) 592-5440

**CANDLEWOOD
SUITES
AIRPORT**
8855 NW 27th St
(33172)
Rates: n/a
(305) 591-9099

**DAYS INN
AIRPORT NORTH**
4767 NW 36th St
(33166)
Rates: $49-$109
(305) 888-3661
(800) 329-7466

**FOUR
SEASONS
HOTEL-KENDALL**
1435 Brickell Ave
(33131)
Rates: $275-$525
(305) 358-3535
(800) 332-3442

**GROVE ISLE
RESORT**
4 Grove Isle Dr
(33133)
Rates: $150-$250+
(305) 858-8300
(800) 884-7683

**HAMPTON INN-
AIRPORT WEST**
3620 NW 79th
Ave (33166)
Rates: $182-$139
(305) 573-0777
(800) 426-7866

**HAMPTON INN
DOWNTOWN-
KEY BISCAYNE
AREA**
2500 Brickell Ave
(33129)
Rates: $110-$120
(305) 854-2070
(800) 426-7866

**HOLIDAY INN-
MIAMI AIRPORT
CENTRAL**
5125 NW 36th St
(33166)
Rates: n/a
(305) 887-2153
(800) 465-4329

AREA CODES - If the local number doesn't connect, check for a new area code.

HOMESTEAD STUDIO SUITES
8720 NW 33rd St (33122)
Rates: $69-$114
(305) 436-1811
(888) 782-9473

HOMESTEAD STUDIO SUITES BLUE LAGOON
6605 NW 7th St (33126)
Rates: $59-$94
(3050 260-0085
(888) 782-9473

HOMEWOOD SUITES
5500 Blue Lagoon Dr (33126)
Rates: $125-$188
(305) 261-3335
(800) 225-5466

LA QUINTA INN
7401 NW 36th St (33166)
Rates: $69-$114
(305) 599-9902
(800) 687-6667

LA QUINTA INN & SUITES AIRPORT WEST
8730 NW 27th St (33172)
Rates: $82-$129
(305) 436-0830
(800) 687-6667

MANDARIN ORIENTAL MIAMI
500 Brickell Key Dr (33131)
Rates: $420-$825
(305) 913-8288
(866) 888-6780

NEWPORT BEACHSIDE RESORT
16701 Collins Ave (33160)
Rates: $100-$249
(800) 327-5476

QUALITY INN SOUTH
14501 S Dixie Hwy (33176)
Rates: $76-$155
(305) 251-2000
(800) 424-6423

RESIDENCE INN BY MARRIOTT AIRPORT
1212 NW 82nd Ave (33126)
Rates: $99-$184
(305) 591-2211
(800) 331-3131

SHERATON BIS-CAYNE BAY HOTEL
495 Brickell Ave (33131)
Rates: $94-$329
(305) 373-6000
(800) 325-3535

SOFITEL MIAMI
5800 Blue Lagoon Dr (33126)
Rates: $69-$149
(305) 264-4888
(800) 258-4888

STAYBRIDGE SUITES-AIRPORT WEST
3265 NW 57th Ave (33172)
Rates: $99-$125
(305) 500-9100
(800) 238-8000

SUMMERFIELD SUITES
5710 Blue Lagoon Dr (33126)
Rates: $89-$149
(305) 269-1922
(800) 833-4353

TOWNEPLACE SUITES
10505 NW 36th St (33178)
Rates: $59-$159
(305) 718-4144
(800) 257-3000

WELLESLEY INN
8436 NW 36th St (33166)
Rates: $58-$72
(305) 892-4799
(800) 444-8888

MIAMI BEACH

ABBEY HOTEL SOUTH BEACH
300 21st Street (33139)
Rates: $79-$185
(305) 531-0031
(888) 612) 2239

ALEXANDER ALL-SUITE OCEANFRONT RESORT
5225 Collins Ave (33140)
Rates: $100-$250+
(305) 865-6500
(800) 327-6121

HISTORIC BREAKWATER HOTEL
940 Ocean Dr (33139)
Rates: $149-$249
(305) 532-1220
(800) 454-1220

BRIGHAM GARDENS B&B
1411 Collins Ave (33139)
Rates: $60-$130
(305) 531-1331

CADET HOTEL
1701 James Ave (33139)
Rates: n/a
(305) 672-6688
(800) 432-2338

CENTURY HOTEL
140 Ocean Dr (33139)
Rates: $85-$155
(305) 674-8855

COMFORT INN ON THE BEACH
6261 Collins Ave (33140)
Rates: $85-$165
(305) 868-1200
(800) 424-6423

CROWN PLAZA ROYAL PALM RESORT
1545 Collins Ave (33139)
Rates: $264-$454
(305) 604-5700
(800) 227-6963

EDEN ROC RENAISSANCE RESORT & SPA
4525 Collins Ave (33140)
Rates: $170-$261
(305) 531-000
(800) 327-8337

FONTAINEBLEAU HILTON RESORT
4441 Collins Ave (33140)
Rates: $239-$355
(305) 538-2000
(800) 548-8886
(800) 221-2424

HOTEL OCEAN
1230 Ocean Dr (33139)
Rates: $179-$600
(305) 672-2579
(800) 783-1725

THE KENT HOTEL
1131 Collins Ave (33139)
Rates: $130-$165
(305) 604-5068

LOEWS MIAMI BEACH HOTEL
1601 Collins Ave (33139)
Rates: $279-$489
(305) 604-1601
(800) 235-6397

THE MARLIN HOTEL
1200 Collins Ave (33139)
Rates: n/a
(305) 604-5063

OCEAN FRONT HOTEL
1230-38 Ocean Dr (33139)
Rates: $125-$335
(305) 672-2579
(800) 783-1725

OCEAN SPRAY MIAMI BEACH
4130 Collins Ave (33139)
Rates: $50-$149
(305) 535-5300

REGAL HOTEL-SOUTH BEACH
436 Ocean Dr (33140)
Rates: $95-$155
(305) 532-7093

SEACOAST SUITE HOTEL
5151 Collins Ave (33140)
Rates: n/a
(305) 865-5152
(800) 523-3671

SUITES OF DORCHESTER
1850 Collins Ave (33139)
Rates: $150-$250+
(305) 531-1443
(800) 327-4739

THE TIDES HOTEL
1220 Ocean Dr (33139)
Rates: $420-$3000
(305) 604-5070

VILLA CAPRI ALL SUITES
3010 Collins Ave (33139)
Rates: n/a
(305) 531-7742

WALDORF TOWERS HOTEL
860 Ocean Dr (33139)
Rates: $109-$219
(305) 531-7684

MIAMI LAKES

WELLESLEY INN
7925 NW 154th St (33016)
Rates: n/a
(305) 821-8274
(800) 444-8888

MAIMI SPRINGS

BAYMONT INN & SUITES
3501 NW Le Jeune Rd (33142)
Rates: $99-$109
(305) 871-1777
(877) 229-6668

COMFORT INN & SUITES-MIAMI AIRPORT
5301 NW 36th St (33166)
Rates: $89-$200
(305) 871-6000
(800) 424-6423

RED ROOF INN MIAMI AIRPORT
3401 NW Le Jeune Rd (33142)
Rates: $70-$100
(305) 871-4221
(800) 843-7663

SLEEP INN MIAMI AIRPORT
105 Fairways Dr (33166)
Rates: $69-$159
(305) 871-7553
(800) 424-6423

MICANOPY
KNIGHTS INN
Rt 2, Box 804 (32667)
Rates: $35-$75
(352) 466-3163
(800) 843-5644

SHADY OAK BED&BREAKFAST
203 Cholokka Blvd, Bx 236 (32667)
Rates: n/a
(352) 466-3476

MILTON
COMFORT INN
4962 SR 87 S (32583)
Rates: $50-$110
(850) 623-1511
(800) 424-6423

RED CARPET INN
4905 Hwy 87 S (32583)
Rates: n/a
(850) 626-7631
(800) 251-1962

MOUNT DORA
LAKESIDE INN
100 N Alexander St (32757)
Rates: $169
(352) 383-4101
(800) 556-5016

NAPLES
BAYMONT INN & SUITES
185 Bedzel Cir (33942)
Rates: $84-$102
(239) 352-8400
(877) 229-6668

CLARION INN & SUITES AT PARK SHORE
4055 Tamiami Tr N (34103)
Rates: $95-$255
(239) 649-5500
(800) 424-6423

COMFORT INN & EXECUTIVE SUITES
3860 Tollgate Blvd (34114)
Rates: $54-$179
(239) 353-9500
(800) 424-6423

HAWTHORN SUITES
3557 Pine Ridge Rd (34109)
Rates: n/a
(239) 593-1300
(800) 527-1133

HOLIDAY INN
1100 Tamiami Tr N (34102)
Rates: n/a
(239) 263-3434
(800) 465-4329

HOTEL ESCALANTE
290 5th Ave S (34102)
Rates: 150-$280
(239) 659-3466
(877) 485-3466

NAPLES BATH & TENNIS CLUB
4995 Airport Rd N (33942)
Rates: $90-$235
(239) 261-5777

QUALITY INN & SUITES GOLF RESORT
4100 Golden Gate Pkwy (34116)
Rates: $79-$209
(239) 455-1010
(800) 424-6423

RESIDENCE INN BY MARRIOTT
4075 Tamiami Tr N (34103)
Rates: $100-$249
(239) 659-1300
(800) 331-3131

STAYBRIDGE SUITES-GULF COAST
4805 Tamiami Tr N (34103)
Rates: $50-$149
(239) 643-8002
(800) 238-8000

WATERSIDE VILLAS
2864 Gulfview Dr (33942)
Rates: $525-$740/ Weekly
(239) 732-2007

WORLD TENNIS CENTER & RESORT
4800 Airport Rd (33942)
Rates: $50-$249
(239) 263-1900
(800) 292-6662

NAVARRE
COMFORT INN
8700 Navarre Pkwy (32566)
Rates: $59-$139
(850) 939-1761
(800) 424-6423

NEW PORT RICHEY
ECONO LODGE
7631 Hwy 19 N (34652)
Rates: $50-$90
(727) 845-4990
(800) 424-6423
(800) 889-9083

MALIBU RESORT MOTEL
17001 Gulf Blvd N (34652)
Rates: n/a
(727) 391-4000
(800) 780-1150

RAMADA INN
5015 Hwy 19 N (34652)
Rates: n/a
(727) 849-8551
(800) 272-6232

NEW SMYRNA BEACH
BUENA VISTA MOTEL
500 N Causeway (32169)
Rates: $35-$60
(386) 428-5565

COQUINA WHARF B&B
704 S Riverside Dr (32169)
Rates: $82-$250
(866) 428-9458

LAPPONIA MOTEL
1157 N Dixie Fwy (32169)
Rates: n/a
(386) 423-3812
(888) 253-8506

LITTLE RIVER INN B&B
532 N Riverside Dr (32168)
Rates: $50-$249
(904) 424-0100
(888) 424-0102

SMYRNA MOTEL
1050 N Dixie Frwy (32168)
Rates: $45-$75
(386) 428-2495

NICEVILLE
COMFORT INN
101 Hwy 85 N (32578)
Rates: $80-$120
(850) 678-8077
(800) 424-6423

HOLIDAY INN EXP
106 Bayshore Dr (32578)
Rates: n/a
(850) 678-9131
(800) 465-4329

NOKOMIS
ROYAL COACHMAN RESORT
1070 Laurel Rd E (34275)
Rates: n/a
(941) 488-9674

OCALA
COMFORT INN
4040 W Silver Springs Blvd (34482)
Rates: $65-$130
(352) 629-8850
(800) 424-6423

DAYS INN
3620 W Silver Springs Blvd (34475)
Rates: $40-$95
(352) 629-0091
(800) 329-7466

DAYS INN
3811 NW Bonnie Heath Rd (34482)
Rates: $50-$135
(352) 629-7041
(800) 329-7466

LA QUINTA INN
3530 SW 36th Ave (34474)
Rates: $75-$109
(352) 861-1137
(800) 687-6667

MOTOR INNS MOTEL & RV RESORT
3601 W Silver Spgs Blvd (34475)
Rates: n/a
(352) 629-6902

QUALITY INN OCALA PLAZA
3721 W Silver Springs Blvd (34470)
Rates: $53-$98
(352) 629-0381
(800) 424-6423

RAMADA INN
3810 NW Bonnie Heath Blvd (34482)
Rates: $55-$85
(352) 732-3131
(800) 272-6232

SOUTHLAND MOTEL
1260 E Silver Sprgs Blvd (34470)
Rates: $19-$39
(352) 351-0113

OCOEE
BEST WESTERN TURNPIKE WEST-ORLANDO
10945 W Colonial Dr (34761)
Rates: $69-$84
(407 656 5050
(800) 528-1234
(800) 327-5429

OKEECHOBEE
WANTA LINGA MOTEL
3225 SE Hwy 441 (34974)
Rates: n/a
(863) 763-1020
(800) 754-0428

OCOEE

**BEST WESTERN
TURNPIKE WEST**
10945 W Colonial
Dr (34761)
Rates: $79-$89
(407) 656-5050
(800) 528-1234

**RED ROOF INN
WEST**
11241 W Colonial
Dr (34761)
Rates: $58-$97
(407) 347-0140
(800) 843-7663

OLD TOWN

**SUWANNEE
GABLES MOTEL**
HC 3, Box 208
(32680)
Rates: $48-$115
(352) 542-7752

ORANGE CITY

DAYS INN
2501 N Volusia
Ave (32763)
Rates: $60-$250
(386) 775-4522
(800) 329-7466

ORANGE PARK

**CLUB
CONTINENTAL
SUITES**
2143 Astor St
(32073)
Rates: $100-$240
(904) 264-6070
(800) 877-6070

COMFORT INN
341 Park Ave
(32073)
Rates: $69-$129
(904) 264-3297
(800) 424-6423

DAYS INN
4280 Eldridge
Loop (32073)
Rates: $69-$350
(904) 269-8887
(800) 329-7466

ORLANDO

BAYMONT INN
2051 Consulate Dr
(32837)
Rates: $64
(407) 240-0500
(877) 229-6668

**CLARION HOTEL
AIRPORT**
3835 McCoy Rd,
Bldg A (32812)
Rates: $59-$89
(407) 859-2711
(800) 424-6423

**CLARION HOTEL
UNIVERSAL**
7299 Universal
Blvd (32819)
Rates: $69-$109
(407) 351-5009
(800) 424-6423

**COMFORT INN
NORTH**
830 Lee Rd
(32810)
Rates: $65-$99
(407) 629-4000
(800) 424-6423

**COMFORT
SUITES-UCF/
RESEARCH PARK**
12101 Challenger
Pkwy (32826)
Rates: $69-$199
(407) 737-7303
(800) 424-6423

**THE COURTYARD
AT LAKE
LUCERNE**
211 N Lucerne
Cir E (32801)
Rates: n/a
(407) 648-5188
(800) 444-5289

**DAYS INN-
DOWNTOWN
DISNEY**
12799 Apopka-
Vineland Rd
(32836)
Rates: $79-$119
(407) 239-4441
(800) 329-7466

**DAYS INN
MAINGATE-
UNIVERSAL
STUDIOS**
5827 Caravan Ct
(32819)
Rates: $35-$109
(407) 351-3800
(800) 329-7466
(800) 327-2111

**DAYS INN-
NORTH OF
UNIVERSAL
STUDIOS**
2500 W 33rd St
(32839)
Rates: $39-$99
(407) 841-3731
(800) 329-7466

**DAYS INN-WEST
OF UNIVERSAL
STUDIOS**
7335 San Lake Rd
(32819)
Rates: $32-$109
(407) 351-1900
(800) 328-7466

**DAYS INN-
SEA WORLD**
9990 Int'l Dr
(32819)
Rates: $39-$109
(407) 352-8700
(800) 329-7466

**DELTA ORLANDO
RESORT**
5715 Major Blvd
(32819)
Rates: $118-$158
(407) 351-3340
(800) 634-4763
(800) 268-1133

**ECONO LODGE
AIRPORT**
3835 McCoy Rd
(32812)
Rates: $39-$99
(407) 581-1394
(800) 424-6423

FLORIDA CONDOS
3905 Coronation
Ct (32839)
Rates: $46-$90
(407) 425-2999
(800) 247-2999

HOLIDAY INN EXP
5323 Int'l Dr
(32819)
Rates: n/a
(407) 351-4430
(800) 465-4329

**HOLIDAY INN
INTERNATIONAL
DRIVE RESORT**
6515 Int'l Dr
(32819)
Rates: $89-$225
(407) 351-3500
(800) 465-4329

**HOLIDAY INN-
MAIN GATE/
UNIVERSAL
STUDIOS**
5905 Kirkman Rd
(32819)
Rates: $89-$109
(407) 351-3333
(800) 465-4329

**HOMES 4U -
DISNEY AREA**
1020 Elmwood St
Suite 6 (32801)
Rates: $100-$149
(407) 898-9758
(888) 746-5446

**HOWARD
JOHNSON
UNIVERSAL
GATEWAY**
7050 Kirkman Rd
(32819)
Rates: $64-$102
(407) 351-2000
(800) 446-4656

**LA QUINTA INN
AIRPORT**
7931 Daetwyler
Dr (32812)
Rates: $85-$105
(407) 857-9215
(800) 687-6667

**LA QUINTA INN
& SUITES
AIRPORT NORTH**
7160 N Frontage
Rd (32812)
Rates: $102-$122
(407) 240-5000
(800) 687-6667

**LA QUINTA INN
& SUITES-UCF**
11805 Research
Pkwy (32812)
Rates: $50-$99
(407) 737-6075
(800) 687-6667

**LA QUINTA INN-
INT'L DRIVE**
8300 Jamaican Ct
(32819)
Rates: $75-$105
(407) 351-1660
(800) 687-6667

MASTERS INN
8222 Jamaican St
(32819)
Rates: $69-$89
(407) 345-1172

**MOTEL 6
UNIVERSAL
STUDIOS**
5909 American
Way (32819)
Rates: $39-$50
(407) 351-6500
(800) 466-8356

**MOTEL 6-
WINTER PARK**
5300 Adanson Rd
(32810)
Rates: $36-$40
(407) 647-1444
(800) 466-8356

QUALITY INN
7600 Int'l Dr
(32819)
Rates: $39-$99
(407) 996-1600
(800) 424-6423
(800) 825-7600

**QUALITY INN
PLAZA**
9000 Int'l Dr
(32819)
Rates: $39-$89
(407) 345-8585
(800) 999-8585
(800) 424-6423

**QUALITY SUITES
UNIVERSAL
ORLANDO**
7400 Canada Ave
(32819)
Rates: $69-$129
(407) 363-0332
(800) 424-6423

RAMADA INN
5858 Int'l Dr
(32819)
Rates: n/a
(407) 351-4410
(800) 272-6232

RED HORSE INN
5825 Int'l Dr
(32819)
Rates: $45-$99
(407) 351-4100
(877) 936-4100

**RENAISSANCE
ORLANDO
RESORT AT
SEAWORLD**
6677 Sea Harbor
Dr (32821)
Rates: $100-$200
(407) 352-5555
(800) 327-6677

AREA CODES - If the local number doesn't connect, check for a new area code.

RODEWAY INN
6327 Int'l Dr
(32819)
Rates: $40-$80
(407) 996-4444
(800) 424-6423
(800) 999-6327

SHERATON SAFARI HOTEL
12205 Apopka-Wineland Rd
(32836)
Rates: $50-$149
(407) 239-0444
(800) 325-3535
(800) 423-3297

SILVER LEAF SUITES
5630 Monterey Dr (32811)
Rates: $79-$119
(407) 295-0883

UNIVERSAL'S HARD ROCK HOTEL
5800 Universal Blvd (32819)
Rates: $150-$275
(407) 503-2000
(800) 232-7827
(888) 856-1955

UNIVERSAL'S PORTOFINO BAY A LOEWS HOTEL
5601 Universak Blvd (32819)
Rates: $250+
(407) 503-1000
(800) 232-7827
(888) 856-1955

UNIVERSAL'S ROYAL PACIFIC A LOEWS HOTEL
6300 Hollywood Way (32819)
Rates: $250+
(407) 503-3000
(800) 232-7827
(888) 856-1955

VERANDA BED & BREAKFAST INN
115 N Summerlin Ave (32801)
Rates: $46-$90
(407) 849-0321
(800) 420-6822

THE WESTIN GRAND BOHEMIAN
325 S Orange Ave (32801)
Rates: n/a
(407) 313-9000
(866) 663-0024

ORMOND BEACH
COMFORT INN ON THE BEACH
507 S Atlantic Ave (32176)
Rates: $75-$200
(386) 677-8550
(800) 424-6423
(800) 456-8550

DAYS INN
1608 N US Hwy 1 (32174)
Rates: $45-$250
(386) 672-7341
(800) 329-7466

DRIFTWOOD BEACH MOTEL
657 S Atlantic Ave (32176(
Rates: $45-$175
(386) 677-1331
(800) 490-8935
z
JAMESON INN
175 Interchange Blvd (32174)
Rates: $49-$104
(386) 672-3675
(800) 526-3766

OSPREY
RAMADA INN
1660 S Tamiami Tr (34229)
Rates: $59-$129
(941) 966-2121
(800) 272-6232

PALATKA
THE OAKS MOTEL
Rt 3, Box 50,
Hwy 17 (32131)
Rates: $50-$89
(904) 328-1545

PALM BAY
JAMESON INN
890 Palm Bay Rd NE (32905)
Rates: $49-$104
(321) 725-2932
(800) 526-3766

MOTEL 6
1170 Malabar Rd
(32909)
Rates: $36-$52
(407) 951-8222
(800) 466-8356

PALM BEACH
THE BRADLEY HOUSE
280 Sunset Ave (33480)
Rates: n/a
(561) 832-7050
(800) 822-4116

BRAZILIAN COURT HOTEL
301 Australian Ave (33480)
Rates: $100-$170
(561) 655-7740
(800) 552-0355

CHESTERFIELD HOTEL
363 Cocoanut Row (33480)
Rates: $229-$450
(561) 659-5800
(800) 243-7871

FOUR SEASONS OCEAN GRAND
2800 S Ocean Blvd (33480)
Rates: $385-$660
(561) 582-2800
(800) 432-2335
(800) 332-3442

HEART OF PALM BEACH HOTEL
160 Royal Palm Way (33480)
Rates: $149-$259
(561) 655-5600
(800) 523-5377

HILTON PALM BEACH OCEANFRONT RESORT
2842 S Ocean Blvd (33480)
Rates: $60-$250+
(800) 445-8667
(800) 433 1718

PLAZA INN
215 Brazilian Ave (33480)
Rates: $125-$285
(561) 832-8666
(800) 233-2632

PALM BEACH GARDENS
DOUBLETREE HOTEL
4431 PGA Blvd (33410)
Rates: $129-$289
(561) 622-2260
(800) 222-8733

INNS OF AMERICA
4123 Northlake Blvd (33410)
Rates: $65-$139
(407) 626-4918
(800) 826-0778

PALM BEACH SHORES
BEST WESTERN SEASPRAY INN-SINGER ISLAND
123 S Ocean Dr (33404)
Rates: $60-$180
(561) 844-0233
(800) 528-1234
(800) 330-0233

THE SAILFISH MARINA & RESORT
98 Lake St (33404)
Rates: $100-$149
(561) 844-1724
(800) 446-4577

PALM COAST
MICROTEL INN & SUITES
16 Kingswood Dr (32137)
Rates: $59-$199
(386) 445-8976
(888) 771-7171

PALM COAST VILLAS
5454 N Oceanshore Blvd (32137)
Rates: $54-$74
(386) 445-3525

PALM HARBOR
BEST WESTERN PALM HARBOR HOTEL
37611 US 19 N (34684)
Rates: $69-$175
(727) 942-0358
(800) 528-1234

KNIGHTS INN
34106 US 19 N (34684)
Rates: $35-$99
(727) 789-2002
(800) 843-5644

RED ROOF INN
32000 US 19 N (34684)
Rates: $45-$96
(727) 786-2529
(800) 843-7663

PALMETTO
BAYSHORE INN
3512 US 41 N (34221)
Rates: $35-$50
(941) 722-7761

LEE'S MOTEL
3311 US Hwy 41 N (34221)
Rates: $30-$50
(941) 729-2676

PELICAN PERCH APARTMENTS
4111 10th St W (34221)
Rates: $50-$100
(941) 729-6653

SEA INN B&B
515 US Hwy 19 N (34221)
Rates: $50-$100
(941) 721-0365

PANAMA CITY
DAYS INN
301 W 23rd St (32405)
Rates: $40-$115
(850) 785-0001
(800) 329-7466

DAYS INN BAYSIDE
711 W Beach Dr (32401)
Rates: $44-$180
(850) 763-4622
(800) 329-7466

DAYS INN CENTRAL
4111 W Hwy 98 (32401)
Rates: $45-$155
(850) 784-1777
(800) 329-7466

ECONO LODGE
4411 W Hwy 98
(32401)
Rates: $35-$150
(850) 785-2700
(800) 424-6423

HOWARD JOHNSON
4601 W Hwy 98
(32401)
Rates: $59-$125
(850) 785-0222
(800) 446-4656

LA QUINTA INN & SUITES
1030 E 23rd St
(32405)
Rates: $93-$122
(850) 914-0022
(800) 687-6667

SUPER 8 MOTEL
207 N Hwy 231
(32405)
Rates: $45-$105
(850) 784-1988
(800) 800-8000

PANAMA CITY BEACH

ADMIRAL IMPERIAL INN MOTEL
16819 Front
Beach Rd (32413)
Rates: n/a
(850) 234-2142

COCONUT GROVE MOTOR INN
9725 Front Beach
Rd (32407)
Rates: $35-$99
(850) 234-3366
(800) 527-6980

CONDO WORLD
8815-A Thomas
Dr (32408)
Rates: $50-$300
(850) 234-5564
(800) 824-5411

DOLPHIN INN AT PINEAPPLE BEACH RESORT
19935 Front
Beach Rd (32413)
Rates: $40-$149
(850) 234-1788
(800) 234-1788

EDGEWATER BEACH RESORT
11212 Front
Beach Rd (32407)
Rates: n/a
(850) 235-4044
(800) 874-8686

PANAMA PALMS MOTEL
5607 Thomas Dr
(32408)
Rates: n/a
(850) 234-2806
(877)310-2267

RIVIERA MOTEL
21504 W Front
Beach Rd (32413)
Rates: $50-$135
(850) 234-2150

SURF HIGH INN ON THE GULF
10611 Front
Beach Rd (32407)
Rates: $35-$61
(850) 234-2129

PEMBROKE PINES

GRAND PALMS GOLF & COUNTRY CLUB RESORT
110 Grand Palms
Dr (33027)
Rates: $135-$155
(954) 431-8800

PENSACOLA

ASHTON INN & SUITES
4 New Warrington
Rd (32506)
Rates: $55-$85
(850) 454-0280

BEST VALUE INN & SUITES
8240 N Davis
Hwy (32514)
Rates: $49-$79
(850) 479-1099
(800) 962-9945

COMFORT INN
8080 N Davis
Hwy (32514)
Rates: $49-$159
(850) 484-8070
(800) 424-6423

COMFORT INN-N.A.S. CORRY
3 New
Warrington Rd
(32506)
Rates: $58-$100
(850) 455-3233
(800) 424-6423

DAYS INN HISTORIC DOWNTOWN
710 Palafox St
(32501)
Rates: $42-$150
(850) 438-4922
(800) 329-7466

DAYS INN NORTH
7051 Pensacola
Blvd (32505)
Rates: $49-$99
(850) 476-9090
(800) 329-7466

HOLIDAY INN
7200 Plantation
Rd (32504)
Rates: $65
(850) 474-0100
(800) 465-4329

HOSPITALITY INN
6900 Pensacola
Blvd (32506)
Rates: $55-$120
(850) 477-2333
(800) 321-0052

LA QUINTA INN
7750 N Davis
Hwy (32514)
Rates: $60-$99
(850) 474-0411
(800) 687-6667

MOTEL 6 EAST
7226 Plantation
Rd (32504)
Rates: $33-$51
(850) 474-1060
(800) 466-8356

MOTEL 6 NORTH
7827 N Davis
Hwy (32514)
Rates: $31-$53
(850) 476-5386
(800) 466-8356

QUALITY INN
6550 Pensacola
Blvd (32505)
Rates: $70-$75
(850) 477-0711
(800) 424-6423

RAMADA INN BAYVIEW
7601 Scenic Hwy
(32504)
Rates $69-$150
(850) 477-7156
(800) 272-6232

RAMADA LTD
8060 Lavalle Way
(32526)
Rates: $40-$100
(850) 944-0333
(800) 272-6232

RED ROOF INN
7340 Plantation
Rd (32504)
Rates: $46-$60
(850) 476-7960
(800) 843-7663

RESIDENCE INN BY MARRIOTT
7230 Plantation
Rd (32524)
Rates: $109
(850) 479-1000
(800) 331-3131

TRAVELODGE INN & SUITES
6950 Pensacola
Blvd (32505)
Rates: $65-$150
(850) 473-0222
(800) 578-7878

PENSACOLA BEACH

BEACHSIDE RESORT
14 Via De Luna
(32561)
Rates: $69-$229
(850) 932-5331
(800) BEACH-16

COMFORT INN
40 Fort Pickens
Rd (32561)
Rates: $69-$185
(850) 934-5400
(800) 424-6423

PERRY

BEST BUDGET INN
2220 S Byron
Butler Pkwy
(32347)
Rates: $38-$46
(850) 584-6231
(800) 458-7215

RAMADA INN
2277 S Byron
Butler Pkwy
(32347)
Rates: $49-$89
(850) 584-5311
(800) 329-7466

GANDY MOTOR LODGE
2239 S Byron
Butler Pkwy
(32347)
Rates: n/a
(850) 584-4947

SOUTHERN INN MOTEL
2238 S Byron
Butler Pkwy
(32347)
Rates: $30-$45
(850) 584-4221

PINELLAS PARK

DAYS INN
9359 US Hwy
19 N (34665)
Rates: $45-$79
(727) 577-3838
(800) 329-7466

HORSE & BUGGY B&B INN
6125 62nd Ave N
(33781)
Rates: n/a
(727) 547-2646
(888) 837-1770

LA QUINTA INN
7500 US 19 N
(34665)
Rates: $69-$100
(727) 545-5611
(800) 687-6667

PLANT CITY

COMFORT INN
2003 S Frontage
Rd (33563)
Rates: $55-$110
(813) 707-6000
(800) 424-6423

RAMADA INN PLANTATION HOUSE
2011 N Wheeler
St Plant City
(33566)
Rates: $64-$130
(813) 752-3141
(800) 272-6232

DAYS INN
2277 S Byron

PLANTATION

HOLIDAY INN
1711 N University
Dr (33322)
Rates: $89-$129
(954) 472-5600
(800) 465-4329

LA QUINTA INN
8101 Peters Rd
(33324)
Rates: $89-$134
(954) 476-6047
(800) 687-6667

**RESIDENCE INN
BY MARRIOTT**
130 N University
Dr (33324)
Rates: $119-$189
(954) 723-0300
(800) 331-3131

**SHERATON
SUITES**
311 N University
Dr (33324)
Rates: $199-$550
(954) 424-3300
(800) 325-3535

**STAYBRIDGE
SUITES**
410 N Pine Island
Rd (33324)
Rates: $105-$195
(954) 577-9696
(800) 465-4329

WELLESLEY INN
7901 SW 6th St
(33324)
Rates: $79-$139
(954) 473-8257
(800) 444-8888

PLANTATION KEY

**TROPIC VISTA
MOTEL**
90701 Overseas
Hwy (33070)
Rates: $38-$95
(305) 852-8799

POMPANO BEACH

**CARIB TERRACE
MOTEL**
552 N Ocean
Blvd (33062)
Rates: n/a
(954) 941-9130

**COTTAGES BY
THE OCEAN**
3309 SE Third St
(33062)
Rates: $50-$149
(954) 956-8999

DAYS INN
1411 NW 31st
Ave (33069)
Rates: $34-$109
(954) 972-3700
(800) 329-7466

**GLENDORI APTS.
OF POMP BEACH**
2441 NE 10th Ct
(33062)
Rates: n/a
(954) 781-0311

MOTEL 6
1201 NW 31st
Ave (33069)
Rates: $39-$67
(954) 977-8011
(800) 466-8356

**SEA CASTLE
RESORT MOTEL**
730 N Ocean
Blvd (33062)
Rates: $48-$149
(954) 941-2570
(800) 331-4666

**WELLESLEY INN
& SUITES**
1401 SW 15th
Ave (33062)
Rates: $67-$118
(954) 783-1050
(800) 444-8888

PONTE VEDRA BEACH

**SAWGRASS
MARRIOTT
RESORT &
BEACH CLUB**
1000 PGA Tour
Blvd (32082)
Rates: $135-$259
(904)285-7777
(800) 228-9290
(800) 457-GOLF

PORT CHARLOTTE

**BANANA BAY
WATERFRONT
MOTEL**
23285 Bay Shore
Rd (33980)
Rates: n/a
(941) 743-4441

DAYS INN
1941 Tamiami Tr
(33948)
Rates: $49-$144
(941) 627-8900
(800) 329-7466

PORT RICHEY

COMFORT INN
11810 US 19
(34668)
Rates: $50-$94
(727) 863-3336
(800) 424-6423

PORT ST. LUCIE

HOLIDAY INN
10120 S Federal
Hwy (34952)
Rates: $50-$230
(772) 337-2200
(800) 465-4329

PORT SALERNO

**PIRATES COVE
RESORT/MARINA**
4307 SE Bayview
St (34992)
Rates: $80-$130
(561) 287-2500
(800) 332-1414

PUNTA GORDA

**BEST WESTERN
WATERFRONT**
300 Retta
Esplanade (33950)
Rates: $69-$138
(941) 639-1165
(800) 528-1234
(800) 525-1022

**HOLIDAY INN-
HARBORSIDE**
33 Tamiami Tr
(33950)
Rates: $69-$250
(941) 639-2167
(800) 465-4329

MOTEL 6
9300 Knights Dr
(33950)
Rates: $32-$68
(941) 639-9585
(800) 466-8356

QUINCY

**ALLISON HOUSE
BED & BREAKFAST**
215 N Madison St
(32351)
Rates: $75-$120
(850) 875-2511
(888) 904-2511

HOLIDAY INN EXP
75 Spooner Rd
(32351)
Rates: n/a
(850) 875-2500
(800) 465-4329

**HOWARD
JOHNSON EXP**
500 W Orange
Ave (32351)
Rates: n/a
(800) 446-4656

**QUINCY
MOTOR LODGE**
368 E Jefferson
(32351)
Rates: n/a
(850) 627-8929

**WHIPPOORWILL
SPRTSMNS LDG**
Rt 3 (32351)
Rates: n/a
(850) 875-2605

REDINGTON BEACH

**ROYAL ORLEANS
CONDOTEL**
16333 Gulf Blvd
(33708)
Rates: n/a
(727) 391-4456

RIDGE MANOR

**RIDGE MANOR
MOTEL**
5205 Treiman
Blvd (33523)
Rates: $34-$49
(352) 583-2109

ROYAL PALM BEACH

ROYAL INN
675 Royal Palm
Beach Blvd
(33411)
Rates: $40-$99
(800) 428-5389

RUSKIN

**MARINER'S CLUB
BAHIA BEACH
RESORT**
611 Destiny Dr
(33570)
Rates: $99-$129
(813) 645-3291
(800) 327-2773

SAFETY HARBOR

**SAFETY HARBOR
RESORT & SPA**
105 N Bayshore
Dr (34695)
Rates: $102-$195
(727) 726-1161
(888) 237-8772

ST.AUGUSTINE

**BEST WESTERN
ST. AUGUSTINE**
2445 SR 16
(32093)
Rates: $49-$110
(904) 829-1999
(800) 528-1234

**CHANNEL
MARKER 71/
BARRIER ISLAND
B&B**
7601 A1A S
(32080)
Rates: n/a
(866) 461-4287
(888) 481 9819

**THE CONCH
HOUSE MARINA
RESORT**
57 Comares Ave
(32085)
Rates: $50-$250+
(904) 829-8646
(800) 940 6256

COZY INN
202 San Marco
Ave (32084)
Rates: $45-$99
(904) 824-2449

**DAYS INN
HISTORIC**
2800 N Ponce de
Leon Blvd
(32084)
Rates: $51-$149
(904) 829-6581
(800) 329-7466
(800) 331-9995

DAYS INN
2560 SR 16
(32092)
Rates: $45-$150
(904) 824-4341
(800) 329-7466
(800) 584-1473

LA QUINTA INN
1300 Ponce de
Leon Blvd
(32084)
Rates: $49-$150
(904) 824-3383
(800) 687-6667

**OCEAN CLUB
CONDOS I**
11 Dondanville
Rd (32084)
Rates: $100-$249
(904) 471-6852
(888) 336-7500

**OCEAN CLUB
CONDOS II**
21 Dondanville
Rd (32084)
Rates: $100-$249
(904) 461-3352
(888) 336-7500

**QUALITY HOTEL
BEACHFRONT**
300 A1A Beach
Blvd (32084)
Rates: $60-$140
(904) 471-2575
(800) 424-6423
(800) 752-4037

RAMADA LIMITED
2535 State
Road16 (32092)
Rates: $54-$145
(904) 829-5643
(800) 272-6232

**ST. FRANCIS
INN B&B**
279 St. George St
(32084)
Rates: $119-$229
(904) 824-6068
(800) 824-6062

SCOTTISH INN
110 San Marco
Ave (32084)
Rates: $45-$100
(904) 824-2871

ST. AUGUSTINE BEACH

**BEACHER'S
LODGE**
6970 A1A S
(32080)
Rates: $50-$240
(904) 471-8849
(800) 527-8849

ECONO LODGE
2365 Hwy 16
(32084)
Rates: $45-$135
(904) 824-4306
(800) 424-6423

**HOLIDAY INN
BEACHSIDE**
860 A1A Beach
Blvd (32084)
Rates: $110-$130
(904) 471-2555
(800) 465-4329
(800) 626-7263

**SUPER 8 BY THE
BEACH**
311 A1A Beach
Blvd (32080)
Rates: $59-$109
(9040 471-2330
(800) 800-8000

ST. CLOUD

BUDGET INN
602 13th St
(34769)
Rates: $35-$45
(407) 892-2858

ST. GEORGE ISLAND

**ANCHOR
VACATION
PROPERTIES**
119 Franklin Blvd
(32328)
Rates: n/a
(904) 927-2625
(800) 824-0416

**PRUDENTIAL
RESORT/VAC
RENTALS**
123 Gulf Beach
Dr W (32328)
Rates: $160-$760/
Two nights
(904) 927-2666
(800) 332-5196

ST. MARKS

**SWEET
MAGNOLIA INN**
803 Port Leon Dr
(32355)
Rates: $50-$125
(850) 925-7670
(800) 779-5214

ST. PETE BEACH

ALL SUITE VILLAS
3751 Gulf Blvd
(33706)
Rates: n/a
(727) 367-7837
(800) 664-7115

BAY PALM RESORT
4237 Gulf Blvd
(33706)
Rates: $55-$99
(727) 360-7642

**BAYVIEW PLAZA
WATERFRONT
RESORT**
4321 Gulf Blvd
(33706)
Rates: n/a
(800) 257-8998

**DON CESAR
BEACH RESORT-
A LOEWS HOTEL**
3400 Gulf Blvd
(33706)
Rates: $219-$499
(727) 360-1881
(800) 235-6397

**LAMARA MOTEL
APARTMENTS**
520 73rd Ave
(33706)
Rates: $50-$99
(727) 360-7521
(800) 211 5108

ST. PETERS- BURG

**HILTON HOTEL
BEACHFRONT**
333 1st St S
(33711)
Rates: $110-$220
(727) 894-5000
(800) 445-8667
(800) 944-5500

LA QUINTA INN
4999 34th St N
(33714)
Rates: $69-$95
(727) 527-8421
(800) 687-6667

**LA VERANDA
B&B**
111 5th Ave N
(33701)
Rates: $50-$275
(727) 824-9997
(800) 484-8423,
Ext. 8417

**MANSION
HOUSE B&B**
105 5th Ave NE
(33701)
Rates: $99-$220
(727) 821-9391

**RAMADA INN
MIRAGE**
5005 34th St N
(33714)
Rates: $49-$85
(727) 525-1181
(800) 272-6232

**VALLEY FORGE
MOTEL**
6825 Central Ave
(33710)
Rates: $35-$99
(727) 345-0135

**VINOY HOUSE
HISTORIC B&B**
532 Beach Dr
(33701)
Rates: $140-$255
(727) 432-6152
(866) 846-6947

SANFORD

**BEST WESTERN
MARINA HOTEL**
530 N Palmetto
Ave (32771)
Rates: $56-$89
(407) 323-1910
(800) 528-1234
(800) 290-1910

DAYS INN
4650 SR 46 W
(32771)
Rates: $55-$115
(407) 323-6500
(800) 329-7466

**ROSE
COTTAGE
INN B&B**
1301 Park Ave
(32771)
Rates: n/a
(407) 323-9448

SANIBEL ISLAND

ANCHOR INN
1245 Periwinkle
Way (33957)
Rates: $50-$240
(239) 395-9688
(866) 469-9543

**BEACH ROAD
INN**
764 Beach Rd
(33957)
Rates: $50-$280
(239) 395-1314
(877) 501-7600

**BEACHVIEW
COTTAGES**
3325 W Gulf Dr
(33957)
Rates: n/a
(239) 472-1202
(800) 860-0532

**CARIBE BEACH
RESORT**
2669 W Gulf Dr
(33957)
Rates: $100-$249
(941) 472-1166
(800) 330-1593

**THE CASTAWAYS
AT BLIND PASS**
6460 Sanibel-
Capitva Rd
(33957)
Rates: $100-$295
(239) 472-1252
(800) 375-0152

**KONA KAI
MOTEL &
COTTAGES**
1539 Periwinkle
Way (33957)
Rates: $50-$235
(239) 472-1001
(800) 820-2385

**PERIWINKLE
COTTAGES OF
SANIBEL**
1431 Jamaica Dr
(33957)
Rates: $79-$249
(239) 472-1880

**SIGNAL INN
BEACH &
RACQUETBALL**
1811 Olde Middle
Gulf Dr (33957)
Rates: $100-$300
(239) 472-4690
(800) 992-4690

AREA CODES - If the local number doesn't connect, check for a new area code.

SUNSHINE ISLAND INN
642 E Gulf Dr (33957)
Rates: $100-$249
(239) 395-2500
(239) 395-2500

TROPICAL WINDS MOTEL & COTTAGES
4819 Tradewinds & Jamaica Dr (33957)
Rates: $119-$269
(239) 472-1765
(866) 646-1731

WATERSIDE INN ON THE BEACH
3033 W Gulf Dr (33957)
Rates: $184-$270
(239) 472-1345
(800) 741-6166

SARASOTA

AMERICINN HOTEL & SUITES
5931 Fruitville Rd (34232)
Rates: $89-$229
(941) 342-8778
(800) 634-3444

COQUINA ON THE BEACH RESORT
1008 Ben Franklin Dr (34236)
Rates: $169-$199
(941) 388-2141
(800) 833-2141

COUNTRY INN & SUITES
5730 Gantt Rd (34233)
Rates: $79-$189
(941) 925-0631
(800) 456-4000

DAYS INN-AIRPORT
4900 N Tamiami Tr (34234)
Rates: $49-$129
(941) 355-9721
(800) 329-7466

HIBISCUS SUITES INN
1735 Stickney Point Rd (34231)
Rates: $100-$750
(941) 921-5797

RAMADA LTD
5774 Clark Rd (34233)
Rates: $70-$139
(941) 921-7812
(800) 272-6232

RITZ-CARLTON
1111 Ritz-Carlton Dr (34236)
Rates: $175-$395
(941) 309-2000
(800) 241-3333

SUNSET LODGE MOTEL
1765 Dawn St (34231)
Rates: $65-$105
(941) 925-1151

THE TIDES INN
1800 Stickney Point Rd (34231)
Rates: $60-$120
(941) 924-7541

SATELLITE BEACH

DAYS INN SPACE COAST
180 Hwy A1A (32937)
Rates: $49-$149
(521) 777-3552
(800) 329-7466

SEBRING

CHATEAU ELAN HOTEL & SPA
150 Midway Dr (33870)
Rates: $119-$149
(863) 655-6252

INN ON THE LAKES
3100 Golfview Rd (33870)
Rates: $69-$109
(863) 471-9400
(800) 531-LAKE

KENILWORTH LODGE
836 SE Lakeview Dr (33870)
Rates: $64-$110
(863) 385-0111

QUALITY INN
6525 Hwy 27 N (33870)
Rates: $60-$290
(863) 385-4500
(800) 424-6423

SEFFNER

MASTERS INN
6010 SR 579 N (33584)
Rates: $30-$99
(813) 621-4681

SIESTA KEY

A BEACH BUNGALOW ON SIESTA KEY
303 Canal Rd (34242)
Rates: n/a
(941) 341-0955

BANANA BAY CLUB
8245 Midnight Pass Rd (34242)
Rates: $75-$249
(941) 346-0113
(888) 622-6229

BEACH PALMS OF SIESTA KEY VILLAGE
153 Beach Rd (34242)
Rates: $150-$249
(941) 349-9000
(888) 241-7009

THE BEACH PLACE
5605 Avenida Del Mare (34242)
Rates: $90-$200
(941) 346-1745
(800) 615-1745

MIRA MAR BEACH APTS
92 Avenida Messina (34242)
Rates: $100-$150
(941) 349-6800
(800) 300-2492

TROPICAL BREEZE RESORT
5150 Ocean Blvd (34242)
Rates: $85-$499
(941) 349-1125

TURTLE BEACH RESORT
9049 Midnight Pass Rd (34242)
Rates: $250-$430
(941) 349-4554

SILVER SPRINGS

DAYS INN
5001 E Silver Spgs Blvd (34488)
Rates: $45-$80
(352) 236-2891
(800) 329-7466

ECONO LODGE
5331 NE Silver Spgs Blvd (34488)
Rates: $45-$105
(352) 236-2383
(800) 424-6423

SUN PLAZA MOTEL
5461 E Silver Spgs Blvd (34489)
Rates: $45-$75
(352) 236-2343

SINGER ISLAND

DAYS INN OCEANFRONT RESORT
2700 N Ocean Dr (33404)
Rates: $89-$229
(561) 848-8661
(800) 329-7466

SOUTH BAY

OKEECHOBEE INN
265 N US Hwy 27 (33493)
Rates: $40-$45
(561) 996-7617

SOUTH PALM BEACH

PALM BEACH HAWAIIAN OCEAN INN
3550 S Ocean Blvd (33480)
Rates: $140-$310
(561) 582-5631

SPRING HILL

BEST WESTERN WEEKI WACHEE RESORT
6172 Commercial Way (34606)
Rates: $59-$89
(352) 596-2007
(800) 528-1234
(800) 490-8268

STARKE

BEST WESTERN MOTOR INN
1290 N Temple Ave (32091)
Rates: $60-$130
(904) 964-6744
(800) 528-1234

DAYS INN
1101 N Temple Ave (32091)
Rates: $55-$200
(904) 964-7600
(800) 329-7466

STEINHATCHEE

STEINHATCHEE LANDING RESORT
228 Hwy 51 N (32359)
Rates: $132-$425
(352) 498-3513
(800) 584-1709

STEINHATCEE RIVER INN
1111 Riverside Dr (32359)
Rates: $60-$89
(352) 498-4049

STUART

HUTCHINSON ISLAND MARRIOTT BEACH RESORT & MARINA
555 NE Ocean Blvd (34996)
Rates: $179-$250
(772) 225-3700
(800) 775-5936

PIRATES COVE RESORT/MARINA
4307 SE Bayview St (34992)
Rates: $145-$249
(772) 287-2500
(800) 332 1414

SUNNY ISLES

OCEAN POINT BEACH RESORT & SPA
17375 Collins Ave (33160)
Rates: n/a
(786) 528-2500
(866) 623-2678

SUNRISE

BAYMONT INN
13651 NW 2nd St
(33325)
Rates: $96-$106
(954) 846-1200
(877) 229-6668

WELLESLEY INN
13600 NW 2nd St
(33325)
Rates: $89-$129
(954) 845-9929
(800) 444-8888

TALLAHASSEE

**BEST WESTERN
PRIDE INN**
2016 Apalachee
Pkwy (32301)
Rates: $59-$139
(850 656-6312
(800) 528-1234
(800) 827-7390

**BEST WESTERN
SEMINOLE INN**
6737 Mahan Dr
(32317)
Rates: $59-$139
(850) 656-2938
(800) 528-1234
(800) 996 6537

DAYS INN
1350 W
Tennessee St
(323040
Rates: $50-$160
(850) 222-3219
(800) 329-7466

**EXECUTIVE SUITE
MOTOR INN**
522 Scotty's Lane
(32303)
Rates: $50
(850) 386-2121
(800) 342-0090
(800) 695-8284

**HOMEWOOD
SUITES**
2987 Apalachee
Pkwy (32301)
Rates: $79-$259
(840) 402-9400
(800) 225-5466

**HOWARD
JOHNSON EXP**
2726 N Monroe
St (32303)
Rates: $49-$69
(850) 386-5000
(800) 446-4656

LA QUINTA INN NORTH
2905 N Monroe
St (32303)
Rates: $59-$92
(850) 385-7172
(800) 687-6667

**LA QUINTA INN
SOUTH**
2850 Apalachee
Pkwy (32301)
Rates: $59-$89
(850) 878-5099
(800) 687-6667

**MOTEL 6
DOWNTOWN**
1027 Apalachee
Pkwy (32301)
Rates: $39-$44
(850) 877-6171
(800) 466-8356

MOTEL 6 NORTH
1481 Timberlane
Rd (32312)
Rates: $43-$44
(850) 668-2600
(800) 466-8356

MOTEL 6 WEST
2738 N Monroe
St (32303)
Rates: $33-$40
(850) 386-7878
(800) 466-8356

SUPER 8 MOTEL
2702 N Monroe
St (32303)
Rates: $40-$65
(850) 386-8818
(800) 800-8000

TAMARAC

**BAYMONT INN
& SUITES**
3800 W
Commercial Blvd
(33309)
Rates: $54-$92
(954) 485-7900
(800) 301-0200

**HOMESTEAD
STUDIO SUITES**
3873 W
Commercial Blvd
(33309)
Rates: $59-$104
(954) 733-6644
(888) 782-9473

TAMPA

**AMERISUITES
AIRPORT**
4811 W Main St
(33607)
Rates: $99-$159
(813) 282-1037
(800) 833-1516

**AMERISUITES
BUSCH
GARDENS**
11408 N 30th St
(33610)
Rates: $109-$125
(813) 979-1922
(800) 833-1516

**AMERISUITES
CORPORATE
PARK**
10007 Princess
Palm Ave (33619)
Rates: $89-$149
(813) 622-8557
(800) 833-1516

**BAYMONT INN
& SUITES-BUSCH
GARDENS**
9202 30th St N
(33612)
Rates: $60-$100
(813) 930-6900
(877) 229-6668

**BAYMONT INN
FAIRGROUNDS**
4811 US Hwy
301 N (33610)
Rates: $69-$76
(813) 626-0885
(877) 229-6668

**BAYMONT INN
& SUITES**
602 S Falkenburg
Rd (33619)
Rates: $85-$92
(813) 684-4007
(877) 229-6668

**BEST WESTERN
ALL SUITES
HOTEL-USF**
3001 University
Center Dr (33612)
Rates: $69-$129
(813) 971-8930
(800) 528-1234
(800) SUNSHINE

BEST WESTERN THE WESTSHORE HOTEL
1200 N
Westshore Blvd
(33607)
Rates: $85-$125
(813) 282-3636
(800) 528-1234
(800) 449-4343

**CHASE SUITE
HOTEL BY
WOODFIN**
3075 N Rocky
Point Rd (33607)
Rates: $85-$229
(813) 281-5677

**CLARION HOTEL
AIRPORT**
5303 W Kennedy
Blvd (33609)
Rates: $79-$159
(813) 289-1950
(800) 424-6423

**DAYS INN-BUSCH
GARDENS NORTH**
701 E Fletcher
Ave (33612)
Rates: $44-$99
(813) 977-1550
(800) 329-7466

HAMPTON INN
5826 W Waters
Ave (33634)
Rates: $99-$139
(813) 901-5900
(800) 426-7866

**HARD ROCK
SEMINOLE
CASINO & HOTEL**
5223 N Orient Rd
(33610)
Rates: $140-$280
(813) 627-7625

**HOLIDAY INN
BUSCH GRDNS**
2701 E Fowler
Ave (33612)
Rates: $72-$130
(813) 971-4710
(800) 465-4329

**HOLIDAY INN
EXPRESS HOTEL**
9402 Corporate
Lake Dr (33634)
Rates: $119-$149
(813) 885-3700
(800) 465-4329

HOLIDAY INN EXPRESS HOTEL
8310 Galbraith
Rd (33647)
Rates: $90-$113
(813) 910-7171
(800) 465-4329

**HOLIDAY INN
EXPRESS HOTEL
STADIUM/AIRPORT**
4732 N Dale
Mabry Hwy
(33614)
Rates: $95-$105
(813) 877-6061
(800) 465-4329

**HOMESTEAD
STUDIO SUITES**
5401 Beamont Ctr
Blvd (33634)
Rates: $59-$105
(813) 243-1913
(888) 782-9473

**LA QUINTA INN
AIRPORT**
4730 Spruce St
(33607)
Rates: $79-$109
(813) 287-0440
(800) 687-6667

**LA QUINTA INN
TAMPA SOUTH**
4620 W Gandy
Blvd (33611)
Rates: $90-$130
(813) 835-6262
(800) 687-6667

**LA QUINTA INN
& SUITES-USF**
3701 E Fowler
Ave (33612)
Rates: $79-$129
(813) 910-7500
(800) 687-6667

**MOTEL 6-BUSCH
GARDENS/
DOWNTOWN**
333 E Fowler Ave
(33612)
Rates: $36-$55
(813) 932-4948
(800) 466-8356

**MOTEL 6
FAIRGROUNDS**
6510 N Hwy 301
(33610)
Rates: $37-$61
(813) 628-0888
(800) 466-8356

AREA CODES - If the local number doesn't connect, check for a new area code.

RED ROOF INN BRANDON
10121 Horace
Ave (33619)
Rates: $66-$89
(813) 681-8484
(800) 843-7663

RED ROOF INN BUSCH GRDNS
2307 E Busch
Blvd (33612)
Rates: $38-$70
(813) 932-0073
(800) 843-7663

RED ROOF INN FAIRGROUNDS
5001 N US 301
(33610)
Rates: $42-$84
(813) 623-5245
(800) 843-7663

RESIDENCE INN BY MARRIOTT
9719 Princess
Palm Ave (33619)
Rates: $109-$179
(813) 627-8855
(800) 331-3131

RESIDENCE INN BY MARRIOTT DOWNTOWN
101 E Tyler St
(33602)
Rates: n/a
(813) 221-4224
(800) 331-3131

SHERATON SUITES HOTEL
4400 W Cypress
St (33607)
Rates: $275-$300
(813) 873-8675
(800) 325-3535

TAHITIAN INN
601 S Dale Mabry
Hwy (33609)
Rates: $104-$209
(813) 877-6721
(800) 876-1397

WELLESLEY INN & SUITES
1805 N
Westshore Blvd
(33607)
Rates: $69-$159
(813) 637-8990
(800) 444-8888

WINGATE INN- USF/BUSCH GARDENS
3751 E Fowler
Ave (33612)
Rates: $99-$114
(813) 979-2828

WYNDHAM WESTSHORE HOTEL
4860 W Kennedy
Blvd (33609)
Rates: $99-$215
(813) 286-4400
(800) 996-3426

TARPON SPRINGS

TAHITIAN RESORT
2337 Hwy 19
(34691)
Rates: $40-$85
(727) 937-4121
(877) 931-0333

TAVARES

BUDGET INN
101 W Burleigh
Blvd (32778)
Rates: $40-$99
(352) 343-4666

INN ON THE GREEN
700 E Burleigh
Blvd (32778)
Rates: $63-$79
(352) 343-6373
(800) 935-2935

TAVERNIER

TAVERNIER HOTEL
91865 Overseas
Hwy (33070)
Rates: n/a
(305) 852-4131
(800) 515-4131

TEMPLE TERRACE

RESIDENCE INN BY MARRIOTT
13420 N Telecom
Pkwy (33637)
Rates: $139-$179
(813) 972-4400
(800) 331-3131

THE VILLAGES

COMFORT SUITES
1202 Avenida
Central N (32159)
Rates: $80-$150
(352) 259-6578
(800) 424-6423

HOLIDAY INN EXPRESS HOTEL
1205 Avenida
Central N (32159)
Rates: n/a
(352) 750-3888
(800) 465-4329

TITUSVILLE

BEST WESTERN SPACE SHUTTLE INN
3455 Cheney
Hwy (32780)
Rates: $69-$135
(321) 269-9100
(800) 523-7654

COMFORT INN
3655 Cheney
Hwy (32780)
Rates: $59-$255
(3210 269-7110
(800) 424-6423

DAYS INN KENNEDY SPACE CTR
3755 Cheney
Hwy (32780)
Rates: $54-$135
(321) 269-4480
(800) 329-7466

HOLIDAY INN KENNEDY SPACE CTR
4951 S
Washington Ave
(32780)
Rates: $99-$179
(321) 269-2121
(800) 465-4329

RAMADA INN KENNEDY SPACE CTR
3500 Cheney
Hwy (32780)
Rates: $94-$149
(321) 269-5510
(800) 272-6232

TREASURE ISLAND

BEST WESTERN SEA CASTLE ALL SUITES
10750 Gulf Blvd
(33706)
Rates: $65-$169
(727) 367-2704
(800) 528-1234
(800) 441-8483

BILMAR BEACH RESORT
10650 Gulf Blvd
(33706)
Rates: $105-$310
(727) 360-5531

LORELEI RESORT
10273 Gulf Blvd
(33706)
Rates: $45-$95
(727) 360-4351
(800) 354-6364

SEA HORSE COTTAGES & APARTMENTS
10356 Gulf Blvd
(33706)
Rates: $35-$105
(727) 367-2291
(800) 741-2291

VENICE

HOLIDAY INN
455 Hwy 41
Bypass N (34285)
Rates: $69-$249
(941) 485-5411
(800) 465-4329
(800) 237-3712

HORSE AND CHASE INN B&B
317 Ponce de
Leon (34285)
Rates: $89-$149
(941) 488-2702

MOTEL 6
281 US Hwy 41
Bypass N (34292)
Rates: $37-$71
(941) 485-8255
(800) 466-8356

PARKVIEW APARTMENTS
505 Menendez St
(34285)
Rates: $69-$150
(941) 484-9615

VERANDA INN & CAFÉ OF VENICE
625 Tamiami Tr S
(34285)
Rates: $50-$240
(941) 484-9559
(800) 345-9559

VERO BEACH

CITRUS MOTEL
3256 US 1 (32960)
Rates: $40-$85
(772) 562-4163

WEEKI WACHEE

BEST WESTERN WEEKI WACHEE RESORT
6172 Commercial
Way (34606)
Rates: $65-$90
(352) 596-2007
(800) 528-1234
(800) 490-8268

WESLEY CHAPEL

MASTERS INN
27807 SR 54W
(33543)
Rates: $39-$63
(813) 973-0155

WEST MELBOURNE

HOWARD JOHNSON
4431 W New
Haven Ave
(32904)
Rates: $69-$99
(321) 768-8877
(800) 446-4656

RAMADA LTD
4500 W New
Haven AVe
(32904)
Rates: n/a
(321) 724-2051
(800) 272-6232

WEST PALM BEACH

COMFORT INN PALM BEACH LAKES
1901 Palm Beach
Lakes Blvd
(33409)
Rates: $59-$129
(561) 689-6100
(800) 424-6423

DAYS INN AIRPORT NORTH
2300 45th St
(33407)
Rates: $39-$149
(561) 689-0450
(800) 329-7466

HIBISCUS HOUSE HISTORIC BED & BREAKFAST
501 30th St
(33407)
Rates: $85-$190
(561) 863-5633
(800) 203-4927

RED ROOF INN
2421 Metro Center Blvd E
(33407)
Rates: $47-$95
(561) 697-7710
(800) 846-7663

RESIDENCE INN BY MARRIOTT
2461 Metro Center Blvd
(33407)
Rates: $114-$154
(561) 687-4747
(800) 331-3131

STUDIO 6 EXTENDED STAY
1535 Centrepeak Dr N (33401)
Rates: $59-$75
(561) 640-3335
(888) 897-0202

WELLESLEY INN
1910 Palm Beach Lakes Blvd
(33409)
Rates: $59-$109
(561) 689-8540
(800) 444-8888

WESTON

AMERISUITES
2201 N Commerce Pkwy
(33326)
Rates: $89-$119
(954) 659-1555
(800) 444-8888

RESIDENCE INN BY MARRIOTT
2605 Weston Rd
(33331)
Rates: $119-$229
(954) 659-8585
(800) 331-3131

TOWNEPLACE SUITES
1545 Three Village Rd
(33326)
Rates: $69-$159
(954) 659-2234
(800) 257-3000

WEWAHITCHKA

MAGNOLIA LODGE
345 S Bass Dr
(32465)
Rates: n/a
(850) 639-6760

WILDWOOD

DAYS INN
551 E SR 44
(34785)
Rates: $50-$90
(352) 748-7766
(800) 329-7466

WILLISTON

WILLISTON MOTOR INN
606 W Noble Ave
(32696)
Rates: $38-$209
(352) 528-4801

WINTER HAVEN

BEST WESTERN ADMIRAL'S INN
5665 Cypress Gardens Blvd
(33884)
Rates: $75-$135
(863) 324-5950
(800) 528-1234
(800) 247-2799

CYPRESS MOTEL
5651 Cypress Gardens Blvd
(33884)
Rates: $44-$80
(863) 324-5867
(800) 729-6706

HOWARD JOHNSON
1300 US 17 SW
(33880)
Rates: $80-$109
(863) 294-7321
(800) 446-4656

RANCH HOUSE MOTOR INN
1911 Cypress Gardens Blvd
(33880)
Rates: $45-$85
(863) 324-5994
(800) 366 5996

YANKEETOWN

RIVERSIDE MARINA & COTTAGES
6451 Riverside Dr (34498)
Rates: n/a
(352) 447-2980

YEEHAW JUNCTION

DESERT INN
5570 S Kenansville Rd
(34972)
Rates: n/a
(407) 436-1054

YULEE

DAYS INN
3250 Hwy 17 N
(32097)
Rates: $40-$80
(904) 225-2011
(800) 329-7466

ZEPHYR HILLS

CRYSTAL SPRINGS MOTOR INN
6736 Gall Blvd
(33541)
Rates: $35-$170
(813) 782-1214

AREA CODES - If the local number doesn't connect, check for a new area code.

GEORGIA

ACWORTH

BEST WESTERN FRONTIER INN
5155 Cowan Rd (30101)
Rates: $50-$65
(770) 974-0116
(800) 528-1234

ECONO LODGE
4980 Cowan Rd (30101)
Rates: $45-$65
(770) 974-1922
(800) 424-6423

RED ROOF INN
5320 Glade Rd (30101)
Rates: $40-$50
(770) 974-5400
(800) 843-7663

SUPER 8 MOTEL
4970 Cowan Rd (30101)
Rates: $40-$79
(770) 966-9700
(800) 800-8000

ADAIRSVILLE

BARNSLEY GARDENS RESORT
597 Barnsley Gardens Rd (30103)
Rates: $125+
(770) 773-7480
(877) 773-2447

COMFORT INN
107 Princeton Blvd (30103)
Rates: $45-$85
(770) 773-2886
(800) 424-6423

RAMADA LIMITED
500 Georgia North Cir (30103)
Rates: $40-$75
(770) 769-9726
(800) 272-6232

ADEL

DAYS INNS
1200 W 4th St (31620)
Rates: $39-$49
(229) 896-4574
(800) 329-7466

HAMPTON INN
1500 W 4th St (31620)
Rates: $68-$72
(229) 896-3099
(800) 426-7866

SUPER 8 MOTEL
1103 W 4th St (31620)
Rates: $39-$52
(229) 896-2244
(800) 800-8000

VILLAGER LODGE
1102 W 4th St (31620)
Rates: $35-$50
(229) 896-4523
(800) 328-7829

ALBANY

ALBANY 8 INN
905 E Ogelthorpe (31705)
Rates: $35-$80
(229) 435-2151

ECONOMY INN & SUITES
422 W Ogelthorpe Blvd (31705)
Rates: $30-$50
(229) 888-2632

HOLIDAY INN-ALBANY MALL
2701 Dawson Rd (31707)
Rates: $50-$120
(229) 883-8100
(800) 465-4329

INN & SUITES
1806 E Ogelthorpe Blvd (31707)
Rates: $35-$80
(229) 883-5544

JAMESON INN
2720 Dawson Rd (31707)
Rates: $49-$104
(229) 435-3837
(800) 541-3268

KNIGHTS INN
1201 Schley Ave (31707)
Rates: $35-$43
(229) 888-9600
(800) 843-5644

MOTEL 6
201 S Thornton Dr (31705)
Rates: $31-$47
(229) 439-0078
(800) 466-8356

REGENCY INN
911 E Ogelthorpe Blvd (31705)
Rates: $35-$80
(229) 883-1650

SUPER 8 MOTEL
2444 N Slappey Blvd (31701)
Rates: $39-$51
(229) 777-8388
(800) 800-8000

WINGATE INN
2735 Dawson Rd (31701)
Rates: $100+
(229) 883-9800
(800) 228-1000

ALMA

DAYS INN
930 S Pierce St (31510)
Rates: $45-$120
(912) 632-7000
(800) 329-7466

SUNSET MOTEL
915 S Pierce St (31510)
Rates: $35-$50
(912) 632-7286

ALPHARETTA

AMERISUITES-CINGULAR
12505 Cingular Way (30004)
Rates: $89-$139
(678) 339-0505
(800) 833-1516

AMERISUITES NORTH POINT MALL
7500 North Point Pkwy (30022)
Rates: $99
(770) 594-8788
(800) 833-1516

AMERISUITES WINDWARD
5595 Windward Pkwy (30004)
Rates: $109-$119
(770) 343-9566
(800) 833-1516

HOMEWOOD SUITES
10775 Davis Dr (30201)
Rates: $89-$139
(770) 998-1622
(800) 225-5466

LA QUINTA INN & SUITES
1350 N Point Dr (30202)
Rates: $69-$104
(770) 754-7800
(800) 687-6667

MARRIOTT SPRINGHILL SUITES
12730 Deerfield Pkwy (30202)
Rates: $81-$120
(770) 751-6900
(888) 287-9400

RESIDENCE INN BY MARRIOTT
5465 Windward Pkwy W (30201)
Rates: $149-$165
(770) 664-0664
(800) 331-3131

SLEEP INN
2925 Jordan Ct (30004)
Rates: $49-$72
(678) 347-0022
(800) 424-6423

STAYBRIDGE SUITES
3980 North Point Pkwy (30005)
Rates: $129-$169
(770) 569-7200
(800) 238-8000

TOWNEPLACE SUITES
7925 Westside Pkwy (30201)
Rates: $81-$104
(770) 664-1300
(800) 257-3000

WELLESLEY INN & SUITES
3329 Old Milton Pkwy (30005)
Rates: $65-$99
(770) 569-1730
(800) 444-8888

WINGATE INN
1005 Kingswood Pl (30004
Rates: $69-$107
(770) 649-0955

AMERICUS

HOLIDAY INN EXP
1607 Hwy 280 E (31709)
Rates: $70-$80
(229) 928-5400
(800) 465-4329

JAMESON INN
1605 E Lamar St (31709)
Rates: $50-$80
(229) 924-2726
(800) 526-3766

1906 PATHWAY INN B&B
501 S Lee St (31709)
Rates: $80-$145
(229) 928-2078
(800) 889-1466

AREA CODES - If the local number doesn't connect, check for a new area code.

ASHBURN

BEST WESTERN ASHBURN INN
820 Shoneys Dr (31714)
Rates: $40-$58
(229) 567-0080
(800) 528-1234

DAYS INN
823 E Washington Ave (31714)
Rates: $38-$55
(229) 567-3346
(800) 329-7466

RAMADA LIMITED
156 Whittle Cir (31714)
Rates: $46-$52
(229) 567-3295
(800) 272-6232

ATHENS

BEST WESTERN COLONIAL INN
170 N Milledge Ave (30601)
Rates: $59-$109
(706) 546-7311
(800) 528-1234
(800) 592-9401

BULLDOG INN
1125 Commerce Rd (30607)
Rates: $38-$59
(706) 543-3611

HOLIDAY INN
197 E Broad St (30603)
Rates: $79-$119
(706) 549-4433
(800) 465-4329

HOLIDAY INN EXP
513 W Broad St (30601)
Rates: $76-$85
(706) 546-8122
(800) 465-4329

MAGNOLIA TERRACE GUESTHOUSE
277 Hill St (30601)
Rates: $95-$135
(706) 548-3860

PERIMETER INN
3791 Atlanta Hwy (30606)
Rates: $35-$80
(706) 548-3999
(800) 934-2963

SUPER 8 MOTEL
3425 Atlanta Hwy (30606)
Rates: $35-$75
(706) 549-0251
(800) 800-8000

ATLANTA

AMERISUITES BUCKHEAD
3242 Peachtree Rd NE (30305)
Rates: $69-$299
(404) 869-6161
(800) 833-1516

AMERISUITES PERIMETER CENTER
1005 Crestline Pkwy (30328)
Rates: $69-$179
(770) 730-9200
(800) 833-1516

BAYMONT INN & SUITES-LENOX/ BUCKHEAD
2535 Chantilly Dr NE (30324)
Rates: $55-$80
(404) 321-0999
(877) 229-6668

BEST WESTERN BEVERLY HILLS INN
65 Sheridan Dr (30305)
Rates: $99-$199
(404) 233-8520
(800) 528-1234
(800) 331-8520

BEST WESTERN GRANADA SUITE HOTEL
1302 W Peachtree St (30309)
Rates: $85-$229
(404) 876-6100
(800) 528-1234
(800) 548-5631

BEST WESTERN INN AT THE PEACHTREES
330 W Peachtree St (30308)
Rates: $81-$229
(404) 577-6970
(800) 528-1234
(800) 242-4642

BEVERLY HILLS INN B&B
54 Sheridan Dr NE (30305)
Rates: $99-$165
(404) 233-8520

CLARION SUITES NORTHEAST
4900 Circle 75 Pkwy (30339)
Rates: $99-$220
(770) 956-1504
(800) 424-6423

CROWNE PLAZA- AIRPORT
1325 Virginia Ave (30344)
Rates: $81-$150
(404) 768-6660
(800) 227-6963

CROWNE PLAZA BUCKHEAD
3377 Peachtree Rd NE (30326)
Rates: $81-$150
(404) 264-1111
(800) 227-6963

CROWNE PLAZA- PERIMETER
6345 Powers Ferry Rd NW (30339)
Rates: $69-$164
(770) 955-1700
(800) 227-6963

FOUR SEASONS
75 14th St (30309)
Rates: $295-$375
(404) 881-9898
(800) 332-3442

GRAND HYATT ATLANTA
3300 Peachtree Rd (30305)
Rates: $119-$275
(404) 365-8100
(800) 233-1234

HAWTHORN SUITES
1500 Parkwood Cir (30339)
Rates: $109-$189
(770) 952-9595
(800) 338-7812

HOLIDAY INN AIRPORT NORTH
1380 Virginia Ave (30344)
Rates: $81-$150
(404) 762-8411
(800) 465-4329

HOLIDAY INN EXPRESS HOTEL
6743 Shannon Pkwy (30291)
Rates: n/a
(770) 969-4567
(800) 465-4329

HOLIDAY INN PERIMETER
4386 Chamblee- Dunwoody Rd (30341)
Rates: $119-$139
(770) 457-6363
(800) 465-4329

HOMESTEAD STUDIO SUITES- NO. DRUID HILLS
1339 Executive Park Dr NE (30329)
Rates: $57-$82
(404) 325-1223
(888) 782-9473

HOMESTEAD STUDIO SUITES- PERIMETER
1050 Hammond Dr (30328)
Rates: $61-$86
(770) 522-0025
(888) 782-9473

HOMEWOOD SUITES BUCKHEAD
3566 Piedmont Rd (30305)
Rates: $116
(404) 365-0001
(800) 225-5466

HOMEWOOD SUITES CUMBERLAND
3200 Cobb Pkwy SW (30339)
Rates: $99-$189
(770) 988-9449
(800) 225-5466

LA QUINTA INN & SUITES
2415 Paces Ferry Rd SE (30326)
Rates: $94-$109
(770) 801-9002
(800) 687-6667

LA QUINTA INN PERIMETER
6260 Peachtree- Dunwoody (30328)
Rates: $79-$99
(770) 350-6177

MICROTEL INN & SUITES
1840 Corporate Blvd (30329)
Rates: $51-$120
(404) 325-4446
(888) 771-7171

OMNI HOTEL- CNN CENTER
100 CNN Center (30303)
Rates: $149-$279
(404) 659-0000
(800) 843-6664

RAMADA INN
418 Armour Dr NE (30324)
Rates: $49-$259
(404) 873-4661
(800) 272-6232

RAMADA INN- SIX FLAGS
4225 Fulton Industrial Blvd (30336)
Rates: $51-$120
(404) 691-4100
(800) 272-6232

RESIDENCE INN BY MARRIOTT DOWNTOWN
134 Peachtree St NW (30303)
Rates: $139-$169
(404) 522-0950
(800) 331-3131

RESIDENCE INN BY MARRIOTT DUNWOODY
1901 Savoy Dr (30341)
Rates: $69-$119
(770) 455-4446
(800) 331-3131

RESIDENCE INN BY MARRIOTT- BUCKHEAD
2960 Piedmont Rd NE (30305)
Rates: $145-$175
(404) 239-0677
(800) 331-3131

RESIDENCE INN BY MARRIOTT- BUCKHEAD/ LENOX
2220 Lake Blvd (30317)
Rates: $134
(404) 467-1660
(800) 331-3131

AREA CODES - If the local number doesn't connect, check for a new area code.

RESIDENCE INN BY MARRIOTT MIDTOWN
1041W Peachtree St (30309)
Rates: $74-$234
(404) 872-8885
(800) 331-3131

RESIDENCE INN MIDTOWN AT 17TH ST.
1365 Peachtree St (30309)
Rates: $99-$299
(404) 745-1000
(800) 331-3131

RITZ-CARLTON BUCKHEAD
3434 Peachtree Rd NE (30326)
Rates: $379-$449
(404) 237-2700
(800) 241-3333

SHERATON ATLANTA
165 Courtland St (30303)
Rates: $99-$139
(404) 659-6500
(800) 325-3535

SHERATON BUCKHEAD
3405 Lenox Rd NE (30326)
Rates: $89-$139
(404) 261-9250
(800) 325-3535

SHERATON GALLERIA
2844 Cobb Pkwy SE (30339)
Rates: $79-$249
(770) 955-3900
(800) 325-3535

SHERATON MIDTOWN AT COLONY SQUARE
188 14th St NE (30361)
Rates: $259-$309
(404) 892-6000
(800) 325-3535

SIERRA SUITES-LENOX
3967 Peachtree Rd (30319)
Rates: $85-$119
(404) 237-9100

SIERRA SUITES PERIMETER
6330 Peachtree-Dunwoody NE (30328)
Rates: $69-$119
(770) 379-0111

STAYBRIDGE SUITES-BUCKHEAD
540 Pharr Rd NE (30305)
Rates: $146-$199
(404) 842-0800
(800) 238-8000

STAYBRIDGE SUITES-PERIMETER
4601 Ridgeview Rd (30338)
Rates: $127
(678) 320-0111
(800) 238-8000

STAYBRIDGE SUITES-MT. VERNON
760 Mt. Vernon Hwy NE (30328)
Rates: $160
(404) 250-0110
(800) 238-8000

STUDIO 6
3601 N Desert Dr (30344)
Rates: $219-$279
(404) 762-5566
(888) 897-0202

SUMMERFIELD SUITES BUCKHEAD
505 Pharr Rd (30305)
Rates: $80-$120
(404) 262-7880
(800) 833-4353

SUPER 8 MOTEL
1641 Peachtree St NE (30309)
Rates: $59-$99
(404) 873-5731
(800) 800-8000

SWISSOTEL ATLANTA
3391 Peachtree Rd NE (30326)
Rates: $125+
(404) 365-0065
(888) 737-9477

TOWNEPLACE SUITES
3300 Northlake Pkwy (30345)
Rates: $51-$120
(770) 938-0408
(800) 257-3000

TRAVEL INN
3701 Presidential Pkwy (30340)
Rates: $39-$50
(770) 458-9009

TRAVELODGE-SIX FLAGS
4265 Shirley Dr (30336)
Rates: $51-$120
(404) 696-4391
(800) 578-7878
(800) 201-7632

UNIVERSITY INN-EMORY
1767 N Decatur Rd (30307)
Rates: $65-$149
(404) 634-7327
(800) 654-8591

W ATLANTA
111 Perimeter Center W (30346)
Rates: $179-$369
(770) 396-6800

WELLESLEY INN & SUITES-WINDY HILL
2225 Interstate North Pkwy (30339)
Rates: $65-$89
(770) 228-0242
(800) 444-8888

WESTIN BUCKHEAD
3391 Peachtree Rd NE (30326)
Rates:n/a
(404) 365-0065
(800) 228-3000

WESTIN NORTH
7 Concourse Pkwy (30328)
Rates: $89-$189
(770) 395-3900
(800) 228-3000

WESTIN PEACHTREE PLAZA
210 Peachtree St (30303)
Rates: n/a
(404) 659-1400
(800) 228-3000

AUGUSTA

ADAMS AFFORDABLE INN
1370 Gordon Hwy (30901)
Rates: $35-$50
(706) 724-0080

AMERISUITES-RIVERWATCH
1062 Claussen Rd (30907)
Rates: $79-$89
(706) 733-4656
(800) 833-1516

AUGUSTA INN
1076 Stevens Crk Rd (30907)
Rates: $49-$79
(706) 738-8811

AUGUSTA SUITES INN
3038 Washington Rd (30907)
Rates: $99
(706) 868-1800

BUDGET INN
441 Broad St (30901)
Rates: $35-$50
(706) 722-0212

COMFORT INN MEDICAL CENTER
1455 Walton Way (30901)
Rates: $64-$250
(706) 722-2224
(800) 424-6423

COMFORT INN W
629 Frontage Rd NW (30907)
Rates: $62-$325
(706) 855-8000
(800) 424-6423

COUNTRY SUITES RIVERWALK
3 9th St (30901)
Rates: $125+
(706) 774-1400
(800) 456-4000

GUEST HOUSE INT'L
3023 Washington Rd (30907)
Rates: $33-$50
(706) 736-2595
(800) 222-2222

GUEST INN
2650 Center West Pkwy (30909)
Rates: $35-$50
(706) 736-2585

HOLIDAY INN AT BOBBY JONES
2155 Gordon Hwy (30909)
Rates: $50-$89
(706) 737-2300
(800) 465-4329

HOWARD JOHNSON
601 Frontage Rd NW (30907)
Rates: $44-$54
(706) 863-2882
(800) 446-4656

LA QUINTA INN
3020 Washington Rd (30907)
Rates: $65-$75
(706) 733-2660
(800) 687-6667

MASTERS INN
3027 Washington Rd (30907)
Rates: $30-$45
(706) 863-5566
(800) 633-3434

PARTRIDGE INN
2110 Walton Way (30904)
Rates: $109-$129
(706) 737-8888
(800) 476-6888

QUALITY INN
4073 Belair Rd (30909)
Rates: $55-$200
(706) 855-2088
(800) 424-6423

QUEEN ANNE INN
406 Greene St (30904)
Rates: $65-$120
(706) 723-0045
(877) 460-0045

AREA CODES - If the local number doesn't connect, check for a new area code.

RADISSON RIVERFRONT HOTEL
2 10th St (30901)
Rates: $129
(706) 722-8900
(800) 333-3333

RAMADA LIMITED
4324 Belair Frontage Rd (30909)
Rates: $45-$200
(706) 860-8840
(800) 272-6232

RED CARPET INN
2050 Gordon Hwy (30909)
Rates: $35-$50
(706) 733-5566
(800) 251-1962

RED ROOF INN & SUITES
4328 Frontage Rd (30907)
Rates: $40-$80
(706) 228-3031
(800) 843-7663

RODEWAY INN WEST
2852 Washington Rd (30909)
Rates: $39-$225
(706) 736-0707
(800) 424-6423

SHERATON HOTEL
2651 Perimeter Pkwy (30909)
Rates: $89-$159
(706) 855-8100
(800) 325-3535

SUBURBAN LODGE
707 Scott Nixon Memorial Dr (30901)
Rates: $35-$80
(706) 865-9711
(800) 951-7829

TRAVELODGE
3039 Washington Rd (30907)
Rates: $35-$50
(706) 868-6939
(800) 578-7878

AUSTELL
LA QUINTA INN SIX FLAGS
7377 Six Flags Dr (30168)
Rates: $69-$95
(770) 944-2110
(800) 687-6667

BAINBRIDGE
CHARTER HOUSE INN
1401 Tallahassee Hwy (31718)
Rates: $41-$50
(229) 246-8550
(800) 768-8550

JAMESON INN
1403 Tallahassee Hwy (31717)
Rates: $49-$104
(229) 243-7000
(800) 526-3766

SUPER 8 MOTEL
751 W Shotwell St (31717)
Rates: $40-$50
(229) 246-0015
(800) 800-8000

BAXLEY
PINE LODGE MOTEL
539 S Main St (31513)
Rates: $32-$46
(912) 367-3622
(800) 841-6052

SCOTTISH INN
1179 Hatch Pkwy S (31513)
Rates: $35-$80
(912) 367-3652
(800) 251-1962

BLAIRSVILLE
EL JOE LODGE MOTEL
1639 El Joe Rd (30512)
Rates: $32-$60
(706) 745-6991

GOOSE CREEK CABINS
7061 Hwy 19 (30514)
Rates: $38-$129
(706) 745-5111

MISTY MTN INN & COTTAGES
4376 Misty Mtn Lane (30514)
Rates: $51-$120
(706) 7454786
(888) 647-8966

SEASONS INN
Box 10, On the Square (30514)
Rates: $35-$80
(706) 745-1631
(800) 901-4422

7 CREEKS CABINS
5109 Horseshoe Cove Rd (30512)
Rates: $55-$250
(706) 745-4753

TOWN CREEK COTTAGES
4863 Seabolt Rd (30512)
Rates: $79-$119
(706) 745-8891
(866) 275-1092

BLUE RIDGE
ABOVE THE REST LUXURY CABINS
P.O. Box 1896, My Mountain (30513)
Rates: $95-$115
(706) 374-2057

BLUE RIDGE MOUNTAIN CABINS
10144 Blue Ridge Dr (30513)
Rates: $85-$135
(706) 632-8999

DOUGLASS INN
1192 Windy Ridge Rd (30513)
Rates: $50-$80
(706) 258-3600

FANNIN INN
1580 Appalachian Hwy (30513)
Rates: $30-$50
(706) 632-2005
(800) 533-9834

TICA CABIN RENTALS
699 E Main St (30513)
Rates: $75-$125
(706) 635-4448

BRASELTON
BEST WESTERN BRASELTON INN
303 Zion Church Rd (30517)
Rates: $69-$145
(706) 654-3081
(800) 528-1234

HOLIDAY INN EXP CHATEAU ELAN LODGE
2069 Hwy 211 (30517)
Rates: $89-$129
(770) 867-8100
(800) 465-4329

BREMEN
DAYS INN
35 Price Creek Rd (30110)
Rates: $40-$85
(770) 537-4646
(800) 329-7466

QUALITY INN & SUITES
1077 Alabama Ave (30110)
Rates: $45-$150
(770) 537-3833
(800) 424-6423

BRUNSWICK
BAYMONT INN & SUITES
165 Warren Mason Blvd (31520)
Rates: $54-$74
(912) 265-7725
(877) 229-6668

BEST WESTERN BRUNSWICK INN
5323 New Jesup Hwy (31523)
Rates: $60-$74
(912) 264-0144
(800) 528-1234

DAYS INN
2307 Gloucester St (31520)
Rates: $48-$129
(912) 265-8830
(800) 329-7466

EMBASSY SUITES
500 Mall Blvd (31520)
Rates: $119-$279
(912) 264-6100
(800) 362-2779

GOLDEN ISLES INN
3302 Glynn Ave H17 (31520)
Rates: $35-$80
(912) 554-0388

HOLIDAY INN
5252 New Jesup Hwy (31523)
Rates: $89-$129
(912) 264-4033
(800) 465-4329

JAMESON INN
661 Scranton Rd (31523)
Rates: $49-$104
(912) 267-0800
(800) 526-3766

KNIGHTS INN
5044 New Jesup Hwy (31523)
Rates: $34-$40
(912) 267-6500
(800) 843-5644

MOTEL 6
403 Butler Dr (31523)
Rates: $34-$55
(912) 264-8582
(800) 466-8356

OAK PARK INN
3104 Glynn Ave (31520)
Rates: $35-$50
(912) 265-9301

RAMADA INN
3040 Scarlet St (31523)
Rates: $89
(912) 264-3621
(800) 272-6232

RED ROOF INN & SUITES
121 Tourist Dr (31520)
Rates: $59-$212
(912) 264-4720
(800) 843-7663

SUPER 8 MOTEL
5280 New Jesup Hwy (31523)
Rates: $50-$76
(912) 264-8800
(800) 800-8000

BUFORD

WINGATE INN-MALL OF GA
1355 Mall of
Georgia Blvd
(30518)
Rates: $81-$120
(678) 714-0248

BYRON

BEST WESTERN INN & SUITES
101 Dunbar Hwy
49 Rd (31008)
Rates: $59
(478) 956-3056
(800) 528-1234

ECONO LODGE
515 Old Mason
Rd (31008)
Rates: $39-$99
(478) 956-5600
(800) 424-6423

ECONO LODGE
12003 Watson
Blvd (31008)
Rates: $45-$49
(478) 956-2800
(800) 424-6423

MEMORIES INN B&B
403 Main St
(31008)
Rates: $60-$120
(478) 956-2498
(800) 671-8111

SUPER 8 MOTEL
305 Hwy 49 N
(31008)
Rates: $51-$80
(478) 956-3311
(800) 800-8000

CAIRO

BEST WESTERN EXECUTIVE INN
2800 US 84 E
(31728)
Rates: $55-$70
(229) 377-8000
(800) 528-1234

DAYS INN
35 US Hwy 84 E
(31728)
Rates: $45-$65
(229) 377-4400
(800) 329-7466

CALHOUN

BEST INN
1438 Hwy 41 N
(30703)
Rates: $35-$60
(706) 625-1511

BUDGET HOST INN-SHEPHERDS
3900 Fairmont
Hwy (30703)
Rates: $37-$49
(706) 629-8644
(800) 666-6878

COMFORT INN
742 Hwy 53 SE
(30701)
Rates: $45-$65
(706) 629-8271
(800) 424-6423

DAYS INN
1220 Red Bud Rd
(30701)
Rates: $35-$65
(706) 629-9191
(800) 329-7466

JAMESON INN
189 Jameson St
SE (30701)
Rates: $49-$104
(706) 629-8133
(800) 541-3268

KNIGHTS INN
2261 Hwy 41 NE
(30701)
Rates: $35-$60
(706) 629-4521
(800) 843-5644

QUALITY INN
915 Hwy 53 E
(30701)
Rates: $60-$75
(706) 629-9501
(800) 424-6423

RAMADA LIMITED
1204 Redbud Rd
NE (30701)
Rates: $45-$99
(706) 629-9207
(800) 272-6232

SCOTTISH INNS
1510 Red Bud Rd
NE (30701)
Rates: $23-$89
(706) 629-8261
(800) 251-1962

CARROLLTON

COUNTRY HEARTH INN
901 S Park St
(30116)
Rates: $50-$80
(770) 834-2001
(888) 443-2784

DAYS INN
180 Centennial
Rd (30117)
Rates: $52-$110
(770) 214-0037
(800) 329-7466

JAMESON INN
700 S Park St
(30116)
Rates: $49-$104
(770) 834-2600
(800) 526-3766

QUALITY INN
160 Centennial
Dr (30116)
Rates: $49-$110
(770) 832-2611
(800) 424-6423

CARTERSVILLE

BEST WESTERN GARDEN INN
5663 Hwy 20 NE
(30121)
Rates: $55-$95
(770) 386-1569
(800) 528-1234

BUDGET HOST INN
851 Cass-White
Rd NW (30120)
Rates: $29-$41
(770) 386-0350
(800) 283-6483

COMFORT INN
28 Hwy 294 SE
(30121)
Rates: $42-$75
(770) 387-1800
(800) 424-6423

COUNTRY INN
43 SR 20 Spur
(30121)
Rates: $85
(770) 386-5888
(800) 456-4000

DAYS INN
5618 Hwy 20 SE
(30120)
Rates: $42-$99
(770) 382-1824
(800) 329-7466

ECONO LODGE
26 SR 20 Spur SE,
I-75, Exit 290
(30120)
Rates: $26-$70
(770) 386-3303
(800) 424-6423

HOWARD JOHNSON EXP
25 Carson Loop
NW (30121)
Rates: $35-$55
(770) 386-0700
(800) 446-4656

KNIGHTS INN
420 E Church St
(30120)
Rates: $40-$70
(770) 386-7263
(800) 843-5644

MOTEL 6
5657 Hwy 20
NE (30120)
Rates: $36-$46
(770) 386-1449
(800) 466-8356

QUALITY INN
235 S Dixie Ave
(30120)
Rates: $52-$61
(770) 386-0510
(800) 424-6423

RED CARPET INN
851 Cass-White
Rd NW (30120)
Rates: $20-$45
(770) 382-8000
(800) 251-1962

SUPER 8 MOTEL
41 SR 20 Spur SE
(30120)
Rates: $37-$60
(770) 382-8881
(800) 800-8000

TRAVELODGE
35 Carson Loop
(30121)
Rates: $40-$45
(770) 387-2696
(800) 578-7878

CEDARTOWN

COUNTRY HEARTH INN
925 N Main St
(30125)
Rates: $45-$85
(770) 749-9951
(888) 443-2784

CHAMBLEE

LODGE ON BUFORD
4815 Buford Hwy
(30341)
Rates: $81-$148
(770) 458-8011

MOTEL 6
2820 Chamblee-Tucker Rd
(30341)
Rates: $39-$48
(770) 458-6626
(800) 466-8356

SAVANNAH SUITES
5280 Peachtree
Industrial Blvd
(30341)
Rates: $51-$120
(678) 805-3400
(866) 367-2766

CHATSWORTH

KEY WEST INN
501 GI Maddox
Pkwy (30705)
Rates: $45-$80
(706) 517-1155
(800) 833-0555

CLAXTON

AMERICAN INN & SUITES
1338 N Duval St
(30417)
Rates: $30-$50
(912) 739-2525

CARRIAGE INN
6 N Duval St
(30417)
Rates: $51-$80
(912) 739-2962
(800) 251-1962

NORTHSIDE INN
8305 Hwy 301
(30417)
Rates: $35-$50
(912) 739-4485

CLAYTON

BEST WESTERN MOUNTAIN CHALET
834 Hwy 441 S
(30525)
Rates: $49-$99
(706) 782-2214
(800) 528-1234
(800) 334-2214

HILLCREST INN
95 Parker Ln
(30525)
Rates: $81-$120
(706) 782-1956

REGAL INN
707 Hwy 441 S
(30525)
Rates: $32-$120
(706) 782-4269

STONEBROOK INN
698 Hwy 441 S
(30525)
Rates: $32-$99
(706) 782-4702
(877) 779-4702

CLEVELAND
CAFFREY SPRINGS INN
1111 Satterfield Rd
(30528)
Rates: $81-$125+
(706) 348-6034

GABBY'S CABINS
3083 Helen Hwy
(30528)
Rates: $65-$140
(706) 865-6772

GATEWAY INN
300 N Main St
(30528)
Rates: $35-$50
(706) 865-3121

SKELTON INN
6394 Duncan
Bridge Rd
(30528)
Rates: $51-$120
(706) 865-6205

COCHRAN
BARKSDALE BOBWHITE PLANTATION
Rt 4, Long Street
Rd (31014)
Rates: $125+
(478) 934-6916

COLLEGE PARK
AMERISUITES AIRPORT
1899 Sullivan Rd
(30337)
Rates: $89-$95
(770) 994-2997
(800) 833-1516

DAYS INN ATLANTA AIRPT
4505 Best Rd
(30337)
Rates: $59-$98
(404) 767-1224
(800) 329-7466

DAYS INN AIRPORT WEST
4979 Old National
Hwy (30349)
Rates: $45-$80
(404) 669-8616
(800) 329-7466

ECONO LODGE AIRPORT
2010 Sullivan Rd
(30337)
Rates: $44-$89
(770) 991-8985
(800) 424-6423

MARRIOTT ATLANTA AIRPT
4711 Best Rd
(30337)
Rates: $89-$189
(404) 766-7900
(800) 228-9290

MOTEL 6 AIRPORT
2471 Old
National Pkwy
(30349)
Rates: $39-$57
(404) 761-9701
(800) 466-8356

SUPER 8 MOTEL
4874 Old
National Hwy
(30337)
Rates: $35-$50
(404) 768-1241
(800) 800-8000

COLUMBUS
BAYMONT INN
2919 Warm
Springs Rd
(31909)
Rates: $65-$100
(706) 323-4344
(877) 229-6668

FOUR POINTS SHERATON AIRPORT
5351 Sidney
Simons Blvd
(31904)
Rates: $89-$129
(706) 327-6868
(800) 325-3535

HERITAGE INN
1325 Veterans
Pkwy (31909)
Rates: $51-$80
(706) 322-2522

HOWARD JOHNSON EXP
1011 Veterans
Pkwy (31901)
Rates: $63-$80
(706) 322-6641
(800) 446-4656

LA QUINTA INN
3201 Macon Rd
(31906)
Rates: $75-$99
(706) 568-1740
(800) 687-6667

MOTEL 6
3050 Victory Dr
(31903)
Rates: $39-$49
(706) 687-7214
(800) 466-8356

SUPER 8 MOTEL
2935 Warm Spgs
Rd (31909)
Rates: $45-$70
(706) 322-6580
(800) 800-8000

COMMERCE
COMFORT INN
165 Eisenhower
Dr (30529)
Rates: $60-$95
(706) 335-9001
(800) 424-6423

HOWARD JOHNSON
148 Eisenhower
Dr (30529)
Rates: $45-$80
(706) 335-5581
(800) 446-4656

RAMADA LIMITED
30537 US 441 S
(30529)
Rates: $39-$89
(706) 335-5191
(800) 272-6232

SCOTTISH INN
30934 US 441 S
(30529)
Rates: $40-$50
(706) 335-5147
(800) 878-0837

SUPER 8 MOTEL
152 Eisenhower
Dr (30529)
Rates: $39-$79
(706) 336-8008
(800) 800-8000

CONYERS
CONYERS MOTOR INN
1056 Dogwood
Dr (30013)
Rates: $30-$50
(770) 483-4724

HAMPTON INN
1340 Dogwood
Dr (30013)
Rates: $75-$95
(770) 483-8838
(800) 426-7866

HOLIDAY INN
1351 Dogwood
Dr (30012)
Rates: $85
(770) 483-3220
(800) 465-4329

JAMESON INN
1164 Dogwood
Dr (30012)
Rates: $49-$104
(770) 760-1230
(800) 526-3766

LA QUINTA INN
1184 Dogwood
Ln (30012)
Rates: $89-$125
(770) 918-0092
(800) 687-6667

RAMADA LTD
1070 Dogwood
Dr (30012)
Rates: n/a
(770) 760-0777
(800) 272-6232

RICHFIELD LODGE
1297 Dogwood
Dr (30012)
Rates: $35-$50
(770) 483-1332

CORDELE
BEST WESTERN COLONIAL INN
1706 16th Ave E
(31015)
Rates: $52-$59
(229) 273-5420
(800) 528-1234
(800) 721-3352

CORDELE INN
566 Farmers
Market Rd
(31015)
Rates: $34-$50
(229) 273-9800

DELUXE INN
1709 E 16th Ave
(31015)
Rates: $35-$50
(229) 271-5000

ECONO LODGE
1711 E 16th Ave
(31015)
Rates: $39-$120
(229) 273-4117
(800) 424-6423

PASSPORT INN
1602 E 16th Ave
(31015)
Rates: $29-$50
(229) 273-4088

PREMIER INN
1609 E 16th Ave
(31015)
Rates: $35-$50
(229) 273-3390

RAMADA INN
2016 E 16th Ave
(31015)
Rates: $60-$70
(229) 273-5000
(800) 272-6232

CORNELIA
HOLIDAY INN EXP
1105 Business 411
(30531)
Rates: $40-$120
(706) 778-3600
(800) 465-4329

TRAVEL INN
109 S Main St
(30531)
Rates: $30-$50
(706) 778-2186

COVINGTON
BEST WESTERN COLONIAL INN
10130 Alcovy Rd
(30209)
Rates: $65-$150
(770) 786-5800
(800) 528-1234

AREA CODES - If the local number doesn't connect, check for a new area code.

CORNERSTONE LODGE OF AMERICA
9161 City Pond Rd (30209)
Rates: $35-$80
(678) 625-1000

HOLIDAY INN EXP
10111 Alcovy Rd (30209)
Rates: $70-$75
(770) 787-4900
(800) 465-4329

CUMMING
COMFORT SUITES
905 Buford Rd (30041)
Rates: $59-$99
(770) 889-4141
(800) 424-6423

HAMPTON INN
915 Baptist Medical Ctr Dr (30041)
Rates: $74-$94
(770) 889-0877
(800) 426-7866

DAHLONEGA
BEND OF THE RIVER CABINS & CHALETS
319 Horseshoe Ln (30533)
Rates: $80-$150
(706) 219-2040

THE CABINS AT HORSESHOE BEND
1104 Horseshoe Bend Rd (30533)
Rates: $135-$150
(770) 518-9942

FOREST HILLS MOUNTAIN RESORT
135 Forest Hills Dr (30533)
Rates: $81-$125+
(706) 864-6456
(800) 654-6313

MOUNTAIN LAUREL CREEK B&B
202 Talmer Grizzle Rd (30533)
Rates: $81-$125+
(706) 867-8134

DALTON
BEST INNS
1529 W Walnut Ave (30720)
Rates: $36-$59
(706) 226-1100
(800) 237-8466

BEST WESTERN DALTON INN
2106 Chattanooga Rd (30720)
Rates: $49-$69
(706) 226-5022
(800) 528-1234

COMFORT INN & SUITES
905 Westbridge Rd (30720)
Rates: $62-$95
(706) 259-2583
(800) 424-6423

DAYS INN
1518 W Walnut Ave (30720)
Rates: $32-$120
(706) 278-0850
(800) 329-7466

ECONO LODGE
2007 Chattanooga Rd (30720)
Rates: $30-$65
(706) 278-4300
(800) 424-6423
(888) 294-6498

HOWARD JOHNSON
2308 Chattanooga Rd (30720)
Rates: $35-$47
(706) 226-4545
(800) 446-4656

JAMESON INN
422 Holiday Dr (30720)
Rates: $49-$104
(706) 281-1880
(800) 526-3766

MOTEL 6
2200 Chattanooga Rd (30720)
Rates: $31-$47
(706) 278-5522
(800) 466-8356

QUALITY INN & SUITES
515 Holiday Dr (30720)
Rates: $59-$79
(706) 278-0500
(800) 424-6423

ROYAL INN
2107 Chattanooga Rd (30720)
Rates: $30-$50
(706) 226-9579

SUPER 8 MOTEL
236 Connector 3 SW (30720)
Rates: $40-$60
(706) 277-9323
(800) 800-8000

TRAVELODGE
911 Market St (30720)
Rates: $40-$120
(706) 275-0100
(800) 578-7878

WINGATE INN
309 Hoilday Dr (30720)
Rates: $51-$120
(706) 272-9099
(800) 228-1000

DARIEN
COMFORT INN
703 Frontage Rd (31305)
Rates: $69-$139
(912) 437-4200
(800) 424-6423

JAYSEN EXECUTIVE INN
Hwy 251 & 195 (31305)
Rates: $51-$80
(912) 437-5373

OPEN GATES B&B
301 Franklin St (31305)
Rates: $85-$150
(912) 437-6985

SUPER 8 MOTEL
Hwy 251 & 195 (31305)
Rates: $37-$58
(912) 437-6660
(800) 800-8000

DAWSONVILLE
BEST WESTERN DAWSON VILLAGE INN
76 North Georgia Ave (30534)
Rates: $55-$119
(706) 216-4410
(800) 528-1234

COMFORT INN
127 Beartooth Pkwy (30534)
Rates: $49-$99
(706) 216-1900
(800) 424-6423

DECATUR
BEST INN & SUITES
4095 Covington Hwy (30032)
Rates: $49-$65
(404) 286-2500

COMFORT INN NORTHEAST
4450 Memorial Dr (30032)
Rates: $49-$79
(404) 298-9255
(800) 424-6423

DAYS INN
4300 Snapfinger Woods Dr (30035)
Rates: $49-$129
(770) 981-5670
(800) 329-7466

GARDEN HOUSE B&B
135 Garden Ln (30035)
Rates: $81-$120
(404) 377 3057

EMORY CONF CENTER HOTEL
1615 Clifton Rd (30032)
Rates: $39-$120
(404) 712-6000

SYCAMORE HOUSE IN OLD DECATUR B&B
624 Sycamore St (30032)
Rates: $121+
(404) 378-0685

DILLARD
DILLARD HOUSE
768 Franklin St (30537)
Rates: $55-$169
(706) 746-5348
(800) 541-0671

RAMADA LTD
3 Best Inn Way (30537)
Rates: $59-$149
(706) 746-5321
(800) 272-6232

DONALSON-VILLE
DAYS INN
Hwy 84, 204 W 3rd St (39845)
Rates: $42-$190
(229) 524-2185
(800) 329-7466

DORAVILLE
MASTERS INN
3092 Presidential Pkwy (30340)
Rates: $39-$63
(770) 454-8373
(800) 633-3434

DOUGLAS
HOLIDAY INN
1750 S Peterson Ave (31533)
Rates: $69-$92
(912) 384-9100
(800) 465-4329

INN AT DOUGLAS
1007 N Peterson Ave (31533)
Rates: $35-$50
(912) 393-3638

WESTERN MOTEL
1700 S Peterson Ave (31533)
Rates: $35-$80
(912) 383-9888

DOUGLAS-VILLE
BEST WESTERN GARDEN INN & SUITES
8304 Cherokee Blvd (30134)
Rates: $49-$99
(800) 528-1234

AREA CODES - If the local number doesn't connect, check for a new area code.

RAMADA LTD
8315 Cherokee
Blvd (30134)
Rates: $35-$50
(770) 949-3090
(800) 272-6232

**ROYAL INN
& SUITES**
8366 Duralee
Lane (30134)
Rates: $40-$80
(770) 942-1036

DUBLIN

**BEST WESTERN
EXECUTIVE INN
& SUITES**
2121 Hwy 441 S
(31040)
Rates: $59-$69
(478) 275-2650
(800) 528-1234
(888) 274-6491

COMFORT INN
2110 Hwy 441 S
(31021)
Rates: $55-$70
(478) 274-8000
(800) 424-6423

ECONO LODGE
2184 Hwy 441 S
(31021)
Rates: $49-$79
(478) 296-1223
(800) 424-6423

JAMESON INN
100 P. M. Watson
Dr (31021)
Rates: $49-$104
(478) 275-3008
(800) 526-3766

DULUTH

**AMERISUITES
JOHN'S CREEK**
11505 Medlock
Bridge Rd (30097)
Rates: $59-$109
(770) 622-5858
(800) 833-1516

**AMERISUITES
GWINNETT MALL**
3530 Venture
Pkwy (30096)
Rates: $89-$109
(770) 623-9699
(800) 833-1516

**CANDLEWOOD
SUITES**
3665 Schackleford
Rd (30096)
Rates: $72-$93
(678) 380-0414
(888) 226-3539

DAYS INN
1920 Pleasant Hill
Rd (30096)
Rates: $70-$100
(770) 476-8700
(800) 329-7466

HAMPTON INN
1725 Pineland Rd
(30096)
Rates: $59-$79
(770) 931-9800
(800) 426-7866

HOLIDAY INN
6310 Sugarloaf
Pkwy (30097)
Rates: $51-$120
(770) 476-2022
(800) 465-4329

LA QUINTA INN
2370 Stephen
Center Dr (30096)
Rates: $79-$89
(678) 957-0500
(800) 687-6667

**RESIDENCE INN
BY MARRIOTT**
1760 Pineland Rd
(30096)
Rates: $134-$179
(770) 921-2202
(800) 331-3131

STUDIO 6
3525 Breckenridge
Blvd (30136)
Rates: $39-$61
(770) 931-3113
(888) 897-0202

WELLESLEY INN
3390 Venture
Pkwy NW (30096)
Rates: $69-$109
(770) 623-6800
(800) 444-8888

EAST DUBLIN

RAMADA LTD
735 Central Dr
(31027)
Rates: $40-$120
(478) 277-9161
(800) 272-6232

EAST ELLIJAY

**BEST WESTERN
MOUNTAIN
VIEW INN**
43 Coosawattee
Dr (30539)
Rates: $60-$150
(706) 515-1500
(800) 528-1234
(866) 515-4550

**STRATFORD
MOTOR INN**
Hwy 515 at
Maddox Dr East
(30539)
Rates: $38-$60
(706) 276-1080
(800) 526-1258

EASTONOLLEE

**APPLE ORCHARD
COUNTRY INN**
Liberty Hill Rd
(30538)
Rates: $51-$120
(706) 779-7292

EAST POINT

**AMERISUITES AIR-
PORT**
3415 Norman
Berry Dr (30344)
Rates: $75-$105
(404) 768-8484
(800) 833-1516

**CROWNE PLAZA
HOTEL & RESORT**
1325 Virginia Ave
(30344)
Rates: $139
(404) 768-6660
(800) 227-6963

**DRURY INN
& SUITES**
1270 Virginia Ave
(30344)
Rates: $73-$123
(404) 761-4900
(800) 378-7946

RED ROOF INN
1200 Virginia Ave
(30344)
Rates: $71-$76
(404) 209-1800
(800) 843-7663

WELLESLEY INN
1377 Virginia Ave
(30344)
Rates: $65-$95
(404) 762-5111
(800) 444-888

EASTMAN

EASTMAN MOTEL
1234 College St
(31023)
Rates: $30-$50
(478) 374-4765

EATONTON

WESTERN MOTEL
926 Oak St (31024)
Rates: $30-$50
(706) 485-1100

EDISON

DAPADY RANCH
Hwy 37 E (31746)
Rates: $125+
(229) 835-2964
(877) 489-7824

ELLIJAY

**BUDGET
HOST INN**
10 Jeff Dr (30540)
Rates: $35-$79
(706) 635-5311
(800)283-4678

ELLIJAY INN
30 S Main St
(30540)
Rates: $34-$65
(706) 635-4615

**OVERLAND
TRAILS LOG
CABIN RENTALS**
Hwy 282 & 76
(30540)
Rates: $95-$150
(706) 276-2211
(877) 474-5647

**SLIDING ROCK
CABINS**
177 Mossy Rock
Ln (30540)
Rates: $135-$145
(706) 636-5895

FITZGERALD

**COUNTRY
HEARTH INN**
125 Stuart Way
(31750)
Rates: $45-$95
(229) 409-9911
(866) 423-7945

**THE INN AT
FITZGERALD**
235 Ocilla Hwy
(31750)
Rates: $35-$65
(229) 423-6661

JAMESON INN
111 Bull Run Rd
(31750)
Rates: $49-$104
(229) 424-9500
(800) 526-3766

FOLKSTON

DAYS INN
1201 S 2nd St
(31537)
Rates: $40-$199
(912) 496-2514
(800) 329-7466

**GEORGIAN
HOTEL**
1900 N 2nd St
(43537)
Rates: $30-$50
(912) 496-7767

FOREST PARK

**DAYS INN
AIRPORT**
5116 Hwy 85
(30297)
Rates: $45-$90
(404) 768-6400
(800) 329-7466

ECONO LODGE
5060 Frontage Rd
(30297)
Rates: $41-$65
(404) 363-6429
(800) 553-2666

SUPER 8 MOTEL
410 Old Dixie
Hwy (30297)
Rates: $39-$55
(404) 363-8811
(800) 800-8000

FORSYTH

**BEST WESTERN
HILLTOP INN**
951 Hwy 42 N
(31029)
Rates: $45-$99
(478) 994-9260
(800) 528-1234

BOERD INN
I-75, Exit 188,
Hwy 42 (31029)
Rates: $30-$50
(478) 994-9333

AREA CODES - If the local number doesn't connect, check for a new area code.

DAYS INN
343 N Lee St
(31029)
Rates: $44-$89
(478) 994-2900
(800) 329-7466

HAMPTON INN
520 Holiday Cir
(31029)
Rates: $63-$80
(478) 994-9697
(800) 426-7866

HOLIDAY INN
480 Holiday Cir
(31029)
Rates: $87
(478) 994-5691
(800) 465-4329

REGENCY INN
325 Cabiness Rd
(31029)
Rates: $30-$50
(478) 994-9383

TRADEWINDS
100 Tradewinds
Dr (31029)
Rates: $30-$50
(912) 994-9383

FORT VALLEY
VALLEY INN
204 Commercial
Hts (31030)
Rates: $36-$80
(912) 822-9090

GAINESVILLE
**GEORGIANA
MOTEL**
1630 Atlanta
Hwy (30504)
Rates: $35-$80
(770) 534-7361

**GUESTHOUSE
INN & SUITES**
520 Queens City
Pkwy (30501)
Rates: $49-$70
(770) 535-8100
(800) 552-4667

MOTEL 6
1585 Monroe Dr
(30507)
Rates: $39-$42
(770) 532-7531
(800) 466-8356

RAMADA LTD
766 Jesse Jewell
Pkwy (30501)
Rates: $40-$120
(770) 287-3205
(800) 272-6232

GARDEN CITY
MASTERS INN
4200 Hwy 21 N
(31408)
Rates: $39-$73
(912) 964-4344

GLENNVILLE
CHEERI-O MOTEL
820 Musgrove St
(30427)
Rates: $35-$42
(912) 654-2176

GLENWOOD
SUPER 8 MOTEL
4600 Glenwood
Rd (30428)
Rates: $35-$50
(404) 289-4940
(800) 800-8000

GOLDEN ISLES
(See: Jekyll Island
& St. Simons Island)

GRAY
DAYS INN
288 W Clinton St
(31032)
Rates: $55-$75
(478) 986-4200
(800) 329-7466

GREENSBORO
MICROTEL INN
2470 Old
Eatonton Rd
(30642)
Rates: $45-$90
(706) 453-7300
(888) 771-7171

**WASHINGTON
GRASS INN B&B**
2281 Fuller Rd
(30642)
Rates: $81-$120
(706) 467-2520

GRIFFIN
**HOWARD
JOHNSON INN**
1690 N Expwy
(30223)
Rates: $45-$189
(770) 227-1516
(800) 446-4656

SCOTTISH INNS
1709 N Expwy
(30223)
Rates: $35-$50
(770) 228-6000
(800) 251-1962

GROVETOWN
MOTEL 6
459 Parkwest Dr
(30813)
Rates: $45-$50
(706) 651-8300
(800) 466-8356

GUYTON
**CLAUDETTE'S
COUNTRY INN**
106 E Central
Blvd (31312)
Rates: $81-$125+
(912) 772 3667
(866) 754-3301

HAHIRA
SUPER 8 MOTEL
1300 Hwy 122 W
(31632)
Rates: $35-$50
(229) 794-8000
(800) 800-8000

HAMILTON
**VALLEY INN
RESORT**
14420 Hwy 27
(31811)
Rates: $50-$80
(706) 628-4454
(800) 944-9393

HAMPTON
**COUNTRY
HEARTH INN**
1078 Bear Crk
Blvd (30228)
Rates: $59-$79
(770) 707-1477
(888) 443-2784

HAPEVILLE
**RESIDENCE INN
BY MARRIOTT**
3401 Intl Blvd
(30354)
Rates: $123-$156
(404) 761-0511
(800) 331-3131

HARTWELL
**BEST WESTERN
LAKE HARTWELL
INN & SUITES**
1357 E Franklin
St (30643)
Rates: $59-$149
(800) 528-1234

**LAKE HARTWELL
B&B**
533 Capri Dr
(30643)
Rates: $81-$125+
(706) 376-1557
(888) 266-8189

HAZELHURST
DAYS INN
312 Coffee St
(31539)
Rates: $35-$55
(912) 375-4527
(800) 329-7466

HELEN
BISCUIT INN B&B
Hwy 356 (30545)
Rates: $51-$120
(706) 892-9837

**BLUE RIDGE
CABIN RENTALS**
2990 Hwy 356
(30571)
Rates: $99-$399
(706) 878-1773

ECONO LODGE
749 Brukenstass
St (30545)
Rates: $35-$250
(706) 878-2141
(800) 424-6423

**HELENDORF
RIVER INN &
TOWERS**
33 Munich
Strasse (30545)
Rates: $34-$160
(706) 878-2271
(800) 445-2271

**HOFBRAUHAUS
RIVERFRONT
MOTEL**
9001 Main St
(30545)
Rates: $51-$125+
(706) 878-2248
(800) 830-3977

**KOUNTRY
PEDDLER
TANGLEWOOD
RESORT**
3387 Hwy 356
(30571)
Rates: $100-$585
(706) 878-3286

**LUND'S
HIDEAWAY
CABINS**
7489 Hwy 75 Alt
(30545)
Rates: n/a
(706) 878-3111

**PREMIER VACA-
TION RENTALS**
5156 Helen Hwy
(30571)
Rates: $85-$595
(706) 348-8323

HIAWASSEE
**ENOTA B&B,
MTN RETREAT**
1000 Hwy 180
(30546)
Rates: $100-$165
(706) 896-9966
(800) 900-8869

**HENSON COVE
PLACE B&B
& CABIN**
1137 Car Miles
Rd (30546)
Rates: $70-$75
(706) 896-6195
(800) 714-5542

**HORNE'S
HIDEAWAY**
1 Hornes
Hideaway
(30546)
Rates: $65-$85
(706) 896-6292

HIAWASSEE INN
193 E Main St
(30546)
Rates: $41-$88
(706) 896-4121
(800) 711-6961

**MOUNTAIN
MEMORIES B&B**
385 Chauncey Dr
(30546)
Rates: $81-$125
(706) 896-8439
(800) 335-8439

SALALE LODGE
1340 Palmer
Place, US 76E
(30546)
Rates: $49-$79
(706) 896-3943

HINESVILLE

DAYS INN-FT. STEWART
738 Oglethorpe
Hwy (31313)
Rates: $45-$65
(912) 368-4146
(800) 329-7466

QUALITY INN
706 Oglethorpe
Hwy (31313)
Rates: $65
(912) 876-4466
(800) 424-6423

HIRAM

COUNTRY INN & SUITES
70 Enterprise
Path (30134)
Rates: $69-$110
(770) 222-0456
(800) 456-4000

HOGANSVILLE

DAYS INN
1630 Bass Cross
Rd (30230)
Rates: $50-$55
(706) 637-5400
(800) 329-7466

ECONO LODGE
1888 E Main St
(30230)
Rates: $40-$90
(706) 637-9395
(800) 424-6423

JASPER

SUPER 8 MOTEL
100 Whitfield Dr
(30143)
Rates: $60-$90
(706) 253-3297
(800) 800-8000

JEKYLL ISLAND

CLARION RESORT BUCCANEER
85 S Beachview
Dr (31527)
Rates: $75-$115
(912) 635-2261
(800) 253-5955

COMFORT INN ISLAND SUITES
711 N Beachview
Dr (31527)
Rates: $69-$369
(912) 635-2211
(800) 424-6423
(800) 204-0202

HOLIDAY INN BEACH RESORT
200 S Beachview
Dr (31527)
Rates: $64-$129
(912) 635-3311
(800) 753-5955

JEKYLL INN
975 N Beachview
Dr (31527)
Rates: $99-$129
(912) 635-2531
(800) 736-1046

QUALITY INN & SUITES
700 N Beachview
Dr (31527)
Rates: $79-$250
(912) 635-2202
(800) 424-6423

VILLAS BY THE SEA HOTEL CONDO
1175 N
Beachview Dr
(31527)
Rates: $84-$239
(912) 635-2521
(800) 841-6262

JESUP

JAMESON INN
205 Hwy 301 N
(31545)
Rates: $49-$104
(912) 427-6800
(800) 526-3766

WESTERN MOTEL
194 Hwy 301 S
(31545)
Rates: $37-$57
(912) 427-7600

JONESBORO

HOLIDAY INN
6288 Old Dixie
Hwy (30236)
Rates: $80-$100
(770) 968-4300
(800) 465-4329

RAMADA INN
6326 Old Dixie
Hwy (30236)
Rates: n/a
(770) 968-4700
(800) 272-6232

SHONEYS INN
6358 Old Dixie
Hwy (30236)
Rates: $49-$63
(770) 968-5018
(800) 222-2222
(800) 552-4667

KENNESAW

BEST WESTERN KENNESAW INN
3375 George
Busbee Pkwy
(30144)
Rates: $59-$95
(770) 424-7666
(800) 528-1234

COUNTRY INN BY CARLSON
3192 Barrett
Lakes Blvd
(30144)
Rates: $79-$125
(770) 423-7105
(800) 456-4000

RAMADA LTD
750 Cobb Place
Blvd (30144)
Rates: $51-$80
(770) 419) 1530
(800) 272-6232

RED ROOF INN-TOWN CENTER
520 Roberts Ct
NW (30144)
Rates: $40-$52
(770) 429-0323
(800) 843-7663

RESIDENCE INN BY MARRIOTT-TOWN CTR
3443 Busbee Dr
(30144)
Rates: $71-$159
(770) 218-1018
(800) 331-3131

RODEWAY INN
1460 George
Busbee Pkwy
(30144)
Rates: $39-$60
(770) 590-0519
(800) 228-2000

TOWNEPLACE SUITES
1074 Cobb Place
Blvd NW (30144)
Rates: $95-$125
(770) 794-8282
(800) 257-3000

KINGSLAND

BEST WESTERN KINGS BAY INN
1353 Hwy 40 E
(31548)
Rates: $73-$89
(912) 729-7666
(800) 728-7666

COMFORT INN
111 Edenfield Rd
(31548)
Rates: $45-$199
(912) 729-6979
(800) 424-6423

DAYS INN
1050 E King Ave
(31548)
Rates: $30-$300
(912) 729-5454
(800) 329-7466

ECONO LODGE
1135 E King Ave
(31548)
Rates: $45-$65
(912) 673-7336
(800) 424-6423

HOMETOWN SUITES INN
2343 Village Dr
(31548)
Rates: $58-$100
(912) 882-3004
(800) 432-6784

JAMESON INN
105 Maycreek Dr
(31548)
Rates: $49-$104
(912) 729-9600
(800) 526-3766

RAMADA INN
930 Hwy 40 E
(31548)
Rates: $49-$79
(912) 729-3000
(800) 272-6232

SUPER 8 MOTEL
120 Edenfield Dr
(31548)
Rates: $35-$85
(912) 729-6888
(800) 800-8000

LA FAYETTE

DAYS INN
2209 N Main St
(30728)
Rates: $50-$150
(706) 639-9362
(800) 329-7466

LA GRANGE

BEST WESTERN LAFAYETTE GARDEN INN
1513 Lafayette
Pkwy (30240)
Rates: $75-$90
(706) 884-6175
(800) 528-1234
(866) 523-2938

DAYS INN-CALLAWAY GARDENS
2606 Whitesville
Rd (30240)
Rates: $45-$75
(706) 882-8881
(800) 329-7466

ECONO LODGE
1601 Lafayette
Pkwy (30241)
Rates: $39-$81
(706) 882-9540
(800) 424-6423

JAMESON INN
110 Jameson Dr
(30241)
Rates: $49-$104
(706) 882-8700
(800) 526-3766

LAKE PARK

DAYS INN
4913 Timber Dr
(31636)
Rates: $45-$55
(229) 559-0229
(800) 329-7466

LAKE PARK INN
6972 Belleville Rd
(31636)
Rates: $35-$80
(229) 559-4939

SUPER 8 MOTEL
4907 Timber Dr
(31636)
Rates: $45-$65
(229) 559-8111
(800) 800-8000

TRAVELODGE
4912 Timber Dr
(31636)
Rates: $38-$60
(229) 559-0110
(800) 578-7878

LAVONIA

BEST WESTERN REGENCY INN & SUITES
13705 Jones St (30553)
Rates: $49-$89
(706) 356-4000
(800) 528-1234

GUESTHOUSE INN
14227 Jones St (30553)
Rates: $40-$80
(706) 356-8848
(800) 214-8378

SOUTHERN OAKS B&B
30 Baker St (30553)
Rates: $51-$80
(706) 356-8382
(888) 850-8178

LAWRENCE-VILLE

A TOUCH OF HOME BED & BREAKFAST
489 Hearth Place (30243)
Rates: $35-$50
(770) 277-3579

DAYS INN
731 Duluth Hwy (30245)
Rates: $51-$90
(770) 995-7782
(800) 329-7466

HAMPTON INN
1135 Lakes Pkwy (30043)
Rates: $59-$89
(770) 338-9600
(800) 426-7866

LINCOLNTON

CULLARS INN
140 Elm St (30817)
Rates: $30-$50
(706) 359-6161

LITHIA SPRINGS

COMFORT INN
850 Crestmark Dr (30122)
Rates: $59-$82
(770) 941-5384
(800) 424-6423

MOTEL 6
920 Bob Arnold Blvd (30122)
Rates: $39-$52
(678) 945-0606
(800) 466-8356

SUITEONE HOTEL
637 Market Cir (30122)
Rates: $49-$99
(770) 948-8331

LITHONIA

AMERISUITES
7900Mall Ring Rd (30038)
Rates: $79-$149
(770) 484-4384
(800) 833-1516

MOTEL 6
2859 Panola Rd (30058)
Rates: $39-$60
(770) 981-6411
(800) 466-8356

LOCUST GROVE

ECONO LODGE
4829 Bill Gardner Pkwy (30248)
Rates: $42-$120
(770) 957-2601
(800) 424-6423

EXECUTIVE INN
4854 Bill Gardner Pkwy (30248)
Rates: $34-$49
(770) 957-2671

RED ROOF INN & SUITES
4832 Bill Gardner Pkwy (30248)
Rates: $54-$89
(678) 583-0004
(800) 843-7663

SCOTTISH INNS
4679 Bill Gardner Pkwy (30248)
Rates: $30-$131
(770) 957-9001

SUNDOWN LODGE
4675 Bill Gardner Pkwy (30248)
Rates: $30-$53
(770) 957-9002

LOUISVILLE

ALLENWOOD MOTEL
525 Hwy 1 Bypass (30434)
Rates: $38+
(478) 625-7205

LOUISVILLE MOTOR LODGE
308 Hwy 1 Bypass (30434)
Rates: $37-$80
(478) 625-7168

MACON

BEST INNS & SUITES
130 Holiday North Dr (31210)
Rates: $39-$55
(478) 405-0106

BEST WESTERN INN & SUITES
4681 Chambers Rd (31206)
Rates: $50-$99
(478) 781-5300
(800) 528-1234

BEST WESTERN RIVERSIDE INN
2400 Riverside Dr (31204)
Rates: $49-$69
(478) 7436311
(800) 528-1234
(888) 454-4565

COMFORT INN
2690 Riverside Dr (31204)
Rates: $49-$69
(478) 746-8855
(800) 424-6423

CROWNE PLAZA HOTEL
108 First St (31201)
Rates: $64-$129
(478) 746-1461
(800) 227-6963

DAYS INN EAST
2856 Jeffersonville Rd (31217)
Rates: $52-$125
(478) 755-9091
(800) 329-7466

DAYS INN N
2737 Sheraton Dr (31204)
Rates: $40-$50
(478) 745-8521
(800) 329-7466

DISCOVERY INN
4604 Chambers Rd (31204)
Rates: $30-$50
(478) 781-2810

ECONO LODGE
4951 Romeiser Rd (31206)
Rates: $32-$45
(478) 474-1661
(800) 424-6423

FAMILY INNS OF AMERICA
4173 Interstate Pkwy (31204)
Rates: $35-$50
(478) 474-8800
(800) 732-8383

HAMPTON INN
3680 Riverside Dr (31210)
Rates: $62-$72
(478) 471-0660
(800) 426-7866

HAWTHORN INN & SUITES
107 Holiday N Dr (31204)
Rates: $59-$73
(478) 471-2121
(800) 527-1133

HOLIDAY INN
3590 Riverside Dr (31210)
Rates: $74-$80
(478) 474-2610
(800) 465-4329

HOWARD JOHNSON
2566 Riverside Dr (31204)
Rates: $50-$65
(478) 746-7671
(800) 446-4656

INN AMBASSADOR
4546 Hartley Bridge Rd (31204)
Rates: $38-$50
(478) 788-7500

JAMESON INN
150 Plantation Inn Dr (31210)
Rates: $49-$104
(478) 474-8004
(800) 526-3766

KNIGHTS INN
4952 Romeiser Dr (31206)
Rates: $32-$48
(478) 471-1230
(800) 843-5644

LA QUINTA INN & SUITES
3944 River Place Dr (31204)
Rates: $59-$89
(478) 475-0206
(800) 687-6667

MASTERS INN
4295 Pio Nono Ave (31206)
Rates: $29-$43
(478) 788-8910
(800) 633-3434

MOTEL 6
4991 Harrison Rd (31206)
Rates: $29-$34
(478) 474-2870
(800) 466-8356

QUALITY INN
4630 Chambers Rd (31206)
Rates: $45-$85
(478) 781-7000
(800) 424-6423

RED ROOF INN
3950 River Place Dr (31210)
Rates: $40-$64
(478) 477-7477
(800) 843-7663

REGENCY INN & SUITES
5009 Harrison Rd (31206)
Rates: $30-$50
(478) 474-0871

RESIDENCE INN BY MARRIOTT
3900 Sheraton Dr (31204)
Rates: $81-$175+
(478) 475-4280
(800) 331-3131

AREA CODES - If the local number doesn't connect, check for a new area code.

RODEWAY INN
4999 Eisenhower
Pkwy (31206)
Rates: $49-$54
(478) 781-4343
(800) 424-6423

SCOTTISH INN
5022 Romeiser Dr
(31206)
Rates: $30-$50
(478) 474-2665
(800) 251-1962

SLEEP INN
140 Plantation
Inn Dr (31210)
Rates: $65-$79
(478) 476-8111
(800) 424-6423

SUPER 8 MOTEL
6007 Harrison Rd
(31206)
Rates: $35-$74
(478) 788-8800
(800) 800-8000

TRAVELODGE
3850 Riverside
Dr (31206)
Rates: $40-$80
(478) 474-9902
(800) 578-7878

MADISON

**BURNETT PLACE
B&B**
317 Old Post Rd
(30650)
Rates: $120+
(706) 342-4034

DAYS INN
2001 Eatonton
Hwy (30650)
Rates: $43-$95
(706) 342-1839
(800) 329-7466

**MADISON FARM
B&B**
1981 Broughton
Rd (30650)
Rates: $120+
(706) 342-9269
(866) 342-9269

RAMADA INN
2020 Eatonton Rd
(30650)
Rates: $44-$85
(706) 342-2121
(800) 272-6232

SUPER 8 MOTEL
2091 Eatonton Rd
(30650)
Rates: $45-$120
(706) 342-7800
(800) 800-8000

MANCHESTER

**DAYS INN
LITTLE WHITE
HOUSE**
2546 Roosevelt
Hwy (31816)
Rates: $55-$95
(706) 846-1247
(800) 329-7466

MARIETTA

DAYS INN
753 N Marietta
Pkwy (30060)
Rates: $52-$120
(676) 797-0233
(800) 329-7466

**DRURY INN
& SUITES**
1170 Powers
Ferry Rd (30067)
Rates: $63-$97
(770) 612-0900
(800) 378-7946

ECONO LODGE
1940 Leland Dr
(30067)
Rates: $44-$109
(770) 952-0052
(800) 424-6423

**HOMESTEAD
STUDIO SUITES**
2239 Powers
Ferry Rd (30067)
Rates: $57-$82
(770) 303-0043
(888) 782-9473

**HOWARD
JOHNSON**
2375 Delk Rd
(30067)
Rates: $48-$88
(770) 951-1144
(800) 446-4656

**HYATT REGENCY
SUITES
PERIMETER**
2999 Windy Hill
Rd (30067)
Rates: $75-$195
(770) 956-1234
(800) 233-1234

LA QUINTA INN
2170 Delk Rd
(30067)
Rates: $65-$81
(770) 951-0026
(800) 687-6667

MASTERS INN
2682 Windy Hill
Rd (30067)
Rates: $39-$63
(770) 951-2005
(800) 633-3434

MOTEL 6
2360 Delk Rd
(30067)
Rates: $35-$40
(770) 952-8161
(800) 466-8356

QUALITY INN
1255 Franklin Rd
(30067)
Rates: $59-$119
(770) 955-0004
(800) 424-6423

**RAMADA
LIMITED SUITES**
630 Franklin Rd
(30067)
Rates: $45-$54
(770) 919-7878
(800) 272-6232

STUDIO 6
2360 Delk Rd,
Suite 301 (30067)
Rates: $199-$259
(770) 952-2395
(888) 897-0202

SUPER 8 MOTEL
610 Franklin Rd
(30067)
Rates: $42-$54
(770) 919-2340
(800) 800-8000

TRAVELERS INN
2500 Delk Rd
(30067)
Rates: $51-$80
(770) 984-1570

**WYNDHAM
GARDEN HOTEL**
1775 Parkway Pl
NW (30067)
Rates: $69-$109
(770) 428-4400
(800) 800-5798

MCCAYSVILLE

**COMPANY
HOUSE B&B INN**
125 Main St
(30555)
Rates: $81-$120
(423) 496-5634
(800) 343-2909

MCDONOUGH

COMFORT INN
80 SR 81 W (30253)
Rates: $65-$155
(770) 954-9110
(800) 424-6423

DAYS INN
744 Hwy 155 S
(30253)
Rates: $48-$160
(770) 957-5261
(800) 329-7466

ECONO LODGE
1279 Hampton
Rd (30253)
Rates: $42-$140
(770) 957-2651
(800) 424-6423

ECONOMY INN
1171 Hampton
Rd (30253)
Rates: $35-$50
(770) 898-5858

HOLIDAY INN
930 Hwy 155 S
(30253)
Rates: $69-$84
(770) 957-5291
(800) 465-4329

**MASTERS
ECONOMY INN**
1311 Hampton
Rd (30253)
Rates: $40-$140
(770) 957-5818
(800) 633-3434

SUPER 8 MOTEL
1170 Hampton
Rd (30253)
Rates: $46-$50
(770) 957-2458
(800) 800-8000

MCRAE

MAGNOLIA INN
750 E Oak St
(31055)
Rates: $35-$50
(229) 868-7431

METTER

METTER INN
850 S Lewis St
(30439)
Rates: $35-$80
(912) 685-2800

MIDWAY

MIDWAY MOTEL
271 N Coastal
Hwy (31320)
Rates: $29-$50
(912) 884-5416

MILLEDGEVILLE

DAYS INN
2551 N Columbia
St (31061)
Rates: $59-$69
(478) 453-8471
(800) 329-7466

**HOLIDAY INN
EXPRESS HOTEL**
1839 N Columbia
St (31061)
Rates: $65-$78
(478) 454-9000
(800) 465-4329

RAMADA LTD
2627 N Columbia
St (31061)
Rates: $40-$120
(478) 452-3502
(800) 272-6232

MONROE

**COUNTRY
HEARTH INN**
1222 W Spring St
(30655)
Rates: $55-$70
(770) 207-1977
(888) 443-2784

MONTEZUMA

**TRAVELERS
REST B&B**
318 N Dooly St
(31063)
Rates: $80-$120
(478) 472-0085

MORROW

**BEST WESTERN
SOUTHLAKE INN**
6347 Jonesboro
Rd (30260)
Rates: $59-$119
(770) 961-6300
(888) 277-5253

AREA CODES - If the local number doesn't connect, check for a new area code.

COMFORT SUITES
South Lake Plaza Dr (30260)
Rates: $60-$169
(800) 424-6423

DAYS INN
1599 Adamson Pkwy (30260)
Rates: $49-$99
(770) 961-6044
(800) 329-7466
(888) 757-3297

DRURY INN & SUITES
6520 S Lee St (30260)
Rates: $62-$102
(770) 960-0500
(800) 378-7946

QUALITY INN SOUTHLAKE
6597 Hwy 54 (30260)
Rates: $45-$160
(770) 960-1957
(800) 424-6423

RED ROOF INN
1348 Southlake Plaza Dr (30260)
Rates: $40-$65
(770) 968-1483
(800) 843-7663

SLEEP INN
2185 Mt. Zion Prkwy (30260)
Rates: $49-$169
(770) 472-9800
(800) 424-6423

MOULTRIE

TOWN TERRACE
600 S Main St (31768)
Rates: $35-$50
(229) 985-3980

NEWNAN

BEST WESTERN SHENANDOAH INN
620 Hwy 34 E (30263)
Rates: $60-$120
(770) 304-9700
(800) 528-1234
(877) 455-1245

JAMESON INN
40 Lakeside Way (30265)
Rates: $49-$104
(770) 252-1236
(800) 526-3766

LA QUINTA INN
600 Bullsboro Dr (30265)
Rates: $40-$80
(770) 502-8688
(800) 687-6667

MOTEL 6
40 Parkway North (30265)
Rates: $39-$46
(770) 251-4580
(800) 466-8356

NORCROSS

AMBERLEY SUITE HOTEL
5885 Oakbrook Pkwy (30093)
Rates: $59-$99
(770) 263-0515
(800) 365-0659

AMERISUITES
5600 Peachtree Pkwy (30092)
Rates: $89-$109
(770) 416-7655
(800) 833-1516

CLUBHOUSE INN & SUITES
5945 Oakbrook Pkwy (30093)
Rates: $59-$89
(770) 368-9400

DAYS INN
5990 Western Hills Dr (30071)
Rates: $49-$79
(770) 368-0218
(800) 329-7466

DRURY INN
5655 Jimmy Carter Blvd (30071)
Rates: $55-$120
(770) 729-0060
(800) 325-8300
(800) 378-7946

GUESTHOUSE INN
2050 Willowtrail Pkwy (30093)
Rates: $49-$69
(770) 564-0492
(800) 214-8378

HILTON HOTEL NORTHEAST
5993 Peachtree Ind Blvd (30071)
Rates: $72-$160
(770) 447-4747
(800) 445-8667

HOMESTEAD STUDIO SUITES
7049 Jimmy Carter Blvd (30092)
Rates: $38-$63
(770) 449-9966
(888) 782-9473

HOMEWOOD SUITES
450 Technology Pkwy (30092)
Rates: $124-$174
(770) 448-4663
(800) 225-5466

LA QUINTA INN
5375 Peachtree Ind. Blvd (30071)
Rates: $60-$70
(770) 449-5144
(800) 687-6667

LA QUINTA INN
6187 Dawson Blvd (30093)
Rates: $60-$75
(770) 448-8686
(800) 687-6667

MOTEL 6
6015 Oakbrook Pkwy (30093)
Rates: $32-$36
(770) 446-2311
(800) 466-8356

RAMADA LTD
6045 Oakbrook Pkwy (30093)
Rates: $59-$99
(770) 449-7322
(800) 272-6232

RED ROOF INN
5171 Brook Hollow Pkwy (30071)
Rates: $36-$54
(770) 448-8944
(800) 843-7663

RED ROOF INN
5395 Peachtree Industrial Blvd (30092)
Rates: $43-$63
(770) 446-2882
(800) 843-7663

RESIDENCE INN BY MARRIOTT PEACHTREE CORNERS
5500 Triangle Dr (30071)
Rates: $51-$120
(770) 447-1714
(800) 331-3131

TOWNEPLACE SUITES
6640 Bay Cir (30071)
Rates: $40-$120
(770) 447-8446
(800) 257-3000

OAKWOOD

ADMIRAL BENBOW INN
4500 Oakwood Rd (30566)
Rates: $58-$79
(770) 531-9929
(800) 451-1986

COUNTRY INN & SUITES
4535 Oakwood Rd (30566)
Rates: $66-$145
(770) 535-8080
(800) 456-4000

JAMESON INN
3780 Merchants Way (30566)
Rates: $49-$104
(770) 533-9400
(800) 526-3766

PEACHTREE CITY

HOLIDAY INN HOTEL & SUITES
203 Newgate Rd (30269)
Rates: $51-$120
(770) 487-4646
(800) 465-4329

PERRY

BEST INN
110 Perimeter Rd (31069)
Rates: $32-$80
(478) 987-4454

BEST WESTERN BRADBURY INN
205 Lect Dr (31069)
Rates: $50-$150
(478) 218 5200
(800) 528-1234

COMFORT INN
1602 Sam Nunn Blvd (31069)
Rates: $44-$150
(478) 987-7710
(800) 424-6423

DAYS INN & SUITES
201 Lect Dr (31069)
Rates: $49-$119
(478) 987-8777
(800) 329-7466

ECONO LODGE
102 Valley Dr (31069)
Rates: $38-$51
(478) 987-2142
(800) 424-6423

GREAT INN
1006 St. Patrick Dr (31069)
Rates: $35-$50
(478) 987-5600
(877) 987-5600

GUESTHOUSE INN
202 Valley Dr (31069)
Rates: $36-$80
(478) 987-2585

HENDERSON VILLAGE
125 S Langston Cir (31069)
Rates: $175-$350
(478) 988-8696
(888) 615-9722

JAMESON INN
200 Market Place Dr (31069)
Rates: $49-$104
(478) 987-5060
(800) 526-3766

KNIGHTS INN
704 Mason Terrace (31069)
Rates: $35-$80
(478) 987-1515
(800) 843-5644

NEW PERRY HOTEL/MOTEL
800 Main St (31069)
Rates: $49-$94
(478) 987-1000
(800) 877-3779

AREA CODES - If the local number doesn't connect, check for a new area code.

QUALITY INN
1504 Sam Nunn
Blvd (31069)
Rates: $55-$95
(478) 987-1345
(800) 424-6423

RAMADA LTD
100 Market Place
Dr (31069)
Rates: $45-$90
(478) 987-8400
(800) 272-6232

RED CARPET INN
105 Gn. Courtney
Hodges Blvd
(31069)
Rates: $37-$35
(478) 987-2200
(800) 251-1962

RELAX INN
103 Marshallville
Rd (31069)
Rates: $30-$50
(478) 987-3200

SANDMAN MOTEL
400 Gn Courtney
Hodges Blvd
(31069)
Rates: $30-$50
(478) 987-2393

SCOTTISH INNS
405 Gn Courtney
Hodges Blvd
(31069)
Rates: $35-$55
(478) 987-3622
(800) 251-1962

SUPER 8 MOTEL
102 Plaza Drive
(31069)
Rates: $46-$60
(478) 987-0999
(800) 800-8000

PHENIX CITY
HOLIDAY INN EXP
1700 US 280
Bypass (36867)
Rates: n/a
(334) 298-9321
(800) 465-4329

PINE MOUNTAIN
DAYS INN
368 S Main Ave
(38122)
Rates: $55-$84
(806) 663-2121
(800) 329-7466

WHITE COLUMNS MOTEL
19727 S US 27
(31822)
Rates: $45-$80
(706) 663-2312
(800) 722-5083

POOLER
BEST WESTERN BRADBURY SUITES
155 Bourne Ave
(31322)
Rates: $69-$159
(912) 330-0330
(800) 528-1234

COMFORT INN & SUITES
301 Govenor
Treutlen Dr
(31322)
Rates: $59-$79
(912) 748-6464
(800) 424-6423

ECONO LODGE
500 E Hwy 80
(31322)
Rates: $56-$130
(912) 748-4124
(800) 424-6423

JAMESON INN
125 Bourne Ave
(31322)
Rates: $49-$109
(912) 748-0017
(800) 526-3766

RAMADA LTD
1016 E Hwy 80
(31322)
Rates: $40-$99
(912) 748-5242
(800) 272-6232

RED ROOF INN
20 Mill Creek Cir
(31322)
Rates: $60-$107
(912) 748-4050
(800) 843-7663

TRAVELODGE SUITES
130 Continental
Blvd (31322)
Rates: $59-$99
(912) 748-6363
(800) 578-7878

RABUN GAP
SYLVAN FALLS MILL B&B
156 Taylor's
Chapel Rd
(30568)
Rates: $81-$120
(706) 746-7138

REGISTER
SCOTTISH INN
2875 Hwy 301 S
(30417)
Rates: $39-$80
(912) 852-5200
(800) 251-1962

RICHLAND
DAYS INN
46 Nicholson St
(31825)
Rates: $40-$100
(229) 887-9000
(800) 329-7466

RICHMOND HILL
A-1 MOTEL
Hwy 17 N (31324)
Rates: $30-$50
(912) 756-2116

DAYS INN
I-95 & Hwy 17,
Exit 87 (31324)
Rates: $50-$100
(912) 756-3371
(800) 329-7466

MOTEL 6
4071 Hwy 17
(31324)
Rates: $29-$34
(912) 756-3543
(800) 466-8356

TRAVELODGE
I-95 & US 17
(31324)
Rates: $51-$100
(912) 756-3325
(800) 578-7878

RINCON
DAYS INN
582 Columbia
Ave (31326)
Rates: $44-$110
(912) 826-6966
(800) 329-7466

RINGGOLD
SUPER 8 MOTEL
5400 Alabama
Hwy (30736)
Rates: $43-$100
(706) 365-7080
(800) 800-8000

ROCKMART
DAYS INN
105 GTM Pkwy
(30153)
Rates: $40-$55
(770) 684-9955
(800) 329-7466

ROME
CLAREMONT HOUSE B&B
906 E Second Ave
(30161)
Rates: $81-$120
(706) 291-0900
(800) 254-4797

COLLEGE INN
2973 Hwy 275
(30161)
Rates: $30-$50
(706) 235-1717

COUNTRY HEARTH & SUITES
1318 Martha
Berry Blvd
(30161)
Rates: $40-$80
(706) 235-4760
(888) 443-2784

HOLIDAY INN-SKYTOP CENTER
20 US Hwy
411 E (30161)
Rates: $80
(706) 295-1100
(800) 465-4329

JAMESON INN
40 Grace Dr
(30616)
Rates: $49-$104
(706) 291-7797
(800) 526-3766

STONE HOUSE AT ZION FARMS
2979 Big Texas
Valley Rd (30616)
Rates: $125+
(706) 235-8002

SUPER 8 MOTEL
390 Dodd Blvd
SE (30161)
Rates: $39-$56
(706) 234-8182
(800) 800-8000

ROSWELL
BAYMONT INN
575 Old Holcomb
Bridge Rd
(30076)
Rates: $59-$69
(770) 552-0200
(877) 229-6668

BEST WESTERN ROSWELL SUITES
907 Holcomb
Bridge (30076)
Rates: $69-$74
(770) 552-5599
(800) 528-1234
(800) 784-8321

BROOKWOOD INN
9995 Old
Dogwood Rd
(30076)
Rates: $45-$59
(770) 587-5161
(888) 253-3609

STUDIO 6
9955 Old
Dogwood Rd
(30076)
Rates: $39-$61
(770) 992-9449
(888) 897-0202

SAINT MARYS
BELLE TARA INN
300 W Conyers St
(31558)
Rates: $81-$120
(912) 882-4199
(877) 749-5974

CUMBERLAND KINGS BAY LODGES
603 Sand Bar Dr
(31558)
Rates: $39-$69
(912) 882-8900
(800) 831-6664

GOODBREAD HOUSE B&B
209 Osborne Rd
(31558)
Rates: $81-$120
(912) 882-7490
(888) 840-1872

AREA CODES - If the local number doesn't connect, check for a new area code.

RIVERVIEW HOTEL
105 Osborne Rd (31558)
Rates: $39-$80
(912) 882-3242

ST. SIMONS ISLAND

NORTH BREAKERS CONDOS
1470 Wood Ave (31522)
Rates: $125+
(912) 638-5450
(800) 627-6850

SEA GATE INN
1014 Ocean Blvd (31522)
Rates: $51-$135
(912) 638-8661
(800) 562-8812

SANDERSVILLE

VILLA SOUTH MOTEL
725 South Harris St (31082)
Rates: $45-$55
(478) 552-1234
(800) 622-7589

SAUTEE

EAGLE'S BROOK B&B
423 Chimney Mtn Rd (30571)
Rates: $51-$120
(706) 878-4607

NACOOCHEE VALLEY GUEST HOUSE
2220 Hwy 17 (30571)
Rates: $59-$100
(706) 878-3830

ROYAL WINDSOR ENGLISH STYLE B&B
4490 Hwy 356 (30571)
Rates: $95-$145
(706) 878-1322

SAVANNAH

BALLASTONE INN HISTORIC B&B
14 E Oglethorpe Ave (31401)
Rates: $215-$395
(912) 236-1484

BAYMONT INN & SUITES
8484 Abercorn St (31406)
Rates: $64-$84
(912) 927-7660
(877) 229-6668

BEST VALUE INN
390 Canebrake Rd (31419)
Rates: $45-$65
(912) 927-2999

BEST WESTERN CENTRAL INN
45 Eisehower Dr (31406)
Rates: $59-$104
(912) 355-1000
(800) 528-1234

CATHERINE WARD HOUSE B&B
118 E Waldburg St (31419)
Rates: $149-$400
(912) 234-8564
(800) 327-4270

CLUBHOUSE INN & SUITES
6800 Abercorn St (31405)
Rates: $75-$109
(912) 356-1234
(800) CLUB-INN

COMFORT SUITES HISTORIC DISTRICT
630 W Bay St (31401)
Rates: $89-$269
(912) 629-2001
(800) 424-6423

DAYS INN
4 Gateway Blvd E (31419)
Rates: $70-$82
(912) 925-3680
(800) 329-7466

EAST BAY INN HISTORIC COUNTRY INN
225 E Bay St (31401)
Rates: $99-$189
(912) 238-1225
(800) 500-1225

ECONO LODGE
7 Gateway Blvd W (31419)
Rates: $49-$129
(912) 925-2280
(800) 424-6423

ECONO LODGE HISTORIC DISTRICT
512 W Oglethorpe Ave (31401)
Rates: $69-$200
(912) 233-9251
(800) 424-6423

EXECUTIVE SUITES AT CHATHAM SQ.
554 E Taylor (31401)
Rates: $81-$150
(912) 232-9175

FORSYTH PARK INN HISTORIC B&B
102 W Hall St (31401)
Rates: $130-$230
(912) 233-6800
(866) 670-6800

FOX HOUSE INN B&B
536 E Harris St (31419)
Rates: $125+
(912) 644-7444

GUEST HOUSE
7312 White Bluff Rd (31419)
Rates: $38-$80
(912) 351-9755

HOMEWOOD SUITES
5820 White Bluff Rd (31405)
Rates: $151-$217
(912) 353-8500
(800) 225-5466

HOWARD JOHNSON EXP
17003 Abercorn St (31419)
Rates: $55-$99
(912) 925-7050
(800) 446-4656

IVY INN B&B
505 E President St (31401)
Rates: $125+
(912) 236-1122

JOAN'S ON JONES B & B
17 W Jones St (31401)
Rates: $145-$160
(912) 234-3863
(888) 989-9806

LA QUINTA INN
6805 Abercorn St (31405)
Rates: $70-$95
(912) 355-3004
(800) 687-6667

LA QUINTA INN
6 Gateway Blvd S (31419)
Rates: $75-$94
(912) 925-9505
(800) 687-6667

THE MANOR HOUSE B&B
201 W Liberty St (31401)
Rates: $145-$250
(912) 233-9597
(800) 462-3595

MASTERS INN
4200 Hwy 21 N (31408)
Rates: $43-$80
(912) 964-4344
(800) 633-3434

OLDE GEORGIAN INN B&B
212 W Hall St (31401)
Rates: $169-$299
(912) 236-2911
(800) 835-6831

OLDE HARBOUR INN B&B
508 E Factors Walk (31401)
Rates: $169-$350
(912) 234-4100
(800) 553-6533

QUALITY INN I-95 SOUTH
3 Gateway Blvd S (31419)
Rates: $49-$139
(912) 925-2770
(800) 424-6423

RED ROOF INN
405 Al Henderson Blvd (31419)
Rates: $46-$87
(912) 920-3535
(800) 843-7663

RESIDENCE INN BY MARRIOTT
5710 White Bluff Rd (31405)
Rates: $99-$179
(912) 356-3266
(800) 331-3131

SAVANNAH INN
100 Travelers Way (31401)
Rates: $38-$80
(912) 965-9555

SUBURBAN LODGE OF SAVANNAH
10614 Abercorn St Exit (31405)
Rates: $40-$80
(912) 920-7700
(800) 951-7829

SUPER 8 MOTEL
15 Fort Argyle Rd (31419)
Rates: $49-$64
(912) 927-8550
(800) 800-8000

TRAVELODGE
1 Fort Argyle Rd (31419)
Rates: $40-$199
(912) 925-2640
(800) 578-7878

WESTIN SAVAN-NAH HARBOR RESORT & SPA
1 Resort Dr (31421)
Rates: $149-$279
(912) 201-2000

SEA ISLAND

CLOISTER HOTEL
100 First St (31561)
Rates: $125+
(912) 638-3611
(800) 732-4752

AREA CODES - If the local number doesn't connect, check for a new area code.

SKY VALLEY

SKY VALLEY LODGING
3608 Hwy 246 N (30537)
Rates: $100-$300
(706) 746-5301
(800) 262-8259

SMYRNA

AMERIHOST INN
5130 S Cobb Dr (30082)
Rates: $69-$89
(404) 794-1600
(800) 434-5800

AMERISUITES GALLERIA
2876 Springhill Pkwy (30080)
Rates: $98-$109
(770) 384-0060
(800) 833-1516

BEST WESTERN INN & SUITES
2221 Corporate Plaza (30080)
Rates: n/a
(770) 541-1499
(800) 528-1234

COMFORT INN & SUITES GALLERIA
2800 Highlands Pkwy (30082)
Rates: $60-$129
(678) 309-1200
(800) 424-6423

HOLIDAY INN EXP
1200 Winchester Pkwy (30080)
Rates: $63-$85
(770) 333-9910
(800) 465-4329

HOMESTEAD SUTDIO SUITES
3103 Sports Ave (30080)
Rates: $47-$72
(770) 432-4000
(800) 225-5466

RED ROOF INN
2200 Corporate Plaza (30080)
Rates: $38-$51
(770) 952-6966
(800) 843-7663

RESIDENCE INN BY MARRIOTT
2771 Cumberland Blvd (30080)
Rates: $74-$149
(770) 433-8877
(800) 331-3131

STATESBORO

BEST WESTERN UNIVERSITY INN
1 Jameson Ave (30458)
Rates: $47-$63
(912) 681-7900
(800) 528-1234

BUDGET INN
109 N Main St (30458)
Rates: $35-$55
(912) 764-5631

DAYS INN
461 S Main St (30458)
Rates: $43-$100
(912) 764-5666
(800) 329-7466

DELUXE INN
225 N Main St (30458)
Rates: $38+
(912) 764-5651

GEORGIA'S B&B
123 S Zetterower Ave (30458)
Rates: $51-$80
(912) 489-6330

HISTORIC STATESBORO INN
106 S Main St (30458)
Rates: $85-$150
(912) 489-8628
(800) 846-9466

HOMETOWN INN
126 Rushing Ln (30458)
Rates: $51-$120
(912) 681-4663
(866) 830-4663

THE LODGE AT STATESBORO
406 Institute St (30458)
Rates: $35-$50
(912) 489-4176

RAMADA INN
230 S Main St (30458)
Rates: $35-$95
(912) 764-6121
(800) 272-6232

TRELLIS GARDEN INN
107 S Main St (30458)
Rates: $51-$120
(912) 489-8781
(800) 475-1380

STOCKBRIDGE

BEST WESTERN ATLANTA SOUTH
619 Hwy 138 (30281)
Rates: $60-$100
(770) 474-8771
(800) 528-1234

MOTEL 6
7233 Davidson Pkwy (30281)
Rates: $39-$57
(770) 389-1142
(800) 466-8356

RED ROOF INN & SUITES
637 Hwy 138 W (30281)
Rates: $40-$80
(678) 782-4100
(800) 843-7663

SHONEY'S INN
110 Hwy 138 W (30281)
Rates: $40-$80
(770) 389-5179
(800) 222-2222

SUPER 8 MOTEL
1451 Hudson Bridge Rd (30281)
Rates: $49-$130
(770) 474-5758
(800) 800-8000

SUCHES

TOCCOA RIVERFRONT CABIN
292 Brown Mt. Dr (30572)
Rates: $225 Three Nights
(352) 237-4335

SUMMERVILLE

COACH INN & SUITES
9785 Rome Blvd (30747)
Rates: $81-$125
(706) 857-7007

SEQUOYAH MOTEL
12384 Hwy 27 N (30747)
Rates: $35-$50
(706) 857-2497

SUWANEE

ADMIRAL BENBOW INN
2955 Hwy 317 (30024)
Rates: n/a
(770) 945-4921

COMFORT INN
2945 Hwy 317 (30024)
Rates: $59-$100
(770) 945-1608
(800) 424-6423

DAYS INN
3103 Hwy 317 (30024)
Rates: $44-$64
(770) 945-8372
(800) 329-7466

PARK INN
2955 Lawrenceville-Suwanee Rd (30024)
Rates: $51-$80
(770) 945-4921
(800) 465-4329

RED ROOF INN & SUITES
77 Swinco Blvd (30024)
Rates: $51-$80
(770) 271-5559
(800) 843-7663

SWAINSBORO

BRADFORD INN
688 S Main St (30401)
Rates: $50-$59
(478) 237-2400

BUDGET INN
322 S Main St (30401)
Rates: $35-$50
(478) 237-4786

COLEMAN HOUSE INN
323 N Main St (30401)
Rates: $55-$90
(478) 237-9100

DAYS INN
654 S Main St (30401)
Rates: $42-$60
(478) 237-9333
(800) 329-7466

NEW SWAINSBORO INN
612 S Main St (30401)
Rates: $35-$50
(478) 237-3577

SYLVESTER

DAYS INN
909 Franklin St (31791)
Rates: $40-$100
(229) 776-9700
(800) 329-7466

TALLAPOOSA

COMFORT INN
778 Hwy 100 & I-20 (30176)
Rates: $50-$200
(770) 574-5575
(800) 424-6423

THOMASTON

BEST WESTERN THOMASTON INN
1207 Hwy 19 N (30286)
Rates: $50-$80
(706) 648-2900
(800) 528-1234

DAYS INN
1215 Hwy 19 N (30286)
Rates: $62-$110
(706) 648-9260
(800) 329-7466

JAMESON INN
1010 Hwy 19 N (30286)
Rates: $49-$104
(706) 648-2232
(800) 526-3766

THOMASVILLE

COMFORT INN
14866 Hwy 19 S (31757)
Rates: $55-$92
(229) 225-9490
(800) 424-6423

AREA CODES - If the local number doesn't connect, check for a new area code.

DAYS INN
15375 US 19 S
(31792)
Rates: $38-$79
(229) 226-6025
(800) 329-7466

JAMESON INN
1670 Remington
Ave (31792)
Rates: $49-$104
(229) 227-9500
(800) 526-3766

**QUALITY INNS
& SUITES CONF
CENTER**
15138 Hwy 19 S
(31792)
Rates: $70-$136
(229) 225-2134
(800) 424-6423

THOMSON
**BEST WESTERN
WHITE COLUMNS
INN**
1890 Washington
Rd (30824)
Rates: $53-$399
(706) 595-8000
(800) 528-1234
(800) 528-9765

DAYS INN
2658 Cobbham
Rd (30824)
Rates: $50-$60
(706) 595-2262
(800) 329-7466

**KNOX
TERRACE MOTEL**
106 Georgia Ave
(30824)
Rates: $30-$50
(706) 595-1202

THOMSON INN
1847 Washington
Rd (30824)
Rates: $30-$50
(706) 595-8700
(800) 526-3766

TIFTON
DAYS INN
1199 Hwy 82 W
(31793)
Rates: $49-$99
(229) 382-8505
(800) 329-7466

ECONO LODGE
1025 W 2nd St
(31794)
Rates: $30-$50
(229) 382-0280
(800) 424-6423

**FAMILY VALUES
INN**
1103 King Rd
(31794)
Rates: $42-$55
(229) 386-9558
(800) 311-5353

HAMPTON INN
720 Hwy 319 S
(31794)
Rates: $82-$97
(229) 382-8800
(800) 426-7866

HOLIDAY INN
1208 Hwy 82 W
(31793)
Rates: $62-$68
(229) 382-6687
(800) 465-4329

MASTERS INN
901 7th St W
(31793)
Rates: $29-$43
(229) 382-8100
(800) 633-3434

**MICROTEL INN &
SUITES**
196 S Virginia
Ave (31794)
Rates: $39-$90
(229) 387-0112
(888) 771-7171

MOTEL 6
579 Old Omega
Rd (30281)
Rates: $34-$38
(229) 388-8777
(800) 466-8356

RAMADA LTD
1211 Hwy 82 W
(31793)
Rates: $48-$85
(229) 382-8500
(800) 272-6232

TOCCOA
**COUNTRY
HEARTH INN**
302 W Savannah
St (30577)
Rates: $40-$80
(706) 297-7799
(888) 443-2784

DAYS INN
(30577)
Rates: $35-$80
(706) 886-9641
(800) 329-7466

TAJ MOTEL
509 W Currahee
St (30577)
Rates: $35-$50
(706) 886-9458

TOWNSEND
DAYS INN
I-95 & GA 57,
Exit 58 (31331)
Rates: $50-$65
(912) 832-4411
(800) 329-7466

**EULONIA LODGE
MOTEL**
RR 3, Box 3350
(31331)
Rates: $30-$50
(912) 832-5175

TRENTON
**EL RANCHO
COURT**
12579 N Main St
(30752)
Rates: $45-$120
(706) 657-4201

TRION
EXPRESS INN
14364 Hwy 27
(30753)
Rates: $35-$80
(706) 734-2117

TUCKER
**COMFORT SUITES
NORTHLAKE**
2060 Crescent Ctr
Blvd (30084)
Rates: $69-$109
(770) 496-1070
(800) 424-6423

**ECONO LODGE
STONE
MOUNTAIN**
1820 Mounain
Ind Blvd (30084)
Rates: $35-$75
(770) 939-8440
(800) 424-6423

MASTERS INN
1435 Montreal Rd
(30084)
Rates: $39-$63
(770) 938-3552
(800) 633-3434

MOTEL 6
1819 Mountain
Ind Blvd (30084)
Rates: $44-$50
(770) 496-1317
(800) 466-8356

RED ROOF INN
2810 Lawrenceville
Hwy (30084)
Rates: $38-$53
(770) 496-1311
(800) 843-7663

STUDIO 6
1795 Crescent Ctr
Blvd (30084)
Rates: $219-$299
(770) 934-4040
(888) 897-0202

TYBEE ISLAND
**BEACHSIDE
COLONY**
404 Butler Ave
(31328)
Rates: $50-$125+
(912) 786-4535
(800) 786-0770

RODEWAY INN
905 Butler Ave
(31328)
Rates: $59-$250
(912) 786-4470
(800) 424-6423

SUPER 8 MOTEL
16 Tybrisia St
(31328)
Rates: $55-$85
(912) 786-8806
(800) 800-8000

**TYBEE
COTTAGES**
14 Captains View
(31328)
Rates: $125+
(912) 786-6746
(877) 524-9819

UNADILLA
RED CARPET INN
101 Robert St
(31091)
Rates: $35-$50
(478) 627-3261
(800) 251-1962

SCOTTISH INN
1062 Pine St
(31091)
Rates: $32-$50
(478) 627-3228
(800) 251-1962

UNION CITY
COMFORT INN
6800 Shannon
Way (30291)
Rates: $49-$109
(770) 306-2677
(800) 424-6423

**MICROTEL INN &
SUITES**
6690 Shannon
Pkwy (30291)
Rates: $40-$46
(770) 306-3800
(888) 771-7171

MOTEL 6
3860 Flat Shoals
Rd (30291)
Rates: $35-$46
(770) 969-0110
(800) 466-8356

RED ROOF INN
6710 Shannon
Pkwy (30291)
Rates: n/a
(770) 306-7750
(800) 843-7669

VALDOSTA
**BEST WESTERN
KING OF THE
ROAD INN**
1403 N St
Augustine Rd
(31601)
Rates: $55-$65
(229) 244-7600
(800) 528-1234

**COMFORT INN
CONFERENCE
CENTER**
2101 W Hill Ave
(31603)
Rates: $62-$150
(229) 242-1212
(800) 424-6423

**COUNTRY INN
& SUITES**
1308 N St.
Augustine Rd
(31601)
Rates: $51-$125
(229) 245-1700
(800) 456-4000

DAYS INN
4958 N Valdosta
Rd (31602)
Rates: $42-$59
(229) 244-4460
(800) 329-7466

AREA CODES - If the local number doesn't connect, check for a new area code.

DAYS INN
1827 W Hill Ave
(316015
Rates: $42-$99
(229) 249-8800
(800) 329-7466

GUESTHOUSE INT'L INN
1828 W Hill Ave
(31601)
Rates: $38-$48
(229) 244-7711
(800) 222-2222

HOLIDAY INN
1309 St Augustine
Rd (31601)
Rates: $69-$89
(229) 242-3881
(800) 465-4329

HOWARD JOHNSON
1330 St. Augustine
Rd (31601)
Rates: $44-$69
(229) 249-8900
(800) 446-4656

JAMESON INN
1725 Gornto Rd
(31601)
Rates: $49-$104
(229) 253-0009
(800) 541-3268

JOLLY INN
1701 Ellis Dr
(31601)
Rates: $35-$50
(229) 244-9500

LA QUINTA INN & SUITES
1800 Clubhouse
Dr (31601)
Rates: $69-$94
(229) 247-7755
(800) 687-6667

MOTEL 6- VALDOSTA STATE UNIV.
2003 West Hill
Ave (31601)
Rates: $29-$36
(229) 333-0047
(800) 466-8356

QUALITY INN NORTH
1209 St Augustine
Rd (31601)
Rates: $45-$85
(229) 244-8510
(800) 424-6423

QUALITY INN SOUTH
1902 W Hill Ave
(31601)
Rates: $45-$75
(229) 244-4520
(800) 424-6423

RAMADA LTD
2008 W Hill Ave
(31601)
Rates: $49-$99
(229) 242-1225
(800) 272-6232

SUPER 8 MOTEL
1825 W Hill Ave
(31601)
Rates: $42-$62
(229) 249-8000
(800) 800-8000

TRAVELERS INN
3470 Madison
Hwy (31601)
Rates: $35-$50
(229) 242-4664

VIDALIA

DAYS INN
1503 Lyons Hwy
(30474)
Rates: $50-$60
(912) 537-9251
(800) 329-7466

GRAND LADY SUITES
103 E Meadows
St (30474)
Rates: $51-$80
(912) 538-8988

HOLIDAY INN EXP
2619 E First St
(30474)
Rates: $69-$75
(912) 537-9000
(800) 465-4329

INN AT VIDALIA
2505 E First St
(30474)
Rates: $30-$50
(912) 537-1282

VILLA RICA

SUPER 8 MOTEL
195 Hwy 61
Connector
(30180)
Rates: $45-$65
(770) 459-8888
(800) 800-8000

WADLEY

WADLEY INN
Hwy 1 Bypass
(30477)
Rates: $35-$81
(478) 252-9393

WARM SPRINGS

BEST WESTERN WHITE HOUSE INN
2526 White House
Pkwy (31830)
Rates: $69-$135
(706) 655-2750
(800) 528-1234
(800) 667-7506

WARNER ROBINS

ADMIRAL BENBOW INN
2079 Watson Blvd
(31093)
Rates: $38-$58
(478) 929-9526
(800) 451-1986

BEST WESTERN PEACH INN
2739 Watson Blvd
(31099)
Rates: $45-$58
(478) 953-3000
(800) 528-1234

COMFORT INN ROBINS AFB
95 S SR 247
(31088)
Rates: $63-$160
(478) 922-7555
(800) 424-6423

COUNTRY INN
220 Margie Dr
(31088)
Rates: $60-$115
(478) 971-1660
(800) 456-4000

GUESTHOUSE INT'L
1440 Watson Blvd
(31093)
Rates: $35-$80
(478) 922-2006
(800) 214-8378

JAMESON INN
2731 Watson Blvd
(31093)
Rates: $49-$104
(478) 953-5522
(800) 526-3766

RAMADA INN
2725 Watson Blvd
(31093)
Rates: $51-$120
(478) 953-3000
(800) 272-6232

SUITE ONE
2103 Moody Rd
(31093)
Rates: $49-$84
(478) 329-9222

WASHINGTON

BABE'S HOUSE B&B
415-Rear E.
Robert Toombs
Ave (30673)
Rates: $81-$120+
(706) 678-2083

HOLLY RIDGE COUNTRY INN
2221 Sandtown
Rd (30673)
Rates: $81-$120
(706) 285-2594

SECOND TIME AROUND MINI FARM B&B
146 Hendry St
(30673)
Rates: $51-$120
(706) 678-4902

WATKINSVILLE

ASHFORD MANOR B&B
5 Harden Hill Rd
(30677)
Rates: $85-$120+
(706) 769-2633

WAVERLY HALL

RAINTREE FARMS B&B
8060 Hwy 208
(31831)
Rates: $125+
(706) 582-3227
(800) 433-0627

WAYCROSS

DAYS INN
2016 Memorial
Dr (31501)
Rates: $45+
(912) 285-4700
(800) 329-7466

HOLIDAY INN
1725 Memorial
Dr (31501)
Rates: $90-$100
(912) 283-4490
(800) 465-4329

JAMESON INN
950 City Blvd
(31501)
Rates: $49-$104
(912) 283-3800
(800) 526-3766

WAYNESBORO

DAYS INN
Hwy 25 S, South
Liberty St (30830)
Rates: $59-$155
(706) 554-9941
(800) 329-7466

JAMESON INN
1436 N Liberty St
(30830)
Rates: $49-$104
(706) 437-0500
(800) 526-3766

WEST POINT

TRAVELODGE
1870 State Rd 18
(31833)
Rates: $50-$105
(706) 643-9922
(800) 578-7878

WHITE

COURTESY ECONOMY INN
2335 Hwy 411 NE
(30184)
Rates: $38+
(770) 382-1122
(877) 434-6834

HOLIDAY INN
2336 Hwy 411 NE
(30184)
Rates: n/a
(770) 386-0830
(800) 465-4329

SCOTTISH INNS
2385 Hwy 411 NE
(30184)
Rates: $25-$100
(770) 382-7011
(800) 251-1962

WHITESBURG

PAPILLON RESORT
1105 Banning Rd
(30185)
Rates: $51-$125
(770) 830-1228

AREA CODES - If the local number doesn't connect, check for a new area code.

WINDER
JAMESON INN
9 Stafford St
(30680)
Rates: $49-$104
(770) 867-1880
(800) 526-3766

WOODSTOCK
COMFORT SUITES
340 Parkway 575
(30188)
Rates: $55-$109
(770) 517-9650
(800) 424-6423

SUITE ONE
470 Pkwy 575
(30188)
Rates: $49-$79
(770) 592-7848

YOUNG HARRIS
CREEKSIDE HIDEAWAY B&B/CABIN
8970 Sharons'
Way (30582)
Rates: $40-$85
(706) 379-1509
(888) 882-7335

HAWAII

SPECIAL NOTE: In the state of Hawaii, pets are not permitted in rooms. In addition, there may be a quarantine on pets arriving from the mainland. If you intend to visit Hawaii with your pet, contact the Hawaii Visitors Bureau, (800) 464-2924 or (808) 923-1811 for additional information.

IDAHO

ALBION
MOUNTAIN MANOR B&B
P. O. Box 128 (83311)
Rates: $45-$50
(208) 673-6642

AMERICAN FALLS
FALLS MOTEL
411 Lincoln (83211)
Rates: $30-$60
(208) 226-9658

HILLVIEW MOTEL
2799 Lakeview Rd (83211)
Rates: $39-$52
(208) 226-5151

ARCO
ARCO INN
540 W Grand Ave (83213)
Rates: $38-$50
(208) 527-3100

D-K MOTEL
316 S Front St (83213)
Rates: $32-$70
(208) 527-8282
(800) 231-0134

LAZY A MOTEL
318 W Grand Ave (83213)
Rates: $28-$50
(208) 527-8263
(800) 388-3679

LOST RIVER MOTEL
405 Highway Dr (83213)
Rates: $30-$65
(208) 527-3600

ASHTON
FOUR SEASONS MOTEL
P. O. Box 848 (83420)
Rates: $32-$50
(208) 652-7769

JENSEN'S B&B & COTTAGES
1146 N 3400 E Hwy 20 (83420)
Rates: $39-$49
(208) 652-3356
(800) 747-3356

LOG CABIN MOTEL
1001 Main (83420)
Rates: $43-$60
(208) 652-3956

RANKIN MOTEL
120 S Yellowstone Hwy (83420)
Rates: $36-$55
(208) 652-3570

SUPER 8 MOTEL TETON TRAVEL PLAZA
164 White Pine Dr (83420)
Rates: $28-$150
(208) 652-7885
(800) 800-8000

ATHOL
CEDAR MTN FARM B&B
25249 N Hatch Rd (83801)
Rates: $90-$135
(208) 683-0572
(866) 683-0572

KELSO LAKE RESORT CABINS
1450 Kelso Lake Rd (83801)
Rates: $40-$45
(208) 683-2297

AVERY
SWIFTWATER MOTEL
645 Old Seibert Rd (83802)
Rates: $35-$75
(208) 245-2845

BANKS
PONDEROSA
HC 76, Box 1010 (83602)
Rates: $25-$30
(208) 793-2700

TRAILS END MOTEL
HC 76, Box 1010 (83602)
Rates: $25-$40
(208) 793-2700

BAYVIEW
BAYVIEW SCENIC MOTEL
34297 N Main St (83803)
Rates: $50-$60
(208) 683-2215

BELLEVUE
HIGH COUNTRY MOTEL
765 Main St S (83313)
Rates: $50-$62
(208) 788-2050
(800) 692-2050

BLACKFOOT
BEST WESTERN BLACKFOOT INN
750 Jensen Grove Dr (83221)
Rates: $49-$89
(208) 785-4144
(800) 528-1234

SUPER 8 MOTEL
1279 Parkway Dr (83221)
Rates: $60-$89
(208) 785-9333
(800) 800-8000

WESTON RIVERISIDE INN
1229 Parkway Dr (83221)
Rates: $42-$95
(208) 785-5000

Y MOTEL
1375 S Broadway (83221)
Rates: $29-$49
(208) 785-1550

BLISS
AMBER INN
17286 US Hwy 30 (83314)
Rates: $36-$46
(208) 352-4441

BOISE
AMERISUITES
925 N Milwaukee St (83709)
Rates: $69-$125
(208) 375-1200
(800) 833-1516

BEST VALUE UNIVERSITY INN
2360 University Dr (83706)
Rates: $56-$78
(208) 345-7170

BEST WESTERN SAFARI MOTOR INN
1070 Grove St (83702)
Rates: $66-$85
(208) 3446556
(800) 528-1234
(800) 541-6556

BUDGET HOST INN
8002 Overland Rd (83709)
Rates: $45-$75
(208) 322-4404
(800) 733-1418

BUDGET INN
2600 Fairview Ave (83702)
Rates: $35-$65
(208) 344-8617
(800) 792-8612

CABANA INN
1600 Main St (83702)
Rates: $35-$60
(208) 343-6000

DOUBLETREE CLUB HOTEL
475 W Parkcenter Blvd (83706)
Rates: $69-$195
(208) 345-2002
(888) 222-8733

DOUBLETREE RIVERSIDE
2900 Chinden Blvd (83714)
Rates: $76-$300
(208) 343-1871
(800) 222-8733

ECONO LODGE
4060 W Fairview Ave (83706)
Rates: $55-$75
(208) 344-4030
(800) 424-6423

EXTENDED STAY AMERICA
2500 S Vista Ave (83705)
Rates: $60-$70
(208) 363-9040

HAMPTON INN
3270 S Shoshone (83705)
Rates: $99-$129
(208) 331-5600
(800) 426-7866

HOLIDAY INN AIRPORT
3300 Vista Ave (83705)
Rates: $89-$109
(208) 344-4900
(800) 465-4329

HOLIDAY MOTEL
5416 Fairview Ave (83706)
Rates: $27-$45
(208) 376-4631

MOTEL 6
2323 Airport Way (83705)
Rates: $41-$62
(208) 344-3506
(800) 466-8356

OWYHEE PLAZA HOTEL
1109 Main St (83702)
Rates: $75-$145
(208) 343-4611
(800) 233-4611

RED LION HOTEL DOWNTOWNER
1800 Fairview Ave (83702)
Rates: $69-$139
(208) 344-7691
(800) 733-5466

RED LION PARKCENTER SUITES
424 E Parkcenter Blvd (83706)
Rates: $59-$125
(208) 342-1044
(800) 342-1044

RESIDENCE INN BY MARRIOTT
1401 Lusk (83706)
Rates: $89-$175
(208) 344-1200
(800) 331-3131

ROBIN'S NEST B&B
2389 W Boise Ave (83706)
Rates: $79-$109
(208) 336-9551

RODEWAY INN
1115 N Curtis Rd (83706)
Rates: $65-$120
(208) 376-2700
(800) 424-6423

SHILO INN AIRPORT
4111 Broadway Ave (83705)
Rates: $52-$109
(208) 343-7662
(800) 222-2244

SHILO INN RIVERSIDE
3031 Main St (83702)
Rates: $49-$92
(208) 344-3521
(800) 222-2244

STATE MOTEL
1115 N 28th St (83702)
Rates: $39-$44
(208) 344-7245

SUPER 8 MOTEL
2773 Elder St (83705)
Rates: $40-$80
(208) 344-8871
(800) 800-8000

WEST RIVER INN
3525 Chinden Blvd (83714)
Rates: $28-$38
(208) 338-1155

WOLFF CORPORATE HOUSING
201 E 41st St, Suite 2 (83714)
Rates: $69-$89
(208) 387-0694
(800) 528-9519

BONNERS FERRY

BEST WESTERN KOOTENAI RIVER INN & CASINO
7169 Plaza St (83805)
Rates: $79-$125
(208) 267-8511
(800) 528-1234
(800) 346-5668

KOOTENAI VALLEY MOTEL
6409 S Main St (83805)
Rates: $35-$105
(208) 267-7567
(888) 292-0490

BUHL

OREGON TRAIL MOTEL
510 S Broadway (83316)
Rates: $38-$50
(208) 543-8814

SIESTA MOTEL
629 S Broadway (83316)
Rates: $26-$45
(208) 543-6427

BURLEY

BEST WESTERN INN & CONV CTR
800 N Overland Ave (83318)
Rates: $55-$103
(208) 678-3501
(800) 528-1234
(800) 599-1849

BUDGET MOTEL
900 N Overland Ave (83318)
Rates: $45-$69
(208) 678-2200
(800) 635-4952

LAMPLITER MOTEL
304 E Main (83318)
Rates: $32-$44
(208) 678-0031

STARLITE MOTEL
500 Overland (83318)
Rates: $25-$45
(208) 678-7766

CALDER

ST. JOE LODGE & RESORT
Rt 3, Box 350 (83808)
Rates: $50
(208) 245-3462

CALDWELL

BEST WESTERN CALDWELL INN
908 Specht Ave (83605)
Rates: $69-$139
(208) 454-7225
(800) 528-1234
(888) 454-3522

HOLIDAY MOTEL
512 Frontage Rd (83606)
Rates: $30+
(208) 455-3550

LA QUINTA INN
901 Specht Ave (83605)
Rates: $65-$90
(208) 454-2222
(800) 687-6667

SUNDOWNER MOTEL
1002 Arthur St (83606)
Rates: $42-$55
(208) 459-1585
(800) 454-9487

CAMBRIDGE

FRONTIER MOTEL
P. O. Box 178 (83610)
Rates: $32-$67
(208) 257-3851

HUNTER'S INN
Hwy 95 & 71 (83610)
Rates: $35-$65
(208) 257-3325

CASCADE

ARROWHEAD CABINS
Hwy 55, P. O. Box 337 (83611)
Rates: $31
(208) 382-4534

CASCADE VACATION RENTALS
Box 942 (83611)
Rates: $85-$300
(208) 382-4600
(866) 382-4800

CHIEF HOTEL & HIGH COUNTRY INN
112 N Main (83611)
Rates: $34-$60
(208) 382-3315

COUGAR MOUNTAIN LODGE
9738 Hwy 55 (83611)
Rates: $55-$65
(208) 382-4464

MOUNTAIN VIEW MOTEL
P. O. Box 1053 (83611)
Rates: $40-$60
(208) 382-4238
(800) 265-7666

PINEWOOD LODGE MOTEL
900 S Main St (83611)
Rates: $50-$72
(208) 382-4948
(866) 382-4941

SILVER PINES MOTEL
403 N Main (83611)
Rates: $40-$60
(208) 382-4370

WHITEWATER GUEST RANCH
HC 83, Frank Church River of No Return Wilderness Area (83611)
Rates: $50-$95
(208) 882-8082

AREA CODES - If the local number doesn't connect, check for a new area code.

CHALLIS

BENJAMIN'S AT GARDEN CREEK INN-COTTAGE & CABINS
Box 1087 (83226)
Rates: $45-$300
(208) 879-5084

HOLIDAY LODGE MOTEL
Hwy 93 N (83226)
Rates: $41-$57
(208) 879-2259
(866) 879-2259

NORTHGATE INN
HC 63, Box 1665
(83226)
Rates: $45-$60
(208) 879-2490

CHUBBUCK

OXBOW MOTOR INN
4333 Yellowstone Ave (83202)
Rates: $34-$39
(208) 237-3100

CLARK FORK

CLARK FORK LODGE
421 E 4th Ave
(83811)
Rates: $45-$79
(208) 266-1716

DIAMOND T GUEST RANCH
5361 River Rd •
(83811)
Rates: $55
(970) 663-4183

RIVER DELTA RESORT
60190 Hwy 200 E
(83811)
Rates: $52-$62
(208) 266-1335

CLAYTON

MAY FAMILY RANCH
60 N Squaw Creek Rd (83227)
Rates: $35-$70
(208) 838-2407

COEUR D'ALENE

BENNETT BAY INN
East 5144 Coeur d'Alene Dr
(83814)
Rates: $55-$150
(208) 664-6168
(800) 368-8609

BEST VALUE INN
330 Appleway Ave (83814)
Rates: $39-$79
(208) 765-3011

BEST WESTERN COEUR D'ALENE INN & CONF CTR
414 W Appleway Ave (83814)
Rates: $79-$149
(208) 765-3200
(800) 518-1234
(800) 251-7829

BOULEVARD MOTEL
2400 Seltice Way
(83814)
Rates: $35-$60
(208) 664-4978
(877) 611-7275

CEDAR MOTEL
319 Coeur d'Alene Lake Dr (83814)
Rates: $29-$92
(208) 664-2278

COEUR D'ALENE KOA CABINS
10588 E Wolf Lodge Bay Rd
(83814)
Rates: $59-$139
(208) 664-4471
(800) 251-7829

COEUR D'ALENE RESORT
115 S 2nd St
(83814)
Rates: $89-$399
(208) 765-4000

COUNTRY RANCH BED & BREAKFAST
1495 S Green Ferry Rd (83814)
Rates: $85-$95
(208) 664-1189

CRICKET ON THE HEARTH B&B
1521 Lakeside Ave
(83814)
Rates: $55-$85
(208) 664-6926

DAYS INN
2200 Northwest Blvd (83814)
Rates: $49-$75
(208) 667-8668
(800) 329-7466

EL RANCHO MOTEL
1915 E Sherman Ave (83814)
Rates: $29-$65
(208) 664-8794
(800) 704-8794

GARDEN MOTEL
1808 Northwest Blvd (83814)
Rates: $40-$100
(208) 664-2743

LA QUINTA INN
280 W Appleway
(83814)
Rates: $60-$113
(208) 765-5500
(800) 687-6667

LA QUINTA INN
2209 E Sherman Ave (83814)
Rates: $39-$179
(208) 667-6777
(800) 667-6667

LAKE DRIVE MOTEL
316 Coeur d'Alene Lake Dr (83814)
Rates: $35-$75
(208) 667-8486

MONTE VISTA MOTEL
320 Coeur d'Alene Lake Dr (83814)
Rates: $26-$75
(208) 765-2369

MOTEL 6
416 W Appleway
(83814)
Rates: $35-$71
(208) 664-6600
(800) 466-8356

O'NEILL'S B&B
1221 Coeur d'Alene Ave
(83814)
Rates: $60
(208) 664-5356

RESORT MANAGEMENT-RENTALS
2120 N 3rd St
(83814)
Rates: $700-$3000 Weekly/Monthly
(208) 667-6035

RODEWAY INN PINES RESORT
1422 Northwest Blvd (83814)
Rates: $49-$92
(208) 664-8244
(800) 424-6423
(800) 651-2510

ROOSEVELT, A B&B INN
105 Wallace Ave
(83816)
Rates: $79-$289
(208) 765-5200
(800) 290-3358

SHILO INN SUITES
702 W Appleway
(83814)
Rates: $69-$179
(208) 664-2300
(800) 222-2244

SQUAW BAY LAKE FRONT RESORT CABINS
5733 Hwy 97 S
(83814)
Rates: $85-$155
(208) 664-6782

STAR MOTEL
1516 Sherman Ave
(83814)
Rates: $35-$90
(208) 664-5035

SUMMER HOUSE BY THE LAKE B&B
1535 Silver Beach Rd (83814)
Rates: $125
(208) 667-9395

SUPER 8 MOTEL
505 W Appleway
(83814)
Rates: $44-$65
(208) 765-8880
(800) 800-8000

COOLIN

BISHOP'S MARINA & RESORT
Box 91 (83821)
Rates: $55-$75
(208) 443-2191

THE INN AT PRIEST LAKE
5310 Dickensheet Rd (83821)
Rates: $50-$150
(208) 443-2447
(800) 443-6240

COTTON WOOD

DOG BARK PARK INN
Hwy 95 at the Dog (83522)
Rates: $85-$105
(208) 962-3647

COUNCIL

STARLITE MOTEL
102 N Dartmouth
(83612)
Rates: $35-$52
(208) 253-4868

DIXIE

DIXIE MOTEL & MERCANTILE
101 Main St
(83525)
Rates: $55-$80
(208) 842-2358

SOUTHERN STAR INN
Box 45 (83525)
Rates: $55-$65
(208) 842-2730

DONNELLY

LONG VALLEY MOTEL
161 S Main St
(83615)
Rates: $40-$65
(208) 325-8271

DOWNEY

DOWNATA HOT SPRINGS
25900 S Downata Rd (83234)
Rates: $50-$250
(208) 897-5736

AREA CODES - If the local number doesn't connect, check for a new area code.

IDAHO

DRIGGS

GRAND VALLEY RENTALS
158 N 1st St E (83422)
Rates: $120-$450
(208) 354-8890
(800) 746-5518

INTERMOUNTAIN LODGE
34 Ski Hill Rd (83422)
Rates: $49-$74
(208) 354-8153

PINES MOTEL-GUEST HAUS
105 South Main (83422)
Rates: $45-$90
(208) 354-2774
(800) 354-2778

RENDEZVOUS SKI TOURS & CHALET
1110 Alta N. Rd (83422)
Rates: $50-$85
(207) 353-2900
(877) 754-4887

DUBOIS

CROSS ROADS MOTEL
391 S Reynolds (83423)
Rates: $28-$40
(208) 374-5258

EDEN

AMBER INN
1132 E 1000 S (83325)
Rates: $37-$60
(208) 825-5200

ELK CITY

BLACKWOOD MANOR B&B
Box 179 (83525)
Rates: $65-$125
(208) 842-2591

BOAR HOAGER INN
309 Main St (83525)
Rates: $50-$55
(208) 842-2735
(800) 842-2292

ELK CITY HOTEL
289 Main St (83525)
Rates: $45-$65
(208) 842-2452

PROSPECTOR CABINS
129 Main St (83525)
Rates: $55-$65
(208) 842-2597

RED RIVER CORRALS/LOG CABINS
HCO 1, Box 18 (83525)
Rates: $55-$129
(208) 842-2228

ELK RIVER

HUCKLEBERRY HEAVEN LODGE
P. O. Box 165 (83827)
Rates: $50-$109
(208) 826-3405

EMMETT

HOLIDAY MOTEL & RV PARK
1111 S Washington Ave (83617)
Rates: $42-$48
(208) 365-4479

FAIRFIELD

COUNTRY INN
P. O. Box 393 (83327)
Rates: $32-$38
(208) 764-2247

FRUITLAND

ELM HOLLOW B&B
4900 Hwy 95 (83619)
Rates: $50-$70
(208) 452-6491

GARDEN VALLEY

GARDEN VALLEY MOTEL
1111 Banks Lowman Rd (83622)
Rates: n/a
(208) 462-2911

IDAHO CABIN KEEPERS
761 S Middle Fork Rd (83622)
Rates: $85-$200
(208) 462-3451
(877) 3 CABINS

SILVER CREEK PLUNGE MOTEL
2345 Silver Creek Rd (83622)
Rates: $40-$78
(208) 890-0586

VALLEY INN
486 S Middle Fork Rd (83622)
Rates: $45-$65
(208) 462-2305

WALK ON THE WILDE SIDE B&B
69 River Ranch Rd, MP 6 (83622)
Rates: $75-$125
(208) 462-8047

GIBBONSVILLE

BROKEN ARROW CABINS
3230 Hwy 93 N (83463)
Rates: $35+
(208) 865-2241

GLENNS FERRY

REDFORD MOTEL
601 W 1st Ave (83623)
Rates: $29-$62
(208) 366-2421

GOODING

COTTAGE INN
1331 S Main St (83330)
Rates: $37-$54
(208) 934-4055

GRANGEVILLE

ELKHORN LODGE
822 SW 1st (83530)
Rates: $35-$48
(208) 983-1500

EVERGREEN B&B
605 E Main #7 (83530)
Rates: $49-$95
(208) 983-2587
(888) 832-5251

JUNCTION LODGE
HC 67, Box 98 (83530)
Rates: $40
(208) 842-2459

MONTY'S MOTEL
700 W Main St (83530)
Rates: $40-$60
(208) 983-2500
(877) 983-1463

SUPER 8 MOTEL
801 SW 1st St (83530)
Rates: $42-$119
(208) 983-1002
(800) 800-8000

HAGERMAN

HAGERMAN VALLEY INN
661 Frog's Landing (83332)
Rates: $49-$69
(208) 837-6196

HAILEY

AIRPORT INN
820 4th Ave S (83333)
Rates: $73-$125
(208) 788-2477

HITCHRACK MOTEL
619 S Main (83333)
Rates: $49-$79
(208) 788-1696
(888) 431-RACK

WOOD RIVER INN
603 N Main (83333)
Rates: $82-$159
(208) 578-0600
(877) 542-0600

HAMMETT

OASIS RANCH MOTEL
HC 63, Box 6 (83627)
Rates: $20-$25
(208) 366-2025

HARRISON

CARLIN BAY RESORT/CABINS
33917 S Hwy 97 (83833)
Rates: $75
(208) 689-3295

LAKEVIEW LODGE
P. O. Box 54 (83833)
Rates: $60-$110
(208) 689-3318

HEYBURN

SUPER 8 MOTEL
336 S 600 W (83336)
Rates: $52-$69
(208) 678-7000
(800) 800-8000

TOPS MOTEL
310 S Hwy 24 (83336)
Rates: $28-$44
(208) 436-4724

HOMEDALE

SUNNYDALE MOTEL
#2 E Colorado (83628)
Rates: $35-$50
(208) 337-3302

HOPE

IDAHO COUNTRY RESORT CABINS
140 Idaho Country Rd (83836)
Rates: $75-$150
(208) 264-5505
(800) 307-3050

HORSESHOE BEND

TRAILS END RESTAURANT & MOTEL
P. O. Box 259 (83629)
Rates: n/a
(208) 793-2700

IDAHO CITY

IDAHO CITY HOTEL
215 Montgomery St (83631)
Rates: $39-$49
(208) 392-4290

KNOTTY PINE CABINS
P. O. Box 624 (83631)
Rates: $60-$105
(208) 392-9976
(800) 440-PINE

PROSPECTOR MOTEL
507 Main St (83631)
Rates: $39-$59
(208) 392-4290

WARM SPRINGS RESORT CABINS
P. O. Box 28 (83631)
Rates: $30-$50
(208) 392-4437

AREA CODES - If the local number doesn't connect, check for a new area code.

IDAHO FALLS

**BEST WESTERN
DRIFTWOOD INN**
575 River Pkwy
(83405)
Rates: $59-$119
(208) 523-2242
(800) 528-1234
(800) 939-2242

COMFORT INN
195 E Colorado
Ave (83402)
Rates: $60-$155
(208) 528-2804
(800) 424-6423

DAYS INN
700 Lindsay Blvd
(83402)
Rates: $49-$75
(208) 523-8900
(800) 329-7466

LE RITZ HOTEL
720 Lindsay Blvd
(83402)
Rates: $89-$209
(208) 528-0880
(800) 813-9266

LITTLETREE INN
888 N Holmes
(83401)
Rates: $39-$79
(208) 523-5993
(800) 521-5993

MOTEL 6
1448 W Broadway
(83402)
Rates: $37-$56
(208) 522-0112
(800) 466-8356

MOTEL WEST
1540 W Broadway
(83402)
Rates: $38-$100
(208) 522-1112
(800) 582-1063

**NATIONAL 9
EXECUTIVE INN**
850 Lindsay Blvd
(83402)
Rates: $56-$99
(208) 523-6260
(800) 852-7829

**RED LION
ON THE FALLS**
475 River Pkwy
(83405)
Rates: $115
(208) 523-8000
(800) 733-5466

**SHILO CONF
HOTEL**
780 Lindsay Blvd
(83402)
Rates: $75-$200
(208) 523-0088
(800) 222-2244

ISLAND PARK

A-BAR MOTEL
3433 Hwy 20
(83429)
Rates: $42-$90
(208) 558-7358
(800) 286-7358

**ELK CREEK GUEST
RANCH**
P. O. Box 2 (83429)
Rates: $85
(208) 558-7404

**MACK'S INN
RESORT**
Box 10 (83429)
Rates: n/a
(208) 558-7272

POND'S LODGE
Box 258 (93429)
Rates: $40-$160
(208) 558-7331
(888) 731-5153

**STALEY SPRINGS
LODGE CABINS**
5398 Henrys Lake
Rd (83429)
Rates: $49-$175
(208) 558-7471

**WILD ROSE
RANCH CABINS**
3778 Hwy 87
(83429)
Rates: $49-$345
(208) 558-7201

JEROME

**BEST WESTERN
SAWTOOTH INN**
2653 S Lincoln
(83338)
Rates: $69-$99
(208) 324-9200
(800) 528-1234

CREST MOTEL
2983 S Lincoln
(83338)
Rates: $42-$60
(208) 324-2670

DAYS INN
1200 Centennial
Spur (83338)
Rates: $45-$85
(208) 324-6400
(800) 329-7466

KAMIAH

**CLEARWATER
12 MOTEL**
Hwy 12 & Cedar
St (83536)
Rates: $40-$60
(208) 935-2671
(800) 935-2671

FLYING B RANCH
2900 Lawyer
Creek Rd (83536)
Rates: $1500-$6500
(208) 935-0755
(800) 472-1945

**LEWIS CLARK
RESORT/MOTEL**
Rt 1, Box 17 (83536)
Rates: $45-$65
(208) 935-2556
(800) 264-9943

KELLOGG

**INN AT SILVER
MOUNTAIN**
305 S Division
(83837)
Rates: $20+
(208) 786-2311
(800) SNOW-FUN

MOTEL-51
206 E Cameron
Ave (83837)
Rates: $25-$40
(208) 786-9441

SILVER SUITES
206 E Cameron
(83837)
Rates: $27-$38
(208) 783-0566
(866) 783-1006

**SILVERHORN
MOTOR INN**
699 W Cameron
Ave (83837)
Rates: $63-$73
(208) 783-1151
(800) 437-6437

SUPER 8 MOTEL
601 Bunker Ave
(83837)
Rates: $47-$92
(208) 783-1234
(800) 800-8000
(800) 785-5443

TRAIL MOTEL
206 W Cameron
Ave (83837)
Rates: $30-$40
(208) 784-1161

KETCHUM

**BEST WESTERN
TYROLEAN
LODGE (SUN
VALLEY AREA)**
260 Cottonwood St
(83340)
Rates: $85-$144
(208) 726-5336
(800) 528-1234
(800) 333-7912

**CHRISTIANIA
MOTOR LODGE**
651 Sun Valley Rd
(83340)
Rates: $89-$105
(208) 726-3351
(800) 535-3241

HEIDLEBERG INN
1908 Warm
Springs Rd
(83340)
Rates: $85-$130
(208) 726-5361
(800) 284-4863

**KETCHUM
KORRAL MOTOR
LODGE**
310 S Main St
(83340)
Rates: $58-$125
(208) 726-3510
(800) 657-2657

RIVER STREET INN
100 W River St
(83340)
Rates: $140-$195
(208) 726-3611
(888) 746-3611

SKI VIEW LODGE
409 S Hwy 75
(83340)
Rates: $40-$70
(208) 726-3441

**TAMARACK
LODGE**
291 Walnut Ave
(83340)
Rates: $82-$159
(208) 726-3344

KINGSTON

**COUNTRY LANE
INN & RESORT**
5972A Old River
Rd (83839)
Rates: $99-$150
(208) 682-2698
(877) 670-5927

**KINGSTON 5
RANCH B & B**
297 Silver Valley
Rd (83839)
Rates: $55-$125
(208) 682-4862
(800) 254-1852

KOOSKIA

**BEAR HOLLOW
B&B**
HC 75, Box 16
(83539)
Rates: $55-$85
(208) 926-7146
(800) 831-3713

IDA-LEE MOTEL
P. O. Box 592
(83539)
Rates: $25-$36
(208) 926-0166

**MOUNT
STUART INN**
Near Clearwater
River/Opera
House Theater
(83539)
Rates: $25-$50
(208) 926-0166

**REFLECTIONS INN
B&B**
Hwy 12, MM 84
& 85 (93539)
Rates: $59-$94
(208) 926-0855

**RYAN'S
WILDERNESS INN**
Lowell Hwy,
MP 97.5 (83539)
Rates: $40-$50
(208) 926-4706
(866) 539-2012

**THREE RIVERS
RESORT &
RAFTING**
HC 75, Box 61,
Hwy 12 (83539)
Rates: $39-$97
(208) 926-4430
(888) 926-4430

AREA CODES - If the local number doesn't connect, check for a new area code.

LAKEFORK

MARY'S CABINS
Box 684 (83635)
Rates: $25+
(208) 634-5527

LAVA HOT SPRINGS

AURA SOMA LAVA
Box 129 (83246)
Rates: $39-$69
(208) 776-5800
(800) 757-1233

DEMPSEY CREEK LODGE
162 E Main
(83246)
Rates: $29-$49
(208) 776-5000

LAVA HOT SPRINGS INN
94 E Portneuf Ave
(83246)
Rates: $69-$225
(208) 776-5830
(800) 527-5830

LAVA RANCH INN MOTEL
9611 Hwy 30
(83246)
Rates: $35-$100
(208) 776-9917

PORTNEUF INN
140 E 1st Alley N
(83246)
Rates: n/a
(208) 776-5050

RIVERSIDE INN & HOT SPRINGS
255 Portneuf Ave
(83246)
Rates: $60-$110
(208) 776-5504
(800) 733-5504

WHITE WOLF B&B
9926 Hwy 30 E
(83246)
Rates: $55-$70
(208) 776-5353
(888) 776-5344

LEADORE

LEADORE INN
401 S Railroad St
(83464)
Rates: $32-$50
(208) 768-2237
(888) 981-6334

LEMHI

MOTEL DELUXE
112 S Church
(83465)
Rates: $32-$48
(208) 756-2231

LEWISTON

BEL AIR MOTEL
2018 N & S Hwy
(83501)
Rates: $22-$27
(208) 743-5946

COMFORT INN
2128 8th Ave
(83501)
Rates: $69-$109
(208) 798-8090
(800) 424-6423

EL RANCHO MOTEL
2240 3rd Ave N
(83501)
Rates: $30-$38
(208) 743-8517

EVERGREEN MOTEL
2125 3rd Ave N
(83501)
Rates: $28-$32
(208) 746-5851

HILLARY MOTEL
2030 North-South
Hwy (83501)
Rates: $25-$54
(208) 743-8514
(800) 856-8514

HOLIDAY INN EXPRESS
2425 Nez Perce Dr
(83501)
Rates: $79
(208) 750-1600
(800) 465-4329

INN AMERICA
702 21st St (83501)
Rates: $44-$99
(208) 746-4600
(800) 469-4667

KIRBY CREEK LODGE
227 Snake River
Ave (83501)
Rates: $100-$360
(208) 746-6276
(800) 262-8874

RED LION HOTEL
621 21st St (83501)
Rates: $69-$203
(208) 799-1000
(800) 733-5466

RIVERVIEW INN
1325 Main St
(83501)
Rates: $39-$60
(208) 746-3311
(800) 806-7666

SACAJAWEA MOTOR INN
1824 Main St
(83501)
Rates: $56-$89
(208) 746-1393

SHEEP CREEK GUEST RANCH
227 Snake River
Ave (83501)
Rates: $85-$280
(208) 746-6276
(800) 262-8874

SNAKE RIVER ADVENTURES
227 Snake River
Ave (83501)
Rates: $85+
(208) 746-6276
(800) 262-8874

SPORTSMAN INN
3001 North-South
Hwy (83501)
Rates: $32-$50
(208) 743-9424

SUPER 8 MOTEL
3120 North
& South Hwy
(83501)
Rates; $35-$54
(208) 743-8808

TRAVEL MOTOR INN
1021 Main St
(83501)
Rates: $30-$49
(208) 743-4501

LOWMAN

NEW HAVEN LODGE
7655 Hwy 21
(83637)
Rates: $38-$110
(208) 259-3344

LUCILE

ACRES FOR KIDS
HC 1, Box 14A
(83542)
Rates: $69-$89
(208) 628-3569
(866) 367-3659

STEELHEAD INN
HC 1, Box 14,
Hwy 95, MP 210
(83542)
Rates: $50-$55
(208) 628-3044
(800) 331-4445

MACKAY

WAGON WHEEL MOTEL
809 W Custer
(83251)
Rates: $38-$80
(208) 588-3331

WHITE KNOB MOTEL
Box 180 (83251)
Rates: $22-$42
(208) 588-2622
(800) 534-2622

MACK'S INN

MACK'S INN RESORT
P. O. Box 10
(83433)
Rates: $20-$110
(208) 558-7272

SAWTELL MOUNTAIN RESORT
P. O. Box 250
(83433)
Rates: $54-$74
(208) 558-9366
(800) 574-0404

MALAD

SOUTH CANYON CABINS
10990 Old Hwy
191 (83252)
Rates: $100-$400
(208) 766-4325
(866) 722-4966

SOURDOUGH LODGE
8406 Hwy 21
(83637)
Rates: $45-$89
(208) 259-3326

VILLAGE INN MOTEL
50 South 300 E
(83252)
Rates: $44-$50
(208) 766-4761

MCCALL

BEST WESTERN
415 N 3rd St
(83638)
Rates: $65-$105
(208) 634-6300
(800) 528-1234

BRUNDAGE BUNGALOWS
308 W Lake St
(83638)
Rates: $59-$169
(208) 634-8573
(800) 643-2009

BRUNDAGE INN
1005 W Lake St
(83638)
Rates: $40-$105
(208) 634-2344
(800) 643-2009

FIRCREST CONDOS
300 Washington,
#107 (83638)
Rates: $59-$149
(208) 634-4528

LAKEFORK LODGE GUEST RANCH
McCall Lick Creek
Rd (83638)
Rates: $150-$175
(208) 634-3713

MCCALL ACCOMMODATION SERVICES
1008 N 3rd St
(83638)
Rates: $85-$800
Weekly/Monthly
(208) 634-7766
(800) 551-8234

SUPER 8 LODGE
303 S 3rd St
(83638)
Rates: $58-$129
(208) 634-4697
(800) 800-8000

AREA CODES - If the local number doesn't connect, check for a new area code.

WOODSMAN MOTEL
402 N 3rd St (83638)
Rates: $32-$58
(208) 634-7671
(888) 578-2658

MELBA

GIVEN'S HOT SPRINGS CABINS
Hwy 78 (83641)
Rates: n/a
(208) 495-2000

MERIDIAN

MOTEL 6
1047 S Progress Ave (83642)
Rates: $49-$60
(208) 888-1212
(800) 466-8356

MONTPELIER

BEST WESTERN CLOVER CREEK INN
243 N 4th St (83254)
Rates: $53-$101
(208) 847-1782
(800) 528-1234

BUDGET MOTEL
240 N 4th St (83254)
Rates: $20-$35
(208) 847-1273

THE FISHER INN
601 N 4th St (83254)
Rates: $27-$62
(208) 847-1772

PARK MOTEL
745 Washington (83254)
Rates: $35-$50
(208) 847-1911

MOSCOW

BEST WESTERN UNIVERSITY INN
1516 Pullman Rd (83843)
Rates: $89-$104
(208) 882-0550
(800) 528-1234
(800) 325-8765

HILLCREST MOTEL
706 N Main (83843)
Rates: $28-$60
(208) 882-7579
(800) 368-6564

JOURNEY'S END B&B
1141 Paradise Ridge Rd (83843)
Rates: $60-$100
(208) 882-4986
(877) 882-5034

MARK IV MOTOR INN
414 N Main St (83843)
Rates: $39-$129
(208) 882-7557
(800) 833-4240

SUPER 8 MOTEL
175 Peterson Dr (83843)
Rates: $44-$85
(208) 883-1503
(800) 800-8000

MOUNTAIN HOME

BEST WESTERN FOOTHILLS MOTOR INN
1080 Hwy 20 (83647)
Rates: $59-$99
(208) 587-8477
(800) 528-1234
(800) 604-8477

HI LANDER MOTEL
615 S 3rd W (83647)
Rates: $35-$49
(208) 587-3311

MAPLE COVE MOTEL
700 E wy 30 (83647)
Rates: $25-$35
(208) 587-2202

MOTEL THUNDERBIRD
910 Sunset Strip (83647)
Rates: $34-$65
(208) 587-7927

SLEEP INN
1180 Hwy 20 (83647)
Rates: $64-$74
(208) 587-9743
(800) 424-6423

TOWNE CENTER MOTEL
410 N 2nd E (83647)
Rates: $24-$40
(208) 587-3373

MOYIE SPRINGS

HEMLOCKS COUNTRY INN & RESORT
Box 554, Hwy 2 (83845)
Rates: $45-$70
(208) 267-9822

MUD LAKE

HAVEN MOTEL
1079 E 1500 N (83450)
Rates: $50
(208) 663-4821

MURPHY

SILVER CITY LODGINGS-GROUP HOSTEL
P. O. Box 56 (83650)
Rates: $40
(208) 583-4111

NAMPA

BUDGET INN
908 3rd St South (83651)
Rates: $35-$45
(208) 466-3594

DESERT INN MOTEL
115 9th Ave S (83651)
Rates: $42-$55
(208) 467-1161
(800) 588-5268

HAMPTON INN IDAHO CENTER
5750 Franklin Rd (83687)
Rates: $99-$129
(208) 442-0036
(800) 426-7866

SHILO INN
617 Nampa Blvd (83687)
Rates: $50-$85
(208) 466-8993
(800) 222-2244

SHILO INN NAMPA SUITES
1401 Shilo Dr (83687)
Rates: $73-$113
(208) 465-3250
(800) 222-2244

STARLITE MOTEL
320 11th Ave N (83651)
Rates: $30-$43
(208) 466-9244

NEW MEADOWS

HARTLAND INN & MOTEL
211 Norris St (83654)
Rates: $59-$150
(208) 347-2114

MEADOWS MOTEL
Box 91, Hwy 95 (83654)
Rates: $35-$55
(208) 347-2175

PINEHURST RESORT COTTAGES
5604 Hwy 95 (83654)
Rates: $45-$70
(208) 628-3323

NORDMAN

ELKINS CABINS ON PRIEST LAKE
404 Elkins Rd (83848)
Rates: $85-$345
(208) 443-2432

KANIKSU RESORT CABINS
485 Jim Low Rd (83848)
Rates: $60+
(208) 443-2609

NORTH FORK

CUMMINGS LAKE LODGE
Box 249 (83466)
Rates: $65
(208) 865-2424

NORTH FORK MOTEL
2046 Hwy 93 N (83466)
Rates: $40-$54
(208) 865-2412

100 ACRE WOOD BED & BREAKFAST
Rt 1, Hwy 93 N (83466)
Rates: $55-$115
(208) 865-2165

RIVER'S FORK INN
2036 Hwy 93 N (83466)
Rates: $52-$62
(208) 865-2301

OAKLEY

POULTON'S B&B
200 E Main (83346)
Rates: $50-$60
(208) 862-3649
(800) 360-7067

OROFINO

HELGESON PLACE HOTEL
125 Johnson Ave (83544)
Rates: $45-$65
(208) 476-5729
(800) 404-5729

KONKOLVILLE MOTEL
2000 Konkolville Rd (83544)
Rates: $50-$65
(208) 476-5584
(800) 616-1964

RIVERSIDE MOTEL
10560 Hwy 12 (83544)
Rates: $25-$39
(208) 476-5711

WHITE PINE MOTEL
222 Brown St (83544)
Rates: $38-$55
(208) 476-7093
(800) 874-2083

PALISADES

PALISADES CABINS
3802 Swan Valley Hwy (83428)
Rates: $45
(208) 483-4485

PARMA

THE COURT MOTEL
712 Grove St (83660)
Rates: $36-$45
(208) 722-5579

AREA CODES - If the local number doesn't connect, check for a new area code.

PIERCE

CEDAR INN MINER'S SHANTY
412 S Main (83546)
Rates: $27-57
(208) 464-2704
(800) 450-0250

KEY BAR HOTEL & CAFE
Box 494 (83546)
Rates: $10-$15
(208) 464-2704

OUTBACK ADVENTURES
Box 383, Main St (83546)
Rates: $40-$125
(208) 464-2171
(800) 538-1754

PIERCE MOTEL
509 Main St (83546)
Rates: $30-$40
(208) 464-2324
(877) 464-2324

PINEHURST

KELLOGG VACATION HOME RENTALS
P. O. Box 944 (83850)
Rates: $50-$200
(208) 786-4261
(800) 435-2588

PLUMMER

HIWAY MOTEL
301 10th St (83851)
Rates: $36-$57
(208) 686-1310

POCATELLO

BACK O'BEYOND B&B
404 S Garfield (83201)
Rates: $60-$65
(208) 232-3825
(888) 232-3820

BEST WESTERN COTTON TREE INN
1415 Bench Rd (83201)
Rates: $69-$129
(208) 237-7650
(800) 528-1234
(800) 662-6886

COMFORT INN
1333 Bench Rd (83201)
Rates: $59-$159
(208) 237-8155
(800) 424-6423

ECONO LODGE UNIVERSITY
835 S 5th Ave (83201)
Rates: $42-$54
(208) 233-0451
(800) 424-6423

HOLIDAY INN
1399 Bench Rd (83201)
Rates: $63-$89
(208) 237-1400
(800) 465-4329

MOTEL 6
291 W Burnside Ave (83202)
Rates: $32-$36
(208) 237-7880
(800) 466-8356

PINE RIDGE INN
4333 Yellowstone Ave (83202)
Rates: $40-$70
(208) 237-3100
(877) 237-3100

RAINBOW MOTEL
3020 S 5th (83201)
Rates: $29-$47
(208) 232-1451

RAMADA INN
133 W Burnside (83202)
Rates: $60-$100
(208) 237-0020
(800) 272-6232

RED LION INN
1555 Pocatello Creek Rd (83201)
Rates: $63-$73
(208) 233-2200
(800) 733-5466
(800) 527-5202

SUPER 8 MOTEL
1330 Bench Rd (83201)
Rates: $49-$73
(208) 234-0888
(800) 800-8000

THUNDERBIRD MOTEL
1415 S 5th Ave (83201)
Rates: $40-$55
(208) 232-6330
(888) 978-2473

POLLACK

NOTHWEST VOYAGEURS' ADVENTURE LODGE
S End #1 Pollock Rd (83547)
Rates: $79-$89
(208) 628-3021
(800) 727-9977

PONDERAY

MONARCH MTN LODGE
363 Bonner Mall Way (83852)
Rates: $42-$95
(208) 263-1222

MOTEL 6
477255 Hwy 95 (83852)
Rates: $40-$56
(208) 263-5383
(800) 466-8356

SUPER 8 MOTEL
476841 Hwy 95 N (83852)
Rates: $33-$66
(208) 263-2210
(800) 800-8000

POST FALLS

HOLIDAY INN EXPRESS
3175 E Seltice Way (83854)
Rates: $72-$139
(208) 773-8900
(800) 465-4329

HOWARD JOHNSON EXPRESS
3647 W 5th Ave (83854)
Rates: $49-$149
(208) 773-4541
(800) 446-4656
(800) 829-3124

RED LION TEMPLIN'S HOTEL ON THE RIVER
414 E 1st Ave (83854)
Rates: $79-$249
(208) 773-1611
(800) 733-5466
(800) 283-6754

SLEEP INN
157 S Pleasant View Rd (83854)
Rates: $59-$149
(208) 777-9394
(800) 424-6423

POTLATCH

ROLLING HILLS BED & BREAKFAST
Rt 1, Box 157 (83855)
Rates: $50-$55
(208) 668-1126

PRESTON

PLAZA MOTEL
427 S Hwy 91 (83263)
Rates: $45-$55
(208) 852-2020

PRIEST LAKE

HILL'S RESORT
4777 W Lake Shore Rd (83856)
Rates: $80-$325
(208) 443-2551

PRIEST LAKE ESCAPES-RENTALS
114 Shelly St (83856)
Rates: $800-$2500 Weekly
(208) 443-0203
(888) 536-4417
(

PRIEST RIVER

EAGLE'S NEST MOTEL
1007 Albeni Hwy (83865)
Rates: $50-$110
(208) 448-2000
(800) 881-6378

SELKIRK MOTEL
1201 Albeni Hwy (83856)
Rates: $35-$61
(208) 448-1112

REXBURG

BEST WESTERN COTTONTREE INN
450 W 4th St S (83440)
Rates: $67-$109
(208) 356-4646
(800) 528-1234
(800) 662-6886

CJ'S MOTEL
357 W 4th St (83440)
Rates: $40-$45
(208) 356-5477

COMFORT INN
858 W Main (83440)
Rates: $55-$99
(208) 359-1311
(800) 424-6423

DAYS INN
271 S 2nd W (83440)
Rates: $51-$73
(208) 356-9222
(800) 329-7466

RIGBY

BLUE HERON INN
4175 E Menan-Lorenzo Hwy (83442)
Rates: $90-$185
(208) 745-9922
(866) 745-9922

RIGGINS

BEST WESTERN SALMON RAPIDS LODGE
1010 S Main St (83549)
Rates: $79-$119
(208) 628-2743
(800) 528-1234
(877) 957-2743

THE LODGE B&B
On Little Salmon River, Hwy 95 (83549)
Rates: $30-$60
(208) 628-3863

RAPID RIVER GUEST RANCH
HC 69, Box 100 (83549)
Rates: $40-$50
(208) 628-3264

RIGGINS MOTEL
615 S Main (83549)
Rates: $38-$110
(208) 628-3001
(800) 669-6739

SALMON RIVER MOTEL
1203 S Hwy 95
(93549)
Rates: $38-$74
(208) 628-3231
(888) 628-3025

TAYLOR MOTEL
206 S Main St
(83549)
Rates: $27
(208) 628-3914

ROGERSON
DESERT HOT SPRINGS MOTEL
General Delivery
(83302)
Rates: $25-$35
(208) 857-2233

RUPERT
FLAMINGO LODGE MOTEL
406 E 8th St
(83350)
Rates: $30-$50
(208) 436-4321

SAGLE
BOTTLE BAY RESORT & MARINA
115 Resort Rd
(83860)
Rates: $80-$145
(208) 263-5916
(866) 268-8532

GARFIELD BAY RESORT CABINS
60 W Garfield Bay
Rd (83860)
Rates: $55
(208) 263-1078

ST. ANTHONY
BEST WESTERN HENRY'S FORK INN
115 S Bridge St
(83445)
Rates: $55-$79
(208) 624-3711
(800) 528-1234

SQUIRREL CREEK ELK RANCH CABINS
109 N 2nd W
(83445)
Rates: $50-$70
(208) 652-3972
(800) 734-7002

ST. MARIES
THE GUEST HOUSE/RENTAL
641 S 10th St
(83861)
Rates: $40-$50
(208) 245-5755

THE PINES MOTEL
1117 Main St
(83861)
Rates: $40-$60
(208) 245-2545

SALMON
MOTEL DELUXE
112 S Church St
(83467)
Rates: $40-$74
(208) 756-2231

SOLAAS B&B
Rt 1, Box 59 (83467)
Rates: $45-$50
(208) 756-3903
(888) 425-5474

SUNCREST MOTEL
705 S Challis St
(83467)
Rates: $33-$65
(208) 756-2294

WAGONS WEST MOTEL
503 hwy 93 N
(83467)
Rates: $45-$75
(208) 756-4281
(800) 756-4281

SANDPOINT
BEST WESTERN EDGEWATER RESORT
56 Bridge St
(83864)
Rates: $74-$146
(208) 263-3194
(800) 528-1234
(800) 635-2534

CHALET MOTEL
3270 Hwy 95 N
(83864)
Rates: $39-$60
(208) 263-3202

COIT HOUSE B&B
502 N 4th Ave
(83864)
Rates: $75-$110
(208) 265-4035

COUNTRY INN
7360 Hwy 95 S
(83864)
Rates: $24-$49
(208) 263-3333
(800) 736-0454

IDAHO COUNTRY RESORT
141 Idaho
Country Rd
(83864)
Rates: $75-$150
(208) 264-5505
(800) 307-3050

INN AT SAND CREEK
105 S 1st Ave
(83864)
Rates: $125-$195
(208) 255-2821
(800) 439-5593

K2 INN AT SANDPOINT
501 N 4th Ave
(83864)
Rates: $30-$109
(208) 263-3441

LA QUINTA INN
415 Cedar St
(83864)
Rates: $89-$139
(208) 263-9581
(800) 687-6667
(800) 282-0660

MOTEL 16
317 Marion Ave
(83864)
Rates: $30-$58
(208) 263-5323

QUALITY INN
807 N 5th Ave
(83864)
Rates: $54-$129
(208) 263-2111
(800) 424-6423

SHOSHONE
GOVERNOR'S MANSION
315 S Greenwood
(83352)
Rates: $30-$65
(208) 886-2858

SHOUP
SHOUP STORE, CAFE & CABINS
1829 Salmon River
Rd (83469)
Rates: $30-$100
(208) 394-2125

SMITH HOUSE B&B
3175 Salmon River
Rd (83469)
Rates: $45-$65
(208) 394-2121
(800) 238-5915

SILVERTON
MOLLY B'DAMM MOTEL
P. O. Box 481
(83867)
Rates: $25-$45
(208) 556-4391

SILVER LEAF MOTEL
Box 151, West
Wallace (83867)
Rates: $25-$30
(208) 752-0222

SODA SPRINGS
CARIBOU LODGE
110 W 2nd S
(83276)
Rates: $28-$55
(208) 547-3377

J-R INN MOTEL
179 W 2nd S
(83276)
Rates: $43-$53
(208) 547-3366

JAMA VILLA B&B
361 E Hooper
(83276)
Rates: n/a
(208) 547-3017

LAKEVIEW MOTEL
341 W 2nd S
(83276)
Rates: $29-$50
(208) 547-4351

SHEEP CREEK GUEST RANCH
Box 44 (93276)
Rates: $150
(208) 540-1513
(877) 787-0301

TRAIL MOTEL
213 E 200 S
(83276)
Rates: $35-$40
(208) 547-0240

SPENCER
SPENCER STAGE STOP CABINS
HC 62, Box 54
(83446)
Rates: $30
(208) 374-5242

SPIRIT LAKE
SILVER BEACH RESORT CABINS
8350 W Spirit
Lake Rd (83869)
Rates: $50-$85
(208) 623-4842

STANLEY
DANNER'S LOG CABIN MOTEL
P. O. Box 196
(83278)
Rates: $50-$125
(208) 774-3539

MOUNTAIN VILLAGE LODGE
US 75 & SR 21
(83278)
Rates: $59-$100
(208) 774-3661
(800) 843-5475

SALMON RIVER CABINS & MOTEL
SR 21 to Jct
US 75 (83278)
Rates: $65-$85
(208) 774-3566

SUNBEAM VILLAGE
HC 67, Box 310
(83278)
Rates: $59-$125
(208) 838-2211
(866) 273-3565

TORREY'S RESORT
HC 67, Box 725
(83278)
Rates: $50
(208) 838-2313
(888) 838-2313

SUN VALLEY
BALD MOUNTAIN LODGE
151 S Main (83353)
Rates: $50-$90
(208) 726-9963
(800) 892-7407

CLARION INN
600 N Main St
(83340)
Rates: $79-$249
(208) 726-5900
(800) 424-6423
(800) 262-4833

HIGH COUNTRY PROPERTIES/ RENTALS
251 S Main St
(83353)
Rates: $90-$3500
(208) 726-1256
(800) 726-7076

LIVING WATERS TOWNHOUSES/ RENTALS
PMB 481, Box 90
(83353)
Rates: $200
(208) 726-5047

SWAN VALLEY
SLEEPY J CABINS
Box 329 (83449)
Rates: $75-$125
(208) 483-0411

TERRETON
B-K'S MOTEL
1073 E 1500 N
(83450)
Rates: $30-$35
(208) 663-4578

TETONIA
TETON MTN VIEW LODGE
510 Egbert Ave
(83452)
Rates: $35-$109
(208) 456-2741
(800) 625-2232

TETON RIDGE RANCH SUITES
200 Valley View Rd (83452)
Rates: $450-$550
(208) 456-2650

TWIN FALLS
BEST WESTERN APOLLO MOTOR INN
296 Addison Ave W (83301)
Rates: $54-$80
(208) 733-2010
(800) 528-1234
(800) 733-6599

COMFORT INN
1893 Canyon Sprgs Rd (83301)
Rates: $69-$139
(208) 734-7494
(800) 424-6423

MOTEL 6
1472 Blue Lake Blvd N (83301)
Rates: $35-$52
(208) 734-3993
(800) 466-8356

RED LION HOTEL-CANYON SPRINGS
1357 Blue Lakes Blvd N (83301)
Rates: $70-$112
(208) 734-5000
(800) 325-4000

SHILO INN SUITES
1586 Blue Lakes Blvd N (83301)
Rates: $79-$159
(208) 733-7545
(800) 222-2244

TWIN FALLS MOTEL
2152 Kimberly Rd (83301)
Rates: $40+
(208) 733-8620

WESTON INN
906 Blue Lake Blvd (83301)
Rates: $40-$70
(208) 733-6095
(800) 551-3505

VICTOR
TETON MOUNTAIN HIDEAWAYS/ RENTALS
219 Highland Way (83455)
Rates: $170-$350
(208) 787-3094

TETON VALLEY CAMPGROUND CABINS
128 Hwy 31 (83455)
Rates: $55
(208) 787-2647
(877) 787-3036

WALLACE
BEST WESTERN WALLACE INN
100 Front St
(83873)
Rates: $66-$94
(208) 752-1252
(800) 528-1234
(800) 643-2386

STARDUST MOTEL
410 Pine St (83873)
Rates: $40-$70
(208) 752-1213
(800) 643-2386

WARM LAKE
NORTH SHORE LODGE CABINS
172 N Shoreline Dr (83611)
Rates: $60-$110
(208) 632-2000
(800) 933-3193

WEIPPE
IRBY'S BLUE SPRUCE LODGE
1090 Lackey Rd (83553)
Rates: $40-$60
(208) 435-4890

WEISER
COLONIAL MOTEL
251 E Main (83672)
Rates: $48-$70
(208) 549-0150
(866) 420-2143

STATE STREET MOTEL
1279 State St
(83672)
Rates: $54-$57
(208) 414-1390

WHITE BIRD
HELLS CANYON JET BOAT TRIPS & LODGING
HC 01, Box 160
(83554)
Rates: $50-$60
(208) 839-2255
(800) 469-8757

WHITE BIRD MOTEL
Hwy 95, Main & Bridge St (83554)
Rates: $32-$65
(208) 839-2308

WINCHESTER
WINCHESTER COUNTRY INN
605 Nez Perce St
(83555)
Rates: $40
(208) 924-7405

WORLEY
COEUR D'ALENE CASINO RESORT HOTEL
27068 S Hwy 95
(83876)
Rates: $60-$275
(208) 686-0248
(800) 523-2464

YELLOW PINE
YELLOW PINE LODGE
P. O. Box 77
(83677)
Rates: $30-$50
(208) 633-3377

ZENA CREEK RANCH
3134 Lick Creek Rd (83677)
Rates: $50-$60
(208) 382-4336

ILLINOIS

ALSIP

BAYMONT INN
12801 S Cicero
Ave (60658)
Rates: $59-$70
(708) 597-3900
(877) 229-6668

DAYS SUITES
5150 W 127th St
(60658)
Rates: $75-$105
(708) 371-5600
(800) 329-7466

**DOUBLETREE
HOTEL**
5000 W 127th St
(60658)
Rates: $79-$159
(708) 371-7300
(800) 222-8733

ALTAMONT

**ALTAMONT
HOTEL**
101 W Cumberland
Rd (62411)
Rates: n/a
(618) 483-6143

KNIGHTS INN
1304 S Main St
(62411)
Rates: n/a
(618) 483-6101
(800) 843-5644

SUPER 8 MOTEL
3091 E Mill Dr
(62411)
Rates: $40-$90
(618) 483-6300
(800) 800-8000

ALTON

**COLLEGE CREST
MOTEL**
Rt 140 & Burling
Dr (62002)
Rates: n/a
(618) 465-3212

COMFORT INN
11 Crossroads Ct
(62002)
Rates: $64-$109
(618) 465-9999
(800) 424-6423

DAYS INN
1900 Homer M
Adams Pkwy
(62002)
Rates: $48-$78
(618) 463-0800
(800) 329-7466

HOLIDAY INN
3800 Homer
Adams Pkwy
(62002)
Rates: n/a
(618) 462-1220
(800) 465-4329

**HOTEL
STRATFORD**
229 Market St
(62002)
Rates: n/a
(618) 465-2700

SUPER 8 MOTEL
1800 Homer M
Adams Pkwy
(62002)
Rates: $45-$79
(618) 465-8885
(800) 800-8000

AMBOY

AMBOY MOTEL
1556 Rt 30 (61310)
Rates: n/a
(815) 857-3916

ANNA

**ANNA PLAZA
MOTEL**
150 E Vienna S E
(62906)
Rates: n/a
(618) 883-5215

SUPER 8 MOTEL
100 Richview Dr
(62906)
Rates: n/a
(618) 833-1888
(800) 800-8000

ANNAWAN

**HOLIDAY INN
EXPRESS**
315 N Canal St
(61234)
Rates: n/a
(309) 935-6565
(800) 465-4329

ANTIOCH

ANTIOCH MOTEL
25324 W Rt 173
(60002)
Rates: n/a
(847) 395-1527
(800) 557-0644

**BEST WESTERN
REGENCY INN**
350 Hwy 173
(60002)
Rates: $69-$145
(847) 395-3606
(800) 528-1234

ARCOLA

ARCOLA INN
236 S Jacques St
(61910)
Rates: n/a
(217) 268-4971
(888) 729-9137

COMFORT INN
610 E Springfield
(61910)
Rates: $36-$99
(217) 268-4000
(800) 424-6423

KNIGHTS INN
640 E Springfield
Rd (61910)
Rates: $34-$55
(217) 268-3031
(800) 283-4678

ARLINGTON
HEIGHTS

AMERISUITES
2111 S Arlington
Hgts Rd (60005)
Rates: $109-$139
(847) 956-1400
(800) 434-5800
(800) 833-1516

BEST VALUE INN
948 E Northwest
Hwy (60004)
Rates: $55-$75
(847) 255-2900

LA QUINTA INN
1415 W Dundee
Rd (60004)
Rates: $89-$109
(847) 253-8777
(800) 687-6667

MOTEL 6

441 W Algonquin
Rd (60005)
Rates: $42-$46
(847) 806-1230
(800) 466-8356

PARK PLAZA
75 W Algonquin
Rd (60005)
Rates: n/a
(847) 364-7600

RED ROOF INN
22 W Algonquin
Rd (60005)
Rates: $66-$95
(847) 228-6650
(800) 843-7663
(800) 773-7663

**SHERATON
CHICAGO
NORTHWEST**
3400 W Euclid
Ave (60005)
Rates: $79-$159
(847) 394-2000
(800) 325-3535

ARTHUR

**ARTHUR'S
COUNTRY INN**
785 E Columbia,
Hwy 133 (61911)
Rates: n/a
(217) 543-3321

ATLANTA

I-55 MOTEL
103 Empire St
(61723)
Rates: $30-$37
(217) 648-2322

AURORA

MOTEL 6
2380 N
Farnsworth Ave
(60504)
Rates: $39-$50
(630) 851-3600
(800) 466-8356

BANNOCK-
BURN

**WOODFIELD
SUITES**
2000 Lakeside Dr
(60015)
Rates: $89-$139
(847) 317-7300
(800) 338-0008

BARRINGTON

DAYS INN
405 W Northwest
Hwy (60010)
Rates: $39-$129
(847) 381-2640
(800) 329-7466

BEACH PARK

**AMERICAN INN
MOTEL**
39-18 N Sheridan
Rd (60083)
Rates: n/a
(847) 746-2095

BEARDSTOWN

SUPER 8 MOTEL
1903 Grand Ave
(62618)
Rates: $40-$60
(217) 323-5858
(800) 800-8000

BELLEVILLE

BELLEVILLE INN
2120 W Main St
(62220)
Rates: n/a
(618) 234-9400

**THE SHRINE
HOTEL**
451 S Demazenod
Dr (62220)
Rates: $62-$67
(618) 397-1162

SUPER 8 MOTEL
600 E Main St
(62220)
Rates: $39-$56
(618) 234-9670
(800) 800-8000

AREA CODES - If the local number doesn't connect, check for a new area code.

TERRACE MOTEL & APARTMENTS
747 S Belt West
(62220)
Rates: n/a
(618) 234-1505

BENTON

DAYS INN
711 W Main St
(62812)
Rates: $45-$169
(618) 439-3183
(800) 329-7466

GRAY PLAZA MOTEL
706 W Main St
(62812)
Rates: n/a
(618) 439-3113

MOTEL BENTON
407 N Main St
(62812)
Rates: n/a
(618) 435-3105

BLOOMING DALE

RESIDENCE INN BY MARRIOTT
295 Knollwood Dr
(60108)
Rates: $99-$149
(630) 893-9200
(800) 331-3131

BLOOMINGTON

THE CHATEAU
1601 Jumer Dr
(61701)
Rates: n/a
(309) 662-2020
(800) 285-8637

COUNTRY INN
923 Maple Hill Rd
(61701)
Rates: $74-$86
(309) 828-7177
(800) 456-4000

COUNTRY INN
2403 E Empire St
(61704)
Rates: $69-$89
(309) 682-3100
(800) 456-4000

DAYS INN
1707 W Market St
(61701)
Rates: $50-$85
(309) 829-6292
(800) 329-7466

EASTLAND SUITES
1801 Eastland Dr
(61701)
Rates: n/a
(309) 662-0000
(800) 537-8483

ECONO LODGE
401 Brock Dr (61701)
Rates: $42-$58
(309) 829-3100
(800) 424-6423

GUESTHOUSE INN
1803 E Empire St
(61701)
Rates: $61-$81
(309) 663-1361
(800) 214-8378

HAWTHORN SUITES
1 Lyon Dr (61701)
Rates: $79-$129
(309) 829-8111
(800) 527-1133

L & L MOTEL
1507 Morrissey Dr
(61701)
Rates: n/a
(309) 663-2361

RADISSON HOTEL
10 Brickyard Dr
(61704)
Rates $89-$119
(309) 664-6446
(800) 333-3333

RAMADA INN
1219 Holiday Dr
(61704)
Rates: n/a
(309) 662-5311
(800) 272-6232

RAMADA LTD
919 Maple Hill Rd
(61704)
Rates: $71-$119
(309) 828-0900
(800) 272-6232

WINGATE INN
1031 Wylie Dr
(61704)
Rates: $79
(309) 820-9990

BOLINGBROOK

HOLIDAY INN HOTEL & SUITES
205 Remington Blvd (60440)
Rates: $116
(630) 679-1600
(800) 465-4329

LA QUINTA INN
225 W South Frontage Rd
(60440)
Rates: $67-$116
(630) 226-0000
(800) 687-6667

BOURBONNAIS

HAMPTON INN
60 Ken Hayes Dr
(60914)
Rates: $80-$127
(815) 932-8369
(800) 426-7866

HOLIDAY INN EXPRESS HOTEL
62 Ken Hayes Dr
(60914)
Rates: n/a
(815) 932-4411
(800) 465-4329

MOTEL 6
1311 Illinois Rt 50 N (60914)
Rates: $35-$50
(815).933-2300
(800) 466-8356

BRADLEY

LEE'S INN
1500 N Rt 50
(60914)
Rates: n/a
(815) 932-8080
(800) 733-5337

QUALITY INN
800 N Kinzie
(60915)
Rates: $75-$175
(815) 939-3501
(800) 424-6423

BRAIDWOOD

SANDS MOTEL
1179 W Kennedy Rd (60408)
Rates: n/a
(815) 458-3401

BREESE

KNOTTY PINE HOTEL
215 N 4th St
(62230)
Rates: n/a
(618) 526-4556

BRIDGEVIEW

EXEL INN
9625 S 76th Ave
(60455)
Rates: $59-$87
(708) 430-1818
(800) 367-3935

BROADVIEW

TRAVEL INN
1150 W Roosevelt Rd (60153)
Rates: n/a
(708) 681-2550

BUNCOMBE

VALLEY VIEW CABINS
7025 Lick Creek Rd (62912)
Rates: n/a
(618) 833-6356

BURBANK

CEZARS INN
5001 W 79th St
(60459)
Rates: n/a
(708) 423-1100

BUREAU

RANCH HOUSE LODGE
Rts 26 & 29
(61315)
Rates: n/a
(815) 659-3361

BURR RIDGE

RAMADA INN
300 S Frontage Rd
(60527)
Rates: n/a
(630) 325-2900
(800) 272-6232

BUSHNELL

BUSHNELL INN
Rt 41 (61422)
Rates: n/a
(309) 772-3172

CACHE

MELTON'S FISHING CAMP
Rural Route
(62913)
Rates: n/a
(618) 776-5504

CAIRO

DAYS INN
I-57, Exit 1, RR 1 Box 10 (62914)
Rates: $34-$70
(618) 734-0215
(800) 329-7466

GARDEN INN
Hwy 51 (62914)
Rates: n/a
(618) 734-9554

RELAX INN
214 Washington Ave (62914)
Rates: n/a
(618) 734-0285

CALUMET CITY

BAYMONT INN
510 East End Ave
(60409)
Rates: $89-$99
(708) 891-2900
(877) 229-6668

CALUMET PARK

BEST WESTERN CHICAGO SOUTHWEST
12800 S Ashland Ave (60827)
Rates: $79-$109
(708) 389-2600
(800) 528-1234

SUPER 8 MOTEL
12808 S Ashland Ave (60827)
Rates: $68-$88
(708) 385-9100
(800) 800-8000

CANTON

CANTON INN
665 W Locust St
(61520)
Rates: n/a
(309) 647-7111

SUPER 8 MOTEL
2110 N Main St
(61520)
Rates: n/a
(309) 647-1888
(800) 800-8000

AREA CODES - If the local number doesn't connect, check for a new area code.

CARBONDALE

HAMPTON INN
2175 Reed Station
Pkwy (62901)
Rates: $79-$119
(618) 549-6900
(800) 426-7866

HORIZON INN
800 E Main St
(62901)
Rates: n/a
(618) 529-1100

MOTEL 6
700 E Main St
(62901)
Rates: $33-$50
(618) 457-5566
(800) 466-8356

**SUN HOTEL &
CONF CENTER**
2400 W Main St
(62901)
Rates: n/a
(618) 529-2424

SUPER 8 MOTEL
1180 E Main St
(62901)
Rates: $42-$79
(618) 457-8822
(800) 800-8000

CARLINVILLE

BEL-AIRE MOTEL
915 E 1st South St
(62626)
Rates: n/a
(217) 854-3287

**CARLIN VILLA-
BEST VALUE INN**
18891 Hwy 4
(62626)
Rates: $37-$68
(217) 854-3201
(888) 315-2378

HOLIDAY INN
19067 W Frontage
Rd (62626)
Rates: $62-$82
(217) 324-2100
(800) 465-4329

CARLYLE

SUPER 8 MOTEL
1371 William Rd
(62231)
Rates: n/a
(618) 594-8888
(800) 800-8000

CARMI

CARMI MOTEL
1008 W Main St
(62821)
Rates: n/a
(618) 382-4121

MIDWEST MOTEL
1719 W Oak St
(62821)
Rates: n/a
(618) 382-2313

CARROLLTON

**GOETTENS
SIERRA MOTEL**
Rt 3 (62016)
Rates: n/a
(217) 942-5012

CARTHAGE

**PRAIRIE WINDS
MOTEL**
Hwy 136 West
(62321)
Rates: n/a
(217) 357-3101

CASEY

COMFORT INN
933 SR 49 62420
Rates: $48-$105
(217) 932-2212
(800) 424-6423

CASEYVILLE

**BEST INNS
OF AMERICA**
2423 Old Country
Inn Rd (62232)
Rates: $59-$72
(618) 397-3300
(800) 237-8466

MOTEL 6
2431 Old Country
Inn Rd (62232)
Rates: $33-$46
(618) 397-8867
(800) 466-8356

CENTRALIA

BELL TOWER INN
200 E Noleman St
(62801)
Rates: $46-$63
(618) 533-1300

**MOTEL
CENTRALIA**
215 S Poplar St
(62801)
Rates: n/a
(618) 532-7357

QUEEN CITY MOTEL
402 N Elm St
(62801)
Rates: n/a
(618) 532-1881

CHAMPAIGN

BAYMONT INN
302 W Anthony
Dr (61821)
Rates: $65-$125
(217) 356-8900
(877) 229-6668

**CHANCELLOR
HOTEL**
1501 S Neil St
(61820)
Rates: n/a
(217) 352-7891
(800) 257-6667

COUNTRY INN
602 W
Marketview
(61822)
Rates: $85
(217) 355-6666
(800) 456-4000

DRURY INN
905 W Anthony
Dr (61821)
Rates: $65-$87
(217) 398-0030
(800) 378-7946

LA QUINTA INN
1900 Center Dr
(61820)
Rates: $65-$85
(217) 356-4000
(800) 687-6667

MICROTEL INN
1615 Rion Dr
(61822)
Rates: $45-$89
(217) 398-4136
(888) 771-7171

PREMIER INN
1501 N Neil St
(61820)
Rates: n/a
(217) 359-1601
(800) 599-7622

RED ROOF INN
212 W Anthony
Dr (61820)
Rates: $40-$76
(217) 352-0101
(800) 843-7663

CHESTER

**BEST WESTERN
REID'S INN**
2150 State St
(62233)
Rates: $64
(618) 826-63034
(800) 528-1234

HI 3 MOTEL
827 Lehman Dr
(62233)
Rates: n/a
(618) 826-4415

CHICAGO

(and Vicinity)

**ALLEGRO
CHICAGO-
A KIMPTON
HOTEL**
171 W Randolph
St (60601)
Rates: $119-$139
(312) 236-0123

**ALLERTON
CROWNE PLAZA**
701 N Michigan
Ave (60611)
Rates: 109-$229
(312) 440-1500
(800) 227-6963

**AMALFI HOTEL
CHICAGO**
20 W Kinzie St
(60610)
Rates: $139-$309
(312) 395-9000
(877) 262-5341

BAYMONT INN
630 N Rush St
(60611)
Rates: n/a
(877) 229-6668

**BEST WESTERN
HAWTHORNE
TERRACE**
3434 N Broadway
Ave (60657)
Rates: $99-$195
(773) 244-3434
(800) 528-1234
(888) 675-2378

**CARLTON INN
MIDWAY**
4944 S Archer Ave
(60632)
Rates: $85-$129
(773) 582-0900

CLARIDGE HOTEL
1244 N Dearborn
Pkwy (60610)
Rates: $139-$225
(312) 787-4980
(800) 245-1258

**CLARION BARCE-
LO HOTEL-
O'HARE**
5615 N
Cumberland Ave
(60631)
Rates: $119-$149
(773) 693-5800
(800) 252-7466

DRAKE HOTEL
140 E Walton Pl
(60611)
Rates: $249-$409
(312) 787-2200
(800) 553-7253

FAIRMONT HOTEL
200 N Columbus
Dr (60601)
Rates: $199-$339
(312) 565-8000
(800) 527-4727

**FOUR SEASONS
HOTEL**
120 E Delaware
Place (60611)
Rates: $360-$3500
(312) 280-8800
(800) 332-3442

**HARD ROCK
HOTEL**
230 N Michigan
Ave (60601)
Rates: $149-$219
(312) 345-1000

**HILTON
CHICAGO**
720 S Michigan
Ave (60605)
Rates: $159-$345
(319) 922-4400
(800) 445-8667

**HILTON
CHICAGO-
O'HARE**
I-190 at O'Hare
Int'l Airport
(66414)
Rates: $109-$324
(773) 686-8000
(800) 445-8667

**HOLIDAY INN/
MART PLAZA-
RIVERVIEW**
350 N Orleans St
(60654)
Rates: $169-$309
(312) 836-5000
(800) 465-4329

**HOLIDAY INN-
O'HARE/
KENNEDY**
8201 W Higgins
Rd (60631)
Rates: n/a
(773) 693-2323
(800) 465-4329

**HOTEL
BURNHAM**
1 W Washington
St (60602)
Rates: $139-$299
(312) 782-1111
(877) 294-9712

HOTEL INDIGO
1244 N Dearborn
St (60610)
Rates: $139-$259
(312) 787-4980

**HOTEL
MONACO**
225 N Wabash Ave
(60611)
Rates: $299-$349
(312) 960-8500
(800) 397-7661

**HOUSE OF BLUES
A LOEWS HOTEL**
333 N Dearborn St
(60610)
Rates: $179-$289
(312) 245-0333
(800) 235-6397

**HYATT ON
PRINTERS ROW**
500 S Dearborn St
(60605)
Rates: $99-$219
(312) 986-1234
(800) 233-1234

**LE MERIDIEN
CHICAGO**
520 N Michigan
Ave (60605)
Rates: $319-$2500
(312) 645-1500
(800) 543-4300

**OMNI
AMBASSADOR
EAST**
1301 N State
Pkwy (60610)
Rates: $199-$289
(312) 787-7200
(800) 843-6664

OMNI HOTEL
676 N Michigan
Ave (60611)
Rates: $329-$1000
(312) 944-6664
(800) 843-6664

**THE PALMER
HOUSE HILTON**
17 E Monroe St
(60603)
Rates: $99-$374
(312) 726-7500
(800) 445-8667

**PARK HYATT
CHICAGO**
800 N Michigan St
(60611)
Rates: $225-$425
(312) 335-1234
(800) 778-7477

**PENINSULA
HOTEL**
108 E Superior St
(60611)
Rates: $445-$890
(312) 337-2888
(866) 288-8889

RADISSON HOTEL
160 E Huron St
(60611)
Rates: $129+
(312) 787-2900
(800) 333-3333

RED ROOF INN
162 E Ontario St
(60611)
Rates: $80-$150
(312) 787-3580
(800) 733-7663

**RENAISSANCE
CHICAGO HOTEL**
1 W Wacker Dr
(60601)
Rates: $219-$350
(312) 372-7200
(800) 228-9290

**RESIDENCE INN
BY MARRIOTT**
201 E Walton Pl
(60611)
Rates: $195-$310
(312) 943-9800
(800) 331-3131

RITZ-CARLTON
160 E Pearson St
(60611)
Rates: $365-$545
(312) 266-1000
(800) 621-6906

**SHERATON
CHICAGO HOTEL
TOWERS**
301 E North Water
St (60611)
Rates: $129-$319
(312) 464-1000
(800) 325-3535

**SOFITEL
CHICAGO
WATER TOWER**
20 E Chestnut St
(60611)
Rates: $329-$399
(312) 324-4000
(877) 813-7700

**SUTTON PLACE
HOTEL**
21 E Bellevue Pl
(60611)
Rates: $169-$289
(312) 266-2100

TRAVELODGE
65 E Harrison St
(60605)
Rates: $59-$89
(312) 427-8000
(800) 578-7878
(800) 211-6706

**W CHICAGO CITY
CENTER**
172 W Adams St
(60603)
Rates: n/a
(312) 332-1200

**W CHICAGO
LAKESHORE**
644 N Lake Shore
Dr (60611)
Rates: $189-$369
(312) 943-9200

**WESTIN
CHICAGO RIVER
NORTH**
320 N Dearborn St
(60610)
Rates: $159-$339
(312) 744-1900
(800) 228-3000

WESTIN HOTEL
909 N Michigan
Ave (60611)
Rates: $129-$324
(312) 943-7200
(800) 228-3000

**WHITEHALL
HOTEL**
105 E Delaware Pl
(60611)
Rates: $149-$389
(312) 944-6300
(800) 948-4255

CHILLICOTHE
SUPER 8 MOTEL
615 S Fourth St
(61523)
Rates: $46-$64
(309) 274-2568
(800) 800-8000

*CLARENDON
HILLS*
**MAYFLOWER
MOTEL**
407 Ogden Ave
(60514)
Rates: n/a
(630) 325-2500

CLINTON
SUNSET INN
Rt 51 Bypass &
Kleeman Dr
(61727)
Rates: n/a
(217) 935-4140
(800) 325-2525

**TOWN &
COUNTRY MOTEL**
1151 Rt 54 W
(61727)
Rates: $25-$32
(217) 935-2121

WYE MOTEL
721 Rt 54 E
(61727)
Rates: $30-$40
(217) 935-3373

COBDEN
**SHAWNEE HILL
B&B**
290 Water Valley
Rd (62902)
Rates: n/a
(618) 893-2211

**BLACK DIAMOND
RANCH**
Rt 3 (62920)
Rates: n/a
(618) 833-7629

COLLINSVILLE
**BEST WESTERN
PEAR TREE INN**
552 Ramada Blvd
(62234)
Rates: $42-$93
(618) 345-9500
(800) 528-1234
(866) 777-8133

DRURY INN
602 N Bluff Rd
(62234)
Rates: $66-$88
(618) 345-7700
(800) 378-7946

HOLIDAY INN
1000 Eastport
Plaza Dr (62234)
Rates: $110
(618) 345-2800
(800) 465-4329

MAGGIE'S B&B
2102 N Keebler
Ave (62234)
Rates: n/a
(618) 344-8283

MOTEL 6
295-A N Bluff Rd
(62234)
Rates: $34-$52
(618) 345-2100
(800) 466-8356

CRESTWOOD
HAMPTON INN
13330 S Cicero
Ave (60455)
Rates: n/a
(708) 597-3330
(800) 426-7866

CRYSTAL LAKE
COMFORT INN
595 E Tracy Tr
(60014)
Rates: $64-$89
(815) 444-0040
(800) 424-6423

SUPER 8 MOTEL
577 Crystal Point
Dr (60014)
Rates: $46-$92
(815) 788-8888
(800) 800-8000

DANVILLE
**BEST WESTERN
REGENCY INN**
360 Eastgate Dr
(61834)
Rates: $50-$75
(217) 446-2111
(800) 528-1234

**BEST WESTERN
RIVERSIDE INN**
57 S Gilbert St
(61832)
Rates: $52-$85
(217) 431-0020
(800) 528-1234

COMFORT INN
383 Lynch Dr
(61832)
Rates: $54-$99
(217) 443-8004
(800) 424-6423

GLO MOTEL
3617 N Vermillion
(61832)
Rates: $31-$45
(217) 442-2086

SLEEP INN, INN
361 Lynch Dr
(61834)
Rates: $59-$199
(217) 442-6600
(800) 424-6423

SUPER 8 MOTEL
377 Lynch Dr
(61834)
Rates: $51-$64
(217) 443-4499
(800) 800-8000

DECATUR
BAYMONT INN
5100 Hickory Pt
Frontage Rd
(62526)
Rates: $60-$65
(217) 875-5800
(877) 229-6668

**BEST VALUE
SHELTON INN**
450 E Pershing
Rd (62526)
Rates: n/a
(217) 877-7255

COUNTRY INN
5150 Hickory Pt
Frontage Rd
(62526)
Rates: $73-$79
(217) 872-2402
(800) 456-4000

DAYS INN
333 N Wyckles Rd
(62522)
Rates: $40-$70
(217) 422-5900
(800) 329-7466

**HOLIDAY INN
SELECT**
4191 W US 36
(62522)
Rates: $95-$110
(217) 422-8800
(800) 465-4329

LAKEVIEW MOTEL
Rt 36 E (62526)
Rates: n/a
(217) 428-4677

RAMADA LTD
355 Hickory Point
Rd (62526)
Rates: $73-$79
(217) 876-8011
(800) 272-6232

SLEEP INN
3920 E
Hospitality Ln
(62521)
Rates: $64-$79
(217) 872-7700
(800) 424-6423

SUPER 8 MOTEL
3141 N Water St
(62526)
Rates: $41-$62
(217) 877-8888
(800) 800-8000

**TRI-MANOR
MOTEL**
3420 N 22nd St
(62526)
Rates: n/a
(217) 877-6900

WINGATE INN
5170 Wingate Dr
(62526)
Rates: $79
(217) 875-5500

DEERFIELD
**RESIDENCE INN
BY MARRIOTT**
530 Lake Cook Rd
(60015)
Rates: $119-$169
(847) 940-4644
(800) 331-3131

DEKALB
BAYMONT INN
1314 W Lincoln
Hwy (60115)
Rates: n/a
(815) 748-4800
(877) 229-6668

**BEST WESTERN
DEKALB INN**
1212 W Lincoln
Hwy (60115)
Rates: $79-$149
(815) 758-8661
(800) 528-1234

**STADIUM INN
MOTEL**
1321 W Lincoln
Hwy (60115)
Rates: $40-$56
(815) 756-1451

SUPER 8 MOTEL
800 W Fairview
Dr (60115)
Rates: n/a
(815) 748-4688
(800) 800-8000

DES PLAINES
**DOUBLETREE
CLUB HOTEL-
O'HARE**
1450 E Touhy Ave
(60018)
Rates: n/a
(847) 296-8866
(800) 222-8733

**TRAVELODGE-
O'HARE**
3003 Mannheim
Rd (60018)
Rates: $84-$169
(847) 296-5541
(800) 578-7878

DIXON
COMFORT INN
136 Plaza Dr
(61201)
Rates: $69-$129
(815) 284-0500
(800) 424-6423

QUALITY INN
154 Plaza Dr
(61021)
Rates: $79-$159
(815) 288-2001
(800) 424-6423

DOWNERS GROVE
**DOWNERS
GROVE MOTEL**
205 Ogden Ave
(60515)
Rates: n/a
(630) 969-7110

RED ROOF INN
1113 Butterfield
Rd (60515)
Rates: $51-$76
(630) 963-4205
(800) 843-7663

DU QUOIN
HUB MOTEL
423 W Main St
(62832)
Rates: n/a
(618) 542-2108

DWIGHT
CLASSIC INN
15 E Northbrook
Dr (60420)
Rates: n/a
(815) 584-1200

SUPER 8 MOTEL
14 E Northbrook
Dr (60420)
Rates: $39-$64
(815) 584-1888
(800) 800-8000

EAST DUBUQUE
**CAPTAIN MERRY
GUEST HOUSE**
399 Sinsinawa Ave
(61025)
Rates: n/a
(815) 747-3644

TIMMERMAN'S HOTEL & RESORT
7777 Timmermans
Dr (61025)
Rates: n/a
(815) 747-3181
(800) 336-3181

EAST HAZEL CREST
RODEWAY INN
17214 S Halsted St
(60429)
Rates: n/a
(708) 957-9233

EAST MOLINE
(see Quad Cities)

EAST PEORIA
MOTEL 6
104 W Camp St
(61611)
Rates: $35-$52
(309) 699-7281
(800) 466-8356

SUPER 8 MOTEL
725 Taylor St
(61611)
Rates: $42-$79
(309) 698-8889

EDDYVILLE
**LITTLE LUSK
TRAIL LODGE**
7390 Hwy 145
(62928)
Rates: n/a
(618) 672-4303

**SAN DAMIANO
RELIGIOUS
RETREAT CENTER**
Rts 146 & 34
(62928)
Rates: n/a
(618) 285-3507

EFFINGHAM
**BEST INNS
OF AMERICA**
1209 N Keller Dr
(62401)
Rates: $38-$55
(217) 347-5141
(866) 252-5141

**BEST WESTERN
RAINTREE INN**
1811 W Fayette
Ave (62401)
Rates: $40-$65
(217) 342-4121
(800) 528-1234

COMFORT INN
1304 W Evergreen
Dr (62401)
Rates: $49-$125
(217) 347-5050
(800) 424-6423

COMFORT SUITES
1310 W Fayette
Ave (62401)
Rates: $52-$140
(217) 342-3151
(800) 424-6423

DAYS INN
1412 W Fayette
Ave (62401)
Rates: $45-$75
(217) 342-9271
(800) 329-7466

ECONO LODGE
1600 W Fayette
Ave (62401)
Rates: $40-$100
(217) 342-4161
(800) 424-6423

**EFFINGHAM
MOTEL**
702 E Fayette Ave
(62401)
Rates: n/a
(217) 342-3991

**HOLIDAY INN
EXPRESS**
1103 Avenue of
Mid America
(62401)
Rates: n/a
(217) 540-1111
(800) 465-4329

**HOWARD
JOHNSON
EXPRESS**
1606 W Fayette
Ave (62401)
Rates: $39-$59
(217) 342-4667
(800) 446-4656

PARADISE INN
1000 W Fayette
Ave (62401)
Rates: $34-$45
(217) 342-2165

SUPER 8 MOTEL
1400 Thelma
Keller Ave (62401)
Rates: $44-$79
(217) 342-6888
(800) 800-8000

EL PASO
DAYS INN
630 W Main (61738)
Rates: $57-$125
(309) 527-7070
(800) 329-7466

SUPER 8 MOTEL
880 W Main (61738)
Rates: $45-$63
(309) 527-4949
(800) 800-8000

ELGIN
**BEST WESTERN
PLAZA HOTEL**
345 W River Rd
(60123)
Rates: $65-$79
(847) 695-5000
(800) 528-1234

DAYS INN
1585 Dundee Ave
(60120)
Rates: $54-$199
(847) 695-2100
(800) 329-7466

QUALITY INN
500 Toll Gate Rd
(60123)
Rates: $50-$80
(847) 931-4800
(800) 424-6423

ELIZABETH
RIDGEVIEW B&B
8833 S Massbach
Rd (61028)
Rates: n/a
(815) 598-3150

ELK GROVE VILLAGE
EXEL INN
1000 W Devon
Ave (60007)
Rates: $61-$84
(847) 895-2085
(800) 367-3935

EXEL INN-O'HARE
2881 W Touhy
Ave (6007)
Rates: $69-$88
(847) 803-9400
(800) 367-3935

HOLIDAY INN
1000 Busse Rd
(60007)
Rates: $64-$109
(847) 437-6010
(800) 465-4329

**LA QUINTA INN-
O'HARE AIRPORT**
1900 Oakton St
(60007)
Rates: $89-$99
(847) 439-6767
(800) 687-6667

MOTEL 6
1601 Oakton St
(60007)
Rates: $36-$40
(847) 981-9766
(800) 466-8356

**SHERATON
SUITES**
121 Northwest
Point Blvd (60007)
Rates: $79-$219
(847) 290-1600
(800) 324-3535

**SUPER 8 MOTEL-
O'HARE**
2951 Touhy Ave
(60007)
Rates: $55-$69
(847) 827-3133
(800) 800-8000

ELMHURST
AMERISUITES
410 W Lake St
(60126)
Rates: $69-$109
(630) 782-6300
(800) 833-1516

HOLIDAY INN
624 N York Rd
(60126)
Rates: $114-$134
(630) 279-1100
(800) 465-4329

**TRAVELERS
REST MOTEL**
572 W Lake St
(60126)
Rates: n/a
(630) 834-3814

ELSAH
**GREEN TREE
INN B&B**
15-17 Mill St
(62028)
Rates: n/a
(618) 374-2821
(800) 701-8003

EVANSTON
**A SOMMER PLACE
BED & BREAKFAST**
1213 Maple Ave
(60201)
Rates: n/a
(847) 869-0543

**HOTEL
ORRINGTON**
1710 Orrington
Ave (60201)
Rates: $162-$252
(847) 866-8700
(800) 529-9100

FAIRVIEW HEIGHTS
DRURY INN
12 Ludwig Dr
(62208)
Rates: $65-$85
(618) 398-8530
(800) 325-8300

RAMADA INN
6900 N Illinois
(62208)
Rates: $69-$85
(618) 632-4747
(800) 272-6232

SUPER 8 MOTEL
45 Ludwig Dr
(62208)
Rates: $42-$79
(618) 398-8338
(800) 800-8000

FARMER CITY
BUDGET MOTEL
825 E Clinton
Ave (61842)
Rates: n/a
(309) 928-2157

FARMERSVILLE
**GLORIA'S FAMILY
RESTAURANT &
MOTEL**
101 Main St
(62533)
Rates: n/a
(217) 227-3566

FINDLAY
THE FINDLAY INN
202 S Main St
(62534)
Rates: n/a
(217) 774-2258

FLORA
**BEST WESTERN
LORSON INN**
201 Gary Hagen
Dr (62839)
Rates: $52-$80
(618) 662 3054
(800) 528-1234

RANCH MOTEL
900 Olive (62839)
Rates: n/a
(618) 662-2181

FORSYTH
COMFORT INN
134 Barnett Ave
(62535)
Rates: $54-$75
(217) 875-1166
(800) 424-6423

FRANKLIN PARK
COMFORT INN
3001 N Mannheim
Rd (60131)
Rates: $79-$109
(847) 233-9292
(800) 424-6423

**SUPER 8 O'HARE
SOUTH**
3010 N Mannheim
Rd (60131)
Rates: $49-$149
(847) 288-0600
(800) 800-8000

FREEPORT
AMERIHOST INN
1060 Riverside Dr
(61032)
Rates: $75-$80
(815) 599-8510
(800) 434-5800

RAMADA INN
1300 E South St
(61032)
Rates: $53-$65
(815) 297-9700
(800) 272-6232

GALENA
**AAAH
TIERRALINDA**
826 S Rocky Hill
Rd (61036)
Rates: n/a
(815) 777-1234

ALLEN'S LOG CABIN GUEST HOUSE
11661 W Chetlain Ln (61036)
Rates: n/a
(815) 777-2845
(866) 847-4637

ALLEN'S VICTORIAN PINES INN & SPA
11383 Hwy 20 W (61036)
Rates: n/a
(815) 777-2043
(866) 847-4637

BEST WESTERN QUIET HOUSE
9915 Rt 20 E (61036)
Rates: $55-$202
(815) 777-2577
(800) 528-1234

CARRIE'S VINTAGE INN
305 N Main St (61036)
Rates: n/a
(815) 777-9125

CHARISMA COUNTRY COTTAGE RENTAL
11868 W Chetlain Ln (61036)
Rates: n/a
(815) 777-1780

CHESTNUT MOUNTAIN RESORT
8700 W Chestnut Rd (61036)
Rates: n/a
(815) 777-1320
(80)0 397-1320

CLORAN MANSION B&B & ANTONIO'S COTTAGE
1237 Franklin St (61036)
Rates: n/a
(815) 777-0583
(866) 234-0583

EAGLE RIDGE RESORT & SPA
444 Eagle Ridge Dr (61036)
Rates: $149-$309
(815) 777-2444

EARLY AMERICAN SETTLEMENT LOG CABINS
9401 Hart John Rd (61036)
Rates: n/a
(815) 777-4200
(800) 366-5647

THE GOLDMOOR B&B
9001 Sand Hill Rd (61036)
Rates: n/a
(815) 777-3925
(800) 255-3925

MAIN STREET INN
404 S Main St (61036)
Rates: n/a
(815) 777-3454

TRIANGLE MOTEL
Rt 20 West (61036)
Rates: n/a
(815) 777-2897
(877) 425-3629

GALESBURG
BEST WESTERN PRAIRIE INN
300 S Soangetaha Rd (61401)
Rates: $59-$86
(309) 343-7151
(800) 528-1234

COMFORT INN
907 W Carl Sandburg Dr (61401)
Rates: $59-$99
(309) 344-5445
(800) 424-6423

HOLIDAY INN EXPRESS
2285 Washington St (61401)
Rates: $60-$127
(309) 343-7100
(800) 465-4329

RAMADA INN
29 Public Sq On Main St (61401)
Rates: $50-$65
(309) 343-9161
(800) 272-6232

SUPER 8 MOTEL
260 W Main St (61401)
Rates: $40-$61
(309) 342-5174
(800) 800-8000

TRAVELER'S REST INN
565 W Main St (61401)
Rates: n/a
(309) 343-3191

GENESEO
SUPER 8 MOTEL
765 W Main St (61254)
Rates: n/a
(309) 945-1898
(800) 800-8000

GENEVA
OSCAR SWAN COUNTRY INN
1800 W State St (60134)
Rates: n/a
(630) 232-0173

GILMAN
BUDGET HOST INN
723 S Crescent St (60938)
Rates: $35-$99
(815) 265-7261
(800) 283-4678
(888) 875-2491

SUPER 8 MOTEL
1301 S Crescent St (60938)
Rates: $49-$69
(815) 265-7000
(800) 800-8000

TRAVEL INN
834 Hwy 24 W (60938)
Rates: $45-$65
(815) 265-7283

GLEN ELLYN
HOLIDAY INN
1250 Roosevelt Rd (60137)
Rates: $89-$129
(630) 629-6000
(800) 465-4329

SUPER 8 FOUR SEASONS MOTEL
675 W Roosevelt Rd (60137)
Rates: n/a
(630) 469-9202
(800) 800-8000

WESLEY INN
675 E Roosevelt Rd (60137)
Rates: n/a
(630) 469-8500
(800) 448-1190

GLENVIEW
BAYMONT INN
1625 Milwaukee Ave (60025)
Rates: $44-$90
(847) 635-8300
(800) 428-3438

MOTEL 6
1535 Milwaukee Ave (60025)
Rates: $41-$50
(847) 390-7200
(800) 466-8356

GODFREY
HIWAY HOUSE MOTOR INN
3023 Godfrey Rd (62035)
Rates: n/a
(618) 466-6676

GOLCONDA
BRIDGEMICKS COTTAGE WEST
Washington Dt (62938)
Rates: n/a
(618) 683-3601

MICHAELS MOTEL
RR 3, Adams St (62938)
Rates: n/a
(618) 683-2424

SMITHLAND POOL LODGING
Main St, Box 435 (62938)
Rates: n/a
(618) 683-2333

GRAFTON
BRAINERD HOUSE B&B
420 E Main St (62037)
Rates: n/a
(618) 786-2340

GRANITE CITY
GRANITE CITY LODGE
1200 19th St (62040)
Rates: n/a
(618) 876-2600

GRAYVILLE
BEST WESTERN WINDSOR OAKS INN
2200 S Court St (62844)
Rates: $68-$104
(618) 375-7930
(800) 528-1234

SUPER 8 MOTEL
2060 Co Rd (62844)
Rates: $74-$79
(618) 375-7288
(800) 800-8000

GREENFIELD
METCALF B&B
607 Garfield St (62044)
Rates: n/a
(217) 368-2428

GREENUP
FIVE STAR MOTEL
US Rt 40 & Rt 130 (62428)
Rates: n/a
(217) 923-5512

GREENVILLE
BEST WESTERN COUNTRY VIEW INN
I-70 & Rt 127 (62246)
Rates: $40-$80
(618) 664-3030
(800) 528-1234

BUDGET HOST INN
1525 SR 127 (62246)
Rates: $28-$47
(618) 664-1950
(800) 283-4678

PRAIRIE HOUSE COUNTRY INN
RR 4, Box 47-AA (62246)
Rates: n/a
(618) 664-3003

2 ACRES MOTEL
I-70 & Rt 127 (62246)
Rates: n/a
(618) 664-3131

UPTOWN MOTEL
323 S Third St (62246)
Rates: n/a
(618) 664-3121

GURNEE

BAYMONT INN
566 N Ridge Rd
(60031)
Rates: $59-$125
(847) 662-7600
(877) 229-6668

COMFORT SUITES
5430 Grand Ave
(60031)
Rates: $59-$149
(847) 782-0890
(800) 424-6423

COUNTRY INN
5420 W Grand
Ave (60031)
Rates: n/a
(847) 625-9700
(800) 456-4000

HAMEL

**INNKEEPER
MOTEL**
418 E State (62234)
Rates: n/a
(618) 633-2111

HAMPSHIRE

SUPER 8 MOTEL
115 Arrowhead Dr
(60140)
Rates: n/a
(847) 683-0888
(800) 800-8000

HARRISBURG

**BUDGET
HOST INN**
411 E Poplar St
(62946)
Rates: $29-$35
(618) 253-7651
(800) 283-4678

HAVANA

**SYCAMORE
MOTOR LODGE**
371 E Dearborn St
(62644)
Rates: n/a
(309) 543-4454

HENRY

**HENRY
HARBOR INN**
208 Cromwell Dr
(61537)
Rates: n/a
(309) 364-2365

HIGHLAND

CARDINAL INN
101 Walnut St
(62249)
Rates: n/a
(618) 654-4433

**HOLIDAY INN
EXPRESS**
20 Central Blvd
(62249)
Rates: $81-$142
(618) 651-1100
(800) 465-4329

HILLSIDE

HOLIDAY INN
4400 Frontge Rd
(60162)
Rates: $98-$103
(708) 544-9300
(800) 465-4329

HINSDALE

GENC MOTEL
16W621 S Frontage
Rd (60521)
Rates: n/a
(630) 323-9567

HOFFMAN ESTATES

BAYMONT INN
2075 Barrington
Rd (60195)
Rates: $73-$80
(847) 882-8848
(877) 229-6668

**CANDLEWOOD
SUITES**
2875 Greenspoint
Pkwy (60195)
Rates: n/a
(847) 490-1686
(888) 226-3539

LA QUINTA INN
2280 Barrington
Rd (60195)
Rates: $95-$109
(847) 882-3312
(800) 687-6667

MARRIOTT HOTEL
4800 Columbine
Blvd (60195)
Rates: n/a
(847) 645-9500
(800) 228-9290

RED ROOF INN
2500 Hassell Rd
(60195)
Rates: $56-$69
(847) 885-7877
(800) 843-7663

HOOPESTON

**DOWNTOWN
MOTEL**
200 E Main St
(60942)
Rates: n/a
(217) 283-6605

HULL

**RAILSPLITTER
INN MOTEL**
Hwy 106 (62343)
Rates: n/a
(217) 432-5417

ITASCA

AMERISUITES
1150 Arlington
Heights Rd
(60143)
Rates: $104-$119
(630) 875-1400
(800) 833-1516

JACKSONVILLE

**BLACKHAWK
VILLAGE INN
& LODGE**
1111 E Morton Rd
(62650)
Rates: n/a
(217) 245-2187

RAMADA INN
1717 W Morton
Ave (62650)
Rates: n/a
(217) 245-9571
(800) 272-6232

STAR LITE MOTEL
1910 W Morton
Ave (62650)
Rates: $38-$48
(217) 245-7184
(800) 489-7773

SUPER 8 MOTEL
1003 W Morton
Ave (62650)
Rates: $39-$70
(217) 479-0303
(800) 800-8000

JERSEYVILLE

SUPER 8 MOTEL
1303 Rt 109
(62052)
Rates: n/a
(618) 498-7888
(800) 800-8000

JOLIET

COMFORT INN N
3235 Norman Ave
(60435)
Rates: $60-$85
(815) 436-5141
(800) 424-6423

**COMFORT INN
CHOICE HOTEL**
135 S Larkin Ave
(60436)
Rates: $75-$100
(815) 744-1770
(800) 424-6423

**HOLIDAY INN
EXPRESS**
411 S Larkin Ave
(60436)
Rates $59-$139
(8150 729-2000
(800) 465-4329

MICROTEL INN
1806 McDonough
St (60435)
Rates: $32-$99
(815) 730-8800
(888) 771-7171

MOTEL 6
1850 McDonough
Rd (60436)
Rates: $30-$45
(815) 729-2800
(800) 466-8356

MOTEL 6
3551 Mall Loop Dr
(60436)
Rates: $33-$42
(815) 439-1332
(800) 466-8356

RED ROOF INN
1750 McDonough
St (60436)
Rates: $47-$64
(815) 741-2304
(800) 843-7663

SUPER 8 MOTEL
3401 Mall Loop Dr
(60436)
Rates: $50-$63
(815) 439-3838
(800) 800-8000

JONESBORO

**TRAIL OF TEARS
LODGE & RESORT**
1575 Fair City Rd
(62952)
Rates: n/a
(618) 833-8697

KANKAKEE

NORMA'S B&B
429 S Fourth
(60901)
Rates: n/a
(815) 937-1533

KEWANEE

**KEWANEE
MOTOR LODGE**
400 S Main St
(61443)
Rates: $45-$50
(309) 853-4000

KNOXVILLE

SUPER 8 MOTEL
737 Knox Hwy 10
(61448)
Rates: n/a
(309) 289-2100
(800) 800-8000

LA GRANGE

**J C COUNTRYSIDE
MOTEL**
6401 Joliet Rd
(60525)
Rates: n/a
(847) 352-3113

LANSING

DAYS INN
17356 S Torrence
Ave (60438)
Rates: $45-$85
(708) 474-6300
(800) 329-7466

RED ROOF INN
2450 E 173rd St
(60438)
Rates: $56-$80
(708) 895-9570
(800) 843-7663

LAWRENCE-VILLE

GAS LITE MOTEL
Rt 1, South on
State St (62439)
Rates: n/a
(618) 943-2374

MR. K'S MOTEL
407 State St
(62439)
Rates: n/a
(618) 943-5112

LE ROY

SUPER 8 MOTEL
1 Demma Dr
(61752)
Rates: $43-$70
(309) 962-4700
(800) 800-8000

LENA

SUGAR MAPLE INN B&B
607 Maple St
(61048)
Rates: n/a
(815) 369-2786

LEWISTON

COTTONWOOD MOTEL
805 S Main St
(61542)
Rates: n/a
(309) 547-3733

LIBERTYVILLE

BEST WESTERN HITCH-INN POST
1765 N
Milwaukee Ave
(60048)
Rates: $59-$109
(847) 362-8700
(800) 528-1234

CANDLEWOOD SUITES
1100 N Hwy 45
(60048)
Rates: $119-$139
(847) 247-9900
(888) 226-3539
(800) 946-6200

DAYS INN
1809 W
Milwaukee Ave
(60048)
Rates: $59-$119
(847) 816-8006
(800) 329-7466

HOLIDAY INN EXPRESS HOTEL
77 Buckley Rd
(60048)
Rates: $94-$106
(847) 549-7878
(800) 465-4329

LINCOLN

BUDGET INN
2011 N Kickapoo
St (62656)
Rates: n/a
(217) 735-1202

COMFORT INN
2811 Woodlawn
Rd (62656)
Rates: $55-$105
(217) 735-3960
(800) 424-6423

HOLIDAY INN EXPRESS
130 Olson Rd
(62656)
Rates: $68
(217) 735-5800
(800) 465-4329

LINCOLNSHIRE

MARRIOTTS RESORT
10 Marriott Dr
(60069)
Rates: $99-$204
(847) 634-0100
(800) 228-9290

STAYBRIDGE SUITES
100 Barclay Blvd
(60069)
Rates: $129-$299
(847) 821-0002
(800) 238-8000

LINCOLNWOOD

RAMADA PLAZA
4500 W Touhy
(60712)
Rates: n/a
(847) 677-1234
(800) 272-6232

LITCHFIELD

BAYMONT INN
1405 W Hudson
Dr (62056)
Rates: $65-$87
(217) 324-4556
(877) 229-6668

BEST VALUE INN-THE GARDENS
224 N Ohren Ln
(62056)
Rates: n/a
(217) 324-2181
(888) 315-2378

COMFORT INN
1010 E Columbia
N Blvd (62056)
Rates: $62-$110
(217) 324-9260
(800) 424-6423

SUPER 8 MOTEL
211 Ohren Ln
(62056)
Rates: $42-$59
(217) 324-7788
(800) 800-8000

LIVINGSTON

COUNTRY INN MOTEL
536 Veterans
Memorial Dr
(62058)
Rates: n/a
(618) 637-2600

LOMBARD

AMERISUITES
2340 S Fountain
Square Dr (60148)
Rates: $89-$99
(630) 932-6501
(800) 833-1516

COMFORT SUITES
530 W North Ave
(60148)
Rates: $79-$129
(630) 268-1300
(800) 424-6423

HOMESTEAD STUDIO SUITES HOTEL
2701 Technology
Dr (60148)
Rates: $69-$89
(630) 928-0202
(888) 782-9473

RESIDENCE INN BY MARRIOTT
2001 S Highland
Ave (60148)
Rates: $113-$175
(630) 629-7800
(800) 331-3131

TOWNEPLACE SUITES BY MARRIOTT
455 E 22nd St
(60148)
Rates: n/a
(630) 932-4400
(800) 257-3000

LOVES PARK

DAYS INN
4313 Bell School
Rd (61111)
Rates: $59-$104
(815) 282-9300
(800) 329-7466

MACOMB

ECONO LODGE
1414 Jackson St
(61455)
Rates: $39-$69
(309) 833-4521
(800) 424-6423

STAR MOTEL
1507 E Jackson St
(61455)
Rates: n/a
(309) 837-4817

SUPER 8 MOTEL
313 University Dr
(61455)
Rates: $45-$130
(309) 836-8888
(800) 800-8000

MANTENO

COMFORT INN
157 Cypress St
(60950)
Rates: $60-$126
(815) 468-8657
(800) 424-6423

COUNTRY INN
380 S Cypress St
(60950)
Rates: $79-$199
(815) 468-2600
(800) 456-4000

MARION

BEST INNS OF AMERICA
2700 W DeYoung
(62959)
Rates: $37-$54
(618) 997-9421
(800) 237-8466

DAYS INN
1802 Bittle Place
(62959)
Rates: $35-$99
(618) 997-1351
(800) 329-7466

DRURY INN
2706 W DeYoung
(62959)
Rates: $54-$78
(618) 997-9600
(800) 378-7946
(800) 325-8300

EXECUTIVE INN
2600 W DeYoung
St (62959)
Rates: n/a
(618) 997-2326
(800) 648-4667

GRAY PLAZA MOTEL

1501 W DeYoung
St (62959)
Rates: n/a
(618) 993-2174

LAKE TREE INN
9600 Lake of
Egypt Rd (62959)
Rates: n/a
(618) 995-1738

MOTEL 6
1008 Halfway Rd
(62959)
Rates: $34-$42
(618) 993-2631
(800) 466-8356

OLD SQUAT INN-ORIGINAL PIONEER LOG CABINS
14160 Liberty
School Rd (62959)
Rates: n/a
(618) 982-2916

RED CARPET INN
8101 Express Dr
(62959)
Rates: n/a
(618) 993-3222
(800) 528-1234

SUPER 8 MOTEL
2601 W DeYoung
St (62959)
Rates: $42-$79
(618) 993-5577
(800) 800-8000

MARSHALL

LINCOLN MOTEL
1002 N 2nd St
(62441)
Rates: n/a
(217) 826-2941

PEAKS MOTOR INN
107 E Trefz Dr
(62441)
Rates: n/a
(217) 826-3031

MARYVILLE

ECONO LODGE
2701 Maryville Rd
(62062)
Rates: $38-$76
(618) 345-5720
(800) 533-2666

MASON CITY

MASON CITY MOTEL
701 W Chestnut St (62664)
Rates: n/a
(217) 482-3003
(877) 482-3003

MATTESON

BAYMONT INN
5210 Southwick Dr (60443)
Rates: $67-$87
(708) 503-0999
(877) 229-6668

MATTOON

BUDGET INN
4134 Hwy 45 (61938)
Rates: n/a
(217) 235-4011

SUPER 8 MOTEL
205 McFall Rd (61938)
Rates: $45-$58
(217) 235-8888
(800) 800-8000

MCLEAN

SUPER 8 MOTEL
500 E South St (61754)
Rates: $44-$95
(309) 874-2366
(800) 800-8000

MENDOTA

COMFORT INN
1307 Kailash Dr (61342)
Rates: $56-$86
(815) 538-3355
(800) 424-6423

METROPOLIS

AMERICAN INN
1502 W 10th St (62960)
Rates: n/a
(618) 524-7431

BEST WESTERN METROPOLIS INN
2119 E 5th St (62960)
Rates: $49-$95
(618) 524-3723
(800) 528-1234
(800) 577-0707

COMFORT INN
2118 E 5th St (62960)
Rates: $60-$110
(618) 524-7227
(800) 424-6423

HOLIDAY INN EXPRESS
2179 E 5th St (62960)
Rates: $79-$125
(618) 524-8899
(800) 465-4329

ISLE OF VIEW B&B
205 Metropolis St (62960)
Rates: $43-$125
(618) 524-5838
(800) 566-7491

OLD BETHLEHEM SCHOOL COTTAGE B&B
6512 Old Marion Rd (62960)
Rates: n/a
(618) 524-4922

SUPER 8 MOTEL
2055 E 5th St (62960)
Rates: $41-$79
(618) 524-8200
(800) 800-8000

MINONK

VICTORIAN OAKS BED & BREAKFAST
435 Locust (61760)
Rates: $59-$104
(309) 432-2771
(800) 621-9970

MOKENA

SUPER 8 MOTEL
9485 W 191st St (60448)
Rates: n/a
(708) 479-7808
(800) 800-8000

MOLINE

(see Quad Cities)

MONEE

BEST WESTERN MONEE INN
5815 W Monee-Manhattan Rd (60449)
Rates: $45-$80
(708) 534-3500
(800) 528-1234

SUPER 8 MOTEL
5825 W Monee-Manhattan Rd (60449)
Rates: $45-$99
(708) 534-1900
(800) 800-8000

MONMOUTH

SUPER 8 MOTEL
1122 N 6th St (61462)
Rates: n/a
(309) 734-8558
(800) 800-8000

MONTICELLO

BEST WESTERN GATEWAY INN
805 Iron Horse Pl (61856)
Rates: $55-$75
(217) 762-9436
(800) 528-1234

MONTROSE

MOTEL MONTAROSA
I-70, Exit 105 (62445)
Rates: n/a
(217) 924-4117

MORRIS

COMFORT INN
70 W Gore Rd (60450)
Rates: $64-$159
(815) 942-1433
(800) 424-6423

DAYS INN
80 Hampton Rd (60450)
Rates: $55-$70
(815) 942-9000
(800) 329-7466

HOLIDAY INN
200 Gore Rd (60450)
Rates: $84-$100
(815) 942-6600
(800) 465-4329

MORTON

BEST WESTERN ASHLAND HOUSE
201 E Ashland Ave (61550)
Rates: $49-$99
(309) 263-5116
(800) 528-1234
(800) 897-7769

COMFROT INN
210 E Ashland St (61550)
Rates: $65-$79
(309) 266-8888
(800) 424-6423

HOLIDAY INN EXPRESS
115 E Ashland Ave (61550)
Rates: $59-$69
(309) 266-8310
(800) 465-4329

WELK-UM INN
101 E Ashland Ave (61550)
Rates: n/a
(309) 266-1600

MORTON GROVE

TRAVELODGE
9424 Waukegan Rd (60053)
Rates: n/a
(847) 965-6400
(800) 578-7878

MOUNT CARMEL

SHAMROCK MOTEL
1303 N Cherry St (62863)
Rates: n/a
(618) 262-4169

SUPER 8 MOTEL
937 Enterprise Ln (62863)
Rates: n/a
(618) 262-4800
(800) 800-8000

TOWN & COUNTRY MOTEL
1515 W 3rd St (62863)
Rates: n/a
(618) 262-4171

MOUNT CARROLL

COUNTRY PALMER HOUSE B&B
17035 Elizabeth Rd (61053)
Rates: n/a
(815) 244-2343

MOUNT MORRIS

THE KABLE HOUSE COUNTRY INN
3160 Sunset Hill (61054)
Rates: n/a
(815) 734-7297

MOUNT MORRIS MOTEL
1691 W Rt 64 (61054)
Rates: n/a
(815) 734-4114

MOUNT STERLING

LAND OF LINCOLN MOTEL
403 E Main St (62353)
Rates: n/a
(217) 773-3311

MOUNT VERNON

BEST INNS OF AMERICA
222 S 44th St (62864)
Rates: $34-$51
(618) 244-4343
(800) 237-8466

DRURY INN
145 N 44th St (62864)
Rates: $55-$75
(618) 244-4550
(800) 325-8300

ECONO LODGE
120 N 44th St (62864)
Rates: $38-$66
(618) 242-6370
(800) 424-6423

HOLIDAY INN
222 Potomac Blvd (62864)
Rates: $75
(618) 244-7100
(800) 465-4329

KNIGHTS INN
750 S 10th St (62864)
Rates: n/a
(618) 244-3224
(800) 843-5644

MOTEL 6
333 S 44th St
(62864)
Rates: $30-$42
(618) 244-2383
(800) 466-8356

SUPER 8 MOTEL
401 S 44th St
(62864)
Rates: $45-$79
(618) 242-8800
(800) 800-8000

THRIFTY INN
100 N 44th St
(62864)
Rates: $44-$62
(618) 244-7750

VILLAGER PREMIER
401 S 44th St
(62864)
Rates:n/a
(618) 244-3670

MUNDELEIN
CROWNE PLAZA NORTH SHORE
510 E Rt 83 (60060)
Rates: $69-$125
(847) 949-5100
(888) 226-3539

SUPER 8 MOTEL
1950 S Lake St
(60060)
Rates: $49-$75
(847) 949-9842
(800) 800-8000

MURPHYS-BORO
APPLE TREE INN
100 North 2nd St
(62966)
Rates: $30-$40
(618) 687-2345
(800) 626-4356

NAPERVILLE
DAYS INN
1350 E Ogden Ave
(60563)
Rates: $52-$71
(630) 369-3600
(800) 329-7466

EXEL INN
1585 N Naperville/
Wheaton Rd
(60563)
Rates: $57-$85
(630) 357-0022
(800) 367-3935

FAIRFIELD INN
1847 W Diehl Rd
(60563)
Rates: $99-$130
(630) 548-0966
(800) 228-2800

HAWTHORN SUITES
1843 W Diehl Rd
(60563)
Rates: $99-$179
(630) 548-0881
(800) 527-1133

HOLIDAY INN SELECT
1801 N Naper
Blvd (60563)
Rates: $69-$149
(630) 505-4900
(800) 465-4329

HOMESTEAD STUDIO SUITES
1827 Centre Point
Circle (60563)
Rates: $69-$95
(630) 577-0200
(888) 782-9473

RED ROOF INN
1698 W Diehl Rd
(60563)
Rates: $71-$81
(630) 369-2500
(800) 843-7663

NASHVILLE
BEST WESTERN U.S. INN
11640 SR 127
(62263)
Rates: $45-$69
(618) 478-5341
(800) 528-1234
(888) 314-5313

NEBO
HEARTLAND LODGE
RR 1, Box 8A
(62355)
Rates: n/a
(800) 717-4868

NEWTON
RIVER PARK MOTEL
10024 Hwy 130
N (62448)
Rates: n/a
(618) 783-2327

TURKEY CREEK LODGE & GAME PRESERVE
13388 N 875th St
(62448)
Rates: n/a
(217) 683-2642
(877) 660-6602

NILES
THRIFTLODGE
7247 N Waukegan
Rd (60714)
Rates: $45-$70
(847) 647-9444
(800) 578-7878
(800) 525-9055

NORMAL
BEST WESTERN UNIVERSITY INN
6 Traders Cir
(61761)
Rates: $69-$99
(309) 454-4070
(800) 528-1234

COMFORT SUITES
310-B Greenbriar
Dr (61761)
Rates: $59-$140
(309) 452-8588
(800) 424-6423

HOLIDAY INN EXPRESS HOTEL
1715 Parkway
Plaza Dr (61761)
Rates: $89-$99
(309) 862-1600
(800) 465-4329

HOLIDAY INN NORTH
8 Traders Cir
(61761)
Rates: $100
(309) 452-8300
(800) 465-4329

MOTEL 6
1600 N Main St
(61761)
Rates: $29-$42
(309) 452-0422
(800) 466-8356

SIGNATURE INN
101 S Veterans
Pkwy (61761)
Rates: $49-$104
(309) 454-4044
(800) 822-5252

SUPER 8 MOTEL
2 Traders Cir
(61761)
Rates: $35-$59
(309) 454-5858
(800) 800-8000

NORTH AURORA
BAYMONT INN
308 S Lincolnway
(60542)
Rates: $74-$109
(630) 897-7695
(877) 229-6668

HOWARD JOHNSON
306 S Lincolnway
(60542)
Rates: $52-$68
(630) 892-6481
(800) 446-4656

NORTHBROOK
RED ROOF INN
340 Waukegan Rd
(60062)
Rates: $70-$100
(847) 205-1755
(800) 843-7663

O'FALLON
COMFORT INN
1100 Eastgate Dr
(62269)
Rates: $65-$129
(618) 624-6060
(800) 424-6423

ECONO LODGE
1409 W Hwy 50
(62269)
Rates: $59-$99
(618) 628-8895
(800) 424-6423

HOWARD JOHN-SON EXPRESS INN
116 Regency Park
(62269)
Rates: $68-$83
(618) 628-1200
(800) 446-4656

OAK BROOK
RESIDENCE INN BY MARRIOTT
790 Jorie Blvd
(60523)
Rates: $149
(630) 571-1200
(800) 331-3131

OAK FOREST
THE TERRACE MOTEL
15353 S Cicero
Ave (60452)
Rates: n/a
(708) 687-7500

OAK LAWN
HOLIDAY INN
4140 W 95th St
(60453)
Rates: $139-$239
(708) 425-7900
(800) 465-4329
(800) 625-5296

OAKBROOK TERRACE
LA QUINTA INN
1S666 Midwest
Rd (60181)
Rates: $55-$105
(630) 495-4600
(800) 687-6667

STAYBRIDGE SUITES
200 Royce Blvd
(60181)
Rates: $139-$159
(630) 953-9393
(800) 238-8000

OGLESBY
HOLIDAY INN EXPRESS
900 Holiday St
(61348)
Rates: $59-$65
(815) 883-3535
(800) 465-4329

OKAWVILLE
SUPER 8 MOTEL
812 N Henhouse
Rd (62271)
Rates: $41-$66
(618) 243-6525
(800) 800-8000

OLIVE BRANCH
HORSESHOE LAKE MOTEL
Rt 3 (62969)
Rates: n/a
(618) 776-5201

OLNEY
ROYAL INN MOTEL
1001 W Main St
(62450)
Rates: n/a
(618) 395-8581
(800) 433-5287

AREA CODES - If the local number doesn't connect, check for a new area code.

TRAVELERS INN MOTEL
1801 E Main St
(62450)
Rates: n/a
(618) 393-2186
(800) 232-0976

OQUAWKA
RIVERBED INN
Hwy 164 E (61469)
Rates: n/a
(309) 867-4321

OREGON
LAKE LADONNA
1302 Harmony Rd
(61061)
Rates: n/a
(815) 732-6804

PINEHILL INN B&B
400 Mix St (61061)
Rates: n/a
(815) 732-2067
(800) 851-0131

ORLAND PARK
COMFORT INN
8800 W 159th St
(60462)
Rates: $80-$226
(708) 403-1100
(800) 424-6423

OTTAWA
COMFORT INN
510 E Etna Rd
(61350)
Rates: $60-$130
(815) 433-9600
(800) 424-6423

HAMPTON INN
4115 Holiday Lane
(61350)
Rates: $84
(815) 434-6040
(800) 426-7866

HOLIDAY INN EXPRESS
120 W Stevenson
Rd (61350)
Rates: $63-$72
(815) 433-0029
(800) 465-4329

OZARK
THE IRISH INN B&B
1 Solomon Lane
(62972)
Rates: n/a
(618) 695-3355

PALATINE
HOLIDAY INN EXPRESS
1550 E Dundee Rd
(60067)
Rates: $64-$84
(847) 934-4900
(800) 465-4329

MOTEL 6
1450 E Dundee Rd
(60067)
Rates: $37-$40
(847) 359-0046
(800) 466-8356

RED GABLES MOTEL
875 W Northwest
Hwy (60067)
Rates: n/a
(847) 358-3443

PANA
LAKE LAWN INN
Hwy 51 & Rt 16 E
(62557)
Rates: n/a
(217) 562-2123

PARIS
SUPER 8 MOTEL
11642 Hwy 150 N
(61944)
Rates: $39-$75
(217) 463-8888
(800) 800-8000

PAXTON
PAXTON INN
980 W Ottawa St
(60957)
Rates: n/a
(217) 379-2316

PEKIN
COMFORT INN
3240 N Vandever
Ave (61554)
Rates: $59+
(309) 353-4047
(800) 424-6423

CONCORD INN
2801 Court St
(61554)
Rates: n/a
(309) 347-5533

PEORIA
AMERICINN LODGE & SUITES
9106 N Lindbergh
Dr (61615)
Rates: $90-$160
(309) 692-9200
(800) 634-3444

BEST WESTERN SIGNATURE INN
4112 N
Brandywine Dr
(61614)
Rates: $59-$129
(309) 685-2556
(800) 528-1234
(800) 822-5252

COMFORT SUITES
1812 War
Memorial Dr
(61614)
Rates: $59-$105
(309) 688-3800
(800) 424-6423

HOLIDAY INN
4400 N
Brandywine Dr
(61614)
Rates: $90-$95
(309) 686-8000
(800) 465-4329

HOLIDAY INN CITY CENTRE
500 Hamilton
Blvd (61602)
Rates: $98-$138
(309) 674-2500
(800) 465-4329

MARK TWAIN HOTEL
225 NE Adams
St (61602)
Rates: $85-$104
(309) 676-3600

RED ROOF INN
4031 N War
Memorial Dr
(61614)
Rates: $46-$56
(309) 684-3911
(800) 843-7663

RESIDENCE INN BY MARRIOTT
4201 N War
Memorial Dr
(61614)
Rates: $130-$140
(309) 681-9000
(800) 331-3131

SLEEP INN, INN
4244 Brandywine
Dr (61614)
Rates: $55-$80
(309) 682-3322
(800) 424-6423

STAYBRIDGE SUITES
300 W Romeo B
Garrett Ave
(61605)
Rates: $129-$199
(309) 673-7829
(800) 238-8000

SUPER 8 MOTEL
4025 W War
Memorial Dr
(61614)
Rates: $47-$79
(309) 688-8074
(800) 800-8000

PERU
ECONO LODGE
1840 May Rd
(61354)
Rates: $45-$75
(815) 224-2500
(800) 424-6423

LA QUINTA INN
4389 Venture Dr
(61354)
Rates: $68-$125
(815) 224-9000
(800) 687-6667

PINCKNEYVILLE
MAINSTREET INN
112 S Main St
(62274)
Rates: $36-$39
(618) 357-2128
(800) 455-7378

PITTSFIELD
HAMMITT'S LAKEVIEW COTTAGES
RR 3 (62363)
Rate: n/a
(217) 285-2998

PINE LAKES RESORT
RR 3 (62363)
Rates: n/a
(21) 285-6719
(877) 808 -7436

POCAHONTAS
POWHATAN MOTEL
I-70 & Exit 36
(62275)
Rates: n/a
(618) 669-2271

TAHOE MOTEL
106 Johnston St
(62275)
Rates: n/a
(618) 669-2404

PONTIAC
COMFORT INN
1821 W Reynolds
St (61764)
Rates: $65-$125
(815) 842-2777
(800) 424-6423

FIESTA MOTEL
951 Reynolds St
(61764)
Rates: n/a
(815) 844-7103

SUPER 8 MOTEL
601 S Deerfield Rd
(61764)
Rates: $41-$58
(815) 844-6888
(800) 800-8000

PONTOON BEACH
BEST WESTERN CAMELOT INN
1240 E Old Chain
of Rocks Rd (62040)
Rates: $46-$73
(618) 931-2262
(800) 528-1234

SUPER 8 MOTEL
4141 Timberlake
Dr (62040)
Rates: $45-$64
(618) 931-8808
(800) 800-8000

PRINCETON
DAYS INN
2238 N Main St
(61356)
Rates: $45-$65
(815) 875-3371
(800) 329-7466

LINCOLN INN
I-80 & Rt 26
(61356)
Rates: $32-$44
(815) 875-3371

PRINCETON MOTOR LODGE
1844 N Main
(61356)
Rates: $36-$44
(815) 875-1121

AREA CODES - If the local number doesn't connect, check for a new area code.

PROSPECT HEIGHTS

EXEL INN
540 Milwaukee Ave (60070)
Rates: $42-$66
(847) 459-0545
(800) 367-3935

QUAD CITIES

BAYMONT INN
400 Jason Way Ct (Davenport 52807)
Rates: $59-$89
(563) 386-1600
(877) 229-6668

BEST WESTERN STEEPLEGATE INN
100 W 76th St (Davenport 52806)
Rates: $79-$169
(563) 386-6900
(800) 373-6900

COMFORT INN
7222 Northwest Blvd (Davenport 52806)
Rates: $49-$140
(563) 391-8222
(800) 424-6423

COMFORT INN
2600 52nd Ave (Moline 61265)
Rates: $55-$90
(309) 762-7000
(800) 424-6423

COUNTRY INN
140 E 55th St (Davenport 52806)
Rates: $64-$99
(563) 388-6444
(800) 456-4000

EXEL INN
6310 N Brady St (Davenport 52806)
Rates: $37-$63
(319) 386-6350
(800) 367-3935

EXEL INN
2501 52nd Ave (Moline 61265)
Rates: $42-$59
(309) 797-5580
(800) 367-3935

HEARTLAND INN
815 Golden Valley Dr (Bettendorf 52722)
Rates: $76-$86
(563) 355-6336
(800) 334-3277

HEARTLAND INN
6605 Brady St (Davenport 52806)
Rates: $76-$86
(563) 386-8336
(800) 334-3277

HOLIDAY INN
5202 Brady St (Davenport 52806)
Rates: $69-$109
(563) 391-1230
(800) 465-4329

HOLIDAY INN-CONVENTION CENTER
6902 27th St (Moline 61265)
Rates: $70
(309) 762-8811
(800) 465-4329

HOLIDAY INN EXPRESS/ AIRPORT AREA
6910 27th St (Moline 61265)
Rates: $59-$75
(309) 762-8300
(800) 465-4329

LA QUINTA INN
5450 27th St (Moline 61265)
Rates: $65-$85
(309) 762-9008
(800) 687-6667

THE LODGE HOTEL
900 Spruce Hills Dr (Bettendorf 52722)
Rates: $95-$105
(563) 359-7141

MOTEL 6
2359 69th Ave (Moline 61265)
Rates: $35-$43
(309) 764-8711
(800) 466-8356

RESIDENCE INN BY MARRIOTT
120 E 55th St (Davenport 52806)
Rates: $99-$149
(563) 391-8877
(800) 331-3131

RHYTHM CITY CASINO BLACK-HAWK HOTEL
200 E 3rd St (Davenport 52801)
Rates: $54-$79
(563) 328-6000

SIGNATURE INN
3020 Utica Ridge Rd (Bettendorf 52722)
Rates: $49-$104
(563) 355-7575

SUPER 8 MOTEL
410 E 65th St (52807)
Rates: $40-$100
(563) 388-9810
(800) 800-8000

SUPER 8 MOTEL
2201 John Deere Expy (East Moline 61244)
Rates: $45-$64
(309) 796-1999
(800) 800-8000

SUPER 8 MOTEL
1191 19th St & 12th Ave (Moline 61265)
Rates: n/a
(309) 764-9644
(800) 800-8000

QUINCY

BEL-AIRE MOTEL
2314 North 12th St (62301)
Rates: n/a
(217) 223-1356

COMFORT INN
4100 Broadway (62301)
Rates: $52-$100
(217) 228-2700
(800) 424-6423

DAYS INN-RIVERSIDE
200 Maine St (62301)
Rates: $30-$110
(217) 223-6610
(800) 329-7466

DIAMOND MOTEL
4703 N 12th St (62301)
Rates: n/a
(217) 223-1436

GARDEN VIEW RETREAT
6104 Lentz Rd (62301)
Rates: n/a
(217) 656-3435

HOLIDAY INN
201 S 3rd St (62301)
Rates: $69-$79
(217) 222-2666
(800) 465-4329

SUPER 8 MOTEL
224 N 36th St (62301)
Rates: $47-$85
(217) 228-8808
(800) 800-8000

TRAVELODGE
200 S 3rd St (62301)
Rates: $45-$75
(217) 222-5620
(800) 578-7878

RANTOUL

BEST WESTERN HERITAGE INN
420 S Murray Rd (61866)
Rates: $49-$75
(217) 892-9292
(800) 528-1234

DAYS INN
801 W Champaign (61866)
Rates: $49-$90
(217) 893-0700
(800) 329-7466

FANMARKER INN
200 Linden Ave (61866)
Rates: n/a
(217) 893-1234

RANTOUL MOTEL
303 N Century Blvd (61866)
Rates: n/a
(217) 893-5500

SUPER 8 MOTEL
207 S Murray Rd (61866)
Rates: $45-$67
(217) 893-8888
(800) 800-8000

RED BUD

RED BUD COUNTRY INN
1617 S Main (62278)
Rates: n/a
(618) 282-4444

RED BUD MOTEL
1103 S Main St (62278)
Rates: n/a
(618) 282-2123

RICHMOND

DRAKE MOTEL
8613 S Rt 12 (60071)
Rates: n/a
(815) 678-3501

ROBINSON

BEST WESTERN ROBINSON INN
1500 W Main St (62454)
Rates: $60-$116
(618) 544-8448
(800) 528-1234

QUAIL CREEK COUNTRY CLUB & RESORT
1010 E Highland Ave (62454)
Rates: n/a
(618) 544-8674
(800) 544-8674

ROCHELLE

COMFORT INN
1133 N 7th St (61068)
Rates: $60-$190
(815) 562-5551
(800) 424-6423

HOLIDAY INN EXPRESS
1240 Dement Rd (61068)
Rates: n/a
(800) 465-4329

ROCK FALLS

HOLIDAY INN
2105 1st Ave (61071)
Rates: $78-$102
(815) 626-5500
(800) 465-4329

AREA CODES - If the local number doesn't connect, check for a new area code.

SUPER 8 MOTEL
2100 1st Ave
(61071)
Rates: $46-$69
(815) 626-8800
(800) 800-8000

ROCKFORD

BAYMONT INN
662 N Lyford Rd
(61107)
Rates: $49-$200
(815) 229-8200
(877) 229-6668

CANDLEWOOD SUITES
7555 Walton St
(61108)
Rates: $84-$104
(815) 229-9300
(888) 226-3539

EXEL INN
220 S Lyford Rd
(61108)
Rates: $44-$64
(815) 332-4915
(800) 367-3935

FOX RUN B&B INN
2815 N Rockton Ave (61108)
Rates: n/a
(815) 963-8151

QUALITY SUITES
7401 Walton Ave
(61108)
Rates: $75-$200
(815) 227-1300
(800) 242-6423

RED ROOF INN
7434 E State St
(61108)
Rates: $63-$76
(815) 398-9750
(800) 843-7663

RESIDENCE INN BY MARRIOTT
7542 Colosseum Dr (61107)
Rates: $89-$129
(815) 227-0013
(800) 331-3131

SLEEP INN
725 Clark Dr
(61107)
Rates: $62-$154
(8150 398-8900
(800) 424-6423

SWEDEN HOUSE LODGE
4605 E State St
(61108)
Rates: $40-$70
(815) 398-4130
(800) 886-4138

ROLLING MEADOWS

MOTEL 6
1800 Winnetka Cir (60008)
Rates: $37-$46
(847) 818-8088
(800) 466-8356

ROMEOVILLE

SUPER 8 MOTEL
1301 Marquette Dr
(60441)
Rates: n/a
(630) 759-8880

ROSEMONT

CROWNE PLAZA CHICAGO O'HARE
5540 N River Rd
(60018)
Rates: $80-$179
(847) 671-6350
(800) 227-6963

DOUBLETREE HOTEL CHICAGO O'HARE
5460 N River Rd
(60018)
Rates: $85-$199
(847) 292-9100
(800) 222-8733

EMBASSY SUITES
5500 N River Rd
(60018)
Rates: $109-$325
(847) 678-4000
(800) 362-2779

RESIDENCE INN BY MARRIOTT
7101 Chestnut St
(60018)
Rates: $139-$189
(847) 375-9000
(800) 331-3131

SHERATON GATEWAY SUITES O'HARE
6501 N Mannheim Rd (60018)
Rates: $89-$259
(847) 699-6300
(800) 325-3535

SOFITEL HOTEL O'HARE
5550 N River Rd
(60018)
Rates: $235-$275
(847) 678-4488
(800) 233-5959

THE WESTIN O'HARE
6100 N River Rd
(60018)
Rates: $99-$289
(847) 698-6000
(800) 228-3000

WYNDHAM O'HARE
6810 N Mannheim Rd (60018)
Rates: $79-$149
(847) 297-1234
(800) 996-3426

RUSHVILLE

CROSSROADS MOTEL
Hwy 67 & 24
(62681)
Rates: n/a
(217) 322-6702

SAINT ANNE

GEORGIAN MOTEL
Rts 1 & 17 (61964)
Rates: n/a
(815) 937-9740

SAINT CHARLES

BEST WESTERN INN
1635 E Main St
(60174)
Rates: $79-$89
(630) 584-4550
(800) 528-1234

HOTEL BAKER
100 W Main St
(60174)
Rates: n/a
(630) 584-2100
(800) 284-0110

SUPER 8 MOTEL
1520 E Main St
(60174)
Rates: $76-$109
(630) 377-8388
(800) 800-8000

SAINT ELMO

WALDORF MOTEL
1000 W Cumberland Rd
(62458)
Rates: n/a
(618) 829-5665

SALEM

CONTINENTAL MOTEL
1600 E Main St
(62881)
Rates: $26-$36
(618) 548-3090

RESTWELL MOTEL
700 W Main St
(62881)
Rates: n/a
(618) 548-2040

SALEM INN
1812 W Main St
(62881)
Rates: n/a
(618) 548-4212

SUPER 8 MOTEL
118 Paragon Rd
(62881)
Rates: $43-$79
(618) 548-5882
(800) 800-8000

SAVANNA

INDIAN HEAD MOTEL
3523 Rt 84 N
(61074)
Rates: n/a
(815) 273-2154

SAVANNA MOTEL
2000 Oakton Rd
(61074)
Rates: n/a
(815) 273-7728

SEVEN EAGLES CAMPGROUND & RESORT
9734 Rt 84 (61074)
Rates: n/a
(815) 273-7301

SUPER 8 MOTEL
101 Valley View Dr (61074)
Rates: n/a
(815) 273-2288
(800) 800-8000

SAVOY

BEST WESTERN PARADISE INN
1001 N Dunlap Ave (61874)
Rates: $57-$77
(217) 356-1824
(800) 528-1234

SCHAUMBURG

AMERISUITES
1851 McConnor Pkwy (60173)
Rates: $89-$154
(847) 330-1060
(800) 833-1516

CANDLEWOOD SUITES
1200 E Bank Dr
(60173)
Rates: n/a
(847) 517-7644
(888) 226-3539

DRURY INN
600 N Martingale Rd (60173)
Rates: $81-$105
(847) 517-7737
(800) 378-7946

HAWTHORN SUITES
1251 E American Ln (60173)
Rates: $69-$149
(847) 706-9007
(800) 527-1133

HOLIDAY INN
1550 N Roselle Rd
(60195)
Rates: $89-$115
(847) 310-0500
(800) 465-4329
(800) 289-8443

HOMESTEAD STUDIO SUITES
51 E State Pkwy
(60173)
Rates: $69-$89
(847) 882-6900
(888) 782-9473

HOMEWOOD SUITES
815 E American Ln (60173)
Rates: $79-$169
(847) 605-0400
(800) 225-5466

LA QUINTA INN
1730 E Higgins Rd
(60173)
Rates: $85-$105
(847) 517-8484
(800) 687-6667

**RESIDENCE INN
BY MARRIOTT**
1610 McConnor
Pkwy (60173)
Rates: $169-$229
(847) 517-9200
(800) 331-3131

**STAYBRIDGE
SUITES**
901 E Woodfield
Office Ct (60173)
Rates: $129-$189
(847) 619-6677
(800) 238-8000

SCHILLER PARK
**CANDLEWOOD
SUITES**
4021 N Manheim
Rd (60176)
Rates: n/a
(847) 671-4663
(888) 226-3539

**COMFORT SUITES
O'HARE AIRPORT**
4200 N River Rd
(60176)
Rates: $79-$159
(847) 233-9000
(800) 424-6423

MOTEL 6
9408 W Lawrence
Ave (60176)
Rates: $47-$60
(847) 671-4282
(800) 466-8356

**TWELVE OAKS
SUITES-O'HARE**
9450 W Lawrence
Ave (60176)
Rates: n/a
(847) 725-2210
(866) 212-6257

SHANNON
**HICKORY HILL
LODGING**
24366 Payne Rd
(61078)
Rates: n/a
(815) 222-1039
(815) 864-2099

SHEFFIELD
DAYS INN
16733 Hwy 40
(61361)
Rates: $40-$125
(815) 454-2361
(800) 329-7466

**HIDDEN LAKE
COUNTRY CLUB
GUEST HOUSES**
Buda on Rt 40
(61361)
Rates: n/a
(815) 454-2603

SHELBYVILLE
**GREGORY'S
RESORT**
RR 4 (62565)
Rates: n/a
(217) 774-4313

JR'S RESORT
RR 4 (62565)
Rates: n/a
(217) 756-3147

SHOREWOOD
JOLIET INN
19747 Frontage Rd
(60436)
Rates: n/a
(815) 725-2180

SKOKIE
COMFORT INN
9333 Skokie Blvd
(60077)
Rates: $89-$149
(847) 679-4200
(800) 424-6423

**HOLIDAY INN
NORTH SHORE**
5300 W Touhy Ave
(60077)
Rates: $130-$150
(847) 679-8900
(800) 465-4329

SOUTH BELOIT
KNIGHTS INN
1710 Gardner St
(61080)
Rates: n/a
(815) 389-2281
(800) 843-5644

SOUTH HOLLAND
MOTEL 6
17301 S Halsted
St (60473)
Rates: $36-$50
(708) 331-1621
(800)466-8356

SOUTH JACKSONVILLE
COMFORT INN
200 Comfort Dr
(62650)
Rates: $79-$100
(217) 245-8372
(800) 424-6423

SPARTA
**BEST WESTERN
SPARTA INN**
1755 N Market
(62286)
Rates: $56-$89
(618) 443-4536
(800) 528-1234

SPARTA MOTEL
700 S St. Louis St
(62286)
Rates: n/a
(618) 443-3614

SPRING VALLEY
RIVIERA MOTEL
I-80 & Rt 89
(61362)
Rates: n/a
(815) 894-2225

SPRINGFIELD
BAYMONT INN
5871 S Sixth St
(62703)
Rates: $65-$72
(217) 529-6655
(877) 229-6668

**BEST INNS
OF AMERICA**
500 N 1st St
(62702)
Rates: $55-$85
(217) 522-1100
(800) 237-8466

**BEST WESTERN
CLEARLAKE
PLAZA**
3440 Clearlake
Ave (62702)
Rates: $65-$149
(217) 525-7420
(800) 528-1234

BUDGET INN
3125 Wide Track
Dr (62702)
Rates: n/a
(217) 789-9471

COMFORT INN
3442 Freedom Dr
(62704)
Rates: $69-$114
(217) 787-2250
(800) 424-6423

DAYS INN
3000 Stevenson Dr
(62703)
Rates: $56-$90
(217) 529-0171
(800) 329-7466

DRURY INN
3180 S Dirksen
Pkwy (62703)
Rates: $65-$85
(217) 529-3900
(800) 378-7946

**HOWARD
JOHNSON INN**
1701 J David Jones
Pkwy (62702)
Rates: $55-$95
(217) 541-8762
(800) 446-4656

MICROTEL INN
2636 Sunrise Dr
(62703)
Rates: $55-$84
(217) 753-2636

MOTEL 6
6011 S 6th St Rd
(62707)
Rates: $35-$50
(217) 529-1633
(800) 466-8356

PEAR TREE INN
3190 S Dirksen
Pkwy (62703)
Rates: $46-$65
(217) 529-9100
(800) 282-8733

**QUALITY INN
& SUITES,
STATE HOUSE**
101 E Adams
(62701)
Rates: $69-$129
(217) 528-5100
(800) 424-6423

RAMADA LIMITED
5970 S 6th St
(62703)
Rates: $49-$90
(217) 529-1410
(800) 272-6232

RED ROOF INN
3200 Singer Ave
(62703)
Rates: $50-$68
(217) 753-4302
(800) 843-7663

SIGNATURE INN
3090 Stevenson Dr
(62703)
Rates: $49-$104
(217) 529-6611
(800) 822-5252

SLEEP INN
3470 Freedom Dr
(62704)
Rates: $45-$129
(217) 787-6200
(800) 424-6423

**STAYBRIDGE
SUITES**
4231 Schooner Dr
(62707)
Rates: n/a
(217) 793-6700
(800) 238-8000

STEVENSON INN
2860 Stevenson Dr
(62703)
Rates: n/a
(217) 585-4002
(888) 993-7378

**SUPER 8 LODGE
SOUTH**
3675 S 6th St
(62703)
Rates: $42-$57
(217) 529-8898
(800) 800-8000

STAUNTON
SUPER 8 MOTEL
1527 Herman Rd
(62088)
Rates: $39-$55
(618) 635-5353
(800) 800-8000

STOCKTON
COUNTRY INN
200 Dillon Ave
(61085)
Rates: $79-$179
(815) 947-6060
(800) 456-4000

CROSS COUNTRY GETAWAY RENTAL
11720 E Wilson Rd (61085)
Rates: n/a
(815) 947-3347

STREATOR
SUPER 8 MOTEL
1705 N Bloomington St (61364)
Rates: n/a
(815) 672-0080
(800) 800-8000

SULLIVAN
GATEWAY INN
1320 S Hamilton St (61951)
Rates: n/a
(217) 728-4314

SYCAMORE
MICROTEL INN
1860 Dekalb Ave (60178)
Rates: $49-$72
(815) 899-6500

TAYLORVILLE
29 WEST MOTEL
709 Springfield Rd (62568)
Rates: $35-$45
(217) 824-2216

TINLEY PARK
BAYMONT INN & SUITES
7255 W 183rd St (60477)
Rates: $68-$92
(708) 633-1200
(877) 229-6668

TONICA
KISHAUWAU ON THE VERMILION
901 N 2129 Rd (61370)
Rates: n/a
(815) 442-8453

TROY
RED ROOF INN
2030 Formosa Rd (62294)
Rates: n/a
(618) 667-2222
(800) 843-7663

VILLAGER LODGE
909 Edwardsville Rd (62294)
Rates: $30-$40
(618) 667-9969

TUSCOLA
COOPER MOTEL
804 E South Line Rd (61953)
Rates: n/a
(217) 253-4743

HOLIDAY INN EXPRESS
1201 Tuscola Blvd (61953)
Rates: $70-$88
(217) 253-6363
(800) 465-4329

SUPER 8 MOTEL
1007 E Hwy 36 (61953)
Rates: $47-$65
(217) 253-5488
(800) 800-8000

ULLIN
BEST WESTERN CHEEKWOOD
128 Cheekwood Lane (62992)
Rates: $55-$75
(618) 845-3773
(800) 528-1234

URBANA
HISTORIC LINCOLN HOTEL
209 S Broadway (61801)
Rates: $75-$94
(217) 384-8800

PARK INN
2408 N Cunningham Ave (61801)
Rates: $55-$60
(217) 344-8000
(800) 437-7275

RAMADA LIMITED
902 W Killaraney (61801)
Rates: $58-$150
(217) 328-4400
(800) 272-6232

SLEEP INN
1908 N Lincoln Ave (61801)
Rates: $58-$115
(217) 367-6000
(800) 424-6423

VANDALIA
DAYS INN
1920 Kennedy Blvd (62471)
Rates: $54-$138
(618) 283-4400
(800) 329-7466

JAY'S INN
720 Gochenour St (62471)
Rates: $38-$60
(618) 283-1200

RAMADA LTD
2707 Veterans Ave (62471)
Rates: $50-$78
(618) 283-1400
(800) 272-6232

TRAVELODGE
1500 N 6th St (62471)
Rates: $37-$70
(618) 283-2363
(800) 578-7878

VERNON HILLS
AMERISUITES
450 N Milwaukee Ave (60061)
Rates: $87-$114
(847) 918-1400
(800) 833-1516

HOMESTEAD STUDIO SUITES
675 Woodland Pkwy (60061)
Rates: $50-$74
(847) 955-1111
(888) 782-9473

VIENNA
BUDGET INN MOTEL
I-24 & Hwy 146 (62995)
Rates: n/a
(618) 658-2802

COUNTRY SCHEMES B&B
3220 Old Metropolis Rd (62995)
Rates: n/a
(618) 658-9044

VILLA PARK
MOTEL 6
10 W Roosevelt Rd (60181)
Rates: $39-$53
(630) 941-9100
(800) 466-8356

WARRENILLE
CANDLEWOOD SUITES
27 W 300 Warrenville Rd (60555)
Rates: n/a
(630) 836-1650
(888) 226-3539

RESIDENCE INN BY MARRIOTT
28500 Bella Vista Pkwy (60555)
Rates: $129-$149
(630) 393-3444
(800) 331-3131

WASHINGTON
SUPER 8 MOTEL
1884 Washington Rd (61571)
Rates: $46-$56
(309) 444-8881
(800) 800-8000

WATSEKA
SUPER 8 MOTEL
710 W Walnut St (60970)
Rates: $52-$71
(815) 432-6000
(800) 800-8000

WATSEKA MOTEL
814 E Walnut St (60970)
Rates: n/a
(815) 432-2426

WAUKEGAN
BEST INNS OF AMERICA
31 N Green Bay Rd (60085)
Rates: $52-$102
(847) 336-9000
(800) 237-8466

BEST WESTERN
411 S Green Bay Rd (60085)
Rates: $59-$149
(847) 244-6100
(800) 528-1234

CANDLEWOOD SUITES
1151 S Waukegan Rd (60085)
Rates: $79-$119
(847) 578-5250
(888) 226-3539

COMFORT INN NAVAL TRAINING CENTER
3031 Belvidere Ave (60085)
Rates: $54-$105
(847) 623-1400
(800) 424-6423

ECONO LODGE
222 Grand Ave (60085)
Rates: $55-$85
(847) 244-7400
(800) 424-6423

RESIDENCE INN BY MARRIOTT
1440 S White Oak Dr (60085)
Rates: $119-$159
(847) 689-9240
(800) 331-3131

SUPER 8 MOTEL
630 N Green Bay Rd (60085)
Rates: n/a
(847) 249-2388
(800) 800-8000

WEST CITY
DAYS INN
711 W Main St (62812)
Rates: $50-$89
(615) 439-3183
(800) 329-7466

SUPER 8 MOTEL
711 1/2 W Main St (62812)
Rates: $50-$89
(615) 438-8205
(800) 800-8000

WEST DUNDEE
TOWNEPLACE SUITES
2185 Marriott Dr (60118)
Rates: $59-$109
(847) 608-6320
(800) 257-3000

WEST FRANKFORT

GRAY PLAZA MOTEL
1010 W Main St
(62896)
Rates: n/a
(618) 932-3116

WESTMONT

CLUBHOUSE INN
630 Pasquinelli Dr
(60559)
Rates: $79
(630) 920-2200
(800) 258-2466

HOMESTEAD STUDIO SUITES
855 Pasquinelli Dr
(60559)
Rates: $60-$80
(630) 323-9292
(888) 782-9473

WHEELING

CANDLEWOOD SUITES
8000 Capital Dr
(60090)
Rates: n/a
(847) 520-1684
(888) 226-3539

WILLOW-BROOK

BAYMONT INN & SUITES
855 W 79th St
(60521)
Rates: $48-$71
(630) 654-0077
(877) 229-6668

RED ROOF INN
7535 Robt Kingery
Hwy (60521)
Rates: $67-$79
(630) 323-8811
(800) 843-7663

WINDSOR

THE DEERFIELD BED & BREAKFAST
RR 1, Box 99-A
(61957)
Rates: n/a
(217) 459-2750

WINTHROP HARBOR

SANDPIPER INN
301 Sheridan Rd
(60096)
Rates: $69-$109
(847) 746-7380

WOODSTOCK

BUNDLING BOARD INN
220 E South St
(60098)
Rates: n/a
(815) 338-7054

CONCORD COUNTRY INN
1122 Cass St
(60098)
Rates: n/a
(815) 338-1100

SUPER 8 MOTEL
1220 Davis Rd
(60098)
Rates: $50-$106
(815) 337-808
(800) 800-8000

YORKVILLE

LIDIA'S MOTEL
10020 Rt 71
(60560)
Rates: n/a
(630) 553-7147

ZION

MOTOR INN MOTEL
41440 Rt 41
(60099)
Rates: n/a
(847) 395-7300

INDIANA

ALEXANDRIA
COUNTRY GAZEBO INN B&B
13867 N 100 W (46001)
Rates: $40-$75
(765) 754-8783

ANDERSON
DAYS INN
5901 Scatterfield Rd (46013)
Rates: $60-$149
(765) 649-0451
(800) 329-7466

ECONO LODGE
2205 E 59th St (46013)
Rates: $40-$99
(765) 644-4422
(800) 424-6423

HAMPTON INN
2312 Hampton Dr (46013)
Rates: $79-$139
(765) 622-0700
(800) 426-7866

LEES INN
2114 E 59th St (46013)
Rates: $59-$129
(765) 649-2500
(800) 733-5337

MARK MOTOR INN
2400 S Scatterfield Rd (46013)
Rates: $29-$45
(765) 642-9966

MOTEL 6
5810 Scatterfield Rd (46013)
Rates: $29-$35
(765) 642-9023
(800) 466-8356

SUPER 8 MOTEL
2215 E 59th St (46013)
Rates: $55-$68
(765) 642-2222
(800) 800-8000

ANGOLA
RAMADA INN
3855 N SR 127 (46703)
Rates: $85-$200
(260) 665-9471
(800) 272-6232

AUBURN
HOLIDAY INN EXPRESS
404 Touring Dr (46706)
Rates: $78-$105
(260) 925-1900
(800) 465-4329

LA QUINTA INN
306 Touring Dr (46706)
Rates: $0-$105
(260) 920-1900
(800) 687-6667

SUPER 8 MOTEL
503 Ley Dr (46706)
Rates: $49-$99
(260) 927-8880
(800) 800-8000
(800) 953-6287

AVON
SUPER 8 MOTEL
8229 E US 36 (46123)
Rates: $60-$135
(317) 272-8789
(800) 800-8000

BATESVILLE
INDIAN LAKES RESORT
7234 Hwy 46 E (47006)
Rates: n/a
(800) 427-3392

BEDFORD
HOLIDAY INN EXPRESS HOTEL
2800 Express Ln (47421)
Rates: $74-$124
(812) 279-1206
(800) 465-4329

MARK III MOTEL
1711 M St (47421)
Rates: $29-$45
(812) 275-5935

PLAZA MOTEL
6843 US 50 E (47421)
Rates: $30-$50
(812) 834-5522

ROSEMOUNT MOTEL
1923 M St (47421)
Rates: $32-$45
(812) 275-5953

SUPER 8 MOTEL
501 Bell Back Rd (47421)
Rates: $59-$99
(812) 275-8881
(800) 800-8000

BLOOMING-DALE
CHEROKEE VILLAGE CAMPING CABINS
RR Box 140 (47832)
Rates: $16-$21
(765) 597-2029

BLOOMINGTON
BEST WESTERN FIRESIDE INN
4501 E Third St (47401)
Rates: $46-$160
(812) 332-2141
(800) 528-1234

DAYS INN
200 Matlock Rd (47401)
Rates: $49-$200
(812) 336-0905
(800) 329-7466

ECONO LODGE
2601 Walnut St (47404)
Rates: $32-$159
(812) 332-9453
(800) 424-6423

HAMPTON INN
2100 N Walnut St (47408)
Rates: $69-$87
(812) 334-2100
(800) 426-7866

LAKE MONROE VILLAGE RESORT
8107 S Fairfax Rd (47408)
Rates: $62-$275
(8120 824-2267

MOTEL 6-UNIVERSITY
1800 N Walnut (47402)
Rates: $33-$46
(812) 332-0820
(800) 466-8356

RAMADA LTD
1722 N Walnut St (47404)
Rates: n/a
(812) 339-1919
(800) 272-6232

TOWNEPLACE SUITES
105 S Franklin Rd (47401)
Rates: $79-$99
(812) 334-1234
(800) 257-3000

BLUFFTON
BUDGET INN
1420 N Main St (46714)
Rates: $35-$45
(219) 824-0820

BOSWELL
BOSWELL MOTEL
307 S Old US 41 (47921)
Rates: $29-$45
(765) 869-5060

BRAZIL
VILLA MOTEL
2186 W Hwy 40 (47834)
Rates: $32-$55
(812) 448-1966

BROWNSBURG
SUPER 8 MOTEL
1100 N Green St (46112)
Rates: $72-$210
(317) 852-5211
(800) 800-8000

CARMEL
COUNTRY INN
9797 N Michigan Rd (46032)
Rates: $89
(917) 876-0333
(800) 456-4000

RESIDENCE INN BY MARRIOTT
11895 N Meridian St (46032)
Rates: $89-$179
(317) 846-2000
(800) 331-3131

SIGNATURE INN
10201 N Meridian St (46032)
Rates: $74-$94
(317) 816-1616
(800) 822-5252

CENTERVILLE
WOODRIDGE INN
3700 Western Ave (47330)
Rates: $57-$120
(765) 825-4800

CHESTERFIELD
SUPER 8 MOTEL
15701 W Commerce Rd (47334)
Rates: $49-$57
(765) 378-0888
(800) 800-8000

CLARKSVILLE
BEST WESTERN GREEN TREE INN
1425 Broadway (47129)
Rates: $49-$89
(812) 288-9281
(800) 528-1234
(800) 950-9281

CLOVERDALE

HOLIDAY INN EXPRESS
1017 N Main St
(46120)
Rates: $69-$99
(765) 795-5050
(800) 465-4329

MIDWEST INN
1010 N Main St
(46120)
Rates: $36-$75
(765) 795-6900

MOTEL 6
924 N Main St
(46120)
Rates: $31-$44
(765) 795-3000
(800) 466-8356

RAMADA INN
1035 N Main St
(46120)
Rates: $39-$64
(765) 795-3500
(800) 272-6232

SUPER 8 MOTEL
1020 N Main St
(46120)
Rates: $50-$70
(765) 795-7373
(800) 800-8000

COLUMBIA CITY

AMERIHOST INN
701 W Connexion Way (46725)
Rates: $79-$99
(260) 248-4551
(800) 434-5800

COLUMBUS

DAYS INN
3445 Jonathan Moore Pike
(47201)
Rates: $49-$89
(812) 376-9951
(800) 329-7466

HOLIDAY INN
2480 Jonathan Moore Pike
(47201)
Rates: $79-$99
(812) 372-1541
(800) 465-4329

RAMADA INN
10330 N US 31
(47201)
Rates: $79-$109
(812) 376-3051
(800) 272-6232

CRAWFORDS-VILLE

COMFORT INN
2991 N Gandhi St
(47933)
Rates: $79-$175
(765) 361-0665
(800) 424-6423

DAVIS HOUSE BED & BREAKFAST
1010 W Wabash Ave (47933)
Rates: $50-$60
(765) 364-0461

GENERAL LEW WALLACE INN
309 W Pike St
(47933)
Rates: $37-$43
(765) 362-8400

HOLIDAY INN
2500 N Lafayette Rd (47933)
Rates: $59-$85
(765) 362-8700
(800) 465-4329

DALE

BAYMONT INN
20857 N US 231
(47523)
Rates: $69-$179
(812) 937-7000
(877) 229-6668

MOTEL 6
20840 N Hwy 231
(47523)
Rates: $43-$80
(812) 937-2294
(800) 466-8356

231 AMBEST PLAZA MOTEL
I-64 at US 231
(47523)
Rates: $25
(812) 937-2816

YELLOW BANKS CABINS
RR 2, Box 160
(47523)
Rates: $55-$65
(812) 567-4703

DECATUR

AMERIHOST INN
1201 S 13th St
(46733)
Rates: $84-$89
(260) 728-4600
(800) 434-5800

COMFORT INN
1302 S 13th St
(46733)
Rates: $69-$99
(260) 724-8888
(800) 424-6423

DAYS INN
1033 N 13th St
(46733)
Rates: $45-$95
(260) 728-2196
(800) 329-7466

DERBY

OHIO RIVER CABINS
13445 N SR 66
(47525)
Rates: $85-$130
(812) 836-2289

DUNREITH

FLAMINGO MOTEL
108 First St (47337)
Rates: $33-$55
(765) 987-7111

EDINBURGH

BEST WESTERN HORIZON INN
11780 N US 31
(46124)
Rates: $49-$139
(812) 526-9883
(800) 528-1234

ELKHART

ECONO LODGE
3440 Cassopolis Rd (46514)
Rates: $34-$135
(574) 262-0540
(800) 424-6423

THE FAIRWAY INN
115 North Pointe Blvd (46514)
Rates: $54-$90
(574) 266-1940
(800) 428-9053

QUALITY INN
3321 Plaza Ct
(46514)
Rates: $69-$165
(574) 264-0404
(800) 424-6423

RAMADA INN
3011 Belvedere Rd
(46514)
Rates: $79-$129
(574) 262-1581
(800) 272-6232

RED ROOF INN
2902 Cassopolis St
(46514)
Rates: $43-$100
(574) 262-3691
(800) 843-7663

SIGNATURE INN
3010 Brittany Ct
(46514)
Rates: $49-$104
(574) 264-7222

SUPER 8 MOTEL
345 Windsor Ave
(46514)
Rates: $54-$68
(574) 264-4457
(800) 800-8000

EVANSVILLE

BAYMONT INN
8005 E Division St
(47715)
Rates: $59-$120
(812) 477-2677
(877) 229-6668

BAYMONT INN
5737 Pearl Dr
(47712)
Rates: $79-$99
(812) 421-9773
(877) 229-6668

BEST WESTERN GATEWAY INN
324 Rusher Creek Rd (47725)
Rates: $64-$99
(812) 868-8000
(800) 528-1234

CASINO AZTAR HOTEL
421 NW Riverside Dr (47708)
Rates: $74-$114
(812) 433-4390
(800) 342-5386

COMFORT INN EAST
8331 E Walnut St
(47715)
Rates: $55-$69
(812) 476-3600
(800) 424-6423

DAYS INN EAST
4819 Tecumseh Ln
(47715)
Rates: $36-$110
(812) 473-7944
(800) 329-7466

DRURY INN & SUITES EAST
100 Cross Pointe Blvd (47715)
Rates: $65-$100
(812) 471-3400
(800) 378-7946

DRURY INN NORTH
3901 US 41 N
(47711)
Rates: $65-$95
(812) 423-5818
(800) 378-7946

ECONO LODGE
5006 E Morgan Ave (47715)
Rates: $45-$99
(812) 477-2211
(800) 424-6423

HOMELIFE STUDIOS
100 S Green River Rd (47715)
Rates: $35-$99
(812) 475-1700

LEES INN
5538 E Indiana St
(47715)
Rates: $59-$129
(812) 477-6663
(800) 733-5337

MICROTEL INN
1930 Cross Pointe Blvd (47715)
Rates: $39-$109
(812) 471-9340

MOTEL 6
4321 Hwy 41 N
(47711)
Rates: $31-$37
(812) 424-6431
(800) 466-8356

QUALITY INN & SUITES EAST
8015 E Division St (47715)
Rates: $59-$99
(812) 471-3414
(800) 424-6423

RESIDENCE INN HOTEL
8283 E Walnut St (47715)
Rates: $105-$165
(812) 471-7191
(800) 331-3131

SIGNATURE INN
1101 N Green River Rd (47715)
Rates: $49-$104
(812) 476-9626
(800) 822-5252

SUPER 8 MOTEL
4600 Morgan Ave (47715)
Rates: $39-$47
(812) 476-4008
(800) 800-8000

FISHERS

COMFORT SUITES
9760 Crosspoint Blvd (46256)
Rates: $74-$119
(317) 578-1200
(800) 424-6423

FREDERICK-TALBOTT INN B&B
13805 Allisonville Rd (46038)
Rates: $99-$179
(317) 578-3600

RAMADA INN
9791 North by Northeast Blvd (46038)
Rates: $84-$200
(317) 558-4100
(800) 272-6232

RESIDENCE INN BY MARRIOTT
9765 Crosspoint Blvd (46256)
Rates: $89-$189
(317) 842-1111
(800) 331-3131

STAYBRIDGE SUITES
9780 Crosspoint Blvd (46038)
Rates: $109-$169
(317) 577-9500
(800) 238-8000

STUDIO 6
8250 North by Northeast Blvd (46038)
Rates: $199-$259
(317) 913-1920
(888) 897-0202

FORT WAYNE

AMERISUITES
111 W Washington Center Rd (46825)
Rates: $69-$94
(260) 471-8522
(800) 833-1516

BAYMONT INN
1005 W Washington Ctr Rd (46825)
Rates: $54-$109
(260) 489-2220
(877) 229-6668

BEST WESTERN LUXBURY INN
5501 Coventry Ln (46804)
Rates: $69-$149
(260) 436-0242
(800) 528-1234

DON HALL'S GUESTHOUSE
1313 W Washington Center Rd (46825)
Rates: $79-$89
(260) 489-2524

ECONO LODGE
2908 Goshen Rd (46808)
Rates: $39-$59
(260) 484-6262
(800) 424-6423

MARRIOTT HOTEL
305 E Washington Center Rd (46825)
Rates: $169-$179
(260) 484-0411
(800) 228-9290

MOTEL 6
3003 Coliseum Blvd W (46808)
Rates: $33-$38
(260) 482-3972
(800) 466-8356

QUALITY HOTEL & FUNDOME
3330 W Coliseum Blvd (46808)
Rates: $65-$104\
(260) 484-7711

RED ROOF INN
2920 Goshen Rd (46808)
Rates: $42-$68
(260) 484-8641
(800) 843-7663

RESIDENCE INN BY MARRIOTT
4919 Lima Rd (46808)
Rates: $89-$149
(260) 484-4700
(800) 331-3131

RESIDENCE INN SOUTHWEST
7811 W Jefferson Blvd (46804)
Rates: $99-$119
(260) 432-8000
(800) 331-3131

FRANKFORT

HOLIDAY INN EXPRESS
592 S CR 200 W (46041)
Rates: $61-$110
(765) 659-4400
(800) 465-4329

SUPER 8 MOTEL
1875 W SR 28 (46041)
Rates: n/a
(765) 654-0088
(800) 800-8000

FRENCH LICK

LANE MOTEL
8483 W SR 56 (47432)
Rates: $45-$75
(812) 936-9919

MICHAEL T'S MOTEL
9633 W SR 56 (47432)
Rates: $40-$50
(812) 936-4656
(877) 228-4812

THE PINES AT PATOKA LAKE VILLAGE
7900 W CR 1025 S (47432)
Rates: $60-$115
(812) 936-9854
(888) 324-5350

GAS CITY

SUPER 8 MOTEL
5172 S Kaybee Dr (46933)
Rates: $50-$80
(765) 998-6800
(800) 800-8000

GEORGETOWN

MOTEL 6
1079 N Luther Rd (47122)
Rates: $43-$99
(812) 923-0441
(800) 466-8356

GOSHEN

BEST WESTERN INN
900 Lncolnway E (46526)
Rates: $64-$74
(574) 533-0408
(800) 528-1234

GREENCASTLE

COLLEGE INN
315 Bloomington St (46135)
Rates: $33-$60
(765) 653-4167

GREENFIELD

LEES INN
2270 N State St (46140)
Rates: $59-$129
(317) 462-7112
(800) 733-5337

GREENSBURG

HOLIDAY INN EXPRESS
915 Ann Blvd (47240)
Rates: $79
(812) 663-5500
(800) 465-4329

LEES INN
2211 N State Rd 3 (47240)
Rates: $59-$129
(812) 663-9998
(800) 733-5337

GREENWOOD

COMFORT INN
110 Sheek Rd (46143)
Rates: $56-$200
(317) 887-1515
(800) 424-6423

LEES INN
1281 S Park Dr (46143)
Rates: $59-$129
(317) 865-0100
(800) 733-5337

RED ROOF INN
110 Sheek Rd (46143)
Rates: $49-$95
(317) 887-1515
(800) 843-7663

HAMMOND

BEST WESTERN NORTHWEST INDIANA INN
3830 179th St (46323)
Rates: $60-$135
(219) 844-2140
(800) 528-1234

MOTEL 6
3840 179th St (46324)
Rates: $35-$56
(219) 845-0330
(800) 466-8356

RESIDENCE INN BY MARRIOTT
7740 Corinne Dr (46324)
Rates: $129-$189
(219) 844-8440
(800) 331-3131

HAUBSTADT

QUALITY INN NORTH
Hwy 41 & I-64 (47639)
Rates: $69-$99
(812) 768-5878
(800) 424-6423

HOWE

SUPER 8 MOTEL
7333 N SR 9 (46746)
Rates: $60-$90
(219) 562-2828
(800) 800-8000

AREA CODES - If the local number doesn't connect, check for a new area code.

HUNTINGBURG
QUALITY INN
406 E 22nd St
(47542)
Rates: $49-$139
(812) 683-2334
(800) 424-6423

HUNTINGTON
AMERIHOST INN
2820 Hotel Ave
(46750)
Rates: $59-$145
(260) 359-9000
(800) 434-5800

COMFORT INN
2205 N Jefferson
St (46750)
Rates: $79-$129
(260) 356-3434
(800) 424-6423

DAYS INN
2996 W Park Dr
(46750)
Rates: $44-$100
(260) 359-8989
(800) 329-7466

INDIANAPOLIS
AMERISUITES
9104 Keystone
Crossing (46240)
Rates: $69-$250
(317) 843-0064
(800) 833-1516

**AMERISUITES
AIRPORT-SPEED-
WAY**
5500 W Bradbury
Ave (46241)
Rates: $59-$89
(317) 227-0950
(800) 883-1516

**BAYMONT INN &
SUITES-
AIRPORT**
2650 Executive Dr
(46241)
Rates: $70-$75
(317) 244-8100
(877) 229-6668

**BAYMONT INN &
SUITES EAST**
2349 Post Dr
(46219)
Rates: $79-$99
(317) 897-2300
(877) 229-6668

**BEST WESTERN
AIRPORT SUITES**
55 S High School
Rd (46241)
Rates: $69-$99
(317) 246-1505
(800) 528-1234

**BEST WESTERN
CASTLETON INN**
8300 Craig St
(46250)
Rates: $59-$299
(317) 842-9190
(800) 232-5757

**CANDLEWOOD
SUITES**
8111 Bash St
(46250)
Rates: n/a
(317) 595-9292
(888) 226-3539

DAYS INN
2150 N Post Rd
(46219)
Rates: $38-$53
(317) 899-1499
(800) 329-7466

DAYS INN
3401 S Keystone
Ave (46237)
Rates: $45-$80
(317) 788-0500
(800) 329-7466

DAYS INN EAST
7314 E 21st St
(46219)
Rates: $39-$125
(317) 359-5500
(800) 329-7466

DAYS INN
8275 Craig St
(46250)
Rates: $54-$96
(317) 841-9700
(800) 329-7466

DRURY INN
9320 N Michigan
Rd (46268)
Rates: $59-$159
(317) 876-9777
(800) 378-7946

**ECONO LODGE
DOWNTOWN
HOTEL**
1530 N Meridian
(46202)
Rates: $40-$195
(317) 634-6100
(800) 424-6423

**ECONO LODGE
NORTH**
3880 W 92nd St
(46268)
Rates: $45-$145
(317) 872-3100
(800) 424-6423

**FOUR POINTS
BY SHERATON**
7701 E 42nd St
(46256)
Rates: $79-$109
(317) 897-4000
(800) 325-3535

**HAWTHORN
SUITES EAST**
7035 Western
Select Dr (46219)
Rates: $89-$109
(317) 322-0011
(800) 527-1133

**HILTON NORTH
HOTEL**
8181 N Shadeland
Ave (46250)
Rates: $99-$259
(317) 849-6668
(800) 445-8667

**HOLIDAY INN
EAST**
6990 E 21st St
(46219)
Rates: $89-$129
(317) 359-5341
(800) 465-4329

**HOLIDAY INN
SOUTHEAST**
5120 Victory Dr
(46203)
Rates: $76-$96
(317) 783-7751
(800) 465-4329

**HOMESTEAD
STUDIO SUITES**
8520 Norhtwest
Blvd (46278)
Rates: $76-$96
(317) 334-7829
(888) 782-9473

**HOMEWOOD
SUITES AT THE
CROSSING**
2501 E 86th St
(46240)
Rates: $124-$164
(317) 253-1919
(800) 225-5466

**INDIANAPOLIS
MOTOR SPEED-
WAY BRICKYARD
CROSSING GOLF
RESORT & INN**
4400 W 16th St
(46202)
Rates: $65-$130
(317) 241-2500

**LA QUINTA INN-
AIRPORT**
5316 W Southern
Ave (46241)
Rates: $79-$129
(317) 247-4281
(800) 687-6777
(800) 221-4731

**LA QUINTA INN-
EAST**
7304 E 21st St
(46219)
Rates: $59-$99
(317) 359-1021
(800) 687-6777
(800) 221-4731

LEES INN
5011 N Lafayette
Rd (46241)
Rates: $59-$129
(317) 297-8880
(800) 733-5337

MARRIOTT HOTEL
7202 E 21st St
(46219)
Rates: $89-$139
(317) 352-1231
(800) 228-9290

**MARTEN HOUSE
HOTEL**
1801 W 86th St
(46240)
Rates: 69-$129
(317) 872-4111

MICROTEL INN
9140 N Michigan
Rd (46268)
Rates: $40-$170
(317) 870-7765

MOTEL 6
5241 W Bradbury
Ave (46241)
Rates: $37-$40
(317) 248-1231
(800) 466-8356

MOTEL 6 EAST
2851 Shadeland
Ave (46219)
Rates: $32-$40
(317) 546-5864
(800) 466-8356

MOTEL 6 SOUTH
5151 Elmwood Dr
(46203)
Rates: $36-$45
(317) 783-5555
(800) 466-8356

MOTEL 6
9402 Haver Way
(46240)
Rates: $35-$38
(317) 848-2433
(800) 466-8356

**OMNI SEVERIN
HOTEL**
40 W Jackson
Place (46225)
Rates: $99-$229
(317) 634-6664
(800) 843-6664

QUALITY INN
4345 Southport
Crossing Way
(46237)
Rates: $64-$199
(317) 859-8888
(800) 424-6423

QUALITY INN
2631 S Lynhurst
Dr (46241)
Rates: $79-$149
(317) 381-1000
(800) 424-6423

**QUALITY INN
EAST**
3525 N Shadeland
Ave (46226)
Rates: $70-$135
(317) 549-2222
(800) 424-6423

**QUALITY INN
SOUTH**
450 Bixler Lane
(46227)
Rates: $59-$219
(317) 788-0811
(800) 424-6423

RAMADA INN
520 E Thompson
Rd (46227)
Rates: n/a
(317) 787-8341
(800) 272-6232

RAMADA LTD
7050 E 21st St
(46219)
Rates: n/a
(317) 352-0481
(800) 272-6232

RAMADA LTD
3851 Shore Dr
(46254)
Rates: n/a
(317) 297-1848
(800) 272-6232

RED ROOF INN SOUTH
5221 Victory Dr
(46203)
Rates: $42-$63
(317) 788-9551
(800) 843-7663

RED ROOF INN SPEEDWAY
6415 Debonair Ln
(46224)
Rates: $41-$62
(317) 293-6881
(800) 843-7663

RESIDENCE INN BY MARRIOTT
350 W New York St (46204)
Rates: $139-$279
(317) 822-0840

RESIDENCE INN BY MARRIOTT
5224 W Southern Ave (46241)
Rates: $89-$159
(317) 244-1500
(800) 331-3131

RESIDENCE INN BY MARRIOTT
6220 Digital Way
(46268)
Rates: $109-$169
(317) 275-6000

RESIDENCE INN BY MARRIOTT
9765 Cross Point Blvd (46256)
Rates: $129-$179
(317) 842-1111
(800) 331-3131

SHERATON HOTEL & SUITES
8787 Keystone Crossing (46240)
Rates: $209-$289
(317) 846-2700
(800) 325-3535

SIGNATURE INN EAST
7610 Old Trails Rd
(46219)
Rates: $49-$104
(317) 353-6966
(800) 822-5252

SIGNATURE INN SOUTH
4402 E Creekview Dr (46237)
Rates: $49-$104
(317) 784-7006
(800) 822-5252

STAYBRIDGE SUITES
9780 Cross Point Blvd (46256)
Rates: n/a
(317) 577-9500
(800) 238-8000

SUPER 8 MOTEL
7202 E 82nd St
(46256)
Rates $55-$59
(317) 841-8585
(800) 800-8000

WELLESLEY INN
5350 W Southern Ave (46241)
Rates: $49-$79
(317) 241-0700
(800) 444-8888

THE WESTIN
50 S Capitol Ave
(46204)
Rates: $159-$199
(317) 262-8100
(800) 228-3000

JASPER
DAYS INN
272 Brucke Strasse
(47547)
Rates: $55-$104
(812) 482-6000
(800) 329-7466

JEFFERSONVILLE
DAYS INN
350 Eastern Blvd
(47130)
Rates: $49-$59
(812) 288-9331

MOTEL 6
2016 Old Hwy 31 E (47130)
Rates: $31-$40
(812) 283-7703
(800) 466-8356

TOWNEPLACE SUITES
703 N Shore Dr
(47130)
Rates: $75-$89
(812) 280-8200
(800) 257-3000

KENDALLVILLE
BEST WESTERN INN
621 Professional Way (46755)
Rates: $69-$129
(260) 347-5263
(800) 528-1234

HOLIDAY INN EXPRESS
1917 Dowling St
(46755)
Rates: $64-$115
(260) 343-0000
(800) 465-4329

KENTLAND
TRI-WAY INN MOTEL
611 E Dunlap St
(47951)
Rates: $35-$51
(219) 474-5141

KNIGHTSTOWN
YOGI BEAR JELLYSTONE PARK CABINS
5964 S SR 109
(46148)
Rates: $45-$65
(765) 737-6585

KOKOMO
BEST WESTERN SIGNATURE INN
4021 S La Fountain St
(46902)
Rates: $65-$115
(765) 455-1000
(800) 528-1234

CLARION HOTEL
1709 E Lincoln Rd
(46902)
Rates: $59-$189
(765) 459-8001
(800) 424-6423

COMFORT INN
522 Essex Dr
(46901)
Rates: $66-$129
(765) 452-5050
(800) 424-6423

DAYS INN
264 S 00 EW
(46902)
Rates: $57-$87
(765) 453-7100
(800) 329-7466

HAMPTON INN
2920 S Reed Rd
(46902)
Rates: $69-$129
(765) 455-2900
(800) 426-7866

MOTEL 6
2808 S Reed Rd
(46902)
Rates: $37-$45
(765) 457-8211
(800) 466-8356

SUPER 8 MOTEL
5110 Clinton St
(46902)
Rates: $49-$81
(765) 455-3288
(800) 800-8000

LAFAYETTE
BEST WESTERN EXECUTIVE PLAZA
4343 SR 26 E
(47905)
Rates: $84-$199
(765) 447-0575
(800) 528-1234

COMFORT SUITES
31 Frontage Rd
(47905)
Rates: $74-$200
(765) 447-0016
(800) 424-6423

DAYS INN
151 Frontage Rd
(47905)
Rates: $49-$159
(765) 446-8558
(800) 329-7466

HOLIDAY INN EXPRESS
201 Frontage Rd
(47905)
Rates: $75-$150
(765) 449-4808
(800) 465-4329

HOMEWOOD SUITES
3939 SR 26E
(47905)
Rates: $124-$189
(765) 448-9700
(800) 225-5466

KNIGHTS INN
4110 SR 26E
(47905)
Rates: $35-$99
(765) 447-4611
(800) 843-5644

LAFAYETTE INN
139 Frontage Rd
(47905)
Rates: $45-$115
(765) 447-7566

LEES INN
4701 Meijer Ct
(47905)
Rates: $59-$129
(765) 447-3434
(800) 733-5337

LOEB HOUSE HISTORIC INN
708 Cincinnati St
(47905)
Rates: $95-$175
(765) 420-7737

MICROTEL INN
151 Frontage Rd
(47905)
Rates: $59-$129
(765) 446-8558
(888) 771-7171

RED ROOF INN
4201 SR 26 E
(47905)
Rates: $40-$62
(765) 448-4671
(800) 843-7663

SIGNATURE INN
4320 SR 26 E
(47905)
Rates: $49-$104
(765) 447-4142
(800) 822-5252

TOWNEPLACE SUITES
163 Frontage Rd
(47905)
Rates: $69-$179
(765) 446-8668
(800) 257-3000

LAWRENCE-BURG
COMFORT INN
765 Eads Pkwy
(47025)
Rates: $55-$129
(800) 424-6423

QUALITY INN & SUITES AT THE CASINOS
1000 Eads Pkwy (47025)
Rates: $69-$239
(812) 539-4770
(800) 424-6423

LEBANON

COMFORT INN
210 Sam Ralston Rd (46052)
Rates: $69-$165
(765) 482-4800
(800) 424-6423

HOLIDAY INN EXPRESS
335 N Mt. Zion Rd (46052)
Rates: $89+
(765) 483-4100
(800) 465-4329

LEES INN
1245 W SR 32 (46052)
Rates: $49-$69
(765) 482-9611
(800) 733-5337

SUPER 8 MOTEL
405 N Mount Zion Rd (46052)
Rates: $50-$60
(765) 482-9999
(800) 800-8000

LINGONIER

MINUETTE B&B
210 S Main St (46767)
Rates: n/a
(219) 894-4494

LOGANSPORT

HOLIDAY INN
3550 E Market St (46947)
Rates: $58-$130
(574) 753-6351
(800) 465-4329

INNTIQUITY, A COUNTRY INN
1075 SR 25 N (46947)
Rates: $50-$90
(574) 722-2398

SUPER 8 MOTEL
3601 E Market St (46947)
Rates: $72-$125
(574) 722-1273

MADISON

BEST WESTERN OF MADISON
700 Clifty Dr, Hwy 62 (47250)
Rates: $62-$136
(812) 273-5151
(800) 528-1234
(800) 497-8863

MARX HOUSE & LOG CABINS
610 & 612 W 3rd St (47250)
Rates: 100-$125
(812) 265-2026

PRESIDENT MADISON MOTEL
906 E 1st St (47250)
Rates: $40-$60
(812) 265-2361
(800) 456-6835

SUPER 8 MOTEL
3767 Clifty Dr (47250)
Rates: $50-$150
(812) 981-7378
(800) 800-8000

MARION

CLARION HOTEL
501 E 4th St (46952)
Rates: $45-$129
(765) 668-8801
(800) 424-6423

COMFORT SUITES
1345 N Baldwin Ave (46952)
Rates: $79-$150
(765) 651-1006
(800) 424-6423

COUNTRY INN
6138 E Corridor Dr (46952)
Rates: $89
(765) 664-5840
(800) 456-4000

MARKLE

SUPER 8 MOTEL
610 Annette Dr (46770)
Rates: $51-$62
(260) 758-8888
(800) 800-8000

MARSHALL

COUNTRY HAVEN COTTAGE
RR 1, Box 188 (47859)
Rates: n/a
(765) 498-2532

MARTINSVILLE

COMFORT INN
50 Bills Blvd (46151)
Rates: $55-$99
(765) 342-1842
(800) 424-6423

MERRILLVILLE

LA QUINTA INN
8210 Louisiana St (46410)
Rates: $65-$95
(219) 738-2870
(800) 687-6667

LEES INN
6201 Opportunity Lane (46410)
Rates: $59-$129
(219) 942-8555

MOTEL 6
8290 Louisiana St (46410)
Rates: $31-$40
(219) 738-2701
(800) 466-8356

RESIDENCE INN BY MARRIOTT
8018 Delaware Place (46410)
Rates: $119-$169
(219) 791-9000
(800) 331-3131

SUPER 8 MOTEL
8300 Louisianna St (46410)
Rates: $35-$65
(219) 736-8383
(800) 800-8000

METAMORA

THORPE HOUSE COUNTRY INN
10949 Clayborne St (47030)
Rates: $70-$125
(765) 647-5425
(888) 427-7932

MICHIGAN CITY

COMFORT INN
3801 N Frontage Rd (46360)
Rates: $55-$170
(219) 879-9190
(800) 424-6423

DAYS INN
3934 N Frontage Rd (46360)
Rates: $40-$85
(219) 879-1150
(800) 329-7466

RED ROOF INN
110 W Kieffer Rd (46360)
Rates: $43-$86
(219) 874-5251
(800) 843-7663

SUPER 8 MOTEL
5724 S Franklin St (46360)
Rates: $40-$65
(219) 879-0411
(800) 800-8000

MONTGOMERY

GASTHOF VILLAGE INN
Box 60, CR 650 E (47558)
Rates: $59-$95
(812) 486-2600

MONTICELLO

BEST WESTERN BRANDYWINE INN
728 S 6th St (47960)
Rates: $75-$210
(574) 583-6333
(800) 528-1234

BIG CHIEF LODGE
501 E Indiana Beach Rd (47960)
Rates: $75-$150
(574) 583-3622

CLEARVIEW RESORT
5070 E Indiana Beach Rd (47960)
Rates: $75-$150
(5740 583-3624

1887 BLACK DOG INN
2830 Untaluti (47960)
Rates: n/a
(574) 583-8297

QUIET WATER B&B
4794 E Harbor Ct (47960)
Rates: $59-$85
(574) 583-6023

MOUNT VERNON

FOUR SEASONS MOTEL
2400 W 4th St (47620)
Rates: $50-$91
(812) 838-4821
(800) 264-1405

SUPER 8 MOTEL
6225 Hwy 69 S (47620)
Rates: $39-$60
(812) 838-8888
(800) 800-8000

MUNCIE

COMFORT INN
4011 W Bethel Ave (47305)
Rates: $54-$120
(765) 282-6666
(800) 424-6423

DAYS INN
3509 N Everbrook Ln (47304)
Rates: $45-$64
(765) 288-2311
(800) 329-7466

LEES INN
3302 N Everbrook Ln (47304)
Rates: $65-$129
(765) 282-7557
(800) 733-5337

RAMADA INN
3400 S Madison St (47302)
Rates: n/a
(765) 288-1911
(800) 272-6232

THE ROBERTS HOTEL
420 S High St (47304)
Rates: $89-$325
(765) 741-7777

SIGNATURE INN
3400 N Chadam Ln (47304)
Rates: $49-$104
(765) 284-4200
(800) 822-5252

SUPER 8 MOTEL
3601 W Fox Ridge Ln (47304)
Rates: $45-$55
(765) 286-4333
(800) 800-8000

AREA CODES - If the local number doesn't connect, check for a new area code.

NASHVILLE

THE STORY INN
6404 S SR 135
(47448)
Rates: $129
(812) 988-2273
(800) 881-1183

NEW ALBANY

HOLIDAY INN EXPRESS
411 W Spring St
(47150)
Rates: $75-$129
(812) 945-2771
(800) 465-4329

NEW CASTLE

BEST WESTERN RAINTREE INN
2836 S SR 3
(47362)
Rates: $65-$131
(765) 521-0100
(800) 528-1234
(800) 521-0015

MIKE & ANGELA'S GUESTHOUSE
2564 E CR 200 S
(47362)
Rates: $100
(765) 354-9461

MULBERRY LANE INN B&B
5256 N CR 75 W
(47362)
Rates: $65-$85
(765) 836-4500

NEW CASTLE INN
2005 S Memorial Dr (47362)
Rates: $31-$45
(765) 529-1670

NOBLES-VILLE

QUALITY INN
16025 Prosperity Dr (46060)
Rates: $59-$159
(317) 770-6772
(800) 424-6423

NORTH VERNON

COMFORT INN
150 FDR Dr
(47265)
Rates: $69-$119
(812) 352-9999
(800) 424-6423

NORTH VERNON'S

RAILROAD INN
302 Summit St
(47265)
Rates: $39-$65
(812) 346-7345

OSGOOD

NEWMAN-VOLLMAR HOUSE B&B
244 S Buckeye St
(47037)
Rates: $68-$155
(812) 689-1535

PAOLI

PATOKA RIVER CABINS
7355 S CR 50 W
(47454)
Rates: $72
(877) 775-5255

PERU

BEST WESTERN CIRCUS CITY INN
2642 Business 31 S
(46970)
Rates: $79-$160
(765) 473-8800
(800) 528-1234

PLAINFIELD

ASHLEY MOTEL
2452 E Main St
(46168)
Rates: $39-$150
(317) 839-6584
(800) 852-9746

DAYS INN
2245 Hadley Rd
(46168)
Rates: $44-$150
(317) 839-5000
(800) 329-7466

LEES INN & SUITES
6010 Gateway Dr
(46168)
Rates: $59-$129
(317) 837-9000
(800) 733-5337

RAMADA LTD
6023 Gateway dr
(46168)
Rates: $43-$49
(317) 837-8360
(800) 272-6232

PLYMOUTH

DAYS INN
2229 N Michigan St (46563)
Rates: $46-$99
(574) 935-4276
(800) 329-7466

RAMADA INN
2550 N Michigan St (46563)
Rates: $73-$90
(574) 936-4013
(800) 272-6232

SUPER 8 MOTEL
2160 N Oak Rd
(46563)
Rates: $52-$130
(574) 936-8856

PORTAGE

COMFORT INN
2300 Willow Creek (46368)
Rates: $69-$129
(219) 763-7177
(800) 424-6423

SUPER 8 MOTEL
6118 Melton Rd
(46368)
Rates: n/a
(219) 762-8857
(800) 800-8000

PORTLAND

HOOSIER INN
1620 Maridian St
(47371)
Rates: $42-$60
(260) 726-7113

PRINCETON

DAYS INN
2110 W Broadway
(47670)
Rates: $49-$100
(812) 386-1200
(800) 329-7466

REMINGTON

SUPER 8 MOTEL
4278 W US 24
(47977)
Rates: $58-$85
(219) 261-2883

RENSSELAER

HOLIDAY INN EXPRESS
4788 Nesbitt Dr
(47978)
Rates: $82-$102
(800) 465-4329
(866) 866-7560

INTERSTATE MOTEL
8530 W St Rd Hwy (47978)
Rates: $30-$40
(219) 866-4164

REYNOLDS

PARK VIEW MOTEL
RR 1, Box 4 (47980)
Rates: $25-$55
(219) 984-5380

RICHMOND

BEST WESTERN IMPERIAL MOTOR LODGE
3020 E Main St
(47374)
Rates: $42-$87
(765) 966-1505
(866) 866-8684

DAYS INN
5775 National Rd East (47374)
Rates: $40-$85
(765) 966-4900
(800) 329-7466

HOLIDAY INN
5501 National Rd East (47374)
Rates: $86-$325
(765) 966-7511
(800) 465-4329

LEES INN
6030 National Rd E (47374)
Rates: $74-$96
(765) 966-6449
(800) 733-5337

MOTEL 6
419 Commerce Dr
(47374)
Rates: $35-$45
(765) 966-6682
(800) 466-8356

RISING SUN

ANDERSON'S RIVIERA INN
119 Industrial Access Rd (47040)
Rates: $89-$99
(812) 438-2121
(888) 243-6446

THE JELLY HOUSE COUNTRY INN B&B
222 S Walnut St
(47040)
Rates: $110-$170
(812) 438-2319
(877) 429-0695

RIVERVIEW COTTAGE
222 S Front St
(47040)
Rates: $55-$75
(812) 438-4057

VICTORIA SUNRISE
318 Short St
(47040)
Rates: $100-$225
(812) 688-4777

ROCKPORT

FRIENDLY FARMS & RIDING STABLES B&B
2354 S 200 W
(47635)
Rates: $85-$125
(812) 649-2668

LOCUST HILL MOTEL
815 S SR 161
(47635)
Rates: $30
(812) 649-9918

ROCKVILLE

BILLIE CREEK VILLAGE & INN
US 36 E, Billie Creek Dr (47872)
Rates: $49-$99
(765) 569-3430

RACOON LAKESIDE LODGE
RR 1, Box 870
(47873)
Rates: $63-$250
(765) 344-1162

ROSELAND

COMFORT SUITES
52939 SR 933 N
(46637)
Rates: $89-$295
(574) 272-1500
(800) 424-6423

QUALITY INN-UNIVERSITY AREA
515 Dixie Way
(46637)
Rates: $70-$100
(574) 272-6600
(800) 424-6423

RAMADA INN
52890 SR 933 N
(46637)
Rates: $69-$99
(574) 272-5220
(800) 272-6232

AREA CODES - If the local number doesn't connect, check for a new area code.

SALEM

DELANEY PARK CABINS
Delaney Park Rd
(47167)
Rates: $29-$45
(812) 883-5101

SCOTTSBURG

BEST WESTERN SCOTTSBURG INN
1525 W McClain
St (47170)
Rates: $63-$107
(812) 752-2212
(800) 528-1234

MARIANN TRAVEL INN
SR 56 & I-65
(47170)
Rates: $48-$58
(812) 752-3396
(800) 648-0662

YOGI BEAR JELLYSTONE PARK CABIN RENTALS
4577 W SR 56
(47170)
Rates: n/a
(812) 752-4062
(812) 752-7046
(800) 437-0566

SELLERSBURG

HOME LODGE
363 Triangle Dr
(47172)
Rates: $299
(812) 246-6332

RAMADA LIMITED
360 Triangle Dr
(47172)
Rates: $109-$129
(812) 246-3131
(800) 272-6232

SEYMOUR

ALLSTATE INN
2603 Outlet Blvd
(47274)
Rates: $28-$40
(812) 522-2666

DAYS INN
302 S Commerce
Dr (47274)
Rates: $36-$89
(812) 522-3678
(800) 329-7466

ECONO LODGE
220 Commerce Dr
(47274)
Rates: $30-$99
(812) 522-8000
(800) 424-6423

HOLIDAY INN
2025 E Tipton St
(47274)
Rates: $66-$129
(812) 522-6767
(800) 465-4329

HOMETOWN INN
207 N Sandy
Creek (47274)
Rates: $25-$45
(812) 522-3523

LEES INN
2075 E Tipton St
(47274)
Rates: $59-$129
(812) 523-1850
(800) 733-5337

MOTEL 6
365 Tanger Blvd
(47274)
Rates: $39-$55
(812) 524-7443
(800) 466-8356

SUPER 8 MOTEL
401 Outlet Blvd
(47274)
Rates: $40-$45
(812)524-2000
(800) 800-8000

SHELBYVILLE

COMFORT INN
36 W Rampart Dr
(46176)
Rates: $59-$129
(765) 398-8044
(800) 424-6423

LEES INN
111 Lee Blvd (46176)
Rates: $59-$129
(765) 392-2299
(800) 733-5337

SHIPSHEWANA

SUPER 8 MOTEL
470 S Van Buren
(46565)
Rates: $55-$110
(260) 768-4004
(800) 800-8000

SOUTH BEND

ECONO LODGE AIRPORT
3233 Lincoln Way
W (46628)
Rates: $45-$169
(574) 232-9019
(800) 424-6423

HOLIDAY INN UNIVERSITY AREA
515 Dixie Way N
(46637)
Rates: $69-$110
(574) 272-6600
(800) 465-4329

MOTEL 6
52624 Hwy 31 N
(46637)
Rates: $33-$48
(574) 272-7072
(800) 466-8356

THE OLIVER INN B&B
630 W Washington
St (46637)
Rates: $95-$165
(888) 697-4466

RESIDENCE INN BY MARRIOTT
716 N Niles (46637)
Rates: $119-$199
(574) 289-5555

SUPER 8 MOTEL
4124 Ameritech
Dr (46628)
Rates: $54-$74
(574) 243-0200

SPEEDWAY

MOTEL 6
6330 Debonair Ln
(46224)
Rates: $31-$36
(317) 293-3220
(800) 466-8356

STACER

BEST WESTERN GATEWAY INN
324 Rusher Creek
Rd (47725)
Rates: $50-$100
(812) 868-8000
(800) 528-1234

HOLIDAY INN EXPRESS
19600 Elpers Rd
(47711)
Rates: $72-$104
(812) 867-1100
(800) 465-4329

SULLIVAN

DAYS INN
907 W SR 154
(47882)
Rates: $40-$70
(812) 268-6391
(800) 329-7466

TAYLORSVILLE

RED ROOF INN
10330 N US 31
(47280)
Rates: $49-$120
(812) 526-9747
(800) 843-7663

TELL CITY

DAYSTOP
17 Hwy 66 E &
14th St (47586)
Rates: $44-$55
(812) 547-3474
(800) 329-7466

HOLIDAY INN EXPRESS HOTEL
310 Orchard Hill
Dr (47586)
Rates: $55-$99
(812) 547-0800
(800) 465-4329

RAMADA LTD
235 Orchard Hill
Dr (47586)
Rates: $59-$99
(812) 547-3234
(800) 272-6232

TERRE HAUTE

COMFORT SUITES
501 E Margaret
Ave (47802)
Rates: $65-$130
(812) 235-1770
(800) 424-6423

DRURY INN
3040 Hwy 41 S
(47802)
Rates: $79-$120
(812) 238-1206
(800) 378-7946

ECONO LODGE
401 E Margaret
Ave (47802)
Rates: $44-$125
(812) 234-9931
(800) 424-6423

HOLIDAY INN
3300 Hwy 41 S
(47802)
Rates: $89-$180
(812) 232-6081
(800) 465-4329

KNIGHTS INN
401 Margaret Ave
(47802)
Rates: $39-$62
(812) 234-9931
(800) 843-5644

MID TOWN MOTEL
400 S 3rd St
(47807)
Rates: $30-$40
(812) 232-0383

MOTEL 6
1 W Honey Creek
Dr (47802)
Rates: $29-$40
(812) 238-1586
(800) 466-8356

PEAR TREE INN
3050 S Hwy 41
(47802)
Rates: $60-$89
(812) 234-4268
(800) 282-8733

RAMADA LTD
101 Margaret Ave
(47802)
Rates: n/a
(812) 232-8006
(800) 272-6232

SUPER 8 LODGE
3089 S 1st St
(47802)
Rates: $42-$60
(812) 232-4890
(800) 800-8000

TOBINSPORT

ROBERTS RIVER CABINS
2696 Tobinsport
Rd (47587)
Rates: $85
(877) 578-4211

VALPARAISO

BEST WESTERN EXPRESSWAY INN
760 Morthland Dr
(46385)
Rates: $49-$139
(219) 464-8555
(800) 528-1234

VERNON

RAYMER'S B&B
10 Jackson Hwy
(47282)
Rates: $50-$70
(812) 346-5658

AREA CODES - If the local number doesn't connect, check for a new area code.

VINCENNES

BEST WESTERN OF OLD VINCENNES
1800 S Old Decker Rd (47591)
Rates: $60-$80
(812) 882-2100
(800) 528-1234
(888) 286-1918

DOLL MOTEL
2015 Old US 41 S
(47591)
Rates: $30
(812) 882-0000

ECONO LODGE
600 Old Wheatland Rd, Bldg A (47591)
Rates: $45-$139
(812) 882-1479
(800) 424-6423

THE EXECUTIVE INN HOTEL
1 Executive Blvd
(47591)
Rates: $45-$100
(812) 886-5000
(800) 457-9154

QUALITY INN
600 Old Wheatland Rd
(47591)
Rates: $55-$169
(812) 886-9900
(800) 424-6423

WABASH

WABASH INN
1950 S Wabash St
(46992)
Rates: $49-$72
(260) 563-7451
(800) 626-7103

WALKERTON

HESTERS CABIN BED & BREAKFST
71880 SR 23
(46574)
Rates: n/a
(219) 586-2105

WARREN

HUGGY BEAR MOTEL
7588 S Warren Rd
(46792)
Rates: $59-$85
(260) 375-2504
(800) 523-5972

LA QUINTA INN
7275 S 75 E
(46792)
Rates: $55-$89
(260) 375-1800
(800) 687-6667

SUPER 8 MOTEL
7281 S 75 E
(46792)
Rates: $40-$45
(260) 375-4688
(800) 800-8000

WARSAW

DAYS INN
2575 E Center St
(46580)
Rates: $49-$99
(574) 269-3344
(800) 329-7466

HAMPTON INN
3328 E Center St
(46580)
Rates: $72-$132
(574) 269-6655
(800) 426-7866

RAMADA PLAZA HOTEL
2519 E Center St
(46580)
Rates: $82-$88
(574) 269-2323
(800) 272-6232

WASHINGTON

BAYMONT INN
7 Cumberland Dr
(47501)
Rates: $62-$92
(877) 229-6668

WEST LAFAYETTE

SUPER 8 MOTEL
2030 Northgate Dr
(47906)
Rates: $50-$70
(765) 567-7100
(800) 800-8000

WHITELAND

WISHING WELL MOTEL
RR 1, Box 93
(46184)
Rates: $21-$25
(317) 535-7548

IOWA

ADAIR

BUDGET INN
100 S 5th St (50002)
Rates: $33-$50
(515) 742-5553

SUPER 8 MOTEL
111 S 5th St (50002)
Rates: $40-$60
(515) 742-5251
(800) 800-8000

ALBIA

INDIAN HILLS INN
100 Hwy 34 E
(52531)
Rates: $44-$66
(515) 932-7181

ALGONA

AMERICINN MOTEL
600 Hwy 18 W
(50511)
Rates: $68-$135
(515) 295-3333
(800) 634-3444

ALTOONA

HEARTLAND INN
5000 NE 56th St
(50009)
Rates: $52-$79
(515) 967-2400
(800) 334-3277

MOTEL 6
3225 Adventureland
Drive (50009)
Rates: $37-$73
(515) 967-5252
(800) 466-8356

SETTLE INN
2101 Adventureland
Dr (50009)
Rates: $59-$89
(515) 967-7888

AMANA COLONIES

HOLIDAY INN
I-80 Exit 225
(52203)
Rates: $84-$100
(319) 668-1175
(800) 465-4329

AMES

AMERICINN
2507 SE 16th St
(50010)
Rates: $69-$109
(515) 233-1005
(800) 634-3444

BAYMONT INN
2500 Elwood Dr
(50010)
Rates: $55-$65
(515) 296-2500
(877) 229-6668

COMFORT INN
1605 S Dayton Ave
(50010)
Rates: $50-$100
(515) 232-0689
(800) 424-6423

COMFORT SUITES
2609 Elwood Dr
(50010)
Rates: $69-$179
(515) 268-8808
(800) 424-6423

HEARTLAND INN
2600 SE 16th St
(50010)
Rates: $140-$150
(515) 233-6060
(800) 334-3277

THE HOTEL AT GATEWAY CNTR
US 30 & Elwood
Dr (50010)
Rates: $129-$179
(515) 292-8600

QUALITY INN & SUITES STARLITE VILLAGE CONF CENTER
2601 E 13th
(50010)
Rates: $59-$149
(515) 232-9260
(800) 424-6423

ANAMOSA

SUPER 7 MOTEL
100 Grant Wood
Dr (52205)
Rates: $47-$70
(319) 462-3888
(800) 800-8000

ANKENY

BEST WESTERN METRO NORTH
133 SE Delaware
(50021)
Rates: $53-$79
(515) 964-1717
(800) 528-1234

DAYS INN
103 NE Delaware
(50021)
Rates: $39-$199
(515) 965-1995
(800) 329-7466

HEARTLAND INN
201 SE Delaware
Ave (50021)
Rates: $76-$86
(515) 964-8202
(800) 334-3277

ARNOLDS PARK

FILLENWARTH BEACH COTTAGES
87 Lake Shore Dr
(51331)
Rates: $290-$4000/Weekly
(712) 332-5646

ATLANTIC

DAYS INN
64968 Boston Rd
(50022)
Rates: $45-$79
(712) 243-4067
(800) 329-7466

SUPER 8 MOTEL
1902 E 7th St
(50022)
Rates: $49-$79
(712) 243-4723

AVOCA

CAPRI MOTEL
Hwy 59 (51521)
Rates: $33-$60
(712) 343-6301
(800) 222-6301

MOTEL 6
7004 N Chestnut
(51521)
Rates: $41-$52
(712) 343-6507
(800) 466-8356

BETTENDORF

(also see Quad
Cities)

ECONO LODGE
2205 Kimberly Rd
(52722)
Rates: $40-$100
(563) 355-6471
(800) 424-6423

HEARTLAND INN
815 Golden Valley
Dr (52722)
Rates: n/a
(563) 355-6336
(800) 334-3277

BLOOMFIELD

SOUTHFORK INN
Hwys 2 & 63
(52537)
Rates: $30-$39
(515) 664-1063
(800) 926-2860

BURLINGTON

BEST WESTERN PZAZZ MOTOR INN
3001 Winegard Dr
(52601)
Rates: $89-$139
(319) 753-2223
(800) 528-1234
(800) 373-1223

COMFORT INN
3051 Kirkwood
Ave (52601)
Rates: $59-$99
(319) 753-0000
(800) 424-6423

SUPER 8 MOTEL
3001 Kirkwood
Ave (52601)
Rates: $50-$72
(319) 752-9806
(800) 800-8000

CARROLL

SUPER 8 MOTEL
1757 US 71 N
(51401)
Rates: n/a
(712) 792-4753
(800) 800-8000

CARTER LAKE

SUPER 8 MOTEL
3000 Airport Dr
(51510)
Rates: $60-$80
(712) 347-5588
(800) 800-8000

CEDAR FALLS

BLACKHAWK MOTOR INN
122 Washington
(50613)
Rates: $36-$39
(319) 271-1161
(888) 577-1161

MIDWEST LODGE
4410 University
Ave (50613)
Rates: n/a
(319) 277-1550

UNIVERSITY INN
4711 University
Ave (50613)
Rates: $39-$120
(319) 277-1412
(800) 962-7784

CEDAR RAPIDS

BEST WESTERN COOPERS MILL HOTEL
100 F Ave NW
(52405)
Rates: $59-$79
(319) 366-5323
(800) 528-1234

BEST WESTERN LONGBRANCH HOTEL
90 Twixt Town Rd
(52402)
Rates: $49-$89
(319) 377-6386
(800) 528-1234
(800) 443-7660

CLARION HOTEL & CONV CTR
525 33rd Ave SW
(52404)
Rates: $65-$120
(319) 366-8671
(800) 424-6423

AREA CODES - If the local number doesn't connect, check for a new area code.

COMFORT INN-NORTH
5055 Rockwell Dr (52402)
Rates: $59-$104
(319) 393-8247
(800) 424-6423

COMFORT INN-SOUTH
390 33rd Ave SW (52404)
Rates: $60-$85
(319) 363-7934
(800) 424-6423

CROWNE PLAZA
350 1st Ave NE (52401)
Rates: $90-$130
(319) 363-8161
(800) 227-6963

DAYS INN
3245 Southgate Place SW (52404)
Rates: $49-$89
(319) 365-4339
(800) 329-7466

ECONO LODGE
622 33rd Ave SW (52404)
Rates: $40-$66
(319) 363-8888
(800) 424-6423

EXEL INN
616 33rd Ave SW (52404)
Rates: $35-$61
(319) 366-2475
(800) 367-3935

GUESTHOUSE INT'L INNS
2215 Blairs Ferry Rd NE (52402)
Rates: $57-$62
(319) 378-3948
(800) 214-8378

HAWTHORN SUITES LTD
4444 Czech Ln NE (52402)
Rates: $92-$98
(319) 294-8700
(800) 527-1133

HEARTLAND INN
3315 Southgate Ct SW (52404)
Rates: $76-$86
(319) 392-9012

HOWARD JOHNSON AIRPORT
700 Wright Brothers Blvd (52404)
Rates: $80-$110
(319) 363-3789
(800) 446-4656

MAINSTAY SUITES
5145 Rockwell Dr NE (52402)
Rates: $69-$145
(319) 363-7829
(800) 424-6423

MARRIOTT CEDAR RAPIDS
1200 Collins Rd NE (52402)
Rates: $125-$145
(319) 393-6600

MOTEL 6
3325 Southgate Ct SW (52404)
Rates: $31-$45
(319) 366-7523
(800) 466-8356

RAMADA LTD
4011 16th Ave SW (52404)
Rates: $65-$75
(319) 396-5000
(800) 272-6232

RAMADA LTD SUITES
2025 Werner Ave NE (52402)
Rates: $65-$85
(319) 378-8888
(800) 272-6232

RESIDENCE INN BY MARRIOTT
1900 Dodge Rd NE (52402)
Rates: $79-$149
(319) 395-0111
(800) 331-3131

SUPER 8 MOTEL
400 33rd Ave SW (52404)
Rates: $45-$60
(319) 363-1755
(800) 800-8000

SUPER 8 MOTEL
720 33rd Ave SW (52404)
Rates: $45-$60
(319) 362-6002
(800) 800-8000

CHARLES CITY

HARTWOOD INN
1312 Gilbert St (50616)
Rates: $35-$55
(641) 228-4352
(800) 972-2335

SLEEP INN, INN
1416 S Grand Ave (50616)
Rates: $40-$70
(641) 257-6700
(800) 424-6423

CHEROKEE

BEST WESTERN LA GRANDE HACIENDA
1401 N 2nd St, Hwy 59N (51012)
Rates: $65-$75
(712) 225-5701
(800) 528-1234
(800) 924-3765

CLARINDA

SUPER 8 MOTEL
1203 S 12th St (51632)
Rates: $50-$70
(712) 542-6333
(800) 800-8000

CLEAR LAKE

BEST WESTERN HOLIDAY LODGE
2023 Hwy 18 (50248)
Rates: $59-$99
(641) 357-5253
(800) 528-1234
(800) 606-3552

BUDGET INN
1306 N 25th St (50428)
Rates: $40-$60
(641) 357-8700
(888) 357-8700

HEARTLAND INN
1603 S Shore Dr (50428)
Rates: $76-$115
(641) 357-5123
(800) 334-3277

LAKE COUNTRY INN
518 Hwy 18 W (50428)
Rates: $30-$70
(641) 357-2184

MICROTEL INN
1305 N 25th St (50428)
Rates: $52-$72
(641) 357-0966
(888) 771-7171

SUPER 8 MOTEL
P. O. Box 340 (50428)
Rates: $44-$60
(641) 357-7521
(800) 800-8000

CLINTON

BEST WESTERN FRONTIER MOTOR INN
2300 Lincolnway (52732)
Rates: $65-$199
(563) 242-7112
(800) 728-7112

COUNTRY INN BY CARLSON
2224 Lincolnway (52732)
Rates: $69-$99
(563) 244-9922
(800) 456-4000

SUPER 8 MOTEL
1711 Lincoln Way (52732)
Rates: $47-$72
(563) 242-8870
(800) 800-8000

CLIVE

BAYMONT INN
1390 NW 118th St (50325)
Rates: $59-$109
(515) 221-9200
(877) 229-6668

CHASE SUITE HOTEL BY WOODFIN
11428 Forest AVe (50325)
Rates: $79-$209
(515) 223-7700

CLIVE HOTEL
11040 Hickman Rd (50325)
Rates: $54-$109
(515) 278-5575

HEARTLAND INN
11414 Forest Ave (50325)
Rates: $76-$86
(515) 226-0414
(800) 334-3277

COLFAX

COMFORT INN
1402 N Walnut St (50054)
Rates: $60-$170
(515) 674-4455
(800) 424-6423

COLUMBUS JUNCTION

COLUMBUS MOTEL
265 Colonels Dr (52738)
Rates: $41-$55
(319) 728-8080

COOK

VERMILLION DAM LODGE
P. O. Box 1105-AA (55723)
Rates: $700-$1040/Weekly
(800) 325-5780

CORALVILLE

AMERICINN
2597 Holiday Dr (53341)
Rates: $65-$155
(319) 625-2400
(800) 634-3444

COMFORT INN
209 W 9th St (52241)
Rates: $64-$99
(319) 351-8144
(800) 424-6423

DAYS INN
205 2nd St (52241)
Rates: $49-$89
(319) 354-4400
(800) 329-7466

HEARTLAND INN
87 2nd St (52241)
Rates: $80-$90
(319) 351-8132
(800) 334-3277

SUPER 8 MOTEL
611 1st Ave (52241)
Rates: $54-$88
(319) 337-8388
(800) 800-8000

AREA CODES - If the local number doesn't connect, check for a new area code.

COUNCIL BLUFFS

BEST WESTERN CROSSROADS OF THE BLUFFS
2216 27th Ave (51501)
Rates: $59-$89
(712) 322-3150
(800) 528-1234
(888) 232-2688

COMFORT SUITES
1801 S 35th St (51503)
Rates: $59-$160
(712) 323-9760
(800) 424-6423

DAYS INN- BY HARRAH'S CASINO
3619 9th Ave (51501)
Rates: $49-$89
(712) 323-2200
(800) 329-7466

DAYS INN LAKE MANAWA
3208 S 7th St (51501)
Rates: $45-$120
(712) 366-9699
(800) 329-7466

HEARTLAND INN
1000 Woodbury Ave (51503)
Rates: $76-$86
(712) 322-8400
(800) 334-3277

MOTEL 6-SOUTH
3032 S Expwy (51501)
Rates: $39-$58
(712) 366-2405
(800) 466-8356

QUALITY INN & SUITES METRO
3537 W Broadway (51501)
Rates: $59-$95
(712) 328-3171
(800) 424-6423

SUPER 8 MOTEL
2712 S 24th St (51501)
Rates: $52-$62
(712) 322-2888
(800) 800-8000

WESTERN INN
1842 Madison Ave (51503)
Rates: $ 65-$93
(712) 322-4499

CRESCO

CRESCO MOTEL
620 2nd Ave SE (42136)
Rates: $41-$73
(563) 547-240

DAVENPORT
(also see Quad Cities)

BAYMONT INN
400 Jason Way Ct (52807)
Rates: $59
(563) 386-1600
(877) 229-6668

BEST WESTERN STEEPLEGATE INN
100 W 76th St (Davenport 52806)
Rates: $79-$169
(563) 386-6900
(800) 528-1234
(800) 373-6900

COMFORT INN
7222 Northwest Blvd (52805)
Rates: $49-$150
(563) 391-8222
(800) 424-6423

DAYS INN
3202 E Kimberly Rd (52807)
Rates: $59-$119
(563) 355-1190
(800) 329-7466

HOLIDAY INN
5202 Brady St (52806)
Rates: n/a
(563) 391-1230
(800) 465-4329

MOTEL 6
6111 N Brady St (52806)
Rates: $29-$46
(563) 391-8997
(800) 466-8356

DE SOTO

EDGETOWNER MOTEL
I-80, Exit 110 (50069)
Rates: $36-$40
(515) 834-2641

DECORAH

HEARTLAND INN
705 Commerce Dr (52101)
Rates: $74-$84
(563) 382-2269
(800) 334-3277

DENISON

DAYS INN
315 Chamberlin Dr (51442)
Rates: $45-$65
(712) 263-2500
(800) 329-7466

SUPER 8 MOTEL
502 Boyer Valley Rd (51442)
Rates: n/a
(712) 263-5081
(800) 800-8000

DES MOINES

AMERICAN INN
5020 NE 14th St (50313)
Rates: $38-$95
(515) 265-7511

ARCHER MOTEL
4965 Hubbell Ave (50317)
Rates: $30-$60
(515) 265-0368

BAVARIAN INN
5220 NE 14th St (50313)
Rates: $49-$69
(515) 265-5611

BROADWAY MOTEL
5100 Hubbell Ave (50317)
Rates: $30-$75
(515) 262-5659

CANDLEWOOD SUITES
7625 Office Plaza Dr N (50266)
Rates: n/a
(515) 221-0001
(888) 226-3539

CLARION HOTEL & CONF CTR
11040 Hickman Rd (50325)
Rates: $69-$109
(515) 278-5575
(800) 424-6423

COMFORT INN
5231 Fleur Dr (50321)
Rates: $65-$134
(515) 287-3434
(800) 424-6423

DAYS INN
10841 Douglas Ave (50322)
Rates: $49-$150
(515) 278-2811
(800) 329-7466

FORT DES MOINES HOTEL
1000 Walnut St (50309)
Rates: $61-$160
(800) 532-1466

FOUR POINTS SHERATON AIRPORT
1810 Army Post Rd (50315)
Rates: $109-$159
(515) 287-6464
(800) 325-3535

HEARTLAND INN AIRPORT
1901 Hackley Ave (50315)
Rates: $80-$90
(515) 256-0603
(800) 334-3277

HICKMAN MOTOR LODGE
6500 Hickman Rd (50322)
Rates: $48-$56
(515) 276-8591

HOLIDAY INN
5000 Merle Hay Rd (50322)
Rates: $79-$109
(515) 278-0271
(800) 465-4329

MARRIOTT HOTEL DOWNTOWN
700 Grand Ave (50309)
Rates: $99-$189
(515) 245-5500
(800) 228-9290

MOTEL 6- AIRPORT
4817 Fleur Dr (50321)
Rates: $33-$46
(515) 287-6364
(800) 466-8356

MOTEL 6-NORTH
4940 NE 14th St (50313)
Rates: $35-$56
(515) 266-5456
(800) 466-8356

QUALITY INN
4995 NW Merle Hay Rd (50322)
Rates: $61-$135
(515) 278-2381
(800) 424-6423

QUALITY INN & SITES STARLITE VILLAGE CONF CENTER
929 3rd St (50309)
Rates: $63-$179
(515) 282-5251
(800) 424-6423

RED ROOF INN
4950 NE 14th St (50313)
Rates: $63-$92
(515) 266-6800
(800) 843-7663

SUPER 8 LODGE
4755 Merle Hay Rd (50322)
Rates: $49-$89
(515) 278-8858
(800) 800-8000

DE SOTO

EDGETOWNER MOTEL
804 Guthrie (50069)
Rates: $38-$60
(515) 834-2641

DUBUQUE

BEST WESTERN INN
3434 Dodge St (52003)
Rates: $69-$119
(563) 556-7760
(800) 528-1234
(800) 747-7760

BEST WESTERN MIDWAY HOTEL
3100 Dodge St (52003)
Rates: $69-$125
(563) 557-8000
(800) 528-1234
(800) 336-4392

COMFORT INN
4055 McDonald
Dr (52003)
Rates: $59-$99
(563) 556-3006
(800) 424-6423

DAYS INN
1111 Dodge St
(52001)
Rates: $49-$149
(563) 583-3297
(800) 329-7466
(800) 772-3297

**HEARTLAND INN
SOUTH**
2090 Southpark Ct
(52003)
Rates: $76-$86
(563) 556-6555
(800) 334-3377

**HEARTLAND INN
WEST**
4025 McDonald
Dr (52003)
Rates: $76-$86
(563) 582-3752
(800) 334-3277

**HOLIDAY INN
FIVE FLAGS**
450 Main St
(52001)
Rates: $89-$109
(563) 556-2000
(800) 465-4329

MAINSTAY SUITES
1275 Associates Dr
(52002)
Rates: $69-$128
(563) 557-7829
(800) 424-6423

DYERSVILLE
COMFORT INN
527 16th Ave SE
(52040)
Rates: $59-$160
(563) 875-7700
(800) 424-6423

SUPER 8 MOTEL
925 15th Ave SE
(52040)
Rates: $51-$68
(563) 875-8885

EARLY
EARLY MOTEL
403 Hwys 71 & 20
(50535)
Rates: $20-$25
(712) 273-5599

ELDORA
VILLAGE MOTEL
2005 E Edgington
Ave (50627)
Rates: $30-$45
(515) 858-3441

ELDRIDGE
QUALITY INN
1000 E Iowa St
(52748)
Rates: $49-$129
(563) 285-4600
(800) 424-6423

ELK HORN
**AMERICINN
MOTEL & SUITES**
4037 Main St
(51531)
Rates: $70-$119
(712) 764-4000
(800) 634-3444

ESTHERVILLE
SLEEP INN
2008 Central Ave
(51334)
Rates: $75-$89
(712) 362-5522
(800) 424-6423

EVANSDALE
RAMADA LTD
450 Evansdale Dr
(50707)
Rates: $69-$79
(319) 235-1111
(800) 272-6232

FAIRFIELD
**BEST WESTERN
FAIRFIELD INN**
2200 W Burlington
(52556)
Rates: $58-$85
(641) 472-2200
(800) 528-1234

FORT DODGE
COMFORT INN
2938 5th Ave S
(50501)
Rates: $55-$140
(515) 573-3731
(800) 424-6423

DAYS INN
3040 5TH Ave S
(50501)
Rates: $45-$64
(515) 576-8000
(800) 329-7466

HOLIDAY INN
2001 Hwy 169 S
(50501)
Rates: $45-$65
(515) 955-3621
(800) 465-4329

SUPER 8 MOTEL
3638 Maple Dr
(50501)
Rates: $60-$80
(515) 576-8788
(800) 800-8000

FORT
MADISON
**MADISON INN
MOTEL**
3440 Ave L (52627)
Rates: $42-$85
(319) 372-7740

SUPER 8 MOTEL
5107 Ave O
(52627)
Rates: $49-$59
(319) 372-8500
(800) 800-8000

GLENWOOD
**LINCOLN BLUFF
VIEW MOTEL**
57902 190 S
(51534)
Rates: $44-$53
(712) 622-8191

GRIMES
**AMERICINN
MOTEL & SUITES**
251 Gateway
(50111)
Rates: $69-$179
(515) 986-9900
(800) 634-3444

GRINNELL
**CLAYTON FARMS
BED & BREAKFST**
621 Newburg Rd
(50112)
Rates: $57-$120
(641) 236-3011
(888) 634-0503
(Horses allowed
only)

DAYS INN
1902 West St S
(50112)
Rates: $55-$199
(641) 236-6710
(800) 329-7466

ECONO LODGE
2210 West St S
(50112)
Rates: $40-$90
(641) 236-6116
(800) 424-6423

HAMPTON
**AMERICINN
MOTEL & SUITES**
702 Central Ave W
(50441)
Rates: $75-$130
(641) 456-5559
(800) 634-3444

HOMESTEAD
**DIE HEIMAT
COUNTRY INN
B&B**
4430 V St (52236)
Rates: $60-$89
(319) 622--3937

HUMBOLT
**CORNER INN
MOTEL-IMA**
1004 13th St N
(50548)
Rates: $36-$53
(515) 332-1672
(800) 341-8000

IDA GROVE
DELUX MOTEL
5981 US 175
(51445)
Rates: $35-$60
(712) 364-3317

INDEPENDENCE
SUPER 8 MOTEL
2000 1st St W
(50644)
Rates: $53-$99
(319) 334-7041
(800) 800-8000

IOWA CITY
MOTEL 6
810 1st Ave
(52241)
Rates: $33-$48
(319) 354-0030
(800) 466-8356

**QUALITY INN
HIGHLANDER**
2525 N Dodge St
(52245)
Rates: $59-$179
(319) 354-2000
(800) 424-6423

**SHERATON
IOWA CITY
PLAZA HOTEL**
210 S Dubuque St
(52240)
Rates: $99-$239
(319) 337-4058
(800) 325-3535

TRAVELODGE
2216 N Dodge St
(52245)
Rates: $69-$139
(319) 351-1010
(800) 578-7878

IOWA FALLS
AMERICINN
810 S Oak St
(50126)
Rates: $65-$71
(641) 648-4600
(800) 634-3444

JEFFERSON
REDWOOD MOTEL
209 E Gallup Rd
(50129)
Rates: $30-$45
(515) 386-3116

JOHNSTON
**BEST INNS
OF AMERICA**
5050 Merle Hay
Rd (50131)
Rates: $49-$87
(515) 270-1111
(800) 237-8466

RAMADA INN
5055 Merle Hay
Rd (50131)
Rates: n/a
(515) 276-5411
(800) 272-6232

KEOKUK
SUPER 8 MOTEL
3511 Main St
(52632)
Rates: $49-$59
(319) 524-3888
(800) 800-8000

LE CLAIRE
(see Quad Cities)

LE MARS
SUPER 8 MOTEL
1201 Hawkeye
Ave SW (51031)
Rates: $50-$80
(712) 546-8800
(800) 800-8000

AREA CODES - If the local number doesn't connect, check for a new area code.

MANCHESTER

SUPER 8 MOTEL
1020 W Main
(52057)
Rates: $51-$96
(563) 927-2533
(800) 800-8000

MAPLETON

MAPLE MOTEL
Hwy 141 & 175
(51034)
Rates: $30-$40
(712) 882-1271

MARION

MICROTEL INN
5500 Dyer Ave
(52302)
Rates: $49-$64
(319) 373-7400

MARQUETTE

THE FRONTIER MOTEL
101 S 1st St
(52158)
Rates: $45-$95
(563) 873-3497

MARSHALL-TOWN

BEST WESTERN REGENCY INN
3303 S Center St
(50158)
Rates: $69-$94
(641) 752-6321
(800) 528-1234
(800) 241-2974

COMFORT INN
2613 S Center St
(50158)
Rates: $58-$88
(641) 752-6000
(800) 424-6423

ECONO LODGE
3315 S Center St
(50158)
Rates: $45-$70
(641) 753-3333
(800) 424-6423

SUPER 8 MOTEL
18 E Berle Rd
(50158)
Rates: n/a
(641) 753-8181
(800) 800-8000

MASON CITY

BEST VALUE INN
24 5th St SW
(50401)
Rates: $40-$69
(641) 424-2910

DAYS INN
2301 4th St SW
(50401)
Rates: $39-$80
(641) 424-0210
(800) 329-7466

HOLIDAY INN
2101 4th St SW
(50401)
Rates: $69-$89
(641) 423-1640
(800) 465-4329

SUPER 8 MOTEL
3010 4th St SW
(50401)
Rates: n/a
(641) 423-8855
(800) 800-8000

MISSOURI VALLEY

DAYS INN
1967 Hwy 30 (51555)
Rates: $49-$99
(712) 642-4003
(800) 329-7466

MONTICELLO

THE BLUE INN
250 N Main St
(52310)
Rates: $56-$100
(319) 465-6116

MOUNT PLEASANT

HEARTLAND INN
Hwy 218 N (52641)
Rates: $73-$83
(319) 385-2102
(800) 334-3277

RAMADA LTD
1200 E Baker St
(52641)
Rates: $50-$125
(319) 385-0571
(800) 272-6232

SUPER 8 MOTEL
1000 N Grand Ave
(52641)
Rates: $46-$85
(319) 385-8888
(800) 800-8000

MOUNT VERNON

SLEEP INN
310 Virgil Ave
(52314)
Rates: $69-$149
(319) 895-0055
(800) 424-6423

MUSCATINE

HOLIDAY INN
2915 N Hwy 61
(52761)
Rates: $69-$109
(563) 264-5550
(800) 465-4329

SUPER 8 MOTEL
2900 N Hwy 61
(52761)
Rates: $46-$69
(563) 263-9100
(800) 800-8000

NEWTON

BEST WESTERN INN
I-80 & Hwy 14
(50208)
Rates: $59-$89
(641) 792-4200
(800) 528-1234
(800) 373-6350

DAYS INN
1605 W 19th St S
(50208)
Rates: $50-$65
(641) 792-2330
(800) 329-7466

HOLIDAY INN EXPRESS
1700 W 19th St S
(50208)
Rates: $40-$65
(641) 792-7722
(800) 465-4329
(888) 249-1468

RAMADA LTD
1405 W 19th St S
(50208)
Rates: $50-$105
(641) 792-8100
(800) 272-2632

RODEWAY INN MAHASKA MOTEL
1315 A Ave S
(52577)
Rates: $40-$85
(641) 673-8351
(800) 424-6423

OKOBOJI

AMERICINN LODGE & SUITES
1005 Brooks Park Dr (51355)
Rates: $69-$195
(712) 332-9000
(800) 634-3444

ARROWHEAD RESORT
1405 US 71 (51355)
Rates: $79-$189
(712) 332-2161

OSCEOLA

AMERICINN LODGE & SUITES
111 Ariel Cir
(50213)
Rates: $79-$144
(641) 342-9400
(800) 634-3444

OSKALOOSA

COMFORT INN
2401 A Ave W
(52577)
Rates: $75-$119
(641) 672-0375
(800) 424-6423

RODEWAY INN
1315 A Ave E
(52577)
Rates: $45-$75
(641) 673-8351
(800) 228-2000

OTTUMWA

COLONIAL MOTOR INN
1534 Albia Rd
(52501)
Rates: $25-$46
(641) 683-1661

HEARTLAND INN
125 W Joseph Ave
(52501)
Rates: $110-$120
(641) 682-8526
(800) 334-3277

PACIFIC JUNCTION

BLUFF VIEW MOTEL
I-29 & Hwy 34
(51561)
Rates: $30-$40
(712) 622-8191
(800) 582-9366

PELLA

AMERIHOST INN
2104 Washington St (50219)
Rates: $69-$129
(641) 628-0085
(800) 434-5800

SUPER 8 MOTEL
105 E Oskaloosa St (50219)
Rates: $45-$59
(641) 628-8181
(800) 800-8000

PERCIVAL

SUPER 8 MOTEL
2103 249th St
(51648)
Rates: $52-$76
(712) 382-2828
(800) 800-8000

QUAD CITIES

BAYMONT INN
400 Jason Way Ct
(Davenport 52807)
Rates: $59-$89
(563) 386-1600
(877) 229-6668

BEST WESTERN STEEPLEGATE INN
100 W 76th St
(Davenport 52806)
Rates: $79-$169
(563) 386-6900
(800) 528-1234
(800) 373-6900

COMFORT INN
7222 Northwest Blvd (Davenport 52806)
Rates: $49-$140
(563) 391-8222
(800) 424-6423

COMFORT INN
902 Mississippi View Ct
(Le Claire 52753)
Rates: $60-$150
(563) 289-4747
(800) 424-6423

COMFORT INN
2600 52nd Ave
(Moline 61265)
Rates: $55-$90
(309) 762-7000
(800) 424-6423

AREA CODES - If the local number doesn't connect, check for a new area code.

COUNTRY INN BY CARLSON
140 E 55th St
(Davenport 52805)
Rates: $64-$99
(563) 388-6444
(800) 456-4000

DAYS INN
3202 E Kimberly
Rd (Davenport
52807)
Rates: $59-$119
(563) 355-1190
(800) 329-7466

ECONO LODGE
2205 Kimberly Rd
(Bettenforf 52722)
Rates: $40-$100
(563) 355-6471
(800) 424-6423

EXEL INNS OF AMERICA
6310 N Brady Ave
(Davenport 52806)
Rates: $39-$63
(563) 386-6350
(800) 367-3935

EXEL INN
2501 52nd Ave
(Moline 61265)
Rates: $37-$63
(309) 797-5580
(800) 367-3935

HEARTLAND INN
815 Golden Valley
Dr (Bettendorf
52722)
Rates: $76-$86
(563) 355-6336
(800) 334-3277

HEARTLAND INN
6605 Brady St
(Davenport 52806)
Rates: $76-$86
(563) 386-8336
(800) 334-3277

HOLIDAY INN
5202 Brady St
(Davenport 52806)
Rates: $69-$157
(563) 391-1230
(800) 465-4329

HOLIDAY INN EXPRESS /ARPT
6910 27th St
(Moline 61265)
Rates: $69-$109
(309) 762-8300
(800) 465-4329

HOLIDAY INN CONVENTION CENTER
6902 27th St
(Moline 61265)
Rates: $52-$129
(309) 762-8811
(800) 465-4329

LA QUINTA INN
5450 27th St
(Moline 61265)
Rates: $65-$102
(309) 762-9008
(800) 687-6667

THE LODGE HOTEL
900 Spruce
Hills Drive
(Bettendorf 52722)
Rates: $95-$104
(3563) 359-7141
(800) 285-8637

MOTEL 6
6111 N Brady St
(Davenport 52806)
Rates: $29-$46
(563) 391-8997
(800) 466-8356

RESIDENCE INN BY MARRIOTT
120 E 55th St
(Davenport 52807)
Rates: $99-$204
(563) 391-8877
(800) 331-3131

RHYTHM CITY CASINO BLACK-HAWK HOTEL
200 E 3rd St
(Davenport 52801)
Rates: $54-$79
(563) 328-6000

SIGNATURE INN
3020 Utica Ridge
Rd (Bettendorf
52722)
Rates: $49-$104
(563) 355-7575

SUPER 8 MOTEL
410 E 65th St
(Davenport 52807)
Rates: $40-$100
(563) 388-9810
(800) 800-8000

SUPER 8 MOTEL
1552 Welcome
Center Rd (Le
Claire 52753)
Rates: $56-$85
(563) 289-5888
(800) 800-8000

TWIN BRIDGES MOTOR INN
221 15th St
(Bettendorf 52722)
Rates: $39-$48
(319) 355-6451

SERGEANT BLUFF
ECONO LODGE
103 Sergeant
Square (51054)
Rates: $30-$65
(712) 943-5079
(800) 424-6423

SHELDON
SHELDON MOTEL
3 Blks W on US 18
(51201)
Rates: $24-$34
(712) 324-2568

SHENANDOAH
COUNTRY INN MOTEL
1503 W Sheridan
Ave (51601)
Rates: $35-$75
(712) 246-1550

SIBLEY
SUPER 8 MOTEL
1108 2nd Ave
(51249)
Rates: $48-$90
(712) 754-3603
(800) 800-8000

SIOUX CITY
AMERICINN LODGE & SUITES
4230 S Lewis Blvd
(51106)
Rates: $75-$80
(712) 255-1800
(800) 634-3444

COMFORT INN
4202 E Lakeport St
(51106)
Rates: $64-$114
(712) 274-1300
(800) 424-6423

ELMDALE MOTEL
US 75 N at 22nd St
(51105)
Rates: $28-$59
(712) 277-1012

MARINA INN
4th & B Sts (51101)
Rates: $64-$74
(800) 798-7980

MOTEL 6
6166 Harbor Dr
(51101)
Rates: $29-$42
(712) 277-3131
(800) 466-8356

PLAZA HOTEL
707 4th St (51101)
Rates: $59-$80
(712) 277-4101

QUALITY INN
1401 Zenith Dr
(51103)
Rates: $49-$69
(712) 277-3211
(800) 424-6423

RIVERBOAT INN
701 Gordon Dr
(51101)
Rates: $55-$75
(712) 277-9400
(800) 236-6146

SUPER 8 MOTEL
4307 Stone Ave
(51106)
Rates: $50-$70
(712) 274-1520

SIOUX RAPIDS
HANSEN HOUSE B&B INN
402 Third St (50585)
Rates: $50-$65
(712) 283-2179
(Pet kennel
provided)

SLOAN
WINNA VEGAS INN
1862 Hwy 141
(51055)
Rates: $53-$58
(712) 428-4280

SPIRIT LAKE
OAKS MOTEL
1701 Chicago
(51360)
Rates: $49-$100
(712) 336-2940

SHAMROCK INN
2231 18th St (51360)
Rates: $49-$109
(712) 336-2668

SUPER 8 MOTEL
2203 Circle Dr W
(51360)
Rates: $55-$120
(812) 336-4901
(800) 800-8000

STORM LAKE
CROSS ROADS MOTEL
Hwys 3 & 71
(50588)
Rates: $23-$38
(712) 732-1456
(800) 383-1456

PALACE MOTEL
E Lake Shore Dr
(50588)
Rates: $30-$50
(712) 732-5753

VISTA ECONOMY INN
1316 N Lake Ave
(50588)
Rates: $28-$44
(712) 732-2342
(800) 826-0778
(800) 451-6261

STORY CITY
COMFORT INN
425 Timberland
Dr (50248)
Rates: $55-$120
(515) 733-6363
(800) 424-6423

VIKING MOTOR INN
West of I-35, Exit
124 (50248)
Rates: $45-$58
(515) 733-4306
(800) 233-4306

STUART
AMERICINN MOTEL & SUITES
420 SW 8th St
(50250)
Rates: $69-$149
(515) 523-9000
(800) 634-3444

SUPER 8 MOTEL
203 SE 7th St
(50250)
Rates: $39-$59
(515) 523-2888

AREA CODES - If the local number doesn't connect, check for a new area code.

TOLEDO

DAYS INN
403 Hwy 30 W
(52342)
Rates: $46-$90
(641) 484-5678
(800) 329-7466

SUPER 8 MOTEL
207 Hwy 30 W
(52342)
Rates: $49-$79
(641) 484-5888
(800) 800-8000

URBANA

SUPER 8 MOTEL
5369 Hutton Dr
(52345)
Rates: $56-$148
(319) 443-8888
(800) 800-8000

URBANDALE

COMFORT INN
5900 Sutton Dr
(50322)
Rates: $59-$99
(515) 270-1037
(800) 424-6423

HOLIDAY INN NORTHWEST
5000 Merle Hay
Rd (50322)
Rates: $76-$84
(515) 278-0271
(800) 465-4329

MICROTEL INN
8711 Plum Dr
(50322)
Rates: $59-$65
(515) 727-5424

SLEEP INN
11211 Hickman Rd
(50322)
Rates: $59-$169
(515) 270-2424
(800) 424-6423

WALCOTT

DAYS INN
2889 N Plainview
Dr (52773)
Rates: $45-$105
(563) 284-6600
(800) 329-7466

WALNUT

SUPER 8 MOTEL
2109 Antique City
Dr (51577)
Rates: $50-$85
(712) 784-2221

WAPELLO

ROY EL MOTEL
405 Hwy 61 S
(52653)
Rates: $28-$38
(319) 523-2991
(877) 523-2111

WASHINGTON

SUPER 8 MOTEL
119 Westview Dr
(52353)
Rates: $43-$63
(319) 653-6621
(800) 800-8000

WATERLOO

COMFORT INN
1945 La Porte Rd
(50702)
Rates: $66-$104
(319) 234-7411
(800) 424-6423

HEARTLAND INN
1809 La Porte Rd
(50702)
Rates: $122-$132
(319) 235-4461
(800) 334-3277

HEARTLAND INN
3052 Marnie Ave
(50701)
Rates: $110-$120
(319) 232-7467
(800) 334-3277

HOLIDAY INN EXPRESS
2141 LaPorte Rd
(50702)
Rates: $82-$105
(319) 233-9191
(800) 465-4329

MOTEL 6
2343 Logan Ave
(50703)
Rates: $45-$50
(319) 236-3238
(800) 466-8356

QUALITY INN
226 W 5th St
(50701)
Rates: $50-$260
(319) 235-0301
(800) 424-6423

RAMADA INN
205 W 4th St
(50701)
Rates: $89-$109
(319) 233-7560
(800) 272-6232

WAVERLY

AMERIHOST INN
404 29th Ave SW
(50677)
Rates: $68-$149
(319) 352-0399
(800) 434-5800

RED FOX INN
1900 Heritage
Way (50677)
Rates: $56-$195
(319) 352-5330

SUPER 8 MOTEL
301 13th Ave SW
(50677)
Rates: $50-$90
(319) 352-0888
(800) 800-8000

WEBSTER CITY

EXECUTIVE INN
1700 Superior St
(50595)
Rates: $40-$75
(515) 832-3631
(800) 322-3631

WEST BEND

WEST BEND MOTEL
West of Hwy 15
(50597)
Rates: $22-$42
(515) 887-3611

WEST BRANCH

PRESIDENTIAL MOTOR INN
711 S Downey
(52358)
Rates: $35-$49
(319) 643-2526

WEST BURLINGTON

AMERICINN MOTEL & SUITES
628 S Gear Ave
(52655)
Rates: $65-$125
(319) 758-9000
(800) 634-3444

WEST DES MOINES

CANDLEWOOD SUITES
7625 Office Plaza
Dr N (50266)
Rates: $75-$119
(515) 221-0001
(888) 226-3539

HAWTHORN SUITES
6905 Lake Dr (50266)
Rates: $ $102-$112
(515) 223-0000
(800) 527-1133

MARRIOTT WEST DES MOINES
1250 Jordan Creek
Pkwy (50266)
Rates: $89-$119
(515) 267-1500
(800) 228-9290

MOTEL 6
7655 Office Plaza
Dr North (50266)
Rates: $37-$56
(515) 267-8885
(800) 466-8356

QUALITY SUITES
1236 74th St (50266)
Rates: $89-$169
(515) 223-9005
(800) 424-6423

SHERATON WEST
1800 50th St (50266)
Rates: $125-$129
(515) 223-1800
(800) 325-3535

VALLEY WEST INN
3535 Westown
Pkwy (50266)
Rates: $59-$119
(515) 225-2524

WEST LIBERTY

ECONO LODGE
1943 Garfield Ave
(52776)
Rates: $47-$70
(319) 627-2171
(800) 424-6423

WEST UNION

ELMS MOTEL
705 Hwy 150
South (52175)
Rates: $30-$60
(319) 422-3841
(800) 422-3843

WILLIAMS

BEST WESTERN NORSEMAN INN
3086 220th St
(50271)
Rates: $44-$68
(515) 854-2281
(800) 528-1234

WILLIAMSBURG

BEST WESTERN QUIET HOUSE
1708 N Highland
St (52361)
Rates: $55-$159
(319) 668-9777
(800) 528-1234

COMFORT INN
2185 U Ave
(52361)
Rates: $55-$115
(319) 668-2700
(800) 424-6423

CREST COUNTRY INN
340 W Evans St
(52361)
Rates: $45-$65
(319) 668-1522

SUPER 8 MOTEL
1708 N Highland
St (52361)
Rates: $70-$100
(319) 668-9718
(800) 800-8000

WINTERSET

VILLAGE VIEW MOTEL
711 Hwy 92 E
(50273)
Rates: $35-$48
(515) 462-1218

WYOMING

SUNSET MOTEL
7032 Hwy 64
(52362)
Rates: $25-$48
(319) 488-2240

AREA CODES - If the local number doesn't connect, check for a new area code.

KANSAS

ABILENE

BEST WESTERN PRESIDENTS INN
2210 N Buckeye (67410)
Rates: $38-$64
(785) 263-2050
(800) 528-1234
(800) 332-2038

BUDGET LODGE INN
101 NW 14th (67410)
Rates: $25-$42
(785) 263-3600
(866) 394-8275

DAYS INN
1709 N Buckeye Ave (67410)
Rates: $35-$85
(785) 263-2800
(800) 329-7466

DIAMOND MOTEL
1407 NW 3rd St (67410)
Rates: $29-$58
(785) 263-2360

HOLIDAY INN EXPRESS HOTEL
110 E Lafayette Ave (67410)
Rates: $67-$99
(785) 263-4049
(800) 465-4329

SUPER 8 MOTEL
2207 N Buckeye (67410)
Rates: $44-$69
(785) 263-4545
(800) 800-8000

ATCHISON

ATCHISON HERITAGE CONF CENTER
710 S 9th (66002)
Rates: $32-$48
(913) 367-1162
(800) 467-1164

COMFORT INN
509 S 9th (66002)
Rates: $54-$90
(913) 367-7666
(800) 424-6423

BALDWIN CITY

LODGE OF BALDWIN CITY
502 Ames (66006)
Rates: $59-$79
(785) 594-3900

BAXTER SPRINGS

BAXTER INN-4 LESS
2451 Military Ave (66713)
Rates: $37-$50
(620) 856-2106

BELLEVILLE

BEST WESTERN BEL VILLA MOTEL
215 US Hwy 36 (66935)
Rates: $55-$69
(785) 527-2231
(800) 528-1234

JEWEL MOTEL
1415 28th St (66935)
Rates: $32-$60
(785) 527-2408

PLAZA MOTEL
901 28th St (66935)
Rates: $40-$50
(785) 527-2228

SUPER 8 MOTEL
1410 28th St (66935)
Rates: $46-$91
(785) 527-2112
(800) 800-8000

BELOIT

MAINLINER INN
RFD 1, Box 47 A (67420)
Rates: $28-$60
(785) 738-3531

SUPER 8 MOTEL
205 W Hwy 24 (67420)
Rates: $49-$75
(785) 738-4300
(800) 800-8000

BURLINGTON

COUNTRY HAVEN INN
207 Cross St (66839)
Rates: $50-$85
(620) 364-8260
(800) 942-8369

CAWKER CITY

OAK CREEK LODGE
1787 Rain Road (67431)
Rates: $55-$85
(913) 263-8755

CHANUTE

GUEST HOUSE MOTOR INN
1814 S Santa Fe (66720)
Rates: $30-$44
(620) 431-0600

HOLIDAY PARK MOTEL
3030 S Santa Fe (66720)
Rates: $40-$65
(620) 431-0850

SAFARI INN
3428 S Santa Fe (66720)
Rates: $38-$63
(620) 431-9460

SKYLINE MOTEL
1216 W Main St (66720)
Rates: $25-$40
(620) 431-1500

CHERRYVALE

BIG HILL LODGE
415 S Liberty (67335)
Rates: $39-$129
(620) 336-2255
(877) 244-4455

CLAY CENTER

CEDAR COURT MOTEL
905 Crawford (67432)
Rates: $40-$65
(785) 632-2148

COFFEYVILLE

APPLETREE INN
820 E 11th (67337)
Rates: $62-$105
(620) 251-0002

REGAL INN
1215 E 3rd St (67337)
Rates: $35-$50
(620) 251-1034

SUPER 8 MOTEL
104 W 11th St (67337)
Rates: $47-$68
(620) 251-2250

COLBY

BEST WESTERN CROWN MOTEL
2320 S Range (67701)
Rates: $48-$79
(785) 462-3943
(800) 528-1234

BUDGET INN
745 W 4th St (67701)
Rates: $40-$70
(785) 462-3338

COMFORT INN
2225 S Range (67701)
Rates: $55-$120
(785) 462-3833
(800) 424-6423

DAYS INN
1925 S Range (6770185
Rates: $50-$85
(785) 462-8691
(800) 329-7466

HOLIDAY INN EXPRESS HOTEL
645 W Willow (67701)
Rates: $70-$120
(785) 462-8787
(800) 465-4329

MOTEL 6
1985 S Range (67701)
Rates: $39-$45
(785) 462-8201
(800) 466-8356

QUALITY INN
1950 S Range (67701)
Rates: $45-$85
(785) 462-3933
(800) 424-6423

SUPER 8 MOTEL
1040 Zelfer Ave (67701)
Rates: $50-$75
(785) 462-8248
(800) 800-8000

COLDWATER

COMANCHE MOTEL
204 S Central (67029)
Rates: $38-$50
(620) 582-2104

CONCORDIA

ECONO LODGE
89 Lincoln St (66901)
Rates: $40-$90
(785) 243-4545
(800) 424-6423

SUPER 8 MOTEL
1320 Lincoln (66901)
Rates: $54-$69
(785) 243-4200
(800) 800-8000

COTTON-WOOD FALLS

GRAND CENTRAL HOTEL & GRILL
215 Broadway (66845)
Rates: $140-$180
(620) 273-6763
(809) 951-6763

COUNCIL GROVE

THE COTTAGE HOUSE HOTEL & MOTEL
25 N Neosho (66846)
Rates: $58-$175
(620) 767-6828
(800) 727-7903

AREA CODES - If the local number doesn't connect, check for a new area code.

DODGE CITY

BEST WESTERN SILVER SPUR LODGE
1510 W Wyatt Earp Blvd (67801)
Rates: $57-$84
(620) 227-2125
(800) 528-1234
(800) 817-2125

BUDGET HOST MOTEL
2200 Wyatt Earp Blvd (67801)
Rates: $30-$65
(620) 227-8146

DODGE HOUSE HOTEL
2408 W Wyatt Earp Blvd (67801)
Rates: $55-$125
(620) 226-9900

ECONO LODGE
1610 W Wyatt Earp Blvd (67801)
Rates: $45-$82
(620) 225-0231
(800) 424-6423

HOLIDAY INN EXPRESS
2320 W Wyatt Earp Blvd (67801)
Rates: $65-$70
(620) 227-5000
(800) 465-4329

HOLIDAY MOTEL
2100 W Wyatt Earp Blvd (67801)
Rates: $33-$38
(620) 227-2169

NENDELS INN
2523 E Wyatt Earp Blvd (67801)
Rates: $62-$80
(620) 225-3000
(800) 547-0106

SUPER 8 MOTEL
1708 W Wyatt Earp Blvd (67801)
Rates: $60-$81
(620) 225-3924
(800) 800-8000

THUNDERBIRD MOTEL
2300 W Wyatt Earp Blvd (67801)
Rates: $35-$50
(620) 225-4143

WYATT EARP INN
2110 E Wyatt Earp Blvd (67801)
Rates: $30-$85
(620) 225-2654

DORRANCE

COUNTRY INN B&B
3871 198th St (67634)
Rates: $40-$80
(785) 6664468

EL DORADO

BEST WESTERN RED COACH INN
2525 W Central (67042)
Rates: $63-$110
(316) 321-6900
(800) 528-1234
(800) 362-2034

HERITAGE INN
2515 W Central Ave (67042)
Rates: $45-$72
(316) 321-6800

ELKHART

ELKHART MOTEL
329 Morton St (67950)
Rates: $35-$57
(620) 697-2168

ELLSWORTH

BEST WESTERN GARDEN INN
1400 N Hwy 156 (67439)
Rates: $55-$73
(785) 472-3116
(800) 528-1234
(800) 234-4240

ELWOOD

CAPRI MOTEL
P. O. Box 97-C
(Wathena 66090)
Rates: $17-$24
(913) 365-0209

EMPORIA

BEST WESTERN HOSPITALITY HOUSE
3021 W Hwy 50 (66801)
Rates: $54-$74
(620) 342-7587
(800) 528-1234
(800) 362-2036

DAYS INN
3032 W Hwy 50 (66801)
Rates: $48-$80
(620) 342-1787
(800) 329-7466

ECONO LODGE
2511 W 18th St (66801)
Rates: $40-$70
(620) 343-7750
(800) 424-6423

KAPP PLACE B&B
630 Rd 145 (66801)
Rates: $59-$69
(620) 342-2992

MOTEL 6
2630 W 18th Ave (66801)
Rates: $34-$37
(620) 343-1240
(800) 466-8356

RAMADA INN & CONF CTR
2700 W 18th Ave (66801)
Rates: $49-$69
(620) 343-2200
(800) 272-6232

SUPER 8 MOTEL
2913 W Hwy 50 (66801)
Rates: $45-$70
(620) 342-7567
(800) 800-8000

ERIE

LAND OF AH'S MOTOR INN
700 W Canville & Hwy 59 (66733)
Rates: $29-$34
(316) 244-5231

FLORENCE

HOLIDAY MOTEL
630 W 5th (66851)
Rates: $22-$31
(316) 878-4246

FORT SCOTT

BEST WESTERN FORT SCOTT INN
101 State St (66701)
Rates: $65-$80
(620) 223-0100
(800) 528-1234
(888) 800-3175

FIRST INTERSTATE INN
2222 1/2 S Main (66701)
Rates: $38-$60
(620) 223-5330
(800) 462-4667

GARDEN CITY

AMERICAN LODGE & SUITES
3020 E Kansas Ave (67846)
Rates: $55-$160
(620) 272-9860
(800) 634-3444

BEST VALUE INN
1818 Commanche (67846)
Rates: $50-$57
(620) 275-5095

BEST WESTERN RED BARON MOTOR INN
US 50 E Side & Hwy 83 (67846)
Rates: $53-$82
(620) 275-4164
(800) 528-1234
(800) 333-4164

BEST WESTERN WHEAT LANDS HOTEL
1311 E Fulton (67846)
Rates: $50-$88
(620) 276-2387
(800) 528-1234
(800) 333-2387

COMFORT INN
2608 E Kansas Ave (67846)
Rates: $87-$115
(620) 275-5800
(800) 424-6423

CONTINENTAL INN
1408 Jones Ave (67846)
Rates: $36-$65
(620) 276-7691

FLAMINGO MOTEL
1612 Jones Ave (67846)
Rates: $32-$55
(620) 276-7601

HOLIDAY INN EXP
2502 E Kansas Ave (67846)
Rates: $67-$75
(620) 275-5900
(800) 465-4329

NATIONAL 9 INN
123 Honey Bee Ct (67846)
Rates: n/a
(620) 275-0677

PLAZA INN
1911 E Kansas Ave (67846)
Rates $66-$120
(620) 275-7471
(800) 875-5201

SUPER 8 MOTEL
2808 N Taylor (67846)
Rates: $42-$62
(620) 275-9625
(800) 800-8000

GLASCO

RUSTIC REMEMBRANCES BED & BRKFAST
616 N 100th Rd (67445)
Rates: $45-$85
(785) 568-2777

GODDARD

EXPRESS INN
19941 W Kellogg Dr (67052)
Rates: $42-$48
(316) 794-3366

GOODLAND

BEST WESTERN BUFFALO INN
830 W Hwy 24 (67735)
Rates: $49-$80
(785) 899-3621
(800) 528-1234
(800) 433-3621

COMFORT INN
2519 Enterprise Rd (67735)
Rates: $65-$110
(785) 899-7181
(800) 424-6423

ECONOMY 9 MOTEL
2420 Commerce Rd (67735)
Rates: $40-$60
(785) 899-5672

AREA CODES - If the local number doesn't connect, check for a new area code.

HOWARD JOHNSON
2218 Commerce Rd (67735)
Rates: $59-$64
(785) 899-3644
(800) 446-4656

MOTEL 7
811 E Hwy 24 (67735)
Rates: $35-$70
(785) 899-6414

SUPER 8 MOTEL
2520 S Hwy 27 (67735)
Rates: $40-$70
(785) 899-7566
(800) 800-8000

GREAT BEND

BALTZELL MOTEL
705 E 10th St (67530)
Rates: $24-$40
(620) 792-4395

BEST WESTERN ANGUS INN
2920 10th St (67530)
Rates: $59-$79
(620) 792-3541
(800) 528-1234
(800) 862-6487

DAYS INN
4701 10th St (67601)
Rates: $42-$110
(620) 792-8235
(800) 329-7466

HIGHLAND HOTEL & CONV CTR
3017 10th St (67601)
Rates: $72-$100
(620) 792-2431

SUPER 8 MOTEL
3500 10th St (67530)
Rates: $42-$57
(620) 793-8486
(800) 800-8000

TRAVELODGE
3200 W 10th St (67530)
Rates: $36-$54
(620) 792-7219
(800) 578-7878

GREENSBURG

BEST WESTERN J-HAWK MOTEL
515 W Kansas Ave (67054)
Rates: $54-$75
(620) 723-2121
(800) 528-1234

HALLOWELL

CLAYTHORNE LODGE
Rt 1, Box 13 (66725)
Rates: n/a
(316) 597-2568

HAYS

BEST WESTERN VAGABOND MOTEL
2524 Vine St (67601)
Rates: $51-$73
(785) 625-2511
(800) 528-1234
(800) 432-2776

BUDGET HOST VILLA INN
810 E 8th (67601)
Rates: $39-$57
(785) 625-2563
(800) 950-5015

DAYS INN
3205 Vine St (67601)
Rates: $57-$120
(785) 628-8261
(800) 329-7466

ECONO LODGE
3503 Vine St (67601)
Rates: $40-$85
(785) 625-4839
(800) 424-6423

HAMPTON INN
3801 Vine St (67601)
Rates: $53-$60
(785) 625-8103
(800) 426-7866

HOLIDAY INN
3603 Vine St (67601)
Rates: $58-$63
(785) 625-7371
(800) 465-4329

MOTEL 6
3404 Vine St (67601)
Rates: $39-$55
(785) 625-4282
(800) 466-8356

HAYSVILLE

HAYSVILLE INN
301 E 71st St (67060)
Rates: $38-$48
(316) 522-1000

HESSTON

AMERICINN LODGE & SUITES
2 Leonard Ct (67062)
Rates: $52-$129
(620) 327-2053
(800) 686-4377

HIAWATHA

COUNTRY SQUIRE MOTEL
2000 Oregon (66434)
Rates: $31-$51
(785) 742-2877

SUNFLOWER MOTEL
406 N 1st (66434)
Rates: $26-$37
(785) 742-4305

HILL CITY

WESTERN HILLS MOTEL
812 W Hwy 24 (67642)
Rates: $25-$45
(785) 421-2141

HILLSBORO

COUNTRY HAVEN INN
804 Western Heights (67063)
Rates: $52-$71
(620) 947-2929
(877) 404-2836

HUGOTON

B & B MOTEL
Jct Hwy 51/56 (67951)
Rates: $30-$45
(620) 544-2466

JACKSON'S MOTEL
615 S Monroe (67530)
Rates: $35
(620) 544-2888

HUTCHINSON

ASTRO MOTEL
15 E 4th (67501)
Rates: $30-$70
(316) 663-1151
(800) 633-1168

BEST WESTERN SUN DOME
11 Des Moines (67505)
Rates: $60-$78
(620) 663-4444
(800) 528-1234
(800) 530-5426

COMFORT INN
1621 Super Plaza (67501)
Rates: $59-$99
(620) 663-7822
(800) 424-6423

ECONO LODGE
15 W 4th Ave (67501)
Rates: $49-$89
(620) 663-1211
(800) 424-6423

HOLIDAY INN EXPRESS HOTEL
1601 Super Plaza (67501)
Rates: $65-$90
(620) 669-5200
(800) 465-4329

MICROTEL INN
1420 N Lorraine St (67501)
Rates: $61-$89
(620) 665-3700
(888) 771-7171

PLAZA HOTEL
1400 N Lorraine St (67501)
Rates: $55-$125
(620) 669-9311
(800) 362-5018

SUPER 8 MOTEL
1315 E 11th Ave (67501)
Rates: $45-$70
(620) 662-6394
(800) 800-8000

TRAILS WEST MOTEL
207 S Main (67501)
Rates: $30-$149
(620) 662-0268
(800) 662-0277

INDEPENDENCE

APPLETREE INN
201 N 8th St (67301)
Rates: $66-$76
(620) 331-5500

GLENDIFF FARM B&B & SPA
448 Glendiff Rd (67301)
Rates: $79-$189
(620) 331-1277
(877) 334-1277

KNIGHTS INN
3222 W Main St (67301)
Rates: $39-$69
(620) 331-7300
(800) 843-5644

MICROTEL INN
2917 W Main St (67301)
Rates: $57-$75
(620) 331-0088
(888) 771-7171

IOLA

BEST WESTERN INN
1315 N State (66749)
Rates: $48-$58
(620) 365-5161
(800) 528-1234
(800) 769-0007

JUNCTION CITY

BEST WESTERN J.C. INN
604 E Chestnut St (66441)
Rates: $59-$89
(785) 210-1212
(800) 528-1234

COURTYARD BY MARRIOTT
310 Hammons Dr (66441)
Rates: $94
(785) 210-1500
(866) 211-4607

DAYS INN
1024 S Washington St (66441)
Rates: $55-$75
(785) 762-2727
(800) 329-7466

DREAMLAND MOTEL
520 E Flint Hills Blvd (66441)
Rates: $26-$36
(785) 238-1108

ECONO LODGE
211 E Flint Hills Blvd (66441)
Rates: $30-$80
(785) 238-8181
(800) 424-4777

GOLDEN WHEAT BUDGET HOST
820 S Washington St (66441)
Rates: $25-$75
(785) 238-5106

HOLIDAY INN EXPRESS
120 N East St (66441)
Rates: $55-$110
(785) 762-4200
(800) 465-4329

MOTEL 6
1931 Lacy Dr (66441)
Rates: $42-$55
(785) 762-2215
(800) 466-8356

RAMADA LTD
1133 S Washington St (66441)
Rates: $39-$79
(785) 238-1141
(800) 272-6232

RED CARPET JAYHAWK INN
110 E Flint Hlls Blvd (66441)
Rates: $40-$75
(785) 238-5188

SUPER 8 MOTEL
1001 E 6th (66441)
Rates: $39-$68
(785) 238-8108
(800) 800-8000

KANSAS CITY

BEST WESTERN INN
501 Southwest Blvd (66103)
Rates: $89-$99
(913) 677-3060
(800) 528-1234
(800) 368-1741

COMFORT INN
234 N 78th St (66112)
Rates: $69-$250
(913) 299-5555
(800) 424-6423

HOLTZE EXEC. VILLAGE
11400 College Blvd (66112)
Rates: $89-$159
(913) 3448100
(800) 446-5893

MICROTEL INN & SUITES/SPEEDWAY
7721 Elizabeth St (66112)
Rates: $49-$106
(913) 334-3028
(888) 771-7171

KINGMAN

BUDGET HOST
1113 Hwy 54 E (67068)
Rates: $35-$60
(620) 532-3118

KOWA

GUEST LODGE
505 Miller (67070)
Rates: $38-$45
(620) 825-4431

LANSING

CONDOTELS SUITES
801 W Eisenhower Rd (66043)
Rates: $73-$199
(913) 727-6590

ECONO LODGE
504 N Main St (66043)
Rates: $45-$75
(913) 727-2777
(800) 424-6423

HOLIDAY INN EXPRESS HOTEL
120 Express Dr (66043)
Rates: $71-$80
(913) 250-1000
(800) 465-4329

LARNED

BEST WESTERN TOWNSMAN INN
123 E 14th St (67550)
Rates: $45-$60
(620) 285-3114
(800) 528-1234
(800) 399-3114

COUNTRY INN MOTEL
135 E 14th St (67550)
Rates: $26-$45
(620) 285-3216

LAWRENCE

BEST VALUE INN
730 Iowa St (66046)
Rates: $54-$99
(785) 841-6500

BEST WESTERN LAWRENCE
2309 Iowa St (66046)
Rates: $62-$99
(785) 843-9100
(800) 528-1234
(800) 235-7997

BISMARK INN
1130 N 3rd St (66046)
Rates: $45-$70
(785) 749-4040
(800) 665-7466

DAYS INN
2309 Iowa St (66046)
Rates: $54-$149
(785) 843-9100
(800) 329-7466

ELDRIDGE HOTEL
701 Massachusetts (66046)
Rates: $79-$139
(785) 749-5011
(800) 527-0909

QUALITY INN
801 N Iowa St (66049)
Rates: $59-$130
(785) 842-5100
(800) 424-6423

RAMADA INN
2222 W 6th St (66049)
Rates: $58-$80
(785) 842-7030
(800) 272-6232

SPRINGHILL SUITES BY MARRIOTT
1 Riverfront Plaza (66049)
Rates: $59-$79
(785) 841-2700
(888) 287-9400

SUPER 8 MOTEL
515 McDonald Dr (66049)
Rates: $45-$78
(785) 842-5721
(800) 800-8000

WESTMINSTER INN & SUITES
2525 W 6th St (66049)
Rates: $49-$79
(785) 841-8410
(888) 937-8646

LEAVENWORTH

DAYS INN
3211 S 4th St (66048)
Rates: $45-$75
(913) 651-6000
(800) 329-7466

RAMADA INN
101 S 3rd St (66048)
Rates: $50-$76
(913) 651-5500
(800) 272-6232

SUPER 8 MOTEL
303 Montana Ct (66048)
Rates: $50-$128
(913) 682-0744
(800) 800-8000

LENEXA

LA QUINTA INN
9461 Lenexa Dr (66215)
Rates: $50-$90
(913) 492-5500
(800) 687-6667

MOTEL 6
9725 Lenexa Dr (66215)
Rates: $36-$46
(913) 541-8558
(800) 466-8356

SUPER 8 MOTEL
9601 Westgate St (66215)
Rates: $49-$65
(913) 888-8899
(800) 800-8000

WELLESLEY INN
8015 Lenaxa Dr (66215)
Rates: $49-$79
(913) 894-5550
(800) 444-8888

LIBERAL

BEST WESTERN LAFONDA MOTEL
229 W Pancake Blvd (67901)
Rates: $43-$60
(620) 624-5601
(800) 528-1234
(800) 550-3111

CIMARRON INN
564 E Pancake Blvd (67901)
Rates: $40-$45
(620) 624-6203

GATEWAY INN
720 E Hwy 54 (67901)
Rates: $44-$72
(620) 624-0242
(800) 833-3391

LIBERAL INN
603 E Pancake Blvd (67901)
Rates: $45-$75
(620) 624-7254
(800) 458-4667

LIBERAL LODGE
405 E Hwy 54 (67901)
Rates: $48-$76
(620) 624-7113

SOUTHWIND INN
619 E Hwy 54 (67901)
Rates: $28-$42
(620) 624-6236

WESTERN HO MOTEL
764 E Hwy 54 (67901)
Rates: $33-$45
(316) 624-1921

LINDSBORG

CORONADO MOTEL & RV
305 N Harrison (67456)
Rates: $36-$66
(785) 227-3943
(800) 747-2793

VIKING MOTEL
446 Harrison (67456)
Rates: $42-$62
(785) 227-3336

LONGTON

SILVER BELL MOTEL
W Hwy 160 (67352)
Rates: $40-$60
(620) 642-6145

LYONS

LYONS INN
817 W Main (67554)
Rates: $45-$55
(620) 257-5185

WAGON WHEEL INN
819 E Hwy 56 (67554)
Rates: $32-$65
(620) 257-2388

MANHATTAN

COMFORT INN
150 E Poyntz Ave
(66502)
Rates: $55-$145
(785) 770-8000
(800) 424-6423

HAMPTON INN
501 E Poyntz Ave
(66502)
Rates: $65-$70
(785) 539-5000
(800) 426-7866

HOLIDAY INN-HOLIDOME
530 Richards Dr
(66502)
Rates: $69-$109
(785) 539-5311
(800) 465-4329

MOTEL 6
510 Tuttle Creek
Blvd (66502)
Rates: $35-$52
(785) 537-1022
(800) 466-8356

RAMADA PLAZA HOTEL
1641 Anderson
Ave (66502)
Rates: $78-$150
(785) 539-7531
(800) 272-6232

MANKATO

DREAMLINER MOTEL
RR 2, Box 3,
Hwy 36 (66956)
Rates: $26-$37
(785) 378-3107

MARION

COUNTRY INN MOTEL
1305 E Main St
(66861)
Rates: $29-$52
(620) 382-2147

MARYSVILLE

BEST WESTERN SURF MOTEL
2105 Center Rd
(66508)
Rates: $39-$64
(785) 562-2354
(800) 528-1234

OAK TREE INN
1127 Pony Express
Hwy (66508)
Rates: $49-$65
(785) 562-1234
(888) 456-8733

SUPER 8 MOTEL
1155 Pony Express
Rd (66508)
Rates: $50-$70
(785) 562-5588
(800) 800-8000

MCPHERSON

BEST WESTERN HOLIDAY MANOR
2211 E Kansas Ave
(67460)
Rates: $54-$77
(620) 241-5343
(800) 528-1234
(888) 841-0038

RED COACH INN
2111 E Kansas Ave
(67460)
Rates: $49-$99
(620) 241-6960
(800) 362-0072

SUPER 8 MOTEL
2110 E Kansas
(67460)
Rates: $52-$72
(620) 241-8881
(800) 800-8000

WHEAT STATE MOTEL
1137 W Kansas
Ave (67460)
Rates: $33-$58
(620) 241-6981
(800) 241-6331

MEADE

DALTON'S BEDPOST MOTEL
519 Carthage
(67864)
Rates: $38-$44
(620) 873-2131

MEDICINE LODGE

BUDGET HOST INN
401 W Fowler
(67104)
Rates: $27-$57
(620) 886-5673

MERRIAM

COMFORT INN
6401 E Frontage
Rd (66202)
Rates: $55-$100
(913) 262-2622
(800) 424-6423

DRURY INN
9009 Shawnee
Mission Pkwy
(66202)
Rates: $60-$100
(913) 236-9200
(800) 378-7946

HOMESTEAD STUDIO SUITES HOTEL
6451 E Frontage
Rd (66202)
Rates: $39-$99
(913) 236-6006

MINNEAPOLIS

ROCK CITY MOTEL
849 Laurel (67467)
Rates: $30-$60
(786) 392-2165
(800) 536-3922

NEODESHA

NEODESHA INN
Rt 2, Box 326 A
(66757)
Rates: $32-$70
(620) 325-2647

NESS CITY

DERRICK INN
Hwy 96 E (67560)
Rates: $36-$85
(913) 798-3617
(800) 561-3409

NEWTON

BEST VALUE INN
1620 E 2nd St
(67114)
Rates: $45-$70
(316) 283-7611

BEST WESTERN RED COACH INN
1301 E 1st St
(67114)
Rates: $44-$109
(316) 283-9120
(800) 777-9120

DAYS INN
105 Manchester
(67114)
Rates: $53-$89
(316) 283-3300
(800) 329-7466

FIRST INTERSTATE INN
1515 E 1st St
(67114)
Rates: $36-$49
(316) 283-8850
(800) 462-4667

NORTON

HILLCREST MOTEL
606 W Holme
(67654)
Rates: $33-$50
(785) 877-3343
(800) 444-8773

R AND M MOTEL
309 E Holme
(67654)
Rates: $30-$32
(785) 877-3541
(800) 848-3541

ROSE OF SHARON B&B
603 E Main (67654)
Rates: $50-$80
(785) 877-3010

OAKLEY

BEST WESTERN GOLDEN PLAINS MOTEL
3506 US 40 (67748)
Rates: $49-$65
(785) 672-3254
(800) 528-1234

FIRST INTERSTATE INN
I-70 & Hwy 40
(67748)
Rates: $34-$49
(785) 672-3203
(800) 462-4667

FIRST TRAVEL INN
708 Center Ave
(67748)
Rates: $33-$60
(785) 672-3226
(800) 994-4667

KANSAS KOUNTRY INN
3538 US 40 (67748)
Rates: $45-$80
(785) 672-3131
(800) 211-6917

OBERLIN

FRONTIER MOTEL
207 E Frontier
Pkwy (67749)
Rates: $35-$49
(785) 475-2203

OBERLIN INN
402 W Frontier
Pkwy (67749)
Rates: $25-$40
(785) 475-2263

OLATHE

DAYS INN
211 Rawhide Dr
(66061)
Rates: $49-$79
(9130 782-4343
(800) 329-7466

RESIDENCE INN BY MARRIOTT
12215 S Strang
Line Rd (66061)
Rates: $79-$179
(913) 829-6700
(800) 331-3131

SLEEP INN
20662 W 151st St
(66061)
Rates: $49-$130
(913) 390-9500
(800) 424-6423

OTTAWA

DAYS INN
1641 S Main
(66067)
Rates: $40-$150
(785) 242-4842
(800) 329-7466

ECONO LODGE
2331 S Cedar Rd
(66067)
Rates: $40-$80
(785) 242-3400
(800) 424-6423

HOLIDAY INN EXPRESS
606 E 23rd St
(66067)
Rates: n/a
(785) 242-2224
(800) 465-4329

SUPER 8 MOTEL
2315 S Oak (66067)
Rates: $50-$65
(785) 242-5551
(800) 800-8000

TRAVELODGE
2209 S Princeton
Rd (66067)
Rates: $44-$69
(785) 242-7999
(800) 578-7878
(888) 540-4024

AREA CODES - If the local number doesn't connect, check for a new area code.

VILLAGE INN MOTEL
2520 S Main
(66067)
Rates: $35-$55
(785) 242-5512

OVERBROOK

PINEMOORE INN
RR 1, Box 44
(66524)
Rates: $60
(913) 453-2304

OVERLAND PARK

AMERISUITES CONVENTION CENTER
5001 W 110th St
(66202)
Rates: $49-$149
(913) 491-9002
(800) 747-8483

AMERISUITS METCALF
6801 W 112th St
(66202)
Rates: $59-$129
(913) 451-2553
(800) 833-1516

CANDLEWOOD SUITES
11001 Oakmont
(66202)
Rates: $49-$119
(913) 469-5557
(888) 226-3539

CHASE SUITE HOTEL BY WOODFIN
6300 W 110th St
(66202)
Rates: $79-$199
(913) 491-3333
(888) 433-9765

CLUBHOUSE INN
10610 Marty
(66202)
Rates: $59-$109
(913) 648-5555
(800) 258-2466

DRURY INN
10963 Metcalf
(66210)
Rates: $60-$120
(913) 345-1500
(800) 379-7946

HOLTZE EXECUTIVE VILLAGE
11400 College
Blvd (66210)
Rates: $82-$165
(913) 344-8110
(888) 446-5893

HOMESTEAD VILLAGE
5401 W 110th St
(66210)
Rates: $49-$75
(913) 661-7111
(888) 782-1473

MICROTEL INN
8750 Ballentine
(66210)
Rates: $45-$79
(913) 541-2664
(888) 771-7171

OVERLAND PARK INN
7200 W 107th St
(66211)
Rates: $76-$92
(913) 648-7858

PEAR TREE INN
10951 Metcalf
(66202)
Rates: $54-$84
(913) 451-0200
(800) 282-8733

RED ROOF INN
6800 W 108th St
(66211)
Rates: $50-$60
(913) 341-0100
(800) 843-7663

RESIDENCE INN BY MARRIOTT
12010 Blue Valley
Pkwy (66202)
Rates: $79-$169
(913) 491-4444
(800) 331-3131

SUPER 8 MOTEL
10750 Barkley St
(66210)
Rates: $49-$60
(913) 341-4440
(800) 800-8000

WELLESLEY INN
7201 W 106th St
(66211)
Rates: $49-$109
(913) 642-2299
(800) 444-8888

WHITE HAVEN MOTOR LODGE
8039 Metcalf Ave
(66204)
Rates: $47-$89
(913) 649-8200
(800) 752-2892

PARK CITY

SUPER 8 MOTEL
6075 Air Cap Dr
(67219)
Rates: $45-$62
(316) 744-2071
(800) 800-8000

PARSONS

BEST WESTERN PARSONS INN
101 E Main St
(67357)
Rates: $59-$99
(620) 423-0303
(800) 528-1234

SUPER 8 MOTEL
229 E Main St
(67357)
Rates: $55-$80
(620) 421-8000
(800) 800-8000

TOWNSMAN MOTEL
1830 Hwy 59
(67357)
Rates: $35-$49
(620) 421-6990

PEABODY

JONES SHEEP FARM B&B
1556 E 59th
(66866)
Rates: $55
(620) 983-2815

PHILLIPSBURG

COTTONWOOD INN
1200 State St
(67661)
Rates: $50-$100
(785) 543-2125
(800) 466-7332

PRATT

BEST WESTERN HILLCREST MOTEL
1336 E 1st St
(67124)
Rates: $41-$68
(620) 672-6407
(800) 528-1234
(800) 336-2279

DAYS INN
1901 E First St
(67124)
Rates: $40-$85
(620) 672-9465
(800) 329-7466

ECONOMY INN
1401 E 1st St
(67124)
Rates: $28-$46
(620) 672-5588

EVERGREEN INN
20001 W Hwy 54
(67124)
Rates: $30-$46
(620) 672-6431

HOLIDAY INN EXPRESS
1401 W Hwy 54
(67124)
Rates: $79-$99
(620) 672-9433
(800) 465-4329

SUPER 8 MOTEL
1906 E 1st St
(67124)
Rates: $40-$53
(620) 672-5945
(800) 800-8000

REXFORD

SHEPHERD'S STAFF CONF/ RETREAT CENTER
315 Main St
(67753)
Rates: $45-$55
(785) 687-2565
(888) 687-2565

RUSSELL

AMERICINN LODGE & SUITES
1430 S Fossil St
(67665)
Rates: $66-$130
(785) 483-4200
(800) 634-3444

DAYS INN
1225 S Fossil St
(67665)
Rates: $44-$71
(785) 483-6660
(800) 329-7466

PRIME 8 INN
2499 E Hwy 40
(67665)
Rates: $40
(785) 483-2200

RUSSELL'S INN
901 S Fossil St
(67665)
Rates: $44-$60
(785) 483-2107

SUPER 8 MOTEL
1405 S Fossil St
(67665)
Rates: $57-$71
(785) 483-2488
(800) 800-8000

SABETHA

SABETHA COUN- TRY INN
1423 S 75 Hwy
(66534)
Rates: $46-$56
(785) 284-2300

ST. JOHN

COUNTRY INN MOTEL
RR 2, Box 135
(67576)
Rates: $24-$37
(316) 549-6604

SALINA

BAYMONT INN
745 Schilling Rd
(67401)
Rates: $50-$90
(785) 493-9800
(877) 229-6668

BEST INN
429 W Diamond
Dr (67401)
Rates: $45-$60
(785) 825-2500
(800) 237-8466

BEST WESTERN MID-AMERICA INN
1846 N 9th St
(67401)
Rates: $50-$72
(785) 827-0356
(800) 528-1234

CANDLEWOOD SUITES HOTEL
2650 Planet Ave
(67401)
Rates: $59-$109
(785) 823-6939
(888) 226-3539

AREA CODES - If the local number doesn't connect, check for a new area code.

COMFORT INN
1820 W Crawford
St (67401)
Rates: $59-$95
(785) 826-1711
(800) 424-6423

FIRST INN GOLD
2403 S 9th St
(67401)
Rates: $40-$60
(785) 827-5511
(800) 462-4667

HOLIDAY INN
1616 W Crawford
St (67401)
Rates: $58-$62
(785) 823-1739
(800) 465-4329

HOLIDAY INN EXPRESS HOTEL
201 E Diamond Dr
(67401)
Rates: $57-$125
(785) 827-9000
(800) 465-4329

MOTEL 6
635 W Diamond
Dr (67401)
Rates: $35-$46
(785) 827-8397
(800) 466-8356

RED COACH INN
2110 W Crawford
St (67401)
Rates: $55-$125
(785) 825-2111

SUPER 8 I-70 MOTEL
120 E Diamond Dr
(67401)
Rates: $45-$65
(785) 823-8808
(800) 800-8000

TRAVELODGE
1949 N 9th St
(67401)
Rates: $45-$65
(785) 825-8211
(800) 578-7878

VAGABOND MOTEL
217 S Broadway
(67401)
Rates: $28-$50
(785) 825-7265
(888) 203-1413

VILLAGE INN
453 S Broadway
(67401)
Rates: $32-$49
(785) 827-4040

SCOTT CITY

96 MOTEL
503 E 5th (67871)
Rates: $33-$47
(620) 872-5560

SENECA

EARSON'S VILLAGE MOTEL
810 North St
(66538)
Rates: $33-$48
(785) 336-3773
(888) 433-2159

SHARON SPRINGS

HEYL'S TRAVELER MOTEL
Jct Hwy 40/27
(67758)
Rates: $32-$50
(785) 852-4293

OAK TREE INN
Jct Hwy 40/27
(67758)
Rates: $59-$75
(785) 852-4664
(888) 456-8733

TUMBLEWEED MOTEL
Jct Hwy 40/27
(67758)
Rates: $27-$48
(785) 852-4223

STAFFORD

HENDERSON HOUSE B&B/ RETREAT CTR
201 N Green
(67578)
Rates: $45-$60
(620) 234-6048
(800) 888-1417

STOCKTON

AMERICANA MOTEL & OUTDOORSMANS LODGE
521 N 1st St
(67669)
Rates: $25-$50
(785) 425-6772
(877) 698-1168

MIDWEST MOTEL
1401 E Main
(67669)
Rates: $29-$47
(785) 425-6706

UNDER THE SON'S B&B
1440 18th Terr
(67669)
Rates: $65-$75
(785) 425-6605

TOPEKA

AMERISUITES
6021 SW 6th Ave
(66615)
Rates: $109
(785) 273-0066
(800) 833-1516

BEST WESTERN CANDLELIGHT INN
2831 SW Fairlawn
Rd (66614)
Rates $49-$110
(785) 272-9550
(800) 528-1234
(800) 223-8892

BEST WESTERN MEADOW ACRES MOTEL
2950 S Topeka
Blvd (66611)
Rates: $48-$78
(785) 267-1681
(800) 528-1234
(800) 432-3949

BEST WESTERN TOPEKA INN
700 SW Fairlawn
St (66606)
Rates; $49-$109
(785) 228-2223
(800) 528-1234
(877) 986-7352

CAPITAL CENTER INN
914 SE Madison
St (66607)
Rates: $40-$80
(785) 232-7721
(888) 421-9020

CAPITAL PLAZA HOTEL
1717 SW Topeka
Blvd (66612)
Rates: $79-$249
(785) 431-7200
(800) 579-7937

CLUBHOUSE INN
924 SW
Henderson
(66615)
Rates: $69-$94
(785) 273-8888
(800) CLUB-INN

COMFORT INN
1518 SW
Wanamaker Rd
(66604)
Rates: $60-$125
(785) 273-5365
(800) 424-6423

COUNTRY INN
6020 SW 10th
(66615)
Rates: $79-$99
(785) 478-9800
(800) 456-4000

DAYS INN
1510 SW
Wanamaker Rd
(66604)
Rates: $45-$89
(785) 272-8538
(800) 329-7466

LIPPINCOTT'S FYSHE HOUSE B&B
8720 W 85th St
(66609)
Rates: $60-$80
(785) 256-2772
(877) 256-3474

MOTEL 6
709 Fairlawn Rd
(66608)
Rates: $35-$42
(785) 272-8283
(800) 466-8356

MOTEL 6
1224 Wanamaker
Rd SW (66604)
Rates: $37-$52
(785) 273-9888
(800) 466-8356

QUALITY INN
1240 SW
Wanamaker Rd
(66604)
Rates: $50-$140
(785) 273-6969
(800) 424-6423

RAMADA INN
420 SE 6th St
(66607)
Rates: $65-$109
(785) 234-5400
(800) 272-6232

RESIDENCE INN BY MARRIOTT
1620 SW Westport
Dr (66604)
Rates: $119-$179
(785) 271-8903
(800) 331-3131

SENATE LUXURY SUITES
900 SW Tyler
(66612)
Rates: $70-$175
(785) 233-5050
(800) 488-3188

ULYSSES

PEDDLERS INN
2093 W Oklahoma
St (67880)
Rates: $36-$50
(620) 356-4021

SANDS MOTEL
622 W Oklahoma
St (67880)
Rates: $35-$40
(620) 356-1404

SINGLE TREE INN
2033 W Oklahoma
St (67880)
Rates: $65-$96
(620) 356-1500
(888) 232-8784

WAGON BED INN
1101 E Oklahoma
St (67880)
Rates: $40-$50
(620) 356-3111

WAKEENEY

BRYANT MOTEL
219 Barclay
(67672)
Rates: $26-$50
(785) 743-5202

BUDGET HOST TRAVEL INN
668 S 13th St
(67672)
Rates: $35-$60
(785) 743-2121
(800) 283-4678

BUTTERFIELD TRAIL BUNKHOUSE B&B
RR 2, Box 86
(67672)
Rates: $40-$60
(785) 743-2322

AREA CODES - If the local number doesn't connect, check for a new area code.

ECONO LODGE-WHEEL MOTEL
705 S 2nd St
(67672)
Rates: $39-$64
(785) 743-5505
(800) 424-6423

KANSAS KOUNTRY INN
223 S 1st St
(67672)
Rates: $32-$50
(785) 743-2129

WAMEGO
SIMMER MOTEL
1215 Hwy 24 W
(66547)
Rates: $37-$70
(785) 456-2304

SUPER 8 MOTEL
Hwy 24 & Lilac St
(66547)
Rates: $48-$60
(785) 458-8888
(800) 800-8000

WASHINGTON
K-MOTEL
112 W 7th (66968)
Rates: $28-$35
(785) 325-2100

WASHINGTON MOTEL
310 W 7th (66968)
Rates: $38-$48
(785) 325-2281

WELLINGTON
OAK TREE INN
1177 Hwy 160 E
(67152)
Rates: $59-$69
(620) 326-8191

WICHITA
BEST WESTERN AIRPORT INN
6815 W Kellogg
(67209)
Rates: $79-$175
(316) 942-5600
(800) 528-1234
(888) 942-5666

BEST WESTERN GOVERNORS INN
4742 S Emporia St
(67216)
Rates: $59-$119
(316) 522-0775
(800) 528-1234
(866) 522-0775

BEST WESTERN WICHITA NORTH/ PARK CITY
915 E 53rd St N
(67219)
Rates: $79-$181
(316) 832-9387
(800) 528-1234

CAMBRIDGE SUITES
711 S Main 67213)
Rates: $89-$145
(316) 263-1061
(800) 946-6200

CANDLEWOOD SUITES-NORTHEAST
3141 N Webb Rd
(67226)
Rates: $39-$85
(316) 634-6070
(888) 226-3539

CLUBHOUSE INN
515 S Webb Rd
(67207)
Rates: $69-$79
(316) 684-1111
(800) CLUB-INN

COMFORT SUITES AIRPORT
658 Westdale
(67209)
Rates: $74-$139
(316) 945-2600
(800) 424-6423

COMFORT INN EAST
9525 E Corporate Hills (67207)
Rates: $50-$85
(316) 686-2844
(800) 424-6423

COMFORT INN SOUTH
4849 S Laura
(67216)
Rates: $55+
(316) 522-1800
(800) 424-6423

DAYS INN
901 E 53rd St N
(67219)
Rates: $53-$72
(316) 832-1131
(800) 329-7466

FOUR POINTS BY SHERATON
5805 W Kellogg
(67209)
Rates: $109
(316) 942-7911
(800) 325-3535

HAMPTON INN
9449 E. Corporate Hills (67207)
Rates: $69-$89
(316) 686-3576
(800) 426-7866

HAWTHORN SUITES AT REFLECTION RIDGE
2405 N Ridge Rd
(67205)
Rates: $81-$101
(316) 729-5700
(800) 527-1133

HOLIDAY INN WICHITA / AIRPORT
5500 W Kellogg
(67209)
Rates: $69-$99
(316) 943-2181
(800) 465-4329
(800) 255-6484

HOLIDAY INN SELECT
549 S Rock Rd
(67207)
Rates: $69-$169
(316) 686-7131
(800) 465-4329
(888) 558-5113

HOLIDAY INN EXPRESS
7824 E 32nd St N
(67226)
Rates: $69-$104
(316) 634-3900
(800) 465-4329

THE INN AT WILLOBEND B&B
3939 Comotara
(67226)
Rates: $89-$109
(316) 636-4032

THE KANSAS INN
1011 N Topeka Ave (67214)
Rates: $55-$58
(316) 269-9999
(888) 539-0123

LA QUINTA INN & SUITES
221 E Kellogg
(67207)
Rates: $99-$179
(316) 269-2090
(800) 687-6667

LA QUINTA INN TOWNE EAST MALL
7700 E Kellogg
(67207)
Rates: $69-$99
(316) 681-2881
(800) 687-6667

MOTEL 6
465 S Webb Rd
(67207)
Rates: $35-$42
(316) 684-6363
(800) 466-8356

MOTEL 6-AIRPORT
5736 W Kellogg
(67209)
Rates: $31-$40
(316) 945-8440
(800) 466-8356

QUALITY INN AIRPORT
600 S Holland
(67209)
Rates: $50-$60
(316) 722-8730
(800) 424-6423

RESIDENCE INN BY MARRIOTT
411 S Webb Rd
(67207)
Rates: $59-$139
(316) 686-7331
(800) 331-3131

SCOTTSMAN INN EAST
465 S Webb Rd
(67207)
Rates: $33-$46
(316) 684-6363
(800) 477-7268

SUPER 8 MOTEL
527 S Webb Rd
(67207)
Rates: $51-$73
(316) 686-3888
(800) 800-8000

TOWNEPLACE SUITES
9444 E 29th St N
(67226)
Rates: $89-$119
(316) 631-3773
(800) 257-3000

WESLEY INN
3343 E Central Ave (67208)
Rates: 68-$78
(316) 858-3343

WINFIELD
COMFORT INN
US 77 at Quail Ridge (67156)
Rates: $63-$155
(316) 221-7529
(800) 424-6423

YATES CENTER
STAR MOTEL
206 S Fry (66783)
Rates: $26-$39
(620) 625-2175

TOWNSMAN MOTEL
609 W Mary
(66783)
Rates: $29-$45
(620) 625-2131

AREA CODES - If the local number doesn't connect, check for a new area code.

KENTUCKY

ALBANY

WISDOM DOCK COTTAGES
Hwy 553 W
(42602)
Rates: $80-$120
(800) 840-8523

WOLF RIVER RESORT CABINS & COTTAGES
Hwy 738 (42602)
Rates: $30-$50
(606) 387-5841

ALLEN

SEASON'S INN
850 KY Rt 1428
(41601)
Rates: $30-$50
(606) 874-2770

ASHLAND

ASHLAND INN
3020 Winchester
Ave (41101)
Rates: $30-$49
(606) 325-0776

BEST WESTERN RIVER CITIES
31 Russell Plaza
Dr (41101)
Rates: $72-$92
(606) 326-0357
(800) 528-1234
(866) 326-9315

DAYS INN
12700 SR 180
(41101)
Rates: $56-$87
(606) 928-3600
(800) 329-7466

DEAN'S INN
539 Summit Rd
(41101)
Rates: $30-$50
(606) 929-9005
(888) 929-9005

KNIGHTS INN
7216 US 60 (41102)
Rates: $38-$48
(606) 928-9501
(800) 843-5644
(800) 497-7560

AUBURN

AUBURN GUEST HOUSE
421 W Main St
(42206)
Rates: n/a
(502) 542-6019

AUGUSTA

JANE'S RIVERVIEW B&B
206 E Riverside Dr
(41002)
Rates: $81-$120
(606) 756-2050

AURORA

CEDAR LANE RESORT COTTAGES
16984 Hwy 68
(42048)
Rates: n/a
(270) 474-8042

EARLY AMERICAN MOTEL
16749 Hwy 68 E
(42048)
Rates: $38-$42
(270) 474-2000

FIN 'N' FEATHER
16695 Hwy 68 E
(42048)
Rates: $30-$50
(270) 474-2351
(800) 486-3961

LAKELAND RESORT
16410 Hwy 68 E
(42048)
Rates: $30-$50
(888) 684-3526

AUSTIN

H & H CABIN RENTALS
Lakeview Rd
(42123)
Rates: $125+
(270) 646-3057

BARBOUR-VILLE

BEST WESTERN WILDERNESS TRAIL INN
US 25-E,
Cumberland Gap
Pkwy (40906)
Rates: $51-$68
(606) 546-8500
(800) 528-1234

BARDSTOWN

BEST WESTERN GENERAL NELSON
411 W Stephen
Foster Ave (40004)
Rates: $59-$79
(502) 348-3977
(800) 225-3977

COMFORT INN
984 Frost Ave
(40004)
Rates: $54-$125
(502) 349-9400
(800) 424-6423

DAYS INN
1875 New Haven
Dr (40004)
Rates: $69-$200
(502) 348-9253
(800) 329-7466

HAMPTON INN
985 Chambers
Blvd (40004)
Rates: $65-$80
(502) 349-0100
(800) 426-7866

OLD BARDSTOWN INN
510 E Stephen
Foster Ave (40004)
Rates: $50-$80
(800) 894-1601

OLD KENTUCKY HOME MOTEL
414 W Stephen
Foster Ave (40004)
Rates: $30-$50
(502) 348-5979
(800) 772-1174

PARKVIEW MOTEL
418 E Stephen
Foster Ave (40004)
Rates: $50-$80
(502) 348-5983
(800) 732-2384

RAMADA INN
523 N 3rd St
(40004)
Rates: $55-$180
(502) 349-0363
(800) 272-6232

BARREN RIVER LAKE

VALLEY ON THE BARREN RETREAT
US 31 E (42156)
Rates: n/a
(502) 646-4672

BEATTYVILLE

LOGO LINDA COTTAGES
850 Black Ridge
Rd (41311)
Rates: $80-$120
(606) 464-2876

THE OLD SCHOOL HOUSE BED & BREAKFST
124 Mt. Paran Rd
(41311)
Rates: $51-$80
(606) 464-9991

TINCHER'S MOTEL
1182 Hwy 11 S
(41311)
Rates: $30-$50
(606) 464-9231

BEAVER DAM

DAYS INN
1750 US Hwy 231
(42320)
Rates: $54-$90
(270) 274-0851
(800) 329-7466

VELLER MOTEL
130 Veller Dr
(42320)
Rates: $50-$80
(270) 274-3431

BENHAM

BENHAM SCHOOL HOUSE INN
100 Central Ave
(40807)
Rates: $50-$80
(800) 231-0627

BENTON

HESTER'S SPOT IN THE SUN COTTAGES
350 Hester Rd
(42025)
Rates: $80-$120
(270) 354-8280
(800) 455-7481

HOLIDAY INN EXPRESS
173 Carroll Rd
(42025)
Rates: $80-$140
(270) 527-5300
(800) 465-4329

KING CREEK RESORT & MARINA
972 King Creek Rd
(42025)
Rates: $475-$850/Weekly
(270) 354-8268
(800) 733-6710

SHAMROCK MOTEL
806 Main (42025)
Rates: $30-$50
(270) 527-1341

SPORTSMAN'S LODGE
12710 US 68 E
(42025)
Rates: $30-$50
(270) 354-8333
(800) 733-6716

BEREA

BOONE TAVERN HOTEL-BEREA COLLEGE
100 Main St
(40403)
Rates: $138
(859) 985-3700

AREA CODES - If the local number doesn't connect, check for a new area code.

COMFORT INN
1003 Paint Lick Rd
(40403)
Rates: $50-$100
(859) 985-5500
(800) 424-6423

DAYS INN
1029 Cooper Dr
(40403)
Rates: $39-$69
(859) 986-7373
(800) 366-9358

ECONO LODGE
1010 Paint Lick Rd
(40403)
Rates: $35-$55
(859) 986-9324
(800) 424-6423

HOLIDAY MOTEL
100 Jane St (40403)
Rates: $45-$55
(859) 986-9311

KNIGHTS INN
715 Chestnut St
(40403)
Rates: $50-$80
(859) 986-2384
(800) 843-5644

SUPER 8 MOTEL
196 Prince Royal
Dr (40403)
Rates: $39-$60
(859) 986-8426
(800) 800-8000

BOWLING GREEN

ALPINE LODGE B&B
5310 Morgantown
Rd (42104)
Rates: $81-$120
(270) 843-4846

BAYMONT INN
165 Three Springs
Rd (42104)
Rates: $49-$99
(270) 843-3200
(877) 229-6668

BEST VALUE INN
250 Cumberland
Trace Rd (42103)
Rates: $40-$70
(270) 781-9594

CONTINENTAL INN
700 Interstate Dr
(42101)
Rates: $45-$65
(270) 781-5200

COUNTRY HEARTH INN
396 Corvette Dr
(42103)
Rates: $50-$85
(270) 783-4443
(888) 294-6491

DAYS INN
4617 Scottsville
Rd (42104)
Rates: $42-$93
(270) 781-6470
(800) 329-7466

DRURY INN
3250 Scottsville
Rd (42103)
Rates: $62-$82
(270) 842-7100
(800) 378-7946

HOLIDAY INN-UNIVERSITY PLAZA HOTEL
1021 Wilkenson
Trace (42104)
Rates: $81-$120
(270) 745-0088
(800) 465-4329

MOTEL 6
3139 Scottsville
Rd (42104)
Rates: $31-$42
(270) 843-0140
(800) 466-8356

NEWS INN OF BOWLING GREEN
3160 Scottsville
Rd (42104)
Rates: $42-$65
(270) 781-3460
(800) 443-3701

QUALITY INN
1919 Mel
Browning St
(42104)
Rates: $45-$149
(270) 846-4588
(800) 424-6423

RAMADA INN
4767 Scottsville
Rd (42104)
Rates: $55-$100
(270) 781-3000
(800) 272-6232

RODEWAY INN
3240 Scottsville
Rd (42104)
Rates: $60-$99
(270) 871-1500
(800) 424-6423

TRAVELODGE
1000 Executive
Way (42104)
Rates: $50-$80
(270) 781-6610
(800) 578-7878

VALUE LODGE
I-65 Exit 28
(42104)
Rates: $30-$50
(270) 781-6181

WESTERN HILLS MOTEL
Hwy 231 & 68
(42101)
Rates: $30-$55
(270) 842-5633

BRANDENBURG

OTTER CREEK PARK MOTEL
850 Otter Creek
Park Rd (40108)
Rates: $50-$80
(502) 574-4583

SUPER 8 MOTEL
196 Prince Royal
Dr (40108)
Rates: $30-$50
(800) 800-8000

BROOKS

COMFORT INN
149 Willabrook Dr
(40109)
Rates: $69
(502) 957-8900
(800) 424-6423

BURKESVILLE

RIVERFRONT LODGE MOTEL
305 Keen St
(42717)
Rates: $40-$48
(270) 864-3300

CADIZ

HOLIDAY INN EXPRESS
153 Broadbent
Blvd (42211)
Rates: $64-$85
(270) 522-3700
(800) 465-4329

KNIGHTS INN
5698 Hopkinsville
Rd (42211)
Rates: $35-$60
(270) 522-9395
(800) 843-5644

PARKVIEW COTTAGES
3535 Blue Springs
Road (42211)
Rates: $50-$80
(270) 924-5351

ROUND OAK INN B&B
8534 Canton Rd
(42211)
Rates: $50-$80
(270) 924-1094

SUPER 8 MOTEL
154 Hospitality Ln
(42211)
Rates: $50-$70
(270) 522-7007
(800) 800-8000
(800) 707-0129

WAYSIDE MOTEL
5511 Canton Rd
(42211)
Rates: $30-$50
(270) 924-1181

CALVERT CITY

FOXFIRE MOTOR INN
3457 US 62 (42029)
Rates: $30-$50
(270) 395-7162

KENTUCKY DAM MOTEL
4020 US 62 (42029)
Rates: $30-$50
(270) 395-5633

CAMPBELLS-VILLE

BEST WESTERN LODGE
1400 E Broadway
(42718)
Rayes: $59-$71
(270) 465-7001
(800) 528-1234
(800) 770-0430

HOLIDAY INN EXPRESS
102 Plantation Dr
(42718)
Rates: $69-$129
(270) 465-2727
(800) 465-4329

LUCKY VISTA MOTEL
1409 S Columbia
(42718)
Rates: $30-$50
(800) 649-4692

CAMPTON

CAMPTON PARKWAY INN
205 Quillens
Chapel Service Rd
(41301)
Rates: $50-$80
(606) 668-7072

KATHY'S B&B
163 N Washington
St (41301)
Rates: $50-$80
(606) 668-6658

CARROLLTON

BEST WESTERN EXECUTIVE INN
10 Slumber Ln
(41008)
Rates: $59-$109
(502) 732-8444
(800) 528-1234

SEPPENFELD HOUSE B&B
714 Highland Ave
(41008)
Rates: $81-$120
(502) 732-9134

DAYS INN
61 Inn Rd (41008)
Rates: $59-$99
(502) 732-9301
(800) 329-7466

SUPER 8 MOTEL
130 Slumber Lane
(41008)
Rates: $49-$55
(502) 732-0252
(800) 800-8000

CAVE CITY

BEST WESTERN KENTUCKY INN
1009 Doyle Ave
(42127)
Rates: $29-$75
(270) 773-3161
(800) 528-1234

BUDGET INN
405 N Dixie Hwy
(42127)
Rates: $30-$50
(270) 773-3444

CAVELAND MOTEL
451 N Dixie Hwy
(42127)
Rates: $50-$80
(270) 773-2321

AREA CODES - If the local number doesn't connect, check for a new area code.

COMFORT INN
801 Mammoth
Cave St (42127)
Rates: $30-$130
(270) 773-2030
(800) 424-6423

DAYS INN
822 Mammoth
Cave St (42127)
Rates: $35-$109
(270) 773-2151
(800) 329-7466

HOWARD JOHNSON
1006A Doyle Ave
(42127)
Rates: $50-$80
(800) 321-4245

PARKVIEW MOTEL
3906 Mammoth
Cave Rd (42127)
Rates: $30-$50
(270) 773-3467
(800) 482-2262

QUALITY INN
102 Gardner Ln
(42127)
Rates: $29-$69
(270) 773-3101
(800) 424-6423

RAMADA LTD
807 Mammoth
Cave Rd (42127)
Rates: n/a
(270) 773-3121
(800) 272-6232

ROSE MANOR B&B
204 Duke St
(42127)
Rates: $81-$120
(270) 773-4402

SCOTTISH INN
414 N Dixie Hwy
(42127)
Rates: $30-$50
(270) 773-3118

SUPER 8 MOTEL
799 Mammoth
Cave St (42127)
Rates: $49-$85
(270) 773-2500
(800) 800-8000

CENTRAL CITY
CARONODA MOTEL
606 S 2nd St (42330)
Rates: $30-$50
(270) 754-1320

CENTRAL MOTEL
300 E Everly
Brothers Blvd
(42330)
Rates: $30-$50
(270) 754-2441

CLARKSON
NOLIN LAKE MOTEL
14088 Peonia Rd
(42726)
Rates: $30-$50
(270 242-9914

CLAY CITY
CLAY CITY INN
6031 Winchester
Rd (40312)
Rates: $50-$80
(606) 663-4042

COLUMBIA
DREAMLAND MOTEL
510 Burkesville St
(42728)
Rates: $30-$50
(270) 384-2131

HOLMES BEND MARINA RESORT COTTAGES
5380 Holmes
Bend Rd (42728)
Rates: $125+
(800) 801-8154

CORBIN
BAYMONT INN
174 Adams Rd
(40701)
Rates: $50-$80
(606) 523-9040
(877) 229-6668

BEST VALUE INN
2615 Cumberland
Falls Rd (40701)
Rates: $30-$50
(606) 528-6301

BEST WESTERN CORBIN INN
2630 Cumberland
Falls Rd (40701)
Rates: $45-$(99
(606) 528-2100
(800) 528-1234
(888) 528-2100

DAYS INN
1860 Cumberland
Falls Rd (40701)
Rates: $35-$75
(606) 528-8150
(800) 329-7466

KNIGHTS INN MOTEL
37 Hwy 770
(40701)
Rates: $33-$75
(606) 523-1500
(800) 843-5644

LANDMARK INN
1891 Cumberland
Gap Pkwy (40701)
Rates: $50-$80
(606) 528-7100

MOM & DAD'S PLACE B&B
53 Corinth Rd
(40701)
Rates: $125+
(513) 625-8270

QUALITY INN
264 W
Cumberland Gap
Pky (40701)
Rates: $46-$125
(606) 528-4802
(800) 424-6423

SUPER 8 MOTEL
171 W
Cumberland Gap
Pkwy (40701)
Rates: $39-$61
(606) 528-8888
(800) 800-8000

CORINTH
K & T MOTEL
Hwy 330 & I-75
Exit 144 (41010)
Rates: n/a
(859) 824-4371

MULLINS LOG CABIN
Scaffold Lick Rd
(41010)
Rates: n/a
(888) 392-5077

THREE SPRINGS SUITES
1550 Owenton Rd
(41010)
Rates: $30-$50
(859) 823-2400

COVINGTON
EMBASSY SUITES AT RIVERCENTER
10 E Rivercenter
Blvd (410118
Rates: $139-$179
(859) 261-8400
(800) 362-2779

CUMBERLAND
CUMBERLAND MOTEL
2203 E Main St
(40823)
Rates: $30-$48
(606) 589-2181
(800) 821-5378

CYNTHIANA
EVERGREEN MOTEL
1528 Hwy 27 N
(41031)
Rates: $30-$50
(859) 234-5460

HAWKS NEST B&B
2433 Hwy 32 W
(41031)
Rates: $50-$80
(859) 235-0440

DANVILLE
BEST WESTERN DANVILLE INN
210 Brenda Ave
(40422)
Rates: $59-$99
(859) 236-5525
(866) 485-0229

BRYANTS CAMP MOTEL
Hwy 34 & 3373
(40422)
Rates: n/a
(606) 236-5601

COUNTRY HEARTH INN
US Bypass 127
(40422)
Rates: $50-$80
(888) 443-2784

GWINN ISLAND RESORT
1200 Gwinn
Island Rd (40422)
Rates: n/a
(606)236-4286

HOLIDAY INN EXPRESS
96 Daniel Dr
(40422)
Rates: $59-$65
(859) 236-8600
(800) 465-4329

MORNING GLORY MANOR B&B
244 E Lexington
Ave (40422)
Rates: $81-$120
(859) 236-1888

OFF-BROADWAY TERRACE
US 127 & 150
(40422)
Rates: n/a
(606) 236-7474

ROYALTY'S FISH CAMP COTTAGES
US 68 & Hwy
342N (40422)
Rates: n/a
(606) 748-5459

SUPER 8 MOTEL
3663 S 150 Danville
Bypass (40422)
Rates: $42-$65
(606) 236-8881
(800) 800-8000

THE COTTAGE
2826 Lexington Rd
(40422)
Rates: $81-$120
(859) 236-9642

DAWSON SPRINGS
SPRINGS INN
207 W Arcadia
Ave (42408)
Rates: $30-$50
(270) 797-2029

DRY RIDGE
DRY RIDGE INN
69 Broadway
(41035)
Rates: $30-$50
(859) 824-7005
(800) 837-5150

HOLIDAY INN EXPRESS
1050 Fashion
Ridge Rd (41035)
Rates: $50-$80
(859) 824-7121
(800) 465-4329

MICROTEL INN
79 Blackburn Lane
(41035)
Rates: $50-$79
(859) 824-2000
(888) 771-7171

EDDYVILLE
EDDY CREEK RESORT & MARI-NA
7612 SR 93 S
(42038)
Rates: $74
(270) 388-2271

HOLIDAY HILLS TOWNHOUSES
5631 KY 93 S
(42038)
Rates: $110-$190
(270) 388-7236
(800) 337-8550

JOURNEY'S END B&B
121 Spring Hill Dr
(42038)
Rates: $81-$120
(270) 388-5117

PALISADES RESORT COTTAGES
1564 Palisades Dr
(42038)
Rates: $50-$80
(800) 890-1374

REGENCY INN
616 Tanner Ave
(42038)
Rates: $30-$50
(270) 388-2281

ELIZABETH-TOWN

BEST WESTERN CARDINAL INN
642 E Dixie Ave
(42701)
Rates: $59-$129
(270) 765-6139
(800) 528-1234

COMFORT INN ATRIUM GARDENS
1043 Executive Dr
(42701)
Rates: $69-$129
(270) 769-3030
(800) 424-6423

DAYS INN
2010 N Mulberry
St (42701)
Rates: $49-$79
(270) 769-5522
(800) 329-7466

E-TOWN MOTEL
616 E Dixie Ave
(42701)
Rates: $30-$50
(270) 765-4312

HOLIDAY INN
1058 N Mulberry
St (42701)
Rates: $50-$80
(270) 769-2344
(800) 465-4329

MOTEL 6
1042 N Mulberry
St (42701)
Rates: $35-$44
(270) 769-3102
(800) 466-8356

THE OLDE BETHLEHEM ACADEMY INN
7051 St John Rd
(42701)
Rates: $65-$150
(270) 862-9003

QUALITY INN
2002 N Mulberry
St (42701)
Rates: $69-$99
(270) 765-4166
(800) 424-6423

SUPER 8 MOTEL
2028 N Mulberry
St (42701)
Rates: $45-$99
(270) 737-1088
(800) 800-8000

ERLANGER

BAYMONT INN
1805 Airport
Exchange Blvd
(41018)
Rates: $79-$110
(859) 746-0300
(877) 229-6668

ECONO LODGE
633 Donaldson
Rd (41018)
Rates: $39-$120
(859) 342-5500
(800) 424-6423

RESIDENCE INN BY MARRIOTT AIRPORT
2811 Circleport
Dr (41018)
Rates: $109-$169
(859) 282-7400
(800) 331-3131

FLORENCE

AMERISUITES AIRPORT
300 Meijer Dr
(41042)
Rates: $89-$139
(859) 647-1170
(800) 833-1516

ASHLEY QUARTERS EXTENDED STAY
4880 Houston Rd
(41042)
Rates: $81-$120
(859) 525-9997
(888) 525-9997

BEST WESTERN FLORENCE INN
7821 Commerce
Dr (41042)
Rates: $49-$95
(859) 525-0090
(800) 528-1234

CROSS COUNTRY INN
7810 Commerce
Dr (41042)
Rates: $38-$59
(859) 283-2030

KNIGHTS INN
8049 Dream St
(41042)
Rates: $47-$60
(859) 371-9711
(800) 843-5644
(800) 210-9759

MOTEL 6
7937 Dream St
(41042)
Rates: $29-$48
(859) 283-0909
(800) 466-8356

QUALITY INN
7915 US Hwy 42
(41042)
Rates: $65-$85
(859) 371-4700
(800) 424-6423

RED ROOF INN
7454 Turfway Rd
(41042)
Rates: $45-$70
(859) 647-2700
(800) 843-7663

SUBURBAN EXTENDED STAY HOTEL
8035 Action Blvd
(41042)
Rates: $40-$50
(859) 746-2400

SUPER 8 MOTEL
7928 Dream St
(41042)
Rates: $55-$70
(859) 283-1221
(800) 800-8000

TRAVELODGE
8075 Steilen Dr
(41042)
Rates: $50-$65
(859) 371-0277
(800) 578-7878

WILDWOOD INN
7809 US 42 (41042)
Rates: $50-$80
(800) 758-2335

FORT MITCHELL

HOLIDAY INN
2100 Dixie Hwy
(41011)
Rates: $69-$129
(859) 331-1500
(800) 465-4329

FORT WRIGHT

RAMADA INN
1939 Dixie Hwy
(41011)
Rates: $50-$80
(859) 331-1400
(800) 272-6232

FRANKFORT

BLUEGRASS INN
635 Versailles Rd
(40601)
Rates: $50-$67
(502) 695-1800
(800) 322-1802

HOLIDAY INN CAPITAL PLAZA
405 Wilkinson
Blvd (40601)
Rates: $80-$120
(502) 227-5100
(800) 465-4329

SUPER 8 MOTEL
1225 US Hwy 127
S (40601)
Rates: $50-$70
(502) 875-3220
(800) 800-8000

FRANKLIN

BEST VALUE INN
3811 Nashville Rd
(42134)
Rates: $37-$43
(270) 586-5090

BEST WESTERN
162 Anand Dr
(42134)
Rates: $40-$75
(270) 598-0070
(800) 528-1234

COLLEGE STREET INN B&B
223 S College St
(42134)
Rates: $50-$80
(270) 586-9352

COMFORT INN
3794 Nashville Rd
(42134)
Rates: $39-$80
(270) 586-6100
(800) 424-6423

DAYS INN
103 Trotter Ln
(42134)
Rates: $40-$70
(270) 598-0163
(800) 329-7466

EXECUTIVE INN
3894 Nashville Rd
(42134)
Rates: $50-$80
(270) 586-3291

FULTON

DERBY MOTEL
200 W Highland
Dr (42041)
Rates: $30-$50
(270) 472-2562

GUEST INN
Purchase Pkwy
& US 52 (42041)
Rates: $50-$80
(270) 472-2342

KINGSWAY MOTEL
806 W Highland
Dr (42041)
Rates: $30-$50
(270) 472-3324

GEORGETOWN

DAYS INN
385 Cherry
Blossom Way
(40324)
Rates: $35-$110
(502) 863-5000
(800) 329-7466

KENTUCKY GAYLA CARRIAGE CLASSIC B&B
3329 Cynthiana
(40324)
Rates: $81-$120
(502) 863-5113

AREA CODES - If the local number doesn't connect, check for a new area code.

MOTEL 6
401 Cherry
Blossom Way
(40324)
Rates: $29-$36
(502) 863-1166
(800) 466-8356

SUPER 8 MOTEL
250 Shoney Dr
(40324)
Rates: $40-$63
(502) 863-4888
(800) 800-8000

GILBERTSVILLE
CLOVERLEAF INN
2237 US 62 (42044)
Rates: $30-$50
(800) 465-9326

INN BY THE LAKE
2184 US 62 (42044)
Rates: $50-$80
(270) 362-4278

**MOORS RESORT
& MARINA**
570 Moors Rd
(42044)
Rates: $81-$120
(270) 362-8361
(800) 626-5472

GLASGOW
COMFORT INN
210 Calvary Dr
(42141)
Rates: $57-$87
(270) 651-9009
(800) 424-6423

**HAPPY
VALLEY INN**
500 Happy Valley
Rd (42141)
Rates: $30-$50
(270) 651-5177

TOWNE MOTEL
604 Happy Valley
Rd (42141)
Rates: $30-$50
(270) 651-2169

GRAND RIVERS
**BARKLEY DAM
MOTEL**
1054 Stringtown
(42045)
Rates: $30-$50
(270) 362-4263
(800) 863-9009

**BEST WESTERN
KENTUCKY-
BARKLEY
LAKES INN**
720 Complex Dr
(42045)
Rates: $52-$84
(270) 928-2700
(800) 528-1234
(800) 928-2711

**GREEN TURTLE
BAY RESORT**
263 Green Turtle
Bay Dr (42045)
Rates: $110-$450
(270) 362-8364
(800) 498-0428

MICROTEL INN
1017 Dover Rd
(42045)
Rates: $35-$79
(270) 928-2740
(888) 771-7171
(877) 890-0111

GRAVEL SWITCH
**LOGAN HILL
LODGE**
Hwy 243 (40328)
Rates: n/a
(502) 692-1741

GRAYSON
SUPER 8 MOTEL
125 Super 8 Ln
(41143)
Rates: $39-$89
(606) 474-8811
(800) 800-8000

GREENUP
WRIGHTS MOTEL
505 Hwy 23
(41144)
Rates: $30-$50
(606) 473-7782

GUTHRIE
HOLIDAY MOTEL
10085 Russelville
Rd (42234)
Rates: $30-$50
(270) 483-2509

HARDIN
**CEDAR LANE
RESORT**
16984 Hwy 68E
(42048)
Rates: $30-$50
(270) 474-8042

HARLAN
**HOLIDAY INN
EXPRESS**
2608 S Hwy 421
(40831)
Rates: $69-$79
(606) 573-3385
(800) 465-4329

**MOUNT AIRE
MOTEL**
355 Skidmore Dr
(40831)
Rates: $30-$50
(800) 988-4660

**VALLEY VIEW
LODGE**
P O Box 832
(40831)
Rates: $30-$50
(606) 573-3808

HARNED
**MOUNTAIN
LAUREL LAKE
RESORT
COTTAGES**
US 60 & Hwy 86
(40144)
Rates: $125+
(502) 756-2737
(888) 263-9150

HARRODS-
BURG
BAUER HAUS B&B
362 N College St
(40330)
Rates: $81-$120
(877) 734-6289

**COUNTRY
HEARTH INN**
105 Commercial
Dr (40330)
Rates: $50-$80
(888) 294-6492

**HADDIX POINT
HIDEAWAY**
1840 Paradise
Camp Rd (40330)
Rates: $125+
(859) 748-9451

**ROYALTY'S FISH
CAMP COTTAGES**
US 68 & Hwy 342
(40330)
Rates: n/a
(859) 748-5459

**STONE
MANOR MOTEL**
774 S College St
(40330)
Rates: $50-$80
(859) 734-4371

HAZARD
SUPER 8 MOTEL
125 Village Ln
(41701)
Rates: $50-$80
(800) 800-8000

HEBRON
**RADISSON INN-
CINCINNATI
AIRPORT**
Cincinnati N KY
Airport (41048)
Rates: $115-$129
(859) 371-6166
(800) 333-3333

HENDERSON
RAMADA INN
2044 US 41 N
(42420)
Rates: $63-$69
(270) 826-6600
(800) 272-6232

SUPER 8 MOTEL
2030 Hwy 41 N
(42420)
Rates: $46-$70
(270) 827-5611
(800) 800-8000
(800) 753-1698

HODGENVILLE
**OLD GAIT
FARM B&B**
7281 Bardstown
Rd (42748)
Rates: $80-$120
(87)7 548-7348

HOPKINSVILLE
**BEST WESTERN
INN**
4101 Fort
Campbell Blvd
(42240)
Rates: $69-$79
(270) 886-9000
(800) 528-1234

HOLIDAY INN
2910 Ft. Campell
Blvd (42240)
Rates: $50-$80
(270) 886-4413
(800) 465-4329

HORSE CAVE
**BUDGET
HOST INN**
I-65 & SR 218
(42749)
Rates: $37-$47
(270) 786-2165
(800) 283-4678

HAMPTON INN
750 Flint Ridge
(42749)
Rates: $50-$80
(270) 786-5000
(800) 426-7866

HURSTBOURNE
**DAYS INN-
AIRPORT/FAIR
& EXPO CTR**
9340 Blairwood
Rd (40222)
Rates: $42-$59
(502) 425-8010
(800) 329-7466

DRURY INN
9501 Blairwood
Rd (40222)
Rates: $70-$100
(502) 326-4170
(800) 378-8946

**HOLIDAY INN
EAST**
1325 S
Hurstbourne
Pkwy (40222)
Rates: $80-$120
(502) 426-2600
(800) 465-4329

**RED ROOF INN-
EAST**
9330 Blairwood
Rd (40222)
Rates: $46-$73
(502) 426-7621
(800) 843-7663
(800) 733-7663

**RESIDENCE INN
BY MARRIOTT**
120 Hurstbourne
Pkwy (40222)
Rates: $92-$120
(502) 425-1821
(800) 331-3131

INEZ
SUPER 8 MOTEL
Hwy 40 E (41224)
Rates: $50-$80
(606) 298-7800
(800) 800-8000

AREA CODES - If the local number doesn't connect, check for a new area code.

IRVINE

OAK TREE INN MOTEL
1075 Richmond
Rd (40336)
Rates: $45-$59
(606) 723-2600

IVEL

ALPIKE MOTEL
4963 Hwy 23 S
(41642)
Rates: $30-$50
(606) 874-2560

JACKSON

JACKSON INN
9 Brewers Dr
(41339)
Rates: $50-$80
(606) 666-7551
(800) 521-5271

JAMESTOWN

RIVERSIDE RETREAT COTTAGES
875 Helm Landing
Rd (42629)
Rates: $80-$120
(270) 343-3777

SASSAFRAS HILLS CABIN RENTALS
310 Kaufman Rd
(42629)
Rates: $125+
(270) 343-4667

JEFFERSON TOWN

AMERISUITES
701 S Hurstbourne
Pkwy (40220)
Rates: $79-$129
(502) 426-0119
(800) 833-1516

BEST WESTERN SIGNATURE INN
1301 Kentucky
Mills Dr (40299)
Rates: $49-$104
(502) 267-8100
(800) 528-1234

CLARION HOTEL
9700 Bluegrass
Pkwy (40299)
Rates: $69-$99
(502) 491-4830
(800) 252-7466

COMFORT SUITES
1850 Resource
Way (40299)
Rates: $64-$81
(502) 266-6509
(800) 424-6423

HOLIDAY INN
1325 S
Hurstbourne
Pkwy (40222)
Rates: $79-$119
(502) 426-2600
(800) 465-4329

HOMESTEAD STUDIO SUITES
1650 Alliant Ave
(40299)
Rates: $49-$79
(502) 267-4454
(888) 782-9473

MICROTEL INN
1221 Kentucky
Mills Dr (40299)
Rates: $50-$65
(502) 266-6590

SLEEP INN
1850 Priority Way
(40299)
Rates: $55-$200
(502) 266-6776
(800) 753-3746

SUPER 8 MOTEL
1501 Alliant Ave
(40299)
Rates: $60-$170
(5020) 267-8889
(800) 800-8000

KENLAKE ST. RESORT PARK

EARLY AMERICAN MOTEL
Rt 1 (Hardin 42048)
Rates: $30-$58
(502) 474-2241

KEVIL

WALDON HUNTING LODGE
779 Colvin Lake
(42053)
Rates: $125+
(270) 224-2020

KUTTAWA

BUZZARD ROCK RESORT & MARINA
985 Buzzard Rock
Rd (42055)
Rates: $80-$120
(800) 826-6238

DAYS INN
139 Days Inn Dr
(42055)
Rates: $50-$90
(270) 388-5420
(800) 329-7466

RELAX INN
224 New Circle
(42055)
Rates: $30-$50
(270) 388-2285
(888) 646-2723

SIDS MOTEL
4975 Hwy 62W
(42055)
Rates: n/a
(270) 388-7601

LA CENTER

BEAVER LODGE
6761 Oscar Rd
(42056)
Rates: n/a
(270) 224-2151

LAGRANGE

COMFORT SUITES
1500 E Crystal Dr
(40031)
Rates: $55-$89
(502) 225-4125
(800) 424-6423

LANCASTER

BRYANT'S COTTAGES
850 Branch Camp
Rd (40444)
Rates: $50-$80
(859) 236-5601

LEBANON

COUNTRY HEARTH INN
720 W Main St
(40033)
Rates: $50-$75
(270) 692-4445

LEITCHFIELD

COUNTRYSIDE INN
315 Commerce Dr
(42754)
Rates: $32-$45
(270) 259-4021

HATFIELD INN
769 White St
(42754)
Rates: $58-$99
(270) 259-0464

MOUNTARDIER RESORT COTTAGES
1990 Mountardier
Rd (42754)
Rates: n/a
(270) 286-4069

LEWISPORT

BEST WESTERN HANCOCK INN
9040 Hwy 60 W
(42351)
Rates: $59
(270) 295-3234
(800) 528-1234

LEXINGTON

BRYAN STATION INN
273 E New Circle
(40505)
Rates: n/a
(859) 299-4162

COMFORT SUITES
5531 Athens-
Boonesboro Rd
(40509)
Rates: $50-$95
(859) 263-0777
(800) 424-6423

COMFORT SUITES
3060 Fieldstone
Way (40513)
Rates: $90-$125
(859) 296-4446
(800) 424-6423

CONTINENTAL INN
801 New Circle
NE (40505)
Rates: n/a
(800) 432-9388

DAYS INN-SOUTH
5575 Athens-
Boonesboro Rd
(40509)
Rates: $40-$65
(859) 263-3100
(800) 329-7466

ECONO LODGE SOUTH
5527 Athens-
Boonesboro Rd
(40509)
Rates: $35-$60
(859) 263-5101
(800) 424-6423

HAMPTON INN
2251 Elkhorn Rd
(40505)
Rates: $55-$149
(859) 299-2613
(800) 426-7866

HOLIDAY INN-NORTH
1950 Newtown
Pike (40511)
Rates: $100-$115
(859) 233-0512
(800) 465-4329

HOLIDAY INN-SOUTH
5532 Athens-
Boonesboro Rd
(40509)
Rates: $65-$99
(859) 263-5241
(800) 465-4329

KNIGHTS INN
1935 Stanton Way
(40511)
Rates: $40-$105
(859) 231-0232
(800) 843-5644

LA QUINTA INN
1919 Stanton Way
(40511)
Rates: $99
(859) 231-7551
(800) 687-6667

MARRIOTT'S GRIFFIN GATE RESORT
1800 Newtown
Pike (40511)
Rates: $139-$169
(859) 231-5100
(800) 228-9290

MICROTEL INN
2240 Buena Vista
Rd (40505)
Rates: $36-$71
(859) 299-9600

MOTEL 6
2260 Elkhorn Rd
(40505)
Rates: $36-$46
(859) 293-1431
(800) 466-8356

QUALITY INN NORTHWEST
750 Newtown
Ct (40511)
Rates: $39-$89
(859) 233-0561
(800) 424-6423

AREA CODES - If the local number doesn't connect, check for a new area code.

RADISSON PLAZA HOTEL
369 W Vine St (40507)
Rates: $159-$179
(859) 231-9000
(800) 333-3333

RAMADA INN & CONF CTR
2143 N Broadway (40505)
Rates: $99-$129
(859) 299-1261
(800) 272-6232

RED ROOF INN-N
1980 Haggard Ln (40505)
Rates: $46-$74
(859) 293-2626
(800) 843-7663

RED ROOF INN-SOUTH
2651 Wilhite Dr (40503)
Rates: $44-$82
(859) 277-9400
(800) 843-7663

RED ROOF INN SOUTHEAST
100 Canebrake Dr (40509)
Rates: $40-$65
(859) 543-1877
(800) 843-7663

RESIDENCE INN
2688 Pink Pigeon Pkwy (40509)
Rates: $99-$149
(859) 263-9979
(800) 331-3131

RESIDENCE INN BY MARRIOTT
1080 Newtown Pike (40511)
Rates: $134-$159
(859) 231-6191
(800) 331-3131

SHONEYS INN
2753 Richmond Rd (40509)
Rates: $53-$71
(859) 269-4999
(800) 552-4667

SILVER SPRING FARM B&B
3710 Leestown Rd (40511)
Rates: $125+
(877) 255-1784

SLEEP INN
1920 Plaudet Pl (40509)
Rates: $49-$104
(859) 543-8400
(800) 424-6423
(800) 543-8400

SUPER 8 MOTEL
2351 Buena Vista Rd (40505)
Rates: $48-$72
(859) 299-6241
(800) 800-8000

LIBERTY

ROYAL INN EXPRESS
579 N Wallace Wilkinson Blvd (42539)
Rates: $38-$44
(606) 787-6224

LONDON

BEST WESTERN HARVEST INN
207 W Hwy 80 (40741)
Rates: $38-$60
(606) 864-2222
(800) 528-1234

BUDGET HOST WESTGATE INN
254 W Daniel Boone Pkwy (40741)
Rates: $36-$49
(606) 878-7330
(800) 283-4678

DAYS INN
2035 W 192 Bypass (40741)
Rates: $45-$95
(606) 864-7331
(800) 329-7466

HOLIDAY INN EXPRESS HOTEL
506 Minton Dr (40741)
Rates: $80-$150
(606) 862-0077
(800) 465-4329

PARK INN
400 Gop St (40741)
Rates: $50-$80
(606) 878-7678
(800) 831-3958

RED ROOF INN
110 Melcon Ln (40741)
Rates: $41-$68
(606) 862-8844
(800) 843-7663

SLEEP INN
105 Melcon Hill Dr (40741)
Rates: $45-$89
(606) 877-9700
(800) 424-6423

SUPER 8 MOTEL
285 W Hwy 80 (40741)
Rates: $39-$59
(606) 878-9800
(800) 800-8000

LOUISA

BEST WESTERN VILLAGE INN
117 E Madison St (41230)
Rates: $45-$60
(606) 638-9417
(800) 528-1234

SUPER 8 MOTEL
US 23 & KY 3 (41230)
Rates: $47-$67
(606) 638-7888
(800) 800-8000

LOUISVILLE
(And vicinity)

ALEKSANDER HOUSE B&B
1213 S 1st St (40203)
Rates: $85-$169
(502) 637-4985

1886 HISTORIC ROCKING HORSE MANOR B&B
1022 S 3rd St (40203)
Rates: $80-$120
(888) 467-7322

BEST WESTERN SIGNATURE INN E
1301 Kentucky Mills Dr (40299)
Rates: $75-$89
(502) 267-8100
(800) 528-1234

BRECKENRIDGE INN
2800 Breckenridge Ln (40220)
Rates: $69-$79
(502) 456-5050

CANDLEWOOD SUITES
1367 Gardiner Ln (40213)
Rates: $80-$120
(502) 357-3577
(888) 226-3539

CANDLEWOOD SUITES-EAST
11762 Commonwealth Dr (40299)
Rates: $80-$120
(502) 261-0085
(888) 226-3539

CLARION HOTEL
9700 Bluegrass Pkwy (40299)
Rates: $70-$300
(502) 491-4830
(800) 424-6423

COMFORT SUITES
1850 Resource Way (40299)
Rates: $69-$270
(502) 266-6509
(800) 424-6423

ECONO LODGE
6109 Preston Hwy (40219)
Rates: $40-$50
(502) 966-5445
(800) 424-6423

EXECUTIVE INN HOTEL
978 Phillips Ln (40209)
Rates: $86-$96
(502) 367-6161
(800) 626-2706

EXECUTIVE WEST HOTEL
830 Phillips Ln (40209)
Rates: $81-$125
(502) 367-2251
(800) 626-2708

HAMPTON INN DOWNTOWN
101 E Jefferson St (40202)
Rates: $79-$149
(502) 585-2200
(800) 426-7866

HOLIDAY INN AIRPORT EAST
4004 Gardiner Point Dr (40213)
Rates: $85-$136
(502) 452-6361
(800) 465-4329

HOLIDAY INN SOUTH-AIRPORT
2715 Fern Valley Rd (40213)
Rates: $105-$145
(502) 964-3311
(800) 465-4329

HOLIDAY INN SOUTHWEST
4110 Dixie Hwy (40216)
Rates: $79-$134
(502) 448-2020
(800) 465-4329

THE INN AT JEWISH HOSPITAL
100 E Jefferson (40202)
Rates: $82-$120
(502) 582-2481
(877) 389-6054

LA QUINTA INN
4125 Preston Hwy (40213)
Rates: $79-$99
(502) 368-0007
(800) 687-6667

MOTEL 6-AIRPORT
3200 Kemmons Dr (40218)
Rates: $36-$43
(502) 473-0000
(800) 466-8356

RED ROOF INN-AIRPORT
4704 Preston Hwy (40213)
Rates: $45-$157
(502) 968-0151
(800) 843-7663
(800) 733-7663

RED ROOF INN-SOUTHEAST
3322 Red Roof Inn Pl (40218)
Rates: $50-$83
(502) 456-2993
(800) 843-7663
(800) 733-7663

AREA CODES - If the local number doesn't connect, check for a new area code.

**RESIDENCE INN
BY MARRIOTT**
700 Phillips Ln
(40209)
Rates: $89-$229
(502) 363-8800
(800) 331-3131

**RESIDENCE INN
BY MARRIOTT NE**
3500 Springhurst
Commons Dr
(40241)
Rates: $139-$149
(502) 412-1311
(800) 331-3131

**RESIDENCE INN
EAST**
120 N
Hurstbourne
Pkwy (40222)
Rates: $89-$134
(502) 425-1821
(800) 331-3131

**SEELBACH
HILTON HOTEL**
500 S 4th St
(40202)
Rates: $179-$274
(502) 585-3200
(800) 445-8667

SIGNATURE INN
6515 Signature Dr
(40213)
Rates: $49-$104
(502) 968-4100
(800) 822-5252

SLEEP INN
1850 Priority Way
(40299)
Rates: $59-$195
(502) 266-6776
(800) 424-6423

**SLEEP INN
SIX FLAGS**
3330 Preston Hwy,
Gate #6 (40213)
Rates: $49-$275
(502) 368-9597
(800) 424-6423

**STAYBRIDGE
SUITES**
11711 Gateworth
Way (40299)
Rates: $109-$149
(502) 244-9511
(800) 238-8000
(888) 269-9590

**SUBURBAN
LODGE**
11405 Westport Rd
(40241)
Rates: $30-$50
(800) 951-7829

**THRIFTY
DUTCHMAN
MOTEL**
2905 Fern Valley
Rd (40213)
Rates: $50-$80
(502) 968-8124

**TRAVELODGE
AIRPORT**
3315 Bardstown
Rd (40218)
Rates: $47-$79
(502) 452-1501
(800) 578-7878

MADISONVILLE
BIG SPRING INN
1750 E Center St
(42431)
Rates: $30-$50
(270) 821-8700

DAYS INN
1900 Lantaff Blvd
(42431)
Rates: $60-$139
(270) 821-8620
(800) 329-7466

VALUE LODGE
1117 E Center St
(42431)
Rates: $30-$50
(270) 281-0364

MAMMOTH
CAVE
NATI'L PARK
(Kennels
provided)

**MAMMOTH CAVE
HOTEL &
COTTAGES**
11 Mi W of Jct I-65
& SR 70 (42259)
Rates: $62-$73
(270) 758-2225

MANCHESTER
**ROCKING
CHAIR INN**
300 Hwy 80
(40962)
Rates: $30-$50
(606) 598-5122

MARION
TOBIN TOURTEL
225 Sturgis Rd
(42064)
Rates: $30-$50
(270) 965-5241

MAYFIELD
DAYS INN
1101 W Housman
St (42066)
Rates: $42-$136
(502) 247-3700
(800) 329-7466

SUPER 8 MOTEL
1100 Links Ln
(42066)
Rates: $48-$80
(502) 247-8899
(800) 800-8000

MAYSVILLE
SUPER 8 MOTEL
550 Tucker Dr
(41056)
Rates: $54-$66
(606) 75-8888
(800) 800-8000

MCKEE
**TOWN &
COUNTRY MOTEL**
390 US 421 S
(40447)
Rates: $30-$50
(606) 287-8235

MIDDLESBORO
BEST WESTERN
1623 Cumberland
Ave (40965)
Rates: $46-$53
(606) 248-5630
(800) 528-1234
(877) 787-1313

MIDWAY
**REBEL'S ROOST
B&B AT
DEARBORN FARM**
1234 Weisenberger
Mill Rd (40347)
Rates: n/a
(859) 846-9799

**SCOTTWOOD
B&B**
2004 E Leestown
Rd (40347)
Rates: $80-$120
(877) 477-0778

MONTICELLO
ANCHOR MOTEL
1077 N Main St
(42633)
Rates: $50-$81
(606) 348-8441

TIFFANY INN
2340 E Hwy 90
Bypass (42633)
Rates: $30-$50
(606) 348-9325

MOREHEAD
**BROWNWOOD
B&B AND CABINS**
46 Carey
Cemetery Rd
(40351)
Rates: $50-$80
(606) 784-8799

COMFORT INN
2650 KY 801 N
(40351)
Rates: $55-$109
(606) 780-7378
(800) 424-6423

**GARVIN'S
COUNTRY
VILLAGE**
1100 Hwy 801 S
(40351)
Rates: $30-$50
(606) 784-3554

**HOLIDAY INN
EXPRESS**
110 Toms Dr
(40351)
Rates: $50-$80
(606) 784-5796
(800) 465-4329

**MOUNTAIN
LODGE**
506 Fraley Dr
(40351)
Rates: $30-$50
(606) 783-1555

MORGAN
TOWN
MOTEL 6
1460 S Main St
(42261)
Rates: $39-$49
(270) 526-9481
(800) 466-8356

MORTON'S
GAP
**BEST WESTERN
PENNYRILE INN**
Pennyrile Pkwy,
Exit 37 (42440)
Rates: $59-$79
(270) 258-5201
(800) 528-1234
(888) 298-2115

MOUNT
STERLING
DAYS INN
705 Maysville Rd
(40353)
Rates: $32-$60
(859) 498-4680
(800) 329-7466

RAMADA LTD
115 Stone Trace Dr
(40353)
Rates: $62-$72
(859) 497-9400
(800) 272-6232

SCOTTISH INN
517 Maysville Rd
(40353)
Rates: $26-$35
(859) 498-3424

MOUNT
VERNON
DAYS INN
1630 Richmond
St (40456)
Rates: $45-$95
(606) 256-3300
(800) 329-7466

ECONO LODGE
1375 Richmond
St (40456)
Rates: $37-$71
(606) 256-4621
(800) 424-6423

**KASTLE INN
MOTEL**
Hwy 25 S (40456)
Rates: $46-$60
(606) 256-5156
(800) 965-4366

MURRAY
**AMERICA'S
PARADISE
RESORT**
1024 Paradise Dr
(42071)
Rates: $80-$120
(270) 436-2767

AREA CODES - If the local number doesn't connect, check for a new area code.

DAYS INN
517 S 12th St
(42071)
Rates: $43-$140
(270) 753-6706
(800) 329-7466

MURRAY PLAZA COURT
504 12th St (42071)
Rates: $33-$39
(270) 753-2682

SHONEY'S INN
1503 N 12th St
(42071)
Rates: $50-$80
(270) 753-5353
(800) 222-2222

NANCY

NANCY'S PLACE
131 Everett Lane
Spur (42544)
Rates: n/a
(606) 341-7789

NEW CONCORD

LAKEVIEW COTTAGES & MARINA
165 Lakeview
Cabin Dr (42076)
Rates: $30-$50
(270) 436-5876

MISSING HILLS RESORT COTTAGES
HC Box 215-A
(42076)
Rates: $50-$80
(270) 436-5519

NEWPORT

HANNAFORD SUITES HOTEL
803 E 6th St
(41071)
Rates: $80-$120
(859) 491-9600

NICHOLASVILLE

CEDAR HAVEN FARM COUNTRY HOME
2380 Bethel Rd
(40356)
Rates: $80-$120
(859) 858-3849

ECONO LODGE
2149 Lexington
Pike (40356)
Rates: $59-$74
(859) 887-8712
(800) 424-6423

OAK GROVE

COMFORT INN
201 Auburn St
(42262)
Rates: $58-$99
(270) 439-3311
(800) 424-6423

DAYS INN-FT. CAMPBELL
212 Auburn St
(42262)
Rates: $41-$99
(270) 640-3888
(800) 329-7466

HOLIDAY INN EXPRESS
12759 Ft Campbell
(42262)
Rates: $50-$80
(270) 439-0022
(800) 465-4329

OWENSBORO

DAYS INN
3720 New Hartford
Rd (42301)
Rates: $42-$59
(270) 684-9621
(800) 329-7466

MOTEL 6
4585 Frederica St
(42301)
Rates: $36-$42
(270) 686-8606
(800) 466-8356

RAMADA INN
3136 W 2nd St
(42302)
Rates: $55-$80
(270) 684-3941
(800) 272-6232

SUPER 8 MOTEL
1027 Goetz Dr
(42301)
Rates: $50-$69
(270) 685-3388
(800) 800-8000

OWENTON

ELK CREEK HUNT CLUB
1860 Georgetown
Rd (40359)
Rates: $50-$80
(502) 484-4569

PADUCAH

BAYMONT INN
5300 Old Cairo Rd
(42001)
Rates: $59-$69
(270) 443-4343
(877) 229-6668

BEST INNS OF AMERICA
5001 Hinckleville
Rd (42002)
Rates: $50-$79
(270) 442-3334
(800) 237-8466

COMFORT INN
5106 Old Cairo Rd
(42001)
Rates: $45-$69
(270) 442-1616
(800) 424-6423

DAYS INN
3901 Hinkleville
Rd (42001)
Rates: $40-$75
(270) 442-7500
(800) 329-7466

DRURY INN
3975 Hinkleville
Rd (42001)
Rates: $59-$86
(270) 443-3313
(800) 378-7946

DRURY SUITES HOTEL
2930 James
Sanders Blvd
(42001)
Rates: $81-$100
(270) 441-0024
(800) 325-8300

EXECUTIVE INN RIVERFRONT
1 Executive Blvd
(42001)
Rates: $50-$80
(800) 866-3636

HAMPTON INN
5006 Hinckleville
Rd (42001)
Rates: $61-$79
(270) 442-4500
(800) 426-7866

HICKORY HOUSE MOTOR INN
2504 Bridge St
(42001)
Rates: $30-$50
(270) 442-1601

HISTORIC ELKS HOME B&B
121 N 5th St
(42001)
Rates: $80-$120
(270) 442-1231

HOLIDAY INN EXPRESS
3994 Hinkleville
Rd (42001)
Rates: $105-$115
(270) 442-8874
(800) 465-4329

KNIGHTS INN
1379 Irvin Cobb
Dr (42001)
Rates: $30-$50
(800) 843-5644

MOTEL 6
5120 Hinkleville
Rd (42001)
Rates: $33-$46
(270) 443-3672
(800) 466-8356

PEAR TREE INN
5002 Hinkleville
Rd (42001)
Rates: $47-$65
(270) 444-7200
(800) 282-8733

RED CARPET INN
2701 HC Mathis
Dr (42001)
Rates: $50-$80
(270) 443-5500
(800) 251-1962

RIVER INN PLACE
4050 Clarks River
Rd (42003)
Rates: n/a
(270) 442-3595

TRAVEL INN
1380 Irvin Cobb
Dr (42001)
Rates: $30-$50
(800) 228-5151

TRINITY HILLS FARM B&B INN/SPA RETREAT
10455 Old
Lovelaceville
(42003)
Rates: $80-$120
(800) 488-3998

VILLAGER LODGE
1234 Broadway St
(42001)
Rates: $30-$50
(800) 328-8929

WESTOWNE INN
3901 Hinkleville
Rd (42003)
Rates: n/a
(270) 442-5666
(800) 329-7466

PAINTSVILLE

BUDGET INN EXPRESS
709 S Mayo Trail
(41240)
Rates: $30-$50
(606) 789-5341

DAYS INN
512 S Mayo Trail
(41240)
Rates: $45-$150
(606) 789-3551
(800) 329-7466

PARIS

CROCKETT'S COLONIAL MOTEL
1493 Main St
(40361)
Rates: $30-$50
(859) 987-3250

PARK CITY

PARKLAND MOTEL
2400 Louisville Rd
(42160)
Rates: n/a
(800) 647-2880

PARKERS LAKE

EAGLE FALLS RESORT
W Hwy 90 (42634)
Rates: $50-$80
(888) 318-2658

HOLIDAY MOTOR LODGE
Hwy 90, Box 300
(42634)
Rates: n/a
(606) 376-2732

PIKEVILLE

DANIEL BOONE MOTOR INN
1040 S Mayo Trail
(41501)
Rates: $30-$50
(606) 432-0365
(800) 432-4564

MODERNE VILLA MOTEL
1066 S Mayo Trail
(41501)
Rates: $30-$50
(606) 432-2188

PRESTONSBURG

SUPER 8 MOTEL
80 Shoppers Path
(41653)
Rates: $44-$59
(606) 886-3355
(800) 800-8000

PROSPECT

MELROSE INN & MOTEL
13306 US 42
(40059)
Rates: $36-$60
(502) 228-1136

RADCLIFF

OTTER CREEK PARK MOTEL & CABINS
US 31 W (40160)
Rates: n/a
(502) 583-3577

SUPER 8 MOTEL
395 Redmar Blvd
(40160)
Rates: $50-$70
(502) 352-1888
(800) 800-8000

RICHMOND

DAYS INN
2109 Belmont Dr
(40475)
Rates: $45-$99
(859) 624-5769
(800) 329-7466

ECONO LODGE
230 Eastern
Bypass (40475)
Rates: $35-$55
(859) 623-8813
(800) 424-6423

HOLIDAY INN EXPRESS
1990 Colby Taylor
Dr (40475)
Rates: $50-$80
(859) 624-4055
(800) 465-4329

JAMESON INN
1007 Colby Taylor
Dr (40475)
Rates: $49-$104
(859) 623-0063
(800) 526-3766

KNIGHTS INN
1688 Northgate Dr
(40475)
Rates: $30-$50
(800) 441-1953

LA QUINTA INN
1751 Lexington Rd
(40475)
Rates: $50-$69
(859) 623-9121
(800) 575-5339

QUALITY QUARTERS
105 N Killarney
Ln (40475)
Rates: n/a
(859) 624-3600

RAMADA LTD
1698 Northgate Dr
(40475)
Rates: n/a
(859) 626-8676
(800) 272-6232

RED ROOF INN
111 Bahama Ct
(40475)
Rates: $45-$70
(859) 625-0084
(800) 843-7663

SUPER 8 MOTEL
107 N Keeneland
(40475)
Rates: $45-$65
(859) 624-1550
(800) 800-8000

RICHWOOD

RICHWOOD MOTEL
10805 Dixie Hwy
(41094)
Rates: n/a
(606) 525-9525

RUSSELL SPRINGS

SHILOH MOTEL
60 W Steve
Warriner Dr
(42642)
Rates: $30-$50
(270) 866-5920
(800) 803-5410

RUSSELLVILLE

HOLLY TREE INN
434 Maple Ln
(42276)
Rates: $50-$80
(270) 725-8865

SCOTTISH INN
815 W 9th St
(42276)
Rates: $30-$50
(270) 726-8351

TOWN MOTEL
485 W 4th St
(42276)
Rates: $30-$50
(270) 726-7665

SALT LICK

JOURNEY'S END LODGE
999 Carrington Dr
(40371)
Rates: $50-$80
(606) 768-2103

SCOTTSVILLE

EXECUTIVE INN
57 Burnley Rd
(42164)
Rates: $55
(270) 622-7770
(800) 530-1705

SHELBYVILLE

BEST WESTERN SHELBYVILLE LODGE
115 Isaac Shelby
Dr (40065)
Rates: $55-$129
(502) 633-4400
(800) 528-1234

DAYS INN
101 Howard Dr
(40065)
Rates: $45-$125
(502) 633-4005
(800) 329-7466

HOLIDAY INN EXPRESS HOTEL
110 Club House
Dr (40065)
Rates: $50-$80
(502) 647-0109
(800) 465-4329

SHEPHERDS-VILLE

BEST WESTERN SOUTH
211 S Lakeview Dr
(40165)
Rates: $55-$79
(502) 543-7097
(800) 528-1234
(877) 543-5080

LOUISVILLE SOUTH KOA COTTAGES
I-65 Exit 1(40165)
Rates: n/a
(502) 543-2041

MOTEL 6
144 Paroquet
Springs Dr (40165)
Rates: $35-$42
(502) 543-4400
(800) 466-8356

SUPER 8 MOTEL
275 Keystone
Crossroad Dr
(40165)
Rates: $30-$50
(800) 800-8000

SLADE

LI'L ABNER MOTEL
1000 Natural
Bridge Rd (40376)
Rates: $30-$50
(606) 663-5384

RED RIVER INN
781 Natural
Bridge Rd (40376)
Rates: $50-$80
(877) 600-5586

SMITHS GROVE

BRYCE INN
592 S Main St
(42171)
Rates: $45-$59
(270) 563-5141

SOMERSET

COMFORT INN
82 Jolin Dr (42503)
Rates: $69-$139
(606) 677-1500
(800) 424-6423

DAYS INN
125 N Hwy 27
(42501)
Rates: $50-$70
(606) 678-2052
(800) 329-7466

LANDMARK INN
1201 S Hwy 27
(42501)
Rates: $30-$50
(606) 678-8115
(800) 585-3503

TRIPLE J & I COTTAGES
Hwy 27 S (42501)
Rates: n/a
(606) 679-7864

STANTON

CHOP CHESTNUT CABIN RENTALS
1886 Chop Chestnut
Rd (40380)
Rates: $81-$120
(606) 424-2935

STEARNS

BIG SOUTH FORK MOTOR LODGE
Bruce St (42647)
Rates: $30-$50
(606) 376-3156

PARKLAND MOTEL
S Hwy 27 (42647)
Rates: $30-$50
(606) 376-5046

TAYLORSVILLE

EAGLES MOTEL
80 Tanglewood Dr
(40071)
Rates: $30-$50
(502) 477-8226

VERSAILLES

1823 HISTORIC ROSE HILL INN B&B
233 Rose Hill
(40383)
Rates: $69-$140
(606) 873-5957
(800) 307-0460

WESTERN FIELDS GUEST HOUSE
5018 Fords Mill
Rd (40383)
Rates: n/a
(800) 600-4935

WALTON

DAYS INN
11777 Frontage Rd
(41094)
Rates: $41-$59
(859) 485-2200
(800) 329-7466

WEST SOMERSET

BECKETT MOTEL
2001 Lees Ford
Dock (42564)
Rates: n/a
(606) 636-6411

WHITESBURG

SUPER 8 MOTEL
107 Medical Plaza
Dr (41858)
Rates: $50-$80
(800) 800-8000

WILLIAMSBURG

SCOTTISH INN
1746 US 25 W
(40769)
Rates: $40-$80
(606) 549-4450

SUPER 8 MOTEL
30W E Hwy 92
(40769)
Rates: $40-$80
(800) 800-8000

WILLIAMSBURG MOTEL
50 Balltown Rd
(40769)
Rates: $40-$80
(606) 549-2300
(800) 426-3267

WILLIAMSTOWN

BEST VALUE INN
10 Skyway Dr
(41097)
Rates: $40-$52
(859) 824-7177

DAYS INN
211 SR 36 W
(41097)
Rates: $45-$85
(859) 824-5025
(800) 329-7466

WILMORE

TURFMOR MOTEL
9110 Harrodsburg
Rd (40390)
Rates: $30-$50
(859) 858-4839

WINCHESTER

BEST WESTERN COUNTRY SQUIRE
1307 W Lexington
Ave (40391)
Rates: $39-$109
(859) 744-7210
(800) 528-1234

SUPER 8 MOTEL
5100 Revilo Rd
(40391)
Rates: $50-$75
(859) 745-0751
(800) 800-8000

AREA CODES - If the local number doesn't connect, check for a new area code.

LOUISIANA

ALEXANDRIA

BEST WESTERN INN & SUITES
2720 W MacArthur Dr (71303)
Rates: $72-$106
(318) 445-5530
(800) 528-1234
(888) 338-2008

CLARION HOTEL
2716 N MacArthur Dr (71303)
Rates: $86-$300
(318) 487-4261
(800) 424-6423

DAYS INN
1146 N MacArthur Dr (71303)
Rates: $49-$59
(318) 443-1841
(800) 329-7466

LA QUINTA INN
6116 W Calhoun Dr (71303)
Rates: $80-$115
(318) 442-3700
(800) 687-6667

MOTEL 6
546 MacArthur Dr (71301)
Rates: $36-$55
(318) 445-2336
(800) 466-8356

RAMADA IMITED
742 MacArthur Dr (71303)
Rates: $55-$70
(318) 448-1611
(800) 272-6232

SUPER 8 MOTEL
700 MacArthur Dr (71301)
Rates: $45-$65
(318) 445-6541
(800) 800-8000

AMITE

BLYTHEWOOD PLANTATION BED & BREAKFAST
400 Daniel St (70422)
Rates: $75-$150
(985) 345-6419

COMFORT INN
1117 W Oak St (70422)
Rates: $60-$72
(985) 748-5550
(800) 424-6423

ARCADIA

DAYS INN
1061 Hazel St (71001)
Rates: $45-$80
(318) 263-3555
(800) 329-7466

BAKER

HOLIDAY INN EXPRESS
430 Main St (70714)
Rates: n/a
(225) 771-1123
(800) 465-4329

BASTROP

COUNTRY INN
1815 E Madison (71220)
Rates: $39-$43
(318) 281-8100

BATON ROUGE

AMERISUITTES
6080 Bluebonnet Blvd (70809)
Rates: $78-$115
(225) 769-4400
(800) 833-1516

BAYMONT INN
10555 Rieger Rd (70809)
Rates: $55-$75
(225) 291-6600
(877) 229-6668

CHASE SUITES BY WOODFIN
5522 Corporate Blvd (70808)
Rates: $144-$179
(225) 927-5630
(800) 237-8811

COMFORT INN UNIVERSITY
2445 S Acadian Thruway (70808)
Rates: $60-$130
(225) 236-4000
(800) 424-6423

LA QUINTA INN
2333 S Acadian Thruway (70808)
Rates: $68-$103
(225) 924-9600
(800) 687-6667

MICROTEL INN
10311 Plaza Americana Dr (70816)
Rates: $40-$50
(225) 927-9997
(888) 771-7171

MOTEL 6
10445 Rieger Rd (70809)
Rates: $37-$53
(2250 291-4912
(800) 466-8356

RESIDENCE INN BY MARRIOTT
10333 N Mall Dr (70809)
Rates: $89-$119
(225) 293-8700
(800) 331-3131

SHERATON BATON ROUGE CONV CTR
102 France St (70802)
Rates: $209
(225) 242-2600
(800) 325-3535

TOWNEPLACE SUITES
8735 Summa Ave (70809)
Rates: $75-$99
(225) 819-2112
(800) 257-3000

BOSCO

BOSCOBEL COTTAGE B&B
185 Cordell Ln (71202)
Rates: $75-$95
(318) 325-1550

BOSSIER CITY

BEST WESTERN AIRLINE MOTOR INN
1984 Airline Dr (71112)
Rates: $65-$95
(318) 742-6000
(800) 528-1234
(800) 635-7639

ECONO LODGE
4300 Industrial Dr (71112)
Rates: $49-$99
(318) 746-5050
(800) 424-6423

HAMPTON INN
1005 Gould Dr (71111)
Rates: $74-$104
(318) 752-1112
(800) 426-7866

LA QUINTA INN
309 Preston Blvd (71112)
Rates: $59-$100
(318) 747-4400
(800) 687-6667

MICROTEL INN
2713 Village Ln (71112)
Rates: $43-$45
(318) 742-7882
(888) 771-7171

MOTEL 6
210 John Wesley Blvd (71112)
Rates: $29-$55
(318) 742-3472
(800) 466-8356

QUALITY INN
2717 Village Ln (71112)
Rates: $79-$150
(318) 742-7890
(800) 424-6423

RESIDENCE INN BY MARRIOTT
1001 Gould Dr (71111)
Rates: $119-$199
(318) 747-6220
(800) 331-3131

SHONEY'S INN
1836 Old Minden Rd (71111)
Rates: $69
(318) 747-7700
(800) 222-2222

BREAUX BRIDGE

BEST WESTERN
2088-B Rees St (70517)
Rates: $65-$250
(337) 332-1114
(800) 528-1234
(888) 783-0007

HOLIDAY INN EXPRESS
2924 H Grand Point Hwy (70517)
Rates: n/a
(337) 667-8913
(800) 465-4329

CHALMETTE

ECONO LODGE
5353 Paris Rd (70043)
Rates: $59-$130
(504) 277-5353
(800) 424-6423

CROWLEY

BEST WESTERN
9571 Egan Hwy (70526)
Rates: $61-$89
(337) 783-2378
(800) 528-1234
(800) 940-0003

CROWLEY INN
2111 N Cherokee Dr (70526)
Rates: n/a
(337) 788-0970
(800) 256-4565

DARROW

TEZCUCO PLANTATION B&B
3138 Hwy 44 (70725)
Rates: $65-$165
(225) 562-3929

AREA CODES - If the local number doesn't connect, check for a new area code.

DELHI
BEST WESTERN DELHI INN
35 Snider Rd
(71232)
Rates: $45-$68
(318) 878-5126
(800) 528-1234

DAYS INN
113 Snider Rd
(71232)
Rates: $55-$75
(318) 878-9000
(800) 329-7466

DERIDDER
STAGECOACH INN
505 E 1st St
(70634)
Rates: $59-$74
(337) 462-0022

EUNICE
SEALE GUESTHOUSE B&B
P. O. Box 568
(70535)
Rates: $65-$75
(318) 457-3753

GRETNA
ECONO LODGE
1411 Claire Ave
(70053)
Rates: $49-$159
(504) 366-4311
(800) 424-6423

LA QUINTA INN
50 Terry Pkwy
(70053)
Rates: $69-$106
(504) 368-5600
(800) 687-6667

HAMMOND
BEST WESTERN HAMMOND HOUSE INN
107 Duo Dr
(70403)
Rates: $60-$95
(985) 419-2001
(800) 528-1234
(877) 598-2001

MICHABELLE-A LITTLE INN
1106 S Holly St
(70403)
Rates: $75-$125
(985) 419-0550

ROCKWOOD INN
42309 S Morrison Blvd (70403)
Rates: n/a
(985) 345-1980

HOUMA
CROCHET HOUSE B&B
301 Midland Dr
(71073)
Rates: $45-$65
(504) 879-3033

IOWA
HOWARD JOHN-SON EXPRESS INN
107 E Frontage Rd
(70647)
Rates: $55-$64
(337) 582-2440
(800) 446-4656

JACKSON
ASPHODEL INN
4626 Hwy 68
(70748)
Rates: $55-$130
(504) 654-6868

JENNINGS
CREOLE ROSE MANOR B & B
214 W Plaquemine
(70546)
Rates: $50-$75
(337) 824-3145

DAYS INN
2002 Port Dr
(70546)
Rates: $50-$75
(337) 824-6550
(800) 329-7466

KENNER
HILTON HOTEL-NEW ORLEANS AIRPORT
901 Airline Dr
(70063)
Rates: $79-$249
(504) 469-5000
(800) 445-8667

LA QUINTA INN
2610 Williams Blvd (70063)
Rates: $79-$111
(504) 466-1401
(800) 687-6667

KINDER
BEST WESTERN INN / COUSHATTA
12102 Hwy 165
(70648)
Rates: $79-$149
(337) 738-4800
(800) 528-1234
(877) 738-4800

HOLIDAY INN EXPRESS HOTEL
11750 US Hwy 165
(70648)
Rates: $79-$150
(337) 738-3381
(800) 465-4329

KROTZ SPRINGS
COUNTRY STORE B & B INN
P. O. Drawer 457
(70750)
Rates: $45-$75
(318) 566-2331

LA PLACE
BEST WESTERN
4289 Main St
(70068)
Rates: $69-$179
(985) 651-4000
(800) 528-1234

LAFAYETTE
BEST SUITES
125 E Kaliste Saloom Rd (70508)
Rates: $79-$159
(337) 235-1367

BEST WESTERN HOTEL ACADIANA
1801 Pinhook Rd
(70508)
Rates: $69-$79
(337) 233-8120
(800) 528-1234
(800) 826-8386

BOIS DES CHENES INN B&B
338 N Sterling
(70501)
Rates: $75-$105
(337) 233-7816

COMFORT INN
1421 SE Evangeline Thruway (70501)
Rates: $76-$89
(337) 232-9000
(800) 424-6423

DAYS INN
1620 N University
(70506)
Rates: $55-$150
(337) 237-8880
(800) 329-7466

HILTON LAFAYETTE & TOWERS
1521 W Pinhook Rd (70503)
Rates: $79-$189
(337) 235-6111
(800) 445-8667

LA QUINTA INN
2100 NE Evangeline Thruway (70501)
Rates: $59-$100
(337) 233-5610
(800) 687-6777

LA QUINTA INN & SUITES-OIL CNTR
1015 W Pinhook Rd (70503)
Rates: $72-$90
(337) 291-1088
(800) 687-6667

MOTEL 6
2724 NE Evangeline Thruway (70507)
Rates: $31-$50
(337) 269-9267
(800) 466-8356

RAMADA INN
120 E Kaliste Saloom Rd (70508)
Rates: $59-$79
(337) 235-0858
(800) 272-6232

RED ROOF INN
1718 N University Ave (70507)
Rates: $36-$67
(337) 233-3339
(800) 843-7663

LAKE CHARLES
BEST SUITES OF AMERICA
401 Lakeshore Dr
(70601)
Rates: $84-$150
(337) 439-2444

LA QUINTA INN
1320 MLK Hwy 171 N (70601)
Rates: $60-$100
(337) 436-5998
(800) 687-6667

LIVONIA
OAK TREE INN
7875 Airline Hwy
(70755)
Rates: $50-$69
(225) 637-2590

MANSFIELD
MANSFIELD INN
1055 Washington Ave (71052)
Rates: $39-$48
(318) 872-5034

METARIE
FOUR POINTS BY SHERATON
6401 Veterans Memorial Blvd (70003)
Rates: $79-$99
(504) 885-5700
(800) 325-3535

LA QUINTA INN CAUSEWAY
3100 I-10 Service Rd (70001)
Rates: $69-$101
(504) 835-8511
(800) 687-6777

LA QUINTA INN
5900 Veterans Memorial Blvd (70002)
Rates: $69-$101
(504) 456-0003
(800) 687-6667

RESIDENCE INN BY MARRIOTT
3 Galleria Blvd (70001)
Rates: $109-$129
(504) 832-0888
(800) 331-3131

MINDEN
BEST WESTERN
1411 Sibley Rd
(71055)
Rates: $60-$70
(318) 377-1001
(800) 528-1234

MONROE
BOSCOBEL COTTAGE B&B
185 Cordell Lane
(71202)
Rates: $65-$95
(318) 325-1550
(800) 254-3529

AREA CODES - If the local number doesn't connect, check for a new area code.

DAYS INN
5650 Frontage Rd
(71202)
Rates: $48-$66
(318) 345-2220
(800) 329-7466

LA QUINTA INN
1035 US 165S
Bypass (71203)
Rates: $59-$89
(318) 322-3900
(800) 687-6667

MOTEL 6
1501 US Hwy 165
Bypass (71202)
Rates: $34-$50
(318) 322-5430
(800) 466-8356

RESIDENCE INN BY MARRIOTT
4960 Millhaven
Rd (71203)
Rates: n/a
(318) 387-0210
(800) 331-3131

MORGAN CITY

DAYS INN
7408 Hwy 90 E
(70380)
Rates: $45-$68
(985) 384-5750
(800) 329-7466

HOLIDAY INN
520 Roderick St
(70381)
Rates: $85-$200
(985) 385-2200
(800) 465-4329

NATCHITOCHES

CLOUTIER TOWN-HOUSE B&B
Front St/Ducoumau
Square (71457)
Rates: $50-$150
(318) 352-5242
(800) 351-7666

DAYS INN
1000 College Ave
(71457)
Rates: $45-$75
(318) 352-4426
(800) 329-7466

HOLIDAY INN EXPRESS
5131 University
Pkwy (71457)
Rates: $66-$88
(318) 354-9911
(800) 465-4329

NEW IBERIA

BEST WESTERN INN & SUITES
2714 Hwy 14
(70560)
Rates: $65-$93
(318) 364-3030
(800) 528-1234
(800) 840-7147

HOLIDAY INN AVERY ISLAND
2915 Hwy 14
(70560)
Rates: $75-$77
(337) 367-1201
(800) 465-4329

LA MAISON B&B
8317 Weeks Island
Rd (70560)
Rates: $75-$140
(318) 364-2970
(800) 225-8671

MAISON MARCELINE B&B
442 E Main (70560)
Rates: $50-$175
(318) 364-5922

NEW ORLEANS
(Includes the
French Quarter)

AMBASSADOR HOTEL
535 Tchoupitoulas
(70130)
Rates: $69-$229
(504) 527-5271
(888) 527-5271

BEST WESTERN PATIO DOWN-TOWN MOTEL
2820 Tulane Ave
(70119)
Rates: $59-$299
(504) 822-0200
(800) 270-6955

CHATEAU SONESTA HOTEL
800 Iberville St
(70112)
Rates: $99-$199
(504) 586-0800
(800) 766-3782

THE 1896 O'MAL-LEY HOUSE B&B
120 S Pierce St
(70119)
Rates: $99-$150
(504) 488-5896

DRURY INN
820 Poydras St
(70112)
Rates: $80-$155
(504) 529-7800
(800) 378-7946

EMBASSY SUITES
315 Julia St
(70130)
Rates: $89-$374
(504) 525-1993
(800) 362-2779

THE FAIRMONT HOTEL
123 Baronne St
(70130)
Rates: $99-$289
(504) 529-7111
(800) 441-1414

FRENCH QUARTER COURTYARD HOTEL
1101 N Rampart St
(70116)
Rates: $69-$229
(504) 522-7333
(800) 290-4233

THE IBERVILLE SUITES
910 Iverbille St
(70112)
Rates: $84-$263
(504) 523-2400

HOTEL MONACO
333 St. Charles
Ave (70130)
Rates: $189-$339
(504) 561-0010

LA QUINTA INN
12001 I-10 Service
Rd (70127)
Rates: $55-$95
(504) 246-3003
(800) 687-6667
(800) 221-4731

LA QUINTA IN
8400 I-10 Service
Rd (70127)
Rates: $69-$89
(504) 246-5800
(800) 687-6667
(800) 221-4731

LA QUINTA INN
301 Camp St
(70130)
Rates: $99-$209
(504) 598-9977
(800) 687-6667
(800) 221-4731

LA MERIDIEN HOTEL
614 Canal St
(70127)
Rates: $270-$285
(504) 525-6500

LE PAPILLON GUESTHOUSE
2011 N Rampart St
(70116)
Rates: $65-$135
(504) 948-4993

LOEWS NEW ORLEANS HOTEL
300 Poydras St
(70120)
Rates: $149-$319
(504) 595-3300
(800) 235-6397

MAISON ESPLANADE GUEST HOUSE B&E
1244 Esplanade
Ave (70116)
Rates: $39-$149
(504) 523-8080
(800) 892-5529

THE MAISON ORLEANS-RITZ CARLTON
904 Iberville St
(70112)
Rates: $410-$509
(504) 670-2900
(800) 241-3333

MOTEL 6
12330 I-10 Service
Rd (70128)
Rates: $41-$60
(504) 240-2862
(800) 466-8356

THE OLIVER ESTATE-A B&B
1425 N Prieur St
(70116)
Rates: $79-$295
(504) 949-9600

OMNI ROYAL CRESCENT HOTEL
535 Gravier St
(70130)
Rates: $109-$209
(504) 527-0006
(800) 843-6664

OMNI ROYAL ORLEANS HOTEL
621 St. Louis St
(70140)
Rates: $99-$399
(504) 529-5333
(800) 843-6664

QUALITY INN
1319 St. Charles
Ave (70130)
Rates: $72-$700
(504) 522-0187
(800) 424-6423

RATHBONE INN B&B
1227 Esplanade
(70116)
Rates: $90-$145
(504) 947-2100
(800) 947-2101

RESIDENCE INN BY MARRIOTT
345 St. Josephs St
(70130)
Rates: $119-$209
(504) 522-1300
(800) 331-3131

RITZ CARLTON NEW ORLEANS
921 Canal St
(70112)
Rates: $109-$276
(504) 524-1331
(800) 241-3333

ROBERT GORDY HOUSE B&B
2630 Bell St
(70119)
Rates: $75-$95
(504) 486-9424
(800) 889-7359

ROYAL SONESTA HOTEL
300 Bourbon St
(70130)
Rates: $109-$329
(504) 586-0300

ST. JAMES HOTEL
330 Magazine St
(70130)
Rates: $59-$149
(504) 304-4000

SHERATON NEW ORLEANS HOTEL
500 Canal St
(70130)
Rates: $449-$549
(504) 525-2500
(800) 325-3535

AREA CODES - If the local number doesn't connect, check for a new area code.

STUDIO 6
12330 I-10 Service Rd (70128)
Rates: $43-$73
(504) 240-9778
(888) 897-0202

SULLY MANSION
2631 Prtania St (70130)
Rates: $50-$150
(504) 891-0457

W FRENCH QUARTER
316 Rue Chartres St (70130)
Rates: $479-$519
(504) 581-1200
(877) 946-8357

W NEW ORLEANS
333 Poydras St (70130)
Rates: $469-$499
(504) 525-9444
(877) 946-8357

WINDSOR COURT HOTEL
300 Gravier St (70140)
Rates: $195-$450
(504) 523-6000

NEW ROADS

RIVER BLOSSOM INN B&B
300 N Carolina St (70760)
Rates: $55-$75
(504) 638-8650

OPELOUSAS

BEST WESTERN OF OPELOUSAS
5791 I-49 Service Rd S (70570)
Rates: $65-$130
(337) 942-5540
(800) 528-1234
(888) 942-5540

DAYS INN
5761 I-49 Service Rd S (70570)
Rates: $71-$86
(337) 407-0004
(800) 329-7466

PORT ALLEN

BEST WESTERN MAGNOLIA MANOR
234 Lobdell Hwy (70767)
Rates: $55
(225) 344-3638
(800) 528-1234

MOTEL 6
2800 I-10 Frontage Rd (70767)
Rates: $34-$50
(225) 343 5945
(800) 466-8356

RAYVILLE

DAYS INN
125 Maxwell Dr (71269)
Rates: $50-$75
(318) 728-4500
(800) 329-7466

RAMADA LIMITED
116 Cottonland (71269)
Rates: $49-$69
(318) 728-5985
(800) 272-6232

RUSTON

ECONO LODGE
1301 Goodwin Rd (71270)
Rates: $49-$79
(318) 255-0354
(800) 424-6423

RAMADA INN
401 N Service Rd (71270)
Rates: $59-$99
(318) 255-5901
(800) 272-6232

ST. FRANCISVILLE

GREEN SPRINGS INN & COTTAGES B&B
7463 Tunica Trace (70775)
Rates: $120-$180
(225) 635-4232

LAKE ROSEMOUND INN B&B
10473 Lindsey Ln (70775)
Rates: $75-$125
(225) 635-3176

ST. MARTINVILLE

MAISON BLEUE B&B
417 N Main St (70582)
Rates: $65-$75
(318) 394-1215

SCOTT

HOWARD JOHNSON
103 Harold Gauthe (70583)
Rates: $60-$70
(337) 593-0849
(800) 446-4656

SHREVEPORT

CLARION HOTEL
1419 E 70th St (71105)
Rates: $109-$139
(318) 797-9900
(800) 252-7466

DAYS INN
4935 W Monkhouse Rd (71109)
Rates: $32-$78
(318) 636-0800
(800) 329-7466

HOLIDAY INN DOWNTOWN
102 Lake St (71101)
Rates: $79-$139
(318) 222-7717
(800) 465-4329

HOWARD JOHNSON EXPRESS
2610 Claiborne Ave (71103)
Rates: $49-$89
(318) 636-0000
(800) 446-4656

JAMESON INN
6715 Rasberry Ln (71129)
Rates: $49-$104
(318) 671-0731
(800) 526-3766

LA QUINTA INN
6700 Financial Cir (71129)
Rates: $79-$109
(318) 671-1100
(800) 687 6667

RED ROOF INN
7296 Greenwood Rd (71119)
Rates: $36-$68
(318) 938-5342
(800) 843-7663

SLIDELL

LA QUINTA INN
794 E I-10 Service Rd (70461)
Rates: $55-$85
(985) 643-9770
(800) 687-6777

MOTEL 6
136 Taos St (70458)
Rates: $33-$40
(985) 649-7925
(800) 466-8356

SLEEP INN
142 Oak Ct (70458)
Rates: $49-$149
(985) 641-2143
(800) 424-6423

SULPHUR

LA QUINTA INN
2600 S Ruth St (70663)
Rates: $54-$94
(337) 527-8303
(800) 687-6667

WINGATE INN
300 Texaco Rd (70665)
Rates: $79-$89
(337) 527-5151

THIBODAUX

OAKES B&B
1418 Himalaya Ave (70301)
Rates: $75-$150
(504) 447-3764

VILLE PLATTE

BEST WESTERN VILLE PLATTE
1919 E Main St (70586)
Rates: $71-$90
(337) 360-9961
(800) 528-1234

WEST MONROE

QUALITY INN
503 Constitution Dr (71292)
Rates: $69-$129
(318) 387-2711
(800) 424-6423

RED ROOF INN
102 Constitution Dr (71292)
Rates: $36-$55
(318) 388-2420
(800) 843-7663

SHONEY'S INN
310 Thomas Rd (71291)
Rates: $39-$49
(318) 325-5780
(800) 222-2222

WINNFIELD

BEST WESTERN OF WINFIELD
700 W Court St (71483)
Rates: $52-$89
(318) 628-3993
(800) 528-1234
(800) 256-4494

WINNSBORO

BEST WESTERN WINNSBORO
4198 Front St (71295)
Rates: $50-$63
(318) 435-2000
(800) 528-1234

AREA CODES - If the local number doesn't connect, check for a new area code.

MAINE

AUBURN

A FIRESIDE INN
1777 Washington
St (04210)
Rates: $70-$120
(207) 777-1777

AUGUSTA

**BEST WESTERN
SENATOR
INN & SPA**
284 Western Ave
(04330)
Rates: $89-$259
(207) 622-5804
(800) 528-1234
(877) 772-2224

**COMFORT INN
CIVIC CENTER**
281 Civic Center
Dr (04330)
Rates: $94-$169
(207) 623-1000
(800) 424-6423

ECONO LODGE
390 Western Ave
(04330)
Rates: $80-$110
(207) 622-6371
(800) 424-6423

HOLIDAY INN
110 Community
Dr (04330)
Rates: $95-$169
(207) 622-4751
(800) 465-4329

MOTEL 6
18 Edison Dr (04330)
Rates: $37-$58
(207) 622-0000
(800) 466-8356

BAILEY ISLAND

**LOG CABIN
LODGING**
Rt 24 (04003)
Rates: $120-$210
(207) 833-5546

BANGOR

BEST INN
570 Main St (04401)
Rates: $75-$120
(207) 947-0566
(800) 237-8466

**BEST WESTERN
WHITE HOUSE**
155 Littlefield Ave
(04401)
Rates: $59-$122
(207) 862-3737
(800) 528-1234

COMFORT INN
750 Hogan Rd
(04401)
Rates: $49-$119
(207) 942-7899
(800) 424-6423

DAYS INN
250 Odlin Rd
(04401)
Rates: $50-$100
(207) 942-8272
(800) 329-7466

ECONO LODGE
327 Odlin Rd
(04401)
Rates: $35-$110
(207) 945-0111
(800) 424-6423

**FOUR POINTS BY
SHERATON**
308 Godfrey Blvd
(04401)
Rates: $129-$159
(207) 947-6721
(800) 325-3535

**HOLIDAY INN
CIVIC CENTER**
500 Main St
(04401)
Rates: $75-$90
(207) 947-8651
(800) 465-4329

**HOLIDAY INN
ODLIN ROAD**
404 Odlin Rd
(04401)
Rates: $73-$89
(207) 947-0101
(800) 465-4329

MAIN STREET INN
480 Main St
(04401)
Rates: $47-$62
(207) 942-5282
(800) 928-9877

MOTEL 6
1100 Hammond St
(04401)
Rates: $29-$59
(207) 947-6921
(800) 466-8356

RAMADA INN
357 Odlin Rd
(04401)
Rates: $49-$99
(207) 947-6961
(800) 272-6232

RIVERSIDE INN
495 State St
(04401)
Rates: $69-$129
(207) 947-3800
(800) 252-4044

TRAVELODGE
482 Odlin Rd
(04401)
Rates: $40-$90
(207) 942-6301
(800) 578-7878

BAR HARBOR

**ANCHORAGE
MOTEL**
51 Mt. Desert St
(04609)
Rates: $54-$129
(207) 288-3959
(800) 336-3959

**A WONDER VIEW
INN & SUITES**
50 Eden St (04609)
Rates: $50-$230
(207) 288-3358
(888) 439-8439

**BALANCE ROCK
INN 1903
HISTORIC B&B**
21 Albert Meadow
(04609)
Rates: $115-$625
(207) 288-2610
(800) 753-0494

**BEST WESTERN
INN BAR HARBOR**
452 State Hwy 3
(04609)
Rates: $74-$140
(207) 288-5823
(800) 528-1234

DAYS INN
120 Eden St
(04609)
Rates: $89-$229
(207) 288-3321
(800) 329-7466

**DREAMWOOD
PINES MOTEL**
389 State Hwy 3
(04609)
Rates: $1560
(207) 288-9717

**HUTCHIN'S
MOUNTAIN VIEW
COTTAGES**
286 SR 3 (04609)
Rates: $46-$98
(207) 288-4833
(800) 775-4833

**LEDGELAWN INN
HISTORIC B&B**
66 Mt. Desert St
(04609)
Rates: $95-$275
(207) 288-4596
(800) 274-5334

**PRIMROSE INN
B&B**
73 Mt. Desert St
(04609)
Rates: $85-$215
(207) 288-4031

BASS HARBOR

**BASS HARBOR
GABLES**
P.O. Box 396
(04653)
Rates: $125
(207) 244-3699

**QUIETSIDE
CAMPGROUND
& CABINS**
P O Box 10 (04653)
Rates: n/a
(207) 244-5992

BATH

**ADMIRAL'S
OCEAN INN**
RR 1, Box 5373
(04915)
Rates: $29-$75
(207) 338-4260

**BELFAST BAY
MEADOWS INN**
192 Northport Ave
(04915)
Rates: $75-$165
(207) 338-5715
(800) 335-2370

FAIRHAVEN INN
North Bath Rd
(04530)
Rates: $60-$90
(207) 443-4391

HOLIDAY INN
139 Richardson
Ave (04530)
Rates: $89-$134
(207) 443-9741
(800) 465-4329

BELFAST

**ADMIRAL'S
OCEAN INN**
RR 1, Box 99A
(04915)
Rates: $48-$75
(207) 338-4260

**BELFAST BAY
MEADOWS INN**
192 Northport Ave
(04915)
Rates: $75-$165
(207) 338-5715
(800) 335-2370

**BELFAST
HARBOR INN**
RR 5, Box 5230
(04915)
Rates: $54-$129
(207) 338-2740
(800) 545-8576

**COMFORT INN
OCEAN'S EDGE**
159 Searsport Ave
(04915)
Rates:$79-$149
(207) 338-2090
(800) 424-6423

GULL MOTEL
196 Searsport Ave
(04915)
Rates: $39-$89
(207) 338-4030

AREA CODES - If the local number doesn't connect, check for a new area code.

SEASCAPE MOTEL & COTTAGES
Rt 1 (04915)
Rates: $49-$123
(207) 338-2130

BETHEL
BETHEL INN & COUNTRY CLUB
1 Bethel Inn Dr (04217)
Rates: $75-$400
(207) 824-2175
(800) 654-0125

THE BRIAR LEA B&B
150 Mayville Rd (04217)
Rates: $59-$129
(207) 824-4717

THE CAMERON HOUSE
Maston St Box 468 (04217)
Rates: n/a
(207) 824-3219

THE INN AT THE ROSTAY
186 Mayville Rd (04217)
Rates: $45-$130
(207) 824-3111

L'AUBERGE HISTORIC COUNTRY INN
22 Mill Hill Rd (04217)
Rates: $99-$247
(207) 824-2774

BINGHAM
BINGHAM MOTOR INN
Route 201 (04920)
Rates: $30-$68
(207) 672-4135

BLUE HILL
DEWING VACA-TION RENTAL
P. O. Box 988 (04614)
Rates: $600 Weekly
(207) 374-2888

BOOTHBAY
HILLSIDE ACRES MOTOR COURT
301 Adams Pond Rd (04537)
Rates: $45-$80
(207) 633-3411

WHITE ANCHOR MOTEL
609 Wiscassat Rd (04537)
Rates: $40-$75
(207) 633-3788

BOOTHBAY HARBOR
(And vicinity)

CATWALK ON THE MILL POND
P.O. Box 447 (East Boothbay 04554)
Rates: $750 Weekly
(207) 633-3270

HARBORSIDE RESORT
P. O. Box 516B (04575)
Rates: $59-$109
(207) 633-5381
(800) 235-5402

LAKEVIEW INN
48 Lakeview Rd (West Boothbay 04575)
Rates: n/a
(207) 633-0353
(866) 851-0450

LAWNMEER INN
350 Townsend Ave (West Boothbay Harbor 04538)
Rates: $95-$175
(207) 633-2544
(800) 633-7645

LEEWARD VILLAGE
Rt 96 Ocean Point Rd (East Boothbay 04544)
Rates: $50-$150
(207) 633-3681

OCEAN POINT CABIN
HC Box 936 (East Boothbay 04544)
Rates: n/a
(207) 633-2981

THE PINES MOTEL
Sunset Rd (04538)
Rates: $70-$90
(207) 633-4555

SMUGGLER'S COVE MOTOR INN
SR 96 (East Boothbay 04544)
Rates: $89-$159
(207) 633-2800
(800) 633-3008

WELCH HOUSE INN B&B
56 McKown St (04538)
Rates: $80-$155
(207) 633-3431
(800) 279-7313

BREWER
BREWER MOTOR INN
359 Wilson St (04412)
Rates: $45-$62
(207) 989-4476

BRIDGTON
PLEASANT MOUNTAIN INN
N High St (04009)
Rates: $60-$125
(207) 647-4505

BROWNFIELD
FOOTHILLS FARM B&B
RR 1, Box 598 (04010)
Rates: n/a
(207) 935-3799

BRUNSWICK
VIKING MOTOR INN
287 Bath Rd (04011)
Rates: $49-$139
(207) 729-6661
(800) 429-6661

BRYANT POND
MOLLYOCKETT MOTEL & SWIM SPA
1132 S Main St (04219)
Rates: $70-$95
(207) 674-2345

BUCKSPORT
BUCKSPORT MOTOR INN
151 Main St (04416)
Rates: $33-$55
(207) 469-3111

SPRING FOUNTAIN MOTEL
RFD 2, Box 710 (04416)
Rates: $34-$75
(207) 469-3139

CALAIS
CALAIS MOTOR INN
293 Main St (04619)
Rates: $44-$84
(207) 454-7111

INTERNATIONAL MOTEL
276 Main St (04619)
Rates: $45-$80
(207) 454-7515

CAMDEN
BLUE HARBOR HOUSE - A VILLAGE INN
67 Elm St (04843)
Rates: $125-$155
(207) 236-3196
(800) 248-3196

CAMDEN HARBOUR INN
83 Bayview St (04843)
Rates: $155-$275
(207) 236-4200

THE CAMDEN RIVERHOUSE HOTEL & INNS
11 Tannery Ln (04843)
Rates: $99-$250
(207) 236-0500

LORD CAMDEN INN B&B
24 Main St (04843)
Rates: $98-$268
(207) 236-4325
(800) 336-4325

CAPE ELIZABETH
INN BY THE SEA
40 Bowery Beach Rd (04107)
Rates: $219-$689
(207) 799-3134
(886) 619-7880

CAPE NEDDICK
COUNTRY VIEW MOTEL & GUESTHOUSE
1521M Rt One (03902)
Rates: n/a
(207) 363-7160
(800) 258-6598

CARIBOU
CARIBOU INN
19 Main St (04736)
Rates: $62-$120
(207) 498-3733

CASTINE
THE HOLIDAY HOUSE
Box 215, Perkins St (04421)
Rates: n/a
(207) 326-4335

THE MANOR
P. O. Box 276 (04421)
Rates: $65-$150
(207) 326-4861

PENTAGOT INN HISTORIC B&B
26 Main St (04421)
Rates: $85-$205
(207) 326-8616

CENTER LOVELL
HEWNOAKS HOUSEKEEPING COTTAGES
RR 1, Box 65 (04016)
Rates: n/a
(207) 925-6051

WESTWAYS ON KEZAR LAKE
Rt 5 (04016)
Rates: $90+
(207) 928-2663

CORNISH
MIDWAY MOTEL
712 S Hiram Rd (04020)
Rates: $49-$99
(207) 625-8835

DAMARISCOTTA
COUNTY FAIR MOTEL
RFD 1, Box 36 (04543)
Rates: $64-$71
(207) 563-3769

EAGLE LAKE

OVERLOOK MOTEL & LAKE-SIDE CABINS
3232 Aroostook
Rd (04739)
Rates: $49-$150
(207) 444-4535

EAST BOOTH-BAY

SMUGGLER'S COVE MOTOR INN
727 Ocean Point
Rd (04544)
Rates: $69-$249
(207) 633-2800
(800) 633-3008

EAST HOLDEN

THE LUCERNE INN
Bar Harbor Rd
(04429)
Rates: $59-$89
(207) 843-5123

EAST WINTHROP

LAKESIDE MOTEL CABINS & MARINA
P. O. Box 236
(04343)
Rates: $35+
(800) 532-6892

EASTPORT

TODD HOUSE
Todd's Head
(04631)
Rates: $45-$80
(207) 853-2328

EDGECOMB

BAYVIEW INN
Rt 1 & Rt 27 S
(04556)
Rates: $60-$90
(207) 882-6911
(800) 530-2445

SHEEPSCOT RIVER INN
306 Eddy Rd
(04556)
Rates: $79-$149
(207) 882-6343
(800) 437-5503

ELLSWORTH

THE COLONIAL INN
321 High St
(04605)
Rates: $54-$160
(207) 667-5548

COMFORT INN
130 High St
(04605)
Rates: $60-$140
(207) 667-1345
(800) 424-6423

HOLIDAY INN
215 High St
(04605)
Rates: $76-$155
(207) 667-0641
(800) 465-4329

JASPERS MOTEL
200 High St
(04605)
Rates: $49-$99
(207) 667-5318

TRAVELODGE
321 High St
(04605)
Rates: $84-$108
(207) 667-5548
(800) 578-7878

TWILITE MOTEL
147 Bucksport Rd
(04605)
Rates: $56-$94
(207) 667-8165
(800) 395-5097

THE WHITE BIRCHES
Thorsen Rd
(04605)
Rates: $50-$200
(207) 667-3621
(800) 435-1287
(800) 660-3621

FARMINGTON

MOUNT BLUE MOTEL
Wilton Rd (04938)
Rates: $44-$60
(207) 778-6004

FREEPORT

BEST WESTERN FREEPORT INN
31 US Rt 1 (04032)
Rates: $69-$149
(207) 865-3106
(800) 528-1234
(800) 998-2583

ECONO LODGE
537 US Rt 1
(04032)
Rates: $49-$159
(207) 865-3777
(800) 424-6423

HARRASKEEKET INN
162 Main St
(04032)
Rates: $135-$289
(207) 865-9377
(800) 342-6423

ISAAC RANDALL HOUSE HISTORIC B&B
5 Independence
Dr (04032)
Rates: $105-$145
(207) 865-9295
(800) 865-9295

MAINE IDYLL MOTOR COURT
325 US Rt 1 N
(04032)
Rates: n/a
(207) 865-4201

GLEN COVE

CLADDAGH MOTEL
US 1 (04846)
Rates: $36-$75
(207) 594-8479

GRAND LAKE STREAM

WEATHERBY'S-THE FISHERMANS RESORT
1 Church St
(04637)
Rates: $152-$240
(207) 796-5558

GREENVILLE

CHALET MOOSE-HEAD LAKE-FRONT MOTEL
12 N Birch St
(04442)
Rates: $67-$130
(207) 695-2950

KINEO VIEW MOTOR LODGE
Overlook Dr
(04441)
Rates: $64-$99
(207) 695-4470
(800) 659-8439

HOULTON

SCOTTISH INNS
239 Bangor St
(04730)
Rates: $45-$70
(207) 532-2236
(800) 251-1962

JACKMAN

BRIARWOOD MOUNTAIN RESORT
P. O. Box 490
(04945)
Rates: $46-$54
(207) 668-7756

SKY LODGE MOTEL/CABINS
U S 201 (04945)
Rates: $50-$165
(207) 668-2171

TUCKAWAY SHORES
Forest St (04945)
Rates: $25
(207) 668-3351

JONESBORO

WINDRISE FARM
Box 47, Evergreen
Pt Rd (04648)
Rates: $250-$500
Weekly
(207) 434-2701

KENNEBUNK

THE LODGE AT KENNEBUNK
95 Alewive Rd
(04043)
Rates: $69-$99
(207) 985-9010
(877) 918-3701

KENNEBUNK-PORT

CABOT COVE COTTAGES
South Main St,
Box 1082 (04046)
Rates: $85-$145
(207) 967-5424
(800) 962-5424

CAPTAIN JEFFERS INN
5 Pearl St (04046)
Rates: $130-$350
(207) 967-2311

THE COLONY RESORT HOTEL
140 Ocean Ave
(04046)
Rates: $175-$427
(207) 967-3331
(800) 552-2363

LODGE AT TURBAT'S CREEK
7 Turbat's Creek
Rd (04046)
Rates: $95-$139
(207) 967-8700
(877) 594-5634

YACHTSMAN LODGE & MARINA
57 Ocean Ave
(04046)
Rates: $199-$314
(207) 967-2511

KITTERY

ENCHANTED NIGHTS B&B
29 Wentworth St
(03904)
Rates: $52-$280
(207) 439-1489

SUPER 8 MOTEL
85 US Rt 1,
Bypass S (03904)
Rates: $35-$94
(207) 439-2000
(800) 800-8000

LEEDS

ANGELL COVE COTTAGES
Box 29, Bishop
Hill Rd (04263)
Rates: $575
Weekly
(207) 524-5041

LEWISTON

CHALET MOTEL
1243 Lisbon St
(04240)
Rates: $50-$70
(207) 784-0600

MOTEL 6
516 Pleasant St
(04240)
Rates: $39-$60
(207) 782-6558
(800) 466-8356

LINCOLN

BRIARWOOD MOTOR INN
P. O. Box 628 (04457)
Rates: $40-$55
(207) 794-6731

LINCOLN HOUSE MOTEL
85 Main St (04457)
Rates: $32-$42
(207) 794-3096

LINCOLNVILLE

ABBINGTONS SEAVIEW MOTEL & COTTAGES
6 Seaview Dr
(04849)
Rates: $60-$130
(207) 236-3471

PINE GROVE COTTAGES
2076 Atlantic Hwy
(04849)
Rates: $50-$150
(207) 236-2929
(800) 530-5265

LUBEC

EASTLAND MOTEL
395 County Rd
(04652)
Rates: $41-$71
(207) 733-5501

MACHIAS

BLUEBIRD MOTEL
Dublin St (04654)
Rates: $54-$70
(207) 255-3332

MACHIAS MOTOR INN
26 E Main St (04654)
Rates: $63-$95
(207) 255-4861

MANSET

SEAWALL MOTEL
Rt 102A (04656)
Rates: $40-$85
(207) 244-9250
(800) 248-9250

MATINICUS

TUCKANUCK LODGE
Shag Hollow Rd
(04851)
Rates: $40-$80
(207) 366-3830

MEDWAY

KATAHDIN SHADOWS MOTEL
I-95, Exit 56
(04460)
Rates: $44-$59
(207) 746-5162
(800) 794-5267

MILFORD

MILFORD MOTEL ON THE RIVER
154 Main Rd
(04461)
Rates: $52-$95
(207) 827-3200
(800) 282-3330

MILLINOCKET

BEST VALUE INN
935 Central St
(04462)
Rates: $69-$89
(207) 723-9777

KATAHDIN INN
740 Central St
(04462)
Rates: $59-$125
(207) 723-4555
(877) 902-4555

PAMOLA MOTOR LODGE
973 Central St
(04462)
Rates: $29-$54
(207) 723-9746

MOODY

NE'R BEACH MOTEL
SR 98 (US 1,
Box 389 (04054)
Rates: $44-$109
(207) 646-2636

MOOSE RIVER

SKY LODGE CABINS & MOTEL
Sky Lodge, Rt 201
(05945)
Rates: n/a
(207) 668-2171
(800) 307-0098

NOBLEBORO

HOUSEKEEPING COTTAGE
RR1, Box 820
(Jefferson, 04348)
Rates: $150-$300
Weekly
(207) 832-7055

NOBLEBORO CABIN
631 W Neck Rd
(04555)
Rates: $500
Weekly
(207) 563-8152
(207) 563-8677

NORTH ANSON

EMBDEN LAKE RESORT
RR 1, Box 3395
(04958)
Rates: $110-$130
(207) 566-7501

NORWAY

LEDGEWOOD MOTEL
RFD 2, Box 30
(04268)
Rates: $38-$60
(207) 743-6347

OGUNQUIT

STUDIO EAST MOTOR INN
267 Main St
(03907)
Rates: $49-$149
(207) 646-7297

OLD ORCHARD BEACH

ALLOUETTE BEACH RESORT
91 E Grand Ave
(04064)
Rates: $49-$265
(207) 934-4151

BEAU RIVAGE MOTEL
54 E Grand Ave
(04064)
Rates: $55-$149
(207) 934-4668
(800) 939-4668

OLD COLONIAL MOTEL
61 W Grand Ave
(04064)
Rates: $70-$220
(207) 934-9862
(888) 225-5989

SEA VIEW MOTEL
65 W Grand Ave
(04064)
Rates: $50-$245
(207) 934-4180
(800) 541-8439

WAVES OCEANFRONT RESORT
87 W Grand Ave
(04064)
Rates: $70-$210
(207) 934-4949

ORONO

BEST WESTERN BLACK BEAR INN
4 Godfrey Dr
(04473)
Rates: $59-$119
(207) 866-7120
(800) 528-1234

UNIVERSITY INN ACADEMIC SUITES
5 College Ave
(04473)
Rates: $59-$82
(207) 866-4921

PATTEN

MT CHASE LODGE & COUNTRY INN
Shin Pond Rd,
Box 281 (04765)
Rates: n/a
(207) 528-2183

SHIN POND VILLAGE
RR 1, Box 280-M
(04765)
Rates: $30-$62
(207) 528-2900

PORTLAND

DOUBLETREE HOTEL
1230 Congress St
(04103)
Rates: $153
(207) 774-5611
(800) 222-8733

EASTLAND PARK HOTEL
157 High St
(04101)
Rates: $99-$159
(207) 775-5411
(888) 671-8008

EMBASSY SUITES HOTEL
1050 Westbrook St
(04103)
Rates: $129-$229
(207) 775-2200
(800) 362-2779

HOLIDAY INN W
81 Riverside St
(04103)
Rates: $114-$143
(207) 774-5601
(800) 465-4329

HOWARD JOHNSON
155 Riverside
(04103)
Rates: $99-$135
(207) 774-5861
(800) 446-4656

MOTEL 6
One Riverside St
(04103)
Rates: $39-$86
(207) 775-0111
(800) 466-8356

PORTLAND HARBOR HOTEL
468 Fore St (04101)
Rates: $169-$245
(207) 775-9090
(888) 798-9090

PRESQUE ISLE

NORTHERN LIGHTS MOTEL
72 Houlton Rd
(04769)
Rates: $40-$70
(207) 764-4441

PRESQUE ISLE INN & CONV CTR
116 Main St (04769)
Rates: $98-$132
(207) 764-3321

RANGELEY

COUNTRY CLUB INN
56 Country Club
Rd (04970)
Rates $79-$116
(207) 864-3831

ROCKLAND

NAVIGATOR MOTOR INN
520 Main St
(04841)
Rates: $59-$139
(207) 594-2131
(800) 545-8026

AREA CODES - If the local number doesn't connect, check for a new area code.

TRADE WINDS MOTOR INN
2 Park Drive
Center (04841)
Rates: $55-$149
(207) 596-6661
(800) 834-3130

ROCKPORT
OAKLAND COT-TAGES & MOTEL
112 Dearborn Ln
(04856)
Rates: n/a
(207) 594-8104

ROCKWOOD
ABNAKI COTTAGES
Abnaki Rd,
P. O. Box 6 (04478)
Rates: n/a
(207) 534-7318

THE BIRCHES RESORT
Box 81 (04478)
Rates: $35-$950
(207) 534-7305

MAYNARDS IN MAINE
P. O. Box 228
(04478)
Rates: n/a
(207) 534-7702

RUMFORD
LINNELL MOTEL
986 Prospect Ave
(04276)
Rates: $55-$75
(207) 364-4511

SACO
HAMPTON INN-OLD ORCHARD BEACH
48 Industrial Park
Rd (04072)
Rates: $69-$159
(207) 282-7222
(800) 426-7866

SACO MOTEL
473 Main St
(04072)
Rates: $40-$80
(207) 284-6952

WAGON WHEEL MOTEL
726 Portland Rd
(04072)
Rates: $40-$95
(207) 284-6387

SANFORD
SUPER 8 MOTEL
1892 Main St
(04073)
Rates: $50-$99
(207) 324-8823
(800) 800-8000

SCARBOROUGH
PRIDE MOTEL & COTTAGES
677 US 1 (04070)
Rates: $40-$105
(207) 883-4816
(800) 424-3350

RESIDENCE INN BY MARRIOTT
800 Roundwood
Dr (04074)
Rates: $139-$229
(207) 883-0400
(800) 331-3131

TOWNEPLACE SUITES
700 Roundwood
Dr (04074)
Rates: $79-$169
(207) 883-6800
(800) 257-3000

SEAL COVE
THE DOCKSIDE
P O Box 124
(04674)
Rates: $60+
(207) 244-5221

SEARSPORT
THE YARDARM MOTEL
172 E Main St
(04974)
Rates: $59-$115
(207) 548-2404

SKOWHEGAN
BREEZY ACRES MOTEL
315 Waterville Rd
(04976)
Rates: $45-$68
(207) 474-2703

SOUTH PORTLAND
BEST WESTERN MERRY MANOR INN
700 Main St
(04106)
Rates: $79-$159
(207) 774-6151
(800) 528-1234

ECONO LODGE
80 John Roberts
Rd (04106)
Rates: $60-$120
(207) 772-3838
(800) 424-6423

HOWARD JOHNSON
675 Main St
(04106)
Rates: $69-$179
(207) 775-5343
(800) 446-4656

MARRIOTT HOTEL
200 Sable Oaks Dr
(04106)
Rates: $109-$229
(207) 871-8000
(800) 228-9290

SABLE OAKS SUITES
303 Sable Oaks Dr
(04106)
Rates: $99-$179
(207) 775-3900

SHERATON SOUTH PORT-LAND
363 Maine Mall
Rd (04106)
Rates: $318
(207) 775-6161
(800) 325-3535

SOUTH PRINCETON
HIDEAWAY ON POCOMOOSHINE LAKE
Mary Wallace, The
Hideaway (04668)
Rates: n/a
(207) 427-6183

SOUTHPORT
LAWNMERE INN
65 Hendricks Hill
Rd (04576)
Rates: $90-$185
(207) 633-2544

SPRUCE HEAD
CRAIGNAIR INN AT CLARK IS.
5 Third St (04859)
Rates: $50-$155
(207) 594-7644

STRATTON
SPILLOVER MOTEL
P. O. Box 427
(04982)
Rates: $42-$68
(207) 246-6571

WATERFORD
WATERFORD INNE
Box 149 (04088)
Rates: $74-$99
(207) 583-4037

WATERVILLE
THE ATRIUM MOTEL
332 Main St
(04901)
Rates: $45-$80
(207) 873-2777

BEST WESTERN INN
356 Main St
(04901)
Rates: $75-$150
(207) 873-3335
(800) 528-1234

BUDGET HOST AIRPORT INN
400 Kennedy
Memorial Dr
(04901)
Rates: $35-$110
(207) 873-3366
(800) 876-2463

ECONO LODGE
455 Kennedy
Memorial Dr
(04901)
Rates: $35-$109
(207) 872-5577
(800) 424-6423

HOLIDAY INN
375 Main St
(04901)
Rates: $75-$105
(207) 873-0111
(800) 465-4329

WELLS
GARRISON SUITES MOTEL & COTTAGES
1099 Post Rd
(04090)
Rates: $35-$110
(207) 646-3497
(800) 646-3497

NE'R BEACH MOTEL
Rt 1 (04090)
Rates: $44-$119
(207) 646-2636

WEST FORKS
INN BY THE RIVER
US Rt 201 (04985)
Rates: $100-$200
(207) 663-2181

WEST KENNEBUNK
ALEWIFE COUNTRY MOTOR INN
P. O. Box 575
(04094)
Rates: $40-$70
(207) 985-6525

WEST TREMONT
QUIETSIDE CAMPGROUND & CABINS
P O Box 8 (04692)
Rates: n/a
(207) 244-5992

WESTPORT
THE SQUIRE TAR-BOX INN
1181 Main Rd
(04578)
Rates: $80-$190
(207) 882-7693

WILTON
WHISPERING PINES MOTEL
183 Lake Rd
(04294)
Rates: $60-$91
(207) 645-3721

YARMOUTH
DOWN-EAST VILLAGE MOTEL
705 US Rt 1
(04096)
Rates: $89-$99
(207) 846-5161
(800) 782-9338

AREA CODES - If the local number doesn't connect, check for a new area code.

MARYLAND

ABERDEEN

DAYS INN
783 W Bel Air Ave
(21001)
Rates: $53-$65
(410) 272-8500
(800) 329-7466

**FOUR POINTS
BY SHERATON**
980 Hospitality
Way (21001)
Rates: $79-$109
(410) 273-6300
(800) 325-3535
(800) 346-3612

**HOLIDAY INN
CHESAPEAKE
HOUSE**
1007 Beards Hill
Rd (21001)
Rates: $95-$125
(410) 272-8100
(800) 465-4329

KEN'S MOTEL
636 S Philadelphia
Blvd (21001)
Rates: n/a
(410) 272-6650

RED ROOF INN
988 Hospitality
Way (21001)
Rates: $48-$71
(410) 273-7800
(800) 843-7663

ANNAPOLIS

**CHARLES INN
B&B**
74 Charles St
(21401)
Rates: n/a
(410) 268-1451

**HOMESTEAD
STUDIO SUITES**
120 Admiral
Cochrane Dr
(21401)
Rates: $81-$106
(410) 571-6600
(800) 660-6246

**JONAS GREEN
HOUSE B&B**
124 Charles St
(21401)
Rates: n/a
(410) 263-5892
(877) 892-4845

**LOEWS
ANNAPOLIS
HOTEL**
126 West St (21401)
Rates: $135-$185
(410) 263-7777
(800) 526-2593

QUALITY INN
1542 Whitehall Rd
(21401)
Rates: $59-$139
(410) 974-4440
(800) 424-6423

RADISSON HOTEL
210 Holiday Ct
(21401)
Rates: $69-$119
(410) 224-3150
(800) 333-3333

**RESIDENCE INN
BY MARRIOTT**
170 Admiral
Cochrane Dr
(21401)
Rates: $160-$184
(410) 573-0300
(800) 331-3131

SCOTLAUR INN
165 Main St
(21401)
Rates: n/a
(410) 268-5665

**SHERATON
BARCELO HOTEL**
173 Jennifer Rd
(21401)
Rates: $89-$259
(410) 266-3131
(800) 325-3535

SUPER 8 MOTEL
74 Old Mill
Bottom Rd N
(21401)
Rates: n/a
(410) 757-2222
(800) 800-8000

ANNAPOLIS JUNCTION

**TOWNEPLAFCE
SUITES**
120 National
Business Pkwy
(20701)
Rates: $59-$139
(301) 498-7477
(800) 257-3000

BALTIMORE

**ADMIRAL FELL
INN**
888 S Broadway St
(21231)
Rates: $199-$239
(410) 522-7377

**BILTMORE SUITES
HOTEL**
205 W Madison St
(21201)
Rates: n/a
(410) 728-6550
(800) 868-5064

**BROOKSHIRE
SUITES**
120 E Lombard St
(21202)
Rates: $179-$209
(410) 625-1300

**CLARION HOTEL-
PEABODY COURT**
612 Cathedral St
(21201)
Rates: $110-$225
(410) 727-7101
(800) 424-6423

**COMFORT INN-
BWI AIRPORT**
6921 Baltimore-
Annapolis Blvd
(21225)
Rates: $79-$139
(410) 789-9100
(800) 424-6423

DAYS INN
5701 Baltimore
National Pike
(21228)
Rates: $79-$129
(410) 747-8900
(800) 329-7466

MOTEL 6
1654 Whitehead
Ct (21207)
Rates: $43-$68
(410) 265-7660
(800) 466-8356

PIER 5 HOTEL
711 Eastern Ave
(21202)
Rates: n/a
(410) 539-2000
(877) 207-9047

**RADISSON HOTEL
AT CROSS KEYS**
5100 Falls Rd
(21210)
Rates: $139-$309
(410) 532-8900
(800) 333-3333

**SHERATON INNER
HARBOR HOTEL**
300 S Charles St
(21201)
Rates: $279-$339
(410) 962-8300
(800) 325-3535

**TREMONT PLAZA
SUITE HOTEL**
222 St. Paul Pl
(21202)
Rates: $115-$155
(410) 727-2222
(800) 873-6668

BEL ALTON

**BEL ALTON
MOTEL**
9295 Crain Hwy
(20611)
Rates: n/a
(301) 934-9505

BETHESDA

MARRIOTT HOTEL
5151 Pooks Hill
Rd (20814)
Rates: $99-$160
(301) 897-9400
(800) 228-9290

**RESIDENCE INN
BY MARRIOTT**
7335 Wisconsin
Ave (20814)
Rates: $209
(301) 718-0200

BOWIE

**RIP'S
COUNTRY INN**
3809 N Crain Hwy
(20717)
Rates: n/a
(301) 262-0900

BUCKEYSTOWN

**CATOCTIN INN &
CONFERENCE
CENTER B&B**
3619 Buckeystown
Pike (21717)
Rates: n/a
(301) 874-5555
(800) 730-5550

CALIFORNIA

**SLEEP INN
LEXINTON PARK**
23428 Three Notch
Rd (20619)
Rates: $89-$170
(301) 737-0000
(800) 424-6423

SUPER 8 MOTEL
22801 Three Notch
Rd (20619)
Rates: $48-$68
(301) 862-9822
(800) 800-8000

CAMBRIDGE

BEST VALUE INN
2831 Ocean
Gateway (21613)
Rates: n/a
(410) 221-0800
(888) 315-2378

**COMMODORE'S
COTTAGE B&B**
215 Glenburn Ave
(21613)
Rates: $85-$100
(410) 228-6938

**HYATT REGENCY
CHESAPEAKE BAY
GOLF RESORT,
SPA & MARINA**
2800 Ocean
Gateway (21613)
Rates: $130-$215
(310) 901-1234
(800) 233-1234

AREA CODES - If the local number doesn't connect, check for a new area code.

CAMP SPRINGS

RAMADA INN
5151 Allentown
Rd (20746)
Rates: n/a
(301) 899-7700
(800) 272-6232

SUPER 8 MOTEL
5151-B Allentown
Rd (20746)
Rates: n/a
(301) 702-0099
(800) 800-8000

CASCADE

**BLUEBIRD ON
THE MOUNTAIN
B&B**
14700 Eyler Ave
(21719)
Rates: n/a
(301) 241-4161
(800) 362-9526

CENTREVILLE

HILLSIDE MOTEL
2630 Centreville
Rd (21617)
Rates: n/a
(410) 758-2270
(800) 705-2270

CHESAPEAKE CITY

**OLD WHARF
COTTAGE B&B**
10 Bohemia Ave
(21915)
Rates: n/a
(410) 885-5040
(877) 582-4049

CHESTERTOWN

DRIFTWOOD INN
609 Washington
Ave (21620)
Rates: n/a
(410) 778-3200

**INN AT PERRY-
PRATT HOUSE**
224 Washington
Ave (21620)
Rates: n/a
(410) 778-2734
(800) 720-8788

**THE PARKER
HOUSE B&B**
108 Spring Ave
(21620)
Rates: n/a
(410) 778-9041

**THE RIVER INN AT
ROLPH'S WHARF**
1008 Rolph's
Wharf Rd (21620)
Rates: n/a
(410) 778-6347
(800) 894-6347

CHEVY CHASE

HOLIDAY INN
5520 Wisconsin
Ave (20815)
Rates: n/a
(3010 656-1500
(800) 465-4329

CLEAR SPRINGS

**CEDAR CREST
COTTAGE B&B-
RUSTIC RETREATS**
12527 Rockdale
Rd (21722)
Rates: n/a
(202) 686-5339
(877) 787-8425

COLUMBIA

**HOMEWOOD
SUITES**
8320 Benson Dr
(21045)
Rates: $99-$199
(410) 872-9200
(800) 225-5466

**RESIDENCE INN
BY MARRIOTT**
4950 Beaver Run
Rd (21043)
Rates: n/a
(410) 997-7200
(800) 331-3131

**SHERATON
COLUMBIA HOTEL**
10207 Wincopin
Cir (21044)
Rates: $99-$235
(410) 730-3900
(800) 325-3535

**STAYBRIDGE
SUITES**
8844 Columbia
200 Pkwy (21045)
Rates: $79-$209
(410) 964-9494
(800) 238-8000

CRISFIELD

BEST VALUE INN
700 Norris Harbor
Dr (21817)
Rates: n/a
(410) 968-1900
(888) 315-2378

CUMBERLAND

**CUMBERLAND
MOTEL**
10900 Mason Rd
(21502)
Rates: n/a
(301) 724-7790

DIPLOMAT MOTEL
17012 McMullen
Hwy (21502)
Rates: n/a
(301) 729-2311

**HOLIDAY INN
DOWNTOWN**
100 S George St
(21502)
Rates: $89-$109
(301) 724-8800
(800) 465-4329

**ROCKY GAP
LODGE & GOLF
RESORT**
16701 Lakeview
Rd NE (21530)
Rates: $89-$195
(301) 784-8400
(800) 724-0828

EASTON

COMFORT INN
8523 Ocean
Gateway (21601)
Rates: $69-$139
(410) 820-8333
(800) 424-6423

DAYS INN
7018 Ocean
Gateway (21601)
Rates: $69-$140
(410) 822-4600
(800) 329-7466

EDGEWOOD

**BEST WESTERN
INVITATION INN**
1709 Edgewood
Rd (21040)
Rates: $59-$89
(410) 679-9700
(800) 528-1234

**MOTEL
EDGEWOOD**
2209 Pulaski Hwy
(21040)
Rates: $36-$42
(410) 676-4466

ELKTON

**GARDEN
COTTAGE AT
SINKING SPRINGS
FARM**
843 Elk Forest Rd
(21921)
Rates: n/a
(410) 398-5566

KNIGHTS INN
262 Belle Hill Rd
(21921)
Rates: $35-$75
(410) 392-6680
(800) 843-5644

**LONG CREEK
VIEW INN &
RETREAT**
1702 Augustine
Herman Hwy
(21921)
Rates: n/a
(410) 885-2012

MOTEL 6
223 Belle Hill Rd
(21921)
Rates: $35-$46
(410) 392-5020
(800) 466-8356

ELLICOTT CITY

FOREST MOTEL
10021 Baltimore
Natl Pike (21042)
Rates: n/a
(410) 465-2090

**RESIDENCE INN
BY MARRIOTT**
4950 Beaver Run
Way (21043)
Rates: $79-$159
(410) 997-7200
(800) 331-3131

EMMITTSBURG

SLEEP INN, INN
501 Silo Hill Pkwy
(21727)
Rates: $59-$169
(301) 447-0044
(800) 424-6423

FAIR HILL

WHITE HALL B&B
67 Poplar Hill Ln
(21921)
Rates: n/a
(410) 392-8751
(800) 230-1818

FLINTSTONE

**ROCKY GAP
LODGE & GOLF
RESORT**
16701 Lakeview
Dr NE (21530)
Rates: n/a
(301) 784-8400
(800) 724-0828

FREDERICK

COMFORT INN
998 W Patrick St
(21702)
Rates: $79-$99
(301) 662-0281
(800) 424-6423

COMFORT INN
Buckeystown
Pike & Executive
(21703)
Rates: $79-$109
(800) 424-6423

ECONO LODGE
6005 Urbana
Pike (21704)
Rates: $49-$74
(301) 698-0555
(800) 424-6423

HAMPTON INN
5311 Buckeystown
Pike (21701)
Rates: $99-$110
(301) 698-2500
(800) 426-7866

**HOLIDAY INN
EXPRESS
FSK MALL**
5579 Spectrum
Dr (21701)
Rates: $74-$94
(301) 695-2881
(800) 465-4329

**HOLIDAY INN-
FT. DETRICK**
999 W Patrick St
(21702)
Rates: $70-$85
(301) 662-5141
(800) 465-4329

**HOLIDAY INN
FRANCIS SCOTT
KEY MALL**
5400 Holiday Dr
(21701)
Rates: $79-$99
(301) 694-7500
(800) 465-4329

AREA CODES - If the local number doesn't connect, check for a new area code.

MAINSTAY SUITES
7310 Executive
Way (21703)
Rates: $89-$129
(301) 668-4600
(800) 424-6423

**QUALITY INN-HISTORIC
FREDERICK**
420 Prospect Blvd
(21701)
Rates: $59-$99
(301) 695-6200
(800) 424-6423

**RESIDENCE INN
BY MARRIOTT**
5230 Westview Dr
(21703)
Rates: $99-$134
(301) 360-0010
(800) 331-3131

FROSTBURG
CHARLIE'S MOTEL
220 W Main St
(21532)
Rates: n/a
(301) 689-6557
(888) 230-9053

FROSTBURG INN
147 E Main St
(21532)
Rates: n/a
(301) 689-3831

**SAVAGE RIVER
LODGE-CABINS**
1600 Mt. Aetna Rd
(21532)
Rates: n/a
(301) 689-3200

GAITHERS-BURG
RED ROOF INN
497 Quince
Orchard Rd
(20878)
Rates: $70-$95
(301) 977-3311
(800) 843-7663

**RESIDENCE INN
BY MARRIOTT**
9721
Washingtonian
Blvd (20879)
Rates: $194
(301) 590-3003
(800) 331-3131

**SUMMERFIELD
SUITES**
200 Skidmore
Blvd (20879)
Rates: $150
(301) 527-6000
(800) 833-4353

**TOWNEPLACE
SUITES BY
MARRIOTT**
212 Perry Pkwy
(20879)
Rates: $59-$109
(301) 590-2300
(800) 257-3000

GERMANTOWN
**HOMESTEAD
VILLAGE GUEST
STUDIOS**
20141 Century
Blvd (20874)
Rates: $69-$104
(301) 515-4500
(888) 782-9473

GLEN BURNIE
DAYS INN
6600 Ritchie Hwy
(21061)
Rates: $75-$139
(410) 761-8300
(800) 329-7466

GRANTSVILLE
GRANTSVILLE INN
2541 Chestnut
Ridge Rd (21536)
Rates: $59-$109
(301) 895-5993

**LITTLE MEADOWS
MOTEL & CAMP-GROUND**
12676 National
Hwy (21536)
Rates: n/a
(301) 895-5142

**WALNUT
RIDGE B&B**
92 Main St (21536)
Rates: $65-$75
(301) 895-4248
(888) 419-2568

GRASONVILLE
**CHESAPEAKE
MOTEL**
107 Hissey Rd
(21638)
Rates: n/a
(410) 827-7272
(800) 822-7272

COMFORT INN
3101 Main St
(21638)
Rates: $79-$179
(410) 827-6767
(800) 424-6423

**LANDS END
MANOR ON THE
BAY B&B**
232 Prospect Bay
Dr (21638)
Rates: n/a
(410) 827-6284

HAGERSTOWN
**CLARION HOTEL
& CONF CENTER
ANTIETAM CREEK**
901 Dual Hwy
(21740)
Rates: $59-$109
(301) 733-5100
(800) 424-6423

**FOUR POINTS
BY SHERATON**
1910 Dual Hwy
(21740)
Rates: $56-$69
(301) 790-3010
(800) 325-3535

MOTEL 6
11321 Massey
Blvd (21740)
Rates: $39-$50
(301) 582-4445
(800) 466-8356

QUALITY INN
1101 Dual Hwy
(21740)
Rates: $69-$109
(301) 733-2700
(800) 424-6423

**SLEEP INN,
INN & SUITES**
18216 Colonel
H K Douglas Dr
(21740)
Rates: $60-$160
(301) 766-9449
(800) 424-6423

SUPER 8 MOTEL
16805 Blake Rd
(21740)
Rates: $42-$55
(301) 582-1992
(800) 800-8000

HANOVER
**RED ROOF INN
BWI PARKWAY**
7306 Parkway Dr
(21076)
Rates: $55-$81
(410) 712-4070
(800) 843-7663

**RESIDENCE INN
BY MARRIOTT**
7035 Arundel
Mills Cir (21076)
Rates: $95-$219
(410) 799-7332
(800) 331-3131

*HAVRE DE
GRACE*
SUPER 8 MOTEL
929 Pulaski Hwy
(21078)
Rates: n/a
(410) 939-1880
(800) 800-8000

**SPENCER SILVER
MANSION B&B**
200 S Union Ave
(21078)
Rates: n/a
(410) 939-1485
(800) 780-1485

HUNTINTOWN
SUPER 8 MOTEL
4694 Indian Head
Hwy (20640)
Rates: n/a
(301) 753-8100
(800) 800-8000

INDIAN HEAD
SUPER 8 MOTEL
4694 Indian Head
Hwy (20640)
Rates: $50-$78
(301) 753-8100
(800) 800-8000

JESSUP
RED ROOF INN
8000 Washington
Blvd (20794)
Rates: $58-$71
(410) 796-0380
(800) 843-7663

JOPPA
SUPER 8 MOTEL
1015 Pulaski Hwy
(21085)
Rates: $60-$76
(410) 676-2700
(800) 800-8000

KEEDYSVILLE
**HOWSERZ
MISTEKE-RUSTIC
RETREATS**
20 N Main st
(21756)
Rates: n/a
(202) 686-5339
(877) 787-8425

LA PLATA
**BEST WESTERN
LA PLATA INN**
6900 Crain Hwy
(20646)
Rates: $69-$119
(301) 934-4900
(800) 528-1234
(877) 356-4900

LAVALE
**OAK TREE INN/
PENNY'S DINER**
12310 Winchester
Rd SW (21502)
Rates: $49-$69
(3010 729-6700
(888) 897-9647

SUPER 8 MOTEL
1301 National
Hwy (21502)
Rates: $46-$54
(301) 729-6265
(800) 800-8000

*LEONARDS
TOWN*
RELAX INN
41655 Park Ave
(20650)
Rates: n/a
(301) 475-3011

*LEXINGTON
PARK*
BEST WESTERN
Rt 235 (20653)
Rates: $69-$92
(301) 862-4100
(800) 528-1234

DAYS INN
21847 Three Notch
Rd (20653)
Rates: $75-$119
(301) 863-6666
(800) 329-7466

AREA CODES - If the local number doesn't connect, check for a new area code.

LINTHICUM HEIGHTS

AMERISUITES-BALITMORE AIR-PORT
940 International Dr (21090)
Rates: $109-$209
(410) 859-3366
(800) 833-1516

CANDLEWOOD SUITES
1247 Winterston Rd (21090)
Rates: $99-$159
(410) 850-9214
(888) 226-3539

COMFORT INN AIRPORT
6921 Baltimore Annapolis Blvd (21225)
Rates: $119-$139
(410) 789-9100
(800) 424-6423

COMFORT INN BWI AIRPORT
815 Elkridge Landing Rd (21090)
Rates: $89-$169
(410) 691-1000
(800) 424-6423

FOUR POINTS BY SHERATON
7032 Elm Rd (21240)
Rates: $89-$239
(410) 859-3300
(800) 325-3535

HAMPTON INN WASHINGTON INTL AIRPORT
829 Elkridge Landing Rd (21090)
Rates: $99-$119
(410) 850-0600
(800) 426-7866

HOLIDAY INN-BWI AIRPORT
890 Elkridge Landing Rd (21240)
Rates: $98-$199
(410) 859-8400
(800) 465-4329
(800) 810-0271

HOMESTEAD STUDIO SUITES
939 International Dr (21090)
Rates: $91-$106
(410) 691-2500
(888) 782-9473

HOMEWOOD SUITES HOTEL BWI AIRPORT
1181 Winterson Rd (21090)
Rates: $139-$174
(410) 684-6100
(800) 225-5466

RED ROOF INN BWI AIRPORT
827 Elkridge Landing Rd (21090)
Rates: $66-$93
(410) 850-7600
(800) 843-7663

RESIDENCE INN-BWI
1160 Winterson Dr (21240)
Rates: $119-$199
(410) 691-0255
(800) 331-3131

SHERATON INTL HOTEL BWI AIRPORT
7032 Elm Rd (21090)
Rates: $79-$225
(410) 859-3300
(800) 325-3535

SLEEP INN & SUITES-BWI
6055 Belle Grove Rd (21240)
Rates: $119-$129
(410) 789-7223
(800) 424-6423

LOTHIAN

DUNCAN'S FAMILY CAMPGROUND CABINS
5381 Sands Rd (20711)
Rates: n/a
(410) 741-9558
(800) 222-2086

MCHENRY

COMFORT INN
2704 Deep Creek Dr (21541)
Rates: $59-$119
(301) 387-4200
(800) 424-6423

GARRETT INN
17848 Garrett Hwy (21541)
Rates: n/a
(301) 387-6696

INNLET MOTOR LODGE
2001 Deep Creek Dr (21541)
Rates: n/a
(301) 387-5596
(800) 540-0763

RAILEY MOUNTAIN LAKE VACATION RENTALS
22491 Garrett Hwy (21541)
Rates: n/a
(301) 387-2124
(800) 846-7368

WISP MOUNTAIN RESROT HOTEL & CONF CTR
290 Marsh Hill Rd (21541)
Rates: $89-$199
(301) 387-5581

MECHANICS-VILLE

WIDE BAY COTTAGE AT DAMERON B&B
28170 Old Village Rd (20659)
Rates: n/a
(301) 884-3254

NORTH EAST

CRYSTAL INN
1 Center Dr (21901)
Rates: $89
(410) 287-7100
(800) 631-3803

TAILWINDS FARM B&B
41 Tailwinds Ln (21901)
Rates: n/a
(410) 658-8187

OAKLAND

BOARD ROOM MOTEL
12678 Garrett Hwy (21550)
Rates: n/a
(301) 334-2126

GLEN HAVEN CHALET
491 Sanders Ln (21550)
Rates: n/a
(31) 334-9616

TIMBER RIDGE MANOR RENTALS
Rt 219 (21563)
Rates: n/a
(703) 591-2107

OCEAN CITY

BAREFOOT MAILMAN MOTEL
35th St & Oceanside (21842)
Rates: n/a
(410) 289-5343
(800) 395-3668

BEST WESTERN SEA BAY INN
6007 Coastal Hwy (21842)
Rates: $29-$404
(410) 524-6100
(800) 528-1234
(800) 888-2229
(pets allowed on a seasonal basis)

CLARION RESORT FONTAINBLEAU HOTEL
10100 Coastal Hwy (21842)
Rates: $139-$369
(410) 524-3535
(800) 424-6423
(800) 252-7466

FENWICK INN
13801 Coastal Hwy (21842)
Rates: $49-$229
(410) 250-1100

OC APARTMENTS
508 Edgewater Ave (21842)
Rates: n/a
(410) 289-4000

SAFARI MOTEL
13th St, Boardwalk (21842)
Rates: n/a
(410) 289-6411
(800) 787-2183

WINDJAMMER APARTMENT MOTEL
4503 Atlantic Ave (21842)
Rates: n/a
(410) 289-9409

OWINGS MILLS

AMERISUITES
4730 Painters Mill Rd (21117)
Rates: $134-$199
(410) 998-3630
(800) 844-1516

OXFORD

COMBSBERRY 1730 INN
4837 Evergreen Rd (21654)
Rates: n/a
(410) 226-5353

PERRYVILLE

RAMADA INN
61 Heather Ln (21903)
Rates: $59-$99
(410) 642-2866
(800) 272-6232

RELAX INN
5271 Pulaski Hwy (21903)
Rates: n/a
(410) 642-2282

POCOMOKE CITY

DAYS INN
1540 Ocean Hwy (21851)
Rates: $55-$130
(410) 957-3000
(800) 329-7466

QUALITY INN
825 Ocean Hwy (21851)
Rates: $56-$100
(410) 957-1300
(800) 424-6423

PORT REPUBLIC

ENCHANTED BAYFRONT HOME RENTAL
10 Governors Run Rd (20676)
Rates: n/a
(703) 620-4408

AREA CODES - If the local number doesn't connect, check for a new area code.

PRINCE FREDERICK

SUPER 8 MOTEL
40 Commerce Ln (20678)
Rates: n/a
(410) 535-8668
(800) 800-8000

PRINCESS ANNE

ECONO LODGE
10936 Market Ln (21853)
Rates: $49-$79
(410) 651-9400
(800) 424-6423

WATERLOO COUNTRY INN
28822 Mt Vernon Rd (21853)
Rates: $100-$225
(410) 651-0883

RAWLINGS

DIPLOMAT MOTEL
17012 McMullen Hwy (21502)
Rates: $35-$48
(301) 729-2311

RIDGE

SCHEIBLE'S MOTEL
48347 Wynne Rd (20680)
Rates: n/a
(301) 872-5175

ROCK HALL

BAY BREEZE INN BED & BREAKFAST
5758 Main St (21661)
Rates: $65-$98
(410) 639-2061

INN AT HUNTINGFIELD CREEK B&B
4928 Eastern Neck Rd (21661)
Rates: $130-$225
(410) 639-7779

MARINERS MOTEL
5681 S Hawthorne Ave (21661)
Rates: $60-$70
(410) 639-2291

ROCKVILLE

RED ROOF INN
16001 Shady Grove Rd (20850)
Rates: $56-$83
(301) 948-0965
(800) 843-7663

WOODFIN SUITES HOTEL
1380 Piccard Dr (20850)
Rates: $124-$179
(301) 590-9880
(800) 237-8811

ST. LEONARD

FISHERMAN'S COTTAGE RENTAL
5863 Hickory Rd in Long Beach (20685)
Rates: n/a
(410) 535-5308

JEFF'S BED & FIX YOUR OWN BREAKFAST RENTAL
6027 Bayview Rd in Long Beach (20685)
Rates: n/a
(410) 535-5308

OSPREY'S NEST RENTAL
6040 Bayview Rd in Long Beach (20685)
Rates: n/a
(410) 535-5308

ST. MICHAELS

CYGNET HOUSE BED & BREAKFAST
201 Carpenter St (21663)
Rates: n/a
(410) 745-2929

FIVE GABLES INN & SPA
209 N Talbot St (21663)
Rates: $130-$375
(410) 745-0100
(877) 466-0100

GEORGE S. BROOKS HOUSE B&B
24500 Rolles Range Rd (21663)
Rates: n/a
(410) 745-0999

INN AT PERRY CABIN
308 Watkins Ln (21663)
Rates: n/a
(410) 745-2200
(800) 722-2949

KEMP HOUSE INN
412 S Talbot St (21663)
Rates: n/a
(410) 745-2243

PARSONAGE INN B&B
210 N Talbot St (21663)
Rates: $125-$195
(410) 745-5519

SALISBURY

BEST VALUE INN
2625 N Salisbury Blvd (21801)
Rates: $66-$120
(410) 742-7194
(800) 446-4656

BEST WESTERN SALISBURY PLAZA
1735 N Salisbury Blvd (21801)
Rates: $49-$140
(410) 546-1300
(800) 528-1234
(800) 636-7554

CHESAPEAKE INN
712 N Salisbury Rd (21801)
Rates: n/a
(410) 219-3399
(800) 709-7155

COMFORT INN
2701 N Salisbury Blvd (21801)
Rates: $59-$139
(410) 543-4666
(800) 424-6423

ECONOMY INN
1500 N Salisbury Blvd (21801)
Rates: n/a
(410) 749-6178

LORD SALISBURY MOTEL
2637 N Salisbury Blvd (21801)
Rates: $39-$75
(410) 742-3251
(800) 299-3232

RAMADA INN
300 S Salisbury Blvd (21801)
Rates: $65-$139
(410) 546-4400
(800) 272-6232
(888) 800-7617

TEMPLE HILL MOTEL
1510 Salisbury Blvd (21801)
Rates: $40-$90
(410) 742-3284
(800) 272-7829

SHARPSBURG

CLIPP'S MILL & WAREHOUSE- RUSTIC RETREAT
110 E Chaplain St (21782)
Rates: n/a
(202) 686-5339
(877) 787-8425

SHERWOOD

LOWES WHARF MARINA INN
21651 Lowes Wharf Rd (21665)
Rates: n/a
(410) 745-6684
(888) 484-9267

SILVER SPRING

LITTLE HOUSE AT WIND SWEPT B&B
17000 Carwell Rd (20905)
Rates: n/a
(301) 384-3336
(800) 861-2434

RAMADA LIMITED
7990 Georgia Ave (20910)
Rates: n/a
(301) 565-3444
(800) 272-6232
(800) 558-6877

SNOW HILL

THE MANSION HOUSE B&B
4436 Bayside Rd, Public Landing (21863)
Rates: n/a
(410) 732-3189

RIVER HOUSE INN BED & BREAKFST
201 E Market St (21863)
Rates: $99-$195
(410) 632-2722

SOLOMONS

COMFORT INN BEACON MARINA
255 Lore Rd (20688)
Rates: $65-$139
(410) 326-6303
(800) 424-6423

LOCUST INN ROOMS B&B
14478 Solomons Island Rd S (20688)
Rates: n/a
(410) 326-9817

SWANTON

ACORN ACRES
932 Beckman Peninsula Rd (21561)
Rates: n/a
(301) 387-9435

TAYLORS ISLAND

BECKY PHIPP'S INN B&B
Taylor's Island Marina Rd, Rt 16 (21669)
Rates: n/a
(410) 221-2911

TAYLORS ISLAND CAMPGROUND APT RENTALS
Bayshore Rd (21669)
Rates: n/a
(410) 397-3275

THURMONT

RAMBLER INN
426 N Church St (21788)
Rates: $38-$92
(301) 271-2424

SUPER 8 MOTEL
300 Tippin Dr (21788)
Rates: $48-$68
(301) 271-7888
(800) 800-8000

TILGHMAN ISLAND

HARRISON'S COUNTRY INN
21551 Chesapeake House Dr (21671)
Rates: n/a
(410) 886-2121

AREA CODES - If the local number doesn't connect, check for a new area code.

TIMONIUM
RED ROOF INN
111 W Timonium
Rd (21093)
Rates: $60-$78
(410) 666-0380
(800) 843-7663

TOWSON
COMFORT INN
8801 Loch Raven
Blvd (21204)
Rates: $99-$179
(410) 882-0900
(800) 424-6423

HOLIDAY INN
1100 Cromwell
Bridge Rd (21286)
Rates: $80-$134
(410) 823-4410
(800) 465-4329

**SHERATON-
BALTIMORE
NORTH**
903 Dulaney
Valley Rd (21204)
Rates: n/a
(410) 321-7400
(800) 433-7619

UPPER
MARLBORO
BRAGG MOTEL
7001 Crain Hwy
(20772)
Rates: n/a
(301) 627-1880

**FOREST HILLS
MOTEL**
2901 Crain Hwy
(20772)
Rates: $45-$55
(301) 627-3969

WALDORF
COMFORT SUITES
11765 Business
Park Dr (20601)
Rates: n/a
(301) 932-4400
(800) 424-6423
(800) 682-3206

ECONO LODGE
11770 Business
Park Dr (20601)
Rates: $59-$129
(301) 645-0022
(800) 424-6423

HAMPTON INN
3750 Crain Hwy
(20603)
Rates: $96-$129
(301) 632-9600
(800) 426-7866

SUPER 8 MOTEL
5050 Hwy 301 S
(20602)
Rates: $45-$59
(301) 932-8957
(800) 800-8000

WESTMINSTER
**BEST WESTERN
WESTMINSTER
CATERING &
CONF CENTER**
451 WMC Dr
(21158)
Rates: $56-$150
(410) 857-1900
(800) 528-1234

BOSTON INN
533 Baltimore
Blvd (21157)
Rates: $36-$70
(410) 848-9095
(800) 634-0846

WHITE MARSH
**RESIDENCE INN
BY MARRIOTT**
4980 Mercantile
Rd (21236)
Rates: $119-$199
(410) 933-9554
(800) 331-3131

WHITEHAVEN
**WHITEHAVEN
B&B**
23844 River St
(21856)
Rates: $75-$100
(410) 873-3294
(888) 205-5921

**WHITEHAVEN
HOTEL**
2685 Whitehaven
Rd (21856)
Rates: n/a
(410) 873-2000
(877) 809-8296

WILLIAMSPORT
RED ROOF INN
310 E Potomac St
(21795)
Rates: $42-$49
(301) 582-3500
(800) 843-7663

WITTMAN
WATERMARK B&B
8956 Tilghman
Island Rd (21676)
Rates: n/a
(410) 745-2892
(800) 314-7734

AREA CODES - If the local number doesn't connect, check for a new area code.

MASSACHUSETTS

AMHERST

LORD JEFFERY INN
30 Boltwood Ave (01002)
Rates: $70-$109
(413) 253-2576
(800) 742-0358

UNIVERSITY LODGE
345 N Pleasant St (01002)
Rates: $65-$105
(413) 256-8111

ANDOVER

COMFORT SUITES
4 Riverside Dr (01810)
Rates: $80-$145
(978) 475-6000
(800) 424-6423

RESIDENCE INN BY MARRIOTT
500 Minuteman Rd (01810)
Rates: $99-$179
(978) 683-0382
(800) 331-3131

STAYBRIDGE SUITES
4 Tech Dr (01810)
Rates: $89-$129
(978) 686-2000
(800) 238-8000

WYNDHAM HOTEL
123 Old River Rd (01810)
Rates: $79-$175
(978) 975-3600
(800) 996-3426

ARLINGTON

HAWTHORN SUITES LTD
1 Massachusetts Ave (02474)
Rates: $119-$229
(781) 643-7258
(800) 527-1133

AUBURN

BAYMONT INN
446 Southbridge St (01501)
Rates: $52-$72
(508) 832-7000
(877) 229-6668

BEST WESTERN YANKEE DRUMMER INN
624 Southbridge St (01501)
Rates: $99-$115
(508) 832-3221
(800) 528-1234

BARRE

HARTMAN'S HERB FARM B&B
1026 Old Dana Rd (01005)
Rates: $70-$109
(978) 355-2015

JENKINS HISTORIC COUNTRY INN
7 West St (01005)
Rates: $165-$195
(978) 355-6444
(800) 378-7373

BERNARDSTON

FOX INN MOTEL
71 Northfield Rd (01337)
Rates: $70-$109
(413) 648-9131
(800) 436-9466

WINDMILL MOTEL
497 Northfield Rd (01337)
Rates: $35-$70
(413) 648-9152

BILLERICA

HOMEWOOD SUITES BY HILTON
35 Middlesex Trpk (01821)
Rates: $70-$149
(978) 670-7111
(800) 225-5466

BOSTON

BOSTON HARBOR HOTEL
70 Rowes Wharf (02110)
Rates: $235-$510
(617) 439-7000
(800) 752-7077

BOSTON PARK PLAZA HOTEL
64 Arlington St (02116)
Rates: $119-$309
(617) 426-2000

CLARION HOTEL
119 Merrimac St (02114)
Rates: $149-$189
(617) 624-0202
(800) 424-6423

COLONNADE HOTEL
120 Huntington Ave (02116)
Rates: $150+
(617) 424-7000
(800) 962-3030

COMFORT INN
900 William T. Morrissey Blvd (02122)
Rates: $99-$189
(617) 287-9200
(800) 424-6423

COPLEY HOUSE INN
239 W Newton St (02116)
Rates: $70-$109
(617) 236-8300
(800) 331-1318

DOUBLETREE GUEST SUITES
400 Soldiers Field Rd (02134)
Rates: $89-$309
(617) 783-0090
(800) 222-8733

THE ELIOT HOTEL
370 Commonwealth Ave (02115)
Rates: $255-$415
(617) 267-1607

EMBASSY SUITES LOGAN AIRPORT
207 Porter St (02128)
Rates: $109-$229
(617) 567-5000
(800) 362-2779

FAIRMONT COPLEY PLAZA HOTEL
138 St James Ave (02116)
Rates: $219-$379
(617) 267-5300
(800) 441-1414

FIFTEEN BEACON HOTEL
15 Beacon St (02108)
Rates: $395-$1400
(617) 670-1500
(877) 982-3226

FOUR SEASONS HOTEL BOSTON
200 Boylston St (02116)
Rates: $465-$610
(617) 338-4400
(800) 332-3442
(800) 268-6282

HILTON-BOSTON LOGAN AIRPORT
85 Terminal Rd (02128)
Rates: $99-$279
(617) 568-6700
(800) 445-8667

HOTEL COMMON-WEALTH
500 Commonwealth Ave (02215)
Rates: $239-$329
(617) 933-5000

HOWARD JOHNSON LODGE
1271 Boylston St (02215)
Rates: $130-$215
(617) 267-8300
(800) 446-4656
(800) 654-2000

HYATT REGENCY FINANCIAL DIST
One Avenue de Lafayette (02111)
Rates: $159-$290
(617) 912-1234
(800) 233-1234

LANGHAM HOTEL
250 Franklin St (02110)
Rates: $333-$370
(617) 451-1900
(800) 791-7761

MIDTOWN HOTEL
220 Huntington Ave (02115)
Rates: $89-$239
(617) 262-1000
(800) 343-1177

OMNI PARKER HOUSE HOTEL DOWNTOWN
60 School St (02108)
Rates: $159-$309
(617) 227-8600
(800) 843-6664

ONYX HOTEL
155 Portland St (02114)
Rates: $209-$309
(617) 557-9955
(866) 660-6699

RAMADA INN
800 Morrissey Blvd (02122)
Rates: $99-$189
(617) 287-9100
(800) 272-6232

RESIDENCE INN BY MARRIOTT
44 Charles River Ave (02129)
Rates: $189-$299
(617) 242-5554
(800) 331-3131

RITZ-CARLTON BOSTON
15 Arlington St (02117)
Rates: $305-$525
(617) 536-5700
(800) 241-3333

RITZ CARLTON-BOSTON COMMON
10 Avery St (02111)
Rates: $320-$505
(617) 574-7100
(800) 241-3333

SEAPORT HOTEL
1 Seaport Lane (02110)
Rates: $169-$299
(617) 385-4000
(877) 732-7678

SHERATON HOTEL
39 Dalton St (02199)
Rates: $309+
(617) 236-2000
(800) 325-3535

UNIVERSITY B&B RESERVATIONS
Box 57166 (02457)
Rates: n/a
(617) 738-1434
(800) 347-5088

THE WESTIN COPLEY PLACE
10 Huntington Ave (02116)
Rates: $260-$355
(617) 262-9600
(800) 937-8461

BOXBOROUG

HOLIDAY INN
242 Adams Pl (01719)
Rates: $129-$219
(978) 263-8701
(800) 465-4329

BRAINTREE

CANDLEWOOD SUITES
235 Wood Rd (02184)
Rates: $50-$109
(781) 849-7450
(800) 946-6200

HOLIDAY INN EXP
190 Wood Rd (02184)
Rates: $99-$200
(781) 848-1260
(800) 465-4329

MOTEL 6
125 Union St (02184)
Rates: $69-$86
(781) 848-7890
(800) 466-8356

SHERATON HOTEL
37 Forbes Rd (02184)
Rates: $140-$179
(781) 848-0600
(800) 325-3535

BROCKTON

RESIDENCE INN BY MARRIOTT
124 Liberty St (02301)
Rates: $89-$209
(508) 583-3600
(800) 331-3131

BROOKLINE

BEECH TREE INN
83 Longwood Ave (02146)
Rates: $40-$109
(617) 277-1620
(800) 544-9660

BERTRAM INN
92 Sewall Ave (02146)
Rates: $70-$164
(617) 566-2234
(800) 295-3822

HOLIDAY INN
1200 Beacon St (02146)
Rates: $169-$199
(617) 277-1200
(800) 465-4329

THE SAMUEL SEWALL INN
143 St. Paul St (02146)
Rates: $70-$150+
(617) 713-0123
(888) 713-2566

BUCKLAND

THE RESTFUL CROW B&B
6 Cross St (01338)
Rates: $70-$149
(413) 625-9507

BURLINGTON

CANDLEWOOD SUITES
130 Middlesex Tpke (01803)
Rates: n/a
(781) 229-4300
(888) 226-3539

FOUR POINTS BY SHERATON
30 Wheeler Rd (01803)
Rates: $110-$149
(781) 272-8800
(800) 325-3535

HOMESTEAD STUDIO SUITES
40 South Ave (01803)
Rates: $95-$117
(781) 359-9099
(888) 782-9473

STAYBRIDGE SUITES
11 Old Concord Rd (01803)
Rates: $126-$171
(781) 221-2233
(800) 238-8000

SUMMERFIELD SUITES HOTEL
2 Van de Graaf Dr (01803)
Rates: $109-$199
(781) 270-0800
(800) 833-4353

BUZZARDS BAY

BAY MOTOR INN
223 Main St (02532)
Rates: $79-$100
(508) 759-3989

FOX RUN B&B
171 PuritanRd (02532)
Rates: $70-$150+
(508) 759-1458

CAMBRIDGE

ALL-NEW WINDSOR HOUSE
283 Windsor St (02139)
Rates: $70-$109
(617) 354-3116

BEST WESTERN HOTEL TRIA'
220 Alewife Brook Pkwy (02138)
Rates: $139-$299
(617) 491-8000
(800) 528-1234
(866)- 33-8742

CAMBRIDGE GATEWAY INN
211 Concord Tpke (02140)
Rates: $70-$109
(617) 661-7800
(800) 258-1980

THE CHARLES HOTEL HARVARD SQUARE
1 Bennett St (02138)
Rates: $350-$575
(617) 864-1200
(800) 882-1818

HOTEL @ MIT
20 Sidney St (02139)
Rates: $109-$399
(617) 577-0200
(800) 445-8667

HOTEL MARLOWE
25 Edwin H Land Blvd (02141)
Rates: $299-$329
(617) 868-8000
(800) 825-7040

HYATT REGENCY CAMBRIDGE
575 Memorial Dr (02139)
Rates: $129-$265
(617) 492-1234
(800) 532-1234

RESIDENCE INN BY MARRIOTT
6 Cambridge Center (02142)
Rates: $179-$399
(617) 349-0700
(800) 331-3131

SHERATON COMMANDER HOTEL
16 Garden St (02138)
Rates: $109-$405
(617) 547-4800
(800) 535-5007

CAPE COD TOWNS

See listings under the following cities:
Barnstable
Bass River
Bourne
Brewster
Buzzards Bay
Centerville
Chatham
Dennis Port
East Falmouth
East Sandwich
Eastham
Falmouth
Harwich Port
Hyannis
Hyannis Port
North Eastham
North Truro
Orleans
Provincetown
Sandwich
South Orleans
South Wellfleet
South Yarmouth
Wellfleet
West Barnstable
West Dennis
West Harwich
West Yarmouth
Yarmouth Port

CENTERVILLE

THE INN AT CENTERVILLE CORNERS
1338 Craigville Beach Rd (02632)
Rates: $115-$130
(508) 775-7223
(800) 242-1137

CHARLEMONT

CHARLEMONT INN
107 Main St (01339)
Rates: $70-$100
(413) 339-5796

THE WARFIELD HOUSE INN B&B
133 Warfield Rd (01339)
Rates: $70-$149
(413) 339-8375
(888) 339-8434

CHARLESTOWN

BUNKER HILL B&B
80 Elm St (02129)
Rates: $110-$149
(617) 241-8067

MARRIOTT RESIDENCE INN-BOSTON HARBOR ON TUDOR WHARF
34-44 Charles River Ave (02129)
Rates: $150+
(617) 242-9000
(866) 297-2296

CHELMSFORD

BEST WESTERN INN
187 Chelmsford St (01824)
Rates: $59-$109
(978) 256-7511
(800) 528-1234
(888) 770-9992

CHICOPEE

MOTEL 6
Rt 291, Burnett Rd (01020)
Rates: $41-$60
(413) 592-5141
(800) 466-8356

SUPER 8 MOTEL
463 Memorial Dr (01020)
Rates: $57-$75
(413) 592-6171
(800) 800-8000

COLRAIN

HIGH POCKET B&B AND BARN
38 Adams Place Rd (01340)
Rates: $70-$109
(413) 624-8988

CONCORD

BEST WESTERN AT HISTORIC CONCORD
740 Elm St (01742)
Rates: $94-$149
(978) 369-6100
(800) 528-1234

NORTH BRIDGE INN B&B
21 Monument St (01742)
Rates: $150+
(978) 772-4300

DANVERS

MOTEL 6
65 Newbury St (01923)
Rates: $59-$70
(978) 774-8045
(800) 466-8356

RESIDENCE INN BY MARRIOTT
51 Newbury St (01923)
Rates: $148-$227
(978) 777-7171
(800) 331-3131

SHERATON FERN-CROFT RESORT
50 Ferncroft Rd (01923)
Rates: $79-$149
(978) 777-2500
(800) 325-3535

TOWNEPLACE SUITES
238 Andover St (01923)
Rates: $79-$129
(978) 777-6222
(800) 257-3000

DARTMOUTH

RESIDENCE INN BY MARRIOTT
181 Faunce Corner Rd (02747)
Rates: $109-$219
(508) 984-5858
(800) 331-3131

DEDHAM

RESIDENCE INN BY MARRIOTT
259 Elm St (02026)
Rates: $149-$169
(781) 407-0999
(800) 331-3131

DEERFIELD

DEERFIELD INN
81 Old Main St (01342)
Rates: $125-$250
(413) 774-5587
(800) 926-3865

RED ROOF INN
Rts 5 & 10 (01342)
Rates: $40-$109
(413) 6657161
(800) 843-7663
(800) 733-7663

DENNIS PORT

ACORN COTTAGES
927 Main St (02639)
Rates: $495-$895
Weekly
(508) 760-2101

BAY LIGHT COTTAGES
235 Division St (02639)
Rates: $100-$750
(508) 398-5989

THE BEACH ROSE COTTAGE
46 Chase Ave (02639)
Rates: $400-$750
Weekly
(508) 760-1140

BETH'S BEACH HOUSE
General Delivery (02639)
Rates: $650
Weekly
(508) 385-4588

GLENDON BEACH COTTAGES
Glendon Rd (02639)
Rates: $110-$149
(508) 394-5832

HURRICANE PINES VACATION RENTAL
94 Old Wharf Rd (02639)
Rates: $200-$400
Weekly
(508) 398-2616

LAMPLIGHTER MOTOR LODGE
329 Main St (02639)
Rates: $28-$55
(508) 398-8469

MARINE LODGE COTTAGES
15 North St (02639)
Rates: $300-$750
Weekly
(508) 398-2963
(888) 398-2963

SEA LORD RESORT MOTEL
Chase Ave (02639)
Rates: $35-$110
(508) 398-6900

TOWN COTTAGES
319 Main St (02639)
Rates: $429
Weekly
(508) 398-8469
(800) 328-8812

UNION WHARF VILLAGE
68 Union Wharf Dr (02639)
Rates: $300-$750
Weekly
(508) 881-1381

DEVENS

DEVENS INN & CONF CENTER
20 10th Mountain Division Rd (01432)
Rates: $40-$70
(978) 772-4300

EAST BOSTON

HILTON-LOGAN AIRPORT
75 Service Rd, Logan Intl Airport (02128)
Rates: $105-$200
(617) 569-9300
(800) 445-8667

EAST FALMOUTH

GREAT BAY MOTEL
485 Teaticket Hwy (02536)
Rates: $50-$109
(508) 548-4114
(866) 448-4114

GREEN HARBOR WATERFRONT MOTOR LODGE
134 Acapesket Rd (02536)
Rates: $89-$150+
(508) 548-4747
(800) 548-5556

EAST SANDWICH

THE EARL OF SANDWICH MOTEL
378 Rt 6A (02537)
Rates: $45-$89
(508) 888-1415
(800) 442-3275

WINGSCORTON FARM INN
Old Kings Hwy (02537)
Rates: $90-$175
(508) 888-0534
(508) 888-0545

EAST WAREHAM

ATLANTIC MOTEL
7 Depot St (02538)
Rates: $59-$189
(508) 295-0210

EASTHAM

COTTAGE GROVE B&B
1975 Rt 6 (02642)
Rates: $70-$149
(508) 255-0500
(877) 521-5522

CRANBERRY COTTAGES
785 State Hwy (02642)
Rates: $45-$85
(508) 255-0602
(800) 292-6631

GIBSON COTTAGES
80 Depot Rd (02642)
Rates: $70-$109
(508) 255-0882

SMITH HEIGHTS COTTAGES
1420 Rt 6 (02642)
Rates: $420-$680
Weekly
(508) 255-5895

EAST HAMPTON

BLOOMSBURY B&B
178 Main St (01027)
Rates: $110-$145
(413) 527-8681
(877) 225-2200

EASTON

EASTON 138 MOTEL
25 Washington St (02356)
Rates: $35-$69
(508) 238-4321

ESSEX

ESSEX RIVER HOUSE MOTEL
132 Main St (01929)
Rates: $70-$149
(978) 768-6800

GEORGE FULLER HOUSE B&B
148 Main St (01929)
Rates: $110-$149
(978) 768-7766
(800) 477-0148

AREA CODES - If the local number doesn't connect, check for a new area code.

FAIRHAVEN

HOLIDAY INN EXP
110 Middle St
(02719)
Rates: $70-$149
(508) 997-1281
(800) 465-4329

THE HUTTLESTON MOTEL
128 Huttleston
Ave (02719)
Rates: $40-$69
(508) 997-7655

FALMOUTH

THE BEACH ROSE INN B&B
17 Chase Rd
(02540)
Rates: $110-$150+
(508) 540-5706
(800) 498-5706

CAPESIDE COTTAGE B&B
320 Woods Hole
Rd (02540)
Rates: $100-$160
(508) 548-6218

FALMOUTH INN
824 Main St
(02540)
Rates: $70-$150+
(508) 540-2500
(800) 255-4157

MARINER MOTEL
555 Main St
(02540)
Rates: $59-$169
(508) 548-1331
(800) 949-2939
(800) 233-2939

FITCHBURG

BEST WESTERN ROYAL PLAZA HOTEL
150 Royal Plaza
Dr (01420)
Rates: $79-$169
(978) 342-7100
(800) 528-1234
(888) 976-9254

FLORIDA

WHITCOMB SUMMIT MOTEL
229 Mohawk Tr
(01247)
Rates: $45-$70
(413) 662-2625
(800) 547-0944

FOXBORO

RESIDENCE INN BY MARRIOTT
250 Foxborough
Blvd (02035)
Rates: $110-$169
(508) 698-2800
(800) 331-3131

FRAMINGHAM

BEST WESTERN INN
130 Worcester Rd
(01702)
Rates: $90-$150
(508) 872-8811
(800) 528-1234
(800) 497-7555

MOTEL 6
1668 Worcester Rd
(01702)
Rates: $55-$60
(508) 620-0500
(800) 466-8356

RED ROOF INN
650 Cochituate Rd
(01701)
Rates: $60-$96
(508) 872-4499
(800) 843-7663

RESIDENCE INN BY MARRIOTT
400 Staples Dr
(01702)
Rates: $159-$199
(508) 370-0001
(800) 331-3131

SHERATON HOTEL
1657 Worcester Rd
(01701)
Rates: $99-$259
(508) 879-7200
(800) 325-3535

FRANKLIN

HAWTHORN SUITES
835 Upper Union
St (02038)
Rates: $99-$220
(508) 553-3500
(800) 527-1133

RESIDENCE INN BY MARRIOTT
4 Forge Pkwy
(02038)
Rates: $99-$189
(508) 541-8188
(800) 331-3131

GARDNER

SUPER 8 MOTEL
22 Pearson Blvd
(01440)
Rates: $65-$105
(978) 630-2888
(800) 800-8000

GLOUCESTER

CAPE ANN MOTOR INN
33 Rockport Rd
(01930)
Rates: $75-$160
(978) 281-2900
(800) 464-8439

GOOD HARBOR BEACH INN
1 Salt Island Rd
(01930)
Rates: $70-$149
(978) 283-1489
(877) 327-4355

THE MANOR INN
141 Essex Ave
(01930)
Rates: $89-$139
(978) 283-0614

OCEAN VIEW INN & RESORT
171 Atlantic Rd
(01930)
Rates: $70-$150+
(978) 283-6200
(800) 315-7557

SAMARKAND GUESTHOUSE
Nautilus and
Harbor Roads
(01930)
Rates: $70-$109
(978) 283-3757

VISTA MOTEL
22 Thatcher Rd
(10930)
Rates: $70-$150+
(978) 281-3410
(866) 847-8262

GREAT BARRINGTON

BARRINGTON COURT MOTEL
400 Stockbridge
Rd (01230)
Rates: $55-$149
(413) 528-2340

CHEZ GABRIELLE B&B
320 State Rd
(01230)
Rates: $110-$180
(413) 528-2799

MONUMENT MOUNTAIN MOTEL
249 Stockbridge
Rd (01230)
Rates: $50-$149
(413) 528-3272

MOUNTAIN VIEW MOTEL
304 State Rd
(01230)
Rates: $45-$125
(413) 528-0250

THE TURNING POINT INN B&B
3 Lake Buel Rd
(01230)
Rates: $70-$150+
(413) 578-4777

GREENFIELD

THE BRANDT HOUSE HISTORIC B&B
29 Highland Ave
(01301)
Rates: $125-$195
(413) 774-3329
(800) 235-3329

CANDLELIGHT MOTOR INN
208 Mohawk Tr
(01301)
Rates: $38-$84
(413) 772-0101
(888) 262-0520

THE HOUSE ON THE HILL B&B
330 Leyden Rd
(01301)
Rates: $110-$149
(413) 774-2070

OLD TAVERN FARM B&B
817 Colrain Rd
(01301)
Rates: $110-$149
(413) 772-0474

HADLEY

HOWARD JOHNSON
401 Russell St
(01036)
Rates: $69-$197
(413) 586-0114
(800) 446-4656

QUALITY INN
237 Russell St
(01035)
Rates: $45-$135
(413) 584-9816
(800) 424-6423

HAMILTON

MILES RIVER COUNTRY INN B&B
823 Bay Rd
(01936)
Rates: $70-$150+
(978) 468-7206

HARWICH PORT

HARBOR WALK B&B
6 Freeman St
(02646)
Rates: $70-$109
(508) 432-1675

HOLLAND

RESTFUL PAWS 70 ALLEN HILL ROAD (01521) 888.430.PAWS .SEE OUR AD ON PAGE 339

HOUSATONIC

BROOK COVE GUEST HOUSE
30 Linda Ln
(01236)
Rates: $70-$95
(413) 274-6653

CHRISTINE'S B&B CARRIAGE HOUSE INN
325 N Plain Rd
(01236)
Rates: $70-$200+
(413) 274-6149
(800) 536-1186

HYANNIS

BEST INN & SUITES
69 Main St (02601)
Rates: $45-$140
(508) 775-2332

AREA CODES - If the local number doesn't connect, check for a new area code.

CASCADE MOTOR LODGE
201 Main St
(02601)
Rates: $39-$70
(508) 775-9717

COMFORT INN
1470 SR 132
(02601)
Rates: $69-$189
(508) 771-4804
(800) 424-6423

GLO-MIN COTTAGES & MOTEL
182 Sea St (02601)
Rates: $59-$149
(508) 775-1423
(800) 696-1423

RAINBOW RESORT MOTEL
Rt 132 (02601)
Rates: $48-$56
(508) 362-3217

SNUG HARBOUR MOTOR LODGE
48 E Main St
(02601)
Rates: $35-$70
(508) 771-0699
(800) 345-0130

HYANNIS PORT

HARBOR VILLAGE
160 Marstons Ave
(02647)
Rates: $90-$150
(508) 775-7581

MARSTON B&B
70 Marston Ave
(02647)
Rates: $70-$109
(508) 775-3334

THE SIMMONS HOMESTEAD INN BED & BREAKFAST
288 Scudder Ave
(02647)
Rates: $175+
(508) 778-4999
(800) 637-1649

KINGSTON

THE INN AT PLYMOUTH BAY
149 Main St
(02364)
Rates: $99-$130
(781) 585-3831
(800) 941-0075

LANESBORO

MT. VIEW MOTEL
499 S Main St
(01237)
Rates: $48-$125
(413) 442-1009

WEATHERVANE MOTEL
475 S Main St
(01237)
Rates: $35-$125
(413) 443-3230

LAWRENCE

HAMPTON INN NORTH
224 Winthrop Ave
(01843)
Rates: $79-$129
(978) 975-4050
(800) 426-7866

LEE

DEVONFIELD COUNTRY INN B&B
85 Stockbridge Rd
(01238)
Rates: $175+
(413) 243-3298
(800) 664-0880

LAUREL HILL MOTEL
200 Laurel St
(01238)
Rates: $55-$150+
(413) 243-0813

LENOX

SEVEN HILLS COUNTRY INN
40 Plunkett St
(01240)
Rates: $85-$325
(413) 637-0060
(800) 869-6518

WALKER HOUSE INN B&B
64 Walker St
(01240)
Rates: $70-$165+
(413) 637-1271
(800) 235-3098

LEOMINSTER

MOTEL 6
48 Commercial St (01453)
Rates: $39-$58
(978) 537-8161
(800) 466-8356

LEXIST PAUNGTON

BATTLE GREEN INN & SUITES
1720 Massachusetts Ave (02173)
Rates: $99-$109
(781) 862-6100
(800) 343-0235

MARY VAN & JIMS "THIS OLD HOUSE" B&B
12 Plainfield St
(02173)
Rates: $50-$109
(781) 861-7057

MORGAN'S REST B&B
205 Follen Rd
(02173)
Rates: $70-$109
(781) 862-2716

SHERATON LEXINGTON HOTEL
727 Marrett Rd
(02173)
Rates: $89-$159
(781) 862-8700
(800) 325-3535

MANSFIELD

HOLIDAY INN
31 Hampshire St
(02048)
Rates: $89-$175
(508) 339-2200
(800) 465-4329

MARBLEHEAD

SEAGULL INN B&B
106 Harbor Ave
(01945)
Rates: $70-$175
(781) 631-1893

MARLBOROUGH

COMFORT INN
880 Donald J Lynch Blvd
(01752)
Rates: $79-$129
(508) 460-1000
(800) 424-6423

EMBASSY SUITES
123 Boston Post Rd W (01752)
Rates: $95-$175
(508) 485-5900
(800) 362-2779

HOMESTEAD STUDIO SUITES
19 Northborough Rd E (01752)
Rates: $92-$117
(508) 490-9911
(888) 782-9473

MARSHFIELD

OCEAN VILLAGE MOTOR INN
875 Ocean St
(02050)
Rates: $70-$90
(781) 837-9901

MARTHA'S VINEYARD

BED & BISCUIT VACATION HOME
20 Jennie Lane
(Edgartown 02539)
Rates: $2000-$2500 Weekly
(508) 627-3666

BRADYS NEWS B&B
8 Canonicus Ave
(Oak Bluffs 02557)
Rates: $110-$150+
(508) 693-9137

DUCK INN B&B
10 Duck Pond Way (Aquinnah 02535)
Rates: $110-$150
(508) 645-9018

ISLAND INN RESORT
Beach Rd, Box 1585
(Oak Bluffs 02557)
Rates: $110-$305
(508) 693-2002
(800) 462-0269

MARTHA'S VINEYARD & NANTUCKET RESERVATIONS
Lagoon Pond Rd, Box 1322
(Vineyard Haven 02568)
Rates: n/a
(508) 693-7200
(800) 649-5671

MARTHA'S VINEYARD SURFSIDE MOTEL
7 Oak Bluffs Ave
(Oak Bluffs 02557)
Rates: $60-$285
(508) 693-2500
(800) 537-3007

SHIRETOWN INN
44 N Water St
(Edgartown 02539)
Rates: $60-$150+
(508) 627-3353
(800) 541-0090

SHIVERICK INN
5 Pease's Point Way (Edgartown 02539)
Rates: $150+
(508) 627-3797
(800) 723-4292

THE VICTORIAN INN
24 S Water St
(Edgartown 02539)
Rates: $150-$295
(508) 627-4784

MEDFORD

AMERISUITES
116 Riverside Ave
(02155)
Rates: $129
(781) 395-8500
(800) 833-1516

MIDDLE BOROUGH

DAYS INN
30 E Clark St
(02346)
Rates: $66-$119
(508) 946-4400
(800) 329-7466

MIDDLEFIELD

BLUE HEAVEN BLUEBERRY FARM
246 Skyline Trail
(01243)
Rates: $100
(413) 623-5519

STRAWBERRY BANKE FARM B&B
Skyline Trail
(01243)
Rates: $70-$109
(413) 623-6481

AREA CODES - If the local number doesn't connect, check for a new area code.

MILFORD

DAYS INN
3 Fortune Blvd
(10757)
Rates: $59-$109
(508) 634-2499
(800) 329-7466

HOLIDAY INN EXP
50 Fortune Blvd
(10757)
Rates: $70-$109
(508) 634-1054
(800) 465-4329

NANTUCKET ISLAND

CORNER HOUSE B&B
49 Centre St
(02554)
Rates: $70-$150+
(508) 228-1530
(866) 228-1409

THE COTTAGES OF THE BOAT BASIN
1 Old South
Wharf (02554)
Rates: $110-$190
(508) 325-1499
(866) 838-9253

SAFE HARBOR B&B
2 Harborview
Way (02554)
Rates: $150+
(508) 228-3222

NATICK

CROWNE PLAZA
1360 Worcester St
(01760)
Rates: $99-$164
(508) 653-8800
(800) 227-6963

TRAVELODGE
1350 Worcester St
(01760)
Rates: $70-$109
(508) 655-2222
(800) 564-7111
(800) 578-7878

NEEDHAM

SHERATON NEEDHAM HOTEL
100 Cabot St
(02494)
Rates: $129-$189
(781) 444-1110
(800) 325-3535

NEPONSET

SUSSE CHALET BOSTON HOTEL
900 Morrissey
Blvd (02122)
Rates: $120-$165
(617) 287-9200
(800) 258-1980

NEW ASHFORD

CARRIAGE HOUSE MOTEL
344 Rt 7 (01237)
Rates: $45-$79
(413) 458-5359

ECONO LODGE THE SPRINGS
Rt 7 (01237)
Rates: $40-$160
(413) 458-5945
(800) 424-6423
(800) 227-0001

NEW BEDFORD

CAPT. HASKELL'S OCTAGON HOUSE B&B
347 Union St
(02740)
Rates: $60-$140
(508) 999-3933

NEWBURYPORT

THE WINDSOR HOUSE B&B
38 Federal St
(01950)
Rates: $110-$149
(978) 462-3778
(888) 873-5296

NEWTON

HOLIDAY INN
399 Grove St
(02462)
Rates: $70-$109
(617) 969-5300
(800) 465-4329

SHERATON HOTEL
320 Washington
St (02158)
Rates: $329-$354
(617) 969-3010
(800) 325-3535

NORTH ATTLEBORO

ARNS PARK MOTEL
515 S Washington
St (02760)
Rates: $55-$70
(508) 695-5102

NORTH CHELMSFORD

HAWTHORN SUITES
25 Research Pl
(01863)
Rates: $89
(978) 256-5151
(800) 527-1133

NORTH DARTMOUTH

RESIDENCE INN BY MARRIOTT
181 Faunce Corner
Rd (02747)
Rates: $70-$149
(508) 984-5858
(800) 331-3131

NORTH EASTHAM

THE BLUE DOLPHIN INN
5950 Rt 6 (02651)
Rates: $79-$149
(508) 255-1159
(800) 654-0504

NORTH TRURO

OUTER REACH RESORT
535 Rt 6 (02652)
Rates: $35-$109
(508) 487-9500
(800) 942-5388

NORTHAMPTON

CLARION HOTEL & CONF CTR
One Atwood Dr
(01060)
Rates: $79-$235
(413) 586-1211
(800) 252-7466

NORTHFIELD

THE PRIOR HOUSE B&B
55 Main St (01360)
Rates: $70-$149
(413) 498-5957

ORANGE

EXECUTIVE INN
110 Daniel Shay's
Hwy (01364)
Rates: $50-$75
(978) 544-8864

TRAVEL INN
180 Daniel Shay's
Hwy (01364)
Rates: $45-$70
(978) 544-8029
(978) 544-2986

ORLEANS

B&B CAPE COD RESERVATION SERVICE
P.O. Box 1312
(02653)
Rates: n/a
(508) 255-3824
(800) 541-6226

SKAKET BEACH MOTEL
203 Cranberry
Hwy (02643)
Rates: $59-$169
(508) 255-1020
(800) 835-0298

OTIS

GROUSE HOUSE INN
Rt 23 (01253)
Rates: $45-$70
(413) 269-0115

PEABODY

HOMESTEAD STUDIO SUITES
200 Jubilee Dr
(01960)
Rates: $85-$120
(978) 531-6632
(888) 782-9473

HOMEWOOD SUITES
57 Newbury St
(01960)
Rates: $99-$159
(978) 536-5050
(800) 225-5466

PETERSHAM

THE INN AT CLAMBER HILL
111 N Main St
(01366)
Rates: $150+
(978) 724-8800
(888) 374-0007

PITTSFIELD

CROWNE PLAZA HOTEL
1 West St (01201)
Rates: $139-$289
(413) 499-2000
(800) 227-6963

HEART OF THE BERKSHIRES MOTEL
970 W Housatonic
St (01201)
Rates: $45-$100
(413) 443-1255

PLYMOUTH

ABSENT INNKEEPER GUEST HOUSE
631 State Rd
(02360)
Rates: $70-$150+
(508) 224-6728

AUBERGE GLADSTONE GUEST HOUSE
8 Vernon St
(02360)
Rates: $85-$135
(508) 830-1890
(866) 722-1890

A BEACH HOUSE OCEANFRONT B&B
45 Black Pond Rd
(02360)
Rates: $110-$150+
(508) 224-3517
(888) 262-2543

HALL'S B&B
3 Sagamore St
(02360)
Rates: $70-$109
(508) 746-2835

HILLSIDE ESTATES B&B
230 Summer St
(02360)
Rates: $70-$109
(508) 747-5690
(866) 747-5690

PROVINCETOWN

THE ARCHER INN
26 Bradford St
(02657)
Rates: $70-$150+
(508) 487-2529
(800) 263-6574

BAYSHORE & CHANDLER CONDOS
493 Commercial St
(02657)
Rates: $95-$295
(508) 487-9133

AREA CODES - If the local number doesn't connect, check for a new area code.

BEACHFRONT WHITE SANDS RESORT
1001 Commercial St (02657)
Rates: $70-$250
(508) 487-0244

BENCHMARK INN & CENTRAL
6 & 8 Dyer St (02657)
Rates: $110-$159+
(508) 487-7440
(888) 487-7440

BREAKWATER MOTEL
716 Commercial St (02657)
Rates: $79-$149
(508) 487-1134
(800) 487-1134

CAPE INN
698 Commercial St (02657)
Rates: $79-$179
(508) 487-1711
(800) 422-4224

THE CAPTAIN & HIS SHIP GUEST HOUSE
164 Commercial St (02657)
Rates: $159+
(508) 487-1850
(800) 400-2278

SURFSIDE HOTEL & SUITES
543 Commercial St (02657)
Rates: $129-$329
(508) 487-1726
(800) 421-1726

WHITE WIND INN B&B
174 Commercial St (02657)
Rates: $80-$235
(508) 487-1526
(888) 449-9463

QUINCY

PRESIDENTS' CITY INN
845 Hancock St (02170)
Rates: $95-$110
(617) 479-6500

RAYNHAM

DAYS INN
164 New State Hwy (02767)
Rates: $49-$99
(508) 824-8647
(800) 329-7466

REHOBOTH

FIVE BRIDGE FARM INN B&B
154 Pine St (02769)
Rates: $88-$145
(508) 252-3190
(508) 252-3770

REVERE

COMFORT INN & SUITES-LOGAN INT'L AIRPORT
85 American Legion Hwy (02151)
Rates: $79-$229
(781) 485-3600
(800) 424-6423

HAMPTON INN
230 Lee Burbank Hwy (02151)
Rates: $89-$179
(781) 286-5665
(800) 426-7866

RICHMOND

A B&B IN THE BERKSHIRES
1666 Dublin Rd (01254)
Rates: $75-$150+
(413) 698-2817
(800) 795-7122

ROCKLAND

HOLIDAY INN EXP
909 Hingham St (02370)
Rates: $119-$150
(781) 871-5660
(800) 465-4329

ROCKPORT

BLUEBERRY COVE BED & BREAKFAST
50 Stockholm Ave (01966)
Rates: $40-$70
(978) 546-2838

CARLSON'S B&B
43 Broadway (01966)
Rates: $40-$70
(978) 546-2770

SANDY BAY MOTOR INN
173 Main St (01966)
Rates: $102-$150
(978) 546-7155
(800) 437-7155

RUTLAND

GENERAL RUFUS PUTNAM HOUSE B&B
344 Main St (01543)
Rates: $110-$150+
(508) 886-0200

SALEM

CLIPPER SHIP INN
40 Bridge St (01970)
Rates: $70-$149
(978) 745-8022

HAWTHORNE HOTEL
18 Washington Sq (01970)
Rates: $140-$189
(978) 744-4080
(800) 729-7829

THE SALEM INN
7 Summer St (01970)
Rates: $160-$290
(978) 741-0680
(800) 446-2995

STEPHEN DANIELS HOUSE INN
1 Daniels St (01970)
Rates: $110-$149
(978) 744-5709

SANDWICH

THE EARL OF SANDWICH MOTEL
378 Rt 6A (02537)
Rates: $55-$109
(508) 888-1415

SANDWICH LODGE & RESORT
54 Rt 6A (02563)
Rates: $59-$170
(508) 888-2275
(800) 282-5353

SAUGUS

RED ROOF INN
920 Broadway (01906)
Rates: $89-$104
(781) 941-1400
(800) 843-7663

SCITUATE

INN AT SCITUATE HARBOR
7 Beaver Dam Rd (02066)
Rates: $72-$149
(781) 545-5550
(800) 368-3818

SEEKONK

MOTEL 6
821 Fall River Ave (02771)
Rates: $54-$75
(508) 336-7800
(800) 466-8356

RAMADA INN
940 Fall River Ave (02771)
Rates: $70-$109
(508) 336-7300
(800) 272-6232

SHEFFIELD

BIRCH HILL B&B
254 S Undermountain Rd (01257)
Rates: $110-$150
(413) 229-2143
(800) 359-3969

RACE BROOK LODGE B&B
864 Undermountain Rd S (01257)
Rates: $70-$150+
(413) 229-2916
(888) 725-6343

SHELBURNE FALLS

RED ROSE MOTEL
1701 Mohawk Trail (01370)
Rates: $35-$69
(413) 526-2666

SOMERSET

QUALITY INN
1878 Wilbur Ave (02725)
Rates: $69-$189
(508) 678-4545
(800) 424-6423

SOUTH DEERFIELD

DEERFIELD GUEST HOUSE B&B
108 N Hillside Rd (01373)
Rates: $70-$149
(413) 665-0922

SOUTH EGREMONT

SWISS HUTTE COUNTRY INN
Rt 23 (01258)
Rates: $70-$150+
(413) 528-6200

SOUTH ORLEANS

OCEAN BAY VIEW COTTAGES
116 Portanimicut Rd (02662)
Rates: n/a
(508) 255-3344

SEA BREEZE MOTEL
13-17 Beach Rd (02662)
Rates: $70-$100
(508) 240-5500

SOUTH YARMOUTH

BRENTWOOD MOTOR INN
961 Main St (02664)
Rates: $35-$65+
(508) 398-8812
(800) 328-8812

CAPTAIN JONATHAN MOTEL
1237 Rt 28 (02664)
Rates: $35-$70
(508) 398-3480
(800) 342-3480

CAVALIER MOTOR LODGE & RESORT
881 Main St (02663)
Rates: $70-$109
(508) 394-6575
(800) 545-3536

MOTEL 6
1314 Rt 28 (02664)
Rates: $44-$93
(508) 394-4000
(800) 466-8356

AREA CODES - If the local number doesn't connect, check for a new area code.

WINDJAMMER MOTOR INN
192 South Shore Dr (02664)
Rates: $49-$100
(508) 398-2370
(800) 448-9744

SOUTHBOROUGH

RED ROOF INN
367 Turnpike Rd (01772)
Rates: $64-$104
(508) 481-3904
(800) 843-7663

SPRINGFIELD

HOLIDAY INN
711 Dwight St (01104)
Rates: $70-$145
(413) 781-0900
(800) 465-4329

SHERATON MONARCH PLACE
1 Monarch Pl (01104)
Rates: $199-$209
(413) 781-1010
(800) 325-3535

STURBRIDGE

BEST WESTERN AMERICAN MOTOR LODGE
350 Main St (01566)
Rates: $69-$109
(508) 347-9121
(800) 528-1234
(877) 738-4801

COMFORT INN & SUITES
215 Charlton Rd (01566)
Rates: $77-$215
(508) 347-3306
(800) 424-6423

DAYS INN
66-68 Haynes St, Old Rt 15 (01566)
Rates: $55-$150
(508) 347-3391
(800) 329-7466

GREEN ACRES MOTEL
2 Shepard Rd (01566)
Rates: $49-$139
(508) 347-3496

PUBLICK HOUSE HISTORIC INN & COUNTRY LODGE
295 Main St (01566)
Rates: $100-$170
(508) 347-3313
(800) 782-5425

QUALITY INN
400 Haynes Rd, Rt 15 (01566)
Rates: $50-$150
(508) 347-1978
(800) 424-6423
(800) 905-0848

RODEWAY INN
172 Main St (01566)
Rates: $55-$140
(508) 347-9673
(800) 424-6423

STURBRIDGE COACH MOTOR LODGE
408 Main St (01566)
Rates: $70-$109
(508) 347-7327

STURBRIDGE HOST HOTEL
366 Main St (01566)
Rates: $119-$179
(508) 347-7393
(800) 582-3232

SUDBURY

CLARION CARRIAGE HOUSE INN
738 Boston Post Rd (01776)
Rates: $139-$179
(978) 443-2223
(800) 424-6423

TEWKSBURY

HOLIDAY INN
4 Highwood Dr (01876)
Rates: $49-$89
(978) 640-9000
(800) 465-4329

MOTEL 6
95 Main St (01876)
Rates: $59-$70
(978) 851-8677
(800) 466-8356

RESIDENCE INN BY MARRIOTT
1775 Andover St (01876)
Rates: $129-$169
(978) 640-1003
(800) 331-3131

TOWNEPLACE SUITES
20 International Pl (01876)
Rates: $84-$129
(978) 863-9800
(800) 257-3000

TYRINGHAM

SUNSET FARM BED & BREAKFAST
74 Tyringham Rd (01264)
Rates: $70-$120
(413) 243-0730

WAKEFIELD

SHERATON COLONIAL HOTEL & GOLF CLUB
1 Audubon Rd (01880)
Rates: $109-$229
(781) 245-9300
(800) 325-3535

WALTHAM

HOMESTEAD STUDIO SUITES
52 Fourth Ave (02154)
Rates: $85-$117
(781) 890-1333
(888) 782-9473

SIERRA SUITES
32 Fourth Ave (02154)
Rates: $80-$149
(781) 622-1900
(800) 474-3772

SUMMERFIELD SUITES
54 Fourth Ave (02154)
Rates: $139-$249
(781) 290-0026
(800) 833-4353

THE WESTIN HOTEL
70 Third Ave (02154)
Rates: $119-$255
(781) 290-5600
(800) 228-3000

WAREHAM

ATLANTIC MOTEL
70 Depot St (East Wareham 02538)
Rates: $55-$150+
(508) 295-0210

LITTLE HARBOR GUEST HOUSE B&B
20 Stockton Shortcut (02571)
Rates: $70-$109
(508) 295-6329

WELLESLEY

WELLESLEY TRAVEL INN
978 Worcester Rd (02482)
Rates: $50-$109
(781) 235-8555

WELLFLEET

GREEN HAVEN COTTAGES
633 State Hwy (02667)
Rates: $475-$925 Weekly
(508) 349-1715

WEST BROOKFIELD

COPPER LANTERN MOTOR LODGE
184 W Main St (01585)
Rates: $40-$75
(508) 867-6441

WEST DENNIS

THE BARNACLE MOTEL
221 Main St (West Dennis 02670)
Rates: $70-$109
(508) 394-8472

CAPTAIN VARRIEUR'S COTTAGES
P.O. Box 1332 (02670)
Rates: $600-$1125+ Weekly
(508) 394-4338
(888) 394-4338

ELMWOOD INN
57 Old Main St (02670)
Rates: $38-$70
(508) 394-2798

PINE COVE INN & COTTAGES
5 Main St (02670)
Rates: $30-$70
(508) 398-8511

WOODBINE VILLAGE ON THE COVE
Rt 28 (02670)
Rates: $300 Weekly
(508) 881-1381

WEST HARWICH

CAPE COD CLADDAGH INN
77 Main St (02671)
Rates: $95-$135
(508) 432-9628
(800) 356-9628

WEST SPRINGFIELD

HAMPTON INN
1011 Riverdale St (01089)
Rates: $70-$149
(413) 732-1300
(800) 426-7866

KNIGHTS INN
1557 Riverdale St (01089)
Rates: $45-$90
(413) 737-9047
(800) 843-5644

QUALITY INN
1150 Riverdale St (01089)
Rates: $59-$159
(413) 739-7261
(800) 424-6423

RED ROOF INN
1254 Riverdale St (01089)
Rates: $52-$87
(413) 731-1010
(800) 843-7663

REGENCY INN & SUITES
21 Baldwin St (01089)
Rates: $50-$150+
(413) 781-2300

RESIDENCE INN BY MARRIOTT
64 Border Way (01089)
Rates: $85-$149
(413) 732-9543
(800) 331-3131

AREA CODES - If the local number doesn't connect, check for a new area code.

WEST STOCKBRIDGE

PLEASANT VALLEY MOTEL
42 Stockbridge Rd (01266)
Rates: $45-$195
(413) 232-8511

SHAKER MILL INN
2 Oak St (01266)
Rates: $70-$175
(413) 232-4600

WEST YARMOUTH

RED ROSE INN
6 New Hampshire Ave (02673)
Rates: $110-$140
(508) 775-2944

WEST-BOROUGH

RESIDENCE INN BY MARRIOTT
25 Connector Rd (01581)
Rates: $89-$199
(508) 366-7700
(800) 331-3131
(888) 533-2774

SIERRA SUITES
1800 Computer Dr (01581)
Rates: $80-$135
(508) 366-6100

WYNDHAM HOTEL
5400 Computer Dr (01581)
Rates: $84-$160
(508) 366-5511
(800) 996-3426

WESTFIELD

COUNTRY COURT MOTEL
480 Southampton Rd (01085)
Rates: $35-$69
(413) 562-9790

WESTFORD

RESIDENCE INN BY MARRIOTT
7 Lain Dr (01886)
Rates: $149-$199
(978) 392-1407
(800) 331-3131

WESTFORD REGENCY INN & CONF CTR
219 Littleton Rd (01886)
Rates: $70-$149
(978) 692-8200
(800) 543-7801

WILLIAMSTOWN

COZY CORNER MOTEL
284 Sand Spring Rd (01267)
Rates: $80-$149
(413) 458-8006

GREEN VALLEY MOTEL
1214 Simonds Rd (01267)
Rates: $70-$109
(413) 458-3864

JERICHO VALLEY INN
2541 Hancock Rd (01267)
Rates: $110-$149
(413) 458-9511
(800) 537-4246

THE VILLAGER MOTEL
953 Simonds Rd (01267)
Rates: $65-$95
(413) 458-4046

WINTHROP

INN AT CRYSTAL COVE
600 Shirley St (02152)
Rates: $70-$109
(617) 846-9217
(877) 966-8447

WOBURN

CROWNE PLAZA HOTEL
2 Forbes Rd (01801)
Rates: $169-$219
(781) 932-0999
(800) 227-6963

RADISSON HOTEL
15 Middlesex Canal Park Rd (01801)
Rates: $110-$149
(781) 935-8760
(800) 333-3333

RED ROOF INN
19 Commerce Way (01801)
Rates: $70-$109
(781) 935-7110
(800) 733-7663
(800) 843-7663

RESIDENCE INN BY MARRIOTT
300 Presidential Way (01801)
Rates: $110-$149
(781) 376-4000
(800) 331-3131

SIERRA SUITES
831 Main St (01801)
Rates: $72-$135
(781) 938-3737

WORCESTER

CROWNE PLAZA HOTEL
10 Lincoln Sq (01608)
Rates: $89-$200
(508) 791-1600
(800) 227-6963

HOLIDAY INN
500 Lincoln St (01608)
Rates: $70-$149
(508) 852-4000
(800) 465-4329

REGENCY SUITES HOTEL
70 Southridge St (01608)
Rates: $99-$150+
(508) 753-3512

YARMOUTH PORT

COLONIAL HOUSE INN
277 Main St (02675)
Rates: $45-$100
(508) 362-4348
(800) 999-3416

AREA CODES - If the local number doesn't connect, check for a new area code.

MICHIGAN

ALANSON

BEST WESTERN CROOKED RIVER LODGE
6845 Hwy 31 N (49706)
Rates: $108-$198
(231) 548-5000
(800) 528-1234
(866) 548-0700

ALGONAC

LINDA'S LIGHTHOUSE INN B&B
5965 Pointe Tremble Rd (48001)
Rates: $85-$135
(810) 794-2992

ALLEGAN

BUDGET HOST SUNSET MOTEL
1580 Lincoln Rd (49010)
Rates: $35-$105
(616) 673-6622
(800) 283-4678

ALLEN PARK

BEST WESTERN GREENFIELD INN
3000 Enterprise Dr (48101)
Rates $79-$140
(313) 271-1600
(800) 528-1234
(800) 342-5802

HOLIDAY INN EXPRESS & SUITES
3600 Enterprise Dr (48101)
Rates: $120-$190
(313) 323-3500
(800) 342-5466
(800) 465-4329

ALLENDALE

SLEEP INN, INN & SUITES
4869 Becker Dr (49041)
Rates: $79-$129
(616) 892-8000
(800) 424-6423

ALPENA

AMBER MOTEL
2052 State St (49707)
Rates: $35-$65
(989) 354-8573

BAY MOTEL
2107 US 23 S (49707)
Rates: $30-$150
(989) 356-6137

DAYS INN
1496 M-32 W (49707)
Rates: $80-$125
(989) 356-6118
(800) 329-7466

FIRESIDE INN
18730 Fireside Hwy (49707)
Rates: n/a
(989) 595-6369

HOLIDAY INN
1000 Hwy 23N (49707)
Rates: $84-$114
(989) 356-2151
(800) 465-4329

PARKER HOUSE MOTEL
11505 Hwy 23N (49707)
Rates: $40-$55
(989) 595-6484

WATERS EDGE MOTEL
1000 State St (49707)
Rates: $28-$49
(989) 354-5495

ANN ARBOR

CANDLEWOOD SUITES
701 Waymarket Dr (48103)
Rates: $74-$169
(734) 663-2818
(888) 226-3539

COMFORT INN
2455 Carpenter Rd (48108)
Rates: $65-$199
(734) 973-6100
(800) 424-6423

EXTENDED STAY AMERICA
1501 Briarwood Circle Dr (48108)
Rates: $66-$71
(734) 332-1980

HAMPTON INN
2300 Green Rd (48105)
Rates: $79-$164
(734) 995-4444
(800) 426-7866

HAWTHORN SUITES
3535 Green Ct (48105)
Rates: $110-$145
(734) 327-0011
(800) 527-1133

MOTEL 6
3764 S State St (48108)
Rates: $43-$58
(734) 665-9900
(800) 466-8356

RED ROOF INN
3621 Plymouth Rd (48105)
Rates: $53-$79
(734) 996-5800
(800) 843-7663

RESIDENCE INN BY MARRIOTT
800 Victors Way (48108)
Rates: $99-$199
(734) 996-5666
(800) 331-3131

SUPER 8 MOTEL
2910 Jackson Ave (48108)
Rates: n/a
(734-741-8888
(800) 800-8000

AU GRES

BEST WESTERN PINEWOOD LODGE
510 W Huron Rd US 23 (48703)
Rates: $69-$84
(989) 876-4060
(800) 528-1234

AUBURN HILLS

AMERISUITES
1545 Opdyke Rd (48326)
Rates: $75-$129
(248) 475-9393
(800) 833-1516

HOMESTEAD STUDIO SUITES
3315 University Dr (48326)
Rates$75-$95
(248) 340-8888
(888) 782-9473

MOTEL 6
1471 Opdyke Rd (48326)
Rates: $42-$50
(248) 373-8440
(800) 466-8356

STAYBRIDGE SUITES
2050 Featherstone Rd (48326)
Rates: $169-$189
(248)322-4600
(800) 238-8000

WELLESLEY INN & SUITES
2100 Featherstone Rd (48326)
Rates: $85-$139
(248) 335-5200
(800) 444-8888

BAD AXE

ECONO LODGE INN & SUITES
898 N Van Dyke Rd (48413)
Rates: $69-$99
(989) 269-3200
(800) 553-2666

BARAGA

SUPER 8 MOTEL
790 Michigan Ave (49908)
Rates: $49-$58
(906) 353-6680
(800) 800-8000

BATTLE CREEK

BAYMONT INN
4725 Beckley Rd (49017)
Rates: $69-$119
(269) 979-5400
(877) 229-6668

DAYS INN
4786 Beckley Rd (49017)
Rates: $35-$99
(269) 979-3561
(800) 329-7466

MOTEL 6
4775 Beckley Rd (49015)
Rates: $29-$42
(269) 979-1141
(800) 466-8356

RAMADA INN
5050 Beckley Rd (49015)
Rates: $55-$120
(269) 979-1100
(800) 272-6232

BAY CITY

AMERICINN
3915 Three Mile Rd (48706)
Rates: $69-$169
(517) 671-0071
(800) 634-3444

HOLIDAY INN
501 Saginaw St (48708)
Rates: $80-$160
(989) 892-3501
(800) 465-4329

BAY VIEW

COMFORT INN
1314 US 31 N (49770)
Rates: $50-$200
(231) 347-3220
(800) 424-6423

AREA CODES - If the local number doesn't connect, check for a new area code.

BEAR LAKE

BELLA VISTA INN
12273 US #31
(49614)
Rates: $55-$99
(616) 864-3000

BELLAIRE

WINDWARD SHORE MOTEL
5812 E Torch Lake Dr (49615)
Rates: n/a
(616) 377-6321

BELLEVILLE

COMFORT INN
45945 S I-94 Service Dr (48111)
Rates: $64-$129
(734) 697-8556
(800) 424-6423

RED ROOF INN METRO AIRPORT
45501 N I-94 Service Dr (48111)
Rates: $53-$73
(734) 697-2244
(800) 843-7663

SUPER 8 MOTEL
45707 S I-94 Service Dr (48111)
Rates: $50-$95
(734) 699-1888
(800) 800-8000

BENTON HARBOR

BEST WESTERN TWIN CITY INN & SUITES
1598 Mall Dr (49022)
Rates: $49-$129
(269) 925-1880
(800) 528-1234
(866) 668-3548

DAYS INN
2699 Michigan Rt 139 (49022)
Rates: $49-$119
(269) 925-7021
(800) 329-7466

MOTEL 6
2063 Pipestone Rd (49022)
Rates: $29-$50
(269) 925-5100
(800) 466-8356

RAMADA INN
798 Ferguson Dr (49022)
Rates: $69-$129
(269) 927-1172
(800) 272-6232

RED ROOF INN
1630 Mall Dr (49022)
Rates: $38-$72
(269) 927-2484
(800) 843-7663

BERGLAND

NORTHWINDS MOTEL & RESORT
1497 W M-28 (49910)
Rates: $22-$69
(906) 575-3557

BEULAH

PINE KNOT MOTEL
171 N Center St (49617)
Rates: $80-$110
(231) 882-7751

SUNNYWOODS RESORT MOTEL
14065 Honor Hwy (49617)
Rates: $30-$80
(616) 325-3952
(800) 347-9728

BIG BAY

BIG BAY DEPOT MOTEL
P. O. Box 61 (49808)
Rates: $50-$55
(906) 345-9350

BIG RAPIDS

HOLIDAY INN
1005 Perry St (49307)
Rates: $76-$95
(231) 796-4400
(800) 465-4329

BIRCH RUN

BEST WESTERN OF BIRCH RUN
9087 Birch Run Rd (48415)
Rates: $49-$179
(989) 625-9395
(800) 528-1234

SUPER 8 MOTEL
9235 Birch Run Rd (48415)
Rates: $47-$72
(989) 624-4440
(800) 800-8000

BIRMINGHAM

BARCLAY IN BIRMINGHAM
34952 Woodward Ave (48009)
Rates: $79-$189
(248) 646-7300

HAMILTON HOTEL
35270 Woodward Ave (48009)
Rates: $151-$161
(248) 642-6200

BLOOMFIELD HILLS

RADISSON KINGSLEY HOTEL
39475 Woodward Ave (48304)
Rates: $119-$199
(248) 644-1400
(800) 333-3333

BOYNE FALLS

BOYNE VUE MOTEL
2711 Railroad, Box 12 (49713)
Rates: $28-$125
(616) 549-2822
(800) 549-2822

BRANCH

LAZY DAYS MOTEL
P. O. Box 104 (49402)
Rates: $32
(616) 898-2252

BREVORT

CHAPEL HILL MOTEL
4422 W US 2 (49760)
Rates: $35-$54
(906) 292-5521

BRIDGEPORT

BAYMONT INN & SUITES
6460 Dixie Hwy (48722)
Rates: $59-$119
(989) 777-3000
(877) 229-6668

BROOKLYN

SUPER 8 MOTEL
155 Wamplers Rd (49250)
Rates: $58-$130
(517) 592-0888
(800) 800-8000

BYRON CENTER

AMERIHOST INN
7625 Caterpillar Ct SW (49548)
Rates: $89-$99
(616) 827-9900
(800) 434-5800

CADILLAC

ECONO LODGE
2501 Sunnyside Dr (49601)
Rates: $50-$110
(231) 775-6700
(800) 424-6423

MCGUIRES RESORT
7880 Mackinaw Tr (49601)
Rates: $79-$199
(231) 775-9947
(800) 662-7302

PILGRIM'S VILLAGE
181 S Lake Mitchell (49601)
Rates: $49
(231) 775-5412

PINE CHATA RESORT
5936 E M 55 (49601)
Rates: $50-$60
(231) 775-4677

PINE KNOLL MOTEL
8072 Mackinaw Tr (49601)
Rates: $35-$65
(231) 775-9471

SOUTH SHORE RESORT
1246 Sunnyside Dr (49601)
Rates: $30-$60
(231) 775-7641

CALUMET

AMERICINN
56925 S 6th St (49913)
Rates: $76-$131
(906) 337-6463
(800) 634-3444

CANTON TOWNSHIP

BAYMONT INN & SUITES
41211 Ford Rd (48187)
Rates: $70-$77
(734) 981-1808
(877) 229-6668

MOTEL 6
41216 Ford Rd (48187)
Rates: $39-$50
(734) 981-5000
(800) 466-8356

SUPER 8 MOTEL
3933 Lotz Rd (48187)
Rates: $49-$89
(734) 722-8880
(800) 800-8000

CARO

KINGS WAY INN
1057 E Caro Rd (48723)
Rates: $27-$65
(517) 673-7511

CASCADE

AMERISUITES
5401 28th St Ct SE (49546)
Rates: $79-$99
(616) 940-8100
(800) 833-1516

COUNTRY INN & SUITES BY CARLSON
5399 28th St (49512)
Rates: $69-$98
(616) 977-0909
(800) 456-4000

BAYMONT INN
2873 Kraft Ave SE (49512)
Rates: $69-$99
(616) 956-3300
(877) 229-6668

CROWNE PLAZA HOTEL
5700 28th St SE (49546)
Rates: $89-$109
(616) 957-1770
(800) 227-6963

DAYS INN AIRPORT
5500 28th St SE (49512)
Rates: $55-$75
(616) 949-8400
(800) 329-7466

EXEL INN
4855 28th St SE (49512)
Rates: $40-$70
(616) 957-3000
(800) 367-3935

HAMPTON INN
4981 28th St SE (495`1)
Rates: $78-$99
(616) 956-9304
(800) 426-7866

HOWARD JOHNSON EXPRESS INN
2985 Kraft Ave SE (49512)
Rates: $69-$109
(616) 940-1777
(800) 446-4656

CASEVILLE
SURF N SAND MTL
6006 Pt Austin Rd (48725)
Rates: $36-$84
(517) 856-4400

CASS CITY
WLDWOOD MOTEL
5986 E Cass City Rd (48726)
Rates: $34
(517) 872-3366

CEDARVILLE
CEDARVILLE INN
106 W M-134 (49719)
Rates: $79-$139
(906) 484-2266

CHARLEVOIX
AMERICINN LODGE & SUITES
11800 US 31 N (49720)
Rates: $79-$149
(231-237-0988
(800) 634-3444

CAPRI MOTEL
1455 S Bridge St (49720)
Rates: $60-$120
(231) 547-2545

THE LODGE MOTEL
US 31 N (49720)
Rates: $30-$160
(231) 547-6565

SLEEP INN
800 Petoskey Ave (49720)
Rates: $49-$210
(231) 547-0300
(800) 424-6423

CHARLOTTE
SUPER 8 MOTEL
828 E Shepherd St (48813)
Rates: $50-$82
(517) 543-8288
(800) 800-8000

CHEBOYGAN
BIRCH HAUS MOTEL
1301 Mackinaw Ave (49721)
Rates: $35-$65
(231) 627-5862

CONTINENTAL INN
613 N Main St (49721)
Rates: $39-$120
(231) 627-7164

PINE RIVER MOTEL
102 Lafayette (49721)
Rates: $30-$80
(231) 627-5119

CHELSEA
COMFORT INN
1645 Commerce Park Dr & Brown Dr (48118)
Rates: $89-$199
(734) 433-8000
(800) 424-6423

CHRISTMAS
PAIR-A-DICE INNE7889 W M-28 (49862)
Rates: $49-$99
(906) 387-3500

CLIO
CINNAMON STICK BED & BREAKFAST
12364 N Genesee Rd (48420)
Rates: $60-$125
(810) 686-8391

COLDWATER
RAMADA INN
1000 Orleans Blvd (49036)
Rates: $59-$189
(517) 278-2017
(800) 272-6232

RED ROOF INN
348 S Willowbrook Rd (49036)
Rates: $49-$89
(517) 279-1199
(800) 843-7663

SUPER 8 MOTEL
600 Orleans Blvd (49036)
Rates: $54-$75
(517) 278-8833
(800) 800-8000

COMSTOCK PARK
SWAN INN MOTEL
5182 Alpine Ave NW (49321)
Rates: $45-$80
(616) 784-1224
(800) 875-7926

COPPER HARBOR
ASTOR HOUSE-MINNETONKA RESORT
P. O. Box 13 (49918)
Rates: $43-$85
(906) 289-4449
(800) 433-2770

BELLA VISTA MOTEL
P. O. Box 26 (49918)
Rates: $38-$50
(906) 289-4213

KING COPPER MOTELS
PO Box 68 (49918)
Rates: $40-$60
(906) 289-4214
(800) 833-2470

LAKE FANNY HOOE RESORT
505 2nd St (49918)
Rates: $69-$99
(906) 289-4451
(800) 426-4451

NORLAND MOTEL
US 41, F #172 (49918)
Rates: $36-$64
(906) 289-4815

CURTIS
SEASONS MOTEL
Main St (49820)
Rates: $30-$43
(906) 586-3078

DEARBORN
ECONO LODGE
23730 Michigan Ave (48124)
Rates: $45-$90
(313) 565-7250
(800) 424-6423

RED ROOF INN
24130 Michigan Ave (48124)
Rates: $61-$94
(313) 278-9732
(800) 843-7663

RITZ CARLTON
Fairlane Plaza, 300 Town Ctr Dr (48126)
Rates: $219-$295
(313) 441-2000
(800) 241-3333

TOWNEPLACE SUITES
6141 Mercury Dr (48126)
Rates: $99-$109
(313) 271-0200
(800) 257-3000

DETROIT
COMFORT INN-DOWNTOWN
1999 E Jefferson Ave (48207)
Rates: $79-$189
(313) 567-8888
(800) 424-6423

HOLIDAY INN EXP
1020 Washington Blvd (48226)
Rates: $80-$170
(313) 887-7000
(800) 465-4329

MARRIOTT HOTEL DETROIT ARPRT
Detroit Metro Airport (48242)
Rates: $139-$160
(313) 941-9400
(800) 228-9290

RAMADA INN
400 Bagley Ave (48226)
Rates: $64-$139
(313) 962-2300
(800) 272-6232

RESIDENCE INN BY MARRIOTT
5777 Southfield Service Dr (48228)
Rates: $59-$199
(313) 441-1700
(800) 331-3131

RIVER PLACE HOTEL
1000 River Pl (48207)
Rates: $99-$159
(313) 259-9500

THE SHORECREST MOTOR INN
1316 E Jefferson (48207)
Rates: $52-$150
(313) 568-3000
(800) 992-9616

SUBURBAN HOUSE
16920 Telegraph (48219)
Rates: $28-$40
(313) 535-9646

WESTIN HOTEL RENAISSANCE CENTER
Renaissance Center (48243)
Rates: $175-$210
(313) 568-8000
(800) 228-3000

DOUGLAS
AMERICINN
2905 Blue Star Hwy (49406)
Rates: $63-$254
(269) 857-8581
(800) 634-3444

PINES MOTEL
56 S Blue Star Hwy (49406)
Rates: $29-$98
(616) 857-5211

DRUMMOND ISLAND

VECHELL'S CEDAR VIEW RESORT
P. O. Box 175
(49726)
Rates: $225-$255
(906) 493-5381

WOODMOOR RESORT COMPLEX
26 Maxton Rd
(49726)
Rates: $69-$109
(906) 493-1000

EAGLE HARBOR

SHORELINE RESORT
201 Front St,
F #2015 (49950)
Rates: $60-$77
(906) 289-4441

EAST JORDAN

WESTBROOK MOTEL
218 Elizabeth St
(49727)
Rates: $45-$55
(616) 536-2674

EAST LANSING

RESIDENCE INN BY MARRIOTT
1600 E Grand River Ave (48823)
Rates: $124-$159
(517) 332-7711
(800) 331-3131

TOWNEPLACE SUITES
2855 Hannah Blvd
(48823)
Rates: $89-$109
(517) 203-1000
(800) 257-3000

EAST TAWAS

HOLIDAY INN TAWAS BAY RESORT
300 E Bay St
(48730)
Rates: $65-$156
(989) 362-8601
(800) 465-4329

EASTPOINTE

EASTLAND MOTEL
21055 Gratiot Ave
(48021)
Rates: $26-$32
(810) 772-1300

ELK RAPIDS

CAMELOT INN
10962 Hwy 31S
(49629)
Rates: $53-$88
(231) 264-8473

EPOUFETTE

WONDERLAND MOTEL
80 West US 2
(49762)
Rates: n/a
(906) 292-5574

ESCANABA

HIAWATHA MOTEL
2400 Ludington St
(49829)
Rates: $35-$60
(906) 786-1341

FARMINGTON HILLS

CANDLEWOOD SUITES
37555 Hills Tech Dr (48331)
Rates: $89-$109
(248) 324-0540
(888) 226-3539

MOTEL 6
38300 Grand River Ave (48335)
Rates: $36-$42
(248) 471-0590
(800) 466-8356

RED ROOF INN
24300 Sinacola Ct
(48335)
Rates: $47-$79
(248) 478-8640
(800) 843-7663

FENTON

HOLIDAY INN EXP HOTEL & SUITES
17800 Silver Pkwy
(48430)
Rates: $70-$160
(810) 714-7171
(800) 465-4329

FLINT

AMERICINN
6075 Hill Dr
(48507)
Rates: n/a
(810) 233-9000
(800) 634-3444

BAYMONT INN & SUITES
4160 Pier North Blvd (48504)
Rates: $40-$64
(810) 732-2300
(877) 229-6668

HOLIDAY INN EXPRESS-CAMPUS AREA
1150 Robert T. Longway Blvd (48503)
Rates: $72-$199
(810) 238-7744
(800) 465-4329

HOWARD JOHNSON EXPRESS
G-3277 Miller Rd
(48507)
Rates: $49-$69
(810) 733-5910
(800) 446-4656

MOTEL 6
2324 Austin Pkwy
(48507)
Rates: $36-$48
(810) 767-7100
(800) 466-8356

RED ROOF INN
G-3219 Miller Rd
(48507)
Rates: $42-$70
(810) 733-1660
(800) 843-7663

RESIDENCE INN BY MARRIOTT
2202 W Hill Rd
(48507)
Rates: $110-$160
(810) 424-7000
(800) 331-3131

FOUNTAIN

CHRISTIE'S LOG CABINS ON ROUND LAKE
6503 E Sugar Grove (49410)
Rates: $45-$80
(616) 462-3218
(800) 209-7385

FRANKEN-MUTH

DRURY INN & SUITES
260 S Main St
(48734)
Rates: $85-$140
(989) 652-2800
(800) 378-7946

FRANKFORT

CHIMNEY CORNERS RESORT
1602 Crystal Dr
(49635)
Rates: $37-$110
(616) 352-7522

HOTEL FRANKFORT B&B
231 Main St
(49635)
Rates: $39-$230
(616) 352-4303

GAYLORD

BEST VALUE ROYAL CREST INN
803 S Otsego Ave
(49735)
Rates: $49-$99
(989) 732-6451
(800) 876-9252

BEST WESTERN ALPINE LODGE
833 W Main St
(49735)
Rates: $59-$119
(989) 732-2431
(800) 528-134
(800) 684-2233

DOWNTOWN MOTEL
208 S Otsego Ave
(49735)
Rates: $46-$66
(989) 732-5010

RED ROOF INN
510 S Wisconsin
(49735)
Rates: $49-$99
(989) 731-6331
(800) 843-7663

TIMBERLY MOTEL
881 S Otsego Ave
(49735)
Rates: $38-$84
(989) 732-5166
(888) 321-2606

GLADWIN

GLADWIN MOTOR INN
1003 W Cedar Ave
(48624)
Rates: $25-$50
(517) 426-9661

GRAND MARAIS

ARBORGATE INN
Randolph Rd
(49839)
Rates: $40-$65
(906) 494-2681

VOYAGEUR'S MOTEL
E Wilson St
(49839)
Rates: $78
(906) 494-2389

GRAND RAPIDS

BAYMONT INN
2873 Kraft Ave SE
(49512)
Rates: n/a
(616) 956-3300
(877) 229-6668

BEST WESTERN MIDWAY HOTEL
4101 28th St SE
(49417)
Rates: $64-$150
(616) 842-4720
(800) 528-1234

CASCADE INN
2865 Broadmoore
(49512)
Rates: $27-$43
(616) 949-0850

COMFORT INN AIRPORT
4155 28th St SE
(49512)
Rates: $65-$99
(616) 957-2080
(800) 424-6423

CROWNE PLAZA
5700 28th St SE
(49546)
Rates: n/a
(616) 958-1770
(800) 227-6963

DAYS INN DOWNTOWN
310 Pearl St NW
(49504)
Rates: $49-$120
(616) 235-7611
(800) 329-7466

AREA CODES - If the local number doesn't connect, check for a new area code.

HAMPTON INN
4981 28th St SE
(49512)
Rates: n/a
(616) 956-9304
(800) 426-7866

**HAWTHORN
SUITES LTD**
2985 Kraft Ave SE
(49512)
Rates: n/a
(616) 940-1777
(800) 527-1133

**HOMEWOOD
SUITES**
3920 Stahl Dr SE
(49546)
Rates: $99-$129
(616) 285-7100
(800) 225-5466

MOTEL 6
3524 28th St SE
(49508)
Rates: $34-$40
(616) 957-3511
(800) 466-8356

**NEW ENGLAND
SUITES HOTEL**
2985 Kraft Ave SE
(49512)
Rates: $55-$75
(616) 940-1777
(800) 784-8371

**QUALITY INN
TERRACE CLUB**
4495 28th St SE
(49512)
Rates: $79-$150
(616) 956-8080
(800) 424-6423

**RADISSON HOTEL
RIVERFRONT**
270 Ann St NW
(49504)
Rates: $79-$129
(616) 363-9001
(800) 333-3333

**STAYBRIDGE
SUITES**
3000 Lake
Eastbrook Blvd SE
(49512)
Rates: n/a
(616) 464-3200
(800) 238-8000

GRANDVILLE

COMFORT SUITES
4520 Kenowa Ave
SW (49418)
Rates: $79-$179
(616) 667-0733
(800) 424-6423

**RESIDENCE INN
BY MARRIOTT**
3451 Rivertown
Point Ct SW
(49418)
Rates: $79-$169
(616) 538-1100
(800) 331-3131

GRAYLING

ECONO LODGE
1232 I-75 Bus
Loop (49738)
Rates: $39-$99
(989) 348-8900
(800) 424-6423

HOLIDAY INN
2650 S I-75 Bus
Loop (49738)
Rates: $109-$129
(989) 348-7611
(800) 465-4329
(800) 292-9055

**NORTH
COUNTRY LODGE**
617 N I-75 Bus
Loop (49738)
Rates: $53-$160
(989) 348-8471
(800) 475-6300

SUPER 8 MOTEL
5828 NA Miles
Pkwy (49738)
Rates: $53-$75
(989) 348-8888
(800) 800-8000

HAGAR SHORE

**SWEET CHERRY
RESORT**
3313 Chestnut
(49038)
Rates: n/a
(616) 849-1233

HANCOCK

**BEST WESTERN
COPPER CROWN
MOTEL**
235 Hancock Ave
(49930)
Rates: $55-$72
(906) 482-6111
(800) 528-1234

HARBOR BEACH

**THE TRAIN
STATION MOTEL**
2044 N Lakeshore
Dr (48441)
Rates: $51-$62
(517) 479-3215

HARBOR SPRINGS

**HARBOR
SPRINGS
COTTAGE INN**
145 Zoll St (49740)
Rates: $90-$100
(231) 526-5431

HARPER WOODS

PARKCREST INN
20000 Harper Ave
(48225)
Rates: $59-$80
(313) 884-8800

HARRISON

**LAKESIDE MOTEL
& COTTAGES**
South Business
#27 (48625)
Rates: $32-$42
(517) 539-3796

**WAGON WHEEL
MOTEL**
4294 North Clare
Ave (48625)
Rates: $30-$40
(517) 539-7065

HARRISVILLE

**WIDOW'S WATCH
BED & BREAKFAST**
401 Lake St
(48740)
Rates: $45-$65
(517) 724-5465
(800) 868-1904

HART

**BUDGET HOST
HART MOTEL**
4143 Polk Rd
(49420)
Rates: $39-$119
(231) 873-1855
(800) 283-4678

COMFORT INN
2248 Comfort Dr
(49420)
Rates: $55-$175
(231) 873-3456
(800) 424-6423

HESSEL

LAKEVIEW MOTEL
P. O. Box 277
(49745)
Rates: $39-$42
(906) 484-2474

HILLSDALE

BAVARIAN INN
1728 Hudson Rd
(49242)
Rates: $27-$34
(517) 437-3367
(800) 779-8033

HOLLAND

**BEST WESTERN
KELLY INN**
2888 W Shore Dr
(49424)
Rates: $99-$159
(616) 994-0400
(800) 528-1234

**RESIDENCE INN
BY MARRIOTT**
631 Southpoint
Ridge Rd (49423)
Rates: $129-$179
(616) 393-6900
(800) 331-3131

HONOR

**SUNNY WOODS
RESORT**
14065 Honor Hwy
(49640)
Rates: $67-$89
(231) 325-3952

HOUGHTON

**BEST VALUE
KING'S INN**
215 Shelden Ave
(49931)
Rates: $69-$110
(906) 482-5000

**BEST WESTERN
FRANKLIN
SQUARE INN**
820 Shelden Ave
(49931)
Rates: $89-$199
(906) 487-1700
(888) 487-1700

HOUGHTON LAKE

**COMFORT SUITES
LAKESIDE**
100 Clearview Dr
(48629)
Rates: $119-$509
(989) 422-4000
(800) 424-6423

HILLSIDE MOTEL
3419 W Houghton
Lake Dr (48629)
Rates: $56-$74
(989) 366-5711

HOLIDAY INN EXP
200 Cloverleaf Ln
(48629)
Rates: $59-$189
(989) 422-7829
(800) 465-4329

SUPER 8 MOTEL
9580 W Lake City
Rd (48629)
Rates: $70-$109
(989) 422-3119
(800) 800-8000

HOWELL

**BEST WESTERN
INN**
1500 Pickney Rd
(48843)
Rates: $69-$115
(517) 548-2900
(800) 528-1234

KENSINGTON INN
124 Holiday Ln
(48843)
Rates: $44-$59
(517) 548-3510

QUALITY INN 125
Holiday Ln
(48843)
Rates: $59-$119
(517) 546-6800
(800) 424-6423

HUDSON

**SUNSET ACRES
MOTEL**
400 S Meridian
US 127 (49247)
Rates: $31-$51
(517) 448-8968

HULBERT

THE LEEJA MOTEL
2000 M28 (49748)
Rates: n/a
(906) 876-2323

IMLAY CITY

DAYS INN
6692 Newark Rd
(48444)
Rates: $55-$119
(810) 724-8005
(800) 329-7466

AREA CODES - If the local number doesn't connect, check for a new area code.

SUPER 8 MOTEL
6951 Newark Rd
(48444)
Rates: $49-$89
(810) 724-8700
(800) 800-8000

INDIAN RIVER

CARAVAN MOTEL COTTAGES
4904 S Straits Hwy
(49749)
Rates: $45-$65
(231) 238-7537

NOR GATE MOTEL
4846 S Straits Hwy
(49749)
Rates: $38-$50
(231) 238-7788

NORTHWOODS LODGE
2390 S Straits Hwy
(49749)
Rates: $44-$98
(231) 238-7729

REIDS MOTOR COURT
3977 S Straits Hwy
(49749)
Rates: $29-$48
(231) 238-9353

STAR GATE MOTEL
4646 S Straits Hwy
(49749)
Rates: $42-$52
(231) 238-7371

WOODLANDS LODGE
5115 S Straits Hwy
(49749)
Rates: $39-$54
(231) 238-4137

IONIA

EVERGREEN MOTEL
2030 N State Rd
(48846)
Rates: $29
(616) 527-0930

MIDWAY MOTEL
7076 S State Rd
(48846)
Rates: $26-$51
(616) 527-2080

SUPER 8 MOTEL
7245 S State Rd
(48846)
Rates: $45-$110
(616) 527-2828
(800) 800-8000

IRON MOUNTAIN

BEST INN
1609 S Stephenson
Ave (49801)
Rates: $50-$250
(908) 776-8000

BUDGET HOST LAKE ANTOINE
1663 N Stephenson
Ave (49801)
Rates: $40-$55
(906) 774-6797
(800) 283-4678

DAYS INN
W 8176 S US 2
(49801)
Rates: $45-$130
(906) 774-2181
(800) 329-7466

EDGEWATER'S COUNTRY CABINS
N4128 N US 2
(49801)
Rates: $44-$70
(906) 774-6244
(800) 236-6244

SUPER 8 MOTEL
2702 N Stephenson
Ave (49801)
Rates: n/a
(906) 774-3400
(800) 800-8000

TIMBERS MOTOR LODGE
200 S Stephenson
Ave (49801)
Rates: $34-$74
(906) 774-7600
(800) 443-8533

WOODLANDS MOTEL
N 3957 North US
2 (49801)
Rates: $30-$40
(906) 774-6106

IRON RIVER

IRON RIVER MOTEL
3073 East US 2
(49935)
Rates: $32
(906) 265-4212

IRONWOOD

AMERICINN
1117 E Cloverland
Dr (49938)
Rates: $69-$149
(906) 932-7200
(800) 634-3444

ARMATA MOTEL
124 W Cloverland
Dr (49938)
Rates: $28-$42
(906) 932-4421

BLUE CLOUD MOTEL
105 W Cloverland
Dr (49938)
Rates: $30-$50
(906) 932-0920

CRESTVIEW MOTEL
424 Cloverland Dr
(49938)
Rates: $35-$75
(906) 932-4845

ROYAL MOTEL
715 W Cloverland
Dr (49938)
Rates: $36-$46
(906) 932-4230

SUPER 8 MOTEL
160 E Cloverland
Dr (49938)
Rates: $58-$98
(906) 932-3395
(800) 800-8000

ISHPEMING

BEST WESTERN COUNTRY INN
850 US 41W
(49849)
Rates: $67-$103
(906) 485-6345
(800) 528-1234

JACKSON

HOLIDAY INN
2000 Holiday Inn
Dr (49202)
Rates: $94-$99
(517) 783-2681
(800) 465-4329

MOTEL 6
830 Royal Dr
(49202)
Rates: $39-$52
(517) 789-7186
(800) 466-8356

JONESVILLE

PINECREST MOTEL
516 W Chicago St
(49250)
Rates: $40-$55
(517) 849-2137

KALAMAZOO

CLARION HOTEL
3600 E Cork St
(49001)
Rates: $59-$179
(269) 385-3922
(800) 252-7466

DAYS INN AIRPORT
3522 Sprinkle Rd
(49001)
Rates: $55-$95
(269) 381-7070
(800) 329-7466

ECONO LODGE & SUITES
3750 Easy St
(49002)
Rates: $40-$50
(269) 388-3551
(800) 424-6423

KNIGHTS INN
1211 S Westnedge
Ave (49008)
Rates: $40-$90
(269) 381-5000
(800) 843-5644

RED ROOF INN-EAST
3701 E Cork St
(49001)
Rates: $45-$77
(269) 382-6350
(800) 843-7663

RED ROOF INN-WEST
5425 W Michigan
Ave (49009)
Rates: $42-$69
(269) 375-7400
(800) 843-7663

KENTWOOD

BEST WESTERN MIDWAY HOTEL
4101 28th St SE
(49512)
Rates: $69-$119
(616) 942-2550
(800) 528-1234

COMFORT INN
4155 28th St SE
(49512)
Rates: $59-$119
(616) 957-2080
(800) 424-6423

RESIDENCE INN BY MARRIOTT
2701 E Beltline SE
(49546)
Rates: $69-$169
(616) 957-8111
(800) 331-3131

STAYBRIDGE SUITES
3000 Lake
Eastbrook Blvd SE
(49512)
Rates: $99-$149
(616) 464-3200
(800) 238-8000

LAKE CITY

NORTHCREST MOTEL
1341 S Lakeshore
(49651)
Rates: $52-$79
(231) 839-2075

LAKE ORION

BEST WESTERN PALACE INN
2755 N Lapeer Rd
(48360)
Rates: $80-$90
(248) 391-2755
(800) 528-1234

LAKESIDE

WHITE RABBIT INN B&B
14634 Red Arrow
Hwy (49116)
Rates: $95-$155
(269) 469-4620
(800) 967-2224

LANSING

BEST WESTERN MIDWAY HOTEL
7711 W Saginaw
Hwy (48917)
Rates: $84-$114
(517) 627-8471
(800) 528-1234
(877) 772-6100

HAMPTON INN
525 N Canal Rd
(48917)
Rates: $69-$89
(517) 627-8381
(800) 426-7866

AREA CODES - If the local number doesn't connect, check for a new area code.

MOTEL 6
7326 W Saginaw
Hwy (48917)
Rates: $39-$50
(517) 321-1444
(800) 466-8356

QUALITY SUITES
901 Delta
Commerce Dr
(48911)
Rates: $89-$129
(517) 886-0600
(800) 424-6423

**RED ROOF
INN EAST**
3615 Dunckel Rd
(48910)
Rates: $52-$73
(517) 332-2575
(800) 843-7663

**RED ROOF
INN WEST**
7412 W Saginaw
Hwy (48917)
Rates: $46-$67
(517) 321-7246
(800) 843-7663

**RESIDENCE INN
BY MARRIOTT**
922 Delta
Commerce Dr
(48917)
Rates: $89-$145
(517) 886-5030
(800) 331-3131

**SHERATON
LANSING INN**
925 S Creyts Rd
(48917)
Rates: $169-$184
(517) 323-7100
(800) 325-3535

LIVONIA

AMERISUITES
19300 Haggerty
Rd (48152)
Rates: $79-$109
(734) 953-9224
(800) 833-1516

**RESIDENCE INN
BY MARRIOTT**
17250 Fox Dr
(48152)
Rates: $139
(734) 462-4201
(800) 331-3131

LUDINGTON

HOLIDAY INN EXP
5323 W US 10
(49431)
Rates: $89-$149
(231) 845-7004
(800) 465-4329

**LUDINGTON
HOUSE B&B**
General Delivery
(49431)
Rates: n/a
(800) 827-7869

**MARINA BAY
MOTOR LODGE**
604 W Ludington
Ave (49431)
Rates: $30-$140
(231) 845-5124
(800) 968-1440

**NADER'S
LAKE SHORE
MOTOR LODGE**
612 N Lakeshore
Dr (49431)
Rates: $50-$85
(231) 843-8757
(800) 968-0109

NOVA MOTEL
472 S Old 31 Hwy
(49431)
Rates: $28-$69
(231) 843-3454

**RAMADA INN
CONV CENTER**
4079 W US 10
(49431)
Rates: n/a
(231) 845-7311
(800) 272-6232

SUPER 8 MOTEL
5005 W US 10
(49431)
Rates: $54-$279
(231) 843-2140
(800) 800-8000

**TIMBERLANE
LONG LAKE
RENOVA MOTEL**
472 S Old 31 Hwy
(49431)
Rates: $28-$69
(231) 843-3454

**TIMBERLANE
LONG LAKE
RESORT**
7410 E US 10
(49458)
Rates: n/a
(231) 757-2142
(800) 227-2142

MACKINAW CITY

**BAYMONT INN
& SUITES**
109 S Nicolet
(49701)
Rates: $99-$129
(231) 436-7737
(877) 229-6668
(866) 331-7737

**BEACHCOMBER
MOTEL ON
THE WATER**
1011 S Huron
(49701)
Rates: $42-$125
(231) 436-8451
(800) 968-1383

**THE BEACH
HOUSE
COTTAGES**
1035 S Huron St
(49701)
Rates: $44-$160
(231) 436-5353
(800) 262-5353

**BUDGET INNS
STARLITE**
116 Old US 31
(49701)
Rates: $26-$129
(231) 436-5959

CAPRI MOTEL
801 S Nicolet St
(49701)
Rates: $29-$89
(231) 436-5498

CHIEF MOTEL
10470 US 23
(49701)
Rates: $39-$99
(231) 436-7961

**DAYS INN
& SUITES-
BRIDGEVIEW
LODGE**
206 N Nicolet St
(49701)
Rates: $39-$249
(231) 436-8961
(800) 329-7466

**DAYS INN
LAKEVIEW**
825 S Huron Ave
(49701)
Rates: $39-$169
(231) 436-5557
(800) 329-7466

HOLIDAY INN EXP
364 Louvingney
(49701)
Rates: $42-$159
(231) 436-7100
(800) 465-4329

KINGS INN
1020 S Nicolet St
(49701)
Rates: $40-$99
(231) 436-5322

MOTEL 6
206 Nicolet St
(49701)
Rates: $45-$96
(231) 436-8961
(800) 466-8356

RAMADA INN
450 S Nicolet
(49701)
Rates: $79-$209
(231) 436-5535
(800) 272-6232

**SUPER 8 MOTEL
BRIDGEVIEW**
601 N Huron Ave
(49701)
Rates: $38-$179
(231) 436-5252
(800) 800-8000

MADISON HEIGHTS

MOTEL 6
32700 Barrington
Rd (48071)
Rates: $37-$48
(248) 583-0500
(800) 466-8356

RED ROOF INN
32511 Concord Dr
(48071)
Rates: $49-$76
(248) 583-4700
(800) 843-7663

**RESIDENCE INN
BY MARRIOTT**
32650 Stephenson
Hwy (48071)
Rates: $159
(248) 583-4322
(800) 331-3131

MANISTEE

HILLSIDE MOTEL
1675 US 31S
(49660)
Rates: $40-$125
(231) 723-2584
(800) 234-1250

MANISTIQUE

**BEACHCOMBER
MOTEL**
795 E Lakeshore
Dr (49854)
Rates: $46-$88
(906) 341-2567

COMFORT INN
726 E Lakeshore
Dr (49854)
Rates: $69-$159
(906) 341-6981
(800) 424-6423

**KEWADIN
CASINO INN**
6596 W US Hwy 2
(49854)
Rates: $47-$70
(906) 341-6911

MANTON

**GREEN MILL
MOTEL**
709 N US 131
(49663)
Rates: $30-$70
(616) 824-3504

IRISH INN MOTEL
415 N Michigan
Ave (49663)
Rates: $31-$41
(616) 824-6988

MARINE CITY

**MARINE BAY
LODGE MOTEL**
6000 River Rd
(E China 48054)
Rates: $30-$62
(810) 765-8877
(810) 765-8878

**PORT SEAWAY
INN**
7623 River Rd
(48039)
Rates: $32-$90
(810) 765-4033

AREA CODES - If the local number doesn't connect, check for a new area code.

MARQUETTE

BIRCHMONT MOTEL
2090 US 41S
(49855)
Rates: $43-$72
(906) 228-7538

ECONO LODGE
2050 US 41S
(49855)
Rates: $49-$129
(906) 225-1305
(800) 424-6423

HOLIDAY INN
1951 US 41W
(49855)
Rates: $79
(906) 225-1351
(800) 465-4329

LAMPLIGHTER MOTEL
3600 US 41W
(49855)
Rates: $22-$44
(906) 228-4004

NORDIC BAY LODGE
1880 US 41 S
(49855)
Rates: $60-$85
(906) 226-7516

RAMADA INN
412 W Washington
(49855)
Rates: $94-$99
(906) 228-6000
(800) 272-6232

TIROLER HOF INN
150 Carp River
Hill (49855)
Rates: $44-$60
(906) 226-7516
(800) 892-9376

TRAVELODGE
1010 M-28 E
(49855)
Rates: $52-$76
(906) 249-1712
(800) 578-7878

MARSHALL

ARBOR INN-HISTORIC MARSHALL
15435 W Michigan
Ave (49068)
Rates: $45-$69
(616) 781-7772
(800) 424-0807

MCMILLAN

INTERLAKEN LODGE
Rt 3, Box 2542
(49853)
Rates: $65-$125
(906) 586-3545

MENOMINEE

ECONO LODGE ON THE BAY
2516 10th St (49858)
Rates: $40-$90
(906) 863-4431
(800) 424-6423

MIDLAND

BEST WESTERN VALLEY PLAZA RESORT
5221 Bay City Rd
(48642)
Rates: $75-$95
(989) 496-2700
(800) 528-1234
(800) 825-2700

FAIRVIEW INN
2200 W Wackerly
St (48640)
Rates: $69-$99
(989) 631-0070
(800) 422-2744

HOLIDAY INN
1500 W Wackerly
St (48640)
Rates: $79-$140
(989) 631-4220
(800) 465-4329
(800) 622-4220

PLAZA SUITES HOTEL
5217 Bay City Rd
(48640)
Rates: $107-$139
(989) 496-0100

SLEEP INN
2100 W Wackerly
St (48640)
Rates: $70-$140
(989) 837-1010
(800) 424-6423
(888) 837-1010

MILFORD

MILFORD'S HURON VALLEY MOTEL
640 N Milford Rd
(48381)
Rates: $35-$45
(810) 685-1020

MIO

MIO MOTEL
415 N Morenci St
(48647)
Rates: $40-$60
(517) 826-3248

MONROE

BEST WESTERN PRESTIGE INN
1900 Welcome
Way (48161)
Rates: $50-$80
(734) 289-2330
(800) 528-1234

COMFORT INN
6500 E Albain Rd
(48161)
Rates: $59-$189
(734) 384-1500
(800) 424-6423

HOMETOWN INN
1885 Welcome
Way (48161)
Rates: $42-$55
(734) 289-1080

MOUNT CLEMENS

COMFORT INN
1 N River Rd
(48043)
Rates: $50-$130
(586) 465-2185
(800) 424-6423

MOUNT PLEASANT

HOLIDAY INN
5665 E Pickard
Ave (48858)
Rates: $89-$159
(989) 772-2905
(800) 465-4329

MUNISING

ALGER FALLS MOTEL
M-28 E (49862)
Rates: $40-$65
(906) 387-3536

BEST WESTERN
SR 28 (M-28)
(49862)
Rates: $59-$119
(906) 387-4864
(800) 528-1234

COMFORT INN
SR 28 (M-28) E
(49862)
Rates: $65-$125
(906) 387-5292
(800) 424-6423

DAYS INN
M-28 E (49862)
Rates: $60-$150
(906) 387-2493
(800) 329-7466

SUNSET MOTEL
1315 Bay St
(49862)
Rates: $45-$78
(906) 387-4574

NEGAUNEE

QUARTZ MTN INN
791 US 41 E
(49866)
Rates: $29-$40
(906) 475-7165

NEW BALTIMORE

COUNTRY HEARTH INN
29101 23-Mile Rd
(48047)
Rates: $40-$70
(810) 949-4520
(800) 282-5711

NEW BUFFALO

ALL SUITES INN
231 E Buffalo
(49117)
Rates: $85-175
(616) 469-1000
(800) 469-7668

EDGEWOOD MOTEL
18716 LaPorte Rd
(49117)
Rates: $33-$43
(616) 469-3345

GRAND BEACH MOTEL
19189 US 12
(49117)
Rates: $25-$70
(616) 469-1555

SANS SOUCI B&B
19265 S Lakeside
Rd (49117)
Rates: $98-$196
(616) 756-3141

NEWBERRY

GATEWAY MOTEL
Rt 4, Box 980,
M123 (49868)
Rates: n/a
(906) 293-5651

GREEN ACRES MOTEL
Rt 1, Box 736 (49868)
Rates: $38-$48
(800) 800-5398

PARK-A-WAY MOTEL
RR 4, Box 966
(49868)
Rates: $30-$60
(906) 293-5771

RAINBOW LODGE
County Rd 423,
P. O. Box 386
(49868)
Rates: $31-$75
(906) 658-3357

NORTON SHORES

BEL AIRE MOTEL
4240 Airline Rd
(49444)
Rates: $56-$72
(231) 733-2196

SEAWAY MOTEL
631 W Norton Ave
(49444)
Rates: $60-$90
(231) 733-1220

NORWAY

AMERICINN
W 6002 US
Hwy 2 (49870)
Rates: $73-$80
(906) 563-7500
(800) 634-3444

NOVI

RESIDENCE INN BY MARRIOTT
27477 Caberet Dr
(48376)
Rates: $99-$599
(248) 735-7400
(800) 331-3131

TOWNEPLACE SUITES
42600 11 Mile Rd
(48376)
Rates: $104-$124
(248) 305-5533
(800) 257-3000

AREA CODES - If the local number doesn't connect, check for a new area code.

OAKS

GUESTHOUSE/
DOGHAVEN
P. O. Box 283
Three (49128)
Rates: $157-$295
(616) 756-3856

ONAWAY
LAKESIDE MOTEL
County Rd 489,
Rt 1 (49765)
Rates: n/a
(517) 733-4298

ONEKAMA
TRAVELERS
MOTEL
5606 Eight Mile,
Box 97 (49675)
Rates: $30-$70
(231) 889-4342
(800) 769-0184

ONTONAGON
RAINBOW MOTEL
& CHALETS
P. O. Box 2900
(49953)
Rates: $36-$70
(906) 885-5348

SCOTT'S
SUPERIOR INN
& CABINS
277 Lakeshore Rd
(49953)
Rates: $39-$58
(906) 884-4866

SUNSHINE MOTEL
& CABINS
1442 M-64 (49953)
Rates: $25-$75
(906) 884-2187

SUPERIOR
SHORES RESORT
1823 M-64 (49953)
Rates: $35-$115
(906) 884-2653
(800) 344-5355

OSCODA
ANCHORAGE
COTTAGES
RESORT
3164 N US 23
(48750)
Rates: $45-$95
(517) 739-7843

**ASPEN MOTOR
INN**
115 N Lake St
(48750)
Rates: $29-$50
(517) 739-9152
(800) 892-7736

BLUE HORIZON
COURT
4208 N US 23,
Box 151 (48750)
Rates: $30-$55
(517) 739-8487
(800) 524-5201

CEDAR LANE
RESORT MOTEL
7404 N US 23
(48750)
Rates: $26-$68
(517) 739-9988

NORTHERN
TRAVELER
5493 N US 23
(48750)
Rates: $34-$58
(517) 739-9261

RAINBOW
RESORT
5764 N US 23
(48750)
Rates: $60-
$400/Weekly
(517) 739-5695

SURFSIDE I & II
CONDO & MOTEL
6504 N US 23
(48750)
Rates: $52-$150
(517) 739-5363

OWOSSO
OWOSSO
MOTOR LODGE
2247 E Main St
(48867)
Rates: $30-$50
(517) 725-7148
(800) 444-7148

PARADISE
TRAVELODGE
M-123 &
Whitefish Rd
(49768)
Rates: $50-$175
(906) 492-3445
(800) 578-7878

PAW PAW
COMFORT INN
153 Ampey Rd
(49079)
Rates: $55-$109
(269) 655-0303
(800) 424-6423

GREEN ACRES
MOTEL
38245 W Red
Arrow (49079)
Rates: n/a
(269) 657-4037

MROCZEK INN
139 Ampey Rd
(49079)
Rates: $31-$40
(269) 657-2578

PELLSTON
HOLIDAY INN EXP
1600 Hwy 31 N
(49769)
Rates: $99-$239
(231) 539-7000
(800) 465-4329

PERRY
HEB'S INN MOTEL
2811 Lansing Rd
(48872)
Rates: $43-$55
(517) 625-7500

PETOSKEY
DAYS INN
1420 US 131 S
(49770)
Rates: $69-$149
(231) 348-3900
(800) 329-7466

PINCONNING
PINCONNING
TRAIL HOUSE
201 S M-13 (48650)
Rates: $32-$75
(517) 879-4219

PLAINWELL
COMFORT INN
622 Allegan St
(49080)
Rates: $74-$180
(269) 685-9891
(800) 424-6423

PLYMOUTH
RED ROOF INN
39700 Ann Arbor
Rd (48170)
Rates: $47-$76
(800) 843-7663

PONTIAC
RESIDENCE INN
BY MARRIOTT
3333 Centerpoint
Pkwy (48341)
Rates: $139-$199
(248) 858-8664
(800) 331-3131

PORT AUSTIN
LAKESIDE
MOTOR LODGE
P.O. Box 358 (48467)
Rates: $35-$60
(517) 738-5201

PORT HURON
MAINSTREET
LODGE
514 Huron Ave
(48060)
Rates: $58-$81
(810) 984-3166
(888) 256-5656

PORTLAND
BEST WESTERN
AMERICAN
HERITAGE INN
1681 Grand River
Ave (48875)
Rates: $69-$84
(517) 647-2200
(800) 528-1234

POWERS
CANDLE LITE
MOTEL
P.O. Box 195 (49874)
Rates: $22-$30
(906) 497-5413

PRUDENVILLE
EAST BAY LODGE
125 12th St (48651)
Rates: $45-$108
(989) 366-5910

RAPID RIVER
RIGHT BOWER
MOTEL
9912 US 2 (49878)
Rates: $23-$36
(906) 474-6078

REDFORD
COACH &
LANTERN MOTEL
25255 Grand River
Ave (48240)
Rates: $29-$42
(313) 533-4020

DORCHESTER
MOTEL
26825 Grand River
Ave (48240)
Rates: $33-$75
(313) 533-8400

**ROCHESTER
HILLS**
RED ROOF INN
2580 Crooks Rd
(48309)
Rates: $52-$85
(248) 853-6400
(800) 843-7663

ROCHESTER
MOTOR LODGE
2070 S Rochester
Rd (48307)
Rates: $38-$48
(248) 651-8591

ROGERS CITY
DRIFTWOOD
MOTEL
540 W Third St
(49779)
Rates: $70-$95
(989) 734-4777

ROMULUS
BAYMONT INN &
SUITES-
AIRPORT
9000 Wickham Rd
(48174)
Rates: $75-$80
(734) 722-6000
(877) 229-6668

DETROIT METRO
AIRPORT
MARRIOTT
30559 Flynn Dr
(48174)
Rates: $79-$169
(734) 729-7555
(800) 228-9290

FOUR POINTS BY
SHERATON
8800 Wickham Rd
(48174)
Rates: $79-$99
(734) 729-9000
(800) 325-3535

SUPER 8 MOTEL
9863 Middlebelt
Rd (48174)
Rates: $49-$79
(734) 946-8808
(800) 800-8000

THE WEST DETROIT METRO AIRPORT
2501 Worldgateway Pl (48242)
Rates: $79-$259
(734) 942-6500
(800) 228-3000

ROSEVILLE
BAYMONT INN & SUITES
20675 13 Mile Road (48066)
Rates: $67-$84
(586) 296-6910
(877) 229-6668

BEST WESTERN GEORGIAN INN
31327 Gratiot Ave (48066)
Rates: $69-$179
(586) 294-0400
(800) 528-1234

COMFORT INN
31960 Little Mack (48066)
Rates: $69-$259
(586) 296-6700
(800) 424-6423

ECONO LODGE
31811 Little Mack Rd (48066)
Rates: $40-$90
(586) 294-6140
(800) 424-6423

RED ROOF INN
31800 Little Mack Rd (48066)
Rates: $43-$75
(586) 296-0310
(800) 843-7663

SAGINAW
BEST WESTERN SAGINAW
1408 S OUter Dr (48601)
Rates: $49-$99
(989) 755-0461
(800) 528-1234

FOUR POINTS BY SHERATON
4960 Towne Center Rd (48604)
Rates: $79
(989) 790-5050
(800) 325-3535

HOWARD JOHNSON PLAZA HOTEL
400 Johnson St (48607)
Rates: $79-$189
(989) 753-6608
(800) 446-4656

MOTEL 6
966 S Outer Dr (48601)
Rates: $35-$40
(989) 754-8414
(800) 466-8356

RAMADA INN & SUITES
3325 Davenport Ave (48602)
Rates: $69-$139
(989) 793-7900
(800) 272-6232

SUPER 8 MOTEL
4848 Town Centre Rd (48603)
Rates: $60-$126
(989) 791-3003
(800) 800-8000

ST. IGNACE
BAY VIEW MOTEL
1133 N State St (49781)
Rates: $32-$76
(906) 643-9444

BLUE BAY MOTEL
1071 N State St (49781)
Rates: $29-$79
(906) 643-7414

BUDGET HOST INN
700 N State St (49781)
Rates: $58-$167
(906) 643-9666
(800) 283-4678

CEDAR'S MOTEL
2040 N Business Loop I-75 (49781)
Rates: $32-$39
(906) 643-9578

COMFORT INN BEACHSIDE
927 N State St (49781)
Rates: $49-$278
(906) 643-7733
(800) 424-6423

THE DRIFTWOOD MOTEL
590 N State St (49781)
Rates: $30-$52
(906) 643-7744

ECONO LODGE INN & SUITES
680 W US 2 (49781)
Rates: $49-$130
(906) 643-9688
(800) 553-2666

QUALITY INN
913 Boulevard Dr (49781)
Rates: $49-$179
(906) 643-9700
(800) 424-6423

ROCKVIEW MOTEL
2055 N Business Loop I-75 (49781)
Rates: $32-$38
(906) 643-8839

SILVER SANDS RESORT
1519 US 2 W (49781)
Rates: $50-$125
(906) 643-8635

WAYSIDE MOTEL
751 N State St (49781)
Rates: $35-$65
(906) 643-8944

ST. JOSEPH
ECONO LODGE
2723 Niles Ave (49085)
Rates: $40-$100
(269) 982-3333
(800) 424-6423

SAULT STE MARIE
ADMIRALS INN
2701 I-75 Business Spur (49783)
Rates: $33-$40
(906) 632-1130

BAMBI MOTEL
1801 Ashmun (49783)
Rates: $34-$65
(906) 632-7881
(800) 289-0864

BAVARIAN ECONOMY INN
2006 Ashmun St (49783)
Rates: $52-$69
(906) 632-6864

BEST WESTERN SAULT STE MARIE
I-75 Business Loop (49783)
Rates: $59-$109
(906) 632-2170
(800) 297-2858
(800) 528-1234

BILTMORE MOTEL
331 E Portage (49783)
Rates: $34-$54
(906) 632-2119
(800) 528-0612

BUDGET HOST CRESVIEW INN
1200 Ashmun St (49783)
Rates: $49-$79
(906) 635-5213
(800) 283-4678

DAYS INN
I-75 Business Spur (49783)
Rates: $55-$90
(906) 635-5200
(800) 329-7466

ECONO LODGE
3525 I-75 Business Spur (49783)
Rates: $55-$90
(906) 632-6000
(800) 424-6423

GRAND MOTEL
1100 E Portage Ave (49783)
Rates: $36-$110
(906) 632-2141

IMPERIAL MOTOR INN
2216 Ashmun St (49783)
Rates: n/a
(906) 632-7334
(800) 859-9898

KING'S INN MOTEL
3755 I-75 Business Spur (49783)
Rates: $28-$60
(906) 635-5061

LA FRANCE TERRACE MOTEL
1608 Ashmun St (49783)
Rates: $38-$75
(906) 632-7823
(888) 458-1144

LAKER INN
1712 Ashmun (49783)
Rates: $42-$46
(906) 632-3581

MID-CITY MOTEL
304 E Portage Ave (49783)
Rates: $36-$58
(906) 632-6832

QUALITY INN
3290 I-75 Business Spur (49783)
Rates: $49-$119
(906) 635-6918
(800) 424-6423

ROYAL MOTEL
1707 Ashmun (49783)
Rates: $38-$64
(906) 632-6323
(800) 978-4454

SUNSET MOTEL
8929 S Mackinaw Tr (49783)
Rates: $42-$48
(906) 632-3906

SUPER 8 MOTEL
3826 I-75 Business Spur (49783)
Rates: $45-$78
(906) 632-8882
(800) 800-8000

SILVER CITY
AMERICINN LODGE & SUITES
120 Lincoln Ave (49953)
Rates: $79-$140
(906) 885-5311
(800) 534-3444

MOUNTAIN VIEW LODGES
237 SR 107 (49953)
Rates: $134-$149
(906) 885-5256

TOMLINSON'S RAINBOW LODGING
2900 M 64 (49953)
Rates: $45-$85
(906) 885-5348

SMYRNA

DOUBLE R RANCH RESORT
4424 Whites Bridge Rd (48887)
Rates: $34-$50
(616) 794-0520

SOUTHFIELD

CANDLEWOOD SUITES
1 Corporate Dr (48076)
Rates: $69-$159
(248) 945-0010
(888) 226-3539

HAWTHORN SUITES LTD
25100 Northwestern Hwy (48075)
Rates: $89-$149
(248) 350-2400
(800) 527-1133

HILTON GARDEN INN
26000 American Dr (48034)
Rates: $69-$169
(248) 357-1100
(800) 445-8667

HOLIDAY INN
26555 Telegraph Rd (48034)
Rates: $65-$149
(248) 353-7700
(800) 465-4329

HOMESTEAD STUDIO SUITES
28500 Northwestern Hwy (48034)
Rates: $69-$89
(248) 213-4500
(888) 782-9473

RED ROOF INN
27660 Northwestern Hwy (48034)
Rates: $60-$80
(248) 353-7200
(800) 843-7663

WESTIN HOTEL
1500 Town Center (48075)
Rates: $89-$270
(248) 827-4000
(800) 228-3000

SOUTHGATE

BAYMONT INN
12888 Reeck Rd (48195)
Rates: $67-$74
(734) 374-3000
(877) 229-6668

BEST VALUE INN
18777 Northline Rd (48195)
Rates: $48-$70
(734) 287-8340

SPRING LAKE

GRAND HAVEN WATERFRONT HOLIDAY INN
940 W Savidge St (49456)
Rates: $89-$185
(616) 846-1000
(800) 465-4329

STANDISH

STANDISH MOTEL
US 23 & M-76 (48658)
Rates: $30-$50
(517) 846-9571

STEPHENSON

STEPHENSON MOTEL
Rt 2, Box 20, Hwy 41 (49887)
Rates: $30-$35
(906) 753-2552

STERLING HEIGHTS

TOWNEPLACE SUITES
14800 Lakeside Cir (48313)
Rates: $89-$119
(586) 566-0900
(800) 257-3000

STEVENSVILLE

BAYMONT INN & SUITES
2601 W Marquette Woods Rd (49127)
Rates: $62-$76
(269) 428-9111
(877) 229-6668

CANDLEWOOD SUITES
2567 Marquette Wood Rd (49127)
Rates: $69-$149
(269) 428-4400
(888) 226-3539

HAMPTON INN
5050 Red Arrow Hwy (49127)
Rates: $69-$99
(269) 429-2700
(800) 426-7866

PARK INN INT'L
4290 Red Arrow Hwy (49127)
Rates: $65-$149
(269) 429-3218
(800) 670-727

STURGIS

BEST VALUE GREEN BRIAR INN
71381 S Centerville Rd (49091)
Rates: $35-$59
(269) 651-2361

SUTTONS BAY

RED LION MOTOR LODGE
4290 S West Bay Shore Rd (49682)
Rates: $49-$135
(231) 271-6694
(800) 547-8010

TAWAS CITY

TAWAS MOTEL & RESORT
1124 US 23S (48764)
Rates: $35-$95
(989) 362-3822

TAYLOR

RED ROOF INN
21230 Eureka Rd (48180)
Rates: $50-$80
(734) 374-1150
(800) 843-7663

TECUMSEH

TECUMSEH INN MOTEL
1445 W Chicago Blvd (49286)
Rates: $49-$150
(517) 423-7401

THREE RIVERS

SUPER 8 MOTEL
711 US 131 (49093)
Rates: $54-$89
(269) 279-8888
(800) 800-8000

TRAVERSE CITY

BEST WESTERN FOUR SEASONS MOTEL
305 Munson Ave (49686)
Rates: $59-$189
(231) 946-8424
(800) 528-1234
(800) 823-7844

DAYS INN & SUITES
420 Munson Ave (49686)
Rates: $44-$199
(231) 941-0208
(800) 329-7466
(800) 982-3297

ECONOMY INN
1582 US 31 N (49686)
Rates: $30-$110
(231) 938-2080

FOX HAUS MOTOR LODGE
704 Munsion Ave (49684)
Rates: $30-$175
(231) 947-4450

HOLIDAY INN
615 E Front St (49684)
Rates: $89-$199
(231) 947-3700
(800) 465-4329
(800) 888-8020

MOTEL 6
1582 US 31 N (49684)
Rates: $35-$94
(231) 938-3002
(800) 466-8356

OLD MISSION INN
18599 Old Mission Rd (49684)
Rates: $250-$500 Weekly
(231) 223-7770

PARK PLACE HOTEL
300 E State St (49684)
Rates: $119-$209
(231) 946-5000
(800) 748-0133

QUALITY INN BY THE BAY
1492 US 31 N (49686)
Rates: $39-$189
(231) 929-4423
(800) 424-6423

TRAVERSE VICTORIAN INN
461 Munson Ave (49686)
Rates: $59-$149
(231) 947-5525

TROUT LAKE

MCGOWAN'S FAMILY MOTEL
M-123 (49793)
Rates: $45-$51
(906) 569-3366

TROY

DRURY INN
575 W Big Beaver Rd (48084)
Rates: $75-$135
(248) 528-3330
(800) 378-7946

HOLIDAY INN
2537 Rochester Ct (48083)
Rates: $79-$139
(248) 689-7500
(800) 465-4329

RED ROOF INN
2350 Rochester Rd (48083)
Rates: $53-$83
(248) 689-4391
(800) 843-7663

RESIDENCE INN BY MARRIOTT
2600 Livernois Rd (48083)
Rates: $134-$179
(248) 689-6856
(800) 331-3131

UTICA

AMERISUITES
45400 Park Ave (48315)
Rates: $69-$149
(586) 803-0100
(800) 833-1516

BAYMONT INN & SUITES
45311 Park Ave (48315)
Rates: $89-$96
(586) 731-4700
(877) 229-6668

AREA CODES - If the local number doesn't connect, check for a new area code.

STAYBRIDGE SUITES
46155 Utica Park Blvd (48315)
Rates: $129-$189
(586) 323-0101
(800) 238-8000

WAKEFIELD

INDIANHEAD MOUNTAIN RESORT
500 Indianhead Rd (49968)
Rates: $58-$160
(906) 229-5181
(800) 346-3426

WALKER

BAYMONT INN & SUITES
2151 Holton Ct NW (49544)
Rates: $69-$99
(616) 735-9595
(877) 229-6668

MOTEL 6
777 Three Mile Rd (49504)
Rates: $37-$46
(616) 784-9375
(800) 466-8356

WARREN

BAYMONT INN & SUITES
30900 Van Dyke (48093)
Rates: $67-$74
(586) 574-0550
(877) 229-6668

HAWTHORN SUITES LTD
7601 Chicago Rd (48093)
Rates: $89
(586) 264-8800
(800) 527-1133

HOMEWOOD SUITES
30180 N Civic Center Blvd (48093)
Rates: $79-$159
(586) 558-7870
(800) 225-5466

MOTEL 6
8300 Chicago Rd (48093)
Rates: $37-$46
(586) 826-9300
(800) 466-8356

RED ROOF INN
26300 DeQuindre Rd (48091)
Rates: $52-$75
(586) 573-4300
(800) 843-7663

WATERFORD

MCGUIRE'S MOTOR INN
120 S Telegraph Rd (48328)
Rates: $46-$52
(248) 682-5100
(800) 545-0454

WATERS

NORTHLAND INN & MOTEL
9311 Old US 27 (49797)
Rates: $40-$70
(517) 732-4470

WATERSMEET

DANCING EAGLES RESORT LAC VIEUX DESERT CASINO
N5384 US Hwy 45 (49969)
Rates: $59-$149
(906) 358-4949

VACATIONLAND RESORT
E 19636 Hebert Rd (49969)
Rates: $60-$160
(906) 358-4380

WEST BRANCH

SUPER 8 MOTEL
2596 Austin Way (48661)
Rates: $75-$179
(989) 345-8488
(800) 800-8000

WHITE PIGEON

PLAZA MOTEL
71410 US 131 S (49099)
Rates: $25-$49
(616) 382-7285

WHITEHALL

LAKE LAND MOTEL
1002 E Colby St (49461)
Rates: $35-$75
(231) 894-5644

WHITMORE LAKE

BEST WESTERN OF WHITMORE LAKE
9897 N Main St (48189)
Rates: $65-$99
(734) 449-2058
(800) 528-1234

LAKES MOTEL
8365 Main St (48189)
Rates: $35-$60
(734) 449-5991

WYOMING

JIM WILLIAMS MOTEL
3821 S Division (49548)
Rates: $28-$46
(616) 241-5461

SUPER 8 MOTEL
727 44th St SW (49509)
Rates: $47-$80
(616) 530-8588
(800) 800-8000

YPSILANT

MAYFLOWER MOTEL
5610 Carpenter (48197)
Rates: $35-$90
(734) 434-2200

MINNESOTA

ADA
NORMAN MOTEL
502 W Thorpe Ave
(56510)
Rates: $27-$47
(218) 784-3781

AITKIN
40 CLUB INN HOTEL
950 2nd St NW
(56431)
Rates: $59-$89
(218) 927-2903
(800) 682-8152

RIPPLE RIVER MOTEL
701 Minnesota
Ave (56431)
Rates: $45-$85
(218) 927-3734
(800) 258-3734

ALBERT LEA
ALBERT LEA COUNTRYSIDE MOTEL
2102 E Main St
(56007)
Rates: $35-$79
(507) 373-2446

BEL AIRE MOTOR INN
700 US Hwy 69 S
(56007)
Rates: $35-$100
(507) 373-3983
(800) 373-4073

COMFORT INN
810 Happy Trails
Ln (56007)
Rates: $49-$129
(507) 377-1100
(800) 424-6423

COUNTRY INN & SUITES
2214 E Main St
(56007)
Rates: $71-$116
(507) 373-5513
(800) 456-4000

DAYS INN
2301 E Main St
(56007)
Rates: $55-$65
(507) 373-8291
(800) 329-7466

ALEXANDRIA
COUNTRY INN & SUITES
5304 Hwy 29 S
(56308)
Rates: $76-$109
(320) 763-9900
(800) 456-4000

HOLIDAY INN
5637 Hwy 29 S
(56308)
Rates: $77-$150
(320) 763-6577
(800) 465-4329

"L" MOTEL
910 Hwy 27 W
(56308)
Rates: $40-$69
(320) 763-5121
(800) 733-1793

SKYLINE MOTEL
605 30th Ave
(56308)
Rates: $39-$59
(320) 763-3175
(800) 467-4096

SUPER 8 MOTEL
4620 Hwy 29 S
(56308)
Rates: $56-$81
(320) 763-6552
(800) 800-8000

VIKING MOTEL & EXTENDED STAY
1903 Aga Dr
(56308)
Rates: $40-$69
(320) 762-3534
(800) 930-3534

ANGLE INLET
NORTHWEST ANGLE RESORT
19637 Crow Creek
Dr NW (56711)
Rates: $30-$40
(218) 223-8511

ANNANDALE
AMERICINN LODGE & SUITES
620 Elm St E
(55302)
Rates: $69-$129
(320) 274-3006
(800) 634-3444

THAYER'S HISTORIC B&B
60 W Elm (55302)
Rates: $62-$245
(320) 274-8222
(800) 944-6595

ANOKA
PIERCE MOTEL
1520 S Ferry
(55303)
Rates: $45-$53
(763) 421-7000

APPLETON
SUPER 8 MOTEL
900 N
Munsterman
(56208)
Rates: $36-$52
(320) 289-2500
(800) 800-8000

ARDEN HILLS
SUPER 8 MOTEL
1125 Red Fox Rd
(55112)
Rates: $59-$89
(651) 484-6557
(800) 800-8000

AUSTIN
AUSTIN MOTEL
805 21st St NE
(55912)
Rates: $39-$59
(507) 433-9254
(800) 433-9254

COUNTRY SIDE INN
3303 Oakland Ave
W (55912)
Rates: $39-$60
(507) 437-7774

DAYS INN
700 16th Ave NW
(55912)
Rates: $50-$75
(507) 433-8600
(800) 329-7466

HOLIDAY INN HOLIDOME
1701 4th St NW
(55912)
Rates: $62-$159
507) 433-1000
(800) 465-4329

BABBITT
TIMBER BAY LODGE & HOUSEBOATS
8347 Timber Bay
Rd (55706)
Rates: $140-$400
(218) 827-3682
(800) 846-6821

BACKUS
MOUNTAIN VIEW RESORT
590 Wood St N
(56435)
Rates: $75-$175
(218) 947-3233

PINE MOUNTAIN INN B&B
P.O. Box 144
(56435)
Rates: $40-$45
(218) 947-3050
(800) 682-2884

BADGER
BADGER MOTEL
Hwy 11 (56714)
Rates: $30-$40
(218) 528-3745

BARNUM
NORTHWOODS MOTEL & COTTAGES
3716 Main St
(55707)
Rates: $33-$75
(218) 389-6951
(800) 228-6951

BAUDETTE
AMERICINN LODGE & SUITES LAKE OF THE WOODS
1179 Main St W
(56623)
Rates: $68-$140
(218) 634-3200
(800) 634-3444

BAUDETTE MOTEL
309 W Main (56623)
Rates: $27-$69
(218) 634-2600
(800) 200-2601

KEN-MAR-KE RESORT CABINS
Box 215, Rt 1
(56623)
Rates: $58+
(218) 634-2072
(800) 535-8155

ROYAL DUTCHMAN RESORT MOTEL
1638 Hwy 11 E
(56623)
Rates: $40-$55
(218) 634-1024
(800) 372-8603

BAXTER
COUNTRY INN BY CARLSON
1220 Delwood Dr
N (56401)
Rates: $79-$107
(218) 828-2161
(800) 456-4000

HAWTHORN INN & SUITES
2300 Fairview Rd
N (56401)
Rates: $89-$349
(218) 822-1133
(800) 527-1133

BEAVER BAY
THE INN AT BEAVER
1017 Main St
(55601)
Rates: $49-$150
(218) 226-4351
(800) 226-4351

AREA CODES - If the local number doesn't connect, check for a new area code.

BECKER

SLEEP INN & SUITES
14435 Bank St (55308)
Rates: $64-$134
(763) 262-7700
(800) 753-3476

BELLE PLAINE

BELLE PLAINE MOTEL
315 S Walnut St (56011)
Rates: $29-$69
(952) 873-2242
(888) 873-6424

BEMIDJI

BALSAM BEACH RESORT
51155 219th Ave (56601)
Rates: $100-$120
(218) 751-5057
(888) 751-5057

BEST WESTERN BEMIDJI INN
2420 Paul Bunyan Dr NW (56601)
Rates: $47-$125
(218) 751-0390
(800) 528-1234
(877) 857-8599

COMFORT INN
3500 Moberg Dr NW (56601)
Rates: $69-$109
(218) 444-7700
(800) 424-6423

LAKESIDE MOTEL
809 Paul Bunyan Dr NE (56601)
Rates: $24-$64
(218) 751-3266
(800) 817-4930

MIDWAY MOTEL
1000 Paul Bunyan Dr NE (56601)
Rates: $40-$65
(218) 751-1180

PAUL BUNYAN MOTEL
915 Paul Bunyan Dr NE (56601)
Rates: $24-$64
(218) 751-1314
(800) 848-3788

RUTTGER'S BIRCHMONT LODGE
7598 Bemidji Rd NE (56601)
Rates: $38-$249
(218) 444-3463
(888) RUTTGER

BENEDICT

BORDE DU LAC LODGE/CABINS
34217 CR 39 (56436)
Rates: $109-$213; $545-$1065 Wkly
(218) 224-2384
(800) 325-5820

BENSON

MOTEL 1
620 Atlantic Ave (56215)
Rates: $28-$38
(320) 843-4434

SUPER 8 MOTEL
600 22nd St S (56215)
Rates: $35-$56
(320) 843-3451
(800) 800-8000

BIG FALLS

BIG FALLS MOTEL
Hwy 71 (56627)
Rates: $25-$38
(218) 276-2261

BIG LAKE

LAKE AIRE MOTEL
340 Jefferson Blvd (55309)
Rates: n/a
(612) 263-2405

BIWABIK

BIWABIK MOTEL
Hwy 135 (55708)
Rates: $25-$30
(218) 865-9980

THE LODGE AT GIANTS RIDGE
6373 Wynne Creek Dr (55708)
Rates: $69-$189
(218) 865-7170

BLACKDUCK

DRAKE MOTEL
305 N Pine (56630)
Rates: $30-$35
(218) 835-4567
(888) 253-8501

BLOOMINGTON

AMERISUITES
7800 International Dr (55425)
Rates: $79-$159
(952) 854-0700
(800) 833-1516

BAYMONT INN AIRPORT
7815 Nicollet Ave S (55420)
Rates: $74-$90
(952) 881-7311
(877) 229-6668

CLARION HOTEL AIRPORT
5151 American Blvd W (55437)
Rates: $59-$109
(952) 830-1300
(800) 424-6423

DAYS INN
7851 Normandale Blvd (55435)
Rates: $59-$90
(952) 835-7400
(800) 329-7466

EXEL INN
2701 E 78th St (55425)
Rates: $61-$85
(952) 854-7200
(800) 367-3935

HILTON HOTEL MINNEAPOLIS-ST PAUL AIRPORT
3800 E 80th St (55425)
Rates: $89-$189
(952) 854-2100
(800) 445-8667

HOMEWOOD SUITES
2261 Killebrew Dr (55425)
Rates: $109-$209
(952) 854-0900
(800) 225-5466

HOSPITALITY INN & SUITES
1601 79th St E (55425)
Rates: $59-$154
(952) 854-1687

PARK INN SUITES
7770 Johnson Ave (55435)
Rates: $95-$120
(952) 893-9999
(800) 670-7275

RAMADA INN AIRPORT
2201 E 78th St (55425)
Rates: $79-$139
(952) 854-3411
(800) 328-1931

RESIDENCE INN BY MARRIOTT
7850 Bloomington Ave S (55425)
Rates: $159-$220
(952) 876-0900
(800) 331-3131

SHERATON HOTEL
7800 Normandale Blvd (55439)
Rates: $89-$229
(952) 835-7800
(800) 325-3535

SOFITEL HOTEL
5601 W 78th St (55439)
Rates: $194-$234
(952) 835-1900
(800) 876-6303

STAYBRIDGE SUITES
5150 American Blvd (55437)
Rates: $109-$139
(952) 831-7900
(800) 238-8000

BLUE EARTH

AMERICINN
1495 Domes Dr (56013)
Rates: $49-$150
(507) 526-4215
(800) 634-3444

SUPER 8 MOTEL
1120 N Grove St (56013)
Rates: $50-$70
(507) 526-7376
(800) 800-8000

BRAINERD

DELLWOOD MOTEL
1302 S 6th St (56401)
Rates: $23-$35
(218) 828-8756

DOWNTOWN MOTEL
507 S 6th St (56401)
Rates: $23-$45
(218) 829-7489

ECONO LODGE
2655 Hwy 371 S (56401)
Rates: $49-$99
(218) 828-0027
(800) 424-6423

RAMADA INN
2115 S 6th St (56401)
Rates: $69-$95
(218) 829-1441
(800) 272-6232

RIVERVIEW INN
324 NW Washington St (56401)
Rates: $30-$70
(218) 829-8771
(800) 850-8771

BRANDON

BERNDT'S KAMP KAPPY RESORT CABINS
13110 Devils Lake Rd NW (56315)
Rates: $75-$110
(320) 524-2225
(800) 845-2566

LAKE COUNTRY MOTEL
305 Central Ave S (56315)
Rates: $42-$65
(320) 524-2786
(866) 524-7867

BRECKENRIDGE

SELECT INN
821 Hwy 75 N (56520)
Rates: $45-$99
(218) 643-9201
(800) 641-1000

BROOKLYN CENTER

BAYMONT INN & SUITES
6415 James Cir N
(55430)
Rates: $74-$89
(763) 561-8400
(877) 229-6668

COMFORT INN
1600 James Cir N
(55430)
Rates: $64-$124
(763) 560-7464
(800) 424-6423

HOLIDAY INN SELECT MINNEAPOLIS NORTH
2200 Freeway
Blvd (55430)
Rates: $82-$100
(763) 566-8000
(800) 465-4329

MOTEL 6
2741 Freeway
Blvd (55430)
Rates: $39-$60
(763) 560-9789
(800) 466-8356

BROOKLYN PARK

SLEEP INN
7011 Northland
Cir (55428)
Rates: $74-$99
(763) 971-8000
(800) 753-3746

BURNSVILLE

RED ROOF INN
12920 Aldrich Ave
S (55337)
Rates: $36-$74
(952) 890-1420
(800) 843-7663

SUPER 8 MOTEL
1101 Burnsville
Pkwy (55337)
Rates: $47-$72
(952) 894-3400
(800) 800-8000

CALEDONIA

AMERICINN
508 N Kruckow
Ave (55921)
Rates: $68-$74
(507) 725-8000
(800) 634-3444

CREST RED CARPET INN
15944 Hwy 76
(55921)
Rates: $39-$52
(507) 724-3311
(800) 845-0904

CANNON FALLS

BEST WESTERN SARATOGA INN
31591 64th Ave
(55009)
Rates: $64-$135
(507) 263-7272
(800) 528-1234

CARAVAN MOTEL
31913 64th Ave
(55009)
Rates: $40-$66
(507) 263-4777

COUNTRY QUIET INN
37295 112th Ave
Way (55009)
Rates: $55-$130
(507) 258-4406
(800) 258-1843

EDGEWOOD MOTEL
7860 365th
Streetway (55009)
Rates: $39
(507) 263-5700

CARLTON

AMERICINN MOTEL
Hwy 210 & I-35,
Box 146 (55718)
Rates: $51-$105
(218) 384-3535
(800) 634-3444

ROYAL PINES MOTEL
1506 CR 61
(55009)
Rates: $32-$110
(218) 384-4242
(800) 788-9622

CASS LAKE

VIEW POINT RESORT COTTAGES
RR 3, Box 642
(56633)
Rates: $500+
Weekly
(218) 335-6746

WHISPERING PINES MOTEL
6318 Hwy 2 NW
(56633)
Rates: $35-$50
(218) 335-8852
(800) 371-8852

CHANHASSEN

AMERICINN HOTEL & SUITES
570 Pond
Promenade
(55317)
Rates: $95-$185
(952) 934-3888
(800) 634-3444

CHISAGO CITY

SUPER 8 MOTEL
11650 Lake Blvd
(55013)
Rates: $42-$77
(612) 257-8088
(800) 800-8000

CLARA CITY

GREEN MEADOW INN
300 Hwy 7 (56222)
Rates: $31-$49
(320) 847-3790
(800) 685-4266

CLEARBROOK

PIPER'S INN MOTEL
223 Hwy 92 SW
(56634)
Rates: $37-$79
(218) 776-2323
(877) 776-2323

CLEARWATER

BUDGET INN
945 SR 24 (55320)
Rates: $31-$58
(320) 558-2221

CLOQUET

AMERICINN MOTEL
111 Big Lake Rd
(55720)
Rates: $58-$103
(218) 879-1231
(877) 879-1522

GOLDEN GATE MOTEL
3202 Rivergate
Ave (55720)
Rates: $35-$74
(218) 879-6752
(800) 732-4241

ROYAL PINES MOTEL
Hwy 210 & I-35
(55718)
Rates: $29-$119
(218) 384-4242
(800) 788-9622

SUNNY SIDE MOTEL
North Hwy 33
(55720)
Rates: $28-$50
(218) 879-4655

SUPER 8 MOTEL
121 Big Lake Rd
(55720)
Rates: $60-$136
(218) 879-1250
(800) 800-8000

COLD SPRING

AMERICINN MOTEL
118 3rd St S
(56320)
Rates: $46-$79
(320) 685-4539
(800) 634-3444

COOK

MOOSEBIRDS ON LAKE VERMILION
3068 Vermilion Dr
(55723)
Rates: $35-$125
(218) 666-2627

COON RAPIDS

COMFORT INN
9052 NW
University (55448)
Rates: $59-$129
(763) 785-4746
(800) 424-6423

COUNTRY SUITES BY CARLSON
155 Coon Rapids
Blvd (55433)
Rates: $92-$99
(763) 780-3797
(800) 456-4000

CRANE LAKE

OLSON'S BORDERLAND
7488 Crane Lake
Rd (55725)
Rates: n/a
(218) 993-2233

PINE POINT LODGE & RESORT
505 Pine Point
(55725)
Rates: $90+
(218) 993-2311
(800) 628-4446

CROOKSTON

COUNTRY CLUB MOTEL
Hwy 2 & 75 NW
(56716)
Rates: $30-$40
(218) 281-1601
(888) 314-0105

GOLF TERRACE MOTEL
1731 University
Ave N (56716)
Rates: $30-$45
(218) 281-2626

NORTHLAND INN
2200 University
Ave (56716)
Rates: $69-$89
(218) 281-5210

DASSEL

DASSEL MOTEL
505 Mn Hwy 15
(55325)
Rates: n/a
(320) 275-3118
(800) 732-9230

DAWSON

THE PICKET FENCE MOTEL
118 1st St (56232)
Rates: $23-$48
(320) 769-4787

DEER RIVER

BAHR'S MOTEL
P. O. Box 614
(56636)
Rates: $27-$42
(218) 246-8271

MILLER'S RESORT
RR 1, Box 266
(56636)
Rates: $275-
$350/Weekly
(218) 246-8951

WILLIAMS NARROWS RESORT
43465 Williams
Narrows Rd
(56636)
Rates: $125-$210
(218) 246-8703
(800) 325-2475

AREA CODES - If the local number doesn't connect, check for a new area code.

DEERWOOD

CAMP HOLIDAY RESORT
17467 Round Lake Rd (56444)
Rates: $60-$90
(218) 678-2495
(800) 450-2495

COUNTRY INN BY CARLSON
115 Front St E (56444)
Rates: $52-$75
(218) 534-3101
(800) 456-4000

DEERWOOD MOTEL
9 W Forest Rd (56444)
Rates: $32-$65
(218) 534-3163

DETROIT LAKES

AMERICINN LODGE & SUITES
777 Hwy 10 E (56501)
Rates: $58-$126
(218) 847-8795
(800) 634-3444

BEST WESTERN HOLLAND HOUSE & SUITES
615 Hwy 10 E (56501)
Rates: $69-$199
(218) 847-4483
(800) 528-1234
(800) 33-TULIP

BUDGET HOST INN
895 Hwy 10 E (56501)
Rates: $42-$89
(218) 847-4454
(800) 888-2124

CASTAWAY INN & RESORT
1226 E Shore Dr (56501)
Rates: $39-$129
(218) 847-4449
(800) 640-3395

SUPER 8 MOTEL
400 Morrow Ave (56501)
Rates: $42-$82
(218) 847-1651
(800) 800-8000

DEXTER

MILL INN MOTEL
I-90 & SR 16 (55926)
Rates: $35-$46
(507) 584-6440

DILWORTH

ECONO LODGE
701 E Center Ave (56529)
Rates: $34-$108
(218) 287-1212
(800) 424-6423

DULUTH

ALLYNDALE MOTEL
510 N 66th Ave W (55807)
Rates: $53-$63
(218) 628-1061
(800) 806-1061

AMERICINN MOTEL & SUITES
185 Hwy 2 (55810)
Rates: $75-$149
(218) 624-1026
(800) 634-3444
(800) 960-2767

BEST WESTERN DOWNTOWN MOTEL
131 W 2nd St (55802)
Rates: $39-$99
(218) 727-6851
(800) 528-1234
(800) 570-9802

BEST WESTERN EDGEWATER
2400 London Rd (55812)
Rates: $67-$169
(218) 728-3601
(800) 528-1234
(800) 777-7925

CHALET MOTEL
1801 Lincoln Rd (55812)
Rates: $35-$78
(218) 728-4238
(800) 235-2957

DAYS INN
909 Cottonwood Ave (55811)
Rates: $49-$155
(218) 727-3110
(800) 329-7466

ECONO LODGE AIRPORT
4197 Haines Rd (55811)
Rates: $39-$159
(218) 722-5522
(800) 424-6423

GRAND MOTEL
4312 Grand Ave (55807)
Rates: n/a
(218) 624-4821
(800) 472-0841

HAWTHORN SUITES AT WATERFRONT PLAZA
325 Lake Ave S (55802)
Rates: $95-$275
(218) 727-4663
(800) 527-1133

LAKEVIEW CASTLE
5135 N Shore Dr (55804)
Rates: n/a
(218) 525-1014

MANOR ON THE CREEK COUNTRY INN B&B
2215 E 2nd St (55812)
Rates: $129-$199
(218) 728-3189
(800) 428-3189

MOTEL 6
200 S 27th Ave W (55806)
Rates: $29-$70
(218) 723-1123
(800) 466-8356

NORTH SHORE COTTAGES
7717 Congdon Blvd (55804)
Rates: $35-$175
(218) 525-2812
(800) 926-6268

RADISSON HOTEL-HARBORVIEW
505 W Superior St (55802)
Rates: $99-$149
(218) 727-8981
(800) 333-3333

SKYLINE COURT MOTEL
4880 Miller Truck Hwy (55811)
Rates: $49-$69
(218) 727-1563
(800) 554-0621

VOYAGEUR LAKEWALK INN
333 E Superior St (55802)
Rates: $35-$175
(218) 722-3911
(800) 258-3911

EAGAN

BEST WESTERN YANKEE SQUARE INN
3450 Washington Dr (55122)
Rates: $79-$130
(651) 452-0100
(800) 528-1234
(800) 624-2888

HOMESTEAD STUDIO SUITES
3015 Denmark Ave (55122)
Rates: $79-$99
(651) 905-1778
(888) 782-9473

MICROTEL INN
3000 Denmark Ave (55121)
Rates: $55-$60
(651) 405-0988

RESIDENCE INN BY MARRIOTT
3040 Eagandale Pl (55121)
Rates: $75-$152
(651) 688-0363
(800) 331-3131

STAYBRIDGE SUITES
4675 Rahncliff Rd (55122)
Rates: $119-$139
(651) 994-7810
(800) 238-8000

TOWNEPLACE SUITES
3615 Crestridge Dr (55122)
Rates: $79-$159
(651) 994-4600
(800) 257-3000

EDEN PRAIRIE

AMERISUITES
11369 Viking Dr (55344)
Rates: $99-$129
(952) 944-9700
(800) 434-5800

HOMESTEAD STUDIO SUITES
11905 Technology Dr (55344)
Rates: $64-$84
(952) 942-6818
(888) 782-9473

RESIDENCE INN BY MARRIOTT
7780 Flying Cloud Dr (55344)
Rates: $89-$159
(952) 829-0033
(800) 331-3131

TOWNEPLACE SUITES
11588 Leona Rd (55344)
Rates: $51-$129
(952) 942-6001
(800) 257-3000

EDINA

RESIDENCE INN
3400 Edinborough Way (55435)
Rates: $161-$199
(952) 893-9300
(800) 331-3131

ELBOW LAKE

COUNTRY INN MOTEL
Hwy 79 E (56531)
Rates: $36-$48
(218) 685-4511

ELK RIVER

AMERICINN LODGE & SUITES
17432 Hwy 10 (55330)
Rates: $75-$149
(763) 441-8554
(800) 634-3444

ELY

BIG LAKE WILDERNESS LODGE
3012 Echo Trail (55731)
Rates: n/a
(218) 365-2125
(800) 446-9080

AREA CODES - If the local number doesn't connect, check for a new area code.

BLUE HERON B&B
827 Kawishiwi
Trail (55731)
Rates: $110-$170
(218) 365-4720

BUDGET HOST-MOTEL ELY
1047 E Sheridan St
(55731)
Rates: $49-$89
(218) 365-3237
(800) 283-4678

CEDAR SHORES RESORT
2024 Grant
McMahan Blvd
(55731)
Rates: $470-$610
Weekly
(218) 365-5775
(847) 678-5398

CUSTOM CABIN RENTALS
14663 Vosburgh
Rd (55731)
Rates: $975-$1250
Weekly
(219) 365-6947
(800) 235-6947

GRAND ELY LODGE RESORT
400 N Pioneer Rd
(55731)
Rates: $90-$175
(218) 365-6565

LA TOURELL'S RESORT
P O Box 239
(55731)
Rates: $100-$360
(218) 365-4531
(800) 365-4531

LODGE OF WHISPERING PINES
2700 Echo Trail
(55731)
Rates: $105+
(218) 365-2129
(800) 510-2947

MOOSE TRACKE CABINS
593 Kawishwi
Trail (55731)
Rates: $110-$150
(218) 365-4106
(800) 777-7091

NORTH COUNTRY LODGE
5865 Moose Lake
Rd (55731)
Rates: $600-$1450
Weekly
(218) 365-4976
(800) 777-4431

OJIBWAY RESORT
Farm Lake, HCR-1
(55731)
Rates: $595
Weekly
(218) 365-4106
(800) 777-7091

OLSON BAY RESORT COTTAGES
2279 Grant
McMahan Blvd
(55731)
Rates: $350-$600
Weekly
(800) 777-4419

PADDLE INN
1314 E Sheridan St
(55731)
Rates: $45-$89
(218) 365-6036
(888) 270-2245

SHAGAWA INN RESORT-ON THE LAKE MOTEL
1973 Shagawa Rd
(55731)
Rates: $55-$73
(218) 365-5154

SILVER RAPIDS LODGE RESORT
HC 1, Box 2992
(55731)
Rates: $50-$180
(218) 365-4877
(800) 950-9425

THREE DEER HAVEN
1850 Deer Haven
Dr (55731)
Rates: $75-$90
(218) 365-6464

TIMBER WOLF LODGE
P O Box 147
(55731)
Rates: $550-$1650
Weekly
(218) 827-3512
(800) 777-8457

WEST GATE MOTEL
110 N 2nd Ave W
(55731)
Rates: $45-$85
(218) 365-4513
(800) 806-4979

ELYSIAN
LOTUS LODGE MOTEL
511 Hwy 60 W
(56028)
Rates: $39-$64
(507) 267-4212

EMILY
WIGWAM MOTEL
43956 Hwy 6
(56447)
Rates: $50-$60
(218) 763-2995
(800) 763-2995

ERSKINE
WIN-E-MAC MOTEL
Box 144 (56535)
Rates: $27-$50
(218) 687-2415
(800) 358-8663

EVELETH
DAYS INN
701 Hat Trick Ave
(55734)
Rates: $49-$129
(218) 744-2703
(800) 329-7466

KOKE'S MOTEL
714 Fayal Rd
(55734)
Rates: $40-$52
(218) 744-4500
(800) 892-5107

SUPER 8 MOTEL
1080 Industrial
Park Dr (55734)
Rates: $56-$127
(218) 744-1661
(800) 800-8000

EXCELSIOR
CHRISTOPHER INN
201 Mill St (55331)
Rates: $80-$155
(612) 474-0605

FAIRFAX
FAIRFAX MOTEL
403 E Lincoln Ave
(55332)
Rates: n/a
(507) 426-7266

FAIRMONT
BUDGET INN
1122 N State St
(56031)
Rates: $32-$42+
(507) 235-3373

COMFORT INN
2225 N State St
(56031)
Rates: $65-$120
(507) 238-5444
(800) 424-6423

HIGHLAND COURT MOTEL
1245 Lake Ave
(56031)
Rates: $23-$49
(507) 235-6686

HOLIDAY INN
1201 Torgerson Dr
(56031)
Rates: $89-$159
(507) 238-4771
(800) 465-4329

SEBASTIANI & EDGEWATER INN
200 S Main (56031)
Rates: $28-$42
(507) 235-5541

SUPER 8 MOTEL
1200 Torgerson Dr
(56031)
Rates: $47-$65
(507) 238-9444
(800) 800-8000

FARIBAULT
AMERICINN MOTEL
1801 Lavender Dr
(55021)
Rates: $75-$150
(507) 334-9464
(800) 634-3444

DAYS INN & SUITES
1920 Cardinal Ln
(55021)
Rates: $50-$89
(507) 334-6835
(800) 329-7466

SELECT INN
4040 Hwy 60 W
(55021)
Rates: $35-$62
(507) 334-2051
(800) 641-1000

WINJUM'S SHADY ACRES RESORT
17759 W 177th St
(55021)
Rates: $375-$900
Weekly
(507) 334-6661
(800) 626-2952

FEDERAL DAM
SUGAR POINT RESORT/CABINS
10125 Sugar Point
Dr NW (56641)
Rates: $107-$240
(218) 654-3150
(800) 733-3150

FERGUS FALLS
AMERICINN LODGE & SUITES
526 Western Ave
N (56537)
Rates: $66-$95
(218) 739-3900
(800) 634-3444

FINLAYSON
BANNING JUNCTION-NORTH COUNTRY INN
60671 State Hwy
23 (55735)
Rates: $45-$90
(320) 245-5284

FOREST LAKE
AMERICINN MOTEL
1291 W Broadway
(55025)
Rates: $64-$95
(651) 464-1930
(800) 634-3444

FOREST LAKE MOTEL
7 NE 6th Ave
(55025)
Rates: $60-$70
(651) 464-4077
(800) 470-4077

FOSSTON
SUPER 8 MOTEL
108 S Amber
(56542)
Rates: $49-$82
(218) 435-1088
(800) 800-8000

AREA CODES - If the local number doesn't connect, check for a new area code.

FRANKLIN

MAPLE HILL COTTAGE
RR 1, Box 12
(55333)
Rates: $45-$55
(507) 557-2403

FRAZEE

MORNINGSIDE MOTEL
31348 County
Hwy 10 (56544)
Rates: $35-$57
(218) 334-5021

GARRISON

COUNTRY INN & SUITES BY CARLSON
9243 Hwy 169
(56450)
Rates: $69-$115
(320) 692-4050
(800) 456-4000

GREGORY'S RESORT/CABINS
HC1, Box 42B
(56540)
Rates: $20+
(320) 692-4415
(800) 689-5108

ROLLING HILLS RESORT
HC1, Box 205A
(56450)
Rates: $56-$82
(320) 692-4348

TWIN PINES RESORT & MOTEL
7827 Hwy 169
(56540)
Rates: $40-$85
(320) 692-4413
(800) 450-4682

GAYLORD

GOLD LEAF INN & SUITES
330 E Main St
(55334)
Rates: $44-$135
(507) 237-5860

GLENCOE

GLENCOE CASTLE BED & BREAKFST
831 13th St E
(55336)
Rates: $65-$175
(320) 864-3043
(800) 517-3334

GLENWOOD

GREEN VALLEY RESORT
17632 N Pelican
Lake Rd (56334)
Rates: $58-$168
(320) 634-4010
(800) 834-4010

SCOTWOOD INN
Hwy 28 & 55
(56334)
Rates: $50-$110
(320) 634-5105

WOODLAWN RESORT
24050 N
Lakeshore Dr
(56334)
Rates: $80-$115
(320) 634-3619
(800) 892-3619

GRAND MARAIS

BEST WESTERN SUPERIOR INN & SUITES
Hwy 61 E (55604)
Rates: $69-$259
(218) 387-2240
(800) 528-1234
(800) 842-8439

CLEARWATER LODGE
355 Gunflint Trail
(55604)
Rates: $595-$625
Weekly
(800) 527-0554

EAST BAY HOTEL
P O Box 220
(55604)
Rates: $26-$155
(218) 387-2800
(800) 414-2807

GOLDEN EAGLE LODGE
325 Gunflint Trail
(55604)
Rates: $89-$120
(218) 388-2203
(800) 346-2203

GUNFLINT LODGE CABINS
143 S Gunflint
Lake (55604)
Rates: $145-$459
(218) 388-2294
(800) 328-3325

GUNFLINT MOTEL
101 W 5th Ave
(55604)
Rates: $39-$89
(218) 387-1454
(800) 439-1311

GUNFLINT PINES RESORT
217 S Gunflint
Trail (55604)
Rates: $130-$195
(218) 388-4454
(800) 533-5814

HUNGRY JACK LODGE/CABINS
372 Hungry Jack
Rd (55604)
Rates: $140+
(218) 388-2265
(800) 338-1566

LITTLE OLLIE LAKE CABIN
590 Gunflint Trail
(55604)
Rates: $110-$125
(218) 388-9972
(800) 322-8327

LUND'S ON THE SCANDINAVIAN RIVIERA
P O Box 126
(55604)
Rates: $48-$108
(218) 387-2155

MOTEL WEDGEWOOD
HC 1, Box 100
(55604)
Rates: $30-$35
(218) 387-2944

NOR' WESTER LODGE & OUTFITTER
7778 Gunflint
Trail (55604)
Rates: $920-$1400/Weekly
(218) 388-2252

OUTPOST MOTEL
2935 SR 61 E
(55604)
Rates: $39-$95
(218) 387-1833

SANDGREN MOTEL
P. O. Box 1056
(55604)
Rates: $30-$45
(218) 387-2975

SEAWALL MOTEL & CABINS
Hwy 61 & 3rd Ave
(55604)
Rates: $42-$72
(218) 387-2095
(800) 245-5806

SUPER 8 MOTEL
1711 Hwy 61 W
(55604)
Rates: $44-$99
(218) 387-2448
(800) 800-8000

TIMBERLUND'S RESORT
Box 312 (55604)
Rates: $45-$95
(218) 387-1147

TOMTEBODA MOTEL
1800 Hwy 61 W
(55604)
Rates: $59-$79
(218) 387-1585

TRAILSIDE CABINS & MOTEL
P O Box 155
(55604)
Rates: $40-$70
(218) 387-1550
(800) 585-2792

WEDGEWOOD MOTEL
1663 Hwy 61 E
(55604)
Rates: $44-$59
(218) 387-2944

GRAND RAPIDS

AMERICANA MOTEL
1915 Hwy 2 W
(55744)
Rates: $33-$75
(218) 326-0369
(888) 326-0369

BUDGET HOST INN
311 E Hwy 2
(55744)
Rates: $45-$78
(218) 326-3457

COUNTRY INN BY CARLSON
2601 Hwy 169 S
(55744)
Rates: $73-$119
(218) 327-4960
(800) 456-4000

ITASCAN MOTEL
610 S Pokegama
Ave (55744)
Rates: $48-$54
(218) 326-3489
(800) 842-7733

SAWMILL INN
2301 S Pokegama
Ave (55744)
Rates: $66-$99
(218) 326-8501

SUPER 8 MOTEL
1702 S Pokegama
Ave (55744)
Rates: $55-$95
(218) 327-1108
(800) 800-8000

GRANITE FALLS

SUPER 8 MOTEL
845 W SR 212
(56241)
Rates: n/a
(320) 564-4075
(800) 800-8000

GREENBUSH

EMERALD INN MOTEL
Hwy 32 S (56751)
Rates: $29-$34
(218) 782-2990

HACKENSACK

GREEN ROOF LODGE ON WOMAN LAKE
945 County 5 NW
(56452)
Rates: $420-$785
Weekly
(218) 682-2399
(800) 366-2399

OWL'S NEST MOTEL & RV
Hwy 371 (56452)
Rates: $28-$49
(218) 675-6141

QUIETWOODS RESORT
4765 Alder Lane
NW (56452)
Rates: $45-$95
(218) 675-6240

HALLOCK

GATEWAY MOTEL
702 S Atlantic
(56728)
Rates: $24-$38
(218) 843-2032

AREA CODES - If the local number doesn't connect, check for a new area code.

HAMPTON

SILVER BELL MOTEL
23380 Emery
Hwy (55031)
Rates: $38-$44
(651) 437-9242

HARMONY

COUNTRY LODGE MOTEL
525 Main Ave N
(55939)
Rates: $45-$65
(507) 886-2515
(800) 870-1710

HASTINGS

COUNTRY INN & SUITES
300 33rd St (55033)
Rates: $65-$89
(651) 437-8870
(800) 456-4000

HENDRICKS

TRIPLE L FARM BED & BREAKFAST
Rt 1, Box 141
(56136)
Rates: $40-$55
(507) 275-3740

HERMAN

LAWNDALE FARM B&B
Rt 2, Box 50
(56248)
Rates: $65
(320) 677-2687

HIBBING

ADAMS HOUSE BED & BREAKFAST
201 E 23rd St
(55746)
Rates: $48-$53
(218) 263-9742
(888) 891-9742

HIBBING PARK HOTEL
1402 E Howard St
(55746)
Rates: $70-$75
(218) 262-3481

SUPER 8 MOTEL
1411 E 40th St
(55746)
Rates: $43-$68
(218) 263-8982
(800) 800-8000

HILL CITY

BLUE MOON RESORT & MOTEL
17090 Hwy 169
(55748)
Rates: $38-$75
(218) 697-8155
(888) 94-MN-FUN

WHITETAIL INN MOTEL
Hwy 169 N
(55748)
Rates: $26-$38
(218) 697-2470

HINCKLEY

DAYS INN
104 Grindstone Ct
(55037)
Rates: $50-$250
(320) 384-7751
(800) 329-7466

HINCKLEY GOLD PINE INN
325 Fire Monument
(55037)
Rates: $45-$109
(320) 384-6112
(888) 384-6112

HOWARD LAKE

HOWARD LAKE MOTEL
210 10th Ave
(55349)
Rates: $29-$34
(320) 543-2186

HUTCHINSON

AMERICINN MOTEL
1115 Hwy 7 E
(55350)
Rates: $59-$139
(320) 587-5515
(800) 634-3444

ECONOMY INN
200 Hwy 7 E
(55350)
Rates: $32-$65
(320) 587-2129

INTERNATIONAL FALLS

DAYS INN
2331 Hwy 53 S
(56649)
Rates: $49-$90
(218) 283-9441
(800) 329-7466

HILLTOP MOTEL
2002 2nd Ave W
(56649)
Rates: $39-$79
(218) 283-2505
(800) 322-6671

HOLIDAY INN
1500 Hwy 71 W
(56649)
Rates: $84-$150
(218) 283-8000
(800) 465-4329

ISLAND VIEW LODGE & MOTEL
1817 Hwy 11E
(56649)
Rates: $47-$195
(218) 266-3511
(800) 777-7856

NORTHERNAIRE FLOATING LODGES
P.O.Box 510 (56649)
Rates: $695-$1895
Weekly
(218) 286-5221

RAMBLER MOTEL
1901 2nd Ave W
(56649)
Rates: n/a
(218) 283-8454

THUNDERBIRD LODGE
2170 CR 139 (56649)
Rates: $65-$89
(218) 286-3151

ISLE

MCQUOID'S INN
1325 Hwy 47 N
(56342)
Rates: $60-$120
(320) 676-3535
(800) 862--3535

SCENIC BAY RESORT & MOTEL
610 W Main St
(56342)
Rates: $36-$50
(320) 676-3274

JACKSON

BUDGET HOST-PRAIRIE WINDS MOTEL
950 N US 71
(56143)
Rates: $29-$56
(507) 847-2020
(800) 283-4678

SUPER 8 MOTEL
2025 Hwy 71 N
(56143)
Rates: $59-$70
(507) 847-3498
(888) 800-2060
(800) 800-8000

KARLSTAD

NORTH STAR MOTOR INN
315 S Main st
(56732)
Rates: $35-$40
(218) 436-2494

KELLIHER

ROYAL SHOOKS MOTEL
35241 Hwy 72
NE (56661)
Rates: $35-$44
(218) 647-8379
(888) 921-5222

LA CRESCENT

RANCH MOTEL
Hwy 14-16-61
(55947)
Rates: $30-$75
(507) 895-4422

LAKE BENTON

STEVE'S RESORT & MOTEL
N Hwys 75 & 14
(56149)
Rates: $30-$37
(507) 368-4399

LAKE BRONSON

LAKE BRONSON MOTEL
P O Box 8 (56734)
Rates: $30-$36
(218) 754-4355

LAKE CITY

EDGE O TOWN MOTEL
1756 Hwy 61 S
(55041)
Rates: $25-$53
(651) 345-2309

LAKE AIRE MOTEL/DIGGERS BOAT RENTAL
917 N Lakeshore
Dr (55041)
Rates: $29-$60
(651) 345-4586

LAKE PEPIN LODGE-MOTEL
620 Central Point
Rd (55041)
Rates: $59-$139
(651) 345-5392
(800) 644-2780

SUNSET MOTEL & RESORT
1515 N Lakeshore
Dr (55041)
Rates: $32-$87
(651) 345-5331
(800) 945-0192

LAKE ELMO

A WILDWOOD LODGE
8511 Hudson Blvd
(55042)
Rates: $149-$159
(651) 714-8068
(866) 294-6250

LAKE GEORGE

LAKE GEORGE PINES MOTEL
37197 US 71
(56458)
Rates: $36-$65
(218) 266-3914

LAKE KABETOGAMA

BIRCH GROVE RESORT
10466 Waltz Rd
(56669)
Rates: $75-$95
(218) 875-2172
(877) 878-4502

CALM BAY'S WHITE EAGLE RESORT
10476 Gamma Rd
(56669)
Rates: $65-$95
(218) 875-2341

LAKEVIEW RESORT
12475 Burma Rd
(56669)
Rates: $80-$90
(218) 875-2471
(877) 422-2471

WATSON'S HARMONY BEACH RESORT & LODGE
10002 Gappa Rd
(56669)
Rates: $35-$145
(218) 875-2811

AREA CODES - If the local number doesn't connect, check for a new area code.

LAKE OF THE WOODS
ZIPPEL BAY RESORT
6080 39th St NW
(56686)
Rates: $45-$100
(800) 222-2537

LAKE SHORE
GULL LAKE MOTEL
7779 Interlachen Rd (56468)
Rates: $50-$85
(218) 963-2208
(800) 599-2208

LAKE VERMILION
FOREST LANE RESORT
1785 Everett Bay Rd (on Lake Vermilion 55079)
Rates: $105-$125
(218) 753-5503
(800) 826-6070

WHITE EAGLE RESORT
3026 Vermilion Dr (55723)
Rates: $550-$1300 Weekly
(218) 666-5500
(800) 542-0365

LAKESHORE
GULL LAKE MOTEL
7779 Interlachen Rd (56468)
Rates: $40-$75
(218) 963-2208
(800) 599-2208

LAKEVILLE
MOTEL 6
11274 210th St
(55044)
Rates: $36-$53
(952) 469-1900
(800) 466-8356

SUPER 8 MOTEL
20800 Kenrick Ave
(55044)
Rates: $59-$111
(952) 469-1134
(800) 800-8000

LAMBERTON
LAMBERTON MOTEL
601 1st Ave W
(56152)
Rates: $35-$55
(507) 752-7242
(888) 785-9762

LE SUEUR
DOWNTOWN MOTEL
510 N Main St
(56058)
Rates: $36-$44
(507) 665-6246

LITCHFIELD
SCOTWOOD MOTEL
1017 E Frontage Rd (55355)
Rates: $49-$145
(320) 693-2496
(800) 225-5489

LITTLE FALLS
CLIFFWOOD MOTEL
1201 N Haven Rd
(56345)
Rates: $30-$48
(320) 632-5488

COUNTRY INN & SUITES BY CARLSON
209 16th St NE
(56345)
Rates: $94-$139
(320) 632-1000
(800) 456-4000

GOODNIGHT INN
RR 6, Box 280
(56345)
Rates: $29-$70
(320) 632-2989
(800) 575-0594

PINE EDGE INN
308 1st St SE
(56345)
Rates: $35-$95
(320) 632-6681
(800) 344-6681

LONG LAKE
LONG LAKE MOTEL
521 Willow Dr
(55356)
Rates: $31-$39
(612) 473-5411

LONG PRAIRIE
BUDGET HOST
417 Lake St (56347)
Rates: $43-$75
(320) 732-6118
(800) 283-4678

LONGVILLE
HOLIDAY HAVEN RESORTS
3529 State 84 N
(56655)
Rates: $60-$96
(218) 363-2473
(800) 279-5372

JOURNEY'S END RESORT
648 Journey's End Lane (56655)
Rates: $495-$1050 Weekly
(218) 363-2601
(800) 429-2523

LONGVILLE INN MOTEL
4959 Hwy 84
(56655)
Rates: $46-$64
(218) 363-2400
(800) 670-0810

PINES MOTEL
5086 Hwy 84
(56655)
Rates: $35-$64
(218) 363-1100
(877) 225-1962

LUTSEN
CASCADE LODGE COUNTRY INN
3719 W Hwy 61
(55612)
Rates: $45-$99
(218) 387-1112

KAH-NEE-TAH GALLERY & COTTAGES
4210 W Hwy 161
(55612)
Rates: $85-$105
(218) 387-2585
(800) 216-2585

THE MOUNTAIN INN AT LUTSEN
360 Ski Hill Rd
(55612)
Rates: $59-$134
(218) 663-7244

SOLBAKKEN RESORT
4874 W Hwy 61
(55612)
Rates: $49-$145
(218) 663-7566
(800) 435-3950

LUVERNE
COZY REST MOTEL
116 S Kniss
(56156)
Rates: $28-$56
(507) 283-4461
(800) 839-1375

SUNRISE MOTEL
I-90, Exit 12
(56156)
Rates: $26-$48
(507) 283-2347
(800) 868-4748

MAHNOMEN
TRAVELERS MOTEL
Hwy 59 & 200
(56557)
Rates: $27-$38
(218) 935-5654
(800) 551-8587

MANKATO
BEST WESTERN HOTEL
1111 Range St
(56601)
Rates: $68-$110
(507) 325-9333
(800) 528-1234

COMFORT INN
131 Apache Pl
(56601)
Rates: $59-$134
(507) 388-5107
(800) 424-6423

DAYS INN
1285 Range St
(56001)
Rates: $40-$130
(507) 387-3332
(800) 329-7466

GRANDSTAY RESIDENTIAL SUITES
1000 Raintree Rd
(56001)
Rates: $99-$119
(507) 388-8688
(877) 388-7829

HOLIDAY INN DOWNTOWN
101 E Main St
(56001)
Rates: $70-$100
(507) 345-1234
(800) 465-4329

SUPER 8 MOTEL
51578 Hwy 169
(56001)
Rates: $53-$60
(507) 387-4041
(800) 800-8000

MANTORVILLE
GRAND OLD MANSION
501 Clay St
(55955)
Rates: $30-$64
(507) 635-3231

MAPLE GROVE
STAYBRIDGE SUITES
7821 Elm Creek Blvd (55369)
Rates: $119-$339
(763) 494-8856
(800) 238-8000

MAPLE PLAIN
MAPLE PLAIN MOTEL
5329 Hwy 12
(55359)
Rates: $28-$40
(612) 479-1434

MARSHALL
BEST WESTERN MARSHALL INN
1500 E College Dr
(56258)
Rates: $67-$99
(507) 532-3221
(800) 528-1234
(800) 422-0897

COMFORT INN
1511 E College Dr
(56258)
Rates: $74-$134
(507) 532-3070
(800) 424-6423

SUPER 8 MOTEL
1106 E Main St
(56258)
Rates: $50-$75
(507) 537-1461
(800) 800-8000

AREA CODES - If the local number doesn't connect, check for a new area code.

TRAVELER'S LODGE
1425 E College Dr (56258)
Rates: $43-$78
(507) 532-5721
(800) 532-5721

MCGREGOR

COUNTRY MEADOWS INN
SR 65 & 210 (55760)
Rates: $60-$99
(218) 768-7378
(888) 331-7378

MENAHGA

SPIRIT LAKE MOTEL
Hwy 71 (56464)
Rates: $25-$39
(218) 564-4151

MERRIFIELD

MISSION BEACH RESORT/ CABINS
26847 CR 19 (56465)
Rates: $250-$570
Weekly
(218) 765-3447
(800) 279-5370

MILLE LACS

ST. ALBANS BAY LODGE
HCr 1 Box 40 (56450)
Rates: $46-$69
(320) 692-4552
(800) 377-2443

MINNEAPOLIS

DOUBLETREE GUEST SUITES
1101 LaSalle Ave (55403)
Rates: $79-$229
(612) 332-6800
(800) 542-5566

ECONO LODGE
2500 University Ave SE (55414)
Rates: $53-$130
(612) 331-6000
(800) 424-6423

HILTON HOTEL
1001 Marquette Ave (55403)
Rates: $95-$339
(612) 376-1000
(800) 445-8667

HOLIDAY INN METRODOME
1500 Washington Ave S (55454)
Rates: $118-$159
(612) 333-4646
(800) 465-4329
(800) 448-3663

MARQUETTE HOTEL
710 Marquette Ave (55402)
Rates: $119-$329
(612) 333-4545
(800) 328-4782

MARRIOTT CITY CENTER
30 S 7th St (55402)
Rates: $199-$239
(612) 349-4000
(800) 228-9290

MILLENIUM HOTEL
1313 Nicollet Mall (55403)
Rates: $89-$141
(612) 332-6000
(866) 866-8086

RADISSON PLAZA HOTEL
35 S 7th St (55402)
Rates: $199-$279
(612) 339-4900
(800) 333-3333

RESIDENCE INN MILWAUKEE ROAD DEPOT
425 S 2nd St (55401)
Rates: $99-$229
(612) 340-1300
(800) 331-3131

MINNESOTA CITY

SUNDOWN MOTEL
RR 2, Box 3A (55959)
Rates: $25-$48
(507) 452-7376
(800) 469-5920

MINNETONKA

MARRIOTT SOUTHWEST
5801 Opus Pkwy (55343)
Rates: $149-$169
(952) 935-5500
(800) 228-9290

SHERATON MINNEAPOLIS WEST HOTEL
12201 Ridgedale Dr (55305)
Rates: $89-$159
(952) 593-0000
(800) 325-3535

MONTEVIDEO

COUNTRY INN & SUITES BY CARLSON
1805 E Hwy 7 (56265)
Rates: $75-$145
(320) 269-8000
(800) 456-4000
(877) 269-8001

FIESTA CITY MOTEL
620 W Hwy 212 (56265)
Rates: $30-$54
(320) 269-8896
(800) 472-6478

SPORTSMEN INN
611 Hwy 212 W (56265)
Rates: $34-$48
(320) 269-8889

VIKING MOTEL
1428 E Hwy 7 (56265)
Rates: $23-$43
(320) 269-6545
(800) 670-0777

MONTICELLO

BEST WESTERN SILVER FOX INN
1114 Cedar St (55362)
Rates: $66-$140
(763) 295-4000
(800) 528-1234

DAYS INN
200 E Oakwood Dr (55362)
Rates: $59-$119
(763) 295-1111
(800) 329-7466

MOORHEAD

DAYS INN
600 30th Ave SW (56560)
Rates: $72-$156
(219) 287-7100
(800) 329-7466

MOTEL 75
810 Belsly Blvd (56560)
Rates: $39-$54
(218) 233-7501
(800) 828-4171

TRAVELODGE
3027 Frontage Rd S (56560)
Rates: $54-$90
(218) 233-5333
(800) 578-7878

MOOSE LAKE

MOOSE LAKE MOTEL
125 S Arrowhead Ln (55767)
Rates: $39-$69
(218) 485-8003
(888) 299-8411

MORA

ANN RIVER SWEDISH MOTEL
1819 S Hwy 65 (55051)
Rates: $95
(320) 679-2972
(800) 679-2973

MOTEL MORA
301 S Hwy 65 (55051)
Rates: $52
(320) 679-3262
(800) 657-0167

MORRIS

BEST WESTERN PRAIRIE INN
200 Hwy 28 E (56267)
Rates: $43-$84
(320) 589-3030
(800) 528-1234
(800) 535-3035

MORTON

THE MORTON INN
400 Kokesch Dr (56270)
Rates: $37-$49
(507) 697-6205
(800) 245-9800

MOTLEY

EASTWOOD INN
900 Hwy 10 S (56466)
Rates: $44-$60
(218) 352-6386
(888) 886-6719

NEVIS

FREMONT'S POINT RESORT CABINS
28104 Junco Dr (56467)
Rates: $825-$895
Weekly
(218) 652-3299
(800) 221-0713

ISLAND VIEW RESORT
RR 2 Box 75 (56467)
Rates: $380-$465
Weekly
(218) 652-3692
(800) 429-1388

PARADISE COVE RESORT
RR 2, Box 123K (56467)
Rates: $450-$685
Weekly
(218) 732-3779
(800) 765-2682

PARK STREET INN HISTORICAL B&B
106 Park St (56467)
Rates: $60-$125
(218) 652-4500
(800) 797-1778

WELCOME INN MOTEL
117 Hwy 34 (56467)
Rates: $33-$45
(218) 652-3600

NEW PRAGUE

HERITAGE INN
410 W Main St (56071)
Rates: $27-$38
(612) 758-4100

NEW ULM

HOLIDAY INN
2101 S Broadway (56073)
Rates: $65-$150
(507) 359-2941
(800) 465-4329

MICROTEL INN & SUITES
424 20th St S (56073)
Rates: $69-$84
(507) 354-9800

AREA CODES - If the local number doesn't connect, check for a new area code.

NEW YORK MILLS
SUNSHINE RESORT
RR 3,Box 256 (56567)
Rates: $315+ Weekly
(218) 346-5487
(888) 346-5487

NISSWA
DAYS INN
24186 Smiley Rd (56468)
Rates: $54-$112
(218) 963-3500
(800) 329-7466

NISSWA MOTEL
1426 Merrill Ave (56468)
Rates: $40-$79
(218) 963-7611
(800) 254-7612

WILDERNESS POINT RESORT
Wilderness Rd (56468)
Rates: $47-$138
(218) 568-5642
(800) 231-4050

NORTH BRANCH
SUPER 8 MOTEL
6010 Main St (55056)
Rates: $44-$84
(651) 277-8000
(866) 277-5718

NORTHFIELD
COLLEGE CITY MOTEL
875 Hwy 3 N (55057)
Rates: $35-$45
(507) 645-4426
(800) 775-0455

OAKDALE
WINGATE INN
970 Helena Ave N (55128)
Rates: $105-$155
(651) 578-8466

OLIVIA
THE SHEEP SHEDDE INN
2425 W Lincoln Ave (56277)
Rates: $50-$65
(320) 523-5000

ONAMIA
ECONO LODGE OF MILLE LACS LAKE
40847 Hwy 169 (56359)
Rates: $35-$110
(320) 532-3838
(800) 424-6423

ORR
AMERICINN LODGE & SUITES
4675 Hwy 53 (55771)
Rates: $80-$230
(218) 757-7613
(800) 634-3444

NORTH COUNTRY INN MOTEL
4483 Hwy 53 (55771)
Rates: $50-$65
(218) 757-3778

PINE ACRES RESORT/CABINS
4498 Pine Acres Rd (55771)
Rates: $450-$900 Weekly
(218) 757-3144
(800) 777-7231

ORTONVILLE
ECONO LODGE
650 Hwy 75 (56278)
Rates: $50-$100
(320) 839-2414
(800) 424-6423

VALI-VU MOTEL
Jct 12 & 75 (56278)
Rates: $25-$42
(320) 839-2558
(800) 841-6236

OSAKIS
BUCK POINT RESORT
21004 Fairfax Ln (56360)
Rates: $65-$150
(320) 859-2530
(800) 543-4179

LINWOOD RESORT/CABINS
17857 Lake St E (56360)
Rates: $$100-$200
(320) 859-2175
(800) 458-5136

OUTING
ROOSEVELT LOG CABIN RESORT & MOTEL
758 State 6 NE (56662)
Rates: $55-$95
(218) 792-5177
(800) 691-1869

OWATONNA
BEST BUDGET INN
1100 I-35 & Hwy 14 (55060)
Rates: $30-$80
(507) 451-0776
(800) 454-2628

MICROTEL INN & SUITES
150 St. John Dr (55060)
Rates: $44-$85
(507) 446-8255
(888) 771-7171

OWATONNA GRAND HOTEL
1212 N I-35 (55060)
Rates: $55
(507) 455-0606

PARK RAPIDS
BAYSIDE RESORT
15597 CR 40 (56470)
Rates: $475-$1275 Weekly
(218) 732-3666
(888) 750-3666

CROW WING CREST LODGE
Rt 2. Box 33 (56433)
Rates: $480-$785 Weekly
(218) 652-3111
(800) 279-2754

HEARTLAND TRAIL B&B
20220 Friar Rd (56470)
Rates: $80-$90
(218) 732-3252

LADY SLIPPER INN
51722 270th St (56470)
Rates: $125
(218) 573-3353
(800) 531-2787

LEE'S RIVERSIDE RESORT-MOTEL
700 N Park (56470)
Rates: $53-$96
(218) 732-9711
(800) 733-9711

LITTLE NORWAY RESORT
HCO 5, Box 145 (56470)
Rates: $475-$760 Weekly
(218) 732-5480

SPIRIT LAKE MOTEL
Hwy 71 (56464)
Rates: $25-$39
(218) 564-4151

TERRACE VIEW MOTOR LODGE
716 N Park (56470)
Rates: $26-$42
(218) 732-1213
(800) 731-1213

PAYNES-VILLE
BLACK SAUCER MOTEL
703 W Main St (56362)
Rates: $30-$65
(320) 243-3774

PELICAN RAPIDS
CROSS POINT RESORT/CABINS
39870 Crosspoint Lane (56572)
Rates: $70-$80
(218) 863-8593
(877) 646-6994

PEQUOT LAKES
AMERICINN LODGE & SUITES
32912 Paul Bunyan Tr Dr (56472)
Rates: $69-$149
(218) 568-8400
(800) 634-3444

BRADMOR MOTEL
Rt 2, Box 440 (56472)
Rates: $27-$52
(218) 568-4366

PERHAM
SUPER 8 MOTEL
106 Jake St SE (56573)
Rates: n/a
(218) 346-7888
(800) 800-8000

PETERSON
HOUSE OF SEVEN GABLES B&B
135 N Church St (55962)
Rates: $65-$100
(507) 875-1000
(800) 442-7969

PINE CITY
CHALET MOTEL
I-35 & Hwy 70 (55063)
Rates: $30-$52
(320) 629-7684

SCHWARTZWALD MOTEL
920 Main St S (55063)
Rates: $50-$55+
(320) 629-2511
(800) 524-2512

PINE ISLAND
PINE MOTEL
106 1st St NE (55963)
Rates: $32-$44
(507) 356-4421

PINE RIVER
CEDARWOOD MOTEL
1st & Maple (56474)
Rates: $38-$48
(888) 390-2208

ECONO LODGE
2684 SR 371 W (56474)
Rates: $56-$100
(218) 587-4499
(800) 424-6423

NORWAY BROOK MOTEL
HCR 77 Box 24 (56474)
Rates: $39-$44
(218) 587-2118
(800) 950-7330

PLYMOUTH

BEST WESTERN KELLY INN
2705 N Annapolis Lane (55441)
Rates: $79-$135
(763) 553-1600
(800) 528-1234

RADISSON HOTEL
3131 Campus Dr (55441)
Rates: $89-$135
(763) 559-6600
(800) 333-3333

RED ROOF INN
2600 Annapolis Ln N (55441)
Rates: $48-$91
(753) 553-1751
(800) 843-7663

PRESTON

INN TOWN LODGE
205 Franklin St (55965)
Rates: $40-$65
(507) 765-4412

THE JAILHOUSE HISTORIC INN
109 Houston St NW (55965)
Rates: $42-$149
(507) 765-2181

PRINCETON

PINE-AIRE MOTEL
3079 90th Ave (55371)
Rates: $38
(612) 389-2812

RUM RIVER MOTEL
510 19th Ave N (55371)
Rates: $36-$45
(612) 389-3120

PROCTOR

AMERICINN
185 US Hwy 2 (55810)
Rates: $55-$130
(218) 624-1026
(800) 634-3444

RANIER

SANDBAY B&B AT TARA'S WHARF
2065 Spruce St Landing (56668)
Rates: $85-$145
(218) 286-5699
(877) 724-6955

RED LAKE FALLS

CHATEAU MOTEL
Hwy 32 N (56750)
Rates: $35-$42
(218) 253-4144

RED WING

BEST WESTERN QUIET HOUSE SUITES
752 Withers Harbor Dr (55066)
Rates: $54-$179
(651) 388-1577
(800) 528-1234

DAYS INN
955 E 7th St (55066)
Rates: $44-$92
(651) 388-3568
(800) 329-7466

PARKWAY MOTEL
3425 Hwy 61 W (55066)
Rates: $35-$50
(651) 388-8231
(800) 776-0934

REDWOOD FALLS

COMFORT INN
1382 E Bridge St (56283)
Rates: $50-$140
(507) 644-5700
(800) 424-6423

SUPER 8 MOTEL
1305 E Bridge St (56283)
Rates: $34-$54
(507) 637-3456
(800) 800-8000

REMER

ANDERSEN'S RESORT
4293 State 6 NE (56672)
Rates: $80+
(218) 566-2555
(800) 458-6707

CEDAR BEACH RESORT
4502 Cedar Trail NE (56672)
Rates: $105-$130
(218) 566-3669
(800) 566-3669

REMER MOTEL
200 Main St (56672)
Rates: $40-$52
(218) 566-2555

RICHFIELD

CANDLEWOOD SUITES
351 W 77th St (55423)
Rates: $59-$120
(612) 869-7704
(888) 226-3539

MOTEL 6
7640 Cedar Ave S (55423)
Rates $39-$56
(612) 861-4491
(800) 466-8356

ROCHESTER

AMERICINN HOTEL & SUITES
5708 Hwy 52 NW (55901)
Rates: $69-$169
(507) 289-3344
(800) 634-3444

BEST VALUE INN
519 3rd Ave SW (55902)
Rates: $39-$59
(507) 288-1855

BLONDELL'S CROWN SQUARE MOTEL
1406 2nd St SW (55902)
Rates: $42-$130
(507) 282-9444
(800) 441-5209

COLONIAL HOTEL
114 2nd St SW (55902)
Rates: $25-$54
(507) 289-3363
(800) 533-2226

COMFORT INN
1625 S Broadway (55904)
Rates: $49-$89
(507) 281-2211
(800) 424-6423

DAYS INN DOWNTOWN
6 First Ave NW (55901)
Rates: $49-$74
(507) 282-3801
(800) 329-7466

DAYS INN SOUTH
111 28th St SE (55904)
Rates: $49-$69
(507) 286-1001
(800) 329-7466

ECONO LODGE S
1850 S Broadway (55904)
Rates: $44-$65
(507) 282-9905
(800) 424-6423

EXECUTIVE SUITES HOTEL & ECONOMY INN
9 3rd Ave NW (55901)
Rates: $80-$110
(507) 289-8646

HILTON GARDEN INN
225 S Broadway (55904)
Rates: $89-$139
(507) 285-1234
(800) 445-8667

HOLIDAY INN SOUTH-MAYO CLINIC AREA
1630 S Broadway (55904)
Rates: $69-$109
(507) 288-1844
(800) 465-4329

THE KAHLER GRAND HOTEL
20 2nd Ave SW (55903)
Rates: $75-$138
(507) 282-2581
(800) 533-1655

MARRIOTT HOTEL
101 1st Ave SW (55902)
Rates: $199
(507) 280-6000
(800) 228-9290

MICROTEL INN
4210 Hwy 52 N (55901)
Rates: $48-$67
(507) 286-8780
(888) 771-7171
(800) 245-9535

MOTEL 6
2107 W Frontage Rd (55901)
Rates: $34-$40
(507) 282-6625
(800) 466-8356

QUALITY INN
1620 1st Ave SE (55904)
Rates: $73-$109
(507) 282-8091
(800) 424-6423

RADISSON PLAZA HOTEL
150 S Broadway (55904)
Rates: $119-$179
(507) 281-8000
(800) 333-3333

SLEEP INN, INN & SUITES
7320 Airport View Dr SW (55902)
Rates: $59-$109
(507) 536-7000
(800) 424-6423

STAYBRIDGE SUITES
1211 Second St SW (55902)
Rates: $129-$209
(507) 289-6600
(800) 238-8000

SUPER 8 MOTEL SOUTH
1230 S Broadway (55904)
Rates: $49-$69
(507) 288-8288
(800) 800-8000

ROGERS

AMERICINN MOTEL
21800 Industrial Blvd (55374)
Rates: $69-$159
(763) 428-4346
(800) 634-3444

ROSEAU

AMERICINN
1090 3rd St NW (56751)
Rates: $49-$86
(218) 463-1045
(800) 634-3444

EVERGREEN MOTEL
304 5th Ave NW (56751)
Rates: $29-$34
(218) 463-1642
(800) 434-7685

ROSEVILLE

RESIDENCE INN
2985 Centre Pointe Dr (55113)
Rates: $139-$179
(651) 636-0680
(800) 331-3131

ROUND LAKE

**THE PRAIRIE
HOUSE B&B**
RR 1, Box 105
(56167)
Rates: $55
(507) 945-8934

RUSHFORD

**WINDSWEPT INN
MOTEL**
207 N Mill St
(55971)
Rates: $30-$36
(507) 864-2545

ST. CLOUD

**AMERICINN
LODGE & SUITES**
4385 Clearwater
Rd (56301)
Rates: $56-$113
(320) 253-6337
(800) 634-3444

**BEST WESTERN
AMERICANNA
INN**
520 S US Hwy 10
(56304)
Rates: $56-$95
(320) 252-8700
(800) 950-8701

**BEST WESTERN
KELLY INN**
1 Sunwood Dr
(56301)
Rates: $69-$199
(320) 253-0606

**COUNTRY
INN & SUITES**
235 S Park Ave
(56301)
Rates: $73-$99
(320) 25-8999
(800) 456-4000

HOLIDAY INN EXP
4322 Clearwater
Rd (56301)
Rates: $54-$72
(320) 240-8000
(800) 465-4329

**HOLIDAY INN
HOTEL & SUITES**
75 37th Ave S
(56302)
Rates: $68-$140
(320) 253-9000
(800) 465-4329

KLEIS MOTEL
30 25th Ave S
(56301)
Rates: $28-$57
(320) 251-7450

MOTEL 6
815 1st St S
(56387)
Rates: $30-$40
(320) 253-7070
(800) 466-8356

QUALITY INN
70 S 37th Ave
(56301)
Rates: $49-$99
(320) 253-4444
(800) 424-6423

RAMADA LTD
121 Park Ave S
(56301)
Rates: $70-$95
(320) 253-3200
(800) 272-6232

SUPER 8 MOTEL
50 Park Ave S
(56301)
Rates: $32-$78
(320) 253-5530
(800) 800-8000

ST. JAMES

SUPER 8 MOTEL
1210 Heckman Ct
(56081)
Rates: $59-$89
(507) 375-4708
(800) 800-8000

ST. LOUIS PARK

LAKELAND INN
4025 Hwy 7 (55416)
Rates: $50-$75
(952) 926-6575

**TOWNEPLACE
SUITES**
1400 Zarthan Ave
S (55416)
Rates: $79-$149
(952) 847-6900
(800) 357-3000

ST. PAUL

**BEST WESTERN
KELLY INN**
161 St Anthony
Ave (55103)
Rates: $89-$129
(651) 227-8711
(800) 528-1234
(800) 937-8376

EXCEL INN
1739 Old Hudson
Rd (55106)
Rates: $40-$76
(651) 771-5566
(800) 367-3935

HOLIDAY INN EXP
1010 Bandana
Blvd W (55108)
Rates: $69-$109
(651) 647-1637
(800) 465-4329

ST. PETER

VIKING JR MOTEL
169 & 90 West
(56082)
Rates: $31-$50
(507) 931-3081
(800) 221-6406

SANBORN

**SOD HOUSE
ON THE PRAIRIE**
Rt 2, Box 75
(56083)
Rates: $75-$135
(507) 723-5138

SANDSTONE

**SANDSTONE
61 MOTEL**
Hwy 23 & 61
(55072)
Rates: $35-$55
(320) 245-5419

SAUK CENTRE

**AMERICINN
LODGE & SUITES**
1230 Timberlane
Dr (56378)
Rates: $65-$129
(320) 352-2800
(800) 634-3444

**GOPHER PRAIRIE
MOTEL**
1222 S Getty
(56378)
Rates: $33-$58
(320) 352-2275
(888) 315-2378

HILLCREST MOTEL
965 Main St
(56378)
Rates: $32-$46
(320) 352-2215
(800) 858-6333

SAVAGE

COMFORT INN
4601 Hwy 13 W
(55378)
Rates: $39-$129
(952) 894-6124
(800) 424-6423

**SAVAGE
MOTOR INN**
7361 Hwy 13 W
(55378)
Rates: $35-$65
(952) 894-4181

SCHROEDER

**LAMB'S RESORT
CABINS**
19 Lamb's Way
(55613)
Rates: $79-$169
(218) 663-7292

**SATELLITE
COUNTRY INN**
9436 W Hwy 61
(55613)
Rates: $45-$80
(218) 663-7574
(800) 700-7574

SEBEKA

SEBEKA MOTEL
Hwy 71, Box 721
(56477)
Rates: $24-$40
(218) 837-5162

SHAKOPEE

**PARK INN
& SUITES**
1244 Canterbury
Rd (55379)
Rates: $49-$139
(952) 445-3644
(877) 291-0622

**SANDALWOOD
STUDIOS &
SUITES**
3910 12th Ave E
(55379)
Rates: $42-$109
(952) 277-0100

SILVER BAY

**AMERICINN
LODGE & SUITES**
150 Mensing Dr
(55614)
Rates: $80-$150
(218) 226-4300
(800) 634-3444

**LITTLE MARAIS
LAKESIDE CABINS**
6476 Hwy 61
(55614)
Rates: $66-$95
(218) 226-3456

MARINER MOTEL
46 Outer Dr
(55614)
Rates: $45-$70
(218) 226-4488

**WHISPERING
PINES MOTEL**
5763 Hwy 61 E
(55614)
Rates: $49-$63
(218) 226-4712
(800) 332-0531

SLAYTON

**RIDOTTO "WACH"
INN MOTEL**
2436 Hwy 59
(56172)
Rates: $36-$48
(507) 836-8511

SLEEPY EYE

**INN OF SEVEN
GABLES**
1100 E Main St
(56085)
Rates: $49-$89
(507) 794-5390
(800) 852-9451

**ORCHID INN &
MOTOR LODGE**
Hwy 14 & 4
(56085)
Rates: $28-$36
(507) 794-3211
(800) 245-4931

SPICER

**NORTHERN INN
HOTEL & SUITES**
154 Lake St (56288)
Rates: $79-$119
(612) 796-2091
(800) 941-0423

SPRING COVE

**STRATFORD-LEE
INN**
RR 1, Box 108
(55974)
Rates: $75-$100
(507) 498-5707

**VILLAGE HOUSE
MOTEL**
265 W Main
(55974)
Rates: $27-$39
(507) 498-3271

AREA CODES - If the local number doesn't connect, check for a new area code.

SPRING VALLEY

66 MOTEL
612 North Huron
Ave (55975)
Rates: $22-$25
(507) 346-9993

SUPER 8 MOTEL
745 N Broadway
(55975)
Rates: $45-$80
(507) 346-7788
(800) 800-8000

STAPLES

SUNSET MOTEL
301 2nd Ave NW
(56479)
Rates: $32-$39
(218) 894-1965

STARBUCK

CEDAR INN OF STARBUCK
604 Main St (56381)
Rates: $39+
(320) 239-4300
(800) 585-8373

STILLWATER

BEST WESTERN INN
1750 Frontage Rd
W (55082)
Rates: $69-$94
(651) 430-1300
(800) 647-4039

SUPER 8 MOTEL
2190 W Frontage
Rd (55082)
Rates: $51-$81
(651) 430-3990
(800) 800-8000

STURGEON LAKE

DAVIDSON'S SAND LAKE RESORT
94154 County
Hwy 61 (55783)
Rates: $79-$119
(218) 485-8164
(877) 314-9252

STURGEON LAKE MOTEL
I-35 & County Rd
46 (55783)
Rates: $32-$47
(218) 372-3194

TAYLORS FALLS

PINES MOTEL
543 River St
(55084)
Rates: $38-$65
(651) 465-3422

THE SPRINGS COUNTRY INN
361 Government
St (55084)
Rates: $45-$95
(651) 465-6565

THIEF RIVER FALLS

BEST WESTERN INN
1060 Hwy 32 S
(56701)
Rates: $69-$99
(218) 681-7555
(800) 569-8123

C'MON INN
1586 Hwy 59 SE
(56701)
Rates: $54-$97
(218) 681-3000
(800) 950-8111

HARTWOOD MOTEL
1010 N Main St
(56701)
Rates: $29-$43
(218) 681-2640

TOFTE

AMERICINN LODGE & SUITES
7261 W Hwy 61
(55615)
Rates: $59-$229
(218) 663-7899
(800) 634-3444

BLUEFIN BAY RESORT ON LAKE SUPERIOR
SR 61 (55615)
Rates: $59-$595
(218) 663-7296
(800) 258-3346

CHATEAU LE VEAUX ON LAKE SUPERIOR
P. O. Box 115
(55615)
Rates: $55-$159
(218) 663-7223
(800) 445-5773

SATELLITE COUNTRY INN
9436 W Hwy 61
(55613)
Rates: $39-$75
(218) 663-7574
(800) 700-7574

SUPERIOR RIDGE RESORT & MOTEL
5041 W Hwy 61
(55615)
Rates: $49-$109
(218) 663-7189
(800) 782-1776

TOWER

THE LURE OF THE LOON RESORT
2162 Birch Point
(55790)
Rates: $75-$195
(218) 753-4732
(800) 832-5988

TWO HARBORS

AMERICINN LODGE & SUITES
1088 SR 61 (55616)
Rates: $65-$220
(218) 834-3000

SUPERIOR SHORES RESORT
1521 Superior
Shores Dr (55616)
Rates: $49-$189
(218) 834-5671
(800) 242-1988

VOYAGEUR MOTEL
1227 7th Ave
(55616)
Rates: $38-$55
(218) 834-3644

TYLER

BABETTE'S INN
308 S Tyler St
(56178)
Rates: $55-$65
(507) 537-1632

VIRGINIA

AMERICINN LODGE & SUITES
5480 Mountain
Iron Dr (55792)
Rates: $69-$162
(218) 741-7839
(800) 634-3444

LAKESHOR MOTOR INN DOWNTOWN
404 N 6th Ave
(55792)
Rates: $39-$89
(218) 741-3360
(800) 569-8131

MIDWAY MOTEL
Hwy 53 & Midway
Rd (55792)
Rates: $36-$60
(218) 741-6145
(800) 777-7956

PARK INN
502 Chestnut St
(55792)
Rates: $58-$82
(218) 749-1000
(800) 670-7275

SKI-VIEW MOTEL
903 N 17th St
(55792)
Rates: $40-$70
(218) 741-8918

WABASHA

AMERICINN LODGE & SUITES
150 Commerce St
(55981)
Rates: $64-$169
(651) 565-5366
(800) 634-3444

COFFEE MILL INN & SUITES
50 Coulee Way
(55981)
Rates: $59+
(651) 565-4561
(877) 775-1366

WABASHA MOTEL
1110 E Hiawatha
Dr (55981)
Rates: $39+
(651) 565-9932
(866) 565-9932

WACONIA

SUPER 8 MOTEL
301 E Frontage Rd
(55387)
Rates: n/a
(952) 442-5147
(800) 800-8000

WADENA

BROOKSIDE MOTEL
1410 Jefferson St
N (56482)
Rates: $33-$43
(218) 631-2930
(800) 929-4603

WADENA INN
500 Ash Ave NW
(56482)
Rates: $45-$65
(218) 631-3725
(877) 439-0495

WAHKON

CJ'S ON THE BAY
550 N Main St
(56386)
Rates: $40-$70
(320) 495-3325

WALKER

ACORN HILL RESORT CABINS
4691 Acorn Hill
Ln NW (56484)
Rates: $595-$1500
Weekly
(218) 547-1015
(800) 237-1015

ADVENTURE NORTH
HCR 84, Box 1207
(56484)
Rates: $625-$1995
Weekly
(218) 547-1532
(800) 294-1532

ANCHOR'S A-WAY RESORT
HCR 73, Box 86
(56484)
Rates: $325-$1095
Weekly
(218) 547-1229
(800) 982-2624

ANDERSON'S CHIPPAWA LODGE
HC 84 Box 376
(56484)
Rates: $300-$2600
Weekly
(218) 836-2437
(800) 416-2216

ANDERSON'S SPIRIT OF THE NORTH
HC 84 Box 392 (56484)
Rates: $75-$105
(218) 836-2357
(800) 516-0077

BAYSIDE RESORT
8039 Onigum Rd NW (56484)
Rates: $115-$172
(218) 547-1350
(800) 484-8056

CHASE MOTOR INN
500 Cleveland Ave W (56484)
Rates: $36-$89
(218) 547-2882
(800) 772-6769

COUNTRY INN & SUITES BY CARLSON
442 Walker Bay Blvd (56484)
Rates: $81-$106
(218) 547-1400
(800) 456-4000

DOC'S LODGE
3425 Stony Point Camp Rd NW (56485)
Rates: $450-$600 Weekly
(218) 547-1772
(800) 753-1529

FOREST INN MOTEL
6615 Hwy 371 NW (56484)
Rates: $28-$48
(218) 547-2400
(800) 738-3639

GRAND VU LODGE
HCR 84 Box 1235 (56484)
Rates: $475-$2400 Weekly
(218) 547-1632
(800) 842-0783

STEAMBOAT BAY RESORT ON LEECH LAKE
6379 Wedgewood Rd NW (56484)
Rates: $95-$255
(218) 547-1575
(800) 705-9925

STONY POINT RESORT
HC 84 Box 942 (56484)
Rates: $92-$224
(218) 547-1665
(800) 338-9303

TIANNA FARMS BED & BREAKFAST
Tianna Farms Rd, Box 968 (56484)
Rates: $45-$125
(218) 547-1306
(800) 842-6620

TRADER'S BAY LODGE
HC 84 Box 1017 (56484)
Rates: $75-$100
(218) 547-1031
(888) 667-7481

WARREN
ELM CREST MOTEL
Hwy 75 N (56762)
Rates: $30-$60
(218) 745-4721

WARROAD
CAN-AM MOTEL
406 Main Ave NE (56763)
Rates: $40-$69
(218) 386-3807
(800) 280-2626

HOSPITAL BAY B&B
620 Lake St NE (56763)
Rates: $40-$60
(218) 386-2627
(800) 568-6028

PATCH MOTEL
SR 11 W (56763)
Rates: $45-$66
(218) 386-2723

WATERTOWN
WANDER INN B&B
2590 Vega Ave (55360)
Rates: $70-$90
(612) 955-2230

WHEATON
WHEATON INN
403 5th St N (56296)
Rates: $27-$45
(320) 563-8236

WHITE BEAR LAKE
BEST WESTERN WHITE BEAR COUNTRY INN
4940 Hwy 61 (55110)
Rates: $89-$225
(612) 429-5393
(800) 528-1234

WILLMAR
COMFORT INN
2200 E US 12 (56201)
Rates: $55-$156
(320) 231-2601
(800) 424-6423

DAYS INN
225 28th St SE (56201)
Rates: $39-$75
(320) 231-1275
(800) 528-1234

HI-WAY 12 MOTEL
609 E Hwy 12 (56201)
Rates: $26-$31
(320) 235-4500
(800) 352-3218

HOLIDAY INN
2100 E Hwy 12 (56201)
Rates: $92-$109
(320) 235-6060
(800) 465-4329

LAKEVIEW INN MOTEL
N Business Hwy 71 & 23 (56201)
Rates: $33-$54
(320) 235-3424
(800) 718-3424

WILLMAR-SPICER
LAKEVIEW MOTEL
15150 Hwy 23 NE (56288)
Rates: $29-$38
(320) 796-2224

WINDOM
GUARDIAN INN MOTEL
1955 1st Ave (56101)
Rates: $54-$82
(507) 831-1809

WINDOM INN
Hwy 60 & 71 N (56101)
Rates: $28-$32
(507) 831-3111

SUPER 8 MOTEL
222 3rd Ave S (56101)
Rates: $39-$59
(507) 831-1120
(800) 800-8000

WINONA
BEST WESTERN RIVERPORT INN
900 Bruski Dr (55987)
Rates: $67-$119
(507) 452-0606
(800) 528-1234
(800) 595-0606

EL RANCHO MOTEL
1429 Gilmore Ave (55987)
Rates: n/a
(507) 454-5920
(800) 469-5920

HOLIDAY INN
1025 Hwy 61 E (55987)
Rates: $99-$179
(507) 453-0303
(800) 465-4329

QUALITY INN
956 Mankato Ave (55987)
Rates: $50-$140
(507) 454-4390
(800) 424-6423

STERLING MOTEL
1450 Gilmore Ave (55987)
Rates: $31-$60
(507) 454-1120
(800) 452-1235

SUGAR LOAF MOTEL
1066 Homer Rd (55987)
Rates: $33-$62
(507) 452-1491

WOODBURY
HAMPTON INN
1450 Weir Dr (55125)
Rates: $75-$110
(651) 578-2822
(800) 426-7866

HOLIDAY INN EXP HOTEL & SUITES
9840 Norma Lane (55125)
Rates: $109
(651) 702-0200
(800) 465-4329

RED ROOF INN
1806 Wooddale Dr (55125)
Rates: $45-$80
(651) 738-7160
(800) 843-7663

WORTHINGTON
AMERICINN LODGE & SUITES
1475 Darling Dr (56187)
Rates: $69-$79
(507) 376-4500
(800) 634-3444

BUDGET INN
1231 Oxford St (56187)
Rates: $28-$40+
(507) 376-6136

DAYS INN
207 Oxford St (56187)
Rates: $46-$129
(507) 376-6155
(800) 329-7466

SUNSET INN
1923 Dover St (56187)
Rates: $32-$75
(507) 376-9494

SUPER 8 MOTEL
850 Lucy Dr (56187)
Rates: $53-$109
(507) 372-7755
(800) 800-8000

TRAVELODGE HOTEL
2015 Humiston Ave N (56187)
Rates: $50-$120
(507) 372-2991
(800) 578-7878

AREA CODES - If the local number doesn't connect, check for a new area code.

MISSISSIPPI

ABERDEEN

BEST WESTERN ABERDEEN INN
801 E Commerce St (39730)
Rates: $55-$75
(662) 369-4343
(800) 528-1234

AMORY

BEST WESTERN AMORY INN
915 Hwy 278 E (38821)
Rates: $55-$65
(662) 256-2120
(800) 528-1234

BATESVILLE

COMFORT INN
290 Power Dr (38606)
Rates: $55-$99
(662) 563-1188
(800) 424-6423

SKYLINE MOTEL
311 Hwy 51S (38606)
Rates: $26-$35
(662) 563-7671

BAY ST. LOUIS

CASINO MAGIC INN
711 Casino Magic Dr (39520)
Rates: $39-$109
(228) 467-9257

KEY WEST INN
1000 Hwy 90 (39521)
Rates: $50-$135
(228) 466-0444
(800) 833-0555

BILOXI

BREAKERS INN
2506 W Beach Blvd (39531)
Rates: $70-$155
(228) 388-6320
(800) 624-5031

BROADWATER BEACH RESORT
2110 Beach Blvd (39531)
Rates: $90-$145
(228) 388-2211
(800) 404-9567

COMFORT INN
7827 Lamar Poole Rd (39532)
Rates: $49-$189
(228) 818-0300
(800) 424-6423

FATHER RYAN HOUSE B&B INN
1196 Beach Blvd (39530)
Rates: n/a
(228) 435-1189

GULF BEACH RESORT HOTEL
2428 Beach Blvd (39530)
Rates: $40-$95
(228) 385-5555

HOLIDAY INN EXPRESS-BEACHFRONT
2416 Beach Blvd (39531)
Rates: $75-$108
(228) 388-1000
(800) 465-4329

LOFTY OAKS INN B&B
17288 Hwy 67 (39532)
Rates: $98-$150
(228) 392-6722

MOTEL 6
2476 Beach Blvd (39531)
Rates: $35-$66
(228) 388-5130
(800) 466-8356

QUALITY INN
11969 Bobby Eleuterus Blvd (39532)
Rates: $49-$100
(228) 396-0100
(800) 424-6423

RAMADA LIMITED
8071 Tucker Rd (39532)
Rates: $54-$149
(228) 872-2323
(800) 272-6232

SEAVIEW RESORT
1870 Beach Blvd (39531)
Rates: $35-$75
(228) 388-5512

BOONEVILLE

SUPER 8 MOTEL
110 Hospitality Ave (38829)
Rates: $55-$65
(662) 720-1688
(800) 800-8000

CANTON

BEST WESTERN
137 Soldier Colony Rd (39046)
Rates: $52-$55
(601) 859-8600
(800) 528-1234

CLARKSDALE

BEST WESTERN EXECUTIVE INN
710 S State St (38614)
Rates: $65-$74
(662) 627-9292
(800) 528-1234

ECONO LODGE
350 S State St (38614)
Rates: $42-$59
(662) 621-1110
(800) 424-6423

CLEVELAND

BEST WESTERN
900 S Davis Ave (38732)
Rates: $54-$64
(662) 846-5404
(800) 528-1234

COMFORT INN
721 N Davis Ave (38732)
Rates: $59-$79
(662) 843-4060
(800) 424-6423

COLUMBIA

COMFORT INN
820 US 98 Bypass (39429)
Rates: $65-$85
(601) 731-9955
(800) 424-6423

COLUMBUS

MASTER HOSTS & INNS
506 Hwy 45 N (39701)
Rates: $49-$64
(662) 328-5202

MOTEL 6
1203 Hwy 45 N (39701)
Rates: $32+
(662) 327-4450
(800) 466-8356

CORINTH

COMFORT INN
2101 Hwy 72 W (38834)
Rates: $39-$99
(662) 287-4421
(800) 424-6423

DIAMOND HEAD

RAMADA INN
103 Live Oak Dr (39525)
Rates: $55-$129
(228) 255-1300
(800) 272-6232

D'IBERVILLE

WINGATE INN
3641 Sangani Dr (39540)
Rates: $49-$99
(228) 396-0036

FOREST

APPLE TREE INN
1846 Hwy 35 S (39074)
Rates: $54-$59
(601) 469-2640

COMFORT INN
1250 Hwy 35 S (39074)
Rates: $55-$60
(601) 469-2100
(800) 424-6423

GREENVILLE

BEST WESTERN REGENCY INN
2428 Hwy 82 E (38701)
Rates: $49-$89
(662) 334-6900
(800) 528-1234

COMFORT INN
3080 Hwy 82 E (38701)
Rates: $59-$129
(662) 378-4976
(800) 424-6423

GREENWOOD

COMFORT INN
401 Hwy 82 W (38930)
Rates: $59-$89
(662) 453-5974
(800) 424-6423

GRENADA

BEST WESTERN
1750 Sunset Dr (38901)
Rates: $46-$69
(662) 226-7816
(800) 528-1234

COUNTRY INN & SUITES
255 SW Frontage Rd (38901)
Rates: $59-$78
(662) 227-8444
(800) 456-4000

DAYS INN
1632 Sunset Dr (38901)
Rates: $39-$119
(662) 226-8888
(800) 329-7466

HOLIDAY INN
1796 Sunset Dr (38901)
Rates: $64-$71
(662) 226-2851
(800) 465-4329

GULFPORT

**BEST WESTERN
SEAWAY INN**
9475 US Hwy 49
& I-10 (39503)
Rates: $45-$120
(228) 864-0050
(800) 528-1234
(800) 822-4141

CRYSTAL INN
9379 Canal Rd
(39503)
Rates: $69-$109
(228) 822-9600
(888) 822 9600

**HOLIDAY INN-
AIRPORT**
9415 Hwy 49
(39503)
Rates: $49-$89
(228) 868-8200
(800) 465-4329

**HOLIDAY INN-
BEACHFRONT**
1600 E Beach
(39501)
Rates: $75-$105
(228) 864-4310
(800) 465-4329

**HOLIDAY INN
EXPRESS-
SPORTSPLEX**
9435 Hwy 49 N
(39503)
Rates: $69-$129
(228) 864-7222
(800) 465-4329

MOTEL 6
9355 US Hwy 49
(39503)
Rates: $33-$66
(228) 863-1890
(800) 466-8356

RAMADA LTD
9375 Hwy 49
(39503)
Rates: $69-$135
(228) 868-8500
(800) 272-6232

HATTIESBURG

**COMFORT INN
UNIVERSITY**
6541 Hwy 49 N
(39402)
Rates: $69-$99
(601) 264-1881
(800) 424-6423

DUNHOPEN INN
3875 Veterans
Memorial Dr
(39401)
Rates: n/a
(601) 543-0707

HAMPTON INN
4301 Hardy St
(39401)
Rates: $76-$84
(601) 264-8080
(800) 426-7866

HOLIDAY INN
6563 Hwy 49 N
(39401)
Rates: $79+
(601) 268-2850
(800) 465-4329

INN ON THE HILL
6595 Hey 49 N
(39401)
Rates: $59-$72
(601) 599-2001

MOTEL 6
6508 Hwy 49 N
(39401)
Rates: $34-$50
(601) 544-6096
(800) 466-8356

HAZLEHURST

DAYS INN
Hwy 28 & I-55,
Exit 61 (39083)
Rates: $50-$65
(601) 894-0388
(800) 329-7466

HOLLY SPRINGS

DAYS INN
120 Heritage Dr
(38635)
Rates: n/a
(662) 252-1120
(800) 329-7466

HAMPTON INN
100 Brooks Rd
(38635)
Rates: $79-$99
(662) 252-5444
(800) 426-7866

HORN LAKE

DAYS INN
801 DeSoto Cove
(38637)
Rates: $49-$149
(662) 349-3493
(800) 329-7466

**DRURY INN
& SUITES**
735 Goodman Rd
W (38637)
Rates: $67-$104
(662) 349-6622
(800) 378-7946

MOTEL 6
701 Southwest Dr
(38637)
Rates: $49-$65
(662) 349-4439
(800) 466-8356

SLEEP INN
708 Desoto Cove
(38637)
Rates: $59-$79
(662) 349-2773
(800) 424-6423

IUKA

**VICTORIAN INN
MOTEL**
199 CR 180 (38852)
Rates: $38-$58
(601) 423-9221
(800) 839-1662

JACKSON

**BEST SUITES OF
AMERICA**
5411 I-55 N
(39206)
Rates: $74-$139
(601) 899-9000
(800) 237-8466

**BEST WESTERN
EXECUTIVE INN**
725 Larson St
(39202)
Rates: $55-$75
(601) 969-6555
(800) 528-1234

**BEST WESTERN
METRO INN**
1520 Ellis Ave
(39204)
Rates: $49-$90
(601) 355-7483
(800) 528-1234
(888) 788-9788

CLARION HOTEL
400 Greymont Ave
(39202)
Rates: $89-$99
(601) 969-2141
(800) 252-7466

CROWNE PLAZA
200 E Amite St
(39201)
Rates: $110-$145
(601) 969-5100
(800) 227-6963

**THE EDISON
WALTHALL HOTEL**
225 E Capitol St
(39201)
Rates: $79-$185
(601) 948-6161
(800) 932-6161

**HOLIDAY INN
HOTEL & SUITES**
5075 I-55 N
(39206)
Rates: $105-$112
(601) 366-9411
(800) 465-4329

JAMESON INN
585 Beasley Rd
(39206)
Rates: $49-$104
(601) 206-8923
(800 526-3766

**LA QUINTA INN
NORTH**
616 Briarwood Rd
(39211)
Rates: $50-$85
(601) 957-1741
(800) 687-6667

MICROTEL INN
614 Monroe St
(39202)
Rates: $50-$68
(601) 352-8282
(888) 771-7171

MOTEL 6
6145 I-55 N
(39213)
Rates: $35-$51
(601) 956-8848
(800) 466-8356

**QUALITY INN
& SUITES**
400 Greymont Ave
(39202)
Rates: $69-$89
(601) 969-2230
(800) 424-6423

**RED ROOF INN
COLISEUM**
700 Larson St
(39202)
Rates: $38-$60
(601) 969-5006
(800) 843-7663

**RESIDENCE INN
BY MARRIOTT**
881 E River Pl
(39202)
Rates: $99-$149
(601) 355-3599
(800) 331-3131

SLEEP INN
2620 Hwy 80 W
(39204)
Rates: $40-$60
(601) 354-3900
(800) 424-6423

KOSCIUSKO

**BEST WESTERN
PARKWAY INN**
1052 Veterans
Memorial Dr
(39090)
Rates: $46-$68
(662) 289-6252
(800) 528-1234

LAUREL

COMFORT SUITES
1820 Jefferson
St (39440)
Rates: $75-$150
(601) 649-2620
(800) 424-6423

**RAMADA INN
& CONV CTR**
1105 Sawmill Rd
(39440)
Rates: $75-$135
(601) 649-9100
(800) 272-6232

LONG BEACH

**RED CREEK
COLONIAL INN**
7416 Red Creek Rd
(39560)
Rates: $39-$69
(228) 452-3080
(800) 729-9670

LOUISVILLE

**BEST WESTERN
RED HILLS INN**
201 Hwy 15 N
(39339)
Rates: $51-$82
(662) 773-9090
(800) 528-1234

MCCOMB

DAYS INN
2298 Delaware
Ave (39648)
Rates: $65-$71
(601) 684-5566
(800) 329-7466

AREA CODES - If the local number doesn't connect, check for a new area code.

HAWTHORN INN & SUITES
2001 Veteran's Blvd (39648)
Rates: $80-$110
(601) 684-8655
(800) 527-1133

MERIDIAN

BAYMONT INN & SUITES
1400 Roebuck Dr (39301)
Rates: $52-$69
(601) 693-2300
(877) 229-6668

DAYS INN
145 US Hwy 80 (39301)
Rates: $48-$89
(601) 483-3812
(800) 329-7466

ECONO LODGE
2405 S Frontage Rd (39301)
Rates: $45-$125
(601) 693-9393
(800) 424-6423

ECONO LODGE NORTHEAST
109 Hwy 11/80 E (39302)
Rates: $43-$70
(601) 485-3254
(800) 424-6423

HOLIDAY INN
111 Hwy 11 & 80 (39301)
Rates: $88-$103
(601) 485-5101
(800) 465-4329

JAMESON INN
524 Bonita Lakes Dr (39301)
Rates: $49-$104
(601) 483-3315
(800) 526-3766

MOTEL 6
2309 S Frontage Rd (39301)
Rates: $35-$40
(601) 482-1182
(800) 466-8356

QUALITY INN
1401 Roebuck Rd (39301)
Rates: $60-$70
(601) 693-4521
(800) 424-6423

MOSS POINT

ECONO LODGE
7205 Tanner Ln (39563)
Rates: $37-$100
(228) 475-9820
(800) 424-6423

HOLIDAY INN EXP
4800 Amoco Dr (39563)
Rates: $59-$89
(228) 474-2100
(800) 465-4329

SHULAR INN
6623 Hwy 63 (39563)
Rates: $45-$54
(228) 475-8444
(800) 962-1820

NATCHEZ

CEDAR GROVE PLANTATION COUNTRY INN
617 Kingston Rd (39120)
Rates: $120-$240
(601) 445-0585

NATCHEZ EOLA HOTEL
110 N Pearl St (39120)
Rates: $98-$145
(601) 445-6000
(866) 445-3652

NEWTON

DAYS INN
261 Eastside Dr (39345)
Rates: $45-$75
(601) 683-3361
(800) 329-7466

OCEAN SPRINGS

DAYS INN
7305 Washington Ave (39564)
Rates: $54-$159
(228) 872-8255
(800) 329-7466

HOLIDAY INN EXP
7304 Washington Ave (39564)
Rates: $79-$149
(228) 875-7555
(800) 465-4329

RAMADA LTD
8011 Tucker Rd (39532)
Rates: $54-$159
(228) 872-2323
(800) 272-6232

OLIVE BRANCH

COMFORT INN
7049 Enterprise Dr (38654)
Rates: $61-$66
(662) 895-0456
(800) 424-6423

HOLIDAY INN EXP
8900 Expressway Dr (38644)
Rates: $89-$129
(662) 893-8700
(888) 465-4329

WHISPERING WOODS HOTEL
11200 E Goodman Rd (38654)
Rates: $139
(662) 895-2941

OXFORD

DAYS INN
1101 Frontage Rd (38655)
Rates: $49-$149
(662) 234-9500
(800) 329-7466

PASCAGOULA

LAFONT INN
2703 Denny Ave (39568)
Rates: $49-$89
(228) 762-7111
(800) 647-6077

SUPER 8 MOTEL
4919 Denny Ave (39568)
Rates: $99-$180
(228) 762-9414
(800) 800-8000

PASS CHRISTIAN

HARBOUR OAKS INN B&B
126 W Scenic Dr (39571)
Rates: $83-$128
(228) 452-9399

PEARL

JAMESON INN
434 Riverwind Dr (39208)
Rates: $49-$104
(601) 932-6030
(800) 526-3766

LA QUINTA INN & SUITES
501 S Pearson Rd (39208)
Rates: $60-$85
(601) 664-0065
(800) 687-6667

MOTEL 6
216 N Pearson Rd (39208)
Rates: $39-$43
(601) 936-9988
(800) 466-8356

RAMADA LTD AIRPORT SOUTH
341 Airport Rd (39208)
Rates: n/a
(601) 933-1122
(800) 272-6232

PHILADELPHIA

DAYS INN
1009 Holland Ave (39350)
Rates: $53-$98
(601) 650-3590
(800) 329-7466

DELUXE INN & SUITES
1004 Central Dr (39350)
Rates: $39-$89
(601) 656-0052

PICAYUNE

DAYS INN
450 S Loften Ave (39466)
Rates: $59-$99
(601) 799-1339
(800) 329-7466

COMFORT INN
550 S Lofton Dr (39466)
Rates: $50-$150
(601) 799-2833
(800) 424-6423

PONTOTOC

DAYS INN
217 Hwy 15 N (38863)
Rates: $48-$95
(662) 489-5200
(800) 329-7466

RICHLAND

DAYS INN
1035 Hwy 49 S (39218)
Rates: $55-$85
(601) 932-5553
(800) 329-7466

EXECUTIVE INN & SUITES
390 Hwy 49 S (39218)
Rates: $45-$59
(601) 664-3456

RIDGELAND

DRURY INN & SUITES
610 E County Line Rd (39157)
Rates: $65-$115
(601) 956-6100
(800) 378-7946

ECONO LODGE
839 Ridgewood Rd (39157)
Rates: $54-$79
(601) 956-7740
(800) 424-6423

HOMEWOOD SUITES
853 Centre St (39157)
Rates: $129
(601) 899-8611
(800) 225-5466

RED ROOF INN
810 Adcock St (39157)
Rates: $40-$57
(601) 956-7707
(800) 843-7663

RIPLEY

BEST WESTERN RIPLEY INN
922 City Ave (38663)
Rates: $54-$61
(662) 837-0002
(800) 528-1234

ROBINSONVILLE

COTTAGE INN
4235 Casino
Centre Dr (38664)
Rates: $65-$95
(601) 363-2900

KEY WEST INN
US 61 (38664)
Rates: $50
(601) 363-0021
(800) 833-0555

SARDIS

KNIGHTS INN
598 E Lee St
(38666)
Rates: $36-$55
(662) 487-2424
(800) 843-5644

SENATOBIA

MOTEL 6
501 E Main St
(38668)
Rates: $38-$42
(662) 562-5241
(800) 466-8356

SOUTHAVEN

SUPER 8 MOTEL
5115 Pepper
Chase Dr (38671)
Rates: n/a
(662) 280-8826
(800) 800-8000

STARKVILLE

BEST WESTERN
119 Hwy 12 W
(39759)
Rates: $59-$110
(662) 324-5555
(800) 528-1234

COMFORT SUITES
801 Russell St
(39759)
Rates: $89-$129
(662) 324-9595
(800) 424-6423

TUNICA

**HISTORIC
HOTEL MARIE**
1195 Main St
(38676)
Rates: $49-$99
(601) 363-0100

TUNICA RESORTS

**BEST WESTERN
TUNICA NORTH**
7500 Casino Strip
Blvd (38664)
Rates: $49-$199
(662) 363-6711
(800) 528-1234
(888) 804-0700

KEY WEST INN
11635 Hwy 61 N
(38664)
Rates: $50-$99
(662) 363-0021

TUPELO

DAYS INN
1015 N Gloster
St (38804)
Rates: $43-$58
(662) 842-0088
(800) 329-7466

EXECUTIVE INN
1011 N Gloster St
(38801)
Rates: $64-$77
(662) 841-2222
(800) 533-3220

**HOWARD JOHN-
SON EXPRESS INN**
923 N Gloster
St (38801)
Rates: $40-$99
(662) 842-8811
(800) 446-4656

JAMESON INN
879 Mississippi Dr
(38804)
Rates: $49-$104
(662) 840-2380
(800) 526-3766

RED ROOF INN
1500 MCullough
Blvd (38801)
Rates: $42-$56
(662) 844-1904
(800) 843-7663

SUPER 8 MOTEL
3898 McCullough
Blvd (38801)
Rates: $47-$58
(662) 842-0448
(800) 800-8000

VICKSBURG

BATTLEFIELD INN
4137 I-20 N
Frontage Rd
(39180)
Rates: $59-$75
(601) 638-5811

**THE
CORNERS B&B**
601 Klein St (39180)
Rates: $80-$130
(601) 636-7421

ECONO LODGE
3330-A Clay St
(39183)
Rates: $39-$74
(601) 634-8766
(800) 424-6423

HAMPTON INN
3330 Clay St
(39180)
Rates: $64-$89
(601) 636-6100
(800) 426-7866

JAMESON INN
3975 S Frontage
Rd (39180)
Rates: $49-$104
(601) 619-7799
(800) 526-3766

MOTEL 6
4127 E Frontage
Rd (39180)
Rates: $40-$76
(601) 638-5077
(800) 466-8356

WAVELAND

**COAST INN
& SUITES**
404 Hwy 90
(39576)
Rates: $59-$69
(228) 467-9261

WIGGINS

**BEST WESTERN
WOODSTONE**
535 Frontage Dr E
(39577)
Rates: $52-$69
(601) 928-1616
(800) 528-1234

YAZOO CITY

COMFORT INN
1600 Jerry Clover
Blvd (39194)
Rates: $48-$75
(662) 746-6444
(800) 424-6423

MISSOURI

AFFTON

OAK GROVE INN
6602 S Lindbergh
Blvd (63123)
Rates: $34-$42
(314) 894-9449

ALBANY

EASTWOOD MOTEL
US 136E (64402)
Rates: $22-$33
(816) 726-5208

ARNOLD

COMFORT INN
3610 W Outer
Rd (63010)
Rates: $74-$139
(636) 296-3000
(800) 424-6423

DRURY INN
1201 Drury Ln
(63010)
Rates: $57-$102
(636) 296-9600
(800) 378-7946

WHITE WING RESORT
P. O. Box 840
(65616)
Rates: $42-$53
(636) 338-2318

AURORA

AURORA INN MOTEL
Rt 3, Box 200
(65605)
Rates: $36-$42
(417) 678-5035

AVA

SUPER 8 MOTEL
1711 S Jefferson St
(65608)
Rates: $55-$65
(417) 683-1343
(800) 800-8000

BETHANY

BEST WESTERN BETHANY INN
496 S 39th St
(64424)
Rates: $58-$80
(660) 425-8006
(800) 528-1234

FAMILY BUDGET INN
4014 Millen
(64424)
Rates: $39-$49
(660) 425-7915

BIRCH TREE

HICKORY HOUSE MOTOR INN
P. O. Box 306
(65438)
Rates: $20-$32
(573) 292-3232

BLUE SPRINGS

DAYS INN
3120 NW Jefferson
St (64015)
Rates: $50-$135
(816) 224-1122
(800) 329-7466

HAMPTON INN
900 NW South
Outer Rd (64015)
Rates: n/a
(816) 220-3844
(800) 426-7866

MOTEL 6
901 W Jefferson
St (64015)
Rates: $29-$40
(816) 228-9133
(800) 466-8356

RAMADA LTD
1110 N 7 Hwy
(64014)
Rates: $40-$85
(816) 229-6363
(800) 272-6232

SLEEP INN
451 NW Jefferson
St (64014)
Rates: $49-$90
(816) 224-1199
(800) 424-6423

BOLIVAR

WELCOME INN
4710 S 128th Rd
(65613)
Rates: $34-$50
(417) 326-5268

BOONVILLE

COMFORT INN
2427 Mid
American
Industrial Dr
(65233)
Rates: $49-$99
(660) 882-5317
(800) 424-6423

BRANSON

BARRINGTON HOTEL
263 Shepherd of
the Hills Expy
(65616)
Rates: $42-$62
(417) 334-8866

BEST WESTERN BRANSON LANDING
403 W Hwy 76
(65616)
Rates: $45-$149
(417) 334-6464
(800) 528-1234
(800) 828-0404

CHATEAU ON THE LAKE RESORT HOTEL
415 N State Hwy
265 (65616)
Rates: $89-$299
(417) 334-1161
(888) 333-5253

DAYS INN
3524 Keeter St
(65616)
Rates: $46-$80
(417) 334-5544
(800) 329-7466

1ST INN GOLD
2719 W Hwy 76
(65616)
Rates: $49-$69
(417) 334-7000

GOOD SHEPHERD INN
1023 W Hwy 76
(65616)
Rates: $29-$60
(417) 334-1695

HALL OF FAME MOTEL
3005 W Hwy 76
(65616)
Rates: $50-$65
(417) 334-5161

HARMONY PLACE MOTEL
3514 W Hwy 76
(65616)
Rates: n/a
(417) 334-5510

HOLIDAY INN EXP HOTEL & SUITES
1970 W Hwy 76
(65616)
Rates: $72-$102
(417) 336-1100
(800) 465-4329

LAKESHORE RESORT
1773 Lakeshore Dr
(65616)
Rates: $80-$150
(417) 334-6262

LIGHTHOUSE INN
2375 Green Mtn
Dr (65616)
Rates: $48-$88
(417) 336-6161

MIDTOWN INN
2330 W Hwy 76
(65616)
Rates: $49-$54
(417) 334-7474

MOTEL 6
2651 Shepherd of
the Hills Expy
(65616)
Rates: $29-$48
(417) 336-6088
(800) 466-8356

OZARK

VALLEY INN
2693 Shephard of
the Hills Expwy
(65616)
Rates: $35-$70
(417) 336-4666
(800) 947-4666

QUALITY INN
3269 Shepherd of
the Hills Expwy
(65616)
Rates: $45-$90
(417) 335-6776
(800) 424-6423

RAMADA INN
1700 Hwy 76 W
(65616)
Rates: $39-$79
(417) 334-1000
(800) 272-6232

RAMADA LTD
2316 Shepherd of
the Hills Expwy
(65616)
Rates: $70-$90
(417) 337-5207
(800) 272-6232

RESIDENCE INN BY MARRIOT
280 Wildwood Dr
S (65616)
Rates: $79-$139
(417) 336-4077
(800) 331-3131

ROCK VIEW RESORT
1049 Parkview Dr
(65672)
Rates: $53-$87
(417) 334-4678

SCENIC HILLS INN
2422 Shepherd of
the Hills Expwy
(65616)
Rates: $39-$59
(417) 336-8855
(888) 800-5577

AREA CODES - If the local number doesn't connect, check for a new area code.

SETTLE INN RESORT
3050 Green Mtn Dr (65616)
Rates: $59-$119
(417) 335-4700
(800) 677-6906

WHITE WING RESORT
1028 Jakes Creek Tr (65616)
Rates: $50-$140
(417) 338-2318

BRANSON WEST

COLONIAL MOUNTAIN INN
US 65 SR 13 (65737)
Rates: $40-$48
(417) 272-8414

ECONO LODGE SILVER DOLLAR CITY AREA
SR 13 (65737)
Rates: $45-$90
(417) 272-3326
(800) 424-6423

SHADY ACRES MOTEL
8722 Hwy 76 (65737)
Rates: $36-$42
(417) 338-2316

BRIDGETON

MOTEL 6
3655 Pennridge Dr (63044)
Rates: $33-$40
(314) 291-6100
(800) 466-8356

RED ROOF INN
3470 Hollenberg Dr (63044)
Rates: $40-$73
(314) 291-3350
(800) 843-7663

BROOKFIELD

BEST WESTERN BROOKFIELD
28622 Hwy 11 (64628)
Rates: $70-$98
(660) 258-4900
(800) 528-1234

COUNTRY INN
800 S Main St (64628)
Rates: $31-$36
(660) 258-7262

BUFFALO

GOODNITE INN
642 S Ash (65622)
Rates: $32-$55
(417) 345-3245

BUTLER

DAYS INN
100 S Fran Ave (64730)
Rates: $40-$70
(660) 679-4544
(800) 329-7466

SUPER 8 MOTEL
1114 W Ft. Scott St (64730)
Rates: $41-$80
(660) 679-6183
(800) 800-8000

CAMDENTON

LAN-O-LAK MOTEL
P. O. Box 619 (65020)
Rates: $38-$55
(573) 346-2256

CAMERON

BEST WESTERN ACORN INN
I-35 & US 36 (644251
(816) 632-2187
(800) 528-1234
(800) 607-2288

COMFORT INN
1803 Comfort Ln (64429)
Rates: $50-$95
(816) 632-5655
(800) 424-6423

ECONO LODGE
220 E Grand (64429)
Rates: $38-$60
(816) 632-6571
(800) 424-6423

SUPER 8 MOTEL
1710 N Walnut St (64429)
Rates: $53-$60
(816) 632-8888
(800) 800-8000

CANTON

COMFORT INN
1701 Oak St (63435)
Rates: $55-$130
(573) 288-8800
(800) 424-6423

CAPE GIRARDEAU

DRURY LODGE
104 S Vantage (63701)
Rates: $78-$98
(573) 334-7151
(800) 378-7946

DRURY SUITES
3303 Campster (63701)
Rates: $88-$108
(573) 339-9500
(800) 378-7946

HAMPTON INN
103 Cape West Pkwy (63701)
Rates: $68-$83
(573) 651-3000
(800) 426-7866

PEAR TREE INN
3248 William St (63701)
Rates: $65-$90
(573) 334-3000
(800) 282-8733

VICTORIAN INN & SUITES
3265 William St (63701)
Rates: $64-$99
(573) 651-4486

CARTHAGE

CARTHAGE INN
2244 Grand Ave (64836)
Rates: $38-$58
(417) 358-2499

ECONO LODGE
1441 W Central (64836)
Rates: $56-$62
(417) 358-3900
(800) 424-6423

SUPER 8 MOTEL
416 W Fir Rd (64836)
Rates: n/a
(417) 359-9000
(800) 800-8000

CASSVILLE

BUDGET INN
Hwy 112/248 (65625)
Rates: $30-$58
(417) 847-4196

SUPER 8 MOTEL
101 S Hwy 37 (656254
Rates: $43-$65
(417) 847-4888
(800) 800-8000

CHARLESTON

CHARLESTON INN
310 S Story (63834)
Rates: $31-$50
(573) 683-2125

CHESTERFIELD

COMFORT INN & SUITES
18375 Chesterfield Arpt. Rd (63005)
Rates: $80-$140
(636) 530-1200
(800) 424-6423

DOUBLETREE HOTEL
16625 Swingley Ridge Rd (63017)
Rates: $79-$169
(636) 532-5000
(800) 222-8733

DRURY PLAZA HOTEL
355 Chesterfield Ctr E (63017)
Rates: n/a
(636) 532-3300
(800) 378-7946

HOMEWOOD SUITES
840 Chesterfield Pkwy W (63017)
Rates: $129-$139
(636) 530-0305
(800) 225-5466

CHILLICOTHE

BEST WESTERN
1020 S Washington (64601)
Rates: $50-$75
(660) 646-0572
(800) 528-1234
(800) 990-9150

SUPER 8 MOTEL
580 Old Hwy 36 E (64601)
Rates: $54-$63
(660) 646-7888
(800) 800-8000

CLARKSVILLE

CLARKSVILLE INN
2nd & Lewis Sts (63336)
Rates: $29-$41
(314) 242-3324

CLAYTON

THE DANIELE HOTEL
216 N Meramec (63105)
Rates: $139
(314) 721-0101

RITZ CARLTON
100 Carondelet Plaza (63105)
Rates: $179-$215
(314) 863-6300
(800) 241-3333

SHERATON CLAYTON PLAZA HOTEL
7730 Bonhomme Ave (63105)
Rates: $99-$129
(314) 863-0400
(800) 325-3535

CLINTON

MOTEL USA
1508 N 2nd St (64735)
Rates: $30-$55
(660) 885-2267

COLUMBIA

BAYMONT INN & SUITES
2500 I-70 Dr SW (65203)
Rates: $59-$67
(573) 445-1899
(877) 229-6668

CANDLEWOOD SUITES
3100 Wingate Ct (65201)
Rates: $79-$179
(573) 817-0525
(888) 226-3539

AREA CODES - If the local number doesn't connect, check for a new area code.

COMFORT INN & SUITES
1740 W Broadway
(65202)
Rates: $59-$107
(800) 424-6423

COMFORT SUITES
3101 Wingate Ct
(65201)
Rates: $79-$149
(800) 424-6423

DAYS INN
1900 I-70 Dr SW
(65203)
Rates: $50-$150
(573) 445-8511
(800) 329-7466

DRURY INN
1000 Knipp St
(65203)
Rates: $72-$117
(573) 445-1800
(800) 378-7946

HOLIDAY INN SELECT-EXECUTIVE CTR
2200 I-70 Dr SW
(65203)
Rates: $109-$129
(573) 445-8531
(800) 465-4329

LA QUINTA INN
901 Conley Rd
(65201)
Rates: $90-$110
(573) 443-4141
(800) 531-5900
(800) 687-6667

MOTEL 6
1800 I-70 Dr SW
(65203)
Rates: $34-$52
(573) 445-8433
(800) 466-8356

MOTEL 6 EAST
3402 I-70 Dr SE
(65201)
Rates: $42-$56
(573) 8150123
(800) 466-8356

QUALITY INN
1612 N
Providence Rd
(65202)
Rates: $59-$149
(573) 449-2491
(800) 424-6423

RED ROOF INN
201 E Texas Ave
(65202)
Rates: $42-$71
(573) 442-0145
(800) 843-7663

TRAVELODGE
900 Vandiver Dr
(65202)
Rates: $49-$99
(573) 449-1065
(800) 578-7878

WINGATE INN
3101 Wingate Ct
(65201)
Rates: $81
(573) 817-0500

CONCORDIA

BEST WESTERN HEIDELBERG INN
406 NW 2nd St
(64020)
Rates: $40-$70
(660) 463-2114
(800) 528-1234

DAYS INN
301 NW 3rd St
(64020)
Rates: $45-$95
(660) 463-7987
(800) 329-7466

CREVE COEUR

DRURY INN & SUITES
11980 Olive Blvd
(63141)
Rates: $73-$133
(314) 989-1100
(800) 378-7946

CUBA

BEST WESTERN CUBA INN
246 Hwy P (65453)
Rates: $45-$75
(573) 885-7707
(800) 528-1234

DEXTER

OAK TREE INN
1608 Hwy
Business 60 W
(63841)
Rates: $42-$56
(573) 624-5800
(800) 223-5555

DONIPHAN

ECONO LODGE AT CURRENT RIVER
Hwy 160 (63935)
Rates: $38-$60
(573) 996-2101
(800) 424-6423

EAGLE ROCK

EAGLE ROCK RESORT
HCR 01, Box 1593
(65641)
Rates: n/a
(417) 271-3222

FLETCHER'S DEVIL'S DIVE RESORT
HCR 01, Box 8
(65641)
Rates: n/a
(417) 271-3396

LAZY EAGLE RESORT
P. O. Box 141 (65641)
Rates: n/a
(417) 271-3390
(800) 232-4783

EARTH CITY

RESIDENCE INN AIRPORT
3290 River Tr S
(63045)
Rates: $134-$169
(314) 209-0995
(800) 331-3131

EDMUNDSON

DRURY INN-AIRPT
10490 Natural
Bridge (63134)
Rates: $60-$121
(314) 423-7700
(800) 378-7946

EL DORADO SPRINGS

EL DORADO MOTEL
102 Hwy 54 East
(64744)
Rates: n/a
(417) 876-6888

ELLINGTON

SCENIC RIVERS MOTEL
231 N 2nd St
(63638)
Rates: $38-$43
(573) 663-7722

EUREKA

HOLIDAY INN SIX FLAGS
4901 Six Flags Rd
(63025)
Rates: $129-$219
(636) 938-6661
(800) 465-4329

FENTON

DRURY INN & SUITES
1088 S Hwy Dr
(63026)
Rates: $66-$105
(636) 343-7822
(800) 378-7946

MOTEL 6
1860 Bowles Ave
(63026)
Rates: $39-$56
(636) 349-1800
(800) 466-8356

PEAR TREE INN
1100 S Hwy Dr
(63026)
Rates: $55-$93
(636) 343-8820
(800) 282-8733

TOWNEPLACE SUITES
1662 Fenton
Business Park Ct
(63026)
Rates: $83-$135
(636) 305-7000
(800) 257-3000

FESTUS

DRURY INN
1001 Veterans
Blvd (63028)
Rates: $60-$96
(636) 933-2400
(800) 378-7946

HOLIDAY INN
1200 Gannon Dr
(63028)
Rates: n/a
(636) 937-0700
(800) 465-4329

FLAT RIVER

ROSENER'S INN
Hwy 67 N (63601)
Rates: $29-$45
(314) 431-4241

FORISTELL

BEST WESTERN WEST 70 INN
12 Hwy West
(63348)
Rates: $55-$75
(636) 673-2900
(800) 528-1234
(888) 869-6990

FREDERICK-TOWN

LONGHORN MOTEL
P. O. Box 721
(63645)
Rates: $31-$50
(573) 783-7200

FRONTENAC

HILTON ST. LOUIS
1335 S Lindbergh
Blvd (63131)
Rates: $79-$229
(314) 993-1100
(800) 445-8667

FULTON

HOLIDAY INN EXP
2205 Cardinal Dr
(65251)
Rates: n/a
(800) 465-4329

LOGANBERRY INN B&B
310 W Seventh St
(65251)
Rates: $89-$189
(573) 642-9229
(888) 866-6661

GRAIN VALLEY

COMFORT INN
210 Jefferson St
(64029)
Rates: n/a
(816) 847-2700
(800) 424-6423

GRAVOIS MILLS

MILLSTONE LODGE RESORT
Rt 1, Box 515
(65037)
Rates: $60-$299
(314) 372-5111

HANNIBAL

DAYS INN
4070 Market St
(63401)
Rates: $32-$95
(573) 248-1700
(800) 329-7466

HANNIBAL INN
4141 Market St
(63401)
Rates: $70-$75
(573) 221-6610

QUALITY INN & SUITES
120 Lindsey Dr,
Hwy 36 (63401)
Rates: $79-$150
(573) 221-4001
(800) 424-6423

TRAVELODGE
502 Mark Twain
Ave (63401)
Rates: $38-$82
(573) 221-4100
(800) 578-7878

HARRISON-VILLE

BEST WESTERN
US 71 & MO 291
(64701)
Rates: $54-$92
(816) 884-3200
(800) 528-1234

BUDGET HOST CARAVAN MOTEL
1705 Hwy 291 N
(64701)
Rates: $33-$60
(816) 884-4100
(800) 283-4678

SLUMBER INN MOTEL
21400 E 275th St
(64701)
Rates: $35-$48
(816) 884-3100

HAYTI

COMFORT INN
I-55 & Hwy 84 E
(63851)
Rates: $50-95
(573) 359-0023
(800) 424-6423

DRURY INN & SUITES
1317 Hwy 84
(63851)
Rates: $60-$129
(573) 359-2702
(800) 378-7946

HAZELWOOD

BAYMONT INN & SUITES
318 Taylor D
(63042)
Rates: $37-$63
(314) 731-4200
(877) 229-6668

LA QUINTA-ARPRT
5781 Campus St
(63042)
Rates: $69-$105
(314) 731-3881
(800) 687-6667

HERMAN

HARBOR HOUSE INN
113 Market St
(65041)
Rates: $45-$125
(573) 486-2222
(888) 942-7529

HIGGINSVILLE

SUPER 8 MOTEL
6471 Oakview Ln
(64037)
Rates: $53-$75
(660) 584-7781
(800) 800-8000

HOLLISTER

ROCK VIEW RESORT
HCR 2, Box 870
(65672)
Rates: $46-$63
(417) 334-4678

HOUSTON

SOUTHERN INN MOTEL
1493 Hwy 63 S
(65483)
Rates: $40-$45
(417) 967-4591

INDEPENDENCE

BEST WESTERN TRUMAN INN
4048 S Lynn Ct
(64055)
Rates: $59-$99
(816) 254-01001
(800) 528-1234

QUALITY INN E
4200 S Noland Rd
(64055)
Rates: $59-$109
(816) 373-8856
(800) 424-6423

RED ROOF INN
13712 E 42nd Ter
(64055)
Rates: $43-$75
(816) 373-2800
(800) 843-7663

SUPER 8 MOTEL
4032 S Lynn Court
Dr (64055)
Rates: $39-$89
(816) 833-1888
(800) 800-8000

ISABELLA

LAKEPOINT RESORT
HCR 1, Box 1152
(65676)
Rates: $42-$47
(417) 273-4343

JACKSON

DRURY INN
225 Drury Ln
(63755)
Rates: $70-$105
(573) 243-9200
(800) 378-7946

JEFFERSON CITY

CAPITOL PLAZA HOTEL
415 W McCarty St
(65101)
Rates: $109-$139
(573) 635-1234

MOTEL 6-SOUTH
1624 Jefferson St
(65109)
Rates: $33-$38
(573) 634-4220
(800) 466-8356

RAMADA INN
1510 Jefferson
(65109)
Rates: $59-$69
(573) 635-7171
(800) 272-6232

SUPER 8 MOTEL
1710 Jefferson St
(65109)
Rates: $50-$89
(573) 636-5456
(800) 800-8000

JOPLIN

BAYMONT INN & SUITES
3510 Range Line
Rd (64804)
Rates: $45-$69
(417) 623-0000
(877) 229-6668

BEST WESTERN OASIS INN
3508 Range Line
Rd (64804)
Rates: $49-$99
(417) 781-6776
(800) 528-1234
(866) 806-4953

CAPRI MOTEL
3401 South Main
(64804)
Rates: n/a
(417) 623-0391

DRURY INN
3601 Range Line
Rd (64804)
Rates: $63-$117
(417) 781-8000
(800) 378-7946

HOLIDAY INN
3615 Range Line
Rd (64804)
Rates: $79-$94
(417) 782-1000
(800) 465-4329

MICROTEL INN & SUITES
4101 Richard
Joseph Blvd
(64804)
Rates: $49-$61
(417) 626-8282

MOTEL 6
3031 S Range Line
Rd (64804)
Rates: $35-$54
(417) 781-6400
(800) 466-8356

SLEEP INN
I-44 & St Hwy 43
S (64803)
Rates: $65-$69
(417) 782-1212
(800) 221-2222

SUPER 8 MOTEL
2830 E 36th St
(64804)
Rates: $45-$95
(417) 782-8765
(800) 800-8000

TROPICANA MOTEL
2417 Range Line
Rd (64804)
Rates: $26-$32
(417) 624-8200

WESTWOOD MOTEL
1700 W 30th St
(64804)
Rates: $33-$39
(417) 782-7212

KANSAS CITY

AMERISUITES KCI AIRPORT
7600 NW 97th Terr
(64153)
Rates: $89-$98
(816) 414-7000
(800) 833-1516

BAYMONT INN & SUITES NORTH
2214 Taney Rd
(64116)
Rates: $61-$68
(816) 221-1200
(877) 229-6668

BAYMONT INN & SUITES SOUTH
8601 Hillcrest Rd
(64136)
Rates: $61-$68
(816) 822-7000
(877) 229-6668

CHASE SUITES BY WOODFIN
9900 NW Prairie
View Rd (64153)
Rates: $89-$159
(816) 891-9009
(800) 237-8811

CLARION HOTEL AIRPORT
11832 Plaza Cir
(64153)
Rates: $49-$119
(816) 464-2345
(800) 424-6423

COMFORT INN & SUITES DOWNTOWN
770 Admiral Blvd
(64106)
Rates: $60-$170
(816) 472-8808
(800) 424-6423

DAYS INN
11120 NW
Ambassador Dr
(64153)
Rates: $65-$190
(816) 746-1666
(800) 329-7466

**DAYS INN-AT
BENJAMIN RANCH**
6101 E 87th St
(64138)
Rates: $55-$100
(816) 765-4331
(800) 329-7466

**DOUBLETREE
HOTEL**
1301 Wyandotte St
(64105)
Rates: $89-$219
(816) 474-6664
(800) 222-8733

**DRURY INN
& SUITES**
3830 Blue Ridge
Cutoff (64133)
Rates: $60-$113
(816) 923-3000
(800) 378-7946

**DRURY INN
& SUITES**
7900 NW Tiffany
Spgs Pky (64153)
Rates: $60-$113
(816) 880-9700
(800) 378-7946

**ECONO LODGE
AIRPORT**
11300 NW
Prarieview Rd
(64153)
Rates: $45-$100
(816) 464-5082
(800) 424-6423

**EMBASSY SUITES
HOTEL-AIRPORT**
7640 NW Tiffany
Spgs Pky (64153)
Rates: $99-$209
(816) 891-7788
(800) 362-2779

**FAIRMONT AT
THE PLAZA**
401 Ward Pkwy
(64112)
Rates: $159-$529
(816) 756-1500
(800) 441-1414

**FOUR POINTS BY
SHERATON
COUNTRY CLUB
PLAZA-**
One E 45th St
(64111)
Rates: $199
(816) 753-7400
(800) 325-3535

**HAMPTON INN-
WORLDS OF FUN**
1051 N
Cambridge/
I-435 (64120)
Rates: $64-$89
(816) 483-7900
(800) 426-7866

HOLIDAY INN
4011 Blue Ridge
Cutoff (64133)
Rates: $89-$100
(816) 353-5300
(800) 465-4329

HOLIDAY INN EXP
801 Westport Rd
(64111)
Rates: $79-$129
(618) 931-1000
(800) 465-4329

**HOMESTEAD
STUDIO SUITES**
4535 Main St
(64153)
Rates: $75-$99
(816) 531-2212
(888) 782-9473

**HOMESTEAD
STUDIO SUITES
AIRPORT**
9701 N Shannon
Ave (64153)
Rates: $52-$76
(816) 891-8500
(888) 782-9473

**HOMEWOOD
SUITES**
7312 N Polo Dr
(64153)
Rates: $79-$179
(816) 880-9880
(800) 225-5466

**INN TOWNE
LODGE**
2620 NE 43rd St
(64117)
Rates: $40-$55
(816) 453-6550

**MARRIOTT
DOWNTOWN**
200 W 12th St
(64105)
Rates: $139-$240
(816) 421-6800
(800) 228-9290

MOTEL 6-NORTH
8230 NW Prairie
View Rd (64152)
Rates: $37-$48
(816) 741-6400
(800) 466-8356

**MOTEL 6-
SOUTHEAST**
6400 E 87th St
(64138)
Rates: $35-$48
(816) 333-4468
(800) 466-8356

**QUALITY INN &
SUITES
AIRPORT**
6901 NW 83rd St
(64152)
Rates: $50-$110
(816) 587-6262
(800) 424-6423

**RADISSON HOTEL
AIRPORT**
11828 NW Plaza
Cir (64153)
Rates: $88-$98
(816) 464-2423
(800) 333-3333

**RED ROOF INN-
NORTH**
3636 NE
Randolph Rd
(64161)
Rates: $43-$76
(816) 452-8585
(800) 843-7663

**RESIDENCE INN
BY MARRIOTT-
UNION HILL**
2975 Main St
(64108)
Rates: $139-$189
(816) 561-3000
(800) 331-3131

**SHERATON
SUITES
COUNTRY CLUB
PLAZA**
770 W 47th St
(64112)
Rates: $145-$165
(816) 931-4400
(800) 325-3535

**SLEEP INN
AIRPORT**
7611 NW 97th
Terrace (64153)
Rates: $50-$119
(816) 891-0111
(800) 424-6423

**WESTIN CROWN
CENTER**
1 Pershing Rd
(64108)
Rates: $104-$169
(816) 474-4400
(800) 228-3000

KEARNEY

ECONO LODGE
505 Shanks Ave
(64060)
Rates: $40-$66
(816) 628-5111
(800) 424-6423

SUPER 8 MOTEL
210 Platte-Clay
Way (64060)
Rates: $56-$100
(816) 628-6800
(800) 800-8000

KENNETT

DAYS INN
110 Independence
Ave (63857)
Rates: $47-$95
(573) 888-9860
(800) 329-7466

KIMBERLING CITY

**KIMBERLING
HEIGHTS
RESORT MOTEL**
HCR 4, Box 980
(65686)
Rates: $39-$59
(417) 779-4158

KINGDOM CITY

DAYS INN
I-70 & US 54
(65262)
Rates: $48-$120
(573) 642-0050
(800) 329-7466

SUPER 8 MOTEL
3370 Gold Ave
(65262)
Rates: $42-$74
(573) 642-2888
(800) 800-8000

KIRKSVILLE

COMFORT INN
2209 N Baltimore
(63501)
Rates: $59-$119
(660) 665-2205
(800) 424-6423

DAYS INN
3805 S Baltimore
(63501)
Rates: $59-$64
(660) 665-8244
(800) 329-7466

SHAMROCK INN
2521 S Business Rt
(63501)
Rates: $40-$50
(660) 665-8352

SUPER 8 MOTEL
1101 Country
Club Dr (63501)
Rates: $43-$75
(660) 665-8826
(800) 800-8000

KIRKWOOD

BEST WESTERN
1200 S Kirkwood
Rd (63122)
Rates: $69-$119
(314) 821-3950
(800) 528-1234
(800) 435-4656

KNOB NOSTER

WHITEMAN INN
2340 W Irish Ln
(65336)
Rates: $44-$75
(660) 563-3000

LAKE OZARK

**HOLIDAY INN
SUNPREE
RESORTS-
OSAGE BEACH**
120 Holiday Lane
(65049)
Rates: $120-$130
(573) 365-2334
(800) 465-4329

MOTEL 6
3703 E Hwy 54
(65049)
Rates: $34-$90
(573) 365-4566
(800) 466-8356

LAKE ST. LOUIS
DAYS INN
10600 Veterans
Memorial Pkwy
(63367)
Rates: $50-$150
(636) 625-1711
(800) 329-7466

LAKEVIEW
**COLONIAL
MOUNTAIN INN**
P. O. Box 2068
(65737)
Rates: $36-$55
(417) 272-8414

**RUSTIC GATE
MOTOR INN**
P. O. Box 1088
(65737)
Rates: $32-$50
(417) 272-3326

LAMAR
BLUE TOP INN
65 SE 1st Ln
(64759)
Rates: $39-$46
(417) 682-3333

LEBANON
**BEST WESTERN
WYOTA INN**
1225 Mill Creek
Rd (65536)
Rates: $55-$65
(417) 532-6171
(800) 528-1234
(866) 996-8246

**BRENTWOOD
MOTEL**
1320 S Jefferson
(65536)
Rates: $29-$41
(417) 532-6131

DAYS INN
2071 W Elm St
(65536)
Rates: $32-$74
(417) 532-7111
(800) 329-7466

ECONO LODGE
2125 W Elm
(65536)
Rates: $32-$69
(417) 588-3226
(800) 424-6423

LEES SUMMIT
COMFORT INN
607 SE Oldham
Pkwy (64063)
Rates: $54-$109
(816) 524-8181
(800) 424-6423

HOLIDAY INN EXP
4825 NE
Lakewood Way
(64064)
Rates: $84-$109
(816) 795-6400
(800) 465-4329

**SUMMIT INN &
SUITES**
625 MW Murray
Rd (64081)
Rates: $62-$72
(816) 525-1400

LEXINGTON
LEXINGTON INN
Jct US 24 & SR 13
(64067)
Rates: $32-$37
(816) 259-4641

LIBERTY
DAYS INN
209 N 291 Hwy
(64068)
Rates: $45-$65
(816) 781-8770
(800) 329-7466

LICKING
BEST VALUE INN
209 S Hwy 63
(65542)
Rates: $41-$46
(573) 674-4809

LOUISIAN
**RIVER'S EDGE
MOTEL**
201 Mansion St
(63353)
Rates: $39-$60
(573) 754-4522

MACON
**BEST WESTERN
INN**
28933 Sunset Dr
(63552)
Rates: $42-$65
(660) 385-2125
(800) 528-1234
(800) 901-2125

SUPER 8 MOTEL
203 E Briggs Dr
(63552)
Rates: $50-$66
(660) 385-5788
(800) 800-8000

MARSHFIELD
HOLIDAY INN EXP
1301 Banning St
(65706)
Rates: $64-$89
(417) 859-6000
(800) 465-4329

MARSTON
SUPER 8 MOTEL
501 SE Outer Rd
(63866)
Rates: $50-$54
(573) 643-9888
(800) 800-8000

*MARYLAND
HEIGHTS*
**CLUBHOUSE
INN & SUITES**
1970 Craig Rd
(63146)
Rates: $69-$149
(314) 205-8000
(800) CLUB-INN

COMFORT INN
12031 Lackland
Rd (63146)
Rates: $60-$96
(314) 878-1400
(800) 424-6423

DRURY INN
12220 Dorsett Rd
(63043)
Rates: $63-$110
(314) 576-9966
(800) 378-7946

RED ROOF INN
11837 Lackland
Rd (63146)
Rates: $42-$75
(314) 991-4900
(800) 843-7663

**STAYBRIDGE
SUITES**
1855 Craigshire
Rd (63146)
Rates: $81-$171
(314) 878-1555
(800) 238-8000

MARYVILLE
SUPER 8 MOTEL
222 Summit Dr
(64468)
Rates: $40-$47
(660) 582-8088
(800) 800-8000

MEHLVILLE
HOLIDAY INN
4234 Butler Hill
Rd (63129)
Rates: $89-$129
(314) 894-0700
(800) 465-4329

MERRIAM
COMFORT INN
6401 E Frontage
Rd (66202)
Rates: $64-$69
(913) 262-2622
(800) 424-6423

**HAMPTON INN
& SUITES**
7400 W Frontage
Rd (66203)
Rates: n/a
(913) 722-0800
(800) 426-7866

MEXICO
VILLA INN
4224 S Clark
(65265)
Rates: $29-$40
(573) 581-8350

MINER
**BEST WESTERN
COACH HOUSE
INN**
220 S Interstate Dr
(63801)
Rates: $55-$130
(573) 471-9700
(800) 528-1234

DRURY INN
2602 E Malone
(63801)
Rates: $70-$106
(573) 471-4100
(800) 378-7946

PEAR TREE INN
2602 E Malone
Rear (63801)
Rates: $52-$76
(573) 471-8660
(800) 282-8733

MOBERLY
**BEST WESTERN
MOBERLY INN**
1200 Hwy 24 E
(65270)
Rates: $60-$127
(660) 263-6540
(800) 830-5152

SUPER 8 MOTEL
300 Hwy 24 E
(65270)
Rates: $42-$75
(660) 263-8862
(800) 800-8000

MONETT
DAYS INN
868 Hwy 60
(65708)
Rates: $49-$80
(417) 235-8039
(800) 329-7466

**HARTLAND
LODGE**
929 Hwy 60E
(65708)
Rates: $37-$43
(417) 235-4000

MONROE CITY
MONROE CITY INN
3 Gateway Square
(63456)
Rates: $37-$50
(573) 735-4200

MOUND CITY
AUDREY'S MOTEL
1211 State St
(64470)
Rates: $30-$51
(816) 442-3191

*MOUNT
VERNON*
**BEL-AIRE
MOTOR INN**
900 E Mt Vernon
Blvd (65712)
Rates: $38-$50
(417) 466-2111

MOTEL USA INN
1015 E Mt. Vernon
Blvd (65712)
Rates: $33-$55
(417) 466-2125

SUPER 8 MOTEL
1200 E Industrial
Blvd (65712)
Rates: $57-$95
(417) 461-0230

AREA CODES - If the local number doesn't connect, check for a new area code.

MOUNTAIN GROVE

BEST WESTERN RANCH HOUSE INN
111 E 17th St (65711)
Rates: $42-$68
(417) 926-3152
(800) 528-1234

DAYS INN
300 E 19th St (65711)
Rates: $38-$68
(417) 926-5555
(800) 329-7466

NEOSHO

BEST WESTERN BIG SPRING LODGE
1810 Southern View Dr (64850)
Rates: $64-$125
(417) 455-2300
(800) 528-1234
(877) 345-9645

HARTLAND LODGE
1400 71 S (64850)
Rates: $47-$50
(417) 451-3784

NEOSHO INN
2500 S 71 Hwy (64850)
Rates: $42-$48
(417) 451-6500

SUPER 8 MOTEL
3085 Gardner/Edgewood Dr (64850)
Rates: $52-$69
(417) 455-1888
(800) 800-8000

NEVADA

DAYS INN
2345 Marvel Rd (64772)
Rates: $50-$95
(417) 667-6777
(800) 329-7466

ECONO LODGE
1401 E Austin Blvd (64772)
Rates: $30-$90
(417) 667-3351
(800) 424-6423

RAMSEY'S NEVADA MOTEL
1514 E Austin Blvd (64772)
Rates: $30-$38
(417) 667-5273

SUPER 8 MOTEL
2301 E Austin (64772)
Rates: $49-$56
(417) 667-8888
(800) 800-8000

NEW FLORENCE

DAYS INN
403 Booneslick Rd (63363)
Rates: $46-$100
(573) 835-7777
(8000 329-7466

NORTH KANSAS CITY

BAYMONT INN &
2214 Taney Rd (64116)
Rates: $59-$99
(816) 221-1200
(877) 229-6668

DAYS INN
2232 Taney St (64116)
Rates: $46-$66
(816) 421-6000
(800) 329-7466

O'FALLON

COMFORT INN & SUITES
100 Comfort Inn Ct (63366)
Rates: $79-$199
(636) 696-8000
(800) 424-6423

OAK GROVE

ECONO LODGE
410 SE 1st St (64075)
Rates: $35-$70
(816) 690-3681
(800) 424-6423

OSAGE BEACH

BEST WESTERN DOGWOOD HILLS RESORT
1252 Hwy KK (65065)
Rates: $46-$129
(573) 348-1735
(800) 220-6571

LAKE CHATEAU RESORT
5066 Hwy 54 (65065)
Rates: $49-$145
(573) 348-2791

SCOTTISH INNS
5404 Hwy 54 (65065)
Rates: $35-$90
(573) 348-3123
(800) 251-1962

OVERLAND PARK

CANDLEWOOD SUITES
1101 Oakmont (66210)
Rates: n/a
(913) 469-5557
(888) 226-3539

HOLIDAY INN
724o Shawnee Mission Pkwy (66202)
Rates: n/a
(913) 262-3010
(800) 465-4329

OZARK

COMFORT INN
1900 W Evangel St (65721)
Rates: $49-$129
(417) 485-6688
(800) 424-6423

PALMYRA

HILLCREST INN
423 E Lafayette (63461)
Rates: $29-$38
(314) 769-2007

PERRYVILLE

BEST WESTERN COLONIAL INN
1500 Liberty St (63755)
Rates: $58-$69
(573) 547-1091
(800) 528-1234
(888) 737-5612

COMFORT INN
1517 S Perryville Blvd (63775)
Rates: $60-$130
(573) 547-1727
(800) 424-6423

PLATTE CITY

BEST WESTERN PRAIRIE VIEW INN & SUITES
2512 NW Prairie View Rd (64079)
Rates: $70-$140
(816) 858-0200

COMFORT INN-KC INT'L AIRPORT
1200 Hwy 92 (64079)
Rates: $62-$140
(816) 858-5430
(800) 424-6423

POPLAR BLUFF

COMFORT INN
2582 N Westwood blvd (63901)
Rates: $68-$105
(573) 686-5200
(800) 424-6423

DRURY INN
2220 N Westwood Blvd (63901)
Rates: $70-$106
(573) 686-2451
(800) 378-7946

PEAR TREE INN
2218 N Westwood Blvd (63901)
Rates: $55-$80
(314) 785-7100
(800) 282-8733

STUGA COTTAGE
900 Nooney St (63901)
Rates: $40
(573) 785-4085

SUPER 8 MOTEL
2831 N Westwood Blvd (63901)
Rates: $45-$55
(573) 785-0176
(800) 800-8000

PORTAGEVILLE

TEROY MOTEL
903 Hwy 61 N (63873)
Rates: $32-$38
(573) 379-5461

REEDS SPRING

KING'S KOVE RESORT
Rt 5, Box 498A (65737)
Rates: $60
(417) 739-4513

RICH HILL

APACHE MOTEL
Rt 3, Box 309A (64779)
Rates: $34-$40
(417) 395-2161

RICHMOND HEIGHTS

RESIDENCE INN BY MARRIOTT-GALLERIA
1100 McMorrow Ave (63117)
Rates: $70-$179
(314) 862-1900
(800) 331-3131

ROCK PORT

ROCK PORT INN
Rt 4, Box 218 (64482)
Rates: $35-$44
(660) 744-6282

ROCKAWAY BEACH

EDEN ROC RESORT
607 Beach Blvd (65740)
Rates: $31-$50
(417) 561-4163
(800) 955-3459

KENNY'S COURT
P. O. Box 87 (65740)
Rates: $31-$75
(417) 561-4131
(800) 942-5557

ROLLA

BEST WESTERN COACHLIGHT
1403 Martin Springs Dr (65401)
Rates: $45-$85
(573) 341-2511
(800) 528-1234
(800) 274-9464

DAYS INN
1207 Kings Hwy (65401)
Rates: $50-$85
(573) 341-3700
(800) 329-7466

DRURY INN
2006 N Bishop (65401)
Rates: $50-$94
(573) 364-4000
(800) 378-7946

ECONO LODGE
1417 Martin
Springs Dr (65401)
Rates: $37-$65
(573) 341-3130
(800) 424-6423

HOLIDAY INN EXP UNIVERSITY AREA
1507 Martin
Springs Dr (65401)
Rates: $60-$90
(573) 364-8200
(800) 465-4329

SUPER 8 MOTEL
1201 Kingshighway
(65401)
Rates: $40-$60
(573) 364-4156
(800) 800-8000

ST. ANN

HAMPTON INN AIRPORT
10820 Pear Tree Ln
(63074)
Rates: $89-$99
(314) 429-2000
(800) 426-7866

PEAR TREE INN AIRPORT
10810 Pear Tree Ln
(63074)
Rates: $50-$101
(314) 427-3400
(800) 282-8733

ST. CHARLES

COMFORT SUITES
1400 S Fifth St
(63301)
Rates: $79-$255
(636) 949-0694
(800) 424-6423

MOTEL 6
3800 Harry S.
Truman Blvd
(63301)
Rates: $39-$53
(636) 925-2020
(800) 466-8356

ST. CLAIR

BUDGET LODGING
866 S Outer Rd
(63077)
Rates: $59-$79
(636) 629-1000

ST. JOSEPH

BEST WESTERN CLASSIC INN
4502 S 169 Hwy
(64507)
Rates: $59-$83
(816) 232-2345
(800) 528-1234
(800) 569-8378

DRURY INN
4213 Frederick
Blvd (64506)
Rates: $50-$93
(816) 364-4700
(800) 378-7946

HOLIDAY INN HISTORIC RIVER-FRONT DISTRICT
102 S Third St
(65401)
Rates: $74-$139
(816) 279-8000
(800) 465-4329

MOTEL 6
4021 Frederick
Blvd (64506)
Rates: $35-$46
(816) 232-2311
(800) 466-8356

RAMADA INN
4016 Frederick
Blvd (64506)
Rates: $60-$90
(816) 233-6192
(800) 272-6232

ST. LOUIS

(and Vicinity)

BAYMONT INN & SUITES
12330 Dorsett Rd
(63043)
Rates: n/a
(3140 878-1212
(877) 299-6668

COMFORT INN
12031 Lackland
Rd (63146)
Rates: $49-$120
(314) 878-1400
(800) 424-6423

DAYS INN
3660 S Lindbergh
(63127)
Rates: $60-$90
(314) 965-9733
(800) 329-7466

DRURY INN
711 N Broadway
(63102)
Rates: $73-$118
(314) 231-8100
(800) 378-7946

DRURY INN UNION STATION HISTORIC MOTOR INN
201 S 20th St
(63103)
Rates: $72-$150
(314) 231-3900
(800) 378-7946

DRURY PLAZA HOTEL-AT THE ARCH
2 S Fourth St
(63102)
Rates: $82-$152
(314) 231-3003
(800) 378-7946

HAMPTON INN AIRPORT
10800 Pear Tree
Lane (63074)
Rates: n/a
(314) 427-3400
(800) 426-7866

HAMPTON INN SOUTHWEST
9 Lambert Drury
Place (63088)
Rates: n/a
(636) 529-9020
(800) 426-7866

HAMPTON INN UNION STATION
2211 Market St
(63103)
Rates: $95-$120
(314) 241-3200
(800) 426-7866

HOLIDAY INN-AIRPORT
4545 N Lindbergh
Blvd (63044)
Rates: n/a
(314) 731-2100
(800) 465-4329

HOLIDAY INN-FOREST PARK
5915 Wilson Ave
(63110)
Rates: $79-$125
(314) 645-0700
(800) 465-4329

HOLIDAY INN SELECT
811 N 9th St
(63101)
Rates: $69-$109
(314) 421-4000
(800) 465-4329

HOLIDAY INN SOUTH
4234 Butler Hill
Rd (63129)
Rates: $99-$145
(314) 894-0700
(800) 465-4329

HOLIDAY INN SOUTHWEST
10709 Watson Rd
(63127)
Rates: n/a
(314) 821-6600
(800) 465-4329

MOTEL 6 AIRPORT
4576 Woodson
Rd (63134)
Rates: $39-$54
(314) 427-1313
(800) 466-8356

MOTEL 6-NORTH
1405 Dunn Rd
(63138)
Rates: $35-$50
(314) 869-9400
(800) 466-8356

MOTEL 6-SOUTH
6500 S Lindbergh
Blvd (63123)
Rates: $44-$56
(314) 892-3664
(800) 466-8356

OMNI MAJESTIC HOTEL
1019 Pine St
(63101)
Rates: $154-$204
(314) 436-2355
(800) 843-6664

RED ROOF INN-HAMPTON
5823 Wilson Ave
(63110)
Rates: $76-$108
(314) 645-0101
(800) 843-7663

RENAISSANCE GRAND HOTEL
800 Washington
Ave (63101)
Rates: $169-$219
(314) 621-9600
(800) 468-3571

RENAISSANCE ST. LOUIS SUITES HOTEL
827 Washington
Ave (63101)
Rates: $189-$229
(314) 621-9700
(800) 468-3571

SHERATON ST. LOUIS CITY CENTER HOTEL & SUITES
400 S 14th St
(63103)
Rates: $299-$439
(314) 231-5007
(800) 325-3535

STAYBRIDGE SUITES
1855 Craigshire
Rd (63146)
Rates: n/a
(314) 878-1555
(800) 238-8000

THE WESTIN ST. LOUIS
811 Spruce St
(63102)
Rates: $334
(314) 621-2000
(800) 228-3000

ST. PETERS

DRURY INN
170 Westfield Dr
(63376)
Rates: $72-$127
(636) 397-9700
(800) 378-7946

ST. ROBERT

BEST WESTERN MONTIS INN
14086 Hwy Z
(65584)
Rates: $49-$79
(573) 336-4299
(800) 528-1234

DAYS INN
14125 Hwy Z
(65584)
Rates: $36-$76
(573) 336-5556
(800) 329-7466

AREA CODES - If the local number doesn't connect, check for a new area code.

ECONO LODGE
309 Hwy Z
(65584)
Rates: $45-$79
(573) 336-7272
(800) 424-6423

MOTEL 6
545 Hwy Z
(65584)
Rates: $49-$56
(573) 336-3610
(800) 466-8356

STE. GENEVIEVE
FAMILY BUDGET INNS
17030 New Bremen (63670)
Rates: $41-$54
(573) 543-2272

SEDALIA
BEST WESTERN STATE FAIR MOTOR INN
3210 S 65 Hwy (65301)
Rates: $59-$99
(660) 826-6100
(800) 528-1234

HOTEL BOTHWELL, A CLARION COLLECTION
103 E 4th St (65301)
Rates: $60-$185
(660) 826-5588
(800) 252-7466

RAMADA INN
3501 W Broadway (65301)
Rates: n/a
(660) 826-8400
(800) 272-6232

SHELL KNOB
BASS HAVEN FAMILY RESORT
HCR 1, Box 4480E (65747)
Rates: $35-$48
(417) 858-6401

SIKESTON
BEST WESTERN COACH HOUSE INN & SUITES
220 S Interstate Dr (63801)
Rates: $55-$150
(573) 471-9700
(800) 528-1234
(877) 471-9700

DAYS INN
1330 S Main St (63801)
Rates: $50-$77
(573) 471-3930
(800) 328-7466

SPRINGFIELD
BAYMONT INN & SUITES
3776 S Glenstone Ave (65803)
Rates: $71-$125
(417) 889-8188
(800) 799-5677

BEST WESTERN COACH HOUSE INN
2535 N Glenstone Ave (65803)
Rates: $44-$149
(417) 862-0701
(800) 528-1234
(800) 287-1476

BEST WESTERN ROUTE 66 RAIL HAVEN
203 S Glenstone Ave (65802)
Rates: $39-$139
(417) 866-1963
(800) 528-1234
(800) 304-0021

CLARION HOTEL
3333 S Glenstone Ave (65804)
Rates: $69-$85
(417) 883-6550
(800) 424-6423
(800) 756-7318

COMFORT SUITES
1260 E Independence St (65804)
Rates: $59-$120
(417) 886-5090
(800) 424-6423

DAYS INN
621 W Sunshine (65807)
Rates: $49-$190
(417) 862-0153
(800) 329-7466

DAYS INN
3260 E Montclair St (65804)
Rates: $39-$99
(417) 882-9484
(800) 329-7466

DRURY INN & SUITES
2715 N Glenstone Ave (65803)
Rates: $70-$102
(417) 863-8400
(800) 378-7946

ECONO LODGE
3404 E Ridgeview (65804)
Rates: $49-$125
(417) 882-2220
(800) 424-6423

HOLIDAY INN NORTH
2720 N Glenstone (65803)
Rates: $93-$126
(417) 865-8600
(800) 465-4329

KRYSTAL AIRE A NON-SMOKING HOTEL
2745 N Glenstone Ave (65803)
Rates: $64-$96
(417) 869-0001
(877) 703-5187

LAMPLIGHTER INN NORTH
2820 N Glenstone AVe (65803)
Rates: $54-$81
(417) 869-3900
(800) 707-0326

LA QUINTA INN
1610 E Evergreen (65803)
Rates: $59-$85
(417) 520-8800
(800) 687-6667

MERIGOLD INN
2006 S Glenstone Ave (65804)
Rates: $38-$68
(417) 881-2833

MOTEL 6-NORTH
3114 N Kentwood (65803)
Rates: $29-$40
(417) 833-0880
(800) 466-8356

QUALITY INN & SUITES
3370 E Battlefield (65804)
Rates: $54-$149
(417) 520-6200
(800) 424-6423

RED ROOF INN
2655 N Glenstone Ave (65803)
Rates: $36-$61
(417) 831-2100
(800) 843-7663

RESIDENCE INN BY MARRIOTT
1303 E Kinglsey St (65804)
Rates: $69-$179
(417) 890-0020
(800) 331-3131

SHERATON HAWTHORN PARK
2431 N Glenstone Ave (65803)
Rates: $79-$99
(417) 831-3131
(800) 325-3535

SLEEP INN
233 E Camino Alto (65810)
Rates: $56-$109
(417) 886-2464
(800) 424-6423

UNIVERSITY PLAZA HOTEL
333 John Q Hammons Pkwy (65806)
Rates: $89-$149
(417) 864-7333

SULLIVAN
ECONO LODGE
307 N Service Rd (63080)
Rates: $35-$70
(573) 468-3136
(800) 424-6423
(800) 361-4185

SUNSET HILLS
HOLIDAY INN-SOUTHWEST
10709 Watson Rd (63127)
Rates: $84-$104
(314) 821-6600
(800) 465-4329

SWEET SPRINGS
PEOPLE'S CHOICE MOTEL
1001 N Locust St (65351)
Rates: $29-$37
(660) 335-6315

SUPER 8 MOTEL
208 W 40 Hwy (65351)
Rates: $50-$70
(660) 335-4888
(800) 800-8000

THEODOSIA
THEODOSIA MARINA-RESORT
HR 5, Box 5020 (65761)
Rates: $32-$50
(417) 273-4444

TIPTON
TWIN PINE MOTEL
442 Hwy 50 W (65081)
Rates: $40-$55
(660) 433-5525

TOWN AND COUNTRY
MARRIOTT WEST
660 Maryville Centre Dr (63141)
Rates: $99-$209
(314) 878-2747
(800) 228-9290

TRENTON
SUPER 8 MOTEL
1845A E 28th St (64683)
Rates: $49-$75
(660) 359-2988
(800) 800-8000

VALLEY PARK
DRURY INN
5 Lambert Drury Pl (63088)
Rates: $75-$130
(636) 861-8300
(800) 378-7946

AREA CODES - If the local number doesn't connect, check for a new area code.

HAMPTON INN
9 Lambert Drury
Pl (63088)
Rates: $92-$112
(636) 529-9020
(800) 426-7866

VILLAGE RIDGE

**BEST WESTERN
DIAMOND INN**
2875 Hwy 100 E
(63089)
Rates: $69-$99
(636) 742-3501
(800) 528-1234
(800) 782-8487

WAPPAPELLO

**MILLERS MOTOR
LODGE**
8920 Hwy T
(63966)
Rates: $48-$89
(573) 222-8579

WARRENSBURG

DAYS INN
204 E Cleveland
(64093)
Rates: $45-$75
(660) 429-2400
(800) 329-7466

UNIVERISTY INN
403 E Russell Ave
(64093)
Rates: $49-$79
(660) 747-5125

WARSAW

SUPER 8 MOTEL
1603 Commercial
St (65355)
Rates: $51-$94
(660) 438-2882
(800) 800-8000

WASHINGTON

SUPER 8 MOTEL
2081 Eckelkamp
Ct (63090)
Rates: $70-$100
(636) 390-0088
(800) 800-8000

WAYNESVILLE

**THE HOME PLACE
BED & BREAKFST**
302 S Benton
(65583)
Rates: $45-$55
(573) 774-6637
(800) 438-3778

WENTZVILLE

ECONO LODGE
1400 Continental
Dr (63385)
Rates: $46-$90
(636) 327-5515
(800) 424-6423

HOLIDAY INN
900 Corporate
Pkwy (63385)
Rates: $96-$129
(636) 327-7001
(800) 465-4329

WEST PLAINS

**BEST WESTERN
GRAND VILLA**
220 Jan Howard
Expwy (65775)
Rates: $56-$77
(417) 257-2711
(800) 528-1234
(800) 391-3977

RAMADA INN
1301 Preacher Roe
Blvd (65775)
Rates: $50-$59
(417) 256-8191
(800) 272-6232

SUPER 8 MOTEL
1210 Porter
Wagoner Blvd
(65775)
Rates: $42-$75
(417) 256-8088
(800) 800-8000

AREA CODES - If the local number doesn't connect, check for a new area code.

MONTANA

ABSAROKEE

STILLWATER LODGE
28 Woodard Ave (59001)
Rates: $40-$60
(406) 328-4899

ALBERTON

RIVER EDGE RESORT
Box 501 (59820)
Rates: $50-$75
(406) 722-3375

ANACONDA

BROWN DERBY
13902 Hwy 1 (59711)
Rates: $50-$75
(406) 563-5788

CELTIC HOUSE INN
23 Main St (59711)
Rates: $30-$50
(406) 563-9471
(800) 866-2593

THE LODGE AT SKYHAVEN
1711 Hwy 48 (59711)
Rates: $30-$50
(406) 563-8342
(800) 563-8089

AUGUSTA

BUNKHOUSE INN
122 Main St (59410)
Rates: $50-$75
(406) 562-3387
(800) 553-4016

BABB

(Also see Glacier National Park)

THRONSON'S MOTEL
US 89, Box 169 (59411)
Rates: $50-$75
(406) 732-5530

BAKER

ROY'S MOTEL
327 W Montana Ave (59313)
Rates: $50-$75
(406) 778-3321
(800) 552-3321

SAGEBRUSH INN
518 US 12 W (59313)
Rates: $50-$75
(406) 778-3341
(800) 638-3708

BASIN

MERRY WIDOW HEALTH MINE
308 E 8th Ave (59631)
Rates: $30-$40
(406) 225-3220
(877) 225-3220

BELGRADE

GALLATIN RIVER LODGE
9105 Thorpe Rd (59718)
Rates: $150-$270
(406) 388-0148

HOLIDAY INN EXP
6261 Jackrabbit Ln (59714)
Rates: $85-$105
(406) 388-0800
(800) 465-4329

LA QUINTA
6445 Jackrabbit Ln (59714)
Rates: $59-$149
(406) 388-2222
(800) 687-6667

SUPER 8 MOTEL
6450 Jackrabbit Ln (59714)
Rates: $53-$104
(406) 388-1493
(800) 800-8000

BIG SANDY

Q'S MOTEL
98 Hwy 236 (59520)
Rates: $30-$40
(406) 378-2389

BIG SKY

BEST WESTERN BUCK'S T-4 LODGE
Hwy 191 (59716)
Rates: $69-$164
(406) 995-4111
(800) 528-1234
(800) 822-4484

COMFORT INN
47214 Gallatin Rd (59716)
Rates: $95-$129
(406) 995-2333
(800) 424-6423

THE HUD CABIN VACATION RENTAL
13730 Portnell Rd (Bozeman 59718)
Rates: $225/Night
Rates: $1575/Wk
(406) 763-5215

320 GUEST RANCH
205 Buffalo Horn Creek Rd (59730)
Rates: $87-$338
(406) 995-4283

BIG TIMBER

BIG TIMBER BUDGET HOST
600 W 2nd St (59011)
Rates: $58-$78
(406) 932-4943

BIG TIMBER INN B&B
Yellowstone River Ln, Box 328 (59011)
Rates: $40-$60
(406) 932-4080

LAZY J MOTEL
Hwy 10 (59011)
Rates: $50-$75
(406) 932-5533

RIPPLING WATERS GUEST HOUSE
P O. Box 1042, Hwy 298 (59011)
Rates: n/a
(406) 932-4718

SUPER 8 MOTEL
20A Big Timber Loop Rd (59011)
Rates: $49-$94
(406) 932-8888
(800) 800-8000

BIGFORK

BAYVIEW RESORT & MARINA
543 Yenne Point Rd (59911)
Rates: $60-$80
(406) 837-4843
(800) 775-3536

HOLIDAY RESORT
17001 E Shore Rd (59911)
Rates: $60-$80
(406) 982-3710
(800) 421-9141

MCCABE'S MOUNTAIN INN
455 Grand Ave (59911)
Rates: $90+
(406) 837-1447

MOUNTAIN LAKE LODGE
1950 Sylvan Dr (59911)
Rates: $85-$265
(406) 837-3800
(877) 823-4923

TIMBERS MOTEL
8540 Hwy 35 (59911)
Rates: $52-$138
(406) 837-6200
(800) 821-4546

WOODS BAY RESORT
26481 E Shore Rt (59911)
Rates: $75-$90
(406) 837-3333

BILLINGS

BEST WESTERN
5610 S Frontage Rd (59101)
Rates: $68-$108
(406) 248-9800
(800) 528-1234

BEST WESTERN PONDEROSA INN
2511 1st Ave N (59101)
Rates: $55-$80
(406) 259-5511
(800) 528-1234
(800) 628-9081

BILLINGS HOTEL
1223 Mullowney Ln (59101)
Rates: $89-$109
(406) 248-7151
(800) 537-7286

CHERRY TREE INN
823 N Broadway (59101)
Rates: $50-$75
(406) 252-5603
(800) 237-5882

COMFORT INN
2030 Overland Ave (59102)
Rates: $55-$100
(406) 652-5200
(800) 424-6423

DAYS INN
843 Parkway Ln (59101)
Rates: $56-$130
(406) 252-4007
(800) 329-7466

DUDE RANCHER LODGE
415 N 29th St (59101)
Rates: $50-$75
(406) 259-5561
(800) 221-3302

HEIGHTS INN MOTEL
1206 Main St (59101)
Rates: $50-$75
(406) 252-8451
(800) 275-8451

HILLTOP INN
1116 N 28th St (59101)
Rates: $58-$72
(406) 245-5000
(800) 878-9282

HISTORIC NORHTERN HOTEL
19 N Broadway (59101)
Rates: $109-$139
(406) 245-5121
(800) 542-5121

HOLIDAY INN GRAND MONTANA
5500 Midland Rd (59101)
Rates: $85-$99
(406) 248-7701
(800) 465-4329

HOWARD JOHNSON EXPRESS INN
101 S 27th St (59101)
Rates: $69-$99
(406) 248-4656
(800) 446-4656

JUNIPER MOTEL
1315 N 27th St (59101)
Rates: $41-$43
(406) 245-4128
(800) 826-7530

KELLY INN
5425 Midland Rd (59101)
Rates: $52-$99
(406) 252-2700
(800) 635-3559

LAZY KT MOTEL
1403 1st Ave N (59101)
Rates: $40
(406) 252-6606
(800) 290-2681

MOTEL 6 SOUTH
5400 Midland Rd, RR 9 (59101)
Rates: $31-$63
(406) 252-0093
(800) 466-8356

QUALITY INN HOMESTEAD
2036 Overland Ave (59102)
Rates: $64-$99
(406) 652-1320
(800) 424-6423

RAMADA LIMITED
1345 Mullowney Ln, Ex 446 (59101)
Rates: $60-$80
(406) 252-2584
(800) 272-6232

RED ROOF INN
5353 Midland Rd (59101)
Rates: $41-$68
(406) 248-7551
(800) 843-7663

RIMROCK INN
1203 North 27th St (59101)
Rates: $40-$60
(406) 252-7107
(800) 624-9770

RIMVIEW INN
1025 N 27th St (59101)
Rates: $50-$72
(406) 248-2622
(800) 551-1418

RIVERSTONE BILLINGS INN
880 N 29th St (59101)
Rates: $58-$72
(406) 252-6800
(800) 231-7782

SHERATON BILLINGS HOTEL
27 N 27th St (59101)
Rates: $115-$135
(406) 252-7400
(800) 588-7666

SUPER 8 MOTEL
5400 Southgate Dr (59102)
Rates: $42-$67
(406) 248-8842
(800) 800-8000

TWIN CUBS MOTEL
1818 Main St (59101)
Rates: $40-$60
(406) 252-9851

WAR BONNET INN
2612 Belknap Ave (59101)
Rates: $40-$60
(406) 248-7761
(888) 242-6023

WESTERN EXECUTIVE INN
3121 King Ave W (59102)
Rates: $75-$100
(406) 294-8888

BOULDER

CASTORIA MOTEL
211 S Monroe (59632)
Rates: $30-$40
(406) 225-3549

O-Z MOTEL
114 N Main St (59632)
Rates: $30-$50
(406) 225-3364

BOZEMAN

AMERICINN LODGE & SUITES
1121 Reeves Rd W (59718)
Rates: $89-$169
(406) 522-8686
(800) 634-3444

BEST VALUE INN
817 Wheat Dr (59715)
Rates: $39-$84
(406) 585-7888

BEST WESTERN GREENTREE INN
1325 N 7th Ave (58715)
Rates: $89-$149
(406) 587-5261
(800) 528-1234
(800) 624-5865

BLUE SKY MOTEL
1010 E Main (59715)
Rates: $50-$75
(406) 587-2311
(800) 845-9032

BOBCAT LODGE
2307 W Main (59715)
Rates: $40-$60
(406) 587-5241
(888) 587-5241

BOZEMAN INN
1235 N 7th Ave (59715)
Rates: $57-$79
(406) 587-3176
(800) 648-7515

BRIDGER MTNS HIGHLAND HOUSE B&B
1540 Nelson Rd (59715)
Rates: $82-$90
(406) 587-0904

COMFORT INN
1370 N 7th Ave (59715)
Rates: $59-$124
(406) 587-2322
(800) 424-6423

DAYS INN
1321 N 7th Ave (59715)
Rates: $49-$149
(406) 587-5251
(800) 329-7466

DOWNTOWN IMPERIAL INN
122 W Main St (59715)
Rates: $40-$60
(406) 586-3354
(800) 880-2383

HOLIDAY INN
5 Baxter Ln (59715)
Rates: $89-$129
(406) 587-4561
(800) 465-4329

THE HUD CABIN/ LOG HOME RENTAL
13730 Portnell Rd (59718)
Rates: n/a
(406) 763-5215

MICROTEL INN & SUITES
612 Nikles Dr (59715)
Rates: $49-$89
(406) 586-3797
(800) 597-3797

RAINBOW MOTEL
510 N 7th Ave (59715)
Rates: $40-$75
(406) 587-4201

RAMADA LIMITED
2020 Wheat Dr (59715)
Rates: $52-$119
(406) 585-2626
(800) 272-6232

RANCH HOUSE MOTEL
1201 E Main St (59715)
Rates: $30-$50
(406) 587-4278

ROYAL "7" BUDGET INN
310 N 7th Ave (59715)
Rates: $45-$66
(406) 587-3103
(800) 587-3103

SUPER 8 MOTEL
800 Wheat Dr (59715)
Rates: $55-$75
(406) 586-1521
(800) 800-8000

TLC INN
805 Wheat Dr (59715)
Rates: $60-$69
(406) 587-2100
(877) 466-7852

WESTERN HERITAGE INN
1200 E Main St (59715)
Rates: $49-$98
(406) 586-8534
(800) 877-1094

BROADUS

BROADUS MOTEL
101 N Park (59317)
Rates: $40-$60
(406) 436-2626

BROWNING

WESTERN MOTEL
121 Central Ave E (59417)
Rates: $45-$98
(406) 338-7572

BUTTE

BEST WESTERN BUTTE PLAZA INN
2900 Harrison Ave (59701)
Rates: $72-$112
(406) 494-3500
(800) 528-1234
(800) 543-5814

COMFORT INN
2777 Harrison Ave (59701)
Rates: $60-$95
(406) 494-8850
(800) 424-6423

AREA CODES - If the local number doesn't connect, check for a new area code.

COPPER KING LODGE & CONV CENTER
4655 Harrison Ave S (59701)
Rates: $55-$109
(406) 494-6666

MOTEL 6
122005 Nissler Rd (59701)
Rates: $39-$54
(406) 782-5678
(800) 466-8356

RAMADA INN COPPER KING
4655 Harrison Ave (59701)
Rates: $89-$109
(406) 494-6666
(800) 332-8600

RED LION HOTEL
2100 Cornell Ave (59701)
Rates: $69-$109
(406) 494-7800
(800) 733-5466
(800) 443-1806

ROCKER INN
122001 W Brown's Gulch Rd (59701)
Rates: $38-$57
(406) 723-5464
(800) 828-5399

SUPER 8 MOTEL
2929 Harrison Ave (59701)
Rates: $49-$92
(406) 494-6000
(800) 800-8000

CAMERON
MADISON RIVER CABINS & RV
1403 Hwy 287 N (59720)
Rates: $50-$75
(406) 682-4890

CASCADE
BADGER MOTEL
132 1st St N (59421)
Rates: $40-$60
(406) 468-9330

RUSSELL'S INN
2468 Old US 91 (59421)
Rates: $70-$90
(406) 468-2855

CHESTER
WHEATSHEAF MOTEL
10 Washington Ave (59522)
Rates: $30-$50
(406) 759-5300

CHINOOK
CHINOOK HOTEL
62 3rd St (59523)
Rates: $30-$40
(406) 357-2231

CHINOOK MOTOR INN
100 Indiana Ave (59523)
Rates: $55-$75
(406) 357-2248

CHOTEAU
BIG SKY MOTEL
209 S Main Ave (59422)
Rates: $38-$60
(406) 466-5318

STAGE STOP INN
1005 N Main Ave (59422)
Rates: $67-$110
(406) 466-5900
(888) 466-5900

CIRCLE
TRAVELERS INN
Hwy 200, Box 78 (59215)
Rates: $30-$50
(406) 485-3323

CLINTON
ROCK CREEK FISHERMAN'S MERC & MOTEL
73 Rock Creek Rd (59825)
Rates: $50-$75
(406) 825-6440

COLSTRIP
FORT UNION INN
73 Dogwood (59323)
Rates: $50-$75
(406) 748-2553
(800) 738-2553

SUPER 8 MOTEL
6227 Main St (59323)
Rates: $55-$70
(406) 748-3400
(800) 800-8000

COLUMBIA FALLS
MEADOW LAKE RESORT
100 St. Andrews Dr (59912)
Rates: $95-$565
(406) 892-8700
(800) 321-GOLF

OL' RIVER BRIDGE INN
7355 Hwy 2 E (59912)
Rates: $50-$75
(406) 892-2181

WESTERN INNS GLACIER MOUNTAIN SHADOWS RESORT
7285 Hwy 2 E (59912)
Rates: $60-$80
(406) 892-7686

COLUMBUS
GLACIER INN MOTEL
1401 2nd Ave E (59912)
Rates: $40-$60
(406) 892-4341

GLACIER MT SHADOWS RESORT
US 2 E & Hwy 206 (59912)
Rates: $40-$60
(406) 892-7686
(800) 766-1137

SUPER 8 MOTEL
602 8th Ave N (59019)
Rates: $50-$75
(406) 322-4101
(800) 800-8000

CONDON
SWAN VALLEY SUPER 8 MOTEL
Hwy 83, Box 1278 (59826)
Rates: $52-$62
(406) 754-2688
(800) 800-8000

CONRAD
CONRAD MOTEL
210 N Main (59425)
Rates: $30-$40
(406) 278-7544

SUPER 8 MOTEL
215 N Main St (59425)
Rates: $50-$75
(406) 278-7676
(800) 800-8000

COOKE CITY
BIG MOOSE RESORT
715 Hwy 212 (59020)
Rates: $50-$75
(406) 838-2393

ELKHORN LODGE
108 Main St (59020)
Rates: $50-$70
(406) 838-2332

HIGH COUNTRY MOTEL
US 212, P. O. Box 1146 (59020)
Rates: $50-$75
(406) 838-2272

CORAM
EVERGREEN MOTEL
US Hwy 2 (59913)
Rates: $60-$80
(406) 387-5365

CULBERTSON
DIAMOND WILLOW INN
104 6th St E (59218)
Rates: $30-$40
(406) 787-6218

CUSTER
D & L MOTEL/CAFE
3rd St, Box 105 (59024)
Rates: $30-$40
(406) 856-4128

CUT BANK
CORNER MOTEL
1201 E Main St (59427)
Rates: $30-$40
(406) 873-5588
(800) 851-5541

GLACIER GATEWAY INN
1121 E Railroad St (59427)
Rates: $46-$74
(406) 873-5544
(800) 851-5541

GLACIER GATEWAY PLAZA
1130 E Main St (59427)
Rates: $59-$84
(406) 873-2566

TERRACE MOTEL
11 9th Ave SE (59427)
Rates: $30-$40
(406) 873-5031

DARBY
ALTA RANCH
9203 West Fork Rd (59829)
Rates: $85-$210
(106) 349-7142
(888) 349-2142

BUD & SHIRLEY'S MOTEL
Main St (59829)
Rates: $40-$60
(406) 821-3401

EL CAPITAN VILLAS
3300 Old Darby Rd (59829)
Rates: $40-$60
(406) 821-3111

HONEY'S MOTEL
3237 US 93 (59829)
Rates: $40-$60
(406) 821-3111

WILDERNESS MOTEL & BUNKHOUSE
308 S Main St (59829)
Rates: $50-$75
(406) 821-3405
(800) 820-2554

DE BORGIA
HOTEL ALBERT B&B
#2 Yellowstone Tr (59830)
Rates: $54-$70
(406) 678-4303

DEER LODGE
COLEMAN FEE MANSION B&B
500 Missouri Ave (59722)
Rates: $65-$150
(406) 846-2922

AREA CODES - If the local number doesn't connect, check for a new area code.

DOWNTOWNER MOTEL
500 4th St (59722)
Rates: $50-$75
(406) 846-1021

SCHARF'S MOTOR INN
819 Main St (59722)
Rates: $50-$75
(406) 846-2810

SUPER 8 MOTEL
1150 N Main St (59722)
Rates: $56-$90
(406) 846-2370
(800) 800-8000

WESTERN BIG SKY INN
210 N Main St (59722)
Rates: $36-$56
(406) 846-2590

DENTON
HOLM MOTEL
106 3rd N (59430)
Rates: $30-$40
(406) 567-2286

DILLON
BEST WESTERN PARADISE INN
650 N Montana St (59725)
Rates: $51-$79
(406) 683-4214
(800) 528-1234

COMFORT INN
450 N Interchange (59725)
Rates: $55-$90
(406) 683-6831
(800) 424-6423

CRESTON MOTEL
335 S Atlantic (59725)
Rates: $30-$50
(406) 683-2341

DILLON BEAVER-HEAD INN
20 Swensen Way (59725)
Rates: $48-$79
(406) 683-6600

GUESTHOUSE INNS & SUITES
580 Sinclair (59725)
Rates: $59-$90
(406) 683-3636
(800) 214-8378

SACAJAWEA MOTEL
775 N Montana St (59725)
Rates: $30-$40
(406) 683-2381

SUNDOWNER MOTEL
500 N Montana St (59725)
Rates: $35-$43
(406) 683-2375
(800) 524-9746

SUPER 8 MOTEL
550 N Montana St (59725)
Rates: $47-$57
(406) 683-4288
(800) 800-8000

DRUMMOND
SKY MOTEL
Front & Broadway (59832)
Rates: $30-$40
(406) 288-3206
(800) 559-3206

WAGON WHEEL CAFE & MOTEL
316 E Front (59832)
Rates: $30-$40
(406) 288-3201

EAST GLACIER PARK
(Also see Glacier National Park)
BISON CREEK RANCH
20722 Hwy 2 W (59434)
Rates: $50-$75
(406) 226-4482
(888) 226-4482

DANCING BEARS INN
40 Montana St (59434)
Rates: $45-$146
(406) 226-4402

EAST GLACIER MOTEL/CABINS
1107 Hwy 49 (59343)
Rates: $50-$75
(406) 226-5593

GLACIER PARK CIRCLE R
402 Hwy 2 E (59343)
Rates: $40-$60
(406) 226-9331

WHISTLING SWAN MOTEL
512 Hwy 2 W (59343)
Rates: $50-$75
(406) 226-4412

ELLISTON
LAST CHANCE MOTEL
26 Hwy 12 S (59728)
Rates: $30-$40
(406) 492-7250

ENNIS
EL WESTERN CABINS & LODGES
4787 Hwy 287 N (59729)
Rates: $75-$185
(406) 682-4127
(800) 831-2773

FAN MTN INN
204 N Main (59729)
Rates: $40-$75
(406) 682-5200
(877) 682-5200

RIVERSIDE MOTEL & OUTFITTERS
346 Main St (59729)
Rates: $75-$90
(406) 682-4240
(800) 535-4139

SILVERTIP LODGE
301 Main St (59729)
Rates: $50-$75
(406) 682-4384

SPORTSMAN'S LODGE
310 US 287 N (59729)
Rates: $40-$100
(406) 682-4242
(800) 220-1690

ESSEX
(Also see Glacier National Park)
THE HALF-WAY MOTEL
Hwy 2, Box 632 (59916)
Rates: $30-$50
(406) 888-5650

MIDDLE FORK RIVER INN
14305 Hwy 2 W (59916)
Rates: $30-$50
(406) 888-5720

EUREKA
CREEK SIDE MOTEL & RV
1333 Hwy 93 N (59917)
Rates: $50-$75
(406) 297-2361

KSANKA MOTOR INN
US 93 & Hwy 37 (59917)
Rates: $40-$60
(406) 297-3127

FAIRVIEW
KORNER MOTEL
217 W 9th (59221)
Rates: $30-$50
(406) 742-5259

FORSYTH
BEST WESTERN SUNDOWNER INN
1018 Front St (59327)
Rates: $64-$759(406) 356-2115
(800) 528-1234
(877) 356-2115

RAILS INN MOTEL
3rd & Front Sts (59327)
Rates: $57-$67
(406) 356-2242
(800) 621-3754

RESTWEL MOTEL
810 Front St (59327)
Rates: $42-$60
(406) 356-2771
(800) 548-3442

WESTWIND MOTOR INN
226 Westwind Lane (59327)
Rates: $55-$65
(406) 356-2038
(888) 356-2038

FORT BENTON
FORT MOTEL
1809 St Charles (59442)
Rates: $40-$60
(406) 622-3312

PIONEER LODGE
1700 Front St (59442)
Rates: $50-$70
(406) 622-5441
(800) 622-6088

FORT PECK
LAKERIDGE MOTEL & TACKLE
HCR 1660 (59223)
Rates: $70-$90
(406) 526-3597
(888) 5548125

GALATA
GALATA MOTEL & RV OVERNITE
Box 31 (59444)
Rates: $30-$40
(406) 432-2352

GALLATIN GATEWAY
CASTLE ROCK INN
65840 Gallatin Gateway (59730)
Rates: n/a
(406) 763-4243

GALLATIN GATEWAY INN
76405 Gallitan Rd, Hwy 191 (59730)
Rates: $90+
(406) 763-4672
(800) 676-3522

MILLERS OF MONTANA B&B
US 191 (59730)
Rates: $50-$75
(406) 763-4102

GARDINER

ABSAROKA LODGE
Box 10, US 89 (59030)
Rates: $70-$90
(406) 848-7414
(800) 755-7414

BEST WESTERN MAMMOTH HOT SPRINGS
Box 646, Hwy 89 S (59030)
Rates: $49-$119
(406) 848-7311
(800) 528-1234
(800) 828-9080

RIVERSIDE COTTAGES
521 Scott St W (59030)
Rates: $75-$90
(406) 848-7719
(877) 774-2836

SUPER 8 MOTEL
Hwy 89 S (59030)
Rates: $39-$99
(406) 848-7401
(800) 800-8000

WESTERNAIRE MOTEL
Hwy 89 S (59030)
Rates: $70-$90
(406) 848-7397
(888) 273-0358

YELLOWSTONE RIVER MOTEL
14 E Park St (59030)
Rates: $45-$85
(406) 848-7303
(888) 797-4837

GLACIER NATIONAL PARK

Also see the following cities for lodging adjacent to the park:
Babb
East Glacier
Essex
St. Mary

GLASGOW

CAMPBELL LODGE
534 3rd Ave S (59230)
Rates: $35-$50
(406) 228-9328

COTTONWOOD INN
45 1st Ave NE (59230)
Rates: $50-$75
(406) 228-8213
(800) 321-8213

KOSKI'S MOTEL
320 US 2 E (59230)
Rates: $30-$40
(406) 228-8282
(888) 238-8282

LACASA MOTEL
238 1st Ave N (59230)
Rates: $30-$40
(406) 228-9311
(877) 228-9311

STAR LODGE MOTEL
903 6th Ave N (59230)
Rates: $30-$40
(406) 228-2494

GLENDIVE

BEST WESTERN JORDAN INN
223 N Merrill Ave (59330)
Rates: $65-$106
(223) 377-5555
(800) 528-1234
(800) 528-1234
(888) 453-6348

BUDGET HOST RIVERSIDE INN
44 Hwy 16 (59330)
Rates: $30-$50
(406) 377-3429
(800) 283-4678

BUDGET MOTEL
1610 N Merrill Ave (59330)
Rates: $30-$50
(406) 377-8334

DAYS INN
2000 N Merrill Ave (59330)
Rates: $32-$74
(406) 365-6011
(800) 329-7466

EL CENTRO MOTEL
112 S Kendrick Ave (59330)
Rates: $25-$35
(406) 365-5211

KINGS INN
1903 N Merrill Ave (59330)
Rates: $30-$40
(406) 365-5636

PARKWOOD MOTEL
1002 W Bell (59330)
Rates: $30-$45
(406) 365-8221

SUPER 8 MOTEL
1904 N Merrill Ave (59330)
Rates: $43-$66
(406) 365-5671
(800) 800-8000

GRASS RANGE

GRASS RANGE MOTEL
570 US 87 S (59032)
Rates: $30-$40
(406) 428-2242

GREAT FALLS

AIRWAY MOTEL
1800 14th St SW (59401)
Rates: $30-$40
(406) 761-8915

ALBERTA MOTEL
1101 Central Ave W (59401)
Rates: $30-$50
(406) 452-3467
(866) 861-1101

BEST WESTERN HERITAGE INN
1700 Fox Farm Rd (59404)
Rates: $79-$119
(406) 761-1900
(800) 528-1234
(800) 548-8256

COMFORT INN
1120 9th St S (59401)
Rates: $75-$100
(406) 454-2727
(800) 424-6423

CRESTVIEW INN
500 13th Ave S (59401)
Rates: $40-$60
(406) 727-8380
(800) 727-8380

DAYS INN
101 14th Ave NW (59404)
Rates: $57-$90
(406) 727-6565
(800) 466-8356

EVERGREEN MOTEL
2531 Vaughn Rd (59401)
Rates: $30-$50
(406) 452-0312

GREAT FALLS INN
1400 28th St S (59405)
Rates: $62-$69
(406) 453-6000
(800) 454-6010

HAMPTON INN
2301 14th St SW (59404)
Rates: $79-$149
(406) 453-2675
(800) 426-7866

HOLIDAY INN
400 10th Ave S (59405)
Rates: $65-$85
(406) 727-7200
(800) 465-4329

HOWARD JOHNSON INN
220 Central Ave (59401)
Rates: $50-$90
(406) 761-3410
(800) 446-4656
(800) 266-3410

IMPERIAL INN
601 2nd Ave N (59401)
Rates: $50-$75
(406) 452-9581
(800) 735-7173
(800) 676-6267

LA QUINTA INN & SUITES
600 River Dr S (59405)
Rates: $79-$99
(406) 761-2600
(800) 687-6668

MID-TOWN MOTEL
526 2nd Ave N (59401)
Rates: $40-$60
(406) 453-2411
(800) 457-2411

MOTEL CENTRAL
715 Central Ave W (59404)
Rates: $50-$70
(406) 453-0161
(800) 794-7433

MOTEL 6
2 Treasure State Dr (59404)
Rates: $46-$65
(406) 453-1602
(800) 466-8356

PLAZA INN
1224 10th Ave S (59405)
Rates: $40-$55
(406) 452-9594
(800) 794-7433

ROYAL MOTEL
1300 Central Ave (59401)
Rates: $30-$40
(406) 452-9548
(800) 794-7433

SKI'S WESTERN MOTEL
2420 10th Ave S (59405)
Rates: $40-$55
(406) 453-3281
(800) 794-7433

SUPER 8 MOTEL
1214 13th St S (59405)
Rates: $44-$55
(406) 727-7600
(800) 800-8000

TOWN & COUNTRY MOTEL
2418 10th Ave S (59405)
Rates: $30-$40
(406) 452-5643

TOWNHOUSE INN
1411 10th St S (59405)
Rates: $80
(406) 761-4600
(800) 442-4667

WAGON WHEEL MOTEL
2620 10th Ave S (59401)
Rates: $40-$60
(406) 761-1300
(800) 800-6483

GREENOUGH

LORAN'S CLEARWATER INN
Hwy 200 & 83,
Box 20 (59836)
Rates: $30-$40
(406) 244-9535

HAMILTON

BITTERROOT MOTEL
408 S 1st St
(59840)
Rates: $30-$40
(406) 363-1142

CITY CENTER MOTEL
W 415 Main
(59840)
Rates: $40-$60
(406) 363-1652

COMFORT INN
1113 N 1st St
(59840)
Rates: $55-$90
(406) 363-6600
(800) 424-6423

DEER CROSSING B&B
396 Hayes Creek
Rd (59840)
Rates: $45-$95
(406) 363-2232
(800) 763-2232

DEFFY'S MOTEL
321 S 1st St
(59840)
Rates: $50-$75
(406) 3631244
(800) 363-1305

RANCH B&B
1615 US 93 S
(59840)
Rates: $40-$60
(406) 363-4739

HARDIN

AMERICAN INN
1324 N Crawford
Ave (59034)
Rates: $45-$90
(406) 665-1870
(800) 582-8094

CAMP CUSTER MOTEL
303 E 4th St
(59034)
Rates: $30-$40
(406) 665-2504

LARIAT MOTEL
709 North Center
Ave (59034)
Rates: $30-$54
(406) 665-2683

SUPER 8 MOTEL
I-90 & Hwy 47 N
(59034)
Rates: $47-$58
(406) 665-1700
(800) 800-8000

WESTERN MOTEL
830 W 3rd St
(59034)
Rates: $28-$75
(406) 665-2296

HARLOWTON

CORRAL MOTEL
US 12 & 191
(59036)
Rates: $40-$55
(406) 632-4331
(800) 392-4723

COUNTRY SIDE INN
309 3rd St NE
(59036)
Rates: $45-$65
(406) 632-4119
(800) 632-4120

TROY MOTEL
106 2nd St NE
(59036)
Rates: $30-$40
(406) 632-4428

HAUGAN

SILVER $ INN
I-90 Exit 16, Box
W (59842)
Rates: $50-$75
(406) 678-4242
(800) 531-1968

HAVRE

BUDGET INN MOTEL
115 9th Ave
(59501)
Rates: $30-$40
(406) 265-8625

CIRCLE INN MOTEL
3565 US 2 E
(59501)
Rates: $30-$40
(406) 265-9655

EL TORO INN
521 1st St (59501)
Rates: $36-$46
(406) 265-5414
(800) 422-5414

HI-LINE MOTEL
20 2nd St (59501)
Rates: $30-$40
(406) 265-5512

RAILS INN
537 2nd St (59501)
Rates: $30-$40
(406) 265-1438
(800) 724-5746

SIESTA MOTEL
600 1st St (59501)
Rates: $40-$60
(406) 265-5863

SUPER 8 MOTEL
166 19th Ave W
(59501)
Rates: $50-$75
(406) 265-1411
(800) 800-8000

TOWNHOUSE INN
601 W 1st St
(59501)
Rates: $59-$84
(406) 265-6711
(800) 442-4667

HELENA

BARRISTER B&B
416 N Ewing
(59601)
Rates: $95-$110
(406) 443-7330
(800) 823-1148

BEST WESTERN GREAT NORTH-ERN HOTEL
835 Great
Northern Blvd
(59601)
Rates: $80-$125
(406) 457-5500
(800) 528-1234
(800) 829-4047

BIRDSEYE B&B
6890 Raven Rd
(59602)
Rates: $65-$85
(406) 449-4380

COMFORT INN
750 Fee St (59601)
Rates: $54-$85
(406) 443-1000
(800) 424-6423

COUNTRY INN & SUITES
2101 11th Ave
(59601)
Rates: $50-$75
(406) 443-2300
(800) 541-2743

DAYS INN
2001 Prospect Ave
(59601)
Rates: $49-$99
(406) 442-3280
(800) 329-7466

ELKHORN MOUNTAIN INN
1 Jackson Creek
(59601)
Rates: $58-$71
(406) 442-6625

HAMPTON INN
3000 Hwy 12 E
(59601)
Rates: $79-$109
(406) 443-5800
(800) 426-7866

HELENA INN
910 N Last Chance
Gulch (59601)
Rates: $40-$60
(406) 442-6080
(877) 387-0102

HOLIDAY INN
22 N Last Chance
Gulch (59601)
Rates: $90+
(406) 443-2200
(800) 465-4329

KNIGHTS REST MOTEL
1831 Euclid
(59601)
Rates: $50-$75
(406) 442-6384
(888) 442-6384

LAMPLIGHTER MOTEL
1006 Madison
(59601)
Rates: $42-$53
(406) 442-9200

MOTEL 6
800 N Oregon
(59601)
Rates: $29-$48
(406) 442-9990
(800) 466-8356

MOUNTAIN VALLEY INN & SUITES
2101 E 11th Ave
(59601)
Rates: $55-$109
(406) 443-2300
(800) 541-2743

RED LION COLONIAL HOTEL
2301 Colonial Dr
(59601)
Rates: $89-$129
(460) 443-2100
(800) 325-4000

SHILO INN
2020 Prospect Ave
(59601)
Rates: $75-$105
(406) 442-0320
(800) 222-2244

SUPER 8 MOTEL
2200 11th Ave
(59601)
Rates: $75-$90
(406) 443-2450
(800) 800-8000

WINGATE INN
2007 N Oakes
(59601)
Rates: $89-$110
(406) 449-3000
(866) 300-7100

HOT SPRINGS

HOT SPRINGS SPA
308 N Springs St
(59845)
Rates: $30-$40
(406) 741-2283

SYMES HOT SPRINGS HOTEL & MINERAL BATHS
209 Wall St (59845)
Rates: $50-$75
(406) 741-2361
(888) 305-3106

HUNGRY HORSE

CROOKED TREE MOTEL
Hwy 2 W (59919)
Rates: $50-$75
(406) 387-5531

AREA CODES - If the local number doesn't connect, check for a new area code.

MINI GOLDEN INNS MOTEL
8955 US 2 E (59919)
Rates: $48-$96
(406) 387-4313
(800) 891-6464

JORDAN

FELLMAN'S MOTEL
Hwy 200 (59337)
Rates: $29-$45
(406) 557-2209
(800) 337-1863

HELL CREEK MARINA
Box 486 (59337)
Rates: $75-$90
(406) 557-2345

KALISPELL

AERO INN
1830 US 93 S (59901)
Rates: $37-$83
(406) 755-3798
(800) 843-6114

BLUE & WHITE MOTEL
640 E Idaho (59901)
Rates: $40-$60
(406) 755-4311
(800) 382-3577

DIAMOND LIL INN
1680 US 93 S (59901)
Rates: $75-$90
(406) 752-3467
(800) 843-7301

FOUR SEASONS MOTOR INN
350 N Main St (59901)
Rates: $43-$98
(406) 755-6123
(800) 545-6399

GLACIER GATEWAY MOTEL
264 N Main St (59901)
Rates: $46-$94
(406) 755-3330

KALISPELL HISTORIC GRAND HOTEL
100 Main St (59901)
Rates: $65-$115
(406) 755-8100
(800) 858-7422

LA QUINTA INN
255 Montclair Dr (59901)
Rates: $59-$159
(406) 752-5255
(800) 687-6667
(888) 870-5552

MOTEL 6
1540 Hwy 93 S (59901)
Rates: $34-$73
(406) 752-6355
(800) 466-8356

RED LION INN
1330 Hwy 2W (59901)
Rates: $69-$141
(406) 755-6700
(800) 733-5466

SUPER 8 MOTEL-AIRPORT
1341 1st Ave E (59901)
Rates: $58-$123
(406) 755-1888
(800) 800-8000

VACATIONER MOTEL
285 7th Ave NE (59901)
Rates: $60-$80
(406) 755-7144
(888) 755-7144

WEST COAST KALISPELL CENTER HOTEL
20 N Main (59901)
Rates: $69-$111
(406) 752-5052
(800) 325-4000

WEST COAST OUTLAW HOTEL
1701 Hwy 93 S (59901)
Rates: $69-$111
(406) 755-6100
(800) 325-4000

LAKESIDE

BAYSHORE RESORT MOTEL
616 Lakeside Blvd (59922)
Rates: $50-$165
(406) 844-3131
(800) 844-3132

SUNRISE VISTA INN
7005 US 93 (59922)
Rates: $80-$125
(406) 844-0231

LAUREL

RUSSELL MOTEL
711 E Main (59044)
Rates: $30-$40
(406) 628-6513
(888) 275-2616

SUPER 8 MOTEL
205 4th ST SE (59044)
Rates: $69-$89
(406) 628-6888
(800) 800-8000

LEWISTOWN

B & B MOTEL
520 E Main St (59457)
Rates: $36-$65
(406) 538-5496
(877) 538-3563

MOUNTAIN VIEW MOTEL
1422 Main St (59457)
Rates: $30-$40
(406) 538-3457
(800) 862-5786

SUNSET MOTEL
115 NE Main (59457)
Rates: $30-$40
(406) 538-8741

TRAIL'S END MOTEL
216 NE Main (59457)
Rates: $30-$40
(406) 538-5468

YOGO INN
211 E Main St (59457)
Rates: $47-$57
(406) 538-8721
(800) 860-9646

LIBBY

CABOOSE MOTEL
714 W 9th (59923)
Rates: $32-$45
(406) 293-6201
(800) 627-0206

EVERGREEN MOTEL
808 Mineral Ave (59923)
Rates: $50-$75
(406) 293-4178

SANDMAN MOTEL
688 Hwy 2 W (59923)
Rates: $35-$62
(406) 293-8831

SUPER 8 MOTEL
448 Hwy 2 W (59923)
Rates: $50-$90
(406) 293-2771
(800) 800-8000

TRAIL 6 RANCH
27506 Hwy 2 S (59923)
Rates: n/a
(406) 293-8665
(horses only)

LIMA

EXIT 15 INN
111 Baily St (59739)
Rates: $50-$75
(406) 276-3535

LINCOLN

BLACKFOOT RIVER INN
At 7UP Ranch, Box 185 (59639)
Rates: $40-$60
(406) 362-4955

HOTEL LINCOLN
101 Sleepy Hollow Ln (59639)
Rates: $50-$75
(406) 362-4396
(888) 362-4396

LEEPER'S PONDEROSA MOTEL
SR 200 & 1st Ave (59639)
Rates: $47-$65
(406) 362-4333

SPORTSMAN MOTEL
Hwy 200 (59639)
Rates: $40-$60
(406) 362-4481
(800) 809-2463

THREE BEARS MOTEL
Hwy 200, Box 1191 (59639)
Rates: $30-$50
(406) 665-1955

LIVINGSTON

BEST WESTERN YELLOWSTONE MOTOR INN
1515 West Park (59047)
Rates: $59-$129
(406) 222-6110
(800) 528-1234
(800) 770-1874

BUDGET HOST PARKWAY MOTEL
1124 W Park (59047)
Rates: $52-$72
(406) 222-3840
(800) 727-7217

COUNTRY MOTOR INN
814 E Park (59047)
Rates: $50-$75
(406) 222-1923
(800) 286-1923

DEL MAR HOTEL
1201 Hwy 10 W (59047)
Rates: $36-$76
(406) 222-3120

ECONO LODGE
111 Rogers Ln (59047)
Rates: $45-$99
(406) 222-0555
(800) 424-6423

GUEST HOUSE MOTEL
105 W Park (59047)
Rates: $50-$75
(406) 222-1460
(888) 222-1460

LIVINGSTON INN MOTEL
5 Rogers Ln (59047)
Rates: $50-$75
(406) 222-3600

MURRAY HOTEL
201 W Park
(59047)
Rates: $70-$90
(406) 222-1350

RAINBOW MOTEL
5574 E Park St
(59047)
Rates: $50-$75
(406) 222-3780
(800) 788-2301

TRAVELODGE
102 Rogers Ln
(59047)
Rates: $49-$110
(406) 222-6320
(800) 578-7878
(800) 437-6291

LOLO

DAYS INN
11225 HWY 93 S
(59847)
Rates: $59-$99
(406) 273-2121
(800) 329-7466

**LOLO TRAIL
CENTER/MTN
LODGING**
38600 Hwy 12 W
(59870)
Rates: $75-$90
(406) 273-2201

MALTA

**GREAT
NORTHERN
MOTEL**
2 S 1st Ave E
(59538)
Rates: $50-$60
(406) 654-2100
(877) 478-6678

RIVERSIDE MOTEL
8 N Central
(59538)
Rates: $30-$40
(406) 654-2310
(800) 854-2310

ROYALS INN
117 N 1st St
(59538)
Rates: $30-$40
(406) 654-1150

**SPORTSMAN
MOTEL**
231 N 1st St E
(59538)
Rates: $30-$50
(406) 654-2300

MARTIN CITY

**MIDDLE FORK
MOTEL**
US 2, P. O. Box
260237 (59926)
Rates: $40-$60
(406) 387-5900

MARTINSDALE

**CRAZY
MOUNTAIN INN**
100 Main St
(59053)
Rates: $30-$40
(406) 572-3307

MCALLISTER

**CROSSROADS
MARKET
& CABINS**
5564 US 287 N,
Box 155 (59740)
Rates: $30-$40
(406) 682-7652

MEDICINE LAKE

**CLUB BAR, HOTEL
& RESTAURANT**
202 W Main St
(59247)
Rates: $30-$50
(406) 789-2208

MELROSE

**SPORTSMAN
MOTEL**
Frontage Rd,
Box 86 (59743)
Rates: $50-$75
(406) 835-2141

MELSTONE

TERRI'S MOTEL
205 Main St
(59054)
Rates: $30-$40
(406) 358-2470

MILES CITY

**BEST WESTERN
WAR BONNET
INN**
1015 S Haynes
Ave (59301)
Rates: $75-$93
(406) 234-4560
(800) 528-1234

BUDGET INN
1006 S Haynes
Ave (59301)
Rates: $30-$50
(406) 874-3550

ECONO LODGE
1209 S Haynes
Ave (59301)
Rates: $45-$105
(406) 232-8880
(800) 424-6423

**GUESTHOUSE
INN & SUITES**
3111 Steel St
(59301)
Rates: $71-$150
(4060 232-3661
(800) 214-8378

**HISTORIC
OLIVE HOTEL**
501 Main (59301)
Rates: $50-$75
(406) 232-2450

MOTEL 6
1314 S Haynes
Ave (59301)
Rates: $29-$35
(406) 232-7040
(800) 466-8356

RED ROCK MOTEL
2700 Valley Dr E
(59301)
Rates: $30-$50
(406) 232-5382

SUPER 8 MOTEL
RR 2, Hwy 59 S
(59301)
Rates: $35-$58
(406) 232-5261
(800) 800-8000

MISSOULA

**BEL AIRE-BEST
VALUE INN**
300 E Broadway
(59802)
Rates: $50-$75
(406) 543-3183
(800) 543-3184

**BEST INN & CONF
CENTER SOUTH**
3803 Brooks St
(59801)
Rates: $65-$89
(406) 251-2665
(800) 272-9500

BEST INN NORTH
4953 N Reserve St
(59802)
Rates: $65-$89
(406) 542-7550
(800) 272-9500

**BEST WESTERN
GRANT CREEK
INN**
5280 Grant Creek
Rd (59801)
Rates: $85-$169
(406) 543-0700
(800) 528-1234
(888) 543-0700

CAMPUS INN
744 E Broadway
(59802)
Rates: $40-$120
(406) 549-5134
(800) 232-8013

COMFORT INN
4545 N Reserve St
(59802)
Rates: $65-$160
(406) 542-0888
(800) 424-6423

CREEKSIDE INN
630 E Broadway
(59802)
Rates: $45-$80
(406) 549-2387
(800) 551-2387

**DAYS INN/
WESTGATE**
8000 Truck Stop
Rd (59802)
Rates: $49-$139
(406) 721-9776
(800) 329-7466

**DOUBLETREE
HOTEL
EDGEWATER**
100 Madison
(59802)
Rates: $99-$285
(406) 728-3100
(800) 222-8733

**DOWNTOWN
MOTEL**
502 E Broadway
(59802)
Rates: $34-$49
(406) 549-5191

EXECUTIVE INN
201 E Main St
(59802)
Rates: $50-$75
(406) 541-7221

FAMILY INN
1031 E Broadway
(59802)
Rates: $52-$78
(406) 543-7371

HAMPTON INN
4805 N Reserve St
(59802)
Rates: $70-$119
(406) 549-1800
(800) 426-7866

**HOLIDAY INN-
MISSOULA
PARKSIDE**
200 S Pattee St
(59802)
Rates: $79-$169
(406) 721-8550
(800) 465-4329

MICROTEL INN
5059 N Reserve St
(59808)
Rates: $55-$110
(406) 543-0959
(888) 771-7171

MOTEL 6
3035 Expo Pkwy
Commerce Ctr
(59802)
Rates: $39-$54
(406) 549-6665
(800) 466-8356

**PONDEROSA
LODGE**
800 E Broadway
(59802)
Rates: $45-$69
(406) 543-3102
(877) 543-3102

RAMADA LIMITED
801 N Orange St
(59802)
Rates: $85+
(406) 721-3610
(800) 272-6232

RED LION INN
700 W Broadway
(59802)
Rates: $54-$200
(406) 728-3300
(800) 733-5466
(800) 547-8010

**REDWOOD
LODGE**
8060 Hwy 93 N
(59802)
Rates: $55-$64
(406) 721-2110
(800) 874-9412

ROYAL MOTEL
338 Washington St
(59802)
Rates: $36-$54
(406) 542-2184
(888) 541-2006

AREA CODES - If the local number doesn't connect, check for a new area code.

RUBY'S INN & CONVENTION CENTER
4825 N Reserve St (59802)
Rates: $65-$120
(406) 541-7829
(800) 221-2057

SLEEP INN
3425 Dore Ln (59801)
Rates: $60-$85
(406) 543-5883
(800) 424-6423

SOUTHGATE INN
3530 Brooks (59802)
Rates: $49-$85
(406) 251-2250
(800) 247-2616

SUPER 8 MOTEL
3901 Brooks St (59801)
Rates: $44-$81
(406) 251-2255
(800) 800-8000

TRAVELERS INN MOTEL
4850 N Reserve St (59802)
Rates: $45-$69
(406) 728-8330
(800) 862-3363

WINGATE INN
5252 Airway Blvd (59808)
Rates: $89-$109
(406) 541-8000
(866) 832-8000

MONARCH
CUB'S DEN MOTEL
5012 US 89 S (59463)
Rates: $40-$60
(406) 236-5922

MONTANA CITY
ELKHORN MOUNTAIN INN
1 Jackson Creek Rd (59634)
Rates: $50-$75
(406) 442-6625
(866) 442-6625

NOXON
AITKEN'S QUIK STOP MOTEL
1402 Hwy 200 (59853)
Rates: $50-$75
(406) 847-2191

NOXON MOTEL
2 Klakken Rd (59853)
Rates: $30-$40
(406) 847-2600
(866) 725-3751

OVANDO
LAKE UPSATA GUEST RANCH
135 Lake Upsala Rd (59854)
Rates: $75-$220
(406) 793-5890
(800) 594-7687

PARK CITY
CJ'S MOTEL
2 S Clark (590630
Rates: $30-$50
(406) 633-2352

PHILIPSBURG
THE INN AT PHILIPSBURG
915 W Broadway (59858)
Rates: $50-$75
(406) 859-3959

PLAINS
CROSSROADS MOTEL & RV
401 E Railroad (59859)
Rates: $50-$75
(406) 826-3623

PLENTYWOOD
GRANDVIEW HOTEL
120 S Main (59254)
Rates: $30-$40
(406) 765-2730

PLAINS MOTEL
626 W 1st Ave (59254)
Rates: $27-$39
(406) 765-1240

SHERWOOD INN
515 W 1st Ave (59254)
Rates: $50-$75
(406) 765-2810

POLARIS
GRASSHOPPER INN & RV
Box 460511 (59746)
Rates: $50-$65
(406) 834-3456

POLSON
BAYVIEW INN
914 Hwy 93 (59860)
Rates: $50-$75
(406) 883-3120
(800) 735-6862

SUPER 8 MOTEL
21 S Shore Rt (59860)
Rates: $39-$67
(406) 883-6266
(800) 800-8000

SWAN HILL B&B
460 Kings Point Rd (59860)
Rates: $75-$150
(406) 883-5292
(800) 537-9489

PRAY
CHICO HOT SPRINGS LODGE
Drawer D, Old Chico Road (59645)
Rates: $36-$275
(406) 333-4933
(800) 468-9232

RED LODGE
(Also see Yellowstone National Park)

BEST WESTERN LUPINE INN
702 S Hauser (59068)
Rates: $59-$99
(406) 446-1321
(888) 567-1321

CHATEAU ROUGE
1505 S Broadway (59068)
Rates: $70-$90
(406) 446-1601
(800) 926-1601

COMFORT INN
612 N Broadway (59068)
Rates: $60-$120
(406) 446-4469
(800) 424-6423

SUPER 8 MOTEL
1223 S Broadway (59068)
Rates: $49-$139
(406) 446-2288
(800) 813-8335

YODELER MOTEL
601 S Broadway (59068)
Rates: $49-$99
(406) 446-1435
(866) 446-1435

RONAN
STARLITE MOTEL
18 Main St SW (59864)
Rates: $52-$79
(406) 676-7000
(800) 823-4403

ROUNDUP
BEST VALUE INN
630 Main St (59072)
Rates: $30-$50
(406) 3231000
(888) 422-1224

BIG SKY MOTEL
740 Main St (59072)
Rates: $30-$40
(406) 323-2303

IDEAL MOTEL
926 Main (59072)
Rates: $29-$43
(406) 323-3371
(888) 323-3371

ST. IGNATIUS
STONEHEART INN B&B
26 N Main (59865)
Rates: $40-$60
(406) 745-4999

SUNSET MOTEL
333 Mountain View (59865)
Rates: $49-$120
(406) 745-3900

ST. MARY
(Also see Glacier National Park)

RED EAGLE MOTEL
Star Rt, Box 896 (59417)
Rates: $45-$75
(406) 732-4453

THE RESORT AT GLACIER
US 89 & Going-to-the-Sun Rd (59417)
Rates: $90+
(406) 732-4431
(800) 368-3689

ST. REGIS
LITTLE RIVER MOTEL
50 Old Hwy 10 (59866)
Rates: $35-$65
(406) 649-2713

ST. REGIS CAMP MOTEL
Old Hwy 10 (59866)
Rates: $35-$50
(406) 649-2428

SUPER 8 MOTEL
9 Old Hwy 10 E (59866)
Rates: $50-$75
(406) 649-2422
(800) 800-8000

SEELEY LAKE
SEELY LAKE MOTOR LODGE
Hwy 83, Box 37 (59868)
Rates: $50-$75
(406) 677-2335
(800) 237-9978

THE EMILY A B&B
SR 83 N, MM 20 (59868)
Rates: $115
(406) 677-3474

WILDERNESS GATEWAY INN
2996 Hwy 83 N (59868)
Rates: $53-$65
(406) 677-2095
(800) 355-5588

SHELBY
COMFORT INN
50 Frontage Rd (59474)
Rates: $60-$95
(406) 434-2212
(800) 220-5150

AREA CODES - If the local number doesn't connect, check for a new area code.

CROSSROADS INN
1200 Roosevelt
Hwy (59474)
Rates: $46-$60
(406) 434-5134
(800) 779-7666

GLACIER MOTEL & RV
744 US 2 (59474)
Rates: $30-$40
(406) 434-5181
(800) 764-5181

O'HAIRE MANOR MOTEL
204 2nd St S
(59474)
Rates: $35-$70
(406) 434-5555
(800) 541-5809

TOTEM MOTEL
730 Oilfield Ave
(59474)
Rates: $30-$40
(406) 434-2930

SHERIDAN
MILL CREEK INN
102 Mill St (59749)
Rates: $40-$60
(406) 842-5422

MORIAH MOTEL
220 S Main (59749)
Rates: $50-$75
(406) 842-5491

SIDNEY
LONE TREE MOTOR INN
900 S Central
Ave (59270)
Rates: $40-$60
(406) 482-4520

PARK PLAZA MOTEL
601 S Central
Ave (59270)
Rates: $30-$39
(406) 482-1520

RICHLAND MOTOR INN
1200 S Centra
Ave (59270)
Rates: $68-$78
(406) 482-6400

SUNRISE MOTEL
2300 S Central
Ave (59270)
Rates: $30-$50
(406) 482-3826

SILVER GATE
GRIZZLY AND ANTLER LODGE
Hwy 212 (59081)
Rates: $50-$75
(406) 838-2219

STEVENSVILLE
HISTORICAL STEVI HOTEL
107 E 3rd St
(59870)
Rates: $50-$75
(406) 777-3087

SUPERIOR
BELLEVUE HOTEL/MOTEL
110 Mullan Rd E
(59872)
Rates: $30-$40
(406) 822-4692

BUDGET HOST BIG SKY MOTEL
103 4th Ave E
(59872)
Rates: $48-$60
(406) 822-4831
(800) 759-0023

HILLTOP MOTEL
201 W Multan Rd
(59872)
Rates: $30-$50
(406) 822-4781

SWAN LAKE
ALPINE CHALET RESTAURANT & MOTEL
71284 Hwy 83
(59911)
Rates: $40-$60
(406) 886-2226

TERRY
DIAMOND MOTEL
118 E Spring (59349)
Rates: $27-$38
(406) 635-5407
(800) 548-6407

KEMPTON HOTEL
204 Spring (59349)
Rates: $28-$35
(406) 635-5543

THOMPSON FALLS
RIMROCK LODGE
4946 Hwy 200 W
(59873)
Rates: $50-$65
(406) 827-3536

RIVERFRONT
4907 Hwy 200 W
(59873)
Rates: $56-$92
(406) 827-3460
(877) 569-0141

THREE FORKS
BROKEN SPUR MOTEL
124 W Elm (59752)
Rates: $40-$68
(406) 285-3237
(888) 354-3048

FORT THREE FORKS MOTEL
10776 Hwy 287
(59752)
Rates: $50-$75
(406) 285-3233
(800) 477-5690

SACAJAWEA HOTEL
5 N Main St (59752)
Rates: $75-$90
(406) 285-6515
(888) 722-2529

TOWNSEND
BEDFORD INN BED & BREAKFAST
7408 US 287
(59644)
Rates: $40-$60
(406) 266-3629

LAKE TOWNSEND MOTEL
413 N Pine (59644)
Rates: $30-$40
(406) 266-3461
(800) 856-3461

MUSTANG MOTEL
412 North Front St
(59644)
Rates: $39-$40
(406) 266-3491

TROUT CREEK
TROUT CREEK MOTEL & RV
2972 Hwy 200
(59874)
Rates: $50-$75
(406) 827-3268

TROY
THE RANCH MOTEL
914 E Missoula
(59935)
Rates: $30-$50
(406) 295-4332

VAUGHN
OFFICE BAR & MOTEL
Hwy 89 (59487)
Rates: $30-$50
(406) 965-9982

VICTOR
WILDLIFE ADVEN-TURES GUEST RANCH
1765 Pleasant
View Dr (59875)
Rates: $90-$170
(406) 642-3262

WEST YELLOWSTONE
BEST WESTERN CROSS WINDS INN
201 Firehole Ave
(59758)
Rates: $49-$130
(406) 646-9557
(877) 446-9557

BEST WESTERN DESERT INN
133 Canyon Ave
(59758)
Rates: $59-$169
(406) 646-7376
(800) 528-1234
(800) 574-7054

BEST WESTERN WESTON INN
103 Gibbon St
(59758)
Rates: $45-$119
(406) 646-7373
(800) 528-1234
(800) 599-9982

GRAY WOLF INN & SUITES
250 S Canyon St
(59758)
Rates: $59-$139
(406) 646-0000
(800) 852-8602

HADLEY'S MOTEL
29 Gibbon Ave
(59758)
Rates: $50-$75
(406) 646-9534

HEBGEN LAKE MOUNTAIN INN
15475 Hebgen
Lake Rd (59758)
Rates: $85-$145
(406) 646-5100

HIBERNATION STATION
212 Gray Wolf Ave
(59758)
Rates: $90+
(406) 646-4200
(800) 580-3557

HO HUM MOTEL
126 Canyon Ave
(59758)
Rates: $30-$50
(406) 646-7746

KELLY INN
104 S Canyon
Ave (59758)
Rates: $59-$149
(406) 646-4544
(800) 635-3559
(800) 259-4672

PINE SHADOWS MOTEL
Hayden & US 20
(59758)
Rates: $40-$60
(406) 646-7541
(800) 624-5291

PIONEER MOTEL
515 Madison
(59758)
Rates: $75-$90
(406) 646-9705

PONY EXPRESS MOTEL & RV
4 Firehole Ave
(59758)
Rates: $40-$60
(406) 646-7644
(800) 323-9708

ROUNDUP MOTEL & DUDE MOTOR INN
3 Madison Ave
(59758)
Rates: $65-$129
(406) 646-7301

STAGE COACH INN
209 Madison Ave
(59758)
Rates: $49-$139
(406) 646-7381
(800) 842-2882

THREE BEAR LODGE
217 Yellowstone
Ave (59758)
Rates: $50-$90
(406) 646-7353
(800) 646-7353

AREA CODES - If the local number doesn't connect, check for a new area code.

TRAVELODGE
236 Dunraven
(59758)
Rates: $75-$90
(406) 646-7681
(800) 578-7878
(877) 439-7377

WHISPERING PINES
321 Canyon Ave
(59758)
Rates: $30-$50
(406) 646-1172

YELLOWSTONE CABINS & RV
504 Hwy 20
(59758)
Rates: $50-$75
(406) 646-9350

YELLOWSTONE COUNTRY INN
234 Firehole
(59758)
Rates: $75-$90
(406) 646-7622
(800) 646-7622

YELLOWSTONE INN
601 Hwy 20
(59758)
Rates: $80+
(406) 646-7633
(800) 858-9224

YELLOWSTONE LODGE
251 Electric St
(59758)
Rates: $59-$139
(406) 646-0020
(877) 239-9298

WHITE SULPHUR SPRINGS

GORDON'S HIGHLAND MOTEL
410 E Main
(59645)
Rates: $30-$40
(406) 547-3880
(877) 201-4292

ALL SEASONS SUPER 8 MOTEL
808 3rd Ave W
(59645)
Rates: $48-$87
(406) 547-8888
(800) 800-8000

TENDERFOOT MOTEL
301 W Main
(59645)
Rates: $30-$40
(406) 547-3303
(800) 898-3303

WHITEFISH

ALLEN'S MOTEL
6540 US 93 S
(59937)
Rates: $40-$60
(406) 862-3995

BAY POINT ON THE LAKE
300 Bay Point Dr
(59937)
Rates: $89-$185
(406) 862-2331
(888) 229-7646

BEST WESTERN ROCKY MOUNTAIN
6510 US 93 S
(59937)
Rates: $69-$189
(406) 862-2569
(800) 528-1234
(800) 862-2569

CHEAP SLEEP MOTEL
6400 Hwy 93 S
(59937)
Rates: $45-$70
(406) 862-5515
(800) 862-3711

CRENSHAW HOUSE B&B
5465 Hwy 93 S
(59937)
Rates: $65-$145
(406) 862-3496
(800) 453-2863

DOWNTOWNER MOTEL & FITNESS CTR
224 Spokane Ave
(59937)
Rates: $50-$75
(406) 862-2535
(888) 325-2535

EAGLE'S ROOST B&B
400 Wisconsin Ave
(59937)
Rates: $65-$100
(406) 862-5198
(888) 750-6378

HOLIDAY INN EXP GLACIER PARK
6390 Hwy 93 S
(59937)
Rates: $90+
(406) 862-4020
(800) 465-4329

KRISTIANNA MOUNTAIN HOMES
3842 Winter Ln
(59937)
Rates: $100-$525
(406) 862-2860

NORTH FORTY RESORT
3765 Hwy 40 W
(59912)
Rates: $69-$215
(406) 862-7740

PINE LODGE
920 Spokane Ave
(59937)
Rates: $70-$139
(460) 862-7600
(800) 305-7463

SUPER 8 MOTEL
800 Spokane Ave
(59937)
Rates: $44-$90
(406) 862-8255
(800) 800-8000

WHITEFISH MOTEL
620 8th St (59937)
Rates: $50-$75
(406) 862-3507

WHITEHALL

CHIEF MOTEL
303 E Legion
(59759)
Rates: $40-$60
(406) 287-3921

RICE MOTEL
7 N "A" St (59759)
Rates: $30-$40
(406) 287-3895
(888) 287-3895

SUPER 8 MOTEL
515 N Whitehall
St (59759)
Rates: $36-$52
(406) 287-5588
(800) 800-8000

WHITEHALL CREEK MOTEL
516 E Legion
(59759)
Rates: $30-$50
(406) 287-5315

WIBAUX

BUDGET HOST INN
400 W 2nd Ave N
(59353)
Rates: $36-$52
(406) 796-2666

NUNBERG'S N HEART RANCH B&B INN
HC 71, Box 7315
(59353)
Rates: n/a
(406) 795-2345

W-V MOTEL
107 W 2nd Ave
(59353)
Rates: $30-$50
(406) 796-2446

WISDOM

NEZ PIERCE MOTEL
Hwy 43, Box 123
(59761)
Rates: $30-$40
(406) 689-3254

SANDMAN MOTEL
Old Hwy 278
(59761)
Rates: $30-$40
(406) 689-3218

WOLF CREEK

CRAIG MADSEN MONTANA RIVER OUTFITTERS LODGING
515 Recreation Rd
(59648)
Rates: $50-$75
(406) 235-4350
(800) 800-4350

WOLF POINT

BIG SKY MOTEL
Hwy 2 E (59201)
Rates: $30-$40
(406) 653-2300

HOMESTEAD INN MOTEL
101 US 2 E (59201)
Rates: $25-$37
(406) 653-1300
(800) 231-0986

SHERMAN MOTOR INN
200 E Main St
(59201)
Rates: $26-$35
(406) 653-1100
(800) 952-1100

YELLOWSTONE NATIONAL PARK, WY
The following accommodations are located near the park entrances:

CANYON VILLAGE LODGE & CABINS
Box 165 (82190)
Rates: $60-$80
(307) 344-7311

LAKE LODGE & CABINS
Box 165 (82190)
Rates: $60-$80
(307) 344-7311

LAKE YELLOWSTONE HOTEL & CABINS
Box 165 (82190)
Rates: $80+
(307) 344-7311

MAMMOTH HOT SPRINGS & HOTEL
Box 165 (82190)
Rates: $60-$80
(307) 344-7311

OLD FAITHFUL LODGE & CABINS
Box 165 (82190)
Rates: $40-$80
(307) 344-7311

OLD FAITHFUL SNOW LODGE
Box 165 (82190)
Rates: $51-$100
(307) 344-7311

ROOSEVELT LODGE
Box 165 (82190)
Rates: $26-$35
(307) 344-7311

ZORTMAN

**BUCKHORN
STORE, CABINS
& RV PARK**
1st & Main Sts,
Box 501 (59546)
Rates: $30-$40
(406) 673-3162
(888) 654-3162

ZORTMAN MOTEL
302 Main St
(59546)
Rates: $30-$40
(406) 673-3160
(800) 517-0372

NEBRASKA

AINSWORTH

AINSWORTH INN BED & BRKFAST
400 N Main (69210)
Rates: $35-$55
(402) 387-0540
(888) 237-0954

COMFORT INN
1124 E 4th St
(69210)
Rates: $69-$84
(402) 387-1050
(800) 424-6423

LAZY A MOTEL
1120 East 4th St
(69210)
Rates: $35+
(402) 387-2600

REMINGTON ARMS MOTEL
1000 E 4th (69210)
Rates: $35-$55
(402) 387-2220
(800) 248-3971

SKINNER'S MOTOR COURT
HC 65 (69210)
Rates: $30-$55
(402) 387-2021

SUPER 8 MOTEL
1025 E 4th St
(69210)
Rates: $44-$51
(402) 387-0700
(800) 800-8000

THE UPPER ROOM BED & BRKFAST
409 N Wilson
(69210)
Rates: $35-$75
(402) 387-0107

ALLIANCE

DAYS INN
First & Cody Ave
(69301)
Rates: $59-$100
(308) 762-8000
(800) 329-7466

SUNSET MOTEL
1210 E Hwy 2
(69301)
Rates: $39-$69
(308) 762-8660
(800) 767-8660

ALMA

SUPER OUTPOST MOTEL
N Hwy 183 & 136
(68920)
Rates: $35+
(308) 928-2116

WESTERN HOLIDAY MOTEL
Rt 1, Box 25-A1
(68920)
Rates: $25-$55
(308) 928-2155
(800) 258-8124

ARAPAHOE

ARAPAHOE MOTEL
W Hwys 6 & 34
(68922)
Rates: $35+
(308) 962-7948

SHADY REST CAMP MOTEL
309 Chestnut
(68922)
Rates: $35-$55
(308) 962-5461

AUBURN

AUBURN INN
517 J St (68305)
Rates: $30-$49
(402) 274-3143
(800) 272-3143

PALMER HOUSE MOTEL
1918 J St (68305)
Rates: $35-$55
(402) 274-3193
(800) 272-3193

AURORA

BUDGET HOST KEN'S MOTEL
1515 11th St
(68818)
Rates: $32-$40
(402) 694-3141
(800) 283-4678

BASSETT

RANCHLAND MOTEL
HC 75, Box 74
(68714)
Rates: $25-$55
(402) 684-3340

BEATRICE

BEATRICE INN
3500 N 6th St
(68310)
Rates: $35-$48
(402) 223-4074
(800) 232-8742

HOLIDAY INN EXP HOTEL & SUITES
4005 N 6th St
(68310)
Rates: $70
(402) 228-7000
(800) 465-4329

HOLIDAY VILLA MOTEL
1820 N 6th St
(68310)
Rates: $35-$55
(402) 223-4036

SUPER 8 MOTEL
3721 N 6th St
(68310)
Rates: $59-$75
(402) 228-8808
(800) 800-8000

BEAVER CITY

FURNAS COUNTY INN
Rt 1, Box 86E
(68926)
Rates: $25-$55
(308) 268-7705

BELLEVUE

BEST WESTERN WHITE HOUSE INN
305 N Fort Crook Rd (68005)
Rates: $54-$99
(402) 293-1600
(800) 528-1234
(800) 962-4601

DAYS INN
SR 370 & Hillcrest
(68005)
Rates: $49-$189
(402) 292-3800
(800) 329-7466

OFFUTT MOTOR COURT
3618 Fort Crook Rd (68005)
Rates: $35+
(402) 291-4333

SETTLE INN & SUITES
2105 Pratt AVe
(68005)
Rates: $59-$200
(402) 292-1155

BIG SPRINGS

BUDGET 8 PANHANDLE INN
P. O. Box 157
(69122)
Rates: $26-$50
(308) 889-3671

BLAIR

BLAIR HOUSE MOTEL
W Hwy 30 (68008)
Rates: $35-$55
(402) 426-4801
(800) 793-9240

ECONO LODGE
1355 Hwy 30
(68008)
Rates: $44-$70
(402) 426-2340
(800) 424-6423

RATH INN
RR 1, Box 268E
(68008)
Rates: $27-$49
(402) 426-8703

BLOOMFIELD

FOUR SEASONS MOTEL
Rt 3, Box 239
(68718)
Rates: $30-$55
(402) 373-2441
(800) 763-1261

BREWSTER

UNCLE BUCK'S LODGE
P. O. Box 100
(68821)
Rates: $35-$55
(308) 547-2210
(800) 239-9190

BRIDGEPORT

BELL MOTOR INN
P. O. Box 854
(69336)
Rates: $29-$38
(308) 262-0557

BRIDGEPORT INN
P. O. Box 1106
(69336)
Rates: $35-$55
(308) 262-0290

GOLDEN ACRES MOTEL & RV PARK
Rt 1, Box 196
(69336)
Rates: $25-$55
(308) 262-0410

BROKEN BOW

WAGON WHEEL MOTEL &
1545 South E St
(68822)
Rates: $26-$35
(308) 872-2433
(800) 770-2433

WM PENN LODGE
853 South E St
(68822)
Rates: $24-$40
(308) 872-2412

BURWELL

CALAMUS COUNTRY MOTEL
HC 79, Box 18A
(68823)
Rates: $35
(308) 346-4729

CALAMUS RIVER LODGE
P.O. Box 305
(68879)
Rates: $25-$35
(308) 346-4331

AREA CODES - If the local number doesn't connect, check for a new area code.

RODEO INN
Hwys 91 & 11
(68823)
Rates: $35-$55
(308) 346-4408
(800) 926-9427

CALLAWAY

CHESLEY'S LODGE
Rt 1, Box 76
(68825)
Rates: $30-$55
(308) 836-2658

**TRAVELERS INN
CALLAWAY
HOUSE**
P. O. Box 189
(68825)
Rates: $35-$70
(308) 836-4414

CAMBRIDGE

**BUNKHOUSE
MOTEL**
E Hwy 6 & 34
(69022)
Rates: $35-$55
(308) 697-4540

**MEDICINE CREEK
LODGE**
Rt 2, Box 93
(69022)
Rates: $35
(308) 697-3774

CENTRAL CITY

**CRAWFORD
MOTEL**
RR 1, Box 270
(68826)
Rates: $18-$25
(308) 946-3051

CREST MOTEL
E Hwy 30 (68826)
Rates: $35
(308) 946-3077
(888) 879-9201

SUPER 8 MOTEL
1701 31st St
(68826)
Rates: $45-$70
(308) 946-5055
(800) 800-8000

CHADRON

**BEST WESTERN
WEST HILLS INN**
1100 W 10th St
(69337)
Rates: $48-$122
(308) 432-3305
(877) 432-3305

BLAINE MOTEL
159 Bordeaux St
(69337)
Rates: $35-$55
(308) 432-5568

**ECONOMY 9
MOTEL**
1201 W Hwy 20
(69337)
Rates: 35-$65
(308) 432-3119

**GRAND WEST-
ERNER MOTEL**
1050 W Hwy 20
(69337)
Rates: $35-$55
(308) 432-5595

**THE OLDE MAIN
STREET INN B&B**
115 Main St
(69337)
Rates: $35-$60
(308) 432-3380

**ROUND UP
MOTEL**
901 E 3rd St
(69337)
Rates: $26-$34
(308) 432-5591

SUPER 8 MOTEL
840 W Hwy 20
(69337)
Rates: $40-$103
(308) 432-4471
(800) 800-8000

**WESTERNER
MOTEL**
300 Oak St (69337)
Rates: $35-$55
(308) 432-5577
(800) 341-8000

CHAPPELL

**EL RANCHO
MOTEL &
CAMPGROUND**
P. O. Box 592
(69129)
Rates: $25-$35
(308) 874-3264

CHESTER

**CHESTER
COUNTRY INN
MOTEL**
Box 3-C (68327)
Rates: $25-$33
(402) 324-8494

CODY

**CODY'S COUNTRY
COTTAGE**
Box 217 (69211)
Rates: $28-$52
(402) 823-4182

COLUMBUS

DAYS INN
371 33rd Ave
(68601)
Rates: $45-$65
(402) 564-2527
(800) 329-7466

GEMBOL'S MOTEL
3220 8th St (68601)
Rates: $35-$55
(402) 564-2729
(800) 288-3658

NEW WORLD INN
265 33rd Ave
(68601)
Rates: $43-$61
(402) 564-1492
(800) 433-1492

ROSEBUD MOTEL
154 Lakeshore Dr
(68601)
Rates: $26-$34
(402) 564-3256

**SEVEN KNIGHTS
MOTEL**
2222 23rd St
(68601)
Rates: $26-$41
(402) 563-3533
(800) 533-8365

**SLEEP INN,
INN & SUITES**
303 23rd St (68601)
Rates: $57-$121
(402) 562-5200
(800) 424-6423

SUPER 8 MOTEL
3324 20th St
(68601)
Rates: $45-$59
(402) 563-3456
(800) 800-8000

COZAD

MOTEL 6
809 S Meridian
(69130)
Rates: $36-$46
(308) 784-4900
(800) 466-8356

CRAWFORD

BUTTE RANCH
803 W Ashcreek
Rd (69339)
Rates: $55
(308) 665-2364

HILLTOP MOTEL
304 McPherson St
(69339)
Rates: $55
(308) 665-1144
(800) 504-1444

**TOWN LINE
MOTEL**
Hwys 2 & 20
(69339)
Rates: $35-$55
(308) 665-1450
(800) 903-1450

CREIGHTON

**THE BLACK
HORSE INN**
408 Rice St (68729)
Rates: $36-$54
(402) 358-3587

CRETE

SUPER 8 MOTEL
1880 W 12th St
(68333)
Rates: $56-$88
(402) 826-3600
(800) 800-8000

CROFTON

BOGNER'S MOTEL
Hwys 12 & 121
(68730)
Rates: $35
(402) 388-4626

DAVID CITY

FIESTA MOTEL
N Hwy 15 (68632)
Rates: $35
(402) 367-3129

DIXON

**THE GEORGES
BED & BREAKFAST**
57759 874 Rd
(68732)
Rates: $30-$55
(402) 584-2625

DONIPHAN

USA INNS
Rt 2, Box 190 E
(68832)
Rates: $33-$60
(308) 381-0111

ELM CREEK

**1ST INTERSTATE
INN**
I-80 & Hwy 183
(68836)
Rates: $30-$40
(308) 856-4652

ELWOOD

J. J.'S MARINA
4 Lakeview Acres
Dr 14 (68937)
Rates: $55+
(308) 785-2836

**THOMPSON'S
RESORT**
20 Bullhead
Expwy, Dr 28
(68937)
Rates: $35-$55
(308) 785-2298

ERICSON

WATSON CABINS
P. O. Box 82
(68637)
Rates: $25-$35
(308) 653-3106

FALLS CITY

CHECK IN MOTEL
1901 Fulton St
(68355)
Rates: $35
(402) 245-2433

**STEPHENSON
MOTEL**
2621 Harlan St
(68355)
Rates: $35-$55
(402) 245-2459

FREMONT

COMFORT INN
1649 E 23rd St
(68025)
Rates: $59-$104
(402) 721-1109
(800) 424-6423

HOLIDAY LODGE
1220 E 23rd St
(68025)
Rates: $60-$80
(402) 727-1110
(800) 743-7666

SLEEP INN
120 W Cathy St
(68025)
Rates: $45-$74
(402) 721-8400
(800) 753-3746

FULLERTON

THE FULLERTON INN
S Hwy 14 (68638)
Rates: $53-$63
(308) 536-2699

FUNK

UNCLE SAM'S HILLTOP LODGE
Rt 1, Box 110
(68940)
Rates: $35-$55
(308) 995-2204

GENOA

REDWOOD MOTEL
336 N Elm St
(68640)
Rates: $25-$55
(402) 993-2817

GERING

CAVALIER MOTEL
3655 N 10th St
(69341)
Rates: $25-$55
(308) 635-3176

CIRCLE S LODGE
400 M St (69341)
Rates: $35-$55
(308) 436-2157

MICROTEL INN & SUITES
1130 M St (69341)
Rates: $60-$65
(308) 436-1950
(888) 771-7171

GIBBON

COUNTRY INN & ANTIQUES
2432 Lowell Rd
(68840)
Rates: $26-$54
(308) 468-5256
(800) 887-6324

GORDON

HACIENDA MOTEL
Rt 1, Box 85
(69343)
Rates: $26-$34
(308) 282-1400

HILLS MOTEL
107 West Hwy 20
(69343)
Rates: $35+
(308) 282-1795

MEADOW VIEW RANCH B&B
HC 91 (69343)
Rates: $40-$55
(308) 282-0679
(800) 484-5753

GOTHENBURG

SUPER 8 MOTEL
401 Platte River Dr (69138)
Rates: $50-$69
(308) 537-2684
(800) 800-8000

GRAND ISLAND

CONOCO MOTEL
2107 W 2nd St
(68803)
Rates: $32-$36
(308) 384-2700

DAYS INN
2620 N Diers Ave
(68803)
Rates: $45-$75
(308) 384-8624
(800) 329-7466

HOLIDAY INN I-80
7838 S US Hwy 281 (68803)
Rates: $49-$67
(308) 384-7770
(800) 465-4329

HOLIDAY INN MIDTOWN
2503 S Locust St
(68801)
Rates: $79-$89
(308) 384-1330
(800) 465-4329

LAZY V MOTEL-IMA
2703 E Hwy 30
(68801)
Rates: $24-$30
(308) 384-0700
(800) 341-8000

OAK GROVE INN
3205 S Locust St
(68801)
Rates: $28-$37
(308) 384-1333
(800) 435-7144

RELAX INN
507 W 2nd St
(68801)
Rates: $27-$50
(308) 483-1000

SUPER 8 MOTEL
2603 S Locust St
(68801)
Rates: $51-$82
(308) 384-4380
(800) 800-8000

TRAVELODGE
1311 S Locust
(68801)
Rates: $45-$57
(308) 382-5003
(800) 578-7878

USA INNS OF AMERICA
7000 S Nine Bridge Rd (68832)
Rates: $45-$60
(308) 381-0111

VALENTINE MOTEL
3518 S Locust St
(68801)
Rates: $29-$35
(308) 384-1740

GRANT

GRANT MOTEL & RV PARK
P. O. Box 400
(69140)
Rates: $25-$34
(308) 352-4844

HARTINGTON

HILLCREST MOTEL
403 Robinson Ave
(68739)
Rates: $27-$54
(402) 254-6850

HASTINGS

HOLIDAY INN
2205 Osborne Dr E (68901)
Rates: $59-$76
(402) 463-6721
(800) 465-4329

MIDLANDS LODGE
910 West J St
(68901)
Rates: $33-$54
(402) 463-2428
(800) 237-1872

RAINBOW MOTEL
1000 West J St
(68901)
Rates: $29-$40
(402) 463-2989
(800) 825-7424

SUPER 8 MOTEL
2200 N Kansas Ave (68901)
Rates: $49-$74
(402) 463-8888
(800) 800-8000

WAYFAIR MOTEL
101 East J St
(68901)
Rates: $35-$55
(402) 463-2434

HAYES CENTER

MIDWAY MOTEL
Hwy 25 (69032)
Rates: $35
(308) 286-3227

HEBRON

ROSEWOOD VILLA MOTEL
140 S 13th St
(68370)
Rates: $24-$33
(402) 768-6524

WAYFARER MOTEL
104 N 13th St
(68370)
Rates: $35
(402) 768-7226

HENDERSON

WAYFARER II MOTOR INN
Jct I-80 & S-93A
(68371)
Rates: $28-$32
(402) 723-5856
(800) 543-0577

HOLDREGE

THE CROW'S NEST B&B INN
503 Grant (68949)
Rates: $44-$55
(308) 995-5440

SUPER 8 MOTEL
420 Broadway
(68949)
Rates: $57-$87
(308) 995-2793
(800) 800-8000

HOWELLS

BERAN B&B
1604 Road 16
(68641)
Rates: $39-$55
(402) 986-1358

KEARNEY

BEST WESTERN INN KEARNEY
1010 3rd Ave
(68848)
Rates: $49-$88
(308) 237-5185
(800) 528-1234
(800) 359-1894

MOTEL 6
101 Talmadge Rd (68847)
Rates: $36-$50
(308) 338-0705
(800) 466-8356

PIONEER MOTEL
917 E 25thSt
(68847)
Rates: $28-$52
(308) 237-3168
(800) 359-6301

RAMADA INN
301 2nd Ave
(68848)
Rates: $69-$99
(308) 237-3141
(800) 272-6232

WESTERN INN SOUTH
510 3rd Ave
(68847)
Rates: $37-$46
(308) 234-1876
(800) 437-8457

KIMBALL

ARABIAN MOTEL
607 E 3rd St
(69145)
Rates: $28-$65
(308) 235-3995

DAYS INN
611 E 3rd St
(69145)
Rates: $53-$135
(308) 235-4671
(800) 329-7466

FINER MOTEL
Rt 1, Box 126
(69145)
Rates: $35-$55
(308) 235-4878

MOTEL KIMBALL
Rt 1, Box 131
(69145)
Rates: $35-$55
(308) 235-4606

AREA CODES - If the local number doesn't connect, check for a new area code.

SLUMBER J MOTEL
Rt 1, Box 126
(69145)
Rates: $27-$34
(308) 235-4878

WESTERN MOTEL
914 W Hwy 30
(69145)
Rates: $55+
(308) 235-4622

LAUREL
BIG RED MOTEL
202 S Hwy 20
(68745)
Rates: $35-$55
(402) 256-9952

LEMOYNE
ADMIRAL'S COVE RESORT
999 Lemoyne Rd
(69146)
Rates: $40-$55
(308) 355-2102
(800) 928-3386

NORTH SHORE LODGE
P. O. Box 237
(69146)
Rates: $42-$70
(308) 335-2222

LEWELLEN
GANDER INN MOTEL
S Main St (69147)
Rates: $35
(308) 778-5616

J'S OTTER CREEK RESORT
1290 Hwy 92 W
(69147)
Rates: $35-$50
(308) 355-5000

LEXINGTON
BUDGET HOST MINUTE MAN MOTEL
801 Plum Creek
Pkwy (68850)
Rates: $35-$50
(308) 324-5544
(800) 283-4678

COMFORT INN
2810 Plum Creek
Pkwy (68850)
Rates: $58-$85
(308) 324-3747
(800) 424-6423

DAYS INN
2506 Plum Creek
Pkwy (68850)
Rates: $40-$85
(308) 324-6440
(800) 329-7466

HOLIDAY INN EXP HOTEL & SUITES
2605 Plum Creek
Pkwy (68850)
Rates: $65-$109
(308)324-9900
(800) 465-4329

TODDLE INN MOTEL
2701 Plum Creek
Pkwy (68850)
Rates: $29-$49
(308) 324-5595
(800) 341-8000

LINCOLN
BAYMONT INN & SUITES
3939 N 26th St
(68521)
Rates: $69-$130
(402) 477-1100
(877) 229-6668

BEST WESTERN CROWN INN
6501 N 28th St
(68503)
Rates: $59-$89
(402) 438-4700
(800) 528-1234
(800) 398-3619

BEST WESTERN VILLAGER COURTYARD & GARDENS
5200 O St (68510)
Rates: $69-$84
(402) 464-9111
(800) 528-1234
(800) 356-4321

CHASE SUITES HOTEL
200 S 68th St Pl
(68510)
Rates: $88-$159
(402) 483-4900

COMFORT INN AIRPORT
2940 NW 12th St
(68521)
Rates: $54-$144
(402) 464-2200
(800) 424-6423

COUNTRY INN & SUITES
5353 N 27th St
(68521)
Rates: $89-$99
(402) 476-5353
(800) 456-4000

DAYS INN
1140 Calvert St
(68502)
Rates: $47-$74
(402) 423-7111
(800) 329-7466

DAYS INN & SUITES
2001 West O St
(68528)
Rates: $45-$99
(402) 477-4488
(800) 329-7466

HOLIDAY INN EXP
1133 Belmont Ave
(68521)
Rates: $54-$90
(402) 435-0200
(800) 465-4329

INN 4 LESS
1140 W
Cornhusker Hwy
(68521)
Rates: $35
(402) 475-4511

MICROTEL INN & SUITES
2505 Fairfield
(68521)
Rates: $40-$56
(402) 476-2591
(888) 569-5070

MOTEL 6
5600 Cornhusker
Hwy (68507)
Rates: $34-$48
(402) 464-5971
(800) 466-8356

MOTEL 6-AIRPORT
3001 NW 12th St
(68521)
Rates: $29-$46
(402) 475-3211
(800) 466-8356

OAK PARK MOTEL
926 Oak St (68521)
Rates: $26-$45
(402) 435-3258

QUALITY INN & SUITES
216 N 48th St
(68504)
Rates: $74-$99
(402) 464-4400
(800) 424-6423

RAMADA INN
1101 W Bond
(68521)
Rates: n/a
(402) 475-4971
(800) 272-6232

RAMADA LIMITED
4433 N 27th St
(68521)
Rates: n/a
(402) 476-2222
(800) 272-6232

RESIDENCE INN BY MARRIOTT
200 S 68th Pl
(68510)
Rates: $93-$143
(402) 483-4900
(800) 331-3131

SETTLE INN & SUITES
2800 Husker Cir
(68521)
Rates: $59-$109
(402) 435-8100

STAYBRIDGE SUITES
2701 Fletcher Ave
(68504)
Rates: $89-$199
(402) 438-7829
(800) 238-8000

SUPER 8 MOTEL
2545 Cornhusker
Hwy (68521)
Rates: $49-$65
(402) 467-4488
(800) 800-8000

SUPER 8 MOTEL
2635 W "O" St
(68528)
Rates: $49-$65
(402) 478-8887
(800) 800-8000

TOWN HOUSE MOTEL
1744 M St (68508)
Rates: $50-$75
(402) 475-3000
(800) 279-1744

LODGEPOLE
LODGEPOLE MOTEL
P. O. Box 114
(69149)
Rates: $25-$35
(308) 483-5890

LONG PINE
THE PINES
P. O. Box 343
(69217)
Rates: $26-$49
(402) 273-4483

LOUP CITY
COLONY INN
Rt 1, Box 184
(68853)
Rates: $35
(308) 745-0164

MCCOOK
BEST WESTERN CHIEF MOTEL
612 West B St
(69001)
Rates: $49-$69
(308) 345-3700
(800) 528-1234
(866) 842-3252

DAYS SUITES
901 N Hwy 83
(69001)
Rates: $45-$120
(308) 345-7115
(800) 329-7466

HOLIDAY INN EXP
1 Holiday Bison
Dr (69001)
Rates: $60
(308) 345-4505
(800) 465-4329

SUPER 8 MOTEL
1103 East B St
(69001)
Rates: $37-$44
(308) 345-1141
(800) 800-8000

MILFORD
MILFORD INN
962 238th St
(68405)
Rates: $26-$34
(402) 761-2151

MINATARE
HARRY'S MOTEL
Box 729 (69356)
Rates: $29-$45
(308) 783-1222

AREA CODES - If the local number doesn't connect, check for a new area code.

MORRILL

OAK TREE INN
80700 Hwy 26
(69358)
Rates: $48-$63
(308) 247-2111

MULLEN

GLIDDEN SANDHILLS MOTEL
P. O. Box 368
(69152)
Rates: $28-$35
(308) 546-2206

MURDOCK

FARM HOUSE B&B
32617 Church Rd
(68407)
Rates: $30-$55
(402) 867-2062

NEBRASKA CITY

APPLE INN
502 S 11th (68410)
Rates: $47-$64
(402) 873-5959
(800) 659-4446

NELIGH

DELUXE MOTEL
101 J St (68756)
Rates: $35-$55
(402) 887-4628

WEST HILLVIEW MOTEL
RR 2, Box 43
(68756)
Rates: $35-$50
(402) 887-4186

NEWMAN GROVE

CRYSTAL KEY INN BED & BRKFAST
P. O. Box 369
(68758)
Rates: $35-$75
(402) 447-2772

NIOBRARA

TWO RIVERS SALOON & HOTEL
254 - 12 Park Ave
(68760)
Rates: $35-$55
(402) 857-3340

NORFOLK

BLUE RIDGE MOTEL
916 S 13th St (68701)
Rates: $35
(402) 371-0530

NORFOLK COUNTRY INN
1201 S 13th St
(68701)
Rates: $56-$62
(402) 371-4430

SUPER 8 MOTEL
1223 Omaha Ave
(68701)
Rates: $49-$59
(402) 379-2220
(800) 800-8000

WHITE HOUSE INN
2206 Market Ln
(68701)
Rates: $55-$60
(402) 371-3133

NORTH PLATTE

BEST VALUE TRAVELERS INN
602 E 4th St (69101)
Rates: $36-$55
(308) 534-4020

BEST WESTERN CHALET LODGE
920 N Jeffers St
(69101)
Rates: $40-$74
(308) 532-2313
(800) 622-2313

BLUE SPRUCE MOTEL
821 S Dewey
(69101)
Rates: $35-$55
(308) 534-2600

CAMINO INN & SUITES
2102 S Jeffers
(69101)
Rates: $50-$66
(308) 532-9090
(800) 760-3333

CEDAR LODGE MOTEL
421 Rodeo Rd
(69101)
Rates: $26-$45
(308) 532-9710

COUNTRY INN
321 S Dewey
(69101)
Rates: $27-$32
(308) 532-8130
(800) 532-8130

HOLIDAY INN EXP HOTEL & SUITES
300 Holiday
Frontage Dr
(69103)
Rates: $57-$79
(308) 532-9500
(800) 465-4329

HOWARD JOHNSON INN
1209 S Dewey
(69101)
Rates: $50-$90
(308) 532-0130
(800) 446-4656

HUSKER INN
721 E 4th St
(69101)
Rates: $25-$35
(308) 534-6960

LA QUINTA INN & SUITES
2600 Eagles Wings
Pl (69101)
Rates: $89-$179
(308) 534-0700
(800) 687-6667

MOTEL 6
1520 S Jeffers
(69101)
Rates: $36-$63
(308) 534-6200
(800) 466-8356

PARK MOTEL
1302 N
Jeffers(69101)
Rates: $26-$37
(308) 532-6834

PIONEER MOTEL
902 S Dewey
(69101)
Rates: $35-$55
(308) 532-8730

QUALITY INN & SUITES
2102 S Jeffers
(6910134
Rates: $59-$84
(308) 532-9090
(800) 424-6423

RAMADA LIMITED
3201 S Jeffers
(69101)
Rates: $47-$76
(308) 534-3120
(800) 272-6232

RAMBLER MOTEL
1420 Rodeo Rd
(69101)
Rates: $25-$35
(308) 532-9290

SANDS MOTOR INN
501 Halligan Dr
(69101)
Rates: $35-$56
(308) 532-0151

STANFORD MOTEL
1400 E 4th St (69101)
Rates: $30-$49
(308) 532-9380
(800) 743-4934

STOCKMAN INN
1402 S Jeffers
(69103)
Rates: $41-$65
(308) 534-3630
(800) 624-4643

OGALLALA

BEST WESTERN STAGECOACH INN
201 Stagecoach Tr
(69153)
Rates: $50-$90
(308) 284-3656
(800) 528-1234
(800) 662-2993

DAYS INN
601 Stagecoach Tr
(69153)
Rates: $49-$85
(308) 284-6365
(800) 329-7466

ECONO LODGE
108 Prospector Dr
(69153)
Rates: $36-$75
(308) 284-2056
(800) 424-6423

ELMS MOTEL
717 W 1st St
(69153)
Rates: $26-$34
(308) 284-3404

HOLIDAY INN EXP
501 Stagecoach
Tr (69153)
Rates: $65-$75
(308) 284-2266
(800) 465-4329

KINGSLEY LODGE
1510 N Hwy 61
(69153)
Rates: $35-$55
(308) 284-2775
(800) 883-2775

LAKEWAY LODGE
918 N Spruce St
(69153)
Rates: $35-$55
(308) 284-4431
(888) 284-4431

LAZY K MOTEL
1501 E 1st St
(69153)
Rates: $28-$40
(308) 284-4085

PLAZA INN
311 E 1st (69153)
Rates: $55-$65
(308) 284-8416

SUNSET MOTEL
1021 W 1st (69153)
Rates: $35
(308) 284-4264

WESTERN PARADISE MOTEL
221 E 1st (69153)
Rates: $35-$55
(308) 284-3684
(800) 733-0899

OMAHA

BAYMONT INN
10760 M St (68127)
Rates: $44-$75
(402) 592-5200
(877) 229-6668

BEST WESTERN KELLY INN
4706 S 108th St
(68137)
Rates: $79-$119
(402) 339-7400
(800) 528-1234

BEST WESTERN REDICK PLAZA HOTEL
1504 Harney St
(68102)
Rates: $99-$169
(402) 342-1500

AREA CODES - If the local number doesn't connect, check for a new area code.

**BEST WESTERN
SETTLE INN**
650 N 109th Ct
(68154)
Rates: $59-$99
(402) 431-1246
(800) 889-0261

**CANDLEWOOD
SUITES**
360 S 108th Ave
(68154)
Rates: $69-$109
(402) 758-2848
(888) 226-3539

**CLARION HOTEL
WEST**
4888 S 118th St
(68137)
Rates: $59-$149
(402) 895-1000
(800) 424-6423

COMFORT INN
9595 S 145th St
(68138)
Rates: $55-$210
(402) 896-6300
(800) 424-6423

**COMFORT INN
SOUTHWEST**
10728 L St (68127)
Rates: $70-$149
(402) 593-2380
(800) 424-6423

COMFORT SUITES
10503 Bedford Ave
(68134)
Rates: $79-$99
(402) 454-0400
(800) 424-6423

**COUNTRYSIDE
SUITES**
9477 S 142nd St
(68138)
Rates: $60-$80
(402) 884-2644

**CROWNE PLAZA
HOTEL &
RESORT-OLD MILL**
5655 N 108th Ave
(68154)
Rates: $79-$189
(402) 496-0850
(800) 227-6963

**DOUBLETREE
GUEST SUITES**
7270 Cedar St
(68124)
Rates: $69-$189
(402) 397-5141
(800) 222-8733

**DOUBLETREE
HOTEL**
1616 Dodge St
(68102)
Rates: $69-$189
(402) 346-7600
(800) 222-8733

ECONO LODGE
7833 W Dodge
Rd(68124)
Rates: $40-$79
(402) 391-7100
(800) 424-6423

EMBASSY SUITES
555 S 10th (68102)
Rates: $119-$289
(402) 346-9000
(800) 362-2779

HAMPTON INN
10728 L St (68127)
Rates: $57-$72
(402) 593-2380
(800) 426-7866

**HAWTHORN
SUITES**
11025 M Street
(68137)
Rates: $89-$99
(402) 331-0101
(800) 527-1133

**HOLIDAY INN EXP
HOTEL & SUITES**
10729 J St (68127)
Rates: $76
(402) 339-8111
(800) 465-4329

**HOMEWOOD
SUITES**
7010 Hascall St
(68106)
Rates: $89-$129
(402) 397-7500
(800) 225-5466

LA QUINTA INN
3330 N 104th Ave
(68134)
Rates: $69-$105
(402) 493-1900
(800) 687-6667

MOTEL 6
10708 M St (68127)
Rates: $37-$60
(402) 331-3161
(800) 466-8356

RAMADA LIMITED
9505 S 142nd St
(68138)
Rates: $55-$85
(402) 896-9500
(800) 272-6232

**RELAX INN
MOTEL & SUITES**
4578 S 60th St
(681117)
Rates: $40-$60
(402) 731-7300

**RESIDENCE INN
BY MARRIOTT**
6990 Dodge St
(68132)
Rates: $126-$132
(402) 553-8898
(800) 331-3131

SATELLITE MOTEL
6006 L St (68117)
Rates: $38-$46
(402) 733-7373

**SHERATON
OMAHA HOTEL**
1615 Howard St
(68102)
Rates: $75-$199
(402) 342-2222
(800) 325-3535

**SUPER 8 MOTEL-
WEST**
11610 W Dodge
Rd (68154)
Rates: $55-$65
(402) 492-8845
(800) 800-8000

**SUPER 8 MOTEL-
WEST**
10829 M St (68137)
Rates: $55-$65
(402) 2339-2250
(800) 800-8000

O'NEILL

ELMS MOTEL
414 Hwy 20 E
(68763)
Rates: $35-$55
(402) 336-3800
(800) 526-9052

GOLDEN HOTEL
406 E Douglas St
(68763)
Rates: $32-$54
(402) 336-4436
(800) 658-3148

HOLIDAY INN EXP
1020 E Douglas
St (68763)
Rates: $68-$85
(402) 336-4500
(800) 465-4329

SUPER 8 MOTEL
106 E Hwy 20
(68763)
Rates: $45-$65
(402) 336-3100
(800) 800-8000

ORCHARD

**DIAMOND E
TROUT RESORT
GUEST RANCH**
P. O. Box B (68764)
Rates: $59-$80
(402) 893-4745
(800) 974-3002

ORCHARD MOTEL
E Hwy 20 (68764)
Rates: $35
(402) 893-2165

OSHKOSH

S & S MOTEL
Hwy 26 & 27
(69154)
Rates: $35
(308) 772-3350

**SHADY REST
MOTEL**
108 Main St
(69154)
Rates: $30-$36
(308) 772-4115

PAWNEE CITY

PAWNEE INN
1021 F St (68420)
Rates: $35-$55
(402) 852-2238

PAXTON

DAYS INN
I-80 Ex 145 (69155)
Rates: $50-$100
(308) 239-4510
(800) 329-7466

PLAINVIEW

HILLCREST MOTEL
P. O. Box 848
(68769)
Rates: $26-$34
(402) 582-3299

PLATTSMOUTH

**BROWN'S
FAMILY MOTEL**
1913 Hwy 34 E
(68048)
Rates: $55-$65
(402) 296-9266

RANDOLPH

CEDAR MOTEL
107 East Hwy 20
(68771)
Rates: $25-$35
(402) 337-0500

RED CLOUD

**MCFARLAND
HOTEL**
137 West 4th Ave
(68970)
Rates: $25-$35
(402) 746-2329

REPUBLICAN CITY

DAVE'S CABINS
RR 1, Box 125
(68971)
Rates: $26-$46
(308) 799-3635

GATEWAY MOTEL
17 Hwy 136
(68971)
Rates: $35
(308) 799-2815

RUSHVILLE

ANTLERS MOTEL
607 East 2nd St
(69360)
Rates: $30-$60
(308) 327-2444

**NEBRASKALAND
MOTEL**
508 East 2nd,
Box 377 (69360)
Rates: $35-$55
(308) 327-2277

ST. PAUL

**KELLER'S KORNER
MOTEL**
1517 2nd St
(68873)
Rates: $35
(308) 754-4451

SUPER 8 MOTEL
116 Howard Ave
(68873)
Rates: $53-$61
(308) 754-4554
(800) 800-8000

AREA CODES - If the local number doesn't connect, check for a new area code.

SCHUYLER

JOHNNIE'S MOTEL
222 W 16th (68661)
Rates: $28-$37
(402) 352-5454

VALLEY COURT MOTEL
320 W 16th St (68661)
Rates: $35
(402) 352-3326

SCOTTSBLUFF

CAPRI MOTEL
2424 Ave I (69361)
Rates: $35-$45
(308) 635-2057
(800) 642-2774

COMFORT INN
1902 21st Ave (69361)
Rates: $56-$85
(308) 632-7510
(800) 424-6423

DAYS INN
1901 21st Ave (69361)
Rates: $54-$68
(308) 635-3111
(800) 329-7466

LAMPLIGHTER MOTEL-AMERICAN INN
606 E 27th St (69361)
Rates: $35-$48
(308) 632-7108

SEWARD

EAST HILL MOTEL
131 Hwy 34 E (68434)
Rates: $35
(402) 643-3679

SUPER 8 MOTEL
1329 Progressive Rd (68434)
Rates: $47-$61
(402) 643-3388
(800) 800-8000

SIDNEY

AMERICINN MOTEL & SUITES
645 Cabela Dr (69162)
Rates: $84-$159
(308) 254-0100
(800) 634-3444

DAYS INN
3042 Silverberg Dr (69162)
Rates: $48-$110
(308) 254-2121
(800) 329-7466

DELUXE MOTEL
2201 Illinois St (69162)
Rates: $25-$34
(308) 254-4666

EL PALOMINO MOTEL
2220 Illinois St (69162)
Rates: $27-$46
(308) 254-5566

FORT SIDNEY INN
935 9th Ave (69162)
Rates: $33-$85
(308) 254-5863
(888) 743-6394

GENERIC MOTEL
11552 Hwy 30 (69162)
Rates: $35-$55
(308) 254-4527
(800) 893-5309

HOLIDAY INN
664 Chase Blvd (69162)
Rates: $75-$80
(308) 254-2000
(800) 465-4329

MOTEL 6
3040 Silverberg Dr (69162)
Rates: $42-$55
(308) 254-5463
(800) 466-8356

SOUTH SIOUX CITY

MARINA INN CONF CENTER
4th & B Sts (68776)
Rates: $84-$109
(402) 494-4000
(800) 798-7980

SPENCER

SKYLINE MOTEL
Hwys 281 & 12 (68777)
Rates: $35
(402) 589-1300
(800) 917-1300

STEINAUER

CONVENT HOUSE BED & BRKFAST
P. O. Box 68 (68441)
Rates: $40-$55
(402) 869-2276

STUART

STUART VILLAGE INN
P. O. Box 238 (68780)
Rates: $26-$35
(402) 924-3133

SUPERIOR

VICTORIAN INN
P. O. Box 407 (68978)
Rates: $27-$34
(402) 879-3245

SUTHERLAND

PARK MOTEL
1110 1st St (69165)
Rates: $35
(308) 386-4384
(800) 437-2565

SUTTON

SUTTON MOTEL
208 N French (68979)
Rates: $25-$35
(402) 773-4803

SYRACUSE

MUSTANG MOTEL
940 Park St (68446)
Rates: $25-$35
(402) 269-2185

SLEEP INN INN & SUITES
130 N 30th Rd (68440)
Rates: $51-$122
(402) 269-2700
(800) 424-6423

THEDFORD

RODEWAY INN
SR 2E (69166)
Rates: $41-$80
(308) 645-2284
(800) 424-6423

TRYON

LONGHORN MOTEL
P. O. Box 94 (69167)
Rates: $26-$34
(308) 587-2345

VALENTINE

BALLARD MOTEL
227 S Hall St (69201)
Rates: $35
(402) 376-2922

DUNES MOTEL
304 E Hwy 20 & 83 (69201)
Rates: $39-$74
(402) 376-3131

HOLIDAY INN EXP
803 E Hwy 20 (69201)
Rates: $65-$99
(402) 376-3000
(800) 465-4329

FOUNTAIN INN
237 S Cherry St (69201)
Rates: $55
(402) 376-2300

MERRITT RESORT
HC 32, Box 23 (69201)
Rates: $60
(402) 376-3437

MOTEL RAINE
616 Hwy 20 W (69201)
Rates: $34-$60
(402) 376-2030
(800) 999-3066

NIOBRARA INN
525 N Main (69201)
Rates: $60-$80
(402) 376-1779

NIOBRARA RIVER RESORT
HC 60, Box 5 (69216)
Rates: $37-$55
(402) 966-3321

TRADE WINDS MOTEL
E Hwy 20 & 83 (69201)
Rates: $40-$69
(402) 376-1600

VERDIGRE

THE VERDIGRE INN
P. O. Box 28 (68783)
Rates: $28-$50
(402) 668-2277

WAHOO

WAHOO HERITAGE INN
950 N Chestnut (68066)
Rates: $50-$79
(402) 443-1288

WAUNETA

WAUNETA MOTEL
P. O. Box 221 (69034)
Rates: $25-$33
(308) 394-5434

WAUSA

COMMERCIAL HOTEL
Main St (68786)
Rates: $35-$55
(402) 586-2377

WAYNE

K-D INN MOTEL
311 East 7th St (68787)
Rates: $30-$55
(402) 375-1770

SPORTS CLUB MOTEL
Rt 2, Box 195 (68787)
Rates: $29-$48
(402) 375-4222

WEST POINT

POINTERS INN MOTEL
534 S Lincoln Hwy (68788)
Rates: $30-$52
(402) 372-2491

WILBER

HOTEL WILBER BED & BREAKFAST
P. O. Box 633 (68465)
Rates: $28-$53
(402) 821-2020
(888) 494-5237

WISNER

MIDWEST MOTEL
1612 Ave E (68791)
Rates: $35-$55
(402) 529-6910

AREA CODES - If the local number doesn't connect, check for a new area code.

WOOD RIVER

WOOD RIVER MOTEL
11774 S Hwy 11
(68883)
Rates: $35
(308) 583-2256
(800) 587-2256

WYMORE

D & M MOTEL
601 S 14th St
(68466)
Rates: $35
(402) 645-3801

YORK

BEST WESTERN PALMER INN
2426 S Lincoln
Ave (68467)
Rates: $38-$90
(402) 362-5585
(800) 528-1234
(800) 452-3185

DAYS INN
3710 S Lincoln
(68467)
Rates: $42-$100
(402) 362-6355
(800) 329-7466

STAEHR MOTEL
RR 4, Box 49
(68467)
Rates: $35-$55
(402) 362-4804

YORKSHIRE INN MOTEL
3402 S Lincoln
Ave (68467)
Rates: $39-$59
(402) 362-6633

AREA CODES - If the local number doesn't connect, check for a new area code.

NEVADA

ALAMO

MEADOW LANE MOTEL
US Hwy 93
(89001)
Rates: $30-$49
(775) 725-3371
(888) 740-8009

AMARGOSA VALLEY

DESERT VILLAGE MOTEL
Rt 373 & Mecca Rd (89020)
Rates: $39-$49
(775) 372-1405

LONGSTREET INN/CASINO & RV PARK
373 Stateline (89020)
Rates: $69-$99
(775) 372-1777
(800) 508-9493

AUSTIN

LINCOLN MOTEL
728 Main (89310)
Rates: $29-$43
(775) 964-2698

PONY CANYON MOTEL
Hwy 50 (89310)
Rates: $34-$52
(775) 964-2605

PONY EXPRESS HOUSE B&B
115 NW Main St (89310)
Rates: $35+
(775) 964-2306

BAKER

BORDER INN
Hwys 50 & 6 (89311)
Rates: $29-$39
(775) 234-7300

HIDDEN CANYON GUEST RANCH
P O Box 180 (89311)
Rates: $44-$124
(775) 234-7267
(888) 711-7552

SILVERJACK MOTEL
Main St (89311)
Rates: $36-$70
(775) 234-7323

BATTLE MOUNTAIN

BIG CHIEF MOTEL
434 W Front St (89820)
Rates: $32-$42
(775) 635-2416

COMFORT INN
521 E Front St (89820)
Rates: $50-$89
(775) 635-5880
(800) 424-6423

BEATTY

AMARGOSA RIVER INN
350 First St (89003)
Rates: $27-$44
(775) 553-2250

BURRO INN
Third St & Hwy 95 (89003)
Rates: $38-$44
(775) 553-2225
(800) 843-2078

EL PORTAL MOTEL
420 Main St (89003)
Rates: $30-$60
(775) 553-2912
(800) 352-3068

MOTEL 6
Hwy 95 N (89003)
Rates: $38+
(775) 553-9090
(800) 466-8356

PHOENIX INN
Hwy 95 & First St (89003)
Rates: $30-$50
(775) 553-2250
(800) 845-7401

STAGECOACH HOTEL & CASINO
Hwy 95 (89003)
Rates: $35-$75
(775) 553-2419
(800) 424-4946

BOULDER CITY

BEST WESTERN LIGHTHOUSE INN & RESORT
110 Vile Dr (89005)
Rates: $49-$99
(702) 293-6444
(800) 528-1234
(800) 934-8282

DESERT INN OF BOULDER CITY
800 Nevada Hwy (89005)
Rates: $40-$120
(702) 293-2827

EL RANCHO BOULDER MOTEL
725 Nevada Way (89005)
Rates: $60-$80
(702) 293-1085

FLAMINGO INN MOTEL
804 Nevada Hwy (89005)
Rates: $27-$60
(702) 293-3565

LAKE MEAD RESORT & MARINA
322 Lakeshore Rd (89005)
Rates: $50-$125
(702) 293-2074
(800) 752-9669

NEVADA INN MOTEL
1009 Nevada Hwy (89005)
Rates: $30-$75
(702) 293-2044
(800) 638-8890

STARVIEW MOTEL
1017 Nevada Hwy (89005)
Rates: $27-$90
(702) 293-1658

SUPER 8 MOTEL
704 Nevada Hwy (89005)
Rates: $50-$100
(702) 294-8888
(800) 800-8000

CALIENTE

CALIENTE HOT SPRINGS MOTEL
Hwy 93 N (89008)
Rates: $34-$75
(775) 726-3777
(888) 726-3777

LONGHORN CATTLE COMPANY GUEST RANCH
Rainbow Canyon Rd (89008)
Rates: $100+
(775) 388-9955

RAINBOW CANYON MOTEL
884 A St (89008)
Rates: $35-$45
(775) 726-3291

SHADY MOTEL
450 Front St (89008)
Rates: $38-$47
(775) 726-3106

CARLIN

CAVALIER MOTEL
10th & State Rt 40 (89822)
Rates: $32-$50
(775) 754-6311

COMFORT INN CENTRAL
1018 Fir St (89822)
Rates: $59-$104
(775) 754-6110
(800) 424-6423

CARSON CITY

BEST VALUE INN
2731 S Carson St (89701)
Rates: $30-$250
(775) 882-2007
(800) 231-6326

BEST WESTERN TRAILSIDE INN
1300 N Carson St (89701)
Rates: $39-$149
(775) 883-7300
(800) 528-1234
(800) 626-1900

CARSON CITY INN
1930 N Carson St (89701)
Rates: $30-$37
(775) 882-1785

DAYS INN
3103 N Carson St (89701)
Rates: $51-$100
(775) 883-3343
(800) 329-7466

DOWNTOWNER MOTOR INN
801 N Carson St (89701)
Rates: $32-$99
(775) 882-1333
(800) 364-4908

FRONTIER MOTEL
1718 N Carson St (89701)
Rates: $25-$179
(775) 882-1377

HOLIDAY INN EXP
4055 N Carson St (89706)
Rates: $89-$269
(775) 283-4055
(800) 465-4329

AREA CODES - If the local number doesn't connect, check for a new area code.

MOTEL 6
2749 S Carson St
(89701)
Rates: $31-$52
(775) 885-7710
(800) 466-8356

NUGGET MOTEL
651 N Stewart St
(89701)
Rates: $40-$75
(775) 882-7711
(800) 948-9111

PIONEER MOTEL
907 S Carson St
(89701)
Rates: $36-$75
(775) 882-3046
(800) 882-3046

RAND AVENUE MOTEL
1464 Rand Ave
(89706)
Rates: $30-$35
(775) 841-7200

ROUND HOUSE INN
1400 N Carson St
(89701)
Rates: $29-$99
(775) 882-3446

SIERRA SAGE MOTEL
801 S Carson St
(89701)
Rates: $25-$60
(775) 882-1419

SIERRA VISTA MOTEL
711 S Plaza St
(89701)
Rates: $30-$75
(775) 883-9500
(800) NEVADA-1

SUPER 8 MOTEL
2829 S Carson St
(89701)
Rates: $28-$199
(775) 883-7800
(800) 800-8000

DENIO

DENIO JUNCTION MOTEL
P. O. Box 10
(89404)
Rates: $40+
(775) 941-0371

ECHO BAY

ECHO BAY RESORT
On Lake Mead
(Overton 89040)
Rates: $85-$115
(702) 394-4000
(800) 752-9669

ELKO

BEST WESTERN GOLD COUNTRY MOTOR INN
2050 Idaho St
(89801)
Rates: $49-$99
(775) 738-8421
(800) 528-1234
(800) 621-1332

COMFORT INN
2970 Idaho St
(89801)
Rates: $59-$89
(775) 777-8762
(800) 424-6423

ELKO MOTEL
1243 Idaho St
(89801)
Rates: $32-$95
(775) 738-4433

ESQUIRE INN
505 Idaho St
(89801)
Rates: $32-$70
(775) 738-3157
(800) 822-7473

HIGH DESERT INN
3015 Idaho St
(89801)
Rates: $59-$109
(775) 738-8425
(888) 394-8303

HOLIDAY MOTEL
1276 Idaho St
(89801)
Rates: $32-$36
(775) 738-7187

KEY MOTEL
650 W Idaho St
(89801)
Rates: $34-$58
(775) 738-8081

LOUIS MOTEL
2100 Idaho St
(89801)
Rates: $26-$108
(775) 738-3536

MANOR MOTOR LODGE
185 Idaho St
(89801)
Rates: $30-$60
(775) 738-3311

MID-TOWN MOTEL
294 Idaho St
(89801)
Rates: $30-$65
(775) 738-3515

MOTEL 6
3021 Idaho St
(89801)
Rates: $29-$36
(775) 738-4337
(800) 466-8356

O.K. 7 MOTEL
291 W Idaho St
(89801)
Rates: $27-$31
(775) 738-4644

OAK TREE INN
95 Spruce Rd
(89801)
Rates: $52-$79
(775) 777-2222
(888) 897-9647

ONCE UPON A TIME B&B
537 14th St (89801)
Rates: $65-$95
(775) 738-1200

RED LION INN & CASINO
2065 Idaho St
(89801)
Rates: $89-$109
(775) 738-2111
(800) 733-5466
(800) 545-0044

RUBY CREST GUEST RANCH
HC 30, Box 197
(89801)
Rates: 150+
(775) 744-2277

RUBY MARSHES GUEST RANCH
HC 30, Box 197
(89801)
Rates: $150+
(775) 744-2277

SHILO INN
2401 Mountain
City Hwy (89801)
Rates: $80-$129
(775) 738-5522
(800) 222-2244

STAMPEDE 7 MOTEL
129 W Idaho St
(89801)
Rates: $30-$50
(775) 738-8471

THUNDERBIRD MOTEL
345 Idaho St
(89801)
Rates: $49-$79
(775) 738-7115

TOWNE HOUSE MOTEL
500 W Oak St
(89801)
Rates: $32-$42
(775) 738-7269

TRAVELERS MOTEL
1181 Idaho St
(89801)
Rates: $26-$38
(775) 738-4048

ELY

BEST WESTERN MAIN MOTEL
1101 Aultman St
(89301)
Rates: $49-$108
(775) 289-4529
(800) 528-1234

BEST WESTERN PARK VUE
930 Aultman St
(89301)
Rates: $49-$79
(775) 289-4497
(800) 528-1234

DESER-EST MOTOR LODGE
1425 Aultman St
(89301)
Rates: $28-$49
(775) 289-8885

EL RANCHO MOTEL
1400 Aultman St
(89301)
Rates: $25-$40
(775) 289-3644

FIRESIDE INN
McGill Hwy
(89301)
Rates: $42-$46
(775) 289-3765
(800) 732-8288

4 SEVENS MOTEL
500 High St
(89301)
Rates: $30-$45
(775) 289-4747

GRAND CENTRAL MOTEL
1498 Lyons Ave
(89301)
Rates: $32-$36
(775) 289-6868

GREAT BASIN INN
701 Ave F (89301)
Rates: $39-$45
(775) 289-4468

HOTEL NEVADA & GAMBLING HALL
501 Aultman St
(89301)
Rates: $30-$85
(775) 289-6665
(888) 406-3055

IDLE INN MOTEL
150 Fourth St
(89301)
Rates: $22-$35
(775) 289-4411

JAILHOUSE MOTEL
Fourth & High Sts
(89301)
Rates: $40-$65
(775) 289-3033
(800) 841-5430

LANE'S RANCH MOTEL
State Rt 318 at
Preston (89301)
Rates: $29-$43
(775) 238-5246

MOTEL 6
770 Ave O (89301)
Rates: $33-$45
(775) 289-6671
(800) 466-8356

AREA CODES - If the local number doesn't connect, check for a new area code.

RAMADA INN COPPER QUEEN HOTEL & CASINO
805 Great Basin Blvd (89301)
Rates: $60-$125
(775) 289-4884
(800) 851-9526
(800) 272-6232

SHAKESPEARE INN
1550 High St (89301)
Rates: $25-$45
(775) 289-2512
(888) 866-8253

WHITE PINE MOTEL
1301 Aultman St (89301)
Rates: $24-$43
(775) 289-3800

EUREKA

COLONNADE HOTEL
Clark & Monroe Sts (89316)
Rates: $25-$44
(775) 237-9988

RUBY HILL MOTEL
Hwy 50 (89316)
Rates: $28-$38
(775) 237-5339

SUNDOWN LODGE
Main St (89316)
Rates: $31-$44
(775) 237-5334

FALLON

COMFORT INN
1830 W Williams Ave (89406)
Rates: $50-$251
(775) 423-5554
(800) 424-6423

FALLON MOTEL
390 W Williams Ave (89406)
Rates: $40-$90
(775) 423-4648

MOTEL 6
1705 S Taylor St (89406)
Rates: $39-$49
(775) 423-2277
(800) 466-8356

OXBOW MOTOR INN
60 S Allen Rd (89406)
Rates: $46-$65
(775) 423-7021

SUPER 8 MOTEL
855 W Williams Ave (89406)
Rates: $45-$50
(775) 423-6031
(800) 800-8000

VALUE INN
180 W Williams Ave (89406)
Rates: $32-$65
(775) 423-5151

WESTERN MOTEL
125 S Carson St (89406)
Rates: $37-$57
(775) 423-5118

FERNLEY

BEST WESTERN FERNLEY INN
1405 E Newlands Dr (89408)
Rates: $59-$110
(775) 575-6776
(800) 528-1234
(877) 576-6776

GABBS

GABBS MOTEL
100 S Main St (89409)
Rates: $28-$45
(775) 285-4019

GARDNERVILLE

BEST WESTERN TOPAZ LAKE INN
3410 Sandy Bowers Ave (89410)
Rates: $45-$139
(775) 266-4661

TOPAZ LODGE & CASINO
1979 Hwy 395 S (89410)
Rates: $29-$79
(775) 266-3338
(800) 962-0732

WESTERNER MOTEL
1353 US 395 N (89410)
Rates: $32-$70
(775) 782-3602

GENOA

GENOA HOUSE INN B&B
180 Nixon St (89411)
Rates: $105-$150
(775) 782-7075

GERLACH

SOLDIER MEADOWS GUEST RANCH & LODGE
Soldier Meadows Rd (89412)
Rates: $50-$120
(530) 233-4881

HAWTHORNE

ANCHOR MOTEL
965 Sierra Way (89415)
Rates: $25-$29
(775) 945-2573

BEST INN & SUITES
1402 E 5th St (89415)
Rates: $55-$60
(775) 945-2660
(800) 237-8466

CLIFF HOUSE LAKESIDE RESORT
1 Cliff House Rd (89415)
Rates: $30-$40
(775) 945-2444
(888) 320-5253

EL CAPITAN RESORT/CASINO
540 F St (89415)
Rates: $50-$55
(775) 945-3321
(800) 922-2311

HAWTHORNE MOTEL
720 Sierra Hwy 95 (89415)
Rates: $25-$30
(775) 945-2544

HOLIDAY LODGE
Fifth & J Sts (89415)
Rates: $26-$32
(775) 945-3316

MONARCH MOTEL
1291 E Fifth St (89415)
Rates: $28-$50
(775) 945-3117

ROCKET MOTEL
694 Sierra Way (89415)
Rates: $22-$25
(775) 945-2143

SAND N SAGE MOTEL
1301 E 5th St (89415)
Rates: $30-$45
(775) 945-3352

WRIGHT MOTEL
W Fifth & I Sts (89415)
Rates: $26-$33
(775) 945-2213

HENDERSON

BOBY MOTEL
2100 S Boulder Hwy (89015)
Rates: $30-$75
(702) 565-9711

GREEN VALLEY RANCH HOTEL
2300 S Paseo Verde Dr (89012)
Rates: $250-$500
(702) 617-7777
(877) 467-2777

HAMPTON INN HOTEL & SUITES
421 Astaire Dr (89014)
Rates: $99-$149
(702) 992-9292
(800) 426-7866

HAWTHORN INN & SUITES
910 S Boulder Hwy (89015)
Rates: $79-$139
(702) 568-7800
(800) 527-1133

HOLIDAY INN EXP
441 Astaire Dr (89014)
Rates: $89-$199
(702) 990-2323
(800) 465-4329

OUTPOST MOTEL
1104 N Boulder Hwy (89015)
Rates: $38-$75
(702) 564-2664

RESIDENCE INN BY MARRIOTT- GREEN VALLEY
2190 Olympic Rd (89014)
Rates: $114-$144
(702) 434-2700
(800) 331-3131

SKY MOTEL
1713 N Boulder Hwy (89015)
Rates: $35-$45
(702) 564-1534

TOWNHOUSE MOTOR LODGE
43 Water St (89015)
Rates: $25-$65
(702) 564-3111

INDIAN SPRINGS

INDIAN SPRINGS MOTOR HOTEL
300 Tonapah Hwy (89018)
Rates: $33-$45
(702) 879-3700

JACKPOT

BARTON'S CLUB 93
Hwy 93 (89825)
Rates: $35-$65
(775) 755-2341
(800) 258-2937

COVERED WAGON MOTEL
1601 Hwy 93 (89825)
Rates: $20-$40
(775) 755-2241
(800) 838-1241

HORSESHU HOTEL & CASINO
1385 Hwy 93, Dice Rd (89825)
Rates: $29-$85
(775) 755-7777
(800) 821-2321

WEST STAR RESORT
Hwy 93 & Poker St (89825)
Rates: $32-$125
(775) 755-2600

AREA CODES - If the local number doesn't connect, check for a new area code.

JARBIDGE

OUTDOOR INN
Main St (89826)
Rates: $30-$75
(775) 488-2311

LAKE LAS VEGAS

RITZ-CARLTON
1610 Lake Las
Vegas Pkwy
(89011)
Rates: $199-$589
(702) 567-4700
(800) 241-3333

LAKE TAHOE

(See additional
listing in California)

**HARRAH'S LAKE
TAHOE HOTEL
& CASINO**
15 Hwy 50
(Stateline 89449)
Rates: $179-$269
(775) 588-6611
(800) 427-7247
(Kennels
provided)

**HORIZON
CASINO RESORT**
P. O. Box C
(89449)
Rates: $69-$200
(775) 588-6211
(800) 322-7723

LAMOILLE

**BREITENSTEIN
HOUSE B&B**
P. O. Box 281381
(89828)
Rates: $55-$125
(775) 753-6356

LAS VEGAS

A FISHERS INN
3565 Boulder Hwy
(89121)
Rates: $25-$65
(702) 457-3900

AMERISUITES
4520 Paradise Rd
(89109)
Rates: $59-$159
(702) 369-3366
(800) 833-1516

**BEST WESTERN
MAIN STREET INN**
1000 N Main St
(89101)
Rates: $39-$149
(702) 382-3455
(800) 528-1234
(800) 851-1414

**BEST WESTERN
NELLIS MOTOR
INN**
5330 E Craig Rd
(89115)
Rates: $49-$200
(702) 643-6111
(800) 528-1234
(800) 546-1119

**BEST WESTERN
PARKVIEW INN**
905 Las Vegas
Blvd N (89101)
Rates: $39-$149
(702) 385-1213
(800) 528-1234
(800) 548-6122

**BLAIR HOUSE
SUITES**
344 E Desert Inn
Rd (89109)
Rates: $45-$125
(702) 792-2222
(800) 553-9111

**BLUE ANGEL
MOTEL**
2110 E Fremont St
(89101)
Rates: $30-$100
(702) 386-9500

**BUDGET SUITES
OF AMERICA**
4625 Boulder Hwy
(89121)
Rates: $49-$69
(702) 454-4625
(800) 752-1501

**BUDGET SUITES
OF AMERICA**
4855 Boulder Hwy
(89121)
Rates: $49-$69
(702) 433-3644

**CANDLEWOOD
SUITES**
4034 S Paradise
Rd (89109)
Rates: $89-$209
(702) 836-3660
(888) 226-3539

**CITY CENTER
MOTEL**
700 E Fremont St
(89101)
Rates: $35-$130
(702) 382-4766

COMFORT INN
910 E Cheyenne
Ave (89030)
Rates: $69-$299
(702) 399-1500
(800) 424-6423

**DAISY MOTEL
& APARTMENTS**
415 S Main St
(89101)
Rates: $29-$35
(702) 382-0707

**FERGUSONS
MOTEL**
1028 E Fremont St
(89101)
Rates: $35-$150
(702) 382-3500
(800) 933-7829

**FOUR SEASONS
HOTEL**
3960 Las Vegas
Blvd S (89193)
Rates: $250-$500
(702) 632-5000
(877) 632-5000

GATEWAY MOTEL
928 Las Vegas
Blvd S (89101)
Rates: $26-$100
(702) 382-2146

**GATEWOOD
MOTEL**
3075 E Fremont St
(89104)
Rates: $25-$125
(702) 457-3600

GLASS POOL INN
4613 Las Vegas
Blvd S (89119)
Rates: $39-$109
(702) 739-6636
(800) 527-7118

**GOLDEN INN
MOTEL**
120 Las Vegas
Blvd N (89101)
Rates: $27-$80
(702) 384-8204

HAMPTON INN
7100 Cascade
Valley Ct (89128)
Rates: $$79-$129
(702) 360-5700
(800) 426-7866

**HAWTHORN
SUITES**
5051 Duke
Ellington Way
(89119)
Rates: $69-$309
(702) 739-7000
(800) 527-1133

**HOLIDAY INN EXP
THE LAKES**
8669 W Sahara
Ave (89117)
Rates: $69-$175
(702) 256-3766
(800) 465-4329

HOLIDAY INN EXP
8669 W Sahara
Ave (89117)
Rates: $79-$169
(702) 256-3766
(800) 465-4329

**HOLIDAY INN EXP
HOTEL & SUITES
N LAS VEGAS**
4540 Donovan
Way (89031)
Rates: $99-$149
(702) 649-3000
(800) 465-4329

**HOMESTEAD
STUDIO SUITES**
3045 S Maryland
Pkwy (89109)
Rates: $64-$84
(702) 369-1414
(888) 782-9473

**HOWARD
JOHNSON
AIRPORT INN**
5100 Paradise Rd
(89119)
Rates: $49-$159
(702) 798-2777
(800) 446-4656

**HOWARD
JOHNSON INN-
LAS VEGAS STRIP**
1401 Las Vegas
Blvd (89104)
Rates: $49-$159
(702) 388-0301
(800) 446-4656

**KING ALBERT
MOTEL**
185 Albert Lane
(89109)
Rates: $39+
(702) 732-1555
(800) 553-7753

LA PALM MOTEL
2512 E Fremont St
(89104)
Rates: $30-$65
(702) 384-5874

**LA QUINTA INN
CONV CENTER**
3970 Paradise Rd
(89109)
Rates: $70-$100
(702) 796-9000
(800) 687-6667

**LA QUINTA INN
NELLS**
4288 N Nellis Blvd
(89115)
Rates: $79-$139
(702) 632-0229
(800) 687-6667

**LA QUINTA INN-
SUMMERLIN TECH
CENTER**
7101 Cascade
Valley Ct (89128)
Rates: $65-$96
(7020 360-1200
(800) 687-6667

**LA QUINTA INN-
TROPICANA**
4975 S Valley
View Blvd (89118)
Rates: $59-$250
(702) 798-7736
(800) 687-6667

**LA QUINTA
SUITES-
WEST/LAKES**
9570 W Sahara
Ave (89117)
Rates: $79-$199
(702) 243-0356
(800) 687-6667

**LAMPLIGHTER
MOTEL**
2805 E Fremont St
(89104)
Rates: $30-$50
(702) 382-8791

AREA CODES - If the local number doesn't connect, check for a new area code.

MEADOWS INN
525 E Bonanza Rd
(89101)
Rates: $35-$55
(702) 366-0456
(800) 932-1499

MOTEL 8/
MR. DELI
3961 Las Vegas
Blvd S (89119)
Rates: $29-$105
(702) 798-7223

MOTEL REGENCY
700 N Main St
(89101)
Rates: $32-$49
(702) 382-2332

MOTEL 6-
BOULDER HIGH-
WAY
4125 Boulder
Hwy (89121)
Rates: $33-$81
(702) 457-8051
(800) 466-8356

MOTEL 6
5085 S Industrial
Rd (89118)
Rates: $35-$60
(702) 739-6747
(800) 466-8356

MOTEL 6
195 E Tropicana
Ave (89109)
Rates: $35-$60
(7020 798-0728
(800) 466-8356

PARADISE
RESORT INN
3450 Paradise Rd
(89109)
Rates: $38-$55
(702) 733-3900

QUALITY INN
220 Convention
Center Dr (89109)
Rates: $36-$200
(702) 735-4151
(800) 424-6423

RAMADA INN-
SPEEDWAY
CASINO
3227 Civic Cir Dr
(89030)
Rates: n/a
(702) 399-3297
(800) 272-6232

RESIDENCE INN
BY MARRIOTT
3225 S Paradise
Rd (891095
Rates: $119-$389
(702) 796-9300
(800) 331-3131
(800) 244-3364

RESIDENCE INN
BY MARRIOTT
370 Hughes Ctr
Dr (89109)
Rates: $99-$300
(702) 650-0040
(800) 331-3131

RESIDENCE INN
LAS VEGAS -S
5875 Industrial Rd
(89118)
Rates: n/a
(702) 795-7378
(800) 331-3131

RODEWAY INN
& SUITES
167 E Tropicana
Ave (89109)
Rates: $36-$209
(702) 795-3311
(800) 424-6423

SILVER QUEEN
MOTEL
1401 E Carson St
(89101)
Rates: $28-$130
(702) 384-8157

ST. TROPEZ ALL
SUITE HOTEL
455 E Harmon
AVe (89109)
Rates: $69-$169
(702) 369-5400

SUPER 8 MOTEL-
LAS VEGAS STRIP
4250 Koval Lane
(89109)
Rates: $61-$225
(702) 794-0888
(800) 800-8000

TRAVEL INN
MOTEL
217 Las Vegas
Blvd N (89101)
Rates: $30-$50
(702) 384-3040

VAGABOND INN
CENTER STRIP
3265 Las Vegas
Blvd S (89109)
Rates: $45-$150
(702) 735-5102
(800) 522-1555
(800) 828-8032

VALLEY MOTEL
1313 E Fremont St
(89101)
Rates: $30-$40
(702) 384-6890

VEGAS CHALET
MOTEL
2401 Las Vegas
Blvd N (89030)
Rates: $35-$125
(702) 642-2115

WALDEN MOTEL
3085 E Fremont
(89104)
Rates: $25-$125
(702) 457-9090

WELLESLEY INN &
SUITES
1550 E Flamingo
Rd (89109)
Rates: $50-$80
(702) 731-3111
(800) 444-8888

WESTIN
CASUARINA
LAS VEGAS
HOTEL & SPA
160 E Flamingo
Rd (89109)
Rates: $139-$299
(702) 836-9775
(866) 837-4215

LAUGHLIN
(Also see Bullhead
City, AZ)
BAY SHORE INN
1955 Casino Dr
(89029)
Rates: $25-$125
(702) 299-9010

DON
LAUGHLIN'S
RIVERSIDE RESORT
HOTEL & CASINO
1650 Casino Dr
(89029)
Rates: $39-$199
(702) 298-2535
(800) 227-3849

EDGEWATER
HOTEL &
CASINO
2020 S Casino Dr
(89029)
Rates: $39-$350
(702) 298-2453

LOVELOCK
CADILLAC INN
1395 Cornell Ave
(89419)
Rates: $20-$42
(775) 273-2798

COVERED
WAGON MOTEL
945 Dartmouth
Ave (89419)
Rates: $38-$45
(775) 273-2961

DESERT PLAZA
INN
1435 Cornell Ave
(89419)
Rates: $35-$55
(775) 273-2500

LOVELOCK INN
55 Cornell Ave
(89419)
Rates: $39-$65
(775) 273-2937

RAMADA INN
STURGEON'S
CASINO
1420 Cornell Ave
(89419)
Rates: $49-$75
(775) 273-2971
(800) 272-6232
(800) 234-6835

SAGE MOTEL
1335 Cornell Ave
(89419)
Rates: $17-$32
(775) 273-0444

SIERRA MOTEL
14th & Dartmouth
Sts (89419)
Rates: $20-$42
(775) 273-2798

MCDERMITT
MCDERMITT
MOTEL
55 Hwy 95 N
(89421)
Rates: $40-$60
(775) 532-8588
(800) 841-3058

MESQUITE
BUDGET INN
& SUITES
390 N Sandhill
(89024)
Rates: $44-$69
(702) 346-7444
(800) 463-6302

DESERT PALMS
MOTEL
Mesquite Blvd
(89024)
Rates: $15-$45
(702) 346-5756

SI REDD'S OASIS
RESORT HOTEL &
CASINO
897 W Mesquite
Blvd (89024)
Rates: $29-$109
(702) 346-5232
(800) 216-2747

VALLEY INN
MOTEL
791 W Mesquite
Blvd (89024)
Rates: $30-$69
(702) 346-5281

VIRGIN RIVER
HOTEL &
CASINO
915 Mesquite Blvd
N (89024)
Rates: $22-$99
(702) 346-7777
(800) 346-7721

MILL CITY
SUPER 8 MOTEL
6000 E Frontage
Rd (89418)
Rates: $39-$53
(775) 538-7311
(800) 800-8000

MINDEN
BEST WESTERN
MINDEN INN
1795 Ironwood Dr
(89423)
Rates: $59-$99
(775) 782-7766
(800) 528-1234
(866) 441-1234

HOLIDAY LODGE
1591 US 395N
(89423)
Rates: $32-$48
(775) 782-2288
(800) 266-2289

MOUNT CHARLESTON

MT. CHARLESTON HOTEL
2 Kyle Canyon Rd (89124)
Rates: $49-$155
(702) 872-5500
(800) 794-3456

MT. CHARLESTON LODGE
Kyle Canyon Rd (89124)
Rates: $125-$220
(702) 872-5408
(800) 955-1314

MOUNTAIN CITY

CHAMBERS' MOTEL
P. O. Box 188 (89831)
Rates: $30-$45
(775) 763-6626

MOUNTAIN CITY MOTEL
Hwy 225 (89831)
Rates: $28-$60
(775) 763-6622

NORTH LAS VEGAS

BARKER MOTEL
26001 Las Vegas Blvd N (89030)
Rates: n/a
(702) 642-1138

COMFORT INN
910 E Cheyenne Rd (89030)
Rates: $55-$250
(702) 399-1500
(800) 424-6423

HOLIDAY INN EXP HOTEL & SUITES
4540 Donovan Way (89031)
Rates: $62-$80
(702) 649-3000
(800) 465-4329

OASIS

OASIS MOTEL
I-80, Exit 378 (89835)
Rates: $23-$45
(702) 478-5113

OLD NEVADA

BONNIE SPRINGS MOTEL
1 Gunfighter Lane (89004)
Rates: $55-$125
(702) 875-4400

OROVADA

ROCKY VIEW INN
Hwy 95 N (89425)
Rates: $30-$40
(775) 272-3337

OVERTON

BEST WESTERN THE NORTH SHORE INN AT LAKE MEAD
520 N Moapa Vly Blvd (89040)
Rates: $49-$75
(702) 397-6000

PAHRUMP

BEST WESTERN PAHRUMP STATION
1101 Hwy 160 N (89041)
Rates: $51-$127
(775) 727-5100
(800) 528-1234
(800) 713-9688

SADDLE WEST HOTEL & CASINO
1220 S Hwy 160 (89041)
Rates: $46-$61
(775) 727-1111

PIOCHE

HUTCHINGS MOTEL
Hwy 93 (89043)
Rates: $35+
(775) 962-5404

MOTEL PIOCHE
100 LaCour St (89043)
Rates: $35+
(775) 962-5551

OVERLAND HOTEL
85 Main St (89043)
Rates: $37-$52
(775) 962-5895

RACHEL

LITTLE A'LE'INN
Hwy 375 (89001)
Rates: $30+
(775) 729-2515

RENO

BONANZA MOTOR INN
215 W Fourth St (89501)
Rates: $38-$125
(775) 322-8632
(800) 808-3303

CITY CENTER MOTEL
365 West St (89501)
Rates: $30-$90
(775) 323-8880

DAYS INN
701 E 7th St (89512)
Rates: $35-$135
(775) 786-4070
(800) 329-7466
(800) 448-4555

DOWNTOWNER MOTOR LODGE
150 Stevenson St (89503)
Rates: $32+
(775) 322-1188

EASY 8 MOTEL
255 W Fifth St (89503)
Rates: $22+
(775) 322-4588

EL RAY MOTEL
330 N Arlington (89501)
Rates: $30-$125
(775) 329-6669

EL TAVERN MOTEL
1801 W Fourth St (89503)
Rates: $30-$40
(775) 322-4504

FLAMINGO MOTEL
520 N Center St (89501)
Rates: $30-$80
(775) 323-3202

GOLD COIN MOTEL
2555 E Fourth St (89512)
Rates: $28-$50
(775) 323-0237

HARRAH'S RENO CASINO/HOTEL
219 Center St (89504)
Rates: $39-$139
(775) 786-3232
(800) HARRAHS
(Kennels provided)

HIGHWAY 40 MOTEL
1750 E Fourth St (89512)
Rates: $25+
(775) 329-1911

HOLIDAY HOTEL & CASINO
111 Mill St (89504)
Rates: $20-$50
(775) 329-0411
(800) 648-5431

HOLIDAY INN DOWNTOWN
1000 E 6th St (89512)
Rates: $79-$109
(775) 786-5151
(800) 465-4329
(800) 648-4877

KAY MARTIN LODGE
6950 S Virginia St (89511)
Rates: $35-$75
(775) 853-6504

KENO MOTEL NO. 1
322 N Arlington Ave (89501)
Rates: $25-$80
(775) 322-6281

LA QUINTA INN
4001 Market St (89501)
Rates: $65-$85
(775) 348-6100
(800) 687-6667

MINER'S INN
1651 N Virginia St (89506)
Rates: $39-$95
(775) 329-3464
(800) 626-1900

MONTE CARLO MOTEL
500 N Virginia St (89501)
Rates: $35-$110
(775) 329-2010

MOTEL 500
500 S Center St (89501)
Rates: $30-$95
(775) 786-2777

MOTEL 6
1400 Stardust St (89503)
Rates: $29-$56
(775) 747-7390
(800) 466-8356

MOTEL 6
866 N Wells Ave (89512)
Rates: $29-$56
(775) 786-9852
(800) 466-8356

MOTEL 6
1901 S Virginia (89502)
Rates: $29-$56
(775) 827-0255
(800) 466-8356

OLYMPIC APARTMENT HOTEL
195 W Second St (89501)
Rates: $30-$60
(775) 323-0726

OX-BOW MOTOR LODGE
941 S Virginia St (89509)
Rates: $30-$95
(775) 786-3777

PONDEROSA HOTEL
515 S Virginia St (89501)
Rates: $29-$70
(775) 786-6820
(800) 228-6820

QUALITY INN SOUTH
1885 S Virginia St (89502)
Rates: $65-$125
(702) 329-1001
(800) 424-6423

RESIDENCE INN BY MARRIOTT
9845 Gateway Dr (89511)
Rates: $112-$149
(775) 853-8800
(800) 331-3131

AREA CODES - If the local number doesn't connect, check for a new area code.

RODEWAY INN
2050 Market St
(89502)
Rates: $39-$99
(775) 786-2500
(800) 424-6423

SAVOY MOTOR LODGE
705 N Virginia St
(89501)
Rates: $28-$55
(775) 322-4477
(877) 200-4099

SEASONS INN
495 West St
(89503)
Rates: $40-$115
(775) 322-6000
(800) 322-8588

SHOWBOAT INN
660 N Virginia St
(89501)
Rates: $35-$125
(775) 786-4032
(800) 648-3960

SILVER DOLLAR MOTOR LODGE
817 N Virginia St
(89501)
Rates: $30-$50
(775) 323-6875

TRUCKEE RIVER LODGE
501 W 1st St
(89503)
Rates: $31-$220
(775) 786-8888
(800) 635-8950

UPTOWN MOTEL
570 N Virginia St
(89501)
Rates: $35+
(775) 323-8906

WHITE POST INN
567 W Fourth St
(89503)
Rates: $38-$55
(775) 322-8181

SEARCHLIGHT
EL REY MOTEL
430 S Hobson
(89046)
Rates: $32-$60
(702) 297-1144

SILVER CITY
HARDWICKE HOUSE B&B
99 Main St (89428)
Rates: $35-$60
(775) 847-0215

SILVER SPRINGS
A SECRET GARDEN B&B
P O Box 1150
(89429)
Rates: $55-$65
(775) 577-0837

PIPERS MOTEL
1190 Hwy 50 W
(89429)
Rates: $35+
(775) 577-2295

SMITH
WALKER RIVER RESORT
Hudson Way, P O
Box 90 (89430)
Rates: $64+
(775) 465-2573
(800) 446-2573

SPARKS
BLUE FOUNTAIN INN
1590 B St (89431)
Rates: n/a
(775) 359-0359

MOTEL 6
2405 Victorian
Ave (89431)
Rates: $29-$56
(775) 358-1080
(800) 466-8356

PONY EXP LODGE
2406 Prater Way
(89431)
Rates: $28-$46
(775) 358-7110

QUALITY INN
55 E Nugget Ave
(89431)
Rates: $49-$150
(775) 358-6900
(800) 424-6423

SUPER 8 MOTEL
1900 E Greg St
(89431)
Rates: $47-$62
(775) 358-8884
(800) 800-8000

WESTERN VILLAGE INN & CASINO
815 E Nichols
Blvd (89432)
Rates: $20-$100
(775) 331-1069
(800) 648-1170

STATELINE
HARRAH'S LAKE TAHOE HOTEL CASINO
15 Hwy 50, Casino
Area (89449)
Rates: $119-$259
(775) 588-6611
(800) 427-7247
(Kennels
provided)

TONOPAH
BEST WESTERN HI-DESERT INN
320 Main St
(89049)
Rates: $59-$89
(775) 482-3511
(800) 528-1234
(877) 286-2208

CLOWN MOTEL
521 N Main St
(89049)
Rates: $35+
(775) 482-5920

GOLDEN HILLS MOTEL
826 E Main St
(89049)
Rates: $24-$65
(775) 482-6238

JIM BUTLER MOTEL
100 S Main St
(89049)
Rates: $34-$55
(775) 482-3577
(800) 635-9455

OK CORRAL MOTEL
Hwy 95 N (89049)
Rates: $24-$47
(775) 482-8202

RAMADA INN TONOPAH STATION
1137 S Main st
(89049)
Rates: n/a
(775) 482-9777
(800) 272-6232

SILVER QUEEN MOTEL
255 Erie Main
(89049)
Rates: $31-$45
(775) 482-6291
(800) 210-9218

SUNDOWNER MOTEL
700 Hwy 95
(89049)
Rates: $27-$34
(775) 482-6224

TONOPAH MOTEL
325 Main St
(89049)
Rates: $27-$33
(775) 482-3987

TOPAZ LAKE
TOPAZ LODGE
1979 US 395 S
(89410)
Rates: $39-$53
(775) 266-3338

UNIONVILLE
OLD PIONEER GARDEN B&B
2805 Unionville
Rd (89418)
Rates: $65-$85
(775) 538-7585

VALMY
VALMY STATION MOTEL
I-80 E, Exit 216
(89438)
Rates: $22-$35
(775) 635-5511

VIRGINIA CITY
SILVER QUEEN HOTEL
28 North C St
(89440)
Rates: $45-$125
(775) 847-0440

SPARGO HOUSE BED & BREAKFST
395 B St (89440)
Rates: $75-$150
(775) 847-7455

WELLS
BEST WESTERN SAGE INN
576 6th St (89835)
Rates: $39-$65
(775) 752-3353
(800) 528-1234
(800) 540-1883

LONE STAR MOTEL
676 6th St (89835)
Rates: $24-$39
(775) 752-3632

MOTEL 6
I-80/US 40 &
Hwy 93 (89835)
Rates: $29-$36
(775) 752-2116
(800) 466-8356

OVERLAND HOTEL
P. O. Box 79
(89835)
Rates: $19-$27
(775) 752-3373

REST INN SUITES MOTEL
1509 E 6th St
(98935)
Rates: $37-$49
(775) 752-2277
(800) 935-5768

SHARON MOTEL
633 6th St (89835)
Rates: $24-$39
(775) 752-3232

SHELL CREST MOTEL
573 6th St (89835)
Rates: $24-$39
(775) 752-3755

WAGON WHEEL MOTEL
340 Sixth St
(89835)
Rates: $19-$37
(775) 752-2151

WENDOVER, UTAH
MOTEL 6
561 E Wendover
Blvd (84083)
Rates: $29-$40
(435) 665-2267
(800) 466-8356

WESTERN RIDGE MOTEL
895 E Wendover
Blvd (84083)
Rates: $26-$80
(435) 665-2211

WINNEMUCCA

BEST WESTERN GOLD COUNTRY INN
921 W Winnemucca
Blvd (89445)
Rates: $69-$119
(775) 623-6999
(800) 528-1234
(800) 346-5306

BUDGET INN
251 E
Winnemucca Blvd
(89445)
Rates: $25-$55
(775) 623-2394

BULL HEAD MOTEL
500 E Winnemucca
Blvd (89445)
Rates: $33-$50
(775) 623-3636

COZY MOTEL
344 E Winnemucca
Blvd (89445)
Rates: $30-$40
(775) 623-2615

DAYS INN
511 W
Winnemucca Blvd
(89445)
Rates: $59-$89
(775) 623-3661
(800) 329-7466

ECONOMY MOTEL
635 W Winnemucca
Blvd (89445)
Rates: $38-$75
(775) 623-5281

FRONTIER MOTEL
410 E Winnemucca
Blvd (89445)
Rates: $38-$65
(775) 623-2915

MOTEL 6
1600 Winnemucca
Blvd (89445)
Rates: $29-$46
(775) 623-1180
(800) 466-8356

PARK MOTEL
740 W Winnemucca
Blvd (89445)
Rates: $30-$40
(775) 623-2810

PONDEROSA MOTEL
705 W Winnemucca
Blvd (89445)
Rates: $28-$59
(775) 623-4898

PYRENEES MOTEL
714 W Winnemucca
Blvd (89445)
Rates: $43-$63
(775) 623-1116

RED LION INN & CASINO
741 W Winnemucca
Blvd (89445)
Rates: $79-$164
(775) 623-2565
(800) 633-6435

SCOTT SHADY COURT
400 First St (89445)
Rates: $35-$75
(775) 623-3646

VAL-U INN MOTEL
125 E Winnemucca
Blvd (89445)
Rates: $62
(775) 623-5248
(800) 443-7777

WINNERS HOTEL & CASINO
185 W Winnemucca
Blvd (89445)
(775) 623-2511
(800) 648-4770

YERINGTON

CASINO WEST
11 N Main St
(89447)
Rates: $34-$60
(775) 463-2481
(800) 227-4661

COPPER INN MOTEL
307 N Main St
(89447)
Rates: $35-$45
(775) 463-2135

IN TOWN MOTEL
111 S Main St
(89447)
Rates: $35-$45
(775) 463-2164

RANCH HOUSE MOTEL
311 W Bridge St
(89447)
Rates: $32-$44
(775) 463-2200

ZEPHYR COVE

TAHOE MANAGEMENT COMPANY RENTALS
601 Hwy 50
P.O. Box 11456
(89448)
Rates: $60-$110
(775) 588-4504
(800) 624-3887

ZEPHYR COVE RESORT
760 Hwy 50
(89448)
Rates: $60-$260
(775) 588-6644

AREA CODES - If the local number doesn't connect, check for a new area code.

NEW HAMPSHIRE

ALTON
EYE JOY COTTAGES
Roberts Cove Rd (03809)
Rates: n/a
(603) 569-4973

ALTON BAY
HORSE & BUGGY COTTAGES
Bay Hill Rd (03810)
Rates: $50-$390
(603) 875-5600

LEMAY'S BY THE BAY
Rt 28A, Box 127 (03810)
Rates: n/a
(603) 875-3629

ANTRIM
MAPLEHURST INN
155 Main St (03440)
Rates: $60-$85
(603) 588-8000

ASHLAND
BLACK HORSE MOTOR COURT
RR 1, Box 46, Rt 3 (03217)
Rates: n/a
(603) 968-7116

BARTLETT
THE VILLAGER MOTEL
Main St, Rt 302 (03812)
Rates: $39-$149
(603) 374-2742
(800) 334-6988

BERLIN
TRAVELER MOTEL
25 Pleasant St (03570)
Rates: $39-$99
(603) 752-2500
(800) 365-9391

BETHLEHEM
THE MULBURN INN B&B
2370 Main St (03574)
Rates: $85-$175
(603) 869-3389

BRADFORD
BRADFORD INN
RFD 1, Box 40 (03221)
Rates: n/a
(603) 938-5309

CAMPTON
GILCREST COTTAGES & MOTEL
RFD 1, Box 927 (03223)
Rates: n/a
(603) 726-3330
(888) 741-0129

PLYMOUTH WHITE MTN HOTEL
Rt 3 (03223)
Rates: $76-$125
(603) 536-3520

CENTER HARBOR
LAKE SHORE MOTEL & COTTAGES
RR 2, Box 16H (03226)
Rates: n/a
(603) 253-6244
(941) 439-6625

THE MEADOWS LAKESIDE LODGING
SR 25 (03226)
Rates: $65-$110
(603) 253-4347

SACO RIVER MOTOR LODGE
Rt 302, P. O. Box 9A (03813)
Rates: $39-$139
(603) 447-3720

WATCH HILL BED & BREAKFAST
P. O. Box 1605 (03226)
Rates: $65+
(603) 253-4334

CHESTERFIELD
CHESTERFIELD COUNTRY INN
399 Cross Rd (03466)
Rates: $110-$250
(603) 256-3211
(800) 365-5515

CHOCORUA
THE LAZY DOG INN B&B
201 White Mountain Hwy (03817)
Rates: $75-$205
(603) 323-8350

CLAREMONT
BEST BUDGET INN
24 Sullivan St (03743)
Rates: $38-$72
(603) 542-9567

CLAREMONT MOTOR LODGE
Beauregard St (03743)
Rates: $45-$60
(603) 542-2540

COLEBROOK
COLEBROOK HOUSE & MOTEL
132 Main St (03576)
Rates: n/a
(603) 237-5521
(800) 626-7331

NORTHERN COMFORT MOTEL
1 Trooper Scott Phillips Hwy (03576)
Rates: $58-$78
(603) 237-4440

CONCORD
BEST WESTERN CONCORD INN & SUITES
97 Hall St (03301)
Rates: $59-$199
(603) 228-4300

BRICK TOWER MOTOR INN
414 S Main St (03301)
Rates: $39-$64
(603) 224-9565

COMFORT INN
71 Hall St (03301)
Rates: $59-$209
(603) 226-4100
(800) 424-6423

CONWAY
SUNNY BROOK COTTAGES
Rt 16, P. O. Box 1429 (03818)
Rates: $49-$59
(603) 447-3922

TANGLEWOOD MOTEL & COTTAGES
Rt 16, Box 108 (03818)
Rates: n/a
(603) 447-5932

WHITE DEER MOTEL
379 White Mtn Hwy (03818)
Rates: $49-$149
(603) 447-5366

DOVER
DAYS INN
481 Central Ave (03820)
Rates: $79-$225
(603) 742-0400
(800) 329-7466

DURHAM
HICKORY POND INN HISTORIC BED & BREAKFST
1 Stagecoach Rd (03824)
Rates: $59-$99
(603) 659-2227

EAST SULLIVAN
POST & BEAM BED & BREAKFST
18 Centre St (03445)
Rates: n/a
(603) 847-3330
(888) 376-6262

EAST SWANZEY
COACH AND FOUR MOTOR INN
755 Monadnock Hwy (03446)
Rates: n/a
(603) 357-3705

EAST WAKEFIELD
LAKE IVANHOE CAMPING & BED & BREAKFAST INN
631 Acton Ridge Rd (03830)
Rates: n/a
(603) 522-8824

EATON CENTER
INN AT CRYSTAL LAKE & RESTAURANT
2356 Eaton Rd (03832)
Rates: $79-$239
(603) 447-2120

EXETER
EXETER INN
90 Front St (03833)
Rates: $73-$135
(603) 772-5901

FITZWILLIAM
THE UNIQUE YANKEE B&B
354 Upper Troy Rd (03447)
Rates: $60-$130
(603) 242-6706

AREA CODES - If the local number doesn't connect, check for a new area code.

FRANCESTOWN

THE INN AT CROTCHED MTN
Mountain Rd
(03043)
Rates: $45-$120
(603) 588-6840

FRANCONIA

FRANCONIA HOTEL
87 Wallace Hill Rd
(03580)
Rates: $69-$139
(603) 823-7422
(888) 669-6777

"FRANCONIA NOTCH VACATIONS" HOME RENTALS
P O Box 906,
Mittersill (03580)
Rates: n/a
(800) 247-5536

GALE RIVER MOTEL
1 Main St (03580)
Rates: $50-$105
(603) 823-5655
(800) 255-7989

LOVETT'S INN BY LAFAYETTE BROOK
1474 Profile Rd
(03580)
Rates: $99-$335
(603) 823-7761
(800) 356-3802

FRANKLIN

D K MOTEL
Rt 3A & 11 (03235)
Rates: n/a
(603) 934-3311

GILMANTON

TEMPERANCE TAVERN HISTORIC BED & BRKFAST
Old Province Rd
(03237)
Rates: $75-$125
(603) 267-7349

GORHAM

COMFORT INN
370 Main St
(03581)
Rates: $36-$125
(603) 466-2732
(800) 424-6423

MOOSE BROOK MOTEL
65 Lancaster Rd
(03581)
Rates: $39-$67
(603) 466-5400

MT. MADISON MOTEL
365 Main St
(03581)
Rates: $37-$124
(603) 466-3622
(800) 851-1136

ROYALTY INN
130 Main St
(03581)
Rates: $51-$104
(603) 466-3312
(800) 437-3529

TOP NOTCH INN
265 Main St
(03581)
Rates: $44-$142
(603) 466-5496
(800) 228-5496

TOWN & COUNTRY MOTOR INN
US Rt 2 (03581)
Rates: $50-$110
(603) 466-3315
(800) 325-4386

HAMPTON

THE INN OF HAMPTON & CONF CTR
815 Lafayette Rd
(03842)
Rates: $99-$189
(603) 926-6771

LAMIE'S INN & TAVERN
490 Lafayette Rd
(03842)
Rates: $95-$135
(603) 926-0330

HAMPTON FALLS

HAMPTON FALLS INN
11 Lafayette Rd
(03844)
Rates: $69-$169
(603) 926-9545
(800) 356-1729

HANOVER

HANOVER INN-DARTMOUTH COLLEGE ON THE GREEN
Main & Wheelocke St
(03755)
Rates: $217-$287
(603) 643-4300
(800) 443-7024

HARTS LOCATION

NOTCHLAND HISTORIC COUNTRY INN
US 302 (03812)
Rates: $165-$245
(603) 374-6131

HILLSBORO

1830 HOUSE MOTEL
626 W Main St
(03244)
Rates: $45+
(603) 478-3135

HOLDERNESS

YANKEE TRAIL MOTEL
Rt 3 (03245)
Rates: $45-$65
(603) 968-3535
(800) 972-1492

INTERVALE

RIVERSIDE INN
Rt 16A (03845)
Rates: $45-$95
(603) 356-9060

SWISS CHALETS VILLAGE INN
Rt 16A (03845)
Rates: $49-$139
(603) 356-2232
(800) 831-2727

JACKSON

THE INN AT JACKSON
Thorn Hill Rd
(03846)
Rates: $99-$209
(603) 383-4321

MOUNTAINSIDE FARM B&B
Carter Notch Rd
(03846)
Rates: $26-$60
(603) 383-6531
(800) 782-4270

THE VILLAGE HOUSE INN
Rt 16 A (03846)
Rates: $26-$50
(603) 383-6666
(800) 972-8343

WHITNEY'S INN
Rt 16-B (03846)
Rates: $135-$155
(603) 383-8916
(800) 677-5737

JAFFREY

WOODBOUND INN
Woodbound Rd
(03452)
Rates: $65-$190
(800) 688-7770

JEFFERSON

APPLEBROOK BED & BREAKFAST
Rt 115-A (03583)
Rates; $55-$90
(603) 586-7713
(800) 545-6504

JEFFERSON NOTCH MOTEL & CABINS
Rt 2, Randolph
(03583)
Rates: $50+
(603) 466-3833
(800) 345-3833

JOSSELYN'S GETAWAY LOG CABINS
RFD 1, Box 51A,
North Rd (03583)
Rates: $56+
(800) 586-4507

KEARSARGE

ISAAC E. MERRILL HOUSE INN B&B
720 Kearsarge Rd
(03847)
Rates: $55-$155
(603) 356-9041
(800) 328-9041

KEENE

BEST WESTERN SOVEREIGN HOTEL
401 Winchester St
(03431)
Rates: $69-$199
(603) 357-3038
(800) 528-1234
(800) 533-6364

HOLIDAY INN EXP
175 Key Rd
(03431)
Rates: $119-$269
(603) 352-7616
(800) 465-4329

THE MOTOR INN MOTEL
921 Main St, Rt 12 S (03431)
Rates: n/a
(603) 352-4138

SUPER 8 MOTEL
3 Ashbrook Rd
(03431)
Rates: $69-$200
(603) 352-9780
(800) 800-8000

VALLEY GREEN MOTEL
379 West St
(03431)
Rates: $30-$69
(603) 352-7350

WINDING BROOK LODGE
Box 372 (03431)
Rates: $34-$50
(603) 352-3111

LACONIA

SUN VALLEY COTTAGES & CONDOS
686 Endicott St N
(03246)
Rates: $45-$60
(603) 366-4945

TIN WHISTLE INN
1047 Union Ave
(03246)
Rates: n/a
(603) 528-4185

LANCASTER

COOS MOTOR INN
209 Main St
(03584)
Rates: $55-$69
(603) 788-3079

LANCASTER MOTOR INN
112 Main St
(03584)
Rates: $39-$55
(603) 788-4921

THE OLD MORSE LODGE B&B
39 Portland St (03584)
Rates: $45-$100
(603) 788-4600

PINETREE MOTEL
RFD 2, Box 281 (03584)
Rates: $28-$40
(603) 636-2479

LEBANON

DAYS INN
135 Rt 120 (03766)
Rates: $89-$189
(603) 448-5070
(800) 329-7466

RESIDENCE INN BY MARRIOTT
32 Centerra Pkwy (03766)
Rates: $119-$219
(603) 643-4511
(800) 331-3131

LINCOLN

COMFORT INN & SUITES
21 Railroad St (03251)
Rates: $99-$199
(603) 745-6700
(800) 424-6423

PARKER'S MOTEL
750 Rt 3 (03251)
Rates: $36-$99
(603) 745-8341
(800) 766-6835

PEMI MOTOR COURT CABINS
RFD 1, Box 97 (03251)
Rates: $50+
(603) 745-8323

LITTLETON

BEAL HOUSE INN
2 W Main St (03561)
Rates: $115-$245
(603) 444-2661

EASTGATE MOTOR INN
335 Cottage St (03561)
Rates: $52-$109
(603) 444-3971

THAYERS INN
111 Main St (03561)
Rates: $59-$99
(603) 444-6469

LOUDON

LOVEJOY FARM B&B
268 Lovejoy Rd (03301)
Rates: $112-$139
(603) 783-4007

LYME

LOCH LYME LODGE
NH 10, RFD 278 (03768)
Rates: $26-$65
(603) 795-2141
(800) 423-2141

MANCHESTER

COMFORT INN
298 Queen City Ave (03102)
Rates: $65-$259
(603) 668-2600
(800) 221-5150

ECONO LODGE
75 W Hancock St (03102)
Rates: $55-$109
(603) 624-0111
(800) 424-6423

HOLIDAY INN EXP HOTEL & SUITES-AIRPORT
1298 S Porter St (03103)
Rates: $99-$119
(603) 669-6800
(800) 465-4329

HOMEWOOD SUITES
1000 N Perimeter Rd (03103)
Rates: $99-$199
(603) 668-2200
(800) 225-5466

RADISSON HOTEL
711 Elm St (03103)
Rates: $99-$189
(603) 625-1000
(800) 333-3333

TOWNEPLACE SUITES
686 Huse Rd (03103)
Rates: $99-$169
(603) 641-2288
(800) 257-3000

MERRIMACK

DAYS INN
242 Daniel Webster Hwy (03054)
Rates: $55-$80
(603) 429-4600
(800) 329-7466

RESIDENCE INN BY MARRIOTT
246 Daniel Webster Hwy (03054)
Rates: $109-$199
(603) 424-8100
(800) 331-3131

MOULTON-BOROUGH

MATTERHORN MOTOR LODGE
340 Rt 25 (03254)
Rates: $95-$125
(603) 253-4314

ROB ROY MOTOR LODGE
P. O. Box 420 (03254)
Rates: $49-$75
(603) 476-5571

MOUNT SUNAPEE

BEST WESTERN SUNAPEE LAKE LODGE
1403 Rt 103 (03255)
Rates: $89-$289
(603) 763-2010
(800) 528-1234
(800) 606-5253

NASHUA

HOLIDAY INN
9 Northeastern Blvd (03062)
Rates: $69-$109
(603) 888-1551
(800) 465-4329

MOTEL 6
2 Progress Ave (03062)
Rates: $43-$60
(603) 889-4151
(800) 466-8356

MARRIOTT HOTEL
2200 Southwood Dr (03063)
Rates: $85-$165
(603) 579-6005
(800) 228-9290

RED ROOF INN
77 Spitbrook Rd (03063)
Rates: $52-$80
(603) 888-1893
(800) 843-7663

SHERATON NASHUA HOTEL
11 Tara Blvd (03062)
Rates: $79-$239
(603) 888-9970
(800) 325-3535

NEWBURY

BEST WESTERN SUNAPEE LAKE LODGE
1403 SR 103 (03255)
Rates: $99-$299
(603) 763-2010
(800) 528-1234

NEW CASTLE

WENTWORTH BY THE SEA MARRIOTT HOTEL & SPA
588 Wentworth Rd (03854)
Rates: $119-$729
(603) 422-7322
(866) 240-6313

NEWPORT

HISTORIC EAGLE INN AT COIT MOUNTAIN
523 N Main St (03773)
Rates: $49-$127
(603) 863-3583
(800) 367-2364

NEWPORT MOTEL
467 Sunapee St (03773)
Rates: $53-$75
(603) 863-1440

NORTH CONWAY

CRANMORE MOUNTAIN LODGE
859 Kearsarge Rd (03860)
Rates: $59-$295
(603) 356-2044
(800) 356-3596

SPRUCE MOOSE LODGE & COTTAGES
B&B
207 Seavey St (03860)
Rates: $49-$159
(603) 356-6239

NORTHWOOD

LAKE SHORE FARM RESORT
275 Jenness Pond Rd (03261)
Rates: $285-$305
(603) 942-5921

OSSIPEE

PINE COVE MOTEL
Rts 16 & 28 (03864)
Rates: $45-$70
(603) 539-4491

PITTSBURG

THE GLEN LODGE
118 Glen Rd (03592)
Rates: $94-$204
(603) 538-6500
(800) 445-4536

LOPSTICK LODGE & CABINS
First Connecticut Lake (03592)
Rates: n/a
(800) 538-6659

SNOWFIELD CABINS
RR 1, Box 94-B, Covill Rd (03592)
Rates: n/a
(603) 538-7008

SPRUCE CONE CABINS
Rt 3, Box 13 (03592)
Rates: $20-$28
(603) 538-6572
(800) 538-6361

AREA CODES - If the local number doesn't connect, check for a new area code.

TALL TIMBER LODGE
Back Lake (03592)
Rates: n/a
(603) 538-6651
(800) 835-6343

TIMBERLAND LODGE & CABINS
First Connecticut Lake (03592)
Rates: $35-$62
(603) 538-6613
(800) 545-6613

PITTSFIELD

APPLE MOUNTAIN LODGE
1301 Upper City Rd (03263)
Rates: n/a
(603) 435-7641

PLYMOUTH

THE COMMON MAN INN & SPA
231 Main St (03264)
Rates: $99-$199
(603) 536-2200
(866) 843-2626

PILGRIM INN & COTTAGES
307 Main St (03264)
Rates: n/a
(603) 536-1319
(800) 216-1900

PORTSMOUTH

MEADOWBROOK INN
549 Hwy 1 Bypass (03801)
Rates: $59-$129
(603) 436-2700

MOTEL 6
3 Gosling Rd (03801)
Rates: $49-$88
(603) 334-6606
(800) 466-8356

RESIDENCE INN BY MARRIOTT
1 Int'l Dr (03801)
Rates: $89-$219
(603) 436-8880
(800) 331-3131

RINDGE

WOODBOUND COUNTRY INN
62 Woodbound Rd (03641)
Rates: $69-$190
(603) 532-8341
(800) 688-7770

ROCHESTER

ANCHORAGE INN
13 Wadleigh Rd (03839)
Rates: $59-$119
(603) 332-3350

SALEM

RED ROOF INN
15 Red Roof Ln (03079)
Rates: $52-$90
(603) 898-6422
(800) 843-7663

SHELBURNE

PHILBROOK FARM INN
881 North Rd (03581)
Rates: $122-$475
(603) 466-3831

SUGAR HILL

THE HILLTOP INN B&B
1348 Main St (03585)
Rates: $80-$195
(603) 823-5695
(800) 770-5695

SUNAPEE

DEXTER'S INN
258 Stagecoach Rd (03782)
Rates: $100-$185
(603) 763-5571
(800) 232-5571

SWANZEY

LOAFER INN AT THE 1792 WHITECOMB HOUSE B&B
27 Main St (03431)
Rates: n/a
(603) 357-6624

TAMWORTH

TAMWORTH HISTORIC COUNTRY INN
15 Cleveland Hill Rd (03886)
Rates: $104-$290
(603) 323-7721
(800) 642-7352

TEMPLE

AUK'S NEST B & B
204 East Road (03084)
Rates: $50-$70
(603) 878-2443

THORNTON

SHAMROCK MOTEL
2913 US 3 (03223)
Rates: $35-$60
(603) 726-3534

TILTON

TILTON MANOR
40 Chestnut St (03276)
Rates: $60-$70
(603) 286-3457

TROY

THE INN AT EAST HILL FARM
Monadnock St (03465)
Rates: $68-$88
(603) 242-6495
(800) 242-6495

TUFTONBORO

19 MILE BAY LODGES
HC 69, Box 110 (03853)
Rates: n/a
(603) 569-3507

TWIN MOUNTAIN

CHARLMONT MOTOR INN
Rt 3, Box G (03595)
Rates: $35-$60
(603) 846-5549

WATERVILLE VALLEY

SNOWY OWL INN
4 Village Rd (03215)
Rates: $102-$430
(603) 236-8383

WEIRS BEACH

CEDAR LODGE AT BRICKYARD MOUNTAIN
Rt 3 (03247)
Rates: n/a
(603) 366-4316
(800) 366-4883

CHANNEL INN & COTTAGES
P O Box 5106 (03247)
Rates: n/a
(603) 366-4673

LANGLEY COVE MOTEL & COTTAGES
563 Weirs Blvd, Rt 3 (03247)
Rates: n/a
(603) 366-5540

WENTWORTH

HILLTOP ACRES BED & BREAKFAST
Eastside & Buffalo Rds (03282)
Rates: $100-$125
(603) 764-5896

WEST LEBANON

ECONOMY INN AIRPORT
45 Airport Rd (03784)
Rates: $50-$115
(603) 298-8888
(800) 845-3557

FIRESIDE INN & SUITES
25 Airport Rd (03784)
Rates: $99-$159
(603) 298-5900
(800) 962-3198

WOLFEBORO

THE LAKE MOTEL
280 S Main St (03894)
Rates: $75-$134
(603) 569-1100

WOODSTOCK

WHEELOCK MOTOR COURT
Rt 3 (03293)
Rates: n/a
(603) 745-8771

WOODSVILLE

ALL SEASONS MOTEL
36 Smith St (03785)
Rates: $45-$95
(603) 747-2157

NOOTKA LODGE
36 Smith St (03785)
Rates: $55-$139
(603) 747-2418

AREA CODES - If the local number doesn't connect, check for a new area code.

NEW JERSEY

ABSECON
COMFORT SUITES
100 E White Horse
Pike (08201)
Rates: $49-$349
(800) 424-6423

ANDOVER
**PANTHER LAKE
CAMPGROUND
CABINS**
6 Panther Lake Rd
(07821)
Rates: $23+
(973) 347-4440
(800) 543-2056

ATLANTIC CITY
(Also see Absecon
and Egg Harbor
Township)

**SHERATON
ATLANTIC CITY
CONV CTR HOTEL**
2 Miss America
Way (08401)
Rates: $79-$399
(609) 344-3535
(800) 325-3535
(888) 627-7212

**SUNSET INN
ON THE BAY**
1600 Albany Ave
(08401)
Rates: $40-$110
(609) 344-2515
(800) 223-6370

(The following pet
care facility is
provided as a
service for pet
owners visiting
the casinos)

**ATLANTIC CITY
BEACH PET CARE
KENNEL**
547 N Trenton Ave
(08401)
Rates: n/a
(609) 348-8660
Website:
www.ackennel.
com

AVENEL
**COMFORT SUITES
AT WOODBRIDG**
1275 US 1 S
(07001)
Rates: $75-$185
(732) 396-3000
(800) 424-6423

BARNEGAT
**SCRUBBLE PINES
FAMILY CABINS**
30 Rt 72 (08005)
Rates: $18-$45
(609) 698-5684
(800) 590-2879

BASKING RIDGE
**THE INN AT
SOMERSET HILLS**
80 Allen Rd
(07920)
Rates: $129-$225
(908) 580-1300

OLDE MILL INN
225 US 202 & N
Maple Ave (07920)
Rates: $169-$199
(908) 221-1100

BAYVILLE
**CEDAR CREEK
CAMPGROUND
CABINS**
1052 Rt 9 (08721)
Rates: n/a
(732) 269-1413

BEACH HAVEN
ENGLESIDE INN
30 Engleside Ave
(08008)
Rates: $90-$417
(609) 492-1251
(800) 762-2214

BRANCHVILLE
**HARMONY
RIDGE FARM &
CAMPGROUND
CABINS**
23 Risdon Dr
(07826)
Rates: $15+
(973) 948-4941
(800) 462-2670

**KYMER
CAMPGROUND
CABINS**
69 Kymer Rd
(07826)
Rates: $20+
(973) 875-3167
(800) 526-2267

BRIDGEPORT
IMPERIAL INN
3312 Rt 206 S
(08505)
Rates: $50-$75
(609) 298-3355

BRIDGEWATER
**HILTON
GARDEN INN**
500 Promenade
Blvd (08807)
Rates: $79-$179
(732) 271-9030
(800) 445-8667

**SUMMERFIELD
SUITES**
530 Rt 22 E
(08807)
Rates: $119-$205
(908) 725-0800
(800) 833-4353

BUENA
**BUENA VISTA
CAMPING PARK
CABINS**
1775 Harding
Hwy Rt (08301)
Rates: $21+
(856) 697-2004

ECONO LODGE
102 Tuckahoe Rd
(08301)
Rates: $35-$125
(856) 697-9000
(800) 424-6423

CAPE MAY
**BEACHCOMBER
CAMPING
RESORT CABINS**
462 Seashore Rd
(08204)
Rates: $29-$35
(800) 233-0150

**MARQUIS DE
LAFAYETTE
HOTEL**
501 Beach Dr
(08204)
Rates: $219-$359
(609) 884-3500
(800) 257-0432

**THE MOFFETT
HOUSE B&B**
715 Broadway
(08204)
Rates: $75-$100
(609) 898-0915
(800) 498-0915

CAPE MAY COURT HOUSE
**BIG TIMBER LAKE
CAMPGROUND
CABINS**
116 Goshen-
Swanton Rd
(08210)
Rates: $31+
(609) 465-4456
(800) 542-CAMP

**THE DOCTORS
INN B&B**
2 N Main St
(08210)
Rates: n/a
(609) 463-9330

**KING NUMMY
TRAIL
CAMPGROUND
CABINS**
205 Rt 47S (08210)
Rates: $19-$23
(609) 465-4242

**NORTH
WILDWOOD
CAMPGROUND
CABINS**
240 W Shellbay
Ave (08210)
Rates: $25+
(609) 465-4440
(800) 752-4882

**SHELLBAY
CABINS**
277 W Shellbay
Ave (08210)
Rates: $25+
(609) 465-4770

CARNEY'S POINT
**HOLIDAY INN EXP
HOTEL & SUITES**
506 Pennsville-
Auburn Rd
(08069)
Rates: $90-$100
(856) 351-9222
(800) 465-4329

CHATSWORTH
**WADING PINES
CAMPGROUND
CABINS**
85 Godfrey Bridge
Rd (08019)
Rates: $25+
(609) 726-1313

CHERRY HILL
HOLIDAY INN
Rt 70 & Sayer Ave
(08002)
Rates: $84-$149
(856) 663-5300
(800) 465-4329

**RESIDENCE INN
BY MARRIOTT**
1821 Old Cuthbert
Rd (08034)
Rates: $169-$219
(856) 429-6111
(800) 331-3131

CLARKESBORO
**TIMBERLANE
CAMPGROUND
CABINS**
117 Timber Lane
(08020)
Rates: $19+
(856) 423-6677

CLERMONT
**AVALON
CAMPGROUND
CABINS**
1917 Rt 9 N
(08210)
Rates: $24+
(609) 624-0075
(800) 814-2267

AREA CODES - If the local number doesn't connect, check for a new area code.

DRIFTWOOD CAMPING RESORT CABINS
1955 Rt 9 & Rt 83 (08210)
Rates: $24+
(609) 624-1899
(800) 624-3743

HIDDEN ACRES CAMPGROUND CABINS
1142 Rt 83 (08210)
Rates: $28+
(609) 624-9015
(800) 874-7576

COLESVILLE
HIGH POINT COUNTRY INN MOTEL
1328 SR 23 N (07461)
Rates: $64-$85
(973) 702-1860

CRANBURY
RESIDENCE INN BY MARRIOTT
2662 Rt 130 (08512)
Rates: $84-$189
(609) 395-9447
(800) 331-3131

STAYBRIDGE SUITES
1272 S River Rd (08512)
Rates: $149-$169
(609) 409-7181
(800) 238-8000

DELAWARE
DELAWARE RIVER CABINS
Rt 46, Box 100 (07833)
Rates: $20+
(908) 475-4517
(800) 543-0271

DENVILLE
HAMPTON INN
350 Morris Ave (07834)
Rates: $79-$159
(973) 664-1050
(800) 426-7866

DEPTFORD
RESIDENCE INN BY MARRIOTT
1154 Hurffville Rd (08096)
Rates: $80-$120
(856) 686-9188
(800) 331-3131

DOROTHY
COUNTRY MOUSE CAMPGROUND CABINS
13 S Jersey Ave (08317)
Rates: $22+
(609) 476-2143
(800) 694-0315

EAST BRUNSWICK
MOTEL 6
244 Rt 18 (08816)
Rates: $57-$63
(732) 390-4545
(800) 466-8356

STUDIO 6
246 Rt 18 (08816)
Rates: $65-$81
(732) 238-3330
(888) 897-0202

EAST HANOVER
RAMADA HOTEL CONF CENTER
130 Rt 10 W (07936)
Rates: $60-$159
(973) 386-5622
(800) 272-6232

EAST RUTHERFORD
HOMESTEAD STUDIO SUITES
300 SR 3 E (07073)
Rates: $91-$116
(201) 939-8866
(888) 782-9473

SHERATON MEADOWLANDS
2 Meadowlands Plaza (07073)
Rates: $169-$194
(201) 896-0500
(800) 325-3535

EATONTOWN
CRYSTAL INN
170 Main St (07724)
Rates: $55-$90
(732) 542-4900
(800) 562-5290

STAYBRIDGE SUITS
4 Industrial Way E (07724)
Rates: n/a
(800) 238-8000

EDISON
RED ROOF INN
860 New Durham Rd (08817)
Rates: $70-$96
(732) 248-9300
(800) 843-7663

SHERATON HOTEL
125 Raritan Center Pkwy (08817)
Rates: $249-$279
(732) 225-8300
(800) 325-3535

WELLESLEY INN & SUITES
831 Rt 1S (08817)
Rates: $65-$110
(732) 287-0171
(800) 444-8888

ELIZABETH
HILTON NEWARK AIRPORT
1170 Spring St (07201)
Rates: $189-$229
(908) 351-3900
(800) 445-8667

RESIDENCE INN BY MARRIOTT
83 Glimcher Realty Way (07201)
Rates: $149-$179
(908) 352-4300
(800) 331-3131

ELMER
YOGI BEAR AT TALL PINES RESORT CABINS
49 Beal Rd (08318)
Rates: $31
(856) 451-7479
(800) 252-2890

ENGLEWOOD
RADISSON HOTEL
401 S Van Brunt St (07631)
Rates: $209-$239
(201) 871-2020
(800) 333-3333

ESTELLE MANOR
PLEASANT VALLEY CAMPGROUND CABINS
60 S River Rd (08319)
Rates: $25+
(609) 625-1238

EGG HARBOR TOWNSHIP
CLARION HOTEL ATLANTIC CITY WEST
6821 Black Horse Pike (08234)
Rates: $55-$299
(609) 272-0200
(800) 424-6423

FAIR LAWN
AMERISUITES
41-01 Broadway (07410)
Rates: $149-$165
(201) 475-3888
(800) 833-1516

FLEMINGTON
RAMADA INN
250 Rts 202 & 31 (08822)
Rates: $89-$102
(908) 782-7472
(800) 272-6232

FRANKLIN-VILLE
THE ROCK AT VILLAGE DOCK CAMPGROUND CABINS
1664 Delsea Dr [(08322
Rates: $20+
(856) 694-4935

HADDONFIELD
HADDONFIELD INN
44 W end Ave (08033)
Rates: $119-$309
(856) 428-2195

HAMMONTON
PARADISE LAKES CAMPGROUND CABINS
500 Paradise Dr (08037)
Rates: $21+
(609) 561-7095

RAMADA LIMITED
308 S White Horse Pike (08037)
Rates: n/a
(609) 561-5700
(800) 272-6232

HAZLET
WELLESLEY INN & SUITES
3215 Hwy 35 N (07730)
Rates: $89-$159
(732) 888-2800
(800) 444-8888

HOPE
THE INN AT MILL-RACE POND B&B
313 Johnsonburg Rd (07844)
Rates: $85-$165
(908) 459-4884
(800 746-6467

ISELIN
SHERATON AT WOODBRIDGE PLACE
515 Rt 1 S (08830)
Rates: $95-$169
(732) 634-3600
(800) 325-3535

JACKSON
BUTTERFLY CAMPGROUND CABINS
360 Butterfly Rd (08527)
Rates: $24+
(732) 928-2107

TIP TAM CAMPING RESORT CABINS
Brewers Bridge Rd (08527)
Rates: $27+
(732) 363-4036

JERSEY CITY
HOLLAND MOTOR LODGE
Holland Tunnel Plaza E (07302)
Rates: $52-$70
(201) 963-6200

AREA CODES - If the local number doesn't connect, check for a new area code.

LAWRENCEVILLE
HOWARD JOHNSON INN
2995 Brunswick Pike (08648)
Rates: $75-$135
(609) 896-1100
(800) 446-4656

RED ROOF INN
3203 Brunswick Pike (08648)
Rates: $56-$85
(609) 896-3388
(800) 843-7663

LEDGEWOOD
DAYS INN
1691 Rt 46 (07852)
Rates: $73-$110
(973) 347-5100
(800) 329-7466

LONG BRANCH
OCEAN PLACE RESORT & SPA
1 Ocean Blvd (07740)
Rates: $98-$251
(732) 571-4000

LYNDHURST
QUALITY INN MEADOWLANDS
10 Polito Ave (07071)
Rates: $79-$179
(201) 933-9800
(800) 424-6423

MAHWAH
COMFORT INN
160 SR 17 S (07430)
Rates: $77-$153
(201) 512-0800
(800) 424-6423

HOMEWOOD SUITES
375 Corporate Dr (07430)
Rates: $159-$199
(201) 760-9994
(800) 225-5466

SHERATON CROSSROADS HOTEL
1 Int'l Blvd (07495)
Rates: $215-$239
(201) 529-1660
(800) 325-3535

MAPLE SHADE
MOTEL 6
Rt 73 N (08052)
Rates: $39-$58
(856) 235-3550
(800) 466-8356

QUALITY INN & CONF CENTER
531 Rt 38 W (08052)
Rates: $74-$250
(856) 235-6400
(800) 424-6423

MARMORA
WHIPPOORWIL CAMPGROUND CABINS
810 S Shore Rd (08223)
Rates: $34+
(609) 390-3458
(800) 424-8275

MAYS LANDING
WINDING RIVER CAMPGROUND CABINS
6752 Weymouth Rd (08330)
Rates: $20+
(609) 625-3191

YOGI BEAR'S JELLYSTONE PARK CABINS
1079 12th Ave (08330)
Rates: $20+
(609) 476-2811
(800) 355-0264

MIDDLETOWN
COMFORT INN
750 Hwy 35 S (07748)
Rates: $99-$172
(732) 671-3400
(800) 424-6423

MILLVILLE
COUNTRY INN BY CARLSON
1125 Village Dr (08332)
Rates: $75-$79
(856) 825-3100
(800) 456-4000

MONMOUTH JUNCTION
RED ROOF INN
208 New Rd (08852)
Rates: $46-$75
(732) 821-8800
(800) 843-7663

RESIDENCE INN BY MARRIOTT
4225 Rt 1 S (08852)
Rates: $169-$179
(732) 329-9600
(800) 331-3131

MONROEVILLE
OLD CEDAR CAMP-GROUND CABINS
274 Richwood Rd (08343)
Rates: $17+
(609) 358-2406
(609) 358-4881

OLDMAN'S CREEK CAMPGROUND CABINS
174 Laux Rd (08343)
Rates: $17+
(609) 478-4502

MONTAGUE
SHIPPEKONK FAMILY CAMPGROUND CABINS
59 River Rd (07827)
Rates: $19+
(973) 293-3383

MORRIS PLAINS
CANDLEWOOD SUITES
100 Candlewood Dr (07950)
Rates: n/a
(973) 984-9960
(888) 226-3539

MORRISTOWN
SUMMERFIELD SUITES
194 Park Ave (07960)
Rates: $109-$199
(973) 971-0008
(800) 833-4353

THE WESTN GOV-ERNOR MORRIS
2 Whippany Rd (07960)
Rates: $229-$239
(973) 539-7300
(800) 228-3000

MOUNT HOLLY
BEST WESTERN BURLINGTON INN
2020 Rt 541 (08060)
Rates: $79-$129
(609) 261-3800
(800) 528-1234
(800) 633-8211

MOUNT LAUREL
AMERISUITES
8000 Crawford Pl (08054)
Rates: $69-$149
(856) 840-0770
(800) 833-1516

CANDLEWOOD SUITES
4000 Crawford Pl (08054)
Rates: $109
(856) 642-7567
(888) 226-3539

DOUBLETREE GUIEST SUITES
515 Fellowship Rd (08054)
Rates: $109-$199
(856) 778-8999
(800) 222-8733

RADISSON HOTEL
915 Rt 73 N (08054)
Rates: $99-$113
(856) 234-7300
(800) 333-3333

RED ROOF INN
603 Fellowship Rd (08054)
Rates: $51-$83
(856) 234-5589
(800) 843-7663

SUMMERFIELD SUITES
3000 Crawford Pl (08054)
Rates: $95-$139
(856) 222-1313
(800) 833-4353

NEPTUNE
DAYS INN
3310 Hwy 33 E (07753)
Rates: $59-$169
(7320 643-8888
(800) 329-7466

NEWARK
HILTON GATEWAY
Raymond Blvd (07114)
Rates: $109-$349
(973) 622-5000
(800) 445-8667

SHERATON HOTEL NEWARK AIRPORT
128 Frontage Rd (07114)
Rates: $99-$269
(973) 690-5500
(800) 325-3535

NORTH BERGEN
COMFORT SUITES
1200 Tonnelle Ave (07047)
Rates: $79-$169
(201) 392-0008
(800) 424-6423

DAYS INN
2750 Tonnelle Ave (07047)
Rates: $99-$250
(201) 348-3600
(800) 329-7466

NORTH BRUNSWICK
COMFORT SUITES
2880 US Rt 1 N (08902)
Rates: $79-$119
(732) 297-7400
(800) 424-6423

OCEAN CITY
CROSSINGS MOTOR INN
3420 Haven Ave (08226)
Rates: $95-$170
(609) 398-4433
(800) 257-8811

OCEAN VIEW

OCEAN VIEW CAMPGROUND CABINS
255 Rt 9, Shore Rd (08230)
Rates: $29+
(609) 624-1675

PINE HAVEN CAMPGROUND CABINS
Rt 9 (08230)
Rates: $27+
(609) 624-3437

SEA GROVE CAMPING RESORT CABINS
2665 Rt 9 (08230)
Rates: $23+
(609) 624-3529
(800) 432-6629

TAMERLANE CAMPGROUND CABINS
2241 Rt 9 (08230)
Rates: $21+
(609) 624-0767

PARK RIDGE

THE RIDGE MARRIOTT HOTEL
300 Brae Blvd (07656)
Rates: $109-$250
(201) 307-0800
(800) 228-9290

PARKERTOWN

BAKER'S ACRES CAMPGROUND CABINS
230 Willets Ave (08087)
Rates: $20+
(609) 296-2664
(800) 648-2227

PARSIPPANY

EMBASSY SUITES
909 Parsippany Blvd (07054)
Rates: $109-$299
(973) 334-1440
(800) 362-2779

RAMADA LTD
949 Rt 46 (07054)
Rates: $95-$120
(973) 263-0404
(800) 272-6232

RED ROOF INN
855 Rt 46 E (07054)
Rates: $68-$86
(973) 334-3737
(800) 843-7663

SHERATON HOTEL
199 Smith Rd (07054)
Rates: $180-$204
(973) 515-2000
(800) 325-3535

SIERRA SUITES HOTEL
299 Smith Rd (07054)
Rates: $89-$209
(973) 428-8875

PHILLIPSBURG

CLARION HOTEL & CONF CENTER
1314 Hwy 22 (08865)
Rates: $80-$100
(908) 454-9771
(800) 424-6423

PILESGROVE

FOUR SEASONS CABIN RENTALS
158 Woodstown-Daretown Rd (08098)
Rates: $18-$20
(856) 769-3635
(888) 372-2267

PISCATAWAY

MOTEL 6
1012 Stelton Rd (08854)
Rates: $55-$60
(732) 981-9200
(800) 466-8356

POMONA

EVERGREEN WOODS CAMPING RESORT CABINS
Rt 575 & Moss Mill Rd (08240)
Rates: $24-$26
(609) 652-1577

PRINCETON

AMERISUITES
3565 US 1 S (08543)
Rates: $149-$179
(609) 720-0200
(800) 833-1516

HOLIDAY INN
100 Independence Way (08540)
Rates: $159
(609) 520-1200
(800) 465-4329

NASSAU INN
10 Palmer Square (08542)
Rates: $178-$288
(609) 921-7500
(800) 862-7728

STAYBRIDGE SUITES
4375 US 1 S (08543)
Rates: n/a
(609) 951-0009
(800) 238-8000

WESTIN PRINCETON AT FORRESTAL VILLAGE
201 Village Blvd (08540)
Rates: $279-$319
(609) 452-7900
(800) 228-3000

RAMSEY

BEST WESTERN INN
1315 Rt 17S (07446)
Rates: $119-$175
(201) 327-6700
(800) 528-1234
(800) 678-5683

WELLESLEY INN & SUITES
946 Rt 17N (07446)
Rates: $79-$109
(201) 934-9250
(800) 444-8888

ROCKAWAY

BEST WESTERN THE INN AT ROCKAWAY
14 Green Pond Rd (07866)
Rates: $99-$149
(973) 625-1200
(800) 528-1234

SECAUCUS

AMERISUITES
575 Park Plaza Dr (07094)
Rates: $169-$179
(201) 422-9480
(800) 833-1516

HOMESTEAD STUDIO SUITES
1 Park Plaza Dr (07094)
Rates: $104-$129
(201) 553-9700
(888) 782-9473

PRIME SUITES
350 Rt 3W, Mill Creek Dr (07094)
Rates: $89-$189
(201) 863-8700

RED ROOF INN
15 Meadowlands Pkwy (07094)
Rates: $83-$110
(201) 319-1000
(800) 843-7663

SHORT HILLS

HILTON SHORT HILLS & SPA
41 John F Kennedy Pkwy (07078)
Rates: $149-$399
(973) 379-0100
(800) 445-8667

SOMERS POINT

RESIDENCE INN BY MARRIOTT AT GREATE BAY GOLF CLUB
900 Mays Landing Rd (08244)
Rates: $139-$309
(609) 927-6400
(800) 331-3131

SOMERSET

COMFORT SUITES
350 Davidson Ave (08873)
Rates: $79-$239
(732) 627-8483
(800) 424-6423

HOLIDAY INN
195 Davidson Ave (08873)
Rates: $149+
(732) 356-1700
(800) 465-4329

RESIDENCE INN BY MARRIOTT
37 World Fair Dr (08873)
Rates: $90-$153
(732) 627-0881
(800) 331-3131

STAYBRIDGE SUITES
260 Davidson Ave (08873)
Rates: $149-$189
(732) 356-8000
(800) 238-8000

SOUTH PLAINFIELD

HOLIDAY INN
4701 Stelton Rd (07080)
Rates: $126-$135
(908) 753-5500
(800) 465-4329

SPRINGFIELD

HOLIDAY INN
304 Rt 22 W (07081)
Rates: $140-$145
(973) 376-9400
(800) 465-4329

TINTON FALLS

HOLIDAY INN
700 Hope Rd (07724)
Rates: $160-$170
(732) 544-9300
(800) 465-4329

RED ROOF INN
11 Centre Plaza-Hope Rd (07724)
Rates: $62-$105
(732) 389-4646
(800) 843-7663

RESIDENCE INN BY MARRIOTT
90 Park Rd (07724)
Rates: $139-$229
(732) 389-8100
(800) 331-3131

SUNRISE SUITES HOTEL
3 Centre Plaza (07724)
Rates: $89-$159
(732) 389-4800
(800) 833-4353

TOMS RIVER

HOWARD JOHNSON HOTEL
955 Hooper Ave (08753)
Rates: $75-$199
(732) 244-1000
(800) 446-4656

AREA CODES - If the local number doesn't connect, check for a new area code.

TUCKERTON

ATLANTIC CITY NORTH BASS RIVER KOA KABINS
Stage Rd (08087)
Rates: $22+
(609) 296-9163
(888) 229-9776

VINELAND

RAMADA INN
2216 W Landis
Ave & Rt 55
(08360)
Rates: $60-$75
(856) 696-3800
(800) 272-6232

WANTAGE

HIGH POINT COUNTRY INN
1328 SR 23 N
(07461)
Rates: $80-$90
(973) 702-1860

WARREN

SOMERSET HILLS HOTEL
200 Liberty
Corner Rd (07059)
Rates: $129-$215
(908) 647-6700

WAYNE

HOLIDAY INN
334 Rt 46 E (07470)
Rates: $81-$108
(973) 256-7000
(800) 465-4329

WELLESLEY INN
1850 Rt 23 (07470)
Rates: $109-$119
(973) 696-8050
(800) 444-8888

WEEHAWKEN

SHERATON SUITES ON THE HUDSON
500 Harbor Blvd
(07087)
Rates: $179-$329
(201) 617-5600
(800) 325-3535

WEST CREEK

SEA PIRATE CAMPGROUND CABINS
154 Rt 9 N (08092)
Rates: $21+
(609) 296-7400
(800) 822-CAMP

WEST ORANGE

RESIDENCE INN BY MARRIOTT
107 Prospect Ave
(07052)
Rates: $199-$299
(973) 669-4700
(800) 331-3131

WESTAMPTON

ECONO LODGE
10 Western Dr
(08060)
Rates: $49-$110
(609) 702-1000
(800) 424-6423

WHIPPANY

HOMESTEAD STUDIO SUITES
125 Rt 10 E (07981)
Rates: $85-$110
(973) 463-1999
(888) 782-9473

SUMMERFIELD SUITES
1 Ridgedale Ave
(07981)
Rates: $109-$189
(973) 605-1001
(800) 833-4353

WELLESLEY INN
1255 Rt 10 (07981)
Rates: $79
(973) 539-8350
(800) 444-8888

WOODBRIDGE

HOMESTEAD STUDIO SUITES
1 Hoover Way
(07095)
Rates: $85-$110
(732) 442-8333
(888) 782-9473

WRIGHTS-TOWN

DAYS INN
507 E Main St
(08562)
Rates: $70-$115
(609) 723-6900
(800) 329-7466

AREA CODES - If the local number doesn't connect, check for a new area code.

NEW MEXICO

ABIQUIU

CASA DEL RIO B&B
Hwy 84, MM
199.46 (87532)
Rates: $90-$125
(505) 753-2035
(horses only)

ALAMOGORDO

ALL AMERICAN INN
508 S White Sands
Blvd (88310)
Rates: $30-$38
(505) 437-1850

BEST WESTERN DESERT AIRE MOTOR HOTEL
1021 S White
Sands Blvd
(88310)
Rates: $52-$68
(505) 437-2110
(800) 528-1234
(800) 565-1988

HOLIDAY INN EXP
1401 S White
Sands Blvd
(88310)
Rates: $65+
(505) 437-7100
(800) 465-4329

MOTEL 6
251 Panorama
Blvd (88310)
Rates: $29-$40
(505) 434-5970
(800) 466-8356

SATELLITE INN
2224 N White
Sands Blvd
(88310)
Rates: $32-$40
(505) 437-8454

SUPER 8 MOTEL
3204 N White
Sands (88310)
Rates: $45-$73
(505) 434-4205
(800) 800-8000

ALBUQUERQUE

AIRPORT UNIVERISTY INN
1901 University
Blvd SE (87106)
Rates: $79-$99
(505) 247-0512

AMERISUITES AIRPORT
1400 Sunport Pl
SE (87106)
Rates: $104-$135
(505) 242-9300
(800) 833-1516

AMERISUITES MIDTOWN
2500 Menaul Blvd
NE (87107)
Rates: $59-$89
(505) 881-0544
(800) 833-1516

AMERISUITES UPTOWN
6901 Arvada Ave
NE (87110)
Rates: $69-$99
(505) 872-9000
(800) 833-1516

BAYMONT INN & SUITES
7439 Pan
American Frwy
NE (87109)
Rates: $55-$66
(505) 345-7500
(877) 229-6668

BEST WESTERN AMERICAN MOTOR INN
12999 Central Ave
NE (87123)
Rates: $49-$109
(505) 298-7426
(800) 528-1234
(800) 366-3252

BEST WESTERN INNSUITES HOTEL
2400 Yale Blvd
SE (87106)
Rates: $69-$139
(505) 242-7022
(800) 528-1234
(877) 771-7810

BEST WESTERN WINROCK INN
18 Winrock Centre
NE (87110)
Rates: $79-$99
(505) 883-5252
(800) 528-1234
(800) 866-5252

BRITTANIA & W. E. MAUGER ESTATE BED & BREAKFAST
701 Roma Ave
NW (87102)
Rates: $89-$209
(505) 242-8755
(800) 719-9189

CANDLEWOOD SUITES
3025 Menaul Blvd
NE (87107)
Rates: $59-$95
(505) 888-3424
(888) 226-3539

CASITA CHAMISA BED & BREAKFAST
850 Chamisal Rd
NW (87107)
Rates: n/a
(505) 897-4644

CLUBHOUSE INN & SUITES
1315 Menaul Blvd
NE (87107)
Rates: $69-$109
(505) 345-0010
(800) CLUB-INN

COMFORT INN AIRPORT
2300 Yale Blvd SE
(87106)
Rates: $49-$105
(505) 243-2244
(800) 424-6423

COMFORT INN
13031 Central Ave
NE (87123)
Rates: $53-$99
(505) 294-1800
(800) 424-6423

COMFORT INN MIDTOWN
2015 Menaul Blvd
NE (87107)
Rates: $49-$110
(505) 881-3210
(800) 424-6423

COMFORT SUITES
900 Louisiana
Blvd NE (87110)
Rates: $49-$279
(505) 255-5566
(800) 424-6423

COMFORT INN & SUITES
5811 Signal Ave
NE (87113)
Rates: $59-$130
(505) 822-1090
(800) 424-6423

COUNTRY INN & SUITES
2601 Mulberry SE
(87106)
Rates: $62-$69
(505) 246-9600
(800) 456-4000

DAYS INN
6031 Iliff Rd NW
(87105)
Rates: $48-$80
(505) 836-3297
(800) 329-7466

DAYS INN
13317 Central Ave
NE (87123)
Rates: $40-$65
(505) 294-3297
(800) 329-7466

DAYS INN
10321 Hotel Ave
NE (87123)
Rates: $52-$90
(505) 275-3297
(800) 329-7466

DE ANZA MOTOR LODGE
4302 Central Ave
NE (87108)
Rates: $20-$37
(505) 255-1654

DRURY INN & SUITES
4310 The 25 Way
NE (87109)
Rates: $73-$103
(505) 341-3600
(800) 378-7946

ECONO LODGE DOWNTOWN
817 Central Ave
NE (87102)
Rates: $46-$70
(505) 243-1321
(800) 424-6423

ECONO LODGE OLD TOWN
2321 Central Ave
NW (87104)
Rates: $40-$99
(505) 243-8475
(800) 424-6423

EQUUS HOTEL SUITES
2401 Wellesley Dr
NE (87107)
Rates: $49-$59
(505) 883-8888

FAIRFIELD INN AIRPORT
2300 Centre Ave
SE (87106)
Rates: $64-$89
(505) 247-1621
(800) 228-2800

GUESTHOUSE INN & SUITES
10331 Hotel Ave
NE (87123)
Rates: $36-$70
(505) 271-8500
(800) 214-8378

HACIENDA ANTIGUA B&B
6708 Tierra Dr
NW (87107)
Rates: $134-$189
(505) 345-5399

HAMPTON INN N
5101 Ellison NE
(87109)
Rates: $60-$110
(505) 344-1555
(800) 426-7866

AREA CODES - If the local number doesn't connect, check for a new area code.

HAWTHORN INN & SUITES
1511 Gibson Blvd SE (87106)
Rates: $64-$189
(505) 242-1555
(800) 527-1133

HOLIDAY INN EXP
10330 Hotel Ave NE (87123)
Rates: $68-$115
(505) 275-8900
(800) 465-4329

HOLIDAY INN EXPRESS-COORS
6100 Iliff Rd (87121)
Rates: $70-$87
(505) 836-8600
(800) 465-4329

HOMEWOOD SUITES BY HILTON
5400 San Antonio Ave NE (87109)
Rates: $79-$149
(505) 998-4663
(800) 225-5466

HOTEL BLUE
717 Central Ave NW (871020
Rates: $69-$109
(505) 924-2400

HOWARD JOHNSON EXPRESS
7630 Pan American Frwy NE (87109)
Rates: $55-$69
(505) 828-1600
(800) 446-4656

HOWARD JOHNSON HOTEL & CONV CENTER
15 Hotel Cir NE (87123)
Rates: $39-$60
(505) 296-4852
(800) 446-4656

LA QUINTA INN
2424 San Mateo Blvd NE (87110)
Rates: $59-$79
(505) 884-3591
(800) 687-6667
(800) 221-4731

LA QUINTA INN-AIRPORT
2116 Yale Blvd SE (87106)
Rates: $75-$95
(505) 243-5500
(800) 687-6667
(800) 221-4731

LA QUINTA INN-NORTH
5241 San Antonio Dr NE (87109)
Rates: $69-$89
(505) 821-9000
(800) 687-6667
(800) 221-4731

LA QUINTA INN WEST
6101 Iliff Rd NW (87212)
Rates: $79-$109
(505) 839-1744
(800) 687-6667
(800) 221-4731

LE BARON COURTYARD & SUITES
2120 Menaul Blvd NE (87107)
Rates: $59-$79
(505) 885-0250

MAGGIE'S RASPBERRY RANCH B&B
9817 Eldridge Rd NW (87114)
Rates: n/a
(505) 897-1523
(800) 897-1523

MCM ELEGANTE HOTEL
2020 Menaul Blvd (87107)
Rates: $61-$154
(505) 884-2511
(866) 650-8900

MICROTEL INN & SUITES
9910 Avalon NW (87121)
Rates: $49-$69
(505) 836-1686
(888) 771-7171

MOTEL 6
3400 Prospect Ave NE (87107)
Rates: $29-$46
(505) 883-8813
(800) 466-8356

MOTEL 6
5701 Iliff Rd NW (87105)
Rates: $29-$52
(505) 831-8888
(800) 466-8356

MOTEL 6-EAST
13141 Central Ave NE (87123)
Rates: $30-$46
(505) 294-4600
(800) 466-8356

MOTEL 6-MIDTOWN
1701 University Blvd NE (87102)
Rates: $29-$46
(505) 843-9228
(800) 466-8356

MOTEL 6-NORTH
8510 Pan American Frwy NE (87109)
Rates: $33-$60
(505) 821-1472
(800) 466-8356

MOTEL 6-STADIUM
1000 Avenida Cesar Chavez SE (87102)
Rates: $35-$55
(505) 243-8017
(800) 466-8356

MOTEL 76
1521 Coors Blvd NW (87121)
Rates: $29-$39
(505) 836-3881

111 BNB JAZZ INN
111 Walter NE (87103)
Rates: $65-$95
(505) 242-1530
(888) JAZZ-INN

PLAZA INN
900 Medical Arts NE (87120)
Rates: $79-$99
(505) 243-5693
(800) 237-1307

QUALITY INN & SUITES
411 McKnight Ave (87102)
Rates: $50-$130
(505) 242-5228
(800) 424-6423

RADISSON HOTEL & CONF CENTER
2500 Carlisle Blvd NE (87110)
Rates: $119-$129
(505) 888-3311
(800) 333-3333

RAMADA LTD
1801 Yale Blvd SE (87106)
Rates: $54-$68
(505) 242-0036
(800) 272-6232

RAMADA LTD
5601 Alameda Ave NE (87113)
Rates: $59-$159
(505) 858-3297
(800) 272-6232

RED ROOF INN
6015 Iliff Rd NW (87121)
Rates: $35-$56
(505) 831-3400
(800) 843-7663

RESIDENCE INN BY MARRIOTT
3300 Prospect Dr NE (87107)
Rates: $79-$199
(505) 881-2661
(800) 331-3131

RESIDENCE INN BY MARRIOTT NORTH
4331 The Lane at 25 NE (87109)
Rates: $109-$149
(505) 761-0200
(800) 331-3131

RODEWAY INN
2108 Menaul Blvd NE (87107)
Rates: $29-$75
(505) 884-2480
(800) 424-6423

ROYAL HOTEL
4119 Central Ave NE (87108)
Rates: $24-$49
(505) 265-3585
(800) 843-8572

SHERATON OLD TOWN
800 Rio Grande Blvd NW (87104)
Rates: $89-$159
(505) 843-6300
(800) 325-3535

SHERATON UPTOWN
2600 Louisiana Blvd NE (87110)
Rates: $79-$189
(505) 881-0000
(800) 252-7772

SILVER MOON LODGE
918 Central Ave SW (87102)
Rates: $59-$63
(505) 243-1773

SLEEP INN AIRPORT
2300 International Ave SE (87106)
Rates: $63-$99
(505) 244-3325
(800) 424-6423

STARDUST INN
801 Central Ave NE (87102)
Rates: $28-$65
(505) 243-2891

STUDIO 6
4441 Osuna Rd NE (87109)
Rates: $199-$289
(505) 344-7744
(888) 897-0202

SUN VILLAGE CORPORATE SUITES-CONDOS
801 Locus NE (87102)
Rates: $60-$90
(505) 842-6640

SUPER 8 MOTEL
2500 University Blvd NE (87107)
Rates: $45-$85
(505) 888-4884
(800) 800-8000

SUPER 8 MOTEL
450 Paisano St NE (87123)
Rates: $48-$75
(505) 271-4807
(800) 800-8000

SUPER 8 MOTEL
6030 Iliff Rd NW (87121)
Rates: $48-$65
(505) 836-5560
(800) 800-8000

AREA CODES - If the local number doesn't connect, check for a new area code.

TOWNEPLACE SUITES
2400 Centre Ave SE (87106)
Rates: $59-$79
(505) 232-5800
(800) 257-3000

TRAVELODGE
13139 Central Ave NE (87123)
Rates: $35-$75
(505) 292-4878
(800) 578-7878

WYNDHAM HOTEL AT INT'L SUNPORT
2910 Yale Blvd SE (87106)
Rates: $79-$130
(505) 843-7000
(800) 996-3426
(800) 227-1117

ALGODONES
HACIENDA VARGAS HISTORIC B&B INN
1431 SR 313 (87001)
Rates: $79-$149
(505) 867-9115

ALTO
HIGH COUNTRY LODGE
N Hwy 48 (88312)
Rates: $89-$130
(505) 336-4321
(800) 845-7265

LA JUNTA GUEST RANCH
P. O. Box 139 (88312)
Rates: $70-$200
(800) 443-8423

RANCHO RUIDOSO CONDOMINIUMS
6 Little Creek Rd (88312)
Rates: $85-$165
(505) 336-8103

ANGEL FIRE
ANGEL FIRE RESORT
1 N Angel Fire Rd (87710)
Rates: $195-$315
(505) 377-6401

ARROYO SECO
ADOBE & STARS BED & BREAKFAST
584 SR 150 (87514)
Rates: $110-$200
(505) 776-2776

ARTESIA
ARTESIA INN
1820 S 1st St (88210)
Rates: $38-$55
(505) 746-9801

HOLIDAY INN EXP
2210 W Main St (88210)
Rates: $75-$95
(505) 748-3904
(800) 465-4329

BELEN
BEST WESTERN BELEN
2111 Camino del Llano (87002)
Rates: $69-$95
(505) 861-3181
(800) 528-1234

HOLIDAY INN EXP
2110 Camino del Llano (87002)
Rates: $73-$89
(505) 861-5000
(800) 465-4329

BERNALILLO
DAYS INN
107 N Camino Del Pueblo Ave (87004)
Rates: $40-$120
(505) 771-7000
(800) 329-7466

LA HACIENDA GRANDE B&B
21 Barros Rd (87004)
Rates: $109-$139
(505) 867-1887

QUALITY INN & SUITES
210 N Hill Rd (87004)
Rates: $46-$125
(505) 771-9500
(800) 424-6423

BLOOMFIELD
SUPER 8 MOTEL
525 W Broadway (87413)
Rates: $46-$50
(505) 632-8886
(800) 800-8000

CARLSBAD
BEST WESTERN STEVENS INN
1829 S Canal St (88220)
Rates: $59-$109
(505) 887-2851
(800) 528-1234
(800) 730-2851

CARLSBAD INN
2019 S Canal St (88220)
Rates: $32-$49
(505) 887-1171

COMFORT INN
2429 W Pierce St (88220)
Rates: $55-$75
(505) 887-1994
(800) 424-6423

CONTINENTAL INN
3820 National Parks Hwy (88220)
Rates: $32-$59
(505) 887-0341

DAYS INN
3910 National Parks Hwy (88220)
Rates: $55-$89
(505) 887-7800
(800) 329-7466

MOTEL 6
3824 National Parks Hwy (88220)
Rates: $27-$36
(505) 885-0011
(800) 466-8356

QUALITY INN
3706 National Parks Hwy (88220)
Rates: $55-$80
(505) 887-2861
(800) 424-6423

STAGECOACH INN
1819 S Canal (88220)
Rates: $34-$52
(505) 887-1148

CHAMA
BRANDING IRON MOTEL
1511 W Main (87520)
Rates: $53-$109
(505) 756-2162

ELK HORN LODGE MOTEL
Rte 1, Box 45 (87520)
Rates: $46-$104
(505) 756-2105
(800) 532-8874

RIVER BEND LODGE
2625 Hwy 64/84 (87520)
Rates: $63-$78
(505) 756-2264

VISTA DEL RIO LODGE
2595 Hwy 84/64 (87520)
Rates: $50-$90
(505) 756-2138

CHIMAYO
CASA ESCONDIDA B&B
64 CR 0100 (87522)
Rates: $85-$145
(505) 351-4805

CIMARRON
CIMARRON INN & RV PARK
212 10th St (87714)
Rates: $40-$55
(505) 376-2268

CLAYTON
BEST WESTERN KOKOPELLI LODGE
702 S First St (88415)
Rates: $69-$189
(505) 374-2589
(800) 528-1234
(800) 392-6691

DAYS INN
1120 S 1st St (88415)
Rates: $69-$139
(505) 374-0133
(800) 329-7466

SUPER 8 MOTEL
1425 S 1st St (88415)
Rates: $45-$70
(505) 374-8127
(800) 800-8000

CLOUDCROFT
THE LODGE
1 Corona Place (88317)
Rates: $99-$319
(505) 682-2566
(866) 595-6343

CLOVIS
COMFORT INN
1616 Mabry Dr (88101)
Rates: $49-$89
(505) 762-4591
(800) 424-6423

ECONO LODGE
1400 E Mabry Dr (88101)
Rates: $49-$109
(505) 763-3439
(800) 424-6423

HOLIDAY INN
2700 Mabry Dr (88101)
Rates: $55-$105
(505) 762-4491
(800) 465-4329

HOWARD JOHNSON EXPRESSWAY INN
2920 Mabry Dr (88101)
Rates: $45-$66
(505) 769-1953
(800) 446-4656

LA QUINTA INN
4521 N Prince St (88101)
Rates: $75-$105
(505) 763-8777
(800) 687-6667

MOTEL 6
2620 Mabry Dr (88101)
Rates: $30+
(505) 762-2995
(800) 466-8356

AREA CODES - If the local number doesn't connect, check for a new area code.

DEMING

BEST WESTERN MIMBRES VALLEY INN
1500 W Pine St (88030)
Rates: $45-$75
(505) 546-4544
(800) 528-1234

DAYS INN
1601 E Pine St (88030)
Rates: $40-$55
(505) 546-8813
(800) 329-7466

GRAND MOTOR INN
1721 E Pine St (88030)
Rates: $40-$48
(505) 546-2632

HOLIDAY INN
4600 Motel Dr (88031)
Rates: $59-$89
(505) 546-2661
(800) 465-4329

MOTEL 6
I-10 & Motel Dr (88031)
Rates: $34+
(505) 546-2623
(800) 466-8356

WAGON WHEEL MOTEL
1109 W Pine St (88030)
Rates: $27-$35
(505) 546-2681

DULCE

BEST WESTERN JICARILLA INN
233 Jicarilla Blvd (87528)
Rates: $50-$110
(505) 759-3663
(800) 528-1234
(800) 742-1938

EDGEWOOD

ALTA MAE'S HERITAGE INN B&B
1950 Old Route 66 (87105)
Rates: $95-$115
(505) 281-5000
(horses only)

ELEPHANT BUTTE

ELEPHANT BUTTE INN
401 Hwy 195 (87935)
Rates: $59-$89
(505) 744-5431

MARINA SUITES MOTEL
200 Country Club Dr (87935)
Rates: $65-$80
(505) 744-5269

ESPAÑOLA

CHAMESA INN
920 N Riverside Dr (87532)
Rates: $53-$63
(505) 753-7291

COMFORT INN
604-B S Riverside Dr (87532)
Rates: $50-$175
(505) 753-2419
(800) 424-6423

DAYS INN
807 S Riverside Dr (87532)
Rates: $42-$90
(505) 747-1242
(800) 329-7466

SUPER 8 MOTEL
811 S Riverside Dr (87532)
Rates: $39-$119
(505) 753-5374
(800) 800-8000

FARMINGTON

BEST WESTERN INN & SUITES
700 Scott Ave (87401)
Rates: $79-$109
(505) 327-5221
(800) 600-5221

COMFORT INN
555 Scott Ave (87401)
Rates: $59-$99
(505) 325-2626
(800) 424-6423

DAYS INN
1901 E Broadway (87401)
Rates: $45-$82
(505) 325-3700
(800) 329-7366

HOLIDAY INN
600 E Broadway (87401)
Rates: $75-$81
(505) 327-9811
(800) 465-4329

HOLIDAY INN EXP
2110 Bloomfield Blvd (87401)
Rates: $69-$75
(505) 325-2545
(800) 465-4329

LA QUINTA INN
675 Scott Ave (87401)
Rates: $65-$91
(505) 327-4706
(800) 687-6667

MOTEL 6
1600 Bloomfield Hwy (87401)
Rates: $29-$36
(505) 326-4501
(800) 466-8356

SUPER 8 MOTEL
1601 Bloomfield Hwy (87401)
Rates: $45-$85
(505) 325-1813

GALLUP

BEST WESTERN INN & SUITES
3009 W Hwy 66 (87301)
Rates: $59-$99
(505) 722-2221
(800) 528-1234
(800) 722-6399

BEST WESTERN ROYAL HOLIDAY MOTEL
1903 W Hwy 66 (87301)
Rates: $49-$100
(505) 722-4900
(800) 528-1234

BLUE SPRUCE LODGE
1119 US 66E (87301)
Rates: $24-$36
(505) 863-5211

COLONIAL MOTEL
1007 W Coal Ave (87301)
Rates: $18-$30
(505) 863-6821

COMFORT INN
3208 US 66 W (87301)
Rates: $45-$99
(505) 722-0982
(800) 424-6423
(888) 722-0982

DAYS INN EAST
1603 US 66 W (87301)
Rates: $32-$63
(505) 863-3891
(800) 329-7466

DAYS INN WEST
3201 US 66 W (87301)
Rates: $45-$75
(505) 863-6889
(800) 329-7466

ECONO LODGE
3101 US 66 W (87301)
Rates: $32-$57
(505) 722-3800
(800) 424-6423

ECONOMY INN
1709 US 66 W (87301)
Rates: $25-$45
(505) 863-9301

EL CAPITAN MOTEL
1300 US 66 E (87301)
Rates: $22-$40
(505) 863-6828

EL RANCHO HOTEL & MOTEL
1000 US 66E (87301)
Rates: $36-$54
(505) 863-9311

MOTEL 6
3306 US 66 W (87301)
Rates: $34-$43
(505) 863-4492
(800) 466-8356

RAMADA LIMITED
1440 W Maloney Ave (87301)
Rates: $39-$59
(505) 726-2700
(800) 272-6232

RED ROOF INN
3304 W Hwy 66 (87301)
Rates: $33-$60
(505) 722-7765
(800) 843-7663

ROAD RUNNER MOTEL
3012 US 66 E (87301)
Rates: $34-$37
(505) 863-3804

ROSEWAY INN
2003 Hwy 66 W (87301)
Rates: $34-$45
(505) 863-9385
(800) 454-5444

SLEEP INN
3820 US 66 E (87301)
Rates: $50-$85
(505) 863-3535
(800) 424-6423

SUPER 8 MOTEL
1715 W US 66 (87301)
Rates: $41-$88
(505) 722-5300

TRAVELODGE
3275 W Hwy 66 (87301)
Rates: $39-$69
(505) 722-2100
(800) 578-7878

GLENWOOD

LOS OLMOS GUEST RANCH HISTORIC COTTAGE
1 Los Olmos Rd (880393)
Rates: $60-$103
(505) 539-2311

GRANTS

BEST WESTERN INN & SUITES
1501 E Santa Fe Ave (87020)
Rates: $59-$89
(505) 287-7901
(800) 528-1234

COMFORT INN
1551 E Santa Fe Ave (87020)
Rates: $39-$99
(505) 287-8700
(800) 424-6423

DAYS INN
1504 E Santa Fe Ave (87020)
Rates: $40-$80
(505) 287-8883
(800) 329-7466

AREA CODES - If the local number doesn't connect, check for a new area code.

ECONO LODGE
1509 E Santa Fe
Ave (87020)
Rates: $32-$57
(505) 287-7700
(800) 424-6423

HOLIDAY INN EXP
1496 E Santa Fe
Ave (87020)
Rates: $59-$89
(505) 285-4676
(800) 465-4329

MOTEL 6
1505 E Santa Fe
Ave (87020)
Rates: $29-$35
(505) 285-4607
(800) 466-8356

SANDS MOTEL
112 McArthur St
(87020)
Rates: $35-$43
(505) 287-2996

SUPER 8 MOTEL
1604 E Santa Fe
Ave (87020)
Rates: $35-$55
(505) 287-8811
(800) 800-800

TRAVELODGE
1608 E Santa Fe
Ave (87020)
Rates: $39-$60
(505) 287-7800
(800) 578-7878

HERNANDEZ
**CASA DEL RIO
BED & BREAKFAST**
Hwy 84,
MM 199.46
(87532)
Rates: $95-$125
(505) 753-2035

HOBBS
**BEST WESTERN
EXECUTIVE INN**
309 N Marland
Blvd (88240)
Rates: $45-$89
(505) 397-7171
(800) 528-1234

DAYS INN
211 N Marland
Blvd (88240)
Rates: $36-$75
(505) 397-6541
(800) 329-7466

ECONO LODGE
619 N Marland
Blvd (88240)
Rates: $37-$60
(505) 397-3591
(800) 424-6423

**HOWARD
JOHNSON**
501 N Marland
Blvd (88240)
Rates: $55-$75
(505) 397-3251
(800) 446-4656

RODEWAY INN
200 N Marland
Blvd (88240)
Rates: $42-$69
(505) 393-4101
(800) 424-6423

LAS CRUCES
**BAYMONT INN
& SUITES**
1500 Hickory Dr
(88005)
Rates: $45-$59
(505) 523-0100
(877) 229-6668

**BEST WESTERN
MESILLA
VALLEY INN**
901 Avenida de
Mesilla (88005)
Rates: $50-$89
(505) 524-8603
(800) 528-1234
(800) 327-3314

**BEST WESTERN
MISSION INN**
1765 S Main St
(88005)
Rates: $52-$82
(505) 524-8591
(800) 528-1234
(800) 390-1440

COMFORT SUITES
2101 S Triviz
(88001)
Rates: $64-$85
(505) 522-1300
(800) 424-6423

HAMPTON INN
755 Avenida de
Mesilla (88005)
Rates: $52-$75
(505) 526-8311
(800) 426-7866

HILTON INN
705 S Telshore
Blvd (88001)
Rates: $79-$94
(505) 522-4300
(800) 445-8667

HOLIDAY INN
201 E University
Ave (88004)
Rates: $68-$95
(505) 526-4411
(800) 465-4329

HOLIDAY INN EXP
2200 S Valley Dr
(88005)
Rates: $49-$149
(505) 527-9947
(800) 465-4329

LA QUINTA INN
790 Avenida de
Mesilla (88005)
Rates: $64-$780
(505) 524-0331
(800) 531-5900

**LUNDEEN INN
OF THE ARTS
HISTORIC B&B**
618 S Alameda
Blvd (88005)
Rates: $65-$77
(505) 526-3326

MOTEL 6
235 La Posada
Ln (88001)
Rates: $36-$55
(505) 525-1010
(800) 466-8356

MOTEL 6
2120 Summit Ct
(88001)
Rates: $39-$46
(505) 525-2055
(800) 466-8356

**ROYAL HOST
MOTEL**
2146 W Picacho St
(88005)
Rates: $34-$42
(505) 524-8536

SLEEP INN
2121 S Triviz
(88001)
Rates: $60-$85
(505) 522-1700
(800) 424-6423

**THE SMITH MAN-
SION B&B**
909 N Alameda
Blvd (88005)
Rates: n/a
(505) 525-2525

SUPER 8 MOTEL
245 La Posada Ln
(88001)
Rates: $37-$47
(505) 523-8695
(800) 800-8000

**TEAKWOOD
INN & SUITES**
2600 S Valley Dr
(88005)
Rates: $40-$100
(505) 526-4441

**TRH SMITH
MANSION B&B**
909 N Alameda
Blvd (88005)
Rates: $89
(505) 525-2525

LAS VEGAS
COMFORT INN
2500 N Grand
Ave (87701)
Rates: $55-$100
(5050 425-1100
(800) 424-6423

EL CAMINO MOTEL
1152 N Grand Ave
(87701)
Rates: $40-$65
(505) 425-5994

**HISTORIC
PLAZA HOTEL**
230 Old Town
Plaza (87701)
Rates: $78-$116
(505) 425-3591
(800) 328-1882

**INN ON THE
SANTA FE TRAIL**
1133 N Grand Ave
(87701)
Rates: $54-$84
(505) 425-6791
(800) 425-6791

PLAZA MOTEL
230 Plaza (87701)
Rates: $68-$124
(505) 425-3591

LORDSBURG
**BEST WESTERN-
WESTERN SKIES
INN**
1303 S Main
(88045)
Rates: $49-$79
(505) 542-8807
(800) 528-1234

HOLIDAY INN EXP
1408 S Main
(88045)
Rates: $67-$74
(505) 542-3666
(800) 465-4329

SUPER 8 MOTEL
110 E Maple
(88045)
Rates: $49-$69
(505) 542-8882
(800) 800-8000

LOS ALAMOS
LOS ALAMOS INN
2201 Trinity Dr
(87544)
Rates: $69-$99
(505) 662-7211

LOS LUNAS
COMFORT INN
1711 Main St SW
(87031)
Rates: $50-$74
(505) 865-5100
(800) 424-6423

DAYS INN
1919 Main St SW
(87031)
Rates: $42-$73
(505) 865-5995
(800) 329-7466

**WESTERN SKIES
INN & SUITES**
2258 Sun Ranch
Village Loop
(87031)
Rates: $54-$69
(505) 865-0001

LOVINGTON
LOVINGTON INN
1600 W Ave D
(88260)
Rates: $49-$74
(505) 396-5346

AREA CODES - If the local number doesn't connect, check for a new area code.

MESILLA

MESON DE MESILLA COUNTRY INN
1803 Avenida de Mesilla (88046)
Rates: $57-$185
(505) 525-9212

MORIARTY

DAYS INN
US 66 W & I-40, Exit 194 (87035)
Rates: $38-$72
(505) 832-4451
(800) 329-7466

ECONO LODGE
1316 Rt 66 W (87035)
Rates: $39-$65
(505) 832-4457
(800) 424-6423

HOLIDAY INN EXP
1507 Rt 66 (87035)
Rates: $74-$95
(505) 832-5000
(800) 465-4329

MOTEL 6
119 Rt 66 E (87035)
Rates: $40+
(505) 832-6666
(800) 466-8356

SUNSET MOTEL
501 Old Rt 66 (87035)
Rates: $33-$49
(505) 832-4234

SUPER 8 MOTEL
1611 W Old Rt 66 (87035)
Rates: $43-$65
(505) 832-6730
(800) 800-8000

PINOS ALTOS

BEAR CREEK MOTEL & CABINS
88 Main St (88053)
Rates: $89-$159
(505) 388-4501

PLACITAS

HACIENDA DE PLACITAS INN OF THE ARTS B&B
491 Hwy 165 (87043)
Rates: $109-$209
(505) 867-0082

POJOAQUE PUEBLO

CITIES OF GOLD HOTEL
10A Cities of Gold Rd (87506)
Rates: $82-$119
(505) 455-0515

RANCHO DE TAOS

BUDGET HOST INN
1798 Paseo Del Pueblo Sur Ave (87557)
Rates: $43-$70
(505) 758-2524
(800) 283-4678

RATON

BUDGET HOST
136 Canyon Dr (87740)
Rates: $38-$54
(505) 445-3655
(800) 283-4678

MOTEL 6
1600 Cedar St (87740)
Rates: $35-$63
(505) 445-2777
(800) 466-8356

THE PASS INN
308 Canyon Dr (87740)
Rates: $36-$52
(505) 445-3641

RED RIVER

BEST WESTERN RIVERS EDGE
301 W River St (87558)
Rates: $72-$130
(505) 754-1766
(800) 528-1234
(877) 600-9990

RIO RANCHO

BEST WESTERN RIO RANCHO INN
1465 Rio Rancho Dr (87124)
Rates: $59-$129
(505) 892-1700
(800) 528-1234
(800) 658-9558

DAYS INN
4200 Crestview Dr (87124)
Rates: $39-$120
(505) 892-8800
(800) 329-7466

RAMADA LIMITED
4081 High Resort Blvd (87124)
Rates: $47-$150
(505) 892-5998
(800) 272-6232

SUPER 8 MOTEL
4100 Barbara Loop SE (87124)
Rates: $46-$61
(505) 896-8888
(800) 800-8000

WELLESLEY INN & SUITES
2221 Rio Rancho Blvd (87124)
Rates: $72-$225
(505) 892-7900
(800) 444-8888

ROSWELL

BEST WESTERN EL RANCHO PALACIO MOTOR LODGE
2205 N Main St (88201)
Rates: $48-$72
(505) 622-2721
(800) 528-1234

BEST WESTERN SALLY PORT INN & SUITES
2000 N Main St (88201)
Rates: $79-$109
(505) 622-6430
(800) 528-1234

BUDGET INN NORTH
2101 N Main St (88201)
Rates: $30-$45
(505) 623-6050
(800) 752-4667

BUDGET INN WEST
2200 W 2nd St (88201)
Rates: $28-$50
(505) 623-3811
(800) 752-4667

COMFORT INN
3595 N Main St (88201)
Rates: $70-$180
(505) 623-4567
(800) 424-6423

DAYS INN
1310 N Main St (88201)
Rates: $50-$80
(505) 623-4021
(800) 329-7466

FRONTIER MOTEL
3010 N Main St (88201)
Rates: $32-$44
(505) 622-1400
(800) 678-1401

LEISURE INN
2700 W 2nd St (88201)
Rates: $32-$65
(505) 622-2575

MOTEL 6
3307 N Main St (88201)
Rates: $39-$43
(505) 625-6666
(800) 466-8356

NATIONAL 9 INN
2001 N Main St (88201)
Rates: $31-$40
(505) 622-0110
(800) 524-9999

RAMADA INN
2803 W 2nd (88201)
Rates: $64-$78
(505) 623-9440
(800) 272-6232

WESTERN INN
2331 N Main St (88201)
Rates: $40-$225
(505) 623-9425

RUIDOSO

BEST WESTERN PINE SPRINGS INN
1420 W Hwy 70 (88345)
Rates: $89-$139
(505) 378-8100
(800) 528-1234

COMFORT INN
2709 Sudderth Dr (88345)
Rates: $59-$139
(505) 257-2770
(800) 424-6423

DAN DEE CABINS
310 Main Rd (88345)
Rates: 484-$240
(505) 257-2165

HAWTHORN SUITES & GOLF RESORT
107 Sierra Blanca Dr (88345)
Rates: $184-$205
(505) 258-5500
(800) 527-1133

MOTEL 6
412 W Hwy 70 (88345)
Rates: $43-$64
(505) 630-1166
(800) 466-8356

TRAVELODGE
159 W Hwy 70 (88345)
Rates: $45-$129
(505) 378-4471
(800) 578-7878

VILLAGE LODGE SUITES CONDOS
1000 Mecham Dr (88345)
Rates: $129-$250
(505) 258-5442

RUIDOSO DOWNS

AMERIHOST INN & SUITES
2191 Hwy 70 W (88346)
Rates: $89-$199
(505) 376-1199
(800) 434-5800

SANTA FE

ALEXANDER'S INN HISTORIC B&B
529 E Palace Ave (87501)
Rates: $85-$190
(505) 986-1431
(888) 321-5123

AREA CODES - If the local number doesn't connect, check for a new area code.

BEST WESTERN INN OF SANTA FE
3650 Cerrillos Rd (87505)
Rates: $40-$110
(505) 438-3822
(800) 528-1234

THE BISHOP'S LODGE RESORT & SPA
N Bishop's Lodge Rd (87501)
Rates: $209-$409
(505) 983-6377
(800) 732-2240

CACTUS LODGE MOTEL
2864 Cerrillos Rd (87505)
Rates: $35-$85
(505) 471-7699

CAMEL ROCK SUITES MOTEL
3007 S St. Frances Dr (87505)
Rates: $79-$99
(505) 989-3600

CASAPUEBLO INN BED & BREAKFST
138 Park Ave (87501)
Rates: $129-$279
(505) 988-4455

COMFORT INN
4312 Cerrillos Rd (87505)
Rates: $69-$179
(505) 474-7330
(800) 424-6423

DANCING GROUND OF THE SUN B&B
711 Paseo de Perlata (87501)
Rates: n/a
(505) 986-9797

EL PARADERO HISTORIC B&B
220 W Manhattan (87501)
Rates: $65-$160
(505) 988-1177

ELDORADO HOTEL
309 W San Francisco St (87501)
Rates: $169-$1500
(505) 988-4455
(800) 955-4455
(800) 385-6073

THE HACIENDA AT HOTEL SANTA FE
1501 Paseo de Peralta (87501)
Rates: $199-$499
(505) 955-7800

HACIENDA NICHOLAS B&B
320 E Marcy St (87501)
Rates: $100-$175
(505) 986-1431
(888) 321-5123

HAMPTON INN
3625 Cerrillos Rd (87505)
Rates: $59-$129
(505) 474-3900
(800) 426-7866

HOTEL PLAZA REAL
125 Washington Ave (87501)
Rates: $139-$299
(505) 988-4900

HOTEL SANTA FE
1501 Paseo De Peralta (87501)
Rates: $119-$499
(505) 982-1200
(800) 210-6441

INN ON THE ALAMEDA
303 E Alameda St (87501)
Rates: $129-$275
(505) 984-2121
(800) 506-9205

LA QUINTA INN
4298 Cerrillos Rd (87505)
Rates: $79-$119
(505) 471-1142
(800) 687-6667

LAS PALOMAS HISTORIC MOTEL
119 Park Ave (87501)
Rates: $129-$239
(505) 988-4455

MOTEL 6-NORTH
3007 Cerrillos Rd (87505)
Rates: $39-$67
(505) 473-1380
(800) 466-8356

PARK INN & SUITES
2907 Cerrillos Rd (87507)
Rates: $74-$84
(505) 471-3000
(800) 670-7275

PECOS TRAIL INN
2239 Old Pecos Trail (87505)
Rates: $79-$149
(505) 982-1943

QUALITY INN
3011 Cerrillos Rd (87501)
Rates: $65-$120
(505) 471-1211
(800) 424-6423

RESIDENCE INN BY MARRIOTT
1698 Galisteo St (87505)
Rates: $139-$239
(505) 988-7300
(800) 331-3131

RIO VISTA SUITES CONDO MOTEL
320 Artist Rd (87501)
Rates: $135-$165
(505) 982-6636
(800) 745-9910

SANTA FE MOTEL & INN
510 Cerrillos Rd (87501)
Rates: $79-$139
(505) 982-1039

SANTA FE PLAZA TRAVELODGE
646 Cerrillos Rd (87501)
Rates: $55-$150
(505) 982-3551
(800) 578-7878

SLEEP INN
8376 Cerillos Rd (87505)
Rates: $59-$179
(505) 474-9500
(800) 424-6423

SANTA ROSA

BEST WESTERN ADOBE INN
1501 E Will Rogers Dr (88435)
Rates: $42-$69
(505) 472-3446
(800) 528-1234

BEST WESTERN SANTA ROSA INN
3022 Historic Rt 66 (88435)
Rates: $49-$70
(505) 472-5877
(800) 528-1234

COMFORT INN
3343 E Will Rogers Blvd (88435)
Rates: $50-$90
(505) 472-5570
(800) 424-6423

DAYS INN
1830 Will Rogers Dr (88435)
Rates: $44-$69
(505) 472-5985
(800) 329-7466

LA QUINTA INN
1701 Rt 66 (88435)
Rates: $60-$90
(505) 472-4800
(800) 687-6667

MOTEL 6
3400 Will Rogers Dr (88435)
Rates: $37-$55
(505) 472-3045
(800) 466-8356

RAMADA INN
3300 Rt 66 (88435)
Rates: $59-$79
(505) 472-5411
(800) 272-6232

SUPER 8 MOTEL
1201 Rt 66 (88435)
Rates: $44-$62
(505) 472-538
(800) 800-8000

SILVER CITY

COMFORT INN
1060 E Hwy 180 (88061)
Rates: $49-$150
(505) 534-1883
(800) 424-6423

DRIFTER MOTEL
711 Silver Heights Blvd (88062)
Rates: $41-$50
(505) 538-2916

ECONO LODGE
1120 Hwy 180 E (88061)
Rates: $44-$71
(505) 534-1111
(800) 424-6423

HOLIDAY INN EXP
1103 Superior St (88061)
Rates: $80-$90
(505) 538-2525
(800) 465-4329

HOLIDAY MOTOR HOTEL
3420 Hwy 180 E (88061)
Rates: $42-$46
(505) 538-3711
(800) 828-8291

SUPER 8 MOTEL
1040 Hwy 180 E (88061)
Rates: $35-$52
(505) 388-1983
(800) 800-8000

SOCORRO

ECONO LODGE
713 California Ave NW (87801)
Rates: $40-$65
(505) 835-1500
(800) 424-6423

HOLIDAY INN EXP
1100 California Ave NW (87801)
Rates: $90-$130
(505) 838-0556
(800) 465-4329

MOTEL 6
807 US Hwy 85 (87801)
Rates: $32-$55
(505) 835-4300
(800) 466-8356

TAOS

ADOBE SUN GOD LODGE
919 Paseo del
Pueblo Sur (87571)
Rates: $49-$99
(505) 758-3162
(800) 821-2437

AMERICAN ARTISTS GALLERY HOUSE B&B
132 Frontier Lane
(87571)
Rates: $95-$225
(505) 758-4446
(800) 532-2041

BROOKS STREET INN B&B
119 Brooks St
(87571)
Rates: $89-$169
(505) 758-1489

BURCH STREET CASITAS
310 Burch St
(87571)
Rates: $69-$139
(505) 737-9038
(800) 954-8267

CASA ENCANTADA B&B
416 Liebert St
(87571)
Rates: $110-$195
(505) 758-7477

CASA EUROPA INN & GALLERY B&B
840 Upper
Ranchitos Rd
(87571)
Rates: $85-$185
(505) 758-9798

EL PUEBLO LODGE
412 Paseo del
Pueblo Norte
(87571)
Rates: $54-$125
(505) 758-8700
(800) 433-9612

FECHIN INN
227 Paseo del
Pueblo Norte
(87571)
Rates: $114-$512
(505) 751-1000
(800) 811-2935

HOLIDAY INN DON FERNANDO DE TAOS
1005 Paseo del
Pueblo Sur (87571)
Rates: $89-$185
(505) 758-4444
(800) 465-4329

INN ON THE RIO
910 E Kit Carson
Rd (87571)
Rates: $79-$129
(505) 758-7199
(800) 859-6752

ORINDA BED & BREAKFAST
461 Valverde
(87571)
Rates: $89-$145
(505) 758-8581

QUALITY INN
1043 Camino del
Pueblo Sur (87571)
Rates: $59-$130
(505) 758-2200
(800) 424-6423
(888) 908-8267

RAMADA INN
615 Paseo del
Pueblo Sur (87571)
Rates: $79-$120
(505) 758-2900
(800) 659-8267

SAGEBRUSH HISTORIC INN
1508 Paseo del
Pueblo Sur (87571)
Rates: $85-$125
(505) 758-2254
(888) 782-8267

SAN GERONIMO LODGE HISTORIC B&B
1101 Witt Rd
(87571)
Rates: $95-$150
(505) 751-3776

THOREAU

ZUNI MOUNTAIN LODGE COUNTRY INN
40 W Perch Dr
(87323)
Rates: $60-$95
(505) 862-7769

TRUTH OR CONSEQUENCES

BEST WESTERN HOT SPRINGS MOTOR INN
2270 N Date St
(87901)
Rates: $57-$75
(505) 894-6665
(800) 528-1234

HOLIDAY IN
2205 N Date St
(87901)
Rates: $60-$85
(505) 894-1660
(800) 465-4329

SUPER 8 MOTEL
2151 N Date St
(87901)
Rates: $53-$61
(505) 894-7888
(800) 800-8000

TUCUMCARI

AMERICANA MOTEL
406 E Tucumcari
Blvd (88401)
Rates: $24-$42
(505) 461-0431

APACHE MOTEL
1106 E Tucumcari
Blvd (88401)
Rates: $20-$34
(505) 461-3367

BEST WESTERN DISCOVERY INN
200 E Estrella
(88401)
Rates: $58-$98
(505) 461-4884
(800) 528-1234

BUCKAROO MOTEL
1315 W Tucumcari
Blvd (88401)
Rates: $18-$22
(505) 461-1650

BUDGET INN
824 W Tucumcari
Blvd (88401)
Rates: $26-$40
(505) 461-4139

COMFORT INN
2800 E Tucumcari
Blvd (88401)
Rates: $51-$89
(505) 461-4094
(800) 424-6423

DAYS INN
2623 S First St
(88401)
Rates: $45-$75
(505) 461-3158
(800) 329-7466

ECONO LODGE
3400 E Tucumcari
Blvd (88401)
Rates: $32-$65
(505) 461-4194
(800) 424-6423

FRIENDS INN MOTEL
315 E Tucumcari
Blvd (88401)
Rates: $24-$40
(505) 461-0330

HOLIDAY INN
3716 E Tucumcari
Blvd (88401)
Rates: $65-$95
(505) 461-3780
(800) 465-4329

HOWARD JOHNSON EXPRESS INN
3604 E Rt 66
(88401)
Rates: $39-$59
(505) 461-2747
(800) 446-4656

MICROTEL INN
2420 S 1st St
(88401)
Rates: $50-$80
(505) 461-0600
(888) 771-7171

MOTEL 6
2900 E Tucumcari
Blvd (88401)
Rates: $35-$48
(505) 461-4791
(800) 466-8356

POW WOW INN
801 W Tucumcari
Blvd (88401)
Rates: $49-$59
(505) 461-0500

RODEWAY INN EAST
1023 E Tucumcari
Blvd (88401)
Rates: $34-$79
(505) 461-0360
(800) 424-6423

SAFARI MOTEL
722 E Tucumcari
Blvd (88401)
Rates: $30-$44
(505) 461-3642

SUPER 8 MOTEL
4001 E Tucumcari
Blvd (88401)
Rates: $45-$75
(505) 461-4444
(800) 800-8000

VAUGHN

BEL-AIR MOTEL
1004 US
54/60/285
(88353)
Rates: $32-$44
(505) 584-2241

OAK TREE INN
Jct US 54/60/285
(88353)
Rates: $59-$64
(505) 584-8733

WHITE ROCK

BANDELIER INN MOTEL
132 SR 4 (87544)
Rates: $62-$69
(505) 672-3838

WHITES CITY

BEST WESTERN CAVERN INN
17 Carlsbad
Caverns Hwy
(88268)
Rates: $65-$105
(505) 785-2291
(800) 528-1234
(800) 228-3767

AREA CODES - If the local number doesn't connect, check for a new area code.

NEW YORK

ACRA
SLEEPY DUTCHMAN
Rt 23, Box 59B (12405)
Rates: n/a
(518) 622-2050

ALBANY
ALBANY MANSION HILL INN B&B
115 Phillip St at Park Ave (12205)
Rates: $175-$215
(518) 465-2038

CRESTHILL SUITES
1415 Washington Ave (12206)
Rates: $129-$229
(518) 454-0007

MOTEL 6
100 Watervliet Ave (12206)
Rates: $45-$70
(518) 438-7447
(800) 466-8356

RAMADA INN
416 Southern Blvd (12209)
Rates: $69-$129
(518) 462-6555
(800) 272-6232

RAMADA INN-DOWNTOWN
300 Broadway (12207)
Rates: $69-$119
(518) 434-4111
(800) 272-6232

TOWNEPLACE SUITES
1379 Washington Ave (12206)
Rates: $100-$180
(518) 435-1900
(800) 257-3000

ALLEGANY
MICROTEL INN & SUITES
3234 SR 417 (14760)
Rates: $39-$89
(716) 373-5333

ALTMAR
BRENDA' S MOTEL & CAMPGROUND
644 CR 48 (13302)
Rates: n/a
(315) 298-2268

CANNON'S PLACE
P. O. Box 209, CR 48 (13302)
Rates: n/a
(315) 298-5054

FOX HOLLOW
2740 SR 13 (13302)
Rates: n/a
(315) 298-2876

JAYHAWKERS BUNKHOUSE
CC Rd, Box 132 (13302)
Rates: n/a
(315) 964-2557

AMAGANSETT
GANSETT GREEN MANOR COTTAGES & APARTMENTS
273 Main St (11937)
Rates: $225-$350
(631) 267-3133

AMENIA
DEER RUN
P O Box 302 (12501)
Rates: $50-$99
(914) 373-9558

AMHERST
BUFFALO MARRIOTT-NIAGARA
1340 Millersport Hwy (14221)
Rates: $99-$179
(716) 689-6900
(800) 228-9290

COMFORT INN
1 Flint Rd (14226)
Rates: $89-$144
(716) 688-0811
(800) 424-6423

LORD AMHERST MOTOR HOTEL
5000 Main St (14226)
Rates: $55-$109
(716) 839-2200
(800) 544-2200

MOTEL 6
4400 Maple Rd (14226)
Rates: $29-$60
(716) 834-2231
(800) 466-8356

RED ROOF INN
42 Flint Rd (14226)
Rates: $43-$88
(716) 689-7474
(800) 843-7663

AMSTERDAM
BEST WESTERN AMSTERDAM INN
10 Market St (12010)
Rates: $65-$99
(518) 843-5760
(800) 528-1234

VALLEY VIEW MOTOR INN
Rts 5 S & 30 (12010)
Rates: $31-$58
(518) 842-5637

ANGELICA
ANGELICA INN BED & BREAKFAST
64 W Main St (14709)
Rates: $75-$150
(585) 466-3295

APALACHIN
THE DOLPHIN INN
7666 SR 434 (13732)
Rates: $50-$75
(607) 625-4441

AUBURN
DAYS INN
37 William St (13021)
Rates: $44-$99
(315) 252-7567
(800) 329-7466

FINGER LAKES INN & SUITES
12 Seminary Ave (13021)
Rates: $79-$149
(315) 253-5000

HOLIDAY INN-FINGER LAKES REGION
75 North St (13021)
Rates: $89-$139
(315) 253-4531
(800) 465-4329

THE IRISH ROSE BED & BREAKFAST
102 South St (13021)
Rates: $55-$95
(315) 255-0196

AVERILL PARK
LA PERLA AT THE GREGORY HOUSE COUNTRY INN
3016 SR 43 (12018)
Rates: $75-$140
(518) 674-3774

AVOCA
CABOOSE MOTEL
8620 State Rt 415 (14809)
Rates: $50-$75
(607) 566-2216

BAINBRIDGE
ALGONKIN MOTEL
262 State Hwy 7 (13733)
Rates: $50-$75
(607) 967-5911

BALDWINS-VILLE
MICROTEL INN & SUITES
131 Downer St (13027)
Rates: $55-$100
(315) 635-9556

BALLSTON LAKE
WESTWOOD MOTEL
1012 Saratoga Rd (12019)
Rates: $45-$80
(518) 339-3612

BATAVIA
BUDGET INN
301 Oak St (14020)
Rates: $40-$99
(585) 343-7921

COMFORT INN
4371 Federal Dr (14020)
Rates: $55-$139
(585) 344-9999
(800) 424-6423

DAYS INN
200 Oak St (14020)
Rates: $49-$119
(585) 343-6000
(800) 329-7466

HOLIDAY INN
8250 Park Rd (14020)
Rates: n/a
(585) 344-2100
(800) 465-4329

RAMADA LTD
8204 Park Rd (14020)
Rates: n/a
(585) 343-1000
(800) 272-6232

BATH
DAYS INN
330 W Morris St (14810)
Rates: $55-$125
(607) 776-7644
(800) 329-7466

AREA CODES - If the local number doesn't connect, check for a new area code.

SUPER 8 MOTEL
333 W Morris St
(14810)
Rates: $56-$96
(607) 776-2187
(800) 800-8000

BELLPORT
**THE GREAT
SOUTH BAY
INN B&B**
160 S Country Rd
(11713)
Rates: $115-$150
(631) 286-8588

BERLIN
**THE SEDGWICK
INN**
17971 Rt 22
(12022)
Rates: $65-$95
(518) 658-2334

BERNHARDS
BAY
SNUG HARBOR
Rt 9, Box 44
(13028)
Rates: n/a
(315) 675-3527

BINGHAMTON
DAYS INN
1000 Front St
(13905)
Rates: $80-$185
(607) 724-3297
(800) 329-7466

ECONO LODGE
690 Front St
(13905)
Rates: $36-$142
(607) 724-1341
(800) 424-6423

**HOLIDAY INN
ARENA**
2-8 Hawley St
(13901)
Rates: $90
(607) 722-1212
(800) 465-4329

MOTEL 6
1012 Front St
(13905)
Rates: $33-$50
(607) 771-0400
(800) 466-8356

**QUALITY INN &
SUITES**
1156 Front St
(13905)
Rates: $50-$200
(607) 722-5353
(800) 424-6423

SAI BLESS INN
65 Front St (13905)
Rates: $49-$99
(607) 724-2412

BLASDELL
CLARION HOTEL
3950 McKinley
Pkwy (14219)
Rates: $59-$129
(716) 648-5700
(800) 252-7466

ECONO LODGE
4344 Milestrip Rd
(14219)
Rates: $45-$99
(716) -825-7530
(800) 553-2666

BOONVILLE
**HEADWATERS
MOTOR LODGE**
13524 Rt 12
(13309)
Rates: $49-$85
(315) 952-4493

BOWMANS-
VILLE
RED ROOF INN
146 Maple Dr
(14026)
Rates: $39-$82
(716) 633-1100
(800) 843-7663

BRIGHTON
**WELLESLEY INN
& SUITES**
797 E Henrietta
Rd (14623)
Rates: $55-$105
(585) 427-0130
(800) 444-8888

BROCKPORT
HOLIDAY INN EXP
4908 Lake Rd S
(14420)
Rates: $83-$143
(585) 395-1000
(800) 465-4329

BUFFALO
**BEST WESTERN
INN-ON THE
AVENUE**
510 Delaware Ave
(14202)
Rates: $79-$149
(716) 886-8333
(800) 528-1234
(888) 868-3033

**HOLIDAY INN-
DOWNTOWN**
620 Delaware Ave
(14202)
Rates: $69-$149
(716) 886-2121
(800) 465-4329

**QUALITY INN
AIRPORT**
4217 Genessee St
(14225)
Rates: $72-$169
(716) 633-5500
(800) 424-6423

CALCIUM
MICROTEL INN
8000 Virginia
Smith Dr (13616)
Rates: $60
(315) 629-5000
(888) 771-7171
(800) 447-9660

CAMBRIDGE
**BLUE WILLOW
MOTEL**
51 S Park St
(12816)
Rates: $35-$65
(518) 677-3552

**CAMBRIDGE INN
BED & BRKFAST**
16 W Main St
(12816)
Rates: $48-$75
(518) 677-5741

**TOWN HOUSE
MOTOR INN**
16 W Main (12816)
Rates: $45-$50
(518) 677-5524

CANANDAIGUA
CAMPUS LODGE
4341 Lakeshore Dr
(14424)
Rates: $50-$95
(585) 394-1250
(800) 836-3299

**CANANDAIGUA
INN ON THE LAKE**
770 S Main St
(14424)
Rates: $89-$304
(585) 394-7800

**ECONO LODGE
MUAR LAKE**
170 Eastern Blvd
(14424)
Rates: $39-$109
(585) 394-9000
(800) 424-6423

**FINGER
LAKES INN**
4343 Rts 5 & 20 E
(14424)
Rates: $50-$75
(585) 394-2800
(800) 727-2775

CANASTOTA
DAYS INN
377 N Peterboro
St (13032)
Rates: $59-$99
(315) 697-3309
(800) 329-7466

CASTLETON
BEL-AIR MOTEL
1036 Rt 9 (12033)
Rates: $40-$55
(518) 732-7744

CATSKILL
**CATSKILL CABIN
RENTAL**
P. O. Box 498
(Grand Gorge
12434)
Rates: $150 Night;
$1050+ Weekly
(212) 532-9322

**QUALITY INN &
CONF CENTER**
I-87/Exit 21 (12414)
Rates: $89-$349
(518) 943-5800
(800) 424-6423

CAZENOVIA
**LINCKLAEN
HOUSE**
79 Albany St
(13035)
Rates: $65-$130
(315) 655-3461

CENTRAL
SQUARE
**TOWN &
COUNTRY MOTEL**
1436 Brewerton
Rd (13036)
Rates: n/a
(315) 668-6751

CHAFFEE
**JOSIE'S
BROOKSIDE
MOTEL**
SR 16 & 39 (14030)
Rates: $29-$45
(716) 496-5057

CHEEKTOWAGA
**HOLIDAY INN EXP
HOTEL & SUITES**
131 Buell Ave
(14225)
Rates: $100-$130
(716) 631-8700
(800) 465-4329

**HOMEWOOD
SUITES**
760 Dick Rd
(14225)
Rates: $124-$199
(716) 685-0700
(800) 225-5466

OAK TREE INN
3475 Union Rd
(14225)
Rates: $46-$105
(716) 681-2600
(800) 456-TREE

**RESIDENCE INN
BY MARRIOTT**
107 Anderson Rd
(14225)
Rates: $69-$169
(716) 892-5410
(800) 331-3131

CICERO
BUDGET INN
901 S Bay Rd
(13039)
Rates: $50-$110
(315) 458-3510

CLARENCE
**ASA RANSOM
HOUSE
HISTORIC COUN-
TRY INN**
10529 Main St
(14031)
Rates: $100-$185
(716-759-2315

CLIFTON

HOWARD JOHNSON INN
680 Rt 3 W (07014)
Rates: $89-$139
(973) 471-3800
(800) 446-4656

CLINTON

THE HEDGES B&B
180 Sanford Ave
(13323)
Rates: $95-$150
(315) 853-3031

COBLESKILL

BEST WESTERN INN
121 Burgin Dr
(12043)
Rates: $79-$179
(518) 234-4321
(800) 528-1234

SUPER 8 MOTEL
955 E Main St
(12043)
Rates: $70-$145
(518) 234-4888
(800) 800-8000

COHOES

INN AT THE CENTURY
997 New Loudon
Rd (12047)
Rates: $72-$110
(518) 785-0931

COLONIE

AMBASSADOR MOTOR INN
1600 Central Ave
(12205)
Rates: $59-$109
(518) 456-8982

SUPER 8 MOTEL
1579 Central Ave
(12205)
Rates: $59-$85
(518) 856-8471
(800) 800-8000

RAMADA LTD
1630 Central Ave
(12205)
Rates: $65-$200
(518) 456-0222
(800) 272-6232

RED ROOF INN
188 Wolf Rd
(12205)
Rates: $56-$83
(518) 459-1971
(800) 843-7663

COOPERS PLAIN

STILES MOTEL
9239 Victory Hwy
(14827)
Rates: $42-$52
(607) 962-5221

CORNING

RADISSON HOTEL
125 Denison Pkwy
E (14870)
Rates: $116-$129
(607) 962-5000
(800) 333-3333

STAYBRIDGE SUITES
201 Townley Ave
(14830)
Rates: $94-$200
(607) 936-7800
(800) 238-8000

CORTLAND

COMFORT INN
2 1/2 Locust Ave
(13045)
Rates: $79-$189
(607) 753-7721
(800) 424-6423

ECONO LODGE
10 Church St
(13045)
Rates: $52-$159
(607) 756-2856
(800) 553-2666

HOLIDAY INN
2 River St (13045)
Rates: $80-$110
(607) 756-4431
(800) 465-4329

QUALITY INN
188 Clinton Ave
(13045)
Rates: $79-$179
(607) 756-5622
(800) 424-6423

WATERFALLS MOTEL
Rt 9A & Furnace
Dock Rd (10520)
Rates: $60-$70
(914) 271-4322

CUBA

CUBA COACH-LIGHT MOTEL
1 N Branch Rd
(14727)
Rates: $44-$69
(585) 968-1992

DANSVILLE

DAYSTOP
1 Commerce Dr
(14437)
Rates: $46-$51
(585) 335-6023
(800) 329-7466

DELHI

BUENA VISTA MOTEL
18718 State Hwy
28 (13753)
Rates: $69-$89
(607) 746-2135

DEPOSIT

ALEXANDER'S INN ON OQUAGA LAKE B&B
770 Oquaga Lake
Rd (13754)
Rates: $59-$99
(607) 467-6023

DEWITT

ECONO LODGE
3400 Erie Blvd E
(13214)
Rates: $55-$130
(315) 446-3300
(800) 424-6423

DOVER PLAINS

OLD DROVERS HISTORIC COUNTRY INN
196 E Duncan Hill
Rd (12522)
Rates: $150-$550
(845) 832-9311

DUNKIRK

BEST WESTERN DUNKIRK INN
3912 Vineyard Dr
(14048)
Rates: $59-$149
(716) 366-7100
(800) 528-1234
(888) 386-5475

COMFORT INN
3925 Vineyard Dr
(14048)
Rates: $64-$179
(716) 672-4450
(800) 424-6423

RAMADA INN
30 Lake Shore Dr
(14048)
Rates: $80-$180
(716) 366-8350
(800) 272-6232

EAST DURHAM

THE CARRIAGE HOUSE B&B & HORSE RANCH
2946 Rt 145 (12423)
Rates: $90-$125
(518) 634-7009

EAST ELMHURST

(See Queens)

EAST GREENBUSH

MOUNT VERNON MOTEL
576 Columbia
Tpke (12061)
Rates: $29-$69
(518) 477-9352
(800) 321-4681

EAST HAMPTON

DUTCH MOTEL
488 Montauk Hwy
(11937)
Rates: $89-$349
(631) 324-4550

EAST HERKIMER

GLEN RIDGE MOTEL
5571 SR 5 (13350)
Rates: n/a
(315) 866-4149
(866) 453-6743

EAST SYRACUSE

COMFORT INN-CARRIER CIRCLE
6491 Thompson
Rd S (13206)
Rates: $72-$90
(315) 437-0222
(800) 424-6423

CRESTHILL SUITES
6410 New Venture
Gear Rd (13057)
Rates: $114-$199
(315) 432-5595

HOLIDAY INN EAST-CARRIER CIRCLE
6555 Old Collamer
Rd (13057)
Rates: $94-$109
(315) 437-2761
(800) 465-4329

MICROTEL INN
6608 Old Collamer
Rd (13057)
Rates: $43-$72
(315) 437-3500
(888) 771-7171
(800) 435-1665

MOTEL 6
6577 Baptist Way
(13057)
Rates: $31-$56
(315) 433-1300
(800) 466-8356

RESIDENCE INN BY MARRIOTT
6420 Yorktown Cir
(13057)
Rates: $154-$174
(315) 432-4488
(800) 331-3131

SUPER 8 MOTEL
6620 Old Collamer
Rd (13057)
Rates: $44-$84
(315) 432-5612
(800) 800-8000

EAST WINDHAM

POINT LOOKOUT MOUNTAIN INN
The Mohican Trail
Rte 23 (12439)
Rates: $55-$125
(518) 734-3381

ELBRIDGE

COZY COTTAGE
4987 Kingston Rd
(13060)
Rates: n/a
(315) 689-2082

ELKA PARK

DIAMOND HORSESHOE RANCH & SKI RESORT
Dale Lane (12427)
Rates: $90-$135
(518) 589-5197
(800) 926-2771

ELLICOTTVILLE

JEFFERSON INN B&B
3 Jefferson St (14731)
Rates: $79-$209
(716) 699-5869

ELMIRA

COACHMAN MOTOR LODGE
908 Pennsylvania Ave (14904)
Rates: $60-$70
(607) 733-5526

ELMSFORD

WELLESLEY INN
540 Saw Mill River Rd (10523)
Rates: $119-$159
(914) 592-3300
(800) 444-8888

ENDICOTT

ECONO LODGE
749 W Main St (13760)
Rates: $40-$150
(607) 754-1533
(800) 424-6423

ENDWELL

KINGS INN
2603 E Main St (13760)
Rates: $39-$100
(607) 754-8020

ERWIN

ERWIN MOTEL
Rt 417 (14870)
Rates: $32-$79
(607) 962-7411

FAIRPORT

TRAIL BREAK MOTOR INN
7340 Pittsford-Palmyra Rd (14450)
Rates: $35-$69
(716) 223-1710

FALCONER

RED ROOF INN
1980 E Main St (14733)
Rates: $48-$73
(716) 665-3670
(800) 843-7663

FARMINGTON

BUDGET INN
6001 Rt 96 (14425)
Rates: $43-$79
(585) 924-5020

ECONO LODGE
6108 Loomis Rd (14424)
Rates: $48-$92
(585) 924-2131
(800) 424-6423
(800) 333-0536

FISHKILL

HOMESTEAD STUDIO SUITES
25 Merritt Blvd (12524)
Rates: $114-$139
(845) 897-2800
(888) 782-9473

RESIDENCE INN BY MARRIOTT
15 Schuyler Blvd (12524)
Rates: $179-$209
(845) 896-5210
(800) 331-3131

WELLESLEY INN & SUITES
20 Schuyler Blvd (12524)
Rates: $99-$119
(845) 896-4995
(800) 444-8888

FLEISCHMANNS

RIVER RUN BED & BRKFAST
882 Main St (12430)
Rates: $60-$119
(845) 254-4884

FREDONIA

DAYS INN
10455 Bennett Rd (14063)
Rates: $50-$144
(716) 673-1351
(800) 329-7466

FULTON

RIVERSIDE INN
930 S 1st St (13069)
Rates: $49-$109
(315) 593-2444

GANSEVOORT

MCGREGOR INN MOTEL
Rt 9 (12831)
Rates: n/a
(518) 587-1394

GARDEN CITY

THE GARDEN CITY HOTEL
45 Seventh St (11530)
Rates: $160-$340
(516) 747-3000
(800) 547-0400

GASPORT

HARTLAND MOTEL
8464 Ridge Rd (14067)
Rates: n/a
(716) 772-2266

GATES

COMFORT INN CENTRAL
395 Buell Rd (14624)
Rates: $49-$85
(585) 436-4400
(800) 424-6423

HOLIDAY INN ROCHESTER AIRPORT
911 Brooks Ave (14624)
Rates: $79-$109
(585) 328-6000
(800) 465-4329

MOTEL 6
155 Buell Rd (14624)
Rates: $39-$60
(585) 436-2170
(800) 466-8356

GENEVA

MOTEL 6
485 Hamilton St (14456)
Rates: $36-$66
(315) 789-4050
(800) 466-8356

99 WILLIAM STREET B&B
99 William St (14456)
Rates: $65
(315) 789-1273

RAMADA INN LAKEFRONT
41 Lakefront Dr (14456)
Rates: $99-$149
(315) 789-0400
(800) 272-6232
(800) 990-0907

GILBERTS-VILLE

SIGNATURE QUILT B&B
6 Commercial St (13776)
Rates: $85+
(607) 783-2722

GOSHEN

COMFORT INN
20 Hatfield Ln (10924)
Rates: $75-$85
(800) 424-6423

GRAND GORGE

GOLDEN ACRES FARM RANCH
Windy Ridge Rd (12076)
Rates: $80-$330
(607) 588-7329

GRAND ISLAND

CHATEAU MOTOR LODGE
1810 Grand Island Blvd (14072)
Rates: $32-$99
(716) 773-2868

GREAT NECK

THE ANDREW HOTEL
75 N Station Plaza (10021)
Rates: $175-$395
(516) 482-2900

INN AT GREAT NECK
30 Cutter Mill Rd (10021)
Rates: $199-$239
(516) 773-2000

GREECE

HAMPTON INN
500 Center Place Dr (14615)
Rates: $89-$119
(585) 663-6070
(800) 426-7866

RESIDENCE INN BY MARRIOTT
500 Paddy Creek Cir (14615)
Rates: $109-$249
(585) 865-2090
(800) 331-3131

WELLESLEY INN & SUITES
1635 W Ridge Rd (14615)
Rates: $55-$105
(585) 621-2060
(800) 444-8888

GREENPORT

SILVER SANDS MOTEL
SR 25, Silvermere Rd (11944)
Rates: $70-$100
(631) 477-0011

GUILDERLAND

BEST WESTERN SOVEREIGN HOTEL ALBANY
1228 Western Ave (12203)
Rates: $89-$149
(518-489-2981
(800) 528-1234

HAMBURG

COMFORT INN & SUITES
3615 Comerce Pl (14075)
Rates: $64-$159
(716) 648-2922
(800) 424-6423

HOLIDAY INN
5440 Camp Rd (14075)
Rates: $64-$129
(716) 649-0500
(800) 465-4329

RED ROOF INN
5370 Camp Rd (14075)
Rates: $37-$82
(716) 648-7222
(800) 843-7663

TALLYHO-TEL
5245 Camp Rd (14075)
Rates: $30-$125
(716) 648-2000

HAMLIN

SANDY CREEK MANOR HOUSE BED & BRKFAST
1960 Redman Rd (14464)
Rates: $60-$95
(716) 964-7528
(800) 594-0400

HANCOCK

SMITHS COLONIAL MOTEL
23085 State Hwy 97 (13783)
Rates: $55-$110
(607) 637-2989

HAUPPAUGE

HYATT REGENCY WINDWATCH HOTEL
1717 Long Island Motor Pkwy (11788)
Rates: $109-$229
(631) 232-9800
(800) 233-1234

RESIDENCE INN BY MARRIOTT
850 Veterans Memorial Hwy (11788)
Rates: $129-$299
(631) 724-4188
(800) 331-3131

SHERATON LONG ISLAND HOTEL SMITHTOWN
110 Vanderbilt Motor Pkwy (11788)
Rates: $104-$166
(631) 231-1100
(800) 325-3535

HENRIETTA

COMFORT SUITES
2085 Hylan Dr (14467)
Rates: $100-$160
(585) 334-6620
(800) 424-6423

DAYS INN THRUWAY
4853 W Henrietta Blvd (14467)
Rates: $45-$95
(585) 334-9300
(800) 329-7466

ECONO LODGE
940 Jefferson Rd (14467)
Rates: $49-$85
(585) 427-2700
(800) 553-2666

HOMEWOOD SUITES
2095 Hyland Dr (14467)
Rates: $109-$149
(585) 334-9150
(800) 225-5466

MICROTEL INN
905 Lehigh Station Rd (14467)
Rates: $39-$69
(585) 334-3400
(888) 771-7171
(800) 999-2005

RAMADA INN
800 Jefferson Rd (14467)
Rates: $69-$119
(585) 175-9190
(800) 272-6232

RED ROOF INN
4820 W Henrietta Rd (14467)
Rates: $44-$75
(585) 359-1100
(800) 843-7663

RESIDENCE INN BY MARRIOTT
1300 Jefferson Rd (14467)
Rates: $149-$205
(585) 272-8850
(800) 331-3131

R I T INN & CONF CENTER
5257 W Henrietta Rd (14467)
Rates: $89-$125
(585) 35-1800

HERKIMER

HERKIMER MOTEL
100 Marginal Rd (13350)
Rates: $59-$68
(315) 866-0490

INN TOWNE MOTEL
227 N Washington St (13350)
Rates: $36-$58
(315) 866-1101

HILLSDALE

LINDEN VALLEY INN
E on NY 23 (12529)
Rates: $115-$145
(518) 325-7100

SWISS HUTTE MOTEL
Rt 23 (12529)
Rates: $75-$179
(518) 325-3333

HORNELL

DAYS INN
Rt 36 & Webb Crossing (14843)
Rates: $49-$110
(607) 324-6222
(800) 329-7466

ECONO LODGE
7462 Seneca Rd N (14843)
Rates: $39-$54
(607) 324-0800
(800) 424-6423

HORSEHEADS

BEST WESTERN MARSHALL MANOR
3527 Watkins Glen Rd (14845)
Rates: $46-$87
(607) 739-3891
(800) 528-1234

HILTON GARDEN INN
35 Arnot Rd (14845)
Rates: $94-$179
(607) 795-1111
(800) 445-8667

HOWARD JOHNSON
2671 Corning Rd (14845)
Rates: $39-$99
(607) 739-5636
(800) 446-4656

MOTEL 6
4133 Rt 17 (14845)
Rates: $32-$54
(607) 739-2525
(800) 466-8356

HUDSON

ST. CHARLES HISTORIC HOTEL
16-18 Park Place (12534)
Rates: $79-$109
(518) 822-9900

HUNTER

EVERGREEN COTTAGES
P.O. Box 161 (12442)
Rates: n/a
(518) 263-4932

HUNTER INN
Rt 23A (12442)
Rates: $79-$285
(518) 263-3777

ILION

WHIFFLETREE MOTEL
345 E Main St (13357)
Rates: $40-$75
(315) 895-7777

ITHACA

BEST WESTERN UNIVERSITY INN
1020 Ellis Hollow Rd (14850)
Rates: $69-$169
(607) 272-6100
(800) 528-1234

CLARION UNIVERSITY HOTEL
1 Sheraton Dr (14850)
Rates: $99-$269
(607) 257-2000
(800) 424-6423
(800) 257-6992

COMFORT INN
356 Elmira Rd (14850)
Rates: $79-$279
(607) 272-0100
(800) 424-6423

COLLEGETOWN MOTOR LODGE
312 College Ave (14850)
Rates: $48-$100
(607) 273-3542
(800) 745-3542

ECONO LODGE
2303 N Triphammer Rd (14850)
Rates: $65-$175
(607) 257-1400
(800) 424-6423

HAMPTON INN
337 Elmira Rd (14850)
Rates: $99-$299
(607) 277-5500
(800) 426-7866

HOLIDAY INN-EXECUTIVE TOWER
222 S Cayuga St (14850)
Rates: $107-$159
(607) 272-1000
(800) 465-4329

LA TOURELLE COUNTRY INN
1150 Danby Rd (14850)
Rates: $99-$299
(607) 273-2734
(800) 765-1492

MEADOW COURT INN
529 S Meadow St (14850)
Rates: $50-$195
(607) 273-3885
(800) 852-4014

RAMADA INN
2310 N Triphammer Rd (14850)
Rates: $99-$199
(607) 257-3100
(800) 272-6232

SPRING WATER MOTEL
1083 Dryden (14850)
Rates: $42-$70
(607) 272-3721
(800) 548-1890

JAMAICA

(See Queens)

JAMESTOWN

COMFORT INN
2800 N Main St (14701)
Rates: $69-$160
(716) 664-5920
(800) 424-6423

AREA CODES - If the local number doesn't connect, check for a new area code.

HOLIDAY INN
150 W Fourth St
(14701)
Rates: $79-$149
(716) 664-3400
(800) 465-4329

JOHNSON CITY
BEST WESTERN
569 Harry L Dr
(13790)
Rates: $55-$115
(607) 729-9194
(800) 528-1234

RED ROOF INN
590 Fairview St
(13790)
Rates: $46-$73
(607) 729-8940
(800) 843-7663

JOHNSTOWN
HOLIDAY INN
308 N Comrie Ave
(12095)
Rates: $60-$91
(518) 762-4686
(800) 465-4329

KENMORE
SUPER 8 MOTEL
1288 Sheridan Dr
(14217)
Rates: $42-$76
(716) 876-4020
(800) 800-8000

KINGSTON
HOLIDAY INN
503 Washington
Ave (12401)
Rates: $119-$159
(845) 338-0400
(800) 465-4329

LAKE GEORGE
**BALMORAL
MOTEL**
444 Canada St
(12845)
Rates: $49-$119
(518) 668-2673
(800) 457-2673

**FORT WILLIAM
HENRY RESORT
HOTEL**
48 Canada St
(12845)
Rates: $89-$359
(518) 668-3081

**GREEN HAVEN
RESORT MOTEL**
3136 Lake Shore
Dr (12845)
Rates: $69-$109
(518) 668-2489
(800) 269-9978

**LAKE GEORGE
ESCAPE-
EVERGREEN
CAMPING
RESORT CABINS**
175 E Schroon
River Rd (12845)
Rates: n/a
(518) 623-3207
(800) 327-3188

**LAKE HAVEN
MOTEL**
442 Canada St
(12845)
Rates: $49-$139
(518) 668-2260

TRAVELODGE
2011 Rt 9N (12845)
Rates: $69-$169
(518) 668-2346
(800) 578-7878
(888) 389-4554

LAKE LUZERNE
LUZERNE COURT
508 Lake Ave
(12846)
Rates: $66-$176
(518) 696-2734

LAKE PLACID
**ART DEVLIN'S
OLYMPIC
MOTOR INN**
350 Main St
(12946)
Rates: $58-$148
(518) 523-3700

**BEST WESTERN
GOLDEN ARROW**
150 Main St
(12946)
Rates: $89-$199
(518) 523-3353
(800) 528-1234
(800) 582-5540

**COMFORT INN
ON LAKE
PLACID**
2125 Saranac Ave
(12946)
Rates: $78-$200
(518) 523-9555
(800) 424-6423

**EDGE OF
THE LAKE MOTEL**
56 Saranac Ave
(12946)
Rates: $49-$139
(518) 523-9430
(800) 523-9430

HILTON RESORT
1 Mirror Lake Dr
(12946)
Rates: $79-$269
(518) 523-4411
(800) 445-8667
(800) 755-5598

**HOLIDAY INN-
LAKE PLACID
RESORT HOTEL
& GOLF CLUB**
1 Olympic Dr
(12946)
Rates: $69-$229
(518) 523-2556
(800) 465-4329
(800) 874-1980

RAMADA INN
8-12 Saranac Ave
(12946)
Rates: $59-$140
(518) 523-2587
(800) 272-6232
(800) 741-7841

SWISS ACRES INN
189 Saranac Ave
(12946)
Rates: $48-$278
(518) 523-3040

LAKEWOOD
STAR MOTEL
270 E Fairmount
Ave (14750)
Rates: $38-$50
(716) 763-8578

LATHAM
**THE CENTURY
HOUSE HOTEL**
997 New Loudon
Rd (12110)
Rates: $115-$225
(518) 785-0931
(888) 674-6873

**COMFORT INN
AIRPORT &**
20 Airport Park
Blvd (12110)
Rates: $75-$135
(518) 783-1900
(800) 424-6423

ECONO LODGE
622 Rt 55 (12110)
Rates: $49-$109
(518) 785-1414
(800) 424-6423

HOLIDAY INN EXP
946 New Loudon
Rd (12110)
Rates: $105-$125
(518) 783-6161
(800) 465-4329

MICROTEL INN
7 Rensselaer Ave
(12110)
Rates: $47-$129
(518) 782-9161
(888) 771-7171

**RESIDENCE INN
BY MARRIOTT**
1 Residence Inn
Dr (12110)
Rates: $199-$249
(518) 783-0600
(800) 331-3131

LIBERTY
DAYS INN
52 Sullivan Ave
(12754)
Rates: $67-$155
(845) 292--7600
(800) 329-7466

LITTLE FALLS
**BEST WESTERN
LITTLE FALLS
MOTOR INN**
20 Albany St
(13365)
Rates: $58-$105
(315) 823-4954
(800) 528-1234

LIVERPOOL
**BEST WESTERN
INN & SUITES**
136 Transistor
Pkwy (13088)
Rates: $79-$169
(315) 701-4400
(800) 528-1234
(800) 681-5405

DAYS INN
400 7th North St
(13088)
Rates: $49-$69
(315) 451-1511
(800) 329-7466

ECONO LODGE
401 7th North St
(13088)
Rates: $42-$99
(315) 451-6000
(800) 424-6423

HOLIDAY INN
441 Electronics
Pkwy (13088)
Rates: $149-$19
(315) 457-1122
(800) 465-4329

**HOMEWOOD
SUITES**
275 Elwood Davis
Rd (13088)
Rates: $139-$219
(315) 451-3800
(800) 225-5466

KNIGHTS INN
430 Electronics
Pkwy (13088)
Rates: $42-$124
(315) 453-6330
(800) 843-5644

SUPER 8 MOTEL
421 7th North St
(13088)
Rates: $59-$99
(315) 451-8888

LOCKPORT
HOLIDAY INN
515 S Transit St
(14094)
Rates: $89-$129
(716) 434-6151
(800) 465-4329

**TWIN OAKS
MOTEL**
4660 Ridge Rd
(14094)
Rates: n/a
(716) 433-2447

LONG ISLAND
(See the
following cities)
Amagansett
Bellport
East Hampton
Garden City
Great Neck
Greenport
Happauge
Plainview
Port Jervis
RiverheadRockvill
e Center
Ronkonkoma
South Hampton
Westbury

AREA CODES - If the local number doesn't connect, check for a new area code.

LONG ISLAND CITY

COMFORT INN
42-24 Crescent St
(11101)
Rates: $89-$209
(718) 303-3700
(800) 424-6423

LONG LAKE

JOURNEY'S END COTTAGES
Deerland Rd,
Rt 30 (12847)
Rates: $500-
$750/Weekly
(518) 624-5381

LONG VIEW LODGE
Deerland Rd,
Rt 30 (12847)
Rates: $65-$110
(518 624-2862

LOWMAN

RED JACKET MOTEL
1744 Rt 17 W
(14861)
Rates: $30-$95
(607) 734-1616

LYONS

KREISS FARM B&B
2097 Highland
Fruit Farm Rd
(14489)
Rates: n/a
(315) 946-9448

MALONE

ECONO LODGE
227 W Main St
(12953)
Rates: $60-$90
(518) 483-0500
(800) 424-6423

FOUR SEASONS MOTEL
206 W Main St
(12953)
Rates: $40-$79
(518) 483-3490

SUNSET INN
3899 US 11 (12953)
Rates: $40-$65
(518) 483-3367

SUPER 8 MOTEL
42 Finny Blvd
(12953)
Rates: $65-$95
(518) 483-8123
(800) 800-8000

MALTA

FAIRFIELD INN
101 Saratoga
Village Blvd
(12020)
Rates: $119-$309
(518) 899-6900
(800) 228-2800

POST ROAD LODGE
2865 Rt 9 (12020)
Rates: n/a
(518) 584-4169
(800) 836-2687

RIVIERA MOTEL
2539 Rt 9 (12020)
Rates: n/a
(518) 899-2600

MASONVILLE

BUDGET MOTOR LODGE/MASON INN
Rt 206, Box 8
(13804)
Rates: $38-$45
(607) 265-3287
(800) 828-3691

MASSENA

BOB'S MOTEL
Rt 2, Box 301
(13662)
Rates: n/a
(315) 769-9497

ECONO LODGE-MEADOW VIEW MOTEL
15054 SR 37
(13662)
Rates: $72-$99
(315) 764-0246
(800) 553-2666

HILLSIDE MOTEL
15 Smith Rd
(13662)
Rates: n/a
(315) 769-5403

PARK INN MOTEL
528 CR 42 (13662)
Rates: n/a
(315) 769-7799

QUALITY INN
10 W Orvis St
(13662)
Rates: $39-$299
(315) 769-2441
(800) 424-6423

MCGRAW

DAYS INN
3775 US Rt 11
(13101)
Rates: $49-$125
(607) 753-7594
(800) 329-7466

MEXICO

STRIKE KING LODGE
286 SR 104B
(13114)
Rates: n/a
(315) 963-7826

WALTON'S MOTEL
3210 US Rt 11, Box
92 (13114)
Rates: n/a
(315) 963-7120

MIDDLE GROVE

DAYBREAK MOTEL
2909 Rt 9 (12850)
Rates: $35-$125
(518) 882-6838

MIDDLEPORT

CANAL COUNTRY INN
4021 Peet St
(14105)
Rates: n/a
(716) 735-7572

MIDDLETOWN

SUPER 8 MOTEL
563 Rt 211 E
(10940)
Rates: $72-$110
(845) 692-5828
(800) 800-8000

MILLBROOK

COTTONWOOD MOTEL
RR2, Box 25 (12545)
Rates: $50-$99
(914) 677-3283

MONTICELLO

RAMADA LIMITED
104 Broadway
(12701)
Rates: n/a
(845) 791-1690
(800) 272-6232

MONTOUR FALLS

FALLS MOTEL
239 N Genesee St
(14865)
Rates: $65-$125
(607) 535-7262

RELAX INN
100 Clawson Blvd
(14865)
Rates: $39-$89
(607) 535-7183

MOUNT KISCO

HOLIDAY INN
1 Holiday Inn Dr
(10549)
Rates: $179-$199
(914) 241-2600
(800) 465-4329

MOUNT TREMPER

LA DUCHESSE ANNE HISTORICAL B&B
1564 Wittenberg
Rd (12457)
Rates: $60-$150
(914) 688-5260

NANUET

DAYS INN
367 Rt 59 (10954)
Rates: $69-$199
(845) 623-4567
(800) 329-7466

NAPLES

LANDMARK RETREAT B&B
6006 Rt 21 (14512)
Rates: $40-$60
(716) 396-2383

NEW HAMPTON

DAYS INN
4939 Rt 17M
(10958)
Rates: $64-$139
(845) 374-2411
(800) 329-7466

NEW HARTFORD

HOLIDAY INN UTICA
1777 Burrstone Rd
(13413)
Rates: $89-$159
(315) 797-2131
(800) 465-4329

NEW YORK CITY

(Manhattan)

AFFINIA 50
155 E 50th St
(10022)
Rates: $189-$399
(212) 751-5710
(866) 233-4642

AFFINIA DUMONT
150 E 34th (10016)
Rates: $189-$399
(212) 481-7600
(866) 233-4642

BEEKMAN TOWER HOTEL
3 Mitchell Pl
(10017)
Rates: $139-$339
(212) 355-7300

THE BENJAMIN HOTEL
125 E 50th St
(10022)
Rates: $219-$459
(212) 715-2500
(888) 423-6526

THE CARLYLE
35 E 76th St
(10021)
Rates: $550-$5000
(212) 744-1600
(800) 227-5737

CROWNE PLAZA UNITED NATIONS
304 E 42nd St
(10017)
Rates: $239-$599
(212) 986-8800
(800) 227-6963
(800) 879-8836

CROWNE PLAZA TIMES SQUARE
1605 Broadway
(10019)
Rates: $199-$249
(212) 977-4000
(800) 227-6963
(800) 243-6969

DOUBLETREE METROPOLITAN HOTEL
569 Lexington Ave
(10022)
Rates: $290-$419
(212) 752-7000
(800) 222-8733

AREA CODES - If the local number doesn't connect, check for a new area code.

EASTGATE TOWER HOTEL
222 E 39th St (10016)
Rates: $139-$319
(212) 687-8000

EMBASSY SUITES HOTEL
102 N End Ave (10282)
Rates: $189-$439
(212) 945-0100
(800) 362-2779
(877) 692-4458

THE ESSEX HOUSE
160 Central Park S (10019)
Rates: $469-$649
(212) 247-0300
(800) 228-3000

FOUR POINTS SHERATON
160 W 25th St (10001)
Rates: $169-$479
(212) 627-1888
(800) 325-3535

FOUR SEASONS HOTEL
57 E 57th St (10022)
Rates: $450-$995
(212) 758-5700
(800) 487-3769
(800) 332-3442

HAMPTON INN-CHELSEA
108 W 24th St (10011)
Rates: $129-$229
(212) 414-1000
(00) 426-7866

HAMPTON INN-SEAPORT/
320 Pearl St (10038)
Rates: n/a
(212) 571-4400
(800) 426-7866

HELMSLEY CARLTON HOUSE
680 Madison Ave (10021)
Rates: $300+
(212) 838-3000

HILTON NEW YORK
1335 Ave of the Americas (10019)
Rates: $169-$305
(212) 586-7000
(800) 445-8667
(877) 692-4458

HILTON TIMES SQUARE
234 W 42nd St (10036)
Rates: $179-$1000
(212) 840-8222
(800) 445-8667
(877) 692-4458

HOLIDAY INN-MARTINIQUE ON BROADWAY
49 W 32nd St (10001)
Rates: $179-$239
(212) 736-3800
(800) 465-4329

HOLIDAY INN-WALL STREET DISTRICT
15 Gold St (10038)
Rates: $219+
(212) 232-7700
(800) 465-4329

HOTEL GANSEVOORT
18 9th Ave (10014)
Rates: $325-$505
(212) 206)-6700

HOTEL PLAZA ATHENEE
37 E 64th St (10021)
Rates: $515-$695
(212) 734-9100
(800) 447-8800

HOTEL STANFORD
43 W 32nd St (10001)
Rates: $119-$165
(212) 563-1500

HOTEL WALES
1295 Madison Ave (10128)
Rates: $375
(212) 876-6000

JOLLY HOTEL MADISON TOWERS
22 E 38th St (10016)
Rates: $220-$275
(212) 802-0600

LE PARKER MERIDIEN
118 W 57th St (10019)
Rates: $430-$555
(212) 245-5000
(800) 543-4300

THE LOWELL
28 E 63rd St (10021)
Rates: $495-$625
(212) 838-1400
(800) 221-4444

LYDEN GARDENS HOTEL
215 E 64th St (10021)
Rates: $179-$339
(212) 355-1230

MANDARIN ORIENTAL NEW YORK
80 Columbus Circle (10023)
Rates: $625+
(212) 805-8800

THE MANSFIELD
12 W 44th St (10036)
Rates: n/a
(212) 944-6050

THE MARK
25 E 77th St (10021)
Rates: $570-$730
(212) 744-4300

MARRIOTT MARQUIS
1535 Broadway (10036)
Rates: $259-$619
(212) 398-1900
(800) 228-9290

METROPOLITAN HOTEL
569 Lexington Ave (10022)
Rates: n/a
(212) 752-7000

MILLENIUM BROADWAY HOTEL
145 W 44th St (10036)
Rates: $319-$499
(212) 768-4400
(800) 622-5569
(866) 866-8086

MILLENIUM HILTON
55 Church St (10007)
Rates: $199-$599
(212) 693-2001
(800) 445-8667
(877) 692-4458

THE MUSE HOTEL
130 W 46th St (10036)
Rates: $289-$349
(212) 485-2400

NEW YORK PALACE HISTORIC HOTEL
455 Madison Ave (10022)
Rates: $450-$690
(212) 888-7000
(800) 697-2522

NOVOTEL NEW YORK
226 W 52nd St (10019)
Rates: $179-$249
(212) 315-0100
(800) 221-3185

OMNI BERKSHIRE PLACE
21 E 52nd St (10022)
Rates: $369-$950
(212) 753-5800
(800) 843-6664

ON THE AVE HOTEL
2178 Broadway (10024)
Rates: $209-$279
(212) 362-1100

THE PENINSULA
700 5th Ave (10019)
Rates: $475-$660
(212) 956-2888
(800) 262-9467

THE PIERRE-A FOUR SEASONS HOTEL
2 E 61st St (10021)
Rates: n/a
(212) 838-8000
(800) 332-3442

RAMADA PLAZA INN & NEW YORKER HOTEL
481 8th Ave at 34th St (10001)
Rates: n/a
(212) 971-0101
(800) 272-6232

THE REGENCY HOTEL
540 Park Ave (10021)
Rates: $249-$509
(212) 759-4100
(800) 233-2356

RENAISSANCE HOTEL
714 7th Ave (10036)
Rates: $219-$569
(212) 765-7676
(800) 228-9892

RITZ CARLTON NEW YORK-BATTERY PARK
Two West St (10004)
Rates: $550-$780
(212) 344-0800
(800) 241-3333

RITZ CARLTON NEW YORK-CENTRAL PARK
50 Central Park S (10019)
Rates: $750-$995
(212) 308-9100
(800) 241-3333

THE ROGER SMITH HOTEL
501 Lexington Ave (10017)
Rates: $260-$320
(212) 755-1400

ROYALTON HOTEL
44 W 44th St (10036)
Rates: $375-$450
(212) 869-4400

AREA CODES - If the local number doesn't connect, check for a new area code.

THE ST. REGIS NEW YORK
2 E 55th St (10022)
Rates: $695-$895
(212) 753-4500

SHELBURNE MUR-RAY HILL HOTEL
303 Lexington Ave (10016)
Rates: $159-$339
(212) 689-5200
(866) 233-4642

SHERATON MAN-HATTAN HOTEL
790 7th Ave (10019)
Rates: $179-$299
(212) 581-3300
(800) 325-3535

SHERATON NEW YORK HOTEL & TOWERS
811 7th Ave (10019)
Rates: $179-$299
(212) 581-1000
(800) 325-3535

SHERATON RUSSELL HOTEL
45 Park Ave (10016)
Rates: $179-$299
(212) 685-7676
(800) 325-3535

THE SHOREHAM HOTEL
33 W 55th St (10019)
Rates: n/a
(212) 247-6700

SOFITEL NEW YORK
45 W 44th St (10036)
Rates: $379-$599
(212) 354-8844
(800) 763-4835

SOHO GRAND HOTEL
310 W Broadway (10013)
Rates: $309-$3500
(212) 965-3000
(800) 965-3000

SOUTHGATE TOWER (AN AFFINIA HOTEL)
371 7th Ave (10001)
Rates: $159-$319
(212) 563-1800
(886) 623-4642

THE STANHOPE-PARK HYATT
995 Fifth Ave (10028)
Rates: $299-$385
(212) 288-5800
(800) 828-1123

SURREY HOTEL
20 E 76th St (10022)
Rates: $259-$435
(212) 288-3700
(800) 637-8483

SWISSOTEL-THE DRAKE
440 Park Ave (10022)
Rates: $270-$430
(212) 421-0900
(800) 372-5369

TRIBECA GRAND HOTEL
2 Ave of the Americas (10013)
Rates: $309-$2300
(212) 519-6600
(877) 519-6000

TRUMP INTERNATIONAL HOTEL & TOWER
1 Central Park W (10023)
Rates: $595-$695
(212) 299-1000

W NEW YORK
541 Lexington Ave (10022)
Rates: $429-$519
(212) 755-1200

W NEW YORK TIMES SQUARE
1567 Broadway at 47th St (10036)
Rates: $429-$519
(212) 930-7400

W NEW YORK-UNION SQUARE
201 Park Ave S (10003)
Rates: $549-$619
(212) 253-9229

W TUSCANY
120 E. 39th St (10016)
Rates: $300+
(212) 686-1600

THE WALL STREET DISTRICT HOTEL
15 Gold St (10038)
Rates: $169-$349
(212) 232-7700

THE WESTIN NEW YORK AT TIMES SQUARE
270 W 43rd St (10036)
Rates: $449-$599
(212) 201-2700
(800) 228-3000

NEWARK

QUALITY INN FINGER LAKES REGION
125 N Main St (14513)
Rates: $79-$170
(315) 331-9500
(800) 424-6423

NEWFANE

LAKE ONTARIO MOTEL
3330 Lockport-Olcott Rd (14108)
Rates: $37-$84
(716) 778-5004
(800) 446-5767

NIAGARA FALLS
(New York, USA)

BEST WESTERN SUMMIT INN
9500 Niagara Falls Blvd (14304)
Rates: $59-$159
(716) 297-5050
(800) 528-1234
(800) 404-8217

BIT O' PARIS MOTEL
9890 Niagara Falls Blvd (14304)
Rates: n/a
(716) 297-1710

BOYLE'S HOUSE BED & BREAKFAST
2478 River Rd (14304)
Rates: n/a
(716) 693-3070

BUDGET HOST INN
6621 Niagara Falls Blvd (14304)
Rates: $59-$239
(716) 283-3839
(888) 493-6861

CARAVAN MOTEL
6730 Niagara Falls Blvd (14304)
Rates: n/a
(716) 236-0752

CLARION HOTEL
7001 Buffalo Ave (14304)
Rates: $69-$299
(716) 283-7612
(800) 424-6423

THE COACHMAN MOTEL
523 Third St (14301)
Rates: $36-$109
(716) 285-2295
(800) 335-2295

DAYS INN
401 Buffalo Ave (14303)
Rates: $40-$180
(716) 285-2541
(800) 329-7466

DUNES MOTEL
5655 Niagara Falls Blvd (14304)
Rates: n/a
(716) 283-6114

FALLS MOTEL
5820 Buffalo Ave (14304)
Rates: n/a
(716) 283-3239

HOWARD JOHNSON LODGE AT THE FALLS
454 Main St (14301)
Rates: $79-$215
(716) 285-5261
(800) 446-4656
(800) 282-5621

JUNIOR'S MOTOR INN
5647 Niagara Falls Blvd (14304)
Rates: n/a
(716) 283-4914

NIAGARA RAINBOW MOTEL
7900 Niagara Falls Blvd (14304)
Rates: $25-$89
(716) 283-1760

PELICAN MOTEL
6817 Niagara Falls Blvd (14304)
Rates: $29-$99
(716) 283-2278
(716) 283-3169

PLAZA COURT MOTEL
7680 Niagara Falls Blvd (14304)
Rates: n/a
(716) 283-2638
(716) 283-3151

QUALITY HOTEL AT THE FALLS
240 Rainbow Blvd (14303)
Rates: $58-189
(716) 282-1212
(800) 424-6423

RODEWAY INN
9900 Niagara Falls Blvd (14304)
Rates: $40-$120
(716) 297-3647
(800) 424-6423

SANDS MOTEL
9393 Niagara Falls Blvd (14304)
Rates: $24-$108
(716) 297-3797

SUNRISE INN
6225 Niagara Falls Blvd (14304)
Rates: n/a
(716) 283-9952

THRIFTLODGE
9401 Niagara Falls Blvd (14304)
Rates: $45-$99
(716) 297-2660
(800) 525-9055

NIAGARA FALLS
(Ontario, Canada)

BEST WESTERN FALLVIEWS
6289 Fallsview Blvd (L2G 3V7)
Rates: $89-$399
(905) 356-0551
(800) 263-2580

AREA CODES - If the local number doesn't connect, check for a new area code.

ECONO LODGE NEW THE FALLS
6000 Stanley Ave (L2G 3Y1)
Rates: $65-$205
(905) 358-6243

FLAMINGO MOTOR INN
7701 Lundy's Ln (L2H 1H3)
Rates: $49-$179
(905) 356-4646
(800) 738-7701

HILLTOP HOTEL
4955 Clifton Hill (L2G 3N5)
Rates: $69-$200
(905) 374-7777

NIAGARA PARKWAY COURT MOTEL
3708 Main St (L2G 6B1)
Rates: $39-$199
(905) 295-3331

PENINSULA INN & RESORT
7373 Niagara Square Dr
Rates: $59-$249
(905) 354-8812

SHERATON FALLSVIEW HOTEL
6755 Fallsview Blvd (L2G 3W7)
Rates: $99-$429
(905) 374-1077
(877) 353-2557

SHERATON ON THE FALLS
5875 Falls Ave (L2E 6W7)
Rates: $99-$999
(905) 374-4445
(888) 263-7135

STANLEY MOTOR INN
6220 Stanley Ave (L2G 3Y4)
Rates: $50-$150
(905) 358-9238

THRIFTLODGE CLIFTON HILL
4945 Clifton Hill (L2G 3N5)
Rates: $59-$299
(905) 357-4330
(800) 578-7878

NORTH CREEK

BLACK MOUNTAIN SKI LODGE & MOTEL
2999 SR 8 (12853)
Rates: $55-$65
(518) 251-2800
(888) 846-4858

THE INN ON GORE MOUNTAIN
Peaceful Valley Rd (12853)
Rates: $59-$75
(518) 251-2111

NORTH SYRACUSE

CANDLEWOOD SUITES
5414 South Bay Rd (13212)
Rates: $99-$149
(315) 315-8999
(888) 226-3539

DOUBLETREE CLUB HOTEL-AIRPORT
6701 Buckley Rd (13212)
Rates: $79-$119
(315) 457-4000
(800) 222-8733
(800) 572-1602

QUALITY INN NORTH
1308 Bucl;eu Rd (13212)
Rates: $69-$169
(315) 451-1212
(800) 424-6423

NORTH TONAWANDA

ROYAL MOTEL
3333 Niagara Falls Blvd (14120)
Rates: n/a
(716) 692-2724
(716) 692-4546

STARFIRE MOTEL
3466 Niagara Falls Blvd (14120)
Rates: n/a
(716) 694-3600

NORWICH

HOWARD JOHNSON
75 N Broad St (13815)
Rates: $75-$199
(607) 334-2200
(800) 446-4656

SUPER 8 MOTEL
6067 State Hwy 12 (13815)
Rates: $55-$115
(607) 336-8880
(800) 800-8000

OGDENSBURG

QUALITY INN GRAN-VIEW
6765 Hwy 37 (13669)
Rates: $69-$175
(315) 393-4550
(800) 424-6423
(800) 392-4550

RAMADA INN RIVER RESORT
119 W River St (13669)
Rates: n/a
(315) 393-2222
(800) 272-6232

STONE FENCE RESORT
7191 SR 37 (13669)
Rates: $72-$89
(315) 393-1545
(800) 253-1545

OLCOTT

BAYSIDE GUEST HOUSE
1572 Lockport-Olcott Rd (14126)
Rates: n/a
(716) 778-7767
(800) 438-2192

OLD FORGE

BEST WESTERN SUNSET INN
Rt 28, Box 261 (13420)
Rates: $49-$239
(315) 369-6836
(800) 528-1234

ONEONTA

HOLIDAY INN-COOPERSTOWN AREA
Rt 23 Southside (13820)
Rates: $199
(607) 433-2250
(800) 465-4329

SUPER 8 MOTEL
4973 Southside (13820)
Rates: $62-$150
(607) 432-9505
(800) 800-8000

OSWEGO

BEST WESTERN THE CAPTAIN'S QUARTERS
26 E First St (13126)
Rates: $68-$166
(315) 342-4040
(800) 528-1234

DAYS INN
101 SR 104 (13126)
Rates: $49-$140
(315) 343-3136
(800) 329-7466

K & G LODGE
94 Creamery Rd (13126)
Rates: n/a
(315) 343-8171

THE THOMAS INN
309 W Seneca St (13126)
Rates: n/a
(315) 343-4900

OWEGO

SUNRISE MOTEL
3778 Waverly Rd (13827)
Rates: $547$73
(607) 687-5667
(800) 806-9074

PAINTED POST

BEST WESTERN LODGE ON THE GREEN
3171 Canada Rd (14870)
Rates: $50-$100
(607) 962-2456
(800) 528-1234

ECONO LODGE
200 Robert Dann Dr (14870)
Rates: $49-$125
(607) 962-4444
(800) 424-6423

LAMPLITER MOTEL
9316 Victory Hwy (14870)
Rates: $30-$43
(607) 962-1184

STILES MOTEL
9239 Victory Hwy (14870)
Rates: $25-$47
(607) 962-5221
(800) 331-3920

PALATINE BRIDGE

ECONO LODGE
93 E Grand St (13428)
Rates: $45-$200
(518) 673-3233
(800) 424-6423

PALENVILLE

HICKORY NOTCH CABINS
P.O. Box 279 (12463)
Rates: n/a
(518) 678-3259

PARISH

MONTCLAIR MOTEL
Rt 69 (13131)
Rates: $39-$44
(315) 625-7100

PARKSVILLE

BEST WESTERN PARAMOUNT
Rt 17 W, Ex 98, Tanzman Rd (12768)
Rates: $60-$230
(845) 292-6700
(800) 528-1234
(800) 922-3498

PEEKSKILL

PEEKSKILL INN
634 Main St (10566)
Rates: $125-$140
(914) 739-1500
(800) 526-9466

AREA CODES - If the local number doesn't connect, check for a new area code.

PEMBROKE

ECONO LODGE-DARIEN LAKES
8493 SR 77 (14036)
Rates: $44-$119
(585) 599-4681
(800) 424-6423

PENN YAN

BEST WESTERN VINEYARD INN & SUITES
142 Lake St
(14527)
Rates: n/a
(315) 531-8391
(800) 528-1234

VIKING MOTEL
680 E Lake Rd
(14527)
Rates: $42-$135
(315) 536-7061

PINE CITY

RUFUS TANNER HOUSE
60 Sagetown Rd
(14871)
Rates: n/a
(607) 732-0213

PINE VALLEY

BEST WESTERN MARSHALL MANOR
3527 Watkins Rd
(14845)
Rates: $48-$87
(607) 739-3891
(800) 528-1234

PLAINVIEW

RESIDENCE INN BY MARRIOTT
9 Gerhard Rd
(11803)
Rates: $189-$209
(516) 433-6200
(800) 331-3131

PLATTSBURGH

BAYMONT INN & SUITES
16 Plaza Blvd
(12901)
Rates: $67-$99
(518) 562-4000
(877) 229-6668

BEST WESTERN-THE INN AT SMITHFIELD
446 Rt 3 (12901)
Rates: $69-$149
(518) 561-7750
(800) 528-1234
(800) 243-4656

MICROTEL INN & SUITES
24 Kennedy Ave
(12901)
Rates: $55-$80
(518) 324-3800

PORT JERVIS

COMFORT INN
2247 Greenville Tpke (12771)
Rates: $69-$199
(845) 856-6611
(800) 424-6423

PORT ONTARIO

MANNING'S PORT ONTARIO
RS 1, Rt 3 (13142)
Rates: n/a
(315) 298-2509

POUGHKEEPSIE

BEST WESTERN INN & CONF CTR
2170 Sout Rd
(12601)
Rates: $90-$140
(845) 462-4600
(800) 528-1234

ECONO LODGE
2625 South Rd
(12601)
Rates: n/a
(845) 452-6600
(800) 424-6423

PULASKI

BIG A SPORT SHOP & LODGE
7542 Salina St
(13142)
Rates: n/a
(315) 298-5509

CLARK'S COTTAGES
RD 2, Lake Rd
(13142)
Rates: n/a
(315) 298-4778

DOUBLE EAGLE LODGE
3268 SR 13 (13142)
Rates: n/a
(315) 298-3326

DRIFTWOOD MOTEL
5240 US Rt 11
(13142)
Rates: n/a
(315) 298-5000

1880 HOUSE BED & BREAKFAST
7536 S Jefferson St
(13142)
Rates: n/a
(315) 298-6088

FISH HAWK LODGE
1091 Albion Cross Rd (13142)
Rates: n/a
(315) 298-5841

GOLDEN FISH CABINS
RD 1, Rt 3 (13142)
Rates: n/a
(315) 298-6556

LAURDON HEIGHTS
7489-90 Lewis St
(13142)
Rates: n/a
(315) 298-6091

MAPLE GROVE SPORT & ANGLER RESORT
2870 SR 13 (13142)
Rates: n/a
(315) 298-7256

PORT LODGE MOTEL
7469 Scenic Hwy
(13142)
Rates: n/a
(315) 298-6876

PORTLY ANGLER LODGE
CR 2A at Rt 13
(13142)
Rates: $50-$75
(315) 298-4773

RAINBOW SHORES HOTEL
RD 2 (13142)
Rates: n/a
(315) 298-9982
(315) 298-5110

RAINBOW SHORES MOTEL
348 Rainbow Shores Rd (13142)
Rates: n/a
(315) 298-4407

REDWOOD MOTEL
3723 SR 13 (13142)
Rates: $40-$75
(315) 298-4717

RUPERT'S TRADING POST
7539 Rome St
(13142)
Rates: n/a
(315) 298-4042

SEQUOIA INN
7686 N Jefferson St (13142)
Rates: n/a
(315) 298-4407
(315) 298-2460

WHITAKERS MOTEL
7700 Rome Rd
(13142)
Rates: n/a
(315) 298-6162

WILD BILL'S LODGE
7453 Lewis St
(13142)
Rates: $18+
(315) 298-2461

PURLING

BAVARIAN MANOR COUNTRY INN
CR 24 (12470)
Rates: n/a
(518) 622-3261

QUEENS

HOLIDAY INN EXP MIDTOWN TUNNEL
38-05 Hunters Point Ave (11101)
Rates: $125-$169
(718) 706-6700
(800) 465-4329

RAMADA PLAZA HOTEL-JFK
Bldg 144/JKF Int'l Airport (11430)
Rates: $109-$149
(718) 995-9000
(800) 272-6232

RHINEBECK

BEEKMAN ARMS & DELAMETER INN
6387 Mill St
(12572)
Rates: $100-$300
(845) 876-7077

RHINEBECK MOTEL
117 Rt 9 (12572)
Rates: $40-$99
(914) 876-5900

WHISTLE WOOD FARM
11 Pells Rd (12572)
Rates: $99-$150
(914) 876-6838

RICHMOND-VILLE

ECONO LODGE
555 Ploss Rd
(12149)
Rates: $49-$200
(518) 294-7739
(800) 424-6423

RIPLEY

BUDGET HOST COLONIAL SQUIRE
Shortman Rd
(14775)
Rates: $49-$55
(716) 736-8000
(800) 283-4678

RIVERHEAD

BEST WESTERN EAST END
1830 Rt 25 (11901)
Rates: $159-$229
(631) 369-2200
(800) 528-1234

ROCHESTER

CLARION HOTEL RIVERSIDE
120 Main St E
(14604)
Rates: $90-$140
(585) 546-6400
(800) 424-6423

COMFORT INN CENTRAL
395 Buell Rd
(14624)
Rates: $40-$125
(585) 436-4400
(800) 424-6423

COMFORT INN WEST
1501 W Ridge Rd (14615)
Rates: $39-$150
(585) 621-5700
(800) 424-6423

ECONO LODGE
940 Jefferson Rd (14623)
Rates: $39-$145
(585) 427-2700
(800) 424-6423

HAMPTON INN
500 Center Place Dr (146215
Rates: n/a
(585) 663-6070
(800) 426-7866

HOLIDAY INN EXP
2200 Goodman St N (14609)
Rates: n/a
(585) 342-0430
(800) 465-4329

RAMADA INN
800 Jefferson Rd (14623)
Rates: n/a
(585) 475-9190
(800) 272-6232

TOWPATH MOTEL
2323 Monroe Ave (14618)
Rates: $40-$46
(585) 271-2147

ROCK HILL
THE LODGE AT ROCK HILL
283 Rock Hill Dr (12775)
Rates: $99-$189
(845) 796-3100

ROCKVILLE CENTRE
BEST WESTERN
173 Sunrise Hwy (11570)
Rates: $159
(516) 678-1300
(800) 528-1234

ROME
ADIRONDACK THIRTEEN PINES MOTEL
7353 River Rd (13440)
Rates: $45-$70
(315) 337-4930

INN AT THE BEECHES
7900 Turin Rd (13440)
Rates: $73-$118
(315) 336-1776

QUALITY INN
200 S James St (13440)
Rates: $49-$200
(315) 336-4300
(800) 424-6423

RONKON-KOMA
COURTYARD BY MARRIOTT
5000 Express Dr S (11779)
Rates: $149-$159
(631) 612-8000
(800) 321-2211

ROSCOE
ROSCOE MOTEL
2054 Old Rt 17 (12776)
Rates: $50-$70
(607) 498-5220

ROTTERDAM
SUPER 8 MOTEL
3083 Carman Rd (11303)
Rates: $45-$85
(518) 355-2190
(800) 800-8000

RYE BROOK
HILTON RYE TOWN
699 Westchester Ave (10573)
Rates: $139-$409
(914) 939-6300
(800) 445-8667

SACKETS HARBOR
ONTARIO PLACE HOTEL
103 General Smith Dr (13685)
Rates: $69-$175
(315) 646-8000
(800) 564-1812

SALAMANCA
HOLIDAY INN EXP HOTEL & SUITES
779 Broad St (14779)
Rates: $100-$160
(716) 945-7600
(800) 465-4329

SANDY CREEK
HARRIS LODGING
P.O. Box 547 (13145)
Rates: n/a
(315) 387-5907
(315) 387-5504

TUG HILL LODGE
216 Salisbury St (13145)
Rates: n/a
(315) 387-5326

SARANAC LAKE
ADIRONDACK MOTEL
23 Lake Flower Ave (12983)
Rates: $60-$160
(518) 891-2116

BEST WESTERN MOUNTAIN LAKE INN
487 Lake Flower Ave (12983)
Rates: $70-$140
(518) 891-1970
(800) 528-1234

HOTEL SARANAC OF PAUL SMITH'S COLLEGE
101 Main St (12983)
Rates: $75-$105
(518) 891-2200
(800) 937-0211

LAKE FLOWER INN
234 Lake Flower Ave (12983)
Rates: $48-$128
(518) 891-2310

THE POINT
HCR 1, Box 65 (12983)
Rates: $825-$1350
(518) 891-5674
(800) 255-3530

SARATOGA SPRINGS
ADIRONDACK INN
230 West Ave (12866)
Rates: $49-$169
(518) 584-3510

COMMUNITY COURT MOTEL
248 Broadway (12866)
Rates: $40-$60+
(518) 584-6666

COUNTRY CLUB MOTEL
306 Church St (12866)
Rates: $55-$175
(518) 882-6838

GRAND UNION MOTEL
120 S Broadway (12866)
Rates: $50-$75
(518) 584-9001

HOLIDAY INN
232 Broadway (12866)
Rates: $219-$279
(518) 584-4550
(800) 465-4329

ROBIN HOOD MOTEL
2205 Rt 50 (12866)
Rates: n/a
(518) 885-8899

SARATOGA MOTEL
440 Church St (12866)
Rates: $69-$189
(518) 584-0920

ST. CHARLES/ ST. FRANCIS MOTEL
160 Broadway (12866)
Rates: $45-$135
(518) 584-2050

UNION GABLES BED & BRKFAST
55 Union Ave (12866)
Rates: $140-$410
(518) 584-1558
(800) 398-1558

SAUGERTIES
COMFORT INN
2790 SR 32 (12477)
Rates: $89-$159
(845) 246-1565
(800) 424-6423

SCHENECTADY
DAYS INN
167 Nott Ter (12308)
Rates: $49-$139
(518) 370-3297
(800) 329-7466

HOLIDAY INN
100 Nott Ter (12308)
Rates: $89-$129
(518) 393-4141
(800) 465-4329

SCHROON LAKE
BLUE RIDGE MOTEL
2455 US Rt 9 (12870)
Rates: $70-$95
(518) 532-7521

DUN ROAMIN CABINS
Rt 9, P. O. Box 535 (12870)
Rates: $40-$75
(518) 532-7277

RAWLINS MOTEL AND CABINS
P.O. Box 9 (12870)
Rates: n/a
(518) 532-7907
(800) 901-5253

SCHUYLER-VILLE
BURGOYNE MOTOR INN
220 Broad St (12871)
Rates: $49-$145
(518) 695-3282

AREA CODES - If the local number doesn't connect, check for a new area code.

SIDNEY

COUNTRY MOTEL
Rt 7 & E of Rt 8
(13838)
Rates: n/a
(607) 563-1035

SKANEATELES

SKANEATELES SUITES
4114 W Genesee St
(13152)
Rates$ 125-$195
(315) 685-7568

SOLVAY

BEST WESTERN FAIRGROUNDS
670 State Fair Blvd
(13209)
Rates: $85-$179
(315) 484-0044
(800) 528-1234

COMFORT INN FAIRGROUNDS
7010 Interstate
Island Rd (13209)
Rates: $79-$159
(315) 453-0045
(800) 424-6423

HOLIDAY INN FARRELL ROAD
100 Farrell Rd
(13209)
Rates: $79-$189
(315) 457-8700
(800) 465-4329

SOUTH WORCESTER

CHARLOTTE VALLEY INN B&B
480 CR 40 (12197)
Rates: $115-$125
(607) 397-8164

SOUTHAMPTON

ATLANTIC HOTEL
1655 County Rd
39A (11968)
Rates: n/a
(631) 283-6100

BENTLEY HOTEL
161 Hill Station
Rd (11968)
Rates: $175+
(631) 283-6100
(631) 283-0908

CAPRI HOTEL
281 County Rd
39A (11968)
Rates: n/a
(631) 283-4220
(631) 283-6100

CONCORD SUITES
161 Hills Station
Rd (11968)
Rates: n/a
(631) 283-1152

SOUTHAMPTON INN
911 Hill St (11968)
Rates: $119-$489
(631) 283-6500
(800) 832-6500

VILLAGE LATCH INN
101 Hill St (11968)
Rates: $295+
(631) 283-2160
(800) 545-2824

SPRING GLEN

GOLD MOUNTAIN CHALET RESORT
36 Tice Rd (12483)
Rates: $100-$150
(914) 647-4332
(800) 395-5200

SPRINGVILLE

MICROTEL INN & SUITES
270 S Cascade Dr
(14141)
Rates: $49-$59
(716) 592-3141

STAMFORD

REXMERE LODGE
5 Lake St (12167)
Rates: $48-$85
(607) 652-7394
(800) 932-1090

STATEN ISLAND

HILTON GARDEN INN
1100 South Ave
(10314)
Rates: $159-$189
(718) 477-2400
(800) 445-8667

THE STATEN ISLAND HOTEL
1415 Richmond
Ave (10314)
Rates: $154-$159
(718) 698-5000

SUFFERN

WELLESLEY INN
17 N Airmont Rd
(10901)
Rates: $99+
(845) 368-1900
(800) 444-8888

SYLVAN BEACH

CINDERELLAS COMFORT SLEEP SUITES
1208 N Main St
(13157)
Rates: 59-179
(315) 762-4280

SYRACUSE

CANDLEWOOD SUITES
5414 S Bay Rd
(13212)
Rates: n/a
(315) 454-8999
(888) 226-3539

CANDLEWOOD SUITES
6550 Baptist Way
(13057)
Rates: n/a
(315) 432-1684
(888) 226-3539

COMFORT INN
6491 Thompson
Rd (13206)
Rates: $59-$124
(315) 437-0222
(800) 424-6423

DAYS INN UNIVERSITY
6609 Thompson
Rd (13206)
Rates: $50-$99
(315) 437-5998
(800) 329-7466

ECONO LODGE UNIVERSITY
454 James St
(13203)
Rates: $39-$149
(315) 425-0015
(800) 424-6423

JOHN MILTON INN
6578 Thompson
Rd (13206)
Rates: $35-$60
(315) 463-8555
(800) 352-1061

QUALITY INN NORTH
1308 Buckley Rd
(13212)
Rates: $69-$139
(315) 451-1212
(800) 424-6423

RADISSON HOTEL & CONF CTR
701 E Genesee St
(13210)
Rates: $99-$189
(315) 479-7000
(800) 333-3333

RAMADA LIMITED UNIVERSITY
6590 Thompson
Rd N (13206)
Rates: $59-$99
(315) 463-0202
(800) 272-6232

RED ROOF INN
6614 Thompson
Rd (13206)
Rates: $56 $85
(315) 437-3309
(800) 843-7663

SHERATON HOTEL
801 University
Ave (13210)
Rates: $139-599
(315) 475-3000
(800) 325-3535

TARRYTOWN

HILTON HOTEL
455 S Broadway
(10591)
Rates: $109-$279
(914) 631-$700
(800) 445-8667

TICONDEROGA

CIRCLE COURT MOTEL
440 Montcalm St
(12883)
Rates: $54-$77
(518) 585-7660

TONAWANDA

DAYS INN
1120 Niagara Falls
Blvd (14150)
Rates: $49-$125
(716) 835-5916
(800) 329-7466

ECONO LODGE
2000 Niagara Falls
Bld (14150)
Rates: $39-$129
(716) 694-6696
(800) 553-2666

MICROTEL INN
1 Hospitality
Centre Way
(14150)
Rates: $45-$71
(716) 693-8100
(888) 771-7171

TROY

BEST WESTERN RENSSELAER INN
1800 6th Ave
(12180)
Rates: $74-$109
(518) 274-3210
(800) 528-1234

TUPPER LAKE

PINE TERRACE MOTEL & TENNIS CLUB
94 Moody Rd
(12986)
Rates: $50-$450
(518) 359-9258

RED TOP INN
90 Moody Rd
(12986)
Rates: $45-$80
(518) 359-9209

SUNSET PARK MOTEL
De Mars Blvd
(12986)
Rates: $44-$56
(518) 359-3995

UPPER SARANAC LAKE

THE WAWBEEK ON UPPER SARANAC LAKE
553 Panther Mtn
Rd (12986)
Rates: $95-$150
(518) 359-2656
(800) 953-2656

UTICA

A-1 MOTEL
238 N Genesee
St (13502)
Rates: $50-$60
(315) 735-6698
(800) 809-6885

AREA CODES - If the local number doesn't connect, check for a new area code.

BEST WESTERN
GATEWAY
ADIRONDACK
INN
175 N Genesee
St (13502)
Rates: $69-$159
(315) 732-4121
(800) 528-1234

HAPPY JOURNEY
MOTEL
300 N Genesee
St (13502)
Rates: $28-$45
(315) 738-1959

MOTEL 6
150 N Genesee
St (13502)
Rates: $37-$77
(315) 797-8743
(800) 466-8356

RADISSON HOTEL
200 N Genesee
St (13502)
Rates: $115-$175
(315) 797-8010
(800) 333-3333

RED ROOF INN
20 Weaver St
(13502)
Rates: $65-$105
(315) 724-7128
(800) 843-7663

VALATIE
BLUE SPRUCE
INN & SUITES
3093 US 9 (12184)
Rates: $60-$95
(518) 758-9711
(888) 261-9823

VESTAL
HOLIDAY INN
4105 Vestal Pkwy
E (13850)
Rates: n/a
(607) 729-6371
(800) 465-4329

RODEWAY INN
900 Vestal Pkwy E
434 (13851)
Rates: $39-$149
(607) 785-3311
(800) 424-6423

VICTOR
HAMPTON INN
7637 SR 95 (14564)
Rates: $119-$149
(585) 924-4400
(800) 426-7866

WADDINGTON
RIVERVIEW
MOTEL &
COTTAGES
RR 1, Box 14
(13694)
Rates: $38-$48
(315) 388-5912

WALLKILL
AUDREY'S FARM
HOUSE B&B
2188 Brunswyck
Rd (12589)
Rates: $90-$110
(914) 895-3440

WARRENSBURG
SUPER 8 MOTEL
3619 SR 9 (12845)
Rates: $60-$150
(518) 623-2811
(800) 800-8000

WATERLOO
HOLIDAY INN
2468 Mound Rd
(13165)
Rates: $119-$139
(315) 539-5011
(800) 465-4329

MICROTEL INN &
SUITES
1966 Rt 5 & 20
(13165)
Rates: $46-$90
(315) 539-8438

WATERTOWN
BEST WESTERN
CARRIAGE
HOUSE INN
300 Washington St
(13601)
Rates: $79-$225
(315) 782-8000
(800) 528-1234

DAVIDSON'S
MOTEL
26177 NYS Rt 3
(13601)
Rates: $50-$54
(315) 782-3861

ECONO LODGE
1030 Arsenal St
(13601)
Rates: $41-$73
(315) 782-5500
(800) 424-6423

NEW PARROT
MOTEL
19325 Washington
St (13601)
Rates: $30-$68
(315) 788-5080
(800) 479-9889

RAINBOW MOTEL
RD 6, Box 20
(13601)
Rates: n/a
(315) 788-2830
(800) 421-8989

RAMADA INN
6300 Arsenal St
(13601)
Rates: $75-$135
(315) 788-0700
(800) 272-6232

ROYAL INN
MOTEL
25791 State Rt 37
(13601)
Rates: $25-$50
(315) 788-2910

THE INN
1190 Arsenal St
(13601)
Rates: $50-$70
(315) 788-6800

*WATKINS
GLEN*
ANCHOR INN &
MARINA
3425 Salt Point Rd
(14891)
Rates: $69-$150
(607) 535-4159

BUDGET INN
435 S Franklin St
(14891)
Rates: $45-$135
(607) 535-4800

CHIEFTAN MOTEL
3815 SR 14 (14891)
Rates: $49-$135
(607) 535-4759

FARM
SANCTUARY BED
& BREAKFAST
P. O. Box 150
(14891)
Rates: $55-$95
(607) 583-2225

WAVERLY
O'BRIENS INN
6312 CR 60
(14892)
Rates: $38-$58
(607) 565-2817

WEEDSPORT
BEST WESTERN
INN
2709 Erie Dr
(13166)
Rates: $59-$150
(315) 834-6623
(800) 528-1234

WELLSVILLE
LONG VUE INN
5081 Rt 417 W
(14895)
Rates: $35-$89
(585) 593-2450

*WEST
COXSACKIE*
BEST WESTERN
NEW BALTIMORE
INN
12600 Rt 9 W
(12192)
Rates: $59-$179
(518) 731 8100
(877) 731-8100

WEST NYACK
NYACK
MOTOR LODGE
Rt 303 (10994)
Rates: $44-$68
(914) 358-4100

WESTBURY
ISLAND INN
Old Country Rd
(11590)
Rates: $99-$350
(516) 228-9500

*WESTMORE-
LAND*
CARRIAGE
MOTOR INN
5370 SR 223
(13490)
Rates: $38-$65
(315) 853-3561

WHEATFIELD
DRIFTWOOD
SUITES
2754 Niagara Falls
Blvd (14304)
Rates: $35-$75
(716) 692-6650

WHITE PLAINS
RENAISSANCE
WESTCHESTER
HOTEL
80 W Red Oak Ln
(10604)
Rates: $130-$239
(914) 694-5400
(800) 468-3571

SUMMERFIELD
SUITES
101 Corporate
Park Dr (10604)
Rates: $139-$189
(914) 251-9700
(800) 833-4353

WHITEHALL
APPLE ORCHARD
INN
Old Fairhaven Rd
(12887)
Rates: $65
(518) 499-0180

WILLIAMSVILLE
MICROTEL INN
50 Freeman Rd
(14221)
Rates: $37-$70
(716) 633-6200
(888) 771-7171

RESIDENCE INN
BY MARRIOTT
100 Maple Rd
(14221)
Rates: $89-$200
(716) 632-6622
(800) 331-3131

WILMINGTON
GRAND VIEW
MOTEL
5941 SR 86 (12987)
Rates: $54-$99
(518) 946-2209

HIGH VALLEY
MOTEL
HCR 2, Box 13
(12997)
Rates: $40-$61
(518) 946-2355

HOLIDAY LODGE
P. O. Box 38
(12997)
Rates: $30-$90
(518) 946-2251

**HUNGRY TROUT
RESORT**
5239 SR 86 (12997)
Rates: $79-$139
(518) 946-2217
(800) 766-9137

**LEDGE ROCK AT
WHITEFACE MTN
MOTEL**
5078 SR 86 (12997)
Rates: $69-$109
(518) 946-2379
(800) 336-4754

**MOUNTAIN
BROOK LODGE**
5712 Rt 86 (12997)
Rates: $60-$99
(518) 946-2262

**NORTH POLE
MOTOR INN**
5636 SR 86 (12997)
Rates: $49-$99
(518) 946-7733
(800) 245-0228

WILSON

**FISHERMAN'S
CHOICE B&B**
4793 E Lake Rd
(14172)
Rates: n/a
(716) 751-9481

YOUNGSTOWN

RIVER LOFT
425 Main St
(14174)
Rates: n/a
(716) 745-3217

TRAVEL NOTES

AREA CODES - If the local number doesn't connect, check for a new area code.

NORTH CAROLINA

ABERDEEN

BEST WESTERN PINEHURST MOTOR INN
1500 Sandhills Blvd (28315)
Rates: $55-$90
(910) 944-2367
(800) 528-1234
(800) 348-3608

INN AT THE BRYANT HOUSE B&B
214 N Poplar St (28315)
Rates: $40-$75
(910) 944-3300
(800) 453-4019

INNKEEPER SOUTHERN PINES
1405 N Sandhills Blvd (28315)
Rates: $48-$71
(910) 944-2324

MOTEL 6
1408 Sandhills Blvd (28315)
Rates: $37-$53
(910) 944-5633
(800) 466-8356

ALBEMARLE

COMFORT INN
735 SR 24/27 Bypass (28001)
Rates: $63-$99
(704) 983-6990
(800) 424-6423

SLEEP INN,
621 SR 24/27 Bypass (28001)
Rates: $60-$80
(704) 983-2770
(800) 424-6423
(800) 426-7866

ANDREWS

HAWKESDENE HOUSE MOUNTAIN RETREAT B&B
381 Phillips Creek Rd (28901)
Rates: $85-$125
(828) 321-6027

APEX

DAYS INN
US 1 S & Hwy 55 (27539)
Rates: n/a
(919) 362-8621
(800) 329-7466

ARCHDALE

COMFORT INN
10123 N Main St (27263)
Rates: $72-$199
(336) 434-4797
(800) 424-6423

ARDEN

COMFORT INN ASHEVILLE AIRPORT
15 Rockwood Rd (28704)
Rates: $39-$149
(828) 687-9199
(8000 424-6423

QUALITY INN & SUITES BILTMORE SOUTH
1 Skyline Inn Dr (28704)
Rates: $69-$199
(828) 684-6688
(800) 424-6423

SUNVALLEY MOTEL
2507 Hendersonville Rd (28704)
Rates: n/a
(828) 684-6944

ASHEBORO

COMFORT INN
242 Lakecrest Rd (27203)
Rates: $64-$130
(336) 626-3680
(800) 424-6423

RAMADA LIMITED
825 W Dixie Dr (27205)
Rates: $45-$95
(336) 626-4414
(800) 272-6232

ASHEVILLE

BEST WESTERN OF ASHEVILLE BILTMORE
22 Woodfin St (28801)
Rates: $69-$134
(828) 253-1851
(800) 528-1234
(888) 854-6897

BLACK WALNUT B&B
288 Montford Ave (28801)
Rates: $195-$250
(828) 254-3878

CAROLINA BED & BREAKFAST
177 Cumberland Ave (28801)
Rates: n/a
(828) 254-3608
(888) 243-3608

COMFORT INN RIVER EDGE
800 Fairview Rd (28803)
Rates: $59-$179
(828) 298-9141
(800) 424-6423
(800) 836-6732

COMFORT SUITES BILTMORE SQUARE MALL
890 Brevard Rd (28806)
Rates: $65-$140
(828) 665-4000
(800) 424-6423

DAYS INN ASHEVILLE MALL
201 Tunnel Rd (28805)
Rates: $35-$179
(828) 252-4000
(800) 329-7466

DAYS INN BILTMORE EAST
1435 Tunnel Rd (28805)
Rates: $35-$169
(828) 298-4000
(800) 329-7466

DOGWOOD COTTAGE INN
40 Canterbury Rd N (28801)
Rates: n/a
(828) 258-9725

HILL HOUSE B&B
120 Hillside St (28801)
Rates: $95-$250
(828) 232-0345
(800) 379-0002

HOLIDAY INN-BILTMORE EAST
1450 Tunnel Rd (28805)
Rates: $59-$159
(828) 298-5611
(800) 465-4329

HOLIDAY INN GREAT SMOKIES SUNSPREE RESORTS
1 Holiday Inn Dr (28806)
Rates: $71-$134
(828) 254-3211
(800) 465-4329
(800) 733-3211

LOG CABIN MOTOR COURT
330 Weaverville Hwy (28804)
Rates: $50-$250
(828) 645-6546
(800) 295-3392

MOTEL 6
1415 Tunnel Rd (28805)
Rates: $33-$55
(828) 299-3040
(800) 466-8356

THE PINES COTTAGES
346 Weaverville Hwy (28804)
Rates: $55-$185
(828) 645-9661
(888) 818-6477

QUALITY INN & SUITES
1430 Tunnel Rd (28805)
Rates: $60-$150
(828) 298-5519
(877) 424-6423

RAMADA PLAZA HOTEL
435 Smoky Park Hwy (28806)
Rates: n/a
(828) 665-2161
(800) 272-6232

RED ROOF INN-WEST
16 Crowell Rd (28806)
Rates: $47-$91
(828) 667-9803
(800) 843-7663

SLEEP INN BILTMORE
117 Hendersonville Rd (28803)
Rates: $69-$189
(828) 277-1800
(800) 424-6423

SLEEP INN BILT-MORE WEST
1918 Old Haywood Rd (28806)
Rates: $75-$143
(828) 670-7600
(800) 424-6423

SUPER 8 MOTEL BILTMORE SQUARE
9 Wedgewood Dr (28806)
Rates: $39-$129
(828) 6708800
(800) 800-8000
(877) 354-8800

SUPER 8 MOTEL CENTRAL
8 Crowell Rd (28806)
Rates: $39-$129
(828) 667-8706
(800) 800-8000

AREA CODES - If the local number doesn't connect, check for a new area code.

SUPER 8 MOTEL-EAST
1329 Tunnel Rd
(28805)
Rates: $39-$199
(828) 298-7952
(800) 800-8000

ATLANTIC BEACH

AMERISUITES
118 Salter Path Rd
(28512)
Rates: n/a
(252) 247-5118
(800) 833-1516

ATLANTIS LODGE OCEANFRONT
MP 5, Salter Path
Rd (28512)
Rates: n/a
(252) 726-5168
(800) 682-7057

SEA GULL MOTEL
102 Henderson
Blvd (28512)
Rates: n/a
(252) 726-3613
(800) 257-2196

AVON

AVON COTTAGES
40279 Younce Rd
(27915)
Rates: n/a
(252) 995-4123

AVON MOTEL
Hwy 12 (27915)
Rates: n/a
(800) 243-5774

COLONY REALTY RENTALS
40197 Bonito Rd
(27915)
Rates: n/a
(252) 995-5891
(800) 962-5256

OUTER BEACHES REALTY RENTALS
Hwy 12 & Tigrone
Blvd (27915)
Rates: n/a
(252) 995-4477
(800) 627-3150

SURF OR SOUND REALTY RENTALS
Hwy 12 (27915)
Rates: n/a
(252) 995-5801
(800) 237-1138

BANNER ELK

BANNER ELK INN B&B
407 Main St E
(28604)
Rates: $95-$175
(828) 898-6223
(800) 295-7851

BEST WESTERN MTN LODGE
1615 Hwy 184
(28604)
Rates: $80-$170
(828) 898-4571
(800) 528-1234
877877-4553

IVY'S SUITES
2489 Beech Mtn
Pkwy (28604)
Rates: n/a
(828) 898-9004
(888) 827-6155

MOUNTAIN CABIN RETRFEAT
4258 Rominger Rd
(28604)
Rates: n/a
(828) 898-9771

BAT CAVE

BURCH VACATION RENTALS
US 64/74A
(28710)
Rates: n/a
(828) 625-8000
(800) 200-2309

ROCKY BROAD COTTAGES
Scenic Hwy 9
(28710)
Rates: n/a
(828) 625-2177
(888) 577-7721

BATTLEBORO

COMFORT INN GOLD ROCK
7048 Hwy 4
(27809)
Rates: $55-$90
(828) 972-9426
(800) 424-6423

DAYS INN GOLD ROCK
6970 Hwy 4
(27809)
Rates: $40-$75
(252) 446-0621
(800) 329-7466

DELUXE INN GOLD ROCK
6956 Hwy 4
(27809)
Rates: n/a
(252) 446-2411

QUALITY INN & SUITES
7688 Hwy 48
(27809)
Rates: $46-$110
(252) 977-0101
(800) 424-6423

RED CARPET INN
6953 Hwy 4
(27809)
Rates: $30-$50
(252) 446-0771
(800) 251-1962

SCOTTISH INNS
7782 Hwy 4
(27809)
Rates: $20-$32
(252) 446-1831
(800) 251-1962

SUPER 8 MOTEL GOLD ROCK
7522 Goldrock Rd
(27809)
Rates: n/a
(252) 442-8075
(800) 800-8000

TRAVELODGE GOLD ROCK
7531 Hwy 48
(27809)
Rates: $30-$50
(252) 977-3505
(800) 578-7878

BEAUFORT

CARTERET COUNTY HOME B&B
299 Hwy 101
(28516)
Rates: n/a
(252) 728-4611

BEECH MOUNTAIN

BEECH MOUNTAIN SLOPESIDE CHALET RENTALS
503 Beech Mtn
Pkwy (28604)
Rates: n/a
(828) 387-4251
(800) 692-2061

BELHAVEN

BELLHAVEN INN B&B
402 E Main St
(27810)
Rates: n/a
(252) 943-6400

BENSON

DAYS INN
202 N Honeycutt
Rd (27504)
Rates: $46-$125
(919) 894-2031
(800) 329-7466

BISCOE

DAYS INN
531 E Main St
(27209)
Rates: $50-$135
(910) 428-2525
(800) 329-7466

BLACK MOUNTAIN

ABBOTT'S CORNER CABIN
514 Blue Ridge Rd
(28711)
Rates: n/a
(828) 664-0922

BLACK MT INN
718 W Old Hwy
70 (28711)
Rates: n/a
(828) 669-6528
(800) 735-6128

THE HAVEN
5 Starlight Dr
(28711)
Rates: n/a
(828) 242-3539

IN THE OAKS EPISCOPAL CENTER RESORT
P O Box 1117
(28711)
Rates: n/a
(828) 669-2117

LONE WOLF ENTERPRISES RENTALS
303 Montreal Rd
(28711)
Rates: $115-$150
(828) 669-1124
(888) 393-7829

MONTE VISTA HOTEL
308 W State St
(28711)
Rates: n/a
(828) 669-2119
(888) 804-8438

SUPER 8 MOTEL
101 Flat Creek Rd
(28711)
Rates: $32-$71
(828) 669-8076
(800) 800-8000

WILDFLOWER COTTAGES
451 N Fork Rd
(28711)
Rates: n/a
(828) 669-0433

BLOWING ROCK

ALTA VISTA MOTEL
Misty Mtn (28605)
Rates: n/a
(828) 730-6630
(866) 730-6410

APPLE RIDGE CABINS
120 Apple Ridge
Ln (28605)
Rates: n/a
(828) 295-6622
(800) 268-4748

PEACOCK RIDGE CABINS
292 Peacock Dr
(28605)
Rates: n/a
(828) 295-3873

PILOT RIDGE INN
8353 Hemlock
Ridge Rd (28605)
Rates: n/a
(828) 295-6509
(828) 964-5420

RIVERSIDE LOG CABIN RENTALS
Hwy 321 &
Mystery Hill
(28605)
Rates: n/a
(828) 263-0507

AREA CODES - If the local number doesn't connect, check for a new area code.

BOONE

THE LION'S DEN B&B & CHALET
109 Red Rhododendron (28607)
Rates: n/a
(828) 863-5785
(800) 963-5785

BRASSTOWN

TROUT COVE CABINS
1629 Trout Cove Rd (28902)
Rates: n/a
(828) 389-3584
(888) 389-3584

BREVARD

ASH GROVE RESORT CABINS
749 E Fork Rd (28712)
Rates: n/a
(828) 885-7216

BLUE RIDGE VISTAS
Rt 1, Box 220A (28712)
Rates: n/a
(828) 233-8080

LAS PRADERAS STABLES & COTTAGES
Rt 1, Box 12A (28712)
Rates: n/a
(828) 883-3375

RAINBOW LAKE
Rainbow Lake Dr (28712)
Rates: n/a
(828) 862-5354

SUNSET MOTEL
415 S Broad St (28712)
Rates: $44-$70
(828) 884-9106

TREEHOUSE AT GOLDEN POND
2190 Reasonover Rd (28712)
Rates: n/a
(828) 877-3530
(888) 729-7329

BRYSON CITY

CREEKSIDE CABINS
1044 W Deep Creek (28713)
Rates: n/a
(828) 488-2235

FONTANA LAKE CABIN RENTALS
1570 Greasy Branch Rd (28713)
Rates: n/a
(828) 488-1935
(877) 366-5253

HIDDEN CREEK CABINS
P. O. Box 973 (28713)
Rates: n/a
(828) 507-5627
(888) 333-5881

LAUREL CREEK CABINS
78 Almond Boat Park Rd (28713)
Rates: n/a
(850) 386-7229

NANTAHALA CABINS
580 Nantahala Ln (28713)
Rates: n/a
(828) 488-1622
(877) 466-1622

NANTAHALA VILLAGE MTN RESORT
9400 Hwy 19 W (28713)
Rates: n/a
(828) 488-2826
(800) 438-1507

ROSE CREEK CABINS
2 Fernwood Dr (28713)
Rates: n/a
(888) 572-7001

POWELL ROOST
850 Peholi Cove Rd (28713)
Rates: n/a
(954) 566-4889

TREE TOP LOG CABINS
630 Watkins Rd (28713)
Rates: n/a
(828) 488-6169

WEST OAK B&B & COTTAGES
101 Fryemont St (28713)
Rates: n/a
(828) 488-2438

BURLINGTON

HOLIDAY INN
2444 Maple Ave (27215)
Rates: $89-$250
(336) 229-5203
(800) 465-4329

MOTEL 6
2155 Hanford Rd (27215)
Rates: $35-$41
(336) 226-1325
(800) 446-8356

RED ROOF INN
2133 W Hanford Rd (27215)
Rates: $40-$105
(336) 227-1270
(800) 843-7663

BURNSVILLE

A NORTH CAROLINA GETAWAY
Cold Springs Rd (28714)
Rates: n/a
(828) 682-3528
(877) 275-5144

ALBERT'S INN & BAVARIAN VILLAGE
20 S Toe River Rd (28714)
Rates: n/a
(828) 675-5011

BOXWOOD LODGE CABINS
Rt 6, Box 615 (28714)
Rates: n/a
(828) 682-9643

CAROLINA COUNTRY MOTEL
600 W Main (28714)
Rates: n/a
(828) 682-6033

SERENDIPITY CABIN
2160 S Toe River Rd (28714)
Rates: $95-$100
(954) 448-8371

7TH HEAVEN
6370 Seven Mile Ridge Rd (28714)
Rates: n/a
(828) 675-4011
(800) 562-9625

WEST RIDGE VACATION RENTAL
19 E (28714)
Rates: n/a
(828) 682-1310
(734) 676-2946

BUXTON

BUXTON BEACH HOTEL
46211 Old Lighthouse Rd (27920)
Rates: $55+
(252) 995-5972

COMFORT INN HATTERAS ISLAND
SR 12 & Old Lighthouse Rd (27920)
Rates: $69-$169
(252) 995-6100
(800) 424-6423

FALCON MOTEL
P. O. Box 633 (27920)
Rates: n/a
(252) 995-5968
(800) 635-6911

OUTER BANKS MOTEL
46577 Hwy 12 (27920)
Rates: n/a
(252) 995-5601

CANDLER

DAYS INN WEST
2551 Smoky Park Hwy (28715)
Rates: $35-$139
(828) 667-9321
(800) 329-7466

CANTON

HERITAGE COVE CABINS
101 Heritage Cove Dr (28716)
Rates: n/a
(828) 648-4020
(800) 646-4020

THE LORALEI INN B&B
659 Lake Dr (28716)
Rates: n/a
(828) 648-6738

RIVERMONT CABINS
162 Rivermont Dr (28716)
Rates: n/a
(828) 648-3066
(888) 648-6373

CAROLINA BEACH

BENSON'S LANDING MOTEL
801 Carolina Beach Ave N (28428)
Rates: n/a
(910) 458-5886
(800) 932-0498

JOY LEE APARTMENTS
317 Carolina Beach Ave N (28428)
Rates: n/a
(910) 458-8361

SANDSTEP MOTEL
619 Carolina Beach Ave N (28428)
Rates: n/a
(910) 458-8387
(800) 934-4076

CARY

BEST WESTERN CARY INN
1722 Walnut St (27511)
Rates: $59-$99
(919) 481-1200
(800) CARY INN

CANDLEWOOD SUITES
1020 Buck Jones Rd (Buck Jones Village 27606)
Rates: $119-$139
(919) 468-4222

COMFORT SUITES
350 Asheville Ave (27511)
Rates: $69-$150
(919) 852-4318
(800) 424-6423

LA QUINTA INN & SUITES
191 Crescent Commons (27511)
Rates: $65-$99
(919) 851-2850
(800) 687-6667

RED ROOF INN
1800 Walnut St (27511)
Rates: $40-$65
(919) 469-3400
(800) 843-7663

RESIDENCE INN BY MARRIOTT
2900 Regency Pkwy (27511)
Rates: $99-$159
(919) 467-4080
(800) 331-3131

TOWNEPLACE SUITES
120 Sage Commons Way (27511)
Rates: n/a
(919) 678-0005
(800) 257-3000

CASHIERS
HIGH HAMPTON INN RESORT
1525 Hwy 107 S (28717)
Rates: $94-$244
(828) 743-2411
(800) 344-2551

LAKESHORE MOUNTAIN HIDE-AWAY
286 Scenic Lake Ln (28717)
Rates: n/a
(828) 743-4252

LAKEVIEW MOUNTAIN CABINS
P O Box 471 (28717)
Rates: n/a
(828) 743-5421

MOUNTAIN VILLAGE VACATION COTTAGES
Hwy 107 S (28717)
Rates: n/a
(828) 743-2377

SHAVER'S SHADY SPOT
416 Evitt Gem Rd (28717)
Rates: n/a
(828) 743-2048

WHITESIDE COVE COTTAGES
5078 Whiteside Cove Rd (28717)
Rates: n/a
(800) 805-3558

CHAPEL HILL
CAROLINA INN
211 Pittsboro St (27516)
Rates: $129-$239
(919) 933-2001
(800) 962-8519

THE COTTAGE AT SPARROW FARM B&B
1224 Old Lystra Rd (27517)
Rates: n/a
(919) 960-6707

HOW SUITE IT IS
#1 Winter Dr (27517)
Rates: n/a
(919) 923-6787

THE SIENA HOTEL
1505 E Franklin St (27514)
Rates: $119-$245
(919) 929-4000
(800) 223-7379

WINDY OAKS INN B&B
1164 Old Lystra Rd (27517)
Rates: n/a
(919) 942-1001

CHARLOTTE
AMERISUITES AIRPORT
2950 Oak Lake Blvd (28206)
Rates: $95-$159
(704) 423-9931
(800) 833-1516

AMERISUITES ARROWHEAD
7900 Forest Point Blvd (28273)
Rates: $94-$159
(704) 522-8400
(800) 833-1516

AMERISUITES COLISEUM
4119 S Stream Blvd (28217)
Rates: $89-$159
(704) 357-8555
(800) 833-1516

ASCOT INN
1025 S Tryon St (28203)
Rates: n/a
(800) 333-9417

BALLANTYNE RESORT
10000 Ballantyne Commons Pkwy (28277)
Rates: $159-$229
(704) 248-4000
(866) 248-4824

BEST VALUE INN & SUITES
3200 S I-85 Service Rd (28208)
Rates: $38-$89
(704) 398-3144

BRADLEY MOTEL
4200 I-85S (28214)
Rates: $27-$36
(704) 392-3206

CANDLEWOOD SUITES
5840 Westpark Dr (28217)
Rates: n/a
(704) 529-7500
(888) 226-3539

CLARION HOTEL-AIRPORT COLISEUM
321 W Woodlawn Rd (28217)
Rates: $69-$200
(704) 523-1400
(800) 424-6423

COMFORT INN CAROWINDS
3725 Ave of the Carolinas (29715)
Rates: $49-$159
(704) 339-0574
(800) 424-6423

COMFORT INN EXECUTIVE PARK
5822 Westpark Dr (28217)
Rates: $69-$129
(704) 525-2626
(800) 424-6423

COMFORT SUITE-UNIVERSITY AREA
7735 University City Blvd (28213)
Rates: $79-$129
(704) 547-0049
(800) 424-6423

COMFORT SUITE AIRPORT
3424 Mulberry Church Rd (28208)
Rates: $69-$199
(704) 971-4400
(800) 424-6423

DAYS INN
118 E Woodlawn Rd (28217)
Rates: $45-$125
(704) 525-5500
(800) 329-7466

DAYS INN
601 N Tryon (28202)
Rates: $49-$135
(704) 333-4733
(800) 329-7466

DAYS INN
1408 W Sugar Creek Rd (28212)
Rates: $34-$65
(704) 597-8110
(800) 329-7466

DAYS INN AIRPORT/ COLISEUM
3101 S I-85 Service Rd (28208)
Rates: $39-$109
(704) 394-3381
(800) 329-7466

DRURY INN & SUITES
415 West WT Harris Blvd (28262)
Rates: $58-$102
(704) 593-0700
(800) 378-7946

HOLIDAY INN AIRPORT
2707 Little Rock Rd (28214)
Rates: $82-$92
(704) 394-4301
(800) 465-4329

HOLIDAY INN UNIVERSITY EXECUTIVE PARK
8520 University Exec Park Dr (28262)
Rates: $99-$139
(704) 547-0999
(800) 465-4329

HOMESTEAD STUDIO SUITES
710 Yorkmont Rd (28217)
Rates: $49-$64
(704) 676-0083
(888) 782-9473

LA QUINTA INN AIRPORT
3100 S I-85 Service Rd (28208)
Rates: $55-$79
(704) 393-5306
(800) 687-6667

LA QUINTA INN COLISEUM
4900 S Tryon St (28202)
Rates: $69-$99
(704) 523-5599
(800) 687-6667

MAINSTAY SUITES
7926 Forest Pine Dr (28273)
Rates: $79-$179
(704) 521-3232
(800) 424-6423

MOTEL 6- COLISEUM
131 Red Roof Dr (28217)
Rates: $32-$35
(704) 529-1020
(800) 466-8356

MOTEL 6- UNIVERSITY PLACE
5116 Reagan Dr (28206)
Rates: $29-$34
(704) 596-8222
(800) 466-8356

MOTEL 6-SOUTH
3430 St. Vardell Ln (28210)
Rates: $29-$34
(704) 527-0144
(800) 466-8356

OMNI CHARLOTTE HOTEL
132 E Trade St (28202)
Rates: $129-$199
(704) 377-0400
(800) 843-6664

QUALITY INN & SUITES CROWN POINT
2501 Sardis Rd N (28227)
Rates: $69-$79
(704) 845-2810
(800) 424-6423

RAMADA LIMITED
5301 N I-85 (28213)
Rates: n/a
(704) 596-9390
(800) 272-6232

RAMADA LIMITED
7900 Nations Ford Rd (28217)
Rates: n/a
(704) 522-7110
(800) 272-6232

RED ROOF INN AIRPORT
3300 S I-85 (28208)
Rates: $42-$73
(704) 392-2316
(800) 843-7663

RESIDENCE INN BY MARRIOTT
8503 N Tryon St (28262)
Rates: $84-$104
(704) 547-1122
(800) 331-3131

RESIDENCE INN BY MARRIOTT
5115 Piper Station Dr (28277)
Rates: $89-$134
(704) 319-3900
(800) 331-3131

RESIDENCE INN BY MARRIOTT
404 S Mint St (28202)
Rates: $149-$199
(704) 340-4000
(800) 331-3131

RESIDENCE INN BY MARRIOTT
5816 Westpark Dr (28216)
Rates: $79-$139
(704) 527-8110
(800) 331-3131

SHERATON AIRPORT PLAZA HOTEL
3315 I-85 S Service Rd (28208)
Rates: $199-$219
(704) 392-1200
(800) 325-3535

SLEEP INN
701 Yorkmont (28217)
Rates: $59-$89
(704) 525-5005
(800) 424-6423

SLEEP INN-UNIVERSITY PLACE
8525 N Tryon St (28262)
Rates: $56-$190
(704) 549-4544
(800) 424-6423

STAYBRIDGE SUITES
7924 Forest Pine Rd (28273)
Rates: n/a
(704) 527-6767
(800) 238-8000

STAYBRIDGE SUITES
15735 John J Delaney Dr (28277)
Rates: $119-$159
(704) 248-5000
(800) 238-8000

STUDIO 6
3420 I-85 Service Rd S (28208)
Rates: $41-$59
(704) 394-4993
(888) 897-0202

SUMMERFIELD SUITES
4920 S Tryon St (28217)
Rates: $79-$109
(704) 525-2600
(800) 833-4353

TOWNEPLACE SUITES
7805 Forest Point Blvd (28217)
Rates: $49-$59
(704) 227-2000
(800) 257-3000

TOWNEPLACE SUITES
8710 Research Dr (28262)
Rates: $56-$94
(704) 548-0388
(800) 258-3000

THE WESTIN CHARLOTTE
601 S College St (28202)
Rates: $249
(704) 375-2600
(800) 228-3000

CHEROKEE

BAYMONT INN
1455 Acquoni Rd (28719)
Rates: $59-$149
(828) 497-2102
(877) 229-6668

BEST WESTERN GREAT SMOKIES
Hwy 441 N & Aquoni (28719)
Rates: $49-$125
(828) 497-2020
(800) 528-1234

MICROTEL INN
674 Casino Tr (28719)
Rates: $39-$119
(828) 497-7800
(888) 771-7171

PIONEER MOTEL
US 19 S (28719)
Rates: $38-$78
(828) 497-2435

CHIMNEY ROCK

FALLS COUNTRY MOTEL
US 64 & 74 A (28720)
Rates: n/a
(828) 625-2771
(877) 808-2771

ROCKY BROAD RIVER COTTAGE
138 Southside Dr (28720)
Rates: n/a
(828) 625-9700

CLAYTON

QUALITY INN
126 Cleveland Crossing Dr (27529)
Rates: n/a
(910) 773-1110
(800) 424-6423

SLEEP INN
105 Commerce Pkwy (27529)
Rates: $50-$70
(910) 772-7771
(800) 424-6423

SUPER 8 MOTEL
101 Leone Ct (27529)
Rates: n/a
(910) 661-1991
(800) 800-8000

CLEMMONS

VILLAGE INN GOLF & CONF CENTER
6205 Ramada Dr (27012)
Rates: $62-$66
(336) 766-9121
(800) 554-6416

CLINTON

DAYS INN
508 SE Blvd (28328)
Rates: $49-$90
(910) 590-0660
(800) 329-7466

CLYDE

GRISTMILL HOUSE
4310 Max Patch Rd (28721)
Rates: n/a
(407) 295-6019

COINJOCK

IDWAY MARINA/MOTEL
157 Coinjock Development Rd (27923)
Rates: n/a
(252) 453-3625

COLUMBUS

LY NAVD HILLS GUEST HOUSE B&B
Rt 2, Box 1723 (28722)
Rates: n/a
(828) 863-2603

CONCORD

COMFORT SUITES
7800 Gateway Ln NW (28027)
Rates: $69-$275
(704) 979-3800
(800) 424-6423

DAYS INN
5125 Davidson Hwy (28027)
Rates: $45-$55
(7040 786-9121
(800) 329-7466

SLEEP INN
1120 Copperfield Blvd (28027)
Rates: $59-$169
(704) 788-2150
(800) 424-6423
(800) 753-3746

SUPER 8 MOTEL
1601 Hwy 29 N (28025)
Rates: n/a
(704) 786-5181
(800) 800-8000

CORNELIUS

BEST WESTERN LAKE NORMAN
19608 Liverpool Pkwy (28031)
Rates: $69-$89
(704) 896-0660
(800) 528-1234
(888) 207-0666

ECONO LODGE LAKE NORMAN
20740 Torrence Chapel Rd (28031)
Rates: $49-$199
(704) 892-3500
(800) 424-6423

HOLIDAY INN LAKE NORMAN
19901 Holiday Ln (28031)
Rates: $65
(704) 892-9120
(800) 465-4329

COROLLA

KITTY DUNES RENTALS
Corolla Light Village Shops (27927)
Rates: n/a
(252) 453-3863
(800) 334-3863

RESORT QUEST OUTER BANKS
1023 Ocean Trail (27927)
Rates: n/a
(252) 453-3033
(800) 962-0201

CRUSO
HERITAGE COVE CABINS
101 Heritage Cove Dr (28716)
Rates: n/a
(828) 648-4020
(800) 646-4020

CULLOWHEE
AWENDAW RIDGE CABIN
Off Hwy 107 N (28723)
Rates: n/a
(828) 743-9856

DILLSBORO
DILLSBORO INN
146 N River Rd (28725)
Rates: n/a
(828) 586-3898

DUCK
DUCK'S REAL ESTATE RENTALS
1232 Duck Rd (27949)
Rates: n/a
(800) 992-2976

DUNN
BUDGET INN
513 Spring Branch Rd (28334)
Rates: n/a
(910) 892-6181

ECONO LODGE
1125 E Broad St (28334)
Rates: $30-$70
(910) 892-1293
(800) 424-6423

EXPRESS INN
510 Spring Branch Rd (28334)
Rates: n/a
(910) 892-1293

JAMESON INN
901 Jackson Rd (29334)
Rates: $49-$104
(910) 891-5758
(800) 526-3766

MIDWAY INN
603 Spring Branch Rd (28334)
Rates: n/a
(910) 892-2162

RAMADA INN
1011 E Cumberland St (28334)
Rates: $34-$59
(910) 892-8101
(800) 272-6232

DURHAM
BEST VALUE CAROLINA DUKE INN
2517 Guess Rd (27705)
Rates: $39-$60
(919) 286-0771
(800) 438-1158

BEST WESTERN SKYLAND INN
5400 US 70 (27705)
Rates: $54-$78
(919) 383-2508
(800) 528-1234

CANDLEWOOD SUITES
1818 E Hwy 54 (27713)
Rates: $81-$99
(919) 484-9922
(888) 226-3539

HOMESTEAD STUDIO SUITES HOTEL
4515 Hwy 55 (27713)
Rates: $59-$74
(919) 544-9991
(888) 782-9473

HOMESTEAD STUDIO SUITES HOTEL-UNIV
1920 Ivy Creek Blvd (27707)
Rates: $59-$74
(919) 402-1700
(888) 782-9473

INNKEEPER SOUTH
4433 Hwy 55 (27713)
Rates: n/a
(919) 544-4579
(800) 466-5337

LA QUINTA INN
1910 W Park Dr (27713)
Rates: $59-$101
(919) 484-1422
(800) 687-6667

LA QUINTA INN & SUITES
4414 Durham-Chapel Hill Blvd (27707)
Rates: $77-$100
(919) 401-9660
(800) 687-6667

RED ROOF INN
5623 Chapel Hill Blvd (27707)
Rates: $51-$78
(919) 489-9421
(800) 843-7663

RED ROOF INN
4405 Hwy 55 E (27713)
Rates: $36-$45
(919) 361-1950
(800) 843-7663

RESIDENCE INN BEST WESTERN
201 Residence Inn Blvd (27713)
Rates: $119-$144
(919) 361-1266
(800) 331-3131

SHERATON IMPERIAL HOTEL
4700 Emperor Blvd (27703)
Rates: $145-$165
(919) 941-5050
(800) 325-3535

SLEEP INN
5208 New Page Rd (27703)
Rates: $79-$99
(919) 993-3393
(800) 424-6423

WELLESLEY INN & SUITES
4919 S Miami Blvd (27703)
Rates: $94-$129
(919) 998-0400
(800) 444-8888

WINGATE INN
5223 Page Rd (27717)
Rates: $59-$155
(919) 941-2854
(800) 228-1000

WYNDHAM GARDEN HOTEL
4620 S Miami Blvd (27703)
Rates: $89-$149
(919) 941-6066
(800) 972-0264

EDEN
JAMESON INN
716 Linden Dr (28288)
Rates: $49-$104
(336) 627-0472
(800) 526-3766

EDENTON
COACH HOUSE INN
823 N Broad St (27932)
Rates: n/a
(252) 482-2107

ELIZABETH CITY
DAYS INN
308 S Hughes Blvd (27909)
Rates: $45-$85
(252) 335-4316
(800) 329-7466

QUALITY INN
522 S Hughes Blvd (27909)
Rates: $65-$176
(252) 338-3951
(800) 424-6423

TRAVELLERS INN
1211 N Road St (27909)
Rates: n/a
(252) 338-5451

EMERALD ISLE
BLUEWATER GMAC RENTALS
200 Mangrove Dr (28594)
Rates: n/a
(252) 354-2323
(888) 258-9287

CENTURY 21 COASTLAND RENTALS
7603 Emerald Dr (28594)
Rates: n/a
(252) 354-2131
(800) 822-2121

FAIRFIELD
HYDE-AWAY MOTEL
6491 Hwy 94 (27826)
Rates: n/a
(252) 926-8101

FAYETTEVILLE
BEST WESTERN FAYETTEVILLE-
2910 Sigman St (28303)
Rates: $79-$125
(910) 485-0520
(800) 528-1234
(877) 485-0520

BUDGET INN
1830 Dunn Rd (28301)
Rates: n/a
(910) 483-9038

COMFORT INN
1957 Cedar Creek Rd (28301)
Rates: $60-$91
(910) 323-8333
(800) 424-6423

DAYS INN
333 Person St (28301)
Rates: $39-$99
(910) 483-0431
(800) 329-7466

ECONO LODGE
1952 Cedar Creek Rd (28301)
Rates: $60-$90
(910) 433-2100
(800) 424-6423

DELUXE INN
2123 Cedar Creek Rd (28301)
Rates: n/a
(910) 484-2666

ECONOMY INN
525 Eastern Blvd (28301)
Rates: n/a
(910) 323-3938

FAYETTEVILLE INN & SUITES
3136 Bordeaux Park Dr (28306)
Rates: $69-$89
(910) 486-8300

AREA CODES - If the local number doesn't connect, check for a new area code.

HOLIDAY INN BORDEAUX
1707 Owen Dr (28304)
Rates: $75-$95
(910) 323-0111
(800) 465-4329

HOLIDAY INN-FT. BRAGG
1706 Skibo Rd (28303)
Rates: $84-$350
(910) 867-6777
(800) 465-4329

HOLIDAY INN SOUTH
1944 Cedar Creek Rd (28312)
Rates: $84-$116
(910) 323-1600
(800) 465-4329

INNKEEPER CROSS CREEK
1720 Skibo Rd (28303)
Rates: $82
(910) 867-7659

KNIGHTS INN-FT. BRAGG
2848 Bragg Blvd (29303)
Rates:n/a
(910) 485-4163
(800) 325-4163

MOTEL 6
2076 Cedar Creek Rd (28301)
Rates: $35-$53
(910) 485-8122
(800) 466-8356

RAMADA LTD
1725 Jim Johnson Rd (28312)
Rates: $49-$75
(920) 485-6866
(800) 272-6232

RED ROOF INN
1569 Jim Johnson Rd (28301)
Rates: $60-$75
(910) 321-1460
(800) 733-7663

STEWARTS CREEK APARTMENTS
690 N Reilly Rd (28303)
Rates: n/a
(910) 864-2126
(800) 334-8416

FLAT ROCK

MOUNTAIN INN & SUITES
755 Upward Rd (28731)
Rates: n/a
(828) 692-7772

FLETCHER

HOLIDAY INN-AIRPORT
550 Airport Rd (28732)
Rates: $72-$99
(828) 684-1213
(800) 465-4329

FONTANA DAM

FONTANA VILLAGE
Hwy 28 N (28733)
Rates: n/a
(828) 498-2211
(800) 849-2258

THE HIKE INN
3204 Fontana Rd (28733)
Rates: $35-$80
(828) 479-3677

FOREST CITY

COMFORT INN
205 Commercial Dr (28043)
Rates: $59-$75
(828) 248-3400
(800) 424-6423

JAMESON INN
164 Jameson Inn Dr (28043)
Rates: $49-$104
(828) 287-8788
(800) 526-3766

RAMADA LIMITED
2600 Hwy 74-A (28043)
Rates: $48-$68
(828) 248-1711
(800) 272-6232

FORT MILL

MOTEL 6
255 Carowinds Blvd (29708)
Rates: $35-$56
(803) 548-9656
(800) 466-8356

FRANKLIN

A LITTLE TOUCH OF HEAVEN
274 Indigo Ln (28734)
Rates: n/a
(828) 497-4563

ALPINE COTTAGES
64 Pennington Dr (28734)
Rates: n/a
(828) 524-2644

BARBER'S MOTEL
3108 S Georgia Rd (28734)
Rates: n/a
(828) 524-2444
(888) 805-1457

CAROLINA MTN TOP HOMES
144 Deer Crossing Rd (28734)
Rates: n/a
(828) 369-3469
(800) 820-1210

COLONIAL INN
3157 Georgia Rd (28734)
Rates: $40-$85
(828) 524-6600
(866) 265-6466

COMFORT INN
313 Cunningham Rd (28734)
Rates: $69-$179
(828) 369-9200
(800) 424-6423

COUNTRY INN TOWN MOTEL
668 E Main St (28734)
Rates: $32-$99
(828) 524-4451
(800) 233-7555

DAYS INN
1320 E Main St (28734)
Rates: $44-$119
(828) 524-6491
(800) 329-7466

DESOTO TRAIL REALTY RENTALS
687 E Main St (28734)
Rates: n/a
(828) 524-8488
(800) 438-8493

FRANKLIN MOTEL INN & SUITES
17 W Palmer St (28734)
Rates: $35-$70
(828) 524-4431

HERITAGE VILLAS
76 Heritage Hollow Dr (28734)
Rates: n/a
(828) 269-6315

MICROTEL INN & SUITES
81 Allman Dr (28734)
Rates: $39-$99
(828) 349-9000
(888) 403-1700

MINI NIAGARA FALLS RENTAL
4912 Wayah Rd (28734)
Rates: n/a
(828) 524-6513

MOUNTAINSIDE VACATION LODGING
8356 Sylva Rd (28734)
Rates: $60-$90
(828) 524-6209

PREFERRED PROPERTY RENTALS
33 Pine Ln (28734)
Rates: n/a
(828) 349-4663
(800) 442-6400

RIVENDELL CABINS
998 Henderson Rd (28734)
Rates: n/a
(828) 349-6087
(800) 994-6462

SLEEPY HOLLOW COTTAGES
130 Sleepy Hollow Ln (28734)
Rates: n/a
(828) 524-4311
(877) 682-8850

TYLER'S MOTEL
7057 Georgia Rd (28734)
Rates: n/a
(828) 524-2919

GARNER

HOLIDAY INN EXP
1595 Mechanical Blvd (27529)
Rates: $85-$100
(919) 662-4890
(800) 465-4329

QUALITY INN
126 Cleveland Crossing Dr (27529)
Rates: $49-$109
(919) 773-1110
(800) 424-6423

SLEEP INN
105 Commerce Pkwy (27529)
Rates: $65+
(919) 772-7771
(800) 424-6423

SUBURBAN LODGE
1491 Hwy 70 E (27529)
Rates: n/a
(919) 662-0101
(800) 951-7829

GASTONIA

DAYS INN
1700 N Chester St (28052)
Rates: $45-$110
(704) 864-9981
(800) 329-7466

MOTEL 6
1721 Broadcast St (28052)
Rates: $33-$36
(704) 868-4900
(800) 466-8356

GOLDSBORO

BEST WESTERN INN
801 US 70 E Bypass (27534)
Rates: $55-$65
(919) 735-7911
(800) 528-1234

HOLIDAY INN EXP
909 N Spence Ave (27534)
Rates: $84-$142
(919) 751-1999
(877) 518-5479

JAMESON INN
1408 Harding Dr (27430)
Rates: $49-$104
(919) 778-9759
(800) 526-3766

AREA CODES - If the local number doesn't connect, check for a new area code.

LODGE INN
2306 Norwood
Ave (27534)
Rates: n/a
(919) 736-0455

MOTEL 6
701 Bypass 70 E
(27534)
Rates: n/a
(919) 734-4542
(800) 466-8656

GRAHAM

TRAVEL INN
640 E Harden St
(27253)
Rates: n/a
(336) 228-0231

GRASSY CREEK

RIVER HOUSE INN
1896 Old Field
Creek Rd (28631)
Rates: n/a
(336) 982-2109

GREENSBORO

AMERISUITES
1619 Stanley Rd
(27407)
Rates: $109-$229
(336) 852-1443
(800) 833-1516

**BEST WESTERN
WINDSOR SUITES**
2006 Veasley St
(27407)
Rates: $80-$195
(336) 294-9100
(800) 528-1234

**BILTMORE
GREENSBORO
HOTEL**
111 W Washington
St (27401)
Rates: $69-$199
(336) 272-3474
(800) 332-0303

**CANDLEWOOD
SUITES**
7623 Thorndike
Rd (27409)
Rates: n/a
(336) 454-0078
(888) 226-3539

COMFORT INN
2001 Veasley St
(27407)
Rates: $65-$161
(336) 294-6220
(800) 424-6423

**CRESTWOOD
SUITES**
5001 Americhase
Dr (27409)
Rates: n/a
(336) 886-1250
(877) 398-3633

DAYS INN-APRT
501 S Regional Rd
(27409)
Rates: $50-$119
(336) 668-0476
(800) 329-7466

**DRURY INN
& SUITES**
3220 High Point
Rd (27407)
Rates: $70-$105
(336) 856-9696
(800) 378-7946

**EXECUTIVE INN
& SUITES**
2701 N.O. Henry
Blvd (27405)
Rates: n/a
(336) 621-6210

FAIRVIEW INN
6452 Burnt Poplar
Rd 927409
Rates: n/a
(336) 668-9400

**HOLIDAY INN-
TRIAD AIRPORT**
6426 Burnt Poplar
Rd (27409)
Rates: n/a
(336) 668-0421
(800) 465-4329

**HOMEWOOD
SUITES BY
HILTON**
201 Centrepoint
Dr (27409)
Rates: n/a
(336) 393-0088
(800) 225-5466

**HOWARD JOHN-
SON COLISEUM**
3030 High Point
Rd (27403)
Rates:n/a
(336) 294-4920

**LA QUINTA
INN & SUITES**
1201 Lanada Rd
(27407)
Rates: $79-$116
(336) 316-0100
(800) 687-6667

**MOTEL 6-
AIRPORT**
605 Regional Rd S
(27409)
Rates: $34-$40
(336) 668-2085
(800) 466-8356

MOTEL 6-SOUTH
831 Greenhaven
Dr (27406)
Rates: $33-$38
(336) 854-0993
(800) 466-8356

**RED ROOF INN-
AIRPORT**
615 Regional Rd
(27409)
Rates: $39-$60
(336) 271-2636
(800) 843-7663

QUALITY INN
120 Seneca Rd
(27406)
Rates: $59-$159
(336) 275-9575
(800) 424-6423

**RESIDENCE INN
BY MARRIOTT**
2000 Veasley St
(27407)
Rates: $89-$144
(336) 294-8600
(800) 331-3131

SUPER 8 MOTEL
2108 W
Meadowview Rd
(27403)
Rates: n/a
(336) 855-8888
(800) 800-8000

TRAVELODGE
2112 W
Meadowview Rd
(27403)
Rates: n/a
(336) 292-2020
(800) 578-7878

GREENVILLE

**HOME-TOWNE
SUITES**
2111 W Arlington
Blvd (27858)
Rates: n/a
(252) 752-3411

JAMESON INN
920 Crosswinds St
(27834)
Rates: $49-$104
(252) 752-7382
(800) 526-3766

TRAVELODGE
3435 S Memorial
Dr (27834)
Rates: $42-$55
(252) 355-5699
(800) 578-7878

HAMILTON

**SOUTHERN
COMFORT B&B**
15909 Hwy 125 N
(27857)
Rates: n/a
(252) 798-7081

HAMPTONVILLE

YADKIN INN
4236 Trails End Rd
(27020)
Rates: n/a
(336) 468-2801

HARKERS ISLAND

**HARKERS ISLAND
FISHING CTR**
1002 Island Rd
(28531)
Rates:n/a
(252) 728-3907

HATTERAS

**MIDGETT REALTY
RENTALS**
Hwy 12 (27943)
Rates: n/a
(252) 986-2841
(800) 527-2903

**SEASIDE
INN B&B**
Hwy 57303
(27943)
Rates: n/a
(252) 986-2700
(866) 986-2700

HAVELOCK

DAYS INN
1220 E Main
(28532)
Rates: $50-$80
(252) 447-1122
(800) 329-7466

HAYESVILLE

**CHATUGE
MOUNTAIN INN**
Hwy 64 (28904)
Rates: $39-$59
(828) 389-9340
(800) 948-2755

DEERFIELD INN
40 Chatuge Ln
(28904)
Rates: $45-$80
(828) 389-8272

**SAWYER COVE
CABIN**
787 Sawyer Cove
Rd (28904)
Rates: n/a
(828) 389-3436

HENDERSON

DAYS INN
1052 Ruin Creek
Rd (27536)
Rates: $40-$90
(252) 492-4041
(800) 329-7466

JAMESON INN
400 N Cooper Dr
(27536)
Rates: $49-$104
(252) 430-0247
(800) 526-3766

LAMPLIGHT INN
1680 Flemington
Rd (27537)
Rates: $70-$120
(252) 438-6311

HENDERSON-VILLE

APPLE INN
1005 White Plne
Dr (28793)
Rates: $69-$139
(828) 693-0107
(800) 615-6611

**BEE HIVE
COTTAGES**
65 Sylvania Dr
(28792)
Rates: n/a
(828) 685-7702

**BEST WESTERN
INN**
I-26 & 64 East
(28793)
Rates: $49-$199
(828) 692-0521
(800) 528-1234
(800) 632-4066

COMFORT INN
206 Mitchell Dr
(28792)
Rates: $45-$149
(828) 693-8800
(800) 424-6423
(800) 882-3843

AREA CODES - If the local number doesn't connect, check for a new area code.

EDGEWATER INN
801 N Lakeside Dr
(28793)
Rates: n/a
(828) 692-6269
(800) 692-6269

MOUNTAIN AIRE SUITES
1351 Asheville
Hwy (28791)
Rates: n/a
(828) 692-9173

QUALITY
201 Sugarloaf Rd
(28792)
Rates: $50-$190
(828) 692-7231
(800) 424-6423

RAMADA LIMITED
I-26, Exit 18A,
Sugarloaf Rd
(28739)
Rates: n/a
(828) 697-0006
(800) 272-6232

WALDROP'S CAROLINA MOTEL
1004 Greenville
Hwy (28792)
Rates: n/a
(828) 692-7460
(800) 616-7411

HERTFORD
BEECHTREE INN COTTAGES
948 Pender Rd
(27944)
Rates: n/a
(252) 426-7815

HICKORY
HICKORY MOTOR LODGE
484 Hwy 70 SW
(28602)
Rates: n/a
(828) 322-1740

JAMESON INN
1120 13th Ave Dr
SE (28602)
Rates: $49-$104
(828) 304-0410
(800) 526-3766

QUALITY INN
1725 13th Ave Dr
NW (28601)
Rates: $68-$99
(828) 431-2100
(800) 424-6423

PARK INN
909 Hwy 70 SW
(28602)
Rates: n/a
(828) 328-5101
(800) 789-0686

RED ROOF INN
1184 Lenoir Rhyne
Blvd (28602)
Rates: $47-$61
(828) 323-1500
(800) 843-7663

SCOTTISH INN
325 Hwy 70 SW
(28602)
Rates: n/a
(828) 328-2111

HIGH POINT
ASHFORD SUITES
3901 Sedgebrook
Dr (27265)
Rates: n/a
(336) 812-8787
(877) 502-9522

CRESTWOOD SUITES
2860 N Main St
(27265)
Rates: n/a
(877) 398-3633

TOAD ALLEY BED & BAGEL
1001 Johnson St
(27262)
Rates: n/a
(336) 886-4773
(800) 409-7946

HIGHLANDS
KELSEY & HUTCHINSON LODGE
450 Spring St
(28741)
Rates: $91-$294
(828) 526-4746
(888) 245-9058

MOUNTAIN HIGH LODGE
200 Main St (28741)
Rates: $49-$109
(828) 526-2790
(800) 445-7293

HILLSBOROUGH
MICROTEL INN
120 Old Dogwood
St (27278)
Rates: $40-$70
(919) 245-3102
(888) 771-7171

HOT SPRINGS
MOUNTAIN SIDE CABINS
441 Rebel Dr
(28743)
Rates: n/a
(828) 622-7647

YE OLDE HIKERHAUS
129 Frisbee St
(28743)
Rates: n/a
(828) 622-7550

HUNTERSVILLE
CANDLEWOOD SUITES
16530 Northcross
Dr (28078)
Rates: n/a
(704) 895-3434
(888) 226-3539

RAMADA LIMITED
16825 Caldwell
Creek Dr (28078)
Rates: $49-$119
(704) 892-6597
(800) 272-6232

RESIDENCE INN BY MARRIOTT
16830 Kenton Dr
(28076)
Rates: n/a
(704) 584-0000
(800) 331-3131

JACKSON SPRINGS
FOXFIRE GOLF & TRAVEL RESORT
9 Foxfire Blvd
(27281)
Rates: n/a
(910) 295-2288
(800) 736-9347

JACKSONVILLE
SUPER 8 MOTEL
2149 N Marine
Blvd (28546)
Rates: $50-$75
(910) 455-6888
(800) 800-8000

JONAS RIDGE
BJ'S BED & BREAKFAST
7348 Joe Johnson
Rd (28641)
Rates: n/a
(828) 733-0342

JONESVILLE
COMFORT INN
1633 Winston Rd
(28642)
Rates: $58-$150
(336) 835-9400
(800) 424-6423

HOLIDAY INN EXP
1713 Hwy 67
(28642)
Rates: $59-$79
(336) 835-6000
(800) 465-4329

ROSE'S VILLAGE MOTEL
407 N Bridge St
(28642)
Rates: n/a
(336) 835-3609

KENLY
DAYS INN
1139 Johnston
Pkwy (27542)
Rates: $34-$70
(919) 284-3400
(800) 329-7466

DELUXE INN
401 US 301 N
(27542)
Rates: n/a
(919) 284-3655

KERNERSVILLE
QUALITY INN
707 Hwy 66 S
(27284)
Rages: $60-$125
(336) 996-3501
(800) 424-6423

KILL DEVIL HILLS
CAVALIER MOTEL
MP 8.5, Beach Rd
(27948)
Rates: n/a
(252) 441-5585

KITTY HAWK RENTALS
2901 N Croatan
Hwy (27948)
Rates: n/a
(252) 441-7166
(800) 635-1559

NAGS HEAD BEACH HOTEL
804 N Virginia
Dare Tr (27948)
Rates: $49-$95
(252) 441-0411
(800) 338-7761

OCEAN VACATIONS
2501 N Croatan
Hwy (27948)
Rates: n/a
(252) 441-3127
(800) 548-2033

RAMADA PLAZA NAGS HEAD BEACH
1701 Virginia Dare
Tr (27948)
Rates: $69-$280
(252) 441-2151
(800) 272-6232

RESORT CENTRAL RENTALS
3120 N Croatan
Hwy, Suite 102
(27984)
Rates: n/a
(800) 624-7432

TRAVELODGE NAGS HEAD BEACH HOTEL
804 N Virginia
Dare Tr (27984)
Rates: $59-$289
(252) 441-0411
(800) 338-7761

KING
ECONO LODGE
109 Vesta St
(27021)
Rates: $48-$80
(336) 983-5600
(800) 424-6423

KINGS MOUNTAIN
COMFORT INN
722 York Rd
(28086)
Rates: $59-$129
(704) 739-7070
(800) 424-6423

TRAVELODGE
728 York Rd
(28086)
Rates: n/a
(704) 739-2544
(800) 578-7878

KINSTON
BEST VALUE INN & SUITES
208 E New Bern
Rd (28504)
Rates: n/a
(252) 527-4155

AREA CODES - If the local number doesn't connect, check for a new area code.

KITTY HAWK

WRIGHT PROPERTY RENTALS
3630 N Croatan
Hwy (27949)
Rates: n/a
(252) 261-2186

KURE BEACH

OCEAN PRINCESS INN
824 Ft. Fisher Blvd
S (28449)
Rates: n/a
(910) 458-6712

SEASHORE MOTOR LODGE
1211 Ft. Fisher
Blvd N (28449)
Rates: n/a
(910) 458-5261
(800) 421-5902

LAKE LURE

CHESTNUT COTTAGES
457 Snug Harbor
Circle (28746)
Rates: n/a
(828) 236-9311

GENEVA RIVERSIDE LODGING
4137 Memorial
Hwy (28746)
Rates: n/a
(828) 625-4121

PINE GABLES
328 Boys Camp
Rd (28746)
Rates: n/a
(828) 625-8846

LAUREL SPRINGS

MOUNTAIN VIEW LODGE & CABIN
P. O. Box 90
(28644)
Rates: n/a
(800) 903-6811

LAURINBURG

HAMPTON INN
115 Hampton Cir
(28352)
Rates: $58-$70
(910) 277-1516
(800) 426-7866

JAMESON INN
14 Jameson Inn Ct
(28352)
Rates: $49-$104
(910) 277-0080
(800) 526-3766

LENOIR

DAYS INN
206 Blowing Rock
Blvd (28645)
Rates: $46-$76
(828) 754-0731
(800) 329-7466

JAMESON INN
350 Wilkesboro
Blvd (28645)
Rates: $49-$104
(828) 758-1200
(800) 526-3766

LEXINGTON

COMFORT SUITES
1620 Cotton Grove
Rd (27292)
Rates: $80-$90
(336) 357-2333
(800) 424-6423

QUALITY INN
418 Piedmont Dr
(27295)
Rates: $60-$114
(336) 249-0111
(800) 424-6423

LINCOLNTON

DAYS INN
614 Clark Dr
(28092)
Rates: $45-$89
(704) 735-8271
(800) 329-7466

LINVILLE

LINVILLE COTTAGE B&B
154 Ruffin St
(28646)
Rates: n/a
(828) 733-6551
(877) 797-1885

LINVILLE FALLS

CROSS CREEK CABINS
P. O. Box 73
(28647)
Rates: n/a
(828) 765-9701

FALLS CABIN
722 Joe Bowman
Rd (28647)
Rates: n/a
(828) 733-6551
(877) 797-1885

HUMPBACK HOLLOW CABINS
16 Luther Franklin
Ln (28647)
Rates: n/a
(828) 766-6555
(888) 263-3632

PARKVIEW LODGE
US 221 & Blue
Ridge Pkwy
(28647)
Rates: n/a
(828) 765-4787
(800) 849-4452

LITTLE SWITZERLAND

SWITZERLAND INN
226A & Blue
Ridge Pkwy,
MP 334 (28749)
Rates: $105-$190
(828) 765-2153
(800) 654-5232

TIMBERLINE PROPERTY RENTALS
P,. O. Box 507
(28749)
Rates: n/a
(828) 766-8900

LUMBERTON

BEST WESTERN INN
201 Jackson Ct
(28358)
Rates: $69-$129
(910) 618-9799
(800) 528-1234

DAYS INN OUTLET MALL
3030 N Roberts
Ave (28359)
Rates: $39-$65
(910) 738-6401
(800) 329-7466

DELUXE INN
3510 Capuano Rd
(28358)
Rates: n/a
(910) 738-4261

ECONO LODGE
3591 Lackey St
(28358)
Rates: $39-$49
(910) 738-7121
(800) 424-6423

MOTEL 6
2361 Lackey Rd
(28358)
Rates: $29-$37
(910) 738-2410
(800) 466-8356

QUALITY INN & SUITES
3608 Kahn Dr
(28358)
Rates: $60-$90
(910) 738-8261
(800) 424-6423

MAGGIE VALLEY

A BIT OF COUNTRY CHARM
99 Sunshine Dr
(28751)
Rates: n/a
(800) 819-9466
(888) 926-6344

A HOLIDAY MOTEL
3289 Soco Rd
(28751)
Rates: n/a
(828) 926-1188
(877) 686-4386

ABBEY INN MOTEL
6375 Soco Rd
(28751)
Rates: n/a
(828) 926-1188
(800) 545-5853

ALAMO MOTEL & COTTAGES
1485 Soco Rd
m(28751)
Rates: n/a
(828) 926-8750
(800) 467-7485

APPLECLOVER INN MOTEL
4077 Soco Rd
(28751)
Rates: $30-$135
(828) 926-9100

CAROLINA MOUNTAIN VACATION HOMES
Soco Rd, P. O
Box 14 (28751)
Rates: n/a
(828) 926-9681

COUNTRY CABINS
171 Bradley St
(28751)
Rates: n/a
(828) 926-0612
(888) 222-4611

COZY CORNER MOTEL
3530 Soco Rd
(28751)
Rates: n/a
(828) 926-9711

COZY CREEK COTTAGES
163 Moody Farm
Rd (28751)
Rates: n/a
(828) 926-1231

CREEK WOOD VILLAGE CABINS
3340 Soco Rd
(28751)
Rates: n/a
(828) 926-3321

ED'S MOTEL
6262 Soco Rd
(28751)
Rates: n/a
(828) 926-1879

JOHNSON BRANCH CABINS
89 Stump Ln
(28751)
Rates: n/a
(828) 926-6032

MAGGIE MOUNTAIN VILLAS & CHALET
60 Twin Hickory
Ln (28751)
Rates: n/a
(828) 452-4285
(800) 308-1808

MEADOWBROOK RESORT
102 Meadowbrook
Loop (28751)
Rates: n/a
(828) 926-1821

MOUNTAIN DREAMS CABINS
P. O. Box 1980
(28751)
Rates: n/a
(828) 926-7839
(877) 529-8690

NELSON CABIN
Cottage #4 on
Shirdash Ln
(28751)
Rates: n/a
(800) 327-5271

**PIONEER
VILLAGE CABINS**
219 Campbell
Creek Rd (28751)
Rates: n/a
(828) 926-1881

QUALITY INN
70 Soco Rd (28751)
Rates: $49-$129
(828) 926-0201
(800) 424-6423

**TEE ROSE
COTTAGE**
236 Soco Rd
(28751)
Rates: n/a
(828) 926-1240
(800) 948-6880

VALLEY INN
236 Soco Rd (28751)
Rates: n/a
(828) 926-1240
(800) 948-6880

MANNS HARBOR
**MANNS HARBOR
MARINA/MOTEL**
Manns Harbor
(27953)
Rates: n/a
(252) 473-5150

MANTEO
**DARE
HAVEN MOTEL**
Hwy 64,
P.O. Box 815
(27954)
Rates: $50-$85
(252) 473-2322

**PIRATE'S COVE
RENTALS**
1 Sailfish Dr
(27954)
Rates: n/a
(252) 473-6800
(800) 537-7245

MARION
**THE BARN
HOUSE INN**
11611 Montford
Cove Rd (28752)
Rates: n/a
(828) 738-4526

**BROOKS &
BROADWELL
CABIN RENTAL**
1020 Sugar Hill
Rd (28752)
Rates: n/a
(828) 652-7757
(800) 842-7253

COMFORT INN
178 Hwy 70 W
(28752)
Rates: $60-$110
(828) 652-4888
(800) 424-6423

**HEATHER GROVE
GOLD & GEM
PANNING**
Rt 5, Box 738
(28752)
Rates: n/a
(828) 738-3573

**INN AT
BLUE RIDGE
COUNTRY CLUB**
Hwy 221 N
(28752)
Rates: n/a
(828) 756-7001
(877) 543-1113

**LOG CABIN
LODGING**
4696 NC 226A
(28752)
Rates: n/a
(828) 746-4339

MARS HILL
**B & B
AT PONDER COVE**
1067 Ponder
Creek Rd (28754)
Rates: $145-$165
(828) 689-7304
(866) 689-7304

MATTHEWS
**COUNTRY
INN & SUITES**
2001 Mount
Harmony Church
Rd (28104)
Rates: $74-$79
(704) 846-8000
(800) 456-4000

MILL SPRING
**MORNING GLORY
FARM COTTAGE**
Hwy 9 S (28756)
Rates: n/a
(828) 894-5595

**SUNCATCHER
FARM CABINS**
5911 Big Level Rd
(28756)
Rates: n/a
(828) 625-8770

**SWISS CHALET
COTTAGES**
730 Hwy 108 E
(28756)
Rates: n/a
(828) 894-8096

MOCKSVILLE
COMFORT INN
1500 Yadkinville
Rd (27028)
Rates: $66-$125
(336) 751-7310
(800) 424-6423

**OLD MOCKS
FIELDS B&B**
1189 Jericho
Church Rd
(27028)
Rates: n/a
(336) 751-2738

MONROE
COMFORT INN
2351 W Roosevelt
Blvd (28110)
Rates: $47-$110
(704) 283-9600
(800) 424-6423

MOTEL 6
305 Venus St
(28112)
Rates: $36-$40
(7040 289-9111
(800) 466-8356

MOREHEAD CITY
**HOLIDAY INN EXP
HOTEL & SUITES**
5063 Executive Dr
(28557)
Rates: $85-$169
(242) 247-5001
(800) 465-4329

MORGANTON
**COMFORT
INN & SUITES**
1273 Burkmount
Ave (28655)
Rates: $49-$159
(828) 430-4000
(800) 424-6423

HOLIDAY INN
2400 S Sterling St
(28655)
Rates: $71-$76
(828) 437-0171
(800) 465-4329

SLEEP INN
2400A Sterling St
(28655)
Rates: $56+
(828) 433-9000
(800) 424-6423

MORRISVILLE
AMERISUITES
200 Airgate Dr
(27560)
Rates: $54-$109
(919) 405-2400
(800) 833-1516

**BAYMONT INN
& SUITES**
1001 Aerial Center
Pkwy (27560)
Rates: $70-$90
(919) 481-3600
(877) 229-6668

**LA QUINTA
INN & SUITES-
AIRPORT**
1001 Hospitality
Ct (27560)
Rates: $69-$132
(919) 461-1771
(800) 687-6667

**RESIDENCE INN
BY MARRIOTT**
2020 Hospitality
Ct (27560)
Rates: n/a
(919) 467-8689
(800) 331-3131

**STAYBRIDGE
SUITES-
AIRPORT**
1012 Airport Bvld
(27560)
Rates: $81-$151
(919) 468-0180
(800) 238-8000

MOUNT AIRY
COMFORT INN
2136 Rockford St
(27030)
Rates: $62-$125
(336) 789-2000
(800) 424-6423

KNIGHTS INN
851 Hwy 52 S
Bypass (27030)
Rates: n/a
(336) 786-8387
(800) 843-5644

MURPHY
**AFTER THE
SNOW CABIN**
37 Grouce Hollow
(28906)
Rates: n/a
(828) 837-3470
(888) 990-3333

BEST WESTERN
1522 Andrews Rd
(28906)
Rates: $69-$99
(828) 837-3060
(800) 528-1234
(866) 466-8774

COMFORT INN
754 US 64 W
(28906)
Rates: $49-$119
(828) 837-8030
(800) 424-6423

**FISH POND
CABINS**
73 Osbourne Ln
(28906)
Rates: n/a
(828) 644-5518

PARK PLACE B&B
54 Hill St (28906)
Rates: n/a
(828) 837-8842

**PINE CREEK
CABINS**
596 Taylor Hensen
Rd (28906)
Rates: n/a
(828) 837-4228

**RIVER COVE
CABINS**
1305 Hill Top Rd
(28906)
Rates: n/a
(828) 644-5979
(800) 779-5979

RIVER'S EDGE CABIN
531 Granite Ln (28906)
Rates: n/a
(248) 330-2726

SCHULTE WATERFRONT CABIN
90 Dreskin Rd (28906)
Rates: n/a
(800) 851-6742

STONE CREEK CABINS
192 Big Canoe Trail (28906)
Rates: $65-$80
(828) 644-9431

NAGS HEAD

ANCHOR COURT COTTAGES
8723 Old Oregon Inlet Rd (27959)
Rates: n/a
(252) 261-3449

COLEMAN'S COTTAGES
500 Sterling Rd (Virginia Beach, VA 23464)
Rates: n/a
(800) 989-4571

COVE REALTY VACATION RENTALS
105 E Dunn St (27959)
Rates: n/a
(252) 441-6391
(800) 635-7007

DOLPHIN OCEANFRONT MOTEL
38017 Old Oregon Inlet Rd (27959)
Rates: $49-$239
(252) 441-7488

NAGS HEAD REALTY VACATION RENTALS
2300 S Croatan Hwy (27959)
Rates: n/a
(252) 441-4311
(800) 222-1531

QUALITY INN SEA OATEL
7123 S Virginia Dare Trail (27959)
Rates: $34-$269
(252) 441-7191
(800) 424-6423
(800) 440-4386

WHALEBONE MOTEL
8201 S Old Oregon Inlet Rd (27959)
Rates: n/a
(252) 441-7423

NANTAHALA

NANTAHALA MOUNTAIN RESORT
115 Franklin Branch Rd (28771)
Rates: n/a
(828) 321-2215
(888) 667-2224

OAK CITY

SOUTHERN COMFORT B&B
15909 Hwy 125 N (27857)
Rates: n/a
(252) 798-7081

OAK ISLAND

OAK ISLAND ACCOMMODATIONS
300 Country Club Dr (28465)
Rates: n/a
(910) 278-6011
(888) 243-8132

OCRACOKE

ANCHORAGE INN
208 Irvin Garrish Hwy (27960)
Rates: $99-$165
(252) 928-1101

OCRACOKE ISLAND RENTALS
1055 Irvin Garrish Hwy (27960)
Rates: n/a
(252) 928-6261
(800) 699-9082

OLD FORT

INN ON MILL CREEK B&B
3895 Mill Creek Rd (28762)
Rates: n/a
(828) 668-1115
(877) 735-2964

OUTER BANKS

(See: Buxton, Duck, Hatteras, Kill Devils Hills, Kitty Hawk, Manteo, Nags Head, Ocracoke)

PENROSE

STANFILLS COUNTRY COTTAGES
Talley Rd (28766)
Rates: n/a
(828) 883-8181

PINEBLUFF

PINE CONE MANOR B&B
450 E Philadelphia Ave (28373)
Rates: n/a
(910) 281-5307

PINEHURST

CONDOTELS OF PINEHURST
1420 Hwy 5 S (28374)
Rates: n/a
(910) 295-8864
(800) 272-8588

HOMEWOOD SUITES
250 Central Park Ave (28374)
Rates: $104-$250
(910) 255-0300
(877) 901-4663

SPRINGHILL SUITES BY MARRIOTT
10024 Hwy 15-501 (28374)
Rates: n/a
(910) 695-0234
(877) 502-3673

PINEVILLE

QUALITY SUITES
9840 Pineville Matthews Rd (28134)
Rates: $79-$149
(704) 889-7095
(800) 424-6423

PINEY CREEK

WEDDEN'S WAY, TOO CABIN
231 Legra Rd (28663)
Rates: n/a
(336) 372-2985

PLEASANT GARDEN

WALNUT LANE B&B INN
7119 Racine Rd (27313)
Rates: n/a
(336) 674-7093

PURLEAR

SLIP AWAY HAVEN
365 Doe Run Rd (28665)
Rates: n/a
(336) 870-6578

RAEFORD

DAYS INN
Hwy 401 Bypass & Teal Dr (28376)
Rates: $50-$95
(910) 904-1050
(800) 329-7466

RALEIGH

AMERISUITES
1105 Navaho Dr (27609)
Rates: $93-$179
(919) 877-9997
(800) 833-1516

BEST WESTERN
2715 Capital Blvd (27604)
Rates: $59-$99
(919) 872-5000
(800) 528-1234
(800) 937-8376

CANDLEWOOD SUITES-CRABTREE
4433 Lead Mine Rd (27612)
Rates: $79
(919) 789-4840
(888) 226-3539

COMFORT SUITES
1309 Corporation Pkwy (27610)
Rates: $59-$150
(919) 212-6900
(800) 424-6423

DAYS INN
6329 Glenwood Ave (27612)
Rates: $49-$79
(919) 781-7904
(800) 329-7466

ECONO LODGE
2641 Appliance Ct (27604)
Rates: $59-$89
(919) 856-9800
(800) 424-5423

HOLIDAY INN-CRABTREE VALLEY
4100 Glenwood Ave (27612)
Rates: $119-$129
(919) 782-8600
(800) 465-4329

HOLIDAY INN-BROWNSTONE DOWNTOWN
1707 Hillsborough St (27605)
Rates: $94-$134
(919) 828-0811
(800) 465-4329

HOLIDAY INN NORTH
2805 Highwoods Blvd (27604)
Rates: $69-$104
(919) 872-3500
(800) 465-4329

HOMESTEAD STUDIO SUITES CRABTREE
4810 Bluestone Dr (27612)
Rates: $49-$64
(919) 510-8551
(888) 782-9473

HOMESTEAD STUDIO SUITES NORTH
3531 Wake Forest Rd (27609)
Rates: $59-$74
(919) 981-7353
(888) 782-9473

HOMESTEAD STUDIO SUITES RALEIGH NE
2601 Appliance Ct (27604)
Rates: $49-$69
(919) 807-9970
(888) 782-9473

AREA CODES - If the local number doesn't connect, check for a new area code.

HOWARD JOHNSON EXPRESS INN
3120 New Bern Ave (27610)
Rates: $38-$58
(919) 231-3000
(800) 446-4656

LA QUINTA INN & SUITES-CRABTREE MALL
2211 Summit Park Ln (27622)
Rates: $65-$129
(919) 785-0071
(800) 687-6667

MILNER INN
1817 Capital Blvd (27604)
Rates: n/a
(919) 834-0717
(888) 331-5500

MOTEL 6-NORTHWEST
3921 Arrow Dr (27612)
Rates: $37-$40
(919) 782-7071
(800) 466-8356

MOTEL 6-SOUTHWEST
1401 Buck Jones Rd (27606)
Rates: $37+
(919) 467-6171
(800) 466-8356

PLANTATION INN RESORT
6401 Capital Blvd (27604)
Rates: $50-$70
(919) 876-1411
(800) 992-9662
(800) 521-1932 (NC)

QUALITY SUITES
4400 Capital Blvd (27604)
Rates: $69-$139
(919) 876-2211
(800) 424-6423

RALEIGH CRABTREE INN
3920 Arrow Dr (27612)
Rates: n/a
(919) 782-7525
(800) 441-4712

RED ROOF INN NORTH
3201 Wake Forest Rd (27609)
Rates: $44-$64
(919) 878-9310
(800) 843-7663

RED ROOF INN SOUTH
1813 S Saunders St (27602)
Rates: $48-$66
(919) 833-6005
(800) 843-7663

RESIDENCE INN BY MARRIOTT CRABTREE
2200 Summit Park Ln (27612)
Rates: $89-$125
(919) 279-300
(800) 331-3131

RESIDENCE INN BY MARRIOTT
1000 Navaho Dr (27609)
Rates: $69-$144
(919) 878-6100
(800) 331-3131

REIDSVILLE

BEST VALUE INN
2100 Barnes St (27320)
Rates: $50-$70
(336) 342-0341

COMFORT INN
2203 Barnes St (27320)
Rates: $50-$205
(336) 634-1275
(800) 424-6423

RESEARCH TRIANGLE PARK

HOLIDAY INN
4810 Page Rd (27709)
Rates: n/a
(919) 941-6000
(800) 465-4329

ROANOKE RAPIDS

JAMESON INN
101 Old Farm Rd (27870)
Rates: $49-$104
(252) 533-0022
(800) 526-3766

MOTEL 6
1911 Julian R Allsbrook Hwy (27870)
Rates: $31-$50
(252) 537-5252
(800) 466-8356

ROBBINSVILLE

HUNDRED ACRE WOOD B&B
P. O. Box 1787 (28771)
Rates: n/a
(828) 479-8884

JIMBO'S FARM CABINS
General Del. (28771)
Rates: n/a
(828) 479-9384

LAKEPOINT COTTAGE
P. O. Box 2059 (28771)
Rates: n/a
(828) 479-4220
(866) 862-4220

MICROTEL INN
111 Rodney Orr Bypass (28771)
Rates: $50+
(828) 479-6772
(888) 771-7171

PHILLIPS MOTEL
290 Main St (28771)
Rates: n/a
(828) 479-3602

TALLULAH CREEK COTTAGE RENTALS
Tallulah Rd (28771)
Rates: n/a
(828) 479-8051

THE TREETOPS & THE RIDGE
3094 Santeetlah Rd (28771)
Rates: n/a
(828) 479-8400

ROCKINGHAM

CHEK INN
307 W Broad Ave (28379)
Rates: n/a
(910) 895-5278

ROCKY MOUNT

BEST WESTERN INN GOLD ROCK
7095 Rt 4 (27809)
Rates: $45-$95
(252) 985-1450
(800) 528-1234

COMFORT INN GATEWAY CTR
200 Gateway Blvd (27804)
Rates: $59-$99
(252) 937-7765
(800) 424-6423
(888) 449-0050

GUESTHOUSE INTL' INN
7797 Hwy 48 (27809)
Rates: $48-$64
(252) 407-8100
(800) 214-8378

RED ROOF INN
1370 N Wesleyan Blvd (27803)
Rates: $36-$63
(252) 984-0907
(800) 843-7663

RESIDENCE INN BY MARRIOTT
230 Gateway Blvd (27803)
Rates: $125-$185
(252) 451-5600
(800) 331-3131

SUPER 8 MOTEL
307 Moseley Ct (27803)
Rates: n/a
(252) 977-2858
(800) 800-8000

RODANTHE

PARADISE-HATTERAS STYLE COTTAGE
Oceanfront (27968)
Rates: n/a
(800) 989-4571

SEA SOUND MOTEL
24224 Sea Sound Rd (27968)
Rates: n/a
(252) 987-2224

SURF OR SOUND RENTALS
Hwy 12 (27968)
Rates: n/a
(252) 987-1444
(888) 919-7686

ROWLAND

HOLIDAY INN EXP
14733 Hwy 301 S (28383)
Rates: $51-$100
(910) 422-3377
(800) 465-4329

ROXBORO

TIMBERLAND MOTEL
720 N Mdison Blvd (27573)
Rates: n/a
(336) 599-2144

RUTHERFORD-TON

DOGWOOD COTTAGES & CABINS
2782 Hwy 64/74A (28139)
Rates: n/a
(919) 929-5553
(800) 770-9055

SALISBURY

HAMPTON INN
1001 Klumac Rd (28144)
Rates: $75-$160
(704) 637-8000
(800) 426-7866

SUPER 8 MOTEL
925 Bendix Dr (28144)
Rates: n/a
(704) 738-8888
(800) 800-8000

SALUDA

SANDY CUT CABINS
Pearson Falls Rd (28773)
Rates: n/a
(828) 749-9555

SPRING POND CABIN
640 E Hwy 176 (28773)
Rates: n/a
(828) 749-9824

TREE BLEW IN RENTAL
87 Smith Hill (28773)
Rates: n/a
(828) 692-3585

AREA CODES - If the local number doesn't connect, check for a new area code.

SALVO
CAPE ESCAPE RENTALS
Hwy 12 (27972)
Rates: n/a
(252) 987-2336
(800) 996-2336

SANFORD
DAYS INN
1217 N Horner Blvd (27330)
Rates: n/a
(919) 776-3150
(800) 329-7466

BEST INN
1143 N Horner Blvd (27330)
Rates: n/a
(919) 776-5121

JAMESON INN
2614 S Horner Blvd (27330)
Rates: $49-$104
(919) 708-7400
(800) 526-3766

SAPPHIRE
STARR'S MOUNTAIN COTTAGE
1 Hemlock Ln (28774)
Rates: n/a
(828) 966-9334

WOODLANDS INN
1305 Hwy 64 W (28774)
Rates: n/a
(828) 966-4709

SCALY
FIRE MOUNTAIN INN & CABINS
700 Happy Hill Rd (28775)
Rates: n/a
(828) 526-4446
(800) 775-4446

SELMA
DAYS INN
419 US 70 E (27576)
Rates: $36-$100
(919) 965-3762
(800) 329-7466

REGENCY INN
300 Graham St (27576)
Rates: n/a
(919) 965-8163

SEVEN DEVILS
FOSCOE COTTAGE RENTALS
1267 Seven Devils Rd (28604)
Rates: n/a
(828) 963-8142
(800) 723-7341

SHALLOTTE
COMFORT INN
360 Whiteville Rd (28459)
Rates: $50-$130
(910) 754-3044
(800) 424-6423

SHELBY
DAYS INN
1431 W Dixon Blvd (28152)
Rates: $40-$69
(704) 482-6721
(800) 329-7466

SUPER 8 MOTEL
1716 E Dixon Blvd (28152)
Rates: n/a
(704) 484-2101
(800) 800-8000

SKYLAND
GLENN & EDNA'S VACATION COTTAGE
P. O. Box 98 (28176)
Rates: n/a
(704) 684-9938

SMITHFIELD
HOWARD JOHNSON EXPRESS INN
220 E Market St (27577)
Rates: $35-$85
(919) 934-7176
(800) 446-4656

JAMESON INN
125 S Equity Dr (27577)
Rates: $49-$104
(919) 989-5901
(800) 526-3766

LOG CABIN MOTEL
2491 Hwy 70 E (27577)
Rates: $45-$47
(919) 934-1534

SUPER 8 MOTEL
735 Industrial Park Dr (27577)
Rates: $53-$99
(919) 989-8988
(800) 800-8000

VILLAGE MOTOR LODGE
198 Mallard Rd (27577)
Rates: n/a
(919) 934-7126
(800) 531-0063

SOUTHERN PINES
FAIRWAY MOTEL
1410 US 1 S (28387)
Rates: n/a
(910) 692-2711

HAMPTON INN
1675 Hwy 1 S (28387)
Rates: $79-$99
(910) 692-9266
(800) 426-7866

HOLIDAY INN
Hwy 1 at Morgantown Rd Exit (28387)
Rates: n/a
(910) 692-8585
(800) 465-4329

MIDLAND ROAD MANOR B&B
1625 Midland Rd (28387)
Rates: n/a
(910) 693-7979

RESIDENCE INN BY MARRIOTT
105 Brucewood Rd (28387)
Rates: n/a
(910) 693-3400
(800) 331-3131
(888) 702-4653

SOUTHERN SHORES
SOUTHERN SHORES RENTALS
5 Ocean Blvd (27949)
Rates: n/a
(252) 261-2000
(800) 334-1000

SPARTA
WEDDEN'S FARM B&B
312 Brookfield Rd (28675)
Rates: n/a
(336) 372-2985

SPINDALE
SUPER 8 MOTEL
210 Reservation Dr (28160)
Rates: n/a
(828) 286-3681
(800) 800-8000

SPRING LAKE
SUPER 8 MOTEL
256 S Main St (29390)
Rates: n/a
(910) 436-8588
(800) 800-8000

SPRUCE PINE
RICHMOND INN B&B
51 Pine Ave (28777)
Rates: $75-$80
(828) 765-6993

SPRUCE PINE MOTEL
423 Oak Ave (28777)
Rates: n/a
(828) 765-9344

STATESVILLE
BEST WESTERN INN
1121 Morland Dr (28677)
Rates: $52-$150
(704) 881-0111
(800) 528-1234

HAMPTON INN
715 Sullivan Rd (28677)
Rates: $61-$74
(704) 878-2721
(800) 426-7866

HOLIDAY INN EXP HOTEL & SUITES
740 Sullivan Rd (28677)
Rates: $69-$129
(704) 872-4101
(800) 465-4329

MASTERS INN
702 Sullivan Rd (28677)
Rates: n/a
(704) 873-5252
(800) 633-3434

MOTEL 6
1137 Moreland Dr (28677)
Rates: $39-$47
(704) 871-1115
(800) 466-8356

RAMADA INN
1023 Salisbury Rd (28677)
Rates: n/a
(704) 872-5215
(800) 272-6232

RED ROOF INN
1508 E Broad St (28677)
Rates: $42-$63
(704) 878-2051
(800) 843-7663

SUPER 8 MOTEL
1125 Greenland Dr (28677)
Rates: $42-$120
(704) 878-9888
(800) 800-8000

SUNSET BEACH
SEA TRAIL GOLF RESORT
211 Clubhouse Rd
Rates: $62-$343
(910) 287-1100

SURF CITY
(On Topsail Island)

SEA STAR INN & BEACH CLUB
2108 N New River Dr (28445)
Rates: n/a
(910) 328-5191
(800) 343-0087

SURF SIDE MOTEL
121 N Shore Dr (28445)
Rates: n/a
(910) 328-4099
(877) 404-9162

WARD RENTALS
116 S Topsail Dr (28445)
Rates: n/a
(910) 328-3221
(800) 782-6216

AREA CODES - If the local number doesn't connect, check for a new area code.

SYLVA

AZALEA MOTEL
97 Skyland Dr
(28779)
Rates: n/a
(828) 586-2051

HEMLOCK HILL LODGE B&B
110 Geranium Dr
(28779)
Rates: n/a
(828) 631-4343

WOODLAND MOTEL
2444 Hwy 441 S
(28779)
Rates: n/a
(828) 586-4331
(800) 366-4331

THOMASVILLE

DAYS INN
895 Lake Rd
(27360)
Rates: $40-$135
(336) 472-6600
(800) 329-7466

RAMADA LIMITED
5 Laura Lane (27360)
Rates: $70-$125
(336) 472-0700
(800) 272-6232

TOPSAIL BEACH
(On Topsail Island)

OCEAN PIER INN
807 Ocean Blvd
(28445)
Rates: n/a
(910) 328-3161

SEA VISTA MOTEL
1521 Ocean Blvd
(28445)
Rates: n/a
(910) 328-2171
(800) 732-8478

TOPSAIL REALTY RENTALS
712 S Anderson
Blvd (28445)
Rates: $694-$1395
Weekly
(910) 328-5241
(800) 526-6432

TRYON

FOXTROT INN
800 Lynn Rd
(28782)
Rates: n/a
(828) 859-9706
(888) 676-8050

THE MELROSE COUNTRY INN
211 Melrose Ave
(28782)
Rates: n/a
(828) 859-7014

PACOLET INN AT LYNN
1213 Lynn Rd
(28782)
Rates: n/a
(828) 859-7668

PINE CREST INN
85 Pine Crest Ln
(28782)
Rates: $90-$199
(828) 859-9135

VALLE CRUCIS

VALLE CRUCIS LOG CABIN RENTALS
Valle Landing,
Hwy 194 (28691)
Rates: n/a
(828) 963-7774

VILAS

BEULAH LAND FARM & GUEST HOUSE
170 Beulah Land
Ln (28692)
Rates: n/a
(828) 297-1329
(888) 550-8006

WADE

DAYS INN
3945 Goldsboro
Hwy (28395)
Rates: $36-$99
(910) 323-1255
(800) 329-7466

WALNUT COVE

MURPHY'S CASTLE B&B
317 Summit St
(27052)
Rates: n/a
(336) 591-5495

SQUIRES INN B&B
1117 Watts Rd
(27052)
Rates: n/a
(336) 591-5653

WASHINGTON

ECONO LODGE NORTH
1220 W 15th St
(27889)
Rates: $38-$75
(252) 946-7781
(800) 424-6423

WAYNESVILLE

COUNTRY CLUB B&B
1366 S Main St
(28786)
Rates: n/a
(828) 452-7764

COZY CABIN RENTALS
797 Ratcliff Cove
Rd (28786)
Rates: n/a
(828) 452-9759

GARDEN BREEZE MOTEL
2541 Dellwood Rd
(28786)
Rates: n/a
(828) 926-1976

GRANGE B&B
355 Grassmere Ln
(28786)
Rates: n/a
(828) 452-0339

HEARTH & HOME INN
3376 Dellwood Rd
(28786)
Rates: n/a
(828) 926-1845
(888) 926-1845

THE LODGE OF WAYNESVILLE
909 Russ Ave
(28786)
Rates: $39-$125
(828) 452-0353

MOUNTAIN CREEK B&B
146 Chestnut
Walk Dr (28786)
Rates: n/a
(828) 456-5509
(800) 557-9766

MOUNTAIN MIST INN B&B CABIN
142 Country Club
Dr (28786)
Rates: n/a
(828) 452-6800
(877) 452-6880

RIVERMONT CABINS
126 Deer Run Dr
(28786)
Rates: n/a
(888) 648-6373

SEVEN SPRINGS CENTER
770 Shelton Cove
Rd (28786)
Rates: n/a
(828) 926-9979
(800) 864-3258

SON COUNTRY CABINS
577 Woodmore Dr
(28786)
Rates: n/a
(828) 926-8767
(800) 790-8767

WEAVERVILLE

OX GLEN VACATION RENTALS
376 Ox Creek Rd
(28787)
Rates: n/a
(828) 645-2974
(800) 326-2373

WELDON

DAYS INN
1611 Roanoke
Rapids Rd (27890)
Rates: $40-$120
(252) 536-4867
(800) 329-7466

INTERSTATE INN
1606 Julian
Allsbrook Hwy
(27890)
Rates: n/a
(252) 536-4111

NEW YORKER MOTEL
Hwy 301 S (27890)
Rates: n/a
(252) 536-3148

WEST JEFFERSON

BARN RIDGE LODGING
1033 Elliot Rd
(28694)
Rates: n/a
(336) 384-9127

CAROLINA MT. RENTALS
8 N Jefferson Ave
(28694)
Rates: n/a
(336) 246-3010
(800) 628-2663

WHITTIER

ADORABLE SAWBUCK FARM & COTTAGES
546 Jericho Rd
(28789)
Rates: n/a
(866) 729-2855

FOLLOWING THE RIVER LOG CABIN
Union Hill Rd
(28789)
Rates: n/a
(877) 803-4724

WILLIAMSTON

HOLIDAY INN
101 East Blvd
(27892)
Rates: $62-$79
(252) 792-3184
(800) 465-4329

WILMINGTON

CAMELLIA COTTAGE B&B
118 S 4th St
(28401)
Rates: n/a
(910) 763-9171
(800) 763-9171

COMFORT INN EXECUTIVE CENTER
151 S College Rd
(28403)
Rates: $60-$165
(910) 791-4841
(800) 424-6423

COMFORT SUITES
4721 Market St
(28405)
Rates: $70-$149
(910) 793-9300
(800) 424-6423

DAYS INN
5040 Market St
(28405)
Rates: $39-$98
(910) 799-6300
(800) 329-7466

4 PORCHES B&B
312 S Third St
(28401)
Rates: n/a
(910) 342-0849

**HILTON HOTEL
RIVERSIDE**
301 N Water St
(28401)
Rates: $109-$250
(910) 763-5900
(800) 445-8667
(888) 324-8170

JAMESON INN
5102 Dunlea Ct
(28405)
Rates: $49-$104
(910) 452-5660
(800) 526-3766

LIVE OAKS B&B
318 S 3rd St
(28401)
Rates: n/a
(910) 762-6733
(888) 762-6732

MAINSTAY SUITES
5229 Market St
(28405)
Rates: $79-$200
(910) 392-1741
(800) 660-6246

MOTEL 6
2828 Market on
US 17/74 (28403)
Rates: $29-$56
(910) 762-0120
(800) 466-8356

**RESIDENCE INN
BY MARRIOTT**
1200 Culbreth Dr
(28405)
Rates: $99-$189
(910) 256-0098
(800) 331-3131

SUPER 8 MOTEL
3604 Market St
(28405)
Rates: $60-$100
(910) 343-9778
(800) 800-8000

**WILMINGTON
INN**
4903 Market St
(28405)
Rates: n/a
(910) 799-1440
(800) 782-9061

WILSON
**HOLIDAY INN EXP
HOTEL & SUITES**
2308 Montgomery
Dr (27893)
Rates: n/a
(252) 246-1588
(800) 465-4329

**MATTHEWS
MOTEL**
2421 Hwy 301 S
(27893)
Rates: n/a
(252) 243-4133
(800) 884-7703

WINDSOR
WINDSOR MOTEL
1523 S King St
(27983)
Rates: n/a
(252) 794-3444

*WINSTON
SALEM*
**AUGUSTUS T
ZEVELY INN
HISTORIC B&B**
803 S Main St
(27101)
Rates: $80-$205
(336) 748-9299
(800) 928-9299

**BEST WESTERN
INN & SUITES**
127 S Cherry St
(27101)
Rates: $75-$129
(336) 725-8561
(800) 528-1234
(800) 533-8760

BUDGET INN
600 Peters Creek
Pkwy (27103)
Rates: n/a
(336) 725-0501

**COMFORT INN
COLISEUM**
531 Akron Dr
(27105)
Rates: $67-$175
(336) 767-8240
(800) 424-6423

DAYS INN
3330 Silas Creek
Pkwy (27103)
Rates: $50-$86
(336) 760-4770
(800) 329-7466

HAWTHORNE INN
420 High St
(27101)
Rates: $59-$98
(336) 777-3000
(800) 972-3774

**HOLIDAY INN
HANES MALL**
2008 S Hawthorne
Rd (27103)
Rates: $59
(336) 765-6670
(800) 465-4329
(888) 834-7733

**HOLIDAY INN
SELECT**
5790 University
Pkwy (27105)
Rates: $99
(336) 767-9595
(800) 465-4329

LA QUINTA INN
2020 Griffith Rd
(27103)
Rates: $79-$105
(336) 765-8777
(800) 687-6667

MOTEL 6
3810 Patterson
Ave (27105)
Rates: $33-$38
(336) 661-1588
(800) 466-8356

**RESIDENCE INN
BY MARRIOTT**
7835 N Point Blvd
(27106)
Rates: $94-$114
(336) 759-0777
(800) 331-3131

**TRAVEL HOST OF
AMERICA**
4191 Patterson
Ave (27105)
Rates: n/a
(336) 767-1930

YANCEYVILLE
DAYS INN
1858 Hwy 86 N
(27379)
Rates: $56-$125
(336) 694-9494
(800) 329-7466

*YAUPON
BEACH*
**OAK ISLAND
VACATION
RENTALS**
300 Country Club
Dr (28465)
Rates: n/a
(910) 278-6011
(800) 243-8132

NORTH DAKOTA

BEACH

BUCKBOARD INN
1191 1st Ave NW
(58621)
Rates: $31-$37
(701) 872-4794
(888) 449-3599

BEULAH

AMERICINN HOTEL & SUITES
2100 2nd Ave NW
(58523)
Rates: $69-126
(701) 873-2220
(800) 634-3444

BISMARCK

BEST WESTERN DOUBLEWOOD INN
1400 E Interchange Ave
(58501)
Rates: $79-$150
(701) 258-7000
(800) 528-1234
(800) 554-7077

BEST WESTERN RAMKOTA HOTEL
800 S 3rd St
(58504)
Rates: $89-$125
(701) 258-7700
(800) 528-1234

COMFORT INN
1030 Interstate Ave (58502)
Rates: $51-$78
(701) 223-1911
(800) 424-6423

COMFORT SUITES
929 Gateway Ave
(58501)
Rates: $53-$102
(701) 223-4009
(800) 424-6423

DAYS INN
1300 Capitol Ave
(58501)
Rates: $44-$119
(701) 223-9151
(800) 329-7466

EXPRESSWAY INN
200 Bismarck Expwy (58504)
Rates: $48-$80
(701) 222-2900
(800) 456-6388

KELLY INN & SUITES
1800 N 12th St
(58501)
Rates: $56-$89
(701) 233-8001
(800) 635-3559

MOTEL 6
2433 State St
(58501)
Rates: $29-$47
(701) 255-6878
(800) 466-8356

RADISSON HOTEL
605 E Broadway Ave (58501)
Rates: $84
(701) 255-6000
(800) 333-3333

SELECT INN
1505 Interchange Ave (58501)
Rates: $40-$72
(701) 223-8060
(800) 641-1000

BOWMAN

NORTH WINDS LODGE
503 Hwy 85 S
(58623)
Rates: $37-$56
(701) 523-5641
(888) 684-9463

CARRINGTON

CHIEFTAIN CONFERENCE CENTER
60 4th Ave S
(58421)
Rates: $50-$85
(701) 652-3131

SUPER 8 MOTEL
101 4th Ave S
(58421)
Rates: $43-$60
(701) 652-3982
(800) 800-8000

DEVILS LAKE

COMFORT INN
215 Hwy 2 E
(58301)
Rates: $56-$85
(701) 662-6760
(800) 424-6423

DAYS INN
1109 Hwy 20 S
(58301)
Rates: $51-$90
(701) 662-5381
(800) 329-7466

TRAILS WEST MOTEL
Hwy 2 W (58301)
Rates: $36-$47
(701) 662-5011
(800) 453-5011

DICKINSON

AMERICINN MOTEL & SUITES
229 15th St W
(58601)
Rates: $66-$130
(701) 225-1400
(800) 634-3444

BEST WESTERN BADLANDS INN
71 Museum Dr
(58601)
Rates: $45-$100
(701) 227-9510
(800) 528-1234
(800) 285-1122

COMFORT INN
493 Elk Dr (58601)
Rates: $68-$165
(701) 264-7300
(800) 424-6423

HARTFIEL INN HISTORIC B&B
509 3rd Ave W
(58601)
Rates: $60-$90
(701) 225-6710

HOLIDAY INN EXP HOTEL & SUITES
103 14th St W
(58601)
Rates: $69-$85
(701) 456-8000
(800) 465-4329

DRAYTON

MOTEL 66
I-29 & Hwy 66
(58225)
Rates: $27-$35
(701) 454-6464

FARGO

AMERICINN LODGE & SUITES
1423 35th St SW
(58103)
Rates: $64-$134
(701) 234-9946
(800) 634-3444

BEST WESTERN DOUBLEWOOD INN
3333 13th Ave S
(58103)
Rates: $79-$173
(701) 235-3333
(800) 528-1234
(800) 433-3235

BEST WESTERN KELLY INN
3800 Main Ave
(58103)
Rates: $54-$97
(701) 282-2143
(800) 528-1234

COMFORT INN EAST
1407 35th St S
(58103)
Rates: $52-$120
(701) 280-9666
(800) 424-6423

COMFORT INN WEST
3825 9th Ave SW
(58103)
Rates: $52-$120
(701) 282-9596
(800) 424-6423

COMFORT SUITES
1415 35th St S
(58103)
Rates: $59-$144
(701) 237-5911
(800) 424-6423

DAYS INN & SUITES AIRPORT/DOME
1507 19th Ave N
(58102)
Rates: $52-$140
(701) 232-0000
(800) 329-7466

ECONO LODGE
1401 35th St S
(58103)
Rates: $34-$69
(701) 232-3412
(800) 424-6423

EXPRESSWAY INN
1340 21st Ave S
(58103)
Rates: $57-$72
(701) 235-3141
(800) 437-0044

HOLIDAY INN
3803 13th Ave
(58106)
Rates: $129-$149
(701) 282-2700
(800) 465-4329

HOLIDAY INN EXP
1040 40th St S
(58103)
Rates: $85-$96
(701) 282-2000
(800) 465-4329

KELLY INN
4207 13th Ave SW
(58106)
Rates: $66-$114
(701) 277-8821
(800) 635-3559

MAINSTAY SUITES
1901 44th St SW
(58103)
Rates: $89-$139
(701) 277-4627
(800) 424-6423

MOTEL 6
1202 36th St S
(58103)
Rates: $35-$42
(701) 232-9251
(800) 466-8356

MOTEL 75
3402 14th Ave S
(58103)
Rates: $39-$54
(701) 232-1321
(800) 828-5962

RADISSON HOTEL
201 5th St N
(58102)
Rates: $79-$109
(701) 232-7363
(800) 333-3333

RODEWAY INN
2202 S University
Dr (58103)
Rates: $49-$79
(701) 239-8022
(800) 424-6423

SELECT INN
1025 38th St SW
(58103)
Rates: $40-$75
(701) 282-6300
(800) 641-1000

SLEEP INN
1921 44th St SW
(58103)
Rates: $59-$79
(701) 281-8240
(800) 424-6423

SUPER 8 MOTEL
3518 Interstate
Blvd (58103)
Rates: $47-$125
(701) 232-9202
(800) 800-8000

GARRISON

**GARRISON
MOTEL**
Frontage Rd &
Hwy 37 (58540)
Rates: $25-$35
(701) 463-2858

GRAFTON

**IRLENE SHIRLEY'S
GINGERBREAD
HOUSE B&B**
603 Eastern Ave
(58237)
Rates: n/a
(701) 352-0856

LEONARD MOTEL
Hwy 17 West
(58237)
Rates: n/a
(701) 352-1730

GRAND FORKS

BEST VALUE INN
1000 N 42nd St
(58203)
Rates: $40-$50
(701) 775-0555

**BEST WESTERN
TOWN HOUSE**
710 1st Ave N
(58203)
Rates: $59-$89
(701) 746-5411
(800) 528-1234
(800) 867-9797

COMFORT INN
3251 30th Ave S
(58201)
Rates: $54-$104
(701) 775-7503
(800) 424-6423

DAYS INN
3101 34th St S
(58201)
Rates: $55-$100
(701) 775-0060
(800) 329-7466

ECONO LODGE
900 N 43rd St
(58201)
Rates: $37-$69
(701) 746-6666
(800) 424-6423

HOLIDAY INN
1210 N 43rd St
(582030)
Rates: $89-$129
(701) 772-7131
(800) 465-4329

TRAVELODGE
2100 S
Washington
(58201)
Rates: $64-$99
(701) 772-8151
(800) 578-7878

JAMESTOWN

COMFORT INN
811 20 St SW
(58401)
Rates: $59-$109
(701) 252-7125
(800) 424-6423

DAYS INN
824 SW 20th St
(58401)
Rates: $52-$150
(701) 251-9085
(800) 329-7466

**RANCH HOUSE
MOTEL**
408 Business Loop
W (58401)
Rates: $35-$45
(701) 252-0222

KENMARE

QUILT INN
1232 Central Ave
N (58746)
Rates: $45-$50
(701) 385-4100

LAKOTA

SUNLAC INN
310 4th Ave SE
(58344)
Rates: $29-$38
(701) 701-2487

LANGDON

**LANGDON
MOTOR INN**
210 Ninth Ave
(58249)
Rates: $26-$34
(701) 256-3600

LINTON

WILLOWS MOTEL
Hwy 83 S (58552)
Rates: $24-$38
(701) 254-4555
(800) 584-9278

MANDAN

**BEST WESTERN
SEVEN SEAS INN**
2611 Old Red Tr
(58554)
Rates: $79-$150
(701) 663-7401
(800) 528-1234
(800) 597-7327

MCCLUSKY

R & H MOTEL
404 Ave (58463)
Rates: n/a
(701) 363-2275

MEDORA

**AMERICINN
MOTEL & SUITES**
75 E River Rd S
(58645)
Rates: $69-$227
(701) 623-4800
(800) 634-3444

MINOT

**BEST WESTERN
KELLY INN**
1510 26th Ave SW
(58701)
Rates: $54-$159
(701) 852-4300
(800) 735-5868

COMFORT INN
1515 22nd Ave SW
(58701)
Rates: $60-$150
(701) 852-2201
(800) 424-6423

DAKOTA INN
US 2 & 52 Bypass
(58701)
Rates: $35-$55
(701) 838-2700

DAYS INN
2100 4th St SW
(58701)
Rates: $41-$80
(701) 852-3646
(800) 329-7466

**HOLIDAY INN
RIVERSIDE**
2200 Burdick
Expy E (58702)
Rates: $55-$89
(701) 852-2504
(800) 465-4329
(800) 468-9968

**INTERNATIONAL
INN**
1505 N Broadway
(58701)
Rates: $58-$95
(701) 852-3161
(800) 735-4493

**SLEEP INN,
INN & SUITES**
2400 10th St SW
(58701)
Rates: $70-$190
(800) 424-6423

NEW TOWN

**4 BEARS CASINO
& LODGE**
SR 23 W (58763)
Rates: $55+
(701) 627-4018
(800) 294-5454

PARSHALL

**PARSHALL
MOTOR INN**
North Main St,
Box 38 (58770)
Rates: n/a
(701) 862-3127

ROLLA

**NORTHERN
LIGHTS**
Hwy 5 East
(58367)
Rates: n/a
(701) 477-6164
(800) 535-6145

RUGBY

ECONO LODGE
US 2 East (58368)
Rates: $45-$69
(701) 776-5776
(800) 424-6423

STEELE

**LONE STEER
MOTEL**
I-94 Hwy #3
(58482)
Rates: n/a
(701) 475-2221
(888) 4L-STEER

O K MOTEL
301 3rd Ave
Northeast (58482)
Rates: n/a
(701) 475-2440

VALLEY CITY

**AMERICINN
LODGE & SUITES**
280 Winter Show
Rd SE (58072)
Rates: $66-$155
(701) 845-5551
(800) 634-3444

SUPER 8 MOTEL
860 11th St SW
(58072)
Rates: $46-$66
(701) 845-1140
(800) 800-8000

**WAGON WHEEL
INN & SUITES**
455 Winter Show
Rd (58072)
Rates: $46-$62
(701) 845-5333

AREA CODES - If the local number doesn't connect, check for a new area code.

WAHPETON

AMERICINN LODGE & SUITES
2029 Two-Ten Dr
(58075)
Rates: $65-$105
(701) 642-8365
(800) 634-3444

COMFORT INN
209 13th St S
(58075)
Rates: $49-$59
(701) 642-1115
(800) 424-6423

HOSPITALITY INN & SUITES
1800 Two-Ten Dr
(58075)
Rates: $49-$99
(701) 642-5000

SUPER 8 MOTEL
995 21st Ave N
(58075)
Rates: $48-$69
(701) 642-8731
(800) 800-8000

WASHBURN

SCOTWOOD MOTEL
1323 Frontage Rd
(58577)
Rates: $35-$46
(701) 462-8191

WATFORD CITY

MCKENZIE INN
132 SW 3rd St
(58854)
Rates: $38-$52
(701) 842-3980

ROOSEVELT INN & SUITES
600 2nd Ave SW
(58854)
Rates: $42-$52
(701) 842-3686

WEST FARGO

DAYS INN
525 E Main Ave
(58078)
Rates: $52-$110
(701) 281-0000
(800) 329-7466

WILLISTON

EL RANCHO MOTOR HOTEL
1623 2nd Ave W
(58802)
Rates: $44-$54
(701) 572-6321
(888) 452-3707

MARQUIS PLAZA & SUITES
1525 9th Ave NW
(58802)
Rates: $53-$110
(701) 774-3250

AREA CODES - If the local number doesn't connect, check for a new area code.

OHIO

AKRON

BEST WESTERN INN & SUITES
160 Montrose
West Ave (44305)
Rates: $69-$199
(330) 670-0888
(800) 528-1234

DAYS INN
3237 Arlington Rd
(44333)
Rates: $40-$70
(330) 644-1204
(800) 329-7466

HOLIDAY INN EXP
2940 Chenoweth
Rd (44312)
Rates: $89-$139
(330) 644-7126
(800) 465-4329

MOTEL 6
99 Rothrock Rd
(44321)
Rates: $35-$45
(330) 666-0566
(800) 466-8356

RED ROOF INN SOUTH
2939 S Arlington
Rd (44312)
Rates: $40-$72
(330) 644-7748
(800) 843-7663

ALLIANCE

COMFORT INN
2500 W State St
(44601)
Rates: $65-$129
(330) 821-5555
(800) 424-6423

HOLIDAY INN EXP HOTEL & SUITES
2341 W State St
(44601)
Rates: $90-$99
(330) 821-6700
(800) 465-4329

SUPER 8 MOTEL
2330 W State St
(44601)
Rates: $44-$77
(330) 821-5688
(800) 800-8000

AMHERST

DAYS INN
934 N Leavitt Rd
(44001)
Rates: $40-$95
(440) 985-1428
(800) 329-7466

MOTEL 6
704 N Leavitt Rd
(44001)
Rates: $29-$58
(440) 988-3266
(800) 466-8356

ASHLAND

DAYS INN
1423 CR 1575
(44805)
Rates: $40-$105
(419) 289-0101
(800) 329-7466

THE SURREY INN
1065 Claremont
Ave (44805)
Rates: $59-$120
(419) 289-7700

ASHTABULA

CEDARS MOTEL
2015 W Prospect
Rd (44004)
Rates: $45-$75
(440) 992-5406

HO HUM MOTEL
3801 N Ridge
West (44004)
Rates: $45-$80
(440) 969-1136

ATHENS

BUDGET HOST COACH INN
100 Albany Rd
(45701)
Rates: $37-$85
(740) 594-2294

DAYS INN
330 Columbus Rd
(45701)
Rates: $50-$150
(740) 592-4000
(800) 329-7466

SUPER 8 MOTEL
2091 E State St
(45701)
Rates: $45-$130
(740) 594-4900
(800) 800-8000

AURORA

WALDEN COUNTRY INN & STABLES
1119 Aurora
Hudson Rd
(44202)
Rates: $225-$500
(330) 562-5508
(888) 808-5003

AUSTINBURG

COMFORT INN
1860 Austinburg
Rd (44010)
Rates: $49-$135
(440) 275-2711
(800) 424-6423

AUSTINTOWN

BEST WESTERN MEANDER INN
870 N Canfield-
Niles Rd (44515)
Rates: $69-$150
(330) 544-2378
(800) 528-1234

ECONO LODGE
5431-1/2 Seventy
Six Dr (44515)
Rates: $40-$95
(330) 270-2865
(800) 424-6423

MOTEL 6
5431 Seventy Six
Dr (44515)
Rates: $39-$55
(330) 793-9305
(800) 466-8356

SUPER 8 MOTEL
5280 76 Dr (44515)
Rates: $44-$89
(330) 793-7788
(800) 800-8000

BATAVIA

FAIRFIELD INN & SUITES
4521 Eastgate
Blvd (45245)
Rates: $70-$96
(513) 947-9402
(800) 228-2800

HAMPTON INN
858 Eastgate
North Dr (45245)
Rates: $71-$109
(513) 752-8584
(800) 426-7866

HOLIDAY INN
4501 Eastgate
Blvd (452415
Rates: $99-$129
(513) 752-4400
(800) 465-4329

BEACHWOOD

HOLIDAY INN
3750 Orange Pl
(44122)
Rates: $69-$109
(216) 831-3300
(800) 465-4329

HOMESTEAD STUDIO SUITES
3625 Orange Pl
(44122)
Rates: $65-$85
(216) 896-5555
(800) 225-5466

RESIDENCE INN BY MARRIOTT
3628 E Park Dr
(44122)
Rates: $169-$299
(216) 831-3030
(800) 331-3131

BEAVERCREEK

RESIDENCE INN BY MARRIOTT
2779 Fairfield
Commons (45431)
Rates: $109-$149
(937) 427-3914
(800) 331-3131

BELLVILLE

DAYS INN
880 SR 97 (44813)
Rates: $35-$85
(419) 886-3800
(800) 329-7466

BLUE ASH

AMERISUITES
11435 Reed-
Hartman Hwy
(45241)
Rates: $79-$129
(513) 489-3666
(800) 833-1516

CANDLEWOOD SUITES
10665 Techwoods
Cir (45242)
Rates: n/a
(513) 733-0100
(888) 226-3539

CLARION HOTEL
5901 Pfeiffer Rd
(45242)
Rates: $70-$110
(513) 793-4500
(800) 252-7466

HOMESTEAD STUDIO SUITES
4630 Creek Rd
(45242)
Rates: $65-$85
(513) 985-9992
(800) 225-5466

RED ROOF INN-NORTHEAST
5900 Pfeiffer Rd
(45242)
Rates: $63-$96
(513) 793-8811
(800) 843-7663

RESIDENCE INN BY MARRIOTT
11401 Reed-
Hartman Hwy
(45241)
Rates: $129-$139
(513) 530-5060
(800) 331-3131

AREA CODES - If the local number doesn't connect, check for a new area code.

TOWNEPLACE SUITES
4650 Cornell Rd (45241)
Rates: $89-$94
(513) 469-8222
(800) 257-3000

BLUE ROCK

MCNUTT FARM
6120 Cutler Lake Rd (43720)
Rates: $40-$45
(614) 674-4555

BLUFFTON

COMFORT INN
117 Commerce Lane (45817)
Rates: $65-$109
(419) 358-6000
(800) 424-6423

KNIGHTS INN
855 State Rt 103 (45817)
Rates: n/a
(419) 358-7000
(800) 843-5644

BOARDMAN

DAYS INN
8392 Market St (44512)
Rates: $36-$165
(330) 758-2371
(800) 329-7466

MICROTEL INN
7393 South Ave (44512)
Rates: $40-$105
(330) 758-1816
(888) 771-7171
(800) 804-8385

RAMADA LTD
9988 Market St (44512)
Rates: $49-$79
(330) 549-0157
(800) 272-6232

BOWLING GREEN

DAYS INN
1550 E Wooster St (43402)
Rates: $51-$109
(419) 352-5211
(800) 329-7466

HOLIDAY INN EXP
2150 E Wooster St (43402)
Rates: $79-$109
(419) 353-5500
(800) 465-4329

QUALITY INN & SUITES
1630 E Wooster St (43402)
Rates: $55-$149
(419) 352-2521
(800) 424-6423

BROADVIEW HEIGHTS

TALLYHO-TEL
4501 E Royalton Rd (44147)
Rates: 34-$59
(440) 526-0640

BROOK PARK

DAYS INN
16161 Brook Park Rd (44135)
Rates: $45-$149
(216) 267-5100
(800) 329-7466

BROOKVILLE

DAYS INN
100 Parkview Dr (45309)
Rates: $50-$60
(937) 833-4003
(800) 328-7466

BRUNSWICK

SLEEP INN
1435 S Carpenter Rd (44212)
Rates: $48-$75
(330) 273-1112
(800) 424-6423

BURBANK

MOTEL PLAZA
Rt 1, Box 8 (44214)
Rates: $27-$32
(216) 624-3012

CAMBRIDGE

BEST WESTERN INN
1945 Southgate Pkwy (43725)
Rates: $39-$79
(740) 439-3581
(800) 528-1234

BUDGET INN
6405 Glenn Hwy (43725)
Rates: $30-$50
(740) 432-2304

COLONEL TAYLOR INN B&B
633 Upland Rd (43725)
Rates: $90-$95
(740) 432-1123

COMFORT INN
2327 Southgate Pkwy (43725)
Rates: $60-$135
(740) 435-3200
(800) 424-6423

DAYS INN
2328 Southgate Pkwy (32725)
Rates: $49-$99
(740) 432-5691
(800) 329-7466

DEER CREEK EXP
2321 Southgate Pkwy (32725)
Rates: $33-$69
(740) 432-6391

HOLIDAY INN
2248 Southgate Pkwy (43725)
Rates: $99+
(740) 432-7313
(800) 465-4329

SUPER 8 MOTEL
8779 Georgetown Rd (43725)
Rates: $39-$89
(740) 432-8080
(800) 800-8000

CANTON

AMERICAS BEST SUITES
4914 Everhard Rd (44718)
Rates: $79-$115
(330) 499-1011
(800) 237-8466

MOTEL 6
6880 Sunset Strip Ave NW (44720)
Rates: $33-$54
(330) 494-7611
(800) 466-8356

RED ROOF INN
5353 Inn Circle Ct NW (44720)
Rates: $46-$74
(330) 499-1970
(800) 843-7663

RESIDENCE INN BY MARRIOTT
5280 Broadmoor Cir NW (44709)
Rates: $99-$129
(330) 493-0004
(800) 331-3131

CARROLLTON

DAYS INN
1111 Canton Rd (44615)
Rates: $65-$120
(330) 627-9314
(800) 329-7466

CEDARVILLE

HEARTHSTONE INN & SUITES
10 S Main St (45314)
Rates: $94-$119
(937) 766-3000

CELINA

COMFORT INN GRAND LAKE
1421 SR 703 E (45822)
Rates: $46-$199
(419) 586-4656
(800) 424-6423

CHERRY GROVE

BEST WESTERN CLERMONT
4004 Williams Dr (45255)
Rates: n/a
(513) 528-7702
(800) 528-1234

RED ROOF INN EAST
4035 Mt Carmel Tobasco Rd (45255)
Rates: $40-$80
(513) 528-2741
(800) 843-7663

CHILLICOTHE

ADENA INN
1250 N Bridge St (45601)
Rates: $59-$79
(740) 775-7000
(800) 329-7466

CHRISTOPHER INN & SUITES
30 N Plaza Blvd (45601)
Rates: $65-$129
(740) 774-6835

COMFORT INN
20 N Plaza Blvd (45601)
Rates: $65-$250
(740) 775-3500
(800) 424-6423

COUNTRY HEARTH INN
1135 E Main St (45601)
Rates: $59-$85
(740) 775-2500

CINCINNATI

BEST WESTERN HOTEL CLERMONT
4004 Williams Dr (45255)
Rates: $59-$95
(513) 528-7702
(800) 528-1234

COMFORT INN
11440 Chester Rd (45246)
Rates: $39-$110
(513) 771-3400
(800) 424-6423

DAYS INN
I-275 & US 42, Ex 46 (45241)
Rates: $45-$140
(513) 554-1400
(800) 329-7466

DAYS INN-EAST
4056 Mt. Carmel-Tobasco Rd (45255)
Rates: $35-$199
(513) 528-3800
(800) 329-7466

FOUR POINTS BY SHERATON
150 W 5th St (45202)
Rates: $59-$169
(513) 357-5800
(800) 325-3535

GARFIELD SUITES HOTEL
2 Garfield Pl (45202)
Rates: $139-$399
(513) 421-3355

AREA CODES - If the local number doesn't connect, check for a new area code.

MILLENIUM HOTEL
141 W 6th St (45202)
Rates: $59-$169
(513) 352-2100
(800) 876-2213

MOTEL 6
5300 Kennedy Ave (45312)
Rates: $39-$55
(513) 531-6589
(800) 466-8356

MOTEL 6-SOUTHEAST
3960 Nine Mile Rd (45255)
Rates: $34-$50
(513) 752-2262
(800) 466-8356

THE VERNON MANOR HOTEL
400 Oak St (45219)
Rates: $115-$225
(513) 281-3300

THE WESTIN
21 E 5th St (45202)
Rates: $153-$295
(513) 621-7700
(800) 228-3000

CLEVELAND

BAYMONT INN & SUITES AIRPORT
4222 W 150th St (44135)
Rates: $68-$80
(216) 251-8500
(877) 229-6668

COMFORT INN DOWNTOWN
180 Euclid Ave (44115)
Rates: $70-$129
(216) 861-0001
(800) 424-6423

INTER-CONTINENTAL HOTEL
9801 Carnegie Ave (44106)
Rates: $209-$349
(216) 707-4100
(800) 424-6835

INTER-CONTINENTAL SUITES HOTEL
8800 Euclid Ave (44106)
Rates: n/a
(216) 707-4300
(800) 424-6835

MARRIOTT AIRPORT
4277 W 150th St (44135)
Rates: $109-$189
(216) 252-5333
(800) 228-9290

RESIDENCE INN BY MARRIOTT
30100 Clemens Rd (44145)
Rates: $99-$169
(216) 892-2254
(800) 331-3131

RITZ CARLTON HOTEL
1515 W 3rd St (44113)
Rates: $259-$279
(216) 623-1300
(800) 241-3333

SHERATON AIRPORT
5300 Riverside Dr (44135)
Rates: $69-$200
(216) 267-1500
(800) 325-3535

CLYDE

RED ROOF INN
1363 W McPherson Hwy (43410)
Rates: $49-$109
(419) 547-6660
(800) 843-7663

COLUMBUS

AMERISUITES
7490 Vantage Dr (43235)
Rates: $89-$118
(614) 846-4355
(800) 833-1516

BAYMONT INN & SUITES
8400 Lyra Dr (43240)
Rates: $79-$159
(614) 791-9700
(877) 229-6668

BEST WESTERN COLUMBUS NORTH
888 E Dublin-Granville Rd (43229)
Rates: $65-$80
(614) 888-8230
(800) 528-1234

CANDLEWOOD SUITES
590 Taylor Rd (43230)
Rates: n/a
(614) 863-4033
(888) 226-3539

CLARION HOTEL
750 Stelzer Rd (43220)
Rates: $69-$149
(614) 237-6360
(800) 424-6423

COMFORT INN NORTH
1213 E Dublin Granville Rd (43229)
Rates: $67-$150
(614) 885-4084
(800) 424-6423

COMFORT SUITES
4270 Sawyer Rd (43219)
Rates: $80-$120
(614) 237-5847
(800) 424-6423

COMFORT SUITES
5547 Keim Cir (43228)
Rates: $74-$89
(614) 870-7658
(800) 424-6423

DAYS INN
1212 E Dublin Granville Rd (43229)
Rates: $42-$69
(614) 885-9696
(800) 329-7466

DAYS INN FAIRGROUNDS
1700 Clara St (43211)
Rates: $45-$80
(614) 299-4300
(800) 329-8466

DAYS INN-WEST
1559 W Broad St (43222)
Rates: $45-$75
(614) 275-0388
(800) 329-7466

DOUBLETREE GUEST SUITES
50 S Front St (43222)
Rates: $99-$169
(614) 228-4600
(800) 222-8733

DRURY INN & SUITES
88 E Nationwide Blvd (43215)
Rates: $94-$145
(614) 221-7008
(800) 378-7946

ECONO LODGE
5950 Scarborough Blvd (43232)
Rates: $45-$85
(614) 864-4670
(800) 424-6423

ECONO LODGE
6125 Zumstein Dr (43229)
Rates: $35-$69
(614) 436-0800
(800) 424-6423

HOLIDAY INN
175 Hutchinson Ave (43235)
Rates: $99-$139
(614) 885-3334
(800) 465-4329

HOLIDAY INN EAST-AIRPORT AREA
4560 Hilton Corporate Dr (43232)
Rates: $99-$209
(614) 868-1380
(800) 465-4329

HOLIDAY INN ON THE LANE-OHIO STATE UNIVERSITY
328 W Lane Ave (43201)
Rates: $92-$99
(614) 294-4848
(800) 465-4329

KNIGHTS INN-EAST
4320 Groves Rd (43232)
Rates: $50-$90
(614) 864-0600
(800) 843-5644

LANSING ST B&B
180 Lansing St (43206)
Rates: $70
(614) 444-8488
(800) 383-7839

MARRIOTT NORTH
6500 Doubletree Ave (43229)
Rates: $99-$169
(614) 885-1885
(800) 228-0290

MICROTEL INN
7500 Vantage Dr (43235)
Rates: $40-$73
(614) 436-0556
(888) 771-7171
(800) 433-3690

MOTEL 6
5500 Renner Rd (43228)
Rates: $34-$37
(614) 870-0993
(800) 466-8356

MOTEL 6-EAST
5910 Scarborough Blvd (43232)
Rates: $29-$40
(614) 755-2250
(800) 466-8356

MOTEL 6
7474 N High St (43235)
Rates: $39-$43
(614) 431-2525
(800) 466-8356

MOTEL 6-NORTH
1289 Dublin-Granville Rd (43229)
Rates: $35-$56
(614) 846-9860
(800) 466-8356

MOTEL 6-OSU
750 Morse Rd (43229)
Rates: $35-$60
(614) 846-8520
(800) 466-8356

AREA CODES - If the local number doesn't connect, check for a new area code.

QUALITY INN N
1001 Schrock Rd
(43229)
Rates: $49-$99
(614) 431-0208
(800) 424-6423

RAMADA LIMITED
6121 Zumstein Dr
(43229)
Rates: n/a
(614) 846-9070
(800) 272-6232

RED ROOF INN
7480 N High St
(43235)
Rates: $50-$70
(614) 846-3001
(800) 843-7663

**RED ROOF INN
DOWNTOWN**
111 Nationwide
Blvd (43215)
Rates: $77-$115
(614) 224-6539
(800) 843-7663

**RED ROOF INN-
OSU**
441 Ackerman Rd
(43202)
Rates: $55-$88
(614) 267-9941
(800) 843-7663

RED ROOF INN-W
5001 Renner Rd
(43228)
Rates: $48-$74
(614) 878-9245
(800) 843-7663

**RESIDENCE INN
BY MARRIOTT**
2084 S Hamilton
Rd (43232)
Rates: $129-$189
(614) 864-8844
(800) 331-3131

**RESIDENCE INN
BY MARRIOTT**
6191 Zumstein Dr
(43229)
Rates: $89-$139
(614) 431-1819
(800) 331-3131

**RESIDENCE INN
BY MARRIOTT**
7300 Huntington
Park Dr (43235)
Rates: $69-$159
(614) 885-0799
(800) 331-3131

**RESIDENCE INN
BY MARRIOTT**
3999 Easton Loop
W (43219)
Rates: n/a
(614) 414-1000
(800) 331-3131

**SHERATON
SUITES**
201 Hutchinson
Ave (43235)
Rates: $99-$200
(614) 436-0004
(800) 325-3535

SIGNATURE INN
6767 Schrock Hill
Ct (43229)
Rates: $49-$104
(614) 890-8111

**TOWNEPLACE
SUITES**
7272 Huntington
Park Dr (43235)
Rates: $89-$109
(614) 885-1557
(800) 257-3000

**UNIVERSITY
PLAZA HOTEL**
3110 Olentangy
River Rd (43202)
Rates: $89-$119
(614) 267-7461

VICTORIAN B&B
78 Smith Pl
(43201)
Rates: n/a
(614) 299-1656

WELLESLEY INN
8555 Lyra Dr
(43240)
Rates: $89-$109
(614) 431-5522
(800) 444-8888

**THE WESTIN
GREAT SO.
COLUMBUS**
310 S High St
(43215)
Rates: $119-$155
(614) 228-3800
(800) 937-8461

CONNEAUT
DAYS INN
600 Days Blvd
(44030)
Rates: $65-$150
(440) 593-6000
(800) 329-7466

*CUYAHOGA
FALLS*
**AKRON
SHERATON
SUITES**
1989 Front St
(44221)
Rates: $114-$214
(330) 929-3000
(800) 325-3535

ECONOMY INN
1070 Graham Rd
(44221)
Rates: $57-$109
(330) 929-8200

DAYTON
**BEST WESTERN
EXECUTIVE HOTEL**
2401 Needmore
Rd (45414)
Rates: $59-$159
(937) 278-5711
(800) 528-1234

COMFORT INN
7125 Miller Ln
(45414)
Rates: $69-$135
(937) 890-9995
(800) 424-6423

**CROWN PLAZA
DAYTON**
33 E Fifth St
(45439)
Rates: $79-$149
(937) 224-0800
(800) 227-6963

HOLIDAY INN EXP
2455 Dryden Rd
(45439)
Rates: n/a
(937) 294-1471
(800) 465-4329

**HOWARD
JOHNSON
EXPRESS**
7575 Poe Ave
(45414)
Rates: $60-$65
(937) 454-0550
(800) 446-4656

MARRIOTT HOTEL
1414 S Patterson
Blvd (45409)
Rates: $79-$140
(937) 223-1000
(800) 228-9290

MOTEL 6-NORTH
7130 Miller Lane
(45414)
Rates: $33-$54
(937) 898-3606
(800) 466-8356

**RAMADA INN
AIRPORT**
4079 Little York
Rd (45414)
Rates: $60-$80
(937) 890-9500
(800) 272-6232

RED ROOF INN-N
7370 Miller Ln
(45414)
Rates: $46-$72
(937) 898-1054
(800) 843-7663

**RESIDENCE INN
BY MARRIOTT**
7070 Poe Ave
(45414)
Rates: $119-$199
(937) 898-7764
(800) 331-3131

DELAWARE
**DELAWARE
HOTEL**
351 S Sandusky St
(43015)
Rates: $49-$129
(740) 363-1262

TRAVELODGE
1001 US 23 N
(43015)
Rates: $52-$140
(740) 369-4421
(800) 578-7878

DOVER
HOSPITALITY INN
889 Commercial
Pkwy (44622)
Rates: $30-$75
(330) 364-7724

DUBLIN
AMERISUITES
6161 Park Center
Cir (43017)
Rates: $79-$129
(614) 799-1913
(800) 833-1516

BAYMONT INN
6145 Park Center
Circle (43017)
Rates: $70-$75
(614) 792-8300
(877) 229-6668

CLARION HOTEL
600 Metro Place N
(43017)
Rates: $79-$159
(614) 764-2200
(800) 252-7466

**DRURY
INN & SUITES**
6170 Park Center
Cir (43017)
Rates: $75-$120
(614) 798-8802
(800) 378-7946

**HOMEWOOD
SUITES**
5300 Parkcenter
Ave (43017)
Rates: $89-$139
(614) 791-8675
(800) 225-5466

**MARRIOTT
NORTHWEST**
5605 Paul Blazer
Mem Pkwy
(43017)
Rates: $159-$189
(614) 791-1000
(800) 228-9290

RED ROOF INN
5125 Post Rd
(43017)
Rates: $57-$82
(614) 764-3993
(800) 843-7663

**RESIDENCE INN
BY MARRIOTT**
435 Metro Place S
(43017)
Rates: $79-$154
(614) 791-0403
(800) 331-3131

**STAYBRIDGE
SUITES**
6095 Emerald
Pkwy (43017)
Rates: $109-$199
(614) 734-9882
(800) 238-8000

**WELLESLEY
INN & SUITES**
5530 Tuttle
Crossing Blvd
(43017)
Rates: $64-$125
(614) 760-0245
(800) 444-8888

AREA CODES - If the local number doesn't connect, check for a new area code.

WOODFIN SUITES HOTEL
4130 Tuller Rd (43017)
Rates: $99-$150
(614) 766-7762
(800) 237-8811

EATON
ECONO LODGE
6161 Hwy 127 N (45320)
Rates: $40-$79
(937) 456-5959
(800) 424-6423

ELYRIA
COMFORT INN
739 Leona St (44035)
Rates: $54-$109
(440) 324-7676
(800) 424-6423

HOLIDAY INN
1825 Lorain Blvd (44035)
Rates: $69-$129
(440) 324-5411
(800) 465-4329

SUPER 8 MOTEL
910 Lorain Blvd (44035)
Rates: $42-$104
(440) 323-7488
(800) 800-8000

ENGLEWOOD
HOLIDAY INN
10 Rockridge Rd (45322)
Rates: $90-$115
(937) 832-1234
(800) 465-4329

MOTEL 6
1212 S Main St (45322)
Rates: $34-$46
(937) 832-3770
(800) 466-8356

RED ROOF INN
9325 N Main St (45322)
Rates: n/a
(937) 836-8339
(800) 843-7663

SUPER 8 MOTEL
15 Rockridge Rd (45322)
Rates: $39-$69
(937) 832-3350
(800) 800-8000

FAIRBORN
COMFORT INN WRIGHT PATTERSON
616 N Broad St (45324)
Rates: $59-$150
(937) 879-7666
(800) 424-6423

HAWTHORN INN & SUITES
730 E Xenia Dr (45324)
Rates: $89-$109
(937) 754-9109
(800) 527-1133

HOMEWOOD SUITES
2750 Presidential Dr (45324)
Rates: $129-$169
(937) 429-0600
(800) 225-5466

RAMADA LTD
2540 University Blvd (45324)
Rates: $72-$110
(937) 490-2000
(800) 272-6232

RED ROOF INN
2580 Col. Glenn Hwy (45324)
Rates: $46-$69
(937) 426-6116
(800) 843-7663

FAIRFIELD
HOLIDAY INN EXP
6755 Fairfield Business Park Dr (45014)
Rates: $87-$105
(513) 860-2900
(800) 465-4329

FAIRLAWN
MOTEL 6
99 Rothrock Rd (44321)
Rates: $36-$53
(330) 666-0566
(800) 466-8356

RESIDENCE INN BY MARRIOTT
120 W Montrose Ave (44321)
Rates: $139-$199
(330) 666-4811
(800) 331-3131

SUPER 8 MOTEL
79 Rochrock Rd (44321)
Rates: $39-$75
(330) 666-8887
(800) 800-8000

FINDLAY
DAYS INN
1305 W Main Cross St (45840)
Rates: $60-$72
(419) 423-7171
(800) 329-7466

ECONO LODGE
316 Emma St (45840)
Rates: $35-$75
(419) 422-0154
(800) 424-6423

HAWTHORN SUITES LTD
2355 Tiffin Ave (45840)
Rates: $79
(419) 425-9696
(800) 527-1133

RED ROOF INN
1951 Broad Ave (45840)
Rates: $50-$80
(419) 424-0466
(800) 843-7663

RODEWAY INN
1901 Broad Ave (45840)
Rates: $42-$65
(419) 424-1133
(800) 424-6423

SUPER 8 MOTEL
1600 Fox St (45840)
Rates: $41-$55
(419) 422-8863
(800) 800-8000

FOREST PARK
AMERISUITES
12001 Chase Plaza Dr (45240)
Rates: $89-$129
(513) 825-9035
(800) 833-1516

LEES INN & SUITES
11967 Chase Plaza Dr (45240)
Rates: n/a
(513) 825-9600
(800) 733-5337

FOSTORIA
COUNTRY CLUB INN & SUITES
737 Independence Rd (44830)
Rates: $43-$75
(419) 435-6511

FREDERICK-TOWN
HEARTLAND COUNTRY B&B
3020 Township Rd 190 (43019)
Rates: $120-$175
(419) 768-9300

FREMONT
COMFORT INN & SUITES
840 Sean Dr (43420)
Rates: $77-$270
(419) 355-9300
(800) 424-6423

FREMONT TURNPIKE MOTEL
520 CR 84E (43420)
Rates: $46-$80
(419) 332-6489

HOLIDAY INN
3422 Port Clinton Rd (43420)
Rates: $79-$149
(419) 334-2682
(800) 465-4329

GAHANNA
HOMEWOOD SUITES
590 Taylor Rd (43230)
Rates: $89-$109
(614) 863-4033
(800) 225-5466

TOWNEPLACE SUITES
695 Taylor Rd (43230)
Rates: $69-$109
(614) 861-1400
(800) 257-3000

GALION
HOMETOWN INN
172 N Portland Way (44833)
Rates: $50-$140
(419) 468-9909

GALLIPOLIS
HOLIDAY INN
577 State Rt 7 N (45631)
Rates: n/a
(740) 446-0090
(800) 465-4329

WILLIAM ANN MOTEL
918 2nd Ave (45631)
Rates: $40-$45
(740) 446-3373

GIRARD
DAYS INN
1610 Motor Inn Dr (44420)
Rates: $35-$149
(330) 759-3410
(800) 329-7466

ECONO LODGE
1615 E Liberty St (44420)
Rates: $35-$75
(330) 759-9820
(800) 424-6423

GREEN
SUPER 8 MOTEL
1605 Corporate Woods Pkwy (44685)
Rates: $60-$130
(330) 899-9888
(800) 800-8000

GREENVILLE
COMFORT INN
1190 Russ Rd (45331)
Rates: $66-$190
(937) 316-5252
(800) 424-6423

GREENVILLE INN
851 E Martin (45331)
Rates: $60-$100
(937) 548-3613

GROVE CITY
BEST WESTERN EXECUTIVE INN
4026 Jackpot Rd (43123)
Rates: $52-$75
(614) 875-7770
(800) 528-1234

AREA CODES - If the local number doesn't connect, check for a new area code.

MOTEL 6
1900 Stringtown
Rd (43123)
Rates: $39+
(614) 875-8543
(800) 466-8356

HAMILTON
**HAMILTONIAN
HOTEL**
1 Riverfront Plaza
(45011)
Rates: $72-$115
(513) 896-6200
(800) 522-5570

HARRISON
COMFORT INN
391 Comfort Dr
(45030)
Rates: $50-$100
(513) 367-9666
(800) 424-6423

HEATH
QUALITY INN
733 Hebron Rd
(4305120
Rates: $55-$110
(740) 522-1165
(800) 424-6423

RAMADA INN
733 Hebron Rd
(43056)
Rates: n/a
(740) 522-1165
(800) 272-6232

HEBRON
RED ROOF INN
10668 Lancaster
Rd SW (43025)
Rates: $53-$63
(740) 467-7663
(800) 843-7663

HILLIARD
COMFORT SUITES
3831 Park Mill
Run Dr (43026)
Rates: $74-$88
(614) 529-8118
(800) 424-6423

**HOMEWOOD
SUITES**
3841 Park Mill Rd
(43026)
Rates: $89-$159
(614) 529-4100
(800) 225-5466

MOTEL 6
3950 Parkway Ln
(43026)
Rates: $29-$40
(614) 771-1500
(800) 466-8356

HOLLAND
**BEST VALUE INN
& SUITES**
1201 E Mall Dr
(43528)
Rates: $46-$64
(419) 866-6565

RED ROOF INN
1214 Corporate Dr
(43528)
Rates: $36-$62
(419) 866-5512
(800) 843-7663

**RESIDENCE INN
BY MARRIOTT**
6101 Trust Dr
(43528)
Rates: $66-$109
(419) 867-9555
(800) 331-3131

HUBER HEIGHTS
**HOLIDAY INN EXP
HOTEL & SUITES**
5612 Merily Way
(45424)
Rates: $84-$109
(937) 235-2000
(800) 465-4329

TRAVELODGE
7911 Brandt Pike
(45424)
Rates: $55-$70
(937) 236-9361
(800) 578-7878

HURON
**PLANTATION
MOTEL**
2815 E Cleveland
Rd (44839)
Rates: $38-$95
(419) 433-4790
(877) 677-2770

INDEPEN-DENCE
AMERISUITES
6025 Jefferson Dr
(44131)
Rates: $114-$134
(216) 328-1060
(800) 833-1516

**BAYMONT INN
& SUITES**
6161 Quarry Ln
(44131)
Rates: $75-$87
(216) 447-1133
(877) 229-6668

CLARION HOTEL
5300 Rockside Rd
(44131)
Rates: $59-$189
(216) 524-0700
(800) 252-7466

RED ROOF INN
6020 Quarry Ln
(44131)
Rates: $72-$100
(216) 447-0030
(800) 843-7663

**RESIDENCE INN
BY MARRIOTT**
5101 W Creek Rd
(44131)
Rates: $99-$179
(216) 520-1450
(800) 331-3131

IRONTON
GRANDVIEW INN
154 County Rd
(45680)
Rates: $40-$75
(614) 377-4388
(800) 424-9849

JACKSON
KNIGHTS INN
404 Chillicothe St
(45640)
Rates: $42-$61
(740) 286-2135
(800) 843-5644

RED ROOF INN
1000 Acy Ave
(45640)
Rates: $55-$70
(740) 288-1200
(800) 843-7663

JEFFERSONVILLE
AMERIHOST INN
11431 Allen Rd
NW (43128)
Rates: $51-$125
(740) 948-2104
(800) 434-5800

KENT
ALDEN INN
4386 SR 43 (44240)
Rates: n/a
(330) 678-9927

DAYS INN
4422 Edson Rd
(44240)
Rates: $59-$85
(330) 677-9400
(800) 329-7466

RAMADA INN
4363 SR 43 (44240)
Rates: $49-$109
(330) 678-0101
(800) 272-6232

SUPER 8 MOTEL
4380 Edson Rd
(44240)
Rates: $45-$85
(330) 678-8817
(800) 800-8000

KINGS ISLAND
HOLIDAY INN EXP
5589 Kings Mills
Rd (45034)
Rates: n/a
(514) 398-8075
(800) 465-4329

LAKEWOOD
DAYS INN
12019 Lake Ave
(44107)
Rates: $49-$79
(216) 226-4800
(800) 329-7466

TRAVELODGE
11837 Edgewater
Dr (44107)
Rates: $59-$79
(216) 221-9000
(800) 578-7878

LANCASTER
**BEST WESTERN
INN**
1858 N Memorial
Dr (43130)
Rates: $69-$95
(740) 653-3040
(800) 528-1234

LIMA
DAYS INN
1250 Neubrecht
Rd (45801)
Rates: $40-$70
(419) 227-6515
(800) 329-7466

ECONO LODGE
1201 Neubrecht
Rd (45801)
Rates: $46-$85
(419) 222-0596
(800) 424-6423

HOLIDAY INN
1920 Roschman
Ave (45804)
Rates: 499-$111
(419) 222-0004
(800) 465-4329

MOTEL 6
1800 Harding
Hwy (45804)
Rates: $35-$40
(419) 228-0156
(800) 466-8356

LOGAN
AMERIHOST INN
12819 SR 664
(43138)
Rates: $55-$199
(740) 385-1700
(800) 434-5800

HOLIDAY INN EXP
12916 Grey St
(43138)
Rates: $89-$159
(740) 385-7700
(800) 465-4329

LONDON
ALEXANDRA'S B&B
117 N Main St
(43140)
Rates: $70-$135
(740) 852-5993

HOLIDAY INN EXP
100 Holiday Trail
NE (43140)
Rates: $79-$89
(740) 852-2700
(800) 465-4329

LOUDONVILLE
**LITTLE BROWN
INN**
940 S Market St
(44842)
Rates: $42-$74
(419) 994-5525

MACEDONIA
**BAYMONT
INN & SUITES**
268 E Highland
Rd (44056)
Rates: $101-$111
(330) 468-5400
(877) 229-6668

KNIGHTS INN
240 E Highland
Rd (44056)
Rates: $39-$75
(330) 467-1981
(800) 843-5644

AREA CODES - If the local number doesn't connect, check for a new area code.

MOTEL 6
311 E Highland
Rd (44056)
Rates: $29-$50
(330) 468-1670
(800) 466-8356

TRAVELODGE
275 Highland Rd
(44056)
Rates: $45-$85
(330) 467-1516
(800) 578-7878

MANSFIELD

AMERIHOST INN
180 E Hanley Rd
(44903)
Rates: $49-$99
(419) 756-6670
(800) 434-5800

**BAYMONT INN
& SUITES**
120 Stander Ave
(44903)
Rates: $43-$61
(419) 774-0005
(877) 229-6668

COMFORT INN
500 N Trimble Rd
(44906)
Rates: $55-$125
(419) 529-1000
(800) 424-6423

ECONO LODGE
1017 Koogle Rd
(44903)
Rates: $38-$60
(419) 589-3333
(800) 424-6423

42 MOTEL
2444 Lexington
Ave (44907)
Rates: $33-$65
(419) 884-1315

KNIGHTS INN
555 N Trimble Rd
(44906)
Rates: $40-$100
(419) 529-2100
(800) 843-5644

SUPER 8 MOTEL
2425 Interstate Cir
(44903)
Rates: $55-$67
(419) 756-8875
(800) 800-8000

TRAVELODGE
90 Hanley W Rd
(44903)
Rates: $45-$90
(419) 756-7600
(800) 578-7878

MARIETTA

BEST VALUE INN
506 Pike St (45750)
Rates: $42-$70
(740) 373-7373

**BEST WESTERN
MARIETTA INN**
279 Muskingum
Dr (45750)
Rates: $55-$79
(740) 374-7211
(800) 528-1234

COMFORT INN
700 Pike St (45750)
Rates: $59-$120
(740) 374-8190
(800) 424-6423

ECONO LODGE
702 Pike St (45750)
Rates: $40-$70
(740) 374-8481
(800) 424-6423

**LAFAYETTE
HOTEL**
101 Front St
(45750)
Rates: $65-$125
(614) 373-5522
(800) 331-9336

SUPER 8 MOTEL
46 Acme St
(45750)
Rates: $45-$57
(740) 374-8888
(800) 800-8000

MARION

COMFORT INN
256 Jamesway
(43302)
Rates: $64+
(740) 398-5552
(800) 424-6423

**HARDING
MOTOR LODGE**
1065 Delaware
Ave (43302)
Rates: $37-$46
(740) 383-6771

MARYSVILLE

DAYS INN
16510 Square Dr
(43040)
Rates: $69-$99
(937) 644-8821
(800) 329-7466

MASON

AMERISUITES
5070 Natorp Blvd
(45040)
Rates: $99-$149
(513) 754-0003
(800) 833-1516

**BAYMONT INN
& SUITES**
9918 Escort Dr
(45040)
Rates: $97-$102
(513) 459-1111
(877) 229-6668

**DAYS INN
KINGS ISLAND**
9735 Mason/Mont-
gomery Rd (45040)
Rates: $49-$149
(513) 398-3297
(800) 329-7466

**THE INN AT
KINGS ISLAND**
5589 Kings Mills
Rd (45030)
Rates: $89-$229
(513) 398-8075
(800) 227-7100

**MICROTEL INN &
SUITES**
5324 Beach Blvd
(45040)
Rates: $39-$159
(513) 754-1500

**RAMADA LIMITED
KINGS ISLAND**
9665 Mason-
Montgomery Rd
(45040)
Rates: $55-$80
(513) 336-7911
(800) 272-6232

**RED ROOF INN
KINGS ISLAND**
9847 Bards Rd
(45040)
Rates: $30-$120
(513) 398-3633
(800) 843-7663

**TOWNEPLACE
SUITES**
9369 Waterstone
Blvd (45040)
Rates: $79-$139
(513) 774-0610
(800) 257-3000

MASSILLON

HAMPTON INN
44 First St SW
(44647)
Rates: $69-$109
(330) 834-1144
(800) 426-7866

MAUMEE

**COMFORT INN
WEST**
1426 S Reynolds
Rd (43537)
Rates: $54-$125
(419) 893-2800
(800) 424-6423

**COUNTRY
INN & SUITES**
541 W Dussel Dr
(43537)
Rates: $75-$110
(419) 893-8576
(800) 456-4000

DAYS INN
1704 Tollgate Dr
(43537)
Rates: $39-$70
(419) 897-6900
(800) 329-7466

ECONO LODGE
150 Dussel Dr
(43537)
Rates: $39-$94
(419) 893-9960
(800) 424-6423

**HOMEWOOD
SUITES HOTEL**
1410 Arrowhead
Rd (43537)
Rates: $89-$129
(419) 897-0980
(800) 225-5466

RED ROOF INN
1570 Reynolds Rd
(43537)
Rates: $42-$76
(419) 893-0292
(800) 843-7663

SUPER 8 MOTEL
1390 Arrowhead
Rd (43537)
Rates: $44-$59
(419) 897-3800
(800) 800-8000

MAYFIELD
HEIGHTS

**BAYMONT INN
& SUITES**
1421 Golden Gate
Blvd (44124)
Rates: $70-$82
(440) 442-8400
(877) 229-6668

MEDINA

BEST VALUE INN
5200 Montville Dr
(44256)
Rates: $53-$89
(330) 722-4335
(888) 315-2378

BEST WESTERN
2875 Medina Rd
(44256)
Rates: $36-$41
(330) 725-4581
(800) 528-1234

MOTEL 6
3122 Eastpointe
Dr (44256)
Rates: $37-$60
(330) 723-3322
(800) 466-8356

MENTOR

**BEST WESTERN
LAWNFIELD INN**
8434 Mentor Ave
(44060)
Rates: $65-$129
(440) 205-7378
(800) 528-1234
(866) 205-REST

COMFORT INN
7701 Reynolds Rd
(44060)
Rates: $65-$99
(440) 951-7333
(800) 424-6423

MOTEL 6
8370 Broadmoor
Rd (44060)
Rates: $34-$54
(440) 953-8835
(800) 466-8356

**RESIDENCE INN
BY MARRIOTT**
5660 Emerald Ct
(44060)
Rates: $99-$139
(440) 392-0800
(800) 331-3131

AREA CODES - If the local number doesn't connect, check for a new area code.

OHIO 467

STUDIO 6
7677 Reynolds Rd
(44060)
Rates: $219-$269
(440) 946-0749
(888) 897-0202

SUPER 8 MOTEL
7325 Palisades
Pkwy (44060)
Rates: $40-$70
(440) 651-8558
(800) 800-8000

MIAMISBURG
ECONO LODGE
185 Byers Rd
(45342)
Rates: $40-$53
(937) 859-8797
(800) 424-6423

HOLIDAY INN
31 Prestige Plaza
Dr (45342)
Rates: $89-$199
(937) 434-8030
(800) 465-4329

HOMEWOOD SUITES
3100
Contemporary
Ln (45342)
Rates: $135
(937) 432-0000
(800) 225-5466

RED ROOF INN
222 Byers Rd
(45342)
Rates: $57-$80
(937) 866-0705
(800) 843-7663

RESIDENCE INN BY MARRIOTT
155 Prestige Pl
(45342)
Rates: $150-$175
(937) 434-7881
(800) 331-3131

SIGNATURE INN
250 Byers Rd
(45342)
Rates: $49-$104
(937) 865-0077
(800) 822-5252

STUDIO 6
8101 Springboro
Pike (45342)
Rates: $199-$259
(937) 434-8750
(888) 897-0202

WELLESLEY INN
155 Monarch Ln
(45342)
Rates: $64-$89
(937) 866-5500
(800) 444-8888

MIDDLEBURG HEIGHTS
CLARION HOTEL AIRPORT WEST
17000 Bagley Rd
(44130)
Rates: $79-$109
(440) 243-4200
(800) 424-6423

COMFORT INN
17550 Rosbough
Dr (44130)
Rates: $59-$129
(440) 234-3131
(800) 424-6423

MOTEL 6
7219 Engle Rd
(44130)
Rates: $37-$50
(440) 234-0990
(800) 466-8356

RAMADA LTD
7233 Engle Rd
(44130)
Rates: $48-$72
(440) 243-2277
(800) 272-6232

RED ROOF INN
17555 Bagley Rd
(44130)
Rates: $45-$83
(440) 243-2441
(800) 843-7663

RESIDENCE INN BY MARRIOTT
17525 Rosbough
Dr (44130)
Rates: $98-$179
(440) 234-6688
(800) 331-3131

TOWNEPLACE SUITES
7325 S Engle Rd
(44130)
Rates: $109-$139
(440) 816-9300
(800) 257-3000

MIDDLETOWN
BEST WESTERN
6475 Culbertson
Rd (45005)
Rates: $65-$145
(513) 424-3551
(800) 528-1234

FAIRFIELD INN
6750 Roosevelt
Pkwy (45044)
Rates: $70-$95
(513) 424-5444
(800) 228-2800

MANCHESTER INN HISTORIC HOTEL
1027 Manchester
Ave (45042)
Rates: $74-$145
(513) 422-5481
(800) 523-9126

RAMADA INN
6147 W SR 122
(45005)
Rates: $73-$85
(513) 424-1201
(800) 272-6232

SUPER 8 MOTEL
3553 Commerce
Dr (45005)
Rates: $49-$69
(513) 422-4888
(800) 800-8000

MILAN
MOTEL 6
11406 Rt 250 N
(44846)
Rates: $34-$130
(419) 499-8001
(800) 466-8356

SUPER 8 MOTEL
11313 Milan Rd
(44846)
Rates: $33-$138
(419) 499-4671
(800) 800-8000

MONTPELIER
ECONO LODGE
13-485 SR 15
(43543)
Rates: $45-$100
(419) 485-3139
(800) 424-6423

RAMADA INN
13508 SR 15
(43543)
Rates:n/a
(419) 485-5555
(800) 272-6232

MORAINE
HOLIDAY INN HOTEL & SUITES
2455 Dryde4329
n Rd (45439)
Rates: $86-$116
(937) 294-1471
(800) 465-4329

SUPER 8 MOTEL
2450 Dryden Rd
(45439)
Rates: $39-$99
(937) 298-0380
(800) 800-8000

MOUNT GILEAD
KNIGHTS INN
5898 SR 95 (43338)
Rates: $39-$80
(419) 946-6010
(800) 843-5644

MOUNT ORAB
BEST WESTERN MT. ORAB INN
100 Leininger St
(45154)
Rates: $59-$99
(937) 444-6666
(800) 528-1234

MOUNT VERNON
AMERIHOST INN
150 Howard St
(43050)
Rates: $64-$125
(740) 392-6886
(800) 434-5800

HOLIDAY INN EXP
11555 Upper
Gillcrest Rd
(43050)
Rates: $68-$74
(740) 392-1900
(800) 465-4329

NELSONVILLE
RAMADA INN
Hwy 33 & SR 691
(45764)
Rates: n/a
(740) 753-3531
(800) 272-6232

NEW PARIS
GOLDEN INN MOTEL
8868 Rt 40 W (45347)
Rates: $35-$50
(937) 437-0722

NEW PHILADELPHIA
HAMPTON INN
1299 W High St
(44663)
Rates: $72-$95
(330) 339-7000
(800) 426-7866

MOTEL 6
181 Bluebell Dr
SW (44663)
Rates: $29-$40
(330) 339-6446
(800) 466-8356

SCHOENBRUNN INN BY CHRISTOPHER
118 McDonald Dr
SW (44663)
Rates: $62-$130
(330) 339-4334

SUPER 8 MOTEL
131 1/2 Bluebell
Dr SW (44663)
Rates: $42-$84
(330) 339-6500
(800) 800-8000

NEWCOMERS-TOWN
HAMPTON INN
200 Morris
Crossing (43832)
Rates: $70-$92
(740) 498-9800
(800) 426-7866

NEWTON FALLS
BUDGET LODGE
4100 SR 5 (44444)
Rates: $45-$65
(330) 872-3833

ECONO LODGE
4248 SR 5 (44444)
Rates: $37-$55
(330) 872-0988
(800) 424-7663

NORTH BALTIMORE
CROWN INN
P. O. Box 82
(45872)
Rates: $35-$40
(419) 257-3821

NORTH CANTON
SUPER 8 MOTEL
3950 Convenience
Cir NW (44718)
Rates: $40-$130
(330) 492-5030
(800) 800-8000

AREA CODES - If the local number doesn't connect, check for a new area code.

NORTH LIMA

LIBERTY INN
10650 Market St
(44452)
Rates: $45-$50
(330) 549-3988

RAMADA LIMITED
9988 Market St
(44452)
Rates: n/a
(330) 549-0157
(800) 272-6232

NORTH OLMSTED

CANDLEWOOD SUITES
24741 Country
Club Blvd (44070)
Rates: n/a
(440) 716-0584
(888) 226-3539

ECONO LODGE AIRPORT WEST
22989 Lorain Rd
(44070)
Rates: $45-$65
(440) 734-1100
(800) 424-6423

HOMESTED STUDIO SUITES
24851 Country
Club Dr (44070)
Rates: $45-$65
(440) 777-8585
(888) 782-9473

RADISSON HOTEL
25070 Country
Club Blvd (44070)
Rates: $89-$139
(440) 734-5060
(800) 333-3333

NORTH-RIDGEVILLE

TRAVELERS INN
32751 Lorain Rd
(44039)
Rates: $40-$62
(216) 327-6311

NORTHWOOD

COMFORT INN SOUTH
2426 Oregon Rd
(43619)
Rates: $50-$80
(419) 666-2600
(800) 424-6423

NORWALK

ECONO LODGE
342 Milan Ave
(44857)
Rates: $39-$139
(419) 668-5656
(800) 424-6423

NORWOOD

HOWARD JOHNSON
5410 Ridge Rd
(45213)
Rates: $60-$74
(513) 631-8500
(800) 446-4656

OBERLIN

OBERLIN INN
7 N Main St
(44074)
Rates: $99-$189
(440) 775-1111

OREGON

COMFORT INN EAST
2930 Navarre Ave
(43616)
Rates: $59-$129
(419) 691-8911
(800) 424-6423

SLEEP INN, INN & SUITES
1761 Meijer Circle
(43616)
Rates: $69-$114
(419) 697-7800
(800) 424-6423

OXFORD

COLLEGE VIEW MOTEL
4000 Oxford-
Millville Rd
(45056)
Rates: $32-$48
(513) 523-6311

PAINESVILLE

RIDER'S INN
792 Mentor Ave
(44077)
Rates: $75-$95
(216) 354-8200

PENINSULA

VIRGINIA MOTEL
5374 Akron-
Cleveland Rd
(44264)
Rates: $29-$50
(216) 650-0449

PERRYSBURG

BAYMONT INN & SUITES
1154 Professional
Dr (43551)
Rates: $65-$72
(419) 872-0000
(877) 229-6668

COMFORT INN
26054 N Dixie
Hwy (43551)
Rates: $35-$55
(419) 872-2902
(800) 424-6423

DAYS INN
10667 Fremont
Pike (43551)
Rates: $55-$85
(419) 874-8771
(800) 329-7466

HOWARD JOHNSON
I-280 & Hanley Rd
(43551)
Rates: $39-$74
(419) 837-5245
(800) 446-4656

PIQUA

COMFORT INN
987 E Ash St
(45356)
Rates: $54-$125
(937) 778-8100
(800) 424-6423

LA QUINTA INN
950 E Ash St
(45356)
Rates: $70-$89
(937) 615-0140
(800) 687-6667

POLAND

RED ROOF INN
1051 Tiffany South
(44514)
Rates: $40-$77
(330) 758-1999
(800) 843-7663

RESIDENCE INN BY MARRIOTT
7396 Tiffany South
(44514)
Rates: $89-$169
(330) 726-1747
(800) 331-3131

PORT CLINTON

BEST WESTERN INN
1734 E Perry St
(43452)
Rates: $39-$149
(419) 734-2274
(800) 528-1234

COMMODORE PERRY INN & SUITES
255 W Lakeshore
Dr (43452)
Rates: $44-$219
(419) 732-2645

COUNTRY HEARTH INN
1815 E Perry St
(43452)
Rates: $40-$95
(419) 732-2111

SUPER 8 MOTEL
1704 E Perry St
(43452)
Rates: $35-$149
(419) 734-4446
(800) 800-8000

PORTSMOUTH

DAYS INN
3762 Hwy 23 N
(45662)
Rates: $50-$70
(740) 354-2851
(800) 329-7466

PUT-IN-BAY

PERRY HOLIDAY HOTEL
99 Concord Ave
(43456)
Rates: $65-$139
(419) 285-2107

REYNOLDS-BURG

DAYS INN & SUITES
2100 Brice Rd
(43068)
Rates: $49-$64
(614) 864-1280
(800) 329-7466

LA QUINTA INN
2447 Brice Rd
(43068)
Rates: $65-$105
(614) 866-6456
(800) 687-6667

RED ROOF INN
2449 Brice Rd
(43068)
Rates: $54-7$83
(614) 864-3683
(800) 843-7663

RICHFIELD

HOLIDAY INN
4742 Brecksville
Rd (44286)
Rates: $89-$119
(330) 659-6151
(800) 465-4329

RIO GRANDE

COLLEGE HILL MOTEL
10987 SR 588
(45674)
Rates: $39-$79
(740) 245-5326

ST. CLAIRSVILLE

BEST VALUE INN
51260 National Rd
(43950)
Rates: $44-$73
(740) 695-5038

ECONO LODGE & SUITES
51659 National Rd
(43950)
Rates: $50-$130
(740) 526-0128
(800) 424-6423

RED ROOF INN
68301 Red Roof
Ln (43950)
Rates: $40-$79
(740) 695-4057
(800) 843-7663

ST. MARYS

AMERIHOST INN
1410 Commerce
Dr (45885)
Rates: $99-$109
(419) 394-2710
(800) 434-5800

BEST VALUE INN & SUITES
1321 Celina Rd
(45885)
Rates: $51-$99
(419) 394-2341

AREA CODES - If the local number doesn't connect, check for a new area code.

SANDUSKY

BEST BUDGET INN
2027 Cleveland
Rd (44870)
Rates: $34-$128
(419) 626-3610

CLARION INN
1119 Sandusky
Mall Blvd (44870)
Rates: $55-$140
(419) 625-6280
(800) 424-6423

KNIGHTS INN
2405 Cleveland
Rd (44870)
Rates: $40-$150
(419) 621-9000
(800) 843-5644

SEVILLE

SUPER 8 MOTEL
6116 Speedway Dr
(44273)
Rates: $50-$100
(330) 769-8880
(800) 800-8000

SHARONVILLE

**ARCADIA
RESIDENTIAL
SUITES**
11180 Dowlin Dr
(45241)
Rates: $89-$169
(513) 354-1000

**HOMEWOOD
SUITES-NORTH**
2670 E Kemper Rd
(45241)
Rates: $89-$139
(513) 772-8888
(800) 225-5466

LIVINN SUITES
11385 Chester Rd
(45246)
Rates: $49-$149
(513) 772-7877

MOTEL 6-EAST
3850 Hauck Rd
(45241)
Rates: $29-$46
(513) 563-1123
(800) 466-8356

MOTEL 6-WEST
2000 E Kemper Rd
(45241)
Rates: $29-$38
(513) 772-5944
(800) 466-8356

RED ROOF INN
2301 E Sharon Rd
(45241)
Rates: $42-$75
(513) 771-5552
(800) 843-7663

**RESIDENCE INN
BY MARRIOTT**
11689 Chester Rd
(45246)
Rates: $88-$209
(513) 771-2525
(800) 331-3131

**WOODFIELD
SUITES**
11029 Dowlin Dr
(45241)
Rates: $99-$189
(513) 771-0300
(800) 338-0008

SIDNEY

COMFORT INN
1459 W Michigan
Ave (45365)
Rates: $69-$129
(937) 492-3001
(800) 424-6423

DAYS INN
420 Folkerth Ave
(45365)
Rates: $50-$119
(937) 492-1104
(800) 329-7466

ECONO LODGE
2009 W Michigan
St (45365)
Rates: $45-$85
(937) 492-9164
(800) 424-6423

HOLIDAY INN
400 Folkerth Ave
(45365)
Rates: $66-$99
(937) 492-1131
(800) 465-4329

SOLON

HAMPTON INN
6035 Enterprise
Pkwy (44139)
Rates: $79-$109
(440) 542-0400
(800) 426-7866

SOUTH POINT

**BEST WESTERN
SOUTHERN HILLS**
803 Solida Rd
(45680)
Rates: $45-$80
(740) 894-3391
(800) 528-1234

**COMFORT
INN & SUITES**
70 Private Rd
(45680)
Rates: $50-$55
(740) 377-2766
(800) 424-6423

SPRINGDALE

**BAYMONT INN
& SUITES**
12150 Springfield
Pike (45246)
Rates: $65+
(513) 671-2300
(877) 229-6668

**BEST WESTERN
HOTEL**
11911 Sheraton Ln
(45246)
Rates: $69-$129
(513) 671-6600
(800) 528-1234

SPRINGFIELD

HOLIDAY INN
383 E Leffel Lane
(45504)
Rates: $99
(937) 323-8631
(800) 465-4329

KNIGHTS INN
2207 W Main St
(45504)
Rates: $41-$60
(937) 325-8721
(800) 843-5644

RAMADA LTD
319 E Leffel Ln
(45504)
Rates: $49-$99
(937) 328-0123
(800) 272-6232

RED ROOF INN
155 W Leffel Ln
(45504)
Rates: $54-$99
(937) 325-5356
(800) 843-7663

STOW

STOW INN
4601 Darrow Rd
(44224)
Rates: $60-$85
(330) 688-3508

STRASBURG

RAMADA LTD
509 S Wooster Ave
(44680)
Rates: $60-$100
(330) 878-1400
(800) 272-6232

STREETSBORO

COMFORT INN
9789 SR 14 (44241)
Rates: $59-$120
(330) 626-5511
(800) 424-6423

MICROTEL INN
9371 SR 14 (44241)
Rates: $56-$106
(330) 422-1234

**TOWNEPLACE
SUITES**
795 Mondial
Pkwy (44241)
Rates: $69-$149
(330) 422-1855
(800) 257-3000

STRONGSVILLE

DAYS INN
9029 Pearl Rd
(44136)
Rates: $40-$65
(440) 234-3575
(800) 329-7466

MOTEL 6
15385 Royalton
Rd (44136)
Rates: $39-$50
(440) 238-0170
(800) 466-8356

SUNBURY

**DAYS INN
& SUITES**
7323 SR 37 E
(43074)
Rates: $55-$70
(740) 362-6159
(800) 329-7466

HAMPTON INN
7329 SR 37 &
US 36 (43074)
Rates: $79-$139
(740) 363-4700
(800) 426-7866

SWANTON

SUPER 8 MOTEL
10753 Airport
Hwy (43558)
Rates: $69
(419) 865-2002
(800) 800-8000

TIFFIN

HOLIDAY INN EXP
78 Shaffer Park Dr
(44883)
Rates: $75
(419) 443-5100
(800) 465-4329

QUALITY INN
1927 S SR 53
(44883)
Rates: $65-$120
(419) 447-6313
(800) 424-5423

TIFFIN MOTEL
315 West Market
St (44883)
Rates: n/a
(419) 447-7411

TOLEDO

**COMFORT INN
NORTH**
445 E Alexis Rd
(43612)
Rates: $59-$99
(419) 476-0170
(800) 424-6423

**HOTEL
SEAGATE**
141 N Summit St
(43604)
Rates: $79-$229
(419) 242-8885

MOTEL 6
5335 Heatherdowns
Blvd (43614)
Rates: $29-$46
(419) 865-2308
(800) 466-8356

RADISSON HOTEL
101 N Summit St
(43504)
Rates: $89
(419) 241-3000
(800) 333-3333

**RED ROOF INN
SECOR**
3530 Executive
Pkwy (43606)
Rates: $44-$78
(419) 536-0118
(800) 843-7663

AREA CODES - If the local number doesn't connect, check for a new area code.

TROY

ECONO LODGE
1210 Brukner Dr
(45373)
Rates: $45-$80
(937) 335-0013
(800) 424-6423

HOLIDAY INN EXP HOTEL & SUITES
60 Troy Town Dr
(45373)
Rates: $94+
(937) 332-1700
(800) 465-4329

RESIDENCE INN BY MARRIOTT
83 Troy Town Dr
(45373)
Rates: $89-$129
(937) 440-9303
(800) 331-3131

TWINSBURG

SUPER 8 MOTEL
8848 Twins Hills
Dr (44087)
Rates: $40-$80
(330) 425-2889
(800) 800-8000

UHRICHSVILLE

BEST WESTERN COUNTRY INN
111 McCauley Dr
(44683)
Rates: $55-$80
(740) 922-0774
(800) 528-1234

URBANA

ECONO LODGE
2551 SR 68 (43078)
Rates: $50-$70
(937) 652-2188
(800) 553-2666

VANDALIA

SUPER 8 MOTEL
550 E National Rd
(45377)
Rates: $45-$89
(937) 898-7636
(800) 800-8000

TRAVELODGE AIRPORT
75 Corporate
Center Dr (45377)
Rates: $39-$90
(937) 898-8321
(800) 578-7878

VERMILION

HOLIDAY INN EXP
2417 State Rd 60
(44089)
Rates: $99-$129
(440) 967-8770
(800) 465-4329

MOTEL PLAZA
4645 Liberty Ave
(44089)
Rates: $50-$89
(440) 967-3191

WADSWORTH

LEGACY INN
810 High St
(44281)
Rates: $35-$51
(330) 336-6671

WAPAKONETA

BEST WESTERN
1510 Saturn Dr
(45895)
Rates: $54-$129
(419) 738-8181
(800) 528-1234

DAYS INN
1659 Bellefontaine
St (45895)
Rates: $40-$80
(419) 738-2184
(800) 329-7466

SUPER 8 MOTEL
1011 Lunar Dr
(45895)
Rates: $49-$55
(419) 738-8810
(800) 800-8000

TRAVELODGE
413 Apollo Dr
(45895)
Rates: $39-$60
(419) 739-9600
(800) 578-7878

WARREN

BEST WESTERN DOWNTOWN MOTOR INN
777 Mahoning Ave
NW (44483)
Rates: $53-$74
(330) 392-2515
(800) 528-1234

COMFORT INN
136 N Park Ave
(44481)
Rates: $60-$125
(330) 393-1200
(800) 424-6423

WARRENS-VILLE HEIGHTS

ECONO LODGE
4353 Northfield
Rd (44128)
Rates: $45-$70
(216) 475-4070
(800) 424-6423

WAUSEON

BEST WESTERN DEL MAR
8319 SH 108
(43567)
Rates: $64-$125
(419) 335-1565
(800) 528-1234
(800) 647-2260

WAYNESVILLE

THE APPLE BARN B&B
88 Plott Valley Rd
(28786)
Rates: $100
(704) 452-1860

THE CABIN
1500 Eagles Nest
Rd (28786)
Rates: $165
(704) 452-7514

WEST CHESTER

SLEEP INN
5944 West Chester
Rd (45069)
Rates: $79-$94
(513) 645-1700
(800) 424-6423

STAYBRIDGE SUITES
8955 Lakota Dr W
(45069)
Rates: $96-$159
(513) 874-1900
(800) 238-8000

WESTERVILLE

CORNELIA'S CORNER B&B
93 W College Ave
(43081)
Rates: $60-$85
(614) 882-2678
(800) 745-2678

WESTLAKE

RED ROOF INN
29595 Clemens Rd
(44145)
Rates: $47-$93
(440) 892-7920
(800) 843-7663

RESIDENCE INN BY MARRIOTT

30100 Clemens Rd
(44145)
Rates: $89-$169
(440) 892-2254
(800) 331-3131

WICKLIFFE

CLARION HOTEL
28500 Euclid Ave
(44092)
Rates: $69-$130
(440) 585-2750
(800) 424-6423

WILLOUGHBY

RED ROOF INN
4166 SR 306
(44094)
Rates: $43-$87
(440) 946-9872
(800) 843-7663

WILMINGTON

HOLIDAY INN EXP
155 Holiday Dr
(45177)
Rates: $74-$125
(937) 382-5858
(800) 465-4329

RAMADA INN
123 Gano Rd
(45177)
Rates: $109
(937) 283-3200
(800) 272-6232

WINCHESTER

BUDGET HOST INN
18760 SR 136
(45697)
Rates: $49-$65
(937) 695-0381

WOOSTER

ECONO LODGE
2137 E Lincoln
Way (44691)
Rates: $48-$69
(330) 264-8883
(800) 424-6423

THE WOOSTER INN
801 E Wayne Ave
(44691)
Rates: $65-$225
(330) 263-2660

XENIA

REGENCY INN
600 Little Main St
(45385)
Rates: $45-$70
(937) 372-9954

YOUNGSTOWN

BEST WESTERN MEANDER INN
870 N Canfield-
Niles Rd (44515)
Rates: $59-$89
(330) 544-2378
(800) 528-1234

QUALITY INN
4055 Belmont Ave
(44515)
Rates: $45-$90
(330) 759-3180
(800) 424-6423

ZANESVILLE

BEST VALUE INN
135 N 7th St
(43701)
Rates: $45-$95
(740) 452-4511

COMFORT INN
500 Monroe St
(43701)
Rates: $59-$149
(740) 454-4144
(800) 424-6423

HOLIDAY INN
4645 E Pike
(43701)
Rates: $74-$109
(740) 453-0771
(800) 465-4329

RED ROOF INN
4929 E Pike
(43701)
Rates: $48-$82
(740) 453-6300
(800) 843-7663

SUPER 8 MOTEL
2440 National Rd
(43701)
Rates: $39-$80
(740) 455-3124
(800) 800-8000

TRAVELODGE
58 N 6th St (43701)
Rates: $45-$70
(740) 453-0611
(800) 578-7878

AREA CODES - If the local number doesn't connect, check for a new area code.

OKLAHOMA

ADA
HOLIDAY INN
400 NE
Richardson Loop
(74820)
Rates: n/a
(580) 332-9000
(800) 465-4329

AFTON
GRAND LAKE COUNTRY INN
I-44, Exit 302
(74331)
Rates: $29-$49
(918) 257-8313

ALTUS
BEST WESTERN ALTUS INN
2804 N Main St
(73521)
Rates: $58-$72
(580) 482-9300
(800) 528-1234
(888) 537-1087

DAYS INN
3202 N Main St
(73521)
Rates: $50-$65
(580) 477-2300
(800) 329-7466

RAMADA INN
2515 E Broadway
(73521)
Rates: $50-$68
(580) 477-3000
(800) 272-6232

ALVA
RANGER INN MOTEL
420 E Oklahoma
Blvd (73717)
Rates: $26-$32
(580) 327-1981

WHARTON'S VISTA MOTEL
1330 W Oklahoma
Blvd (73717)
Rates: $20-$29
(580) 327-3232

ARDMORE
BEST WESTERN INN
6 Holiday Dr
(73401)
Rates: $58-$75
(580) 223-7525
(800) 528-1234

COMFORT INN
2700 W Broadway
(73401)
Rates: $64-$125
(580) 226-1250
(800) 424-6423

DAYS INN
2614 W Broadway
(73401)
Rates: $55-$72
(580) 226-1761
(800) 329-7466

HOLIDAY INN
2705 W Broadway
(73401)
Rates: $63-$89
(580) 223-7130
(800) 465-4329

LA QUINTA INN
2432 Veterans
Blvd (73401)
Rates: n/a
(580) 223-7976
(800) 687-6667

MOTEL 6
120 Holiday Dr
(73401)
Rates: $29-$37
(580) 226-7666
(800) 466-8356

MICROTEL INN & SUITES
1904 Cooper Dr
(73401)
Rates: $43-$52
(580) 224-2600

SUPER 8 MOTEL
2120 Veterans
Blvd (73401)
Rates: $36-$50
(580) 223-2201
(800) 800-8000

ATOKA
BEST WESTERN ATOKA INN
2101 S Mississippi
(74525)
Rates: $59-$69
(580) 889-7381
(800) 528-1234

BARTLESVILLE
BEST WESTERN WESTON INN
222 SE
Washington Blvd
(74006)
Rates: $49-$79
(918) 335-7755
(800) 528-1234
(800) 336-2415

ECONO LODGE
3910 SE Nowata
Rd (74006)
Rates: $49-$89
(918) 333-0710
(800) 424-6423

HOLIDAY INN
1410 SE
Washington Blvd
(74006)
Rates: $55-$76
(918) 333-8320
(800) 465-4329

SUPER 8 MOTEL
211 SE
Washington Blvd
(74006)
Rates: $48-$54
(918) 335-1122
(800) 800-8000

BIG CABIN
SUPER 8 MOTEL
30954 S Hwy 69
(74301)
Rates: $43-$54
(918) 783-5888
(800) 800-8000

BLACKWELL
COMFORT INN
1201 N 44th St
(74631)
Rates: $50-$80
(580) 363-7000
(800) 424-6423

BOISE CITY
TOWNSMAN MOTEL
1205 E Main
(73933)
Rates: $27-$35
(580) 544-2506

BROKEN ARROW
HOLIDAY INN
2600 N Aspen
(74012)
Rates: $66-$84
(918) 258-7085
(800) 465-4329

BROKEN BOW
BROKEN BOW LAKE CABIN & BOAT RENTALS
P O Box 234
(74728)
Rates: $85
(580) 494-6349

CHARLES WESLEY MOTOR LODGE
302 N Park Dr
(74728)
Rates: $30-$37
(580) 584-3303

END OF TRAIL MOTEL
11 N Park Dr
(74728)
Rates: n/a
(580) 584-3350

MICROTEL INN
1701 S Park Dr
(74728)
Rates: $49-$59
(580) 584-7708

CATOOSA
SUPER 8 MOTEL
19250 Timbercrest
Dr (74015)
Rates: $33-$60
(918) 266-7000
(800) 800-8000

CHANDLER
ECONO LODGE
600 N Price
(74834)
Rates: $40-$49
(405) 258-2131
(800) 424-6423

CHECOTAH
DAYS INN
Hwy 69 & 150
(74426)
Rates: $46-$65
(918) 689-3999
(800) 329-7466

LAKE EUFAULA INN
I-40 & S Hwy 150
(74426)
Rates: $49-$79
(918) 473-2376

SHARPE HOUSE BED & BREAKFAST
301 NW 2nd
(74426)
Rates: $35-$50
(918) 473-2832

CHEROKEE
CHEROKEE INN
1720 S Grand
(73728)
Rates: $57-$60
(580) 596-2828

CHICKASHA
BEST WESTERN INN
2101 S 4th (73018)
Rates: $50-$70
(405) 224-4890
(800) 528-1234
(877) 489-0647

CLAREMORE
BEST WESTERN WILL ROGERS INN
940 S Lynn Riggs
Blvd (74017)
Rates: $54-$69
(918) 341-4410
(800) 528-1234
(800) 644-WILL

CLAREMORE MOTOR INN
1709 N Lynn Riggs (74017)
Rates: $33-$42
(918) 342-4545

DAYS INN
1720 S Lynn Riggs (74017)
Rates: $50-$80
(918) 343-3297
(800) 329-7466

MICROTEL INN & SUITES
10600 E Mallard Lake Rd (74017)
Rates: $52-$58
(918) 343-2868

SUPER 8 MOTEL
100 E Will Rogers Blvd (74017)
Rates: $49-$69
(918) 341-2323
(800) 800-8000

TRAVEL INN
812 E Will Rogers Blvd (74017)
Rates: $30-$50
(918) 341-3254

CLINTON

BEST WESTERN TRADE WINDS COURTYARD INN
2128 Gary Blvd (73601)
Rates: $48-$66
(580) 323-2610
(800) 528-1234
(800) 321-2209

DAYS INN
1200 S 10th (73601)
Rates: $65+
(580) 323-5550
(800) 329-7466

RAMADA INN
2140 Gary Blvd (73601)
Rates: n/a
(580) 323-2010
(800) 272-6232

DEL CITY

LA QUINTA INN
5501 Tinker Diagonal (73115)
Rates: $79-$99
(405) 672-0067
(800) 687-6667

DUNCAN

CHISHOLM SUITE HOTEL
1204 N Hwy 81 (73553)
Rates: $59-$77
(580) 255-0551

DUNCAN INN
3402 N Hwy 81 (73533)
Rates: $25-$36
(580) 252-5210

HERITAGE INN
1515 S Hwy 81 (73533)
Rates: $30-$43
(580) 252-5612

HILLCREST MOTEL
1417 S 81 Bypass (73533)
Rates: $18-$20
(580) 255-1640
(800) 710-7788

HOLIDAY INN
1015 N Hwy 81 (73533)
Rates: $43-$53
(580) 252-1500
(800) 465-4329

DURANT

COMFORT INN
2112 W Main St (74701)
Rates: $67-$79
(580) 924-8881
(800) 424-6423

QUALITY INN
2121 W Main st (74701)
Rates: $60-$65
(580) 924-5432
(800) 424-6423

EDMOND

BEST WESTERN EDMOND INN & SUITES
2700 E Second St (73034)
Rates: $55-$125
(405) 216-0300
(800) 528-1234
(877) 584-1550

RAMADA PLAZA HOTEL
930 E Second St (73034)
Rates: $69-$79
(405) 341-3577
(800) 272-6232

EL RENO

BEST WESTERN INN
2701 S Country Club Rd (73036)
Rates: $45-$70
(405) 262-6490
(800) 528-1234
(800) 263-3844

COMFORT INN
1707 SW 27th St (73036)
Rates: $51-$66
(405) 262-3050
(800) 424-6423

DAYS INN
2700 S Country Club Rd (73036)
Rates: $40-$56
(405) 262-8720
(800) 329-7466

ELK CITY

BEDFORD INN MOTEL
2004 S Main St (73644)
Rates: $50-$75
(580) 225-6775

DAYS INN
2500 S Main St (73644)
Rates: $52-$68
(580) 225-0305
(800) 329-7466

ECONO LODGE
108 Meadow Ridge (73644)
Rates: $39-$59
(580) 225-5120
(800) 424-6423

HOLIDAY INN
101 Meadow Ridge (73648)
Rates: $55-$67
(580) 225-6637
(800) 465-4329

MOTEL 6
2604 E Hwy 66 (73644)
Rates: $32-$40
(580) 225-2541
(800) 466-8356

RAMADA INN
102 BJ Hughes Access Rd (73644)
Rates: $58
(580) 225-8140
(800) 272-6232

TRAVELODGE
2500 E Hwy 66 (73644)
Rates: $35-$49
(580) 225-6661
(800) 578-7878

ENID

BEST WESTERN ENID INN
2818 S Van Buren (73703)
Rates: $65-$75
(580) 242-7110
(800) 378-6308

COMFORT INN
202 N Van Buren (73703)
Rates: $71-$135
(580) 234-1200
(800) 424-6423

DAYS INN
2901 S Van Buren (73703)
Rates: $50-$80
(580) 237-6000
(800) 329-7466

MOTEL 6
2523 Mercer Dr (73701)
Rates: $44+
(580) 237-3090
(800) 466-8356

RAMADA INN
3005 W Garriot Rd (73703)
Rates: $42-$62
(580) 234-0440
(800) 272-6232

ERICK

COMFORT INN
1001 N Sheb Wooley (73645)
Rates: $70-$109
(580) 526-8124
(800) 4240-423

DAYS INN
Rt 1, I-40 & Hwy 30 (73645)
Rates: $47-$98
(580) 526-3315
(800) 329-7466

FREDERICK

SCOTTISH INNS
1015 S Main St (73542)
Rates: $35-$59
(580) 335-2129
(800) 251-1962

GLENPOOL

BEST WESTERN INN
14831 S Casper St (73033)
Rates: $52-$63
(918) 322-5201
(800) 528-1234
(800) 678-5201

GROVE

BEST WESTERN TIMBERRIDGE INN
120 E 18th St (74344)
Rates: $63-$125
(918) 786-6900
(800) 528-1234
(877) 785-6725

GUTHRIE

BEST WESTERN TERRITORIAL INN
2323 Territorial Tr (73044)
Rates: $61-$71
(405) 282-8831
(800) 528-1234
(888) 282-8831

HARRISON HOUSE INN B&B
124 West Harrison (73044)
Rates: $52-$87
(405) 282-1000
(800) 375-1001

TOWN HOUSE MOTEL
223 E Oklahoma Ave (73044)
Rates: $27-$39
(405) 282-2400

GUYMON

AMBASSADOR INN
1909 NW US 54 (73942)
Rates: $50-$80
(580) 338-5555

BEST WESTERN TOWNSMAN INN
212 NE Hwy 54 (73942)
Rates: $55-$95
(580) 338-6556
(800) 528-1234
(800) 245-0335

AREA CODES - If the local number doesn't connect, check for a new area code.

ECONO LODGE
923 Hwy 54 E
(73942)
Rates: $38-$45
(580) 338-5431
(800) 424-6423

SUPER 8 MOTEL
1201 Hwy 54 NE
(73942)
Rates: $50-$90
(580) 338-0507
(800) 800-8000

HEAVENER

GREEN COUNTRY INN
Hwy 59 North
(74937)
Rates: $49-$59
(918) 653-7801

HENRYETTA

GREEN COUNTRY INN
2004 Old Hwy 75 W (74437)
Rates: $35-$42
(918) 652-9988

HOOKER

SUNSET MOTEL
710 Hwy 54
(73945)
Rates: $23-$30
(405) 652-3250

IDABEL

COMFORT SUITES
400 SE Lincoln Blvd (74745)
Rates: $70-$85
(580) 286-9393
(800) 424-6423

MICROTEL INN
2906 NW Texas St
(74745)
Rates: $49-$64
(580) 286-4466

KINGSTON

LAKE TEXOMA RESORT
US 70 E (73439)
Rates: $62-$96
(580) 564-2311
(800) 654-8240

LAWTON

BAYMONT INN & SUITES
1203 NW 40th St
(73506)
Rates: $69-$89
(580) 353-5581
(877) 229-6668

BEST WESTERN HOTEL
1125 E Gore Blvd
(73501)
Rates: $78-$88
(580) 353-0200
(800) 528-1234

DAYS INN
3110 Cache Rd
(73505)
Rates: $45-$150
(580) 353-3104
(800) 329-7466

MOTEL 6
202 SE Lee Blvd
(73501)
Rates: $39-$45
(580) 355-9765
(800) 466-8356

RAMADA INN
601 NW 2nd St
(73507)
Rates: $54-$64
(580) 355-7155
(800) 272-6232

RED LION HOTEL
3134 NW Cache Rd (73505)
Rates: $68-$77
(580) 353-1682
(800) 733-5466

LONE WOLF

QUARTZ MTN RESORT
Rt 1 (73655)
Rates: $50-$88
(800) 654-8240

McALESTER

BEST WESTERN INN
1215 George Nigh Expwy (74501)
Rates: $51-$74
(918) 426-0115
(866) 229-5139

DAYS INN
1217 S George Nigh Expwy (74501)
Rates: $49-$70
(918) 426-5050
(800) 329-7466

ECONO LODGE
731 S George Nigh Expwy (74501)
Rates: $50-$65
(918) 426-4420
(800) 424-6423

HOLIDAY INN EXP HOTEL & SUITES
650 George Nigh Expwy (74501)
Rates: $91-$129
(918) 302-0001
(800) 465-4329

MICROTEL INN
1400 S George Nigh Expwy (74501)
Rates: $49-$65
(918) 429-0910

SUPER 8 MOTEL
2400 S Main Bus 69 (74501)
Rates: $45-$65
(918) 426-5400
(800) 800-8000

MIAMI

BEST WESTERN INN
2225 E Steve Owens Blvd (74354)
Rates: $54-$79
(918) 542-6681
(800) 528-1234
(877) 884-5422

MIDWEST CITY

AMERISUITES
5701 Tinker Diagonal Rd (73110)
Rates: $89-$99
(405) 737-7777
(800) 833-1516

MOTEL 6
6166 Tinker Diagonal Rd (73110)
Rates: $32-$44
(405) 737-6676
(800) 466-8356

STUDIO 6
5801 Tinker Diagonal Rd (73110)
Rates: $45-$62
(405) 737-8851

MOORE

BEST WESTERN GREENTREE INN & SUITES
1811 N Moore Ave (73160)
Rates: $70-$150
(405) 912-8882
(800) 528-1234

MICROTEL INN & SUITES
2400 S Service Rd (73160)
Rates: $50-$69
(405) 799-8181

MOTEL 6
1417 N Moore Ave (73160)
Rates: n/a
(405) 799-6616
(800) 466-8356

SUPER 8 MOTEL
1520 N Service Rd (73160)
Rates: $44-$71
(405) 794-4030
(800) 800-8000

MUSKOGEE

DAYS INN
900 S 32nd St
(74401)
Rates: $49-$79
(918) 683-3911
(800) 329-7466

ECONO LODGE
2018 W Shawnee Ave (74401)
Rates: $49-$79
(918) 683-0101
(800) 424-6423

MOTEL 6
903 S 32nd St
(74401)
Rates: $29-$38
(918) 683-8369
(800) 466-8356

MUSKOGEE INN
2360 E Shawnee Ave (74401)
Rates: $46-$51
(918) 683-6551

RAMADA INN
800 S 32nd St
(74401)
Rates: $50-$95
(918) 682-4341
(800) 272-6232

NORMAN

DAYS INN
609 N Interstate Dr (73069)
Rates: $50-$65
(405) 360-4380
(800) 329-7466

ECONO LODGE
100 26th Dr NW
(73069)
Rates: $55-$75
(405) 364-5554
(800) 424-6423

HOLIDAY INN
1000 N Interstate Dr (73069)
Rates: $164
(405) 364-2882
(800) 465-4329

LA QUINTA INN
930 Ed Noble Dr
(73069)
Rates: $79-$99
(405) 579-4000
(800) 687-6667

QUALITY INN
100 SW 26th Dr
(73069)
Rates: $60-$85
(405) 364-5554
(800) 424-6423

RESIDENCE INN BY MARRIOTT
2681 Jefferson St
(73072)
Rates: $89-$119
(405) 366-0900
(800) 331-3131

OKLAHOMA CITY

AMERISUITES AIRPORT
1818 S Meridian Ave (73108)
Rates: $99-$104
(405) 682-3900
(800) 833-1516

AMERISUITES QUAIL SPRINGS
3201 W Memorial Dr (73134)
Rates: $99-$104
(405) 749-1595
(800) 833-1516

BEST WESTERN MEMORIAL INN & SUITES
NW Quadrant of W Memorial Rd & Western Ave (73114)
Rates: $60-$110
(800) 528-1234

BEST WESTERN SADDLEBACK INN
4300 SW 3rd St (73108)
Rates: $74-$94
(405) 947-7000
(800) 528-1234
(800) 228-3903

BEST WESTERN TRADE WINDS CENTRAL INN
1800 E Reno (73117)
Rates: $55-$70
(405) 235-4531
(800) 528-1234
(800) 615-2647

CANDLEWOOD SUITES
4400 River Park Dr (73108)
Rates: $79-$98
(405) 680-8770
(888) 226-3539

CLARION HOTEL AIRPORT
737 S Meridian Ave (73108)
Rates: $59-$99
(405) 942-8511
(800) 424-6423

COMFORT INN
4240 W I-40 Service Rd (73108)
Rates: $65-$70
(405) 943-4400
(800) 424-6423

COMFORT INN AT FOUNDERS TOWER
5704 Mosteller Dr (73112)
Rates: $62-$99
(405) 810-1100
(800) 424-6423

COMFORT INN NORTH
4625 NE 120th St (73131)
Rates: $59-$130
(405) 478-7282
(800) 424-6423

COMFORT INN & SUITES
5405 N Lincoln Blvd (73105)
Rates: $49-$69
(405) 528-7563
(800) 424-6423

DAYS INN NORTH
12013 I-35 N Service Rd (73131)
Rates: $49-$135
(405) 478-2554
(800) 329-7466

DAYS INN NORTHWEST
2801 NW 39th St (73112)
Rates: $45-$80
(405) 946-0741
(800) 329-7466

DAYS INN SOUTH
2616 I-35 S (73129)
Rates: $45-$75
(405) 677-0521
(800) 329-7466

DAYS INN WEST
504 S Meridian (73108)
Rates: $54-$64
(405) 942-8294
(800) 329-7466

ECONO LODGE
4601 SW Third St (73128)
Rates: $42-$46
(405) 942-5955
(800) 424-6423

ECONO LODGE
8200 W I-40 Service Rd (73128)
Rates: $40-$50
(405) 787-7051
(800) 424-6423

EMBASSY SUITES
1815 S Meridian Ave (73108)
Rates: $99-$179
(405) 682-6000
(800) 362-2779

FOUR POINTS BY SHERATON
6300 Terminal Dr (73159)
Rates: $90
(405) 681-3500
(800) 325-3535

HILTON HOTEL NORTHWEST
2945 NW Expwy (73112)
Rates: $69-$154
(405) 848-4811
(800) 445-8667

HOLIDAY INN EXP
13520 Plaza Terrace (73120)
Rates: $60-$85
(405) 755-8686
(800) 465-4329

HOLIDAY INN HOTEL & SUITES
6200 N Robinson (73118)
Rates: $77
(405) 843-5558
(800) 465-4329

HOWARD JOHNSON EXP
400 S Meridian Ave (73108)
Rates: $47-$68
(405) 943-9841
(800) 446-4656

LA QUINTA INN AIRPORT
800 S Meridian Ave (73108)
Rates: $79-$99
(405) 942-0040
(800) 687-6667

LA QUINTA INN-SOUTH
8315 I-35 S (73149)
Rates: $69-$89
(405) 631-8661
(800) 687-6667

LA QUINTA INN & SUITES
4829 NW Expwy (73131)
Rates: $89-$109
(4050 773-5575
(800) 687-6667

MARRIOTT HOTEL
3233 NW Expwy (73112)
Rates: $132-$169
(405) 842-6633
(800) 228-9290

MOTEL 6
12121 NE Expwy (73131)
Rates: $31-$42
(405) 478-4030
(800) 466-8356

MOTEL 6-AIRPORT
820 S Meridian Ave (73108)
Rates: $34-$42
(405) 946-6662
(800) 466-8356

MOTEL 6-WEST
4200 W I-40 (73108)
Rates: $36-$44
(405) 947-6550
(800) 466-8356

QUALITY INN NORTH
12001 N I-25 Service Rd (73131)
Rates: $50-$100
(405) 478-0400
(800) 424-6423

QUALITY INN SOUTHWEST
7800 C A Henderson Blvd (73139)
Rates: $69-$85
(405) 632-6666
(800) 424-6423

RAMADA LTD
2727 I-44 W Service Rd (73117)
Rates: $48-$73
(405) 948-8000
(800) 272-6232

RAMADA LTD
1400 63rd St (73111)
Rates: $49-$79
(405) 478-5221
(800) 272-6232

RENAISSANCE HOTEL
10 N Broadway Ave (73102)
Rates: $189-$209
(405) 228-8000
(800) 468-3571

RESIDENCE INN BY MARRIOTT
4361 W Reno (73107)
Rates: $105-$135
(405) 942-4500
(800) 331-3131

RESIDENCE INN BY MARRIOTT CROSSROADS MALL
1111 E I240 Service Rd (73149)
Rates: $109-$145
(405) 634-9696
(800) 331-3131

RODEWAY INN WEST
720 S MacArthur Blvd (73128)
Rates: $45-$55
(405) 943-2393
(800) 424-6423

SHERATON HOTEL
One N Broadway Ave (73102)
Rates: $199-$239
(405) 235-2780
(800) 325-3535

SLEEP INN, INN & SUITES
12024 122nd St (73131)
Rates: $60-$90
(405) 478-9898
(800) 424-6423

STUDIO 6
5801 Tinker Diagonal (73110)
Rates: $209-$269
(405) 737-8851
(888) 897-0202

THE WATERFORD MARRIOTT
6300 Waterford Blvd (73118)
Rates: $71-$195
(405) 848-4782
(800) 228-9290

OKMULGEE
BEST WESTERN INN
3499 N Wood Dr (74447)
Rates: $61-$71
(918) 756-9200
(800) 528-1234
(800) 552-9201

DAYS INN
1221 S Wood Dr (74447)
Rates: $50-$60
(918) 758-0660
(800) 329-7466

PAULS VALLEY
AMISH INN MOTEL
3101 W Grant Ave (73075)
Rates: $26-$36
(405) 238-7545

DAYS INN
3203 W Grant Ave
(73075)
Rates: $55-$80
(405) 238-7548
(800) 329-7466

GARDEN INN MOTEL
S Hwy 19 & I-35
(73075)
Rates: $22-$31
(405) 238-7313

PERRY

**BEST WESTERN
CHEROKEE STRIP
MOTEL**
I-35 Exit 185 (73077)
Rates: $48-$60
(580) 336-2218
(800) 528-1234

DAN-D-MOTEL
515 Fir St (73077)
Rates: $18-$24
(580) 336-4463

PONCA CITY

HOLIDAY INN
2215 N 14th St
(74601)
Rates: $79-$108
(580) 762-8311
(800) 465-4329

POTEAU

**BEST WESTERN
TRADERS INN**
3111 N Broadway
(74953)
Rates: $50-$75
(918 647-4001
(800) 528-1234
(888) 264-5838

PRYOR

**COMFORT
INN & SUITES**
307 Mid America
Dr (74361)
Rates: $59-$119
(918) 476-6660
(800) 424-6423

DAYS INN
Hwy 69 S & 69A
(74362)
Rates: $40-$70
(918) 825-7600
(800) 329-7466

MICROTEL INN
315 Mid America
Dr (74361)
Rates: n/a
(918) 476-4661

**PRYOR HOUSE
MOTOR INN**
123 S Mill (74361)
Rates: $32-$42
(918) 825-6677

PURCELL

ECONO LODGE
2500 Hwy 74 S
(73080)
Rates: $45-$60
(405) 527-5603
(800) 424-6423

ROLAND

DAYS INN
207 Cherokee
Blvd (74954)
Rates: $60-$65
(918) 427-1000
(800) 329-7466

SALLISAW

**BEST WESTERN
BLUE RIBBON INN**
706 S Kerr Blvd
(74955)
Rates: $60-$100
(918) 775-6294
(800) 528-1234

DAYS INN
1700 W Cherokee
(74955)
Rates: $36-$65
(918) 775-4406
(800) 329-7466

ECONO LODGE
2403 E Cherokee
(74955)
Rates: $35-$46
(918) 775-7981
(800) 424-6423

**GOLDEN
SPUR INN**
601 S Kerr Blvd
(74955)
Rates: $26-$34
(918) 775-4443

**MICROTEL INN &
SUITES**
710 S Kerr Blvd
(74955)
Rates: $43-$64
(918) 774-0400

MOTEL 6
1300 E Cherokee
(74955)
Rates: $30-$38
(918) 775-6000
(800) 466-8356

SAND SPRINGS

BEST WESTERN INN
211 S Lake Dr
(74063)
Rates: $59-$99
(918) 245-4999
(800) 528-1234
(888) 297-7466

DAYS INN
1110 Charles Page
Blvd (74063)
Rates: $30-$72
(918) 245-0283
(800) 329-7466

SAPULPA

SUPER 8 MOTEL
1505 New Sapulpa
Rd (74066)
Rates: $45-$54
(918) 227-3300
(800) 800-8000

SAVANNA

TRAVELODGE
Hwy 69 & Panola
St (74565)
Rates: $35-$75
(918) 548-3506
(800) 578-7878

SAYRE

**AMERICINN
LODGE & SUITES**
2405 S El Camino
Rd (73662)
Rates: $70-$137
(580) 928-2700
(800) 634-3444

SHAWNEE

MOTEL 6
4981 N Harrison
St (74801)
Rates: $37-$47
(405) 275-5310
(800) 466-8356

RAMADA INN
4900 N Harrison
St (74801)
Rates: $58-$75
(405) 275-4404
(800) 272-6232

STILLWATER

**BEST WESTERN
INN**
600 E McElroy
(74075)
Rates: $65-$99
(405) 377-7010
(800) 528-1234
(800) 353-6894

DAYS INN
5010 W 6th St
(74074)
Rates: $35-$70
(405) 743-2570
(800) 329-7466

HOLIDAY INN
2515 W 6th St
(74074)
Rates: $45-$62
(405) 372-0800
(800) 465-4329

MOTEL 6
5122 W 6th
(74074)
Rates: $34+
(405) 624-0433
(800) 466-8356

STROUD

**BEST WESTERN
STROUD MOTOR
LODGE**
1200 N 8th Ave
(74079)
Rates: $49-$62
(918) 968-9515
(800) 528-1234

TAHLEQUAH

**OAK HILL
MOTEL SUITES**
2600 S Muskogee
(74464)
Rates: $51-$70
(918) 458-1200

TONKAWA

WESTERN INN
I-35 & US 60
(74653)
Rates: $34-$44
(580) 628-2577

TULSA

AMERISUITES
7037 S Zurich Ave
(74136)
Rates: $104-$139
(918) 491-4010
(800) 833-1516

**BAYMONT INN
& SUITES**
4530 E Skelly Dr
(74135)
Rates: $55-$61
(918) 488-8777
(877) 229-6668

**BEST WESTERN
TRADEWINDS
CENTRAL INN**
3141 E Skelly Dr
(74105)
Rates: $55-$80
(918) 749-5561
(800) 528-1234
(800) 685-4564

COMFORT SUITES
8338 E 61st St
South (74133)
Rates: $65-$99
(918) 254-0088
(800) 424-6423

DAYS INN
5525 W Skelly Dr
(74107)
Rates: $34-$60
(918) 446-1561
(800) 329-7466

DAYS INN EAST
8201 E Skelly Dr
(74129)
Rates: $47-$62
(918) 665-6800
(800) 329-7466

**DOUBLETREE
HOTEL**
6110 S Yale Ave
(74136)
Rates: $79-$189
(918) 495-1000
(800) 222-8733

**DOUBLETREE
HOTEL-DOWN-
TOWN**
616 W 7th St
(74127)
Rates: $79-$179
(918) 587-8000
(800) 222-8733

**ECONO LODGE
& SUITES**
3217 S 79th E
(74145)
Rates: $41-$69
(918) 624-2800
(800) 424-6423

**HILTON
SOUTHERN HILLS**
7902 S Lewis
(74136)
Rates: $69-$169
(918) 492-5000
(800) 445-8667

AREA CODES - If the local number doesn't connect, check for a new area code.

HOLIDAY INN INT'L AIRPORT
1010 N Garnett Rd (74116)
Rates: $96-$116
(918) 437-7660
(800) 465-4329

HOLIDAY INN SELECT
5000 E Skelly Dr (74135)
Rates: $129
(918) 622-7000
(800) 465-4329

HOLIDAY INN EXP WOODLAND HILLS
9010 E 71st St (74133)
Rates: $65-$90
(918) 459-5321
(800) 465-4329

HOTEL AMBASSADOR
1324 A Main St (74119)
Rates: $149-$240
(918) 587-8200

LA QUINTA INN
10829 E 41st St (74146)
Rates: $69-$79
(918) 665-0220
(800) 687-6667

LA QUINTA INN-AIRPORT
35 N Sheridan Rd (74115)
Rates: $64-$82
(918) 836-3931
(800) 687-6667

LA QUINTA INN CENTRAL
6030 E Skelly Dr (74135)
Rates: $65-$89
(918) 665-2630
(800) 687-6667

LA QUINTA INN-S
12525 E 52nd St (74146)
Rates: $69-$89
(918) 254-1626
(800) 687-6667

MICROTEL INN & SUITES
4531 E 21st St (74114)
Rates: $39-$65
(918) 858-3775
(888) 771-7171

MICROTEL INN
16518 E Admiral Pl (74116)
Rates: $41-$65
(918) 234-9100
(888) 771-7171

MOTEL 6-EAST
1011 S Garnett Rd (74128)
Rates: $29-$36
(918) 234-6200
(800) 466-8356

MOTEL 6-WEST
5828 W Skelly Dr (74107)
Rates: $29-$36
(918) 445-0223
(800) 466-8356

RAMADA INN
3131 E 51st St (74105)
Rates: $60-$85
(918) 743-9811
(800) 272-6232

RAMADA INN
8181 E Skelly Dr (74119)
Rates: n/a
(918) 663-4541
(800) 272-6232

RED ROOF INN
4717 S Yale Ave (74135)
Rates: $47-$90
(918) 622-6776
(800) 843-7663

RENAISSANCE HOTEL & CONV CTR
6808 S 107th E Ave (74133)
Rates: $98-$189
(918) 307-2600

RESIDENCE INN BY MARRIOTT
11025 E 73rd St (74133)
Rates: $89-$119
(918) 250-4850
(800) 331-3131

RODEWAY INN & SUITES
8181 E 41st St (74145)
Rates: $55-$95
(918) 664-7241
(800) 228-2000

SHERATON HOTEL
10918 E 41st St (74105)
Rates: $99-$165
(918) 627-5000
(800) 325-3535

SLEEP INN, INN & SUITES CENTRAL
8021 E 33rd St South (74145)
Rates: $73-$109
(918) 663-2777
(800) 424-6423

STAYBRIDGE SUITES
11111 E 73rd St South (74133)
Rates: $105-$110
(918) 461-2100
(800) 238-8000

SUPER 8 MOTEL
5811 S 49th West Ave (74107)
Rates: $33-$60
(918) 446-6000
(800) 800-8000

VINITA

PARK HILLS MOTEL
Rt 4, Box 292 (74301)
Rates: $20-$28
(918) 256-5511

WAGONOR

INDIAN LODGE MOTEL
SH 51 E (74467)
Rates: $32-$70
(918) 485-3184

WESTERN HILLS GUEST RANCH
SH 51 (74477)
Rates: $45-$98
(918) 772-2545

WATONGA

ROMAN NOSE RESORT
Rt 1 (73772)
Rates: $45-$68
(580) 623-7281

WEATHERFORD

BEST WESTERN MARK MOTOR HOTEL
525 E Main St (73096)
Rates: $48-$79
(580) 772-3325
(800) 528-1234
(800) 598-3089

COMFORT INN & SUITES
Main St & Washington St NE (73096)
Rates: $55-$100
(580) 772-1900
(800) 424-6423

WOODWARD

DAYS INN
1212 NW Hwy 270 (73801)
Rates: $40-$60
(580) 256-1546
(800) 329-7466

NORTHWEST INN
Hwy 270 & 1st St (73801)
Rates: $65-$85
(580) 256-7600

RED COUNTRY INN
2314 8th St (73801)
Rates: $30-$39
(580) 254-9147

WAYFARER INN
2901 Williams Ave (73801)
Rates: $35-$52
(580) 256-5553

YUKON

BEST WESTERN INN & SUITES
11440 W I-40 Service Rd (73099)
Rates: $55-$80
(405) 265-2995
(800) 528-1234
(877) 429-4795

AREA CODES - If the local number doesn't connect, check for a new area code.

OREGON

AGNESS

**SINGING
SPRINGS RESORT**
34501 Agness
Illahe Rd (97406)
Rates: $45-$85
(541) 247-6162

ALBANY

**BEST WESTERN
INN**
315 Airport Rd SE
(97321)
Rates: $59-$99
(541) 928-6322
(800) 528-1234
(866) 890-0519

**DAYS INN
& SUITES**
1100 Price Rd SE
(97321)
Rates: $49-$145
(541) 928-5050
(800) 329-7466

**LA QUINTA INN &
SUITES**
251 Airport Rd SE
(97321)
Rates: $69-$89
(541) 928-0921
(800) 687-6667

MOTEL 6
2735 E Pacific
Blvd (97321)
Rates: $43-$50
(541) 926-4233
(800) 466-8356

**PHOENIX INN
SUITES**
3410 Spicer Rd SE
(97322)
Rates: $69-$99
(541) 926-5696
(888) 889-0208

ARLINGTON

**VILLAGE INN
MOTEL**
410 Beech St
(97812)
Rates: $40-$60
(541) 454-2646

ASHLAND

**ASHLAND
SPRINGS
HISTORIC HOTEL**
212 E Main St
(97520)
Rates: $89-$209
(541) 488-5400
(800) 426-0670

**ASHLAND
PATTERSON
HOUSE B&B**
639 N Main St
(97520)
Rates: $70-$105
(541) 482-9171
(888) 482-9171

**ASHLAND
TIMBERS MOTEL**
1450 Ashland St
(97520)
Rates: n/a
(541) 482-4242
(866) 550-4400

**BEST WESTERN
BARD'S INN**
132 N Main St
(97520)
Rates: $72-$184
(541) 482-0049
(800) 528-1234
(800) 533-9627

**BEST WESTERN
WINDSOR INN**
2520 Ashland St
(97520)
Rates: $79-$139
(541) 488-2330
(800) 528-1234
(800) 334-2330

**CEDARWOOD
INN**
1801 Siskiyou
Blvd (97520)
Rates: $59-$105
(541) 488-2000
(800) 547-4141

FLAGSHIP INN
1193 Siskiyou
Blvd (97520)
Rates: $59-$109
(541) 482-2641

**KNIGHTS INN
MOTEL**
2359 Hwy 66
(97520)
Rates: $52-$88
(541) 482-5111
(800) 843-5644

**LA QUINTA
INN & SUITES**
434 Valley View
Rd (97520)
Rates: $65-$129
(541) 482-6932
(800) 687-6667

**PLAZA INN &
SUITES AT
ASHLAND CREEK**
98 Central Ave
(97520)
Rates: $69-$249
(541) 488-8900
(888) 488-0358

SUPER 8 MOTEL
2350 Ashland St
(97520)
Rates: $50-$110
(541) 482-8887
(800) 800-8000

TIMBERS MOTEL
1450 Ashland St
(97520)
Rates: $46-$97
(541) 482-4242

**WINDMILL'S
ASHLAND HILLS
INN & SUITES**
2525 Ashland St
(97520)
Rates: $53-$250
(541) 482-8310
(800) 547-4747

ASTORIA

**BEST WESTERN
ASTORIA INN**
555 Hamburg
(97103)
Rates: $79-$259
(503) 325-2205
(800) 528-1234
(800) 621-0641

CLEMENTINE'S B&B
847 Exchange St
(97103)
Rates: $65-$150
(503) 325-2005
(800) 521-6801

CREST MOTEL
5366 Leif Erickson
Dr (97103)
Rates: $65-$138
(503) 325-3141
(800) 421-3141

**HISTORIC
HOTEL ELLIOTT**
357 12th St (97103)
Rates: $105-$135
(503) 325-2222
(877) 378-1924

**HOLIDAY INN EXP
HOTEL & SUITES**
204 W Marine Dr
(97103)
Rates: $89-$239
(503) 325-6222
(800) 465-4329
(888) 898-6222

RED LION INN
400 Industry St
(97103)
Rates: $69-$129
(503) 325-7373
(800) 733-5466

**ROSE RIVER INN
B&B**
1510 Franklin Ave
(97103)
Rates: $80-$140
(503) 325-7175
(800) 876-0028

BAKER CITY

**BAKER CITY
MOTEL**
880 Elm St (97814)
Rates: $28-$37
(541) 523-6391
(800) 931-9229

**BEST WESTERN
SUNRIDGE INN**
1 Sunridge Ln
(97814)
Rates: $69-$180
(541) 523-6444
(800) 233-2368

**BRIDGE
STREET INN**
134 Bridge St (97814)
Rates: $32-$65
(541) 523-6571
(800) 932-9220

ELDORADO INN
695 Campbell
(97814)
Rates: $45-$80
(541) 523-6494
(800) 537-5756

**GEISER GRAND
HISTORIC HOTEL**
1996 Main St
(97814)
Rates: $79-$209
(541) 523-1889
(888) 434-7374

**GREEN GABLES
MOTEL**
2533 10th St (97814)
Rates: $30+
(541) 523-5588

**OREGON
TRAIL MOTEL**
211 Bridge St (97814)
Rates: $35-$70
(541) 523-5844
(800) 628-3982

**POWDER RIVER
BED & BREAKFAST**
HCR 87, Box 500
(97814)
Rates: $60-$65
(541) 523-7143
(800) 600-7143

RODEWAY INN
810 Campbell St
(97814)
Rates: $45-$80
(541) 523-2242
(800) 424-6423

TRAIL MOTEL
2815 10th St
(97814)
Rates: n/a
(541) 523-4646

AREA CODES - If the local number doesn't connect, check for a new area code.

WARNERS SLOUGH HOUSE B & B
Rt 2, Box 135 (97814)
Rates: n/a
(541) 523-6196

WELCOME INN
175 Campbell St (97814)
Rates: $47-$63
(541) 523-3431

THE WESTERN MOTEL
3055 10th St (97814)
Rates: $30-$35
(541) 523-3700
(800) 481-3701

BANDON

BANDON WAYSIDE MOTEL
1175 2nd St SE (97411)
Rates: $40-$80
(541) 347-3421

BEST WESTERN INN AT FACE ROCK
3225 Beach Loop Rd (97411)
Rates: $88-$254
(541) 347-9441
(800) 528-1234
(800) 638-3092

CAPRICE MOTEL
Rt 1, Box 530 (97411)
Rates: $34-$60
(541) 347-4494

DRIFTWOOD MOTEL
460 Hwy 101 (97411)
Rates: $45-$100
(541) 347-9022

GORMAN MOTEL AT COQUILLE PT
1110 11th St SW (97411)
Rates: $65-$95
(541) 347-9451
(866) 347-9451

HARBOR VIEW MOTEL
355 Hwy 101 (97411)
Rates: $69-$129
(541) 347-4417
(800) 526-0209

LA KRIS MOTEL
Hwy 101 S at 9th St (97411)
Rates: $42-$85
(541) 347-3610
(888) 496-3610

SHOOTING STAR MOTEL
1640 Oregon Ave SW (97411)
Rates: $55-$75
(541) 347-9192

SUNSET OCEANFRONT LODGING
1865 Beach Loop Dr SW (97411)
Rates: $55-$175
(541) 347-2453
(800) 842-2407

TABLE ROCK MOTEL
840 Beach Loop Rd (97411)
Rates: $40-$235
(541) 347-2700
(800) 457-9141

BEATTY

BEATTY MOTEL
Hwy 140, P.O.Box 335 (97621)
Rates: n/a
(541) 533-2689

BEAVERTON

ALOHA JUNCTION INN & GARDEN B&B
5085 SW 170th Ave (97007)
Rates: $59-$75
(503) 642-7236
(888) 832-5251

BEST WESTERN GREENWOOD INN & SUITES
10700 SW Allen Blvd (97005)
Rates: $69-$109
(503) 643-7444
(800) 528-1234
(800) 289-1300

BUDGET INN
12255 SW Canyon Rd (97005)
Rates: $40-$55
(503) 643-6621
(866) 286-9661

COMFORT INN & SUITES WEST
13455 SW Canyon Rd (97005)
Rates: $59-$139
(503) 643-9100
(800)424-6423

HOMEWOOD SUITES BY HILTON
15525 NW Gateway Ct (97005)
Rates: $109-$119
(503) 614-0900
(800) 225-5466

PEPPERTREE INN
10720 SW Allen Blve (97005)
Rates: $49-$69
(503) 641-7477
(800) 453-6219

BEND

ARLINE MCDONALD'S VACATION HOMES
1530 NW Jacksonville (97701)
Rates: $150-$250
(541) 382-4534

BEST WESTERN INN & SUITES
721 NE 3rd St (97701)
Rates: $69-$129
(541) 382-1515
(800) 528-1234

CASCADE MOTEL LODGE
420 SE 3rd St (97702)
Rates: $85
(541) 382-2612
(800) 852-6031

CASCADE VIEW RANCH GUEST HOUSE
60435 Tekampe Rd (97702)
Rates: $150-$285
(541) 388-5658

CHALET MOTEL
510 SE 3rd St (97702)
Rates: $29-$40
(541) 382-6124

CIMARRON NORTH
437 NE 3rd St (97701)
Rates: $39-$54
(541) 382-7711
(800) 304-4050

CRICKETWOOD B&B & COTTAGE
63520 Cricketwood Rd (97701)
Rates: $90-$130
(541) 330-0747
(877) 330-0747

CULTUS LAKE RESORT
P.O. Box 262 (97709)
Rates: $52-$89
(541) 389-3230

ECONO LODGE
3705 N US Hwy 97 (97701)
Rates: $35-$89
(541) 382-2211
(800) 424-6423

ENTRADA LODGE
19221 Century Dr (97702)
Rates: $69-$109
(541) 382-4080

FAIRFIELD INN & SUITES
1626 NW Hill St (97701)
Rates: $79-$149
(541) 318-1747
(800) 228-2800

GUEST HOUSE B&B
20020 Glen Vista Rd (97702)
Rates: n/a
(541) 382-8565

HAMPTON INN
15 NE Butler Market Rd (97701)
Rates: $69-$99
(541) 388-4114
(800) 426-7866

HOLIDAY INN EXP HOTEL & SUITES
20615 Grandview Dr (97701)
Rates: $80-$199
(541) 317-8500
(800) 465-4329

HOLIDAY MOTEL
880 SE 3rd St (97702)
Rates: $34-$38
(541) 382-4620
(800) 252-0121

INN OF THE SEVENTH MOUNTAIN
18575 SW Century Dr (97702)
Rates: $89-$125
(541) 382-8711

LA QUINA INN & SUITES
61200 S Business Hwy 97 (97702)
Rates: $69-$119
(541) 388-2227
(800) 687-6667

MOTEL 6
201 NE 3rd St (97701)
Rates: $45-$60
(541) 382-8282
(800) 466-8356

MOTEL WEST
228 NE Irving (97701)
Rates: $36-$50
(541) 389-5577
(800) 282-5577

QUALITY INN
20600 Grandview Dr (97701)
Rates: $45-$99
(541) 318-0848
(800) 424-6423

RED LION-NORTH
1415 NE 3rd St (97701)
Rates: $64-$99
(541) 382-7011
(800) 733-5466

RED LION-SOUTH
849 NE 3rd St (97701)
Rates: $84-$99
(541) 382-8384
(800) 733-5466

THE RIVERHOUSE RESORT HOTEL
3075 N Business 97 (97701)
Rates: $67-$125
(541) 389-3111
(866) 557-6574

AREA CODES - If the local number doesn't connect, check for a new area code.

RODEWAY INN
3705 N Hwy 97
(97701)
Rates: $39-$89
(541) 382-2211
(800) 424-6423
(800) 507-2211

SCANDIA PINES LODGE
61405 S Hwy 97
(97702)
Rates: $39-$89
(541) 389-5910
(800) 500-5910

SHILO SUITES HOTEL
3105 O B Riley Rd
(97701)
Rates: $89-$225
(541) 389-9600
(800) 222-2244

SLEEP INN
600 NE Bellevue
(97701)
Rates: $59-$89
(541) 330-0050
(800) 424-6423

SONOMA LODGE
450 SE 3rd St
(97702)
Rates: $32-$89
(541) 382-4891

SUPER 8 MOTEL
1275 S Hwy 97
(97702)
Rates: $59-$97
(541) 388-6888
(800) 800-8000

SWALLOW RIDGE BED & BREAKFAST
65711 Twin
Bridges Rd (97701)
Rates: $50-$70
(541) 389-1913

WESTWARD HO MOTEL
904 SE 3rd St
(97702)
Rates: $30-$99
(541) 382-2111
(800) 999-8143

BLUE RIVER

HOLIDAY FARM RESORT B&B
54455 McKenzie
River Dr (97413)
Rates: $135-$375
(541) 822-3715
(800) 823-3715

MCKENZIE RIVER CONF CENTER
54705 McKenzie
Hwy (97413)
Rates: $20-$40
(541) 431-4667
(800) 844-4947

BOARDMAN

DODGE CITY INN
100 NW 1st St
(97818)
Rates: $43-$68
(541) 481-2451

ECONO LODGE
105 Front St SW
(97818)
Rates: $50-$80
(541) 481-2375
(800) 424-6423

RIVERVIEW MOTEL
200 Front St (97818)
Rates: $32-$42
(541) 481-2775

BRIGHTWOOD

MT. HOOD HIDEAWAYS
63045 E
Brightwod Loop
#539 (97049)
Rates: $110-$180
(503) 348-3967

MT. HOOD RIVER-FRONT CABINS
70386 E Zigzag
(97049)
Rates: $70-$200
(503) 939-9491
(800) 524-9251

BROOKINGS

BEST WESTERN BEACHFRONT INN
16608 Boat Basin
Rd (97415)
Rates: $109-$285
(541) 469-7779
(800) 528-1234
(800) 468-4081

BEAVER STATE MOTEL
437 Chetco Ave
(97415)
Rates: $39-$55
(541) 469-5361

CHART HOUSE OUTFITTERS
15833 Pedrioli Rd
(97415)
Rates: $38-$75
(541) 469-3867
(800) 290-6208

PACIFIC SUNSET INN
1144 Chetco Ave
(97415)
Rates: $34-$58
(541) 469-2141
(800) 469-2141

SEA DREAMER INN B&B
15167 McVay Ln
(97415)
Rates: $38-$75
(541) 469-6629
(800) 408-4367

WESTWARD MOTEL
1026 Chetco Ave
(97415)
Rates: $55-$150
(541) 469-7471

WHALESHEAD BEACH RESORT
19921 Whaleshead
Rd (97415)
Rates: n/a
(541) 469-7446
(800) 943-4325

BURNS

BEST INN
999 Oregon Ave
(97720)
Rates: $52-$60
(541) 573-1700
(800) 237-8466

DAYS INN
577 W Monroe
(97720)
Rates: $36-$50
(541) 573-2047
(800) 329-7466

SILVER SPUR MOTEL
789 N Bdwy
(97720)
Rates: $39-$62
(541) 573-2077
(800) 400-2077

CAMP SHERMAN

BLACK BUTTE RESORT MOTEL
25635 SW Forest
Service Rd (97730)
Rates: $60-$70
(541) 595-6514
(877) 595-6514

COLD SPRINGS RESORT
25615 Cold
Springs Resort Ln
(97730)
Rates: $103-$145
(541) 595-6271

LAKE CREEK LODGE
13375 SW Forest
Service Rd #1419
(97730)
Rates: n/a
(541) 595-6331
(800) 797-6331

TWIN VIEW RESORT
13860 SW FS Rd
1419 (97730)
Rates: $66-$98
(541) 595-6125

CANNON BEACH

CANNON BEACH ECOLA CREEK LODGE
208 5th St (97110)
Rates: $109-$219
(503) 436-2776
(800) 873-2749

CANNON VILLAGE MOTEL
3163 S Hemlock St
(97110)
Rates: $40-$130
(503) 436-2317

ECOLA INN RESORT MOTEL
1164 Ecola Ct
(97110)
Rates: $81-$86
(503) 436-2457

HALLMARK RESORT
1400 S Hemlock St
(97110)
Rates: $69-$299
(503) 436-1566
(888) 448-4449

HAYSTACK RESORT MOTEL
3339 S Hemlock St
(97110)
Rates: $119-$189
(503) 436-1577
(800) 499-2220

INN AT CANNON BEACH
3215 S Hemlock
(97110)
Rates: $99-$229
(503) 436-9085
(800) 321-6304

MCBEE MOTEL COTTAGES
888 S Hemlock St
(97110)
Rates: $35-$135
(503) 436-2569
(800) 238-4107

THE OCEAN LODGE
2864 S Pacific St
(7110)
Rates: $159-$289
(503) 436-2241
(888) 777-4047

QUIET CANNON LODGINGS
372 N Spruce St
(97110)
Rates: $95-$105
(503) 436-1405

SANDCASTLE MOTEL CONDOS
3188 S Hemlock
(97110)
Rates: $65-$235
(503) 436-2021
(877) 386-3402

SURF SAND RESORT
148 W Gower
(97110)
Rates: $129-$319
(503) 436-2274
(800) 547-6100

TOLOVANA INN
3400 S Hemlock St
(97110)
Rates: $65-$289
(503) 436-2211
(800) 333-8890

AREA CODES - If the local number doesn't connect, check for a new area code.

**VAN BUREN
LIGHTHOUSE INN**
963 S Hemlock
(97110)
Rates: $59-$159
(503) 436-2929
(866) 265-1686

CANYONVILLE
**BEST WESTERN
CANYONVILLE
INN & SUITES**
200 Creekside Rd
(97417)
Rates: $63-$159
(541) 839-4200
(800) 528-1234

RIVERSIDE LODGE
1786 Stanton Park
Rd (97417)
Rates: $35-$75
(541) 839-4557

CASCADE
LOCKS
**BEST WESTERN
COLUMBIA RIVER
INN**
735 Wanapa St
(97014)
Rates: $69-$159
(541) 374-8777
(800) 528-1234
(800) 595-7108

**SCANDIAN
MOTOR LODGE**
25 Oneonta St
(97014)
Rates: $32-$48
(541) 374-8417

CAVE
JUNCTION
**COUNTRY HILLS
RESORT**
7901 Caves Hwy
(97523)
Rates: $49-$70
(541) 592-3406
(800) 997-8464

**RUSK RANCH
COUNTRY
COTTAGE**
27742 Redwood
Hwy, Box 270
(97523)
Rates: $48-$75
(541) 592-4658

CHARLESTON
**CAPTAIN JOHN'S
MOTEL**
63360 Kingfisher
Dr (97420)
Rates: $40-$125
(541) 888-4041

CHEMULT
CHEMULT MOTEL
Hwy 97 (97731)
Rates: $38-$44
(541) 365-2228

**CRATER LAKE
MOTEL**
109482 Hwy 97
(97731)
Rates: $35-$89
(541) 365-2241

**DAWSON HOUSE
LODGE**
109455 Hwy 97 N
(97731)
Rates: $50-$100
(541) 365-2232
(888) 281-8375

FEATHERBED INN
108915 Hwy 97 N
(97731)
Rates: $30-$120
(541) 365-2235

**HOLIDAY
VILLAGE MOTEL**
Hwy 97, Milepost
209 (97731)
Rates: $32-$85
(541) 365-2394

**SINGING PINES
RANCH MOTEL**
Hwy 97, Box 117
(97731)
Rates: n/a
(541) 365-9909

**WHISPERING
PINES MOTEL**
Hwy 138 & 97
(97604)
Rates: n/a
(541) 365-2259

CHILOQUIN
**AGENCY LAKE
RESORT**
37000 Modoc Rd
(97624)
Rates: $30-$45
(541) 783-2489

MELITA'S MOTEL
39500 Hwy 97 N
(97624)
Rates: $26-$53
(541) 783-2401

**SPORTSMAN'S
MOTEL**
27627 Hwy 97 N
(97624)
Rates: $27-$45
(541) 783-2867
(888) 905-9074

**SPRING CREEK
RANCH MOTEL**
47600 Hwy 97 N
(97624)
Rates: $28-$34
(541) 783-2775
(800) 626-1292

**WILLIAMSON
RIVER RESORT**
31900 Modoc Rd
(97624)
Rates: $25-$50
(541) 783-2071

CHRITSMAS
VALLEY
**LAKESIDE
TERRACE MOTEL**
Spruce St (97641)
Rates: n/a
(541) 576-2309

CLACKAMAS
**CLACKAMAS INN
SUITES**
16010 SE 82nd Dr
(97266)
Rates: $49-$100
(503) 650-5340
(800) 874-6560

CLATSKANIE
**NORTHWOODS
INN**
945 E Columbia
River Hwy
(97016)
Rates: n/a
(503) 728-4311

COLUMBIA
RIVER GORGE
See Cascade
Locks, Hood River,
The Dalles,
Portland and
Troutdale for addi-
tional lodging.

CONDON
CONDON MOTEL
216 N Washington
(97823)
Rates: $38-$60
(541) 384-2181

**HOTEL
CONDON**
202 S Main St
(97823)
Rates: $70-$105
(541) 384-4624
(800) 201-6706

COOS BAY
**BEST WESTERN
HOLIDAY MOTEL**
411 N Bayshore Dr
(97420)
Rates: $69-$159
(541) 269-5111
(800) 528-1234
(800) 228-8655

**COOS BAY
MANOR B&B**
955 S 5th St
(97420)
Rates: $65-$100
(541) 269-1224
(800) 269-1224

EDGEWATER INN
275 E Johnson St
(97420)
Rates: $76-$159
(541) 267-0423
(800) 233-0423

LAZY J MOTEL
1143 Hill St
(97420)
Rates: n/a
(541) 269-9666

MOTEL 6
1445 N Bayshore
Dr (97420)
Rates: $37-$62
(541) 267-7171
(800) 466-8356

PLAINVIEW MOTEL
91904 Cape Arago
Hwy (97420)
Rates: $40-$95
(541) 888-5166
(800) 962-2815

RED LION INN
1313 N Bayshore
Dr (97420)
Rates: $67-$135
(541) 267-4141
(800) 733-5466

**TIMBER LODGE
MOTEL**
1001 N Bayshore
Dr (97420)
Rates: n/a
(541) 267-7066
(800) 782-7592

COQUILLE
**MYRTLE LANE
MOTEL**
787 N Central
Blvd (97423)
Rates: $39-$69
(541) 396-2102

CORVALLIS
DAYS INN
1113 NW 9th St
(97330)
Rates: $60-$85
(541) 754-7474
(800) 329-7466

ECONO LODGE
345 NW 2nd St
(97330)
Rates: $44-$52
(541) 752-9601
(800) 424-6423

HOLIDAY INN EXP
781 NE 2nd St
(97330)
Rates: $65-$149
(541) 752-0800
(800) 465-4329

JASON INN
800 NW 9th St
(97330)
Rates: $36-$48
(541) 753-7326
(800) 346-3291

MOTEL 6
935 NW Garfield
(97330)
Rates: $42-$52
(541) 758-9125
(800) 466-8356

RAMADA INN
1550 NW 9th
(97330)
Rates: n/a
(541) 753-9151
(800) 272-6232

SUPER 8 MOTEL
407 NW 2nd St
(97330)
Rates: $69-$90
(541) 758-8088
(800) 800-8000

AREA CODES - If the local number doesn't connect, check for a new area code.

COTTAGE GROVE

CITY CENTER MOTEL
737 Hwy 99 S (97424)
Rates: $30-$35
(541) 942-8322

COMFORT INN
845 Gateway Blvd (97424)
Rates: $54-$150
(541) 942-9747
(800) 424-6423
(800) 944-0287

HOLIDAY INN EXP
1601 Gateway Blvd (97424)
Rates: $58-$125
(541) 942-1000
(800) 465-4329

RELAX INN
1030 Pacific Hwy 99 N (97424)
Rates: $30-$48
(541) 942-5132

RIVER COUNTRY INN
71864 London Rd (97424)
Rates: $65
(541) 942-9334

VILLAGE GREEN
725 Row River Rd (97424)
Rates: $59-$129
(541) 942-2491
(800) 343-7666

CRESCENT

WOODSMAN COUNTRY LODGE
136740 Hwy 97 (97733)
Rates: $37-$89
(541) 433-2710

CRESCENT LAKE JUNCTION

CRESCENT CREEK COTTAGES
Hwy 58, Milepost 71 (97425)
Rates: $30-$50
(541) 433-2324

CRESCENT LAKE LODGE & RESORT
P.O. Box 73 (97425)
Rates: $45-$120
(541) 433-2505

ODELL LAKE LODGE & RESORT
Hwy 58, Milepost 67 (97425)
Rates: $50-$240
(541) 433-2540
(800) 434-2540

SHELTER COVE RESORT
W Odell Lake Rd, Hwy 58 (97425)
Rates: $65-$85
(541) 433-2548

WILLAMETTE PASS INN
Hwy 58, Milepost 69 (97425)
Rates: $58-$88
(541) 433-2211

CRESWELL

BEST WESTERN CRESWELL INN
345 E Oregon Ave (9742149
Rates: $49-$55
(541) 895-3341
(800) 626-1900
(877) 895-3341

CURTIN

STARDUST MOTEL
455 Bear Creek Rd (97428)
Rates: $28-$38
(541) 942-5706
(888) 657-2527

DALLAS

BEST WESTERN DALLAS INN & SUITES
250 Orchard Dr (97338)
Rates $69-$150
(503) 623-6000
(800) 528-1234

RIVERSIDE INN
517 Main St (97338)
Rates: $40-$50
(503) 623-8163
(866) 740-2830

DEADWOOD

CEDARHILL GETAWAY RENTAL
92201 W Fork Rd (97430)
Rates: $20-$25 (per person)
(541) 345-1619
(877) 345-1633

DEPOE BAY

ROWN PACIFIC INN
50 NE Bechill St (97341)
Rates: $85-$105
(541) 765-7773
(877) 765-7773

GRACIE'S SEA HAG INN B&B
235 SE Bay View Ave (97341)
Rates: $85-$135
(541) 765-2322
(800) 228-0448

INN AT ARCH ROCK
70 NW Sunset St (97341)
Rates: $69-$269
(541) 765-2560
(800) 767-1835

TROLLERS LODGE MOTEL & VACATION HOMES
355 SW Hwy 101 (97341)
Rates: $63-$300
(541) 765-2287
(800) 472-9335

DETROIT

ALL SEASONS MOTEL
130 Breitenbush Rd (97342)
Rates: $40-$80
(503) 854-3421

DIAMOND LAKE

DIAMOND LAKE RESORT
350 Resort Dr (97731))
Rates: $85-$250
(541) 793-3333
(800) 733-7593

ELGIN

MINAM MOTEL
72601 Hwy 82 (97827)
Rates: $27-$48
(541) 437-4475

ELKTON

THE BIG K GUEST RANCH
20029 Hwy 138 W (97436)
Rates: $130-$225
(541) 584-2295
(800) 390-2445

ENTERPRISE

BOUCHER GUEST COTTAGE
83162 W Dorrance Ln (97828)
Rates: $55+
(541) 426-3209

PONDEROSA MOTEL
102 Greenwood SE (97828)
Rates: $54-$64
(541) 426-3186

WILDERNESS INN
301 W North St (97828)
Rates: $51-$66
(541) 426-4535
(800) 965-1205

EUGENE

BEST VALUE INN
1140 W 6th Ave (97402)
Rates: $39-$74
(541) 343-0730

BEST WESTERN GREENTREE INN
1759 Franklin Blvd (97403)
Rates: $68-$150
(541) 485-2727
(800) 528-1234

BEST WESTERN NEW OREGON MOTEL
1655 Franklin Blvd (97403)
Rates: $68-$150
(541) 683-3669
(800) 528-1234

BUDGET HOST MOTOR INN
1190 W 6th Ave (97402)
Rates: $37-$55
(541) 342-7273
(800) 554-9822

CLASSIC RESIDENCE INN
1140 W 6th Ave (97402)
Rates: $33-$70
(541) 343-0730
(877) 646-2466

COUNTRY SQUIRE INN
33100 Van Duyn Rd (97401)
Rates: $39-$100
(541) 484-2000

COURTESY INN
345 W 6th Ave (97401)
Rates: $35-$65
(541) 345-3391
(888) 259-8481

DAYS INN
1859 Franklin Blvd (97403)
Rates: $54-$112
(541) 342-6383
(800) 329-7466

EXPRESS INN & SUITES
990 W 6th Ave (97401)
Rates: $50-$65
(541) 868-1520

FRANKLIN INN
1857 Franklin Blvd (97403)
Rates: $40-$69
(541) 342-4804
(800) 424-5213

HILTON HOTEL
66 E 6th & Oak Sts (97401)
Rates: $120-$212
(541) 342-2000
(800) 445-8667
(800) 937-6660

LA QUINTA INN & SUITES - WATERFRONT
155 Day Island Rd (97401)
Rates: $89-$170
(541) 344-8335
(800) 687-6667

MOTEL 6
3690 Glenwood Dr (97403)
Rates: $39-$56
(541) 687-2395
(800) 466-8356

NITE INN
1522 W 6th Ave (97402)
Rates: $30-$49
(541) 686-2060

AREA CODES - If the local number doesn't connect, check for a new area code.

**QUALITY INN
& SUITES**
2121 Franklin
Blvd (97403)
Rates: $57-$105
(541) 342-1243
(800) 424-6423

RAMADA INN
225 Coburg Rd
(97401)
Rates: $49-$108
(541) 342-5181
(800) 272-6232
(800) 917-5500

RED LION INN
205 Coburg Rd
(97401)
Rates: $65-$110
(541) 342-5201
(800) 733-5466

**RESIDENCE INN
BY MARRIOTT**
25 Club Rd
(97401)
Rates: $79-$159
(541) 342-7171
(800) 331-3131

SIXTY-SIX MOTEL
755 E Broadway
(97403)
Rates: $35-$55
(541) 342-5041

**THE VALLEY
RIVER INN**
1000 Valley River
Way (97440)
Rates: $170-$300
(541) 687-0123
(800) 543-8266

**VALUE INN
MOTEL**
595 Hwy 99 N
(97402)
Rates: $38-$69
(541) 688-2733

FLORENCE
**LE CHATEAU
MOTEL**
1084 Hwy 101 N
(97439)
Rates: $45-$84
(541) 997-3481

LIGHTHOUSE INN
155 Hwy 101
(97439)
Rates: $40-$125
(541) 997-3221

**MERCER LAKE
RESORT**
88875 Bay Berry
Ln (97439)
Rates: $65-$95
(541) 997-3633
(800) 355-3633

**MONEY SAVER
MOTEL**
170 Hwy 101
(97439)
Rates: $59-$69
(541) 997-7131

**OCEAN BREEZE
MOTEL**
85165 Hwy 101 S
(97439)
Rates: $49-$129
(541) 997-2642
(800) 753-2642

OLD TOWN INN
170 Hwy 101
(97439)
Rates: $49-$79
(541) 997-7131
(800) 579-0490

PARK MOTEL
85034 Hwy 101 S
(97439)
Rates: $49-$139
(541) 997-2634
(800) 392-0441

FOREST GROVE
**BEST VALUE
INN & SUITES**
3306 Pacific Ave
(97116)
Rates: $49-$69
(503) 357-9000

**BEST WESTERN
UNIVERSITY INN
& SUITES**
3933 Pacific Ave
(97116)
Rates: $69-$129
(503) 992-8888
(800) 528-1234

HOLIDAY MOTEL
3224 Pacific Ave
(97116)
Rates: $45-$60
(503) 357-7411

FORT KLAMATH
**CRATER LAKE
RESORT &
CABINS**
50711 Hwy 62,
Milepost 92
(97626)
Rates: $50-$80
(541) 381-2349

**SUN PASS RANCH
BED & BREAKFST**
52125 Hwy 62
(97626)
Rates: n/a
(541) 381-2259

**WILSON'S
COTTAGES**
57997 Hwy 62
(97626)
Rates: $60-$70
(541) 381-2209

FOSSIL
**BRIDGE CREEK
FLORA INN B&B**
828 Main St
B(97830)
Rates: $60-$75
(541) 763-2355

GARIBALDI
BAYSHORE INN
227 Garibaldi Ave
(97118)
Rates: $64-$125
(503) 322-2552
(877) 537-2121

HARBOR VIEW INN
302 S 7th St (97118)
Rates: $30-$55
(503) 322-3251

**INN AT
GARIBALDI**
Hwy 101 (97118)
Rates: $59-$159
(503) 322-3338
(800) 547-0106

TILLA-BAY MOTEL
805 Garibaldi Ave
(97118)
Rates: $39+
(503) 322-3405

GEARHART
**GEARHART
BY THE SEA
RESORT**
1157 N Marion
(97138)
Rates: $65-$260
(503) 738-8331
(800) 547-0115

**GEARHART
OCEAN INN**
67 N Cottage Ave
(97138)
Rates: $49-$119
(503) 738-7373
(800) 352-8034

**SURFSIDE
CONDOS ON
THE BEACH**
P.O. Box 2591
(97138)
Rates: $69-$145
(503) 738-6384

**WINDJAMMER
MOTEL**
4253 Hwy 101 N
(97138)
Rates: $48-$117
(503) 738-3250
(800) 479-5191

GILCHRIST
GILCHRIST INN
3 Mississippi Dr
(97737)
Rates: $60-$75
(541) 433-2878

GLADSTONE
OXFORD SUITES
75 82nd Dr (97027)
Rates: $69-$99
(503) 722-7777
(877) 558-7710

GLENEDEN BEACH
**BEACHCOMBERS
HAVEN**
7045 NW Glen
Ave (97388)
Rates: $62-$250
(541) 764-2252
(800) 428-5533

**SALISHAN LODGE
& GOLF RESORT**
7760 Hwy 101 N
(98388)
Rates: $195-$365
(541) 764-2371
(800) SALISHAN

GLIDE
**STEELHEAD
RUN B&B**
23049 N Umpqua
Hwy, Box 639
(97443)
Rates: $56-$180
(541) 496-0563
(800) 348-0563

GOLD BEACH
**BREAKERS GOLD
BEACH MOTEL**
29171 Ellensburg
Ave (97444)
Rates: $45-$139
(541) 247-6606

**CITY CENTER
MOTEL**
94200 Harlow St
(97444)
Rates: $32-$95
(541) 247-6675

**CLEAR SKY
LODGING**
29350 Clear Sky
Ln (97444)
Rates: $65-$150
(541) 247-6456

DRIFT IN MOTEL
94250 Port Dr
(97444)
Rates: $25-$75
(541) 247-4547
(800) 424-3833

ECONO LODGE
29171 Ellensburg
Ave (97444)
Rates: $40-$125
(541) 247-6606
(800) 424-6423

GOLD BEACH INN
29346 Ellensburg
Ave (97444)
Rates: $48-$119
(541) 247-7091

**INN OF THE
BEACHCOMBER**
29266 Ellensburg
Ave (97444)
Rates: $55-$180
(541) 247-6691
(888) 690-2378

**IRELAND'S RUSTIC
LODGES**
29330 Ellensburg
Ave S (97444)
Rates: $45-$80
(541) 247-7718

AREA CODES - If the local number doesn't connect, check for a new area code.

JOT'S RESORT & CONDOS
94360 Wedderburn Loop Rd (97444)
Rates: $85-$195
(541) 247-6676
(800) 367-5687

MOTEL 6
94433 Jerry's Flat Rd (97444)
Rates: $38-$70
(541) 247-4533
(800) 466-8356
(800) 759-4533

OREGON TRAIL LODGE
29855 N Ellensburg Ave (97444)
Rates: $45-$65
(541) 247-6030

ROGUE LANDING
94749 Jerry's Flat Rd (97444)
Rates: $20-$50
(541) 247-6105

SAND 'N SEA MOTEL
29362 Ellensburg Ave (97444)
Rates: $49-$119
(541) 247-6658
(800) 808-SAND

SHORE CLIFF INN
29346 Ellensburg Ave (97444)
Rates: $45-$80
(541) 247-7091
(888) 663-0608

WHIMSEY VACATION HOUSE
94249 Third St (97444)
Rates: $95
(541) 247-2661
(888) 401-0344

GOVERNMENT CAMP
COLLINS LAKE RESORT
P. O. Box 280 (97028)
Rates: $180-$260
(971) 404-7599
(877) MTHOOD3

MT. HOOD INN
87450 E Govt Camp Loop (97028)
Rates: $149-$169
(503) 272-3205
(800) 443-7777

SUMMIT MEADOW CABINS
P.O. Box 235 (97028)
Rates: $140-$250
(503) 272-3494

GRANTS PASS
BEST WESTERN GRANTS PASS INN
111 NE Agness Ave (97526)
Rates: $70-$141
(541) 476-1117
(800) 528-1234
(800) 553-7666

BEST WESTERN INN AT THE ROGUE
8959 Rogue River Hwy (97527)
Rates: $55-$99
(541) 582-2200
(800) 528-1234
(800) 238-0700

COMFORT INN
1889 NE 6th St (97526)
Rates: $56-$114
(541) 479-8301
(800) 424-6423

FLAMINGO INN
728 NW 6th St (97526)
Rates: $30-$42
(541) 476-6601

HOLIDAY INN EXP
105 NE Agness (97526)
Rates: $83-$94
(541) 471-6144
(800) 465-4329
(800) 838-7666

KNIGHTS INN MOTEL
104 SE 7th St (97526)
Rates: $45-$55
(541) 479-5595
(800) 826-6835

LA QUINTA INN & SUITES
243 NE Morgan Ln (97526)
Rates: $64-$88
(541) 472-1808
(800) 687-6667

MOTEL DEL ROGUE
2600 Rogue River Hwy (97527)
Rates: $55-$125
(541) 479-2111
(866) 479-2111

MOTEL 6
1800 NE 7th St (97526)
Rates: $39-$58
(541) 474-1331
(800) 466-8356

REDWOOD MOTEL
815 NE 6th St (97526)
Rates: $58-$92
(541) 476-0878

RIVERSIDE INN RESORT
971 SE 6th St (97526)
Rates: $65-$350
(541) 476-6873
(800) 334-4567

ROD & REEL MOTEL
7875 Rogue River Hwy (97527)
Rates: $40-$75
(541) 582-1516
(800) 516-5557

ROGUE RIVER INN
6285 Rogue River Hwy (97527)
Rates: $43-$79
(541) 582-1120

ROGUE VALLEY MOTEL
7799 Rogue River Hwy (97527)
Rates: $42-$72
(541) 582-3762

SHILO INN
1880 NW 6th St (97526)
Rates: $42-$109
(541) 479-8391
(800) 222-2244

SUNSET INN
1400 NW 6th St (97526)
Rates: $45-$135
(541) 479-3305

SUPER 8 MOTEL
1949 NE 7th St (97526)
Rates: $54-$76
(541) 474-0888
(800) 800-8000

SWEET BREEZE INN
1627 NE 6th St (97526)
Rates: $48-$110
(541) 471-4434

TRAVELODGE
1950 NW Vine St (97526)
Rates: $49-$81
(541) 479-6611
(800) 578-7878

GRESHAM
BEST WESTERN PONY SOLIDER INN
1060 NE Cleveland (97030)
Rates: $69-$89
(503) 665-1591
(800) 634-7669

HAWTHORN INN & SUITES
2323 NE 181st Ave (97230)
Rates: $85-$109
(503) 492-4000
(800) 527-1133

SLEEP INN
2261 NE 181st Ave (97230)
Rates: $58-$119
(503) 618-8400
(800) 753-3746

SUPER 8 MOTEL
121 NE 181st Ave (97230)
Rates: $49-$69
(503) 661-5100
(888) 599-5100

HALFWAY
CLEAR CREEK FARM B&B
Rt 1, Box 138 (97834)
Rates: $55-$60
(541) 742-2238
(800) 742-4992

PINE VALLEY LODGE
163 N Main St (97834)
Rates: $65-$105
(541) 742-2027

HALSEY
BEST WESTERN PIONEER LODGE
33180 Hwy 228 (97348)
Rates: $59-$81
(541) 369-2804
(800) 528-1234

HARBOR
BEST WESTERN BEACHFRONT INN
16008 Boat Basin Rd (97415)
Rates: $95-$195
(541) 469-7779
(800) 528-1234
(800) 468-4081

HEPPNER
NORTHWESTERN MOTEL
389 N Main (97836)
Rates: $45-$65
(541) 676-9167
(888) 851-8436

HERMISTON
ECONOMY INN
835 N 1st St (97838)
Rates: $42-$100
(541) 567-5516
(888) 567-9521

OAK TREE INN
1110 SE 4th St (97838)
Rates: $59-$69
(541) 567-2330

OXFORD SUITES
1050 N 1st St (97838)
Rates: $69-$115
(541) 564-8000
(888) 545-7848

THE WAY INN
635 S Hwy 395 (97838)
Rates: $32-$34
(541) 567-5561
(888) 564-8767

HILLSBORO

CANDLEWOOD SUITES
3133 NE Shute Rd (97124)
Rates: $69-$118
(503) 681-2121
(888) 226-3539

THE DUNES MOTEL
452 SE 10th Ave (97124)
Rates: $38-$55
(503) 648-8991

LARKSPUR LANDING HOTEL
3133 NE Shute Rd (97214)
Rates: $69-$129
(502) 681-2121

RED LION HOTEL
3500 NE Cornell Rd (97124)
Rates: $62-$105
(503) 648-3600
(800) 733-5466

RESIDENCE INN PORTLAND WEST
18855 NW Tanasbourne Dr (97124)
Rates: $79-$149
(503) 531-3200
(800) 331-3131

TOWNEPLACE SUITES BY MARRIOTT
6550 NE Brighton St (97124)
Rates: $59-$109
(503) 268-6000
(800) 257-3000

WELLESLEY INN & SUITES
19311 NW Cornell Rd (97124)
Rates: $85-$105
(503) 439-0706
(800) 444-8888

HINES

COMFORT INN
504 N Hwy 20 (97738)
Rates: $64-$87
(541) 573-3370
(800) 424-6423

HOOD RIVER

BERYL HOUSE B&B
4079 Barrett Dr (97031)
Rates: $60-$70
(541) 386-5567

BEST WESTERN HOOD RIVER INN
1108 E Marina Way (97031)
Rates: $79-$139
(541) 386-2200
(800) 528-1234
(800) 828-7873

COLUMBIA GORGE HOTEL
4000 Westcliff Dr (97031)
Rates: $179-$399
(541) 386-5566
(800) 345-1921

HACKETT HOUSE B&B
922 State St (97031)
Rates: $45-$75
(541) 386-1014

HOOD RIVER VACATION RENTALS
823 Cascade Ave (97031)
Rates: n/a
(541) 387-3113

LOST LAKE RESORT
Mt. Hood Nat'l Forest, End of Lost Lake Rd (97031)
Rates: $50-$125
(541) 386-6366

PLEASANT VALLEY ORCHARDS B&B
3890 Acree Dr (97031)
Rates: n/a
(431) 386-2803
(877) 386-2337

VAGABOND LODGE
4070 Westcliff Dr (97031)
Rates: $48-$90
(541) 386-2992

IDLEYLD PARK

IDLEYLD LODGE INN
23834 N Umpqua Hwy (97447)
Rates: $39-$99
(541) 496-0088

NORTH UMPQUA RESORT
23885 N Umpqua Hwy (97447)
Rates: $29-$65
(541) 496-0149
(800) 350-1028

SWIFTWATER GUEST HOUSE
119-121 Tioga Ln (97447)
Rates: n/a
(888) 454-9696

JACKSONVILLE

JACKSONVILLE INN HISTORIC HOTEL
175 E California St (97530)
Rates: $113-$245
(541) 899-1900
(800) 321-9344

THE STAGE LODGE
830 N 5th St (97530)
Rates: $82-$180
(541) 899-3953
(800) 253-8254

JOHN DAY

BEST WESTERN JOHN DAY INN
315 W Main St (97845)
Rates: $65-$143
(541) 575-1700
(800) 528-1234

BUDGET INN
250 E Main St (97845)
Rates: $45-$55
(541) 575-2100
(800) 854-4442

DREAMERS LODGE
144 N Canyon Blvd (97845)
Rates: $44-$54
(541) 575-0526
(800) 654-2849

SONSHINE BED & BREAKFAST
210 NW Canton (97845)
Rates: $55-$65
(541) 575-1827

SUNSET INN
390 W Main St (97845)
Rates: $44-$58
(541) 575-1462
(800) 452-4899

TRAVELLER'S MOTEL
755 S Canyon Blvd (97845)
Rates: $30+
(541) 575-2076

JORDAN VALLEY

SAHARA MOTEL
607 Main St (97910)
Rates: $42-$44
(541) 586-2810
(800) 828-4432

JOSEPH

COLLETTS' CABINS
84681 Ponderosa Lane (97846)
Rates: $60-$115
(541) 432-2391
(866) 432-2391

DRAGON MEADOWS B&B
504 N Lake St (97846)
Rates: $65+
(541) 432-1027

EAGLE CAP CHALETS
59879 Wallowa Lake Hwy (97846)
Rates: $50-$145
(541) 432-4704

MOUNTAIN VIEW MOTEL
83450 Joseph Hwy (97846)
Rates: $35-$75
(541) 4322982
(866) 262-9891

TAMARACK PINES INN
60073 Wallowa Lake Hwy (97846)
Rates: $87
(541) 432-2920
(866) 200-8804

JUNCTION CITY

GUEST HOUSE MOTEL
1335 Ivy St (97448)
Rates: $49-$69
(541) 998-6524
(800) 835-5170

JUNTURA

THE OASIS CAFE & MOTEL
5838 Hwy 20 (97911)
Rates: $30-$60
(541) 277-3605

KENO

GREEN SPRINGS BOX R RANCH
16799 Hwy 66 (97627)
Rates: $110-$150
(541) 482-1873

KERBY

HOLIDAY MOTEL
24810 Redwood Hwy (97531)
Rates: $50-$60
(503) 592-3003

KING CITY

BEST WESTERN NORTHWIND INN & SUITES
16105 SW Pacific Hwy (97224)
Rates: $79-$89
(503) 431-2100
(800) 528-1234

KLAMATH FALLS

A-1 BUDGET MOTEL
3844 Hwy 97 N (97601)
Rates: $30-$60
(541) 884-8104

BEST WESTERN KLAMATH INN
4061 S 6th St (97603)
Rates: $55-$73
(541) 882-1200
(800) 528-1234
(877) 882-1200

AREA CODES - If the local number doesn't connect, check for a new area code.

CIMARRON MOTOR INN
3060 S 6th St (97603)
Rates: $45-$65
(541) 882-4601
(800) 742-2648

CRYSTALWOOD LODGE
38625 Westside Rd (97601)
Rates: n/a
(541) 381-2322
(866) 381-2322

ECONO LODGE
75 Main St (97601)
Rates: $35-$72
(541) 884-7735
(800) 424-6423

GOLDEN WEST MOTEL
6402 S 6th St (97601)
Rates: $36-$56
(541) 882-1758

HARRIMAN SPRINGS RESORT
26661 Rocky Point Rd (97601)
Rates: n/a
(541) 356-2331

HIGH CHAPARRAL MOTEL
5440 Hwy 97 N (97601)
Rates: $22-$90
(541) 882-4675

HILL VIEW MOTEL
5543 S 6th St (97601)
Rates: $40-$60
(541) 883-7771

LA VISTA MOTEL
3939 Hwy 97 N (97601)
Rates: $32-$48
(541) 882-8844

LAKE OF THE WOODS RESORT
950 Harriman Rd (97601)
Rates: $55-$80
(541) 949-8300

MAJESTIC INN & SUITES
5543 S 6th St (97501)
Rates: $36-$65
(541) 883-7771
(866) 488-0088

MAVERICK MOTEL
1220 Main St (97601)
Rates: $39-$59
(541) 882-6688
(800) 404-6690

MOTEL 6
5136 S 6th St (97601)
Rates: $35-$58
(541) 884-2110
(800) 466-8356

OREGON MOTEL 8
5225 Hwy 97 N (97601)
Rates: $39-$63
(541) 883-3431

QUALITY INN
100 Main St (97601)
Rates: $59-$119
(541) 882-4666
(800) 424-6423
(800) 732-4666

RED LION INN
3612 S 6th St (97603)
Rates: $69-$139
(541) 882-8864
(800) 733-5466

ROCK-WOOD MOTEL
2005 Biehn St (97601)
Rates: n/a
(541) 882-9992

ROCKY POINT RESORT
28121 Rocky Point Rd (97601)
Rates: $48-$89
(541) 356-2287

RUNNING Y RANCH RESORT
5500 Running Y Rd (97501)
Rates: $119-$269
(541) 850-5500
(888) 850-0275

SOUTH ENTRANCE MOTEL
9339 Hwy 97 S (97601)
Rates: n/a
(541) 883-1994

SUPER 8 MOTEL
3805 Hwy 97 N (97601)
Rates: $58-$73
(541) 884-8880
(800) 800-8000

LA GRANDE

GREENWELL MOTEL
305 Adams Ave (97850)
Rates: $25-$30
(541) 963-4134
(800) 772-0991

MOON MOTEL
2116 Adams Ave (97850)
Rates: n/a
(541) 963-2724

ORCHARD MOTEL
2206 Adams Ave (97850)
Rates: $30-$39
(541) 963-6160

ROYAL MOTOR INN
1510 Adams Ave (97850)
Rates: $28-$44
(541) 963-4154
(800) 990-7575

STARDUST LODGE
402 Adams Ave (97850)
Rates: $27-$50
(541) 963-4166

TRAVELODGE
2215 Adams Ave (97850)
Rates: $44-$74
(541) 963-7116
(800) 578-7878

LA PINE

BEST WESTERN NEWBERRY STATION
16515 Reed Rd & Hwy 97 (97739)
Rates: $79-$129
(541) 536-5130
(800) 528-1234
(800) 210-8616

DIAMOND STONE GUEST LODGE B&B
16693 Sprague Loop (97739)
Rates: $75-$120
(541) 536-6263
(800) 600-6263

EAST LAKE RESORT
22430 East Lakes Rd (97739)
Rates: $50-$150
(541) 536-2230

HIGHLANDER MOTEL
51511 Hwy 97 S (97739)
Rates: $30-$51
(541) 536-2131

LAMPLITER MOTEL
51526 Hwy 97 S (97739)
Rates: $32-$36
(541) 536-2931

PAULINA LAKE RESORT
P.O. Box 7 (97739)
Rates: $65-$135
(541) 536-2240

QUALITY INN
52560 Hwy 97 S (97739)
Rates: $39-$69
(541) 536-1737
(800) 424-6423

WEST VIEW MOTEL
51371 Hwy 97 S (97739)
Rates: $35-$55
(541) 536-2115

LAKE OSWEGO

CROWNE PLAZA HOTEL
14811 Kruse Oaks Blvd (97035)
Rates: $59-$180
(503) 624-8400
(800) 227-6963

PHOENIX INN & SUITES
14905 SW Bangy Rd (97035)
Rates: $79-$109
(503) 624-7400
(800) 824-9992

RESIDENCE INN PORTLAND SOUTH
15200 SW Bangy Rd (97035)
Rates: $119-$199
(503) 684-2603
(800) 331-3131

LAKESIDE

LAKESHORE LODGE
290 S 8th St (97449)
Rates: $34-$49
(541) 759-3161
(800) 759-3951

SEADRIFT MOTEL
11022 Coast Hwy 101 (97449)
Rates: $36-$44
(541) 759-3102

LAKEVIEW

BEST VALUE INN -LAKEVIEW LODGE
301 North G St (97630)
Rates: n/a
(541) 947-2181
(888) 315-2378

BEST WESTERN SKYLINE MOTOR LODGE
414 North G St (97630)
Rates: $69-$149
(541) 947-2194
(800) 528-1234

BUDGET INN
411 North F St (97630)
Rates: $38-$45
(541) 947-2201

INTERSTATE 8 MOTEL
354 North K St (97630)
Rates: $38-$52
(541) 947-3341

RIM ROCK MOTEL
727 South F St (97630)
Rates: $30-$32
(541) 947-2185

AREA CODES - If the local number doesn't connect, check for a new area code.

LEBANON

SHANICO INN
1840 Main St
(97355)
Rates: $44-$75
(541) 259-2601
(888) 815-4408

VALLEY INN
2885 S Santiam
Hwy (97355)
Rates: n/a
(541) 258-8184

LINCOLN CITY

**ALL SEASONS
VACATION
RENTALS**
1116 SW 51st St
(97367)
Rates: n/a
(541) 996-3549
(800) 362-5229

**ANCHOR MOTEL
AND LODGE**
4417 SW Hwy 101
(97367)
Rates: $40-$60
(541) 996-3810
(800) 582-8611

BEL-AIRE MOTEL
2945 NW Hwy
101 (97367)
Rates: n/a
(541) 994-2984

**BUDGET INN
MOTEL**
1713 NW 21st St
(97367)
Rates: $32-$89
(541) 994-5281

**CAPTAIN
COOK INN**
2626 NE Hwy 101
(97367)
Rates: $55-$109
(541) 994-2522
(800) 809-6805

COHO INN
1635 NW Harbor
(97367)
Rates: $62-$160
(541) 994-3684

**CROWN PACIFIC
INN EXPRESS**
1070 SE 1st St
(97367)
Rates: $45-$85
(541) 994-7559
(800) 359-7559

EDGECLIFF MOTEL
3733 SW Hwy 101
(97367)
Rates: $60-$190
(541) 996-2055
(888) 750-3636

ESTER LEE MOTEL
3803 SW Hwy 101
(97367)
Rates: $83-$128
(541) 996-3606
(888) 996-3606

**HIDEAWAY
OCEANFRONT
MOTEL**
810 SW 10th St
(97367)
Rates: n/a
(541) 994-8874

**LINCOLN CITY
INN**
1091 SE 1st St
(97367)
Rates: $50-$99
(541) 996-4400

**LOOKING GLASS
INN**
861 SW 51st St
(97367)
Rates: $59-$129
(541) 996-3996
(800) 843-4940

MOTEL 6
3517 NW Hwy
101 (97367)
Rates: $41-$66
(541) 996-9900
(800) 466-8356

O'DYSIUS HOTEL
120 NW Inlet Ct
(97367)
Rates: $149-$299
(541) 994-4121
(800) 869-8160

**OVERLOOK
MOTEL**
3521 SW Anchor
(97367)
Rates: $52-$115
(541) 996-3300

**SAILOR JACK'S
OCEANFRONT
MOTEL**
1035 NW Harbor
Ave (97367)
Rates: n/a
(541) 994-3696
(888) 432-8346

SEA ECHO MOTEL
3510 NE Hwy 101
(97367)
Rates: $39-$65
(541) 994-2575

**SEA HORSE
OCEANFRONT**
2039 N Harbor Dr
(97367)
Rates: $45-$170
(541) 994-2101
(800) 662-2101

**SEAGULL
BEACHFRONT
MOTEL**
1511 NW Harbor
Ave (97367)
Rates: $46-$199
(541) 994-2948
(800) 422-0219

**SHILO INN
SUITES HOTEL**
1501 NW 40th Pl
(97367)
Rates: $69-$309
(541) 994-3655
(800) 222-2244

**WHISTLING
WINDS**
3264 NW Jetty
Ave (97367)
Rates: n/a
(541) 994-6155

LONG CREEK

**LONG CREEK
LODGE**
171 W Main on
Hwy 395 (97856)
Rates: n/a
(541) 421-9212

MADRAS

**BEST WESTERN
RAMA INN**
12 SW 4th (97741)
Rates: $69-$89
(541) 475-6141
(800) 528-1234

JUNIPER MOTEL
414 N Hwy 26
(97741)
Rates: $39-$89
(541) 475-6186
(800) 244-1399

**ROYAL DUTCH
MOTEL**
1101 SW Hwy 97
(97741)
Rates: $32+
(541) 475-2281

MANZANITA

SAN DUNE INN
428 Dorcas Ln
(97130)
Rates: $55-$140
(503) 368-5163
(888) 368-5163

**SUNSET SURF
MOTEL**
248 Ocean Rd
(97130)
Rates: $50-$119
(503) 368-5224
(800) 243-8035

MAUPIN

**IMPERIAL RIVER
COMPANY**
304 Bakeoven Rd
(97037)
Rates: $50-$150
(541) 395-2404
(800) 395-3903

**THE OASIS
RESORT**
609 Hwy 197
(97037)
Rates: $50-$70
(541) 395-2611

MCKENZIE BRIDGE

**BELKNAP LODGE
& HOT SPRINGS
CABINS**
59296 Belknap
Spgs Rd (97413)
Rates: n/a
(541) 822-3512

**THE COUNTRY
PLACE**
56245 Delta Dr
(97413)
Rates: $75-$220
(541) 822-6008

McMINNVILLE

PARAGON MOTEL
2065 Hwy 99 W
(97128)
Rates: $46-$53
(503) 472-9493
(800) 525-5469

**RED LION INN &
SUITES**
2535 NE Cumulus
Ave (97128)
Rates: $97-$134
(503) 472-1500
(800) 733-5466

MEDFORD

**BEST WESTERN
HORIZON INN**
1154 Barnett Rd
(97504)
Rates $75-$159
(541) 779-5085
(800) 528-1234
(800) 452-2255

CAPRI MOTEL
250 Barnett Rd
(97501)
Rates: $33-$42
(541) 773-7796

**CEDAR LODGE
MOTOR INN**
518 N Riverside
Ave (97501)
Rates: $45-$78
(541) 773-7361
(800) 282-3419

**COMFORT INN
NORTH**
1100 Hilton Rd
(97504)
Rates: $72-$109
(541) 772-9500
(800) 424-6423

KNIGHTS INN
500 N Riverside
Ave (97051)
Rates: $50-$70
(541) 773-3676
(800) 843-5644

**MEDFORD INN
& SUITES**
1015 S Riverside
Ave (97501)
Rates: $55-$98
(541) 773-8266

MOTEL 6 NORTH
2400 Biddle Rd
(97504)
Rates: $45-$62
(541) 779-0550
(800) 466-8356

MOTEL 6 SOUTH
950 Alba Dr (97504)
Rates: $39-$58
(541) 773-4290
(800) 466-8356

RED LION HOTEL
200 N Riverside
Ave (97501)
Rates: $69-$79
(541) 779-5811
(800) 733-5466

AREA CODES - If the local number doesn't connect, check for a new area code.

RESTON HOTEL
2300 Crater Lake
Hwy (97504)
Rates: $69-$130
(541) 779-3141
(800) 779-7829

SHILO INN
2111 Biddle Rd
(97504)
Rates: $59-$84
(541) 770-5151
(800) 222-2244

**WAVERLY
COTTAGES
& SUITES**
314 S Holly
(97501)
Rates: n/a
(541) 779-4716

WINDMILL INN
1950 Biddle Rd
(97504)
Rates: $84
(541) 779-0050
(800) 547-4747

MERLIN
**DOUBLETREE
RANCH-CABINS
ON THE RIVER**
6000 Abegg Rd
(97523)
Rates: $85-$125
(541) 476-1686

**ROGUE
FOREST B&B**
12035 Galice Rd
(97523)
Rates: $125-$175
(541) 472-1052

MERRILL
MERRILL MOTEL
P.O. Box 323
(97633)
Rates: n/a
(541) 798-5598

MILTON FREEWATER
OUT WEST MOTEL
84040 Hwy 11
(97862)
Rates: $40-$65
(541) 938-6647
(800) 881-6647

MILWAUKIE
**ECONO LODGE
SUITES INN**
17330 SE
McLoughlin Blvd
(97222)
Rates: $49-$69
(503) 654-2222
(800) 553-2666

**OCEANVIEW
VACATION
RENTALS**
9981 SE 32nd Ave
(97222)
Rates: $60-$70
(503) 653-8378

MOLALLA
**STAGECOACH
INN MOTEL**
415 Grange St
(97038)
Rates: $46-$61
(503) 829-4382

MONMOUTH
**COLLEGE INN
MOTEL**
235 S Pacific Ave
(97361)
Rates: $35-$58
(503) 838-1711

COURTESY INN
270 N Pacific Hwy
(97361)
Rates: $49-$69
(503) 838-4438

MONUMENT
**MONUMENT
MOTEL & RV
PARK**
760 Hwy 402
(97864)
Rates: $45-$60
(541) 934-2242

MOSIER
**HEWETT'S BED
& BREAKFAST**
501 Third St
(97040)
Rates: $45-$75
(541) 478-3455

MOUNT HOOD
MT. HOOD INN
87450 E Govt
Camp Loop
(97028)
Rates: $130-$160
(503) 272-3205
(800) 443-7777

**SHAMROCK
FOREST INN**
59550 E Hwy 26
(97028)
Rates: $38-$69
(503) 622-4003

MOUNT VERNON
**BLUE
MOUNTAIN
LODGE MOTEL**
150 W Main St
(97865)
Rates: $36-$75
(541) 932-4461

MYRTLE CREEK
**QUICK STOP
MOTEL &
MARKET**
6453 Dole Rd
(97457)
Rates: $34-$45
(541) 863-7267

MYRTLE POINT
**MYRTLE TREES
MOTEL**
1010 8th St (97458)
Rates: $48-$58
(541) 572-5811

NESIKA BEACH
**BREAKER HOUSE
AT NESIKA
BEACH**
32864 Nesika
Beach Rd (97444)
Rates: $80-$145
(541) 247-6670

NESKOWIN
**THE BREAKERS
CONDOS**
48060 Breakers
Blvd (97149)
Rates: $110-$255
(503) 392-3417

NETARTS
**EDGEWATER
MOTEL**
First St (97143)
Rates: $72-$82
(503) 842-1300

**SAMS VACATION
RENTALS**
1035 5th St Loop
(97143)
Rates: $55
(503) 842-5814

**TERIMORE
LODGING
BY THE SEA**
5105 Crab Ave
(97143)
Rates: $45-$105
(503) 842-4623
(800) 635-1821

THREE CAPES INN
4800 Netarts Hwy
W (97141)
Rates: $39-$95
(503) 842-4003

NEWBERG
**SHILO INN
& SUITES**
501 Sitka Ave
(97132)
Rates: $59-$99
(503) 537-0303
(800) 222-2244

**TRAVELODGE
SUITES**
2816 Portland Rd
(97132)
Rates: $59-$64
(541) 537-5000
(800) 578-7878

NEWPORT
**AGATE BEACH
OCEAN FRONT
MOTEL**
175 NW Gilbert
Way (97365)
Rates: $90-$100
(541) 265-8746
(800) 755-5674

**THE
ANCHORAGE**
7743 N Coast
Hwy (97365)
Rates: $60-$66
(541) 265-5463

**BEST WESTERN
AGATE BEACH INN**
3019 N Coast
Hwy (97365)
Rates: $79-$152
(541) 265-9411
(800) 465-4329
(800) 547-3310

**CITY CENTER
MOTEL**
538 SW Coast
Hwy (97365)
Rates: $38-$65
(541) 265-7381
(800) 628-9665

**DRIFTWOOD
VILLAGE MOTEL**
7947 N Coast
Hwy (97365)
Rates: $55-$125
(541) 265-5738

ECONO LODGE
606 SW Coast
Hwy (97365)
Rates: $49-$104
(541) 265-7723
(800) 424-6423

**HALLMARK
RESORT**
744 SW Elizabeth
St (97365)
Rates: $79-$179
(541) 265-2600
(888) 448-4449

**LA QUINTA INN &
SUITES**
45 SE 32nd (98365)
Rates: $59-$169
(541) 867-7727
(800) 687-6667

**MONEY SAVER
MOTEL**
861 SW Coast
Hwy 101 (97365)
Rates: $44-$85
(541) 265-2277
(877) 428-4393

**PENNY SAVER
MOTEL**
710 N Hwy 101
(97365)
Rates: $30-$60
(541) 265-6631

**SANDS MOTOR
LODGE**
206 N Coast Hwy
(97365)
Rates: $36-$48
(541) 265-5321

SHILO INN HOTEL
536 SW Elizabeth
(97365)
Rates: $88-$412
(541) 265-7701
(800) 222-2244

AREA CODES - If the local number doesn't connect, check for a new area code.

STARFISH POINT CONDOS
140 NW 48th St
(97365)
Rates: $115-$190
(541) 265-3751

SURF 'N SAND MOTEL
8143 N Hwy 101
(97365)
Rates: $58-$89
(541) 265-2215

TIDES INN MOTEL
715 SW Bay St
(97365)
Rates: $38-$55
(541) 265-7202

VAL-U-INN MOTEL
531 SW Fall St
(97365)
Rates: $50-$100
(541) 265-6203
(800) 443-7777

VIKINGS COTTAGES
729 NW Coast St
(97365)
Rates: $65-$80
(541) 265-2477
(800) 480-2477

WAVES MOTEL & VACATION RENTALS
820 NW Coast St
(97365)
Rates: $48-$118
(541) 265-4661
(800) 282-6993

WEST WIND MOTEL
747 SW Coast St
(97365)
Rates: $40-$55
(541) 265-5388
(800) 305-5388

WHALER MOTEL
155 SW Elizabeth
(97365)
Rates: $79-$129
(541) 265-9261
(800) 433-9444

WILLER'S MOTEL
754 SW Coast Hwy (97365)
Rates: $38-$80
(541) 265-2241
(800) 945-5377

NORTH BEND
BAY BRIDGE MOTEL
66304 Hwy 101
(97459)
Rates: $49-$70
(541) 756-3151
(800) 557-3156

CITY CENTER MOTEL
750 Connecticut Ave (97459)
Rates: $35-$70
(541) 756-5118

ITTY BITTY INN B&B
1504 Sherman Ave (97459)
Rates: $40-$49
(541) 756-6398

PARKSIDE MOTEL
1480 Sherman Ave (97459)
Rates: n/a
(541) 756-4124

NORTH POWDER
POWDER RIVER MOTEL
850 2nd St (97867)
Rates: $25-$38
(541) 898-2829

OAKLAND
BEST WESTERN RICE HILL
621 Long John Rd (97462)
Rates: $50-$100
(541) 849-3335
(800) 528-1234

RANCH MOTEL
581 John Long Rd (97462)
Rates: $27-$75
(541) 849-2126

OAKRIDGE
ARBOR INN
48229 Hwy 58
(974632
Rates: $27-$46
(541) 782-2611

BEST WESTERN OAKRIDGE INN
47433 Hwy 58
(97463)
Rates: $59-$79
(541) 782-2212
(800) 528-1234

CASCADE MOTEL
47487 Hwy 58
(97463)
Rates: $38-$48
(541) 782-2489
(800) 718-2489

OAKRIDGE MOTEL
48197 Hwy 58 E
(97463)
Rates: $26-$30
(541) 782-2432

ODELL LAKE
SHELTER COVE RESORT
Hwy 58, W Odell Lake Rd (97044)
Rates: $60-$85
(541) 433-2548

OLALLIE LAKE SCENIC AREA
OLALLIE LAKE RESORT CABINS
Mt. Hood National Forest (97760)
Rates: $30-$80
(541) 504-1010

ONTARIO
BUDGET INN
1737 N Oregon St
(97914)
Rates: $35-$40
(541) 889-3101
(800) 905-0024

ECONOMY INN MOTEL
88 N Oregon St
(97914)
Rates: $25-$45
(541) 889-6449

HOLIDAY INN
1249 Tapadera Ave (97914)
Rates: $63-$85
(541) 889-8621
(800) 465-4329

HOLIDAY MOTEL
615 E Idaho Ave
(97914)
Rates: $44-$56
(541) 889-9188

MOTEL 6
275 NE 12th St
(97914)
Rates: $29-$40
(541) 889-6617
(800) 466-8356

OREGON TRAIL MOTEL
92 E Idaho Ave
(97914)
Rates: $25-$55
(541) 889-8633
(800) 895-7945

PLAZA MOTEL
1144 SW 4th Ave
(97914)
Rates: $25-$95
(541) 889-9641

STOCKMAN'S MOTEL
81 SW 1st St
(97914)
Rates: $35-$50
(541) 889-4446

OREGON CITY
RIVERSHORE HOTEL
1900 Clackamette Dr (97045)
Rates: $78-$125
(503) 655-7141
(800) 443-7777

OTTER ROCK
ALPINE CHALETS
7045 Otter Crest Loop Rd (97369)
Rates: $90-$180
(541) 765-2572
(800) 825-5768

PACIFIC CITY
ANCHORAGE MOTEL
6585 Pacific Ave
(97135)
Rates: $52-$135
(503) 965-6773
(800) 941-6250

INN AT CAPE KIWANDA
33105 Cape Kiwanda Dr
(97135)
Rates: $109-$309
(503) 965-7001
(888) 965-7001

INN AT PACIFIC CITY
35215 Brooten Rd
(97135)
Rates: $75-$119
(503) 965-6366
(888) 722-2489

PACIFIC CITY INN
35280 Brooten Rd
(97135)
Rates: $59-$79
(503) 965-6464
(866) 567-3466

SEA VIEW VACATION RENTALS
P.O. Box 1049
(97135)
Rates: $75-$235
(503) 965-7888

PARKDALE
OLD PARKDALE INN
4932 Baseline Rd
(97041)
Rates: $110-$135
(541) 352-5551

PENDLETON
BEST WESTERN PENDLETON INN
400 SE Nye Ave
(97801)
Rates: $60-$125
(541) 276-2135
(800) 528-1234

ECONO LODGE
620 SW Tutuilla Rd (97801)
Rates: $39-$62
(541) 276-8654
(800) 424-6423

HOLIDAY INN EXP
600 SE Nye Ave
(97801)
Rates: $59-$250
(541) 966-6520
(800) 465-4329

LET 'ER BUCK MOTEL
205 SE Dorion Ave
(97801)
Rates: $28-$42
(541) 276-3293

MOTEL 6
325 SE Nye Ave
(97801)
Rates: $33-$43
(541) 276-3160
(800) 466-8356

OXFORD SUITES
2400 SW Court Pl
(97801)
Rates: $89-$159
(541) 276-6000

AREA CODES - If the local number doesn't connect, check for a new area code.

RED LION INN
304 SE Nye Ave
(97801)
Rates: $66-$86
(541) 276-6141
(800) 733-5466

SUPER 8 MOTEL
601 SE Nye Ave
(97801)
Rates: $57-$77
(541) 276-8881
(800) 800-8000

TRAVELODGE
411 SW Dorion
Ave (97801)
Rates: $49-$120
(541) 276-7531
(800) 578-7878

**WILDHORSE
RESORT HOTEL**
72779 Hwy 331
(97801)
Rates: $63-$140
(541) 276-0355
(800) 654-WILD

PHOENIX
SUPER 8 MOTEL
300 Pear Tree Ln
(97535)
Rates: $55-$95
(541) 535-4445
(800) 800-8000

PILOT ROCK
**PILOT ROCK
MOTEL**
362 NE 4th St
(97868)
Rates: $30-$53
(541) 443-2851

PISTOL RIVER
**ARCADIA ON THE
OREGON COAST
VACATION HOME**
23154 Hwy 101
(97444)
Rates: n/a
(888) 227-1963

PORT ORFORD
**CASTAWAY
BY-THE-SEA
MOTEL**
545 W 5th St
(97465)
Rates: $45-$145
(541) 332-4502

SEA CREST MOTEL
44 Hwy 101
(97465)
Rates: n/a
(541) 332-3040
(888) 332-3040

**SHORELINE
MOTEL**
206 6th St (97465)
Rates: n/a
(541) 332-2903

PORTLAND
**THE BENSON
HOTEL**
309 SW Broadway
(97205)
Rates: $119-$269
(503) 228-2000
(888) 523-6766

**BEST WESTERN INN
AT THE MEADOWS**
1215 N Hayden
Meadows Dr
(97217)
Rates: $69-$109
(503) 286-9600
(800) 528-1234

**COUNTRY INN &
SUITES**
7205 NE
Alderwood Rd
(97218)
Ratews: $89
(503) 255-2700
(800) 456-4000

CYPRESS INN
809 SW King St
(97205)
Rates: $45-$80
(503) 226-6288
(800) 532-9543

DAYS INN NORTH
9930 N Whitaker
Rd (97217)
Rates: $50-$90
(503) 289-1800
(800) 329-7466
(800) 833-1800

**DOUBLETREE
COLUMBIA RIVER**
1401 N Hayden
Island Dr (97215)
Rates: $79-$139
(503) 283-2111
(800) 222-8733

**DOUBLETREE
JANTZEN BEACH**
909 N Hayden
Island Dr (97217)
Rates: $79-$139
(503) 283-4466
(800) 222-8733

ECONO LODGE
3800 NE Sandy
Blvd (97232)
Rates: $45-$70
(503) 460-9000
(800) 424-6423

**FIFTH AVENUE
SUITES HISTORIC
HOTEL**
521 SW 5th Ave
(97204)
Rates: $109-$250
(503) 222-0001
(800) 711-2971

**FOUR POINTS BY
SHERATON**
50 SW Morrison
(97204)
Rates: $69-$159
(503) 221-0711
(888) 627-8263

**FOURTH AVENUE
MOTEL**
1889 SW 4th Ave
(97201)
Rates: $40-$45
(503) 226-7646

**HEATHMAN
HOTEL**
1001 SW
Broadway (97205)
Rates: $150-$775
(503) 241-4100
(800) 551-0011

**HILTON PORT-
LAND & EXECU-
TIVE TOWER**
921 SW 6th Ave
(97204)
Rates: $99-$175
(503) 226-1611
(800) 445-8667

HOSPITALITY INN
10155 SW Capitol
Hwy (97219)
Rates: $68-$89
(503) 244-6684

HOTEL LUCIA
400 SW Broadway
(97205)
Rates: $130-$575
(503) 225-1717

**LA QUINTA INN
AIRPORT**
11207 NE Holman
St (97220)
Rates: $59-$89
(503) 382-3820
(800) 687-6667
(877) 620-1002

**LA QUINTA INN
(LLOYD CENTER)**
431 NE
Multnomah St
(97232)
Rates: $84-$104
(503) 233-7933
(800) 687-6667

**LA QUINTA INN &
SUITES**
4319 NW Yeon
(97210)
Rates: $65-$96
(503) 497-9044
(800) 687-6667

MADISON SUITES
3620 NE 82nd Ave
(97220)
Rates: $40-$50
(503) 257-4981
(800) 945-4425

**MALLORY
HISTORIC HOTEL**
729 SW 15th Ave
Rates: $110-$165
(503) 223-6311
(800) 228-8657

**THE MARK
SPENCER HOTEL**
409 SW 11th Ave
(97205)
Rates: $69-$149
(503) 224-3293
(800) 548-3934

**MARRIOTT
CITY CENTER**
520 SW Broadway
(97205)
Rates: $89-$179
(503) 226-6300
(800) 228-9290

**MOTEL 6
AIRPORT**
9225 SE Stark St
(97216)
Rates: $39-$53
(503) 255-0808
(800) 466-8356

**MOTEL 6
CENTRAL**
3104 SE Powell
Blvd (97202)
Rates: $37-$58
(503) 238-0600
(800) 466-8356

MOTEL 6 NORTH
1125 N Schmeer
Rd (97217)
Rates: $44-$55
(503) 247-3700
(800) 466-8356

OXFORD SUITES
12226 N Jantzen
Dr (97217)
Rates: $75-$149
(503) 283-3030
(800) 548-7848

**PARAMOUNT
HOTEL**
808 SW Taylor
(97205)
Rates: $109-$195
(503) 223-9900

**PARK LANE
SUITES**
809 SW King Ave
(97205)
Rates: $89-$179
(503) 226-6288

**PORTLAND
CENTER
APARTMENTS**
200 SW Harrison
St (97201)
Rates: n/a
(503) 224-3030

**THE
PORTLANDER INN**
10350 N
Vancouver Way
(97211)
Rates: $69
(503) 345-0300
(800) 523-1193

**QUALITY INN
AIRPORT**
8247 NE Sandy
Blvd (97220)
Rates: $55-$89
(503) 256-4111
(800) 424-6423
(800) 246-4649

RAMADA INN ROSE QUARTER
10 N Weidler (97227)
Rates: n/a
(503) 287-9900
(800) 272-6232

RANCH INN MOTEL
10138 SW Barbur Blvd (97219)
Rates: $33-$50
(503) 246-3375

RED LION HOTEL CONV CENTER
1021 NE Grand Ave (97232)
Rates: $89-$159
(503) 235-2100
(800) 343-1822

RED LION INN & SUITES AIRPORT
5019 NE 102nd Ave (97220)
Rates: $69-$109
(503) 252-6397
(800) 735-5466

RESIDENCE INN BY MARRIOTT-LLOYD CENTER
1710 NE Multnomah St (97232)
Rates: $129-$199
(503) 288-1400
(800) 331-3131

RESIDENCE INN BY MARRIOTT RIVERPLACE
2115 SW River Pkwy (97201)
Rates: $109-$209
(503) 552-9500
(800) 331-3131

RIVERPLACE HOTEL
1510 SW Harbor Way (97201)
Rates: $149-$499
(503) 228-3233
(800) 227-1333

RODEWAY INN & SUITES
3828 NE 82nd Ave (97220)
Rates: $55-$66
(503) 256-2550
(800) 424-6423

ROSE MANOR INN
4546 SE McLoughlin Blvd (97202)
Rates: $30-$51
(503) 236-4175
(800) 252-8222

ROSE MOTEL
8920 SW Barbur (97219)
Rates: $35-$65
(503) 244-0107

SHERATON PORTLAND AIRPORT
8235 NE Airport Way (97220)
Rates: $178-$204
(503) 281-2500
(800) 325-3535

SHILO INN HOTEL
9900 SW Canyon Rd (97225)
Rates: $59-$195
(503) 297-2551
(800) 222-2244

SLEEP INN EAST
2261 NE 181st Ave (97230)
Rates: $52-$99
(503) 618-8400
(800) 424-6423

STAYBRIDGE SUITES
11936 NE Glenn Widing Dr (97220)
Rates: n/a
(503) 262-8888
(800) 238-8000

SULLIVAN'S GULCH B&B
1744 NE Clackamas St (97232)
Rates: $70-$85
(503) 331-1104

TRAVELODGE SUITES
7740 SE Powell Blvd (97206)
Rates: $63-$81
(503) 788-9394
(800) 578-7878

TRAVELODGE SUITES AIRPORT
11936 NE Glenn Widing Dr (97220)
Rates: n/a
(503) 262-8888
(800) 578-7878

VINTAGE PLAZA HISTORIC HOTEL
422 SW Broadway (97205)
Rates: $109-$300
(503) 228-1212
(800) 243-0555

THE WESTIN PORTLAND
750 SW Alder St (97205)
Rates: $99-$285
(503) 294-9000
(888) 627-8401

PRAIRIE CITY

STRAWBERRY MOUNTAIN INN B&B
940 Hwy 26 E (97869)
Rates: $65-$125
(541) 820-4522
(800) 545-6913

PRINEVILLE

BEST WESTERN PRINEVILLE INN
1475 NE 3rd St (97754)
Rates: $68-$125
(541) 447-8080
(800) 528-1234

CITY CENTER MOTEL
509 E 3rd St (97754)
Rates: $32-$50
(541) 447-5522

EXECUTIVE INN
1050 NE 3rd St (97754)
Rates: n/a
(541) 447-4152
(888) 447-4152

LITTLE PINE MOTEL
251 N Deer St (97754)
Rates: $32-$55
(541) 447-3440

OCHOCO INN
123 NE 3rd St (97754)
Rates: $32-$70
(541) 447-6231
(888) 800-9948

STAFFORD INN
1773 NE 3rd St (97754)
Rates: $69-$109
(541) 447-4185
(877) 744-7100

PROSPECT

PROSPECT HISTORICAL HOTEL/MOTEL
391 Mill Creek Dr (97536)
Rates: $50-$95
(541) 560-3664
(800) 944-6490

UNION CREEK RESORT
56484 Hwy 62 (97536)
Rates: n/a
(541) 560-3565
(866) 560-3565

RAINIER

BUDGET INN
120 "A" St W (97048)
Rates: $35-$85
(503) 556-4231
(800) 263-5658

REDMOND

COMFORT SUITES AIRPORT
2243 SW Yew Ave (97756)
Rates: $69-$174
(541) 504-8900
(800) 424-6423

EAGLE CREST RESORT
1522 Cline Falls Rd (97756)
Rates: $69-$340
(541) 923-2453
(800) 682-4786

HUB MOTEL SUPER VALUE INN
1128 N Hwy 97 (97756)
Rates: $35-$48
(541) 548-2101
(800) 784-3482

MOTEL 6
2247 S Hwy 97 (97756)
Rates: $45-$66
(541) 923-2100
(800) 466-8356

REDMOND INN
1545 Hwy 97 N (97756)
Rates: $40-$75
(541) 548-1091
(800) 833-3259

SUPER 8 MOTEL
3629 21st Pl SW (97756)
Rates: $52-$68
(541) 548-8881
(800) 800-8000

REEDSPORT

ANCHOR BAY INN
1821 Winchester Ave (97467)
Rates: $37-$150
(541) 271-2149
(800) 767-1821

BEST WESTERN SALBASGEON INN & SUITES
1400 Hwy Ave 101 (97467)
Rates: $67-$175
(541) 271-4831
(800) 528-1234
(800) 965-8808

ECONOMY INN
1593 Highway Ave (97467)
Rates: $36-$80
(541) 271-3671
(800) 799-9970

FIR GROVE MOTEL
2178 Winchester Ave (97467)
Rates: $49+
(541) 271-4848

SALBASGEON INN OF THE UMPQUA
45209 Hwy 38 (97467)
Rates: $64-$180
(541) 271-2025

SALTY SEAGULL MOTEL
1806 Winchester Ave (97467)
Rates: $29-$44
(541) 271-3729
(800) 476-8336

ROCKAWAY BEACH

COASTAL HIDEAWAYS
216 Hwy 101 N (97136)
Rates: $65-$125
(503) 355-2229

GETAWAY OCEANFRONT LODGING
621 S Pacific Ave (97136)
Rates: $65-$125
(503) 355-2501
(800) 756-5552

OCEAN LOCOMOTION MOTEL
19130 Alder Ave (97136)
Rates: $50-$125
(503) 355-2093

101 MOTEL
530 N Hwy 101 (97136)
Rates: $35-$55
(503) 355-2420
(888) 878-3973

SAND DOLLAR MOTEL
105 NW 23rd Ave (97136)
Rates: $45-$100
(503) 355-2301

SEA TREASURES INN
301 N Miller St (97136)
Rates: $45-$99
(503) 355-8220
(800) 444-1864

SILVER SANDS MOTEL
215 S Pacific St (97136)
Rates: $75-$154
(503) 355-2206
(800) 457-8972

SURFSIDE OCEANFRONT RESORT MOTEL
101 NW 11th Ave (97136)
Rates: n/a
(503) 355-2312
(800) 243-7786

TRADEWINDS MOTEL
523 N Pacific St (97136)
Rates: $47-$246
(503) 355-2112
(800) 824-0938

ROSEBURG

BEST WESTERN GARDEN VILLA
760 NW Garden Valley Blvd (97470)
Rates: $59-$99
(541) 672-1601
(800) 528-1234
(800) 547-3446

BUDGET 16 MOTEL
1067 NE Stephens St (97470)
Rates: $30-$57
(541) 673-5556
(800) 414-1648

CASA LOMA MOTEL
1107 NE Stephens St (97470)
Rates: $27-$35
(541) 673-5569

CITY CENTER MOTEL
1321 SE Stephens St (97470)
Rates: $30-$40
(541) 673-6134

COMFORT INN
1539 Mullholland Dr (97470)
Rates: $64-$114
(541) 957-1100
(800) 424-6423

DUNES MOTEL
610 W Madrone St (97470)
Rates: $39-$60
(541) 672-6684
(800) 260-9973

ECONO LODGE
760 NW Garden Valley Blvd, Suite 125 (97470)
Rates: $44-$85
(541) 673-6000
(800) 424-6423

HOLIDAY INN EXP
375 W Harvard Blvd (97470)
Rates: $89-$105
(541) 673-7517
(800) 465-4329
(800) 898-ROOM

HOWARD JOHNSON EXPRESS INN
978 NE Stephens St (97470)
Rates: $52-$82
(541) 673-5082
(800) 446-4656

MOTEL 6
3100 NW Aviation (97470)
Rates: $39-$50
(541) 464-8000
(800) 466-8356

QUALITY INN CENTRAL
427 NW Garden Valley Blvd (97470)
Rates: $45-$129
(541) 673-5561
(800) 424-6423

ROSE CITY MOTEL
1142 NE Stephens St (97470)
Rates: $30-$50
(541) 673-8209

SHADY OAKS MOTEL
2954 Old Hwy 99 S (97470)
Rates: $34-$49
(541) 672-2608

SLEEP INN
2866 NW Edenbower Blvd (97470)
Rates: $54-$94
(541) 464-8338
(800) 753-3746

SUPER 8 MOTEL
3200 NW Aviation Dr (97470)
Rates: $48-$65
(541) 672-8880
(800) 800-8000

SYCAMORE MOTEL NATIONAL 9
1627 SE Stephens St (97470)
Rates: n/a
(541) 672-3354
(800) 524-9999

SLEEP INN, INN & SUITES
2855 NW Edenbower Blvd (97470)
Rates: $49-$89
(541) 464-8338
(800) 424-6423

TRAVELODGE
315 W Harvard Blvd (97470)
Rates: $58-$78
(541) 672-4836
(800) 578-7878

VISTA MOTEL
1183 NE Stephens St (97470)
Rates: $30-$40
(541) 673-2736

WINDMILL INN
1450 NW Mulholland Dr (97470)
Rates: $80-$102
(541) 673-0901
(800) 547-4747

RUFUS

DINTY'S MOTOR INN
P.O. Box 136 (97050)
Rates: n/a
(541) 739-2596

TYEE MOTEL
304 1/2 E 1st St (97050)
Rates: $40-$45
(541) 739-2310

ST. HELENS

BEST WESTERN OAK MEADOWS INN
585 S Columbia River Hwy (97501)
Rates: $69-$109
(503) 397-3000
(800) 528-1234

VILLAGE INN MOTEL
535 S Hwy 30 (97501)
Rates: n/a
(503) 397-1490

SALEM

BEST WESTERN NEW KINGS INN
1600 Motor Court NE (97301)
Rates: $74-$134
(503) 581-1559
(800) 528-1234
(877) 594-1110

BEST WESTERN PACIFIC HIGHWAY INN
4646 Portland Rd NE (97305)
Rates: $62-$88
(503) 390-3200
(800) 528-1234
(800) 832-8905

CITY CENTER MOTEL
510 Liberty St SE (97301)
Rates: $40-$60
(503) 364-0121
(800) 289-0121

EAGLE CREST B&B
4401 Eagle Crest NW (97301)
Rates: $55
(503) 364-3960

HOLIDAY INN EXP
890 Hawthorne Ave SE (97301)
Rates: $59-$129
(503) 391-7000
(800) 465-4329
(866) 391-7222

HOLIDAY LODGE
1400 Hawthorne Ave NE (97301)
Rates: $40-$90
(503) 585-2323

MAR DON MOTEL
3355 Portland Rd NE (97301)
Rates: $30-$45
(503) 585-2089

MOTEL 6
1401 Hawthorne Ave NE (97302)
Rates: $37-$58
(503) 371-8024
(800) 466-8356

OREGON

CAPITAL INN
745 Commercial St
SE (97308)
Rates: $34-$49
(503) 363-2451

**PHOENIX INN
SUITES-NORTH**
1590 Weston Ct
NE (97301)
Rates: $79-$99
(503) 581-7004
(888) 239-9593

**PHOENIX INN
SUITES-SOUTH**
4370 Commercial
SE (97308)
Rates: $79-$99
(503) 588-9220
(800) 445-4498

RED LION HOTEL
3301 Market St NE
(97301)
Rates: $59-$99
(503) 370-7888
(800) 733-5466

**RESIDENCE INN
BY MARRIOTT**
640 Hawthorne
Ave SE (97301)
Rates: $100-$120
(503) 585-6500
(800) 331-3131

**SALEM COMFORT
SUITES**
630 Hawthorne
Ave SE (97301)
Rates: $89-$99
(503) 585-9705

SALEM INN
1775 Freeway CT
NE (97303)
Rates: $59-$119
(503) 588-0515
(888) 305-0515

SUPER 8 MOTEL
1288 Hawthorne
NE (97301)
Rates: $54-$79
(503) 370-8888
(800) 800-8000

SHILO INN SUITES
3304 Market St NE
(97301)
Rates: $59-$149
(503) 581-4001
(800) 222-2244

TIKI LODGE MOTEL
3705 Market St NE
(97301)
Rates: $39-$59
(503) 581-4441
(800) 438-8458

**TRAVELERS INN
MOTEL**
3230 Portland Rd
NE (97303)
Rates: $32-$59
(503) 581-2444
(800) 740-3900

**TRAVELODGE-
SALEM
CAPITAL**
1555 State St
(97301)
Rates: $39-$69
(503) 581-2466
(800) 578-7878
(866) 471-9912

SANDY

**BEST WESTERN
SANDY INN**
37465 Hwy 26
(97055)
Rates: $72-$95
(503) 668-7100
(800) 528-1234
(888) 882-1214

BROOKSIDE B&B
45232 SE Paha
Loop (97055)
Rates: $40-$70
(503) 668-4766

SCAPPOOSE

**MALARKEY
RANCH B&B**
55948 Columbia
River Hwy (97056)
Rates: n/a
(503) 543-5244

SEASIDE

A RIVERSIDE INN
430 S Holladay Dr
(97138)
Rates: $49-$129
(503) 738-8254

**BEST WESTERN
OCEAN VIEW
RESORT**
414 N Promenade
(97138)
Rates: $75-$375
(503) 738-3334
(800) 528-1234
(800) 234-8439

CITY CENTER MOTEL
250 1st Ave
(97138)
Rates: $48-$149
(503) 738-6377
(800) 479-5191

COAST RIVER INN
800 S Holladay Dr
(97138)
Rates: n/a
(503) 738-8474

**COLONIAL
MOTOR INN**
1120 N Holladay
Dr (97138)
Rates: $47-$210
(503) 738-6295

**COMFORT INN
BOARDWALK**
545 Broadway
(97138)
Rates: $69-$279
(503) 738-3011
(800) 424-6423

MOTEL 6
2369 S Roosevelt
(97138)
Rates: $41-$68
(503) 738-6269
(800) 466-8356

**ROGERS INN
& VACATION
HOMES**
436 S Downing
(97138)
Rates: $65-$395
(503) 738-7367
(888) 717-7367

**SEA SIDE OCEAN-
FRONT INN B&B**
581 S Promenade
(97138)
Rates: $95-$305
(503) 738-6403
(800) 772-7766

SEASIDE INN
441 2nd Ave
(97138)
Rates: $99-$189
(503) 738-9581
(800) 699-5070

SEASIDER MOTEL
110 5th Ave
(97138)
Rates: $50-$75
(503) 738-7764
(800) 840-7764

**SEASIDER II
MOTEL**
210 N Downing St
(97138)
Rates: $45-$75
(503) 738-7622

SEAVIEW INN
120 9th Ave
(97138)
Rates: $54-$84
(503) 738-5371
(800) 479-5191

**SHILO INN
SEASIDE EAST**
900 S Holladay
(97138)
Rates: $49-$159
(503) 738-0549
(800) 222-2244

SHADY COVE

**EDGEWATER INN
ON THE ROGUE
RIVER**
7800 Rogue River
Dr (97539)
Rates: $74-$109
(541) 878-3171
(888) 811-3171

SISTERS

**ASPEN
MEADOW LODGE**
68733 Junipine Ln
(97759)
Rates: $89-$129
(541) 549-4312
(866) 549-4312

**BEST WESTERN
PONDEROSA
LODGE**
500 Hwy 20 W
(97759)
Rates: $79-$169
(541) 549-1234
(800) 528-1234
(888) 549-4321

BLUE LAKE RESORT
Blue Lake Dr,
Hwy 20/126
(97759)
Rates: $68-$108
(541) 595-6671

COMFORT INN
540 Hwy 20 W
(97759)
Rates: $80-$105
(541) 549-7829
(800) 424-6423

**CONKLIN'S
GUEST
HOUSE B&B**
69013 Camp Polk
Rd (97759)
Rates: $90-$150
(541) 549-0123
(800) 549-4262

**RAGS TO
WALKERS
GUEST RANCH**
17045 Farthing Ln
(97759)
Rates: $95-$150
(541) 548-7000
(800) 422--5622

SQUAW CREEK B&B
68733 Junipine Ln
(97759)
Rates: $80-$90
(541) 549-4312
(800) 930-0055

SUN RANCH INN
69013 Camp Polk
Rd (97759)
Rates: $70-$150
(541) 549-0123

SOUTH BEACH

**SOLACE BY THE
SEA B&B**
9602 S Coast Hwy
(97366)
Rates: $110-$175
(541) 867-3566
(800) 4-SOLACE

**THIEL SHORES
MOTEL**
9812 S Coast Hwy
(97366)
Rates: $55-$75
(541) 867-4305

SPRINGFIELD

**BEST WESTERN
GRAND MANOR
INN**
971 Kruse Way
(97477)
Rates: $79-$110
(541) 726-4769
(800) 528-1234

CLARION HOTEL
3280 Gateway Rd
(97477)
Rates: $62-$139
(541) 726-8181
(800) 424-6423

COMFORT SUITES
969 Kruse Way
(97477)
Rates: $59-$145
(541) 746-5359
(800) 424-6423

HOLIDAY INN EXP
3480 Hutton St
(97477)
Rates: $89-$119
(541) 746-8471
(800) 465-4329

MOTEL 6
3752 International
Ct (97477)
Rates: $37-$52
(541) 741-1105
(800) 466-8356

**SHILO
INN & SUITES**
3350 Gateway St
(97477)
Rates: $59-$109
(541) 747-0332
(800) 222-2244

SUPER 8 MOTEL
3315 Gateway St
(97477)
Rates: $45-$67
(541) 746-1314
(800) 800-8000

**VILLAGE INN
MOTEL**
1875 Mohawk
Blvd (97477)
Rates: $62-$82
(541) 747-4546
(800) 327-6871

STAYTON
**GARDNER HOUSE
BED & BREAKFST**
633 N 3rd Ave
(97383)
Rates: $55-$67
(503) 769-5478

SUBLIMITY
**BEST WESTERN
SUNRISE INN**
300 Sublimity
Blvd (97385)
Rates: $69-$99
(503) 769-9579
(800) 528-1234

**SILVER
MOUNTAIN B&B**
4672 Drift Creek
Rd SE (97385)
Rates: $60-$75
(503) 769-7127
(800) 952-3905

SUMMER LAKE
**THE LODGE AT
SUMMER LAKE**
36980 Hwy 31
(97640)
Rates: $50-$72
(541) 943-3993
(866) 943-3993

**SUMMER
LAKE INN**
47531 Hwy 31
(97640)
Rates: $105-$265
(541) 943-3983
(800) 261-2778

SUMPTER
SUMPTER B&B
344 NE Columbia
St (97877)
Rates: n/a
(541) 894-2229
(800) 640-3184

SUNNY VALLEY
**SUNNY VALLEY
MOTEL**
352 Sunny Valley
Loop (97497)
Rates: $30-$45
(541) 476-9217

SUNRIVER
**SUNRAY
VACATION
RENTALS**
P.O. Box 4518
(97707)
Rates: n/a
(541) 593-3225
(800) 531-1130

**SUNRIVER
RESORT**
1 Center Dr
(97707)
Rates: $119-$199
(541) 593-1000
(888) 547-2603

**TWIN LAKES
RESORT**
11200 S Century
Dr (97707)
Rates: $72-$106
(541) 593-6526

**VILLAGE VACA-
TION RENTALS**
P.O. Box 3055
(97707)
Rates: $80-$350
(541) 593-1653
(800) 786-7483

SUTHERLIN
SUTHERLIN INN
1400 Hospitality
Pl (97479)
Rates: $40-$90
(541) 459-6800

**TOWN &
COUNTRY MOTEL**
1386 W Central
Ave (97479)
Rates: $34-$44
(541) 459-9615
(800) 459-9615

**UMPQUA
REGENCY INN**
150 Myrtle St
(97479)
Rates: $56-$79
(541) 459-1424

SWEET HOME
SWEET HOME INN
805 Long St
(97386)
Rates: $45-$125
(541) 367-5137

THE DALLES
**AMERICAN
HOSPITALITY INN**
200 W 2nd St
(97058)
Rates: $40-$65
(541) 296-9111

**BEST WESTERN
RIVER CITY INN**
112 W 2nd St
(97058)
Rates: $49-$99
(541) 296-9107
(800) 528-1234
(888) 935-2378

**CAPTAIN GRAY'S
GUEST HOUSE**
210 W 4th St
(97058)
Rates: $60-$90
(541) 298-2222
(800) 448-4729

COMFORT INN
351 Ln Pine Dr
(97058)
Rates: $55-$119
(541) 298-2800
(800) 424-6423
(800) 955-9626

**COUSINS COUN-
TRY INN**
351 Lone Pine Dr
(97058)
Rates: $62-$99
(541) 298-5161
(800) 848-9378

**INN AT THE
DALLES**
3550 SE Frontage
Rd (97058)
Rates: $28-$60
(541) 296-1167
(800) 982-3496

SHILO INN
3223 Bret
Clodfelter Way
(97058)
Rates: $59-$185
(541) 298-5502
(800) 222-2244

SUPER 8 MOTEL
609 Cherry
Heights Rd
(97058)
Rates: $55-$84
(541) 296-6888
(800) 800-8000

TIGARD
DAYS INN
11455 SW Pacific
Hwy (97223)
Rates: $55-$75
(503) 246-8451
(800) 329-7466

**EMBASSY
SUITES HOTEL**
9000 SW
Washington Sq Rd
(97223)
Rates: $89-$159
(503) 644-4000
(800) 586-5455

**HOMESTEAD
STUDIO SUITES
HOTEL**
13009 SW 68th
Pkwy (97223)
Rates: $56-$104
(503) 670-0555
(888) 782-9473

MOTEL 6
17950 McEwan
Rd SW (97224)
Rates: $39-$48
(503) 620-2066
(800) 466-8356

RAMADA LIMITED
17993 Lower
Boones Ferry Rd
(97224)
Rates: n/a
(503) 620-2030
(800) 272-6232

**SHILO INN-
WASHINGTON
SQUARE**
10830 SW
Greenburg Rd
(97223)
Rates: $49-$99
(503) 620-4320
(800) 222-2244

TILLAMOOK
MAR-CLAIR INN
11 Main Ave
(97141)
Rates: $60-$80
(503) 842-7571
(800) 331-6857

**SHILO
INN & SUITES**
2515 N Main Ave
(97141)
Rates: $59-$189
(503) 842-7971
(800) 222-2244

TRAIL
**OBSTINATE
J RANCH**
29680 Hwy 62
(97541)
Rates: $80-$110
(541) 878-2718

TROUTDALE
**COMFORT INN
& SUITES**
477 NW Phoenix
Dr (97060)
Rates: $60-$150
(503) 669-6500
(800) 424-6423

HOLIDAY INN EXP
1000 NW
Gresham Rd
(97060)
Rates: $69-$89
(503) 492-2900
(800) 465-4329

AREA CODES - If the local number doesn't connect, check for a new area code.

MOTEL 6
1610 NW Frontage
Rd (97060)
Rates: $43-$48
(503) 665-2254
(800) 466-8356

TRAVELODGE
23705 NE Sandy
Blvd (97060)
Rates: $36-$69
(503) 666-6623
(877) 753-3794

TUALATIN
**COMFORT INN &
SUITES**
7640 SW Warm
Springs St (97062)
Rates: $79-$149
(503) 612-9952
(800) 424-6423

**SWEETBRIER
INN & SUITES**
7125 SW Nyberg
Rd (97062)
Rates: $75-$115
(503) 692-5800
(800) 551-9167

UMATILLA
**DESERT
RIVER INN**
705 Willamette
Ave (97882)
Rates: $58-$81
(541) 922-1000
(877) 922-1500

**UMATILLA
INN & SUITES**
1370 6th St, Hwy
730 (97882)
Rates: $45-$55
(541) 922-3271
(800) 423-9913

UNION
**ANGLE FARM
COUNTRY INN
BED & BREAKFST**
1782 S Main St
(97883)
Rates: n/a
(541) 562-5671

UNION CREEK
**UNION CREEK
RESORT**
56484 Hwy 62
(97536)
Rates: $38-$80
(541) 560-3565

VALE
**1900 SEARS &
ROEBUCK HOME
B&B**
484 N 10th (97918)
Rates: $50-$95
(541) 889-9009

VERNONIA
VERNONIA INN
900 Madison Ave
(97064)
Rates: $49-$95
(503) 429-4006
(800) 354-9494

VIDA
**EAGLE ROCK
LODGE B&B**
49198 McKenzie
Hwy (97488)
Rates: $75-$195
(541) 822-3630
(888) 733-4333

**MCKENZIE RIVER
INN B&B & CABINS**
49164 McKenzie
Hwy (97488)
Rates: $89-$145
(541) 822-6260

**WAYFARER
RESORT
COTTAGES**
46725
Goodpasture Rd
(97488)
Rates: $65-$250
(541) 896-3613
(800) 627-3613

WALDPORT
**ALSEA MANOR
MOTEL**
190 SW Hwy 101
(97394)
Rates: $65-$79
(541) 563-3249
(888) 700-0503

**EDGEWATER
COTTAGES**
3978 SW Pacific
Coast Hwy
(97394)
Rates: $90-$205
(541) 563-2240

**SUNDOWN
MOTEL**
5050 SW Pacific
Coast Hwy
(97394)
Rates: $41-$95
(541) 563-3018

WALLOWA
**CHEROKEE
MINGO MOTEL**
102 N Alder
(97885)
Rates: $40+
(541) 886-2021

WARRENTON
RAY'S MOTEL
45 NE Skipanon
Dr (97146)
Rates: $32-$43
(503) 861-2566
(800) 348-2566

WELCHES
**MT. HOOD
VILLAGE RESORT**
65000 E Hwy 26
(97067)
Rates: n/a
(503) 622-4011
(800) 255-3069

**OLD WELCHES
INN B&B**
26401 E Welches
Rd (97067)
Rates: $106-$162
(503) 622-3574

**OREGON ARK
MOTEL**
61700 E Hwy 26
(97067)
Rates: $30-$50
(503) 622-3121

**THE RESORT AT
THE MOUNTAIN**
68010 E Fairway
Ave (97067)
Rates: $99-$450
(503) 622-3101

WESTLAKE
**SILTCOOS LAKE
RESORT**
82855 Fir St
(97493)
Rates: $35-$65
(541) 997-3741

WESTON
**TAMARACK INN
B&B**
62388 Hwy 204
(97886)
Rates: $75-$110
(541) 566-9348
(800) 662-9348

WESTPORT
**WESTPORT
MOTEL**
Hwy 30, East of
Astoria
Rates: $48-$80
(503) 455-2212

WHEELER
**WHEELER ON
THE BAY LODGE
& MARINA**
580 Marine Dr
(97147)
Rates: $50-$145
(503) 368-5858

WILSONVILLE
**BEST WESTERN
WILLAMETTE INN**
30800 SW
Parkway Ave
(97070)
Rates: $70-$90
(503) 682-2288
(800) 528-1234
(888) 682-0101

**BURNS WEST
MOTEL**
8750 SW Elligsen
Rd (97070)
Rates: n/a
(503) 682-2123
(800) 909-2876

COMFORT INN
8855 SW Citizen
Dr (97070)
Rates: $59-$109
(503) 682-9000
(800) 424-6423

**DAYS INN
& SUITES**
8815 SW Sun
Place (97070)
Rates: $45-$79
(503) 682-3184
(800) 329-7466

HOLIDAY INN
25425 SW 95th
Ave (97070)
Rates: $71-$125
(503) 682-2211
(800) 465-4329

WINSTON
**SWEET BREEZE
INN II**
251 NE Main St
(97496)
Rates: $55-$70
(541) 579-2420

WOOD VILLAGE
TRAVELODGE
23705 E Sandy
Blvd (97060)
Rates: $38-$89
(503) 666-6623
(800) 578-7878

WOODBURN
**BEST WESTERN
WOODBURN INN**
2887 Newberg
Hwy (97071)
Rates: $59-$149
(503) 982-6515
(800) 528-1234
(800) 766-6433

LA QUINTA INN
120 NE Arney Rd
(97071)
Rates: $75-$125
(503) 982-1272
(800) 687-6667

WOODBURN INN
1025 N Pacific
Hwy (97071)
Rates: $40-$55
(503) 982-9741

YACHATS
**THE ADOBE
RESORT**
1555 Hwy 101
(97498)
Rates: $65-$400
(541) 547-3141
(800) 522-3623

**BEACHCOMBER'S
MOTEL**
95500 Hwy 101 S
(97498)
Rates: $30-$100
(541) 547-3432

**THE DUBLIN
HOUSE**
251 W 7th St
(97489)
Rates: $49-$160
(541) 547-3200

**FIRESIDE RESORT
MOTEL**
1881 Hwy 101 N
(97498)
Rates: $75-$130
(541) 547-3636
(800) 336-3573

AREA CODES - If the local number doesn't connect, check for a new area code.

GRACE COVE RENTAL
466 Ocean View
Dr (97498)
Rates: $115
(541) 547-4111

OCEAN COVE INN
180 Prospect Ave
(97498)
Rates: $75-$130
(541) 547-3900

RAVEN'S RETREAT RENTAL
228 Jennifer
(97498)
Rates: $90-$120
(541) 547-4111

ROCK PARK COTTAGES
431 West 2nd St
(97498)
Rates: $65-$115
(541) 547-3214

SEE VUE MOTEL
95590 Hwy 101
(97498)
Rates: $49-$65
(541) 547-3227

SHAMROCK LODGETTES
105 Hwy 101 S
(97498)
Rates: $59-$200
(541) 547-3312

SHORE PINES COTTAGE RENTAL
88 Trout St (97498)
Rates: $70
(541) 547-4111

SILVER SURF MOTEL
3767 Hwy 101 N
(97498)
Rates: $59-$159
(541) 547-3175
(800) 281-5723

WILDWOOD LODGE VACATION RENTAL
1430 King St
(97498)
Rates: $250-$495+
(541) 465-9010

YA-TEL MOTEL
640 Hwy 101
(97498)
Rates: $45-$95
(541) 547-3225
(800) 406-1338

YACHATS INN
331 Hwy 101 S
(97498)
Rates: $80-$125
(541) 547-3456
(888) 270-3456

YACHATS VACATION RENTAL HOME
c/o Sweetland
Properties
P. O. Box 525
(Waldport 97394)
Rates: $100 Night
$550 Weekly
(541) 563-5913

YACHATS VILLAGE RENTALS
P.O. Box 44
(97498)
Rates: n/a
(541) 547-3501

YAMHILL

FLYING M GUEST RANCH
23029 NW Flying
M Rd (97148)
Rates: $60-$200
(503) 662-3222

PENNSYLVANIA

ABBOTTSTOWN

THE ALTLAND HOUSE
Center Sq Rt 30 (17901)
Rates: $99-$150
(717) 259-9535

ADAMSTOWN

THE BARNYARD INN B&B & SUITES
2145 Old Lancaster Pike (17569)
Rates: $85-$100
(717) 484-1111

BLACK FOREST INN
2828 N Reading Rd (19501)
Rates: $49-$109
(717) 484-4801

ALLENTOWN

ALLENWOOD MOTEL
1058 Hausman Rd (18104)
Rates: $49-$125
(610) 395-3707

COMFORT INN LEHIGH VALLEY WEST
7625 Imperial Way (18106)
Rates: $69-$129
(610) 391-0344
(800) 424-6423

CROWN PLAZA HOTEL
904 Hamilton St (18101)
Rates: $94-$169
(610) 433-2221
(800) 424-6423
(800) 227-6963

DAYS INN
1151 Bulldog Dr (18104)
Rates: $49-$145
(610) 395-3731
(800) 329-7466
(888) 395-5200

FOUR POINTS BY SHERATON HOTEL & SUITES
3400 Airport Rd (18109)
Rates: $79-$159
(610) 266-1000
(800) 325-3535

HOLIDAY INN
7736 Adrienne Dr (18103)
Rates: $54-$95
(610) 391-1000
(800) 465-4329

MICROTEL INN
1880 Steelstone Rd (18103)
Rates: $35-$139
(610) 266-9070
(888) 771-7171
(800) 647-7280

QUALITY INN
1033 Airport Rd (18109)
Rates: $39-$199
(610) 434-9550
(800) 424-6423

RED ROOF INN
1846 Catasauqua Rd (18103)
Rates: $48-$98
(610) 264-5404
(800) 843-7663

STAYBRIDGE SUITES
1787 A Airport Rd (18109
Rates: $89-$169
(610) 443-5000
(800) 238-8000

SUPER 8 MOTEL
1715 Plaza Ln (18104)
Rates: $65-$95
(610) 435-7880
(800) 800-8000

ALTOONA

ECONO LODGE
2906 Pleasant Vly Blvd (16601)
Rates: $50-$66
(814) 944-3555
(800) 424-6423

MOTEL 6
1500 Sterling St (16601)
Rates: $39-$47
(814) 946-7601
(800) 466-8356

SUPER 8 MOTEL
3535 Fairway Dr (16601)
Rates: $44-$60
(814) 942-5350
(800) 800-8000

ALUM BANK

WEST VU MOTEL
4158 Quaker Valley Rd (15521)
Rates: $32-$45
(814) 839-2632

BARKEYVILLE

COMFORT INN
137 Gibb Rd (16038)
Rates: $55-$85
(814) 786-7901
(800) 424-6423

SUPER 8 MOTEL
1010 Dholu Rd (16038)
Rates: $48-$69
(814) 786-8375
(800) 800-8000

BARTONS-VILLE

(See Pocono Mountains Area)

BEAVER FALLS

HOLIDAY INN
7195 Eastwood Rd (15010)
Rates: $89
(724) 846-3700
(800) 465-4329

BEDFORD

BEST WESTERN BEDFORD INN
4517 Business Rt 220 N (15522)
Rates: $57-$86
(814) 623-9006
(800) 528-1234
(800) 752-8592

BUDGET HOST INN
4378 Business Rt 220 (15522)
Rates: $29-$85
(814) 623-8107
(800) 283-4678

ECONO LODGE
141 Hillcrest Dr (15522)
Rates: $36-$90
(814) 623-5174
(800) 424-6423

JANEY LYNN MOTEL
3567 Business Rt 220 N (15522)
Rates: $29-$75
(814) 623-9515

MOTEL TOWN HOUSE
200 S Richard St (15522)
Rates: $32-$65
(814) 623-5138
(800) 879-8696

QUALITY INN
4407 Business Rt 220 N (15522)
Rates: $57-$125
(814) 623-5188
(800) 424-6423

SUPER 8 MOTEL
4498 Business Rt 220 N (15522)
Rates: $50-$60
(814) 623-5880
(800) 800-8000

TRAVELODGE
4721 Business Rt 220 (15522)
Rates: $39-$109
(814) 623-7800
(800) 578-7878

BENSALEM

HOLIDAY INN
3499 Street Rd (19020)
Rates: $119-$139
(215) 638-1500
(800) 465-4329

SLEEP INN, INN & SUITES
3427 Street Rd (19020)
Rates: $69-$149
(215) 244-2300
(800) 424-6423

BENTON

THE RED POPPY HISTORIC B&B
RR 2, Box 82 (17814)
Rates: $55-$85
(570) 925-5823

BERWICK

RED MAPLE INN
RR 3, Rt 11 (18603)
Rates: $40-$70
(717) 752-6220

BERWYN

RESIDENCE INN BY MARRIOTT
600 W Swedesford Rd (19312)
Rates: $169
(610) 640-9494
(800) 331-3131

BETHEL

COMFORT INN MIDWAY
41 Diner Rd (19507)
Rates: $69-$129
(717) 933-8888
(800) 424-6423

BETHEL PARK

HOLIDAY INN SELECT
164 Ft. Couch Rd (15241
Rates: $99-$242
(412) 833-5300
(800) 465-4329

BETHLEHEM

COMFORT INN
3191 Highfield Dr (18017)
Rates: $69-$139
(610) 865-6300
(800) 424-6423

COMFORT SUITES
120 W 3rd St
(18017)
Rates: $69-$149
(610) 882-9700
(800) 424-6423

HOLIDAY INN
300 Gateway Dr
(18017)
Rates: $99-$129
(610) 866-5800
(800) 465-4329

RESIDENCE INN BY MARRIOTT
2180 Motel Dr
(18018)
Rates: $139-$209
(610) 317-2662
(800) 331-3131

BLAKESLEE
(See Pocono Mountains Area)

BLOOMSBURG
ECONO LODGE
189 Columbia Mall Dr (17815)
Rates: $66-$169
(570) 387-0490
(800) 424-6423

THE INN AT TURKEY HILL
991 Central Rd
(17815)
Rates: $102-$119
(570) 387-1500

MAGEE'S MAIN STREET
20 W Main St
(17815)
Rates: $55-$150
(800) 331-9815

BLUE BELL
KORMANSUITES EXTENDED STAY
1707 Meadow Dr
(17506)
Rates: n/a
(610) 275-5265
(800) 567-6268

BLUE MOUNTAIN
KENMAR MOTEL
17788 Cumberland Hwy
(17240)
Rates: $45-$75
(717) 423-5915

BOYERTOWN
MEL-DOR MOTEL
494 Swamp Creek Rd (19545)
Rates: $51-$54
(610) 367-2626

BRADFORD
BEST WESTERN BRADFORD INN
100 Davis St
(16701)
Rates: $70-$159
(814) 362-4501
(800) 528-1234
(800) 344-4656

COMFORT INN
76 Elm St (16701)
Rates: $69-$121
(814) 368-6772
(800) 424-6423

GLENDORN-A LODGE IN THE COUNTRY
1032 W Coryden
(16701)
Rates: $395-$795
(814) 362-6511

BREEZEWOOD
BEST WESTERN PLAZA MOTOR LODGE
16407 Lincoln Hwy (15533)
Rates: $52-$70
(814) 735-4352
(866) 768-7256

HERITAGE INN
16550 Lincoln Hwy (15533)
Rates: $49-$79
(814) 735-2200

RAMADA INN
16620 Lincoln Hwy (15533)
Rates: $41-$79
(814) 735-4005
(800) 272-6232

WILTSHIRE MOTEL
140 S Breezewood Rd (15533)
Rates: $34-$50
(814) 735-4361

BRIDGEVILLE
KNIGHTS INN
111 Hickory Grade Rd (15017)
Rates: $50-$55
(412) 221-8110
(800) 843-5644

BROOKVILLE
BUDGET HOST GOLD EAGLE INN
250 W Main St
(15825)
Rates: $45-$75
(814) 849-7344
(800) 283-4678

DAYS INN
230 Allegheny Blvd (15825)
Rates: $50-$90
(814) 849-8001
(800) 329-7466

HOLIDAY INN EXP
235 Allegheny Blvd (15825)
Rates: $59-$79
(814) 849-8381
(800) 465-4329

SUPER 8 MOTEL
251 Allegheny Blvd (15825)
Rates: $45-$65
(814) 849-8840
(800) 800-8000

BUTLER
COMFORT INN
1 Comfort Ln
(16001)
Rates: $69-$149
(724) 287-7177
(800) 424-6423

SUPER 8 MOTEL
138 Pittsburgh Rd
(16001)
Rates: $50-$65
(724) 287-8888
(800) 800-8000

CAMBRIDGE SPRINGS
RIVERSIDE INN-HISTORIC COUNTRY INN
1 Fountain Ave
(16403)
Rates: $65-$170
(814) 398-4645

CANONSBURG
SUPER 8 MOTEL
8 Curry Ave
(15317)
Rates: $58-$69
(724) 873-8808
(800) 800-8000

CARLISLE
COMFORT SUITES
10 S Hanover St
(17013)
Rates: $79-$209
(717) 960-1000
(800) 424-6423

DAYS INN
101 Alexander Springs Rd
(17013)
Rates: $70-$170
(717) 258-4147
(800) 329-7466

ECONO LODGE
1460 Harrisburg Pike (17013)
Rates: $39-$149
(717) 249-7775
(800) 424-6423

HAMPTON INN
1164 Harrisburg Pike (17013)
Rates: $69-$159
(717) 240-0200
(800) 426-7866

HOLIDAY INN
1450 Harrisburg Pike (17013)
Rates: $55-$104
(717) 245-2400
(800) 465-4329

HOTEL CARLISLE
1700 Harrisburg Pike (17013)
Rates: $74-$169
(717) 243-1717
(800) 293-4243

HOWARD JOHNSON INN
1245 Hamburg Pike (17013)
Rates: $49-$139
(717) 243-5411
(800) 446-4656

MOTEL 6
1153 Harrisburg Pike (17013)
Rates: $29-$42
(717) 249-7622
(800) 466-8356

PHEASANT FIELD B&B
150 Hickorytown Rd (17013)
Rates: $90-$175
(717) 258-0717

QUALITY INN
1255 Harrisburg Pike (17013)
Rates: $60-$130
(717) 243-6000
(800) 424-6423

RAMADA LTD
1252 Harrisburg Pike (17013)
Rates: $65-$79
(717) 243-8585
(800) 272-6232

RODEWAY INN
1239 Harrisburg Pike (17013)
Rates: $45-$125
(717) 249-2800
(800) 424-6423

SLEEP INN
5 E Garland Dr
(17013)
Rates: $70-$137
(717) 249-8863
(800) 424-6423

SUPER 8 MOTEL-NORTH
1800 Harrisburg Pike (17013)
Rates: $29-$129
(717) 249-7000
(800) 800-8000

SUPER 8 MOTEL-SOUTH
100 Alexander Spring Rd (17013)
Rates: $42-$68
(717) 245-9898
(800) 800-8000

CHADDS FORD
BRANDYWINE RIVER HOTEL
US 1 & SR 100
(19317)
Rates: $125-$169
(610) 388-1200

CHALK HILL
HISTORIC SUMMIT INN
101 Skyline Dr
(Farmington 15421)
Rates: $89-$211
(724) 438-8594

LODGE AT CHALK HILL
Rt 40E, Box 240
(15421)
Rates: $49-$84
(724) 438-8880
(800) 833-4283

AREA CODES - If the local number doesn't connect, check for a new area code.

CHAMBERS-BURG

BEST WESTERN
211 Walker Rd
(17201)
Rates: $50-$139
(717) 262-4994
(877) 292-4262

COMFORT INN
3301 Black Gap
Rd (17201)
Rates: $59-$129
(717) 263-6655
(800) 424-6423

DAYS INN
30 Falling Springs
Rd (17201)
Rates: $59-$109
(717) 263-1288
(800) 329-7466

ECONO LODGE
1110 Sheller Ave
(17201)
Rates: $39-$99
(717) 264-8005
(800) 424-6423

TRAVELODGE
565 Lincoln Way E
(17201)
Rates: $30-$89
(717) 264-4187
(800) 578-7878

CLARION

HOLIDAY INN
45 Holiday Inn
Rd (16214)
Rates: $95+
(814) 226-8850
(800) 465-4329

MICROTEL INN & SUITES
151 Hotel Dr
(16214)
Rates: $54-$74
(814) 227-2700

SUPER 8 MOTEL
135 Hotel Rd
(16214)
Rates: $39-$80
(814) 226-4550
(800) 800-8000

CLARKS SUMMIT

COMFORT INN
811 Northern Blvd
(18411)
Rates: $55-$150
(570) 586-9100
(800) 424-6423

THE INN AT NICHOLS VILLAGE
1101 Northern
Blvd (18411)
Rates: $89-$220
(570) 587-1135
(800) 642-2215

RAMADA PLAZA HOTEL
820 Northern Blvd
(18411)
Rates: $89-$169
(570) 586-2732
(800) 272-6232

CLEARFIELD

BUDGET INN
6321 Woodland
Hwy (16830)
Rates: $32-$62
(814) 765-2639

COMFORT INN
1821 Industrial
Park Rd (16830)
Rates: $55-$150
(814) 768-6400
(800) 424-6423

DAYS INN
Rt 879 & I-80
(16830)
Rates: $45-$125
(814) 765-5381
(800) 329-7466

RAMADA INN
150 Hotel Heights
(16830)
Rates: n/a
(814) 765-2441
(800) 272-6232

SUPER 8 MOTEL
14597 Clearfield/
Shawville Hwy
(16830)
Rates: $46-$81
(814) 768-7580
(800) 800-8000

CONSHO-HOCKEN

RESIDENCE INN BY MARRIOTT
191Washington St
(19428)
Rates: $99-$229
(610) 828-8800
(800) 331-3131

COOKSBURG

CLARION RIVER LODGE RESORT & SPA
River Rd (16217)
Rates: $122-$551
(814) 744-8171
(800) 252-7466

COOPERSBURG

ECONO LODGE
321 S 3rd St
(18036)
Rates: $53-$89
(610) 282-1212
(800) 424-6423

CORAOPOLIS

COMFORT SUITES
750 Aten Rd
(15108)
Rates: $89+
(412) 494-5750
(800) 424-6423

EMBASSY SUITES
550 Cherrington
Pkwy (15108)
Rates: $89-$199
(412) 269-9070
(800) 362-2779

HAMPTON INN AIRPORT
8514 University
Blvd (15108)
Rates: $89-$99
(412) 264-0020
(800) 426-7866

HOLIDAY INN INT'L AIRPORT
8256 University
Blvd (15108)
Rates: $119-$139
(412) 262-3600
(800) 465-4329

LA QUINTA INN AIRPORT
8507 University
Blvd (15108)
Rates: $75-$106
(412) 269-0400
(800) 687-6667

MOTEL 6 AIRPORT
1170 Thorn Run
Rd (15108)
Rates: $29-$36
(412) 269-0990
(800) 466-8356

SLEEP INN
2500 Market Place
Blvd (15108)
Rates: $69-$139
(412) 859-4000
(800) 424-6423

COUDERSPORT

BIG MOORE'S RUN LODGE
2218 Big Moore's
Run Rd (16915)
Rates: $60-$80
(814) 647-5300

CRANBERRY TOWNSHIP

AMERISUITES
136 Emeryville Dr
(16066)
Rates: $89-$125
(724) 779-7900
(800) 833-1516

HAMPTON INN
210 Executive Dr
(16066)
Rates: $104
(724) 776-1000
(800) 426-7866

HOLIDAY INN EXP
20003 Rt 19
(16066)
Rates: $74-$79
(724) 772-1000
(800) 465-4329

RED ROOF INN
20009 Rt 19
(16066)
Rates: $40-$76
(724) 776-5670
(800) 843-7663

DANVILLE

HAMPTON INN
97 Valley School
Rd (17821)
Rates: $99-$199
(570) 271-2500
(800) 426-7866

QUALITY INN & SUITES
15 Valley West Rd
(17821)
Rates: $69-$149
(570) 275-5100
(800) 424-6423

DELMONT

SUPER 8 MOTEL
180 Sheffield Dr
(15626)
Rates: $48-$60
(724) 468-4888
(800) 800-8000

DENVER

BLACK HORSE LODGE & SUITES
2180 N Reading
Rd (17517)
Rates: $59-$159
(717) 336-7563

COMFORT INN
2015 N Reading
Rd (17517)
Rates: $59-$159
(717) 336-4649
(800) 424-6423

HOLIDAY INN
1 Denver Rd
(17517)
Rates: $69-$159
(717) 336-7541
(800) 465-4329

PENNSYLVANIA DUTCH MOTEL
2275 N Reading
Rd (17517)
Rates: $36-$50
(717) 336-5559

DICKSON CITY

(See Pocono
Mountains Area)

DOUGLASS-VILLE

ECONO LODGE
387 Ben Franklin
Hwy (19518)
Rates: $50-$145
(610) 385-3016
(800) 424-6423

DU BOIS

HOLIDAY INN
US 219 & I-80
(15801)
Rates: $75-$83
(814) 371-5100
(800) 959-3412

DUBLIN

STONE RIDGE FARM B&B
956 Bypass Rd
(18944)
Rates: $99-$225
(215) 249-9186

DUNCANSVILLE
COMFORT INN
130 Patchway Rd
(16635)
Rates: $75-$115
(814) 693-1800
(800) 424-6423

DUNMORE
(See Pocono
Mountains Area)

EAST NORRITON
SUMMERFIELD SUITES BY WYNDHAM
501 E
Germantown Pike
(19401)
Rates: $119-$149
(610) 313-9990
(800) 833-4353

EAST STROUDSBURG
(See Pocono
Mountains Area)

EASTON
BEST WESTERN EASTON INN
185 S 3rd St
(18042)
Rates: $69-$129
(610) 253-9131
(800) 528-1234
(800) 882-0113

DAYS INN
2555 Nazareth Rd
(18042)
Rates: $49-$150
(610) 253-0546
(800) 329-7466

EBENSBURG
COMFORT INN
111 Cook Rd
(15931)
Rates: $58-$125
(814) 472-6100
(800) 424-6423

THE COTTAGE
RD 4, Box 50
(15931)
Rates: $48-$64
(814) 472-8002

EMLENTON
WHIPPLE TREE INN & FARM B&B
Big Bend Rd (16373)
Rates: $50-$60
(724) 867-9543

ENTRIKEN
RAYSTOWN RESORT & LODGE
Rt 994 (16638)
Rates: n/a
(814) 658-3500

EPHRATA
SMITHTON COUNTRY INN HISTORIC B&B
900 W Main St
(17522)
Rates: $85-$150
(717) 733-6094

ERIE
BEST WESTERN ERIE INN
7820 Perry Hwy
(16509)
Rates: $52-$129
(814) 864-1812
(800) 528-1234

BEST WESTERN PRESQUE ISLE COUNTRY INN
6467 Sterrettania
Rd (16415)
Rates: $49-$99
(814) 838-7647
(800) 528-1234

COUNTRY INN & SUITES
8040 Oliver Rd
(16509)
Rates: $49-$129
(814) 864-5810
(800) 456-4000

DAYS INN
7415 Schultz Rd
(16509)
Rates: $40-$100
(814) 868-8521
(800) 329-7466

HAMPTON INN
8050 Old Oliver
Rd (16509)
Rates: $74-$139
(814) 866-6800
(800) 426-7866

HOMEWOOD SUITES
2084 Interchange
Rd (16565)
Rates: $89-$149
(814) 866-8292
(800) 225-5466

MICROTEL INN
8100 Peach St
(16509)
Rates: $42-$77
(814) 864-1010
(888) 771-7171
(800) 975-4400

MOTEL 6
7575 Peach St (16509)
Rates: $42-$90
(814) 864-4811
(800) 466-8356

QUALITY INN
8040 Perry Hwy
(16509)
Rates: $45-$170
(814) 864-4911
(800) 424-6423

RED ROOF INN
7865 Perry Hwy
(16509)
Rates: $40-$78
(814) 868-5246
(800) 843-7663

RESIDENCE INN BY MARRIOTT
8061 Peach St
(16509)
Rates: $129-$299
(814) 864-2500
(800) 331-3131

RODEWAY INN
2540 W 8th St
(16505)
Rates: $45-$90
(814) 838-2081
(800) 424-6423

SUPER 8 MOTEL
8040 B Perry Hwy
(16506)
Rates: $42-$99
(814) 864-9200
(800) 800-8000

ERWINNA
HISTORIC GOLDEN PHEASANT COUNTRY INN
763 River Rd
(18920)
Rates: $95-$225
(610) 294-9595

ESSINGTON
COMFORT INN AIRPORT
53 Industrial Hwy
(19029)
Rates: $59-$125
(610) 521-9800
(800) 424-6423

HOLIDAY INN AIRPORT
45 Industrial Hwy
(19029)
Rates: $119-$129
(610) 521-2400
(800) 465-4329

MOTEL 6 AIRPORT
43 Industrial
Hwy (19029)
Rates: $53-$66
(610) 521-6650
(800) 466-8356

RED ROOF INN AIRPORT
49 Industrial Hwy
(19029)
Rates: $75-$95
(610) 521-5090
(800) 843-7663

EXTON
HAMPTON INN
4 N Pottstown
Pike (19341)
Rates: $83-$89
(610) 363-5555
(800) 426-7866

HOLIDAY INN EXP
120 N Pottstown
Pike (19341)
Rates: $77-$109
(610) 524-9000
(800) 465-4329

FAYETTEVILLE
RITE SPOT SCOT-TISH INN
5651 Lincoln Way
E (17222)
Rates: $35-$70
(717) 352-2144

FOGELSVILLE
CLOVERLEAF MOTEL
327 Star Rd
(18051)
Rates: $40-$50
(610) 395-3367

COMFORT INN W
7625 Imperial Way
(Allentown
(18106)
Rates: $80-$120
(610) 391-0344
(800) 42406423

GLASBERN HISTORIC COUNTRY INN
2141 Packhouse
Rd (18051)
Rates: $125-$260
(610) 285-4723

HOLIDAY INN
7736 Adrienne Dr
(18031)
Rates: $89-$159
(610) 391-1000
(800) 465-4329

SLEEP INN
327 Star Rd
(18106)
Rates: $59-$99
(610) 395-6603
(800) 753-3746

FRACKVILLE
ECONO LODGE
501 S Middle St
(17931)
Rates: $40-$125
(570) 874-3838
(800) 424-6423

GRANNY'S MOTEL & RESTAURANT
115 W Coal St
(17931)
Rates: $39-$48
(570) 874-0408

MOTEL 6
701 Altamont
Blvd (17931)
Rates: $39-$45
(570) 874-1223
(800) 466-8356

FRANKLIN
FRANKLIN MOTEL
1421 Liberty St
(16323)
Rates: n/a
(814) 437-3061

SUPER 8 MOTEL
847 Allegheny Ave
(16323)
Rates: $60-$65
(814) 432-2102
(800) 800-8000

FRYSTOWN
MOTEL OF FRYSTOWN
90 Fort Motel Dr (17067)
Rates: $35-$45
(717) 933-4613

GALETON
OX YOKE INN
RD 1, Route 6 (16922)
Rates: n/a
(814) 435-6522

PINE LOG MOTEL
5156 US Rt 6 W (16922)
Rates: $45-$75
(814) 435-6400

GETTYSBURG
AMERICA'S BEST INN
301 Steinwher Ave (17325)
Rates: $38-$136
(717) 334-1188
(800) 237-8466

COMFORT INN
871 York Rd (17325)
Rates: $59-$154
(717) 337-2400
(800) 424-6423

HERITAGE MOTOR INN
613 Baltimore St (17325)
Rates: $81-$99
(717) 334-9281

HOLIDAY INN-BATTLEFIELD
516 Baltimore Pike (17325)
Rates: $98-$200
(717) 334-6211
(800) 465-4329

HOLIDAY INN EXP
869 York Rd (17325)
Rates: $59-$117
(717) 337-1400
(800) 465-4329

RED CARPET INN-PERFECT REST MOTEL
2450 Emmitsburg Rd (17325)
Rates: $40-$130
(717) 334-1345
(800) 336-1345

TRAVELODGE
613 Baltimore St (17325)
Rates: $59-$165
(717) 334-9281
(800) 578-7878

GIBSONIA
COMFORT INN
5137 SR 8 (15044)
Rates: $55-$125
(724) 444-8700
(800) 424-6423

GIRARD
THE GREEN ROOF INN
8790 Rt 16 (16417)
Rates: $45-$80
(814) 774-7072

GLEN MILLS
SWEETWATER FARM BED & BREAKFAST
50 Sweetwater Rd (19342)
Rates: n/a
(610) 459-4711
(800) 793-3892

GLEN ROCK
ROCKY RIDGE MOTEL
Rt 216, Steaks Run Rd (17327)
Rates: $28-$38
(717) 235-5646

GORDONVILLE
MOTEL 6
2959 Lincoln Hwy E (17529)
Rates: $45-$81
(717) 687-3880
(800) 446-8356

GRANTVILLE
ECONO LODGE
252 Bow Creek Rd (17028)
Rates: $49-$119
(717) 469-0631
(800) 424-6423

HOLIDAY INN
604 Station Rd (17028)
Rates: $99-$199
(717) 469-0661
(800) 465-4329

GREEN TREE
HAMPTON INN
555 Trumbull Dr (15205)
Rates: $74-$94
(412) 922-0100
(800) 426-7866

HAWTHORNE SUITES
700 Marshfield Ave (15205)
Rates: $99-$149
(412) 279-6300
(800) 527-1133

HOLIDAY INN
401 Holiday Dr (15205)
Rates: $79-$109
(412) 922-8100
(800) 465-4329

GREENCASTLE
COMFORT INN
50 Pine Dr (17225)
Rates: $57-$80
(717) 597-8164
(800) 424-6423

ECONO LODGE
735 Buchanan Trail E (17225)
Rates: $39-$75
(717) 597-5255
(800) 424-6423

GREENSBURG
COMFORT INN
1129 E Pittsburgh St (15601)
Rates: $79-$170
(724) 832-2600
(800) 424-6423

FOUR POINTS BY SHERATON
100 Sheraton Dr (15601)
Rates: $129-$149
(724) 836-6060
(800) 325-3535

KNIGHTS INN
1215 S Main St (15601)
Rates: 53-$85
(724) 836-7100
(800) 843-5644

HAMBURG
MICROTEL INN
50 Industrial Dr (19526)
Rates: $50-$140
(610) 562-4234

HAMLIN
(See Pocono Mountains Area)

HANOVER
HOWARD JOHNSON INN
1080 Carlisle St (17331)
Rates: $39-$119
(717) 646-1000
(800) 446-4656

HARMARVILLE
DAYS INN
6 Landings Dr (15238)
Rates: $50-$75
(412) 828-5400
(800) 329-7466

HARRISBURG
BAYMONT INN & SUITES
990 Eisenhower Blvd (17111)
Rates: $64-$71
(717) 939-8000
(877) 229-6668

BEST WESTERN CAPITAL PLAZA
150 Nationwide Dr (17110)
Rates: $74-$86
(717) 545-9089
(800) 528-1234

BEST WESTERN HERSHEY HOTEL & SUITES
I-81 Exit 72 (17112)
Rates: $64-$130
(717) 652-7180
(800) 528-1234

COMFORT INN
7744 Linglestown Rd (17112)
Rates: $69-$159
(717) 540-8400
(800) 424-6423

COMFORT INN EAST
4021 Union Deposit Rd (17109)
Rates: $89-$129
(717) 561-8100
(800) 424-6423

COMFORT INN RIVERFRONT
525 S Front St (17104)
Rates: $59-$149
(717) 233-1611
(800) 424-6423

CROWN PLAZA
23 S 2nd St (17101)
Rates: $99-$209
(717) 234-5021
(800) 227-6963

DAYS INN
800 S Eisenhower Blvd S (17057)
Rates: $94-$99
(717) 939-4147
(800) 329-7466

DAYSTOP
7848 Linglestown Rd (17112)
Rates: $50-$70
(717) 652-9578
(800) 329-7466

GREENLAWN MOTEL
7490 Allentown Blvd (17112)
Rates: $59-$79
(717) 652-1530

HOLIDAY INN EAST-AIRPORT AREA
4751 Lindle Rd (17111)
Rates: $102-$114
(717) 939-7841
(800) 465-4329

HOLIDAY INN EXP HOTEL & SUITES
5680 Allentown Blvd (17112)
Rates: $69-$189
(717) 657-2200
(800) 465-4329

HOWARD JOHNSON INN
7930 Linglestown Rd (17112)
Rates: $49-$179
(717) 540-9100
(800) 446-4656

QUALITY INN
200 N Mountain Rd (17112)
Rates: $60-$105
(717) 540-9339
(800) 424-6423

AREA CODES - If the local number doesn't connect, check for a new area code.

RAMADA LTD
7965 Jonestown
Rd (17112)
Rates: $69-$119
(717) 545-6944
(800) 272-6232

RED ROOF INN-N
400 Corporate Cir
(17110)
Rates: $40-$79
(717) 657-1445
(800) 843-7663

RED ROOF INN-S
950 Eisenhower
Blvd (17111)
Rates: $40-$79
(717) 939-1331
(800) 843-7663

RESIDENCE INN BY MARRIOTT
4480 Lewis Rd
(17111)
Rates: $169-$269
(717) 561-1900
(800) 331-3131

SLEEP INN
7930 Linglestown
Rd (17112)
Rates: $59-$179
(717) 540-9100
(800) 424-6423

SUPER 8 MOTEL-N
4125 N Front St
(17110)
Rates: $55-$139
(717) 233-5891
(800) 800-8000

WYNDHAM HOTEL
4650 Lindle Rd
(17111)
Rates: $149-$159
(717) 564-5511
(800) 996-3426

HAWLEY
(See Pocono
Mountains Area)

HAZLETON
(See Pocono
Mountains Area)

HERMITAGE
QUALITY INN
3200 S Hermitage
Rd (15148)
Rates: $55-$90
(724) 981-1530
(800) 424-6423

ROYAL MOTEL
301 S Hermitage
Rd (16148)
Rates: $33-$39
(724) 347-5546
(800) 831-8348

HERSHEY
BEST WESTERN INN
US 422 & Sipe Ave
(17033)
Rates: $89-$229
(717) 533-5665
(800) 528-1234
(800) 233-0338

COMFORT INN AT THE PARK
1200 Mae St
(17036)
Rates: $80-$270
(717) 566-2050
(800) 424-6423

DAYS INN
350 W Chocolate
Ave (17033)
Rates: $89-$199
(717) 534-2162
(800) 329-7466

ECONO LODGE
115 Lucy Ave
(17033)
Rates: $49-$169
(717) 533-2515
(800) 424-6423

HAMPTON INN & SUITES
749 E Chocolate
Ave (17033)
Rates: $169-$250
(717) 533-8400
(800) 426-7866

HERSHEY TRAVEL INN
905 E Chocolate
Ave (17033)
Rates: $40-$95
(717) 533-7950

HOLIDAY INN EXP
610 Walton Ave
(17036)
Rates: $89-$219
(717) 583-0500
(800) 465-4329

HONESDALE
(See Pocono
Mountains Area)

HONEY BROOK
WAYNESBROOK INN HISTORIC B&B
Main St (19344)
Rates: $58-$205
(610) 273-2444

HORSHAM
DAYS INN
245 Easton Rd
(19044)
Rates: $89-$119
(215) 674-2500
(800) 329-7466

HOMESTEAD STUDIO SUITES
537 Dresher Rd
(19044)
Rates: $95-$110
(215) 956-9966
(888) 782-9473

RESIDENCE INN BY MARRIOTT
3 Walnut Grove
Dr (19044)
Rates: $164-$184
(215) 443-7330
(800) 331-3131

HUNTINGDON
COMFORT INN
4th St (16652)
Rates: $60-$110
(814) 643-1600
(800) 424-6423

HUNTINGDON MOTOR INN
Motor Inn Rd
(16652)
Rates: $41-$65
(814) 643-1133

JENNY SPRINGS CABIN RENTAL
Rothrock State
Forest (16652)
Rates: n/a
(814) 627-5311

INDIANA
BEST WESTERN UNIVERSITY INN
1545 Wayne Ave
(15701)
Rates: $49-$99
(724) 349-9620
(800) 528-1234
(888) 299-9620

HOLIDAY INN
1395 Wayne Ave
(15701)
Rates: $59-$89
(724) 463-3561
(800) 477-3561

JOHNSTOWN
COMFORT INN & SUITES
455 Theatre Dr
(15904)
Rates: $65-$135
(814) 266-3678
(800) 424-6423

ECONO LODGE
430 Napoleon
Place (15901)
Rates: $49-$85
(814) 536-1114
(800) 424-6423

HOLIDAY INN-DOWNTOWN
250 Market St
(15901)
Rates: $90-$100
(814) 535-7777
(800) 465-4329

HOLIDAY INN EXP
1440 Scalp Ave
(15904)
Rates: $85-$109
(814) 266-8789
(800) 465-4329

SLEEP INN
453 Theatre Dr
(15904)
Rates: $55-$95
(814) 262-9292
(800) 424-6423

SUPER 8 MOTEL
627 Solomon Run
Rd (15904)
Rates: $40-$59
(814) 535-5600
(800) 800-8000

JONESTOWN
DAYS INN
3 Everest Lane
(17038)
Rates: $78-$160
(717) 865-4064
(800) 329-7466

RED CARPET INN & SUITES
16 Marsenna Ln
(17038)
Rates: $45-$100
(717) 865-6600

STRAWBERRY PATCH B&B
115 Moore Rd
(17046)
Rates: $85-$189
(717) 865-7219

KANE
KANE VIEW MOTEL
Rt 6 (16735)
Rates: $38-$52
(814) 837-8600

KEMPTON
HAWK MTN INN BED & BREAKFST
RD 1, Box 186
(19529)
Rates: n/a
(215) 756-4224

KING OF PRUSSIA
HOMESTEAD STUDIO SUITES
400 American Ave
(19406)
Rates: $76-$101
(610) 962-9000
(888) 782-9473

MAINSTAY SUITES
440 American Ave
(19406)
Rates: $139-$189
(484) 690-3000
(800) 424-6423

MOTEL 6
815 W Dekaib
Pike (19406)
Rates: $55-$60
(610) 265-7200
(800) 466-8356

SHERATON PARK RIDGE HOTEL
480 N Gulph Rd
(19406)
Rates: $110-$195
(610) 337-1800
(800) 325-3535

SLEEP INN
440 American Ave
(19406)
Rates: $79-$129
(484) 690-2000
(800) 424-6423

KINTNERSVILLE

**LIGHTFARM
HISTORIC B&B**
2042 Berger Rd
(18930)
Rates: $79-$150
(610) 847-3276

KITTANNING

COMFORT INN
13 Hilltop Plaza
(16201)
Rates: $59-$109
(724) 543-5200
(800) 424-6423

**QUALITY INN
ROYLE**
405 Butler Rd
(16201)
Rates: $55-$95
(724) 543-1159
(800) 424-6423

RODEWAY INN
Rd 6, US 422 E
(16201)
Rates: $50-$63
(724) 543-1100
(800) 424-6423

KULPSVILLE

**BEST WESTERN
THE INN AT
TOWAMENCIN**
1750 Sumneytown
Pike (19443)
Rates: $110-$125
(215) 368-3800
(800) 528-1234
(800) 277-3615

KUTZTOWN

CAMPUS INN
15080 Kutztown
Rd (19530)
Rates: $50-$75
(610) 683-8721

LINCOLN MOTEL
12 Lincoln Dr
(19530)
Rates: $45-$70
(610) 683-3456

LAKE HARMONY

(See Pocono
Mountains Area)

LAMAR

COMFORT INN
31 Comfort Inn Ln
(17751)
Rates: $70-$150
(570) 726-4901
(800) 424-6423

LANCASTER

**BEST WESTERN
EDEN RESORT
INN
& SUITES**
222 Eden Rd
(17601)
Rates: $59-$199
(717) 569-6444
(800) 528-1234
(888) 477-7726

**HAWTHORN INN
& SUITES**
2045 Lincoln Hwy
E (17602)
Rates: $69-$139
(717) 290-7100
(800) 527-1133

**HOLIDAY INN
VISITORS CTR**
531 Greenfield Rd
(17601)
Rates: $80-$89
(717) 299-2551
(800) 465-4329

**LANCASTER
HOST HOTEL**
2300 E Lincoln
Hwy (17602)
Rates: $99-$179
(717) 299-5500
(800) 238-0121

RAMADA INN
151 N Queen St
(17603)
Rates: $75-$105
(717) 397-4801
(800) 272-6232

TRAVELODGE
1492 Lititz Pike
(17603)
Rates: $49-$99
(717) 393-0771
(800) 578-7878

LANDENBERG

**TIPTREE LODGE
APT RENTALS**
308 Buttonwood
Rd (19350)
Rates: n/a
(302) 234-9872

LANGHORNE

RED ROOF INN
3100 Cabot Blvd
W (19047)
Rates: $59-$121
(215) 750-6200
(800) 843-7663

**SHERATON
BUCKS COUNTY
HOTEL**
400 Oxford Valley
Rd (19047)
Rates: $209-$279
(215) 547-4100
(800) 325-3535

LANSDALE

KORMAN SUITES
1203 A Cross Hill
Ct (19446)
Rates: n/a
(215) 542-1777
(800) 567-6268

LEBANON

**QUALITY INN
LEBANON VALLEY**
625 Quentin Rd
(17042)
Rates: $89-$149
(717) 273-6771
(800) 424-6423

LENHARTSVILLE

TOP MOTEL
RD 1, Box 834
(19534)
Rates: n/a
(215) 756-6021

LEVITTOWN

COMFORT INN
6401 Bristol Pk
(19057)
Rates: $59-$129
(215) 547-5000
(800) 424-6423

LEWISBURG

BRYNWOOD INN
Rt 15 & 45 (17837)
Rates: $50-$73
(570) 524-2121

DAYS INN
US Rt 15 (17837)
Rates: $77-$110
(570) 523-1171
(800) 329-7466

ECONO LODGE
651 Rt 15 (17837)
Rates: $40-$125
(570) 523-1106
(800) 424-6423

LIGONIER

**LADY OF THE
LAKE B&B**
157 Rt 30 E (15658)
Rates: $65-$135
(724) 238-6955

LINCOLN FALLS

**MORGAN
CENTURY FARM
B&B**
Rt 154 (18616)
Rates: $75-$125
(570) 924-4909

LIONVILLE

HAMPTON INN
4 N Pottstown
Pike (19341)
Rates: $79-$119
(610) 363-5555
(800) 426-7866

**RESIDENCE INN
BY MARRIOTT**
10 N Pottstown
Pike (19341)
Rates: $100-$200
(610) 594-9705
(800) 331-3131

LITITZ

**GENERAL
SUTTER HISTORIC
COUNTRY INN**
14 E Main St (17543)
Rates: $66-$120
(717) 626-2115

LOCK HAVEN

**BEST WESTERN
LOCK HAVEN INN**
101 E Walnut St
(17745)
Rates: $75-$115
(570) 748-3297
(800) 528-1234

MALVERN

**HOMEWOOD
SUITES**
12 E Swedesford
Rd (19355)
Rates: $89-$149
(610) 296-3500
(800) 225-5466

**SHERATON
GREAT VALLEY
HOTEL**
707 Lancaster Pike
(19355)
Rates: $139-$159
(610) 524-5500
(800) 325-3535

STAYBRIDGE SUITES
20 Morehall Rd
(19355)
Rates: $99-$199
(610) 296-4343
(800) 238-8000

MANHEIM

RODEWAY INN
2931 Lebanon Rd
(17545)
Rates: $40-$72
(717) 665-2755
(800) 424-6423

MANSFIELD

COMFORT INN
300 Gateway Dr
(16933)
Rates: $69-$129
(570) 662-3000
(800) 424-6423
(800) 822-5470

MANSFIELD INN
26 S Main St
(16933)
Rates: $54-$75
(570) 662-2136

**WEST'S DELUXE
MOTEL**
2848 S Main St
(16933)
Rates: $40-$65
(570) 659-5141
(800) 995-9378

MARS

**COMFORT INN
CRANBERRY TWP**
924 Sheraton Dr
(16046)
Rates: $64-$105
(724) 772-2700
(800) 424-6423

MOTEL 6
19025 Perry Hwy
(16046)
Rates: $39-$53
(724) 776-4333
(800) 466-8356

MARSHALLS CREEK

(See Pocono
Mountains Area)

MATAMORAS

(See Pocono
Mountains Area)

MEADVILLE
DAVID MEAD INN
455 Chestnut St
(16335)
Rates: n/a
(814) 336-1692

DAYS INN
18360 Conneaut
Lake Rd (16335)
Rates: $45-$149
(814) 337-4264
(800) 329-7466

MOTEL 6
11237 Shaw Ave
(16335)
Rates: $47-$90
(814) 724-6366
(800) 466-8356

SUPER 8 MOTEL
17259 Conneaut
Lake Rd (16335)
Rates: $52-$75
(814) 333-8883
(800) 800-8000

**MECHANICS-
BURG**
COMFORT INN
1012 Wesley Dr
(17055)
Rates: $69-$199
(717) 766-3700
(800) 424-6423

HAMPTON INN
4950 Ritter Rd
(17055)
Rates: $86-$98
(717) 691-1300
(800) 426-7866

HOLIDAY INN
5401 Carlisle Pike
(17055)
Rates: $94-$134
(717) 697-0321
(800) 465-4329

HOMEWOOD
SUITES
5001 Ritler Rd
(17055)
Rates: $109-$128
(701) 697-4900
(800) 225-5466

MERCER
COLONIAL INN
MOTEL
383 N Perry Hwy
(16137)
Rates: $33-$40
(724) 662-5600

**HOWARD
JOHNSON**
835 Perry Hwy
(16137)
Rates: $84-$90
(724) 748-3030
(800) 446-4656

MIDDLETOWN
DAYS INN
800 S Eisenhower
Blvd (17057)
Rates: $49-$99
(717) 939-4147
(800) 329-7466

MIFFLINVILLE
SUPER 8 MOTEL
3rd Street (18631)
Rates: $35-$89
(570) 759-6778
(800) 800-8000

MILESBURG
HOLIDAY INN
971 N Eagle Valley
Rd (16853)
Rates: $90-$260
(814) 355-7521
(800) 465-4329

MILFORD
(See Pocono
Mountains Area)

MILL HALL
COMFORT INN
31 Comfort Inn
Ln (17751)
Rates: $74-$199
(570) 726-4901
(800) 424-6423

MONACA
HOLIDAY INN EXP
HOTEL & SUITES
105 Stone Quarry
Rd (15061)
Rates: n/a
(724 728-5121
(800) 465-4329

MONROEVILLE
COMFORT INN
699 Rodi Rd
(15146)
Rates: $79-$119
(412) 244-1600
(800) 424-6423

DAYS INN
2727 Mosside
Blvd (15146)
Rates: $41-$66
(412) 856-1610
(800) 329-7466

HAMPTON INN
3000 Mosside
Blvd (15146)
Rates: $99-$109
(412) 380-4000
(800) 426-7866

HOLIDAY INN
2750 Mosside
Blvd (15146)
Rates: $139
(412) 372-1022
(800) 465-4329

RED ROOF INN
2729 Mosside
Blvd (15146)
Rates: $50-$74
(412) 856-4738
(800) 843-7663

SUPER 8 MOTEL
1807 Rt 286
(15146)
Rates: $49-$57
(724) 733-8008
(800) 800-8000

**MONTGOMERY-
VILLE**
QUALITY INN
CONF CENTER
969 Bethlehem
Pike (18936)
Rates: $89-$119
(215) 699-8800
(800) 424-6423

RESIDENCE INN
BY MARRIOTT
1110 Bethlehem
Pike (18936)
Rates: $99-$169
(215) 468-0111
(800) 331-3131

MONTROSE
(See Pocono
Mountains Area)

MOON RUN
AMERISUITES
AIRPORT
6011 Campbells
Run Rd (15205)
Rates: $99-$109
(412) 494-0202
(800) 833-1516

COMFORT INN
7011 Old
Steubenville Pike
(15205)
Rates: $99-$109
(412) 494-0202
(800) 424-6423

COMFORT SUITES
750 AtenRd
(15108)
Rates: $79-$89
(412) 787-2600
(800) 424-6423

MAINSTAY SUITES
1000 Park Lane Dr
(15275)
Rates: $72-$82
(412) 490-7343
(800) 660-6246

MOTEL 6
211 Beecham Dr
(15205)
Rates: $29-$45
(412) 922-9400
(800) 466-8356

RED ROOF INN
AIRPORT
6404 Steubenville
Pike (15205)
Rates: $54-$78
(412) 787-7870
(800) 843-7663

RESIDENCE INN
AIRPORT
1500 Park Lane Dr
(15275)
Rates: $139-$189
(412) 787-3300
(800) 331-3131

SLEEP INN
2500 Marketplace
Blvd (15108)
Rates: $59-$129
(412) 859-4000
(800) 753-3746

WYNDHAM-APRT
777 Aten Rd
(15108)
Rates: $99-$159
(412) 788-8800
(800) 996-3426

**MOON
TOWNSHIP**
HAMPTON INN
8514 University
Blvd (15108)
Rates: n/a
(412) 264-0020
(800) 426-7866

MOOSIC
RODEWAY INN
4130 Birney Ave
(18507)
Rates: $36-$125
(570) 457-6713
(800) 424-6423

**MORGAN-
TOWN**
CONESTOGA
WAGON MOTEL
Rt 23 (19543)
Rates: n/a
(215) 286-5061

HOLIDAY INN
6170 Morgantown
Rd, Rt 10 (19543)
Rates: $89-$109
(610) 286-3000
(800) 465-4329

MOUNTVILLE
MAINSTAY SUITES
314 Primrose Ln
(17554)
Rates: $85-$185
(717) 285-2500
(800) 424-6423

**NEW
BERLINVILLE**
MEL-DOR MOTEL
P. O. Box 349
(19545)
Rates: $35-$45
(610) 367-2626

NEW CASTLE
COMFORT INN
1740 New Butler
Rd (16101)
Rates: $59-$84
(724) 658-7700
(800) 424-6423

**NEW
COLUMBIA**
COMFORT INN
330 Commerce
Park Dr (17856)
Rates: $70-$120
(570) 568-8000
(800) 424-6423

HOLIDAY INN EXP
160 Commerce
Park Dr (17856)
Rates: $91-$189
(570) 568-1100
(800) 465-4329

**NEW
CUMBERLAND**
DAYS INN
353 Lewisberry
Rd (17070)
Rates: $59-$95
(717) 774-4156
(800) 329-7466

HOLIDAY INN
148 Sheraton Dr
(17070)
Rates: $129-$189
(717) 774-2721
(800) 465-4329

MOTEL 6
200 Commerce Dr
(17070)
Rates: $29-$44
(717) 774-8910
(800) 466-8356

RODEWAY INN
110 Limekiln Rd
(17070)
Rates: $39-$109
(717) 774-1100
(800) 424-6423

NEW HOLLAND
THE HOLLANDER MOTEL
320 E Main St
(17557)
Rates: $52-$65
(717) 354-4377

NEW HOPE
AARON BURR HOUSE B&B
80 W Bridge St
(18938)
Rates: $95-$275
(215) 862-2520

BEST WESTERN INN
6426 Lower York Rd (18938)
Rates: $89-$169
(215) 862-5221
(800) 528-1234
(800) 467-3202

NEW HOPE MOTEL IN THE WOODS
400 W Bridge St
(18938)
Rates: $95-$265
(215) 862-2570

WEDGEWOOD INN B&B
111 W Bridge St
(18938)
Rates: $90-$265
(215) 862-2520

NEW KENSINGTON
CLARION HOTEL
300 Tarentum Bridge Rd (15068)
Rates: $69-$99
(724) 335-9171
(800) 424-6423

NEW STANTON
HOWARD JOHNSON INN
112 W Byers Ave (15672)
Rates: $45-$99
(724) 925-3511
(800) 446-4656

QUALITY INN
110 N Main St (15672)
Rates: $60-$90
(724) 925-6755
(800) 424-6423

SUPER 8 MOTEL
103 Blair Blvd (15672)
Rates: $50-$77
(724) 925-8915
(800) 800-8000

NORTH EAST
SUPER 8 MOTEL
11021 Side Hill Rd (16428)
Rates: $48-$78
(814) 725-4567
(800) 800-8000

NORTH HAZELTON
(See Pocono Mountains Area)

OAKDALE
COMFORT INN
7011 Old Stuebenville Pike (15071)
Rates: $55-$120
(412) 787-2600
(800) 424-6423

PALMYRA
RED CARPET INN & SUITES
977 E Main St (17078)
Rates: $39-$129
(717) 838-5466

PHILADELPHIA
BEST WESTERN CENTER CITY HOTEL
501 N 22nd St (19130)
Rates: $115-$145
(215) 568-8300
(800) 528-1234

BEST WESTERN INDEPENDENCE PARK INN
235 Chestnut St (19106)
Rates: $135-$205
(215) 922-4443
(800) 528-1234
(800) 624-2988

DOUBLETREE HOTEL
237 Broad St (19107)
Rates: $129-$219
(215) 893-1600
(800) 222-8733

FOUR POINTS BY SHERATON
4101 Island Ave (19153)
Rates: $189
(215) 492-0400
(800) 325-3535

FOUR SEASONS HOTEL
1 Logan Sq (19103)
Rates: $320-$500
(215) 963-1500
(800) 332-3442

HAMPTON INN CITY CENTER
1301 Race St (19107)
Rates: $89-$169
(215) 665-9100
(800) 426-7866

HOLIDAY INN-STADIUM
900 Packer Ave (19148)
Rates: $109
(215) 755-9500
(800) 465-4329

LOEWS HOTEL
1200 Market St (19107)
Rates: $129-$304
(215) 627-1200
(800) 235-6397

MARRIOTT HOTEL
1201 Market St (19107)
Rates: $239-$269
(215) 625-2900
(800) 228-9290

RADISSON PLAZA-WARWICK HOTEL
1701 Locust St (19103)
Rates $119-$169
(215) 735-6000
(800) 333-3333

RESIDENCE INN BY MARRIOTT
1 E Penn Square (19107)
Rates: $189-$349
(215) 557-0005
(800) 331-3131

RESIDENCE INN BY MARRIOTT
4630 Island Ave (19153)
Rates: $199
(215) 492-1611
(800) 331-3131

RITTENHOUSE HOTEL & CONDO RESIDENCES
210 W Rittenhouse Sq (19103)
Rates: $355-$420
(215) 546-9000

RITZ-CARLTON
Ten Avenue of the Arts (19102)
Rates: $249-$519
(215) 523-8000
(800) 241-3333

SHERATON SOCIETY HILL
One Dock St (19106)
Rates: $289
(215) 238-6000
(800) 325-3535

SHERATON SUITES
4101 Island Ave (19153)
Rates: $225
(215) 365-6600
(800) 325-3535

SHERATON UNIVERSITY CITY
36th & Chestnut Sts (19104)
Rates: $279-$299
(215) 387-8000
(800) 325-3535

SOFITEL HOTEL
120 S 17th St (19103)
Rates: $199
(215) 569-8300

THE WESTIN
99 S 17th St (19103)
Rates: $139-$259
(215) 563-1600
(800) 228-3000

WYNDHAM AT FRANKLIN PLAZA
2 Franklin Plaza (19103
Rates: $99-$199
(215) 448-2000
(800) 996-3426

PHILIPSBURG
MAIN LINER MOTEL
1896 Philipsburg Bigler Hwy (16866)
Rates: $33-$59
(814) 342-2004

PIGEON
THE FOREST LODGE
HC 2, Box 68 (Marienville 16239)
Rates: $45-$60
(814) 927-8790

PINE GROVE
COMFORT INN
I-81 & SR 443 (17963)
Rates: $59-$139
(570) 345-8031
(800) 424-6423

ECONO LODGE
419 Suedberg Rd (17963)
Rates: $39-$65
(570) 345-4099
(800) 424-6423

AREA CODES - If the local number doesn't connect, check for a new area code.

PITTSBURGH

BEST WESTERN UNIVERSITY CTR
3401 Blvd of the Allies (15213)
Rates: $81-$105
(412) 683-6100
(800) 254-4444

COMFORT INN
4770 Steubenville Pike (15205)
Rates: $59-$79
(412) 922-7555
(800) 424-6423

COMFORT INN
699 Rodi Rd (15235)
Rates: $59-$149
(412) 244-1600
(800) 424-6423

COMFORT INN & SUITES
2898 Banksvile Rd (15216)
Rates: $49-$150
(412) 343-3000
(800) 424-6423

DAYS INN
6 Landings Dr (15238)
Rates: $50-$125
(412) 826-5400
(800) 329-7466

DAYS INN
1150 Banksville Rd (15216)
Rates: $49-$150
(412) 531-8900
(800) 329-7466

ECONO LODGE
4800 Steubenville Pike (15205)
Rates: $39-$79
(412) 922-6900
(800) 424-6423

HAMPTON INN UNIVERSITY CTR
3315 Harriet St (15213)
Rates: $99-$119
(412) 681-1000
(800) 426-7866

HAMPTON INN
555 Trumbull Dr (15205)
Rates: n/a
(412) 922-0100
(800) 426-7866

HILTON HOTEL
600 Commonwealth Pl (15222)
Rates: $94-$234
(412) 391-4600
(800) 445-8667

HOLIDAY INN CENTRAL
401 Holiday Dr (15220)
Rates: n/a
(412) 922-8100
(800) 465-4329

HOLIDAY INN HOTEL & SUITES
180 Gamma Dr (15238)
Rates: n/a
(412) 963-0600
(800) 465-4329

HOLIDAY INN-NORTH HILLS
4859 McKnight Rd (15237)
Rates: $129-$149
(412) 366-5200
(800) 465-4329

HOLIDAY INN-PARKWAY EAST
915 Brinton Rd (15221)
Rates: n/a
(412) 247-2700
(800) 465-4329

HOLIDAY INN SELECT
100 Lytton Ave (15213)
Rates: $135-$170
(412) 682-6200
(800) 465-4329

MAINSTAY SUITES
1000 Park Lane Dr (15275)
Rates: $59-$99
(412) 490-7343
(800) 424-6423

MOTEL 6
211 Beecham Dr (15205)
Rates: $29-$32
(412) 922-9400
(800) 466-8356

OMNI WILLIAM PENN
530 William Penn Pl (15219)
Rates: $189-$209
(412) 281-7100
(800) 843-6664

QUALITY INN UNIVERSITY CENTER
3401 Blvd of the Allies (15213)
Rates: $80-$90
(412) 683-6100
(800) 424-6423

RESIDENCE INN BY MARRIOTT
3896 Bigelow Blvd (15213)
Rates: $159-$179
(412) 621-2200
(800) 331-3131

SHERATON STATION SQUARE HOTEL
300 W Station Square St (15219)
Rates: $119-$239
(412) 261-2000
(800) 325-3535

THE WESTIN
1000 Penn Ave (15222)
Rates: $109-$249
(412) 281-3700
(800) 228-3000

WYNDHAM GARDEN HOTEL
3454 Forbes Ave (15213)
Rates: $109-$189
(412) 683-2040
(800) 996-3426

PITTSTON TOWNSHIP

KNIGHTS INN
310 Rt 315 (18640)
Rates: $35-$75
(570) 654-6020
(800) 843-5644

SUPER 8 MOTEL
307 Rt 315 (18640)
Rates: $45-$150
(570) 654-3301
(800) 800-8000

VICTORIA INNS & SUITES
400 Rt 315 (18640)
Rates: $89-$167
(570) 655-1234

PLYMOUTH MEETING

DOUBLETREE GUEST SUITES
640 W Germantown Pike (19462)
Rates: $89-$249
(610) 834-8300
(800) 222-8733

POCONO MOUNTAIN AREA

BEST WESTERN INN
Route 115 (Blakeslee 18610)
Rates: $80-$215
(570) 646-6000
(800) 528-1234
(888) 296-2466

BEST WESTERN GENETTI MOTOR LODGE
32nd & N Church (Hazleton 18201)
Rates: $55-$110
(570) 454-2494
(800) 528-1234

BEST WESTERN GENETTI HOTEL
77 E Market St (Wilkes-Barre 18701)
Rates: $69-$104
(570) 823-6152
(800) 528-1234
(800) 833-6152

BEST WESTERN INN AT HUNT'S LANDING
120 Rt 6 & 209 (Matamoras 18336)
Rates: $59-$179
(570) 491-2400
(800) 528-1234

BLUE BERRY MTN INN B&B
Thomas Rd (Blakeslee 18610)
Rates: $110-$125
(717) 646-7144

BUDGET MOTEL
I-80, Exit 51 (East Stroudsburg 18301)
Rates: $59-$94
(570) 424-5451
(800) 233-8144

COMFORT INN
I-84 & SR 191 (Hamlin 18436)
Rates: $70-$220
(570) 689-4148
(800) 424-6423

DAYS INN
1946 Scranton-Carbondale Hwy (Dickson City 18508)
Rates: $68-$120
(570) 383-9979
(800) 329-7466

DAYS INN
1226 O'Neill Hwy (Dunmore 18512)
Rates: $55-$195
(570) 348-6101
(800) 329-7466

DAYS INN
760 Kidder St (Wilkes-Barre 18702)
Rates: $51-$65
(570) 826-0111
(800) 329-7466

ECONO LODGE INN & SUITES
SR 940 (Lake Harmony 18661)
Rates: $69-$99
(570) 443-0391
(800) 424-6423

ECONO LODGE
1075 Wilkes-Barret Twp Blvd (Wilkes-Barre 18702)
Rates: $48-$140
(570) 823-0600
(800) 424-6423

THE FALLS PORT INN
330 Main Ave (Hawley 18428)
Rates: $70-$120
(570) 226-2609

FIFE & DRUM MOTOR INN
100 Terrace St (Honesdale 18431)
Rates: $35-$79
(570) 253-1392

HAZELTON MOTOR INN
615 E Broad St (Hazleton 18201)
Rates: $35-$50
(570) 459-1451

AREA CODES - If the local number doesn't connect, check for a new area code.

HOLIDAY INN
200 Tigue St
(Dunmore 18512)
Rates: $135
(570) 343-4771
(800) 465-4329
(800) 959-3412

HOLIDAY INN
880 Kidder St
(Wilkes-Barre
18702)
Rates: $84
(570) 824-8901
(800) 465-4329

**HOST INN
RESIDENTIAL
SUITES**
860 Kidder St
(Wilkes-Barre
18702)
Rates: $109-$199
(570) 270-4678

MILFORD MOTEL
591 Rt 6 & 209
(Milford 18337)
Rates: $45-$95
(570) 296-6411

**MOUNT LAUREL
MOTEL**
1039 S Church St
(Hazleton 18201)
Rates: $38-$55
(570) 455-6391

MYER MOTEL
600 Rt 6 & 209
(Milford 18337)
Rates: $50-$88
(570) 296-7223

**POCONO
MT. LODGE**
SR 940
(White Haven
18661)
Rates: $50-$68
(800) 443-4049

RAMADA INN
Rt 940 (Lake
Harmony 18624)
Rates: $65-$125
(570) 443-8471
(800) 272-6232

RAMADA INN
Rt 309
(North Hazleton
18201)
Rates: $69-$99
(570) 455-2061
(800) 272-6232

RED CARPET INN
240 Rt 6
(Milford 18337)
Rates: $55-$115
(570) 296-9444
(800) 251-1962

RED ROOF INN
1035 Hwy 315
(18702)
Rates: $43-$62
(570) 829-6422
(800) 843-7663

**RESIDENCE INN
BY MARRIOTT**
947 Viewmont Dr
(Dickson City
18519)
Rates: $79-$169
(570) 343-5121
(800) 331-3131

**RIDGE HOUSE
HISTORIC B&B**
6 Ridge St
(Montrose 18801)
Rates: $40-$55
(717) 278-4933

SCOTTISH INNS
274 Rt 6 & 209
(18337)
Rates: $45-$95
(570) 491-4414

**SLEEP INN,
INN & SUITES**
102 Monahan Ave
(Dunmore 18512)
Rates: $69-$99
(800) 424-6423

SUPER 8 MOTEL
340 Green Tree DrE
(East Stroudsburg
18301)
Rates: $58-$82
(570) 424-7411
(800) 800-8000

**TOURIST VILLAGE
MOTEL**
Pike US 6 & 209
(Milford 18337)
Rates: $48-$78
(570) 491-4414

POTTSTOWN

COMFORT INN
99 Robinson St
(19464)
Rates: $69-$99
(610) 326-5000
(800) 424-6423

DAYS INN
29 High St (19464)
Rates: $37-$70
(610) 970-1101
(800) 329-7466

MOTEL 6
78 Robinson st
(19464)
Rates: $49-$55
(610) 819-1288
(800) 466-8356

QUALITY INN
61 W King St
(19464)
Rates: $64-$99
(610) 326-6700
(800) 424-6423

*PUNXSU-
TAWNEY*

**COUNTRY VILLA
MOTEL**
Rt 119 (15767)
Rates: $30-$44
(814) 938-8330

**PANTALL
HISTORIC HOTEL**
135 E Mahoning
(15767)
Rates: $49-$105
(814) 938-6600
(800) 872-6825

QUAKERTOWN

HAMPTON INN
1915 John Fries
Hwy (18951)
Rates: n/a
(215) 536-7779
(800) 426-7866

RODEWAY INN
1920 SR 663
(18951)
Rates: $55-$75
(215) 536-7600
(800) 424-6423

READING

**BEST WESTERN
DUTCH COLONY
INN & SUITES**
4635 Perkiomen
Ave (19606)
Rates: $86-$145
(610) 779-2345
(800) 528-1234
(800) 828-2830

**ECONO LODGE
NORTHEAST**
2310 Fraver Dr
(19605)
Rates: $40-$75
(610) 378-1145
(800) 424-6423

QUALITY INN
2017 Bernville Rd
(19601)
Rates: $60-$70
(610) 736-0400
(800) 424-6423

RAMADA INN
2545 N 5th St
Hwy (19605)
Rates: n/a
(610) 929-4741
(800) 272-6232

RIDGEWAY

ROYAL INN
Boot Jack Rd
(15853)
Rates: $39-$55
(814) 773-3153

ST. MARYS

COMFORT INN
976 S St. Mary's
Rd (15857)
Rates: $61-$80
(814) 834-2030
(800) 424-6423

**TOWNE HOUSE
INN**
138 Center St
(15857)
Rates: $53-$85
(814) 781-1556

SAXTON

**THE BRYAN
HOUSE VACA-
TION RENTAL**
1101A Church St
(16678)
Rates: n/a
(814) 635-2828

SCRANTON

(Endless
Mountain Area)

DAYS INN
1946 Scranton-
Carbondale Hwy
(18508)
Rates: $68-$120
(570) 383-9979
(800) 329-7466

ECONO LODGE
1175 Kane St
(18505)
Rates: $40-$125
(570) 348-1000
(800) 424-6423

SELINSGROVE

COMFORT INN
710 S US Hwy
11/15 (17870)
Rates: $59-$169
(570) 374-8880
(800) 424-6423

**HAMPTON INN-
SHAMOKIN DAM**
Hwy 11 & 15
(17870)
Rates: $70-$110
(570) 743-2223
(800) 426-7866

SEWICKLEY

**SEWICKLEY
COUNTRY INN**
801 Ohio River
Blvd (15143)
Rates: $64-$80
(412) 741-4300
(800) 835-6072

*SHAMOKIN
DAM*

HAMPTON INN
3 Stettler Ave
(17870)
Rates: $119-$179
(570) 743-2223
(800) 426-7866

QUALITY INN
2 Susquehanna Dr
(17876)
Rates: $59-$199
(570) 743-1111
(800) 424-6423

SHARTLESVILLE

BUDGET INN
Roadside Dr
(19554)
Rates: $39-$125
(610) 488-1578

DUTCH MOTEL
1 Motel Rd (19554)
Rates: $40-$65
(610) 488-1479

AREA CODES - If the local number doesn't connect, check for a new area code.

SHICKSHINNY
THE BLUE HERON BED & BREAKFST
RR 2, Box 2212
(18655)
Rates: $60-$90
(570) 864-3740

SLIPPERY ROCK
EVENING STAR MOTEL
915 New Castle Rd (16057)
Rates: $46-$55
(724) 794-3211

SOMERSET
BEST WESTERN EXECUTIVE INN
165 Water Works Rd (15501)
Rates: $50-$130
(814) 445-3996
(800) 528-1234
(888) 859-0609

BUDGET HOST INN
799 N Central Ave (15501)
Rates: $40-$85
(814) 445-7988
(800) 283-4678

BUDGET INN
736 N Center Ave (15501)
Rates: $30-$75
(814) 443-6441

DAYS INN
220 Water Works Rd (15501)
Rates: $35-$125
(814) 445-9200
(800) 329-7466

DOLLAR INN
1146 N Center Ave (15501)
Rates: $30-$75
(814) 445-2977
(800) 250-1505

GLADES PIKE INN
2684 Glades Pike (15501)
Rates: $60-$125
(814) 443-4978

HOLIDAY INN
202 Harmon St (15501)
Rates: $79-$119
(814) 445-9611
(800) 465-4329
(800) 354-7405

INN AT GEORGIAN PLACE HISTORIC B&B
800 Georgian Place Dr (15501)
Rates: $95-$185
(814) 443-1043

KNIGHTS INN
585 Ramada Rd (15501)
Rates: $40-$71
(814) 445-8933
(800) 843-5644

RAMADA INN
215 Ramada Rd (15501)
Rates: $59-$109
(814) 443-4646
(800) 272-6232

SUPER 8 MOTEL
125 Lewis Dr (15501)
Rates: $40-$88
(814) 445-8788
(800) 800-8000

SOUTH WILLIAMSPORT
QUALITY INN
234 Montgomery Pike (17702)
Rates: $59-$139
(570) 323-9801
(800) 424-6423

RIDGEMONT MOTEL
637 Rt 15 Hwy (17702)
Rates: $39-$53
(570) 321-5300

STATE COLLEGE
AUTOPORT MOTEL
1405 S Atherton St (16801)
Rates: $49-$95
(814) 237-7666

BREWMEISTER'S B&B MOTEL
2070 Cato Ave (16801)
Rates: $40-$70
(814) 238-0015

DAYS INN-PENN STATE
240 S Pugh St (16801)
Rates: $49-$260
(814) 238-8454
(800) 329-7466

HAPPY VALLEY MOTOR INN
1245 S Atherton St (16801)
Rates: $36-$85
(814) 234-1111

MOTEL 6 PENN STATE UNIV
1274 N Atherton St (16801)
Rates: $54-$60
(814) 234-1600
(800) 466-8356

NITTANY BUDGET MOTEL
2070 Cato Ave (16801)
Rates: $35-$50
(814) 238-0015

RAMADA INN
1450 S Atherton St (16801)
Rates: $95-$175
(814) 238-3001
(800) 272-6232

SUPER 8 MOTEL
1663 S Atherton St (16801)
Rates: $44-$89
(814) 237-6005
(800) 800-8000

STRASBURG
CARRIAGE HOUSE MOTOR INN
144 E Main St (17579)
Rates: $49-$99
(717) 687-7691
(800) 872-0201

NETHERLANDS INN & SPA
One Historic District Dr (17579)
Rates: $69-$169
(717) 687-7691
(800) 872-0201

STROUDSBURG
CLARION HOTEL
1220 W Main St (18360)
Rates: $59-$260
(570) 420-1000
(800) 424-6423

TOWANDA
(Endless Mountain Region)

COMFORT INN
RR 6, Box 6167A (18848)
Rates: $79-$125
(570) 265-5691
(800) 424-6423

TOWANDA MOTEL & RESTAURANT
383 York Ave (18848)
Rates: $44-$79
(570) 265-2178

TOWN HILL
DAYS INN BREEZEWOOD
9650 Old 126 (17267)
Rates: n/a
(814) 735-3860
(800) 329-7466

TREVOSE
KNIGHTS INN
2707 Super Hwy (19053)
Rates: $45-$99
(215) 639-4900
(800) 843-3559

RADISSON HOTEL
2400 Old Lincoln Hwy (19053)
Rates: $119-$126
(215) 638-8300
(800) 333-3333

RED ROOF INN
3100 Lincoln Hwy (19053)
Rates: $55-$88
(215) 244-9422
(800) 843-7663

TURTLE CREEK
JAMES STREET BED & BREAKFAST
553 James St (15145)
Rates: $35-$55
(412) 372-8060

ULYSSES
PINE LOG MOTEL
Rt 1, Box 15 (16948)
Rates: $32-$38
(814) 435-6400

UNIONTOWN
HOLIDAY INN
700 W Main St (15401)
Rates: $79-$129
(724) 437-2816
(800) 258-7238

WARFORDS BURG
DAYS INN
9648 Old 126 (17267)
Rates: $40-$69
(814) 735-3860
(800) 329-7466

WARREN
HOLIDAY INN
210 Ludlow St (16365)
Rates: $80-$100
(814) 726-3000
(800) 465-4329

SUPER 8 MOTEL
204 Struthers St (16365)
Rates: $63-$72
(814) 723-8881
(800) 800-8000

WASHINGTON
HOLIDAY INN MEADOW LANDS
340 Race Track Rd (15301)
Rates: $79-$139
(724) 222-6200
(800) 465-4329

LONGSTRETCH HARBOUR HISTORIC B&B
951 National Pike E (15301)
Rates: $40-$75
(724) 223-8283

MOTEL 6
1283 Motel 6 Dr (15301)
Rates: $38-$50
(724) 223-8040
(800) 466-8356

AREA CODES - If the local number doesn't connect, check for a new area code.

RAMADA INN
1170 W Chestnut
St (15301)
Rates: $65-$97
(724) 225-9750
(800) 272-6232

RED ROOF INN
1399 W Chestnut
St (15301)
Rates: $50-$69
(724) 228-5750
(800) 843-7663

WATSON-TOWN

ALOHA MOTEL
16 W Brimmer
Ave (17777)
Rates: $50-$60
(717) 538-5979

WAYNESBORO

BEST WESTERN INN
239 W Main St
(17268)
Rates: $55-$75
(717) 762-9113
(800) 528-1234
(877) 333-1986

WAYNESBURG

COMFORT INN
100 Comfort Lane
(15370)
Rates: $59-$159
(724) 627-3700
(800) 424-6423

ECONO LODGE
350 Miller Ln
(15370)
Rates: $41-$72
(724) 627-5544
(800) 424-6423

SUPER 8 MOTEL
80 Miller Ln
(15370)
Rates: $45-$95
(724) 627-8880
(800) 800-8000

WELLSBORO

COACH STOP INN
4755 US Rt 6 S
(16901)
Rates: $55-$89
(570) 724-5361

FOXFIRE B&B
RD 2, Box 439
(16901)
Rates: $36-$65
(570) 724-5175

PENN WELLS LODGE
4 Main St (16901)
Rates: $50-$100
(570) 724-3463

WEST CHESTER

ABBEY GREEN MOTOR LODGE
1036 Wilmington
Pike (19382)
Rates: $39-$57
(610) 692-3310

MICROTEL INN & SUITES
500 Willowbrook
Ln (19382)
Rates: $69-$84
(610) 738-9111
(888) 771-7171
(888) 619-9292

WEST HAZELTON

COMFORT INN
58 SR 93 (18201)
Rates: $90-$175
(570) 455-9300
(800) 424-6423

FOREST HILL INN
18202 SR 93
(18201)
Rates: $55-$60
(570) 459-2730
(800) 736-2730

WEST MIDDLESEX

SUPER 8 MOTEL
3369 New Castle
Rd (16159)
Rates: $50-$80
(724) 528-3888
(800) 800-8000

WHITE HAVEN

(See Pocono
Mountain Area)

WILKES-BARRE

(See Pocono
Mountain Area)

WILLIAMSPORT

BING'S MOTEL
2961 Lycoming
Creek Rd (17701)
Rates: $28-$34
(570) 494-0601

CITY VIEW INN
RD 4, Box 550
(17701)
Rates: $42-$48
(570) 326-2601

ECONO LODGE
2401 E 3rd St
(17701)
Rates: $52-$100
(570) 326-1501
(800) 424-6423

GENETTI HISTORIC HOTEL & SUITES
200 W 4th St
(17701)
Rates: $95-$175
(570) 326-6600
(800) 321-1388

HOLIDAY INN
1840 E 3rd St
(17701)
Rates: $69-$79
(570) 326-1981
(800) 465-4329

QUALITY INN
234 Rt 15 Hwy
(17701)
Rates: $54-$189
(570) 323-9801
(800) 424-6423

RADISSON INN
100 Pine St (17701)
Rates: $109-$119
(570) 327-8231
(800) 333-3333

WIND GAP

TRAVEL INN
499 E Moorestown
Rd (18091)
Rates: $40-$90
(610) 863-4146

WORMLEYS BURG

ECONO LODGE
860 N Front St
(17043)
Rates: $55-$90
(717) 763-7086
(800)) 424-64234

WYOMISSING

ECONO LODGE
635 Spring St
(19610)
Rates: $54-$129
(610) 378-5105
(800) 424-6423

THE INN AT READING
1040 Park Rd
(19610)
Rates: $69-$149
(610) 372-7811

SHERATON READING HOTEL
1741 W Papermill
Rd (19610)
Rates: $119-$169
(610) 376-3811
(800) 325-3535

WELLESLEY INN
910 Woodland
Ave (19610)
Rates: $89-$129
(610) 374-1500
(800) 444-8888

WYSOX

COMFORT INN
US 6 (18854)
Rates: $99-$125
(570) 265-5691
(800) 424-6423

YORK

BEST WESTERN-WESTGATE
1415 Kenneth Rd
(17404)
Rates: $82-$88
(717) 767-6931
(800) 528-1234

DAYS INN
222 Arsenal Rd
(17402)
Rates: $49-$79
(717) 843-9971
(800) 329-7466

FOUR POINTS BY SHERATON
1650 Toronita St
(17402)
Rates: $149-$159
(717) 846-4940
(800) 325-3535

HOLIDAY INN
334 Arsenal Rd
(17402)
Rates: $92-$110
(717) 845-5671
(800) 465-4329

HOLIDAY INN
2000 Loucks Rd
(17402)
Rates: $124
(717) 846-9500
(800) 465-4329

MOTEL 6
125 Arsenal Rd
(17404)
Rates: $33-$46
(717) 846-6260
(800) 466-8356

QUALITY INN & SUITES
2600 E Market St
(17402)
Rates: $60-$100
(717) 755-1966
(800) 424-6423

RED ROOF INN
323 Arsenal Rd
(17402)
Rates: $40-$79
(717) 843-8181
(800) 843-7663

SUPER 8 MOTEL
40 Arsenal Rd
(17404)
Rates: $45-$90
(717) 852-8686
(800) 800-8000

AREA CODES - If the local number doesn't connect, check for a new area code.

RHODE ISLAND

BLOCK ISLAND

**BLUE DORY INN
BED & BREAKFST**
Dodge St (02807)
Rates: n/a
(401) 466-5891
(800) 992-7290

**EASTGATE
HOUSE B&B**
Spring St (02807)
Rates: n/a
(401) 465-2164

BRISTOL

**JOSEPH
REYNOLDS
HOUSE INN B&B**
956 Hope St
(02809)
Rates: n/a
(401) 254-0230
(800) 754-0230

CHARLESTOWN

**KRYSTAL
PENGUIN MOTEL**
5399 Post Rd
(02813)
Rates: n/a
(401) 364-0062
(888) 879-8106

CRANSTON

DAYS INN
101 New London
Ave (02920)
Rates: $69-$109
(401) 942-4200
(800) 329-7466

EAST
PROVIDENCE

**NEW YORKER
MOTOR LODGE**
400 Newport Ave
(02916)
Rates: n/a
(401) 434-8000

MIDDLETOWN

BARTRAM'S B&B
94 Kane Ave
(02842)
Rates: n/a
(401) 846-2259

**THE BAY
WILLOWS INN**
1225 Aquidneck
Ave (02842)
Rates: $39-$179
(401) 847-8400
(800) 838-5642

**HOWARD
JOHNSON INN**
351 W Main Rd
(02842)
Rates: $99-$244
(401) 849-2000
(800) 654-2000

**SEAVIEW INN
MOTEL**
240 Aquidneck
Ave (02842)
Rates: $59-$229
(401) 846-5000
(800) 495-2046

NEWPORT

**ANNA'S
VICTORIAN
CONNECTION**
5 Fowler Ave
(02840)
Rates: n/a
(401) 849-2489

**B&B
INTERNATIONAL**
21 Dearborn St
(02840)
Rates: n/a
(401) 846-7716

**BANNISTER'S
WHARF MARINA
& GUEST ROOMS**
Bannister's Wharf
(02840)
Rates: n/a
(401) 846-4500

**BEECH TREE
INN B&B**
34 Rhode Island
Ave (02840)
Rates: $115-$350
(401) 847-9794

**HARBOR-BASE
PINEAPPLE INN**
372 Coddington
Hwy (02840)
Rates: $25-$70
(401) 847-2600

**THE HOTEL
VIKING**
One Bellevue Ave
(02840)
Rates: $139-$349
(401) 847-3300

MOTEL 6
249 J T Connell
Hwy (02840)
Rates: $39-$90
(401) 848-0600
(800) 466-8356

**1 MURRAY HOUSE
BED & BREAKFAST**
Murray Pl (02840)
Rates: n/a
(401) 846-3337

**SANFORD-
COVELL VILLA
MARINA B&B**
72 Washington St
(02840)
Rates: n/a
(401) 847-0206

NORTH
KINGSTOWN

COVE MOTEL
7825 Post Rd
(02904)
Rates: n/a
(401) 294-4853

**HAMILTON VIL-
LAGE INN MOTEL**
642 Boston Neck
Rd (02904)
Rates: $79-$119
(401) 295-0700

**THE WICKFORD
HOUSE B&B**
68 Main St (02904)
Rates: n/a
(401) 294-6479

PORTSMOUTH

**FOUNDER'S
BROOK
MOTEL & SUITES**
314 Boyd's Ln
(02871)
Rates: $59-$159
(401) 683-1244

PROVIDENCE

**PROVIDENCE
BILTMORE HOTEL**
Kennedy Plaza
(02903)
Rates: $149-$249
(401) 421-0700
(800) 294-7799

**THE WESTIN
HOTEL**
1 W Exchange St
(02903)
Rates: $419-$444
(401) 598-8000
(800) 228-3000

SOUTH
KINGSTOWN

CAPTAIN'S B&B
2 Heather Hollow
Rd (02879)
Rates: n/a
(401) 782-3445

**THE HOLLY
HOUSE B&B**
522 Main St
(02879)
Rates: n/a
(401) 783-5454
(800) 275-5450

WAKEFIELD

**THE KING'S ROSE
B&B INN**
1747 Mooresfield
Rd (02879)
Rates: $100-$170
(401) 783-5222

WARWICK

CROWNE PLAZA
801 Greenwich
Ave (02886)
Rates: $119-$209
(401) 732-6000
(800) 227-6963

**HAMPTON
INN & SUITES**
2100 Post Rd
(02886)
Rates: $95-$150
(401) 739-8888
(800) 426-7866

**HOLIDAY INN EXP
HOTEL & SUITES**
901 Jefferson Blvd
(02886)
Rates: $89-$159
(401) 736-5000
(800) 465-4329

**HOMESTEAD
STUDIO SUITES
HOTEL**
268 Metro Center
Blvd (02886)
Rates: $95-$117
(401) 732-6667
(888) 782-9473

MOTEL 6
20 Jefferson Blvd
(02888)
Rates: $55-$90
(401) 467-9800
(800) 466-8356

**REDWOOD
LODGE MOTEL**
2282 Post Rd
(02886)
Rates: n/a
(401) 739-1150
(800) 874-4114

**RESIDENCE INN
BY MARRIOTT**
500 Kilvert St
(02886)
Rates: $79-$209
(401) 737-7100
(800) 331-3131

**SHERATON
PROVIDENCE
AIRPORT HOTEL**
1850 Post Rd
(02886)
Rates: $129-$179
(401) 738-4000
(800) 557-2050

WEST
WARWICK

**LEPRECHAUN
MOTEL**
325 Quaker Lane
(02893)
Rates: n/a
(401) 828-1509

AREA CODES - If the local number doesn't connect, check for a new area code.

WESTERLY

**FRANKLIN
GARDENS MOTEL**
129 Franklin St
(02891)
Rates: n/a
(401) 596-2705
(888) 596-2705

**THE PINE LODGE
COTTAGES**
92 Old Post Rd
(02891)
Rates: $68-$104
(401) 322-0333

**SANDPIPER
MOTEL**
55 Winnapaug Rd
(02891)
Rates: n/a
(401) 596-7920

SEA SHELL MOTEL
19 Winnapaug Rd
(02891)
Rates: n/a
(401) 348-8337

WOONSOCKET

**HOLIDAY INN EXP
HOTEL & SUITES**
194 Fortin Dr
(02895)
Rates: $107-$145
(401) 769-5000
(800) 465-4329

WYOMING

**STAGECOACH
HOUSE INN B&B**
1136 Main St
(02898)
Rates: $99-$129
(401) 539-9600

AREA CODES - If the local number doesn't connect, check for a new area code.

SOUTH CAROLINA

AIKEN

BEST WESTERN EXECUTIVE INN
3560 Richland Ave W (29801)
Rates: $42-$250
(803) 649-3968
(800) 528-1234

DAYS INN
1204 Richland Ave W (29801)
Rates: $45-$175
(803) 649-5524
(800) 329-7466

DAYS INN
2654 Columbia Hwy N (29801)
Rates: $38-$150
(803) 642-5692
(800) 329-7466

DELUXE INN
1919 Edgefield Hwy (29801)
Rates: $27-$44
(803) 642-2840

HOLIDAY INN EXP
155 Colony Pkwy (29803)
Rates: $100
(803) 648-0999
(800) 465-4329

QUALITY INN
3608 Richland Ave W (29801)
Rates: $55-$80
(803) 641-1100
(800) 424-6423

RAMADA LIMITED
1850 Richland Ave W (29801)
Rates: $49-$54
(803) 648-6821
(800) 272-6232

SLEEP INN
1002 Monterey Dr (29803)
Rates: $49-$219
(803) 644-9900
(800) 424-6423

ANDERSON

DAYS INN
1007 Smith Mill Rd (29625)
Rates: $57-$149
(864) 375-0375
(800) 329-7466

HOLIDAY INN EXP
103 Anderson Business Park (29621)
Rates: $69-$159
(864) 231-0231
(800) 465-4329

LA QUINTA INN
3430 Clemson Blvd (29621)
Rates: $59-$80
(864) 225-3721
(800) 687-6667

ROYAL AMERICAN MOTOR INN
4515 Clemson Blvd (29621)
Rates: $33-$42
(864) 226-7236
(800) 524-9823

BEAUFORT

BATTERY CREEK INN
102 B Marina Blvd (29902)
Rates: $70+
(843) 521-1441

ECONO LODGE
2221 Boundary St (29902)
Rates: $45-$70
(843) 521-1555
(800) 424-6423

RAMADA LIMITED
2001 Boundary St (29902)
Rates: $59-$199
(843) 524-2144
(800) 272-6232

BENNETTSVILLE

HOLIDAY INN EXP
213 Hwy 15/401 Bypass E (29512)
Rates: $65-$85
(843) 479-1700
(800) 465-4329

BLUFFTON

COMFORT SUITES
Hwy 278 at Simmonsville Rd (29910)
Rates: $69-$119
(800) 424-6423

HOLIDAY INN EXP
35 Bluffton Rd (29910)
Rates: $79-$139
(843) 757-2002
(800) 465-4329

CAMDEN

COLONY INN
2020 W DeKalb St (29020)
Rates: $49-$59
(803) 432-5508

CAYCE

RAMADA LTD ARPT
3020 Charleston Hwy (29033)
Rates: $50-$59
(803) 794-7500
(800) 272-6232

RIVERSIDE INN
111 Knox Abbott Dr (29033)
Rates: $55-$65
(803) 939-4688

CHARLESTON

BEST WESTERN SWEETGRASS INN
1540 Savannah Hwy (29407)
Rates: $49-$189
(843) 571-6100
(800) 528-1234

CHARLESTON PLACE HOTEL
205 Meeting St (29401)
Rates: $179-$499
(843) 722-4900

COMFORT INN COLISEUM
5055 N Arco Ln (29418)
Rates: $45-$109
(843) 554-6485
(800) 424-6423

DAYS INN-AIRPORT
2998 W Montague Ave (29418)
Rates: $49-$119
(843) 747-4101
(800) 329-7466

HOWARD JOHNSON RIVERFRONT
250 Spring St (29403)
Rates: $59-$149
(843) 722-4000
(800) 446-4656

INDIGO INN HISTORIC B&B
1 Maiden Ln (29401)
Rates: $140-$236
(843) 577-5900
(800) 845-7639

MIDDLETON INN
Ashley River Rd (29414)
Rates: $109-$139
(843) 556-0500
(800) 543-4774

MOTEL 6-SOUTH
2058 Savannah Hwy (29407)
Rates: $35-$56
(843) 556-5144
(800) 466-8356

ORCHARD INN
4725 Saul White Blvd (29418)
Rates: $36-$57
(843) 747-3671

RESIDENCE INN BY MARRIOTT
90 Ripley Point Dr (29407)
Rates: $89-$229
(843) 571-7979
(800) 331-3131

TOWN & COUNTRY INN
2008 Savannah Hwy (29407)
Rates: $69-$119
(843) 571-1000
(800) 334-6660

CHERAW

DAYS INN
820 Market St (29520)
Rates: $50-$110
(843) 537-5554
(800) 329-7466

JAMESON INN
885 Chesterfield Hwy (29520)
Rates: $49-$104
(843) 537-5625
(800) 526-3766

CLEMSON

COMFORT INN
1305 Tiger Blvd (29631)
Rates: $73-$261
(864) 653-3600
(800) 424-6423

RAMADA INN
1310 Tiger Blvd (29631)
Rates: $64-$89
(864) 654-7501
(800) 272-6232

CLINTON

COMFORT INN
105 Trade St (29325)
Rates: $52-$95
(864) 833-5558
(800) 424-6423

DAYS INN
12374 Hwy 56 N (29325)
Rates: $49-$85
(864) 833-6600
(800) 329-7466

RAMADA INN
Hwy 56 & I-26 (29325)
Rates: $59-$89
(864) 833-4900
(800) 272-6232

COLUMBIA

AMERISUITES
7525 Two Notch Rd (29223)
Rates: $99-$119
(803) 736-6666
(800) 833-1516

AREA CODES - If the local number doesn't connect, check for a new area code.

BAYMONT INN & SUITES EAST
1538 Horseshoe Dr (29204)
Rates: $49-$75
(803) 736-6400
(877) 229-6668

BEST INN
1335 Garner Ln (29210)
Rates: n/a
(803) 798-9590

BEST WESTERN JACKSON
240 E Exchange Blvd (29209)
Rates: $69-$99
(803) 695-0666
(800) 528-1234

BEST WESTERN GOVERNOR'S HOUSE HOTEL
1301 Main St (29201)
Rates: $53-$95
(803) 779-7790
(800) 528-1234

CHESTNUT COTTAGE B&B
1718 Hampton St (29201)
Rates: $95-$225
(803) 256-1718

COLUMBIANA HOTEL & CONF CENTER
2100 Bush River Rd (29210)
Rates: $84-$209
(803) 731-0300

DAYS INN
133 Plumbers Rd (29203)
Rates: $55-$69
(803) 754-4408
(800) 329-7466

DAYS INN
911 Bush River Rd (29210)
Rates: $45-$75
(803) 798-5101
(800) 329-7466

ECONO LODGE
4486 Fort Jackson Blvd (29209)
Rates: $52-$65
(803) 738-0510
(800) 424-6423

HOLIDAY INN EXP HOTEL & SUITES
1011 Clemson Frontage Rd (29223)
Rates: $70
(803) 419-3558
(800) 465-4329

HOLIDAY INN-NE
7510 Two Notch Rd (29223)
Rates: $89-$99
(803) 736-3000
(800) 465-4329

MICROTEL INN
1520 Barbara Dr (29223)
Rates: $45-$55
(803) 736-3237
(888) 771-7171

MOTEL 6 EAST
7541 Nates Rd (29223)
Rates: $37-$53
(803) 736-3900
(800) 466-8356

MOTEL 6 WEST
1776 Burning Tree Rd (29210)
Rates: $29-$40
(803) 798-9210
(800) 466-8356

QUALITY INN
1144 Bush River Rd (29210)
Rates: $46-$120
(803) 798-2100
(800) 424-6423

RAMADA PLAZA HOTEL
8105 Two Notch Rd (29223)
Rates: $79-$99
(803) 736-5600
(800) 272-6232

RED ROOF INN-WEST
10 Berryhill Rd (29210)
Rates: $37-$64
(803) 798-9220
(800) 843-7663

RESIDENCE INN BY MARRIOTT
150 Stoneridge Dr (29210)
Rates: $89-$179
(803) 779-7000
(800) 331-3131

SUPER 8 MOTEL
773 St. Andrews Rd (29210)
Rates: $55-$120
(803) 772-7275
(800) 800-8000

TOWNEPLACE SUITES
350 Columbiana Dr (29212)
Rates: $44-$79
(8030 781-9391
(800) 257-3000

DILLON
DAYS INN
818 Radford Blvd (29536)
Rates: $55-$125
(843) 774-6041
(800) 329-7466

ECONO LODGE
1223 Radford Blvd (29536)
Rates: $36-$140
(843) 774-4181
(800) 424-6423

DUNCAN
DAYS INN
1386 E Main St (29334)
Rates: $44-$74
(864) 433-1122
(800) 329-7466

QUALITY INN
1391 E Main St (29334)
Rates: $50-$60
(864) 433-1333
(800) 424-6423

EASLEY
JAMESON INN
211 Dayton School Rd (29642)
Rates: $49-$104
(864) 306-9000
(800) 526-3766

FLORENCE
COMFORT INN
1916 W Lucas St (29501)
Rates: $46-$99
(843) 665-4558
(800) 424-6423

COUNTRY HEARTH INN
831 S Irby St (29501)
Rates: $39-$58
(843) 662-9421
(888) 443-2784

DAYS INN NORTH
2111 W Lucas St (29501)
Rates: $150
(843) 665-4444
(800) 329-7466

ECONO LODGE
1811 W Lucas St (29501)
Rates: $39-$69
(843) 665-8558
(800) 424-6423

HOLIDAY INN EXP
150 Dunbarton Dr (29501)
Rates: n/a
(843) 664-2400
(800) 465-4329

HOLIDAY INN HOTEL & SUITES
1819 W Lucas St (29501)
Rates: $69
(843) 665-4555
(800) 465-4329

HOWARD JOHNSON EXP
3821 Bancroft Rd (29503)
Rates: $54-$95
(843) 664-9494
(800) 446-4656

MOTEL 6
1834 W Lucas Rd (29501)
Rates: $31-$51
(843) 667-6100
(800) 466-8356

RAMADA INN
2038 W Lucas (29501)
Rates: $69-$75
(843) 669-4241
(800) 272-6232

RED ROOF INN
2690 David McLeod Blvd (29501)
Rates: $35-$55
(843) 678-9000
(800) 843-7663

RODEWAY INN
3024 T.V. Rd (29501)
Rates: $32-$126
(843) 669-1715
(800) 424-6423

THUNDERBIRD INN
2004 W Lucas Rd (29502)
Rates: $39-$53
(843) 669-1611
(800) 522-9552

FORT MILL
COMFORT INN AT CAROWINDS
3725 Ave of the Carolinas (29715)
Rates: $59-$149
(704) 339-0574
(800) 424-6423

GAFFNEY
COMFORT INN
143 Corona Dr (29341)
Rates: $60-$129
(864) 487-4200
(800) 424-6423

JAMESON INN
101 Stuard St (29341)
Rates: $49-$104
(864) 489-0240
(800) 526-3766

GEORGETOWN
CAROLINIAN INN
706 Church St (29440)
Rates: $54-$79
(843) 546-5191

JAMESON INN
120 Church St (29440)
Rates: $49-$104
(843) 546-6090
(800) 526-3766

WINYAH BAY INN B&B
3030 S Island Rd (29440)
Rates: $65-$135
(843) 546-0464

GOOSE CREEK
DAYS INN
1430 Redbank Rd (29445)
Rates: $50-$70
(843) 797-6000
(800) 329-7466

GREENVILLE
AMERISUITES
40 W Orchard Park Rd (29615)
Rates: $71-$119
(864) 232-3000
(800) 833-1516

AREA CODES - If the local number doesn't connect, check for a new area code.

COMFORT INN
831 Congaree Rd
(29607)
Rates: $55-$125
(864) 288-6221
(800) 424-6423

COMFORT INN EXEC CTR
540 N
Pleasantburg Dr
(29607)
Rates: $54-$125
(864) 271-0060
(800) 424-6423

CROWNE PLAZA
851 Congaree Rd
(29607)
Rates: $98-$149
(864) 297-6300
(800) 227-6963

DAYS INN
2756 Laurens Rd
(29607)
Rates: $55-$79
(864) 288-6900
(800) 329-7466

GUESTHOUSE INTL' SUITES PLUS
48 McPrice Ct
(29615)
Rates: n/a
(864) 297-0099
(800) 214-8378

HILTON GREENVILLE
45 W Orchard
Park DR (29615)
Rates: $99-$169
(864) 232-4747
(800) 445-8667

HOLIDAY INN
4295 Augusta Rd
(29605)
Rates: $78-$108
(864) 277-8921
(800) 465-4329

HOLIDAY INN EXP
2681 Dry Pocket
Rd (29650)
Rates: $88
(864) 213-9331
(800) 465-4329

HOLIDAY INN EXP HOTEL & SUITES
1036 Woodruff Rd
(29607)
Rates: $90-$127
(864) 678-5555
(800) 465-4329

LA QUINTA INN
31 Old Country
Rd (29607)
Rates: $59-$75
(864) 297-3500
(800) 687-6667

LA QUINTA INN
65 W Orchard
Park Dr (29615)
Rates: $64-$89
(864) 233-8018
(800) 687-6667

MAINSTAY SUITES PELHAM ROAD
2671 Dry Pocket
Rd (29650)
Rates: $74-$84
(864) 987-5566
(800) 424-6423

MARRIOTT HOTEL AIRPORT
1 Parkway E
(29615)
Rates: $66-$115
(864) 297-0300
(800) 228-9290

MICROTEL INN
1024 Woodruff Rd
(29607)
Rates: $52-$63
(864) 297-3811
(888) 771-7171

MOTEL 6
224 Bruce Rd
(29605)
Rates: $29-$32
(864) 277-8630
(800) 466-8356

PHOENIX INN
246 N
Pleasantburg Dr
(29606)
Rates: $65-$109
(864) 233-4651
(800) 257-3529

RED ROOF INN
2801 Laurens Rd
(29607)
Rates: $36-$61
(864) 297-4458
(800) 843-7663

SLEEP INN
231 N
Pleasantburg Dr
(29607)
Rates: $54-$109
(864) 240-2006
(800) 424-6423

GREENWOOD

DAYS INN
230 Birchtree Dr
(29649)
Rates: $50-$55
(864) 223-1818
(800) 329-7466

GREER

SUPER 8 MOTEL
1515 Hwy 101 S
(29651)
Rates: $50-$55
(864) 848-1626
(800) 800-8000

HARDEEZVILLE

COMFORT INN
Hwy 17 & I-95
(29927)
Rates: $49-$79
(843) 784-2188
(800) 424-6423

QUALITY INN
19000 Whythe
Hardee Blvd
(29927)
Rates: $55-$110
(843) 784-7060
(800) 424-6423

SLEEP INN
I-95 & Hwy 17
(29927)
Rates: $59-$109
(843) 784-7181
(800) 424-6423

HARTSVILLE

LANDMARK INN
1301 S 4th St
(29550)
Rates: $52-$68
(843) 332-2611
(800) 628-9108

HILTON HEAD ISLAND

COMFORT INN FOREST BEACH
2 Tanglewood Dr
(29928)
Rates: $49-$183
(843) 842-6662
(800) 424-6423

HOLIDAY INN EXP
40 Waterside Dr
(29928)
Rates: $60-$200
(843) 842-8888
(800) 465-4329

MOTEL 6
830 Wm Hilton
Pkwy (29928)
Rates: $39-$61
(843) 785-2700
(800) 466-8356

QUALITY INN
200 Museum St
(29926)
Rates: $50-$150
(843) 681-3655
(800) 424-6423

RED ROOF INN
5 Regency Pkwy
(29928)
Rates: $43-$88
(843) 686-6808
(800) 843-7663

IRMO

AMERISUITES
1130 Kinley Rd
(29063)
Rates: $99-$119
(803) 407-1560
(800) 883-1516

WELLESLEY INN
1170 Kinley Rd
(29063)
Rates: $89-$109
(803) 781-8590
(800) 444-8888

LAKE CITY

DAYS INN
170 S Ron McNair
Blvd (29560)
Rates: $49-$89
(843) 394-3269
(800) 329-7466

LANCASTER

JAMESON INN
114 Commerce
Blvd (29720)
Rates: $49-$104
(803) 283-1188
(800) 526-3766

LANDRUM

THE RED HORSE INN COTTAGES
310 N Campbell
Rd (29356)
Rates: $105-$210
(864) 895-4968

LITTLE RIVER

HOLIDAY INN
722 Hwy 17 N
(29566)
Rates: $39-$299
(843) 281-9400
(800) 465-4329

LUGOFF

BEST WESTERN CAMDEN WEST
Hwy 1 & 601 S
(29078)
Rates: $62-$99
(803) 438-9441
(800) 528-1234
(800) 344-1545

RAMADA LIMITED
542 Hwy 601 S
(29078)
Rates: $59+
(803) 438-1807
(800) 272-6232

MANNING

BEST WESTERN PALMETTO INN
2825 Paxville
Hwy (29102)
Rates: $59-$89
(803) 473-4021
(800) 528-1234

COMFORT INN
3031 Paxville
Hwy (29102)
Rates: $59-$79
(803) 473-7550
(800) 424-6423

RAMADA LIMITED
2816 Paxville
Hwy (29102)
Rates: $54-$130
(803) 473-5135
(800) 272-6232

MOUNT PLEASANT

COMFORT INN EAST
310 Hwy 17
Bypass (29464)
Rates: $59-$159
(843) 884-5853
(800) 424-6423

GUILDS INN HISTORIC B&B
101 Pitt St (29464)
Rates: $85-$140
(843) 881-0510
(800) 331-0510

HOMEWOOD SUITES
1998 Riviera Dr
(29464)
Rates: $99-$189
(843) 881-6950
(800) 225-5466

AREA CODES - If the local number doesn't connect, check for a new area code.

MAINSTAY SUITES
400 McGrath
Darby Blvd
(29464)
Rates: $59-$169
(843) 881-1722
(800) 660-9246

RED ROOF INN
301 Johnnie
Dodds Blvd
(29464)
Rates: $44-$83
(843) 884-1411
(800) 843-7663

**RESIDENCE INN
BY MARRIOTT**
1116 Isle of Palms
Connector (29464)
Rates: $89-$199
(843) 881-1599
(800) 331-3131

SLEEP INN
299 Wingo Way
(29646)
Rates: $49-$139
(843) 856-5000
(800) 424-6423

MYRTLE BEACH
**A SUMMER WIND
MOTEL**
1903 S Ocean Blvd
(29577)
Rates: $31-$159
(843) 946-6960

**EL DORADO
MOTEL**
2800 S Ocean Blvd
(29577)
Rates: $35-$135
(843) 626-3559

**HURL ROCK
MOTEL**
2010 S Ocean Blvd
(29577)
Rates: $22-$98
(843) 626-3531

LA QUINTA INN
1561 21st Ave N
(29577)
Rates: $69-$185
(843) 916-8801
(800) 687-6667

**MARINER
APARTMENT
MOTEL**
7003 N Ocean
Blvd (29572)
Rates: $29-$149
(843) 449-5281

THE PALM HOUSE
4010 Halyard Way
(29572)
Rates: $495-$1395
Weekly
(843) 236-6623

RED ROOF INN
1601-B Hwy 17 N
(29582)
Rates: n/a
(843) 280-4555
(800) 843-7663

RED ROOF INN
2801 S Kings Hwy
(29577)
Rates: $32-$99
(843) 626-4444
(800) 843-7663

ST JOHN'S INN
6803 N Ocean
Blvd (29572)
Rates: $36-$99
(843) 449-5251
(800) 845-0624

**SEA MIST OCEAN-
FRONT RESORT**
1200 S Ocean Blvd
(29577)
Rates: $26-$192
(843) 448-1551
(800) 654-5613

**STAYBRIDGE
SUITES-FANTASY
HARBOUR**
3163 Outlet Blvd
(29579)
Rates: $69-$169
(843) 903-4000
(800) 238-8000

NEWBERRY
**BEST WESTERN
INN**
11701 S Hwy 34
(29108)
Rates: $50-$70
(803) 276-5850
(800) 528-1234

NORTH CHARLESTON
**BEST WESTERN
CHARLESTON
AIRPORT HOTEL**
6099 Fain St
(29406)
Rates: $59-$99
(843) 744-1621
(800) 528-1234

**COMFORT INN
COLISEUM**
5055 N Arco Ln
(29418)
Rates: $60-$80
(843) 554-6485
(800) 424-6423

**HOMESTEAD STU-
DIO SUITES ARPT**
5045 N Arco Ln
(29418)
Rates: $89-$104
(843) 740-3440
(888) 782-9473

LA QUINTA INN
2499 La Quinta Ln
(29418)
Rates: $60-$95
(843) 797-8181
(800) 687-6667

MOTEL 6
2551 Ashley
Phosphate Rd
(29418)
Rates: $37-$53
(843) 572-6590
(800) 466-8356

RED ROOF INN
7480 Northwoods
Blvd (29418)
Rates: $45-$69
(843) 572-9100
(800) 843-7663

**RESIDENCE INN
BY MARRIOTT**
7645 Northwoods
Blvd (29418)
Rates: $126-$166
(843) 572-5757
(800) 331-3131

**RESIDENCE INN
BY MARRIOTT**
5035 Intl' Blvd
(29418)
Rates: $89-$199
(843) 266-3434
(800) 331-3131

**SHERATON
HOTEL**
4770 Goer Dr
(29406)
Rates: $89-$109
(843) 747-1900
(800) 325-3535

SLEEP INN
7435 Northside Dr
(29420)
Rates: $49-$149
(8430 572-8400
(800) 424-6423

SUPER 8 MOTEL
2311 Ashley
Phosphate Rd
(29406)
Rates: $54-$119
(843) 572-2228
(800) 800-8000

ORANGEBURG
COMFORT INN
3671 St. Matthews
Rd (29118)
Rates: $73-$160
(803) 531-9200
(800) 424-6423

DAYS INN
3402 Five Chop Rd
(29115)
Rates: $56-$86
(803) 534-0500
(800) 329-7466

DAYS INN
3691 St. Mathews
Rd (29118)
Rates: $50-$150
(803) 531-2590
(800) 329-7466

JAMESON INN
2350 Chestnut St
NE (29115)
Rates: $49-$104
(803) 534-1611
(800) 526-3766

PICKENS
**THE SCHELL HAUS,
A RESORT B&B**
117 Hiawatha Tr
(29671)
Rates: $90-$165
(864) 878-0078

POINT SOUTH
HOLIDAY INN EXP
138 Frampton Dr
(29945)
Rates: $73-$85
(843) 726-9400
(800) 465-4329

RIDGELAND
COMFORT INN
200 James F Taylor
Blvd (29936)
Rates: $92+
(843) 726-2121
(800) 424-6423

DAYS INN
516 E Main St
(29936)
Rates: $40-$92
(843) 726-5553
(800) 424-6423

RIDGEWAY
RAMADA LIMITED
6173 S Hwy 34 E
(29130)
Rates: n/a
(803) 337-7575
(800) 272-6232

**RIDGEWAY
MOTEL**
Hwy 34 (29130)
Rates: $26-$29
(803) 337-3238

ROCK HILL
**BEST WESTERN
INN**
1106 Anderson Rd
(29730)
Rates: $55-$135
(803) 329-1330
(800) 528-1234

**THE BOOK &
SPINDLE B&B**
626 Oakland Ave
(29730)
Rates: $75-$425
(803) 328-1913

HOLIDAY INN
2640 N Cherry
Rd (29730)
Rates: $71-$89
(803) 329-1122
(800) 465-4329

ST. GEORGE
BEST VALUE INN
125 Motel Dr
(29477)
Rates: $31-$66
(843) 563-2360

**BEST WESTERN
INN**
I-95 & Hwy 78
(29477)
Rates: $55-$109
(843) 563-2277
(800) 528-1234

COMFORT INN
139 Motel Dr
(29477)
Rates: $60-$90
(843) 563-4180
(800) 424-6423

ECONO LODGE
5971 W Jim Bilton
Blvd (29477)
Rates: $40-$80
(843) 563-4195
(800) 424-6423

AREA CODES - If the local number doesn't connect, check for a new area code.

QUALITY INN
6014 W Jim Bilton
Blvd (29477)
Rates: $54-$69
(843) 563-4581
(800) 424-6423

ST. STEPHEN
ECONO LODGE
3986 Byrnes Dr
(29479)
Rates: $61-$76
(843) 567-7397
(800) 424-6423

SANTEE
COMFORT INN
249 Britain St
(29142)
Rates: $50-$125
(803) 854-3221
(800) 424-6423

DAYS INN
9074 Old Hwy 6
(29142)
Rates: $45-$60
(803) 854-2175
(800) 329-7466

HOWARD JOHN-
SON EXP
9112 Old Hwy 6
(29142)
Rates: $48-$62
(803) 854-3870
(800) 446-4656
(800) 827-4539

SUPER 8 MOTEL
9125 Old Hwy 6
(29142)
Rates: $50-$55
(803) 854-3456
(800) 800-8000

SENECA
JAMESON INN
226 Hi-Tech Rd
(29678)
Rates: $49-$104
(864) 888-8300
(800) 526-3766

SIMPSONVILLE
DAYS INN
45 Ray East
Talley Ct (29680)
Rates: $55-$187
(864) 963-7701
(800) 329-7466

SPARTANBURG
BROOKWOOD
INN
4930 College Dr
(29303)
Rates: n/a
(864) 576-6080

HOLIDAY INN EXP
895 Spartan Blvd
(29301)
Rates: $89-$105
(864) 699-7777
(800) 465-4329

MOTEL 6
105 Jones Rd
(29303)
Rates: $29-$35
(864) 573-6383
(800) 466-8356

SUMMERTON
DAYS INN
18 Buff Blvd
(29148)
Rates: $40-$75
(843) 485-2865
(800) 329-7466

SUMMERVILLE
COMFORT INN
1005 Jockey Ct
(29483)
Rates: $60-$105
(843) 851-2333
(800) 424-6423

ECONO LODGE
110 Holiday Dr
(29483)
Rates: $45-$100
(843) 875-3022
(800) 424-6423

HOLIDAY INN EXP
120 Holiday Dr
(29483)
Rates: $62-$82
(843) 875-3300
(800) 465-4329

WOODLANDS
RESORT & INN
125 Parsons Rd
(29483)
Rates: $295-$450
(843) 875-2600

SUMTER
MAGNOLIA
HOUSE B&B
230 Church St
(29151)
Rates: $75-$105
(803) 775-6694

RAMADA INN
226 N Washington
St (29151)
Rates: $69-$85
(803) 775-2323
(800) 272-6232

TURBEVILLE
DAYS INN
I-95 & Hwy 378,
Exit 135 (29162)
Rates: $39-$95
(843) 659-8060
(800) 329-7466

KNIGHTS INN
7840 Myrtle Beach
Hwy (29162)
Rates: $35-$45
(843) 659-2175
(800) 843-5644

WALTERBORO
BEST WESTERN INN
1428 Snider's Hwy
(29488)
Rates: $49-$99
(843) 538-3600
(800) 528-1234

ECONO LODGE
1145 Snider's
Hwy (29488)
Rates: $45-$89
(843) 538-3830
(800) 424-6423

HOWARD
JOHNSON EXP
1286 Sniders Hwy
(29488)
Rates: $49-$55
(843) 538-5473
(800) 446-4656

RAMADA INN
1245 Snider's
Hwy (29488)
Rates: $60-$70
(843) 538-5403
(800) 272-6232

RICE PLANTERS INN
97 Ladson St
(29488)
Rates: $30-$40
(843) 538-8964
(800) 647-4831

SUPER 8 MOTEL
1972 Bells Hwy
(29488)
Rates: $39-$65
(843) 538-5383
(800) 800-8000

THUNDERBIRD
INN
1142 Snider's
Hwy (29488)
Rates: $30-$39
(843) 538-2503
(800) 538-2473

WEST COLUMBIA
RAMADA INN
114 McSwain Dr
(29169)
Rates: $66-$75
(803) 796-2700
(800) 272-6232

SLEEP INN
AIRPORT
2208-A Edmund
Hwy (29170)
Rates: $66-$76
(803) 926-9260
(800) 424-6423

WINNSBORO
DAYS INN
1894 Hwy 321
Bypass (29180)
Rates: $38-$85
(803) 635-1447
(800) 329-7466

FAIRFIELD MOTEL
56 US 321 Bypass
S (29180)
Rates: $35-$55
(803) 635-3458

YEMASSEE
DAYS INN
Jct US 17 & I-95
(29945)
Rates: $36-$64
(843) 726-8156
(800) 329-7466

PALMETTO LODGE
12 Lane St (29945)
Rates: $20-$32
(843) 589-2361

HOLIDAY INN EXP
138 Frampton Dr
(29945)
Rates: n/a
(843) 726-9400
(800) 465-4329

YORK
DAYS INN
1568 Alexander
Love Hwy (29745)
Rates: $55-$110
(803) 684-2525
(800) 329-7466

AREA CODES - If the local number doesn't connect, check for a new area code.

SOUTH DAKOTA

ABERDEEN

**AMERICINN
LODGE & SUITES**
310 Centennial St
(57401)
Rates: n/a
(605) 225-4565
(800) 634-3444

**BEST WESTERN
RAMKOTA INN**
1400 8th Ave
NW (57401)
Rates: $69-$94
(605) 229-4040
(800) 528-1234

COMFORT INN
2923 6th Ave SE
(57401)
Rates: $65-$139
(605) 226-0097
(800) 424-6423

FOOTE CREEK B&B
12841 383rd Ave
(57401)
Rates: $60-$150
(605) 225-1617

**HOLIDAY INN EXP
HOTEL & SUITES**
3310 7th Ave SE
(57401)
Rates: $85-$250
(605) 725-4000
(800) 465-4329

RAMADA INN
2727 6th Ave SE
(57401)
Rates: $61-$120
(605) 225-3600
(800) 272-6232

**SUPER 8 MOTEL-
EAST**
2405 6th Ave SE
(57401)
Rates: $50-$131
(605) 229-5005
(800) 800-8000

**SUPER 8 MOTEL-
NORTH**
770 NW Hwy 281
(57401)
Rates: $43-$92
(605) 226-2288
(800) 800-8000

**SUPER 8
MOTEL-WEST**
714 S Hwy 281
(57401)
Rates: $43-$97
(605) 225-1711
(800) 800-8000

BELLE FOURCHE

ACE MOTEL
109 6th Ave
(57717)
Rates: $25-$50
(605) 892-2612

LARIAT MOTEL
1033 Elkhorn
(57717)
Rates: $25-$45
(605) 892-2601

MOTEL 6
1815 5th Ave
(57717)
Rates: $39-$50
(605) 892-6663
(800) 466-8356

BERESFORD

**CROSSROADS
MOTEL**
1409 W Cedar
(57004)
Rates: $22-$32
(605) 763-2020

SUPER 8 MOTEL
1410 W Cedar
(57004)
Rates: $47-$58
(605) 763-2001
(800) 800-8000

BLACK HAWK

SUPER 8 MOTEL
7900 Stagestop Rd
(57718)
Rates: n/a
(605) 787-4844
(800) 800-8000

BRANDON

HOLIDAY INN EXP
1105 N Spillrock
Blvd (57005)
Rates: $73-$139
(605) 582-2901
(800) 465-4329

BROOKINGS

HOLIDAY INN EXP
3020 LeFevre Dr
(57006)
Rates: $75-$125
(605) 592-9060
(800) 465-4329

STAR MOTEL
108 6th St (57006)
Rates: n/a
(605) 692-6345
(800) 884-2518

SUPER 8 MOTEL
3034 LeFevre Dr
(57006)
Rates: $48-$73
(605) 692-6920
(800) 800-8000

WAYSIDE MOTEL
1430 6th St (57006)
Rates: $26-$30
(605) 692-4831
(800) 658-4577

BUFFALO

TIPPERARY LODGE
604 1st St W
(57720)
Rates: $40-$48
(605) 375-3721

CANISTOTA

**BEST WESTERN
U-BAR MOTEL**
130 Ash St (57012)
Rates: $37-$80
(605) 296-3466
(800) 528-1234
(800) 566-8227

CANOVA

**SKOGLUND FARM
BED & BRKFAST**
Rt 1, Box 45
(57321)
Rates: n/a
(605) 247-3445

CHAMBERLAIN

**AMERICINN
LODGE & SUITES**
1981 E King St
(57325)
Rates: $80-$160
(605) 734-0985
(800) 634-3444

BEL AIRE MOTEL
312 E King St
(57325)
Rates: $35-$64
(605) 734-5595

**BEST WESTERN
LEE'S MOTOR INN**
220 West King
(57325)
Rates: $40-$85
(605) 734-5575
(800) 528-1234

**CEDAR SHORE
RESORT**
1500 Shoreline Dr
(57325)
Rates: $80-$150
(605) 734-6376
(888) 697-6363

HOLIDAY INN EXP
100 W Hwy 16
(57365)
Rates: $70-$150
(605) 734-5593
(800) 465-4329

**LAKE SHORE
MOTEL**
115 N River St
(57365)
Rates: $25-$64
(605) 234-5566

OASIS INN
1100 E Hwy 16
(57365)
Rates: $45-$119
(605) 734-6061
(800) 635-3559

CORSICA

**PARKWAY
MOTEL-IMA**
Hwy 281 (57328)
Rates: $21-$35
(605) 946-5230
(800) 341-8000

CUSTER

**AMERICAN
PRESIDENTS
CABINS &RESORT**
Hwy 16A,
P O Box 446
(57730)
Rates: $49-$77
(605) 673-3373

**AMERICAN
PRESIDENTS
MOTEL**
Hwy 16A,
P O Box 446
(57730)
Rates: $27-$68
(605) 673-3373

**BAVARIAN INN
MOTEL**
1000 N 5th St
(57730)
Rates: $46-$116
(605) 673-2802
(800) 657-4312

**BLUE BELL
LODGE & RESORT**
HCR 83, Box 63
(57730)
Rates: $75-$100
(605) 255-4531
(800) 265-4531

CHIEF MOTEL
120 Mt. Rushmore
Rd (57730)
Rates: $49-$93
(605) 673-2318

**LEGION LAKE
RESORT**
HCR 83, Box 67
(57730)
Rates: $69-$110
(605) 255-4521
(800) 658-3530

**ROCK CREST
LODGE**
15 W Mt.
Rushmore Rd
(57730)
Rates: $45-$99
(605) 673-4323
(866) 464-4557

ROCKET MOTEL
211 Mt. Rushmore
Rd (57730)
Rates: $36-$64
(605) 673-4401

**THE ROOST
RESORT COTTAGES**
US 16 A-E (57730)
Rates: $46-$86
(605) 673-2326
(800) 294-4603

AREA CODES - If the local number doesn't connect, check for a new area code.

SUPER 8 MOTEL
415 W Mt.
Rushmore Rd
(57730)
Rates: $55-$109
(605) 673-2200
(800) 800-8000

VALLEY MOTEL
Hwy 16A (57730)
Rates: n/a
(605) 673-4819
(800) 252-2446

CUSTER STATE PARK

DOUBLE L B&B & HORSECAMP
HC 83, Box 1041
(57730)
Rates: n/a
(605) 673-2558

DE SMET

SUPER 8 MOTLE
288 Hwy 14 E
(57231)
Rates: $59-$129
(605) 854-9388
(800) -800-8000

DEADWOOD

FIRST GOLD HOTEL
270 Main St
(57732)
Rates: $65-$195
(605) 578-3979
(800) 274-1876

DELL RAPIDS

SUPER 8 MOTEL
510 N Hwy 77
(57022)
Rates: $49-$72
(605) 428-4288
(800) 800-8000

EDGEMONT

RAINBOW MOTEL
Hwy 18 & 471
(57735)
Rates: n/a
(605) 662-7244

EUREKA

LAKEVIEW MOTEL
RR 1, Box 49
(57437)
Rates: $24-$35
(605) 284-2400
(888) 666-9306

FAITH

PRAIRIE VISTA INN
Hwy 212 & E 1st
St (57626)
Rates: $60-$85
(605) 967-2343
(800) 341-8000

FAULKTON

SUPER 8 MOTEL
700 Main St
(57438)
Rates: $40-$62
(605) 598-4567
(800) 800-8000

FLANDREAU

ROYAL RIVER CASINO & HOTEL
607 S Veterans St
(57028)
Rates: $55-$99
(605) 997-3746
(800) 833-8666

FORT PIERRE

FORT PIERRE MOTEL
211 S First St
(57532)
Rates: $48-$60
(605) 223-3111
(800) 286-0895

HOLIDAY INN EXP HOTEL & SUITES
110 E Stanley Rd
(57532)
Rates: $65-$85
(605) 223-9045
(800) 465-4329

FREEMAN

FENSEL'S MOTEL
Hwy 81 (57029)
Rates: n/a
(605) 925-4204
(800) 658-3319

SUPER 8 MOTEL
1019 S Hwy 81
(57029)
Rates: $45-$55
(605) 925-4888
(800) 800-8000

GETTYSBURG

HARER LODGE BED & BREAKFST
RR 1, Box 87A
(57442)
Rates: n/a
(605) 765-2167
(800) 283-3356

TRAIL MOTEL-IMA
211 E Garfield
(57442)
Rates: $23-$38
(605) 765-2482
(800) 341-8000

HERMOSA

HERMOSA HILLS BED & BRKFAST
HCR 89, Box 62
(57744)
Rates: n/a
(605) 255-4278
(800) 247-4404

HILL CITY

BEST WESTERN GOLDEN SPIKE INN & SUITES
106 Main St
(57745)
Rates: $45-$169
(605) 574-2577
(800) 528-1234

LANTERN INN MOTEL
131 Main St
(57745)
Rates: $44-$120
(605) 574-2582
(800) 456-0520

LODGE AT PALMER GULCH
12620 SR 244
(57745)
Rates: $57-$150
(605) 574-2525
(800) 562-8503

HOT SPRINGS

BEST VALUE INN BY THE RIVER
602 W River
(57757)
Rates: $39-$160
(605) 745-4292

BEST WESTERN SUNDOWNER INN
737 S 6th St
(57757)
Rates: $59-$169
(605) 745-7378
(800) 528-1234

BUDGET HOST HILLS INN
640 S 6th St
(57747)
Rates: $49-$144
(605) 745-3130
(888) 445-7546

COMFORT INN
737 S 6th St
(57747)
Rates: $59-$159
(605) 745-7378
(800) 424-6423

HOLIDAY INN EXP
1401 Hwy 18
(57747)
Rates: $89-$295
(605) 745-4411
(800) 465-4329

MUELLER HOUSE BED & BREAKFAST
201 S 6th St
(57747)
Rates: n/a
(888) 268-8259

RODEWAY INN
402 Battle
Mountain Ave
(57747)
Rates: $60-$90
(605) 745-3182
(800) 228-2000

SUPER 8 MOTEL
800 Mammoth St
(57747)
Rates: $53-$121
(605) 745-3888
(800) 800-8000

HURON

BEST WESTERN INN
2000 Dakota Ave S
(57350)
Rates: $49-$93
(605) 352-2000
(800) 528-1234
(888) 816-0317

CROSSROADS HOTEL
100 4th St SW
(57350)
Rates: $75-$145
(605) 352-3204
(800) 876-5858

HOLIDAY INN EXP
100 21st St SW
(57250)
Rates: $69-$85
(605) 352-6655
(800) 465-4329

TRAVELER MOTEL
241 Lincoln NW
(57350)
Rates: n/a
(605) 352-6401

INTERIOR

BADLANDS BUDGET HOST MOTEL
900 SD Hwy 377
(57750)
Rates: $46-$58
(605) 433-5335
(800) 283-4678

CEDAR PASS LODGE HISTORIC COTTAGE
1 Cedar St, Box 5
(57750)
Rates: $35-$45
(605) 433-5460

KADOKA

BEST VALUE DAKOTA INN-
106 SD Hwy 73
(57543)
Rates: $40-$70
(605) 837-2151

BEST WESTERN H & H EL CENTRO
105 E Hwy 16
(57543)
Rates: $50-$115
(605) 837-2287
(800) 528-1234

HILLTOP MOTEL
225 Hwy 16 E
(57543)
Rates: $45-$70
(605) 837-2216
(800) 582-4356

WEST MOTEL
306 Hwy 16 W
(57543)
Rates: $32-$70
(605) 837-2427
(800) 830-9378

KENNEBEC

KING'S MOTEL
HC 81, Box 30
(57544)
Rates: $25-$38
(605) 869-2270

KEYSTONE

B & B INN
208 1st St (57751)
Rates: $75-$84
(605) 666-4490
(888) 833-4490

FIRST LADY INN
702 Hwy 16A
(57751)
Rates: $49-$169
(605) 666-4990
(800) 252-2119

HIILLSIDE HISTORIC COUNTRY COTTAGES
13315 S Hwy 16 (57701)
Rates: $34-$60
(605) 342-4121

MINER'S MOTEL
#522 Hwy 16A, PO Bx 157 (57751)
Rates: $35-$109
(605) 666-4638
(800) 727-2421

MT. RUSHMORES WHITE HOUSE RESORT
111 Swanzey St (57751)
Rates: $40-$100
(605) 666-4917
(866) 996-6835

POWDER HOUSE LODGE
24125 Hwy16 A (57751)
Rates: $65-$200
(605) 666-4646
(800) 321-0692

SUPER 8 MOTEL
250 Winter St (57751)
Rates: $49-$149
(605) 666-6666
(800) 800-8000

TRIPLE R RANCH
Hwy 16A (57751)
Rates: n/a
(605) 666-4605
(888) RRRANCH

LEAD

GOLDEN HILLS INN
900 Miners Ave (57754)
Rates: $49-$150
(605) 584-1800

WHITE HOUSE INN
395 Glendale Dr (57754)
Rates: $40-$115
(605) 584-2000
(800) 654-5323

LEMMON

PRAIRIE MOTEL
115 E 10th (57638)
Rates: $25-$32
(605) 374-3304
(800) 619-0030

LOWER BRULE

GOLDEN BUFFALO RESORT-IMA
120 Crazy Horse St (57548)
Rates: $40-$60
(605) 473-5506
(800) 341-8000

MADISON

LAKE PARK MOTEL
1515 NW 2nd St (57042)
Rates: $40-$52
(605) 256-3524

SUPER 8 MOTEL
Jct Hwy 34 & 81 (57042)
Rates: $36-$47
(605) 256-6931
(800) 800-8000

MILBANK

LANTERN MOTEL
S Hwy 15 (57252)
Rates: $28-$42
(605) 432-4591
(800) 627-6075

MANOR MOTEL
E Hwy 12 (57252)
Rates: $39-$49
(605) 432-4527

MILLER

DEW DROP INN
HC 64, Bx 140, N Hwy14/45 (57362)
Rates: $27-$50
(605) 853-2431
(888) DEWDROP

MISSION

QUALITY INN ROSEBUD CASINO
Hwy 83 (57555)
Rates: $62-$86
(605) 378-3360
(800) 424-6423

MITCHELL

AMERICINN MOTEL & SUITES
1421 S Burr St (57301)
Rates: $63-$100
(605) 996-9700
(800) 634-3444

COACHLIGHT MOTEL
1000 W Havens St (57301)
Rates: $37-$48
(605) 996-5686

ECONO LODGE
1313 S Ohlman St (57301)
Rates: $39-$99
(605) 996-6647
(800) 424-6423

HAMPTON INN
1920 Highland Way (57301)
Rates: $64-$123
(605) 995-1575
(800) 426-7866

HOLIDAY INN
1525 W Havens St (57301)
Rates: $100-$110
(605) 996-6501
(800) 465-4329

KELLY INN
1010 Cabela Dr (57301)
Rates: $59-$119
(605) 995-0500
(800) 665-2906

MOTEL 6
1309 S Ohlman St (57301)
Rates: $35-$50
(605) 996-0530
(800) 466-8356

THUNDERBIRD LODGE
1601 S Burr St (57301)
Rates: $39-$89
(605) 996-6645

MOBRIDGE

BEST VALUE WRANGLER INN
820 W Grand Crossing (57601)
Rates: $55-$79
(605) 845-3641

MURDO

ANDERSON MOTEL
408 Lincoln (57559)
Rates: n/a
(605) 669-2448

BEST WESTERN GRAHAM'S
301 W 5th St (57559)
Rates: $38-$106
(605) 669-2441
(800) 528-1234

DAYS INN RANGE COUNTRY
302 W 5th (57559)
Rates: $65-$125
(605) 669-2425
(800) 329-7466

NORTH SIOUX CITY

COMFORT INN
1311 River Dr (57049)
Rates: $54-$154
(605) 232-3366
(800) 424-6423

ECONO LODGE
110 Sodrac Dr (57049)
Rates: $40-$74
(605) 232-9600
(800) 424-6423

HAMPTON INN
101 S Sodrac Dr (57049)
Rates: $62-$99
(605) 232-9739
(800) 426-7866

SUPER 8 MOTEL
1300 River Dr (57049)
Rates: $42-$116
(605) 232-4716
(800) 800-8000

OACOMA

COMFORT INN
203 E Hwy 16 (57365)
Rates: $49-$119
(605) 734-4222
(800) 424-6423

DAYS INN
I-90, Exit 260 (57365)
Rates: $34-$110
(605) 734-4100
(800) 329-7466

HOLIDAY INN EXP
I-90, Exit 260 (57365)
Rates: n/a
(605) 734-5593
(800) 465-4329

PICKSTOWN

FORT RANDALL INN
103 Hwy 18/281 (57367)
Rates: $40-$57
(605) 487-7801
(800) 340-7801

PIEDMONT

ELK CREEK RESORT & LODGE
Elk Creek Rd (57769)
Rates: $99-$119
(605) 787-4884
(800) 846-2267

PIERRE

BEST WESTERN RAMKOTA INN
920 W Sioux Ave (57501)
Rates: $79-$94
(605) 224-6877
(800) 528-1234

CAPITOL INN MOTEL
815 Wells Ave (57501)
Rates: $28-$35
(800) 658-3055

COMFORT INN
410 W Sioux Ave (57501)
Rates: $69-$120
(605) 224-0377
(800) 424-6423

DAYS INN
520 W Sioux Ave (57501)
Rates: $49-$185
(605) 224-0411
(800) 329-7466

GOVERNOR'S INN
700 W Sioux Ave (57501)
Rates: $59-$109
(605) 224-4200

KELLY INN
713 W Sioux (57501)
Rates: $47-$62
(605) 224-4140
(800) 635-3559

SUPER 8 MOTEL
320 W Sioux (57501)
Rates: $35-$75
(605) 224-1617

AREA CODES - If the local number doesn't connect, check for a new area code.

PLANKINTON

SUPER 8 MOTEL
801 S Main,
RR 3 (57368)
Rates: $45-$80
(605) 942-7722
(800) 800-8000

PLATTE

KINGS INN MOTEL
Hwy 44 (57369)
Rates: $22-$34
(605) 337-3385
(800) 337-7756

PRESHO

HUTCH'S MOTEL
930 E 9th St
(57568)
Rates: $26-$60
(605) 895-2591

RAPID CITY

A ROSEMARY REMEMBRANCE COUNTRY INN
815 Main St
(57701)
Rates: n/a
(800) 577-3952

ALEX JOHNSON HOTEL
523 6th St (57701)
Rates: $59-$160
(605) 342-1210
(800) 888-2539

BEST WESTERN RAMKOTA HOTEL
2111 N LaCrosse
St (57701)
Rates: $79-$149
(605) 343-8550
(800) 528-1234
(877) 666-5383

BIG SKY MOTEL
4080 Tower Rd
(57701)
Rates: $43-$48
(605) 348-3200
(800) 318-3208

CASTLE INN
15 E North St
(57701)
Rates: $29-$90
(603) 348-4120
(800) 658-5464

COMFORT INN
1550 N LaCrosse
(57701)
Rates: $49-$329
(603) 348-2221
(800) 424-6423

ECONO LODGE
625 E Disk Dr
(57701)
Rates: $45-$235
(605) 342-6400
(800) 424-6423

FAIR VALUE INN
1607 LaCrosse St
(57701)
Rates: $38-$75
(605) 342-8118
(800) 954-8118

FAMILY INN
3737 Sturgis Rd
(57702)
Rates: n/a
(605) 342-2892
(800) 349-2892

FOOTHILLS INN
1625 LaCrosse St
(57701)
Rates: $29-$329
(605) 348-5640
(800) 348-5640

GOLD STAR MOTEL
801 E North
(57701)
Rates: $29-$68
(605) 341-7051

HOLIDAY INN EXP HOTEL & SUITES
645 E Disk Dr
(57701)
Rates: $81-$158
(605) 355-9090
(800) 465-4329

HOLIDAY INN-RUSHMORE PLAZA
505 N Fifth St
(57701)
Rates: $89-$140
(605) 348-4000
(800) 465-4329

MICROTEL INN
1740 Rapp St
(57701)
Rates: $52-$114
(605) 348-2523
(888) 591-32585

MOTEL 6
620 E Latrobe St
(57701)
Rates: $29-$73
(605) 343-3687
(800) 466-8356

QUALITY INN
1902 LaCrosse St
(57701)
Rates: $49-$299
(605) 342-3322
(800) 424-6423

RAMADA INN GOLD KEY
1721 N LaCrosse
St (57701)
Rates: $69-$349
(605) 342-1300
(800) 272-6232

RED ROOF INN
620 Howard St
(57701)
Rates: $40-$120
(605) 343-5434
(800) 843-7663

RODEWAY INN
2208 Mt. Rushmore
Rd (57701)
Rates: $45-$189
(605) 342-1303
(800) 424-6423

SUPER 8 MOTEL-I90
2124 LaCrosse St
(57701)
Rates: $40-$175
(605) 348-8070
(800) 800-8000

SUPER 8 MOTEL-S
2520 Tower Rd
(57701)
Rates: $40-$180
(605) 342-4911
(800) 800-8000

THRIFTY MOTOR INN
1303 LaCrosse St
(57701)
Rates: $38-$75
(605) 342-0551
(800) 318-0551

ROCKERVILLE

ROCKERVILLE TRADING POST
13525 Main St
(57701)
Rates: $45-$75
(605) 341-4880
(800) 450-0496

SIOUX FALLS

AYMONT INN
3200 Meadow Ave
(57106)
Rates: $62-$106
(605) 362-0835
(877) 229-6668

BEST WESTERN RAMKOTA INN
3200 W Maple St
(57107)
Rates: $79-$129
(605) 336-0650
(800) 528-1234

BRIMARK INN
3200 W Russell St
(57101)
Rates: $39-$58
(605) 332-2000
(800) 658-4508

CLUBHOUSE HOTEL & SUITES
2320 S Louise Ave
(57106)
Rates: $99-$59
(605) 361-8700
(866) 534-8700

COMFORT INN-NORTH
5100 N Cliff Ave
(57104)
Rates: $50-$120
(605) 331-4490
(800) 424-6423

COMFORT INN-SOUTH
3216 S Carolyn
Ave (57106)
Rates: $59-$140
(605) 361-2822
(800) 424-6423

COMFORT SUITES
3208 S Carolyn
Ave (57106)
Rates: $65-$134
(605) 362-9711
(800) 424-6423

COUNTRY INN
200 E 8th St (57103)
Rates: $69-$179
(605) 373-0153
(800) 456-4000

DAYS INN
5001 N Cliff Ave
(57104)
Rates: $56-$140
(605) 331-5959
(800) 329-7466

ECONO LODGE
1300 W Russell St
(57104)
Rates: $42-$60
(605) 331-5800
(800) 424-6423

HOMEWOOD SUITES
3620 W Avera Dr
(57108)
Rates: $99-$209
(605) 338-8585
(800) 225-5466

KELLY INN
3101 W Russell
St (57107)
Rates: $62-$80
(605) 338-6242
(800) 635-3559

MICROTEL INN
2901 S Carolyn
Ave (57106)
Rates: $49-$85
(605) 361-7484

MOTEL 6
3009 W Russell
St (57107)
Rates: $31-$55
(605) 336-7800
(800) 466-8356

RAMADA LIMITED
407 South Lyons
Ave (57106)
Rates: $65-$85
(605) 330-0000
(800) 272-6232

RED ROOF INN
3500 S Gateway
Blvd (57106)
Rates: $42-$75
(605) 361-1864
(800) 843-7663

RESIDENCE INN BY MARRIOTT
4509 W Empire Pl
(57106)
Rates: $100-$200
(605) 361-2202
(800) 331-3131

SHERATON HOTEL
1211 N West Ave
(57104)
Rates: $129-$149
(605) 331-0100
(800) 325-3535

AREA CODES - If the local number doesn't connect, check for a new area code.

SLEEP INN
1500 N Kiwanis
Ave (57104)
Rates: $49-$85
(605) 339-3992
(800) 424-6423

SUPER 8 MOTEL-AIRPORT
4808 N Cliff Ave
(57104)
Rates: $50-$90
(605) 339-9212
(800) 800-8000

SUPER 8 MOTEL
4100 W 41st St
(57106)
Rates: $49-$65
(605) 361-9719
(800) 800-8000

SUPER 8 MOTEL
2616 E 10th St
(57103)
Rates: $49-$110
(605) 338-8881
(800) 800-8000

TONWEPLACE SUITES
4545 W Homefield
Dr (57106)
Rates: $79-$139
(605) 361-2626
(800) 257-3000

SISSETON

HOLIDAY MOTEL
E of Jct US 127
(57262)
Rates: $22-$30
(605) 698-7644
(888) 460-9548

VIKING MOTEL
W. Hwy 10 (57262)
Rates: n/a
(605) 698-7663
(800) 823-7669

SPEARFISH

BEST WESTERN BLACK HILLS LODGE
540 E Jackson
Blvd (57783)
Rates: $50-$109
(605) 642-2795
(800) 528-1234

DAYS INN
240 Ryan Rd (57783)
Rates: $57-$102
(605) 642-7101
(800) 329-7466

HOLIDAY INN-NORTHERN BLACK HILLS
305 N 27th St (57783)
Rates: $70-$110
(605) 642-4683
(800) 465-4329
(800) 999-3541

HOWARD JOHNSON EXP INN
323 S 27th St
(57783)
Rates: $50-$80
(605) 642-8105
(800) 446-4656

QUEEN'S MOTEL
305 Main St (57783)
Rates: $25-$49
(605) 642-2631

ROYAL REST MOTEL
444 Main St (57783)
Rates: $40-$55
(605) 642-3842

SHADY PINES CABINS
514 Mason St
(57783)
Rates: n/a
(800) 551-8920

SHERWOOD LODGE
231 West Jackson
Blvd (57783)
Rates: n/a
(605) 642-4688
(800) 234-2032

SPEARFISH CANYON LODGE
10619 Roughlock
Falls Rd (57784)
Rates: $89-$159
(605) 584-3435
(877) 975-6343

TRAVELODGE
346 W Kansas St
(57783)
Rates: $35-$120
(605) 642-4676
(800) 578-7878

STURGIS

BEST WESTERN INN
2431 S Junction
Ave (57785)
Rates: $45-$109
(605) 347-3604
(800) 528-1234
(800) 611-3569

DAYS INN
I-90 Exit 30 &
Hwy 14 (57785)
Rates: $49-$125
(605) 347-3027
(800) 329-7466

JUNCTION INN
1802 S Junction
Ave (57785)
Rates: $29-$69
(605) 347-5675

STAR LITE MOTEL
2426 Junction Ave
(57785)
Rates: $35-$70
(605) 347-2506

VERMILLION

COMFORT INN
701 W Cherry St
(57069)
Rates: $58-$120
(605) 624-8333
(800) 424-6423

HOLIDAY INN EXP
1200 N Dakota St
(57069)
Rates: $69-$149
(605) 624-7600
(800) 465-4329

WALL

BEST WESTERN PLAINS MOTEL
712 Glenn St
(57790)
Rates: $45-$150
(605) 279-2145
(800) 528-1234

DAYS INN
I-90 Ex 110 &
Hwy 240 (57790)
Rates: $45-$140
(605) 279-2000
(800) 329-7466

ECONO LODGE
804 Glenn St
(57790)
Rates: $60-$150
(605) 279-2121
(800) 424-6423

SUNSHINE INN
608 Main St
(57790)
Rates: $63-$75
(605) 279-2178
(800) 782-2613

WATERTOWN

BEST WESTERN RAMKOTA INN
1901 9th Ave SW
(57201)
Rates: $69-$84
(605) 886-8011
(800) 528-1234

COMFORT INN
800 35th St Cir
(57201)
Rates: $69-$114
(605) 886-3010
(800) 424-6423

COUNTRY INN
3400 8th Ave SE
(57201)
Rates: $79-$129
(605) 886-8900
(800) 456-4000

DAYS INN
2900 9th Ave SE
(57201)
Rates: $56-$100
(605) 886-3500
(800) 329-7466

DRAKE MOTOR INN
Jct 212 & 81 (57201)
Rates: $27-$37
(605) 886-8411
(800) 252-4532

GUEST HOUSE MOTOR INN
101 N Broadway
(57201)
Rates: $32-$37
(605) 886-8061
(800) 356-7979

HOLIDAY INN EXP
3900 9th Ave SE
(57201)
Rates: $69-$149
(605) 882-3636
(800) 465-4329

TRAVEL HOST MOTEL
1714 9th Ave SW
(57201)
Rates: $38-$64
(605) 886-6120
(800) 658-5512

TRAVELERS INN MOTEL
920 14th St SE
(57201)
Rates: $43-$50
(605) 882-2243

WINNER

BUFFALO TRAIL MOTEL
950 W 1st St
(57580)
Rates: $111-$120
(605) 842-2212

HOLIDAY INN EXP HOTEL & SUITES
1360 E Hwy 44
(57580)
Rates: $69-$129
(605) 842-2255
(800) 465-4329

WARRIOR INN MOTEL
Hwys 44 & 118
(57580)
Rates: $34-$70
(605) 842-3121
(800) 658-4705

YANKTON

BEST WESTERN KELLY INN
1607 E Hwy 50
(57078)
Rates: $59-$99
(605) 665-2906
(800) 528-1234

BROADWAY MOTEL
1210 Broadway
(57078)
Rates: $25-$33
(605) 665-7805

DAYS INN
2410 Broadway
(57078)
Rates: $45-$125
(605) 665-8717
(800) 329-7466

LEWIS & CLARK RESORT MOTEL
43496 Lake Shore
Dr (57078)
Rates: $50-$210
(605) 665-2680

MULBERRY INN B&B
512 Mulberry St
(57078)
Rates: $25-$48
(605) 665-7116

RAMADA LIMITED
2118 Broadway
(57078)
Rates: n /a
(605) 665-8053
(800) 272-6232

AREA CODES - If the local number doesn't connect, check for a new area code.

TENNESSEE

ADAMSVILLE
DEERFIELD INN
414 E Main St
(38310)
Rates: n/a
(731) 632-2100

ALCOA
COMFORT SUITES AIRPORT
140 Cusick Rd
(37701)
Rates: $59-$99
(865) 984-9840
(800) 424-6423

DAYS INN AIRPORT
2962 Alcoa Hwy
(37701)
Rates: $39-$98
(865) 970-3060
(800) 329-7466

EXECUTIVE LODGE MOTEL
215 Hall Rd (37701)
Rates: n/a
(865) 984-9958

HOLIDAY INN EXP HOTEL & SUITES
130 Associates Blvd (37701)
Rates: $93
(865) 981-9008
(800) 465-4329

JAMESON INN
206 Corporate Place (37701)
Rates: $49-$104
(865) 984-6800

MAINSTAY SUITES AIRPORT
361 Fountain View Circle (37701)
Rates: $59-$139
(865) 379-7799
(800) 424-6423

ALPINE
EAST PORT MARINA & RESORT
5652 E Port Rd
(38543)
Rates: $30-$150+
(800) 736-7951

ALTAMONT
1885 MANOR B&B
1830 Courthouse Cabin (37301)
Rates: n/a
(931) 692-3153

THE WOODLEE HOUSE B&B
10 Cumberland St
(37301)
Rates: n/a
(931) 692-2368

ANTIOCH
DAYS INN-HICKORY HOLLOW
501 Collins Park Dr (37013)
Rates: $49-$90
(615) 731-7800
(800) 329-7466

HOLIDAY INN-THE CROSSINGS
201 Crossings Pl
(37013)
Rates: $75-$78
(615) 731-2361
(800) 465-4329
(888) 683-8883

KNIGHTS INN
1111 Bell Rd N
(37013)
Rates: $30-$49
(615) 713-3205
(800) 843-5644

ASHLAND CITY
DEERFIELD INN
1212 N Main St
(37015)
Ratews: $50-$99
(615) 792-4331

ATHENS
DAYS INNS
2541 Decatur Pike (37302)
Rates: $45-$75
(423) 745-5800
(800) 329-7466

HOMESTEAD INN W
2808 Decatur Pike
(37303)
Rates: $36-$150+
(423) 745-9002
(877) 745-9002

KNIGHTS INN
2620 Decatur Pike
(37303)
Rates: $30-$59
(423) 744-8200
(800) 843-5644

MOTEL 6
2002 Whitaker Rd
(37307)
Rates: $33-$37
(423) 745-4441
(800) 466-8356

RAMADA LTD
115 County Rd
247 (37303)
Rates: $59-$99
(423) 745-1212
(800) 272-6232

BELLS
MOTEL 6
9740 Hwy 70 E
(38006)
Rates: $31-$36
(901) 772-9500
(800) 466-8356

BIG SANDY
NANNIE REE'S OAK TREE RESORT
7905 Lick Creek Rd (38221)
Rates: n/a
(731) 593-5685

BLOUNTVILLE
ROCKY TOP CABINS
496 Pearl Ln
(37617)
Rates: n/a
(423) 323-2535
(800) 452-6456

BOLIVAR
ARISTOCRAT MOTOR INN
108 Porter St
(38008)
Rates: n/a
(731) 658-6451

THE BOLIVAR INN
626 W Market St
(38008)
Rates: $35-$40
(731) 658-3372

RODEWAY INN
916 W Market St
(38008)
Rates: $45-$85
(731) 658-7888
(800) 424-6423

BON AQUA
MORNING STAR STABLES B&B
11375 Back Piney Rd (37025)
Rates: n/a
(931) 670-5052

BRENTWOOD
AMERISUITES
202 Summit View Dr (37027)
Rates: $79-$109
(615) 661-9477
(800) 833-1516

BAYMONT INN
111 Penn Warren Dr (37027)
Rates: $65-$74
(615) 376-4666
(877) 229-6668

CANDLEWOOD SUITES
5129 Virginia Way
(37027)
Rates: $63
(615) 309-0600
(888) 226-3539

COMFORT INN
5566 Franklin Pike Cir (37027)
Rates: $65-$85
(615) 221-5001
(800) 424-6423

HILTON SUITES
9000 Overlook Blvd (37027)
Rates: $115-$189
(615) 370-0111
(800) 445-8667

MAINSTAY SUITES
107 Brentwood Blvd (37027)
Rates: $50-$100
(615) 371-8477
(800) 424-6423

RESIDENCE INN BY MARRIOTT
206 Ward Cir
(37027)
Rates: $109-$139
(615) 371-0100
(800) 331-3131

SLEEP INN
1611 Service Merchandise Blvd
(37027)
Rates: $59-$79
(615) 376-2122
(800) 424-6423

BRISTOL
BEST WESTERN
111 Holiday Dr
(37620)
Rates: $62-$210
(423) 968-1101
(800) 528-1234
(877) 968-1101

DAYS INN
3281 W State St
(37620)
Rates: $45-$400
(423) 968-9119
(800) 329-7466

REGENCY INN
975 Volunteer Pkwy (37620)
Rates: $38-$135
(423) 968-9474

BROWNSVILLE
BEST WESTERN TRAVELLERS IN
110 Sunny Hill Cove (38012)
Rates: $45-$62
(731) 779-2389
(800) 528-1234

COMFORT INN
2600 Anderson AVe (38012)
Rates: $42-$82
(731) 772-4082
(800) 424-6423

DAYS INN
2530 Anderson Ave (38012)
Rates: $42-$79
(731) 772-3297
(800) 329-7466

AREA CODES - If the local number doesn't connect, check for a new area code.

HOLIDAY INN EXP
120 Sunny Hill
Cove (38012)
Rates: $58
(731) 772-4030
(800) 465-4329

SUNRISE INN
328 W Main St
(38012)
Rates: $30-$49
(731) 772-1483

BUCHANAN
CYPRESS BAY
RESORT
110 Cypress
Resort Loop
(38222)
Rates: n/a
(731) 232-8221

FISH TALE LODGE
14725 Hwy 79
(38222)
Rates: n/a
(731) 642-7113

PARIS LANDING
MOTEL
15515 Hwy 79 N
(38222)
Rates: $35-$99
(731) 642-0217

SHAMROCK
RESORT
220 Shamrock Rd
(38222)
Rates: n/a
(731) 232-8211
(800) 852-7885

BUCKSNORT
TRAVEL INN
5032 Hwy 230 W
(37140)
Rates: $32-$51
(615) 729-5450

BULLS GAP
COMFORT INN
50 Speedway Ln
(37711)
Rates: $46-$180
(423) 235-9111
(800) 424-6423
*
SUPER 8 MOTEL
90 Speedway Ln
(37711)
Rates: $40-$89
(423) 235-4112
(800) 800-8000

BUTLER
CREEKSIDE
CHALET
138 Moreland Dr
(37640)
Rates: $150+
(888) 781-2399

HEAD FOR THE
HILLS RESORT
631 Cowan Town
Rd (37640)
Rates: n/a
(423) 768-3346
(800) 705-7724

IRON
MOUNTAIN
INN B&B
138 Moreland Dr
(37640)
Rates: $165-$250
(423) 768-2446
(888) 781-2399

LAKEVIEW
TERRACE LODGE
1024 Lakeview
(37640)
Rates: $50-$149
(877) WATAUGA

MOUNTAIN
WILDERNESS
RESORT
166 Wilderness
Trail (37640)
Rates: n/a
(800) 381-6751

CAMDEN
BIRDSONG
RESORT/
MARINA &
CABINS
255 Marina Rd
(38320)
Rates: n/a
(731) 584-7880
(800) 225-7469

DAYS INN
30 Old Rt One
(38320)
Rates: $39-$57
(731) 584-3111
(800) 329-7466

CARTHAGE
DEFEATED CREEK
MARINA
156 Marina Ln
(37030)
Rates: n/a
(615) 774-3131

CARYVILLE
BUDGET HOST INN
115 Woods Ave
(37714)
Rates: $27-$36
(423) 562-9595
(800) 283-4678

FAMILY INNS OF
AMERICA
I-75 & 25 W
(37714)
Rates: n/a
(800) 251-9752

SUPER 8 MOTEL
200 John McGhee
Blvd (37714)
Rates: $44-$60
(423) 562-8476
(800) 800-8000

CELINA
CEDAR HILL
RESORT
2371 Cedar Hill
Rd (38551)
Rates: $35-$110
(931) 243-3201
(800) 872-8393

HUNTER'S LODGE
CABINS
970 Bill Hunter Rd
(38551)
Rates: n/a
(931) 243-3459

CENTERVILLE
DAYS INN
634 David St (37033)
Rates: $45-$99
(931) 729-5600
(800) 329-7466

CHATTANOOGA
ALPINE LODGE
MOTEL
4328 Cummings
Hwy (37419)
Rates: $150+
(423) 821-2546

BAYMONT INN
3540 Cummings
Hwy (37419)
Rates: $45-$110
(423) 821-1090
(877) 229-6668

BEST HOLIDAY
TRAV-L-PARK
1709 Mack Smith
Rd (37412)
Rates: n/a
(800) 693-2877

BEST INN-HAMIL-
TON MALL
7717 Lee Hwy
(37412)
Rates: $36-$90
(423) 894-5454

BEST INN
6521 Ringgold Rd
(37412)
Rates: $48-$89
(423) 894-6720

BEST
VALUE INN
6639 Capehart Ln
(37412)
Rates: $35-$50
(800) 272-6232

BEST WESTERN
HERITAGE INN
7641 Lee Hwy
(37412)
Rates: $49-$89
(423) 899-3311
(800) 528-1234

BEST WESTERN
ROYAL INN
3644 Cummings
Hwy (37419)
Rates: $60-$99
(423) 821-6840
(800) 528-1234

COMFORT INN
3109 Parker Ln
(37419)
Rates: $49-$125
(423) 821-1499
(800) 424-6423

DAYS INN
AIRPORT
7725 Lee Hwy
(37421)
Rates: n/a
(423) 899-2288
(800) 329-7466

DAYS INN
LOOKOUT MTN
3801 Cummings
Hwy (37419)
Rates: $48-$78
(423) 821-6044
(800) 329-7466

ECONO LODGE
1417 St.Thomas St
(37412)
Rates: $29-$59
(423) 894-1417
(800) 424-6423

LA QUINTA INN
7015 Shallowford
Rd (37421)
Rates: $65-$89
(423) 855-0011
(800) 687-6667

LOOKOUT
LAKE B&B
3408 Elder Mtn Rd
(37419)
Rates: n/a
(423) 821-8088

MARRIOTT AT
THE CONV CTR
2 Carter Plaza
(37402)
Rates: $94-$113
(423) 753-0002
(800) 228-9290

MICROTEL INN
7014 McCutcheon
Rd (37421)
Rates: $35-$54
(423) 510-0761
(888) 771-7171
(800) 874-8507

MOTEL 6
7707 Lee Hwy
(37421)
Rates: $33-$36
(423) 892-7707
(800) 466-8356

MOTEL 6
DOWNTOWN
2440 Williams St
(37408)
Rates: $33-$50
(4230 265-7300
(800) 466-8356

QUALITY INN
5505 Brainerd Rd
(37411)
Rates: $45-$58
(423) 894-2040
(800) 424-6423

RAMADA INN
100 W 21st St
(37408)
Rates: n/a
(423) 265-3151
(800) 272-6232
(866) 349-3333

RAMADA LIMITED
30 Birmingham
Hwy (37419)
Rates: n/a
(423) 821-7162
(800) 272-6232

RAMADA LIMITED
6650 Ringgold Rd (37412)
Rates: n/a
(423) 894-1860
(800) 272-6232

RED ROOF INN
7014 Shallowford Rd (37421)
Rates: $36-$62
(423) 899-0143
(800) 843-7663

RESIDENCE INN BY MARRIOTT
215 Chestnut St (37402)
Rates: $99-$109
(423) 266-0600
(800) 331-3131

SLEEP INN
3117 Parker Ln (37419)
Rates: $49-$125
(423) 822-7322
(800) 424-6423

STAYBRIDGE SUITES
1300 Carter St (37402)
Rates: n/a
(423) 267-0900
(800) 238-8000

SUPER 8 MOTEL-AQUARIUM
20 Birmingham Rd (37419)
Rates: $50-$67
(423) 821-8880
(800) 800-8000

CLARKSVILLE
COMFORT INN
1112 SR 76 (37043)
Rates: $40-$75
(931) 358-2020
(800) 424-6423

DAYS INN
1100 Hwy 76, Connector Rd (37043)
Rates: $45-$80
(931) 358-3194
(800) 329-7466

DAYS INN NORTH
130 Westfield Ct (37040)
Rates: $50-$66
(931) 552-1155
(800) 329-7466

HACHLAND HILL INN & RETREAT
1601 Madison St (37043)
Rates: $50-$99
(931) 647-4084

HOLIDAY INN
3095 Wilma Rudolph Blvd (37040)
Rates: $63-$75
(931) 648-4848
(800) 465-4329

HOME-TOWNE SUITES
129 Westfield Ct (37040)
Rates: $50-$99
(931) 551-7711

MICROTEL INN
241 Holiday Dr (37040)
Rates: $39-$59
(931) 905-1505
(888) 771-7171

MID TOWN INN
890 Kraft St (37040)
Rates: n/a
(931) 647-6536

MOTEL 6
254 Holiday Dr (37040)
Rates: $36-$43
(931) 552-2663
(800) 466-8356

QUALITY INN DOWNTOWN
803 N 2nd St (37040)
Rates: $39-$89
(931) 645-9084
(800) 424-6423

RAMADA LIMITED
3100 Wilma Rudolph Blvd (37040)
Rates: $35-$60
(931) 552-0098
(800) 272-6232

RED ROOF INN
197 Holiday Dr (37040)
Rates: $41-$79
(931) 905-1555
(800) 843-7663

SHONEY'S INN
190 Holiday Rd (37040)
Rates: $35-$99
(800) 552-4667

SUPER 8 MOTEL
635 Huntco Dr (37043)
Rates: $50-$69
(931) 358-0810
(800) 800-8000

VACATION MOTOR HOTEL
650 Providence Blvd (37042)
Rates: $35-$49
(931) 645-6483

CLEVELAND
COMFORT INN
153 James Asbury Dr (37312)
Rates: $50-$90
(423) 478-5265
(800) 424-6423

DAYS INN
2550 Georgetown Rd (37311)
Rates: $30-$75
(423) 476-2112
(800) 329-7466

DOUGLAS INN & SUITES
2600 Westside Dr NW (37312)
Rates: $40-$99
(423) 559-5579

ECONO LODGE
2655 Westside Dr NW (37312)
Rates: $40-$70
(423) 472-3281
(800) 553-2666

HOLIDAY INN-MOUNTAIN VIEW
2400 Executive Park Dr (37320)
Rates: $110
(423) 472-1504
(800) 465-4329

JAMESON INN
360 Paul Huff Pkwy (37312)
Rates: $49-$104
(423) 614-5583
(800) 526-3766

QUALITY INN CHALET
2595 Georgetown Rd (37311)
Rates: $49-$125
(423) 476-8511
(800) 424-6423

RAMADA LIMITED
156 James Asbury Dr (37312)
Rates: $55-$80
(423) 472-5566
(800) 272-6232

SUPER 8 MOTEL
163 Bernham Dr (37312)
Rates: $45-$55
(423) 476-5555
(800) 800-8000

TRAVEL INN
3000 Valley Hills Tr NW (37311)
Rates: $30-$45
(615) 472-2185
(800) 838-9998

CLINTON
BEST WESTERN CLINTON INN
720 Park Place (37716)
Rates: $44-$120
(865) 457-2311
(800) 528-1234

HOLIDAY INN EXP
141 Buffalo Rd (37716)
Rates: $79-$109
(865) 457-2233
(800) 465-4329

SKUNK RIDGE FARM B&B
1203 Mountain Rd (37716)
Rates: n/a
(865) 548-1646

SUPER 8 MOTEL
2317 N Seviers Blvd (37716)
Rates: $60-$125
(854) 457-0565
(800) 800-8000

COKER CREEK
SHADY PINES COTTAGES
12135 Hwy 68 S (37314)
Rates: n/a
(423) 261-2242

COLLIERVILLE
COMFORT INN
1230 W Poplar (38017)
Rates: $60-$125
(901) 853-1235
(800) 424-6423

COLUMBIA
BEST VALUE INN
1548 Bear Creek Pike (38401)
Rates: $39-$49
(931) 381-1410

DAYS INN
1504 Nashville Hwy (38401)
Rates: $38-$49
(931) 381-3297
(800) 329-7466

HOLIDAY INN EXP
1554 Bear Creek Pike (38401)
Rates: $75-$83
(931) 380-1227
(800) 465-4329

THE HONORS INN
1208 Nashville Hwy (38401)
Rates: $40-$99
(800) 574-6112

JAMES K POLK MOTEL
1111 Nashville Hwy (38401)
Rates: $35-$40
(931) 388-4913

OAK SPRINGS INN & GALLERY
1512 Williamsport Pike (38401)
Rates: n/a
(931) 388-7539
(800) 542-7698

RELAX INN
1547 Bear Creek Pk (38401)
Rates: n/a
(931) 388-8539

RICHLAND INN
2405 Hwy 31 S (38401)
Rates: n/a
(800) 828-4832

COOKEVILLE
ALPINE LODGE
2021 E Spring St (38506)
Rates: $36-$52
(931) 526-3333
(800) 213-2016

BAYMONT INN
1151 S Jefferson (38506)
Rates: $69-$99
(931) 525-6668
(877) 229-6668

BEST WESTERN THUNDERBIRD MOTEL
900 S Jefferson Ave (38501)
Rates: $40-$90
(931) 526-7115
(800) 528-1234

COMFORT SUITES
1035 Interstate Dr (38501)
Rates: $54-$89
(931) 372-1881
(800) 424-6423

DAYS INN
1292 S Walnut Ave (38501)
Rates: $30-$70
(931) 528-1511
(800) 329-7466

ECONO LODGE
1100 S Jefferson Ave (38506)
Rates: $30-$85
(931) 528-1040
(800) 424-6423

HAMPTON INN
1025 Interstate Dr (38501)
Rates: $60-$70
(931) 520-1117
(800) 426-7866

HOLIDAY INN
970 S Jefferson Ave (38501)
Rates: $69-$75
(931) 526-7125
(800) 465-4329

KEY WEST INN
663 S Willow Ave (38501)
Rates: n/a
(931) 525-1110
(800) 253-9937

KNIGHTS INN
1814 Salem Rd (38501)
Rates: $30-$49
(800) 843-5644

STAR MOTOR INN
1115 S Willow Ave (38501)
Rates: $35-$99
(931) 526-9511
(800) 842-1685

COPPERHILL

COPPERHILL COUNTRY CABINS
496 Deal Rd (37317)
Rates: $50-$99
(423) 496-5225

CORDOVA

QUALITY SUITES
8166 Varnavas Dr (38018)
Rates: $79-$165
(901) 386-4600
(800) 424-6423

CORNERSVILLE

ECONO LODGE
3731 Pulaski Hwy (37047)
Rates: $59-$125
(931) 293-2111
(800) 424-6423

COSBY

COSBY CREEK CABINS
4378 Cosby Hwy (37722)
Rates: $50-$149
(800) 508-8844

CUB MOTEL
4344 Cosby Hwy (37722)
Rates: $30-$50
(423) 487-4344
(888) 853-9370

FOX DEN MOTEL
311 S Hwy 32 (37722)
Rates: n/a
(888) 369-3361

LITTLE CREEK CABINS
173 Stonebrook Dr (37722)
Rates: n/a
(423) 908-7147
(800) 201-0932

SERENITY FALLS CABIN RENTALS
4555 Redwood Way (37722)
Rates: $50-$149
(423) 487-2900

WILDWOOD ACRES LOG CABINS
4410 Wildwood Dr (37722)
Rates: n/a
(800) 423-2030

COVINGTON

COMFORT INN
901 Hwy 51 N (38019)
Rates: $62-$85
(901) 475-0380
(800) 424-6423

CROSSVILLE

CHEROKEE LODGE & RESORT
324 Trails End Rd (38571)
Rates: n/a
(931) 277-5140

DAYS INN
305 Executive Dr (38556)
Rates: $45-$70
(931) 484-9691
(800) 329-7466

RAMADA INN
4083 Hwy 127 N (38571)
Rates: $69-$89
(931) 484-7581
(800) 272-6232

SCOTTISH INNS
3406 N Main St (38555)
Rates: $30-$60
(931) 484-8122
(800) 251-1962

CRUMP

RIVER HEIGHTS MOTEL
3950 Hwy 64 (38372)
Rates: $30-$49
(731) 632-4535

CUMBERLAND GAP

RAMADA INN
Hwy 58 & US 25 E (37724)
Rates: $65-$71
(423) 869-3631
(800) 272-6232

DANDRIDGE

COMFORT INN
620 Green Valley Dr (37225)
Rates: $54-$199
(865) 397-2090
(800) 424-6423

D & D MCARTHUR COTTAGE
2515 Hills Chapel Rd (37225)
Rates: $50-$149
(865) 397-5207

HOLIDAY INN EXP
119 Sharon Dr (37225)
Rates: n/a
(865) 397-1910
(800) 465-4329

INDIAN CREEK DOCK & CABINS
2321 Norman Way (37225)
Rates: n/a
(865) 397-7286

MOUNTAIN HARBOR INN B&B
1199 Hwy 139 (37725)
Rates: $60-$135
(865) 397-3345
(866) 249-1050

TENNESSEE MOUNTAIN INN
531 Patriot Dr (37225)
Rates: $29-$129
(865) 397-9437

DAYTON

BEST WESTERN
7835 Rhea Cty Hwy (37321)
Rates: $65-$105
(423) 775-6560
(800) 528-1234
(800) 437-9604

DAYS INN
3914 Rhea County Hwy (37321)
Rates: $45-$85
(423) 775-9718
(800) 329-7466

DECATUR

COTTON PORT FISH 'N' CAMP MOTEL
County Rd 235 (37322)
Rates: n/a
(423) 334-4999

DECATURVILLE

MERMAID MARINA CABINS
110 Lagoon Ln (38329)
Rates: $50-$99
(800) 506-0008

DECHERD

JAMESON INN
1836 Decherd Blvd (37324)
Rates: $49-$104
(931) 962-0139
(800) 526-3766

DEL RIO

BEAR'S DEN LOG CABIN RENTAL
651 Odyssey Rd (37727)
Rates: n/a
(423) 487-4419

GANNON'S FRENCH BROAD OUTPOST RANCH CABINS
461 Old River Rd (37727)
Rates: n/a
(423) 487-3120
(800) 995-POST

DICKSON

BEST WESTERN EXECUTIVE INN
2338 Hwy 46 S (37055)
Rates: $40-$60
(615) 446-0541
(800) 528-1234

COMFORT INN
1025 E Christi Dr (37055)
Rates: $50-$80
(615) 441-5252
(800) 424-6423

DAYS INN
2415 Hwy 46 S (37055)
Rates: $40-$80
(615) 446-7561
(800) 329-7466

HIGHLAND MOTEL
1414 Hwy 70 E (37055)
Rates: $30-$49
(615) 446-8025

HOLIDAY INN
2420 Hwy 46 S (37055)
Rates: $59-$84
(615) 446-9081
(800) 465-4329

AREA CODES - If the local number doesn't connect, check for a new area code.

MOTEL 6
2325 Hwy 46 S
(37055)
Rates: $36-$40
(615) 446-2423
(800) 446-8356

SUPER 8 MOTEL
150 Suzanne Dr
(37055)
Rates: $70-$85
(615) 446-1923
(800) 800-8000

DOVER
DOVER INN
1545 Donelson
Pkwy (37058)
Rates: n/a
(931) 232-5556

SUNSET MOTOR INN
314 Hwy 79 (37058)
Rates: $35-$89
(931) 232-5102

DRESDEN
DRESDEN MOTOR INN
8563 Hwy 22
(83225)
Rates: n/a
(901) 364-3151

DUNLAP
B&B GUEST RANCH
Rt 1, Box 454A
(37327)
Rates: n/a
(423) 554-4677

DYERSBURG
BEST WESTERN DYERSBURG INN & SUITES
770 Hwy 51
Bypass W (38024)
Rates: $64-$69
(731) 285-8601
(866) 285-8601

COMFORT INN
815 Reelfoot Dr
(38024)
Rates: $59-$74
(731) 285-6951
(800) 424-6423

HAMPTON INN
2750 Mall Loop
Rd (38024)
Rates: $74-$89
(731) 285-4778
(800) 426-7866

PLAZA MOTEL
1170 Hwy 51 S
Bypass (38024)
Rates: $30-$49
(731) 286-8001

EAST RIDGE
BEST VALUE INN
639 Camp Jordan
Pkwy (37412)
Rates: $34-$59
(423) 894-6110

HOWARD JOHNSON PLAZA HOTEL
6700 Ringgold Rd
(37412)
Rates: $60-$80
(423) 892-8100
(800) 446-4656

RAMADA LTD
6650 Ringgold Rd
(37412)
Rates: $45-$100
(423) 894-1860
(800) 272-6232

ELIZABETHTON
AMERICOURT HOTEL
1515 US 19 E
(37643)
Rates: $59-$99
(800) 228-5150

DAYS INN
505 W Elk Ave
(37643)
Rates: $44-$175
(423) 543-3344
(800) 329-7466

ELKTON
BEST VALUE INN
I-65 & Bryson Rd
(38455)
Rates: $30-$49
(888) 315-BEST

ERWIN
HOLIDAY INN EXP
2002 Temple Hill
Rd (37650)
Rates: $70-$94
(423) 743-4100
(800) 465-4329

SUPER 8 MOTEL
1101 N Buffalo St
(37650)
Rates: $30-$50
(800) 800-8000

ETOWAH
ETOWAH MOTEL
330 N Tennessee
Ave (37331)
Rates: n/a
(423) 263-7618

HOLIDAY TERRACE MOTEL
324 N Tennessee
Ave (37331)
Rates: n/a
(423) 263-7618

FAIRVIEW
DEERFIELD INN
1407 Hwy 96 N
(37062)
Rates: $39-$69
(615) 799-4700

SWEET ANNIE'S BED,BREAKFAST
7201 Cumberland
Dr (37062)
Rates: n/a
(615) 799-8833

FARRAGUT
BAYMONT INN
11341 Campbell
Lakes Dr (37922)
Rates: $60-$96
(865) 671-1010
(877) 229-6668

SUPER 8 MOTEL
11748 Snyder Rd
(37932)
Rates: $44-$95
(865) 675-5566
(800) 800-8000

FAYETTEVILLE
BEST WESTERN
3021 Thornton
Taylor Pkwy
(37334)
Rates: $57-$68
(931) 433-0100
(800) 528-1234

DAYS INN
1653 Huntsville
Hwy (37334)
Rates: $49-$79
(931) 433-6121
(800) 329-7466

FRANKLIN
AMERISUITES
650 Bakers Bridge
Ave (37067)
Rates: $89-$129
(615) 771-8900
(800) 833-1516

BAYMONT INN
4207 Franklin
Commons Ct
(37064)
Rates: $60-$65
(615) 791-7700
(877) 229-6668

BEST WESTERN
1308 Murfreesboro
Rd (37064)
Rates: $35-$80
(615) 790-0570
(800) 251-3200

BLUE MOON FARM, PRIVATE COTTAGE B&B
4441 N Chapel Rd
(37067)
Rates: n/a
(800) 493-4518

COMFORT INN
4206 Franklin
Common Ct (37064)
Rates: $54-$130
(615) 791-6675
(800) 424-6423

DAYS INN
4217 S Carothers
Rd (37064)
Rates: $50-$200
(615) 790-1140
(800) 329-7466

HOLIDAY INN EXP HOTEL & SUITES
4202 Franklin
Commons Ct
(37067)
Rates: $99
(615) 591-6660
(800) 465-4329

HOMESTEAD STUDIO SUITES
680 Bakers Bridge
Ave (37076)
Rates: $49-$74
(615) 771-7600
(888) 782-9473

NAMASTE ACRES COUNTRY RANCH INN B&B
5436 Leipers
Creek (37064)
Rates: $85-$95
(615) 791-0333

RAMADA LIMITED
6210 Hospitality
Dr (37064)
Rates: $58
(615) 791-4004
(800) 272-6232

SUPER 8 MOTEL
1307 Murfreesboro
Rd (37064)
Rates: $45-$75
(615) 794-7591
(800) 800-8000

FRANKWING
HOLLOW POND FARM B&B
P O Box 775, Tight
Bark Hollow Rd
(38459)
Rates: n/a
(931) 424-8535
(800) 463-0154
(Horses allowed only)

OUTBACK HIDEAWAY CABINS
64 Endsley Rd
(38459)
Rates: n/a
(931) 732-4297

GALLATIN
COMFORT INN
354 Summer Hall
Dr (37066)
Rates: $45-$135
(615) 230-8300
(800) 424-6423

JAMESON INN
1001 Village Green
Crossing (37066)
Rates: $49-$104
(615) 451-4494
(800) 526-3766

SHONEY'S INN
221 W Main St
(37066)
Rates: n/a
(615) 452-5433
(800) 552INNS

GATLINBURG
ABOVE THE SMOKIES CABINS
201 Parkway
(37738)
Rates: $50-$150+
(888) 436-4121

BARBARA'S CHALET & CABIN S
523 Cherokee
Orchard Rd
(37738)
Rates: n/a
(800) 346-3195

BON AIR LODGE
950 Parkway
(37738)
Rates: $43-$95
(800) 523-3919

CHERRY HILL CABIN
302 Newman Rd
(37738)
Rates: n/a
(865) 436-5881
(888) 737-4295

COBLEY NOB RENTALS INC
3722 E Parkway
(37738)
Rates: $75-$150
(865) 436-5298
(865) 834-8196

DUDLEY CREEK MOTEL & CABINS
804 E Parkway
(37738)
Rates: $39-$149
(865) 436-4347
(888) 430-5867

FAMILY INNS OF AMERICA SUITES
218 Ski Mountain
Rd (37738)
Rates: n/a
(865) 436-3300
(800) 468-6326

GRAND PRIX MOTEL
235 Ski Mountain
Rd (37738)
Rates: n/a
(800) 732-2802

GRANDVIEW CABIN & COTTAGES
335 E Holly Ridge
Rd (37738)
Rates: $80-$100
(865) 436-3161
(800) 578-4330

GREENBRIER VALLEY RESORTS CABINS
3629 E Parkway
(37738)
Rates: $100-$450
(865) 436-2015
(800) 546-1144

HOLIDAY INN SUNSPREE RESORTS
520 Airport Rd
(37738)
Rates: $79-$139
(865) 436-9201
(800) 465-4329
(800) 435-9201

LAURELWOOD MOTEL
115 Willow Lane
(37738)
Rates: $40-$99
(865) 436-4155

MAPLES PREMIER CHALETS
1670 E Parkway
(37738)
Rates: n/a
(865) 430-3985
(800) 878-8981

MICROTEL INN
211 Airport Rd
(37738)
Rates: $59-$94
(865) 436-0107
(888) 771-7171
(800) 266-3500

MIDTOWN LODGE
805 Parkway
(37738)
Rates: $50-$149
(800) 633-2446

MOUNTAIN HERITAGE INN HOTEL
575 River Rd
(37738)
Rates: $35-$149
(865) 436-3474
(800) 343-7953

MOUNTAIN VIEW CHALETS
General Delivery
(37738)
Rates: $50-$150+
(865) 436-0983
(800) 548-3872

OGLE'S VACA-TION MOTEL
310 E Parkway
(37738)
Rates: $35-$99
(800) 634-2595

THE PARK VISTA HOTEL
705 Cherokee
Orchard Rd
(37738)
Rates: $40-$169
(865) 436-9211
(800) 421-PARK

QUALITY INN CREEKSIDE
125 LeConte
Creek Dr (37738)
Rates: $59-$159
(865) 436-4865
(800) 424-6423

RAMADA INN FOUR SEASONS HOTEL
756 Parkway
(37738)
Rates: $54-$139
(865) 436-7881
(800) 272-6232

RIVER TERRACE RESORT
240 River Rd
(37728)
Rates: $59-$109
(865) 436-5161
(800) 251-2070

SMOKY TOP CABIN RENTALS
604 King Branch
(37738)
Rates: $50-$150+
(865) 436-5749
(800) 468-6813

STONY BROOK MOTEL
167 Parkway
(37738)
Rates: $35-$99
(800) 276-1526

TERRACE MOTEL
396 Parkway
(37738)
Rates: $30-$89
(865) 436-4965

TRENT MOTOR LODGE
919 Parkway
(37738)
Rates: n/a
(865) 436-4807
(800) 251-9752

THE VILLAS OF GATLINBURG
201 Parkway
(37738)
Rates: $50-$150+
(800) 223-6264

GERMANTOWN

COMFORT INN
7787 Wolf River
Blvd (38138)
Rates: $59-$129
(901) 757-7800
(800) 424-6423

HOMEWOOD SUITES
7855 Wolf River
Blvd (38138)
Rates: $129
(901) 751-2500
(800) 225-5466

RESIDENCE INN BY MARRIOTT
9314 Poplar Pike
(38138)
Rates: $113-$124
(901) 751-2500
(800) 331-3131

GOODLETTSVILLE

BAYMONT INN
120 Cartwright St
(37072)
Rates: $55-$120
(615) 851-1891
(877) 229-6668

BEST WESTERN FAIRWINDS INN
100 Northcreek
Blvd (37072)
Rates: $45-$99
(615) 851-1067
(800) 528-1234

MOTEL 6
323 Cartwright St
(37072)
Rates: $31-$38
(615) 859-9674
(800) 466-8356

RED ROOF INN
110 Northgate Dr
(37072)
Rates: $35-$54
(615) 859-2537
(800) 843-7663

RODEWAY INN
650 Wade Cir
(37072)
Rates: $30-$50
(615) 859-1416
(800) 424-6423

SUPER 8 MOTEL
622 Rivergate
Pkwy (37072)
Rates: $35-$89
(800) 800-8000

GORDONS-VILLE

COMFORT INN
479 Gordonsville
Hwy (38563)
Rates: $55-$80
(615) 683-1300
(800) 424-6423

GREENEVILLE

COMFORT INN
1790 E Andrew
Johnson Hwy
(37745)
Rates: $65-$199
(423) 639-4185
(800) 424-6423

DAYS INN
935 E Andrew
Johnson Hwy
(37743)
Rates: $39-$185
(423) 639-2156
(800) 329-7466

HAMPSHIRE

RIDGETOP B&B
2141 Columbia
Hwy (38461)
Rates: n/a
(800) 377-2770

HARRIMAN

BEST WESTERN SUNDANCER MOTOR LODGE
120 Childs Rd
(37748)
Rates: $42-$60
(865) 882-6200
(800) 528-1234

HOLIDAY INN EXP
1845 S Roane St
(37748)
Rates: $59-$69
(865) 882-5340
(800) 465-4329

SUPER 8 MOTEL
1867 S Roane St
(37748)
Rates: $45-$55
(865) 882-6600
(800) 800-8000

AREA CODES - If the local number doesn't connect, check for a new area code.

HENDERSON
CHICKASAW CHALET
115 Chalet Ln (38340)
Rates: $50-$99
(731) 983-6000

HENDERSON-VILLE
AMERISUITES
330 E Main St (37075)
Rates: $79-$99
(615) 826-4301
(800) 747-8483

MORNING STAR B&B
460 Jones Ln (37075)
Rates: n/a
(615) 264-2614

HERMITAGE
BEST INN
5770 Old Hickory Blvd (37076)
Rates: $42-$65
(615) 889-8940
(800) BEST-INN

COMFORT INN
5768 Old Hickory Blvd (37076)
Rates: $59-$85
(615) 889-5060
(800) 424-6423

HERMITAGE INN
4144 Lebanon Rd (37076)
Rates: $48-$73
(615) 883-7444

HIXSON
HOME AWAY EXTENDED STAY STUDIOS
1949 North Point Blvd (37343)
Rates: $59-$69
(423) 643-4663

HOHENWALD
EMBASSY INN
235 E Main St (38462)
Rates: $35-$89
(931) 796-1500

HOLLADAY
DAYS INN
13845 Hwy 641 N (38341)
Rates: $50-$80
(731) 847-2278
(800) 329-7466

HORNBEAK
BOARDMAN RESORT
813 Lake Dr (38232)
Rates: n/a
(901) 538-2112

HAMILTON'S RESORT
4992 Hamilton Rd (38232)
Rates: n/a
(901) 538-2325

HUNTINGDON
BEST WESTERN HUNTINGDON INN
11790 Lexington St (38344)
Rates: $51-$62
(731) 986-2281
(800) 528-1234

HUNTSVILLE
GRAND VISTA HOTEL
11597 Scott Hwy (37756)
Rates: $50-$99
(888) 854-6300

HURRICANE MILLS
BEST WESTERN INN
15542 Hwy 13 S (37078)
Rates: $55-$100
(931) 296-4251
(800) 528-1234

BUFFALO RIVER KOA CABINS
473 Barren Hollow Rd (37078)
Rates: n/a
(931) 296-1306
(800) KOA-0832

DAYS INN
15415 Hwy 13 S (37078)
Rates: $40-$60
(931) 296-7647
(800) 329-7466

HOLIDAY INN EXP
15368 Hwy 13 (37078)
Rates: $54-$65
(931) 296-2999
(800) 465-4329

JACKSON
BAYMONT INN
2370 N Highland Ave (38305)
Rates: $49-$54
(731) 664-1800
(877) 229-6668

BEST WESTERN INN & SUITES
1936 Hwy 45 Bypass (38305)
Rates: $50-$75
(731) 664-3030
(800) 528-1234

COMFORT INN
1963 Hwy 45 Bypass (38305)
Rates: $60-$130
(731) 668-4100
(800) 424-6423

DAYS INN
1919 Hwy 45 Bypass (38305)
Rates: $32-$50
(731) 668-3444
(800) 329-7466

DAYS INN-WEST
2239 N Hollywood Dr (38305)
Rates: $34-$70
(731) 668-4840
(800) 329-7466

DOUBLETREE HOTEL
1770 Hwy 45 Bypass (38305)
Rates: $79-$109
(731) 664-6900
(800) 222-8733

EXECUTIVE INN
2318 N Highland Ave (38305)
Rates: $35-$140
(731) 668-0490

HIGHLAND PLACE B&B INN
519 N Highland Ave (38301)
Rates: n/a
(877) 614-6305

JAMESON INN
1292 Vann Dr (38305)
Rates: $50-$99
(731) 660-8651
(800) 526-03766

MOTEL 6
1940 Hwy 45 Bypass (38305)
Rates: $38-$45
(731) 661-0919
(800) 446-8356

OLD HICKORY INN
1849 Hwy 45 Bypass (38305)
Rates: $39-$59
(316) 668-4222
(800) 53-SUITE

RAMADA LIMITED
2262 N Highland Ave (38305)
Rates: n/a
(731) 668-1066
(800) 272-6232

JAMESTOWN
EAST FORK STABLES
3598 S York Hwy (38556)
Rates: n/a
(800) 97-TRAIL

JORDAN MOTEL
2904 S York Hwy (38556)
Rates: n/a
(931) 879-4421

LAUREL FORK RUSTIC RETREAT CABINS
1364 Oby Blevins Rd (38556)
Rates: n/a
(865) 281-7495

QUILT COUNTRY INN B&B
1457 N York Hwy (38556)
Rates: n/a
(931) 879-2001

WILDWOOD COUNTRY CABINS
3636 Pickett Park Hwy (38556)
Rates: $50-$99
(931) 879-9454

JASPER
ACUFF COUNTRY INN MOTEL
1156 Hwy 28 (37347)
Rates: $35-$50
(423) 942-6370
(800) 782-7217

JEFFERSON CITY
HEARTHSTONE B&B
2308 N Ridge Dr (37760)
Rates: $50-$149
(865) 475-6992

JELLICO
BEST WESTERN HOLIDAY PLAZA MOTEL
133 Holiday Dr (37762)
Rates: $36-$85
(423) 784-7241
(800) 528-1234

DAYS INN
I-75 & 25 W, Exit 160 (37762)
Rates: $39-$55
(423) 784-7281
(800) 329-7466

JOELTON
DAYS INN
201 Gifford Pl (37080)
Rates: $45-$65
(615) 876-3261
(800) 329-7466

HACHLAND HILL SPRING CREEK INN
1601 Madison Ct (37080)
Rates: $50-$149
(615) 876-1500

JOHNSON CITY
AMERICAN CLASSIC EFFICIENCY SUITES
121 Lynn Rd (37604)
Rates: $40-$99
(423) 926-6200

BEST WESTERN HOTEL
2406 N Roan St (37601)
Rates: $68-$99
(423) 282-2161
(877) 504-1007

AREA CODES - If the local number doesn't connect, check for a new area code.

CARNEGIE HOTEL
1216 State of
Franklin Rd
(37604)
Rates: n/a
(866) 757-8277

COMFORT INN
1900 S Roan St
(37604)
Rates: $54-$250
(423) 928-9600
(800) 424-6423

DAYS INN
2312 Brown's Mill
Rd (37601)
Rates: $35-$235
(423) 282-2211
(800) 329-7466

HOLIDAY INN
101 W
Springbrook Dr
(37604)
Rates: $81-$87
(423) 282-4611
(800) 465-4329

JAMESON INN
119 Pinnacle Dr
(37604)
Rates: $49-$104
(423) 282-0488
(800) 526-3766

JOHNSON INN
2700 W Market St
(37604)
Rates: $30-$50
(423) 926-8145

RED ROOF INN
210 Broyles Dr
(37601)
Rates: $47-$74
(423) 282-3040
(800) 843-7663

SLEEP INN
2020 Franklin
Terr Ct (37604)
Rates: $51-$300
(423) 915-0081
(800) 424-6423

JONES-BOROUGH

**CHEROKEE
MOUNTAIN
LLAMA B&B**
201 Charlie Hicks
Rd (37659)
Rates: n/a
(423) 913-2781

KIMBALL

DAYS INN
130 Main St
(37347)
Rates: $36-$70
(423) 837-7933
(800) 329-7466

KINGSPORT

COMFORT INN
100 Indian Center
Ct (37660)
Rates: $45-$200
(423) 378-4418
(800) 424-6423

JAMESON INN
3004 Bays Meadow
Pl (37663)
Rates: $50-$149
(423) 230-0534
(800) 526-3766

LA QUINTA INN
10150 Airport
Pkwy (37663)
Rates: $53-$73
(423) 323-0500
(800) 687-6667

**RED
CARPET INN**
9980 Airport
Pkwy (37663)
Rates: $35-$49
(423) 279-7111
(800) 251-1962

SLEEP INN
200 Hospitality Pl
(37663)
Rates: $49-$300
(423) 279-1811
(800) 424-6423

WESTSIDE INN
1017 W Stone Dr
(37660)
Rates: n/a
(423) 247-2176
(888) 882-2176

KINGSTON

COMFORT INN
905 Kentucky St
(37763)
Rates: $45-$75
(865) 376-4965
(800) 424-6423

DAYS INN
495 Gallaher Rd
(37763)
Rates: $46-$89
(865) 376-2069
(800) 329-7466

KNIGHTS INN
1200 N Kentucky
St (37763)
Rates: 30-$99
(865) 376-3477

KINGSTON SPRINGS

**BEST WESTERN
HARPETH INN**
116 Luyben Hills
Rd (37082)
Rates: $39-$79
(615) 952-3961
(800) 528-1234

ECONO LODGE
123 Luyben Hills
Rd (37082)
Rates: $45-$75
(615) 952-2900
(800) 424-6423

KNOXVILLE

BAYMONT INN W
11341 Campbell
Lakes Dr (37922)
Rates: $47-$71
(865) 671-1010
(877) 229-6668

BEST WESTERN
500 Lovell Rd
(37932)
Rates: $45-$85
(865) 675-7666
(800) 528-1234

**CANDLEWOOD
SUITES**
10206 Parkside Dr
(37922)
Rates: n/a
(865) 777-0400
(888) 226-3539

CLARION INN
5634 Merchants
Center Blvd
(37912)
Rates: $59-$110
(865) 687-8989
(800) 424-6423

CLUBHOUSE INN
208 Market Place
Ln (37922)
Rates: $69-$109
(865) 531-1900

DAYS INN WEST
326 Lovell Rd
(37922)
Rates: $42-$59
(865) 966-5801
(800) 329-7466

**ECONO LODGE
WEST**
9240 Park West
Blvd (37923)
Rates: $39-$125
(865) 693-6061
(800) 424-6423

**FAMILY INNS OF
AMERICA**
300 Merchants Dr
(37912)
Rates: n/a
(865) 689-2200
(800) 303-0089

**FAMILY INNS OF
AMERICA**
4300 Rutledge
Pike (37914)
Rates: n/a
(865) 546-3910
(800) 362-8383

**HAMPTON
INN-WEST**
9128 Executive
Park Blvd (37923)
Rates: $74-$84
(865) 693-1011
(800) 426-7866

**HIGHWAY HOST
INN & SUITES**
5005 Central Ave
Pk (37912)
Rates: $40-$99
(865) 688-8886

HILTON HOTEL
501 W Church St
(37902)
Rates: $84
(865) 523-2300
(800) 445-8667

HOLIDAY INN
1315 Kirby Rd
(37909)
Rates: $99-$189
(865) 584-3911
(800) 465-4329

**HOLIDAY INN
SELECT**
304 Cedar Bluff
Rd (37923)
Rates: $50-$149
(865) 693-1011
(800) 465-4329

KNIGHTS INN
114 Dante Rd
(37918)
Rates: $35-$99
(865) 687-3500
(800) 276-7697

LA QUINTA INN
258 Peters Rd N
(37923)
Rates: $73-$91
(865) 690-9777
(800) 221-4731

MICROTEL INN
309 N Peters Rd
(37922)
Rates: $37-$69
(865) 531-8041
(888) 771-7171
(800) 579-1683

MOTEL 6
402 Lovell Rd
(37922)
Rates: $33-$42
(865) 675-7200
(800) 466-8356

MOTEL 6 NORTH
5640 Merchants
Center Blvd
(37912)
Rates: $33-$44
(865) 689-7100
(800) 446-8356

QUALITY INN N
6712 Central Ave
Pike (37912)
Rates: $45-$110
(865) 689-6600
(800) 424-6423

RADISSON
401 W Summit
Hill Dr (37902)
Rates: $129-$139
(865) 522-2600
(800) 333-3333

**RAMADA
LIMITED EAST**
722 Brakebill Rd
(37924)
Rates: $49-$110
(865) 546-7271
(800) 272-6232

**RAMADA
LIMITED SUITES**
5317 Pratt Rd
(37912)
Rates: $99-$149
(865) 687-9922
(800) 272-6232

RED ROOF INN-WEST
209 Advantage Pl
(37922)
Rates: $36-$70
(865) 691-1664
(800) 843-7663

AREA CODES - If the local number doesn't connect, check for a new area code.

SUPER 8 MOTEL DOWNTOWN
6200 Papermill Rd (37919)
Rates: $44-$70
(865) 584-8511
(800) 800-8000

KODAK

BEST WESTERN DUMPLIN VALLEY INN
3426 Winfield Dunn Pkwy (37764)
Rates: $38-$118
(865) 933-3467
(800) 528-1234
(888) 377-9888

HOLIDAY INN EXP
2863 Winfield Dunn Pkwy (37764)
Rates: n/a
(865) 939-9448
(800) 465-4329

MOTEL 6
184 E Dumplin Valley Rd (37764)
Rates: $32-$74
(865) 933-8141
(800) 446-8356

LA FOLLETTE

SHANGHAI RESORT & MARINA
1042 Shanghai Rd (37766)
Rates: n/a
(423) 562-8650
(800) 245-7651

LAKE CITY

BLUE HAVEN MOTEL
445 N Main St (37769)
Rates: n/a
(865) 426-2433

DAYS INN
221 Colonial Ln (37769)
Rates: $50-$70
(865) 426-2816
(800) 329-7466

LAMB'S INN MOTEL
620 N Main (37769)
Rates: $29-$53
(865) 426-2171

MOUNTAIN LAKE MARINA & CABINS
136 Campground Rd (37769)
Rates: n/a
(887) MTN-CAMP

LAKELAND

DAYS INN
9822 Huff & Puff Rd (38002)
Rates: $45-$65
(901) 388-7120
(800) 329-7466

SUPER 8 MOTEL
9779 Huff & Puff Rd (38002)
Rates: $50-$75
(901) 372-4575
(800) 800-8000

LAWRENCE- BURG

BEST WESTERN VILLA INN
2126 N Locust Ave (38464)
Rates: $59-$89
(931) 762-4448
(800) 528-1234
(800) 838-4552

LEBANON

BEST VALUE INN & SUITES
822 S Cumberland St (37087)
Rates: $37-$129
(615) 449-5781

BEST WESTERN EXECUTIVE INN
631 S Cumberland St (37087)
Rates: $42-$102
(615) 444-0505
(800) 528-1234

COMFORT INN
829 S Cumberland St (37087)
Rates: $39-$149
(615) 444-1001
(800) 424-6423

COUNTRY INN
140 Dixie Ave (37087)
Rates: $65-$78
(615) 470-1001
(800) 456-4000

DAYS INN
914 Murfreesboro Rd (37087)
Rates: $30-$80
(615) 444-5635
(800) 329-7466

HAMPTON INN
704 S Cumberland St (37087)
Rates: $69-$85
(615) 444-7400
(800) 426-7866

KNIGHTS INN
903 Murfreesboro Rd (37087)
Rates: $35-$79
(800) 843-5644

SHONEYS INN
822 S Cumberland St (37087)
Rates: $35-$89
(800) 552-INNS

SLEEP INN,
150 S Eastgate Ct (37090)
Rates: $50-$190
(615) 449-7005
(800) 424-6423

SUPER 8 MOTEL
914 Murfreesboro Rd (37090)
Rates: $45-$65
(615) 444-5637
(800) 800-8000

WILD TURKEY RANCH
5750 E Richmond Shop Rd (37090)
Rates: n/a
(615) 286-2610

LENOIR CITY

DAYS INN
1110 Hwy 321 N (37771)
Rates: $55-$75
(865) 986-2011
(800) 329-7466

ECONO LODGE
1211 Hwy 321 N (37771)
Rates: $45-$80
(865) 986-0295
(800) 424-6423

INN OF LENOIR MOTOR LODGE
503 Hwy 321 N (37771)
Rates: $30-$50
(865) 986-8043
(888) 471-0042

KINGS INN MOTEL
1031 Hwy 321 N (37771)
Rates: n/a
(865) 986-9091

LEWISBURG

CELEBRATION INN
1234 Nashville Hwy (37091)
Rates: n/a
(931) 359-7490

THE WALKING HORSE LODGE
255 N Ellington Pkwy (37091)
Rates: $40-$99
(800) WH-LODGE

LEXINGTON

WESTERN SHORES LODGE
732 W Church St (38351)
Rates: $35-$99
(731) 968-0171

LIMESTONE

SNAPP INN B&B
1990 Davy Crockett Park Rd (37681)
Rates: n/a
(423) 257-2482

LOUDON

KNIGHTS INN
15100 Hwy 72 N (37774)
Rates: $40-$60
(423) 458-5855
(800) 843-5644

SUPER 8 MOTEL
12452 Hwy 72 N (37774)
Rates: $35-$99
(865) 458-5669
(800) 800-8000

MADISONVILLE

MOTOR INNS OF AMERICA
4740 Hwy 68 (37354)
Rates: $30-$50
(423) 442-9045

MANCHESTER

AMBASSADOR INN
925 Interstate Dr (37355)
Rates: $40-$99
(800) 237-9228

COUNTRY INN
126 Expressway Dr (37355)
Rates: $65-$85
(931) 728-7551
(800) 456-4000

DAYS INN
2259 Hillsboro Blvd (37355)
Rates: $40-$105
(931) 728-9530
(800) 329-7366

ECONO LODGE
890 Interstate Dr (37355)
Rates: $30-$70
(931) 728-6023
(800) 424-6423

RAMADA INN
2314 Hillsboro Blvd (37355)
Rates: $33-$89
(931) 728-0800
(800) 272-6232

SCOTTISH INNS
2457 Hillsboro Blvd (37355)
Rates: $29-$69
(931) 728-0506
(800) 251-1962
(800) 765-4936

MARTIN

DAYS INN
800 University St (38237)
Rates: $50-$125
(731) 587-9577
(800) 329-7466

ECONO LODGE
853 University St (38237)
Rates: $55-$149
(731) 587-4241
(800) 424-6423

OUR BACKYARD TOWN B&B
520 N College St (38237)
Rates: n/a
(731) 587-1918

AREA CODES - If the local number doesn't connect, check for a new area code.

MARYVILLE

411 MOTEL
2651 Hwy 411 S
(37801)
Rates: n/a
(865) 982-5361

HIDEAWAY COTTAGES & LOG CABINS
102 Oriole Lane
(37803)
Rates: n/a
(865) 984-1700

THE OWL'S HOOT CHALET
102 Oriole Lane
(37803)
Rates: n/a
(865) 984-1700

MCKENZIE

BEST WESTERN MCKENZIE INN
16180 Highland
Dr (38201)
Rates: $54-$65
(731) 352-1083
(800) 528-1234

MCMINNVILLE

MCMINNVILLE INN
2545 Sparta St
(37110)
Rates: $40-$99
(931) 473-7338

SCOTTISH INNS
1105 Sparta St
(37110)
Rates: $23-$34
(931) 473-2181
(800) 251-1962

MEMPHIS

AIRPORT INN
1441 E Brooks
Rd (38116)
Rates: $30-$49
(901) 398-9211
(866) 398-9211

AMERISUITES
7905 Giacosa Pl
(38133)
Rates: $109-$119
(901) 371-0010
(800) 833-1516

AMERISUITES
1220 Primacy
Pkwy (38119)
Rates: $89-$109
(901) 680-9700
(800) 434-5800

BAYMONT INN & SUITES AIRPORT
3005 Millbranch
Rd (38116)
Rates: $59-$89
(901) 396-5411
(877) 229-6668

BAYMONT INN
6020 Shelby Oaks
Dr (38134)
Rates: $64-$72
(901) 377-2233
(877) 229-6668

BEST WESTERN TRAVELERS INN
5024 Hwy 78
(38118)
Rates: $60-$140
(901) 363-8430
(800) 528-1234
(800) 891-6016

CLARION HOTEL AIRPORT
1471 E Brooks Rd
(38116)
Rates: $72-$123
(901) 332-3500
(800) 424-6423

COMFORT INN AIRPORT / GRACELAND
1581 E Brooks Rd
(38116)
Rates: $50-$89
(901) 345-3344
(800) 424-6423

COMFORT INN I-40 EAST
1335 McRee St
(38134)
Rates: $50-$100
(901) 372-2700
(800) 424-6423

COMFORT SUITES
2427 N
Germantown
Pkwy (38108)
Rates: $74-$99
(901) 213-3600
(800) 424-6423

COMFORT SUITES
2575 Thousand
Oaks Cove (38118)
Rates: $75-$165
(901) 365-2575
(800) 424-6423

DAYS INN
2889 Old Austin
Peay Hwy (38128)
Rates: $39-$129
(901) 386-0033
(800) 329-7466

DAYS INN AIRPORT
2715 Cherry Rd
(38118)
Rates: $69-$139
(901) 366-0000
(800) 329-7466

DAYS INN-GRACELAND
3839 Elvis Presley
Blvd (38116)
Rates: $55-$95
(901) 346-5500
(800) 329-7466

DRURY INN
1556 Sycamore
View (38134)
Rates: $60-$95
(901) 373-8200
(800) 378-7946

ECONO LODGE AIRPORT
3456 Lamar Ave
(38118)
Rates: $35-$54
(901) 365-7335
(800) 424-6423

ECONO LODGE
2315 S Service Rd
(W Memphis, AR
72303)
Rates: $44-$69
(870) 732-2830
(800) 424-6423

HAMPTON INN
962 S Shady
Grove Rd (38120)
Rates: $109-$129
(901) 762-0056
(800) 426-7866

HAWTHORN SUITES
1070 Ridge Lake
Blvd (38120)
Rates: $79-$149
(901) 682-1722
(800) 527-1133

HOLIDAY INN
6101 Shelby Oaks
Dr (38134)
Rates: $50-$149
(901) 388-7050
(800) 465-4329

HOLIDAY INN
3700 Central Ave
(38152)
Rates: $115-$125
(901) 678-8200
(800) 465-4329

HOMESTEAD STUDIO SUITES
2541 Corporate
Ave E (38132)
Rates: $64-$89
(901) 344-0010
(800) 225-5466

HOMESTEAD STUDIO SUITES
6500 Poplar Ave
(38119)
Rates: $59-$89
(901) 767-5522
(800) 225-5466

HOMEWOOD SUITES
5811 Poplar Ave
(38119)
Rates: $89-$149
(901) 763-0500
(800) 225-5466

HOMEWOOD SUITES
3583 Hacks Cross
Rd (38125)
Rates: $119-$179
(901) 758-5018
(800) 225-5466

KNIGHTS INN AIRPORT
2949 Airways
Blvd (38131)
Rates: $30-$79
(800) 843-5644

LA QUINTA INN
1236 Primacy
Pkwy (38119)
Rates: $69-$99
(901) 374-0330
(800) 687-6667

MARRIOTT HOTEL DOWNTOWN
250 N Main St
(38103)
Rates: $129-$249
(901) 527-7300
(800) 228-9290

MOTEL 6
4000 Hwy 78
(38118)
Rates: $41-$56
(901) 365-7999
(800) 466-8356

MOTEL 6-EAST
1321 Sycamore
View Rd (38134)
Rates: $36-$42
(901) 382-8572
(800) 466-8356

MOTEL 6-GRACELAND EAST
1117 E Brooks Rd
(38116)
Rates: $36-$40
(901) 346-0992
(800) 466-8356

MOTEL 6 MEDICAL CENTER
210 S Pauline
(38104)
Rates: $37-$46
(901) 528-0650
(800) 466-8356

QUALITY INN
1541 Sycamore
View Rd (38134)
Rates: $50-$140
(901) 388-1300
(800) 424-6423

RAMADA INN
6068 Macon Cove
Rd (38134)
Rates: $49-$89
(901) 382-2323
(800) 272-6232

RED ROOF INN-E
6055 Shelby Oaks
Dr (38134)
Rates: $40-$60
(901) 388-6111
(800) 843-7663

RESIDENCE INN BY MARRIOTT
6141 Old Poplar
Pike (38119)
Rates: $79-$159
(901) 685-9595
(800) 331-3131

RIDGEWAY INN
5679 Poplar Ave
(38119)
Rates: n/a
(901) 766-4000
(800) 822-3360

SLEEP INN
5119 American
Way (38115)
Rates: $65-$99
(901) 363-4800
(800) 424-6423

AREA CODES - If the local number doesn't connect, check for a new area code.

SLEEP INN
2855 Old Austin
Peay Hwy (38128)
Rates: $49-$79
(901) 312-7777
(800) 424-6423

STUDIO 6
4300 American
Way (38118)
Rates: $189-$279
(901) 366-9333
(888) 897-0202

SUPER 8 MOTEL
340 W Illinois St
(38106)
Rates: $35-$89
(800) 800-8000

WELLESLEY INN
2520 Horizon
Lake Dr (38133)
Rates: $84-$94
(901) 380-1525
(800) 444-8888

MILLERSVILLE

**HOLIDAY REST
MOTOR INN**
1204 Louisville
Hwy (37072)
Rates: n/a
(615) 859-1313

MONTEAGLE

**BEST WESTERN
SMOKE HOUSE
LODGE**
850 W Main St
(37356)
Rates: $57-$175
(931) 924-2091
(800) 528-1234
(800) 489-2091

DAYS INN
742 Dixie Lee
Ave (37356)
Rates: $30-$100
(931) 924-2900
(800) 329-7466

**SMOKE HOUSE
GETAWAY CABINS**
I-24, Exit 134
(37356)
Rates: $50-$149
(800) 489-2091

MORRISTOWN

**CHEROKEE LAKE
CABINS**
9617 Hwy 11 W
(37811)
Rates: n/a
(423) 272-3333

COMFORT SUITES
3660 W Andrew
Johnson Hwy
(37814)
Rates: $55-$139
(423) 585-4000
(800) 424-6423

DAYS INN
2512 E Andrew
Johnson Hwy
(37814)
Rates: $42-$65
(423) 587-2200
(800) 329-7466

HOLIDAY INN
3304 W Andrew
Johnson Hwy
(37814)
Rates: $50-$99
(423) 581-8700
(800) 465-4329

**HOLIDAY INN
& CONF CTR**
5435 S Davy
Crockett Pkwy
(37813)
Rates: $59-$120
(423) 587-2400
(800) 465-4329

MOTEL 6
5984 W Andrew
Johnson Hwy
(37814)
Rates: $33-$40
(423) 586-4666
(800) 466-8356

PARKVIEW CABINS
3643 Brights Pk
(37814)
Rates: $35-$99
(423) 586-5096

SUPER 8 MOTEL
5400 S Davy
Crockett Pkwy
(37813)
Rates: $44-$59
(423) 318-8888
(800) 800-8000

MT. JULIET

MICROTEL INN
1000 Herschel Dr
(37122)
Rates: $40-$99
(615) 773-3600
(888) 771-7171

**NATUREVIEW INN
B&B**
3354 Old Lebanon
Dirt Rd (37122)
Rates: $50-$149
(615) 758-4439
(800) 758-7972

MOUNTAIN CITY

**BROOKSIDE
MOUNTAIN COTTAGES**
579 Trout Run Rd
(37683)
Rates: n/a
(866) 220-2111

MURFREESBORO

BEST INN & SUITES
2135 S Church St
(37130)
Rates: $50-$99
(615) 890-1006

BEST VALUE INN
1954 S Church St
(37130)
Rates: $35-$79
(615) 896-6030
(800) 214-8378

**BEST WESTERN
CHAFFIN INN**
168 Chaffin Pl
(37129)
Rates: $45-$89
(615) 895-3818
(800) 528-1234

**CARRIAGE LANE
INN**
411 N Maney Ave
(37130)
Rates: n/a
(800) 357-2827

**DOUBLETREE
HOTEL**
1850 Old Fort
Pkwy (37129)
Rates: $79-$119
(615) 895-5555
(800) 222-8733

HAMPTON INN
2230 Armory Dr
(37129)
Rates: $59-$139
(615) 896-1172
(800) 426-7866

**HOWARD
JOHNSON
EXPRESS INN**
2424 S Church St
(37130)
Rates: $30-$85
(615) 896-5522
(800) 446-4656

KNIGHTS INN
2036 S Church St
(37130)
Rates: $50-$99
(615) 893-1090
(800) 843-5644

MOTEL 6
148 Chaffin Pl
(37129)
Rates: $29-$40
(615) 890-8524
(800) 466-8356

QUALITY INN
118 Westgate
Blvd (37130)
Rates: $35-$89
(615) 848-9030
(800) 424-6423

RAMADA LIMITED
1855 S Church St
(37130)
Rates: $40-$100
(615) 896-5080
(800) 272-6232

RED ROOF INN
2282 Old Fort
Pkwy (37130)
Rates: $35-$99
(615) 893-0104
(800) 843-7663

SCARLET HOTELS
2227 Old Fort
Pkwy (37130)
Rates: $75-$99
(615) 896-2420

NASHVILLE

**AMERISUITES
AIRPORT**
721 Royal Pkwy
(37214)
Rates: $79-$129
(615) 493-5200
(800) 833-1516

AMERISUITES
220 Rudy's Circle
Dr (37214)
Rates: $99-$129
(615) 872-0422
(800) 833-1516

**BAYMONT INN/
OPRYLAND/
AIRPORT**
531 Donelson Pike
(37214)
Rates: $66-$76
(615) 885-3100
(877) 229-6668

BEST VALUE INN
2403 Brick Church
Pike (37207)
Rates: $49-$89
(615) 226-9805

**BEST WESTERN
AIRPORT INN**
701 Stewarts Ferry
Pike (37214)
Rates: $39-$125
(615) 889-9199
(800) 528-1234
(888) 528-6828

**BEST WESTERN
MUSIC ROW**
1407 Division St
(37203)
Rates: $59-$129
(615) 242-1631
(800) 528-1234

CAPSTONE INN
341 Harding Pl
(37211)
Rates: $60-$80
(615) 834-7170

CLUBHOUSE INN
2435 Atrium Way
(37214)
Rates: $69-$139
(615) 883-0500
(800) CLUBINN

COMFORT INN
2407 Brick Church
Pike (37207)
Rates: $59-$100
(615) 226-3300
(800) 424-6423

COMFORT INN
1501 Demonbreun
St (37203)
Rates: $49-$129
(615) 255-9977
(800) 424-6423

COMFORT INN
412 White Bridge
Pl (37209)
Rates: $65-$99
(615) 356-0888
(800) 424-6423

AREA CODES - If the local number doesn't connect, check for a new area code.

COMFORT INN OPRYLAND AREA
2516 Music Valley Dr (37214)
Rates: $59-$100
(615) 889-0086
(800) 424-6423

CRESTWOOD SUITES
665 Myatt Dr (37115)
Rates: $49-$54
(615) 860-8500

CROCKER SPRINGS B&B
2382 Crocker Spgs Rd (37072)
Rates: n/a
(877) 541-4612

DAYS INN
1400 Brick Church Pike (37207)
Rates: $35-$60
(615) 228-5977
(800) 329-7466

DAYS INN
821 Murfreesboro Rd (37217)
Rates: $55-$70
(615) 399-0017
(800) 329-7466

DAYS INN BELL ROAD
510 Collins Park Dr (37103)
Rates: $49-$69
(615) 731-7800
(800) 329-7466

DAYS INN VANDERBILT
1800 W End Ave (37203)
Rates: $72-$114
(615) 327-0922
(800) 329-7466

DAYS INN WEST
269 White Bridge Rd (37209)
Rates: $39-$88
(615) 356-9100
(800) 329-7466

DOUBLETREE HOTEL
315 Fourth Ave N (37219)
Rates: $50-$150
(615) 244-8200
(800) 222-8733

DRURY INN
555 Donelson Pike (37214)
Rates: $65-$110
(615) 902-0400
(800) 378-7946

EMBASSY SUITES
10 Century Blvd (37214)
Rates: $129-$169
(615) 871-0033
(800) 362-2779

FAMILY INNS OF AMERICA
3430 Percy Priest Dr (37214)
Rates: n/a
(615) 889-5090
(800) 457-2299

FIDDLERS INN
2410 Music Valley Dr (37214)
Rates: $50-$80
(615) 885-1440
(800) 847-9102

GUESTHOUSE INT'L INN
2420 Music Valley Dr (37214)
Rates: $50-$99
(615) 885-4030
(800) 21-GUEST

HAMPTON INN-OPRYLAND
2350 Elm Hill Pike (37214)
Rates: $75-$91
(615) 871-0222
(800) 426-7866

HAMPTON INN & SUITES-UNIVERSITY
2330 Elliston Pl (37203)
Rates: $109-$169
(615) 320-6060
(800) 426-7866

HERMITAGE HOTEL
231 Sixth Ave N (37219)
Rates: $199-$279
(615) 244-3121
(888) 888-9414

HILLSBORO HOUSE B&B
1933 20th Ave S (37212)
Rates: $85-$95
(615) 292-5501
(800) 228-7851

HOLIDAY INN CROSSINGS
201 Crossings Pl (37013)
Rates: $69-$99
(615) 731-2361
(800) 465-4329

HOLIDAY INN SELECT-VANDERBILT DOWNTOWN
2613 West End Ave (37203)
Rates: $129-$179
(615) 327-4707
(800) 465-4329

HOMEWOOD STUDIO SUITES
727 McGavock Pike (37214)
Rates: $39-$69
(615) 316-9020
(800) 225-5466

HOMEWOOD SUITES
2640 Elm Hill Pike (37210)
Rates: $50-$149
(615) 884-8111
(800) 225-5466

HOWARD JOHNSON INN
6834 Charlotte Pike (37209)
Rates: $48-$70
(615) 352-7080
(800) 446-4656

LA QUINTA INN-AIRPORT
2345 Atrium Way (37214)
Rates: $65-$90
(615) 885-3000
(800) 687-6667

LA QUINTA INN-SOUTH
4311 Sidco Dr (37204)
Rates: $55-$82
(615) 834-6900
(800) 687-6667

LOEWS VANDERBILT PLAZA HOTEL
2100 W End Ave (37203)
Rates: $119-$159
(615) 320-1700
(800) 235-6397
(800) 336-3335

MARRIOTT AT VANDERBILT
2555 West End Ave (37203)
Rates: $189-$279
(615) 321-1300
(800) 228-9290

MICROTEL INN & SUITES
100 Coley Davis Ct (37221)
Rates: $35-$79
(615) 662-0004
(888) 771-7171

MOTEL 6-AIRPORT
420 Metroplex Dr (37211)
Rates: $31-$38
(615) 833-8887
(800) 466-8356

MOTEL 6-NORTH
311 W Trinity Ln (37207)
Rates: $31-$34
(615) 227-9696
(800) 466-8356

MOTEL 6-SOUTH
95 Wallace Rd (37211)
Rates: $29-$36
(615) 333-9933
(800) 466-8356

PEAR TREE INN
343 Harding Pl (37211)
Rates: $50-$70
(615) 834-4242
(800) 282-8733

THE QUARTERS MOTOR INN
1100 Bell Rd (37103)
Rates: $49-$125
(615) 731-5990

RED ROOF INN
2460 Music Valley Dr (37214)
Rates: $49-$79
(615) 889-0090
(800) 843-7663

RED ROOF INN AIRPORT
510 Claridge Dr (37214)
Rates: $40-$55
(615) 872-0735
(800) 843-7663

RED ROOF INN SOUTH
4271 Sidco Dr (37204)
Rates: $40-$65
(615) 832-0093
(800) 843-7663

RESIDENCE INN BY MARRIOTT
2300 Elm Hill Pike (37214)
Rates: $85-$114
(615) 889-8600
(800) 331-3131

RODEWAY INN
893 Murfreesboro Rd (37217)
Rates: $35-$75
(615) 361-6830
(800) 424-6423

SHERATON MUSIC CITY HOTEL
777 McGavock Pike (37214)
Rates: $149-$169
(615) 885-2200
(800) 325-3535

STADIUM INN
10 Interstate Dr (37213)
Rates: n/a
(615) 244-6050

SUPER 8 MOTEL
350 Harding Pl (37211)
Rates: $49-$69
(615) 834-0620
(800) 800-8000

SUPER 8 MOTEL WEST
6924 Charlotte Pike (37209)
Rates: $45-$80
(615) 356-6005
(800) 800-8000

UNION STATION-WYNDHAM HISTORIC HOTEL
1001 Broadway (37203)
Rates: $99-$169
(615) 726-1001
(800) 331-2123

AREA CODES - If the local number doesn't connect, check for a new area code.

NEW JOHN-SONVILLE
ANCHOR INN
Hwy 70 (37134)
Rates: n/a
(931) 535-2897

NEW MARKET
BARRINGTON INN
1174 McGuire Rd
(37820)
Rates: n/a
(889) 205-8482

NEWPORT
BEST WESTERN NEWPORT INN
1015 Cosby Hwy
(37822)
Rates: $39-$129
(423) 623-8713
(800) 251-4022

BRYANT TOWN MOTEL
766 Cosby Hwy
(37861)
Rates: $35-$99
(423) 623-6006

COMFORT INN
1149 Smokey Mtn
Ln (37821)
Rates: $40-$200
(423) 623-5355
(800) 424-6423

FAMILY INNS OF AMERICA
1311 Hwy 25/70
W (37821)
Rates: n/a
(423) 623-2626
(800) 362-8282

HOLIDAY INN
1010 Cosby Rd
(37821)
Rates: $54-$119
(423) 623-8622
(800) 465-4329

MOTEL 6
255 Heritage
Blvd (37821)
Rates: $29-$64
(423) 623-1850
(800) 466-8356

NORMANDY
PARIS PATCH FARM & INN
1100 Cortner Mill
(37360)
Rates: n/a
(931) 857-3017
(800) 876-3017

OAK RIDGE
COMFORT INN
433 S Rutgers Ave
(37830)
Rates: $70-$90
(865) 481-8200
(800) 424-6423

DAYS INN
206 S Illinois (37830)
Rates: $44-$65
(865) 483-5615
(800) 329-7466

DOUBLETREE
215 S Illinois
(37830)
Rates: n/a
(865) 481-2468
(800) 2228733

OAKLAND
DAYS INN
6805 Hwy 64
(38060)
Rates: $47-$85
(901) 465-5630
(800) 329-7466

ONEIDA
BIG SOUTH FORK WILDNERESS RESORTS
4800 Station
Camp Rd (37841)
Rates: n/a
(423) 569-9847

GALLOWAY INN
299 Galloway Dr
(37841)
Rates: $35-$43
(423) 569-8835

OOLTEWAH
SUPER 8 MOTEL
5111 Hunter Rd
(37363)
Rates: $39-$49
(423) 238-5951
(800) 800-8000

PARIS
AVALON MOTEL
1315 Wood St
(38242)
Rates: n/a
(901) 642-4121

HAMPTON INN
1510 E Wood St
(38242)
Rates: $65-$89
(731) 642-2838
(800) 426-7866

KNIGHTS INN
409 Tyson Ave
(38242)
Rates: $30-$49
(800) 843-5644

SUPER 8 MOTEL
1309 E Wood St
(38242)
Rates: $30-$49
(731) 644-7008
(800) 800-8000

TERRACE WOODS TRAVEL LODGE
1190 N Market St
(38242)
Rates: n/a
(731) 642-2642

PARROTTS-VILLE
MEADOW CREEK MOUNTAIN FARM
959 Browns
Chapel Rd (37843)
Rates: n/a
(423) 623-7543

PARSONS
DEERFIELD INN
863 Tennessee Ave
N (38363)
Rates: $50-$79
(731) 847-4700

PICKWICK DAM
PICKWICK LANDING STATE PARK INN
220 Playground
Loop (38365)
Rates: $50-$99
(800) 250-8615

PIGEON FORGE
BAYMONT INN
2179 Parkway
(37863)
Rates: $40-$149
(866) 896-2950

FAMILY INNS OF AMERICA EAST
3785 Parkway
(37863)
Rates: n/a
(865) 453-5573
(800) 251-9752

FAMILY INNS OF AMERICA NORTH
3239 Parkway
(37863)
Rates: n/a
(865) 453-7151
(800) 251-9752

FAMILY INNS OF AMERICA SOUTH
4112 Parkway
(37863)
Rates: n/a
(865) 453-5549
(800) 251-9752

FAMILY INNS OF AMERICA TWIN MALLS
2647 Parkway
(37863)
Rates: n/a
(800) 251-9752

FAMILY INNS OF AMERICA WEST
3144 Parkway
(37863)
Rates: $40-$99
(865) 453-4905
(800) 272-1177

GRAND INNS OF AMERICA
3206 Parkway
(37863)
Rates: n/a
(4865) 453-0056
(800) 251-9752

GRAND RESORT HOTEL
3171 Parkway
(37863)
Rates: $70-$130
(865) 453-1000
(800) 251-4444

HEARTHSIDE CABIN RENTALS
1191 Wears Valley
Rd (37863)
Rates: $100-$160
(865) 429-0955
(888) 993-7655

HOLIDAY INN RESORT
3230 Parkway
(37868)
Rates: $50-$140
(865) 428-2700
(800) 465-4329
(800) 782-3119

MICROTEL
202 Emert St (37863)
Rates: $59-$94
(865) 429-0150
(888) 771-7171
(800) 431-7666

MICROTEL SUITES MUSIC ROAD
2045 Parkway
(37863)
Rates: $35-$120
(865) 453-1116
(888) 771-7171

MOTEL 6
336 Henderson
Chapel Rd (37863)
Rates: $25-$90
(865) 908-1244
(800) 466-8356

NATIONAL PARKS RESORT LODGE
2385 Parkway
(37863)
Rates: $30-$120
(865) 453-4106

RIVERS LANDING HOTEL
4025 Parkway
(37863)
Rates: n/a
(800) 345-6799

RIVIERA MOTEL
4035 Parkway
(37863)
Rates: n/a
(865) 453-4677
(800) 251-9752

SMOKY SHADOWS MOTEL
4215 Parkway
(37863)
Rates: $29-$99
(865) 453-7155
(800) 282-2121

TIMBERS LOG MOTEL
134 Wears Valley
Rd E (37863)
Rates: $35-$150
(865) 428-5216
(800) 445-1803

PIKEVILLE
MOUNTAIN TOP RETREAT B&B
Hwy 127 N
(37367)
Rates: n/a
(888) 396-7099

AREA CODES - If the local number doesn't connect, check for a new area code.

POWELL
COMFORT INN
323 E Emory Rd
(37849)
Rates: $49-$99
(423) 938-5500
(800) 424-6423

PULASKI
COMFORT INN
1140 W College St
(38478)
Rates: $72-$99
(931) 424-1600
(800) 424-6423

RICHLAND INN
1020 W College St
(38478)
Rates: $50-$99
(800) 833-9472

STAR MOTEL
1749 Elkton Pk
(38478)
Rates: n/a
(931) 363-3185

SUPER 8 MOTEL
2400 Hwy 64
(38478)
Rates: $40-$70
(931) 363-4501
(800) 800-8000

RELIANCE
LOST CREEK CABINS
328 Lost Creek Rd
(37369)
Rates: $50-$149
(888) 495-7350

WEBB BROTHERS GUEST HOUSE B&B
Childers Creek Rd
(37369)
Rates: n/a
(877) 932-7238

WHISPERING RIDGE CABINS
180 Yellow Jacket
Dr (37369)
Rates: $100-$150
(888) 299-9262

RICEVILLE
RELAX INN
3803 Hwy 39 W
(37370)
Rates: $20-$25
(615) 745-5893

RIPLEY
DAYS INN
555 Hwy 51
Bypass (38063)
Rates: $45-$75
(731) 635-7378
(800) 329-7466

ROAN MOUNTAIN
SAFE HAVEN FARM CABINS
336 Stanley
Hollow Rd
(37687)
Rates: n/a
(423) 725-4262

ROCKWOOD
BRIGADOON RESORT
159 Eagle Lodge
Rd (37854)
Rates: $50-$150+
(865) 354-0202

BUDGET MOTEL
608 S Gateway
Ave (37854)
Rates: $30-$49
(865) 354-2515

ROGERVILLE
HOLIDAY INN EXP
7139 Hwy 11 W
(37857)
Rates: $73-$83
(423) 272-1842
(800) 465-4329

SANDMAN MOTEL
4319 Hwy 66 S
(37857)
Rates: n/a
(423) 272-6800

SAMBURG
BILL NATION'S CAMP
244 W Lakeview
Dr (38232)
Rates: n/a
(731) 538-2177

BOARDMAN'S RESORT
813 Lake Dr
(38232)
Rates: n/a
(731) 538-2112

DUCK INN
218 Church (38254)
Rates: n/a
(731) 538-2364

HAMILTON'S RESORT
4992 Hamilton Rd
(38232)
Rates: n/a
(731) 538-2325

SAMBURG MOTEL
100 Lakeview St
(38254)
Rates: $35-$99
(731) 538-2385

SAVANNAH
SAVANNAH MOTEL
105 Adams St
(38372)
Rates: $30-$49
(731) 925-3392

SHAWS KOMFORT MOTEL
2302 Wayne Rd
(38372)
Rates: $30-$49
(731) 925-3977

SELMER
SUPER 8 MOTEL
644 Mulberry Ave
(38375)
Rates: $50-$60
(901) 645-8880
(800) 800-8000

SEVIERVILLE
BEST WESTERN DUMPLIN VALLEY INN
3426 Winfield
Dunn Pkwy
(37862)
Rates: $39-$125
(865) 933-3467
(800) 528-1234
(888) 377-9888

"CALL OF THE WILD" CABIN
2314 Foxwell Way
(37862)
Rates: $135-$155
(800) 644-4859

COMFORT INN MOUNTAIN RIVER SUITES
860 Winfield
Dunn Pkwy
(37876)
Rates: $49-$149
(865) 428-5519
(800) 424-6423

ENGLISH MOUNTAIN CONDO RESORT
1081 Cove Rd
(37876)
Rates: n/a
(865) 453-1071
(800) 842-6415

HIGH VALLEY RENTALS
630 Thomas Loop
Rd (37876)
Rates: $85-$95
(865) 428-0608
(800) 636-0608

HOLIDAY INN EXP HOTEL & SUITES
2863 Winfield
Dunn Pkwy
(37864)
Rates: $59-$149
(865) 933-9448
(800) 465-4329

HUCKLEBERRY INN B&B
1754 Sandstone
Way (37876)
Rates: n/a
(800) 704-3278

MIZE MOTEL
804 Parkway
(37862)
Rates: $30-$89
(800) 239-9117

SEYMOUR
WAY-OMA MOTEL
10240 Chapman
Hwy (37865)
Rates: n/a
(423) 577-7995
(877) 480-9758

SHELBYVILLE
BEST WESTERN CELEBRATION INN
724 Madison St
(37160)
Rates: $55-$195
(931) 684-2378
(800) 528-1234

OLDE GORE HOUSE BED & BREAKFAST
410 Belmont Ave
(37160)
Rates: n/a
(931) 685-0636

SUPER 8 MOTEL
317 N Cannon
Blvd (37160)
Rates: $49-$60
(931) 684-6050
(800) 800-8000

SILVER POINT
HIDEAWAYS AT CENTER HILL LAKE
337 Hurricane Ln
(38582)
Rates: n/a
(931) 858-3687

SMITHVILLE
CENTER HILL MOTEL
4867 Sparta Hwy
(37166)
Rates: n/a
(615) 597-4226

LAKESIDE RESORT CABINS
358 Relax Dr
(37166)
Rates: n/a
(888) 839-4799

SMYRNA
DAYS INN
1300 Plaza Dr
(37167)
Rates: $45-$150
(615) 355-6161
(800) 329-7466

SOMERVILLE
PLEASANT RETREAT
420 Hotel St
(38076)
Rates: n/a
(901) 465-4599
(901) 465-3916

SPARTA
ROYAL INN
803 Valley View
Dr (38583)
Rates: n/a
(931) 738-8585

SPENCER
LOST COVE CABINS
12512 SR Hwy 111
(38585)
Rates: $30-$140
(866) 578-2683

AREA CODES - If the local number doesn't connect, check for a new area code.

SPRING CITY

ARROWHEAD RESORT
261 Bennet Dr (37381)
Rates: $50-$150+
(423) 365-6484

SPRING HILL

STEEPLECHASE INN
104 Kedron Rd (37174)
Rates: n/a
(877) 486-2234

SPRINGFIELD

BEST WESTERN
2001 Memorial Blvd (37172)
Rates: $57-$105
(615) 384-1234
(800) 528-1234

SPRINGVILLE

BUCHANAN RESORT
785 Buchanan Resort Rd (38256)
Rates: n/a
(731) 642-2828

MANSARD ISLAND RESORT & MARINA
60 Mansard Island Dr (38256)
Rates: n/a
(731) 642-5590
(800) 533-5590

PLEASANT VIEW RESORT CABINS
289 Pleasant View Resort Rd (38256)
Rates: $100-$149
(731) 593-5511
(877) 593-5511

SWEETWATER

BEST WESTERN
1421 Murray's Chapel Rd (37874)
Rates: $69-$105
(423) 337-3541
(800) 528-1234
(800) 647-3529

BUDGET HOST INN
207 Hwy 68 (37874)
Rates: $35-$59
(423) 337-9357

COMFORT INN
731 S Main St (37874)
Rates: $40-$59
(423) 337-6646
(800) 424-6423

COMFORT INN W
249 Hwy 68 (37874)
Rates: $50-$80
(423) 337-3353
(800) 424-6423

DAYS INN
229 Hwy 68 (37874)
Rates: $39-$150
(423) 337-4200
(800) 329-7466

QUALITY INN
1116 Hwy 68 (37874)
Rates: $65-$200
(423) 337-4900
(800) 424-6423

TAZEWELL

TAZEWELL MOTOR LODGE
2357 Hwy 25 E (37879)
Rates: n/a
(423) 626-7229

TELLICO PINES

CANEY CREEK VILLAGE CABINS
5859 Hwy 360 (37385)
Rates: $35-$99
(800) 251-9658

TEN MILE

BAYSIDE MARINA & RESORT
134 Bayside Dr (37880)
Rates: n/a
(865) 376-7031

TENNESSEE LAKE-FRONT COTTAGES
136 Branham Rd (37880)
Rates: $50-$150+
(800) 597-1952

TIPTONVILLE

BLUE BASIN COVE B&B
Blue Basin Rd (38079)
Rates: n/a
(731) 253-9064

BOYETTE'S RESORT
30 Boyette Rd (38079)
Rates: n/a
(731) 253-6523
(888) 465-6523

CYPRESS POINT RESORT & WHITE'S LANDING
3535 Hwy 21 E (38079)
Rates: n/a
(800) 394-1886

REELFOOT LAKE INN
1520 Hwy 21 E (38079)
Rates: $50-$99
(731) 253-6845

REELFOOT LAKE SPORTSMANS RESORT-N
100 Sportsmans Resort Ln (38079)
Rates: $50-$99
(731) 253-6581

TOWNSEND

BEST WESTERN VALLEY VIEW LODGE
7726 E Lamar Alexander Pkwy (37882)
Rates: $45-$100
(865) 448-2237
(800) 528-1234
(800) 282-4844

BLACK BEAR HOLLOW CABINS
182 Cave Creek Way (37882)
Rates: $50-$150+
(866) 686-2327

BLUE SMOKE MOUNTAIN CABINS
11233 Carrs Creek Rd (37882)
Rates: $50-$99
(865) 448-3068

COMFORT INN PARKSIDE
7824 E Lamar Alexander Pkwy (37882)
Rates: $39-$179
(865) 448-9000
(800) 424-6423

GOODE NIGHT VACATION RENTALS
608 Rudd Hollow Rd (37882)
Rates: $50-$149
(865) 448-6842
(877) SMOKY15

HIDEAWAY COTTAGES & LOG CABINS
Black Mash Hollow Rd (37882)
Rates: n/a
(865) 984-1700

MAPLE LEAF LODGE & CABINS
137 Apple Valley Way (37882)
Rates: n/a
(865) 448-6000
(800) 369-0111

MOUNTAIN LAUREL CABINS
146 Black Mash Hollow Rd (37882)
Rates: n/a
(865) 448-9657

THE OWL'S HOOT CABIN RENTAL
139 Black Mash Hollow (37882)
Rates: n/a
(865) 984-1700

PEARLS OF THE MTNS CABINS
7717 E Lamar Alexander Pkwy (37882)
Rates: n/a
(865) 448-8001
(800) 324-8415

PILGRIM CABIN RENTAL
7207 Old Tuckaleechee Rd (37882)
Rates: n/a
(865) 448-6878

ROADSEDGE CABIN RENTAL
333 Black Mash Hollow Rd (37882)
Rates: n/a
(865) 982-9975

STRAWBERRY PATCH INN
7509 Old Hwy 73 (37882)
Rates: $50-$149
(865) 448-6306

THE WRIGHT CABINS
136 Black Mash Hollow Rd (37882)
Rates: $50-$149
(865) 448-9090
(888) 461-1885

TULLAHOMA

EXECUTIVE INN
1410 N Jackson St (37388)
Rates: $40-$99
(931) 455-4501

JAMESON INN
2113 N Jackson St (37388)
Rates: $49-$104
(931) 455-7891
(800) 526-3766

VERANDA HOUSE
100 W Lincoln St (37388)
Rates: $40-$99
(931) 455-7033

UNICOI

FAMILY INNS OF AMERICA
100 Country Club Dr (37692)
Rates: n/a
(423) 743-9181
(800) 545-3311

UNION CITY

COUNTRY HEARTH INN
2009 W Reelfoot Ave (38261)
Rates: $35-$99
(731) 885-7774

VONORE

GRAND VISTA HOTEL & SUITES
117 Grand Vista Dr (37885)
Rates: $90
(423) 885-8850
(866) 484-7111

AREA CODES - If the local number doesn't connect, check for a new area code.

WALLAND
TWIN VALLEY B&B HORSE RANCH
2848 Old
Chillhowee Rd
(37886)
Rates: n/a
(423) 984-0980
(800) 872-2235

WATTS BAR DAM
WATTS BAR RESORT
6767 Watts Bar
Hwy (37381)
Rates: n/a
(800) 365-9598

WAVERLY
CLYDETON DOCK RESORT
10669 Clydeton
Rd (37185)
Rates: $40-$99
(931) 296-2211

MASON'S\ BOAT DOCK
10275 Clydeton
Rd (37185)
Rates: n/a
(931) 296-9165

NOLAN HOUSE B&B
375 Hwy 13 N
(37185)
Rates: n/a
(931) 296-2511

WHITE HOUSE
COMFORT INN
340 Hester Lane
(37188)
Rates: $59-$69
(615) 672-8850
(800) 424-6423

DAYS INN
1009 Hwy 76
(37188)
Rates: $42-$60
(615) 672-3746
(800) 329-7466

HOLIDAY INN EXP
354 Hester Lane
(37188)
Rates: $54-$65
(615) 672-7200
(800) 465-4329

WHITE PINE
DAYS INN
3670 Roy Messer
Hwy (37890)
Rates: $49-$149
(865) 674-2573
(800) 329-7466

TWIN PINES MOTEL
Hwy 25 E (37890)
Rates: n/a
(865) 674-0706

WHITEVILLE
SUPER 8 MOTEL
2040 Hwy 65
(38075)
Rates: $50-$60
(901) 254-8884
(800) 800-8000

WILDERSVILLE
BEST WESTERN CROSSROADS INN
21045 Hwy 22 N
(38388)
Rates: $34-$56
(731) 968-2532
(800) 528-1234

WINCHESTER
BEST WESTERN INN
1602 Dinah Shore
Blvd (37398)
Rates: $55-$99
(931) 967-9444
(800) 528-1234

TIMS FORD MARI-NA & RESORT
175 Marina Ln
(37398)
Rates: $35-$140
(800) 722-1164

WINCHESTER INN MOTEL
700 S College St
(37398)
Rates: $24-$50
(931) 967-3846

TEXAS

ABILENE

AMBASSADOR SUITES HOTEL
4250 Ridgemont Dr (79606)
Rates: $99-$109
(325) 698-1234
(800) 897-9644

ANTILLEY INN
6550 S Hwy 83 (70606)
Rates: $43-$70
(325) 695-3330
(800) 959-1001

BEST WESTERN MALL SOUTH
3950 Ridgemont Dr (79606)
Rates: $61-$68
(325) 695-1262
(800) 528-1234
(800) 346-1574

BEST WESTERN INN & SUITES
350 W IH-20 (79601)
Rates: $59-$89
(325) 672-5501
(800) 528-1234

BUDGET HOST COLONIAL INN
3210 Pine St (79601)
Rates: $42-$50
(325) 677-2683
(800) 283-4678

CIVIC PLAZA HOTEL
505 Pine St (79601)
Rates: $49-$125
(325) 676-0222

COMFORT SUITES
3165 S Danville Dr (79606)
Rates: $84-$164
(325) 795-8500
(800) 424-6423

DAYS INN
1702 E I-20 (79601)
Rates: $45-$60
(325) 672-6433
(800) 329-7466

ECONO LODGE
1633 W Stamford (79601)
Rates: $40-$60
(325) 673-5424
(800) 424-6423

EXECUTIVE INN
1650 E I-20 (79601)
Rates: $35-$70
(325) 677-2200

KIVA HOTEL & CONFERENCE CENTER
5403 S 1st St (79605)
Rates: $67-$79
(325) 695-2150

LA QUINTA INN
3501 W Lake Rd (79601)
Rates: $70-$85
(325) 676-1676
(800) 687-6777

MOTEL 6
4951 W Stamford (79603)
Rates: $33-$43
(325) 672-8462
(800) 466-8356

REGENCY INN
3450 S Clack St (79606)
Rates: $49-$79
(325) 695-7700

ROYAL INN
5695 S 1st St (79605)
Rates: $27-$55
(325) 692-3022
(800) 588-4386

SUPER 8 MOTEL
1525 E I-20 (79601)
Rates: $45-$70
(325) 673-5251
(800) 800-8000

WHITTEN INN EXPO
840 E Hwy 80 (79601)
Rates: $45-$64
(325) 677-8100

WHITTEN INN UNIVERSITY
1625 SR 351 (79601)
Rates: $39-$65
(325) 673-5271

ADDISON

BEST WESTERN HOTEL & SUITES- GALLERIA
15200 Addison Rd (75001)
Rates: $69-$129
(972) 386-4800
(800) 528-1234

COMFORT INN GALLERIA
14975 Landmark Blvd (75240)
Rates: $49-$99
(972) 701-0881
(800) 424-6423

COMFORT SUITES
4555 Belt Line (75001)
Rates: $49-$69
(972)-503-6500
(800) 424-6423

CROWNE PLAZA GALLERIA
14315 Midway Rd (75244)
Rates: $109-$199
(972) 980-8877
(800) 227-6963

HOMEWOOD SUITES BY HILTON
4451 Beltline Rd (75244)
Rates: $109-$129
(972) 788-1342
(800) 225-5466

LA QUINTA INN
14925 Landmark Blvd (75244)
Rates: $60-$100
(972) 404-0004
(800) 687-6777

MAINSTAY SUITES
15200 Addison Rd (75001)
Rates: $49-$99
(972) 340-3001
(800) 660-MAIN

MOTEL 6
4325 Beltline Rd (75244)
Rates: $46-$61
(972) 386-4577
(800) 466-8356

RESIDENCE INN BY MARRIOTT
14975 Quorum Dr (75254)
Rates: $89-$179
(972) 866-9933
(800) 331-3131

SUITES OF AMERICA
4004 Belt Line Rd (75001)
Rates: $59-$99
(877) 822-5272

SUMMERFIELD SUITES HOTEL
4900 Edwin Lewis Dr (75244)
Rates: $129-$159
(972) 661-3113
(800) 833-4353

SUPER 8 MOTEL
4150 Beltway Dr (75001)
Rates: $39-$89
(972) 233-2525
(800) 800-8000

ALAMO

ALAMO INN B&B
801 Main St (78516)
Rates: $45-$89
(866) 7821-9912

SUPER 8 MOTEL
714 N Alamo Rd (78516)
Rates: $39-$79
(956) 787-9444
(800) 800-8000

ALBANY

ALBANY MOTOR INN
Hwy 180 @ 283 N (76430)
Rates: $47-$69
(888) 525-2269

OLE NAIL HOUSE INN
357 S 3rd St (76430)
Rates: $50-$80
(800) 245-5163

ALICE

DAYS INN
555 N Johnson St (78332)
Rates: $55-$81
(361) 664-6616
(800) 329-7466

KINGS INN MOTEL
815 Hwy 281 S (78332)
Rates: $35-$40
(361) 664-4351

ALPINE

ANTELOPE LODGE
2310 W Hwy 90 (79830)
Rates: $34-$64
(800) 880-8106

BEST WESTERN ALPINE CLASSIC INN
2401 E Hwy 90 (79830)
Rates: $70-$80
(432) 837-1530
(800) 528-1234

THE CORNER HOUSE B&B
801 E Avenue (79830)
Rates: $27-$65
(432) 837-7161
(800) 585-7795

GRANDMA & GRANDPA'S TRAILS B&B
P. O. Box 1207 (79831)
Rates: $85-$100
(432) 386-3382

HIGHLAND INN & APARTMENTS
1404 E Hwy 90 (79830)
Rates: $40-$66
(432) 837-5811

AREA CODES - If the local number doesn't connect, check for a new area code.

HISTORIC HOLLAND HOTEL
209 W Holland Ave (79830)
Rates: $45-$175
(800) 535-8040

LONGHORN RANCH MOTEL
HC 65, P. O. Box 267 (79830)
Rates: $45-$55
(432) 371-2541

MOTEL BIEN VENIDO
809 E Holland Ave (79830)
Rates: $29-$36
(432) 837-3454

OAK TREE INN
2407 E Hwy 90 (79830)
Rates: $65-$78
(432) 837-5711

RAMADA LTD
2800 W Hwy 90 (79830)
Rates: $80-$140
(432) 837-1100
(800) 272-6232

SUNDAY HOUSE INN MOTEL
2010 E Hwy 90 (79830)
Rates: $35-$80
(432) 837-3363
(800) 510-3363

WILD HORSE STATION CABINS
HC 65, Box 276 C (79830)
Rates: $60-$120
(432) 371-2526

ALVIN

COMFORT INN
1535 S Bypass 35 (77511)
Rates: $59-$99
(281) 756-8800
(800) 424-6423

COUNTRY HEARTH INN
1588 S Hwy 35 Bypass (77511)
Rates: $50-$58
(281) 331-0335
(888) 325-7815

DAYS INN
110 E Hwy 6 (77511)
Rates: $49-$69
(281) 331-5227
(800) 329-7466

AMARILLO

AMBASSADOR HOTEL
3100 W I-40 (79102)
Rates: $69-$169
(806) 358-6161
(800) 817-0521

BEST WESTERN AMARILLO INN
1610 Coulter Dr (79106)
Rates: $72-$92
(806) 358-7861
(800) 528-1234

BEST WESTERN SANTA FE INN
4600 I-40 E (79120)
Rates: $75-$85
(806) 372-1885
(800) 528-1234

BIG TEXAN INN
7701 I-40 E (79120)
Rates: $40-$65
(806) 372-5000
(800) 657-7177

BRONCO MOTEL
6005 Amarillo Blvd W (79106)
Rates: $37-$45
(806) 355-3321

CLARION HOTEL AIRPORT
7090 E I-40 (79104)
Rates: $75-$89
(806) 373-3303
(800) 252-7466
(800) 424-6423

COACHLIGHT INN #3
2115 I-40 E (79102)
Rates: $38-$55
(806) 376-5911

COACHLIGHT INN #4
6810 I-40 E (79104)
Rates: $45-$52
(806) 373-6871

COMFORT INN AIRPORT
1515 I-40 E (79102)
Rates: $49-$119
(806) 376-9993
(800) 424-6423

DAYS INN EAST
1701 I-40 E (79102)
Rates: $49-$79
(806) 379-6255
(800) 329-7466

DAYS INN
2102 S Coulter Dr (79106)
Rates: $69-$109
(806) 359-9393
(800) 329-7466

DAYS INN SOUTH
8601 Canyon Dr (79110)
Rates: $50-$79
(806) 468-7100
(800) 329-7466

ECONO LODGE
2915 I-40 E (79104)
Rates: $45-$75
(806) 372-8101
(800) 424-6423

HAMPTON INN
1700 I-40 E (79103)
Rates: $49-$109
(806) 372-1425
(800) 426-7866

HOLIDAY INN EXP
3411 I-40 W (79109)
Rates: $109-$139
(806) 356-6800
(800) 465-4329

HOLIDAY INN I-40
1911 I-40 at Ross-Osage (79102)
Rates: $119-$125
(806) 372-8741
(800) 465-4329

LA KIVA HOTEL
2501 I-40 E (79104)
Rates: $89
(806) 379-6555

LA QUINTA INN EAST/AIRPORT
1708 I-40 E (79103)
Rates: $69-$89
(806) 373-7486
(800) 687-6667

LA QUINTA INN WEST/MEDICAL CENTER
2108 S Coulter St (79106)
Rates: $69-$89
(806) 352-6311
(800) 687-6667

MICROTEL INN
1501 S Ross St (79102)
Rates: $59-$99
(806) 372-8373

MOTEL 6-CENTRAL
2032 Paramount Blvd (79109)
Rates: $33-$45
(806) 355-6554
(800) 466-8356

MOTEL 6-EAST
3930 I-40 E (79103)
Rates: $31-$39
(806) 374-6444
(800) 466-8356

MOTEL 6-WEST
6030 I-40 W (79106)
Rates: $31-$39
(806) 359-7651
(800) 466-8356

QUALITY INN
1515 I-40 E (79102)
Rates: $49-$109
(806) 376-9993
(800) 424-6423

QUALITY INN
1803 Lakeside Dr (79120)
Rates: $79-$159
(806) 335-1561
(800) 847-6556

QUALITY INN & SUITES WEST
6800 I-40 W Service Rd (79102)
Rates: $69-$119
(806) 358-7943
(800) 424-6423

RAMADA LIMITED
1620 I-40 E (79103)
Rates: $47-$76
(806) 374-2020
(800) 272-6232

RESIDENCE INN BY MARRIOTT
6700 I-40 W (79106)
Rates: $130-$164
(806) 354-2978
(800) 331-3131

RITZ PLAZA HOTEL AIRPORT
7909 I-40 E (79118)
Rates: $40-$70
(806) 373-3303
(800) 241-3333

SLEEP INN
2401 I-40 E (79104)
Rates: $65-$120
(806) 372-6200
(800) 753-3746

SUPER 8 MOTEL
2909 I-40 E (79104)
Rates: $35-$75
(800) 800-8000

TRAVELODGE-EAST
3205 I-40 E, Tee Anchor Blvd (79104)
Rates: $48-$70
(806) 372-8171
(800) 578-7878

TRAVELODGE-WEST
2035 Paramount Blvd (79109)
Rates: $30-$62
(806) 353-3541
(800) 578-7878

ANGLETON

BEST VALUE INN
1235 N Velasco (77515)
Rates: $55-$68
(979) 849-2465

BEST WESTERN ANGLETON INN
1809 N Velasco (77515)
Rates: $60-$110
(979) 849-5822
(800) 528-1234

ANTHONY

HOLIDAY INN EXP
9401 S Desert Blvd (79821)
Rates: $79-$89
(915) 886-3333
(800) 465-4329

AREA CODES - If the local number doesn't connect, check for a new area code.

SUPER 8 MOTEL WEST
100 Park North Dr (79821)
Rates: $41-$60
(915) 886-2888
(800) 800-8000

ARANSAS PASS
HOMEPORT INN
1515 W Wheeler Ave (78336)
Rates: $35-$42
(361) 758-3213

TRAVELODGE
545 N Commercial (78336)
Rates: $38-$58
(361) 758-5305
(800) 578-7878

ARLINGTON
AMERISUITES
2380 East Rd to Six Flags Dr (76011)
Rates: $59-$129
(817) 649-7676
(800) 833-1516

BAYMONT INN
2401 Diplomacy Dr (76011)
Rates: $49-$99
(817) 633-2400
(800) 301-0200

BEST WESTERN GREAT SOUTH-WEST INN
3501 E Division St (76011)
Rates: $49-$95
(817) 640-7722
(800) 528-1234
(800) 346-2378

CANDLEWOOD SUITES
2221 Brookhollow Plaza Dr (76006)
Rates: n/a
(817) 649-3336
(888) 226-3539

COUNTRY INN & SUITES BY CARLSON
1075 West N Wild Way (76011)
Rates: $59-$149
(817) 715-3292
(800) 456-4000

DAYS INN
1901 W Pleasant Ridge (76011)
Rates: $55-$79
(817) 557-5828
(800) 329-7466

DAYS INN BALLPARK AT ARLINGTON-SIX FLAGS
910 N Collins St (76011)
Rates: $35-$95
(817) 261-8444
(800) 329-7466

HAWTHORN SUITES HOTEL
2401 Brookhollow Plaza Dr (76011)
Rates: $79-$199
(817) 640-1188
(800) 225-5466
(800) 527-1133

HOMESTEAD STUDIO SUITES
1221 N Watson Rd (76011)
Rates: $44-$59
(817) 633-7588
(888) 782-9473

HOMEWOOD SUITES
2401 East Rd to Six Flags Dr (76011)
Rates: $109-$159
(817) 633-1594
(800) 225-5466

HOWARD JOHNSON EXP
2001 E Copeland Rd (76011)
Rates: $49-$99
(817) 461-1122
(800) 446-4656

LA QUINTA INN CONFERENCE CENTER
825 N Watson Rd (76011)
Rates: $70-$115
(817) 640-4142
(800) 687-6667

LA QUINTA INN
4001 Scott's Legacy (76011)
Rates: $96-$131
(817) 467-7756
(800) 687-6667

LESTER MOTOR INN
2725 W Division St (76012)
Rates: $28-$42
(817) 275-5496

MICROTEL INN
1740 Oak Village Blvd (76013)
Rates: $50-$85
(817) 557-8400
(888) 771-7171

MOTEL 6
2626 E Randol Mill Rd (76011)
Rates: $42-$58
(817) 649-0147
(800) 466-8356

OASIS MOTEL
818 W Division St (76011)
Rates: $26-$52
(817) 274-1616

PARKWAY INN
703 Benge Dr (76013)
Rates: $50-$60
(817) 860-2323
(800) 437-7275

QUALITY INN DFW AIRPORT SOUTH
1607 N Watson Rd (76006)
Rates: n/a
(817) 640-4444
(800) 424-6423

RESIDENCE INN BY MARRIOTT
1050 Brookhollow Plaza Dr (76006)
Rates: $129-$199
(817) 649-7300
(800) 331-3131

SLEEP INN-MAIN GATE/SIX FLAGS
750 Six Flags Dr (76004)
Rates: $66-$110
(817) 649-1010
(800) 753-3746

STUDIO 6-SOUTH
1980 W Pleasant Ridge Rd (76011)
Rates: $199-$279
(817) 465-8500
(888) 897-0202

TOWNEPLACE SUITES BY MARRIOTT
1709 E Lamar Ave (76006)
Rates: $79-$89
(817) 861-8728
(800) 257-3000

WHITTEN INN
121 I-20 E (76018)
Rates: $59-$69
(817) 467-3535

ATHENS
BUDGET INN
305 Dallas Hwy (75751)
Rates: $35-$40
(903) 675-5194

SPANISH TRACE INN MOTEL
716 E Tyler St (75751)
Rates: $44-$95
(903) 675-5173
(800) 488-5173

SUPER 8 MOTEL
205 Dallas Hwy 175 (75751)
Rates: $39-$85
(903) 675-7511
(800) 800-8000

VICTORIAN INN
1803 E Hwy 31 (75751)
Rates: $34-$70
(903) 677-1470

ATLANTA
THE BUTLER'S INN
1100 W Main St (75551)
Rates: $38-$65
(903) 796-8235
(800) 338-0297

AUSTIN
AMERICAN INN
7300 I-35 N (78752)
Rates: $45-$57
(512) 452-9371

AMERISUITES-AIRPORT
7601 Ben White Blvd (78741)
Rates: $60-$79
(512) 386-7600
(800) 833-1516

AMERISUITES-ARBORETUM
3612 Tudor Blvd (78759)
Rates: $149-$179
(512) 231-8491
(800) 833-1516

AMERISUITES-NORTH CENTRAL
7522 N I-35 (78752)
Rates: $99-$129
(512) 323-2121
(800) 833-1516

AUSTIN EXECUTIVE LODGING
809 W MLK Blvd (78701)
Rates: $49-$175
(800) 494-2261

AUSTIN FOLK HOUSE B & BT
506 West 22nd St (78705)
Rates: $79-$139
(512) 472-6700
(866) 472-6700

BAYMONT INN
150 Parker Dr (78728)
Rates: $69-$129
(512) 246-2800
(800) 301-0200

BEST VALUE INN
2525 I-35 S (78741)
Rates: $45-$50
(512) 441-0143

BEST VALUE INN
6911 I-35 N (78752)
Rates: $60-$80
(512) 459-4251
(800) 306-4629

BEST WESTERN ATRIUM NORTH
7928 Gessner Dr (78753)
Rates: $49-$99
(512) 339-7311
(800) 528-1234
(800) 468-3708

BEST WESTERN SEVILLE PLAZA INN
4323 I-35 S (78744)
Rates: $55-$89
(512) 447-5511
(800) 528-1234

AREA CODES - If the local number doesn't connect, check for a new area code.

BRAVA HOUSE B&B
1108 Blanco St (78744)
Rates: $89-$195
(512) 478-5034
(888) 545-8200

CANDLEWOOD SUITES-NW
9701 Stonelake Blvd (78759)
Rates: $72-$89
(512) 338-1611
(800) 465-4329

CANDLEWOOD SUITES-SOUTH
4320 S I-35 (78745)
Rate: $105-$157
(512) 444-8882
(800) 465-4329

CARRINGTON'S BLUFF B&B
1900 David St (78705)
Rates: $89-$149
(888) 290-6090

CLARION INN & SUITES CONF CTR
2200 S I-35 (78704)
Rates: $69-$149
(512) 444-0561
(800) 252-7466
(800) 424-6423

COMFORT INN
700 Delmar Ave (78752)
Rates: $62-$95
(512) 302-5576
(800) 424-6423

COMFORT SUITES DOWNTOWN S
1701 E St. Elmo Rd (78744)
Rates: $79-$129
(512) 444-6630
(800) 424-6423

CORPORATE HOUSING/ APARTMENT RENTALS
2007 Mountain View (78734)
Rates: n/a
(800) 845-6343

COUNTRY COTTAGE
2008 Travis Hghts Blvd (78765)
Rates: $100-$400
(512) 479-0073

CROWN PLAZA HOTEL
500 N I-35 (78753)
Rates: $109-$159
(512) 480-8181
(800) 227-6963

DAYS INN NORTH
820 E Anderson Ln (78752)
Rates: $49-$67
(512) 835-4311
(800) 329-7466

DAYS INN UNIVERSITY-DOWNTOWN
3105 N I-35 (78722)
Rates: $55-$99
(512) 478-1631
(800) 329-7466

DOUBLETREE CLUB HOTEL
1617 I-35 N (78702)
Rates: $79-$149
(512) 479-4000
(800) 222-8733

DOUBLETREE GUEST SUITES
303 W 15th St (78701)
Rates: $109-$249
(512) 478-7000
(800) 222-8733

DOUBLETREE HOTEL
6505 I-35 N (78752)
Rates: $89-$179
(512) 454-3737
(800) 222-8733

THE DRISKILL
604 Brazos St (78701)
Rates: $195-$380
(512) 474-5911

DRURY INN HIGHLAND MALL
919 E Koenig Ln (78751)
Rates: $72-$102
(512) 454-1144
(800) 378-7946

DRURY INN & SUITES NORTH
6511 I-35 N (78752)
Rates: $79-$109
(512) 467-9500
(800) 378-7946

ECONO LODGE
6201 Hwy 290 E (78723)
Rates: $49-$99
(512) 458-4759
(800) 424-6423

EMBASSY SUITES HOTEL
300 S Congress Ave (78704)
Rates: $109-$219
(512) 469-9000
(800) 362-2779

EXEL INN
2711 I-35 S (78741)
Rates: $40-$79
(512) 462-9201
(800) 367-3935

FOUR POINTS HOTEL BY SHERATON
7800 N I-35 (78753)
Rates: $112-$128
(512) 836-8520
(800) 325-3535

FOUR SEASONS HOTEL
98 San Jacinto Blvd (78701)
Rates: $245-$395
(512) 478-4500
(800) 332-3442

GREENSHORES ON LAKE AUSTIN
6900 Greenshores Rd (78730)
Rates: $70-$130
(512) 346-0011

HABITAT SUITES HOTEL
500 Highland Mall Blvd (78752)
Rates: $127-$187
(512) 467-6000
(800) 535-4663

HAMPTON INN-ARBORETUM/ NORTHWEST
3908 W Braker Ln (78759)
Rates: $79-$109
(512) 349-9898
(800) 426-7866

HAWTHORN SUITES LTD-AIRPORT
7800 E Riverside Dr (78744)
Rates: $69-$149
(512) 247-6166
(800) 527-1133

HAWTHORN SUITES CENTRAL
935 La Posada Dr (78752)
Rates: $79-$164
(512) 459-3335
(800) 527-1133

HAWTHORN SUITES-NORTHWEST
8888 Tallwood Dr (78759)
Rates: $79-$129
(512) 343-0008
(800) 527-1133

HAWTHORN SUITES-SOUTH
4020 I-35 S (78704)
Rates: $59-$138
(512) 440-7722
(800) 527-1133

HEART OF TEXAS MOTEL
5303 US 290 W (78735)
Rates: $50-$65
(512) 892-0644

HEARTHSIDE SUITES BY VILLAGER
12989 Research Blvd (78729)
Rates: $59-$99
(512) 652-4300

HEARTHSIDE SUITES BY VILLAGER
7101 N I-35 (78752)
Rates: $59-$99
(512) 452-9332

HILTON AUSTIN NORTH
6000 Middle Fiskville Rd (78752)
Rates: $89-$179
(512) 451-5757
(800) 445-8667
(800) 347-0330

HOLIDAY INN AIRPORT SOUTH
3401 I-35 S (78741)
Rates: $89-$99
(512) 448-2444
(800) 465-4329

HOLIDAY INN NORTHWEST PLAZA
8901 Business Park Dr (78759)
Rates: $59-$109
(512) 343-0888
(800) 465-4329

HOLIDAY INN TOWN LAKE
20 N I-35 (78701)
Rates: $129
(512) 472-8211
(800) 465-4329

HOMESTEAD STUDIO SUITES
507 S 1st St (78701)
Rates: $69-$84
(512) 476-1818
(888) 782-9473

HOMESTEAD STUDIO SUITES/ ARBORETUM
9100 Waterford Centre Blvd (78758)
Rates: $49-$64
(512) 837-6677
(888) 782-9473

HOMEWOOD SUITES ARBORE-TUM
10925 Stonelake Blvd (78759)
Rates: $129
(512) 349-9966
(800) 225-5466

HOMEWOOD SUITES-SOUTH
4143 Governors Row ((78744)
Rates: $119-$129
(512) 445-5050
(800) 225-5466

HYATT REGENCY
208 Barton Springs (78704)
Rates: $109-$239
(512) 477-1234
(800) 233-1234

AREA CODES - If the local number doesn't connect, check for a new area code.

LA QUINTA INN-BEN WHITE
4200 I-35 S (78745)
Rates: $65-$86
(512) 443-1774
(800) 687-6667

LA QUINTA INN-CAPITOL
300 E 11th St
(78701)
Rates: $90-$130
(512) 476-1166
(800) 687-6667

LA QUINTA INN-HIGHLAND MALL/AIRPORT
5812 I-35 N
(78751)
Rates: $65-$86
(512) 459-4381
(800) 687-6667

LA QUINTA INN-N
7100 I-35 N (78752)
Rates: $65-$86
(512) 452-9401
(800) 687-6667

LA QUINTA INN-OLTORF
1603 E Oltorf Blvd
(78741)
Rates: $65-$86
(512) 447-6661
(800) 687-6667

LA QUINTA INN
11901 N Mo-Pac
Blvd (78759)
Rates: $76-$120
(512) 832-2121
(800) 687-6667

LA QUINTA INN & SUITES-AIRPORT
7625 E Ben White
Blvd (78704)
Rates: $70-$100
(512) 386-6800
(800) 687-6667

LA QUINTA INN SOUTH WEST
4424 S Loop 1
(78735)
Rates: $110-$140
(512) 899-3000
(800) 687-6667

LAKE AUSTIN SPA RESORT
1705 Quinlan Park
Rd (78732)
Rates: $295-$450
(512) 266-2444
(800) 847-5637

LAKEWAY INN RESORT
101 Lakeway Dr
(78734)
Rates: $99-$250
(800) LAKEWAY

THE MANSION AT JUDGE'S HILL
1900 Rio Grande
(78705)
Rates: $99-$295
(512) 495-1800
(800) 311-1619

MARRIOTT HOTEL AT THE CAPITOL
701 E 11th St
(78701)
Rates: $129-$199
(512) 478-1111
(800) 228-9290

MOTEL 6 CENTRAL NORTH
8010 I-35 N
(78753)
Rates: $37-$51
(512) 837-9890
(800) 466-8356

MOTEL 6 CENTRAL SOUTH
5330 I-35 N(78751)
Rates: $37-$55
(512) 467-9111
(800) 466-8356

MOTEL 6-NORTH
9420 I-35 N
(78753)
Rates: $35-$56
(512) 339-6161
(800) 466-8356

MOTEL 6 SOUTH AIRPORT
2707 Interregional
Hwy S (78741)
Rates: $42-$58
(512) 444-5882
(800) 466-8356

NORTHPARK EXECUTIVE SUITE HOTEL
7685 Northcross
Dr (78757)
Rates: $75-$129
(512) 452-9391

OMNI AUSTIN HOTEL & SUITES
700 San Jacinto
Blvd (78701)
Rates: $139-$379
(512) 476-3700
(800) 843-6664

OMNI AUSTIN HOTEL SOUTHPARK
4140 Governor's
Row (78744)
Rates: $129-$179
(512) 448-2222
(800) 843-6664

QUALITY INN CENTRAL
909 E Koenig Ln
(78751)
Rates: $54-$89
(512) 452-4200
(800) 424-6423

QUALITY SUITES AUSTIN NORTH
14620 N I-35
(78728)
Rates: $79-$109
(512) 251-9110
(800) 424-6423

RAMADA LIMITED NORTH
9121 N I-35
(78753)
Rates: $45-$99
(512) 836-0079
(800) 272-6232

RAMADA INN AIRPORT SOUTH
1212 W Ben White
Blvd (78704)
Rates: $59-$89
(512) 447-0151
(800) 272-6232

RAMADA LIMITED UNIVERSITY NORTH
5526 N I-35
(78751)
Rates: n/a
(512) 451-7001
(800) 272-6232

RED LION HOTEL AIRPORT
6121 I-35 N
(78752)
Rates: $69-$99
(512) 323-5466
(800) 733-5466

RED ROOF INN NORTH
8210 N I-35
(78753)
Rates: $34-$54
(512) 835-2200
(800) 843-7663

RED ROOF INN SOUTH
4701 S I-35 (78744)
Rates: $39-$59
(512) 448-0091
(800) 843-7663

RENAISSANCE AUSTIN HOTEL
9721 Arboretum
Blvd (78759)
Rates: $179-$199
(512) 343-2626
(800) 468-3571

RESIDENCE INN BY MARRIOTT-ARBORETUM
3713 Tudor Blvd
(78759)
Rates: $89-$199
(512) 502-8200
(800) 331-3131

RESIDENCE INN BY MARRIOTT NORTH
12401 N Lamar
Blvd (78753)
Rates: $119-$169
(512) 977-0544
(800) 331-3131

RESIDENCE INN BY MARRIOTT SOUTH
4537 S I-35 (78744)
Rates: $119-$159
(512) 912-1100
(800) 331-3131

RODEWAY INN NORTH
5656 I-35 N
(78751)
Rates: $38-$79
(512) 452-1177
(800) 424-6423

STAYBRIDGE SUITES HOTEL
10201 Stonelake
Blvd (78759)
Rates: $69-$161
(512) 349-0888
(800) 238-8000

STUDIO 6-MIDTOWN
6603 I-35 (78752)
Rates: 199-$289
(512) 458-5453
(888) 897-0202

STUDIO 6 NORTHWEST
11901 Pavillion
Blvd (78759)
Rates: $199-$289
(888) 897-0202

SUMMERFIELD SUITES
7685 Northcross
Dr (78757)
Rates: $69-$119
(512) 452-9391
(800) 833-4353

SUPER 8 MOTEL
6000 Middle
Fiskville Rd
(78752)
Rates: $40-$74
(512) 467-8163
(800) 800-8000

SUPER 8 MOTEL CENTRAL
1201 N I-35
(78702)
Rates: $55-$89
(512) 472-8331

SUPER 8 MOTEL NORTH
8128 N I-35
(78753)
Rates: $45-$77
(512) 339-1300
(800) 800-8000

TRAVELODGE
8300 N I-35
(78753)
Rates: $39-$89
(512) 835-5050
(800) 578-7878

WALNUT FOREST MOTEL
11506 I-35 N
(78753)
Rates: $26-$35
(512) 835-0864

WELLESLEY INN & SUITES-MOPAC
2700 Gracy Farms
Ln (78758
Rates: $65-$75
(512) 833-0898
(800) 444-8888

WELLESLEY INN & SUITES-NORTH
8221 N I-35
(78753)
Rates: $62
(512) 339-6005
(800) 444-8888

WELLESLEY INN & SUITES-NW
12424 Research Blvd (78759)
Rates: $63-$72
(512) 219-6500
(800) 444-8888

WELLESLEY INN & SUITES-TOWN LAKE
1001 S I-35 (78744)
Rates: $75-$115
(512) 326-0100
(800) 444-8888

BAIRD
BAIRD MOTOR INN
500 I-20 E (79504)
Rates: $40-$55
(325) 854-2527

BALLINGER
BALLINGER CLASSIC MOTEL
1005 Hutchins (76821)
Rates: $34-$40
(325) 365-5717

DESERT INN MOTEL
Hwy 67 W (76821)
Rates: $28-$40
(325) 365-2518

STONEWALL MOTEL
201 N Broadway (76821)
Rates: $26-$36
(325) 365-3524

BANDERA
BACKROADS RESERVATIONS
1107 Cedar St (78003)
Rates: $85-$175
(866) 796-0660

BANDERA LODGE MOTEL
700 Hwy 16S (78003)
Rates: $55-$90
(830) 796-3093
(800) 796-3514

COOL WATER ACRES B&B
3301 FM 470 (78003)
Rates: $70-$90
(830) 796-4866

MANSION AT BANDERA B&B
1007 Hackberry St (78003)
Rates: $60-$155
(830) 796-4590

RIVER FRONT MOTEL
1004 Maple (78003)
Rates: $59-$74
(830) 460-3690
(800) 870-5671

RIVER OAK INN & RESTAURANT
1203 Main St (78003)
Rates: $39-$109
(830) 796-7751

BASTROP
DAYS INN
4102 Hwy 71 E (78602)
Rates: $50-$95
(512) 321-1157
(800) 329-7466

HOLIDAY INN EXP HOTEL & SUITES
491 Agnes St (78602)
Rates: $71-$80
(512) 321-1900
(800) 465-4329

PECAN STREET INN B&B
1010 Pecan St (78602)
Rates: $75-$135
(512) 321-3315

SCHAEFFER HOUSE B&B
608 Pecan St (78602)
Rates: $65-$100
(512) 303-2734

BAY CITY
BAY CITY INN
101 W 7th St (77414)
Rates: $32-$79
(979) 245-0985

ECONO LODGE
3712 7th St (77414)
Rates: $49-$99
(979) 245-5115
(800) 424-6423

BAYTOWN
BAYMONT INN
5215 I-10 E (77521)
Rates: $54-$74
(281) 421-7300
(800) 301-0200

HOLIDAY INN EXP
5222 I-10 E (77521)
Rates: $79-$89
(281) 421-7200
(800) 465-4329

LA QUINTA INN
4911 I-10 E (77521)
Rates: $60-$82
(281) 421-5566
(800) 687-6667

MOTEL 6
8911 Hwy 146 (77520)
Rates: $37-$55
(281) 576-5777
(800) 466-8356

QUALITY INN
300 S Hwy 146 (77520)
Rates: $55-$150
(281) 427-7481
(800) 424-6423

BEAUMONT
BEST WESTERN BEAUMONT INN
2155 N 11th St (77703)
Rates: $53-$59
(409) 898-8150
(800) 528-1234

BEST WESTERN JEFFERSON INN
1610 I-10 S (77707)
Rates: $50-$62
(409) 842-0037
(800) 528-1234

GRAND DUERR MANOR B&B
2298 McFaddin at 7th (77701)
Rates: $99-$159
(409) 833-9600

HILTON HOTEL
2355 I-10 S (77705)
Rates: $79-$109
(409) 842-3600
(800) 445-8667

HOLIDAY INN ATRIUM PLAZA
3950 I-10 S (77705)
Rates: $89-$99
(409) 842-5995
(800) 465-4329

HOLIDAY INN MIDTOWN
2095 N 11th St (77703)
Rates: $100-$109
(409) 892-2222
(800) 465-4329

HOWARD JOHN-SON EXP INN
2615 I-10 E (77703)
Rates: $69-$109
(409) 832-0666
(800) 446-4656

J & J MOTEL
6675 Eastex Frwy (77705)
Rates: $24+
(409) 892-4241

LA QUINTA INN
220 I-10 N (77702)
Rates: $63-$82
(409) 838-9991
(800) 687-6667

LA QUINTA INN
5820 Walden Rd (77707)
Rates: $83
(409) 842-0002
(800) 687-6667

MOTEL 6
1155 I-10 S (77701)
Rates: $37-$41
(409) 835-5913
(800) 466-8356

RAMADA LIMITED
4085 I-10 South (77705)
Rates: $49-$67
(409) 842-1111
(800) 272-6232

SUPER 8 MOTEL
2850 I-10 E (77703)
Rates: $41-$48
(409) 899-3040
(800) 800-8000

BEDFORD
COMFORT INN
2904 Crystal Spgs St (76095)
Rates: $69-$120
(817) 545-2555
(800) 424-6423

HOLIDAY INN AIRPORT WEST
3005 W Airport Frwy (76021)
Rates: $59-$69
(817) 267-3181
(800) 465-4329

LA QUINTA INN
1450 W Airport Frwy (76022)
Rates: $60-$82
(817) 267-5200
(800) 687-6667

SUPER 8 MOTEL
1800 Airport Frwy (76022)
Rates: $50-$55
(817) 545-8108
(800) 800-8000

BEEVILLE
BEEVILLE INN
400 SE Bypass 181 (78102)
Rates: $49-$54
(361) 358-4000

BEST WESTERN TEXAN INN
2001 Hwy 59 (78102)
Rates: $65-$95
(361) 358-9999
(800) 528-1234

EL CAMINO MOTEL
1500 N Washington (78102)
Rates: $32-$39
(361) 358-2141

BELLMEAD
MOTEL 6
1509 Hogan Ln (76705)
Rates: $35-$50
(254) 799-4957
(800) 466-8356

BELLVILLE
TEXAS RANCH LIFE
Tottenham Road at Cactus (77418)
Rates: $135-$160
(866) TEXASRL
(Dude Ranch)

BELTON
BUDGET HOST INN
1520 I-35 S (76513)
Rates: $35-$52
(254) 939-0744
(800) 283-4678

RAMADA LIMITED
1102 E 2nd Ave (76513)
Rates: $51-$72
(254) 939-3745
(800) 272-6232

AREA CODES - If the local number doesn't connect, check for a new area code.

RIVER
FOREST INN
1414 E 6th Ave
(76513)
Rates: $40-$75
(254) 939-5711

BENBROOK
BEST WESTERN
WINSCOTT INN
590 Winscott Rd
(76126)
Rates: $79-$189
(817) 249-0076
(800) 528-1234

MOTEL 6
8601 Benbrook
Blvd (76126)
Rates: $44-$75
(817) 249-8885
(800) 466-8356

BIG BEND
NAT'L PARK
CHISOS
MOUNTAINS
LODGE
Basin Rural
Station (79834)
Rates: $76-$92
(432) 477-2291

BIG SPRING
DAYS INN
2701 S Gregg St
(79720)
Rates: $45-$60
(432) 267-5237
(800) 329-7466

ECONO LODGE
804 I-20 W (79720)
Rates: $49-$79
(432) 263-5200
(800) 424-6423

MOTEL 6
600 I-20 W (79720)
Rates: $30-$51
(432) 267-1695
(800) 466-8356

SUPER 8 MOTEL
700 W I-20 (79720)
Rates: $40-$108
(432) 267-1601
(800) 800-8000

BLUFF DALE
THE HIDEAWAY
COUNTRY LOG
CABINS B&B
1022 Private Rd
1250 (76433)
Rates: $94-$105
(254) 823-6606

TRICKLE CREEK
CABINS
3501 CR 196
(76433)
Rates: $115-$135
(254) 396-0000

BOERNE
BEST WESTERN
TEXAS COUNTRY
INN
35150 I-10 W
(78006)
Rates: $63-$90
(830) 249-9791
(800) 528-1234
(800) 299-9791

BOERNE B&B
RESERVATION
SERVICE
132 S Main St
(78066)
Rates: $85-$160
(866) 336-3809

BOERNE LAKE
LODGE B&B
RESORT
310 Lakeview Dr
(78006)
Rates: $150-$250
(830) 816-6060
(800) 809-5050

KEY TO THE
HILLS MOTEL
1228 S Main St
(78006)
Rates: $52-$65
(830) 249-3562
(800) 690-5763

BONHAM
5 STAR INN
1515 Old Ector Rd
(75418)
Rates: $46-$58
(903) 583-3121

BORGER
BEST WESTERN
BORGER INN
206 S Cedar
(79007)
Rates: $73-$120
(806) 274-7050
(800) 528-1234

HERITAGE INN
100 Bulldog Blvd
(79007)
Rates: $35-$59
(806) 273-9556

BOWIE
DAYS INN
2436 S Hwy 287
(76230)
Rates: $45-$65
(940) 872-5426
(800) 329-7466

PARK'S INN
708 W Wise St
(76230)
Rates: $37-$60
(940) 872-1111

BRADY
BEST WESTERN
BRADY INN
2200 S Bridge St
(76825)
Rates: $45-$75
(325) 597-3997
(800) 528-1234

DAYS INN
2108 S Bridge St
(76825)
Rates: $39-$79
(325) 597-0789
(800) 329-7466

GOLD KEY INN
2023 S Bridge St
(76825)
Rates: $30-$41
(325) 597-2185

BRECKENRIDGE
RIDGE MOTEL
Hwy 180 (76424)
Rates: $30-$44
(817) 559-2244
(800) 462-5308

BRENHAM
BEST WESTERN
INN
1503 Hwy 290 E
(77833)
Rates: $65-$109
(979) 251-7791
(800) 528-1234

BRENHAM HOUSE
BED & BREAKFST
705 Clinton St
(77833)
Rates: $75
(979) 830-0477
(800) 259-8367

COMFORT SUITES
2350 S Day St
(77833)
Rates: $62-$107
(979) 421-8100
(800) 424-6423

DAYS INN
201 Hwy 290
Loop East (77833)
Rates: $45-$80
(979) 830-1110
(800) 329-7466

BROADDUS
COUNTRY
INN MOTEL
Hwy 147 N
(75929)
Rates: $35-$70
(936) 872-3691

HARVEY'S CABINS
Rt 1, Box 255,
Hwy 147 (75929)
Rates: n/a
(936) 872-3644

BRONTE
TERLINGUA
HOUSE
P. O. Box 657
(76933)
Rates: $200-$225
(325) 473-4400

BROOKSHIRE
EXPRESS INN
217 Waller Ave
(77423)
Rates: $36-$49
(281) 934-3122

TRAVELERS INN
542 FM 1489 Rd
(77423)
Rates: n/a
(281) 934-4477

BROWNFIELD
BEST WESTERN
CAPROCK INN
321 Lubbock Rd
(79316)
Rates: $50-$65
(806) 637-9471
(800) 528-1234

BROWNSVILLE
COMFORT INN
825 N Expressway
(78520)
Rates: $69-$250
(956) 504-3331
(800) 424-6423

FOUR POINTS
BY SHERATON
3777 N Expressway
(78520)
Rates: $99-$129
(956) 547-1500
(800) 325-7385

HAWTHORN
SUITES
3759 N Expressway
(78520)
Rates: $119-$149
(956) 574-6900
(800) 527-1133

LA QUINTA INN
1225 N Expressway
(78520)
Rates: $69-$119
(800) 687-6667

MOTEL CITRUS
2054 Central Blvd
(78520)
Rates: $35-$80
(956) 550-9077

MOTEL 6
2255 N Expressway
(78521)
Rates: $34-$48
(956) 546-4699
(800) 466-8356

PLAZA SQUARE
MOTOR LODGE
2255 Central Blvd
(78520)
Rates: $29-$35
(956) 546-5104

RED ROOF INN
2377 N Expressway
83 (78520)
Rates: $49-$113
(956) 504-2300
(800) 843-7663

RESIDENCE INN
BY MARRIOTT
3975 N Expressway
(78520)
Rates: $105-$169
(956) 350-8100
(800) 331-3131

BROWNWOOD
BEST WESTERN
BROWNWOOD
410 E Commerce
(76801)
Rates: $44-$69
(325) 646-3511
(800) 528-1234
(877) 646-3513

DAYS INN
515 E Commerce
(76801)
Rates: $44-$74
(325) 646-2551
(800) 329-7466
(877) 500-2600

AREA CODES - If the local number doesn't connect, check for a new area code.

GATE I
MOTOR INN
4410 Hwy 377 S
(76801)
Rates: $40-$65
(325) 643-5463
(800) 400-8300

LAKE
BROWNWOOD
BED & BREAKFST
9321 CR 558
(76801)
Rates: $75-$95
(325) 784-7729

STAR OF
TEXAS B & B
650 Morelock Ln
(76801)
Rates: $95-$115
(325) 646-4128
(800) 850-2003

TIN TOP RANCH
1400 FM 586 E
(76801)
Rates: $80-$100
(325) 646-4156

BRYAN
PREFERENCE INN
1601 S Texas Ave
(77802)
Rates: $40-$99
(979) 822-6196

BUFFALO
BEST WESTERN
CRAIG'S INN
I-45 & US 79
(75831)
Rates: $59-$85
(903) 322-5831
(800) 528-1234

BURLESON
COMFORT SUITES
321 S Burleson
Blvd (76028)
Rates: $69-$89
(817) 426-6666
(800) 424-6423

DAYS INN
329 S Burleson
Blvd (76028)
Rates: $55-$75
(817) 447-1111
(800) 329-7466

SUPER 8 MOTEL
151 E Alsbury St
(76028)
Rates: $55-$120
(817) 447-0011
(800) 800-8000

BURNET
BEST WESTERN
POST OAK INN
908 Buchanan Dr
(78611)
Rates: $45-$95
(512) 756-4747
(800) 528-1234

CANYON OF THE
EAGLES LODGE
16942 Ranch Rd
2341 (78611)
Rates: $99-$179
(512) 756-8787
(800) 977-0081

ROCKY REST
COUNTRY INN
404 S Water St
(78611)
Rates: $55-$60
(512) 756-2600

CALDWELL
CALDWELL MOTEL
1819 W Hwy 21
(77836)
Rates: n/a
(979) 567-4000

SUNSET INN
MOTEL
705 Hwy 36 N
(77836)
Rates: $33-$49
(979) 567-4661

THE SURREY INN
403 E Hwy 21
(77836)
Rates: $37-$40
(979) 567-3221

CAMERON
VARSITY MOTEL
1004 E 1st St
(76520)
Rates: $34-$40
(254) 697-6446

CANTON
BEST WESTERN
CANTON INN
2251 N Trade
Days Blvd (75103)
Rates: $49-$169
(903) 567-6591
(800) 528-1234

DAYS INN
17299 S I-20
(75103)
Rates: $48-$145
(903) 567-6588
(800) 329-7466

HOLIDAY INN EXP
2406 N Trade
Days Blvd (75103)
Rates: $55-$165
(903) 567-0909
(800) 465-4329

SUPER 8 MOTEL
110 N I-20 (75103)
Rates: $45-$63
(903) 567-6567
(800) 800-8000

CANYON
COUNTRY HOME
BED & BREAKFAST
Rt 1, Box 447 (79015)
Rates: $55-$85
(806) 655-7636
(800) 664-7636

HOLIDAY INN EXP
HOTEL & SUITES
2901 4th Ave
(79015)
Rates: $72-$130
(806) 655-4445
(800) 465-4329

CANYON LAKE
MARICOPA
RANCH RESORT
12915 FM 306
(78130)
Rates: $45-$105
(830) 964-3731
(800) 460-8891

CARRIZO
SPRINGS
BALIA INN
S Hwy 83 (78834)
Rates: $40-$70
(830) 876-3583

CARROLLTON
RED ROOF INN
1720 S Broadway
(75006)
Rates: $33-$61
(972) 245-1700
(800) 843-7663

CARTHAGE
CARTHAGE MOTEL
321 S Shelby (75633)
Rates: $28-$35
(903) 693-3814

CEDAR PARK
COMFORT INN
300 E Whitestone
Blvd (78613)
Rates: $65-$100
(512) 259-1810
(800) 424-6423

CENTER
BEST WESTERN
CENTER INN
1005 Hurst St
(75935)
Rates: $52-$75
(936) 598-3384
(800) 528-1234

CENTER POINT
MARIANNE'S
COUNTRY B&B
Rt 1, Box 527
(78010)
Rates: $75-$110
(830) 634-7489
(800) 634-7489

CENTERVILLE
DAYS INN
Hwy 7 & I-45,
Exit 164 (75833)
Rates: $44-$86
(9030 536-7175
(800) 329-7466

CHANNELVIEW
BEST WESTERN
HOUSTON EAST
15919 I-10 E
(77530)
Rates: $46-$80
(281) 452-1000
(800) 528-1234

BUDGET LODGE
17011 I-10 E (77530)
Rates: $44-$165
(281) 457-2966

TRAVELODGE
SUITES
15831 2nd St
(77520)
Rates: $60-$65
(281) 862-0222
(800) 578-7878

CHILDRESS
BEST WESTERN
CLASSIC INN
1805 Ave "F" NW
(79201)
Rates: $60-$80
(940) 937-6353
(800) 528-1234
(800) 346-1576

COMFORT INN
1804 Ave "F" NW
(79201)
Rates: $69-$94
(940) 937-6363
(800) 424-6423

DAYS INN
2220 Ave "F" (79201)
Rates: $59-$84
(940) 937-0622
(800) 329-7466

ECONO LODGE
1612 Ave "F" NW
(79201)
Rates: $38-$70
(940) 937-3695
(800) 424-6423

HOLIDAY INN EXP
2008 Ave "F" NW
(79201)
Rates: $59-$99
(940) 937-3434
(800) 465-4329

SUPER 8 MOTEL
411 Ave "F" NE
(79201)
Rates: $60-$100
(940) 937-8825
(800) 800-8000

CISCO
BEST WESTERN
INN CISCO
1898 Hwy 206 W
(76437)
Rates: $59-$64
(254) 442-3735
(800) 621-2457

CISCO MOTOR INN
204 I-20 W (76437)
Rates: $30-$50
(254) 442-3040

OAK MOTEL
300 I-20 E (76437)
Rates: $25-$32
(254) 442-2100

CLARENDON
BAR H WORKING
DUDE RANCH
P O Box 1191
(79226)
Rates: n/a
(806) 874-2634
(800) 627-9871

IT'LL DO MOTEL
403 W 2nd St (79226)
Rates: n/a
(806) 874-3471

WESTERN SKIES
MOTEL
800 W 2nd St
(79226)
Rates: $35-$50
(806) 874-3501

AREA CODES - If the local number doesn't connect, check for a new area code.

CLAUDE

L A MOTEL
200 E 1st St
(79019)
Rates: $35-$50
(806) 226-4981

CLEBURNE

ANGLIN ROSE B&B
808 S Anglin
(76031)
Rates: $90-$100
(817) 641-7433

COMFORT INN
2117 N Main St
(76031)
Rates: $79-$89
(817) 641-4702
(800) 424-6423

DAYS INN
101 N Ridgeway Dr (76031)
Rates: $50-$80
(817) 645-8836
(800) 329-7466

SAGAMAR INN
2107 N Main
(76031)
Rates: $56-$60
(817) 556-3631

CLIFTON

CLIFFVIEW RESORT CABINS
180 CR 1802
(76634)
Rates: $71-$120
(866) 821-6040

RIVER'S BEND BED & BREAKFAST
P. O. Box 228
(76634)
Rates: $95-$150
(254) 675-4936

CLUTE

BEST WESTERN INN & SUITES
900 Hwy 332
(77531)
Rates: $69-$129
(979) 388-0055
(800) 528-1234

LA QUINTA INN
1126 Hwy 332 W
(77531)
Rates: $65-$87
(979) 265-7461
(800) 687-6667

MAINSTAY SUITES
1003 Hwy 332 W
(77531)
Rates: $90-$140
(979) 388-9300
(800) 660-6246
(800) 424-6423

MOTEL 6
1000 Hwy 332 W
(77531)
Rates: $34-$39
(979) 265-4764
(800) 466-8356

COLDSPRING

SAN JACINTO INN
13815 Hwy 150 W
(77331)
Rates: $40-$43
(936) 653-3008

COLEMAN

BEST WESTERN COLEMAN INN
1401 Hwy 84 Bypass (76834)
Rates: $55-$75
(325) 625-4176
(800) 528-1234

COLLEGE STATION

HILTON HOTEL & CONFERENCE CENTER
801 E University Dr (77840)
Rates: $69-$125
(979) 693-7500
(800) 445-8667

HOLIDAY INN
1503 Texas Ave S
(77840)
Rates: $79
(979) 693-1736
(800) 465-4329

HOWARD JOHNSON EXP
3702 Hwy 6 S
(77845)
Rates: $40-$125
(800) 446-4656

LA QUINTA INN
607 Texas Ave S
(77840)
Rates: $70-$96
(979) 696-7777
(800) 687-6667

MANOR HOUSE INN
2504 Texas Ave S
(77840)
Rates: $60-$99
(979) 764-9540
(800) 231-4100

MOTEL 6
2327 Texas Ave S
(77840)
Rates: $37-$57
(979) 696-3379
(800) 466-8356

RAMADA INN
1502 Texas Ave S
(77840)
Rates: $59-$63
(979) 693-9891
(800) 272-6232

SUPER 8 MOTEL
301 Texas Ave
(77840)
Rates: $65-$109
(979) 846-8800
(800) 800-8000

TOWNEPLACE SUITES BY MARRIOTT
1300 E University Dr (77840)
Rates: $89-$131
(979) 260-8500
(800) 257-3000

COLORADO CITY

RELAX INN
1041 Westpoint Ave (79512)
Rates: n/a
(325) 728-5742

VILLA INN MOTEL
2310 Hickory St
(79512)
Rates: $32-$44
(325) 728-5217

COLUMBUS

COLUMBUS INN
2208 Hwy 71 S
(78934)
Rates: $50-$65
(979) 732-5723

COUNTRY HEARTH INN
2436 Hwy 71 S
(78934)
Rates: $62-$80
(979) 732-6293
(888) 325-7817

HOLIDAY INN EXP HOTEL & SUITES
4321 I-10 (78934)
Rates: $69-$89
(979) 733-9300
(800) 465-4329

COMANCHE

GUEST HOUSE-HERITAGE HILL BED & BREAKFAST
Hwy 36 E, Rt 3 Box 221 (76442)
Rates: $70-$100
(915) 356-3397

COMFORT

IDLEWILDE B & B
115 Hwy 473
(78013)
Rates: $63-$93
(830) 995-3844

KLEINA HIMMUL BED & BREAKFAST
Rt 1, Box 127-B
(78013)
Rates: $75-$85
(830) 995-2003

MOTOR INN AT COMFORT
32 N Hwy 87
(78013)
Rates: $60-$140
(830) 995-3822

COMMERCE

HOLIDAY INN EXP
2207 Culver St
(75428)
Rates: $66-$82
(903) 886-4777
(800) 465-4329

CONCAN

B.E.N.T. RIVER RETREAT CABINS
1000 CR 350
(78838)
Rates: $100-$180
(888) 388-3707

FRIO ACRES CABINS
1047 CR 350
(78838)
Rates: $90-$145
(877) 635-4848

SEVEN BLUFF CABINS
3rd Crossing - River Rd (78838)
Rates: $90-$400
(800) 360-5260

CONROE

BAYMONT INN
1506 I-45 S (77301)
Rates: $69-$84
(936) 539-5100
(800) 301-0200

LA QUINTA INN
4006 Sprayberry Ln (77303)
Rates: $69-$109
(936) 228-0790
(800) 687-6667

MOTEL 6
820 I-45 S (77304)
Rates: $36-$45
(926) 760-4003
(800) 466-8356

CONWAY

BUDGET HOST INN S&S MOTEL
I-40 & Hwy 207
(79068)
Rates: $35-$47
(806) 537-5111
(800) 283-4678

COPPERAS COVE

HOWARD JOHNSON EXPRESS INN
302 W Hwy 190
(76522)
Rates: $54-$69
(254) 547-2345
(800) 446-4656

CORPUS CHRISTI

ANCHOR RESORT CONDOMINIUMS
14300 S Padre Island Dr (78418)
Rates: $69-$129
(800) 460-8770

BAYFRONT INN
601 N Shoreline Blvd (78401)
Rates: $49-$125
(361) 883-7271
(800) 456-2293

BEST VALUE INN
6255 Corn Products Rd
(78409)
Rates: $29-$159
(361) 289-0991

BEST WESTERN GARDEN INN
11217 I-37 (78410)
Rates: $59-$139
(361) 241-6675
(800) 528-1234

BEST WESTERN MARINA GRAND HOTEL
300 N Shoreline Dr (78401)
Rates: $69-$195
(361) 883-5111
(800) 528-1234
(800) 883-5119

BEST WESTERN ON THE ISLAND
14050 S Padre Island Dr (78418)
Rates: $59-$150
(361) 949-2300
(800) 528-1234

BEST WESTERN PARADISE INN
6301 S Padre Island Dr (78412)
Rates: $74-$145
(361) 992-3100
(800) 528-1234

CHRISTY ESTATE SUITES
3942 Holly Rd (78415)
Rates: $109-$189
(361) 854-1091
(800) 6-SUITE

CLARION HOTEL
5224 I-37, N Navigation Blvd (78407)
Rates: $60-$130
(361) 883-6161
(800) 252-7466
(800) 424-6423

COMFORT INN
3838 Hwy 77 (78410)
Rates: $69-$120
(361) 241-6363
(800) 424-6423

DAYS INN
901 Navigation Blvd (78408)
Rates: $40-$130
(361) 888-8599
(800) 329-7466

DAYS INN-SOUTH
2838 S Padre Island Dr (78415)
Rates: $59-$169
(361) 854-0005
(800) 329-7466

DRURY INN
2021 N Padre Island Dr (78408)
Rates: $62-$92
(361) 289-8200
(800) 378-7946

GULF BEACH-II MOTOR INN
3500 Surfside Blvd (78402)
Rates: $40-$90
(361) 882-3500

HOLIDAY INN EMERALD BEACH
1102 S Shoreline Blvd (78401)
Rates: $115-$179
(361) 883-5731
(800) 465-4329

HOLIDAY INN-PADRE IS. DRIVE
5549 Leopard St (78408)
Rates: $79-$129
(361) 289-5100
(800) 465-4329

HOMEWOOD SUITES
5202 Crosstown Expresswy (78417)
Rates: $99-$129
(361) 854-1331
(800) 225-5466

LA QUINTA INN-N
5155 I-37 N (78408)
Rates: $63-$129
(361) 888-5721
(800) 687-6667

LA QUINTA INN-SOUTH
6225 S Padre Island Dr (78412)
Rates: $69-$129
(361) 991-5730
(800) 687-6667

MOTEL 6-LANTANA
845 Lantana St (78408)
Rates: $29-$53
(361) 289-9397
(800) 466-8356

MOTEL 6-SPI DRIVE
8202 S Padre Island Dr (78412)
Rates: $33-$55
(361) 991-8858
(800) 466-8356

QUALITY INN & SUITES SANDY SHORES
3202 Surfside Blvd (78402)
Rates: $69-$199
(361) 883-7456
(800) 424-6423

RED ROOF INN AIRPORT
6301 I-37 (78409)
Rates: $37-$175
(361) 289-6925
(800) 843-7663

RESIDENCE INN BY MARRIOTT
5229 Blanche Moore Dr (78411)
Rates: $89-$159
(361) 985-1113
(800) 331-3131

SURFSIDE CONDOMINIUM APARTMENTS
15005 Windward Dr (78418)
Rates: $120-$155
(361) 949-8128
(800) 548-4585

CORSICANA

DAYS INN
2018 Hwy 287 S (75110)
Rates: $37-$90
(903) 872-0659
(800) 329-7466

RAMADA INN
2000 S Hwy 287 (75110)
Rates: $49-$69
(903) 874-7413
(800) 272-6232

CROCKETT

CROCKETT FAMILY RESORT & MARINA
Rt 3, Box 460 (75835)
Rates: $40-$60
(877) 544-8466

CROCKETT INN
1600 Loop 304 E (75835)
Rates: $35+
(936) 544-5611
(800) 633-9518

EMBERS MOTOR INN
1401 Loop 304 E (75835)
Rates: $25-$36
(936) 544-5681

CROWELL

CYNTHIA ANN PARKER COUNTRY INN
915 N 2nd St (79227)
Rates: $55-$65
(940) 684-1915

CRYSTAL CITY

RIATA INN
1531 N Hwy 83 (78839)
Rates: $40-$70
(830) 374-5665

CUERO

SANDS MOTEL & RV PARK
2117 N Esplanade (77954)
Rates: $32-$38
(512) 275-3437

DALHART

BEST WESTERN NURSANICKEL MOTEL
102 Scott Ave (79022)
Rates: $48-$78
(806) 249-5637
(800) 528-1234
(800) 309-2399

BUDGET INN
415 Liberal St (79022)
Rates: $36-$69
(806) 244-4557

COMFORT INN
1110 Hwy 54 E (79022)
Rates: $65-$100
(806) 249-8585
(800) 424-6423

DAYS INN
701 Liberal St (79022)
Rates: $69-$149
(806) 244-5246
(800) 329-7466

ECONO LODGE
123 Liberal St (79022)
Rates: $50-$90
(806) 244-6464
(800) 424-6423

HOLIDAY INN EXP
801 Liberal St (79022)
Rates: $79-$99
(806) 249-1145
(800) 465-4329

SANDS MOTEL
301 Liberal St (79022)
Rates: $25-$70
(806) 244-4568

SUPER 8 MOTEL
403 Tanglewood Rd (79022)
Rates: $49-$65
(806) 249-8526
(800) 800-8000

DALLAS
(and Vicinity)

THE ADOLPHUS
1321 Commerce St (75202)
Rates: $130-$415
(214) 742-8200

AMERISUITES GALLERIA
5229 Spring Valley Rd (75240)
Rates: $99-$109
(972) 716-2001
(800) 833-1516

AMERISUITES PARK CENTRAL
12411 N Central Expressway (75243)
Rates: $99-$119
(972) 456-1224
(800) 833-1516

AMERISUITES WEST END
1907 N Lamar St (75202)
Rates: $149-$159
(214) 999-0500
(800) 833-1516

BEST WESTERN TELECOM AREA SUITES
13636 Goldmark Dr (75240)
Rates: $79-$89
(972) 669-0478
(800) 528-1234

AREA CODES - If the local number doesn't connect, check for a new area code.

BUDGET SUITES-MARKET CENTER
8150 Stemmons Frwy (75247)
Rates: $59-$79
(877) 822 -5272

CANDLEWOOD SUITES-MARKET CENTER
7930 N Stemmons (75247)
Rates: $74-$144
(214) 631-3333
(800) 465-4329

CANDLEWOOD SUITES-GALLERIA
13939 Noel Rd (75240)
Rates: $49-$119
(972) 233-6888
(800) 465-4329

CANDLEWOOD SUITES-NORTH
12525 Greenville Ave (75243)
Rates: $69-$99
(972) 669-9606
(800) 465-4329

CLARION INN MARKET CENTER
7138 N Stemmons Frwy (75247)
Rates: $69-$109
(214) 461-2677
(800) 424-6423

COMFORT INN GALLERIA
14975 Landmark Blvd (75240)
Rates: $69-$125
(972) 701-0881
(800) 424-6423

COMFORT INN SOUTH
8541 S Hampton Rd (75232)
Rates: $69-$120
(972) 572-1020
(800) 424-6423

COMFORT INN & SUITES MARKET CENTER
7138N Stemmons Frwy (75247)
Rates: $69-$129
(214) 461-2677
(800) 424-6423

COUNTRY INN
13185 N Central Expressway (75243)
Rates: $63-$81
(972) 907-9500
(800) 456-4000

CROWNE PLAZA HOTEL & RESORT MARKET CENTER
7050 Stemmons Frwy (75247)
Rates: $119-$179
(214) 630-8500
(800) 227-6963

CROWNE PLAZA SUITES & RESORT- DALLAS PARK
7800 Alpha Rd (75240)
Rates: $79-$139
(972) 233-7600
(800) 227-6963

DOUBLETREE CLUB HOTEL
8102 LBJ Frwy (75251)
Rates: $59-$89
(972) 960-6555
(800) 222-8733

DRURY INN & SUITES-DALLAS NORTH
2421 Walnut Hill Ln (75229)
Rates: $63-$97
(972) 484-3330
(800) 378-7946

ECONO LODGE
2275 Valley View Lane (75234)
Rates: $45-$65
(972) 243-5500
(800) 424-6423

EMBASSY SUITES HOTEL-DALLAS/PARK CENTRAL
13131 N Central Expressway (75243)
Rates: $89-$143
(972) 234-3300
(800) 362-2779

EMBASSY SUITES MARKET CENTER
2727 Stemmons Frwy (75207)
Rates: $99-$219
(214) 630-5332
(800) 362-2779

FAIRMONT HOTEL
1717 N Akard St (75201)
Rates: $129-$309
(214) 720-2020
(800) 527-4727

HAWTHORN SUITES-MARKET CENTER
7900 Brookriver Dr (75247)
Rates: $79-$159
(214) 688-1010
(800) 527-1133

HEARTHSIDE SUITES BY VILLAGER
12301 N Central Expressway (75243)
Rates: $59-$99
(972) 716-0600

HEARTHSIDE SUITES BY VILLAGER
10326 Finnell St (75220)
Rates: $59-$99
(214) 904-9666

HOLIDAY INN EXP
13185 N Central Expressway (75243)
Rates: $59-$75
(972) 907-9500
(800) 465-4329

HOLIDAY INN EXP-LOVE FIELD
2370 W Northwest Hwy (75220)
Rates: $69-$99
(214) 350-5577
(800) 465-4329

HOLIDAY INN SELECT
11350 LBJ Frwy (75238)
Rates: n/a
(214) 341-5400
(800) 465-4329

HOLIDAY INN SELECT DALLAS CENTRAL
10650 N Central Expressway (75231)
Rates: $129-$350
(214) 373-6000
(800) 465-4329

HOMESTEAD STUDIO SUITES
17425 N Dallas Pkwy (75287)
Rates: $39-$54
(972) 447-1800
(888) 782-9473

HOMESTEAD STUDIO SUITES
12121 Coit Rd (75251)
Rates: $49-$64
(972) 663-1800
(888) 782-9473

HOMESTEAD STUDIO SUITES/PLANO
18470 N Dallas Pkwy (75287)
Rates: $64-$79
(972) 248-2233
(888) 782-9473

HOMEWOOD SUITES BY HILTON
2747 N Stemmons Frwy (75207)
Rates: $86
(214) 819-9700
(800) 225-5466

HOMEWOOD SUITES BY HILTON
9169 Markville Dr (75243)
Rates: $109
(972) 437-6966
(800) 225-5466

HOTEL CRESCENT COURT
400 Crescent Court (75201)
Rates: $365-$2500
(214) 871-3200
(800) 654-6541

HOTEL DALLAS MOCKINGBIRD
1893 W Mockingbird Ln (75235)
Rates: $49-$109
(214) 634-8850

HOTEL ST. GERMAIN
2516 Maple Ave (75201)
Rates: $290-$650
(214) 871-2516

HOTEL ZAZA
2332 Leonard St (75201)
Rates: $259-$350
(214) 468-8399

LA QUINTA INN-DALLAS CITY PLACE
4440 N Central Expresswy (75206)
Rates: $80-$100
(214) 821-4220
(800) 687-6667

LA QUINTA INN-DALLAS EAST
8303 E R L Thornton Frwy (75228)
Rates: $60-$81
(214) 324-3731
(800) 687-6667

LA QUINTA INN LOVE FIELD
1625 Regal Row (75247)
Rates: $50-$80
(214) 630-5701
(800) 687-6667

LA QUINTA INN RICHARDSON
13685 N Central Expresswy (75243)
Rates: $50-$70
(972) 234-1016
(800) 687-6667

LA QUINTA INN & SUITES NORTHPARK
10001 N Central Expresswy (75231)
Rates: $80-$121
(214) 361-8200
(800) 687-6667

LA QUINTA INN & SUITES NORTHWEST
2380 W Northwest Hwy (75220)
Rates: $59-$79
(214) 904-9955
(800) 687-6667

MAGNOLIA HOTEL DALLAS
1401 Commerce St (75201)
Rates: $159-$230
(214) 915-6500

AREA CODES - If the local number doesn't connect, check for a new area code.

**THE MANSION
ON TURTLE CREEK**
2821 Turtle Creek
Blvd (75219)
Rates: $400-$2400
(214) 559-2100
(800) 527-5432

**MARRIOTT SUITES
MARKET CENTER**
2493 N Stemmons
Frwy (75207)
Rates: $79-$199
(214) 905-0050
(800) 228-9290

**THE MELROSE
HOTEL**
3015 Oak Lawn
Ave (75219)
Rates: $249-$279
(214) 521-5151

MOTEL 6
8108 E R L
Thornton Frwy
(75228)
Rates: $41-$65
(214) 388-8741
(800) 466-8356

MOTEL 6
10335 Gardner Rd
(75220)
Rates: $36-$54
(972) 506-8100
(800) 466-8356

MOTEL 6 NORTH
2753 Forest Ln
(75234)
Rates: $35-$51
(972) 620-2828
(800) 466-8356

MOTEL 6-NE
10921 Estate Lane
(75238)
Rates: $34-$40
(214) 340-2299
(800) 466-8356

MOTEL 6 SOUTH
2660 Forest Ln
(75234)
Rates: $33-$56
(972) 484-9111
(800) 466-8356

MOTEL 6-SE
4220 Indepen-
dence Dr (75237)
Rates: $35-$42
(972) 296-3331
(800) 466-8356

**QUALITY INN
DALLAS MARKET
CENTER**
1955 Market
Center Blvd
(75207)
Rates: $79-$119
(214) 747-9551
(800) 424-6423

**RADISSON HOTEL
CENTRAL/DALLAS**
6060 N Central
Expressway (75206)
Rates: $139-$159
(214) 750-6060
(800) 333-3333

RADISSON HOTEL
2330 W Northwest
Hwy (75220)
Rates: $149-$169
(214) 351-4477
(800) 333-3333

**RED ROOF INN
MARKET CENTER**
1550 Empire
Central Dr (75235)
Rates: $39-$59
(214) 638-5151
(800) 843-7663

**RED ROOF INN-
NORTHWEST**
10335 Gardner Rd
(75220)
Rates: $45-$60
(972) 506-8100
(800) 843-7663

**RENAISSANCE
HOTEL
MARKET CENTER**
2222 Stemmons
Frwy (75207)
Rates: $89-$199
(972) 631-2222
(800) 228-9898

**RESIDENCE INN
BY MARRIOTT/
CENTRAL-N.PARK**
10333 N Central
Expressway (75231)
Rates: $126-$165
(214) 750-8220
(800) 331-3131

**RESIDENCE INN
BY MARRIOTT-
MARKET CENTER**
6950 N Stemmons
Frwy (75247)
Rates: $79-$119
(214) 631-2472
(800) 331-3131

**RESIDENCE INN
BY MARRIOTT-
PARK CENTRAL**
7642 LBJ Frwy
(75251)
Rates: $69-$159
(972) 503-1333
(800) 331-3131

RODEWAY INN
8541 S Hampton
Rd (75232)
Rates: n/a
(972) 572-1030
(800) 228-2000

**SHERATON
BROOKHOLLOW
HOTEL**
1241 W
Mockingbird Ln
(75247)
Rates: $59-$119
(214) 630-7000
(800) 325-3535

**SHERATON
SUITES MARKET
CENTER**
2101 Stemmons
Frwy (75207)
Rates: $219-$229
(214) 747-3000
(800) 325-3535

**STAYBRIDGE
SUITES-PARK
CENTRAL**
7880 Alpha Rd
(75240)
Rates: $129-$169
(972) 391-0000
(800) 238-8000

**STERLING HOTEL
DALLAS**
1055 Regal Row
(75247)
Rates: $69-$79
(214) 634-8550

**STONELEIGH
HOTEL**
2927 Maple Ave
(75201)
Rates: $119-$199
(800) 255-9299

STUDIO 6
2395 Stemmons Tr
(75220)
Rates: $199-$269
(214) 904-1400
(888) 892-0202

STUDIO 6
9801 Adleta Ct
(75243)
Rates: $179-$299
(214) 342-5400
(888) 892-0202

**WELLESLEY INN
& SUITES PARK
CENTRAL**
9019 Vantage
Point Rd (75243)
Rates: $69-$79
(972) 671-7722
(800) 444-8888

**WESTIN-CITY
CENTER DALLAS**
650 N Pearl St
(75201)
Rates: $109-$149
(214) 979-9000
(800) 228-3000

**WESTIN HOTEL
GALLERIA
DALLAS**
13340 Dallas
Pkwy (75240)
Rates: $199-$359
(972) 934-9494
(800) 228-3000

**WESTIN HOTEL
PARK CENTRAL**
12720 Merit Dr
(75251)
Rates: $239-$259
(972) 385-3000
(800) 228-3000

WINGATE INN
8650 N Stemmons
Frwy (75247)
Rates: $89-$109
(214) 267-8400

DE SOTO
RED ROOF INN
1401 N Beckley Dr
(75115)
Rates: $36-$54
(972) 224-7100
(800) 843-7663

DECATUR
BEST WESTERN INN
1801 Hwy 287 S
(76234)
Rates: $55-$85
(940) 627-5982
(800) 528-1234
(800) 399-1553

COMFORT INN
1709 Hwy 287 S
(76234)
Rates: $54-$110
(940) 627-6919
(800) 424-6423

DAYS INN
1900 S Trinity St
(76234)
Rates: $60-$105
(940) 627-2463
(800) 329-7466

**DECATUR MANOR
GUEST HOUSE**
500 W Walnut St
(76234)
Rates: $59-$99
(940) 627-3079

MOTEL 6
1600 S Hwy
81/287 (76234)
Rates: $39-$52
(940) 627-0250
(800) 466-8356

**PAINTED VALLEY
RANCH B&B**
1724 W Preskitt
Rd (76234)
Rates: $89-$129
(940) 627-8056
(888) 817-6377

DEER PARK
COMFORT SUITES
1501 Center St
(77536)
Rates: $69-$129
(281) 930-8888
(800) 424-6423

DEL RIO
**AMISTAD
LODGE MOTEL**
Hwy 90 W (78840)
Rates: $31+
(830) 775-8591

**ANGLER'S
LODGE MOTEL**
Hwy 90 W (78840)
Rates: $27+
(830) 775-1586

**BEST WESTERN
INN OF DEL RIO**
810 Veterans Blvd
(78840)
Rates: $59-$135
(830) 775-7511
(800) 528-1234
(800) 336-3537

COMFORT INN
3616 Veterans Blvd (78840)
Rates: $50-$88
(830) 775-2933
(800) 424-6423

DAYS INN
3808 Veterans Blvd (78840)
Rates: $49-$79
(830) 775-0585
(800) 329-7466

LA QUINTA INN
2005 Veterans Blvd (78840)
Rates: $63-$83
(830) 775-7591
(800) 687-6667

LAKEVIEW INN DIABLO EAST
Hwy 90 W, HCR 3, Box 38 (78840)
Rates: $29-$48
(830) 775-9521

MOTEL 6
2115 Veterans Blvd (78840)
Rates: $31-$49
(830) 774-2115
(800) 466-8356

RAMADA INN
2101 Veterans Blvd (78840)
Rates: $79-$105
(830) 775-1511
(800) 272-6232

ROUGH CANYON INN MOTEL
Hwy 277 N, RR 2 (78840)
Rates: $27+
(830) 774-6266

WESTERN MOTEL
1203 Ave F (78840)
Rates: $24-$56
(830) 774-4661

DENISON
HOLIDAY INN EXP
801 Hwy 75 N (75020)
Rates: n/a
(903) 464-0340
(800) 465-4329

MOTEL 6
615 N Hwy 75 (75020)
Rates: $37-$44
(903) 465-4446
(800) 466-8356

TEXOMA INN
1600 S Austin Ave (75021)
Rates: $39-$66
(903) 465-6800

DENTON
DESERT SANDS MOTOR INN
611 S I-35 E (76205)
Rates: $28-$50
(940) 387-6181

EXEL INN
4211 N I-35 E (76201)
Rates: $38-$65
(940) 383 1471
(800) 367-3935

THE HERITAGE INNS B&B
815 N Locust (76201)
Rates: $65-$135
(940) 565-6414
(888) 565-6414

HOLIDAY LODGE
1112 E University (76205)
Rates: $25-$31
(940) 382-9688

LA QUINTA INN
700 Fort Worth Dr (76201)
Rates: $66-$95
(940) 387-5840
(800) 687-6667

MOTEL 6
4125 N I-35 (76207)
Rates: $37-$56
(940) 566-4798
(800) 466-8356

RADISSON HOTEL & EAGLE POINT GOLF CLUB
2211 I-35E N (76205)
Rates: $129-$169
(940) 565-8499
(800) 333-3333

DIBOLL
BEST WESTERN INN
910 N Temple Dr (75941)
Rates: $56-$89
(936) 829-2055
(800) 528-1234

DONNA
HOWARD JOHNSON EXPRESS INN
602 N Victoria Rd (78537)
Rates: $72-$109
(956) 464-7801
(800) 446-4656

DUMAS
BEST WESTERN WINDSOR INN
1701 S Dumas Ave (79029)
Rates: $52-$89
(806) 935-9644
(800) 528-1234
(800) 661-7626

DUMAS INN MOTEL
1712 S Dumas Ave (79029)
Rates: $52-$80
(806) 935-6441
(800) 396-8831

ECONO LODGE OLD TOWN INN
1719 S Dumas Ave (79029)
Rates: $49-$96
(806) 935-9098
(800) 424-6423

HOLIDAY INN EXP
1525 S Dumas Ave (79029)
Rates: $69-$99
(806) 935-4000
(800) 465-4329

PHILLIPS MANOR MOTEL
1821 S Dumas Ave (79029)
Rates: $28-$44
(806) 935-9281

SUPER 8 MOTEL
119 W 17th (79029)
Rates: $59-$89
(806) 935-6222
(800) 800-8000

DUNCANVILLE
MOTEL 6
202 Jellison Rd (75116)
Rates: $35-$55
(972) 296-0345
(800) 466-8356

EAGLE LAKE
THE FARRIS 1912 INN
201 N McCarty St (77434)
Rates: $40-$95
(979) 234-2546

EAGLE PASS
BEST WESTERN EAGLE PASS
1923 Loop 431 (78852)
Rates: $84-$90
(830) 758-1234
(800) 992-3245

HOLIDAY INN EXP
2007 Loop 431 (78852)
Rates: $85-$99
(830) 757-3050
(800) 465-4329

HOLLY INN
2421 E Main St (78852)
Rates: $39-$44
(830) 773-9261
(800) 424-8125

LA QUINTA INN
2525 E Main St (78852)
Rates: $65-$86
(830) 773-7000
(800) 687-6667

SUPER 8 MOTEL
2150 N Hwy 277 (78852)
Rates: $50-$65
(830) 773-9531
(800) 272-9786

EARLY
POST OAK INN
606 Early Blvd (76802)
Rates: $55-$75
(325) 643-5621

EASTLAND
BUDGET HOST INN
2001 I-20 W (76448)
Rates: $38-$50
(254) 629-3324

RAMADA INN-DALLAS SW
711 E Camp Wisdom Rd (75116)
Rates: $59-$69
(972) 298-8911
(800) 272-6232

THE EASTLAND B&B
112 N Lamar St (76448)
Rates: $70-$135
(254) 629-8397

RAMADA INN
2501 I-20 East (76448)
Rates: $45-$65
(254) 629-2655
(800) 272-6232

SUPER 8 MOTEL
3900 I-20 E (76448)
Rates: $49-$79
(254) 629-3336
(800) 800-8000

EDINBURG
ECHO HOTEL
1903 S Closner Blvd (78539)
Rates: $47-$91
(800) 422-0336

LA COPA INN
1210 E Canton Rd (78539)
Rates: $49-$79
(956) 381-8888

SUPER 8 MOTEL
202 N Hwy 81 (78541)
Rates: $49-$79
(956) 381-1688

EL CAMPO
BEST WESTERN EXECUTIVE INN
1022 Hwy 59 W (77437)
Rates: $55-$120
(979) 543-7033
(800) 528-1234

EL CAMPO INN
210 W Hwy 59 (77437)
Rates: $37-$52
(979) 543-1110

EL PASO
AMERICANA INN
14387 Gateway Blvd W (79927)
Rates: $38-$52
(915) 852-3025

AMERISUITES-EL PASO AIRPORT
6030 Gateway Blvd E (79905)
Rates: $79-$115
(915) 771-0022
(800) 833-1516

AREA CODES - If the local number doesn't connect, check for a new area code.

BAYMONT INN
7620 N Mesa St
(79912)
Rates: $54-$79
(915) 585-2999
(800) 789-4103

BAYMONT INN
7944 Gateway
Blvd E (79915)
Rates: $54-$79
(915) 591-3300
(800) 789-4103

**BEST WESTERN
AIRPORT INN**
7144 Gateway
Blvd E (79915)
Rates: $59-$68
(915) 779-7700
(800) 295-7276

**BEST WESTERN
SUNLAND PARK
INN**
1045 Sunland Park
Dr (79922)
Rates: $54-$69
(915) 587-4900
(800) 528-1234

**BUDGET LODGE
MOTEL**
1301 N Mesa St
(79902)
Rates: $28-$38
(915) 533-6821

**CAMINO REAL
HOTEL**
101 S El Paso St
(79901)
Rates: $99-$170
(915) 534-3099
(800) 722-6466

**CHASE SUITES
BY WOODFIN**
6791 Montana Ave
(79925)
Rates: $95-$170
(915) 772-8000
(800) 237-8811

COMFORT INN
7651 N Mesa St
(79912)
Rates: $55-$94
(915) 845-1906
(800) 424-6423

**COMFORT INN
AIRPORT EAST**
900 N Yarborough
St (79915)
Rates: $45-$95
(915) 594-9111
(800) 424-6423
(800) 497-1347

COMFORT SUITES
949 Sunland Park
Dr (79922)
Rates: $69-$90
(915) 587-5300
(800) 424-6423

DAYS INN
5035 S Desert Blvd
(79932)
Rates: $70-$80
(915) 845-3500
(800) 329-7466

**ECONO LODGE
FORT BLISS**
6363 Montana St
(79925)
Rates: $50-$60
(915) 778-3311
(800) 424-6423

**EL PASO
RESIDENT INN**
6355 Gateway
Blvd W (79925)
Rates: $119-$129
(915) 771-0504

HAWTHORN INN
6789 Boeing St
(79925)
Rates: $120-$140
(915) 778-6789
(800) 527-1133

**HILTON-EL PASO
AIRPORT**
2027 Airway Blvd
(79925)
Rates: $114-$147
(915) 778-4241
(800) 445-8667
(800) 742-7248

**HOLIDAY INN
SUNLAND PARK**
900 Sunland Park
Dr (79922)
Rates: $92-$104
(915) 833-2900
(800) 465-4329
(800) 658-2744

**HOWARD
JOHNSON EXP**
500 Executive
Center Blvd
(79902)
Rates: $55-$86
(915) 532-8981
(800) 446-4656

**HOWARD
JOHNSON INN**
8887 Gateway
Blvd W (79925)
Rates: $60-$80
(915) 591-9471
(800) 446-4656

**LA QUINTA INN-
AIRPORT**
6140 Gateway
Blvd E (79905)
Rates: $63-$84
(915) 778-9321
(800) 687-6667

**LA QUINTA INN-
CIELO VISTA**
9125 Gateway
Blvd W (79925)
Rates: $60-$89
(915) 593-8400
(800) 687-6667

**LA QUINTA INN-
LOMALAND**
11033 Gateway
Blvd W (79935)
Rates: $46-$75
(915) 591-2244
(800) 687-6667

**LA QUINTA INN-
EL PASO WEST**
7550 Remcon Cir
(79912)
Rates: $63-$85
(915) 833-2522
(800) 687-6667

**MICROTEL INN &
SUITES AIRPORT**
2001 Airway Blvd
(79925)
Rates: $49-$93
(915) 772-3650
(888) 771-7171

MICROTEL INN
6185 Desert Blvd S
(79932)
Rates: $40-$60
(915) 584-2026
(888) 771-7171

**MICROTEL INN &
SUITES EAST**
1221 Gateway W
(79936)
Rates: $40-$66
(915) 858-1600
(888) 771-7171

MOTEL 6
1330 Lomaland Dr
(79935)
Rates: $34-$44
(915) 592-6386
(800) 466-8356

MOTEL 6-CENTRAL
4800 Gateway
Blvd E (79905)
Rates: $34-$39
(915) 533-7521
(800) 466-8356

**PEAR TREE
CORPORATE
APARTMENTS**
222 Bartlett
(79912)
Rates: $50-$85
(915) 833-7327

QUALITY INN
6099 Montana Ave
(79925)
Rates: $64-$89
(915) 772-3300
(800) 424-6423

**RED ROOF
INN EAST**
11400 Chito
Samaniego (79936)
Rates: $35-$45
(915) 599-8877
(800) 843-7663

**RED ROOF
INN WEST**
7530 Remcon Cir
(79912)
Rates: $36-$61
(915) 587-9977
(800) 843-7663

**RESIDENCE INN
BY MARRIOTT**
6355 Gateway
Blvd W (79925)
Rates: $122-$139
(915) 771-0504
(800) 331-3131

SLEEP INN
953 Sunland Park
Dr (79922)
Rates: $49-$94
(915) 585-7577
(800) 753-3746

STUDIO 6
11049 Gateway
Blvd W (79935)
Rates: $179-$239
(915) 594-8533
(888) 897-0202

TRAVELODGE
7815 N Mesa St
(79932)
Rates: $45-$70
(915) 833-2613
(800) 578-7878

**TRAVELODGE
HOTEL
CITY CENTER**
409 E Missouri St
(79901)
Rates: $45-$90
(915) 544-3333
(800) 578-7878

**TRAVELODGE
LA HACIENDA
AIRPORT**
6400 Montana Ave
(79925)
Rates: $37-$77
(915) 772-4231
(800) 578-7878

ELGIN
**RAGTIME RANCH
BED & BREAKFAST**
P. O. Box 575
(78621)
Rates: $95-$125
(800) 800-9743

ELMENDORF
**COMFORT INN
BRAUNIG LAKE**
13800 I-37 S
(78112)
Rates: $50-$89
(210) 633-1833
(800) 424-6423

ENNIS
QUALITY INN
107 Chamber of
Commerce Dr
(75119)
Rates: $59-$79
(972) 875-9641
(800) 424-6423

EULESS
DAYS INN
13954 Trinity Blvd
(76040)
Rates: $49-$129
(817) 399-9500
(800) 329-7466

**LA QUINTA INN-
DFW AIRPORT W**
1001 W Airport
Frwy (76040)
Rates: $60-$85
(817) 540-0233
(800) 687-6667

MICROTEL INN
901 W Airport
Frwy (76040)
Rates: $47-$70
(817) 545-1111
(888) 771-7171
(888) 545-1112

AREA CODES - If the local number doesn't connect, check for a new area code.

MOTEL 6
110 W Airport
Frwy (76039)
Rates: $35-$50
(817) 545-0141
(800) 466-8356

FAIRFIELD

REGENCY INN
903 W Hwy 84
(75840)
Rates: $38-$51
(903) 389-4440

FALFURRIAS

DAYS INN
2116 Hwy 281 S
(78355)
Rates: $52-$60
(361) 325-2515
(800) 329-7466

FARMERS BRANCH

BEST WESTERN DALLAS NORTH
13333 N
Stemmons Frwy
(75234)
Rates: $59-$104
(972) 241-8521
(800) 528-1234
(800) 308-4593

COMFORT INN
14040 Stemmons
Rd (75234)
Rates: $45-$129
(972) 406-3030
(800) 424-6423

DALLAS HOTEL PARK WEST
1590 LBJ Frwy
(75234)
Rates: $99-$209
(972) 869-4300

DAYS INN DALLAS NORTH
13313 N
Stemmons Frwy
(75234)
Rates: $39-$69
(972) 488-0800
(800) 329-7466

DOUBLETREE CLUB HOTEL
11611 Luna Rd
(75234)
Rates: $59-$149
(972) 506-0066
(800) 222-8733

LA QUINTA INN NORTHWEST
13235 N
Stemmons Frwy
(75234)
Rates: $50-$79
(972) 620-7333
(800) 687-6667

FLORESVILLE

BEST WESTERN FLORESVILLE INN
1720 S 10th St
(78114)
Rates: $59-$79
(830) 393-0443
(800) 528-1234
(800) 847-4364

FOREST HILL

COMFORT INN
3232 SE Loop 820
(76140)
Rates: $56-$99
(817) 551-5200
(800) 424-6423

FORNEY

FORNEY INN
103 W Hwy 80
(75126)
Rates: $50-$65
(972) 552-3888

FORT DAVIS

FORT DAVIS MOTOR INN
Hwy 17 N (79734)
Rates: $55-$65
(800) 80-DAVIS

HISTORIC LIMPIA HOTEL
100 Main St,
On the Town
Square (79734)
Rates: $79-$175
(432) 426-3237
(800) 662-5517

HISTORIAL PRUDE GUEST RANCH
Hwy 118 N
(79734)
Rates: $50-$75
(432) 426-3202

WILDFLOWER VACATION HOMES & COTTAGES
210 Webster Ave
(79734)
Rates: $75-$125
(800) 752-4145

FORT HANCOCK

FORT HANCOCK MOTEL
I-20, Exit 72
(79839)
Rates: $38-$52
(915) 769-3981

FORT STOCKTON

ATRIUM WEST INN HOTEL
1305 N Hwy 285
(79735)
Rates: $59-$129
(432) 336-6666

BEST WESTERN SWISS CLOCK INN
3201 W Dickinson
Blvd (79735)
Rates: $58-$99
(432) 336-8521
(800) 528-1234

BUDGET INN
801 E Dickinson
Blvd (79735)
Rates: $59-$99
(432) 336-3311

COMFORT INN
3200 W Dickinson
Blvd (79735)
Rates: $56-$85
(432) 336-8531
(800) 424-6423

DAYS INN
1408 N Hwy 285
(79735)
Rates: $46-$79
(432) 336-7500
(800) 329-7466

ECONO LODGE
800 E Dickinson
Blvd (79735)
Rates: $39-$79
(432) 336-9711
(800) 424-6423

HOLIDAY INN EXP
1308 N Hwy 285
(79735)
Rates: $58-$95
(432) 336-5955
(800) 465-4329

LA QUINTA INN
1537 N Hwy 285
(79735)
Rates: $53-$68
(432) 336-9781
(800) 687-6667

MOTEL 6
3001 W Dickinson
Blvd (79735)
Rates: $31-$34
(432) 336-9737
(800) 466-8356

SANDS MOTEL
1801 W Dickinson
Blvd (79735)
Rates: $26-$30
(432) 336-2274

TOWN & COUNTRY MOTEL
1505 W Dickinson
Blvd (97935)
Rates: $21-$30
(432) 336-2651

FORT WORTH

AMERISUITES CITY VIEW
5900 City View
Blvd (76132)
Rates: $105-$115
(817) 361-9797
(800) 833-1516

THE ASHTON HOTEL
610 Main St
(76102)
Rates: $250-$770
(817) 332-0100

BEST WESTERN INN
6700 Fossil Bluff
Dr (76137)
Rates: $59-$89
(817) 847-8484
(800) 528-1234

BEST WESTERN INN & SUITES
2000 Beach St
(76103)
Rates: $62-$119
(817) 534-4801
(800) 528-1234

CANDLEWOOD SUITES
5201 Endicott Ave
(76137)
Rates: $69-$99
(817) 838-8229
(800) 465-4329

CARAVAN MOTOR HOTEL
2601 Jacksboro
Hwy (76114)
Rates: $33-$42
(817) 626-1951

CLARION HOTEL
600 Commerce St
(76102)
Rates: $89-$129
(817) 332-6900
(800) 424-6423

COMFORT INN
2425 Scott Ave
(76103)
Rates: $47-$69
(817) 535-2591
(800) 424-6423

COMFORT INN NORTH
4850 North Frwy
(76137)
Rates: $49-$99
(817) 834-4001
(800) 424-6423

COMFORT SUITES NORTH
3751 Tanacross Dr
(76137)
Rates: $69-$179
(817) 222-2333
(800) 424-6423

DAYS INN
4213 S I-35 W
Fwy (76115)
Rates: $40-$65
(817) 923-1987
(800) 329-7466

DAYS INN
1551 University
Dr (76107)
Rates: $45-$65
(817) 336-9823
(800) 329-7466

DAYS INN WEST
8500 I-30 & Las
Vegas Tr (76108)
Rates: $32-$59
(817) 246-4961
(800) 329-7466

GREEN OAKS INN & CONF CENTER
6901 W Frwy
(76116)
Rates: $61-$98
(817) 738-7311
(800) 433-2174
(800) 772-7341

HAMPTON INN
13600 North Frwy
(76178)
Rates: $79
(817) 439-0400
(800) 426-7868

AREA CODES - If the local number doesn't connect, check for a new area code.

HAMPTON INN WEST
2700 Cherry Ln (76116)
Rates: $72-$99
(817) 560-4180
(800) 426-7866

HOLIDAY INN
100 Altamesa Blvd E (76134)
Rates: $70-$100
(817) 293-3088
(800) 465-4329

HOLIDAY INN NORTH
2540 Meacham Blvd (76106)
Rates: $69-$199
(817) 625-9911
(800) 465-4329

HOLIDAY INN EXP HOTEL & SUITES
4609 City Lake Blvd W (76109)
Rates: $74-$164
(817) 292-4900
(800) 465-4329

HOLIDAY INN EXP HOTEL & SUITES-W
2730 Cherry Ln (76116)
Rates: $89-$129
(817) 560-4200
(800) 465-4329

HOMESTEAD STUDIO SUITES
1601 River Run (76107)
Rates: $59-$74
(817) 338-4808
(888) 782-9473

LA QUINTA INN & SUITES NORTH
4700 North Frwy (76137)
Rates: $80-$106
(817) 222-2888
(800) 687-6667

LA QUINTA INN & SUITES-SOUTHWEST
4900 Bryant Irvin Rd (76132)
Rates: $90-$116
(817) 370-2700
(800) 687-6667

LA QUINTA INN-MEDICAL CENTER
7888 I-30 W (76108)
Rates: $66-$80
(817) 246-5511
(800) 687-6667

MD RESORT BED & BREAKFAST
601 Old Base Rd (76078)
Rates: $79-$350
(817) 489-5150

MICROTEL INN
3740 Tanacross Dr (76137)
Rates: $59-$89
(817) 222-3740
(888) 771-7171

MOTEL 6-EAST
1236 Oakland Blvd (76103)
Rates: $38-$56
(817) 834-7361
(800) 466-8356

MOTEL 6-NORTH
3271 W I-35 (76106)
Rates: $38-$56
(817) 625-4359
(800) 466-8356

MOTEL 6-SOUTH
6600 S Frwy (76134)
Rates: $38-$56
(817) 293-8595
(800) 466-8356

MOTEL 6-WEST
8701 W I-30 (76116)
Rates: $35-$51
(817) 244-9740
(800) 466-8356

RAMADA INN-MIDTOWN
1401 S University Dr (76107)
Rates: $57-$80
(817) 336-9311
(800) 272-6232

RENAISSANCE WORTHINGTON HOTEL
200 Main St (76102)
Rates: $142-$225
(817) 870-1000
(800) 468-3571
(800) 433-5677

RESIDENCE INN BY MARRIOTT
1701 S University Dr (76107)
Rates: $138-$179
(817) 870-1011
(800) 331-3131

RESIDENCE INN-ALLIANCE AIRPORT
13400 North Frwy (76177)
Rates: $69-$250
(817) 750-7000
(800) 331-3131

RESIDENCE INN-FOSSIL CREEK
5801 Sandshell (76137)
Rates: $69-$114
(817) 439-1300
(800) 331-3131

STOCKYARDS HOTEL
109 E Exchange Ave (76106)
Rates: $89-$360
(817) 625-6427
(800) 423-8471

TOWNEPLACE SUITES BY MARRIOTT
4200 International Plaza Dr (76109)
Rates: $67-$109
(817) 732-2224
(800) 257-3000

FREDERICKS-BURG

ALFRED HAUS B&B
231 W Main St (78624)
Rates: $74+
(830) 997-5612
(866) 427-8374

BE MY GUEST LODGING SVS
110 N Milam (78624)
Rates: $61-$135
(830) 997-7227
(800) 314-8555

BECKERS B & B & BICYCLES
404 W Hackberry St (78624)
Rates: $75-$85
(830) 990-9157

BEST WESTERN
324 E Highway St (78624)
Rates: $79-$135
(830) 992-2929
(888) 908-2929

BUDGET HOST DELUXE INN
901 E Main St (78624)
Rates: $45-$79
(830) 997-3344

COMFORT INN
908 S Adams St (78624)
Rates: $75-$90
(830) 997-9811
(800) 424-6423

COMFORT INN
723 S Washington St (78624)
Rates: $90-$95
(830) 990-2552
(800) 424-6423

COUNTRY INN MOTEL
Hwy 290 W (78624)
Rates: $38-$62
(830) 997-2185

DAS KEIDEL INN B&B
Main St (78624)
Rates: $98-$195
(830) 997-5612
(866) 427-8374

DIETZEL MOTEL
1141 W Hwy 290 (78624)
Rates: $45-$79
(830) 997-3330

FIRST CLASS B&B RESERVATION SVS
909 E Main St (78624)
Rates: $75-$195
(888) 991-6749

FRONTIER INN
1704 US Hwy 290 West (78624)
Rates: $46-$150
(830) 997-4389

THE FULL MOON INN B&B
3234 Luckenbach Rd (78624)
Rates: $150-$200
(830) 997-2205
(800) 997-1124

THE GARDEN HOUSE B & B
104 N Adams St (78624)
Rates: $69
(830) 990-8455
(800) 745-3591

HOFFMAN HAUS GUESTHOUSE
608 E Creek St (78624)
Rates: $120-$190
(830) 997-6739
(800) 899-1672

HOLIDAY INN EXP
1220 N Hwy 87 (78624)
Rates: $84-$109
(830) 990-4200
(800) 465-4329

HOME ON THE RANGE B&B AT STONEWALL VALLEY RANCH
7490 Ranch Rd 2721 (78624)
Rates: $95-$60
(800) 460-2380

MILLERS INN MOTEL
910 E Main St (78624)
Rates: $35-$85
(830) 997-2244

MISS TOODLES INN B&B
104 N Adams St (78624)
Rates: $115+
(830) 990-8455
(800) 745-3591

PEACH TREE INN
401 S Washington (78624)
Rates: $40-$100
(830) 997-2117
(800) 843-4666

QUALITY INN
908 S Adams St (78624)
Rates: $64-$99
(830) 997-9811
(800) 424-6423

ROCK HOUSE ON ACORN B&B
231 W Main St (78624)
Rates: $85+
(830) 997-5612
(866) 427-8374

AREA CODES - If the local number doesn't connect, check for a new area code.

ROCKY TOP
BED & BREAKFAST
7910 Ranch Rd
965 (78624)
Rates: $85
(830) 997-8145

SCHMIDT BARN
BED & BREAKFAST
231 W Main St
(78624)
Rates: $65-$140
(830) 997-5612
(866) 427-8374

SETTLERS
CROSSING
HISTORIC GUEST
HOUSES
104 Settlers
Crossing Rd
(78624)
Rates: $90-$125
(830) 997-2722
(800) 874-1020

STONEWALL
VALLEY
RANCH HOUSE
104 N Adams St
(78624)
Rates: $85
(830) 990-8455
(800) 745-3591

STRACKBEIN-
ROEDER
SUNDAY HAUS
BED & BREAKFAST
231 W Main St
(78624)
Rates: $100+
(830) 997-5612
(866) 427-8374

SUNDAY HOUSE
INN & SUITES
501 E Main St
(78624)
Rates: $69-$150
(830) 997-4484
(800) 274-3762

SUNSET INN
900 S Adams St
(78624)
Rates: $54-$69
(830) 997-9581

SUPER 8 MOTEL
514 E Main St
(78624)
Rates: $59-$110
(830) 997-6568
(800) 800-8000
(877) 776-7283

WEST MAIN HAUS
BED & BREAKFAST
231 W Main St
(78624)
Rates: $75+
(830) 997-5612
(866) 427-8374

WOLF CREEK
BARN B&B
231 W Main St
(78624)
Rates: $98+
(830) 997-5612
(866) 427-8374

FREEPORT

ANCHOR MOTEL
1302 Bluewater
Hwy (77541)
Rates: $35-$55
(979) 239-3543

BEACH RESORT
SERVICES-
RENTALS
409 E Hwy 332,
#2 (77541)
Rates: $75-$350
(800) 382-9283

COUNTRY
HEARTH INN
1015 W 2nd St
(77541)
Rates: n/a
(979) 39-1602

FRISCO

WESTIN STONE-
BRIAR RESORT
1549 Legacy Dr
(75034)
Rates: $119-$329
(972) 668-8000
(800) 228-3000

FULTON

BAY FRONT
COTTAGES
309 S Fulton
Beach Rd (78382)
Rates: $45-$54
(361) 729-6693

BEST WESTERN
INN BY THE BAY
3902 N Hwy 35
(78358)
Rates: $80-$95
(361) 729-8351
(800) 528-1234
(800) 235-6076

HARBOR LIGHTS
COTTAGES
108 Laurel (78358)
Rates: $45+
(361) 729-6770

INN AT FULTON
HARBOR
215 N Fulton
Beach Rd (78358)
Rates: $94-$119
(866) 301-5111

PELICAN BAY
RESORT
4206 N Hwy 35
(78358)
Rates: $69-$275
(866) 729-7177

GAINESVILLE

BEST WESTERN
SOUTHWINDS
2103 I-35 N
(76240)
Rates: $49-$79
(940) 665-7737
(800) 731-1501

BUDGET
HOST INN
1900 I-35 N
(76240)
Rates: $40
(940) 665-2856
(800) 283-4678

DELUXE INN/
SUPER 8
1936 I-35 N (76240)
Rates: $54-$61
(940) 665-5599
(800) 800-8000

RAMADA LIMITED
600 Fair Park Blvd
(76240)
Rates: $59-$119
(940) 665-8800
(800) 272-6232

GALVESTON

AVENUE O BED
& BREAKFAST
2323 Ave O (77550)
Rates: $85-$145
(866) 762-2868

COTTAGE BY THE
BEACH RENTAL
810 Ave L (77550)
Rates: $90-$250
per night/
$500+ weekly/
$900 monthly
(409) 770-9332

ECONO LODGE
3924 Ave U (77550)
Rates: $40-$200
(409) 750-9400
(800) 424-6423

GALVESTON-
APTS.COM
1811 Moody (21st)
#5 (77550)
Rates: $40-$125
(409) 765-6916

LA QUINTA INN
1402 Seawall Blvd
(77550)
Rates: $70-$199
(409) 763-1224
(800) 687-6667

THE MAGNOLIA
HOUSE-VACA-
TION RENTAL
812 Ave L (77550)
Rates: $120-$195
per night/
$800-$1600
monthly
(409) 770-9332

MOTEL 6
7404 Ave J -
Broadway (77554)
Rates: $33-$69
(409) 740-3794
(800) 466-8356

GARLAND

BEST WESTERN
LAKEVIEW INN
1635 E I-30 at
Chaha Rd (75043)
Rates: $49-$89
(972) 303-1601
(800) 276-7462

COMFORT INN
12670 E Northwest
Hwy (75228)
Rates: $45-$53
(972) 613-5000
(800) 424-6423

DAYS INN
6222 Broadway
Blvd (75043)
Rates: $40-$49
(972) 226-7621
(800) 329-7466

HOLIDAY INN
SELECT
11350 LBJ Frwy
(75238)
Rates: $89-$109
(214) 341-5400
(800) 465-4329

LA QUINTA INN
NORTHEAST
12721 I-635 (75041)
Rates: $60-$86
(972) 271-7581
(800) 687-6667

MICROTEL INN
1901 Pendleton Dr
(75041)
Rates: $40-$85
(972) 270-7200
(888) 771-7171

MOTEL 6
436 W I-30 &
Beltline (75043)
Rates: $33-$53
(972) 226-7140
(800) 466-8356

GATESVILLE

BEST WESTERN
CHATEAU VILLE
MOTOR INN
2501 E Main St
(76528)
Rates: $49-$69
(254) 865-2281
(800) 528-1234
(888) 451-4521

KEENER
HOUSE BED
& BREAKFAST
1308 W Main
(76528)
Rates: $60-$70
(254) 865-6476

GEORGE WEST

BEST WESTERN
EXECUTIVE INN
208 N Nueces St
(78022)
Rates: $65-$90
(361) 449-3300
(800) 528-1234

GEORGETOWN

COMFORT INN
1005 Leander Rd
(78628)
Rates: $54-$89
(512) 863-7504
(800) 424-6423

HOLIDAY INN EXP
HOTEL & SUITES
600 San Gabriel
Village Blvd
(78628)
Rates: n/a
(512) 868-8555
(800) 465-4329

AREA CODES - If the local number doesn't connect, check for a new area code.

LA QUINTA INN
333 I-35 N
(78628)
Rates: $60-$86
(512) 869-2541
(800) 687-6667

GIDDINGS

RAMADA LIMITED
4002 E Austin St
(78942)
Rates: $75-$85
(979) 542-9666
(800) 272-6232

SANDS MOTEL
1600 E Austin
(78942)
Rates: $37-$50
(979) 542-3111

SUPER 8 MOTEL
3556 E Austin
(78942)
Rates: $44-$61
(979) 542-5791
(800) 800-8000

GILMER

EXECUTIVE INN
1200 Hwy 271 S
(75644)
Rates: $55-$80
(903) 843-6099

GLEN ROSE

BEST WESTERN DINOSAUR VALLEY INN
1311 NE Big
Bend Trail (76043)
Rates: $85-$375
(254) 897-4818
(800) 528-1234

COUNTRY WOODS INN B&B
420 Grand Ave
(76043)
Rates: $90-$150
(254) 279-3002
(888) 849-6637

GLEN HOTEL
201 Barnard St
(76043)
Rates: $35-$60
(254) 897-2420

GLEN ROSE INN
300 SW Big Bend
Trail (76043)
Rates: $49-$99
(800) 577-2540

THE HAYLOFT B&B AT ROLLING ROCK RANCH
County Rd 2009
(76043)
Rates: n/a
(254) 897-3094

HIDEAWAY COUNTRY LOG CABIN B & B
P. O. Box 430
(76043)
Rates: $95-$140
(254) 823-6606

QUAIL RIDGE RANCH B&B
P. O. Box 900
(76043)
Rates: $195-$350
(866) 897-3618

ROUGH CREEK LODGE EXECUTIVE RETREAT/RESORT
P O Box 2400
(76043)
Rates: $199-$1200
(800) 864-4705

TRES RIOS RIVER RESORT
2322 CR 312 (76043)
Rates: $56-$175
(254) 897-4253
(888) 4-CAMPRV

GONZALES

BOOTH HOUSE B & B
706 St. George St
(78629)
Rates: $85-$140
(830) 672-7509

LUXURY INN
1804 Sarah DeWitt
Dr (78629)
Rates: $50-$93
(830) 672-9611

GRAHAM

GATEWAY INN
1401 Hwy 16 S
(76450)
Rates: $38-$45
(940) 549-0222

RODEWAY INN
1919 Hwy 16 S
(76450)
Rates: $49-$65
(940) 549-8320
(800) 424-6423

GRANBURY

COMFORT INN
1201 Plaza Dr N
(76048)
Rates: $70-$190
(817) 573-2611
(800) 424-6423

DAYS INN
1339 N Plaza Dr
(76048)
Rates: $49-$99
(817) 573-2691
(800) 329-7466
(800) 858-8607 (TX)

PLANTATION INN ON THE LAKE
1451 E Pearl St
(76048)
Rates: $60-$95
(817) 573-8846
(800) 422-2402

THE BAKER-CARMICHAEL HOUSE SOUTHERN COUNTRY INN
226 E Pearl St
(76048)
Rates: $89-$149
(866) 476-8631

GRAND PRAIRIE

AMERISUITES
1542 N Hwy 360
(75050)
Rates: $109-$119
(972) 988-6800
(800) 833-1516

BUDGET SUITES OF AMERICA
2270 N Hwy 360
(75050)
Rates: $59-$99
(877) 822-5272

DAYS INN
2615 Sara Jane
Pkwy (75050)
Rates: $54-$145
(972) 623-1998
(800) 329-7466

HOWARD JOHNSON EXPRESS INN
1114 E Main St
(75050)
Rates: $45-$65
(800) 446-4656

LA QUINTA INN SIX FLAGS
1410 NW 19th St
(75050)
Rates: $60-$95
(972) 641-3021
(800) 687-6667

MOTEL 6
406 E Safari Pkwy
(75050)
Rates: $29-$53
(972) 642-9424
(800) 466-8356

QUALITY INN
3891 S Great
Southwest Pkwy
(75052)
Rates: $55-$85
(972) 602-9400
(800) 424-6423

GRAPEVINE

AMERISUITES-DFW AIRPORT N
2220 Grapevine
Mills Circle W
(76051)
Rates: $89-$119
(972) 691-1199
(800) 833-1516

BAYMONT INN DFW AIRPORT N
301 Capital St
(76051)
Rates: $79-$89
(817) 329-9300
(877) 229-6668

EMBASSY SUITES OUTDOOR WORLD
2401 Bass Pro Dr
(76051)
Rates: $109-$229
(972) 724-2600
(800) 362-2779

HOMEWOOD SUITES
2214 Grapevine
Mills Circle W
(76051)
Rates: $125-$134
(972) 691-2427
(800) 225-5466

SUPER 8 MOTEL
250 E Hwy 114
(76051)
Rates: $59-$79
(972) 329-7222
(800) 800-8000

GREENVILLE

AMERICAN INN
I-30 & US 69
(75401)
Rates: $30-$45
(903) 455-9600

BEST WESTERN INN & SUITES
1216 I-30 W
(75402)
Rates: $64-$74
(903) 454-1792
(800) 528-1234
(800) 795-2300

HOLIDAY INN EXP HOTEL & SUITES
2901 Mustang
Crossing (75402)
Rates: $89-$125
(903) 454-8680
(800) 465-4329

MOTEL 6
5109 I-30 & US 69
(75402)
Rates: $34-$52
(903) 455-0515
(800) 466-8356

SUPER 8 MOTEL
5010 Hwy 69 S
(75402)
Rates: $48-$69
(903) 454-3736
(800) 800-8000

GROVES

MOTEL 6
5201 E Pkwy
(77619)
Rates: $29-$35
(409) 962-6611
(800) 466-8356

HALLETTSVILLE

AUNT CAROL'S BED & BREAKFST
749 CR 244
(77964)
Rates: $65-$75
(361) 798-4674
(888) 556-6582

HAMILTON

HAMILTON GUEST HOTEL B&B
109 N Rice (76351)
Rates: $49-$79
(254) 386-8977
(800) 876-2502

AREA CODES - If the local number doesn't connect, check for a new area code.

VALUE LODGE INN MOTEL
Rt 3, Box 319
(76351)
Rates: $25-$40
(254) 386-8959

WESTERN MOTEL
1208 S Rice St
(76351)
Rates: $31-$37
(254) 386-3141

HARLINGEN

COMFORT INN
406 N Expressway
77 (78552)
Rates: $53-$120
(956) 412-7771
(800) 424-6423

COUNTRY INN
3825 S Expressway
83 (78550)
Rates: $59-$120
(956) 428-0043
(800) 456-4000

HOWARD JOHNSON INN
6779 W Expressway
83 (78552)
Rates: $55-$67
(956) 425-7070
(800) 446-4656

LA QUINTA INN
1002 S Expressway
83 (78552)
Rates: $75-$101
(956) 428-6888
(800) 687-6667

MOTEL 6
205 N Expressway
77 (78550)
Rates: $42-$50
(956) 423-9292
(800) 466-8356

SUPER 8 MOTEL
1115 S Expressway
83
(78550)
Rates: $45-$59
(956) 412-8873
(800) 800-8000

HASKELL

BEVERS HOUSE BED & BREAKFAST
311 N Ave F
(79521)
Rates: $60-$85
(940) 864-3284
(800) 580-3284

HEARNE

EXECUTIVE INN
Hwy 6 at FM 485
(77859)
Rates: $45-$69
(979) 279-5345

OAK TREE INN
1051 N Market St
(77859)
Rates: $75-$125
(979) 279-5599

HEBBRONVILLE

EXECUTIVE INN
1302 N Smith
(78361)
Rates: $45-$69
(361) 527-4082
(800) 870-7689

HENDERSON

BEST WESTERN INN
1500 Hwy 259 S
(75652)
Rates: $65-$85
(903) 657-9561
(800) 528-1234

HEREFORD

BEST WESTERN RED CARPET INN
830 W 1st St (79045)
Rates: $60-$75
(806) 364-0540
(800) 528-1234

HOIDAY INN EXP
1400 W 1st St (79045)
Rates: n/a
(806) 364-3322
(800) 465-4329

HILLSBORO

BEST WESTERN HILLSBORO INN
307 I-35 (76645)
Rates: $59-$71
(254) 582-8465
(800) 528-1234

DAYS INN
I-35 & Hwy 22
(76645)
Rates: $41-$65
(254) 582-3493
(800) 329-7466

MOTEL 6
1506 Hillview Dr
(76645)
Rates: $43-$57
(254) 580-9000
(800) 466-8356

HONDO

HONDO EXECUTIVE INN
102 E 19th St
(78861)
Rates: $35-$65
(830) 426-2535

WHITETAIL LODGE
401 Hwy 90 E
(78861)
Rates: $45-$86
(830) 426-3031
(800) 375-4065

HORSESHOE BAY

MARRIOTT HORSESHOE BAY RESORT
200 Hi Circle
North (78657)
Rates: $99-$159
(512) 404-6939
(800) 228-9290

HOUSTON

AMERICAS INN
10552 Southwest
Frwy (77074)
Rates: $46-$50
(713) 270-9559

AMERISUITES HOBBY AIRPORT
7922 Mosley Rd
(77061)
Rates: $99-$109
(713) 943-1713
(800) 833-1516

AMERISUITES-HOUSTON AIR-PORT
300 Ronan Park Pl
(77060)
Rates: $109-$129
(281) 820-6060
(800) 833-1516

BAYMONT INN
12701 North Frwy
(77060)
Rates: $59-$71
(281) 875-2000
(800) 301-0200

BAYMONT INN & SUITES-NW
11130 NW Frwy
(77092)
Rates: $64-$79
(713) 680-8282
(800) 301-0200

BAYMONT INN & SUITES-SW
6790 SW Frwy
(77074)
Rates: $59-$84
(713) 784-3838
(800) 301-0200

BEST WESTERN GREENWAY PLAZA INN
2929 SW Freeway
(77098)
Rates: $59-$89
(713) 528-6161
(800) 528-1234

BEST WESTERN PARK PLACE SUITES-HOUSTON MEDICAL
1400 Old Spanish
Trail (77054)
Rates: $89-$189
(713) 796-1000
(800) 528-1234

BEST WESTERN WINDSOR SUITES
13371 FM 1960 W
(77065)
Rates: $79-$135
(800) 528-1234

CANDLEWOOD SUITES-CLEAR LAKE
2737 Bay Area
Blvd (77058)
Rates: $49-$136
(281) 461-3060
(888) 226-3539

CANDLEWOOD SUITES-GALLERIA
4900 Loop Central
Dr (77081)
Rates: $129-$159
(713) 839-9411
(888) 226-3539

CANDLEWOOD SUITES-TOWN & COUNTRY
10503 Town &
Country Way
(77024)
Rates: $87-$101
(713) 464-2677
(888) 226-3539

CANDLEWOOD SUITES-WESTCHASE
4033 W Sam
Houston Pkwy S
(77042)
Rates: $49-$109
(713) 780-7881
(800) 226-3539

CHAMPIONS LODGE MOTEL
4726 FM 1960 W
(77069)
Rates: $42-$57
(281) 587-9171

CLARION HOTEL
1301 NASA Rd
One (77058)
Rates: $59-$99
(281) 488-0220
(800) 424-6423

COMFORT INN DOWNTOWN
5820 Katy Frwy
(77007)
Rates: $49-$189
(713) 869-9211
(800) 424-6423

COMFORT INN GALLERIA-WESTCHASE
9041 Westheimer
Rd (77063)
Rates: $69-$89
(713) 783-1400
(800) 424-6423

COMFORT INN WEST/ENERGY CORRIDOR
715 SR 6 S (77079)
Rates: $79-$169
(281) 493-0444
(800) 424-6423

COMFORT SUITES GALLERIA
6221 Richmond
Ave (77057
Rates: $99-$206
(713) 787-0004
(800) 424-6423

COMFORT SUITES NORTH
150 Overland Tr
(77090)
Rates: $59-$149
(281) 440-4448
(800) 424-6423

CROWNE PLAZA HOTEL/RESORT-BROOKHOLLOW
12801 Northwest
Frwy (77040)
Rates: $149
(713) 462-9977
(800) 227-6963

DAYS INN
9353 Katy Frwy
(77024)
Rates: $44-$59
(713) 467-4411
(800) 329-7466

DAYS INN-NORTH
9025 N Frwy
(77037)
Rates: $44-$55
(281) 820-1500
(800) 329-7466

DAYS INN
1303 NASA Road
One (77058)
Rates: $59-$89
(281) 286-0434
(800) 329-7466

DAYS INN
7887 W Tidwell
(77040)
Rates: n/a
(713) 690-1493
(800) 329-7466

**DAYS INN
INTERCON-
TINENTAL
AIRPORT**
12500 N I-45
(77060)
Rates: $42-$64
(281) 876-3888
(800) 329-7466

**DOUBLETREE
GUEST SUITES**
5353 Westheimer
Rd (77056)
Rates: $89-$239
(713) 961-9000
(800) 222-8733
(800) 772-7666

**DOUBLETREE
HOTEL AT ALLEN
CENTER**
400 Dallas St
(77002)
Rates: $139-$339
(713) 759-0202
(800) 222-8733
(800) 772-7666

**DRURY INN-
GALLERIA**
1615 W Loop 610
S (77027)
Rates: $105-$120
(713) 963-0700
(800) 378-7946

**DRURY INN
HOUSTON
HOBBY**
7902 Mosley Rd
(77017)
Rates: $81-$111
(713) 941-4300
(800) 378-7946

**DRURY INN
I-10 WEST**
1000 N Hwy 6
(77079)
Rates: $72-$106
(281) 558-7007
(800) 378-7946

**EXECUTIVE INN
& SUITES-HOBBY
AIRPORT**
6711 Telephone Rd
(77061)
Rates: $45-$180
(713) 645-7666
(866) 888-1755

**FOUR SEASONS
HOTEL**
1300 Lamar St
(77010)
Rates: $295-$350
(713) 650-1300
(800) 332-3442

**GRANTS PALM
COURT INN**
8200 S Main St
(77025)
Rates: $55-$75
(713) 668-8000
(800) 255-8904

**GUESTHOUSE
INN-ASTRODOME**
2364 South Loop
W (77054)
Rates: $68-$93
(713) 799-2436

**HAMPTON INN
I-10 EAST**
828 Mercury Dr
(77013)
Rates: $69-$92
(713) 673-4200
(800) 426-7866

**HEARTHSIDE
SUITES BY
VILLAGER**
12925 Northwest
Frwy (77040)
Rates: $59-$99
(713) 895-8888

**HEARTHSIDE
SUITES BY
VILLAGER**
15385 Katy Frwy
(77094)
Rates: $59-$99
(281) 398-6500

**HILTON HOTEL-
AMERICAS/
DOWNTOWN**
1600 Lamar St
(77010)
Rates: $159-$404
(800) 236-2905

HOLIDAY INN
18818 Tomball
Pkwy (77070)
Rates: n/a
(281) 970-4888
(800) 465-4329

HOLIDAY INN
14996 NW Frwy
(77040)
Rates: n/a
(713) 939-9955
(800) 465-4329

**HOLIDAY INN EXP
HOTEL & SUITES**
8080 Main St
(77025)
Rates: n/a
(713) 665-4439
(800) 465-4329

**HOLIDAY INN EXP
HOTEL & SUITES-
INTERCONTINENTAL**
1330 N Sam
Houston Pkwy
(77032)
Rates: $89-$109
(281) 372-1000
(800) 465-4329

**HOLIDAY INN-
GALLERIA**
7787 Katy Frwy
(77024)
Rates: $119-$139
(713) 681-5000
(800) 465-4329

**HOLIDAY INN
HOUSTON
AIRPORT**
15222 JFK Blvd
(77032)
Rates: $79-$159
(281) 449-2311
(800) 465-4329

**HOLIDAY INN-
NASA/
CLEAR LAKE**
1300 NASA Pkwy
(77058)
Rates: $69-$159
(800) 682-3193

**HOLIDAY INN
SELECT GREEN-
WAY PLAZA**
2712 Southwest
Frwy (77098)
Rates: $65-$160
(713) 523-8448
(800) 465-4329

**HOLIDAY INN EXP
HOTEL & SUITES-W**
10137 North Frwy
(77037)
Rates: $71-$80
(832) 554-5000
(800) 465-4329

**HOLIDAY INN
SELECT WEST**
14703 Park Row
(77079)
Rates: $130-$188
(281) 558-5580
(800) 465-4329

**HOMESTEAD
STUDIO SUITES-
GALLERIA**
2300 W Loop S
(77092)
Rates: $69-$89
(713) 960-9660
(888) 782-9473

**HOMESTEAD
STUDIO SUITES-
MEDICAL CENTER**
7979 Fannin St
(77054)
Rates: $53-$78
(713) 797-0000
(888) 782-9473

**HOMESTEAD
STUDIO SUITES-
WILLOWBROOK**
13223 Champions
Center Dr (77069)
Rates: $45-$64
(281) 397-9922
(888) 782-9473

**HOMEWOOD
SUITES**
401 Bay Area Blvd
(77058)
Rates: $139-$189
(281) 486-7677
(800) 225-5466

**HOMEWOOD
SUITES
WESTCHASE**
2424 Rogerdale
Rd (77042)
Rates: $112-$124
(713) 334-2424
(800) 225-5466

**HOMEWOOD
SUITES HOTEL-
WILLOWBROOK**
7655 W FM 1960
(77070)
Rates: $119-$169
(281) 955-5200
(800) 225-5466

HOTEL DEREK
2525 W Loop S
(77027)
Rates: $90+
(713) 961-3000

HOTEL SOFITEL
425 N Sam
Houston Pkwy E
(77060)
Rates: $89-$209
(281) 445-9000

**HOWARD
JOHNSON EXP**
9604 S Main St
(77025)
Rates: $49-$96
(800) 446-4656

**HOWARD JOHN-
SON EXP INN**
6 N Sam Houston
Pkwy E (77060)
Rates: $50-$60
(281) 447-6888
(800) 446-4656

**INTER-
CONTINENTAL
HOUSTON**
2222 W Loop S
(77027)
Rates: $259-$515
(713) 627-7600
(800) 424-6835

**INTERSTATE
MOTOR LODGE**
13213 I-10 E
(77015)
Rates: $42-$47
(713) 453-6353

**LA QUINTA INN-
ASTRODOME**
9911 Buffalo
Speedway (77054)
Rates: $70-$107
(713) 668-8082
(800) 687-6667

AREA CODES - If the local number doesn't connect, check for a new area code.

LA QUINTA INN-BROOKHOLLOW
11002 Northwest Frwy (77092)
Rates: $60-$81
(713) 688-2581
(800) 687-6667

LA QUINTA INN-CYFAIR
13290 FM 1960W (77065)
Rates: $70-$93
(281) 469-4018
(800) 687-6667

LA QUINTA INN GREENWAY PLAZA
4015 Southwest Frwy (77027)
Rates: $70-$100
(713) 623-4750
(800) 687-6667

LA QUINTA INN HOBBY AIRPORT
9902 Gulf Frwy (77034)
Rates: $65-$82
(713) 941-0900
(800) 687-6667

LA QUINTA INN-EAST
11999 E Frwy (77029)
Rates: $60-$80
(713) 453-5425
(800) 687-6667

LA QUINTA INN-LOOP 1960
17111 N Frwy (77090)
Rates: $60-$82
(281) 444-7500
(800) 687-6667

LA QUINTA INN & SUITES-BUSH AIRPORT
15510 JFK Blvd (77032)
Rates: $100-$130
(281) 219-2000
(800) 687-6667

LA QUINTA INN & SUITES-GALLERIA
1625 W Loop S (77027)
Rates: $70-$150
(713) 355-3440
(800) 687-6667

LA QUINTA INN & SUITES-NORTH
10137 North Frwy (77037)
Rates: $79-$99
(800) 687-6667

LA QUINTA INN & SUITES-PARK 10
15225 Katy Frwy (77094)
Rates: $80-$110
(281) 646-9200
(800) 687-6667

LA QUINTA INN-WILCREST
11113 Katy Frwy (77079)
Rates: $60-$80
(713) 932-0808
(800) 687-6667

LA QUINTA INN-WIRT RD
8017 Katy Frwy (77024)
Rates: $63-$87
(713) 688-8941
(800) 687-6667

LANCASTER HISTORIC HOTEL
701 Texas at Louisiana (77002)
Rates: $200-$350
(713) 228-9500
(800) 231-0336

THE LOVETT INN HISTORIC B&B
501 Lovett Blvd (77006)
Rates: $85-$275
(713) 522-5224
(800) 779-5224

MARRIOTT-BY THE GALLERIA
1750 W Loop S (77027)
Rates: $76-$229
(713) 960-0111
(800) 228-9290

MARRIOTT-HOBBY AIRPORT
9100 Gulf Frwy (77017)
Rates: $179-$199
(713) 943-7979
(800) 228-9290

MARRIOTT-HOUSTON MEDICAL CENTER
6580 Fannin St (77030)
Rates: $89-$199
(713) 796-0080
(800) 228-9290

MOTEL 6
16884 Northwest Frwy (77040)
Rates: $40-$56
(713) 937-7056
(800) 466-8356

MOTEL 6
5555 W 34th St (77092)
Rates: $38-$44
(713) 682-8588
(800) 466-8356

MOTEL 6
9638 Plainfield Rd (77036)
Rates: $38-$54
(713) 778-0008
(800) 466-8356

MOTEL 6 HOBBY AIRPORT
8800 Airport Blvd (77061)
Rates: $37-$45
(713) 941-0990
(800) 466-8356

MOTEL 6-WEST
14833 Katy Frwy (77094)
Rates: $37-$42
(281) 497-5000
(800) 466-8356

MOTEL 6 WESTCHASE
2900 W Sam Houston Pkwy S (77042)
Rates: $46-$62
(713) 334-9188
(800) 466-8356

OMNI HOUSTON
4 Riverway (77056)
Rates: $315-$399
(713) 871-8181
(800) 843-6664

OMNI HOUSTON WESTISDE
13210 Katy Frwy (77079)
Rates: $71-$184
(281) 558-8338
(800) 843-6664

PALM COURT INN
8200 S Main St (77025)
Rates: $55-$75
(713) 668-8000

PARK PLAZA RELIANT CENTER
8686 Kirby Dr (77054)
Rates: $95-$155
(713) 748-3221

PARKVIEW INN
9000 S Main (77085)
Rates: $49-$76
(713) 666-4151

QUALITY INN-AIRPORT
6115 Will Clayton Pkwy (77205)
Rates: $69-$120
(281) 446-9131
(800) 424-6423
(800) 231-6134

QUALITY INN HOBBY AIRPORT
7775 Airport Blvd (77061)
Rates: $65-$150
(713) 644-3800
(800) 424-6423

RADISSON HOTEL ASTRODOME
8686 Kirby Dr (77054)
Rates: $129-$279
(713) 795-8477
(800) 333-3333

RAMADA LIMITED S.H. 249
18836 Tomball Pkwy (77070)
Rates: $80-$90
(281) 970-5000
(800) 272-6232

RAMADA PLAZA HOTEL/GALLERIA
7611 Katy Frwy, Hwy 10 W (77024)
Rates: $90-$121
(713) 688-2222
(800) 272-6232

RED ROOF INN HOBBY AIRPORT
9005 Airport Blvd (77061)
Rates: $39-$61
(713) 943-3300
(800) 843-7663

RED ROOF INN NORTHWEST
12929 Northwest Frwy (77040)
Rates: $39-$64
(713) 939-0800
(800) 843-7663

RED ROOF INN W
15701 Park Ten Place (77084)
Rates: $39-$62
(281) 579-7200
(800) 843-7663

RED ROOF INNS
2960 W Sam Houston Pkwy S (77042)
Rates: $44-$63
(713) 785-9909
(800) 843-7663

RENAISSANCE HOUSTON HOTEL GREENWAY PLAZA
6 Greenway Plaza E (77046)
Rates: $89-$189
(713) 629-1200
(800) 468-3571

RESIDENCE INN BY MARRIOTT
2500 McCue (77056)
Rates: $99-$299
(713) 840-9757
(800) 331-3131

RESIDENCE INN BY MARRIOTT-ASTRODOME
7710 S Main St (77030)
Rates: $139-$179
(713) 660-7993
(800) 331-3131

RESIDENCE INN HOUSTON-CLEAR LAKE
525 Bay Area Blvd (77058)
Rates: $139-$179
(281) 486-2424
(800) 331-3131

RESIDENCE INN BY MARRIOTT-WEST UNIVERSITY
2939 Westpark Dr (77005)
Rates: $79-$134
(713) 661-4660
(800) 331-3131

AREA CODES - If the local number doesn't connect, check for a new area code.

RESIDENCE INN BY MARRIOTT-WESTCHASE
9965 Westheimer (77042)
Rates: $132-$180
(713) 974-5454
(800) 331-3131

RESIDENCE INN BY MARRIOTT-WILLOWBROOK
7311 W Greens Rd (77064)
Rates: $120-$170
(832) 237-2002
(800) 331-3131

ROBIN'S NEST B&B INN
4104 Greeley (77006)
Rates: $89-$150
(713) 528-5821
(800) 622-8343

RODEWAY INN-SW FREEWAY
3135 Southwest Frwy (77098)
Rates: $52-$73
(713) 526-1071
(800) 424-6423

SAM HOUSTON HOTEL
1117 Prairie (77002)
Rates: $159-$299
(832) 200-8800
(877) 348-8800

SHERATON HOUSTON BROOKHOLLOW
3000 N Loop W (77092)
Rates: $229-$259
(713) 688-0100
(800) 325-3535
(888) 627-8196

SHERATON N. HOUSTON HOTEL
15700 John F Kennedy Blvd (77032)
Rates: $199-$299
(281) 442-5100
(800) 325-3535

SHERATON SUITES HOUSTON GALLERIA
2400 W Loop S (77027)
Rates: $89-$279
(713) 586-2444
(800) 325-3535

SLEEP INN BUSH AIRPORT
15675 John F. Kennedy Blvd (77032)
Rates: $65-$75
(281) 442-7770
(800) 424-6423

SPRINGHILL SUITES HOUSTON HOBBY
7922 Mosley Rd (77061)
Rates: $99-$109
(713) 943-1713

THE ST. REGIS HOUSTON
1919 Briar Oaks Ln (77027)
Rates: $430
(713) 840-7600

STAYBRIDGE SUITES-GALLERIA
5190 Hidalgo St (77056)
Rates: $79-$149
(713) 355-8888
(800) 348-8000

STUDIO 6
1255 Hwy 6 N (77084)
Rates: $199-$279
(281) 579-6959
(888) 897-0202

STUDIO 6-CYPRESS STATION
220 Bammel-Westfield Rd (77090)
Rates: $199-$279
(281) 580-2221
(888) 897-0202

STUDIO 6-HOBBY SOUTH
12700 Featherwood (77034)
Rates: $209-$289
(281) 929-5400
(888) 897-0202

STUDIO 6-NORTHWEST
14255 Northwest Frwy (77040)
Rates: $199-$279
(713) 895-2900
(888) 897-0202

STUDIO 6-WESTCHASE
3030 W Sam Houston Pkwy S (77042)
Rates: $229-$309
(713) 785-8550
(888) 897-0202

SUPER 8 MOTEL
609 W FM 1960 (77090)
Rates: $60-$109
(281) 866-8686
(800) 800-8000

SUPER 8 MOTEL GESSNER
8201 Southwest Frwy (77074)
Rates: $45-$59
(713) 772-3626
(800) 800-8000

TOWNEPLACE SUITES BY MARRIOTT
15155 Katy Frwy (77024)
Rates: $60-$120
(281) 646-0058
(800) 257-3000

TOWNEPLACE SUITES BY MARRIOTT- NW
12820 Northwest Frwy (77040)
Rates: $60-$90
(713) 690-4035
(800) 257-3000

TRAVELERS INN
17607 Eastex Fwy & Will Clayton Fwy (77396)
Rates: $49-$69
(281) 446-4611

THE WARWICK
5701 S Main St (77005)
Rates: $129-$350
(713) 526-1991

WELLESLEY INN & SUITES-MEDICAL CENTER
1301 S Braeswood (77030)
Rates: $109-$119
(713) 794-0800
(800) 444-8888

WELLESLEY INN MEMORIAL
7855 Katy Frwy (77024)
Rates: $55-$159
(713) 263-9770
(800) 444-8888

THE WESTIN GALLERIA
5060 W Alabama St (77056)
Rates: $129-$349
(713) 960-8100
(800) 228-3000

THE WESTIN OAKS
5011 Westheimer Rd (77056)
Rates: $129-$349
(713) 960-8100
(800) 228-3000

HUMBLE

ECONO LODGE
9821 W FM 1960 (77338)
Rates: $55-$72
(281) 548-2900
(800) 424-6423

HOLIDAY INN EXP HOTEL & SUITES
7014 Will Clayton Pkwy (77396)
Rates: $129-$139
(281) 446-9997
(800) 465-4329

MOTEL 6
15319 Eastex Frwy (77396)
Rates: $37-$44
(281) 441-7887
(800) 466-8356

HUNTSVILLE

GATEWAY INN
606 I-45 S (77340)
Rates: $35-$80
(936) 295-7595

HOLIDAY INN EXP
201 W Hill Park Circle (77340)
Rates: $62-$99
(936) 293-8800
(800) 465-4329

LA QUINTA INN
124 I-45 N (77340)
Rates: $62-$79
(936) 295-6454
(800) 687-6667

MOTEL 6
122 I-45 N (77340)
Rates: $33-$39
(936) 291-6927
(800) 466-8356

SAM HOUSTON PLACE
3296 I-45 S, Exit 114 (77340)
Rates: $48-$59
(936) 295-9151
(800) 395-9151

HURST

AMERISUITES
1601 Hurst Town Center Dr (76054)
Rates: $89-$99
(817) 577-3003
(800) 833-1516

HYE

HERITAGE FARMS B&B
P. O. Box 232 (78635)
Rates: $80-$105
(830) 868-4204

INGLESIDE

BEST WESTERN-NAVAL STATION INN
2025 State Hwy 361 (78362)
Rates: $65-$150
(361) 776-2767
(800) 528-1234

INGRAM

HUNTER HOUSE MOTOR INN
310 Hwy 39 W (78025)
Rates: $44-$99
(830) 367-2377
(800) 655-2377

IRVING

AMERISUITES LAS COLINAS-HIDDEN RIDGE
333 W John Carpenter Frwy (75039)
Rates: $89-$119
(972) 910-0302
(800) 833-1516

AMERISUITES LAS COLINAS-WALNUT HILL
5455 Green Park Dr (75038)
Rates: $69-$109
(972) 550-7400
(800) 833-1516

AREA CODES - If the local number doesn't connect, check for a new area code.

CANDLEWOOD LAS COLINAS
5300 Green Park
Dr (75038)
Rates: $95-$114
(972) 714-9990
(800) 465-4329

CLARION INN
5000 W John
Carpenter Frwy
(75063)
Rates: $67-$129
(972) 929-5757
(800) 424-6423

COMFORT INN DFW AIRPORT
8205 Esters Blvd
(75063)
Rates: $49-$99
(972) 929-0066
(800) 424-6423

COMFORT SUITES
1223 Greenway
Cir (75038)
Rates: $55-$99
(972) 518-0606
(800) 424-6423

DRURY INN-DFW AIRPORT
4210 W Airport
Frwy (75062)
Rates: $65-$104
(972) 986-1200
(800) 378-7946

ECONO LODGE
3135 E John
Carpenter Fwy
(75062)
Rates: $36-$109
(972) 894-1900
(800) 424-6423

FOUR SEASONS RESORT & CLUB
4150 N Mac-Arthur
Blvd (75038)
Rates: $315-$460
(972) 717-0700
(800) 332-3442

HAMPTON INN-DFW AIRPORT
4340 W Airport
Frwy (75061)
Rates: $92-$112
(972) 986-3606
(800) 426-7866

HARVEY HOTEL-DFW AIRPORT
4545 W John
Carpenter Frwy
(75063)
Rates: $119-$149
(972) 929-4500
(800) 922-9222

HARVEY SUITES-DFW AIRPORT
4550 W John
Carpenter Frwy
(75063)
Rates: $110-$152
(972) 929-4499
(800) 922-9222

HOLIDAY INN SELECT-DFW AIRPORT
4440 W Airport
Frwy (75062)
Rates: $69-$99
(972) 399-1010
(800) 465-4329

HOMESTEAD STUDIO SUITES-LAS COLINAS
5315 Camaby St
(75038)
Rates: $49-$64
(972) 756-0458
(800) 225-5466

HOMEWOOD SUITES-LAS COLINAS
4300 Wingren Rd
(75039)
Rates: $139-$199
(972) 556-0665
(800) 225-5466

KNIGHTS INN
120 W Airport
Frwy (75062)
Rates: $35-$45
(800) 843-5644

LA QUINTA INN DFW AIRPORT-N
4850 W John
Carpenter Frwy
(75063)
Rates: $70-$106
(972) 915-4022
(800) 687-6667

LA QUINTA INN DFW AIRPORT-S
4105 W Airport
Frwy (75062)
Rates: $70-$106
(972) 252-6546
(800) 687-6667

MAINSTAY SUITES DFW AIRPORT-S
2323 Imperial Dr
(75062)
Rates: $69-$99
(972) 257-5400
(800) 660-6246

MOTEL 6
510 S Loop 12
(75060)
Rates: $33-$49
(972) 438-4227
(800) 466-8356

MOTEL 6-DFW NORTH
7800 Heathrow Dr
(75063)
Rates: $37-$58
(972) 915-3993
(800) 466-8356

MOTEL 6-DFW SOUTH
2611 W Airport
Frwy (75062)
Rates: $29-$55
(972) 570-7500
(800) 466-8356

OMNI MANDALAY LAS COLINAS
221 E Las Colinas
Blvd (75039)
Rates: $109-$249
(972) 556-0800
(800) 843-6664

QUALITY INN & SUITES-DFW N
4100 W John
Carpenter Frwy
(75063)
Rates: $49-$119
(972) 929-4008
(800) 424-6423

RADISSON HOTEL DFW AIRPORT-N
4600 W Airport
Frwy (75062)
Rates: $99-$139
(972) 513-0800
(800) 333-3333

RED ROOF INN-DFW AIRPORT
8150 Esters Blvd
(75063)
Rates: $39-$92
(972) 929-0020
(800) 843-7663

RESIDENCE INN BY MARRIOTT LAS COLINAS
950 Walnut Hill
Ln (75038)
Rates: $132-$149
(972) 580-7773
(800) 331-3131

RESIDENCE INN BY MARRIOTT-DFW IRVING
8600 Esters Blvd
(75063)
Rates: $94-$159
(972) 871-1331
(800) 331-3131

SHERATON GRAND HOTEL
4440 W Carpenter
Frwy (75261)
Rates: $75-$170
(972) 929-8400
(800) 325-3535
(800) 345-5251 (TX)

STAYBRIDGE SUITES-LAS COLINAS
1201 Executive
Circle (75038)
Rates: $120-$150
(972) 465-9400
(800) 465-4329
(800) 238-8000

SUMMERFIELD SUITES-LAS COLINAS
5901 N
MacArthur Blvd
(75039)
Rates: $65-$148
(972) 831-0909
(800) 833-4353

SUPER 8 MOTEL DFW NORTH
4770 W John
Carpenter Frwy
(75063)
Rates: $49-$65
(214) 441-9000
(800) 800-8000

TOWNEPLACE SUITES LAS COLINAS
900 W Walnut Hill
Ln (75038)
Rates: $80
(972) 550-7796
(800) 257-3000

WELLESLEY INN
5401 Green Park
Dr (75038)
Rates: $79-$149
(972) 751-0808
(800) 444-8888

JACKSBORO

JACKSBORO INN
704 S Main St
(76458)
Rates: $34-$43
(940) 567-3751

JACKSONVILLE

HOLIDAY INN EXP
1848 S Jackson St
(75766)
Rates: $80-$110
(903) 589-8400
(800) 465-4329

RAMADA INN
1407 E Rusk
(75766)
Rates: n/a
(903) 586-9841
(800) 272-6232

JASPER

BEST WESTERN INN
205 W Gibson
(75951)
Rates: $53-$59
(409) 384-7767
(800) 528-1234

RAMADA INN
239 E Gibson
(75951)
Rates: $55-$79
(409) 384-9021
(800) 272-6232

SWAN HOTEL BED & BREAKFAST
250 N Main St
(75951)
Rates: $59-$99
(409) 489-9010

JEFFERSON

INN OF JEFFERSON
400 S Walcott
(75657)
Rates: $42-$68
(903) 665-3983

BUDGET INN
Hwy 59 S (75657)
Rates: $30-$54
(903) 665-2581

JOHNSON CITY

CAROLYNE'S COTTAGE B&B
103 Live Oak (78636)
Rates: $90+
(830) 868-4548

EXOTIC RESORT ZOO & LODGING
235 Zoo Trail (78636)
Rates: $100-$120
(830) 868-4357

SAVE INN MOTEL
107 Hwy 281 & 290 S (78636)
Rates: $40-$60
(830) 868-4044

JUNCTION

DAYS INN
111 S Martinez St (76849)
Rates: $62-$70
(325) 446-3730
(800) 329-7466

ECONO LODGE OF SEGOVIA
311 S Segovia Access Rd (76849)
Rates: $59-$69
(325) 446-2475
(800) 768-1872

THE HILLS MOTEL
1520 N Main St (76849)
Rates: $34-$42
(325) 446-2567

KATY

BEST WESTERN HOUSTON WEST
22455 I-10 W (77450)
Rates: $59-$78
(281) 392-9800
(800) 528-1234

HOLIDAY INN EXP
22105 Katy Fwy (77450)
Rates: $62-$67
(281) 395-4800
(800) 465-4329

SUPER 8 MOTEL
22157 Katy Frwy (77450)
Rates: $45-$55
(281) 395-5757
(800) 800-8000

KAUFMAN

BEST WESTERN-LA HACIENDA INN
200 E Hwy 175 (75142)
Rates: $45-$65
(972) 962-6272
(800) 528-1234

KEMAH

THE SCULPTURED GARDEN B&B
710 Bradford (77565)
Rates: $75-$300
(281) 334-2517

KENEDY

DAYS INN
453 N Sunset Strip (78119)
Rates: $45-$85
(830) 583-2521
(800) 329-7466

KERRVILLE

BEST WESTERN SUNDAY HOUSE INN
2124 Sidney Baker St (78028)
Rates: $60-$109
(830) 896-1313
(800) 528-1234
(800) 677-9477

BUDGET INN
1804 Sidney Baker St (78028)
Rates: $40-$65
(830) 896-8200
(800) 219-8158

COMFORT INN
2001 Sidney Bkaer St (78028)
Rates: $64-$149
(830) 792-7700
(800) 424-6423

DAYS INN
2000 Sidney Baker St (78028)
Rates: $59-$94
(830) 896-1000
(800) 329-7466

ECONO LODGE
2145 Sidney Baker St (78028)
Rates: $39-$129
(830) 896-1711
(800) 424-6423

FLAGSTAFF INN
906 Junction Hwy (78028)
Rates: $40+
(830) 792-4449

HILLCREST INN
1508 Sidney Baker St (78028)
Rates: $36-$80
(830) 896-7400
(800) 221-0251

LA REATA RANCH BED & BREAKFAST
2555 Sheppard Rees Rd (78028)
Rates: $75+
(830) 896-5503

MOTEL 6
1810 Sidney Baker St (78028)
Rates: $37-$62
(830) 257-1500
(800) 466-8356

TURTLE CREEK LODGE
689 Upper Turtle Creek (78028)
Rates: $150-$250
(210) 828-0377

Y.O. RANCH RESORT HOTEL & CONF CENTER
2033 Sidney Baker St (78028)
Rates: $98-$119
(830) 257-4440
(800) 531-2800
(877) YO-RESORT

KILGORE

BEST WESTERN INN
1411 N Hwy 259 (75662)
Rates: $67
(903) 986-1195
(800) 528-1234

DAYS INN
3505 N Hwy 259 (75662)
Rates: $35-$52
(903) 983-2975
(800) 329-7466

RAMADA INN
3501 N Hwy 259 (75662)
Rates: $48-$66
(903) 983-3456
(800) 272-6232

KILLEEN

HOLIDAY INN EXP
1602 E Center Expressway (76541)
Rates: $59-$95
(254) 554-2727
(800) 465-4328

LA QUINTA INN
1112 S Ft Hood St (76541)
Rates: $70-$86
(254) 526-8331
(800) 687-6667

MOTEL 6
800 E Central TX Expresswy (76542)
Rates: $41-$46
(254) 634-4151
(800) 466-8356

KINGSVILLE

BUDGET INN
716 S 14th St (78363)
Rates: $27-$50
(361) 592-4322

ECONOMY INN
1415 S 14th St (78363)
Rates: $28-$55
(361) 592-5214

HOLIDAY INN
3430 Hwy 77 S (78363)
Rates: $52-$65
(361) 595-5753
(800) 465-4329

MOTEL 6
101 Hwy 77 N (78363)
Rates: $34-$37
(361) 592-5106
(800) 466-8356

QUALITY INN
221 S Hwy 77 (78363)
Rates: $59-$99
(361) 592-5251
(800) 424-6423

SUPER 8 MOTEL
105 S 77 Bypass (78363)
Rates: $49-$79
(361) 592-6471
(800) 800-8000

KINGWOOD

HOMEWOOD SUITES
23320 Hwy 59 N (77339)
Rates: $79-$259
(281) 358-5566
(800) 225-5466

LA QUINTA INN
22790 Hwy 59 N (77339)
Rates: $69-$119
(800) 687-6667

KOUNTZE

LITTLE HOUSE ON TIMBER RIDGE
Hwy 92 & 1943 (77625)
Rates: $75+
(409) 246-3107

LA GRANGE

BED & BREAKFAST ON MAIN
512 S Main St (78945)
Rates: $70-$75
(979) 968-9535

LA PORTE

LA QUINTA INN
1105 Hwy 146 S (77571)
Rates: $65-$87
(281) 470-0760
(800) 687-6667

LAGUNA VISTA

EXECUTIVE INN
1411 E Hwy 100 (78578)
Rates: $43-$62
(956) 943-7866

LAJITAS

LAJITAS THE ULTIMATE HIDEOUT RESORT
1 Main St (79852)
Rates: $235-$451
(432) 424-5000

LAKE JACKSON

CHEROTEL BRAZOSPORT HOTEL
925 Hwy 332 (77566)
Rates: $132-$161
(979) 297-1161
(800) 544-2119

AREA CODES - If the local number doesn't connect, check for a new area code.

SUPER 8 MOTEL
915 Hwy 332 W
(77566)
Rates: $55-$65
(979) 297-3031
(800) 800-8000

LAKE LBJ

TROPICAL HIDEAWAY BEACH RESORT
604 Highcrest Dr
(78654)
Rates: $85-$250
(210) 598-9896
(800) 662-4431

VALENTINE LAKESIDE RESORT
814 Euel Moore
Dr (Kingsland
78639)
Rates: $68-$250
(915) 388-4418

LAKEWAY

LAKEWAY INN CONFERENCE RESORT
101 Lakeway Dr
(78734)
Rates: $109-$290
(512) 261-6600
(800) 525-3929

LAMESA

BUDGET HOST INN
901 S Dallas Ave
(79331)
Rates: $32-$46
(806) 872-2118
(800) 283-4678

SHILOH INN
1707 Lubbock
Hwy (79331)
Rates: $35-$53
(806) 872-6721
(800) 222-2244

LAMPASAS

COUNTRY INN
1502 S Key Ave
(76550)
Rates: $40-$52
(512) 556-6201
(800) 556-2322

HOLIDAY INN EXP
1200 Central Texas
Expresswy (76550)
Rates: $79-$149
(512) 556-9292
(800) 465-4329

SARATOGA MOTEL
1408 S Key Ave
(76550)
Rates: $30-$60
(512) 556-6244

LAREDO

FAMILY GARDEN INN & SUITES
5830 San Bernardo
Ave (78041)
Rates: $49-$79
(956) 723-5300
(800) 292-4053

LA QUINTA INN
3610 Santa Ursula
Ave (78041)
Rates: $83-$106
(956) 722-0511
(800) 687-6667

MOTEL 6-NORTH
5920 San Bernardo
Ave (78041)
Rates: $46-$64
(956) 722-8133
(800) 466-8356

MOTEL 6-SOUTH
5310 San Bernardo
Ave (78041)
Rates: $46-$63
(956) 725-8187
(800) 466-8356

RED ROOF INN
1006 W Calton Rd
(78041)
Rates: $49-$74
(956) 712-0733
(800) 843-7663

RIO GRANDE PLAZA HOTEL
1 S Main Ave (78040)
Rates: $79-$125
(956) 722-2411
(800) 446-4656

LEAKEY

LEAKEY SPRINGS CABINS
P. O. Box 610 (78873)
Rates: $75-$125
(830) 232-6351

WHISKEY MTN INN BED & BREAKFAST
HCR 1, Box 555
(78873)
Rates: $60-$125
(830) 232-6797
(800) 370-6797

LEON VALLEY

SUPER 8 SEA-WORLD AREA
5336 Wurzbach
Rd (78238)
Rates: $45-$99
(210) 520-0888
(800) 800-8000

LEWISVILLE

COMFORT SUITES
755A Vista Ridge
Mall Dr (75067)
Rates: $59-$75
(9720 315-6464
(800) 424-6423

COUNTRY INN
755B Vista Ridge
Mall Dr (75067)
Rates: $59-$79
(972) 315-6565
(800) 456-4000

DAYS INN
200 N Stemmons
Frwy (75067)
Rates: $49-$65
(972) 434-1000
(800) 329-7466

HEARTHSIDE SUITES BY VILLAGER
1920 Lakepointe
Dr (75057)
Rates: $59-$99
(972) 459-7777

LA QUINTA INN
1657 N Stemmons
Frwy (75067)
Rates: $55-$86
(972) 221-7525
(800) 687-6667

MICROTEL INN
881 S Stemmons
Frwy (75067)
Rates: $42-$83
(972) 434-0447
(888) 642-7685

MOTEL 6
1705 Lakepointe
Dr (75057)
Rates: $34-$52
(972) 436-5008
(800) 466-8356

RAMADA LIMITED AIRPORT
1102 Texas St (75057)
Rates: $48-$80
(972) 221-2121
(800) 272-6232

RESIDENCE INN BY MARRIOTT
755C Vista Ridge
Mall Dr (75067)
Rates: $125-$130
(972) 315-3777
(800) 331-3131

SUPER 8-DALLAS NORTH AIRPORT
1305 S Stemmons
Frwy (75067)
Rates: $45-$50
(972) 221-7511

LINDALE

DAYS INN
13307 CR 472 E
(75771)
Rates: $40-$70
(903) 882-7800
(800) 329-7466

LITTLEFIELD

CRESCENT PARK MOTEL
2000 Hall Ave
(79339)
Rates: $36-$65
(806) 385-4464
(800) 658-9960

LIVE OAK

LA QUINTA INN TOPPERWEIN
12822 I-35 N
(78233)
Rates: $69-$109
(210) 657-5500
(800) 687-6667

LIVINGSTON

LAKE LIVINGSTON INN
2500 Hwy 59 S
(77351)
Rates: $37-$45
(936) 327-2525

LLANO

THE BADU HOUSE HISTORIC B&B
601 Bessemer St
(78643)
Rates: $60-$70
(325) 247-1207

BEST WESTERN LLANO INN
901 W Young St
(78643)
Rates: $51-$79
(325) 247-4101
(800) 528-1234
(800) 346-1578

CHAPARRAL MOTOR INN
700 W Young
(78643)
Rates: $38-$65
(325) 247-4111

LOCKHART

BEST WESTERN PLUM CREEK INN
2001 Hwy 183 S
(78644)
Rates: $75-$95
(512) 398-4911
(800) 528-1234

LOCKHART INN
1207 Hwy 183 S
(78644)
Rates: $29-$39
(512) 398-5201

LONGVIEW

BEST WESTERN INN
3119 Estes Pkwy
(75602)
Rates: $69-$150
(903) 758-0700
(800) 528-1234

ECONO LODGE
3120 Estes Pkwy
(75602)
Rates: $45-$49
(903) 753-4884
(800) 424-6423

HAMPTON INN
112 S Access Rd
(75603)
Rates: $68-$80
(903) 758-0959
(800) 426-7866

LA QUINTA INN
502 S Access Rd
(75602)
Rates: $63-$79
(903) 757-3663
(800) 687-6667

LONGVIEW INN
605 Access Rd
(75602)
Rates: $40-$80
(903) 753-0350
(800) 933-1139

MOTEL 6
110 S Access Rd
(75603)
Rates: $33-$38
(903) 758-5256
(800) 466-8356

LUBBOCK

BARCELONA COURT HOTEL
5215 S Loop 289 (79424)
Rates: $65-$85
(800) 222-1122

BEST WESTERN WINDSOR INN
5410 I-27 (79412)
Rates: $69-$109
(806) 762-8400
(800) 528-1234

CIRCUS INN MOTEL
150 Slaton Hwy I-27 (79404)
Rates: $35-$65
(888) 745-5677

COMFORT INN
5828 I-27 (79404)
Rates: $60-$169
(806) 763-6500
(800) 424-6423

DAYS INN-TEXAS TECH
2401 4th St (79415)
Rates: $49-$89
(806) 747-7111
(800) 329-7466

ECONO LODGE
5401 Ave Q (79412)
Rates: $45-$99
(806) 747-3525
(800) 424-6423

FOUR POINTS SHERATON HOTEL
505 Ave Q (79401)
Rates: $99-$200
(806) 747-0171
(800) 325-3535

HOLIDAY INN-PARK PLAZA
3201 Loop 289 S (79423)
Rates: $72-$82
(806) 797-3241
(800) 465-4329

KOKO INN
5201 Ave Q (79412)
Rates: $45-$85
(800) 782-3254

LA QUINTA INN-CIVIC CENTER
601 Ave Q (79412)
Rates: $65-$83
(806) 763-9441
(800) 687-6667

LA QUINTA INN-MEDICAL CENTER
4115 Brownfield Hwy (79407)
Rates: $69-$96
(806) 792-0065
(800) 687-6667

MOTEL 6
909 66th St (79412)
Rates: $35-$55
(806) 745-5541
(800) 466-8356

QUALITY INN
5706 I-27 (79404)
Rates: $59-$109
(806) 749-1090
(800) 424-6423

RAMADA INN & CONF CENTER
6624 I-27 (79404)
Rates: $54-$95
(806) 745-2208
(800) 272-6232

RESIDENCE INN BY MARRIOTT
2551 S Loop 289 (79423)
Rates: $114
(806) 745-1963
(800) 331-3131

SUPER 8 MOTEL
501 Ave Q (79401)
Rates: $44-$67
(806) 762-8726
(800) 800-8000

TOWNEPLACE SUITES
5310 W Loop 289 (79424)
Rates: $99-$139
(806) 799-6226
(800) 257-3000

LUFKIN

DAYS INN
2130 S 1st St (75901)
Rates: $67-$87
(936) 639-3301
(800) 329-7466

EXPO INN
4200 N Medford Dr (75901)
Rates: $47-$66
(936) 632-7300

HOLIDAY INN
4306 S 1st St (75901)
Rates: $60-$85
(936) 639-3333
(800) 465-4329

LA QUINTA INN
2119 S 1st St (75901)
Rates: $66-$86
(936) 634-3351
(800) 687-6667

MOTEL 6
1110 S Timberland Dr (75901)
Rates: $32-$55
(936) 637-7850
(800) 466-8356

LULING

COACHWAY INN
1908 E Pierce St (78648)
Rates: $35-$52
(830) 875-5635

LYTLE

DAYS INN
19525 McDonald St (78052)
Rates: $36-$60
(830) 772-4777
(800) 329-7466
(800) 833-5243

MADISONVILLE

WESTERN LODGE
2007 E Main St (77864)
Rates: $40-$50
(936) 348-7654

MANOR

QUALITY INN
11301 Hwy 290 E (78653)
Rates: $75-$155
(512) 272-9373
(800) 424-6423

MANSFIELD

COMFORT INN
Hwy 287 & E Broad St (76063)
Rates: $65-$140
(817) 453-8848
(800) 424-6423

MARATHON

CAPTAINS SHEPARD'S INN
P. O. Box 46 (79842)
Rates: $99-$125
(800) 844-4243

THE GAGE HOTEL
102 Hwy 90 W (79842)
Rates: $69-$155
(432) 386-4205
(800) 884-4243

HEATH CANYON RANCH
P. O. Box 386 (79842)
Rates: $30-$125
(432) 371-2235

MARATHON MOTEL/RV PARK
P. O. Box 141 (79842)
Rates: $55-$85
(432) 386-4241

MARBLE FALLS

BEST WESTERN MARBLE FALLS INN
1403 Hwy 281 N (78654)
Rates: $49-$109
(830) 693-5122
(800) 528-1234

MARFA

RIATA INN
Hwy 90 E (79843)
Rates: $40-$70
(432) 729-3800

THE HOTEL PAISANO
207 N Highland (79843)
Rates: $79-$275
(866) 729-3669

MARSHALL

BEST WESTERN EXECUTIVE INN
5201 E End Blvd S (75672)
Rates: $69-$99
(903) 935-0707
(800) 528-1234

DAYS INN
100 I-20 W (75672)
Rates: $45-$90
(903) 927-1718
(800) 329-7466

LA MAISON MALFACON COUNTRY INN
700 E Rusk St (75670)
Rates: $45-$60
(903) 938-3600

LA QUINTA INN
5301 East End Blvd (75672)
Rates: $59-$89
(903) 927-0009
(800) 687-6667

MOTEL 6
300 I-20 E (75670)
Rates: $34-$48
(903) 935-4393
(800) 466-8356

QUALITY INN
5555 E End Blvd S (75670)
Rates: $65-$100
(903) 935-1941
(800) 424-6423

MASON

HILL COUNTRY INN
454 Ft. McKavitt St (76856)
Rates: $32-$66
(325) 347-6317

MATHIS

MATHIS MOTOR INN
1223 N Front St (78368)
Rates: $30-$39
(361) 547-3272
(800) 251-7531

MCALLEN

DRURY INN
612 W Expresswy 83 (78501)
Rates: $67-$101
(956) 687-5100
(800) 378-7946

DRURY SUITES
228 W Expresswy 83 (78501)
Rates: $93-$113
(956) 682-3222
(800) 378-7946

HAMPTON INN
300 W Expresswy 83 (78501)
Rates: $82-$112
(956) 682-4900
(800) 426-7866

HOLIDAY INN CIVIC CENTER
200 W Expressway 83 (78501)
Rates: $69-$94
(956) 686-2471
(800) 465-4329

LA COPA INN
1010 W Houston Ave (78501)
Rates: $49-$99
(956) 682-1190

LA QUINTA INN
1100 S 10th St (78501)
Rates: $68-$72
(956) 687-1101
(800) 687-6667

MOTEL 6
700 Expressway 83 (78501)
Rates: $38-$45
(956) 687-3700
(800) 466-8356

POSADA ANA INN
620 W Expressway 83 (78501)
Rates: $55-$75
(956) 631-6700

RAMADA LIMITED AIRPORT
1505 S 9th St (78501)
Rates: $55-$65
(956) 686-4401
(800) 272-6232

RENAISSANCE CASA DE PALMAS HOTEL & SUITES
101 N Main St (78501)
Rates: $69-$239
(800) 228-9290

RESIDENCE INN BY MARRIOTT
220 W Expressway 83 (78501)
Rates: $89-$94
(956) 994-8626
(800) 331-3131

STUDIO 6
700 W Savannah (78503)
Rates: $249-$359
(956) 668-7829
(888) 897-0202

MCKINNEY

A TARTAN THISTLE BED & BREAKFAST
513 W Louisiana St (75069)
Rates: $65-$135
(214) 680-2744

DAYS INN
2104 N Central Expressway (75070)
Rates: $55-$75
(972) 548-8888
(800) 329-7466

HOLIDAY INN
1300 N Central Expressway (75069)
Rates: n/a
(972) 542-9471
(800) 465-4329

MCKINNEY INN
1431 N Tennessee St (75070)
Rates: $31-$48
(972) 542-4469

MOTEL 6
2125 White Ave (75069)
Rates: $40-$70
(972) 542-8600
(800) 466-8356

SUPER 8 MOTEL
910 N Central Expressway (75070)
Rates: $51-$75
(972) 658-8880
(800) 800-8000

MCLEAN

CACTUS INN MOTEL
101 Pine St (79057)
Rates: $33-$52
(806) 779-2346

MEMPHIS

EXECUTIVE INN
1600 Boykin Dr (79245)
Rates: $39-$60
(806) 259-3583

MERCEDES

EXECUTIVE INN
Mile 2 W & Expresswy 83 (78570)
Rates: $45-$77
(956) 565-3121

MESQUITE

COMFORT SUITES
2100 N Beltline Rd (75150)
Rates: $74-$119
(972) 329-9400
(800) 424-6423

COUNTRY INN
118 Hwy 80 E (75150)
Rates: $55-$125
(972) 216-7460
(800) 456-4000

HAMPTON INN
1700 Rodeo Dr (75149)
Rates: $84-$106
(972) 329-3100
(800) 426-7866

RODEO INN
3601 Hwy 80 E (75150)
Rates: $40-$55
(972) 279-6561

SPANISH TRAILS INN
1129 Gross Rd (75149)
Rates: $49-$69
(972) 226-9800

SUPER 8 MOTEL
121 Grand Junction (75149)
Rates: $44-$66
(972) 289-5481
(800) 800-8000

MIDLAND

BEST WESTERN ATRIUM INN
3904 W Wall St (79703)
Rates: $59-$89
(432) 694-7774
(800) 528-1234

COMFORT INN
302 I-20 W (79701)
Rates: $69-$104
(432) 683-1111
(800) 424-6423

DAYS INN
1003 S Midkiff Rd (79701)
Rates: $50-$86
(432) 697-3155
(800) 329-7466

HOLIDAY INN
4300 W Wall St (79703)
Rates: $59-$64
(432) 697-3181
(800) 465-4329

LA QUINTA INN
4130 W Wall St (79703)
Rates: $59-$79
(432) 697-9900
(800) 687-6667

PLAZA INN
4108 N Big Spring (79705)
Rates: $65
(432) 686-8733

RAMADA LIMITED
3100 W Wall St (79701)
Rates: $59-$69
(432) 699-4144
(800) 272-6232

SLEEP INN
3828 W Wall St (79703)
Rates: $50-$79
(432) 689-6822
(800) 753-3746

SUPER 8 MOTEL
1000 I-20 W (79701)
Rates: $38-$59
(432) 684-8888
(800) 800-8000

TRAVELODGE
2500 Commerce Dr (79703)
Rates: $49-$99
(432) 694-1300
(800) 578-7878

MIDLOTHIAN

BEST WESTERN MIDLOTHIAN INN
220 N Hwy 67 (76065)
Rates: $59-$74
(972) 775-1891
(800) 528-1234

MINERAL WELLS

AMERICAN INN
3701 E Hubbard (76067)
Rates: $45-$85
(940) 325-6961

BEST WESTERN CLUBHOUSE INN & SUITES
4410 Hwy 180 E (76067)
Rates: $79-$159
(940) 325-2270
(800) 528-1234

BUDGET HOST INN MESA HOTEL
3601 E Hwy 180 (76067)
Rates: $39-$56
(940) 325-3377
(800) 283-4678

EXECUTIVE INN
2809 Hwy 180 W (76067)
Rates: $42-$55
(940) 328-1111

MISSION

EL ROCIO RETREAT CENTER
2519 S Inspiration Rd (78572)
Rates: $60-$175
(956) 584-7432

EXECUTIVE INN
1786 W Hwy 83 (78572)
Rates: $45-$60
(956) 581-7451

HAWTHORN SUITES LTD
3700 Plantation Grove Blvd (78572)
Rates: $69-$109
(956) 519-9696
(800) 527-1133

INDIAN RIDGE B&B
N Bentsen Palm Dr & W 2 Mile Rd (78574)
Rates: $75-$175
(956) 519-3305

MONAHANS

BEST WESTERN COLONIAL INN
702 I-20 W (79756)
Rates: $43-$64
(432) 943-4345
(800) 528-1234

SUPER 8 MOTEL
1420 E Jackson Ave (78503)
Rates: $59-$99
(956) 682-1190
(800) 800-8000

AREA CODES - If the local number doesn't connect, check for a new area code.

MOUNT PLEASANT

BEST WESTERN MT. PLEASANT INN
102 E Burton St (75455)
Rates: $74-$84
(903) 572-5051
(800) 528-1234

DAYS INN
2501 W Ferguson (75455)
Rates: $50-$72
(903) 577-0152
(800) 329-7466

HOLIDAY INN EXP HOTEL & SUITES
2306 Greenhill Rd (75455)
Rates: $76-$110
(903) 577-3800
(800) 465-4329

RAMADA INN
2502 W Ferguson Rd (75455)
Rates: $49-$55
(903) 572-6611
(800) 272-6232

SUPER 8 MOTEL
204 Lakewood Dr (75455)
Rates: $45-$70
(903) 572-9808
(800) 800-8000

TANKERSLEY GARDENS B&B
Rt 7, Box 696 (75455)
Rates: $45-$110
(903) 572-0567

MOUNT VERNON

SUPER 8 MOTEL
401 W I-30 (75457)
Rates: $45-$59
(903) 588-2882
(800) 800-8000

MOUNTAIN HOME

Y.O. RANCH
1736 Y O Ranch Rd NW (78058)
Rates: $70-$100
(830) 640-3222
(800) 967-2624

MULESHOE

ECONOMY INN
2701 W American Blvd (79347)
Rates: $38-$46
(806) 272-4261

HERITAGE HOUSE INN
2301 W American Blvd (79347)
Rates: $44-$75
(806) 272-7575
(800) 253-5896

NACOGDOCHES

COMFORT INN
3400 South St (75964)
Rates: $49-$159
(936) 569-8100
(800) 424-6423

THE FREDONIA HISTORIC HOTEL
200 N Fredonia St (75961)
Rates: $65-$100
(936) 564-1234
(800) 594-5323

HARDEMAN GUEST HOUSE-HISTORIC B&B
316 N Church St (75961)
Rates: $75-$95
(936) 569-1947
(800) 884-1947

LA QUINTA INN
3215 South St (75961)
Rates: $60-$76
(936) 560-5453
(800) 687-6667

VICTORIAN INN & SUITES
3612 North St (75961)
Rates: $42-$65
(800) 935-0676

NASSAU BAY

HOLIDAY INN HOUSTON-NASA
1300 NASA Rd One (77058)
Rates: $69-$159
(281) 333-2500
(800) 465-4329

NAVASOTA

SUPER 8 MOTEL
9460 Hwy 6 South (77868)
Rates: $39-$79
(409) 825-7775
(800) 800-8000

NEDERLAND

BEST WESTERN AIRPORT INN
200 Memorial Hwy 69 (77627)
Rates: $55-$70
(409) 727-1631
(800) 528-1234

NEW BOSTON

BEST WESTERN INN OF NEW BOSTON
1024 N Center (75570)
Rates: $59-$99
(903) 628-6999
(800) 528-1234

NEW BRAUNFELS

ACORN HILL B&B
250 School House (78132)
Rates: $100-$175
(800) 525-4618

ALTA VISTA COMAL RESORTS
350 S Union (78130)
Rates: $99-$325
(800) 227-5883

BEST VALUE INN
375 Hwy 46 S (78130)
Rates: $36-$169
(830) 625-6282

BEST WESTERN INN
1493 I-35 N (78130)
Rates: $49-$149
(830) 625-7337
(800) 528-1234

EDELWEISS INN
1063 I-35 N (78130)
Rates: $45-$99
(830) 629-6967

EXECUTIVE INN
808 Hwy 46 S (78130)
Rates: $39-$199
(830) 625-3932

FOUNTAIN MOTEL
1210 N Business I-35 (78130)
Rates: $32-$99
(830) 625-2821

HOLIDAY INN
1051 I-35 E (78130)
Rates: $109-$199
(830) 625-8017
(800) 465-4329

KUEBLER-WALDRIP HAUS BED & BREAKFAST
1620 Hueco Springs Loop (78132)
Rates: $120-$200
(830) 625-8372
(800) 299-8372

LA QUINTA INN
356 S Hwy 46 (78130)
Rates: $69-$99
(830) 687-6667

MOTEL 6
1275 I-35 (78130)
Rates: $34-$129
(830) 626-0600
(800) 466-8356

RODEWAY INN
1209 I-35 E (78130)
Rates: $49-$129
(830) 629-6991
(800) 424-6423
(800) 967-1168

SUPER 8 MOTEL
510 Hwy 46 S (78130)
Rates: $44-$129
(830) 629-1155
(800) 800-8000

NOCONA

NOCONA HILLS MOTEL & RESORT
100 E Huron Circle (76255)
Rates: $34-$46
(940) 825-3161

NORTH PADRE ISLAND

MOTEL 6
8202 S Padre Island Dr (78412)
Rates: $39-$59
(361) 991-8858
(800) 466-8356

N. RICHLAND HILLS

BENISON INN
5151 Thaxton Pkwy (86180)
Rates: $59-$129
(817) 268-6879

LEXINGTON INN-DFW WEST
8709 Airport Frwy (76180)
Rates: $62-$85
(817) 656-8881
(800) 656-8886

MOTEL 6
7804 Bedford-Euless Rd (76180)
Rates: $38-$54
(817) 485-3000
(800) 466-8356

RAMADA LIMITED
7920 Bedford-Euless Rd (76180)
Rates: $40-$69
(817) 485-2750
(800) 272-6232

STUDIO 6
7450 NE Loop 820 (76180)
Rates: $199-$279
(817) 788-6000
(888) 897-0202

ODEM

DAYS INN
1505 S Hwy 77 (78370)
Rates: $50-$110
(361) 368-2166
(800) 329-7466

ODESSA

BEST WESTERN GARDEN OASIS
110 W I-20 (79761)
Rates: $50-$110
(432) 337-3006
(800) 528-1234
(877) 524-9231

CLASSIC SUITES
3031 E Hwy 80 (79761)
Rates: $27-$32
(432) 333-9678

COMFORT SUITES
4801 E 50th St (79762)
Rates: $69-$129
(432) 362-1500
(800) 424-6423

AREA CODES - If the local number doesn't connect, check for a new area code.

DAYS INN
3075 E Business
Loop 20 (79761)
Rates: $50-$64
(432) 335-8000
(800) 329-7466

HOLIDAY INN HOTEL & SUITES
6201 E Business
Loop I-20 (79760)
Rates: $64
(432) 362-2311
(800) 465-4329

LA QUINTA INN
5001 E Business
Loop I-20 (79761)
Rates: $64-$80
(432) 333-2820
(800) 687-6667

MGM GRANDE HOTEL-FUN DOME
6201 E Business I-20 (79762)
Rates: $63-$75
(432) 362-2311
(866) 362-2311

MOTEL ONE
2925 E Hwy 80
(79761)
Rates: $27-$33
(432) 332-4500

MOTEL 6
200 E I-20 Service
Rd (79766)
Rates: $31-$48
(432) 333-4025
(800) 466-8356

PARKWAY INN
3071 Hwy 80 E
(79761)
Rates: $32-$39
(432) 332-4224
(800) 480-0761

QUALITY INN
3001 E Business
Loop I-20 (79760)
Rates: $69-$129
(432) 333-3931
(800) 424-6423

VILLA WEST INN
300 W Pool Road
(79760)
Rates: $27-$39
(432) 335-5055

ORANGE
BEST VALUE INN
2208 Lutcher Dr
(77630)
Rates: $35-$45
(409) 883-6701

BEST WESTERN ORANGE INN
2630 I-10 (77630)
Rates: $80-$125
(409) 883-6616
(800) 528-1234

CAROLINE'S B&B
808 6th St (77630)
Rates: $75-$85
(409) 883-5860

EXECUTIVE INN
4301 27th St (77632)
Rates: $29-$69
(409) 883-9981

LEXINGTON INN
2900 I-10 (77632)
Rates: $50-$70
(409) 988-0110

MOTEL 6
4407 27th St (77630)
Rates: $29-$34
(409) 883-4891
(800) 466-8356

RAMADA INN
2610 I-10 W
(77630)
Rates: $65-$150
(409) 883-0231
(800) 272-6232

THE ROGERS HOUSE B&B
907 Pine Ave
(77630)
Rates: $40-$95
(409) 697-0911

SUPER 8 MOTEL
2710 I-10 W
(77630)
Rates: $50-$59
(409) 882-0888
(800) 800-8000

OZONA
BEST VALUE INN
820 11th St (76943)
Rates: $39-$60
(325) 392-2631

SUPER 8 MOTEL
3330 I-10 E (76943)
Rates: $62-$95
(325) 392-2611
(800) 800-8000

TRAVELODGE
8 11th St (76943)
Rates: $45-$65
(325) 392-2656
(800) 578-7878

PALESTINE
BEST WESTERN PALESTINE INN
1601 W Palestine
Ave (75801)
Rates: $42-$70
(903) 723-4655
(800) 523-0121

EXPRESS INN
1100 E Palestine
Ave (75801)
Rates: $35-$135
(903) 729-3151
(800) 944-1143

RAMADA INN
1101 E Palestine
Ave (75801)
Rates: $59-$85
(903) 723-7300
(800) 272-6232

PANHANDLE
S & S MOTOR INN
I-40 & SR 207
(79068)
Rates: $35-$47
(806) 537-5111

PARIS
BEST WESTERN INN OF PARIS
3755 NE Loop
286 (75460)
Rates: $50-$68
(903) 785-5566
(800) 528-1234

HOLIDAY INN
3560 NE Loop 286
(75460)
Rates: $64
(903) 785-5545
(800) 465-4329

VICTORIAN INN OF PARIS
425 NE 35th St
(75460)
Rates: $45-$66
(903) 785-3871
(800) 935-0863

PASADENA
RAMADA INN
114 S Richy
(77506)
Rates: $57-$89
(713) 477-6871
(800) 272-6232

PEARLAND
BEST WESTERN INN
1855 N Main St
(77581)
Rates: $65-$79
(281) 997-2000
(800) 528-1234

PEARSALL
EXECUTIVE INN
613 North Oak
(78061)
Rates: $35-$55
(830) 334-3693

PECOS
BEST WESTERN SWISS CLOCK INN
900 W Palmer
(79772)
Rates: $59-$86
(432) 447-2215
(800) 528-1234

LAURA LODGE
1000 E Business 20
(79772)
Rates: $35-$48
(432) 445-4924

MOTEL 6
3002 S Cedar St
(79772)
Rates: $30-$51
(432) 445-9034
(800) 466-8356

OAK TREE INN
22 N Frontage Rd
(79772)
Rates: $59-$91
(432) 447-0180

QUALITY INN
4002 S Cedar St
(79772)
Rates: $56-$86
(432) 445-5404
(800) 424-6423

PHARR
LA QUINTA INN & SUITES-RIO GRAND VALLEY
4603 N Cage
(78577)
Rates: $70-$120
(800) 687-6667

MOTEL 6
4701 N Cage
(78577)
Rates: $39-$43
(956) 781-7202
(800) 466-8356

RAMADA LIMITED SUITES
1130 E Expressy
83 (78577)
Rates: $59-$75
(956) 702-3330
(800) 272-6232

SUPER 8 MOTEL
4401 N Cage
(78577)
Rates: $65-$82
(956) 782-8880
(800) 800-8000

PIPE CREEK
LIGHTNING RANCH
818 FM 1283
(78063)
Rates: $85-$135
(800) 994-7373
(Dude Ranch)

PITTSBURG
CARSON HOUSE INN & GRILLE
302 Mt Pleasant St
(75686)
Rates: $69-$79
(903) 856-2468

PLAINVIEW
BEST WESTERN CONESTOGA INN
600 I-27 N (79072)
Rates: $37-$99
(806) 293-9454
(800) 528-1234

BUDGET INN
2001 W 5th St
(79072)
Rates: $27-$39
(806) 293-2578

DAYS INN
3600 Olton Rd
(79072)
Rates: $41-$70
(806) 293-2561
(800) 329-7466

HOLIDAY INN EXP
4213 W 13th St
(79072)
Rates: $90-$150
(806) 296-9900
(800) 465-4329

PLAINVIEW HOTEL
4005 Olton Rd
(79072)
Rates: $55-$70
(806) 293-4181

AREA CODES - If the local number doesn't connect, check for a new area code.

WARRICK INN
800 Broadway
(79072)
Rates: $32-$49
(806) 293-4266

PLANO

AMERISUITES
3100 Dallas Pkwy
(75093)
Rates: $89-$109
(972) 378-3997
(800) 833-1516

**BEST WESTERN
PARK SUITES
HOTEL**
640 Park Blvd E
(75074)
Rates: $85-$100
(972) 578-2243
(800) 528-1234

**CANDLEWOOD
SUITES**
4701 Legacy Dr
(75024)
Rates: $69-$99
(972) 618-5446
(800) 465-4329

COMFORT INN
5021 W Plano
Pkwy (75093)
Rates: $49-$89
(972) 733-4700
(800) 424-6423

HAMPTON INN
4901 Old
Shepherd Place
(75093)
Rates: $79-$89
(972) 519-1000
(800) 426-7866

**HEARTHSIDE
SUITES BY
VILLAGER**
4704 W Plano
Pkwy (75093)
Rates: $59-$99
(972) 758-8888

**HOLIDAY INN EXP
HOTEL & SUITES**
700 Central Pkwy
E (75074)
Rates: $89-$119
(972) 881-1881
(800) 465-4329

**HOMESTEAD
STUDIO SUITES-
LEGACY PARK**
4709 W Plano
Pkwy (75093)
Rates: $64-$84
(972) 596-9955
(800) 782-9473

**HOMEWOOD
SUITES**
4705 Old Shepard
Pl (75093)
Rates: $129
(972) 758-8800
(800) 225-5466

LA QUINTA INN
1820 N Central
Expresswy (75074)
Rates: $55-$75
(972) 423-1300
(800) 687-6667

LA QUINTA INN
4800 W Plano
Pkwy (75091)
Rates: $60-$110
(972) 599-0700
(800) 687-6667

MOTEL 6
2550 N Central
Expresswy (75074)
Rates: $35-$61
(972) 578-1626
(800) 466-8356

RED ROOF INN
301 Ruisseau Dr
(75032)
Rates: $34-$70
(972) 881-8191
(800) 843-7663

**RESIDENCE INN
BY MARRIOTT**
5001 Whitestone
Ln (75024)
Rates: $132-$189
(972) 473-6761
(800) 331-3131

SLEEP INN
4801 W Plano
Pkwy (75093)
Rates: $49-$89
(972) 867-1111
(800) 753-3746

**SOUTHFORK
HOTEL**
1600 N Central
Expresswy (75074)
Rates: $69-$79
(972) 578-8555

SUPER 8 MOTEL
1704 N Central
Expresswy (75074)
Rates: $45-$59
(972) 423-8300

**TOWNEPLACE
SUITES**
5005 Whitestone
Ln (75024)
Rates: $84-$94
(972) 943-8200
(800) 257-3000

WELLESLEY INN
2900 Dallas Pkwy
(75093)
Rates: $79-$109
(972) 378-9978
(800) 444-8888

PORT ARANSAS

**BEACH HOUSE
RENTALS**
2122 On The
Beach (78373)
Rates: $135-$250
(361) 749-5434

BELLE'S INN MOTEL
710 S Station
(78373)
Rates: $35-$65
(361) 749-6138

**CAPTAIN'S QUAR-
TERS INN**
235 W Cotter
(78373)
Rates: $59-$129
(361) 749-6005

**HARBORVIEW
MOTEL**
121 W Cotter
(78373)
Rates: $35
(361) 749-6391

LONE PALM MOTEL
306 S Alister (78373)
Rates: $28-$80
(361) 749-5450

**PARADISE ISLE
MOTEL**
314 Cutoff Rd
(78373)
Rates: $40
(361) 749-6993

ROCK COTTAGES
603 E Ave G
(78373)
Rates: $39-$45
(361) 749-6360

SEA HORSE LODGE
503 E Ave G (78373)
Rates: $65-$95
(361) 749-5513

**SEA & SANDS
COTTAGES**
410 10th St (78373)
Rates: $65-$110
(361) 749-5191

SEASIDE MOTEL
841 Sandcastle Dr
(78373)
Rates: $39-$180
(361) 749-4105
(800) 765-3101

SUNDAY VILLAS
1900 S 11th St
(78373)
Rates: $70
(361) 749-6113

**TROPIC ISLAND
MOTEL**
315 Cutoff Rd
(78373)
Rates: $55-$105
(361) 749-6128

PORT ARTHUR

RAMADA INN
3801 Hwy 73
(77642)
Rates: $55-$69
(409) 962-9858
(800) 272-6232

STUDIO 6
3000 Jimmy
Johnson Blvd
(77642)
Rates: $249-$329
(409) 729-6611
(888) 897-0202

PORT ISABEL

**FAMILY COURTS
& MARINA**
133 Bridge St
(78578)
Rates: n/a
(956) 943-7881

SOUTHWIND INN
600 Davis St (78578)
Rates: $40-$120
(956) 943-3392

**YACHT CLUB
HOTEL**
700 Yturria St
(78578)
Rates: $39-$102
(956) 943-1301

PORT LAVACA

**BEST WESTERN
PORT LAVACA
INN**
2202 N I-35
(77979)
Rates: $59-$87
(361) 553-6800
(800) 528-1234

DAYS INN
2100 N I-35
(77979)
Rates: $45-$90
(361) 552-4511
(800) 329-7466

PORT MANSFIELD

**CASA GRANDE
MOTEL**
1144 S Port Dr
(78598)
Rates: $50-$200
(956) 944-2182

PORTLAND

COMFORT INN
1703 N Hwy 181
(78374)
Rates: $70-$120
(361) 643-2222
(800) 424-6423

POST

**BEST WESTERN
POST INN**
1011 N Broadway
(79356)
Rates: $65-$70
(806) 4956-9933
(800) 528-1234

PRESIDIO

RIATA INN
N Hwy 67 (79788)
Rates: $40-$70
(432) 229-2528

QUANAH

**CASA
ROYALE INN**
1500 W 11th St
(79252)
Rates: n/a
(940) 663-6341

**QUANAH
PARKER INN**
1415 W 11th St
(79252)
Rates: $29-$43
(940) 663-6366

AREA CODES - If the local number doesn't connect, check for a new area code.

QUEEN CITY

EXPRESS INN
301 Hwy 59
(75572)
Rates: $36-$55
(903) 796-7195

RANGER

DAYS INN
I-20 Ex 349,
Box 160-C (76470)
Rates: $50-$69
(254) 647-1176
(800) 329-7466

RANKIN

RIATA INN
509 E Hwy 67
(79778)
Rates: $40-$70
(432) 693-2300

RAYMOND-VILLE

**BEST WESTERN
EXECUTIVE INN**
118 N Expressway
77 (78580)
Rates: $59-$89
(956) 689-4141
(800) 528-1234

RICHARDSON

HAMPTON INN
1577 Gateway
Blvd (75080)
Rates: $59-$89
(972) 234-5400
(800) 426-7866

**HOMESTEAD
STUDIO SUITES**
901 E Campbell
Rd (75080)
Rates: $64-$79
(972) 479-0500
(800) 782-9473

**RENAISSANCE
HOTEL**
900 E Lookout Dr
(75082)
Rates: $139-$270
(972) 367-2000
(800) 468-3571
(800) 228-9290

**RESIDENCE INN
BY MARRIOTT**
1040 Waterwood
Dr (75081)
Rates: $99-$159
(972) 669-5888
(800) 331-3131

SLEEP INN
2458 N Central
Expresswy (75081)
Rates: $44-$65
(972) 470-9440
(800) 753-3746

RICHMOND

EXECUTIVE INN
26035 Southwest
Frwy (77469)
Rates: $35-$45
(281) 342-5387

ROANOKE

COMFORT SUITES
801 Byron Nelson
Blvd (76262)
Rates: $69-$300
(817) 490-1455
(800) 424-6423

**SLEEP INN
& SUITES-
SPEEDWAY**
13471 Raceway Dr
(76262)
Rates: $60-$90
(817) 491-3120
(800) 753-3746

ROBSTOWN

DAYS INN
320 Hwy 77 S
(78380)
Rates: $45-$100
(361) 387-9416
(800) 329-7466

ROCKPORT

ANCHOR MOTEL
1114 E Market
(78382)
Rates: $40-$60
(361) 729-3249

**ANTHONY'S BY
THE SEA B&B**
732 S Pearl St (78382)
Rates: $75-$95
(361) 729-6100
(800) 460-2557

DAYS INN
1212 Laurel
(78382)
Rates: $50-$150
(361) 729-6379
(800) 329-7466

**HOLIDAY LODGE
MOTEL**
1406 I-35 N
(78382)
Rates: $34-$40
(361) 729-3433

**HUNT'S CASTLE-
WATERFRONT**
725 S Water St
(78382)
Rates: $85-$169
(361) 729-5002
(888) 345-4868

**KEY ALLEGRO
ISLAND CONDO
RENTALS**
1798 Bayshore
(78382)
Rates: $125+
(361) 729-2333
(800) 348-1627

**KONTIKI BEACH
RESORT**
2290 N Fulton
Beach Rd (78382)
Rates: $55-$205
(361) 729-4975
(800) 388-0649

**LAGUNA REEF
CONDO HOTEL-
ON THE BAY**
1021 Water St
(78382)
Rates: $80-$350
(361) 729-1742
(800) 248-1057

**OCEAN VIEW
MOTEL**
1131 S Water St
(78382)
Rates: $35-$65
(361) 729-3326

ROCKPORT INN
813 S Church St
(78382)
Rates: $40
(361) 729-9591

**ROD AND REEL
MOTEL**
1105 E Market St
(78382)
Rates: $31-$54
(361) 729-2028
(888) 729-2028

**SANDOLLAR
RESORT MOTEL**
919 N Fulton
Beach Rd (78382)
Rates: $44-$59
(361) 729-2381

**SANDRA BAY
COTTAGES**
1801 Broadway
(78382)
Rates: $45+
(361) 729-6257

SEAVIEW MOTEL
1155 I-35 N (78382)
Rates: $35-$55
(361) 729-9112

SUN-TAN MOTEL
1805 Broadway
(78382)
Rates: $39-$60
(361) 729-2179

**THE VILLAGE
INN MOTEL**
503 N Austin St
(78382)
Rates: $55-$120
(361) 729-6370
(800) 338-7539

ROCKWALL

SUPER 8 MOTEL
1130 I-30 (75087)
Rates: $44-$55
(972) 722-9922
(800) 800-8000

ROSENBERG

**HOLIDAY INN EXP
HOTEL & SUITES**
27927 Southwest
Frwy (77471)
Rates: $69-$89
(281) 342-7888
(800) 465-4329

ROUND ROCK

AMERISUITES
2340 I-35 N
(78681)
Rates: $69-$139
(512) 733-2599
(800) 833-1516

BAYMONT INN
150 Parker Dr
(78728)
Rates: $74-$129
(512) 246-2800
(800) 301-0200

**BEST WESTERN
EXECUTIVE INN**
1851 N I-35
(78664)
Rates: $55-$79
(512) 255-3222
(800) 528-1234
(888) 821-5578

**CANDLEWOOD
SUITES**
521 S I-35 (78664)
Rates: $64-$109
(512) 828-0899
(800) 465-4329

DAYS INN
1802 I-35 S (78681)
Rates: $49-$89
(512) 246-0055
(800) 329-7466
(877) 295-3189

HOLIDAY INN
230 N I-35 (78681)
Rates: $74-$94
(512) 733-2630
(800) 465-4329

LA QUINTA INN
2004 I-35 N (78681)
Rates: $70-$90
(512) 255-6666
(800) 687-6667

RED ROOF INN
1990 N I-35 (78681)
Rates: $42-$77
(512) 310-1111
(800) 843-7663

**RESIDENCE INN
BY MARRIOTT**
2505 S I-35 (78664)
Rates: $89-$119
(512) 733-2400
(800) 331-3131

**STAYBRIDGE
SUITES**
520 I-35 S (78681)
Rates: $109-$179
(512) 733-0942
(800) 238-8000

WINGATE INN
1209 N I-35
(78664)
Rates: $69-$125
(512) 341-7000

ROUND TOP

**ROUND TOP INN
BED & BREAKFST**
102 Bauer
Rummell (78954)
Rates: $95-$145
(979) 249-5294
(888) 356-8946

ROWLETT

**COMFORT SUITES
LAKE RAY
HUBBARD**
8701 E Interstate,
I-30 (75088)
Rates: $79-$149
(972) 463-9595
(800) 424-6423

AREA CODES - If the local number doesn't connect, check for a new area code.

SAN ANGELO

BENCHMARK-COMFORT INN
2502 Loop 306 (76904)
Rates: $70-$105
(325) 944-2578
(800) 424-6423

BEST VALUE INN
1601 S Bryant Blvd (76904)
Rates: $60-$70
(325) 944-2578

BEST WESTERN SAN ANGELO
3017 W Loop 306 (76904)
Rates: $65-$75
(325) 223-1273
(800) 528-1234

DAYS INN
4613 S Jackson (76903)
Rates: $45-$75
(325) 658-6594
(800) 329-7466

EL PATIO MOTEL
1901 W Beauregard St (76901)
Rates: $25-$40
(325) 655-5711
(800) 677-7735

EXECUTIVE INN
4205 S Bryant Blvd (76903)
Rates: $48-$75
(325) 653-6966

HOLIDAY INN CONVENTION CENTER HOTEL
441 Rio Concho Dr (76903)
Rates: $109-$169
(325) 658-2828
(800) 465-4329

HOWARD JOHNSON
415 W Beauregard St (76901)
Rates: $54-$65
(325) 653-2995
(800) 446-4656

INN OF THE CONCHOS
2021 N Bryant Blvd (76903)
Rates: $59-$89
(325) 658-2811
(800) 621-6041

LA QUINTA INN
2307 Loop 306 (76904)
Rates: $54-$91
(325) 949-0515
(800) 687-6667

MOTEL 6
311 N Bryant Blvd (76903)
Rates: $34-$52
(325) 658-8061
(800) 466-8356

RAMADA LIMITED
2201 N Bryant (76903)
Rates: n/a
(325) 653-8442
(800) 272-6232

SANTA FE JCT MOTOR INN
410 W Ave L (76903)
Rates: $29-$60
(325) 655-8101
(800) 634-2599

SUPER 8 MOTEL
1601 S Bryant Blvd (76903)
Rates: $44-$57
(325) 653-1323
(800) 800-8000

SAN ANTONIO

A BASIC HOME-VACATION RENTAL
7423 Dell Oak (78218)
Rates $99-$195
(800) 227-5883

A BLANSETT BARN GUEST HOUSE
206 Madison St (78204)
Rates: $125-$250
(800) 221-1412

ALAMO TRAVELODGE-RIVERWALK
405 Broadway (78205)
Rates: $45-$149
(210) 222-1000
(800) 578-7878

ALOHA INN
1435 Austin Hwy (78209)
Rates: $40-$70
(210) 828-0933
(800) 752-6354

AMERISUITES AIRPORT
7615 Jones Maltsberger Rd (78216)
Rates: $69-$135
(210) 930-2333
(800) 833-1516

AMERISUITES NORTHWEST
4325 AmeriSuites Dr (78230)
Rates: $89-$129
(210) 561-0099
(800) 833-1516

AMERISUITES RIVERWALK
601 S St. Mary's St (78205)
Rates: $109-$199
(210) 227-6854
(800) 833-1516

ANTONIO INN
2131 N I-35 (78208)
Rates: $55-$165
(210) 354-2998

ARBOR HOUSE INN B & B
109 Arciniega St (78205)
Rates: $95-$225
(210) 472-2005
(888) 272-6700

BEST WESTERN FIESTA INN
13535 I-10 W (78249)
Rates: $50-$130
(210) 696-2400
(800) 528-1234
(800) 662-9607

BEST WESTERN INGRAM PARK INN
6855 NW Loop 410 (78238)
Rates: $50-$130
(210) 520-8080
(800) 528-1234
(888) 889-3444

BEST WESTERN LACKLAND INN & SUITES
6815 Hwy 90 W (78227)
Rates: $59-$120
(210) 675-9690
(800) 528-1234
(888) 227-2313

BEST WESTERN NORTHEAST
11939 N I-35 (78236)
Rates: $69-$159
(210) 599-0999
(800) 528-1234

BEST WESTERN POSADA ANA INN
8600 Jones Maltsberger Rd (78216)
Rates: $73-$120
(210) 342-1400
(800) 528-1234

BEST WESTERN POSADA ANA INN-MEDICAL CENTER
9411 Wurzbach Rd (78240)
Rates: $67-$110
(210) 561-9300
(800) 528-1234

BEST WESTERN SHETLAND INN
3602 SE Military Dr (78223)
Rates: $55-$95
(210) 798-5000
(800) 528-1234

BRACKENRIDGE HOUSE B&B
230 Madison St (78204)
Rates: $110-$200
(210) 271-3342
(800) 221-1412

BUDGET SUITES MEDICAL DISTRICT
7880 Fredericksburg Rd (78240)
Rates: $49-$59
(877) 822-5272

CANDLEWOOD SUITES HOTEL
9350 I-10 W (78230)
Rates: $89-$109
(210) 615-0550
(800) 465-4329

CLARION HOTEL RIVERWALK
110 Lexington Ave (78205)
Rates: n/a
(210) 223-9461
(800) 424-6423

CLARION SUITES
13101 E Loop 1604 N (78233)
Rates: $69-$159
(210) 655-9491
(800) 424-6423

CLASSIC INN
9603 I-35 N (78233)
Rates: $29-$89
(210) 655-2120

COACHMAN INN BROOKS FIELD
3180 Gollard Rd (78223)
Rates: $39-$56
(210) 337-7171

COMFORT INN ET
4403 I-10 E (78219)
Rates: $43-$175
(210) 33-9430
(800) 424-6423

COMFORT INN-FIESTA PARK/SIX FLAGS
6755 N Loop 1604 W (78249)
Rates: $59-$149
(210) 696-4766
(800) 424-6423

COMFORT INN SEA WORLD
4 Plano Pl (78229)
Rates: $55-$175
(210) 684-8606
(800) 424-6423

COMFORT INN & SUITES AIRPORT
Laurel Hurst & Greenbrier (78209)
Rates: $75-$99
(800) 424-6423

COMFORT SUITES CENTRAL
6901 I-10 W (78213)
Rates: $64-$114
(210) 738-1100
(800) 424-6423

COUNTRY HEARTH INN
7500 Louis Pasteur (78229)
Rates: $54-$78
(210) 616-0030
(888) 325-7821

DAYS INN
1500 S Laredo St (78204)
Rates: $49-$109
(210) 271-3334
(800) 329-7466

DAYS INN/ COLISEUM
3443 I-35 N (78219)
Rates: $50-$110
(210) 225-4040
(800) 329-7466
(800) 548-262

DAYS INN-EAST
4039 E Houston
St (78220)
Rates: $29-$69
(210) 333-9100
(800) 329-7466

DAYS INN-WINDCREST
9401 I-35 N (78233)
Rates: $40-$110
(210) 650-9779
(800) 329-7466

DELUX INN
3370 I-35 N (78219)
Rates: $35-$99
(210) 271-3100

DRURY INN EAST
8300 I-35 N (78239)
Rates: $70-$100
(210) 654-1144
(800) 378-7946

DRURY INN & SUITES/AIRPORT
95 NE Loop 410 (78216)
Rates: $72-$107
(210) 308-8100
(800) 378-7946

DRURY INN NORTHEAST
8300 I-35 N (78230)
Rates: $71-$140
(210) 561-2510
(800) 378-7946

DRURY INN & SUITES-NORTHWEST
9806 I-10 W (78230)
Rates: $75-$122
(210) 561-2510
(800) 378-7946

ECONO LODGE
6023 I-10 W (78201)
Rates: $50-$200
(210) 737-1855
(800) 424-6423

ECONO LODGE
2635 NE Loop 410 (78217)
Rates: $47-$74
(210) 247-4774
(800) 424-6423

ECONO LODGE
3817 N I-35, Bldg C (78219)
Rates: $43-$110
(210) 224-5114
(800) 424-6423

THE FAIRMOUNT HISTORIC HOTEL
401 S Alamo St (78205)
Rates: $199-$555
(210) 224-8800

FOUR POINTS BY SHERATON/ RIVERWALK N.
110 Lexington Ave (78205)
Rates: $89-$119
(210) 223-9461

GARDENIA INN B&B
307 Beauregard St (78204)
Rates: $90-$140
(800) 356-1605

HAMPTON INN AIRPORT
8818 Jones Maltsberger Rd (78216)
Rates: $80-$120
(210) 366-1800
(800) 426-7866

HAMPTON INN NORTHWOODS
2127 Gold Canyon Dr (78232)
Rates: n/a
(210) 404-1144
(800) 426-7866

HAMPTON INN SIX FLAGS AREA
11010 I-10 W (78230)
Rates: $89-$124
(210) 561-9058
(800) 426-7866
(877) 731-4331

HAWTHORN SUITES RIVERWALK
830 N St. Marys Street (78205)
Rates: $119-$189
(210) 527-1900
(800) 527-1133

HILL COUNTRY INN
2383 NE Loop 410 (78217)
Rates: $56-$66
(210) 599-4204

HILTON PALACIO DEL RIO
200 S Alamo St (78205)
Rates: $98-$256
(210) 222-1400
(800) 445-8667

HILTON SAN ANTONIO AIRPORT
611 NW Loop 410 (78216)
Rates: $79-$265
(210) 340-6060
(800) 445-8667

HOLIDAY INN-CROCKETT HOTEL
320 Bonham (78205)
Rates: $89-$189
(210) 225-6500
(800) 465-4329
(800) 292-1050

HOLIDAY INN-DOWNTOWN-MARKET SQUARE
318 W Durango (78204)
Rates: $119-$139
(210) 225-3211
(800) 465-4329

HOLIDAY INN EXP
11939 N I-35 (78233)
Rates: $69-$209
(210) 599-0999
(800) 465-4329

HOLIDAY INN EXP AIRPORT
91 NE Loop 410 (78216)
Rates: $93-$123
(210) 308-6700
(800) 465-4329

HOLIDAY INN NORTHEAST
3855 I-35 N (78219)
Rates: $94-$99
(210) 226-4361
(800) 465-4329

HOLIDAY INN RIVERWALK
217 N St. Mary's St (78205)
Rates: $149-$179
(210) 224-2500
(800) 465-4329

HOLIDAY INN SELECT-INT'L AIRPORT
77 NE Loop 410 (78216)
Rates: $109-$129
(210) 349-9900
(800) 465-4329

HOMEGATE STUDIOS & SUITES-AIRPORT
11221 San Pedro Ave (78216)
Rates: $49-$89
(210) 342-4800
(888) 456-4283

HOMESTEAD STUDIO SUITES/ AIRPORT
1015 Central Pkwy S Loop 410 (78232)
Rates: $50-$74
(210) 491-9009
(888) 782-9473

HOWARD JOHNSON COLISEUM
2755 N Pan Am Expresswy (78208)
Rates: $50-$120
(210) 229-9220
(800) 446-4656

HOWARD JOHNSON EXP INN FIESTA
13279 IH-10 W (78249)
Rates: $49-$99
(210) 558-7152
(800) 446-4656

KNIGHTS INN WINDSOR PARK
6370 I-35 N (78218)
Rates: $49-$89
(210) 646-6336
(800) 843-5644

LA MANSION DEL RIO HOTEL
112 College St (78205)
Rates: $219-$369
(210) 518-1000
(800) 531-7208
(800) 292-7300

LA QUINTA INN
1001 E Commerce St (78205)
Rates: $105-$155
(210) 222-9181
(800) 687-6667

LA QUINTA INN INGRAM PARK
7134 NW Loop 410 (78238)
Rates: $55-$122
(210) 680-8883
(800) 687-6667

LA QUINTA INN-LACKLAND
6511 Military Dr W (78227)
Rates: $65-$91
(210) 674-3200
(800) 687-6667

LA QUINTA INN MARKET SQUARE
900 Dolorosa St (78207)
Rates: $79-$139
(210) 271-0001
(800) 687-6667

LA QUINTA INN SAN ANTONIO AIRPORT
850 Halm (78216)
Rates: $89-$109
(210) 342-3738
(800) 687-6667

LA QUINTA INN SOUTH PARK
7202 S Pan Am Expresswy (78224)
Rates: $65-$90
(800) 687-6667

LA QUINTA INN TOPPERWEIN
12822 N I-35 (78233)
Rates: $70-$90
(800) 687-6667

LA QUINTA INN VANCE JACKSON
5922 NW Expresswy (78201)
Rates: $65-$95
(210) 734-7931
(800) 687-6667

LA QUINTA INN WINDSOR PARK
6410 I-35 N (78218)
Rates: $65-$101
(210) 653-6619
(800) 687-6667

AREA CODES - If the local number doesn't connect, check for a new area code.

LA QUINTA INN-WURZBACH
9542 I-10 W (78230)
Rates: $69-$99
(210) 593-0338
(800) 687-6667

LITTLE FLOWER INN B&B
225 Madison St
(78204)
Rates: $85-$110
(210) 354-3116

MARRIOTT PLAZA HOTEL
555 S Alamo (78205)
Rates: $99-$274
(210) 229-1000
(800) 228-9290
(800) 727-3239

MARRIOTT RIVERCENTER
101 Bowie St (78205)
Rates: $129-$324
(210) 223-1000
(800) 228-9290
(800) 648-4462

MARRIOTT RIVERWALK
711 E Riverwalk
(78205)
Rates: $129-$324
(210) 224-4555
(800) 228-9290
(800) 648-4462

MOTEL 6-ALAMO DOME S
748 Hot Wells Blvd
(78223)
Rates: $42-$64
(210) 533-6667
(800) 466-8356

MOTEL 6-EAST
138 N WW White
Rd (78219)
Rates: $37-$53
(210) 333-1850
(800) 466-8356

MOTEL 6-FIESTA
16500 I-10 W
(78257)
Rates: $35-$60
(210) 697-0731
(800) 466-8356

MOTEL 6 NE
4621 E Rittiman
Rd (78218)
Rates: $31-$55
(210) 653-8088
(800) 466-8356

MOTEL 6 -FT. SAM HOUSTON
5522 N Pan Am
Expresswy (78218)
Rates: $31-$50
(210) 661-8791
(800) 466-8356

MOTEL 6-NORTH
9503 I-35 N (78233)
Rates: $33-$51
(210) 650-4419
(800) 466-8356

MOTEL 6-NW MEDICAL CENTER
9400 Wurzbach
Rd (78240)
Rates: $39-$59
(210) 593-0013
(800) 466-8356

MOTEL 6-RIVERWALK
211 N Pecos St
(78207)
Rates: $39-$71
(210) 225-1111
(800) 466-8356

MOTEL 6 SOUTH
7950 S Pan Am
Expresswy (78224)
Rates: $36-$69
(210) 928-2866
(800) 466-8356

MOTEL 6-WEST SEA WORLD
2185 SW Loop 410
(78227)
Rates: $42-$58
(210) 673-9020
(800) 466-8356

O'CASEYS BED & BREAKFAST
225 W Craig Place
(78212)
Rates: $69-$115
(800) 738-1378

OMNI HOTEL SAN ANTONIO
9821 Colonnade
Blvd (78230)
Rates: $89-$169
(210) 669-5884
(800) 843-6664

PAINTED LADY INN ON BROADWAY B&B
620 Broadway
(78215)
Rates: $79-$189
(210) 220-1092

PEAR TREE INN
143 NE Loop 410
(78216)
Rates: $68-$94
(210) 366-9300
(800) 282-8733

PLAZA SAN ANTONIO-A MARRIOTT HOTEL
555 S Alamo St
(78205)
Rates: $169-$500
(210) 229-1000
(800) 421-1172
(800) 727-3239

QUALITY INN
222 South W W
White Rd (78219)
Rates: $45-$129
(210) 359-7200
(800) 424-6423

QUALITY INN & SUITES COLISEUM
3817 I-35 N (78219)
Rates: $49-$89
(210) 224-3030
(800) 424-6423

QUALITY INN NORTHWOOD
1505 Bexar
Crossing (78232)
Rates: $69-$139
(210) 545-5400
(800) 424-6423

RADFORD INN
13575 I-10 W
(78201)
Rates: n/a
(210) 690-5500

RADISSON RESORT HILL COUNTRY
9800 Westover
Hills Blvd (78251)
Rates: $129-$189
(210) 509-9800
(800) 333-3333

RAMADA LIMITED SBC CENTER
3939 E Houston
St (78220)
Rates: n/a
(210) 359-1111
(800) 272-6232

RED ROOF INN AIRPORT
333 Wolf Rd &
US 281 (78216)
Rates: $48-$73
(210) 340-4055
(800) 843-7663

RED ROOF INN DOWNTOWN
1011 E Houston St
(78205)
Rates: $49-$94
(210) 229-9973
(800) 843-7663

RED ROOF INN LACKLAND
6861 Hwy 90 W
(78227)
Rates: $39-$66
(210) 675-4120
(800) 843-7663

RED ROOF INN NW-SEAWORLD
6880 NW Loop
410 (78238)
Rates: $46-$78
(210) 509-3434
(800) 843-7663

RELAY STATION MOTEL
5530 I-10 E (78219)
Rates: $32-$47
(210) 662-6691
(800) 735-2981

RESIDENCE INN BY MARRIOTT AIRPORT
1014 NE Loop 410
(78209)
Rates: $134-$229
(210) 805-8118
(800) 331-3131

RESIDENCE INN BY MARRIOTT
628 S Santa Rosa
Blvd (78204)
Rates: $149-$299
(210) 231-6000
(800) 331-3131

RESIDENCE INN BY MARRIOTT-ALAMO PLAZA
425 Bonham St
(78205)
Rates: $169-$236
(210) 212-5555
(800) 331-3131

RESIDENCE INN NW-SIX FLAGS
4041 Bluemel Rd
(78240)
Rates: $109-$199
(210) 561-9660
(800) 331-3131

RODEWAY INN DOWNTOWN
900 N Main Ave
(78212)
Rates: $72-$108
(210) 223-2951
(800) 424-6423

RODEWAY INN SIX FLAGS-FIESTA
19793 I-10 W
(78257)
Rates: $58-$109
(210) 698-3991
(800) 242-6423

SEVEN OAKS RESORT
1400 Austin Hwy
(78209)
Rates: $50-$65
(210) 824-5371
(800) 346-5866

SHERATON GUNTER HIS-TORIC HOTEL
205 E Houston St
(78205)
Rates: $189-$199
(210) 227-3241
(800) 325-3535

SLEEP INN NW MEDICAL CENTER
8318 I-10 W (78230)
Rates: $50-$95
(210) 344-5400
(800) 753-3746

STAYBRIDGE SUITES BY HOLIDAY INN NW COLONNADE
4320 Spectrum
One (78230)
Rates: $96-$208
(210) 558-9009
(800) 238-8000

STAYBRIDGE SUITES AIRPORT
66 NE Loop 410
(78216)
Rates: $138-$178
(210) 341-3220
(800) 238-8000

STUDIO 6-MEDICAL CENTER
7719 Louis
Pasteur Ct (78229)
Rates: $209-$299
(210) 349-3100
(888) 897-0202

AREA CODES - If the local number doesn't connect, check for a new area code.

**STUDIO 6-
SIX FLAGS**
11802 I-10 W
(78230)
Rates: $209-$299
(210) 691-0121
(888) 897-0202

SUPER 8 MOTEL
11027 I-35 N
(78233)
Rates: $35-$85
(210) 637-1033
(800) 800-8000

**SUPER 8 MOTEL
DOWNTOWN**
3617 N Pan Am
Expresswy (78219)
Rates: $42-$88
(210) 227-8888
(800) 800-8000

**SUPER 8-SIX
FLAGS FIESTA**
5319 Casa Bella
(78249)
Rates: $54-$94
(210) 696-6916
(800) 800-8000

VILLAGER LODGE
1126 E Elmira St
(78212)
Rates: $34-$50
(800) 584-0800

**WELLESLEY INN
AIRPORT**
2635 NE Loop 410
(78217)
Rates: $55-$95
(210) 653-9110
(800) 444-8888

**WESTIN
RIVERWALK
HOTEL**
420 W Market St
(78205)
Rates: $329-$419
(210) 224-6500
(800) 228-3000

**WOODFIELD
SUITES-
DOWNTOWN**
100 W Durango
Blvd (78204)
Rates: $79-$169
(210) 212-5400
(800) 338-0008
(877) 211-0103

SAN AUGUSTINE

**SAN
AUGUSTINE INN**
1009 Hwy 21 W
(75972)
Rates: $36-$46
(936) 275-3452

SAN BENITO

DAYS INN
1451 W
Expresswy 83 &
77 (78586)
Rates: $38-$125
(956) 399-3891
(800) 329-7466

**VIEH'S BED
& BREAKFAST**
18413 Landrum
Park Rd (78586)
Rates: $65-$95
(956) 425-4651

SAN MARCOS

**BEST WESTERN
SAN MARCOS**
917 I-35 N (78666)
Rates: $59-$99
(512) 754-7557
(800) 528-1234

DAYS INN
1005 I-35 N
(78666)
Rates: $35-$125
(512) 353-5050
(800) 329-7466

LA QUINTA INN
1619 I-35 N (78666)
Rates: $60-$105
(512) 392-8800
(800) 687-6667

**LONESOME DOVE
BED & BREAKFAST**
407 Oakwood
Loop (78666)
Rates: $65-$85
(512) 392-2921

MOTEL 6
1321 I-35 N
(78666)
Rates: $34-$55
(512) 396-8705
(800) 466-8356

RAMADA LIMITED
1701 I-35 N
(78667)
Rates: $34-$129
(512) 395-8000
(800) 272-6232

RED ROOF INN
817 I-35 N (78666)
Rates: $39-$149
(512) 754-8899
(800) 843-7663

STRATFORD INN
1601 I-35 N (78666)
Rates: $39-$79
(512) 396-3700

SUPER 8 MOTEL
1429 I-35 N (78666)
Rates: $69-$75
(512) 396-0400
(800) 800-8000

UNIVERSITY INN
1507 I-35 N
(78666)
Rates: $29-$100
(512) 396-6060

SANDERSON

BUDGET INN
Hwy 90 E (79848)
Rates: $28-$48
(432) 345-2541

DESERT AIR MOTEL
806 W Oak (79848)
Rates: $30-$39
(432) 345-2572

**OUTBACK
OASIS MOTEL**
800 W Hwy 90
(79848)
Rates: $29-$59
(888) 466-8822

SANDIA

**KNOLLE FARM &
RANCH- B&B**
Rt 1, Box 681
(78387)
Rates: $85-$175
(361) 547-2546

SCHULENBURG

**OAKRIDGE
MOTOR INN**
I-10 & Hwy 77
(78956)
Rates: $42-$64
(979) 743-4192

SEALY

**BEST WESTERN
INN**
2107 Hwy 36 S
(77474)
Rates: $61-$65
(979) 885-3707
(800) 528-1234

RODEWAY INN
2021 Hwy 36 S
(77474)
Rates: $39-$65
(979) 885-7407
(800) 424-6423

SEGOVIA

ECONO LODGE
311 S Segovia Exp.
Rd (76849)
Rates: n/a
(325) 446-2475
(800) 424-6423

SEGUIN

**BEST WESTERN
OF SEGUIN**
1603 I-10, Hwy 46
(78155)
Rates: $55-$99
(830) 379-9631
(800) 528-1234

HOLIDAY INN
2950 N123 Bypass
(78155)
Rates: $86-$116
(830) 372-0860
(800) 465-4329

SUPER 8 MOTEL
1525 N Hwy 46
(78155)
Rates: $45-$120
(830) 379-6888
(800) 800-8000

SEMINOLE

**RAYMOND
MOTOR INN**
301 W Ave A
(79360)
Rates: $37-$45
(432) 758-3653

SEMINOLE INN
2200 Hobbs Hwy
(79360)
Rates: $42-$57
(432) 758-9881

SEYMOUR

SAGAMAR INN
1101 N Main St
(76380)
Rates: $40-$65
(940) 888-5507

SHAFTER

**CIBOLO CREEK
RANCH RESORT**
US Hwy 67 N
(79850)
Rates: n/a
(432) 229-3737

SHAMROCK

**BUDGET HOST
BLARNEY INN**
402 E 12th St
(79079)
Rates: $28-$45
(806) 956-2101
(800) 283-4678

ECONO LODGE
1006 E 12th St
(79079)
Rates: $45-$70
(806) 256-2111
(800) 424-6423

IRISH INN
301 I-40 E (79079)
Rates: $45-$58
(806) 256-2106
(800) 538-6747

**THE WESTERN
MOTEL**
104 E 12th St
(79079)
Rates: $39-$59
(806) 256-3244

SHENANDOAH

LA QUINTA INN
28673 N I-45
(77384)
Rates: $69-$75
(281) 367-7722
(800) 687-6667

SPRING INN
29007 N I-45
(77381)
Rates: $39-$90
(281) 363-3933

SHERMAN

**COMFORT SUITES
OF SHERMAN**
2900 Hwy 75 N
(75090)
Rates: $79-$129
(903) 893-0499
(800) 424-6423

**CROSSROADS
INN MOTEL**
2424 Texoma
Pkwy (75090)
Rates: $30+
(903) 893-0184

DAYS INN
1831 Texoma
Pkwy (75090)
Rates: $45-$66
(903) 892-0433
(800) 329-7466

EXECUTIVE INN
2105 Texoma
Pkwy (75090)
Rates: $49-$77
(903) 892-2161
(800) 723-4194

HOLIDAY INN
3605 Hwy 75 S
(75090)
Rates: $59-$72
(903) 868-0555
(800) 465-4329

LA QUINTA INN
2912 Hwy 75 N
(75090)
Rates: $80-$110
(903) 870-1122
(800) 687-6667

SUPER 8 MOTEL
111 E Hwy 1417
(75090)
Rates: $40-$55
(903) 868-9325
(800) 800-8000

SMITHVILLE
**THE KATY HOUSE
BED & BREAKFAST**
201 Ramona St
(78957)
Rates: $90-$140
(512) 237-4262
(800) 843-5289

**9E RANCH BED
& BREAKFAST**
21558 Hwy 304
(78957)
Rates: $95-$135
(512) 497-9502

PINE POINT INN
1503 Dorothy
Nichols Ln (78957)
Rates: $50-$70
(512) 237-2040

SNYDER
BEACON LODGE
1900 E Hwy 180
(79549)
Rates: $39-$47
(325) 573-8526

**BEST WESTERN
SNYDER INN**
810 E Coliseum Dr
(79549)
Rates: $65-$95
(325) 574-2200
(800) 528-1234

DAYS INN
800 E Coliseum Dr
(79454)
Rates: $42-$55
(325) 573-1166
(800) 329-7466

**PURPLE SAGE
MOTEL**
1501 E Coliseum
Dr (79549)
Rates: $48-$70
(325) 573-5491
(800) 545-5792

WILLOW PARK INN
1137 E Hwy 180
& 84 (79549)
Rates: $45-$75
(325) 573-1961
(800) 854-6818

SOMERVILLE
SUPER 8 MOTEL
152 Ave B South
(77879)
Rates: $45-$85
(979) 596-3884
(800) 800-8000

SONORA
**BEST VALUE INN-
TWIN OAKS MOTEL**
907 N Crockett
Ave (76950)
Rates: $36-$50
(325) 387-2551

**BEST WESTERN
SONORA INN**
270 Hwy 277 N
(76950)
Rates: $64-$90
(325) 387-9111
(800) 528-1234

COMFORT INN
311 N Hwy 277
(76950)
Rates: $69-$89
(325) 387-5800
(800) 424-6423

**DAYS INN-
DEVIL'S RIVER**
1312 N Service Rd
(76950)
Rates: $49-$69
(325) 387-3516
(800) 329-7466

**HOLIDAY HOST
MOTEL**
127 Loop 467
(76950)
Rates: $34-$50
(325) 387-2532

SOUTH PADRE ISLAND
**ALL ON BEACH-
VACATION
RENTALS**
2700 Gulf Blvd
(78597)
Rates: $99-$395
(800) 227-5883

**BEST WESTERN
FIESTA ISLES**
5701 Padre Blvd
(78597)
Rates: $39-$249
(956) 761-4913
(800) 528-1234

**CASA DE SIESTA
B&B INN**
4610 Padre Blvd
(78597)
Rates: $99-$150
(956) 761-5656

**CASTAWAYS
CONDOMINIUMS**
3700 Gulf Blvd
(78597)
Rates: $95+
(956) 761-1903
(800) 892-6278

COMFORT SUITES
912 Padre Blvd
(78597)
Rates: $79-$249
(956) 772-9020
(800) 424-6423

**CONTINENTAL
CONDOMINIUMS**
4908 Gulf Blvd
(78597)
Rates: $84+
(956) 761-1306
(800) 426-6530

DAYS INN
3913 Padre Blvd
(78597)
Rates: $59-$250
(956) 761-7831
(800) 329-7466

ECONO LODGE
3813 Padre Blvd
(78597)
Rates: $29-$299
(956) 761-8500
(800) 424-6423

**HOWARD JOHN-
SON INN RESORT**
1709 Padre Blvd
(78597)
Rates: $39-$249
(956) 761-5658
(800) 446-4656

**ISLAND INN
ON THE BEACH**
5100 Gulf Blvd
(78597)
Rates: $59-$249
(956) 761-7677

**LA COPA BEACH
RESORT**
350 Padre Blvd
(78597)
Rates: $39-$299
(958) 761-6000
(866) 452-2672

**LA
INTERNATIONAL**
5008 Gulf Blvd
(78597)
Rates: $75+
(956) 761-1306
(800) 426-6530

LA QUINTA INN
7000 Padre Blvd
(78597)
Rates: $49-$349
(956) 772-7000
(800) 687-6667

MOTEL 6
4013 Padre Blvd
(78597)
Rates: $37-$75
(956) 761-7911
(800) 466-8356

PALMS RESORT
3616 Gulf Blvd
(78597)
Rates: $44+
(956) 761-1316
(800) 221-5218

RAMADA LTD
4109 Padre Blvd
(78597)
Rates: $49-$209
(956) 761-4097
(800) 272-6232

**SAND CASTLE
MOTEL**
208 W Kingfish
(78597)
Rates: $46-$64
(956) 761-1321
(800) 426-6530

**SOUTH
BEACH INN**
120 E Jupiter
(78597)
Rates: $39-$99
(956) 761-2471

**SOUTH PADRE
BEACH HOUSES**
5009 Padre Blvd
(78597)
Rates: $80-$360
(956) 761-6554

SUPER 8 MOTEL
4205 Padre Blvd
(78597)
Rates: $40-$340
(956) 761-6300
(800) 800-8000

**THE TIKI
CONDOMINIUM
HOTEL**
6608 Padre Blvd
(78597)
Rates: $79-$155
(956) 761-2694

TRAVELODGE
6200 Padre Blvd
(78597)
Rates: $39-$295
(956) 761-4744
(800) 578-7878

**TRES PALMAS
BEACH HOUSE
RENTALS**
116 E Kingfish
(78597)
Rates: $95-$200
per night/
$550-$1100 wk/
$900-$2200 month
(956) 761-5607

SPRING
MOTEL 6
19606
Cypresswood Ct
(77388)
Rates: $37-$46
(281) 350-6400
(800) 466-8356

STAFFORD
**BEST WESTERN
FORT BEND INN**
11206 W Airport
Blvd (77477)
Rates: $60
(281) 575-6060
(800) 528-1234

AREA CODES - If the local number doesn't connect, check for a new area code.

COMFORT SUITES
4820 Techniplex
Dr (77477)
Rates: $75-$139
(281) 565-5566
(800) 424-6423

DAYS INN
4630 Techniplex
Dr (77477)
Rates: $38-$45
(281) 240-8100
(800) 329-7466

LA QUINTA INN
12727 Southwest
Frwy (77477)
Rates: $60-$86
(281) 240-2300
(800) 687-6667

**RESIDENCE INN
BY MARRIOTT**
12703 Southwest
Frwy (77477)
Rates: $129
(281) 277-0770
(800) 331-3131

STUDIO 6
12827 Southwest
Frwy (77477)
Rates: $199-$279
(281) 240-6900
(888) 897-0202

WELLESLEY INN
4726 Sugar Grove
Blvd (77477)
Rates: $79-$89
(241) 240-0025
(800) 444-8888

STEPHENVILLE
**BEST WESTERN
CROSS TIMBERS**
1625 S Loop (76401)
Rates: $50-$85
(254) 968-2114
(800) 528-1234

COMFORT INN
2925 W Washington
(76401)
Rates: $59-$99
(254) 965-7162
(800) 424-6423

DAYS INN
701 E South Loop
(76401)
Rates: $48-$74
(254) 968-3392
(800) 329-7466

HOLIDAY INN
2865 W Washington
(76401)
Rates: $89-$99
(254) 968-5256
(800) 465-4329

TEXAN INN
3030 W Washington
(76401)
Rates: $36-$46
(254) 968-5003

STONEWALL
**COUNTRY
CABINS B&B**
P. O. Box 421
(78671)
Rates: $95-$130
(830) 868-7447

STRATFORD
STRATFORD INN
402 Texas Ave
(79084)
Rates: $39-$59
(806) 366-5574

SUGAR LAND
DRURY INN
13770 Southwest
Frwy (77478)
Rates: $81-$111
(281) 277-9700
(800) 378-7946

**HEARTHSIDE
SUITES BY
VILLAGER**
13420 Southwest
Frwy (77478)
Rates: $59-$99
(281) 494-6699

HOLIDAY INN EXP
14444 Southwest
Frwy (77478)
Rates: $79
(281) 565-6655
(800) 465-4329

STUDIO 6
12827 Southwest
Frwy (77477)
Rates: $46-$63
(888) 897-0202

SULPHUR SPRINGS
**BEST WESTERN
TRAIL DUST INN**
1521 Shannon Rd
(75482)
Rates: $74-$109
(903) 885-7515
(800) 980-2378

COMFORT SUITES
1521 E Industrial
(75483)
Rates: $74-$99
(903) 438-0918
(800) 424-6423

HOLIDAY INN
1495 E Industrial
(75482)
Rates: $79-$99
(903) 885-0562
(800) 465-4329

SWEETWATER
COMFORT INN
216 S Georgia St
(79556)
Rates: $59-$125
(325) 235-5234
(800) 424-6423

HOLIDAY INN
500 NW Georgia
St (79556)
Rates: $79-$119
(325) 236-6887
(800) 465-4329

MOTEL 6
510 NW Georgia
St (79556)
Rates: $31-$40
(325) 235-4387
(800) 466-8356

**MULBERRY
MANSION B&B**
1400 Sam Houston
(79556)
Rates: $65-$225
(325) 235-3811
(800) 235-3911

RAMADA INN
701 SW Georgia St
(79556)
Rates: $50-$60
(325) 235-4853
(800) 272-6232

**RANCH HOUSE
MOTEL**
301 SW Georgia St
(79556)
Rates: $39-$65
(325) 236-6341
(800) 622-5361

**TRAVELERS
MOTEL**
1413 E Broadway
(79556)
Rates: $25-$35
(325) 235-2850

TAYLOR
REGENCY INN
2007 N Main
(76574)
Rates: $40-$49
(512) 352-2666

TEMPLE
DAYS INN
1104 N General
Bruce Dr (76504)
Rates: $59-$79
(254) 774-9223
(800) 329-7466

ECONO LODGE
1001 N General
Bruce Dr (76504)
Rates: $39-$79
(254) 771-1688
(800) 424-6423

**HOWARD JOHN-
SON EXP INN**
1912 S 31st St
(76504)
Rates: $59-$64
(254) 778-5521
(800) 446-4656

LA QUINTA INN
1604 W Barton
Ave (76504)
Rates: $60-$85
(254) 771-2980
(800) 687-6667

MOTEL 6
1100 N General
Bruce Dr (76504)
Rates: $34-$50
(254) 778-0272
(800) 466-8356

**STRATFORD
HOUSE INN**
1602 N General
Bruce Dr (76502)
Rates: $75+
(254) 771-1495

SUPER 8 MOTEL
5505 S General
Bruce Dr (76502)
Rates: $45-$60
(254) 778-0962
(800) 800-8000

TRAVELODGE
802 N General
Bruce Dr (76504)
Rates: $40-$70
(254) 778-4411
(800) 578-7878

TERLINGUA
**BIG BEND
MOTOR INN**
300 N Jim Wright
Frwy (79852)
Rates: $70-$87
(432) 371-2218
(800) 848-2363

**CHISOS MINING
COMPANY MOTEL**
Box 228, Hwy 170
(79852)
Rates: $40-$75
(432) 371-2254

**EL DORADO
MOTEL**
P. O. Box 394
(79852)
Rates: $89-$150
(432) 371-2111

**LAJITAS ON THE
RIO GRANDE B&B**
Star Rt 70, Box 400
(79852)
Rates: $48-$65
(432) 424-3471

**TERLINGUA
RANCH LODGE**
HC 65, Box 600
(79830)
Rates: $42-$59
(432) 371-2416

TERRELL
BEST INN
309 I-20 E (75160)
Rates: $45-$65
(972) 563-2676
(800) 237-8466

**BEST WESTERN
COUNTRY INN**
1604 Hwy 34 W
(75160)
Rates: $52-$62
(800) 528-1234
(800) 346-1580

COMFORT INN
103 Mira Place
(75160)
Rates: $55-$150
(972) 524-5590
(800) 424-6423

DAYS INN
1618 Hwy 34 S
(75160)
Rates: $48-$120
(972) 551-1170
(800) 329-7466

MOTEL 6
101 Mira Place
(75160)
Rates: $39-$47
(972) 563-0300
(800) 466-8356

SUPER 8 MOTEL
1705 Hwy 34 S
(75160)
Rates: $50-$99
(972) 563-1511
(800) 800-8000

TEXARKANA, ARKANSAS
BAYMONT INN
5102 N State Line
Ave (71854)
Rates: $46-$89
(870) 773-1000
(800) 301-0200

BEST WESTERN KINGS ROW INN
4200 N State Line
Ave (71854)
Rates: $55-$65
(870) 774-3851
(800) 528-1234

HOLIDAY INN-HOLIDOME
5100 N State Line
Ave (71854)
Rates: $98
(870) 774-3521
(800) 465-4329

HOUSE OF WADLEY
618 Pecan (71854)
Rates: $99-$129
(870) 773-7093

QUALITY INN
5210 N State Line
Ave (71854)
Rates: $49-$79
(870) 772-0070
(800) 424-6423

TEXARKANA TEXAS
BEST WESTERN NORTHGATE MOTOR LODGE
400 W 53rd St
(75502)
Rates: $55-$69
(903) 793-6565
(800) 528-1234
(800) 262-0048

COMFORT INN
5105 State Line
Ave (75501)
Rates: $69-$79
(903) 792-6688
(800) 424-6423

ECONO LODGE
4505 N State Line
Ave (75503)
Rates: $39-$79
(903) 793-5546
(800) 424-6423

FOUR POINTS HOTEL SHERATON
5301 N State Line
Ave (75503)
Rates: $75-$105
(903) 792-3222
(800) 325-3535

HOLIDAY INN EXP
5401 N State Line
Ave (75503)
Rates: $71-$79
(903) 792-3366
(800) 465-4329

LA QUINTA INN
5201 N State Line
Ave (75503)
Rates: $65-$81
(903) 794-1900
(800) 687-6667

MOTEL 6-WEST
1924 Hampton Rd
(75503)
Rates: $35-$50
(903) 793-1413
(800) 466-8356

RAMADA INN
I-30 at Summerhill
Rd (75503)
Rates: n/a
(903) 794-3131
(800) 272-6232

TEXAS CITY
ECONO LODGE
1902 Texas Ave
(77590)
Rates: $49-$69
(409) 945-7727
(800) 424-6423

LA QUINTA INN
1121 Hwy 146 N
(77590)
Rates: $65-$85
(409) 948-3101
(800) 687-6667

THE COLONY
COMFORT SUITES STONE BRIAR MALL
4796 Memorial Dr
(75056)
Rates: $79-$150
(972) 668-5555
(800) 424-6423

THE WOODLANDS
BUDGET INN
19565 N I-45
(77384)
Rates: $55-$69
(936) 298-8140

DRURY INN
28099 I-45 N
(77381)
Rates: $72-$102
(281) 362-7222
(800) 378-7946

HOLIDAY INN EXP HOTEL & SUITES
24888 I-45 N
(77386)
Rates: $77
(281) 681-8088
(800) 465-4329

LA QUINTA INN
28673 I-45 N
(77380)
Rates: $62-$79
(281) 367-7722
(800) 687-6667

RED ROOF INN
24903 I-45 N
(77380)
Rates: $48-$65
(281) 367-5040
(800) 843-7663

RESIDENCE INN I BY MARRIOTT
1040 Lake Front
Cr (77380)
Rates: $105
(281) 292-3252
(800) 331-3131

RESIDENCE INN II BY MARRIOTT
9333 Six Pines Dr
(77380)
Rates: $79-$159
(281) 419-1542
(800) 331-3131

THREE RIVERS
BEST WESTERN
900 N Harborth
Ave (78071)
Rates: $65-$85
(361) 786-2000
(800) 528-1234

NOLAN RYAN'S BASS INN
Hwy 72 W (78071)
Rates: $37-$99
(361) 786-3521
(800) 803-3340

TOMBALL
LA QUINTA INN
14000 Medical
Complex Dr
(77377)
Rates: $69-$109
(800) 687-6667

TRINITY
WHISPERING PINES DUDE RANCH
933 FM 230
(75862)
Rates: $175-$300
(936) 594-3986

TULIA
SELECT INN
Rt 1, Box 60
(79088)
Rates: $49-$64
(806) 995-3248

TYLER
BEST WESTERN INN & SUITES
2828 W NW Loop
323 (75702)
Rates: $65-$99
(903) 595-2681
(800) 528-1234
(800) 298-9537

CANDLEWOOD SUITES
315 Rieck Rd
(75703)
Rates: $70-$85
(903) 509-4131
(888) 226-3539

COMFORT SUITES
303 E Rieck Rd
(75703)
Rates: $79-$129
(903) 534-0999
(800) 424-6423

DAYS INN
12732 Hwy 155
N (75708)
Rates: $38-$75
(903) 877-9227
(800) 329-7466

ECONO LODGE
2739 WMW Loop
323 (75702)
Rates: $49-$99
(903) 531-9513
(800) 424-6423

HOLIDAY INN SELECT
5701 S Broadway
(75703)
Rates: $129-$139
(903) 561-5800
(800) 465-4329

LA QUINTA INN
1601 W SW Loop
323 (75701)
Rates: $70-$99
(903) 561-2223
(800) 687-6667

MOTEL 6
3236 Gentry Pkwy
(75702)
Rates: $31-$45
(903) 595-6691
(800) 466-8356
(

QUALITY HOTEL
2843 W NW Loop
323 (75702)
Rates: $69-$89
(903) 597-1301
(800) 424-6423

RAMADA TYLER
3310 Troup Hwy
(75701)
Rates: $48-$109
(903) 593-3600
(800) 272-6232

RESIDENCE INN BY MARRIOTT
3303 Troup Hwy
(75701)
Rates: $76-$125
(903) 595-5188
(800) 331-3131

STRATFORD HOUSE INN MOTEL
2600 W NW Loop
323 (75702)
Rates: $31-$35
(903) 597-2756

UNCERTAIN

MOSSY BRAKE LODGE B&B
151 Mossy Brake Dr S (75661)
Rates: $65+
(903) 789-3440
(800) 607-6002

SPATTERDOCK GUEST HOUSE
168 Mossy Brake D (75661)
Rates: $100
(903) 789-3268

UNIVERSAL CITY

CLARION SUITES HOTEL
13191 E Loop, 1604 N (78233)
Rates: $69-$159
(210) 655-9491
(800) 424-6423

UTOPIA

BEAR CREEK CABINS
P. O. Box 453, Hwy 1050 (78884)
Rates: $85-$95
(800) 483-7593

UVALDE

BEST WESTERN CONTINENTAL INN
701 E Main St (78801)
Rates: $55-$80
(830) 278-5671
(800) 528-1234

FRIDAY RANCH
P O Box 1 (78802)
Rates: $110-$225
(830) 597-2257
(877) 374-3298
(Working ranch)

HOLIDAY INN
920 E Main St (78801)
Rates: $47-$57
(830) 278-4511
(800) 465-4329

VAN

VAN INN
P. O. Box 956 (75790)
Rates: $32-$70
(903) 963-8381

VAN HORN

BEST WESTERN AMERICAN INN
1309 W Broadway (79855)
Rates: $49-$95
(432) 283-2030
(800) 528-1234
(800) 621-2478

BEST WESTERN INN VAN HORN
1705 W Broadway (79855)
Rates: $45-$89
(432) 283-2410
(800) 528-1234
(800) 367-7589

BUDGET INN
1303 W Broadway (79855)
Rates: $25-$45
(432) 283-2019

COMFORT INN
1601 W Broadway (79855)
Rates: $45-$99
(432) 283-2211
(800) 424-6423

DAYS INN
600 E Broadway St (79855)
Rates: $52-$62
(432) 283-1007
(800) 329-7466

ECONOMY INN
1500 W Broadway St (79855)
Rates: $25-$55
(432) 283-2754
(800) 826-0778

HOLIDAY INN EXP
1905 SW Frontage Rd (79855)
Rates: $69-$99
(432) 283-7444
(800) 465-4329

MOTEL 6
1805 W Broadway St (79855)
Rates: $45-$55
(432) 283-2992
(800) 466-8356

RAMADA LIMITED
200 Golf Course Dr (79855)
Rates: $48-$88
(432) 283-2780
(800) 272-6232

SUPER 8 MOTEL
1807 E Service Rd (79855)
Rates: $52-$62
(432) 283-2282
(800) 800-8000

VEGA

BEST WESTERN COUNTRY INN
1800 W Vega Blvd (79092)
Rates: $59-$89
(806) 267-2131
(800) 528-1234

COMFORT INN
1005 S Main St (79092)
Rates: $69-$120
(806) 267-0126
(800) 424-6423

VERNON

BEST WESTERN VILLAGE INN
1615 Expressway (76384)
Rates: $59-$69
(940) 552-5417
(800) 528-1234
(800) 600-5417

DAYS INN
311- Frmtage Rd (76384)
Rates: $40-$75
(940) 552-9982
(800) 329-7466

ECONO LODGE
4100 Hwy 287 NW (76384)
Rates: $32-$75
(940) 553-3384
(800) 424-6423

SUPER 8 MOTEL
1829 Express Hwy 287 (76384)
Rates: $36-$52
(940) 552-9321
(800) 800-8000

WESTERN MOTEL
715 Wilbarger St (76384)
Rates: $28-$45
(940) 552-2531

VICTORIA

COMFORT INN
1906 Houston Hwy (77901)
Rates: $50-$150
(361) 574-9393
(800) 424-6423

HOLIDAY INN HOLIDOME
2705 E Houston Hwy (77901)
Rates: $90-$145
(361) 575-0251
(800) 465-4329

LA QUINTA INN
7603 N Navarro St (77904)
Rates: $65-$91
(361) 572-3585
(800) 687-6667

QUALITY INN
3112 Houston Hwy (77901)
Rates: $69-$129
(361) 578-2030
(800) 424-6423

WACO

BEST WESTERN OLD MAIN LODGE
I-35 & 4th St (76706)
Rates: $84-$99
(254) 753-0316
(800) 299-9226

CLARION HOTEL
801 S 4th St (76706)
Rates: $59-$149
(254) 757-2000
(800) 752-7466
(800) 424-6423

DAYS INN
1504 I-35 N (76705)
Rates: $69-$89
(254) 799-8585
(800) 329-7466

HAWTHORN SUITES
1508 I-35 N (76705)
Rates: $85-$110
(254) 799-9989
(800) 527-1133

HOLIDAY INN
1001 Martin Luther King Blvd (76704)
Rates: $90-$100
(254) 753-0261
(800) 465-4329

LA QUINTA INN
1110 S 9th St (76706)
Rates: $70-$99
(254) 752-9741
(800) 687-6667

RESIDENCE INN BY MARRIOTT
501 S University Parks Dr (76706)
Rates: $120
(254) 714-1386
(800) 331-3131

RODEWAY INN
3912 Jack Kultgen Frwy (76709)
Rates: $39-$79
(254) 662-3320
(800) 424-6423

SUPER 8 MOTEL
1320 S Jack Kultgen Frwy (76706)
Rates: $59-$79
(254) 754-1023

WAXAHACHIE

BEST WESTERN GINGERBREAD INN
200 N I-35 E (75165)
Rates: $66-$82
(972) 937-4202
(800) 528-1234

BONNYNOOK INN B&B
414 W Main (75165)
Rates: $75-$105
(972) 938-7207
(800) 486-5936

RAMADA LIMITED
795 S I-35 E (75165)
Rates: $38-$155
(972) 937-4982
(800) 272-6232

SUPER 8 MOTEL
400 I-35 E (75165)
Rates: $60-$75
(972) 938-9088

WEATHERFORD

BEST WESTERN SANTA FE INN
1927 Santa Fe Dr (76086)
Rates: $69-$89
(817) 594-7401
(800) 229-3400

COMFORT SUITES
210 Alford Dr (76086)
Rates: $79-$140
(817) 599-3300
(800) 424-6423

AREA CODES - If the local number doesn't connect, check for a new area code.

DAYS INN
1106 W Park Ave
(76087)
Rates: $49-$159
(817) 594-3816
(800) 329-7466

ECONO LODGE
2207 Old Dennis
Rd (76087)
Rates: $40-$50
(800) 424-6423

HAMPTON INN
2524 S Main St
(76087)
Rates: $70-$150
(817) 599-4800
(800) 426-7866

HOLIDAY INN EXP
2500 S Main St
(76087)
Rates: $70-$160
(817) 599-3700
(800) 465-4329

LA QUINTA INN
1915 Wall St (76086)
Rates: $79-$129
(800) 687-6667

MOTEL 6
220 Alford Dr
(76086)
Rates: $39-$45
(817) 594-1740
(800) 466-8356

RAMADA LIMITED
809 Palo Pinto St
(76086)
Rates: n/a
(817) 599-8683
(800) 272-6232

SUPER 8 MOTEL
720 Adams Dr
(76087)
Rates: $50-$70
(817) 598-0852

WEBSTER
COMFORT INN
NASA
750 W NASA Rd
One (77598)
Rates: $55-$99
(281) 332-1001
(800) 424-6423

WELLESLEY INN
720 W Bay Area
Blvd (77598)
Rates: $85-$139
(281) 338-7711
(800) 444-8888

WEIMAR
SUPER 8 MOTEL
102 Townsend Ln
(78962)
Rates: 55-$85
(979) 725-9788

WELLINGTON
CHEROKEE INN
1105 Houston
(79095)
Rates: $32-$48
(806) 447-2508

WESLACO
BEST WESTERN
PALM AIRE
MOTOR INN
415 S Int'l Blvd
(78596)
Rates: $48-$111
(956) 969-2411
(800) 248-6511

DELUXE INN
601 N Westgate Dr
(78596)
Rates: $35-$75
(956) 968-0606

SUPER 8 MOTEL
1702 E Expressway
83 (78596)
Rates: $45-$69
(956) 969-9920
(800) 800-8000

W. COLUMBIA
BEST WESTERN
INN
714 Columbia Dr
(77486)
Rates: $55-$68
(800) 528-1234
(888) 325-7819

WESTLAKE
MARRIOTT
SOLANA
DALLAS/FW
5 Village Cir
(76262)
Rates: $75-$151
(817) 430-3848
(800) 228-9290

WICHITA FALLS
BEST WESTERN
WICHITA FALLS
INN
1032 Central Frwy
(76305)
Rates: $59-$136
(940) 766-6881

COMFORT INN
1740 Maurine St
(76304)
Rates: $69-$99
(940) 767-5653
(800) 424-6423

ECONO LODGE
1700 Fifth St (76301)
Rates: $55-$70
(940) 761-1889
(800) 424-6423

HAMPTON INN
1317 Kenley Ave
(76305)
Rates: $59-$89
(940) 766-3300
(800) 426-7866

HAWTHORN
SUITES LTD
1917 N Elmwood
Ave (76308)
Rates: $84-$149
(940) 692-7900
(800) 527-1133

KINGS INN
1211 Central
Expresswy (76305)
Rates: $36-$55
(940) 723-5541

LA QUINTA INN
1128 Central
Frwy N (76305)
Rates: $63-$79
(940) 322-6971
(800) 687-6667

MOTEL 6
1812 Maurine St
(76304)
Rates: $39-$57
(940) 322-8817
(800) 466-8356

QUALITY INN
1750 Maurine St
(76306)
Rates: $59-$69
(940) 322-2477
(800) 424-6423

RADISSON HOTEL
100 Central Frwy
(76305)
Rates: $79-$99
(940) 761-6000
(800) 333-3333

RAMADA LIMITED
3209 Northwest
Frwy (76305)
Rates: $55
(940) 855-0085
(800) 272-6232

TOWNE CREST INN
1601 8th St (76301)
Rates: $37-$49
(940) 322-1182

WIMBERLEY
A CREEK RUNS
THROUGH IT
GUESTHOUSE
3200 FM3237
(78676)
Rates: $95-$225
(512) 847-6887
(877) 327-9138

HOMESTEAD
COTTAGES
BED & BREAKFAST
RR 2 at Scudder
Ln (78676)
Rates: $85-$99
(512) 847-8788
(800) 918-8788

LONESOME DOVE
RIVER INN AT
CLIFFSIDE B&B
600 River Rd
(78676)
Rates: $85+
(512) 392-2921
(800) 690-3683

7A RANCH
RESORT
333 Wayside Dr
(78676)
Rates: $50-$86
(512) 847-2517

SINGING CYPRESS
GARDENS
400 Mill Race Ln
(78676)
Rates: $75-$150
(512) 847-9344
(800) 827-1913

SOUTHWIND B&B
INN AND CABINS
2701 FM 3237
(78676)
Rates: $75-$90
(800) 508-5277

WINNIE
BEST WESTERN
GULF COAST INN
46318 I-10 East
(77665)
Rates: $50-$75
(409) 296-9292
(800) 528-1234

WINNIE INN
205 Spur 5, Hwy
124 (77665)
Rates: $45-$65
(409) 296-2947

WINNSBORO
THEE HUBBELL
HOUSE B & B
307 W Elm St
(75494)
Rates: $89-$175
(800) 227-0639

WOODVILLE
WOODVILLE INN
201 N Magnolia
(75979)
Rates: $36-$45
(409) 283-3741

WOODWAY
HOLIDAY INN EXP
HOTEL & SUITES
6808 Woodway Dr
(76712)
Rates: n/a
(254) 772-2227
(800) 465-4329

YOAKUM
BUDGET HOST
LA MANCHA INN
606 S Hwy 77A
(77995)
Rates: $40-$75
(361) 293-5211
(800) 283-4678

ZAPATA
BEACON LODGE
313 Lakeshore Dr
(78076)
Rates: n/a
(956) 765-4616

BEST WESTERN
INN BY THE LAKE
Hwy 83 S (78076)
Rates: $68-$85
(956) 765-8403
(800) 528-1234
(800) 399-1558

FALCON
MOTOR HOTEL
Hwy 83 S (78076)
Rates: n/a
(956) 765-4373

SIESTA MOTEL
Hwy 73 & 5th St
(78076)
Rates: n/a
(956) 765-4362

AREA CODES - If the local number doesn't connect, check for a new area code.

UTAH

ALTAMONT
MOON LAKE RESORT
P.O. Box 70 (Mtn Home 84001)
Rates: $50-$75
(435) 454-3475

AMERICAN FORK
AMERICAN FORK BED & BREAKFAST
1021 N 150 W (84003)
Rates: $49-$75
(801) 756-9459

QUALITY INN
712 S Utah Valley Dr (84003)
Rates: $59-$129
(801) 763-8383
(800) 424-6423

BEAVER
BEST WESTERN BUTCH CASSIDY INN
161 S Main St (84713)
Rates: $55-$105
(435) 438-2438
(800) 528-1234

BEST WESTERN PARADISE INN
1451 N 300 (84713)
Rates: $51-$79
(435) 438-2455
(800) 528-1234

COUNTRY INN
1450 N 300 W (84713)
Rates: $39-$45
(435) 438-2484
(800) 754-2484

DELANO MOTEL
480 N Main St (84713)
Rates: $29-$42
(435) 438-2418
(800) 537-2165

GRANADA INN
75 S Main St (84713)
Rates: $40-$49
(435) 438-2292

MOTEL 6
1345 N 450 W (84713)
Rates: $35-$46
(435) 438-1666
(800) 466-8356

QUALITY INN
781 W 1800 S (84713)
Rates: $49-$69
(435) 438-5426
(800) 424-6423

SLEEPY LAGOON MOTEL
882 S Main St (84713)
Rates: $35-$60
(435) 438-5681

SUPER 8 MOTEL
626 W 1400 N (84713)
Rates: $35-$79
(435) 438-3888
(800) 800-8000

BICKNELL
AQUARIUS MOTEL
240 W Main St (84715)
Rates: $35-$48
(435) 425-3835
(800) 833-5379

SUNGLOW MOTEL
63 E Main St (84715)
Rates: $27-$37
(435) 425-3821

BIG WATER
CLIFF PALACE MOTEL
132 S Main (84741)
Rates: $50-$75
(435) 678-2264
(800) 553-8093

HIGHWAY HOST MOTEL
Hwy 89, Box 4 (84741)
Rates: $50-$75
(435) 675-3731
(800) 748-5034

WARM CREEK MOTEL
Hwy 89, Box 410004 (84741)
Rates: $50-$75
(435) 675-9199
(800) 748-5065

BLANDING
BEST WESTERN GATEWAY INN
88 E Center St (84511)
Rates: $39-$89
(435) 678-2278
(800) 528-1234
(866) 921-2279

FOUR CORNERS INN
131 E Center St (84511)
Rates: $46-$66
(435) 678-3257
(800) 574-3150

SUNSET INN
88 W Center St (84512)
Rates: $40-$49
(435) 678-3323

BLUFF
KOKOPELLI INN
161 E Main St (84512)
Rates: $38-$48
(435) 672-2322
(800) 541-8854

RECAPTURE LODGE
220 E Main St (84512)
Rates: $34-$56
(435) 672-2281

BOULDER
BOULDER MOUNTAIN LODGE
20 N Hwy 12 (84716)
Rates: $75-$186
(435) 335-7460
(800) 556-3446
(800) 765-7787

BOULDER MOUNTAIN RANCH
Hell's Backbone Road, Box 1373 (84716)
Rates: $50-$75
(435) 335-7480

CIRCLE CLIFFS MOTEL
225 N Hwy 12 (84716)
Rates: $40-$49
(435) 335-7333

EAGLESTAR RANCH B&B
330 E Boulder Pines Rd (84716)
Rates: n/a
(435) 335-7438

BOUNTIFUL
COUNTRY INN
999 N 500 W (84010)
Rates: $69-$159
(801) 292-8100
(800) 456-4000

BRIAN HEAD
LODGE AT BRIAN HEAD
314 Hunter Ridge Rd (84719)
Rates: $65-$250
(435) 677-3222
(800) 386-5634

BRIGHAM CITY
CRYSTAL INN
480 Westland Dr (84302)
Rates: $59-$99
(435) 723-0440

HOWARD JOHNSON INN
1167 S Main St (84302)
Rates: $46-$70
(435) 723-8511
(800) 446-4656

BRYCE CANYON NATIONAL PARK
(Also see Cannonville, Hatch, Panguitch & Tropic)

BEST WESTERN RUBY'S INN
Hwy 63 (84764)
Rates: $49-$115
(435) 834-5341
(800) 528-1234
(800) 468-8660

BRYCE CANYON RESORT
13500 E Hwy 12 (84717)
Rates: $39-$120
(435) 834-5351
(800) 834-0043

BRYCE VIEW LODGE
UT Hwy 63 (84764)
Rates: $45-$70
(435) 834-5180
(888) 279-2304

HAROLDS PLACE CABINS
3066 Hwy 12 (84764)
Rates: $60
(435) 676-2350

CANNONDALE
GALLOPING TORTOISE B&B
250 N Hwy 12 (84718)
Rates: $50-$75
(435) 679-8664

CANNONVILLE
GRAND STAIRCASE INN & COUNTRY STORE
105 N Kodachrome Dr (84718)
Rates: $39-$89
(435) 679-8400
(877) 472-6346

AREA CODES - If the local number doesn't connect, check for a new area code.

CASTLE DALE

VILLAGE INN MOTEL
375 E Main St (84513)
Rates: $40-$49
(435) 381-2309

CEDAR BREAKS NATIONAL MONUMENT

ASPEN WHISPERING PINES LODGE
P. O. Box 1001 (84762)
Rates: $85-$135
(801) 682-2378

CEDAR CITY

BEST VALUE INN
323 S Main St (84720)
Rates: $27-$79
(435) 586-6557
(888) 315-2378

CEDAR REST MOTEL
479 S Main St (84720)
Rates: $30-$70
(435) 586-9471

COMFORT INN
250 N 1100 W (84720)
Rates: $42-$95
(435) 586-2082
(800) 424-6423
(800) 627-0374

CRYSTAL INN
1575 W 200 N (84720)
Rates: $59-$99
(435) 586-8888
(888) 787-6661

DAYS INN
1204 S Main St (84720)
Rates: $54-$89
(435) 867-8877
(800) 329-7466

ECONOMY MOTEL
443 S Main St (84720)
Rates: $21-$42
(435) 586-4461

HOLIDAY INN EXP
1555 S Old Hwy 91 (84720)
Rates: $89-$149
(435) 865-7799
(800) 465-4329

MOTEL 6
1620 W 200 N (84720)
Rates: $32-$50
(435) 586-9200
(800) 466-8356

RAMADA LIMITED
281 S Main St (84720)
Rates: $39-$99
(435) 586-9916
(800) 272-6232

SUPER 7 MOTEL
190 S Main St (84720)
Rates: $30-$80
(435) 586-6566

SUPER 8 MOTEL
145 N 1550 W (84720)
Rates: $48-$69
(435) 586-8880
(800) 800-8000

VALU INN
344 S Main St (84720)
Rates: $25-$45
(435) 586-9114

WILLOW GLEN INN B&B
3308 N Bulldog Rd (84720)
Rates: $59-$195
(435) 586-3275

CENTRAL

DIXIE DEER LODGE
148 E Center Rd (84722)
Rates: $39-$49
(435) 574-2650

CLEARFIELD

SUPER 8 MOTEL
572 N Main (84015)
Rates: $40-$85
(801) 825-8000
(800) 800-8000

COALVILLE

A COUNTRY PLACE
99 S Main (84017)
Rates: $40-$75
(435) 336-2451
(800) 371-2451

BEST WESTERN HOLIDAY HILLS
210 S 200 W (84017)
Rates: $49-$109
(435) 336-4444
(800) 528-1234
(866) 922-7278

COTTONWOOD HEIGHTS

CANDLEWOOD SUITES HOTEL
6990 S Park Centre Dr (84121)
Rates: $77-$129
(801) 567-0111
(888) 226-3539

RESIDENCE INN BY MARRIOTT
6425 S 3000 E (84121)
Rates: $109-$269
(801) 453-0430
(888) 226-3539

DELTA

BEST WESTERN MOTOR INN
527 E Topaz Blvd (84624)
Rates: $47-$72
(435) 864-3882
(800) 528-1234
(800) 354-9378

BUDGET MOTEL
75 South 350 E (84624)
Rates: $25-$45
(435) 864-4533

DIAMOND "D" MOTOR LODGE
234 W Main (84624)
Rates: $29-$49
(435) 864-2041

DRAPER

HOLIDAY INN EXP
12033 S Factory Outlet Dr (84020)
Rates: $59-$79
(801) 571-2511
(800) 465-4329

RAMADA LIMITED
12605 S Minuteman Dr (84020)
Rates: $45-$75
(801) 571-1122
(800) 272-6232

DUCK CREEK VILLAGE

DUCK CREEK VILLAGE INN
Hwy 14 (84762)
Rates: $49-$84
(435) 682-2565

FALCON'S NEST CABINS
60 Movie Ranch Rd (84762)
Rates: $50-$75
(435) 682-2556
(800) 240-4930

INN AT CEDAR MOUNTAIN
116 Color Country Rd (84762)
Rates: $79-$125
(435) 682-2378
(800) 897-4995

MEADOW VIEW LODGE/CABINS
Movie Ranch Rd Box 1331 (84762)
Rates: $50-$75
(435) 682-2495
(800) 332-0568

PINEWOODS RESORT
125 Color Country Rd (84762)
Rates: $90-$150
(435) 682-2512
(800) 848-2525

WHISPERING PINES LODGE
116 Color Country Rd (84762)
Rates: $75-$150
(435) 682-2378

DUTCH JOHN

RED CANYON LODGE
790 Red Canyon Rd in Flamingo Gorge (84023)
Rates: $40-$150
(435) 889-3759

ECHO

KOZY CAFE & MOTEL
24 Echo Main St (84024)
Rates: $30-$49
(435) 336-5641

EPHRAIM

IRON HORSE MOTEL
670 N Main (84627)
Rates: $50-$125
(435) 283-4223
(800) 339-4201

ESCALANTE

CIRCLE D MOTEL
475 W Main (84726)
Rates: $40-$75
(435) 826-4297

RAINBOW COUNTRY B&B
585 E 300 S (84726)
Rates: $40-$75
(435) 826-4567
(800) 252-8824

FAIRVIEW

SKYLINE MOTEL
236 N State St (84629)
Rates: $40-$49
(435) 427-3312

FILLMORE

BEST WESTERN PARADISE INN
905 N Main St (84631)
Rates: $51-$79
(435) 743-6895
(800) 528-1234
(800) 937-8376

FILLMORE MOTEL
61 N Main St (84631)
Rates: $32-$43
(435) 743-5454

INN AT APPLE CREEK
940 S Hwy 99 (84631)
Rates: $45-$76
(435) 743-4334

AREA CODES - If the local number doesn't connect, check for a new area code.

FRY CANYON

FRY CANYON LODGE
90 W Hwy 95 (84533)
Rates: $74-$89
(435) 259-5334

GARDEN CITY

BEAR LAKE MOTOR LODGE
50 S Bear Lake Blvd (84028)
Rates: $50-$75
(435) 946-3271
(800) 756-0795

BLUE WATER RESORT
2126 S Bear Lake Blvd (84028)
Rates: $75-$150
(435) 946-3333
(800) 756-0795

CANYON COVE INN
315 W Logan Hwy (84028)
Rates: $45-$125
(435) 946-3565
(877) 232-7525

EAGLE FEATHER INN B&B
135 S Bear Lake Blvd (84028)
Rates: $50-$75
(435) 946-2846
(877) 977-2846

HARBOR VILLAGE RESORT
900 N Bear Lake Blvd (84028)
Rates: $75-$300
(435) 946-3448
(800) 324-6840

GLENDALE

HISTORIC SMITH HOTEL B&B
295 N Main St (84729)
Rates: $44-$70
(435) 648-2156
(800) 528-3558

GREEN RIVER

BOOK CLIFF LODGE
395 E Main (84525)
Rates: $30-$125
(435) 564-3406

GREEN RIVER INN-NATIONAL 9 INN
456 W Main (84525)
Rates: $40-$49
(435) 564-8237
(800) 474-3304

HOLIDAY INN EXP
965 E Main St (84525)
Rates: $55-$85
(435) 564-4439
(800) 465-4329

MOTEL 6
946 E Main (84525)
Rates: $35-$48
(435) 564-3436
(800) 466-8356

RAMADA LIMITED
1117 E Main St (84525)
Rates: $45-$75
(435) 564-8441
(800) 272-6232

ROBBER'S ROOST MOTEL
225 W Main (84525)
Rates: $29-$49
(435) 564-3452

SUPER 8 MOTEL
1248 E Main (84525)
Rates: $39-$70
(435) 564-8888
(800) 800-8000

HANKSVILLE

BEST VALUE INN
322 E 100 N (84734)
Rates: $40-$49
(435) 542-3471

HATCH

NEW BRYCE INN & CAFE
227 W Main (84735)
Rates: $37-$47
(435) 735-4265
(800) 370-5272

RIVERSIDE RESORT & RV
594 Hwy 98 (84735)
Rates: $40-$80
(435) 735-4223
(800) 824-5651

HEBER CITY

DANISH VIKING LODGE
989 S Main (84032)
Rates: $39-$250
(435) 654-2202
(800) 544-4066

NATIONAL 9 HIGH COUNTRY INN
1000 S Main (84032)
Rates: $49-$66
(435) 654-0201

SWISS ALPS INN
167 S Main (84032)
Rates: $40-$90
(435) 654-0722

HUNTINGTON

VILLAGE INN MOTEL
307 S Main (84528)
Rates: $40-$49
(435) 687-9888

HUNTSVILLE

JACKSON FORK INN B&B
7345 E 900 S (84317)
Rates: $75-$125
(435) 745-0051
(800) 255-0672

HURRICANE

DAYS INN
40 N 2600 W (84737)
Rates: $39-$110
(435) 635-0500
(800) 329-7466

MOTEL 6
650 W State St (84737)
Rates: $54-$75
(435) 635-4010
(800) 466-8356

PAH TEMPE HOT SPRINGS RESORT B&B
825 N 800 E (84737)
Rates: $50-$75
(435) 635-2353
(888) 726-8367

SUPER 8 MOTEL
65 S 700 W (84737)
Rates: $39-$78
(435) 635-0808
(800) 800-8000

TRAVELODGE
280 W State St (84737)
Rates: $32-$89
(435) 635-4647
(800) 578-7878

JUNCTION

JUNCTION MOTEL
300 S Main (84740)
Rates: $40-$49
(435) 577-2629

KANAB

AIKENS LODGE-NATIONAL 9
9 W Center St (84741)
Rates: $30-$57
(435) 644-2625
(800) 524-9999

BEST WESTERN RED HILLS INN
125 W Center (84741)
Rates: $49-$119
(435) 644-2675
(800) 528-1234
(800) 830-2675

BON-BON INN
171 W 200 S (84741)
Rates: $25-$65
(435) 644-3069

BRANDON MOTEL BED & BREAKFST
223 West Center St (84741)
Rates: $50-$75
(435) 644-2631
(800) 839-2631

CLARION HOTEL VICTORIAN CHARM INN
190 N Hwy 89 (84741)
Rates: $79-$159
(435) 644-8660
(800) 424-6423

COLOR COUNTRY INN
1550 S Hwy 89A (84741)
Rates: $50-$75
(435) 644-2164
(800) 473-2164

FOUR SEASONS MOTEL
36 North 300 W (84741)
Rates: $35-$79
(435) 644-5841

HOLIDAY INN EXP
815 E Hwy 89 (84741)
Rates: $80-$89
(435) 644-8888
(800) 465-4329
(800) 574-4061

KANAB MISSION MOTEL
386 E 300 S (84741)
Rates: $37-$47
(435) 644-5373

PARRY LODGE
89 E Center St (84741)
Rates: $35-$78
(435) 644-2601
(800) 748-4104

QUAIL PARK LODGE
125 Hwy 89 N (84741)
Rates: $25-$65
(435) 644-5094
(800) 644-8115

SHILO INN
296 W 100 N (84741)
Rates: $45-$95
(435) 644-2562
(800) 222-2244

SUN-N-SAND MOTEL
347 S 100 E (84741)
Rates: $34-$75
(435) 644-5050
(800) 654-1868

SUPER 8 MOTEL
70 S 200 W (84741)
Rates: $41-$78
(435) 644-5500
(800) 800-8000

TREASURE TRAIL MOTEL
150 W Center St (84741)
Rates: $40-$58
(435) 644-2687
(800) 603-2687

KOOSHAREM

GRASS VALLEY GUEST RANCH MOTEL & CAFE
138 N Main St (84744)
Rates: $40-$49
(435) 638-7322

AREA CODES - If the local number doesn't connect, check for a new area code.

LAKE POWELL

CITY CENTER MOTEL
Hwy 276 (84533)
Rates: $89-$149
(435) 684-7000

DEFIANCE HOUSE LODGE/BULL-FROG MARINA
SR 276, Bullfrog Marina (84533)
Rates: $108-$128
(435) 684-3000
(800) 528-6154

HALLS CROSSING FAMILY UNITS
Hwy 276 at Halls Crossing Marina (84533)
Rates: $76-$125
(435) 684-7000
(800) 528-6154

HITE MARINA FAMILY UNITS
Hwy 95 at Hite Marina (84533)
Rates: $76-$125
(435) 684-2278
(800) 528-6154

LAYTON

COMFORT INN
877 N 400 W (84041)
Rates: $50-$75
(801) 544-5577
(800) 424-6423

HAMPTON INN
1702 N Woodland Park Dr (84041)
Rates: $79-$89
(801) 775-8800
(800) 426-7866

HOLIDAY INN EXP
1695 Woodland Park Dr (84041)
Rates: $79-$129
(801) 773-3773
(800) 465-4329

LA QUINTA INN
1965 N 1200 West (84041)
Rates: $55-$125
(801) 776-6700
(800) 687-6667

TOWNEPLACE SUITES
1743 Woodland Park Blvd (84041)
Rates: $79-$99
(801) 779-2422
(800) 257-3000

VALLEY VIEW MOTEL
1560 N Main St (84041)
Rates: $40-$49
(801) 825-1632

LEHI

BEST WESTERN TIMPANOGOS INN
195 S 850 E (84043)
Rates: $45-$85
(801) 768-1400
(800) 528-1234
(866) 444-1218

MOTEL 6
210 S 1200 E (84043)
Rates: $29-$36
(801) 768-2668
(800) 466-8356

SUPER 8 MOTEL
125 S 850 E (84043)
Rates: $45-$79
(801) 768-8800
(800) 800-8000

LOGAN

BEST WESTERN WESTON INN
250 N Main (84321)
Rates: $49-$99
(435) 752-5700
(800) 528-1234
(800) 532-5055

DAYS INN
364 S Main (84321)
Rates: $36-$92
(435) 753-5623
(800) 329-7466

RAMADA LIMITED
2002 S Hwy 89/91 (84321)
Rates: $47-$75
(435) 787-2060
(800) 272-6232

SUPER 8 MOTEL
865 S Hwy 89/91 (84321)
Rates: $39-$80
(435) 753-8883
(800) 800-8000

MANILA

RIANBOW INN
Hwy 43 (84046)
Rates: $35-$47
(435) 784-3117

VACATION INN
Hwy 43 (84046)
Rates: $43-$59
(435) 784-3259
(800) 662-4327

MANTI

MANTI COUNTRY VILLAGE MOTEL
145 N Main St (84642)
Rates: $48-$82
(435) 835-9300
(800) 452-0787

MANTI MOTEL
445 N Main St (84642)
Rates: $50-$75
(435) 835-8533

MARYSVALE

BIG ROCK CANDY MTN RESORT
4479 N Hwy 89 (84750)
Rates: $59-$99
(435) 326-2000
(888) 560-7625

LIZZY & CHARLIE'S CABINS
300 E Rio Grande Ave (84750)
Rates: $29-$49
(435) 326-4213

MEXICAN HAT

BURCH'S MOTEL
Hwy 163/Main St (84531)
Rates: $50-$125
(435) 683-2221

SAN JUAN INN
Hwy 163 & San Juan River (84531)
Rates: $38-$72
(435) 683-2220
(800) 447-2022

MIDVALE

BEST WESTERN EXECUTIVE INN
280 W 7200 S (84047)
Rates: $59-$89
(801) 566-4141
(800) 528-1234
(800) 253-0512

LA QUINTA INN
530 Catalpa Rd (84047)
Rates: $59-$79
(801) 566-3291
(800) 687-6667

MOTEL 6
7263 S Catalpa Rd (84047)
Rates: $40+
(801) 561-0058
(800) 466-8356

NATIONAL 9 DISCOVERY INN
380 W 7200 South (84047)
Rates: $39-$74
(801) 561-2256
(866) 399-8299

SUPER 8 MOTEL
7048 S 900 E (84047)
Rates: $49-$74
(801) 255-5559

MILFORD

MILFORD STATION MOTEL
485 S 100 W (84751)
Rates: $50-$75
(435) 387-2481

OAK TREE INN
777 W Hwy 21 (84751)
Rates: $50-$60
(435) 387-5266

MOAB

ADVENTURE INN
512 N Main St (84532)
Rates: $40-$70
(435) 259-6122

APACHE MOTEL
166 S 400 E (84532)
Rates: $29-$89
(435) 259-5727
(800) 228-6882

BEST INN
988 N Main St (84532)
Rates: $35-$65
(435) 259-8848
(877) 238-7626

BIG HORN LODGE
550 S Main St (84532)
Rates $30-$89
(435) 259-6171
(800) 325-6171

BOWEN MOTEL
169 N Main St (84532)
Rates: $30-$65
(435) 259-7132
(800) 874-5439

CEDAR BREAKS CONDOS
400 E & Center St (84532)
Rates: $55-$95
(435) 259-7830
(800) 505-5343

COMFORT SUITES
800 S Main St (84532)
Rates: $70-$159
(435) 259-5252
(800) 424-6423

DAYS INN
426 N Main St (84532)
Rates: $40-$95
(435) 259-4468
(800) 329-7466

ENTRADA RANCH
1000 E Entrada Rd (84532)
Rates: $50-$150
(435) 259-5796

THE GONZO INN
100 W 200 S (84532)
Rates: $80-$299
(435) 359-2515
(800) 791-4044

HOTEL OFF CENTER
96 E Center (84532)
Rates: $50-$75
(801) 259-4244

KOKOPELLI LODGE
72 S 100 E (84532)
Rates: $53-$75
(435) 259-7615
(888) 530-3134

LA QUINTA INN
815 S Main St (84532)
Rates: $50-$106
(435) 259-8700
(800) 687-6667

MOAB LODGING
50 E Center St (84532)
Rates: n/a
(435) 259-5125
(800) 505-5343

MOAB

VALLEY INN
711 S Main St
(84532)
Rates: $57-$135
(435) 259-4419
(800) 831-6622

MORRIS' LAST RESORT
5501 S Hwy 191
(84532)
Rates: n/a
(435) 259-5000
(888) 820-8525

MOTEL 6
1089 N Main St
(84532)
Rates: $30-$70
(435) 259-6686
(800) 466-8356

PACK CREEK RANCH
La Sal Mtn Loop
Rd (84532)
Rates: $90-$200
(435) 259-5505

PIONEER SPRINGS B&B
1275 S Boulder
(84532)
Rates: $50-$125
(435) 259-4663

RAMADA INN
182 S Main St
(84532)
Rates: $35-$135
(435) 259-7141
(800) 272-6232

RED CLIFFS ADVENTURE LODGE
MP 14 Hwy 128
(84532)
Rates: $79-$169
(435) 259-2002
(866) 812-2002

RED ROCK LODGE
51 N 100 W (84532)
Rates: $29-$95
(435) 259-5431
(877) 207-9708

RED STONE INN
535 S Main St
(84532)
Rates: $30-$80
(435) 259-3500
(800) 772-1972

RIVER CANYON LODGE-EXTENDED STAY INN
71 W 200 N
(84532)
Rates: $32-$135
(435) 259-8838
(866) 486-6738

RUSTIC INN MOTEL
120 E 100 S
(84532)
Rates: $30-$75
(435) 259-6177
(800) 231-8184

SILVER SAGE INN
840 S Main St
(84532)
Rates: $22-$54
(435) 259-4420
(888) 774-6622

SLEEP INN
1051 S Main St
(84532)
Rates: $36-$129
(435) 259-4655
(800) 424-6423

SLICKROCK CABINS
1301 1/2 N Hwy
191 (84532)
Rates: $30-$45
(435) 259-7660
(800) 488-8873

SUNSET MOTEL
41 W 100 N
(84532)
Rates: $50-$150
(801) 259-5191
(800) 421-5614

SUPER 8 MOTEL
889 N Main St
(84532)
Rates: $30-$99
(435) 259-8868
(800) 800-8000

VIRGINIAN MOTEL
70 E 200 S (84532)
Rates: $25-$79
(435) 259-5951
(800) 261-2063

MONTICELLO

BEST WESTERN WAYSIDE INN
173 E Central St
(84535)
Rates: $45-$75
(435) 587-2261
(800) 528-1234

CANYONLANDS MOTOR INN
97 N Main (84535)
Rates: $50-$75
(435) 587-2266
(800) 952-6212

GO WEST INN
649 N Main
(84535)
Rates: $39-$68
(435) 587-2489
(877) 246-9378

MOUNT CARMEL JUNCTION

BEST WESTERN THUNDERBIRD RESORT
Hwy 9 & 89
(84755)
Rates: $49-$102
(435) 648-2203
(800) 528-1234
(888) 848-6358

GOLDEN HILLS MOTEL
4473 S State St
(84755)
Rates: $28-$49
(435) 648-2268
(800) 648-2268

MT. CARMEL MOTEL
Hwy 89 Muddy
Creek Bridge
(84755)
Rates: $29-$49
(435) 648-2323

MURRAY

HOLIDAY INN EXP
4465 S Century Dr
(84123)
Rates: $63-$90
(801) 268-2533
(800) 465-4329

PAVILION INN
5335 College Dr
(84123)
Rates: $69-$79
(801) 264-1054
(800) 231-9710

STUDIO 6
975 E 6600 S
(84123)
Rates: $43-$59
(801) 685-2102
(888) 897-0202

NEPHI

BEST WESTERN PARADISE INN
1025 S Main
(84648)
Rates: $40-$68
(435) 623-0624
(800) 528-1234

MOTEL 6
2195 S Main St
(84648)
Rates: $35-$43
(435) 623-0666
(800) 466-8356

ROBERTA'S COVE MOTOR INN
2250 S Main St
(84648)
Rates: $40-$50
(435) 623-2629
(800) 456-6460

SAFARI MOTEL
413 S Main
(84648)
Rates: $31-$47
(435) 623-1071

NORTH SALT LAKE

BEST WESTERN COTTONTREE INN
1030 N 400 E
(84054)
Rates: $69-$139
(801) 292-7666
(800) 528-1234
(800) 662-6886

OAKLEY

GRAYSTONE LODGE & GUESTHOUSE
40 W Boulderville
Rd (84055)
Rates: $76-$125
(435) 783-5744
(800) 675-8397

PEOA VACATION COTTAGE
5880 N Hwy 32
(Peoa 84061)
Rates: $76-$125
(435) 783-5339

OGDEN

BEST REST INN
1206 W 21st St
(84401)
Rates: $49-$69
(801) 393-8644
(800) 343-8644

BEST WESTERN HIGH COUNTRY INN
1335 W 12th St
(84404)
Rates: $59-$79
(801) 394-9474
(800) 528-1234
(800) 594-8974

COLONIAL MOTEL
1269 Washington
Blvd (84404)
Rates: $40-$49
(801) 399-5851

COMFORT SUITES
2250 S 1200 W
(84401)
Rates: $60-$150
(801) 621-2545
(800) 424-6423

DAYS INN
3306 Washington
Blvd (84403)
Rates: $45-$79
(801) 399-5671
(800) 329-7466

HAMPTON INN
2401 Washington
Blvd (84401)
Rates: $69-$129
(801) 394-9400
(800) 426-7866

HOLIDAY INN EXP HOTEL & SUITES
2245 S 1200 West
(84401)
Rates: $69-$150
(801) 392-5000
(800) 465-4329

MILLSTREAM MOTEL
1450 Washington
Blvd (84404)
Rates: $50-$75
(801) 394-9425

MOTEL 6-DOWNTOWN
1455 Washington
Blvd (84404)
Rates: $33-$40
(801) 627-4560
(800) 466-8356

OGDEN LODGE
2110 Washington
Blvd (84401)
Rates: $32-$45
(801) 394-4563

OGDEN PLAZA HOTEL-ECCLES CENTER
2401 Washington Blvd (84401)
Rates: $59-$199
(801) 394-9400

RED ROOF INN
1500 W Riverdale Rd (84405)
Rates: $39-$54
(801) 627-2880
(800) 843-7663

SUPER 8 MOTEL
1508 W 2100 S (84401)
Rates: $37-$54
(801) 731-7100
(800) 800-8000

WESTERN COLONY INN
234 24th St (84401)
Rates: $30-$40
(801) 627-1332

WESTERN INN
1155 S 1700 W (84404)
Rates: $52-$68
(801) 731-6500

OLD LA SAL
MT. PEALE INN & SPA B&B
1415 E Hwy 46 (84530)
Rates: $65-$95
(435) 686-2284

OREM
LA QUINTA INN
1100 W 780 N (84057)
Rates: $49-$89
(801) 235-9555
(800) 687-6667

LA QUINTA INN
521 W 1300 (84058)
Rates: $65-$85
(801) 226-0440
(800) 687-6667

PANGUITCH
ADOBE SANDS MOTEL
390 N Main St (84759)
Rates: $30-$52
(435) 676-8874
(800) 497-9261

BRYCE JUNCTION INN
3068 E Hwy 12 (84759)
Rates: n/a
(435) 676-2221
(800) 437-4361

BRYCE WAY MOTEL
429 N Main St (84759)
Rates: $35-$55
(435) 676-2400
(800) 225-6534

CAMERON HOTEL
78 W Center St (84759)
Rates: $50-$75
(435) 676-8840
(800) 537-9212

COLOR COUNTRY MOTEL
526 N Main St (84759)
Rates: $28-$62
(435) 676-2386
(800) 225-6518

HAROLD'S PLACE CABINS
3066 Hwy 12 (84759)
Rates: $45-$60
(435) 676-2350

HAROLD'S PLACE LODGE
3068 Hwy 12 (84759)
Rates: $55-$65
(435) 676-8886

HORIZON MOTEL
730 N Main St (84759)
Rates: $35-$99
(435) 676-2651
(800) 776-2651

MARIANNA INN MOTEL
699 N Main (84759)
Rates: $25-$75
(435) 676-8844
(800) 331-7407

PATRIARCHS MOTEL & CABINS
12120 W Hwy 9 (84759)
Rates: $29-$49
(435) 648-2154

PURPLE SAGE MOTEL
104 E Center St (84759)
Rates: $50-$125
(435) 676-2659
(800) 241-6889

ROCKING HORSE INN
2762 N Hwy 89 (84759)
Rates: $29-$49
(435) 676-2287

SILVERADO WILD WEST "MOVIE TOWN" MOTEL
3800 S Hwy 89 (84759)
Rates: $69-$108
(435) 676-8770
(888) 687-4339

PANGUITCH LAKE
BEAR PAW LAKE VIEW RESORT
905 S Hwy 143 (84759)
Rates: $50-$75
(435) 676-2650
(888) 553-8439

PANGUITCH LAKE RESORT
796 S Lake Shore Dr (84759)
Rates: $50-$125
(435) 676-2657

PARK CITY
BEST WESTERN LANDMARK INN
6560 N Landmark Dr (84060)
Rates: $49-$199
(435) 649-7300
(800) 528-1234
(800) 548-8824

HOLIDAY INN EXP HOTEL & SUITES
1501 W Ute Blvd (84098)
Rates: $164-$210
(435) 658-1600
(800) 465-4329

RADISSON INN
2121 Park Ave (84060)
Rates: $69-$215
(435) 649-5000
(800) 333-3333

WESTGATE PARK CITY RESORT & SPA
3000 The Canyons Resort Dr (84098)
Rates: $99-$599
(435) 940-9444
(888) 433-3704

PAROWAN
ACE MOTEL
82 N Main (84761)
Rates: n/a
(435) 477-3384

CRIMSON HILLS MOTEL
400 S Hwy 91 (84761)
Rates: $39-$49
(435) 477-8662

DAYS INN
625 W 200 S (84761)
Rates: $42-$90
(435) 477-3326
(800) 329-7466

PAYSON
COMFORT INN
830 N Main (84651)
Rates: $66-$100
(801) 465-4861
(800) 424-6423

PINE VALLEY
PINE VALLEY LODGE
960 E Main St (84722)
Rates: $50-$75
(435) 574-2544

PRICE
BUDGET HOST
145 N Carbonville Rd (84501)
Rates: $36-$59
(435) 637-2424
(800) 283-4678

PRICE RIVER INN-NATIONAL 9
641 W Price River Dr (84501)
Rates: $36-$75
(435) 637-7000
(800) 524-9999

PROVO
COLONY INN SUITES-NAT'L 9
1380 S University Ave (84601)
Rates: $39-$62
(801) 374-6800
(866) 776-8699

DAYS INN
1675 North 200 W (84604)
Rates: $44-$74
(801) 375-8600
(800) 329-7466

ECONO LODGE AIRPORT
1625 W Center St (84601)
Rates: $39-$89
(801) 373-0099
(800) 424-6423

HAMPTON INN
1511 S 40 E (84601)
Rates: $69-$89
(801) 377-6396
(800) 426-7866

LA QUINTA INN
1555 N Canyon Rd (84604)
Rates: $65-$69
(801) 374-6020
(800) 687-6667

RESIDENCE INN BY MARRIOTT
252 W 2230 N (84604)
Rates: $99-$129
(801) 374-1000
(800) 331-3131

SLEEP INN
1505 S 40th E (84601)
Rates: $50-$55
(801) 377-6597
(800) 424-6423

SUPER 8 MOTEL
1555 N Canyon Rd (84601)
Rates: $49-$79
(801) 374-6020
(800) 800-8000

TRAVELERS INN
469 W Center St (84601)
Rates: $35-$70
(801) 373-8248

VALLEY INN MOTEL
1425 S State St (84606)
Rates: $40-$49
(801) 377-3804

AREA CODES - If the local number doesn't connect, check for a new area code.

RICHFIELD

BEST WESTERN APPLE TREE INN
145 S Main St (84701)
Rates: $45-$79
(435) 896-5481
(800) 528-1234

BUDGET HOST NIGHTS INN
69 S Main St (84701)
Rates: $33-$48
(435) 896-8228
(800) 525-9024

DAYS INN
333 N Main St (84701)
Rates: $55-$100
(435) 896-6476
(800) 329-7466

LUXURY INN
1335 N Main St (84701)
Rates: $34-$79
(435) 893-0100

NEW WEST MOTEL
447 S Main St (84701)
Rates: $27-$37
(435) 896-5450
(800) 278-4076

ROMANICO INN
1170 S Main St (84701)
Rates: $30-$44
(435) 896-8471
(800) 948-0001

TRAVELODGE
647 S Main St (84701)
Rates: $48-$82
(435) 896-9271
(800) 578-7878
(800) 549-8208

ROOSEVELT

FRONTIER MOTEL
75 S 200 E (84066)
Rates: $40-$55
(435) 722-2201
(800) 248-1014

WESTERN HILLS MOTEL
737 E 200 S (84066)
Rates: $29-$45
(435) 722-5115

ST. GEORGE

AN OLDE PENNY FARTHING INN BED & BREAKFAST
278 N 100 W (84770)
Rates: $60-$130
(435) 673-7755

ATKIN'S SINGLETREE INN
260 E St. George Blvd (84770)
Rates: $42-$129
(435) 673-6161
(800) 528-8890

BEST VALUE INN
60 W St. George Blvd (84770)
Rates: $29-$99
(435) 673-4666

THE BLUFFS INN
1140 S Bluff (84770)
Rates: $39-$99
(435) 628-6699
(800) 832-5833

BUDGET INN
1221 S Main (84770)
Rates: $35-$142
(435) 673-6661
(800) 929-0790

CORONADA INN
559 E St. George Blvd (84770)
Rates: $36-$99
(435) 628-4436

CRYSTAL INN ST. GEORGE
1450 S Hilton Dr (84770)
Rates: $99-$139
(435) 688-7477
(800) 438-0170

DAYS INN
150 N 1000 E (84770)
Rates: $46-$149
(435) 673-6123
(800) 329-7466

ECONO LODGE
460 E St. George Blvd (84770)
Rates: $35-$89
(435) 673-4861
(800) 424-6423

GREEN VALLEY SPA & COYOTE INN/RESORT
1871 W Canyon View Dr (94770)
Rates: $295-$395
(435) 628-8060
(800) 237-1068

HOLIDAY INN
850 S Bluff St (84770)
Rates: $72-$140
(435) 628-4235
(800) 465-4329

HOWARD JOHNSON EXP INN & SUITES
1040 S Main St (84770)
Rates: $44-$135
(435) 628-8000
(800) 446-4656

MOTEL 6
205 N 1000 E St (84770)
Rates: $30-$46
(435) 628-7979
(800) 466-8356

RED CLIFFS INN
912 Red Cliffs Dr (84780)
Rates: $44-$129
(435) 673-3537
(888) 733-2543

SANDS MOTEL
581 E St. George Blvd (84770)
Rates: $50-$150
(435) 673-3501

SEVEN WIVES INN
217 N 100 W (84770)
Rates: $85-$250
(435) 628-3737
(800) 600-3737

SUNTIME INN
420 E St. George Blvd (84770)
Rates: $29-$79
(435) 673-6181
(800) 237-6253

SUPER 8 MOTEL
915 S Bluff St (84770)
Rates: $39-$78
(435) 688-8383
(800) 800-8000

SALINA

HENRY'S HIDEAWAY
60 N State St (84654)
Rates: $35-$65
(435) 529-7467
(800) 354-6468

LUXURY INN
1400 S State St (84654)
Rates: $34-$79
(435) 529-1300

RANCH MOTEL
80 N State St (84654)
Rates: $32-$48
(435) 529-7789

SAFARI MOTEL
1425 S State St (84654)
Rates: $35-$75
(435) 529-7447

SUPER 8 MOTEL SCENIC HILLS
75 East 1500 S (84654)
Rates: $45-$62
(435) 529-7483
(800) 800-8000

SALT LAKE CITY

ALLSTAR TRAVEL INN
754 W North Temple (84116)
Rates: $40-$49
(801) 531-7300

ALPINE EXECUTIVE SUITES
164 S 900 E (84102)
Rates: $99-$109
(801) 533-8184
(800) 733-8184

BEST INN& SUITES
1009 S Main (84111)
Rates: $60-$99
(801) 355-4567
(800) 237-8466
(888) 500-9192

BEST WESTERN AIRPORT INN
315 N Admiral Byrd Rd (84116)
Rates: $69-$89
(801) 539-5005
(800) 528-1234

BEST WESTERN GARDEN INN
154 West 600 S (84101)
Rates: $55-$119
(801) 521-2930
(800) 528-1234
(800) 521-9997

BEST WESTERN SALT LAKE PLAZA
122 W So Temple (84101)
Rates: $69-$119
(801) 521-0130
(800) 528-1234
(800) 366-3684

CANDLEWOOD SUITES
2170 W North Temple (84116)
Rates: $69-$99
(801) 359-7500
(888) 226-3539

CANDLEWOOD SUITES- FORT UNION
6990 S Park Centre Dr (84121)
Rates: n/a
(801) 567-0111
(888) 226-3539

CHASE SUITE HOTEL BY WOODFIN
765 E 400 S (84102)
Rates: $98-$128
(801) 532-5511
(800) 237-8811

CITY CREEK INN MOTEL
230 W N Temple (84103)
Rates: $41-$74
(801) 533-9100
(866) 533-4898

COLONIAL VILLAGE
1530 S Main (84115)
Rates: $40-$49
(801) 486-8171

COMFORT INN AIRPORT
200 N Admiral Byrd Rd (84116)
Rates: $69-$119
(801) 746-5200
(800) 424-6423

AREA CODES - If the local number doesn't connect, check for a new area code.

DAYS INN AIRPORT
1900 W N Temple St (84116)
Rates: $67-$169
(801) 539-8538
(800) 329-7466

DAYS INN CENTRAL
315 W 33rd South (84115)
Rates: $49-$99
(801) 486-8780
(800) 329-7466

ECONO LODGE
715 W N Temple (84116)
Rates: $49-$89
(801) 363-0062
(800) 424-6423

HILTON AIRPORT
5151 Wiley Post Way (84116)
Rates: $69-$159
(801) 539-1515
(800) 999-3736

HILTON CITY CENTER
255 S W Temple (84101)
Rates: $69-$179
(801) 328-2000
(800) 445-8667

HOLIDAY INN DOWNTOWN
999 S Main St (84111)
Rates: $110-$145
(801) 359-8600
(800) 465-4329

HOLIDAY INN EXP
4465 S Century Dr (84116)
Rates: n/a
(800) 465-4329

HOMESTEAD STUDIO SUITES
1220 E 2100 S (84116)
Rates: $67-$92
(801) 474-0771
(888) 782-9473

HOTEL MONACO
15 W 200 S (84116)
Rates: $199-$220
(801) 595-0000
(877) 294-9710

HOWARD JOHNSON EXP INN
121 N 300 W (84103)
Rates: $54-$99
(801) 521-3450
(800) 446-4656

LA QUINTA INN & SUITES AIRPORT
4905 W Wiley Post Way (84116)
Rates: $59-$99
(801) 366-4444
(800) 687-6667

LOG CABIN ON THE HILL B&B
2275 E 6200 S (84121)
Rates: $50-$150
(801) 272-2969
(888) 639-2969

METROPOLITAN INN
524 SW Temple (84101)
Rates: $59-$119
(801) 531-7100

MICROTEL INN
61 N Tommy Thompson Rd (84116)
Rates: $43-$68
(801) 236-2800
(888) 771-7171

QUALITY INN MIDVALLEY
4465 Century Dr (84123)
Rates: $50-$100
(801) 268-2533
(800) 424-6423

RAMADA LIMITED
2455 S State St (84115)
Rates: n/a
(801) 486-2400
(800) 272-6232

RED LION HOTEL DOWNTOWN
161 W 600 S (84101)
Rates: $159-$169
(801) 521-7373
(800) 733-5466

RENAISSANCE SUITES
267 W Broadway (84101)
Rates: $94-$174
(801) 534-8500

RESIDENCE INN BY MARRIOTT AIRPORT
4883 W Douglas Corrigon Way (84116)
Rates: $107-$152
(801) 532-4101
(800) 331-3131

RESIDENCE INN BY MARRIOTT CITY CENTER
285 W 300 S (84101)
Rates: $109-$209
(801) 355-3300
(800) 331-3131

RESIDENCE INN BY MARRIOTT COTTONWOODS
6425 S 3000 E (84121)
Rates: $71-$239
(801) 453-0430
(800) 331-3131

RESIDENCE INN BY MARRIOTT UNIVERSITY PARK
480 Wakara Way (84108)
Rates: $149
(801) 581-1000
(800) 331-3131

SALT CITY INN
1025 N 900 W (84101)
Rates: n/a
(801) 364-1035

SALTAIR BED & BREAKFAST
164 S 900 E (84102)
Rates: $55-$109
(801) 533-8184

SHERATON CITY CENTRE
150 W 500 S (84101)
Rates: $70-$119
(801) 401-2000
(800) 325-3535
(800) 401-2000

SHILO INN HOTEL
206 SW Temple (84101)
Rates: $70-$140
(801) 521-9500

THE SKYLINE INN
2475 E 1700 S (84108)
Rates: $49-$77
(801) 582-5350

SLEEP INN
3440 S 2200 W (84119)
Rates: $49-$99
(435) 975-1888
(800) 424-6423

STUDIO 6
975 E 6600 S (84121)
Rates: $219-$299
(801) 685-2102
(888) 897-0202

SUPER 8 MOTEL AIRPORT
223 N Jimmy Doolittle Rd (84116)
Rates: $45-$79
(801) 533-8878

TRAVELODGE CITY CENTER
524 S W Temple St (84101)
Rates: $59+
(801) 531-7100
(800) 578-7878

TRAVELODGE AT TEMPLE SQUARE
144 W N Temple St (84103)
Rates: $45-$75
(801) 533-8200
(800) 578-7878

WASATCH FRONT SKI CONDOS
2020 E 3300 S, #23 (84109)
Rates: $76-$125+
(801) 486-4296
(800) 762-7606

SANDY

BEST WESTERN COTTON TREE
10695 S Auto Mall Dr (84054)
Rates: $84-$149
(801) 523-8484
(800) 662-6886

COMFORT INN
8955 S 255 W (84070)
Rates: $65-$120
(801) 255-4919
(800) 424-6423

COUNTRY INN
10499 S Jordan Gate Way (84095)
Rates: $92
(801) 553-1151
(800) 456-4000

MAJESTIC ROCKIES MOTEL
8901 S State (84111)
Rates: $40-$49
(801) 255-2313

RESIDENCE INN BY MARRIOTT
270 W 10000 South (84070)
Rates: $109-$209
(801) 561-5005
(800) 331-3131

SANDY COMFORT SUITES
10680 S Auto Mall Dr (4070
Rates: $65-$85
(801) 495-1317

SLEEP INN
10676 S 300 W (84095)
Rates: $50-$79
(801) 572-2020
(800) 424-6423

SUPER 8 MOTEL
10722 S 300 W (84095)
Rates: $45-$79
(801) 553-8888
(800) 800-8000

SCIPIO

HOTEL SCIPIO
195 N State, Box 75 (84656)
Rates: $40-$49
(435) 758-2450

SUPER 8 MOTEL
230 W 400 N (84656)
Rates: $50-$65
(435) 758-9188
(800) 800-8000

SOUTH JORDAN

SLEEP INN
10676 S 300 W (84095)
RatesL $49-$79
(801) 572-2020
(800) 424-6423

SUPER 8 MOTEL
10722 S 300 W
(84095)
Rates: $59-$110
(801) 553-8888
(800) 800-8000

SOUTH SALT LAKE CITY

DAYS INN CENTRAL
315 W 3300 S
(84115)
Rates: $49-$89
(8010 486-8780
(800) 329-7466

RAMADA LIMITED
2455 S State St
(84115)
Rates: $69-$75
(801) 486-2400
(800) 272-6232

SPANISH FORK

IDEAL MOTEL
150 S Main St
(84660)
Rates: $40-$49
(801) 798-1900

WESTERN INN
632 Kirby Ln
(84660)
Rates: $54-$65
(801) 798-9400
(888) 700-5335

SPRINGDALE

BEST WESTERN ZION PARK INN
1215 Zion Park
Blvd (84767)
Rates: $62-$109
(435) 772-3200
(800) 528-1234
(800) 934 7275

CANYON RANCH MOTEL
668 Zion Park
Blvd (84767)
Rates: $68-$88
(435) 772-3357

CANYON VISTA BED & BREAKFST
2175 Zion Park
Blvd (84767)
Rates: $76-$125
(435) 772-3801

DRIFTWOOD LODGE
1515 Zion Park
Blvd (84767)
Rates: $62-$109
(435) 772-3262
(888) 801-8811

EL RIO LODGE IN ZION CANYON
995 Zion Park
Blvd (84767)
Rates: $50-$75
(435) 772-3205
(888) 772-3205

MAJESTIC VIEW LODGE
2400 Zion Park
Blvd (84767)
Rates: $89-$199
(435) 772-0665
(866) 772-0665

SPRINGVILLE

BEST WESTERN COTTONTREE INN
1455 N 1750 W
(84663)
Rates: $54-$79
(801) 489-3641
(800) 528-1234
(800) 662-6886

DAYS INN
520 S 2000 W
(84663)
Rates: $49-$109
(801) 491-0300
(800) 329-7466

TAYLORSVILLE

HOMESTEAD STUDIO SUITES HOTEL
5683 S Redwood
Rd (84123)
Rates: $45-$70
(801) 269-9292
(800) 782-9473

TICABOO

TICABOO RESORT
84533 Hwy 276
(84533)
Rates: $49-$99
(435) 788-2110
(877) 842-2267

TOQUERVILLE

YOUR INN B&B
650 Spring Dr
(84774)
Rates: $40-$150
(435) 635-9964

TORREY

CACTUS HILL RANCH MOTEL
830 S 1000 E
(84744)
Rates: $38-$75
(435) 425-3578

CAPITOL REEF INN & CAFE
360 W Main St
(84744)
Rates: $35-$75
(435) 425-3271

COMFORT INN
2424 E Hwy 24
(84775)
Rates: $39-$109
(435) 425-3866
(800) 424-6423

DAYS INN
675 E Hwy 24
(84775)
Rates: $40-$100
(435) 425-3111
(800) 329-7466

RIM ROCK INN
2523 E Hwy 24
(84774)
Rates: $45-$59
(435) 425-3398
(888) 447-4676

SUPER 8 MOTEL
600 E Hwy 24
(84775)
Rates: $39-$78
(435) 425-3688
(800) 800-8000

TORREY TRADING POST & CABINS
75 W Main St
(84774)
Rates: $40-$49
(435) 425-3716

WONDERLAND INN MOTEL
Jct Hwys 12 & 24
(84774)
Rates: $36-$70
(435) 425-3775
(800) 458-0216

TREMONTON

SANDMAN MOTEL
585 W Main St
(84337)
Rates: $45-$60
(435) 257-7149

TROPIC

BRYCE PIONEER VILLAGE
80 S Main
(84776)
Rates: $50-$125
(435) 679-8654
(800) 222-0381

DOUGS COUNTRY INN MOTEL
141 N Main St
(84776)
Rates: $25-$50
(435) 679-8632
(800) 993-6847

WORLD HOST BRYCE VALLEY INN
199 N Main St
(84776)
Rates: $47-$89
(435) 679-8811
(800) 422-1890

VERNAL

ECONO LODGE DOWNTOWN
311 E Main
(84078)
Rates: $39-$75
(435) 789-2000
(800) 424-6423

RODEWAY INN
590 W Main
(84078)
Rates: $35-$69
(435) 789-8172
(800) 424-6423

SAGE MOTEL
54 W Main
(84078)
Rates: $35-$80
(435) 789-1442
(800) 760-1442

WASHINGTON

RED CLIFF INN
912 Red Cliff Dr
(84780)
Rates: $50-$75
(435) 673-3537
(800) 438-6465

WELLINGTON

NATIONAL 9 INN
50 S 700 E (84542)
Rates: $40-$59
(435) 637-7980
(800) 524-9999

WENDOVER

DAYS INN
685 E Wendover
Blvd (84083)
Rates: $39-$149
(435) 665-2215
(800) 329-7466

ECONO LODGE
245 E Wendover
Bvd (84083)
Rates: $36-$99
(435) 665-2226
(800) 424-6423

WESTERN RIDGE MOTEL
895 E Wendover
Blvd (84083)
Rates: $20-$64
(435) 665-2211

W. VALLEY CITY

BAYMONT INN
2229 W City
Center Ct (84119)
Rates: $66-$71
(801) 886-1300
(800) 307-0200

LA QUINTA INN
3540 S 220 W
(84119)
Rates: $49-$99
(801) 954-9292
(800) 687-6667

PARKWAY SUITES
3580 W Parkway
Blvd (84119)
Rates: $69-$79
(801) 977-0800

SLEEP INN
3440 S 2200 W
(84119)
Rates: $55-$59
(801) 975-1888
(800) 424-6423

W. WENDOVER

SUPER 8 MOTEL
1325 Wendover
Blvd (89883)
Rates: $40-$100
(775) 664-2888

WOODS CROSS

HAMPTON INN
2393 South 800
West (84087)
Rates: $69-$80
(801) 296-1211
(800) 426-7866

AREA CODES - If the local number doesn't connect, check for a new area code.

TRAVEL NOTES

AREA CODES - If the local number doesn't connect, check for a new area code.

VERMONT

ADDISON

WHITFORD HOUSE INN
912 Grandey Rd (05491)
Rates: $110-$175
(802) 758-2704
(800) 746-2704

ALBURG

AUBERGE ALBURG
54 S Main St (05440)
Rates: $20-$75
(802) 796-3169

HENRY'S SPORTSMAN'S COTTAGES
218 Poor Farm Rd (05440)
Rates: $380-$460
(802) 796-3616

RANSOM BAY INN
4 Center Bay Rd (05440)
Rates: $70-$95
(802) 796-3399

YE OLDE GRAYSTONE B&B
RFD 1, Box 76 (05440)
Rates: $50-$55
(802) 796-3911

ANDOVER

INN AT HIGH VIEW
753 East Hill Rd (05143)
Rates: $135-$195
(802) 875-2724

ARLINGTON

(Also see Sunderland)

CUTLEAF MAPLES MOTEL & LODGE
3420 Rt 7A (05250)
Rates: $40-$80
(802) 375-2725

ROARING BRANCH HOUSEKEEPING CABINS
Sunderland Hill Rd (05250)
Rates: $700-$800 Weekly
(802) 375-6401

VALHALLA MOTEL
Historic Rt 7A (05250)
Rates: $38-$70
(802) 375-2212
(800) 258-2212

AVERILL

QUIMBY COUNTRY COTTAGES
Rt 114 Forest Lake Rd (05901)
Rates: $99-$145
(802) 822-5533

BARNARD

THE FAN HOUSE B&B
P.O. Box 294, Rt 12 N (05031)
Rates: $100-$180
(802) 234-9096

BARNET

INN AT MAPLEMONT FARM
2742 Rt 5 S (05821)
Rates: $75-$100
(802) 633-4880
(800) 230-1617

BARRE

HOLLOW INN & MOTEL
278 S Main St (05641)
Rates: $70-$140
(802) 479-9313
(800) 998-9444

BARTON

PINE CREST MOTEL
RR 1, Box 279 (05822)
Rates: $35-$50
(802) 525-3472

ROUTE 16 BED & BREAKFAST
3922 Willoughby Lake Rd (05822)
Rates: $80
(802) 525-3954

BELLOWS FALLS

EVERYDAY INN
593 Rockingham Rd (05101)
Rates: $49-$139
(802) 463-4536
(800) 255-4756

WHIPPOWIL COTTAGES
US Rt 5 (05101)
Rates: n/a
(802) 463-3442

BENNINGTON

APPLEY VALLEY INN & CAFE
Rt 7 (05201)
Rates: $59-$85
(802) 442-6588

BENNINGTON MOTOR INN
143 W Main St (05201)
Rates: $73-$108
(802) 442-5479
(800) 359-9900

DARLING KELLY'S MOTEL
357 Rt 7 S (05201)
Rates: $43-$87
(802) 442-2322
(877) 447-1364

FIFE 'N DRUM MOTEL
693 US Rt 7 S (05201)
Rates: $47-$112
(802) 442-4074

HARWOOD HILL MOTEL
864 Harwood Hill Rd (05201)
Rates: $48-$80
(802) 442-6278

KNOTTY PINE MOTEL
130 Northside Dr (05201)
Rates: $50-$82
(802) 442-5487

PLEASANT VALLEY MOTEL
Pleasant Valley Rd (05201)
Rates: $40-$48
(802) 442-6222

SOUTH GATE MOTEL
124 Elm St (05201)
Rates: $54-$89
(802) 447-7525

VERMONTER MOTOR LODGE
2968 West Rd (05201)
Rates: $50-$129
(802) 442-2529
(800) 382-3175

BETHEL

GREENHURST HISTORICAL INN
River St, RD 2 Box 60 (05032)
Rates: $50-$100
(802) 234-9474
(800) 510-2553

POPLAR MANOR BED & BRKFAST
Rt 107 & 12 (05032)
Rates: $42-$44
(802) 234-5426

BOLTON VALLEY

BLACK BEAR INN
4010 Bolton Access Rd (05477)
Rates: $89-$205
(802) 434-2126
(800) 395-6335

TRAILSIDE CONDOS
HC 33, Box 751 (05477)
Rates: $190-$454
(802) 434-2769
(800) 451-5025

BONDVILLE

ALPENROSE INN
261 Winhall Hollow Rd (05340)
Rates: $95-$180
(802) 297-2750
(877) 206-9343

BROMLEY

VIEW INN
Rt 30, Box 161 (05340)
Rates: $60-$90
(802) 297-1459
(800) 297-1459

BRADFORD

BRADFORD MOTEL
Rt 5 (05033)
Rates: $48-$70
(802) 222-4467

BRANDON

BRANDON MOTOR LODGE
2095 Franklin St (05733)
Rates: $55-$95
(802) 247-9594
(800) 675-7614

GINGERBREAD HOUSE FINE ARTS BED & BRKFAST
RR 3, Rt 73 E Box 3241 (05733)
Rates: $60-$150
(802) 247-3380

HIVUE B&B TREE FARM
Highpond Rd (05733)
Rates: $50+
(802) 247-3042
(800) 880-3042

THE LILAC INN-HISTORIC COUNTRY INN
53 Park St (05733)
Rates: $140-$325
(802) 247-5463
(800) 221-0720

AREA CODES - If the local number doesn't connect, check for a new area code.

BRATTLEBORO

COLONIAL MOTEL & SPA
889 Putney Rd
(05301)
Rates: $60-$95
(802) 257-7733
(800) 239-0032

ECONO LODGE
515 Canal St (05301)
Rates: $40-$130
(802) 254-2360
(800) 424-6423

40 PUTNEY RD B&B
40 Putney Rd
(05301)
Rates: $99-$230
(802) 254-6268
(800) 941-2413

MOTEL 6
1254 Putney Rd
(05301)
Rates: $39-$60
(802) 254-6007
(800) 466-8356

QUALITY INN
1380 Putney Rd
(05301)
Rates: $56-$169
(802) 254-8701
(800) 424-6423

SUPER 8 MOTEL
1043 Putney Rd
(05301)
Rates: $50-$159
(802) 254-8889
(800) 800-8000

BRIDGEWATER CORNERS

CORNERS INN
Rt 4 & Upper Rd
(05035)
Rates: $45-$85
(802) 672-9968

BRIDPORT

CHAMPLAIN VALLEY FARMSTAY
326 Fiddlers Lane
(05734)
Rates: $35-$200
(802) 758-3276

BRISTOL

BRISTOL COMMONS INN
Jct 17 & 116
(05443)
Rates: $39-$68
(802) 453-2326

FIREFLY B&B
P. O. Box 152
(05443)
Rates: $70-$79
(802) 453-2223

BROWNSVILLE

BURTON FARM LODGE B&B
RFD 1, Box 558
(05089)
Rates: $60-$70
(802) 484-3300

MILLBROOK B&B
1328 Rt 44 (05037)
Rates: $80-$140
(802) 484-7283

THE POND HOUSE FARM B&B
P. O. Box 234
(05037)
Rates: $150-$200
(802) 484-0011
(Horses & dogs welcome)

BURKE

(Also see East Burke)

OLD TIME B&B
P. O. Box 244
(05871)
Rates: $30-$50
(800) 507-9873

BURLINGTON

(Also see South Burlington)

BEL-AIRE MOTEL
111 Shelburne Rd
(05401)
Rates: $36-$85
(802) 863-3116

HO HUM MOTEL
1660 Williston Rd
(05401)
Rates: $32-$96
(802) 863-4551

SHERATON HOTEL
870 Williston Rd
(05403)
Rates: $145-$200
(802) 865-6600
(800) 325-3535

TOWN & COUNTRY MOTEL
490 Shelburne Rd
(05401)
Rates: $59-$139
(802) 862-5786

CANAAN

LAKE WALLACE MOTEL
Rt 114 (05903)
Rates: n/a
(802) 266-3311

CAVENDISH

CLARION HOTEL AT CAVENDISH POINTE
2940 SR 103
(05142)
Rates: $69-$269
(802) 226-7688
(800) 424-6423

CHESTER

MOTEL IN THE MEADOW
936 Rt 11 W
(05143)
Rates: $64-$90
(802) 875-2626

CHITTENDON

FOX CREEK INN
49 Dam Rd
(05737)
Rates: $190-$409
(802) 483-6213
(800) 707-0017

THE MOUNTAIN TOP INN & RESORT
195 Mountain Top Rd (05737)
Rates: $130-$235
(802) 483-2311

COLCHESTER

DAYS INN
23 College Pkwy
(05446)
Rates: $45-$185
(802) 655-0900
(800) 329-7466

HAMPTON INN
42 Lower Mountain View Dr (05446)
Rates: $99-$114
(802) 655-6177
(800) 426-7866

MOTEL 6
74 South Park Dr (05446)
Rates: $39-$70
(802) 654-6860
(800) 466-8356

CRAFTSBURY COMMON

THE INN ON THE COMMON
1162 N Craftsbury Rd (05827)
Rates: $240-$340
(802) 586-7720
(800) 521-2233

DERBY

THE BORDER MOTEL
135 N Main (05829)
Rates: $42-$49
(802) 766-2088
(800) 280-1898

DORSET

BARROWS HOUSE
Rt 30 (05251)
Rates: $155-$250
(802) 867-4455
(800) 639-1620

EAST BURKE

(Also see Burke)

THE B&B MOOSE CROSSING
2171 Rt 114
(05832)
Rates: $55-$85
(802) 626-0989

VILLAGE INN
Rt 114 (05832)
Rates: $75-$85
(802) 626-3161

EAST ST. JOHNSBURY

ECHO LEDGE FARM INN
P.O. Box 75
(05838)
Rates: $95
(802) 748-4750

ENOSBURG FALLS

BERKSON FARMS B&B
1205 W Berkshire Rd, Rt 108 N
(05450)
Rates: $55-$65
(802) 933-2522

ESSEX JUNCTION

BIRCHCLIFF B&B
205 Chapin Rd
(05452)
Rates: $89-$149
(802) 879-1685

THE INN AT ESSEX
70 Essex Way
(05452)
Rates: $109-$269
(802) 878-1100
(800) 727-4295

THE WILSON INN
10 Kellog Rd
(05452)
Rates: $89-$209
(802) 879-1515
(800) 521-2234

FAIRFAX

THE INN AT BUCK HOLLOW FARM B&B
2150 Buck Hollow Rd (05454)
Rates: $63-$98
(802) 849-2400

FAIRLEE

SILVER MAPLE LODGE & COTTAGES B&B
Rt 5 (05045)
Rates: $64-$98
(802) 333-4326
(800) 666-1946

FRANKLIN

FAIR MEADOWS FARM B&B
Box 430, Rt 235
(05457)
Rates: n/a
(802) 285-2132

GLOVER

LAKESIDE HAVEN LODGING
76 Maynard Dr
(05839)
Rates: $75-$85
(802) 525-3196

GRAFTON

THE HAYES HOUSE
Bear Hill Rd
(05146)
Rates: n/a
(802) 843-2461

AREA CODES - If the local number doesn't connect, check for a new area code.

GRAND ISLE

BY THE LAKE MOTEL
Lakeshore Blvd (05458)
Rates: $60-$70
(802) 372-6134
(802) 879-4015

HANCOCK

OLD HANCOCK HOTEL
3 Vt Rte 125 (05748)
Rates: $55-$85
(802) 767-4976

ISLAND POND

CLYDE RIVER HOTEL
5 Cross St (05846)
Rates: $35-$100
(802) 723-5663

JAMAICA

THREE MTN INN
3732 Main St (05343)
Rates: $145-$345
(802) 874-4140
(800) 532-9399

JEFFERSON-VILLE

DEER RUN MOTOR INN
80 Deer Run Loop (05464)
Rates: $70-$85
(802) 644-8866
(800) 354-2728

HIGHLANDER MOTEL
RR 1, Box 436 (05464)
Rates: $42-$64
(802) 644-2725
(800) 367-6471

JEFFERSON HOUSE
Main St, Box 288 (05464)
Rates: $55-$75
(802) 644-2030

JERICHO

HOMEPLACE B&B
Old Pump Rd (05465)
Rates: $65-$75
(802) 899-4694

KILLINGTON

BUTTERNUT ON THE MTN
63 Weathervane Rd (05751)
Rates: $56-$120
(802) 422-2000
(800) 524-7654

CASCADES LODGE
58 Old Mill Rd (05751)
Rates: $81-$229
(802) 422-3731
(800) 214-8459

CEDARBROOK MOTOR INN/SUITES
US 4 & SR 100 S (05751)
Rates: $34-$114
(802) 422-9666
(800) 446-1088

CORTINA INN & RESORT
103 Rt 4 (05751)
Rates: $104-$199
(802) 773-3333
(800) 451-6108

HAPPY BEAR MOTEL
1784 Killington Rd (05751)
Rates: $50-$125
(802) 422-3305
(800) 518-4468

INN AT LONG TRAIL
Rt 4, Sherburne Pass (05751)
Rates: $68-$250
(802) 775-7181
(800) 325-2540

MENDON MOUNTAINVIEW RESORT LODGE
78 Rt 4 (05751)
Rates: $46-$169
(802) 773-4311
(800) 368-4311

VAL ROCK MOTEL
8006 Rt 4 (05751)
Rates: $64-$150
(802) 422-3881
(800) 238-8762

LANDGROVE

LANDGROVE INN
132 Landgrove Rd (05148)
Rates: $90-$235
(802) 824-6673
(800) 669-8466

LINCOLN

THE OLD HOTEL B&B
233 E River Rd (05443)
Rates: $65-$95
(802) 453-2567

LONDONDERRY

FROG'S LEAP INN
RR 1, Box 107, Rt 100 (05148)
Rates: $120-$275
(802) 824-3019
(877) 376-4753

WHITE PINE LODGE
Rt 11 West (05148)
Rates: $50-$110
(802) 824-3909

LUDLOW

CLARION CAVENDISH POINTE HOTEL
Rt 103 (05142)
Rates: $89-$149
(802) 226-7688
(800) 438-7908

THE COMBES FAMILY INN
953 E Lake Rd (05149)
Rates: $65-$160
(802) 228-8799
(800) 822-8799

OKEMO MTN VACATION CENTER RENTALS
44 Pond St (05149)
Rates: n/a
(802) 228-8255
(800) 829-8205

TIMBER INN MOTEL
112 Rt 103 S (05149)
Rates: $69-$149
(802) 228-8666
(877) 606-1479

MANCHESTER

AVALANCHE MOTOR LODGE
Rt 11 & 30 (05254)
Rates: $55-$75
(802) 362-2622
(800) 592-2622

BRITTANY INN MOTEL
Rt 7A, Box 760 (05255)
Rates: $51-$72
(802) 362-1033
(800) 298-4650

MARLBORO

WHETSTONE INN
Off Hwy 9 (05344)
Rates: $30-$85
(802) 254-2500

MENDON

CORTINA INN
103 US Rt 4 (05701)
Rates: $99-$229
(802) 773-3333
(800) 451-6108

ECONO LODGE KILLINGTON AREA
51 Rt 4 E (05701)
Rates: $50-$160
(802) 773-6644
(800) 424-6423
(800) 992-9067

EDELWEISS RED CARPET INN
119 US Rt 4 (05751)
Rates: $44-$125
(802) 775-5577
(800) 479-2863

MENDON MTN ORCHARDS MOTEL
16 US Rt 4 (05701)
Rates: $42-$47
(802) 775-5477

RED CLOVER HISTORIC COUNTRY INN
7 Woodward Rd (05701)
Rates: $185-$450
(802) 775-2290
(800) 752-0571

MIDDLEBURY

FAIRHILL B&B
Rd 3, Box 2300 (05753)
Rates: n/a
(802) 388-3044

MIDDLEBURY B&B
Washington St (05753)
Rates: $55-$85
(802) 388-4851

MIDDLEBURY COUNTRY INN
14 Courthouse Square (05753)
Rates: $78-$385
(802) 388-4961
(800) 842-4666

SUGARHOUSE MOTOR INN
Rt 7 (05753)
Rates: $50-$60
(802) 388-2770
(800) 784-2746

MONTPELIER

ECONO LODGE
101 Northfield St (05602)
Rates: $49-$98
(802) 223-5258
(800) 424-6423

MOUNT TABOR

MOUNT TABOR INN & TAVERN
217 Troll Hill Rd (05739)
Rates: $75-$125
(802) 293-5907

NEWFANE

FOUR COLUMNS INN
22 West St (05345)
Rates: $175-$400
(802) 365-7713

RIVER BEND LODGE
1086 SR 30 (05345)
Rates: $50-$60
(802) 365-7952

NEWPORT

TOP O' THE HILLS MOTEL & INN
HCR 61, Box 14 (05855)
Rates: $75-$95
(802) 334-2452
(800) 258-6748

WATER'S EDGE B&B
324 Wishing Well Ave (05855)
Rates: $70-$120
(802) 334-7726

AREA CODES - If the local number doesn't connect, check for a new area code.

NORTH HERO
SHORE ACRES INN
237 Shore Acres
Dr (05475)
Rates: $75-$199
(802) 372-8722

NORTH SPRINGFIELD
THE ABBY-LYN MOTEL
RD 1, Box 80
(05150)
Rates: $60-$75
(802) 886-2223

ORLEANS
GREEN ACRES CABINS
1051 Rt 5A (05860)
Rates: n/a
(802) 525-3722

WILLOUGH-VALE INN
793 Rt 5A (05860)
Rates: $79-$229
(802) 525-4123
(800) 594-9102

ORWELL
BUCKSWOOD B&B
633 Rt 73E
(05760)
Rates: $55-$65
(802) 948-2054

PERKINSVILLE
GWENDOLYN'S B&B INN
Rt 106 (05151)
Rates: $55-$92
(802) 263-5248

PERU
JOHNNY SEE-SAW'S LODGE
SEE AD BELOW

PITTSFIELD
CLEAR RIVER INN
Rt 100 (05762)
Rates: $38-$85
(802) 746-7916
(800) 746-7916

POULTNEY
STONEBRIDGE INN B&B
3 Beaunau St
(05764)
Rates: $60-$84
(802) 287-9849
(800) 308-7001

PUTNEY
PUTNEY INN
57 Putney
Landing Rd
(05346)
Rates: $78-$158
(802) 387-5517
(800) 653-5517

QUECHEE
QUALITY INN
5817 Woodstock
Rd (05059)
Rates: $79-$180
(802) 295-7600
(800) 732-4376

READING
BAILEY'S MILLS B&B
1347 Bailey's Mill
Rd (05062)
Rates: $100-$165
(802) 484-7809
(800) 639-3437

RICHMOND
MAMA BOWER'S BED & BREAKFST
P O Box 22
(05477)
Rates: $40-$65
(802) 434-2632

ROCHESTER
HARVEY'S MTN VIEW INN
RR 1, Box 53
(05767)
Rates: $625 Wk
(802) 767-4273

ROXBURY
JOHNNYCAKE FLATS B&B
47 Carrie Howe
Rd (05669)
Rates: $105-$125
(802) 485-8961

RUTLAND
COMFORT INN TROLLEY SQUARE
19 Allen St (05701)
Rates: $58-$189
(802) 775-2200
(800) 424-6423

HIGHLANDER MOTEL
203 N Main St
(05701)
Rates: $50-$100
(802) 773-6069
(800) 884-6069

HOLIDAY INN
476 SR 7 S (05701)
Rates: $140-$218
(802) 775-1911
(800) 465-4329
(800) 462-4810

RAMADA LIMITED
253 S Main St
(05701)
Rates: $69-$151
(802) 773-3361
(800) 272-6232

RED ROOF INN
401 US Hwy 7 S
(05701)
Rates: $59-$159
(802) 775-4303
(800) 843-7663

RODEWAY INN
138 N Main St
(05701)
Rates: $42-$139
(802) 775-2575
(800) 424-6423

ROYAL MOTEL
115 Woodstock
Ave (05701)
Rates: $42-$109
(802) 773-9176

TYROL MOTOR INN
RR 2, Box 7602
(05701)
Rates: $40-$106
(802) 773-7485

ST. ALBANS
CADILLAC MOTEL
213 Main St
(05478)
Rates: $43-$70
(802) 524-2191

COMFORT INN
813 Fairfax Rd
(05478)
Rates: $69-$149
(802) 524-3300
(800) 424-6423

ECONO LODGE
287 S Main St
(05478)
Rates: $49-$99
(802) 524-5956
(800) 424-6423

OLD MILL RIVER PLACE B&B
6206 Georgia
Shore Rd (05478)
Rates: $55-$65
(802) 524-7211

ST. JOHNSBURY
AIME'S MOTEL
46 VT Rt 18
(05819)
Rates: $55-$70
(802) 748-3194
(800) 504-6663

FAIRBANKS INN
401 Western Ave
(05819)
Rates: $79-$279
(802) 748-5666

HOLIDAY MOTEL
222 Hastings St
(05819)
Rates: $59-$139
(802) 748-8192

MAPLE CENTER MOTEL
20 Hastings St
(05819)
Rates: $42-$85
(802) 748-2393

SAXTONS RIVER
THE INN AT SAXTONS RIVER
27 Main St (05154)
Rates: $98-$108
(802) 869-2110

SHAFTSBURY
BAYBERRY MOTEL
Rt 7A, Box 137
(05262)
Rates: $38-$75
(802) 447-7180

Johnny Seesaw's

Rated Five Bones

LODGING AND DINING
Cottages with Fireplace • Family Suites • Award Winning Restaurant
Ten Secluded Acres • Swimming Pool • Clay Tennis Court
Route 11, Bromley Mountain, Peru, Vermont
www.johnnyseesaw.com   email: gary@jseesaw.com
(802) 824-5533 • (800) 424-CSAW

GOVERNOR'S ROCK MOTEL
4325 SR 7A
Rates: $49-$85
(802) 442-4734

HILLBROOK MOTEL
Historic SR 7A
(05262)
Rates: $40-$70
(802) 447-7201

KIMBERLY COTTAGE
Myers Rd, Box 345
(05262)
Rates: $85-$185
(802) 442-4354

SERENITY MOTEL
4379 Rt 7A (05262)
Rates: $55-$80
(802) 442-6490
(800) 644-6490

SHARON
COLUMNS MOTOR LODGE
Rt 14 (05065)
Rates: $38-$46
(802) 763-7040

SHELBURNE
ECONO LODGE
3164 Shelburne
Rd (05482)
Rates: $39-$150
(802) 985-3377
(800) 424-6423

SHOREHAM
INDIAN TRAIL FARM B&B
Box 49, Smith St
(05770)
Rates: $50+
(802) 897-5292

SOUTH BURLINGTON
(Also see Burlington)

ANCHORAGE INN
108 Dorset St
(05403)
Rates: $49-$117
(802) 863-7000
(800) 336-1869

BEST WESTERN
1076 Williston Rd
(05403)
Rates: $85-$195
(802) 853-1125
(800) 371-1125

CLARION HOTEL
1117 Williston Rd
(05403)
Rates: $79-$225
(802) 658-0250
(800) 424-6423

COMFORT INN
1285 Williston Rd
(05403)
Rates: $59-$159
(802) 865-3400
(800) 424-6423

ETHAN ALLEN MOTEL
1611 Williston Rd
(05403)
Rates: $42-$84
(802) 863-4573
(866) 316-6835

HAWTHORN SUITES HOTEL
401 Dorset St
(05403)
Rates: $119-$179
(802) 860-1212
(886) 337-1616

HOLIDAY INN
1068 Williston Rd
(05403)
Rates: $115-$146
(802) 863-6363
(800) 465-4329

MAINSTAY SUITES
1702 Shelburne Rd
(05403)
Rates: $89-$239
(802) 860-1986
(800) 424-6423

SHERATON HOTEL
870 Williston Rd
(05403)
Rates: $189-$249
(802) 865-6600
(800) 325-3535

SMART SUITES HOTEL
1700 Shelburne Rd
(05403)
Rates: $79-$159
(802) 860-9900
(877) 862-6800

SOUTH HERO
SANDBAR MOTOR INN
US Rt 2 (05486)
Rates: $48-$85
(802) 372-6911

SOUTH WOODSTOCK
KEDRON VALLEY HISTORIC INN
Rt 106 (05071)
Rates: $111-$329
(802) 457-1473
(800) 836-1193

SPRINGFIELD
THE HARTNESS HOUSE COUNTRY INN
30 Orchard St
(05156)
Rates: $90-$195
(802) 885-2115

HOLIDAY INN EXP
818 Charlestown
Rd (05156)
Rates: $119-$179
(802) 885-4516
(800) 465-4329

PA-LO-MAR MOTEL
2 Linhale Dr
(05156)
Rates: $30-$56
(802) 885-4142

STARKSBORO
MILLHOUSE B&B
394 State Prison
Hollow Rd
(05487)
Rates: $35-$40
(802) 453-2008
(800) 859-5758

STOCKBRIDGE
CHASE INN B&B
Rt 100 (05772)
Rates: $20-$40
(802) 746-8972
(800) 746-8972

STOWE
ANDERSEN LODGE
3430 Mountain Rd
(05672)
Rates: $75-$135
(802) 253-7336
(800) 336-7336

BURGUNDY ROSE INN
Rt 100, P. O.
Box 488 (05672)
Rates: $45-$79
(802) 253-7768
(800) 989-7768

COMMODORES INN
231 Main St
(05672)
Rates: $98-$168
(802) 253-7131
(800) 447-8693

COVERED BRIDGE B&B
12 Chandler Farm
Rd (05672)
Rates: $85-$150
(802) 253-8221

EDSON HILL MANOR INN
1500 Edson Hill
Rd (05672)
Rates: $89-$219
(802) 253-7371

EDSON HILL VIEW BED & BREAKFST
903 Edson Hill Rd
(05672)
Rates: $65-$110
(802) 253-4337
(800) 559-4337

1860 HOUSE B&B
P.O. Box 276
(05672)
Rates: n/a
(802) 253-7351
(800) 248-1860

GREEN MTN COUNTRY INN
18 S Main St
(05672)
Rates: $115-$695
(802) 253-7301
(800) 253-7302

HOB KNOB INN
2364 Mountain Rd
(05672)
Rates: $95-$195
(802) 253-8549
(800) 245-8540

HONEYWOOD LODGE & INN
4527 Mountain Rd
(05672)
Rates: $89-$199
(802) 253-4124
(800) 659-6289

INNSBRUCK INN
4361 Mountain Rd
(05672)
Rates: $69-$169
(802) 253-8582
(800) 225-8582

MIGUEL'S STOWE AWAY B&B INN
3148 Mountain Rd
(05672)
Rates: $35-$120
(802) 253-7574
(800) 245-1240

THE MOUNTAIN ROAD RESORT
1007 Mountain Rd
(05672)
Rates: $105-$325
(802) 253-4566
(800) 367-6873

MOUNTAINEER INN
3343 Mountain Rd
(05672)
Rates: $59-$105
(802) 253-7525

NOTCH BROOK CONDOS
1229 Notch Brook
Rd (05672)
Rates: $66-$275
(802) 253-4882
(800) 253-4882

RASPEBERRY PATCH B&B
606 Randolph Rd
(05672)
Rates: $50-$95
(802) 253-4145
(800) 624-0639

RIVERSIDE INN
1965 Mountain Rd
(05672)
Rates: $49-$130
(802) 253-4217
(800) 966-4217

SALZBURG INN
Mountain Rd,
Rt 108 (05672)
Rates: $58-$78
(802) 253-8541
(800) 448-4554

SEASON'S PASS INN
613 S Main St
(05672)
Rates: $62-$105
(802) 253-7244

STOWE INN
123 Mountain Rd
(05672)
Rates: $78-$198
(802) 253-4030
(800) 256-4030

**TEN ACRES
COUNTRY INN**
14 Barrows Rd
(05672)
Rates: $165-$350
(802) 253-7638
(800) 327-7357

**TOPNOTCH
AT STOWE**
4000 Mountain Rd
(05672)
Rates: $180-$525
(802) 253-8585
(800) 451-8686

**TWO DOG LODGE
& CHALETS**
3576 Mountain Rd
(05672)
Rates: $89-$400
(802) 253-8555
(800) 339-2DOG

**WALKABOUT
CREEK LODGE B&B**
199 Edson Hill Rd
(05672)
Rates: $70-$150
(802) 253-7354
(800) 426-6697

**YE OLDE
ENGLAND INNE**
433 Mountain Rd
(05672)
Rates: $119-$345
(802) 253-7558
(800) 477-3771

*STRATTON
MOUNTAIN*
**LIFTLINE LODGE
RESORT HOTEL**
Stratton Mtn Rd
(05155)
Rates: $59-$145
(802) 297-2600
(800) 597-5438

SUNDERLAND
**ARCADY AT THE
SUNDERLAND**
6249 Rt 7A
(Arlington 05250)
Rates: $70-$130
(802) 362-1176
(800) 362-1151

GREEN RIVER INN
3402 Sandgate Rd
(05250)
Rates: $90-$200
(802) 375-2272
(888) 648-2212

SWANTON
BLUE FORD MOTEL
325 N River Rd
(05488)
Rates: $35-$75
(802) 868-4147

**COUNTRY
ESSENCE B&B**
641 Rt 7 N (05488)
Rates: $60+
(802) 868-4247

TAFTSVILLE
APPLEBUTTER B&B
Happy Valley Rd
(05073)
Rates: $40-$65
(802) 457-4158

TOWNSHEND
**BOARDMAN
HOUSE B&B**
On the Green
(05353)
Rates: $65-$85
(802) 365-4086

UNDERHILL
4 PAUSE B&B
354 Pleasant
Valley Rd (05489)
Rates: $55-$70
(802) 899-3927

VERGENNES
**BASIN HARBOR
CLUB RESORT**
4800 Basin Harbor
Rd (05491)
Rates: $115-$255
(802) 475-2311
(800) 622-4000

**HILLCREST
COTTAGES**
686 Basin Harbor
Rd (05491)
Rates: $45
(802) 475-2343

WAITSFIELD
**GARRISON
MOTEL & CONDOS**
Rt 17, Box 539
(05673)
Rates: $65-$525
(802) 496-2352
(800) 766-7829

HYDE AWAY INN
1428 Millbrook Rd
(05673)
Rates: $69-$159
(802) 496-2322
(800) 777-4933

MILLBROOK INN
533 Millbrook Rd
(05673)
Rates: $90-$150
(802) 496-2405
(800) 477-2809

**WEATHERTOP
LODGE**
755 Millbrook Rd
(05673)
Rates: $95-$250
(802) 496-4909
(800) 800-3625

WARREN
**GOLDEN LION
RIVERSIDE INN**
Sugarbush Access
Rd, Rt 100 (05674)
Rates: $26-$44
(802) 496-3084

**POWDERHOUND
INN & CONDOS**
203 Powderhound
Rd (05674)
Rates: $84-$149
(802) 496-5100
(800) 548-4022

*WATERBURY
CENTER*
1836 CABINS
Box 128-T, Rt 100,
Stowe Rd (05677)
Rates: $99-$149
(802) 244-8533

WELLS RIVER
**BIRCHWOOD
MOTOR INN**
RR 1, Box 2 (45081)
Rates: n/a
(802) 757-2274
(800) 895-2277

*WEST
BRATTLEBORO*
**MOLLY STARK
MOTEL**
829 Marlboro Rd
(05301)
Rates: $40-$80
(802) 254-2440

*WEST
DANVILLE*
**INDIAN JOE
COURT CABINS**
US Rt 2, Box 126
(05873)
Rates: $40-$75
(802) 684-3430

**POINT COMFORT
COTTAGES**
3182 Rt 2 (05873)
Rates: n/a
(802) 684-3379

WEST DOVER
ANDIRONS LODGE
183 Rt 100 (05356)
Rates: $75-$150
(802) 464-2114
(800) 445-7669

GRAY GHOST INN
290 Rt 100 N
(05356)
Rates: $49-$137
(802) 464-2474

RED OAK INN
45 Rt 100 (05356)
Rates: $70-$260
(802) 464-8817
(866) 5-REDOAK

**SNOW GOOSE
INN B&B**
259 Rt 100 (05356)
Rates: $115-$395
(802) 464-3984

WESTMORE
**WILLOUGHVALE
INN ON LAKE
WILLOUGHBY**
793 VT Rt 5A
(05860)
Rates: $75-$224
(802) 525-4123

WESTON
**THE DARLING
FAMILY INN**
815 Rt 100 (05161)
Rates: $80-$125
(802) 824-3223

*WHITE RIVER
JUNCTION*
**BEST WESTERN
AT THE JUNCTION**
306 N Hartland
Rd (05001)
Rates: $59-$169
(802) 295-3015
(800) 370-4656

COMFORT INN
8 Sykes Ave
(05001)
Rates: $82-$249
(802) 295-3051
(800) 424-6423

REGENCY
259 Holiday Dr
(05001)
Rates: $60-$160
(802) 295-3000
(800) 648-3754

WILDER
WILDER MOTEL
319 Hartford Ave
(05088)
Rates: $45-$65
(802) 295-9793

WILLIAMSTOWN
AUTUMN CREST INN
RFD 1, Box 1540
(05679)
Rates: $88-$148
(802) 433-6627
(800) 339-6627

**AUTUMN
HARVEST
COUNTRY INN**
118 Clark Rd
(05679)
Rates: $89-$159
(802) 433-1355

WILLISTON
**TOWNE PLACE
SUITES**
66 Zephyr Rd
(05495)
Rates: $79-$129
(802) 872-5900
(800) 257-3000

WILMINGTON
**INN AT QUAIL
RUN B&B**
106 Smith Rd
(05363)
Rates: $105-$220
(802) 464-3362
(800) 343-7227

**THE VINTAGE
MOTEL**
195 Rt 9 W (05363)
Rates: $55-$90
(802) 464-8824
(800) 899-9660

WOODSTOCK
BRAESIDE MOTEL
432 Rt 4 E (05091)
Rates: $68-$118
(802) 457-1366
(800) 303-1366

**THE WINSLOW
HOUSE B&B**
492 Woodstock Rd
(05091)
Rates: $100-$175
(802) 457-1820

AREA CODES - If the local number doesn't connect, check for a new area code.

VIRGINIA

ABINGDON

QUALITY INN & SUITES
930 E Main St (24210)
Rates: $99-$129
(276) 676-9090
(800) 424-6423

ALDIE

THE CASTLE
Rt 15, Box 28K
Rates: n/a
(703) 327-4113

ALEXANDRIA

ALEXANDRIA SUITES HOTEL
420 N Van Dorn St (22303)
Rates: $99-$119
(703) 370-1000

CLASSIC B&B
6216 Saddle Tree Dr (22340)
Rates: $100
(703) 922-7836

EXECUTIVE CLUB SUITES
610 Bashford Ln (22314)
Rates: $110-$130
(703) 739-2582
(800) 535-2582

ALTAVISTA

COMFORT SUITES
1558 Main St (24517)
Rates: $58-$147
(434) 369-4000
(800) 424-6423

AMHERST

CRUMPS MTN COTTAGE
2150 Indian Creek Rd (24521)
Rates: n/a
(804) 277-5563

FAIRVIEW B&B
Rt 4, Box 117 (25421)
Rates: $65-$70
(804) 277-8500

APPOMATTOX

SUPER 8 MOTEL
Rt 4, Box 100 (24522)
Rates: $52-$66
(434) 352-2339
(800) 800-8000

ARLINGTON

BEST WESTERN ROSSLYN-KEY BRIDGE
1850 N Ft. Myer Dr (22209)
Rates: $135-$150
(703) 522-0400
(800) 528-1234
)800) 539-2743

HOMESTEAD STUDIO SUITES
4504 Brookfield Corp Dr (22309)
Rates: $89-$134
(703) 263-3361
(888) 782-9473

QUALITY HOTEL COURTHOUSE PLAZA
1200 N Courthouse Rd (22201)
Rates: $85-$175
(703) 524-4000
(800) 424-6423

RESIDENCE INN- PENTAGON CITY
550 Army-Navy Dr (22201)
Rates: n/a
(703) 413-6630
(800) 331-3131

RITZ CARLTON- PENTAGON CITY
1250 S Hayes St (22201)
Rates: n/a
(703) 415-5000
(800) 241-3333

SHERATON CRYSTAL CITY
1800 Jefferson Davis Hwy (22201)
Rates: n/a
(703) 521-1900
(800) 325-3535

VIRGINIA SUITES
1500 Arlington Rd (22201)
Rates: n/a
(703) 522-9600

ASHLAND

DAYS INN
806 England St (23005)
Rates: $50-$100
(804) 798-4262
(800) 329-7466

ECONO LODGE
103 N Carter Rd (23005)
Rates: $35-$117
(804) 798-9221
(800) 424-6423

THE HENRY CLAY INN
114 N Railroad Ave (23005)
Rates: $90
(804) 798-3100

QUALITY INN & SUITES
810 England St (23005)
Rates: $60-$150
(804) 798-4231
(800) 424-6423

SLEEP INN, INN & SUITES
I-95 & Hwy 54 (23005)
Rates: $69-$89
(800) 424-6423

ATKINS

COMFORT INN
5558 Lee Hwy (24311)
Rates: $55-$195
(276) 783-2144
(800) 424-6423

BASYE

SKY CHALET COUNTRY INN
P O Box 300 (22810)
Rates: n/a
(504) 856-2147

BEDFORD

DAYS INN
921 Blue Ridge Ave (24523)
Rates: $45-$90
(540) 586-8286
(800) 329-7466

BERRYVILLE

BLUE RIDGE B&B RESERVATIONS
Rt 2, Box 3895 (22611)
Rates: n/a
(703) 955-1246
(800) 296-1246

BIG STONE GAP

COUNTRY INN MOTEL
627 Gilley Ave (24219)
Rates: $45-$50
(276) 523-0374

BLACKSBURG

BEST WESTERN RED LION INN
900 Plantation Rd (24060)
Rates: $59-$95
(540) 552-7770
(800) 528-1234

COMFORT INN
3705 S Main St (24060)
Rates: $55-$150
(540) 951-1500
(800) 424-6423

DONALDSON BROWN RESORT & CONF CENTER
201 Otey St (24061)
Rates: n/a
(540) 231-9485
(877) 200-3360

RAMADA LIMITED
3503 Holiday Lane (24060)
Rates: $50-$110
(540) 951-1330
(800) 272-6232

BLACKSTONE

EPES HOUSE BED & BREAKFST
210 College Ave (23824)
Rates: n/a
(804) 292-7941

BLAND

BIG WALKER MOTEL
P. O. Box 155 (24315)
Rates: $34-$48
(540) 688-3331

BOWLING GREEN

MANSION VIEW BED & BREAKFAST
P. O. Box 787 (22427)
Rates: n/a
(804) 633-2202
(800) 251-9335

WEBB'S MOTEL
18080 A.P. Hill Blvd (22427)
Rates: n/a
(804) 633-6755

BOYDTON

SOUTHERN HERITAGE BED & BREAKFAST
1100 Jefferson St (23917)
Rates: n/a
(804) 738-0167

BRANDY STATION

BLUE HAVEN BED & BREAKFAST
14648 Carrico Mills Rd (22714)
Rates: $65-$85
(540) -825-0716

BRISTOL

ECONO LODGE
912 Commonwealth Ave (24201)
Rates: $34-$65
(276) 466-2112
(800) 424-6423

HOLIDAY INN HOTEL & SUITES
3005 Linden Dr (24202)
Rates: $99
(276) 466-4100
(800) 465-4329

LA QUINTA INN
1014 Old Airport Rd (24201)
Rates: $62-$95
(276) 669-9353
(800) 687-6667

MICROTEL INN & SUITES
131 Bristol Rd E (24201)
Rates: $54-$64
(276) 669-8164

MOTEL 6
21561 Clear Creek Rd (24201)
Rates: $42-$60
(276) 466-6060
(800) 466-8356

RAMADA INN
2221 Euclid Ave (24201)
Rates: n/a
(276) 669-7171
(800) 272-6232

SKYLAND MOTEL
15545 Lee Hwy (24201)
Rates: $20-$45
(276) 669-0166

SUPER 8 MOTEL
2139 Lee Hwy (24201)
Rates: $44-$275
(276) 466-8800
(800) 800-8000

BUENA VISTA

BUENA VISTA MOTEL
477 E 29th St (24416)
Rates: $35-$70
(540) 261-2138

BUFFALO JUNCTION

THE LITTLE RETREAT
877 Riverview Ave (24592)
Rates: n/a
(800) 843-0633

BURGESS

BAILEY-COCKRELL HOUSE B&B
P O Box 296 (22432)
Rates: n/a
(804) 453-5900

BURKEVILLE

COMFORT INN
419 N Agnew St (23922)
Rates: $55-$115
(434) 767-3750
(800) 424-6423

CALLAO

STRANGERS IN GOOD COMPANY BED & BREAKFST
170 Bell's Cove Rd (22435)
Rates: n/a
(804) 529-5132

CAPE CHARLES

BEST WESTERN SUNSET BEACH RESORT
32246 Lankford Hwy (23310)
Rates: $64-$109
(757) 331-1776
(800) 528-1234
(800) 899-4786

DAYS INN
29106 Lankford Hwy (23310)
Rates: $49-$89
(757) 331-1000
(800) 329-7466

SUNSET BEACH INN
Rt 13 (23310)
Rates: n/a
(757) 331-4786

CARMEL CHURCH

DAYS INN
24320 Rogers Clark Blvd (22546)
Rates: $45-$99
(804) 448-2011
(800) 328-7466

RED ROOF INN
23500 Welcome Way Dr (22546)
Rates: $49-$85
(804) 448-2828
(800) 843-7663

CHAMPLAIN

LINDEN HOUSE B&B PLANTATION
11770 Tidewater Trail (22438)
Rates: $95
(804) 443-1170

CHARLES CITY

RIVER'S REST MOTEL & MARINA
9100 Willcox Neck Rd (23030)
Rates: $49-$69
(804) 829-2753

CHARLOTTES-VILLE

BEST WESTERN CAVALIER INN
105 Emmet St (22905)
Rates: $75-$109
(434) 296-8111
(800) 528-1234
(888) 882-2129

CAMPS & COTTAGES OF CHARLOTTESVILLE
Rt 6, Box 260A (22902)
Rates: n/a
(434) 293-2529

COMFORT INN
1807 Emmet St (22901)
Rates: $65-$149
(434) 293-6188
(800) 424-6423

DAYS INN
1600 Emmet St (22901)
Rates: $49-$139
(434) 293-9111
(800) 329-7466

DOUBLETREE HOTEL
990 Hilton Heights Rd (22901)
Rates: $79-$136
(434) 973-2121
(800) 222-8733

ECONO LODGE
400 Emmet St (22903)
Rates: $41-$160
(434) 296-2104
(800) 424-6423

HOLIDAY INN
1200 5th St (22902)
Rates: $70-$90
(434) 977-5100
(800) 465-4329

OMNI HOTEL
235 W Main St (22901)
Rates: $119-$179
(434) 971-5500
(800) 843-6664

QUALITY INN
1600 Emmet St (22901)
Rates: $45-$150
(434) 971-3746
(800) 424-6423

RED ROOF INN
1309 W Main St (22903)
Rates: $69-$100
(434) 295-4333
(800) 843-7663

RESIDENCE INN BY MARRIOTT
1111 Millmont St (22903)
Rates: $119-$149
(434) 923-0300
(800) 331-3131

SLEEP INN, INN & SUITES
1185 5th St SW (22902)
Rates: $65-$99
(434) 244-9969
(800) 424-6423

SUPER 8 MOTEL
390 Greenbrier Dr (22901)
Rates: $49-$89
(434) 973-0888
(800) 800-8000

CHESAPEAKE

DAYS INN
1439 N George Washington Hwy (23323)
Rates: $55-$95
(757) 487-8861
(800) 329-7466

ECONO LODGE
4725 Military Hwy W (23321)
Rates: $36-$90
(757) 488-4963
(800) 424-6423

MOTEL 6
701 Woodlake Dr (23320)
Rates: $36-$60
(757) 420-2976
(800) 466-8356

RED ROOF INN
724 Woodlake Dr (23320)
Rates: $42-$74
(757) 523-0123
(800) 843-7663

SUPER 8 MOTEL
3216 Churchland Blvd (23320)
Rates: $52-$77
(757) 686-8888
(800) 800-8000

TOWNPLACE SUITES BY MARRIOTT
2000 Old Greenbriar Rd (23320)
Rates: $79-$139
(757) 523-5004
(800) 257-3000

CHESTER

CLARION HOTEL
2401 W Hundred Rd (23831)
Rates: $59-$99
(804) 748-6321
(800) 424-6423

COMFORT INN
2100 W Hundred Rd (23831)
Rates: $59-$125
(804) 751-000
(800) 424-6423

DAYS INN
2410 W Hundred Rd (23831)
Rates: $55-$85
(804) 748-5871
(800) 329-7466

QUALITY INN
12711 Old Stage Rd (23831)
Rates: $59-$169
(804) 796-5200
(800) 424-6423

CHINCO-TEAGUE

BAYSIDE RETREAT
4215 Main St (23336)
Rates: n/a
(757) 336-6798

AREA CODES - If the local number doesn't connect, check for a new area code.

EAST SIDE RENTALS
7462 East Side Rd (23336)
Rates: n/a
(757) 336-6861

ISLAND PROPERTY ENTERPRISES
4065 Main St (23336)
Rates: n/a
(800) 346-2559

MAIN STREET HOUSE B&B
4356 MainSt (23336)
Rates: n/a
(757) 336-6030

SEA BREEZE RENTALS
6755 Maddox Blvd (23336)
Rates: n/a
(800) 795-3931

SEA TAG LODGE
7486 E Side Dr (23336)
Rates: n/a
(757) 336-5555

CHRISTIANS-BURG
DAYS INN
2635 Roanoke St (24073)
Rates: $41-$99
(540) 382-0261
(800) 329-7466

ECONO LODGE
2430 Roanoke St (24073)
Rates: $40-$169
(540) 382-69161
(800) 553-2666

SUPER 8 MOTEL
55 Laurel St NE (24073)
Rates: $52-$84
(540) 382-5813
(800) 800-8000

CLARKSVILLE
BAYVIEW EFFICIENCIES
405 4th St (23927)
Rates: n/a
(434) 374-9216

BEST WESTERN ON THE LAKE
103 Second St (23927)
Rates: $69-$114
(434) 374-5023
(800) 528-1234

CLIFTON FORGE
LONGDALE INN
6209 Longdale Furnace Rd (24422)
Rates: n/a
(540) 862-0892
(800) 862-0386

COLLINSVILLE
FAIRYSTONE MOTEL
626 Virginia Ave (24078)
Rates: $37-$48
(5276 647-3941

KNIGHTS INN
2357 Virginia Ave (24078)
Rates: $55-$65
(276) 647-3716
(800) 843-5644

QUALITY INN DUTCH INN
2360 Virginia Ave (24078)
Rates: $74-$89
(276) 647-3721
(800) 424-6423

COLONIAL BEACH
DAYS INN-ON THE POTOMAC
30 Colonial Ave (22443)
Rates: $55-$100
(804) 224-0404
(800) 329-7466

COLONIAL HEIGHTS
DAYS INN
2310 Indian Hill Rd (23834)
Rates: $42-$85
(804) 520-1010
(800) 329-7466

COVINGTON
BEST WESTERN MOUNTAINVIEW
820 E Madison St (24426)
Rates: $79-$96
(540) 962-4951
(800) 528-1234

COMFORT INN
203 Interstate Dr (24426)
Rates: $77-$100
(540) 962-2141
(800) 424-6423

HIGHLAND MOTEL
720 S Highland Ave (24426)
Rates: n/a
(540) 962-3901

KNIGHTS COURT
908 Valley Ridge Rd (24426)
Rates: $53-$73
(540) 962-7600
(800) 843-5644

MILTON HALL B&B INN
207 Thorny Ln (24426)
Rates: n/a
(540) 965-0196

CROZET
YANCY MILLS BED & BREAKFAST
6334 Hillsboro Lane (22932)
Rates: n/a
(804) 823-4839

CULPEPER
COMFORT INN
890 Willis Lane (22701)
Rates: $63-$125
(540) 825-4900
(800) 424-6423

CUMBERLAND
RT. 60 MOTEL
Rt 60, Box 162 (23040)
Rates: n/a
(804) 492-4119

DALEVILLE
HOWARD JOHN-SON EXPRESS
437 Roanoke Rd (24083)
Rates: $65-$72
(540) 992-1234
(800) 446-4656
(800) 628-1958

DAMASCUS
APPLE TREE B&B
115 E Laurel Ave (24236)
Rates: $60-$85
(276) 475-5261

DANVILLE
COMFORT INN & SUITES
100 Tower Dr (24540)
Rates: $69-$139
(434) 793-2000
(800) 424-6423

DAYS INN
1390 Piney Forest Dr (24540)
Rates: $45-$75
(434) 836-6745
(800) 329-7466

INNKEEPER DANVILLE NORTH
1030 Piney Forest Rd (24540)
Rates: $52-$62
(434) 836-1700

RAMADA INN
2500 Riverside Dr (24540)
Rates: $55-$116
(434) 793-2500
(800) 272-6232

SUPER 8 MOTEL
2385 Riverside Dr (24540)
Rates: $49-$65
(434) 799-5845
(800) 800-8000

DOSWELL
BEST WESTERN-KINGS QUARTERS
16102 Theme Park Way (23047)
Rates: $34-$189
(804) 876-3321
(800) 528-1234

DUBLIN
COMFORT INN
4424 Cleburne Blvd (24084)
Rates: $59-$155
(540) 674-1100
(800) 424-6423
(800) 424-6423

DUMFRIES
HOLIDAY INN EXP
17133 Dumfries Rd (22026)
Rates: $65-$85
(703) 221-1141
(800) 465-4329

BEST WESTERN EMPORIA INN
1100 W Atlantic St (23847)
Rates: $55-$77
(434) 634-3200
(800) 528-1234

COMFORT INN
1411 Skippers Rd (23847)
Rates: $48-$70
(434) 348-3282
(800) 424-6423

DAYS INN
921 W Atlantic St (23847)
Rates: $45-$85
(434) 634-9481
(800) 329-7466

HAMPTON INN
1207 W Atlantic St (23847)
Rates: $60-$75
(434) 634-9200
(800) 426-7866

KNIGHTS INN
3173 Sussex Dr (23847)
Rates: $30-$64
(434) 535-8535
(800) 843-5644

RESTÉ MOTEL
3190 Sussex Dr (23847)
Rates: $30-$50
(434) 535-8505

ETLAN
DULLANEY HOLLOW /OLD RAG MTN
Rt 6, Box 214 (22719)
Rates: n/a
(540) 923-4470

FAIRFIELD
FOX HILL ORDINARY
4383 Borden Grant Trail (24435)
Rates: n/a
(888) 440-4383

FANCY GAP
CASCADE MOUNTAIN INN
96 Cascade Trail (24328)
Rates: $50-$85
(276) 728-2300

DOE RUN LODGE
MM 189.2 on Blue
Ridge Pkwy
(24328)
Rates: $99-$234
(276) 398-2212

FARMVILLE
SUPER 8 MOTEL
Hwy 15 S (23901)
Rates: $45-$105
(434) 392-8196
(800) 800-8000

FERRUM
**OLD SPRING
FARM B&B**
7629 Charity Hwy
(24088)
Rates: n/a
(540) 930-3404

FORT HAYWOOD
**INN AT TABB'S
CREEK LANDING**
P.O. Box 219 (23138)
Rates: n/a
(804) 725-5136

FORT MONROE
**CHAMBERLIN
HOTEL**
General Delivery
(23651)
Rates: n/a
(757) 723-6511
(800) 582-8975

FRANKLIN
COMFORT INN
1620 Armory Dr
(23851)
Rates: $56-$74
(757) 569-0018
(800) 424-6423

DAYS INN
1660 Armory Dr
(23851)
Rates: $55-$85
(757) 562-2225
(800) 328-7466

FREDERICKS BURG
**BEST WESTERN
INN**
2205 William St
(22401)
Rates: $59-$79
(540) 371-5050
(800) 528-1234

**BEST WESTERN
CENTRAL PLAZA**
3000 Plank Rd
(22401)
Rates: $50-$79
(540) 786-7404
(800) 528-1234

DAYS INN-NORTH
14 Simpson Rd
(22405)
Rates: $30-$71
(540) 373-5340
(800) 329-7466

DAYS INN-SOUTH
5316 Jefferson
Davis Hwy
(22401)
Rates: $30-$71
(540) 898-6800
(800) 329-7466

**DUNNING
MILLS INN ALL
SUITES HOTEL**
2305-C Jefferson
Davis Hwy
(22401)
Rates: $69-$90
(540) 373-1256

ECONO LODGE
5321 Jefferson
Davis Hwy
(22408)
Rates: $44-$85
(540) 898-5440
(800) 424-6423

ECONO LODGE
2809 Plank Rd
(22404)
Rates: $36-$65
(540) 786-8374
(800) 424-6423

HAMPTON INN
2310 William St
(22401)
Rates: $64-$86
(540) 371-0330
(800) 426-7866

**HOLIDAY INN
SELECT**
2801 Plank Rd
(22404)
Rates: $59-$99
(540) 786-8321
(800) 465-4329

HOLIDAY INN-N
564 Warrenton Rd
(22405)
Rates: $67-$82
(540) 371-5550
(800) 465-4329

**HOWARD
JOHNSON**
5327 Jefferson
Davis Hwy
(22408)
Rates: $59-$109
(540) 898-1800
(800) 446-4656

MOTEL 6
401 Warrenton
Rd (22405)
Rates: $30-$52
(540) 371-5443
(800) 466-8356

QUALITY INN
543 Warrenton Rd
(22406)
Rates: $49-$99
(540) 373-0000
(800) 424-6423

RAMADA INN
5324 Jefferson
Davis Hwy
(22408)
Rates: $39-$109
(540) 898-1102
(800) 272-6232

FRONT ROYAL
BLUEMONT INN
1525 N
Shenandoah Ave
(22630)
Rates: $47-$195
(540) 635-9191
(800) 461-1720

BUDGET INN
1122 N Royal St
(22630)
Rates: $39-$75
(540) 635-2196
(800) 766-6748

PIONEER MOTEL
541 S Royal Ave
(22630)
Rates: n/a
(540) 635-4784

RELAX INN
1801 N
Shenandoah Ave
(22630)
Rates: $40-$75
(540) 635-4101
(877) 487-3529

SCOTTISH INNS
533 S Royal Ave
(22630)
Rates: $44-$79
(540) 636-6168
(800) 251-1962

TWI-LITE MOTEL
53 W 14th St
(22630)
Rates: $35-$89
(540) 635-4148
(800) 230-7349

GALAX
**CREST HAVEN
FARM**
114 Deerfield Rd
(24333)
Rates: n/a
(540) 236-4436

GLADE SPRING
**SWISS INN MOTEL
& SUITES**
33361 Lee Hwy
(24340)
Rates: $39-$65
(276) 429-5191

GLEN ALLEN
AMERISUITES
4100 Cox Rd
(23060)
Rates: $99-$159
(804) 747-9644
(800) 833-1516

**CANDLEWOOD
SUITES**
4120 Brookriver
Dr (23060)
Rates: $89-$109
(804) 364-2000
(888) 226-3539

**HOMESTEAD
STUDIO SUITES**
10961 W Broad St
(23060)
Rates: $54-$99
(804) 747-8898
(888) 782-9473

**HOMEWOOD
SUITES BY
HILTON**
4100 Innslake Dr
(23060)
Rates: $109-$159
(804) 217-8000
(800) 225-5466

**RESIDENCE INN
BY MARRIOTT**
3940 Westerre
Pkwy (23060)
Rates: $129-$179
(804) 762-9852
(800) 331-3131

**TOWNPLACE
SUITES BY
MARRIOTT**
4231 Park Place Ct
(23060)
Rates: $59-$89
(804) 747-5253
(800) 257-3000

**THE VIRGINIA
CLIFFE INN**
2900 Mountain Rd
(23060)
Rates: n/a
(804) 266-1661

GLOUCESTER
COMFORT INN
6639 Forest Hill
Dr (23061)
Rates: $69-$109
(804)) 695-1900
(800) 424-6423

GLOUCESTER POINT
**TIDEWATER
MOTEL**
Rt 17 (23072)
Rates: n/a
(804) 642-2155

GORDONS-VILLE
**NORFIELDS FARM
BED & BREAKFAST**
1982 James Madison
Hwy (22942)
Rates: n/a
(540) 832-2952
(800) 754-0105

ROCKLANDS B&B
17439 Rocklands
Dr (22942)
Rates: n/a
(540) 832-7176

**SLEEPY HOLLOW
FARM B&B**
16280 Blue Ridge
Turnpike (22942)
Rates: $85
(540) 832-5555
(800) 215-4804

GOSHEN
**BIG RIVER GUEST
LODGE**
1800 Big River Rd
(24439)
Rates: n/a
(800) 997-2745

HUMMINGBIRD INN
30 Wood Lane (24439)
Rates: $95-$155
(540) 997-9065
(800) 397-3214

GREENVILLE

BUDGET HOST-HISTORIC HESSIAN HOUSE
3554 Lee Jackson Hwy (24401)
Rates: $35-$75
(540) 337-1231

GRUNDY

COMFORT INN
US 460 & Main St (24614)
Rates: $60-$141
(276) 935-5050
(800) 424-6423
(800) 561-2291

HAMPTON

ARROW INN
7 Semple Farm Rd (23666)
Rates: $46-$67
(757) 865-0300
(800) 833-2520

CANDLEWOOD SUITES
401 Butler Farm Rd (23666)
Rates: $59-$189
(757) 766-8976
(888) 226-3539

CHAMBERLIN HOTEL
2 Fenwick Rd (23651)
Rates: n/a
(757) 723-6511

COLISEUM INTERSTATE INN
2000 W Mercury Blvd (23666)
Rates: n/a
(757) 838-7070

HOLIDAY INN
1815 W Mercury Blvd (23666)
Rates: $99-$129
(757) 838-0200
(800) 465-4329

LA QUINTA INN
2138 W Mercury Blvd (23666)
Rates: $69-$144
(757) 827-8680
(800) 687-6667

QUALITY INN & SUITES CONF CTR
1215 W Mercury Blvd (23666)
Rates: $89-$139
(757) 838-5011
(800) 424-6423

SUPER 8 MOTEL
1330 Thomas St (23669)
Rates: $48-$85
(757) 723-2888
(800) 800-8000

HARDYSVILLE

RIVER'S RISE B&BS
Rte 652,
PO Box 18 (23070)
Rates: n/a
(804) 776-7521

HARRISONBURG

BELLE MEADE RED CARPET INN
3210 S Main St (22801)
Rates: $40-$70
(540) 434-6704
(800) 251-1962

COMFORT INN
1440 E Market St (22801)
Rates: $60-$175
(540) 433-6066
(800) 424-6423

DAYS INN
1131 Forest Hill Rd (22801)
Rates: $45-$160
(540) 433-9353
(800) 329-7466

ECONO LODGE
1703 E Market St (22801)
Rates: $45-$200
(540) 433-2576
(800) 424-6423

FOUR POINTS BY SHERATON
1400 E Market St (22801)
Rates: $89-$139
(540) 433-2521
(800) 325-3535

MOTEL 6
10 Linda Ln (22801)
Rates: $39-$50
(540) 433-6939
(800) 466-8356

RAMADA INN
1 Pleasant Valley Rd (22801)
Rates: $45-$85
(540) 434-9981
(800) 272-6232

ROCKINGHAM MOTEL
4035 S Main St (22801)
Rates: $33-$39
(540) 433-2538

SUPER 8 MOTEL
3330 S Main (22801)
Rates: $35-$200
(540) 433-8888
(800) 800-8000

VILLAGE INN
4979 S Valley Pike (22801)
Rates: $60-$74
(540) 434-7355
(800) 736-7355

HILLSVILLE

DOE RUN AT GROUNDHOG MOUNTAIN
MP 189, Blue Ridge Pkwy (24343)
Rates: $109-$275
(276) 398-2212

HOLIDAY INN EXP
85 Airport Rd (24343)
Rates: $69-$150
(276) 728-2120
(800) 465-4329

RED CARPET INN
2666 Old Galax Pike (24343)
Rates: $38-$131
(276) 728-9118

HOPEWELL

CANDLEWOOD SUITES
5113 Plaza Dr (23860)
Rates: $69-$79
(804) 541-0200
(888) 226-3539

ECONO LODGE
4096 Oaklawn Blvd (23860)
Rates: $59-$99
(804) 541-4849
(800) 424-6423

HOT SPRINGS

ROSELOE MOTEL
590 US 220 N (24445)
Rates: $60-$80
(540) 839-5373

HUME

ANTERBURY COTTAGE ON PENDRAGON LAKE
12055 Crest Hill Rd (22639)
Rates: n/a
(540) 364-3970

INDEPENDENCE

BLUE RIDGE VIEWS VACATION RENTALS
751 Mtn View Rd (24348)
Rates: n/a
(540) 773-2496

CLIFFHANGER
288 Tarnywood Rd (24348)
Rates: n/a
(757) 868-7948
(336) 372-2293

THE FARMHOUSE ON ELK CREEK
6957 Peach Bottom Rd (24348)
Rates: n/a
(540) 655-4413

NEW RIVER RETREAT CABIN
538 Old River Lane (24348)
Rates: n/a
(540) 773-3946

IRVINGTON

THE HOPE AND GLORY INN B&B
634 King Carter Dr (22480)
Rates: $190-$350
(804) 438-6053

TIDES INN
480 King Center Dr (22480)
Rates: $199-$375
(804) 438-5000
(800) 843-3746

TIDES LODGE
#1 St. Andrews Lane (22480)
Rates: $105-$325
(804) 438-6000

KESWICK

KESWICK HALL AT MONTICELLO RESORT HOTEL
701 Club Dr (22947)
Rates: $295-$795
(434) 979-3440

KEYSVILLE

SHELDON'S MOTEL
1450 Four Locust Hwy (23947)
Rates: $41-$75
(434) 736-8434

LAWRENCEVILLE

BRUNSWICK MINERAL SPRINGS B&B CIRCA 1786
14910 Western Mill Rd (23868)
Rates: $85-$155
(434) 848-4010

LEESBURG

COLONIAL INN
21 S King St (22075)
Rates: n/a
(703) 777-5000

DAYS INN
721 E Market St (22075)
Rates: $59-$81
(703) 777-6622
(800) 329-7466

LAUREL BRIGADE INN
20 W Market St (22075)
Rates: n/a
(703) 777-1010

LEESBURG WESTPARK HOTEL
59 Club House Dr SW (22075)
Rates: n/a
(703) 777-1910

AREA CODES - If the local number doesn't connect, check for a new area code.

LITTLE ROCK MOTEL
Rt 4, Box 608
(22075)
Rates: n/a
(703) 777-3499

NORRIS HOUSE INN
108 Loudoun St
SW (20175)
Rates: n/a
(703) 777-1806
(800) 644-1806

PIEDMONT MOTEL
Rt 2, Box 230
(22075)
Rates: n/a
(703) 777-3361

LEXINGTON
APPLEWOOD INN & LLAMA TREKKING
242 Tarn Beck
Lane (24450)
Rates: n/a
(540) 463-1962
(800) 463-1902

BEST WESTERN AT HUNT RIDGE
25 Willow Springs
Rd (24450)
Rates: $54-$150
(540) 464-1500
(800) 528-1234
(800) 464-1501

COMFORT INN-VIRGINIA HORSE CENTER
62 Comfort Way
(24450)
Rates: $55-$89
(540) 463-7311
(800) 424-6423

DAYS INN-KEYDET GENERAL
325 W Midland
Trail (24450)
Rates: $40-$89
(540) 463-2143
(800) 329-7466

ECONO LODGE
66 Econo Lane
(24450)
Rates: $40-$90
(540) 463-7371
(800) 424-6423

GREYSTONE CABIN
1288 Collierstown
Rd (24450)
Rates: n/a
(540) 463-5906

HOLIDAY INN EXP
850 N Lee Hwy
(24450)
Rates: $65-$104
(540) 463-7351
(800) 465-4329

HOWARD JOHNSON
2836 N Lee Hwy
(24450)
Rates: $60-$135
(540) 463-9181
(800) 446-4656

RAMADA INN
2814 N Lee Hwy
(24450)
Rates: $52-$68
(540) 463-6400
(800) 272-6232

THE KEEP
116 Lee Ave
(24450)
Rates: n/a
(540) 463-3560

THRIFTY INN
820 S Main St
(24450)
Rates: $29-$49
(540) 463-2151

LINCOLN
CREEK CROSSING FARM
37768 Chappelle
Hill Rd (22078)
Rates: n/a
(540) 338-4548

LOCUST DALE
INN AT MEANDER PLANTATION
HC 5, Box 460
(22948)
Rates: n/a
(540) 672-4912
(800) 385-4936

LOUISA
GINGER HILL B&B
47 Holly Springs
Dr (23093)
Rates: $75-$130
(703) 967-3260

LURAY
BEST WESTERN LURAY
410 W Main St
(22835)
Rates: $60-$110
(540) 743-6511
(800) 528-1234

CARDINAL MOTEL
US Bus 211
(22835)
Rates: n/a
(540) 743-5010

DAYS INN
138 Whispering
Hill Rd (22835)
Rates: $49-$159
(540) 743-4521
(800) 329-7466

DEERLANE COTTAGES
P O Box 188
(22835)
Rates: n/a
(540) 743-3344
(800) 696-3337

INTOWN MOTEL
410 W Main St
(22835)
Rates: $38-$85
(540) 743-6511

LION & CROW LODGE & CABINS
244 Forest Rd
(22835)
Rates: n/a
(540) 743-6605
(877) 833-6515

THE MAYNEVIEW B&B
439 Mechanic St
(22835)
Rates: $110-$150
(540) 743-7921

MIMSLYN INN
401 W Main St
(22835)
Rates: n/a
(540) 743-5105
(800) 296-5105

STONE MOUNTAIN CABIN
1680 Egypt Bend
Rd (22835)
Rates: n/a
(540) 843-4944

LYNCHBURG
BEST WESTERN
2815 Candlers
Mtn Rd (224502)
Rates: $69-$150
(434) 237-2986
(800) 528-1234

COMFORT INN
3125 Albert
Lankford Dr
(24506)
Rates: $65-$149
(434) 847-9041
(800) 424-6423

DAYS INN
3320 Candlers
Mtn Rd (24502)
Rates: $59-$129
(434) 847-8655
(800) 329-7466

ECONO LODGE
2400 Stadium Rd
(24501)
Rates: $46-$130
(424) 847-1045
(800) 553-2666

HOLIDAY INN SELECT
601 Main St
(24504)
Rates: $69-$89
(434) 528-2500
(800) 465-4329

LYNDHURST
CABIN CREEKWOOD
Rt 1, Box 444-J
(22952)
Rates: n/a
(540) 943-8552

MADISON
DULANEY HOLLOW AT OLD RAG MTN COTTAGES
Rt 6, Box 215
(22727)
Rates: n/a
(540) 923-4470

MADISONVILLE
MADISONVILLE FARM INN
HC 1, Box 35
(23958)
Rates: n/a
(804) 248-9020

MANASSAS
BEST WESTERN BATTLEFIELD INN
10820 Bals Ford
Rd (22109)
Rates: $59-$125
(703) 361-8000
(800) 528-1234
(800) 775-4548

SUNRISE HILL FARM B&B
5590 Old Farm
Lane (20109)
Rates: n/a
(703) 754-8309

MARION
BEST WESTERN
1424 N Main St
(24354)
Rates: $59-$74
(276) 783-3193
(800) 528-1234
(800) 322-8857

HUNGRY MOTHER STATE PARK CABINS
2854 Park Blvd
(24354)
Rates: n/a
(276) 782-9032
(800) 933-7275

VIRGINIA HOUSE MOTOR INN
1419 N Main St
(24354)
Rates: $44-$49
(276) 783-5112

MARTINSVILLE
BEST LODGE
1985 Virginia Ave
(24114)
Rates: $40-$65
(276) 647-3941

BEST WESTERN INN
1755 Virginia Ave
(24114)
Rates: $59-$109
(276) 632-5611
(800) 528-1234
(800) 388-3934

SUPER 8 MOTEL
1044 N Memorial
Blvd (24114)
Rates: $49-$65
(276) 666-8888
(800) 800-8000

MAX MEADOWS

COMFORT INN
2594 E Lee Hwy
(24362)
Rates: $69-$200
(276) 637-4281
(800) 424-6423

SUPER 8 MOTEL
194 Ft. Chiswell
Rd (24360)
Rates: $50-$140
(276) 637-4027
(800) 800-8000

MCLEAN

HILTON TYSONS CORNER
7920 Jones Branch
Dr (22102)
Rates: n/a
(703) 847-5000
(800) 445-8667

MEADOWS OF DAN

PRIMELAND RESORT
4621 Busted Rock
Rd (24120)
Rates: n/a
(540) 251-8012

WOODBERRY INN
MP 908, Blue
Ridge Pky (24120)
Rates: n/a
(540) 593-2567

MELFA

CAPT'S QUARTERS MOTEL
Rt 13, Box D (23410)
Rates: n/a
(757) 787-4545

MIDDLEBURG

BRIAR PATCH B&B
23130 Briar Patch
Ln (22117)
Rates: $105-$235
(703) 327-5911
(866) 327-5911

MIDDLEBURG COUNTRY INN & HORSE BOARDING
209 E Washington
St (22117)
Rates: n/a
(800) 262-6082

RED FOX INN
2 E Washington St
(22117)
Rates: n/a
(540) 687-6301

MIDDLETOWN

SUPER 8 MOTEL
2120 Reliance Rd
(22645)
Rates: $55-$165
(540) 868-1800
(800) 800-8000

MILLBORO

DOUTHAT STATE PARK CABINS
Rt 1, Box 212
(24460)
Rates: n/a
(540) 862-8100

FORT LEWIS LODGE
HCR 3, Box 21A
(24460)
Rates: n/a
(703) 925-2314

MINT SPRING

DAYS INN
372 White hill Rd
(24463)
Rates: $49-$129
(540) 337-3031
(800) 329-7466

RED CARPET INN
210 White Hill Rd
(24463)
Rates: n/a
(540) 337-2611

MONTEREY

BOBBIE'S B&B
HC-02, Box 5
(24465)
Rates: n/a
(540) 468-2308

MONTVALLEE MOTEL
P O Box 25 (24465)
Rates: n/a
(540) 468-2500

MONTROSS

THE INN AT MONTROSS
P. O. Box 908,
Courthouse Sq
(22520)
Rates: $65-$125
(804) 493-0573
(800) 321-0979

MOUNT JACKSON

BEST WESTERN SHENANDOAH VALLEY
250 Conickville
Rd (22842)
Rates: $50-$82
(540) 477-2911
(800) 528-1234

THE WIDOW KIP'S COUNTRY INN
335 Orchard Dr
(22842)
Rates: $90-$95
(540) 477-2400
(800) 478-8714

MOUTH OF WILSON

CABIN ON THE RIDGE
548 York Ridge Rd
(24363)
Rates: n/a
(540) 579-4452

WILSON CREEK DELIGHT
61 Red Fox Lane
(24363)
Rates: n/a
(540) 579-6763

NASSAWADOX

ANCHOR MOTEL
7120 Lankford
Hwy (23413)
Rates: $60-$77
(757) 442-6363

NELLYSFORD

ACORN INN
P. O. Box 431
(22958)
Rates: n/a
(804) 361-9357

NEW CHURCH

THE GARDEN & THE SEA INN
4188 Nelson Rd
(23415)
Rates: $75-$205
(757) 824-0672
(800) 824-0672

NEW MARKET

BUDGET INN
2192 Old Valley
Pike (22844)
Rates: $29-$79
(540) 740-3105
(800) 296-6835

DAYS INN
9360 George C
Collins Pkwy
(22844)
Rates: $39-$149
(540) 740-4100
(800) 329-7466

NEWPORT NEWS

AMERICAN TUDOR INN
15540 Warwick
Blvd (23602)
Rates: n/a
(757) 887-0180

CAPRI COUNTRY INN
12880 Jefferson
Ave (23608)
Rates: n/a
(757) 877-7000
(877) 622-9901

COMFORT INN
12330 Jefferson
Ave (23602)
Rates: $89-$159
(757) 249-0200
(800) 424-6423

DAYS INN
14747 Warwick
Blvd (23602)
Rates: $55-$95
(757) 874-0201
(800) 329-7466

DAYS INN-OYSTER POINT
11829 Fishing Pt
Dr (23606)
Rates: $69-$119
(757) 873-6700
(800) 329-7466

HOST INN
985 J. Clyde Morris
Blvd (23601)
Rates: $45-$90
(757) 599-3303
(888) 599-3303

KING JAMES MOTOR HOTEL
6045 Jefferson Ave
(23605)
Rates: $30-$50
(757) 245-2801

MOTEL 6
797 J. Clyde Morris
Blvd (23601)
Rates: $37-$54
(757) 595-6336
(800) 466-8356

NEWPORT NEWS INN

6128 Jefferson Ave
(23605)
Rates: $39-$60
(757) 826-4500

TDY INN
15910 Warwick
Blvd (23608)
Rates: n/a
(757) 888-6667
(800) 282-8849

THE-RIFT INN
6129 Jefferson Ave
(23605)
Rates: n/a
(757) 838-6852

NORFOLK

ANCHORAGE INN
929 E Ocean View
Ave (23503)
Rates: n/a
(757) 583-2605

BEACHCOMBER MOTEL
2090 E Ocean
View Ave (23503)
Rates: n/a
(757) 583-2605

CLARION HOTEL JAMES MADISON
345 Granby St
(23504)
Rates: $79-$139
(757) 622-6682
(800) 424-6423

DAYS INN-MARINA/ BEACHFRONT
1631 Bayville St
(23503)
Rates: $49-$99
(757) 583-4521
(800) 329-7466

ECONO LODGE AIRPORT
3343 N Military
Hwy (23518)
Rates: $49-$150
(757) 855-3116
(800) 424-6423

ECONO LODGE MILITARY CIRCLE
865 N Military
Hwy (23502)
Rates: $37-$125
(757) 461-4865
(800) 424-6423

ECONO LODGE OCEAN VIEW W
9601 4th View St (23503)
Rates: $35-$100
(757) 480-9611
(800) 424-6423

LAFAYETTE HOTEL
4233 Granby St (23504)
Rates: n/a
(757) 622-5383

MOTEL 6
853 N Military Hwy (23502)
Rates: $41-$65
(757) 461-2380
(800) 466-8356

THE PAGE HOUSE INN-HISTORIC B&B
323 Fairfax Ave (23502)
Rates: $140-$225
(757) 625-5033

QUALITY INN LAKE WRIGHT
6280 Northampton Blvd (23502)
Rates: $89-$179
(757) 461-6251
(800) 424-6423

RADISSON HOTEL
700 Monticello Ave (23510)
Rates: $129-$166
(757) 627-5555
(800) 333-3333

RESIDENCE INN BY MARRIOTT-AIRPORT
1590 N Military Hwy (23502)
Rates: $79-$159
(757) 333-3000
(800) 331-3131

SHERATON WATERSIDE HOTEL
777 Waterside Dr (23510)
Rates: $79-$179
(757) 622-6664
(800) 325-3535

SLEEP INN LAKE WRIGHT
6280 Northampton Blvd (23502)
Rates: $69-$139
(757) 461-1133
(800) 424-6423

NORTON
DAYS INN
375 Wharton Ln (24273)
Rates: $49-$76
(276) 679-5340
(800) 329-7466

HOLIDAY INN
551 Hwy 58 E (24273)
Rates: $79-$115
(276) 679-7000
(800) 465-4329

ONLEY
ANCHOR MOTEL
P.O. Box 69 (23418)
Rates: $42-$58
(757) 787-8000

ORANGE
WILLOW GROVE INN
14079 Plantation Way (22960)
Rates: n/a
(540) 672-5982
(800) 949-1778

PAMPLIN
MADISONVILLE FARM B&B
11055 Thomas Jefferson Hwy (23958)
Rates: $95-$145
(434) 248-9020

PETERSBURG
BEST WESTERN STEVEN KENT
12205 S Crater Rd (23803)
Rates: $45-$90
(804) 733-0600
(800) 528-1234
(800) 628-9393

CALIFORNIA INN
2214 Country Dr (23803)
Rates: n/a
(804) 732-5500

COMFORT INN
11974 S Crater Rd (23805)
Rates: $56-$95
(804) 732-2900
(800) 424-6423

DAYS INN
12208 S Crater Rd (23805)
Rates: $49-$80
(804) 733-4400
(800) 329-7466

ECONO LODGE-S
16905 Parkdale Rd (23805)
Rates: $39-$130
(804) 862-2717
(800) 424-6423

THE HIGH STREET INN B&B
405 High St (23803)
Rates: $75-$110
(804) 733-0505
(888) 733-0505

QUALITY INN
405 E Washington St (23803)
Rates: $65-$120
(804) 733-1776
(800) 424-6423

STAR MOTEL
39 S Crater Rd (23803)
Rates: n/a
(804) 733-3600

PORT HAYWOOD
INN AT TABB'S CREEK LNDNG
Rt 14, P. O. Box 219 (23138)
Rates: n/a
(804) 725-5136

PORT ROYAL
BROWN'S MOTEL
25550 A.P. Hill Blvd (22535)
Rates: n/a
(804) 742-5523

PORTSMOUTH
HOLIDAY INN-OLDE TOWN WATERFRONT
8 Crawford Pkwy (23704)
Rates: $99-$135
(757) 393-2573
(800) 465-4329

HARBOR TOWER APARTMENTS
One Harbor Ct (23704)
Rates: n/a
(757) 393-1600
(800) 897-1601

PULASKI
DAYS INN
3063 Old Rt 100 Rd (24301)
Rates: $45-$125
(540) 980-2230
(800) 329-7466

PUNGOTEAGUE
PUNGOTEAGUE JUNCTION B&B
General Delivery (23422)
Rates: n/a
(757) 442-3581

RADFORD
THE ALLEGHANY INN
1123 Grove Ave (24141)
Rates: $65-$95
(540) 731-4466

BEST WESTERN INN
1501 Tyler Ave (24141)
Rates: $69-$95
(540) 639-3000
(800) 528-1234
(800) 628-1955

DOGWOOD LODGE
7073 Lee Hwy (24141)
Rates: $30-$38
(540) 639-9338

RAPHINE
DAYS INN
584 Oakland Cr (24472)
Rates: $49-$109
(540) 377-2604
(800) 329-7466

REEDVILLE
MORRIS HOUSE
Main St (22539)
Rates: n/a
(804) 453-7016

RICHMOND
AMERISUITES
201 Arboretum Pl (23236)
Rates: $104-$139
(804) 560-1566
(800) 833-1516

BEST WESTERN EXECUTIVE HOTEL
7007 W Broad St (23294)
Rates: $59-$89
(804) 672-7007
(800) 528-1234

CANDLEWOOD SUITES
4301 Commerce Rd (23234)
Rates: $84-$109
(804) 271-0016
(888) 226-3539

COMFORT INN EXECUTIVE CTR
7201 W Broad St (232940
Rates: $75-$150
(804) 672-1108
(800) 424-6423

COMMON-WEALTH PARK SUITES
901 Bank St (23219)
Rates: $93-$123
(804) 343-7300

DAYS INN
1600 Robin Hood Rd (23220)
Rates: $45-$75
(804) 353-1287
(800) 329-7466

DAYS INN
2100 Dickens Rd (23230)
Rates: $59-$129
(804) 282-3300
(800) 329-7466

DAYS INN
6910 Midlothian Tpk (23225)
Rates: $55-$199
(800) 329-7466

ECONO LODGE-SOUTH
2125 Willis Rd (23237)
Rates: $40-$115
(804) 271-6031
(800) 424-6423

ECONO LODGE-WEST
6523 Midlothian Tpk (23225)
Rates: $37-$100
(804) 276-8241
(800) 424-6423

AREA CODES - If the local number doesn't connect, check for a new area code.

ECONOMY HOUSE MOTEL
2302 Willis Rd (23237)
Rates: n/a
(804) 275-1412

HOLIDAY INN CENTRAL
3207 N Boulevard (23230)
Rates: $89-$119
(804) 359-9441
(800) 465-4329

HOLIDAY INN-N
801 E Parham Rd (223227)
Rates: $79-$139
(804) 266-8753
(800) 465-4329

HOMESTEAD STUDIO SUITES
241 Arboretum Place (23236)
Rates: $58-$83
(804) 272-1800
(888) 782-9473

THE JEFFERSON HOTEL
101 W Franklin St (23220)
Rates: $265-$335
(804) 788-8000
(866) 247-2303

MOTEL 6
100 Greshamwood Pl (23225)
Rates: $37-$46
(804) 745-0600
(800) 466-8356

OMNI RICHMOND HOTEL
100 S 12th St (23219)
Rates: $220-$240
(804) 344-7000
(800) 843-6664

QUALITY INN
201 E Cary St (23219)
Rates: $79-$159
(804) 788-1600
(800) 424-6423

QUALITY INN
5701 Chamberlayne Rd (23227)
Rates: $55-$149
(804) 266-7616
(800) 424-6423

QUALITY INN WEST END
8008 W Broad St (23294)
Rates: $69-$96
(804) 346-0000
(800) 424-6423

RADISSON HOTEL-HISTORIC RICHMOND
301 W Franklin St (23220)
Rates: $89-$109
(804) 644-9871
(800) 333-3333

RAMADA INN - SOUTH
2126 Willis Rd (23237)
Rates: $59-$85
(804) 271-1281
(800) 272-6232

RAMADA INN WEST
Parham & Quioccasin Rds (23229)
Rates: n/a
(804) 285-9061
(800) 272-6232

RAMADA LIMITED
5701-B Chamberlayne Rd (23227)
Rates: n/a
(804) 266-3739
(800) 272-6232

RESIDENCE INN BY MARRIOTT
2121 Dickens Rd (23230)
Rates: $101-$162
(804) 285-8200
(800) 331-3131

RICHMOND HOTEL & CONF CENTER
6531 W Broad St (23234)
Rates: $89-$139
(804) 285-9951

SHERATON RICHMOND WEST
6624 W Broad St (23234)
Rates: $81-$109
(804) 285-2000
(800) 325-3535

WYNDHAM RICHMOND AIRPORT
4700 S Laburnum Ave (23231)
Rates: $89-$119
(804) 226-4300
(800) 996-3426

RINER

RIVER'S EDGE B&B
6208 Little Camp Rd (24149)
Rates: n/a
(540) 381-4147
(888) 786-9413

ROANOKE

AMERISUITES
5040 Valley View Blvd (24012)
Rates: $109-$179
(540) 366-4700
(800) 833-1516

BEST WESTERN INN AT VALLEY VIEW
5050 Valley View Blvd (24012)
Rates: $59-$149
(540) 362-2400
(800) 528-1234

CLARION HOTEL AIRPORT
3315 Ordway Dr (24017)
Rates: $69-$134
(540) 362-4500
(800) 424-6423

COMFORT INN AIRPORT
5070 Valley View Blvd (24012)
Rates: $64-$169
(540) 527-2020
(800) 424-6423

DAYS INN AIRPORT
818 Plantation Rd (24019)
Rates: $48-$129
(540) 366-0341
(800) 329-7466

DAYS INN CIVIC CENTER
535 Orange Ave NE (24016)
Rates: $55-$125
(540) 342-4551
(800) 329-7466

MAINSTAY SUITES AIRPORT
5080 Valley View Blvd (24012)
Rates: $54-$175
(540) 527-3030
(800) 424-6423

MOTEL 6
3695 Thirlane Rd (23019)
Rates: $44-$50
(540) 563-0229
(800) 466-8356

PATRICK HENRY HOTEL
617 S Jefferson St (24016)
Rates: n/a
(540) 345-8811

RAMADA INN-RIVER'S EDGE
1927 Franklin Rd SW (24014)
Rates: $45-$85
(540) 343-0121
(800) 272-6232

RAMADA LIMITED
6520 Thirlane Rd (24014)
Rates: $48-$70
(540) 563-2871
(800) 272-6232

RODEWAY INN-CIVIC CENTER
526 Orange Ave NE (24016)
Rates: $35-$100
(540) 981-9341
(800) 424-6423

SUPER 8 MOTEL
6616 Thirlane Rd (24019)
Rates: $46-$68
(540) 563-8888
(800) 800-8000

VILLAGER LODGE
6510 Thirlane Rd (24019)
Rates: $35-$60
(540) 265-7600

WYNDHAM ROANOKE AIRPORT
2801 Hershberger Rd (24017)
Rates: $79-$229
(540) 563-9300
(800) 996-3426

ROCKY MOUNT

FRANKLIN MOTEL
20281 Virgil H. Goode Hwy (24151)
Rates: $37-$80
(540) 483-9962
(800) 775-3506

ROSSLYN

EXECUTIVE CLUB SUITES
1730 Arlington Blvd (22209)
Rates: n/a
(703) 525-2582
(800) 535-2582

RUTHER GLEN

HOLIDAY INN EXP
24011 Ruther Glen Rd (22546)
Rates: n/a
(804) 448-2608
(800) 465-4329

SALEM

BLUE JAY BUDGET HOST INN
5399 W Main St (24153)
Rates: $28-$80
(540) 380-2080
(800) 283-4678

COMFORT SUITES INN AT RIDGE-WOOD PARK
2898 Keagy Rd (24153)
Rates: $54-$129
(540) 375-4800
(800) 424-6423

ECONO LODGE
301 Wildwood Rd (24153)
Rates: $32-$89
(540) 389-0280
(800) 424-6423

QUALITY INN
179 Sheraton Dr (24153)
Rates: $50-$129
(540) 562-1912
(800) 424-6423

SANDSTON

DAYS INN- ARPRT
5500 Williamsburg Rd (23150)
Rates: $45-$71
(804) 222-2041
(800) 329-7566

AREA CODES - If the local number doesn't connect, check for a new area code.

ECONO LODGE-AIRPORT
5408 Williamsburg Rd (23150)
Rates: $37-$150
(804) 222-1020
(800) 424-6423

HOLIDAY INN AIRPORT
5203 Williamsburg Rd (23150)
Rates: $79-$169
(804) 222-6450
(800) 465-4329

LEGACY INN
5252 Airport Square Ln (23150)
Rates: $30-$46
(804) 226-4519

MICROTEL INN
6000 Audubon Dr (23150)
Rates: $59-$80
(804) 737-3322
(888) 771-7171

MOTEL 6
5704 Williamsburg Rd (23150)
Rates: $30-$48
(804) 222-7600
(800) 466-8356

WINGATE INN
491 Int'l Centre Dr (23150)
Rates: $89
(804) 222-1499

SCOTTSVILLE
CHESTER INN
Rt 4, Box 57 (24590)
Rates: n/a
(804) 286-2218

HIGH MEADOWS VINEYARD & MOUNTAIN SUNSET INN
High Meadows Ln (24590)
Rates: $82-$285
(804) 286-2218
(800) 232-1832

SKIPPERS
ECONO LODGE
1200 Moore's Ferry Rd (23879)
Rates: $32-$66
(434) 634-6124
(800) 424-6423

SMITHFIELD
FOUR SQUARE PLANTATION B&B
13357 Four Square Rd (23430)
Rates: n/a
(757) 365-0749

MANSION ON MAIN B&B
36 Main St (23430)
Rates: n/a
(757) 357-0006

SOUTH BOSTON
HOLIDAY INN EXP
1074 Bil Tuck Hwy (24592)
Rates: $90
(434) 575-4000
(800) 465-4329

QUALITY INN
2001 Seymour Dr (24592)
Rates: $49-$139
(434) 572-4311
(800) 424-6423

SOUTH HILL
BEST WESTERN SOUTH HILL
Hwy 58 & I-85 (23970)
Rates: $48-$82
(434) 447-3123
(800) 528-1234
(800) 296-3123

COMFORT INN
918 E Atlantic St (23970)
Rates: $45-$70
(434) 447-2600
(800) 424-6423

ECONO LODGE
623 E Atlantic St (23970)
Rates: $40-$75
(434) 447-7116
(800) 424-6423

SUPER 8 MOTEL
250 Thompson St (23950)
Rates: $47-$91
(434) 447-2313
(800) 800-8000

SPERRYVILLE
THE CONYERS HOUSE B&B
Rt 1, Box 157 (22740)
Rates: $90-$195
(703) 987-8025

SPRINGFIELD
HAMPTON INN
6550 Loisdale Ct (22150)
Rates: $89-$129
(703) 924-9444
(800) 426-7866

SPOTSYLVANIA
ROXBURY MILL BED & BREAKFST
6908 Roxbury Mill Rd (22553)
Rates: n/a
(540) 582-6611

STAFFORD
DAYS INN
2868 Jefferson Davis Hwy (22554)
Rates: $73-$89
(540) 659-0022
(800) 329-7466

HOLIDAY INN EXP
28 Greenspring Dr (22554)
Rates: $99-$119
(540) 657-5566
(800) 465-4329

STANARDS-VILLE
THE LAFAYETTE HOTEL
146 Main St (22973)
Rates: n/a
(804) 985-6345

STANLEY
JORDAN HOLLOW FARM INN
Rt 2, Box 375 (22851)
Rates: n/a
(703) 778-2209

STAUNTON
ARMSTRONG MOTEL
Rt 2, Box 412-B (24401)
Rates: n/a
(540) 337-2611

ASHTON COUNTRY HOUSE B&B
1205 Middlebrook Ave (24401)
Rates: $80-$140
(540) 885-7819

BEST WESTERN STAUNTON INN
92 Rowe Rd (24401)
Rates: $49-$129
(540) 885-1112
(800) 528-1234
(800) 752-9471

COMFORT INN
1302 Richmond (24401)
Rates: $75-$120
(540) 886-5000
(800) 424-6423

DAYS INN
273-D Bells Lane (24402)
Rates: $40-$110
(540) 248-0888
(800) 329-7466

ECONO LODGE
1031 Richmond (24401)
Rates: $57-$85
(540) 885-5158
(800) 424-6423

HOLIDAY INN GOLF
152 Fairway Lane (24401)
Rates: $64-$200
(540) 248-6020
(800) 465-4329

INGLESIDE RESORT & CONF CENTER
US 11 (24401)
Rates: n/a
(540) 248-1201

QUALITY INN
96 Baker Lane (24402)
Rates: $54-$95
(540) 248-5111
(800) 424-6423

SLEEP INN
222 JeffersonHwy (24401)
Rates: $45-$125
(540) 887-6500
(800) 424-6423

SUPER 8 MOTEL
1015 Richmond Rd (24401)
Rates: $54-$99
(540) 886-2888
(800) 800-8000

STEPHENS CITY
COMFORT INN
167 Town Run Lane (22655)
Rates: $60-$90
(540) 869-6500
(800) 424-6423

STERLING
HAMPTON INN DULLES AIRPORT
45440 Holiday Dr (22170)
Rates: n/a
(703) 471-4300
(800) 426-7866

STONY CREEK
HAMPTON INN
10476 Blue Star Hwy (23882)
Rates: $79-$129
(434) 246-5500
(800) 426-7866

SLEEP INN, INN & SUITES
11019 Blue Star Hwy (23882)
Rates: $56-$155
(434) 246-5100
(800) 424-6423

STRASBURG
HOTEL STRASBURG
201 Holliday St (22657)
Rates: $78-$149
(540) 465-9191
(800) 348-8327

VALLEY VIEW MOTEL
29156 Old Valley Pike (22657)
Rates: n/a
(540) 465-8510

SUFFOLK
HOLIDAY INN
2864 Pruden Blvd (23434)
Rates: $80
(757) 934-2311
(800) 465-4329

SYRIA

GRAVES MOUNTAIN LODGE
Hwy 670 (22743)
Rates: $75-$200
(540) 923-4231

TAPPAHANNOCK

DAYS INN
1414 Tappahannock Blvd (22560)
Rates: $50-$80
(804) 443-9200
(800) 329-7466

SUPER 8 MOTEL
1800 Tappahannock Blvd (22560)
Rates: $50-$76
(804) 443-3888
(800) 800-8000

THORNBURG

HOLIDAY INN EXP
6409 Dan Bell Lane (22565)
Rates: $69-$89
(540) 582-1097
(800) 465-4329

TRIANGLE

US INN
4502 Inn St (22172)
Rates: n/a
(703) 221-1115

TROUTDALE

FOX HILL B&B
Rt 2, (24378)
Rates: n/a
(703) 677-3313
(800) 874-3313

HIDDEN HOLLOW HIDEAWAY
670 Grange Hall Rd (24378)
Rates: n/a
(888) 698-9907

TROUTVILLE

COMFORT INN
2654 Lee Hwy S (24175)
Rates: $62-$108
(540) 992-5600
(800) 424-6423

TRAVELODGE N
2619 Lee Hwy S (24378)
Rates: $40-$85
(409) 992-6700
(800) 578-7878

VERONA

RAMADA LIMITED
70 Lodge Lane (24482)
Rates: $50-$85
(540) 248-8981
(800) 272-6232

VIENNA

VIENNA WOLFTRAP MOTEL
430 Maple Ave W (22180)
Rates: n/a
(703) 281-2330

VIRGINIA BEACH

ANGIE'S GUEST COTTAGE
302 24th St (23451)
Rates: n/a
(757) 428-4690

CLARION HOTEL TOWN CENTER
4453 Bonney Rd (23452)
Rates: $79-$229
(757) 472-1700
(800) 424-6423

CORAL SAND MOTEL
23rd & Pacific (23451)
Rates: n/a
(757) 425-0872

DAYS INN AIRPORT
5708 Northhampton Blvd (23455)
Rates: $39-$149
(757) 460-2205
(800) 329-7466

DOUBLETREE HOTEL
1900 Pavilion Dr (23451)
Rates: $59-$229
(757) 422-8900
(800) 222-8733

ECONO LODGE BAY BEACH
2968 Shore Dr (23451)
Rates: $35-$300
(757) 481-7992
(800) 424-6423

ECONO LODGE TOWN CENTER
3637 Bonney Rd (23452)
Rates: $36-$150
(757) 486-5711
(800) 424-6423

EXECUTIVE INN
717 S Military Hwy (23464)
Rates: $29-$69
(757) 420-2120
(800) 678-3466

FLAGSHIP INN
512 Atlantic Ave (23451)
Rates: $59-$155
(757) 425-6422

HOLLY KOVE EFFICIENCIES
395 Norfolk Ave (23451)
Rates: n/a
(757) 425-8374

LA COQUILLE MOTEL
314 16th St (23451)
Rates: $45-$88
(757) 422-3889

LA QUINTA INN
192 Newtown Rd (23462)
Rates: $69-$145
(757) 497-6620
(800) 687-6667

LAKESIDE MOTEL
2572 Virginia Beach Blvd (23452)
Rates: n/a
(757) 340-3211

LOTUS POND B&B
1324 Sandbridge Rd (23456)
Rates: n/a
(757) 426-7164

MARDI GRAS MOTEL
28th & Atlantic (23451)
Rates: n/a
(757) 428-3434

RAMADA PLAZA HOTEL
Atlantic Ave & 57th St (23458)
Rates: $85-$260
(757) 428-7025
(800) 272-6232

RED ROOF INN
196 Ballard Ct (23462)
Rates: $42-$105
(757) 490-0225
(800) 843-7663

RED ROOF INN AIRPORT
5745 Northampton Blvd (23455)
Rates: $50-$176
(757) 460-6700
(800) 843-7663

SANDPIPER MOTEL
1112 Pacific Ave (23451)
Rates: n/a
(757) 422-0001

SEA MIST MOTEL
27th & Pacific Ave (23451)
Rates: n/a
(757) 428-4926

SHERATON OCEANFRONT HOTEL
3501 Atlantic Ave (23451)
Rates: $69-$179
(757) 425-9000
(800) 325-3535

STARGATE ATLANTIC
28th & Atlantic (23451)
Rates: n/a
(757) 428-3434

STARGATE OCEANFRONT MOTEL
1909 Atlantic Ave (23451)
Rates: n/a
(757) 425-0650

SUNDOWNER MOTEL
27th & Pacific Ave (23451)
Rates: n/a
(757) 428-3011

SUNTIDE MOTEL
6607 Atlantic Ave (23451)
Rates: n/a
(757) 428-6404

THUNDERBIRD MOTOR LODGE
3410 Atlantic Ave (23451)
Rates: $65-$135
(757) 428-3024
(800) 633-6669

TOWNPLACE SUITES BY MARRIOTT
5757 Cleveland St (23451)
Rates: $94=-$180
(757) 490-9367
(800) 257-3000

WACHAPREAGUE

WACHAPREAGUE MOTEL & MARINA
General Delivery (23480)
Rates: n/a
(757) 787-2105

WARM SPRINGS

ANDERSON COTTAGE B&B
B7B Old Germantown Rd (24484)
Rates: n/a
(540) 839-2975

MEADOW LANE LODGE
Star Rt A, Box 110 (24484)
Rates: n/a
(703) 839-5959

THREE HILLS INN
Rt 220, P.O. Box 9 (24484)
Rates: $49-$149
(540) 839-5381

WARRENTON

CHESWICK MOTEL
394 Broadview Ave (22186)
Rates: n/a
(540) 349-1901

COMFORT INN
7379 Comfort Inn Dr (22186)
Rates: $79-$109
(540) 349-8900
(800) 424-6423

AREA CODES - If the local number doesn't connect, check for a new area code.

HAMPTON INN
501 Blackwell Rd
(22186)
Rates: $63-$79
(540) 349-4200
(800) 426-7866

HOWARD JOHNSON INN
6 Broadview Ave
(22186)
Rates: $70-$110
(540) 347-4141
(800) 446-4656

WARSAW
BEST WESTERN WARSAW
4522 Richmond
Rd (22572)
Rates: $74-$90
(804) 333-1700

SIMONSON HOUSE & COTTAGE
2883 Simonson Rd
(22572)
Rates: n/a
(804) 333-3347

WASHINGTON
GAY STREET INN
160 Gay St (22747)
Rates: n/a
(540) 675-3288

WATERFORD
MILLTOWN FARMS INN
14163 Milltown
Rd (22190)
Rates: n/a
(540) 882-4470

WAYNESBORO
COMFORT INN
15 Windi Grove
Dr (22980)
Rates: $62-$98
(540) 932-3060
(800) 424-6423

DAYS INN
2060 Rosser Ave
(22980)
Rates: $49-$89
(540) 943-1101
(800) 329-7466

QUALITY INN
640 W Broad St
(22980)
Rates: $59-$109
(540) 942-1171
(800) 424-6423

SUPER 8 MOTEL
2045 Rosser Ave
(22980)
Rates: $54-$125
(540) 943-3888
(800) 800-8000

WHITETOP
BLUFF MOUNTAIN CABIN
634 Bluff Mtn Rd
(24292)
Rates: n/a
(540) 388-3838

ENCHANTED LODGE
420 Old Park Rd
(24292)
Rates: n/a
(540) 466-4044

WILLIAMSBURG
BEST WESTERN
7411 Pocahantas
Trail (23187)
Rates: $69-$129
(757) 229-3003
(800) 528-1234
(800) 446-9228

BEST WESTERN-COLONIAL CAPITOL INN
111 Penniman Rd
(23187)
Rates: $59-$129
(757) 253-1222
(800) 528-1234
(800) 446-9228

BEST WESTERN-PATRICK HENRY INN
249 E York St (23187)
Rates: $49-$179
(757) 229-9540
(800) 528-1234
(800) 446-9228

BEST WESTERN WILIAMSBURG WESTPARK HOTEL
1600 Richmond
Rd (23185)
Rates: $29-$99
(757) 229-1134
(800) 528-1234
(800) 446-1062

CLARION HOTEL CONF CENTER-HISTORIC DISTRICT
500 Merrimac
Trail (23185)
Rates: $59-$139
(757) 220-1410
(800) 424-6423

COMFORT INN HISTORIC AREA
706 Bypass Rd
(23185)
Rates: $39-$129
(757) 229-9230
(800) 424-6423

DAYS INN
902 Richmond Rd
(23185)
Rates: $40-$159
(757) 229-5060
(800) 329-7466

FOUR POINTS BY SHERATON HOTEL & SUITES
351 York St
(23185)
Rates: $59-$169
(757) 229-4100
(800) 325-3535

HERITAGE INN
1324 Richmond
Rd (23185)
Rates: $80
(757) 229-6220
(800) 782-3800

HOLIDAY INN PATRIOT
3032 Richmond
Rd (23185)
Rates: $79-$129
(757) 565-2600
(800) 465-4329

HOTEL COLONIAL AMERICA
6483 Richmond
Rd (23185)
Rates: n/a
(757) 565-1000

LA QUINTA INN-HISTORIC AREA
119 Bypass Rd
(23185)
Rates: $45-$135
(757) 253-1663
(800) 283-1663

MOTEL ROCHAMBEAU
929 Capitol
Landing Rd
(23185)
Rates: $24-$56
(757) 229-2851
(800) 368-1055

MOTEL 6
3030 Richmond
Rd (23185)
Rates: $30-$63
(757) 565-3433
(800) 466-8356

QUARTERPATH INN
620 York St
(23185)
Rates: $65-$119
(757) 220-0960
(800) 446-9222

RAMADA INN
725 Bypass Rd
(23185)
Rates: $49-$129
(757) 220-1776
(800) 272-6232

RAMADA INN & SUITES CENTRAL
5351 Richmond
Rd (23185)
Rates: $32-$92
(757) 565-2000
(800) 272-6232

RESIDENCE INN BY MARRIOTT
1648 Richmond
Rd (23185)
Rates: $59-$359
(757) 941-2000
(800) 331-3131
(888) 259-9222

THOMAS JEFFERSON INN
7247 Pocahontas
Trail (23185)
Rates: n/a
(757) 220-2000

WILLIAMSBURG CENTER HOTEL
600 Bypass Rd
(23185)
Rates: n/a
(757) 220-2800
(800) 492-2855

WILLIS WHARF
BALLARD HOUSE BED & BREAKFST
12527 Ballard Dr
(23486)
Rates: $50
(757) 442-2206

WINCHESTER
BEST WESTERN LEE-JACKSON MOTOR INN
711 Millwood Ave
(22601)
Rates: $52-$70
(540) 662-4154
(800) 528-1234

DAYS INN
2951 Valley Ave
(22601)
Rates: $49-$69
(540) 667-1200
(800) 329-7466

ECHO VILLAGE MOTEL
US Rt 11 (22603)
Rates: n/a
(703) 869-1900

MOHAWK MOTEL
2754 Northwestern
Pike (22603)
Rates: $48-$53
(540) 667-1410

QUALITY INN EAST
603 Millwood Ave
(22601)
Rates: $56-$80
(540) 667-2250
(800) 424-6423

RED ROOF INN
991 Millwood
Pike (22601)
Rates: $58-$79
(540) 667-5000
(800) 843-7663

SUPER 8 MOTEL
1077 Millwood
Pike (22601)
Rates: $49-$60
(540) 665-4450
(800) 800-8000

TOURIST CITY MOTEL
214 Millwood Ave
(22601)
Rates: $31-$42
(540) 662-9011

AREA CODES - If the local number doesn't connect, check for a new area code.

TRAVELODGE
160 Front Royal
Pike (22602)
Rates: $76-$85
(540) 665-0685
(800) 578-7878

WISE
BEST WESTERN OF WISE
124 Woodland Dr
(24293)
Rates: 59-$77
(276) 328-3500
(800) 528-1234

WOODBRIDGE
FRIENDSHIP INN
13964 Jefferson
Davis Hwy (22191)
Rates: $44-$80
(703) 494-4144
(800) 453-4511

WOODSTOCK
BUDGET HOST INN
1290 S Main St
(22664)
Rates: $40-$52
(540) 459-4086
(800) 283-4678

COMFORT INN
1011 Motel Dr
(22664)
Rates: $60-$150
(540) 459-7600
(800) 424-6423

RAMADA INN
11360 Motel Dr
(22664)
Rates: $59-$99
(540) 459-5000
(800) 272-6232

WYTHEVILLE
BEST WESTERN WYTHEVILLE INN
355 Nye Rd
(24382)
Rates: $50-$89
(276) 228-7300
(800) 528-1234
(800) 224-9172

BUDGET HOST INN/ INTERSTATE INN
705 Chapman Rd
(24382)
Rates: $29-$150
(276) 228-8618
(800) 283-4678

DAYS INN
150 Malin Dr
(24382)
Rates: $40-$75
(276) 228-5500
(800) 329-7466

ECONO LODGE
1160 E Main St
(24382)
Rates: $34-$115
(276) 228-5517
(800) 424-6423

HOLIDAY INN
1800 E Main St
(24382)
Rates: $89
(276) 228-5483
(800) 465-4329

MOTEL 6
220 Lithia Rd
(24382)
Rates: $30-$50
(276) 228-7988
(800) 466-8356

RAMADA INN
955 Pepper's
Ferry Rd (24382)
Rates: $49-$95
(276) 228-6000
(800) 272-6232

RED CARPET INN
280 Lithia Rd
(24382)
Rates: $40-$130
(276) 228-5525
(800) 251-1962

SUPER 8 MOTEL
130 Nye Cir
(24382)
Rates: $48-$67
(276) 228-6620
(800) 800-8000

TRAVELODGE
140 Lithia Rd
(24382)
Rates: $65-$120
(276) 228-3188
(800) 578-7878

YORKTOWN
CANDLEWOOD SUITES
329 Commonwealth
Dr (23693)
Rates: $69-$169
(757) 952-1120
(888) 266-3539

MARL INN BED & BREAKFAST
220 Church St
(23690)
Rates: n/a
(757) 898-9268

TOWNEPLACE SUITES
200 Cybernetics
Way (23693)
Rates: $125-$139
(757) 874-8884

AREA CODES - If the local number doesn't connect, check for a new area code.

WASHINGTON

ABERDEEN

CENTRAL PARK MOTEL
6504 Olympic Hwy (98520)
Rates: $30-$45
(360) 533-1210

GUESTHOUSE INT'L INN
701 E Heron St (98520)
Rates: 75-$95
(360) 537-7460
(800) 214-8378

NORDIC INN
1700 S Boone St (98520)
Rates: $35-$64
(360) 533-0100
(800) 442-1010

OLYMPIC INN
616 W Heron St (98520)
Rates: $55-$95
(360) 533-4200
(800) 562-8618

RED LION INN
521 W Wishkah St (98520)
Rates: $74-$99
(360) 532-5210
(800) 547-8010

THUNDERBIRD MOTEL
410 W Wishkah St (98520)
Rates: $46-$64
(360) 532-3153

TRAVELURE MOTEL
623 W Wishkah St (98520)
Rates: $37-$62
(360) 532-3280

AIRWAY HEIGHTS

HEIGHTS MOTEL
13504 W Hwy 2 (99001)
Rates: $25
(509) 244-2072

LANTERN PARK MOTEL
13820 W Sunset Hwy (99001)
Rates: $29-$57
(509) 244-3653

AMANDA PARK

AMANDA PARK MOTEL
8 River Dr (98526)
Rates: $60+
(360) 288-2237
(800) 410-2237

LOCHAERIE RESORT
638 N Shore Rd (98526)
Rates: $60+
(360) 288-2215

ANACORTES

ANACO INN
905 20th St (98221)
Rates: $59-$119
(360) 293-8833
(877) 299-3320

ANACORTES INN
3006 Commercial Ave (98221)
Rates: $60-$85
(360) 293-3153

CAP SANTE INN
906 9th St (98221)
Rates: $58-E85
(369) 293-0602
(800) 852-0456

FIDALGO COUNTRY INN
1250 Hwy 20 (98221)
Rates: $79-$169
(360) 293-3494
(800) 244-4179

ISLANDS INN
3401 Commercial Ave (98221)
Rates: $83-$130
(360) 293-4644

OLD BROOK INN BED & BREAKFAST
530 Old Brook Ln (98221)
Rates: $80-$90
(360) 293-4768
(800) 503-4768

SAN JUAN MOTEL
1103 6th St (98221)
Rates: $35-$56
(360) 293-5105
(800) 533-8009

SHIP HARBOR INN
5316 Ferry Terminal Rd (98221)
Rates: $65-$95
(360) 293-5177
(800) 852-8568

ARLINGTON

ARLINGTON MOTOR INN
2214 SR 530 (98223)
Rates: $47-$59
(360) 652-9595

QUALITY INN
5200 172nd St NE (98223)
Rates: $69-$99
(360) 403-7222
(800) 424-6423

SMOKEY POINT MOTOR INN
17329 Smokey Point Dr (98223)
Rates: $45-$75
(360) 659-8561

ASHFORD

CABINS AT THE BERRY
37221 SR 706 E (98304)
Rates: $65-$125
(360) 569-2628

GATEWAY INN RESORT
38820 SR 706 E (98304)
Rates: $30-$60
(360) 569-2506

STORM KING & SPA AT MT. RAINIER
37311 SR 706 E (98304)
Rates: $155-$175
(360) 569-2964

ASOTIN

ASOTIN MOTEL
P.O. Box 188 (99402)
Rates: $34-$40
(509) 243-4888

AUBURN

DAYS INN
521 D St NE (98002)
Rates: $50-$85
(253) 939-5950
(800) 329-7466

NENDEL'S VALU INN
102 15th St NE (98802)
Rates: $55-$85
(253) 833-8007
(866) 833-8007

TRAVELODGE SUITES
Nine 16th St W (98001)
Rates: $45-$79
(253) 833-7171

VAL-U INN
Nine 14th Ave NW (98001)
Rates: $59-$79
(253) 735-9600
(800) 443-7777

BAINBRIDGE ISLAND

BAINBRIDGE INN BED & BREAKFAST
9200 Hemlock Ave NE (98110)
Rates: n/a
(206) 842-7564

FROG ROCK INN B&B
15576 Washington Ave NE (98110)
Rates: $60-$75
(206) 842-2761

ISLAND COUNTRY INN
920 Hildebrand Ln NE (98110)
Rates: $89-$179
(206) 842-6861
(800) 842-8429

MONARCH MANOR B&B
7656 Yeomalt Pt Dr NE (98110)
Rates: $75-$250
(206) 780-0112

BEAVER

BEAR CREEK MOTEL/RV PARK
205860 Hwy 101 (98305)
Rates: $45+
(360) 327-3660

EAGLE POINT INN
MP 202, Hwy 101 W (98305)
Rates $42-$48
(360) 327-3660

BELFAIR

BELFAIR MOTEL
23322 Hwy 3 NE (98528)
Rates: $50-$60
(360) 275-4485

BELLEVUE

BELLEVUE CLUB HOTEL
11200 SE 6th St (98004)
Rates: $130-$315
(425) 454-4424

CANDLEWOOD SUITES
15805 SE 37th St (98006)
Rates: $79-$135
(425) 373-1212
(888) 226-3539

AREA CODES - If the local number doesn't connect, check for a new area code.

COAST BELLEVUE HOTEL
625 116th Ave NE (98004)
Rates: $104-$135
(425) 455-9444
(800) 426-0670

DAYS INN
3241 156th Ave SE (98007)
Rates: $60-$106
(425) 643-6644
(800) 329-7466

EMBASSY SUITES
3225 158th Ave SE (98008)
Rates: $89-$209
(425) 644-2500
(800) 362-2779

HOMESTEAD STUDIO SUITES
3700 132nd Ave SE (98006)
Rates: $79-$99
(425) 865-8680
(888) 782-9473

HOMESTEAD STUDIO SUITES-MICROSOFT
15805 NE 28th St (98006)
Rates: $47-$66
(425) 885-6675
(888) 782-9473

LA QUINTA INN
10530 NE Northup Way (98033)
Rates: $79-$115
(425) 828-6585
(800) 687-6667

LA RESIDENCE SUITE HOTEL
475 100th Ave SE (98004)
Rates: $95-$145
(425) 455-1475

LARKSPUR LANDING HOTEL
15805 SE 37th St (98006)
Rates: $79-$169
(425) 373-1212
(877) LARKSPUR

RAMADA INN BELLEVUE CENTER
818 112th Ave NE (98004)
Rates: $65-$85
(425) 455-1515
(800) 272-6232

RED LION INN
11211 Main St (98004)
Rates: $89-$159
(425) 455-5240
(800) 733-5466

RESIDENCE INN BY MARRIOTT
14455 NE 29th Pl (98007)
Rates: $199-$299
(425) 882-1222
(800) 331-3131

BELLINGHAM
BEST WESTERN LAKEWAY INN
714 Lakerway Dr (98226)
Rates: $74-$129
(360) 671-1011
(800) 528-1234
(888) 671-1011

CASCADE INN
208 N Samish Way (98225)
Rates: n/a
(360) 733-2520

THE CHRYSALIS INN & SPA
804 10th St (98225)
Rates: $155-$199
(360) 756-1005

COACHMAN INN
120 N Samish Way (98225)
Rates: $45-$70
(360) 671-9000
(800) 962-6641

DAYS INN
125 E Kellogg Rd (98226)
Rates: $59-$145
(360) 671-6200
(800) 329-7466

FAIRHAVEN VILLAGE INN
1200 10th St (98225)
Rates: $99-$159
(360) 733-1311
(877) 733-1100

HOLIDAY INN EXP
4160 Meridian St (98226)
Rates: $89-$124
(360) 671-4800
(800) 465-4329

HOTEL BELLWETHER
1 Bellwether Way ((98225)
Rates: $99-$800
(360) 392-3100

LIONS INN MOTEL
2419 Elm St (98225)
Rates: $44-$48
(360) 733-2330

MOTEL 6
3701 Byron (98225)
Rates: $37-$60
(360) 671-4494
(800) 466-8356

QUALITY INN BARON SUITES
100 E Kellogg Rd (98226)
Rates: $75-$195
(360) 647-8000
(800) 424-6423

RODEWAY INN
3710 Meridian St (98225)
Rates: $39-$95
(360) 738-6000
(800) 424-6423

SHANGRI-LA DOWNTOWN MOTEL
611 E Holly St (98225)
Rates: $35-$49
(360) 733-7050

TRAVEL HOUSE INN
3750 Meridian St (98225)
Rates: $38-$89
(360) 671-4600

VAL-U INN
805 Lakeway Dr (98226)
Rates: $59-$85
(360) 671-9600
(800) 443-7777

BINGEN
CITY CENTER MOTEL
208 W Steuben (98605)
Rates: $32-$53
(509) 493-2445

BIRCH BAY
BEV'S BEACH RESORT
8126 Birch Bay Dr (98230)
Rates: $75-$125
(360) 371-2756

BIRCH BAY BUNGALOWS
8226 Birch Bay Dr (98230)
Rates: $60-$70
(360) 371-2851

BLAINE
THE INN AT SEMI-AH-MOOA WYNDHAM RESORT
9565 Semiahmoo Pkwy (98230)
Rates: $99-$409
(360) 371-2000
(800) 770-7992

MOTEL INTNL
758 Peace Portal Dr (98231)
Rates: n/a
(360) 332-8222

WESTVIEW MOTEL
1300 Peace Portal Dr (98230)
Rates: n/a
(360) 332-5501

BOTHELL
RESIDENCE INN BY MARRIOTT
11920 NE 195th St (98011)
Rates: $139-$199
(425) 485-3030
(800) 331-3131

BREMERTON
BEST WESTERN
4303 Kitsap Way (98312)
Rates: $78-$174
(360) 405-1111
(800) 528-1234
(800) 776-2291

THE CHIEFTAN MOTEL
600 National Ave N (98312)
Rates: $35-$45
(360) 479-3111

DUNES MOTEL
3400 11th St (98312)
Rates: $45-$65
(360) 377-0093
(800) 828-8238

FLAGSHIP INN
4320 Kitsap Way (98312)
Rates: $59-$99
(360) 479-6566
(800) 447-9396

ILLAHEE MANOR B&B
6680 Illahee Rd NE (98311)
Rates: $115-$290
(360) 698-7555

MIDWAY INN
2909 Wheaton Way (98310)
Rates: $59-$99
(360) 479-2909
(800) 231-0575

OYSTER BAY INN
4412 Kitsap Way (98312)
Rates: $69-$80
(360) 377-5510
(800) 393-3862

SUPER 8 MOTEL
5068 Kitsap Way (98310)
Rates: $57-$77
(360) 377-8881
(800) 800-8000

BREWSTER
BREWSTER MOTEL
801 S Bridge St (98812)
Rates: $32-$60
(509) 689-2625

BUCKLEY
MOUNTAIN VIEW INN
29405 Hwy 410 (98321)
Rates: $75-$95
(360) 829-1100
(800) 582-4111

WEST MAIN MOTOR INN
466 W Main (98321)
Rates: n/a
(360) 829-2400

BURLINGTON
COCUSA MOTEL
370 W Rio Vista (98233)
Rates: $60-$125
(360) 757-6044

AREA CODES - If the local number doesn't connect, check for a new area code.

CARSON

SANDHILL COTTAGES
932 Hot Springs Ave (98610)
Rates: $55-$75
(509) 427-3464

WIND RIVER MOTEL &CABINS
1261 Wind River Hwy (98610)
Rates: $50-$75
(509) 527-7777

CASHMERE

VILLAGE INN MOTEL
229 Cottage Ave (98815)
Rates: $45-$65
(509) 782-3522

CASTLE ROCK

MOTEL 7 WEST
864 Walsh Ave NE (98611)
Rates: $36-$58
(360) 274-7526

TIMBERLAND INN
1271 Mt. St. Helens Way (98611)
Rates: $59-$110
(360) 274-6002
(888) 900-6335

CATHLAMET

NASSA POINT MOTEL
851 E Hwy 4 (98612)
Rates: $28-$45
(360) 795-3941

CENTRALIA

FERRYMAN'S INN
1003 Eckerson Rd (98531)
Rates: $45-$52
(360) 330-2094

MOTEL 6
1310 Belmont Ave (98531)
Rates: $29-$46
(360) 330-2057
(800) 466-8356

PARK MOTEL
1011 Belmont Ave (98531)
Rates: $29-$38
(360) 736-9333

PEPPERTREE WEST MOTOR INN
1208 Alder St (98531)
Rates: $35-$46
(360) 736-1124
(800) 795-1124

CHEHALIS

BEST WESTERN PARK PLACE INN & SUITES
201 SW Interstate Ave (98532)
Rates: $70-$95
(360) 748-4040
(877) 748-0008

HOWARD JOHNSON INN
122 Interstate Ave (98532)
Rates: $65-$80
(360) 748-0101
(800) 446-4656

CHELAN

BEST WESTERN LAKESIDE LODGE
2312 W Woodin Ave (98816)
Rates: $79-$319
(509) 682-4396
(800) 468-2781

BRICKHOUSE INN BED & BREAKFAST
304 Wapato St (98816)
Rates: n/a
(509) 682-4791
(800) 799-2332

CABANA MOTEL
420 Manson Rd (98816)
Rates: $68-$117
(509) 682-2233
(800) 799-2332

KELLY'S RESORT
12801 S Lakeshore Rd (98816)
Rates: $80-$160
(509) 687-3220
(800) 561-8978

LAKE CHELAN MOTEL
2044 W Woodin Ave (98816)
Rates: $35+
(509) 682-2742

CHENEY

BUNKERS RESORT WILLIAMS LAKE
S 36402 Bunker Landing Rd (99004)
Rates: $45-$55
(509) 235-5212

ROSEBROOK INN
304 W 1st (99004)
Rates: $34-$51
(509) 235-6538

WILLOW SPRINGS MOTEL
5 B St (99004)
Rates: $37-$45
(509) 235-5138

CHEWELAH

NORDLIG MOTEL
101 W Grant St (99109)
Rates: $49-$61
(509) 935-6704

CLALLAM BAY

WINTER'S SUMMER INN B&B
16651 Hwy 112 (98326)
Rates: $60-$95
(360) 963-2264

CLARKSTON

ASTOR MOTEL
1201 Bridge St (99403)
Rates: n/a
(509) 758-2509

GOLDEN KEY MOTEL
1376 Bridge St (99403)
Rates: n/a
(509) 758-5566

HACIENDA LODGE MOTEL
812 Bridge St (99403)
Rates: n/a
(509) 758-8853
(800) 600-5583

HIGHLAND HOUSE B&B
707 Highland (99403)
Rates $40-$85
(509) 758-3126

MOTEL 6
222 Bridge St (99403)
Rates: $35-$46
(509) 758-1631
(800) 466-8356

CLE ELUM

ASTER INN
521 E 1st St (98922)
Rates: $40-$95
(509) 674-2551
(888) 616-9722

CHALET MOTEL
800 E First St (98922)
Rates: $35-$55
(509) 674-2320

STEWART LODGE
805 W First St (98922)
Rates: $40-$78
(509) 674-4548

TIMBER LODGE INN
301 W First St (98922)
Rates: $50-$75
(509) 674-5966
(800) 589-1133

TRAVELERS INN
1001 E First St (98922)
Rates: $34-$100
(509) 674-5535

WIND BLEW INN MOTEL
811 Hwy 970 (98922)
Rates: $50-$570
(509) 674-2294

CLINTON

(See Whidbey Island for lodging)

COLFAX

BEST WESTERN WHEATLAND INN
701 N Main St (99111)
Rates: $69-$109
(509) 397-0397
(800) 528-1234

UNION CREEK RANCH
2501 Upper Union Flat Rd (99111)
Rates: $55-$75
(509) 397-3292

COLVILLE

BEAVER LODGE RESORT
2430 Hwy 20 East (99114)
Rates: n/a
(509) 684-5657

BENNY'S COLVILLE INN
915 S Main St (99114)
Rates: $40-$105
(509) 684-2517
(800) 680-2517

COMFORT INN
166 NE Canning Dr (99114)
Rates: $61-$125
(509) 684-2010
(800) 424-6423

DOWNTOWN MOTEL
369 S Main St (99114)
Rates: $28-$48
(509) 684-2565

MAPLE AT SIXTH BED & BREAKFAST
407 E 6th (99114)
Rates: $45-$55
(800) 446-2750

CONCONULLY

CONCONULLY LAKE RESORT
102 Sinlahekin Rd (98819)
Rates: $25-$48
(509) 826-0813
(800) 850-0813

CONCONULLY MOTEL
P.O. Box 181 (98819)
Rates: n/a
(509) 826-1610

GIBSON'S NORTH FORK LODGE
100 W Boone (98819)
Rates: n/a
(509) 826-1475

JACK'S MOTEL
116 A Ave (98819)
Rates: n/a
(509) 826-0132
(800) 893-5668

AREA CODES - If the local number doesn't connect, check for a new area code.

KOZY CABINS
111 E Broadway
(98819)
Rates: $35-$42
(509) 862-6780

LIAR'S COVE RESORT
1835 A Conconully
Rd (98819)
Rates: $40-$50
(509) 826-1288
(800) 830-1288

SHADY PINES RESORT
125 W Fork Salmon
Cr Rd (98819)
Rates: $54-$60
(800) 552-2287

CONCRETE
OVENELL'S HERITAGE B&B
46276 Concrete
Sauk Valley Rd
(98237)
Rates: $90-$120
(360) 853-8494

CONNELL
M & M MOTEL
730 S Columbia
Ave (99326)
Rates: $46-$59
(509) 234-8811
(800) 353-09981

TUMBLEWOOD MOTEL
433 S Columbia
Ave (99326)
Rates: $23-$38
(509) 234-2081

COPALIS BEACH
BEACHWOOD RESORT
SR 109, PO Box
116 (98535)
Rates: n/a
(360) 289-2177

ECHOES OF THE SEA MOTEL
3208 SR 109
(98535)
Rates: $38-$78
(360) 289-3358
(800) 578-ECHO

IRON SPRINGS RESORT
3707 Hwy 109
(98535)
Rates: n/a
(360) 276-4230

LINDA'S LOW TIDE MOTEL
14 McCullough
Rd (98535)
Rates: $30-$60
(360) 289-3450

ROD'S BEACH RESORT
2961 SR 109 (98535)
Rates: n/a
(360) 289-2222

TIDELANDS RESORT
2991 Hwy 109
(98535)
Rates: n/a
(360) 289-8963

COUGAR
LONE FIR RESORT MOTEL
16806 Lewis River
Rd (98616
Rates: $140-$85
(360) 238-5210

COULEE CITY
ALA COZY MOTEL
9988 Hwy 2 E
(99115)
Rates: $42-$67
(509) 632-5703

BLUE TOP MOTEL
109 N 6th St (99115)
Rates: $27-$48
(509) 632-5596

COULEE LODGE RESORT
33017 Park Lake
Rd NE (99115)
Rates: $27-$53
(509) 632-5565

LAKEVIEW MOTEL
HCR 1, Box 11
(99115)
Rates: n/a
(509) 632-5792

LAUREN'T SUN VILLAGE RESORT
33575 Park Lake
Rd NE (99115)
Rates: $42-$95
(509) 632-5664

SUN LAKES PARK RESORT
34228 Park Lake
Rd NE (99115)
Rates: $58-$91
(509) 632-5291

COULEE DAM
COULEE HOUSE INN & SUITES
110 Roosevelt Way
(99116)
Rates: $50-$132
(509) 633-1101
(800) 715-7767

COUPEVILLE
(See Whidbey
Island for lodging)

CURLEW
BLUE COUGAR MOTEL
18081 Hwy 21 N
(99118)
Rates: n/a
(509) 779-4817

CUSICK
BLUESLIDE RESORT
40041 Hwy 20
(99119)
Rates: $35-$44
(509) 445-1327

THE OUTPOST RESORT/RV PARK
405351 Hwy 20
(99119)
Rates: $40-$60
(509) 445-1317

DARRINGTON
STAGE COACH INN
1100 Seeman St
(98241)
Rates: $60-$75
(360) 436-1776

DAYTON
BLUE MOUNTAIN MOTEL
414 W Main St
(99328)
Rates: n/a
(509) 382-3040

THE PURPLE HOUSE B&B
415 E Clay St
(99328)
Rates: $85-$125
(509) 382-3159
(800) 486-2574

THE WEINHARD HISTORIC HOTEL
235 E Main St
(99328)
Rates: $75-$150
(509) 382-4032

DEER PARK
LOVE'S VICTORIAN B&B
North 31317
Cedar Rd (99006)
Rates: $74-$98
(509) 276-6939

DEMING
THE GUEST HOUSE B&B
5723 Schombush
Rd (98244)
Rates: $45-$60
(360) 592-2343

THE LOGS RESORT
9002 Mt. Baker
Hwy (98244)
Rates: $75+
(360) 599-2711

DES MOINES
KING'S ARMS MOTEL APARTMENT
23226 30th Ave S
(98198)
Rates: $27-$59
(253) 824-0300

DUPONT
GUESTHOUSE INN & SUITES
1609 McNeil St
(98327)
Rates: $79-$150
(253) 912-8900
(800) 214-8378

EAST WENATCHEE
CEDARS INN
80 Ninth St NE
(98802)
Rates: $64-$87
(509) 886-8000
(877) 358-2074

MICKEY O'REILLY'S INN AT THE RIVER
580 Valley Mall
Pkwy (98802)
Rates: n/a
(509) 884-1474

EATONVILLE
HENLEY'S SILVER LAKE RESORT
40718 S Silver
Lake Rd E (98328)
Rates: n/a
(360) 832-3580

MILL VILLAGE MOTEL
210 Center St E
(98328)
Rates: $60-$90
(360) 832-3200

MOUNTAIN VIEW CEDAR LODGE
36203 Pulford Rd
E (98328)
Rates: $85-$115
(360) 832-8080
(800) 903-5636

EDMONDS
HARBOR INN
130 W Dayton St
(98020)
Rates: $79-$159
(425) 771-5021
(800) 441-8033

HUDGENS HAVEN BED & BREAKFAST
9313 190th St SW
(98020)
Rates: $60-$65
(425) 776-2202

K & E MOTOR INN
23921 Hwy 99
(98020)
Rates: $49-$64
(425) 778-2181
(800) 787-2181

TRAVELODGE
23825 Hwy 99
(98026)
Rates: $59-$109
(425) 771-8008
(800) 578-7878

ELBE
HOBO INN
54104 Mountain
Hwy E (98330)
Rates: $70-$85
(360) 569-2500

ELK
JERRY'S LANDING RESORT
N 41114 Lakeshore
(99009)
Rates: n/a
(509) 292-2337

ELLENSBURG
BEST WESTERN LINCOLN INN
211 N Umptanum
Rd (98921)
Rates: $69-$159
(509) 925-4244
(800) 528-1234
(866) 925-4288

AREA CODES - If the local number doesn't connect, check for a new area code.

COMFORT INN
1722 Canyon Rd
(98926)
Rates: $70-$170
(509) 925-7037
(800) 424-6423

ELLENSBURG INN
1700 Canyon Rd
(98926)
Rates: $55-$89
(509) 925-9801

HAROLDS MOTEL
601 N Water (98926)
Rates: $28-$48
(509) 925-4141

I-90 INN MOTEL
1390 Dollar Way
Rd N (98926)
Rates: $46-
$670(509) 925-9844

NITES INN MOTEL
1200 S Ruby (98926)
Rates: $50-$59
(509) 962-9600

ENUMCLAW
**BEST WESTERN
PARK CTR HOTEL**
1000 Griffin Ave
(98022)
Rates: $75-$85
(360) 825-4490
(800) 528-1234

KING'S VALU INN
1334 Roosevelt
Ave E (98022)
Rates: $48-$89
(360) 825-1626
(888) 886-5118

EPHRATA
**COLUMBIA
MOTEL**
1257 Basin St SW
(98823)
Rates: $35-$60
(509) 754-5226

LARIAT MOTEL
1639 Basin St SW
(98823)
Rates: n/a
(509) 754-2437

TRAVELODGE
31 Basin St SW
(98823)
Rates: $40-$75
(509) 754-4651
(800) 578-7878

EVERETT
**BEST WESTERN
CASCADIA INN**
2800 Pacific Ave
(98201)
Rates: $59-$129
(425) 258-4141
(800) 822-5876

**COMFORT INN
& SUITES**
101 108th St SE
(98208)
Rates: $82-$102
(425) 425-2900
(800) 424-6423

DAYS INN
1602 SE Everett
Mall Way (98208)
Rates: $49-$145
(425) 355-1570
(800) 329-7466

EVERETT INN
12619 4th Ave W
(98204)
Rates: $40-$105
(425) 347-9099

**INN AT PORT
GARDNER**
1700 W Marine
View Dr (98201)
Rates: $89-$109
(425) 252-6779

MOTEL 6 NORTH
10006 Everett Way
(98204)
Rates: $35-$50
(425) 347-2060
(800) 466-8356

MOTEL 6 SOUTH
224 128th St SW
(98204)
Rates: $37-$50
(425) 353-8120
(800) 466-8356

QUALITY INN
101 128th ST SE
(98208)
Rates: $84-$104
(800) 424-6423
(800) 256-8137

**ROYAL MOTOR
INN**
952 N Broadway
(98201)
Rates: $44+
(425) 259-5177

**TOWNE PLACE
SUITES**
8521 Mukilteo
Speedway (98275)
Rates: $69-$89
(425) 551-5900
(800) 257-3000

**WELCOME
MOTOR INN**
1205 Broadway
(98201)
Rates: $39-$49
(800) 252-5512

FEDERAL WAY
**BEST WESTERN
EXECUTEL**
31611 20th Ave S
(98003)
Rates: $69-$119
(253) 941-6000
(800) 648-3311

COMFORT IN
31622 Pacific Hwy
S (98003)
Rates: $59-$149
(253) 529-0101
(800) 225-5150

LA QUINTA INN
32124 25th Ave S
(98003)
Rates: $69-$109
(253) 529-4000
(800) 687-6667

QUALITY INN
1400 S 348th St
(98003)
Rates: $69-$129
(253) 835-4141
(800) 424-6423

**ROADRUNNER
MOTEL**
1501 350th St S
(98003)
Rates: $30-$38
(800) 828-7202

**STEVENSON
MOTEL**
33330 Pacific Hwy
S (98003)
Rates: n/a
(253) 927-2500

SUPER 8 MOTEL
1688 348th St S
(98003)
Rates: $52-$72
(253) 838-8808
(800) 800-8000

FERNDALE
EXECUTIVE INN EXP
5370 Barrett Rd
(98248)
Rates: $99-$139
(360) 380-4600

**SCOTTISH LODGE
MOTEL**
5671 Riverside Dr
(98248)
Rates: $30
(360) 384-4040

SUPER 8 MOTEL
5788 Barrett Ave
(98248)
Rates: $52-$74
(360) 384-8881
(800) 800-8000

FIFE
**BEST WESTERN
FIFE HOTEL**
5700 Pacific Hwy
E (98424)
Rates $74-$119
(253) 922-3555
(800) 528-1234
(888) 820-3555

COMFORT INN
5601 Pacific Hwy
E (98424)
Rates: $56-$90
(253) 926-2301
(800) 424-6423

DAYS INN
3021 Pacific Hwy
E (98424)
Rates: $50-$73
(253) 922-3500
(800) 329-7466

**ECONO LODGE
INN & SUITES**
3100 Pacific Hwy
E (98424)
Rates: $47-$62
(253) 922-9520
(800) 553-2666

HOMETEL INN
3520 Pacific Hwy
E (98424)
Rates: $40-$60
(253) 922-0555
(800) 258-3520

**KINGS
MOTOR INN**
5115 Pacific Hwy
E (98424)
Rates: $36
(253) 922-3636
(800) 929-3509

MOTEL 6
5201 20th St E
(98424)
Rates: $37-$50
(253) 922-1270
(800) 466-8356

PARADISE MOTEL
1618 59th Ave
Court E (98424)
Rates: n/a
(253) 922-5158

QUALITY INN
5601 Pacific Hwy
E (98424)
Rates: $55-$145
(253) 926-2301
(800) 424-6423

RAMADA LIMITED
3501 Pacific Hwy
E (98424)
Rates: $59-$74
(253) 926-1000
(800) 272-6232

**ROYAL
COACHMAN INN**
5805 Pacific Hwy
E (98424)
Rates: $45-$140
(253) 922-2500
(800) 422-3051

FIR ISLAND
**SOUTH FORK
MOORAGE BED
& BREAKFAST**
2187 Mann Rd
(98238)
Rates: $95-$115
(360) 445-4803

FORKS
**BAGBY'S
TOWN MOTEL**
1080 Forks Ave S
(98331)
Rates: $30-$45
(360) 374-6231
(800) 742-2429

DEW DROP INN
100 Fernhill Rd
(98331)
Rates: $42-$65
(360) 374-4055

FORKS MOTEL
351 Forks Ave S
(98331)
Rates: $52-$95
(360) 374-6243
(800) 544-3416

AREA CODES - If the local number doesn't connect, check for a new area code.

HOH HUMM RANCH B&B
171763 Hwy 101 (98331)
Rates: $65+
(360) 374-5337

MANITOU LODGE B&B
813 Kilmer Rd (98331)
Rates: $90-$120
(360) 374-6295

MILL CREEK INN BED & BREAKFAST
Hwy 101 S (98331)
Rates: $45+
(360) 374-5873

MILLER TREE INN BED & BREAKFAST
654 E Division St (98331)
Rates: $55-$125
(360) 374-6806
(800) 943-6563

OLSON'S CABINS
2423 Mora Rd (98331)
Rates: $45+
(360) 374-3142

OLYMPIC SUITES INN
800 Olympic Dr (98331)
Rates: $43-$99
(360) 374-5400
(800) 262-3433

PACIFIC INN MOTEL
352 US 101 (98331)
Rates: $45-$68
(360) 374-9400

RIVER INN B&B
2596 Bogachiel Way (98331)
Rates: $60+
(360) 374-6526

THREE RIVERS RESORT CABINS
7764 LaPush Rd (98331)
Rates: $45+
(360) 374-5300

WESTWARD HOH RESORT
5692 Upper Ho Rd (98331)
Rates: $45+
(360) 374-6657

FREELAND
(See Whidbey Island for lodging)

FRIDAY HARBOR
(See San Juan Island for lodging)

GIG HARBOR
BEST WESTERN WESLEY INN
6575 Kimball (98335)
Rates: $109-$194
(253) 858-9690
(800) 528-1234
(888) 462-0002

HARBORSIDE B&B
8708 Goodman Dr NW (98332)
Rates: $115
(253) 851-1795

THE INN AT GIG HARBOR
3211 56th St NW (98335)
Rates: $118-$129
(253) 858-1111

NO CABBAGES B&B
10319 Sunrise Beach Dr NW (98332)
Rates: $55
(253) 858-7797

WESTWYND MOTEL & SUITES
6703 144 St NW (98332)
Rates: $55-$80
(253) 857-4047
(800) 468-9963

GLACIER
GLACIER CREEK LODGE
10036 Mt. Baker Hwy (98244)
Rates: $48-$185
(360) 599-2991
(800) 719-1414

MOUNT BAKER CHALET RESORT
9857 Mt. Baker Hwy (98244)
Rates: $50-$180
(360) 599-2405

MOUNT BAKER LODGING
7463 Mt. Baker Hwy (98244)
Rates: $85-$495
(800) 709-7669

GOLDENDALE
BARCHRIS MOTEL
128 N Academy (98620)
Rates: n/a
(509) 773-4325

PONDEROSA MOTEL
775 E Broadway St (98620)
Rates: $40-$70
(509) 773-5842

GRAND COULEE
TRAIL WEST MOTEL
108 Spokane Way (99133)
Rates: $32-$70
(509) 633-3155

GRANDVIEW
GRANDVIEW MOTEL
522 E Wine Country Rd (98930)
Rates: $26-$39
(509) 882-1323

GRANITE FALLS
MOUNTAIN VIEW INN MOTEL
32005 Mt. Loop Hwy (98252)
Rates: $35-$60
(360) 691-6668

GRAYLAND
GRAYLAND MOTEL & COTTAGES
2013 SR 105 S (98547)
Rates: n/a
(360) 267-2395
(800) 292-0845

OCEAN GATE RESORT
1939 SR 105 S (98547)
Rates: n/a
(360) 267-1956
(800) 473-1956

OCEAN SPRAY MOTEL
1757 SR 105 S (98547)
Rates: $45-$70
(360) 267-2205

SURF MOTEL
2029 SR 105 S (98547)
Rates: $56-$67
(360) 267-2244

WALSH MOTEL
1593 SR 105 S (98547)
Rates: $40+
(360) 267-2191

GREEN ACRES
ALPINE MOTEL
18815 E Cataldo (99016)
Rates: $40-$66
(509) 928-2700

GREENWATER
ALTA CRYSTAL RESORT / MT. RAINIER
68317 SR 410 E (98022)
Rates: $69-$159
(360) 663-2500
(800) 277-6475

THE INN AT THE RANCH CABIN
16423 Mountainside Dr (98022)
Rates: $75-$150
(360) 663-2667

HANSVILLE
GUEST HOUSE AT TWIN SPITS BED & BREAKFAST
2570 NE Twin Spits Rd (98340)
Rates: $60-$75
(360) 638-1001

HOME VALLEY
HOME VALLEY B&B
P.O. Box 377 (98648)
Rates: n/a
(509) 427-7070

WIND MOUNTAIN RESORT
50561 Hwy 14 (98648)
Rates: $69-$99
(509) 427-5152

HOODSPORT
CANAL CREEK MOTEL
N 27131 Hwy 101 (98548)
Rates: $38-$52
(360) 877-6770

SUNRISE MOTEL & RESORT
N 24520 Hwy 101 (98548)
Rates: n/a
(360) 877-5301

HOQUIAM
LYTLE HOUSE B&B
509 Chenault Ave (98550)
Rates: $60+
(360) 533-2320
(800) 677-2320

SNORE & WHISKER MOTEL
3031 Simpson Ave (98550)
Rates: $35-$65
(360) 532-5060

TIMBERLINE INN
415 Perry Ave (98550)
Rates: $35-$75
(360) 533-8048

WESTWOOD INN
910 Simpson Ave (98550)
Rates: $42-$85
(360) 532-8161
(800) 562-0994

ILWACO
A-CO-HO MOTEL & CHARTERS
Port of Ilwaco, P.O. Box 268 (98624)
Rates: n/a
(360) 642-3333
(800) 339-2646

COL-PACIFIC MOTEL
P.O. Box 34 (98624)
Rates: n/a
(360) 642-3177

HEIDI'S INN MOTEL
126 Spruce St (98624)
Rates: $35-$125
(360) 642-2387
(800) 576-1032

AREA CODES - If the local number doesn't connect, check for a new area code.

INCHELIUM

HARTMAN'S LOG CABIN RESORT
5744 S Twin Lakes Access Rd (99138)
Rates: $36-$50
(509) 722-3543

RAINBOW BEACH RESORT
HC1, Box 146, Twin Lakes Rd (99138)
Rates: n/a
(509) 722-5901

INDEX

THE CABIN AT INDEX BED & BREAKFAST
52525 Riverside Rd (98256)
Rates: $80-$95
(360) 827-2102

IONE

PEND OREILLE INN
107 Riverside (99139)
Rates: n/a
(509) 442-3418

PLAZA MOTEL
103 S 2nd Ave (99139)
Rates: $30-$40
(509) 442-3534

ISSAQUAH

MOTEL 6
1885 15th Pl NW (98027)
Rates $49-$66
(425) 392-8405
(800) 466-8356

MOUNTAINS & PLAINS BED & BREAKFAST
100 Big Bear Place NW (98027)
Rates: $38-$80
(800) 231-8068

KALALOCH

(Near Forks)

KALALOCH LODGE
157151 Hwy 101 (98331)
Rates: $119-$273
(360) 962-2271
(866) 525-2562

KALAMA

BEST VALUE KALAMA RIVER INN
602 NE Frontage Rd (98625)
Rates: $30-$39
(360) 673-2855
(888) 412-2855

KELSO

BEST WESTERN ALADDIN MOTOR INN
310 Long Ave (98626)
Rates: $63-$88
(360) 425-9660
(800) 528-1234
(800) 764-7378

GUESTHOUSE INN & SUITES
501 Three Rivers Dr (98626)
Rates: $70-$80
(360) 414-5953
(800) 214-8378

MOTEL 6
106 Minor Rd (98626)
Rates: $35-$57
(360) 425-3229
(800) 466-8356

RED LION HOTEL
510 Kelso Dr (98626)
Rates: $59-$89
(360) 636-4400
(800) 733-5466

SUPER 8 MOTEL
250 Kelso Dr (98626)
Rates: $48-$77
(360) 423-8880
(800) 800-8000

KENNEWICK

BEST VALUE CLEARWATER INN
5616 W Clearwater Ave (99336)
Rates: $68
(509) 735-2242

BEST WESTERN INN
4001 W 27th St (99336)
Rates: $75-$140
(509) 586-1332
(800) 528-1234

CASABLANCA BED & BREAKFAST
94806 E Granada Ct (99337)
Rates: $85-$115
(888) 627-0676

CLOVER ISLAND INN
435 Clover Island Dr (99336)
Rates: $69-$109
(866) 586-0542

COMFORT INN
7801 W Quinault Ave (99336)
Rates: $55-$129
(509) 783-8396
(800) 424-6423

DAYS INN
2811 W 2nd Ave (99336)
Rates: $55-$95
(509) 735-9511
(800) 329-7466

ECONO LODGE
300 N Ely St #`A (99336)
Rates: $49-$120
(509) 783-6191
(800) 553-2666

GREEN GABLE MOTEL
515 W Columbia Dr (99336)
Rates: n/a
(509) 582-5811

LA QUINTA INN & SUITES
4220 W 27th Pl (99336)
Rates: $79-$139
(509) 736-3326
(800) 687-6667

RED LION HOTEL AT COLUMBIA CENTER
1101 N Columbia Center Blvd (99336)
Rates: $85-$99
(509) 783-0611
(800) 733-5466

TRAVELODGE EXTENDED STAY
321 N Johnson St (99336)
Rates: $49-$68
(509) 735-6385
(800) 578-7878

KENT

COMFORT INN
22311 84th Ave S (98032)
Rates: $79-$169
(253) 872-2211
(800) 424-6423

CYPRESS INN
22218 84th Ave S (98032)
Rates: $67-$89
(253) 395-0219
(800) 752-9991

DAYS INN SOUTH
1711 W Meeker St (98032)
Rates: $55-$80
(253) 854-1950
(800) 329-7466

GOLDEN KENT MOTEL
22203 84th Ave S (98032)
Rates: $40-$55
(253) 872-8372

HAWTHORN SUITES
6329 S 212th (98032)
Rates: $89-$129
(253) 395-3800
(800) 527-1133

HOWARD JOHNSON INN
1233 N Central (98032)
Rates: $69-$129
(253) 852-7224
(800) 446-4656

RAMADA INN
25100 7th Ave S (98032)
Rates: $69-$99
(253) 520-6670
(800) 272-6232

ROYAL SKIES APARTMENTS
25907 27th Pl S (98032)
Rates: n/a
(253) 941-7788

TOWNEPLACE SUITES
18123 72nd Ave S (98032)
Rates: $109-$119
(253) 796-6000
(800) 257-3000

VAL-U INN
22420 84th Ave S (98032)
Rates: $60-$89
(253) 872-5525
(800) 443-7777

KETTLE FALLS

BARNEY'S CAFE & MOTEL
395 & 20 Jct (99141)
Rates: n/a
(509) 738-6546

BULL HILL RANCH & RESORT
3738 Bull Hill Rd (99141)
Rates: $85-$140
(509) 732-4355

GRANDVIEW INN MOTEL
978 Hwy 395 N (99141)
Rates: n/a
(509) 738-6733

KETTLE FALLS BEST VALUE NN
205 E 3rd St, Hwy 395 (99141)
Rates: $43-$59
(509) 738-6514
(888) 315-2378

KINGSTON

KINGSTON HOUSE B&B
26117 Ohio Ave NE (98346)
Rates: $85-$180
(360) 297-8818

SMILEY'S COLONIAL MOTEL
11067 Hwy 104 (98346)
Rates: $30-$59
(360) 297-3622

KIRKLAND

BEST WESTERN KIRKLAND INN
12223 116th NE (98034)
Rates: $75-$97
(425) 822-2300
(800) 528-1234
(800) 332-4200

AREA CODES - If the local number doesn't connect, check for a new area code.

LA QUINTA INN
10530 NE
Northup Way
(98033)
Rates: $94-$144
(425) 828-6585
(800) 687-6667

MOTEL 6
12010 120th Place
NE (98034)
Rates: $49-$62
(425) 821-5618
(800) 466-8356

THE WOODMARK HOTEL ON LAKE WASHINGTON
1200 Carillon
Point (98033)
Rates: $225-$1800
(425) 822-3700

LA CONNER

ART'S PLACE B&B
511 Talbott St
(98257)
Rates: $60
(360) 466-3033

KATY'S INN B&B
503 S 3rd St
(98257)
Rates: $79-$159
(360) 466-9909

LA CONNER COUNTRY INN
107 S 2nd St
(98257)
Rates: $95-$135
(360) 466-3101

LA PUSH

LA PUSH OCEAN PARK RESORT
770 Main St
(98350)
Rates: $45+
(360) 374-5267
(800) 487-1267

LACEY

QUALITY INN & SUITES
120 College St
SE (98503)
Rates: $55-$85
(360) 493-1991
(800) 424-6423

LAKE BAY

RANSOM'S POND OSTRICH FARM BED & BREAKFAST
3915 Mahnke Rd
KPS (98351)
Rates: $75-$95
(206) 884-5666

LAKE CRESCENT

HISTORIC LAKE CRESCENT LODGE RESORT
416 Lake Crescent
Rd (Port Angeles
98362)
Rates: $64-$114
(360) 928-3211

LAKEWOOD

BEST VALUE INN
4215 Sharondale
St (98499)
Rates: $62-$85
(253) 584-2212

BEST WESTERN LAKEWOOD INN
6125 Motor Ave
SW (98499)
Rates: $61-$82
(253) 584-2212
(800) 528-1234
(888) 844-6656

MADIGAN MOTEL
12039 Pacific Hwy
SW (98499)
Rates: $30-$60
(253) 588-8697

NIGHTS INN
9325 S Tacoma
Way (98499)
Rates: $32-$44
(253) 582-7550

RAMADA INN
9920 S Tacoma
Way (98499)
Rates: $59-$99
(253) 588-5241
(800) 272-6232

LANGLEY

(See Whidbey
Island for lodging)

LEAVENWORTH

ALPINE CHALETS
3601 Allen Ln
(98826)
Rates: $82-$125
(509) 548-5674
(800) 548-5011

ALPINE RIVERS INN
1505 Alpensee
Strasse (98826)
Rates: $69-$79
(509) 548-5875
(800) 873-3960

BAVARIAN RITZ HOTEL
633 Front St
(98826)
Rates: $89-$199
(509) 548-5455

BEDFINDERS
305 8th St (98826)
Rates: $95-$195
(509) 548-4410
(800) 323-2920

BINDLESTIFFS RIVERSIDE CABINS
1600 Hwy 2
(98826)
Rates: $79-$109
(509) 548-1685

DER RITTERHOF MOTOR INN
190 US 2 (98826)
Rates: $87-$170
(509) 548-5845
(800) 255-5845

EVERGREEN INN
1117 Front St
(98826)
Rates: $75-$135
(509) 548-5515
(800) 327-7212

HOWARD JOHNSON EXPRESS
405 W US 2
(98826)
Rates: $69-$129
(509) 548-4326
(800) 423-9380

LAKE WENATCHEE HIDE-A-WAYS
19944 US 207
(98826)
Rates: $95-$135
(509) 548-9074
(800) 883-2611

LANGSTON INN & SUITES
185 US 2 (98826)
Rates: $69-$119
(509) 548-7992

NATAPOC LODGING
12348 Bretz Rd
(98826)
Rates: $140+
(509) 763-3313
(888) 628-2762

OBERTAL MOTOR INN
922 Commercial St
(98826)
Rates: $59-$139
(509) 548-5204
(800) 537-9382

PHIPPEN'S B & B
10285 Ski Hill Dr
(98826)
Rates: $70-$90
(800) 666-9806

RIVER'S EDGE LODGE
8401 US 2 (98826)
Rates: $75-$125
(509) 548-7612
(800) 451-5285

RODEWAY INN & SUITES
185 Hwy 2 (98826)
Rates: $69-$199
(509) 548-7992
(800) 424-6423

SAIMON'S HIDE-A-WAYS
16408 River Rd
(98826)
Rates: $145-$295
(509) 763-3213
(800) 845-8638

SQUIRREL TREE INN
15251 Hwy 2 (98826)
Rates: $50
(509) 763-3157

LIBERTY LAKE

COMFORT INN
2327 N Madson
Rd (99019)
Rates: $60-$89
(509) 340-3333
(800) 424-6423

LILLIWAUP

MIKE'S BEACH RESORT
N 38470 Hwy 101
(98555)
Rates: $45-$95
(360) 877-5324
(800) 231-5324

LONG BEACH PENINSULA

ANCHORAGE COTTAGES
2209 N Blvd
(98631)
Rates: $64-$120
(360) 642-2351
(800) 646-2351

ARCADIA COURT MOTEL
401 N Ocean
Beach Blvd (98631)
Rates: $41-$85
(360) 642-2613

BOULEVARD MOTEL
301 N Ocean Blvd
(98631)
Rates: $55-$95
(360) 642-2434
(888) 454-0346

THE BREAKERS MOTEL
26th St & Hwy 103
(98631)
Rates: $48-$160
(800) 219-9833

CHAUTAUQUA LODGE
304 N 14th (98631)
Rates: $69-$179
(360) 642-4401
(800) 869-8401

EDGEWATER INN MOTEL
409 10th St (98631)
Rates: $94
(360) 642-2311
(800) 561-2456

LIGHTHOUSE MOTEL
12415 Pacific Way
(98631)
Rates: $47-$59
(360) 642-3622

LONG BEACH MOTEL
1200 Pacific Hwy
S (98631)
Rates: n/a
(360) 642-3500

OCEAN LODGE
101 Bolstad Ave
(98631)
Rates: $50-$150
(360) 642-2777

AREA CODES - If the local number doesn't connect, check for a new area code.

**OUR PLACE
AT THE BEACH**
1309 S Blvd
(98631)
Rates: $42-$89
(360) 642-3793
(800) 538-5107

**PACIFIC VIEW
MOTEL**
203 Bolstad St
(98631)
Rates: $55-$160
(360) 642-2415
(800) 238-0859

SAND LO MOTEL
1910 N Pacific
Hwy (98631)
Rates: n/a
(360) 642-2600
(800) 676-2601

**THE SANDS
MOTEL**
12211 Pacific Way
(98631)
Rates: $33-$50
(360) 642-2100

SHAMAN MOTEL
115 3rd St SW
(98631)
Rates: $54-$109
(360) 642-3714
(800) 753-3750

SUPER 8 MOTEL
500 Ocean Beach
(98631)
Rates: $59-$99
(360) 642-8988
(800) 800-8000
(888) 478-3297

**THUNDERBIRD
MOTEL**
201 N Blvd
(98631)
Rates: $30-$80
(360) 642-2412

LONGVIEW

**HUDSON
MANOR INN**
1616 Hudson St
(98632)
Rates: $48-$70
(360) 425-1100

RAMADA LIMITED
723 7th Ave
(98632)
Rates: $60-$90
(360) 414-1000
(800) 272-6232

**TOWN CHALET
MOTOR HOTEL**
1822 Washington
Way (98632)
Rates: $31-$46
(360) 423-2020

**TOWNHOUSE
MOTEL**
744 Washington
Way (98632)
Rates: $38-$57
(360) 423-7200

LOON LAKE

**INN AT WHITE
PINE BED
& BARN**
3848 White Pine
Rd (99148)
Rates: $65-$85
(509) 233-2971
(Horse stables
available)

LOPEZ ISLAND

**LOPEZ ISLANDER
RESORT &MARINA**
2864 Fisherman
Bay Rd
(Lopez, 98261)
Rates: $79-$190
(360) 468-2233
(800) 736-3434

LYLE

LYLE HOTEL
100 7th St (98635)
Rates: $54-$64
(509) 365-5953

LYNNWOOD

**EMBASSY SUITES
HOTEL**
20610 44th Ave W
(98036)
Rates: $89-$159
(425) 775-2500
(800) 362-2779

LA QUINTA INN
4300 Alderwood
Mall Blvd (98036)
Rates: $69-$99
(425) 775-7447
(800) 687-6667

**RESIDENCE INN
BY MARRIOTT**
18200 Alderwood
Mall Pkwy (98037)
Rates: $79-$139
(425) 771-1100
(800) 331-3131

ROSE MOTEL
20222 Hwy 99
(98036)
Rates: n/a
(425) 744-5616

MAPLE FALLS

**YODELER INN
BED & BREAKFAST**
7485 Mt. Baker
Hwy (98266)
Rates: $65
(800) 642-9033

MARYSVILLE

**BEST WESTERN
TULALIP INN**
6128 Marine Dr
(98271)
Rates: $59-$109
(360) 659-4488
(800) 528-1234
(800) 481-4804

**VILLAGE INN &
SUITES**
235 Beach St
(98270)
Rates: $49-$71
(360) 659-0005

*METALINE
FALLS*

CIRCLE MOTEL
HC2, Box 616,
Hwy 31 (99153)
Rates: $30-$45
(509) 446-4343

MOCLIPS

**BARNACLE
MOTEL**
4816 Pacific Ave
(98562)
Rates: $45-$65
(360) 276-4318

**HI-TIDE OCEAN
BEACH RESORT
CONDOS**
4890 Railroad Ave
(98562)
Rates: $95-$150
(360) 276-4142
(800) 662-5477

MOCLIPS MOTEL
4852 Pacific Ave
(98562)
Rates: n/a
(360) 276-4228

**MOONSTONE
BEACH MOTEL**
4849 Pacific Ave
(98562)
Rates: $56-$72
(360) 276-4346
(888) 888-9063

**OCEAN CREST
RESORT**
4651 SR 109 N,
Sunset Beach
(98562)
Rates: $69-$159
(360) 276-4465
(800) 684-8439

THE SPINDRIFT
4807 Pacific Ave
(98562)
Rates: $105-$155
(800) 645-8443

MONROE

**BEST WESTERN
BARON INN**
19233 Hwy 2
(98272)
Rates: $65-$130
(360) 794-3111
(800) 528-1234

**BROOKSIDE
MOTEL**
19930 Hwy 2
(98272)
Rates: n/a
(360) 794-8832

**FAIRGROUNDS
INN MOTEL**
18950 Hwy 2
(98272)
Rates: $35-$60
(360) 794-5401

MONTESANO

**MONTE SQUARE
MOTEL**
518 1/2 South 1st
St (98563)
Rates: $59-$99
(360) 249-4424

MORTON

**EVERGREEN
MOTEL**
121 Front St (98356)
Rates: $27-$45
(360) 496-5407

**RESORT OF THE
MOUNTAINS**
1130 SR 7 (98356)
Rates: n/a
(360) 496-5885

SEASONS MOTEL
200 A Westlake
(98356)
Rates: $55-$70
(360) 496-6835
(877) 496-6835

STILTNER MOTEL
250 Morton Rd
(98356)
Rates: n/a
(360) 496-5103

MOSES LAKE

AMERIHOST
1157 N Stratford
Rd (98831)
Rates: $69-$89
(509) 764-7500
(800) 434-5800

**BEST VALUE
EL RANCHO
MOTEL**
1214 S Pioneer
Way (98837)
Rates: $40-$70
(509) 765-9173

**BEST WESTERN
HALLMARK INN**
3000 Marina Dr
(98837)
Rates: $74-$99
(509) 765-9211
(800) 528-1234
(888) 448-4449

HERITAGE SUITES
511 S Division
(98837)
Rates: $48-$89
(800) 457-0271

HOLIDAY INN EXP
1745 E Kittleson
(98837)
Rates: $79-$105
(509) 766-2000
(800) 465-4329

IMPERIAL MOTEL
905 W Broadway
(98837)
Rates: $35-$55
(509) 765-8626

**INN AT
MOSES LAKE**
1741 E Kittleson
Rd (98837)
Rates: $59-$75
(800) 576-7500

AREA CODES - If the local number doesn't connect, check for a new area code.

INTERSTATE INN
2801 W Broadway
(98837)
Rates: $30-$55
(509) 765-1777
(800) 777-5889

LAKESHORE MOTEL
3206 W Lakeshore
Dr (98837)
Rates: $28-$35
(509) 765-9201

MAPLES MOTEL
1006 W 3rd
(98837)
Rates: $40-$55
(509) 765-5665

MOTEL OASIS INN
466 Melva Ln
(98837)
Rates: $39-$49
(509) 765-8636
(800) 456-0708

MOTEL 6
2822 Driggs Dr
(98837)
Rates: $30-$56
(509) 766-0250
(800) 466-8356

SAGE "N" SAND MOTEL
1011 S Pioneer
Way (98837)
Rates: $25-$55
(509) 765-1755
(800) 336-0454

SHILO INN SUITES
1819 E Kittleson
(98837)
Rates: $68-$113
(509) 765-9317
(800) 222-2244

SUNLAND MOTOR INN
309 E Third Ave
(98837)
Rates: $25-$55
(509) 765-1170
(800) 220-4403

SUPER 8 MOTEL
449 Melva Lane
(98837)
Rates: $50-$65
(509) 765-8886
(800) 800-8000

TRAVELODGE
316 S Pioneer Way
(98837)
Rates: $49-$89
(509) 765-8631
(800) 578-7878
(800) 255-3050

MOSSYROCK

MOSSYROCK INN
118 E State St
(98564)
Rates: n/a
(360) 983-8641

MOUNT VERNON

BEST WESTERN COLLEGE WAY INN
300 W College
Way (98273)
Rates: $68-$93
(360) 424-4287
(800) 528-1234
(800) 793-4024

BEST WESTERN COTTONTREE INN
2300 Market St
(98273)
Rates: $84-$154
(360) 428-5678
(800) 528-1234
(800) 662-6886

COMFORT INN
1910 Freeway Dr
(98273)
Rates: $59-$129
(360) 428-7020
(800) 424-6423

DAYS INN CASINO AREA
2009 Riverside Dr
(98273)
Rates: $50-$150
(360) 424-4141
(800) 329-7466

HILLSIDE MOTEL
2300 Bonnie View
Rd (98273)
Rates: n/a
(360) 445-3252

TULIP INN
2200 Freeway Dr
(98273)
Rates: $55-$80
(360) 428-5969

WEST WINDS MOTEL
2020 Riverside Dr
(98273)
Rates: $32-$50
(360) 424-4224

WHISPERING FIRS BED & BREAKFAST
1957 Kanako Ln
(98273)
Rates: $65-$95
(360) 428-1990
(800) 428-1992

MOUNTLAKE TERRACE

STUDIO 6
6017 244th St SW
(98043)
Rates: $49-$69
(425) 771-3139
(888) 897-0202

MT. BAKER

MT. BAKER LODGING
800.709.7669
SEE OUR AD ON
PAGE 627

MUKILTEO

TOWNEPLACE SUITES
8521 Mukilteo
Speedway (98275)
Rates: $59-$89
(425) 551-5900
(800) 257-3000

NACHES

APPLE COUNTRY BED & BREAKFAST
4561 Old Naches
Hwy (98937)
Rates: $65+
(509) 965-0344

SILVER BEACH RESORT
40380 Hwy 12
(98937)
Rates: n/a
(509) 672-2500

SQUAW ROCK RESORT
15070 SR 410
(98937)
Rates: $65-$79
(509) 658-2926

TROUT LODGE
27090 Hwy 12
(98937)
Rates: $40-$55
(509) 672-2211

NAHCOTTA

MOBY DICK HOTEL & OYSTER FARM
25814 Sundridge
Rd (98637)
Rates: $85-$135
(360) 665-4543

OUR HOUSE IN NAHCOTTA / OYSTERVILLE B&B
P.O. Box 33
(98637)
Rates: $85-$95
(360) 665-6667

NASELLE

SLEEPY HOLLOW MOTEL
1032 SR 4 (98638)
Rates: $35-$40
(360) 484-3232

NEAH BAY

CAPE MOTEL
1500 Bayview Ave
(98357)
Rates: $45-$74
(360) 645-2250

SILVER SALMON RESORT
1280 Bayview Ave
(98357)
Rates: $45+
(360) 645-2388
(888) 713-6477

SNOW CREEK RESORT
691 Hwy 112 W
(98357)
Rates: $45-$74
(360) 645-2284
(800) 883-1464

TYEE MOTEL
Bayview Ave
(98357)
Rates: $45-$100
(360) 645-2233

NEWPORT

GOLDEN SPUR MOTOR INN
924 W Hwy 2
(99156)
Rates: $38-$54
(509) 447-3823

THE LAZY J HIDEAWAY
3792 Deer Valley
Rd (99156)
Rates: $60
(509) 447-2535
(800) 898-3412

NEWPORT CITY INN
220 N Washington
(99156)
Rates: $38-$60
(509) 447-3463

OAK HARBOR
(See Whidbey
Island for lodging)

OCEAN CITY

NORTH BEACH MOTEL
2601 SR 109
(98569)
Rates: $30-$55
(360) 289-4116
(800) 640-8053

PACIFIC SANDS MOTEL & RESORT
2687 SR 109
(98569)
Rates: $40-$56
(360) 289-3588

WEST WINDS RESORT MOTEL
2537 SR 109
(98569)
Rates: $36-$66
(360) 289-3448
(800) 867-3448

OCEAN PARK

COASTAL COTTAGES OF OCEAN PARK
P.O. Box 888
(98640)
Rates: $50-$69
(360) 665-4658
(800) 200-0424

HARBOR VIEW MOTEL
3306 281st St
(98640)
Rates: $40-$60
(360) 665-4959

OCEAN PARK RESORT
25904 "R" St
(98640)
Rates: $69-$100
(360) 665-4585
(800) 835-4634

SHAKTI COVE COTTAGES
253rd Place
(98640)
Rates: $60-$75
(360) 665-4000

AREA CODES - If the local number doesn't connect, check for a new area code.

SUNSET VIEW RESORT
25517 Park Ave (98640)
Rates: $64-$159
(360) 665-4494

WESTGATE MOTEL
20803 Pacific Hwy (98640)
Rates: $42-$55
(360) 665-4211

OCEAN SHORES

BEACH FRONT VACATION RENTALS
759 Ocean Shores Blvd (98569)
Rates: $65-$225
(800) 544-8887

CASA DEL ORO MOTEL
667 Point Brown Ave NW (98569)
Rates: $85-$120
(360) 289-2281
(800) 291-2281

CHALET VILLAGE CABINS
659 Ocean Shores Blvd (98569)
Rates: $85-$95
(360) 289-4297
(800) 303-4297 (WA)

DISCOVERY INN
1031 Discovery Ave SE (98569)
Rates: $52-$78
(360) 289-3371
(800) 882-8821

GREY GULL CONDO MOTEL
651 Ocean Shores Blvd SW (98569)
Rates: $120-$355
(360) 289-3381
(800) 562-9712 (WA)

LINDE'S LANDING
648 Ocean Shores Blvd NW (98569)
Rates: n/a
(800) 448-2433

NAUTILUS CONDO HOTEL
835 Ocean Shores Blvd (98569)
Rates: $70-$150
(360) 289-2722
(800) 221-4541

OCEAN SHORES MOTEL
681 Ocean Shores Blvd N (98569)
Rates: $40-$125
(360) 289-3351
(800) 464-2526 (WA)

POLYNESIAN CONDO RESORT
615 Ocean Shores Blvd (98569)
Rates: $99-$179
(360) 289-3361
(800) 562-4836

THE SANDS RESORT
801 Ocean Shores Blvd (98569)
Rates: $49-$125
(360) 289-2444
(800) 841-4001

SANDS ROYAL PACIFIC MOTEL
801 Ocean Shores Blvd NW (98569)
Rates: $39-$129
(360) 289-3306
(800) 562-9748

SILVER KING MOTEL
1070 Discovery Ave SE (98569)
Rates: $35-$90
(360) 289-3386
(800) 562-6001 (WA)

SURFVIEW CONDOS
757 Ocean Court NW (98569)
Rates: $65-$85
(360) 289-3077
(800) 544-8887 (WA)

WESTERLY MOTEL
870 Ocean Shores Blvd NW (98569)
Rates: $30-$50
(360) 289-3711

ODESSA

ODESSA MOTEL
601 E First Ave (99159)
Rates: $35-$47
(509) 982-2412

OKANOGAN

CEDARS INN
One Apple Way (98840)
Rates: $45-$57
(509) 422-6431

PONDEROSA MOTOR LODGE
1034 S 2nd Ave (98840)
Rates: $46-$55
(509) 422-0400
(800) 732-6702

U & I RIVERS EDGE MOTEL
838 2nd St N (98840)
Rates: $28-$35
(509) 422-2920

OLALLA

OLALLA ORCHARD B&B
12530 Orchard Ave SE (98359)
Rates: $95
(253) 857-5915

OLYMPIA

BAILEY MOTOR INN
3333 Martin Way (98506)
Rates: n/a
(360) 491-7515

BEST WESTERN ALADDIN MOTOR INN
900 S Capitol Way (98501)
Rates: $69-$100
(360) 352-7200
(800) 367-7771

THE CINNAMON RABBIT B&B
1304 7th Ave W (98502)
Rates: $60-$75
(360) 357-5520

DEEP LAKE RESORT
12405 Tilley Rd S (98512)
Rates: $53-$85
(360) 352-7388

LEE STREET SUITES
348 Lee St SW (98501)
Rates: n/a
(360) 943-8391

RAMADA INN GOVERNOR HOUSE
621 S Capitol Way (98501)
Rates: $130-$160
(360) 352-7700
(800) 272-6232

RED LION HOTEL
2300 Evergreen Park Dr SW (98502)
Rates: $85-$105
(360) 943-4000
(866) 896-4000

TYEE HOTEL
500 Tyee Dr (98502)
Rates: $70-$78
(360) 352-0511
(800) 648-6440
(800) 386-8933

OLYMPIC NATIONAL PARK

LAKE CRESCENT LODGE
416 Lake Crescent Rd (98362)
Rates: $85-$211
(360) 928-3211

LOG CABIN RESORT
3183 E Beach Rd (Port Angeles 98363)
Rates: $75-$127
(360) 928-3325

OMAK

LEISURE VILLAGE MOTEL
630 Okoma Dr (98841)
Rates: $36-$47
(509) 826-4442
(800) 427-4495 (WA)

MOTEL NICHOLAS
527 E Grape St (98841)
Rates: $42-$46
(509) 826-4611

OMAK INN
912 Koala Dr (98841)
Rates: $67-$77
(509) 826-3822

RODEWAY INN & SUITES
122 Main St (98841)
Rates: $44-$130
(509) 826-0400
(800) 424-6423

ROYAL MOTEL
514 E Riverside Dr (98841)
Rates: $28-$44
(509) 826-5715

STAMPEDE MOTEL
215 W 4th St (98841)
Rates: n/a
(800) 639-1161

ORCAS ISLAND

BARTWOOD LODGE
178 Fossil Bay Dr (Eastsound 98245)
Rates: $59-$189
(360) 376-2242
(866) 666-2242

DEER HARBOR INN
33 Inn Ln (Deer Harbour 98243)
Rates: $125-$325
(360) 376-4110

DOE BAY VILLAGE RESORT
P.O. Box 437 (Olga 98279)
Rates: $40+
(360) 376-2291

HARRISON HOUSE SUITES
235 C St (Friday Harbor 98250)
Rates: $89-$300
(800) 407-7933

NORTH SHORE COTTAGES
P.O. Box 1273 (Eastsound 98245)
Rates: $120
(360) 376-5131

OUTLOOK INN
171 Main St (Eastsound 98245)
Rates: $74-$165
(360) 376-2200
(888) OUTLOOK

AREA CODES - If the local number doesn't connect, check for a new area code.

SMALL ISLAND FARM & INN
Rt 1, Box 76
(Eastsound 98245)
Rates: $70-$95
(360) 376-4292

WEST BEACH RESORT
Rt 1, Box 510
(Eastsound 98245)
Rates: $105-$150
(360) 376-2240

OROVILLE
CAMARY MOTEL
1815 Main St
(98844)
Rates: $36-$55
(509) 476-3694

EDEN VALLEY GUEST RANCH
31 Eden Valley Rd
(98844)
Rates: $85-$95
(509) 485-4002

OTHELLO
BEST WESTERN LINCOLN INN
1020 E Cedar St
(99344)
Rates: $59-$119
(509) 488-5671
(800) 528-1234
(800) 240-7865

MAR DON RESORT
8198 Hwy 262 E
(99344)
Rates: $38-$55
(509) 346-2651

THE RAMA INN
1450 E Main St
(99344)
Rates: n/a
(509) 488-6612

PACIFIC BEACH
SAND DOLLAR MOTEL
53 Central (98571)
Rates: $43-$100
(360) 276-4525

SANDPIPER BEACH RESORT CONDOS
4159 SR 109 (98571)
Rates: $60-$120
(360) 276-4580
(800) 567-4737

SHORELINE MOTEL
12 1st St South
(98571)
Rates: $45-$75
(360) 276-4433

PACKWOOD
INN OF PACKWOOD
13032 Hwy 12
(98361)
Rates: $45-$145
(360) 494-5500
(877) 496-9666

MOUNTAIN VIEW LODGE MOTEL
13163 Hwy 12
(98361)
Rates: $40-$100
(360) 494-5555

TATOOSH MEADOWS RESORT
102 E Main (98361)
Rates: $125+
(800) 294-2311

WOODLAND MOTEL
11890 Hwy 12
(98361)
Rates: $40-$50
(360) 494-6766

PASCO
AIRPORT MOTEL
2532 N 4th St
(99301)
Rates: $27-$38
(509) 545-1460

AMERISUITES
4525 Convention Place (99301)
Rates: $89-$125
(609) 542-9521
(800) 833-1516

BEST WESTERN PASCO INN
NE corner St. Andrews Loop
(99301)
Rates: $89-$159
(509) 543-7722
(800) 528-1234

BUDGET INN
1520 N Oregon ST
(99301)
Rates: $41-$44
(509) 546-2010

KING CITY TRUCK STOP MOTEL
2100 E Hillsboro Rd (99301)
Rates: $38-$48
(509) 547-8511

RED LION HOTEL PASCO
2525 N 20th Ave
(99301)
Rates: $99-$119
(509) 547-0701
(800) 733-5466

SAGE 'N SUN MOTEL
1232 S 10th St
(99301)
Rates: $28-$48
(800) 391-9188

SLEEP INN
9930 Bedford St
(99301)
Rates: $55-$119
(509) 545-9554
(800) 424-6423

THUNDERBIRD MOTEL
414 W Columbia
(99301)
Rates: n/a
(509) 547-9506

TRI-MARK MOTEL
720 W Lewis St
(99301)
Rates: n/a
(509) 547-7766

THE VINEYARD INN
1800 W Lewis
(99301)
Rates: $39-$55
(509) 547-0791
(800) 824-5457

PATEROS
LAKE PATEROS MOTOR INN
115 Lakeshore Dr
(98846)
Rates: $51-$59
(509) 923-2207
(800) 444-1985

PESHASTIN
TIMBERLINE HOTEL
8284 Hwy 2
(98847)
Rates: n/a
(509) 548-7415

POINT ROBERTS
CEDAR HOUSE INN B&B
1534 Gulf Rd
(98281)
Rates: $36-$49
(360) 945-0284

POMEROY
PIONEER MOTEL
1201 Main St,
Box 579 (99347)
Rates: $35-$50
(509) 843-1559

PORT ANGELES
BLUE MOUNTAIN LODGE B&B
380 Lewis Rd
(98362)
Rates: 60+
(360) 457-8540

CHINOOK MOTEL
1414 E 1st St (98362)
Rates: $45-$80
(360) 452-2336

INDIAN VALLEY MOTEL
235471 Hwy 101
(98362)
Rates: $45+
(360) 928-3266

LOG CABIN RESORT
3183 E Beach Rd
(98363)
Rates: $62-$100
(360) 928-3325

NORTHWEST MANOR B&B
1320 Marie View
(98362)
Rates: $75+
(360) 452-5839
(888) 229-7052

OCEAN CREST B&B
402 S "M" (98362)
Rates: $60+
(360) 452-4832
(877) 413-2169

THE POND MOTEL
1425 W US 101
(98363)
Rates: $33-$70
(360) 452-8422

PORTSIDE INN
1510 E Front St
(98362)
Rates: $79-$99
(360) 452-4015
(877) 438-8588

QUALITY INN UPTOWN
101 E 2nd St
(98362)
Rates: $59-$199
(360) 457-9434
(800) 424-6423
(800) 858-3812

RED LION HOTEL
221 N Lincoln St
(98362)
Rates: $95-$139
(360) 452-9215
(800) 733-5466

RIVIERA INN
535 E Front St
(98362)
Rates: $35-$139
(360) 417-3955

ROYAL VICTORIAN MOTEL
521 E 1st St
(98362)
Rates: $45+
(360) 452-2316

RUFFLES MOTEL
812 E 1st St
(98363)
Rates: $45+
(360) 457-7788

SUPER 8 MOTEL
2104 E 1st St
(98362)
Rates: $45-$61
(360) 452-8401
(800) 800-8000

THOR TOWN INTERNATIONAL HOSTEL
316 N Race St
(98362)
Rates: 45+
(360) 452-0931

UPTOWN INN
101 E 2nd St
(98362)
Rates: $45+
(360) 457-9434
(800) 858-3812

AREA CODES - If the local number doesn't connect, check for a new area code.

PORT HADLOCK

HADLOCK MOTEL
175 B Chimacum
Rd (98339)
Rates: $65-$90
(888) 360-3111

**INN AT PORT
HADLOCK**
310 Hadlock Bay
Rd (98339)
Rates: $79-$249
(800) 785-2030

**THE OLD
ALCOHOL PLANT**
310 Alcohol Loop
Rd (98339)
Rates: $59-$250
(360) 385-7030
(800) 785-7030

**VALLEY VIEW
CABINS**
12775 Hwy 30
(98339)
Rates: $45-$50
(360) 385-1666
(800) 280-1666

**PORT
LUDLOW**

**BEAVERS POND
RETREAT**
1 Beaver's Pond
Trail (98365)
Rates: $75+
(888) 399-6533

**HERON BEACH
INN ON
LUDLOW BAY**
1 Heron Rd (98365)
Rates: $135-$450
(360) 437-0411

**JULIANNA'S
COTTAGE B&B**
3851 Larson Lake
Rd (98365)
Rates: $75+
(888) 399-6533

**PORT
ORCHARD**

**CEDAR
HOLLOW GUEST
HOUSE B&B**
3875 Locker Rd
(98366)
Rates: $75
(360) 871-1527

DAYS INN
220 Bravo Terrace
(98366)
Rates: $79-$159
(360) 895-7818
(800) 329-7466

HOLIDAY INN EXP
1121 Bay St (98366)
Rates: $65-$99
(360) 895-2666
(800) 465-4329

VISTA MOTEL
1090 Bethel (98366)
Rates: $30-$59
(360) 876-8046

**PORT
TOWNSEND**

**ALADDIN
MOTOR INN**
2333 Washington
St (98368)
Rates: $50-$99
(360) 385-3747
(800) 281-3747

**ANNAPURNA
RETREAT & SPA**
338 Adams St
(98368)
Rates: $65-$125
(360) 385-2909

**BISHOP
VICTORIAN HOTEL**
714 Washington St
(98368)
Rates: $95-$205
(360) 385-6122
(800) 824-4738

**CABIN VACATION
RENTAL**
839 Jacob Miller
(98368)
Rates: $95
(360) 385-5571

**HARBORSIDE
INN MOTEL**
330 Benedict St
(98368)
Rates: $72-$150
(360) 385-7909
(800) 942-5960

**HERON HILL LOFT
GUEST COTTAGE**
241 Sand Rd
(98368)
Rates: $100-$115+
(Weekly &
Monthly rates too)
(360) 379-3105

**NORTH BEACH
RETREAT RENTAL**
510 56th St (98368)
Rates: $50+
(360) 385-1621

**THE HISTORIC
PALACE HOTEL**
1004 Water St
(98368)
Rates: $69-$229
(360) 385-0733
(800) 962-0741

**PILOT HOUSE
RENTAL**
327 Jackson St
(98368)
Rates: $60-$95
(360) 379-0811

**POINT HUDSON
RESORT/MARINA**
103 Hudson St
(98368)
Rates: $45-$90
(360) 385-2828
(800) 826-3854

**PORT TOWNSEND
INN**
2020 Washington
St (98368)
Rates: $68-$175
(360) 385-2211
(800) 216-4985

THE SWAN HOTEL
216 Monroe St
(98368)
Rates: $115-$475
(360) 385-6122
(800) 776-1718

TIDES INN MOTEL
1807 Water St
(98368)
Rates: $58-$124
(360) 385-0595
(800) 822-8696

**VALLEY VIEW
MOTEL**
162 Hwy 20 (98368)
Rates: $45-$60
(360) 385-1666
(800) 280-1666

POULSBO

HOLIDAY INN EXP
19801 7th Ave NE
(98370)
Rates: n/a
(360) 697-4400
(800) 465-4329

**POULSBO
INN & SUITES**
18680 Hwy 305
(98370)
Rates: $90-$115
(360) 779-3921

**SANDY HOOK
BEACH SHACK**
14532 Sandy Hook
Rd. NE, Cabin #2
(98370)
Rates: $50-$70
(206)842-4260 or
(360)394-3632

PROSSER

**BEST WESTERN
PROSSER INN**
225 Merlot Dr
(99350)
Rates: $79-$109
(509) 786-7977
(800) 528-1234

**INN AT HORSE
HEAVEN**
259 Merlot Dr
(99350)
Rates: $79-$109
(509) 786-7090

PROSSER MOTEL
1206 Wine Country
Rd (99350)
Rates: $30-$48
(509) 786-2555

PULLMAN

**AMERICAN
TRAVEL INN**
515 S Grand Ave
(99163)
Rates: $47-$64
(509) 334-3500

HAWTHORN INN
928 NW Olsen St
(99163)
Rates: $79-$119
(509) 332-0928
(800) 527-1133

HOLIDAY INN EXP
SE 1190 Bishop
Blvd (99163)
Rates: $79-$109
(509) 334-4437
(800) 465-4329

**MANOR LODGE
MOTEL**
SE 455 Paradise
(99163)
Rates: $39-$59
(509) 334-2511

**QUALITY INN
PARADISE CREEK**
SE 1400 Bishop
(99163)
Rates: $54-$114
(509) 332-0500
(800) 424-6423

PUYALLUP

**BEST WESTERN
PARK PLACE**
620 S Hill Park Dr
(98373)
Rates: $114-$169
(253) 848-1500
(800) 528-1234
(888) 204-5804

**HOLIDAY INN EXP
HOTEL & SUITES**
812 S Hill Park Dr
(98373)
Rates: $119-$129
(253) 848-4900
(800) 465-4329

MOTEL PUYALLUP
1412 S Meridian St
(98371)
Rates: $44-$54
(253) 845-8825
*800) 921-2700

**NORTHWEST
MOTOR INN**
1409 S Meridian St
(98371)
Rates: $60-$73
(253) 841-2600
(800) 845-9490

QUILCENE

**LELAND LAKE
HOUSE**
47 Munn Rd
(98376)
Rates: $75+
(360) 308-0325
(888) 337-9090

**MAPLE GROVE
MOTEL**
61 Maple Grove
Rd (98376)
Rates: $45-$60
(360) 765-3410

**MOUNT
WALKER INN**
295433 Hwy 101
(98376)
Rates: $50-$70
(360) 765-3410

AREA CODES - If the local number doesn't connect, check for a new area code.

QUINAULT

LAKE QUINAULT LODGE
345 S Shore Rd (98575)
Rates: $68-$360
(360) 288-2900
(800) 562-6672

QUINCY

SUNDOWNER MOTEL
414 F St SE (98848)
Rates: n/a
(509) 787-3587

TRADITIONAL INNS
500 F St SW (98848)
Rates: $53-$67
(509) 787-3525

RAINIER

7 C'S GUEST RANCH
11123 128th St SE (98576)
Rates: $30-$100
(360) 446-7957

RANDLE

MEDICI MOTEL
471 Cispus Rd (98377)
Rates: $45
(360) 497-7700
(800) 697-7750

WOODLAND MOTEL
11890 US 12 (98377)
Rates: $40-$50
(360) 494-6766

RAYMOND

MAUNU'S MOUNTCASTLE MOTEL
524 3rd St (98577)
Rates: $40-$55
(360) 942-5571

WILLIS MOTEL
425 3rd St (98577)
Rates: $40+
(360) 942-5313

REDMOND

RESIDENCE INN TOWN CENTER
7575 164th Ave NE (98052)
Rates: $199-$249
(425) 497-9226
(800) 331-3131

RENTON

BEST VALUE INN
3700 E Valley Rd (98055)
Rates: $59-$79
(425) 251-9591

ECONO LODGE
4710 Lake Washington Blvd (98055)
Rates: $54-$69
(425) 228-2858
(800) 553-2666

HOLIDAY INN SELECT
One South Grady Way (98055)
Rates: $79-$129
(425) 226-7700
(800) 465-4329

REPUBLIC

THE NORTHERN INN
852 S Clark Ave (99166)
Rates: $28-$33
(509) 775-3371

FISHERMAN'S COVE RESORT
15 Fisherman's Cove Rd (99166)
Rates: $25-$85
(509) 775-3641

K-DIAMOND-K CATTLE & GUEST RANCH
15661 Hwy 21 S (99166)
Rates: $60-$100
(509) 775-3536

KLONDIKE MOTEL
150 N Clark Ave (99166)
Rates: $36-$44
(509) 775-3555

PROSPECTOR INN MOTEL
979 S Clark Ave (99166)
Rates: $48-$115
(509) 775-3361
(888) 844-6480

TIFFANYS RESORT
1026 Tiffany Rd (99166)
Rates: $43-$115
(509) 775-3152

RICHLAND

BALI HI MOTEL
1201 George Washington Way (99352)
Rates: $39-$45
(509) 943-3101

CLARION HOTEL & CONF CENTER
1515 George Washington Way (99352)
Rates: $69-$89
(509) 946-4121
(800) 252-7466

DAYS INN
615 Jadwin Ave (993520
Rates: $54-$79
(509) 943-4611
(800) 329-7466

ELK CITY HOTEL
1426 Potter Ave (99352)
Rates: $25-$48
(208) 842-2452

MOTEL 6
1751 Fowler St (99352)
Rates: $39-$52
(509) 783-1250
(800) 466-8356

RED LION INN HANFORD HOUSE
802 George Washington Way (99352)
Rates: $79-$99
(509) 946-7611
(800) 733-5466

SHILO INN
50 Comstock St (99352)
Rates: $74-$199
(509) 946-4661
(800) 222-2244

RIMROCK

GAME RIDGE MOTEL-LODGE
27350 Hwy 12 (98937)
Rates: $65-$130
(509) 672-2212
(800) 301-9354

RITZVILLE

BEST WESTERN BRONCO INN
105 Galbreath Way (99169)
Rates: $79-$109
(509) 659-5000
(800) 528-1234

COLWELL BEST VALUE INN
501 W 1st St (99169)
Rates: $42-$54
(509) 659-1620
(888) 315-2378

COTTAGE MOTEL
508 E 1st Ave (99169)
Rates: n/a
(509) 659-0721

EMPIRE MOTEL
101 W 1st Ave (99169)
Rates: $27-$47
(509) 659-1030

LA QUINTA INN
1513 Smitty's Blvd (99169)
Rates: $39-$79
(509) 659-1007
(800) 687-6667

TOP HAT MOTEL
210 E 1st St (99169)
Rates: $38-$49
(509) 659-1100

ROCKPORT

CLARK'S SKAGIT RIVER CABINS
5675 Hwy 20 (98283)
Rates: $56-$140
(360) 386-4437
(800) 273-2606

TOTEM TRAIL MOTEL
5551 Hwy 20 (98283)
Rates: $35-$50
(360) 873-4535

ROSLYN

THE LITTLE ROSLYN INN
106 5th St (98941)
Rates: $38-$90
(925) 649-2936

THE ORIGINAL ROSLYN INN
102 5th St (98941)
Rates: $190
(925) 649-2936

THE ROSLYN "INN BETWEEN"
104 5th St (98941)
Rates: $290
(925) 649-2936

SAN JUAN ISLAND

B&B ASSN. OF SAN JUAN ISLAND
P. O. Box 3016 (Friday Harbor 98250)
Rates: $59-$325
(866) 645-3030

BEAVERTON VALLEY FARM B&B
4144 Beaverton Valley Rd (Friday Harbor 98250)
Rates: $80-$100
(877) 378-3276

BLAIR HOUSE B&B
345 Blair Ave (Friday Harbor 98250)
Rates: $75-$125
(360) 378-5907
(800) 899-3030

THE FRIDAY HARBOR INN
410 Spring St (Friday Harbor 98250)
Rates: $69-$195
(360) 378-4000
(800) 793-4576

HARRISON HOUSE SUITES
235 C St (Friday Harbor 98250)
Rates: $89-$300
(360) 378-3587
(800) 407-7933

LAKEDALE RESORT
4313 Roche Harbor Rd (Friday Harbor 98250)
Rates: $120-$267
(360) 378-2350
(800) 617-2267

AREA CODES - If the local number doesn't connect, check for a new area code.

SAN JUAN INN
50 Spring St
(98250)
Rates: $70-$175
(360) 378-2070
(800) 742-8210

SAN JUAN ISLAND VACATION RENTALS
P O Box 1133
(Friday Harbor 98250)
Rates: $80-$300
(360) 378-3190
(888) 367-5211

SNUG HARBOR RESORT & MARINA
1997 Mitchell Bay Rd (98250)
Rates: $30-$200
(360) 378-4762

TUCKER HOUSE BED & BREAKFAST
260 B St (98250)
Rates: $70-$135
(360) 378-2783
(800) 965-0123

WESTWINDS B&B
4909 H-Hannah Rd (98250)
Rates: $165-$245
(360) 378-5283

WHARFSIDE B&B ON THE JACQUELINE
Slip K-13 (98250)
Rates: $80-$95
(360) 378-5661

SAN JUAN ISLANDS
(For lodging, see individual island listings - Lopez Island, San Juan Island, Shaw Island and Orcas Island)

SEABECK
SUMMER SONG BED & BREAKFAST
P.O. Box 82
(98380)
Rates: n/a
(360) 830-5089

SEATAC
AIRPORT PLAZA HOTEL
18601 Pacific Hwy S (98188)
Rates: $60-$65
(206) 433-0400

CLARION MOTEL
3000 S 176th St (98188)
Rates: $69-$149
(206) 242-0200
(800) 424-6423

COAST GATEWAY HOTEL
18415 Int'l Blvd (98188)
Rates: $77-$99
(206) 248-8200

DOUBLETREE AIRPORT HOTEL
18740 Int'l Blvd (98188)
Rates: $69-$149
(206) 246-8600
(800) 222-8733

HILTON HOTEL SEATTLE AIRPORT
17620 Pacific Hwy S (98188)
Rates: $89-$199
(206) 244-4800
(800) 445-8667

HOLIDAY INN EXP HOTEL & SUITES
19621 Int'l Blvd (98188)
Rates: $79-$129
(206) 824-3200
(800) 465-4329

HOLIDAY INN SEA-TAC INT'L AIRPORT
17338 Int'l Blvd (98188)
Rates: $129-$159
(206) 248-1000
(800) 465-4329

LA QUINTA INN SEATAC INTL
2824 S 188th St (98188)
Rates: $89-$1034(206) 241-5211
(800) 687-6667

MARRIOTT SEA-TAC AIRPORT
3201 S 176th St (98188)
Rates: $79-$183
(206) 241-2000
(800) 228-9290

MOTEL 6 SEA-TAC AIRPORT
16500 Pacific Hwy S (98188)
Rates: $39-$52
(206) 246-4101
(800) 466-8356

MOTEL 6 SEA-TAC AIRPORT SOUTH
18900 47th Ave S (98188)
Rates: $39-$52
(206) 241-1648
(800) 466-8356

MOTEL 6
20651 Military Rd (98198)
Rates: $39-$59
(206) 824-9902
(800) 466-8356

QUALITY INN SEA-TAC AIR-PORT
2900 S 192nd St (98188)
Rates: $62-$82
(206) 241-9292
(800) 424-6423

RADISSON HOTEL AIRPORT
17001 Pacific Hwy S (98188)
Rates: $79-$109
(206) 244-6000
(800) 333-3333

RED LION HOTEL SEATTLE AIRPORT
18220 Int'l Blvd (98188)
Rates: $89-$149
(206) 246-5535
(800) 733-5466

RED ROOF INN
16838 Int'l Blvd (98188)
Rates: $53-$82
(206) 248-0901
(800) 843-7663

RODEWAY INN
2930 S 176th St (98188)
Rates: $45-$70
(206) 246-9300
(800) 424-6423

SEA-TAC CREST MOTOR INN
18845 Int'l Blvd (98188)
Rates: $42-$59
(206) 433-0999
(800) 554-0300

SLEEP INN SEATAC ARPT
20406 Int'l Blvd (98198)
Rates: $59-$89
(206) 878-3600
(800) 424-6423

SUPER 8 MOTEL
3100 S 192nd (98188)
Rates: $59-$89
(206) 433-8188
(800) 800-8000

SEATTLE
(For additional lodging in the Seattle area, see listings under: Bellevue, Bainbridge Island, Bothell, Bremerton, Camano Island, Issaquah, Mercer Island, Redmond, Renton, SeaTac, Shoreline, Whidbey Island.)

ACE HOTEL
2423 1st Ave (98121)
Rates: $65-$200
(206) 448-4721

THE ALEXIS HISTORIC HOTEL
1007 First Ave (98104)
Rates: $175-$370
(206) 624-4844
(888) 850-1155

AURORA SEAFAIR INN
9100 Aurora Ave N (98103)
Rates: $65-$100
(206) 524-3600
(800) 445-9297

B&B ON BROADWAY
722 Broadway Ave E (98102)
Rates: $85-$115
(206) 329-8933
(888) 329-8933

BEECH TREE MANOR INN B&B
1405 Queen Anne Ave N (98109)
Rates: $45-$79
(206) 281-7037

BELLEVUE PLACE BED & BREAKFAST
1111 Bellevue Place E (98102)
Rates: $85-$95
(206) 325-9253
(800) 325-9253

BEST VALUE INN & SUITES
225 Aurora Ave N (98109)
Rates: $69-$169
(206) 728-7666

BEST WESTERN AIRPORT EXECUTEL
20717 Int'l Blvd S (98198)
Rates: $69-$119
(206) 878-3300
(800) 528-1234
(800) 648-3311

BEST WESTERN EVERGREEN INN
13700 Aurora Ave N (98133)
Rates: $72-$149
(206) 361-3700
(800) 528-1234
(800) 213-6308

BEST WESTERN EXECUTIVE INN
200 Taylor Ave N (98109)
Rates: $79-$165
(206) 448-9444
(800) 528-1234
(800) 351-9444

COMFORT SUITES DOWNTOWN SEATTLE CENTER
601 Roy St (98109)
Rates: $79-$179
(206) 282-2600
(800) 424-6423

CONTINENTAL PLAZA INN
2500 Aurora Ave N (98109)
Rates: $54-$78
(206) 284-1900

CROWNE PLAZA-DOWNTOWN
1113 6th Ave (98101)
Rates: n/a
(206) 464-1980
(800) 227-6963

DAYS INN
2205 7th Ave (981210)
Rates: $69-$139
(206) 448-3434
(800) 329-7466

EASTLAKE INN
2215 Eastlake E (98102)
Rates: n/a
(206) 322-7726

ECONO LODGE SEATAC AIRPORT
13910 Int'l Blvd (98168)
Rates: $59-$89
(206) 244-0810
(800) 424-6423

EDGEWATER
Pier 67, 2411 Alaskan Way (98121)
Rates: $179-$415
(206) 728-7000
(800) 624-0670

EXEC. PACIFIC PLAZA HOTEL
400 Spring St (98104)
Rates: $109-$129
(206) 623-3900

THE FAIRMONT OLYMPIC HOTEL
411 University St (98101)
Rates: $199-$365
(206) 621-1700
(800) 8218106

GEISHA MOTOR INN
9613 Aurora Ave N (98103)
Rates: n/a
(206) 524-8880

HOMEWOOD SUITES
206 Western Ave W (98119)
Rates: $89-$189
(206) 281-9393
(800) 225-5466

HOTEL MONACO
1101 Fourth Ave (98101)
Rates: $219-$299
(206) 621-1770
(800) 945-2240

HOTEL VINTAGE PARK
1100 Fifth Ave (98101)
Rates: $239
(206) 624-8000

LA QUINTA INN
2824 S 188th St (98188)
Rates: $85-$108
(206) 241-5211
(800) 687-6667

LEGEND MOTEL
22204 Pacific Hwy S (98198)
Rates: n/a
(206) 878-0366

MOTEL 6-SOUTH
20651 Military Rd (98188)
Rates: $39-$54
(206) 824-9902
(800) 466-8356

PARAMOUNT HOTEL
724 Pine (98101)
Rates: n/a
(206) 292-9500

PAR GARDENS B&B
14716 26th Ave NE (98155)
Rates: $60-$75
(206) 367-1437
(888) 742-2632

PENSIONE NICHOLAS B&B
1923 First Ave (98101)
Rates: $60-$80
(206) 441-7125
(800) 440-7125

RAMADA INN NORTHGATE
2140 N Northgate Way (98133)
Rates: $109-$129
(206) 365-0700
(800) 272-6232

RED LION ON FIFTH AVE
1415 Fifth Ave (98101)
Rates: $129-$199
(206) 971-8000
(800) 733-5466

RED LION HOTEL AIRPORT
18220 Int'l Blvd (98188)
Rates: $69-$89
(206) 246-5535
(800) 733-5466

RED LION HOTEL SOUTH
11244 Pacific Hwy S (98168)
Rates: $79-$99
(206) 762-0300
(800) 733-5466

RED ROOF INN
16838 Int'l Blvd (98188)
Rates: $49-$69
(206) 248-0901
(800) 843-7663

RENAISSANCE SEATTLE HOTEL
515 Madison St (98104)
Rates: $139-$299
(800) 278-4159

RESIDENCE INN BY MARRIOTT
800 Fairview Ave N (98109)
Rates: $129-$199
(206) 624-6000
(800) 331-3131

SANDPIPER CORP SUITES
11000 1st Ave SW (98146)
Rates: $39-$59
(206) 242-8883

SHADOW MOTEL
2930 S 176th (98188)
Rates: $32-$50
(206) 246-9300

SHERATON SEATTLE HOTEL
1400 6th Ave (98101)
Rates: $159-$249
(206) 621-9000
(800) 325-3535

SORRENTO HOTEL
900 Madison (98104)
Rates: $294-$2600
(206) 622-6400

TRAVELODGE SPACE NEEDLE
200 6th Ave N (98109)
Rates: $79-$159
(206) 441-7878
(800) 578-7878

UNIVERSITY INN
4140 Roosevelt Way N (98105)
Rates: 85-$105
(206) 632-5055

VANCE HOTEL
620 Stewart St (98101)
Rates: $79-$139
(206) 956-8500

W SEATTLE HOTEL
1112 4th Ave (98101)
Rates: $239-$315
(206) 264-6000

THE WESTIN HOTEL
1900 5th Ave (98101)
Rates: $149-$249
(206) 728-1000
(800) 228-3000

SEAVIEW
THE LIONS PAW INN B&B
3310 Pacific Hwy S (98644)
Rates: $100-$150
(360) 642-2481
(800) 972-1046

SEAVIEW COHO MOTEL
3701 Pacific Way (98644)
Rates: $55-$110
(360) 642-2531
(800) 681-8153

SOU'WESTER LODGE & CABINS
Beach Access Rd-38th Pl (98644)
Rates: $39-$109
(360) 642-2542

SEDRO WOOLLEY
SKAGIT MOTEL
1977 Hwy 20 (98284)
Rates: n/a
(360) 856-6001

THREE RIVERS INN MOTEL
210 Ball St (98284)
Rates: $59-$79
(360) 855-2626
(800) 221-5122

SEKIU
BAY MOTEL & MARINA
15562 Hwy 112 W (98381)
Rates: $45-$75
(360) 963-2444

CURLEY'S RESORT & DIVE CENTER
291 Front St (98381)
Rates: $45-$80
(360) 963-2281
(800) 542-9680

HERB'S MOTEL
411 Front St (98381)
Rates: $45-$74
(360) 963-2346

SEQUIM
ECONO LODGE
801 E Washington St (98382)
Rates: $55-$119
(360) 683-7113
(800) 424-6423

GREATHOUSE MOTEL
740 E Washington St (98382)
Rates: $45+
(877) 683-7272

GROVELAND COTTAGE B&B
4861 Sequim-Dungeness Way (98382)
Rates: $75-$120
(360) 683-3565
(800) 879-8859

AREA CODES - If the local number doesn't connect, check for a new area code.

RAMADA LTD
1095 E
Washington
(98382)
Rates: $49-$100
(360) 683-1775
(800) 272-6232

RED RANCH INN
830 W
Washington St
(98382)
Rates: $50-$100
(360) 683-4195
(800) 777-4195

SEQUIM BAY LODGE
268522 Hwy 101
(98382)
Rates: $59-$113
(360) 683-0691
(800) 622-0691

SEQUIM BAY RESORT
2634 W Sequim
Bay Rd (98382)
Rates: $45+
(360) 681-3853

SEQUIM WEST INN
740 W
Washington St
(98382)
Rates: $59-$115
(360) 683-4144
(800) 528-4527

SUNDOWNER MOTEL
364 W
Washington St
(98382)
Rates: $69-$79
(360) 683-5532
(800) 325-6966

SHELTON

CANAL SIDE RESORT MOTEL
N 21660 Hwy 101
(98584)
Rates: $38-$48
(360) 877-9422

CITY CENTER BEST RATES MOTEL
128 E Alder
(98584)
Rates: $36-$54
(360) 426-3397

LAKE NAHWATZEL RESORT
W 12900 Shelton-
Matlock Rd
(98584)
Rates: $30-$50
(360) 426-8323

RESTFULL FARM B&B
W 2230 Shelton
Valley Rd (98584)
Rates: $60-$70
(360) 426-8774

SHELTON INN
628 Railroad Ave
(98584)
Rates: $48-$68
(360) 426-4468
(800) 451-4560

SUPER 8 MOTEL
2943 Northview
Circle (98584)
Rates: $51-$80
(360) 426-1654
(800) 800-8000

SILVER CREEK

LAKE MAYFIELD MOTEL
2911 US Hwy 12
(98585)
Rates: n/a
(360) 985-2484

SILVER LAKE

SILVER LAKE MOTEL & RESORT
3201 Spirit Lake
Hwy (98645)
Rates: $54-$115
(360) 274-6141

SILVERDALE

CIMARRON MOTEL
9734 NW
Silverdale Way
(98315)
Rates: $69-$89
(360) 692-7777
(800) 273-5076

RED LION HOTEL
3073 NW Bucklin
Hill Rd (98315)
Rates: $89-$123
(360) 698-1000
(800) 733-5466

SEABREEZE COTTAGES & SPA
16609 Olympic
View Rd NW
(98315)
Rates: $76-$169
(360) 692-4648

SKYKOMISH

SKYKOMISH HOTEL
102 Railroad Ave
(98288)
Rates: n/a
(360) 677-8105

SKYRIVER INN
333 River Dr E
(98288)
Rates: 78-$83
(360) 677-2261
(800) 367-8194

SNOHOMISH

INN AT SNOHOMISH
323 2nd St (98290)
Rates: $65-$105
(360) 568-2208
(800) 548-9993

SNOHOMISH GRAND HOTEL B&B
901 1/2 1st St
(98290)
Rates: $60-$75
(360) 568-8854

SNOHOMISH GRAND VALLEY INN
11910 Springetti
Rd (98290)
Rates: n/a
(360) 568-8854

SNOQUALMIE PASS

BEST WESTERN SUMMITT INN
603 SR 906 (98068)
Rates: $109-$299
(425) 434-6300
(800) 528-1234
(800) 557-7829

SOAP LAKE

NOTARAS LODGE
236 E Main Ave
(98851)
Rates: $58-$250
(509) 246-0462

ROYAL VIEW MOTEL
Hwy 17 & 4th Sts
(98851)
Rates: n/a
(509) 246-1831

TOLO VISTA COTTAGE
22 N Daisy
(98851)
Rates: n/a
(509) 246-1512

SOUTH BEND

H & H MOTEL
Hwy 101,
PO Box 613
(98586)
Rates: $34-$49
(360) 875-5523

THE RUSSELL HOUSE HISTORIC B&B
902 E Water St
(98586)
Rates: $50-$250
(360) 875-6487

SEAQUEST MOTEL
801 W 1st St
(98586)
Rates: $54-$74
(360) 875-5349

SPOKANE

ALPINE MOTEL
18815 E Cataldo
(99201)
Rates: $50-$60
(509) 928-2700

APPLE TREE INN
9508 N Division St
(99218)
Rates: $50-$59
(509) 466-3020
(800) 323-5796

BEL AIR MOTEL 7
1303 E Sprague
Ave (99202)
Rates: $33-$49
(509) 535-1677

BELL MOTEL
9030 W Sunset
Hwy (99204)
Rates: $30-$43
(800) 223-1388

BEST VALUE THUNDERBIRD INN
120 W Third Ave
(99201)
Rates: $49-$79
(509) 747-2011

BEST WESTERN PEPPER TREE AIRPORT INN
3711 S Geiger
(99204)
Rates: $69-$179
(509) 624-4655
(800) 799-3933

BEST WESTERN PHEASANT HILL
12415 E Mission
(99216)
Rates: $59-$199
(509) 926-7432
(800) 269-0061

BEST WESTERN TRADE WINDS
3033 N Division St
(99207)
Rates: $64-$109
(509) 326-5500
(800) 621-8593

BROADWAY MOTEL
6317 E Broadway
(99212)
Rates: $66-$74
(509) 535-2442

BUDGET INN
110 E 4th Ave
(99202)
Rates: $39-$99
(509) 838-6101

BUDGET SAVER MOTEL
1234 E Sprague
Ave (99202)
Rates: $26-$59
(509) 534-0669

CLINIC CENTER INN
702 S McClellan
(99204)
Rates: $38-$46
(509) 747-6081

COMFORT INN NORTH
7111 N Division St
(98208)
Rates: $47-$175
(509) 467-7111
(800) 424-6423

AREA CODES - If the local number doesn't connect, check for a new area code.

THE DAVENPORT HOTEL & SPA
10 S Post St
(99201)
Rates: $155-$1950
(509) 455-8888

DAYS INN - ARPT
4212 W Sunset
Blvd (99204)
Rates: $59-$149
(509) 747-2021
(800) 329-7466

DOUBLETREE SPOKANE CITY CENTER
322 N Spokane
Falls Ct (99201)
Rates: $109-$159
(509) 455-9600
(800) 222-8733

ECONO LODGE
120 W 3rd Ave
(99201)
Rates: $37-$89
(509) 747-2011
(800) 553-2666

HOLIDAY INN AIRPORT
1616 S Windsor Dr
(99224)
Rates: $89
(509) 838-1170
(800) 465-4329

HOLIDAY INN EXP
9220 E Mission
(99206)
Rates: n/a
(509) 927-7100
(800) 465-4329

HOWARD JOHNSON INN
211 S Division St
(99202)
Rates: $45-$95
(509) 838-6630
(800) 446-4656

LA QUINTA INN
3808 N Sullivan
Rd (99216)
Rates: $69-$89
(509) 893-0955
(800) 687-6667

MADISON INN
15 W Rockwood
Blvd (99204)
Rates: $64-$69
(509) 474-4200
(800) 538-0375

MAPLETREE MOTEL
4824 E Sprague
Ave (99212)
Rates: $26-$48
(509) 535-5810

MICROTEL INN & SUITES
1215 S Garfield Rd
(99001)
Rates: $44-$69
(509) 242-1200

MOTEL 6
1919 N
Hutchinson Rd
(99212)
Rates: $33-$54
(509) 926-5399
(800) 466-8356

MOTEL 6 AIRPORT
1508 S Rustle St
(99204)
Rates: $29-$48
(509) 459-6120
(800) 466-8356

OXFORD SUITES
15015 E Indiana
(99206)
Rates: $89-$159
(509) 847-1000

OXFORD SUITES
115 W North
River Dr (99201)
Rates: $89-$149
(509) 353-9000

PARK LANE MOTEL & SUITES
4412 E Sprague
Ave (99212)
Rates: $57-$62
(509) 535-1626
(800) 533-1626

QUALITY INN OAKWOOD
7919 N Division St
(98208)
Rates: $65-$250
(509) 467-4900
(800) 424-6423

QUALITY INN VALLEY SUITES
8923 E Mission
Ave (99212)
Rates: $87-$250
(509) 928-5218
(800) 424-6423

RAMADA INN & SUITES
9601 N Newport
Hwy (99218)
Rates: $59-$89
(509) 468-4201
(800) 272-6232

RAMADA LIMITED
123 S Post St
(99204)
Rates: $44-$64
(509) 838-8504
(800) 272-6232

RANCH MOTEL
1609 S Lewis St
(99204)
Rates: $25-$32
(509) 456-8919
(800) 871-8919

RED LION HOTEL AT THE PARK
303 W North
River Dr (99201)
Rates: $85-$125
(509) 326-8000
(800) 733-5466

RED LION RIVER INN
700 N Division St
(99202)
Rates: $79-$110
(509) 326-5577
(800) 733-5466

RED TOP MOTEL
7217 E Trent Ave
(99212)
Rates: $42-$105
(509) 926-5728

RODEWAY INN
901 W 1st Ave
(99201)
Rates: $42-$84
(509) 747-1041
(800) 424-6423

ROYAL SCOT MOTEL
20 W Houston
(99208)
Rates: n/a
(509) 467-6672
(888) 467-7268

SHANGRI-LA MOTEL
2922 W Government
Way (99204)
Rates: $41-$76
(509) 747-2066
(800) 234-4941

SHILO INN
923 E 3rd Ave
(99202)
Rates: $72-$105
(509) 535-9000
(800) 222-2244

THE SPOKANE HOUSE HOTEL
4301 W Sunset
Blvd (99224)
Rates: $64-$69
(509) 838-1471

SUPER 8 MOTEL WEST
11102 W Westbow
Blvd (99204)
Rates: $69-$99
(509) 838-8800
(800) 800-8000

TRADE WINDS MOTEL
907 W 3rd Ave
(99204)
Rates: $50-$70
(509) 838-2091
(800) 586-5397

TRAVELODGE
33 W Spokane
Falls Blvd (99201)
Rates: $60-$180
(509) 623-9727
(800) 578-7878

TRAVELODGE HOTEL
4301 Sunset Blvd
(99224)
Rates: $50-$80
(509) 838-1471
(800) 578-7878

WEST COAST RIDPATH HOTEL
515 W Sprague
Ave (99201)
Rates: $59-$69
(509) 838-2711
(800) 325-4000

SPOKANE VALLEY

BEST WESTERN PHEASANT HILL
12415 E Mission
(99216)
Rates: $69-$129
(509) 926-7432
(800) 528-1234

BROADWAY INN
6309 E Broadway
(99212)
Rates: $49-$89
(509) 535-7185

COMFORT INN VALLEY
905 N Sullivan Rd
(99037)
Rates: $39-$150
(509) 924-3838
(800) 424-6423

HOLIDAY INN EXP-VALLEY
9220 E Mission
(99206)
Rates: $89-$189
(509) 927-7100
(800) 465-4329

LA QUINTA INN & SUITES
3808 N Sullivan
Rd (99216)
Rates: $59-$109
(509) 893-0955
(800) 687-6667

MIRABEAU PARK HOTEL
1100 N Sullivan
Rd (99037)
Rates: $89-$149
(509) 924-9000
(866) 584-4MPH

OXFORD SUITES-VALLEY
15015 E Indiana
Ave (99216)
Rates: $85-$159
(509) 847-1000

QUALITY INN VALLEY SUITES
8923 E Mission
(99212)
Rates: $69-$90
(509) 928-5218
(800) 424-6423

RESIDENCE INN BY MARRIOTT
15915 E Indiana
(99216)
Rates: $89-$169
(509) 892-9300
(800) 331-3131

AREA CODES - If the local number doesn't connect, check for a new area code.

SUPER 8 MOTEL
2020 Argonne Rd (99212)
Rates: $45-$89
(509) 928-4888
(800) 800-8000

SPRAGUE

LAST ROUNDUP MOTEL
312 E First (99032)
Rates: $36-$54
(509) 257-2583

PURPLE SAGE MOTEL
405-9 First (99032)
Rates: $28-$42
(509) 257-2507

STEVENSON

COLUMBIA GORGE RIVERSIDE LODGE
200 W Cascade Ave (98648)
Rates: $55-$89
(866) 427-5650

DOLCE SKAMANIA LODGE
1131 Skamania Lodge Way (98648)
Rates: $129-$299
(509) 427-7700
(800) 221-7117

SULTAN

DUTCH CUP MOTEL
918 Main St (98294)
Rates: $51-$70
(360) 793-2215
(800) 844-0488

SUMAS

BB BORDER INN MOTEL
121 Cleveland (98295)
Rates: n/a
(360) 988-5800

SUMNER

SUMNER MOTOR INN
15506 E Main St (98380)
Rates: $50-$66
(253) 863-3250

SUNNYSIDE

RODEWAY INN
3209 Picard Pl (98944)
Rates: $79-$109
(509) 837-5781
(800) 424-6423

SUN VALLEY INN
724 Valley Hwy (98944)
Rates: $25-$75
(509) 837-4721

TOWN HOUSE MOTEL
509 Yakima Valley Hwy (98944)
Rates: $38-$52
(509) 837-5500
(800) 342-4435

TACOMA

BEST WESTERN TACOMA INN
8726 S Hosmer St (98444)
Rates: $89-$169
(253) 535-2880
(800) 305-2888

BLUE SPRUCE MOTEL
12715 Pacific Ave (98444)
Rates: n/a
(253) 531-6111

BUDGET INN-SOUTH TACOMA
9915 S Tacoma Way (98499)
Rates: $36+
(253) 588-6615

COMFORT INN
8620 S Hosmer St (98444)
Rates: $99-$161
(253) 538-7998
(800) 424-6423

CORPORATE SUITES
219 Division Ct E (98404)
Rates: $57-$99
(253) 473-4105

DAYS INN
6802 Tacoma Mall Blvd (98409)
Rates: $62-$90
(253) 475-5900
(800) 329-7466

HIDDEN MAPLE B&B
4616 N 46th (98407)
Rates: $75-$95
(253) 756-2094

HOWARD JOHNSON INN
8726 S Hosmer St (98444)
Rates: $89-$119
(253) 535-2880
(800) 446-4656

LA QUINTA INN
1425 E 27th St (98421)
Rates: $83-$99
(253) 383-0146
(800) 687-6667

MOTEL 6 SOUTH
1811 S 76th St (98408)
Rates: $39-$58
(253) 473-7100
(800) 466-8356

RAMADA INN TACOMA DOME
2611 East E St (98421)
Rates: $62-$110
(253) 572-7272
(800) 272-6232

ROYAL COACHMAN INN
5805 Pacific Hwy E (98424)
Rates: $73-$84
(253) 922-2500
(800) 422-3051

SHERATON TACOMA HOTEL
1320 Broadway Plaza (98402)
Rates: $199-$219
(253) 572-3200
(800) 325-3535

SHILO INN
7414 S Hosmer St (98408)
Rates: $72-$109
(253) 475-4020
(800) 222-2244

VALLEY MOTEL
1220 Puyallup Ave (98421)
Rates: n/a
(253) 272-7720

VICTORY MOTEL
10801 Pacific Hwy SW (98499)
Rates: $23-$50
(253) 588-9107

TENINO

OFFUT LAKE RESORT
4005 120th Ave SE (98589)
Rates: $27-$45
(360) 264-2438

THORP

CIRCLE H HOLIDAY RANCH RESORT
810 Watt Canyon Rd (98946)
Rates: n/a
(509) 964-2000

TOKELAND

TRADEWINDS ON THE BAY MOTEL
4305 Pomeroy Ave (98590)
Rates: n/a
(360) 267-7500

TOLEDO

COWLITZ MOTEL
162 Cowlitz Loop Rd (98591)
Rates: n/a
(360) 864-6611

TONASKET

BONAPARTE LAKE RESORT
615 Bonaparte Lake Rd (98855)
Rates: n/a
(509) 486-2491

RAINBOW RESORT
761 Loomis Hwy (98855)
Rates: $26-$60
(509) 223-3700
(800) 347-4375

RED APPLE INN
Hwy 97 & 1st St (98855)
Rates: $37-$47
(509) 486-2119

SPECTACLE LAKE RESORT
10 McCammon Rd (98855)
Rates: $30-$105
(509) 223-3433

TOPPENISH

BEST WESTERN
515 S Elm St (98948)
Rates: $59-$159
(509) 865-7444
(877) 509-7444

EL CORRAL MOTEL
61731 Hwy 97 (98948)
Rates: $34-$39
(509) 865-2365

OXBOW INN
511 S Elm St (98948)
Rates: $31-$49
(509) 865-5800
(800) 222-3161

TROUT LAKE

KELLY'S TROUT CREEK INN B&B
25 Mt. Adams Rd (98650)
Rates: $65
(509) 395-2769

TUKWILA

COMFORT SUITES
7200 Fun Center Way (98188)
Rates: $75-$160
(425) 227-7200
(800) 424-6423

ECONOLODGE
13910 Tukwila Int'l Blvd (98168)
Rates: $54-$69
(206) 244-0810
(800) 553-2666

HOMESTEAD STUDIO SUITES
15635 W Valley Hwy (98188)
Rates: $55-$65
(425) 235-7160
(888) 782-9473

HOMEWOOD SUITES HOTEL
6955 Fort Dent Way (98188)
Rates: $99-$129
(425) 433-8000
(800) 225-5466

RAMADA LIMITED
13900 Int'lBlvd (98168)
Rates: $69-$99
(425) 244-8800
(800) 272-6232

AREA CODES - If the local number doesn't connect, check for a new area code.

RED LION HOTEL
11244 Tukwila
Int'l Blvd (98168)
Rates: $72-$85
(206) 762-0300
(800) 733-5466

**RESIDENCE INN
BY MARRIOTT**
16201 W Valley
Hwy (98188)
Rates: $150-$200
(425) 226-5500
(800) 331-3131

**SOUTH CITY
MOTEL**
14242 S Pacific
Hwy (98168)
Rates: n/a
(425) 243-0222

TUMWATER
**BEST WESTERN
TUMWATER INN**
5188 Capitol Blvd
(98501)
Rates: $70-$85
(360) 956-1235
(800) 848-4992

COMFORT INN
1620 7th Ave SW
(98512)
Rates: $70-$139
(360) 352-0691
(800) 424-6423

GUESTHOUSE INN
1600 74th Ave SW
(98512)
Rates: $88-$135
(360) 943-5040
(800) 214-8378

MOTEL 6
400 W Lee St
(98501)
Rates: $37-$46
(360) 754-7320
(800) 466-8356

SHALIMAR SUITES
5895 Capitol Blvd
S (98501)
Rates: n/a
(360) 943-8391

TWISP
**IDLE-A-WHILE
MOTEL**
505 N Hwy 20
(98856)
Rates: $46-$85
(509) 997-3222

**SPORTSMAN
MOTEL**
1010 E Hwy 20
(98856)
Rates: $29-$45
(509) 997-2911

**WAGON WHEEL
MOTEL**
HCR 73, Box 57
(98856)
Rates: n/a
(509) 997-4671

UNION
**ALDERBROOK
RESORT**
7101 E SR 106
(98592)
Rates: $135-$170
(360) 898-2200
(800) 622-9370

**ROBIN HOOD
VILLAGE**
6780 E SR 106
(98592)
Rates: $75-$85
(360) 898-2163

UNION GAP
**BEST WESTERN
AHTANUM INN**
2408 Rudkin Rd
(98903)
Rates: $109-$139
(509) 248-9700
(800) 528-1234
(800) 348-9701

QUALITY INN
12 E Valley Mall
(98903)
Rates: $59-$119
(509) 248-6924
(800) 424-6423

SUPER 8 MOTEL
2605 Rudkin Rd
(98903)
Rates: $58-$80
(509) 248-8880
(800) 800-8000

USK
THE HOTEL USK
410 River Rd (99180)
Rates: $25-$57
(509) 445-1526

VALLEY
**TEAL'S WAITTS
LAKE RESORT**
3365 Waitts Lake
Rd (99181)
Rates: n/a
(509) 937-2400

VANCOUVER
**BEST INN
& SUITES**
7001 NE Hwy 99
(98665)
Rates: $59-$69
(360) 696-0516
(888) 696-0516

COMFORT INN
13207 NE 20th
Ave (98686)
Rates: $59-$129
(360) 574-6000
(800) 424-6423

DAYS INN
221 NE Chkalov
Dr (98684)
Rates: $49-$95
(360) 256-7044
(800) 329-7466

FERRYMAN'S INN
7901 NE 6th Ave
(98665)
Rates: $54-$68
(360) 574-2151

**HOMEWOOD
SUITES**
701 SE Columbia
Shores Blvd
(98661)
Rates: $109-$139
(360) 750-1100
(800) 225-5466

QUALITY INN
7001 NE Hwy 99
(98665)
Rates: $69-$99
(360) 696-0516
(800) 424-6423

**RED LION HOTEL
AT THE QUAY**
100 Columbia St
(98660)
Rates: $59-$109
(360) 694-8341
(800) 733-5466
**RED LION INN AT
SALMON CREEK**
1500 NE 134th St
(98685)
Rates: $89
(360) 566-1100
(800) 733-5466

**RESIDENCE INN
BY MARRIOTT**
8005 NE Parkway
Dr (98662)
Rates: $79-$119
(360) 253-4800
(800) 331-3131

RIVERSIDE MOTEL
4400 Columbia
House Blvd (98661)
Rates: n/a
(360) 693-3677

**SHILO INN
DOWNTOWN**
401 E 13th St
(98686)
Rates: $68-$99
(360) 696-0411
(800) 222-2244

**SHILO INN
HAZEL DELL**
13206 Hwy 99
(98686)
Rates: $50-$110
(360) 573-0511
(800) 222-2244

SLEEP INN
9201 NE
Vancouver Mall
Dr (98662)
Rates: n/a
(360) 254-0900
(800) 753-3746

**STAYBRIDGE
SUITES**
7301 NE 41st St
(98662)
Rates: $79-$169
(360) 891-8282
(800) 238-8000

**SUNNYSIDE
MOTEL**
12200 NE Hwy 99
(98686)
Rates: n/a
(360) 573-4141

VALUE MOTEL
708 NE 78th St
(98665)
Rates: n/a
(360) 574-2345

**VANCOUVER
LODGE**
601 Broadway
(98660)
Rates: $40-$75
(360) 693-3668

*VASHON
ISLAND*
**ANGELS OF THE
SEA B&B**
26431 99th Ave
SW (98070)
Rates: $65-$85
(206) 463-6980
(800) 798-9249

CASTLE HILL B&B
26734 94th Ave
SW (98070)
Rates: $65+
(206) 463-5491

**SWALLOW'S NEST
GUEST
COTTAGES**
6030 248th St SW
(98070)
Rates: $65-$250
(206) 463-2646
(800) 269-6378

WALLA WALLA
**BEST WESTERN
WALLA WALLA** 7
E Oak St (99362)
Rates: $69-$119
(509) 525-4700
(800) 528-1234

BUDGET INN
305 N 2nd Ave
(99362)
Rates: $45-$95
(509) 529-4410

CAPRI MOTEL
2003 Melrose St
(99362)
Rates: $32-$65
(509) 525-1130

**CITY CENTER
MOTEL**
627 W Main St
(99362)
Rates: $32-$50
(509) 529-2660
(800) 453-3160

HOLIDAY INN EXP
1433 W Pine St
(99362)
Rates: $69-$99
(509) 525-6200
(800) 465-4329

**HOWARD
JOHNSON EXP**
325 E Main St
(99362)
Rates: $79-$119
(509) 529-4360
(800) 446-4656

LA QUINTA INN
520 N 2nd Ave
(99362)
Rates: $79-$119
(509) 525-2522
(800) 687-6667

AREA CODES - If the local number doesn't connect, check for a new area code.

SICYON GALLERY BED & BREAKFAST
1283 Star (99362)
Rates: n/a
(509) 525-2964

SUPER 8 MOTEL
2315 Eastgate St N (99362)
Rates: $56-$76
(509) 525-8800
(800) 800-8000

TRAVELODGE
421 E Main St (99362)
Rates: $48-$95
(509) 529-4940
(800) 578-7878

WHITMAN INN
107 N 2nd St (99362)
Rates: $39-$115
(509) 525-2200
(800) 237-4436

WENATCHEE
AVENUE MOTEL
720 N Wenatchee Ave (98801)
Rates: $50-$85
(509) 663-7161
(800) 733-8981

COAST CENTER HOTEL
201 N Wenatchee Ave (98801)
Rates: $89-$125
(509) 662-1234

COMFORT INN
815 N Wenatchee Ave (98801)
Rates: $65-$124
(509) 662-1700
(800) 424-6423

FORGET ME NOT BED & BREAKFAST
1133 Washington St (98801)
Rates: n/a
(509) 663-6114

HILL CREST MOTEL
2921 School St (98801)
Rates: $25-$40
(509) 663-5157

HOLIDAY INN EXP
1921 N Wenatchee Ave (98801)
Rates: $89-$169
(509) 663-6355
(800) 465-4329

HOLIDAY LODGE
610 N Wenatchee Ave (98801)
Rates: $38-$75
(509) 663-8167
(800) 722-0852

LA QUINTA INN
1905 N Wenatchee Ave (98801)
Rates: $79-$119
(509) 664-6565
(800) 687-6667

LYLE'S MOTEL
924 N Wenatchee Ave (98801)
Rates: $30-$75
(509) 663-5155
(800) 582-3788

ORCHARD INN
1401 N Miller Ave (98801)
Rates: $49-$77
(509) 662-3443
(800) 368-4571

RED LION HOTEL
1225 N Wenatchee Ave (98801)
Rates: $79-$109
(509) 663-0711
(800) 733-5466

SUPER 8 MOTEL
1401 N Miller St (98801)
Rates: $69-$89
(509) 662-3443
(800) 800-8000

UPTOWNER MOTEL
101 N Mission St (98801)
Rates: $40-$55
(509) 663-8516
(800) 288-5279

VALUE INN
1640 N Wenatchee Ave (98801)
Rates: $42-$79
(509) 663-8115
(800) 668-1862

WELCOME INN
232 N Wenatchee Ave (98801)
Rates: $40-$55
(509) 663-7121
(800) 561-8856

WESTPORT
ALASKAN MOTEL
708 N First (98595)
Rates: n/a
(360) 268-9133

BREAKERS MOTEL
971 N Montesano St (98595)
Rates: $52-$70
(360) 268-0848

CHINOOK MOTEL
707 N Montesano St (98595)
Rates: n/a
(360) 268-9623

CRANBERRY MOTEL
920 S Montesano St (98595)
Rates: $30+
(360) 268-0807

GARDENS RESORT
725 S Montesano St (98595)
Rates: $42-$108
(360) 268-9200

GLENACRES INN B&B
222 N Montesano St (98595)
Rates: n/a
(360) 268-9391

HARBOR RESORT
871 Neddie Rose Dr (98595)
Rates: n/a
(360) 268-0169

ISLANDER MOTEL & CHARTERS
421 Westhaven & Neddie Rose (98595)
Rates: $50
(360) 268-9166
(800) 322-1740

MARINERS COVE
303 Ocean Ave (98595)
Rates: $49-$60
(360) 268-0531

OCEAN AVENUE INN
275 W Ocean Ave (98595)
Rates: $50-$145
(360) 268-9278
(888) 692-5262

WINDJAMMER HOTEL
461 E Pacific Ave (98595)
Rates: $40-$90
(360) 268-9351

WHIDBEY ISLAND
(Clinton)

HOME BY THE SEA COTTAGES
2388 E Sunlight Beach Rd (98236)
Rates: $155-$175
(360) 321-2964

NORTHWEST VACATION HOMES
6497 E Hunziker Ln (98236)
Rates: $100-$275
(360) 341-5005
(800) 544-4304

SUNSET COTTAGES
7358 /7359 Maxwelton Rd (98236)
Rates: 85-$175
(360) 579-1590

(Coupeville)

THE VICTORIAN HISTORIC B&B
602 N Main St (98239)
Rates: $65-$100
(360) 678-5305

(Freeland)

HARBOUR INN MOTEL
1606 E Main St (98249)
Rates: $65-$88
(360) 331-6900

(Langley)

DRAKE'S LANDING B&B
203 Wharf St (98260)
Rates: $65+
(360) 221-3999

THE INN AT LANGLEY
400 1st St (98260)
Rates: $235-$260
(360) 221-3033

ISLAND TYME B&B
4940 S Bayview Rd (98260)
Rates: $85-$140
(360) 221-5078
(800) 898-8963

(Oak Harbor)

ACORN MOTOR INN
3150 Hwy 20 (98277)
Rates: $44-$98
(360) 675-6646
(800) 280-6646

BEST WESTERN HARBOR PLAZA
33175 SR 20 (98277)
Rates: $99-$149
(360) 679-4567
(800) 927-5478

WHITE PASS
GAME RIDGE MOTEL & LODGE
27350 Hwy 12 (98937)
Rates: $39-$82
(509) 672-2212

WHITE SALMON
INN OF THE WHITE SALMON BED & BREAKFAST
172 W Jewett (98672)
Rates: $75-$115
(509) 493-2335
(800) 972-5226

WINLOCK
SUNRISE MOTEL
663 SR 505 (98596)
Rates: $38
(360) 785-4343

WINTHROP
BEST WESTERN CASCADE INN
960 Hwy 20 (98862)
Rates: $60-$179
(509) 996-3100
(800) 468-6754

PINE-NEAR MOTEL
350 Castle Ave (98862)
Rates: n/a
(509) 996-2391

RIVER RUN INN
27 Rader Rd (98862)
Rates: $70-$155
(509) 996-2173
(800) 757-2709

AREA CODES - If the local number doesn't connect, check for a new area code.

THE VIRGINIAN
808 N Cascade
Hwy (98862)
Rates: $75-$95
(509) 996-2535
(800) 854-2834

WINTHROP INN
960 SR 20 (98862)
Rates: $60-$95
(509) 996-2217

WOLFRIDGE RESORT
412B Wolf Creek
Rd (98862)
Rates: $44-$149
(509) 996-2828

WOODINVILLE
WILLOWS LODGE
14580 NE 145th St
(98072)
Rates: $260
(425) 424-3900

WOODLAND
LEWIS RIVER INN
1100 Lewis River
Rd (98674)
Rates: $49-$76
(360) 225-6257
(800) 543-4344

SCANDIA MOTEL
1123 Hoffman St
(98674)
Rates: $32-$42
(360) 225-8006

YAKIMA
BALI HAI MOTEL
710 N 1st St (98901)
Rates: $23-$43
(509) 452-7178

BEST WESTERN AHTANUM INN
2408 Rudkin Rd
(98903)
Rates: $79-$209
(509) 248-9700
(800) 348-9701

BEST WESTERN PEPPERTREE INN
1614 N 1st St
(98901)
Rates: $69-$179
(509) 453-8898
(800) 834-1649

CEDARS INN AND SUITES
1010 E A St
(98901)
Rates: $40-$65
(509) 452-8101

CLARION HOTEL
1507 N 1st St
(98901)
Rates: $49-$109
(509) 248-7850
(800) 252-7466

COMFORT SUITES
3702 Fruitvale
Blvd (98901)
Rates: $89-$149
(509) 249-1900
(800) 424-6423

DOUBLETREE INN YAKIMA VALLEY
1507 N 1st St
(98901)
Rates: $72-$109
(509) 248-7850
(800) 222-8733

HOLIDAY INN EXP
1001 East A St
(98901)
Rates: $74-$98
(509) 249-1000

NENDEL'S INN
1405 N 1st St
(98901)
Rates: $32-$66
(509) 453-8981
(800) 547-0106

NISKA'S INNS OF AMERICA
1022 N 1st St
(98901)
Rates: $35+
(509) 453-5615

OXFORD INN
1603 E Yakima
Ave (98901)
Rates: $65-$85
(509) 457-4444

OXFORD SUITES
1701 E Yakima
Ave (98901)
Rates: $95-$99
(509) 457-9000

QUALITY INN
12 E Valley Mall
Blvd (98903)
Rates: $59-$139
(509) 248-6924
(800) 424-6423

RAMADA LIMITED
418 N 1st St
(98901)
Rates: $69-$109
(509) 453-0391
(800) 272-6232

RED LION HOTEL-
607 E Yakima Ave
(98901)
Rates: $72-$129
(509) 248-5900
(800) 733-5466

SUN COUNTRY INN
1700 N 1st St
(98901)
Rates: $57-$76
(509) 248-5650

YELM
OG HOUSE BED & BREAKFAST
11249 Bald Hill Rd
(98597)
Rates: $95-$150
(360) 458-4385

PRAIRIE HOTEL
701 Prairie Park
Ln (98597)
Rates: $55-$110
(360) 458-8300

ZILLAH
COMFORT INN
911 Vintage Valley
Pkwy (98953)
Rates: $80-$161
(509) 829-3399
(800) 424-6423

AREA CODES - If the local number doesn't connect, check for a new area code.

WEST VIRGINIA

BARBOURS-VILLE

COMFORT INN
249 Mall Rd
(25504)
Rates: $53-$90
(304) 73702122
(800) 424-6423

BECKLEY

BECKLEY HOTEL
1940 Harper Rd
(25801)
Rates: $65-$200
(800) 274-6010

BEST WESTERN FOUR SEASONS INN
1939 Harper Rd
(25801)
Rates: $54-$99
(304) 252-0671
(800) 528-1234

CHARLES HOUSE MOTEL
223 S Heber St
(25801)
Rates: n/a
(304) 253-8318

COMFORT INN
1909 Harper Rd
(25801)
Rates: $49-$110
(304) 255-2161
(800) 424-6423

COUNTRY INN & SUITES
2120 Harper Rd
(25801)
Rates: $83-$160
(304) 252-5100
(800) 458-4000

HOWARD JOHNSON EXPRESS INN
1907 Harper Rd
(25801)
Rates: $70-$110
(304) 255-5900
(800) 446-4656

MICROTEL INN
2130 Harper Rd
(25801)
Rates: $49-$89
(304) 256-2000

PARK INN & SUITES
134 Harper Park Dr (25801)
Rates: $49-$89
(304) 255-9091
(800) 670-7275

BERKELEY SPRINGS

THE GATEHOUSE VACATION RENTAL AT SLEEPY CREEK
126 Camp Harmison Dr (25411)
Rates: n/a
(304) 258-9282

PARK HAVEN MOTOR LODGE
Rt 1, Box 298,
Rt 522 S (25411)
Rates: n/a
(304) 258-1734

BLUEFIELD

EAST RIVER MOUNTAIN INN
3175 E Cumberland Rd (24701)
Rates: $56-$62
(304) 325-5421

ECONO LODGE
3400 Cumberland Rd (24701)
Rates: $37-$135
(304) 327-8171
(800) 424-6423

HOLIDAY INN ON THE HILL
3350 Big Laurel Hwy (24701)
Rates: $100
(304) 325-6170
(800) 465-4329

BRIDGEPORT

HEDGES MOTEL
Rt 50 East (26330)
Rates: n/a
(304) 842-2811

HOLIDAY INN
100 Lodgeville Rd (26330)
Rates: $79-$90
(304) 842-5411
(800) 465-4329

KNIGHTS INN
1235 W Main St (26330)
Rates: $52-$86
(304) 842-7115
(800) 843-5644

SLEEP INN
115 Tolley Rd (26330)
Rates: $59-$99
(304) 842-1919
(800) 753-3746

BUCKHANNON

BAXA HOTEL-MOTEL
21 N Kanawha St (26201)
Rates: $29-$38
(304) 472-2500

COLONIAL MOTEL
24 N Kanawha St (26201)
Rates: n/a
(304) 472-3000

BURNSVILLE

BURNSVILLE MOTEL
5th & Main (26335)
Rates: $26-$31
(304) 853-2918

CHAPMANVILLE

RODEWAY INN
SR 10 & US 119 (25508)
Rates: $48-$85
(304) 855-7182
(800) 424-6423

CHARLES TOWN

NORTH GATE INN
188 Patrick Henry Way (25414)
Rates: n/a
(304) 725-1402

CHARLESTON

COMFORT SUITES
107 Alex Ln (25304)
Rates: $79-$139
(304) 925-1171
(800) 424-6423

COUNTRY INN & SUITES
105 Alex Ln (25304)
Rates: $84-$119
(304) 925-4300
(800) 456-4000

DAYS INN
6400 MacCorkle Ave (25304)
Rates: $50-$85
(304) 925-1010
(800) 329-7466

HOLIDAY INN EXP CIVIC CENTER
100 Civic Center Dr (25301)
Rates: $99
(304) 345-0600
(800) 465-4329

KNIGHTS INN
6401 MacCorkle Ave SE (25304)
Rates: $39-$58
(304) 925-0451
(800) 843-5644

MOTEL 6
6311 MacCorkle Ave SE (25304)
Rates: $35-$50
(304) 925-0471
(800) 466-8356

RED ROOF INN
6305 MacCorkle Ave SE (25304)
Rates: $45-$67
(304) 925-6953
(800) 843-7663

SLEEP INN
2772 Pennsylvania Ave (25302)
Rates: $59-4129
(304) 345-5111
(800) 424-6423

CLARKSBURG

TERRACE MOTEL
1202 E Pike St (26301)
Rates: n/a
(304) 622-6161

CROSS LANES

COMFORT INN
102 Racer Dr (25313)
Rates: $65-$150
(800) 798-7886
(800) 424-6423

MOTEL 6
330 Goff Mountain Rd (25313)
Rates: $37-$50
(304) 776-5911
(800) 466-8356

DAVIS

DEERFIELD VILLAGE RESORT-CANAAN VALLEY
Cortland Lane (26260)
Rates: $140-$275
(304) 866-4698
(800) 342-3217

ELKINS

BEST COUNTRY INN & SUITES
Rt 219 & 250 S (26241)
Rates: $51-$120
(304) 636-7711

CHEAT RIVER LODGE & INN
Rt 1, Box 115 (26241)
Rates: $68-$83
(304) 636-2301

AREA CODES - If the local number doesn't connect, check for a new area code.

DAYS INN
1200 Harrison Ave
(26241)
Rates: $63-$99
(304) 637-4667
(800) 329-7466

ECONO LODGE
US 33 E (26241)
Rates: $45-$75
(304) 636-5311
(800) 424-6423

**MOUNTAIN
SPLENDOR INN**
P. O. Box 1802
(26241)
Rates: n/a
(304) 636-8111

SUPER 8 MOTEL
350 Beverly Pike
(26241)
Rates: $49-$65
(304) 636-6500
(800) 800-8000

FAIRMONT
DAYS INN
228 Middletown
Rd (26554)
Rates: $44-$90
(304) 366-5995
(800) 329-7466

HOLIDAY INN
930 E Old Grafton
Rd (26554)
Rates: $72-$109
(304) 366-5500
(800) 465-4329

RED ROOF INN
50 Middletown
Rd (26554)
Rates: $45-$61
(304) 366-6800
(800) 843-7663

SUPER 8 MOTEL
2208 Pleasant
Valley Rd (26554)
Rates: $51-$79
(304) 363-1488
(800) 800-8000

FALLING WATERS
HOLIDAY INN EXP
1220 TJ Jackson Dr
(25419)
Rates: $69-$79
(304) 274-6100
(800) 465-4329

FAYETTEVILLE
**COMFORT INN-
NEW RIVER**
US 19 & Laurel
Creek Rd (25840)
Rates: $40-$109
(304) 574-3443
(800) 424-6423

**WHITE HOUSE
BED & BREAKFST**
120 Fayette Ave
(25840)
Rates: $70-$110
(304) 574-1400

FRANKLIN
MT. STATE MOTEL
Rt 220 North
(26807)
Rates: n/a
(304) 358-2084

FROST
**THE INN AT
MOUNTAIN
QUEST**
Rt 92 Frost (24954)
Rates: $85-$140
(304) 799-7267

HARPERS FERRY
**QUALITY INN &
CONFERENCE
CENTER**
4328 William L
Wilson Frwy
(25425)
Rates: $70-$158
(304) 535-6302
(800) 424-7423

HILLSBORO
THE CURRENT
Denmar Rd
(24946)
Rates: n/a
(304) 653-4722

HUNTINGTON
RED ROOF INN
5190 US 60 E
(25705)
Rates: $40-$74
(304) 733-3737
(800) 843-7663

HURRICANE
RED ROOF INN
500 Putnam
Village Dr (25526)
Rates: $40-$55
(304) 757-6392
(800) 843-7663

SUPER 8 MOTEL
419 Hurricane
Creek Rd (25526)
Rates: $50
(304) 562-3346
(800) 800-8000

JANE LEW
**WILDERNESS
PLANTATION INN**
Rt 7, Berlin Rd
(26378)
Rates: $49-$70
(304) 884-7806

KEYSER
KEYSER INN
Rt 220 S (26726)
Rates: $54-$65
(304) 788-0913

LEWISBURG
BRIER INN
540 N Jefferson St
(24901)
Rates: $54-$80
(304) 645-7722

DAYS INN
635 N Jefferson St
(24901)
Rates: $50-$140
(304) 645-2345
(800) 329-7466

**ECONO LODGE
FORT SAVANNAH**
204 N Jefferson St
(24901)
Rates: $49-$129
(304) 645-3055
(800) 424-6423

RODEWAY INN
107 W Fair St
(24901)
Rates: $45-$65
(304) 645-7070
(800) 424-6423

SUPER 8 MOTEL
550 N Jefferson St
(24901)
Rates: $51-$84
(304) 647-3188
(800) 800-8000

MARLINTON
**MARLINTON
MOTOR INN**
US 219 N (24954)
Rates: $38+
(304) 799-4711

MARTINSBURG
DAYS INN
209 Viking Way
(25401)
Rates: $59-$79
(304) 263-1800
(800) 329-7466

ECONO LODGE
5595 Hammonds
Mill Rd (25401)
Rates: $52-$62
(304) 274-2181
(800) 424-6423

ECONOMY INN
1193 Winchester
(25401)
Rates: $38-$60
(304) 267-2994

HAMPTON INN
975 Foxcroft Ave
(25401)
Rates: $59-$75
(304) 267-2900
(800) 426-7866

HOLIDAY INN
301 Foxcroft Ave
(25401)
Rates: $69-$89
(304) 267-5500
(800) 465-4329

KNIGHTS INN
1599 Edwin Miller
Blvd (25401)
Rates: $47-$75
(304) 267-2211
(800) 843-5644

KRISTA LITE MOTEL
Rt 1 (25401)
Rates: $35-$39
(304) 263-0906

PIKESIDE MOTEL
2138 Winchester
Ave (25401)
Rates: n/a
(304) 263-5189

QUALITY INN
94 McMillan Ct
(25401)
Rates: $59-$109
(304) 263-8811
(800) 424-6423

RELAX INN
1022 Winchester
(25401)
Rates: $30-$59
(304) 263-0831

SCOTTISH INNS
1024 Winchester
Ave (25401)
Rates: $35-$59
(304) 267-2935
(800) 251-1962

MINERAL WELLS
MICROTEL INN
104 Old Nicolette
Rd (26150)
Rates: $43-$65
(304) 489-3892
(888) 771-7171

MORGAN-TOWN
COMFORT INN
225 Comfort Inn
Dr (26508)
Rates: $59-$140
(304) 296 9364
(800) 424-6423

**ECONO LODGE
COLISEUM**
3506 Monongahela
Blvd (26505)
Rates: $49-$120
(304) 599-8181
(800) 424-6423

FRIENDS INN
452 Country Club
Rd (26505)
Rates: $45-$75
(304) 599-4850
(800) 453-4511

RAMADA INN
US Rt 119 at
I-79 & 68 (26505)
Rates: $75-$115
(304) 296-3431
(800) 272-6232

NEW CREEK
**TOLL GATE
MOTEL**
HC 72, Box 121
(26743)
Rates: $27-$34
(304) 788-5100

NITRO
ECONO LODGE
4115 1st Ave
(25143)
Rates: $39-$65
(304) 755-8341
(800) 424-6423

AREA CODES - If the local number doesn't connect, check for a new area code.

OCEANA

OCEANA MOTEL
Cook Parkway
(24870)
Rates: n/a
(304) 682-6186

PARKERSBURG

ECONO LODGE
1954 E 7th St
(26101)
Rates: $44-$125
(304) 428-7500
(800) 424-6423

EXPRESSWAY MOTOR INN
6333 Emerson Ave
(26101)
Rates: $38-$56
(304) 385-1851

MOTEL 6
3604 7th St (26101)
Rates: $37-$55
(304) 424-5100
(800) 466-8356

RED ROOF INN
3714 E 7th St
(26101)
Rates: $50-$66
(304) 485-1741
(800) 843-7663

THE STABLES LODGE
3604 7th St (26101)
Rates: n/a
(304) 424-5100

PENCE SPRINGS

PENCE SPRINGS HOTEL
P. O. Box 90
(24962)
Rates: $45-$300
(304) 445-2606

PHILIPPI

PHILIPPI LODGING
Rt 250 (26416)
Rates: $45-$64
(304) 457-5888

PRINCETON

DAYS INN
347 Meadowfield
Ln (24740)
Rates: $48-$78
(304) 425-8100
(800) 329-7466

SLEEP INN
1015 Oakvale Rd
(24740)
Rates: $50-$125
(304) 431-2800
(800) 424-6423

TOWN-N-COUNTRY MOTEL
805 Oakvale Rd
(24740)
Rates: $33-$55
(304) 425-8156

RICHWOOD

FOUR SEASONS LODGE
39-55 Rt Marlinton
Rd (26261)
Rates: n/a
(304) 846-4605

RIPLEY

BEST WESTERN MCCOYS INN
701 W Main St
(25271)
Rates: $59-$79
(304) 372-9122
(800) 528-1234
(800) 288-9122

SUPER 8 MOTEL
102 Duke Dr (25271)
Rates: $48-$70
(304) 372-8880
(800) 800-8000

SEEBERT

GREENBRIER RIVER CABINS
Greenbrier River
Bike Trail (24946)
Rates: n/a
(304) 653-4646
(800) 225-5982

SOUTH CHARLESTON

RAMADA PLAZA HOTEL
400 2nd Ave
(25303)
Rates: $85-$94
(304) 744-4641
(800) 272-6232

STAR CITY

ECONO LODGE-COLISEUM
3506 Monongahela
Blvd (26505)
Rates: $59-$66
(304) 599-8181
(800) 553-2666

HOLIDAY INN
1400 Saratoga Ave
(26505)
Rates: $63-$129
(304) 599-1680
(800) 465-4329

SUMMERSVILLE

BEST WESTERN SUMMERVILLE LAKE MOTOR LODGE
1203 S Broad St
(26651)
Rates: $45-$85
(304) 872-6900
(800) 528-1234
(800) 214-9551

COMFORT INN
903 Industrial Dr
N (26651)
Rates: $60-$145
(304) 872-6500
(800) 424-6423

SLEEP INN
701 Professional
Park Dr (26651)
Rates: $44-$105
(304) 872-4500
(800) 424-6423

SUPER 8 MOTEL
306 Merchants
Walk (26651)
Rates: $49-$64
(304) 872-4888
(800) 800-8000

SUTTON

ELK MOTOR CT
35 Camden Ave
(26601)
Rates: n/a
(304) 765-7173

TRIADELPHIA

HOLIDAY INN EXP
I-70 Exit 11 Dallas
Pike (26059)
Rates: $69-$129
(304) 547-1380
(800) 465-4329

WEIRTON

HOLIDAY INN
350 Three Springs
Dr (26062)
Rates: $99-$159
(304) 723-5522
(800) 465-4329

WESTON

COMFORT INN
2906 US 33 E
(26452)
Rates: $53-$99
(304) 269-7000
(800) 424-6423

SUPER 8 MOTEL
12 Market Pl
(26452)
Rates: $50-$66
(304) 269-1086
(800) 800-8000

WHEELING

DAYS INN
I-70 & Dallas Pike,
Ex 11 (26059)
Rates: $45-$100
(304) 547-0610
(800) 329-7466

WHITE SULPHUR SPRINGS

THE HISTORIC JAMES WYLIE HOUSE
208 E Main
St (24986)
Rates: n/a
(304) 536-9444
(800) 870-1613

OLD WHITE MOTEL
865 E Main St
(24986)
Rates: $30-$65
(304) 536-2441

AREA CODES - If the local number doesn't connect, check for a new area code.

WISCONSIN

ABBOTSFORD

CEDAR CREST MOTEL
207 N 4th St (54405)
Rates: $24-$38
(715) 223-3661

HOME MOTEL
412 N 4th St (54405)
Rates: $34-$45
(715) 223-6343

SLEEP INN
300 E Elderberry Rd (54405)
Rates: $49-$89
(715) 223-3337
(800) 424-6423

ABRAMS

FOSTER FARM HOUSE VACATION HOME
4991-Hwy 41 (54101)
Rates: $50-$75
(414) 826-7570

ALGOMA

ALGOMA BEACH MOTEL & CONDOS
1500 Lake St (54201)
Rates: $59-$259/ $594-$1554 Wkly
(920) 487-2828
(888) 254-6621

BARBIE ANN MOTEL
533 4th St (54201)
Rates: $30-$45
(920) 487-5561

RIVER HILLS MOTEL
820 N Water St (54201)
Rates: $45-$70
(920) 487-3451
(800) 236-3451

SCENIC SHORE INN MOTEL
2221 Lake St (54201)
Rates: $44-$59
(920) 487-3214

WEST WIND SHORES COTTAGES
N6870 Hwy 42 (54201)
Rates: $52-$87
(920) 487-5867

ALLENTON

ADDISON HOUSE BED & BREAKFAST
6373 Hwy 175 (53002)
Rates: $45-$85
(262) 629-9993

ALMA

TRITSCH HOUSE BED & BREAKFAST
601 S 2nd St (54610)
Rates: $65-$115
(608) 685-4090

AMBERG

ITALIAN INN
N14835 Hwy 141 (54104)
Rates: $35-$45
(715) 759-5231

ANTIGO

SUPER 8 MOTEL
535 Century Ave (54409)
Rates: $49-$99
(715) 623-4188
(800) 800-8000

APPLETON

BEST WESTERN MIDWAY HOTEL
3033 W College Ave (54914)
Rates: $75-$114
(920) 731-4141
(800) 528-1234
(800) 482-3879

BUDGETEL INN
3920 W College Ave (54914)
Rates: $89-$199
(920) 734-6070

CANDLEWOOD SUITES
4525 W College Ave (54914)
Rates: $65-$95
(920) 739-8000

COMFORT SUITES-COMFORT DOME
3809 W Wisconsin Ave (54914)
Rates: $89-$250
(920) 730-3800
(800) 424-6423

COUNTRY INN
355 Fox River Dr (54915)
Rates: $79-$179
(920) 830-3240
(800) 456-4000

EXEL INN
210 N Westhill Blvd (54914)
Rates: $35-$80
(920) 733-5551
(800) 367-3935

MICROTEL INN
321 Metro Dr (54915)
Rates: $44-$78
(920) 997-3121
(888) 771-7171

RESIDENCE INN BY MARRIOTT
310 Metro Dr (54915)
Rates: $110-$145
(920) 954-0570
(800) 331-3131

ROADSTAR INN
3623 W College Ave (54914)
Rates: $37-$85
(920) 731-5271

SNUG INN MOTEL
3437 N Richmond (54914)
Rates: $40-$70
(920) 739-7316
(800) 236-4444

WOODFIELD SUITES
3730 W College Ave (54914)
Rates: $89-$209
(920) 734-7777
(800) 338-0008

ARBOR VITAE

BUCKHORN LODGE & MOTEL
1720 Buckhorn Rd (54568)
Rates: $50-$150/ $330-$830 Wkly
(715) 356-5090

ARCADIA

RKD MOTEL
915 E Main St (54612)
Rates: $40-$60
(608) 323-3338
(888) 812-3338

ASHLAND

AMERICINN
3009 E Lakeshore Dr (54806)
Rates: $79-$199
(715) 682-9950
(800) 634-3444

ASHLAND MOTEL
2300 W Lakeshore Dr (54806)
Rates: $33-$73
(715) 682-5503
(877) 682-5503

BAYVIEW MOTEL
2419 E Lakeshore Dr (54806)
Rates: $25-$55
(715) 682-5253
(800) 249-3200

CREST MOTEL
115 Sanborn Ave (54806)
Rates: $35-$65
(715) 682-6603
(800) 657-1329

HOTEL CHEQUAMEGON
101 W Lakeshore Dr (54806)
Rates: $60-$155
(715) 682-9095
(800) 946-5555

LAKE AIRE MOTOR INN
101 E Lakeshore Dr (54806)
Rates: $45-$95
(715) 682-4551

LAKESIDE MOTEL
1706 W Lakeshore Dr (54806)
Rates: $20-$60
(715) 682-4575

SUPER 8 MOTEL
1610 W Lakeshore Dr (54806)
Rates: $53-$145
(715) 682-9377
(800) 800-8000

TOWN MOTEL
920 W Lakeshore Dr (54806)
Rates: $39-$59
(715) 682-5555

BAILEYS HARBOR

BAILEYS HARBOR RIDGES RESORT & LAKEVIEW SUITE
8252 Hwy 57 (54202)
Rates: $52-$210
(920) 839-2127
(800) 328-1710

JOURNEY'S END MOTEL
8271 Journey's End Lane (54202)
Rates: $50-$150
(920) 839-2887
(800) 944-3582

SANDS RESORT MOTEL
2371 Ridges Dr (54202)
Rates: $50-$110
(414) 839-2401

BALDWIN

AMERICINN
500 Baldwin Plaza Dr (54002)
Rates: $69-$154
(715) 684-5888
(800) 634-3444

AREA CODES - If the local number doesn't connect, check for a new area code.

SUPER 8 MOTEL
2110 10th Ave
(54002)
Rates: $63-$78
(715) 684-2700
(800) 800-8000

BALSAM LAKE

BALSAM LAKE MOTEL
501 W Main St
(54810)
Rates: $34-$45
(715) 485-3501

FOX DEN MOTEL & RESORT
101 County Rd 1
(54810)
Rates: $35-$80
(715) 485-3400

SUNSET VIEW RESORT
701 Pearson Rd
(54810)
Rates: $55-$75
(715) 485-3178

BARABOO

CAMPUS INN MOTEL
750 W Pine St
(53913)
Rates: $49-$200
(608) 356-8366
(800) 421-4748

DEVIL'S LAKE RESORT
S 5798 Old Lake Rd (53913)
Rates: $80-$160/
$395-$700 Wkly
(608) 356-6757

4 WINDS MOTEL
S 4090 A Hwy 12
(53913)
Rates: $35-$100
(608) 356-9481

GARDEN GATE B&B
220 8th St (53913)
Rates: $65-$120
(608) 356-0963

LOG LODGE MOTEL
830 W Pine St
(53913)
Rates: $40-$140
(608) 356-6552

NORDIC PINES RESORT & CAMP-GROUND
E11740 Cty. DL
(53913)
Rates: $76-$148
(608) 356-5810

PARK PLAZA HOTEL
626 W Pine St
(53913)
Rates: $76-$123
(608) 356-6422

SILVER DALE RESORT
E11878 Hwy DL
(53913)
Rates: $67-$97/
$300-$485 Wkly
(608) 356-4004

SPINNING WHEEL MOTEL
809 8th St (53913)
Rates: $30-$95
(608) 356-3933
(800) 360-5003

SUNSET RESORT B&B
HCR 61 Box 6325
(54873)
Rates: $55-$65
(608) 795-2449

SWANSON'S DOWNTOWN MOTOR COURT
414 8th Ave
(53913)
Rates: $29-$60
(608) 356-4005

THUNDERBIRD MOTOR INN
1013 8th St (53913)
Rates: $40-$125
(608) 356-7757
(800) 233-0827

BAYFIELD

APPLE TREE INN B&B
Rt 1, Box 251
(54814)
Rates: $85-$95
(715) 779-5572
(800) 400-6532

BAY VILLA MOTEL
Rte 1 Box 33
(54814)
Rates: $48-$84
(715) 779-3252

HARBOR'S EDGE MOTEL
33 N Front St
(54814)
Rates: $59-$129
(715) 779-3962

MORNING GLORY B&B
119 S 6th St
(54814)
Rates: $60-$77
(715) 779-5621

SEAGULL BAY MOTEL
325 S 7th St
(54814)
Rates: $60-$90
(715) 779-5558

SUPERIOR BEACH-SIDE COTTAGES
83650 Hwy 13 S
(54814)
Rates: $69-$250
(715) 779-5123
(800) 379-0564

WINFIELD INN & GARDENS
1225 E Lynde Ave
(54814)
Rates: $48-$220
(715) 779-3252

BEAVER DAM

AMERICINN LODGE & SUITES
325 Seippel Blvd
(53916)
Rates: $70-$147
(920) 356-9000
(800) 634-3444

GRAND VIEW MOTEL
1510 N Center
(53916)
Rates: $24-$40
(920) 885-9208

SUPER 8 MOTEL
711 Park Ave
(53916)
Rates: $50-$77
(920) 887-8880
(800) 800-8000

BELGIUM

THE LAKE CHURCH INN
680 County Rd D
(53004)
Rates: $42-$62
(262) 285-3475

QUARRY INN MOTEL
690 Hwy D
(53004)
Rates: $29-$57
(414) 285-3475

BELOIT

BELOIT INN
500 Pleasant St
(53511)
Rates: $89-$139
(608) 362-8800

COMFORT INN
2786 Milwaukee Rd (53511)
Rates: $54-$109
(608) 362-2666
(800) 424-6423

DRIFTWOOD MOTEL
1826 Riverside Dr
(53511)
Rates: $26-$36
(608) 364-4081

ECONO LODGE
2956 Milwaukee Rd (53511)
Rates: $42-$59
(608) 364-4000
(800) 424-6423

IKE'S MOTEL
114 Dearborn Ave
(53511)
Rates: $30-$60
(608) 362-3423

SUPER 8 MOTEL
3002 Milwaukee Rd (53511)
Rates: $54-$79
(608) 365-8680
(800) 800-8000

BERLIN

BEST WESTERN COUNTRYSIDE
227 Ripon Rd
(54923)
Rates: $69-$119
(920) 361-4441
(800) 528-1234
(800) 555-7954

BIRCHWOOD

BIRCHWOOD MOTEL
601 E Hwy 48
(54817)
Rates: $55-$60
(715) 354-7706

LINCOLNWOOD RESORT
N 1075 Eastside Rd (54817)
Rates: $95-$150/
$500-$810 Wkly
(715) 354-3533

BLACK RIVER FALLS

BEST WESTERN-ARROWHEAD LODGE & SUITES
600 Oasis Rd
(54615)
Rates: $53-$199
(715) 284-9471
(800) 528-1234
(800) 284-9471

DAYS INN
919 Hwy 54
(54615)
Rates: $59-$135
(715) 284-4333
(800) 329-7466

FALLS ECONOMY MOTEL
512 E 2nd St
(54615)
Rates: $35-$125
(715) 284-9919

PINES MOTOR LODGE
I-94 & Hwy 12 N
(54615)
Rates: $35-$50
(715) 284-5311
(800) 345-7463

RIVER CREST RESORT
N 6978 Hwy 12
(54615)
Rates: $59-$79/
$285-$385 Wkly
(715) 284-4763
(800) 863-4764

BLOOMER

BLOOMER INN & SUITES
Hwy 53 & 40
(54724)
Rates: $40-$105
(715) 568-3234
(800) 322-7995

OASIDE MOTEL
2407 Woodard Dr
(54724)
Rates: $36-$75
(715) 568-3234
(800) 322-7995

AREA CODES - If the local number doesn't connect, check for a new area code.

TWI-LITE MOTEL
18981 Hwy 40
(54724)
Rates: $30-$45
(715) 568-5200

BOSCOBEL
HUBL'S MOTEL
41120 Hwy 60
(53805)
Rates: $39-$79
(608) 375-4277

SANDS MOTEL
Hwy 61 N (53805)
Rates: $30-$61
(608) 375-4167

BOULDER JUNCTION
EVERGREEN LODGE
6235 Evergreen Ln
(54512)
Rates: $65-$170/
$500-$1215 Wkly
(715) 385-2132

WHITE BIRCH VILLAGE RESORT COTTAGES
8746 Hwy K East
(54512)
Rates: $700-$1600
Weekly
(715) 385-2182

WILDCAT LODGE
10016 Kitten Ln
(54512)
Rates: $75-$140/
$525-$1420 Wkly
(715) 385-2421

ZASTROWS LYNX LAKE LODGE
Hwy B (54512)
Rates: $249
(715) 686-2249
(800) 882-5969

BRANTWOOD
PALMQUIST'S FARM
Rt 1, Box 134
(54513)
Rates: $49-$59
(715) 564-2558

BRILLION
SANDMAN MOTEL
550 W Ryan St
(54110)
Rates: $40-$65
(920) 756-2106

BROOKFIELD
BAYMONT INN & SUITES
20391 W
Bluemound Rd
(53045)
Rates: $69-$159
(262) 782-9100
(877) BAYMONT

HOMESTEAD STUDIO SUITES
325 N Brookfield
Rd (53005)
Rates: $64-$784
(262) 782-9300
(888) 782-9473

MOTEL 6
20300 W
Bluemound Rd
(53045)
Rates: $36-$54
(262) 786-7337
(800) 466-8356

SHERATON HOTEL
375 S Moorland
Rd (53005)
Rates: $79-$209
(262) 786-1100
(800) 325-3535

TOWNEPLACE SUITES
600 N Calhoun Rd
(53005)
Rates: $59-$119
(262) 784-8450
(800) 257-3000

CABLE
LAKEWOODS RESORT & GOLF
21540 Cty Hwy M
(54821)
Rates: $52-$500
(715) 794-2561
(800) 255-5937

MOGASHEEN RESORT
23380 Missionary
Point Dr (54821)
Rates: $85-$250
(715) 794-2113

PILOT FISH INN MOTEL
Hwy M & Telemark
Rd (54821)
Rates: n/a
(715) 798-3474
(877) 798-3474

TELEMARK RESORT & CONV CTR
42225 Telemark
Rd (54821)
Rates: $69-$99
(715) 798-3999
(877) 798-4718

CADOTT
COUNTRYSIDE MOTEL
Hwys 29 & 27
(54727)
Rates: $38-$90
(715) 289-4000

CAMBRIDGE
BISON TRAIL B&B
W9443 E
Kroghville Rd
(53523)
Rates: $55-$75
(920) 648-5433

CAMERON
VIKING MOTEL
201 S 1st St (54822)
Rates: $60-$65
(715) 458-2111

CAMP DOUGLAS
K & K MOTEL
219 Hwy 12 & 16
(54618)
Rates: $45-$65
(608) 427-3100

CAMPBELSPORT
INN THE KETTLES B&B
W 977 Hwy F
(53010)
Rates: $70-$140
(920) 533-8602

NEWCASTLE PINES
N1499 Hwy 45
(53010)
Rates: $75-$95
(920) 533-5252

CASCADE
FOUR SEASONS RESORT
W9029 Crooked
Lake Dr (53011)
Rates: $70-$400
(262) 626-2934

TIMBERLAKE INN B&B
311 Madison Ave
(53011)
Rates: $75-$100
(920) 528-8481
(888) 528-8481

CASSVILLE
SAND BAR MOTEL
1115 E Bluff St
(53806)
Rates: $40-$60
(608) 725-5300

CECIL
FIRESIDE INN
400 Lake St
(54111)
Rates: $30-$119
(715) 745-6444
(800) 325-5289

CHETEK
RED LODGE RESORT
400 Russell St
(54728)
Rates: $80-$200
(715) 924-4113

TJ'S TIMBERLINE RESORT
1189 N Potato
Lake Rd (54728)
Rates: $70-$350
(715) 353-2238

WILDWOOD RESORT
865 - 23 3/4 St
(54728)
Rates: $50-$175
(715) 924-3259

CHILTON
BEST WESTERN STANTON INN
1101 E Chestnut St
(53014)
Rates: $70-$90
(920) 849-3600
(866) 855-5216

EAST SHORE INN
N3049 Hwy 151
(53014)
Rates: $80-$195
(920) 849-4230

THUNDERBIRD MOTEL
121 E Chestnut St
(53014)
Rates: $39-$70
(920) 849-4216

CHIPPEWA FALLS
AMERICINN MOTEL & SUITES
11 W South Ave
(54729)
Rates: $74-$134
(715) 723-5711
(800) 634-3444

COUNTRY VILLA MOTEL
Rt 3 Box 40
(54729)
Rates: $26-$40
(715) 288-6376

INDIANHEAD MOTEL
501 Summit Ave
(54729)
Rates: $38-$70
(715) 723-917
(800) 306-3049

LAKE AIRE MOTEL & MICRO MART
5732 Sandburst Ln
(54729)
Rates: $30-$50
(715) 723-2231
(800) 236-2231

PARK INN
1009 W Park Ave
(54729)
Rates: $69-$129
(715) 723-2281
(800) 446-9320

CLEAR LAKE
ATHLETIC CLUB MOTEL
200 Digital Dr
(54005)
Rates: $35-$65
(715) 263-3111

CLINTONVILLE
CLINTONVILLE MOTEL
297 S Main St
(54929)
Rates: $32-$48
(715) 823-6565

LANDMARK MOTEL
5 N Main St
(54929)
Rates: $43-$70
(715) 823-7899
(866) 830-6115

AREA CODES - If the local number doesn't connect, check for a new area code.

COLUMBUS

SUPER 8 MOTEL
219 Industrial Dr
(53925)
Rates: $54-$97
(920) 623-8800
(800) 800-8000

CRANDON

**MAIN
STREET INN**
400 S Lake Ave
(54520)
Rates: n/a
(715) 478-242
(866) 478-2210

CRIVITZ

**BONNIE BELL
MOTEL**
1450 US Hwy 141
(54114)
Rates: $31-$63
(715) 854-7395

THE PINES MOTEL
N 7968 Hwy 141
(54114)
Rates: $30-$60
(715) 854-7987

**SHAFFER PARK
MOTEL**
N 7217 Shaffer Rd
(54114)
Rates: $49-$135
(715) 854-2186

CROSS PLAINS

**BBB FARM BED &
BREAKFAST**
3883 Observatory
Rd (53528)
Rates: $80-$95
(608) 798-1123

CUMBERLAND

**ISLAND INN
MOTEL**
Hwy 63 N (54829)
Rates: $42-$90
(715) 822-8540

**WILD IRIS
SHORES**
2741 11th St
(54829)
Rates: $95-$120
(715) 822-8594

DANBURY

**DES MOINES
LAKE CABINS**
3119 Cherry Ln
(54830)
Rates: $65-$85
(715) 259-7931

DARLINGTON

**WALKER'S
TOWNE MOTEL**
245 W Harriet St
(53530)
Rates: n/a
(608) 776-2661

DE FOREST

HOLIDAY INN EXP
7184 Morrisonville
Rd (53532)
Rates: $69-$109
(608) 846-8686
(800) 465-4329

DE PERE

KRESS INN
300 Grant St
(54115)
Rates: $104-$139
(920) 403-5100

DELAFIELD

**BAYMONT INN
& SUITES**
2801 Hillside Dr
(53018)
Rates: $57-$125
(262) 646-8500
(877) 229-6668

DICKEYVILLE

PLAZA MOTEL
203 S Main (53808)
Rates: $32-$60
(608) 568-7562
(800) 545-4061

DODGEVILLE

**BEST WESTERN
QUIET HOUSE**
1130 N Johns St
(53533)
Rates: $54-$159
(608) 935-7739
(800) 528-1234

**PINE RIDGE
MOTEL**
405 CR YZ (53533)
Rates: $25-$65
(608) 935-3386

SUPER 8 MOTEL
1308 Johns St
(53533)
Rates: $45-$100
(608) 935-3888
(800) 800-8000

DRESSER

VALLEY MOTEL
211 State Rd 35
(54009)
Rates: $40-$85
(715) 755-2781
(800) 545-6107

DUNBAR

**RICHARDS'
MOTEL**
11466 W Hwy 8
(54119)
Rates: $28-$38
(715) 324-5444

DURAND

DURAND MOTEL
610-11th Ave
(54736)
Rates: $22-$35
(715) 755-2781
(800) 545-6107

DYCKESVILLE

**HIAWATHA
MOTOR INN**
1982 N Hwy 45
(54217)
Rates: $30-$80
(920) 479-6431
(800) 645-4370

**PINE-AIRE
RESORT**
4443 Chain
O'Lakes Rd
(54217)
Rates: $75-$200
(920) 479-9208
(800) 597-6777

**SUNSET BEACH
MOTEL & CONDO**
8931 N Hwy 57
(54217)
Rates: $39-$129
(920) 866-2978

EAGLE RIVER

**BEST WESTERN
DERBY INN**
Hwy 45 N (54521)
Rates: $70-$170
(715) 479-1600
(800) 528-1234
(888) 499-0403

DAYS INN
844 N Railroad St
(54521)
Rates: $64-$101
(715) 479-5151
(800) 329-7466
(800) 356-8018

**EDGEWATER INN &
RESORT**
5054 Hwy 70 W
(54521)
Rates: $40-$77
(715) 479-4011
(888) 334-3987

**GYPSY VILLA
RESORT**
950 Circle Dr
(54217)
Rates: $59-$488
(715) 479-8644
(800) 232-9714

**PINE-AIRE
RESORT &
CAMPGROUND
COTTAGES**
4443 Chain
O'Lakes Rd
(54521)
Rates: $88-$260
(715) 479-9208
(800) 597-6777

**RIVERSIDE MOTEL
RESORT**
5012 Hwy 70
(54521)
Rates: n/a
(800) 530-0019

**7 MILE PINECREST
RESORT**
11899 Knapp Rd
(54521)
Rates: $65-$230
(715) 479-8118
(800) 358-4467

**TRAVELERS' INN
MOTEL**
309 Wall St (54521)
Rates: $45-$80
(715) 479-4403
(800) 344-1194

**WHITE EAGLE
MOTEL**
4948 Hwy 70 W
(54521)
Rates: $40-$60
(715) 479-4426
(800) 782-6488

EAST TROY

COUNTRY INN
2921 O'Leary Ln
(53120)
Rates: $74-$135
(262) 642-2100
(800) 456-4000

MITTEN FARM B&B
W2452 County Rd
J (53120)
Rates: $60
(262) 642-5530

EAU CLAIRE

**AMERICINN
MOTEL & SUITES**
620 Texaco Dr
(54703)
Rates: $79-$149
(715) 874-4900
(800) 634-3444

**BEST WESTERN
WHITE HOUSE
INN**
1828 S Hastings
Way (54701)
Rates: $59-$130
(715) 832-8356
(877) 213-1600

COMFORT INN
3117 Craig Rd
(54701)
Rates: $59-$119
(715) 833-9798
(800) 424-6423

DAYS INN-WEST
6319 Traux Ln
(54703)
Rates: $59-$130
(715) 874-5550
(800) 329-7466

EAU CLAIRE MOTEL
3210 E Clairemont
Ave (54701)
Rates: $27-$41
(715) 835-5148
(800) 624-3763

ECONO LODGE
4608 Royal Dr
(54701)
Rates: $39-$125
(715) 833-8818
(800) 424-6423

EXEL INN
2305 Craig Rd
(54701)
Rates: $38-$110
(715) 834-3193
(800) 367-3935

AREA CODES - If the local number doesn't connect, check for a new area code.

**GRANDSTAY RESI-
DENTIAL SUITES**
5310 Prill Rd
(54701)
Rates: $67-$129
(715) 834-1700

GREEN TREE INN
516 Galloway St
(54703)
Rates: $35-$110
(715) 832-3411
(800) 236-3411

HEARTLAND INN
4075 Common-
wealth Ave (54701)
Rates: $65-$80
(715) 839-7100
(800) 334-3277

HIGHLANDER INN
1135 W MacArthur
Ave (54701)
Rates: $27-$35
(715) 835-2261

**HOLIDAY INN
CAMPUS AREA**
2703 Craig Rd
(54701)
Rates: $62-$129
(715) 835-2211
(800) 465-4329

**MAPLE MANOR
MOTEL**
2507 S Hastings
Way (54701)
Rates: $30-$45
(715) 834-2618
(800) 624-3763

**PARK INN
& SUITES**
3340 Mondovi Rd
(54701)
Rates: $69-$149
(715) 838-9989
(888) 634-5330

**PLAZA HOTEL
SUITES**
1202 W
Clairemont Ave
(54701)
Rates: $69-$199
(715) 834-3181
(800) 482-7829

**RAMADA INN
CONV CENTER**
205 S Barstow Ave
(54701)
Rates: $55-$110
(715) 835-6121
(800) 272-6232

EDGERTON
COMFORT INN
11102 Goede Rd
(53534)
Rates: $49-$149
(608) 884-2118
(800) 424-6423

**TOWNE EDGE
MOTEL**
1104 N Main St
(53534)
Rates: $30-$60
(608) 884-9328

EGG HARBOR
**COTTAGE
RETREAT**
4355 Cty T (54209)
Rates: $50-$360
(920) 743-0967

ELCHO
**KATCH'S PINE
POINT RESORT**
N12065 Post Lake
Dr (54428)
Rates: $70
(715) 275-4600

ELLISON BAY
**ANDERSON'S
RETREAT
COTTAGES**
12621 Woodland
Dr (54210)
Rates: $65-$95/
$495-$550 Wkly
(920) 854-2746

**MAPLE GROVE
MOTEL**
809 State Rd 42
(54210)
Rates: $55-$85
(920) 854-2587
(877) 448-4484

**TESKIE'S
COTTAGES**
970 Cottage Rd
(54210)
Rates: $88-$120
(920) 854-4063

ELLSWORTH
DAVID MOTEL
W7670 Hwy 10
(54011)
Rates: $50-$65
(715) 273-3333

ELM GROVE
**SLEEPY HOLLOW
MOTEL**
12600 W
Bluemound Rd
(53122)
Rates: $39-$110
(414) 782-8333
(800) 341-8000

ELROY
**ELROY VALLEY
INN**
Hwy 80 & 82
(53929)
Rates: $30-$50
(608) 462-8251

FENNIMORE
**FENMORE HILLS
MOTEL**
5814 Hwy 18 W
(53809)
Rates: $59-$135
(608) 822-3281

NAPPS MOTEL
645 12th St (53809)
Rates: $30-$50
(608) 822-3226
(888) 806-3226

FERRRYVILLE
**GRANDVIEW
MOTEL**
14812 Hwy 35
(54628)
Rates: $45-$85
(608) 734-3235

**MISSISSIPPI
HUMBLE BUSH
BED & BRAKFAST**
Hwy 35, Main St
(54628)
Rates: $65-$85
(608) 734-3022

FIFIELD
**BOYD'S MASON
LAKE RESORT**
N12351 Boyd's Rd
(54524)
Rates: $70-$112
(715) 762-3469

FISH CREEK
**JULIE'S PARK
CAFE & MOTEL**
4020 Hwy 42
(54212)
Rates: $41-$106
(920) 868-2999

FITCHBURG
**QUALITY INN &
SUITES**
2969 Cahill Main
(53711)
Rates: $79-$139
(608) 274-7200
(800) 424-6423

FOND DU LAC
**BAYMONT INN
& SUITES**
77 Holiday Lane
(54935)
Rates: $69-$250
(920) 921-4000
(877) 229-6668

BEST VALUE INN
738 W Johnson St
(54935)
Rates: $35-$100
(920) 923-6990

DAYS INN
107 N Pioneer Rd
(54937)
Rates: $35-$160
(920) 923-6790
(800) 329-7466

ECONO LODGE
649 W Johnson St
(54935)
Rates: $49-$120
(920) 923-2020
(800) 424-6423

**FOND DU LAC
KOA CMPGRND
COTTAGES**
W 5099 Hwy B
(54935)
Rates: $38
(920) 477-2300
(800) KOA-3912

HOLIDAY INN
625 W Rolling
Meadows Dr
(54935)
Rates: $90-$200
(920) 923-1440
(800) 465-4329

**LITTLE LAKE HOUSE
PROPERTIES**
N7921 Lakeshore
Dr (54935)
Rates: $150-$300/
$600-$2500 Wkly
(920) 923-9636

**MICROTEL INN
& SUITES**
US 41 & 151
(54935)
Rates: $44-$97
(920) 929-4000
(888) 771-7171

**NORTHWAY
MOTEL**
301 S Pioneer Rd
(54935)
Rates: $35-$65
(920) 921-7975

PIONEER MOTEL
195 N Pioneer Rd
(54935)
Rates: $30-$75
(920) 921-2181

**RAMADA PLAZA
HOTEL**
1 N Main St
(54935)
Rates: $59-$249
(920) 923-3000
(800) 272-6232
(800) 274-1712

**STRETCH,
EAT & SLEEP
MOTEL**
Hwy 41 & 100 E
(54935)
Rates: $27-$53
(920) 923-3131

SUPER 8 MOTEL
391 N Pioneer Rd
(54935)
Rates: $50-$125
(920) 922-1088
(800) 800-8000

FONTANA
**FONTANA
COUNTRY INN
& SUITES**
W 5869 Brick
Church Rd (53125)
Rates: $95-$195
(262) 275-2878

FORT ATKINSON
**BEST WESTERN
COURTYARD INN**
1225 Janesville
Ave (53538)
Rates: $55-$79
(920) 5636444
(800) 528-1234
(800) 992-6789

AREA CODES - If the local number doesn't connect, check for a new area code.

VILLA INN HOTEL
1255 Whitewater
Ave (53538)
Rates: $39-$99
(920) 568-4552

FRIENDSHIP

CAMELOT MOTEL
2262 Ctr Rd Z
(53934)
Rates: $36-$60
(608) 339-7505
(800) 668-3555

**DUCK CREEK
LODGE MOTEL**
1870 Duck Creek
Dr (53934)
Rates: $28-$48
(608) 339-3502
(800) 311-3502

**ISLAND RESORT
COTTAGES**
306 Hillwood
Lane (53934)
Rates: $60-$125
(608) 339-6725

GALESVILLE

SONIC MOTEL
W21278 Hwy 93
& 54 (54630)
Rates: $47-$65
(608) 582-2281
(800) 718-3886

GAYS MILLS

**UPPER PLACE
VACATION
COTTAGE**
RR 2 (54631)
Rates: $120-$200/
$525-$565 Wkly
(608) 588-7187

GERMANTOWN

HOLIDAY INN EXP
W 177 N9675
Riversbend Ln
(53022)
Rates: $89-1$59
(262) 255-1100
(800) 465-4329

SUPER 8 MOTEL
N96 W17490
County Line Rd
(53022)
Rates: $50-$75
(262) 255-0880
(800) 800-8000

GILLETT

**SLEEPY
HOLLOW MOTEL**
5 Hwy 22 E
(54124)
Rates: $40-$58
(920) 855-2727

GILLS ROCK

**HARBOR HOUSE
INN B&B**
12666 Hwy 42
(54210)
Rates: $69-$185
(920) 854-5196

**MAPLE GROVE
MOTEL**
809 SR 42 (54210)
Rates: $55-$85
(920) 854-2587

**WINDSIDE
COTTAGES**
12714 Hwy 42
(54210)
Rates: $75-$100
(920) 854-4871
(866) 518-3892

GLENDALE

**BAYMONT INN
NORTHEAST**
5110 N Port
Washington Rd
(53217)
Rates: $66-$100
(414) 964-8484
(877) 229-6668

**EXEL INN
NORTHEAST**
5485 N Port
Washington Rd
(53217)
Rates: $50-$91
(414) 961-7272
(800) 367-3935

**RESIDENCE INN
BY MARRIOTT**
7275 N Port
Washington Rd
(53217)
Rates: $149-$199
(414) 352-0070
(800) 331-3131

**WOODFIELD
SUITES**
5423 N Port
Washington Rd
(53217)
Rates: $100-$160
(414) 962-6767
(800) 338-0008

GORDON

**STRONG'S
RESORT**
13933 S Resort Rd
(54838)
Rates: $80-$120
(715) 376-2382

GRAFTON

**PORT MOTEL
OF GRAFTON**
2340 E Sauk Rd
(53024)
Rates: $30-$55
(262) 284-9964

GRANTSBURG

**CEDAR POINT
RESORT**
12480 Cedar Point
Ln (54840)
Rates: $75+
(715) 488-2224

**WOOD RIVER INN
MOTEL**
703 Hwy 70
(54840)
Rates: $45-$55
(715) 463-2541

GREEN BAY

A-1 TOWER MOTEL
2625 Humboldt
Rd (54311)
Rates: $36-$60
(920) 468-1242

AMERICINN
2032 Velp Ave
(54303)
Rates: $60-$140
(920) 434-9790
(800) 634-3444
(866) 889-9790

ARENA MOTEL
871 Lombardi Ave
(54311)
Rates: $40-$54
(920) 494-5636

BAY MOTEL
1301 S Military
Ave (54304)
Rates: $39-$70
(920) 494-3441
(888) 775-7590

BAYMONT INN
2840 S Oneida
(54304)
Rates: $63-$88
(920) 494-7887
(877) 229-6668

**BEST WESTERN
MIDWAY HOTEL**
780 Packer Dr
(54304)
Rates: $69-$150
(920) 499-3161
(800) 528-1234
(800) 482-3885

**BEST WESTERN
WASHINGTON
STREET INN**
321 S Washington
St (54301)
Rates: $69-$109
(920) 437-8771
(800) 528-1234
(800) 252-2952

COMFORT INN
2641 Ramada Way
(54304)
Rates: $60-$160
(920) 498-2060
(800) 424-6423

**COUNTRY INN
& SUITES**
2945 Allied St
(54304)
Rates: $74-$154
(920) 336-6600
(800) 456-4000

**DAYS INN-
CITY CENTER**
406 N Washington
St (54301)
Rates: $60-$125
(920) 435-4484
(800) 329-7466

**DAYS INN-
LAMBEAU FIELD**
1978 Holmgren
Way (54304)
Rates: $59-$116
(920) 498-8088
(800) 329-7466

EXEL INN
2870 Ramada Way
(54304)
Rates: $43-$110
(920) 499-3599
(800) 367-3935

**HOLIDAY INN-
CITY CENTRE**
200 Main St
(54301)
Rates: $92-$119
(920) 437-5900
(800) 465-4329

KRESS INN
300 Grant St
(54115)
Rates: $69-$139
(920) 403-5100
(800) 221-5070

MOTEL 6
1614 Shawano Ave
(54303)
Rates: $32-$44
(920) 494-6730
(800) 466-8356

**REGENCY SUITES
HOTEL**
333 Main St
(54302)
Rates: $85-$160
(920) 432-4555
(800) 236-3330

**RESIDENCE INN
BY MARRIOTT**
335 W St. Joseph
St (54301)
Rates: $99-$159
(920) 435-2222
(800) 331-3131

SUPER 8 MOTEL
2868 S Oneida St
(54304)
Rates: $53-$77
(920) 494-2042
(800) 800-8000

VALLEY MOTEL
116 N Military
Ave (54303)
Rates: $35-$44
(920) 494-3455

GREEN LAKE

DARTFORD INN
N 6264 Lawson Dr
(54941)
Rates: $35-$80
(920) 294-6546

HARSHAW

**SMITTY'S
IDLEWILD RESORT**
5320 Lakewood
Rd (54529)
Rates: $50-$65
(715) 277-2314

HARTFORD

SUPER 8 MOTEL
1539 E Sumner St
(53027)
Rates: $50-$95
(262) 673-7431
(800) 800-8000

AREA CODES - If the local number doesn't connect, check for a new area code.

HAYWARD

AMERICINN
15601 US Hwy 63 (54843)
Rates: $60-$140
(715) 634-2700
(800) 634-3444

BEST WESTERN NORTHERN PINE INN
9966 N State Rd 27 (54843)
Rates: $49-$119
(715) 634-4959
(800) 528-1234
(800) 777-7996

COMFORT SUITES
15586 County Rd B (54843)
Rates: $70-$165
(715) 634-0700
(800) 424-6423

EMPIRE LODGE
13180 N Empire Rd (54843)
Rates: $95-$130
(715) 462-3772

GHOST LAKE LODGE
Rt 7, Box 74501 (54843)
Rates: $95-$300
(715) 462-3939

HERMAN'S LANDING COTTAGES
8255 N Cty Rd CC (54843)
Rates: $90-$190/ $400-$940 Wkly
(715) 462-3626

MOOSE LAKE RESORT
7685 W Pine Point Rd (54843)
Rates: $160-$225
(715) 462-3706
(888) 462-3706

NELSON LAKE LANDING
13045 N Dam Rd (54843)
Rates: $72-$115
(715) 634-4175

NORTHLAND LODGE
9181 W Brandt Rd (54843)
Rates: $108-$359
(715) 462-3379

NORTHWOODS MOTEL
9854 N State Hwy 27 (54843)
Rates: $40-$105
(715) 634-8088
(800) 232-9202

PINE CREST RESORT COTTAGES
12459 N Town Hall Rd (54843)
Rates: $65-$105
(715) 462-3297

ROSS' TEAL LAKE LODGE
12425 N Ross Rd (54843)
Rates: $150-$590
(715) 462-3631

SUNSET LODGE-TEAL LAKE
Rt 7, Box 7405 (54843)
Rates: $65-$165
(715) 462-3757

SUPER 8 MOTEL
10444 N Hwy 27 S (54843)
Rates: $46-$90
(715) 634-2646
(800) 800-8000

TOTEM POLE LODGE & RESORT
9216 W Brandt Rd W (54843)
Rates: $110-$150
(715) 462-3757

VIRGIN TIMBER RESORT COTTAGES
10820 N Moose Lake Rd (54843)
Rates: $90-$162
(715) 462-3269

WHIPLASH LAKE RESORT
12721 N Upper "A" Rd (54843)
Rates: $118+
(715) 462-4302

WILDERNESS HAVEN RESORT COTTAGES
Rt 9, Box 9442 (54843)
Rates: $55-$85
(715) 634-1060

HAZELHURST

HAZELHURST INN
6941 Hwy 51 (54531)
Rates: $49-$60
(715) 356-6571

HILES

LITTLE PINE MOTEL & RESORT
RR 2, Box 655, Hwy 32 (54511)
Rates: $32-$75
(715) 649-3431

HILLSBORO

SLEEP INN
1212 High Ave (54634)
Rates: $58-$95
(608) 489-3000
(800) 424-6423

TIGER INN
629 High Ave (54634)
Rates: $49-$62
(608) 489-2918

HIXTON

MOTEL 95 & CAMPGROUND
I-94 & Hwy 95 (54635)
Rates: $28-$50
(715) 963-4311
(888) 668-3595

HORICON

ROYAL OAKS MOTEL
W4419 Hwy 33 (53032)
Rates: $30-$50
(920) 485-4489

HUDSON

COMFORT INN
811 Dominion Dr (54016)
Rates: $45-$120
(715) 386-6355
(800) 424-6423

ESCAPE BY THE LAKE B&B
922 Sally's Alley N (54016)
Rates: $129
(715) 381-2871

J.R. RANCH MOTEL
736 Hwy 12 (54016)
Rates: $30-$95
(715) 386-6190
(800) 386-6190

JEFFERSON-DAY HOUSE B&B
1109 3rd St (54016)
Rates: $99-$189
(715) 386-7111

ROYAL INN MOTEL
1509 Coulee Rd (54016)
Rates: $41-$80
(715) 386-2366

SUPER 8 MOTEL
808 Dominion Dr (54016)
Rates: $68-$160
(715) 386-8800
(800) 800-8000

HURLEY

DAYS INN
850 N 10th Ave (54534)
Rates: $59-$107
(715) 561-3500
(800) 329-7466

EAGLE BLUFF CONDO RENTALS
990 10th Ave N (54534)
Rates: $49-$258
(715) 561-2787
(800) 336-0973

HAVEN NORTH CONDOS
1075 LaRue Ct (54534)
Rates: $49-$249/ $239-$329 Wkly
(715) 561-5626
(888) 404-2836

IOLA

NORSEMAN HOUSE MOTEL
410 N Main St (54945)
Rates: $34-$65
(715) 445-3300

IRON RIVER

DELTA LODGE COTTAGES
Rt 2, Box 161 (54847)
Rates: $75-$250
(715) 372-4299

HERMITAGE SUPPER CLUB & RESORT
Rt 2, Box 48 (54847)
Rates: $69-$99
(715) 372-4580

JACKSON

COMFORT INN & SUITES
W227 N16890 Tillie Lake Ct (53037)
Rates: $69-$129
(262) 677-1133
(800) 424-6423

JANESVILLE

BAYMONT INN & SUITES
616 Midland Rd (53546)
Rates: $62-$70
(608) 758-4545
(877) 229-6668

BEST WESTERN OF JANESVILLE
3900 Milton Ave (53546)
Rates: $64-$179
(608) 756-4511
(800) 528-1234
(800) 334-4271

MICROTEL INN
3121 ,Wellington Pl (53546)
Rates: $ 46-$66
(608) 752-3121

MOTEL 6
3907 Milton Ave (53546)
Rates: $31-$37
(608) 756-1742
(800) 466-8356

REDWOOD MOTEL
3912 N Hackbarth Rd (53545)
Rates: $50-$85
(608) 756-4501

AREA CODES - If the local number doesn't connect, check for a new area code.

SCARLETT HOUSE VICTORIAN B&B
825 E Court St (53545)
Rates: $55-$120
(608) 754-8000

SELECT INN
3520 Milton Ave (53545)
Rates: $36-$60
(608) 754-0251

JEFFERSON

RODEWAY INN
1456 S Ryan Ave (53549)
Rates: $50-$190
(920) 674-4404
(800) 424-6423

JOHNSON CREEK

COLONIAL INN MOTEL
Hwy 26 & B (53038)
Rates: $24-$50
(414) 699-3518

DAYS INN
W 4545 Linmar Ln (53038)
Rates: $68-$90
(920) 699-8000
(800) 329-7466

KING ARTHUR'S INN
1 Hartwig Dr (53038)
Rates: $51-$99
(920) 699-4141

KAUKAUNA

SETTLE INN
1201 Maloney Dr (54130)
Rates: $50-$99
(920) 766-0088
(800) 831-4785

KENOSHA

COUNTRY INN
7011 122nd Ave (53140)
Rates: $80-$135
(262) 857-3680
(800) 456-4000

HOLIDAY INN EXP
5125 6th Ave (53140)
Rates: $89-$110
(262) 658-3281
(800) 465-4329

VALUE INN
7221 122nd Ave (53142)
Rates: $48-$80
(262) 857-2622

KEWASKUM

COUNTRY RIDGE INN B&B
4134 Ridge Rd (53040)
Rates: $55-$70
(262) 626-4853

THE DOCTORS INN B&B
1121 Fond du Lac Ave (53040)
Rates: $55-$75
(262) 626-2666

KEWAUNEE

COHO MOTEL
705 Main St (54216)
Rates: $35-$75
(920) 388-3565

THE HISTORIC KARSTEN INN
122 Ellis St (54216)
Rates: $59-$149
(920) 388-3800
(800) 277-2132

LA CROSSE

BEST WESTERN MIDWAY HOTEL
1836 Rose St (54603)
Rates: $64-$129
(608) 781-7000
(800) 528-1234
(877) 688-9260

BLUFF VIEW INN
3715 Mormon Coulee Rd (54601)
Rates: $27-$75
(608) 788-0600

DAYS INN
101 Sky Harbour Dr (54603)
Rates: $79-$94
(608) 783-1000
(800) 329-7466

EAGLE BLUFF MOTEL
2344 State Rd 16 (54603)
Rates: $39-$55
(608) 781-7381

EDGEWATER MOTEL
N5326 Hilltop Dr (54603)
Rates: $25-$60
(608) 783-2286

EXEL INN
2150 Rose St (54603)
Rates: $39-$100
(608) 781-0400
(800) 367-3935

GRANDSTAY RESIDENTIAL SUITES
525 Front St N (54601)
Rates: $80-$159
(608) 796-1615
(877) 388-STAY

GUEST HOUSE MOTEL
810 S 4th St (54601)
Rates: $45-$70
(608) 784-8840
(800) 274-6873

HEROLD'S MOTEL
3827 Mormon Coulee Rd (54603)
Rates: $30-$42
(608) 788-1065

MEDARY MOTEL
2344 SR 16 (54601)
Rates: $35-$42
(608) 781-7381

RADISSON HOTEL
200 Harborview Plaza (54601)
Rates: $89-$169
(608) 784-6680
(800) 333-3333

LA FARGE

BUCKEYE VIEW GUEST HOUSE & CABINS
S 3099 Wirts Rd (54639)
Rates: $65-$125
(608) 625-6212

LA POINTE

WOODS MANOR BED & BREAKFAST
933 Nebraska Row (54850)
Rates: $140-$250
(715) 747-3102
(800) 966-3756

LAC DU FLAMBEAU

DILLMAN'S BAY RESORT
3305 Sand Lake Ln (54538)
Rates: $55-$400
(715) 588-3143

TIMBER BAY RESORT
3315 Sand Lake Lodge (43438)
Rates: n/a
(715) 588-1207
(888) 395-0757

YMCA FAMILY CAMP NAWAKWA
13400 Camp Nawakwa Ln (54538)
Rates: $89-$129
(715) 588-7422

LADYSMITH

AMERICINN MOTEL & SUITES
800 W College AVe (54848)
Rates: $59-$129
(715) 532-6650
(800) 634-3444

BEST WESTERN EL RANCHO MOTEL
8500 W Flambeau Ave (54848)
Rates: $55-$80
(715) 532-6666
(800) 528-1234

DAVIS MOTEL
820 Miner Ave W & Hwy 7 (54848)
Rates: $34-$80
(715) 532-5576

HI-WAY 8 MOTEL
420 E Edgewood Ave (54848)
Rates: $32-$60
(715) 532-3346

LAKE DELTON

HO-CHUNK LODGE
131 Canyon Rd (53940)
Rates: $79-$149
(608) 254-2584
(800) 303-0265

PLAYDAY MOTEL
1781 Wisconsin Dells Pky (53940)
Rates: $59-$135
(608) 253-3961
(888) 339-3063

TRAVELODGE
10892 Fern Dell Rd (59340)
Rates: $45-$69
(608) 355-0700
(800) 578-7878

LAKE GENEVA

ALPINE MOTEL
682 Wells St (53147)
Rates: $35-$125
(262) 248-4264

BOULEVARD MOTEL
722 Wells St (53147)
Rates: $40-$110
(262) 248-8374

ELEVEN GABLES INN ON THE LAKE
493 Wrigley Dr (53147)
Rates: $89-$258
(262) 248-8393

LAKE GENEVA MOTEL
524 Wells St (53147)
Rates: $49-$125
(262) 248-3464

MARIA'S B&B
512 S Wells St (53147)
Rates: $100-$250
(262) 249-0632
(877) 249-0632

PINE TREE MOTEL
903 Wells St (53147)
Rates: n/a
(262) 248-4988

PLAZA MOTEL
304 Wells St (53147)
Rates: $40-$100
(262) 248-3049

ROSES BED & BREAKFAST
429 S Lake Shore Dr (53147)
Rates: $95-$155
(262) 248-4344
(888) 767-3262

LAKE NEBAGAMON

R & M CABINS
6873 S Eastlake Rd
(54849)
Rates: $45-$90
(715) 374-3184

LAKEWOOD

NORTH STAR MOTEL
15698 Hwy 32
(54138)
Rates: $39-$125
(715) 276-6351

WAUBEE LODGE RESORT MOTEL
18398 Waubee
Park Ln (54138)
Rates: $80-$110
(715) 276-6091
(800) 492-8233

LANCASTER

MARTHA'S B&B
7867 University
Farm Rd (53813)
Rates: $60
(608) 723-4711

PINE GROVE MOTEL
1415 S Madison St
(53813)
Rates: $40-$55
(608) 723-6411

LAND O' LAKES

SUNRISE LODGE
5894 W Shore Dr
(54540)
Rates: $55-$187
(715) 547-3684
(800) 221-9689

WHISPERING PINES RESORT
5932 W Shore Rd
(54540)
Rates: $60-$105
(715) 547-3600

LODI

BEST WESTERN COUNTRYSIDE INN
W 9250 Prospect
Dr (53555)
Rates: $59-$95
(608) 592-1450
(800) 528-1234

LODI VALLEY SUITES MOTEL
N 1440 Hwy 113
(53555)
Rates: $59-$125
(608) 592-7452

PRAIRIE GARDEN B&B
W13172 Hwy 188
(53555)
Rates: $55-$115
(608) 592-5187
(800) 380-8427

SUNSET RESORT COTTAGES
N2849 Lake Point
Dr (53555)
Rates: $65-$85
(608) 592-4880

LUBLIN

DEER TRAIL CABINS
W1030 County
Hwy A (54447)
Rates: $65-$85
(715) 669-3464
(888) 353-0828

LUCK

LUCK COUNTRY INN MOTEL
10 Robertson St
(54853)
Rates: $61-$94
(715) 472-2000
(800) 544-7396

LYNDON STATION

CROCKETT'S RESORT COTTAGES
N2884 28th Ave
(53944)
Rates: $16-$48
(608) 666-2040
(888) 621-4711

MADISON

AMERICINN LODGE & SUITES
101 W Broadway
(53716)
Rates: $75-$170
(608) 222-8601
(800) 634-3444

BAYMONT INN
8102 Excelsior Dr
(53717)
Rates: $75-$129
(608) 831-7711
(877) 229-6668

BEST WESTERN EAST TOWNE SUITES
4801 Annamark
Dr (53704)
Rates: $65-$95
(608) 244-2020
(800) 528-1234
(800) 950-1919

BEST WESTERN WEST TOWNE SUITES
650 Grand Canyon
Dr (53719)
Rates: $40-$109
(608) 833-4200
(800) 528-1234
(800) 8 47-7919

CLARION SUITES CENTRAL
2110 Rimrock Rd
(53713)
Rates: $84-$249
(608) 284-1234
(800) 424-6423

COLLINS HOUSE B&B
704 E Gorham St
(53703)
Rates: $85-$160
(608) 255-4230

COMFORT SUITES
1253 John Q
Hammons Dr
(53704)
Rates: $79-$240
(608) 836-3033
(800) 424-6423

CROWNE PLAZA-EAST TOWNE
4402 E
Washington Ave
(53704)
Rates: $89-$189
(608) 244-4703
(800) 227-6963
(800) 404-7630

DAYS INN
4402 E Broadway
Svc Rd (53704)
Rates: $68-$138
(608) 223-1800
(800) 329-7466

ECONO LODGE
4726 E
Washington Ave
(53704)
Rates: $39-$83
(608) 241-4171
(800) 424-6423

EXEL INN
4202 E Towne
Blvd (53704)
Rates: $44-$115
(608) 241-3861
(800) 367-3935

EXPO INN MOTEL
910 Ann St (53713)
Rates: $35-$47
(608) 251-6555

GRANDSTAY RESIDENTIAL SUITES
5317 High
Crossing Blvd
(53718)
Rates: $89-$139
(608) 241-2500

HOLIDAY INN
3841 E
Washington Ave
(53704)
Rates: $79-$138
(608) 244-2481
(800) 465-4329

HOLIDAY INN EXP
722 John Nolen Dr
(53713)
Rates: $74-$130
(608) 255-7400
(800) 465-4329

IVY INN HOTEL
2355 University
Ave (53705)
Rates: $68-$89
(608) 233-9717
(877) 489-4661

KNIGHTS INN
3438 Hwy 12 & 18
(53718)
Rates: $34-$64
(608) 226-9999
(800) 843-5644

MAYFLOWER MOTEL & LOUNGE
2500 Perry St
(53713)
Rates: $31-$59
(608) 256-0272

MERRILL SPRINGS INN MOTEL
5117 University
Ave (53704)
Rates: $34-$62
(608) 233-5357

MICROTEL INN
2139 E Springs Dr
(53704)
Rates: $40-$84
(608) 242-9000
(888) 771-7171
(888) 258-1283

MOTEL 6-NORTH
1754 Thierer Rd
(53704)
Rates: $34-$56
(608) 241-8101
(800) 466-8356

QUALITY INN & SUITES
2969 Cahill Main
(53711)
Rates: $69-$139
(608) 274-7200
(800) 424-6423

QUALITY INN-SOUTH
4916 E Broadway
(53716)
Rates: $69-$209
(608) 222-5501
(800) 424-6423

RED ROOF INN
4830 Hayes Rd
(53704)
Rates: $53-$72
(608) 241-1787
(800) 843-7663

RESIDENCE INN BY MARRIOTT
4862 Hayes Rd
(53704)
Rates: $95-$150
(608) 244-5047
(800) 331-3131

RESIDENCE INN BY MARRIOTT
501 D'Onofrio Dr
(53719)
Rates: $79-$170
(608) 833-8333
(800) 225-5466

ROADSTAR-WEST TOWNE
6900 Seybold Rd
(53719)
Rates: $44-$76
(608) 274-6900

SELECT INN
4845 Hayes Rd
(53704)
Rates: $44-$89
(608) 249-1815
(800) 641-1000

AREA CODES - If the local number doesn't connect, check for a new area code.

STAYBRIDGE SUITES
3301 City View Dr (53718)
Rates: $99-$129
(608) 241-2300
(800) 238-8000

SUPER 8 MOTEL
1602 W Beltline Hwy (53713)
Rates: $59-$99
(608) 258-8882
(800) 800-8000

WINGATE INN
3510 Mill Pond Rd (53704)
Rates: $79-$109
(608) 224-1500

WOODFIELD SUITES
5217 E Terrace Dr (53718)
Rates: $69-$149
(608) 245-0123
(800) 338-0008

MANITOWISH WATERS

BUTLER'S FOUR SEASONS RESORT
535 Alder Cir (54545)
Rates: $75-$95
(715) 543-2955

CHIPPEWA RETREAT
37 Deer Park Rd (54545)
Rates: n/a
(715) 543-8111

SLEIGHT'S WILDWOOD MOTEL
HC 2, Box 166 Wildwood Rd (54545)
Rates: $25-$100
(715) 543-2140

VOSS' BIRCHWOOD LODGE
P. O. Box 456 (54545)
Rates: $52-$79
(715) 543-8441

MANITOWOC

BIRCH CREEK INN
4626 Calumet Ave (54220)
Rates: $45-$125
(920) 684-3374
(800) 424-6126

COMFORT INN
2200 S 44th St (54220)
Rates: $49-$115
(920) 683-0220
(800) 424-6423

HERITAGE INN
908 Washington St (54220)
Rates: n/a
(920) 682-8271
(888) 717-8980

HOLIDAY INN
4601 Calumet Ave (54220)
Rates: $140-$160
(920) 682-6000
(800) 465-4329

INN ON MARITIME BAY
101 Maritime Dr (54220)
Rates: $95-$135
(920) 682-7000
(800) 654-5353

MARINETTE

CHALET MOTEL
1301 Marinette Ave (54143)
Rates: $34-$44
(715) 735-6687
(800) 341-8000

THE DOME RESORT
751 University Dr (54143)
Rates: n/a
(715) 735-0533

MARSHFIELD

BEST VALUE INN-7 STAR MOTEL
2121 W Veterans Pkwy (54449)
Rates: $28-$50
(715) 387-2511
(888) 887-5255

BEST WESTERN CLEARWATERS HOTEL
2700 S Roddis Ave (54449)
Rates: $49-$134
(715) 387-1761
(800) 528-1234
(800) 227-1761

HILLCREST MOTEL
504 St. Joseph Ave (54449)
Rates: $32-$49
(715) 387-1234
(866) 387-1235

HOLIDAY INN HOTEL & SUITES
750 S Central Ave (54449)
Rates: $69-$134
(715) 486-1500
(800) 465-4329

MARSHFIELD INN
116 W Ives (54449)
Rates: $42-$62
(715) 387-6381
(800) 851-8669

PARK MOTEL
1806 S Roddis Ave (54449)
Rates: $35-$46
(715) 387-1741

STARDUST MOTEL
1801 S Roddis AVe (54449)
Rates: $33-$42
(715) 387-1191

MAUSTON

ALASKAN MOTOR INN
I-90/94 & Hwy 82 (53948)
Rates: $35-$86
(608) 847-5609
(800) 835-8268

CASTLE ROCK HIDEAWAY
N6187 Cty Hwy G (53948)
Rates: $53-$118
(608) 847-4475

CITY CENTER MOTEL
315 E State St (53948)
Rates: $26-$48
(608) 847-5634

COUNTRY INN BY CARLSON
1001 SR 82 (53948)
Rates: $75-$96
(608) 847-5959
(800) 456-4000

SUPER 8 MOTEL
1001 A Hwy 82 E (53948)
Rates: $69-$179
(608) 847-2300
(800) 800-8000

WILLOWS MOTEL
1035 E state St (53948)
Rates: $45-$65
(608) 847-6800

WOODSIDE RANCH RESORT
W 4015 Hwy 82 (53948)
Rates: $179-$202
(608) 847-4275
(800) 626-4275

MAYVILLE

AUDUBON INN
45 N Main St (53050)
Rates: $120-$200
(920) 387-5858

MAZOMANIE

BEL AIRE MOTEL
10291 Hwy 14 (53560)
Rates: $30-$50
(608) 795-2806

MEDFORD

MEDFORD INN
321 N 8th St (54451)
Rates: $38-$47
(715) 748-4420
(800) 748-0650

MENOMONIE

BEST WESTERN INN
1815 N Broadway (54751)
Rates: $49-$139
(715) 235-9651
(800) 528-1234
(800) 622-0504

BOLO COUNTRY INN B&B
207 Pine Ave W (54751)
Rates: $55-$85
(715) 235-5596
(800) 553-2656

CEDAR TRAIL GUESTHOUSE
E4761 County Rd C (54751)
Rates: $50-$70
(715) 664-8828

COUNTRY INN & SUITES
320 Oak Ave (54751)
Rates: $99-$189
(715) 235-5664
(800) 456-4000

MOTEL 6-UNIVERSITY OF WISCONSIN
2100 Stout St (54751)
Rates: $34-$45
(715) 235-6901
(800) 466-8356

SUPER 8 MOTEL
1622 N Broadway (54751)
Rates: $49-$69
(715) 235-8889
(800) 800-8000

MEQUON

BEST WESTERN QUIET HOUSE & SUITES
10330 N Port Washington Rd (53092)
Rates: $76-$194
(262) 241-3677
(800) 528-1234

CHALET MOTEL
10401 N Port Washington Rd (53092)
Rates: $59-$150
(262) 241-4510
(800) 343-4510

PORT ZEDLER MOTEL
10036 N Port Washington Rd (53092)
Rates: $40-$90
(262) 241-5850

MERCER

GREAT NORTHERN MOTEL
Hwy 51S (54547)
Rates: $39-$59
(715) 476-2440

PINE NOEL RESORT
3307 Goettsche Rd (54547)
Rates: $440-$490 Weekly
(715) 476-2539

VOYAGEUR INN
4514 Lake of the Falls Rd (54547)
Rates: $40-$100
(715) 476-0013

MERRILL

AMERICINN LODGE & SUITES
3300 E Main St (54452)
Rates: $79-$139
(715) 536-797
(800) 634-3444

BRICK HOUSE B&B
108 S Cleveland St (54452)
Rates: $40-$60
(715) 536-3230

MERRILL VIEW MOTEL
703 S Center Ave (54452)
Rates: $34-$57
(715) 536-5555

PINE RIDGE INN
200 S Pine Ridge Ave (54452)
Rates: $39-$75
(715) 536-9526
(888) 220-5160

SUPER 8 MOTEL
3209 E Main St (54452)
Rates: $55-$130
(715) 536-6880
(800) 800-8000

MERRILLAN

LIGHTHOUSE INN
Hwys 12/27 & 95 (54754)
Rates: $27-$50
(715) 333-2801

MERRIMAC

MOON VALLEY RESORT
E13105 Hwy 78 (53561)
Rates: $100-$170
(608) 493-2226

MIDDLETON

COUNTRY INN & SUITES
2212 Deming Way (53561)
Rates: $79-$179
(608) 831-6970
(800) 456-4000

MARRIOTT MADISON WEST
1313 John Q Hammons Dr (53562)
Rates: $109-$179
(608) 831-2000
(800) 228-9290

STAYBRIDGE SUITES
7790 Elmwood Ave (53562)
Rates: $109-$159
(608) 664-5888
(800) 238-8000

MILTON

CHASE ON THE HILL B&B
11624 State Rd 26 (53563)
Rates: $45-$60
(608) 868-6646

MILWAUKEE

THE ACANTHUS INN B&B
3009 W Highland Blvd (53208)
Rates: $85-$120
(414) 342-9788

AMBASSADOR HOTEL
2308 W Wisconsin Ave (53233)
Rates: $99-$199
(414) 342-8400

AMERISUITES WEST
11777 W Silver Spring Dr (53225)
Rates: $79-$109
(414) 462-3500
(800) 833-1516

BAYMONT INN & SUITES
5442 N Lovers Ln (53225)
Rates: $75-$93
(414) 535-1300
(877) 229-6668

BEST WESTERN INN TOWNE
710 N Old World Third St (53203)
Rates: $59-$119
(414) 224-8400
(800) 528-1234
(877) 484-6835

BEST WESTERN AIRPORT HOTEL
5105 S Howell Ave (53207)
Rates: $59-$111
(414) 769-2100
(800) 528-1234
(877) 461-8547

BILLER HOTEL
725 N 22nd St (53233)
Rates: $44-$79
(414) 933-6000

COUNTY CLARE AN IRISH INN
1234 N Astor St (53202)
Rates: $119-$139
(414) 272-5273
(800) 942-5273

THE EXECUTIVE INN
2301 W Wisconsin Ave (53203)
Rates: $69-$109
(414) 342-0000

EXEL INN - NE
5485 N Port Washington Rd (53217)
Rates: $50-$80
(414) 961-7272
(800) 367-3935

HOTEL METRO
411 E Mason St (53202)
Rates: $149-$279
(414) 272-1937
(877) 638-7620

HOTEL WISCONSIN
720 N Old World Third St (53203)
Rates: $59-$105
(414) 271-4900

THE KILBOURN GUEST HOUSE
2825 W Kilbourn Ave (53208)
Rates: $69-$149
(414) 344-3167

MOTEL 6
5037 S Howell Ave (53207)
Rates: $33-$50
(414) 482-4414
(800) 466-8356

PORT MOTEL
9717 W Appleton Ave (53225)
Rates: $33-$46
(414) 466-4728

RAMADA INN SOUTH AIRPORT
6401 S 13th St (53221)
Rates: n/a
(414) 764-5300
(800) 272-6232

MINERAL POINT

CHESTNUT CORNER COTTAGE
899 N Chestnut (53565)
Rates: $99-$169
(608) 987-3933
(800) 987-3977

COMFORT INN
1345 Business Park Rd (53565)
Rates: $55-$149
(608) 987-4747
(800) 424-6423

MINOCQUA

AMERICINN
700 Hwy 51 (54548)
Rates: $69-$179
(715) 356-3730
(800) 634-3444

AQUA AIRE MOTEL
806 Hwy 51 N (54548)
Rates: $36-$89
(715) 356-3433

BAY VIEW LODGE
8555 Hwy 51 (54548)
Rates: $39-$115
(715) 356-9610
(877) 215-8051

CLOUDNINE BAR & RESORT
5678 Lakewood Rd (54548)
Rates: $400-$500 Weekly
(715) 277-2662

COMFORT INN
8729 Hwy 51 N (54548)
Rates: $59-$109
(715) 358-2588
(800) 424-6423
(800) 876-8422

CROSS TRAILS MOTOR LODGE
8644 Hwy 51 N (54548)
Rates: $30-$69
(715) 356-5202
(800) 841-5261

LAKEVIEW MOTOR LODGE
311 E Park Ave
Rates: n/a
(715) 356-5208

MOTEL MINOCQUA
7528 Hwy 51 S (54548)
Rates: $30-$70
(715) 356-3090
(888) 218-9650

SUPER 8 MOTEL
8730 Hwy 51 N (54548)
Rates: $54-$102
(715) 356-9541
(800) 800-8000

MONONA

AMERICINN
101 W Broadway (53716)
Rates: $79-$99
(608) 222-8601
(800) 634-3444

MONROE

LUDLOW MANSION B&B
1421 Mansion Dr (53577)
Rates: $90-$140
(608) 325-1219

MONTELLO

HILLTOP MOTEL
131 Church St (53949)
Rates: $38-$52
(608) 297-2090
(800) 760-9960

PUCKAWAY LANDING
N 3152 Lotus Dr (53949)
Rates: $65-$85
(920) 295-4197

AREA CODES - If the local number doesn't connect, check for a new area code.

SUNDOWNER MOTEL
510 Underwood
Ave (53949)
Rates: $35-$76
(608) 297-2121

TNT HORSE RANCH B&B
N4649 18th Rd
(53949)
Rates: n/a
(608) 297-2056

MOSINEE

COMFORT INN
1510 County
Hwy XX (54455)
Rates: $59-$119
(715) 355-4449
(800) 424-6423

LAKEVIEW LOG CABIN RESORT
1095 Wambold Dr
(54455)
Rates: $70-$125
(715) 693-2595
(800) 545-9388

MOUNTAIN

SPUR OF THE MOMENT RANCH
14221 Helen Ln
(54149)
Rates: $35-$80
(715) 276-3726
(800) 644-8783

NEENAH

FOX VALLEY INN
2000 Holly Rd
(54956)
Rates: $24-$65
(920) 734-9872

HOLIDAY INN RIVERWALK
123 E Wisconsin
Ave (54956)
Rates: $93-$129
(920) 725-8441
(800) 465-4329

PARKWAY MOTEL
1181 Gillingham
Rd (54956)
Rates: $30-$80
(920) 725-3244

NEILLSVILLE

FANNIES MOTEL
W3741 US Hwy 10
(54456)
Rates: $30-$45
(715) 743-2169

HEARTLAND MOTEL
7 S Hewett St
(54456)
Rates: $40-$60
(715) 743-4004

NEKOOSA

SHERMALOT MOTEL
1148 Queens Way
(54457)
Rates: $45-$52
(715) 325-2626

NEW AUBURN

SUNNY'S CLEAR LAKE RESORT
N207 Park Dr
(54757)
Rates: $65-$95
(715) 967-2562

NEW BERLIN

BAYMONT INN & SUITES
15300 W Rock
Ridge Rd (53151)
Rates: $59-$149
(262) 717-0900
(877) BAYMONT

NEW GLARUS

SWISS-AIRE MOTEL
1200 Hwy 69
(53574)
Rates: $49-$79
(608) 527-2138
(800) 798-4391

NEW HOLSTEIN

STARLITE MOTEL
1321 Milwaukee
Dr (53061)
Rates: $36-$51
(920) 898-4265

NEW LISBON

EDGE O' THE WOOD MOTEL
W 7396 Frontage
Rd (53950)
Rates: $37-$80
(608) 562-3705
(800) 638-4929

TRAVELODGE
1700 E Bridge St
(53950)
Rates: $47-$99
(608) 562-5141
(800) 578-7878
(888) 895-6200

NEW LONDON

AMERICINN LODGE & SUITES
1404 N Shawano
St (54961)
Rates: $59-$165
(920) 982-5700
(866) 459-1659

RAINBOW MOTEL
1140 N Shawano
St (54961)
Rates: $45-$70
(920) 982-4550
(888) 588-9147

RIDGEMARK INNS
1409 N Shawano
St (54961)
Rates: $49-$115
(920) 982-5820
(888) 321-7907

NEW RICHMOND

AMERICINN MOTEL
1020 S Knowles
Ave (54017)
Rates: $55-$125
(715) 246-3993
(800) 634-3444

SUPER 8 MOTEL
Hwy 65 S (54017)
Rates: $57-$99
(715) 246-7829
(800) 800-8000

NORTHFIELD

TRIPLE R RESORT
N11818 Hixton-
Levis Rd (54635)
Rates: $41-$112
(715) 964-8777
(888) 963-8777

OAK CREEK

BAYMONT \INN & SUITES
7141 S 13th St
(53154)
Rates: $70-$87
(414) 762-2266
(877) 229-6668

COMFORT SUITES AIRPORT
6362 S 13th St
(53154)
Rates: $79-$119
(414) 570-1111
(800) 424-6423

EXEL INN SOUTH
1201 W College
Ave (53154)
Rates: $39-$125
(414) 764-1776
(800) 367-3935

MAINSTAY SUITES
1001 W College
Ave (53154)
Rates: $69-$329
(414) 571-8800
(800) 424-6423

RED ROOF INN
6360 S 13th St
(53154)
Rates: $49-$71
(414) 764-3500
(800) 843-7663

VALUE INN
9420 S 20th St
(53154)
Rates: $40-$90
(414) 761-3807

OCONOMOWOC

INN AT PINE TERRACE
351 E Lisbon Rd
(53066)
Rates: $69-$129
(262) 567-7463

OLYMPIA RESORT
1350 Royale Mile
Rd (53066)
Rates: $135-$265
(262) 369-4999
(800) 558-9573

OCONTO

OCONTO MOTEL
5680 Hwy 41 S
(54153)
Rates: $39-$47
(920) 834-2000

OCONTO FALLS

COACHLIGHT INN
248 N Main
(54154)
Rates: $39-$225
(920) 846-3424

OGEMA

HIGH POINT VILLAGE INN
W3075 Cnty RR
(54459)
Rates: $65-$150
(715) 767-5287

ONALASKA

BAYMONT INN
3300 N Kinney
Coulee Rd (54650)
Rates: $69-$184
(608) 783-7191
(877) 229-6668

CLEARWATER CABINS
W7605 CTH ZB
(54650)
Rates: $65-$110
(608) 781-1716

COMFORT INN
1223 Crossing
Meadows Dr
(54650)
Rates: $59-$144
(608) 781-7500
(800) 424-6423

COZY CORNER COTTAGES
W8071 CTH ZB
(54650)
Rates: $70+
(608) 781-3792

EDGEWATER MOTEL
N5326 State Rd 35
(54650)
Rates: $30-$50
(608) 783-2286

HOLIDAY INN EXP
9409 Hwy 16
(54650)
Rates: $71-$129
(608) 783-6555
(800) 465-4329
(800) 411-3712

MICROTEL INN
3240 N Kinney
Coulee Rd (54650)
Rates: $459$80
(608) 783-0833
(888) 818-2359

ONALASKA INN
651 2nd Ave S
(54650)
Rates: $30-$80
(608) 783-2270
(888) 359-2619

SHADOW RUN LODGE
710 2nd Ave N
(54650)
Rates: $35-$70
(608) 783-0020
(800) 657-4749

ONTARIO

**THE INN AT
WILDCAT
MOUNTAIN**
Hwy 33,
P.O. Box 112
Rates: $50-$75
(608) 337-4352

OSCEOLA

**RIVER VALLEY INN
& SUITES**
1030 Cascade St
(54020)
Rates: $72-$120
(715) 294-4060
(888) 791-2200

OSHKOSH

BAYMONT INN
1950 Omro Rd
(54901)
Rates: $60-$135
(920) 233-4190
(877) 229-6668

**HAWTHORN INN
& SUITES**
3105 S Washburn
St (54904)
Rates: $99-$299
(920) 303-1133
(800) 527-1133

**HOLIDAY INN EXP
HOTEL & SUITES**
2251 Westowne
Ave (54901)
Rates: $109-$185
(920) 303-1300
(800) 465-4329

RAMADA INN
500 S Koeller
(54901)
Rates: $59-$89
(920) 235-3700
(800) 272-6232

TRAVELODGE
1015 S Washburn
St (54409)
Rates: $41-$51
(920) 233-4300
(800) 578-7878

OSSEO

RED CARPET INN
Hwy 10/I-94,
Exit 88 (54758)
Rates: $37-$69
(715) 597-3175
(866) 228-1950

TEN SEVEN INN
12554 Gunderson
Rd (54758)
Rates: $36-$48
(715) 597-3114

OXFORD

**CROSSROADS
MOTEL**
W6330 Hwy 23
(53952)
Rates: $40-$65
(608) 589-5151
(866) 589-5151

PARK FALLS

**BRIGHAM'S EDGE
O' TOWN MOTEL**
900 4th Ave N
(54552)
Rates: $45-$60
(715) 744-1700
(866) 744-1700

MASON MOTEL
798 S 4th Ave
(54552)
Rates: $30-$50
(715) 762-3780

**NORTHWAY
MOTOR LODGE**
1113 Hwy 13S
(54552)
Rates: $58-$84
(715) 762-2406
(800) 844-7144

SUPER 8 MOTEL
1212 Hwy 13S
(54552)
Rates: $50-$77
(715) 762-3383
(800) 800-8000

**WOJCIESZAK'S
FLAMBEAU
RESORT**
N15355 East Rd
(54552)
Rates: $100-$150
(715) 762-2178
(888) 438-4629

PELICAN LAKE

**WEAVER'S
RESORT &
CAMPGROUND**
1001 Weaver Rd
(54463)
Rates: $80-$110
(715) 487-5217

PEMBINE

GRAND MOTEL
N18379 Hwy 141
(54156)
Rates: $32-$64
(715) 324-5417

**ROCKY INN
RESORT**
W4814 Hiltop Dr
(54156)
Rates: $500-$1000
Weekly
(715) 434-8966

PHELPS

**AFTERGLOW
LAKE RESORT**
5050 Sugar Maple
Rd (54554)
Rates: $100-$350/
$500-$2000 Wkly
(715) 545-2560

PHILLIPS

**HIDDEN
VALLEY INN
& RESORT**
W7724 Co. Hwy
W (54555)
Rates: $48-$165
(715) 339-2757

**RED PINE
MOTEL/RESORT**
850 Elk Lake Dr
(54555)
Rates: $85-$350
(715) 339-4333
(800) 651-4333

SKYLINE MOTEL
804 N Lake Ave
(54555)
Rates: $39-$75
(715) 339-3086
(800) 596-0407

SUPER 8 MOTEL
726 S Lake Ave
(54555)
Rates: $45-$70
(715) 339-2898
(800) 800-8000

TIMBER INN
606 N Lake Ave
(54555)
Rates: $43-$49
(715) 339-3071
(800) 844-4521

PLATTEVILLE

**GOVERNOR
DODGE HOTEL**
300 Hwy 151
(53818)
Rates: $64-$89
(608) 348-2301

**MOUND
VIEW INN**
1755 E Hwy 151
(53818)
Rates: $40-$98
(608) 348-9518

SUPER 8 MOTEL
100 Hwy 80/81 S
(53818)
Rates: $47-$90
(608) 348-8800
(800) 800-8000

**VISION
BY THE LAKE**
683 Joes Lane
(53818)
Rates: $150-$200
(608) 943-8375

PLEASANT PRAIRIE

BAYMONT INN
7540 117th Ave
(53158)
Rates: $75-$85
(262) 857-7911
(877) 229-6668

**HAWTHORN
SUITES LTD**
7887 94th Ave
(53158)
Rates: $79-$149
(262) 942-6000
(800) 527-1133

PLOVER

ELIZABETH INN
5246 Harding Ave
(54467)
Rates: $45-$80
(715) 341-4414
(800) 280-0778

PLYMOUTH

**BEVERLY'S LOG
GUEST HOUSE**
W6926 Stoney
Ridge Ln (53073)
Rates: $65-$75
(920) 892-6064

**HARMONY HILLS
IN THE HOLOW
B&B**
W7625 Cty Rd N
(53073)
Rates: $70-$90
(920) 528-8233

**PLYMOUTH INN
HOTEL**
606 E Mill St
(53073)
Rates: $65-$150
(920) 893-5623
(888) 779-5623

PORT WASHINGTON

**DRIFTWOOD
MOTEL**
3415 N Green Bay
Rd (53024)
Rates: $32-$54
(262) 284-4413

**THE GRAND INN
B&B**
832 W Grand Ave
(53024)
Rates: $100-$125
(262) 284-6719

**HOLIDAY INN
HARBORVIEW**
135 E Grand Ave
(53024)
Rates: $75-$149
(262) 284-9461
(800) 465-4329

PORTAGE

LAMP-LITE MOTEL
Hwy 51/16
(53901)
Rates: $30-$45
(608) 742-6365

**PORTERHOUSE
MOTEL**
1721 New Pinery
Rd (53901)
Rates: $26-$69
(608) 742-2186

**RIDGE MOTOR
INN**
2900 New Pinery
Rd (53901)
Rates: $55-$160
(608) 742-5306
(877) 742-5306

AREA CODES - If the local number doesn't connect, check for a new area code.

SUPER 8 MOTEL
3000 New Pinery
(53901)
Rates: $49-$59
(608) 742-8330
(800) 800-8000

POYNETTE

BAYVIEW LODGE RESORT
N3135 County
Hwy V (53955)
Rates: $70+
(608) 635-4089

LAKE WISCONSIN RESORT
W10941 Corning
Rd (53955)
Rates: $85-$195
(608) 635-7291

HAPPY HOLLOW RESORT
N3769 Tipperary
Rd (53955)
Rates: $80-$95
(608) 635-4032

JAMIESON HOUSE INN
407 N Franklin St
(53955)
Rates: $70-$155
(608) 635-4100
(888) 462-3216

PRAIRIE DU CHIEN

BEST WESTERN QUIET HOUSE SUITES
37268 Hwy 18
(53821)
Rates: $54-$169
(608) 326-4777
(800) 528-1234

BRIDGEPORT INN
Hwy 18, 35 & 60
(53821)
Rates: $79-$129
(608) 326-6082
(800) 234-6082

BRISBOIS MOTOR INN
533 N Marquette
Rd (53821)
Rates: $54-$99
(608) 326-8404
(800) 356-5850

HIDDEN VALLEY LODGE
1833 S Marquette
Rd (53821)
Rates: $45-$125
(608) 326-8476
(800) 349-8476

RODEWAY INN/ WINDSOR PLACE INN
1936 S Marquette
Rd (53821)
Rates: $79-$100
(608) 326-7799
(800) 424-6423

SUPER 8 MOTEL
1930 S Marquette
Rd (53821)
Rates: $62-$89
(608) 326-8777
(800) 800-8000

PRAIRIE DU SAC

SKYVIEW MOTEL
S9645 Hwy 12
(53578)
Rates: $38-$65
(608) 643-4344
(888) 643-4344

PRENTICE

COUNTRYSIDE MOTEL
W5370 E
Greenberg Rd
(54556)
Rates: $42-$75
(715) 428-2333

PRINCETON

ACORN RIDGE MOTEL
W3910 Hwy
23/73 (54968)
Rates: $48-$89
(920) 295-6533

RACINE

DAYS INN
3700 Northwestern
Ave (53405)
Rates: $50-$220
(262) 637-9311
(800) 329-7466

KNIGHTS INN
1149 Oakes Rd
(53406)
Rates: $43-$99
(262) 886-6667
(800) 843-5644

MARRIOTT HOTEL
7111 Washington
Ave (53406)
Rates: $69-$153
(262) 886-6100
(800) 228-9290

MICROTEL INN
5419 Durand Ave
(53406)
Rates: $54-$75
(262) 554-8855

SUPER 8 MOTEL
1150 Oakes Rd
(53406)
Rates: $50-$160
(262) 884-0486
(800) 800-8000

REEDSBURG

COPPER SPRINGS MOTEL
E7278 Hwy 23
& 33 (53959)
Rates: $39-$68
(608) 524-4312

MOTEL REEDSBURG
1133 E Main St
(53959)
Rates: $29-$68
(608) 524-2306
(800) 526-6835

RHINELANDER

AMERICINN
648 W Kemp (54501)
Rates: $57-$110
(715) 369-9600
(800) 734-3444

BEST WESTERN CLARIDGE MOTOR INN
70 N Stevens St
(54501)
Rates: $69-$129
(715) 362-7100
(800) 528-1234
(800) 427-1377

BREKKE'S FIRE-SIDE RESORT
4268 Hwy 8 E
(54501)
Rates: $70-$120
(715) 369-3112

BUCK HAVEN RESORT
4743 Wilderness
Ln (54529)
Rates: $60-$90
(715) 277-2341

COMFORT INN
1490 Lincoln St
(54501)
Rates: $51-$159
(715) 369-1100
(800) 424-6423

FEASES' SHADY REST LODGE
8440 Shady Rest
Rd (54501)
Rates: $60-$400
(715) 282-5231
(800) 477-3229

HOLIDAY ACRES RESORT ON LAKE THOMPSON
4060 S Shore Dr
(54501)
Rates: $69-$299
(715) 369-1500
(800) 261-1500

HOLIDAY INN EXP
668 W Kemp St
(54501)
Rates: $74-$174
(715) 369-3600
(800) 465-4329

KAFKA'S RESORT
4281 W Lake
George Rd (54501)
Rates: $75-$150
(715) 369-2929
(800) 426-6674

MERRY DALE RESORT
4150 Satuit Ln,
Lake George
(54501)
Rates: $80-$150
(715) 362-3794
(800) 315-3990

MILLER'S SHORE-WOOD VISTA
4239 W Lake
George Rd (54501)
Rates: n/a
(715) 362-4818

RIB LAKE

LAKEVIEW RESORT
N9503 Spirit Lake
Rd (54470)
Rates: n/a
(715) 427-3344

RICE LAKE

CURRIER'S LAKEVIEW RESORT MOTEL
2010 E Sawyer
St (54868)
Rates: $49-$149
(715) 234-7474
(800) 433-5253

MICROTEL INN
2771 Decker Dr
(54868)
Rates: $45-$85
(715) 736-2010
(888) 202-4223

STARLIGHT MOTEL
1710 S Main St
(54868)
Rates: $40-$55
(715) 234-4444
(800) 992-1669

RICHLAND CENTER

CANDLEWOOD CABIN IN THE WOODS
29493 Hwy 80
(53581)
Rates: $125-$150
(608) 647-5720

LITTLEDALE B&B
21925 County
Hwy ZZ (53581)
Rates: $45-$55
(608) 647-7118

RIVERSIDE MOTEL
28299 Hwy 14
(53581)
Rates: $47-$99
(608) 647-6420

SUPER 8 MOTEL
100 Foundry Dr
(53581)
Rates: $58-$85
(608) 647-8988
(800) 800-8000

RIVER FALLS

KINNI CREEK LODGE & B&B
545 N Main St
(54022)
Rates: $115-$135
(715) 425-7378
(877) 504-9705

AREA CODES - If the local number doesn't connect, check for a new area code.

RIVER FALLS MOTEL
1300 S Main St (54022)
Rates: $30-$60
(715) 425-8181

SUPER 8 MOTEL
1207 St. Croix St (54022)
Rates: $65-$92
(715) 425-8388
(800) 800-8000

ROTHSCHILD
BUDGE INN MOTEL
1106 E Grand Ave (54474)
Rates: $29-$50
(715) 359-5986

ST. CROIX FALLS
DALLES HOUSE MOTEL
726 Vincent (54024)
Rates: $53-$130
(715) 483-3206
(888) 725-6913

HOLIDAY INN EXP HOTEL & SUITES
2190 E US Hwy 8 (54024)
Rates: $75-$95
(715) 483-5775
(800) 465-4329

ST. GERMAIN
NORTHWOODS REST MOTEL
8083 Hwy 70 E (54558)
Rates: $42-$52
(715) 479-8770

RUSTIC MANOR MOTOR LODGE
6343 Hwy 70 E (54558)
Rates: $55-$129
(715) 479-9776
(800) 272-9776

ST. GERMAIN MOTEL
170 Hwy 70 (54558)
Rates: $50-$120
(715) 542-3535

TWIN WATERS RESORT
8560 Inlet Rd (54558)
Rates: $75-$150
(715) 542-3486

SAUK CITY
RAY'S RIVERSIDE RESORT
7554 Hwy 12 (53583)
Rates: $40-$75
(608) 643-3243

SAYNER
FROELICH'S SAYNER LODGE
P. O. Box 100 (54560)
Rates: $60-$100
(715) 542-3261
(800) 553-9695

WOODLANDS RESORT ON PLUM LAKE
8553 Camp Highland Rd (54560)
Rates: $75-$125
(715) 542-2474

SCHOFIELD
NITE INN/INTERIM LODGING
425 Grand Ave (54476)
Rates: $29-$55
(715) 355-1641

SHAWANO
AMERICINN
1330 E Green Bay St (54166)
Rates: $59-$129
(715) 524-5111
(800) 634-3444

SUPER 8 MOTEL
211 Waukechon St (54166)
Rates: $41-$80
(715) 526-6688
(800) 800-8000

SHEBOYGAN
AMERICINN MOTEL & SUITES
3664 S Taylor Dr (53081)
Rates: $70-$180
(920) 208-8130
(800) 634-3444

BAYMONT INN
2932 Kohler Memorial Dr (53081)
Rates: $69-$119
(920) 457-2321
(877) 229-6668

COMFORT INN
4332 N 40th St (53083)
Rates: $59-$199
(920) 457-7724
(800) 424-6423

PARKWAY MOTEL
3900 Motel Rd (53081)
Rates: $42-$64
(920) 458-8338
(800) 341-8000

SLEEP INN
3912 Motel Rd (53081)
Rates: $65-$170
(920) 694-0099
(800) 424-6423

SUPER 8 MOTEL
3402 Wilgus Rd (53081)
Rates: $54-$79
(920) 458-8080
(800) 800-8000

SHEBOYGAN FALLS
PINEHURST INN
600 hWY 32 n (53085)
Rates: $58-$120
(920) 467-4314
(800) 845-8106

SHELL LAKE
AMERICAINN
315 Hwy 63 S (54871)
Rates: $36-$199
(715) 468-4494
(800) 634-3444

AQUA VISTA RESORT & MOTEL
412 E Hwy B (54871)
Rates: $35-$110
(715) 468-2256
(800) 889-2256

RIVARD'S BASHAW LAKE RESORT
3215 Lakeview Church Rd (54871)
Rates: $53+
(715) 468-2310
(877) 306-3501

SIREN
THE LODGE AT CROOKED LAKE HOTEL
24271 SR 35 N (54872)
Rates: $79-$250
(715) 349-2500
(877) 843-5634

PINE WOOD MOTEL
23862 Hwy 35 (54872)
Rates: $45-$55
(715) 349-5225

SISTER BAY
EDGE OF TOWN MOTEL
11092 Hwy 42 (54234)
Rates: $40-$80
(920) 854-2012

SCANDIA COTTAGES
11062 Beach Rd (54234)
Rates: $60-$150
(920) 854-2447

SPARTA
BEST NIGHTS INN
303 W Wisconsin St (54656)
Rates: $29-$139
(608) 269-3066
(800) 201-0234

BEST WESTERN SPARTA TRAIL LODGE
4445 Theatre Rd (54656)
Rates: $69-$149
(608) 269-2664
(800) 528-1234
(800) 780-7234

COUNTRY INN BY CARLSON
737 Avon Rd (54656)
Rates: $71-$119
(608) 269-3110
(800) 456-4000

DOWNTOWN MOTEL
509 S Water St (54656)
Rates: $28-$48
(608) 269-3138

GRAPEVINE LOG CABINS B&B
19149 Jade Rd (54656)
Rates: $125-$175
(608) 269-3619

HERITAGE MOTEL
704 W Wisconsin St (54656)
Rates: $30-$50
(608) 269-6991

JUSTIN TRAILS COUNTRY INN & NORDIC SKI CENTER
7452 Kathryn Ave (54656)
Rates: $80-$300
(608) 269-4522
(800) 488-4521

SPARTAN MOTEL
1900 W Wisconsin St (54656)
Rates: $33-$48
(608) 269-2770

SUNSET MOTEL
1009 W Wisconsin St (54656)
Rates: $25-$60
(608) 269-2140

SUPER 8 MOTEL
716 Avon Rd (54656)
Rates: $58-$168
(608) 269-8489
(800) 800-8000

SPOONER
BEST WESTERN AMERICAN HERITAGE INN
101 Maple St (54801)
Rates: $64-$109
(715) 635-9770
(800) 528-1234

COUNTRY HOUSE MOTEL
717 S Hwy 63 S (54801)
Rates: $50-$120
(715) 635-8721

GREEN ACRES MOTEL
N 4809 Hwy 63 S
& 253 (54801)
Rates: $49-$79
(715) 635-2177

TREGO INN MOTEL
Hwy 53 & 63
(54801)
Rates: $40-$70
(715) 635-3204
(800) 681-5939

SPRING GREEN
GERMANIA COUNTRY INN
E4867 Hwy 14
(53588)
Rates: $28-$98
(608) 588-2222
(800) 588-8566

THE SILVER STAR B&B COUNTRY INN
3852 Limmex Hill
Rd (53588)
Rates: $95-$135
(608) 935-7297

SPRING GREEN MOTEL
Hwy 14 (53577)
Rates: $28-$79
(608) 588-2141
(888) 647-4410

STAR LAKE
RISMON'S LODGE
Hwy K 8080
(54561)
Rates: $36
(715) 542-3682

STEVENS POINT
BAYMONT INN & SUITES
4917 Main St
(54481)
Rates: $57-$95
(715) 344-1900
(877) 229-6668

COUNTRY INN & SUITES
301 Division St N
(54481)
Rates: $54-$109
(715) 345-7000
(800) 456-4000

HOLIDAY INN
1501 N Point Dr
(54481)
Rates: $99-$119
(715) 341-1340
(800) 465-4329

POINT MOTEL
209 Division St
(54481)
Rates: $33-$70
(715) 344-8312

ROADSTAR INN
159 N Division St
(54481)
Rates: $35-$80
(715) 341-9000
(800) 445-4667

STOCKHOLM
PINE CREEK LODGE
N447 244th St
(54769)
Rates: $85
(715) 448-3203

STODDARD
WATER'S EDGE MOTEL
201 N Pearl St
(54658)
Rates: n/a
(608) 457-2126

STOUGHTON
CHOSE FAMILY INN
1124 W Main St
(53589)
Rates: $55-$72
(608) 873-0330

STURGEON BAY
CARL'S OLD BRIDGE MOTEL
114 N Madison
Ave (54235)
Rates: $30-$70
(920) 743-1245

CHERRYLAND MOTEL & COTTAGES
1309 Green Bay
Rd (54235)
Rates: $65-$125
(920) 743-3289
(800) 313-9019

HOLIDAY MOTEL
29 N 2nd Ave
(54235)
Rates: $29-$81
(920) 743-5571

NAUTICAL INN B&B
234 Kentucky St
(54235)
Rates: $55
(920) 743-3399

NIGHTENGALE MOTEL
1547 Egg Harbor
Rd (54235)
Rates: $27-$62
(920) 743-7633

PEMBROKE INN B&B
410 N 4th Ave
(54235)
Rates: $80-$120
(920) 746-9776

QUIET COTTAGE
4608 Glidden Dr
(54235)
Rates: $160-$185
(920) 743-4526

SNUG HARBOR INN & MARINA
1627 Memorial Dr
(54235)
Rates: $50-$169
(920) 743-2337
(800) 231-5767

SUPER 8 MOTEL
409 Green Bay Rd
(54235)
Rates: $44-$101
(920) 743-9211
(800) 800-8000

WHITE BIRCH INN
1009 S Oxford Ave
(54235)
Rates: $49-$129
(920) 743-3295

STURTEVANT
BEST WESTERN GRANDVIEW INN
910 S Sylvania Ave
(53177)
Rates: $54-$109
(262) 886-0385
(800) 528-1234

HOLIDAY INN EXP
13339 Hospitality
Ct (53177)
Rates: $74-$94
(262) 884-0200
(800) 465-4329

SUN PRAIRIE
MCGOVERN'S MOTEL & SUITES
820 W Main St
(53590)
Rates: $46-$100
(608) 837-7321
(888) 837-7321

SUPERIOR
BARKERS ISLAND INN
300 Marina Dr
(54880)
Rates: $69-$210
(715) 392-7152

BAY MOTEL
306 E 3rd St
(54880)
Rates: $20-$150
(715) 392-5166
(888) 668-5229

BEST WESTERN BAY WALK INN
1405 Susquehanna
Ave (54880)
Rates: $55-$109
(715) 392-7600
(800) 528-1234

BEST WESTERN BRIDGEVIEW MOTOR INN
415 Hammond
Ave (54880)
Rates: $49-$129
(715) 392-8174
(800) 528-1234
(800) 777-5572

DAYS INN
110 Harborview
Pkwy (54880)
Rates: $49-$159
(715) 392-4783
(800) 329-7466

DRIFTWOOD MOTEL
2200 E 2nd St
(54880)
Rates: $24-$75
(715) 398-6661

STOCKADE MOTEL
1610 E 2nd St
(54880)
Rates: $30-$75
(715) 398-3585

SUNSHINE MOTEL
1807 N 58th St
(54880)
Rates: $20-$150
(715) 394-7055
(888) 786-8355

SUPERIOR INN
525 Hammond
Ave (54880)
Rates: $49-$120
(715) 394-7706

THORP
AMERICINN LODGE & SUITES
203 1/2 W Hill St
(54771)
Rates: $55-$110
(715) 669-5959
(866) 279-8180

THREE LAKES
MAPLE SHORES RESORT
1660 Superior St
(54562)
Rates: $45-$125
(715) 546-3111

TOMAH
AMERICINN LODGE & SUITES
750 Vandervort St
(54660)
Rates: $80-$175
(608) 372-4100
(800) 634-3444

BRENTWOOD INN
24318 Gopher Ave
(54660)
Rates: $50-$75
(608) 372-4500

COMFORT INN
305 Wittig Rd
(54660)
Rates: $50-$150
(608) 372-6600
(800) 424-6423

CRANBERRY COUNTRY LODGES
319 Wittig Rd
(54660)
Rates: $59-$199
(608) 374-2801
(800) 243-9874

ECONO LODGE
2005 N Superior
Ave (54660)
Rates: $49-$140
(608) 372-9100
(800) 424-6423

HOLIDAY INN
1017 E McCoy
Blvd (54660)
Rates: $69
(608) 372-3211
(800) 465-4329

LARK INN
229 N Superior
Ave (54660)
Rates: $47-$84
(608) 372-5981
(800) 447-5275

REST WELL MOTEL
25491 Hwy 12
(54660)
Rates: $39-$65
(608) 372-2471
(

SUPER 8 MOTEL
1008 E McCoy
Blvd (54660)
Rates: $52-$90
(608) 372-3901
(800) 800-8000

TOMAHAWK

ALAMO PLAZA MOTEL
411 Southgate Dr
(54487)
Rates: $36-$60
(715) 453-2196

COMFORT INN
8900 Comfort Dr
(54487)
Rates: $75-$250
(715) 453-8900
(800) 424-6423

PINE POINT RESORT COTTAGES
W4249 Sandy
Lane (54487)
Rates: $70
(715) 453-4930

SUPER 8 MOTEL
108 W Mohawk
Dr (54487)
Rates: $46-$79
(715) 453-5210
(800) 800-8000

TOMAHAWK LODGE & RESORT
N10985 County
CC (54487)
Rates: $60-$80
(715) 453-3452

TREMPEALEAU

INN ON THE RIVER
11321 Main St
(54661)
Rates: $50-$100
(608) 534-7784

PLEASANT KNOLL INN
11451 Main St
(54661)
Rates: $50-$75
(608) 534-6615
(888) 210-8790

TREVOR

STATE LINE MOTEL
23610 128th St
(53179)
Rates: n/a
(414) 396-9561

TWO RIVERS

COOL CITY MOTEL
3009 Lincoln Ave
(54241)
Rates: $21-$51
(920) 793-2244
(800) 729-1520

LAKEVIEW MOTEL
2802 Memorial Dr
(54241)
Rates: $30-$56
(920) 793-2251

LIGHTHOUSE INN ON THE LAKE
1515 Memorial Dr
(54241)
Rates: $75-$115
(920) 793-4524

VILLAGE INN & SUITES
3310 Memorial Dr
(54241)
Rates: $55-$175
(920) 794-8818
(800) 551-4795

VERONA

SUPER 8 MOTEL
131 Horizon Dr
(53593)
Rates: $60-$106
(608) 848-7829
(800) 800-8000

VIROQUA

MIDWAY MOTEL
850 N Main
(54665)
Rates: $40-$139
(608) 637-2929

VIROQUA HERITAGE INN B&B
217 & 220 E
Jefferson St
(54665)
Rates: $60-$120
(508) 637-3306
(888) 443-7466

WABENO

SAFARI MOTEL
4454 N Branch St
(54566)
Rates: $28-$36
(715) 473-3521

WASHBURN

REDWOOD MOTEL & CHALETS
26 W Bayfield St
(54891)
Rates: $50-$78
(715) 373-5512

WASHINGTON ISLAND

THE DOR CROS INN
Box 259, Lobdell
Point Rd (54246)
Rates: $55-$135
(920) 847-2126

FINDLAY'S HOLIDAY INN
Detroit Harbor
(54246)
Rates: $60-$100
(414) 847-2526

VIKING VILLAGE MOTEL
P. O. Box 135
(54246)
Rates: $48-$85
(414) 847-2551

WATERFORD

BAYMONT INN & SUITES
750 Fox Ln (53185)
Rates: $59-$150
(262) 534-4100
(877) 229-6668

WATERTOWN

CANDLE-GLO MOTEL
1200 N 4th St
(53098)
Rates: $33-$50
(920) 261-2281

ECONO LODGE
700 E Main St
(53094)
Rates: $45-$140
(920) 261-9010
(800) 424-6423

FLAGS INN MOTEL
N627 Hwy 26
(53094)
Rates: $35-$65
(920) 261-9400
(800) 288-5875

HOLIDAY INN EXP
101 Aviation Way
(43095)
Rates: $80-$99
(920) 262-1910
(800) 465-4329

KARLSHUEGEL INN
749 N Church St
(53098)
Rates: $60-$85
(920) 261-3980

SUPER 8 MOTEL
1730 S Church St
(53094)
Rates: $73-$93
(920) 261-1188
(800) 800-8000

WAUKESHA

BEST WESTERN WAUKESHA GRAND HOTEL
2840 N
Grandview Blvd
(53072)
Rates: $79-$90
(262) 524-9300
(800) 528-1234
(800) 574-3935

SELECT INN
2510 Plaza Ct
(53072)
Rates: $46-$125
(262) 786-6015
(800) 641-1000

WAUPACA

BEST WESTERN GRAND SEASONS HOTEL
110 Grand Seasons
Dr (54981)
Rates: $77-$179
(715) 258-9212
(800) 528-1234

COMFORT SUITES AT FOXFIRE
199 Foxfire Dr
(54981)
Rates: $69-$139
(715) 942-0500
(800) 424-6423

PARK MOTEL & LIBRARY LOUNGE
E 3621 Hwy 10/49
(54981)
Rates: $34-$99
(715) 258-3225

VILLAGE INN MOTEL
1060 W Fulton St
(54981)
Rates: $67-$115
(715) 258-6526
(800) 626-6391

WINDMILL MANOR B&B
N2919 Hwy QQ
(54981)
Rates: $85-$135
(715) 256-1770

WAUPUN

INN TOWN MOTEL
27 S State St
(53963)
Rates: $38-$78
(920) 324-4211
(800) 433-6231

WAUSAU

ACE MOTEL
2211 Stewart Ave
(54401)
Rates: n/a
(715) 845-4261

BAYMONT INN
1910 Stewart Ave
(54401)
Rates: $54-$99
(715) 842-0421
(877) 229-6668

BEST WESTERN MIDWAY HOTEL
2901 Martin Ave (54401)
Rates: $69-$115
(715) 842-1616
(800) 528-1234
(800) 482-3770

BUDGET INN MOTEL
1106 E Grand Ave (54474)
Rates: $32-$48
(715) 359-5986

DAYS INN
4700 Rib Mtn Rd (54401)
Rates: $59-$140
(715) 355-5501
(800) 329-7466

EXEL INN
116 S 17th Ave (54401)
Rates: $39-$100
(715) 842-0641
(800) 367-3935

MARJON MOTEL
512 S 3rd Ave (54401)
Rates: $34-$42
(715) 845-3125

PARK INN
2101 N Mountain Rd (54401)
Rates: $79-$119
(715) 842-0711
(800) 928-7281

PLAZA HOTEL & SUITES
201 N 17th Ave (54401)
Rates: $75-$199
(715) 845-4341

RIB MOUNTAIN INN
2900 Rib Mtn Way (54401)
Rates: $55-$300
(715) 848-2802
(877) 960-8900

STEWART INN B&B
521 Grant St (54403)
Rates: $130-$170
(715) 849-5858

SUPER 8 MOTEL
2006 Stewart Ave (54401)
Rates: $45-$75
(715) 848-2888
(800) 800-8000

WAUSAU INN
2001 N Mountain Rd (54401)
Rates: $65-$73
(715) 842-0711
(800) 928-7281

WAUSAUKEE
BEAR POINT MOTEL
W5154 Hwy 180 (54177)
Rates: $30-$45
(715) 856-5921

WAUTOMA
AMERICINN MOTEL
W7696 Hwys 21/73 (54982)
Rates: $55-$125
(920) 787-5050
(800) 634-3444

SUPER 8 MOTEL
W7607 Hwy 21E (54982)
Rates: $55-$100
(920) 787-4811
(800) 800-8000

WAUWATOSA
EXEL INN WEST
115 N Mayfair Rd (53226)
Rates: $44-$125
(414) 257-0140
(800) 367-3935

WEBB LAKE
DES MOINES LAKE CABINS
3119 Cherry Ln (54830)
Rates: $65-$105
(715) 259-7931

ROSENTHAL'S RESORT
30925 Namekagon Rd (54830)
Rates: $95-$150
(715) 259-3363

WEBSTER
WAGNER'S PORT SAND RESORT
4904 State Hwy 70 (54893)
Rates: $50
(715) 349-2395

WEBSTER MOTEL
Hwy 25 & Main St (54893)
Rates: $24-$44
(715) 866-8951

WEST SALEM
AMERICINN
125 Buol Rd (54669)
Rates: $65-$131
(608) 786-3340
(800) 634-3444

WESTBY
OLD TOWNE MOTEL
Hwy 27 & 14 & 61 S (54667)
Rates: $35-$50
(608) 634-2111
(800) 605-0276

WESTFIELD
MARTHA'S ETHNIC B&B
259 2nd St (53964)
Rates: $45-$65
(608) 296-3361

SANDMAN MOTEL
N6820 Harris Ct (53964)
Rates: $35-$70
(608) 296-2565

WEYER-HAEUSER
COUNTRY VIEW MOTEL
W14691 Hwy 8 (54895)
Rates: $24-$30
(715) 353-2780

WHITE LAKE
JESSE'S HISTORIC WOLF RIVER LODGE
W2119 Taylor Rd (54491)
Rates: $80-$160
(715) 882-2182

WHITE LAKE
JESSE'S HISTORIC WOLF RIVER LODGE
W2119 Taylor Rd (54491)
Rates: $100-$320
(715) 882-2182

WHITEHALL
OAK PARK INN & HISTORIC HOPKINS HOUSE
18224 Ervin St (54773)
Rates: $58-$78
(715) 538-4858
(877) 479-7024

WHITEWATER
AMERIHOST INN & SUITES
1355 W Main St (53190)
Rates: $69-$84
(262) 472-9400
(800) 434-5800

BLACK STALLION INN
Rt 1 US Hwy 12 (53190)
Rates: n/a
(414) 473-7700

SUPER 8 MOTEL
917 E Milwaukee St (53190)
Rates: $39-$199
(262) 473-8818
(800) 800-8000

WHITE HORSE INN MOTEL
W4890 Tri County Line Rd (53190)
Rates: $40-$50
(414) 473-4777

WILLARD
THE BARN OF CLARK COUNTY
N7890 Bachelors Ave (54493)
Rates: $59-$79
(715) 267-3215

SUNSET PINES RESORT
W9210 Rock Creek Rd (54493)
Rates: $65-$120
(715) 267-6989

WINDSOR
DAYS INN
6311 Rostad Dr (53598)
Rates: $49-$120
(608) 846-7473
(800) 329-7466

SUPER 8 MOTEL
4506 Lake Cir (53598)
Rates: $50-$75
(608) 846-3971
(800) 800-8000

WINTER
HOWE'S NORTHERN HIDEAWAY
W5284 Log Lodge Rd (54896)
Rates: $44-$125
(715) 266-5953

WISCONSIN DELLS
BAKERS SUNSET BAY RESORT
921 Canyon Rd (53965)
Rates: $49-$205
(608) 254-8406
(800) 435-6515

BLACKHAWK MOTEL
720 Race St (53965)
Rates: $40-$165
(608) 254-7770

BRIDGE VIEW MOTEL
1020 River Rd (53965)
Rates: $35-$220
(608) 254-6114

DAY'S END MOTEL
N604 Hwy 12-16, Exit 85 (53965)
Rates: $34-$132
(608) 254-8171
(888) 315-2378

DELTON OAKS MOTEL RESORT
730 E Hiawatha Dr (53965)
Rates: $60-$200
(608) 253-4092
(888) 374-6257

AREA CODES - If the local number doesn't connect, check for a new area code.

HOWARD JOHNSON HOTEL & ANTIQUA BAY WATERPARK
655 Frontage Rd (53965)
Rates: $77-$170
(608) 254-8306
(800) 54-DELLS

INTERNATIONAL MOTEL
1311 E Broadway (53965)
Rates: $30-$140
(608) 254-2431

KING'S INN MOTEL
31 Whitlock St (53965)
Rates: $35-$150
(608) 254-2043

PINE AIR MOTEL & SUITES
511 Wisconsin Dells Pky (53965)
Rates: $48-$275
(608) 254-2131
(800) 635-8627

RODEWAY INN
350 W Munroe St (53965)
Rates: $55-$149
(608) 254-6492
(800) 424-6423

SANDS MOTEL
124 Wisc Dells Pkwy S (53965)
Rates: n/a
(608) 254-7447

SPRING BOOK VACATION RENTALS
420 Birchwood Rd #1 (53965)
Rates: $90-$400
(608) 254-4349
(877) 228-8686

STAR MOTEL-RESORT
1531 Wisc Dells Pkwy (53965)
Rates: $40-$150
(608) 254-2051

SUPER 8 MOTEL
800 County Hwy H (53965)
Rates: $57-$88
(608) 254-6464
(800) 800-8000

SURFSIDE MOTEL
231 Wisc Dells Pkwy (53965)
Rates: $49-$180
(608) 254-7594

THUNDER VALLEY INN
W15344 Waubeek Rd (53965)
Rates: $65-$135
(608) 254-4145

TWI-LITE MOTEL
111 Wisc Dells Pkwy S (53965)
Rates: $35-$105
(608) 253-1911

WISCONSIN RAPIDS

BEST WESTERN RAPIDS MOTOR INN
911 Huntington Ave (54494)
Rates: $52-$72
(715) 423-3211
(800) 528-1234

HOTEL MEAD
451 E Grand Ave (54494)
Rates: $62-$204
(715) 423-1500
(800) 843-6323

SUPER 8 MOTEL
3410 8th St S (54494)
Rates: $48-$73
(715) 423-8080
(800) 800-8000

WITTENBERG

COMFORT INN & WILDERNESS
W17267 Red Oak Ln (54499)
Rates: $70-$188
(715) 253-3755
(800) 424-6423

WOODVILLE

WOODVILLE MOTEL
543 Cty Rd B (54028)
Rates: $45-$65
(715) 698-2481

AREA CODES - If the local number doesn't connect, check for a new area code.

WYOMING

AFTON

THE CORRAL CABINS
161 S Washington (83110)
Rates: $45-$60
(307) 886-5424

HIGH COUNTRY INN
689 S Washington St (83110)
Rates: $75-$100
(307) 885-3856

LAZY B MOTEL
219 Washington (83110)
Rates: $50-$75
(307) 886-3187

MOUNTAIN INN
83542 Hwy 89 (83110)
Rates: $55-$80
(307) 886-3156

ALPINE

ALPINE INN
Box 263 (83128)
Rates: $35-$99
(307) 654-7644

BEST WESTERN FLYING ADDLE LODGE
118878 Hwy 26 & 89 (83128)
Rates: $65-$180
(307) 654-7561
(800) 528-1234
(866) 666-2937

LAKESIDE MOTEL
Box 238 (83128)
Rates: $30-$50
(307) 654-7507

ROYAL RESORT
Hwy 89 & 26 (83128)
Rates: $70-$100
(307) 654-7545
(800) 343-6755

THREE RIVERS MOTEL
US Hwy 89 (83128)
Rates: $26-$50
(307) 654-7551

ATLANTIC CITY

ATLANTIC CITY MERCHANTILE
100 Main St (82520)
Rates: $25-$50
(307) 332-5143
(888) 257-0215

MINER'S DELIGHT BED & BREAKFST
290 Atlantic Rd (82520)
Rates: n/a
(307) 332-0248
(888) 292-0248

BAGGS

DRIFTERS INN
Hwy 789 (82321)
Rates: $25-$49
(307) 383-2015

BASIN

LILAC MOTEL
710 W C St (82410)
Rates: $26-$45
(307) 568-3355

BEULAH

WINDY ACRES RANCH B&B
5480 Hwy 14 (82712)
Rates: n/a
(307) 283-2664

BIG HORN

BOZEMAN TRAIL B&B
304 Hwy 335 (82833)
Rates: $75-$99
(307) 672-2381

BONDURANT

HOBACK VILLAGE MOTEL
14272 Hwy 189-191 (82922)
Rates: $30-$60
(307) 733-3631

SMILING S MOTEL
33 Mi S of Jackson, Box 171 (82922)
Rates: $25-$50
(307) 733-3457

BUFFALO

ARROWHEAD MOTEL
749 Fort St (82834)
Rates: $35-$60
(307) 684-9453

BIG HORN MOTEL
209 N Main St (82834)
Rates: $38-$75
(307) 684-7822

BLUE GABLES MOTEL
662 N Main St (82834)
Rates: $26-$100
(307) 684-7822
(800) 684-2574

BUFFALO MOTEL
370 N Main St (82834)
Rates: $37-$59
(307) 684-0753
(888) 684-0753

CANYON MOTEL
997 Fort St (82834)
Rates: $32-$60
(307) 684-2957
(800) 231-0742

COMFORT INN
65 US 16 E (82834)
Rates: $45-$130
(307) 684-9564
(800) 424-6423

COWBOY TOWN MOTEL
181 Hwy 16 E (82834)
Rates: $37-$99
(307) 684-0603
(888) 323-2865

CROSSROADS INN
75 N Bypass (82834)
Rates: $45-$94
(307) 684-2256
(800) 852-2302

ECONO LODGE
333 E Hart St (82834)
Rates: $49-$109
(307) 684-2219
(800) 424-6423

MOTEL 6
100 Flat Iron Dr (82834)
Rates: $39-$70
(307) 684-7000
(800) 466-8356

MOUNTAIN VIEW CABINS
585 Fort St (82834)
Rates: $35-$100
(307) 684-2881

SOUTH FORK INN
Hwy US 16 (82834)
Rates: $26-$45
(307) 684-9609

SUPER 8 MOTEL
655 E Hart St (82834)
Rates: $49-$116
(307) 684-2531
(800) 800-8000

WYOMING MOTEL
610 E Hart St (82834)
Rates: $27-$113
(307) 684-5505
(800) 666-5505

Z-BAR MOTEL
626 Fort St (82834)
Rates: $34-$69
(307) 684-5535
(888) 313-1227

CASPER

ALL AMERICAN INN
5755 Cy Ave (82601)
Rates: $25-$50
(307) 235-6688

DAYS INN
301 East E St (82601)
Rates: $62-$89
(307) 234-1159
(800) 329-7466

ELK VALLEY INN
3256 N Fork Hwy (82601)
Rates: $51-$85
(307) 587-4149

FIRST INTERSTATE INN
205 E Wyoming Blvd (82601)
Rates: $29-$45
(307) 234-9125

HOLIDAY INN
300 W F St (82601)
Rates: $79-$129
(307) 235-2531
(800) 465-4329

MOTEL 6
1150 Wilkins Cir (82601)
Rates: $33-$48
(307) 234-3903
(800) 466-8356

NATIONAL 9 INN
100 West F St (82601)
Rates: $23-$56
(307) 235-2711
(800) 524-9999

PARKWAY PLAZA
123 W East St (82601)
Rates: $80-$109
(307) 235-1777
(800) 270-7829

QUALITY INN
821 N Poplar (82601)
Rates: $55-$161
(307) 266-2400
(800) 424-6423

RADISSON HOTEL
800 N Poplar (82601)
Rates: $84-$94
(307) 266-6000
(800) 333-3333

RANCH HOUSE MOTEL
1130 E F St (82601)
Rates: $25-$50
(307) 266-4044

ROYAL INN
440 East A St (82601)
Rates: $35-$55
(307) 234-3501
(800) 967-6925

AREA CODES - If the local number doesn't connect, check for a new area code.

SKYLER INN
111 S Wilson St
(82601)
Rates: $68-$106
(307) 232-5100

SUPER 8 MOTEL
3838 Cy Ave
(82604)
Rates: $55-$70
(307) 266-3480
(888) 266-0497

TOPPER MOTEL
728 E A St (82601)
Rates: $25-$50
(307) 237-8407

VIRGINIAN MOTEL
830 E A St (82601)
Rates: $25-$50
(307) 266-9731

WESTRIDGE MOTEL
955 Cy Ave (82601)
Rates: $38-$58
(307) 234-8911
(800) 341-8000

YELLOWSTONE MOTEL
1610 E Yellowstone
(82601)
Rates: $25-$49
(307) 234-9174
(800) 531-9257

CENTENNIAL
CENTENNIAL VALLEY TRADING POST
2755 Hwy 130
(82055)
Rates: $26-$49
(307) 721-5074

FRIENDLY FLY STORE & MOTEL
Hwy 130, Box 195
(82055)
Rates: $51-$100
(307) 742-6033

THE OLD CORRAL MOUNTAIN LODGE
Main St (82055)
Rates: $51-$100
(307) 745-5918

SARAH ROSE HOTEL
2747 Hwy 130
(82055)
Rates: $61-$100
(307) 742-5476
(888) 400-9953

SNOWY MOUNTAIN LODGE
3474 Hwy 130
(82055)
Rates: n/a
(307) 742-7669

CHEYENNE
ADVENTURERS COUNTRY B&B
3803 I-80 S Service
Rd (82001)
Rates: n/a
(307) 632-4087

ATLAS MOTEL
1524 W
Lincolnway
(82001)
Rates: $25-$50
(307) 632-9214

BEST WESTERN HITCHING POST
1700 W Lincolnway
(82001)
Rates: $79-$225
(307) 638-3301
(800) 528-1234
(800) 221-0125

BIT-O-WYO RANCH B&B
470 Happy Jack
Rd (82001)
Rates: n/a
(307) 638-8340
(Horses allowed only)

CHEYENNE MOTEL
1601 E
Lincolnway
(82001)
Rates: $25-$50
(307) 778-7664

COMFORT INN
2245 Etchepare Dr
(82007)
Rates: $49-$200
(307) 638-7202
(800) 424-6423

DAYS INN
2360 W
Lincolnway
(82003)
Rates: $39-$145
(307) 778-8877
(800) 329-7466

DRUMMOND'S RANCH B&B
399 Happy Jack
Rd (82007)
Rates: $65-$175
(307) 634-6042

EXPRESS INN
2512 W
Lincolnway
(82003)
Rates: $40-$70
(307) 632-7556

FIREBIRD MOTEL
1905 E
Lincolnway
(82001)
Rates: $25-$50
(307) 632-5505

FLEETWOOD MOTEL
3800 E
Lincolnway
(82001)
Rates: $40-$59
(307) 638-8908
(800) 634-7763

FRONTIER MOTEL
1400 W
Lincolnway
(82001)
Rates: $26-$48
(307) 634-7961

HOLIDAY INN
204 W Fox Farm
Rd (82007)
Rates: $86-$100
(307) 638-4466
(800) 465-4329

HOME RANCH MOTEL
2414 E Lincolnway
(82001)
Rates: $27-$47
(307) 634-3575

HOWDY PARDNER B&B
1920 Tranquility
Rd (82009)
Rates: n/a
(406) 259-7993
(307) 634-6493

LA QUINTA INN
2410 W
Lincolnway
(82001)
Rates: $74-$115
(307) 632-7117
(800) 687-6667

LINCOLN COURT
1700 W
Lincolnway
(82001)
Rates: $55-$85
(307) 638-3302
(800) 221-0125

MOTEL 6
1735 Westland Rd
(82001)
Rates: $30-$80
(307) 635-6806
(800) 466-8356

NAGLE WARREN MANSION B&B
222 E 17th St
(82001)
Rates: $118-$168
(307) 637-3333
(800) 811-2610

OAK TREE INN
1625 Stillwater
Ave (82001)
Rates: $55-$100
(307) 778-6620

THE PLAINS HOTEL
1600 Central Ave
(82001)
Rates: $49-$159
(307) 638-3311
(866) 275-2467

PORCH SWING B&B
712 E 20th St
(82001)
Rates: $75-$85
(307) 778-7182

QUALITY INN
5401 Walker Rd
(82001)
Rates: $39-$159
(307) 632-8901
(800) 424-6423
(800) 876-8901

RAINSFORD INN BED & BREAKFST
219 E 18th St
(82001)
Rates: n/a
(307) 638-2337

RANGER MOTEL
909 W 16th St
(82001)
Rates: $27-$48
(307) 634-7995

RODEO INN
3839 E Lincolnway
(82001)
Rates: $35-$60
307) 634-2171

ROUNDUP MOTEL
403 S Greeley
Hwy (82001)
Rates: $25-$50
(307) 634-7741

SAPP BROS.BIG C
I-80 & Archer
(82001)
Rates: $24-$50
(307) 632-6000
(800) 788-4671

TWIN CHIMNEYS MOTEL
2405 E
Lincolnway
(82001)
Rates: $27-$48
(307) 632-8921

WINDY HILLS GUEST HOUSE B&B
393 Happy Jack
Rd (82007)
Rates: $99-$280
(307) 632-6423

WYOMING MOTEL
1401 W Lincolnway
(82001)
Rates: $25-$50
(307) 632-8104

CHUGWATER
SUPER 8 MOTEL
100 Buffalo Dr
(82210)
Rates: $39-$80
(307) 422-3248
(800) 800-8000

CLEARMONT
RBL BISON GUEST RANCH B&B
4355 US Hwy
14-16 E (82835)
Rates: $48-$78
(307) 758-4387
(800) 597-0109

CODY
BEARTOOTH INN OF CODY
2513 Greybull
Hwy (83414)
Rates: $49-$150
(307) 527-5505
(800) 807-8522

AREA CODES - If the local number doesn't connect, check for a new area code.

BEST BET INN
1701 17th St
(82414)
Rates: $24-$46
(307) 587-9009

BEST WESTERN SUNSET MOTOR INN
1601 8th St (82414)
Rates: $55-$145
(307) 587-4265
(800) 528-1234
(800) 624-2727

BIG BEAR MOTEL
139 W
Yellowstone Hwy
(82414)
Rates: $39-$75
(307) 587-3117
(800) 325-7163

CARTER MOUNTAIN MOTEL
1701 Central
(82414)
Rates: $25-$50
(307) 587-4295

CODY MOTOR LODGE
1455 Sheridan Ave
(82414)
Rates: $45-$120
(307) 527-6291
(800) 340-2639

ELK VALLEY INN
3256 Yellowstone
Hwy (82414)
Rates: $30-$45
(307) 587-4149

GATEWAY MOTEL
203 Yellowstone
Ave (82414)
Rates: $25-$50
(307) 587-2561

GREEN GABLES INN
1636 Central Ave
(82414)
Rates: $54-$108
(307) 587-6886

HIGH COUNTRY MOTOR INN
405 Yellowstone
Ave (82414)
Rates: $52-$98
(307) 587-5960
(800) 835-7427

HOUSE OF BURGESS B&B
1508 Alger Ave
(82414)
Rates: n/a
(307) 527-7208

KELLY INN
2513 Greybull
Hwy (82414)
Rates: $92-$112
(307) 527-5505
(800) 635-3559

MOUNTAIN VIEW INN
N Fork Star Rt
(82414)
Rates: $45-$100
(307) 587-2081

PARKWAY INN
720 Yellowstone
Ave (82414)
Rates: $88-$98
(307) 587-4208

QUESTION CREEK B&B
311 Lane 17 (82414)
Rates: n/a
(307) 754-3249

SEVEN K'S MOTEL
232 W Yellowstone
Ave (82414)
Rates: $23-$45
(307) 587-5890
(800) 223-9204

SKYLINE MOTOR INN
1919 17th St
(82414)
Rates: $35-$74
(307) 587-4201
(800) 843-8809

STAGE STOP
502 Yellowstone
Ave (82414)
Rates: $52-$97
(307) 527-5065

STREAMSIDE INN
Yellowstone Hwy
14, 16 & 20 (82414)
Rates: $61-$100
(307) 587-8242
(800) 285-1282

SUNRISE MOTOR INN
1407 8th St (82414)
Rates: $39-$129
(307) 587-5566
(877) 587-5566

SUPER 8 MOTEL
730 Yellowstone
Ave (82414)
Rates: $85-$135
(307) 527-6214
(800) 800-8000

TRAIL INN & MOTEL
2750 N Fork Hwy
(82414)
Rates: $25-$50
(307) 587-3741

TROUT CREEK INN
Yellowstone Hwy
W (82414)
Rates: $28-$64
(307) 587-6288
(800) 341-8000

UPTOWN MOTEL
1562 Sheridan Ave
(82414)
Rates: $25-$50
(307) 587-4245

WESTERN 6 GUN MOTEL
423 Yellowstone
Ave (82414)
Rates: $54-$99
(307) 587-4835

WISE CHOICE INN
2908 N Fork Hwy
(82414)
Rates: $66-$75
(307) 587-5004

YELLOWSTONE VALLEY INN
3324 N Fork Hwy
(82414)
Rates: $52-$97
(307) 587-3961
(888) 705-7703

COKEVILLE

HIDEOUT MOTEL
245 S Hwy 30 N
(83114)
Rates: $23-$44
(307) 279-3281

VALLEY HI MOTEL
Hwy 30 & 89
(83114)
Rates: $25-$48
(307) 279-3251

DAYTON

FOOTHILLS MOTEL
101 N Main
(82836)
Rates: $25-$50
(307) 655-2547

DOUGLAS

ALPINE INN
2310 E Richards
(82633)
Rates: $40-$60
(307) 358-4780

BEST WESTERN DOUGLAS INN
1450 Riverbend
Dr (82633)
Rates: $65-$105
(307) 358-9790
(800) 528-1234
(800) 344-2113

CARRIAGE HOUSE B&B
413 Center St
(82633)
Rates: n/a
(307) 358-2752

CHIEFTAIN MOTEL
815 Richards
(82633)
Rates: $29-$43
(307) 358-2673

FIRST INTERSTATE INN
2349 E Richards
(82633)
Rates: $27-$44
(307) 358-2833
(800) 992-9026

4 WINDS MOTEL
615 E Richards
(82633)
Rates: $25-$50
(307) 358-2322

PLAINS MOTEL
628 Richards E
(82633)
Rates: $25-$49
(307) 358-4484

SUPER 8 MOTEL
314 Russell Ave
(82633)
Rates: $37-$61
(307) 358-6800
(800) 800-8000

VAGABOND MOTEL
430 E Richards
(82633)
Rates: $25-$50
(307) 358-9414

DUBOIS

BALD MOUNTAIN INN
1349 W Ramshorn
St (82513)
Rates: $49-$110
(307) 455-2844
(800) 682-9323

BLACK BEAR COUNTRY INN
505 N Ramshorn
St (82513)
Rates: $30-$60
(307) 455-2344
(800) 873-2327

BRANDING IRON INN
401 N Ramshorn
St (82513)
Rates: $40-$90
(307) 455-2893

CHINOOK WINDS MTN LODGE
640 S 1st St
(82513)
Rates: $40-$75
(307) 455-2987

PINNACLE BUTTES LODGE
3577 Hwy 26 W
(82513)
Rates: $50-$160
(307) 455-2506

RIVERSIDE INN
5810 Hwy 26
(82513)
Rates: $30-$50
(307) 455-2337

STAGECOACH MOTOR INN
103 E Ramshorn
St (82513)
Rates: $40-$78
(307) 455-2303
(800) 455-5090

TRAILS END MOTEL
511 Ramshorn St
(82513)
Rates: $35-$100
(307) 455-2540
(888) 455-6660

WIND RIVER MOTEL
519 W Ramshorn St (82513)
Rates: $25-$50
(307) 455-2611
(877) 455-2621

EDGERTON

TEAPOT MOTOR LODGE
727 Hwy 387 (82635)
Rates: $25-$48
(307) 437-6541

ENCAMPMENT

RIVERSIDE CABINS
Star Rt, Box 15 (82325)
Rates: $25-$50
(307) 327-5361

RUSTIC MOUNTAIN LODGE B&B
Star Rt, Box 49 (82325)
Rates: $45-$65
(307) 327-5539

VACHER'S BIGHORN LODGE
508 McCaffrey Ave (82325)
Rates: $25-$50
(307) 327-5110
(888) 327-5110

EVANSTON

ALEXANDER MOTEL
Box 181 (82930)
Rates: $25-$50
(307) 789-2346

COMFORT INN
1931 Harrison Dr (82930)
Rates: $50-$225
(307) 789-7799
(800) 424-6423

ECONOMY INN
1710 Harrison Dr (82930)
Rates: $30-$49
(307) 789-2777

HILLCREST DX MOTEL
1725 Harrison Dr (82930)
Rates: $25-$50
(307) 789-1111

MOTEL 6
261 Bear River Dr (82930)
Rates: $36-$40
(307) 789-0791
(800) 466-8356

NATIONAL 9 INN
1724 Harrison Dr (82930)
Rates: $25-$50
(307) 789-9610
(800) 524-9999

PRAIRIE INN MOTEL
264 Bear River Dr (82930)
Rates: $40-$65
(307) 789-2920

SUPER 8 MOTEL
70 Bear River Dr (82930)
Rates: $34-$47
(307) 789-7510
(800) 800-8000

WESTON PLAZA HOTEL
1983 Harrison Dr (82930)
Rates: $44-$49
(307) 789-0783
(800) 255-9840

WESTON SUPER BUDGET INN
1936 Harrison Dr (82930)
Rates: $25-$50
(307) 789-2810
(800) 255-9840

EVANSVILLE

COMFORT INN
480 Lathrop (82601)
Rates: $69-$99
(307) 235-3038
(800) 424-6423

SUPER 8 MOTEL
269 Miracle Dr (82636)
Rates: $75-$169
(307) 237-8100
(800) 800-8000

FARSON

SITZMAN'S MOTEL
Box 25 (82932)
Rates: $25-$50
(307) 273-9241

FORT BRIDGER

WAGON WHEEL MOTEL
270 N Main (82933)
Rates: $25-$50
(307) 782-6361

GILLETTE

BEST WESTERN TOWER WEST LODGE
109 N Hwy 14-16 (82716)
Rates: $44-$148
(307) 686-2210
(800) 528-1234
(800) 762-7375

CLARION WESTERN PLAZA
2009 S Douglas Hwy (82718)
Rates: $71-$160
(307) 686-3000
(800) 424-6423

CIRCLE L MOTEL
410 E 2nd (82716)
Rates: $25-$46
(307) 682-9375

COMFORT INN
1607 W 2nd St ((82716)
Rates: $50-$209
(307) 685-2223
(800) 424-6423

DAYS INN
910 E Boxelder Rd (82716)
Rates: $45-$110
(307) 682-3999
(800) 329-7466

ECONO LODGE
409 Butler-Spaeth Rd (92716)
Rates: $40-$120
(307) 682-4757
(800) 424-6423

HOLIDAY INN EXP
1908 Cliff Davis Dr (82718)
Rates: $89-$189
(307) 686-9576
(800) 686-3368

MOTEL 6
2105 Rodgers Dr (82716)
Rates: $35-$60
(307) 686-8600
(800) 466-8356

MUSTANG MOTEL
922 E 3rd St (82716)
Rates: $25-$50
(307) 682-4784

NATIONAL 9 INN
1020 Hwy 51 E (82716)
Rates: $36-$56
(307) 682-5111
(800) 524-9999

SUPER 8 MOTEL
208 S Decker Ct (82716)
Rates: $30-$72
(307) 682-8078
(800) 800-800

THRIFTY INN
1004 E Hwy 14-16 (82716)
Rates: $25-$50
(307) 621-2616
(800) 621-2182

GLENDO

GLENDO MARINA MOTEL
383 Glendo Park Rd (82213)
Rates: $35-$58
(307) 735-4216

GLENROCK

ALL AMERICAN INN
500 W Aspen (82637)
Rates: $30-$240
(307) 436-2772

GLENROCK MOTEL
108 S 3rd St (82637)
Rates: $25-$50
(307) 436-2772

GRAND TETON NATIONAL PARK

FLAGG RANCH RESORT
Hwy 89 & US 191, (P O Box 187, Moran 83013)
Rates: $155-$170
(307) 543-2861
(800) 443-2311

HATCHEL RESORT
US 26 & 287 (Moran 83013)
Rates: $90-$180
(307) 543-2413

JACKSON LAKE LODGE
US 89 & 287
P O Box 240 (Moran 83013)
Rates: $115-$198
(307) 543-2855
(307) 543-2811
(800) 628-9988

SIGNAL MOUNTAIN LODGE
US 89, 191 & 287, P O Box 50 (Moran 83013)
Rates: $99-$265
(307) 543-2831
(800) 672-6012

GREEN RIVER

DESMOND MOTEL
140 N 7th W (82935)
Rates: $26-$36
(307) 875-3701

FLAMING GORGE MOTEL
316 E Flaming Gorge Way (82935)
Rates: $25-$50
(307) 875-4190

OAK TREE INN
1170 W Flaming Gorge Way (82935)
Rates: $59-$79
(307) 875-3500

SUPER 8 MOTEL
280 W Flaming Gorge Way (82935)
Rates: $42-$56
(307) 875-9330
(800) 800-8000

WESTERN MOTEL
890 Flaming Gorge Way (82935)
Rates: $33-$40
(307) 875-2840

GREYBULL

A MAVERIK MOTEL
625 N 6th St (82426)
Rates: $40-$65
(307) 765-4626

ANTLER MOTEL
1116 N 6th St
(82426)
Rates: $35-$60
(307) 765-4404

K-BAR MOTEL
300 Greybull Ave
(82426)
Rates: $24-$54
(307) 765-4426
(877) 765-4426

SAGE MOTEL
1009 N 6th St
(82426)
Rates: $36-$48
(307) 765-4443

YELLOWSTONE MOTEL
247 Greybull Ave
(82426)
Rates: $50-$79
(307) 765-4456

GUERNSEY
ANNETTE'S B&B
Box 31 (82214)
Rates: n/a
(307) 836-2148

BUNKHOUSE MOTEL
350 W Whalen
(82214)
Rates: $40-$69
(307) 836-2356

HANNA
GOLDEN RULE MOTEL
305 S Adams
(82327)
Rates: $25-$50
(307) 325-6525

HELL'S HALF ACRE
HELL'S HALF ACRE MOTEL
Hwys 20 & 26
(82648)
Rates: n/a
(307) 472-0018

HULETT
DIAMOND L GUEST RANCH
Box 70 (82720)
Rates: $90+
(307) 467-5236
(800) 851-5909

HULETT MOTEL
202 Main St
(82720)
Rates: $65-$85
(307) 467-5220
(800) 451-4332

MOTEL PIONEER
119 Hunter
(82720)
Rates: $24-$39
(307) 467-5656
(800) 231-6335

PINE RIDGE RANCH B&B
979 New Haven Rd (82720)
Rates: n/a
(307) 467-5519

JACKSON HOLE
ALPINE MOTEL
70 Jean St (83001)
Rates: $24-$38
(307) 739-3200

ANTLER INN
43 W Pearl St
(83001)
Rates: $76-$115
(307) 733-2535
(800) 4-TETONS

CACHE CREEK MOTEL
390 N Glenwood
(83001)
Rates: $51-$100
(307) 733-7781
(800) 843-4788

COTTAGE AT SNOW KING
470 King St (83001)
Rates: $25-$50
(307) 733-3480

COWBOY VILLAGE RESORT CABINS
120 S Flat Creek Dr (83002)
Rates: $70-$180
(307) 733-3121
(800) 962-4988

DON'T FENCE ME INN
2350 N Moose-Wilson Rd (83001)
Rates: n/a
(307) 733-7979

ELK COUNTRY INN
480 W Pearl St
(83001)
Rates: $56-$156
(307) 733-2364
(800) 4-TETONS

FLAT CREEK MOTEL
1935 N US 89
(83001)
Rates: $65-$95
(307) 733-5276
(800) 438-9338

FRIENDSHIP INN ANTLER MOTEL
43 W Pearl St
(83001)
Rates: $62-$125
(307) 733-2535
(800) 453-4511

JACKSON HOLE LODGE
420 W Broadway
(83001)
Rates: $79-$124
(307) 733-2992
(800) 604-9404

JACKSON HOLE RACQUET CLUB RESORT
Star Rt 362A
(83001)
Rates: $51-$100
(307) 733-3990
(800) 443-8616

MAD DOG RANCH
6 mi NW of Jackson,
Box 7737 (83001)
Rates: $51-$100
(307) 733-3729

MOTEL 6
600 S Hwy 89
(83001)
Rates: $34-$90
(307) 733-1620
(800) 466-8356

PAINTED BUFFALO INN
400 W Broadway
(83001)
Rates: $60-$149
(307) 733-5430
(800) 288-3866

PROSPECTOR MOTEL
155 N Jackson St
(83001)
Rates: $45-$125
(307) 733-4858
(800) 851-0070

QUALITY INN & SUITES/49'ER
330 W Pearl St
(83001)
Rates: $58-$210
(307) 733-7550
(800) 424-6423

RANCH INN
45 E Pearl St
(83001)
Rates: $40-$250
(307) 733-6363
(800) 348-5599

RAWHIDE MOTEL
75 S Millward
(93001)
Rates: $51-$150
(307) 733-1216
(800) 835-2999

SNOW KING RESORT
400 E Snow King Ave (83001)
Rates: $130-$750
(307) 733-5200
(800) 522-5464

TETON GABLES MOTEL
Jct 191-189-22
(83001)
Rates: $51-$99
(307) 733-3723

TWIN MOUNTAIN RIVER RANCH BED & BREAKFST
Star Rt 40 (83001)
Rates: n/a
(307) 733-1168

WESTERN MOTEL
225 S Glenwood
(83001)
Rates: $51-$98
(307) 733-3291
(800) 845-7999

JELM
WOODS LANDING
9 State Hwy 10
(82063)
Rates: $25-$50
(307) 745-9638

KAYCEE
CASSIDY INN MOTEL
346 Nolan Ave
(82426)
Rates: $25-$50
(307) 738-2250

GRAVES B&B COWBOY BUNKHOUSES
1729 Barnum Rd
(82639)
Rates: n/a
(307) 738-2319

RIVERSIDE INN
120 2nd St (82639)
Rates: $35-$55
(307) 738-2659

SIESTA MOTEL
255 Nolan Ave
(82639)
Rates: $25-$48
(307) 738-2291

KEMMERER
ANTLER MOTEL
419 Coral St
(83101)
Rates: $30-$50
(307) 877-4461

BON RICO MOTEL
Hwy 189, Box 150
(83101)
Rates: $25-$50
(307) 877-4503

FAIRVIEW MOTEL
61 Hwy N 30 at
189 (83101)
Rates: $30-$44
(307) 877-3938
(800) 247-3938

FOSSIL BUTTE MOTEL
1424 Central Ave
(83101)
Rates: $27-$48
(307) 877-3996

LAKE VIVA NAUGHTON MARINA MOTEL
Hwy 233 (83101)
Rates: n/a
(307) 877-9669

RAILWAY INN MOTEL
1427 W 5th Ave
(83101)
Rates: $25-$50
(307) 877-3544

AREA CODES - If the local number doesn't connect, check for a new area code.

LANDER

BEST WESTERN THE INN AT LANDER
260 Grand View Dr (82520)
Rates: $56-$140
(307) 332-2847
(800) 528-1234

BUDGET HOST PRONGHORN LODGE
150 E Main St (82520)
Rates: $45-$125
(307) 332-3940
(800) 283-4678

THE BUNK HOUSE B&B
2024 Mortimore Ln (82520)
Rates: n/a
(307) 332-5624
(800) 582-5262

COTTAGE HOUSE AT SQUAW CREEK B&B
72 Squaw Creek Ct (82520)
Rates: n/a
(307) 332-5003

DOWNTOWN MOTEL
569 Main St (82520)
Rates: $25-$50
(307) 332-3171

HOLIDAY LODGE
210 McFarlane Dr (82520)
Rates: $45-$55
(307) 332-2511
(800) 624-1974

MAVERICK MOTEL
808 Main St (82520)
Rates: $25-$47
(307) 332-2300
(877) 622-2300

PIECE OF CAKE B&B
2343 Baldwin Crk Rd (82520)
Rates: $70-$90
(307) 332-7608

ROCK SHOP INN
4260 Hwy 28 (82520)
Rates: $35-$80
(307) 332-7396

SILVER SPUR MOTEL
1240 Main St (82520)
Rates: $35-$90
(307) 332-5189
(800) 922-7831

TETON MOTEL
586 W Main St (82520)
Rates: $26-$48
(307) 332-3582

LARAMIE

BEST WESTERN CENTER HOTEL
2313 Soldier Springs Rd (82070)
Rates: $79-$199
(307) 742-6611
(800) 528-1234

DAYS INN
1368 McCue St (82070)
Rates: $49-$159
(307) 745-5678
(800) 329-7466

ECONO LODGE
1370 McCue St (82070)
Rates: $55-$105
(307) 745-8900
(800) 424-6423

1ST INN GOLD
421 Boswell (82070)
Rates: $46-$70
(307) 742-3721
(800) 642-4212

GAS LITE INN MOTEL
960 N 3rd St (82070)
Rates: $40-$66
(307) 742-6616

MOTEL 6
621 Plaza Ln (82070)
Rates: $29-$56
(307) 742-2307
(800) 466-8356

MOTEL 8
501 Boswell Dr (82070)
Rates: $25-$49
(307) 745-4856

NORMAN HOUSE BED & BREAKFST
100 S 8th St (82070)
Rates: n/a
(307) 742-2899

PRAIRIE BREEZE BED & BREAKFST
718 Ivinson Ave (82070)
Rates: n/a
(307) 745-5482
(800) 840-2170

RAMADA INN
2313 Soldier Springs Rd (82070)
Rates: $84-$114
(307) 742-6611
(800) 272-6232

RANGER MOTEL
453 N 3rd (82070)
Rates: $25-$50
(307) 742-6677

SUNSET INN
1104 S 3rd St (82070)
Rates: $45-$75
(307) 742-3741

THUNDERBIRD LODGE
1369 N 3rd (82070)
Rates: $25-$48
(307) 745-4871

TRAVELODGE
165 N 3rd St (82070)
Rates: $39-$74
(307) 742-6671
(800) 578-7878

UNIVERSITY INN
1720 Grand Ave (82070)
Rates: $35-$69
(307) 721-8855
(800) 869-9466

WYCOTO LODGE
4039 Hwy 230 (82070)
Rates: $25-$50
(307) 742-4230

LOVELL

CATTLEMAN MOTEL
470 Montana Ave (82431)
Rates: $38-$52
(307) 548-2296

HORSESHOE BEND MOTEL
375 E Main St (82431)
Rates: $36-$58
(307) 548-2221

SUPER 8 MOTEL
595 E Main St (82431)
Rates: $34-$57
(307) 548-2725
(800) 800-8000

WESTERN MOTEL
180 W Main St (82431)
Rates: $35-$250
(307) 548-2781

LUSK

RAWHIDE MOTEL
805 S Main St (82225)
Rates: $26-$49
(307) 334-2440
(888) 679-2558

SAGE & CACTUS VILLAGE TEPEE B&B
Box 158, Star Rt 1 (82225)
Rates: n/a
(307) 663-7653

TOWN HOUSE MOTEL
525 S Main St (82225)
Rates: $35-$90
(307) 334-2376

TRAIL MOTEL
305 W 8th St (82225)
Rates: $52-$62
(307) 334-2530

LYMAN

VALLEY WEST MOTEL
Main St (82937)
Rates: $25-$50
(307) 787-3700

LYSITE

DEER CREEK GUEST RANCH
Box 3 (82642)
Rates: n/a
(307) 457-2451

MANDERSON

HARMONY RANCH COTTAGE BED & BREAKFAST
182 Hwy 31 (82432)
Rates: n/a
(307) 568-2514

MEDICINE BOW

TRAMPAS LODGE
Box 66 (82329)
Rates: $25-$50
(307) 379-2280

VIRGINIAN HOTEL
404 Lincoln Hwy, Box 127 (82329)
Rates: $25-$50
(307) 379-2377

MEETEETSE

OASIS MOTEL
1702 State St (82433)
Rates: $51-$99
(307) 868-2551

VISION QUEST MOTEL
2207 State St (82433)
Rates: $25-$50
(307) 868-2512
(888) 281-9866

MILLS

RED ARROW MOTEL
West Yellowstone & Wyoming Blvd (82644)
Rates: $25-$50
(307) 234-5293

MOORCROFT

COZY MOTEL
219 W Converse St (82721)
Rates: $35-$99
(307) 756-3486

KEYHOLE MARINA & MOTEL
215 McKean Rd (82721)
Rates: $23-$38
(307) 756-9529

AREA CODES - If the local number doesn't connect, check for a new area code.

MOORCOURT MOTEL
Hwy 14 & Devils Tower Rd (82721)
Rates: $35-$65
(307) 756-3411

WYOMING MOTEL
112 E Converse St (82721)
Rates: $35-$58
(307) 756-3452

NEWCASTLE

AUTO INN MOTEL
2503 W Main (82701)
Rates: $32-$69
(307) 746-2734
(877) 228-8646

FLYING V CAMBRIA INN
23726 Hwy 85 (82701)
Rates: $52-$99
(307) 746-2096

FOUNTAIN MOTOR INN
2 Fountain Plaza (82701)
Rates: $42-$62
(307) 746-4426
(800) 882-8858

FOUR CORNER, DINER & INN
24714 US Hwy 85 N (82701)
Rates: $35-$100
(307) 746-4776

HILLTOP MOTEL
1121 S Summit (82701)
Rates: $25-$50
(307) 746-4494

MORGAN MOTEL
205 S Spokane (82701)
Rates: $25-$50
(307) 746-2715

PINES MOTEL
248 E Wentworth (82701)
Rates: $38-$100
(307) 746-4334
(800) 946-4334

SAGE MOTEL
1227 S Summit Ave (82701)
Rates: $36-$60
(307) 746-2724

SUNDOWNER INN
451 W Main (82701)
Rates: $23-$37
(307) 746-2796

PAHASKA TEPEE

(Yellowstone National Park area)

ELEPHANT HEAD LODGE CABINS
1170 Yellowstone Hwy (82450)
Rates: $95-$139
(307) 587-3980

PAINTER

HUNTER PEAK RANCH
4027 Crandall Rd (82414)
Rates: $121-$158
(307) 587-3711

PINE BLUFFS

GATOR'S TRAVELYN MOTEL
515 W 7th St (82082)
Rates: $25-$50
(307) 245-3226

SUNSET MOTEL
316 W 3rd (82082)
Rates: $25-$50
(307) 245-3591

PINEDALE

BEST WESTERN PINEDALE INN
850 W Pine St (82941)
Rates: $60-$119
(307) 367-6869
(800) 528-1234

BOULDER LAKE LODGE
Box 1100 (82941)
Rates: n/a
(307) 537-4300

CAMP O'THE PINES MOTEL
38 N Fremont (82941)
Rates: $23-$45
(307) 367-4536

CHAMBERS HOUSE B&B
111 W Magnolia St (82041)
Rates: n/a
(307) 367-2168
(800) 567-2168

HALF MOON LODGE MOTEL
46 N Sublett Ave (82941)
Rates: $51-$100
(307) 367-2851

LAKESIDE LODGE RESORT/MARINA
99 FS 111 on Fremont Lake (82941)
Rates: $75-$139
(307) 367-2221

THE LODGE AT PINEDALE
1054 W Pine St (82941)
Rates: $65-$105
(307) 367-8800

LOG CABIN MOTEL
49 E Magnolia (82941)
Rates: $50-$65
(307) 367-4579

PINE CREEK INN
650 W Pine St (82941)
Rates: $25-$47
(307) 367-2191

POLE CREEK RANCH B&B
244 Pole Creek Rd (82941)
Rates: $50-$55
(307) 367-4433

RIVERA LODGE
442 W Marilyn (82941)
Rates: $52-$97
(307) 367-2424

SUN DANCE MOTEL
148 E Pine (82941)
Rates: $50-$140
(307) 367-4336

TETON COURT MOTEL
123 E Magnolia St (82941)
Rates: $27-$47
(307) 367-4317

WINDOW ON THE WINDS B&B
10151 Hwy 191 (82941)
Rates: $60-$95
(307) 367-2600
(888) 367-1345

POWDER RIVER

HELL'S HALF ACRE MOTEL & CAMPGROUND
Hell's Half Acre (82648)
Rates: $24-$36
(307) 472-0018

POWELL

BEST CHOICE MOTEL
337 E 2nd St (82435)
Rates: $25-$50
(307) 754-2243
(800) 308-8447

THE JOANN RANCH B&B
137 Rd 8VE (82435)
Rates: n/a
(307) 645-3109

KINGS INN
777 E 2nd St (82435)
Rates: $54-$76
(307) 754-5117

RANCHESTER

HISTORIC OLD STONE HOUSE B&B
135 Wolf Creek Rd (82839)
Rates: $50-$100
(307) 655-9239

WESTERN MOTEL
350 Dayton St (82839)
Rates: $45-$65
(307) 655-2212

RAWLINS

BEST WESTERN COTTONTREE INN
2221 W Spruce St (82301)
Rates: $69-$114
(307) 324-2737
(800) 662-6886

BRIDGER INN
1904 E Cedar St (82301)
Rates: $26-$34
(307) 328-1401

DAYS INN
2222 E Cedar St (82301)
Rates: $60-$92
(307) 324-6615
(800) 329-7466

THE LODGE AT RAWLINS
1801 E Cedar St (82301)
Rates: $50-$80
(307) 324-2783
(877) RAWLINS

RAWLINS MOTEL
905 W Spruce St (82301)
Rates: $28-$42
(307) 324-3456

SLEEP INN
1400 Higley Blvd (82301)
Rates: $59-$80
(307) 328-1732
(800) 424-6423

RIVERSIDE

BEAR TRAP BAR, CAFE & CABINS
120 E Riverside Ave (82325)
Rates: $25-$45
(307) 327-5277

LAZY ACRES MOTEL
Hwy 230 (82325)
Rates: $25-$35
(307) 327-5968

RIVERSIDE CABINS
Star Rt, Box 15 (82325)
Rates: $61-$100
(307) 327-5361

AREA CODES - If the local number doesn't connect, check for a new area code.

RIVERTON

COTTONWOOD RANCH B&B
951 Missouri Valley Rd (82501)
Rates: n/a
(307) 856-3064

DAYS INN
909 W Main St (82501)
Rates: $35-$90
(307) 856-9677
(800) 329-7466

DRIFTWOOD INN
611 W Main St (82501)
Rates: $30-$40
(307) 856-4811

HI-LO MOTEL
414 N Federal Blvd (82501)
Rates: $24-$33
(307) 856-9223

HOLIDAY INN CONV CTR
900 E Sunset (82501)
Rates: $49-$119
(307) 856-8100
(800) 465-4329

INN EL RANCHO
221 S Federal Blvd (82501)
Rates: $30-$45
(307) 856-7455

MOUNTAIN VIEW MOTEL
720 W Main St (82501)
Rates: $27-$47
(307) 856-2418

PAINTBRUSH MOTEL
1550 N Federal Blvd (82501)
Rates: $36-$49
(307) 856-9238

ROOMER'S MOTEL
319 N Federal (82501)
Rates: $35-$50
(307) 857-1735
(800) 857-4097

SUNDOWNER STATION MOTEL
1616 N Federal Blvd (82501)
Rates: $50-$65
(307) 856-6503
(800) 874-1116

SUPER 8 MOTEL
1040 N Federal Blvd (82501)
Rates: $40-$75
(307) 857-2400
(800) 800-8000

THUNDERBIRD MOTEL
302 E Fremont (82501)
Rates: $38-$56
(307) 856-9201

ROCK RIVER

LONGHORN LODGE
Rt 287 (82083)
Rates: $25-$50
(307) 378-2555

ROCK SPRINGS

BUDGET HOST INN
1004 Dewar Dr (82901)
Rates: $36-$75
(307) 362-6673

COMFORT INN
1670 Sunset Dr (82901)
Rates: $55-$80
(307) 382-9490
(800) 424-6423

DAYS INN
1545 Elk St (82901)
Rates: $43-$85
(307) 362-5646
(800) 329-7466

HOLIDAY INN
1675 Sunset Dr (82901)
Rates: $80-$100
(307) 382-9200
(800) 465-4329

THE INN AT ROCK SPRGS
2518 Foothill Blvd (82901)
Rates: $44-$80
(307) 362-9600
(800) 442-9692

LA QUINTA INN
2717 Dewar Dr (82901)
Rates: $70-$106
(307) 362-1770
(800) 687-6667

MOTEL 6
2615 Commercial Way (82901)
Rates: $37-$57
(307) 362-1850
(800) 466-8356

MOTEL 8
108 Gateway Blvd (82901)
Rates: $25-$50
(307) 362-8200
(888) 362-8200

RAMADA LIMITED
2717 Dewar Dr (82901)
Rates: n/a
(307) 362-1770
(800) 272-6232

SPRINGS MOTEL
1525 9th St (82901)
Rates: $38-$64
(307) 362-6683

THUNDERBIRD MOTEL
1556 9th St (82901)
Rates: $35-$55
(307) 362-3739

SARATOGA

BROOKSONG B&B
HC 63, Box 9L (82331)
Rates: n/a
(307) 326-8744

CARY'S SAGE & SAND MOTEL
311 S 1st (82331)
Rates: $25-$50
(307) 326-8339

HACIENDA MOTEL
1116 S 1st St (82331)
Rates: $46-$76
(307) 326-5751

RIVIERA LODGE
303 N 1st (82331)
Rates: $25-$50
(307) 326-5651

SILVER MOON
412 E Bridge (82331)
Rates: $25-$50
(307) 326-5974

SHELL

HAP'S TRAPPER CREEK B&B
4046 Trapper Crk Rd (82441)
Rates: n/a
(307) 765-9685

MAYLAND RANCH LODGE & CABINS
P. O. Box 215 (82441)
Rates: $50-$75
(307) 765-2669

TRAPPER'S REST B&B
4351 Trapper Crk Rd (82441)
Rates: $50-$90
(307) 765-9239
(800) 826-8872

WAGON WHEEL LODGE
Hwy 14 (82441)
Rates: $23-$38
(307) 765-2561

SHERIDAN

ALAMO MOTEL
1326 N Main (82801)
Rates: $25-$37
(307) 672-2455

APPLE TREE INN
1552 Coffeen Ave (82801)
Rates: $32-$45
(307) 672-2428
(800) 670-2428

ASPEN INN
1744 N Main St (82801)
Rates: $35-$58
(307) 672-9064

BEST WESTERN SHERIDAN CENTER
612 N Main (82801)
Rates: $69-$139
(307) 674-7421
(800) 528-1234
(877) 437-4326

BRAMBLE MOTEL
2366 N Main (82801)
Rates: $24-$38
(307) 674-4902

BUDGET HOST INN
2007 N Main (82801)
Rates: $35-$70
(307) 674-7496
(800) 283-4678

DAYS INN
I-90, Ex 25, Brundage Ln (82801)
Rates: $45-$199
(307) 672-2888
(800) 329-7466

EVERGREEN INN
580 E 5th St (82801)
Rates: $25-$40
(307) 672-9757
(800) 771-4761

FOOTHILLS RANCH B&B
521 Pass Creek Rd (Parkman 82838)
Rates: n/a
(307) 655-9362

HOLIDAY INN ATRIUM & CONV CTR
1809 Sugarland Dr (82801)
Rates: $99-$135
(307) 672-8931
(800) 465-4329

HOLIDAY LODGE
625 Coffeen Ave (82801)
Rates: $25-$50
(307) 672-2407

LARIAT MOTEL
2068 Coffeen Ave (82801)
Rates: $35-$60
(307) 672-6475

MOTEL 6
911 Sibley Circle (82801)
Rates: $39-$70
(307) 673-9500
(800) 466-8356

AREA CODES - If the local number doesn't connect, check for a new area code.

PARKWAY MOTEL
2112 Coffeen Ave
(82801)
Rates: $24-$47
(307) 674-7259

RANCH WILLOW B&B
501 Hwy 14 E
(82801)
Rates: n/a
(307) 674-1510
(800) 354-2830

ROCK TRIM MOTEL
449 Coffeen Ave
(82801)
Rates: $40-$60
(307) 672-2464

STAGE STOP MOTEL
2167 N Main
(82801)
Rates: 35-$50
(307) 672-3459

SUPER SAVER INN
1789 N Main
(82801)
Rates: $23-$35
(307) 672-0471

TRAILS END MOTEL
2125 N Main St
(82801)
Rates: $34-$52
(307) 672-2477

TRIANGLE MOTEL
540 CoffeenAve
(82801)
Rates: $34-$49
(307) 674-8031

XL MOTEL
907 N Broadway
(82801)
Rates: $24-$30
(307) 674-6458

SHOSHONI

DESERT INN MOTEL
605 W 2nd (82649)
Rates: $30-$100
(307) 876-2273

SHOSHONI MOTEL
503 W 2nd (82649)
Rates: $35-$60
(307) 876-2216

SMOOT

ROCKING P B&B
Box 127 (83126)
Rates: n/a
(307) 886-0455
(Horses allowed only)

STORY

STORY PINES INN
46 N Piney Rd
(82842)
Rates: $61-$100
(307) 683-2120
(800) 596-6297

WAGON BOX SUPPER CLUB INN
Box 248 (82842)
Rates: $30-$48
(307) 683-2444
(800) 308-2444

SUNDANCE

BEAR LODGE MOTEL-IMA
218 Cleveland Ave (82729)
Rates: $48-$64
(307) 283-1611
(800) 341-8000

BEST WESTERN INN/SUNDANCE
2719 E Cleveland Ave (82729)
Rates: $49-$119
(307) 283-2800
(800) 528-1234
(800) 238-0965

BUDGET HOST ARROWHEAD MOTEL
214 Cleveland Ave (82729)
Rates: $36-$69
(307) 283-3307
(800) 283-4678

DEAN'S PINEVIEW MOTEL
117 N 8th St
(82729)
Rates: $28-$34
(307) 283-2262

SUNDANCE INN
2719 E Cleveland (82729)
Rates: $44-$99
(307) 283-1100

SUNDANCE MOUNTAIN INN
26 Hwy 585
(82729)
Rates: $50-$83
(307) 283-3737

TEN SLEEP

FLAGSTAFF MOTEL
Box 376 (82442)
Rates: $25-$32
(307) 366-2745

LOG CABIN MOTEL
Box 50 (82442)
Rates: $24-$30
(307) 366-2320

MEADOWLARK LAKE RESORT
26 mi E on Hwy 16, Box 86 (82442)
Rates: n/a
(307) 366-2424
(800) 858-5672

TETON VILLAGE

(Grand Teton National Park area)

THE ALPENHOF LODGE
3255 W Village Dr
(83025)
Rates: $109-$539
(307) 733-3242
(800) 732-3244

CRYSTAL SPRINGS INN
3285 W McCollister Dr
(83025)
Rates: $46-$84
(307) 733-4423

FOUR SEASONS RESORT
7680 Granite Loop Rd (83025)
Rates: $275-$4000
(307) 732-5000
(800) 332-3442

THE HOSTEL
Box 546 (83025)
Rates: $25-$50
(307) 733-3415

THAYNE

SWISS MOUNTAIN MOTEL
119 Wright St
(83127)
Rates: $35-$50
(307) 883-2227

THERMOPOLIS

BROADWAY INN B&B
342 Broadway
(82443)
Rates: n/a
(307) 864-2636
(888) 821-9759

CACTUS INN MOTEL
605 S 6th (82443)
Rates: $26-$32
(307) 864-3155

COACHMAN INN
112 Hwy 20, South Yellowstone
(82443)
Rates: $27-$40
(307) 864-3141
(888) 864-3854

EL RANCHO MOTEL
924 Shoshoni Rd
(82443)
Rates: $25-$42
(307) 864-2341
(800) 283-2777

HOLIDAY INN OF THE WATERS
115 E Park (82443)
Rates: $81-$139
(307) 864-3131
(800) 465-4329

JURASSIC INN
501 S 6th (82443)
Rates: $29-$38
(307) 864-2325

RAINBOW MOTEL
408 Park St
(82443)
Rates: $24-$33
(307) 864-2129
(800) 544-8815

ROUNDTOP MOUNTAIN MOTEL
412 N 6th (82443)
Rates: $28-$33
(307) 864-3126

WIND RIVER MOTEL
501 S 6th St
(82443)
Rates: $24-$34
(307) 864-2325

TORRINGTON

BLUE LANTERN MOTEL
1402 S Main
(82240)
Rates: $25-$49
(307) 532-8999

HOLIDAY INN EXP HOTEL & SUITES
1700 East Valley Rd (82240)
Rates: $60-$165
(307) 532-7600
(800) 465-4329

KING'S INN
1555 S Main
(82240)
Rates: $49-$85
(307) 532-4011

MAVERICK MOTEL
4577 Hwy 26 & 85
(82240)
Rates: $40-$48
(307) 532-4064

OREGON TRAIL LODGE
710 East Valley Blvd (82240)
Rates: $26-$47
(307) 532-2101

UCROSS

THE RANCH AT UCROSS
2673 Hwy 14 E
(82835)
Rates: $299
(307) 737-2281
(800) 447-0194

UPTON

UPTON MOTEL
440 1st St (82730)
Rates: $32-$45
(307) 468-9282

WESTON INN MOTEL
1601 Hwy 16
(82730)
Rates: $35-$46
(307) 468-2401

AREA CODES - If the local number doesn't connect, check for a new area code.

WAPITI
(Yellowstone National Park area)

ABSAROKA MOUNTAIN LODGE
1231 E Yellowstone Hwy (82450)
Rates: $66-$110
(307) 587-3963

GOFF CREEK LODGE
995 E Yellowstone Hwy (82414)
Rates: $95-$115
(307) 587-3753
(800) 859-3985

GREEN CREEK INN
2908 Yellowstone Hwy (82414)
Rates: 35-$75
(307) 587-5004
(877) 587-5004

SHOSHONE LODGE RANCH
349 Yellowstone Hwy (82414)
Rates: $99-$189
(307) 587-4044

WHEATLAND
BEST WESTERN TORCHLIGHT MOTOR INN
1809 N 16th St (82201)
Rates: $44-$80
(307) 322-4070
(800) 528-1234
(800) 662-3968

BLACKBIRD INN B&B
1101 11th St (82201)
Rates: n/a
(307) 322-4540

HOMESTEAD B&B
431 E Havely Rd (82201)
Rates: $50-$74
(307) 322-3316

MOTEL 6
95 16th St (82201)
Rates: $34-$65
(307) 322-1800
(800) 466-8356

MOTEL WEST WINDS
1756 South Rd (82201)
Rates: $35-$64
(307) 322-2705

PLAINS MOTEL
208 16th St (82201)
Rates: $25-$50
(307) 322-3416

VIMBO'S MOTEL
203 16th St (82201)
Rates: $37-$45
(307) 322-3842

WYOMING MOTEL
1101 9th St (82201)
Rates: $25-$49
(307) 322-5383

WILSON
(Grand Teton National Park area)

SASSY MOOSE INN B&B
3859 Miles Rd (83014)
Rates: $129-$149
(307) 733-1277
(800) 356-1277

WORLAND
DAYS INN
500 N 10th (82401)
Rates: $55-$95
(307) 347-4251
(800) 329-7466

SUPER 8 MOTEL
2500 Big Horn Ave (82401)
Rates: $42-$55
(307) 347-9236
(800) 800-8000

TOWN & COUNTRY MOTEL
1021 Russell Ave (82401)
Rates: $24-$36
(307) 347-3249

TOWN HOUSE MOTOR INN
119 N 10th (82401)
Rates: $28-$32
(307) 347-2426

YELLOWSTONE NATIONAL PARK
The following accommodations are located near the park entrances:

CANYON VILLAGE LODGE & CABINS
Box 165 (82190)
Rates: $60-$80
(307) 344-7311

LAKE LODGE & CABINS
Box 165 (82190)
Rates: $60-$80
(307) 344-7311

LAKE YELLOWSTONE HOTEL & CABINS
Box 165 (82190)
Rates: $80+
(307) 344-7311

MAMMOTH HOT SPRINGS & HOTEL
Box 165 (82190)
Rates: $60-$80
(307) 344-7311

AREA CODES - If the local number doesn't connect, check for a new area code.

HOTEL/MOTEL 800 NUMBERS

ACCENT INNS
800-663-0298

AMERICINN
800-634-3444

AMERIHOST
800-434-5800

AMERISUITES
800-833-1516

BAYMONT INNS
877-229-6668

BEST INNS OF
AMERICA
800-237-8466

BEST WESTERN
800-528-1234

BUDGET HOST
800-283-4678

CANDLEWOOD
SUITES
888-226-3539

CHOICE HOTELS
(CANADA)
800-228-1222

CHOICE HOTELS
(USA)
800-424-6423

CLARION INNS
800-252-7466

COMFORT INNS
800-228-5150

COUNTRY
HEARTH
888-443-2784

COUNTRY
INN & SUITES
800-456-4000

COURTYARD
BY MARRIOTT
800-321-2211

CROWNE PLAZA
800-227-6963

DAYS INN
800-329-7466

DELTA HOTELS
800-268-1133

DOUBLETREE
800-222-8733

DRURY INNS
800-378-7946

ECONO LODGE
800-553-2666

EMBASSY SUITES
800-362-2779

EXEL INNS
800-367-4935

FAIRFIELD INN
800-228-2800

FAIRMONT
HOTELS
800-527-4727

FOUR SEASONS
800-332-3442

GUESTHOUSE
INN & SUITES
800-214-8378

HAMPTON INNS
800-426-7866

HARVEY HOTELS
800-922-9222

HAWTHORN
SUITES
800-527-1133

HEARTLAND
INNS
800-334-3277

HILTON HOTELS
800-445-8667

HOLIDAY INNS
800-465-4329

HOMESTEAD
GUEST SUITES
888-782-9473
800-225-5466

HOWARD
JOHNSON
800-446-4656

HYATT HOTELS
800-233-1234

INN SUITES
800-842-4242

INTER-
CONTINENTAL
800-327-0200

JAMESON INNS
800-526-3766

KELLY INNS
800-635-3559

KNIGHTS INNS
800-843-5644

LA QUINTA INNS
800-687-6667

LOEWS HOTELS
800-235-6397

HOTEL/MOTEL 800 NUMBERS

MAINSTAY SUITES
800-660-6246

MARRIOTT HOTELS
800-228-9290

MICROTEL INNS
888-771-7171

MOTEL 6
800-466-8356

OMNI HOTELS
800-843-6664

PARKS INNS INTERNATIONAL
800-670-7275

PEAR TREE INNS
800-282-8733

QUALITY INNS
800-228-5151

RADISSON SUITES
800-333-3333

RAMADA INNS
800-272-6232

RED LION INNS
800-733-5466

RED ROOF INNS
800-843-7663

RENAISSANCE HOTELS
800-468-3571

RESIDENCE INN BY MARRIOTT
800-331-3131

RITZ-CARLTON
800-241-3333

RODEWAY INNS
800-228-2000

SANDMAN INNS
800-726-3626

SHERATON HOTELS
800-325-3535

SHILO INNS
800-222-2244

SHONEY'S INNS
800-222-2222

SLEEP INNS
800-753-3746

STAYBRIDGE SUITES
800-238-8000

SUMMERFIELD SUITES
800-833-4353

SUPER 8 MOTELS
800-800-8000

THRIFTLODGE
800-525-9055

TOWNEPLACE SUITES
800-257-3000

TRAVELODGE
800-578-7878

VAGABOND INNS
800-522-1555

VALUE INNS
800-442-7777

W HOTELS
877-946-8357

WELLESLEY INNS
800-444-8888

WESTIN HOTELS
800-228-3000

WINDMILL INNS
800-547-4747

WOODFIN SUITES
800-237-8811

WYNDHAM HOTELS
800-996-3426

STATE DEPARTMENTS OF TOURISM

ALABAMA	KENTUCKY	NORTH DAKOTA
800-252-2262	800-225-8747	800-435-5663
ALASKA	LOUISIANA	OHIO
907-929-2200	800-334-8626	800-282-5393
ARIZONA	MAINE	OKLAHOMA
888-520-3434	88-624-6345	800-652-6552
ARKANSAS	MARYLAND	OREGON
800-628-8725	800-543-1036	800-547-7842
CALIFORNIA	MASSACHUSETTS	PENNSYLVANIA
800-862-2543	800-447-6277	800-847-4872
COLORADO	MICHIGAN	RHODE ISLAND
800-265-6723	800-543-2937	800-556-2484
CONNECTICUT	MINNESOTA	SOUTH CAROLINA
800-282-6863	800-657-3700	803-734-0122
DELAWARE	MISSISSIPPI	SOUTH DAKOTA
800-441-8846	800-927-6378	800-732-5682
DIST. OF COLUMBIA	MISSOURI	TENNESSEE
202-789-7000	800-877-1234	800-836-6200
FLORIDA	MONTANA	TEXAS
888-735-2872	800-847-4868	800-452-9292
GEORGIA	NEBRASKA	UTAH
800-847-4842	800-228-4307	801-538-1030
HAWAII	NEVADA	VERMONT
800-464-2924	800-638-2328	800-837-6668
IDAHO	NEW HAMPSHIRE	VIRGINIA
800-635-7820	800-386-4664	800-847-4882
ILLINOIS	NEW JERSEY	WASHINGTON
800-223-0121	800-537-7397	360-586-2088
INDIANA	NEW MEXICO	WEST VIRGINIA
800-289-6646	800-545-2040	800-225-5982
IOWA	NEW YORK	WISCONSIN
800-345-4692	800-225-5697	800-432-8747
KANSAS	NORTH CAROLINA	WYOMING
800-252-6727	800-847-4862	800-225-5996

CANADIAN DIRECTORY OF PET-FRIENDLY LODGING

TRAVELING BETWEEN THE UNITED STATES AND CANADA

Dogs and cats

If you intend to travel into Canada with either a dog or a cat, your animal must have a certificate signed by a licensed veterinarian. This certificate must clearly describe the animal and validate that the animal has been vaccinated against rabies within the past 36 months. The certificate will also be needed for your animal's re-entry into the United States. Make certain that the rabies vaccination does not expire while you're touring Canada. Exemptions from this rule: Seeing eye dogs, puppies and kittens under three months, provided they are healthy at the time of importation.

Passports and proof of citizenship

United States citizens are not required to have a passport to enter Canada or return to the United States. Proof of citizenship in the form of a birth certificate, voter's certificate or baptismal certificate are normally all you'll need. If you're a naturalized citizen, carry your naturalization papers. U.S. resident aliens must have an Alien Registration Receipt Card. If minors are traveling with you, or on their own, they must present a notarized letter of consent signed by both parents or guardians in addition to providing proof of citizenship.

You should know that Canadian customs can stop a person traveling with a minor from entering Canada if customs has been advised that a divorced or separated parent is attempting to cross the border with a minor child without the written permission of the absent parent.

The Canadian GST

Beginning January 1, 1991, the Canadian government established a 7% Goods and Services Tax (GST) which is levied on most items sold and most services rendered. Non-Canadians may apply for a rebate on many items, among them short-term accommodations. There is a minimum rebate claim of $7 and evidence of purchase is required. Penalties apply and vary by province and territory. Be prepared and avoid penalties and delays.

Brochures explaining the GST and containing a rebate form are available in Canada at the land border as well as in airport duty-free shops, information centers, custom offices and many individual hotels. For additional information, write: Revenue Canada, Visitor Rebate Program, Summerside Tax Centre, Summerside, PE, Canada C1N 6C6; phone (902) 432-5608 or call (800) 668-4748 toll-free in Canada.

Personal baggage may be brought into Canada on a temporary basis without payment of duties and taxes. Infrequently, a refundable security deposit may be required by customs at the time of your entry. All items brought into the country must accompany you on your departure.

Personal baggage can include clothing, personal effects, sporting goods, cars, vessels, aircraft, snowmobiles, cameras, food products and those items that would be considered appropriate for the purpose and length of your stay.

There are some limitations as follows: Tobacco products are limited to 50 cigars, 200 cigarettes and 400 grams (14 oz.) of tobacco per person. Alcoholic beverages are limited to 1.14 litres (40 oz.) of liquor or wine or 8.5 litres (300 oz.) of beer or ale, (the equivalent of 24 bottles/cans). A minimum stay of 24 hours is normally required when transporting liquor or tobacco products into Canada.

Liquor and tobacco products exceeding the allowable quantities are subject to federal duty and taxes as well as provincial liquor fees. In addition, you must be 18 or 19 (depending on the province or territory) to bring alcohol into Canada and be at least 16 to import tobacco and related products.

Gifts

With the exception of tobacco, alcoholic beverages and advertising matter, gifts taken into or mailed to Canada are allowed free entry as long as the value of the gift doesn't exceed $60 (Canadian currency). Gifts with a higher value are subject to duty and taxes on the excess amount.

Plants and fruits

House plants may be admitted into Canada. Other plants and plant material need a permit from Agriculture Canada and a state or federal phytosanitary certificate obtained from the plant health authority of origin.

Fresh fruits and vegetables not typically grown in Canada, i.e., tropical and subtropical items, may be imported. However, they may be inspected by a plant health inspector at the time of entry. Fresh fruit and vegetables commonly grown in Canada, may be refused entry, depending on the original and final destination of the fruits or vegetables. For further information, contact the Plant Health Division, Food Production and Inspection Branch, Agriculture Canada, Ottawa, ON, Canada K1A 0C6.

Employment of visitors

Without employment authorization prior to entry into Canada, employment of visitors is not permitted. In order to secure employment, a permit for a specific job for a specific period of time must be obtained from the Canadian Department of Manpower and Immigration. You will be denied entry into Canada if it is your intention to finance your visit by seeking a paying job.

U.S. Customs regulations

Exemptions granted to returning residents of the United States include a $400 exemption if not used within the prior 30 days for residents who have been in Canada no less than 48 hours. Based on retail value, the exemptions apply only to goods acquired for personal or household use or as gifts - not intended for resale. Exemptions for a family can be combined, i.e. a family of four would be entitled to a $1,600 duty-free exemption on one declaration even if the articles declared by one member of the family exceeded that individual's $400 exemption.

Evidence of retail value will be needed. Keep all sales slips. The goods for which the exemption is claimed must be with you at the time of re-entry.

You can also send gifts to friends and relatives in the United States free of duty and taxes. However, the retail value of any one gift may not exceed more than $40. Only one gift per day can be received by any one recipient. Tobacco products, alcoholic beverages and perfume containing alcohol with a value of more than $5 retail are excluded from this provision. The package containing the gift must be marked "Unsolicited Gift" and include the contents and retail value on the outside of the package. These gifts are not considered part of your $400 exemption. You do not have to declare them upon your return to the United States.

If you qualify for the $400 exemption, you may include 100 cigars and 200 cigarettes duty free. Cigarettes may be subject to state or local tax. If you're over 21, you may include 1 litre in your $400 exemption from tax and duty. In all cases, state liquor laws are enforced by customs.

When your stay in Canada has been less than 48 hours, you may return with duty and tax free merchandise that has a maximum value of $25. This exemption must not include more than 50 cigarettes, 10 cigars, 150 millilitres of alcohol or 150 millilitres of perfume containing alcohol. Members of a family unit may NOT combine their purchases under this exemption. All goods must be declared.

National Park entrance fees

Daily or annual permits are available for visiting Canada's National Parks. The entrance fees vary according to the park and the age of the visitor. The annual permit admits a vehicle and all occupants to all national parks. The daily permit is valid only on the date of purchase.

The main number for Canadian National Park information is (888) 773-8888. The PARKS CANADA NATIONAL OFFICE address is 25 Eddy Street, Hull, Quebec, Canada K1A 0M5 . The website for the Canadian National Parks is very informative and gives rates for all the parks. You can access it at http://www.parkscanada.gc.ca.

FOR YOUR INFORMATION:

Seat Belts: The use of seat belts is mandatory in all vehicles traveling in or through Canada.

Radar Detectors: The possession and use of radar detection devices is illegal in Manitoba, Newfoundland, Northwest Territories, Ontario, Prince Edward Island, Quebec and Yukon Territory.

Currency: Prices and admission fees are in Canadian dollars. It is financially advantageous to use Canadian currency when traveling in Canada. You can obtain the official exchange rate of U.S. funds at a bank in Canada or purchase traveler's checks in Canadian currency.

Legal Questions: Persons with felony convictions, DWI's or other offenses may be denied entry into Canada. For further info, contact the Department of Citizenship and Immigration at (613) 995-6486 or call (888) 242-2100 toll-free inside Canada. For additional information refer to: http://www.cic.gc.ca.

ALBERTA

AIRDRIE

SUPER 8 MOTEL
815 E Lake Blvd
(T4B 2A2)
(403) 948-4188
(800) 800-8000

ATHABASCA

BEST WESTERN ATHABASCA INN
5211 41 Ave
(T9S 1A5)
(780) 675-2294
(800) 528-1234
(800) 567-5718

BANFF

BANFF ROCKY MOUNTAIN RESORT
1029 Banff Ave
(T1L 1A2)
(403) 762-5531

BEST WESTERN SIDING 29 LODGE
453 Marten St
(T0L 0C0)
(403) 762-5575
(800) 528-1234

CANADIAN PACIFIC BANFF SPRINGS HOTEL
405 Spray Ave
(403) 762-2211
(800) 441-1414

CASTLE MOUNTAIN CHALETS
Box 1655 (T0L 0C0)
(403) 762-3868
(800) 661-1315

THE FAIRMONT BANFF SPRINGS
405 Spray Ave
(T1L 1J4)
(403) 762-2211

JOHNSTON CANYON RESORT
Hwy 1A (T1L 1A9)
(403) 762-2971

PTARMIGAN INN
337 Banff Ave
(403) 762-2207

RED CARPET INN
425 Banff Ave
(T0L 0C0)
(403) 762-4184

BROOKS

BEST WESTERN BROOKS INN
115 Fifteenth Ave W (T1R 1C4)
(403) 363-0080
(800) 528-1234

THE DOUGLAS COUNTRY INN
Hwy 873 (T0J 0J0)
(403) 362-2873

HERITAGE INN
1303 2nd St W
(T1R 1B8)
(403) 362-6666

HOLIDAY INN EXPRESS HOTEL
1307 2nd St W
(T1R 1B3)
(403) 362-7440
(800) 465-4329

TRAVELODGE
1240 Cassils Rd E
(T1R 1B6)
(403) 362-8000
(800) 578-7878

CALGARY

BEST WESTERN HOSPITALITY INN
135 Southland Dr SE (T2J 5X5)
(403) 278-5050
(800) 528-1234
(877) 278-5050

BEST WESTERN SUITES DOWNTOWN
1330 8 St SW
(T2R 1B6)
(403) 228-6900
(800) 528-1234
(800) 981-2555

BEST WESTERN VILLAGE PARK INN
1804 Crowchild Trail NW (T2M 3Y7)
(403) 289-0241
(800) 528-1234
(888) 774-7716

BLACKFOOT INN
5940 Blackfoot Trail SE (T2H 2B5)
(403) 252-2253
(800) 661-1151

CALGARY MARRIOTT HOTEL
110 9th Ave SE (T2G 5A6)
(403) 266-7331
(800) 627-7468

CALGARY WESTWAYS GUEST HOUSE
216 25th Ave SW (T2S 0L1)
(403) 229-1758

CARRIAGE HOUSE INN
9030 Macleod Trail S (T2H 0M4)
(403) 253-1101
(800) 661-9566

THE COAST PLAZA HOTEL
1316 33rd St NE (T2A 6B6)
(403) 248-8888

DAYS INN AIRPORT
2799 Sunridge Way NE (T1Y 7K7)
(403) 250-3297
(800) 329-7466

DAYS INN S
3828 Macleod Trail S (T2G 2R2)
(403) 243-5531
(800) 329-7466

DAYS INN WEST
1818 16th Ave NW (T2M 0L8)
(403) 289-1961
(800) 329-7466

DELTA BOW VALLEY HOTEL
209 4th Ave SE (T2G 0C6)
(403) 266-1980
(800) 268-1133

DELTA CALGARY AIRPORT
2001 Airport Rd NE (T2E 6Z8)
(403) 291-2600

ECONO LODGE SOUTH
7505 MacLeod Tr S (T2H 0L8)
(403) 252-4401
(800) 553-2666

ECONO LODGE WEST
101 St & Trans-Canada Hwy 1 W (T2M 4N3)
(403) 288-4436
(800) 553-2666

ELBOW RIVER INN & CASINO
1919 Macleod Trail SE (T2G 4S1)
(403) 269-6771
(800) 661-1463

EXECUTIVE ROYAL INN
2828 23rd St NE (T2E 8T4)
(403) 291-2003

GLENMORE INN
2720 Glenmore Tr SE (T2C 2E6)
(403) 279-8611

GREENWOOD INN HOTELS
3515 26th St NE (T1Y 7E3)
(403) 250-8855

HAWTHORN HOTEL & SUITES
618 5th Ave SW (T2P 0M7)
(403) 263-0520
(800) 527-1133

HOLIDAY INN AIRPORT
1250 McKinnon Dr NE (T2E 7T7)
(403) 230-1999
(800) 465-4329

HOLIDAY INN DOWNTOWN
119 12th Ave SW (T2R 2G8)
(403) 266-4611
(800) 465-4329

HOLIDAY INN EXPRESS HOTEL DOWNTOWN
1020 8th Ave SW (T2P 1J2)
(403) 269-8262
(800) 465-4329

HOLIDAY INN EXPRESS HOTEL S
12025 Lake Fraser Dr SE (T2J 7G5)
(403) 225-3000
(800) 465-4329

HOLIDAY INN EXPRESS UNIVERSITY
2227 Banff Trail NW (T2M 4L2)
(403) 289-6600
(800) 465-4329

INTERNATIONAL HOTEL CALGARY
220 4th Ave SW (T2P 0H5)
(403) 265-9600

THE PALLISER FAIRMONT HOTEL/RESORT
133 9th Ave SW
(403) 262-1234
(800) 527-4727

QUALITY HOTEL
3828 Macleod Trail (T2G 2R2)
(403) 243-5531
(800) 228-5151

QUALITY INN AIRPORT
4804 Edmonton Tr
NE (T2E 3V2)
(403) 276-3391
(800) 228-5151

QUALITY INN MOTEL VILLAGE
2359 Banff Trail NW
(T2M 4L2)
(403) 289-1973
(800) 228-5151

RADISSON HOTEL AIRPORT
2120 16th Ave NE
(T2E 1L4)
(403) 291-4666
(800) 333-3333

RESIDENCE INN BY MARRIOTT
2622 39th Ave NE
(T1Y 7J9)
(403) 735-3336
(800) 331-3131

SANDMAN HOTEL DOWN-TOWN CALGARY
888 7th Ave SW
(T2P 3J3)
(403) 237-8626

SANDMAN HOTEL SUITES & SPA
25 Hopewell Way
NE (T3J 4V7)
(403) 219-2475

SHERATON CAVALIER HOTEL
2620 32nd Ave
NE (T1Y 6B8)
(403) 291-0107
(800) 325-3535

SHERATON SUITES CALGARY EAU CLAIRE
255 Barclay Parade SW (T2P 5C2)
(403) 266-7200
(800) 325-3535

SUPER 8 MOTEL AIRPORT
3030 BarlowTrail NE
(T1Y 1A2)
(403) 291-9888
(800) 800-8000

SUPER 8 MOTEL-MOTEL VILLAGE
1904 Crowchild Tr NW (T2M 3Y7)
(403) 289-9211
(800) 800-8000

SUPER 8 MOTEL
60 Shawville Rd SE (T2R 1J4)
(403) 254-8878
(800) 800-8000

TRAVELODGE AIRPORT
2750 Sunridge Blvd NE
(T1Y3C2)
(403) 291-1260
(800) 578-7878

TRAVELODGE
9206 Macleod Trail S
(T2J 0P5)
(403) 253-7070
(800) 578-7878

WESTIN HOTEL
320 4th Ave SW
(T2P 2S6)
(403) 266-1611
(800) 228-3000

WINGATE INN
400 Midpark Way
(T2X 3S4)
(403) 514-0099

CAMROSE
NORSEMEN INN
6505 48th Ave
(T4V 3K3)
(780) 672-9171

THE TRAVELLERS INN
6216 48th Ave
(T4V 0K6)
(780) 672-3377

CANMORE
BANFF BOUND-ARY LODGE
1000 Harvie Hgts Rd T1W 2W2)
(403) 678-9555

BEST WESTERN GREEN GABLES
1602 2nd Ave
(T1W 1M8)
(403) 678-5488
(800) 528-1234
(800) 661-2133

BEST WESTERN POCATERRA INN
1725 Mountain Ave
(T1W 2W1)
(403) 678-4334
(800) 528-1234
(888) 678-6786

CANADIAN ROCKIES CHALETS
1206 Bow Valley Trail (T1W 1N6)
(403) 678-3799

HOWARD JOHNSON
1402 Bow Valley Trail (T1W 1N5)
(403) 609-4656
(800) 446-4656

MYSTIC SPRINGS CHALETS & HOT POOLS
140 Kananaskis Way (T1W 2X2)
(403) 609-0333
(866) 446-9784

RADISSON HOTEL
511 Bow Valley Trail (T1W 1N7)
(403) 678-3625
(800) 333-3333

RESIDENCE INN BY MARRIOTT
91 Three Sister Dr (T1W 2X4)
(403) 678-3400
(800) 331-3131

ROCKY MOUN-TAIN SKI LODGE
1711 Bow Valley Trail (T1W 2T8)
(403) 678-5445
(800) 665-6111

RUNDLE MOUNTAIN LODGE
1723 Bow Valley Trail (T1W 1L7)
(403) 678-5322

RUNDLE RIDGE CHALETS
1100 Harvie Hghts Rd (T1W 2W2)
(403) 678-5387
(800) 332-1299

THE STOCKADE LOG CABINS
1050 Harvie Hghts Rd (T1W 2W2)
(403) 678-5212

WINDTOWER LODGE & SUITES
160 Kananaskis Way (T1W 3E2)
(403) 609-6600
(866) 609-6600

CARDSTON
FLAMINGO MOTEL
848 Main St S
(403) 653-3952

HOWARD JOHNSON EXPRESS INN
37 8th Ave W
(T0K 0K0)
(403) 653-4481
(800) 446-4656

CLARESHOLM
BLUEBIRD MOTEL
5505 Main St S
(T0L 0T0)
(403) 625-3395
(800) 661-4891

COCHRANE
BEST WESTERN HARVEST COUN-TRY INN
11 West Side Dr
(T4C 1M1)
(403) 932-1410
(800) 528-1234

BOW RIVER INN
3 West Side Dr
(T4C 1M1)
(403) 932-7900

SUPER 8 MOTEL
10 West Side Dr
(T4C 1M1)
(403) 932-6355
(800) 800-8000

COLD LAKE
NEW FRONTIER MOTEL
1002 8th Ave
(780) 639-3030

DEAD MAN'S FLATS
PIGEON MOUNTAIN MOTEL
250 1st Ave
(T1W 2T8)
(403) 678-5756

DRAYTON VALLEY
SUPER 8 MOTEL
3727 50th St
(T7A 1S4)
(780) 542-9122
(800) 800-8000

DRUMHELLER
BEST WESTERN JURASSIC INN
1103 Hwy 9 S
(T0J 0Y0)
(403) 823-7700
(800) 528-1234
(888) 823-3466

INN AT THE HEARTWOOD MANOR
320 N Railway Ave E (T0J 0Y4)
(403) 823-6495

SUPER 8 MOTEL
600 - 680 2nd St SE (T0J 0Y0)
(403) 823-8887
(800) 800-8000
(888) 823-8882

EDMONTON
ALBERTA PLAZA SUITE HOTEL
10049 103rd St
(T5J 2W7)
(780) 423-1565

ARGYLL PLAZA HOTEL
9933 63rd Ave
(T6E 6C9)
(780) 438-5876
(800) 661-6454

BEST WESTERN CEDAR PARK INN
5116 Calgary Tr N (T6H 2H4)
(780) 434-7411
(800) 528-1234
(800) 661-9461

CHATEAU EDMONTON HOTEL & SUITES
7230 Argyll Rd
(T6C 4A6)
(780) 465-7931

CHATEAU LOUIS HOTEL
11727 Kingsway
(T5G 3A1)
(780) 452-7770
(800) 661-9843

COMFORT INN
17610 100th Ave
(T5S 1S9)
(780) 484-4415
(800) 228-5150

CROWNE PLAZA CHATEAU LACOMBE
10111 Bellamy Hill
(T5J 1N7)
(780) 428-6611
(800) 227-6963

DELTA EDMONTON CENTRE SUITE HOTEL
10222 102nd St
(T5J 4C5)
(780) 429-3900

DELTA EDMONTON SOUTH HOTEL
4404 Calgary Tr
(780) 434-6415
(800) 268-1133

EDMONTON INN
11830 Kingsway Ave
(780) 454-9521

EXECUTIVE ROYAL INN WEST
10010 178th St
(T5S 1T3)
(780) 484-6000

THE FAIRMONT HOTEL MACDONALD
10065 100th St
(T5J 0N6)
(780) 424-5181

GREENWOOD INN HOTELS
4485 Gateway Blvd (T6H 5C3)
(780) 431-1100

HOLIDAY INN & CONV CENTRE
4520 76th Ave
(T6B 0A5)
(780) 468-5400
(800) 465-4329

HOLIDAY INN THE PALACE
4235 Calgary Tr N (T6J 5H2)
(780) 438-1222
(800) 465-4329

HOTEL MACDONALD
10065 100th St
(780) 424-5181

MAYFIELD INN
16615 109 Ave
(T5P 4K8)
(780) 484-0821

THE MET HOTEL
10454 82nd Ave
(T6E 4Z7)
(780) 465-8150

RAMADA INN & CONF CENTRE
11834 Kingsway Ave (T56 3J5)
(780) 454-5454
(800) 272-6232

RODEWAY INN
10425 100th Ave
(T5J 0A3)
(780) 423-5611
(800) 228-2000

ROSSLYN INN
13620 97 St
(T5E 4E2)
(780) 476-6241

SUPER 8 HOTEL
3610 Gateway Blvd (T6J 7H6)
(780) 433-8688
(800) 800-8000

THE SUTTON PLACE HOTEL
10235 101st St
(T5J 3E9)
(780) 428-7111

TRAVELODGE
10320 45th Ave S
(T6H 5K3)
(780) 436-9770
(800) 578-7878

TRAVELODGE BEVERLY CREST
3414 118th Ave
(T5W 0Z4)
(780) 474-0456
(800) 578-7878

TRAVELODGE-W
18320 Stony Plain Rd (T5S 1A7)
(780) 483-6031
(800) 661-9563

THE VARSCONA HOTEL
8208 106th St
(T6E 6R9)
(780) 434-6111

WESTIN HOTEL
10135 100th St
(T5J 0N7)
(780) 426-3636
(800) 228-3000

WINGATE INN W
18220 100th Ave
(T5S 2V2)
(780) 443-1000

EDSON

BEST WESTERN HIGH ROAD INN
300 52nd St
(T7V 1E8)
(780) 712-2378
(800) 528-1234
(888) 895-1444

GUEST HOUSE INN & SUITES
4411 4th Ave
(T7E 1B8)
(780) 723-4486

SUPER 8 MOTEL
4300 2nd Ave
(T7E 1B8)
(780) 723-2500
(800) 800-8000

FORT MACLEOD

FORT MOTEL
451 Main St
(T0L 0Z0)
(403) 553-3606

SUNSET MOTEL
104 Hwy 3W
(T0L 0Z0)
(403) 553-4448

FORT MCMURRAY

QUALITY HOTEL
424 Gregoire Dr
(T9H 3R2)
(780) 791-7200
(800) 424-6423

SUPER 8 MOTEL
321 Sakitaww Tr
(T9H 5E7)
(780) 799-8450
(800) 800-8000

TRAVELODGE HOTEL
9713 Hardin St
(T9H 1L2)
(780) 743-3301
(800) 578-7878

FORT SASKATCHE-WAN

BEST WESTERN FORT INN & SUITES
10115 88th Ave
(T8L 2T3)
(780) 998-7888
(800) 528-1234
(877) 998-7493

GRAND PRAIRIE

AMERIHOST INN & SUITES
11710 102nd St
(T8V 7S7)
(780) 831-2999
(800) 434-5800

BEST WESTERN GRANDE PRAIRIE HOTEL & SUITES
10745 117th Ave
(T8V 7N6)
(780) 402-2378
(800) 528-1234

QUALITY HOTEL & CONF CENTRE
11201 100th Ave
(T8V 5M6)
(780) 539-6000
(800) 424-6423

SERVICE PLUS INNS & SUITES
10810 107th A Ave (T8V 7A9)
(780) 538-3900

STANFORD INN
11401 100th Ave
(T8V 5M6)
(780) 539-5678

SUPER 8 MOTEL
10050 116th Ave
(T8V 4K5)
(780) 532-8288
(800) 800-8000

HANNA

BEST WESTERN HANA INN
113 Palleser Tr
(T0J 1P0)
(403) 854-2400
(800) 528-1234
(888) 854-2401

HIGH RIVER

HERITAGE INN
1104 11th Ave SE
(T1V 1M4)
(403) 652-3834

SUPER 8 MOTEL
1601 13th Ave SE
(T1V 1M6)
(403) 652-4448
(800) 800-8000

HINTON

BEST WESTERN WHITE WOLF INN
828 Carmichael Ln (T7V 1T1)
(780) 865-7777
(800) 528-1234

RAMADA LIMITED SUITES
500 Smith St
(T7V 2A1)
(780) 865-2575
(800) 272-6232

SUPER 8 MOTEL
284 Smith St
(T7V 2A1)
(780) 817-2228
(800) 800-8000

JASPER

AMETHYST LODGE
200 Connaught Dr (T0E 1E0)
(780) 852-3394

THE FAIRMONT JASPER PARK LODGE
Lodge Road
(780) 852-3301
(800) 654-9977

JASPER INN ALPINE RESORT
98 Geikie St
(T0E 1E0)
(780) 852-4461
(800) 661-1933

LOBSTICK LODGE
94 Geikie St
(T0E 1E0)
(780) 852-4431
(800) 661-9317

MARMOT LODGE
86 Connaught Dr
(T0E 1E0)
(780) 852-4471
(800) 661-6521

PATRICIA LAKE BUNGALOWS
Pyramid Lake Rd
(T0E 1E0)
(780) 852-3560

PYRAMID LAKE RESORT
Pyramid Lake Rd
(T0E 1E0)
(780) 852-4900

THE SAWRIDGE INN & CONF CENTRE
82 Connaught Dr
(TOE 1E0)
(780) 852-5111

SUNWAPTA FALLS RESORT
Hwy 93 (T0E 1E0)
(780) 852-4852
(888) 828-5777

TEKARRA LODGE
Hwy 93 A
(780) 852-3058

KANANASKIS
DELTA LODGE
P. O. Box 240,
Kananaskis
Village (T0L 2H0)
(403) 591-7711
(882) 244-8666

LAKE LOUISE
THE FAIRMONT CHATEAUX LAKE LOUISE
111 Lake Louise Dr (T0L 1E0)
(403) 522-3511
(800) 441-1414

LAKE LOUISE INN
P. O. Box 209
(T0L 1E0)
(403) 522-3791
(800) 661-9237

LEDUC
EXECUTIVE ROYAL INN HOTEL
8450 Sparrow Dr
(T9E 7G4)
(780) 986-1840

SUPER 8 MOTEL
8004 Sparrow Crescent (T9E 7G1)
(780) 986-8898
(800) 800-0000

LETHBRIDGE
COMFORT INN
3226 Fairway Plaza Rd S (T1K 7T5)
(403) 320-8874
(800) 424-6423

DAYS INN
100 3rd Ave S
(T1J 4L2)
(403) 327-6000
(800) 329-7466

ECONO LODGE
1124 Mayor McGrath Dr S
(T1K 2P8)
(403) 328-5591
(800) 553-2666

HOLIDAY INN EXPRESS HOTEL & SUITES
120 Stafford Dr S
(T1J 4W4)
(403) 394-9292
(800) 465-4329

LETHBRIDGE LODGE HOTEL
320 Scenic Dr
(T1J 4B4)
(403) 328-1123

QUALITY INN
1030 Mayor Magrath Dr (T1K 2P8)
(403) 328-6636
(800) 228-5151

RAMADA HOTEL
2375 Mayor Magrath Dr (T1K 7M1)
(403) 380-5050
(800) 272-6232

SOUTH COUNTRY INN
2225 Mayor Magrath Dr (T1K 7M1)
(403) 380-6677

THRIFTLODGE
1142 Mayor Magrath Dr (T1K 2P8)
(403) 328-4436

LLOYDMIN-STER
BEST WESTERN WAYSIDE INN
5411 44th St
(T9V 0A9)
(780) 875-4404
(800) 528-1234

TROPICAL INN
5621 44th St
(T9V 0B2)
(780) 875-7000

MEDICINE HAT
BEST WESTERN INN
722 Redcliff Dr
(T1A 5E3)
(403) 527-3700
(800) 528-1234

DAYS INN
3216 13th Ave SE
(T1B 1H8)
(403) 526-7487
(800) 329-7466

IMPERIAL INN
3282 13th Ave SE
(T1B 1H8)
(403) 527-8811
(800) 661-5322

MEDICINE HAT LODGE HOTEL
1051 Ross Glen Dr SE (T1B 3T8)
(403) 529-2222
(800) 661-8095

RANCHMAN MOTEL
1617 Bomford Crescent SW
(T1A 5E7)
(403) 527-2263

SUPER 8 MOTEL
1280 Trans-Canada Way
(T1B 1J5)
(403) 528-8888
(800) 800-8000

TRAVELODGE
1100 Redcliff Dr SW (T1A 5E5)
(403) 527-2275
(800) 578-7878

NISKU
HOLIDAY INN EXPRESS-AIRPORT
1102 4th St (T9E 8E2)
(780) 955-1000
(800) 465-4329

NISKU INN & CONF CENTRE
1103 4th St (T9E 7N1)
(780) 955-7744

OKOTOKS
BEST WESTERN OKOTOKS LODGE
22 Southridge Dr
(T1S 1N1)
(403) 938-7400
(800) 528-1234

OKOTOKS COUNTRY INN
59 River Side Gate
(403) 938-1999

PEACE RIVER
TRAVELLER'S MOTOR HOTEL
9510 100th St
(T8S 1S9)
(780) 624-3621

PINCHER CREEK
HERITAGE INN
919 Waterton Ave
(T0K 1W)
(403) 627-5000

RED DEER
CAPRI HOTEL TRADE
3310 50th Ave
(T4N 3X9)
(403) 346-2091

HOLIDAY INN
6500 67th Ave
(T4P 1A2)
(403) 342-6567
(800) 465-4329

HOLIDAY INN EXPRESS
2803 50th Ave
(T4R 1H1)
(403) 343-2112
(800) 465-4329

RED DEER LODGE & CONF CENTRE
4311 49th Ave
(T4N 5Y7)
(403) 346-8841

SANDMAN HOTEL
2818 Gaetz Ave
(T4R 1M4)
(403) 343-7400

SERVICE PLUS INN & SUITES
6853 66th St
(T4P 3T5)
(403) 342-4445

STANFORD INN
4707 Ross St
(T4N 1X3)
(403) 347-5551

ROCKY MOUNTAIN HOUSE
CHINOOK INN
5321 59th Ave
(T4T 1J4)
(403) 845-2833

HOLIDAY INN EXPRESS
4715 45th St
(T4T 1B1)
(403) 8452871
(800) 465-4329

SUPER 8 MOTEL
4406 41st Ave
(T4T 1J6)
(403) 846-0088
(800) 800-8000

SHERWOOD PARK

FRANKLIN'S INN
2016 Sherwood
Dr (T8A 3X3)
(780) 467-1234

RAMADA LTD EAST
30 Broadway
Blvd (T8H 2A2)
(780) 467-6727
(800) 272-6232

ROADKING INNS
26 Strathmoor Dr
(T8H 2B6)
(780) 464-1000

SPRUCE GROVE

ROYAL INN EXPRESS HOTEL
20 Westgrove Dr
(T7X 3X3)
(780) 962-6050

STETTLER

BEST WESTERN CRUSADER INN
6020 50th Ave
(T0C 2L0)
(403) 742-3371
(800) 528-1234
(888) 742-5808

SUPER 8 MOTEL
5720 44th Ave
(T0C 2L0)
(403) 742-3391
(800) 800-8000
(888) 742-8008

STONY PLAIN

RAMADA INN & SUITES
3301 43rd Ave
(T7Z 1L1)
(780) 963-9222
(800) 272-6232

STONY CONVENTION INN
4801 48 St
(T7Z 1L4)
(780) 963-3444

STRATHMORE

BEST WESTERN STRATHMORE INN
550 Hwy 1
(T1P 1M6)
(403) 934-5777
(800) 528-1234

SUPER 8 MOTEL
450 Westlake Rd
(T1P 1H8)
(403) 934-1808
(800) 800-8000

TRAVELODGE
350 Ridge Rd
(T1P 1B5)
(403) 901-0000
(800) 578-7878

TABER

HERITAGE INN
4830 46th Ave
(T0K 2G0)
(403) 223-4424

THREE HILLS

SUPER 8 MOTEL
208 18th Ave N
(T0M 2A0)
(403) 443-8888
(800) 800-8000

VERMILION

SUPER 8 MOTEL
5108 47th Ave
(T9X 1J6)
(403) 853-4741
(800) 800-8000

WATERTON PARK

BAYSHORE INN
111 Waterton Ave
(T0K 2M0)
(403) 859-2211
(888) 527-9555

WATERON LAKES LODGE
101 Clematis Ave
(T0K 2M0)
(403) 859-2151
(888) 856-343

WESTLOCK

HIGHWAY MOTOR INN
East Service Rd
(T0G 2L0)
(780) 349-3138

WETASKIWIN

BEST WESTERN WAYSIDE INN
4103 56th St
(T9A 1V2)
(780) 352-6681
(800) 528-1234

FORT ETHIER LODGE
3802 56th St
(T9A 2B2)
(780) 352-9161

SUPER 8 MOTEL
3820 56th St
(T9A 2B2)
(780) 361-3808
(800) 800-8000

WHITECOURT

QUALITY INN
5420 47th Ave
(T7S 1P3)
(780) 778-5477
(800) 228-5151

SUPER 8 MOTEL
4121 Kepler St
(T7S 1P6)
(780) 778-8908
(800) 800-8000

TRAVELODGE HOTEL
5003 50th St
(T7S 1N3)
(780) 778-2216
(800) 578-7878

BRITISH COLUMBIA

ABBOTSFORD

ABBOTSFORD HOTEL
2020 Sumas Way (V2S 2C7)
(504) 853-1880
(800) 663-9842

ALPINE MOTOR INN
32111 Marshall Rd (V2T 1A3)
(604) 859-3171

BEST WESTERN BAKERVIEW INN
1821 Sumas Way (V2S 4L5)
(604) 859-1341
(800) 528-1234

COMFORT INN
2073 Clearbrook Rd (V2T 2X1)
(604) 859-6211
(800) 424-6423

RAMADA INN
36035 N Parallel Rd (V3G 2C6)
(604) 870-1050
(800) 272-6232

SUPER 8 MOTEL
1881 Sumas Way (V2S 4L5)
(604) 853-1141
(800) 800-8000

ALDERGROVE

BEST WESTERN COUNTRY MEADOWS
3070 264th St (V4W 3E1)
(604) 856-9880
(800) 528-1234
(800) 834-0833

BARRIERE

MOUNTAIN SPRINGS MOTEL
4253 Yellowhead Hwy (V-E 1E0)
(250) 672-0090

BLUE RIVER

GLACIER MTN LODGE
869 Shell Rd (V0E 1J0)
(250) 673-2393

MIKE WIEGELE HELICOPTER SKIING RESORT HOTEL
1 Harrwood Dr (V0E 1J0)
(250) 673-8381

BOSWELL

DESTINY BAY RESORT
11935 Hwy 3A
(250) 223-8234

BOWEN ISLAND

WILDWOOD LANE COTTAGES
1291 Adams Rd (V0N 1G0)
(604) 947-2253

BURNABY

ACCENT INNS
3777 Hennings Dr (V5C 6N5)
(604) 473-5000
(800) 663-0298

BEST WESTERN KINGS INN &
5411 Kingsway (V5H 2G1)
(604) 438-1383
(800) 528-1234
(800) 211-1122

HILTON METROTOWN
6083 McKay Ave (V5H 2W7)
(604) 438-1200
(800) 916-2221
(800) 445-8667

LAKE CITY MOTOR INN
5415 Lougheed Hwy (V5H 2B3)
(604) 294-5331
(800) 694-6860

CACHE CREEK

BONAPARTE MOTEL
1395 Hwy 97 N (V0K 1H0)
(250) 457-9693

CAMPBELL RIVER

BEST WESTERN AUSTRIAN CHALET
462 S Island Hwy (V9W 1A5)
(250) 923-4231
(800) 528-1234
(800) 6677207

CAMPBELL RIVER LODGE FISHING RESORT
1760 Island Hwy
(250) 287-7446

CASTLEGAR

BEST WESTERN FIRESIDE INN
1810 8th Ave (V1N 2Y2)
(250) 365-2128
(800) 499-6399

DAYS INN
651 18th St (V1N 2N1)
(250) 365-2700
(800) 329-7466

CHASE

CHASE COUNTRY INN MOTEL
576 Coburn St (V0E 1M0)
(250) 679-3333

QUAAOUT LODGE RESORT
Trans Canada Hwy 1
(250) 679-3090

CHEMAINUS

FULLER LAKE MOTEL
9300 Trans Canada Hwy
(250) 246-3282

CHILLIWACK

BEST WESTERN RAINBOW COUNTRY INN
43971 Industrial Way (V2R 3A4)
(604) 795-3828
(800) 528-1234
(800) 665-1030

COMFORT INN
45405 Luckakuck Way (V2R 3C7)
(604) 858-0636
(800) 228-5150

ECONO LODGE
8600 Young Rd (V2P 4P4)
(604) 795-9155
(800) 553-2666

RHOMBUS DOWNTOWN
45920 1st Ave (V2P 7K1)
(604) 795-4788

RAINBOW MOTOR INN
45620 Yale Rd W (V2P 2N2)
(604) 792-6412

CHRISTINA LAKE

NEW HORIZON MOTEL
2037 Hwy 3 (V0H 1E0)
(250) 447-9312

CLEARWATER

JASPER WAY MOTEL ON BEAUTIFUL DUTCH LAKE
57 E Old N Thompson Hwy (V0E 1N0)
(250) 674-3345

COQUITLAM

BEST WESTERN CHELSEA INN
725 Brunette Ave (V3K 1C3)
(604) 525-7777
(800) 528-1234
(866) 525-7779

HOLIDAY INN
631 Lougheed Hwy (V3K 3S5)
(604) 931-4433
(800) 465-4329

COURTENAY

BEST WESTERN COLLINGWOOD
1675 Cliffe Ave (V9N 2K6)
(250) 338-1464
(800) 528-1234
(800) 663-7922

COAST WESTERLY HOTEL
1590 Cliffe Ave (V9N 2K4)
(250) 338-7741

KINGFISHER OCEANSIDE RESORT & SPA
4330 S Island Hwy (V9N 8H9)
(250) 338-1323

TRAVELODGE
2605 S Island Hwy (V9N 2L8)
(250) 334-4491
(800) 578-7878

COWICHAN BAY

HOWARD JOHNSON RESOR
1681 Cowichan Bay Rd (V0R 1N0)
(250) 748-6222
(800) 446-4656

CRANBROOK

DELTA ST. EUGENE MISSION RESORT
7731 Mission Rd (V1C 7E5)
(250) 420-2000
(888) 244-8666

HERITAGE INN OF THE SOUTH
803 Cranbrook St N (V1C 3S2)
(250) 489-4301

MODEL A INN
1908 Cranbrook
St N (V1C 3T1)
(250) 489-4600

SUPER 8 MOTEL
2370 Cranbrook
St N (V1C 3T2)
(250) 489-8028
(800) 800-8000

CRESTON

**DOWNTOWNER
MOTOR INN**
1218 Canyon St
(V0B 1G0)
(250) 428-2238
(800) 665-9904

**SUMMERHORN
INN**
2711 Hwy 3
(V0B 1G0)
(250) 428-4009

SUNSET MOTEL
2705 Hwy 3
(V0B 1G0)
(250) 428-2229

DAWSON CREEK

RAMADA LIMITED
1748 Alaska Ave
(V1G 4H7)
(250) 782-8595
(800) 272-6232

SUPER 8 MOTEL
1440 Alaska Ave
(V1G 1Z5)
(250) 782-8899
(800) 800-8000

DELTA

**THE COAST
TSAWWASSEN INN**
1665 56th St
(V4L 2B2)
(604) 943-8221
(800) 943-8221

**RIVER RUN
COTTAGES**
4551 River Rd W
(V4K 1R9)
(604) 946-7778

DUNCAN

**BEST WESTERN
COWICHAN INN**
6464 Trans
Canada Hwy
(V9L 6C6)
(250) 748-2722
(800) 927-6199

DAYS INN
5325 Trans
Canada Hwy
(V9L 3X5)
(250) 748-0661
(800) 329-7466

**FALCON NEST
MOTEL**
5867 Trans
Canada Hwy
(250) 748-8188

**TRAVELODGE
SILVER BRIDGE
INN**
140 Trans Canada
Hwy (V9L 3P7)
(250) 748-4311
(800) 578-7878

ENDERBY

**HOWARD JOHN-
SON FORTUNES
LANDING**
1902 George St
(V0E 1V0)
(250) 838-6825
(800) 446-4656

FERNIE

**BEST WESTERN
FERNIE MOUN-
TAIN LODGE**
1622 7th Ave
(V0B 1M0)
(250) 4235500
(800) 528-1234

FERNIE LOG INN
141 Commerce
Rd (V0B 1M5)
(250) 423-6222

**PARK PLACE
LODGE**
742 Hwy 3 (V0B
1M0)
(250) 423-6871

**RIVERSIDE
MOUNTAIN
LODGE**
100 Riverside
Way (V0B 1M1)
(250) 423-5000
(877) 423-5600

SUPER 8 MOTEL
2021 Hwy #3
(V0B 1M1)
(250) 423-6788
(800) 800-8000

FORT NELSON

TRAVELODGE
4711 50th Ave
(V0E 1R0)
(250) 774-3911
(800) 578-7878

FORT ST. JOHN

**BEST WESTERN
COACHMAN INN**
8540 Alaska Rd
(V1T 5L6)
(250) 787-0651
(800) 528-1234
(888) 388-9408

**QUALITY INN
NORTHERN
GRAND**
9830 100th Ave
(V1T 1Y5)
(250) 787-0521
(800) 424-6423

RAMADA LIMITED
10103 98 Ave
(V1J 1P8)
(250) 787-0779
(800) 272-6232

SUPER 8 MOTEL
9500 Alaska Hwy
(V1J 6S7)
(250) 785-7588
(800) 800-8000

FORT STEELE

**BULL RIVER
GUEST RANCH**
Ft. Steele-Wardner
Rd (V1C 3S2)
(250) 429-3760

GIBSONS

CEDAR'S INN
895 Sunshine Coast
Hwy (V0N 1V0)
(604) 886-3008

GOLD BRIDGE

**MORROW
CHALETS**
General Delivery
(250) 238-2462

GOLDEN

**BEST WESTERN
MOUNTAINVIEW
INN**
1024 - 11th St N
(V0A 1H0)
(250) 344-2333
(800) 528-1234

**GOLDEN GATE
MOTEL**
1408 Golden
View Rd (V0A
1H0)
(250) 344-2252

**GOLDEN RIM
MOTOR INN**
1416 Golden View
Rd (V0A 1H0)
(250) 344-2216

**HILLSIDE LODGE
& CHALETS**
1740 Seward
Frontage Rd
(V0A 1H0)
(250) 344-7281

**QUANTUM LEAPS
LODGING LTD**
2119 Blaeberry Rd
(V0A 1H1)
(250) 344-2114

RONDO MOTEL
824 Park Dr (V0A
1H0)
(250) 344-5295

GRAND FORKS

IMPERIAL MOTEL
7389 Riverside,
Box 2558
(V0H 1H0)
(250) 442-8236

RAMADA LIMITED
2729 Central Ave
(V0H 1H2)
(250) 442-2127
(800) 593-0511

**WESTERN
TRAVELLER
MOTEL**
1591 Central Ave
(V0H 1H0)
(250) 442-5566

HARRISON HOT SPRINGS

**HARRISON HOT
SPRINGS RESORT**
100 Esplanade
(V0M 1K0)
(604) 796-2244
(800) 663-2266

QUALITY HOTEL
190 Lillooet Ave
(V0M 1K0)
(604) 796-5555
(800) 228-5151

HOPE

ALPINE MOTEL
505 Old Hope-
Princeton Hwy
(V0X 1L0)
(604) 869-9931

**BEST CONTINEN-
TAL MOTEL**
860 Fraser Ave
(V0X 1L0)
(604) 869-9726

**INN-TOWNE
MOTEL**
510 Trans Canada
Hwy 1 (V0X 1L0)
(604) 869-7276

QUALITY INN
350 Old Hope-
Princeton Hwy
(V0X 1L0)
(604) 869-9951
(800) 228-5151

INVERMERE

**BEST WESTERN
INVERMERE INN**
1310 7th Ave
(V0A 1K0)
(250) 342-9246
(800) 528-1234

KAMLOOPS

ACCENT INNS
1325 Columbia St
W (V2C 6P4)
(250) 374-8877
(800) 663-0298

**BEST VALUE
SUPER VIEW INN**
1200 Rogers Way
(V1S 1N5)
(250) 374-8100

**CASA MARQUIS
MOTOR INN**
530 Columbia St
(V2C 2V1)
(250) 372-7761

COURTESY MOTEL
1773 E Trans
Canada Hwy
(V2C 3Z6)
(250) 372-8533

DAYS INN
1285 W Trans
Canada Hwy
(V2E 2J7)
(250) 374-5911
(800) 329-7466

DREAM LODGE
1855 Rogers Place
(250) 314-9889

GRANDVIEW MOTEL
463 Grandview
Terr (V2C 3Z3)
(250) 372-1312
(800) 210-6088

HOSPITALITY INN
500 W Columbia
St (V2C 1K6)
(250) 374-4164

HOWARD JOHNSON EXP. INN
610 Columbia St
(V2C 1L1)
(250) 374-1515
(800) 446-4656

RAMADA INN
555 W Columbia
St (V2C 1K7)
(250) 374-0358
(800) 272-6232

RANCHLAND MOTEL
2357 Trans
Canada Hwy E
(V2C 4A8)
(250) 828-8787
(800) 663-4902

SCOTT'S INN & RESTAURANT
551 11th Ave
(V2C 3Y1)
(250) 372-8221

STAY'N SAVE INNS
1325 Columbia St
W
(250) 374-8877
(800) 663-0298

SUPER 8 MOTEL
1521 Hugh Allan
Dr (V1S 1P4)
(250) 374-8688
(800) 800-8000

THOMPSON HOTEL
650 Victoria St
(250) 374-1999

THRIFT INN
2459 Trans
Canada Hwy E
(V2C 4A9)
(250) 374-2488

KELOWNA

ACCENT INNS
1140 Harvey Ave
(V1Y 6E7)
(250) 862-8888
(800) 663-0298

BEST WESTERN INN
2402 Hwy 97 N
(V1X 4J1)
(250) 860-1212
(800) 528-1234
(888) 860-1212

COMFORT INN
1655 Westgate Rd
(V1Z 3P1)
(250) 769-2355
(800) 424-6423

THE GRAND OKANAGAN LAKEFRONT RESORT
1310 Water St
(V1Y 9P3)
(250) 763-4500

PANDOSY INN
3327 Lakeshore Rd
(V1W 3S9)
(250) 762-5858

RAMADA LODGE HOTEL
2170 Harvey Ave
(V1Y 6G8)
(250) 860-9711
(800) 272-6232

THE ROYAL ANNE HOTEL
348 Bernard St
(V1Y 6N5)
(250) 763-2277

SIESTA MOTOR INN
3152 Lakeshore Rd
(250) 763-5013

STAY'N SAVE INN
1140 Harvey Ave
(250) 862-8888
(800) 663-0298

TOWN & COUNTRY MOTEL
2629 Hwy 97 N
(V1X 4J6)
(250) 860-7121

VINEYARD INN
2486 Hwy 97 N
(V1X 4J3)
(250) 860-5703

KIMBERLEY

QUALITY INN
300 Wallinger
Ave (V1A1Z4)
(250) 427-2266
(800) 228--5151

TRICKLE CREEK RESIDENCE INN BY MARRIOTT
500 Sternwinder
Dr (V1A 2Y6)
(250) 427-5175
(800) 331-3131

LADYSMITH

SEAVIEW MARINE RESORT
11111 Chemainus
Rd
(250) 245-3768

LANGLEY

BEST VALUE WESTWARD INN
19650 Fraser Hwy
(V3A 4C7)
(604) 534-9238

BEST WESTERN LANGLEY INN
5978 Glover Rd
(V3A 4H9)
(604) 530-9311
(888) 530-9311

HOLIDAY INN EXPRESS HOTEL
8750 204th St
(V1M 2Y5)
(604) 882-2000
(604) 859-6211
(800) 465-4329

SANDMAN HOTEL
8855 202nd St
(V1M 2N9)
(604) 888-7263

SLEEP INN
6722 Glover Rd
(V2Y 1S6)
(604) 5143111

TRAVELODGE-LANGLEY MOTOR INN
20470 88th Ave
(V1M 2Y6)
(604) 888-4891
(800) 578-7878

LOGAN LAKE

LOGAN LAKE LODGE
111 Chartrand
Ave (V0K 1W)
(250) 523-9466

MADEIRA PARK

SUNSHINE COAST RESORT
12695 Sunshine
Coast Hwy (V0N
2H0)
(640) 883-9177

MALAHAT

MALAHAT BUNGALOWS MOTEL
Malahat Dr
(V0R 2L0)
(250) 478-3011
(800) 665-8066

MANNING PARK

MANNING PARK RESORT
Hwy 3, Crowsnest
(V0X 1R)
(250) 840-8822

MAPLE RIDGE

TRAVELODGE
21650 Lougheed
Hwy (V2X 2S1)
(604) 467-1511
(800) 578-7878

MCBRIDE

NORTH COUNTRY LODGE
868 N Frontage
Rd (V0J 2E0)
(250) 560-0001

MERRITT

BEST WESTERN NICOLA INN
4025 Walters St
(V1K 1K1)
(250) 378-4253
(800) 528-1234
(888) 663-2830

MERRITT MOTOR INN
3561 Voght St
(V0K 2B0)
(250) 378-9422

RAMADA LIMITED
3571 Voght St
(V0K 1C5)
(250) 378-3567
(800) 272-6232

TRAVELODGE
3581 Voght St
(V1K 1C5)
(250) 378-8830
(800) 578-7878

MISSION

BEST WESTERN MISSION CITY LODGE
32281 Lougheed
Hwy (V2V 6B2)
(604) 820-5500
(888) 552-5542

NAKUSP

THE SELKIRK INN
210 6th Ave W
(V0G 1R0)
(250) 265-3666

NANAIMO

BEST WESTERN DORCHESTER 70
Church St
(V9R 5H4)
(250) 754-6835
(800) 661-2449

BEST WESTERN NORTH GATE
6450 Metral Dr
(V9T 2L8)
(250) 390-2222
(800) 528-1234

DAYS INN-HARBORVIEW
809 Island Hwy S
(V9R 5K1)
(250) 754-8171
(800) 329-7466

RAMADA LIMITED ON THE LAKE
4700 Island Hwy
N (V9T 1W6)
(250) 758-1144
(800) 272-6232

TRAVELODGE
96 Terminal Ave
N (V9S 4J2)
(250) 754-6355
(800) 578-7878

NANOOSE BAY

FAIRWINDS SCHOONER COVE RESORT & MARINA
3521 Dolphin Dr
(V9P 9J7)
(250) 468-7691

NARAMATA

THE VILLAGE MOTEL
244 Robinson Dr
(V0H 1N0)
(250) 496-5535

NELSON

**BEST WESTERN
BAKER STREET**
153 Baker St
(V1L 4H1)
(250) 352-3525
(800) 528-1234
(888) 255-3525

NEW DENVER

**SWEET DREAMS
GUESTHOUSE &
DINING**
702 Eldorado St
(V0G 1S0)
(250) 358-2415

NORTH VANCOUVER

**HOLIDAY INN
HOTEL & SUITES**
700 Old Lillooet
Rd (V7J 2H5)
(604) 985-3111
(877) 985-3111

**LIONSGATE
TRAVELODGE**
2060 Marine Dr
(V7P 1V7)
(604) 985-5311
(800) 578-7878

**OLD ENGLISH
B&B REGISTRY**
1226 Silverwood
Crescent (V7P 1J3)
(604) 986-5069

**RAMADA INN
NORTH SHORE**
1800 Capilano Rd
(V7P 3B6)
(604) 987-4461
(800) 663-4055

OLIVER

**SOUTHWIND
MOTOR INN**
34017 Hwy 97S
(V0H 1T0)
(250) 498-3442

100 MILE HOUSE

RAMADA LIMITED
917 Alder Rd
(V0K 2E0)
(250) 3952777
(800) 272-6232

RED COACH INN
170 N Cariboo
Hwy (V0K 2E0)
(250) 295-2266
(800) 663-8422

SUPER 8 MOTEL
989 Alder Ave
(V0K 2E0)
(250) 395-8888
(800) 800-8000

108 MILE HOUSE

108 RESORT
4816 Telqua Dr
(V0K 2Z0)
(250) 791-5211
(800) 667-5233

OSOYOOS

**WESTRIDGE
MOTOR INN**
9913 Hwy 3
(V0H 1V0)
(250) 495-7322

PARKSVILLE

**BEST WESTERN
BAYSIDE INN**
240 Dogwood St
(V9P 2H5)
(250) 248-8333
(800) 663-4232

SKYLITE MOTEL
459 E Island Hwy
(V9P 2G5)
(250) 248-4271

**TIGH-NA-MARA
SEASIDE SPA
RESORT**
1095 E Island
Hwy (V9P 2G5)
(250) 248-2072

TRAVELODGE
424 W Island
Hwy (V9P 2G3)
(250) 248-2232
(800) 578-7878

V.I.P. MOTEL
414 W Island
Hwy (V9P 2G3)
(250) 248-3244
(800) 663-7300

PARSON

**TIMBER INN-
CHALET**
3483 Hwy 95
(V0A 1L0)
(250) 348-2228

PEACHLAND

**HATHEUME LAKE
RESORT**
P. O. Box 490
(V0H 1X0)
(250) 767-2642

PEMBERTON

**PEMBERTON
VALLEY LODGE**
1490 Portage Rd
(V0N 2L0)
(604) 8942000

PENDER ISLAND

**POETS COVE
RESORT & SPA**
9801 Spalding Rd
(South Pender
Island V0N 2M3)
(250) 629-2100

PENTICTON

**BEST WESTERN
INN AT PENTICTON**
3180 Skaha Lake
Rd (V2A 6G4)
(250) 493-0311
(800) 668-6746

DAYS INN
152 Riverside Dr
(V2A 5Y4)
(250) 493-6616
(800) 329-7466

**GOLDEN
SANDS RESORT**
1028 Lakeshore
Dr (V2A 1C1)
(250) 492-4210

**PENTICTON
LAKESIDE RESORT**
21 Lakeshore Dr
W (V2A 7M5)
(250) 493-8221
(800) 663-1144

**PENTICTON
SLUMBER LODGE**
274 Lakeshore Dr
W
(V2A 7M5)
(250) 492-4008

RAMADA INN
1050 Eckhardt
Ave W (V2A 2C3)
(250) 492-8926
(800) 272-6232

**SPANISH
VILLA RESORT**
890 Lakeshore Dr
W (V2A 1C1)
(250) 492-2922

SUPER 8 MOTEL
1706 Main St
(V2A 5G8)
(250) 492-3829

TRAVELODGE
950 Westminster
Ave W (V2A 1L2)
(250) 492-0225
(800) 578-7878

WATERFRONT INN
3688 Parkview St
(V2A 6H1)
(250) 492-8228
(800) 563-6006

PORT ALBERNI

**BEST WESTERN
BARCLAY HOTEL**
4277 Stamp Ave
(V9Y 7X8)
(250) 724-7171
(800) 528-1234

**COAST HOSPI-
TALITY INN**
3835 Redford St
(V9Y 3S2)
(250) 723-8111
(800) 663-6677

RIVERSIDE MOTEL
5065 Roger St
(V9Y 3Y9)
(250) 724-9916

PORT COQUITLAM

**BEST WESTERN
POCO INN**
1545 Lougheed
Hwy (V3B 1A5)
(604) 941-6216
(800) 930-2235

PORT HARDY

AIRPORT INN
4030 Byng Rd
(V0N 2P0)
(250) 949-9434

GLEN LYON INN
6435 Hardy Bay
Rd (V0N 2P0)
(250) 949-7115

PIONEER INN
4965 Byng Rd,
Box 699 (V0N
2P0)
(250) 949-7271

POWELL RIVER

**POWELL RIVER
TOWN CENTRE
HOTEL**
4660 Joyce Ave
(V8A 3B6)
(604) 485-3000

**PRINCE
GEORGE
BEST WESTERN
CITY CENTRE**
910 Victoria Dr
(V2L 2K8)
(250) 563-1267
(800) 528-1234

**P. G. HI-WAY
MOTEL**
1737 20th Ave
(V2L 4B9)
(250) 564-6869

PRINCE RUPERT

ALEEDA MOTEL
900 3rd Ave W
(V8J 1M8)
(250) 627-1367

**HOWARD
JOHNSON
HIGHLINER
PLAZA HOTEL**
815 1st Ave W
(V8J 1B3)
(250) 624-9060
(800) 446-4656

PRINCETON

**BEST WESTERN
PRINCETON INN**
169 Hwy 3
(V0X 1W0)
(250) 295-3537
(888) 295-3537

ECONO LODGE
244 4th St (V0X
1W0)
(250) 295-6996
(800) 424-6423

QUADRA ISLAND

TAKU RESORT
616 Taku Rd
(V0P 1H0)
(250) 285-3031

QUALICUM BEACH

**OLD DUTCH INN
BY THE SEA**
2690 Island Hwy
(V9K 1T3)
(250) 752-6914

QUALICUM HERITAGE INN
427 College Rd
(V9K 2G4)
(250) 752-9262

QUESNEL

TALISMAN INN
753 Front St
(V2J 2Y2)
(250) 992-7247

RADIUM HOT SPRINGS

CEDAR MOTEL
7593 Main St W
(V0A 1M0)
(250) 347-9463

THE CHALET EUROPE
5063 Madsen Rd
(V0A 1M0)
(250) 347-9305

LIDO MOTEL
4876 McKay St
(V0A 1M0)
(250) 347-9533

SUNRISE SUITES MOTEL
7371 Prospector Ave (V0A 1M0)
(250) 347-0008

SUNSET MOTEL
4883 McKay St
(V0A 1M0)
(250) 347-9863

REVELSTOKE

BEST WESTERN WAYSIDE INN
1901 Laforme Blvd (V0E 2S0)
(250) 837-6161
(800) 528-1234
(800) 663-5307

THE COAST HILLCREST RESORT HOTEL
2100 Oak Dr
(V0E 2S0)
(250) 837-3322

MONASHEE LODGE
1601 3rd St W
(V0E 2S0)
(250) 837-6778

THE REGENT INN
112 First St E
(V0E 2S0)
(250) 837-2107

SWISS CHALET MOTEL
1101 Victoria Rd
(V0E 2S0)
(250) 837-4650

RICHMOND

ACCENT INNS
10551 St. Edwards Dr
(V6X 3L8)
(604) 273-3311
(800) 663-0298

BEST WESTERN ABERCORN INN
9260 Bridgeport Rd (V6X 1S1)
(604) 270-7576
(800) 663-0085

BEST WESTERN RICHMOND INN
7551 Westminster Hwy (V6X 1A3)
(604) 273-7878
(800) 663-0299

COMFORT INN AIRPORT
3031 #3 Rd &
Sea Island Way
(V6X 2B6)
(604) 278-5161
(800) 228-5150

DELTA VANCOUVER AIRPORT
3500 Cessna Dr
(V7B 1C7)
(604) 278-1241
(800) 268-1133

THE FAIRMONT HOTEL AIRPORT
3111 Grand McConachie Way
(V7B 1X9)
(604) 207-5200
(800) 441-1414

HOLIDAY INN EXPRESS
9351 Bridgeport Rd (V6X 1S3)
(604) 273-8080
(800) 465-4329

HOWARD JOHNSON HOTEL
9020 Bridgeport Rd (V6X 1S1)
(604) 270-6030
(800) 446-4656

LA QUINTA INN
8640 Alexandra Rd (V6X 1C4)
(604) 276-2711
(800) 531-5900

MARRIOTT HOTEL AIRPORT
7571 Westminster Hwy (V6X 1A3)
(604) 276-2112
(800) 228-9290

PARK PLAZA
10251 St. Edwards Dr (V6X 2M9)
(604) 278-9611
(866) 482-8444

RAMADA INN AIRPORT
7188 Westminster Hwy (V6X 1A1)
(604) 207-9000
(800) 272-6232

SANDMAN HOTEL
3233 St. Edwards Dr (V6X 3K4)
(604) 303-8888

STAY'N SAVE INNS
10551 St. Edwards Dr
(604) 273-3311
(800) 663-0298

ROSSLAND

THRIFTLODGE
1199 Nancy Green Hwy (V0G 1Y0)
(250) 362-7364
(800) 525-9055

SAANICHTON

QUALITY INN-WADDLING DOG
2476 Mt. Newton Cross Rd (V8M 2B8)
(250) 652-1146
(800) 228-5151

SUPER 8 MOTEL
2477 Mt. Newton Cross Rd (V8M 2B7)
(250) 652-6888
(800) 800-8000

SALMON ARM

THE COAST SHUSWAP LODGE
200 Trans Canada Hwy W (V1E 4P6)
(250) 832-7081
(800) 661-4355

HOLIDAY INN EXPRESS HOTEL
1090 22nd St NE
(V1E 2V5)
(250) 832-7711
(800) 465-4329

SUPER 8 MOTEL
2901 10th Ave NE
(V1E 4N1)
(250) 832-8812

SALTSPRING ISLAND

HARBOUR HOUSE HOTEL
121 Upper Ganges Rd
(V8K 2S2)
(250) 537-5571

SEABREEZE INN MOTEL
101 Bittancourt Rd (V8K 2K2)
(250) 537-4145

SECHELT

BELLA BEACH MOTOR INN
4748 Hwy 101
(V0N 3A0)
(604) 885-7191

DRIFTWOOD INN
5454 Trail Ave
(V0N 3A0)
(604) 885-5811

SICAMOUS

SUPER 8 MOTEL
1122 Riverside Ave (V0E 2V0)
(250) 836-4988
(800) 800-8000

SIDNEY

BEST WESTERN EMERALD ISLE
2306 Beacon Ave
(V8L 1X2)
(250) 656-4441
(800) 528-1234
(800) 315-3377

CEDARWOOD INN & SUITES
9522 Lochside Dr
(V8L 1N8)
(250) 656-5551

SHOAL HARBOUR INN
2328 Harbour Rd
(V8L 2P8)
(250) 656-6622

TRAVELODGE-VICTORIA ARPT
2280 Beacon Ave
(V8L 1X1)
(250) 656-1176
(800) 578-7878

SILVERTON

WILLIAM HUNTER CABINS
303 Lake Ave
(V0B 2G0)
(250) 358-2844

SMITHERS

ASPEN MOTOR INN
4268 Yellowhead Hwy (V0J 2N0)
(250) 847-4551
(800) 663-7676

SOOKE

OCEAN WILDERNESS COUNTRY INN
109 W Coast Rd
(V0S 1N0)
(250) 646-2116
(800) 323-2116

SOOKE HARBOUR HOUSE
1528 Whiffen Spit Rd (V0S 1N0)
(250) 642-3421

SQUAMISH

SEA TO SKY HOTEL
40330 Tantalus Way (V0N 1T0)
(604) 898-4874
(800) 531-1530

SUMMERLAND

SUMMERLAND MOTEL
2107 Tait St
(V0H 1Z0)
(250) 494-4444

SUN PEAKS

DELTA SUN PEAKS RESORT
3240 Village Way
(V0E 1Z1)
(250) 578-6000
(888) 244-8666

SURREY

DAYS HOTEL-SURREY CENTRE
9850 King George Hwy (V3T 4Y3)
(604) 588-9511

RAMADA HOTEL
10410 158th St
(V4N 5C2)
(604) 930-4700
(800) 272-6232

RAMADA LTD
19225 Hwy 10
(V3S 8V9)
(604) 576-8388
(800) 272-6232

SHERATON GUILDFORD HOTEL
15269 104th Ave
(V3R 1N5)
(604) 582-9288
(800) 325-3535

SUPER 8 MOTEL AT SKY TRAIN STATION
13893 Fraser Hwy (V3T 4E6)
(604) 581-7122
(800) 800-8000

TERRACE
BEST WESTERN TERRACE INN & CONF CENTRE
4553 Greig Ave
(V8G 1M7)
(250) 635-0083
(800) 488-1898

COAST INN OF THE WEST
4620 Lakelse Ave
(V8G 1R1)
(250) 638-8141
(800) 772-5555

TOFINO
BEST WESTERN TIN WIS RESORT LODGE
1119 Pacific Rim Hwy (V0R 2Z0)
(250) 725-4445
(800) 528-1234

CRYSTAL COVE BEACH RESORT
1165 Cedarwood Place (V0R 2Z0)
(250) 725-4213

LONG BEACH LODGE RESORT
1441 Pacific Rim Hwy (V0R 2Z0)
(250) 725-2442

WICKANINNISH INN
Osprey Lane at Chesterman Beach (V0R 2Z0)
(250) 725-3100

VALEMOUNT
BEST WESTERN CANADIAN LODGE
1501 5th Ave
(V0E 2Z0)
(250) 566-8222
(800) 811-5808

CANOE MOUNTAIN LODGE
1465 5th Ave
(V0E 2Z0)
(250) 566-9171

CHALET CONTINENTAL MOTEL
1450 5th Ave
(V0E 2Z0)
(250) 566-9787

HOLIDAY INN HOTEL & SUITES
1950 Hwy 5 S
(V0E 2Z0)
(250) 566-0086
(800) 465-4329

VANCOUVER
BEST WESTERN CHATEAU GRANVILLE
1100 Granville St
(V6B 2B6)
(604) 669-7070
(800) 528-1234

BEST WESTERN DOWNTOWN
718 Drake St
(V6Z 2W6)
(604) 669-9888
(888) 669-9888

BEST WESTERN SANDS
1755 Davie St
(V6G 1W5)
(604) 682-1831
(800) 528-1234
(800) 661-7887

BOSMAN'S MOTOR HOTEL
1060 Howe St
(V6Z 1P5)
(604) 682-3171
(800) 663-7840

COMFORT INN
654 Nelson St
(V6B 6K4)
(604) 605-4333
(800) 424-6423

CROWNE PLAZA HOTEL GEORGIA
801 W Georgia St
(V6C 1P7)
(604) 682-5566
(800) 227-6963

DELTA VANCOUVER SUITES
550 W Hastings St (V6B1L6)
(604) 689-8188
(800) 268-1133

THE FAIRMONT HOTEL
900 W Georgia St
(V6C 2W6)
(604) 684-3131

THE FAIRMONT WATERFRONT
900 Canada Place Way (V6C 3L5)
(604) 691-1991

FOUR SEASONS HOTEL
791 W Georgia St
(V6C 2T4)
(604) 689-9333
(800) 332-3442

THE GEORGIAN COURT HOTEL
773 Beatty St
(V6B 2M4)
(604) 682-5555
(800) 663-1155

GRANVILLE ISLAND HOTEL
1253 Johnston St
(V6H 3R9)
(604) 683-7373

HOLIDAY INN EXPRESS
2889 E Hastings St (V5K 2A1)
(604) 254-1000
(800) 465-4329

HOLIDAY INN
1110 Howe St
(V6Z 1R2)
(604) 684-2151
(800) 465-4329

HOLIDAY INN VANCOUVER CTR
711 W Broadway Ave (V5Z 3Y2)
(604) 879-0511
(800) 465-4329

HOTEL LE SOLEIL
567 Hornby St
(V6C 2E8)
(604) 632-3000

HOWARD JOHNSON HOTEL
1176 Granville St
(V6Z 1L8)
(604) 688-8701
(888) 654-6336

THE LONDON GUARD MOTEL
2227 Kingsway
(V5N 2T6)
(604) 430-4646

MARRIOTT PINNACLE DOWNTOWN
1128 W Hastings St (V6E 4R5)
(604) 684-1128
(800) 228-9290

METROPOLITAN HOTEL
645 Howe St
(V6C 2Y9)
(604) 687-1122

PACIFIC PALISADES HOTEL
1277 Robson St
(V6G 1C1)
(604) 688-0461

THE PAN PACIFIC VANCOUVER
999 Canada Place
(V6C 3B5)
(604) 662-8111
(800) 663-1515

QUALITY INN-FALSE CREEK
1335 Howe St
(V6Z 1R7)
(604) 682-0229
(800) 424-6423
(800) 228-5151

RAMADA INN DOWNTOWN
1221 Granville St
(V6Z 1M6)
(604) 685-1111
(866) 685-1112
(800) 272-6232

RENAISSANCE HOTEL HARBOURSIDE
1133 W Hastings St (V6E 3T3)
(604) 689-9211
(800) 468-3571

RESIDENCE INN BY MARRIOTT
1234 Hornby St
(V6Z 1W2)
(604) 688-1234
(800) 331-3131

SANDMAN HOTEL DOWNTOWN
180 W Georgia St
(V6B 4P4)
(604) 681-2211

SHERATON VANCOUVER WALL CENTRE HOTEL
1088 Burrard St
(V6Z 3R9)
(604) 331-1000
(800) 663-9255
(800) 325-3535

THE SUTTON PLACE HOTEL
845 Burrard St
(V6Z 2K6)
(604) 682-5511
(866) 3-SUTTON

SYLVIA HOTEL
1154 Gilford St
(V6G 2P6)
(604) 681-9321

2400 MOTEL
2400 Kingsway
(V5R 5G9)
(604) 434-2464

THE WESTIN BAYSHORE RESORT & MARINA
1601 Bayshore Dr
(V6G 2V4)
(604) 682-3377
(800) WESTIN-1

VERNON
BEST WESTERN LODGE & CONF CENTRE
3914 32 St
(V1T 5P1)
(250) 545-3385
(800) 528-1234
(800) 663-4422

BEST WESTERN VILLAGER INN
5121 26th St
(V1T 8G4)
(250) 549-2224
(800) 549-2270

COMFORT INN
4204 32nd St
(V1T 5P4)
(250) 542-4434
(800) 228-5150

HOLIDAY INN EXPRESS HOTEL
4716 34th St
(V1T 5Y9)
(250) 550-7777
(800) 465-4329

THE MARIA ROSE B & B
8083 Aspen Rd
(250) 549-4773

SCHELL MOTEL
2810 35th St
(V1T 6B5)
(250) 545-1351

TIKI VILLAGE MOTOR INN
2408 34th St
(V1T 5W8)
(250) 503-5566

TRAVELODGE
3000 28th Ave
(V1T 1W1)
(250) 545-2101
(800) 578-7878

VICTORIA
ABIGAIL'S HOTEL B&B
906 McClure St
(V8V 3E7)
(250) 388-5363
(800) 561-6565

ACCENT INNS
3233 Maple St
(V8X 4Y9)
(250) 475-7500
(800) 663-0298

ADMIRAL MOTEL
257 Belleville St
(V8V 1X1)
(250) 388-6267
(888) 823-6472

BLUE RIDGE INNS
3110 Douglas St
(V8Z 3K4)
(250) 388-4345

CHATEAU VICTORIA HOTEL
740 Burdett Ave
(V8W 1B2)
(250) 382-4221
(800) 663-5891

COMFORT INN
101 Island Hwy
(V9B 1E8)
(250) 388-7861
(800) 424-6423

DASHWOOD SEASIDE MANOR
1 Cook St
(V8V 3W6)
(250) 385-5517

DAYS INN ON THE HARBOUR
427 Belleville St
(V8V 1X3)
(250) 386-3451
(800) 665-3024

DELTA VICTORIA OCEAN POINTE RESORT & SPA
45 Songhees Rd
(V9A 6T3)
(250) 360-2999
(888) 244-8666

EXECUTIVE HOUSE HOTEL
777 Douglas St
(V8W 2B5)
(250) 388-5111
(800) 663-7001

THE FAIRMONT EMPRESS
721 Government St (V8W 1W5)
(250) 384-8111
(888) 270-8853

HARBOUR TOWERS HOTEL
345 Quebec St
(V8V 1W4)
(250) 385-2405
(800) 663-5896

HOTEL GRAND PACIFIC
463 Belleville St
(V8V 1X3)
(250) 386-0450
(800) 663-7550

HOWARD JOHNSON HOTEL
4670 Elk Lake Dr
(V8Z 5M2)
(250) 704-4656
(800) 446-4656

HOWARD JOHNSON INN-CITY CENTRE
310 Gorge Rd
(V8T 2W2)
(250) 382-2151
(800) 446-4656

THE MAGNOLIA HOTEL & SPA
623 Courtney St
(V8W 1B8)
(250) 381-0999
(877) 624-6654

MARRIOTT INNER HARBOUR
728 Humboldt St
(V8W 3Z5)
(250) 381-8439
(800) 228-9290

OXFORD CASTLE INN
133 Gorge Rd E
(V9A 1L4)
(250) 388-6431

QUALITY INN HARBOURVIEW
455 Belleville St
(V8V 1X3)
(250) 386-2421
(800) 228-5151

RAMADA HOTEL
330 Quebec St
(V8V 1W3)
(250) 381-3456
(800) 663-7557

ROBIN HOOD MOTEL
136 Gorge Rd E
(V9A 1L4)
(250) 388-4302

RYAN'S B & B
224 Superior St
(250) 389-0012

TRAVELLER'S INN-IN TOWN
3025 Douglas St
(250) 978-1000

TRAVELODGE
229 Gorge Rd E
(V9A 1L1)
(250) 388-6611
(800) 565-3777

WESTBANK
HOLIDAY INN
2569 Dobbin Rd
(V4T 2J6)
(250) 768-8879
(800) 465-4329

WHISTLER
BEST WESTERN LISTEL WHISTLER HOTEL
4121 Village Green (V0N 1B4)
(604) 932-1133
(800) 528-1234
(800) 663-5472

CRYSTAL LODGE
4154 Village Green
(V0N 1B0)
(604) 932-2221
(800) 667-3363

DELTA WHISTLER VILLAGE SUITES
4308 Main St
(V0N 1B7)
(604) 905-3987
(800) 268-1133

EDGEWATER LODGE
8841 Hwy 99
(V0N 1B0)
(604) 932-0688
(888) 870-9065

THE FAIRMONT CHATEAU
4599 Chateau Blvd
(V0N 1B4)
(604) 938-8000
(800) 606-8244

FOUR SEASONS RESORT
4591 Blackcomb Way (V0N 1B4)
(604) 9358-3400

RESIDENCE INN BY MARRIOTT
4899 Painted Cliff Rd (V0N 1B4)
(604) 905-3400
(800) 331-3131

SUMMIT LODGE & SPA
4359 Main St
(V0N 1B4)
(604) 932-2778

SUNDIAL BOUTIQUE HOTEL
4340 Sundial Cir
(V0N 1B4)
(604) 932-2321

TANTALUS RESORT CONDO LODGE
4200 Whistler Way
(V0N 1B4)
(604) 932-4146

WHISTLER VILLAGE RESORT
4050 Whistler Way
(V0N 1B4)
(604) 932-1982

WHITE ROCK
OCEAN PROMENADE HOTEL
15611 Marine Dr
(V4B 1E1)
(604) 542-0102

WILLIAMS LAKE
DRUMMOND LODGE MOTEL
1405 Cariboo Hwy
(V2G 2W3)
(250) 392-5334
(800) 667-4555

SUPER 8 MOTEL
1712 Broadway Ave S
(V2G 2W4)
(250) 398-8884
(800) 800-8000

YALE
FORT YALE MOTEL
31265 Trans Canada Hwy
(V0K 2S0)
(604) 863-2216

(

MANITOBA

BRANDON

COMFORT INN
925 Middleton
Ave (R7C 1A8)
(204) 727-6232
(800) 228-5150

DAYS INN
2130 Currie Blvd
(R7B 4E7)
(204) 727-3600
(800) 329-7466

RODEWAY INN
300 18th St N
(R7A 6Z2)
(204) 728-7230
(800) 228-2000

ROYAL OAK INN
3130 Victoria Ave
(R7A 5Z7)
(204) 728-5775

SUPER 8 MOTEL
1570 Highland Ave
(R7C 1A7)
(204) 729-8024
(800) 800-8000

VICTORIA INN
3550 Victoria Ave
W (R7A 5Z4)
(204) 725-1532

CHURCHILL

POLAR INN
15 Franklin St
(R0B 0E0)
(204) 675-8878

THE TUNDRA INN
34 Franklin St
(R0B 0E0)
(204) 675-8831

DAUPHIN

CANWAY INN
1601 Main St S
(R7N 2V4)
(204) 638-5102

SUPER 8 MOTEL
1457 Main St S
(R7N 3B3)
(204) 638-0800
(800) 800-8000

FLIN FLON

VICORIA INN-N
160 Hwy 10A N
(R8A 1M9)
(204) 687-7555

HECLA VILLAGE

**SOLMUNDSON
GESTA HUS**
Hwy 8, Hecla
Provincial Park
(Riverton, R0C
2R0)
(204) 279-2088

MORRIS

SUPER 8 MOTEL
400 Main St
(R0G 1K0)
(204) 746-6879

NEEPAWA

BAY HILL INNS
160 Main St W
(R0J 1H0)
(204) 476-8888

PORTAGE LA PRAIRIE

SUPER 8 MOTEL
Trans Canada
Hwy 1A
(204) 857-8883

**WESTGATE INN
MOTEL**
1010 Saskatchewan
Ave E (R1N 0K1)
(204) 239-5200

RUSSELL

**RUSSELL INN
HOTEL**
Hwy 16 & 83
(R0J 1W0)
(204) 773-2186

STEINBACH

DAYS INN
75 Hwy 12 N
(R5G 1T3)
(204) 320-9200

THE PAS

KILIWAK INN
Hwy 10 N
(R0B 2J0)
(204) 623-1800

SUPER 8 MOTEL
1717 Gordon Ave
(R9A 1K3)
(204) 623-1888
(800) 800-8000

WESCANA INN
439 Fischer Ave
(R9A 1M3)
(204) 623-5446

THOMPSON

COUNTRY INN
70 Thompson Dr
N (R8N 0C3)
(204) 778-8879
(800) 456-4000

WINKLER

**HEARTLAND
RESORT**
851 Main St N
R6W 4A4)
(204) 325-4381

WINNIPEG

CARLTON INN
220 Carlton St
(R3C 1P5)
(204) 942-0881

**CANAD INNS
EXPRESS
FORT GARRY**
1792 Pembina
Hwy
(R3T 2G2)
(204) 269-6955
(888) 332-2623

**CANAD INNS
POLO PARK**
1405 St.
Matthews Ave
(R3G 0K5)
(204) 775-8791
(888) 332-2623

CLARION HOTEL
1445 Portage Ave
(R3G 3P4)
(204) 774-5110

COMFORT INN
3109 Pembina
Hwy (R3T 4R6)
(204) 269-7390
(800) 228-5150

**COMFORT INN-
AIRPORT**
1770 Sargent Ave
(R3H 0C8)
(204) 783-5627
(800) 228-5150

COUNTRY INN
730 King Edward
St (R3H 1B4)
(204) 783-6900
(800) 456-4000

DAYS INN
550 McPhillips St
(R2X 2H2)
(204) 586-8525
(800) 329-7466

DELTA WINNIPEG
350 St. Mary's
Ave (R3C 3J2)
(204) 942-0551

**THE FAIRMONT
WINNIPEG**
2 Lombard Pl
(R3B 0Y3)
(204) 957-1350

**GORDON
DOWNTOWNER
MOTOR HOTEL**
330 Kennedy St
(204) 943-5581

**GREENWOOD
INN**
1715 Wellington
Ave (R3H 0G1)
(204) 775-9889

**HILTON SUITES
WINNIPEG-ARPT**
1800 Wellington
Ave (R3H 1B2)
(204) 783-1700

**HOLIDAY INN
WINNIPEG S**
1330 Pembina
Hwy (R3T 2B4)
(204) 452-4747
(800) 465-4329

**HOWARD JOHN-
SON HOTEL**
1740 Ellice Ave
(R3H 0B3)
(204) 775-7131
(800) 446-4656

**PLACE LOUIS
RIEL ALL-SUITE
HOTEL**
190 Smith St
(R3C 1J8)
(204) 947-6961

QUALITY INN
635 Pembina
Hwy (R3M 2L4)
(204) 453-8247
(800) 228-5151

**RADISSON
HOTEL WINNIPEG
DOWNTOWN**
288 Portage Ave
(R3C 0B8)
(204) 956-0410

**RAMADA MARL-
BOROUGH HOTEL**
331 Smith St
(R3B 2G9)
(204) 942-6411
(800) 272-6232

**SHERATON
HOTEL**
161 Donald St
(R3C 1M3)
(204) 942-5300
(866) 782-7737

SUPER 8 MOTEL
1485 Niakwa Rd
E (R2J 3T3)
(204) 253-1935
(800) 800-8000

TRAVELODGE
20 Alpine Ave
(R2M 0Y5)
(204) 255-6000

**TWIN PILLARS
B & B**
235 Oakwood
Ave (R3L 1E5)
(204) 284-7590

VICTORIA HOTEL
1808 Wellington
Ave (R3H 0G3)
(204) 786-4801

**VISCOUNT
GORT HOTEL**
1670 Portage Ave
(R3J 0C9)
(204) 775-0451

NEW BRUNSWICK

BATHURST

ATLANTIC HOST HOTEL
1450 Vanier Blvd
(506) 548-3335

BEST WESTERN DANNY'S INN & CONF CENTRE
St. Peter Ave W
(E2A 3Z2)
(506) 546-6621
(800) 528-1234
(800) 200-1350

COMFORT INN
1170 St. Peter Ave
(E2A 2Z9)
(506) 547-8000
(800) 228-5150

COUNTRY INN & SUITES
777 St. Peter Ave
(E2A 1Y9)
(506) 548-4949
(800) 456-4000

KEDDY'S LE CHATEAU BATHURST
80 Main St
(506) 546-6691

CAMPBELLTON

COMFORT INN
111 Val D'Amour Rd (E3N 3G9)
(506) 753-4121
(800) 228-5150

HOWARD JOHNSON HOTEL
157 Water St
(E3N 3H2)
(506) 753-4133
(800) 446-4656

COCAGNE

COCAGNE MOTEL
Hwy 11
(506) 576-6657

DALHOUSIE

BEST WESTERN MANOIR ADELAIDE
385 Adelaide
(E8C 1B4)
(506) 684-5681
(800) 528-1234
(800) 934-5444

EDMUNDSTON

COMFORT INN
5 Bateman Ave
(E3V 3L1)
(506) 739-8361
(800) 228-5150

HOWARD JOHNSON PLAZA HOTEL
100 Rice St
(E3V 1T4)
(506) 739-7321
(800) 446-4656

FLORENCEVILLE

FLORENCEVILLE MOTOR INN
239 Burnham Rd
(R0J 1K0)
(506) 392-6053

FREDERICTON

CARRIAGE HOUSE INN
230 University Ave
(506) 452-9924

COMFORT INN
255 Prospect St
W (E3B 5Y4)
(506) 453-0800
(800) 228-5150

COUNTRY INN & SUITES
665 Prospect St
(506) 459-0035
(800) 456-4000

HOLIDAY INN
35 Mactaquac Rd
(French Village
E3E 1L2)
(506) 363-5111
(800) 465-4329

HOWARD JOHNSON HOTEL
Lower St. Mary's,
Trans Canada
Hwy #2 (E3B
5E3)
(506) 460-5500
(800) 446-4656

KEDDY'S INN
368 Forest Hill
Rd (E3B 5G2)
(506) 454-4461
(800) 561-7666

LORD BEAVERBROOK HOTEL
659 Queen St
(506) 455-3371

GRAND FALLS

AUBERGE PRES-DU-LAC INN
Trans Canada
Hwy #2
(E0J 1M0)
(506) 473-1300

MIRAMICHI

COMFORT INN
201 Edward St
(506) 622-1215
(800) 228-5150

COUNTRY INN & SUITES
333 King George
Hwy
(506) 627-1999
(800) 456-4000

RODD MIRAMICHI RIVER-A RODD SIGNATURE HOTEL
1809 Water St
(506) 773-3111
(800) 565-7633

MONCTON

BEACON LIGHT MOTEL
1062 Mountain
Rd
(506) 384-1734

BEST WESTERN CRYSTAL PALACE HOTEL
499 Paul St
(Montcon/Dieppe
, E1A 6S5)
(506) 858-8584
(800) 528-1234
(800) 561-7108

BRUNSWICK HOTEL
1005 Main St
(506) 854-6340

COLONIAL INNS
42 Highfield St
(E1C 8T6)
(506) 382-3395
(800) 561-4667

COMFORT INN EAST
20 Maplewood
Dr (E1A 6P9)
(506) 859-6868
(800) 228-5150

COMFORT INN MAGNETIC HILL
2495 Mountain
Rd (E1C 8K2)
(506) 384-3175
(800) 228-5150

COUNTRY INN
2475 Mountain
Rd (E1C 8J3)
(506) 852-7000
(800) 456-4000

ECONO LODGE
1905 W Main St
(E1E 1H9)
(506) 382-2587
(800) 553-2666

HOLIDAY INN EXPRESS
2515 Mountain
Rd (E1C BR7)
(506) 384-1050
(800) 465-4329

KEDDY'S MOTOR INN
1510 Shediac Rd
(E1C 8K1)
(506) 854-2210
(800) 561-7666

NOR-WEST MOTEL
1325 Mountain Rd
(506) 384-1222

RODD PARK HOUSE INN
434 Main St
(506) 382-1664
(800) 565-7633

TRAVELODGE
434 Main St
(E1C 1B9)
(506) 382-1664
(800) 578-7878

NEWCASTLE

COMFORT INN
201 Edward St
(E1V 2Y7)
(506) 622-1215
(800) 228-5150

SACKVILLE

MARSHLANDS INN
55 Bridge St
(E0A 3C0)
(506) 536-0170

SAINT JOHN

COLONIAL INNS
175 City Rd
(E2L 3T5)
(506) 652-3000
(800) 561-4667

COMFORT INN
1155 Fairville
Blvd
(E2M 5T9)
(506) 674-1873
(800) 228-5150

COUNTRY INN & SUITES
1011 Fairville
Blvd
(E2M 4Y2)
(506) 635-0400
(800) 456-4000

DELTA BRUNSWICK
39 King St
(E2L 4W3)
(506) 648-1981
(800) 268-1133

FORT HOWE HOTEL
10 Portland St
at Main St
(506) 657-7320

HOWARD JOHNSON HOTEL
400 Main St,
Chelsey Dr
(E2K 4N5)
(506) 642-2622
(800) 446-4656

ISLAND VIEW MOTEL
1726
Manawagonish
Rd (E2M 3Y5)
(506) 672-1381

REGENT MOTEL
2121 Ocean West
Way (E2M 5H6)
(506) 672-8273

SAINT JOHN HILTON
1 Market Square
(506) 693-8484
(800) 445-8667

SHADOW LAWN COUNTRY INN
3180 Rothesay Rd
(506) 847-7539

ST. LEONARD
DAIGLE'S MOTEL
68 rue DuPont
(E0L 1M0)
(506) 423-6351

ST. ANDREWS
CANADIAN PACIFIC THE ALGONQUIN
184 Adolphus St,
Off Hwy 127
(506) 529-8823
(800) 441-1414

KINGSBRAE ARMS HOTEL
219 King St
(E5B 1Y1)
(506) 529-1897
(877) 529-1897

ST. GEORGE
GRANITE TOWN HOTEL & COUNTRY INN
79 Main St
(506) 755-6415

LAKE DIGDEGUASH FOUR SEASONS CHALETS
148 Pleasant St
(E3L 2X2)
(506) 755-2737

ST. STEPHEN
LEON BAY LODGE
Rt 3
(506) 466-1240

ST. STEPHEN INN
99 King St (E3L 2C6)
(506) 466-1814

SUSSEX
ECONO LODGE
1015 Main St
(E4E 2M6)
(506) 433-2220
(800) 553-2666

PINE CONE MOTEL
Hwy 114 (E0E 1P0)
(506) 433-3958

QUALITY INN FAIRWAY
Trans Canada
Hwy #2
(E4E 5L6)
(506) 433-3470
(800) 228-5151

WOODSTOCK
AUBERGE WANDLYN INN
Trans Canada
Hwy #2 (E0J 2B0)
(506) 328-8876
(800) 561-0000

PANORAMA MOTEL
Trans Canada
Hwy #2 (E0J 2B0)
(506) 328-3315

STILES MOTEL HILLVIEW
827 Main St
(E0J 2B0)
(506) 328-6671

YOUNGS COVE ROAD
MCCREADY'S MOTEL
Young's Cove
Rd, Centre (E0E 1S0)
(506) 362-2916

NEWFOUNDLAND

CORNER BROOK

BEST WESTERN MAMATEEK INN
Maple Valley Rd
Box 787 (A1H 6G7)
(709) 639-8901
(800) 528-1234
(800) 563-8600

COMFORT INN
41 Maple Valley Rd (A2H 6P2)
(709) 639-1980
(800) 228-5150

HOLIDAY INN
48 West St
(A2H 2Z2)
(709) 634-5381
(800) 465-4329

GANDER

ALBATROSS MOTEL
Trans Canada Hwy #1
(A1V 1W8)
(709) 256-3956

COMFORT INN
112 Trans Canada Hwy #1 (A1V 1P8)
(709) 256-3535
(800) 228-5150

HOTEL GANDER
100 Trans Canada Hwy (A1V 1P5)
(709) 256-3931

SINBAD'S HOTEL & SUITES
Bennett Dr
(A1V 1W8)
(709) 651-2678
(800) 563-4900

GRAND FALLS

MOUNT PETYON MOTOR HOTEL
214 Lincoln Rd
(A2A 1P8)
(709) 489-2251
(800) 563-4900

ST. JOHN'S

THE BATTERY HOTEL & SUITES
100 Signal Hill Rd
(709) 576-0040

BEST WESTERN TRAVELLERS INN
199 Kenmount Rd (A1B 3P9)
(709) 722-5540
(800) 528-1234
(800) 261-5540

DELTA ST. JOHNS HOTEL
120 New Gower St (A1C 6K4)
(709) 739-6404
(800) 268-1133

HOLIDAY INN GOVERNMENT CENTRE
180 Portugal Cove Rd (A1B 2N2)
(702) 722-0506
(800) 465-4329

STEPHENVILLE

HOLIDAY INN
44 Queen St
(A2N 2M5)
(709) 643-6666
(800) 465-4329

NORTHWEST TERRITORIES

BAKER LAKE

IGLU HOTEL
Box 179
(X0C 0A0)
(867) 793-2801

FORT PROVIDENCE

SNOWSHOE INN
(X0E 0L0)
(867) 699-3511

HAY RIVER

MACKENZIE PLACE
Box 1880
(X0E 0R0)
(867) 874-2535

MIGRATOR MOTEL
Box 1847
(X0E 0R0)
(867) 874-6792

PTARMIGAN INN
Box 1000 (X0E 0R0)
(867) 874-6781

HOLMAN

ARCTIC CHAR INN
General Delivery
(X0E 0S0)
(867) 396-3531

IQALUIT

NAVIGATOR INN
P. O. Box 158
(X0A 0H0)
(867) 979-6201

NORMAN WELLS

RAYUKA INN
Box 308
(X0E 0V0)
(867) 587-2354

YELLOWKNIFE

FRASER TOWER SUITE HOTEL
5303 52nd St
(X1A 1V1)
(867) 873-8700

SUPER 8 MOTEL
308 Old Airport Rd (X1A 3G3)
(867) 669-8888
(800) 800-8000

YELLOWKNIFE INN
P. O. Box 490
(X1A 2N4)
(867) 873-2601

NOVA SCOTIA

AMHERST
AUBERGE WANDLYN INN
Box 275, Hwy 104 (B4H 3Z2)
(902) 667-3331
(800) 561-0000

COMFORT INN
143 S Albion St (B4H 2X2)
(902) 667-0404
(800) 228-5150

ANTIGONISH
MARITIME INN
158 Main St (B2G 2B7)
(902) 863-4001

AULDS COVE
COVE MOTEL & MARINER DINING ROOM
Hwy 104
(902) 747-2700

BADDECK
MCINTYRE'S HOUSEKEEPING COTTAGES
8908 Hwy 105 (B0E 1B0)
(902) 295-1133

SILVER DART LODGE
259 Hwy 205 (B0E 1B0)
(902) 295-2340

BEDORD
ESQUIRE MOTEL
771 Bedford Hwy
(902) 835-3367

TRAVELERS MOTEL
773 Bedford Hwy (B4A 1A4)
(902) 835-3394

BLACK POINT
GRAND VIEW MOTEL
Hwy 3 (B0J 1B0)
(902) 857-9776

BRIDGETOWN
BRIDGETOWN MOTOR HOTEL
396 Granville St E (B0S 1C0)
(902) 665-4403

BRIDGEWATER
AUBERGE WANDLYN INN
50 North St, Box 40 (B4V 2W6)
(902) 543-7131
(800) 561-0000

COMFORT INN
49 North St (B4V 2V7)
(902) 543-1498
(800) 228-5150

CHESTER
WINDJAMMER MOTEL
4070 Rt 3 (B0J 1J0)
(902) 275-3567

CHETICAMP
CABOT TRAIL SEA & GOLF CHALETS
71 Fraser Doucet Ln
(902) 224-1777

LAURIE'S MOTOR INN
15456 Main St
(902) 224-2400

CHURCH POINT
LA MANOIR SAMSON INN
1768 Rt 1
(902) 769-2526

DARTMOUTH
BEST WESTERN MIC MAC HOTEL
313 Prince Albert Rd (B2Y 1N3)
(902) 469-5850
(800) 528-1234
(800) 565-1275

COMFORT INN
456 Windmill Rd (B3A 1J7)
(902) 463-9900
(800) 228-5150

COUNTRY INN & SUITES
101 Yorkshire Ave (B2Y 3Y2)
(902) 465-4000
(800) 456-4000

FUTURE INNS
20 Highfield Park Dr (B3A 4S8)
(902) 465-6555

HOLIDAY INN HARBOURVIEW
99 Wyse Rd (B3A 1L9)
(902) 463-1100
(800) 465-4329

KEDDY'S DARTMOUTH INN
9 Braemer Dr (B2H 3H6)
(902) 469-0331
(800) 561-7666

RAMADA PARK PLACE PLAZA HOTEL
240 Brownlow Ave (B3B 1X6)
(902) 468-8888
(800) 272-6232

DIGBY
ADMIRAL DIGBY INN
441 Shore Rd (B0V 1A0)
(902) 245-2531

DINGWALL
MARKLAND COASTAL RESORT
802 Dingwall Rd
(902) 383-2246

HALIFAX
AUBERGE WANDLYN INN
50 Bedford Hwy (B3M 2J2)
(902) 443-0416
(800) 561-0000

CHEBUCTO INN
6151 Lady Hammond Rd
(902) 453-4330

CITADEL HOTEL
1960 Brunswick St (B3J 2G7)
(902) 422-1391
(800) 565-7162

DELTA BARRINGTON HOTEL
1875 Barrington St (B3J 3L6)
(902) 429-7410
(800) 268-1133

DELTA HALIFAX
1990 Barrington St (B3J 1P2)
(902) 425-6700
(800) 268-1133
(800) 828-7447

ECONO LODGE
560 Bedford Hwy (B3M 2L8)
(902) 443-0303
(800) 553-2666

HOLIDAY INN EXPRESS
133 Kearney Lake Rd (B3M 4P3)
(902) 445-1100
(800) 465-4329

HOLIDAY INN SELECT HALIFAX CENTRE
1980 Robie St (B3H 3G5)
(902) 423-1161
(800) 465-4329

KEDDY'S HALIFAX HOTEL
20 St. Margarets Bay Rd (B3N 1J4)
(902) 477-5611
(800) 561-7666

THE LORD NELSON HOTEL
1515 S Park St, Box 700 (B3J 2T3)
(800) 565-2020

THE PRINCE GEORGE HOTEL
1725 Market St (B3J 3N9)
(902) 425-1986
(800) 565-1567

SHERATON HALIFAX HOTEL
1919 Upper Water St
(902) 421-1700
(800) 325-3535

TRAVELODGE
374 Bedford Hwy, (B3M 2L1)
(902) 443-1576
(800) 578-7878

THE WESTIN NOVA SCOTIAN
1181 Hollis St (B3H 2P6)
(902) 421-1000
(800) 228-3000

INGONISH BEACH
KELTIC LODGE
Middle Head Peninsula (B0C 1L0)
(902) 285-2880

KENTVILLE
ALLEN'S MOTEL
384 Park St (B4N 1M9)
(902) 678-2683

AUBERGE WANDLYN INN
3230 Hwy 1 (B4N 1M9)
(902) 678-8311
(800) 561-0000

SUN VALLEY MOTEL
905 Park St (B4N 1M9)
(902) 678-7368

LISCOMB
LISCOMB LODGE
Hwy 7,
Guysborough
Cnty
(902) 779-2307

LUNENBURG
BOSCAWEN INN
150 Cumberland
St (B0J 2C0)
(902) 634-3325

**HOMEPORT
MOTEL & INN**
167 Victoria Rd
(B0J 2C0)
(902) 634-8234

MAHONE BAY
**BAYVIEW PINES
COUNTRY INN**
678 Oakland Rd
(902) 624-9970

**THE MANSE AT
MAHONE BAY
COUNTRY INN**
88 Orchard St
(902) 624-1121

MARGAREE
VALLEY
**THE NORMAWAY
INN**
691 Egypt Rd
(902) 248-2987

MAVILLETTE
**CAPE VIEW
MOTEL
& COTTAGES**
Rt 1
(902) 645-2258

NEW
GLASGOW
COMFORT INN
740 Westville Rd
(B2H 2J8)
(902) 755-6450
(800) 228-5150

**COUNTRY INN
& SUITES**
700 Westville Rd
(B2H 2J8)
(902) 928-1333
(800) 456-4000

NORTH
SYDNEY
**BEST WESTERN
NORTH STAR
INN**
39 Forrest St
(B2A 3M3)
(902) 794-8581
(800) 528-1234
(800) 561-8585

**CLANSMAN
MOTEL**
Peppett St
(B2A 3M3)
(902) 794-7226

PORT
HASTINGS
KEDDY'S INN
Trans Canada
Hwy 105
(902) 625-0460
(800) 561-7666

**MACPUFFIN
MOTEL**
Hwy 4
(902) 625-0621

SKYE LODGE
353 Port Hastings
(B0E 2T0)
(902) 625-1300

PORT
HAWKESBURY
MARITIME INN
717 Reeves St,
Box 759 (B0E
2V0)
(902) 625-0320

SCOTSBURN
**STONEHAME
CHALETS**
Trans Canada
Hwy 104
(902) 485-3468

SHELBURNE
**MACKENZIE'S
MOTEL &
COTTAGES**
260 Water St
(B0T 1W0)
(902) 875-2842

SMITHS COVE
**HEDLEY HOUSE
MOTEL**
RR 1
(902) 245-2500

**MOUNTAIN GAP
INN**
Hwy 101
(902) 245-5841

SYDNEY
COMFORT INN
368 Kings Rd
(B1S 1A8)
(902) 562-0200
(800) 228-5150

DAYS INN
480 Kings Rd
(B1S 1A8)
(902) 539-6750
(800) 329-7466

**DELTA SYDNEY
HOTEL**
300 Esplanade
(902) 562-7500
(800) 268-1133

SYDNEY MINES
**GOWRIE HOUSE
COUNTRY INN**
139 Shore Rd
(B1V 1A6)
(902) 544-1050

TRURO
**BEST WESTERN
GLENGARRY
TRADE &
CONV CENTRE**
150 Willow St
(B2N 4Z6)
(902) 893-4311
(800) 528-1234
(800) 567-4276

COMFORT INN
12 Meadow Dr
(B2N 5V4)
(902) 893-0330
(800) 228-5150

KEDDY'S INN
437 Prince St
(B2N 1E6)
(902) 895-1651
(800) 561-7666

**PALLISER
RESORT**
Tidal Bore Rd
(902) 893-8951

WESTERN
SHORE
**OAK ISLAND
INN & MARINA**
55 Vaughn Rd
(B0J 3M0)
(902) 627-2600
(800) 565-5075

WHITE POINT
**WHITE POINT
BEACH RESORT**
White Point
Beach,
Hwy 103
(902) 354-2711

YARMOUTH
**BEST WESTERN
MERMAID MOTEL**
545 Main St
(B5A 1J6)
(902) 742-7821
(800) 528-1234
(800) 772-2774

CAPRI MOTEL
8-12 Herbert St
(B5A 1J6)
(902) 742-7168

COMFORT INN
96 Starrs Rd
(B5A 2T5)
(902) 742-1119
(800) 228-5150

**LAKELAWN
MOTEL**
641 Main St
(902) 742-3588

**RODD COLONY
HARBOUR INN**
6 Forrest St
(B5A 3K7)
(902) 742-9194
(800) 565-7633

**RODD GRAND
YARMOUTH-A
RODD
SIGNATURE
HOTEL**
417 Main St
(B5A 4B2)
(902) 742-2446
(800) 565-7633

ONTARIO

AURORA

HOWARD JOHNSON
15520 Yonge St
(L4G 1P2)
(905) 727-1312
(800) 446-4656

BANCROFT

BEST WESTERN SWORD MOTOR INN
146 Hastings St
(K0L 1C0)
(613) 332-2474
(800) 528-1234

BARRIE

BEST WESTERN ROYAL OAK INN
35 Hart Dr
(L4N 5M3)
(705) 721-4848
(800) 528-1234

COMFORT INN
75 Hart Dr
(L4N 5M3)
(705) 722-3600
(800) 228-5150

HOLIDAY INN
20 Fairview Rd
(L4M 6E7)
(705) 728-6191
(800) 465-4329

TRAVELODGE
55 Hart Dr
(L4N 5M3)
(705) 734-9500
(800) 578-7878

TRAVELODGE
300 Bayfield St
(L4M 3B9)
(705) 722-4466
(800) 578-7878

BARRY'S BAY

MOUNTAIN VIEW MOTEL
Box 101, RR 2
(K0J 1B0)
(613) 756-2757

BAYFIELD

THE LITTLE INN OF BAYFIELD
Main St
(519) 565-2611

BELLEVILLE

BEST WESTERN INN
387 Front St N
(K8P 3C8)
(613) 969-1112
(800) 528-1234

COMFORT INN
200 Park St N
(K8P 2Y9)
(613) 966-7703
(800) 228-5150

QUALITY INN
407 Front St N
(K8P 3C8)
(613) 962-9211
(800) 228-5151

RAMADA INN ON THE BAY
11 Bay Bridge Rd,
Hwy 62 (K8N 4Z1)
(613) 968-3411
(800) 272-6232

BLENHEIM

QUEEN'S MOTEL
Hwy 3, Talbots Trail
(519) 676-5477

BOWMANVILLE

HOWARD JOHNSON CLARINGTON HOTEL
143 Duke St
(L1C 2W4)
(905) 623-3373
(800) 446-4656

BRACEBRIDGE

BELLWOOD MOTEL
133 Manitoba St
(705) 645-4424

ISLANDER INN
320 Taylor Rd
(705) 645-2235

BRAMPTON

COMFORT INN
5 Rutherford Rd
(L6W 3J3)
(905) 452-0600
(800) 228-5150

HOLIDAY INN
30 Peel Centre Dr
(L6T 4G3)
(905) 792-9900
(800) 465-4329

BRANTFORD

COMFORT INN
58 King George
Rd (N3R 5K4)
(519) 753-3100
(800) 228-5150

DAYS INN
460 Fairview Dr
(N3R 7A9)
(519) 759-2700
(800) 329-7466

RAMADA INN
664 Colborne St
(N3S 3P8)
(519) 758-9999
(800) 272-6232

BRIGHTON

PRESQUILE BEACH MOTEL
243 Main St W,
RR 4 (K0K 1H0)
(613) 475-1010

BROCKVILLE

BEST WESTERN WHITE HOUSE MOTEL
1843 Hwy 2 E
(K6V 5T1)
(613) 345-1622
(800) 528-1234

COMFORT INN
7777 Kent Blvd
(K6V 6N7)
(613) 345-0042
(800) 228-5150

SUPER 8 MOTEL
7789 Kent Blvd
(K6V 6N7)
(613) 345-3900
(800) 800-8000

BURLINGTON

COMFORT INN
3290 S Service Rd
(L7N 3M6)
(905) 639-1700
(800) 228-5150

HOLIDAY INN
3063 S Service Rd
(L7N 3E9)
(905) 639-4443
(800) 465-4329

TOWN & COUNTRY MOTEL
517 Plains Rd E
(L7T 2E2)
(905) 634-2383

TRAVELODGE HOTEL
2020 Lakeshore Rd
(L7S 1Y2)
(905) 681-0762
(800) 578-7878

CAMBRIDGE

BEST WESTERN CAMBRIDGE HOTEL
730 Hespeler Rd
(519) 623-4600
(800) 528-1234

COMFORT INN
220 Holiday Inn Dr
(N3C 1Z4)
(519) 658-1100
(800) 228-5150

GATEWAY INN
650 Hespeler Rd
(N1R 6J8)
(519) 622-1070

HOLIDAY INN
200 Holiday Inn Dr
(N3C 1Z4)
(519) 658-4601
(800) 465-4329

LANGDON HALL COUNTRY HOUSE HOTEL & SPA
RR 3
(519) 740-2100

CHAPLEAU

RIVERSIDE MOTEL
116 Cherry St,
Box 699 (P0M 1K0)
(705) 864-0440

CHATHAM

COMFORT INN
1100 Richmond St
(N7M 5J5)
(519) 352-5500
(800) 228-5150

LUXURY INN
25 Michener Rd
(N7L 4B8)
(519) 354-3366

TRAVELODGE
555 Bloomfield Rd
(N7M 5J5)
(519) 436-1200
(800) 578-7878

CHATSWORTH

KEY MOTEL
RR 3, Hwy 6 & 10
(N0H 1G0)
(519) 794-2350

COBOURG

BEST WESTERN COBOURG INN & CONV CENTRE
930 Burnham St
(K3A 2X9)
(905) 372-2105
(800) 528-1234

COMFORT INN
121 Densmore Rd
(K9A 4J9)
(905) 372-7007
(800) 228-5150

CORNWALL

BEST WESTERN PARKWAY INN & CONV CENTRE
1515 Vincent Massey Dr (K6H 5R6)
(613) 932-0451
(800) 528-1234
(800) 874-2595

DAYS INN
1541 Vincent
Massey Dr (K6J
5K6)
(613) 937-3535
(800) 329-7466

ECONO LODGE
1142 Brookdale
Ave (K61 4P4)
(613) 936-1996
(800) 553-2666

HOLIDAY INN
1625 Vincent
Massey Dr (K6H
5R6)
(613) 937-0111
(800) 465-4329

RAMADA INN & CONF CENTRE
805 Brookdale
Ave (K6J 4P3)
(613) 933-8000
(800) 272-6232

DOWNSVIEW
MONTECASSINO
HOTEL &
BANQUET HALLS
3710 Chesswood
Dr
(416) 630-8100

DRYDEN
BEST WESTERN
MOTOR INN
349 Government
Rd (P8N 2Z5)
(807) 223-3201
(800) 528-1234
(888) 394-2378

COMFORT INN
522 Government
Rd (P8N 2P5)
(807) 223-3893
(800) 228-5150

ELLIOT LAKE
DUNLOP LAKE
LODGE
75 Dunlop Lake
Rd (P5A 2J7)
(705) 848-8090

ELMSDALE
FERN GLEN INN
BED & BREAK-
FAST
RR 1
(705) 636-1391

ETOBICOKE
HOLIDAY INN
TORONTO
AIRPORT
970 Dixon Rd
(M9W 1J9)
(416) 675-7611
(800) 465-4329

QUALITY SUITES-
AIRPORT
262 Carlingview
Dr (M9W 5G1)
(416) 674-8442
(800) 228-5151

QUALITY HOTEL
& SUITES-
AIRPORT EAST
2180 Islington
Ave (M9P 3P1)
(416) 240-9090
(800) 228-5151

RAMADA HOTEL -
TORONTO
AIRPORT
2 Holiday Dr
(M9C 2Z7)
(416) 621-2121
(800) 272-6232

TRAVELODGE
HOTEL
445 Rexdale Blvd
(M9W 6K5)
(416) 740-9500
(800) 578-7878

TRAVELODGE
HOTEL
925 Dixon Rd
(M9W 1J8)
(416) 674-2222
(800) 578-7878

FONTHILL
HIPWELL'S MOTEL
299 Hwy 10 W,
Box 253 (L0S 1E0)
(905) 892-3588

FORT ERIE
COMFORT INN
1 Hospitality Dr
(L2A 6G1)
(905) 871-8500
(800) 228-5150

GANANOQUE
COUNTRY
SQUIRE RESORT
715 King St E
(K7G 1H4)
(613) 382-3511

GLOUCESTER
COMFORT INN
1252 Michael St
(613) 744-2900
(800) 228-5150

TRAVELODGE
1486 Innes Rd
(K1B 3V5)
(613) 745-1133
(800) 578-7878

GRAVENHURST
HOWARD
JOHNSON INN
1165 Muskoka Rd
S (P1P 1K6)
(705) 687-7707
(800) 446-4656

GRIMSBY
HOWARD
JOHNSON INN
2 Windward Dr
(905) 309-7171
(800) 446-4656

GUELPH
BEST WESTERN
EMERALD INN
106 Carden St
(NiH 3A3)
(519) 836-1331
(800) 528-1234

COMFORT INN
480 Silvercreek
Pkwy (N1H 7R5)
(519) 763-1900
(800) 228-5150

HOLIDAY INN
601 Scottsdale Dr
(N1G 3E7)
(519) 836-0231
(800) 465-4329

SUPER 8 MOTEL
281 Woodlawn
Rd (N1H 7K7)
(519) 836-5850
(800) 800-8000

HAMILTON
COMFORT INN
183 Centennial
Pkwy N (L8E
1H8)
(905) 560-4500
(800) 228-5150

HOWARD JOHN-
SON PLAZA
HOTEL
112 King St E
(L8N 1A8)
(905) 546-8111
(800) 446-4656

RAMADA
PLAZA HOTEL
150 King St E
(L8N 1B2)
(905) 528-3451
(800) 272-6232

SHERATON
HAMILTON
HOTEL
116 King St W
(L8P 4V3)
(905) 529-5515
(800) 325-3535

HAWKESBURY
BEST WESTERN
MOTEL
L'HERITAGE
1575 Tupper St
(K6A 3E1)
(613) 632-5941
(800) 528-1234

HILTON BEACH
HILTON HARBOR
RESORT
3117 Marks St
(705) 246-0063
(800) 445-8667

HUNTSVILLE
COMFORT INN
86 King William
St
(P0A 1K0)
(705) 789-1701
(800) 228-5150

HIGHLAND
COURT MOTEL
208 W Main St
(P0A 1K0)
(705) 789-4424

TULIP MOTOR
INN
1661 Muskoka
Rd 3 N (P0A 1K0)
(705) 789-4001
(800) 565-4001

INGERSOLL
TRAVELODGE
20 Samnah Cres
(N5C 3J7)
(519) 425-1100
(800) 578-7878

IRON BRIDGE
RED TOP
MOTOR INN
Hwy 17 (P0R
1H0)
(705) 843-2100

JORDAN
BEST WESTERN
BEACON
HARBORSIDE
RESORT &
CONF CENTRE
2793 Beacon Blvd
(905) 562-4155
(800) 528-1234
(888) 823-2266

KAPUSKASING
COMFORT INN
172 Government
Rd E
(P5N 2W9)
(705) 335-8583
(800) 228-5150

KENORA
BEST WESTERN
LAKESIDE INN &
CONV CENTRE
470 1st Ave S
(P9N 1W5)
(807) 468-5521
(800) 528-1234
(800) 465-1120

COMFORT INN
1230 Hwy 17 E
(P9N 1L9)
(807) 468-8845
(807) 228-5150

DAYS INN
920 Hwy 17 E
(P9N 3X1)
(807) 468-2003
(800) 329-7466

SUPER 8 MOTEL
240 Lakeview Dr
(P9N 3W7)
(807) 468-8016
(800) 800-8000

TRAVELODGE
800 Sunset Strip
(P9N 1N9)
(807) 468-3155
(800) 578-7878

WHISPERING
PINES MOTEL
Hwy 17 E
(P0X 1H0)
(807) 548-4025

KINGSTON

COMFORT INN
55 Warne Crescent
(K7L 4V4)
(613) 546-0500
(800) 228-5150

COMFORT INN MIDTOWN
1454 Princess St
(K7M 3E5)
(613) 549-5550
(800) 228-5150

ECONO LODGE
2327 Princess St
(K7M 3G1)
(613) 531-8929
(800) 553-2666

EXECUTIVE MOTEL
794 Hwy 2 E
(K7L 4V1)
(613) 549-1620

HOLIDAY INN KINGSTON WATERFRONT
1 Princess St
(K7L 1A1)
(613) 549-8400
(800) 465-4329

HOWARD JOHNSON CONFEDERATION PLACE HOTEL
237 Ontario St
(K7L 2Z4)
(613) 549-6300
(800) 446-4656

THE NORTH NOOK B & B
83 Earl St
(613) 547-8061

PEACHTREE INN
1187 Princess St
(613) 546-4411

SUPER 8 MOTEL
720 Princess St
(K7L 1G2)
(613) 542-7395
(800) 800-8000

KIRKLAND LAKE

COMFORT INN
455 Government
Rd W (P0K 1A0)
(705) 567-4909
(800) 228-5150

SUPER 8 MOTEL
50 Government
Rd E (P2N 1A5)
(705) 567-3241
(800) 800-8000

KITCHENER

ARAM'S "ROOTS & WINGS" B&B
11 Sunbridge
Cres
(519) 743-4557

COMFORT INN
2899 King St E
(N2A 1A6)
(519) 894-3500
(800) 228-5150

THE CONESTOGA HOWARD JOHNSON HOTEL
1333 E Weber St
(N2A 1C2)
(519) 893-1234
(800) 446-4656

FOUR POINTS HOTEL SHERATON
105 King St E
(N2G 3W9)
(519) 744-4141
(800) 325-3535

HOLIDAY INN
30 Fairway Rd S
(N2A 2N2)
(519) 893-1211
(800) 465-4329

RADISSON HOTEL
2960 King St E
(N2A 1A9)
(519) 849-9500
(800) 333-3333

RODEWAY SUITES CONESTOGA
55 New Dundee
Rd (N2G 3W5)
(519) 895-2272
(800) 228-2000

LEAMINGTON

COMFORT INN
279 Erie St S
(N8H 3C4)
(519) 326-9071
(800) 228-5150

DAYS INN

Hwy 18 S,RR 1
(N8H 3V4)
(519) 326-8646
(800) 329-7466

LINDSAY

RAMADA INN & CONV CENTRE
1754 Hwy 7 W
(K9V 4R2)
(705) 328-1743
(800) 272-6232

LONDON

BEST WESTERN LAMPLIGHTER INN
591 Wellington
Rd S
(N6C 4R3)
(519) 681-7151
(800) 528-1234
(888) 232-6747

DELTA LONDON ARMOURIES HOTEL
325 Dundas St
(N6B 1T9)
(519) 679-6111
(800) 268-1133

HOWARD JOHNSON INN
1150 Wellington
Rd S (N6E 1M3)
(519) 681-1550
(800) 446-4656

QUALITY INN
1156 Wellington
Rd
(N6E 1M3)
(519) 685-9300
(800) 228-5151

QUALITY SUITES
1120 Dearness Dr
(N6E 1N9)
(519) 680-1024
(800) 228-5151

STATIONPARK ALL SUITE HOTEL
242 Pall Mall St
(N6A 5P6)
(519) 642-4444

SUPER 8 MOTEL
636 York St
(N5W 2S7)
(519) 433-8161
(800) 800-8000

MARATHON

PENINSULA INN
Hwy 17 (P0T 2E0)
(807) 229-0651

MARKHAM

COMFORT INN
8330 Woodbine
Ave
(L3R 2N8)
(905) 477-6077
(800) 228-5150

MIDLAND

COMFORT INN
980 King St
(L4R 4K5)
(705) 526-2090
(800) 228-5150

MILTON

QUALITY INN
161 Chisholm Dr
(L9T 4A6)
(905) 875-3818
(800) 228-5151

MISSISSAUGA

BEST WESTERN ADMIRAL HOTEL & SUITES
40 Admiral Blvd
& Hwy 10 (L5T 2W1)
(800) 528-1234

COMFORT INN
1500 Matheson
Blvd (L4W 3Z4)
(905) 624-6900
(800) 228-5150

DELTA MEADOW-VALE RESORT & CONF CENTRE
6750 Mississauga
Rd
(905) 821-1981
(800) 268-1133

FOUR POINTS HOTEL SHERATON TORONTO AIRPORT
5444 Dixie Rd
(905) 624-1144
(800) 325-3535

HAMPTON INN
7040 Edward
Blvd (L2S 1Z1)
(905) 564-2122
(800) 426-7866

HILTON HOTEL TORONTO AIRPORT

5875 Airport Rd
(905) 677-9900
(800) 445-8667

HOLIDAY INN TORONTO WEST
100 Britannia Rd
(L4Z 2G1)
(905) 890-5700
(800) 465-4329

HOWARD JOHNSON EXPRESS INN
2420 Surveyor Rd
(L5N 4E6)
(905) 858-8600
(800) 446-4656

NOVOTEL HOTEL
3670 Hurontario
St (L5B 1P3)
(905) 896-1000
(800) 668-6835

RADISSON HOTEL
2501 Argentia Rd
(L5N 4G8)
(905) 858-2424
(800) 333-3333

SANDALWOOD HOTEL & SUITES
5050 Orbitor Dr
(905) 238-9600

SHERATON GATEWAY HOTEL TORONTO INT'L AIRPORT
Box 3000
(905) 672-7000
(800) 325-3535

MONTEVILLE

MEMQUISIT LODGE
Hwy 64 &
Memquisit Lodge
Rd
(705) 898-2355

MOUNT HOPE

SUPER 8 MOTEL HAMILTON AIRPORT
2975 Homestead
Dr (L0R 1W0)
(905) 679-3355
(800) 800-8000

NEPEAN

MONTEREY INN RESORT
2259 Hwy 16
(K2E 6Z8)
(613) 226-5813

RIDEAU HEIGHTS MOTOR INN
72 Rideau
Heights Rd
(613) 226-4152

NEW LISKEARD

ECONO LODGE
Hwy 11 N (P0J 1P0)
(705) 647-6705
(800) 553-2666

QUALITY INN
Hwy 11 N (P0J 1P0)
(705) 647-7357
(800) 228-5151

NEWMARKET

COMFORT INN
1230 Journey's
End Cir (L3Y 7V1)
(905) 895-3355
(800) 228-5150

NIAGARA FALLS

BEST WESTERN FALLSVIEW MOTOR HOTEL
5551 Murray St
(L2G 2J4)
(905) 356-0551
(800) 528-1234
(800) 263-2580

CAMELOT INN
5640 Stanley Ave
(L2G 3X5)
(905) 354-3754

FLAMINGO MOTOR INN
7701 Lundy's Ln
(L2H 1H3)
(905) 356-4646
(800) 738-7701

GLENGATE MOTEL
5534 Stanley Ave
(L2G 3X2)
(905) 357-1333

HOLIDAY INN BY THE FALLS
5339 Murray Hill
(905) 356-1333
(800) 465-4329

HOWARD JOHNSON PLAZA HOTEL
5905 Victoria Ave
(L2G 3L8)
(905) 357-4040
(800) 446-4656

INN ON THE NIAGARA PARKWAY
7857 Niagara
River Pkwy
(905) 295-4371

NIAGARA PARKWAY COURT MOTEL
3708 Main St
(L2G 6B1)
(905) 295-3331

PENINSULA INN & RESORT
7373 Niagara
Square Dr
(905) 354-8812

SHERATON INN
6045 Stanley Ave
(L2G 3Y3)
(905) 374-4142
(800) 325-3535
(800) 267-5439

STANLEY MOTOR INN
6220 Stanley Ave
(905) 358-92138

SUNSET INN
5803 Stanley Ave
(L2G 3X8)
(905) 354-7513

THRIFTLODGE
6000 Stanley Ave
(L2G 3Y1)
(905) 358-6243
(800) 578-7878

NIAGARA-ON-THE-LAKE

COUNTRYSIDE BED & BREAKFAST
RR 2, Line 1 Rd
(L0S 1J0)
(905) 684-6218
(866) 684-6218

GATE HOUSE HOTEL
142 Queen St
(905) 468-3263

NORTH BAY

BEST WESTERN NORTH BAY INN
700 Lakeshore Dr
(P1A 2G4)
(705) 474-5800
(800) 528-1234
(800) 461-6199

COMFORT INN
676 Lakeshore Dr
(P1A 2G4)
(705) 494-9444
(800) 228-5150

COMFORT INN
1200 O'Brien St
(P1B 9B3)
(705) 476-5400
(800) 228-5150

TRAVELODGE
800 Sunset Strip
(P9N 1L9)
(705) 468-3155
(800) 578-7878

TRAVELODGE
718 Lakeshore Dr
(P1A 2G4)
(705) 472-7171
(800) 578-7878

OAKVILLE

QUALITY HOTEL & EXEC SUITES
754 Bronte Rd
(L6J 4Z3)
(905) 847-6667
(800) 228-5151

RAMADA INN & CONV CENTRE
360 Oakville Place
Dr (L6H 6K8)
(905) 845-7561
(800) 272-6232

ORILLIA

COMFORT INN
75 Progress Dr
(L3V 6V7)
(705) 327-7744
(800) 228-5150

TRAVELODGE HOTEL
600 Sundial Dr
(L3V 6H3)
(705) 325-2233
(800) 578-7878

OSHAWA

COMFORT INN
605 Bloor St W
(L1J 5Y6)
(905) 434-5000
(800) 228-5150

HOLIDAY INN
1011 Bloor St E
(L1H 7K6)
(906) 576-5101
(800) 465-4329

OTTAWA

ALBERT HOUSE INN B&B
478 Albert St
(613) 236-4479

COMFORT INN
1252 Michael St
(K1J 7T1)
(613) 744-2900
(800) 228-5150

DAYS INN DOWNTOWN
319 Rideau St
(K1N 5Y4)
(613) 789-5555
(800) 329-7466

DELTA OTTAWA HOTEL & SUITES
361 Queen St
(K1R 7S9)
(613) 238-6000
(800) 268-1133

HOWARD JOHNSON HOTEL
140 Slater St
(K1P 5H6)
(613) 238-2888
(800) 446-4656

LES SUITES HOTEL
130 Besserer St
(613) 232-2000

LORD ELGIN HOTEL
100 Elgin St
(K1P 5K8)
(613) 235-3333
(800) 267-4298

MARRIOTT HOTEL
100 Kent St
(K1P 5R7)
(613) 238-1122
(800) 228-9290

NOVOTEL HOTEL OTTAWA
33 Nicholas St
(K1N 9M7)
(613) 230-3033
(800) 668-6835

QUALITY HOTEL DOWNTOWN
290 Rideau St
(K1N 5Y3)
(613) 789-7511
(800) 228-5151

RAMADA HOTEL & SUITES
111 Cooper St
(K2P 2E3)
(613) 238-1331
(800) 272-6232

SHERATON HOTEL
150 Albert St
(K1P 5G2)
(613) 238-1500
(800) 325-3535

SOUTHWAY INN
2431 Bank St
(K1V 8R9)
(613) 737-0811

TRAVELODGE
2098 Montreal Rd
(K1J 6M8)
(613) 745-1531
(800) 578-7878

TRAVELODGE HOTEL
402 Queen St
(K1R 5A7)
(613) 236-1133
(800) 578-7878

TRAVELODGE HOTEL
1376 Carling Ave
(K1Z 7L5)
(613) 722-7600
(800) 578-7878

WEBB'S MOTEL
1705 Carling Ave
(K2A 1C8)
(613) 728-1881

WESTIN HOTEL
11 Colonel By Dr
(K1N 9H4)
(613) 560-7000
(800) 228-3000

OWEN SOUND

COMFORT INN
955 9th Ave E
(N4K 6N4)
(519) 371-5500
(800) 228-5150

CRYSTAL MOTEL
672 10th St W
(519) 372-2929

OWEN SOUND MOTOR INN
485 9th Ave E
(N4K 3E2)
(519) 371-3011

TRAVELODGE
880 10th St E
(N4K 1T4)
(519) 371-9297
(800) 578-7878

PARRY SOUND

BEST WESTERN GEORGIAN INN
48 Joseph St
(P2A 2G5)
(705) 746-5837
(800) 528-1234

COMFORT INN
120 Bowes St
(P2A 2L7)
(705) 746-6221
(800) 228-5150

JOLLY ROGER INN
Hwy 69
(705) 378-2461

SUNNY POINT COTTAGES & INN
Box P, Rosseau
Rd (P0C 1K0)
(705) 378-2505
(800) 265-0432

PEMBROKE

BEST WESTERN PEMBROKE INN & CONF CENTRE
1 International
Dr
(K8A 6X9)
(613) 735-0131
(800) 528-1234
(800) 567-2378

COLONIAL FIRESIDE INN
1350 Pembroke St
W (K8A 7A3)
(613) 732-3623

COMFORT INN
959 Pembroke St
E (K8A 3M3)
(613) 735-1057
(800) 228-5150

PETERBOROUGH

COMFORT INN
1209 Landsdowne
St (K9J 7M2)
(705) 740-7000
(800) 228-5150

HOLIDAY INN WATERFRONT
150 George St N
(K9J 3G5)
(705) 743-1144
(800) 465-4329

KING BETHUNE HOUSE B&B
270 King St
(705) 743-4101

QUALITY INN
1074 Landsdowne
St (K9J 1Z9)
(705) 748-6801
(800) 228-5151

ROBYN'S MOTEL
1136 Hwy 7E
(705) 745-3225

PICKERING

COMFORT INN
533 Kingston Rd
(L1V 3N7)
(905) 831-6200
(800) 228-5150

PLANTAGENET

MOTEL DE CHAMPLAIN
200 Hwy 17
(K0B 1L0)
(613) 673-5220

PORT ELGIN

SUPER 8 MOTEL
Hwy 21 S
(N0H 2C0)
(519) 832-2058

PORT HOPE

THE CARLYLE INN
86 John St (L1A
3V9)
(905) 885-8686

COMFORT INN
Hwy 401 & 28
(L1A 3V9)
(905) 885-7000
(800) 228-5150

THE HILL & DALE MANOR B&B
47 Pine St S
(L1A 3V9)
(905) 885-8686

PROVIDENCE BAY

HURON SANDS MOTEL
5216 Hwy 551,
General Delivery
(P0P 1T0)
(705) 377-4616

RICHARDS LANDING

THE CLANSMEN MOTEL
Hwy 548
(705) 246-2581

RICHMOND HILL

BEST WESTERN PARKWAY INN
600 Hwy 7 E
(L4B 1B2)
(905) 881-2600
(800) 668-0101

ROSSPORT

THE WILLOWS INN B & B
1 Main St
(807) 824-3389

ST. CATHARINES

COMFORT INN
2 Dunlop Dr
(L2R 1A2)
(905) 687-8890
(800) 228-5150

HOLIDAY INN
2 N Service Rd
(L2N 4G9)
(905) 934-8000
(800) 465-4329

HOWARD JOHN-SON HOTEL & CONF CTR
89 Meadowvale
Dr (L2N 3Z8)
(905) 934-5400
(800) 446-4656

RAMADA PARKWAY INN
327 Ontario St
(L2R 5L3)
(905) 688-2324
(800) 272-6232

ST. THOMAS

COMFORT INN
100 Centennial
Ave
(N5R 5B2)
(519) 633-4082
(800) 228-5150

SARNIA

BEST WESTERN GUILDWOOD INN
1400 Venetian
Blvd
(N7T 7W6)
(519) 337-7577
(800) 528-1234

DRAWBRIDGE INN
283 N Christina
St
(519) 337-7571

HOLIDAY INN
1498 Venetian
Blvd (N7T 7W6)
(519) 336-4130
(800) 465-4329

SAULT STE. MARIE

AMBASSADOR MOTEL
1275 Great
Northern Rd
(P6A 5K7)
(705) 759-6199

BEL-AIR MOTEL
398 Pim St (P6B
2V1)
(705) 945-7950

COMFORT INN
333 Great
Northern Rd
(P6B 4Z8)
(705) 759-8000
(800) 228-5150

GLENVIEW VACATION COTTAGES
2611 Great
Northern Rd
(705) 759-3436

HOLIDAY INN WATERFRONT
208 St. Mary's
River Dr (P6A
5V4)
(705) 949-0611
(800) 465-4329

NORTHLANDER MOTEL
243 Great
Northern Rd
(705) 254-6452

RAMADA INN & CONV CENTER
229 Great Northern
Rd (P6B 4Z2)
(705) 942-2500
(800) 262-6232

SATELITE MOTEL
248 Great
Northern Rd
(P6B 4Z6)
(705) 759-2897

SLEEP INN
727 Bay St
(P6A 1X6)
(705) 253-7533
(800) 753-3746

TRAVELODGE SUITES
332 Bay St,
(P6A 1X1)
(705) 759-1400
(800) 578-7878

SIMCOE

BEST WESTERN LITTLE RIVER INN
203 Queensway
W (N3Y 2M9)
(519) 426-2125
(800) 528-1234

COMFORT INN
85 Queensway
E (N3Y 4M5)
(519) 426-2611
(800) 228-5150

SUDBURY

BEST WESTERN DOWNTOWN SUDBURY CENTRE-VILLE
151 Larch St
(P3E 1C3)
(705) 673-7801
(800) 387-0697

COMFORT INN
440 2nd Ave N
(P3A 4S9)
(705) 560-4502
(800) 228-5150

COMFORT INN
2171 Regent St S
(P3E 5V3)
(705) 522-1101
(800) 228-5150

DAYS INN
117 Elm St
(P3C 1T3)
(705) 674-7517
(800) 329-7466

HOWARD JOHNSON HOTEL
390 Elgin St S
(P3B 1B4)
(705) 675-1273
(800) 446-4656

RAMADA INN CITY CENTRE
85 Ste. Anne Rd
(P3E 4S4)
(705) 675-1123
(800) 272-6232

SUPER 8 MOTEL
1956 Regent St S
(P3E 3Z9)
(705) 522-7600
(800) 800-8000

TRAVELODGE
1401 Paris St
(P3E 3B6)
(705) 522-1100
(800) 578-7878

THESSALON
CAROLYN BEACH MOTEL
1 Lakeside Dr
(P0R 1L0)
(705) 842-3330

THOROLD
NIAGARA SUITES HOTEL
3530 Schmon Pkwy
(905) 984-8484

THUNDER BAY
BEST WESTERN CROSSROADS MOTOR INN
655 W Arthur St
(P7E 5R6)
(807) 577-4241
(800) 528-1234
(800) 265-3253

BEST WESTERN NOR'WESTER RESORT HOTEL
2080 Hwy 61
(P7J 1B8)
(807) 473-9123
(800) 528-1234
(888) 473-2378

COMFORT INN
660 W Arthur St
(P7E 5R8)
(807) 475-3155
(800) 228-5150

PINEBROOK BED & BREAKFAST
134 Mitchell Rd
(807) 683-6114

RITZ MOTEL
2600 Arthur St E
(807) 623-8189

SUPER 8 MOTEL
439 Memorial Ave
(P7B 3Y6)
(807) 344-2612
(800) 800-8000

TRAVELODGE
450 Memorial Ave
(P7B 3Y7)
(807) 345-2343
(800) 578-7878

TRAVELODGE HOTEL
698 W Arthur St
(P7E 5R8)
(807) 473-1600
(800) 578-7878

TILLSONBURG
SUPER 8 MOTEL
92 Simcoe St
(N4G 2J1)
(519) 842-7366
(800) 800-8000

TIMMINS
BEST WESTERN HOTEL & CONF CENTRE
1800 Riverside Dr (P4N 7J5)
(705) 267-6241
(800) 528-1234

COMFORT INN BY JOURNEY'S END
939 Algonquin Blvd E (P4N 7J5)
(705) 264-9474
(800) 228-5150

SUPER 8 MOTEL
730 Algonquin Blvd E (P4N 7G2)
(705) 268-7171
(800) 800-8000

TRAVELODGE
1136 Riverside Dr
(P4R 1A2)
(705) 360-1122
(800) 578-7878

TORONTO
(Metro Area)

BEST WESTERN ROSEHAMPTON HOTEL & SUITES
808 Mt. Pleasant Rd
(M4P 2L2)
(416) 487-5101
(800) 528-1234
(800) 387-8899

CANADIAN PACIFIC SKY-DOME HOTEL
1 Blue Jays Way
(M5V 3B4)
(416) 341-7100
(800) 441-1414

CARLINGVIEW AIRPORT INN
221 Carlingview Dr
(M9W 5E8)
(416) 675-3303

COLONY HOTEL
89 Chestnut St
(M5G 1R1)
(416) 977-0707

COMFORT INN
66 Norfinch Dr
(M3N 1X1)
(416) 736-4700
(800) 228-5150

DAYS INN DOWNTOWN
30 Carlton St
(M5B 2E9)
(416) 977-6655
(800) 329-7466

DELTA CHELSEA HOTEL
33 Gerrard St W
(M5G 1Z4)
(416) 595-1975
(800) 268-1133

DELTA TORONTO AIRPORT
801 Dixon Rd
(M9W 1J5)
(416) 675-6100
(800) 268-1133

DELTA TORONTO EAST
2035 Kennedy Rd
(M1T 3G2)
(416) 299-1500
(800) 268-1133

FAIRMONT ROYAL YORK
100 Front St W
(M5J 1E3)
(416) 368-2511

FOUR SEASONS HOTEL
21 Avenue Rd
(M5R 2G1)
(416) 964-0411
(800) 332-3442

HILTON TORONTO
145 Richmond St W
(416) 869-3456
(800) 445-8667

HOLIDAY INN ON KING
370 King St W
(M5V 1J9)
(416) 599-4000
(800) 465-4329

HOTEL INTER-CONTINENTAL
220 Bloor St W
(M5S 1T8)
(416) 960-5200

HOWARD JOHNSON PLAZA HOTEL NORTH YORK
2737 Keele St
(M2M 2E9)
(416) 636-4656
(800) 446-4656

LE ROYAL MERIDIEN KING EDWARD HOTEL
37 King St E
(M5C 1E9)
(416) 863-3131

METROPOLITAN HOTEL
108 Chestnut St
(416) 977-5000

NOVOTEL NORTH YORK HOTEL
3 Park Home Ave
(M2N 6L3)
(416) 733-2929
(800) 221-4542

NOVOTEL-TORONTO AIRPORT
135 Carlingview Dr
(M9W 5E7)
(416) 798-9800
(800) 221-4542

NOVOTEL-TORONTO CENTRE
45 The Esplanade
(M5E 1W2)
(416) 367-8900
(800) 221-4542

PARK HYATT HOTEL
4 Avenue Rd
(M5R 2E8)
(416) 924-1234

QUALITY HOTEL-DOWNTOWN
111 Lombard St
(M5C 2T9)
(416) 367-5555
(800) 228-5151

QUALITY HOTEL-MIDTOWN
280 Bloor St W
(M5S 1V8)
(416) 968-0010
(800) 228-5151

RADISSON PLAZA HOTEL ADMIRAL-HARBOUR FRONT
249 Queen's Quay W
(416) 203-3333
(800) 333-3333

RADISSON SUITE HOTEL AIRPORT
640 Dixon Rd
(416) 242-7400
(800) 333-3333

RAMADA HOTEL AIRPORT EAST
1677 Wilson Ave
(M3L 1A5)
(416) 249-8171
(800) 272-6232

VALHALLA INN
1 Valhalla Inn Rd
(M9B 1S9)
(416) 239-2391

THE WESTIN HARBOUR CASTLE
One Harbour Square
(M5J 1A6)
(416) 869-1600
(800) 228-3000

TRENTON
COMFORT INN
68 Monogram Pl
(K8V 6S3)
(613) 965-6660
(800) 228-5150

DAYS INN
10 Trenton St
(K8V 4M9)
(613) 392-9291
(800) 329-7466

HOLIDAY INN
99 Glen Miller Rd
(K8V 5R1)
(613) 394-4855
(800) 465-4329

TWEED
PARK PLACE MOTEL
43 Victoria St
(K0K 3J0)
(613) 478-3134

WALLACEBURG
SUPER 8 MOTEL
76 McNaughton Ave (N8A 1R9)
(519) 627-0781
(800) 800-8000

WASAGA BEACH
BON AIR MOTEL
268 Main St (L0L 2P0)
(705) 429-6364

KINGSBRIDGE INN
268 Main St (L0L 2P0)
(705) 429-6364

WATERLOO
COMFORT INN
190 Weber St N
(N2J 3H4)
(519) 747-9400
(800) 228-5150

WATERLOO INN
475 King St N
(519) 884-0220

WAWA
KINNIWABI PINES MOTEL/ COTTAGES
Hwy 17 (P0S 1K0)
(705) 856-7302

PARKWAY MOTEL
Box 784, Hwy 17 (P0S 1K0)
(705) 856-7020

SPORTSMAN'S MOTEL
45 Mission Rd, Box 219 (P0S 1K0)
(705) 856-2272

WAWA NORTHERN LIGHTS MOTEL
Box 124, Hwy 17 N (P0S 1K0)
(705) 856-1900

WELLAND
BEST WESTERN ROSE CITY SUITES
300 Prince Charles Dr (L3C 7B3)
(905) 732-0922
(800) 528-1234
(800) 387-8186

COMFORT INN
870 Niagara St (L3C 1M3)
(905) 732-4811
(800) 228-5150

WHITBY
QUALITY SUITES
1700 Champlain Ave
(L1N 6A7)
(905) 432-8800
(800) 228-5151

WHITEFISH FALLS
THE ISLAND LODGE
Box 87, Hwy 6
(705) 285-4343
(Phone for boat)

WINDSOR
COMFORT INN
2955 Dougall Ave (N9E 1S1)
(519) 966-7800
(800) 228-5150

HILTON WINDSOR
277 Riverview Dr W
(N9A 5K4)
(519) 973-5555
(800) 445-8667

HOLIDAY INN SELECT
1855 Huron Church Rd (N9C 2L6)
(519) 966-1200
(800) 465-4329

HOWARD JOHNSON PLAZA HOTEL
430 Ouellette Ave (N9A 1B2)
(519) 256-4656
(800) 446-4656

IVY ROSE MOTOR INN
2885 Howard Ave
(519) 966-1700

QUALITY SUITES-DOWNTOWN
250 Dougall Ave (N9A 7C6)
(519) 977-9707
(800) 228-5151

RADISSON RIVERFRONT HOTEL
333 Riverside Dr W
(519) 977-9777
(800) 333-3333

WOODSTOCK
QUALITY INN & CONV CENTRE
580 Bruin Blvd (N4V 1E5)
(519) 537-5586
(800) 228-5151

SUPER 8 MOTEL
560 Norwich Ave (N4V 1C6)
(519) 421-4588
(800) 800-8000

WYOMING
COUNTRY VIEW MOTEL & RESORT
Hwy 22
(519) 845-3394

PRINCE EDWARD ISLAND

CAVENDISH

**BAY VISTA
MOTOR INN**
RR 1 (C0A 1N0)
(902) 963-2225

**CAVENDISH
BOSOM BUDDIES
COTTAGES**
RR 1 (C0A 1N0)
(902) 963-3449

**CAVENDISH
MAPLES
COTTAGES**
(Rt 6 & 13 (C0A
1N0)
(902) 963-2818

CHARLOTTE TOWN

**BEST WESTERN
CHARLOTTE-
TOWN**
238 Grafton St
(C1A 1L5)
(902) 892-2461
(800) 528-1234

COMFORT INN
112 Trans Canada
Hwy (C1E 1E7)
(902) 566-4424
(800) 228-5150

**DELTA PRINCE
EDWARD HOTEL**
18 Queen St
(C1A 8B9)
(902) 566-2222
(800) 268-1133

**HOLIDAY INN
EXPRESS HOTEL
& SUITES**
Trans Canada
Hwy 1
(902) 892-1201
(800) 465-4329

**QUALITY INN
ON THE HILL**
150 Euston St
(C1A 1W5)
(902) 894-8572
(800) 228-5151

**RODD
CHARLOTTE-
TOWN-A RODD
SIGNATURE
HOTEL**
Kent & Pownal
Sts
(902) 894-7371
(800) 565-7633

**RODD
CONFEDERATION
INN & SUITES**
Trans Canada
Hwy
(C1A 7L3)
(902) 892-2481
(800) 565-7633

**RODD ROYALTY
INN & CONF
CENTER**
Intersection of
Hwys
1 & 2 (C1A 8C2)
(902) 894-8566
(800) 565-7633

THRIFTLODGE
Highway 1
(C1A 7L3)
(902) 892-2481
(800) 578-7878

CORNWALL

**SUNNY KING
MOTEL**
Centre on Hwy 1
(C0A 1H0)
(902) 566-2209

MAYFIELD

QUALITY INN
Rt 13 (C0A 1N0)
(902) 963-2213
(800) 228-5151

MONTAGUE

**RODD MARINA
INN & SUITES**
115 Sackville st
(C0A 1R0)
(902) 838-4075
(800) 565-7633

NORTH RUSTICO

**ST. LAWRENCE
MOTEL**
PEI National
Park on Gulf
Shore Road
(902) 963-2053

ROSENEATH

**RODD
BRUDENELL
RIVER-A RODD
SIGNATURE
RESORT**
Rt 4 & 3
(902) 652-2332
(800) 565-7633

STRATFORD

**ANNE'S OCEAN
VIEW HAVEN
B&B**
Kinloch R
(902) 569-4644

SUMMERSIDE

**QUALITY INN
GARDEN OF
THE GULF**
618 Water St E
(C1N 2V5)
(902) 436-2295
(800) 228-5151

WOODSTOCK

**RODD MILL
RIVER-A RODD
SIGNATURE
HOTEL**
Rt 136 (C0B 1V0)
(902) 859-3555
(800) 565-7633

QUEBEC

ALMA
COMFORT INN
870 Ave du Pont
Sud (G8B 2V8)
(418) 668-9221
(800) 424-6423

ANCIENNE LORETTE
COMFORT INN-WEST
1255 Boul
Duplessis
(G2G 2B4)
(418) 872-5900
(800) 424-6423

AYLMER
CHATEAU CARTIER RESORT
1170 Chemin
Aylmer
(819) 778-0000

BAIE-ST-PAUL
HOTEL BAIE-SAINT-PAUL
911 Boul Mgr
Laval
(418) 435-3683

BEAUPORT
COMFORT INN-EAST
240 Boul Sainte-Anne (G1E 3L7)
(418) 666-1226
(800) 424-6423

BOUCHERVILLE
COMFORT INN-SOUTH SHORE
96 Boul de
Mortagne
(J4B 5M7)
(450) 641-2880
(800) 424-6423

BROSSARD
COMFORT INN SOUTH
7863 Boul
Taschereau
(J4Y 1A4)
(450) 678-9350
(800) 424-6423

CHICOUTIMI
COMFORT INN
1595 Boul Talbot
(G7H 4C3)
(418) 693-8686
(800) 424-6423

LE NOUVEL HOTEL LA SAGUENEENNE
250 des
Saguenéens
(G7H 3A4)
(418) 545-8326

DORVAL
COMFORT INN-AEROPORT
340 Ave Michel-Jasmin (H9P 1C1)
(514) 636-3391
(800) 424-6423

QUALITY HOTEL-DORVAL AEROPORT
7700 Cote de
Liesse
(H4T 1E7)
(514) 731-7821
(800) 228-5151

TRAVELODGE DORVAL AIR-PORT
1010 Herron Rd
(H9S 1B3)
(514) 631-4537
(800) 578-7878

DRUMMOND-VILLE
COMFORT INN
1055 Rue Hains
(J2C 6G6)
(819) 477-4000
(800) 424-6423

GASPE
MOTEL ADAMS
20 Rue Adams
(G0C 1R0)
(418) 368-2244

QUALITY INN DES COMMANDANTS
178 Rue De La
Reine(G0C 1R0)
(418) 368-3355
(800) 228-5151

GATINEAU
COMFORT INN
630 Boul la
Gappe
(J8T 9Z6)
(819) 243-6010
(800) 424-6423

GRANBY
HOTEL LA CASTEL
901 Rue
Principale
(450) 378-9071

HULL
HOLIDAY INN
2 Montcalm St,
(J8X 4B4)
(819) 778-3880
(800) 465-4329

L'ANCIENNE LORETTE
COMFORT INN
1255 Boul
Duplessis
(G2G 2B4)
(418) 872-5900
(800) 424-6423

LA MALBAIE POINTE AU PIC
ECONO LODGE
250 Boul de
Comporte
(G5A 1T1)
(418) 665-3733
(800) 553-2666

LA MANOIR REICHELIEU
181 Rue
Richelieu
(418) 665-3703

LA POCATIERE
MOTEL LA POCATOIS
235 Rt 132
(G0R 1Z0)
(418) 856-1688

LAC BROME (KNOWLTON)
AUBERGE LAKEVIEW INN
50 Rue Victoria
(450) 243-6183

LAVAL
COMFORT INN
2055 Autoroute
des Laurentides
(H7S 1Z6)
(450) 686-0600
(800) 424-6423

ECONO LODGE
1981 Blvd Cure
Labelle (H7T
1L4)
(450) 681-6411
(800) 553-2666

HOTEL PRESIDENT LAVAL
2225 Autoroute
des Laurentides
(450) 682-2225

QUALITY SUITES
2035 Autoroute
des Laurentides
(H7S 1Z6)
(450) 686-6777
(800) 228-5151

TRAVELODGE HOTEL
2900 Boul le
Carrefour
(H7T 2K9)
(450) 682-9000
(800) 578-7878

LEBEL SUR LENNOXVILLE
LA PAYSANNE MOTEL
42 Queen (J1M
1H9)
(819) 569-5585

LEVIS
COMFORT INN
10 du Vallon est
(G6V 9J3)
(418) 835-5605
(800) 424-6423

LONGUEUIL
DAYS INN
2800 Boul Marie
Victorian (J4G
1P5)
(450) 677-8911
(800) 329-7466

HOLIDAY INN
900 Rue St-Charles
(J4K 2T1)
(450) 646-8100
(800) 465-4329

LOUISVILLE
GITE DU CAR-REFOUR AND MAISON HISTORIQUE J.L.L. HAMELIN
11 Ave St-Laurent
Ouest
(819) 228-4932

MARIA
QUALITY INN HONGUEDO
546 Boul Perron
(6OC 1Y0)
(418) 759-3488
(800) 228-5151

MATANE
MOTEL LA MARINA
1032 Ave Du
Phare Ouest
(418) 562-3234

QUALITY INN INTER-RIVES MATANE
1550 Ave Du
Phare Ouest
(G4W 3M6)
(418) 562-6433
(800) 228-5151

MONT LAURIER

COMFORT INN
700 Blvd Paquette
(J9L 1L4)
(819) 623-6465
(800) 424-6423

MONTEBELLO

**LE CHATEAU
MONTEBELLO**
392 Rue Notre-
Dame
(819) 423-6341

MONTREAL

(Metro Area)

**BEST WESTERN
EUROPA
DOWNTOWN**
1240 Rue
Drummond
(H3G 1V7)
(514) 866-6492
(800) 528-1234
(800) 361-3000

**CHATEAU
VERSAILLES
HOTEL**
1659 Rue
Sherbrooke
Ouest
(514) 933-3611

**CROWNE PLAZA-
METRO CENTRE**
505 Rue
Sherbrooke East
(H2L 1K2)
(514) 842-8581
(800) 227-6963

**DELTA
MONTREAL**
475 Ave President
Kennedy (H3A
2T4)
(514) 286-1986
(800) 268-1133

**HILTON
MONTREAL
BONAVENTURE**
1 Place
Bonaventure
(514) 878-2332
(800) 445-8667

**HOLIDAY INN
MIDTOWN**
420 Rue
Sherbrooke
Ouest (H3A 1B4)
(514) 842-6111
(800) 465-4329

**HOTEL AUBERGE
UNIVERSAL**
5000 Rue
Sherbrooke E
(514) 253-3365

**HOTEL
INTERCONTI-
NENTAL**
360 Rue St-
Antoine Ouest
(514) 987-9900

**HOTEL LORD
BERRI**
11 Rue Berri
(514) 845-9236

**HOTEL OMNI
MONTREAL**
1050 Rue
Sherbrooke
Ouest (H3A 2R6)
(514) 284-1110
(800) 843-6664

**LA CENTRE
SHERATON**
1201 Boul Rene-
Levesque Ouest
(514) 878-2000
(800) 325-3535

**LOEWS HOTEL
VOGUE**
1425 Rue de la
Montagne
(514) 285-5555
(800) 235-6397

NOVOTEL
1180 Rue de la
Montagne
(H3G 1Z1)
(514) 861-6000
(800) 668-6835

QUALITY HOTEL
3440 Ave Du Parc
(H2X 2H5)
(514) 849-1413
(800) 228-5151

**RENAISSANCE
HOTEL DU PARC**
3625 Ave du Parc
(H2X 3P8)
(514) 288-6666
(800) 468-3571

**RESIDENCE INN
BY MARRIOTT**
2056 Rue Peel
(514) 982-6064
(800) 331-3131

**SHERATON
FOUR POINTS
MONTREAL**
475 Rue
Sherbrooke
Quest (H3A 2L9)
(514) 842-3961
(800) 325-3535

**TRAVELODGE
HOTEL**
50 Boul René-
Lévesque Ouest
(H2Z 1A2))
(514) 874-9090
(800) 578-7878

NEW RICHMOND

**HOTEL MOTEL
FRANCIS**
210 Pandiac
(G0C 2B0)
(418) 392-4485

PASPEBIAC

MOTEL CAROL
127 Boul Gerard
D Levesque
CP1035
(418) 752-3158

PERCE

**AU PIC DE L'AU-
RORE**
1 Rt 132
(418) 782-2166

**BONAVENTURE
PAVILLON COTE
SURPRISE**
367 Rt 132
(418) 782-2166

**HOTEL MOTEL
MANOIR DE
PERCE**
212 Rt 132
(418) 782-2022

PINE HILL

**HOTEL DU LAC
CARLING**
2255 Rt 327
(450) 533-9211

POINTE CLAIRE

**COMFORT INN-
WEST ISLAND**
700 Boul Saint-
Jean
(H9R 3K2)
(514) 697-6210
(800) 424-6423

HOLIDAY INN
6700 Trans
Canada Hwy
(H9R 1C2)
(514) 697-7110
(800) 465-4329

**QUALITY SUITES-
WEST ISLAND**
6300 Trans
Canada Hwy
(H9R 1B9)
(514) 426-5060
(800) 228-5151

QUEBEC CITY

(Metro Area)

**CHATEAU
GRANDE-ALLEE**
601 Grande-Allee E
(418) 647-4433

HILTON QUEBEC
1100 Boul Rene-
Levesque E
(418) 647-2411
(800) 445-8667

**HOTEL CHATEAU
BELLEVUE**
16 Rue de La Porte
(418) 692-2573

**HOTEL CHATEAU
LAURIER**
1220 George V W
(418) 522-8108

**HOTEL LA
MANOIR
LAFAYETTE**
661 Rue Grande
Allee
(418) 522-2652

**L'HOTEL DU
VIEUX QUEBEC**
1190 Rue St-Jean
(418) 692-1850

**LOEWS
LE CONCORDE**
1225 Place
Montcalm
(G1R 4W6)
(418) 647-2222
(800) 235-6397

**QUALITY HOTEL
DOWNTOWN**
330 rue de la
Couronne (G1K
6E6)
(418) 649-1919
(800) 228-5151

QUALITY SUITES
1600 Rue Bouvier
(G2K 1N8)
(418) 622-4244
(800) 228-5151

**RAMADA HOTEL
DOWNTOWN**
395 Rue De La
Couronne (G1K
7X4)
(418) 647-2611
(800) 272-6232

RIMOUSKI

COMFORT INN
455 Boul St-
Germain Ouest
(G5L 3P2)
(418) 724-2500
(800) 424-6423

**HOTEL
L'EMPRESS**
360 Monte
Industrielle
(418) 723-6944

RIVIERE-DU-LOUP

COMFORT INN
85 Boul Cartier
(G5R 4X4)
(418) 867-4162
(800) 424-6423

DAYS INN
182 Rue Fraser
(G2R 1C8)
(418) 862-6354
(800) 329-7466

ROBERVAL

**HOTEL CHATEAU
ROBERVAL**
1225 Boul
St-Dominique
(418) 275-7511

ROCK FOREST

COMFORT INN
4295 Boul
Bourque
(J1N 1C3
(819) 564-4400
(800) 424-6423

ROUYN-NORANDA

COMFORT INN
1295 Rue
Lariviere
(J9X 6M6)
(819) 797-1313
(800) 424-6423

SALABERRY DE VALLEYFIELD

HOTEL VALLEY-FIELD BY DELTA
40 Ave du
Centenaire
(450) 373-1990
(800) 268-1133

ST.-ANTOINE-DE-TILLY

MANOIR DE TILLY COUNTRY INN
3854 Chemin de
Tilly
(418) 886-2407

ST-FAUSTIN-LAC CARRE

MOTEL SUR LA COLLINE
357 Rt 117
(819) 688-2102

ST-FELICIEN

HOTEL DU JARDIN
1400 Boul du
Jardin
(418) 679-8422

ST. GEORGES DE BEAUCE

ECONO LODGE
16525 Boul
Lacroix
(G5V 2G2)
(418) 227-1227
(800) 553-2666

ST-HYACINTHE

HOTEL GOU-VERNEUR ST-HYACINTHE
1200 Johnson
(450) 774-3810

ST-JEAN-PORT-JOLI

AUBERGE DU FAUBOURG
280 Ave de Gaspe
Ouest
(418) 598-6455

ST. JEAN-SUR RICHELIEU

COMFORT INN
700 Rue Gadbois
(J3A 1V1)
(450) 359-4466
(800) 424-6423

HOTEL GOUVERNEUR
725 Boul du
Seminaire nord
(450) 348-7376

ST. LAURENT

HOLIDAY INN AEORPORT
6500 Cote de
Liesse (H4T 1E3)
(514) 739-3391
(800) 465-4329

QUALITY HOTEL DORVAL
7700 Cote de Liesse
(514) 731-7821
(800) 228-5151

RAMADA HOTEL MONTREAL AIRPORT
7300 Cote de
Liesse (H4T 1E7)
(514) 733-8818
(800) 272-6232

ST. LEONARD

ECONO LODGE
4645 Metropolitan
E (H1R 1Z4)
(514) 725-3671
(800) 553-2666

ST. LIBOIRE

ECONO LODGE
110 Charlotte
(J0H 1R0)
(450) 793-4444
(800) 553-2666

STE-AGATHE-NORD

AUBERGE DE LA SAUVAGINE
1592 Rt 329 Nord
(819) 326-7673

STE-ANNE-DES-MONTS

MOTEL BEAURIVAGE
245 1 Ere Ave
Ouest
(418) 763-2291

STE. FOY

COMFORT INN WEST
7320 Boul
Wilfred-Hamel
(G2G 1C1)
(418) 872-5038
(800) 424-6423

HOLIDAY INN
3125 Boul
Hochelaga (G1V
4A8)
(418) 653-4901
(800) 465-4329

MOTEL L'ABITATION
2828 Boul Laurier
(G1V 2M1)
(418) 653-7267
(800) 567-7267

MOTEL ONCLE SAM
7025 Boul
Wilfred-Hamel
(G2G 1B6)
(418) 872-1488

STE. HELENE DE BAGOT

DAYS INN
410 Couture
(J0H 1M0)
(450) 791-2580
(800) 329-7466

STE-MARTHE

AUBERGE DES GALLANT
1171 Chemin St-Henri
(450) 459-4241

SEPT-ILES

COMFORT INN
854 Boul Laure
(G4R 1Y7)
(418) 968-6005
(800) 424-6423

SHAWINIGAN

AUBERGE ESCAPADE
3383 Rue Garnier
(819) 539-6911

SHAWINIGAN SUD

MOTEL SAFARI
4500 12e Ave
(G9N 6T5)
(819) 536-2664

SHERBROOKE

DELTA SHER-BROOKE HOTEL & CONF CENTRE
2685 Rue King
Ouest
(819) 822-1989
(800) 268-1133

MOTEL LA RESERVE
4235 Rue King
Ouest
(819) 566-6464

THETFORD MINES

COMFORT INN
123 Boul Smith S
(G6G 7S7)
(418) 338-0171
(800) 424-6423

TRACY

HOTEL LE DAUPIN
8200 Rue
Industrielle
(450) 743-2791

TROIS-RIVIERES

DELTA TROIS-RIVIERES HOTEL & CONF CENTRE
1620 Rue Notre-Dame
(819) 376-1991
(800) 268-1133

TROIS-RIVIERES OUEST

BEST WESTERN TROIS-RIVIERES
3600 Boul Royal
(G9A 4M3)
(819) 379-3232
(800) 528-1234
(800) 463-4620

COMFORT INN
6255 Rue Corbeil
(G8Z 4P9)
(819) 371-3566
(800) 424-6423

DAYS INN
3155 Boul St. Jean
(G9A 5E1)
(819) 377-4444
(800) 329-7466

VAL D'OR

COMFORT INN
1665 3 Ieme Ave
(J9P 1V9)
(819) 825-9360
(800) 424-6423

SASKATCHEWAN

CARONPORT

THE PILGRIM INN
310 College Dr
(S0H 0S0)
(306) 756-5002

ELBOW

**LAKEVIEW
LODGE MOTEL**
447 Saskatchewan
St (S0H 1J0)
(306) 854-4444

ESTEVAN

BEEFEATER INN
1305 9th St
(S4A 2H7)
(306) 634-6456

**PERFECT
INNS & SUITES**
134 2nd Ave
(S4A 2W6)
(306) 634-8585

FOAM LAKE

LA VISTA MOTEL
Hwy 16 & 310
(S0A 1A0)
(306) 272-3341

KINDERSLEY

**BEST WESTERN
WESTRIDGE
MOTOR INN**
100 12 Ave NW
(S0L 1S0)
(306) 463-4687
(800) 528-1234

MOOSE JAW

**CAPONE'S
HIDEAWAY
MOTEL**
1 Main St N
(S6H 0V6)
(306) 692-6422

COMFORT INN
155 Thatcher Dr
W (S6J 1M1)
(306) 692-2100
(800) 228-5150

DAYS INN
1720 Main St N
(S6J 1L4)
(306) 691-5777
(800) 329-7466

HERITAGE INN
1590 Main St N
(S6H 7N7)
(306) 693-7550

**PRAIRIE OASIS
MOTEL**
955 Thatcher Dr
E (S6H 4N9)
(306) 693-8888

SUPER 8 MOTEL
1706 Main St N
(S6H 4P1)
(306) 692-8888
(800) 800-8000

NORTH BATTLEFORD

SUPER 8 MOTEL
1006 Hwy 16
Bypass (S9A
3W2)
(306) 446-8888
(800) 800-8000

TROPICAL INN
1001 Hwy 16
Bypass
(S9A 2W3)
(306) 446-4700

PRINCE ALBERT

COMFORT INN
3863 2nd Ave W
(S6W 1A1)
(306) 763-4466
(800) 228-5150

SUPER 8 MOTEL
4444 2nd Ave W
(S6V 5R5)
(306) 953-0088
(800) 800-8000

TRAVELODGE
3551 2nd Ave W
(S6V 5G1)
(306) 764-6441
(800) 578-7878

REGINA

COMFORT INN
3221 E Eastgate
Dr (S4Z 1A4)
(306) 789-5522
(800) 228-5150

COUNTRY INNS & SUITES
3321 E Eastgate
Bay (S4Z 1A4)
(306) 789-9117
(800) 456-4000

DAYS INN
3875 Eastgate Dr
(S4Z 1A4)
(306) 522-3297
(800) 329-7466

DELTA REGINA
1919 Saskatchewan
Dr (S4P 4H2)
(306) 525-5255

**HOWARD
JOHNSON**
4255 Albert St S
(S4S 3R6)
(306) 584-8800

**RADISSION
PLAZA HOTEL**
2125 Victoria Ave
(S4P 0S3)
(306) 522-7691

**RAMADA HOTEL
& CONV CENTRE**
1818 Victoria Ave
(S4P 0R1)
(306) 569-1666
(800) 272-6232

**REGINA INN
HOTEL**
1975 Broad St
(S4P 1Y2)
(306) 525-6767

**SANDMAN
HOTEL**
1800 Victoria Ave
E (S4N 6E6)
(306) 757-2444

**TRAVELODGE
REGINA EAST**
1110 Victoria Ave
E (S4N 7A9)
(306) 565-0455

SASKATOON

**BEST WESTERN
INN & SUITES**
1715 Idylwyld Dr
N (S7L 1B4)
(306) 244-5552
(888) 244-5552

**COLONIAL
SQUARE MOTEL
& SUITES**
1301 8th St E
(S7H 0S7)
(306) 343-1676

COMFORT INN
2155 Northridge
Dr (S7L 6X6)
(306) 934-1122
(800) 228-5150

**COUNTRY
INNS & SUITES**
617 Cynthia St
(S7L 6B7)
(306) 934-3900
(800) 456-4000

**DELTA
BESSBOROUGH**
601 Spadina Cres
E (S7K 3G8)
(306) 244-5521
(800) 268-1133

HERITAGE INN
102 Cardinal
Crescent
(S7L 6H6)
(306) 665-8121

**HOLIDAY INN
EXPRESS HOTEL
& SUITES**
315 Idylwyld Dr
N (S7L 0Z1)
(306) 384-8844
(800) 465-4329

QUALITY HOTEL
90 - 22nd St E
(S7K 3X6)
(306) 244-2311

**RADISSON
HOTEL**
405 20th St E
(S7K 6X6)
(306) 665-3322
(800) 333-3333

RAMADA HOTEL & GOLF DOME
806 Idylwyld Dr
N
(S7L 0Z6)
(306) 665-6500

**SANDMAN
HOTEL**
310 Circle Dr W
(S7L 2Y5)
(306) 477-4844

**SASKATOON
INN HOTEL &
CONFERENCE
CENTRE**
2002 Airport Dr
(S7L 6M4)
(306) 242-1440

**SHERATON
CAVALIER**
612 Spadina
Crescent E (S7L
3G9)
(306) 652-6770

SUPER 8 MOTEL
705 Circle Dr
(S7K 3T7)
(306) 384-8989
(800) 800-8000

THRIFTLODGE
1825 Idylwyld
Dr N (S7L 1B6)
(306) 244-2191

**TRAVELODGE
HOTEL**
106 Circle Dr W
(S7L 4L6)
(306) 242-8881
(800) 578-7878

SHAUNAVON

**HIDDEN HILTEN
MOTEL**
352 5th St W
(S0N 2M0)
(306) 297-4166

SWIFT CURRENT

CARAVEL MOTEL
705 N Service Rd
(S9H 3X6)
(306) 773-8385

COMFORT INN
1510 S Service Rd
E (S9H 3X6)
(306) 778-3994
(800) 228-5150

GREEN HECTARES RANCH/B&B
Waker Rd
(S9H 4M7)
(306) 773-7632

RODEWAY INN
1200 S Service Rd
(S9H 3X6)
(306) 773-4664
(800) 228-2000

SAFARI MOTEL
810 Begg St E
(S9H 3X6)
(306) 773-4608

SUPER 8 MOTEL
405 N Service Rd
E (S9H 3X6)
(306) 778-6088
(800) 800-8000

TRAVELODGE
Trans Canada
Hwy 1 E (S9H 3X6)
(306) 776-3101

WESTWIND MOTEL
155 Begg St W
(S9H 3S8)
(306) 773-1441

WEYBURN

PERFECT INNS SUITES
238 Sims Ave
(S4H 2J8)
(306) 842-2691

WEYBURN INN
5 Government
Rd (S4H 0N8)
(306) 842-6543

YORKTON

COMFORT INN & SUITES
22 Dracup Ave
(S3N 3W1)
(306) 783-0333
(800) 424-6423

HOWARD JOHNSON INN
207 Broadway
E (S3N 2V6)
(306) 783-6581

TRAVELODGE
345 Broadway W
(S3N 0N8)
(306) 783-6571
(800) 578-7878

YUKON

BEAVER CREEK

WESTMARK INN
Alaska Hwy,
MP 1202
(867) 862-7501

DAWSON CITY

BONANZA GOLD MOTEL
Hwy 2 (Y0B 1G0)
(867) 993-6789

KLONDIKE KATES CABINS & RESTAURANT
1103 3rd Ave &
King St (Y0B 1G0)
(867) 993-6527

WESTMARK INN
5th & Harper
Sts (Y0B 1G0)
(867) 993-5542

WHITE RAM MANOR BED & BREAKFAST
7th & Harper
Sts (Y0B 1G0)
(867) 993-5772

HAINES JUNCTION

ALCAN MOTOR INN
Alaska &
Haines Hwys,
P.O. Box 5460
(Y0B 1L0)
(867) 634-2371

WHITEHORSE

BEST WESTERN GOLD RUSH INN
411 Main St
(Y1A 2B6)
(867) 668-4500
(800) 528-1234

HIGH COUNTRY INN
4051 4th Ave
(Y1A 1H1)
(867) 667-4471
(800) 554-4471

THE TOWN & MOUNTAIN HOTEL
401 Main St
(Y1A 2B6)
(867) 668-7644

WESTMARK WHITEHORSE HOTEL
201 Wood St
(Y1A 2E4)
(867) 393-4900

TRAVEL NOTES